o the House of the God of Jacob and He will teach us
d shall go forth the Law and the word of the lord from
em

ENCYCLOPAEDIA
JUDAICA

VOLUME 13
P-REC

ENCYCLOPAEDIA
JUDAICA

ENCYCLOPAEDIA JUDAICA JERUSALEM

Library of Congress Catalog Card Number: 72–90254

Second printing, 1973

Produced and printed in Jerusalem, Israel

A Clal Project

GLOSSARY

Asterisked terms have separate entries in the Encyclopaedia.

Actions Committee, early name of the Zionist General Council, the supreme institution of the World Zionist Organization in the interim between Congresses. The Zionist Executive's name was then the "Small Actions Committee."

***Adar,** twelfth month of the Jewish religious year, sixth of the civil, approximating to February-March.

***Aggadah,** name given to those sections of Talmud and Midrash containing homiletic expositions of the Bible, stories, legends, folklore, anecdotes, or maxims. In contradistinction to **halakhah.*

***Agunah,** woman unable to remarry according to Jewish law, because of desertion by her husband or inability to accept presumption of death.

***Aḥaronim,** later rabbinic authorities. In contradistinction to **rishonim* ("early ones").

Ahavah, liturgical poem inserted in the second benediction of the morning prayer *(*Ahavah Rabbah)* of the festivals and/or special Sabbaths.

Aktion (Ger.), operation involving the mass assembly, deportation, and murder of Jews by the Nazis during the *Holocaust.

***Aliyah,** (1) being called to Reading of the Law in synagogue; (2) immigration to Ereẓ Israel; (3) one of the waves of immigration to Ereẓ Israel from the early 1880s.

***Amidah,** main prayer recited at all services; also known as *Shemoneh Esreh* and *Tefillah.*

***Amora** (pl. **amoraim**), title given to the Jewish scholars in Ereẓ Israel and Babylonia in the third to sixth centuries who were responsible for the **Gemara.*

Aravah, the *willow; one of the *Four Species used on *Sukkot ("festival of Tabernacles") together with the **etrog, hadas,* and **lulav.*

***Arvit,** evening prayer.

Asarah be-Tevet, fast on the 10th of Tevet commemorating the commencement of the siege of Jerusalem by Nebuchadnezzar.

Asefat ha-Nivḥarim, representative assembly elected by Jews in Palestine during the period of the British Mandate (1920–48).

***Ashkenaz,** name applied generally in medieval rabbinical literature to Germany.

***Ashkenazi** (pl. **Ashkenazim**), German or West-, Central-, or East-European Jew(s), as contrasted with *Sephardi(m).

***Av,** fifth month of the Jewish religious year, eleventh of the civil, approximating to July-August.

***Av bet din,** vice-president of the supreme court *(bet din ha-gadol)* in Jerusalem during the Second Temple period; later, title given to communal rabbis as heads of the religious courts (see **bet din*).

***Badḥan,** jester, particularly at traditional Jewish weddings in Eastern Europe.

***Bakkashah** (Heb. "supplication"), type of petitionary prayer, mainly recited in the Sephardi rite on Rosh Ha-Shanah and the Day of Atonement.

Bar, "son of . . ."; frequently appearing in personal names.

***Baraita** (pl. **beraitot**), statement of **tanna* not found in *Mishnah.

***Bar mitzvah,** ceremony marking the initiation of a boy at the age of 13 into the Jewish religious community.

Ben, "son of . . ."; frequently appearing in personal names.

Berakhah (pl. **berakhot**), *benediction, blessing; formula of praise and thanksgiving.

***Bet din** (pl. **battei din**), rabbinic court of law.

***Bet ha-midrash,** school for higher rabbinic learning; often attached to or serving as a synagogue.

***Bilu,** first modern movement for pioneering and agricultural settlement in Ereẓ Israel, founded in 1882 at Kharkov, Russia.

***Bund,** Jewish socialist party founded in Vilna in 1897, supporting Jewish national rights; Yiddishist, and anti-Zionist.

Cohen (pl. **Cohanim**), see Kohen.

***Conservative Judaism,** trend in Judaism developed in the United States in the 20th century which, while opposing extreme changes in traditional observances, permits certain modifications of *halakhah* in response to the changing needs of the Jewish people.

***Consistory** (Fr. *consistoire*), governing body of a Jewish communal district in France and certain other countries.

***Converso(s),** term applied in Spain and Portugal to converted Jew(s), and sometimes more loosely to their descendants.

***Crypto-Jew,** term applied to a person who although observing outwardly Christianity (or some other religion) was at heart a Jew and maintained Jewish observances as far as possible (see Converso; Marrano; Neofiti; New Christian; Jadīd al-Islām).

***Dayyan,** member of rabbinic court.

Decisor, equivalent to the Hebrew *posek* (pl. **posekim*), the rabbi who gives the decision (*halakhah*) in Jewish law or practice.

***Devekut,** "devotion"; attachment or adhesion to God; communion with God.

***Diaspora,** Jews living in the "dispersion" outside Ereẓ Israel; area of Jewish settlement outside Ereẓ Israel.

Din, a law (both secular and religious), legal decision, or lawsuit.

Divan, diwan, collection of poems, especially in Hebrew, Arabic, or Persian.

Dunam, unit of land area (1,000 sq. m., c. 1/4 acre), used in Israel.

Einsatzgruppen, mobile units of Nazi S.S. and S.D.; in U.S.S.R. and Serbia, mobile killing units.

***Ein-Sof,** "without end"; "the infinite"; hidden, impersonal aspect of God; also used as a Divine Name.

***Elul,** sixth month of the Jewish religious calendar, 12th of the civil, precedes the High Holiday season in the fall.

Endloesung, see *Final Solution.

***Ereẓ Israel,** Land of Israel; Palestine.

***Eruv,** technical term for rabbinical provision permitting the alleviation of certain restrictions.

***Etrog,** citron; one of the *Four Species used on *Sukkot together with the **lulav, hadas,* and *aravah.*

Even ha-Ezer, see Shulḥan Arukh.

***Exilarch,** lay head of Jewish community in Babylonia (see also *resh galuta*), and elsewhere.

***Final Solution** (Ger. *Endloesung*), in Nazi terminology, the Nazi-planned mass murder and total annihilation of the Jews.

***Gabbai,** official of a Jewish congregation; originally a charity collector.

***Galut,** "exile"; the condition of the Jewish people in dispersion.
***Gaon** (pl. **geonim**), head of academy in post-talmudic period, especially in Babylonia.
Gaonate, office of *gaon.
***Gemara,** traditions, discussions, and rulings of the *amoraim, commenting on and supplementing the *Mishnah, and forming part of the Babylonian and Palestinian Talmuds (see Talmud).
***Gematria,** interpretation of Hebrew word according to the numerical value of its letters.
General Government, territory in Poland administered by a German civilian governor-general with headquarters in Cracow after the German occupation in World War II.
***Genizah,** depository for sacred books. The best known was discovered in the synagogue of Fostat (old Cairo).
Get, bill of *divorce.
***Ge'ullah,** hymn inserted after the **Shema* into the benediction of the morning prayer of the festivals and special Sabbaths.
***Gilgul,** metempsychosis; transmigration of souls.
***Golem,** automaton, especially in human form, created by magical means and endowed with life.
***Ḥabad,** initials of *ḥokhmah, binah, da'at*: "wisdom, understanding, knowledge"; ḥasidic movement founded in Belorussia by *Shneur Zalman of Lyady.
Hadas, *myrtle; one of the *Four Species used on Sukkot together with the **etrog*, **lulav*, and *aravah*.
***Haftarah** (pl. **haftarot**), designation of the portion from the prophetical books of the Bible recited after the synagogue reading from the Pentateuch on Sabbaths and holidays.
***Haganah,** clandestine Jewish organization for armed self-defense in Ereẓ Israel under the British Mandate, which eventually evolved into a people's militia and became the basis for the Israel army.
***Haggadah,** ritual recited in the home on *Passover eve at *seder* table.
Haham, title of chief rabbi of the Spanish and Portuguese congregations in London, England.
***Ḥakham,** title of rabbi of *Sephardi congregation.
***Ḥakham bashi,** title in the 15th century and modern times of the chief rabbi in the Ottoman Empire, residing in Constantinople (Istanbul), also applied to principal rabbis in provincial towns.
Hakhsharah ("preparation"), organized training in the Diaspora of pioneers for agricultural settlement in Ereẓ Israel.
***Halakhah** (pl. **halakhot**), an accepted decision in rabbinic law. Also refers to those parts of the *Talmud concerned with legal matters. In contradistinction to **aggadah*.
Ḥaliẓah, biblically prescribed ceremony (Deut. 25:9–10) performed when a man refuses to marry his brother's childless widow, enabling her to remarry.
***Hallel,** term referring to Psalms 113–18 in liturgical use.
***Ḥalukkah,** system of financing the maintenance of Jewish communities in the holy cities of Ereẓ Israel by collections made abroad, mainly in the pre-Zionist era (see *kolel*).
Ḥalutz (pl. **ḥalutzim**), pioneer, especially in agriculture, in Ereẓ Israel.
Ḥalutziyyut, pioneering.
***Ḥanukkah,** eight-day celebration commemorating the victory of *Judah Maccabee over the Syrian king *Antiochus Epiphanes and the subsequent rededication of the Temple.
Ḥasid, adherent of *Ḥasidism.
***Ḥasidei Ashkenaz,** medieval pietist movement among the Jews of Germany.
***Ḥasidism,** (1) religious revivalist movement of popular mysticism among Jews of Germany in the Middle Ages; (2) religious movement founded by *Israel ben Eliezer Ba'al Shem Tov in the first half of the 18th century.
***Haskalah,** "Enlightenment"; movement for spreading modern European culture among Jews c. 1750–1880. See *maskil*.
***Havdalah,** ceremony marking the end of Sabbath or festival.
***Ḥazzan,** precentor who intones the liturgy and leads the prayers in synagogue; in earlier times a synagogue official.
***Ḥeder** (lit. "room"), school for teaching children Jewish religious observance.
Heikhalot, "palaces"; tradition in Jewish mysticism centering on mystical journeys through the heavenly spheres and palaces to the Divine Chariot (see Merkabah).
***Ḥerem,** excommunication, imposed by rabbinical authorities for purposes of religious and/or communal discipline; originally, in biblical times, that which is separated from common use either because it was an abomination or because it was consecrated to God.
Ḥeshvan, see Marḥeshvan.
***Ḥevra kaddisha,** title applied to charitable confraternity (**ḥevrah*), now generally limited to associations for burial of the dead.
***Ḥibbat Zion,** see Ḥovevei Zion.
***Histadrut** (abbr. for Heb. **Ha-Histadrut ha-Kelalit shel ha-Ovedim ha-Ivriyyim be-Ereẓ Israel**). Ereẓ Israel Jewish Labor Federation, founded in 1920; subsequently renamed Histadrut ha-Ovedim be-Ereẓ Israel.
***Holocaust,** the organized mass persecution and annihilation of European Jewry by the Nazis (1933–1945).
***Hoshana Rabba,** the seventh day of *Sukkot on which special observances are held.
Ḥoshen Mishpat, see Shulḥan Arukh.
Ḥovevei Zion, federation of *Ḥibbat Zion, early (pre-*Herzl) Zionist movement in Russia.
Illui, outstanding scholar or genius, especially a young prodigy in talmudic learning.
***Iyyar,** second month of the Jewish religious year, eighth of the civil, approximating to April-May.
I.Z.L. (initials of Heb. ***Irgun Ẓeva'i Le'ummi**; "National Military Organization"), underground Jewish organization in Ereẓ Israel founded in 1931, which engaged from 1937 in retaliatory acts against Arab attacks and later against the British mandatory authorities.
***Jadīd al-Islām** (Ar.), a person practicing the Jewish religion in secret although outwardly observing Islam.
***Jewish Legion,** Jewish units in British army during World War I.
***Jihād** (Ar.), in Muslim religious law, holy war waged against infidels.
***Judenrat** (Ger. "Jewish council"), council set up in Jewish communities and ghettos under the Nazis to execute their instructions.
***Judenrein** (Ger. "clean of Jews"), in Nazi terminology the condition of a locality from which all Jews had been eliminated.
***Kabbalah,** the Jewish mystical tradition:
Kabbalah iyyunit, speculative Kabbalah;
Kabbalah ma'asit, practical Kabbalah;
Kabbalah nevu'it, prophetic Kabbalah.
Kabbalist, student of Kabbalah.
***Kaddish,** liturgical doxology.
Kahal, Jewish congregation; among Ashkenazim, *kehillah*.
***Kalām** (Ar.), science of Muslim theology; adherents of the Kalām are called *mutakallimūn*.
***Karaite,** member of a Jewish sect originating in the eighth century which rejected rabbinic (*Rabbanite) Judaism and claimed to accept only Scripture as authoritative.
***Kasher,** ritually permissible food.
Kashrut, Jewish *dietary laws.
***Kavvanah,** "intention"; term denoting the spiritual concentration accompanying prayer and the performance of ritual or of a commandment.
***Kedushah,** main addition to the third blessing in the reader's repetition of the *Amidah* in which the public responds to the precentor's introduction.
Kefar, village; first part of name of many settlements in Israel.
Kehillah, congregation; see *kahal*.
Kelippah (pl. **kelippot**), "husk(s)"; mystical term denoting force(s) of evil.
***Keneset Yisrael,** comprehensive communal organization of the Jews in Palestine during the British Mandate.
Keri, variants in the masoretic (*masorah) text of the Bible between the spelling (*ketiv*) and its pronunciation (*keri*).
***Kerovah** (collective plural (corrupted) from **kerovez**), poem(s) incorporated into the **Amidah*.
Ketiv, see *keri*.
***Ketubbah,** marriage contract, stipulating husband's obligations to wife.
Kevuẓah, small commune of pioneers constituting an agricultural settlement in Ereẓ Israel (evolved later into *kibbutz).
***Kibbutz** (pl. **kibbutzim**), larger-size commune constituting a settlement in Ereẓ Israel based mainly on agriculture but engaging also in industry.
***Kiddush,** prayer of sanctification, recited over wine or bread on eve of Sabbaths and festivals.
***Kiddush ha-Shem,** term connoting martyrdom or act of strict integrity in support of Judaic principles.

***Kinah** (pl. **kinot**), lamentation dirge(s) for the Ninth of Av and other fast days.

***Kislev,** ninth month of the Jewish religious year, third of the civil, approximating to November-December.

Klaus, name given in Central and Eastern Europe to an institution, usually with synagogue attached, where *Talmud was studied perpetually by adults; applied by Ḥasidim to their synagogue ("*kloyz*").

***Knesset,** parliament of the State of Israel.

K(c)ohen (pl. **K(c)ohanim**), Jew(s) of priestly (Aaronide) descent.

***Kolel,** (1) community in Ereẓ Israel of persons from a particular country or locality, often supported by their fellow countrymen in the Diaspora; (2) institution for higher Torah study.

Kosher, see *kasher*.

***Kristallnacht** (Ger. "crystal night," meaning "night of broken glass"), organized destruction of synagogues, Jewish houses, and shops, accompanied by mass arrests of Jews, which took place in Germany and Austria under the Nazis on the night of Nov. 9–10, 1938.

***Lag ba-Omer,** 33rd (Heb. **lag**) day of the **Omer* period falling on the 18th of *Iyyar; a semi-holiday.

Leḥi (abbr. for Heb. ***Loḥamei Ḥerut Israel,** "Fighters for the Freedom of Israel"), radically anti-British armed underground organization in Palestine, founded in 1940 by dissidents from *I.Ẓ.L.

Levir, husband's brother.

***Levirate marriage** (Heb. *yibbum*), marriage of childless widow *(yevamah)* by brother *(yavam)* of the deceased husband (in accordance with Deut. 25:5); release from such an obligation is effected through *ḥaliẓah*.

LḤY, see Leḥi.

***Lulav,** palm branch; one of the *Four Species used on *Sukkot together with the **etrog, hadas,* and *aravah*.

***Ma'aravot,** hymns inserted into the evening prayer of the three festivals, Passover, Shavuot, and Sukkot.

Ma'ariv, evening prayer; also called **arvit*.

***Ma'barah,** transition camp; temporary settlement for newcomers in Israel during the period of mass immigration following 1948.

***Maftir,** reader of the concluding portion of the Pentateuchal section on Sabbaths and holidays in synagogue; reader of the portion of the prophetical books of the Bible (**haftarah*).

***Maggid,** popular preacher.

***Maḥzor** (pl. **maḥzorim**), festival prayer book.

***Mamzer,** bastard; according to Jewish law, the offspring of an incestuous relationship.

***Mandate, Palestine,** responsibility for the administration of Palestine conferred on Britain by the League of Nations in 1922; mandatory government: the British administration of Palestine.

***Maqāma** (Ar., pl. **maqamāt**), poetic form (rhymed prose) which, in its classical arrangement, has rigid rules of form and content.

***Marḥeshvan,** popularly called Ḥeshvan; eighth month of the Jewish religious year, second of the civil, approximating to October-November.

***Marrano(s),** descendant(s) of Jew(s) in Spain and Portugal whose ancestors had been converted to Christianity under pressure but who secretly observed Jewish rituals.

Maskil (pl. **maskilim**), adherent of *Haskalah ("Enlightenment") movement.

***Masorah,** body of traditions regarding the correct spelling, writing, and reading of the Hebrew Bible.

Masorete, scholar of the masoretic tradition.

Masoretic, in accordance with the masorah.

Meliẓah, in Middle Ages, elegant style; modern usage, florid style using biblical or talmudic phraseology.

Mellah, *Jewish quarter in North African towns.

***Menorah,** candelabrum; seven-branched oil lamp used in the Tabernacle and Temple; also eight-branched candelabrum used on *Ḥanukkah.

Me'orah, hymn inserted into the first benediction of the morning prayer (*Yoẓer ha-Me'orot*).

***Merkabah,** *merkavah,* "chariot"; mystical discipline associated with Ezekiel's vision of the Divine Throne-Chariot (Ezek. 1).

Meshullaḥ, emissary sent to conduct propaganda or raise funds for rabbinical academies or charitable institutions.

***Mezuzah** (pl. **mezuzot**), parchment scroll with selected Torah verses placed in container and affixed to gates and doorposts of houses occupied by Jews.

***Midrash,** method of interpreting Scripture to elucidate legal points (*Midrash Halakhah*) or to bring out lessons by stories or homiletics (*Midrash Aggadah*). Also the name for a collection of such rabbinic interpretations.

***Mikveh,** ritual bath.

***Minhag** (pl. **minhagim**), ritual custom(s); synagogal rite(s); especially of a specific sector of Jewry.

***Minḥah,** afternoon prayer; originally meal offering in Temple.

***Minyan,** group of ten male adult Jews, the minimum required for communal prayer.

***Mishnah,** earliest codification of Jewish Oral Law.

Mishnah (pl. **mishnayot**), subdivision of tractates of the Mishnah.

Mitnagged (pl. ***Mitnaggedim**), originally, opponents of *Ḥasidism in Eastern Europe.

***Mitzvah,** biblical or rabbinic injunction; applied also to good or charitable deeds.

Mohel, official performing circumcisions.

***Moshav,** smallholders' cooperative agricultural settlement in Israel, see moshav ovedim.

Moshavah, earliest type of Jewish village in modern Ereẓ Israel in which farming is conducted on individual farms mostly on privately owned land.

Moshav ovedim ("workers' moshav"), agricultural village in Israel whose inhabitants possess individual homes and holdings but cooperate in the purchase of equipment, sale of produce, mutual aid, etc.

***Moshav shittufi** ("collective moshav"), agricultural village in Israel whose members possess individual homesteads but where the agriculture and economy are conducted as a collective unit.

Mostegab (Ar.), poem with biblical verse at beginning of each stanza.

***Muqaddam** (Ar., pl. **muqaddamūn**), "leader," "head of the community."

***Musaf,** additional service on Sabbath and festivals; originally the additional sacrifice offered in the Temple.

Musar, traditional ethical literature.

***Musar movement,** ethical movement developing in the latter part of the 19th century among Orthodox Jewish groups in Lithuania; founded by R. Israel *Lipkin (Salanter).

***Nagid** (pl. **negidim**), title applied in Muslim (and some Christian) countries in the Middle Ages to a leader recognized by the state as head of the Jewish community.

Nakdan (pl. **nakdanim**), "punctuator"; scholar of the 9th to 14th centuries who provided biblical manuscripts with masoretic apparatus, vowels, and accents.

***Nasi** (pl. **nesi'im**), talmudic term for president of the Sanhedrin, who was also the spiritual head and, later, political representative of the Jewish people; from second century a descendant of Hillel recognized by the Roman authorities as patriarch of the Jews. Now applied to the president of the State of Israel.

***Negev,** the southern, mostly arid, area of Israel.

***Ne'ilah,** concluding service on the *Day of Atonement.

Neofiti, term applied in southern Italy to converts to Christianity from Judaism and their descendants who were suspected of maintaining secret allegiance to Judaism.

***Neology; Neolog; Neologism,** trend of *Reform Judaism in Hungary forming separate congregations after 1868.

***Nevelah** (lit. "carcass"), meat forbidden by the *dietary laws on account of the absence of, or defect in, the act of **sheḥitah* (ritual slaughter).

***New Christians,** term applied especially in Spain and Portugal to converts from Judaism (and from Islam) and their descendants; "Half New Christian" designated a person one of whose parents was of full Jewish blood.

***Niddah** ("menstruous woman"), woman during the period of menstruation.

***Nisan,** first month of the Jewish religious year, seventh of the civil, approximating to March-April.

Niẓoẓot, "sparks"; mystical term for sparks of the holy light imprisoned in all matter.

Nosaḥ (nusaḥ), "version"; (1) textual variant; (2) term applied to distinguish the various prayer rites, e.g., *nosaḥ Ashkenaz;* (3) the accepted tradition of synagogue melody.

***Notarikon,** method of abbreviating Hebrew words or phrases by acronym.

Novella(e) (Heb. **ḥiddush(im)*), commentary on talmudic and later rabbinic subjects that derives new facts or principles from the implications of the text.

***Nuremberg Laws,** Nazi laws excluding Jews from German citizenship, and imposing other restrictions.

Ofan, hymns inserted into a passage of the morning prayer.

***Omer,** first sheaf cut during the barley harvest, offered in the Temple on the second day of Passover.

Omer, Counting of (Heb. *Sefirat ha-Omer*), 49 days counted from the day on which the *omer* was first offered in the Temple (according to the rabbis the 16th of Nisan, i.e., the second day of Passover) until the festival of Shavuot; now a period of semi-mourning.

Oraḥ Ḥayyim, see Shulḥan Arukh.

***Orthodoxy** (Orthodox Judaism), modern term for the strictly traditional sector of Jewry.

***Pale of Settlement,** 25 provinces of czarist Russia where Jews were permitted permanent residence.

***Palmaḥ** (abbr. for Heb. *peluggot maḥaẓ;* "shock companies"), striking arm of the *Haganah.

***Pardes,** medieval biblical exegesis giving the literal, allegorical, homiletical, and esoteric interpretations.

***Parnas,** chief synagogue functionary, originally vested with both religious and administrative functions; subsequently an elected lay leader.

Partition plan(s), proposals for dividing Ereẓ Israel into autonomous areas.

Paytan, composer of **piyyut* (liturgical poetry).

***Peel Commission,** British Royal Commission appointed by the British government in 1936 to inquire into the Palestine problem and make recommendations for its solution.

Pesaḥ, *Passover.

***Pilpul,** in talmudic and rabbinic literature, a sharp dialectic used particularly by talmudists in Poland from the 16th century.

***Pinkas,** community register or minute-book.

***Piyyut** (pl. **piyyutim**), Hebrew liturgical poetry.

***Pizmon,** poem with refrain.

Posek (pl. ***posekim**), decisor; codifier or rabbinic scholar who pronounces decisions in disputes and on questions of Jewish law.

***Prosbul,** legal method of overcoming the cancelation of debts with the advent of the *sabbatical year.

***Purim,** festival held on Adar 14 or 15 in commemoration of the delivery of the Jews of Persia in the time of *Esther.

Rabban, honorific title higher than that of rabbi, applied to heads of the *Sanhedrin in mishnaic times.

***Rabbanite,** adherent of rabbinic Judaism. In contradistinction to *Karaite.

Reb, rebbe, Yiddish form for rabbi, applied generally to a teacher or ḥasidic rabbi.

***Reconstructionism,** trend in Jewish thought originating in the United States.

***Reform Judaism,** trend in Judaism advocating modification of *Orthodoxy in conformity with the exigencies of contemporary life and thought.

Resh galuta, lay head of Babylonian Jewry (see exilarch).

Responsum (pl. ***responsa**), written opinion (*teshuvah*) given to question (*she'elah*) on aspects of Jewish law by qualified authorities; pl. collection of such queries and opinions in book form *(she'elot u-teshuvot)*.

***Rishonim,** older rabbinical authorities. Distinguished from later authorities (**aḥaronim*).

***Rishon le-Zion,** title given to Sephardi chief rabbi of Ereẓ Israel.

***Rosh Ha-Shanah,** two-day holiday (one day in biblical and early mishnaic times) at the beginning of the month of *Tishri (September-October), traditionally the New Year.

Rosh Ḥodesh, *New Moon, marking the beginning of the Hebrew month.

Rosh Yeshivah, see *Yeshivah.

***R.S.H.A.** (initials of Ger. *Reichssicherheitshauptamt*: "Reich Security Main Office"), the central security department of the German Reich, formed in 1939, and combining the security police (Gestapo and Kripo) and the S.D.

***Sanhedrin,** the assembly of ordained scholars which functioned both as a supreme court and as a legislature before 70 C.E. In modern times the name was given to the body of representative Jews convoked by Napoleon in 1807.

***Savora** (pl. **savoraim**), name given to the Babylonian scholars of the period between the **amoraim* and the **geonim,* approximately 500–700 C.E.

S.D. (initials of Ger. *Sicherheitsdienst*: "security service"), security service of the *S.S. formed in 1932 as the sole intelligence organization of the Nazi party.

Seder, ceremony observed in the Jewish home on the first night of Passover (outside Ereẓ Israel first two nights), when the **Haggadah* is recited.

***Sefer Torah,** manuscript scroll of the Pentateuch for public reading in synagogue.

***Sefirot, the ten,** the ten "Numbers"; mystical term denoting the ten spheres or emanations through which the Divine manifests itself; elements of the world; dimensions, primordial numbers.

Selektion (Ger.), (1) in ghettos and other Jewish settlements, the drawing up by Nazis of lists of deportees; (2) separation of incoming victims to concentration camps into two categories—those destined for immediate killing and those to be sent for forced labor.

Seliḥah (pl. ***seliḥot**), penitential prayer.

***Semikhah,** ordination conferring the title "rabbi" and permission to give decisions in matters of ritual and law.

Sephardi (pl. ***Sephardim**), Jew(s) of Spain and Portugal and their descendants, wherever resident, as contrasted with *Ashkenazi(m).

Shabbatean, adherent of the pseudo-messiah *Shabbetai Ẓevi (17th century).

Shaddai, name of God found frequently in the Bible and commonly translated "Almighty."

***Shaḥarit,** morning service.

Shali'aḥ (pl. **sheliḥim**), in Jewish law, messenger, agent; in modern times, an emissary from Ereẓ Israel to Jewish communities or organizations abroad for the purpose of fund-raising, organizing pioneer immigrants, education, etc.

Shalmonit, poetic meter introduced by the liturgical poet *Solomon ha-Bavli.

***Shammash,** synagogue beadle.

***Shavuot,** Pentecost; Festival of Weeks; second of the three annual pilgrim festivals, commemorating the receiving of the Torah at Mt. Sinai.

***Sheḥitah,** ritual slaughtering of animals.

***Shekhinah,** Divine Presence.

Shelishit, poem with three-line stanzas.

***Sheluḥei Erez Israel** (or **shadarim**), emissaries from Ereẓ Israel.

***Shema** ([Yisrael]; "hear . . . [O Israel]," Deut. 6:4), Judaism's confession of faith, proclaiming the absolute unity of God.

Shemini Aẓeret, final festal day (in the Diaspora, final two days) at the conclusion of *Sukkot.

Shemittah, *Sabbatical year.

Sheniyyah, poem with two-line stanzas.

***Shephelah,** southern part of the coastal plain of Ereẓ Israel.

***Shevat,** eleventh month of the Jewish religious year, fifth of the civil, approximating to January-February.

***Shi'ur Komah,** Hebrew mystical work (c. eighth century) containing a physical description of God's dimensions; term denoting enormous spacial measurement used in speculations concerning the body of the **Shekhinah.*

Shivah, the "seven days" of *mourning following burial of a relative.

***Shofar,** horn of the ram (or any other ritually clean animal excepting the cow) sounded for the memorial blowing on *Rosh Ha-Shanah, and other occasions.

Shoḥet, person qualified to perform **sheḥitah.*

Shomer, *Ha-Shomer, organization of Jewish workers in Ereẓ Israel founded in 1909 to defend Jewish settlements.

***Shtadlan,** Jewish representative or negotiator with access to dignitaries of state, active at royal courts, etc.

***Shtetl,** Jewish small-town community in Eastern Europe.

***Shulḥan Arukh,** Joseph *Caro's code of Jewish law in four parts:
Oraḥ Ḥayyim, laws relating to prayers, Sabbath, festivals, and fasts;
Yoreh De'ah, dietary laws, etc;
Even ha-Ezer, laws dealing with women, marriage, etc;
Ḥoshen Mishpat, civil, criminal law, court procedure, etc.

Siddur, among Ashkenazim, the volume containing the daily prayers (in distinction to the **maḥzor* containing those for the festivals).

***Simḥat Torah,** holiday marking the completion in the synagogue of the annual cycle of reading the Pentateuch; in Ereẓ Israel observed on Shemini Aẓeret (outside Ereẓ Israel on the following day).

***Sinai Campaign,** brief campaign in October-November 1956 when Israel army reacted to Egyptian terrorist attacks and blockade by occupying the Sinai peninsula.

Sitra aḥra, "the other side" (of God); left side; the demoniac and satanic powers.

***Sivan,** third month of the Jewish religious year, ninth of the civil, approximating to May-June.

***Six-Day War,** rapid war in June 1967 when Israel reacted to Arab threats and blockade by defeating the Egyptian, Jordanian, and Syrian armies.

***S.S.** (initials of Ger. *Schutzstaffel*: "protection detachment"), Nazi formation established in 1925 which later became the "elite" organization of the Nazi Party and carried out central tasks in the "Final Solution."

***Status quo ante** community, community in Hungary retaining the status it had held before the convention of the General Jewish Congress there in 1868 and the resultant split in Hungarian Jewry.

***Sukkah,** booth or tabernacle erected for *Sukkot when, for seven days, religious Jews "dwell" or at least eat in the *sukkah* (Lev. 23:42).

***Sukkot,** festival of Tabernacles; last of the three pilgrim festivals, beginning on the 15th of Tishri.

Sūra (Ar.), chapter of the Koran.

Ta'anit Esther (Fast of *Esther), fast on the 13th of Adar, the day preceding Purim.

Takkanah (pl. ***takkanot**), regulation supplementing the law of the Torah; regulations governing the internal life of communities and congregations.

***Tallit (gadol),** four-cornered prayer shawl with fringes *(ẓiẓit)* at each corner.

***Tallit katan,** garment with fringes *(ẓiẓit)* appended, worn by observant male Jews under their outer garments.

***Talmud,** "teaching"; compendium of discussions on the Mishnah by generations of scholars and jurists in many academies over a period of several centuries. The Jerusalem (or Palestinian) Talmud mainly contains the discussions of the Palestinian sages. The Babylonian Talmud incorporates the parallel discussion in the Babylonian academies.

Talmud torah, term generally applied to Jewish religious (and ultimately to talmudic) study; also to traditional Jewish religious public schools.

***Tammuz,** fourth month of the Jewish religious year, tenth of the civil, approximating to June-July.

Tanna (pl. ***tannaim**), rabbinic teacher of mishnaic period.

***Targum,** Aramaic translation of the Bible.

***Tefillin,** phylacteries, small leather cases containing passages from Scripture and affixed on the forehead and arm by male Jews during the recital of morning prayers.

Tell (Ar. "mound," "hillock"), ancient mound in the Middle East composed of remains of successive settlements.

***Terefah,** food that is not **kasher*, owing to a defect in the animal.

***Territorialism,** 20th century movement supporting the creation of an autonomous territory for Jewish mass-settlement outside Ereẓ Israel.

***Tevet,** tenth month of the Jewish religious year, fourth of the civil, approximating to December-January.

Tikkun ("restitution," "reintegration"), (1) order of service for certain occasions, mostly recited at night; (2) mystical term denoting restoration of the right order and true unity after the spiritual "catastrophe" which occurred in the cosmos.

Tishah be-Av, Ninth of *Av, fast day commemorating the destruction of the First and Second Temples.

***Tishri,** seventh month of the Jewish religious year, first of the civil, approximating to September-October.

Tokheḥah, reproof sections of the Pentateuch (Lev. 26 and Deut. 28); poem of reproof.

***Torah,** Pentateuch or the Pentateuchal scroll for reading in synagogue; entire body of traditional Jewish teaching and literature.

Tosafist, talmudic glossator, mainly French (12th–14th centuries), bringing additions to the commentary by *Rashi.

***Tosafot,** glosses supplied by tosafist.

***Tosefta,** a collection of teachings and traditions of the *tannaim*, closely related to the Mishnah.

Tradent, person who hands down a talmudic statement in the name of his teacher or other earlier authority.

***Tu bi-Shevat,** the 15th day of Shevat, the New Year for Trees; date marking a dividing line for fruit tithing; in modern Israel celebrated as arbor day.

***Uganda Scheme,** plan suggested by the British government in 1903 to establish an autonomous Jewish settlement area in East Africa.

***Va'ad Le'ummi,** national council of the Jewish community in Ereẓ Israel during the period of the British *Mandate.

***Wannsee Conference,** Nazi conference held on Jan. 20, 1942, at which the planned annihilation of European Jewry was endorsed.

Waqf (Ar.), (1) a Muslim charitable pious foundation; (2) state lands and other property passed to the Muslim community for public welfare.

***War of Independence,** war of 1947–49 when the Jews of Israel fought off Arab invading armies and ensured the establishment of the new State.

***White Paper(s),** report(s) issued by British government, frequently statements of policy, as issued in connection with Palestine during the *Mandate period.

***Wissenschaft des Judentums** (Ger. "Science of Judaism"), movement in Europe beginning in the 19th century for scientific study of Jewish history, religion, and literature.

***Yad Vashem,** Israel official authority for commemorating the *Holocaust in the Nazi era and Jewish resistance and heroism at that time.

Yeshivah (pl. ***yeshivot**), Jewish traditional academy devoted primarily to study of rabbinic literature; *rosh yeshivah*, head of the yeshivah.

YHWH, the letters of the holy name of God, the Tetragrammaton.

Yibbum, see levirate marriage.

Yiḥud, "union"; mystical term for intention which causes the union of God with the **Shekhinah*.

Yishuv, settlement; more specifically, the Jewish community of Ereẓ Israel in the pre-State period. The pre-Zionist community is generally designated the "old yishuv" and the community evolving from 1880, the "new yishuv."

Yom Kippur, Yom ha-Kippurim, *Day of Atonement, solemn fast day observed on the 10th of Tishri.

Yoreh De'ah, see Shulḥan Arukh.

Yozer, hymns inserted in the first benediction *(Yoẓer Or)* of the morning **Shema*.

***Ẓaddik,** person outstanding for his faith and piety; especially a ḥasidic rabbi or leader.

Ẓimẓum, "contraction"; mystical term denoting the process whereby God withdraws or contracts within Himself so leaving a primordial vacuum in which creation can take place; primordial exile or self-limitation of God.

***Zionist Commission (1918),** commission appointed in 1918 by the British government to advise the British military authorities in Palestine on the implementation of the *Balfour Declaration.

Ẓiyyonei Zion, the organized opposition to Herzl in connection with the *Uganda Scheme.

***Ẓiẓit,** fringes attached to the **tallit* and **tallit katan*.

***Zohar,** mystical commentary on the Pentateuch; main textbook of *Kabbalah.

Zulat, hymn inserted after the **Shema* in the morning service.

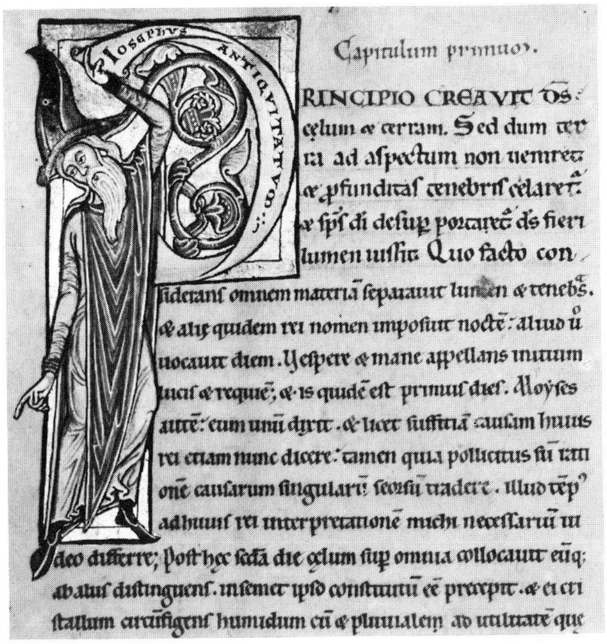

Initial letter "P" of the word *Principio* in a Latin manuscript of *The Antiquities of the Jews* by Josephus Flavius, France, 12th century. The figure in the illuminated letter is wearing the medieval Jewish pointed hat. Paris, Bibliothèque Nationale, Cod. Lat. 5047, fol. 2, column 2. Photo Bildarchiv Foto Marburg, Marburg-Lahn.

PABIANICE (Rus. **Pabyanitse**), city in Lodz province, central Poland. One of Poland's most ancient towns, Pabianice was officially granted municipal status in the 14th century. The prohibition against Jewish residents, based on a privilege *de non tolerandis Judaeis*, appears to have been abrogated when the town came under Prussian domination. Jews then began to settle in the old city of Pabianice. The growth of the Jewish population was closely tied to the development of the local textile industry, and the spinning mills which were set up under subcontract for the textile factories of Lodz. In 1850 steam-powered machines were introduced into the Jewish-owned factories and large numbers of Jewish workers were employed in them from that time on, although Jews were compelled to compete against Polish workers who sought vigorously to supplant them. In 1913 the Polish workers of one Jewish-owned factory declared a strike because the owner hired four Jewish workers. The number of Jews increased from 27 in 1808 to 5,017 in 1897 (18% of the total population). Because Pabianice was in a battle region during World War I, the activity of the spinning mills was almost entirely interrupted and many Jews left, but they returned immediately after the armistice. In 1921 the Jews numbered 7,230, about 33% of the population. Their relative number, however, decreased so that in 1938 the 8,357 Jews in town constituted only 16% of the total population. Economic competition between the Poles and Jews led to an encroachment on Jewish enterprises and during the 1930s Jewish poverty became widespread. Many Jews actually suffered from hunger.

The Jews of Pabianice were greatly influenced by *Ḥasidism, the *ẓaddikim* of *Sochaczew, *Radoshits, and *Komarno having lived in the city. One of the rabbis of Pabianice was Mendele Alter, a brother of the Rabbi of Gur. After R. Alter left to become rabbi of Kalish, his position was filled by his son, R. Abraham. The community's synagogue was first built by Jewish workers in 1847. Restored in 1880, it was famous for its frescoes and wooden engravings and the artistic construction of its Ark. Many organizations were active in the community between the world wars. The *Mizrachi organization was founded in 1918, and Revisionists began their activities in 1927. The *Po'alei Agudat Israel and Ẓe'irei Emunei Israel of the community were affiliated with *Agudat Israel. A large school, Or Torah, which also served as a cultural center for adults, was established by Agudat Israel. In 1919 the Zionists organized a Hebrew high school. [Sh.L.K.]

Holocaust Period. German forces entered the city on Sept. 8, 1939, and immediately introduced a series of repressive acts against the Jewish population. On Rosh Ha-Shanah the synagogue was destroyed and the building converted into a stable. On the Day of Atonement an intensive campaign of kidnapping was carried out in the streets and in the clandestine places of worship. In November many Jews were brutally evicted from their homes, in order to make room for Germans. At the same time the chairman and three other members of the *Judenrat were arrested and two of them murdered. In February 1940 a ghetto was formed in the old district of the town into which 8,000–9,000 Jews were crowded. Contact with the non-Jewish population was still possible and anyone could leave or enter the ghetto at will. Jewish artisans continued to earn wages, and thus supplement the meager rations allocated by the Germans. However, as a result of internal dissension, several members of the Judenrat, including its chairman, Jehiel Rubinstein, were denounced by a group of Jews, resulting in their arrest and dispatch to concentration camps in Germany where they met their death.

The synagogue of Pabianice, Poland, built in 1847. Courtesy Yad Vashem Archives, Jerusalem.

In February 1942 the Germans carried out a medical examination of all the Jews in Pabianice of ten years of age and older. The able-bodied were stamped "A," while the elderly and sick were marked "B." The liquidation of the ghetto took place on May 16, 1942. Some 3,500 Jews in the "A" category and a few children were sent to the *Lodz ghetto. The 150 patients in the hospital were murdered on the spot, 180 tailors were detained in Pabianice to finish the work they had started, while the rest of the Jewish population—the "B" category—were sent to death in the *Chelmno camp. After the liquidation of the ghetto, some 250 Pabianice Jews were employed in the large storehouse located nearby in Dombrowa where the clothing of the murdered Jewish population of western Poland (*Warthegau*) was processed, sorted, and repaired.

A memorial book, *Sefer Pabianice* (1956) was published in Yiddish in Tel Aviv by the society of immigrants from Pabianice. [DE.D.]

Bibliography: Dąbrowska, in: BZIH, nos. 13–14 (1955); idem (ed.), *Kronika getta lodzkiego*, 1 (1965), passim.

PABLO DE SANTA MARIA (el Burguense; c. 1350–1435), one of the most prominent apostates of Christian Spain, bishop, and theologian. He was born Solomon Halevi, a member of a distinguished Jewish family of *Burgos which had produced several tax farmers and financiers of the Castilian kingdom. In his youth he belonged to the circle of Jewish scholars whose most outstanding members were his relative Don Meir *Alguades, Joseph *Orabuena, and Don Benveniste de la *Cavallería. During the early 1380s he corresponded with R. *Isaac b. Sheshet on questions of ritual law (Responsa Ribash, ch. 187–92) and from this may be deduced his familiarity with *halakhah*. He had some knowledge of Jewish and Arabic philosophy and had read Christian theological works. From a humorous letter written in Hebrew to Meir Alguades in honor of the festival of Purim, it appears that he was in "England" in 1389. Some believe that he was detained there as a Castilian hostage but the more logical assumption is that his stay was connected with a diplomatic mission and that the reference is not to England itself but to Acquitaine, then under English rule.

The circumstances of Pablo's apostasy are obscure: according to Christian tradition he was baptized on July 21, 1390, but from a letter sent him after his conversion by his disciple Joshua *Lorki, also known as Geronimo de Sante Fe, there is reason to assume that he was converted after the outbreak of the riots of 1391 (see *Spain). It is in any case clear that he was already perplexed over questions of faith several years prior to his apostasy. His conversion to Christianity was to a certain extent a protest against the Averroistic views advanced by a considerable number of Jewish intellectuals in Spain. There is no doubt that he was vitally influenced by the apostate *Abner of Burgos, whom he frequently quotes in his own works. His four sons, his daughter, and his three brothers were baptized together with him. At first his wife refused to follow his example, but she accepted baptism a few years later. After his conversion, which left a powerful imprint on Jewish intellectuals, he sent a letter to Joseph Orabuena explaining the reasons that prompted his conversion to Christianity. This letter, which was widely circulated, also reached his disciple Joshua Lorki, who was converted some years later. In a lengthy letter, addressed to Pablo, Lorki asked him the reasons for his decision and expressed fundamental reservations on the messianic role of Jesus. Only the last part of Pablo's reply has been preserved; it includes the idea that it is incumbent upon every Jew to delve into the Bible and the Oral Law so as to discern the messianism of Jesus.

To increase his knowledge of Christian theology, Pablo traveled to Paris, where he studied until 1394 and was ordained a priest. On completing his studies, he settled in Avignon, where he became one of the favorites of Pope *Benedict XIII and one of his staunchest supporters. It was during this period that he began his anti-Jewish activity, when he attempted to induce King John I of Aragon to issue anti-Jewish laws. His ascent in the Catholic hierarchy was rapid: in 1396 he was appointed archdeacon of Trevinno, in 1403 bishop of Cartagena, and from 1415 until his death, he was bishop of Burgos. He also held the position of *canciller mayor* to the king of Castile from 1407.

Pablo left a number of works: the first, *Scrutinium Scripturarum*, was completed in 1432. The first part describes a dialog between the Jew Saul and the Christian Paul. The Jew argues against the tenets of Christianity and the Christian refutes all his objections. In the second part, an apostate asks his teacher to elucidate a number of points of Christian dogma which are not sufficiently clear to him. In 1429 Paulus completed the *Aditiones ad postillam Magistri Nicolai Lyra* ("Additions to the Biblical Commentary of *Nicholas de Lyra"). He also wrote a historical poem, *Las Siete edades del Mundo* or *Edades trovadas*, as well as a work on the history of Spain from antiquity until 1412, *Suma de las crónicas del mundo*. Toward the end of his life, he wrote a book on his origins and genealogy. His brothers held important positions in Castilian society: PEDRO JUÁREZ became governor of Burgos and ALVAR GARCÍA the notary of the royal office. This was also the case with his sons: GONZALO GARCIA DE SANTA MARÍA rose to the rank of bishop; ALONSO OF CARTAGENA succeeded his father as bishop of Burgos and wrote *Defensorium unitatis christianae* in defense of the Conversos; PEDRO DE CARTAGENA became a military commander of the kings of Castile, and ALVAR SÁNCHEZ DE CARTAGENA was a diplomat in the service of the kingdom.

Bibliography: Baer, Spain, index; I. Abrahams, in: JQR, 12 (1900), 255–63; P. L. Serrano, *Los conversos Pablo de Santa María y Alfonso de Cartagena* (1942); F. Cantera, *La conversión del célebre talmudista Salomón Leví* (1933); idem, *Alvar García de Santa María y su familia de conversos* (1952), index; idem, in: *Homenaje a Millás-Vallicrosa*, 1 (1954), 301–7.

[J.KA.]

PACHECO, RODRIGO BENJAMIN MENDES (d. 1749), early U.S. merchant. Pacheco, whose place of birth is unknown, went to New York City early in his career and was made freeman of the city in 1712. Increasingly prominent as his mercantile business flourished, Pacheco petitioned the authorities in 1728 with others for the right to purchase land for a Jewish cemetery. He was instrumental in the erection of the Shearith Israel synagogue on Mill Street, in 1729–30. In 1731 Pacheco was appointed colonial agent for the province. Around 1740 he did a brisk business in shipping supplies to the new colony of Georgia, where his contact was the Nunezes family. A more extensive enterprise was carried on there by a competitor, Jacob *Franks, who, unlike Pacheco, was Ashkenazi. In the wake of a bitter legal entanglement over his business affairs, Pacheco settled permanently in London in 1731.

Bibliography: J. R. Marcus, *Early American Jewry*, 1 (1951), 158; 2 (1953), 293; L. Hershkowitz and I. S. Meyer (eds.), *Lee Max Friedman Collection of American Colonial Correspondence* (1968); M. Stern, *Americans of Jewish Descent* (1960). [L.He.]

PACHT, ISAAC (1890–), U.S. attorney, judge, and community leader. Pacht, who was born in Millie, Austria, was taken to the U.S. while a boy. After his graduation from Brooklyn Law School in 1912, he moved to Los Angeles and in 1913 was admitted to the California bar. Pacht was a practicing attorney except for the periods when he served as judge of the Superior Court (1931–32) and judge of the California District Court of Appeal (1932–35). He was deeply involved in California prison reform and served for a number of years as president of the State Board of Prison Directors (1940–50), under appointment by Governor Culbert Olson. Governor Earl Warren appointed Pacht chairman of the California Commission on Criminal Law and Procedure (1947–49). Extremely active in Los Angeles Jewish affairs, Pacht's posts included: chairman (the first) of the the United Jewish Welfare Fund (1932–34); president of the Jewish Institute of Religion of Los Angeles; and president of the Los Angeles Jewish Community Council (1949–51). He also served as president or director of the Vista Del Mar Child Care Service for more than 40 years. [M.V.]

PACIFICI, ALFONSO (1889–), Italian lawyer and thinker. Born in Florence, he came under the influence of Rabbi S. H. *Margulies and became the leader of the group who attempted to revitalize Jewish life in Italy through "integral" Judaism, combining religion, culture, and Zionism. A remarkable orator with a striking appearance and great personal charm, he exercised a considerable influence on a whole generation of Jews in Italy, even those who subsequently disagreed with his increasingly uncompromising orthodoxy. In 1916, he founded (with Dante *Lattes) the weekly *Israel.* He settled in 1934 in Ereẓ Israel, where he continued his activities, mainly for Orthodox educational institutions. His ideas are expressed in such works as *Discorsi sullo Shemà* (1953), *Israel Segullà* (1955), and its semi-autobiographical sequel *Interludio* (1959).

Bibliography: *Israel* (June 5, 1969); Roth, in: *Menorah Journal*, 47 (1959), 41–49; RMI, 35 (1969), 233f. [C.R.]

PACIFICI, RICCARDO (1904–c. 1943), Italian rabbi and scholar. Born in Florence and trained there at the Collegio Rabbinico Italiano, Pacifici served as assistant rabbi in Venice in 1928–31. He was the head of the rabbinical seminary (and later rabbi) in Rhodes, and in 1936 was appointed rabbi of Genoa. His published works (1929–36) include monographs on Venetian Jewish history (including a volume on the inscriptions in the Jewish cemetery in the Lido; 1929), historical accounts of the Jews of Rhodes (1933, 1935) and of the Genoese community (1939, 1948), and a selection of sermons and addresses, *Discorsi sulla Torà* (1968). At the height of Nazi and Fascist persecution he published a Midrash anthology. After making great efforts to assist the victims of the Nazi terror (DELASEM; Delegazione Assistenza Emigranti Ebrei), he was arrested and deported by the Germans in 1943, his subsequent fate being unknown.

Bibliography: Milano, Bibliotheca, index; A. Segre, in: R. Pacifici, *Discorsi sulla Torà* (1968), xii–xxxiii; A. Luzzatto, *Riccardo Pacifici* (1967), incl. bibl. [A.M.R.]

PACIFICO, DAVID (called **"Don Pacifico"**; 1784–1854), merchant and diplomat. Born in Gibraltar, Pacifico was a British subject. In 1812 his business activities took him to Lagos, Portugal, where he was appointed Portuguese consul to Morocco (1835–37) and to Greece (1837–42). In 1847 the Greek minister, Coletti, in deference to one of the Rothschilds who happened to be in Athens at the time, prohibited the populace of Athens from burning a wooden effigy of Judas Iscariot on the Friday before Easter as was the yearly custom. Riot broke out and Pacifico was attacked and his house destroyed. Pacifico demanded a sum of 800,000 drachmas (then equivalent to £26,618) as compensation. The Greek government refused to consider his claim and even confiscated Pacifico's real estate. In order to defend his interests as a British subject, the British Admiral Park—upon the instruction of the prime minister, Palmerston—blockaded the port of Piraeus and captured 200 Greek ships. The Greek government was compelled to pay 120,000 drachmas and £500. Pacifico retired to London, where he died. The incident was important in its time as Palmerston had to defend himself for having supported the lawsuit of a Jew. Palmerston replied that it was not right that because "a man is of Jewish persuasion" he should be outraged.

Bibliography: *Hansard Parliamentary Reports* (June 25, 1850), cols. 380–444; M. Molho, in: *Joshua Starr Memorial Volume* (1953). [S.Mar.]

PADDAN-ARAM (Heb. פַּדַּן אֲרָם), place mentioned only in Genesis and prominently associated with the lives of the Patriarchs. Paddan-Aram seems to have been either identical with, or included within, the area of Aram-Naharaim and is described by Abraham as "the land of my birth" to which he sent his servant to find a wife for Isaac (24:4, 10; 25:20). It is most frequently mentioned in connection with Jacob's flight from Esau and his residence with his uncle Laban, the brother of Rebekah his mother. All but one of the tribes of Israel originated there (28:2–7; 31:18; 33:18; 35:9, 26; 46:15; 48:7).

Paddan-Aram must have been situated in northern Mesopotamia since it included the city of Haran (28:10; 29:4). The repeated description of Laban as an Aramean (25:20; 28:5; 31:20, 24) would imply an Aramean population speaking the Aramaic language (31:47). In fact, the name is generally accepted as deriving from the Aramaic *paddânâ*, "a field, or plain," and meaning "the Plain of Aram," corresponding to the Hebrew *sedeh Aram* (Hos. 12:13).

Bibliography: Albright, Stone, 180; B. Maisler, in: *Zion*, 11 (1946), 3. [N.M.S.]

PADERBORN, town in N.W. Germany. The earliest documentary source reflecting the presence of Jews in the city of Paderborn dates from 1342; the existence of a stone house belonging to them at this time attests to their wealth. In a dispute between Bishop Herman von Spiegel in 1378 and the city of Paderborn, the bishop referred to "his Jews" who were under his protection. Nevertheless an organized Jewish community came into being in the city only in 1590.

A prayer room was opened in the 17th century. In 1640 seven Jewish families were permitted to live in Paderborn; by 1652 the number had increased to 14 families. The Jews of the city were mentioned among those benefiting from a general letter of protection granted in 1661. They played a leading role in the federation of Jewish communities in the bishopric. Numbers remained fairly constant until the end of the 18th century. By 1764 a synagogue is noted in the city; a cemetery plot was purchased in 1728. In 1778 there were 19 "protected" Jews in the town and in 1803, 26, in addition to two communal employees. In the course of the 19th century the community grew from 288 persons in 1840 to 389 in 1913. A new synagogue was built in 1881 (destroyed by the Nazis in 1938). Together with the synagogue the community also maintained a religious school. After 1938 the prayer room of the Jewish orphanage (consecrated in 1863) was used as the cultural center for the continuously declining community. In 1932 there were still 310 Jews in Paderborn, but in 1939 only 123 remained, the greater part of whom were later deported. In July 1942 the staff and children of the orphanage (founded 1856) were also deported. From the summer of 1939 until March 1943 the town contained a so-called "Jewish Retraining Center" for some 100 people who were forcibly employed by the Nazi authorities in Paderborn. On March 1, 1943, all the inmates of the center were deported to Auschwitz; only ten survived. After World War II a community was reestablished in Paderborn including the districts of Bueren, Hoexter, Lippstadt, *Soest, and Warburg, and in 1962 numbered 55 members. The new synagogue was dedicated in 1950. [B.Br.]

Province (formerly bishopric) of Paderborn. The presence of Jews in the bishopric of Paderborn is first mentioned as early as 1258; in 1281 they were put under the protection of the bishop who intervened actively, following the murder of Jews in Bueren in 1292. Sources remain scanty until the 17th century. In the intervening years Jewish communities were slowly built in the towns of the bishopric. Jurisdiction over the Jews had passed to the municipalities, who restricted Jewish economic activity to trading in unredeemed pawned articles, gold, and jewels, so as not to compete with local merchants. In the 16th century the Jews of Warburg were permitted to engage in *moneylending and restricted commercial activity, providing it did not interfere with the guilds. In the beginning of the 17th century jurisdiction over the Jews reverted to the bishop. By 1646 there were 67 Jewish families in the bishopric, and by 1677, 144. From 1619 the rabbinate for the **Landjudenschaft* of the bishopric was located in Warburg, the largest Jewish community till the emancipation. In 1661 a general letter of protection was addressed by Bishop Ferdinand von Fuerstenberg to the Jewries of Warburg, Paderborn, Beverungen, Peckelsheim, and Borgentreich (among others), granting them liberal privileges. In part as a result of the need to defend themselves against the municipalities and in part due to the need for funds to support a rabbi and maintain a cemetery, a federation of Jewish communities in the bishopric was organized in 1628, responsible directly to the bishop. At the head of the community was an *Obervorgaenger* at whose suggestion the other officials were appointed by the bishop. During 1649–50 the office was filled by Solomon Levi, in the following year by the Court Jew, Behrend *Levi, later accused of embezzlement and removed. Some of his successors in the well-paid position were likewise corrupt and in 1677 three non-salaried officials took over the duties of the head of the community. A Diet (*Va'ad Gadol*) met once every three years in varying places. During the 18th century the Diet elected the community's elders. Among the duties of the organized community tax assessment was perhaps the most important; the community was often divided over the inequities of the tax system and the domination of the federation by a few wealthy families. The rabbinate was given a free hand in ritual matters; dues collected through taxation of *se'udot mitzvah* went to the support of Ereẓ Israel.

The economic condition of the Jews in the bishopric steadily improved as restrictions on their economic activity were removed. In 1661 they were granted permission to engage in retail trade in dry goods; permission for peddling was granted in 1687. They became prominent in the import trade in tobacco as well as the leasing of the salt monopoly. All restrictions were lifted in 1704 and Jews expanded their commercial activity still more, trading in agricultural produce and playing a leading role in establishing Warburg as a grain center. They were among the prominent merchants at the *Leipzig fairs. In 1802 the bishopric was secularized and in 1803 became a province of Prussia. Emancipation, introduced during the Napoleonic invasion, was eclipsed during the reaction that followed and came into its own only toward the end of the century. In the period following the Franco-Prussian War, Jews took an increasingly active part in the economic and social life of the province as well as coming into prominence in the arts and sciences, a development that came to an end only with the liquidation of Jewish life by the Nazis. [A.Sha.]

Bibliography: *Baun wir doch aufs neue das alte Haus—juedisches Schicksal in Paderborn* (1964), incl. bibl.; *Westfalia Judaica*, ed. by B. Brilling, 1 (1967), 119, 213; Germ Jud, 2 pt. 2 (1968), 643f.; *Aus Geschichte und Leben der Juden in Westfalen*, ed. by H. Ch. Meyer (1962), 45–46, 254 (bibl.); M. Kreutzberger, *Katalog*, 1 (1970), 203; B. Altmann, in: JSOS, 3 (1941), 159–88; 5 (1943), 163–86; idem, *Die Juden im ehemaligen Hochstift Paderborn zur Zeit des 17. und 18. Jahrhunderts* (1923), unpublished dissertation, University of Freiburg in Breisgau; M. Grunwald, in: ZGJD, 7 (1937), 112–4.

PADUA, capital of Padua province, N. Italy. In documents dated 1134 and 1182 two or three persons with the surname Judaeus are mentioned, although some scholarly opinion holds that they were not Jews. In 1289 the physician Jacob Bonacosa, a Jew, translated *Averroes' *Colliget*, a medical text. Several loan banks were founded by Jews who came from various parts of Italy, such as Pisa, Roma, Bologna, and Ancona in the 1360s, and in the 1380s and 1390s from Germany and Spain as well. In 1380 Jewish bankers were responsible for three powerful loan and trading concerns with a capital investment of 20,000 ducats. Taxation imposed by Padua's rulers, the Carraras, was not heavy, and the populace was normally tolerant of the Jews. The community grew rapidly in wealth and social position; there was a synagogue and cemetery. In 1405 Padua became part of the Venetian republic. In 1415 an attempt was made by the Venetian authorities at the request of the Paduan city council to lower the interest rate of Jewish loan bankers to between 12% and 15%. The attempt was opposed vigorously by the Jewish bankers who closed their places of business in retaliation. The strike was backed by students who were deprived of their source of credit. During the first years of Venetian rule Jewish economic progress continued at a rapid pace. Their situation deteriorated, however, in the second quarter of the century. In part due to internal difficulties within the Venetian republic increasing pressure was directed against the economic status and legal position of the Jewish community. In 1420 the authorities imposed a lower rate of interest.

The situation of the loan bankers gradually worsened and they were expelled from the city in 1456. A major role in the expulsion of the bankers was taken by John

Figure 1. *Bimah* of the "Italian" synagogue in Padua built in the second half of the 16th century, and by 1970 the city's only synagogue. Drawing by Georges Lukomski, 1934.

*Capistrano and his followers. The rest of the community was not expelled, however, and a Jewish loan banker returned to the city by 1468. Jewish moneylending was officially permitted again in 1483. In 1475, when rumors spread about a blood libel at *Trent, the Jews of Padua were set upon by the mob, despite appeals by the senate. Tempers rose again in 1491 when the populace was incited by *Bernardino de Feltre and other Franciscan monks. Influenced by the monks, the town council sought several times to expel the Jews. The opening of the first *Monte di Pietà in 1492 did not adversely affect the economic status of the loan bankers. In 1509, led by Maximilian I of Hapsburg, the Lansquenets descended upon Italy. Jewish property was sacked, first by Austrians and afterward by the returning Venetian soldiers. Two leading bankers, Vita Meshullam and Naphtali Herz Wertheim, were completely ruined and Jewish loans ran to a total of about 15,000 ducats. The development of the community's inner life continued during the 16th century and its legal status was strengthened despite the numerous ways in which Jews were publicly degraded. In 1547 the republic of Venice ordered Jewish banks closed so as not to compete with the local Monte di Pietà. The Jews successfully turned to commerce; there were Jewish proprietors in many of the town shops, especially those dealing in jewelry, cloth, and drapery.

Early in the 16th century the Jews were ordered to live in their own quarter, but they were not completely restricted to a ghetto and some of the wealthier families lived among Christians on the most elegant streets. The idea of establishing a ghetto similar to those in Rome or Venice was decided on between 1581 and 1584 but not actually put into effect until 1601. The district itself centered around a small square where the synagogue was situated. There were five gates to the ghetto, one of which was surmounted by a tablet with an inscription in Latin and Hebrew prohibiting both Jews and Christians from coming near the ghetto's gates at night. Until 1715 Jews were compelled to listen to malevolent anti-Jewish sermons in the churches. Giving in to various pressures, the town council allowed the burning of the Talmud and other Hebrew books in 1556. Nevertheless, Padua remained an important center for Hebrew studies by virtue of its rabbinical academies and the fact that Jews were drawn there from all over Europe to study in its university.

In 1616 the Jewish population of Padua numbered 665, chiefly engaged in the silk industry. The community suffered gravely from a plague, 421 of the 721 Jews dying in 1630–31. In 1688 the community of Padua helped ransom 600 Jews of Belgrade who had been captured and maltreated by the Imperial troops. Hostility toward the Jews grew in the 17th century during the wars waged by Venice against the Turks. Because of rumors that the Jews had given help to Buda (see *Budapest) during the siege by the Austrian and Venetian armies, on Aug. 20, 1684, the populace sacked the ghetto. Loss of life was narrowly prevented by the intervention of the army and the town authorities. As a result of the outbreak, the death penalty was established for causing riots. To commemorate the community's rescue, a day of thanksgiving (the *Purim di-Buda*) was celebrated each year. Another "Purim" was celebrated in 1795 to commemorate the putting out of a fire which might otherwise have destroyed the community. Disturbances occasionally arose because medical students sought to perform autopsies on dead Jews, despite the fact that the Jews paid up to 100 lire annually to the *studium patavinum* in order to prevent this. Incidents connected with this problem occurred in the 16th and 17th centuries until a fixed itinerary for Jewish funerals was worked out by the authorities.

When the French troops entered Padua on April 29, 1797, the Jews were temporarily emancipated; in August the central government decreed that Jews were free to reside wherever they wished. The ghetto was renamed Via Libera ("Liberty Way") and its gates taken down. From 1805 to 1814 Padua was part of Napoleon's kingdom of Italy; R. Isaac Raphael b. Elisha *Finzi took part in the Paris *Sanhedrin convened by the emperor. However, when the Austrians entered Padua in January 1814, the populace attacked the Jews, who were considered friends of the French. Having to appear satisfied with the change of regime, the Jews celebrated the entrance of the Austrians in the German synagogue. After the Treaty of Vienna (in 1815), when Padua again came under Austrian rule, the Jews were allowed to enjoy practically all rights, except that of serving in public office. In 1840 the Jewish population of Padua numbered 910. Full emancipation was obtained only in 1866, when Padua once more became part of the kingdom of Italy. By 1881, the Jewish population had risen to 1,378; thereafter, however, the cultural and social life of the community deteriorated and by 1911 the number had decreased to 881. Because of discrimination affecting all Italian Jewry, the Jews of Padua either left for other Italian centers or emigrated to other countries, among them Ereẓ Israel; by 1938 their number had further declined to 586.

There were three synagogues in Padua. One of German rite, which was opened in 1525, served also as a *bet midrash* for the whole community from 1682. In the same year the Ashkenazi synagogue, or Scuola grande was inaugurated. In 1892 the Scuola adopted the Italian rite. In 1943 the building was severely damaged by a bomb, and in 1960 its huge Ark was taken to the Yad Eliyahu Synagogue in Tel-Aviv. The third synagogue, of Sephardi rite, built in 1617 on the initiative of the influential *Marini family, was closed down in 1892. In 1958 its ark was taken to Hechal Shelomo in Jerusalem. The synagogue of Italian rite, built in 1548 and completed later in the 16th century, closed down in 1892. It was reopened after World War II and in 1970 was the only synagogue in the city.

Figure 2. Renaissance laver at the "Italian" synagogue, Padua. Photo Gislon, Padua.

Community Life. Until the close of the 18th century the administrators of the Jewish community were chosen according to their country of origin; in 1577 there was a "general assembly" *(capitolo generale)*, a "directional council" *(capitolo ristretto)*, and three *parnassim* or *memunim*. Internal laws for all aspects of life, social or spiritual, were based on talmudic law until the French conquest. A statute was drawn up by the community in 1815 (revised in 1826 and recognized by Venice in 1828), requiring members to pay taxes proportionate to their incomes. The statute was modified again in 1832, 1841, and 1866, and finally thoroughly revised on the initiative of S. D. Luzzatto. The new regulations took effect from Jan. 27, 1894, and remained in use until replaced by a comprehensive law for all the Jewish communities in 1930. The community maintained relations with Ereẓ Israel, especially through emissaries sent to Jerusalem, Hebron, Safed, and Tiberias. In 1713 a philanthrophic society, the fraternity of Lomedei Torah ve-Shomerei Mitzvah was founded, whose members paid a relatively high admission fee and made a fixed annual contribution. In return, in case of illness members received medical and surgical assistance, plus a daily allowance for the duration of illness; expenses for funerals and burial were also defrayed by the fraternity. This fraternity was still in existence in 1970, side by side with the brotherhood Malbish Arumim, the "S. D. Luzzatto Cultural Circle," and branches of various Zionist movements.

Of particular importance in the Padua community was academic activity. Jews studied medicine simultaneously with Torah. From 1519 to 1619 about 80 Jews obtained degrees in medicine in Padua, and from 1619 to 1721, 149 Jews graduated as physicians. Numbers of Jews from Germany, Poland, and the Levant also came to study in Padua. Some pressure was exerted by Christian doctors and the ecclesiastical authorities, so that the senate prohibited Jewish doctors from practicing outside the ghetto, but this was not too strictly applied. Jewish medical students were allowed to wear the black beret of their colleagues, rather than the yellow one required of other Jews (see Jewish *Badge). Among those students who distinguished themselves particularly were Elijah b. Moses Abba *Delmedigo, physician and philosopher, and Abraham b. Meir de *Balmes of Lecce.

In the field of Hebrew studies, Padua was of particular importance in the second half of the 15th century, under the guidance of Judah *Minz, one of the major rabbinical authorities of that period. Judah was followed by his son, Aaron Minz, and by his brother-in-law, Meir *Katzenellenbogen, whose responsa constitute a vital source for the history of the Jews of that time. Other prominent figures in Padua were Meir b. Ezekiel ibn *Gabbai, Menahem Delmedigo, Johanan b. *Treves, Raphael b. Joshua Ẓarefati, Jacob b. Moses Levi, Benzion b. Raphael, and Judah b. Moses Fano (16th century); Isaac Ḥayyim Cantarini, Samuel de *Archivolti, Aryeh and Abraham Cattalani, Benedetto Luzzatto, Judah b. Samuel Cantarini, Samuel and Ḥayyim Moses *Cantarini, Solomon and Shabbetai b. Luzzatto, Judah b. Samuel Cantarini, Samuel and Ḥayyim Moses *Cantarini, Solomon and Shabbetai b. Isaac Marini, Aaron Romanin, Samuel David b. Jehiel *Ottolengo (17th century); Moses Ḥayyim Luzzatto, Michael Terni, Abraham Shalom, Solomon Nizza, Jacob Raphael Ezekiel *Forti, Solomon Eliezer Ghirondi and Benzion Ghirondi (18th century); Isaac Raphael b. Elisha *Finzi, Israel Conian, Mordecai Samuel b. Benzion Aryeh *Ghirondi, Ephraim Raphael Ghirondi, Leone Osimo, Graziadio Viterbi, Giuseppe *Basevi, Eudi Lolli, Alessandro Zammatto, Filosseno Luzzatto, Giuseppe *Almanzi, Eugenia Gentilomo, Gabriele Trieste, Marco Osimo (19th century); and Gustavo Castelbolognesi, Paolo Nissim, and Dante *Lattes (20th century). Padua had one last touch of splendor in the 19th century with the inauguration of the *Istituto Superiore Rabbinico*, later known as the *Collegio Rabbinico Italiano, the first rabbinical seminary in Europe to combine secular and traditional Jewish study. The institute was initiated by Isacco Samuel *Reggio, and Lelip *Della Torre and S. D. *Luzzatto were among the rectors. The institute itself (transferred to Rome in 1870) exerted a considerable influence on the spiritual life of Italian Jews. From 1962 to 1965 Dante Lattes edited the journal *Rassegna Mensile di Israel* in Padua. Some Hebrew works were printed in Padua.

Printing. In 1563 Meir b. Ezekiel b. Gabbai's *Derekh Emunah* was printed by Lorenzo Pasquato of Padua, with Samuel Boehm serving as proofreader. This was followed by Shem Tov b. Shem Tov's *Derashot ha-Torah* in 1567. A conference of Italian communities convened at Padua in 1585 to consider a new approach to Pope Sixtus V on the question of printing the Talmud, then available only in a censored and emasculated edition. In 1622 Hebrew printing was continued in Padua by Gaspare (later Giulio) Crivellari, who printed Jacob Heilprin's *Naḥalat Ya'akov*, followed in the same year by the printing of *Kinot Eikhah*, printed by Abraham Catalono, and Leon de Modena's Hebrew-Italian dictionary, *Galut Yehudah* (1640–42). In the 19th century Antonio Bianchi printed S. D. Luzzatto's *Isziah* (1885) and other works, between 1834 and 1879. Francesco Sacchetto printed Luzzatto's Pentateuch commentary in 1872.

Modern Period. In 1931 the community of Padua had a Jewish population of 586. In 1941 the interior of the Scuolo grande was desecrated by Fascist bands. Between 1943 and 1945 more than 85 Jews, among whom was Rabbi Eugenio Cohen Sacerdoti, were sent to extermination camps. After the war (1948) there were 269 Jews in Padua and their number had declined to 220 by 1970.

Bibliography: A. Ciscato, *Gli Ebrei in Padua* (1801); Milano, Bibliotheca, index s.v. *Padova;* Milano, Italia, index; G. Gabrieli, *Italia Judaica* (1924), index; Roth, Italy, index; C. Roth, *Venice* (1930), index; U. Cassuto, *Gli Ebrei a Firenze* (1918), index; J. Pinkerfeld, *Battei Keneset be-Italyah* (1954), index; D. Carpi, *Ha-Yehudim be-Padova bi-Tekufat ha-Renaissance* (unpublished doctoral dissertation, Hebrew, Jerusalem, 1967), Fr. summary; idem, in: RMI, 28 (1962), 47–60; 32 (1966), nos. 9–10, 1–306; P. C. I. Zorattini, *ibid.*, 34 (1968), 582–91; A. Modena and E. Morpurgo, *Medici e Chirurgi Ebrei . . . nell'Università di Padova . . .* (1967); C. Roth, *Il Purim di Buda* (1934); U. Nahon, *Aronot Kodesh . . .* (1970); Z. Shazar, *Ha-Tikvah li-Shenat HaTaK* (1970); D. W. Amram, *Makers of Hebrew Books in Italy* (1909), index; Ḥ. D. Friedberg, *Toledot ha-Defus ha-Ivri be-Italyah* (1956²), 83f.

[A.M.R.]

PADWAY, JOSEPH ARTHUR (1891–1947), U.S. labor lawyer and politician. Padway, who was born in Leeds, England, went to Milwaukee in 1905. Admitted to the Wisconsin bar in 1912, he was appointed legal counsel for the Wisconsin State Federation of Labor three years later. He was elected state senator on the Socialist ticket and served in the 1925 session of the legislature. Padway was twice appointed to the Milwaukee civil court bench (1924, 1926). After 1927 he was associated with the Progressive Republicans in Wisconsin. Padway played a major role in shaping Wisconsin labor legislation between 1915 and 1935. Upon his appointment as the first general counsel of the American Federation of Labor, he moved to Washington where he served until his death. In this capacity, he successfully defended the constitutionality of the National Labor Relations (Wagner) Act before the United States Supreme Court.

Bibliography: L. J. Swichkow and L. P. Gartner, *The History of the Jews of Milwaukee* (1963), 163, 253–4. [L.J.Sw.]

PAGEL, JULIUS LEOPOLD (1851–1912), German physician and medical historian. Pagel was born in Pomerania, and practiced medicine in Berlin and was appointed professor of history of medicine at the University of Berlin. He wrote over 100 books and articles dealing mainly with medical history. These included many medical biographies taken from unpublished manuscripts and a full description of methods of therapy used in the 19th century. He edited *Biographisches Lexikon hervorragender Aerzte des 19. Jahrhunderts* (1901) and coedited with Max Neuburger the *Handbuch der Geschichte der Medizin* (1902–05).

His youngest son, WALTER PAGEL (1898–), pursued two careers—he was a pathologist and a famous historian of science. Born in Berlin he was lecturer in pathology and medical history at Heidelberg (1928–33). With the advent of Hitler he left for England where he became pathologist, first at the Central Middlesex County Hospital, London, and from the beginning of World War II, at Clare Hall Hospital, Hertfordshire.

He published books and articles in the fields of pathology, bacteriology, tuberculosis, and allergic phenomena. On medical history, his publications include: *Jo. Bapt. van Helmont; Einfuehrung in die philosophische Medizin des Barock* (1930); *The Religious and Philosophical Aspects of Van Helmont's Science and Medicine* (1944); and *William Harvey, Some Neglected Aspects of Medical History* (1944).

Bibliography: S. R. Kagan, *Jewish Medicine* (1952), 242–3, 556.

[S.M.]

°**PAGNINI, SANTES (Xanthus Pagninus;** 1470–1536), Italian Hebraist and Bible scholar. Born in Lucca, Pagnini entered the Dominican order in 1487 and, under the direction of Savonarola, later studied Hebrew, his teacher being the Spanish convert Clement Abraham. Pagnini became one of the foremost Hebraists of the age and, at the request of Pope Leo X, taught in Rome for many years before settling in Lyons, where from 1524 until death he combated French heterodoxy. His greatest achievement was his *Utriusque instrumenti nova translatio* (Lyons, 1528), of which the Old Testament portion was the first since Jerome to be based directly on the original Hebrew. This Bible, the prefaces to which include two letters from Giovanni *Pico della Mirandola, reputedly took 25 years to prepare; and its notation of the biblical text according to chapter and verse has been retained until the present day. Pagnini's Latin translation inspired the Italian Bible of the Florentine reformer Antonio Brucioli (Venice, 1532) and the later Italian Protestant Bible of Geneva (1562).

Other works by Pagnini were *Institutionum hebraicarum abbreviatio* (Lyons, 1528; Paris, 1556); the authoritative and pioneering *Thesaurus linguae sanctae sive Lexicon hebraicum* (Lyons, 1529); and *Isagogae ad sacras literas, liber unicus. Ejusdem isagogae ad mysticos Sacrae Scripturae sensus, libri decem et octo* (Lyons, 1536). He also wrote a commentary on the Psalms. Pagnini's Bible and Hebrew grammar were widely consulted in the 16th century.

Bibliography: C. Roth, *Jews in the Renaissance* (1959), 146f.; F. Secret, *Les Kabbalistes chrétiens de la Renaissance* (1964), index; *New Catholic Encyclopedia*, 10 (1967), 862. [G.E.S.]

PAIVA, JACQUES (d. 1687), London diamond merchant originally from Holland, one of the earliest Jewish settlers in Fort St. George (*Madras). He was authorized by the East India Company in London to travel to Madras in 1684, taking with him "one man-servant, one Christian maid, and one Jewish servant to attend on his wife in his voyage to the port, he paying the charge of their transportation." During his stay in Madras, Paiva was one of the representatives of the "Hebrew" merchants. While on a trip to the diamond mines in Golconda in 1687, he fell dangerously ill and was taken back to Fort St. George, where he died. He was buried in the cemetery at the Memorial Hall in Peddenaipetam, which apparently had been acquired with Paiva's help. His will throws remarkable light on the gem trade between England and India in the 17th century. His widow subsequently lived with Elihu Yale, the governor of Madras after whom Yale University is named.

Bibliography: Fischel, in: *Journal of the Economic and Social History of the Orient*, 3 (1960), 78–107, 175–95; C. Roth, *Anglo-Jewish Letters* (1938), 78–81; H. D. Love, *Vestiges of Old Madras*, 4 vols. (1913).

[W.J.F.]

PAKISTAN, Islamic republic, S. Asia, established in 1947 after the partition of India. At the beginning of the 20th century, the largest city, Karachi (now in West Pakistan), had about 2,500 Jews engaged as tradesmen, artisans, and civil servants. Their mother tongue was Marathi, indicating their *Bene Israel origin. In 1893 the Jews of Karachi built the Magen Shalom Synagogue (D. S. Sassoon, *Ohel Dawid*, 2 (1932), 576), and in 1936 one of the leaders of the Jewish community, Abraham Reuben, became the first Jewish councillor on the city corporation. The Jews lived primarily in Karachi, but there was a small community served by two synagogues in Peshawar in the northwest frontier province. The following Jewish organizations existed at that time: the Young Men's Jewish Association, founded in 1903, whose aim was to encourage sports as well as religious and social activities of the Bene Israel in Karachi; the Karachi Bene Israel Relief Fund, established to support poor Jews in Karachi; the Karachi Jewish syndicate, formed in 1918, to provide homes to poor Jews at reasonable rents.

The foundation of an Islamic state immediately prior to

Entrance to the Magen Shalom Synagogue, Karachi, West Pakistan, built in 1893. Courtesy Union of American Hebrew Congregations, New York.

the establishment of the State of Israel created a rising feeling of insecurity within the Jewish community; this anxiety was later exacerbated by the disturbances and demonstrations directed against the Jews during the Arab-Israel wars in 1948, 1956, and 1967. A large number of Jews moved from Pakistan to India, which became for some the stepping stone to a further migration to Israel and the United Kingdom. The small community in Peshawar ceased to exist, and the synagogues were closed. By 1968 the total number of Jews in Pakistan had decreased to 250, almost all of whom were concentrated in Karachi, where there was one synagogue, a welfare organization, and a recreational organization. Out of Muslim solidarity with the Arab states Pakistan did not establish any ties with Israel and frequently joined in anti-Israel moves in the United Nations and the boycott initiated by the Arab states.

Bibliography: World Jewish Congress, Institute of Jewish Affairs, *Jewish Communities of the World* (1971), 72.

[W.J.F./P.Go./E. Eli.]

PAKS, town in W. central Hungary. Jews first settled there in 1720, and in 1770 numbered 64. Initially they were mainly peddlers and small traders, who paid only a small protection tax to the estate owners. In 1844 a meeting of rabbis was held in Paks which tried unsuccessfully to effect a compromise between the Orthodox and the adherents of Reform. Finally there was a split, and although the community remained Orthodox, a separate status quo ante congregation was established. In 1788, on instructions from Emperor *Joseph II, a Jewish school with German as the language of instruction was founded, changed to Hungarian by the community in 1870. The school was closed down in 1919. The Jewish population numbered 1,129 in 1869, 1,011 in 1900, 891 in 1920, 782 in 1930, and 730 in 1941.

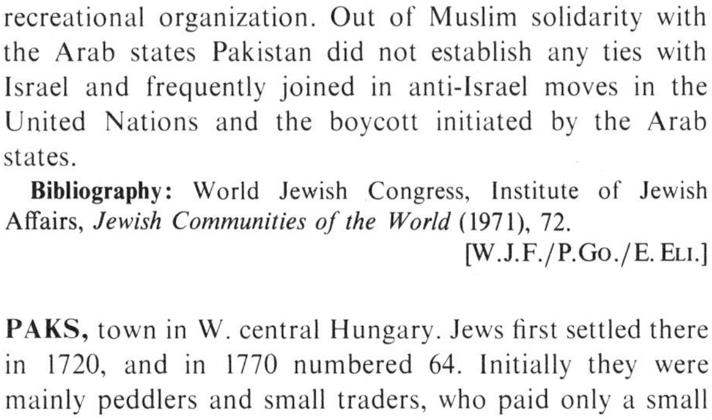

The synagogue of Paks, Hungary. Courtesy C.A.H.J.P., Jerusalem.

Rabbis of the community included Solomon Beer (Solomon Lazar; appointed 1746), Jehiel Ze'ev (1780), Isaac Krishaber (1795), Ezekiel *Banet (1825), and Paul (Feiwel) Horovitz (1844).

After the German occupation (March 19, 1944), about 730 members of the community were deported to *Auschwitz. There were 180 Jews living in Paks in 1946.

Bibliography: *Magyar Zsidó Szemle* (1898), 378ff; (1899), 142ff.

[B.Y.]

PALACHE (Pallache, Palacio, de Palatio, al-Palas, Pallas, Palaggi, Balyash, etc.), family whose name first occurs in Spain as Palyāj. The historian Ibn Daud relates (in his *Sefer ha-Qabbalah,* ed. by G. D. Cohen (1967), 66, no. 64 Eng. sect.), "R. Moses the Rabbi (one of the *Four Captives) allied himself by marriage with the Ibn Falija (Palyāj) family, which was the greatest of the families of the community of Córdoba, and took from them a wife for his son R. *Ḥanokh." Moses al-Palas (b.c. 1535), an outstanding rabbi and orator, was born in Marrakesh. He later lived in Tetuán, where his sermons attracted large audiences, including many former Marranos. When he returned to Marrakesh, he delivered a lengthy discourse on the ethics of the Jewish religion—at the request and in the presence of the Spanish ambassador. This success encouraged him to undertake a journey through the countries inhabited by the descendants of the victims of the Spanish Expulsion in order to preach to them. He visited the Balkans, Turkey, and Palestine and lived in Salonika for a time. He appears to have finally settled in Venice, where he published *Va-Yakhel Moshe* (1597) and *Ho'il Moshe* (1597), which includes homilies, eulogies, and sermons, as well as a biography of the author. R. Isaac Palache was a distinguished rabbi in Fez in about 1560. He had two sons, Samuel Palache (d. 1616) and Joseph (see below). They and their children held an important place in the economic life of that period and from the beginning of the 17th century became active at the courts of Europe, particularly the Netherlands which maintained relations with Morocco. In Madrid, the Inquisition probably suspected them of inciting the Marranos to leave the country and return to Judaism. In order to escape prosecution, they took asylum in the house of the French ambassador, and offered their services to King Henry IV; they left Spain a short while later. According to some historians, Samuel was the first Jew to settle in the Netherlands as a declared Jew. He was responsible for obtaining the authorization for his coreligionists to settle. He gathered the first *minyan* in Amsterdam at his home for Day of Atonement prayers in 1596. Palache is also said to have built the first synagogue in that country. According to documents in the Netherlands archives, the right to settle in the country was refused to him, and during the same year, 1608, he was appointed ambassador to The Hague by the Moroccan sultan Mulay Zidan. In 1610 he successfully negotiated the first treaty of alliance between a Christian state (the Netherlands), and a Muslim state (Morocco). In 1614 he personally assumed the command of a small Moroccan fleet which seized some ships belonging to the king of Spain, with whom Morocco was at war. The Spanish ambassador, who was very influential in London, had him arrested when he was in England. He accused him of piracy; reverberations of his trial were widespread. Once acquitted, he returned to the Netherlands. When he died in the Hague, Palache was given an imposing funeral attended by Prince Maurice of Nassau. Samuel Palache's two sons, Isaac and Jacob-Carlos, also engaged in diplomatic work. The former was entrusted with Dutch interests in Morocco from 1624, and the latter represented the sultan in Copenhagen. Samuel's brother, Joseph Palache (d. after

1638), succeeded him in his diplomatic position. Joseph Palache's five sons held very important offices. One of them, Isaac Palache (d. 1647) was known as "the lame." His variegated career included a mission to the Turkish sultan (1614–1), important negotiations in Danzig (1618–19), a professorship in Hebrew at the University of Leiden, and missions to Morocco and Algiers in 1624 on behalf of the Dutch. In 1639 he was called upon to redeem the Christian captives who were held by the famous marabout of Tazerwalt. He became involved in a violent conflict with his brothers over succession rights and converted to Christianity. Another son, Moses Palache (d. after 1650), was secretary to his uncle Samuel at the French court, interpreter and secretary to the sultan of Morocco, and the de facto—but not official—foreign minister of four successive Moroccan sovereigns; his name was cited by Manasseh Ben Israel to Oliver Cromwell as an example of the loyalty of the Jews when he sought authorization for them to settle in England. Joshua Palache (d. after 1650) and his son Samuel Palache were merchants of international status and tax farmers of the leading Moroccan port, Safi. David Palache (d. 1649), another of Joseph's sons, was a diplomat. Entrusted with a mission to Louis XIII of France, various accusations were brought against him. His innocence was finally proven and he reassumed his position as Moroccan ambassador to the Netherlands. Abraham Palache (d. after 1630) was a financier in Morocco and diplomat. The descendants of the main branch of the Palache family lived in Amsterdam, where Isaac Palache was elected chief rabbi in 1900. His son Judah Lion *Palache was professor of Semitic languages at the University of Amsterdam and died in an extermination camp. Another branch lived in Izmir, where Ḥayyim *Palache and his son Abraham Palache were noted rabbis in the 19th century.

Bibliography: SIHM, ser. 1., index vol. s.v. *Pallache;* H. I. Bloom, *The Economic Activities of the Jews in Amsterdam* (1937, repr. 1969), 75–82; D. Corcos, in: *Zion*, 25 (1960), 122–33; J. Caillé, in: *Hespéris-Tamuda*, 4 (1963), 5–67; Hirschberg, Afrikah, 2 (1965), 228–42.

[D.Co./H.Z.H.]

PALACHE (Palaggi), ḤAYYIM (also called by the acronym **Ḥabif;** 1788–1869), rabbi and *ḥakham bashi.* Born in Izmir (Smyrna), Palache, a member of the distinguished *Palache family, was the grandson on his mother's side of Joseph Raphael *Ḥazzan (author of *Ḥikrei Lev*) and was a disciple of Joseph Gatenio (author of *Beit Yiẓḥak*). He became *av bet din* in 1837. In 1847 he was appointed as *rav sheni* ("second rabbi") with the title *dayyan,* authorized to render judgement alone, and later was awarded the rabbinical title *marbiẓ Torah* (see Abraham Palache, *Ḥelkam ba-Ḥayyim,* 1874). His position as *marbiẓ Torah* is attested by Ḥayyim Palache himself: "I, the *marbiẓ Torah* of this place, the town of Izmir . . . and its environs" (*Male Ḥayyim; Ha-Takkanot,* 42, 74), i.e., the neighboring towns of Izmir as well, such as Tiriya, Manissa, Bergama. In 1855 he was appointed as *rav kolel* ("chief of the rabbis"; *Ḥayyim ba-Yad* (1873), nos. 63, 74, 75). In 1865, at the age of 77, he was appointed *ḥakham bashi* of *Izmir. Because of Palache's advanced age, some of his colleagues took charge of the community and administered it according to their will. At the end of November 1865 the Jews of Izmir elected an administrative committee composed of a president and nine members. At their first meeting the members of the committee invited Palache to appear alone, without his advisers and followers, and compelled him to sign a declaration stating that he would not sign any document without prior authorization by the majority of the members of the committee. Palache signed, but the administrative committee did not function for a long time. At that time the administrators of the community bought the monopoly of the *gabella* (tax) for the sale of wine, alcohol, and salt for the ridiculously low price of 10,000–12,000 francs. When the people complained, they decided to pay 44,000 francs for the monopoly, but when the community demanded an accounting of its financial situation, the officials refused to comply. In order to put an end to this situation, Palache repealed this tax. The entire group of Gabelleros, as well as those interested in leasing monopolies, swore to remove the aged rabbi. Following the argument which broke out in the community, the government ordered the *ḥakham bashi* of Istanbul (Constantinople), Yakir Gueron, to send someone to Izmir to restore order. In December 1866 R. Samuel Danon, secretary of Gueron, was sent. He convinced Gueron that the only solution to these complicated intrigues was to remove Palache and that he himself should be appointed in the former's place. Gueron responded affirmatively to the report of his secretary, which was only signed by 60 of Izmir's inhabitants. He requested that the government remove Palache, and the vizier's order of removal was sent to Izmir. Most of the Jewish inhabitants of Izmir, however, so strongly opposed the order that the pasha of Izmir had to consult a higher authority. According to a new order, the pasha was supposed to delay the execution of the vizier's first order, to remove Palache only temporarily, and to appoint Danon in his place. This began a series of requests—for and against Palache—to Gueron. The supporters of Palache eventually succeeded in October 1867 in having him returned to his rabbinic post and recognized as the chief rabbi of the Izmir community. Palache did not exploit his victory for revenge, and he dealt mercifully with the Gabelleros, who asked for his pardon. One of the conditions of his reelection was that immediately on assuming the post, administrative procedures would be instituted *(Nizamnamé du Hakham-Hané).* However, Palache's death prevented his fulfilling his promise.

Palache was a prolific writer. Many of his manuscripts were burned and a great number were not published, but 26 works were printed, among them: *Darkhei Ḥayyim* (Izmir, 1821), on *Pirkei Avot; Lev Ḥayyim* (vol. 1, Salonika, 1823; vols. 2–3, Izmir, 1874–90), responsa, interpretations, and comments on the Shulḥan Arukh; *Nishmat Kol Ḥai* (2 vols., Salonika, 1832–37), responsa; *Ẓedakah Ḥayyim* (Izmir, 1838); *Ḥikekei Lev* (2 vols., Salonika, 1840–53), homilies and eulogies; *Nefesh Ḥayyim* (1842); *Torah ve-Ḥayyim* (1846); *Kaf ha-Ḥayyim* (1859); *Mo'ed le-Khol Ḥai* (1861); *Ḥayyim ve-Shalom* (2 vols., 1857–72); *Sefer Ḥayyim* (1863); and *Ginzei Ḥayyim* (1871).

Abraham Palache (1809–1899), son of Ḥayyim, was also a distinguished rabbinical scholar. Four months after Ḥayyim Palache's death the *ḥakham bashi* of Istanbul appointed Joseph Ḥakim, chief rabbi of Manissa, as *ḥakham bashi* of Izmir. This was done in order to satisfy the demands of the older generation, but Ḥakim was elected by only a small minority. Three-quarters of the Jews of Izmir opposed him, and their objections were intensified by his opposition to the teaching of languages in Jewish schools. Many people in Izmir then approached the local ruler, Ishmael Pasha, to appoint Abraham Palache to the post of *ḥakham bashi,* but their request was rejected. Several French, English, and Italian Jews who were in Izmir then turned to their local consuls, asking that a request, signed by 15,000 Izmir Jews, be sent to the sultan demanding, among other things, the appointment of Palache as *ḥakham bashi.* The Italian consul took the necessary steps with his ambassador in Istanbul, as well as with Ishmael Pasha, and succeeded in having the request fulfilled. In August 1869, according to a supreme order, Joseph Ḥakim was removed and the following year, 1870, Palache was appointed as *ḥakham bashi* of the Izmir community and served in this post for almost 30 years.

Palache wrote numerous works in Hebrew and one in Ladino: *Shama Avraham* (Salonika, 1850), responsa; *Berakh et Avraham* (Salonika, 1857), homilies; *Shemo-Avraham* (2 vols., 1878–96), ethics and homilies; *Va-Yikra Avraham* (1884); *Va-Yashkem Avraham* (1885), studies in Psalms; *Va-Ya'an Avraham* (1886), responsa; *Avraham Anokhi,* studies on the Torah (1889); *Avraham Ezkor* and *Yemaher Avraham* (1889); *Ve-Avraham Zaken* (1899), homilies; and in Ladino, *Ve-Hokhi'aḥ Avraham* (2 vols., 1853–62).

Bibliography: M. D. Gaon, *Yehudei ha-Mizraḥ be-Ereẓ Yisrael,* 2 (1938), 560f., I. I. Ḥasida, *Rabbi Ḥayyim Palaggi u-Sefarav* (1968); Y. Y. Kohen, in: *Yad la-Koré,* 9 (1968), 66–68. [Y.GEL.]

PALACHE, JUDAH LION (1886–1944), orientalist and teacher. Palache was born in Amsterdam, a son of Isaac Palache, the *ḥakham* of the Spanish-Portuguese congregation. He studied at the Ets-Ḥayyim rabbinical seminary and at Amsterdam and Leyden universities and was a student of Snouck-Hurgronje. From 1925 he was professor of Bible and Semitic languages at the University of Amsterdam. Though no longer Orthodox, he served as *parnas* of the Spanish-Portuguese congregation and was active in some of

Judah L. Palache, Dutch orientalist.

its institutions. During World War II Palache was deported to Theresienstadt and later sent to an extermination camp. A great part of a major work he was compiling on Hebrew semantics was lost during the war.

Palache's scholarly interests lay in Judaism and Islam as well as in comparative Semitic philology. Among Palache's published works are *Het Heiligdom in de voorstelling der semietische volken* (1920); *Inleiding in de Talmoed,* an introduction to the Talmud (Dutch, 1922, 1954²), *Introduction to the Talmud,* 1934); *De Hebreeuwsche literatuur*... (with A. S. Levisson and S. Pinkhof, 1935); *The ʿEbed-Jahveh enigma in Pseudo-Isaiah* (1934); and posthumously: *Sinai en Paran,* ed., with an introduction by M. Reisel (1959), and *Semantic Notes on the Hebrew Lexicon* (translated from Dutch and ed. by R. J. Z. Werblowsky, 1959).

Bibliography: M. Reisel, in: J. L. Palache, *Sinai en Paran* (1959), 9–12; R. J. Z. Werblowsky, in: J. L. Palache, *Semantic Notes on the Hebrew Lexicon* (1959), 7–9 (introd.). [ED.]

PALÁGYI, LAJOS (1866–1933), Hungarian poet. Palágyi, who was born at Óbecse, was a brother of the philosopher Menyhért *Palágyi. Palágyi had a hard struggle against poverty, and in order to be able to devote himself to the writing of poetry earned his living as an instructor at teachers' seminaries and later as a journalist. He was one of the writers who engaged in the struggle which resulted in 1895 in the official recognition of the Jewish religion in Hungary. Palágyi belonged to the group of Hungarian philosophical poets influenced by the German philosopher Schopenhauer. His poems won several prizes, but never enjoyed wide popularity. Several of them deal with Jewish themes, including *Bibliai emlékek* ("Biblical Reminiscences," 1896). He also published *Magányos úton* ("On the Lonely Road," 1893); *Költemények* ("Poems," 1907); the dramatic *A rabszolgák* ("Slaves," 1899); and the epic *Az anyaföld* ("Mother Earth," 1921). He translated Goethe's *Faust* into Hungarian (1909). Palágyi was at first regarded as a socialist poet but he never acutally joined the socialist

Lajos Palágyi, Hungarian poet. Jerusalem, J.N.U.L., Schwadron Collection.

movement since, in his own words, "the sufferings of humanity cannot be cured by institutions. Hearts and brains must be renewed." He turned his back on society and his opposition to socialism grew progressively stronger. Nevertheless in 1920, following the Hungarian revolution, he was expelled from the distinguished Petőfi literary society and deprived of his pension. Eleven years later he published a pamphlet in self-justification, telling the story of his persecution.

Bibliography: *Magyar Zsidó Lexikon* (1929), 678–9; *Magyar Irodalmi Lexikon,* 2(1965), 420–1; J. Sporer, *Palágyi Lajos élete és költészete* (1937). [B.Y.]

PALÁGYI, MENYHÉRT (Melchior; 1859–1924), philosopher; brother of the poet Lajos *Palágyi, Palágyi taught at the University of Kolozsvár (Cluj). When Kolozsvár was seized by Rumania in 1919 he moved to Germany.

His *Neue Theorie des Raumes und der Zeit* (1901) anticipated Einstein and Minkowski. His works on logic (1902 and 1903) against psychologism were criticized by Husserl. His *Kant und Bolzano* (1902) revived interest in Bolzano. Palágyi also worked in epistemology, aesthetics, and natural philosophy (where he worked out a system of world mechanics). His later work appears in *Ausgewaehlte Werke,* 3 vols. (1924–25).

Bibliography: Kövesi, in: *Encyclopedia of Philosophy,* 6 (1967), 18–19; Boyce Gibson, in: *Journal of Philosophical Studies,* 3 (1928), 15–28. [R.H.P.]

PALANGA (Ger. **Polangen**), resort town on the Baltic Sea in Lithuanian S.S.R. Jews were granted privileges of town dwellers in Palanga by the Polish king Sigismund III (1587–1632), and were permitted to own land and to engage in crafts and commerce. These privileges were confirmed by subsequent rulers in 1639 and 1742. There were 398 Jews living in Palanga and the vicinity in 1765. At the beginning of the 1820s, Palanga was included in the Russian province of *Courland. The community numbered 729 in 1850, 925 in 1897 (43% of the total population), 455 in 1923, and approximately 700 in 1939. The production of decorative objects and jewelry made from amber found on the seashore, for which Palanga is famous, was formerly a Jewish industry. Many Jews also earned their livelihood by providing various services for summer vacationers. Soon after the outbreak of the German-Soviet war on June 22, 1941, Palanga was occupied by the Germans and all the Jews were murdered, the men at once, and the women and children a month later.

Bibliography: Mark, in: *Lite,* 1 (1951), 1454–74; *Yahadut Lita,* 1 (1959), 45, 54; Gar, in: *Algemeine Entsiklopedie,* 6 (1963), 366, 367, 374. [JO.GA.]

PALATINATE (Ger. **Pfalz**), region in W. Germany, also known as Western or Rhenish Palatinate. In the Middle Ages it was the domain of the counts and electors of the Palatinate who were closely connected with the ruling house of the duchy of Bavaria. The first mention of Jews in the region is as residents of *Speyer in 1084. Communities existed in *Weinheim, *Kaiserslautern, *Heidelberg, and *Landau, all of which suffered during the *Black Death (1348) persecutions. To the indignation of the populace, Elector Rupert I (1329–90) permitted refugees from the massacres perpetrated in *Worms and Speyer to settle in Heidelberg and other nearby localities. Heidelberg eventually emerged as the leading Jewish community and in 1369 authorities granted it permission to enlarge its cemetery. The nephew of Rupert I, Rupert II (1390–98), and his son Rupert III (1398–1410), king of Germany and Holy Roman Emperor (1400), expelled Jews from the Palatinate. In the course of the 14th and 15th centuries, however, Jews expelled from German cities managed to return and to settle in the villages of the Palatinate. An official inquiry of 1550 revealed the presence of 155 Jewish heads of families. These constituted a **Landjudenschaft* which convened fairly regularly to discuss the problem of tax distribution (which in 1554 was fixed at 1,000 florins annually for a period of six years). Charles Louis (1632–80) introduced taxes on circumcision, burial, and marriage. He also granted the Portuguese and Ashkenazi communities in *Mannheim extraordinary privileges (1660). Mannheim rapidly became the largest Jewish community in the Palatinate, with 63 families in 1697, while Heidelberg had only eight. The increasing Jewish population of the Palatinate, which overflowed into other German states where there were fewer Jews, resulted in the use by Jews of such names as Landau, Weinheim, Mannheim, and Oppenheim which had their origin in Palatinate localities. The leading Austrian families of *Court Jews, the *Wertheimers and *Oppenheimers, were originally from the Palatinate, as was the *Seligmann-Eichthal family. The electors of the Palatinate employed many Court Jews, purveyors, and military *contractors. One of them, Lemle Moses Reinganum, established a 100,000 florin endowment for Talmud study, the renowned Mannheim *Klaus* (1706), which remained in existence for more than two centuries.

The number of Jews in the Palatinate continued to increase despite a temporary setback caused by the devastations of the wars of conquest (1688–89) of Louis XIV. In 1722 there were 535 registered Jewish families in the Palatinate, 160 of them in Mannheim. The first **Landrabbiner* served in 1706 and the third, David Ullmann (Ulmo), a member of an influential family, was recognized as *Landrabbiner* in 1728 despite his youth. Although the *Landjudenschaft* had opposed his nomination, ignored his authority, and demanded that he be examined by three eminent rabbis, Ullmann nevertheless served with official support until 1762. His successor, Naphtali Hirsch *Katzenellenbogen (d. 1800), was also *Oberrabbiner* (chief rabbi) of the Mannheim *Klaus*. Elector Charles Theodore (1742–99) attempted to restrict the Jewish population of the Palatinate to 300 after a 1743 inquiry revealed the presence of 488 Jewish families and protracted negotiations over the payment of the 45,000 florins tax burden were conducted with the *Landjudenschaft*. All "honorable" professions, that of butcher in particular, were declared open to Jews; and Jews were allowed to open cemeteries. The majority of Palatinate Jews were livestock merchants, peddlers, and dealers in wine, hops, tobacco, and other agricultural products. By 1775 the number of Jewish families was 823; one-fourth of them lived in Mannheim.

Under French rule (1792–1814) the Jews enjoyed equality, but lost it on the return to Bavaria. In 1818 *Napoleon's "Infamous Decree" (1808) was extended indefinitely in the Palatinate. The struggle for Jewish emancipation was led by Elias Gruenebaum (b. 1807), rabbi of Landau (1836–93), an energetic advocate of Reform Judaism in both liturgy and education. Emancipation was granted only in 1848 and 1851. Anti-Jewish disturbances broke out in the villages of the Palatinate in 1819 (see *Hep! Hep!), the early 1830s, and in 1849.

The Jewish population of Rheinbayern (Rhenish Bavaria), which numbered some 2,000 families in 1821, grew to 13,526 persons in 1833 and to 15,412 in 1840 (2.65% of the total population), after which it began to decline (to 10,108 in 1900 and to 6,487 in 1933). In 1840 the population was distributed among 180 localities, 40 of which had at least 100 Jews. Ingenheim, one of the largest, had 551 Jews (one-third of the total population). By October 1937 4,300 Jews remained in 67 localities, only nine of which contained more than 100 persons. Those communities which grew after World War I were Ludwigshafen (1,400 in 1931) and Pirmasens (800 in 1931), both of which were themselves part of developing industrial cities. After 1933 the Jews of the primarily rural communities suffered from a relentless campaign to exclude them from the trade in livestock, wine, tobacco, leather, hops, etc., all of which were traditional Jewish occupations. During the *Kristallnacht* (November 1938) many synagogues of the Palatinate were burned down and hundreds of male Jews were arrested. Jews were also evicted from the villages to the cities and subsequently deported during World War II. In 1970 668 Jews lived in the federal state of Rheinland-Pfalz (300 in Neustadt).

Bibliography: H. Arnold, *Von den Juden in der Pfalz* (1967); H. Schnee, *Die Hoffinanz und der moderne Staat*, 4 (1963), 178–86; M. Stern, *Koenig Ruprecht von der Pfalz in seinen Beziehungen zu den Juden* (1898); L. Loewenstein, *Geschichte der Juden in der Kurpfalz* (1895); R. Herz, *Die Juden in der Pfalz* (1937); B. Rosenthal, in: MGWJ, 79 (1935), 443–50.

[H.W.]

"Painting of a girl" by Israel Paldi, 1967. Photo J. Agor, Bat Yam.

PALDI (Feldman), ISRAEL (1892–), Israel painter. Paldi was born at Berdyansk, Russia, and emigrated to Palestine in 1909. He spent the years 1910–20 in Europe. On his return to Palestine he exhibited in David's Tower in Jerusalem (1923) and was a leader of the "Modern Artists" in Tel Aviv (1927).

Paldi's work is extremely individual in style. In the 1920s he was an expressionist, and his work was full of stormy color and movement. Later it became simple, restrained, and even naive under the influence of the School of *Paris. In 1942 Paldi did pioneer work in making colored abstract plaster reliefs, using unusual materials such as sand, and in the late 1950s his painting became almost monochrome. Thereafter his work was characterized by an effort to integrate color and form, often by decorative methods.

Bibliography: Roth, Art, 907–8; H. Gamzo, *Painting and Sculpture in Israel* (1958), 41, plate 43. [Y.Fi.]

PALENCIA, city in N. central Spain in the province of Palencia, Castile. Palencia had an important Jewish community, which is thought to have started as early as the 11th century. However, the earliest available information on Jewish settlement in Palencia dates from 1175, when Alfonso VIII delivered 40 Jews to the bishop of the town and placed them under his jurisdiction (this agreement was reratified in 1351). In 1192 Alfonso VIII exempted all Jews and Moors in the town from the payment of royal taxes, as they were already paying their share of the town's revenues. During the 13th century the population remained at 40 families and the community continued to prosper, as did many of the communities in Castile. In 1295 the Jews participated in the revolt against the king and the destruction of the bishop's palace. At the beginning of the 14th century *Asher b. Jehiel, giving his verdict (Responsa 21, § 8) concerning the *eruv* arrangements introduced by R. Jacob b. R. Moses Debalincia (Palencia), decreed that the latter was to retract his instructions because he had misled the public. R. Asher demanded that R. Jacob be considered a "rebellious scholar" and banned from the Jewish community.

The community of Palencia suffered during the civil war between Pedro of Castile and Henry of Trastamara: according to the testimony of R. Samuel Ẓarẓa in his *Mekor Ḥayyim,* Henry claimed a large sum from the community; in R. Samuel's words, "they were in great distress." The community of Palencia was not spared during the persecutions of 1391 and it also had its *Conversos. Palencia and its surrounding region, however, witnessed the appearance of a popular prophet, who at the beginning of the 15th century called for repentance and announced the forthcoming redemption.

In 1480 the Jews and Conversos were separated into distinct quarters. A new quarter was allocated to them on Maria Gutiérrez Street (now Martín Calleja). After the 1492 Expulsion the name of the street was changed to Santa Fé and a fine was to be imposed on anyone who referred to the street as *judería* (*Jewish Quarter). In 1485 the Jews were ordered to wear a distinctive sign and Christians were forbidden to lodge in Jewish houses, although they could work for them by day. The Jews were called upon to contribute 501,183 maravedis toward the redemption of the prisoners of Malaga. It is known that during the Expulsion period—as early as May 1492—a decree was issued to sell the synagogue located on the present-day Street of San Marcos. The proceeds of this sale were given to poor Jews to assist their departure from Palencia. Another synagogue was converted into a hospital in November 1492. There is little information available on the Conversos of Palencia. The prophetic movement of the Maiden Inés was formed in 1500 in the region of Palencia, at *Herrera de Pisuerga.

Bibliography: Baer, Spain, index; Baer, Urkunden, 2 (1936), index; J. González, *El Reino de Castilla a la época de Alfonso VIII* (1960), 129f., 132; F. Cantera, in: *Sefarad,* 22 (1962), 93ff.; P. León Tello, *Los judíos de Palencia* (1967). [H.B.]

PALE OF SETTLEMENT (Rus. **Cherta [postoyannoy yevreyskoy] osedlosti**), territory within the borders of czarist Russia wherein the residence of Jews was legally authorized. Limits for the area in which Jewish settlement was permissible in Russia came into being when Russia was confronted with the necessity of adjusting to a Jewish element within its borders, from which Jews had been excluded since the end of the 15th century. These limitations were consonant with the general conception of freedom of movement of persons which then applied. At the time, most of the inhabitants of Russia, not only the serfs but also townsmen and merchants, were deprived of freedom of movement and confined to their places of residence.

After the first partition of Poland in 1772, when masses of Jews living within the former country came under Russian rule, it was decided (1791) to permit the presence of the Jews not only in their former regions of residence, but also in the new areas which had then been annexed from Turkey on the Black Sea shore, in whose rapid colonization the Russian government was interested. On the other hand, Jewish merchants were prohibited from trading in the provinces of inner Russia. These decrees were intended to serve the national and economic interests of the state by preventing competition of the Jewish with Russian merchants and encouraging settlement in the desolate steppes of southern Russia; after a time these formed the provinces of *Kherson, *Dnepropetrovsk (Yekaterinoslav), and Taurida (*Crimea). The Russian government also sought thus to reduce the excess of Jews in the branches of commerce and innkeeping within the territory annexed from Poland. In 1794 the earlier decree was ratified and applied to the regions which had been annexed with the second partition of Poland (1793) also—the provinces of *Minsk, *Volhynia, and *Podolia—as well as to the region to the east of the River Dnieper (the provinces of *Chernigov and *Poltava).

With the third partition of Poland (1795), the law was also applied to the provinces of *Vilna and *Grodno. In 1799 *Courland was added to the Pale of Settlement. In the "Jewish Statute" promulgated in 1804, the province of *Astrakhan and the whole of the northern Caucasus were added to the regions open to Jews. In 1812, upon its annexation, *Bessarabia was included also. The "Kingdom of Poland," incorporated into Russia in 1815, which included ten provinces that later became known as the "Vistula Region," was not officially included within the Pale of Settlement, and until 1868 the transit of Jews through it to the Lithuanian and Ukrainian provinces was prohibited by law. In practice, however, the provinces of the Vistula Region were generally included within the Pale of Settlement.

To sum up, it was the intention of the Russian legislators of the reigns of Catherine II and Alexander I to extend the Pale of Settlement beyond the regions acquired from Poland only to those areas where Jews could serve as a colonizing element. However, from the reign of Alexander II the restrictive aspects of the Pale of Settlement became accentuated; for while freedom of movement for non-Jews in Russia increased, in particular after the emancipation of the serfs, the restrictions on the movement of Jews beyond the Pale remained in force, and became explicitly underlined within the Pale itself. This was accomplished both by anti-Jewish enactments on the part of the government and by the growing impatience of Jewish society and liberal public opinion with these disabilities.

Czar Nicholas I (under whom the term "Pale of Settlement" was coined) removed Courland from the Pale in 1829; however, the rights of the Jews already settled and registered there were maintained. In 1835 the provinces of Astrakhan and the northern Caucasus were excluded from the Pale. In 1843 Nicholas I ordered the expulsion of the Jews from a strip of 50 versts (about 33 mi.) in width extending along the border with Prussia and Austria. Many difficulties were encountered in the application of this law, and in 1858 it was redrafted to apply only to those Jews who would wish to settle in the border zone after that year. A similar law which had applied to the provinces of Russian Poland (where the border zone closed to Jewish residence was 21 versts in width) was abrogated in 1862. In 1827 severe restrictions were imposed on the residence of Jews in Kiev, the largest town in southern Russia, that served as an important commercial center for the surrounding regions which had a dense Jewish population.

Under Alexander II, rights of residence beyond the Pale began to be granted to various classes of the Jewish population: in 1859 to merchants able to pay the registration fees of the First Guild, in 1861 to university graduates, as well as those engaged in medical professions (dentists, male and female nurses, midwives, etc., from 1879), and in 1865 to various craftsmen. The right of residence throughout Russia was also granted to *Cantonists who had remained Jews and to their offspring (the so-called "Nicholas soldiers"). The Jews hoped that these regulations would prove to be the first steps toward the complete abolition of the Pale of Settlement. However, they were disappointed when these alleviations came to a complete halt after 1881, as part of the general reaction in Russia at this period. The "Temporary (*May) Laws" of 1881 prohibited any new settlement by Jews outside towns and townlets in the Pale of Settlement (this law did not apply to the Vistula Region). Jews who had been living in villages before the publication of the decree were authorized to reside in those same villages only. The peasants were granted the right of demanding the expulsion of the Jews who lived among them. These decrees were bound up with intensified administrative pressure, brutality by local authorities, and the systematic acceptance of bribery on the part of the lower administrative ranks. Occasionally, new places were excluded from the Pale of Settlement, such as *Rostov and *Taganrog (1887) and the spa town of *Yalta (1893). During the years 1891–92, thousands of Jewish craftsmen and their families were expelled from *Moscow.

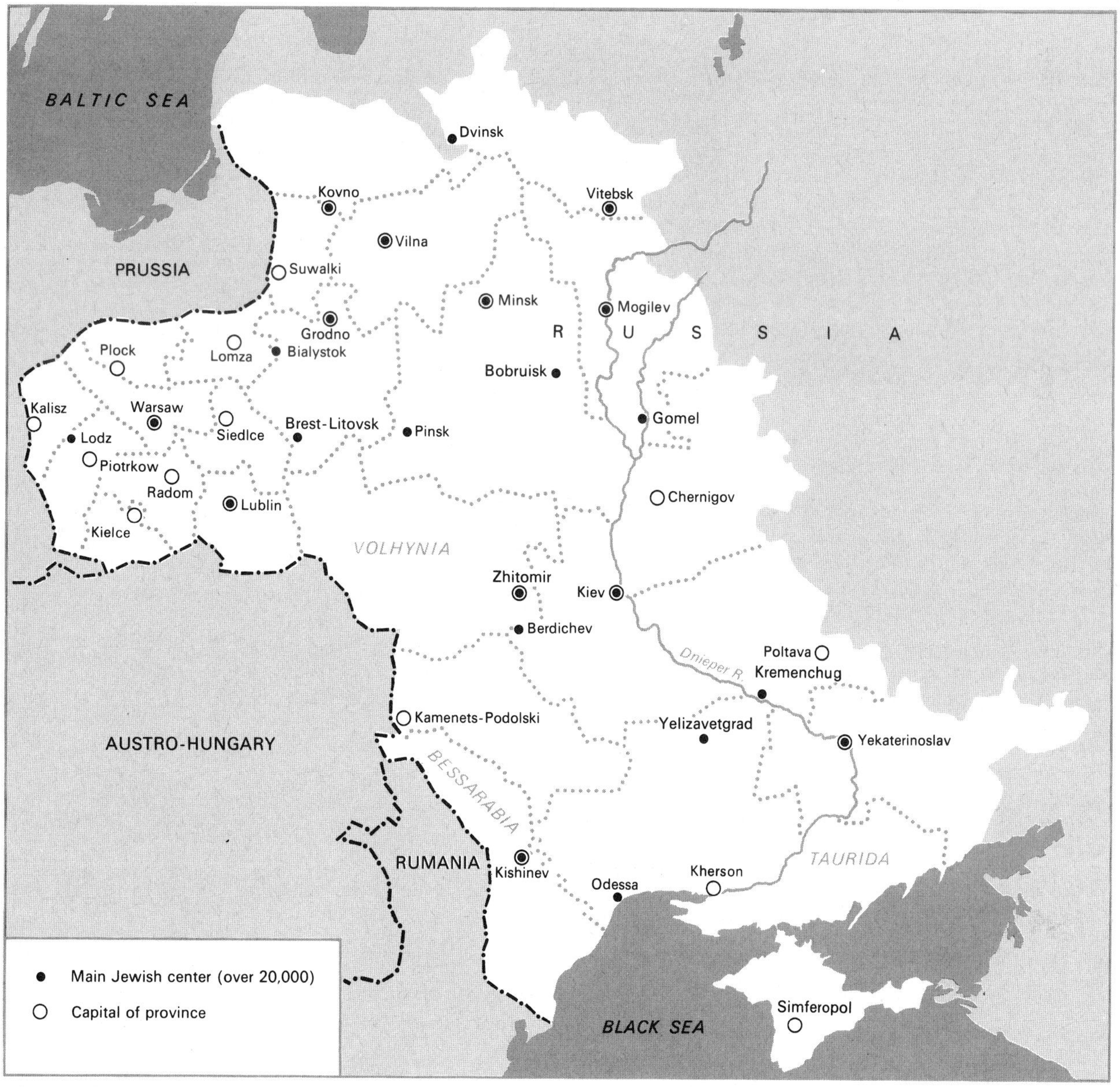

The Pale of Settlement at the end of the 19th century.

At the beginning of the 20th century political and economic pressure on the Russian government intensified, and in various places alleviations in the "Temporary Laws" occurred. From 1903 some village settlements which had assumed an urban character were given the status of townlets, and the Jews were thus granted the legal right of living in them. Up to the outbreak of World War I some 300 settlements were thus opened for Jewish residence. In 1904 instructions were issued that all the Jews authorized to reside outside the Pale of Settlement could also settle in the rural areas there.

In 1910 the Jewish members of the *Duma, N. *Friedman and L. *Nisselovich, with the support of the Constitutional-Democratic Party, proposed a bill for the abolition of the Pale of Settlement. However, the balance of power in the Duma between the liberals and reactionaries made the proposal of demonstrative value only. The extreme Right retorted with a counter-motion "to expel the Jews from Russia"; the original motion was voted upon in February 1911 and transferred to the commission for personal freedom, where it fell into oblivion and was no longer mentioned in plenary session of the Duma. In August 1915, when many thousands of expelled and refugee Jews from the battle zones streamed into the interior of Russia, the government was compelled to permit the residence of these refugees in the towns of inner Russia, with the exception of St. Petersburg and Moscow; thus the existence of the Pale of Settlement in practice was brought to an end. After the Revolution of February 1917 the provisional government abolished the Pale of Settlement among the rest of the anti-Jewish restrictions.

The Pale covered an area of about 1,000,000 sq. km. (386,100 sq. mi.) from the Baltic Sea to the Black Sea. According to the census of 1897, 4,899,300 Jews lived there, forming 94% of the total Jewish population of Russia and c. 11.6% of the general population of this area. The largest of the other nations living within the area of the Pale were the Ukrainian, Polish, Belorussian, Russian, Lithuanian, Moldavian (mostly in Bessarabia), and German. These (with the exception of the Germans) were essentially concentrated in their own territorial regions, where they formed the majority of the population. The Jews were a minority in every province (from 17.5% in the province of Grodno to 3.8% in the province of Taurida); 82% of the Jews lived in the towns and townlets of the Pale and their concentration in these was prominent: they formed 36.9% of the urban population, and in nine provinces they formed the majority of the urban population (province of Minsk—58.8%; Grodno—57.7%; Mogilev—52.4%; etc.). In the townlets and many small towns all the inhabitants or the overwhelming majority were Jews. The ten largest communities were *Warsaw (219,149 persons); *Odessa (138,915); *Lodz (98,677); *Vilna (64,000); *Kishinev (50,237); *Minsk (47,562); *Bialystok (41,900); *Berdichev (41,617); Yekaterinoslav (*Dnepropetrovsk; 40,009); and *Vitebsk (34,470).

It was, however, not only the limitation of their residential area which oppressed the Jews. By force of historical circumstances they were also restricted in their occupations. They were concentrated in commerce (38.6% of the Jews gainfully occupied) and crafts (35.4%); 72.8% of the total of persons engaged in commerce within the Pale of Settlement were Jews, as well as 31.4% of those engaged in crafts. Jewish artisans concentrated in certain branches of crafts (tailoring; shoemaking). Very few had the possibility of engaging in agriculture. The competition among the merchants, shopkeepers, and craftsmen was intense and gave rise to pauperization and the development of a Jewish proletariat which could not be integrated. This situation, together with the incessant anti-Jewish decrees and the waves of pogroms, especially during the years 1881–84 and 1903–06, resulted in a constant stream of Jewish emigration from the Pale of Settlement to Western Europe and the United States. Even this great emigration was, however, insufficient to counterbalance the natural growth of the Jews in the Pale of Settlement.

The language spoken by the Jews in the Pale of Settlement was Yiddish (according to the census of 1897 by 99% of the Jews). Most Jewish children received a Jewish education in the *ḥeder* and the yeshivah. Jewish literature and newspapers in Yiddish, Hebrew, Russian, and Polish circulated in many thousands of copies. The masses of Ḥasidim were attached to the "courts" of their spiritual leaders in *Lubavich (Ḥabad), *Stolin, *Talnoye (Talna), *Gora Kalwaria (Gur), *Aleksandrow, etc. More modern movements such as *Ḥibbat Zion and Zionism, the *Bund and the socialist parties were also active in the towns and townlets of the Pale, either openly or illegally underground.

World War I, the disintegration of the Russian Empire, the Revolution, and the civil war in Russia, destroyed the foundations of this Jewish world, which was finally annihilated in the Holocaust. With the perspective of time, assessment of the Pale of Settlement has changed; it is necessary to consider not only its negative aspects but also its positive, unintended results, as forming a framework for an independent Jewry, as the area of settlement of a whole Jewish nation in which generations of Jews developed their own culture, and as the source of the establishment and development of large Jewish centers in America, South Africa, and many other countries, as well as Israel.

Bibliography: Yu. Hessen, in: YE, 7 (c. 1910), 590–7; J. Bikerman, *Cherta yevreyskoy osedlosti* (1911); Dubnow, Hist Russ, 3 (1920), index; J. Lestschinsky, *Dos Yidishe Folk in Tsifern* (1922), 13–84; B. Dinur, in: *Zion*, 23 (1958), 93–101; I. Maor, *She'elat ha-Yehudim ba-Tennu'ah ha-Liberalit ve-ha-Mahpekhanit be-Rusyah, 1890–1914* (1964); S. W. Baron, *The Russian Jew under Tsars and Soviets* (1964), index; Y. Slutsky, in: *He-Avar*, 13 (1966), 41–58; S. Ettinger, *Toledot Am Yisrael*, 3 (1969), index s.v. *Teḥum ha-Moshav*.

[Y.S.]

PALERMO, capital of Sicily. Jews apparently lived there in Roman times. Evidence of their presence is first supplied by Pope *Gregory I. His intervention in 598 with Bishop Victor of Palermo, who had requisitioned the synagogue and hospice, indicates that the community had by then attained some prosperity. The Jews could not resume possession of the buildings since they had been consecrated as churches, but they were indemnified and the religious objects restored to them. During the Saracenic period the community was augmented by Jews who had been sold as slaves in Sicily and ransomed by their coreligionists. Like the other Jews in Sicily at this period those of Palermo had to pay a poll tax (*jizya*) and an impost on real estate (*khārāj*). These and other restrictions, however, did not prevent them from prospering. With the establishment of Norman rule in Sicily (1072) the Jews in Palermo came under the jurisdiction of the sovereign, who continued collecting the *jizya* from them in addition to the impost they paid to the local archbishop in 1089. However, the Jews were recognized as full citizens with the right to own property, excepting slaves, and free to engage in a variety of crafts. A prominent number were fishermen, and Jews had virtually a monopoly of the silk and dyeing industry. The art of silk weaving was developed in Palermo by Jews brought there as prisoners from Greece by Roger II in 1147; they later settled throughout Italy, leading in this craft for four centuries. In 1211 a tax was collected for the right to practice dyeing by the ecclesiastical curia in Palermo. According to *Benjamin of Tudela, 1,500 Jews (or Jewish families) were living in Palermo around 1172. In 1312 Frederick II revoked a former decree confining the Jews to a special quarter outside the city walls. Before 1393 the Jews of Palermo had been allowed to wear a distinguishing *badge much smaller than the size stipulated for the other Sicilian Jews.

The Jews of Palermo had to attend missionary sermons. The incitement of fanatical preachers frequently resulted in bloodshed, as in a riot which occurred in Palermo in 1339. Besides paying taxes levied by the royal administration, the Jews in Palermo sometimes had to contribute funds to rebut libels; in 1437 they paid 150 gold ounces to defray the expenditure of the war against the Kingdom of Naples, and in 1475 they paid 500 gold ounces to silence a false accusation. In 1450 Alfonso V issued a decree permitting the Jews of Palermo to reside outside the ghetto, and in 1453 he reconfirmed their former privileges which had been abolished by the church authorities. This enabled them again to acquire houses and land, to lease property, to maintain schools and synagogues, and to acquire cemeteries; the king also prohibited anti-Jewish preaching.

The Palermo community was the largest and most important of the Sicilian communities, paying one-seventh of the total taxes levied on the city. Obadiah *Bertinoro, who spent some months in Palermo in 1487–88, gives a vivacious description of the community which he estimated at 850 families, mainly coppersmiths, ironworkers, laborers, and porters, much despised by the Christians because of their ragged clothing. The main synagogue, with its sweet-voiced cantors and its elaborate subsidiary buildings, was the most beautiful he had ever seen.

Twelve *proti* (from the Greek πρῶτοι) or notables assisted by councillors were in charge of the communal administration (see *Sicily). In 1393, by a decree issued by King Martin I, the Giudecca, or Jewish community body of Palermo, was given the function of acting as a court of appeal in legal disputes among the Sicilian Jews. Outstanding among those who contributed to the cultural life of the community were the physician Master Busach; *Moses of Palermo, translator of works from Arabic, who served at court; the poet Saul b. Nafusi of Palermo; the *dayyan* Anatol b. Joseph who spent about ten years in Palermo (1170–80); the poet and physician *Ahitub b. Isaac to whom Solomon b. Abraham *Adret of Barcelona addressed a polemic against the kabbalist Abraham *Abulafia; the poet and physician Moses *Remos, who was unjustly sentenced to death and wrote a moving poem on the eve of his execution as his moral testament to posterity; and Joseph *Abenafia, born in Syracuse, physician at the court of Martin I and the first **dienchelele* of the Jewish communities of the realm. In 1491 the intervention of the Jews in Palermo prevented Jewish refugees from Provence who had arrived in Sicily from being sold as slaves.

After the decree of expulsion of 1492 was issued the Jews of Palermo, then numbering about 5,000, were obliged to leave the island. When the Jews were temporarily readmitted to the Kingdom of the Two Sicilies, in 1695–1702 and 1740–46, a few presumably came to Palermo. In the early 1920s a *minyan* could be obtained, at the most, composed of Jews from Central or Eastern Europe who had acquired Italian citizenship. Two of them, Philippsohn and Beretvas, lectured at the faculty of medicine. Most had left Sicily before 1938, when Mussolini's racial laws deprived them of Italian citizenship. There were seven Jewish families living in Palermo in 1970.

Bibliography: C. Roth, *Gleanings* (1969); Milano, Bibliotheca, index. [J.S.S.]

PALESTINE, one of the names of the territory known as the Land of *Israel or the Holy Land. The name "Palestine" was originally an adjective derived from Heb. פְּלֶשֶׁת, *Peleshet*. It is first mentioned by Herodotus in the form of Συρία ἡ Παλαιστίνη, i.e., "the Philistine Syria"; subsequently, the name was shortened and the adjective "Palaistinei" became a proper noun. Philo identifies "Palaistinei" with biblical *Canaan. In talmudic literature Palestine is used as the name of a Roman province, adjoining the provinces of *Finukyah* (Phoenicia) and *Aruvyah* (Arabia; Gen. R. 90:6). From the fourth century, however, the three provinces into which the Land of Israel was divided were referred to as the "first," "second," and "third Palestine" respectively.

The Arabs used the term "Filasṭīn" فلسطين for the "first Palestine" only, differentiating between it and "Urdunn" (أردن -Jordan); but these designations soon fell into disuse, as the Arabs generally referred to provinces by the names of their capital cities. The crusaders renewed the use of the "three Palestines," the borders of which, however, differed from those of the Roman provinces. After the fall of the crusader kingdom, Palestine was no longer an official designation, but it was still used in non-Jewish languages as the name of the "Holy Land" on both sides of the Jordan. It was not an administrative unit under the Ottoman Empire, when it was part of the province of Syria.

This was the situation until 1922, when the British, who had received the Mandate over Palestine on both sides of the Jordan from the League of Nations, practically restricted the application of the name to the part west of the Jordan, while east of the Jordan and south of the Yarmuk they established the emirate of Transjordan, which in 1946 became a kingdom. In 1948 the State of Israel was established in a part of western Palestine, its territory demarcated in the *Armistice agreements of 1949 with the neighboring Arab countries. Transjordan annexed the Arab-inhabited part of western Palestine occupied by the Jordanian army and changed its own name to the Hashemite Kingdom of *Jordan, and Egypt retained and administered the *Gaza Strip. Thus, Palestine as a political entity ceased to exist. During the *Six-Day War (1967) the Israel army occupied the whole of Palestine west of the Jordan, including the Gaza Strip, as well as the *Sinai Peninsula and the *Golan Heights. See also: *Israel, Land of, Names.

[A.J.Br./Ed.]

PALESTINE, INQUIRY COMMISSIONS, a series of commissions and committees that conducted inquiries into the internal developments, system of government, and political status of Palestine against the background of British and international commitments to assist in the establishment of a National Home for the Jewish people (see *Balfour Declaration). The first of these endeavors, the King-Crane Commission (1919), was appointed by the United States. Four commissions were appointed by the British government during the period of the Mandate, after the outbreaks of Arab violence in 1921, 1929, and 1936. After World War II, a joint Anglo-American Committee was appointed by the British and U.S. governments in 1945, and the UN Special Committee on Palestine (UNSCOP) was appointed by the United Nations in 1947.

King-Crane Commission (1919). After World War I the United States, Great Britain, and France agreed, on President Wilson's suggestion, to appoint a special committee to visit the regions of the former Ottoman Empire involved in recent agreements, negotiations, and declarations "to acquaint themselves as fully as possible with the shade of opinion there . . . with the social, racial, and economic conditions . . . and to form as definite an opinion as the circumstances and the time at your disposal will permit of the divisions of territory and assignment of mandates." As a result of obstruction by France and the lukewarm attitude of Britain, however, the only members actually appointed were two Americans, H. C. King, president of Oberlin College, Ohio, and C. R. Crane, a Chicago business man with many connections in the Near East, particularly Turkey.

In their report, presented only to the American Peace Commission (published in a somewhat condensed form in December 1922 and officially published only in 1947), King and Crane recommended the preservation of the unity of Syria, including both Lebanon and Palestine, which should be granted a reasonable measure of local autonomy; and that a Mandate over Syria be entrusted to the United States or, if that seemed impracticable, to Great Britain. The commission further recommended "a serious modification of the extreme Zionist program for Palestine of unlimited immigration of Jews, looking finally to making Palestine distinctly a Jewish State." Policy toward Palestine should be governed by the principle laid down by President Wilson on July 4, 1918: "The settlement of every question on the basis of the free acceptance of that settlement by the people immediately concerned." Since, according to the commission's findings, the non-Jewish population of Palestine—

nearly 90% of the whole—were "emphatically against the entire Zionist program," their wishes should be respected.

The commission declared that the Zionist claim "that they have a 'right' to Palestine, based on an occupation of two thousand years ago, can hardly be seriously considered." A further consideration was the fact that, since Palestine was the Holy Land for Jews, Christians, and Moslems alike, the Jews could not be proper guardians of the holy places. The complete Jewish occupation of Palestine "would intensify, with a certainty like fate, the anti-Jewish feeling both in Palestine and in all other portions of the world which look to Palestine as 'the Holy Land.'"

In view of all these considerations, the commission recommended that "Jewish immigration to Palestine should definitely be limited and that the project for making Palestine distinctly a Jewish commonwealth should be given up." The commission's report was never submitted to the Paris Peace Conference, and its recommendations were never acted upon.

Haycraft Commission of Inquiry (1921). A commission of inquiry into the disturbance of May 1921 (see *Israel, Land of, Historical Survey) was appointed by Sir Herbert *Samuel, then high commissioner for Palestine, "to inquire into the recent disturbances in the town and neighbourhood of Jaffa and to report thereon." It was headed by Sir W. Haycraft, chief justice of Palestine, and its members were H. C. Luke, assistant governor of Jerusalem, and J. N. Stubbs of the Legal Department. The commission found that the immediate reason for the riots (in which 47 Jews and 48 Arabs were killed and 146 Jews and 73 Arabs wounded) was a clash between Jewish Communist and the general Jewish labor movement May Day demonstrations in Jaffa, which served as "a spark igniting explosive material." However, the commission stated that "the racial strife was begun by Arabs," while "the police were, with few exceptions, half-trained and inefficient, in many cases indifferent and in some cases leaders of or participators in violence." The fundamental cause of the disturbances, the commission found, was the Arab feeling of discontent with, and hostility to, the Jews due to political and economic causes and connected with Jewish immigration and with their conception of Zionist policy as derived from Jewish exponents. Much could be done, the commission suggested, to allay hostility between Arabs and Jews if responsible people on both sides would sit together to discuss the questions arising between them in a "reasonable spirit," on the basis that the Arabs should implicitly accept the government's policy on the subject of the Jewish National Home and "that the Zionist leaders should abandon and repudiate all pretensions that go beyond it."

Commission on the Palestine Disturbances of 1929 (The Shaw Commission). This commission was appointed by the British colonial secretary, Lord Passfield, after the serious disturbances of August 1929, which broke out in connection with the question of Jewish rights at the *Western (Wailing) Wall. In the disturbances 133 Jews were killed and 339 wounded, mainly in Jerusalem and Hebron; Arab casualties, chiefly from police action, were 116 killed and 232 wounded. The commission's terms of reference were "to enquire into the immediate causes which led to the recent outbreak in Palestine and to make recommendations as to the steps necessary to avoid a recurrence." It consisted of Sir Walter Shaw, former chief justice of the Straits Settlements, as chairman, and three members of parliament Sir H. Betterton (Conservative), R. H. Morris (Liberal), and H. Snell (Labour).

Although Prime Minister Ramsay MacDonald stated that matters of major policy were definitely outside its terms of reference, the commission went into Arab political and economic grievances in considerable depth and detail. It found that the outbreak in Jerusalem was from the beginning "an attack by Arabs on Jews" and apportioned "a share in the responsibility" to Al-Hajj Amin *Husseini, the mufti of Jerusalem. In dealing with the causes of the trouble, the commission stated: "There can be no doubt that racial animosity on the part of the Arabs, consequent upon the disappointment of their political and national aspirations and fear for their economic future, was the fundamental cause of the outbreak of August last," and that the Churchill White Paper of 1922 (see *White Papers) charged the Palestine government with the primary duty of "holding the balance between the two parties in the country." It considered the policy of the government to be of a dual nature and that it had succeeded in steering a middle course between the conflicting policies proposed by the two parties.

The commission accepted most of the Arab claims and recommended that a new statement of policy should be issued, containing "a definition in clear and positive terms" of the meaning of the passages in the Mandate providing for "the safeguarding of the rights of the non-Jewish communities." It recommended: that immigration policy be reviewed to prevent a repetition of what the commission described as the excessive immigration of 1925 and 1926; that a special inquiry should be undertaken into the prospects of introducing improved methods of cultivation and that a new land policy be introduced, having regard for the natural increase in the present rural population; and that a special commission be appointed to determine rights and claims in connection with the Western Wall.

In a long note of reservations, Harry Snell attributed a greater share in the responsibility for the disturbances to the mufti, blamed the government for not having issued an official denial that the Jews had designs on the Muslim holy places, ascribed the outbreaks mainly to fears and antipathies fostered by the Arab leaders for political needs, and declared that what was needed was not so much a change of policy, as a change of mind on the part of the Arab population.

The British government appointed Sir John Hope-Simpson to report on questions of immigration, land settlement, and development and issued a preliminary statement accepting the substance of the Shaw Commission Report. In reply to trenchant criticism of the report by the Permanent Mandates Commission of the *League of Nations, the government further defended the commission's conclusions. The Hope-Simpson report, which was issued on Oct. 21, 1930, simultaneously with the Passfield White Paper (see *White Papers), stated that: if all the cultivable land in Palestine were divided up among the Arab agricultural population, there would not be enough to provide every family with a decent livelihood; until further development took place and the Arabs adopted better methods of cultivation, "there is no room for a single additional settler, if the standard of life of the fellaheen is to remain at its present level"; and that with thorough development of the country, there would be room "for no less than 20,000 families of settlers from outside."

Palestine Royal Commission (Peel Commission; 1937). The commission was appointed by the British government on Aug. 7, 1936, with very wide terms of reference. "(1) To ascertain the underlying causes of the disturbances which broke out in Palestine in the middle of April. (2) To inquire into the manner in which the Mandate for Palestine is being implemented in relation to the obligations of the Mandatory towards the Arabs and Jews respectively. (3) To ascertain whether, upon a proper construction of the terms of the Mandate, either the Arabs or the Jews have any legitimate grievances upon account of the way in which the Mandate has been, or is being implemented. (4) If the Commission is satisfied that any such grievances are well founded, to make recommendation for their removal and for the prevention of their recurrence."

The commission was headed by Earl Peel, a former secretary of state for India, and its members were Sir H. G. M. Rumbold, Sir E. L. L. Hammond, Sir W. M. Carter, Sir H. Morris, and Professor R. Coupland. The commission's report, issued on July 7, was the most thorough study of the problem conducted by any of the inquiry commissions and committees. It started with a comprehensive survey of the history of Palestine and the connection of Jews and Arabs with it, as well as a bird's-eye view of Jewish history in the Diaspora, showing a deep and sympathetic understanding of the Zionist movement and its aims. After a thorough study of British promises to Jews and Arabs during World War I and of the terms of the Mandate, it reached the conclusion that "the primary purpose of the Mandate . . . is to promote the establishment of the Jewish National Home." The commission found that the Jewish National Home was now a "going concern" and that its establishment had been to the economic advantage of the Arabs as a whole. At the same time, however, "with almost mathematical precision the betterment of the economic situation in Palestine meant the deterioration of the political situation." The underlying causes of the disturbances in 1936 were, therefore, found to be the desire of the Arabs for national independence and their hatred and fear of the establishment of the Jewish National Home, the same causes that had led to the disturbances in the past.

"It is impossible," the commission commented "to see the National Home and not to wish it well. It has meant so much for the relief of unmerited suffering. It displays so much energy and enterprise and devotion to a common cause. In so far as Britain has helped towards its creation, we would claim, with Lord Balfour, that to that extent, at any rate, Christendom has shown itself not oblivious of all the wrong it has done, but at the same time the difficulties which confront the National Home should not be underestimated, and it must be admitted that the situation in Palestine has reached a deadlock." The solution of the problem of Palestine must be a drastic one. All other recommendations would be but palliatives. "We cannot—in Palestine as it now is—both concede the Arab claim to self-government and secure the establishment of the Jewish National Home," the report declared. "The disease is so deep-rooted that the only hope of a cure lies in a surgical operation." This operation was to be the partitioning of the country and the establishment of separate Jewish and Arab states, while Jerusalem and Bethlehem, with a corridor to the sea at Jaffa, and Nazareth would remain under British Mandate (see *Palestine, Partition; *Israel, State of, Historical Survey, 1880–1948).

Palestine Partition Commission (The Woodhead Commission; 1938). This commission was appointed on Jan. 4, 1938, to recommend boundaries for the Arab and Jewish areas and the enclaves to be retained permanently or under British Mandate as proposed by the Peel Commission. In effect it reported that Partition was impracticable (see *Palestine, Partition and Partition Plans for a more detailed account).

Anglo-American Committee of Enquiry Regarding the Problems of European Jewry and Palestine (1946). The terms of reference of the committee, appointed by the governments of the United States and Britain in November 1945 to examine political, economic, and social conditions in Palestine as they bore upon the problem of Jewish immigration and settlement therein and the well-being of the peoples now living therein; to examine the position of the Jews in those countries in Europe where they had been the victims of Nazi and Fascist persecution . . . and to make estimates of those who wished or would be impelled by their conditions to migrate to Palestine or other countries outside Europe; and to make recommendations for *ad interim* handling of these problems, as well as for their permanent solution.

This committee differed from its predecessors in two important respects. First, it represented both Britain and the United States. Of its 12 members, six were British (J. E. Singleton, W. F. Crick, R. H. S. Crossman, F. Leggett, R. E. Manningham-Buller, and Lord Morrison) and six were Americans (J. C. Hutcheson, F. Aydelotte, F. W. Buxton, B. C. Crum, J. G. *MacDonald, and W. Phillips), with Singleton and Hutcheson as joint chairmen. Secondly, it connected, for the first time, the problem of world Jewry with that of the Jews in Palestine, thereby tacitly admitting that the Jewish problem and the problem of the Jewish National Home must be seen as one. The committee therefore visited Germany, Poland, Czechoslovakia, Austria, Italy, and Greece, even before it carried out its investigations in Palestine.

In its unanimous report and recommendations, the committee found that no country other than Palestine was ready to give substantial assistance in finding homes for Jews wishing or impelled to leave Europe, but that Palestine alone could not solve their emigration needs. It therefore recommended that the U.S. and British governments should endeavor to find new places for the *Displaced Persons, in addition to Palestine, and that 100,000 certificates for immigration to Palestine be authorized immediately for the Jewish victims of Nazi and Fascist persecution. Future immigration to Palestine should be regulated according to the Mandate, and the Land Transfers Regulation of 1940 should be annulled and replaced by new ones based on "a policy of freedom in the sale, lease, or use of land, irrespective of race, community, or creed." As for long-term policy, the committee recommended the guiding principle that Palestine should be neither a Jewish state nor an Arab state, and that Jew should not dominate Arab nor Arab dominate Jew. Until the hostility between Jews and Arabs disappeared, the government of Palestine should be continued under the Mandate. In effect, therefore, the committee proposed de facto abrogation of the 1939 White Paper policy (see *White Papers). The British government's rejection of the committee's recommendations (in particular the proposal for the issue of 100,000 certificates), despite President Truman's acceptance of the report, led to a further deterioration in the Palestine situation; consequently, the British government turned the whole problem over to the United Nations, which appointed the UN Special Committee on Palestine (UNSCOP).

United Nations Special Committee on Palestine (UNSCOP; 1947). The General Assembly of the United Nations, at a special meeting convened in April 1947 at the request of the British government, appointed this committee to prepare a report on Palestine. It consisted of 11 members: representatives of Australia (J. D. Hood), Canada (I. C. Rand), Czechoslovakia (K. Lisicky), Guatemala (J. G. Granados), India (A. Rahman), Iran (N. Entezam), the Netherlands (N. S. Blom), Peru (A. Ulloa), Sweden (E. Sandstrom), Uruguay (E. R. Fabregat), and Yugoslavia (V. Simic), with the Swedish delegate, Justice Emil Sandstrom, as chairman and Alberto Ulloa of Peru, vice-chairman. Its terms of reference gave the committee "the widest powers to ascertain and record facts, and to investigate all questions and issues relevant to the problems of Palestine." In its report, published on Aug. 31, 1947, it recommended unanimously that the Mandate for Palestine should be terminated at the earliest possible date and that independence should be granted in Palestine at the earliest practical date. The majority, composed of the representatives of Canada, Czechoslovakia, Guatemala, the Netherlands, Peru, Sweden, and Uruguay, proposed the partitioning of Palestine into a Jewish state, an Arab state, and a special international regime for Jerusalem and its environs (see *Palestine, Partition and Partition Plans). The minority, consisting of the representatives of India, Iran, and Yugoslavia proposed the establishment of a binational federal state. The majority proposals were adopted by a special meeting of the General Assembly on Nov. 29, 1947: 33 member states (including the United States and the U.S.S.R.) voted in favor, 13 against (including all the Arab states) and ten (including Great Britain) abstained.

See also *Israel, Historical Survey; *Palestine, Partition and Partition Plans: *White Papers; *Zionism, Zionist Policy.

For bibliography see *White Papers. [D.Ef.]

PALESTINE, PARTITION AND PARTITION PLANS.

The first partition of Palestine took place in 1922, when the British government excluded Transjordan from the area to which the provisions of the *Balfour Declaration would apply. The Zionist Executive reluctantly acquiesced in this decision. The *Revisionist movement, established in 1925, hotly opposed the separation of Transjordan; its basic slogan was "a Jewish state on both sides of the Jordan." The idea of partitioning western Palestine between Jews and Arabs was first broached officially in 1937 by the Palestine Royal Commission (see *Palestine, Inquiry Commissions, Peel Commision) as a method of enabling each nation to exercise sovereignty and achieve its principal national aims in part of the country while maintaining a British foothold centered in Jerusalem. The proposal was at first approved by the British government and accepted in principle, after a vigorous controversy, by the majority of the *yishuv* and the Zionist movement. The British withdrew their support, however, after the Palestine Partition Commission (the Woodhead Commission, see below) had failed to produce a "practicable" partition plan, and instead adopted in 1939 the White Paper policy (see *White Papers), which would ultimately have created an independent Palestinian state with a permanent Arab majority.

The abortive Morrison-Grady scheme of 1946 (see below), which would have left more than two-fifths of the country in British hands and given neither Arabs nor Jews more than limited autonomy, was rejected by both sides, and it was not until Britain put the problem before the United Nations that a new partition plan was evolved. This was done by the UN Special Committee on Palestine (UNSCOP, see below), which recommended the establishment of a Jewish and an Arab state joined in an economic union, with Jerusalem and its environs as a separate international enclave. This proposal was accepted by the Jews and rejected by the Arabs, while the British refused to play any part in implementing it.

The partition of western Palestine was not merely a theoretical proposal, but one of the possibilities inherent in the situation created by two generations of Zionist settlement before and during the British *Mandate. Jewish land purchases, mainly by the *Jewish National Fund, and the establishment of Jewish towns and villages had created areas of contiguous Jewish settlement, with a self-reliant and economically viable community that was prepared and able to defend itself and institutions of self-government based upon the voluntary allegiance of the Jewish population. Without such a *yishuv,* fortified by the moral, political, and financial support of Jews around the world, no decision by any external body could have been implemented. Ultimately, the partition of western Palestine was the result of two forces: the capacity of the *yishuv* to hold its own by force against the attacks of Palestinian Arabs and the surrounding Arab states on the one hand, and the inability of the *yishuv* to gain control of the whole of western Palestine, on the other. The following are the details of the partition plans presented by the various commissions and committees.

Palestine Royal Commission (see *Palestine, Inquiry Commissions). This commission, often referred to as the Peel Commission, published its report on July 7, 1937. It came to the conclusion that partition was the best solution for both sides. Although this proposal meant neither Jews nor Arabs would get all they wanted, the commission believed that it offered many advantages to both sides. The Arabs would obtain national independence and finally be delivered from fear of ultimate subjection to Jewish rule. By converting the Jewish National Home into a Jewish state, the Jews would not only be free of the fear of Arab rule, but they "will attain the primary objective of Zionism—a Jewish nation, planted in Palestine, giving its nationals the same status in the world as other nations give theirs. They will cease at last to live a 'minority life.' A new sense of confidence and security would replace the existing feeling of fear and suspicion and both Jews and Arabs would obtain the inestimable boon of peace."

The commission therefore proposed that Palestine be divided into (1) a Jewish state, comprising the whole of Galilee and the Jezreel Valley, most of the Beth-Shean Valley, and the Coastal Plain from Ras el-Nakura (Rosh ha-Nikrah) on the Lebanese border to Be'er Tuviyyah in the south; (2) an Arab state comprising Transjordan, the hill country of Samaria and Judea, and the Negev; (3) a British zone under permanent Mandate, consisting of Jerusalem, Bethlehem, and their environs, a corridor to the coast at Jaffa, and Nazareth. British treaties of alliance with the Jewish and the Arab state would guarantee the protection of minorities, facilities for British forces, etc., and the Jewish state would pay a subvention to the Arab state. (For details of proposed boundaries, see *Israel, State of: Frontiers.)

The 20th Zionist Congress (Zurich, Aug. 3–17, 1937) declared that the Peel Commission's scheme was "unacceptable," but empowered the Executive to negotiate with the British government on "precise terms" for the establishment of "a Jewish state," provided that any scheme that might emerge would be submitted for approval to a newly elected Congress.

Palestine Partition Commission. In 1938 the British government appointed the Palestine Partition Commission (generally known as the Woodhead Commission, after its chairman Sir John Woodhead) "to recommend boundaries for the proposed Arab and Jewish areas and the British enclaves that would (a) afford a reasonable prospect of the eventual establishment . . . of self-supporting Arab and Jewish states; (b) necessitate the inclusion of the fewest possible Arabs and Arab enterprises in the Jewish area and vice versa; and (c) enable the British government to carry out its 'Mandatory responsibilities.' " The commission, whose report was published in October 1938, found that the Peel Commission's scheme (Plan A) was impracticable. One member favored Plan B, which would have excluded Galilee and a small area in the south from the Jewish state as proposed in Plan A; two others preferred Plan C, which provided for small Jewish and Arab states, with Galilee, a Jerusalem enclave, and the Negev under British mandate; and a fourth rejected all three plans. The commission, therefore, was unable to recommend boundaries that would meet its terms of reference, and the British government came to the conclusion that partition was impracticable.

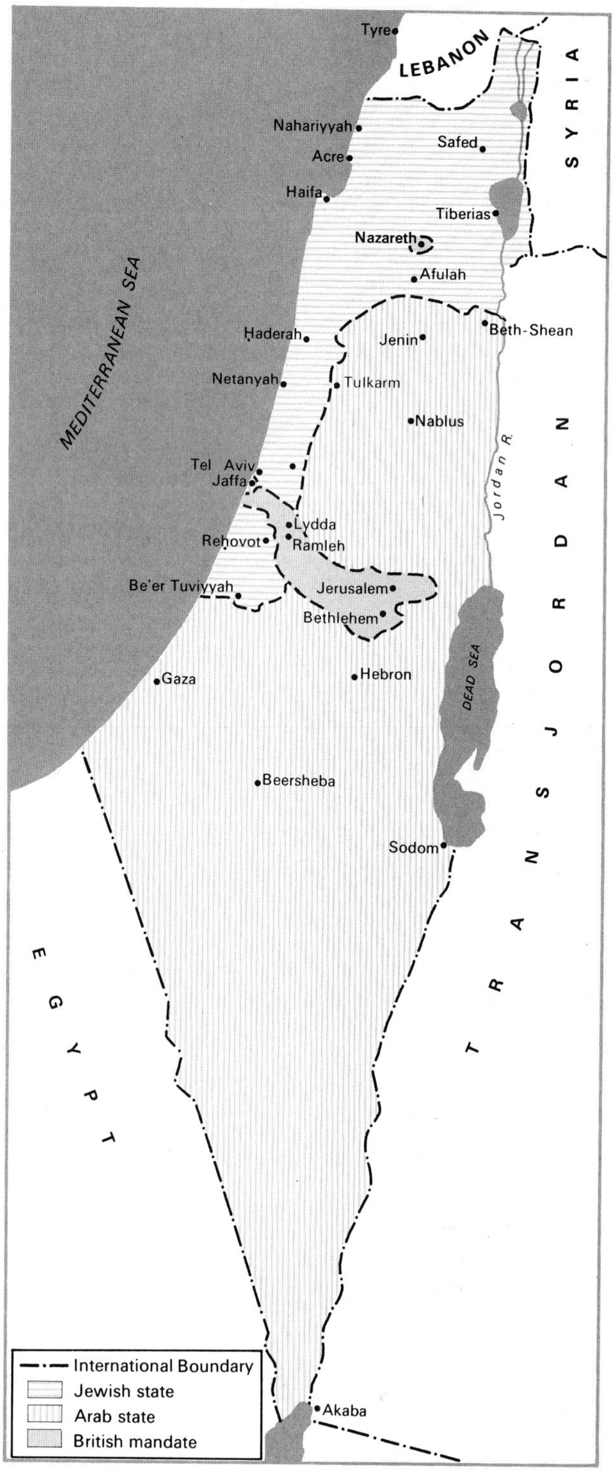

Map 1. The Peel Partition Plan, 1937. After Zev Vilnay, *The New Israel Atlas,* Jerusalem, 1968.

The Morrison-Grady Scheme. This was a plan evolved in July 1946 by British and American representatives, headed by Herbert Morrison, then lord president of the council, and T. Grady of the U.S. State Department. It purported to be based on the report of the Anglo-American Committee (see *Palestine, Inquiry Commissions), but actually had little or nothing in common with it. The scheme provided for the division of Palestine into four provinces: an Arab province, consisting of about 40% of the area; a Jewish province, with 17%, and two British provinces—the Jerusalem district and the Negev—covering 43% of the area. A British high commissioner, assisted by a nominated executive council, would head the central government. The Arab and Jewish provinces would have elected legislatures, with executives appointed by the high commissioner from among their members. The powers of these executives would be very limited: defense, foreign relations, and customs and excise would be controlled by the central government, and bills passed by the provincial legislatures would require the high commissioner's assent. The Land Transfer Regulations of the 1939 White Paper would be repealed. The Arab legislature would be free to permit or refuse Jews permission to buy lands in its province, while the Jews would be permitted to buy land in their own area. Final control over immigration would rest with the high commissioner, who would act according to the recommendations of the provincial governments, provided the economic absorptive capacity was not exceeded (see *White Papers). As for the future, the plan left the way open for either partition or for federal unity. The U.S. government declined to accept the plan as a basis for consideration, and it was rejected by the Zionist Congress.

UN Special Committee on Palestine (UNSCOP). UNSCOP was appointed by the UN General Assembly in May 1947 after Britain had submitted the Palestine problem to the UN (see *Palestine Inquiry Commissions). The seven-member majority called for the

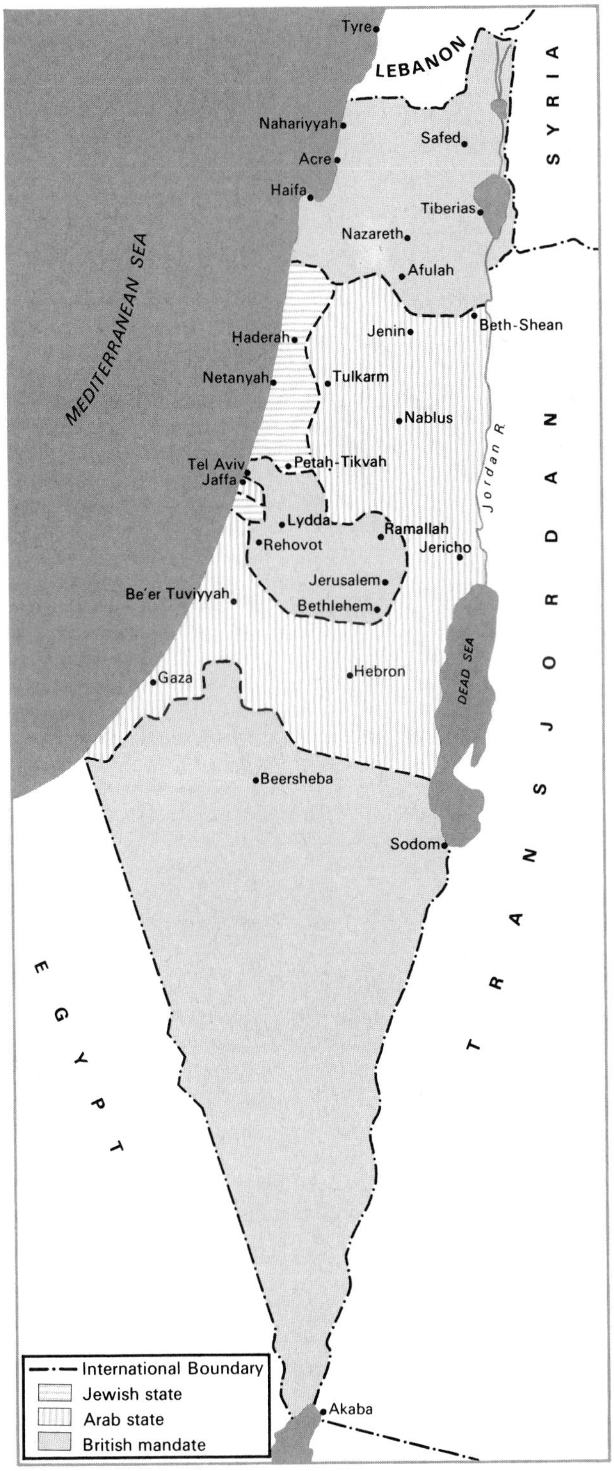

Map 2. "Plan C" examined by the Woodhead Palestine Partition Commission, 1938. After Zev Vilnay, *The New Israel Atlas*, Jerusalem, 1968.

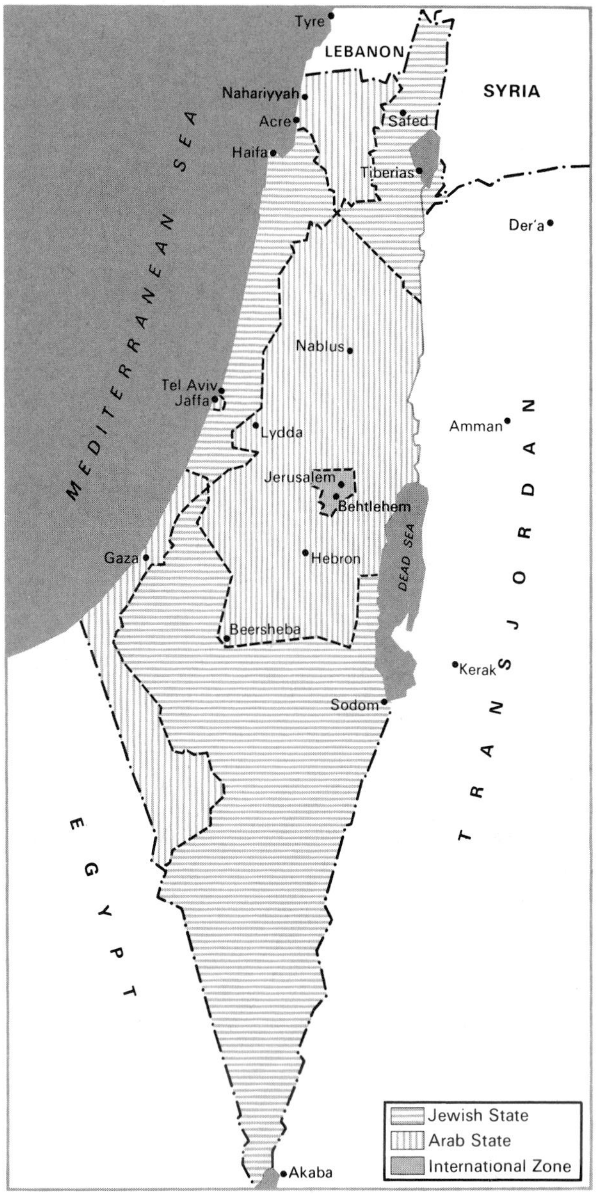

Map 3. The UNSCOP Partition Plan, 1947. After Zev Vilnay, *The New Israel Atlas*, Jerusalem, 1968.

partition of Palestine into an Arab state, a Jewish state, and a "Special International Regime" for Jerusalem, all three to be linked in an economic union. The minority proposed the establishment of a binational federal state, while the Australian representative abstained.

The majority proposals, with slight territorial modifications, were adopted by a special meeting of the General Assembly on Nov. 19, 1947. The Arab state was to comprise western Galilee, the hill country of Samaria and Judea (excluding Jerusalem), and the Coastal Plain from Isdud (Ashdod) to the Sinai frontier; the Jewish state would include eastern Galilee, the Jezreel Valley, most of the Coastal Plain, and the Negev. Each state was thus to consist of three sections linked at two crossing points. The Jerusalem enclave was to be under UN trusteeship. (For details of proposed boundaries, see *Israel, State of: Frontiers.)

The proposals were accepted by the Jews and rejected by the Arabs, who announced that they would do all in their power to bring about the collapse of the plan, while the British stated that they would do nothing to enforce it. In the end, the United Nations decision was implemented by the *Haganah and the Israel Defense Forces, which repelled attacks against Jewish centers and enabled the *yishuv* to establish the State of Israel, with its legislature, government, and administration in effective control of its territory. The de facto boundaries of the State of Israel, which were determined by the *Armistice agreements concluded in 1949 with Egypt, Lebanon, Jordan, and Syria, were roughly similar to those proposed in the UN resolution, with the addition of western

Galilee and a broad corridor from the coast to western Jerusalem. The special international regime for Jerusalem could not be implemented and the city was divided along the cease-fire lines between Israel and Jordan.

The question of partition came to the fore again after the *Six-Day War of June 1967, as a result of which Israel found itself in control of the entire area that had constituted western Palestine. In Israel, some of those (headed by *Ḥerut leaders) who were opposed to any withdrawal from the new cease-fire lines, especially the Palestinian areas, based their attitude on the total negation of any "renewed partition of Ereẓ Israel." The majority of Israel opinion, however, supported the policy of withdrawing from a part of the newly occupied territories in exchange for effective peace treaties with the neighboring Arab states, which would put an end to the Israel-Arab conflict and grant Israel "defensible borders." This policy guided the Israel government in 1970–71 in its negotiations with Egypt and Jordan under the auspices of UN representative Gunnar Jarring, in accordance with the Security Council resolution of Nov. 22, 1967.

See also *Zionist Policy; State of *Israel, Historical Survey; *War of Independence; *Six-Day War and After; *Palestine, Inquiry Commissions. For bibliography see *White Papers.

[D.EF./ED.]

PALESTINE ECONOMIC CORPORATION (now known as **PEC Israel Economic Corporation**), a public company, incorporated in the United States through the merger of two agencies interested in the economic development of Palestine. According to its charter, its principal purpose was "to afford financial aid to commercial, banking, credit, industrial, and agricultural enterprises, cooperative or otherwise, in or relating to Palestine." In 1922 a group of prominent Jews headed by Robert *Szold formed a corporation called Palestine Cooperative Co., Inc. In 1926 another group of non-Zionist American Jews, headed by Bernard *Flexner, formed the Palestine Economic Corporation under the laws of the State of Maine. The purpose was to combine the assets of Palestine Cooperative Company, Inc. and the assets in Palestine of the Reconstruction Committee of the *American Jewish Joint Distribution Committee into a single corporation. Flexner and Szold both had a close personal relationship with Louis D. *Brandeis, and his urgings and inspiration were probably the most important factor leading to the foundation of the company. The initial authorized capital was $3,000,000. The object was to establish an organization to which American Jews might give material aid on a business basis for productive enterprises in Palestine. At first the corporation invested and operated through the Central Bank of Cooperative Institutions in Palestine, Palestine Mortgage and Credit Bank Ltd., Palestine Water Company Ltd., Bayside Land Corporation Ltd., and Loan Bank Ltd.

The Central Bank for Cooperatives was a major factor in financing diversified cooperative institutions and furthering the cooperative movement in Palestine. For many years, it was the only credit institution dealing solely with kibbutzim and cooperative societies introducing tested cooperative principles developed in Western Europe. Apart from building low-cost housing and developing large urban areas, the Bayside Land Corporation was responsible for the preparation of a master plan by eminent British town planners for the future development of the city of Haifa, which was subsequently adopted by the Palestine government and is the plan pursuant to which the modern city of Haifa has been developed. The Mortgage and Credit Bank engaged in the construction and financing of houses for workers, both urban and rural. It was instrumental in reducing costs of construction, through competitive bidding, supervision, inspection of building materials and methods, and building houses in large groups. The Loan Bank made loans to artisans, farmers, and small businesses. The Water Company introduced modern American well-boring machinery and greatly contributed to the enlargement of new wells for domestic and agricultural use. The company also engaged in geological, hydrographical, and geophysical investigations of the country and trained early settlers. It participated in the initial capital of the Palestine Electric Company and in the formation of Palestine Potash Ltd., which received the concession for the exploitation of mineral deposits in the Dead Sea. Over the years these activities have been expanded, and by 1971 the company had investments in some 50 different corporations engaged in industry, construction, transport, marketing finance, and agriculture in Israel.

Its stock was purchased by investors throughout the United States. In 1931 it increased its authorized capital to $10,030,000 and this was subsequently increased to $25,030,000. As of the end of 1970, its capital and surplus was close to $25,000,000 and its stockholders numbered many thousands. The company paid regular dividends from 1933, with the exception of the years of World War II. In 1969 Albert Levinson was president of the corporation, Robert Szold honorary chairman, and Joseph Meyerhoff chairman of the board. [JU.W.]

PALESTINE EXPLORATION FUND, a British society for the exploration of the Holy Land, founded in 1865 under the patronage of Queen Victoria; the first president and secretary were, respectively, the archbishop of York and G. Grove. The society was to be conducted strictly on scientific principles, not subject to any religious dogma. The quarterly statement of the society, first published in 1869, was still appearing in 1971. Between 1911 and 1970, six volumes of an Annual were published. After World War I it joined forces with the British School of Archaeology in Jerusalem.

The first activities of the fund included a survey of Jerusalem. It maintained C. *Warren's expedition to Jerusalem, where work was carried out mainly around the enclosure wall of the Temple. From 1874 to 1882, the fund was engaged in its second large project: the survey of the region west of the Jordan. This work was completed by C. R. *Conder, C. W. *Wilson, and H. H. H. *Kitchener and included a 26-sheet map and *Memoirs* (5 vols.). At about the same time, the society supported C. S. *Clermont-Ganneau's researches in Palestine and made a partial survey of Transjordan. In 1890 the fund resumed excavations: at Tell el-Ḥesi, directed by W. M. F. *Petrie and F. J. *Bliss; in Jerusalem, directed by Bliss and Dickie; and in the hills of the Shephelah, directed by Bliss and R. A. S. *Macalister. From 1905 to 1909, it financed Macalister's large excavations at *Gezer and afterward started work at *Beth Shemesh, under the direction of Duncan and Mackenzie. After World War I, the fund took part in the work on the hill of Ophel, directed by Mackenzie, Macalister, and J. W. *Crowfoot, and in the excavations at Samaria, under the direction of Crowfoot. After World War II, it participated in the excavations of K. *Kenyon in Jericho and Jerusalem. In addition to its field work, the Palestine Exploration Fund has published a series of English translations of oriental sources and the accounts of ancient pilgrims. It has an excellent library and archives at the London headquarters.

[M.A.-Y.]

PALESTINE OFFICE, the name of a Zionist institution whose meaning and function was entirely different before World War I and after it. (1) In 1908 a Palestine office (*Palaestinaamt*) was established in Ereẓ Israel, with its seat in Jaffa, by the executive of the World Zionist Organization. Headed by Arthur *Ruppin, it served under the Ottoman regime as the central agency for Zionist settlement activities, including land purchase and aiding immigration. (2) After World War I the name Palestine Offices was applied to Zionist "consulates" in the Diaspora countries charged with the organization, regulation, and implementation of Jewish immigration to Palestine. The first Palestine Office of this kind was set up in Vienna in 1918. Subordinated from 1921 to the Immigration Department of the Zionist Executive, which functioned under the provisions of the Mandate as the *Jewish Agency for Palestine, the Palestine offices were run in every country by a commission (*Palaestinaamtskommission*) composed of representatives of various Zionist parties, on the basis of parity or according to their strength at the last Zionist

Congress, frequently with a preponderance of Labor Zionists and always with a strong representation of pioneering youth movements. The composition and functions of the Palestine offices were governed by the resolutions of Zionist Congresses, particularly the 12th, 13th, and 14th (1921–25).

In the 1920s and 1930s the Palestine Office distributed the immigration "certificates" issued by the Mandatory government to the Jewish Agency; dealt with *hakhsharah* (i.e., agricultural training of *ḥalutzim*); provided information to prospective immigrants; prepared and provided the necessary travel documents; and served as a link to the British consulates and the authorities of the country concerned. In those years Palestine offices existed in most European capitals (the largest being in Warsaw), as well as in exit ports to Palestine (like Trieste), and large provincial towns of some countries with a dense Jewish population (like Poland). After the outbreak of World War II, the Geneva Palestine Office engaged in rescuing Jews from Axis-dominated territories and transferring them to Palestine. In later stages of the war, the offices in Istanbul and Teheran—and after its end, those in Vienna, Munich, Rome, and Marseilles—acquired particular importance in these rescue operations. After World War II the Palestine offices unofficially assisted the "*illegal" immigration to Palestine of refugees and survivors of the Holocaust.

With the establishment of the State of Israel (1948), the jurisdiction and activities of these offices underwent considerable change. They were named offices of the Immigration Department of the Jewish Agency and, mostly administered by emissaries from Israel, were charged with nongovernmental functions complementary to those of the consulates of the Israel government, as, e.g., the promotion and organization of Jewish immigration to Israel and particularly the transport of immigrants needing the Jewish Agency's assistance.

See also Arthur *Ruppin.

Bibliography: World Zionist Organization *Protocols of the Zionist Congresses,* esp. of the 12th, 13th, and 14th; Zionist Organization, *Executive Report . . . to the 22nd Zionist Congress* (1946); JL, s.v. *Palestina-Aemter.* [A.Z.]

PALEY, WILLIAM SAMUEL (1901–), U.S. radio and television executive. Born in Chicago, Paley joined his father Samuel Paley's cigar manufacturing business, in which he served as vice-president from 1922 to 1928. In the

William S. Paley, founder of Columbia Broadcasting System. Courtesy CBS, New York.

course of advertising cigars over the airwaves Paley became impressed with the potential of the radio medium and in 1928 bought a financially unsuccessful chain of 16 eastern U.S. radio stations which he renamed the Columbia Broadcasting System (CBS). Under his direction CBS grew into one of the three giant coast-to-coast radio networks in the United States. After World War II Paley led CBS into the field of television, where it once again established itself as one of the three great national networks. As chairman of the board of CBS from 1946 on, he revolutionized the television industry by taking control of all programming away from the advertising agencies and investing it in the network itself. By the mid-1960s CBS television led both NBC and ABC on all national ratings, and the initial $400,000 investment with which Paley had bought the chain in 1928 was reputedly worth close to $70,000,000.

During World War II he served as deputy chief of the psychological warfare division of the Allied command (SHAEF) in Europe. Paley established the William S. Paley Foundation, Inc., and as president was responsible for the foundation's generous donations to the Weizmann Institute of Science, Reḥovot, as well as other Israel institutions and funds. He was also a trustee and board member of many public institutions and amassed one of the largest known private collections of French postimpressionist art. [Ed.]

PALGRAVE, English family. Sir Francis (1788–1861) was an English historian. The son of a London stockbroker named Meyer Cohen, Palgrave was an infant prodigy and, at the age of eight, made a French translation of *The Battle of the Frogs and the Mice,* a Greek classic attributed to Homer, which was published by his father (1797). When he married a non-Jew in 1823 he became a Christian and adopted his mother-in-law's maiden name. In 1827 he

Francis Palgrave, English historian. Jerusalem, J.N.U.L., Schwadron Collection.

qualified as a barrister, but displayed increasing interest in English history and his plans for the publication of the national records were officially approved. Knighted in 1832, Palgrave became first deputy keeper of the Public Records in 1838, retaining the post until his death. In this capacity he was in effect the chief organizer of the Public Record Office and distinguished himself as the first English historian to make systematic use of medieval records. His two outstanding works were *The Rise and Progress of the English Commonwealth* (1832) and *The History of Normandy and England* (4 vols., 1851–64). Francis Palgrave's four sons also gained renown in various spheres. Sir Francis Turner (1824–1897) became assistant secretary of education (1855–84). A close friend of the poet Tennyson, he is remembered for his classic anthology, *The Golden Treasury of the Best Songs and Lyrical Poems in the English Language* (1861; revised 1896), which went through dozens of editions. Between 1885 and 1895 F. T. Palgrave was professor of poetry at Oxford. William Gifford (1826–1888) was for some time a Jesuit missionary in Syria and Arabia. He renounced Catholicism to become a diplomat and ended his career as British minister-resident in Montevideo. He published a *Narrative of a Year's Journey through Central and Eastern Arabia, 1862–1863* (1865). Sir Robert Harry Inglis (1827–1919), a successful banker, edited *The Economist* (1877–83) and *The Dictionary of Political Economy* (3 vols., 1894–99). He also published his father's collected historical works (1919). The youngest son, Sir Reginald Francis Douce (1829–1904), who was clerk of the House of Commons (1886–1900), edited the *Rules, Orders and Forms of Procedure of the House of Commons* (1886–96), and wrote *The Chairman's Handbook* (1877).

Bibliography: DNB, and supplements; R. H. Emden, *Jews of Britain* (1943), 77–82; Edwards, in: J. M. Shaftesley (ed.), *Remember the Days. Essays... Presented to Cecil Roth* (1966), 303–22; E. Elath, *Britanniah u-Netiveha le-Hodu* (1971), 164–5.

[Ed.]

°**PALLIÈRE, AIMÉ** (1875–1949), French writer and theologian. Born into a devout Catholic family, as an adolescent Pallière intended to take holy orders but instead his spiritual odyssey led him first into the Salvation Army and eventually—as the result of a chance visit to the Lyons synagogue on the Day of Atonement—toward Judaism. Although he wished to become a Jew, he was persuaded by the Liberal Italian rabbi, E. *Benamozegh, who became his spiritual mentor, to settle for the status of a Noachide, without full conversion to Judaism. Nevertheless, he lived the life of an ardent and ascetic Jew. Although he recognized only Orthodox Judaism as authentic, Pallière became a spiritual guide to the Paris Liberal (i.e., Reform) synagogue and the French *Reform movement. He was much sought after as a lecturer and was for some time president of the World Union of Jewish Youth. He edited its periodical *Chalom* and also contributed to *Foi et Réveil.* Toward the end of his life, Pallière drew closer to the religion of his birth. Among his published works the best known is the autobiographical *Le Sanctuaire Inconnu* (1926, *The Unknown Sanctuary,* 1928). He also wrote *Bergson et le Judaïsme* (1932); *L'Ame Juive et Dieu* (n.d.); *Le Voile Soulevé* (1936); and some of his sermons were published. In 1914 he edited Benamozegh's *Israël et l'Humanité.*

Bibliography: E. Fleg, in: A. Pallière, *The Unknown Sanctuary* (1928); *Le Rayon* (Jan. 1950).

[C.S.]

PALM (biblical Heb. תָּמָר, mishnaic Heb. דֶּקֶל), the *Phoenix dactylifera.* In the Bible the word *tamar* refers only to the tree; it refers to the fruit also only in rabbinic literature. According to rabbinic tradition the "honey" enumerated among the seven species with which Israel is blessed (Deut. 8:8) is the honey of the date. The date palm is tall and straight (Song 7:8–9), and the righteous are compared to its straight trunk and evergreen foliage (Ps. 92:13). In its shade the prophet Deborah judged the people (Judg. 4:5). Because of the arched appearance of the tree top, it is also called *kippah,* symbolizing the "head" (Isa. 9:13, 19:15). Its long leaves are called the *kappot* of the palm tree and are one of the *four species taken on the feast of Tabernacles (Lev. 23:40). According to the rabbis the "*kappot* of palm" means the *lulav,* this being the stage when the leaves are close together (*kafut,* Suk. 32a). The tradition of using the closed leaves and not the open ones termed *ḥarut* may originate in the potential danger from the prickly leaflets of the latter, especially during festival processions (cf. Suk. 4:6). The palm needs a hot climate for its fruit to ripen and grows mainly in the valley of Jericho, the lowland of the southern coast, and the plains of the wilderness, so that Rabban Simeon b. Gamaliel asserted that "palms are an indication of valleys" (Pes. 53a). It does grow in the mountains but does not produce edible fruit there, whence the rebuke, "You are a mountain palm" (Sifra, ed. by J. H. Weiss (1862), 68a). It was therefore laid down that first fruits may not be brought from mountain palms (Bik. 1:3), but only from those growing in Jericho (Tosef. *ibid.* 1:5, cf. Deut. 34:3). Dates were a valuable export (Dem. 2:1), and Pliny refers to the reputation of the Jericho dates and their excellent quality (*Natural History* 13:45). He describes four varieties of dates, which are also mentioned in the Mishnah (Av. Zar. 1:5). In the Bible a number of places are named after the palm: Hazazon Tamar (Gen. 14:7), Ba'al Tamar (Jud. 20:33); Tadmor (Palmyra, I Kings 9:18). Three

Palm on a carved stone frieze of the synagogue at Capernaum (Kefar Naḥum) in Galilee, second–fourth centuries C.E. Courtesy Government Press Office, Tel Aviv.

women were named *Tamar: Judah's daughter-in-law, David's daughter, and Absalom's daughter. Its beautiful form was used as a model for sculpture (cf. Jer. 10:5). There were ornaments like *timmorot* ("palm trees") in the Temple (I Kings 6:29; cf. Ez. 40:16, *timmorim*). The *aggadah* compares Isaac and Rebekah (Lev. R. 30:10), Moses and Aaron (Targ. to Song 2:12), David and the Messiah with the palm tree (PdRE 19). The Hasmoneans took the palm as an emblem of their victory (I Macc. 13:37; II Macc. 14:4), and it appears on their coins. The Romans also engraved the image of captive Judea—*Judea capta*—sitting in mourning beneath the palm. A palm branch symbolizes the victory of the Jew against his accusers (Lev. R. 30:2): "dreaming of palm trees is a sign that one's sins have come to an end"; "dreaming of a *lulav* ["palm branch"] indicates that one is serving God wholeheartedly" (Ber. 57a).

Rabbinic literature contains much information about the growing of palm trees. Among other things, it mentions that there are male and female palms, that it is necessary to pollinate the female from the male blossom in order to obtain fruit, and that this must be done during a limited number of days (cf. Pes. 4:8). It is asserted that "the palm has desire," and in that connection the story is told of a female palm in the vicinity of Tiberias which longed for a palm in Jericho, and only began to yield fruit after being pollinated by it (Gen. R. 41:1). Of its many uses the Midrash (*ibid.*) says: "As no part of the palm has any waste, the dates being eaten, the branches used for *Hallel,* the twigs for covering [booths], the bast for ropes, the leaves for besoms, and the planed boards for ceiling rooms, so are there none worthless in Israel..."

Bibliography: Loew, Flora, 2 (1924), 306–62; H. N. and A. L. Moldenke, *Plants of the Bible* (1952), index; J. Feliks, *Olam ha-Ẓome'aḥ ha-Mikra'i* (1968[2]), 40–47.

[J.F.]

PLATE 1. The *ushpizin* prayer in the form of a *sukkah* decoration. *Ushpizin* (Aramaic for guests) is an invitation to the souls of Abraham, Isaac, Jacob, Joseph, Moses, Aaron, and David to come and spend the evening in the tabernacle. Moses and Aaron are depicted in this papercut. Germany, 18th century, parchment, $12\frac{1}{2}\times8\frac{1}{4}$ in. (32×21.2 cm.). Jerusalem, Israel Museum. Photo David Harris, Jerusalem.

PLATE 2. *Kimpetbriefel* including Ps. 121 and magic names. Germany (?), 19th century, stamped and cut-out paper, 9×11 in. (22.5×28.5 cm.). Jerusalem, Israel Museum. Photo David Harris,

PLATE 3. *Mizraḥ* with the names of the Patriarchs and of Moses, Aaron, David and Solomon on the Moorish arches. The decoration includes the Oriental open-palmed charm (*ḥamsa*). N. Africa, early 19th century, paper mounted on colored metal, 18¼×24 in. (46.5×61 cm.). Paris, Musée d'Art Juif.

PLATE 4. *Kimpetbriefel,* a protective amulet for a woman in childbirth. It was also known as a *shirha-malechl* because it was inscribed with the text of Psalm 121, beginning with the words *shir ha-ma'alot* ("a song of ascents"). E. Europe, 18th century, $6\frac{1}{2}\times8$ in. (1.6×20.5 cm.). Jerusalem, Israel Museum. Photo David Harris, Jerusalem.

PLATE 5. *Shivviti* page, with medallions giving three names of the Deity surrounded by birds and foliage. Poland, 18th–19th century, parchment, $3\frac{1}{4}\times4\frac{1}{4}$ in. (8.5×11 cm.). Jerusalem, Israel Museum. Photo David Harris, Jerusalem.

PLATE 6. *Omer* calendar, with the first day, including the benediction, placed in the center and the other 48 days in the medallions around the border. The ornamentation includes a stylized *menorah* flanked by two stags, birds, and flowers. Poland, 1866, 23×20½ in. (59×52 cm.). Jerusalem, Israel Museum. Photo David Harris, Jerusalem.

PALMA, LA, city in Andalusia, near Córdoba, S.W. Spain. The only information available on a Jewish settlement there dates from the end of the period of Jewish residence in Spain. The town was located on the estate of Don Luis de Puertocarrero, who granted refuge to the *Conversos of Córdoba when they fled to La Palma after the riots of 1473. The small community reached the high point of its history with the arrival of another large group of Conversos who had fled from *Ciudad Real on the outbreak of further anti-Converso riots in 1474. In La Palma the Conversos once again returned to Judaism, calling upon the services of a rabbi who later himself became converted to Christianity (adopting the name Fernando de Trujillo) and who, upon entering the service of the *Inquisition in Ciudad Real in 1483, denounced the whole community by revealing the details of its return to Judaism. In 1485, upon payment of 60 castellanos, its share in the expenses of the war against Granada, the community of La Palma was incorporated into that of *Córdoba.

Bibliography: Baer, Spain, index; H. Beinart, in: *Zion*, 20 (1957), 13ff.; idem, *Anusim be-Din ha-Inkvizizyah* (1964), index; Suárez Fernández, Documentos, 256. [H.B.]

PALMAḤ (abbreviation for *peluggot maḥaz;* "assault companies"), the permanently mobilized striking force of the *Haganah and later, until its dissolution, part of the Israel Defense Forces (IDF). The Palmaḥ was established by an emergency order of the Haganah's national command on May 19, 1941, when the Axis forces were nearing the approaches to Palestine. In view of the worsening situation, nine assault companies were to be established and placed in a state of readiness: three in northern Galilee, two in central Galilee, three in southern Galilee, and one in the Jerusalem area. They were to consist of volunteers from existing Haganah units prepared to report for active service on 24 hours' notice and serve in any capacity whenever and wherever required. The Palmaḥ was to serve as a national and regional fighting reserve. For purposes of administration and training the companies would be under the orders of the area commander, but for operational purposes, they were to be directly subordinate to the Haganah's high command, which would appoint a commander for each company on a permanent basis. A staff officer was appointed to supervise training and organization through the area commanders.

Yiẓḥak *Sadeh was appointed general staff officer for Palmaḥ affairs and set about establishing the first six companies, which were to be composed entirely of volunteers, in coordination with the area commanders of the Haganah. While it was in the process of formation, the

Figure 1. Some of the 23 members of the crew of the vessel "Sea Lion," who were lost on a mission to Tripoli in 1941. Courtesy Haganah Historical Archives, Tel Aviv.

Figure 2. The "German Squad" of the Palmaḥ on a training march, summer 1942. Courtesy Haganah Historical Archives, Tel Aviv.

Palmaḥ was called upon to participate in special operations in advance of the Allied invasion of Syria and Lebanon, which were under the command of the Vichy French. On the day before the official establishment of the Palmaḥ, a boat carrying 23 men, with a British liaison officer, sailed in secrecy to sabotage the refineries in Tripoli (Lebanon), but all traces of the detachment were lost. Scores of Arabic-speaking members of the Palmaḥ crossed the frontier dressed as Arabs and carried out intelligence and sabotage work in these countries. The first units of A and B companies participated in the invasion of Syria and Lebanon in June 1941 as saboteurs, guides, scouts, and intelligence men.

Gradually, the number of companies grew to 12, which were combined into battalions and, together, constituted a corps. Sadeh became its commander, with a staff of the type usual in such a force. The commander of the Palmaḥ was directly subordinate to the Haganah chief of staff. The Palmaḥ assumed the character and function of a commando unit and, in addition to the infantry, prepared a special naval force to carry out tasks that would be required in connection with "*illegal" immigration: sabotage and small engagements at sea. It also established the nucleus of an air force disguised as a civilian flying club, in which pilots were trained to fly light planes, which were more than once engaged as fighters against enemy forces. The Palmaḥ achieved high standards in physical fitness, field training, and guerilla fighting by day and night. It was the first of the Haganah forces to establish the battalion as a tactical and administrative unit. It developed high-level intelligence, sabotage, and scouting. Special attention was paid to educational activity and ideological guidance. On the principle of training every fighting man according to his ability, more section and platoon commanders were trained than were needed for current operations, on the assumption that in an emergency the Palmaḥ would widen its framework and absorb many recruits.

As the mobilized units of the Haganah until the *War of Independence, the Palmaḥ served, in effect, as a kind of laboratory for experiments in training methods and operational, tactical, and administrative concepts. Although stationed in different parts of the country, it made up a national army not restricted to local self-defense. It was given six main tasks: (1) to prepare during World War II for guerilla warfare against German and Italian invasion forces if these reached Syria, Lebanon, and Palestine; (2) to carry out, after the war, the main military operations, on land and sea, against the British Mandatory regime; (3) to play a central role in halting a possible Arab military invasion; (4) to punish Arab terrorist units that attacked the Jewish population; (5) to assume the offensive at the first suitable opportunity; (6) to establish settlements in strategically and politically important areas. The general staff of the Haganah decided in June 1941 that in the event that the front reached Palestine, the Palmaḥ would operate in strategic areas distant from Jewish centers.

At first the Allies financed part of the maintenance of the Palmaḥ units, but when the danger of foreign invasion passed, they went underground. For lack of a national budget, the fighters maintained themselves by working in settlements, mainly kibbutzim, and in the ports. In 14 days' work per month, they earned their keep for the rest of the month, which was mainly given over to training. No wages were customary in the Palmaḥ: the men received small sums for pocket-money, traveling expenses, and clothes. It fostered a comradeship in arms between officers and men, which stood the test of fire. Discipline was founded on personal conviction. According to a special decision of the staff, the men went into the reserves: privates after two years' service, squad commanders (equivalent to corporal or sergeant) after three years, and platoon commanders after four years.

In 1945, when Yiẓḥak Sadeh was appointed chief of the Haganah general staff, his deputy, Yigal *Allon, was appointed to command the Palmaḥ. In August 1948, when Allon became the commander of the southern front with the rank of *aluf* (brigadier general), his deputy, Uri Brenner, was appointed acting commander of the Palmaḥ, retaining the post until the corps was disbanded in 1948.

In 1947, when the security situation of the *yishuv* was becoming graver, units of the Palmaḥ operated in Upper Galilee, western Galilee, the Jezreel Valley, the Eẓyon Bloc, and the Negev. Others provided covering forces for convoys in hilly regions or Arab-populated areas in Upper Galilee, the road to Jerusalem, and the Negev. In the War of Independence, when the reservists were called up and the Palmaḥ received new recruits, it operated in three brigades: Yiftaḥ, under Shemu'el (Mula) Cohen; Harel, under Yosef Tabenkin; and the Negev, under Naḥum Sarig. The Palmaḥ was an integral part of the Israel Defense Forces and played a major role in all stages of the war, from the defense of isolated settlements and dangerous supply routes in strategic areas to important offensives which liberated parts of the country. Yiftaḥ led Operation Yiftaḥ to liberate Upper Galilee and Safad and repulse invading Syrian and Lebanese forces. At a later stage it fought on the southern front, the Negev, and Sinai. Harel bore the brunt of Operation Harel for the establishment and widening of the Jerusalem corridor, the liberation of the Jerusalem suburbs and Mount Zion, and the breaking through to the Jewish Quarter of the Old City. It was also active in the operations that led to the liberation of the Negev and the occupation of northern Sinai.

Figure 3. The origins of Palavir, the Palmaḥ air unit: Haganah members organized under the guise of an amateur gliders' club, 1936. Courtesy Haganah Historical Archives, Tel Aviv.

At the beginning of August 1948 Allon was appointed commander of the southern front. The question of whether the Palmaḥ should continue to preserve its special character under the command of its own special staff was raised by David *Ben-Gurion, prime minister and minister of defense in the provisional government, and others who argued that all units must be under the direct command of the IDF general staff in all respects. The leaders of the Palmaḥ, on the other hand, believed that the separate framework was necessary in order to enable it to continue to make its own special contribution to the war effort and character of the IDF. The provisional government accepted Ben-Gurion's view and decided on Nov. 7, 1948, to disband the separate staff of the Palmaḥ. In May 1948 the three Palmaḥ brigades were merged with other IDF units.

Many of the leading officers of the IDF rose from service in the Palmaḥ. To mention only the generals, they included, in addition to Yiẓḥak Sadeh and Yigal Allon, three chiefs of staff—Moshe *Dayyan, Yiẓḥak *Rabin, and Haim *Bar-Lev—as well as Yoḥai Bin-Nun, Avraham Eden, David Elazar, Yeshayahu Gavish, Mordecai Hod, Yitzḥak Hofi, Amos Ḥorev, Uzzi Narkis, El'ad Peled, Mattityahu Peled, Ezer Weizman, Ẓvi Zamir, and Raḥavam Ze'evi: This is only one indication of the Palmaḥ's special contribution to the building of the IDF, in addition to its major role in the main operations during the Haganah period and the War of Independence.

See also State of *Israel, Historical Survey, Defense; *Haganah.

Bibliography: Y. Allon, *Shield of David; the Story of Israel's Armed Forces* (1970); idem, *The Making of Israel's Army* (1970); Y. Bauer, *From Diplomacy to Resistance* (1970); *Sefer ha-Palmaḥ*, ed. by Z. Gilead, 2 vols. (1953); Y. Sadeh, *Mah Ḥiddesh Palmaḥ* (1950); Y. Allon, *Ma'arekhot Palmaḥ* (1966). [Y.A.]

°**PALMER, EDWARD HENRY** (1840–1882), English orientalist. Born in Cambridge, he took part in the 1867 Sinai Survey Expedition of the Palestine Exploration Fund. In 1869/70 he traveled with Tyrwhitt Drake in the desert of Tih, Edom, Moab, and the Lebanon, and this resulted in a two-volume work, *Desert of the Exodus* (1871), in which he described the discovery of—*inter alia*—the site of Kurnub in the Negev. He was appointed professor of Arabic in 1871. In 1881 he left Cambridge and edited the *Arabic and English Name Lists* of the *Survey of Western Palestine* (1881) in which his excellent knowledge of Arabic and other oriental languages served him well. In 1882 he was dispatched on a secret mission to Sinai in connection with British operations in Egypt against Arabi Pasha; he was assassinated there by Bedouins. His works include *Jerusalem: the City of Herod and Saladin*, written jointly with W. Besant (1888). [M.A.-Y.]

PALOMBO, DAVID (1920–1966), Israel sculptor. He was born in Jerusalem and studied sculpture, restoration, and mosaics under Ze'ev *Ben-Zvi, later teaching at the Bezalel School of Art, Jerusalem. He made his home on Mount Zion, where he founded a studio for the production of mosaics, wrought-iron work, and jewelry. In his small sculpture he moved from simplified representation to total abstraction using a diversity of materials including wood and rough or cut stone. Wrought iron attracted him and his talent was well-suited to large-scale works as part of an architectural concept. His first monumental work was the entrance gate to the *Yad Vashem Memorial in Jerusalem (1961). This embodied a rhythmic composition of welded iron bars and steel electroplatings, a technique which he subsequently repeated. The impact of these works springs from the contrast of simple but expressive elements against

"Burning Bush," a sculpture by David Palombo at the Knesset, Jerusalem. Courtesy Government Press Office, Tel Aviv.

the starkness of concrete walls. Palombo worked on other projects, of which the most important, the gates of the Knesset building in Jerusalem (1966), was finished shortly before his death in a road accident on Mount Zion.

Bibliography: Spencer, in: *Ariel* (Autumn 1967), 58–61, includes plates; B. Tammuz, *Art In Israel* (1966), 153–4. [Y.Fi.]

PALTI (**Paltiel;** Heb. פַּלְטִי, a hypocoristicon of a name like פַּלְטִיאֵל ; "God is [my] deliverance"), son of Laish from Gallim in Benjamin. Saul's daughter *Michal, who had been given in marriage to *David, was given in marriage to Palti when David incurred Saul's jealousy and had to flee the court to save his life. After Saul's death, *Abner, angered by Saul's son Ish-Bosheth, secretly offered David to win over the men of Israel for him. David, however, refused to even begin negotiations unless he brought Michal to him. It was probably under pressure of the powerful Abner that Ish-Bosheth took Michal away from Palti and returned her to David. It is related that the unhappy Palti followed Michal in tears until Abner ordered him to turn back (II Sam. 3:15–16). [Ed.]

PALTIEL (d. 975), astrologer, physician, and statesman in the court of the Fatimid caliph, al-Muʿizz. Paltiel is referred to in two Hebrew sources. Ahimaaz, his relative, lists him in his genealogy (*Megillat Aḥima'az*, ed. B. Klar (1944), 35–45), indicating that in 962, with al-Muʿizz's conquest of the south Italian city of Oria, which was Paltiel's birthplace, the caliph was taken with Paltiel's astrological skills and appointed him as his chief aide. The *Sefer Ḥasidim* of *Judah b. Samuel of Regensburg notes that Paltiel was captured during the conquest of Ora, and that he became the physician of the Fatimid ruler. Ahimaaz describes how during the conquest of Egypt by the caliph (969), Paltiel was charged with provisioning the army. It appears that Paltiel was *Wāsiṭa* (somewhat lower than vizier). He appears to have served as state secretary, or in some similar position, and in connection with this office he handled matters of military administration. Ahimaaz refers to him by the title **nagid* on three occasions. For this reason, J. *Mann and others presume that he was the first to bear this title in Egypt. However, it has already been shown that his public office had no connection with duties performed for his coreligionists, as was the case with a *nagid* at a later date.

Other scholars have tried to identify Paltiel with well-known personalities of his generation. M. J. de Goeje (in: ZDMG, 52 (1898), 75–80) stated that Paltiel was none other than al-Jawhar, a well-known Fatimid military leader. Thus, he concluded that Jawhar must have been a Jew. D. Kaufmann and W. J. Fischel sought to identify him with a Jewish convert to Islam, Yaʿqūb *ibn Killis, the first of the Fatimid viziers of Egypt. A. *Marx maintains the view of de Goeje on the basis of the *Sefer Ḥasidim* reference. It has been established, however, that neither of these identifications is correct. B. *Lewis identified him with Mūsā ibn Eleazar, who was captured during the Fatimid conquest of Oria, and of whom it is known that he became the physician of the caliph al-Muʿizz, and was with him during his conquest of Egypt. A number of Mūsā's medical writings are extant, and he was also a friend of Yaʿqūb ibn Killis. After Paltiel's death, the office of court physician to the Fatimid caliphate was filled for four generations by Paltiel's descendants.

Bibliography: Marx, in: JQR, 1 (1910/11), 78–85; Mann, Egypt, index; Fischel, Islam, 65–68; Neustadt, in: *Zion*, 4 (1939), 135–43; Hirschberg, *ibid.*, 23–24 (1958/59), 166f.; Hirschberg, Afrikah, 1 (1965), 152–4; Lewis, in: *Bulletin of the School of Oriental and African Studies*, 30 (1967), 177–81. [A.D.]

PALTOI BAR ABBAYE, *gaon* of Pumbedita from 842 to 857; father of *Ẓemaḥ Gaon. Paltoi was a powerful, energetic, and strong-minded personality. His appointment heralded a new era of prominence for the gaonate of Pumbedita. His authority was such that the exilarch had to come to his academy in order to convene a public assembly. During his gaonate the ties with the outside communities were strengthened and increased. Paltoi and Ẓemaḥ were the first *geonim* to establish contact with the community of North Africa. A community in Spain sent a request to Paltoi "to write the Talmud and its explanations for them," basing their request on the grounds that "the majority of the people have recourse to digests of the *halakhah (hilkhot ketu'ot)* and say 'what need have we for the difficulties of the Talmud?' " Paltoi vigorously protested against this. "They are not acting correctly, and it is forbidden to do this. They thereby cause a decline in the study of the Torah, causing it to be forgotten." His extant responsa, which are to be found in most collections of geonic responsa, as well as being quoted in the works of the **posekim*, only represent a minority of those he wrote. New fragments were published by A. N. Z. Roth.

Bibliography: Abramson, Merkazim, 10, 16; Assaf, Ge'onim, 52f., 171; A. N. Z. Roth, in: *Tarbiz*, 25 (1956), 140–8; M. Margolioth, *ibid.*, 149–53. [M.H.]

PAM, HUGO (1870–1930), U.S. jurist and Zionist leader. Pam, who was born in Chicago, practiced law in that city with his brother Max. In 1911 he was elected to the Cook County Superior Court, on which he served for 20 years. As a judge he developed a special interest in the psychology of criminal behavior, which led him to be chosen vice-president of the Illinois Society of Mental Hygiene. He also served for three years as president of the American Institute of Criminal Law and Criminology. Pam became active in organized Jewish life in 1912, when he joined the Federation of American Zionists, of which he was later vice-president. He took part in the founding of the *American Jewish Congress in 1916. After World War I, he traveled to Russia and Poland on behalf of HIAS (Hebrew Sheltering and Immigrant Aid Society—see *HICEM) to survey conditions in the Jewish communities there. [A.Li.]

PAMIERS, town in the department of Ariège, France. The earliest evidence of the presence of Jews in Pamiers goes back to 1256. They were then under the authority of the abbot of Saint Antonin of Pamiers who, in 1274, protested against the Jews having to pay the royal poll tax and claimed their contributions belonged to him alone. The community appears to have been relatively well established by 1279; in that year a series of internal regulations (concerning the restriction of private expenditures, religious discipline, and mutual assistance) were drawn up and immediately approved by the abbot of Saint Antonin. The text of these regulations, the oldest of their type, has been preserved. The community was administered by two or more trustees and internal taxes were levied. The subsequent abbots of Saint Antonin continued to assure the relatively favorable condition of the Jews. When Saint Antonin became a bishopric, the Jews were still protected from the excesses of the inquisitors (1298). However, the bishop was unsuccessful in his opposition to the expulsion order of 1306. A community was reconstituted between 1315 and 1322. Although Bishop Jacques Fournier ordered a relentless search for volumes of the Talmud so as to have them burnt (see *Talmud, Burning of), he nevertheless protected his Jewish subjects from the persecutions of the Pastoureaux to the extent that many Jews from the rest of the region sought refuge in the town. After the expulsion of 1322, Jews occasionally passed through Pamiers and are thus mentioned in the toll tariffs of 1327 and 1340. A third community was formed after 1359. At the close of the 19th century, a Hebrew seal of a certain Solomon Vidal b. Pourtaya was found and survives as the only material trace of the Jews of Pamiers.

Bibliography: G. Saige, *Juifs en Languedoc*... (1881), index; Gross, Gal Jud, 438; J. de Lahondes, in: *Annales de Pamiers*, 1 (1882), 38, 86, 144; J. Ourgaud, *Notice historique sur... Pamiers* (1865), 108, 130, 255; J. A. Blanchet, in: REJ, 18 (1889), 139–41; E. Ferran, in: *Bulletin philologique et historique* (1903), 184ff.; J. M. Vidal, *Le Tribunal d'inquisition à Pamiers* (1906), 67, 80; B. Blumenkranz, in: *Archives Juives*, 5 (1968–69), 38ff., 47ff.

[B.BL.]

PAMPHYLIA, region in the southern part of Asia Minor. According to a Roman decree quoted in I Maccabees (15:16ff.), Pamphylia was among those countries notified by the Roman consul Lucius (142 B.C.E.) of the renewed pact of friendship between the Roman Senate and the Jewish nation under the high priest Simeon. Numerous scholars have deduced from this document that a Jewish community existed in Pamphylia (cf. F.-M. Abel, *Les Livres des Maccabées* (1949), 269) as well as the other districts mentioned in the decree. There is, however, only sparse information on Jewish communities in Pamphylia. There is some information about the Jews in Pamphylia in the city of Side in I Maccabees 15:23 (cf. also a late inscription from the Byzantine period from Side (*Journal of Hellenic Studies*, 28 (1908), 195)), and also mention of Jews in Pamphylia in Philo's *Legatio ad Gaium*, 281, and in Acts 2:10. Josephus makes no mention of such a community, and refers to the area primarily in connection with Herod, who was nearly shipwrecked not far from Pamphylia on his way to Rome in 40 B.C.E. (Ant. 14:377; Wars 1:280).

Bibliography: Schuerer, Gesch, 3 (1909[4]), 22; Juster, Juifs, 1 (1914), 192.

[I.G.]

PAMPLONA (Pomplona, Pampeluna), city in N. Spain; capital of the former kingdom of Navarre. Pamplona's Jewish community appears to have been founded during the renewed Christian domination of the peninsula after the Muslim conquest. The earliest information, however, on the Jews in the city dates from the tenth century. In 958 *Ḥisdai ibn Shaprut visited Pamplona on a diplomatic mission to confer with Sancho I, king of León, who had found refuge there. At that time there was already a Jewish quarter in the section of the city known as the Navarrería. Even though there is no extant information, there is no doubt that a Jewish community continued to exist in Pamplona throughout the 11th and 12th centuries. In 1277 anti-Jewish riots occurred, the Jewish quarter was apparently destroyed, and the community's property confiscated. In 1280 the town was ordered to restitute the property and allocate space for the erection of Jewish homes. Nonetheless, only after the suppression of the French *Pastoureaux (1320) was the community able to start rebuilding the quarter.

Numerous accounts and receipts involving the Jews of Pamplona in the 14th century are extant in the archives of the town. A considerable part of the documents are written in Hebrew and bear the signatures of royal agents, physicians, and merchants who were involved in royal transactions. Among other occupations, the Jews of Pamplona owned vineyards and farms or traded with communities in Navarre, Aragon, and Castile. King Charles II of Navarre (1349–87) even exempted the Jews of Pamplona from the prohibition of bringing grapes into the town as they were for private use and the taxes from Jews were based on their incomes from wine. As evidenced from the tax accounts, the community possessed considerable means but, nevertheless, was—like the other communities of Navarre—in a state of crisis and decline. Pamplona was the site of the disputation on Dec. 26, 1375, between R. Shem Tov b. Isaac Shaprut and Pedro de Luna, who later became the anti-pope *Benedict XIII. Toward the close of the 14th century R. Ḥayyim *Galipapa, the author of *Emek Refa'im*, was rabbi of Pamplona.

At the beginning of the 15th century there were over 200 Jewish families living in Pamplona; this increase in the Jewish population was probably due to refugees from the persecutions of 1391 which took place in the kingdoms of Aragon and Castile. In 1400 the king gave Isaac Alburji, who was probably a goldsmith in the employ of the court, 345 gold florins from the taxes collected in the community. Other Jews were employed as purveyors to the court. In 1407, however, Charles III ordered the sale of Jewish property and notables of the community were imprisoned. During 1410–11 a plague ravaged Pamplona and many members of the community were among the victims; the community, however, appears to have recovered. In 1469 Leonor, the daughter of John II—in her function as regent of the kingdom—ordered that a strict watch be kept over the Jews to assure that they only lived in their quarter of town. When the Jews were expelled from Spain in 1492, some of them went to Pamplona. They suffered the same fate as the rest of the community, however, when the Jews of the kingdom of Navarre were expelled in 1498.

Bibliography: Baer, Spain, index; Baer, Urkunden, 1 (1929), index; M. Kayserling, *Juden in Navarra*... (1861), index; J. Ma. Sanz Artibucilla, in: *Sefarad*, 5 (1945), 339; F. Cantera y Burgos, *Sinagogas españolas* (1955), 263.

[H.B.]

PANĂ, SAŞA (originally **Alexander Binder;** 1902–), Rumanian poet and author. Born in Bucharest, Pană qualified as a physician and, while serving as an army medical officer, achieved a reputation as a writer.

Generally considered the most fanatical propagator of avant-garde literary trends, he was the guiding spirit of the literary review *Unu* (1928–32), Rumania's most important avant-garde magazine. Pană's blunt manifesto begins with the words: "Reader, disinfect your brains." His own poems are notable for their scorn of literary conformism. He wrote essays and, after World War II, sketches and short stories inspired by army life mainly satirizing the behavior of officers. Pană also wrote some short plays and translations from Paul Eluard and Ilarie *Voronca. Between 1926 and 1968 he published some 30 volumes. In the collection of verse entitled *Pentru libertate* ("For Freedom," 1945) there is a poem about the transportation of Rumanian Jews to Transnistria and the crimes committed by the SS. Another volume on the same theme, *Poeme fără imaginaţie* ("Poems Without Imagination," 1948) was dedicated "to all the victims of the Nazi brutes... to Benjamin Fordane and Ilarie Voronca..." Pană edited *Uliţa evreească* ("The Jewish Street," 1946), a volume of reproductions of wood carvings by Aurel Mărculescu, and an album by the same author (1967) depicting scenes from life in the Transnistrian camps to which the artists had been transported. In 1969 Pană published an anthology of Rumania's avant-garde literature *(Anthologia literaturii române de avangard)*.

Bibliography: G. Calinescu, *Istoria Literaturii Române*... (1941), 803, 922; L. Cristescu, in: *Contemporanul* (July 2, 1965).

[D.L.]

PANAMA, Central American republic. The general population of Panama in 1960 was 1,075,571. A census conducted in the same year by the B'nai B'rith found 1,807 Jews in Panama, 1,387 of whom lived in the capital, Panama; 257 in Colon; 163 in other areas; and 200 American Jews in the Canal Zone under the control of the United States. At the end of the Spanish Colonial Administration in 1821, Panama became attached to *Colombia. At that time several Sephardi Jews from Jamaica and Ashkenazi Jews from Central Europe settled in the provinces. Because of a lack of a Jewish environment, they intermarried and assimilated. In the middle of the 19th century, a number of immigrants of Sephardi origin from the Caribbean region and a few Ashkenazim from Europe, who arrived at the time of the gold rush in California—especially after the completion of the railroad in 1855—settled in the city of Panama. A new wave of Sephardi immigrants arrived after the earthquake in St. Thomas in 1867. The first Jewish community, Kol Shearith Israel, was founded in 1876. A synagogue was established, as well as a cemetery and a mutual-assistance organization. About the same time, in Colon, another Jewish organization was established. After the construction of the Panama Canal, the census of 1911 found 505 declared Jews. Owing to intermarriages the Kol Shearith Israel congregation diminished considerably. It was affiliated with the Reform movement and descendants of many of its founders have turned away from Judaism. The wave of conversions along with reemigration was the reason that in spite of the immigration of a large number of Sephardim after World War I as well as Ashkenazi Jews from Eastern and Western Europe, the total of Panamanian Jewry was estimated in 1936 at only 600 persons. The largest Jewish congregation in Panama, Shevet Aḥim, has an Orthodox synagogue and consists of Jews of Levantine origin. The third congregation, Beth El, also has an Orthodox synagogue and consists of a small group of Ashkenazi Jews who arrived in the 1930s from Nazi-dominated Europe. A central council acts as a unifying body of the three congregations to represent the affairs of the community and raise funds for Israel. It is affiliated with the Federation of Jewish Communities of Central America. The Jewish day school, Instituto Alberto Einstein (founded in 1954), consists of pre-primary, primary, and secondary grades, and provides secular and Jewish education on high academic standards to almost all Jewish children. A community center, B'nai B'rith, *WIZO, and a students' club are the other major Panamanian Jewish institutions. In spite of their limited numbers, the Jews of Colon organized into two separate communities, Ashkenazi and Sephardi. These communities are also affiliated with the central council.

The laws that limited the rights of aliens, allowing only 25% of them to work in some companies, and difficulties in the process of attaining citizenship made it difficult for Jewish immigrants to solve their economic problems. In spite of these obstacles, however, Jews succeeded in integrating. They are engaged mainly in commerce, banking, and light industry, in which they were pioneers. Some have coffee plantations, farms, and cattle ranches, and the young generation goes into professions in which many have distinguished themselves. Jewish contribution to Panamaian culture has had a great impact, especially in music and education. Jews cherish their political rights and occupy high positions in the Republic. From 1964–68 Max Delvalle was the first vice-president of the Republic and also acted as president for a time. There are three rabbis in the country. Religious life is centered around the different communities, some of which have their own cemeteries. The synagogue in the Canal Zone was maintained by the Jewish Welfare Board.

Relations with Israel. Relations between Panama and Israel were cordial, especially after 1960, when the two countries first exchanged ambassadors. Panama consistently supported Israel in the United Nations. Israel extended experts to Panama, particularly in cattle raising, fruit orchards, agricultural produce for industrial processes, and the organization of consumer cooperation. Israel exports to Panama, composed mainly of consumer goods and ships, reached $2,200,000 in 1969.

Bibliography: A. Monk and J. Isaacson, *Communidades Judías de Latinoamérica* (1968), 102–6, 227–8, 279; H. Klepfisz, *Realidad y Vision* (1965); idem, *Un Año en el Instituto Alberto Einstein* (1962); J. Beller, *Jews in Latin America* (1969), 52–57.

[H.Kl.]

PANET, EZEKIEL BEN JOSEPH (1783–1845), Transylvanian rabbi. He was born in Bielitz (Bielsko), Silesia. Under the *Familiants Laws, as the second son of his father, he was forbidden to marry in the country and went to Linsk in Poland. He continued his studies in Linsk until 1807, when he was appointed rabbi of Ostrik in Galicia, and in 1813 became rabbi of Tarcal in Hungary. Panet held the ḥasidic rabbis in high esteem and maintained close contacts with them. While in Tarcal he became particularly intimate with the ḥasidic rabbi Isaac *Taub, the rabbi of Nagykallo. According to the inscription on his tombstone, Panet also engaged in Kabbalah. After the death of R. Mendel, the rabbi of Alba-Iulia, in 1823, the community asked R. Moses *Sofer to recommend a successor. Panet was one of three candidates recommended by Sofer, and he was elected, serving until his death. From 1754 to 1868 the rabbi of this ancient community was regarded as the chief rabbi of Transylvania, and in fact his seal bore the Latin inscription: *Supperabi Transilvaniae-sigil-Ezechiel Panet.*

The Jewish population of the district was small at the time, and religious life was at a low ebb. Panet acted energetically in bringing about a religious revival. Since there were practically no other rabbis in the whole province, he supervised the religious life of the whole area, making regular and repeated journeys for this purpose to the smallest and most isolated communities. During his period of office the community of Alba-Iulia gradually went over from the Sephardi rite, which had hitherto prevailed, to the Ashkenazi. Although according to a family tradition Panet left about 18 bound volumes in manuscript, only one of his works was published (posthumously): the responsa *Mareh Yeḥezkel u-She'arei Ẓiyyon* (1875). It is the first volume of responsa of a Transylvanian rabbi, and in addition to its halakhic value is important as a source for the contemporary history of the Jews of Transylvania. Panet also collected funds for the Hungarian **kolel* in Ereẓ Israel. Panet's descendants (some of whom spelled their name Paneth) were well-known rabbis in the Orthodox communities of Transylvania and Hungary. A genealogical table of his descendants and where they served as rabbis appears in the work of his descendant Philip Paneth (see bibl.). One of his sons, Menahem Mendel (d. 1884), founded the Dej ḥasidic dynasty.

Bibliography: *"Toledot Yeḥezkel,"* in: H. B. Panet, *Derekh Yivḥar* (1894); M. Eisler, in: IMIT (1901), 241–3; P. Paneth, *Rabbenu Jecheskël* (Eng., 1927); J. J. Cohen, in: *Ha-Ma'yan*, 4 no. 2 (1964), 34–45.

[Y.M.]

PANETH, FRIEDRICH ADOLF (1887–1958), Austrian physical and radioactivity chemist. Paneth, a son of Joseph Paneth, a physiologist who discovered certain histological cells which still bear his name, was born in Vienna. Both his parents were born Jews, but they brought up their children as Protestants. Paneth worked from 1912 to 1917 at the Institute for Radium Research in Vienna, where with the Hungarian chemist George Hevesy he carried out the first use of radioactive tracers to measure physical properties. From 1918 he held professorships successively at the Prague Institute of Technology, and Hamburg, Berlin, Koenigsberg universities. When the Nazis came to power in 1933 he went to London, where he worked first at the Imperial College and then as reader in atomic chemistry in the University of London. In 1939 he was appointed professor of chemistry at Durham University, where he remained for 14 years. During this time he was chairman of the chemistry division of the British Canadian atomic energy team in Montreal (1943–45). In 1947 he was elected a fellow of the Royal Society. On his retirement from Durham in 1953 he returned to Germany as director of the Max Planck Institute for Chemistry at Mainz.

Paneth's prolific output of scientific papers dealt mainly with radioactive tracers, free radicals, and neutron radiation. He developed new methods for the analysis of helium and used them to determine the age and origin of meteorites. His books include *Radio-Elements as Indicators, and Other Selected Topics in Inorganic Chemistry* (1928) and *The Origin of Meteorites* (1940).

Bibliography: H. Dingle et al. (eds.), *Chemistry and Beyond* (1964); H. J. Emeléus, in: Royal Society of London, *Biographical Memoirs,* 6 (1960), 227–46; *Chemiker-Zeitung,* 81 (1957), 618.

[S.A.M.]

PANEVEZYS (**Panevezhis;** Lith. **Panevežys;** Rus. **Ponevezh**), city in N. Lithuanian S.S.R. In 1766 the Jewish community numbered 254; in 1847, 1,447 Jews were registered, and in 1897, 6,627 Jews (50% of the total population) lived in Panevezys. An ancient *Karaite community is also known to have existed there. A number of noted rabbis officiated in Panevezys, among them Isaac Jacob Rabinovich (Itzele *Ponevezher), Joseph Sh. *Kahaneman, and Jeroham Leibovich. The Hebrew poet Judah Leib *Gordon served as a teacher in the city from 1853 to 1860. Naphtali *Friedman, a noted advocate, served as delegate from Panevezys to the third *Duma.

In May 1915, during World War I, the Jews of Panevezys were sent along with other Lithuanian Jews to the interior of Russia by the Russian military authorities. Most of them returned after the Russian Revolution. In 1923 there were 6,845 Jews living in Panevezys (35% of the total population), most of them occupied in small trade and crafts and some in larger business enterprises and industry.

The community had an active social and cultural life. Its educational institutions included Hebrew and Yiddish primary schools, two Hebrew secondary schools (one belonging to the Zionist-orientated *Tarbut educational system and the other, for girls, to the religious *Yavneh), a Jewish pro-gymnasium, and libraries.

The Panevezys Yeshivah, which had a high reputation, was founded by Liebe Miriam Gavronsky, daughter of K. Z. Wissotszky. When the Jews were expelled during World War I, the yeshivah was first moved to *Ludza in Vitebsk province and then to Mariupol (*Zhdanov) in the Ukraine. After World War I Rabbi Kahaneman founded the great Ohel Yiẓḥak yeshivah in Panevezys with about 200 students. In 1944 the yeshivah was reestablished by Rabbi Kahaneman in *Bene Berak, Israel.

Panevezys was occupied by the Germans in 1941 a few days after the outbreak of the German-Soviet war. A ghetto was established from which Jews were transported and murdered in September 1941. They were buried in 12 mass graves. In 1968 the Jewish cemetery at Panevezys was destroyed.

Bibliography: *Lite,* 1 (1951), index; 2 (1965), index; *Yahadut Lita,* 1 (1959), index; 3 (1967), 335–7; J. Gar, in: *Algemeyne Entsiklopedie: Yidn,* 6 (1964), index. [Jo.Ga.]

Faculty and students of the Panevezys Yeshivah, 1929. Courtesy Yad Vashem Archives (Y. Kamson Collection), Jerusalem.

PANIGEL, ELIYAHU MOSHE (1850–1919), Sephardi chief rabbi of Ereẓ Israel. Orphaned in childhood, Panigel was raised by his uncle, the Sephardi chief rabbi of Ereẓ Israel *(rishon le-Zion),* Rabbi Raphael Meir *Panigel. He was sent on fund-raising missions to Algeria by the Misgav la-Dakh Hospital in Jerusalem and to North Africa, Italy, India, the Caucasus and Bokhara, by the Jerusalem community. An outstanding preacher and cantor, he eulogized Herzl in Jerusalem upon his death in 1904. In 1907 he was appointed *ḥakham bashi* (chief rabbi of the Ottoman Empire) and Sephardi chief rabbi of Ereẓ Israel. When Jerusalem was captured by the British in 1917, he publicly welcomed General Allenby and the Jewish Legion.

Bibliography: M. D. Gaon, *Yehudei ha-Mizraḥ be-Ereẓ Yisrael,* 1 (1928), 527–30. [G.B.-Y.]

PANIGEL, RAPHAEL MEIR BEN JUDAH (1804–1893), chief rabbi of Jerusalem. Panigel was born in Bulgaria, but when he was three years old his parents, who were well-to-do, immigrated to Ereẓ Israel. In 1828 and in 1863 he went as an emissary of Jerusalem to the countries of North Africa, remaining there on both occasions for several years. In 1845 he went to Italy as an emissary of Hebron. While in Rome he succeeded in making peace between two rival factions in the community. He was also received with great respect at the Vatican by Pope Gregory XVI. In 1866 he supported Ludwig August *Frankl in his endeavor to establish a modern school in Jerusalem. In 1880 he was appointed **rishon le-Zion,* and in 1890 the Turkish authorities appointed him *ḥakham bashi* (head of the Jewish community of Ereẓ Israel). He was acceptable to all the communities and esteemed by the authorities. He was the author of *Lev Marpe* (the initials of his name; 1887), talmudic novellae, responsa, and homilies. Some of his novellae were published in the Jerusalem *Me'assef* and in *Torah mi-Ẓiyyon*. His other works have remained in manuscript.

Bibliography: A.M. Luncz, in: *Yerushalayim*, 4 (1892), 214–5 (Heb. pt.); Frumkin-Rivlin, 3 (1929), 312; M. D. Gaon, *Yehudei ha-Mizraḥ be-Ereẓ Yisrael*, 2 (1937), 533–4; Yaari, Sheluḥei, index, s.v. [A.D.]

PANKEN, JACOB (1879–1968), judge and U.S. Socialist leader. Born in the Ukraine, Panken was taken to the United States as a child. He worked in leather factories in New York City and attended school in the evenings. Panken was admitted to the bar in 1905. In 1917, he was elected a judge of New York City's Municipal Court and served until 1928. In 1934 he was appointed a judge of the Domestic Relations Court, a post which he held for 20 years. Panken was attracted to the labor movement from his youth. At the age of 18 he organized a leather goods union and later helped found the Ladies Garment Workers Union (1900). In those days, gangsters had ties with employers as well as with politicians in New York's East Side. Thus, prominent figures in the socialist movement were the objects of violence. Panken was shot at in 1904 and assaulted by thugs in 1906.

Panken represented U.S. Socialists at a number of international congresses and at the same time maintained association with Jewish movements. When World War I broke out, he was one of the organizers of the People's Relief Committee to aid the Jews of Eastern Europe. Later, he helped to organize the American branch of *ORT and for many years was its president. He was also president of the *Jewish Daily Forward* from 1917 to 1925. His writings include *Socialism in America* (1931) and *The Child Speaks: The Prevention of Juvenile Delinquency* (1941). [CH.R.]

PANOFSKY, ERWIN (1892–1968), U.S. art historian. Born in Hanover, Germany, he fled to the U.S. in 1934. He was appointed visiting professor of fine arts at New York University and at Princeton University, where he remained as a professor in the Institute for Advanced Studies. He was a man of many gifts and for a year in 1947 was the Charles Eliot Norton professor of poetry at Harvard. While there

Erwin Panofsky, U.S. art historian. Courtesy Harvard College Archives, Cambridge, Mass.

he developed understanding and interest in "Netherlandish Painting" and also exposed several frauds in works attributed to such Dutch masters as Jan Van Eyck. As an authority on old movies he published in 1937 "Style and Medium in the Moving Pictures" which is still regarded as a classic film commentary. As a leading art historian he published, with Dora Panofsky, *Pandora's Box, The Changing Aspects of a Mythical Symbol* (1956), and a collection of papers: *Meaning in the Visual Arts* (1957).

Bibliography: M. Meiss (ed.), *Essays in Honor of Erwin Panofsky*, 2 vols. (1961), incl. bibl.; D. Wildenstein et al., in: *Gazette des Beaux-Arts*, 71 (1968), 257–68, incl. bibl. [ED.]

PAP, ARTHUR (1921–1959), philosopher. Born and brought up in Zurich, where his father was a successful businessman, he moved to New York in 1941. He taught at the University of Chicago, where he was greatly influenced by Rudolf Carnap, one of the founders of the Vienna school of Logical Positivism. Pap assumed a teaching position at Yale University in the mid-1950s.

Considered one of the ablest philosophers of his generation, Pap developed a modified, flexible type of logical positivism. The flexible approach that characterized his work is clearly seen in his five books and numerous articles, particularly in *Semantics and Necessary Truth* (1958), which is perhaps the most careful and meticulous inquiry into the notion of necessary proof. His *Elements of Analytic Philosophy* (1949) and *An Introduction to the Philosophy of Science* (1962) reflect his desire to make science philosophically accurate in its formulations and to make philosophy scientific in its approach.

Bibliography: *New York Times* (Sept. 8, 1959), 35. [ED.]

PAP, KÁROLY (1897–1945), Hungarian author. Born in Sopron, where his father Miksa *Pollák was the rabbi of the Neolog community, Pap was an officer in the Austro-Hungarian army during World War I and was decorated for bravery. After demobilization, he joined Béla *Kun's October Revolution and became a Hungarian Red Army commander. On the collapse of the revolution he was arrested, reduced to the ranks, and condemned to 18 months' imprisonment. After his release he left the country until 1925. Then, settling in Budapest, he began writing poetry and stories. He soon became known as a short story writer, but wishing to remain independent, he refused to take any employment.

Pap's first novel, *Megszabaditottál a haláltól* ("Thou Hast Delivered Me from Death," 1932), which dealt with a popular Jewish Messiah in the time of Jesus, was enthusiastically received by liberal and radical writers, notably the great Hungarian author, Zsigmond Móricz, who gave him much encouragement. The character of Jesus and the period in which he lived recur constantly in Pap's writings, not because of any attraction to Christianity but because, in his opinion, this "classical" period of Judaism retained traces of the Divinity, and at the same time presented social contrasts and gave Jews the taste of suffering. His great autobiographical novel, *Azarel* (1937), which portrayed his father's house through the eyes of a child, aroused a great indignation among Jewish readers because of the cruel frankness of the description. In his sensational essay, *Zsidó sebek és bűnök* ("Jewish Wounds and Sins," 1935), Pap made a thorough and candid analysis of his Jewish and non-Jewish social surroundings. He traced the history of the Jews, particularly of Hungarian Jewry, in order to expose conventional lies, especially those concerning emancipation. He found only one solution to the Jewish problem: acceptance of the fate of a national minority. He himself was fanatically attached to all aspects of Jewish life and was uncompromising in his loyalty.

During World War II the Budapest Jewish Theater performed two biblical plays by Pap: *Bathsheba* (1940) and *Moses* (1944). In May 1944 he was sent to a labor camp. From there he refused to escape and was deported to Buchenwald, and is presumed to have died in Bergen-Belsen. Three works which appeared posthumously were *A szűziesség fátylai* ("The Veils of Chastity," 1945), *A hószobor* ("The Snow Statue," 1954) and *B városában történt* ("It Happened in the City B," 2 vols., 1964).

Bibliography: *Magyar Irodalmi Lexikon*, 2 (1965), 433–4; D. Keresztúry, in: Pap Károly, *A hószobor* (1954), introd.; A. Komlós, in: *Nyugat*, 2 (1935), 41–43. [B.Y.]

PAPA (c. 300–375), Babylonian *amora*. Papa studied under *Rava (Er. 51a) and Abbaye (Ber. 20a). After the latter's death he founded an academy at *Naresh (near Sura), where he held the post of *resh metivta* (head of the academy) (Ta'an. 9a) for 19 years, until his death. Although some of Rava's former pupils expressed dissatisfaction with Papa's teaching *(ibid.)*, his academy was famous for the number of its pupils (Ket. 106a). The extent of Papa's learning is revealed by the number of occasions in which he participated in halakhic disputes. The manner in which Papa's rulings are often given points to him as one of the editors of the Talmud. His opinion is frequently the last one quoted and it takes the form of reconciling and accepting conflicting opinions (Meg. 21b; Ta'an. 29b; Ḥul. 46a). In these cases he prefaces his decision with the word *hilkakh* "therefore." In other cases he uses the expression *shema mina,* "from this we can deduce" (the *halakhah* in a certain matter; Yoma 28b; Yev. 103a).

Papa belonged to a wealthy family and increased his fortune by his own successful business ventures (Pes. 113a). He engaged in the sale of poppy seeds (Git. 73a) and in the expert brewing of date beer (Ber. 44b; Pes. 113a; BM 65a). Rava commented on his wealth by adapting Ecclesiastes 8:14, stating "Happy are the righteous, who prosper in this world" (Hor. 10b). On one occasion Papa had to defend himself against a charge of practicing usury (BM 65a). On another, however, his action in returning some land which he had bought from a man who needed the money was praised as going beyond the strict requirements of the law (Ket. 97a). Papa was renowned for his impartiality in judgment (BM 69a) and his piety (Shab. 118b; Nid. 12b). He also had a deep respect for his fellow scholars (MK 17a) and made a point of visiting the local rabbi of any town he visited (Nid. 33b). He once undertook a self-imposed fast in atonement for speaking unkindly of a scholar (Sanh. 100a), although fasting did not agree with him (Ta'an. 24b). On another occasion, when he heard a particularly wise decision from a student, he offered him his daughter's hand in marriage (Hor. 12b). His deepest affections were reserved for his colleague Huna ben Joshua (Shab. 89a), the friendship dating from their student days (Pes. 111b; Hor. 10b). Huna served as Papa's deputy at Naresh (Ber. 57a; *Sherira Ga'on* 3:3) and was his business partner (Git. 73a). It is related that the two refused to part even for a journey (Yev. 85a).

In the course of his many business travels, Papa collected numerous popular sayings which he often quoted in discussion. Among them are: "If you hear that your neighbor has died, believe it; if you hear that he has become rich, do not believe it" (Git. 30b); "Sow corn for your use that you should not be obliged to purchase it; and strive to acquire landed property" (Yev. 63a). He also suggested advice on family relationships: "If your wife is short bend down to hear her whisper," i.e., always consult her, even though she is less important than you are (BM 59a). Papa's second wife was the daughter of Abba of Sura (Ket. 39b).

The formula to be recited at a **hadran* on the completion of the study of a tractate includes the recitation of the names of ten "sons of Papa." Although all are mentioned in the Talmud, some of them are definitely not the sons of this Papa (e.g., Surḥav and Daru). Among the various reasons that have been given for this recital is that it assists the memory.

Bibliography: Hyman, Toledot, s.v.; J. Newman, *The Agricultural Life of the Jews in Babylonia* (1932), index s.v. *R. Pappa;* Ḥ. Albeck, *Mavo la-Talmudim* (1969), 417–80.

[Ed.]

PAPA (Hung. **Pápa**), town in N.W. Hungary. A few families first settled in Papa under the protection of the Esterházy family; by 1714 the first synagogue was built. At that time the tax collector of the city was a Jew. A new synagogue was built in 1743. In 1748 Count F. Esterházy authorized Jews to settle in Papa and organize a community. A Bikkur Ḥolim society was founded in 1770. The first Jewish private school was opened in 1812, and the community school, founded in 1826, had 504 pupils in 1841. In 1899 the first junior high school was founded. The synagogue erected in 1846 was an important step toward the introduction of Reform: space was left for an organ although none was installed; the **bimah* was set in front of the Ark and not in the center of the synagogue. After the religious schism in Hungarian Jewry in 1869 the Neologists (see *Neology) left the community, but returned five years later. During the *Tiszaeszlar blood libel case (1882) anti-Jewish riots broke out in Papa but they were suppressed by the authorities.

The synagogue of Papa, Hungary, built in 1846. From I. Heller and Z. Vajda, *The Synagogues in Hungary,* New York, 1968.

The first rabbi of the community was Bernard Isaac, followed by Selig Bettelheim. The Orthodox rabbi Paul (Feiwel) Horwitz initiated the meeting of rabbis in *Paks in 1844. Leopold *Loew (1846–50) was the first rabbi to introduce Reform. Moritz *Klein, rabbi from 1876 to 1880, translated part of *Maimonides' *Guide of the Perplexed* into Hungarian. He was followed by Solomon *Breuer (1880–83). The last rabbi was J. Haberfeld, who perished with his congregation in the Holocaust.

The anti-Jewish laws of 1938–39 caused great hardship in the community, and from 1940 the young Jewish men were sent to forced-labor battalions, at first within Hungary, but later to the Russian front (1942). The Jewish population in Papa increased from 452 in 1787 to 2,645 in 1840 (19.6% of the total population), and 3,550 in 1880 (24.2%). After the beginning of the 20th century a gradual decline began; there were 3,076 Jews in 1910 (15.3%), 2,991 in 1920, 2,613 in 1941 (11%) and 2,565 in 1944. After the German occupation on March 19, 1944, the Jews were confined in a ghetto on May 24 and from there moved to a concentration camp which was set up in a factory in the town. On July 4 and 5 2,565 Jews of the city plus 300 from the vicinity were deported to Auschwitz, from which less than 10% returned. In 1946 there were 470 Jews in the town (2% of the population) and by 1970 the number had fallen to 40.

Bibliography: J. Barna and F. Csukási, *A magyar zsidó felekezet . . . iskoláinak monográfiája* (1896); *Zsidó Világkongresszus Magyarországi Képviselete Statisztikai Osztályának Közleményei,* 4 (1947); 8–9 (1948); 13–14 (1949); *Új Élet,* 25 (1970), 1.

[L.H.]

PAPER-CUTS. Jewish paper-cuts present an interesting branch of traditional folk art which fulfilled a specific part in the life of the community. The subjects of Jewish paper-cuts were connected with customs and ceremonies, and associated with holidays and family life. They were encountered widely among the Jews of Poland and Russia in the 19th and the early years of the 20th centuries; Jewish

Figure 1. Paper-cut *Mizraḥ* from Drohobycz, Galicia, 1875. Motifs include a double-headed eagle, a *menorah*, animals, and foliage. 14×11 in. (36×28 cm.). Courtesy Gisa Frankel, Haifa.

paper-cuts were also known in Germany and probably in Holland; some Italian Jewish parchment marriage contracts (see *ketubbot) of the late 17th, 18th, and 19th centuries were decorated with cut-outs as well as some elaborate scrolls of *Esther. Paper-cuts are also to be found—with some characteristic style differences—in North Africa and the Middle East. But most information available concerns the East European cut-outs.

The cut-out is basically a pattern cut out of paper, often tinted and mounted on a layer of different color. Sheets of paper were usually folded, with half a design drawn on one side. The folded sheet was then fastened with thin nails to a wooden board and the design cut out with a sharp knife. By unfolding the paper a symmetrical design was obtained. Circular or multilateral designs were folded several times and asymmetrical compositions were cut out separately.

Paper-cuts present a rich variety of forms and motifs with texts drawn from the Holy Scriptures.

Motifs. In the center there is usually the seven-branched *menorah*, the Ten Commandments, or a Torah scroll; at the top they are decorated with a crown, Magen David, or an eagle. They are surrounded by motifs from the animal world and plant life, or geometrical forms. Among the animals the most frequent are lions, deer, eagles, tigers, which have a symbolic connotation (Avot 5:23). Sometimes bears, camels, and a wide selection of birds are used; mythological figures such as winged gryphons, cherubs, and leviathans; or the old motif of the tree of life; the symbols of the 12 signs of the Zodiac are also frequently used.

Types. Mizraḥ and Shivviti. The *Mizraḥ* ("East") was the most impressive and intricate form of Jewish paper-cuts hung up in homes and in synagogues on the eastern wall to indicate the direction of prayer (to Jerusalem). The *Mizraḥ* in the synagogue was generally called *Shivviti* according to the saying *"Shivviti Adonai le-Negdi Tamid"* ("I have set the Lord always before me"; Ps. 16:8) which appears mostly on these paper-cuts. Usually rectangular and framed under glass, they were made of white paper, almost always tinted with water colors and inscribed with biblical sayings. These paper-cuts presented the artist with vast opportunities to exercise his skill, and are often admired for their delicacy and finesse.

"Shevuoslekh" and *"Royselekh"* represent another widely encountered type of paper-cuts, rectangular or circular, used to decorate the windows on Shavuot; *"Shevuosl"* from the name of the holiday; *"Roysele"* from rosette or flower. It was customary on this holiday to decorate the doors with greenery, while these paper-cuts were stuck onto the glass panes of the small windows of Jewish homes. Thus they were smaller than the *Mizraḥ*, made of white paper, seldom colored, and often displayed the short text *"Ḥag ha-Shavuot ha-Zeh"* ("this holiday of Shavuot"). While most of them show the usual motifs, some depict soldiers and cavalrymen, a subject which seems to have excited the imagination of the Talmud students poring over their books. Visible from the street, they must have been familiar to non-Jews as well. "Torah Flags," carried by children at the Simḥat Torah processions, were often decorated with these cuts. At the top of the flag stick, candles were fixed inside apples or potatoes. The motifs of the flags were symbols of the 12 tribes or contained inscriptions suitable for the festival of Simḥat Torah. They were two-sided and made of colored paper.

A *"Kimpetbriv"* or *"Shir-Hamales"* was a kind of amulet put up on the four walls of the birth room to protect the mother and her newborn child against the evil power of the witch *Lilith, who, according to ancient beliefs, snatched the infants away. Texts included "Let the witch perish," "God will destroy devils," etc. The center always featured a psalm beginning with the words *"Shir ha-Ma'alot"* ("A song of degrees"; cf. Ps. 120), from which the amulet took its name. The expression *kimpet* derives from the old Yiddish-German *kindbett* ("childbed"), while *brivl* means "letter" or "note." Others were calendars, to count the days of the Omer,

Figure 2. A *menorah,* with inscriptions on each of its seven branches, as the central decorative element in an 18th-century paper-cut from Syria. Parchment, 5×3 in. (11.5×8 cm.). Jerusalem, Israel Museum. Photo David Harris, Jerusalem.

Figure 3. Paper-cut *Mizraḥ* with the Decalogue and pillars as its central design, from Wieliczka, Poland, 1925, 26½×20 in. (68×51 cm.). Original destroyed in World War II. Courtesy Gisa Frankel, Haifa.

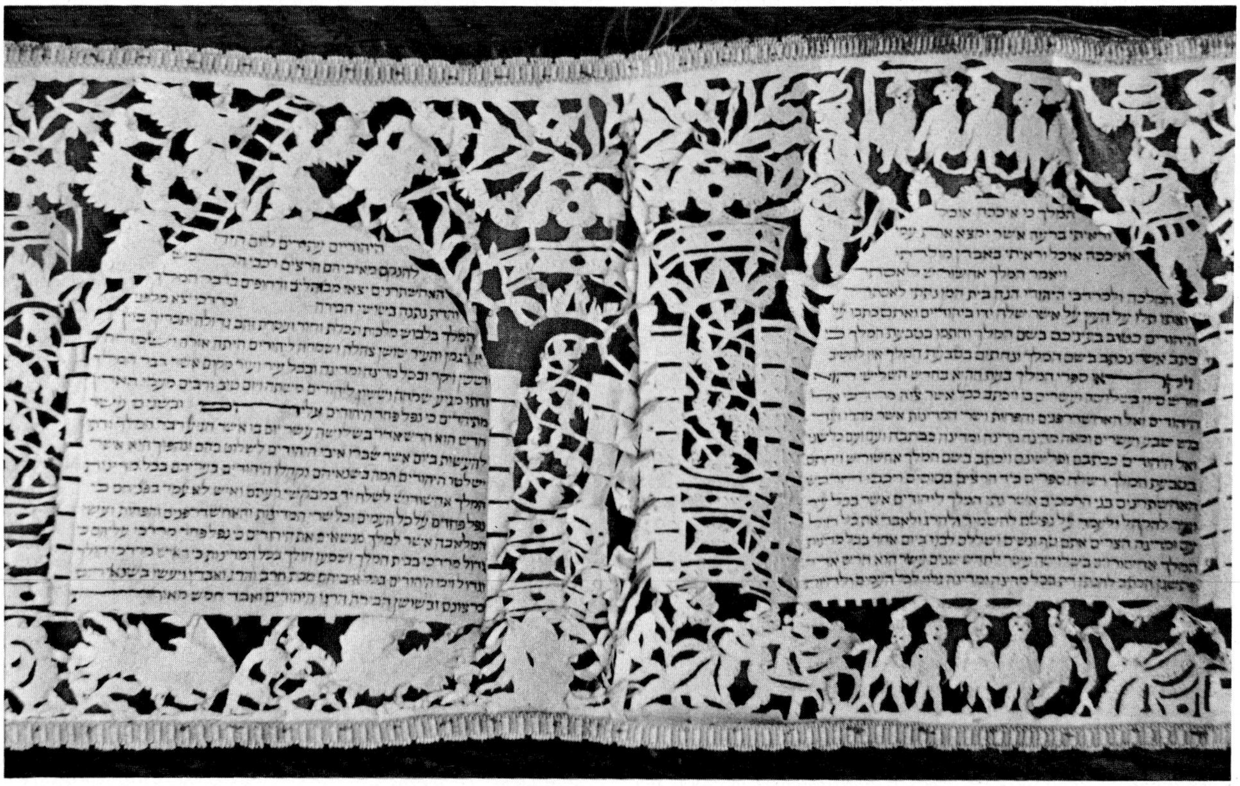

Figure 4. Italian 17th-century Esther scroll, parchment, height 4½ in. (11½ cm.). Top right, the hanging of Haman's sons; left, Jacob's dream. Cecil Roth Collection. Photo Werner Braun, Jerusalem.

Figure 5. *"Shevuosl"* from Yavorov, Galicia, 19th century. This paper-cut, used to decorate windows on the festival of Shavuot, shows two leviathans flanking a synagogue. 5½×8 in. (13.5×20 cm.). Tel Aviv, Mrs. G. Kadouri Collection.

"Ushpizin" to hang up in the *sukkah; "Mi-she-Nikhnas Adar,"* displayed on the walls of the synagogue during the month of Adar, etc. Paper lanterns whose sides were decorated with cut-outs were lit during open air weddings or on memorial days of great rabbis.

The beginning of the 20th century saw the disappearance of the Jewish paper-cuts and only old people remembered the art of their youth. Many of those preserved were destroyed during World War II and relatively few remain in public or private collections.

The paper-cuts from North Africa and the Middle East were called *Menorah,* because the *menorah,* one or more, always appeared as the central motif. They included many inscriptions, mostly on the arms of the candelabras. The underlayer of these cut-outs was made from thin, colored metal sheets. Two groups stand out. The first group is a counterpart of the *Mizraḥ* and the second includes smaller paper-cuts used as charms. The motifs are the same as in European paper-cuts but they have a specific oriental style. Very often the *ḥamsa* ("the five-finger hand"), unknown in Europe, appears on these paper-cuts.

Origin. It would be difficult to determine when the first Jewish paper-cuts originated. Information dating from as far back as the 17th and 18th centuries points to the fact that the European Jews of this time were acquainted with this type of art. The fact, however, that Jewish paper-cuts can be traced to Syria, Iraq, and North Africa, and that there is a similarity in the cutting techniques (with a knife) between those of East European Jews, and those of the Chinese, in their ancient folk craft, may indicate that the origin goes back even further.

Bibliography: B. W. Segel, in: *Globus,* 61 (1892), 235; R. Lilienthal, *Święta żydowskie* (1909), 249; J. Reizes, in: *Das Zelt,* 1 (1924), pt. 2; G. Frankel, in: *Lud,* 8 (Pol., 1929); idem, in: Haifa, Museum of Ethnology and Folklore, *Catalog* (Heb. and Eng., 1959); idem, in: JC (Dec. 11, 1964); idem, in: *Polska Sztuka Ludowa,* 3 (1965); idem, in: *Jewish Heritage* (Fall, 1967); M. Narkis, in: *Ofakim,* 2 (1944); F. Landesberger, in: HUCA, 26 (1955), 516; Mayer, Art, index. [Gi.F.]

PAPERNA, ABRAHAM BARUCH (d. 1863), Italian Hebrew writer and anthologist. Born in Leghorn where he also served as rabbi, Paperna was primarily interested in modern Hebrew poetry in Italy. His anthology of this poetry, *Kol Ugav* (1846), contains an appendix with biobibliographical data on the poets. He possessed a collection of manuscripts of authors whose works are reproduced in the anthology, as well as of other writers he mentions. He also contributed introductions to several books that were published in Leghorn. One of his pupils was Sabato *Morais. Ḥ. N. *Bialik (*Iggerot,* 3 (1938), 155) was deeply impressed by his anthology. [G.K.]

PAPERNA, ABRAHAM JACOB (1840–1919), Hebrew writer and critic. Paperna, who was born in Kapuli, Russia, was brought up in the spirit of the moderate Haskalah which prevailed in his father's house. In 1861 he started publishing articles and poems in *Ha-Meliẓ* and *Ha-Karmel.* He studied in the government rabbinical seminaries of Zhitomir (1863–64) and Vilna (1864–67). At the same time he became acquainted with Russian literature and was particularly influenced by Russian literary criticism. In 1867 he published a collection of articles entitled *Kankan Ḥadash Male Yashan* ("A New Vessel Full of Old [Wine]"), in which he criticized the Hebrew literature of the Haskalah in the realistic manner introduced by Uri *Kovner. Paperna's aim was to give the Hebrew reader elementary concepts in literary theory and to point out the main weaknesses of the Hebrew literature of his day. The latter included dilettantism, exaggerated use of pompous and ornate language, and versification instead of poetry. At the same time he acknowledged the achievements of contemporary Hebrew literature and paid tribute to some of its leading figures. A bitter controversy arose over Paperna's second brochure *Ha-Dramah bi-Khelal ve-ha-Ivrit bi-Ferat* ("Drama in General and Hebrew Drama in Particular," 1868). The brochure opens with an explanation of the basic concepts of poetry and concentrates upon tragedy, bringing examples from Greek and English drama. It then gives an account of the history of Hebrew drama from M. Ḥ. *Luzzatto to A. D. *Lebensohn's *Emet ve-Emunah.* In *Ha-Meliẓ* (1869), Paperna published an essay on *Mendele Mokher Seforim's *Ha-Avot ve-ha-Banim.* This was to be part of a larger article on the development of the novel but the fierce controversy which this essay engendered apparently deterred him from continuing this work. Upon his graduation from the rabbinical seminary in 1867, he was appointed teacher in the government school in Zakroczym, Poland, and in 1869 he moved to Plotsk where he worked as a teacher for some 45 years. During this time he wrote a number of Hebrew-Russian text books. After a lapse of almost 20

Abraham Jacob Paperna, Hebrew writer and critic. Jerusalem, J.N.U.L., Schwadron Collection.

years Paperna returned to the field of Hebrew literature, probably under the influence of the national revival among the Jews in Russia. He wrote poems and essays, as well as two booklets, *Siḥot Ḥayyot ve-Ofot* (1892), and *Mishlei ha-Zeman* (1893), which were sharp satires on modern civilization with allusions to the particular situation of the Jews in Russia. His memoirs appeared in the Russian-Jewish anthology *Perezhitaje.* His works were edited by Y. Zmora and published in Tel Aviv in 1952. Together with his contemporaries Uri Kovner and Mendele Mokher Seforim, Paperna raised Hebrew literary criticism from the level of personal invective directed against the author to systematic analysis guided by principles of literary forms and aesthetic theory.

Bibliography: Klausner, Sifrut, 4 (1954²), 176–89; I. Averbuch, in: *Orlogin,* 9 (1953), 166–87; A. Sha'anan, *Ha-Sifrut ha-Ivrit ha-Ḥadashah li-Zerameha,* 1 (1962), 262–6; Waxman, Literature, index s.v. *Papirno.* [Y.S.]

PAPI, name of two *amoraim.* Papi I, Babylonian *amora* of the fourth century. A disciple of Rava, the greatest *amora* of his time, he became the son-in-law of R. *Isaac Nappaḥa (Ḥul. 110a) and the head of an academy, attended, among others, by Rav *Ashi (Ḥul. 77a; 82a; RH 29b) and Mar *Zutra (Suk. 46a). He was apparently a well-to-do landowner, and, after reciting the sanctification of the Sabbath for his family and students, he would repeat the ceremony for the benefit of his tenants who arrived later from the field (RH 29b). Papi was on friendly terms with the exilarch Mar Samuel, at whose home he would sometimes dine (Beẓah 14b). When the exilarch ordered the case of a certain Bar Ḥama who was charged with murder to be investigated, Papi successfully defended the accused, whereupon the latter "kissed his [Papi's] feet and undertook to pay his poll tax for him for the rest of his life" (Sanh. 27a–b).

PAPI II, Palestinian *amora* of the fourth century, somewhat later than the above. His teacher was Joshua of Sikhnin, and his few recorded sayings are for the most part aggadic traditions in the name of his teacher or in the name of R. Levi, whose traditions were chiefly transmitted by Joshua of Sikhnin. Among the statements cited by him is a prediction that the future rebuilt Jerusalem would be three times or even 30 times as large as the old city (BB 75b).

Bibliography: Hyman, Toledot, s.v.; Ḥ. Albeck, *Mavo la-Talmudim* (1969), 418–19. [M.A.]

PAPIERNIKOV, JOSEPH (1897–), Yiddish poet. Born in Warsaw of poor parents, at the age of 15 he had to leave school to become an errand boy. Because of his fine voice and sensitive ear for music, he was accepted as choir boy in Cantor Gershon *Sirota's Tlomacka Synagogue in Warsaw. He joined the Left Po'alei Zion party at an early age and there he found the first audiences for his lyrics. I. M. *Weissenberg introduced him to the wider circle of Warsaw writers and, as editor of Warsaw journals, published his first poems in 1918. Other editors then accepted his lyrics for Left Po'alei Zion publications such as *Di Arbayter Tsaytung* and *Yunger Dor.* In 1924 Papiernikov left for Palestine, where he remained except for a sojourn in Warsaw (1929–33).

Papiernikov is the author of works including *In Zunikn Land* ("In the Sunny Land," 1927) and *Mayn Shir Hashirim* ("My Song of Songs," 1967). These are chiefly lyric volumes but also include translations from the Hebrew and the Russian, short stories, and memoirs. His lyric "I Build my Castles in the Air." to which he also composed the music, became a popular folk song. He was honored with several literary awards, and a volume of tributes to him was published on the fortieth anniversary of his settling in Israel. Papiernikov is the faithful lyric recorder of Israel's pioneering period and expresses his unabating love for the *ḥalutzim* who lived lives of hardship and poverty to build the Jewish homeland.

Bibliography: Rejzen, Leksikon, 2 (1927), 870–1; M. Ravitch, *Mayn Leksikon,* 1 (1945), 159–61. [I.H.B.]

PAPO, SAMUEL SHEMAIAH (1708–after 1774), Italian rabbi. Papo was apparently born in Ragusa where his father, Abraham David Papo, the teacher of David *Pardo, was rabbi. Many of his father's responsa are preserved in the *Shemesh Ẓedakah* of Samson *Morpurgo. In his early youth Papo moved to Ancona and studied in the *bet midrash* of Joseph Lehava (Fiammetta) and, after the latter's death, in that of his son-in-law, Samson Morpurgo. He also studied under Moses Ḥayyim Morpurgo, son of Samson; Jehiel ha-Kohen; and Isaac Costantini. In July 1758, on the recommendation of Costantini, he was granted the title *ḥakham* by the communal council. From 1756 to 1761 he served as **dayyan* of the town and signed all the documents of the *bet din.* From 1761 to 1774 his name no longer appears in the records of the sessions of the *bet din.* He may have left Ancona for business reasons or waived his right to participate in the local *bet din* because of disagreements that broke out between him and Isaac Shabbetai Fiano, rabbi and *av bet din.* In 1753 during Ḥ. J. D. *Azulai's first mission to Italy, Papo exerted himself to extend every honor and esteem to Azulai during his stay in Ancona (from Ḥeshvan 24 to the Kislev 12). In his diary, the *Ma'gal Tov* (ed. by A. Freimann (1921), 6), Azulai refers to Papo in terms of respect and admiration; "master of the Talmud," "the luminary," etc. The close ties of friendship thus formed grew stronger with the passage of time, as is testified by a correspondence still in manuscript. Papo endured much suffering and many troubles during his life because of his unswerving integrity. Many halakhic responsa by him are preserved in manuscript, all testifying to his erudition and acumen.

Bibliography: Roth, in: *Sinai,* 21 (1947), 326; Wilensky, *ibid.,* 25 (1949), 80–81. [G.La.]

PAPPENHEIM, BERTHA (1859–1936), social worker and leader of the German Jewish feminist movement. Born in Vienna to a wealthy Orthodox family, Bertha Pappenheim was treated by Josef *Breuer, a colleague of Sigmund *Freud, who regarded her case ("Anna O.") as a major breakthrough in psychoanalysis. She subsequently moved to Frankfort and became the headmistress of an orphanage in 1895. In 1904 she founded the *Juedischer Frauenbund (and edited its periodical), affiliated to the German women's movement. She visited Galicia, Rumania, and

"Bertha Pappenheim, helper of humanity," stamp issued by the West German Post Office, 1954. Jerusalem, B. M. Ansbacher Collection.

Russia, organizing relief work and aid to refugees. Her major efforts were directed against white slavery, prostitution, and illegitimacy. In 1914 she founded an institute at Neu-Isenburg (near Frankfort) for unwed mothers, prostitutes, and delinquent women, and later for children as well. Bertha Pappenheim directed her organization with a firm hand and led study groups on the ethics of social work at the Frankfort Lehrhaus. She was a vigorous opponent of Zionism and of emigration from Germany, due to its disruptive effect on family life. She died soon after she was interrogated by the Gestapo. She translated into German the memoirs of (her ancestor) *Glueckel of Hameln (1910), the *Ẓe'enah u-Re'enah* (1930), and the *Maaseh Buch* (1929), and wrote under the pen name of Paul Berthold.

Bibliography: D. Edinger (ed.), *Bertha Pappenheim: Leben und Schriften* (1963); idem, in: JSOS, 20 (1958), 180–6; E. Jones, *Sigmund Freud,* 1 (1953), 245–8. [Ed.]

PAPPENHEIM, SOLOMON (1740–1814), Hebrew linguist and poet. Born in Zuelz (Germany), Pappenheim served as a *dayyan* in Breslau till his death. He first became known as a linguist in his three-part *Yeri'ot Shelomo* (1784, 1811, and 1831), a study of synonyms. Although an ardent advocate of the Haskalah, Pappenheim opposed religious reforms and David *Friedlaender's proposal (1812) that education be entrusted to the government.

His contribution to modern Hebrew literature is his small book, *Aggadat Arba Kosot* ("Legend of Four Glasses"; Berlin, 1790 and often reprinted), a work influenced by family tragedies and by the *Night Thoughts* by the English poet Edward Young. Pappenheim's book, which begins with sorrow and ends with exultation and faith, is written in poetic prose. The poet, on the one hand, writes in a classical, rationalist vein from the standpoint of the structure and spirit of the work, and he preaches and believes in reason and morality. On the other hand, he is influenced by the sentimentalism which had begun to affect contemporary literature, which cried out against fate and yearned for nature and night. *Aggadat Arba Kosot* is one of the foundations of Hebrew lyricism, and its influence may be seen in the poetry of A. D. B. (Adam ha-Kohen) *Lebensohn and his son, M. J. *Lebensohn.

Bibliography: H. A. Wolfson, in: *Jewish Studies... Israel Abrahams* (1927), 427–40; F. Delitzsch, *Zur Geschichte der juedischen Poesie* (Leipzig, 1836), 110; Lachower, Sifrut, 1 (1963), 96–99; Klausner, Sifrut, 1 (1952), 254–60; H. G. Shapira, *Toledot ha-Sifrut ha-Ivrit ha-Ḥadashah* (1939), 346–54; Zinberg, Sifrut, 5 (1959), 114–6; Zeitlin, Bibliotheca, index.

[El.K.]

PAPPUS AND JULIANUS (Lulianus; second century C.E.), patriot brothers, perhaps from Laodicea. According to rabbinic tradition the two brothers, "when the government ordered the Temple to be rebuilt," set up (exchange-?) tables from Acre to Antioch to provide for those who came from the Exile (Gen. R. 64). It is also related that they were captured in Laodicea and condemned to death by *Trajan, the sentence being carried out immediately (Ta'an. 18b; Sifra, Emor, 9:5) or, according to an alternative account (Mekh. SbY to 21:13; Sem. 8:15), only after their judge—either Trajan or Lusius *Quietus, governor of Judea—had himself been killed. Rashi, who identifies Pappus and Julianus with the "Martyrs of Lydda" mentioned in the Talmud, indicated that they sacrificed themselves by claiming to have killed a princess for whose murder the whole of Jewry was held responsible (*Sefer ha-Arukh*, s.v. הרג ; Rashi, Ta'an. 18b). Despite attempts to make them appear to transgress the commandments, Pappus and Julianus chose death rather than comply (TJ, Sanh. 3:6, 21b; TJ. Shev, 42:2, 35a). From these various sources it would seem that Trajan gave permission to rebuild the Temple, in commemoration of which a holiday was instituted. Later, after the execution of Pappus and Julianus, which might coincide with the Trajanic persecutions of 117 C.E., the holiday was abolished.

Bibliography: Lieberman, in: JQR, 36 (1945/46), 243–6; Allon, Toledot, 1 (1958[3]), 260f.; L. Finkelstein, *Akiba* (Eng., 1936), 231–4, 313–6.

[L.Ro.]

PAPPUS BEN JUDAH (end of the first and beginning of the second century C.E.), *tanna* and aggadist. A contemporary of Rabban Gamaliel and R. Joshua (TJ, Ber. 2:9 according to the correct reading of the *Kaftor va-Feraḥ;* cf. L. Ginzberg, *Perushim ve-Ḥiddushim ba-Yerushalmi*, 1 (1941), 410), Pappus was imprisoned with Akiva at the time of the Hadrianic persecutions. Before their imprisonment Pappus had attempted to deter Akiva from continuing to teach his disciples, fearing the spies that were all around them. Thereupon Akiva told him the famous fable of the fox and the fish which illustrated that the Jewish people without Torah would be like fish out of water and would suffer a spiritual death. When Pappus later found himself in prison with Akiva, he said to him: "It is well with thee, Akiva, who hast been imprisoned for studying Torah, but woe to Pappus who has been imprisoned for vain, worldly things" (Ber. 61b). Pappus was distinguished for his pious character, and conducted himself with special stringency. He would lock his wife indoors when he went out so that she would not talk to other people (Git. 90a). This behavior was compared by Meir to a man who when finding a fly in his drink would throw away both fly and drink. Pappus' aggadic interpretation of Genesis 3:23 to the effect that man is equal to the angels was rejected by Akiva (Gen. R. 21:5). A long aggadic discussion between him and Akiva occurs in *Mekhilta Be-Shallaḥ*, 6.

[Ed.]

PAPYRI. Papyri mentioning Jews and Judaism have been found in excavations at *Masada (dating to the period of the Jewish War against Rome in the first century C.E.), in caves in the Judean desert at *Qumran and Murabba'at (from the first and second centuries C.E., with the dramatic exception of one document thought to be from the eighth century B.C.E.; see *Dead Sea Scrolls; *Bar Kokhba), and in Egypt. The languages used are Greek, Latin, Aramaic, Hebrew, and Nabatean. Another important discovery was the *Nash papyrus discovered by L. W. Nash and published in 1903. The earliest Jewish papyri from Egypt are written in an Aramaic not greatly different from biblical Aramaic. Such papyri, dating from the late sixth through the fifth centuries B.C.E., have been found at various sites including *Elephantine, Memphis, and, most recently, Hermopolis Magna. At Elephantine, a Jewish and Samaritan military colony, dating from the seventh or sixth century, provides an important source of papyri from the fifth century, when Egypt was under Persian domination. Most of these papyri are legal documents concerning marriage, divorce, manumission of slaves, loans, business contracts, litigation, and sales or gifts of property. Certain private letters are found on papyri and ostraca. The papyri attest to the existence of a Temple of YHWH, and the celebration of a Feast of Unleavened Bread, though possibly not in the form which is familiar from the Bible; evidence for the observance of the Sabbath is less certain. Geographical and racial considerations made it necessary for the Jews of Elephantine to tolerate and recognize other deities. The Temple was destroyed in 410, but certainly restored a few years later. The colony seems to have survived the change from Persian to Saitic rule, but seems to have disappeared finally in the course of the fourth century B.C.E. The Greco-Roman material from the Ptolemaic and the two Roman periods (323 B.C.E.–641/2 C.E.) which has been collected in Tcherikover, et al. *CPJ* (1957–60), contains over 500 documents, both papyri and ostraca, concerning Jews from many parts of Egypt, particularly the towns of the Fayum. The criteria taken by the editors for deciding whether a document is "Jewish" are, broadly: the occurrence of specifically Jewish institutions, Jewish names, and places of exclusively Jewish settlement, though the editors state the difficulty of identifying Jewish names, and have accordingly omitted many uncertain cases (*ibid.*, 1 introduction). The papyri, in conjunction with ostraca and *inscriptions, give a full picture of the social and economic state of the Jews in towns and villages throughout Egypt. Jews are found negotiating loans, participating in contracts, paying taxes in the same way as the other inhabitants of Egypt, fitting into the existing legal and bureaucratic structure, and even adopting Greek, Roman, and Egyptian names. The papyri provide religious information attesting to the existence of synagogues and the affirmation, at certain times, of the right of Jews to practice their religion. Evidence of the spread of Jewish religious and cultural influence can be seen in some demotic papyri and magical texts, and in the practice, among non-Jews, of adopting names connected with the Sabbath. The reliability of the papyri in points of detail provides valuable historical evidence which can be used to supplement and sometimes correct the evidence of *Philo and *Josephus, who drew their material from the richer and socially superior Alexandrian Jews. Papyri give evidence, for instance, of the spread of the Jewish Revolt of 115–7 C.E. in Egypt, information which is given by no other source.

Bibliography: Tcherikover, Corpus; idem, in: *Sefer Magnes* (1938), 199ff. (English summary); idem, *Ha-Yehudim be-Miẓrayim ba-Tekufah ha-Hellenistit ha-Romit le-Or ha-Papirologyah* (1963[2]); idem and F. Heichelheim, in: HTR, 35 (1942), 25–44; idem, *Auswaertige Bevoelkerung im Ptolemaeerreich* (1925, 1963[2]), 100ff.; A. E. Cowley (ed. and tr.), *Aramaic Papyri of the Fifth Century B.C.* (1923); G. R. Driver (ed.), *Aramaic Documents of the Fifth Century B.C.* (1957); E. G. Kraeling, *Brooklyn Museum Aramaic Papyri* (1953); R. Yaron, *Introduction to the Law of the Aramaic Papyri* (1961); H. Cazelles, in: *Syria*, 32 (1955), 75–100 (Fr.); H. I. Bell, *Cults and Creeds in Graeco-Roman Egypt* (1953), 27–33; W. F. Albright, in: JBL, 56 (1937), 145–76 (includes the Nash papyrus Ms.); idem, in: BASOR, no 115 (1949), 10–19 (facs. of Nash papyrus).

[A.K.B.]

PAPYRUS. The plant *Cyperus papyrus* grows in the swamps of Israel. It was formerly very widespread in Lower Egypt and in old Egyptian drawings symbolized the region. The use of papyrus was very varied; it was employed for boats, utensils, shoes, and paper, and its soft stalks were also used as food. In the Bible it is called *gomë* (גֹּמֶא) or *eveh* (אֵבֶה), and in the Mishnah *papir* or *neyar*. *Gomë* was used for making the ark of Moses (Ex. 2:3). Boats which sailed beyond the rivers of Ethiopia were made of it (Isa. 18:2). Together with the *reed *(kaneh)* it grew near marshes and swamps, and Isaiah (35:7) prophesied that both would grow in the desert. The Book of Job (8:11–12) notes that papyrus cannot grow without swamp, that it shrivels up in the winter when the grass begins to go green, and that then it is ready for harvesting. The Tosefta speaks of papyrus vessels being more valuable than those made of plaited wicker (Kel. BM 5:15). Papyrus barrels were also made (Kel. 2:5), as well as clothes, "a shirt of papyrus" (Tosef., Kel. BB 5:2) serving as clothes for the poor (Gen. R. 37:8). The main use of papyrus was in the manufacture of paper, especially in the era of the Mishnah and Talmud. Paper was made from the stalk, which bears the inflorescence, and which was cut into fine strips and stuck together in length and in breadth with glue—the *kolon shel soferim* ("scribes' glue": Gr. κόλλα, glue) which contained leaven and was therefore forbidden on Passover (Pes. 3:1, 42b). The Jerusalem Talmud (Pes. 3:1, 29d) notes that in Alexandria this glue was prepared in large vessels. According to Josephus (Ant., 14:33) there was a place called Papyron near the Jordan. *Gemi* is frequently mentioned in the Mishnah and Talmud as material for the making of baskets, mats, and ropes. It is possible that papyrus *(gomë)* is also included in this name (cf. Rashi to Ex. 2:3), though it seems that it generally refers to the fibers of other plants also. The Bible once mentions *eveh* ships as being light and swift (Job 9:25–26). This word is connected with the Akkadian *apu*, the name of swamp plants used for weaving, including the papyrus.

Papyrus *(Cyperus papyrus)* growing in Lake Ḥuleh. Courtesy Government Press Office, Tel Aviv.

Nowadays papyrus has almost disappeared from lower Egypt. In Israel it used to grow over the large expanse of the Ḥuleh swamp, where the Arab villagers earned their livelihood by weaving mats from it. With the draining of these swamps only a few acres of papyrus remain in the local nature reserve. The papyrus is a perennial, growing to a height of up to 15 feet. The triple shaft of the inflorescence is $2\frac{1}{2}$–$3\frac{1}{2}$ inches thick at the base and from it the papyrus strips were made. The plant dies in winter, and the stalks rot. The peat in the Ḥuleh is formed from the layers of the rotted plants.

Bibliography: Loew, Flora, 1 (1926), 558–71; J. Feliks, *Olam ha-Ẓome'aḥ ha-Mikra'i* (1968[2]), 294–7; H. N. and A. L. Moldenke, *Plants of the Bible* (1952), 318 (index), s.v.

[J.F.]

PARABLE, from the Greek παραβολή (lit., "juxtaposition"), the usual Septuagint rendering of Hebrew *mashal* ("comparison," "saying," and "derived meanings"). No distinction is made in biblical usage between parable, allegory, and fable; all are forms of the *mashal* and have the same functions of illustration and instruction. The comparison may be explicit or implied. It may take the form of declarative or interrogative sentences (e.g., Prov. 26:1; 27:4). When developed into a short story, an interpretation or application is usually appended.

The story-parable, often introduced by "like" or "as," is told in terms drawn from ordinary experiences and usually makes one principal point. Some examples are Nathan's parable (II Sam. 12:1–5), and the parables of the Surviving Son (II Sam. 14:5b–7), the Escaped Prisoner (I Kings 20: 39–40), the Disappointing Vineyard (Isa. 5:1b–6) and the Farmer's Skill (Isa. 28:24–29). All but the last-named are followed by explicit interpretations. The rhetorical question with which the Book of Jonah ends may suggest that the book was intended as a parable. Ruth, too, may be a parable, with its more subtle point underlined by the appended genealogy.

The allegory-*mashal* is a more artificial narrative having individual features which are independently figurative, so that it becomes a kind of riddle. The one of the Eagles and the Vine (Ezek. 17:3–10) is described as both *ḥidah* ("riddle") and *mashal*. The oracular Laments of the Lioness (*ibid.* 19:2–9) and the Transplanted Vine (*ibid.* 19:10–14) and the stories of the Harlot Sisters (*ibid.* 23:2–21) and the Cooking-Pot (*ibid.* 24:3b–5) are allegorical. A third type of *mashal* is the fable, where animals or inanimate objects are made to speak and act like men. Judges 9:8–15 and II Kings 14: 9–10 are examples; in each case the moral is made explicit.

A riddle *(ḥidah)* is a kind of parable whose point is deliberately obscured so that greater perception is needed to interpret it; Samson's riddle (Judg. 14:14) is an example. *Mashal* and *ḥidah* are used almost synonymously in Ezekiel 17:2; Habakkuk 2:6; Psalms 49:5 and 78:2; and Proverbs 1:6. Certain proverbs are in effect parable-riddles, e.g., Proverbs 30:15a, 15b–16, 18–19, and 21–31.

Other biblical forms related to the parable type of *mashal* are: prophetic oracles where a metaphor is extended into a lively description, e.g., Isaiah 1:5–6; Hosea 2:2–15; 7: 8–9, 11–12; Joel 4:13; and Jeremiah 25:15–29; prophetic oracles proclaimed through symbolic actions, e.g., I Kings 11:29; II Kings 13:15–19, and Isaiah 20:2–6; extended personifications as of Wisdom and Folly in Proverbs 1:20–33; 8:1–36; 9:1–6, 13–18; and revelatory dreams and visions having symbolism which the sequel interprets as allegorical, e.g., Genesis 37:6–11; 40:9–13, 16–19; Zechariah 1:8–11; 2:1–4; and Daniel 2:31–45.

See also *Allegory; *Fable; *Hebrew Literature; *Wisdom, Wisdom Literature. [R.B.Y.S.]

IN THE TALMUD AND MIDRASH

The rabbis made extensive use of parables as a definitive method of teaching in the Talmud, and especially in the Midrash. Jesus, in his parables, was employing a well-established rabbinic form of conveying ethical and moral lessons. There are 31 parables in the New Testament, some of which are found in a slightly different version in rabbinical literature (cf. Shab. 153a with Matt. 25:1–12; and TJ, Ber. 2:8, 5c, the parable given by R. Zeira in his funeral oration on the death of R. Avin, the son of R. Ḥiyya, with Matt. 20:1–16), which contains thousands of examples, and a comparison between the parallel parables reveals the greater beauty and detail of the latter. The word *mashal* in rabbinical literature refers nearly always to the parable; only in such phrases as *ha-mashal omer* or its Aramaic equivalent *matla amra* ("the *mashal* says"; cf. Ex. R. 21:7 and Lev. R. 19:6) and in the phrase *mashal hedyot* ("a folk *mashal*") does it bear the meaning which it does in the Bible of a proverb (see also *Proverbs, Talmudic). The standard formula, however, always introduces a full parable. That the use of parables was a distinct and recognized method of moral instruction is clear from the statements that "fox fables and fuller fables" (see below) were among the attainments of Rabban Johanan b. Zakkai (Suk. 28a; BB 134a) and that R. Meir consistently divided his discourses into three parts, *halakhah, aggadah,* and parables (Sanh. 38b). It is in this context that R. Johanan refers to the 300 animal parables of R. Meir (see *Animal Tales).

The rabbis not only used the parable extensively; they also emphasized its great value in opening a door to an understanding of the spirit of the Torah. Both of these aspects are reflected in a passage in the Midrash. Regarding the word *mashal* in Ecclesiastes 12:9 in the sense of parable, "and Koheleth . . . taught the people knowledge; yea he pondered and set out many *meshalim,*" the Midrash ascribes the first use of parables to Solomon. On this the Midrash gives five parables, to illustrate the manner in which the parable aids the understanding of the Bible. R. Naḥman gives two, one of the "thread of Ariadne," which he applies to a palace of many doors, and the other of a man cutting a path through the jungle. R. Yose compares the parable to a handle with which an otherwise unwieldy basket can be carried; R. Shila gives the parable of a jug of boiling water carried by the same method; while R. Ḥanina, of a bucket let down to a well of cold and sweet water. The passage concludes "Let not the parable be lightly esteemed in thine eyes, since by its means one can master the whole of the words of the Torah." Realizing that the parable may not be the most profound or weighty means of instruction, the passage adds that just as one uses a candle, which is almost worthless, to find a precious stone which has been lost, "a parable should not be lightly esteemed in thine eyes, since by means of it a man arrives at the true meaning of the words of the Torah" (Songs R. 1:1, no. 8).

The parable is usually introduced by the phrase, *Mashal; le-mah ha-davar domeh le* . . . "A parable; to what can this matter be compared to . . ."), but so characteristic a picture is it of rabbinical teaching that the phrase is often omitted and the parable is introduced merely with the prefix *le* ("to").

The material is so vast that only some of the most salient features and of the most striking parables can be given.

King Parables. One of the most frequent motifs is the king (i.e., God), of which there are many permutations.

The King as Ruler, With Mankind as His Subjects. This, for instance, is the basis of the parable of R. Johanan b. Zakkai to illustrate the verse "at all times let thy garments be white, and let not thy head lack ointment" (Eccles. 9:8), which he interprets to mean that man should ever be prepared to meet his Maker. It is the parable of a king who announced a forthcoming banquet without stating the time. Those who were prescient dressed for the occasion and waited; those who were foolish went about their ordinary work, confident that they would be informed of the time. Suddenly the summons came. The wise entered properly dressed, while the fools had to come in their soiled garments. The king was pleased with the former, but was angry with the latter (Shab. 153a).

The King as Father, With Israel as the Sometimes Wayward But Beloved Son. A king left his wife before her child was born and went overseas, remaining there many years. The queen bore a son who grew up. When the king returned she brought the son into his presence. The son looked at a duke, and then at a provincial governor and said successively of them, "This is my father." The king said, "Why do you gaze at them? From them you will have no benefit. You are my son, and I am your father." (PR 21:104). Many of these parables have the same theme as the New Testament parable of the prodigal son.

The King as the Husband and Israel as the Wife. To emphasize the honor due to God, the Midrash tells the parable of the king who had a number of children with a *matrona* ("a noble lady"—the term usually used in these parables for the king's consort). She was undutiful to him and he announced his intention of divorcing her and remarrying. When she discovered the name of the woman whom he intended to marry she called her children together and told them, hoping that they would intercede with their father because they found her objectionable. When they answered that they did not mind, she then said, "I appeal to you in the name of the honor of your father" (Deut. R. 3:11). One of these "family" parables calls for special mention. R. Simeon b. Yoḥai asked R. Eleazar b. Yose ha-Gelili whether his father, a noted aggadist, had ever explained to him the verse: "(and gaze upon Solomon) even upon the crown wherewith his mother hath crowned him" (Song 3:11). Eleazar answered in the affirmative with a parable of a king who had an especially beloved daughter. At first he called her "my daughter," but as his affection for her increased he called her "sister," and finally he used to refer to her as "mother." So Israel is referred to as a daughter (Ps. 45:11), then as a sister (Song 5:2), and then as a mother (reading *le'ummi;* "my nation," in Isa. 51:4 as *le'immi,* "to my mother"). On hearing this explanation R. Simeon b. Yoḥai arose and kissed him on his head" (Ex. R. 52:5). The reason for R. Simeon's enthusiasm is probably to be found in the fact that the rabbis found themselves in a grave theological quandary. If the king of the Song of Songs is the Almighty, how can his mother be referred to, and his parable answered it by explaining that "mother" was but an endearing term for "daughter."

The King and His Subjects, of Whom Israel is the Favorite. Thus the Midrash explains the striking difference between the 70 bullocks offered during the first seven days of Sukkot (Num. 29:12–34) which are regarded as expiations for the *seventy nations and the single bullock offered on the eighth day (v. 36) which represents Israel with the parable of a king who made a banquet for seven days to which all the people were invited. At the conclusion of the seven days he said to his close intimate, "We have now done our duty to all the people; let us both have an intimate meal with whatever comes to hand, a piece of meat, or fish, or even vegetables" (Num. R. 21:24).

So standard is the motif of the king in parables that it is frequently used without any connotation of royalty, and it could be substituted for the word "man" without affecting the parable. Thus the above-mentioned parable of searching for a precious stone with a candle is made to refer to a king. Similarly there is the parable of R. Judah ha-Nasi in which he explained to Antoninus the responsibility shared by body and soul for transgressions— to the effect that a king had a beautiful orchard bearing choice fruit. In order to prevent pilfering of the fruit by the watchmen, he appointed one who was lame, and thus could not climb the tree, and one who was blind, who could not see it. The lame watchman, however, arranged for the blind one to carry him to the fruit. When the theft was discovered each pleaded physical inability to steal the fruit, but the king, realizing how they had acted, placed the blind man on the shoulders of the lame and punished them as one man. "So will the Holy One, blessed be He, replace the soul in the body and punish both for their sins" (Sanh. 91a/b). It is obvious that in this passage the word "king" is a mere literary device.

Animal Parables. Parables taken from the animal world, especially fox fables, are very popular (see *Animal Tales). R. Akiva explained to Pappus b. Judah why he continued to teach Torah at the risk of his life by the parable of the fox who invited the fish to leave the water to avoid being caught in the fishermen's nets. The fish replied that while in the water it was in its natural element where it might die but might also live, whereas out of its element it would surely die (Ber. 61b). R. Joshua b. Hananiah dissuaded the Jews from breaking out in revolt against the Romans by telling them the parable of the crane which extracted a thorn from the tongue of a lion, and when it asked for its reward, was told that it had been sufficiently rewarded by the lion not closing its jaws on it after it had extracted the thorn (Gen. R. 64:10). The doctrine that later and greater troubles cause the former and lesser ones to be forgotten is illustrated by the parable of the man who, saved from a wolf, told all his friends about his escape. Subsequently avoiding a similar fate from a lion, he made this escape the subject of his story, until he was delivered from the poisonous sting of a snake, and then told the story of that deliverance (Ber. 13a). Many of the fables have new origin or parallel in the fables of other ancient peoples.

It is not certain what are the "parables of *kovesim*" which are mentioned together with Fox Fables among the accomplishments of Johanan ben Zakkai. It is usually rendered "fables of launderers" ("fullers") and, in fact, the launderer is a well-known figure in Roman comedy. No such parables, however, exist in rabbinic literature.

Parables from Nature. Every phenomenon of nature or of plants is made the subject of parables. The rabbis point out that there is hardly a fruit which is not regarded as a parable of Israel (Ex. R. 36:1), and the most sustained and extensive parables in the Midrash are on the vine, the palm (cf. Num R. 3:1), the cedar, etc. One of the most beautiful in this class is the blessing which R. Isaac of Palestine invoked upon his host R. Naḥman in Babylon when he took leave of him. When Naḥman asked for his blessing R. Isaac claimed that it was difficult to think of a subject for blessing, since Naḥman had been blessed with all the blessings of this world, wealth, health, honor, and children, and he continued: "Let me tell you a parable. A man was journeying in the wilderness. He was hungry, thirsty, and weary and he lighted on a tree which had sweet fruits, pleasant shade, and a stream of water flowing beneath it. He ate of the fruit, drank of the water, and rested under its shade. When about to resume his journey he said, "O Tree, with what shall I bless thee? With the blessing of sweet fruit? Thou already has it. That thy shade be pleasant? It already is. That water shall flow by thee? It does. May it be God's will that all the shoots taken from thee be like thee," and he proceeded to explain, "May all thy children be like thee" (Ta'an, 5b–6a).

Many of the parables are taken from daily life, and are a rich source for social history. R. Levi gives a parable to explain the verse, "Better the day of death than the day of one's birth" (Eccles. 7:1). It is the parable of two ships sailing in the Mediterranean. One was leaving the harbor and the other coming in. Everyone was happy at the ship which was leaving, while the ship which had completed its journey slipped in without incident. There was an intelligent man there, who said, "I see something topsy-turvy. There is no point in rejoicing at the ship which is leaving, since they know not what conditions she may meet, what seas she may encounter, and what wind she may have to face, whereas all should rejoice for this ship which has successfully completed its voyage" (Ex. R. 48:1). An essentially earthy parable is given to explain the fact that the 70 bullocks sacrificed on the seven days of Sukkot are made up of 13 the first day, decreasing in number by one each day. "It is to teach you the way of the world (*derekh ereẓ,* usually meaning "etiquette," but here obviously to be translated literally). "A man is given hospitality by a friend. On the first day he gives him poultry, on the second meat, on the third fish, on the fourth vegetables. So daily he gives him less luxurious food, until in the end he feeds him on pulse" (Num. R. 21:25). An almost daring example of this type of parable is the one in which R. Huna in the name of R. Johanan interprets Exodus 32:11, "thy people that thou hast brought out of the Land of Egypt," as the retort of Moses to God that He was to blame for the idolatrous tendencies of the children of Israel. The parable says: "A wise man opened a cosmetic shop for his son in the street of the harlots. The site played its part, the trade played its part, and the young man—in his prime—played his part. He got into evil ways and his father came and caught him with a harlot. His father began to shout at him, saying 'I'll kill you!' But a friend who was with him, said to him, 'You have ruined him and yet you shout at him! You disregarded all occupations and taught him only to be a cosmetician. You abandoned all other sites and opened a shop for him only in the street of the harlots.' So said Moses, 'Lord of the Universe, thou didst disregard the whole world and enslaved thy children in Egypt, where they worship lambs, and thus thy children learned from them and made a golden calf'" (Ex. R. 43:7).

POST-TALMUDIC PERIOD

Medieval writers also had recourse to parables in their works. These included *Baḥya ibn Paquda in his *Ḥovot ha-Levavot* and *Judah Halevi in the *Kuzari,* both of whom use the standard formula of the parable of the king, and both of a "king in India" (*Ḥovot ha-Levavot* 3:9; *Kuzari* 1:109; cf. also Ḥovot 2:6); Samuel ha-Nagid in his *Ben Mishlei* and the *Mishlei Shu'alim* of Berechiah ha-Nakdan. In ḥasidic literature the most striking parables are the tales in *Naḥman of Bratzlav's *Sefer Ma'asiyyot.* Parables, most of them popular, and all striking, were especially characteristic of the method of preaching of Jacob *Krantz, the *maggid* of Dubnow.

See also *Fables. [L.I.R.]

Bibliography: O. Eissfeldt, *Der Maschal im Alten Testament* (1913); A. Bentzen, *Introduction to the Old Testament*, 1 (1952[2]), 167–77; Johnson, in: VT, Supplement, 3 (1955), 162–9; Haran, in: EM, 5 (1968), 548–53 (incl. bibl.). IN TALMUD AND MIDRASH: Ziegler, *Die Koenigsgleichnisse des Midrasch beleuchtet durch die roemische Kaiserzeit* (1903); I. J. Weissberg, *Mishlei Kadmonim* (1950[2]). For a collection of parables see: Ḥ. N. Bialik and J. H. Rawnitzki, *Sefer ha-Aggadah* (1908–) and C. G. Montefiore and H. Loewe, *A Rabbinic Anthology* (1938), passim. W. Bacher, *Die exegetische Terminologie der juedischen Traditionsliteratur*, 1 (1899), 121f., 2 (1905), 120f.; S. Lieberman, *Greek in Jewish Palestine* (1942), 144–60.

PARADISE. The English derivative of Παράδεισος, Greek for "garden" in the Eden narrative of Genesis 2:4b–3:24 (see *Garden of Eden). One of the best-known and most widely interpreted pericopes in the Bible, this narrative is at the same time one of the most problematic. While on the surface the narrative unfolds smoothly, its deeper meaning, its composition and literary affinities, and many of its allusions, assumptions, and implications raise questions that are presently insoluble.

CONTENTS OF THE NARRATIVE

The pericope divides naturally into two sections, one relating God's beneficent acts in creating man and placing him in a paradise; the other, man's disobedience and consequent banishment from paradise. The masoretic *parashah* division considers 2:4a ("This is the story of heaven and earth when they were created") the beginning of this narrative, but most scholars today take 4a as the conclusion of the first creation story (1:1–2:4a), the opening verse of which it echoes, and begin the Eden narrative with 2:4b. More ambiguous is the position of 2:25 ("The two of them were naked, the man and his wife, yet they felt no shame"): some, accepting the present chapter division, consider it the climax of the perfect state created by God before man's disobedience; others (including NJPS) see that climax in 2:23–24 and take 2:25 as the introduction, which sets the theme, to the section on the "fall" in which awareness of nakedness and the making of clothing are prominent (3:7, 10–11, 21).

After the Lord God had made earth and heaven, but before the appearance of grasses and shrubbery, God created man out of lumps of soil and breathed life into him (man thus combines both earthly and divine elements). As man's home He created a garden in Eden filled with fruit-bearing trees, including the tree of life and the tree of knowledge of good and bad, which man was prohibited to eat on pain of death. God then created, also out of earth, all the animals and the birds of the sky and brought them to Adam to be named. God then fashioned a woman out of one of Adam's ribs, and Adam found her a fitting helper. The two were naked, but were unashamed of the fact. The serpent convinced the woman that God's threat of death for eating from the tree of knowledge was idle and that in fact its fruit would make the couple like divine beings who know good and bad. The woman and then the man ate some of the forbidden fruit and became aware of their nakedness; they then sewed some fig leaves into loincloths for themselves. Each participant in this act of disobedience was punished by God. The serpent was condemned to a life of crawling on its belly, and of enmity with mankind. The woman was condemned to painful pregnancy and childbirth, further, she would be dominated by her husband. The man was condemned to a life of struggling to eke out a living from the earth. To prevent him from eating from the tree of life, too, and acquiring the attribute of immortality, the Lord banished the man and his wife from the garden and set up *cherubim and "the fiery ever-turning sword" to guard the way to the tree of life.

SPECIFIC PROBLEMS

Many details of the narrative are elusive or troublesome.

The Location of the Garden. The text states that the garden is located "in Eden, in the east" (2:8), and that "a river issues from Eden to water the garden, and it then divides and becomes four branches: . . . Pishon, . . . which winds through the whole land of Havilah . . . Gihon, . . . which winds through the whole land of Cush . . . the Tigris, . . . and . . . the Euphrates" (2:10–14, NJPS translation). Starting from what is clear, the Tigris and the Euphrates, scholarly opinion has divided into two schools. The first reasons that the two unknown rivers must be great world rivers on the scale of the Tigris and Euphrates; this view is supported by the Gihon's association with Cush, which usually means Nubia in the Bible, from which it is concluded that the Gihon is the Nile. Accordingly the fourth river is thought to be the Indus or the Ganges. These views, and their many variants, would locate the garden at some hypothetical common point of origin of the Tigris, Euphrates, Nile, and Indus or Ganges. The second school reasons that the two unknown rivers must be near the Tigris and the Euphrates. The Gihon's association with Cush presents no problem for this view since the Ancient Near East also had another area known as Cush, the land of the Kassites (Akk. *Kaššû/Kuššu-*, Greek *Kossaîoi*) in present-day Luristan, east of the Tigris (cf. also the Mesopotamian associations of Cush in Gen. 10:8–10). This accords well with the Samaritan version's translation of Gihon as *ʾAsqop*, apparently the river Choaspes, modern Kerkha—in Luristan! If, following the apparent order of the biblical text, one then looks further east for the Pishon, the Karûn in Elam becomes a candidate. However, this school also admits other possibilities, e.g., that the Gihon is the Diyala and Pishon the Kerkha or even the Arabian Wadi er-Rumma (for other aspects of this problem see *Havilah). According to any of these views, since the common meeting point of these rivers in antiquity was, or was believed to be, the Persian Gulf, the latter would be the undivided river mentioned in Genesis 2:10a (but could it ever be referred to as a river?). This would conform with the implication of Genesis 11:2, 9 that the garden was located east of Shinar (probably Sumer) and Babylon. Since Sumerian tradition (the Eden story has many Mesopotamian affinities) located its paradise in Dilmun, somewhere in or along the Persian Gulf, this school seems to be on the right track. Often associated with this school is the explanation of "Eden" (traditionally connected with Heb. *ʿeden* pl. *ʿadanim*, "luxury, delight") as the Sumerian *edin* ("plain"), a term which is often used as a geographic designation for the plain between the Tigris and Euphrates in southern Mesopotamia. However, this does not conform precisely to the text's suggestion that the garden is east of the Mesopotamian plain. Furthermore, the assumption of this view that Genesis 2:10 speaks of four rivers flowing into one, rather than vice versa, is debatable. It is at least equally possible that the single source river is understood to be located at the head of the Tigris and the Euphrates in the north, in which case the identification of Pishon and Gihon remains problematic. The location of Eden and its rivers clearly remains an open question.

The Trees of Life and Knowledge. As elusive as the identification of the rivers of paradise is the meaning of "the tree of knowledge of good and bad" (*ʿeẓ ha-daʿat tov wa-raʿ*; for the syntax cf. *ha-daʿat ʾoti* in Jer. 22:16). Several theories have been proposed over the centuries, but none has won general acceptance.

MORAL DISCERNMENT. This view takes "good and bad" in the moral sense of right and wrong (cf. Isa. 5:20; Amos 5:14; Micah 3:2) and "knowledge" as the ability to distinguish (cf. II Sam. 19:36; Isa. 7:15) the one from the other. Critics of this view note that the very prohibition presumes that man knows the rightness of obedience and the wrongness of disobedience, and ask how the biblical God can be conceived as wishing to withhold moral discernment from man.

SEXUAL KNOWLEDGE. The main evidence supporting this interpretation is the frequent use of "to know" (not only in Hebrew and other ancient Near Eastern languages) in the sense of "to be intimate with;" it also finds a distinction between homosexual and heterosexual indulgence in the phrase "to know good and bad," ignoring the objective case of the nouns. Another argument for interpreting "knowledge of good and bad" in the Garden of Eden story as "sexual awareness" is the use of "to know good and bad" in contexts which may conceivably refer (actually they are far more embracing) to the sexual urge (Deut. 1:39, before it develops; Manual of Discipline 1: 9–11, when it develops; II Sam. 19:36, after it has faded). Indeed, the immediate consequence of eating from the tree is awareness of nakedness, and the first action reported after the expulsion from the garden is Adam's "knowing" Eve (4:1). As regards the latter, however, *we-ha-ʾadam yadaʿ* (instead of *wa-yedaʿ ha-ʾadam*) can indicate the past perfect tense and could be interpreted as "Now the man had known," which suggests that Adam knew his wife before eating from the tree. Further, critics of the sexual awakening theory cite God's declaration to the heavenly court in 3:22 that through this knowledge "man has become like one of us." It is inconceivable that the Bible would attribute sexuality to God; and the answer that the reference here is to human procreation as the counterpart of divine creativity seems forced. Genesis 2:23–24 seems naturally to include sexuality as established already before eating from the tree. Furthermore, eating from this tree was prohibited even before the woman was created.

Universal Knowledge. This view understands "good and bad" as a merism, expressing totality by two extremes (cf. II Sam. 14:17 and 22, where David is said in one verse to resemble an angel [cf. Gen. 3:22] in "understanding [lit. "hearing"] good and bad" and in the other to be as "wise as an angel . . . in knowing all that is on the earth"; cf. also "good and bad," meaning "anything at all," Gen. 24:50; 31:24, 29; II Sam. 13:22). Against this interpretation it is pointed out that man did not, in fact, gain universal knowledge.

Mature Intelligence. This view notes passages where knowledge of good and bad is said to be absent in children (Deut. 1:39; Isa. 7:15; cf. Manual of Discipline 1: 9–11), and notes that unconcern with nakedness is typical of early childhood, while shame comes with maturation. Critics argue that Adam's ability to name the animals and God's holding him responsible for disobedience assume something beyond childlike intelligence. These objections, however, may not be decisive, and there may be some significance in the fact that this interpretation was assumed by certain *tannaim* (Gen. R. 15:7, cf. Ber. 40a; Sanh. 70b).

Civilizing Human Rationality. This view identifies the knowledge acquired by eating from the tree as the mental capacity which distinguishes man from beast and is the source of civilization. Critics point out that man's assignment "to till the garden and tend it" (2:15) itself constitutes civilized behavior; that the only change reported in the text is awareness of nakedness; and that the arts and crafts of civilization for the most part originate only with Adam's descendants (4:20ff.). However, Adam himself, not only his descendants, became a farmer (3:19, 23), a typically civilized occupation. Becoming aware of nakedness is also a distinguishing mark of civilization and may be only the first of many civilized acts.

The latter point, like this interpretation as a whole, may claim some support in comparative Ancient Near Eastern literature. The beginning of the Mesopotamian *Gilgamesh Epic* (Pritchard, Texts, 72–99, 503–7) describes the early life of Gilgamesh's friend Enkidu; he lived with and in the manner of, wild animals, knowing nothing of civilized ways. His rise to civilization began when a harlot seduced him. After a week of cohabitation Enkidu "now had [wi]sdom, [br]oader understanding," and the harlot described his change as having "become like a god" (*ibid.*, p. 75c, lines 29, 34), much as Adam and Eve became "like divine beings who know good and bad" (Gen. 3:5, 22; if the beginning of the last-quoted line from the Gilgamesh Epic is really to be restored, "Thou art [wi]se," the parallel with Gen. 3:5, 22 would be even more complete; however, a restoration "Thou art [beauti]ful" is also possible; cf. Pritchard, Texts, 77a, line 11). Subsequently the harlot clothed Enkidu and introduced him to human food and drink and other aspects of civilization. Clearly the change in Enkidu was far more than sexual, as some have held. The text stresses Enkidu's resultant alienation from his erstwhile animal companions and his acquisition of human ways. The "wisdom" and "understanding" he gained constitute human intelligence. (A sort of commentary on this passage appears in Dan. 4:29–30, which describes Nebuchadnezzar's life while exiled in terms reminiscent of Enkidu's early life (some literary relationship between the two passages must be presumed), while Dan. 4:13 states explicitly that the change is from a human mind (lit. "*heart") to an animal mind, and verse 31 specifies a loss of "knowledge" (*mandaʿ*)). Some parts of the Enkidu narrative are known to be modeled on creation myths, and the narrative of his civilization may similarly reflect an as yet unknown text about the first man. Be that as it may, this narrative supports the view that the knowledge gained from the tree of knowledge was human rationality (cf. below, for knowledge in the "Myth of Adapa"). However, such comparative literary support cannot be considered an infallible guide to the biblical meaning, since literature often undergoes reinterpretation when transferred from one society to another. Far less problematic, but still not lacking in ambiguity, is the "tree of life." Clearly it confers immortality (3:22, "he might also take from the tree of life and eat, and live forever!"). It is not included in God's prohibition (2:16–17), so it may be that God originally intended Adam to live forever; only after man had disobeyed and obtained the divine prerogative of "knowing good and bad" was this boon revoked (3:19, 22–24). It is not clear whether immortality would have been conferred by eating this tree's fruit once or only by continuous eating. Since Adam had access to the tree before the expulsion, the fact that he had not already gained immortality suggests that the fruit had to be eaten continuously, but the urgency of the expulsion (3:22–24) suggests that a single eating may have sufficed.

The Serpent. The text is at pains to point out the creatureliness of the serpent, describing it as one "of all the wild beasts that the Lord God had made" (3:1, 14); it is distinguished from the other beasts only by its shrewdness (3:1). Its insignificance is underlined in 3:9–19, where God interrogates Adam and Eve, and both respond, while the serpent is not questioned and does not respond. In view of the prominent role played by serpents in Ancient Near Eastern religion and mythology this treatment of the serpent amounts to desecration and demythologization, quite possibly intentional. As a result, the source of evil is denied divine or even demonic status: evil is no independent principle in the cosmos, but stems from the behavior and attitudes of God's creatures.

From early times the serpent has been seen as a symbol, whose meaning is widely debated. Some have stressed the serpent's well-known phallic symbolism and fertility associations, taking the narrative to reflect an attitude toward human sexuality, fertility cults, and the like. Others see the serpent as representing man's own shrewdness. Since in Ancient Near Eastern mythology the forces of chaos which oppose the forces of creation and cosmos are widely represented as serpents, many see the serpent here, too, as a personification of the forces of chaos. According to this view, disobeying God undermines the cosmic order. Alternatively, the serpent may represent ethical evil in general, a meaning that serpentine mythological motifs are given elsewhere in the Bible (e.g., Isa. 26:21–27:1).

Mythological Features. Certain details of the narrative seem not to conform to "classical" biblical religion, but rather to reflect more primitive notions and premises. The very need to withhold immortality from man bespeaks divine jealousy: God and the divine beings are unwilling to have man acquire both of the distinctive characteristics of divinity, "knowledge of good and bad" and immortality (even if they may be willing to have man acquire immortality alone). The Eden narrative is deeply rooted in Ancient Near Eastern and folkloristic traditions. In spite of some adaptation of these traditions to biblical theological tenets, it seems that some of the primitive notions of these traditions resisted adaptation.

LITERARY COMPOSITION

Critics generally hold that the Eden narrative stems from a different source than the preceding creation narrative (Gen. 1:1–2:4a or 4b). Divergent authorship is indicated, according to the documentary hypothesis, by the two narratives' contradictory orders of creation (ch. 1: trees, animals, man and woman; ch 2: man, trees, animals, woman). On the basis of vocabulary and content the first narrative is assigned to the Priestly Document (P), while the second is assigned to the Jehovist, or Yahwist, Document (J; for a contrary view see Cassuto, *Genesis I*, ad loc.).

The Eden pericope in itself appears to combine more than one narrative of the same events. Many doublets in the text point to at least two parallel recensions. The following are some of the doublets which have been suggested: 2:5 and 6 (primordial irrigation), 2:8 and 9 (planting the garden), 2:8 and 15 (placing man in it), 2:23 and 3:20 (naming the woman), 3:7 and 21 (clothing the couple), 3:18b and 19a (man's future food), 3:18a and 17c, d, 19a (man's future occupation), 3:19b and 19c (man's return to the earth), 3:23 and 24 (expulsion from paradise). Other seemingly disjunctive elements are 2:9b (the two trees clumsily seem attached to the verse) and 10–14 (the rivers). On these points there is general agreement, at least in principle. However there is no unanimity at all when it comes to regrouping the variants in order to reconstruct the hypothetical earlier recensions.

LITERARY AND FOLKLORISTIC AFFINITIES

The Eden narrative's affinities with primitive folklore and other biblical and Ancient Near Eastern, especially Mesopotamian, compositions are many, yet there is no single piece of ancient literature which resembles the narrative as a whole, either in its details or theological significance.

The primordial absence of produce and standard forms of irrigation resemble the immediately postdiluvian conditions, which presumably duplicate primordial conditions in the Sumerian "Rulers of Lagās" (in: JCS, 21 (1967), 283). The notion of a divine garden, paradigm of fertility, is mentioned elsewhere in the Bible (Gen. 13:10; Isa. 51:3; Ezek. 36:35; Joel 2:3); a fragmentary passage in the Gilgamesh Epic (Pritchard, Texts, p. 89c) and a fuller passage in Ezekiel 28:11–19 speak of its jewel-bearing trees; the Ezekiel passage is a narrative and reflects a different version of the Eden story (cf., also Ezek. 31:5–9, 16–18). Yet another paradise narrative is the Sumerian tale of "Enki and Ninhursag" (Pritchard, Texts, 37–41), which describes the land (or island) of Dilmun, east of Sumer, as a pure, clean, and bright land, where there is neither sickness nor death, and where the animals live in harmony. One episode in the narrative involves the sun-god's watering Dilmun with fresh water brought up from the earth, thus making it fertile. The earth-goddess Ninhursag gives birth to eight plants, which the water-god Enki proceeds to devour. This leads Ninhursag to curse Enki; this nearly causes the latter's death, but ultimately Ninhursag is made to heal him. Aside from the Eden narrative's manifest similarities to these stories, the differences are also significant; most noticeable is the far more natural configuration of the narrative in Genesis 2–3, in contrast to the fantastic or supernatural nature of the other accounts, including Ezekiel's. Placing man in the garden "to till and tend it" faintly echoes the Mesopotamian creation stories according to which man was created to free the gods from laboring to produce their own food (Pritchard, Texts, 68; cf. W. G. Lambert, *Atrahasis* (1969), 42–67; A. Heidel, *The Babylonian Genesis* (1942) 69–71; S. N. Kramer, *The Sumerians* (1963), 149–50). In the Bible this is not seen as the purpose of man's creation—in fact, the creation of man and the placing of him in the garden are separated by several verses; and there is no suggestion at all that God or the other heavenly beings benefit from man's labor. The theme of lost immortality appears briefly near the end of the Gilgamesh Epic. From the bottom of the sea Gilgamesh brought up a plant which contained the power of rejuvenating the aged; he called it "The Man Becomes Young in Old Age," declaring, "I myself shall eat [it], and thus return to the state of my youth" (in Pritchard, Texts, 96). Later, however, Gilgamesh set the plant down while bathing, and a serpent made off with it and subsequently shed its skin (11. 285–9; in 1. 296 the serpent is referred to as "ground-lion"; some take this as simply an epithet of the serpent, but others, following the testimony of Akkadian lexical texts, take "ground-lion" as "chameleon" (which etymologically means "ground-lion")). The belief that snakes, or lizards, regain their youth when they cast their skins is common among primitive peoples (cf., the analogous belief about molting eagles in Isa. 40:31; Ps. 103:51). This is a reflex of the well-known folklore motif of how the serpent cheated man out of immortality, for the significance of which see below. The loss of immortality is treated in great detail in the Akkadian Myth of Adapa (Pritchard, Texts, 101–3). Priest and sage of the city of Eridu, Adapa had been given "wise understanding . . . to teach the patterns of the land" (A, 3 (this apparently means to teach mankind the patterns of civilization), had been shown "the heart of the heaven and the earth" (B, 57–58)). The god Ea "had given him wisdom, eternal life he had not given him" (A, 4). While he was fishing in the Persian Gulf to supply Ea's temple at Eridu with fish, the south wind swamped Adapa's boat, so Adapa broke its wing with a curse. As Adapa was summoned before the chief god Anu in heaven to account for this behavior, Ea warned him not to eat and drink the bread and water of death that would be presented to him there. However, Anu had been disposed favorably to Adapa by another of Ea's strategems, so that he in fact desired to supplement Adapa's wisdom by offering him the bread and food of life. Unaware, Adapa refused it, accepting only a garment and some anointing oil Ea had approved; and so he lost (eternal) life. Adapa is to be identified with Oannes, known from other sources to have been the first of approximately seven antediluvian sages who taught humanity civilization, paralleling the culture-founding Cainite genealogy from Adam through Lamech's children (Gen. 4), with Oannes-Adapa occupying the position of Adam. To this some have added the evidence of an Akkadian synonym list which supposedly equates Adapa, written *a-da-ap/b,* with "man" (E. A. Speiser in Pritchard, Texts, 101 n. 1; see also M. Civil (ed.), *Materials for the Sumerian Lexicon,* vol. 12, p. 93 line 20); however it is doubtful that this is Adapa, whose name is not written this way, and the very significance of the equation is uncertain. Not all details of the relationship of the Myth of Adapa to the Eden narrative are clear or necessarily convincing, but some relationship does seem indicated. The contrasts, aside from obviously wide divergence in details and plot, are most profound and characteristic in the area of underlying religious outlook. Although the Myth of Adapa does not make it clear whether Ea simply erred or purposely deceived Adapa, it expresses in either case a resigned acceptance of death as a situation beyond rational human control. The biblical narrative, on the other hand, assumes that death and other forms of misfortune in this world are the earned results of human behavior whose consequences man knew in advance. The theme of man's being cheated out of immortality by the serpent or some other skin-sloughing animal appears in the folklore of several peoples. Another frequently occurring motif is that of the perverted message, wherein God sent to man a message of immortality which the messenger perverted into a message of mortality, thus dooming mankind ever since. At times these two motifs are combined: God's message instructed man to rejuvenate himself by casting off his old skin, but the faithless messenger gave this information to the serpent instead, and told man that his life would end in death. On the basis of these motifs, J. G. Frazer surmised that an earlier version of the Eden narrative related as follows: The garden contained two trees—the tree of life and the tree of death (cf. the food and drink offered Adapa). God sent a message, through the serpent, that man should eat from the tree of life, not the tree of death. The clever serpent, however, reversed the message, leading the human couple to eat from the tree of death (cf. the deception of Adapa), while he himself ate from the tree of life and thus gained immortality (cf. Pritchard, Texts, 96 referred to above).

The material surveyed above leads to the conclusion that the biblical Eden narrative has roots in Ancient Near Eastern literature. Yet, as noted above, these parallels are fragmentary, dealing with only a few motifs each, and the discrepancies in detail are often great. How these gaps were bridged cannot be said with certainty, presumably because of ignorance of the process of transmission of Ancient Near Eastern literature to the Bible. Quite possibly these stories became known to the biblical authors in proto-Israelite versions which they molded, with creative editorial skill, into a unique narrative with a wholly new meaning. [J.H.T.]

PARADISE AND HELL IN LATER JEWISH THOUGHT

Paradise and Hell, the places of reward for the righteous and punishment for the wicked after death, are traditionally referred to as the Garden of Eden and *Gehinnom respectively. In the Bible these two names never refer to the abode of souls after death; nevertheless, the idea of a fiery torment for the wicked may have been suggested by Isaiah 66:24. The earliest possible allusion to Gehinnom in the new sense is found in the Apocrypha, in which the general phrase "accursed valley" is used to describe the place where the wicked will be judged and punished (I En. 27:1ff.). The name Gehenna (= Gehinnom) first appears in the New Testament (e.g., Matt. 5:22, 29ff.), as does "Paradise," the abode of the blessed (e.g., Luke 23:43). The word *pardes* ("park," "orchard") occurs in biblical and talmudic sources, but rarely, if ever, in the sense of "heavenly abode." The oldest Jewish source to mention Gan (=Garden of) Eden and Gehinnom is probably a statement of Johanan b. Zakkai at the end of the first century C.E.: "There are two ways before me, one leading to Paradise and the other to Gehinnom" (Ber. 28b). Jewish teaching about a future life was never systematized, and the varied statements in rabbinic literature cannot be combined into a consistent whole. "Days of the Messiah" and "World to Come" are sometimes sharply distinguished, sometimes virtually identified. Some passages indicate that the righteous and wicked will enter Gan Eden and Gehinnom only after the resurrection and last judgment; in others, the departed take their assigned places immediately after death. Other descriptions of future bliss and punishment make no mention of locale.

APOCALYPTIC LITERATURE

The apocalypses frequently mention the punishment of the wicked by fire (I En. 90:26ff., IV Ezra 7:36; Testament of Abraham (A) 12). In II Enoch 10 the places of reward and punishment are located in the third heaven; usually Hell is underground, as in II Enoch 40:12. Hell is sometimes identified with *Sheol (I En. 22:8ff.). In the Bible, however, Sheol was the abode of all the dead, and it was not a place of retribution. Now it becomes to some extent a place of punishment. The Apocalypses of Baruch and Ezra come closer to the old notion: Sheol is the temporary abode of souls between death and the last judgment (II Bar. 23:5, IV Ezra 4:41); but reward and punishment may begin during this period (II Bar. 36:11). The punishment at the end of time is final, and there is no hope of any further change or repentance (*ibid.* 85:12). The sources also describe the rewards of the righteous; Assumption of Moses 10:10 includes among the satisfactions of the righteous that they will see the wicked suffering in Gehenna.

RABBINIC LITERATURE

Gehinnom and Gan Eden existed even before the world was created (Pes. 54a), Gehinnom at the left hand of God, Gan Eden at His right (Mid. Ps. 90:12).

Gehinnom. So vast is Hell, it may be compared to a pot of which the rest of the universe forms the lid (Pes. 94a). Gehinnom is not only for punishment, but also for purgation. According to Bet Shammai, those whose merits and sins are evenly balanced will be purified in the flames of Gehinnom, and thus rendered fit to enter Gan Eden. *Bet Hillel held that such marginal persons would, by God's mercy, escape the ordeal (Tosef., Sanh. 13:3; RH 16b–17a). A widely held view was that the wicked will be punished in Gehinnom for 12 months only, after which they will be annihilated, to suffer no more. Only a limited group, chiefly those who by word and deed have repudiated their loyalty to the Jewish people and the basic doctrines of Jewish faith, will endure endless torment (Tosef., Sanh. 12:4, 5; RH 17a). However, R. Akiva cited Isaiah 66:23 concerning the 12-month sentence, indicating that even the wicked after having atoned for their sins in purgatory will join the righteous in Gan Eden (Eduy. 10). The severity of Gehinnom was mitigated in rabbinic thought. It was widely believed that all Israel, except for a few arch sinners, would have a share in the world to come, and so could not be unconditionally doomed to Hell (Sanh. 10). Abraham was said to stand at the entrance of Gehinnom and prevent his circumcised descendants from being incarcerated there (Er. 19a; cf. the reference to "Abraham's bosom" in Luke 16:23). Moreover, all the condemned, including gentiles, would have respite from punishment on the Sabbath (Sanh. 65b). The possibility that the reprobates might repent, acknowledge the justness of their punishment, and thus open the way to their redemption is mentioned in several places (Er. loc. cit.; on the sons of Korah, see Ginzberg, Legends, 6 (1928), 103, n. 586). That the piety of a son may mitigate the punishment of a deceased parent is implied in Kiddushin 31b (cf. II Macc. 12:42ff.) and stated explicitly in a post-talmudic story (*Kallah Rabbati,* 2:9, ed. Higger, 202ff.). The special effectiveness of the recital of **Kaddish* for this purpose is mentioned in medieval writings (e.g. *Baḥya ben Asher, Deut. 21:8). Some Palestinian rabbis denied that there is, or will be, a place called Gehinnom. They held that at the final judgment sinners will be destroyed by the unshielded rays of the sun or by a fire issuing from their own bodies (Gen. R. 6:6; 26:6).

Gan Eden. A place is reserved for every Israelite in both Gan Eden and Gehinnom. Before being assigned to their proper abode, the wicked are shown the place they might have occupied in Heaven, and the righteous, the place they might have occupied in Hell (Mid. Ps. 6:6; 31:6). In contrast to passages that depict the righteous sitting at golden tables (Ta'an. 25a) or under elaborate canopies (Ruth 3:4) and participating in lavish banquets (BB 75a), Rav (third century C.E.) declared that in the world to come—Gan Eden is not specifically mentioned—there will be no sensual enjoyment and no transaction of business or competition, but the righteous will sit crowned, enjoying the radiance of the Divine Presence (Ber. 17a). Some 11 persons, mostly biblical figures, entered Paradise alive (Ginzberg, Legends, 5 (1925), 5–96) and legend tells in detail how R. Joshua b. Levi accomplished this feat (Ket. 77b). See also *Garden of Eden.

MEDIEVAL LITERATURE

A number of post-talmudic writings give longer and more fully elaborated descriptions of Gan Eden and Gehinnom, which are in substantial agreement with the briefer accounts in the Talmud and classic Midrashim. Among these writings are tractate *Gan Eden* and tractate *Gehinnom,* the *Iggeret of R. Joshua b. Levi, Midrash Konen,* and *Otiyyot de-R. Akiva.* They generally picture Heaven and Hell each divided into seven sections; souls are assigned to the several sections in accordance with the level of their merits or the heinousness of their sins. The Jewish accounts of Hell are tame compared to those in medieval Christian literature, as is apparent from Dante's *Divine Comedy,* written in the 14th century. On the other hand, Gan Eden is not pictured as a place of completely static bliss: the Messiah is there awaiting the day of the redemption (according to *Midrash Konen,* suffering for the sins of Israel), and he enlists the help of the righteous souls in urging God to speed the final deliverance (see J. D. Eisenstein, *Oẓar Midrashim,* 1 (1915), 85, 87). In the 13th–14th centuries the poet *Immanuel b. Solomon of Rome wrote the fullest account of Paradise and Hell in Hebrew literature; it is entitled *Tophet and Eden* and is the last section of his *Maḥbarot.* It was possibly suggested by Dante's *Divine Comedy,* but possesses little literary power or religious depth. Its most notable feature is the inclusion of a section in Eden for pious gentiles in accordance with the prevailing Jewish teaching. Moreover, unlike Dante, Immanuel did not mention reprobates in *Tophet* by name. Some medieval philosophers explained earlier references to Paradise and Hell as figures of speech. Heaven meant the joy of communion with God, and Hell meant to be deprived of eternal life (Maim. Yad, Teshuvah, 8:1, 5). To Joseph *Albo, Hell is the state of the soul which, having sought only material gratifications in this life, has no means of obtaining satisfaction in the non-material life beyond the grave (*Ikkarim* 4:33). The Kabbalists developed and adapted the relatively simple notions of Gan Eden and

Gehinnom to fit into their complex systems, and especially in order to reconcile them with the doctrine of reincarnation (see *Gilgul).

MODERN PERIOD

Moses *Mendelssohn flatly rejected the idea of Hell as incompatible with the mercy of God (*Gesammelte Schriften,* 3 (1843), 345–7). Modern Jews of all religious viewpoints, including those who vigorously uphold the belief in personal immortality, have generally discarded the idea that Paradise and Hell exist literally. Since these concepts, though once widely accepted, were never regarded as dogmatically binding, the rejection of them has not occasioned any strain, even on Orthodoxy.

See also *Eschatology; *Resurrection of the Dead; *World to Come. For Islam see *Eschatology. [B.J.B.]

Bibliography: J. Frazer, *Folklore in the Old Testament,* 1 (1919), 45–77; Th. C. Vriezen, *Orderzoek naar de paradijs-voorstelling bij de oude Semietische Volken* (1937), incl. bibl.; P. Humbert, *Etudes sur le récit du paradis et de la chute dans la Genèse* (1940), incl. bibl.; U. Cassuto, in: *Studies in Memory of M. Schorr* (1944), 248–58; J. L. McKenzie, in: *Theological Studies,* 15 (1954), 541–72; E. A. Speiser, in: BASOR, 140 (1955), 9–11; idem, in: *Festschrift Johannes Friedrich* (1959), 473–85; R. Gordis, in: JBL, 76 (1957), 123–38; B. S. Childs, *Myth and Reality in the Old Testament* (1962[2]), 43–50; N. M. Sarna, *Understanding Genesis* (1966), 23–28; T. H. Gaster, *Myth, Legend and Custom in the Old Testament* (1969), 6–50, 327–71; J. A. Bailey, in: JBL, 89 (1970), 137–50. See also Commentaries to Genesis 2:4–3. IN JEWISH PHILOSOPHY: R. H. Charles, *Eschatology* (1963[2]); K. Kohler, *Heaven and Hell in Comparative Religion* (1923); H. Strack and P. Billerbeck, *Kommentar zum Neuen Testament,* 4 (1928), 1928), 1016–65.

PARAF, PIERRE (1893–), French author, editor and broadcasting executive. Born in Paris, Paraf, a graduate in law, was an officer in the French army during World War I, then took up journalism, and from 1930 until 1939 was literary editor of the Paris daily *La République.* He later worked for the left-wing daily *Combat* and for the monthly *L'Europe.* In 1936 he joined the French radio service and eventually became chief editor of French Radio-Television. After the French military collapse in 1940, he fought with the underground until the liberation in 1944. Paraf showed strong Jewish loyalties in his work and writings. In one of his early books, *Quand Israël Aima* (1929), he expressed his pride in belonging to the Jewish people. With the writer Bernard *Lecache, he founded in 1927 the Ligue internationale contre le Racisme et l'Antisémitisme. He was president of the Mouvement contre le Racisme, l'Antisémitisme et pour la Paix and a member of the executive of the League for the Rights of Man. After World War II he directed the monthly review *Amitié France-Israël* and wrote books on Jewish and Zionist themes. Among them were *Israël dans le monde* (1947) and *L'Etat d'Israël dans le monde* (1960). Other of his books were *Les cités du bonheur* (1945), *L'Ascension des peuples noirs* (1958), *Les démocraties populaires* (1962), and *Le Racisme dans le monde* (1964). [G.E.S.]

PARAGUAY, South American republic. A few isolated Jews came to Paraguay from France, Switzerland, and Italy toward the end of the 19th century and merged with the native population without ever establishing a Jewish community. On the eve of World War I a number of Sephardi Jews immigrated from Palestine. The families Arditi, Cohenca, Levi, Mendelzon, and Varzan formed the first *hevra kaddisha* (Alianza Israelita) in 1917 and established the first synagogue with other Sephardim from Turkey and Greece. A second immigration in the early 1920s brought Jews from the Ukraine and Poland who founded the Ashkenazi community, Unión Hebraica. Between 1933 and 1939 between 15,000 and 20,000 Jews from Germany, Austria, and Czechoslovakia took advantage of Paraguay's liberal immigration laws to escape from Nazi Europe. Most of them used Paraguay or their Paraguayan visas as stepping stones to Argentina, Brazil, and Uruguay where immigration laws were more severe. The small fraction that remained in Paraguay established the Unión de Israelitas pro Socorro Mutuo. This group built the main synagogue, later located within the premises of the Unión Hebraica. After World War II a last group of immigrants, mostly survivors from the concentration camps, arrived. In 1968 the Jewish community was estimated at some 300 families or 1,000 persons. The size of the community is decreasing through emigration to Argentina and Brazil, but there are also occasional immigrants from those countries, especially due to marriage. There is a continuous trickle of emigrants to Israel, and some 50 people have settled there.

Most Paraguayan Jews engage in commerce or industry. There are about 25 Jewish professionals, most of whom studied in Paraguay. The community supports a Jewish school, named "Escuela Integral Estado de Israel," in which Hebrew is taught in addition to the Paraguayan curriculum. About 50 Jewish students are enrolled at the university, in addition to others who study abroad. The Jewish community is heavily outnumbered by the richer and more influential Arab colony, whose members engage in Paraguayan politics and have intermarried with the country's most important families. There are also some 40,000 Germans or people of German descent, many of whom had openly supported the Nazis before and during World War II. A number of prominent Nazis, among them Dr. J. *Mengele of *Auschwitz, found temporary shelter in Paraguay. There were some short-lived anti-Semitic decrees in 1936 and some anti-Semitic incidents prior to the establishment of the strong-arm regime of General Alfredo Stroessner in 1954. After that time, Jews were not disturbed. Paraguay voted in 1947 for the UN Resolution on the partition of Palestine and has been friendly to Israel ever since. The population, which lost two-thirds of its members in the war against an array of larger nations between 1865 and 1870, tends to empathize with Israel. An Israel Embassy was established in 1968. The Consejo Representativeo Israelita del Paraguay represents the Jewish community vis-à-vis the public and authorities. There is also a sports club, a *B'nai B'rith, *Wizo chapter, and a *Ha-No'ar ha-Ẓiyyoni movement. In 1968 another youth organization, Centro Israelita Juvenil, was established.

Bibliography: Associación Filantrópica Israelita, Buenos Aires, *Zehn Jahre Aufbauarbeit in Suedamerika* (Ger. and Sp., 1943),

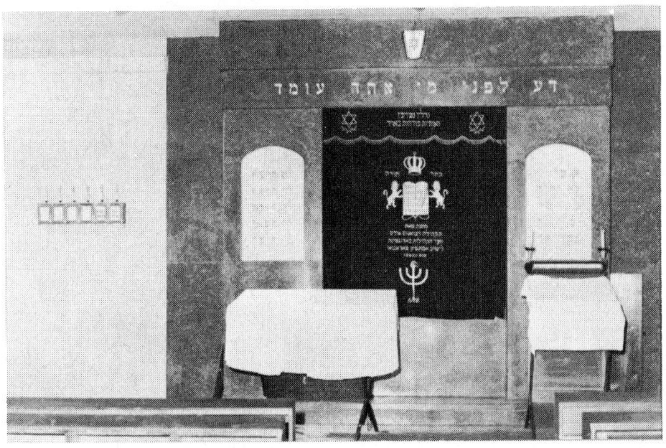

Ashkenazi synagogue in Asunción, Paraguay. Courtesy Central Institute of Cultural Relations, Israel-South America, Spain, and Portugal, Jerusalem.

293–9; A. Monk and J. Isaacson, *Comunidades Judías de Latinoamérica* (1968), 107–8; J. Shatzky, *Comunidades Judías en Latinoamérica* (1952), J. Beller, *Jews in Latin America* (1969), 204–9.
[B.VA.]

PARAH (Heb. פָּרָה; "heifer"), name of the fourth treatise in the Mishnah and the Tosefta in the order of **Tohorot*. This tractate is based upon the pentateuchal law of the burning of the *red heifer as set forth in Numbers 19:1–22.

The tractate is divided into 12 chapters whose subject matter is the proper age for the validity of the heifer and other sacrificial animals; the type of work that invalidates the heifer (3:1, 3, 4); the degree of redness required (2:2, 5); the preparation of the priest prior to the burning of the heifer (3:1, 5, 8); the manner of bringing the spring water (3:3, 4); the procedure of the bringing and burning of the heifer (3:6, 7, 9–11; 4:2, 3); irrelevant intentions at the time of the slaughtering of the heifer (4:1, 3); defilement of those engaged in the preparation and burning of the heifer (4:4); qualifications for vessels containing the purifying waters (5); laws pertaining to work done with the spring water and the procedure of its mingling with the ashes of the heifer (6; 7; 8:1, 2; 9:4); the type and condition of spring water considered fit for the purifying waters (8:8–11; 9:1–3); status of the mixture after defilement (9:5–9); ritual uncleanness of objects coming in contact with the purifying waters or their vessels (10); cases of doubt if the purifying waters were defiled (11:1–2); laws of the hyssop used in the sprinkling of the purifying waters (11:7–9; 12:2, 6); procedure in the sprinkling on the ritually unclean (12:3–5, 11).

It is stated that until the destruction of the Temple no more than nine heifers were actually prepared (3:5), and the names of those who prepared them are given. Of significance is chapter 3 outlining extreme measures instituted by the rabbis to guarantee the ritual purity of the priest who was to burn the heifer. These were enacted as safeguards from certain opposing views of the Sadducees. The tractate includes discussion on some general principles of ritual uncleanness, not directly related to the major theme (8:4–7; 11:4–6; 12:8–10).

The Tosefta *Parah* consists of twelve chapters, which embody and supplement in detail the laws contained in the Mishnah.

Engraving for the tractate *Parah,* which deals with the ritual burning of a red heifer. From a title page of the Hebrew-Latin Mishnah illustrated by Mich. Richey, Amsterdam, 1700–04. Jerusalem, J.N.U.L.

Noteworthy is the section on laws pertaining to the different standards of ritual purity between a **ḥaver* and an **am-ha-areẓ* (4:12–5:3). There is no *Gemara* on the tractate in the Babylonian Talmud nor in the Jerusalem Talmud.

Bibliography: P. Blackman, *Mishnayot,* 6 (Eng., 1955), 401–5; H. Danby, *Mishnah* (Eng., 1933), 697–714; H. L. Strack, *Introduction to the Talmud and Midrash* (1931), 61–62.
[J.KE.]

PARAH, PERATH (Heb. פָּרָת, פָּרָה), town (Parah) listed among the cities of Benjamin with Avvim and Ophrah (Josh. 18:23). Jeremiah was bidden by the Lord to hide his girdle by the Perath (AV translation: Euphrates); when the girdle was later removed, it was found spoiled, as a prophetic sign (Jer. 13:4, 7). It is now generally assumed that these references are to the ancient settlement at Tell Fāra and to the Wadi Fāra, a deep gorge near Jeremiah's birthplace Anathoth. In Hasmonean times, Bacchides fortified the place (I Macc. 9:50; as Pharathon). The Zealot leader Bar Giora camped at Ain near the river Pheretai in the First Jewish War (Jos., Wars 4:512). The Wadi Fāra contains many remains of the Byzantine period. Its main source, ʿAyn Fāra (1,135 cu.m. daily), supplied Herodian Jericho with water by means of a rock-cut channel; during the British Mandate this water was pumped to Jerusalem.

Bibliography: Avi-Yonah, Geog, 36–37, 105; Abel, Geog, 2 (1938), 404.
[M.A.-Y.]

PARAN (Heb. פָּארָן), biblical appellation for the main desert in the eastern Sinai peninsula. Its boundaries can be reconstructed by means of a number of biblical references. In their campaign against Canaan, the kings of Shinar, Ellasar, Elam, and Golim reached El-Paran, "which is by the wilderness" (Gen. 14:6), a place generally identified with Elath on the Red Sea. Moses spoke to Israel "in the Arabah, near Suph [Red Sea?], between Paran and Tophel" (Deut. 1:1). The Red Sea, therefore, was probably the southern extremity of the Paran wilderness. On the other hand, when Ishmael was cast out with Hagar by Abraham, presumably from Beer-Sheba, he dwelt in the wilderness of Paran (Gen. 21:21). The twelve spies of Moses were sent from the wilderness of Paran, to Canaan, and returned to "the wilderness of Paran, to Kadesh" (Num. 13:3, 26), which is usually described in the Bible as situated in the wilderness of Zin. Paran, therefore, extended as far north as Kadesh and even the periphery of Beer-Sheba. David went to the wilderness of Paran in his wanderings (I Sam. 25:1) and came into contact with Nabal, "a man in Maon," which is in southern Judah. Thus it also extended to the northeast. The Israelites entered it from the wilderness of Sinai (Num. 10:12), or, more specifically, from Hazeroth. If the identification of Hazeroth with ʿAyn al-Ḥaḍra near Jebel Ḥillāl is correct (rather than with ʿAyn Ḥaḍra in southeastern Sinai, as some have suggested), Paran would be limited to the Tih Desert in the northeastern part of the Sinai Peninsula, which agrees roughly with the story of Hadad, the Edomite pretender, who fled from Midian to Egypt by way of Paran (I Kings 11:18). An element of doubt is created, however, by the juxtaposition of Mt. Paran with Mt. Sinai and Mt. Seir in Deuteronomy 33:2 and Habakkuk 3:3; some interpreters regard this mountain as synonymous with Mt. Sinai, while others look for a separate Mt. Paran at a site called Jebel Fārān, a place mentioned by some travelers, but not located by others. It can perhaps best be defined as the eastern part of the Tih Desert, placed between the desert of Shur near Egypt and the desert of Zin near the Judean Mountains. It is crossed by the eastern confluents of the Brook of Egypt (Wadi al-ʿArīsh).

In later times, the name occurs as that of a tribe

Figure 1. Seventeenth-century map of the Paran Desert. From T. Fuller, *A Pisgah-sight of Palestine and confines thereof with the Historie of the old and new Testament acted thereon,* London, 1650. Jerusalem, Sir Isaac and Lady Wolfson Museum in Hechal Shlomo. Photo David Harris, Jerusalem.

(Ptolemy, *Geographia,* 3:5, 17), and in the Byzantine period, in the description of the area in which St. Nilus searched for his son, who had been kidnapped by the Saracens (PG, vol. 79, pp. 667ff.).

Bibliography: Aharoni, Land, index; Glueck, in: AASOR, 15 (1935), 104. [M.A.-Y.]

Figure 2. The Paran Desert. Courtesy J.N.F., Jerusalem.

PARAPET (Heb. מַעֲקֶה). Ancient roofs were flat and in general use (cf. Josh. 2:6; Judg. 16:27; I Sam. 9:25f; Isa. 22:1; et al.), and the Bible enjoins "when thou buildest a new house, then thou shalt make a parapet for thy roof, that thou bring not blood upon thy house, if any man fall from thence" (Deut. 22:8). The parapet must be not less than ten handbreadths high and strong enough to keep a person who leans on it from falling (Sif. Deut. 229; Maim. Yad, Roẓe'aḥ 11:3). The law was given a far wider application, however, and made to include the need to remove any object that constitutes a public or a private hazard. Such precautions include fencing or covering a well or a pit (Maim. *ibid.,* 11:4) and not keeping a savage dog or a shaky ladder in one's house (BK 15b). The statement of R. Eleazar (BK 4:9), that "No precaution is adequate [for a vicious ox] save the slaughterer's knife," is based by Abbaye on this same law (BK 46a). For the same reason one who keeps a wild dog or cat in his house is placed under the ban (Ket. 41b). Even if only the owner is endangered and he is willing to take the risk, he is forbidden and forcibly prevented if necessary (Maim. *ibid.,* 4f.). [H.FR.]

PARCZEW, district capital in the province of Lublin, E. Poland. Since it was lying on the border of the kingdom of Poland and the Duchy of Lithuania, it served as the seat of the sessions of the Sejm until 1564, a fact which greatly affected the sources of livelihood of the Jews living there. An organized Jewish community existed from the beginning of the 16th century. In 1564, 11 houses were owned by Jews. Between 1563 and 1570 a violent struggle was waged between the Jewish community and the municipal council, which sought to move Jewish merchants and craftsmen from the center of the town to its suburbs. In 1591 a compromise was reached: the Jews were to remain in their former place of residence in exchange for their consent to bear an equal share of obligations imposed on the town, an arrangement ratified by the king in 1623. In 1654 King John

II Casimir authorized the Jews to build houses, to engage in commerce within the boundaries of the town, and to manufacture alcoholic liquor for their own needs. In 1674 among the 331 townsmen who paid the poll tax, 84 were Jews. The town was severely damaged in the Northern War (1700–21), and by 1718 only four Jews remained in Parczew. In the course of time Jews made an important contribution to the development of the town and its economy. In 1762 Jews owned 47 houses. In 1765 there were 303 Jews who paid the poll tax, including nine bakers, six tailors, six hatters, and one locksmith. In the 29 villages in the vicinity 151 Jews paid the poll tax. Between 1790 and 1795 Jews established tanneries in the town. Under Russian rule there were no restrictions against the residence of Jews in Parczew. In 1827 the community numbered 1,079 (37% of the total population), and by 1857 had increased to 1,692 (about 50% of the total). During the second half of the 19th century, Jews earned their livelihood mainly from tailoring, weaving, and carpentry, as well as from the retail trade in agricultural produce. During this period the influence of *Ḥasidism intensified. In 1921 there were 4,005 Jews (51% of the population) in the town. Between the two world wars, branches of the Zionist parties and youth organizations as well as the *Agudat Israel were active in Parczew. [A.Cy.]

Holocaust Period. On the outbreak of World War II there were 5,000 Jews in Parczew. On Sept. 19, 1942, the Germans began to deport the town's Jewish population to the *Treblinka death camp. During this deportation, as well as those from a number of places in the vicinity, several thousand people fled to the Parczew forest (Lasy Parczewskie). Most of them were shot by German armed units that searched the woods frequently, but a few hundred managed to establish themselves within the forest in a family camp called Altana. A guerrilla battalion under the command of a Jewish officer, Alexander Skotnicki, operated in the Parczew forest. Its largest detachment was a Jewish guerrilla company commanded by Jechiel Grynszpan. When the Parczew region was liberated (at the end of July 1944), about 150 Jewish partisans and about 200 survivors of the Jewish family camp, which existed thanks to the defense provided by the Jewish partisans, left the forest. [S.Kr.]

Bibliography: R. Mahler, *Yidn in Amolikn Poyln in Likht fun Tsifern* (1958), index; Warsaw, Archiwum Główne Akt Dawnych, *Lustracje woj. lubelskiego* (1660), pp. 49, 58; ibid. for. (1762), p. 40; Lodz, Archiwum Państwowe, *Archiwum Kossowskich z Glogowy*, no. V-29/1; W. A. P. Lublin, *Księgi gródzkie lubelskie księgi miasta Parczewa* (=C.A.H.J.P., HM 7049, 6706); B. Wasiutyński, *Ludność żydowska w Polsce w wiekach XIV i XX* (1930), 34; I. Schiper (ed.), *Dzieje handlu żydowskiego na ziemiach polskich* (1937), index; M. Zakrzewska-Dubasowa, *Parczew w XV–XVIII wieku* (1962), 26, 27, 28, 40, 46–48; T. Brustin-Bernstein, in: *Bleter far Geshikhte*, 3, no. 1–2 (1950), 51–78.

PARDES (Heb. פַּרְדֵּ״ס), in the Middle Ages the word *pardes* was used as a mnemonic for the four types of biblical exegesis, an acronym of **peshat* ("the literal meaning"), *remez* ("hint," i.e., veiled allusions such as **gematria*, and **notarikon*), **derash* ("homiletical interpretation"), and *sod* ("mystery," i.e., the esoteric interpretation), the word being made up of the initial letters of these words. For the meaning of the word in mysticism, see *Kabbalah. [Ed.]

PARDES ḤANNAH-KARKUR (Heb. פַּרְדֵּס חַנָּה – כַּרְכּוּר), predominantly rural community in the northern Sharon, Israel, about 4 mi. (7 km.) N.E. of Ḥaderah, created in 1969 through the amalgamation of Pardes Ḥannah and Karkur. Karkur was founded in 1913 by a group of English Jews, "Aḥuzzat London," on land acquired the year before by the Palestine Land Development Company

and guarded by members of *Ha-Shomer who remained and worked on the place, together with other Jewish laborers, until the 1920s. In 1919 building began, but a part of the English group arrived only in 1925–26. In 1927 Karkur already numbered 300 inhabitants, and the initially hard conditions improved after abundant groundwater was found. The moshav, based mainly on citrus, had 900 inhabitants in 1948; its population increased to 3,000 in 1952, but has since remained the same. Most inhabitants are from Eastern Europe; others are from Yemen. It is the site of a *dew research station.

Pardes Ḥannah was established in 1929 by the Palestine Jewish Colonization Association for the settlement of veteran farm laborers. In 1939 the moshavah was enlarged to include the neighboring village of Meged founded in 1933. During the 1930s, immigrants from Central Europe joined Pardes Ḥannah, some of whom erected the Tel Shalom quarter. In 1947 a housing project was set up named Neveh Asher, after Selig *Brodetsky. During World War II, the British authorities expropriated Pardes Ḥannah lands to build large military camps which after 1948 became two large **ma'barot*, bringing the population from 2,350 inhabitants to over 10,000. When the *ma'barot* were closed down at the end of the 1950s, only some of their inhabitants remained and were transferred to local housing. The population figure then shrank to 7,500 but slowly rose again to 13,400 in 1970. The economy of Pardes Ḥannah-Karkur is based on highly intensive and fully irrigated farming as well as on industry. There are several large schools, including the agricultural high school of the Farmers' Union (Hitaḥadut ha-Ikkarim) and No'am, the combined yeshivah high school. "Pardes Ḥannah," meaning "Hannah's Citrus Grove," commemorates a cousin of Baron Edmond de *Rothschild.

Bibliography: A. Ever-Hadani (ed.), *Aḥuzzah Alef London-Karkur 1913–1968* (1969), with Eng. summ. [E.O.]

PARDESIYYAH (Heb. פַּרְדֵּסִיָּה), Jewish village with municipal council status, in central Israel, about 4 mi. (6 km.) S.E. of Netanyah. Founded in 1940, it initially housed a few families of Jewish laborers originating from Yemen who were employed in the citrus groves in the vicinity. The village expanded greatly in the 1950s, as it was in the neighborhood of large *ma'barot* (immigrant camps) part of whose area was included in Pardesiyyah's municipal boundary. The village had 332 inhabitants in 1955, 1,587 in 1961, and 800 in 1970. [E.O.]

PARDO, family which apparently originated in Prado del Rey, Castile, and which flourished during the 16th–18th centuries in the Ottoman Empire, Italy, the Netherlands, England, and America. The more celebrated members of the family are dealt with under separate entries.

David (d. 1657), son of Joseph *Pardo, served as rabbi in Amsterdam. He was born in Salonika and moved to Amsterdam with his father. In 1618 he was appointed rabbi of the Beth Israel congregations. After the three Sephardi congregations had amalgamated into the Talmud Torah congregation (1639), he was appointed one of its four rabbis and trustee of the cemetery. He published an edition in Latin characters of Ẓaddik b. Joseph Formon's Ladino translation of *Ḥovot ha-Levavot* by Baḥya ibn Paquda (Amsterdam, 1610). His son, Josiah, was a disciple and son-in-law of Saul Levi *Morteira. After teaching in the

Yesiba de los Pintos of Rotterdam, which was transferred to Amsterdam in 1669, he emigrated to Curaçao (Antilles). From 1674 he was *ḥakham* of the community there and appears to have founded the local yeshivah, Eẓ Ḥayyim ve-Ohel Ya'akov. In 1683 he left for Jamaica, where he also served as rabbi. David Pardo (d. c. 1717), the rabbi of the Portuguese community of Surinam, was probably his son.

The Pardo family was scattered throughout North America, where they became known as Brown (or Browne; although the actual meaning of Pardo is "grey"). Saul Pardo (d. 1708), known as Saul Brown, was the first *ḥazzan* of the Jewish community of New York. He held this office in the She'erit Israel synagogue until 1682.

Bibliography: Kayserling, Bibl, index; L. Blau, *Leo Modenas Briefe und Schriftstuecke* (1907), 79ff.; J. Mendes dos Remedios, *Os Judeus Portuguesesem Amsterdam* (1911), 9, 13, 16, 41; J. S. da Silva Rosa, *Geschiedenis der Portugeesche Joden te Amsterdam* (1925), index; C. Roth, *A Life of Menasseh Ben Israel* (1934), index; H. I. Bloom, *The Economic Activities of Jews of Amsterdam* (1937), index; Brugmans-Frank, 211ff.; H. B. Grinstein, *The Rise of the Jewish Community of New York* (1945), 484, 488; J. R. Marcus, *Early American Jewry,* 1 (1951), 35, and index s.v. *Brown;* Wiznitzer, in: HJ, 20 (1958), 110f., 117f.; Emmanuel, in: AJHSP, 44 (1954–55), 216f., 221, 225 n.; Hershkowitz, *ibid.,* 55 (1965–66), 324ff. and index s.v. *Brown, Browne.* [Ed.]

PARDO, DAVID SAMUEL BEN JACOB (1718–1790), rabbinical author and poet. Born in Venice, he went to Sarajevo for a time as a result of a dispute over an inheritance, and from there to Spalato, in Dalmatia. From approximately 1738 he was a teacher of children, at the same time studying under the local rabbi, Abraham David Papo. Eventually Pardo was appointed rabbi of the town. From 1760 he was rabbi of Sarajevo. From 1776 to 1782 he traveled to Ereẓ Israel, settling in Jerusalem where he served as head of the yeshivah Ḥesed le-Avraham u-Vinyan Shelomo. Pardo was regarded as one of Jerusalem's great rabbis. Of his many works his series of commentaries and novellae on tannaitic literature are especially original. His first work was *Shoshannim le-David* (Venice, 1752), a commentary on the Mishnah. The somewhat sharp language he employed in the first part in criticizing contemporary scholars gave rise to friction between him and David Corinaldi and Mas'ud Rokeaḥ in Leghorn. But after he mitigated his language in the second part and published an apology, a reconciliation took place.

Pardo's *Ḥasdei David* (Leghorn, 1776–90; Jerusalem, 1890) on the Tosefta is considered the most important commentary on this work (the portion on *Tohorot,* the manuscript of which is in the National Library of Jerusalem, has not been published). He completed the work in Jerusalem on his 68th birthday. Portions of it were published in the Romm Vilna edition of the Talmud with the text of the Tosefta. Similarly, his *Sifrei de-Vei Rav* (Salonika, 1799), which he commenced in 1786 and was published by his son Abraham after his death, is the most important commentary on the *Sifrei.* In it he makes use of commentaries of Hillel b. Eliakim, Solomon ibn Okhana, and Eliezer ibn Nahum, all of which he had in manuscript. Other works he wrote are *Mikhtam le-David* (Salonika, 1772), halakhic decisions and responsa; *Maskil le-David* (Venice, 1761), a supercommentary on Rashi's biblical commentary; *La-Menaẓẓe'aḥ le-David* (Salonika, 1765), on those talmudic passages where alternative explanations are given; *Mizmor le-David* (Leghorn, 1818), notes on the *Perot Ginnosar* of Hezekiah da Silva and Ḥayyim ibn Attar on Shulḥan Arukh, *Even ha-Ezer.* Pardo's liturgical poems and prayers are included in the Sephardi daily and festival prayer books. His arrangement of the *Avodah* for the Day of Atonement, which was adopted in the Sephardi rite, appeared in his *Shifat Revivim* (Leghorn, 1788).

Of his sons, Jacob Pardo became chief rabbi of Ragusa and died in Jerusalem. He was a noted talmudist and well versed in Kabbalah. His chief works were *Kohelet Ya'akov* (Venice, 1784), a commentary on the early prophets; *Appe Zutre* (*ibid.,* 1797), on *Hilkhot Ishut* of the Shulḥan Arukh *Even ha-Ezer,* and *Minḥat Aharon* (*ibid.,* 1809), which deals mainly with the laws of prayer. A second son, Isaac, was rabbi of Sarajevo, while a third, Abraham, who married the daughter of Ḥ. J. D. *Azulai, became head of the yeshivah Ḥesed le-Avraham u-Vinyan Shelomo after his father-in-law's death. Pardo's disciples included Shabbetai b. Abraham Ventura, who succeeded him as rabbi of Spalato, David Pinto, and Abraham Penso.

Bibliography: Frumkin-Rivlin, 3 (1929), 95–98; Rosanes, Togarmah, 5 (1938), 117–22, 175–7; M. D. Gaon, *Yehudei ha-Mizraḥ be-Ereẓ Yisrael,* 2 (1938), 539–40; M. Benayahu, *Ḥ. J. D. Azulai* (Heb., 1959), 71–72, 357–60. [S.Z.H.]

PARDO, JOSEPH (d. 1619), Italian rabbi and merchant. Pardo was born in Salonika, but went to Venice before 1589, and there he served as rabbi to the Levantine community and also engaged in business. He and Judah Leib *Saraval made themselves responsible for the collection of money from the Jews of Italy for the poor of Ereẓ Israel. He also financed the publication of several books: *Genesis Rabbah* (Venice, 1597–1606) with the commentary *Yefeh To'ar* of Samuel Jaffe Ashkenazi. He was unsuccessful in his plan to publish a number of intended publications, one an edition of the Talmud which was to have been published in Salonika, and another the *Ma'amar Yayin ha-Meshummar* which was later published by Nathan *Shapira with his own additions (Venice, 1660). In 1601 Pardo wanted to publish a new commentary on the Pentateuch consisting of literal interpretations culled from the works of the classical commentators. The work of preparing the commentary was given to Leone de *Modena, who, as he states in his introduction to the commentary (which is still in manuscript) succeeded in preparing the sections only on the weekly portions of *Bereshit, Pinḥas, Mattot,* and *Masei.* He also relates there that Pardo became bankrupt and moved to Amsterdam (probably toward the end of 1608 or the beginning of 1609). From 1609 until his death Pardo served as rabbi of the Beit Ya'akov congregation of Amsterdam. One of the regulations he introduced was that every member was obliged to pay a fixed sum yearly for the communities of Jerusalem and Safed. Two **bakkashot* he composed were published in the *Imrei No'am* (Amsterdam, 1628, pp. 158–9).

His grandson Joseph Pardo (d. 1677) was the reader of the Spanish and Portuguese congregation in London; he died in Amsterdam. He was the author of *Shulḥan Tahor,* on *Oraḥ Ḥayyim* and *Yoreh De'ah,* which is written with the maximum of brevity. It was published a number of times, first by his son David Pardo in 1686 in London; in 1689 it was published with a Spanish translation. Apparently it lost its popularity with scholars in the course of time because of its excessive brevity.

Bibliography: A. Neubauer, in: REJ, 22 (1891), 82–84; J. Blau, *Kitvei ha-Rav Yehudah Aryeh mi-Modena* (1905), 79–81, 127, 139, 190; S. Seeligman, *Bibliographie en Historie . . . Sepharadim in Amsterdam* (1927), 26–30; I. Solomons, in: JHST, 12 (1928–1931), 88–90; Ch. Tchernowitz, *Toledoth ha-Poskim* 3 (1947), 297–99; I. S. Emmanuel, in: *Sefunot,* 6 (1962), 401–402; I. Sonne, *Kobez al-Jad,* 5 (1950), 215–216. [A.D.]

PARDO, MOSES BEN RAPHAEL (d. 1888), rabbi and rabbinical emissary. Pardo was born in Jerusalem. After serving as rabbi in Jerusalem for many years, he left the city in 1870, traveling to North Africa on a mission on behalf of Jerusalem. On his return trip in 1871 he stopped at Alexandria and accepted an offer to serve as the rabbi of the Jewish community there, a post which he retained until his death. Pardo was the author of *Hora'ah de-Veit Din* (Izmir,

1872), on divorce laws; *Shemo Moshe* (*ibid.*, 1874), responsa; and *Ẓedek u-Mishpat* (*ibid.*, 1874), novellae to *Ḥoshen Mishpat*.

Bibliography: Frumkin-Rivlin, 3 (1929), 312; M. D. Gaon, *Yehudei ha-Mizraḥ be-Ereẓ Yisrael*, 2 (1937), 541f.; J. M. Landau, *Ha-Yehudim be-Miẓrayim* (1967), index. [Ed.]

PARENT AND CHILD.

STATUS OF THE CHILD

In Jewish law, there is no discrimination against a child because of the mere fact that he is born out of lawful wedlock. While the said fact may complicate the question of establishing paternity, once the identity of the father is clearly known there is no distinction in law so far as the parent-child relationship is concerned, between such a child and one born in lawful wedlock. This is also the position with regard to a **mamzer*. On the status of a child with one non-Jewish parent, see below. For further details, see **Yuḥasin*.

PARENTAL RIGHTS

Except as detailed below, the principle in Jewish law is that parents have no legal rights in respect of their children, neither as to their person nor their property (Ket. 46b–47a; Sh. Ar., ḤM 424:7). So far as male children are concerned, the father is entitled to the finds of his son even if the latter is a *gadol* (i.e., beyond the age until which his father is obliged by law to maintain him), provided that the son is dependent on him (lit. "seated at his table"); this is "for the reason of enmity," i.e., in order to avoid the enmity which might arise between father and son if the former, who supports his son without even being obliged to by law, was not even entitled to the finds that come to the son without any effort or investment on his part (BM 12a–b; Sh. Ar., ḤM 270:2 and commentaries). For the same reason the father is entitled to the income of his dependent son (*Rema*, ḤM 270:2). Hence a father who is obliged by law to maintain his son—for example, because he has so undertaken in a divorce agreement—has no claim to the finds or income of the son and therefore he is entitled to set them off against his liability to maintain him (*Taz*, ḤM 270:2; PDR 3:329). As regards his daughter, the father is entitled to everything mentioned above, even if she is not dependent on him, until she becomes a major (*bogeret*), since until then she remains under his authority. For the same reason, until she reaches her majority, the father will be entitled to her handiwork and to give her in *marriage (Ket. 46a–47a; Yad, Ishut 3:11; see also Avadim 4:2). The mother has none of these rights in respect of her children since in law she has no pecuniary obligations toward them (see below).

PARENTAL OBLIGATIONS

The general rule is that the legal obligations toward their children are imposed on the father alone and not on the mother (*Maggid Mishneh*, Ishut, 21:18).

Maintenance. Obligations of the Father. The father's duty to maintain his son embraces the responsibility of providing for all the child's needs, including his daily care (Yad, Ishut 13:6; Sh. Ar., EH 73:6, 7). The rules concerning the duty of maintenance also apply with regard to the father's duty to educate his son and to teach him Torah, to see that he learns a trade or profession, and to bear all the necessary expenses connected with this (Kid. 29b, 30; Sh. Ar., YD 245:1, 4). Until the son reaches the age of six years (see below) these obligations must be borne by the father even if he has limited means and the son has independent means of his own, e.g., acquired by inheritance (Sh. Ar., EH 71:1). These obligations are imposed on the father by virtue of his paternity, whether or not he is married to the child's mother and therefore notwithstanding termination of the marriage between the child's parents, by death or divorce, or the fact that the child was born out of wedlock (Resp. Ribash no. 41; Resp. Rosh 17:7; contrary to Ran, on Rif at end of Ket. ch. 5, who is of the opinion that the father's obligation to support his children is linked with his obligation to maintain his wife).

Obligation of the Mother. The mother has no legal obligation to maintain her children even if she is able to do so out of her own property or income (*Ba'er Heitev*, EH 71, n. 1). She may only be obliged to do so on the strength of the rules of *ẓedakah* ("charity") if, after providing in full for her own needs, she is able to satisfy the needs of her children when they have no property or income of their own and the father, being poor, is unable to support them (*Pitḥei Teshuvah*, EH 82 n. 3; PDR 2:3). The position is different, however, if the mother has undertaken to maintain her children, for example in a divorce agreement. In this event, if the mother has the means to support her children at a time when the father is not legally obliged to do so (i.e., because they are above the specified age), she alone will have to maintain them as she is obliged to do by virtue of law (her undertaking); the father's duty in this case is based on the rules of *ẓedakah* only, and since the children have property of their own (the right to be maintained by the mother) they are no longer in need of *ẓedakah* (PDR 3:170; 4:3, 7). On the wife's duty to take care of her children as part of her marital duties toward her husband, see *Husband and Wife.

If the child's mother is not entitled to maintenance from the father—e.g., because the parties are divorced—and the child is in need of her care so that she can no longer continue to work and support herself, there will be legal grounds for obliging the father to maintain her to a certain extent, including payment of the rental for her dwelling. Because it is in the interests of the child to be with the mother, she must dwell with him, and because the expenses necessary for taking care of the child devolve on the father, he has to bear them within the limits of the remuneration he would otherwise be called upon to pay any other woman for taking care of the child. This would include the cost of the child's dwelling (with the mother)—notwithstanding the fact that the mother is in a position to defray all the said expenses out of her own means (PDR 1:118f.; 2:3, 5f.). After being divorced, the mother may also claim from the child's father any of the said expenses she incurred before she filed her claim for them, since, unlike the case of a married woman, there is no room for considering that she has waived this claim (PDR 1:230, 234; 2:164f.; Resp. Maharsham, pt. 2, no. 236).

The Standard of Maintenance. Unlike maintenance for a wife (see *Husband and Wife), the standard of maintenance to which children are entitled is determined by their actual needs and not by the financial status of their father (Yad, Ishut 13:6; Sh. Ar., EH 73:6). For this purpose the needs of a child will not be limited to an essential minimum, but they may vary according to whether the child is from a rich or a poor family. Certainly under the laws of *ẓedakah* a wealthy father may be made liable to maintain his children as befits them and not merely as absolutely necessary, although in a case where a child has other sources of income, and thus is not in need of *ẓedakah*, he will not be entitled to maintenance (Sh. Ar. EH 82:7; PDR 2:3, 8; 4:3, 7). On the other hand, in determining the essential minimum attention will be paid to what the father is capable of earning and not merely to his actual income.

Additional Obligations Toward Daughters. In addition to maintaining his daughter, the father has to see to her marriage to a worthy husband, and, if the need arises, to provide her with a dowry sufficient at least—if his means permit—to cover a year's raiment (*Ḥelkat Meḥokek* 58, n. 1). Although the father is not legally obliged to give a dowry in accordance with his means, it is a *mitzvah* for him and he should do so (Ket. 68a; Sh. Ar., EH 58:1 and 71:1, *Rema*, ad loc. n. 4). On the father's death, and in the absence of a testamentary disposition depriving his daughter of a dowry, his heirs are bound to give the daughter a dowry based on an assessment of what her father would have given her had he been alive; in the absence of data that might form the basis for such assessment, the heirs have to give her one-tenth of his estate for the purpose of her marriage (see *Succession; Ket. 68a; Sh. Ar., EH 113:2, 10).

Children Entitled to Maintenance Until a Certain Age. An opinion that a *takkanah* of the *Sanhedrin (i.e., the *Takkanat Usha*) laid down that the father must maintain his children as long as they are minors (sons until the age of 13 and daughters until 12) was not followed, and the *halakhah* was laid down to the effect that the father's legal obligation is only to maintain his children until they reach the age of six full years (Ket. 49b, 65b; Sh. Ar., EH 71:1); above this age the obligation flows merely from the laws of *ẓedakah*, and, insofar as they are applicable (see above), fulfillment of the obligation will be compulsory. Since it concerns a person's own children the charitable duty is more stringent in this case than it is with ordinary *ẓedakah*, and therefore the father will be required to exert himself to the utmost in order to satisfy his children's needs (Ket. and Sh. Ar. loc. cit.; Yad, Ishut 12:14, 15:21:17, *Maggid Mishneh;* Sh. Ar., YD 251:4). In the course of time it became apparent that the legal position as described above did not adequately protect the interests of children above six years of age, as the father tried to evade his duty. Hence it was ordained in a *takkanah* of the Chief Rabbinate of Palestine (1944) that the father shall be bound to maintain his sons and daughters until they reach the age of 15 years, provided they have no independent means of support (see Freimann, bibl.).

Maintenance out of the Deceased's Estate. The father's obligation to maintain his children is imposed on him as father and terminates upon his death without being transmitted to his heirs as a charge on the estate. Hence the minor heirs cannot demand from the others that they should be maintained out of the estate in addition to their normal share of the legacy; the estate will therefore be divided amongst all the heirs, each of them, regardless of age, being given his righful share (BB 139a; Sh. Ar., ḤM 286:1). The position is different, however, with regard to the maintenance of the daughters of the deceased. Jewish law excludes daughters from succession to their father's estate when he is survived by sons or their descendants (see *Succession), and instead, in such a case, entitles daughters to be maintained out of the estate until their majority or marriage—whichever comes first—to the same extent as they were entitled during their father's lifetime (i.e., in accordance with their needs; Ket. 52b, 53b; Sh. Ar., EH 112:16). This right of the daughter flows from the conditions of her mother's *ketubbah* as her independent right and therefore she cannot be deprived of it without her own consent, neither by her father's testamentary disposition nor by her mother's waiver of the respective condition of the *ketubbah* in an agreement with the father, and it remains in force notwithstanding the divorce of her parents (Ket. loc. cit., Yad, Ishut 12:2; 19:10; *Rema*, EH 112:1). If the assets of the estate are not sufficient to satisfy both the daughters' right of maintenance and the heirs' rights of succession (*nekhasim mu'atim*), the daughters' right takes preference (Ket. 108b; Sh. Ar., EH 112:11); even if the assets of the estate should suffice for both (*nekhasim merubbim*) but there is established reason to fear that the sons might squander them and thus endanger the daughters' maintenance, the court will have power to take any steps it may deem fit for the preservation of the daughters' right (*Rema* loc. cit.).

Custody of Children. The law deals here with the determination of a child's abode, taking into account the responsibility of the parents for his physical and spiritual welfare, his raising, and his education. The rule is that the child's own interest is always the paramount consideration and his custody is a matter of a parental duty rather than a right, it being a right of the child vis-à-vis his parents.

Different Rules for Boys and Girls. In pursuance of this rule, the halakhic scholars laid down that children below the age of six years must be in the custody of their mother, since at this tender age they are mainly in need of physical care and attention. Above the age of six, boys must be with their father, since at this age they are in need of education and religious instruction, a task imposed by law upon the father, and girls with their mother ("the daughter must always be with her mother"), since they are in need of her instruction in the ways of modesty (Ket. 102b, 103a; Yad, Ishut, 21:17; Sh. Ar., EH 82:7). As these rules are directed at serving the welfare of the child, the court may diverge from them if in a proper case it considers it necessary in the interests of the child and even order that he be removed from both his parents and be kept in a place where, in the court's opinion, his interests are better served (*Rema*, EH 82:7; *Pitḥei Teshuvah* ad loc., n. 6, in the name of Radbaz). The custody of the child is a matter not of the rights of the parents but of the rights of the child in respect of his parents. The principle of the matter is that the rule establishing the right that the daughter be always with her mother establishes the daughter's right and not the mother's; similarly in the case of the son until the age of six, it is the son's right which is established and not the father's (Resp. Maharashdam, EH 123; see also Resp. Radbaz, no. 123). As Ereẓ Israel is looked upon as the best possible place for bringing up and educating a Jewish child, his removal abroad will generally not be approved, but the court may nevertheless permit this to the mother or father if it is satisfied that in the circumstances it is necessary in the better interests of the child (PDR 1:103–7, 173–8).

Relation Between Custody and Duty of Maintenance. The rules concerning the custody of children have no influence on the parental obligation to maintain them. Hence the fact that the children are with their mother in accordance with these rules does not relieve the father from his obligation to maintain them—whether this is based on law or the rules of *ẓedakah* (Sh. Ar., EH 82:7). Moreover, the mother is not obliged to accept the children inasmuch as, on principle, the duty to take care of them is imposed on the father only; should she therefore refuse to take them, she may send them to him and he will not be entitled to reject them (Yad, Ishut 21:18; Sh. Ar., EH 82:8). However, if a boy above the age of six should be with his mother contrary to law, i.e., without the consent of the father or permission of the court, the father will be entitled to refuse to pay for the boy's maintenance for any period he is not with him (*ibid*).

Access of the Non-Custodian Parent. The custodian parent has no right to deprive the other of access to their child, nor the child of access to the other parent, since the child is entitled to derive education and care from both his parents and to maintain his natural tie with both of them so as not to grow up as if orphaned of one of them. For the purpose of realization of this right of the child, it is incumbent on the parents to come to an understanding between themselves, failing which the court will decide the question of access on the basis of the child's interest rather than those of his parents. Since for each of the parents it is a matter of a duty (not of a right) toward their child, they will not be entitled to make performance of the one's obligation dependent upon performance of the other's. Thus the fact that the mother refuses to allow her son to visit his father, or the father to have access to him, in defiance of an agreement or order of the court to this effect, will not entitle the father to withhold the son's maintenance for as long as the mother persists in her attitude; nor will the mother be entitled to refuse the father access to the child because the father withholds the latter's maintenance (PDR 1:113, 118, 158, 176).

Custody in Case of Death of Either or Both Parents. In this case too the decisive question is the welfare of the child. On the death of either parent, it is presumed to be best served by leaving the child with the surviving parent, while in principle no special right of custody exists in favor of the parents of the deceased. Only when clearly indicated in the interests of the child, having the regard for all the circumstances including the care of teaching him Torah, will the court order otherwise (PDR 1:65–77). On the death of both parents, custody of the child will generally be given to the grandparents on the side of the parent who would have been entitled to custody had both been alive (*Rema,* EH 82:7 and *Ḥelkat Meḥokek* ad loc., n. 11; Resp. Radbaz no. 123).

AGREEMENTS BETWEEN PARENTS CONCERNING THEIR CHILDREN

An agreement between parents as to maintenance or custody of their child will not avail to affect his rights unless proved to be in his best interest, nor will it preclude him, since he is represented by one parent, from claiming their enforcement against the other. The child is not party to an agreement between the parents and the rule is that "no obligation can be imposed on a person in his absence" (BM 12a; PDR 2:3). Hence the father, in a claim against him by the child for maintenance, will not escape liability on a plea that he is free of such a liability by virtue of an agreement made with the mother in which she took this liability upon herself (PDR 2:171–7; 5:171, 173). The effect, if any, of such agreement is merely that it may possibly give the father the right to recover from the mother any amount he may have to expend on the child's maintenance, but toward the child it is of no effect (PDR 5:171). Similarly, a divorce agreement in which the mother waives the right to custody of her children below the age of six, or the father to custody of his sons above this age, will not preclude the children from claiming through the other parent that the court should disregard the terms of the agreement and decide the matter in their own best interest only, in the light of all the circumstances. For this purpose, the question of whether the change of his abode may detrimentally affect the child's mental well-being will be a weighty consideration (PDR 1:177) and, in a proper case, if the court considers it just to do so, it will also pay due regard to the child's own wishes (*Ḥelkat Meḥokek* 82, n. 10 and *Ba'er Heitev* ad loc., n. 6). The court's approval of such an agreement will not preclude a fresh approach to the court owing to the fact that the circumstances have later changed, nor an application for the reconsideration of the case with regard to the child's best interests in the light of such a change (Resp. Radbaz no. 123; PDR 4:332–6).

CHILDREN OF PARENTS WHO ARE NOT BOTH JEWISH

Unless both parents are Jewish, the father has no legal standing in relation to the children, neither as regards maintenance nor custody. If the father is Jewish and the mother not, the child will be considered a non-Jew while, halakhically speaking, the non-Jewish father will not be considered his father (see **Yuḥasin*). Since the duty of maintenance, like all other paternal duties, is only imposed on the person halakhically recognized as the father—toward his halakhically recognized child—there is therefore no room for the imposition of any recognized legal obligation incumbent on the father of a child qua father except if he and the mother are both Jewish. A different, and so far apparently unsupported, opinion was expressed by R. Ben Zion Ouziel (*Mishpetei Uziel,* EH no. 4).

IN THE STATE OF ISRAEL

Matters of child maintenance by Jewish parents are governed by Jewish law (s. 3 of the Family Law Amendment (Maintenance) Law, 1959; see also no. 507/61 in PD 16 (1962), 925, 928; no. 426/65, PD 20, pt. 2 (1966), 21). Other matters, including custody—in the case of Jewish parents—are also governed by Jewish law, except as otherwise provided in the Capacity and Guardianship Law, 1962. For their greater part both the above-mentioned laws are based on principles of Jewish law (see Elon, bibl.), and they regulate the legal position of both parents as regards maintenance and custody of their children even where one parent is a non-Jew.

For social and ethical relationship between parent and child see *Family; *Parents, Honor of.

Bibliography: Gulak, Yesodei, 3 (1922), 66–70; A. Aptowitzer, in: *Ha-Mishpat ha-Ivri,* 2 (1926/27), 9–23; A. H. Freimann, in: *Sinai,* 14 (1943/44), 254–62; ET, 1 (1951^3), 5–7, 228; 2 (1949), 22f., 378; 4 (1952), 744f.; 6 (1954), 329–32; M. Elon, in: ILR, 3 (1968), 430–2; 4 (1969), 119–26; Elon, Mafte'aḥ, 8–11; B. Schereschewsky, *Dinei Mishpaḥah* (1967^2), 359–94.

[B.-Z. Sch.]

PARENTS, HONOR OF (Heb. כִּבּוּד אָב וָאֵם; lit. "the honoring of father and mother"), the fifth commandment in the *Decalogue. The importance attached by the Bible to this precept is apparent from the fact that the declared reward for its observance is the lengthening of "thy days . . . upon the land which the Lord thy God giveth thee" (Ex. 20:12). The rabbis also emphasized that the observer of this commandment would enjoy reward both in this world and in the next (Pe'ah 1:1). Viewing it as a reflection of the godliness in man, they declared that the Bible equated the honor due to parents with that due to God (Ex. 20:12; Prov. 3:9) since "there are three partners in man, the Holy One blessed be He, the father, and the mother." According to the rabbis, when a man honors his father and his mother, God declares, "I ascribe merit to them as though I had dwelt among them and they had honored Me" (Kid. 30b). Further, they stated that since a child intuitively honors his mother more than his father because she is usually kinder to him, the Pentateuch placed the honor of the father before that of the mother (Ex. 20:12). A child, however, fears his father more than his mother, and the Pentateuch accordingly placed the fear of the mother before that of the father (Lev. 19:3; Kid. 30b–31a).

If his parents are in need, the son fulfills the commandment by sustaining them with such items as food, drink, clothing, and blankets, and guides them in old age. Fear of parents is to be expressed in that the son must neither stand nor sit in their usual place, contradict them nor support their opponents in a scholarly dispute (Kid. 31b; Rashi ad loc.). During the first 12 months after his father's death, the son should say, "Thus said my father, my teacher, for whose resting place may I be an atonement." After the initial 12 months, the son says, "His memory be for a blessing, for the life of the world to come" (Kid. 31b). The rabbis differed concerning the monetary expenses to which the son was obliged to go in fulfillment of the fifth commandment. One viewpoint was that the father had to reimburse the son for his actual expenditure, but not for his loss of time. Another opinion was that it was always at the son's personal expense. The *halakhah* declared that the *mitzvah* must be fulfilled at the father's expense, the son, however, being obliged to utilize his own funds when his father was impoverished (Kid. 32a; Sh. Ar., YD 240:5). Receiving great emphasis is the gracious attitude which the son must display in discharging this obligation. It was stated that a son may give his father pheasants as food and yet this act, if performed begrudgingly, will cause the son to lose his portion in the world to come. Yet another may gain the world to come by requesting, in a spirit of kindness and respect, that his father undertake difficult work such as grinding flour in a mill (Kid. 32a; TJ, Kid. 1:7, 61b). A father, however, could renounce the honor due to him and thereby relieve his son of his responsibilities (Kid. 32a). The rabbis held that this commandment had been revealed to the Jews at Marah (Ex. 15:25), before the revelation at Sinai (Sanh. 56b). Individuals, whether Jew or gentile, who excelled in the performance of this precept were praised. The heathen Dama, son of Netina of Ashkelon, refused to awaken his father although he needed the key that was lying under his father's pillow to conclude a transaction which would have brought him a profit of 600,000 gold coins (Kid. 31a). When R. Tarfon's mother wished to climb into bed, he would bend down to let her ascend by stepping upon him. R. Joseph, on hearing his mother's footsteps, would say, "I will arise before the approaching *Shekhinah*" (Kid. 31a–b). Married women were exempted from fulfilling this precept if it conflicted with their husband's wishes (Kid. 30b; Sh. Ar., YD 240:17). A child was obligated to honor his stepfather, stepmother, and eldest brother (Ket. 103a; Sh. Ar., YD 240:21, 22). It is not permitted for a child to transgress a prohibition at his father's request since both father and son are obligated to observe the divine commandments (Yev. 6a).

See also *Family; *Fertility and Barrenness. For legal obligations see *Parent and Child.

Bibliography: I. Abrahams, *Jewish Life in the Middle Ages* (1932²), 123f.; H. Loewe and C. G. Montefiore, *A Rabbinic Anthology* (1938, repr. 1960, 1963), ch. XXII and XXIV. [A.Ro.]

PARENZO, 16th–17th-century family of Hebrew printers in Venice. JACOB (d. 1546) had come to Venice from Parenzo, on the Dalmatian coast of Italy, whence the family name, but was probably of German origin. His son MEIR (d. 1575) probably learned the printing trade at the *Bomberg press, where he worked together with Cornelio *Adelkind in 1545, and his own productions compare favorably in beauty and elegance with those of his masters.

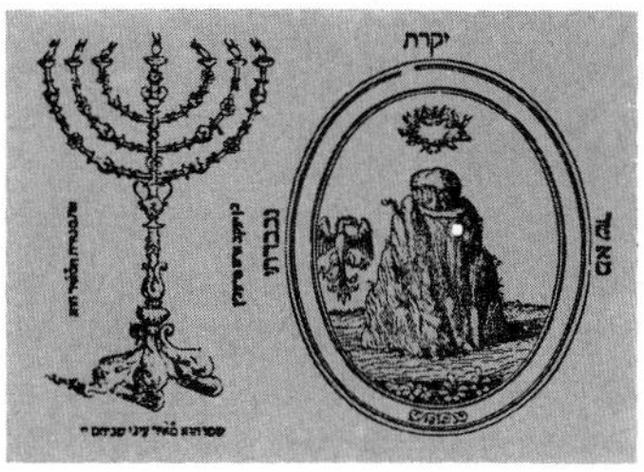

Printers' marks of Meir Parenzo (left) and his brother Asher. From A. Yaari, *Hebrew Printers' Marks,* Jerusalem, 1943.

Parenzo worked for some time as a typesetter and corrector at the press owned by Carlo Querini. During 1546–48 he worked on his own, publishing five works, and later an edition of the Mishnah with Bertinoro's commentary for Querini, although from about 1550 his main work was with Alvise *Bragadini. The Parenzos used various *printer's marks: Meir, a seven-branch *menorah,* and a rather daring design with Venus directing arrows at a seven-headed dragon; and his brother, ASHER, a mountain rising from the sea, with a laurel wreath above and a flying eagle at the left. Meir's *colophons abound in editions prepared by him. In 1547 the great French engraver and typecutter Guillaume *Le Bé, and later Jacob of Mantua, produced Hebrew type for him. At Meir's death (1575), his brother Asher took over working for the Venetian printer Giovanni di *Gara, as well as for Bragadini, until 1596. GERSHON BEN MOSES, probably a nephew of Meir and Asher, descendants of Jacob Parenzo, worked for the Venetian printer Giovanni di Gara during 1599–1609 as did his son Moses in 1629.

Bibliography: Steinschneider, Cat Bod, 2842 (7818); 2984 (8761); H. D. Friedberg, *Toledot ha-Defus ha-Ivri be-Italyah* (1956²), 69ff.; A. M. Habermann, in: *Aresheth,* 1 (1959), 61–90; A. Yaari, *Diglei ha-Madpisim ha-Ivriyyim* (1944), nos. 14, 35, 36; idem, in: KS, 30 (1955), 113–7; D. W. Amram, *Makers of Hebrew Books in Italy* (1909), index. [ED.]

PARḤON, SALOMON BEN ABRAHAM IBN (12th century), lexicographer. Born in Qal'a, Spain, he was a student of *Judah Halevi and Abraham *ibn Ezra. Parḥon emigrated to Italy, where in 1160 at Salerno he completed his *Maḥberet he-Arukh,* a biblical lexicon written in Hebrew and his only extant work. On the one hand, the title is reminiscent of *Menaḥem b. Jacob ibn Saruq's dictionary and, on the other, of *Nathan b. Jehiel's. *Maḥberet he-Arukh* comprises the whole of medieval Hebrew lexicography after *Ibn Janaḥ and is, as Parḥon states in his introduction, an epitome of Ibn Janaḥ's *Book of Roots* (*Sefer ha-Shorashim,* 1896). Parḥon also acknowledges the use of excerpts from Ibn Janaḥ's other books and from Judah b. David *Ḥayyuj, the Hebrew translator of Ibn Janaḥ's *Book of Roots.* Ten years after Parḥon's dictionary appeared Judah ibn *Tibbon claimed it was merely a plagiarism of Ibn Janaḥ's lexicon. However, this claim is unjust because in addition to the necessity of taking into consideration the rather liberal medieval attitude toward utilizing the works of others, *Maḥberet he-Arukh* contains original material in its own right. For example, material pertaining to the development of religious ritual, which is of considerable historical interest, and original explanations of biblical passages are found in the work. The introduction to the dictionary comprises a compendium of biblical Hebrew grammar and terminates with a short excursus on medieval Hebrew prosody. Its appendix (appearing immediately after the introduction in S. G. Stern's 1844 edition) is entitled "About biblical matters, as to which one has to dispel one's doubts," and deals with problems of style and syntax following Ibn Janaḥ's *Kitab al-luma'* (*Sefer ha-Rikmah,* 1964). The major importance of *Maḥberet he-Arukh,* however, was that, being written in Hebrew, it transferred to Christian countries the advances in Hebrew philology made under the influence of Arabic linguists in Spain. In his introduction Parḥon asserts this to be one of his aims since he found that in Italy only the *Maḥberet* of Menaḥem ibn Saruq was known. Accordingly, he followed the example of his teacher, Abraham ibn Ezra, the most important popularizer of Spanish scholarship in Christian lands. The *Maḥberet he-Arukh* became an extremely popular work, not least because of the fluency, lucidity, and purity of Parḥon's Hebrew style, a style befitting a pupil of Abraham ibn Ezra.

Bibliography: S. G. Stern (ed.), Salomon ben Abraham ibn Parḥon, *Maḥberet he-Arukh* (1844); W. Bacher, in: J. Winter and A. Wuensche, *Juedische Literatur,* 2 (1897), 190; idem, in: ZAW, 11 (1891), 35–99. [Y.BL.]

PARIENTE, Moroccan family of Spanish origin. JACOB (early to mid-16th century) was a leader of the community of Spanish exiles in Fez, a signatory of its *takkanot,* and a liturgical poet. A tradition holds that he was king of that part of Morocco called the Rif. ABRAHAM (early to mid-16th century) represented the Safi community before David *Reubeni in Portugal. The wealthy merchant and diplomat SOLOMON (mid-17th century) served as interpreter and negotiator for four English governors in Tangiers and leader of its Jewish community. In additon to extensive commercial negotiations, Pariente also negotiated a peace treaty in which he is suspected of inserting a clause favoring the Moors. In 1662 he apparently supported King Mulay Muhammad b. al-Sharif, though not his successor Mulay al-Rashid. The merchant JACOB (mid-17th century) served as the interpreter for Roland Frejus on his voyages from Marseilles to Morocco in 1666 and 1671. He helped increase the commercial ties between the two countries by means of his friendship with Aaron Carsinet, the Jewish goldsmith and banker of Mulay al-Rashid. The descendants of JUDAH BEN ABRAHAM (late 18th century) of Rabat founded the Pariente bank in Tangiers, which was important until the mid-20th century. In the early 20th century the philanthropist JOSEPH lived in Tangiers and SAMUEL was a Hebrew scholar and collector of antiquities and manuscripts in Tetuán.

Bibliography: J. M. Toledano, *Ner ha-Ma'arav* (1911), 78–79; Hirschberg, Afrikah, 2 (1965), 254, 281; idem, in: H. J. Zimmels et al. (eds.), *Essays Presented to Chief Rabbi Israel Brodie* . . . (1967), 157; I. Laredo, *Memorias de un viejo tangerino* (1935), 180–4; J. Ben-Naim, *Malkhei Rabbanan* (1931), 17, 64; D. Corcos, in: *Sefunot*, 10 (1968), 55ff.

[ED.]

PARIS, capital of *France. In 582, the date of the first documentary evidence of the presence of Jews in Paris, there was already a community owning at least a synagogue, situated in the neighborhood of the present church of St. Julien le Pauvre. The murder of the Jew *Priscus, purveyor to King Chilperic, was avenged by a Christian mob—proof of the good relationship existing between the two religious groups. However, the sixth Council of Paris (614 or 615) decided that Jews who held public office, and their families, must convert to Christianity. When giving the council's decisions the force of law, King Clothaire II ignored the baptism clause, reiterating the ban on Jews holding public office and laying down severe penalties for any breach of this. Although these two documents are proof not only that there were Jews living in Paris but also that their social standing was high, there is no reason to believe than one Solomon, who is mentioned as a toll-collector in Paris in 633, was a Jew or even an apostate. In the tenth and 11th centuries the Jews appear to have lived in the present Rue de la Harpe, between the Rue de la Huchette and Rue Saint Sévérin, and a street later known as the Rue de la Vieille Juiverie which lies between Rue Saint Sévérin and Rue Monsieur le Prince. In the tenth century a synagogue stood at the intersection of these two streets. From 1119 at the latest there was a *Jewish quarter, the *vicus Judaeorum*, situated right in the center of Paris on the Ile de la Cité; its boundaries were the present Rue de la Cité (the central part of which was called Rue des Juifs), the Quai de la Corse, and the Rue de Lutèce. The synagogue, which was 8 meters wide and 31 meters long, was built on the site of the present Marché aux Fleurs; after the expulsion of 1182 it was converted into the St. Madeleine Church. According to Rigord, biographer of *Philip Augustus and one of the sources of *Joseph ha-Kohen's *Emek ha-Bakha*, Paris Jews owned about half the land in Paris and the vicinity. They employed many Christian servants, and the objects they took in pledge included even church vessels; jealousy of their prosperity gave rise to the rumor that they used the latter as wine goblets at table.

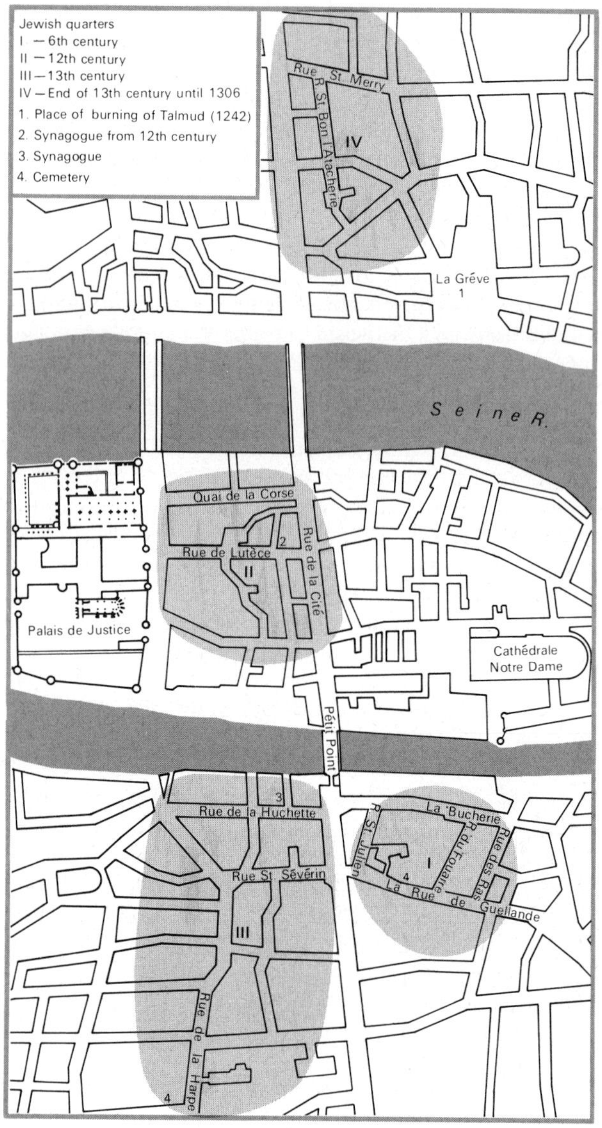

Jewish quarters in Paris during the Middle Ages.

Far more portentous was the *blood libel which arose against the Jews of *Blois in 1171, appeared simultaneously in a number of other places, and reached the region of Paris. Even though *Louis VII, in answer to the intervention of the leaders of the Paris community, promised to take care that no similar accusation arose in the future and above all that no persecution resulted from it, he was unable to prevent this slander from being deeply engrained in the public mind, even among children. Thus Philip Augustus was told by a playmate when he was only six years old that Jews killed Christian children; according to his biographer, the hatred he conceived at this time was the origin of his expulsion order of 1182. On this occasion, the crown confiscated the houses of the Jews as well as the synagogue and the king gave 24 of them to the drapers of Paris and 18 to the furriers.

Rabbinical questions were addressed to the scholars of Paris from Rome around 1125. About 20 years later the rabbis of Paris took part in a *synod convened by *Solomon b. Meir (Rashbam) and Jacob b. Meir *Tam. In the second half of the 12th century Mattathias Gaon was head of a yeshivah in Paris; his son was the *posek* Jehiel. Among the other scholars of Paris before 1182 were the tosafists Yom Tov and *Ḥayyim b. Hananel ha-Kohen, the commentator Moses, the *posek* Elijah b. Judah, and Jacob b. Simeon, known for his activities in various fields. That the secular sciences were also studied is attested by the 12th-century epitaph (discovered in the 15th century) of one

Figure 1. The Great Synagogue of Paris, on the Rue de la Victoire, completed in 1877. Photo M. Ninio, Jerusalem.

Zour, physician and astrologer. This stone points to the existence of a Jewish cemetery in Rue Pierre Sarrazin, behind Rue de la Harpe.

When the Jews were permitted to return to the kingdom of France in 1198 they settled in Paris in and around the present Rue Ferdinand Duval, which, coincidentally, became the Jewish quarter once again in the modern era. Around the end of the 12th century they lived especially in the present Rue de Moussy, Rue du Renard Saint Merry, Rue de la Tacherie, and on the Petit Pont; they were probably restricted to the Petit Pont in 1294, the date when residence in Jewish quarters became obligatory. However, the number of streets in Paris where Jews actually lived in the Middle Ages, as well as places named after them (Moulin aux Juifs, Ile aux Juifs, Cour de la Juiverie, etc.), was actually much greater; an exhaustive study of the Jewish settlement in Paris with precise dates is still lacking. The first scholarly history of Paris, written by Henri Sauval (1623–1676), barrister in the *parlement* of Paris, contained an important chapter devoted to the Jews (vol. 2, book 10, 508–32). Although permission to publish the *Histoire de Paris* was granted in 1654, it was not in fact published until 1724.

In the reign of *Louis IX, after the denunciations of Nicholas *Donin and Pope *Gregory IX's order that Jewish books be examined, the famous *disputation on the Talmud was held in Paris in 1240. The Jewish delegation was led by *Jehiel b. Joseph of Paris. After the condemnation of the Talmud, 24 cart-loads of Jewish books were burned in public in the Place de Grève, now the Place de l'Hôtel de Ville (see *Talmud, Burning of). A Jewish moneylender called Jonathan was accused of desecrating the *Host in 1290, his supposed crime being revealed by various miracles. A commemorative chapel was speedily erected on the site of this alleged desecration (of which not only Jonathan and his family but also the whole Jewish community were accused) and the tale was spread in stories and pictures. It is said that this was the main cause of the expulsion of 1306.

Tax rolls of the Jews of Paris in 1292 and 1296 give a good picture of their economic and social status. One striking fact is that a great many of them originated from the provinces. In spite of the prohibition on the settlement of Jews expelled from England (1290), a number of recent arrivals from that country are listed. As in many other places, the profession of physician figures most prominently among the professions noted. The majority of the rest of the Jews engaged in *moneylending and commerce. In the space of only four years, as witnessed by the amount of the tax imposed on them, the Jews became considerably impoverished. During the same period the composition of the Jewish community, which numbered at least 100 heads of families, changed to a large extent through migration and the number also declined to a marked degree. One of the most illustrious Jewish scholars of medieval France, *Judah b. Isaac, known as Sir Leon of Paris, headed the yeshivah of Paris in the early years of the 13th century. He was succeeded by Jehiel b. Joseph, the Jewish leader at the 1240 disputation. After the wholesale destruction of Jewish books on this occasion until the expulsion of 1306, the yeshivah of Paris produced no more scholars of note.

After the return in 1315 the number of Jews who settled in the city and region of Paris—to judge from their contribution to the enormous fine imposed on the Jews of France a year before the expulsion of 1322—was little greater than those who had lived there before. However, these few were left untouched by both the *Pastoureaux persecutions and accusations of having poisoned the wells. Relative to this community, the new one formed in Paris from 1359 was quite large. Notables of this period included *Manessier de Vesoul, *procureur-général* and *commissaire* of the Jews of Langue-d'oyl; his associate *Jacob of Pont-Sainte-Maxence; Mattathias b. Joseph, chief rabbi of France and head of the yeshivah (1360–85); and his successor, his son Jonathan, whose authority was contested by one of his father's former pupils, Isaiah b. Abba Mari, also known as Astruc de Savoy. Although Hugues Aubriot, the provost of Paris, took the Jews under his protection, this was to no avail against the murderous attacks and looting in 1380 and 1382 perpetrated by a populace in revolt against the tax burden. King Charles VI relieved the Jews of responsibility for the valuable pledges which had been stolen from them on this occasion and granted them other financial concessions; but the community was unable to recover from those blows, either financially or in number. Not many years later, in 1394, it was further struck by the Denis de *Machaut affair. Machaut, a Jewish convert to Christianity, had disappeared and the Jews were accused of having murdered him or, at the very least, of having imprisoned him until he agreed to return to Judaism. Seven Jewish notables were condemned to death, but their sentence was commuted to a heavy fine allied to imprisonment until Machaut reappeared. This affair was a prelude to the "definitive" expulsion of the Jews from France in 1394.

There is no evidence of Jews in Paris, not even of lone individuals, in the 15th and 16th centuries. In 1611 the physician Elijah of Montalto was called to the court of

Marie de Médicis; though he had some contact with Concini, Marshal of Ancre, and his mistress L. Galigaï, there is no reason for supposing that either of these was a Jew. Still less should the old clothes dealers of Paris be taken for secret Jews just because their guild was known as the "synagogue"; in 1652 they murdered a citizen who used this term with reference to them. From the beginning of the 18th century the Jews of *Metz applied to the authorities for permission to enter Paris on their business pursuits; gradually the periods of their stay in the capital increased and were prolonged. At the same time the city saw the arrival of Jews from *Bordeaux (the "Portuguese") and from *Avignon. From 1721 to 1772 a police inspector was given special charge over the Jews, an office which the successive holders used to extort what they could from them in money and goods. After the discontinuation of the office, the trustee of the Jews from 1777 was Jacob Rodrigues *Pereire, a Jew from Bordeaux, who had charge over a group of Spanish and Portuguese Jews, while the German Jews (from Metz, Alsace, and Lorraine) were led by Moses Eliezer Liefman *Calmer, and those from Avignon by Israel Salom. The German Jews lived in the poor quarters of Saint-Martin and Saint-Denis, and those from Bordeaux, *Bayonne, and Avignon inhabited the more luxurious quarters of Saint Germain and Saint André. Large numbers of the Jews eked out a miserable living in peddling and selling secondhand clothes and rags. The more well-to-do were moneylenders, military purveyors (especially of horses), and traded in jewels. There were also some craftsmen among them: jewelers, painters, engravers, designers, and embroiderers. Inns preparing kosher food existed from 1721; these also served as prayer rooms since otherwise services could only be held in private houses—in either case strictly forbidden by the police. From at least 1736 an innkeeper from La Villette allowed his garden to be used for burials; after 1780 the Portuguese community acquired an adjoining plot of land which could officially be used for a cemetery. Soon after the Ashkenazim also acquired a cemetery, in Montrouge. Neither continued in use for very long but both were still in existence in 1971. The first publicly acknowledged synagogue was opened in Rue de Brisemiche in 1788. The number of Jews in Paris just before the Revolution was probably no greater than 500. On Aug. 26, 1789 they presented the Constituent Assembly with a petition asking for the rights of citizens. The Paris commune came to the defense of its Jewish residents, sending a deputation to the assembly to plead for them; full citizenship rights were granted to the Spanish, Portuguese, and Avignon Jews on Jan. 28, 1790.

After the freedom of movement brought about by emancipation, a large influx of Jews arrived in Paris, numbering 2,908 in 1809. These Jews were exempt from the general Jewish disablilities imposed by *Napoleon in 1808. Most of them lived in the present third and fourth *arondissements*. In 1819, when the Jewish population of Paris had reached between 6,000 and 7,000 persons, the *consistory began to build the first Great Synagogue, in Rue Notre Dame de Nazareth. It stood for no more than 30 years and had barely been rebuilt when, in 1852 (the year of the foundation of the Rothschild Hospital), it became apparent that it was not large enough for a Jewish population which had reached 20,000. General difficulties beset the building of new synagogues (those in Rue de la Victoire and Rue des Tournelles were completed in 1877), but local difficulties led to the transfer of the Rabbinical Seminary of Metz to Paris in 1859. The consistory had established its first primary school in 1819; a second school was added in 1846, and three others between 1864 and 1867. At the same time charitable associations increased; their

Figure 2. Ark of the Law in the synagogue of the Rue Pavée, rebuilt after World War II. Photo M. Ninio, Jerusalem.

buildings frequently also served as prayer rooms for immigrant Jews. The capital was the seat of the Central Consistory of France (as well as the Consistory of Paris) and from 1860 of the *Alliance Israélite Universelle. Two Jewish journals serving all France were published in Paris: *L'Univers Israélite* and the *Archives Israélites*. The 30,000 or so Jews who lived in Paris in 1869 constituted about 40% of the Jewish population of France. The great majority originated from Metz, Alsace, Lorraine, and Germany, and there were already a few hundreds from Poland. Apart from a very few wealthy capitalists, the great majority of the Jews belonged to the middle economic level. Alongside the peddlers, merchants, and dealers in secondhand goods, the proportion of craftsmen—painters, hat-makers, tailors, and shoemakers—was increasing. Many organizations and societies—the first dating from 1825—encouraged young Jewish men and women to acquire an aptitude for and pride in manual work. The liberal professions also attracted numerous Jews; the community included an increasing number of professors, lawyers, and physicians.

With the loss of Alsace and Lorraine in 1871, the Jewish population of France numbered only 60,000 persons, almost two-thirds of whom lived in Paris. After 1881 their numbers were augmented by refugees from Poland, Russia, and the Slav provinces of Austria and Rumania; this influx led to a noticeable increase in the percentage of manual workers among Parisian Jews. At the same time there was a marked increase in the anti-Semitic movement, particularly with the foundation of the journal *La *Croix* in 1883 and the agitation of E. A. *Drumont. The *Dreyfus affair, from 1894, split the intellectuals of Paris into "Dreyfusards" and "anti-Dreyfusards" who frequently clashed on the streets, especially in the Latin Quarter. With the law separating church and state in 1905, the Jewish consistories lost their official status, becoming no more than private religious associations. The growing numbers of Jewish immigrants to Paris resented the heavy hand of a consistory, which was largely under the control of Jews from Alsace and Lorraine, now a minority group.

These immigrants formed the greater part of the 13,000 "foreign" Jews who enlisted in World War I. Especially after 1918, Jews began to arrive from North Africa, Turkey, and the Balkans, and in greatly increased numbers from Eastern Europe. Thus in 1939 there were around 150,000 Jews in Paris (over half the total in France), the overwhelming majority Yiddish-speaking recent immigrants. The Jews lived all over the city but there were large concentrations in the north and east. More than 150 Landmanschaften composed of immigrants from Eastern Europe and many charitable societies united large numbers of Jews, while at this period the Paris Consistory (which retained the name with its changed function) had no more than 6,000 members. Only one of the 19th-century Jewish primary schools was still in existence in 1939, but a few years earlier the system of Jewish education—which was strictly private in nature—acquired a secondary school and a properly supervised religious education, for which the consistory was responsible, in the synagogues, prayer rooms, and also in a few state high schools. As well as the French Jewish journals, the Yiddish press became increasingly important. Many great Jewish scholars were born and lived in Paris in the modern period. They included the Nobel prizewinners René *Cassin and A. *Lwoff. In the plastic arts Jews played an especially prominent part in the School of *Paris. [B.Bl.]

Hebrew Printing. The first books containing Hebrew type issued in Paris were printed by A. Gourmont from 1508; and other works were printed during the next half-century. Robert Stephanus produced particularly beautiful Bibles between 1539 and 1556. Hebrew printing was resumed in 1620 by S. Cramoisy. When Louis XIII established a printing press in 1640, it had a Hebrew department, of which, however, little use was subsequently made. Under Napoleon I the printer Setier issued some liturgical items. From the middle of the 19th century until the present day the firm of E. Durlacher, the first Jewish printer in Paris, has printed mainly liturgies. [Ed.]

Holocaust Period. On June 14, 1940, the Wehrmacht entered Paris, which was proclaimed an open city. Most Parisians left, including the Jews. However, the population returned in the following weeks. The German-imposed census of Jewish persons and businesses in November 1940 recorded a total of 149,734 Jews (over 6 years of age), 7,737 Jewish businesses (private), and 3,456 companies considered Jewish. The Jewish population figure was similar to the prewar one, but large numbers of Parisian Jews had preferred to remain in the southern, unoccupied French territory and a sizable number of well-known Jews fled to England and the U.S. (André *Maurois, Georges Gombault, Pierre Lazareff), while some, e.g., René *Cassin and Gaston Palewski, joined General De Gaulle's Free French movement in London. In August 1940 a number of Jewish shops on the Champs Elysées were stoned by French Nazis under German protection. The anti-Jewish measures which followed (see *France, Holocaust Period) first affected the Parisian Jews. Jews were active from the very first in *Résistance movements. The march to the Etoile on Nov. 11, 1940, of high school and university students, the first major public manifestation of resistance, included among its organizers Francis Cohen, Suzanne Djian, and Bernard Kirschen (see also *Partisans, Jewish, in General Resistance in France).

The first major roundups of Parisian Jews of foreign nationality took place in 1941: about 5,000 "foreign" Jews were deported on May 14, about 8,000 "foreigners" in August, and about 100 "intellectuals" on December 13. On July 16, 1942, 12,884 Jews were rounded up in Paris (including about 4,000 children). The Parisian Jews represented over half the 85,000 Jews deported from France to extermination camps in the East; most of them were sent to Compiègne or *Drancy and from there to *Auschwitz, while about three convoys, in March 1943, were despatched to *Majdanek and one transport, in May 1944, to Kovno (*Kaunas). During the night of Oct. 2–3, 1941, seven Parisian synagogues were attacked. After an attempt to place the blame on the Jews themselves, it rapidly transpired that the attacks were instigated by the German S.D. (security police) in Paris (see *Gestapo) and carried out by French Fascists, led by Eugène Deloncle, with explosives supplied by the S.D. *SS-Brigadefuehrer* Max Thomas, R. T. *Heydrich's representative to Belgium and France, was then recalled to Berlin, but his Paris subordinate, *Standarten-fuehrer* Helmut Knochen, kept his position and was even promoted.

Several scores of Jews fell in the Paris insurrection in August 1944. Many streets in Paris and the outlying suburbs bear the names of Jewish heroes and martyrs of the Holocaust period and the Memorial to the Unknown Jewish Martyr, a part of the *Centre de Documentation Juive Contemporaire, was erected in 1956 in the heart of Paris. [L.St.]

Contemporary Period. In 1968 Paris and its suburbs contained about 60% of the Jewish population of France. Between 1945 and 1950 the Jewish population of the area grew from 125,000 to 150,000, and in 1968 it was estimated at between 300,000 and 350,000 (about 5% of the total population). In 1950 two-thirds of the Jews were concentrated in about a dozen of the poorer or commercial districts in the east of the city. The social and economic advancement of the second generation of East European

Figure 3a and b. Scenes from the *"Pletzel,"* the major Jewish neighborhood of Paris.

immigrants, the influx of North Africans, and the gradual implementation of the urban renewal program caused a considerable change in the once Jewish districts and the dispersal of the Jews throughout other districts of Paris. The greatest change took place in the neighborhoods that in 1956–57 were still inhabited by artisans and small traders of East European origin. By 1968 the inhabitants of these neighborhoods had been replaced by the most impoverished of the North African immigrants. Between 1945 and 1968, the urbanization of the Paris region became accelerated. In 1941 10% of the Jews of Paris resided in the inner suburbs of the city; by 1966 about 20% were living outside the city limits. North African Jews were partly relocated in the large housing developments reserved for repatriated citizens. Between 1957 and 1966 the number of Jewish communities in the Paris region rose from 44 to 148. Like other suburban inhabitants, the Jews were employed mostly in Paris.

Paris is the center of Jewish activities in France, as all the major institutions have their headquarters there. The Paris Consistory, traditionally presided over by a member of the *Rothschild family, officially provides for all religious needs. Approximately 20 synagogues and meeting places for prayer observing Ashkenazi or Sephardi (North African) rites are affiliated with the consistory, which also provides for the religious needs of new communities in the suburbs. This responsibility is shared by traditional Orthodox elements, who, together with the reform and other independent groups, maintain another 30 or so synagogues. The Orientation and Information Office of the Fonds Social Juif Unifié has advised or assisted over 100,000 refugees from North Africa. It works in close cooperation with government services and social welfare and educational institutions of the community. The numerous educational and cultural activities of various kinds include efforts to draw young people and intellectuals back into the Jewish community. From 1957 the *World Jewish Congress held an annual French-language colloquium of intellectuals. The Centre Universitaire d'Etudes Juives (C.U.E.J.) exists for the purpose of introducing university students to Jewish culture. Paris was one of very few cities in the Diaspora with a full-fledged Israel-type school, conducted by Israel teachers according to the Israel curriculum. It served the relatively large colony of Israelis, as well as some French Jews who aspired to give their children a genuine Hebrew education. Numerous cultural and Zionist associations also present varied programs for the Jewish public each evening. However, only one-third of the Jewish population maintains any relations with community institutions. The *Six-Day War (1967), which drew thousands of Jews into debates and pro-Israel demonstrations, was an opportunity for many of them to reassess their personal attitude toward the Jewish people. During the "students' revolution" of 1968 in nearby Nanterre and in the Sorbonne, young Jews played an outstanding role in the leadership of left-wing activists (see *New Left) and often identified with Arab anti-Israel propaganda extolling the Palestinian organizations, particularly the terrorist Popular Front, as an example of the Third World struggle against imperialism. Eventually, however, when the "revolutionary" wave subsided, it appeared that the bulk of Jewish students in Paris, including many supporters of various New Left groups, remained loyal to Israel and strongly opposed Arab terrorism, although many of them criticized the Israel government for "ignoring the right of the Palestinian people to self-determination." The tension created by the Six-Day War also exacerbated frictions and led to several violent clashes between North African Arabs and Jews in lower middle class and proletarian quarters of Paris. Young

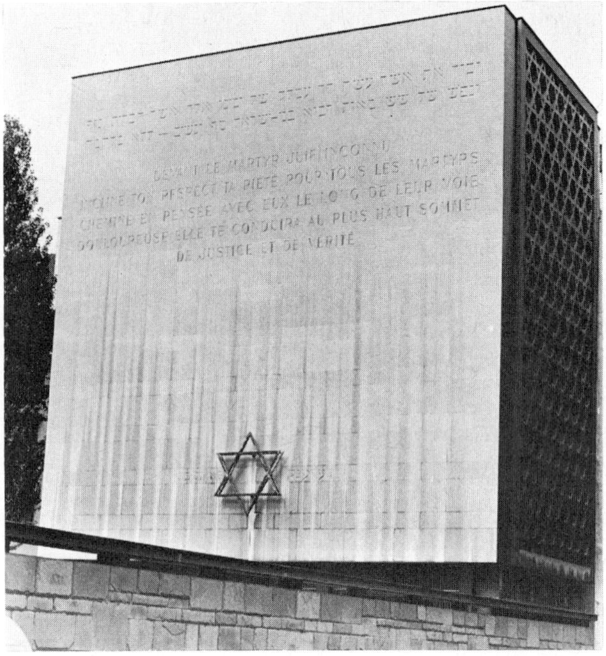

Figure 5. The Memorial to the Unknown Jewish Martyr, erected in Paris in 1956. Photo M. Ninio, Jerusalem.

Jews began to organize for self-defense against physical attacks, but the clashes ceased mainly through the intervention of the local police.

See also *France. [D.Bs.]

Bibliography: Gross, Gal Jud, 496ff.; B. Blumenkranz, *Bibliographie des Juifs en France* (1963), s.v. *L. Kahn* for 10 works and many periodical articles; J. Hillairet, *Evocation du vieux Paris,* 1 (1951), 361f.; idem, *Dictionnaire historique des rues de Paris* (1964²), index; idem, *L'Ile de la Cité* (1969), 34–37; I. Loeb, in: REJ, 1 (1880), 60–71; M. Ginsburger, *ibid.*, 78 (1924), 156ff.; P. Hildenfinger, *Documents sur les Juifs à Paris au XVIIIe siècle* (1913); L. Berman, *Histoire des Juifs de France* (1937), passim; Z. Szajkowski, in: *Yidn in Frankraykh* (1942), passim; idem, *Franco-Judaica* (1962), index; idem, *Analytical Franco-Jewish Gazetteer 1939–1945* (1966), index; R. Anchel, *Les Juifs de France* (1946), passim; U. Issembert-Gannat, *Guide de Judaïsme à Paris* (1964); C. Korenchandler, *Yidn in Paris* (1970). Holocaust Period: J. Billig, *Le Commissariat Général aux questions Juives,* 3 vols. (1955–60), incl. bibl. index; L. Steinberg, *Les autorités allemandes en France occupée* (1966), incl. bibl. index; C. Lévy and P. Tillard, *Betrayal at the Vel d'Hiv* (1969); Centre de Documentation Juive Contemporaine Bibliothèque, *Catalogue No. 1: La France . . .* (1964), index; G. Reitlinger, *Final Solution* (1968²), 327–51 and passim; L. Steinberg, *La révolte des Justes* (1970), incl. bibl. 1945–1970: M. Roblin, *Juifs de Paris* (1952); C. Roland, *Du ghetto à l'Occident* (1962).

PARIS SCHOOL OF ART (Jewish School of). In the history and criticism of 20th-century painting "School of Paris" has become a widely used term, generally designating a style which is not necessarily nor typically French, but which is followed by a large number of foreign-born artists living in France. It was only in the third decade of the 20th century, however, that this term began to be accepted. Because of the great number of foreign-born artists who had settled permanently in Paris or who had lived there briefly but been profoundly influenced by French art, it became necessary to refer to most of them as artists of the School of Paris rather than of the French School.

The Jewish School. As many of these foreign artists, especially between 1910 and 1940, happened also to be of East European Jewish origin, the term "Jewish School of Paris" was then coined to refer more specifically to a school of painting which gravitated only peripherally around the main schools of modern art of France, such as fauvism,

Figure 1. "Young Girl Asleep," a Fauvist painting by Sonia Delaunay-Terk, 1907, oil on canvas, 18×22 in. (46×55 cm.). Paris, Musée National d'Art Moderne.

cubism, or surrealism, but which had developed certain features of its own. Some of these features, however, can also be detected in the work of non-Jewish and even French-born painters of the School of Paris, who associated closely with the artists of the so-called "Jewish School." The latter has therefore been more properly called by some critics and art historians, the "School of Montparnasse," because it was in this Left Bank neighborhood that many of the artists concerned lived and worked, or congregated in their leisure hours. Nationalist or anti-Semitic French critics and publicists have often argued that the main trends of 20th-century avant-garde French art were dictated or dominated by foreigners and, more specifically, by Jews, who thus, they claimed, exerted a disruptive influence on French traditions. In fact the influence of Jewish artists, whether French or foreign-born, on the major schools of contemporary French painting has been, on the whole, very modest.

Fauvist School. Among the Fauvist painters who began to attract attention in 1905, only Russian-born Sonia *Delaunay-Terk and a group of Hungarian-born painters—Béla *Czobel, Robert Berény (1887–1954), Bertalan Pór (1880–1964), Lajos Tihanyi (1885–1939), Vilmos Perlrott-Csaba (1879–1954), and István Farkas (1887–1944)—were Jews of foreign origin, and these were never leading figures in the Fauvist group. Among the French-born Fauvists, Léopold Levy (1882–1967) was a painter of great distinction, but he somehow failed to achieve the reputation he deserved. Nevertheless, he exerted a decisive influence on Turkish painting as a teacher for many years at the School of Fine Arts in Istanbul. Between 1910 and 1914, the French Fauvist master Matisse was an influential figure in German expressionist painting, mainly through a few German-Jewish artists who had been his pupils in Paris and who subsequently achieved eminence in Germany and Israel. The two most important were Rudolf Levy (1875–1944) and Jakob *Steinhardt.

The Cubists. Among the Paris cubists, Sonia Delaunay-Terk, a convert from Fauvism, was slow to gain recognition as an artist of great significance. Her later transition to an idiom of abstract art ensures her place in art history as one of the pioneers of what was subsequently known as op art. Henryk Berlewi (1894–1967), a Pole, was another pioneer of op art. Other Jewish artists who achieved some prominence among the Paris cubists, or as one-time disciples of cubism, are German-born Otto *Freundlich, Polish-born Henri Hayden (1883–) and Louis Marcoussis (1883–1941), French-born Henry Valensi (1883–1960) and Marcelle Cahn (1895–), and Russian-born Nechama Szmuszkowicz (1895–), Serge Charchoune (1889–), and Jacques Pailes (1895–). Hungarian-born Alfred Reth (1884–1965) was one of the first painters to formulate the cubist idiom in Paris, though he was never an active member of the cubist group. The French poet and painter Max *Jacob, a close friend of Picasso and the other cubist masters, played an important part as a representative of cubist poetry, but was never a cubist in his painting. Although he was also a member of the group between 1910 and 1914 and was influenced to some extent by its style, Marc *Chagall denied any allegiance to cubism. Without ever being a true cubist, except in his sculpture, Amedeo *Modigliani was closely associated with the Paris cubists. Three Russian-born artists, Chana *Orloff, Ossip *Zadkine, and Jacques *Lipchitz earned worldwide fame as masters of cubist sculpture. Jules *Pascin, a Bulgarian, was a prominent figure in the Paris art world in the heyday of cubism, although he was not a true cubist in his own drawings and paintings. The same can be said of Polish-born Moise *Kisling. Though influenced by his close friend Modigliani and by cubist theory, Kisling was never an orthodox cubist.

The Surrealists. There were no Jewish artists of real significance among the Paris dadaists of 1917 to 1922, although Marcel *Janco (1895–) had been a leader in the original Zurich dada group. After 1922, Rumanian-born Victor Brauner (1903–1966) and Jacques Herold (1910–) slowly came to the fore as representatives of French surrealist paintings. By the time he died, Brauner was generally recognized as one of the major surrealists. Meret Oppenheim (1913–), a German, achieved historical importance as the inventor of a number of famous surrealist objects. Kurt Seligmann (1900–1962), a Swiss artist who sank into undeserved neglect, achieved prominence as a surrealist both in Paris and in New York and produced many of the finest surrealist engravings. Rumanian-born Grégoire Michonze (1902–), a close associate and friend of Max Ernst and other major surrealists, excelled in dreamworld allegories rather than in surrealism.

Figure 2. "Portrait of Guillaume Apollinaire," a cubist lithograph by Louis Marcoussis. Courtesy Editions Pierre Cailler, Pully, Switzerland. Photo Ivan Bettex, Pully.

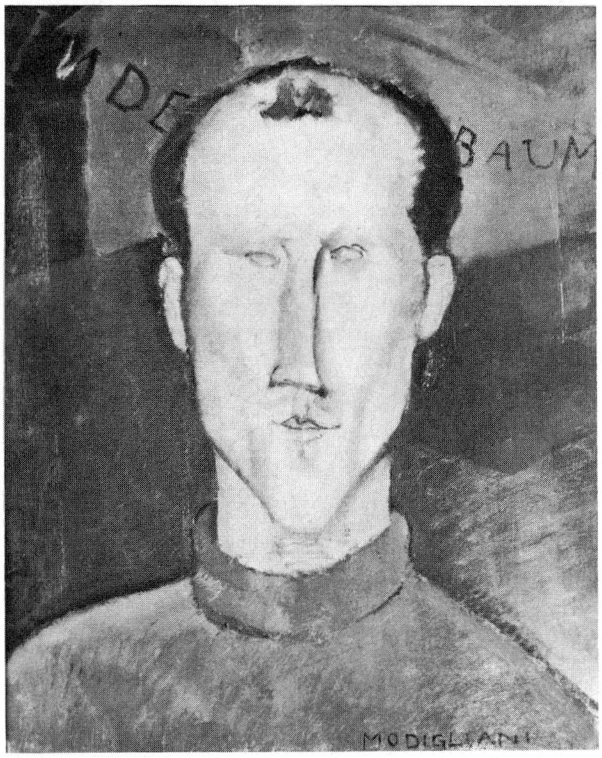

Figure 3. "Portrait of Leon Indenbaum," by Amedeo Modigliani, 1916, oil on canvas, $21\frac{1}{2}\times18$ in. (54×46 cm.). New York, H. Pearlman Collection.

Closely allied at one time to the surrealist group, the Paris neoromantics who flourished around 1930 included almost more painters of Jewish origin than any other 20th-century school of French painting, but can scarcely be said to constitute a Jewish School of Paris. These neoromantic painters, widely scattered by Nazism throughout Western Europe and the United States, at one time included: from Russia, Eugene Berman (1899–) and his brother Leonid (1896–), Philippe Hosiasson (1898–), and Léon Zack (1892–); from Austria, Victor Tischler (1890–1950), Joseph Floch (1896–), and Georg Merkel (1881–); from Egypt, Josiah Victor Ades (1893–); from Poland, Jacques Zucker (1900–); and from the United States, Maurice Grosser (1905–). The Jewish School of Paris or School of Montparnasse thus appears to have developed as a somewhat marginal phenomenon that was never too closely associated with any of the major movements of contemporary French art, but was influenced by most of these movements in turn. Around 1910, large numbers of foreign-born painters began to choose the cafés of the Boulevard Montparnasse, especially the Café du Dôme, as their leisure-time headquarters. Until 1914, these foreign artists included a considerable number of Germans, among whom the sculptor Wilhelm Lehmbruck subsequently proved to be one of the most important. His many Jewish friends, who met him regularly at the Café du Dôme, included Jules Pascin, Otto Freundlich, Rudolf Levy, Georges Kars (1880–1945), and Eugen von Kahler (1882–1911), the last two from Czechoslovakia. Of the many gifted Paris painters who have not yet been granted the recognition they deserved, Kars is certainly one of the finest; under the influence of Cézanne and of cubist theory rather than cubist style, he achieved, especially in his drawings, a rare synthesis of romantic feeling and classical form. Eugen von Kahler is now remembered mainly as a promising participant in some of the early activities of the Munich Blaue Reiter (Blue Rider) School, in which he associated with Klee and Kandinski.

Montparnasse and La Ruche. During World War I and the years that immediately followed it, social and political upheavals in Eastern Europe, especially in Russia, Poland, Rumania, and Hungary, brought about a great increase in the numbers of refugee artists who became permanent or semipermanent residents of Paris. Many of these artists were Jews, refugees from persecution or from other limitations, such as a lack of interested collectors, in their native country. Some American Jewish artists, such as Abraham *Rattner, also went to live in Paris and began to associate, in Montparnasse, with French or other foreign-born artists. Even before 1914, many of these foreign-born Jewish artists had been living in a couple of ramshackle old studio buildings located in the tangle of narrow streets that extended behind Montparnasse railway station, especially in the studios of La Ruche, where Chagall had lived before 1914, and of the Cité Falguière, where Modigliani lived at one time. Russian-born Chaim *Soutine remains a legendary representative of this earlier period of the Jewish School of Paris and of the whole history of Montparnasse as an art colony. Montparnasse's almost slum-like little ghettos of more or less improvised studios, however, were also occupied at one time or another by a number of non-Jewish artists, such as the cubist master Fernand Léger, so that they never constituted purely Jewish enclaves in the Left Bank art world. The painter Jacques *Chapiro published a nostalgic and somewhat romanticized historical record of La Ruche and its inmates, among whom the Polish-born sculptor Léon Indenbaum (1890–) stands out as an artist who deserves to be more widely known.

The major representatives of the so-called Jewish School of Paris would now appear to be Pinkus Krémègne (1890–), Michel Kikoine (1892–1968), *Mané-Katz (1894–1962), Balgley (1891–1934), Adolphe Milich (1891–1944), Adolf Feder (1887–1943), Isaac Dobrinsky (1891–), Maurice Blond (1899–), Abraham Mintchine (1898–1931), Joseph Pressmane (1904–1967), Zygmund Landau (1898–1962), Zygmund Schreter (1896–), David Seifert (1896–), Marc Sterling (1898–), Charles Tcherniawsky (1900–), and Isaac Antscher (1899–). Most of them were born in Russia, Poland, or other former provinces of the czarist empire, including Lithuania and Bessarabia. To these names should be added those of a number of former Paris residents on whose subsequent work the School of Montparnasse left a lasting mark and who later achieved distinction elsewhere, such as Max Band (1900–) in the U.S. and Josef Iser (1881–1963) in Rumania. The Jewish School of Paris is distinguished, in general, by its expressionist insistence on communicating emotion or mood rather than formal relationships or effects of light and color. Nevertheless, many of its members, especially Mané-Katz, Kikoine, and Feder, are noted for their effects of color and texture. The more typical painters of the school tended to rely heavily on impasto effects obtained by using a heavily loaded brush or palette knife in such a way as to create the impression that they actually drew with their pigment or even modeled it, as a sculptor might, in low relief. Several Jewish painters of the School of Montparnasse, including some of those already mentioned, refrained from allowing themselves the kind of exuberance or sensuality that characterizes, above all, the still life and landscape painting of Mané-Katz, Feder, and Kikoine. Thus Leopold *Gottlieb (1883–1934), a much younger brother of the famous 19th-century Polish painter Mauricy *Gottlieb, stood out as a representative of an almost classical pictorial refinement, always avoiding effects of color or texture that might appear over rich. The Russian-born painter Joseph Lubitch (1908–) likewise remains, in a minor key, a belated disciple of French impressionism, often delighting in effects that recall Whistler. Another Russian, Arbit Blatas (1908–), tempers the neo-primitive violence of

Figure 4. "La Ronde" by Gregoire Michanze, 1938/39, oil on canvas, $25\frac{1}{2}\times12$ in. (65×31 cm.). London, Alexander Margulies Collection.

Fauvism by handling its style in an elegiac, intimate, and almost neoromantic mood.

Victims of Nazism. In 1940 the Nazi occupation of Paris decimated the city's Jewish population. Among the more prom-

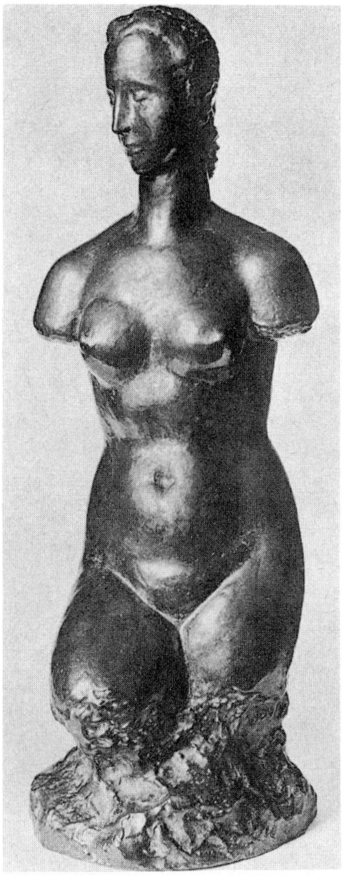

Figure 5. "Young Girl," bronze by Wilhelm Lehmbruk. Boston, Museum of Fine Arts.

inent artists who died as victims of Nazi extermination camps were Otto Freundlich, Henri (Chaim) Epstein, Adolf Feder, Tobias Haber (1906–1943), Abram Weinbaum (1890–1943), Alice Hoherman (1902–1943), Abrami Mordkin (1874–1943), Georges Ascher (1884–1943), Jacques Gotko (1900–1943), Samuel Granovsky (1889–1942), David Goychmann (1900–1942), David Michael Krever (1904–1941), Jacob Macznik (1905–1944), Ephraim Mandelbaum (1884–1942), Leon Weissberg (1893–1943), Lajos Tihanyi, and Istvan Farkas. These martyred artists were gifted with such outstanding and diverse talents that it would now be as unfair to try to force them all into a Jewish school as it was, under the Nazi regime, to deny them their human rights because they were Jews. One who deserves particular mention is the Russian-born sculptor Moyshe Kogan (1879–1942). Before migrating from Germany to Paris, he had already distinguished himself in Munich as the only sculptor of the Blue Rider Group.

After World War II. After 1945, the School of Paris soon began again to attract many foreign-born Jewish painters and sculptors, though now mainly from the U.S., Israel, French North Africa, and, of course, from among the East European survivors of the Holocaust. The Algerian-born abstract painter Jean *Atlan soon achieved prominence as a recognized master of postwar French painting. In the same school of non-geometrical and more lyrical abstract painting, Philippe Hosiasson and Léon Zack, both former neoromantics, also came to be recognized as masters. Rumanian-born Robert Helman (1910–) and Turkish-born Albert Bitran (1931–) also came to the fore after 1950, each with a distinctive idiom of non-geometrical abstraction. Russian-born Alexander Garbell (1903–), a master of elegant brush work and of subtle color harmonies and textures, experimented for a while with an abstract idiom but soon returned to a style of revised post-impressionism better suited to his temperament. Of the small group of abstract painters hailing from Hungary, the most outstanding in the late sixties was Zsigmund Kolozsvari, known professionally as Kolos-Vari (1889–). Alfred Aberdam (1894–1963), who was born in Austrian Galicia, began to attract attention in Paris only after 1945. A painter of unusual refinement, he revealed in his mature work a surprising affinity with some Italian mannerist and baroque masters of the later Renaissance, though he expressed himself in a pictorial idiom that seems to have derived from the neoromantic painters of the 1930s.

As public interest in modern art grew after World War II, artists all over the world found themselves free to cater to a much wider variety of tastes than formerly, and after 1945 French painting and that of the School of Paris came to be characterized by an ever increasing diversity of styles. There is even less justification to use the term "Jewish School" for this later generation of Jewish painters than between the two world wars. Polish-born Marek Halter (1932–), for instance, might well be classed among the new realists, although his work reveals a far greater refinement of draftsmanship and painterly discretion than that of Bernard Buffet. A native Parisian, Jacques Winsberg (1929–) also attracted attention as a new realist or "misérabiliste," concerning himself, like Buffet, mainly with effects of pathos. Another Frenchman, Gabriel Zendel (1906–), on the other hand, brought new life to the moribund idiom of cubism by exploiting it with a more varied sense of color and of texture. Though born in Russia, Chapoval (1912–1953) was educated in France and, as an early representative of French tachisme or lyrical and non-geometrical abstraction, immediately achieved considerable prominence. Polish-born Georges Goldkorn (1907–), Felicia Pacanowska (1907–), and Abram Krol (1884–) came to the fore mainly as outstanding graphic artists, Goldkorn and Pacanowska in the field of etching, Krol in woodcuts. Krol, a gifted French poet as well as an artist, became well known among bibliophiles all over the world as a remarkable creator of beautiful books. German-born Johnny Friedlaender (1912–) likewise earned an international reputation as a virtuoso of rare technical brilliance, especially in his color etchings.

In addition to Jean Atlan, Algeria gave Paris three other painters of note. Smadja, after studying with the cubist master Fernand Léger, developed a lyrical, non-geometric abstract style of his own. The expressionist Corsia (1915–) succeeded in infusing a truly Mediterranean sensuality and sense of color into an idiom inherited from Van Gogh. A Mediterranean sense of color and light is also typical of Assus, a belated post-impressionist. Two Moroccan artists worthy of mention are André Elbaz, whose North African Jewish themes are handled in an expressionist idiom previously used mainly for East European Jewish subjects, and Hasdai Elmosnino, who was profoundly influenced by French painting before emigrating to a new home in Canada. Among other painters of North African origin is Tunisian-born Jules Lellouche (1903–1965), a post-impressionist who was often haunted by nostalgic memories of classical Venetian painting. Among Polish-born survivors of the Holocaust who distinguished themselves as painters in Paris after 1945, Maryan (1927–), who eventually moved to New York, proved to be a worthy heir to the great tradition of East European Jewish visionary fantasy that first obtained international recognition in the early works of Chagall, Issachar Ryback, and Yankel Adler. But Maryan's art is disturbed

Figure 6. "Landscape" by Adolphe Feder, Jerusalem, Joseph Leron Collection. Photo Erde, Tel Aviv.

Figure 7. "Epicier" by Mané-Katz, 1927–29, oil on canvas, 50×35½ in. (126×90 cm.). Kefar Shemaryahu, Y. Sahar Collection.

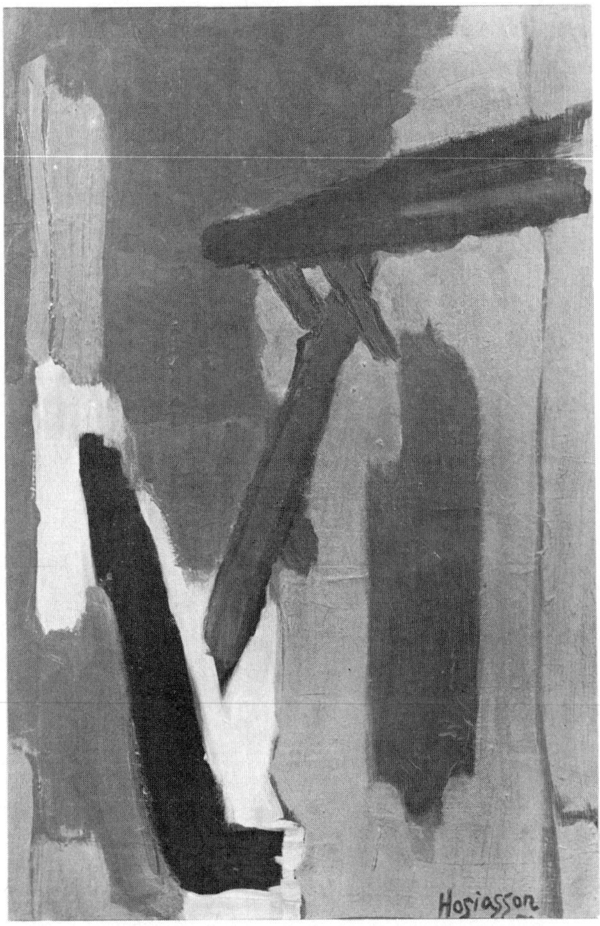

Figure 8. "Paysage Ombres Rouges," by Philippe Hasiasson, oil on canvas, 21½×15 in. (55×38 cm.). London, Alexander Margulies Collection.

by macabre memories, transmuted into a peculiarly sardonic and bitter kind of clowning.

Traditionalists and Individualists. In addition to all the artists who have been named, a number of other Jewish painters, several of them French-born, distinguished themselves in Paris in the 20th century, but in the traditional schools of strictly French art rather than in any of its more experimental innovations. Several other Jewish artists, moreover, attracted attention at various times as individualists whose work fails to fit into any of the categories of contemporary criticism. Russian-born Eugène Zak (1884–1926), for example, achieved a curious synthesis of mildly cubist stylization and almost Pre-Raphaelite idealism that is perhaps unique. Frenel (1898–), who was born in Ereẓ Israel as Frenkel, is a somewhat mystical or romantic painter of Jewish themes whose work expresses little of the anguish and turbulence of Mané-Katz and other East European Paris painters who have handled similar themes. In this respect, Frenel belongs rather with Balgley and with Polish-born J. D. Kirszenbaum (1900–1954), an artist whose work likewise escapes classification under any of the usual headings of contemporary painting. Arthur Kolnick (1890–) is notable for his tender and poetic paintings of traditional types and scenes recalled from the ḥasidic communities of his native Galicia. Emma Stern (1878–1967), who fled to Paris from Nazi Germany, began painting late in life. With her scenes of a happy childhood in small towns in the Saarland, she was soon acclaimed as a new Grandma Moses. When Simon Segal (1898–1970) left Russia for Berlin, he was profoundly influenced by German expressionism; but in France he developed a style of his own in which a new kind of realism suggests a mysterious affinity with Permeke and the Flemish expressionists. Finally, in the late 1960s, the American-born painter and sculptor Zev, originally named Dan Harris (1914–), injected an element of "Alice in Wonderland" nonsense into traditional surrealist fantasy, which he thus enriched with some novel, individual, and technically refined sculpture. It would probably be correct to say that most of the Jewish painters of the School of Paris settled in the French capital in order to escape from more traditional or Orthodox Jewish backgrounds, especially in Eastern Europe, as much as from the limitations imposed on them by persecution or by their status as Jews. In their work as artists as well as in their lives as members of the Paris bohemian community, most of these artists were cultural assimilationists, though many of them were also haunted from time to time by nostalgic memories of the life from which they had chosen to escape. In the work of Soutine, for instance, there are practically no direct memories of his Russian-Jewish background. In the works of most other painters of the so-called Jewish School of Paris, such memories appear only occasionally, and generally in an idealized and almost idyllic form; they then seem to express nostalgia for the past, or even guilt feelings about having abandoned it. Following the great commercial success of Chagall's Jewish themes, some of these artists reverted to similar themes, handled with great pathos or nostalgic humor, in what can only be regarded as deliberate exploitation of a new fashion for such memories of a vanished world.

Bibliography: Edouard Roditi Archives, Leo Baeck Institute, New York; W. George, in: Roth, Art, 639–718. [E.R.]

PARKER, DOROTHY (1893–1967), U.S. poet and author. Daughter of a Jewish father and a Scottish mother, she began her career by writing reviews for *Vogue* and *Vanity*

Dorothy Parker, U.S. satirist. Wide World Photos, New York.

Fair (who found her reviews too harsh) and then for *The New Yorker*. Her first book of verse, *Enough Rope* (1926), was a best seller, and was followed by two others, all three later being collected in *Not So Deep As a Well* (1936). She also became known as a short story writer, her prizewinning tale, *Big Blond* (1929), being generally considered her best. Collected short stories appeared in *Laments for the Living* (1930), *After Such Pleasures* (1933), and *Here Lies* (1939); in 1944 a collection of her prose and verse appeared as *The Portable Dorothy Parker,* with an introduction by W. Somerset Maugham. Dorothy Parker was witty, sardonic, elegant, and often profound. She also wrote Hollywood screenplays, and a drama in which she collaborated with Arnaud d'Usseau, *Ladies of the Corridor* (1953), was successfully staged in New York.

Bibliography: J. Keats, *You Might as Well Live* (1970); N. W. Yates, *American Humorist* (1964), 262–73; S. J. Kunitz, *Twentieth Century Authors, first supplement* (1955); Paris Review, *Writers at Work* (1958), 69–82. [S.L.]

°**PARKES, JAMES WILLIAM** (1896–), English theologian and historian. A member of the Church of England, Parkes was ordained in 1926 and from 1928 to 1934 was study secretary of the International Student Service in Geneva. Actively aware of the anti-Semitism prevalent in the Central and Eastern European universities, he wrote his earliest book, *The Jew and His Neighbour* (1930, 1938²). He

James Parkes (left) receiving an honorary fellowship from Jacob Katz, rector of the Hebrew University, 1970. Photo David Harris, Jerusalem.

then embarked on what was planned as a comprehensive history of anti-Semitism, the chief responsibility for which he saw in the policy of the Christian Church (*The Conflict of the Church and the Synagogue,* 1934; *The Jew in the Medieval Community,* 1938). He wrote a long series of other works on anti-Semitism, the origins of Christianity, the history of Palestine, etc., in all of which he demonstrated a strong sympathy with the Jewish people and appreciation of Judaism as a religious system. Parkes collaborated with many Jewish organizations and was president of the Jewish Historical Society of England (1949–51). His important private library on Jewish history and Jewish-Gentile relations, which he collected at his home in Barley (near Cambridge) and was incorporated in 1956 as a center for the study of relations between the Jewish and non-Jewish worlds, was sold to Southampton University, where he established a research fellowship for the study of the relations of Jewish and non-Jewish communities. In 1967 Parkes published *Arabs and Jews in the Middle East—A Tragedy of Errors.* Parkes' autobiography, *Voyage of Discoveries,* appeared in 1969. [C.R.]

PARLAMENTSKLUB, JUEDISCHER, Jewish caucus active in the Austrian House of Deputies *(Reichsrat)* during the legislative period 1907–11, the first Austrian parliament elected by equal ballot. It consisted of the deputies of the Jewish national parties of Galicia and Bukovina, not including Jews of other parties. Three of its members, Adolf *Stand, Heinrich Gabel, and Arthur *Mahler, were elected in Galicia, where a number of Jewish deputies also were elected as Poles. The fourth member and chairman, Benno Straucher, came from Bukovina. The Jewish caucus issued a declaration demanding national autonomy for the Jews as well as a democratic and sound social policy in general. Straucher became a forceful speaker for the rights of Austrian Jews. Despite its small membership the Jewish caucus became a political factor in parliament, although it was frequently paralyzed by the antagonism of the Polish caucus *(Polenklub).* In 1911 only Straucher of all the initial members was reelected. A Jewish caucus existed also in the provincial diet *(Landtag)* of Bukovina.

Bibliography: A. Boehm, *Die zionistische Bewegung,* 1 (1935), 344. [Hu.K.]

PARMA, city in N. Italy, capital of the province and former duchy of the same name. Jews are mentioned in Parma around the middle of the 14th century when the town was ruled by the Visconti dukes of Mantua. When the *Black Death was raging in 1348, the Jews were accused of poisoning wells and fountains, and some were put to death. Under the Visconti, Jewish moneylenders were able to carry on business in Parma. In 1440 Elias, physician and lecturer at the medical school of Pavia, was appointed physician to the duke of Parma; among other physicians who practiced there were Giacobb, who may be identical with Giacobbe who treated Duke Erede I of Este in 1467, and Abraham, son of Moses of Prato (1480).

Under the rule of the Sforza, about the middle of the 15th century, the Jews enjoyed the protection of the dukes against oppression by the municipal authorities. The Franciscan *Bernardino da Feltre instigated the expulsion of some Jewish women who had given dancing lessons to aristocratic women in Parma. In 1488 Bernardino succeeded in having a Christian loan-bank *(*Monte di Pietà)* established there; the Jewish loan-bankers began to leave the town, taking refuge in Piacenza and the smaller centers of the duchy. Following the bull "cum nimis absurdum" issued by Pope *Paul IV in July 1555, Jews were no longer permitted to carry on their moneylending activities or to reside in Parma. Under Paul's successor, Pius IV, the Jews were permitted in 1562 to open loan-banks in 16 smaller centers in the duchy of Parma and Piacenza (at Colorno, Roccabianca, Soragna, Borgo San Donnino (now Fidenza), Busseto, San Secondo Parmense, and Sissa). The concession, valid for a duration of 12 years, was later renewed for eight centers only; these included the first five mentioned above. Renewals were granted every 12 years, the last dating from 1669. The loan-banks were a necessity for the predominantly agricultural population. The Jews were accorded political equality on July 12, 1803 by the French commissaire Moreau de Saint-Méry, but this was rescinded in 1816 by the archduchess Marie Louise. Jews were now beginning to resettle in Parma itself. Publication of a *Rivista Israelitica* was begun in Parma in 1845, but lasted only for three years. Emancipation followed the inclusion of Parma in the Kingdom of Sardinia. In 1866 the renewed community of Parma drew up its constitution and arranged for the building of a synagogue. Rabbis of Parma include Donato Camerini (1866–1921), editor of a prayer book according to the Italian rite (Parma, 1912). The community numbered 510 in 1840, and 684 in 1881, declining to 415 in 1911.

[A.M.R.]

In 1931 there were 232 Jews in the community of Parma. During the Holocaust at least 12 were sent to extermination

Street in Parma, Italy, with the synagogue on the left. Courtesy Italian Synagogue, Jerusalem.

camps. After the war the community had a membership of 86, which declined to 60 by 1969. [S.D.P.]

Palatina Library. The Palatina Library in Parma contains one of the richest collections of Hebrew manuscripts and incunabula in the world, among them many valuable illuminated manuscripts. Included in the collection are early Bible codices, and it is especially rich in liturgical manuscripts. Important manuscripts of Midrashim and rabbinical works include the commentaries of Menahem b. Solomon *Meiri. In 1816 Marie-Louise, Napoleon's wife, bought the G. B. de' *Rossi collection of more than 1,500 manuscripts. In 1846 the library acquired over 100 Hebrew manuscripts from the collection of M. B. *Foa of Reggio Emilia. The codices are amply described by G.B. de' Rossi in his *Manuscripti codices Hebraici bibliothecae* (3 vols., 1803); the 55 manuscripts later acquired by de'Rossi were described by M. Steinschneider in: HB, 6–7 (1863–64); 12 (1872); 14 (1874) and by P. *Perreau (*Catologo dei Codici ebraici de . . . non descritti dal de' Rossi,* 1880). G. Tamani described the library's illuminated manuscripts (in: *La Bibliofilia,* 70 (1968), 39–139). [A.M.R.]

Bibliography: Roth, Italy, index; Milano, Italia, index; V. Rovè, *L'Educatore Israelita,* 18 (1870); A. Orvieto, in: *Il Vessillo Israelitico,* 43 (1895), 323–7, 357–60; E. Loevinson, in: RMI, 7 (1932), 350–8; G. Bachi, *ibid.,* 12 (1938), 204–5; 28 (1962), 37 (statistics); P. Colbi, *ibid.,* 29 (1963), 438–45; E. Urbach, in: MGWJ, 80 (1936), 275–81; M. A. Szulwas, *Ḥayyei ha-Yehudim be-Italyah . . .* (1955), index. PALATINA LIBRARY: Zunz, Gesch, 240; G. Gabrieli, *Manoscritti . . .* (1930); idem, in: RMI, 7 (1932–33), 167–75; E. Loevinson, *ibid.,* 477–92; U. Cassuto, *I Manoscritti Palatini ebraici della Biblioteca apostolica Vaticana . . .* (1935); G. Tamani, *Studii nell Oriente e le Bibbie* (1967), 201–26.

PARNAS (Heb. פַּרְנָס; "leader"; also called *rosh*), head of the community. The *parnas* was usually elected, sometimes for life but more customarily for a definite term of one year or three years. In larger communities in the later Middle Ages and early modern times, there were several *parnasim* who led the community in rotation, each for one month; they were then called *parnas ha-ḥodesh* ("the *parnas* of the month"; this system is described in detail in the *takkanot* of Cracow for 1595). The leaders of the territorial autonomy structure also used this title, which was later attached to partial, functional leadership, when a distinction was made between the *parnas ha-kahal* ("of the community"), *parnas ha-galil* ("of the province"), *parnas ha-shuk* ("of the market"), the *parnasim* of the guilds and the like. In modern times the title Parnas is employed for the president of a community or a congregation (in the Spanish and Portuguese congregation of London he is called Parnas—Presidente). See also *Elders.

Bibliography: Baron, Community, 3 (1942), index s.v. *Parnasim.*
[N.E.]

PARNAS, ḤAYYIM NAḤMAN (d. 1854), Lithuanian scholar. Parnas was born in Dubnov. After the death of his first wife, Parnas remarried and settled in Vilna. It was his practice to study wrapped in *tallit* and *tefillin* until mid-afternoon each day in his father-in-law's *bet ha-midrash* and to continue studying for the rest of the day at home. By means of his extraordinary diligence he achieved a mastery of both *halakhah* and Kabbalah. He delivered daily discourses on Isaac *Alfasi and the commentary on him by *Nissim b. Reuben Gerondi before the leading figures of the community in the *bet ha-midrash.* In 1850 he established a yeshivah in Vilna. In his prayers he followed the ritual of the "Ari" (Isaac *Luria), and every Sabbath, before the reading of the Law, when the congregation was going over the weekly portion, he studied the Zohar on it.

Parnas took an active interest in communal affairs and was himself widely esteemed. For many years he administered the distribution of Vilna's philanthropic funds, including those for indigent Jews residing in Ereẓ Israel. His approbations appear in a number of contemporary works. The last section of the *Sha'agat Aryeh* printed in the Slavuta edition (1833) contains some novellae of Parnas which display talmudic erudition. He concerned himself with the needs of the community as a whole and of the individuals in it, and because of his grasp of worldly matters many turned to him for advice on their problems.

Bibliography: S. J. Fuenn, *Kiryah Ne'emanah* (1915), 257; Ḥ. N. Maggid-Steinschneider, *Ir Vilna* (1900), 63, 185; H. Brawermann, *Anshei Shem* (1892), 36a.
[SH.A.H./ED.]

PARODY, HEBREW.

Parody in Early Hebrew Literature. Parody is the use of a recognizable literary form as a vehicle to ridicule or mock something or someone. The writer takes a well-known, serious work as his model and invests it with new and amusing contents, at times in order to deride the original or its author, at others to express his views and criticisms of contemporary political and social issues. This technique is used in order to grasp the attention of the reader who will easily recognize the parodied text. Parody, though it uses different forms, is in fact a literary genre in its own right and one of the keenest weapons of satire. In Hebrew literature, parody is an ancient genre. Although mockery for its own sake is not among the things allowed a Jew, the mockery of idolatry is permitted (Meg. 25b) and by inference, the mocking of anything morally or legally defective. Evidence of this concealed form of derision is found already in the Bible: "Elijah mocked them [the prophets of the Baal]) and said: Cry aloud; for he is a god; either he is musing, or he is gone aside, or he is on a journey, or peradventure he sleepeth, and must be awaked" (I Kings 18:27) and, incidentally, in various places in the Talmud and the

Midrash. It is not always possible to identify the source which is being imitated; however, the meter and rhythm of the work make it almost certain that it is a parody on something.

Well known among the fables of Simeon Bar-Kappara, many of which are parodies, is the riddle Bar-Kappara puts in the mouth of the son-in-law of Judah ha-Nasi, Ben-Elasah, who was rich but ignorant and did not participate in the learned conversation of the wise men gathered in Judah's house. The riddle had two objects: first, to mock the rich ignoramus, and secondly, to criticize Judah himself for leading the people with a "high hand." Judah immediately realized that Bar-Kappara was behind his son-in-law's riddle and was angry with the true author. The "riddle" was in fact a parody on the fables of Solomon or of Ben-Sira and is one of the gems of early Hebrew satire:

The netherworld looked down from heaven
Turbulence at the sides of her house
Scaring all winged creatures
The young men saw me and hid themselves
And the aged rose up and stood;
He who flees shall say: Alas, alas!
And he who is trapped is trapped by his own sin (TJ, MK 3:1).

Generally it may be said that the use of such allegoric or heroic language for mundane trivia should be considered parody, even if it is difficult to identify its source. An unusual homily in the Talmud itself should also be regarded as a kind of parody in talmudic *pilpul* style: "Where is Haman [of the Book of Esther] mentioned in the Torah? It

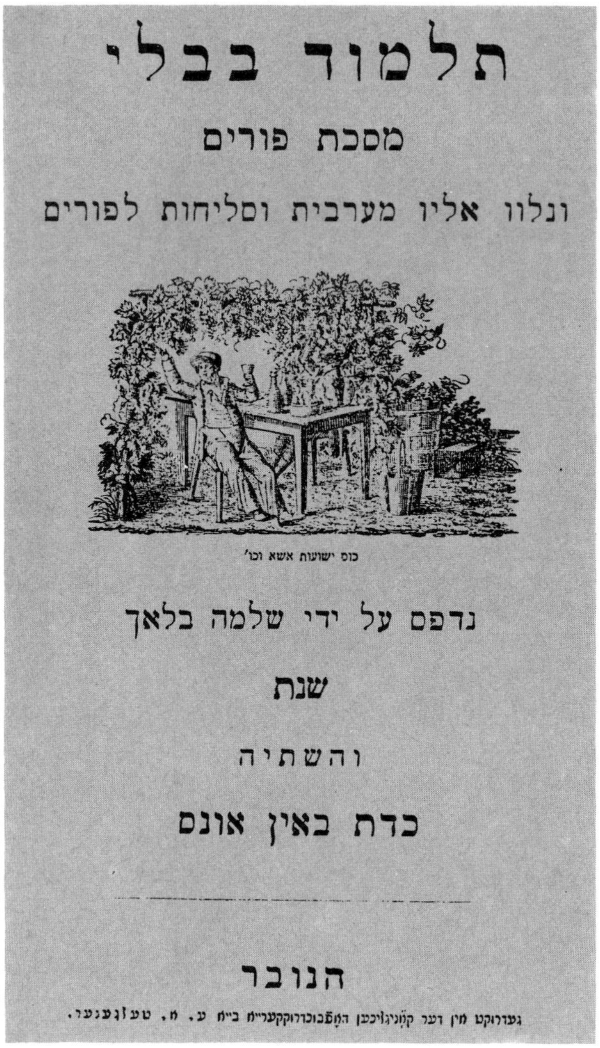
תלמוד בבלי
מסכת פורים
ונלוו אליו מערבית וסליחות לפורים
כוס ישועות אשא וכו'
נדפס על ידי שלמה בלאך
שנת
והשתיה
כדת באין אונס
הנובר
געדרוקט מין דער קעניגליכען האפבוכדרוקקעריי ביי ע. ח. טעלגענער.

Figure 1. Title page of an edition of *Massekhet Purim*, together with other Purim parodies, published in Hanover in 1844. Jerusalem, J.N.U.L.

is written, Hast thou eaten of the tree, whereof I commanded thee that thou shouldest not eat?" (Gen. 3:11). It cannot be assumed that anyone would have thought that that question which Adam was asked hinted even faintly at Haman in the Book of Esther. The novelty consists not only in the fact that the Hebrew letters of "Haman" and *Ha-Min* are identical but also in the juxtaposition of the evil Haman and the "tree" on which he was hanged. This witticism is in fact an imitation of more serious homilies, sometimes hair-splitting in their attempts to make a point, which were common in the Babylonian academies, and thus displays one of the most obvious characteristics of parody.

Parody Since the 12th Century. Hebrew parody as an established literary form is post-talmudic, dating for the most part from the 12th century. It first appeared in Spain, then in Provence and Italy, from where it passed to the literary centers of the Netherlands, Germany, and Eastern Europe. Among the secular poems of the Spanish and Italian *paytanim* are many excellent parodies on diverse subjects. The poem *Al ha-Zevuvim* ("On Flies") by Abraham *ibn Ezra, who was one of the cleverest satirists of Hebrew poetry, is clearly an imitation of an epic. It begins with witty rhymes and pretentious language:

To whom shall I flee for help from my oppression?
Whom shall I implore against the devastation of the flies?
Which will not give me respite
With all their power they oppress me like enemies
And flutter over my eyes and eyelids,
Reciting passionate love songs in my ears;
I venture to eat my meal alone
And they partake of it like wolves,
And even drink out of my glass of wine as though
I had invited them like lovers or friends.

By using such thundering sentences when speaking merely of tiny flies, Ibn Ezra forcefully achieves the amusing effect of parody.

The *Ma'ariv le-Furim*, written by *Menahem b. Aaron (who lived in 14th-century Toledo), is an amusing parody on the *piyyut Leil Shimmurim Hu Zeh ha-Laylah* ("This is the Night of Vigil"), by *Meir b. Isaac, included in the *Ma'ariv* prayer for the first day of Passover. This parody was unaccountably included in a serious edition of the festival prayers and *piyyutim*. With light and boisterous rhymes the author of the parody includes all creation in the joy of Purim:

On this night all creatures get drunk
To remember the law established on Purim
And damned be the man who lifts his hands
To drink abominable water.

and so on, in similar style. Apart from its relevance to Purim, this parody is apparently also a protest against the abundance of *piyyutim* composed by the *paytanim* of that period, many of which have been included in the prayer book and especially in the prayer books for holidays.

The poems by Joseph *ibn Zabara (who lived in 12th-century Spain) on the subjects of doctors and women, specify in a typically medical jargon all the remedies for the fever and other illnesses. They are obviously caricatures of Hippocrates' "collections." One of the masters of Hebrew satire and parody was the Spanish *paytan* Judah *Al-Ḥarizi. His amusing book of **maqāmāt*, *Taḥkemoni*, is written in the spirit of the Arab poet Abu Muhammad al-Qasem Al-Ḥariri (1054–1122), whose book of *maqāmāt* Al-Ḥarizi translated into Hebrew. The *Taḥkemoni* abounds in droll parodies on contemporary personalities and on customs which Al-Ḥarizi found amusing. For example, he ridicules the ceremony of **kapparot* on the eve of the Day of Atonement by relating the words of a cock, who for fear of being killed had escaped to the roof of the synagogue. The style of the cock's speech is biblical although there is a

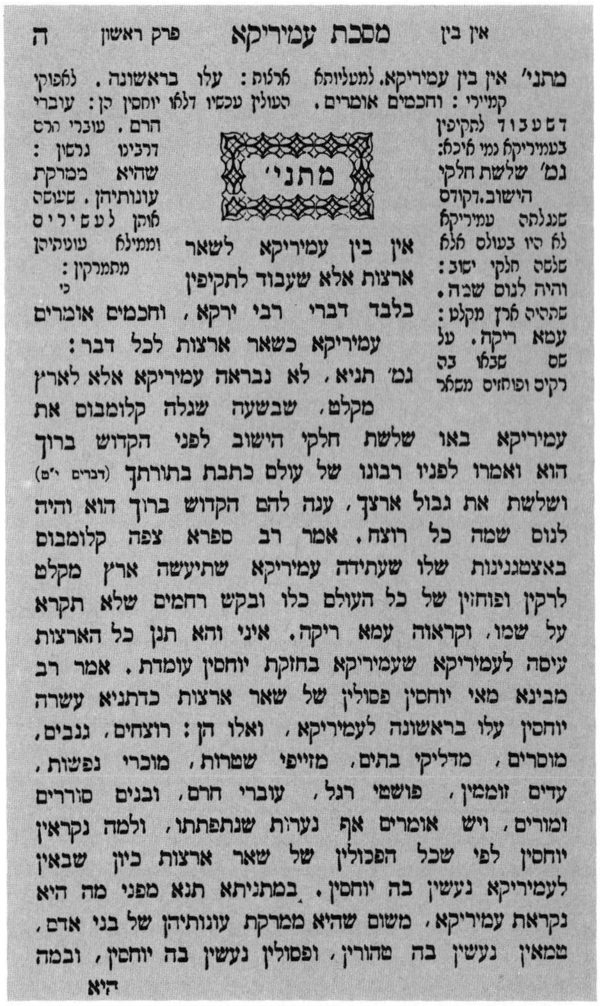

אין בין מסכת עמיריקא פרק ראשון ה

מתני' אין בין עמיריקא. למטליותא ארצות: עלו בראשונה. לאפוקי
קמיירי: וחכמים אומרים. העולין עכשיו דלאו יוחסין הן: עוברי
דשעבוד לתקיפין
בעמיריקא נמי איכא:
גמ' שלשת חלקי
הישוב. דקודם
שנגלתה עמיריקא
לא היו בעולם אלא
שלשה חלקי ישוב:
והיה לנוס שמה.
שתהיה ארץ מקלט:
עמא ריקה. על
שם שבאו בה
רקים ופוחזים משאר

הרם. עוברי הרס
דרכינו גרשון:
שהיא ממרקת
עונותיהן. שעושה
אותן לעשירים
וממילא עונותיהן
מתמרקין:
כי

מתני'

אין בין עמיריקא לשאר ארצות אלא שעבוד לתקיפין בלבד דברי רבי ירקא, וחכמים אומרים עמיריקא כשאר ארצות לכל דבר:

גמ' תניא, לא נבראה עמיריקא אלא לארץ מקלט, שבשעה שגלה קלומבוס את עמיריקא באו שלשת חלקי הישוב לפני הקדוש ברוך הוא ואמרו לפניו רבונו של עולם כתבת בתורתך (דברים י"ט) ושלשת את גבול ארצך, ענה להם הקדוש ברוך הוא והיה לנוס שמה כל רוצח. אמר רב ספרא צפה קלומבוס באצטגנינות שלו שעתידה עמיריקא שתיעשה ארץ מקלט לרקין ופוחזין של כל העולם כלו ובקש רחמים שלא תקרא על שמו, וקראוה עמא ריקה. איני והא תנן כל הארצות עיסה לעמיריקא שעמיריקא בחזקת יוחסין עומדת. אמר רב מבינא מאי יוחסין פסולין של שאר ארצות כדתניא עשרה יוחסין עלו בראשונה לעמיריקא, ואלו הן: רוצחים, גנבים, מוסרים, מדליקי בתים, מזייפי שטרות, מוכרי נפשות, עדים זוממין, פושטי רגל, עוברי חרם, ובנים סוררים ומורים, ויש אומרים אף נערות שנתפתתו, ולמה נקראין יוחסין לפי שכל הפסולין של שאר ארצות כיון שבאין לעמיריקא נעשין בה יוחסין. במתניתא תנא מפני מה היא נקראת עמיריקא, משום שהיא ממרקת עונותיהן של בני אדם, טמאין נעשין בה טהורין, ופסולין נעשין בה יוחסין, ובמה היא

Figure 2. Opening page of *Massekhet Amerika* from the collection *Talmud Yanka'i* by Gershon Rosenzweig, Vilna, 1894. The work is dedicated to *Dodi R. Shmuel ha-Nagid* (Uncle Sam). Jerusalem, J.N.U.L.

suggestion too of the style of the contemporary preachers whom Al-Ḥarizi mocks in other places.

Another of the early Hebrew parodists was *Judah b. Isaac ibn Shabbetai, born in Toledo or Burgos in the 13th century. He was the author of *Minḥat Yehudah Sone ha-Nashim* ("The Tribute of Judah the Misogynist"), a satire on bachelors and women-haters in the style of the Bible and of medieval stories. He also wrote *Milḥemet ha-Ḥokhmah ve-ha-Osher* ("The War of Wisdom and Wealth," 1214) and *Divrei ha-Alah ve-ha-Niddui* ("The Words of the Curse and the Ban," date unknown).

KALONYMUS B. KALONYMUS. While the *paytanim* of the Golden Age in Spain wrote in biblical Hebrew, they employed Arabic meters. The contents of their poetry, especially the secular, was also influenced by contemporary poetry in general and by Arabic poetry in particular. Their parodies, too, were mostly imitations of contemporary literature (e.g., epic poems, love songs, and medical treatises). Gradually satire ceased to be the concern only of poets, rhetoricians, and rhymists, and scholars began to take a casual interest in it. Parody in talmudic style was welcomed on those days when jesting was allowed, the days which "Jews ordained, and took upon them, and upon their seed, and upon all such as joined themselves unto them, so as it should not fail, that they would keep these two days according to the writing thereof, and according to the appointed time thereof, every year" (Esth. 9:27).

The father of parody in the style of the Talmud was Kalonymus b. Kalonymus, who was born in 1286 and lived in Italy from 1318, and who was one of the outstanding physicians of his time. Besides his profound knowledge of Torah and rabbinic literature, he mastered several languages and translated a selection of medical and philosophical books from Arabic into Latin at the request of the Italian King Robert, a lover of art and literature. His translations served as a bridge between the knowledge of East and West. His most famous work is *Massekhet Purim*, "Tractate Purim," written in the language and form of a talmudic tractate. Its four chapters contain a humorous debate regarding food, drink, and drunkenness on Purim. At the end of the tractate the author says that it was his intention "to gladden people on Purim and the reader will not lose but [will gain] like him who reads a book of medicine and of matters that benefit the body and do not harm the soul, because I, Kalonymus, invented this essay, the mishnah and the gemara and I call to witness R. Shakran ("Liar") and his brother R. Kazvan ("Deceiver"), who are mentioned at the end of the tractate." A literary masterpiece in style, presentation, and contents, *Massekhet Purim* serves as more than a mere jest, for much can be learned from it regarding the life, customs, and food, etc., of the 13th-century Italian Jews. Among the Purim customs which Kalonymus mentions are: horse riding in the streets of the town, waving pine branches, and dancing around a rag puppet which symbolized the figure of Haman. *Massekhet Purim* also specifies 24 Italian dishes, popular among the Jews, some of which are otherwise unknown. The 24 dishes represent the 24 "contributions to the priests" donated by the people at the time of the Temple in Jerusalem and the 24 books of the Bible.

Although other works by the same author met with no opposition, Kalonymus' *Massekhet Purim* was frowned upon by extremist rabbis who considered a parody in talmudic style to be a sacrilege. They banned reading the book and even condemned it to be burned. Samuel ben Abraham *Aboab, in his *Devar Shemu'el*, wrote: "He who reads that book called *Massekhet Purim* will be grieved for by all God-fearing people, who saw, and straight away were amazed, how the author dared print it and felt no remorse—hopefully the book will be put away and will become like something which has been lost, so that it shall not be seen and shall not be found, . . ." It therefore became rare and passed from hand to hand in manuscript. In the 19th century it was printed anonymously by various publishers, sometimes supplemented by other facetious Purim parodies of a later date. Jonah *Wilheimer, who published it in Vienna in 1871, relates in his preface that he copied it from an old manuscript found in a collection of books (including some formerly belonging to Jacob *Emden) which he bought from an Amsterdam bookseller. He writes: "I hereunder publish *Megillat Setarim* and *Massekhet Purim* without inquiring into who wrote these books or whose spirit collected them, but rather hailing this delightful treasure, because the author(s) have made a jest to cheer the readers with their sweet language in the style of the authors of the Talmud, and so as not to withhold what is good from its rightful owners, I publish them."

Massekhet Purim served as a blueprint for other imitations of talmudic tractates and also of liturgical literature in all its forms; prayers, *seliḥot*, lamentations for the Ninth of Av, and especially the Passover *Haggadah*. Steinschneider lists three Purim tractates in his list of 31 parodies and hundreds of other comic works, and Davidson mentions a further 21 in his list of 500 parodies in Hebrew and other languages (see bibliography). In a list of Hebrew manuscripts in Offenbach, Germany, a *Massekhet Purim* with Latin translation is mentioned, but it was apparently never printed. One *Massekhet Purim*, together with other Purim parodies collected from the large anonymous Purim literature, appeared in 1844, published by Solomon b. Ephraim Bloch, at the "Royal Court Press" in Hanover, where Jews had lived since the 13th century. A novel feature of this edition is its illustrations—one of a drunkard in the shade of trees in the innyard, and one of four people, including a woman, in festive fancy dress.

Most of the later editions of *Massekhet Purim* are followed by *Megillat Setarim,* which consists of three chapters. It begins in the style of *Pirkei Avot:*

> Ḥavakbuk received instruction (in drinking) from Karmi, who handed it down to Noah, and Noah to Lot and Lot to Joseph's brothers (apparently by virtue of the "cup" found in Benjamin's sack, Gen. 44:12), and Joseph's brothers to Nabal the Carmelite (who was "very drunken," I Sam. 25:36), and Nabal the Carmelite to Ben Hadad (king of Aram in Ahab's time, of whom it is said, who "was drinking himself drunk," I Kings 20:16), and Ben Hadad to Belshazzar (who "drank wine before the thousand," Dan 5:1), and Belshazzar to Ahasuerus (thanks to whose feast blessed with "royal wine in abundance" the festival of Purim came about), and Ahasuerus to Rabbi Bibi (according to Shab. 80b, a certain Rabbi Bibi "got drunk," as a result of which he became a central figure in *Megillat Setarim*).

The characters of *Ḥavakbuk ha-Navi* and Karmi figure in *Sefer Ḥavakbuk ha-Navi* which was appended to a number of editions of *Massekhet Purim,* beginning with the Venice edition of 1551. It is a parody in a pure and precise biblical style (of the books of the prophets) in praise of wine on Purim. The modification of the prophet's name from "Ḥavakkuk" to "Ḥavakbuk" ("he embraced the bottle") is the sort of humorous pun which recurs throughout the parody. All personal and place names are derived from the Bible, and with a change of meaning, are made to recall wine and everything connected with it:

> Karmi (a biblical first name, here meaning a vineyard); Boẓrah (the town Basra; here it alludes to the vintage); Be'eri (a biblical first name, here meaning a water well); Ha-Tiroshta (appelation of Nehemiah, "because he was allowed to drink the king's wine"; here the allusion is to *tirosh,* new wine); *kos* ("glass"); *enav* ("grape"); and *bakbuk* ("bottle"). In the parody, Karmi, king of Israel from Boẓrah and Be'eri contend for the kingship. The prophet Ḥavakbuk brings the word of God to the waverers between Karmi and Be'eri. Influenced by Ḥavakbuk's powerful words, the people forsake Be'eri and "return to Karmi with all their heart," after the prophecy was fulfilled that "at midnight God directed a very strong east wind and dried up the sea, the rivers and lakes and destroyed the canals and wells." The parody ends with a sentence based on Deuteronomy 34:10; "And there hath not arisen a prophet since in the house of Karmi, like unto Ḥavakbuk in all the signs and wonders, which he wrought in the sight of Israel."

Both *Megillat Setarim* and *Sefer Ḥavakbuk ha-Navi* were erroneously attributed to Kalonymus b. Kalonymus since they were appended to most editions of his *Massekhet Purim.* Other writers, Lavi ha-Levi (known also as Leon de Blautes (de Valentibus)) and Elijah Baḥur *Levita, were also credited with their authorship. Neubauer and Davidson, however, established that the actual author of these parodies was *Levi b. Gershom.

MASSEKHET ḤANUKKAH. Ḥanukkah, like Purim, is a festival of celebration and games, but very little entertaining literature has been written for it. What there is consists mainly of songs, riddles, and witticisms concerning food and drink, in particular various local Ḥanukkah dishes, all of which symbolize historical events connected with Ḥanukkah. Although the Scroll of Antiochus, which relates the Jewish victory in Hasmonean times and the miracle of Ḥanukkah, is an imitation of the style of the Book of Esther, it is in no way a parody. There are, however, three special Ḥanukkah "tractates," modeled on the *Massekhet Purim* and concentrating especially on the secular aspects of the festival—the food and entertainment. The first, the author of which is unknown, was found in manuscript in the collection of David *Franco-Mendes and published, with an introduction by A. Z. Ben-Yishai in *Aresheth,* 3 (1964), 173–92. It is written as a profound talmudic discussion on the essence of the festival, its joys, and its "laws." It details the quantity of the special Ḥanukkah delicacies a Jew must eat "until he is nauseated" or until "he breathes his last." There are actual descriptions of local color, for which no other source is extant, obviously written by a person who was observant of his environment. It tells of the pastimes current among the well-to-do, cultured Jews of that day, which goes far to explain the reprimands of the great rabbis of the 18th century, Jacob Emden, Moses Ḥagiz, and Ẓevi Hirsch Kaidonover among them, who in their writings admonished their contemporaries "who spend their days going to the theaters and circuses, in dancing, card-playing, and even hunting." Another Ḥanukkah tractate, by Joshua Calinari, appeared in Venice, and later in Salonika, while the third, by Jacob Segre, remained in manuscript.

PARODIES AGAINST CATHOLICS, APOSTATES, AND FALSE MESSIAHS. In the defensive war against incitement or coercion of Jews to convert (mainly on the part of the Catholics), and against the false messiah Shabbetai Ẓevi, satiric parodies came to be written which were circulated in manuscript for fear of the authorities, and which were preserved in various archives. Some of these parodies were printed only hundreds of years later, in countries enjoying a free press. One of the bitterest of those directed against the Catholics is *Pilpul al Zeman, Zemannim, Zemanneihem* by Jonah ha-Kohen Rafa, which was printed in London in 1908, some 226 years after the author's death, from a manuscript in the Montefiore collection. It is a derisive imitation of Jewish ritual style, in the manner of the Passover *Haggadah,* and of the *Avodah* (the Temple service of the Day of Atonement). The descriptions of the Christian *carnival, of gluttony and drunkenness, and of other gratifications of the flesh, point at the debauchery of the Catholic priests of those days, which was far removed from the holy and ascetic life preached by the Church. The author's sharp, unrestrained pen, and his insight into contemporary church and monastery life, highlight the suffering and distress of the Jewish community confronted with religious incitement or coercion.

A parody of a different kind is *Iggeret Al Tehi ka-Avotekha* ("Be not as your fathers"), written by Isaac Efodi (Profiat *Duran) in the 15th century to his friend Bonat Bongiorno, who had apostatized. Written in the mild language of the pastoral epistles of Christian preachers, Duran equivocally advises his friend "to remain in the

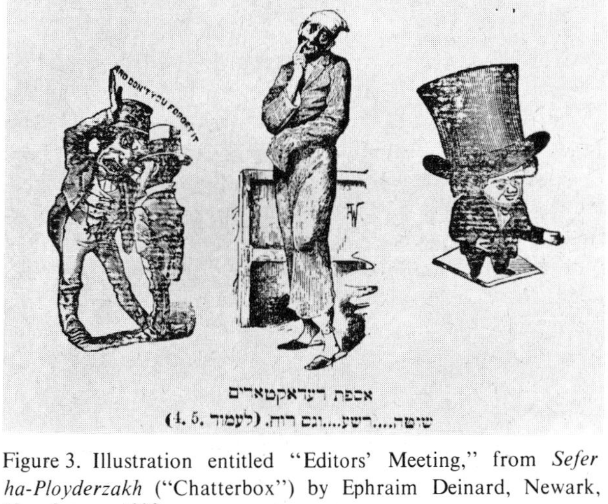

Figure 3. Illustration entitled "Editors' Meeting," from *Sefer ha-Ployderzakh* ("Chatterbox") by Ephraim Deinard, Newark, New Jersey, 1892.

Christian faith." By pretending to prove the mistakes of the Jews, as it were, he actually mocks Christianity and its preachers and, by inference, the apostates. The name of the parody and its flattering style misled many into thinking that this really was an epistle of the Church, until they came to the end and its conclusions.

The opposition to the false Messiah, Shabbetai Ẓevi, and to his movement in the 17th and 18th centuries, produced an extensive polemical literature in Hebrew, both in poetry and in prose. The Italian poets, Jacob and Emanuel Frances, published a book of satiric poems called *Ẓevi Mudaḥ*, directed at him. The parody *Haggadah le-Tishah be-Av* is also attributed to the two brothers. (The Ninth of Av was chosen for the recital of the *"Haggadah"* parody because Shabbetai Ẓevi "abolished" the fast on that day and turned it into a feast.) Two versions of this parody, preserved in manuscript, were published by A. M. Habermann, in *Kobez al Jad* 13, pt. 2 (1940), 185–206. Using the framework of the Passover *Haggadah*, including instructions for the various *seder* customs connecting the different sections, the author unleashes his sarcasm and contempt, curses and abuse upon the false messiah. For example, his version of *Dayyeinu* ("It would have been enough"):

> Had he made himself false Messiah
> And not abolished the fast of the Fourth,
> It would have been enough.
> Had he abolished the Fast of the Fourth and not abolished the fast of the Fifth,
> It would have been enough.
> Had he abolished the Fast of the Fifth and not
> turned it into a regular feast,
> It would have been enough.
> Had he turned it into a regular feast and not eaten
> and distributed forbidden fats,
> It would have been enough.
> Had he eaten and distributed forbidden fats and not
> desecrated the Sabbath,
> It would have been enough.
> Had he desecrated the Sabbath and not uttered the
> Ineffable Name,
> It would have been enough.
> Had he uttered the Ineffable Name and not permitted
> murder,
> It would have been enough.
> Had he permitted murder and not apostatized,
> It would have been enough.
> Had he apostatized and not desecrated the name of
> God in public, to the hazard of all the Jews of the
> Diaspora,
> It would have been enough.

The Early Haskalah. One of the fathers of Hebrew parody of the Haskalah was Judah Leib *Ben Ze'ev, one of the early *maskilim* and Hebrew philologists. His *Meliẓah le-Furim*, based on the prayers of the Day of Atonement, is a paeon of praise to wine and utter abandon. The uncurbed Purim joy, permitted according to the *halakhah*, served as a cover for the freedom of drinking and gluttony. At the same time the *Meliẓah* also utilized sacred prayers to convey profane ideas, without which no work by a *maskil* of that generation was complete. Parodies of a different kind are Ben Ze'ev's erotic poems, which were never published, but passed from hand to hand like secret pamphlets. One of the poems *Derekh Gever be-Almah* (a play on the word *almah*; the title can mean "The Way of a Certain Man" or "The Way of a Man with a Maiden") is a precise description of sexual intercourse, in a garbled combination of fractions of biblical verses. Through this erotic parody Ben Ze'ev wanted to prove that classical Hebrew could express not only holy and exalted ideas, but even intimate, earthy matters.

Not only the Bible and the Talmud served as a framework for amusing parodies at times of festivity, but the Zohar also was used. One of the parodies of the Zohar is *Zohar Ḥadash le-Furim*, whose author was the Polish writer Tobias *Feder. *Zohar Ḥadash* was published in *Oẓar ha-Sifrut*, 3 (1887–90). Even the names of chapters are borrowed from the Zohar. In a language comprehensible only to those familiar with the original, it deals with the festivity of Purim and the purpose of drinking, utilizing biblical verses in a display of homiletics and a pseudo-mysticism. Like the amusing names of the *tannaim* in Kalonymus' *Massekhet Purim*, in the *Zohar Ḥadash* there are also names alluding to Purim dishes and to inebriating drinks.

Another Hebrew philologist, Ẓevi Hirsch Sommerhausen, who lived in Holland and Belgium, was the author of one of the best Hebrew parodies which has retained its popularity, *Haggadah le-Leil Shikkorim*, a parody of the traditional Passover *Haggadah*. It is reminiscent of the classical wine-songs in the Hebrew poetry of Spain and in the poetry of the other peoples—the Greek Anacreon and the Persian Omar Khayyam. Sommerhausen's *Haggadah* begins with these Anacreonic rhymes:

> Drink and eat, eat and drink,
> Dissipate every heart-ache
> Eat and drink, drink and eat
> Till you don't know black from white.

At the end is a German poem by the author (in Hebrew letters) in praise of wine, even specifying particular types.

Another booklet of this period "including all the intoxication rules of Purim" is *Even Shetiyyah* (1861). The name originally refers to the foundation rock in the Temple, but may also be translated "drinking stone." The rules which the anonymous author gives include those "forbidding water on Purim":

> (a) it is forbidden to touch, carry, or look at a vessel which contains water or is used for water; (b) he who finds water in his house on Purim should cover it with earth, and he who has a well in his yard should invalidate it with three partitions; (c) laundrymen and all who work with water are forbidden to join the congregation on Purim; (d) it is forbidden to walk on the river bank on Purim; (e) it is forbidden to sail a boat on the river; (f) it is forbidden to drink wine mixed with water on Purim, even if it was mixed before the feast; (g) it is forbidden to walk outside in the rain; (h) it is forbidden to lick salt on Purim, and similar prohibitions.

Parodies Directed Against Ḥasidism and Extreme Orthodoxy. There was hardly a poet or author among the early *maskilim* who did not, on some occasion, attempt to write parody, principally as a weapon of derision against his "ideological" adversaries. In particular they mocked Ḥasidism, its customs, and its way of life. Joseph *Perl was a Ḥasid in his youth but, after his stay at the centers of the Haskalah, he became a fanatical adversary of Ḥasidism and a militant *maskil*. He wrote classical parodies directed against ḥasidic literature, in particular the *Shivḥei ha-Besht*, and the stories of *Naḥman of Bratslav. These allegorical stories, which are today considered gems of Hebrew literature were, at the time of their publication, derided by the linguistically pedantic *maskilim* for their confused language and strange contents. So successful were the parodies that they deceived many innocent Ḥasidim into thinking that they had really been written by ḥasidic authors. In *Megalleh Temirin* ("Revealer of Secrets," 1819), written in the form of 151 epistles which the "obscurantist" Jews were supposed to have exchanged, Perl gives a biased caricature of Ḥasidism in Volhynia and Galicia, and of the *ẓaddikim* whom he despised, and whom he describes as swindlers and avaricious men. It is written in a corrupt Hebrew, spiced with Yiddish idioms and Slavic expressions. His second book, *Boḥen Ẓaddik* (1838), also in the form of letters, is a continuation and explanation of the first. Another satirical work aimed at the Ḥasidim of Galicia is *Ha-Ẓofeh le-Veit Yisrael* (1858) by Isaac *Erter, written in biblical language and in the spirit of Haskalah.

Some of the parodies against Ḥasidism were written in Yiddish poetry and prose. A very popular parody in its time was *Tsvey Khasidimlekh* by N. Goldberg, modeled on *Heine's *Die Grenadiere.*

It tells of two Ḥasidim traveling to the *ẓaddik* Israel of Ruzhin to celebrate the feast of Sukkot and "to listen to his talk with the Divine Guests *(ushpizin).*" On the way, they hear of the rabbi's arrest and imprisonment together with others suspected of plotting rebellion. The dialogue between the two Ḥasidim is modeled directly on that of Heine's grenadiers, who return from Russian captivity, and while on their way hear of the defeat of Napoleon and his imprisonment. The two Ḥasidim are deeply shaken when they hear of the rabbi's arrest, and the more sentimental of them begs his friend (like Napoleon's grenadier) that if he die of chagrin, he be buried at the rabbi's town, Ruzhin, and covered with its earth. In one hand of the deceased, who is to wear a *tallit* and *tefillin,* they should place a *shofar* and in the other a bottle of brandy. When the rabbi is released and treads on the Ḥasid's tomb, the latter will arise, blow a prolonged blast, and drink to the health of the rabbi.

Another parody directed against Ḥasidism and popular in its time was *Dos Lid fun'm Kugil* (1863), on the model of *Schiller's poem *The Bell.* It was written by Abraham *Gottlober, a popular and prolific Hebrew and Yiddish author who published many such satiric works both in poetry and in prose, mainly against Ḥasidism, in the spirit of the Haskalah.

Sefer ha-Kundas (1824) is a witty parody in the style and form of the Shulḥan Arukh. The book is divided into paragraphs and the paragraphs into sections, which determine, in a style typical of the Shulḥan Arukh, how the true prankster must behave in order to justify his title. It is a satire on the severe way of life, which robbed young children of the joy of living by prematurely imposing ritualistic duties upon them. In many cases they rebelled against the severe restrictions by complete licentiousness. The author also wanted to prove how common this type of prankster was among the youth of good families in Vilna. There are differences of opinion as to the identity of the author of *Sefer ha-Kundas.* It is often ascribed to Aaron of Berdichev, whose exact identity is unknown, but according to Zinberg and others, it was Abraham Isaac, the son of Rabbi Ḥayyim Landa, a learned young man who was familiar with the teaching of the *maskilim.* Pressed by the hostile environment, Landa was compelled to divorce his wife. In order to avenge himself on his former father-in-law and on the leaders of the Vilna community, he wrote *Sefer ha-Kundas* relating "the prankster's deed, ruses and actions and his doings from the beginning of the year to its end." *Kundas* (perhaps related to the Polish word *kondys*—a farmer's dog, lacking manners) is a common appellation in the Yiddish of East European Jews for a mischievous, prankish boy, or a social outcast who uses vulgar and obscene language, affronting the dignitaries and appearing wherever there is a crowd. The dignitaries of Vilna considered *Sefer ha-Kundas* to be a dangerous pamphlet, and banned it soon after its publication, burning all available copies so that it should not be circulated. Only individual copies survived, one of which was published 88 years later by the student of Jewish folklore David *Maggid in 1913, with an introduction by the publisher about the parody and its author.

In recent generations, remote from the controversies of the Haskalah, evaluation of the works written in the heat of the polemics of that time have changed, and literary critics now regard *Sefer ha-Kundas* as a "gay sunbeam peeping through the dark clouds of seriousness" of the Haskalah period (see S. Niger, *Bleter far Geshikhte fun der Yidisher Literatur,* 1954). According to this view, this was the first book in the Hebrew literature of the 19th century, which was amusing for its own sake and without any polemical or didactic aim. This seems also to have been the view of Ḥ. N. *Bialik, who, in writing a children's poem describing a merry, mischievous boy, admitted to having been influenced by the 19th-century *Sefer ha-Kundas.*

Isaac Dov *Levinsohn was one of the early Russian *maskilim.* He was the author of several parodies, including *Divrei Ẓaddikim,* similar to Joseph Perl's *Megalleh Temirin,* concerning *ẓaddikim* and Ḥasidim, and *Oto ve-et Beno,* a tractate in talmudic style, protesting against unfair trade practices, etc. Judah Leib *Gordon, the greatest Hebrew poet of the late Haskalah, who successfully tried his hand at all literary forms, also attempted parody, especially in his *Shirim le-Et Meẓo.* It includes *maqāmāt,* epigrams, and a long and witty parodic poem in Aramaic called *Be-Niggun Akdamot.* Gordon derides the conduct of the provincial Jewish tradesmen in the 1800s who came on business to St. Petersburg, where no one knew them "with the aim of making great profits and stuffing their bellies with delicious food and other delights." With all his reservation toward Yiddish, Gordon tried his hand at writing poems in that language collected in a volume with the Hebrew title of *Siḥat Ḥullin.* The majority of the poems are humorous imitations of naive folktales, which may be considered parodies. One of them, *Eliyahu ha-Navi min ha-Nahar Ridevka* ("The Prophet Elijah of the river Ridevka"), is the story of a pretty shopkeeper, the wife of a yeshivah student, who suddenly becomes rich thanks to "the prophet Elijah" who enters through the window while her good-for-nothing husband studies Torah at the *bet ha-midrash* until late at night. The "Elijah" is a gentile lover who is a public official and who bestows many presents upon the pretty shopkeeper in return for her favors. This is a parody on those Jewish folktales which attribute any obscure success in the life of the individual to miraculous events and to the "appearance of Elijah." The Haskalah orientation of this parody and of similar poems is obvious.

The jesters *(*badḥanim),* whose job it was to entertain the bride and bridegroom on their wedding day, composed many entertaining parodies in Yiddish, interspersed with Hebrew words and phrases. Most have been forgotten, while some have been preserved in Jewish folklore, though the sources which inspired the jesters are not always identifiable.

Modern Times. Parody as a Socialist Weapon. With the development of political movements in the late 19th and early 20th centuries, the war against religious Orthodoxy and the "obscurantists" slackened and new battles broke out in Jewish society on nationalistic and socialistic issues. The *maskilim* began to employ satirical parody as a weapon against unfair trade, widespread ignorance, and the miserable social position of religious personnel, particularly of teachers and yeshivah students. Themes from the life of Jewish society which did not receive adequate treatment in journalism or in serious literature were reflected gaily in an exaggerated and biased light in satire. These satires were modeled on the common liturgy which was well known to all Jews in those days, and were thus intelligible even to people not used to reading belles lettres for their own sake. Not only "professional" authors but also adroit dabblers in writing engaged in such parody. Many of the writers are anonymous and it is almost impossible to identify them, despite the effort of literary scholars to decipher and identify some of their pen names. But even as anonymous amateurs these writers make a substantial contribution to the knowledge of Jewish social life in various periods; these descriptions cannot be ignored in the study of all classes of Jewish life, at differing times and in diverse countries. The language of this "unofficial" literature also contributed in its own way to the development and crystallization of modern Hebrew.

Massekhet Aniyyut ("A Tractate on Poverty," 1878), by Isaac Meir Dick, considered the "father of the Yiddish folktale," is one of the most successful parodies in Hebrew literature. It severely critizes the poor social and economic conditions of Lithuanian Jews at that time. It also contains autobiographical elements: in those years the school where Dick taught was closed down, and a state school was opened in its stead to which Dick could not adjust, and he thus remained jobless. Sachs published the parody unknown to its author and it made a great impression, reflecting as it did the reality of Jewish society at the time.

The parody *Kiẓẓur Shulḥan Arukh li-Melammedim u-le-Morim* by Joseph *Brill of Minsk, whose pen name was Iyov, printed in *Oẓar ha-Sifrut,* 3 (1889), also belongs to the class of "socialistic" parodies. An outstanding parodist, he described in a lively, biting, and comical fashion the miserable position in Jewish society of "the educators of the generation"—the *melammedim* of the old system and the teachers of the new.

Even with the change in the contents and purpose of parodies, traditional books of worship, such as the festival prayers and in particular the Passover *Haggadah,* continued to serve as a model for topical parodies. The authors directed their satire against local affairs, such as profiteering, exploitation of the poor, cultural emptiness, excessive materialism, and similar negative phenomena. When the aim of the parody was to protest against the decrees and restrictions of unjust authorities, the disguise of stories and prayers was used in order to circumvent censorship. The *Mah Nishtanah* questions of the *Haggadah* and the recurring answer "We were the slaves of . . ." would be given new topical contents each year. The same was done to the chorus of the song *Ḥad Gadya.* In addition to parodies on traditional liturgical literature, parodies on popular contemporary works, Jewish and gentile, eventually came to be written.

The following parodies are of a salient socialistic orientation: *Seder Haggadah li-Melammedim* (1882), with a commentary by Levi Reuben Zimlin, a teacher in Odessa, imitates the Passover *Haggadah* "imbued with moral lessons for *melammedim* and for landlords who inspire them with awe for a loaf of bread that does not satiate." The book contains recommendations by Gottlober, Lilienblum, and others. *Seder Haggadah le-Ḥoveshei Beit ha-Midrash* ("Haggadah of Bet Midrash Students," 1899), by Elijah Ḥayyim Zayantshik, describes the miserable state of students ("he will divide the food he eats into two shares, so that one remains for the morrow, because a miracle does not occur every day, and the second share is the **afikoman,* because after that there is nothing to eat or drink but water"), and bitterly criticizes the treasurers, supervisors, and landlords who neglect the students. *Massekhet Soḥarim* ("Traders' Tractate," 1900) by Abraham Shelomo Melamed (1862–1951), a Hebrew teacher in Feodosia, in the Crimean Peninsula, is a parody in the style of the Mishnah and Gemara and a bitter satire on the various tradesmen ("wheat tradesmen, wood tradesmen, contractors and shopkeepers") who engaged in unfair trade, profiteering, international bankruptcy, and arson in order to collect the insurance money. *Massekhet Shetarot* ("Bills' Tractate," 1894) by "La-Saifa ve-la-Safra" (pen name of Abraham Abba Rokovsky, born in Poland, who translated many books from various languages into Hebrew, including *Alroy* by Disraeli), is also a parody in talmudic style "depicting the world of trade, its customs, stratagems and wicked impulses" (from the publisher's introduction to the book).

Hebrew Parody in the U.S. At the time of the large-scale immigration to U.S. from Russia and other East European countries during the late 19th century, the newcomers were able to give vent to their feelings through parody. They had immigrated to the new country to seek their fortune and discovered only chaos in Jewish life. Far from the old *bet ha-midrash* tradition, many of the Jews in the U.S. had largely abandoned Jewish tradition, and satire was a convenient genre for adroit writers to express their anger and bitterness at this development. Abraham Kotlier, born near Kovno, immigrated to the United States in 1880 and lived in Cleveland as a bookseller for over 50 years, before moving in his old age to Ereẓ Israel. His first parody, *Massekhet Derekh Ereẓ ha-Ḥadashah* ("Tractate on the Way of Life of the New Country"), was a devastating attack on Jewish immigrants living in the U.S., their faults and vices, and on the Jewish administrators and "Reform" leaders who corrupted Jewish life. It was first published serially in the Yiddish weekly *Folks Fraynd,* and later on its own in St. Petersburg (1893). It also appeared in Warsaw in 1898 together with *Maḥzor Katan—Hagaddah le-Fesaḥ,* a volume of *piyyutim* and a *Haggadah* "according to the American custom." A third edition was published in Tel Aviv in 1927.

Gershon *Rosenzweig, born in Russian Poland, was a teacher who went to the U.S. in 1888. He contributed to the Hebrew and Yiddish press, specializing mainly in parodies and aphorisms. He also edited and published some of the Hebrew periodicals: *Ha-Ivri* (1892–1902), *Kadimah* (1899), and *Ha-Devorah* (1912). In a series of "tractates" first published in *Ha-Ivri* and then in the collection *Talmud Yanka'i,* Rosenzweig satirizes U.S. Jewish life. According to Rosenzweig, Columbus refused to have the country he discovered called after him and it was therefore called "America," deriving from the Aramaic *Amma-Reika* ("an empty people"). There is hardly an aspect of Jewish life in America that Rosenzweig does not touch upon. He pours out his protest against the low standards of education, the neglect of the younger generation, and the Reform rabbis. He attacks the fact that most synagogues are mortgaged, that ignorance among Jews was becoming even more widespread; he criticizes the prevalence of card games, and touches also on the inferior state of Jewish writers, and the mediocre Yiddish press which fed its readers on cheap sensations and trash." In *Massekhet Okẓin* ("Tractate Sarcasm") Rosenzweig treats the subject of plagiarisms which were then very common. In yet another tractate, *Massekhet Maḥaloket mi-Talmud Ẓivoni* ("Tractate Discord, from the Colored Talmud"), Rosenzweig discusses the quarrels between Portuguese Jews and German Jews in Philadelphia.

During the period of "prohibition" in the United States Gershon Kiss published *Massekhet Prohibishon* (1929), in which he depicted humorously, in talmudic style, the many and diverse maneuvers carried out in order to circumvent the laws of prohibition, as well as all the mishaps occurring due to the consumption of noxious drinks. Here is an excerpt from one of the chapters:

> Mishnah. How does one hide the drinks? One hides them in the walls and under the floor, in pits, ditches and caves, in toilets, bathrooms, and any place out of reach of the city guardians. Gemara. The rabbis have taught: The pious men of olden days used to hide the drinks in the walls and under the floor and in pits, bushes, and caves, but pious men of recent times have decided once and for all that there is no hope of storing them, so they immediately store them in their stomachs.

Ephraim *Deinard, born in Russian Latvia, was a scholar,

traveler, and bookseller who lived in the U.S. for many years. He published several satires in parodic form, including one called *Sefer ha-Kundas* ("The Book of the Prankster," 1900), and *Sefer ha-Ployderzakh* ("The Chatterbox"), a caricature of contemporary Jewish newspapers in America. The title page describes it as "a general gazette for everyone, and the attentive reader will merit life in this world, and I am positive he will not have to read any other gazette."

Hebrew Parody in Communist Russia. During the early years in post-1917 Russia, when Judaism, the Zionist movement, and Hebrew culture generally were the subjects of persecution, many bitter satirical parodies were written attacking the oppressive regime and its supporters. In particular, the "Yevsektsia," the department of the Communist Party responsible for the liquidation of Jewish communities and institutions and the suppression of the various Jewish parties, and especially the Zionist ones, came under protest. As these parodies could not appear in print they passed from hand to hand as "underground literature." They were modeled on well-known prayers and folksongs in Hebrew, Yiddish, and Russian. One of the most successful parodies on the Bolshevik regime was *Massekhet Admonim min-Talmud Bolshevi* ("Tractate of the Reds from the Bolshevik Talmud") signed by Avshalom Bar-Deroma, the pen name of A. S. Melamed (see above). It was brought out of Russia by the author in the early 1920s, and was published in Tel Aviv in 1923.

Parody in Modern Ereẓ Israel. Jewish settlement in Ereẓ Israel from the second half of the 19th century onward, gave rise to many varied social conflicts which were reflected in mostly verbal satire, such as new words sung to old and familiar tunes. During the period of Turkish rule hardly any satires had been written due to the despotism of the regime. Those which were circulated, treated only of internal affairs of the Jewish *yishuv*. One of the major conflicts within the *yishuv* before World War I was the struggle for the place of Hebrew as the language of the people. When the Hilfsverein founded the Technion in Haifa, it declared its intention of having German as the language of instruction. The protagonists of Hebrew carried their struggle to the press and published, among other items, a parody in talmudic style, *Massekhet Bava Tekhnikah* (1910), by Kadish Yehudah Leib *Silman. Silman was a teacher and journalist, born in Russia, who wrote and edited textbooks, and published various humorous works. Another "internal" parody, an anonymous satire against the plague of anniversary celebrations prevalent in the *yishuv* among the communal workers and writers of the time, was called *Ha-Yabbelet* ("The Ulcer," 1914).

Under the semi-democratic rule of the British Mandate in Ereẓ Israel between 1918 and 1948, there was a greater degree of freedom of criticism, and political satire against the regime was allowed to develop. During the 29 years of the Mandate many humorous and satirical papers appeared, most of them of one issue only, usually for holidays and festivals, especially Purim. A political parody which had a great impact was *Haggadah shel ha-Bayit ha-Le'ummi* ("*Haggadah* of the National Home") by "Afarkeset," a regular columnist in the daily *Haaretz*. It appeared for Passover 1930, when a British commission was visiting the country to investigate the bloody riots of the Arabs a year earlier and the slaughter of the Jews of Hebron and other towns. It begins with *Mah Nishtannah:*

> How does the present rule [the British] differ from the former [Turkish] rule? Under the former regime we settled to the west of the Jordan as well as to its east, while this regime has completely closed the land of Gad and of Reuben to us. Under the former regime we bought lands and received *kushans* [sales certificates], while this regime hinders the buying of new lands and invalidates old *kushans*. Under the former regime there were no riots, while under this one they have occurred four times. Under the former regime we were residents enjoying the protection of consuls, while under this regime we are all citizens and we lack protection and defense.

The following chant appears in the same parody, based on the *Dayyeinu* of the Passover *Haggadah:*

> What a long line of kindnesses has John Bull bestowed on us: Had he given us the Balfour Declaration and not appended a second part that contradicts the first—it would have been enough. Had he appended a second part that contradicts the first and not given us an alien police force—it would have been enough. Had he given us an alien police force and not ignored Arab incitement—it would have been enough. Had he ignored Arab incitement and not distributed high positions to the inciters—it would have been enough. Had he distributed high positions to the inciters and not negotiated with them regarding the future of the country—it would have been enough. Had he negotiated with the inciters and not sent us a commission to investigate sabotage—it would have been enough. Had he sent us a commission to investigate sabotage and it had not interviewed various land specialists—it would have been enough. Had it interviewed various land specialists and not drawn conclusions and not closed the country to Jewish immigration—it would have been more than enough.

Under the British Mandate theatrical troupes were also established, a large part of whose program consisted in satires against the regime, only some of which have appeared in print. The unique life during the Mandate and the contrasts between the three elements in the population—Jews, Arabs, and British—is reflected to some extent in *Palestine Parodies* (Eng., 1930). Tel Aviv, the largest town in Ereẓ Israel, became the subject of a special parodic *Haggadah* on its 25th anniversary. Its author did not spare the eminent status of "the first Hebrew town," and severely criticized the leaders of the town for their many words and few actions. The citizens, too, came under fire for their lack of social etiquette, and the confusion of foreign languages rivalling Hebrew. Nor was the British regime spared.

The life of the State of Israel, its new parliament, austerity at home, and international adventures all gave rise to an improvised satirical literature, much of it concentrated in the Friday and holiday supplements of the daily press. It featured too in the entertainment programs of the radio. The Talmud, which was studied in the secondary schools as well as in the many yeshivot, continued to be a popular model on which to build parodies. In *Massekhet Yamim Tovim* ("Tractate of Holidays," 1959), M. Y. Bar-On, a journalist and translator, wittily criticized the faults of the state and of the different strata of its society, alluding to various public scandals.

Parodies of Writers on Writers. Hebrew parody through the ages was mostly of the sort which used easily recognizable literary forms as a vehicle for social, religious, or political themes. Such were, of course, the works of Kalonymus b. Kalonymus, Ben Ze'ev, Sommerhausen, and the extensive Purim literature, all intended mainly for entertainment. However, there were also examples of the type of parody designed to deride the very work or literary form which it emulates. Among these were the writings of Joseph Perl against the early books of Ḥasidism, mocking not only the ḥasidic movement but also its literature, with its entangled style, faulty syntax, and confused presentation. This was the start of parodies of "writers on writers." Some of the work of Joseph Brill (see above) also belongs to this category.

Brill's *"Midrash Soferim"* ("Midrash of Writers," in: *Ha-Shaḥar*, 10; 1880–81) is a witty satire directed against

הגדה של הבית הלאומי
בפסח תר״ץ
ערוכה ומסודרת בידי אזרח וגר
יוצר הבית הלאומי בגן־העדן
זאב נבון
הרצל (לבלפור, שהגיע זה עכשיו לגן־העדן): שלום עליך, רבי בלפור.
משום מה נחפזת כל־כך להסתלק מן העולם? ומה שלום הכרזת־בלפור?
בלפור (כשפניו מביעים עצבות): מתוך הפירוש החדש על הכרזת־
בלפור שהכינה ועדת־החקירה, ראיתי והנה עוד מעט ולא ישאר מהכרזתי כלום.
אמרתי: במקום שישאר בלפור בלי הכרזה, מוטב שתשאר ההכרזה בלי בלפור...
הוצאת „ים המלח" (בעריכת אפרכסת)
תל־אביב
פסח תר״ץ

Figure 4. Title page of *Haggadah shel ha-Bayit ha-Le'ummi* ("*Haggadah* of the National Home"), a parody aimed at British rule in Palestine. The illustration by Zeev Navon shows Herzl interviewing Lord Balfour in paradise. Tel Aviv, 1930.

various literary types. Of contemporary newspaper editors he writes: "There are three who eat and do not labor—a son-in-law supported by his father-in-law, a soldier on guard and a boorish editor." He lashes out at "the scholars and historians who peck like hens, and who prefer one grain of barley on the mound of an ancient hill, already rotten and mouldy, to all the precious stones and jewels glittering in the valley of the present."

Well-known Hebrew authors and poets of the 20th century, among them Frischmann, Bialik, Tchernichowsky, Shneour, Berkowitz, Shlonsky, and Hameiri, occasionally wrote parodies on other writers and on literary works, some of them simply for amusement and entertainment, others for genuine criticism. They appeared mostly under pen names, scattered in newspapers, appearing for festivals, especially Purim, in Russia, Poland, the U.S., and Israel. The Hebrew stage, which became firmly established towards the middle of the 20th century, and especially the smaller, entertainment theaters, produced many topical satires which however, seldom appeared in print. Some well-known Yiddish authors also wrote occasional parodies mostly anonymously or under a pen name. Joseph *Tunkel was a prominent Yiddish humorist and parodist. A regular columnist of Yiddish papers in Poland, he published special collections of parodies, including *Mitn Kop Arop* (1931), *Di Royte Hagode* (1917), *Di Bolshevistishe Hagode* (1918), and some on writers and on literature: *Der Krumer Shpigl* (1911), and *Kataves* (1923). Small theatrical troupes in Yiddish, in countries where Yiddish was spoken and Yiddish newspapers appeared, also owed much of their popularity to topical parodies.

Bibliography: I. Davidson, *Parody in Jewish Literature* (1907), incl. list of 500 parodies; J. Chotzner, *Humour and Irony of the Bible* (1883); idem, *Hebrew Satire* (1911); N. S. Leibowitz, *Ha-Shome'a Yizḥak; Mivḥar ha-Ḥiddud ve-ha-Hittul* (1907); M. Steinschneider, *Gesammelte Schriften*, 1 (1925), 196–214; idem, in: MGWJ, 46 (1902); 47 (1903); 48 (1904); Zinberg, Sifrut, passim; Waxman, Literature, 2 (1960), 603ff., and passim; W. Jerrold and R. M. Leonard (eds.), *Century of Parody and Imitation* (1963); J. Kabakoff, *Ḥalutzei ha-Sifrut ha-Ivrit ba-Amerikah* (1967), 211–66.

[A.Z.B.-Y.]

°**PARROT, ANDRÉ** (1901–), French archaeologist. He directed the French excavations at Tello and Larsa in Iraq from 1931 to 1933 and at *Mari in Syria (1933–64). He was curator in chief of the French national museums from 1946 and professor at the Ecole du Louvre and the Protestant Theology Faculty of Paris (both institutions from 1936). His contributions in the field of Near Eastern archaeology are highlighted by his excavations of the palace of Mari. His recovery of more than 20,000 tablets of the Mari royal archives, composed mainly during the reign of Zimrilim (18th century B.C.E.), immeasurably increased the historical understanding of Western Asia, especially as regards the Patriarchial Age.

His contributions on Mari include: *Une Bille Perdue* (1945); an assortment of studies appearing in *Syria*, a French quarterly on Oriental art and archaeology, and the series *Archives Royales de Mari* (vols. 1–9, 1950–60), and *Mission archéologique de Mari* (3 vols., 1956–67), all scholarly publications which he has helped edit. He wrote voluminously on ancient Near Eastern history, literature, architecture, philology, and similar subjects. Many of his semipopular works, marked by clarity, humor, and enthusiasm, are concerned with the problems of the biblical past and its oriental background.

[Z.G.]

PARTISANS. Jewish partisans composed part of the resistance movement and the guerrilla war in Europe against Nazi Germany during World War II. The first nuclei of partisans were composed of individuals or groups that were forced to flee from the Nazis and their collaborators; soldiers who were thrown into areas that were occupied by the enemy; and prisoners of war who escaped from camps. Their natural bases were the forests and swamps of eastern *Poland, Lithuania, Belorussia, and the Ukraine, the mountainous areas of the Alps, *Yugoslavia, Slovakia, and *Greece. While the partisan movement as a whole became a substantial force in the military and political battles of World War II the motivations, organizational forms, and development of the Jewish partisan movement was basically different. Unlike the non-Jews in occupied areas, the Jews were condemned by the Nazis to total extermination. As a result of this situation, two unique aspects of the movement stand out: Jews joined the partisan struggle as a path of revenge on the murderous enemy; they also wished to combine partisan fighting with attempts to save themselves and other Jews.

Jews participated in the partisan movement throughout occupied Europe—from Briansk in the east of the U.S.S.R. to *France, Italy, Yugoslavia, and Greece. It is impossible to arrive at exact numbers of Jews in partisan units, but it is possible to conjecture that tens of thousands of Jews fought in the partisan struggle as a whole. The number of Jews who actually fought, however, was only a tiny proportion of the European Jews who wished to participate in and had access

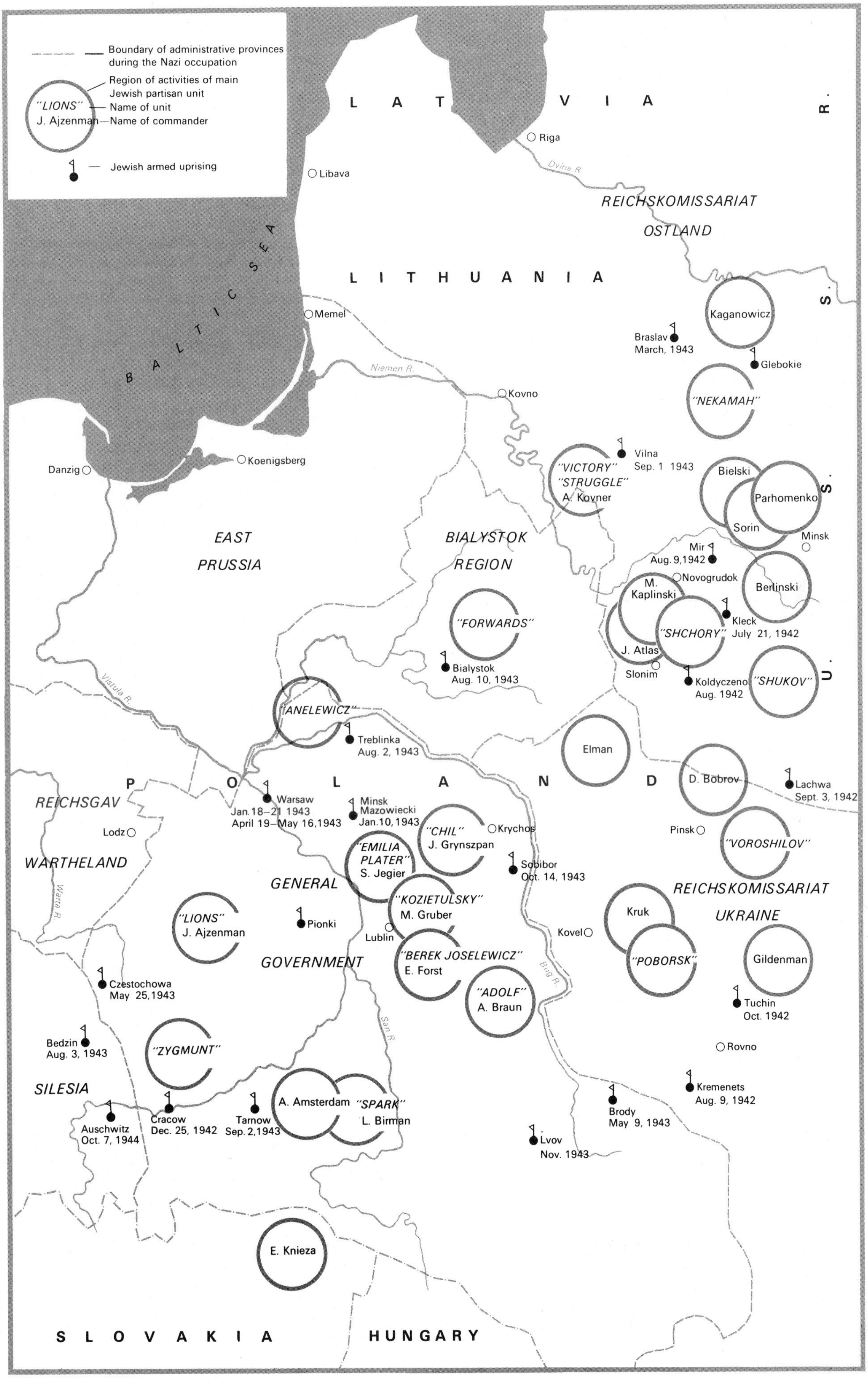
Boundary of administrative provinces during the Nazi occupation
Region of activities of main Jewish partisan unit
"LIONS" — Name of unit
J. Ajzenman — Name of commander
Jewish armed uprising
L A T V I A
R. S. S. U.
Riga
Dvina R.
Libava
REICHSKOMISSARIAT OSTLAND
BALTIC SEA
LITHUANIA
Memel
Kaganowicz
Braslav March, 1943
Glebokie
Niemen R.
Kovno
"NEKAMAH"
Vilna Sep. 1 1943
"VICTORY" "STRUGGLE" A. Kovner
Bielski
Parhomenko
Sorin
Minsk
Danzig
Koenigsberg
EAST PRUSSIA
BIALYSTOK REGION
Mir Aug. 9,1942
Novogrudok
M. Kaplinski
Berlinski
"FORWARDS"
Kleck July 21, 1942
"SHCHORY"
J. Atlas
Slonim
Bialystok Aug. 10, 1943
Koldyczeno Aug. 1942
"SHUKOV"
Vistula R.
"ANELEWICZ"
Treblinka Aug. 2, 1943
Elman
D. Bobrov
Lachwa Sept. 3, 1942
P O L A N D
REICHSGAV WARTHELAND
Warsaw Jan. 18–21 1943 April 19–May 16,1943
Minsk Mazowiecki Jan.10,1943
Lodz
"CHIL" J. Grynszpan
Krychos
Pinsk
"VOROSHILOV"
"EMILIA PLATER" S. Jegier
Sobibor Oct. 14, 1943
GENERAL GOVERNMENT
REICHSKOMISSARIAT UKRAINE
Warta R.
"KOZIETULSKY" M. Gruber
Kruk
"LIONS" J. Ajzenman
Pionki
Lublin
Kovel
"BEREK JOSELEWICZ" E. Forst
"POBORSK"
Gildenman
Bug R.
Czestochowa May 25,1943
"ADOLF" A. Braun
Tuchin Oct. 1942
San R.
Bedzin Aug. 3, 1943
"ZYGMUNT"
Rovno
SILESIA
Kremenets Aug. 9, 1942
A. Amsterdam
"SPARK" L. Birman
Brody May 9, 1943
Auschwitz Oct. 7, 1944
Cracow Dec. 25, 1942
Tarnow Sep. 2,1943
Lvov Nov. 1943
E. Knieza
S L O V A K I A
HUNGARY

Major Jewish partisan units and armed uprisings, 1941–44.

Figure 1. Jewish partisan unit commanded by Captain Grynszpan, Poland. Courtesy Yad Vashem Archives, Jerusalem.

to the partisans, but were prevented from doing so for a number of reasons. One should distinguish between subjective obstacles to their participation, which resulted from the nature of the condition of Jewish life in Eastern Europe, and obstructions that resulted from their objective situation and attitude of the non-Jewish environment.

The Jews were a classically urban element. Existence in dense forest, in the wilds of nature, was alien and frightening to them. In addition, the traditionally strong family ties that held them together also held them back from leaving their homes. The youth, who were the prime candidates for escape into the forests, were sometimes the only source of support of the family under conditions of a bitter struggle for physical survival and uncertainty about the future. Moreover, the consolidation of Jews or other groups in the forests was conditional upon a priori factors. A central condition for the establishment of any partisan force was contacts with the inhabitants of the surrounding area. The partisans were in need of safe places of refuge in the event of emergency, loyal sources of intelligence, and the supply of food, horses, etc. All these things could be obtained from villagers who lived near the partisan camps. The villagers would provide the necessary services either out of fear or because they believed that cooperation would be to their benefit in the future. However, the Polish, Lithuanian, Belorussian, and Ukrainian countryside was hostile toward the Jews. The villagers, with the exception of those few who remained loyal to Jews under the most difficult conditions, not only refused to aid the Jews in establishing themselves in the forests, but often turned escaped Jews over to the Germans or murdered Jews who managed to reach the forests and looted their property.

The chances of being accepted into a partisan unit were conditional upon physical strength, military experience, and the possession of arms. The sources of arms were those left by retreating armies and passed into the hands of the movements through the underground or they were private property. Such arms were not given to Jews, who were thus forced to acquire weapons from the enemy by illegal purchase, robbery, or acquisition in battle. By these means, it was possible to acquire only the most minimal store of weapons.

The partisan movement itself was not free of anti-Semitism. The extreme right-wing factions of the Polish underground viewed the Jews as "bandits" prowling around the forests. They took arms away from the Jews and even murdered many of them. The leftist groups took a less hostile stand toward the Jews. In Lithuania, Belorussia, and the Ukraine, anti-Semitism was somewhat restrained after permanent contact had been established between the partisan areas and the Soviet high command; but the Soviet command did not approve of the existence of separate Jewish partisan units and obligated the Jews to integrate into the multinational partisan frameworks.

The very act of leaving the ghetto for the forests was bound up with many obstacles and difficulties. The Jewish population in central Poland was far from the areas of dense forest. The attempts by the Jewish Fighting Organization in *Warsaw, *Częstochowa, and Zagłębie to establish contact with Polish underground organizations and smuggle groups of Jewish fighters into the forests most often ended in failure; the fighters were captured or murdered before they could reach their destination or early in their stay in the forest. In the large ghettos in Warsaw, *Vilna, and *Bialystok, a sharp dispute took place among the members of the Jewish Fighting Organization over which path to choose: resistance inside the ghetto or escape to the forests and carrying on the struggle within the ranks of the partisan movement. In Warsaw it was finally decided to concentrate all forces for resistance within the ghetto; in Vilna and Bialystok a two-pronged method was arrived at, i.e., after the uprising in the ghetto the surviving fighters turned to the forests.

The most important obstacle that prevented the mass escape of the Jews to the forests was a chronological factor. The expansion and strengthening of the partisan movement began only during 1943. By then most of the Jews in Europe had already been deported to or exterminated in the Nazi death camps. Although the Jews had in many cases been the first who paved the way in the forests, these pioneer partisans had only limited chances of absorbing large groups of people and maintaining their existence for a longer period.

In Western Europe the obstacles were of a different nature, for there the Germans succeeded in deceiving the Jews by well thought-out devices. The resistance movement mostly took the form of an urban underground, which was not to the benefit of the Jews.

However, despite all the obstacles and stumbling blocks, tens of thousands of Jews reached the ranks of the partisan movement. Many Jews fought as individuals (sometimes hiding their Jewish identity) in mixed partisan units, while others belonged to separate Jewish units or groups of Jews united in larger partisan frameworks. Many Jewish partisans rose to commanding ranks and were among the parachutists sent by the Soviet High Command to organize and command partisan camps in large areas. A number received medals for their leadership, and their names and feats of heroism became legendary.

Among the Jewish groups were some that had organized earlier in the Jewish Fighters' Organizations in the ghettos (the *Fareinkte Partizaner Organizatsie* [F.P.O.] in Vilna, the organizations in Bialystok, the remnants of the Jewish

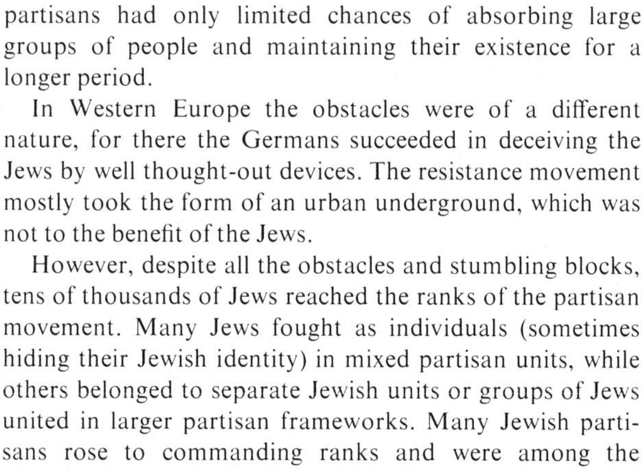

Figure 2. Jewish partisan group, operating in the vicinity of Vilna, commanded by Abba Kovner (standing, center). Courtesy Yad Vashem Archives, Jerusalem.

Figure 3. Misha Gildenman, known as "Uncle Misha," commander of a Jewish partisan unit in Volhynia, Russia. Courtesy Yad Vashem Archives, Jerusalem.

Fighting Organization after the Warsaw ghetto uprising). They were equipped and trained during their stay in the ghetto, and their later struggle in the forests was but a logical continuation of the path they had chosen. There were also groups and camps of Jews, mostly from small townlets, who had escaped in whole families or individually during the deportations or from a camp. Together with the youth who were engaged in actual fighting were Jewish family camps in the forests. These camps absorbed women and children, the aged and sick, and a small number of fighters who protected them and provided for their indispensable needs. Most of the time these family camps existed under the aegis of fighting Jewish units or large partisan battalions whose commanders demonstrated a humane attitude and sensitivity toward Jews.

Many Jewish fighters tried to combine their war against the enemy with extending aid to the surviving Jews who were still hiding in the ghettos and in taking revenge against people who were known to have murdered Jews or turned them over to the Nazis. In many cases, Jewish units that established themselves in the forests became the focal point for uniting prisoners of war and members of other nationalities and constituted the beginning of a powerful partisan center. There were about 15,000–20,000 Jewish partisans in the area under the control of the Soviet command. A large partisan concentration existed in the forests of Rudnik around Vilna. Groups of fighters from the F.P.O. reached this area in September 1943 and formed the fighting Jewish Brigade, which consisted of four battalions, under the command of Abba *Kovner. Earlier, a group of fighters under the command of Josef Glazman, had left the ghetto and merged with an existing Jewish group to form the fighting group Nekamah ("Revenge") in the forests of Navocz. The commander of the unit, which was later disbanded, was B. Boyarski. Members of the *Kovno ghetto underground also reached the forests of Rudnik. These partisans crystallized into a Jewish bloc in the "Lithuanian Brigade," which consisted mostly of Jews.

During 1943 those in the forests surrounding Bialystok were practically all Jews. A group of young women active in the underground in the city helped to supply them. Surrounding *Slonim in the forests of Lipiczansk were a number of Jewish units and Jewish family camps. The most famous of these units was that under the command of Jehezkiel *Atlas, who cooperated with the Pobeda ("Victory") unit. Atlas' company gained much experience in battle. In the forests of Lipiczansk, an area of western Belorussia, the group under the command of Hirsch Kaplinski, which numbered more than 100 people—most of them from the town of *Zhetil (*Dyatlovo)—was also active. In central Belorussia, in the forest area of Naliwki, was a large camp of Jewish fighters. In the autumn of 1943 its membership reached more than 1,000, some of whom were fighters and the rest members of the family camp. This camp functioned under the leadership of the Bielski brothers and was composed of simple people from the tiny townlets in the area. Later on, the camp was divided into a fighting company named after *Ordzhonikidze and a family camp named after Kalinin.

In the swamplands of Polesie, Jews were active in general units and separate Jewish ones. The Jewish units were formed by the escapees from the townlets. In a small townlet in the center of Polesie, *Lachva, about 600 Jews revolted and fled in the direction of the forests. Only about 120 of the youth succeeded in reaching the forests with one rifle and one revolver among them. In Volhynia, Jews were among the first fighters in the forests. The emissary Konishtschook who arrived from the Minsk area to organize partisan action in Volhynia, united Jewish youth from the neigboring townlet. The most daring military offensives were those of the unit commanded by M. Gildenman, which was a branch of Suborov's forces.

An important chapter in the annals of the partisan movement was contributed by the Jews of *Minsk. The Jews who organized the underground in the Minsk ghetto were among the key organizers of the partisan movement in Soviet territory. There were also a number of Jews in many Soviet brigades. Many Jews were in positions of command and in the ranks of the fighters in the Kovpak camp. Jewish survivors from the *Skalat ghetto joined this camp during its march over the Carpathians and established the 7th Jewish Brigade of the Kovpak camp.

Within the boundaries of the Polish General Government, Jewish units were active in cooperation with the leftist People's Army. Most of these units were active in the *Lublin and Kielce areas. Many individual Jews filtered through to the units of the military underground of the

Figure 4. Jewish partisan unit in Yugoslavia. Courtesy Yad Vashem Archives, Jerusalem.

Figure 5. Procession of Belgian Jewish partisans to honor fallen members of their ranks, following the liberation of Brussels, November 1944. Courtesy Yad Vashem Archives, Jerusalem.

Polish government-in-exile in London, but this organization did not encourage the escape of Jews into the forests, and its extremists even pursued and murdered Jews.

About 2,000 Jews fought in the ranks of Tito's partisan movement, and a number of Jewish groups even existed independently for a period of time. Moshe Pijade was one of Tito's first and closest collaborators. In September 1943 a group containing a few hundred fighters and a substantial number of nurses formed the Jewish "Rab Battalion" within the Italian concentration camp on the Adriatic island by that name. They joined the partisans as a well-organized unit, but later dispersed and fought in various units. According to official figures, 250 Jews fought with general partisan units in Bulgaria. In Italy as well Jews were scattered among the Italian fighters. Eugenio Caló from Pisa was the founder of a partisan unit in the Val di Piana, and among its members was Emmanuele Artom. Another Italian Jew, Giulio Bolaffi, from Turin, founded and commanded the "4th Alpine Battalion" that was active in the area of the Vale d'Suza in Piedmont.

Jews were among the founders of the partisan movement in Slovakia. The beginnings of this movement were in 1942, but the partisan struggle in Slovakia became a full-scale war in the summer of 1944 with the national Slovak rebellion. Members of many national groups fought in this uprising, including about 2,500 Jews. Two Jewish labor camps—Sered and Novaky—were in the area liberated by the partisans and organized Jewish units, and the inmates of these camps joined the rebellion. At the height of the uprising, four parachutists from Palestine reached Slovakia; two of them remained in Slovakia and the other two passed into Hungary. The two who remained in Slovakia fell into the hands of the Nazis on their way to the last center of the rebels in Banska Bystrica; both were shot in November 1944. After the rebellion was suppressed in October 1944, the partisans retreated to the mountains. There were 2,000 Jews (out of a total of 15,000) in the ranks of the Slovak partisan movement after the uprising.

The participation of Jews in the French Resistance was substantial—constituting only about 1% of the total population of France, at one stage Jews composed about 15–20% of the Resistance. It is necessary to distinguish between Jews who joined general organizations and units of the Resistance and those who formed independent Jewish units.

In contrast to the situation in several East European countries, Judaism was not an obstacle to accepting candidates into the ranks of the French Resistance. Nonetheless, most Jewish fighters preferred to suppress the fact of their origin, either for security reasons or because they felt their identity as Frenchmen more important than their identity as Jews.

The role of Jews both in the ranks of the Resistance and in positions of leadership and command was outstanding. Among the six men who founded the organization called Libération were three Jews. At the time of the liberation of France, there were at least three Jews among the 16 members of the National Committee, the highest institution of the underground. Jean-Pierre Lévy was the founder of the Franc Tireurs. The commander of the Franc Tireurs et Partisans Français (F.T.P.) in the Paris region in 1942–43 was "Colonel Gilles" (the underground name of Joseph Epstein of Warsaw). The leader of the F.T.P. in Toulouse, who fell during the uprising toward the end of the fight for liberation, was "Captain Philippe" (Ze'ev Gustman). The French underground hero, Jacques Bingen, whose name was commemorated on a stamp bearing his image, left France in 1940, joined De Gaulle's forces, and was returned to France in 1943 as the head of the Free French delegation in the northern region.

Among the independent Jewish groups, a distinction should be drawn between Jewish Communists from Eastern Europe and Jewish groups that united on the basis of national and religious motives. The groups of Jewish Communists, opposing the party line of alliance with Hitler (until June 22, 1941), formed a number of commando units that operated in Paris in 1942–43. These groups of the F.T.P., and, in the south, groups of the Jewish Organization for Resistance and Mutual Aid engaged in daring and efficient actions, such as the execution of Nazi officers and collaborators, mining railroad tracks, and raids on enemy arms' depots.

A distinct nationalist Jewish character was the sign of a movement whose nucleus was composed of members of the Jewish Scouts, Zionist youth movements, and members of the *He-Ḥalutz from Holland who had reached France. The movement of Jewish Scouts at first engaged in welfare activities and "passive resistance." It aided in the evacuation of Jewish children from Paris to provincial towns, forging documents, and smuggling Jews over borders, but eventually it did not content itself with these activities and together with the Armée Juive, established the Organization Juive de Combat (O.J.C.).

Figure 6. Robert Gamzon, founder of the Jewish Maquis, which aided in the fight against the Nazis in France. Courtesy Yad Vashem Archives, Jerusalem.

Robert Gamzon established the Jewish Maquis. This unit entered into action with the landing of the Allies on French shores, attacking the retreating German forces and capturing an armed German train. Other groups of the O.J.C., whose headquarters were in Toulouse, were established in Paris, Lyons, Grenoble, Marseilles, Chombron,

Nice, and other cities. The O.J.C. testified to carrying out 1,925 actions, including 750 instances of sabotaging trains, destroying 32 factories that worked for the enemy, and blowing up 25 bridges. It also executed 152 militiamen, traitors, and secret agents (including General Phillipo, a German spy). In 175 actions against the Germans, it killed 1,085 of the enemy's men. In addition, as a result of the organization's activities, the German army lost seven planes (blown up on the ground), 286 trucks, and more than 2,000,000 liters of gasoline. Groups of the O.J.C. also participated in the battles for the liberation of Marseilles and Grenoble.

At the end of the war, the Zionist partisans were among the first to plan and organize the "illegal" immigration to bring the remnants of the Holocaust out of Eastern Europe and over the borders to Palestine. On their way to Palestine, the Jewish partisans organized a unique group known as "Partisans, Soldiers, Pioneers" (P.Ḥ.Ḥ.). An organization of partisans and ghetto fighters exists in Israel, and in 1970 it began to expand into a worldwide Jewish organization.

Bibliography: Y. Suhl (ed.), *They Fought Back* (1968); J. Robinson, *And the Crooked Shall be Made Straight* (1965), 213–26 and index; *European Resistance Movements 1939–1945*, 1 (1960), 2 (1964), passim; *Sefer Milḥamot ha-Getta'ot* (1954² = *The Fighting Ghettos*, partial trans. by M. Barkai, 1962); M. Kahanovich, in: *Yad Vashem Studies*, 1 (1957), 153–67; A. Z. Bar-On, *ibid.* (1960), 167–89; J. Ariel, *ibid.*, 6 (1967), 221–50; H. Michel, *ibid.*, 7 (1968), 1–16; *Sefer ha-Partizanim ha-Yehudim*, 2 vols. (1958); A. Lidowski, *Ba-Ye'arot* (1946); R. Korchak, *Lehavot ba-Efer* (1956); A. Z. Bar-On and D. Levin, *Toledoteha shel Maḥteret* (1962); K. Nir, *Shevilim be-Ma'gal ha-Esh* (1967); B. West, *Hem Hayu Rabbim* (1968); Y. Yelinek, in: *Yalkut Moreshet*, 1 no. 1 (1963), 47–67 (Eng. summ.); H. Smolar, *Yidn in Gele Lates* (1952²); D. Knout, *Contribution à l'histoire de la résistance juive en France, 1940–1944* (1967).

[I.GU.]

PARTNERSHIP.

Formation. The earliest form of commercial partnership in Jewish law was partnership in property, or joint ownership. Craftmen or tradesmen who wished to form a partnership were required to place money in a common bag and lift it or execute some other recognized form of *kinyan* for movables (Ket. 10:4; Yad, Sheluḥin 4:1). The need for executing a *kinyan* precluded an agreement concerning a future matter (Maim., *ibid.* 4:2), since there can be no acquisition of a thing that is not yet in existence (see *Acquisition). In later times this difficulty was overcome when the *halakhot* concerning the need for acquisition formalities were interpreted as having reference only to the formation of the partnership and not to matters in continuation thereof (Maharik Resp. no. 20).

From the tenth century onward, new developments became acknowledged with regard to the manner of forming a partnership. Thus the German and French scholars recognized formation of a partnership by mere agreement between the contracting parties (*Ha-Ittur*, vol. 1, s.v. *Shittuf; Mordekhai* BK 176; Resp. Rosh no. 89:13). A second development was recognition of each partner as the agent of his other partners (*Haggahot Maimuniyyot*, Gezelah 17:3 n. 4), which offered the possibility of partnership formed solely by verbal agreement (see *Agency, Law of). A further development, that of recognizing each partner as the hireling of his other partners (*Hassagot Rabad*, Sheluḥin, 4:2), facilitated partnership agreement with reference also to further activities. The drawback of partnership by way of agency or hire is that each partner has the power to dissolve the partnership at any time. Another method was formation of a partnership by personal undertaking, each partner taking a solemn oath to perform certain acts on behalf of the partnership (Ribash Resp. no. 71).

Partnership formation by agreement alone was most prevalent from the 16th to the 19th centuries, particularly in the communities of the Spanish exiles, in reliance on the principle of accepted trade customs (e.g., *kinyan sitomta:* see BM 74a and codes; see also **Minhag*). It was on the basis of a trade custom that formation of a partnership through verbal agreement alone was recognized, even by the mere recital of the single word *"beinenu"* (*Rosh Mashbir*, ḤM no. 31; *Kerem Shelomo*, Ribbit, 8) or by implication (*Shemesh Ẓedakah*, ḤM 35). Texts of the standard partnership deeds developed over the years indicate that, in general, formation of the partnership agreement rested on a number of elements, mainly *kinyan sudar* (acquisition by the kerchief), personal undertaking, and hire (see e.g., *Darkhei No'am*, ḤM, 54). In this way it was possible to form a partnership with a minimum of formalities, valid also in respect of future activities and not retractable from prior to expiry of the specified period (see *Contract).

It may be noted that the fraternal heirs are deemed to be partners until the inheritance is divided among them (see *Succession).

Distribution of Profits and Losses. In the earliest discussions of partnership in Jewish law, the question of distribution of profits was treated in cases of an unequal capital investment by the individual partners (Ket. 10:4). In the first *halakhot* two conflicting opinions were expressed: in the Mishnah, distribution in proportion to the amount invested; in the Tosefta, equal distribution of the partnership profits. In the Talmud, application of the mishnaic *halakhah* was limited to cases of capital gain or those in which it was impossible to make a physical division (TJ, BK 4:1, and Ket. 10:4; Ket. 93). Talmudic sources reflect no hard and fast rule concerning the distribution of profit deriving from commercial activity. For a long period of time, from the geonic period until the 19th century, these *halakhot* were applied by the scholars in both fashions discussed above. In centers of Jewish life where there was a great deal of activity in commerce and the crafts, the tendency was to decide in favor of an equal distribution of profits in all cases; in centers were there were many loan transactions the tendency was to decide in favor of a distribution pro rata to investment. Thus in the 12th and 13th centuries the principle of an equal distribution was followed in Spain, whereas the German and French scholars took the view that in general the gain, whenever divisible, should be shared in proportion to the investment of each partner.

In general, profit earned by a partner in an unlawful manner, for example, through theft, has not been considered as belonging to the partnership (*Ha-Ittur*, vol. 1, s.v. *Shittuf; Siftei Kohen*, ḤM, 176 n. 27). A contrary ruling with regard to partnership gains from theft was laid down in Germany and France in the 14th century, as an outcome of the persecution of the Jews (*Haggahot Maimuniyyot*, Sheluḥin 5:9 no. 4; see also *Contract, on the attitude of Jewish law to illegal contracts). From the 17th century onward the application of this *halakhah* came to be confined to cases of necessity on account of danger (*Siftei Kohen*, loc. cit.) or those in which an act, although illegal, falls within the scope of the partnership business (*Arukh ha-Shulḥan* ḤM 176:60).

A tax waiver in favor of one partner benefits the whole partnership, except when a waiver is granted at the taxing authority's own initiative (ḤM 178:1). A condition that all profits shall belong to the partnership has been interpreted in accordance with the *ejusdem generis* rule, so as to exclude therefrom all unusual or unforeseeable profits (Rosh, Resp. no. 89:15). A partner who salvages part of the partnership assets from a robbery does so for the benefit of the partnership in the absense of his prior stipulation to the contrary (BK 116b and codes). The partners may not deal in goods whose use is prohibited, for example, for reasons of ritual impurity (Maim. Yad, Sheluḥin 5:10).

Until the end of the 12th century, any loss attributable to a partner's personal fault had to be borne by the partner himself, on the principle that an agent is liable for the consequences of a departure from his mandate (Yad, Sheluḥin 5:2; see also *Agency). From the 13th century onward, the general trend has been toward collective partnership responsibility for a loss occasioned by one of its members. At first it was laid down that the partnership bear such a loss as if the member's liability were that of bailee for reward (see **Shomerim*); later it was ruled that a partner be regarded as a gratuitous bailee for this purpose; and later still that the partnership bear the loss occasioned by a member even if it was the result of his own negligence (Mordecai BB 538). The partner himself must bear any loss occasioned through his own acquiescence or active participation (Mabit, Resp. vol. 2, pt. 2, no. 158).

Each partner is responsible as a surety for the undertakings made by his other partners in respect of a partnership matter (Yad, Malveh 25:9). This liability is secondary however, as is usual in simple *suretyship in Jewish law, and effective only upon default of the principal debtor (*Sefer ha-Terumot,* 44). According to another opinion, one partner is a surety for the other only when he has expressly subjected his person and assets as a surety for the undertaking, in which event he becomes the principal debtor (Rosh, Resp. no. 89:3).

Powers and Duties of the Partners. The rule is that a partner may not deviate from the regular course of activities of the partnership, and his powers, if not defined by agreement, are governed by trade custom (*Ha-Ittur,* vol. 1, s.v. *Shittuf;* Yad, Sheluḥin 5:1; Rosh. Resp. no. 89:14). When the intention of the partners cannot be ascertained, a number of activities have been recorded as constituting deviation from the partnership. In the course of time the early partnership *halakhot* came to be interpreted in favor of wider powers for the individual partner. Thus, with regard to the rule that a partner might not transact partnership business away from the place of the partnership (Yad, loc. cit.), it was decided that the restriction did not apply to a market place situated in the same area (*Netivot ha-Mishpat, Mishpat ha-Kohanim* 176 n. 35) nor to the case in which one partner provided the other partners with suitable indemnities against possible loss (*Arukh ha-Shulḥan* ḤM 176:46–47).

The question of whether a partnership member has power to execute credit transactions was already disputed in geonic times. One approach tended to recognize the power of a partner to sell on credit in all cases, because it was considered that he was bound to be careful about securing the repayment of money in which he had a personal stake (*Sha'arei Ẓedek,* 4:8, 4). A second approach denied a partner the power to sell on credit unless this accorded with a custom followed by all local traders (Rif., Resp. no. 191) and, by way of compromise, it was laid down that it sufficed if the custom was followed by a majority of local traders (Rosh. Resp. no. 89:14). It was also laid down that a partner is exempted from liability if an overall profit results from all his transactions (*Ḥokhmat Shelomo* ḤM 176:10).

A partner may not introduce outsiders into the partnership activities as partners (Yad, Sheluḥin 5:2), but may employ them on his own behalf and at his own responsibility (Rashdam, ḤM, 190). It was ruled that a member of a partnership might not engage in private transactions *(ibid.),* but this was later permitted when the same kind of merchandise as the partnership dealt in was involved (*Matteh Yosef* vol. 1 ḤM no. 9) or in association with an outsider (*Sma,* ḤM 176 n. 32). Partnership merchandise may not be sold before the appointed season for its sale (Git. 31b and codes).

In general, a partnership member is not entitled to remuneration for his services (Reshakh, Resp. pt. 1 no. 139), but some of the *posekim* allowed this in the case of unusually onerous services (*She'ilat Yaveẓ* no. 6; *Simḥat Yom Tov* no. 23). Similarly, a partner is not entitled to a refund of the amount expended on his subsistence while on partnership business (ḤM 176:45), except for extraordinary expenses (*Taz,* ad loc.). A partner who is unable to participate in the partnership activities on account of illness, or for some other personal reason, is not entitled to share in the profits earned by the partnership during his absence and must also defray his medical expenses, etc., out of his own pocket, unless local custom decrees otherwise (BB 144b and codes). If partnership property is later found in the possession of one of the partners, his possession will not avail against any of the other partners (Alfasi, BB 1; see **Ḥazakah*). Each partner may compel the other to engage in the partnership activities and also to invest additional amounts therein (*Netivot ha-Mishpat, Mishpat ha-Urim,* ḤM 176:32).

The act of a partner may be validated by subsequent ratification, which may also be implied from the silence of the remaining partners (Maharik, Resp. no. 24). Far-reaching powers are afforded a partnership member through application of the principle that an act may be "for the benefit of the partnership." In the opinion of a number of scholars, a partner may deviate from the customary framework of the partnership activities when he considers this to be necessary in the interests of the partnership, provided that the terms of the partnership agreement expressly permit him to trade in all kinds of merchandise and that there is no radical departure from the customary partnership practices (Resp. Maharashdam, ḤM 166; *Ne'eman Shemu'el* no. 100). One partner may oblige another who is suspected of an irregularity with regard to a partnership matter to deliver an oath in accordance with a rabbinical enactment (Shevu. 7:8). For this reason it was originally forbidden for a Jew to take a gentile as a partner, as the latter was likely to make an idolatrous reference in swearing his oath, but this is permissible now because of "their belief in the Maker of heaven and earth" (Ran on Rif, Git. 5).

Representation of the Partnership by One of its Members. In talmudic law the principle was established that only when all the partners are in the same town can they be represented by the partner who is plaintiff in an action, this even without their express power of attorney (Ket. 94a and codes). From the 13th century onward, the following guiding rules came to be laid down: one partner represents the others when there is an equal division of profits between them; partners who have not been joined as plaintiffs may not thereafter renew the action in their own names unless they plead new issues; one partner represents the others only when he makes a claim against the defendant and not a waiver in his favor (*Shitah Mekubbeẓet,* Ket. 94). Other scholars expressed opinions in favor of the reverse situation, i.e., that one partner represents the others only if there is no denial of liability on the defendant's part and there is no dispute between them (Maharit, Resp., vol. 2 ḤM no. 16); the plaintiff partner represents the remaining partners once the latter have knowledge of the suit, even if they are not all present in the same town (Resp. Solomon b. Isaac ha-Levi, ḤM no. 41); the partner who is on the scene may sue in all cases, but may not recover the shares of his absent partners (*Piskei ha-Rosh,* Ket. 10:12); the absent partners have the right to sue in their own names if they do so immediately after their return to the town in question, but lose this right after a certain period of delay (*Mikhtam le-David,* ḤM no. 31; *Edut bi-Yhosef* vol. 2 no. 38). The partners may each plead in turn, or empower one of them to represent all (Maharam of Rothenburg, Resp., ed. Prague, nos. 332, 333). A partner has authority to collect debts owing to the partnership in terms of a bond of indebtedness of which he is the holder (Rashba, Resp. vol. 1, no. 1137). One partner generally does not represent the remaining partners as defendant in an action unless empowered by them to do so (*Mordekhai,* Ket. 239). The defendant does, however, represent his absent partners if he is in possession of the subject matter of the claim (Tur, ḤM 176:31). See also Agency; *Practice and Procedure.

Dissolution of Partnership. The activities of a partnership formed for an unspecified period of duration may be terminated at any time at the instance of any of its members, except if this is sought when it is not the season for the sale of its merchandise and provided there are no outstanding partnership debts for which all partners are liable. A partnership formed for a specified period may not—according to the majority of the *posekim*—be dissolved before the stipulated date (Yad, Sheluḥin 4:4). The existence of a partnership is also terminated when its capital has been exhausted, its defined tasks completed and on the death of any of its members. Improper conduct on the part of a member—such as theft—does not, in the opinion of the majority of the *posekim,* serve to terminate the partnership. On dissolution of a partnership, division of its monies—if in the same currency—may be made by the partner in possession thereof and this need not necessarily be done before the court. Division of the partnership assets must be made before three persons, who need only be knowledgeable in the matter (Yad, Sheluḥin 5:9).

Iska ("In Commendam" Transactions). Freedom to contract a partnership is limited to some extent in the case where one party provides the capital and the other the work. In order to avoid a situation in which the party furnishing the capital ultimately receives an increment on his investment which is in the nature of interest, there was evolved a form of transaction known as *iska,* i.e., "business," in which half of the furnished capital constitutes a loan to the "businessman," or active partner, and the other half is held by him in the form of a deposit (BM 104b and codes). The parties to an *iska* are free to stipulate as they please, provided that they observe the principle that the "businessman" must enjoy some greater benefit than the "capitalist," by way of remuneration for his services (BM 5:4). It would seem that the profits from the loan part of the capital belong to the businessman and the profit from the deposit part, after deduction of the former's remuneration, belong to the capitalist. Unless otherwise agreed upon, the businessman is to receive wages as a regular worker if he devotes himself entirely to the affairs of the business, and if not, he may be paid a token amount. Another possibility, if nothing is stipulated, is that the businessman receives two-thirds of the profits, and bears one-third of the losses (Yad, Sheluḥin 6:3) or, according to another opinion, one-half of the losses (*Hassagot Rabad* thereto). The businessman's liability in respect of the loan half of the capital is absolute, whereas his liability in respect of the deposit half is that of a gratuitous bailee (Yad, Sheluḥin 6:2) or according to another opinion, that of a bailee for reward *(Hassagot Rabad, ibid.).*

According to one school, an *iska* is constituted whenever the partnership arrangement involves an active as well as an inactive partner, and it makes no difference whether the inactive partner alone or both of them contribute the capital (Yad, Sheluḥin, 6:1); according to another school, there is no *iska* unless the distinction between an investing but inactive and an active but noninvesting partner is clearly maintained in the partnership arrangement (*Beit Yosef,* YD 177). The capital-investing partner takes no share in the profits of a prohibited *iska* (*Piskei ha-Rosh,* BM 8:7).

That an *iska* is essentially a legal device designed to avoid the prohibition against *usury may be seen from the fact that a nominal remuneration may be agreed upon for the active partner and from the rule that the latter may not distinguish between the loan and the deposit parts but must put to work the whole amount of the capital invested (Yad, Sheluḥin 7:4). In most respects the law of *iska* follows the law of partnership but the following basic differences may be noted: the "businessman," unlike a partner in a regular partnership, may retract from the contract at any time, as in the case of a worker (Tur ḤM 176:28) and he must receive remuneration for his services (*Mishpat Ẓedek,* vol. 2, no. 16, et al.).

Joint Ownership. As already indicated, the *halakhot* of partnership developed mainly from the law of joint ownership. Characteristic of this is the power of each part-owner to compel the others to carry out the usual and required activities with regard to the common property—such as the construction of a gate to the premises—or to refrain from any unusual use of the property, such as keeping an animal on the premises; similarly, each part-owner may bring about a dissolution of the partnership by compelling a partition of the common property provided that thereupon each share still fits the original description of the property and, in the case of immovable property, that it is possible to erect a partition against exposure to the sight of neighbors. If the common property does not allow for proper subdivision, the interested partner may offer to sell his share to the remaining partners or to purchase their shares from them; if the matter cannot be settled in this manner, the property must be sold, or let to a third party, or an arrangement must be made for its joint use by the partners, simultaneously or successively, all in terms of detailed rules on the subject (BB 1–3, and codes).

A Legal Persona. A cooperative body in modern legal systems is an entity with rights and obligations quite apart from those of its component members (see G. Procaccia, Ha-Ta'agid Mahuto . . . vi-Yẓirato (1965), p. 39). According to the law of the State of Israel, a registered partnership is a legal persona, capable of suing and being sued (The Partnerships Ordinance, 1930, sec. 61 (1)). However, this approach is foreign to Jewish law, the *halakhah* recognizing man alone—whether individually or in cooperation with others—as the subject-matter of the law, so that it does not accord an association a separate personality (see Gulak, Yesodei (1922), 50). It is for this reason that the word "partners" rather than "partnership" is the more commonly employed halakhic term. Thus a suit brought by the partners against one of their number, e.g., arising out of fraud (see **Ona'ah*), is not the suit of the partnership but of its individual members (Yad, Sheluḥin, 5:6; Sh. Ar. ḤM 176:4). Nevertheless, even though the partnership as such does not have the status of an independent legal persona, the moment a person is recognized as a partnership member his rights and obligations change and no longer correspond to those attaching to the individual or to an agent. Thus one partner represents his fellow partners vis-à-vis third parties, and unlike an agent, renders them bound by the consequences of his acts in certain circumstances, even without having been appointed as their representative (Yad,

Sheluḥin, 3:3); Similarly, if jointly owned property is later found in the possession of one of the co-owners, the latter's possession will not be recognized, despite the rule that the onus of proof is on the person seeking to recover from the neighbor (BB 4a and codes); subsequent ratification of a fellow partner's acts amounting to deviation from the customary partnership activities suffices to absolve the latter from liability for such deviation—according to some of the *posekim* even if they are only passed over in silence without protest (*Shenei ha-Me'orot ha-Gedolim* no. 26). Thus the special standing which the law affords a partner to some extent lends a partnership the coloring of a legal persona.

In the State of Israel. The laws of partnership are governed by the above-mentioned mandatory partnership ordinance, which is based on the British Partnership Act, 1890, but differs from it mainly in that it necessitates registration of a partnership to which it lends the character of a legal persona (sec. 61 (1)). Still unclear is the position as regards the standing of an unregistered partnership (PD 15:1246; Pesakim Meḥoziyyim, 56:362). Case law shows that the *halakhah* is sometimes quoted with regards to problems left unresolved within the framework of the Partnership Ordinance (e.g., on the questions of dissolution of partnership (PD 21:576) and the share of each of the spouses in the profits and losses deriving from their common enterprise (Pesakim Meḥoziyyim, 23:418)). In cases where the parties agree to submit their dispute to a rabbinical court, the issue will be decided in accordance with Jewish law (see PDR 2:376, 5:310).

Bibliography: J. S. Zuri, *Mishpat ha-Talmud,* 4 (1921), 55–59; 5 (1921), 154–6; idem, *Arikhat ha-Mishpat ha-Ivri . . . Ḥok Ḥevrat ha-Shutafut* (1940); Gulak, Yesodei, 1 (1922), 135–7; 2 (1922), 192–8; Gulak, Oẓar, 147f., 217–23; E. E. Hildesheimer, *Das juedische Gesellschaftsrecht . . .* (1930); Herzog, Instit, 1 (1936), 213–23; 2 (1939), 155–66; Elon, Mafte'aḥ, 321–41. [S.D.R.]

PARTOS, OEDOEN (1909–), Israel composer. Partos studied the violin and viola, and composition (with Zoltán Kodály) at the academy in his native Budapest. In 1924 he became first violinist of the Lucerne orchestra, then appeared as soloist in Hungary and Germany, and from 1936 to 1938 taught violin and composition at the conservatory in Baku. In 1938 he went to Palestine and joined the Palestine (later Israel Philharmonic) Orchestra as first viola player until 1950. He also became active as teacher and composer and in 1953 was appointed director of the Israel (later Rubin) Conservatory and Academy of Music in Tel Aviv. In the same year he received the Israel Prize for his symphonic fantasia *En Gev.*

Oedoen Partos, Israel composer.

Partos' interest in Near Eastern musical subjects and techniques had already been aroused during his stay in Baku. In Palestine he was confronted with the added musical traditions of the Oriental Sephardi and Yemenite Jews, toward which he was drawn by Bracha *Zefira, for whose recitals he prepared several imaginative settings of such tunes.

His works include: *Shir Tehillah,* concerto for viola and orchestra (1945); *Yizkor,* for viola and string orchestra (1946), also in versions for violin or viola or cello and piano, based on an East Ashkenazi synagogal chant and commemorating the Holocaust; *En Gev,* symphonic fantasia (1951), on the motive E-G-B (Israel Prize, 1953); *String Quartet No. 2—Tehillim* (1960); *Ḥezyonot,* for flute, piano, and string orchestra (1957), also performed as a ballet *The Mythical Hunter;* a quintet for flute and strings (1958); a violin concerto (concluded 1958); *Nebulae* for woodwind quintet (1967); and several cantatas and choral works, some of which were published as *Shirei Makhelah* (1953), including the well-known *Ein Addir ka-Adonai,* based on a Sephardi melody.

Bibliography: P. E. Gradenwitz, *Music and Musicians in Israel* (1959), 73–78, 152–3; *Who Is Who in ACUM* (1965), 63; I. Shalita *Enẓiklopedyah le-Musikah* (1950²), cols. 750–2. [B.B.]

PARTRIDGE (Heb. חָגְלָה, *ḥoglah*), bird. Two species of the partridge are found in Israel, the see-see partridge *(Ammoperdix heyi)* and the chukar partridge *(Alectoris graeca).* The latter is called *ḥajel* in Arabic, which is the *ḥoglah* mentioned as the name of one of Zelophehad's daughters (Num. 26:33) and as the place-name Beth-Hoglah (Josh. 15:6). These two species of partridge, which are kosher birds, are extensively hunted because of their delicious meat. They belong to the family of pheasants, like the *pheasant and the *quail, which are both included in the Talmud among four species of game birds, the best of which is stated to be the שִׂכְלִי *(shikhli),* apparently the chukar partridge, and the least tasty the quail (Yoma 75b). The two species of partridge mentioned above are distinguished by the intensive cries of the male during the breeding season, so that the biblical name קוֹרֵא (*kore,* "calling") is appropriate for both of them, although it is applied nowadays only to the see-see partridge. This bird is found in large flocks in the Judean Desert and the Negev. In the breeding season the partridges separate into pairs, and the female lays between five and 14 eggs in a nest. Sometimes two females lay eggs in the same nest, in which case one gains the upper hand and drives the other away; however her small body is unable to keep such a large number of eggs warm, so that eventually the embryos die. It was to this that the proverb referred when speaking of one who robs another of his possessions without ultimately deriving any benefit: "As the partridge that broodeth over young which she hath not brought forth, so is he that getteth riches, and not by right; in the midst of his days he shall leave them" (Jer. 17:11). A similar phenomenon occurs sometimes in the chukar partridge's nest. These two species of partridge feed on seeds and on insects which they hunt, a circumstance referred to in David's question when he asked Saul why he was hunting him "as the partridge hunts" (the flea; I Sam. 26:20). In the Mishnah (Ḥul. 12:2) the *kore* is mentioned as a kosher bird, the male of which also sits on the eggs, as is indeed done by the partridge. Some (Rashi and others) identified the *kore* with the cuckoo, but this identification is incorrect and was rejected already by the *tosafot* (to Ḥul. 63a s.v. *neẓ*).

Bibliography: J. Feliks, *Animal World of the Bible* (1962), 56f. [J.F.]

PARVAIM (Heb. פַּרְוָיִם), the region from which Solomon is said to have obtained gold for the ornamentation of his Temple (II Chron. 3:6). The word may possibly derive from the Sanskrit *pûrva,* "eastern." Some scholars identify Parvaim with Sāq al-Farwayn near Mt. Shammar in northwest Arabia; others, with Farwa in southern Arabia.

Bibliography: S. J. Simons, *Geographical and Topographical Texts of the Old Testament* (1959), 346, n.869. [Ed.]

PARVEH (Heb. and Yid. פַּרְוֶה), term applied to foods which cannot be classified as milk or meat, and which may therefore be eaten with either without infringing the *dietary laws. Fish, vegetables, and eggs are included in this category. *Parveh* utensils are kept apart from meat or milk vessels.

The origin of the word is problematic. It may be derived from the Hebrew root ערב ("mixed"). The Mishnah refers to *bet ha-parvah* (spelled פַּרְוָה), a courtyard, to which the high priest was taken for ritual immersion, distinguished by being neither holy nor profane (Yoma 3:3). In the *Gemara* the word, used in a derogatory sense to indicate a bird which it is forbidden to eat, was derived from the name of a wicked magician (Ḥul. 62b). It has also been posited that *parveh* originates from the Latin *parvus* ("small"). The Yiddish word *pare* ("steam") has also been suggested. Finally, there is a theory that the word is of Slavonic origin ("a pair"): the Czech *párové,* for instance, denotes an item that may have a dual purpose.

Bibliography: JC (Jan. 17, 24, 31; Feb. 7; March 7, 27, 1964).

[Ed.]

°**PASCAL, BLAISE** (1623–1662), French religious philosopher, writer, and scientist. Pascal, an ardent Christian, was a member of the austere Catholic group known as the Jansenists. He is famous for his *Pensées sur la religion* (1670), fragments intended to form part of an *Apologie de la religion chrétienne.* An authoritative modern edition is that published in 1908–14 by the Jewish scholar Léon *Brunschvicg. In the *Pensées,* Pascal sought to convince the unbeliever of the existence of God and the superiority of the Christian religion by showing that only through God and Jesus could man surmount the misery of the human condition and understand the mystery of his own dual nature. His proofs and arguments include the biblical prophecies and the survival and role of the Jewish people. He studied the Bible closely and found himself drawn to talmudic and midrashic literature in order to penetrate the deeper message of the prophecies. He quoted the Midrash, the Talmud, and Maimonides, though he had only secondhand access to the sources through the medieval *Pugio Fidei* of the Spanish Dominican, Raymond *Martini.

Meditation on the Bible led Pascal to ponder the role of the Jewish people. Just as he saw the Hebrew prophets as the harbingers of Christianity, so he saw Israel as a symbolic forerunner of the Messiah, its survival bearing witness to the divine scheme of salvation. Thus Israel was both glorious and lowly: glorious as God's elect, lowly because of its rejection of Jesus. But Pascal did not content himself with this traditional Christian view of the Jewish people. He delved deeper and was impressed by the loyalty of the Jews to their religion. He admired Jewish law for its strictness, its perfection, and its durability. He also noted the unique bond of brotherhood which links Jews. He marveled even more at a phenomenon "without precedent or equal in the world": that Jews love deeply, unreservedly, to the point of martyrdom, the book in which their leader, Moses, chastised them for their ingratitude to God, predicting their downfall and dispersal among the nations. This loyalty to religion, against their own "honor," exists, in Pascal's view, only among the Jews.

While Pascal admired the faithfulness and obstinate survival of the Jews, he rejected the "excessive formalism" of Jewish law, and condemned the Jews for their lack of spirituality and for their blindness to Christian truth; but equally, he condemned "unspiritual" Christians. Ardently desiring a purified spiritual religion for Jews and Christians alike, Pascal wrote: "The Messiah, according to unspiritual Jews, must be a great temporal prince. Christ, according to unspiritual Christians, came to exempt us from loving God . . . Neither view represents Christianity or Judaism. True Jews and true Christians have always waited for a Messiah who would make them love God, and, through this love alone, triumph over their enemies."

Bibliography: J. Mesnard, *Pascal, his Life and Works* (1952); M. V. Hay, *The Prejudices of Pascal . . .* (1962); Lovsky, in: *Cahiers Sioniens,* 5 (1951), 355–66; L. Goldmann, *Le Dieu Caché* (1955); C. Lehrmann, *L'Elément juif dans la littérature française,* 1 (1960[2]), 120–5.

[Li.C.]

PASCANI, town in Jassy province in Moldavia, N.E. Rumania. The town may have been founded by Jews, since in 1859, ten years after its foundation, 86 Jews and only five Christians lived there. The ground for the synagogue, the Jewish cemetery (opened in 1870), and the ritual bath (founded in 1872) was granted by the owner of the estate on which the town was established. The locality began to develop after 1879, when the railway from Jassy to Cernauti (Chernovtsy) and Lemberg was built. Pascani was also a railway junction for Bucharest. In 1899 there were 1,862 Jews (14.7% of the total population) in Pascani, six religious schools *(ḥadarim),* and four synagogues; by the eve of World War I the latter had increased to five. In 1900 a modern primary school was opened by the community at the suggestion of a Christian pharmacist who donated money for this purpose. A second school was opened in 1911 with the aid of the *Jewish Colonization Association. During the Peasants' Revolt of 1907 a Jew was killed and many Jewish houses were plundered. Between 1880 and 1913 proposals were made for changing the status of the town to a city, but these were rejected by parliament on the ground that the situation of the Jews might thereby be improved. By 1910 the Jewish population had decreased to 1,543. Pascani was a ḥasidic center in Rumania, as the *ẓaddik* M. L. Friedman, son of I. Friedman (of the *Ruzhin dynasty), the rabbi of Buhusi, lived there.

In World War II most Pascani Jews were deported to Bostosam and some to Roman. In 1947 the Jewish population numbered 870, decreasing to 500 in 1950. In 1969 only about 20 Jewish families had remained. There was one synagogue.

Bibliography: PK Romanyah, 195–7; E. Schwarzfeld, *Impopularea, reîmpopularea şi întemeierea tîrgurilor şi tîrguţoarelor în Moldova* (1914), 40, 41, 98; V. Tufescu, *Tirguşoarele din Moldova şi importanţa lor economícă* (1942), 93, 94, 114, 116, 124, 129, 138.

[T.L.]

PASCHELES, WOLF (**Ze'ev;** 1814–1857), author, publisher, and bookseller. Born in Prague, Pascheles published—while in his teens—*Deutsche Gebete fuer Frauen* (1828) of which several editions appeared under various titles. With the money earned on the first edition, he opened the first Jewish bookstore in Prague.

He wrote a biography of Solomon *Heine together with one of the Viennese merchant Herrmann Tedesco (1845). In 1857 he edited and published E. Bondi's *Mikhtevei Sefat Kodesh,* a Hebrew chrestomathy (including biographies of famous Jews) with interlinear German translation. Pascheles' great success were his collections of legends and biographies, medieval and modern, under the title *Sippurim* (1846/47) which went through many editions. Among the contributors were I. M. *Jost, Solomon Kohn, R. J. *Fuerstenthal, and S. J. *Kaempf. A popular edition was published (1888, 1909[3]) by his son-in-law Jacob Brandeis. Adaptations of the *Sippurim* were prepared by S. Schmitz (1921,1926) and H. Pollitzer (*Die goldene Gasse,* 1937) as well as a selection and translation into English by C. Field (*Jewish Legends . . .,* n.d.). Pascheles' miniature Pentateuch, with German translation by H. *Arnheim, and his *Illustrierter israelitischer Volkskalender,* which appeared from 1860 to 1935, was also popular. He also published a popular series called *Juedische Universal-Bibliothek,* which included works on Jewish history, biographies, and contemporary events. After Pascheles' death these were edited by his son Jacob and his son-in-law, J. Brandeis, who continued the book-selling and publishing firm (catalogs appeared 1879–94).

Bibliography: Society for the History of Czechoslovak Jews, New York, *Jews of Czechoslovakia,* 1 (1968), 341, 533. [ED.]

PASCIN, JULES (1885–1930), painter. Pascin was born in Viddin, Bulgaria, the son of a Sephardi grain merchant, Marcus Pincus. In 1891 the family settled in Bucharest. After leaving high school, Pascin traveled, taking courses at several art academies. On his return, his clever drawings earned him a contract with the Munich satirical weekly *Simplicissimus.* He changed his name to Pascin. In 1905 he went to Paris and there became a celebrated figure on the Left Bank. During World War I he left for the United States and became a U.S. citizen. In 1920 he returned to Paris and, in spite of a life of dissipation, produced about 500 oils as well as drawings, prints, colors, and a few small sculptures. Suffering from incurable cirrhosis of the liver, he committed suicide by hanging himself in his studio, leaving bizarre instructions for a Jewish funeral.

His acute draftsmanship can be seen in his *Simplicissimus* cartoons and in his humorous and often savage illustrations of books, among them an edition of Heinrich Heine's *Die Memoiren des Herrn von Schnabelewopski.* This draftsmanship was the basis of all his compositions and some critics claimed that his oils were only "drawings heightened by paint." His paintings have a quasi-surrealist quality. Pascin also made prints using a sharp needle directly on copper (similar to drawing) for preserving impressions of travel, suburban scenes, and café life. Though most of his work depicts women singly or in groups, he was also a keen observer of many milieus and he drew or painted children at play, circus artists, and nightclub scenes. He was fascinated by figures from folklore and the Bible including the Prodigal Son, Salome, and Bathsheba.

Bibliography: A. Werner, *Pascin* (Eng., 1962); G. Diehl, *Pascin* (Fr., 1968). [A.W.]

Portrait by Jules Pascin, 1914. Oil on canvas, 14×15 in. (46×38 cm.). Jerusalem, Israel Museum. Photo R. Milon, Jerusalem.

PASHHUR (Heb. פַּשְׁחוּר), son of Immer, priest and chief officer in the Temple during the last years of the kingdom of Judah (Jer. 20:1–6). Pashhur was deputy to the high priest and responsible for the maintenance of order in the Temple. In the narrative of Jeremiah 20:1–6 it is related that he beat Jeremiah and put him in the stocks as a punishment for his harsh prophecy against Judah and Jerusalem (Jer. 19:15). Jeremiah responded by declaring "The Lord does not call your name Pashhur, but Terror (Heb. *magor*) on every side." One interpretation of this play on words derives the name Pashhur from the Aramaic root *pwš* ("to rest") and the Aramaic word *seḥor* ("round about"), i.e., where formerly there was peace and quiet, there will now be terror all about. Jeremiah prophesied that Pashhur would be taken into exile and would die in a foreign land: "And you, Pashhur, and all who dwell in your house, shall go into captivity, to Babylon you shall go; and there you shall die, and there you shall be buried . . . " (Jer. 20:6).

Bibliography: de Vaux, Anc Isr, 378–9; Waechter, in: ZAW, 74 (1962), 57–62. [Jo.S.]

PASMANIK, DANIEL (1869–1930), Zionist writer and leader. Born in Gadyach, Ukraine, Pasmanik studied medicine in Switzerland and Bulgaria and from 1899 served as an instructor in medicine at Geneva University. He joined the Zionist Movement in 1900 and became one of its leading publicists and theoreticians. In 1905, upon his return to Russia, he joined the editorial board of the monthly *Yevreyskaya Zhizn* and later of the weekly *Razsvet.* He advocated the evolutionary concept of Zionism, practical work in Ereẓ Israel, and active Zionist participation in Diaspora life (see *Helsingfors Program). Pasmanik's articles appeared in Russian, Yiddish, German, Hebrew, Polish, and Croat periodicals; several were published in pamphlet and book form. An entire Zionist generation was educated largely on Pasmanik's writings. He also contributed articles to *Die *Welt,* to the non-Zionist *Yevreyskiy Mir,* and to the *Yevreyskaya Entsiklopediya.* In 1905 (January–October) he published pseudonymously, in *Yevreyskaya Zhizn,* a much-discussed, largely autobiographical novel, *"Istoriya odnogo yevreyskago intelligenta"* ("The Story of a Jewish Intellectual"). He was also among the first theoreticians of *Po'alei Zion, with his *Teorie un Praktike fun Poalei Zionizmus* (1906). During the civil war in Russia (1917–21), Pasmanik sided with the counterrevolutionary White armies of generals Denikin and Wrangel, who were responsible for innumerable anti-Jewish pogroms. In 1919 he emigrated to Paris, where in 1920–22 he was coeditor of the Russian émigré paper *Obshcheye Delo.* Association with these circles estranged Pasmanik from the Zionist movement.

Daniel Pasmanik, Zionist theoretician. Pen and ink drawing by Nathan Altman. Jerusalem, J.N.U.L., Schwadron Collection.

Pasmanik's main writings include: *Kritika "teoriy" Bunda* ("A Critique of the 'Theories' of the Bund," 1906); *Sudby yevreyskago naroda: problemy yevreyskoy obshchestvennosti* ("The Destiny of the Jewish Nation . . .," 1917); and *Russkaya revolyutsiya i yevreystvo: bolshevizm i iudaizm* ("Jewry and the Russian Revolution . . .," 1923). His study *Stranstvuyushchiy Izrail: psikhologiya yevreystva v razseyanii* ("The Wandering Jew: the Psychology of Diaspora Jewry," 1910) was also published in German (1911) and Yiddish (1918). Pasmanik's last book, *Qu'est-ce que le judaïsme?*, was published in 1930. Several studies on medical topics appeared in specialized German and French publications. [J.B.SCH.]

PASSAIC-CLIFTON, twin cities 12 mi. E. of New York City in N.E. New Jersey; total population of Passaic, 55,000 (1970), total population of Clifton, 81,787 (1970), combined Jewish population estimated at 10,500 (1970). Passaic is bordered on three sides by Clifton and their Jewish population is normally considered as a single unit. No systematic demographic study has been taken of the area since 1949, but it seems apparent that for the period 1950–70 the Jewish population of Passaic has decreased considerably, although Jewish businesses continue to be located there, and that Clifton's Jewish population has developed since 1945 at Passaic's expense.

Passaic was founded by Dutch settlers in the late 17th century, but until the 1860s was little more than a transportation hub. In 1859, however, the advent of waterpower there led to its transformation into an industrial city. Incorporated as a village in 1869, Passaic, three years later, achieved the status of city. Up until the 1860s, however, it had no Jewish residents. Significantly, the first sustained industrial enterprise at Passaic was a mill owned by a Jewish man. Jacob Basch & Co. opened in 1862, and eventually it was joined by additional woolen and worsted establishments; by 1910 Passaic's well-known worsted mills employed nearly 43% of all its industrial employees. Unfortunately, when the woolen industry abandoned the city after World War II, its earlier prosperity was severely undermined. Inasmuch as the textile industry traditionally attracted cheap labor, Passaic became a haven for European immigrants. By 1910 just over half of the city's 54,773 people were foreign born; an estimated 3,500 were Jewish, although the great preponderance was Slavic. During the first decade of the 20th century, moreover, Passaic became overcrowded, leading newcomers to make their residences beyond its borders in Acquackanonk Township, which in 1917 was incorporated as Clifton, as well as in the towns of Garfield and Wallington, which are also adjacent to the city. As a result of the textile industry's demise, the offspring of Passaic's white population began to move away, their places being filled by nonwhite minorities.

While Jacob Basch, the mill owner, was the city's original Jewish settler, a onetime itinerant peddler named Moses Simon undertook to organize its Jewish community. Although the Simon family supposedly had settled near Passaic in 1870, communal activity did not begin until 1885, by which time the pattern of immigration had shifted. Passaic's Jewish population was originally largely occupied in small retail businesses that serviced the ethnic neighborhoods. By 1900, however, members of the community were also involved in legal and financial affairs as well. A sociological survey conducted in 1937 reported that 43% of the gainfully employed Jews in Passaic were engaged in commercial trade, 22% in manufacturing, and 12% in professional services; a more recent study, made in 1949, found 40% in trade, 30% in the professions, and only 12% in manufacturing.

Almost from its inception, members of the Jewish community also participated in civic life as well, a tradition that began with Jacob Basch's son Henry, who took an active interest in municipal affairs beginning in the 1880s. As early as 1892 Jews gained minor elective offices, such as election judge; in 1904 Joseph Spitz was elected as a council representative from his ward, and in 1919 Abram Preiskel, in being elected to the board of commissioners, became the first Jew to win a city-wide political contest. Passaic's first Jewish mayor, Morris Pashman, was elected in 1951; in 1967 Bernard D. Pinck was elected mayor, and he was succeeded by Gerald Goldman in 1971. Clifton's first Jewish councilman, Fred Friend, was elected in 1931, and in 1962 Ira Schoem was elected as that city's first Jewish mayor. In both cities members of the Jewish community have long been active in the deliberations of the respective boards of education. [M.H.E.]

Passaic's first Jewish congregation, B'nai Jacob (Orthodox), was founded in 1889; by 1911 it had been joined by six others, all Orthodox. More Orthodox congregations were established after World War I, and eventually some have been rebuilt in the newer sections of the city. Passaic's single Conservative synagogue, Temple Emanuel (1923), quickly became the city's leading congregation. The Clifton Jewish Center (1943, Conservative) and Beth Sholom Reform Temple (1959) were established to serve the population which had shifted to the suburbs of Passaic from the early 1940s. The Jewish Community Council of Passaic-Clifton (organized in 1933) administers the United Jewish Appeal and coordinates all community bodies, which include the Passaic-Clifton YM-YWHA, the Beth Israel Hospital, and The Daughters of Miriam Home for the Aged, as well as a variety of other fraternal and service groups. The Hillel Academy (1945), an Orthodox day school, offers intensive Jewish education. The Passaic-Clifton Board of Rabbis (founded in 1953) directs the Va'ad HaKohol, which supervises *kashrut* in the community. A unique institution is the Passaic United Hebrew Burial Association *(ḥevra kaddisha)* which built the Jewish Memorial Chapel in 1949. It is one of two such nonprofit institutions in the United States and is owned and administered by the Jewish community. [E.N.S.]

Bibliography: *Jewish Roots: A History of the Jewish Community of Passaic and Environs* (1959); S. M. Robinson, in: S. M. Robinson and J. Starr (eds.), *Jewish Population Studies* (1943), 22–36; B. B. Seligman, *Jewish Population of Passaic, New Jersey, 1949: A Demographic Study* (1951).

PASSAU, city in Bavaria, W. Germany. Jews are mentioned in an early tenth-century local customs regulation (Raffelsteten). Documentary evidence for their presence in the city of Passau, however, dates only from 1210, when Bishop Mangold compensated the Jews of the city after they had been robbed. In 1206 they were released from paying customs and taxes in return for their aid in helping the bishop collect his tithes. They earned their livelihood in moneylending. A *Judenstrasse* is first mentioned in 1328, a synagogue in 1314, and a cemetery in 1418. (Before 1418 Jews were buried in Regensburg.) The *Black Death persecutions of 1349 caused considerable loss to the community, but Jews were again resident in Passau in 1390. In March 1478 a petty thief "confessed" to having stolen and sold the Host to Jews. On being tortured, ten Jews confessed to having stabbed the Host and caused its blood to flow. All (including the witness) were sentenced to death. Concomitantly approximately 40 Jews accepted Christianity while the rest were expelled; the synagogue and Jewish homes were demolished. A church erected on the site became the object of pilgrimages. Small numbers of Jews were permitted to reside in Passau in later centuries. The Jewish settlement reached 73 in 1910 and 48 in 1932, and was affiliated with the Straubing community. In 1968, 13 Jews were recorded as residents of Passau.

Bibliography: Germ Jud, 1 (1963), 266–7; 2 (1968), 647–8; M. Stern, in : *Jeschurun*, 15 (1928), 541–60, 647–76; W. M. Schmid, in: ZGJD, 1 (1929), 119–35; PK, Germanyah; M. Pfamholz, in: *Festschrift fuer Lorenz Spindler (196?)*; J. R. Marcus, *Jew in the Medieval World* (1965), 155–8.

[Ed.]

PASSI, DAVID (16th century), Turkish statesman. Passi was born in Portugal a Marrano, lived for a time in Venice, and then settled as a Jew in Constantinople. French, English, Venetian, and Neapolitan envoys all highly appreciated his services, which were largely toward forming an Anglo-Turkish alliance against Spain. The sultan is reported to have said that he had slaves like the grand vizier in abundance, but none like Passi. According to a report of 1585, he was invested with the Duchy of Naxos, like Joseph *Nasi before him. He worked, generally, in close cooperation with the physician Moses Benveniste. In 1589 these two were responsible for the schemes for currency reform, and when the janissaries subsequently attacked the divan, Passi was wounded. In 1591, as a result of a defamatory letter which he wrote to the chancellor of Poland about the grand vizier Sinan Pasha, he was put in chains and exiled to Rhodes; he returned after Sinan's death shortly thereafter, but played no further part in public life.

Bibliography: C. Roth, *The House of Nasi: The Duke of Naxos* (1948), 204–12; *Times Literary Supplement* (July 6, 1922); Wolf, in: JHSET, 11 (1924–27), 26–28, 63–64, 85ff.

[C.R.]

PASSOVER (Heb. פֶּסַח, **Pesaḥ**), a spring festival, beginning on the 15th day of Nisan, lasting seven days in Israel and eight in the Diaspora. It commemorates the Exodus from Egypt. The first and seventh days (the first two and last two in the Diaspora) are *yom tov* (a "festival" on which work is prohibited) and the other days *ḥol ha-mo'ed* ("intermediate days" on which work is permitted).

Names and History. The biblical names for the festival are: *ḥag ha-Pesaḥ* ("the feast of the Passover," Ex. 34:25), so called because God "passed over" (or "protected") the houses of the children of Israel (Ex. 12:23), and *ḥag ha-Maẓẓot* ("the feast of Unleavened Bread"; Ex. 23:15; Lev. 23:6; Deut. 16:16). Pesaḥ is the paschal lamb, offered as a sacrifice on the eve of the feast (14th Nisan) in Temple times; it was eaten in family groups after having been roasted whole (Ex. 12:1–28, 43–49; Deut. 16:1–8). A person who was unable (because of ritual impurity or great distance from the Sanctuary) to keep the "first Passover" could keep it a month later—*Pesaḥ Sheni* ("the Second Passover," also called "Minor Passover," Num. 9:1–14).

According to tradition, the Passover rites were divinely ordained as a permanent reminder of God's deliverance of His people from Egyptian bondage. The critical view points to two distinct festivals in the Bible; the feast of unleavened bread, a pastoral feast, and the Passover, an agricultural feast (see below).

In the Book of Joshua (5:10–11), it is said that the Israelites led by Joshua kept the feast at Gilgal. The Book of Kings relates that Passover was kept with special solemnity in King Josiah's reign in the seventh century B.C.E.: "The king commanded all the people, saying: 'Keep the passover unto the Lord your God, as it is written in this book of the covenant. For there was not kept such a passover from the days of the judges that judged Israel, nor in all the days of the kings of Israel, nor of the kings of Judah; but in the eighteenth year of King Josiah was this passover kept to the Lord in Jerusalem'" (II Kings 23:21–23).

As far as can be ascertained, the Passover festival was kept throughout the period of the Second Temple. Josephus records contemporary Passover celebrations in which he

Figure 1. Preparation of utensils for Passover by immersion in boiling water. Illustration from a 14th-century *Haggadah* from Spain. London, British Museum, Or. Ms. 2737.

estimates that the participants who gathered in Jerusalem to perform the sacrifice in the year 65 C.E., were "not less than three millions" (Jos., Wars, 2:280). The Talmud (Pes. 64b) similarly records: "King Agrippa once wished to take a census of the hosts of Israel. He said to the high priest, 'Cast your eyes on the Passover offerings.' He took a kidney from each, and 600,000 pairs of kidneys were found there, twice as many as those who departed from Egypt, excluding those who were unclean and those who were on a distant journey; and there was not a single paschal lamb for which more than ten people had not registered; and they called it: 'The Passover of the dense throngs.'" Allowing for hyperbole, the account of immense crowds assembled to offer the paschal lamb cannot be too far from historical reality.

The Samaritans considered all the biblical rules regarding the sacrifice of the lamb in Egypt (Ex. 12) to be applicable for all time. The practice, as recorded in the Mishnah (Pes. 9:5), is that only *Pesaḥ Miẓrayim* ("Passover of Egypt") required the setting aside of the lamb four days before the festival, the sprinkling of the blood on lintel and doorposts, and that the lamb be eaten in "haste." The Mishnah (Pes. 10:5) explains the commands of the lamb sacrifice and the eating of **mazzah* ("unleavened bread") and *maror* ("bitter herbs") as follows: the lamb is offered because God "passed over" *(pasaḥ)*; the unleavened bread is eaten because God redeemed the Israelites from Egypt (Ex. 12:39); and the bitter herbs, because the Egyptians embittered their lives (Ex. 1:14).

With the destruction of the Temple, the offering of the paschal lamb came to an end, although it is possible that for a time the sacrifice was continued in modified form in some circles (Guttman, in: HUCA, 38 (1967), 137–48). The other rites and ceremonies of the Passover festival continued as before. The Samaritans, however, still sacrifice the paschal lamb in a special ceremony on Mt. Gerizim near Shechem. The Last Supper, mentioned in the New Testament (Mark 14, Matt. 26, Luke 22), may be the *seder* meal. Early Christians observed Easter on Passover and Roman Christians on the Sunday after Passover. Later the *blood libel against Jews was frequently connected with the Passover festival.

The Seder. The special home ceremony on the first night of Passover, the *seder* ("order"), is based on the injunction to parents to inform their children of the deliverance from Egypt: "And thou shalt tell thy son in that day, saying: It is because of that which the Lord did for me when I came forth out of Egypt" (Ex. 13:8). The Mishnah (Pes. 10:4) gives a formula of four questions (see **Mah Nishtannah*) which are asked by the child and to which the father replies "according to the son's intelligence" (see *Four Sons).

Figure 2. Passover scenes from the *Golden Haggadah*, Spain, c. 1320. Upper register: right, Miriam dancing with a drum; left, a father distributing *mazzot;* lower register: right, searching for leaven; left, preparation of the paschal lamb. London, British Museum, Add. Ms. 27210, fol. 15r.

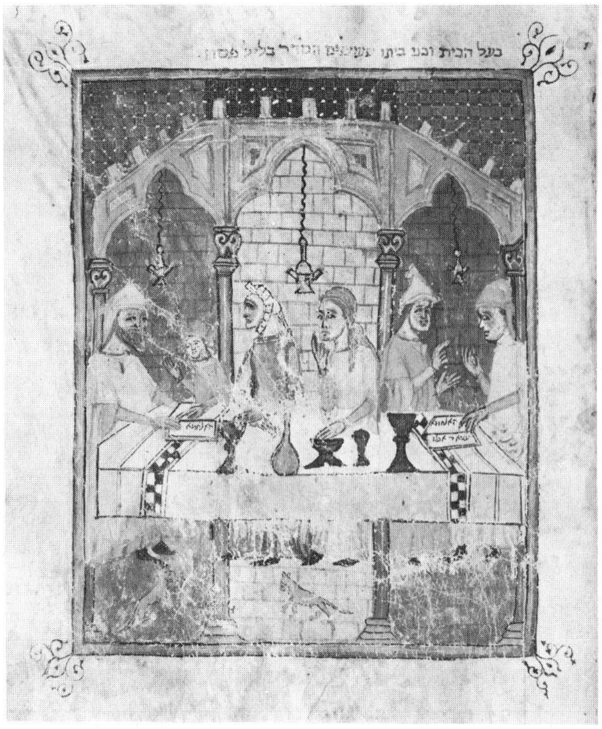

Figure 3. The Passover *seder,* shown in an illustration from a 14th-century *Haggadah* from Spain. London, British Museum, Or. Ms. 2884, fol. 18a.

During the Middle Ages a special order of service for the *seder* was adapted with a formal reply to the questions (culled from various rabbinic sources) and with supplementary material such as table hymns and jingles calculated to appeal to children. These are recorded in the Passover **Haggadah.* The Mishnah (Pes. 10:1) rules that even the poorest man in Israel must not eat on the first night of Passover unless he reclines. In mishnaic times, free men would normally recline at meals and on this night all must demonstrate that they are free. In the Middle Ages, in many communities, the custom of reclining at meals during the year was abandoned, but it became a duty to recline at the *seder.* During the *seder,* one must partake of four cups of wine (Pes. 10:1; see **Arba Kosot*). These were interpreted symbolically as corresponding to the four expressions of redemption in the Book of Exodus (6:6–7) or the four cups mentioned in the Book of Genesis (40:11–13) in connection with the dream of the chief butler (TJ, Pes. 10:1, 37c).

On the *seder* table are the following items: three (in some rites two) cakes of *mazzot* placed one on top of the other; a roasted egg and shankbone or other bone (as reminders of the paschal lamb and the festival offering in Temple times); a dish of salt water (for "dipping" and as a symbol of the Israelites' tears); **maror* such as lettuce (or horseradish) for "dipping"; and **haroset* ("clay"), a paste made from almonds, apples, and wine (Pes. 10:3) for the purpose of sweetening the bitter herbs and as a symbol of the mortar the Israelites used when building under the lash of their taskmasters.

The *seder* follows this standard order: (1) *kaddesh* ("sanctification"): the festival is introduced by the *Kiddush* benediction in which God is praised for giving the festivals to Israel; (2) *rehaz* ("wash"): the hands are washed in accordance with the ancient practice of ritual purification before partaking of anything dipped in liquid; (3) *karpas* ("greens"): the parsley is dipped in salt water; (4) *yahaz* ("division"): the middle *mazzah* is broken in two and one half is hidden. This latter portion is known as the **afikoman* ("the after-meal") and is eaten at the end of the meal, as a reminder of the paschal lamb which was eaten at the end so that its taste would remain in the mouth. It is customary for children to look for the *afikoman,* a prize being given to the successful finder; (5) *maggid* ("recitation"): the *Haggadah* is recited; (6) *rahzah* ("washing"): the ritual washing of the hands before breaking bread; (7) *mozi* ("bringing forth"): Grace before Meals is recited: "Blessed art Thou . . . who bringest forth *[ha-mozi]* bread . . ."; (8) *mazzah:* pieces of the top *mazzah* and the broken middle one are eaten; (9) *maror:* the bitter herbs are dipped in the *haroset* and eaten; (10) *korekh* ("binding"): a sandwich is made of pieces of the bottom *mazzah* and bitter herbs and eaten. This is a reminder of Hillel's practice in Temple times, based on the verse: "They shall eat it [the paschal lamb] with unleavened bread and bitter herbs" (Num. 9:11); (11) *shulhan arukh* ("prepared table"): the festive meal is eaten; (12) *zafun* ("hidden"): the *afikoman* is found and eaten; (13) *barekh* ("blessing"): Grace after Meals is recited; (14) *Hallel* ("psalms of praise"): Psalms 115–8 are recited. It was customary in Temple times to recite these psalms at the time of the offering of the paschal lamb (Pes. 5:7); (15) *nirzah* ("acceptance").

It is customary to have on the *seder* table a full cup of wine known as "*Elijah's cup." Reflections on past deliverance awaken hope for the final redemption, and Elijah, being the herald of the Messiah (Mal. 3:23), is welcomed; toward the end of the *seder,* the front door of the house is opened to demonstrate that this is a "night of watching" (Ex. 12:42) on which Israel knows no fear. In the Diaspora the *seder* is repeated on the second night. On the second night of Passover the counting of the *omer is begun. The laws of Passover in the Talmud occur in the talmudic tractate **Pesahim.* In the United States several additional prayers have been suggested by different groups.

Figure 4. Reclining on Passover, illustrated in the *Bird's Head Haggadah,* S. Germany, c. 1300. The human figures have birds' heads to comply with the commandment forbidding graven images. Jerusalem, Israel Museum, Ms. 180/57, fol. 8a.

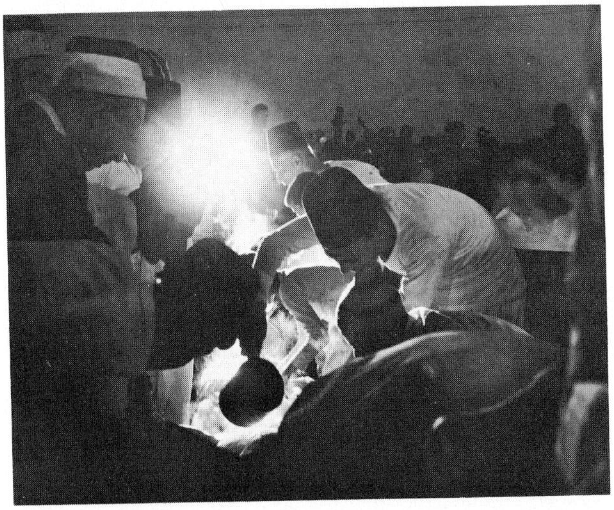

Figure 5. The sacrifice of the paschal lamb by the Samaritans on Mt. Gerizim, 1968. A sheep is being plucked with the aid of boiling water. Courtesy Government Press Office, Tel Aviv.

These include a prayer on behalf of the Holocaust victims, one for Russian Jewry, and a prayer of thanksgiving for the State of Israel, usually combined with a fifth cup of wine.

The Laws and Customs of Passover. No *ḥamez* ("leaven") is to be found in the house or owned during Passover (Ex. 12:15, 19). On the night before the festival, the house is thoroughly searched for *ḥamez* (Pes. 1:1). All leaven found in the house is gathered together in one place and burned on the following day before noon (see **Bedikat Ḥamez;* **Ḥamez,* Sale of).

According to rabbinic authorities, the obligation to eat *mazzah* applies only to the first night (Pes. 120a); it is customary, therefore, to prepare special *mazzot,* the wheat of which has been under observation from the time of reaping or grinding *(mazzah shemurah),* for it. During the remainder of the festival, though leaven may not be eaten, there is no obligation to eat *mazzah.* Some rabbinic authorities were opposed to the use of *mazzot* baked by machine.

Utensils in which leaven has been cooked, baked, or boiled must be specially treated before they can be used on Passover. The method is to immerse them in a caldron of boiling water, or, if they are utensils used on a fire, to heat them in a fire until they glow. However, not all vessels can be treated so. Unlike other forbidden food which becomes neutralized and may be eaten if mixed in 60 times its bulk, on Passover, the smallest admixture of *ḥamez* is enough to render a dish forbidden (see *Dietary Laws).

On the first day of Passover in the synagogue, a special prayer for dew *(tal)* is recited and the phrase *morid ha-geshem* is not said. On the Sabbath of Passover, the Song of Songs is read in the synagogue (Ashkenazi rite). Full **Hallel* is recited on the first day (two days in the Diaspora) and half-*Hallel* the rest of the festival. On the last day **Hazkarat Neshamot* is recited. When the liturgy refers to the festival, it does so as "the period of our freedom." *Ḥerut* ("freedom"), is, in fact, the dominant note of Passover.

See **Haggadah;* **Ḥamez;* **Mazzah;* *Festivals; *First-born, Fast of the. [L.J.]

Critical View. The feast of Passover consists of two parts: The Passover ceremony and the Feast of Unleavened Bread. Originally both parts existed separately; but at the beginning of the Exile they were combined.

Passover was originally not a pilgrimage feast, but a domestic ceremony consisting of the slaughtering and eating of the paschal animal. This animal—according to Exodus 12:21 (J) a sheep or goat, according to Deuteronomy 16:2, either a sheep or a bovine animal, according to Exodus 12:5 (P; cf. II Chron. 35:7), a year-old lamb or kid—was killed, in accordance with later texts (Ex. 12:6; Lev. 23:5; Num. 9:3–5; 28:16 (33:3); Josh. 5:10: Ezek. 45:21; Ezra 6:19; II Chron. 35:1), on the 14th of the first month (i.e., the 14th of Nisan, March/April), "between the evenings" (Ex. 12:6b; Lev. 23:5; Num. 9:3, 5, 11; 28:4, 8), i.e., at the setting of the sun. The early texts, Exodus 23:15 and 34:18, however, place the Festival of Unleavened Bread in "the season of the *ḥodesh* of Abib, since it was at the *ḥodesh* of Abib that you went free from Egypt," and Deuteronomy 16:1ff. places the slaughtering of the Passover sacrifice in "the *ḥodesh* of Abib, seeing that it was in this *ḥodesh* of Abib that you went free from Egypt at night . . ., so that you may remember the day you went free from Egypt"; and it has been argued that the last cited passage in particular makes poor sense unless *ḥodesh* designates not a 30-day period ("month") but a single day, i.e., the New Moon. (Both senses of *ḥodesh* are well attested; which is intended in this case can be confirmed only from the context.) The rite of touching the lintel and the doorposts of the house (formerly the tent) with blood from the paschal animal was connected with the slaughter (Ex. 12:7, 13 [P], 22 [J]). The flesh of the animal was boiled, according to Deuteronomy 16:7; but later—by II Chronicles 35:13a—this was interpreted in light of the P (Ex. 12:8–9) to mean broiling (cf. LXX, Deut. 16:7), and this is the rabbinic *halakhah* (Pes. 5:10). The flesh was then eaten with unleavened bread and bitter herbs (Ex. 12:8b; cf. Deut. 16:3a), during the night (Ex. 12:8a), in a community meal, in which the whole family or a combination of families (Ex. 12:4), but no uncircumcised persons (Ex. 12:48b; cf. 12:44–45, 48a [P]), took part. No flesh was allowed to remain until the next day (Deut. 16:4b).

Nothing is found in the Bible about the original meaning of the Passover rite. There is no clue in the name "Passover" (Heb. *pesaḥ*) because its etymology is uncertain. The assumption that the Passover was originally a sacrifice of the firstborn (G. Beer and others) is incorrect (1) because according to Exodus 22:28–29 and Leviticus 22:27, the firstborn of the sheep, ox, and goat was to be offered on the eighth day, (2) because according to PC (Ex. 12:5), the Passover animal had to be a year old, and (3) because the regulations about the firstborn in Exodus 34:19, 20a and 13:11–13 are connected with the eating of *mazzot* (Ex. [34:18]; 13:3–10), but not with the Passover (Ex. [34:25]; 12:24–27a; Kutsch, Segal).

Originally the Passover was celebrated by transient breeders of sheep and goats, later by the Israelites, to secure protection for their flocks prior to leaving the desert winter pasture for cultivated regions (Rost). The rite of the blood (see above) as well as the regulation, which was later still in force (Ex. 12:46b; cf. Num. 9:12), whereby no bone of the Passover animal was to be broken had an apotropaic significance. The oldest literary record in Exodus 12:21 (J) already presupposes the Passover. Hence the old nomadic custom is "historicized" by being connected with the main event in the Israelite salvation history, the Exodus. The reason for this connection was, from a traditional-historical standpoint, the situation of departure which belonged also to the Passover. Moreover, the rite of the blood made it possible to connect the Passover with the story of the killing of the Egyptian firstborn (Ex. 12:23), which was also inserted into the tradition of the Exodus as the reason why the Pharaoh let the Israelites go (Ex. 11:4aβ–8; Kutsch). This "historicization" has determined the character of the Passover: it became the feast commemorating the Exodus (cf. Ex. 12:11–14aα[P]; Deut. 16:1, 3). Originally, the Passover was celebrated among the families (Ex. 12:21 [J]) in tents, after the territorial occupation, in houses. After the cultic centralization of King Josiah, the celebration of the Passover was transferred to the central Sanctuary in Jerusalem (Deut. 16:2, 7; II Kings 23:21–23). The requirement that the slaughtering, preparing, and eating of the paschal animals was to take place in the forecourts of the Temple was maintained after the Exile (II Chron. 30:1–5; 35:13–14; Jub. 49:16, 20). Later, because of the large numbers of participants, the paschal animal was killed at the Temple place, but boiled and eaten in the houses of Jerusalem (e.g., Pes. 5:10; 7:12). The transfer of the Passover feast to the Temple entailed the end of the rite of blood; the blood of the paschal animals was, like other sacrificial blood, now poured on the base of the altar (II Chron. 30:16; 35:11).

The reason for the institution of a second Passover on the 14th day of the second month (Num. 9:10–12 [P^{s}]), which is wrongly ascribed in II Chronicles 30 to King Hezekiah of Judah, is not a difference in calendar between Judah and Northern Israel (cf. S. Talmon, in: VT, 8 (1958), 48–74) but the possibility that a Jew might be prevented from taking part in the feast on the 14th day of the first month because of uncleanness or a distant journey.

Feast of the Unleavened Bread. Unlike the Passover, the seven-day Feast of Unleavened Bread, which was celebrated in the month of Abib (Ex. 13:4; 23:15; 34:18), is probably taken over from the Canaanites. The main custom of the feast is the eating of unleavened bread or *maẓẓot* (e.g., Ex. 23:15; 34:18). The required pilgrimage (Ex. 23:14–15, 17; 34:23; Deut. 16:16), originally to a local sanctuary, later—after the cult centralization of Josiah—to Jerusalem, is secondary to the eating of *maẓẓot*.

Originally the feast extended over a week beginning not on the day following the Paschal night but on a "morrow after the Sabbath." The counting of the seven weeks until the "Feast of Weeks" (Pentecost; Lev. 23:11, 15–16). In Deuteronomy 16:9 it is described as the day on which the Israelites "first put the sickle to the standing grain" and the grain harvest is begun. Because of its proximity to the traditional date of the Exodus, the *maẓẓot* feast was also connected with the Exodus and thus "historicized" (e.g., Ex. 12:29–34, 37–39 [J]; cf. 12:15–20; 23:15; 34:18 [P]; Deut. 16:3b). A yearly celebration of the march through the Jordan (according to Josh. 3–4) on the Feast of Unleavened Bread (Kraus, Soggin) cannot be derived from the late text Joshua 5:10–12; and the thesis that therefore the *maẓẓot* feast was celebrated in older times as an "election feast" in Gilgal (Wildberger) is contradictory to the fact that the Exodus was also remembered in the celebration of the Passover. Until shortly before the Exile (Deut. 16:7b), the participants in the celebration of the Passover returned home after the celebration at the Temple (the instructions about the *maẓẓot* feast in Deut. 16:3aβ, 3b, 4a, 8 and 16 are a secondary enlargement [Horst]; even then the Passover and *maẓẓot* feasts (as pilgrimages) were still celebrated separately. To fix a common date for the Jews in Babylonia the *maẓẓot* feast after 587 B.C.E. was given a fixed date, the 15th to 21st of the first month, and thus connected with the Passover (first mentioned Ezek. 45:21; Lev. 23:5,6; Num. 28:16, 17; Josh. 5:10, 11; Ezra 6:19, 22; II Chron. [30:15, 13 21–22] 35:17a, 17b; cf. also the Passover papyrus from Elephantine).

Passover in the New Testament. The combined Passover-*Maẓẓot* Feast is also presupposed in the New Testament. The name here refers a) to the celebration of the Passover (Matt. 26:18; Mark 14:1; Heb. 11:28); b) to the whole feast (Matt. 26:2; Luke 2:41; 22:1; Acts 12:4; especially in John 2:13, 23, et al.; for this name "[feast of] unleavened bread" [Mark 14:1, 12; Luke 22:1, 7; Acts. 12:3; 20:6] is also used), and c) as in the Old Testament (e.g., Ex. 12:21), to the Passover lamb (Mark 14:12, 14, 16; Luke 22:8, 15; John 18–28; II Cor. 5:7). The connection of the death of Jesus with the Passover is important. According to the synoptic gospels, Jesus was crucified on the 15th day of Nisan, the first day of the feast; they understand the last supper of Jesus as a Passover meal, during which the salvational meaning of Jesus' death is disclosed (Mark 14:22, 24). The gospel of John, on the other hand, dates the death of Jesus to the 14th of Nisan (John 19:14; cf. 18:28), to the hour of the Passover slaughtering (cf. John 19:14, 31; Mark 15:33–34, 37; cf. Pes. 5:1; Jos. Wars, 6:423), and the meal to the night of the 13th of Nisan. This does not have calendaric

(Jaubert), but theological reasons. Unlike the synoptic gospels, John interprets Jesus as the Passover lamb (John 1:29; 19:36; cf. e.g., otherwise I Cor. 5:7; I Pet. 1:19; Rev. 5:6).   [Er.K]

Passover Cookery. Leaven, grain (except in the form of *maẓẓot* and *maẓẓah* meal), and pulses are forbidden in some rites during the Passover week. Ashkenazim also refrain from eating rice. The ceremonial food placed on the *seder* table varies little from community to community, although the ingredients in the *ḥaroset* change in different localities. The basic recipe of honey, wine, nuts, fruit, and spices is however common to all.

Although *maẓẓah*-meal dumplings *(kleys, kneydlekh)* are considered a typical Passover dish, Ashkenazi ultra-Orthodox Jews do not eat them, in case they should ferment slightly; the same applies to the *maẓẓah*-and-chocolate layer cake, popular in Israel among all communities at Passover. Lithuanian Jews, even the ultra-Orthodox, eat a fermented beet soup called *risel borsht*. Other Ashkenazim also eat borsht and *khreyn*, a condiment prepared from grated horseradish which is colored with beet juice. Sephardim and North Africans have lamb as the main course at the *seder* meal, and serve stuffed lamb intestines during the week. Among the North Africans, white truffles are considered a Passover delicacy. Sephardim generally do not cook with *maẓẓah* meal but use *maẓẓah* with eggs and in meat dishes. All communities adapt year-round recipes to Passover, substituting in dishes such as pancakes potato flour and or *maẓẓah* meal for flour. Ashkenazi desserts include: cinnamon balls, *teyglekh* (honey cakes), *plava* cake (a sponge cake in which ground almonds replace the flour), coconut cakes, and candies containing carrots, cinnamon, or ginger. Sephardim eat a sponge cake called *bisquitte pané d'Espagne,* and the North Africans, cakes of honey, almonds, and cinnamon, as well as French-style doughnuts *(beignets)* made with *maẓẓah* meal. Among Moroccan Jews a feast is held at the end of Passover called *Maimuna.   [ED.]

In Art. While the Haggadah, by its presence and use, dominates the *seder* table, other manifestations of the artistic impulse are by no means lacking. The table itself is a center of attraction as an object around which to gather and feast. The most important item on the Passover table is the *seder* plate, or a basket. A special Passover plate *(ke'arah)* is mentioned in mishnaic times, and throughout history, but no indication of its actual decoration is known in early times. Illuminated medieval *Haggadot* illustrate a large round plate on the table in Ashkenazi ones, and a wicker basket in some Sephardi and Italian manuscripts. A custom of placing the basket on a child's head when reciting *Ha Laḥma* was illustrated in the Barcelona Haggadah (British Museum, Add. Ms. 14761).

Extant *seder* plates from the time of the Renaissance and onward were made of practically every material: wood, copper, brass, pewter, porcelain, faience, stoneware, and plastics. Many of the old simple plates are of pewter because it shines like silver when well kept, cleaned, and polished, and also lends itself easily to engraving. The motif most usually found on these pewter plates is the paschal lamb; another favorite is a five- or six-pointed star in the center. Plates are frequently adorned with scenes from the Passover story: the *seder* meal, the rabbis at Bene-Berak, the four sons, the story of the *Ḥad Gadya,* or the order of the *seder* ceremony. Hebrew inscriptions are another typical and popular decorative scheme. The favorite, usually in the center, consists of the *Kiddush,* or an important citation from the *Haggadah* such as the *Ha Laḥma.* There is often a well-loved psalm or the grace after meals.

The earliest ceramic plates for Passover were probably made in Spain. In the ceramic group, the most important plates were made in the 16th century of majolica in Italian workshops, some by Isaac Cohen Modon. Fourteen such plates are known and were all executed in dark brown decorated with colored pictures illustrating Passover rituals and figures. There are also blue Delft plates for Passover use inscribed *"Pesaḥdic"* or *"Yontefdic."* An interesting type of *seder* plate is the three-tiered open one, on which the

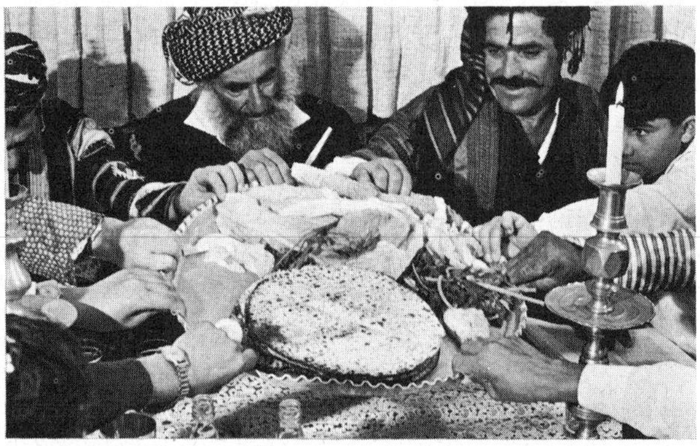

Figure 6. Passover *seder* of Kurdish Jews in Jerusalem. The ceremonial *seder* plate is being raised. Photo David Harris, Jerusalem.

Passover

PLATE 1. Delft *seder* dish by Albrest de Kerser, 1642. Diameter $9\frac{1}{4}$ in. (23.5 cm.). Jerusalem, Israel Museum. Photo David Harris, Jerusalem.

PLATE 2. Majolica *seder* dish, Spain, c. 1450. Diameter $22\frac{1}{4}$ in. (56.5 cm.). Jerusalem, Israel Museum. Photo Jacob Goren, Jerusalem.

4

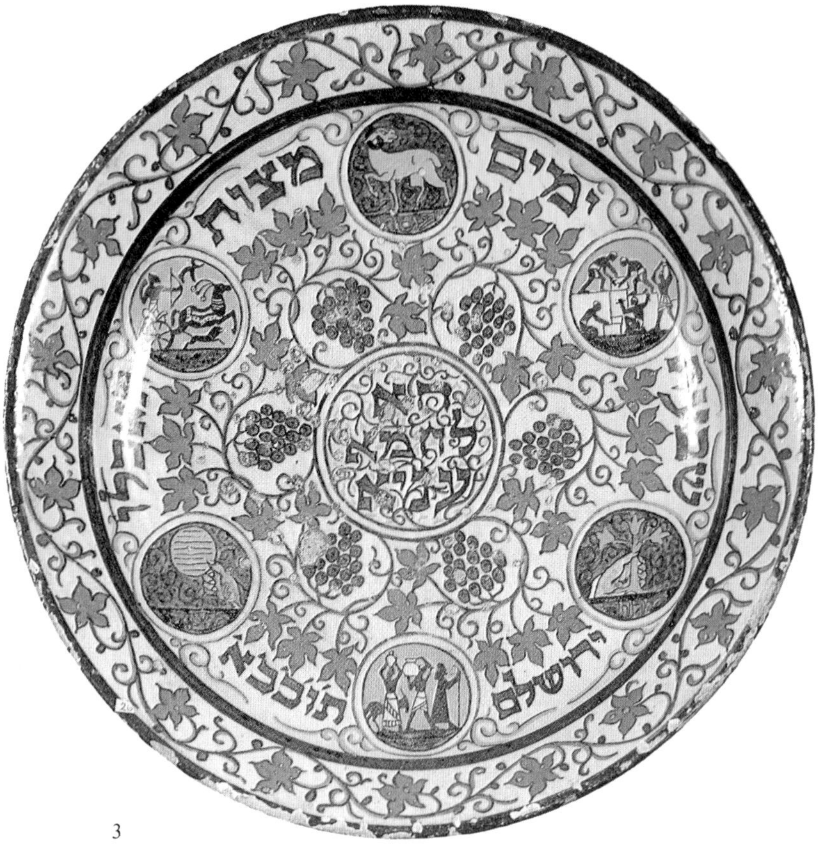

3

5

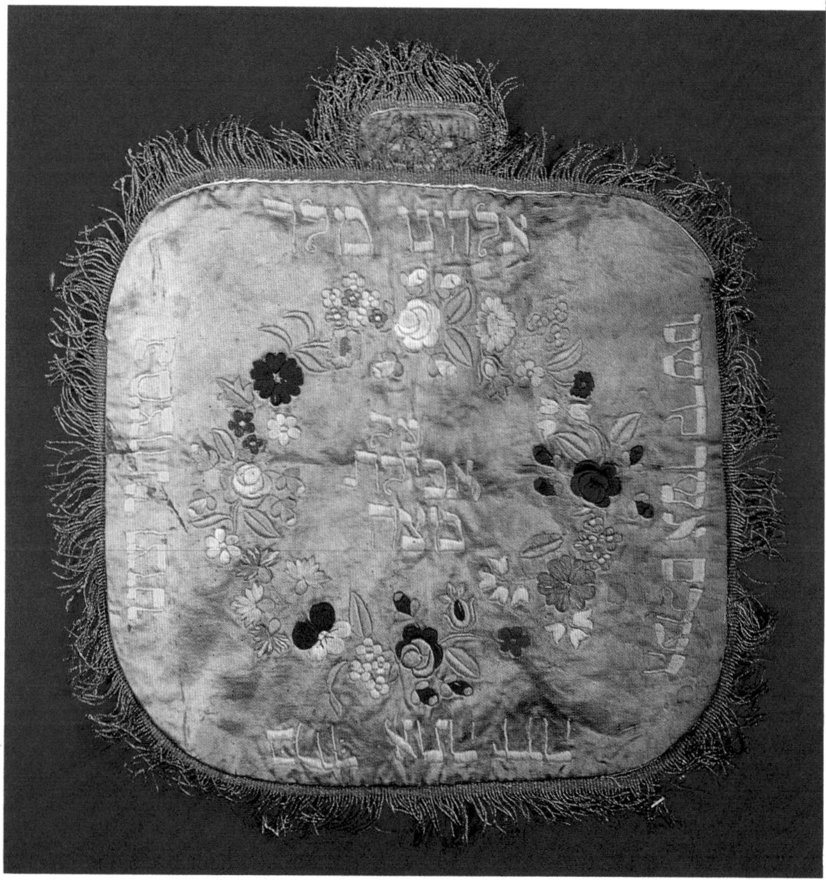

PLATE 3. Glazed ceramic *seder* dish, Ereẓ Israel, 19th century. Diameter 13⅓ in. (34 cm.). Jerusalem, Sir Isaac and Lady Wolfson Museum in Hechal Shlomo. Photo David Harris, Jerusalem.

PLATE 4. Painted linen Passover banner, showing Adam and Eve in the Garden of Eden. Germany, early 19th century. Length 40 in. (101.6 cm.). New York, Central Synagogue of N.Y.

PLATE 5. Embroidered *mazzah* cover, Germany, late 19th or early 20th century. Jerusalem, Michael Kaufman Collection. Photo David Harris, Jerusalem.

6

PLATE 6. Faience *seder* dish by Isaac Cohen, Padua, Italy, 1673. Diameter 16¾ in. (42.5 cm.). Jerusalem, Israel Museum. Photo David Harris, Jerusalem.

PLATE 7. Ceramic *seder* dish, Hungary, early 19th century. Diameter 15½ in. (39.4 cm.). Jerusalem, Sir Isaac and Lady Wolfson Museum in Hechal Shlomo. Photo David Harris, Jerusalem.

PLATE 8. Majolica *seder* dish, Czechoslovakia, 19th century. Cleveland, Joseph B. and Olyn Horwitz Collection.

7

8

PLATE 9. *Seder* in an 18th-century Bohemian home. Frontispiece to the *"Sister" to the Van Geldern Haggadah,* written and illuminated by the Moravian artist, Moses Leib b. Wolf of Trebitsch, 1716–17. Cincinnati, Hebrew Union College.

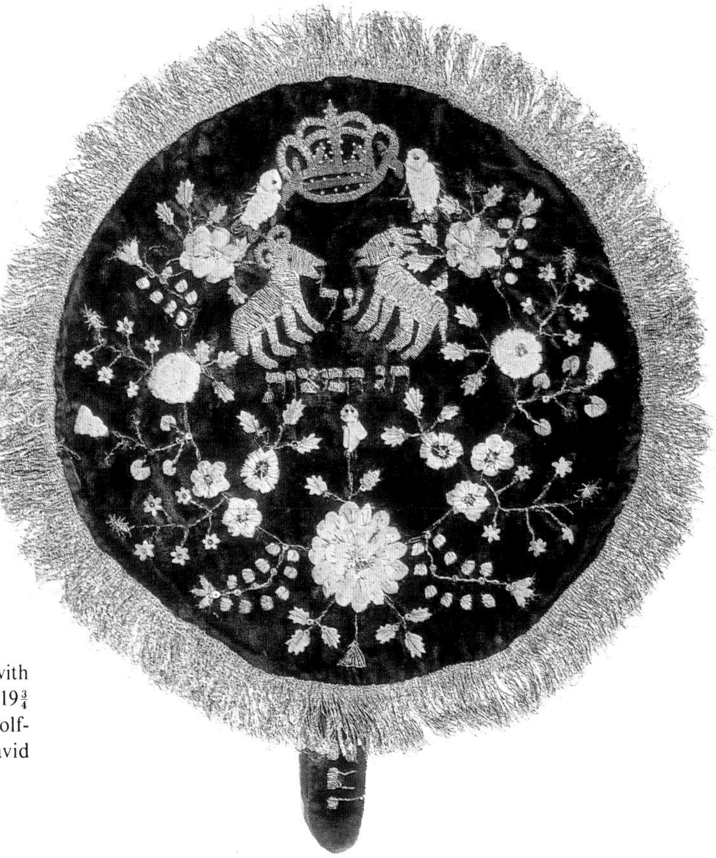

PLATE 10. Velvet *mazzah* cover embroidered with fish scales, Hungary, 19th century. Diameter $19\frac{3}{4}$ in. (50 cm.). Jerusalem, Sir Isaac and Lady Wolfson Museum in Hechal Shlomo. Photo David Harris, Jerusalem.

three *mazzot* are placed. This type was probably invented in the 18th century, in order to overcome the problem of the *mazzot* covering the decorated plate, and the different items placed on top of the *mazzot*. Many of these plates, executed in Eastern Europe, were made of silver frame and glass tiers. They are round or square, with decorated tops, some with decorative receptacles for the five items. A traditional modern *seder* plate of the same type was made by Ludwig Wolpert of contemporary materials—a silver frame supporting three glass partitions in which the three ceremonial *mazzot* are clearly visible. The *maror, ḥaroset,* roast egg, and shankbone, in glass dishes, rest on top of the upper partition.

In addition to the *seder* plate there are wine cups for *Kiddush*, a special cup for the prophet Elijah, and others for drinking the ritual four cups of wine. The most splendid of all cups is reserved for the prophet Elijah. The favorite theme on these vessels is the return of Zion. One features the Messiah entering Jerusalem on a donkey, led by Elijah blowing a ram's horn, while David is playing his harp.

The *seder* has inspired other ceremonial objects of particular artistic quality: a cloth to cover the *mazzot;* a hand towel for washing of the hands; a pillow for the father to lean on; and a white robe for him to wear. [AB.K.]

Bibliography: P. Goodman, *The Passover Anthology* (1961), incl. bibl.; I. Levy, *A Guide to Passover* (1958); M. M. Kasher, *Haggadah Shelemah* (1967[3]); J. B. Segal, *The Hebrew Passover* (1963); Schauss, *Guide of Jewish Holy Days* (1966[4]), 38–85; T. Gaster, *Passover: Its History and Traditions* (1949); S. J. Zevin, *Ha-Mo'adim ba-Halakhah* (1963[10]), 215–91. CRITICAL VIEW: F. Horst, *Das Privilegrecht Jahres...* (1930), 81ff.; L. Rost, in: ZDPV, 66 (1943), 205–16; J. Jeremias, in: *Theologisches Woerterbuch zum Neuen Testament,* 5 (1954), 895–903; A. Jaubert, *La date de la Cène* (1957); E. Auerbach, in: VT, 8 (1958), 1–18; E. Kutsch, in: *Zeitschrift fuer Theologie und Kirche,* 55 (1958), 1–35; H. Haag, in: *Dictionnaire de la Bible, Suppléments,* 6 (1960), 1120–49; H. Wildberger, *Jahwes Eigentumsvolk* (1960); H.-J. Kraus, *Gottesdienst in Israel...* (1962[2]); J. A. Soggin, in: VT Supplement, 15 (1966), 263–77; P. Grelot, in: VT, 17 (1967), 201–7; A. B. Ehrlich, *Randglossen zur hebraeischen Bibel,* 1 (1968), 312–3. IN THE ARTS: Mayer, Art, index.

PASSOVER, ALEXANDER (1840–1910), Russian jurist. The son of an army surgeon, Passover was born in Uman, Ukraine, and graduated from Moscow University in 1861. He was denied a professorship because of his refusal to renounce Judaism, and became a prosecutor's secretary at the Moscow District Court. Passover was admitted to the Odessa bar in 1871 and after the Odessa pogrom of that year was one of several Jewish lawyers who represented the victims in court proceedings against the perpetrators. From 1874 he practiced in St. Petersburg, where he founded a seminary for law students and where he acquired a reputation as an outstanding jurist and an authority on Russian and foreign law. His advice on civil-law matters was sought by public bodies and his interpretations of judicial rulings in Russian legal journals were sometimes adopted by the Supreme Court. For some years, he sat on the board of the St. Petersburg Bar Association, but resigned in 1889 when the board gave the Ministry of Justice statistics on Jews in the legal profession.

Passover was an active figure in the Jewish community and initiated research projects on the economic situation of the Jews in Russia. He bequeathed his large library, containing a huge amount of anti-Jewish literature, to the St. Petersburg Academy of Sciences.

Bibliography: S. Ginsburg, *Amolike Peterburg* (1944), 101–10; *Russian Jewry 1860–1917* (1966), index. [D.B.-R.-H.]

PASSOVER, SECOND (Heb. פֶּסַח שֵׁנִי, *Pesaḥ Sheni*), According to the Bible (Num. 9:6–13) every person unable to offer the *Passover sacrifice on the 14th of Nisan because of ritual defilement or because of unavoidable absence from Jerusalem was bound to observe the Passover ritual for one day, one month later, on the 14th of Iyyar. The only biblical reference to the actual observance of the Second Passover is to the time of *Hezekiah, and occurs in II Chronicles 30:1–27. Since the date of the Second Passover falls during the mourning period of the counting of the **Omer* and only four days before *Lag ba-Omer, no special ritual is now observed except the omission of the **Taḥanun* in the liturgy. Some people eat unleavened bread on Second Passover, as a symbolic remembrance. [ED.]

PASSOW, AARON HARRY (1920–), U.S. educator. Passow's major efforts focused on curriculum appraisal, particularly in programs for the gifted and for the socially disadvantaged. Born in Liberty, New York, he studied at the New York State College for Teachers at Albany, and at Teachers College, Columbia University. He later taught at both universities, and became a professor at the latter. He directed the Talented Youth Project at Columbia, which studied programs for the gifted in various parts of the United States. In 1965 he became chairman of the Teachers College Committee on Urban Education and directed a comprehensive study of the Washington, D.C., public schools (1966–67), a major analysis of problems facing public education in an urban depressed area. He published *Secondary Education for All: The English Approach* (1961); *Developing a Curriculum for Modern Living* (1957); *Education in Depressed Areas* (1963); and together with others: *Education of the Disadvantaged* (1967). [A.J.T.]

PASTERNAK, BORIS LEONIDOVICH (1890–1960), Soviet Russian poet and novelist. A son of the painter Leonid *Pasternak, the younger Pasternak ultimately became one of the very few Soviet writers whose work is essentially Christian in spirit. Born and educated in Moscow, he also studied at the University of Marburg, Germany. He is chiefly remembered as one of the truly

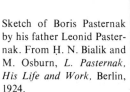

Sketch of Boris Pasternak by his father Leonid Pasternak. From Ḥ. N. Bialik and M. Osburn, *L. Pasternak, His Life and Work,* Berlin, 1924.

great Russian poets of all time, his exquisitely polished verse being highly intellectual, erudite, and occasionally obscure. His prose, too, is essentially poetic in nature, emphasizing language, structure, and style. Among Pasternak's favorite subjects are the wholesomeness of nature, the artificiality of man-made ideas, and the futility of ideologies. A recurrent theme is the irrelevance of politics to human happiness, and the inability of truly sensitive and intelligent men to choose sides at times of political upheaval because unquestioning allegiance to any political grouping requires renunciation of one's intellectual and ethical independence and a willingness to condone violence perpetrated in the name of a noble cause. Pasternak's verse collections include *Poverkh baryerov* ("Over the Barriers," 1917, 1931[2]), *Sestra moya—zhizn* ("My Sister—Life," 1922), *Devyatsot pyaty god* ("The Year 1905," 1927), and

Vtoroye rozhdeniye ("Second Birth," 1932). After World War II he published a number of outstanding translations of world classics, mainly drama.

Pasternak's abhorrence of violence and consequent flight from political realities in search of individual happiness forms the leitmotif of his most famous work, the novel *Doctor Zhivago,* which was smuggled out of the U.S.S.R. and first published in Italy in 1957 (Eng. tr., 1958). The event became a major political, as well as literary, sensation. In 1958 Pasternak was awarded the Nobel Prize for Literature, but the political storm in the U.S.S.R., during which it was suggested that he be expelled from the country, forced him to decline the award. After his death, he was halfheartedly reinstated into the pantheon of Soviet poetry, and some of his verse was reprinted. *Doctor Zhivago,* however, continued to be banned. The novel reveals Pasternak's total estrangement from Judaism and his faith in the superiority of Christianity. The best Soviet appreciation of Pasternak was written by Andrei Sinyavsky (see Yuli *Daniel).

Bibliography: P. S. R. Payne, *The Three Worlds of Boris Pasternak* (1962), incl. bibl.; G. Ruge, *Pasternak: a Pictorial Biography* (1959); G. R. A. Conquest, *The Pasternak Affair; Courage of a Genius; a Documentary Report* (1962); J. Stora, in: *Cahiers du Monde Russe et Soviétique* (July–Dec., 1968), 353–64.
[M.F.]

PASTERNAK, LEONID OSIPOVICH (1862–1945), Russian artist. Born in Odessa, Pasternak studied medicine in Moscow, but in 1883 went to Munich to enroll at the Academy of Art. Returning to Odessa, he did a full year's military service, then met and married the pianist Rosa Kaufmann. In 1888 his first large canvas, "Letter from Home," was bought by the Tretyakov Gallery, Moscow. The Pasternaks moved to Moscow, where he opened a school of painting, edited a periodical, *The Artist,* and for some years taught at the Moscow School of Painting,

Self-portrait by Leonid Pasternak. From Ḥ. N. Bialik and M. Osborn, *L. Pasternak, His Life and Work,* Berlin, 1924.

Sculpture, and Architecture. He was a close friend of Leo Tolstoy, whom he often portrayed. His illustrations of Tolstoy's *Resurrection* were exhibited at the Paris World Exhibition, 1900. In 1921 Pasternak, with his wife, went to Paris, and in 1938 emigrated to England, spending his last years in Oxford. Pasternak was at his best not as an oil painter but as a draftsman, whose portrait studies superbly catch the sitter's character. He painted portraits of outstanding Zionists, among them Bialik, Sokolow, Tchernichowsky, and Weizmann. In 1924 he visited Palestine, where he made drawings and watercolors of the countryside. He was the father of the novelist, Boris *Pasternak.

Bibliography: Russell, in: *Studio,* 161 (1961), 98–101; Bialik, in: *Saturday Review* (April 4, 1959), 18–21.
[A.W.]

PASTOUREAUX ("Shepherds"), the name given to the participants in two popular Crusades in France called against the Muslims in Spain. The first movement emerged in Picardy in 1251, inspired by a leader who called himself the "ruler of Hungary." Claiming to have had a vision in which the Virgin Mary ordered him to take up the cross, he rapidly gathered 30,000 adherents, mainly young men and women, who marched toward the south. This group of Pastoureaux did not attack the Jews until they arrived in Bourges: there they broke into synagogues, destroyed books, and robbed the Jews. At Bordeaux they were turned back by the seneschal of Gascony and dispersed.

A similar movement arose in the southwest in 1320. Jewish chroniclers (Solomon *ibn Verga, *Joseph ha-Kohen, and Samuel *Usque) telescoped these two movements by attributing to the second the beginnings of the first. This time the religious aim of waging war against the Muslims in Spain was accompanied by a social revolt against the rich and the higher clergy. Thus, the civil and religious authorities swiftly intervened against the crusaders, and *Philip V the Tall and Pope *John XXII called on them to protect the Jews. In fact, the Pastoureaux turned first against the Jews, intending to use their riches to purchase weapons; they also put to death those Jews who refused to accept baptism. The anti-Jewish persecutions first began in *Agen or Agenais, *Bordeaux or Bourdeilles, *Gascony and Bigorre, Mont-de-Marsan and Condom, Auch, Rabastens, Gaillac, *Albi, Lézat, and especially Verdun-sur-Garonne and *Castelsarrasin, where several hundreds of Jews were killed or committed suicide. The events at *Toulouse were reported by an eyewitness, the German Jew Baruch, who was employed as a teacher by the local Jewish community. The viscount of Toulouse, who had been informed of the massacre perpetrated by the Pastoureaux in Castelsarrasin and the neighboring localities between June 10 and 12, set out at the head of an armed detachment in order to check their advance. He returned with 24 cartloads of Pastoureaux, intending to imprison them in a castle of the town, but the populace came to their assistance and released them. At once they invaded the Jewish quarter, looting the houses and putting to death anyone who refused baptism. When they marched toward *Carcassone, extremely severe repressive measures were taken against them. A number succeeded in reaching Aragon, where they persecuted the Jews anew, particularly in *Montclus. King James II of *Aragon ordered the suppression of the Pastoureaux, and on this occasion many of them were slaughtered.

According to Jewish chroniclers, 120 communities suffered at the hands of the Pastoureaux, and this appears to be an accurate estimate. Baruch also relates that although the pope called upon the authorities to protect the Jews, the Inquisition would not allow those who had been forcibly baptized to return to Judaism.

Bibliography: C. de Vic and J. J. Vaissete, *Histoire générale de Languedoc...* (1730), passim; S. Grayzel, in: HJ, 17 (1955), 89–120; J. Duvernoy (ed.), *Registre d'inquisition de Jacques Fournier, évêque de Pamiers* (1965). [B.BL.]

PAT, JACOB (1890–1966), Jewish labor leader, teacher, author, and journalist. Pat was born in *Bialystok into a working-class family, was an outstanding student in the *Musar yeshivot, and joined the Zionist socialist circles of his native town on the eve of the 1905 revolution. He was a member of the *Zionist-Socialist Workers' Party and from 1917 of the *United Jewish Socialist Workers' Party. In 1920 he joined the Bund and at first adhered to its left wing. He began his pedagogic career as a Hebrew teacher and was later headmaster of several schools, as well as an active proponent of Yiddish culture. After World War I he acted as secretary of the Democratic Jewish Community of Bialystok. From 1921 to 1939 he lived in Warsaw. He served as secretary of the center of the Yiddish school network (CYSHO; 1921–29). He was a recognized spokesman of the Bund and in 1929 he became a member of the editorial board of its daily organ *Folkstsaytung*. Pat was also a member of the Jewish community council of Warsaw. On the eve of World War II he arrived in the United States as a member of the Bund delegation, and remained there. He was a member of the body representing the Polish Bund in the U. S. until its dissolution (1947), but his main activity was within the *Jewish Labor Committee, of which he was the general secretary until 1963. Though formerly an outspoken anti-Zionist, Pat headed the new trend in the Bund which called for a change in the attitude toward the Jewish state in Palestine, even before its establishment. He was an ardent orator and a versatile lecturer. He began to write Hebrew novels in 1905, later changing to Yiddish, and he was a prolific author and publicist who dealt with a wide range of subjects. In the United States Pat was coeditor of the monthly *Zukunft*. His writings include *Bundistn* 1–2 (1926–29) and *Ashes and Fire* (1947).

Bibliography: I. S. Hertz (ed.), *Doyres Bundistn*, 3 (1968), 61–65. [M.M.]

PATAI, JÓZSEF (1882–1953), Hungarian and Hebrew poet, translator, and editor. Patai, who was born in Gyöngyöspata, taught at a Budapest municipal high school (1908–19).

He published a Hebrew verse collection, *Sha'ashu'ei Alumim* ("The Pleasures of Youth," 1902), and two anthologies of Hungarian poetry *Babilon vizein* ("By the Waters of Babylon," 1906) and *Sulamit látod a lángot?* ("Shulamit, Do You See the Flame?" 1919). A selection of his poems also appeared in English

József Patai, Hungarian and Hebrew writer.

(1920). He published Hungarian versions of the Hebrew poetry of many eras, his translations eventually appearing in five volumes entitled *Héber költők* ("Hebrew Poets," 1910–12; 1921²). Three of his most important works were his volume of early recollections, *A középső kapu* ("The Middle Gate," 1927); *A föltámadó Szentföld* ("The Holy Land Restored," 1926), on his first visit to Palestine; and his biography of Theodor *Herzl (1931; *Star over Jordan*, 1946).

Patai also distinguished himself as editor of the Zionist monthly *Mult és Jövő*, which he founded in 1912 and edited for 27 years. By publishing good translations of major Jewish writers from many countries, he imbued Hungarian Jewish intellectuals with an appreciation for Jewish literature, art, and thought. Patai also combated the anti-Zionists, he and some associates founding the Magyar Zsidók Pro Palestina Szövetsége ("League of Hungarian Jews for Palestine"), and organizing annual pilgrimages to Ereẓ Israel.

In 1938 Patai emigrated to Palestine. At first he lived in Jerusalem, but later settled in Givatayim. His subsequent publications include the three-volume selection of his writings *Mivḥar Kitvei Yosef Patai* (1943); and a volume based on his lectures at the Hebrew University (*Mi-Sefunei ha-Shirah*, 1939).

His wife, EDITH (Ehrenfeld) PATAI (1889–), author and lyric poet, wrote works of Jewish and Zionist inspiration, notably *Engem is hív a föld* ("The Land Calls Me Too," 1927) and a novel, *Szent szomjúság* ("Sacred Thirst," 1936). His sons were the folklore authority Raphael *Patai, and Shaul Patai (1918–), professor of chemistry at the Hebrew University of Jerusalem.

Bibliography: *Magyar Irodalmi Lexikon*, 2 (1965), 448–9; I. Pap, *Patai Edith, a költő* (1936). [B.Y.]

PATAI, RAPHAEL (1910–), anthropologist, biblical scholar, and editor. A son of József *Patai, he was born in Budapest, Hungary. In 1933 he settled in Palestine, where he was awarded the first Ph.D. degree of the Hebrew University in 1936. Returning to Budapest for a brief period, he was ordained at the rabbinical seminary. In 1938 Patai became an instructor in Hebrew at the Hebrew University. In 1942–43 he served as academic secretary of the Haifa Technion. In 1944 Patai founded the Palestine Institute of Folklore and Ethnology in Jerusalem and served as its director of research until 1948. In 1945 he launched and edited the journal of the institute, *Edoth (Communities); a Quarterly of Folklore and Ethnology*. In 1949 he began editing a series of books for the institute entitled *Studies in Folklore and Ethnology* (5 vols.) and another series *Social Studies* (2 vols.).

In 1947 he went to the U.S. and in 1948–57 was professor of anthropology at Dropsie College. From 1966 he was professor of anthropology at Fairleigh Dickinson University, Rutherford, New Jersey. During 1956–68 Patai served as president of the American Friends of the Tel Aviv University in New York. In 1956 he became director of research of the Herzl Institute, New York, and from 1957 also editor of the Herzl Press.

His main contribution to scholarship resides in two fields—the culture of the ancient Hebrews and Jews and that of the modern Middle East including Israel.

He published several hundred articles and more than two dozen books, among them: *Ha-Mayim* (A Study in Palestinology and Palestinian Folklore, 1936); *Ha-Sappanut ha-Ivrit* ("Jewish Seafaring in Ancient Times," 1938); *Man and Earth in Hebrew Custom, Belief and Legend* (2 vols., 1942–43); *Madda ha-Adam* ("An Introduction to Anthropology," 2 vols., 1947–48); *Man and Temple in Ancient Jewish Myth and Ritual* (1947, 1967²); *Israel Between East and West* (1953, 1970²); *Sex and Family in the Bible and the Middle East* (1959); *Golden River to Golden Road: Society, Culture and Change in the Middle East* (1962, 1967, 1969, 1971); *Hebrew Myths* (with Robert Graves, 1964); and *The Hebrew Goddess* (1967).

Patai also edited a number of important publications, such as: *The Republic of Syria* (2 vols., 1956); *The Republic of Lebanon* (2 vols., 1956); *The Kingdom of Jordan* (1956⁸); *Herzl Year Book* (1958–65); *The Complete Diaries of Theodor Herzl* (5 vols., 1960); *Studies in Biblical and Jewish Folklore* (with Francis Lee Utley and Dov Noy, 1960); *Women in the Modern World* (1967); and *Encyclopedia of Zionism and Israel* (2 vols., 1971). [T.P.]

PATERSON, city in N.E. New Jersey. Jews first settled in Paterson about 1844. In 1904 there were 1,250 Jews in the city, and the Jewish population increased to 24,000 in 1940. However, their number declined to about 15,000 in the latter 1960s.

The Jewish settlers of the 1840s were primarily tailors and merchants from Germany, Bohemia, and Hungary. In 1847 a group of them organized Congregation B'nai Jeshurun, the first Jewish congregation in New Jersey. In the early 1890s a new synagogue was built, largely due to the generosity of Nathan *Barnert.

Late in the 1870s Barnert served two terms as alderman, and was twice elected mayor during the 1880s. Nevertheless, there was growing antagonism toward Jews and other "new immigrants" at this time. Newspaper editorials clearly indicated that undesirable Europeans were those from southern and Eastern Europe, including the Jews then beginning to arrive from Russia and Poland. These new Jewish immigrants, who had fled the Russian pogroms, especially those in the Polish textile centers of Lodz and Bialystok in 1905 and 1906, were attracted to the "Silk City," as Paterson was then known. A sampling of Russian Jews in Paterson reported by the U.S. Immigration Commission in 1911 indicated that more than 91% had worked in textile mills prior to coming to the United States. The new Jewish immigrants moved into a troubled silk industry. New and improved machinery had made it possible for employers to replace skilled, expensive English, German, and Irish labor, with less skilled and cheaper Jewish, Italian, and other "new immigrant" labor, creating anti-Jewish feeling in the city. These Jewish workers' experience in radical ideas, labor organization, and strikes in Europe helped to continue Paterson's long tradition of labor troubles. Consequently many silk manufacturers moved their factories to Pennsylvania coal-mining towns and to the South, and many Polish Jews acquired machinery during the 1920s and opened small shops often with only one or two employees. During the 1920s as many as 90% of the silk manufacturing shops in Paterson were operated by Polish Jews. Competition was intense; few shops prospered. By the end of World War II the silk industry in Paterson had virtually disappeared, while the city's other important sources of employment and economic activity, in addition to manufacturing, retail, and wholesale establishments, began a period of stagnation.

After 1920 Paterson's total population increased only a little, while the number of Jews living there declined. In the same period, and especially after 1940, the city's suburbs, Clifton to the south, Fair Lawn to the east, and Wayne to the north, grew substantially, as did their Jewish populations. The number of Jewish congregations in Paterson declined after 1945. Among those still in existence are the three oldest in the city: Congregation B'nai Jeshurun Barnert Memorial, Temple Emanuel (organized in 1904), and Congregation B'nai Israel (founded 1886), which in the 1960s merged with Congregation Ahawath Joseph. Other institutions which serve Paterson and its suburban Jewish communities are the YM-YWHA, founded in 1925 to carry on cultural, social, and physical education work, and the Jewish Community Council, founded in 1933 to coordinate the work of various organizations in their local and national fund-raising campaigns. Distinguished Jewish residents, or former residents of Paterson include father-and-son poets Louis and Allen *Ginsberg, and former Democratic congressman Charles S. Joelson, from 1969 a judge of the Superior Court of New Jersey.

Bibliography: W. N. Jamison, *Religion in New Jersey* (1964); R. J. Vecoli, *People of New Jersey* (1965); U.S. Immigration Commission, *Immigrants in Industries,* Pt. 5: *Silk Goods* ... (1911); W. Nelson and C. A. Shriner, *History of Paterson and Its Environs,* 3 vols. (1920); J. Haberman, *Jews in New Jersey* (Ms. Rutgers University); M. W. Garber, *Silk Industry of Paterson New Jersey* (1968; unpublished Ph.D. dissertation. Rutgers University).

[M.W.G.]

PATHROS (Heb. פַּתְרוֹס), region mentioned five times in the Bible (Isa. 11:11; Jer. 44:1,15; Ezek. 29:14; 30:14), either in connection with Miẓrayim (see *Egypt) or with a city of Lower Egypt (Nof=Memphis or *Zoan=Tanis). The name is derived, like the Greek Παθουρης, Φαθωρης (LXX, Jer. 51:1, 15; Ezek. 29:14; 30:14), from the Egyptian expression *pa to resy* ("the Southern Land"), i.e., Upper Egypt. In the Bible, Pathros is named as a region where Jewish communities existed, both before and after the fall of Jerusalem in 587. According to Ezekiel 29:14, Pathros is considered the original home of the Egyptians.

Bibliography: A. Erman, in: ZAW, 10 (1890), 118–9; G. Steindorf, in: *Beitraege zur Assyriologie und semitischer Sprachwissenschaft,* 1 (1890), 344.

[AL.R.S.]

PATINKIN, DON (1922–), Israel economist and educator. He was born in Chicago and after teaching at the University of Chicago (1947–48) and at the University of Illinois (1948–49), he settled in Israel in 1949 and began teaching at the Hebrew University in Jerusalem (full professor, 1957). In 1956 he became director of research at the Falk Institute for Economic Research in Israel. Patinkin's principal fields of interest were the theory of money, monetary influences on an economy, and the general economic development of the State of Israel. He wrote *Keynesian Economics and the Quantity Theory* (1954), *Money, Interest and Prices* (1956, 1965[2]), *The Israel Economy: The First Decade* (1959), and *On the Nature of the Monetary Mechanism* (1967). In 1970 he was awarded the Israel Prize in economics.

[ED.]

PATRAS, port city in N. Peloponnesus, Greece. There were Jews living in Patras in ancient times, as can be assumed from the Hebrew inscriptions found in the local church of St. Anastasius; *Benjamin of Tudela reported the presence of 50 Jews there in the 12th century. Under Byzantine rule the Jews owned land and farms. When the Venetians conquered the town in 1532, they took Jewish prisoners whom they sold as slaves in Italy. Sailors from Naples and Sicily, who attacked Patras in 1595, plundered and murdered Jews. Already in the 16th century there were four synagogues in the city, one Ashkenazi and three Sephardi. Many noted scholars lived there: Moses Alashkar (d. after 1535), author of responsa; Shem Tov b. Jacob Melammed, author of *Keter Shem Tov;* David Vital, author of *Mikhtam le-David* and *Keter Torah;* Jacob ha-Levi (d. 1636), author of responsa; Meir Melammed, author of *Mishpetei Ẓedek;* and others. In the 17th century, during the Turko-Venetian War, the Jews fled the town, returning in 1715 when Turkish rule was reestablished. Jewish silk merchants from Patras traveled as far as Persia for their purchases. The Jewish community ceased to exist at the time of the Greek Revolution (1821–29) and was renewed only in 1905. In 1923 there were 40 to 50 Jews living in the town, most of them merchants or commission agents. In 1943, 242 Jews fled from the town in order to escape the Nazis; others were deported. In 1948 there were 150 Jews in Patras, by 1958 their number had dwindled to 37, and 19 Jews were registered in 1967.

Bibliography: J. Starr, *Jews in the Byzantine Empire* (1939), 229; idem, *Romania* (1949), 73–76; J. Nehama, *In Memoriam,* ed. by M. Molho, 2 (1949), 57, 164; M. Molho and J. Nehama, *Sho'at Yehudei Yavan* (1965), index.

[S.MAR.]

PATRIA, ship bearing "illegal" Jewish immigrants to Palestine which sank in Haifa Bay. Early in November 1940, the steamers *Milos* and *Pacific,* together carrying 1,771 Jewish refugees from Central Europe, arrived in Haifa (see "*Illegal" Immigration). The passengers were transferred on board the 12,000-ton French liner, *Patria,* which had been chartered by the British, to be deported to the island of *Mauritius, by order of the British Mandatory government in accordance with the Defense Regulations (Entry Prohibition; 1940). They were not to be permitted entry to Palestine at any time. On the morning of November 25, when the transshipment of the passengers of the *Atlantic*—another ship with about 1,800 "illegal" immigrants—was in progress and some 130 of them were already on the *Patria,* the ship blew up and sank within 15 minutes inside Haifa Bay with a loss of life of about 260 persons; the number of bodies finally recovered was 209. This disaster was caused by the ignition of explosives brought aboard in an attempt to sabotage the engines and thus prevent the deportation. The survivors of the *Patria* were permitted to remain in Palestine and were interned for some time at the detention camp at *Athlit. They were released by groups in the course of 1941. However, the remaining passengers of the *Atlantic,* about 1,600 persons, mostly from Austria, Czechoslovakia, and Poland, were deported to Mauritius and interned there until August 1945.

Bibliography: M. M. Mardov, *Strictly Illegal* (1964) 56–83; B. Ḥabas, *Gate Breakers* (1963), 126–49; G. E. Steiner, *Patria* (Heb., 1964); Yad Vashem, *Ha-Sho'ah ve-ha-Gevurah be-Aspaklar-yah shel ha-Ittonut ha-Ivrit,* 2 (1966), 11842–884. [A.Z.]

PATRIARCHS, THE, the founding fathers of the people of Israel, *Abraham, *Isaac, and *Jacob.

History and Use of the Term. IV Maccabees 7:19 refers to "our patriarchs, Abraham, Isaac, and Jacob" (*οἱ πατριάρχαι ἡμῶν*), but the same work (16:25) also speaks of, "Abraham and Isaac and Jacob and all the patriarchs" (*καὶ πάντες οι πατριάρχαι*). The New Testament applies the term to Abraham (Heb. 7:4), to the twelve sons of Jacob, and to David (Acts 7:8–9 and 2:29). However, the rabbinic restriction of the designation to Abraham, Isaac, and Jacob (Ber. 16b) follows the biblical Hebrew pattern which frequently features this triad and never extends it to include others.

The development of the concept may be traced through the *Genesis narratives (28:13; 32:9) to its first usage in Exodus 2:24. The Hebrew term *ha-avot* in its absolute form, meaning "the [three] fathers," par excellence, is never used in the Hebrew Bible, only the possessive suffixed form, either in conjunction with the three names (Deut. 1:8; 6:10; 9:5; 29:12; 30:20; I Chron. 29:18. Not quite analogous is the usage in Ex. 3:6, 15, 16; 4:5), or alone in unambiguous reference to the Divine promises (Deut. 1:21, 35 and passim 26 times; Ex. 13:5, 11; Num. 14:23; Josh. 1:6; 5:6; 21:41; Judg. 2:1; Jer. 11:5; 32:22; Ezek. 20:42; 47:14). In fact, mention of the patriarchs in the Bible is predominantly in this connection.

The Chronological Background. The joint lifetimes of the three patriarchs cover a period of just over 300 years (Gen. 21:5; 25:26; 47:28). However, in the absence of external synchronistic controls, their place within the framework of history depends upon the date of the Exodus and the duration of the Egyptian slavery, neither of which can be determined with certainty. The first half of the second millennium B.C.E. is favored by the religious situation, the urban distribution presupposed by the wanderings, the onomasticon, the history of the Jordan rift and of nomadism in Transjordan, the simplicity of life as opposed to later feudalism in Canaan, and the complete absence of the horse.

The Mesopotamian Background. One of the peculiarities of the patriarchal narratives is the consistent association with *Mesopotamia. The family originated in Ur (Gen. 11:28; 15:7; Neh. 9:7; cf. Josh. 24:2–3), then moved to Haran in the north (Gen. 11:31). Abraham found a wife for Isaac there (24:4ff.) and Jacob fled there from Esau's wrath (28:2, 10). He spent a good part of his adult life there and all the tribes except Benjamin originated in that area. This association ends abruptly with Jacob. Since there can be no reason for the invention of the tradition or for its discontinuance, it must be assumed to represent a historic memory.

The Onomasticon. The patriarchs are descended from Shem son of Noah through the line of Eber (Gen. 10:21–32; 11:10–32). Of 38 names connected with the family, 27 never recur in the Bible. A large number conform to the onomastic patterns common to the Western Semites during the first half of the second millennium B.C.E. Of special interest is the identity of the personal names, Peleg (10:25; 11:16–19), Serug (11:20–23), Nahor (11:22–27; 24:10), and Terah (11:24–32), with place names in the vicinity of Haran, mentioned in the *Mari texts.

Patriarchal Society. The patriarchs are essentially ass-nomads (Gen. 12:16; 22:3, 5), constantly on the move, primarily raisers of sheep and cattle (12:16; et al.), and, as such, restricted in the scope of their wanderings (33:13). They are tent-dwellers (12:8, et al.), but their travels take place between great urban centers into which they rarely venture. These peregrinations are confined to sites in the sparsely populated central hill country and the Negev, viz., Shechem, Beth-El, Hebron, Beer-Sheba, Gerar, and, in the case of Jacob, also central Gilead, The patriarchs seem to have been in the first stages of agriculture (26:12; cf. 37:7). They were all buried in the cave of Machpelah (49:29–30; 50:13).

With few exceptions their contacts with their neighbors are peaceful. They make pacts with them (14:13; 21:22–32; 26:28–31) and purchase land from them (23:2–30; 33:19), and there is little sign of the hostility to the Arameans, Canaanites, Philistines, and Egyptians that marks the later history of Israel.

Peculiar to this period are social institutions reflected in the narratives. Many are known to have been characteristic of Hurrian society (of which the city of Haran was part), as recorded in the archives from the city of *Nuzi. The thrice-repeated wife-sister motif (12:11–20; 20:1–18; 26:6–11) is probably a refracted echo of a socio-legal status conferring superior privileges and protection. Concubinage in cases of childlessness (16:2; 30:2) is well attested, as is also service-adoption, an institution that well explains the relationship of Eliezer to Abraham (15:2–4) and of Jacob to Laban (29–31). Fratriarchy is probably behind Laban's show of authority in the marriage negotiations of his sister (24:29, 50, 53ff.; 25:20). In addition, marriage by consent (24:57–58), transference of the birthright (25:29–34; 27:1–29, contrast Deut. 21:15ff.), and the validity of the oral testament (Gen. 27:28–29, 39–40) are all paralleled in the Nuzi tablets.

The Religion of the Patriarchs. The Bible does not explicitly represent the patriarchs as religious innovators. In fact, the narratives record no religious tension between them and their neighbors. The war on idolatry, the leading motif of post-Mosaic religion, is conspicuously absent. Nevertheless, there is much evidence linking the patriarchal period with a distinct stage in the religious history of Israel. The tradition of Joshua 24:2 mentions the idolatry of Abraham's forebears (cf. Gen. 31:19, 30, 32; 35:2–4). The appellation, "the God of my [your/his] father" is peculiar to this time; the possessive suffix is used in reference to each and all of the patriarchs (Gen. 26:24; 28:13; 31:42; 32:10; 46:1, 3; 50:17; Ex. 3:6), but is never employed by or to Abraham in respect of Terah.

The patriarchal narratives are extraordinary, too, in the preservation of experiences in direct variance with the moral and religious ideas and cultic norms of a later period. Abraham married his paternal half-sister (Gen. 20:12; contrast Lev. 18:9, 11); Jacob was simultaneously married to two sisters (contrast Lev. 18:18); Abraham planted a sacred tree (Gen. 21:33; contrast Deut. 16:21); Jacob set up sacred stone pillars (Gen. 28:18, 22; 31:13, 45–52; 35:14; contrast Ex. 23:24); there are no festivals; and the fathers build altars, never using existing ones, and they offer sacrifices without priest or temple (Gen. 12:7–8; 13:4, 18; 22:9, 13; 26:25; 31:54; 30:20; 35:1, 3, 7; 46:1).

The religion of the patriarchs is further differentiated from the Mosaic stage by the absence of any national-territorial framework, by the non-existence of apostolic prophecy, and by the tradition of Exodus 6:2–3, supported by the narratives themselves, that the prominence of YHWH as the divine name was not characteristic of the period. In fact, the patriarchal accounts are distinguished by the employment of numerous divine names, several of them unique (see Names of *God): *El Elyon* (Gen. 14:18, 22), *El Ro'i* (16:13), *El Olam* (21:33), *El Beth-El* (31:13; 35:7), *El Elohei Yisrael* (33:19–20), and, most frequent of all, *El Shaddai* (17:1; 28:3; 35:11; 43:14; 48:3; Ex. 6:3). In addition, one finds *Paḥad Yiẓḥak* (Gen. 31:42; cf. 31:53) and *Abbir Ya'akov* (49:24). It should be pointed out that the *El* element is a widespread Semitic word for God and occurs as a component in theophoric names beyond the Canaanite sphere. In the patriarchal narratives it always appears as a generalized name which becomes personalized only in combination with an identifying element. For these reasons, it is unlikely to be identical with the proper name El, designating the head of the Canaanite pantheon. It is significant that Genesis, unlike the rest of the Bible, contains no reference either to Baal or to fertility cults, indicating that the narratives reflect an early phase of Canaanite religious history. [N.M.S.]

Patriarchs and Matriarchs in the Aggadah. Only Abraham, Isaac, and Jacob may be designated as the patriarchs, and *Sarah, *Rebekah, *Rachel, and *Leah, the matriarchs (Ber. 16b; Sem. 1:14). Sarah conceived on Rosh Ha-Shanah (Ber. 29a). The patriarchs were born and died in Tishri (R. Eliezer) or Nisan (R. Joshua, RH 11a) except for Isaac, who was born on Passover. They were indeed the "Fathers of the world" (Shek. 8a). Although they eventually begot children they were originally sterile (Yev. 64b). The matriarchs were also at first barren because the Almighty longed for their prayers (Song R. 2:14, no. 8). The merit and faith of the patriarchs were great. The Almighty rebuked Moses by contrasting his lack of faith with their unwavering faith (Sanh. 111a). They were the first to make the Almighty known to man (Men. 53a), and they instituted the daily services (Ber. 26b). All three patriarchs were on an equal spiritual level (Gen. R. 1:15). Yet in a sense Jacob was the choicest of the patriarchs: Abraham and Isaac both begot wicked sons—Ishmael and Esau, respectively—whereas all Jacob's sons were loyal to God ("his bed was complete"; Lev. R. 36:5; Zohar, Gen. 119b). The three patriarchs were tested in many ways, including by famine, so that their descendants would be worthy of receiving the Torah (Midrash Sam. 28:2). Neither the *yeẓer ha-ra* (the "evil inclination"—hypostasized) nor the Angel of Death had mastery over them, and in death they were not touched by worms; they were given a foretaste of the bliss of the hereafter here on earth (BB 17a). They constituted the divine chariot of Ezekiel's vision (Gen. R. 47:6). God turned their meditations into the key that opened the road to freedom for their descendants (Gen. R. 70:6), and it was for the sake of the patriarchs and matriarchs that He liberated the Israelites from Egypt (RH 11a).

The virtue of the patriarchs stood their descendants in good stead; and it was for their sake that God hastened their redemption (RH 11a; see also *Zekhut Avot*). When the Israelites sinned with the golden calf, Moses prayed for forgiveness on their behalf, but only when he recalled the patriarchs were they forgiven (Shab. 30a; Deut. R. 3:11).

There are differences of opinion whether "Merit of the Fathers" (*zekhut avot*) would always operate in favor of their descendants. One view is that it would continue forever (Lev. R. 36:6), while another held that it would come to an end, and that it had even ceased already (*ibid.*); another view boldly declared that labor was more precious than the "Merit of the Fathers" (Gen. R. 74:12). Mamre-Hebron was called Kiriath-Arba ("the City of Four"; Gen. 35:27) because four couples were buried there: Adam and Eve; Abraham and Sarah; Isaac and Rebecca; and Jacob and Leah (Eruv. 53a). [H.Fr.]

Bibliography: Albright, Stone, 200–72; Alt, Kl Schr, 1 (1953), 1–78; F. M. T. Boehl, *Opera Minora* (1953), 26–49; Cross, in: HTR, 55 (1962), 225–59; Gibson, in JSS, 7 (1962), 44–62; C. H. Gordon, *The Ancient Near East* (1945), 113–33; idem, in: BA, 3 (1940), 1–12; Haran, in: *Sefer D. Ben-Gurion* (1964), 40–70; idem, in: *Annual of the Swedish Theological Institute,* 4 (1965), 30–55; J. M. Holt, *The Patriarchs of Israel* (1964); Kaufmann Y., Toledot, 2 (1960), 1–32; Rowley, in: BJRL, 32 (1949), 44–79; N. M. Sarna, *Understanding Genesis* (1966), 81–231; Segal, in: JQR, 52 (1961/62), 41–68; de Vaux, in: RB, 53 (1946), 321–46; 55 (1948), 321–47; 56 (1949), 7–36; G. E. Wright, *Biblical Archaeology* (1962), 36–52; Yeivin, in: RSO, 38 (1963), 277–302. Patriarchs and Matriarchs in the Aggadah: Ginzberg, Legends, index; B. Mazar (ed.), *World History of the Jewish People,* 2 (1970).

PATRIARCHS, TESTAMENTS OF THE TWELVE, an early Jewish pseudepigraphic work, giving the last words of the 12 sons of Jacob to their descendants who assembled before their deaths. Although there are Christian passages in the book, with clear hints at salvation through Jesus and in some versions even a reference to Paul (Test. Patr., Ben. 11), which led some scholars to believe that the Testaments are a Christian work, the opinion of most scholars today is that the Testaments are Jewish and that the Christian passages are later interpolations.

The book had been preserved in Slavonic, Armenian, and Greek versions, the last being the original and not a translation from Hebrew or Aramaic. The book seems to have been written before Paul, because he apparently quotes (I Thess. 2:16) the present Testament of Levi (6:11). It is likely that all the 12 Testaments, with the probable exception of the Testament of Asher in which hatred of sinners and even their killing is preached (in contrast to the other Testaments where compassion to enemies is recommended), were written by one Jewish author, but even this difference can be explained by the different sources of this Testament. The individual Testaments contain mostly aggadic descriptions of incidents in the lives of the sons of Jacob, especially Joseph, profound ethical teachings, and eschatological prophecies as in apocalyptical literature.

It is unlikely that the Greek work is based on a single Hebrew or Aramaic pseudepigraphon no longer extant, but on the other hand it is certain that the Testaments derive from Jewish Palestinian literature and thought. The Greek book is a product of a final stage of rich literary output of pseudepigraphic testaments of the individual sons of Jacob. One source was the Aramaic Testament of *Levi and another a Hebrew Testament of *Naphtali, one fragment of which has been found among the *Dead Sea Scrolls. Another Testament of Naphtali is preserved in medieval Hebrew translation, most probably from the Greek, and shows literary affinity to the Testament of Naphtali in the actual book and the same ethical approach as the Testaments of the Twelve Patriarchs. It is clear, however, that this Testament of Naphtali is not one of its sources, though it is close to them in content and approach. The material about the wars of Jacob and his sons, included in the Book of Jubilees, in the actual Testament of Judah, and in Hebrew medieval narrative (see **Midrash Va-Yissa'u*), points to the conclusion that there existed an ancient Hebrew (or Aramaic) Testament of Judah, which contained descriptions of these wars of the sons of Jacob, and it was used both by the author of the Book of Jubilees and the present Greek Testament of Judah. It is unknown if there were also other Hebrew or Aramaic Testaments of the sons of Jacob, which could have served as direct or indirect sources of the Testaments; the Jewish Palestinian material could have reached the author by other channels. There is also a Greek influence, both ethical and literary, in the Testaments of the Patriarchs.

It is important to note that the known sources of the Testaments have a connection with the Dead Sea Scrolls; not only have fragments of the Aramaic Testament of Levi (which is quoted in the Damascus Document) and a fragment of the Hebrew Testament of Levi and fragments of the Book of Jubilees been found in Qumran, but also the doctrines propagated in the Testaments are close to the doctrines of the Dead Sea sect and the author often refers to prophecies of *Enoch, ideas in the Book of Enoch being close to those of the Dead Sea sect. Like the literature of the Dead Sea sect, the Testaments of the Patriarchs show a strong dualistic tendency, both moral and spiritual, and the ethics both of the Dead Sea Scrolls and the Testaments are based on it (see Manual of Discipline 3, 25 and Test. Patr., Reu. 2:3). In the Scrolls and in the Testaments the demonic leader of the evil spirits is named Belial. The main difference is that while in the Dead Sea sect the dualism is sharper—humanity being divided between the Sons of Light and Sons of Darkness and their lots preordained—in the Testaments of the Patriarchs the doctrine of predestination is absent and the struggle between good and evil has to be fought by man himself. This is also the opinion of the Testament of Asher, although it is nearer to the Dead Sea sect than the other Testaments because it too preaches hatred against sinners, while the other Testaments differ from the sect in their humanistic approach. These affinities and differences between the Testaments and the Dead Sea sect can be explained by the suggestion that the author of the Testaments was a member of a movement in Judaism of which the Dead Sea sect was a part. It is very probable that his spiritual, and possible also literary, tradition originated in a fusion between that of the Dead Sea sect and similar groups and the Pharisaic outlook. Thus, for instance, the Testaments mention the belief in the resurrection of the dead, while the sectarian documents speak only about an afterlife of the soul. The extremely humanistic approach of the Testaments (with the exception of that of Asher) is a development from the precept of nonviolence toward the wicked world outside and temporary obedience to it, an idea known from the Scrolls; in the Testaments nonviolence and the humility of spirit in the face of the wicked is unconditional and linked with compassion, and all hatred is eliminated. The love of God and fellow men, central doctrines of the Testaments, are found in rabbinic literature. The two precepts are combined and united in the Testaments of the Patriarchs, in the teachings of Jesus, and in the Jewish source of the early Christian Didache (the Jewish "Two Ways"). A similar fusion of elements from the Dead Sea sect and doctrines found in rabbinic sources and a similar ethical approach as in the Testaments (and the Jewish source of the Didache) is typical of Jesus' message. There is even an important parallel to Jesus' beatitudes and woes (Math. 5, 3–12, Luke 6, 20–26) in the Testament of Judah (ch. 25). Thus, the Testaments of the Patriarchs, though originally written in Greek, are one of the most important sources for the understanding of Jesus' message. In the context of the history of Jewish thought, they are one of the most sublime documents of Jewish ethics in antiquity.

The eschatology of the Testaments is often obscured by Christian interpolations which destroy the original context and meaning. Even so, it is clear that the messianic belief of the author was similar to that of the Dead Sea sect and of the Book of Jubilees and similar ideas must have already appeared in the sources of the Testaments: Levi and Judah are exalted and preference is given to Levi above Judah, the priesthood being more important than the monarchy; in the Testament of Naphtali, Levi is compared to the sun and Judah to the moon. Like the Dead Sea sect, the author of the Testaments looked forward to two eschatological figures: a levitic high priest and a king from Judah; these are the Messiahs from Aaron and from Israel of the Dead Sea sect.

The Testaments of the Patriarchs were translated from a Greek manuscript by Robert Grosseteste bishop of Lincoln, into Latin (c. 1175–1253; this version was translated into English by A. Gilby in 1581). The argument of the supremacy of the priesthood of Levi, the sun, over Judah, the moon, was used and developed in favor of the papacy against the power of the emperor and Dante, an adherent of monarchy, denounced this ideology in *De Monarchia* 3:4–5.

Bibliography: EDITORS AND TRANSLATIONS: R. H. Charles (ed.), *The Greek Versions of the Testaments of the Twelve Patriarchs* (1908, repr. 1960); M. de Jonge (ed.), *Testamenta XII Patriarcharum* (1964); R. H. Charles, *The Testaments of the Twelve Patriarchs Translated from the Editor's Greek Text* (1908); M. E. Stone, *The Testament of Levi, A First Study of the Armenian Mss.* (1969). BIBLIOGRAPHY: M. de Jonge, *The Testaments of the Twelve Patriarchs* (1953); R. Eppel, *Le Piétisme juif dans les Testaments des douze Patriarches* (1930); A. S. van des Woude, *Die messianischen Vorstellungen der Gemeinde von Qumrân* (1957), esp. ch. 2; J. Becker, *Untersuchungen zur Entstehungsgeschichte der Testamente der zwoelf Patriarchen* (1970); M. Braun, *History and Romance in Graeco—Oriental Literature* (1938), 44ff.; C. Burchard, J. Jervell, and J. Thomas, *Studien zu Testamenten der zwoelf Patriarchen* (1969); M. Philonenko, *Les Interpolations Chrétiennes des Testaments des douze Patriarches et les Manuscrits de Qoumran* (1960); A. Dupont-Sommer, in: *Semitica*, 4 (1951–52), 33–53; J. Liver, in: HTR, 52 (1959), 149–85; F. M. Braun, in: RB, 67 (1960), 516–69; D. Flusser, *Jesus* (Eng., 1969), 76–82; idem, in: HTR, 61 (1968), 107–27; idem, in: A. J. Toynbee (ed.), *The Crucible of Christianity* (1969), 227. [D.FL.]

PATTERSON, DAVID (1922–), English scholar. Patterson, who was born in Liverpool, was appointed lecturer in post-Biblical Hebrew at the University of Oxford in 1956. He has also taught Hebrew literature at Cornell University, New York. He served as general editor of the Modern Hebrew Literature series, published by the Cornell University Press and the East and West Library.

As literary historian, Patterson applied modern critical theories and standards to the major and minor Hebrew novels, short stories, and dramas of the early phases of modern Hebrew belles lettres. His primary interest was with the intrinsic aesthetic qualities of these compositions. His translation of Moshe *Shamir's novel *Melekh Basar va-Dam*, published as *King of Flesh and Blood* (1958), and the English renditions that illustrate and substantiate his conclusions in his *Abraham Mapu, Creator of the Modern Hebrew Novel* (1964) and *Hebrew Novel in Czarist Russia* (1964) convey the subtleties and flavor of the originals. [AV.HO.]

°**PATTERSON, JOHN HENRY** (1867–1947), British soldier and author; commanding officer of the Zion Mule Corps and the *Jewish Legion. Born in Dublin, Ireland, into a Protestant family, Patterson's education included the study of the Bible. He was employed as an engineer in the construction of bridges in the British colonies of East Africa, and he described some of his experiences there in his books, *The Man-eaters of Tsavo* (1907) and *In the Grip of the Nyika* (1909). In the Boer War he commanded the 33rd Battalion of the Imperial Yeomanry and in 1915 he was appointed commander of the Zion Mule Corps. With the rank of lieutenant-colonel, he went through the entire Gallipoli campaign with Joseph *Trumpeldor and the Jewish volunteers from Ereẓ Israel. From that time he became an ardent supporter of the Zionist idea. When the Gallipoli campaign ended and the unit broke up, Patterson associated himself with Vladimir *Jabotinsky's efforts in London for the formation of a Jewish Legion which would fight with the British for the liberation of Palestine from Turkish rule. With this objective in mind he wrote his book *With the Zionists in Gallipoli* (1916). When the first battalion of the Jewish Legion was created in Britain, Patterson became its commander with the rank of colonel and accompanied it to the battle front of Samaria and the Jordan Valley, remaining in command until a year after World War I. He described this experience in his book *With the Judeans in the Palestine Campaign* (1922). From then on Patterson became attached to the Zionist Movement and maintained particularly close relations with Jabotinsky. In 1939 he violently condemned the *White Paper policy of

John Henry Patterson (left) with Vladimir Jabotinsky in Palestine, 1929. Courtesy Jabotinsky Institute, Tel Aviv.

Malcolm MacDonald in the press, defining it as a betrayal. In 1940 he participated in Jabotinsky's campaign in the United States for the formation of a Jewish army to fight the Nazis.

Bibliography: V. Jabotinsky, *Story of the Jewish Legion* (1946), index; R. N. Salaman, *Palestine Reclaimed* (1920), index. [Y.S.]

PAUKER (née Rabinsohn), ANA (1890–1960), Rumanian communist leader and cabinet minister. Born into a religious family in Bucharest, she received a traditional Jewish education and became a Hebrew teacher at an elementary school run by the Jewish community. In 1920, influenced by her future husband, Marcel Pauker, she joined the illegal Communist party. She was imprisoned from 1936 to 1941, and on her release she went to the Soviet Union, returning in 1944 with the Russian forces.

After World War II Ana Pauker was the organizer of the Rumanian Democratic Front and became minister of foreign affairs in 1947. She also held the posts of secretary of the party central committee and first deputy prime minister in the cabinet of Petre Groza. In 1952, however, she was expelled from the party, deprived of all her posts, and put under house arrest for several years. Among the charges against her was the accusation that she favored mass emigration to Israel between 1948 and 1951, but this

Ana Pauker, Rumanian foreign minister, with Reuven Rubin, Israel minister (left) and Mihail Sadoveanu, president of the Rumanian parliament, Bucharest, 1948. Courtesy Yad Vashem Archives, Jerusalem.

charge was not substantiated. Long before her death Ana Pauker severed any ties she may have had with the Jewish community, although many of her own close relatives were among the first Rumanian settlers in the State of Israel.

Bibliography: *New York Times* (June 15, 1960), 41. [I.BE.]

°**PAUL I** (1754–1801), emperor of Russia, son of Catherine II and Peter III; ascended the throne in 1796. His decrees concerning the Jews testify that he acted tolerantly toward them. The dispute between Christians and Jews in *Kaunas (Kovno) which continued for decades, was settled by the decree that the Jews be allowed to remain in the city and that no obstacles be placed in their way in following their trades and handicrafts. Paul I also opposed the expulsion of the Jews from *Kamenets-Podolski and *Kiev.

During the discussion, at the end of the 18th century, between the *Courland authorities and the Senate which took an extremely negative stand toward the Jews, Paul I asked Baron Heiking to handle the problem. On Heiking's advice, the privilege of citizenship to the Jews of Courland was granted on March 14, 1799, and thus also municipal rights. The czar opposed G. R. *Derzhavin's advice to question the validity of the oath of the Jews before the courts. In addition, Paul I took a stand in the struggle between the *Ḥasidim and **Mitnaggedim* by liberating the head of the former, Zalman *Shneur of Lyady, and he rejected all *blood libel accusations leveled against the Jews.

Paul's policy toward the Jews was at first a continuation of Catherine's policy to develop craftsmanship and trade, but in the few years of his reign Paul made numerous concessions to the aristocracy which resulted in the imposition of many restrictions upon the Jews. Paul I was murdered in 1801 before he had time to examine the proposals of Senator Derzhavin's report, containing 88 slanders against the Jews, but they were taken up by his successor, Czar *Alexander I, who made them the foundation of his Jewish legislation.

Bibliography: I. Gessen, *Yevrei v Rossii*, 1 (1916), 201–7; Dubnow, Hist Russ, 1 (1916), 321–34; R. Mahler, *Divrei Yemei Yisrael—Dorot Aḥaronim*, 3 (1955), 116–29. [ED.]

°**PAUL IV** (1476–1559), pope from 1555; born **Giovanni Pietro Caraffa.** Even before his election he was a leading spirit in the Counter-Reformation and staunch enemy of all forms of heresy. Because of this, he was extremely hostile to the Jews, as shown by his zeal as head of the *Inquisition from 1542. Scarcely had he been elected pope than he bore down upon the Jews in the Papal States with implacable ruthlessness. He was mainly responsible for the burning of the Talmud in 1553. In his Bull *Cum nimis absurdum* of July 14, 1555, he decreed that in every town the Jews were to gather together in one street or one quarter, which was to be locked at night (the ghetto), and all synagogues except one were to close. Jews were to sell all their houses and landed property, confine themselves to trading in second-hand clothing and rags, and avoid all contact with Christians. They were forbidden to employ Christian wet nurses or domestic servants, and were ordered to wear the Jewish *badge on their clothes. He directed his hatred in particular against the Marranos of *Ancona, who had been invited there by previous popes in order to develop trade between Ancona and Turkey. Paul IV had some hundred of the Marranos of Ancona thrown into prison; 50 were sentenced by the tribunal of the Inquisition and 25 of these were burned at the stake. Paul IV may be considered the instigator of one of the most wretched periods in the history of the Jews in Italy—the period of the ghettos, which dragged on for three centuries.

Bibliography: Milano, Italia, index s.v. *Paolo IV;* idem, *Ghetto di Roma* (1964), index s.v. *Paolo IV;* Roth, Italy, index; J. Sonne, *Mi Paolo ha-Revi'i ad Pius ha-Ḥamishi* . . . (1954). [A.Mil.]

°**PAUL VI** (1897–), pope from 1963. Born **Giovanni Battista Montini** in Concesio, near Brescia, he was ordained in 1920. In 1922 he joined the Vatican Secretariat of State and in 1937 was appointed surrogate to the secretary of state, Cardinal Pacelli (later Pope Pius XII). He was in daily contact with *Pius XII until 1954 and thus was a primary source of evidence for the latter's conduct during the war and his attitude toward the Jews. Montini was appointed prosecretary of state in 1952, archbishop of Milan in 1954, and became a cardinal in 1958. The second Vatican Council, convoked by his predecessor, *John XXIII, was brought to a conclusion by Paul VI (see *Church Councils). According to reliable sources, his personal intervention led to the approval of the *Nostra aetate* declaration on the attitude of the Church to the non-Christian religions by those bishops who had been reluctant to give the declaration their approval even in its modified form. Paul VI promulgated the declaration in 1965. The pontificate of Paul VI is noted for the extensive trips undertaken by the pontiff. During his first major journey, a pilgrimage to the Holy Land (January 4 to 6, 1964), he spent 12 hours in Israel, but avoided the use of the word "Israel" in all the addresses he made on this occasion. While his attitude toward the State of Israel was reserved, it appeared to have modified after the 1967 *Six-Day War. In 1969 the pope officially received for the first time Israel's foreign minister, Abba *Eban. On the other hand, Paul's sermons were not always in line with the council's declaration, especially his reference to the part played by the Jews in the death of Jesus in his sermon on Palm Sunday in 1965, which seemed to indicate a reversal to pre-council theological attitudes.

Bibliography: G. Schwaiger, *Geschichte der Paepste im 20. Jahrhundert* (1968); M. Serafian, *The Pilgrim* (1964); X. Rynne, *Second Session* (1964), *Third Session* (1965), *Fourth Session* (1966). [W.P.E.]

PAULI, JOHANNES (c. 1455–c. 1535), German friar and humorist. Born in Pfeddersheim, Alsace, Pauli abandoned Judaism in his youth and entered the Franciscan order. From 1479 he taught in various church institutions and became a popular preacher. A chance meeting with the Christian Hebraist Conrad *Pellicanus in 1496 led "Paul Feddersheimer" (as the former called Pauli) to promise Pellicanus the gift of some Hebrew manuscripts bequeathed to him by his father. These texts (of Isaiah, Ezekiel, and the Minor Prophets) were duly dispatched from Mainz.

Pauli is remembered for one major work, *Schimpf und Ernst* (Thann, 1522) a collection of 693 jests and moral anecdotes drawn from ancient and medieval sources and from oral tradition. Some 60 editions of this work were printed before 1700. Although he mocked at human failings, Pauli invariably gave an ethical point to his graphic stories, which partly inspired the Elizabethan era's *Hundred Merry Tales,* a source much read and exploited by William *Shakespeare.

Bibliography: H. Oesterley, in: Johannes Pauli, *Schimpf und Ernst* (1866), 1–12; B. Riggenbach (ed.), *Das Chronikon des Konrad Pellikan* (1877); H. Oesterley, in: ADB, 25 (1887), 261–2 (incl. bibl.); J. Bolte, *Schimpf und Ernst,* 2 vols. (1923); C. Roth, *Jewish Contribution to Civilization* (1956), 80, 84; F. Secret, *Les Kabbalistes chrétiens de la Renaissance* (1964), 142. [G.E.S.]

PAUL OF TARSUS (d. c. 65 C.E.), the "Apostle to the Gentiles." The sources for Paul's life and doctrines are in the New Testament—in the Acts of the Apostles and in the seven Pauline epistles known to be genuine (which are the oldest part of the New Testament). The Epistle to the Hebrews does not even pretend to be written by Paul, the three so-called Pastoral Epistles (the two Epistles to Timothy and the Epistle to Titus) are pseudepigrapha, and there are doubts about the authorship of the Epistle to the Ephesians, the Epistle to the Colossians, and the second Epistle to the Thessalonians.

His Life. Paul was a Jew, born during the first years of the common era. His original name was Saul and he was a native of Tarsus in Cilicia and possessed Roman citizenship, but according to Jerome (De Viris Illustribus, ch. 5), his family originated from Giscala (Gush Ḥalav) in Galilee. This may explain his adherence to the Pharisaic form of Judaism (Acts 26:5) and his studies in Jerusalem, where, according to Acts 22:3, he was a pupil of Rabban *Gamaliel the Elder; however, neither his Jewish nor his Greek learning was extensive or deep. Initially, he was a fanatical persecutor of the Christians and, according to the account in the New Testament, he was sent to Damascus on the authority of the high priest in order to arrest any Christians that he found there and bring them to Jerusalem for trial; on the way he had a vision of *Jesus and he converted to Christianity and was baptized in Damascus.

He made three missionary journeys, converting gentiles to Christianity and founding Christian communities. He visited among other places Cyprus, Asia Minor, and Antioch; he went to Greece and stayed for a long time in Corinth and later spent two years in Ephesus in Asia Minor. It was from Greece that he set out for Jerusalem together with delegates from the churches of Asia and Greece carrying contributions that had been collected to relieve the poverty of the mother Church of Jerusalem.

Paul was not the first to preach Christianity to gentiles, but he was the most important of these missionaries. The first followers of Jesus formed a group within Judaism, and gentile Christians became a serious problem for the mother Church. Finally, it adopted the position that the Mosaic Law was not to be imposed upon them (Acts 15) and permitted Paul's mission to the gentiles (Gal. 2:6–9). But not only did Paul refuse to restrict his activities to gentiles; he also strongly opposed the observance of all Jewish practices in his gentile Christian communities. The complexity of the situation became evident during Paul's last visit to Jerusalem. He had in his previous missionary activities already been persecuted by gentiles as well as by Jews, who were well aware of his teachings. So it began to be said in Jerusalem that he was teaching "the Jews who are among the gentiles to forsake Moses, telling them not to circumcise their children or observe the customs" (Acts 21:21). Although the leaders in Jerusalem succeeded in appeasing the local community, Jews from Asia instigated violent riots against Paul when he visited the Temple. In the end, he was rescued by Roman soldiers, who put him under protective arrest; he spent two years in detention in Caesarea and was then sent for a decision on his case to Rome, where he passed a further two years in custody. According to a well-established tradition, he was slain there during the Neronian persecution of Christians.

His Attitude Toward the Jewish Law. Although Paul's assertion that "no human being will be justified by the works of the law" (Rom. 3:20) can be understood in a broader theological and philosophical sense, what he was chiefly opposing was the Law of the Jews. Paul's concept that Christ's death abolished the Mosaic Law cannot be explained as a new development of the eschatological idea which sometimes occurs in later rabbinic sources, namely that in the world to come the commandments will no longer be valid; of this idea there is no trace in his teachings.

Paul's attitude toward the Jewish Law is extreme and cannot be explained as stemming only from his theology of the Cross. For him the old Mosaic covenant was "a dispensation of death, carved in letters on stone ... a dispensation of condemnation ... [which] ... fadeth away," in comparison with the new covenant, which is the "dispensation of the Spirit" (II Cor. 3:6–11). "For the law brings wrath, but where there is no law there is no transgression" (Rom. 4:15), and "all who rely on works of the law are under a curse" (Gal. 3:10–14).

Sometimes Paul's argument against the commandments of Judaism comes close to a rationalistic, liberal approach. Thus he says "Eat whatever is sold in the meat market without raising any question on the ground of conscience, for the earth is the Lord's and everything in it" (I Cor. 10:23–26). But Paul's argumentation often goes beyond a purely liberal attitude and is not based solely on christological grounds. For him, there is no essential difference between the days of the week and the different kinds of food.

It seems clear from all his assertions that Paul's conversion meant for him liberation from the yoke of the Jewish law. The new covenant of Christianity was freedom from the law.

Paul could not say in so many words that the Jewish Law had also ceased to have validity for Jews converted to Christianity, not only because he maintained that he who accepts the validity of the law and transgresses it, is condemned, and because he did not want to shame the "weak brethren," but also because it was obviously unwise to provoke the wrath of the mother Church in Jerusalem. He thought, moreover, that "everyone should remain in the state in which he was called" (I Cor. 7:17–20). Although for the purpose of winning over Jews to Christianity, he tended to "become as a Jew" (I Cor. 19–21), to the Jews themselves it seemed that he was unwilling to fulfill the commandments of the law in his private life.

Paul's numerous expressions of his attitude toward the law could not be fully accepted by later Christianity since they imply opposition to all religious legal obligations; but, although he was not the only early Christian who, by abrogation of the Jewish *halakhah,* paved the way for the separation of Christianity from Judaism, his arguments against the Jewish way of life had a very strong impact upon the development of gentile Christianity. As the Apostle to the Gentiles and an opponent to the Jewish religious way of life, he aroused opposition from all groups of Jewish Christians, who were united in their polemics against him.

In contrast to Paul's hostile attitude toward the law, he always—with the exception of an anti-Jewish passage in his earliest letter (I Thess. 2:14–16)—showed a positive attitude toward the Jews themselves. He was certain that the election of Israel was not abrogated and that, after the gentiles had accepted the new faith, Israel would also become Christian, and so "all Israel will be saved" (Rom. 9–11).

Bibliography: W. Wrede, *Paulus* (Ger., 1905, Eng., 1908); A. Schweitzer, *Paul and his Interpreters* (1912); K. Barth, *Der Roemerbrief* (1929); W. L. Knox, *St. Paul* (1932); J. Klausner, *From Jesus to Paul* (1943); H. J. Schoeps, *Theologie und Geschichte des Judenchristentums* (1949); idem, *Paul, the Theology of the Apostle in the Light of Jewish Religious History* (1961); idem, *Das Judenchristentum* (1964); M. Buber, *Zwei Glaubensweisen* (1950); L. Baeck, in: JJS, 3 (1952), 93–110; A. D. Nock, *St. Paul* (1955); W. D. Davies, *Paul and the Rabbinic Judaism* (1955[2]); A. Schweitzer, *The Mysticism of Paul the Apostle* (1956); S. Sandmel, *The Genius of Paul* (1958); G. Strecker, *Das Judenchristentum in den Pseudoklementinen* (1958); D. Flusser, in: *Scripta Hierosolymitana,* 4 (1958), 215–66; S. Pines, *The Jewish Christians of the Early Centuries of Christianity According to a New Source* (1966); G. Bornkamm, *Paulus* (1969); S. Ben-Chorin, *Paulus* (Ger., 1970).

[D.Fl.]

°**PAVELIĆ, ANTE** (1889–1959), Nazi-appointed ruler of Croatia during World War II. Born in Mostar (Herzegovina), Pavelić was an obscure Zagreb lawyer who came into prominence in 1929, when he founded the extreme right-wing Croatian separatists, Ustaše. In 1934, from his place of exile in Italy, he organized the assassination in Marseilles of King Alexander I of Yugoslavia (who was killed together with French Foreign Minister Louis Barthou) during the king's state visit to France (October 1934). After the German invasion of Yugoslavia in April 1941, the Nazis proclaimed him "Poglavnik" (leader) of the Independent State of Croatia. He created a fascist-racialist regime, repressing all opposition and instituting ruthless persecution of the Serbs and other minorities living in Croatia, particularly Jews, through arbitrary arrests, deportations, killing of thousands of innocent people, the destruction of Orthodox Serb churches, forcible conversions of Serbs to Catholicism, and exile with plunder of property. Pavelić was a fierce anti-Semite, and together with his aides Eugen Kvaternik and his minister of the interior, Andrija Artuković (still living in the United States in 1970, although extradition proceedings were introduced by Yugoslavia), he was instrumental in exterminating about 35,000 Jews. These Jewish victims were not sent to Poland, but were exterminated in local concentration camps. Under Pavelić's aegis, a Croatian Muslim division was formed in Bosnia and was visited by the Jerusalem Mufti, Hajj Amin al-Husseini. After the Axis' defeat, Pavelić found his way to Argentina, via Austria and Italy. He lived under assumed names and died in Spain.

See *Yugoslavia, Holocaust Period; *Zagreb. [Z.Lo.]

PAVIA, city in N. Italy. In 750 the Jew Lullo took part in a religious *disputation in Pavia with the Christian Peter of Pisa. In the ninth century a Jewish scholar named Moses, whose name is associated with the diffusion of mystical lore in Europe, left *Oria to settle in Pavia; his relationship to the 11th century R. *Moses of Pavia is obscure. In 1225 the Jews were expelled from Lombardy, including Pavia. In 1389 Jewish loan-bankers reappeared in the city. They were so violently attacked in the sermons of *Bernardino da Feltre between 1480 and 1494 that the inhabitants demanded their expulsion. However, Duke Giangaleazzo Sforza refused to comply. Popular agitation for the exclusion of the Jews nevertheless continued. When Pavia was besieged by the French in 1527 its inhabitants solemnly vowed that if they surmounted the catastrophe they would "cleanse" the town of Jews. However, the efforts of the numerous delegations later dispatched to the authorities in Milan to obtain their agreement came to nothing.

The physician *Elijah b. Shabbetai taught medicine at the University of Pavia at the beginning of the 15th century— the only authenticated case of a Jewish university teacher in Europe at this period. A chair of Hebrew was established at the end of the 15th century and was renewed in 1521, the first incumbent being the erudite apostate Paolo *Riccio. The duchy of Milan came under Spanish rule in 1535, and the Jews in Pavia obtained short residence permits for a time. In 1558 only seven Jewish families remained in Pavia, and they left during the series of expulsions between 1565 and 1597 which drove all Jews from the duchy of Milan.

Bibliography: Invernizzi, in: *Bollettino della Società pavese di storia patria*, 5 (1905), 191–240, 281–319; Roth, Italy, index; Milano, Italia, index; Milano, Bibliotheca, index; Roth, Dark Ages, index. [A.Mil.]

PAVLOGRAD, city in Dnepropetrovsk oblast, Ukrainian S.S.R. Jews began to settle in Pavlograd shortly after its establishment in 1780. In 1803 there were 167 Jews, 21 of them merchants. During the 19th century Pavlograd became an important center for the grain and flour industry, which helped to support a considerable increase in the Jewish population. There were 979 Jews registered in the community in 1847, increasing to 4,382 (27.8% of the total) in 1897. The 1926 census showed 3,921 Jews (20.9% of the total population). The community was destroyed during the Nazi occupation of 1941. After the war Jews returned to Pavlograd and in 1970 there were about 1,000 Jews there. [Y.S.]

PAVOLOCH, townlet in Zhitomir oblast, Ukrainian S.S.R. A Jewish community is first known to have existed in the townlet at the beginning of the 17th century. In 1736 the *Haidamacks carried out a pogrom in Pavoloch, massacring 35 Jews and engaging in plunder. Records of 1765 show 1,041 Jews as paying the poll tax in Pavoloch and its vicinity. Jews numbered 2,113 in 1847, and in 1897 the number rose to 3,391 (42% of the total population). During the Civil War the townlet declined and most of its inhabitants left. Jewish residents numbered 1,837 (88.2% of the population) in 1926. The Jews who remained in Pavoloch during the Nazi occupation in World War II were exterminated. There is no information on Jews living in Pavoloch after World War II. [Y.S.]

°**PAWLIKOWSKI, JÓZEF** (c. 1768–1829), Polish nobleman, Jacobin, publicist, and lawyer. During the period of the Great Sejm (1788–92) Pawlikowski discussed Jewish problems in anonymous pamphlets. The pamphlet "About the Polish subjects" (1788) sharply critcizes Jewish innkeepers for making the peasants drink heavily; his study *Myśli Politiczne o Polsce* (Political Thoughts of Poland, 1789) insists on barring Jews from leasing taverns but formulates an extremely liberal reform program of the social and political laws for the benefit of the Jews. Pawlikowski was the only representative of the Polish Enlightenment who accorded equal importance to social emancipation of the peasants, townsmen, and Jews. In contradistinction to others he did not consider the Jews to be exploiters as a whole, but saw them as an oppressed and largely poor people. He felt that it was unrealistic to direct the majority of the Jews toward agriculture. Espousing the necessity of complete tolerance and the granting of all urban rights to the Jews, he stated that the introduction of these changes was subject to the Jews gaining a secular education. He therefore proposed the transfer of the Jewish schools to the National Education Commission, adding that "one cannot demolish anything belonging to their religion"; he also warned, "let us not act like the old Spaniards." In 1826 Pawlikowski was imprisoned in Warsaw and died there.

Bibliography: B. Leśnodorscy, *Polscy jakobini* (1958); E. Rostworowski, *Legendy i fakty XVIII w.* (1963); *Bibel*, 1 (1968), 312–3. [J.Go.]

PAZ, DUARTE DE (d. c. 1542), representative in Rome of Portuguese Marranos. Of Marrano descent, Duarte began a career in diplomacy as the Portuguese military attaché for North Africa. He won the confidence of King John III, who knighted him in 1532 and sent him on a secret mission. Instead he went to Rome to enlist the Curia's intercession for the Marranos. He had a cool and cunning style and plied the cardinals and Pope Clement VII with money made available for this purpose by the Marranos. His initial success was the issuance on Oct. 17, 1532 of a papal decree abrogating the bull *Cum ad nihil magis* of 1531, which had introduced the Inquisition into Portugal. His second success, on April 7, 1533, was the issuance of a bull pardoning the Marranos for "lapses" into Judaism on the ground that their forced conversions were not valid (see *Inquisition, *Portugal). Continuing his activities under Pope Paul III (1534–49), Duarte achieved another success on Oct. 2, 1535, when a papal bull extended the civil rights of Marranos, resulting in the immediate release of 1,800 Marranos from Portuguese dungeons. By this time King John had taken furious notice of Duarte's insubordinate activities and ordered him stripped of commission and honor. In January 1536 Duarte was attacked by masked men, stabbed fourteen times, and left for dead on the road. Because of concealed armor he was wearing and the subsequent careful nursing by the pope's doctors, he recovered and accused King John of having ordered his assassination. John denied the accusation, and in any event, since Duarte was no longer in a position to defend his constituents effectively, he proceeded to bring his affairs to a close. When the Marranos questioned Duarte accusingly about a missing 4,000 ducats, enraged, he turned completely against them and denounced both them and their new representative, Diogo Antonio, in many courts in Europe. While on a visit to *Ferrara he was taken by surprise and imprisoned. On his release, he openly espoused Judaism and migrated to Turkey, where, shortly before his death, he reportedly became a Muslim.

Bibliography: Baron, Social, index; M. A. Cohen (trans.), *Usque's Consolation for the Tribulations of Israel* (1965), 1–9; Graetz, Hist, 4 (1894), 512–20; Roth, Marranos, index. [Ed.]

PE (Heb. פֵּא, פ), the 17th letter of the Hebrew alphabet; its numerical value is 80. In the proto-Sinaitic inscriptions this letter seems to be represented by the drawing of either a mouth *(peh)* or corner *(pê'āh)*: ᒪ, ᓗ. In the eleventh and tenth centuries B.C.E., its form was ᒣ(which presumably was the prototype of Greek (Γ)→and Latin (P). The later West-Semitic variants are: Hebrew ᒧ (Samaritan ᑐ), Phoenician) and Aramaic ɔ→ɔ in medial and ͻ in final positions. The latter forms are the ancestors of the Jewish (modern Heb.) פ and ף. From the Nabatean ʃ (final)→ᑫ (medial) developed the Arabic ڡ (the single diacritic mark distinguishes it from ق which developed from the *qaf*).

See *Alphabet. [Jo.Na.]

PEACE (Heb. שָׁלוֹם, *shalom*).

In the Bible. The verb *shalem* (so both the perfect, Gen. 15:16, and the participle, Gen. 33:18) in the *qal* means "to be whole, complete, or sound."

"Peace." The range of nuances is rather wide. That the iniquity of the Amorites has not yet become *shalem* (Gen. 15:16) means that it is not yet complete. That Jacob arrived *shalem* in the city of Shechem (Gen. 33:18) means that he arrived there safe. To be *shalem* with somebody means to be loyal to him (Gen. 34:21; I Kings 8:61; 11:4; etc.), and one's *sholem* (Ps. 7:5) is one's ally. Although recent translations show a great improvement in this regard, the noun *shalom* is still interpreted to mean "peace" more often than is warranted. It, of course, very frequently means health and/or well-being: Genesis 29:6 (twice); 37:14 (twice); 43:28. In this sense, *shalom* is frequently equivalent to a sentence, "It is well," and *le* may be added to express the English "with"; *shalom* is used alone in this way in II Samuel 18:28, and with *le* II Samuel 18:29, 32. In Genesis 43:23 and Judges 19:20, "It is well with you" is equivalent to "Don't worry about that," referring in the second case to a roof under which to spend the night (the last clause in verse 18). That the antithesis in Isaiah 45:7 is not between "peace" and "evil" but between prosperity *(shalom)* and adversity *(raᶜ)* has happily long been the dominant view (cf. *shalom, tov, yeshuᶜah,* Isa. 52:7). It needs to be noted, however, that still not "peace" but safety is the meaning of *shalom* in Leviticus 26:6 (cf. verses 25bb–26: within the land, they shall dwell secure—with never a savage beast or an invader—but only because the enemy will be kept out by dint of successful warfare); Jeremiah 12:12; Zechariah 8:10; and elsewhere. In the above-cited verse Isaiah 52:7, *shalom* stands in synonymous parallelism with *ṭov* in the sense of physical good; it likewise shares with *ṭov* the sense of moral good. Thus *ṭov* has the former meaning in Psalm 34:13 and the latter one in verse 15—where it is paralleled by *shalom.* Translate: (13) Is there anyone among you who desires life, is eager for longevity and to experience well-being *(ṭov)*? (14) Then guard your tongue against evil and your lips against speaking deceit. (15) Shun evil and do good *(ṭov)*; seek and pursue integrity/equity *(shalom).* For the interpretation of Psalm 37:37b, it makes no difference whether or not one reads in 37a *shemor ṭov u-reᶜeh yosher,* "practice probity and cultivate equity" (in light of verse 3 where conversely *shekhon ereẓ* is to be emended to *shemor ẓedek (ẓedeq),* "practice righteousness," in light of the preceding "do good" and the following "cultivate honesty" as well as the *shemor* of this verse): 37b must in any case be translated "for there is a happy future for the man of integrity." Similarly, in Zechariah 8:16, in which the second *ʾemet* is obviously an erroneous repetition of the first, the sense is: "Speak the truth to each other, and judge equitably (lit. judge judgment of equity *[shalom]*) in your gates." And again in verse 19: ". . . The Fast of the Fourth Month, and the Fast of the Fifth Month, and the Fast of the Seventh Month, and the Fast of the Tenth Month shall become [occasions of] rejoicing and gladness and happy seasons for the House of Judah—only love truth and equity *[shalom].*" (Alluding to this verse, Esth. 9:30 characterizes Queen Esther's ordinance for the observation of the new holidays—the Purim of the provinces and the Purim of Shushan—as "an ordinance of equity and truth.") The parallelism alone would not suffice to tip the balance in favor of this meaning of *shalom* in Psalm 72:3, 7, for in Isaiah 60:17 the context precludes any interpretation of *shalom/ẓedaqah* other than "prosperity/success" (see *Righteousness). In Psalm 72:3, however, the context points once again to "equity." The prosperity of the country (in contrast to that of the king) is actually treated only in one corrupt verse near the end (verse 16). Finally, Y. Muffs has pointed out that, in light of the Akkadian idiom *šalmeš atalluku (maḫar X), be-shalom u-ve-mishor halakh itti,* Malachi 2:6, means "he served me with integrity and equity" (more idiomatically, "loyally and conscientiously"—H. L. Ginsberg). Even apart from the Akkadian evidence, the sense of Malachi 2:6 is clear from the foregoing and from the context: Levi, the ancestor of the priestly caste, saved the masses *(rabbim),* or laity by his conscientiousness in making *torah* rulings, from committing ritual offenses; his unworthy descendants, by being lax in this regard, often out of partiality, make the masses *(rabbim),* or laity, stumble by their rulings *(torah).*

PEACE AND THE LIKE. Of course *shalom* does mean "peace" too. But first it must be pointed out that it often approaches this meaning without quite reaching it. YHWH's *berit* (covenant) of *shalom* with Phinehas (Num. 25:12) and with Zion (Isa. 54:10) were, for pity's sake, neither peace treaties terminating previous wars nor nonaggression pacts to refrain from starting new ones. They were solemn—actually unilateral—promises of divine grace. So too the *priestly blessing (Num. 6:24–26), after wishing YHWH's blessing, protection, friendliness, favor, and benignity, ends not, bathetically, with "and may He grant you peace" but, appropriately, "and may He extend grace *(shalom)* to you." In Jeremiah 16:5, YHWH's grace *(shalom)* is explicated as "kindness *(ḥesed)* and mercy *(raḥamim)*"; and in light of that passage it is probable that a *vav* has been lost at the end of Num. 6:24–26 before the initial *vav* of verse 27, so that *shelomo,* is to be read "His grace." In line with this is the phrase "intentions of *shalom*" for "gracious kind, intentions" (on the part of YHWH) in Jeremiah 29:11. A step closer to mere "peace" is "friendship" (or "alliance"), which sense *shalom* has in Judges 4:17: "there was *shalom* between King Jabin of Hazor and the family of Heber the Kenite," so that Jabin's general Sisera, fleeing from the Israelites, believed that he would find safety in the tent of Heber. So, too, one's *shalom*-men are one's friends or allies; Jeremiah 20:10; 38:22; Obadiah 7. Finally, *shalom* obviously means precisely "peace" in I Kings 2:5; Psalm 120:7; Ecclesiastes 3:8; Job 15:21, in which passage it stands in antithesis to war or marauding; but the cases in which this sense can be attributed to the word in good conscience are a small proportion of the total number of its occurrences. Thus it is not true that in Deuteronomy 20:10 the Torah required Israel to invite its adversary "to settle the dispute amicably" "before the commencement of hostilities." The Israelite army has already been mobilized, verse 2a, and has already marched up to an enemy city (not necessarily the first), verse 10a, and it now invites the city not "to settle the dispute amicably" but to surrender on ignominious terms in order to avoid a worse fate (verses 10–17). *Shalom* here means not peace but submission, and the verb *hishlim* definitely means not "to make peace" but "to submit," not only in Deuteronomy 20:12 but also in Joshua 10:1, 4; 11:19; II Samuel 10:19; I Chronicles 19:19; and presumably also I Kings 22:45; Proverbs 16:7. *Isaiah's vision of an age where there would be no more war between nations, Isaiah 4:2–4 (Micah 4:1ff.), is unparallelled. It should not, however, be confused with pacifism. The reason for his opposition to alliances is explained in the Book of *Isaiah. It does not mean that he believed that self-defense was wrong. On the contrary, he predicts that in a penitent Judah those charged with defense (so long as defense, despite 2:2–4, remains necessary) will be endowed with charismatic valor (Isa. 28:6). [H.L.G.]

In the Talmud. With the possible exception of *justice, peace is the most exalted ideal of the rabbis of the Talmud. No words of praise are too exaggerated to emphasize the importance of this ideal. On the statement of Rabban Simeon b. Gamaliel, "By three things the world is preserved, by truth, by judgment, and by peace" (Avot 1:18), the Talmud declares that they are in effect one, since "if judgment is executed, truth is vindicated, and peace prevails" (TJ, Ta'an. 4:2, 68a). The rabbis interpret Hosea 4:17 to teach that "even if Israel is tied to idols, leave him, as long as peace prevails within it" (Gen. R. 38:6). The role of the scholars is to increase peace in the world (Ber. 64a) and it is to bring the rule of peace that Elijah will come (Eduy. 8:7). There is not a blessing or prayer in the liturgy, the *Amidah*, the *Kaddish*, the Priestly Blessing, and the Grace after Meals, which does not conclude with the prayer for peace (Lev. R. 9:9). *"Shalom"* is the standard greeting among Jews both on meeting and on saying farewell, so that the phrase for greeting and for answering the greeting is "to enquire of the peace of" and to "answer the peace of" (Ber. 2:1, 4b). *Shalom* is one of the names of God (Shab. 10b; Lev. R. 9:9). "The Holy One, blessed be He, found no vessel more worthy of retaining a blessing within it than peace" (Uk. 3:12).

It is permitted to deviate from the strict line of truth in order to establish peace (Yev. 65b) and the Talmud declares with regard to Numbers 5:23 "if in order to establish peace between husband and wife the Name of God, which was written in holiness, may be blotted out, how much more so to bring about peace for the world as a whole" (TJ, Sot. 1:4, 16d). It will be seen that the ideal of peace encompasses the whole gamut of human relationship, between man and his fellowman, and between nation and nation, bringing about the ideal of universal peace.

*Aaron is regarded as the prototype of the ideal of peace (Avot 1:12; cf. Yoma 71b) and in the parallel passage in *Avot de-Rabbi Nathan* (12, p. 48) there is a loving and detailed account of the manner in which he used to devote himself to the bringing about of his ideal. In this Aaron stands in contrast to his brother Moses, who exemplifies the ideal of justice. Aaron's assent to the demand of the people to fashion the golden calf is contrasted with Moses' demands as the rival claims of the ideals of peace and justice when they clash, and the one can be achieved only at the price of the denial of the other, Moses maintaining, "Let justice pierce the mountain" (cf. *"Fiat Justitia, Ruat Coelum"*) whereas Aaron maintained the love and pursuit of peace at all cost. In similar vein is the homily of Rabban Johanan b. Zakkai on the injunction that no iron tool was to be used in the building of the altar, which had to be made of "whole stones" (*"avanim shelemot"* interpreted as "stones which bring peace" Deut. 27:5–6; cf. Ex. 20:22). Is it not an a fortiori argument? If the stones of the altar which can neither see nor hear nor speak, but because they bring peace between Israel and their Father in Heaven, the Holy One, blessed be He said, 'thou shalt lift up no iron tool upon them'; how much more so he who brings about peace between man and his fellow, between husband and wife, between city and city, between nation and nation, between government and government, and between family and family" (Mekh., Ba-Ḥodesh, II). Abbaye's favorite maxim was "man should always strive to increase peace with his brother, his relations, with every other man, even with the heathen in the market place, in order that he be beloved on high and well-liked on earth, and acceptable to his fellowman" (Ber. 17a; SER 26), and there is a whole series of enactments and adjustments of the law made "in the interest of peace" *(mi-penei darkhei shalom)*.

Nevertheless, Judaism is not uncompromisingly pacifist in its outlook. It sees universal peace as an ideal which will be achieved only in the messianic age, and Maimonides concludes his famous Code with the declaration that in that era there will be "neither famine nor war, neither jealousy nor strife." Judaism believes that war is sometimes morally justified and divides war into "the war of *mitzvah,*" "the obligatory war" (*milḥemet ḥovah*; the war of the two are sometimes identified), and the optional war (cf. Maim. Yad, Melakhim 5–7; see *Mitzvah). Nevertheless, the whole weight of the ethics of the rabbis recoiled from the glorification of war. This attitude is strikingly expressed in a Mishnah (Shab. 6:4) which lays it down that a man may not go out wearing his arms on the Sabbath, and "if he did so he is obligated to bring a sin-offering." In answer to the opposite opinion that they can be regarded as adornments, the rabbis indignantly retorted, "they are nought but a reproach, as it is written, 'and they shall beat their swords into plowshares and their spears into pruning-hooks. Nation shall not lift up sword against nation, neither shall they learn war any more' " (Isa. 2:4). [L.I.R.]

In Post-Talmudic Jewish Thought. The medieval Jewish thinkers discuss peace under the two headings of world peace and of the avoidance of internal strife and contention in the Jewish community. Jews in the Middle Ages had no voice in international affairs. World peace in the here and now was for them a purely academic question. Their discussions of it, consequently, are in a messianic context. Saadiah (*Emunot ve-Deot* 7:10) points to the continuing wars among nations, including wars of religion, to demonstrate that the prophetic vision of peace on earth can only apply to the messianic age. Maimonides (Yad, Melakhim 12:5) similarly considers the establishment of peace for all mankind to be an accomplishment of the Messiah. David Kimḥi (to Isa. 2:4) states that the nations will bring their disputes to the Messiah for arbitration. He will decide so wisely and justly that war between nations will be purposeless. It has frequently been pointed out that in medieval illustrated *Haggadot* the wicked son is depicted as a warrior, the wise son as a peace-loving sage.

Joseph Albo (*Sefer ha-Ikkarim* 4:51) defines peace as the harmony of opposites. There is no virtue in one extreme predominating over another but only in the harmony between the irascible and the patient, the niggardly and the extravagant, and so on. Peace of mind means the attainment of harmony among the different parts of the soul. Isaac Arama (*Akedat Yiẓḥak,* 74) holds that the conventional view of peace as a mere negation of strife fails to do justice to the richness of the concept. Peace is a positive thing, the essential means by which men of differing temperaments and opinions can work together for the common good. Pearls of individual virtue would be dim in isolation were it not for the string of peace that binds them together and so increases their luster. That is why peace is a name of God for it is He who gives unity to the whole of creation.

The rabbinic teachings regarding the importance of peace in the home and the community were given full emphasis in medieval moralistic literature. The moralistic treatises contain whole sections on this theme (e.g., Isaac Aboab's *Menorat ha-Ma'or* 2:7, 61–65) in the form of rabbinic quotations on the value of peace and the harm done by dissension together with the author's elaborations. However, the record of fierce rabbinic debates in which no holds were barred demanded that reservations be made in connection with study and generally where religious principles were at stake. The "controversy for the sake of heaven" was held to be good since it helped to promote truth. Such a controversy would endure, it was taught, each of the protagonists holding relentlessly to his position (Bertinoro to Avot 5:17). To combat heresy was in any event considered to be a virtue. Peace with unbelievers was not held to be a desirable goal.

In the Kabbalah the pursuit of peace has a cosmic significance. Man's deeds determine whether or not there is harmony in the realm of the *Sefirot*. The virtuous man assists the supernal peace between the Holy One, blessed be He, and His *Shekhinah* (Zohar 3, 113b–114a). More specifically, *shalom,* "peace," is the name given to the *Sefirah Yesod,* "Foundation." In erotic symbolism favored by the Kabbalah, "peace on earth" represents the supernal unification in which *Yesod* carries the flow of blessing into earth, the *Sefirah Malkhut,* "Sovereignty" (Naḥmanides and Baḥya to Lev. 26:6).

While the Ḥasidim, like all other Jews, saw peace as a high value, the conflicts between the Ḥasidim and their opponents, as well as the rivalries between the ḥasidic dynasties themselves, encouraged an extension of the idea of the "controversy for the sake of heaven." R. Naḥman of Bratzlav, a controversial figure all his life, went so far as to argue that only the *ẓaddik* who has enemies, and therefore something for which to struggle, is able to lead his followers to the worship of God (*Sefer ha-Middot, Merivah,* 2:18).

Modern Jewish Thought. Modern Jewish thought. without any denominational differences, except, possibly, on the question of religious toleration, is unanimous on the great value of peace. Morris Joseph (*Judaism as Creed and Life* (1903), 456–7) is typical of the whole modern trend when he writes that only the peace-loving Jew is a true follower of the prophets, that the greatest sacrifices should be made to avoid war, that a Jew cannot consistently belong to a war party, and that the Jew's religion, history, and mission all pledge him to a policy of peace, as a citizen as well as an individual. A. I. Kook, commenting on the ruling that the office of the priest "anointed for war" (Deut. 20:2–4) is not a hereditary one, remarks that the idea of a hereditary position is to express permanence in human affairs. However, peace is the only state deserving of permanence. Consequently, there can be no question of a hereditary appointment for a functionary connected with warfare, but only for one who operates in times of peace (Zevin: *Le-Or ha-Halakhah* (1946), 27–28). The Reform *Union Prayer Book* contains this prayer: "Grant us peace, Thy most precious gift. O Thou eternal source of peace, and enable Israel to be its messenger unto the peoples of the earth. Bless our country that it may ever be a stronghold of peace, and its advocate in the council of nations." [L.J.]

Bibliography: In the Bible: Koehler-Baumgartner, 973–4; Y. Muffs, *Studies in the Aramaic Legal Papyri from Elephantine* (1969), 203–4. In Talmud: G. F. Moore, *Judaism,* 2 (1927), 195–7; J. S. Kornfeld, *Judaism and International Peace* (193ff.); A. Cronbach, in: CCARY, 46 (1936), 198–221; M. Wald, *Jewish Teaching on Peace* (1944); L. I. Rabinowitz, in: JQR, 58 (1967/68), 148 no. 20.

PEACH (mishnaic Heb. פַּרְסֵק or אֲפַרְסֵק), the tree and the fruit of the *Persica vulgaris (Prunus persica).* This tree was first grown in Ereẓ Israel during the Greco-Roman era, hence its name *afarsek,* i.e., "Persian apple" in the Mishnah (Gr. *μῆλον περσικόν*). Characteristic of the peach are the red fibers extending from a deeply grooved kernel. The Mishnah accordingly lays it down that peaches become liable for tithing "after they begin to show red veins" (Ma'as, 1:2). Under suitable conditions, peaches can grow to a substantial size, and the *aggadah* states that it happened that a single peach became large enough to provide more than a meal for a man and his ass (TJ, Pe'ah 7:4, 20a). The Mishnah states that the peach used to be grafted on the almond (as it is today) and forbids the practice since it constitutes *kilayim* ("*mixed species"; Kil. 1:4). On the other hand, the statement (TJ, Kil. 27a according to the reading of the Mussafia in his additions to the *Arukh*) that the grafting of a walnut tree on a peach produces the fruit *karyah-persikah* ("Persian walnuts"), a sort of crossbreed between the walnut and the peach, belongs to agricultural folklore.

The name *nucipersica* ("Persian nut") occurs on an inscription discovered in a Roman villa and this name entered into the botanical literature of the Middle Ages for a species of peach with a skin as smooth as that of the outer husk of the walnut. It is certain that these two unrelated species cannot be grafted and no hybrid can be produced from them. After the ruin of Jewish agriculture in Ereẓ Israel at the end of the talmudic era, peach plantations all but disappeared. During recent years, however, they have been planted in large numbers and are found in abundance.

Bibliography: Loew, Flora, 3 (1924), 159–63; J. Feliks, *Kilei Zera'im ve-Harkavah* (1967), 101–3. [J.F.]

PEACOCK, bird called *ταως* in Greek and *tavvas* in the Mishnah. The peacock *(Pavo cristatus)* is a ritually clean bird (see *Dietary Laws) belonging to the pheasant family. In mishnaic times some wealthy people in Ereẓ Israel bred the peacock as an ornamental bird and even ate it on occasion, its head in particular being regarded as a great delicacy (Shab. 130a). According to the Tosefta (Kil. 1:8), "chicken, peacock, and pheasant, although resembling one another, are each heterogeneous with the other." A poetic comment on the peacock's beauty is given in the Midrash (Tanḥ. B., Lev. 33; cf. Gen. R. 7:4): "Although the peacock comes from a drop of white matter, it has 365 different colors, as many as the days in a year." The peacock originates from India, from where, it is suggested, Alexander the Great imported it into Europe. The *tukkiyyim* conveyed to Solomon in ships of Tarshish (I Kings 10:22; II Chron. 9:21) are most probably to be identified with peacocks, called in Tamil *togai, tokai,* an identification found also in ancient translations. In modern Hebrew *tukki* is mistakenly used to denote a parrot.

Bibliography: Lewysohn, Zool, 189f., no. 241; F. S. Bodenheimer, *Animal and Man in Bible Lands* (1960), 121, 125; J. Feliks, *Kilei Zera'im ve-Harkavah* (1967), 118f., 129–32; idem, *Animal World of the Bible* (1962), 60. [J.F.]

PE'AH (Heb. פֵּאָה; "corner"), name of the second treatise of the Mishnah, in the order of *Zera'im.* Despite its name, this tractate deals with the laws of all the different dues to the poor, namely: *pe'ah, leket* ("gleaning of grapes"), *peret* ("fallen grapes"), *ma'aser ani* ("poor man's tithe") which are enjoined in Leviticus 19:9, 10, and Deuteronomy 24:19; 14:28, 29.

The tractate is divided into eight chapters whose contents are: required amount and size of field to which the law of *pe'ah* applies (1:1, 2; 3:6); the type of field and agricultural produce from which

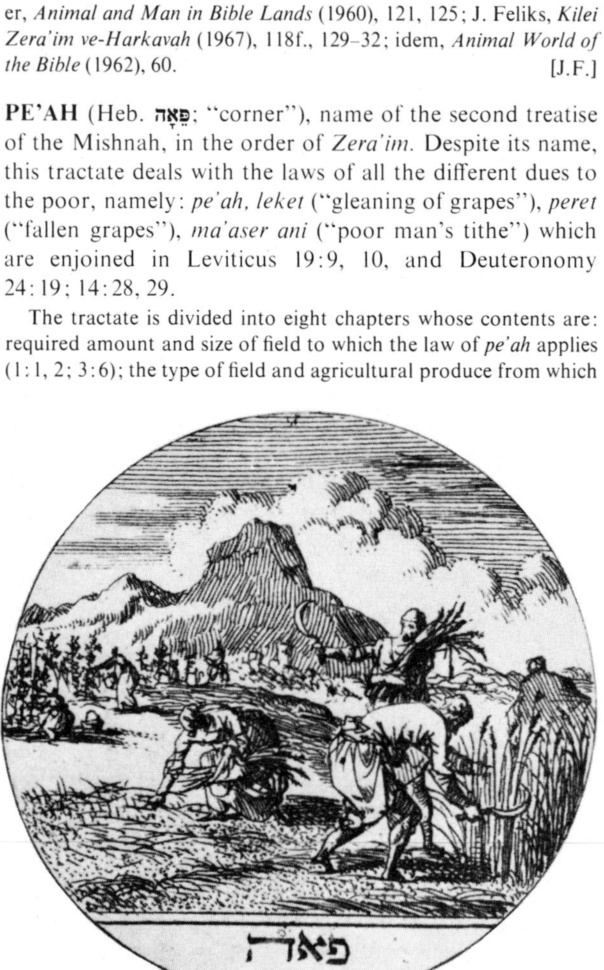

Engraving showing a poor man gleaning wheat, representing the tractate *Pe'ah.* From a title page of the Hebrew-Latin Mishnah illustrated by Mich. Richey, Amsterdam, 1700–04. Jerusalem, J.N.U.L.

pe'ah may be given (1:4, 5; 3:4); modes of division in a field (2:1–4; 3:1, 2); procedure in giving *pe'ah* (4:1–5); type of gleanings which constitute *leket* (4:10, 11; 5:1, 2); type of harvest, position of leftover sheaves and amount of sheaves that require the giving of *shikhḥah* (5:7, 8; 6:2–11; 7:1, 2); laws of *peret* and *olelot* (7:3–7); laws of *ma'aser ani* (8:2, 5–7); obligation of consecrated land to the Temple in connection with dues to the poor (1:6; 4:6–9; 7:8). Thus 1–4:9 deal with the laws of *pe'ah;* 4:10–5:6 with *leket;* 5:7–7:2 with *shikhḥah;* 7:3 with *peret;* 7:4–7, 8 with *olelot;* 8, especially from Mishnah 5 onward, with *ma'aser ani* and charity. A number of topics unrelated to the immediate subject of the tractate are included: enumeration of *mitzvot* having no fixed measure (1:1); legal transactions involving small amounts of land (3:6, 7); laws of renunciation of ownership (1:6; 6:1). The first of these has been included (with variant readings) in the prayer book as part of the morning introductory prayers.

The Tosefta has four chapters, which, besides complementing and interpreting the Mishnah, include several interpretations and emendations based on the Talmud (Tosef., 1:6; 2:2; see Epstein, Tanna'im, 252). The Tosefta also contains some aggadic passages, such as, "The Almighty combines a good intention with an action, but an evil intention the Almighty does not combine with an action" (1:4). In the last chapter, in which charity is highly praised, it is stated that charity and deeds of lovingkindness equal all the *mitzvot* in the Torah (4:19), that he who shuts his eyes to charity is like one who practices idolatry (4:20). There is no *Gemara* on the tractate in the Babylonian Talmud but there is in the Jerusalem Talmud, which includes much aggadic literature (see **Leket, Shikhḥah, Pe'ah).*

Bibliography: H. L. Strack, *Introduction to the Talmud and Midrash* (1931), 29–30; P. Blackman (ed. and tr.), *Mishnayot,* 1 (1951); J. D. Herzog (ed. and tr.), *Mishnayot,* 2 (1947). [J.KE.]

PEAR (mishnaic Heb. אַגָּס), *Pyrus communis.* Although it is first mentioned in rabbinic literature this does not necessarily mean that the pear was not grown in Ereẓ Israel in biblical times. A member of the same genus, the Syrian pear *Pyrus syriaca* (mishnaic Heb. *ḥizrar*), grows wild in Ereẓ Israel in Upper Galilee (Kil. 1:4). The same Mishnah mentions a variety of pear called *krostomlin* which is regarded as belonging to the same species. The reference is to the pear called by Pliny (*Natural History,* 15:53) *crustumina.* It seems that during the time of the Mishnah they began to grow this excellent species in Ereẓ Israel, hence its Roman name. In modern Israel the Arabs used to grow small local pears, but excellent large species have been introduced by the Jews in recent years, and today pears are found in abundance.

Bibliography: Loew, Flora, 3 (1924), 235–40; J. Feliks, *Kilei Zera'im ve-Harkavah* (1967), 93–95. [J.F.]

PECHERSKY, ALEXANDER (1919–), Jewish lieutenant in the Soviet army who organized and successfully led the revolt in the Nazi extermination camp of *Sobibór.The uprising was a heroic chapter in the history of anti-Nazi resistance. Born in Rostov-on-Don, Pechersky was drafted into the Soviet army when German forces invaded Soviet Russia in the summer of 1941. In October 1941 he was captured by the Germans, but managed to escape. He was caught again and sent to Sobibór in September 1943, when the Germans discovered that he was a Jew. There, together with six other Jews, he immediately started to prepare a detailed plan for a revolt, which was executed on October 14, 1943. Pechersky's men attacked the German officers, killing ten of them. With the weapons taken from the dead officers the prisoners killed or wounded 38 Ukrainian guards. Of the 600 camp inmates, almost 400 escaped, but about half of them were killed in the surrounding minefields or as a result of the large-scale manhunt organized by the Germans and by Polish fascists. Pechersky and a group of his comrades succeeded in escaping and reaching the Soviet partisans. Later he rejoined the Soviet army and was seriously wounded in August 1944. He was demobilized and returned to his hometown.

Bibliography: Y. Suhl (ed.), *They Fought Back* (1967), 7–50; Ainsztein, in: JSOS, 28 (1966), 19–24; idem, in: *Jewish Observer and Middle East Review* (April 23, 1965), 14–22; Lev, in: *Sovetish Heymland,* 2 (1964), 78–93; V. Tomin and A. Sinelnikov, *Vozvrashcheniye nezhelatel'no* (1964). [Y.GU.]

°**PÉCHI, SIMON** (c. 1567–c. 1639), Hungarian statesman, poet, and author, leader of the Judaizing "Sabbatarian" sect. Born in Transylvania, Péchi was at first employed as tutor of A. Eössy's children; Eössy, the founder of the sect, introduced him to the court of the prince Stephen Báthory. As emissary of Báthory, Péchi set out on his political travels to Rumania and Turkey and even reached Italy and Africa. There he probably acquired a knowledge of Hebrew. From 1613 he was chancellor of Transylvania under the rule of the prince Gabriel Bethlen. In 1621 he was imprisoned for reasons which are unknown but was subsequently set free. During the reign of the prince George Rákóczy his position was so strong that he was even authorized to propagate his views in public.

In a description of the usages of the sect it is reported that in addition to the observance of the Sabbath, the wives of the members of this sect adopted the Jewish dietary laws. At the height of the sect's success about 20,000 Transylvanian Hungarians of the "Székely" tribe were among its members (1635). After a brief period and a change of political circumstances, a law was passed in Transylvania which rendered the members of the sect liable to the death penalty and confiscation of their property if they did not return to Christianity within one year. Péchi remained steadfast in his beliefs until 1638 but finally converted to Calvinism. Although death penalties were not applied, the property of the members of the sect was seized.

Péchi was a talented poet and author, and according to the opinion of S. *Kohn, historian of Hungarian Jewry and researcher on the "Sabbatarians," his works are of exceptional value. Péchi's translations from Psalms and the Jewish prayer book are of special importance, being the first in this area.

Bibliography: Á. Szilády (ed.), *Péchi Simon Psalteriuma* (1913); S. Kohn, *A szombatosok* (1889); M. Guttmann and S. Harmos, *Péchi Simon szombatos imádságos könyve* (1914). [B.Y.]

PECHINA (Arabic, **Bajjāna**), village located N. of *Almeria on the S. coast of Spain. Until 922, when it was incorporated into Andalusia by ʿAbd al-Raḥmān III, Pechina was a separate state under Umayyad protection. During its period of independence (ninth–tenth centuries), Pechina was a prosperous, busy seaport which was settled by Arabs from the *Yemen. The Jews also shared in its prosperity, and for the most part were merchants. When *Saadiah Gaon addressed the important Jewish communities of southern Spain, Pechina was included among them in his letter (Abraham ibn Daud, *Sefer ha-Qabbalah—The Book of Tradition,* ed. by G. D. Cohen (1967), 79; see also index). Even in the late tenth century, as the town declined, a large and important Jewish community existed there. Its leader, Samuel ha-Kohen b. Josiah of Fez, Morocco, was a learned scholar who corresponded with *Sherira Gaon and supported *Ḥanokh b. Moses in his struggle against *Joseph ibn Abitur who also visited Pechina for the religious authority in Cordoba. Samuel's leadership virtually marks the final greatness of the Pechina community, most of whose members moved to developing Almeria in the tenth century. Pechina is considered by some scholars to be identical with the Spanish town of Calsena.

Bibliography: E. Lévi-Provençal, *La Péninsule Ibérique au Moyen-Age* (1938), 47–50; Ashtor, Korot, 1 (1966^2), 207–10. [ED.]

PECS (Hung. **Pécs;** Ger. **Fuenfkirchen**), town in S. Hungary. The celebrated Turkish traveler Evlia Cselebi found Jews there (1663). During the conversionary activities of the Catholic Church at the end of the 17th century, following the end of the Turkish conquest, the Jews were expelled from the city; the city council then solemnly pledged (1692) that no Jews would set foot in Pecs again. It was not until 1788 that Jews were again permitted to settle there. Among the first to arrive was the *Engel family who were among the leaders of the Jewish community for over a century. An organized community was formed in Pecs in 1840, but it already had a cemetery in 1827. The first synagogue was built in 1843 and the second in 1869; the latter, which was declared to be an architectural monument, still exists. Rabbis of Pecs were Israel Loew (officiated 1842–57); Alexander *Kohut, author of *Arukh ha-Shalem* (1872–80); A. Perls (1889–1914), one of the most notable Jewish preachers in Hungary; and Z. Wallenstein (1923–44). The Jewish population numbered 72 in 1840, 385 in 1850, 4,126 in 1910, 4,030 in 1930 and 3,486 in 1940. Up to World War I the Jews in Pecs were prosperous and included several industrialists, as well as merchants, contractors, wage earners, and artisans. After the enactment of the anti-Jewish laws in Hungary of 1938 and 1939, many who were thus deprived of their livelihood turned to crafts. The Jews in Pecs assisted refugees from Germany both from their own resources and with the aid of the "Wanderfuersorge." A number of Jewish doctors who had served in the Polish army arrived in Pecs after the German occupation (on March 19, 1944) and were also helped by the community. In May of that year the Jews in Pecs were concentrated into ghettos and at the end of June were sent to Auschwitz under conditions of extreme cruelty.

After the war 414 Jewish survivors returned. In 1945 the community was reorganized, and in 1971 numbered approximately 500.

Bibliography: A. Scheiber, in: MHJ, 8 (1965), 80; J. Schweitzer, *A pécsi izraelita hitközség története* (1966); idem, in: *Guttenberg Jahrbuch* (1966). [Jo.Sch.]

The Pecs synagogue built in 1869 by Karoly Gerster and Lajos Frey. From I. Heller and Z. Vajda, *The Synagogues of Hungary*, New York, 1968.

Figure 1. Etching of a Jewish peddler in Nuremberg, by A. Gabler, 1790. Nuremberg, Germanisches Nationalmuseum.

PEDDLING, the retail sale of wares or trade services and the buying up of agricultural and village produce by an itinerant seller, craftsman, or buyer who made relatively short trips, usually recurrent, to the places where his clients or employers lived. From the Middle Ages it was an important source of livelihood for Jews in many countries. In the Muslim Near East many Jews were engaged either in peddling their crafts, as shown by the evidence of the ninth-century Karaite *Benjamin of Nahavend, or in peddling wares, e.g., in 12th-century Egypt, as revealed in the responsa of *Maimonides. Peddling wares and crafts remained the source of income for many Jews up to the 20th century. It is difficult to determine to what extent the traders buying from and selling to feudal lords in 11th-century Western Europe could be considered as peddlers. With the predominance of *moneylending there from the 12th century onward, the Jews ceased to engage in peddling until the 15th century; a new situation then obtained, a combination of general economic trends, the tendency of Jews expelled from cities to settle in nearby villages and estates, and the movement of Jews from the west eastward. Expulsions and the development of an economy based on great landed estates created similar conditions for peddling in Bohemia. Jews were permitted to settle on these estates, the express condition of this settlement being the *"Versilbern,"* i.e., their obligation to purchase at a fixed price, the total agricultural produce of the estate. The Jewish leaseholder would pass on the produce to customers through Jewish peddlers, who also sold spices, tobacco, textiles, and manufactured utensils—again supplied to them by the leaseholder—to the peasants. The leaseholder often maintained a warehouse and processing plant and concentrated on wholesale commerce. The peddler was thus dependent, economically, legally, and socially, on the wholesaler from whom he received and offered wares on credit. By means of this system *Court Jews, who were often military contractors as well, were able to tap the economy of the country at its roots to supply immense amounts of grain, fodder, and livestock for the army. The Jewish peddler was a fixture of Bohemian rural life until well into the 19th century, when his role as intermediary in the purchase of agricultural produce declined: he sold hardware, haberdashery, sewing articles, and trinkets, and bought the peasants' by-products: feathers, furs, and hides. Poorer peddlers also bought old clothes, rags, bones, and junk. The peddler lived amicably among his Christian neighbors, to whom he was identical in dialect, dress, and manners. Generally a strict observer of the dietary laws, he adopted a special diet of eggs, cheese, onions, and bread on his Sunday till Friday peddling excursions. The hard lot of the peddler was depicted by L. *Kompert in several stories, especially *"Der Dorfgeher,"* the name by which the peddler was generally known. Many Bohemian and Moravian communities were founded by peddlers, a prominent example being that of *Carlsbad. There were communities in the south of Bohemia and Moravia, such as *Kolodeje, which consisted mainly of peddlers doing business in upper and lower Austria, where Jews were not permitted to settle.

In Germany, following the expulsions of the 15th and 16th centuries, many Jews settled in villages and on estates of the gentry where they gradually adapted themselves to peddling from house to house (known in German as *hausieren*), becoming to a certain degree the itinerant middlemen between estates and villages on the one hand and towns on the other. The large estate *(Gut)* looked for intermediaries to bring its increasing amount of produce to the townspeople free of the limitations imposed by town and guilds. The activity of the Jewish peddlers was viewed with suspicion and animosity by feudal circles and townsfolk, who were wary of the changes the proliferation of peddlers was making in the relationship between the town and its surroundings. Legislation was enacted against the peddlers in several German principalities. From the second half of the 17th century the situation was exacerbated by the continuous emigration of Jews from Poland to Germany, many of whom turned to peddling. The traveling peddler was sometimes identified with wandering Jewish beggars *(Betteljuden)*, as well as with vagabonds in general; smuggling also came naturally to be associated with his mobility, in particular near borders. Frequently **Schutzjuden* employed their unlicensed brethren as peddlers, thereby offering them legal protection and security. Thus, in Luebeck (1658) the first of a continuous series of complaints lodged against Jewish *Hausierer* accused them of buying up precious metals, probably for reminting by the *Schutzjuden* *mintmasters. When the Jews were compelled to leave

Figure 2. Watercolor and ink drawing of Florentine Jewish peddlers, c. 18th century. Cecil Roth Collection.

Luebeck in 1699, they settled in nearby Moisling, but complaints against the activity of Jewish peddlers in the city of Luebeck continued to be made up to the mid-19th century.

In Prussia it was objected in 1672 that Jewish peddlers "are not ashamed to go around buying and selling on holy Sunday, going to villages and entering the public houses offering their wares" (S. Stern, *Der Preussische Staat und die Juden,* I Akten, p. 29). Innumerable laws prohibiting all forms of *hausieren* were passed in many German principalities and towns. Measures taken against peddling in 1819 were one cause for thousands of Jews to emigrate from Bavaria to the U.S. Similar laws against peddling were enacted in Baden, Hesse, and Wuerttemberg. In these states emancipation was made conditional on the Jews abandoning peddling. The rapid development of 19th-century Germany gradually made the peddler's role obsolete, though he persisted in agricultural or remote regions. In the main, *Alsace-Lorraine was similar to Germany, and from there peddlers penetrated into those parts of France prohibited to Jews. The rural peddler, who was found mainly in southern Germany in the middle and late 19th century, generally lived amicably among his Christian neighbors. A staunch upholder of Orthodoxy, he often had special cooking utensils, inscribed *"kasher,"* reserved for his use in the local inns.

In the variegated Jewish economic life of Poland-Lithuania, various forms of peddling were common, including market hawkers and rural peddlers engaged in buying and selling; women were often found among them. In Lvov there was even a guild of Jewish street vendors. However, major cities passed laws prohibiting peddling, which was blamed for unbusiness-like practices and regarded as endangering the livelihood of Christians. Established Jewish traders, too, often opposed the competition of the mobile peddlers. In the *Pale of Settlement of Czarist Russia peddling was an important means of livelihood up to 1917, particularly in the eastern part of the region. A rapidly growing population in the townlets and expulsion from the villages led many to take up peddling. Numerous Jewish craftsmen left their homes on Sunday, worked all week in villages, and returned home on Friday; because of this they were known as *Wochers.* More important than the peddler who brought wares to sell was the one who bought up agricultural produce, in particular goods (like flax and hemp) which could be supplied to industrial centers at home or exported to Germany. In the large cities there were also many Jewish hawkers. Peddling could not, of course, survive in a Communist economy, but in Poland and the Baltic states it continued up to the Holocaust.

Jewish rural peddlers, immigrants from Alsace-Lorraine and the Rhineland, began to appear in England toward the middle of the 18th century, becoming common in most of southern England in the late 18th and early 19th century. The poet Robert Southey stated in 1807: "You meet Jew peddlers everywhere, traveling with boxes of haberdashery at their backs, cuckoo-clocks, sealing wax . . . miserable prints of King and Queen . . . even the Nativity and Crucifixion." Some Jews were also street vendors in London and other large cities. The influx of East European Jews in the 1880s caused a sudden resurgence in street vending in London and other major cities. Penniless immigrants, immediately off the boat, began hawking wares bought on credit; in 1906, 600 of *Glasgow's 6,000 Jews were engaged in peddling and the percentage in *Edinburgh was even higher. Street vending was the springboard to other commercial occupations; the father of Simon *Marks, founder of Marks and Spencer's, proudly exhibited the cart from which he conducted his first business. After

Figure 3. Shoelace seller in New York at Wall St. and Broadway, 1896. Courtesy Staten Island Historical Society, Staten Island, N.Y. Photo Alice Austen.

World War II the life of the East End, and including that of the Jewish street vendor, was depicted in the writings of H. Pinter, A. Wesker, W. Mankowitz, and Bernard Kops. The latter portrays this vanishing world in his play *The Hamlet of Stepney Green.*

In the Netherlands peddling and street vending received a fresh impetus with the arrival of Ashkenazim in the early 20th century. In 1921 31.6% of Amsterdam's 6,500 peddlers were Jews. The situation was identical in Belgium where there were about 1,600 Jewish market vendors in 1937, primarily in Brussels.

North America. The vast areas of North America made peddling important generally till about the middle of the 19th century. Sephardi peddlers appeared as early as 1655. Of licenses granted to peddlers in Pennsylvania, one out of 18 was to a Jew in 1771, five out of 49 in 1772, and four out of 27 in 1773. Trade in calico, cutlery, snuff, and similar goods was often conducted by barter in return for skins and furs. Peddlers frequently traded with Indians, who learned to respect the peaceful and peculiar Jewish peddler with his strange dietary laws: some Cherokees named one "the eggeater." The wares of the peddler, those he sold and those he purchased for sale, were generally handled by a wealthy wholesale trader with sufficient capital, like David *Franks, Joseph Simon, or the *Gratz family. Business was conducted through frontier entrepôts where furs and skins were exchanged for cash and additional negotiable goods. Occupational hazards were financial failure and murder on the highway.

In the second and third decades of the 19th century mass emigration of Jews from southern Germany and Prussian Poland brought many of them to peddling in the United States. They dealt mainly in consumer goods, haberdashery, trinkets, and jewelry. Carrying a pack sometimes weighing around 100 lb., the peddler served the farmers' stores and sold to him at his home. About one-half of all Jewish peddlers in the period 1820–80 arrived in this immigration wave, settling predominantly in the west, beyond the Appalachians in the Middle West, and after 1865 in the Far West. Many new colonists knew German, which helped the German-Jewish peddler. In order to operate properly in these newly developed areas, the peddler needed a store to replenish his supplies, but here the functions were complementary, unlike in Europe where they were fiercely competitive. An enterprising peddler, often the first in the vicinity, opened a store to supply fellow peddlers, thus moving up economically and socially. After settling, peddlers became the nucleus of a community. The Jewish population of Cincinnati grew from a handful in 1818 to 3,300 in 1850, a large percentage of whom were peddlers, future peddlers, and former peddlers. Immediately after the 1849 gold rush Jewish peddlers arrived to ply the mines, and communities were soon founded in San Francisco and Sacramento, the supply center for the mining area. One such man was Levi *Strauss, manufacturer of the original blue jeans; many others founded stores. The Jewish peddler was present throughout the far west: the *Goldwater department stores of Arizona were founded by a peddler: Meyer *Guggenheim began his meteoric career as a peddler in the west. The *Seligman family of New York were peddlers from Baiersdorf, Bavaria. Other successful peddlers were Adam *Gimbel, Moses and Caesar *Cone, and Nathan *Straus.

The Chicago Jewish community leader Abraham Kohn (d. 1871) described in his diary his way of life on becoming a peddler within a week of his arrival from Bavaria: "Leading such a life that none of us is able to observe the smallest commandment. Thousands of peddlers wander about America: young, strong men, they waste their strength by carrying heavy loads in the summer's heat; they lose their health in the icy cold of winter. And thus forget completely their Creator. They no longer put on the phylacteries; they pray neither on working day nor on the Sabbath. In truth, they have given up their religion for the pack which is on their backs" (AJA, 3 (1951) p. 99). He

Figure 4. English Derby-ware figure of a Jewish peddler, c. 1800. London, Jewish Museum. Courtesy Warburg Institute, London.

found consolation in the many acquaintances from Bavaria he encountered in his rise to financial success—within two years he owned a store in Chicago. The turnover in the profession was rapid; the average peddling term being between one and five years and the average age 18–25. Unlike in Europe, where peddling was a traditional continuous occupation, in the U.S. the individual Jew used peddling as a short-term step to more stable commercial ventures. After amassing some capital he tended to enter into a partnership with a compatriot, being especially inclined to enter the clothing trade and open a shop. Country peddling became obsolete with the growth of retail trade. The mail-order business, developed especially by Julius *Rosenwald's Sears-Roebuck Co., struck hard.

Jewish vendors appeared in strength on American streets with the mass emigration from Eastern Europe in the late 19th and early 20th centuries. The Lower East Side of New York witnessed the emergence of open air markets and pushcart traders and peddlers offering every conceivable type of merchandise. The situation in Chicago was similar. In 1890–93 a census conducted in New York among 23,801 Jewish families revealed that peddling was the second most common occupation (after *tailoring), with 2,440 full-time peddlers. Their ranks were swelled in times of economic crisis and unemployment. The great number of peddlers at any one given moment barely suggested the multitudes who had passed through this apprenticeship. A vivid picture of the East Side peddler was given by Harry *Golden and other Jewish authors.

Bibliography: BOHEMIA: R. Kestenberg-Gladstein, in: *Zion,* 12 (1947), 49–65, 160–185; idem, *Neuere Geschichte der Juden in den boehmischen Laendern* (1969), 96ff., 350f.; S. H. Lieben, in: *Afike Jehuda Festschrift* (1930) 39ff.; O. Donath, *Boehmische Dorfjuden* (1926); I. Ziegler, *Dokumente zur Geschichte der Juden in Karlsbad* (1913). GERMANY: M. Grunwald, *Hamburg's deutsche Juden bis zur Aufloesung der Dreigemeinden* (1904), 23, 57, 60, 150; F. Nienhaus, *Die Juden im ehemaligen Herzogtum Cleve* (1914), 24–28; A. Mueller, *Geschichte der Juden in Nuernberg* (1968), 61, 105ff., 123ff.; S. Stern, *Der Preussische Staat und die Juden,* 1 (1962), Akten, no. 2, 23, 27, 28, 144, 156, 165, 213, 377, 419, 441, 455; 2 (1962), Akten no. 187, 201, 549, 551, 553, 602, 609, 611, 660; A. Kapp, in: ZGJD, 6 (1935), 45–47; H. Schwab, *Jewish Rural Communities in Germany* (1956); E. Baasch, in: *Vierteljahreshefte fuer Sozial- und Wirtschaftspolitik,* 16 (1922), 370–98; D. A. Winter, *Geschichte der juedischen Gemeinde in Moisling/Luebeck* (1968), 1–85; S. Schwarz, *Die Juden in Bayern* (1963), 125, 195–205; H. Gonsiorowski, *Die Berufe der Juden Hamburgs* (1927), 39f., 48ff., 65f., 74–77; L. Kahn, *Geschichte der Juden in Sulzburg* (1969); C. Rixen, *Geschichte und Organisation der Juden im ehemaligen Stift Muenster* (1906), 52–57; A. Taenzer, *Die Geschichte der Juden in Jebenhausen und Goeppingen* (1927), 102–43; A. Welder-Steinberg, *Geschichte der Juden in der Schweiz* (1966); M. Aschkewitz, *Zur Geschichte der Juden in Westpreussen* (1967), 85ff., 95f.; T. Oelsner, in: JSOS, 4 (1942), 241–68, 349–98; B. Brilling, *Geschichte der Juden in Breslau* (1960), 22f.; F. Kynass, *Der Jude im deutschen Volkslied* (1934), 84f., 90f., 135–8; A. Blum, *Die wirtschaftliche Lage der juedischen Landbevoelkerung im Grossherzogtum Baden* (1901), 31f. AUSTRIA: D. Herzog, *B'nai B'rith Mitteilungen fuer Oesterreich,* 33 (1933), 341–6; L. Moses, *Geschichte der Juden in Niederoesterreich* (1935), 91ff.; G. Wolf, in: *Neuzeit,* 27 (1887), 87f. POLAND: R. Mahler, *Toledot ha-Yehudim be-Polin* (1946), s.v. index *Rokhelim;* S. Dubnow (ed.), *Pinkas ha-Medinah* (1925), 60, 70, 258f. W. H. Glicksman, *In the Mirror of Literature* (1966), 170ff., 189ff., 192, 198; J. Jacobson, in: MGWJ, 64 (1920), 222ff.; L. Shelomowitch, in: *Yidishe Ekonomik,* 3 (1939), 194–209; I. Schiper (ed.) *Dzieje handlu żydowskiego na ziemiach polskich* (1937). THE LOW COUNTRIES: K. Liberman, in: *Yidishe Ekonomik,* 2 (1938), 250–65; S. Kleerekoper, in: *Studia Rosenthaliana,* 1 (1967), 73ff.; H. Bloom, *Economic Activity of the Jews of Amsterdam* (1937), index. FRANCE: Z. Szajkowski, *Poverty and Social Welfare among French Jews (1800–1880)* (1954), 30f.; idem, *The Economic Status of the Jews in Alsace, Metz, and Lorraine (1648–1789)* (1954), 62ff.; idem, *Franco-Judaica* (1962), index; idem, in: JSOS, 8 (1946), 307f. ENGLAND: A. M. Jacob, in: JHSET, 17 (1953), 63–72; J. Rumney, *ibid.,* 13 (1936), 336ff.; V. D. Lipman, *Social History of the Jews in England, 1850–1950* (1954), 28–32; L. P. Gartner, *The Jewish Immigrant in England, 1870–1914* (1960), index; C. Roth, *Essays and Portraits in Anglo-Jewish History* (1962), 130–9; A. Rubens, in: JHSET, 19 (1960). U.S.; M. Whiteman, in: JQR, 53 (1963), 306–21; idem in: *Studies and Essays in Honor of A. A. Neuman* (1962), 503–15; F. S. Fierman, in: *Password,* 8 (1963), 43–55; O. Handlin, *Adventure in Freedom* (1954), index; R. Glanz, *The Jew in Old American Folklore* (1961), 122–46; idem, in: JSOS, 7 (1945), 119–36; idem, *The Jews of California* (1960); W. J. Parish, in: *New Mexico Historical Review,* 35 (1960), 1–29; M. Freund, *Jewish Merchants in Colonial America* (1939); S. Stern, in: E. E. Hirschler (ed.), *Jews from Germany in the United States* (1955), 36–39; H. L. Golden, *Forgotten Pioneer* (1963); M. Rischin, *The Promised City* (1962), index; A. Schoener (ed.), *Portal to America: The Lower East Side 1870–1925* (1967); AJA, 8 (1956), 87–89; 19 (1967), 6–8; A. V. Goodman, *ibid.,* 3 (1951), 81–111; W. L. Provol, *ibid.,* 16 (1964), 26–34; L. M. Friedman, in: AJHSP, 44 (1955/56), 1–7; AJHSP, 38 (1948/49), 22ff.; 40 (1950/51), 59ff., 327; 53 (1963/64), 271; 54 (1964/65), 488–90; 56 (1966/67), 296–300; L. Berg, in: *Commentary* (July 1965), 63–67; J. R. Marcus (ed.), *Memoirs of American Jews,* 3 vols. (1955).

[H.W.]

°**PEDERSEN, JOHANNES** (1883–), Danish Semitist, religious historian, and biblical scholar. From 1916 to 1921 he was a lecturer on the Old Testament, and from 1921 to 1950 professor of Semitic philology, at Copenhagen University. Among his works on Semitic philology are a Hebrew grammar (*Hebraeisk Grammatik,* 1926), a treatise of fundamental importance on the Keret text from Ras Shamra (*Die Krt-Legende,* 1941), and a translation and commentary on the Karatepe texts (in: *Acta Orientalia,* 21 (1950–53), 35–56). He published a number of treatises on Islam in Danish. Of singular importance are Pedersen's achievements in biblical research. In 1920 he published the first volume of *Israel* (*Israel: its Life and Culture,* Eng. tr., 1926), in which he endeavors to describe Israelite thinking and social life in terms of the mentality and behavior of a primitive civilization, thus making an attempt to extricate himself from the preconceived theological and philosophic notions that have influenced the interpretation of the old Israelite texts since Hellenistic times. In the second volume, published in 1934 (Eng. tr., 1940), Pedersen traces the development of Israelite civilization from the period of Judges until the Exile. The foundation of the religious development was the spontaneous experience of a cooperation between the divine forces and man himself; with David, purposefulness took the place of spontaneity in the relation to God, and the deity was looked upon as the strong will of personality. The preaching of the prophets emphasized the overwhelming greatness of God and the inferiority of man, thus preparing the way for Judaism's ideas of God and man. From the point of view of social development, the contact with the Canaanite way of life and urbanization resulted in a crisis in the ancient pattern of life.

In *Israel* and in his articles "Die Auffassung vom Alten Testament" (in: ZAW, 49 (1931), 161–81) and "Passahfest und Passahlegende" (*ibid.,* 52 (1934), 161–76), Pedersen condemned Higher Criticism's distinction of sources in the Pentateuch. He does not deny that there are discernible layers in the Pentateuch, yet he maintains that these cannot be distinguished and dated: "All sources are both pre-Exilic and post-Exilic." In 1931 Pedersen published *Scepticisme israélite,* a study of Ecclesiastes, and in Festschriften to Mowinckel (1955, pp. 62–72) and Rowley (1955, pp. 238–46), he shed light on the problems behind Genesis 2–3, with the help of late Jewish texts and old oriental myths, especially the Adapa myth.

Bibliography: Two festschriften published in honor of Pedersen's 60th and 70th birthdays: *Mélanges d'histoire des religions... J. Pedersen,* 1–3 (1944–47); *Studia Orientalia Joanni Pedersen* (1953).

[ED.N.]

PEEL COMMISSION, name commonly used for the Royal Commission on Palestine under the chairmanship of Earl Peel, appointed by the British government on Aug. 7, 1936, to study the underlying causes of the Arab riots. In July 1937 the commission presented its report recommending the partitioning of Palestine into a Jewish state, an Arab state, and a British mandatory enclave, but its recommendations were not implemented.

See also *Israel, Historical Survey; *Palestine, Inquiry Commissions; *Palestine Partition and Partition Plans; *Zionism, Zionist Policy. [ED.]

PEERCE, JAN (originally **Jacob Pincus Perelmuth;** 1904–), U.S. operatic tenor. Born in New York he first studied medicine, and began his musical career as a dance band violinist and occasional singer. In 1933 he obtained a long-term engagement as a singer at Radio City Music Hall,

Jan Peerce, U.S. tenor. Courtesy Israel Philharmonic Orchestra, Tel Aviv. Photo Boris Goldenberg, New York.

New York. Toscanini heard him and chose him to sing with the N.B.C. Symphony Orchestra in 1938. After his operatic debut in Philadelphia and a recital in New York, he was cast by the Metropolitan Opera in 1941 to sing the leading tenor role in "La Traviata." Peerce was acclaimed for his colorful quality, his sensitive interpretations, and a temperament suited both to the Italian and German lieder. Retaining his interest in Jewish life, he appeared in cantorial recitals, and made recordings of cantorial works and Jewish folksongs. He toured widely in America and Europe, London and West Germany, toured the U.S.S.R. under U.S. State Department auspices in 1956 (again in 1963), and sang in Israel many times.

Bibliography: Biancolli, in: *Opera News,* 30 (Jan. 29, 1966), 26. [C.AB.]

°**PÉGUY, CHARLES-PIERRE** (1873–1914), French Catholic poet, editor, and essayist. Born in Orleans, Péguy studied at the Ecole Normale Supérieure in Paris, where he came under the influence of Henri *Bergson. Politically a radical, he puzzled men of both the left and the right with his unique fusion of socialism and Catholicism. His abiding sympathy for the Jewish people is to be seen in his activities, his writings, and his circle of friends. From 1893, he helped to rally student support for the retrial of *Dreyfus, for socialism, and for the defense of the republic. In 1900 he launched his celebrated *Cahiers de la Quinzaine,* which popularized the works of many Jewish authors, including André *Spire, Edmond *Fleg, André *Suarès, and the English novelist Israel *Zangwill. Jewish subscribers played a major part in keeping the journal alive. Péguy's bookshop near the Sorbonne became a rendezvous for liberal writers and intellectuals. A man of stern convictions, Péguy cherished four great spiritual traditions: Hebrew, Greek, Christian, and French. He believed that, while the Catholics had read for only two centuries and the Protestants since Calvin, Israel—the "eternally anguished people"—had read for 2,000 years. He adhered to the Catholic view that the Old Testament prefigured the New, but regarded the Jewish people as "the only race to have given prophets . . . to be of the race of prophets." Thus, Péguy considered his friend, Bernard *Lazare, though an atheist, "a prophet of Israel," because of his quest for justice. For Péguy, Israel's vocation was to remain faithful to itself and pursue its historic mission of prophecy, and he hinted that Israel's divine mission had not ended with the Christian revelation. In *Notre jeunesse* (1910), Péguy criticized the reactionary turncoat Daniel *Halévy, who had once been his friend. *Notre Patrie* (1905), *Portrait de Bernard Lazare* (1928), and *L'Argent* (1913) reflect other aspects of his philo-Semitism. Péguy's thought seems to have been influenced by Jewish messianism. This is particularly apparent in his poem, *Le Mystère de la Charité de Jeanne d'Arc* (1910 and many subsequent editions), in which Joan, fighting for both the soul and the homesteads of France, becomes the symbol of mankind's struggle for temporal salvation and his "eternal need for spiritual salvation." Péguy died in action on the Marne at the beginning of World War I.

Bibliography: A. Salomon, *In Praise of Enlightenment* (1963), 375–86; A. Suarès, *Péguy* (Fr., 1915); D. Halévy, *Charles Péguy et les Cahiers de la Quinzaine* (1918); Rabi, in: *Esprit,* 32 no. 8–9 (1964), 331–42; Prajs, in: *Cahiers Paul Claudel,* no. 7 (1968), 387–404. [JA.K.]

PEIERLS, SIR RUDOLF ERNST (1907–), British physicist. Peierls, who was born in Berlin, held an appointment at the Federal Institute of Technology in Zurich from 1929 to 1932. In 1933 he went to England and pursued research at Manchester University for four years. He became professor of applied mathematics at Birmingham University and worked on the atomic energy project there from 1940 to 1943. In the latter year he went to the U.S., and was for three years one of the leading scientists on the Manhattan Project at the Los Alamos Laboratory. In 1946 he returned to Birmingham, where he remained until 1963 when appointed professor of physics at Oxford. He was elected a Fellow of the Royal Society in 1945 and was knighted in 1968.

From the outset of his academic life Peierls was deeply involved in the development of atomic energy. At Birmingham at the outbreak of World War II, he and Otto *Frisch considered the theoretical questions involved in chain reaction and concluded that the energy liberated by a five-kilogram bomb would be equivalent to several thousand tons of dynamite. In a short paper which also outlined a possible thermal diffusion method for the separation of uranium 235 and suggested how the bomb could be detonated, they were the first in the world to enunciate the practical possibility of the atom bomb with scientific precision. The Peierls-Frisch paper was one of the factors that influenced the British Government to begin an atomic energy program prior to the Manhattan Project. Peierls' publications included: *Quantum Theory of Solids* (1955) and *Laws of Nature* (1955).

Sir Rudolph's son, RONALD FRANK PEIERLS (1935–), was also a physicist. Born in Manchester, he went to the United States and had posts at the Institute for Advanced Study at Princeton, N.J. and Cornell University before being appointed to the physics division at Brookhaven national laboratory, Long Island, N.Y. in 1966. His main interest was the nature and properties of interactions between elementary particles. [J.L.M.]

PEIPER, TADEUSZ (1891–), Polish poet, playwright, and literary theorist. Born in Cracow, Peiper spent the years 1914–20 in Spain, returning to Poland in 1921, when he organized the Awangarda Cracow group of poets whose leading theorist he then became. During the years 1922–23 and 1926–27 Peiper edited the group's official periodical *Zwrotnica.* Believing that human progress depends on man's conquest of nature, he called for artistic glorification of the machine, technology, and invention as weapons in this struggle. Peiper also maintained that the poet's task was creative and utilitarian and that his duty was to write about organized human society in order to improve it. Although he did not succeed in founding a school, Peiper made a valuable contribution to Polish literature between the world wars. After the Nazi invasion, he fled to Moscow, where he contributed to the weekly *Wolna Polska* and to *Nowe Horyzonty*, returning to Warsaw after the defeat of Nazi Germany.

His works include verse collections such as *A* (1924), *Żywe linie* ("Living Lines," 1924), and *Poematy* (1935); *Nowe usta* ("The New Mouth," 1925), a lecture on poetry; *Tędy* ("This Way," 1930), collected articles, essays, and sketches; plays such as *Skoro go nie ma* ("Since He is Not Here," 1933); and the novel *Krzysztof Kolumb, odkrywca* ("Christopher Columbus the Discoverer," 1949).

Bibliography: *Słownik współczesnych pisarzy polskich*, 2 (1964), 639–42. [S.W.]

PEIXOTTO, U.S. family of Sephardi origin. DANIEL LEVI MADURO PEIXOTTO (1800–1843), a physician, was born in Amsterdam, and was taken to New York in 1807 by his father MOSES LEVI MADURO PEIXOTTO (1767–1828), a merchant who served as *ḥazzan* of New York's Congregation Shearith Israel from 1820 until his death. Daniel Peixotto graduated from Columbia College in 1816 and became a leading physician in New York City, serving as editor of the *New York Medical and Physical Journal* and as a founder of the New York Academy of Medicine. He was an active Jacksonian Democrat and a leader and intellectual mentor of the Jewish community. From 1835 until 1841 he was a professor at the newly founded medical school of Willoughby University near Cleveland, Ohio, a forerunner of the Case-Western Reserve University Medical School.

His son, BENJAMIN FRANKLIN PEIXOTTO (1834–1890), was a lawyer, diplomat, and Jewish communal leader. Born in New York City, he was brought by his family to Cleveland, then back to New York, later resettling in Cleveland during 1847–66. There he became a clothing merchant, and also frequently wrote editorials for the daily *Cleveland Plain Dealer*. Peixotto was a founder and president of the Mercantile Library Association and Lyceum, and a follower of Democratic Senator Stephen A. Douglas of Illinois, under whose guidance he studied law. A trustee and founder of the Sunday School at Congregation Tifereth Israel (now The Temple), he served as Grand Sar (president) of *B'nai B'rith during 1863–64 and was the prime mover for its Jewish Orphan Asylum (now Bellefaire) established in Cleveland in 1869. In 1866 Peixotto moved to New York to practice law, then transferred to San Francisco in 1869.

Benjamin Franklin Peixotto, U.S. diplomat and communal leader. Courtesy B'nai B'rith, Washington, D.C.

Early in 1870, moved by the Rumanian persecution of Jews, Peixotto succeeded in becoming the first U.S. consul in Bucharest, appointed by President Grant through the intervention of the *Seligmans. His financial needs in the unpaid position, as well as political support, were provided, not always reliably, by a group of wealthy U.S. Jews, along with the *B'nai B'rith, the *Board of Delegates of American Israelites, and prominent French and English Jews led by Sir Francis *Goldsmid. In Bucarest Peixotto pressed vigorously for Jewish emancipation, to which Rumanian Jews were legally entitled by the Treaty of Paris of 1856, and also took the initiative in founding Jewish schools, cultural societies, and Rumanian B'nai B'rith, as part of his plan to modernize Jewish life in that country. Although he accomplished little toward emancipation, his well-publicized presence inhibited new anti-Semitic legislation and avoided or mitigated several pogroms. His unofficial inquiry in the summer of 1872 about the possibility of large-scale Rumanian Jewish emigration to the U.S. was loudly endorsed by that regime, but scandalized most of Peixotto's backers and was rejected by them as a policy. Although much embarrassed, he continued to endorse emigration privately while serving in Bucharest until 1876. From 1877 to 1885 Peixotto was U.S. consul in Lyons, and then lived in New York City, engaging in law, Republican politics, and Jewish communal affairs until his death.

His son was GEORGE DA MADURO PEIXOTTO (1859–1937), a painter. Born in Cleveland, he received his art education in Dresden during his father's service in Rumania. He became a notable portrait painter, executing portraits from life of Cardinal Manning, President McKinley, Chief Justice Waite, and John Hay, among others. His "Grandchildren of Mark Hopkins" won wide praise, and his "Family Group" was exhibited at the Paris Salon in 1893. Peixotto's portrait of Sir Moses *Montefiore at the latter's centenary in 1884 hung in the Corcoran Gallery, and his painting of Julius *Bien hangs in the National Museum, Washington, D.C. Murals by him decorated the New Amsterdam Theater and the Criterion Club in New York City.

Bibliography: J. L. Blau and S. W. Baron, *Jews of the United States 1790–1840*, 2 (1964), 437–9, 469–75, 597–601; M. U. Schappes, *Documentary History of the Jews in the United States* (1951^2), 611; D. de Sola Pool, *Portraits Etched in Stone* (1952), 428–32; L. P. Gartner, in: AJHSQ, 58 (1968/69), 25–117; AJYB, 6 (1904/05), 163; I. J. Benjamin, *Three Years in America 1859–1862*, 1 (1956), 51–52; *New York Times* (Oct. 13, 1937). [L.P.G.]

PEKAH (Heb. פֶּקַח; "He [God] has opened [His eyes]," i.e., given heed), son of Remaliah, king of Israel from 735 to 732 B.C.E. (II Kings 15:27–32). In the inscriptions of Tiglath-Pileser III, his name appears in the form *Pa-qa-ḫa*. It is stated that Pekah was the *shalish* (apparently, "army commander") of high rank of Pekahiah son of Menahem and that he conspired against his royal master in Samaria with the aid of "fifty men of the Gileadites and . . . slew him, and reigned in his stead" (II Kings 15:25). The statement in the Bible that Pekah reigned for 20 years (II Kings 15:27) can hardly be accepted as it stands, since he was killed by *Hoshea son of Elah (II Kings 15:30) in 732 B.C.E. at the very latest, while *Menahem son of Gadi is still mentioned in Tiglath-Pileser III's inscriptions as king of Samaria in 738 (or 743, at the earliest). For this reason, some scholars think that Pekah reigned in Gilead (cf. II Kings 15:25), for a certain period overlapping the reigns of the kings in Samaria, and seized the throne in Samaria only in 736, most probably with the aid of *Rezin, king of Aram. From both the biblical sources and the Assyrian documents it is clear that the military and political alliance of Pekah and Rezin operated against Judah, on the one hand, and against Assyria, on the other. The stronger partner in the alliance was Rezin (cf. Isa. 7:2), whose help Pekah evidently needed against rivals to his throne.

According to II Kings 15:37, Pekah and Rezin first attacked Judah in the reign of Jotham and continued the war into the reign of Ahaz (II Kings 16; II Chron. 28). In the opinion of most commentators the occasion for the war was an attempt by Aram and Israel to force Ahaz to join an anti-Assyrian alliance led by Aram-Damascus and supported by Egypt. The armies of Aram and Israel invaded Judah (II Chron. 28:5–15) and laid siege to Jerusalem (II Kings 16:5; Isa. 7:2). The allies intended to contract the kingdom of Judah's territory to the advantage of the kingdom of Israel, to depose the Davidic dynasty, and to install as king in Jerusalem a certain "son of Tabeel," possibly a Transjordanian and an ancestor of the *Tobiads. But the course of events was completely changed by the appearance of Tiglath-Pileser III in southern Syria and Palestine. In 734 B.C.E. the Assyrian armies undertook an expedition against Philistia, along the Phoenician coast, and it is possible that during his campaign Tiglath-Pileser III detached the coastal region (the Dor district and the Sharon region) from the kingdom of Israel. In 733 B.C.E. the Assyrian army besieged Damascus, at the same time conquering northern Transjordan, Gilead, and Galilee and deporting the population of these areas to Assyria (II Kings 15:29). Tiglath-Pileser III himself mentions, in his Annals, the capture of (Ramoth) Gilead and cities in Galilee and the deportation of their populations. In the following year (732 B.C.E.) the Assyrian armies apparently invaded the hill country of Ephraim and threatened to capture the capital, Samaria. According to the biblical narrative, Hoshea son of Elah then conspired against Pekah and usurped the throne (II Kings 15:30). Pekah's policy, in contrast to that of Menahem and his son Pekahiah, apparently showed allegiance to Assyria, had grave consequences for the Kingdom of Israel, and marked the beginning of the process which culminated in the fall of Samaria about a decade later. The most fertile areas of the kingdom were conquered by the Assyrians and turned into the Assyrian provinces of *Gilead, *Megiddo, and *Dor (cf. Isa. 8:23).

Bibliography: Bright, Hist, 254–60; Albright, in: BASOR, 140 (1955), 34–35; J. Cook, in: VT, 14 (1964), 121–35; Oded, in: *Tarbiz,* 38 (1968/69), 205ff.; Mazar, in: IEJ, 7 (1957), 137–45; Tadmor, in: H. H. Ben-Sasson (ed.), *Toledot Am Yisrael bi-Ymei Kedem* (1969), 134–5.

[B.O.]

PEKAHIAH (Heb. פְּקַחְיָה; "YHWH has opened [the eyes]"), the son of *Menahem; ruled Israel in Samaria for two years (c. 737/6–735/4 B.C.E.) during the reign of Uzziah, son of Amaziah, over Judah (II Kings 15:22–24). The Bible provides no information about Pekahiah's acts or about the condition of the northern kingdom in his day, apart from the formulaic comment, "He did what was evil in the sight of the Lord . . . " (II Kings 15:24). It may be presumed that Pekahiah continued the policy of his father, Menahem, and displayed his loyalty to Assyria. In the second year of his reign he fell victim to a conspiracy led by his army commander *Pekah, son of Remaliah, who killed him with the support of 50 Gileadites and took his place on the throne (II Kings 15:25).

Bibliography: Bright, Hist, 254.

[B.O.]

PEKELIS, ALEXANDER HAIM (1902–1946), jurist and communal worker. Born in Odessa, Russia, Pekelis studied at various European universities. In 1932 he was appointed lecturer in jurisprudence at the University of Florence but the local Fascist party had him removed. He became professor of jurisprudence at the University of Rome in 1935 where he founded and edited a review, *Il Massimario Della Corte Toscana.* Pekelis left Italy following the enactment of the anti-Semitic laws in 1938 and settled in Paris where he practiced law. Just before the Nazi occupation of France in June 1940, Pekelis went with his wife and five children to Lisbon and in 1941 emigrated to the United States. He lectured at the New School for Social research in New York City and at the same time studied at the Columbia University Law School, where he was editor in chief of the *Columbia Law Review.* In 1945, he became chief consultant to the Commission on Law and Social Action of the American Jewish Congress, a post he held until his death in an airplane accident at Shannon, Ireland, while returning from an international Zionist conference as a representative of the Labor Zionist movement.

Pekelis made an important contribution to the struggle against anti-Semitism with the formulation of a bold new program for the American Jewish Congress entitled "Full Equality in a Free Society—A Program for Jewish Action." He drafted the bill, enacted two years after his death, which ultimately eliminated the numerus clausus in the medical schools of New York state. Pekelis contributed many articles urging a "jurisprudence of welfare," the submission of "private governments" to constitutional requirements, the establishment of a "Human Rights Agency" by the United Nations and an annual "Supreme Court Yearbook" which would critically examine that court's decisions. Many of his proposals were subsequently adopted.

Bibliography: M. R. Konvits, ed., *Law and Social Action: Selected Essays of Alexander H. Pekelis* (1950).

[WI.M.]

PEKERIS, CHAIM LEIB (1908–), mathematician. Born in Alytus, Lithuania, Pekeris emigrated to the United States in his late teens. He did research at the Massachussetts Institute of Technology from 1936 to 1940, and from 1941 to 1946 headed the mathematics-physics group in the war research division at Columbia University. After two years at the Institute for Advanced Study at Princeton, he went to Israel in 1948, to establish the department of applied mathematics at the Weizmann Institute of Science. Under his direction, an eight-year gravimetrical and seismic mapping survey of the country was undertaken, and methods of prospecting were developed which laid the basis for Israel's petroleum-boring programs.

Pekeris' own main interests were the internal constitution of the earth, including the study of the origin and nature of earthquakes, theoretical seismology, the calculation of ocean tides, and the way fluids flow through pipes and around obstacles.

[J.L.M.]

PEKI'IN (Heb. פְּקִיעִין), village in Upper Galilee; noted for its tradition of continuous Jewish settlement throughout the ages. Peki'in can possibly be identified with Baca (Jos., Wars 3:39), the town which marked the boundary between the Upper and Lower Galilee. Fragments of reliefs with Jewish symbols are found dispersed in the village, dating from the late Roman period. According to the *Pesikta de-Rav Kahana,* Beqa' was the place where R. *Simeon b. Yoḥai and his son R. Eleazar lived in a cave for 13 years during the Hadrianic persecution of Jews which followed the Bar Kokhba War (132–35). In the *Midrash Kohelet Rabbah* (10:11), which is the main source of the story, the place is called Peki'in. During their stay in the cave they lived from the fruits of an old mulberry tree. Above the cave stood a giant carob tree and a spring was located below it. Votive gifts and oil lamps were placed in the crevice of the cave by Jews and non-Jews alike. Additional places of importance

The synagogue of Peki'in, restored in 1873. Courtesy Government Press Office, Tel Aviv.

in the village included the marked grave of the talmudic scholar R. *Oshayah of Tiria, which was located near the spring of Ein Tiria to the west of Peki'in and surrounded by large and hallowed trees, referred to by the Jews of the village as the "groves." Also located there was the tomb of R. Yose of Peki'in, which is mentioned in the Zohar and other sources. The antiquity, mystery, and wonder surrounding the Jews of Peki'in were added to by the presence of Jewish fellaheen in this outlying corner of Upper Galilee and their claim of being the last group of Jews who were never exiled. Their features, their clothing, their language, and their Arabic village life until the second third of the 20th century all added to the character of the village.

The Jews of Peki'in are first mentioned in the travel book of R. Moses *Basola (1522). He refers to them as *"fallaḥim"* ("workers of the land") and to the village by its Arabic name, "Bukayyᶜa." Responsa of the Safed rabbis of the 16th century dealing with mitzvot to be fulfilled only in the Land (of Israel), the priestly tithes, the levitical tithes, and the Sabbatical Year, all of which concern Jewish farm workers in Galilee, also testify to the existence of Jewish agriculture in Bukayyᶜa. The Jews of the village were also engaged in the breeding of silkworms. Sixteenth-century Turkish tax registers from the Istanbul archives which mention the number of taxable Jewish families in ten Galilee villages during the years 1525–73 include 33 to 45 Jewish families in Bukayyᶜa. From time to time groups of Jews engaged in commerce and the leasing and tilling of lands; other groups engaged in the study of Torah and the Zohar "under the carob tree of R. Simeon b. Yohai." Peki'in was also a summer resort for urban Jews, especially for those from Tiberias. The Jews of the towns sought refuge there when plagues broke out. In 1602 R. Joseph *Trani of Safed visited Peki'in to instruct the local Jews, who were cultivating mulberries for silkworms.

The name Peki'in again appears during the 18th century. In 1742, the kabbalist R. Ḥayyim *Attar, who during the same year had emigrated to Ereẓ Israel with his disciples, lived there for about two months. After the severe earthquakes of 1759, many of the victims from Safed fled there. The rabbis of Safed also established a yeshivah for some time in the village. The refugees included the son of Rabbi Jacob of Vilna, who was from the group led by R. *Judah he-Ḥasid, which had emigrated to Ereẓ Israel. R. Joseph Sofer, author of *Edut bi-Yhosef,* lived and died in Peki'in. R. Reuben Satanov, author of *Ahavat Ẓiyyon,* also lived and studied the Zohar there. In 1783 some members of the ḥasidic *aliyah* from Russia and Poland established themselves there after leaving Safed and Jerusalem.

In 1820 only 20 families of Jews were left in Peki'in; their number rose to 50 (numbering 300 persons) in 1832—mainly Sephardim. In 1856, 50 Jews remained in Peki'in and in 1900, 11 families of farmers (93 persons). During the riots of 1929, the Jews of Peki'in were compelled to abandon their village out of fear of the Arab gangs. Upon their return to the village, they were occasionally compelled to seek work in the Jewish settlements. After the riots of 1936–39, only one family returned to the village. In 1948 Peki'in's population included 800 Druzes, 242 Christians, 68 Muslims, and one Jewish family, Zeynati (from the old inhabitants). In 1948 Peki'in was incorporated into Israel; part of the Arab inhabitants left and Jews—new immigrants—were settled there. The ancient synagogue and the cemetery were renovated with the assistance of I. *Ben-Zvi and are considered historical sites. The traditional tombs of R. Oshayah of Tiria and R. Yose of Peki'in were also repaired. In 1955, the moshav Peki'in ha-Ḥadashah ("New Peki'in") was established above Ein Tiria. The new settlers arrived from Spanish and French Morocco, from Tangier, Fez, and Marrakesh. In 1968, "Old" Peki'in had 2,070 inhabitants, about three-quarters Druze and the rest Christian Arabs, mostly of the Greek Orthodox denomination. In the synagogue of Peki'in (built in 1873) and on the walls of some of the houses of the village are incorporated fragments of reliefs, showing Jewish symbols such as the seven-branched candlestick *(menorah),* the *shofar* and *lulav,* the vine, etc. These remains prove the existence of a synagogue in the village during the talmudic period.

Bibliography: J. Braslavski (Braslavi), *Le-Ḥeker Arẓenu* (1954), index; idem, in: BJPES, 3 (1935/36), 24–29; idem, in: *Ma'aravo shel-Galil ve-Ḥof ha-Galil* (1965), 137ff.; B. Lewis, *Notes and Documents from the Turkish Archives* (1952), 9, 20–21; Goodenough, Symbols, 218–9, 572–3; I. Ben-Zvi, *She'ar Yashuv* (1965), index.

[M.A.-Y./Jo.Br.]

PEKING, capital of China. In the second half of the 13th century Marco Polo reported the presence of Jews in Peking among the followers of the Mongol emperor Kublai Khan. The Scottish traveler, John Bell, who visited Peking in 1720–21, found a few Jews, supposedly descendants of these early arrivals. This remnant disappeared and no Jews settled in Peking until modern times. During World War II there were about 100 Jews of various nationalities (or stateless) in Peking, mostly European refugees. All of them left the Chinese capital after the war.

Bibliography: I. Cohen, *Journal of a Jewish Traveller* (1925), 189–94.

[R.L.]

PEKOD (Heb. פְּקוֹד), Aramean tribe (see *Aram) that once inhabited the eastern bank of the Lower Tigris, and is identified with the Puqudu mentioned in Assyrian texts beginning with the time of Tiglath-Pileser III. The Pekod tribe was organized and put under the jurisdiction of the governor of Arrapha. However, the tribe participated in many revolts and was subsequently deported. Many individuals of this tribe are known from the sources. In the Bible, Pekod is mentioned in Jeremiah's prophecy against Babylon (Jer. 50:21) in a wordplay: *pqd,* "to punish." The Babylonian king is called to go up against well-known enemies (see *Chaldea), such as the tribe of Pekod which was practically unconquerable, and thus exhaust himself and bring upon himself punishment and doom. Ezekiel 23:23 mentions Pekod as a typical representative of the Babylonian "mobile" administration. The verse speaks of peoples sent to conquered territories to fill various posts or as settler-deportees. Pekod (like similar tribes) could act as a police force or fill other posts.

Bibliography: E. Forrer, *Die Provinzeinteilung des assyrischen Reiches* (1920), 96, 98ff.; Luckenbill, Records, index; J. Bright, *Jeremiah* (1965), 359; J. A. Brinkman, *A Political History of Post-Kassite Babylonia* (1968), index. For further bibl. see *Aram, Arameans. [P.A.]

PELICAN, one of the largest of water birds. Three species of the pelican (genus *Pelecanus*) are occasionally seen in Israel in the nature preserve that was formerly part of the Ḥuleh swamps, as well as in fish ponds. The pelican may be the שַׁקְנַאי *(saknai)* mentioned in the Talmud (Ḥul 63a) as a bird that was eaten in some places but not in others since there were doubts as to its *kashrut*. Its Hebrew name is derived from the pouch *(sak)* under its lower bill jaw used for storing the fish it catches. The Septuagint identifies the pelican with the קָאַת (*ka'at;* Lev. 11:18; Isa. 34:11; et al.), which was apparently the view, too, of an *amora* (Ḥul. loc. cit.), who identified the *ka'at* with the *kik* (Ḥul. loc. cit with the reading of the Arukh) said to be found in the neighborhood of seas and to be very fatty (Shab. 21a). But the identification of *ka'at* with the pelican, a waterfowl, is improbable, since it is mentioned in the Bible as a bird that inhabits the desert and ruins, and is a species of *owl. This identification has, however, passed into modern Hebrew.

Bibliography: Lewysohn, Zool, 184f., 368; F.S. Bodenheimer, *Animal and Man in Bible Lands* (1960), 64; M. Dor, *Leksikon Zo'ologi* (1965), 343. [J.F.]

PELLA or **PAḤAL,** ancient city situated east of the Jordan River, 8 mi. (c. 13 km.) S.E. of Beth-Shean. The present name of the site is Khirbet Faḥil. The first mention of it occurs in the Egyptian Execration texts, dating to the late 19th century B.C.E. as Pi-ḥi-lim. It is mentioned as well in almost all Egyptian sources relating to Canaan, appearing in the list of Canaanite cities of Thutmosis III as *Phr;* in Anastasi Papyri (3 and 4) as a center for the manufacture of chariots; in the Beth-Shean stele of Seti I as a place which revolted against Egypt and besieged Rehob, and was subsequently subdued in one day by the first regiment of the Amon brigade; and in the list of Ramses II. From El-Amarna letter 148, it appears that Hazor and Tyre contended for possession of Piḥili, whose prince at that time was Motbaal. After 1300 B.C.E. the place is not mentioned in extant sources; however, Late Bronze and Iron Age pottery was found there. It revived in the Hellenistic period, when it was known as Pella, after the Macedonian capital. The city was captured by Antiochus III in 218 B.C.E (Polybius 5:70, 12) and later by Alexander Yannai, who destroyed it (Jos., Ant., 13:397). Pompey restored it and incorporated it into the Decapolis league. Prior to Jerusalem's siege by Titus, its Christian community moved to Pella. Some Christians, including the author Aristion of Pella, remained there afterward. In Byzantine times it was the seat of a bishop. The hot baths located there (Ḥamta di Paḥal) are mentioned in the Jerusalem Talmud (Shev. 6:1, 36c). In 635/636 Muslim Arabs defeated the Byzantine forces near Pella and took the city, which continued to exist for some time with a mixed Greek and Arab population. Ruins on the site include two temples, a triapsidal basilica, colonnaded streets, a necropolis, and a theater near baths.

Excavations on the site were carried out by an American expedition in 1958 and in later years. Pottery of the tenth century B.C.E. and Israelite houses and walls of the eighth century were uncovered. Above these were remains of the Hellenistic and Arab periods; dating to the latter period are the remains of a church.

Bibliography: G. Schumacher, *Pella* (Eng., 1888); D. C. Steuernagel, *Der ʿAdschlūn* (1925), 398ff.; J. Richmond, in: PEFQS, 166 (1934), 18ff.; Funk and Richardson, in: BA, 21 (1958), 82ff.; H. Seyrig, in: *Syria,* 36 (1959), 68ff.; Press, Ereẓ, s.v. [M.A.-Y.]

PELLEG (POLLAK), FRANK (1910–1968), Israel musician. Born in Prague, Pelleg conducted at the Prague Opera before going to Palestine in 1936. There he initiated chamber music concerts at the Tel Aviv Museum. After the War of Independence Pelleg headed the Music Department of the Ministry of Education (1948–52). In 1951 he moved to Haifa, where he managed the affairs of the Haifa Philharmonic Orchestra and was its musical adviser. He also served the Haifa Theatre in the same capacity. A well-known pianist and harpsichordist, Pelleg traveled widely and was noted for his interpretation of Bach.

Frank Pelleg, Israel musician.

He lectured at the Tel Aviv Museum and at the Samuel Rubin Israel Academy of Music, Tel Aviv University, at the Technion and at the University of Haifa. He composed for the piano and for chamber orchestras, and wrote vocal music and also incidental music for the theater. Pelleg wrote a number of works on music, among them: *Da et ha-Muzikah* (1946) and *Kelei ha-Neginah* (1965). [YE.G.]

°**PELLICANUS (Pellikan), CONRAD (Kursiner, Kuers(ch)ner,** also known as **Pellicanus Rubeaquensis:** 1478–1556), German Hebraist and Bible scholar. Born in Rouffach, Alsace, Pellicanus entered the Franciscan order in 1493. He first obtained Hebrew manuscripts of the Prophets from the convert Johannes *Pauli, an eminent Rhenish preacher, and it was the laborious study of these manuscripts which determined his subsequent scholarly career. In Tuebingen he met Johann *Reuchlin, and on his encouragement began copying Hebrew texts; later he learned Aramaic and translated books on grammar and Kabbalah. One of the pioneer Christian Hebraists of Northern Europe, Pellicanus was the first Christian to publish a Hebrew grammar, *De modo legendi et intelligendi Hebraeum* (Strasbourg, 1504), a forerunner of Reuchlin's *De rudimentis Hebraicis.* After teaching Bible in Basle (1502–07) and Rouffach (1508–11), he became a wandering scholar for some years. He visited the library of *Trithemius in Sponheim, he met Jacques Lefèvre d'Etaples in Paris, and he copied and acquired Hebrew books. Sebastian *Muenster was one of his pupils in Basle, where he again taught from 1519 until 1523, when he was deposed as local superior because of his suspect opinions. He was then appointed professor of Bible at Basle University, but in 1526 he accepted a call from the Swiss reformer Huldreich

(Ulrich) Zwingli, an old friend and colleague, to become professor of Hebrew at Zurich. By then he had married, and formally embraced Protestantism.

Pellicanus was a prominent collaborator in the Zwinglian Bible translations into German; he published a voluminous *Commentaria Bibliorum* (Zurich, 1532–39), which reveals his wide reading in the Christian Kabbalah. He translated many rabbinic works, including *Genesis Rabbah* and commentaries on the Pentateuch by Abraham ibn Ezra and Baḥya b. Asher, as well as part of Guillaume *Postel's version of the Zohar on Genesis. He also copied Gerard *Veltwyck's *Shevilei Tohu* and Postel's kabbalistic treatise on the Candelabrum *(Or Nerot ha-Menorah)*, both of which he translated into Latin. These have been preserved in manuscript in Zurich.

Bibliography: M. Adam, *Vitae germanorum theologorum* (Frankfort, 1653[2]), 262–99; E. Silberstein, *Conrad Pellicanus; ein Beitrag zur Geschichte des Studiums der hebraeischen Sprache in der ersten Haelfte des XVI. Jahrhunderts* (1900); F. Secret, *Le Zôhar chez les kabbalistes chrétiens de la Renaissance* (1964[2]), index; idem, in: *Bibliothèque d'Humanisme et Renaissance*, 22 (1960), 389ff.; idem, *Les kabbalistes chrétiens de la Renaissance* (1964), index; idem, *G. Postel (1510–1581) et son Interprétation du Candélabre de Moyse en hébreu, latin, italien et français* (1966), introd. and 33ff.; Baron, Social[2], 13 (1969), 164, 166, 169, 394–5; G. E. Weil, *Élie Lévita, Humaniste et Massorète (1469–1549)* (1963), 10–25, 248–54.

[G.E.S.]

PELTIN, SAMUEL HIRSH (1831–1896), Polish author. Peltin settled in Warsaw in 1855, and established there in 1865 the Polish weekly *Izraelita. In this journal, which he edited until his death, he wrote articles on religion, ethics, and Jewish history, and defended the Jewish cause against anti-Semitic attacks. He also wrote a number of tales of Jewish life, and translated the works of Leopold *Kompert and other writers. In his youth he compiled a Polish textbook, especially designed for Jewish children. He left many works in manuscript, including a book on Jewish history entitled "Historia Zydow." Peltin was active in the Reform Temple in Warsaw and attempted to give a Polish rather than a German orientation to the service and the sermon, and invest it with the character suited to an enlightened Polish Jewish intellectual.

Bibliography: N. Sokolow (ed.), *Sefer Zikkaron* (1889), 91; J. Shatzky, *Di Geshikhte fun Yidn in Varshe*, 3 (1953), 165–71.

[ED.]

PELTZ, ISAC (1899–), Rumanian novelist. Born in Bucharest, Peltz first wrote essays, prose poems, sketches, and stories, which appeared in several volumes between 1916 and 1924. His prizewinning first novel, *Viaţa cu haz şi fără a numitului Stan* ("The Humorous and Not-So Humorous Life of Stan," 1929) heralded the career of one of the most prolific and highly praised writers in Rumanian literature. For the first time, Jewish ghetto life with all its color and its drama was given artistic form in Rumanian literature. Peltz's novels told the full story of the Jewish slums. Painting immense frescoes of the people of the ghetto—artisans, tradesmen, peddlers, unsuccessful poets and writers, prostitutes, tramps, and beggars—he showed partiality for the poverty-stricken.

Outstanding among the novels of this type are *Calea Văcăreşti* (1934) and *Foc în Hanul cu Tei* ("Fire at the Linden Inn," 1935), which were republished several times. A dramatic adaptation of the former was staged in 1942. Other pre-World War II novels include *Horoscop* (1932) and *Nopţile Domnişoarei Mili* ("The Nights of Miss Mili," 1937). Peltz described the horrors of the Nazi period and the sufferings of the Jews in the novel *Israel însîngerat* ("Bleeding Israel," 1946). His postwar novel *Maz şi lumea lui* ("Max and his World," 1957), conforming to the norms of the Stalinist period, was a satire directed against the Rumanian Jewish bourgeoisie. His other works include: *De-a viaţa şi de-a moartea* ("Playing Life and Death," 1942), *Inimi sbuciumat* ("Anguished Souls," 1962), short stories, and *Cum i-am cunoscut* ("How I Knew Them," 1964).

Bibliography: G. Călinescu, *Istoria Literaturii Romîne . . .* (1941), 708–10; E. Lovinescu, *Memorii*, vol. 3, 40–42; C. Baltazar, *Scriitor şi Om* (1946), 107–12; Şerbu, in: *Viaţa Romînească* (1957), no. 7; V. Rapeanu, *Foc în Hanul cu Tei* (1961), introd.; V. Ardeleanu, *Calea Văcăreşti* (1966), introd.

[A.FE.]

PENAL LAW.

Principles of Legality. Under talmudic law, no act is a criminal offense and punishable as such unless laid down in express terms in the Bible (the Written Law). For this purpose, it is not sufficient that there should be a provision imposing a specified penalty in respect of any given act *(onesh)*—e.g., the murderer shall be killed (Num. 35:16–21), or the adulterers shall be killed (Lev. 20:10)—so long as the commission of the act has not first distinctly been prohibited *(azharah)*—e.g., you shall not murder (Ex. 20:13; Deut. 5:17), or you shall not commit adultery *(ibid.)*. Where such prohibition is lacking, even the availability of a penal provision will not warrant the imposition of the penalty provided (Zev. 106a–b, et al.); the penal provision is a *nuda lex*, which may be interpreted as a threat of *divine punishment, in respect of which no prior prohibition is required (Mak. 13b).

All biblical injunctions are either positive *(mitzvot aseh)* or negative *(mitzvot lo ta'aseh)*, i.e., either to do or to abstain from doing a certain thing. Any negative injunction qualifies as prohibition for the purposes of penal legislation (Maim. Comm. to Mishnah, Mak. 3:1). But no prohibition may be inferred, *e contrario*, from any positive injunction (Tem. 4a). The prohibitory provision is required not only for capital offenses (Sanh. 54a–b), but also for offenses punishable by *flogging (Mak. 4b; Ket. 46a), and even for offenses punishable by *fines (Sifra, *Kedoshim*, 2, 1). A prohibition may not be inferred, either by analogy or by any other form of logical deduction; from the prohibition on intercourse, for instance, with the daughter of one's father or of one's mother (Lev. 18:9), the prohibition on intercourse with one's full sister could not be inferred, but had to be stated expressly (Lev. 18:11).

Similarly, the penal provision must be explicit as applying to an offense constituted of certain factual elements, and may not be extended to cover other offenses, whether by way of analogy or by way of other logical deductions. Thus, for instance, malicious witnesses who commit *perjury by testifying that an innocent man has committed a capital offense are to be executed only if the accused has not yet been executed himself: for it is written, "you shall do to him as he schemed to do to his fellow" (Deut. 19:19), and not as has been done already to his fellow, and the latter may not be inferred, *a fortiori*, from the former (Mak. 5b). The reason underlying this seemingly hairsplitting precaution has been said to be that if the punishment laid down by law were the right and proper one for the lesser crime or the lesser evil, it could not be the right and proper punishment for the graver one (Maharsha to Sanh. 64b), and the Divine Legislator having seen fit to penalize the lesser offense, no human legislator should presume to improve on or rectify His action, least of all by human logic (*Korban Aharon, Middot Aharon*, 2:13). This strict legality already gave rise to practical difficulties in talmudic times. "Not in order to contravene the law, but in order to make fences around the law" (Sanh. 46a; Yev. 90b; Yad, Sanh. 24:4), were the courts empowered to impose punishments even where the principle of legality could not be observed (see *Extraordinary Remedies). Such extralegal sanctions were imposed not only at the discretion of the courts, but also by virtue of express penal legislation (see *Takkanot*).

Parties to Offenses. As a general rule, only the actual

perpetrator of an offense is criminally responsible in Jewish law. Thus no responsibility attaches to procurers, counsellors, inciters, and other such offenders who cause the offense to be committed by some other person (except, of course, where the incitement as such constitutes the offense, as, e.g., incitement to idolatry: Deut. 13:7–11).

PRINCIPALS AND AGENTS. Even where a person hires another to commit a crime, criminal responsibility attaches only to the agent who actually commits it, and not to the principal who made him commit it (Kid. 42b–43a; BK 51a, 79a; BM 8a, 10b; et al.). Where the commission of the offense entails some enjoyment, as the consumption of prohibited food or consummation of prohibited intercourse, it is clear that he who has the enjoyment pays the penalty (Kid. 43a); but even where the agent derives no enjoyment at all from the commission of the offense, it is he who is responsible, because as a person endowed with free will he has to obey God rather than men (Kid. 42b). There are several exceptions to this rule: first, where the agent is not capable of criminal responsibility, whether because he is a minor, or insane, or otherwise exempt from responsibility, his principal is responsible (BM 10b; *Rema*, ḤM 182:1, 348:8); or, where the actual perpetrator is an innocent agent, that is, ignorant of the fact that it is an offense he commits (Tos. to Kid. 42b s.v. *amai;* Tos. to BK 79a s.v. *natnu; Mordekhai*, BM 1, 237; and cf. Redak, II Sam. 12:9). Further exceptions apply to particular offenses and are derived from biblical exegesis, such as stealing trust money (Ex. 22:6), slaughtering and stealing oxen or sheep (Ex. 21:37), or trespass on sacred things (Lev. 5:15)—for all of which the principal and not the agent is criminally responsible (Kid. 42b–43a). However, the blameworthiness of the procurer did not escape the talmudic jurists: everybody agrees that he is liable to some punishment, lesser *(dina zuta)* or greater (*dina rabba;* Kid. 43a), and the view generally taken is that he will be visited with divine punishment (Kid. 43a; Yad, Roẓe'aḥ 2:2–3). The matter is very distinctly put apropos the biblical injunction that where a woman committed bestiality both she and the beast should be killed (Lev. 20:16): "The woman has sinned, but what sin did the beast commit? But because it caused mischief, it must be stoned—and if a beast which does not know any difference between good and evil is stoned because of the mischief it caused, a fortiori must a man who caused another to commit a capital offense be taken by God from this world" (Sifra, Kedoshim, 10:5). Maimonides goes even further, allowing not only for divine punishment but also for human capital punishment, whether by the king by virtue of his royal prerogative (see *Extraordinary Remedies), or by the court in exercise of its emergency powers, wherever circumstances of time and place so require (Yad, Roẓe'aḥ 2:4); and indeed capital punishment was actually imposed on a father who had ordered his son to commit homicide (Ribash, Resp. no. 251). But short of capital punishment, courts are at any rate admonished to administer "very hard floggings" and impose severe imprisonment for long periods, so as to deter and threaten potential criminals that they may not think they can commit with impunity their crimes by the hands of others (Yad, Roẓe'aḥ 5). See also *Agency, Law of.

JOINT OFFENDERS. As a general rule, a criminal offense is committed by a single person acting alone, and not by two or more acting together (Sifra, Va-Yikra, 7; Shab. 92b). Thus, where an offense is committed by joint offenders, all are liable only if the offense could not have been committed otherwise than by all of them together; if the offense could have been committed by any one (or more) of them, they are all entitled to the benefit of the doubt that none of them did actually complete the offense (Yad, Shab. 1:15–16). Where, therefore, a man is beaten to death by several people, none of them would be criminally liable (Sanh. 78a); but where the death was clearly caused by the last stroke, the man who struck last would be guilty of murder (Yad, Roẓe'aḥ 4:6–7). It might be otherwise where death could not have ensued unless by the combined action of all attackers together: in such a case they would all be liable (Rashba, Nov., BK 53b). Like accessories before and at the offense, so are accessories after the fact free from responsibility for the offense—except, again, in the case of incitement to idolatry, where the protection of the offender is made an offense (Deut. 13:9).

Attempts and Inchoate Offenses. From the foregoing it is already apparent that, as a rule, no offense is committed unless it is completed: he who completes the offense is guilty; he who commits only part of the offense, or does not achieve the criminal result, is not guilty (Sifra, Va-Yikra, 7, 9; Shab. 92b–93a). No criminal intent, however far-reaching, suffices to render any act punishable which is not the completed offense defined by law (Kid. 39b; Ḥul. 142a). In exceptional cases, however, the attempt as such constitutes the completed offenses, e.g., malicious perjury (Deut. 19:16), where the false witnesses are liable only if the result intended by them had not yet been achieved (Mak. 1:6). But, again, the potential turpitude of the attempt to commit an offense has not escaped juridical notice: he who raises a hand against another, even without striking him, is not only wicked, but should (according at least to one great scholar) have his hand cut off, if he is prone to strike frequently (Sanh. 58b and Rashi). Extralegal punishments have indeed been inflicted time and again on attempts, especially of murder (e.g., Maharam of Rothenburg, Resp., ed. Prague, no. 383; and cf. *Darkhei Moshe*, ḤM 421, n.7).

Criminal Responsibility. No person is criminally responsible for any act unless he did that act willfully (Av. Zar. 54a; BK 28b; Yad, Yesodei ha-Torah 5:4; Sanh. 20:2). Willfulness is excluded by duress *(*ones)*, a concept much wider in Jewish than in other systems of law. For the purpose of penal law, it can be roughly divided into five categories: (1) coercion; (2) threats of death, including governmental decrees threatening criminal prosecution; (3) torture; (4) *force majeure*, including sickness and other happenings beyond one's control; and (5) mistakes of fact and unconsciousness. As distinguished from duress for the purposes of civil law, generally no duress is recognized in criminal law which flows from any monetary cause, as, e.g., the necessity to save any property from perdition (*Beit Yosef*, ḤM 388; *Rema*, ḤM 388:2).

DURESS BY COERCION. The coercion by violence of a married woman to commit *adultery (nowadays known as rape) exempts her from any criminal responsibility (Deut. 22:26). No such coercion is recognized in regard to the male adulterer, because he cannot physiologically be raped (Yev. 53b). Where the woman is in an isolated spot ("in the open country": Deut. 22:25), or otherwise incapable of summoning help, she will be presumed to have been coerced against her will (Naḥmanides ad loc.; Sif. Deut. 243), even where she could have resisted by striking back, but failed to do so in the belief she was not allowed to, she is deemed to have been raped (Naḥmanides, *ibid.*). It is irrelevant that, after having been forced to submit, she eventually acquiesced: it is the duress of human urges and human nature that then compel her to surrender (Yad, Issurei Bi'ah 1:9).

DURESS BY THREATS. There are three grave offenses of which it is said that a man must let himself be killed rather than commit any of them, namely, idolatry, adultery or *incest *(gillui arayot)*, and *homicide (Sanh. 74a; Yad, Yesodei ha-Torah 5:2; Sh. Ar., YD 157:1). This rule has sometimes been wrongly interpreted as excluding the defense of duress by threats of death in the case of any of these offenses; as a matter of law, however, where the rule is disobeyed and any such offense is committed in order to escape death, the offender is not criminally responsible, however reprehensible he may be morally or religiously (Yad, *ibid.* 4). It is irrevocably presumed that where a man acts under threat of immediate death and in order to save his life, any criminal intent in respect of that act is excluded or superseded, and he cannot be criminally responsible for it.

In the Middle Ages, the threat of prosecution and death became a very effective inducement to denounce Judaism and outwardly embrace another religion. So long as a man did only what was really required to save his life, the transgression was recognized as being committed under duress; as soon as he did anything not so required, it was deemed to be done willfully, however strong the initial duress may have been (*Rema*, YD 124:9; Ribash, Resp. nos. 4, 11, 12).

Duress by Torture is closely related to the two foregoing categories; on the one hand, it entails physical force, and the sheer force applied may be sufficient to deprive the victim of his free will; on the other hand, it entails threats of death, or of ever more torture to come until death may ensue, and hence any criminal intent will be replaced or superseded by the wish to have the torture terminated (cf. Ket. 33b for an instance of torture to compel to idolatry).

Duress by Force Majeure, as an instance of duress, is well illustrated by the case of a man who fell ill, and his doctors prescribed for his cure the consumption of prohibited food: while partaking of such food is a criminal offense, the patient will not be liable to punishment, as his intent was not criminal but medical (Yad, *ibid.* 6). It is, however, made clear that this defense would not hold good for all offenses: thus, a man cannot be heard to say that for medical reasons and in order to save his life, he had to commit adultery (Yad, *ibid.* 9) or even a lesser indecency (Sanh. 75a). Other unforeseen circumstances which may make a man act unlawfully, contrary to his real intentions, are, e.g., attacks by wild beasts (cf. BM 7:9), or accidents such as fire (BM 47b, 49b) and other like dangers: the defense of duress in these cases is closely related to that of self-defense or self-help (see below). It is noteworthy that in English and Israel law, the commission of an offense in order to avoid grievous harm or injury which could not otherwise be avoided is excused by reason of "necessity" (Sec. 18, Criminal Code Ordinance, 1936).

Duress by Mistake or Unconsciousness. A lesser form of duress is the "duress of sleep" (cf. Ber. 4b): a man who has fallen asleep is not criminally (as distinguished from civilly; BK 2:6) responsible for anything he did while asleep, for the reason that he acted without any criminal (or other) intent. The same applies to acts of automatism or anything done in a state of unconsciousness, however induced. Jewish law—again, as distinguished from other systems of law—includes within this category, as a species of duress, also the common mistake of fact: it is regarded as the "duress of the heart" (Shev. 26a) if a man acts under a misapprehension of relevant facts, and any criminal intent may be excluded by such other intent as is warranted by the facts mistakenly believed to exist. If a man acts under such factual misapprehension, it is as if he acted outside the physical world as it really exists, hence the analogy with sleep and unconsciousness. Similarly, the forgetfulness of old age may constitute duress (Ber. 8b).

The Deaf and Dumb, Lunatics, Infants, and the Blind. Apart from these forms of duress, which are applicable to all persons, there are special categories of persons who are wholly exempt from criminal responsibility for reason of the duress inherent in their infirmity or deficiency, namely, the deaf and dumb, the insane, and infants—all regarded in law as devoid of reason (Yev. 99b; Ḥag. 2b; Git. 23a; et al.; and see *Legal Capacity). Persons who are both deaf and dumb (Ter. 1:2) are equated with infants for all purposes of the law (cf. Tur, ḤM 235:19), and the law exempting infants from criminal responsibility is derived from scriptural exegesis (Mekh. Mishpatim 4; Sanh. 52b, 54a, 68b). It is not quite settled at what age infancy ends for purposes of criminal law: there are dicta to the effect that divine punishment is not imposed for sins committed before the age of 20 (TJ, Bik. 2:1, 64c: TJ, Sanh. 11:7, 30b; Shab. 89b; Tanḥ. Koraḥ 6), and it is said that where Heaven exempts from punishment, men ought not to punish (cf. Sanh. 82b); on the other hand, with the age of 13 for the male and 12 for the female, the age of reason is reached (Nid. 45b; Yad, Ishut 2:1, 10), and there would no longer be any rational cause for exemption from responsibility. Some scholars hold that while human beings are criminally responsible as from the age of 13 and 12 respectively, no capital punishment would be imposed until they reached the age of 20. However that may be, we find exhortations to punish infants by flogging, even below the age of reason, not because of their responsibility, but only in order to deter them from further crime (Yad, Genevah 1:10). As far as sexual crimes are concerned, an infant girl is deemed to be so easily tempted as to deprive her of any willfulness (Yev. 33b, 61b; TJ, Sot. 1:2, 16c).

The insane is a person whose mind is permanently deranged (Yad, Edut 9:9). Monomaniacs who "go around alone at nights, stay overnight in cemeteries, tear their clothes, and lose everything they are given" (Ḥag. 3b; Tosef., Ter. 1:3), as well as idiots who are so retarded as to be unable to differentiate between contradictory matters (Yad, *ibid.* 10; ḤM 35:10), are presumed to be insane. They are not criminally responsible for any of their acts (BK 87a; cf. Git. 22b), and it is—in contradistinction to modern systems of law—irrelevant whether any causal connection can be established between the disease and the offense: once insanity is shown, criminal responsibility is excluded. Persons who suffer from transient attacks of insanity, such as epileptics, are criminally responsible only for acts committed during lucid intervals (cf. Yad, *ibid.* 9; ḤM 35:9). Apart from being devoid of reason, the insane are also devoid of will—hence any sexual offense committed by an insane woman is deemed to have been committed unwillfully (*Mishneh la-Melekh*, Ishut 11:8).

Opinions were divided among talmudic jurists in regard to the criminal responsibility of the blind (BK 86b; Tosef., Mak. 2:9), but the rule eventually evolved that blindness does not affect such responsibility, any more than the obligation to obey all the laws; but a blind person who kills inadvertently is exempt from exile to a *city of refuge, because his act is near to duress (Yad, Roẓe'aḥ 6:14). The blind man differs from the deaf and dumb in that he freely expresses himself, while with the latter one never knows whether he is in possession of his mental and volitive faculties or not, and Jewish law does not recognize any presumption of sanity.

Intoxication. Self-induced intoxication as such is not regarded as duress sufficient to exempt from criminal responsibility for acts committed while drunk (Tosef., Ter. 3:1), except where the intoxication amounts to the "drunkenness of Lot" (Gen. 19:33–35), that is to say, to virtual unconsciousness (Er. 65a).

Ignorance of Law. Talmudic law differs from most (if not all) other systems of law also in one further respect: namely, that ignorance of law is a good defense to any criminal charge. Not only is nobody punishable for an offense committed bona fide, i.e., in the mistaken belief that his act was lawful, but it is incumbent upon the prosecution to show that the accused was, immediately before the commission of the offense, expressly warned by two competent witnesses that it would be unlawful for him to commit it, and that if he committed it he would be liable to that specific penalty provided for it by law (Sanh. 8b; et al.; and see *Evidence, *Practice and Procedure). It is this antecedent warning that enables the court to distinguish between the intentional *(mezid)* and the unintentional *(shogeg)* offender (Yad, Sanhedrin 12:2 and Issurei Bi'ah 1:3), the latter category comprising not only those acting "with a claim of right" in ignorance of the law, but also those who by accident or misadventure achieved any criminal result without intending it (Yad, Roẓe'aḥ 6:1–9), or who achieved any result (however criminal) different from the criminal result they intended to achieve (*ibid.* 4:1). Within the category of unintentional offenders, a distinction is made between those nearer to duress and those nearer to criminality: the former acted without negligence, and their conduct was in no way blameworthy; the latter acted recklessly and in disregard of common standards of behavior (the most striking example is the man who maintained that it was perfectly lawful to kill). While neither is, as a matter of law, criminally responsible, the one nearer to criminality may not be entitled to resort to cities of refuge (Yad, *ibid.* 6:10) and is liable to be flogged and imprisoned for purposes of deterrence (Yad, *ibid.* 2:5 and Sanh. 24:4). Previous warning of illegality was held to be unnecessary where the nature of the offense or its planning rendered the warning impracticable, such as in cases of perjury (Ket. 32a) or burglary at night (Sanh. 72b), or where it was redundant, as in the case of the *rebellious elder (Sanh. 88b) or of recidivists (Sanh. 81b; and cf. Maim. Yad, Sanhedrin 18, 5). Some scholars held the warning unnecessary also where the offender was a man learned in the law (Sanh. 8b).

Self-Defense and Rescue. Another important cause of exemption from criminal responsibility is the right and duty of defense against unlawful attack and of protection from danger; where any person (including an infant) pursues another with the manifest intent to kill him, everybody is under a duty to rescue the victim, even by killing the pursuer (Sanh. 8:7; Yad, Roẓe'aḥ 1:6). This general rule has been extended to cover the killing of an embryo endangering the life of the mother (Yad, *ibid.* 9; and see *Abortion) and the killing of a rapist caught before completion of his offense, if he could not otherwise be induced to desist (Yad, *ibid.* 10). It would be as unlawful to kill the pursuer where the victim could be rescued by some other means (though even then the killer would not be guilty of murder (Yad, *ibid.* 13)), as it would be unlawful not to kill the pursuer if the victim could not otherwise be rescued (Yad, *ibid.* 14–16). Thus the nature of this defense is not just duress; here the criminal intent is superseded by the intent to fulfill a legal duty, and hence the defense is one of justification.

Justification. In the more technical sense of the term, justification exempts from criminal responsibility the following three categories of persons: officers of the court who kill or injure any person (or property) in the course of performing their official duties (cf. Mak. 3:14; Yad, Sanhedrin 16:12); any person lawfully engaged in the execution of convicts (Lev. 24:16; Deut. 13:10, 17:7, 21:21, 22:21, 24); and any person who acts upon the advice or instruction of the court as to what is the law (Sifra, Va-Yikra, 7, 1–2; Hor. 2b, 3b).

Bibliography: ET, 1 (1951), 162–72, 193–5, 303–5, 321–4; 11 (1965), 291–314; J. D. Michaelis, *Mosaisches Recht,* 6 vols. (1770–75); M. Duschak, *Das mosaisch-talmudische Strafrecht* (1869); H. B. Fassel, *Ve-Shaftu ve-Hizzilu: Das mosaisch-rabbinische Strafgesetz und strafrechtliche Gerichts-Verfahren* (1870); S. Mayer, *Geschichte der Strafrechte* (1876); B. Berger, *Criminal Code of the Jews* (1880); S. Mendelsohn, *Criminal Jurisprudence of the Ancient Hebrews* (1891; repr. 1968); G. Foerster, *Das mosaische Strafrecht in seiner geschichtlichen Entwicklung* (1900); H. Vogelstein, in: MGWJ, 48 (1904), 513–33; J. Steinberg, in: *Zeitschrift fuer vergleichende Rechtswissenschaft,* 25 (1911), 140–97; I. S. Zuri, *Mishpat ha-Talmud,* 1 (1921); 6 (1921); S. Assaf, *Ha-Onshin Aḥarei Ḥatimat ha-Talmud* (1922); H. Cohen, in: *Jeschurun,* 9 (1922), 272–99; V. Aptowitzer, in: JQR, 15 (1924/25), 55–118; idem, in: HUCA, 3 (1926), 117–55; J. Manen, in: HHY, 10 (1926), 200–8; L. Kantor, *Beitraege zur Lehre von der strafrechtlichen Schuld im Talmud* (1926); M. Higger, *Intention in Talmudic Law* (1927); P. Dykan, *Dinei Onshin,* 1 (1938; 1955[2]); 2 (1947; 1962[2]); 3 (1953); idem, in: *Sinai,* 60 (1966), 51–62; H. E. Goldin, *Hebrew Criminal Law and Procedure* (1952); J. Ginzberg, *Mishpatim le-Yisrael* (1956); M. Minkowitz, *Ha-Maḥashavah ha-Pelilit ba-Mishpat ha-Talmudi u-va-Mishpat ha-Mekubbal ha-Angli* (1961); D. Daube, *Collaboration with Tyranny in Rabbinic Law* (1965); M. Elon, in: ILR, 3 (1968), 94–97; Elon, Mafte'aḥ s.v. *Onshin, Dinei.*

[H.H.C.]

PENINNAH (Heb. פְּנִנָּה; possibly "coral"), second wife of *Elkanah (I Sam. 1:1–2). Peninnah had sons and daughters, while *Hannah, Elkanah's first wife, was barren (1:2). In I Samuel 1, which deals with Samuel's birth, Peninnah plays a secondary role. She seems to have been her husband's less favored wife (cf. 1:5) and is portrayed as a rather unkind woman who made life difficult for Hannah, her rival (1:6–7).

In the Aggadah. The *aggadah* elaborates on the manner in which Peninnah taunted Hannah on account of her childlessness. Every morning she would mockingly ask whether Hannah had washed her sons' faces, and in the afternoon would sarcastically enquire when she expected them home from school (PR 43, 181b). According to one tradition, this cruelty had a righteous intent; Peninnah hoped thereby that she would encourage Hannah to pray for children (BB 18a; Mid. Ḥag. to Gen. 22:1). She was nevertheless ultimately punished. Two of her children died whenever Hannah gave birth; and she thus witnessed the death of eight of her ten children. The last two were spared solely as a result of Hannah's intercession with the Almighty on her behalf (PR, *ibid.,* 182a).

Bibliography: In the Aggadah: Ginzberg, Legends, 4 (1913), 58, 60; 6 (1928), 216–8, 220; I. Ḥasida, *Ishei ha-Tanakh* (1964), 363f.

[Ed.]

PENN, ALEXANDER (1906–1972), Hebrew poet. Born in Nizhne-Kolymsk, Russia, he came under the influence of Mayakovski, Yesenin, and *Pasternak, and wrote poetry in Russian. In 1927 he settled in Palestine where he founded, together with Nathan Axelrod, the first film studio. In 1929, encouraged by A. *Shlonsky, he began to publish his poems which were mostly lyrical, inspired by the Israel landscape. He was also, however, a pioneer of the topical political *chanson.* His poems were published in *Ketuvim, Moznayim, Davar,* and *Turim.* According to his own testimony, 1934 was a turning point in his literary work, when he cut down on his lyrical poetry and devoted himself increasingly to poems of political and social message, which he published mainly in the Marxist press. From 1947 he served as editor of the literary and art supplement of the Communist daily, *Kol ha-Am.* A selection from his poetry was published in Russian translation in the Soviet Union (1965), the collection of translations from modern Hebrew poetry published in Russian in the Soviet Union. After the 1967 Six-Day War, Penn left Maki, the Israel Communist Party, because of its "nationalistic regression."

Bibliography: Kressel, Leksikon, 2 (1967), 643–5. [G.K.]

PENNSYLVANIA, one of the 13 original states of the U.S.; general population 11,663,300 (1970), Jewish population 444,000 (est.). Pennsylvania has nearly 110 cities and towns numbering over 100 Jews each, 17 of which have over 1,000. Approximately 175 rabbis served over 250 congregations and five collegiate Hillel Foundations at Pennsylvania State University, Temple University, and the universities of Pennsylvania and *Pittsburgh. Jewish institutions of higher education in the state included *Gratz College, *Dropsie College, and the *Reconstructionist Rabbinical School, all in *Philadelphia.

Following the first permanent settlement in Pennsylvania in 1643, the colony passed through Dutch (1655) and English (1664) rule until 1681, when William Penn acquired the territory. By 1656 New Amsterdam Jews traded along the Delaware River on Pennsylvania's eastern border, and by 1681 several Jews probably settled in the southeastern area. While most of these Jews were of Spanish-Portuguese origin, during the 18th century many came from Central Europe. Isaac Miranda (d. 1732) of Tuscany, a prominent Philadelphia landowner and public official, was the first Jew to settle in *Lancaster, where he died a convert to Christianity. His son George traded with the Shawnee Indians along the Allegheny River. By 1747—when ten Jewish families lived in Lancaster—a cemetery was purchased by Isaac Nunez Ricus (Henriques) and Joseph *Simon, the leading merchant who had a trading outpost at Fort Pitt (later Pittsburgh). An early Jewish resident of Lancaster, Isaac Cohen, was Pennsylvania's first physician.

Jews settled at an early date in the port of Philadelphia, where many of them, such as the traders David *Franks and Nathan *Levy, engaged in shipping by the 1750s. Michael *Gratz arrived in 1759 from London and joined the mercantile enterprises of his brother Barnard. Franks, Levy, Andrew Levy, and Joseph Simon speculated in western land, suffering damages from Indian raids. Franks, Barnard Gratz, and Aaron *Levy were among the purchasers of land from the Illinois Indians in 1773. Levy became a landowner in nearly every county and founded Aaronsburg, which he named for himself, in 1786. Another early Jewish settlement was at Easton, north of Philadelphia on the Delaware. The merchant Myer Hart de Shira (Texeira) was among its founders, and by 1750 11 Jewish families lived there. Some lived in Reading from 1753 and in York from 1758. By the end of the American Revolution (1783), in which Jews played military and financial roles, about 800 Jews lived in the state. They enjoyed political rights, except that of membership in the General Assembly, although

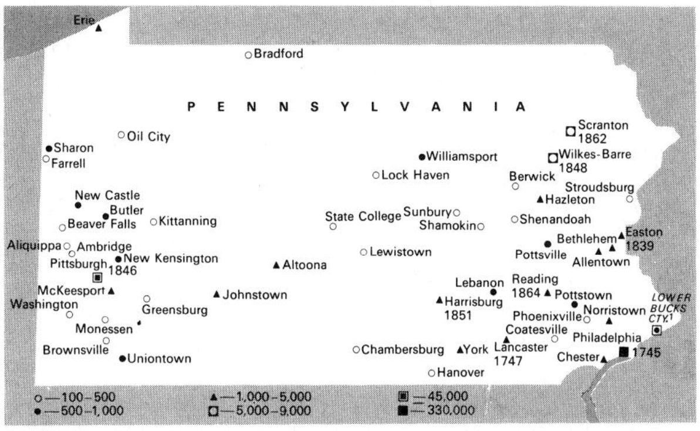

Total Jewish population of Pennsylvania	443,595
% of Jews in general population of Pennsylvania	3.78
% of Pennsylvania Jews in Jewish population of U.S.A.	7.56

[1] Includes Bensalem Township, Bristol, Langhorne, Levittown, New Hope, Newtown, Penndel, Warrington, and Yardley.

Jewish communities in Pennsylvania and dates of establishment. Population figures for 1968.

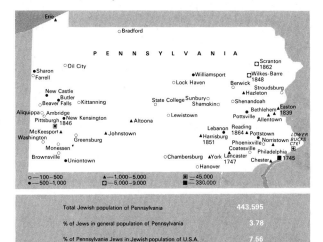

Synagogue of Temple Keneseth Israel, Allentown, Pennsylvania.

before the revolution David Franks (1748) and Benjamin *Cohen (1755) sat in that body.

Few Jews lived in western Pennsylvania until numbers of German Jews settled there after 1825. Jewish communities were formed in Pittsburgh, Reading, Pottsville, and Wilkes-Barre during the 1830s, in Harrisburg, *Scranton, Erie, and Allentown during the 1840s, in Honesdale from 1849—where the smallest synagogue in the U.S. was built—and in Hazelton, Altoona, and Uniontown during the 1860s. There were only nine congregations in Pennsylvania in 1856, which grew by 1877 to 26 for approximately 17,000 Jews. Between 1889 and 1910 over 100,000 East European Jews immigrated to the state, so that by 1917 there were 320,000 Jews. New Jewish communities arose in Bethlehem, Greensburg, Johnstown, McKeesport, Mt. Carmel, New Kensington, Shamokin, Sharon, Sunbury, and Washington during the 1880s and in Braddock and West Chester during the next decade. By 1927 there were 405,000 Jews, the number growing moderately thereafter. Most Jews settled in large cities, but many settled in the state's numerous mining and industrial towns as merchants. From the mid-1950s they tended to move to the developing suburbs. Thus, many Jews left Philadelphia for the western, northeastern, and northwestern suburbs of the city. On the other hand, Pittsburgh, second in size and importance to Philadelphia, was suburbanized very little.

Jewish communal life centralized during the 20th century, and Jewish welfare federations were organized in Allentown (1948), Altoona (1920), Butler (1938), Easton (1939), Erie (1946), Harrisburg (1933), Johnstown (1938), Lancaster (1928), Levittown (1956), New Castle and Norristown (1936), Philadelphia (1901), Pittsburgh (1912), Pottsville (1935), Reading (1935), Scranton (1945), Sharon (1940), Uniontown (1939), Wilkes-Barre (1935), and York (1928). Jewish newspapers were published in Philadelphia and Pittsburgh.

Jews have attained prominence in all professions in Pennsylvania and have held high federal and state offices. U.S. Congressmen have included: Lewis Charles Levin (1845–51), Henry M. Phillips (1857–59), Myer Strouse (1863–67), Benjamin Golder (1925–33), Henry Ellenbogen (1933–39), Leon Sacks (1937–43), Samuel A. Weiss (1941–47), and Joshua Eilberg (1967–71). Milton *Shapp became the state's governor in 1969, while Horace Stern was chief justice of the State Supreme Court from 1952 to 1957.

Bibliography: AJYB (1918–70), passim; H. S. Linfield, *Statistics of Jews and Jewish Organizations* (1939); J. R. Marcus, *Early American Jewry* (1955), 3–164.

[E.GR.]

PENSO DE LA VEGA, JOSEPH (1650–1692), *Marrano writer and merchant. Joseph was born in Amsterdam. His father Isaac Penso Felix, a native of Espejo, Spain, had been imprisoned by the *Inquisition in Spain, and supposedly vowed to embrace Judaism openly within a year of his release. When freed he fled with his family to Antwerp and then to Amsterdam, and formally returned to Judaism at Middleburg. A charitable man, Isaac was said to have distributed 80,000 guldens as tithes from his profits.

Joseph Penso spent a short period in Leghorn, but lived mainly in Amsterdam, where he was a member of several literary academies and produced many and varied works. Besides funeral orations, wedding verses, and similar occasional pieces, he claimed to have written more than 200 epistles to different European statesmen. One of his earliest efforts was a Hebrew drama, *Asirei ha-Tikvah* (Amsterdam, 1673), an allegorical depiction of the victory of the will over the passions.

His Spanish books, all published in Amsterdam, include the *Triunfos del Aguila* (1683), on the relief of Vienna by John Sobieski; *Retrato de la Prudencia* (1690), which eulogized William of Orange when he became king of England; a collection of *Discursos académicos, morales, retóricos y sagrados* (1685), which he delivered at the Academia de los Floridos in Amsterdam; and *Rumbos Peligrosos* (1684), containing three short novels. These works, particularly the last named, enjoyed considerable vogue, but suffer the defects of the period: excessive display of erudition, digressions, and baroque floridness. One of his outstanding works is *Confusión de Confusiones* (1688), the first book to treat the workings of the stock exchange. It is still considered one of the best descriptions of dealings in stocks and shares. In the form of four dialogues between a "fastidious philosopher," a "prudent merchant" and an "erudite stockholder," Penso explains what stocks are, how they are bought and sold, the use of options, speculative maneuvers, and so on, and describes the operations of the Dutch trading companies. In spite of its serious subject, the work is enlivened by whimsical explanations of the origins of this kind of dealing and ironic descriptions of the bourse, of Amsterdam's coffee houses, and of the life of stock traders. Selections of it were translated into English by H. Kellenbenz and published under the same title in 1957.

Bibliography: Roth, Marranos, 336–7; M. B. Amzalak, *Joseph de la Vega e o seu livro Confusión de Confusiones* (1925); idem, *As Operações de Bolsa segundo Joseph de la Vega* (1926); idem, *Trois précurseurs Portugais* (193–?); J. Caro Baroja, *Los Judios en la España moderna y contemporánea*, 2 (1962), 157–9.

[K.R.S.]

PENTATEUCH. This article is arranged according to the following outline:

- Name
- Canonization
- The Critical View
    - Extent and Nature of the Corpus
    - Date and Composition
        - Sources
            - J and E Sources
            - P Source
            - D Source
        - Chronology of the Sources
        - The Problem of the Date of P
            - Wellhausen's View
            - Kaufmann's View
        - The Historical Narrative of P
    - P and D—Theological Outlines
    - Laws Common to P and D
        - Ritual
        - Social Matters
            - The Resident Alien
            - Care of the Poor
        - Laws of Asylum
        - Priestly Donations
    - P and D—Comparison of Tradition and Style
        - The Peroration
        - Levitical Priests
        - Stylistic and Idiomatic Differences
    - Relation of P to JE
    - Relation of D to JE
    - The Tradition Underlying the Sources—Form Criticism
        - The Patriarchal Theme
        - The Exodus
        - Law and Covenant—The Sinai Theme
- The Traditional View

NAME

The so-called "law of Moses" (cf. I Kings 2:3; II Kings 14:6; Ezra 3:2; 7:6, etc.) has long been divided into five books, hence the Hebrew *ḥummash* (חֻמָּשׁ) or *ḥamishah ḥumshei Torah* (חֲמִשָּׁה חֻמְשֵׁי תּוֹרָה) and the Latin *Pentateuch* derived from the Greek *πεντάτευχος*. Though it is not known when the division was made, it seems that it was in existence long before the destruction of the Second Temple. The Greek names of the five books of the Torah: *Γένεσις*, *Ἔξοδος*, *Λευιτικόν*, *Ἀριθμοί*, *Δεύτερονομιον* bear the character of titles given to the books, while the common Hebrew names *Bereshit* (בְּרֵאשִׁית), *Shemot* (שְׁמוֹת), *Va-Yikra (Wa-Yiqra)*; (וַיִּקְרָא), *Be-Midbar* (בְּמִדְבַּר), *Devarim* (דְּבָרִים), are taken from the opening words of each book. The prevalent Hebrew nomenclature, however, was not the exclusive one. The Mishnah contains the name *Torat Kohanim* (תּוֹרַת כֹּהֲנִים; "priestly law") for Leviticus (Meg. 3:5), *Ḥummash ha-Pequdim* "[the fifth part] of the numbered or mustered [referring to the census described at the beginning]" for Numbers (Yoma 7:1; Sot. 7:7), and *Mishneh Torah* (מִשְׁנֵה תּוֹרָה; "the repeated law") for Deuteronomy (Sif. Deut. 160) which attests to the fact that titles like those of the Septuagint were also used in Palestine, and may have originated there. However, the system of naming a literary creation after its incipit is very ancient, as may be learned from Mesopotamia, and it is quite possible, therefore, that the common Hebrew nomenclature is the original one.

The division into five books could have been motivated by technical reasons, as, for example, the length of the scroll needed for convenient reading. It should, however, be recognized that the division is not a purely external one but is inherent in Scripture. Thus, Genesis deserves a separate book by virtue of its extraordinary nature (the history of the Hebrews as a family and not a people); Exodus has a prologue and an epilogue (1:1–7; 40:36–38) which separate it from the other books (see *Exodus); Leviticus is concerned with priestly legislative matters and has a definite conclusion; while Numbers is earmarked by its particular concern with the events in the desert. Deuteronomy is separate from the other books from the point of view of style and rhetoric as well as content (see *Deuteronomy).

CANONIZATION

The "Book of the Torah" as a sanctified work recited before the people is encountered for the first time in Israel's history at Josiah's reform. This book was undoubtedly the Book of *Deuteronomy, as may be learned from the references to its contents in II Kings 22–23. Indeed, whenever the terms "Book of the Torah" or the "Book of Moses" are mentioned in the literature of the Exilic period (i.e., Deuteronomic literature), it is clear from the context that Deuteronomy is referred to (cf. Josh. 1:8 with Deut. 17:19–20; Josh. 8:32, 34 with Deut. 27:8 and 31:11–12; Josh. 23:6 with Deut. 5:29 and 17:20; II Kings 14:6 with Deut. 24:16). The other four books of the Pentateuch (Tetrateuch) were apparently canonized at the time of Ezra and Nehemiah. The "Book of the Torah" introduced by Ezra (Ezra 7) already contained passages from the Book of Leviticus (cf. Neh. 8:14, 15, 18b with Lev. 23:39ff.) and Numbers (cf. Neh. 10:38–39 with Num. 15:20 and 18:8ff.), in addition to the passages from Deuteronomy (cf. Neh. 13:1–2 with Deut. 23:4–5, etc.). In the Pentateuch itself, the term "the Book of the Torah" occurs only in Deuteronomy where it always refers to Deuteronomy itself. Only after the four books were added to Deuteronomy did the term acquire a broader application and become the title of the whole Pentateuch.

THE CRITICAL VIEW

Extent and Nature of the Corpus. The Pentateuch contains the history of Israel from its beginning to the death of Moses. The first 11 chapters, it is true, seem to be dealing with the history of mankind; in fact, however, they serve as an introduction to the people of Israel through a brief sketch of their genealogy and do not pretend to present world history as such. The main purpose of the pentateuchal history is to describe the "golden age" or the "salvation history" of Israel. In this period, God revealed Himself to the Patriarchs and established a covenantal relationship with them. It is at this period that God brought the children of Israel out of the hcuse of bondage, gave them the Law at Mt. Sinai, and led them to the Promised Land. This is why the Pentateuch has always been considered the prime religious-literary creation of ancient Israel, and thus the pentateuchal period became the "canonical period" of Israel's history. It is no wonder that the history of this "golden age" has been told and retold in so many versions.

At one time it was customary to speak of the "Hexateuch" instead of the "Pentateuch"—the Hexateuch consisting of the Pentateuch plus Joshua—and there are still some who do so. The reasons for including Joshua are: (1) that the Exodus was only the preparation for the conquest and one would expect, therefore, to find in this history something about the realization of the promises to the Patriarchs, with which the history opened. (2) In the Book of Joshua it is possible to discern the sources found in the Pentateuch, i.e., JE, P, and D (see below), thus this book might be seen as the direct continuation of the Five Books of Moses. In spite of these arguments, however, there is no justification for the postulation of a "Hexateuch," because the Book of Joshua, unlike the books of the Pentateuch, constitutes an organic part—from the point of view of editorial-literary activity—of the so-called *Deuteronomic history that was edited at the times of the Exile. It cannot, therefore, be considered as a part of the Pentateuch, the composition of which was made along completely different lines. Furthermore, the traditions of Joshua reveal a slavish dependence upon the pentateuchal traditions (cf., e.g., Josh. 14–21 with Num. 26:52–56 and 34:1–35:34; Josh. 23:16 with Deut. 11:16–17) and in some places even a mixture of the pentateuchal sources may be recognized (cf. Josh. 20 with Num. 35:9ff. and Deut. 19:1–13). Affinities with the pentateuchal sources are, of course, found in Joshua, but the same exists in respect to the other books of the Former Prophets and no scholar today would extend the limits of the Pentateuch beyond Joshua (it was only G. Hoelscher (see bibl.) who traced the pentateuchal sources down to the Book of Kings but his hypothesis was never accepted by anyone).

Date and Composition. The pentateuchal literature originated no earlier than the period of the Monarchy. This can be learned from a number of allusions found in different places in the Pentateuch, e.g., Genesis 36:31 (a king in Israel), Exodus 15:17 (Temple), Numbers 24:7 (Agag; cf. 24:20–21). These allusions are doubly significant since they are interspersed, especially the two latter, in poetical pieces which are accepted as being more ancient than the prose sections. Moreover, the sources in the Pentateuch and in the Former Prophets include poetic sections from earlier works: "the Book of the Wars of the Lord" (Num. 21:14) and "the *Book of Jashar" (Josh. 10:13, II Sam. 1:18; cf. LXX, I Kings 8:13). Although these books contain songs from the period of the Conquest and the Judges, they too were apparently not formed into complete literary works before the Monarchy. "The Book of Jashar," which is similar in nature to "the Book of the Wars of the Lord"—and there are some who even identify the two—was evidently not edited before the period of the Monarchy since it includes David's lamentation for Saul and Jonathan (II Sam. 1:18) as well as the Song of Solomon during the dedication of the Temple (LXX, I Kings 8:13). It may, therefore, be assumed that although the traditions that serve as the basis of the pentateuchal literature began to be crystallized, whether by way of oral accounts or by way of written narratives, as early as the period of the Judges, they did not acquire their final form before the time of the Monarchy.

Sources. The opinion accepted in contemporary biblical research is that the pentateuchal literature is composed of four major sources: J, E, P, and D. The postulation of additional documents like L (O. Eissfeldt), K (J. Morgenstern), and S (R. H. Pfeiffer) has not been generally accepted in pentateuchal criticism. The basis of this division into sources is literary-critical, i.e., it is based on topical and stylistic-linguistic distinctions. The distinction between J and E is based primarily on the different usage of the divine name in these sources: YHWH in J and *ʾElohim* ("God") in E. P is the Priestly Source and D the Deuteronomic. The different usage of the divine name is not only a matter of form but relates to the type of attitude taken to the history of the religion of Israel. According to J, YHWH, the Lord of Israel, was worshiped as early as the time of Enosh (Gen. 4:26), while according to E, YHWH, i.e., the true name of the God of Israel, was first revealed to Moses at the burning bush (Ex. 3:6ff.). P, which holds a similar attitude, gives explicit expression to this division: "I appeared to Abraham, Isaac, and Jacob as *ʾEl Shaddai,* but I did not make Myself known to them by My name YHWH" (Ex. 6:3). The controversy in modern scholarship as to whether monotheism began in the time of Moses or whether it was a continuation of the belief of the Patriarchs is foreshadowed in pentateuchal literature. J notes a religious continuity beginning with the time of Enosh and continuing through the period of the Patriarchs to Moses. In contrast, E and P, while admitting that the God who was revealed to the Patriarchs is the God who was revealed to Moses, maintain that the Patriarchs did not know Him by His true name, and there is doubtless theological significance to this lack of knowledge. Furthermore, P, which places great emphasis on the religious chasm between the period of the Patriarchs and that of Moses, does not consider the possibility of legitimate worship of God (sacrifices) before the revelation in the time of Moses.

J and E Sources. The difference between J and E is most evident in Genesis, where it is based on an explicit criterion: YHWH in J as opposed to *ʾElohim* in E. The distinction becomes more difficult in the subsequent books of the Pentateuch since after the Exodus E also uses the Tetragrammaton. For this reason the JE source is often referred to, thus obviating the necessity to make the distinction. This distinction between J and E in Genesis explains repetitions and inconsistencies in the accounts. The distinction between the two sources is based on the different usage of the divine name, as has been indicated, as well as the different usage of Jacob's name (Jacob, in contrast to Israel). There is also a difference of religious ideology between these two sources. J presents the contact between God and the Patriarchs as being direct, while E tends to dilute and refine this contact by introducing the dream and the angel as an intermediary factor (20:3ff.; 28:12; 31:11–13, etc.), though this difference should not be viewed as an absolute and decisive factor. The difficulties inherent in the distinction between J and E originate from the fact that the editor who put these sources together attempted to reconcile the details and create a uniform composition. Thus the impression is sometimes given that these are not two independent sources but rather one source (J) to which was added a later source (E).

P Source. The uniqueness of this source is more

pronounced than that of J and E. P is marked by a distinct style and by characteristic linguistic usages which facilitate its identification, such as: *toledot* (תּוֹלְדוֹת; "genealogy"), *pereh u-reveh* (פְּרֵה וּרְבֵה; "increased and multiplied"), *be-ezem ha-yom ha-zeh* (בְּעֶצֶם הַיּוֹם הַזֶּה; "in this very day"), *le-dorotam le-dorotekhem* (לְדֹרֹתָם לְדֹרֹתֵיכֶם; "for their/your generations"), *ʾereẓ megurehem* (אֶרֶץ מְגוּרֵיהֶם; "the land of their sojourn"), *ʾaḥuzzah* (אֲחֻזָּה; "possession"), *kehal (qehal) goyim* (קְהַל גּוֹיִם; "a congregation of nations"), *be-moshevotekhem* (בְּמוֹשְׁבוֹתֵיכֶם; "in all your dwelling places"), etc. The sections belonging to P in accordance with the above principle are: Genesis 1:1–2:3; 5:1–32; 6:9–22; 7:6–9; 9:1–17; 11:10–22; 17:1–27; 25:1–18; 28:1–9; 36:1–43; Exodus 1:1–7; 6:1–30; 12:1–20, 43–51; chapters 25–31; chapters 35–40; all of Leviticus; Numbers 1:1–10:28; chapters 13–14, 15–16, 17:19, 26–36. This source displays a system and a religious ideology which do not exist in JE. As has already been indicated, P gives explicit expression to the idea that God had not revealed Himself in His true name before Moses (Ex. 3:6ff.), and it accordingly describes the time of the Patriarchs as a period in which there is no real worship of God (sacrifices). The priestly version of the flood story thus eliminates the distinction between pure and impure animals (Gen. 6:9–22; 7:6–9) which is established in J. In contrast, circumcision and the Sabbath play a central role in this source (Gen. 2:1–3; 17:1ff.; Ex. 12:44, 48; 16:1ff.; 31:12–17; 35:1–3, etc.).

It is only natural for a priestly sect to concern itself with these ritualistic matters, which give practical expression of the uniqueness of Israel. Moreover, circumcision and the Sabbath, together with the rainbow in the cloud (Gen. 9:1–17), belong, in accordance with P, to the set of signs which symbolize the covenants contracted between God and humanity and the Patriarchs of Israel. Actually, the priestly material in Genesis serves only the priestly and sacred purpose of emphasizing the basis for the sanctity of Israel and its institutions and so do the priestly sections of Exodus, Leviticus, and Numbers. The main focus of P is the Tabernacle and everything connected with it. This matter plays such a major role in the priestly literature that it overshadows even such an important matter as the covenant between God and Israel at Mt. Sinai. Unlike JE and D, P relates nothing about the revelation at Mt. Sinai. However, it does describe the theophany during the dedication of the Tabernacle, where a fire emanating from God consumes the burnt offering and the fat on the altar (Lev. 9:24), which symbolized the descent of the *Shekhinah* among Israel (see Divine *Presence). The material of P contains essentially matters of sanctification and ritual such as sacrifices (Lev. 1–10), purity and impurity (Lev. 11–16), festivals and appointed seasons (Lev. 23; Num. 28–29), Sabbatical and Jubilee Years (Lev. 25), the sanctity of the land and its preservation (Num. 32ff.), etc. While it does present a description of the past such as the accounts of creation (Gen. 1:1–2:4a), the covenants with Noah and Abraham (Gen. 9:1–17; 17:1ff.), and descriptions of the Exodus from Egypt, these are marked by the sacred institutions of Israel, such as the Sabbath, circumcision, the prohibition against the eating of blood, and the Passover sacrifice. The laws contained in this source that appear to be concerned with women or civil matters, such as the laws of adultery in Leviticus 18 and 20 and the episode of the daughters of Zelophehad in Numbers 27 and 36, are not aimed at presenting legal problems pertaining to family law and inheritance, found in Deuteronomy (21–22), but at enhancing the sanctity of the family and the land.

D Source. Another source which from a literary standpoint constitutes an organic creation is Deuteronomy (see *Deuteronomy). This book is structured in the form of a farewell address by Moses (delivered in the Plains of Moab), presented in autobiographical fashion (Deut. 1–31), marked by a particular style and a distinctive phraseology. This book, through its ideas and linguistic forms, influenced the editor of the Former Prophets and especially the editor of Kings and Jeremiah. This source served as a point of departure for establishing the chronology of the sources of the Pentateuch in general. In 1805 W. W. M. L. de Wette developed the theory, which has been accepted by most biblical scholars, that Deuteronomy in its content and form reflects the period of Hezekiah-Josiah. He thus paved the way for a chronological historical arrangement of the pentateuchal sources concerning whose existence there was a consensus of opinion as early as the 18th century. De Wette sought a historical basis for the Pentateuch's development, which he found in the description of the discovery of a Book of the Torah in II Kings 22–23. The description of the discovery of the book, its contents, and the ensuing events prove that this refers to Deuteronomy. The most important proof is the concentration of the cult in Jerusalem; according to the Book of Kings, the first king to unite the cult in Jerusalem was Hezekiah (II Kings 18:4); before him no one had even thought of this. On the contrary, the prophet Elijah regarded the destruction of altars of the God of Israel as a sin (I Kings 19:10, 14). The only law in the literature commanding the unity of the cult is that in Deuteronomy (cf. Deut. 12 and other laws based on the principle of unification). It may thus be assumed that these laws began to take form in the time of Hezekiah, and were embodied in book form when discovered in the time of Josiah. In addition to the criterion of the unity of the cult, there are two other criteria for the dating of D: (1) Style—the style found in D does not appear before the time of Josiah, while from this time onward it begins to dominate biblical literature (Kings, Jeremiah, and later prophets). (2) Deuteronomy, which is structured in the form of a covenant between a lord and a vassal (historical introduction, conditions of the covenant, obligations, blessings and curses), incorporates a host of literary forms and means of expression which are known from contemporary Assyrian literature (eighth–seventh centuries B.C.E.) and especially from contracts signed by Assyrian kings with their vassals (see *Deuteronomy).

CHRONOLOGY OF THE SOURCES. The period established for the composition of D serves as a criterion for fixing the time of the other pentateuchal sources. The sources which assume decentralized worship (Ex. 20:24–26 [21–23]) clearly belong to the time before Hezekiah and Josiah, while those which reflect a centralized cult are from a later period. On the basis of this criterion it is evident that JE is earlier than Deuteronomy. It can be seen from the general background of the JE sources, especially from Genesis, that a period of national growth and development is reflected, and, according to all the characteristics, including style, it seems that this was the period of the United Kingdom in the time of David and Solomon. The JE sources view Israel's national and religious reality in its land as the realization of God's promises (prophecies) to the Patriarchs and the fulfillment of the religious message propounded by Moses, the greatest prophet. The promise of the land given to the Patriarchs, which is the leading motif of the Book of Genesis, can be properly understood against the background of the United Kingdom. The ideal of "a great nation" *goi gadol* (גּוֹי גָּדוֹל) that characterizes the promise to the Patriarchs (Gen. 12:2; 18:18; 46:3; Ex. 32:10; Num. 14:12) has to be understood in the physical sense, i.e., as meaning a "large nation," as is clear, for example, from Genesis 18:18: "Abraham is to become a great and populous nation." The promise of a great nation occurs also in the revelation to Hagar concerning Ishmael (Gen. 21:18; cf. 17:20), and it is clear that the promise to Ishmael does not involve any kind of spiritual message. The ideal of a great nation is embodied in three kinds of promises scattered throughout the Book of Genesis: (1) extended territory (13:14–15; 15:18–21; 26:3; 28:14); (2) numerous progeny (13:16 "as dust of the earth"; 15:5 "as the stars of the heaven"; 22:17 "as the stars of the heaven and sands on the seashore"; 24:60; 26:4, 24; 28:14; 32:12; 48:16, 19); and (3) military victory which means political expansion (22:17; 24:60; 25:23; 27:29; 28:14; 48:19; 49:10). These three promises are interwoven, generally occur together, and actually serve one aim: numerous progeny is needed in order to fight their enemies, control their territories, and thus expand the land which extends to the Euphrates. This is even explicitly said in verses such as: "I will make your descendants as numerous as the stars of the heaven and the sands on the seashore; and your descendants shall seize the gates of their foes" (22:17); "May you grow into thousands of myriads; may your offspring seize the gates of their foes" (24:60); or "Your descendants shall be as the dust of the earth; you shall spread out to the west and to the east, to the north and to the south" (28:14). That numerous descendants assure victory in battle may be learned from Psalm 127:3–5. A large population, expanded territory, and the subjugation of enemies, together make the nation great. It is not without significance that the term used in this context is *goi* ("nation") and not *ʿam* ("people"). In contradistinction to *ʿam*—used in Deuteronomy (see below)—which has a familial connotation, suggesting blood ties, *goi* is a political concept embracing all the men living on a common territorial base (see E. A. Speiser, in: JBL, 79 (1960), 157–63).

It was during the period of the United Kingdom that all those prophecies and promises became true. It was in David's period that Israel's borders reached the Euphrates (II Sam. 8:3; I Chron. 18:3; cf. I Kings 5:1, 4), as promised to Abraham in Genesis 15:18. It was at this period that Israel dominated "peoples and nations" as predicted in the blessings of Isaac to Jacob (Gen. 27:29) and of Jacob to his children (Gen. 49:10). The promise for progeny "as numerous as the sands of the seashore" (Gen. 22:17, etc.) is explicitly mentioned in I Kings 4:20 in the passage describing Solomon's kingdom. The promise of a "great nation" (גּוֹי גָּדוֹל) and a "great name" (וַאֲגַדְּלָה שְׁמֶךָ), as well as the idea of blessings for nations with which J opens the history of Israel (Gen. 12:1–3), can also be well understood against the background of the Davidic epoch. "Greatness of name" means "fame" and, in this case, international reputation which is, in fact, ascribed to David in connection with overcoming his enemies (II Sam. 7:9) and establishing his empire (II Sam. 8:13). This same term is attested to in an Akkadian letter from Mari (*Archives royales de Mari,* 1 (1950), no. 69, reverse lines 13–16: *sumam rabem,* "a great name") in the context of military victories. The dictum "and you shall be a blessing" or "all the families of the earth shall bless themselves by you" in the passage under discussion is none other than a standard by which a blessing is invoked. Everybody who sees the success of Israel will exclaim: "Would it be that I might acquire such success." Therefore this idea has nothing to do with the universal-eschatological ideals of classical prophecy. Israel as "the treasured possession *(segullah)* of God among all the peoples" and as a "kingdom of priests," i.e., the aristocracy of mankind (Ex. 19:4ff.), can also be best understood against the background of an established kingdom in Israel, i.e., the United Kingdom. *Goi* and *mamlakhah* found in this passage (19:6) denote a nation and state (cf. I Kings 18:10; Jer. 18:7, 9), in contrast to *ʿam* which is limited to a group of individuals tied by blood (see above). The term *segullah* is attested to in a Ugaritic text (*Palais royal d'Ugarit,* 5 (1965), 84 no. 60:12), where it specifies an especially privileged vassal, so that like *goi/mamlakhah* it belongs to the political vocabulary befitting the reality of the United Kingdom. The expansive and domineering mood in the JE source is reflected in the Balaam oracles (cf., e.g., Agag in Num. 24:7). These contain metaphors identical with those of Genesis 49, as for example: "Lo, a people that rises like a lion and leaps up like a king of beasts, it does not lie down until it devours prey and drinks the blood of the slain" (Num. 23:24), or in another pericope: "he crouches, lies down like a lion . . . who dare rouse him" (24:9). These verses are close in wording and in ideas to the blessing of Jacob to Judah: "Judah is a lions' whelp, on prey, my son, have you grown, he crouches, lies down like a lion, who dare rouse him" (Gen. 49:9). The theme of subjugating nations is also elaborated there: "They shall devour enemy nations, crush their bones, and smash their arrows" (Num. 24:8) or "a star rises from Jacob, a meteor comes forth from Israel, it smashes the brow of Moab, the pate [or foundation] of all children of Seth; Edom becomes a possession . . ." (Num. 24:16–19).

Though some of these phrases might be clichés prevalent in the pre-monarchical period, they were undoubtedly applied to Judah and Israel at the time of great military and political success. However, it is not only the political situation of the United Kingdom which is reflected in the JE sources; "justice and righteousness" *(mishpat-ẓedakah (ẓedaqah))* in which David's kingdom excelled (II Sam. 8:15; I Kings 10:9; cf. Isa. 9:6; 16:5; Jer. 23:5; 33:15) is postulated in Genesis 18:19 as the purpose of Abraham's election. Indeed, "justice and righteousness" occurs side by side with political success in the royal psalms and is especially salient in the Solomonic psalm mentioned, which opens with the entreaty: "O God, give Your justice to the king and your righteousness to the king's son; let him judge Your people with righteousness and Your poor ones with justice" (72:1–2). The implementation of *ẓedaqah* and *mishpat* is ascribed to Moses (Deut. 33:21), a tradition which seems also to underlie Moses' codification of law in Israel. The historical reality which gave rise to the national ideology of JE, delineated above, may be thrown in bolder relief when compared with the national ideology of Deuteronomy which was crystallized about 300 years later.

The Book of Deuteronomy, the product of seventh-century Israel, does not use the term *goi* when referring to Israel but prefers the usage of *ʿam,* "people." As has been indicated above, *goi* is a political concept whereas *ʿam* is a familial term relating to a people bound by blood ties. Moreover, Deuteronomy does not speak about the physical greatness of Israel and the subjugation of other peoples as does its predecessor, the JE source. Israel in this period is quite aware that it is "the smallest of peoples" (Deut. 7:7) and cannot, therefore, see itself as a large nation. Its "greatness" is now expressed by its laws and rules and by its closeness to the one God (4:6–8), not by territorial expansion and large numbers of children. In line with this view, Deuteronomy demands the respect of other nations' rights and warns against encroachment on their territories. These warnings were delivered often while the Israelites were passing through eastern Transjordan when it was feared that they might provoke other nations in the vicinity (Edom, Ammon, and Moab). When the people pass through the border territory of Edom, Moses commands them "not to start a fight with them. For I will not give you of their land so much as a foot can tread on; I have given the hill country of Seir as a possession to Esau" (Deut. 2:5). Similar warnings are pronounced also in relation to

Ammon and Moab (2:9, 19). Together with these warnings is the historical justification for these national territorial rights: "Seir was formerly inhabited by the Horites; but the descendants of Esau dispossessed them, wiping them out and settling in their place, just as Israel did in the land they were to possess" (2:12). This means that the Edomites established their ownership of the land of Seir to the same extent that the Israelites established their ownership of Canaan; and the case is the same for the Ammonites (2:21). For this reason their territorial rights must be respected. The special position of Deuteronomy in this matter becomes more evident when compared with Numbers 21:24, which states: "and [Israel] took possession of their land [of Sihon], from the Arnon to the Jabbok, as far as the Ammonites, for the boundary of the Ammonites was strong," i.e., the strength of Ammon's border prevented the Israelites from invading this land.

In contrast, Deuteronomy justifies the fact that Ammon was not conquered on the grounds that it had been given as an inheritance to the descendants of Lot (Deut. 2:19) and this national right is not to be harmed. This dating, however, cannot be considered as absolute. The Davidic-Solomonic background alluded to is to be found mostly in the J stratum of Genesis, and since the literary and chronological relationship between J and E, especially in the books of Exodus-Numbers, is still unclear, this dating cannot be seen as valid for the whole literary corpus designated as JE. What seems certain is that the J editor of Genesis was active at the time of the United Kingdom. If this editor continued his work in Exodus-Numbers—which is commonly assumed—the same chronological background is to be supposed for the whole J source.

The Problem of the Date of P. De Wette, who had established the chronological setting of D, still assumed that D was the last book of the Pentateuch in terms of its chronological development. It was the Graf-Kuenen-Wellhausen school that introduced the theory that P was later than D, and that it originated during the Second Temple, in the period of the consolidation of Judaism, established by Ezra and Nehemiah. The most comprehensive basis for this theory was offered by J. Wellhausen in his *Prolegomena to the History of Ancient Israel.*

Wellhausen's View. J. Wellhausen held that the Jewish religion underwent a development from a religion rooted in the life of nature to a religion divorced from nature and that the P source embodied the peak of this development. According to Wellhausen, it was the rule of the hierocracy of the Second Temple period that was reflected in the Priestly Code. His view may be summarized as follows:

(1) P assumed the centralization of the cult as a self-evident fact. The worship of God is indeed linked in this source to the Tent of Meeting which is an exclusive cultic institution.

(2) In the period preceding the reform of Josiah, cultic activities were conducted everywhere, and people who were not priests served in the various temples and altars (see Ex. 20:24–26 [21–23]). With the centralization of the cult by Josiah the provincial cultic places were abolished and the Temple in Jerusalem became the exclusive temple in which only priests from the house of Zadok officiated; the priests who served in the high places and provincial temples became, in the course of time, secondary cultic officials (cf. Ezek. 44:9ff.), and these were the levites of P. According to Wellhausen, the high priest found in P is a reflection of the head of the religious community in the Second Temple period.

(3) The numerous sacred institutions found in P express the power of the priestly circle during the period of the Second Temple. This is the reason for the large number of sacrifices and gifts to the priesthood which are not mentioned in earlier literature, such as the daily and festival offerings (Num. 28–29); sin and guilt offerings (Lev. 4–5); tithe for the Levites (Num. 18:21–24); tithe from the tithe for the priests (Num. 18:25–32); the firstborn given to the priests (Num. 18:15–20); levitical cities (Num. 35:1–8); etc.

(4) Laws of purity and impurity, which are so characteristic of P, such as the laws regarding the impurity of the dead (Num. 19), the leper, and male and female discharges (Lev. 13–15), childbirth (Lev. 12), impure animals, carcasses, and swarming creatures (Lev. 11), result from the sacred intensification of the hierocracy of the Second Temple period. The numerous admonitions regarding the desecration of the Temple are also included (Lev. 21–22).

(5) During this period there is increasing entrenchment of religious institutions which are not dependent on the land, such as the Sabbath and circumcision, which, in effect, became the distinguishing mark of the Jews in Exile (Gen. 1:1–2:3; 17:1ff.; Ex. 16:1ff.; 31:12–17; 35:1–3; Num. 15:32–34).

(6) The festivals which were connected with the agricultural seasons in Palestine became historical festivals given specified times and stripped of the agricultural milieu, which by its very nature could not be bound by a strict chronological framework. During this period two festivals came into being: Rosh Ha-Shanah and the Day of Atonement (Lev. 23:17ff.; 23:23–32; Num. 29:1–11) which have no connection with the natural-agricultural life of the people and which express the supreme spirituality of Second Temple Judaism and the sense of sin inherent in it.

(7) The Tent of Meeting, described in detail in P (Ex. 25–30; 35–40; Num. 1–4; 7–8), is a fictional creation of the Jerusalem priesthood of the Second Temple period and is only a reflection of the Temple of Jerusalem. All the ancient history related in P underwent, in effect, schematic editing in accordance with the religious reality of the Second Temple.

Kaufmann's View. Y. Kaufmann, in his *Toledot ha-Emunah ha-Yisre'elit,* opposed Wellhausen's thesis, showing that it is impossible to explain the development of P against the background of the Second Temple period. Increasing information about the cult of the peoples of the Ancient Near East corroborate Kaufmann's approach, and this material will be referred to insofar as is possible within the framework of this article.

(1) The Tent of Meeting is the prototype of the Temple (according to Kaufmann, perhaps also of a high place, which in M. Weinfeld's view is untenable) and is not necessarily a central temple. In the wilderness period the community is concentrated in one place, and thus there is no necessity for more than one temple. In addition, there are several basic laws in P which in no way allow for the assumption of the centralization of the cult: (a) In light of the law for the centralization of the cult, Deuteronomy permits secular slaughtering (Deut. 12:15–16; 20:24), which had previously been prohibited (cf. I Sam. 14:31–35). However, P prohibits secular slaughter (Lev. 17:1–7), a prohibition which could not have been in effect during a period of centralized worship. According to P, shedding the blood of a living thing is a sin which is expiated by means of pouring blood over the altar (Lev. 17:11) or by covering it (in the case of the blood of an animal or bird, 17:13–14), while in D it is permitted to pour the blood over the ground like water (Deut. 12:16, 24). It must, therefore, be said that this law precedes Josiah's reform. (b) The blood rites of the Passover sacrifice, according to JE (Ex. 12:21–23) and P (Ex. 12:1–14), are performed in the house, while D, which commands the performance of the Passover sacrifice "at the place where the Lord your God will choose," dispenses with

these house rites and turns the Passover sacrifice into a public ceremony (Deut. 16:5–6). It can hardly be supposed that after the Passover sacrifice became public it regained its domestic character. (c) According to P, the firstborn of animals is given to the priest (Num. 18:17–18) and the tithe to the levite (Num. 18:21–24) or the Temple (Lev. 27:30–33). According to JE, too, the firstborn belongs to God, i.e., the Temple (Ex. 13:2, 12–13; 22:28). According to D, the firstborn and the tithe are eaten by their owners in Jerusalem (Deut. 14:22–29; 15:19–23). The removal of the firstborn and the tithe from the realm of the sancta and their transfer to the owners can be explained as resulting from the centralization of the cult, but it is unlikely that the opposite would have occurred, i.e., that the firstborn and the tithe which had been allotted to their owners would again be given to the priests.

(2) (a) The levites existed throughout the First Temple period, while during the Second Temple period they were very few (Ezra 8:15–19). It is impossible that this minority merited such great and numerous gifts exceeding those earmarked for the priests (tithe for the levite and only a tithe of a tithe for the priest, levitical cities). (b) The office of the high priest is mentioned explicitly during the First Temple period, and there is no justification to date those sections in which he appears to a later period (II Kings 12:11; 22:4, 8; 23:4). High priests, descended from ancient and distinguished families, as is the case of Aaron and his sons, are known from Assyria and Babylonia. There is even similarity in professional terminology. Thus, for example, the chief priest in Assyria is called the "big brother" *(abu rabû),* which is, in fact, the manner of referring to the high priest in Leviticus 21:10: *we-ha-kohen ha-gadol me-ʾeḥaw* (וְהַכֹּהֵן הַגָּדוֹל מֵאֶחָיו; "and the priest who is the highest [lit. biggest] of his brothers"). The priest who replaces Aaron is called *ha-kohen taḥtaw* (הַכֹּהֵן תַּחְתָּיו; "he [among his sons] who becomes priest in his stead"; Ex. 29:30), an expression which is literally equivalent to the Assyrian title *(kūmussu),* which designates the priest who replaces the high priest in Assyria. There is no basis, therefore, for Wellhausen's view that the high priest in P is an artificial imitation of a royal figure.

(3) The cultic complex delineated by P existed during the First Temple period (II Kings 16:15 (daily offering); 12:17 (sin and guilt offerings)), while various Ancient Near Eastern texts attest the existence of this complex throughout the Ancient Near East (Mesopotamia, Ugarit, and Hittites) and even in the pre-Israelite period. A daily offering, in the morning and evening, is explicitly mentioned in Mesopotamian texts (*Mémoires de la Délégation archéologique de Perse,* 4 (1902), pl. 2, 2:14–15). Different kinds of sacrifices are mentioned in Phoenician texts (the so-called Carthago Price List) and sacred cities are known from Mesopotamia and the Hittites.

(4) There are allusions to laws of purity and impurity in the literature of the Monarchy (I Sam. 21:6; II Sam. 11:4; II Kings 7:3; Hos. 9:9). In addition, it is known that these laws were carefully observed by all the peoples of the Ancient Near East. Of major significance in this connection are the cultic prescriptions of the Hittites (Pritchard, Texts, 207–10; cf. laws of menstruating women, in: AFO, 17 (1954–56), 276:46–47).

(5) Circumcision and the Sabbath are known in Israel from very ancient times (Gen. 34; Ex. 4:24–26; II Kings 4:23; Amos 8:5, etc.), and they were particularly emphasized in the priestly literature in which sacral and ritual institutions played a central role. The emphasis on the Sabbath in the literature of the period of the Exile and the Restoration, rather than pointing to the crystallization of these institutions during that period, results from the weakening of this institution (Neh. 13:15–22; cf. Jer. 17:21–27). On the contrary, in the period of the Monarchy, the Sabbath was observed even by the oppressors against whom the prophet inveighs (Amos 8:5). The difference between the conception of the Sabbath in P and that of the period of Exile and Restoration can be learned from the fact that in P only the nonobservance of the Sabbatical Year leads to exile and destruction (Lev. 26:34), while according to Ezekiel 20:13, 21, 24; Jeremiah 17:24; and Nehemiah 13:15–22, desecration of the Sabbath causes exile and destruction (see *Sabbath).

(6) Festivals in the large sanctuaries must be linked to fixed dates and to specific texts, and this, indeed, is the case with the neighboring peoples. The fact that it is P which preserves a system of fixed dates can be explained in that the priests—who were responsible for the composition of this source—must have been especially concerned with this matter which was central to their activities. The non-priestly sources JE and D have no need for fixed dates as they do not need the description of the ceremonies and sacrifices which are the concern of the priests alone. The claim that the festivals in P are stripped of their natural settings is unfounded. It is precisely in Leviticus 23 that the complete details of the agricultural ceremonies of the different festivals are found: the waving of the *ʿomer* at the beginning of the harvest; the offering of the two baked loaves at the end of the harvest; the celebration of the Feast of the Tabernacles in booths and the taking of the four species on this festival. Rosh Ha-Shanah and the Day of Atonement were Temple festivals in which the priest played an important role while the people were passive. This was also the case in Mesopotamia, where the festivals of the New Year lasted around 12 days, and the major concern was with the purification of and atonement for the Temple (cf. Thureau-Dangin, *Rituels accadiens* (1921); cf. Ezek. 45:18ff.). It was for this reason that there is no place for these festivals in the popular sources and not because they were not celebrated during the First Temple period.

(7) Concerning the Tent of Meeting, there is evidence in I Samuel 2:22 and II Samuel 7:6 that the tradition of the "tent" and the "tabernacle" had been rooted in Israel for a long period, and there is, thus, no justification for rejecting it and viewing the Tent of Meeting as a figment of priestly imagination from the Second Temple period. According to many scholars, the priestly description of the Tent of Meeting was influenced by the tabernacle of Shiloh (see Josh. 18:1; cf. M. Haran, in: JBL, 81 (1962), 14–24) or by the Davidic tent (II Sam. 6:17; cf. F. M. Cross, in: BA, 10 (1947), 45–65). It is possible that the Tent of Meeting included aspects of the Jerusalem Temple but the existence of an ark and a Tent during the period of the wanderings cannot be doubted.

The Historical Narrative of P. The sacral character of the Israelite history in P does not stem from the fact that Judea was under foreign rule during the Second Temple period and that the regime was then hierocratic as Wellhausen contended. It is rather to be explained by the nature of the circle responsible for the composition of this source. The Jerusalemite priesthood viewed everything from a sacral perspective and in this manner it described the past as well. It was not concerned with representing history as such, but rather with seeking the basis of the Israelite sacral institutions through their connection with history. Thus, for example, the creation in Genesis was recorded by P with the intention of giving the *raison d'être* of the institution of the Sabbath (Gen. 1); the covenant with Noah after the Flood is distinguished by the prohibition against the shedding of human blood and the consuming of animal blood (Gen. 9:1–17); the covenant with Abraham is essentially the establishment of the rite of circumcision (Gen. 17). In the description of the events on Mt. Sinai the building of the Sanctuary plays a central role (Ex. 25ff.), as do the various laws concerning sacrifice and purity and impurity (Lev.) and the dismantling of the Sanctuary and its reconstruction during the wanderings of the Israelites in the wilderness (Num. 1:1–10:28). According to P, the central theme of the spies' sin is the defamation of the Holy Land (13:22ff.) and not necessarily their demoralization of the people (cf. Deut. 1:28); the sin of Korah and his followers is essentially the undermining of the priestly hierarchy and not the actual rebellion against the leadership of Moses, as it is described in JE (Num. 16:12–15) and in Deuteronomy (11:6). Even the punishment is different. According to JE and D, Dothan and Abiram and their followers were swallowed up by the ground (Num. 16:26ff.; Deut. 11:6), but according to P, Korah and his followers were burned by the fire sent by God while they were offering the incense (Num. 16:16–19, 35).

The events in eastern Transjordan are described in P against the background of the passion of Phinehas, son of Eleazar the priest (Num. 25:10ff.); the Israelites' census and their preparation for the Conquest (Num. 26) under Joshua's leadership was conducted under the divine inspiration of Eleazar the priest (27:15–23). The war against the Midianites was conducted under the leadership of Phinehas, son of Eleazar the priest (Num. 31:6), and in accordance with the distinct purity customs (31:13ff.). No one was killed in the war (31:49) and part of the spoil was set aside for the levites and for the Tent of Meeting as a remembrance before God (31:47ff.).

This is, therefore, the sacred history of Israel as befits the priestly sect for whom the institutions reflected in this history played a central role. Therefore, Wellhausen's contention that P is late does not stand. On the contrary, evidence can be found for its antiquity. The covenant with Abraham in P includes promises like: "Kings shall stem from him" or "Father of the host of nations" (Gen. 17:4–6; cf. 28:3; 35:11; 48:4), which could hardly have been born in the post-Exilic period. These promises can rather be viewed against the background of the Monarchy in its expanding and flourishing phase. Since P is an accumulative priestly work, composed of laws, genealogical lists, and sacred traditions of the pre-monarchical as well as the monarchical period, the dating of P is difficult. It seems that this source is a product of a priestly scholastic circle that was active for hundreds of years. The final crystallization of the work, however, seems to have taken place sometime in the seventh century B.C.E. This may be deduced from the fact that P was the one who edited the JE traditions, or, in other words, the one responsible for the composition of the Tetrateuch, which means that his editorial activity cannot be dated earlier than the time of the composition of J and E (tenth–eighth centuries B.C.E.). On the other hand, it has not preserved any traces of Deuteronomy, which is unanimously dated at the end of the seventh century B.C.E. This may, therefore, serve as the terminus ad quem for P.

P and D—Theological Outlines. The bulk of the laws found in the priestly source centers on the divine Tabernacle and all that relates to its construction and to the ministrations performed in it. It is the pervading presence of God (see Divine *Presence) in the midst of Israel (i.e., the Sanctuary) that gives meaning to the Israelite scene. Remove the divine immanence, and the entire Priestly Code collapses. Not only would the worship of God cease but laws relating to the social sphere would become inoperative. The laws of asylum, for instance, are inconceivable without a high priest (Num. 35:25); the laws of warfare are unimaginable without the participation of sacral persons who march forth with their holy trumpets in hand (Num. 31:6; cf. 10:9); the law of suspected conjugal infidelity could not be implemented without a sanctuary (Num. 5:11ff.); military operations could not be conducted without the presence of the high priest bearing the Urim (Num. 27:21); and so forth. These laws do not presuppose the post-Exilic theocracy, as Wellhausen believed, because post-Exilic Judea did not conduct wars, nor were its leaders appointed by the congregation (*ʿadat Yisraʾel*). Nor is it possible to speak of the presence of God in a temple, when the Ark, upon which the Glory of God dwelt between the cherubim and to which the ritual of the Sanctuary was oriented, was at that time nonexistent.

The reality reflected in the Priestly Code accords more with the ancient life of Israel, grounded on sacral dogma and prescriptions, which continued to mold the life of the Israelites even after the establishment of the Monarchy. The reality depicted in the ancient narratives, which are not tendentious, is, indeed, similar to that reflected in the priestly document. Thus, Saul and David conduct their military campaigns according to the instructions provided by the Urim; holy wars resound with the blast of trumpets and horns (Josh. 6; Judg. 7:18); the priestly class participates in military expeditions (Josh. 6; Judg. 10:26–28; I Sam. 4); and the booty is brought to the house of God (Josh. 6:24; II Sam. 8:11; II Kings 12:19; cf. Num. 31:50–54).

The regime of holiness and taboo underlying the priestly document is not the product of the theological ruminations of priests of the post-Exilic period but derives from the Israelite reality prevailing during the times of the Judges and in the monarchical period. The sacral institutions, which occupy a central place in the priestly theology, are known to us from early biblical literature. Thus the Sabbath, for example, or the New Moon, the "days of solemn rest" (*shabbaton*, שַׁבָּתוֹן), and the "holy convocations (*Miqra qodesh*, מִקְרָא קֹדֶשׁ) are not peculiar to P. Like the priestly document, the early sources also speak of days on which one refrained from work (Amos 8:5), days on which one partook of holy meals (I Sam. 20:24–32), made pilgrimages to holy men (II Kings 4:22–23), gathered in sacral assemblies and holy convocations (Isa. 1:13), offered sacrifices and poured libations (Hos. 9:4–5).

Matters affecting purity and defilement, concerning which the priestly document provides such detailed regulations, are also known to us from early biblical literature. The participants in a sacral event must purify themselves and cleanse their garments (Gen. 35:2; Ex. 19:10; I Sam. 16:5); Israelite warriors must observe sexual continence and consecrate their utensils before departing for war (I Sam. 21:6); women must cleanse themselves of menstrual impurity (II Sam. 11:4); lepers are ejected from the city (II Kings 7:3ff.); and persons defiled by contact with the dead are forbidden to enter the house of YHWH (Hos. 9:4). The same is true of matters concerning the Temple and holy taboos. The danger that ensues from approaching the divine sanctum, which is so frequently mentioned in the priestly document, is also alluded to in the early sources (I Sam. 6:19; II Sam. 6:6–9).

These old sources, furthermore, contain regulations for sacrifices and alimentary offerings to God (Ex. 23:18; 34:25; I Sam. 2:13–17; 21:7, the bread of the Presence; Amos 4:5; cf. Lev. 7:13) and describe cultic practices, which also figure as an essential part of priestly teaching. The early sources also contain references to holy consecrations, communal sacrifices, and sin and guilt offerings. The institution of the Nazirite, which is one of the most ancient in Israel, is mentioned, remarkably enough, only in the priestly document (Num. 6) and nowhere else in the

Pentateuch. Nonsacrificial slaughter, which is prohibited by the Holiness Code (Lev. 17) and which is designated as "eating with the blood" (Lev. 19:26), is mentioned in I Samuel 14:32–35: "Behold the people are sinning against YHWH by eating with the blood," i.e., by eating without first sprinkling the blood upon the altar.

While much can be learned about the character of P from a knowledge of what it contains, much more can be discovered about its world view by considering what is missing from this source. Most astonishing is the marked absence from the priestly document of civil-social ordinances and regulations pertaining to conjugal life, which occupy so great a place in the Book of Deuteronomy. Even when we do encounter laws dealing with such matters in P, they always appear in a sacro-ritual light. Thus the incest prohibitions are set forth in the same context as the prohibitions concerning menstrual uncleanness, bestiality, Moloch worship (Lev. 18:21–23), necromancy, and clean and unclean animals (20:6, 25). Incest, then, is conceived as a distinctly sacral matter and not as one which concerns civil law. The Sabbatical Year, which in the Book of Deuteronomy has a patently social character, figures in P as a sacral institution: "The land shall keep a Sabbath of YHWH" (Lev. 25:2), which is to say that the obligation to rest falls upon the land, so that if the land does not fulfill this duty while the nation dwells thereon, it must pay back this obligation during its years of desolation when the people are in exile: "Then shall the land make up for its sabbath years . . . throughout the time that it is desolate it shall observe the rest that it did not observe in your sabbath years while you were dwelling upon it" (Lev. 26:34–35). Here, in contradistinction to the Book of Deuteronomy, which makes mention only of the remission of debts (Deut. 15:1–11), there is no reference to the year of release, which cancels the debts of the poor. It must be pointed out that as far as actual practice was concerned the two laws were not mutually exclusive, which is to say that it is quite likely that both were observed or, at any rate, that both were regarded as obligatory, and that nevertheless there was a connection between them. The way in which the two laws appear in the sources sheds light on the ideology of the respective writers. Thus, for example, the priestly writer is concerned with the taboo of the seventh year and with the sacral implications of this taboo, while the author of Deuteronomy is concerned with the social aspect of this law and completely ignores the sacral side.

This recalls the manner in which the Sabbath is presented in each of these two sources. In P the rationale for the Sabbath is that God worked six days in creating the world and rested on the seventh (Gen. 2:1–3; Ex. 31:17), which is to say that man, by his Sabbath rest, reenacts, so to speak, God's rest on the seventh day of creation—a point of view appropriate to the priestly circle, which, by means of its ritual in the Sanctuary, reenacts what takes place in the divine sphere. As against this, Deuteronomy supplies another reason for the Sabbath: the Israelite is obligated to rest on the Sabbath not because God rested on this day but rather to provide a respite for his servants: "so that your male and female slave may rest as you do" (Deut. 5:14). Alongside the social motivation there appears the religious one: "Remember that you were a slave in the land of Egypt and YHWH your God freed you from there with a mighty hand and an outstretched arm; therefore YHWH your God has commanded you to observe the Sabbath day" (Deut. 5:15). Thus God derives the Sabbath not from creation, as in P, but from the Exodus. As in the case of the Sabbatical Year so in the case of the Sabbath, it is possible that the social motivation existed alongside the sacral and that they were both able to coexist. It is a fact that the Sabbath is given a social motivation in Exodus 23:12. However, there is, no doubt, some significance to the fact that the author of P selected specifically the sacral motivation and developed it in his own way, while the Book of Deuteronomy chose the social motivation and formulated it in its own unique way, i.e., humanistically (see *Deuteronomy).

Another example which demonstrates the different theologies of the two compositions under consideration is the law concerning going forth to war. According to the priestly literature, when the people go forth to battle, the priests are to blow trumpets (Num. 10:9). At the end of the war the soldiers must undergo purifacatory rites (Num. 31:19–20) and must give an offering to the sacral domain from the booty (Num. 31:50–54). The Book of Deuteronomy, on the other hand, makes no mention of the blowing of trumpets or of purificatory rites; it speaks rather of a priest, who, before the war, speaks to the people to encourage them and to implant in them the spirit of valor (Deut. 20:1–9). Regulations as to conduct within the battle line contain provisions which are bound up with the maintenance of cleanliness and health no less than they are with the preservation of the sacral state of the camp (Deut. 23:10–15).

Another matter which provides information about the different theologies of these compositions is the law of retaliation. This law, the *lex talionis,* which stands by itself in the Covenant Code (Ex. 21:23b–25; cf. Alt, Kl Schr, 1 (1953), 278ff.), appears in various contexts in P and D. In P it appears in connection with the law of the blasphemer (Lev. 24:16–22), while in Deuteronomy it is found in connection with the law of the false witness (Deut. 19:21), i.e., in the context of civil and criminal legislation. Just as P concerns itself with codifying sacral legislation, so does Deuteronomy occupy itself with laws belonging to the civil-secular sphere.

Not only do we encounter institutions of a manifestly secular character such as the judiciary (Deut. 16:18–20; 17:8–13), the monarchy (17:14ff.), the military (Deut. 20), and civil and criminal laws, which treat of the family and inheritance (21:18–23; 22:13–29; 24:1–4; 25:5–9), loans and debts (15:1–18; 24:10–13), litigations and quarrels (25:1–3, 11–12), trespassing (19:14), false testimony (19:15–21) and the like, but even institutions and practices, which were originally sacral in character, have here been recast in secularized forms. Thus, for example, the piercing of the slave's ear, which, according to the Covenant Code, must be done "before God" (i.e., in the Temple; Ex. 21:6), is to be done near any door without any connection to a sanctuary, according to Deuteronomy (Deut. 15:17). Similarly, the cities of refuge which, according to P, are levitical cities, i.e., cities which belong to the sacral realm, are transformed in Deuteronomy to serve the pragmatic purpose of holding the manslayer in protective custody from the avenger of blood, and nothing more. In P, on the other hand, the manslayer, who is required to dwell in the city of refuge until the death of the high priest (Num. 35), achieves the expiation of his sin by dwelling in the city of refuge.

The absence of sacral institutions in the Book of Deuteronomy is no less surprising than the absence of sociolegal institutions in the priestly document. The very book which makes "the chosen place" such a central concern completely ignores the sacral institutions, which the chosen place must necessarily imply and without which the conduct of sacral worship is unimaginable. The holy ministrations, which involve the presentation of the shewbread, the kindling of candles, the burning of incense, the offering of the suet, the daily and seasonal sacrifices, and the reception and disposal of the holy donations, in short, the most essential charges and rites of the Israelite cult, find no mention whatsoever in the Book of Deuteronomy. The exhortations regarding the awe and reverence with which the sanctity of the Temple must be treated and the restrictions imposed to avert the desecration of the sanctum are familiar to us from the early Israelite literature and figure prominently in the priestly document but find no mention whatsoever in the Book of Deuteronomy. Even if the author of Deuteronomy presupposed these regulations, he should still have given some intimation of their existence when setting forth the ordinances concerning the chosen place. The fact that he did not allude to them implies that these regulations were of no concern to him. Particularly obvious is the absence from Deuteronomy of the sacral law (Lat. *fas*), to which such an important place is dedicated in P. In Deuteronomy there is no warning whatsoever against blasphemy, the most heinous of sins in Israel, which is dealt with in the Covenant Code (Ex. 22:27) and in P (Lev. 24:15–16; Num. 30; I Kings 21:13).

Sorcery, the worship of Moloch, and necromancy, which, according to P, the *Holiness Code, and the testimony of the historical books, were punishable by death (Ex. 22:17; Lev. 18:21; 20:1–6, 27; I Sam. 28:3, 9), are, of course, forbidden by Deuteronomy, but without any particular punishment specified. On the other hand, in the Book of Deuteronomy capital punishment is prescribed in two cases where the other codes had not employed it. These are the cases of the rebellious elder (Deut. 17:12) and of the one who instigates idolatry (Deut. 13:2–12). The nonsacral character of the legal conception of Deuteronomy is also manifest in the fact that severe religious and cultic offenses, which are punishable, according to P, by *karet*, do not even appear in Deuteronomy, for all of these offenses are connected with the sphere of sacral legislation (Lat. *fas*) while Deuteronomy deals with the jus. These religious and cultic offenses include the eating of fat or blood (Lev. 7:25–27), the consumption of the flesh of sacrificed animals in a state of impurity (Lev. 7:20–21), the defilement of the Sanctuary and its appurtenances (Lev. 22:3; Num. 19:13, 20), the breach of the covenant of circumcision (Gen. 17:14), failure to offer the paschal sacrifice (Num. 9:13), and failure to practice self-denial on Yom Kippur (Lev. 23:29).

Up to this point the selective purposes of the two sources P and D have been dealt with. Mention has to be made of the implications of the different selection with reference to the question of the concept of holiness. Holiness in the Book of Deuteronomy seems to have more of a national than a cultic aspect. It is a condition that derives from the relationship existing between God and Israel. Israel is holy because God has chosen and set Israel apart from all other nations: "For you are a people holy to YHWH your God and YHWH has chosen you to be a people for His own possession out of all the peoples that are on the face of the earth" (Deut. 14:2). According to the Book of Deuteronomy, therefore, holiness devolves automatically upon every Israelite, who, consequently, must not profane it by defilement. This is very different from P's conception of holiness as contingent upon physical proximity to the divine presence and upon the preservation of that proximity through ritual means. Thus, according to the Holiness Code, only the priests are forbidden to eat *nevelah* ("carcasses," Lev. 22:8; cf. Ezek. 44:31); lay Israelites are not prohibited from eating *nevelah*, though they must undergo ritual purification afterward if they do so (Lev. 11:39–40; cf. 17:15), as must a person who carries a carcass. Deuteronomy (14:21), on the other hand, forbids all Israelites to eat *nevelah*, because it makes no distinction between priests and laity in matters concerning holiness. Similarly, the Book of Deuteronomy applies the prohibition against self-mutilation to all Israelites (Deut. 14:1), while P restricts it to the priests (Lev. 21:5). The reason for this divergency between the laws is that the priestly document regards the priests as an essential part of the Sanctuary or the divine sphere and as possessing, therefore, a greater degree of holiness than the lay Israelites. As a result, the priests are to be treated as holy persons (Lev. 21:8). Deuteronomy, on the other hand, regards all the people of Israel as holy, not by reason of their physical proximity to the tangible sanctity of the Deity but by virtue of their election by God.

Laws Common to P and D. Although the P and D sources differ, as has been shown, in their purpose and methods of presentation, they have in common several matters which do not occur in JE altogether. When these matters are considered, especially the institutions and laws common to both, it can be seen that in most cases P is the primary and original source. Following is a brief survey of these laws:

Ritual. (1) Deuteronomy 24:8 commands that a leper be dealt with according to the instructions of the priests and Levites. It is doubtless referring to the instructions relating to the various forms of leprosy as they appear in Leviticus 13–14. There is no reason to assume that the laws, as such, did not exist at the time of the formulation of D, although it is not certain that they existed then in their present form.

(2) The section on pure and impure animals in Deuteronomy 14:3–21 is paralleled in Leviticus 11, and Deuteronomy 14:13–18a has been shown recently to have been borrowed from the Priestly Source (W. L. Moran, in: CBQ, 28 (1966), 271ff.). However, while in Leviticus 11 there is also a detailed description of impure swarming things and the manner in which they transfer impurity (11:24ff.), D comprises mainly matters relating to eating and does not place special emphasis on the impurity of a carcass, with which the priests were particularly concerned.

(3) The laws of hybrid species in Leviticus 19 include hybrid cattle, hybrid seeds, and hybrid clothing (19:19). D includes these laws and even presents and explains them in detail (Deut. 22:9–11). The lateness of these laws in D may be indicated by the explanation of the word *sha'atnez* (שַׁעַטְנֵז). In Leviticus this word is not explained since, apparently, it was well known, while D found it necessary to add the explanatory phrase: "wool and linen together."

(4) A law which in D is close to the law of hybrid species is that of *gedilim* (גְּדִלִים; 22:12), which in P are called *ẓiẓit* (צִיצִת; "fringes"; Num. 15:37–41). Both expressions are identical in meaning and refer to the threads woven in the hem of the garment in the shape of a flower, etc. (cf. I Kings 6:18, 29, 32, 35: פְּטוּרֵי צִצִּים; I Kings 7:17: גְּדִלִים מַעֲשֵׂה שַׁרְשְׁרוֹת, both of which are intended to beautify and embellish the Temple; cf. also Akk. *gidiltu* and *ṣiṣtu*). P dwells upon the religious significance of this custom. The "fringes" are considered a "sign" (there are some who amend וְהָיָה לָכֶם לְצִיצִת, "that shall be your fringe," to וְהָיָה לָכֶם לְאוֹת, "and shall be a sign unto you," in Num. 15:39) that will serve as a reminder to fulfill the commandments (15:39, 40), and indeed the "sign for remembrance" is very characteristic of P's theology; note: the "sign of the covenant of the Sabbath" (Ex. 31:13), the rainbow (Gen. 9:12, 17), circumcision (Gen. 17:11), Passover (Ex. 12:13), and others (e.g., Num. 17:3, 25).

(5) In relation to the festivals, D is apparently dependent on P, since it enjoins the observance of Sukkot for seven days and enjoins the Israelites to rejoice on these days, as does Leviticus 23:39–40. Like P (H=Holiness Code), Deuteronomy also names the festival "the Feast of Tabernacles [Booths]." The name is explained in P(H) by the commandment appearing there regarding dwelling in booths (23:42), which is not mentioned in JE. The author of Deuteronomy preserved the name of this festival but ignored the commandment about dwelling in booths since

such a custom was possible only at the provincial sanctuaries situated in the neighborhood of the fields and vineyards where the festivities took place. The same applies to the decorative flora which has to be brought, according to P, for the festive procession (Lev. 23:40). This could hardly be required from the farmer living at a considerable distance from the "chosen place." Deuteronomy also commands the "counting" of seven weeks from the beginning of the harvest to the festival of Shavuot, which covers—according to P—the period between the waving of the *ʿomer* at the beginning of the harvest and bringing the "new offering," the two baked loaves, at its end (Lev. 23:9–21). While D does preserve the period of seven weeks, it does not mention the ceremonies which are the basis for this counting, since these ceremonies, originally intended for the private farmer, could not be performed after the centralization of the cult.

(6) The pagan institutions, such as the Moloch (or in D: "he who passes his son and daughter through fire"), divination and soothsaying, ghosts and familiar spirits (Lev. 18:21; 19:26, 31; 20:1–6, 27) are prohibited in Deuteronomy too (18:10–11), but to these are added the magician (קֹסֵם), one who casts spells (חֹבֵר חָבֶר), and the one who inquires of the dead (דֹּרֵשׁ אֶל הַמֵּתִים).

SOCIAL MATTERS. *The Resident Alien.* Like P and the Holiness Code (included in P; Lev. 19:10, 33–34; 23:22), D also enjoins helping and loving the stranger (Deut. 10:19). There are differences, however, in regard to obligations devolving on the stranger in P and D. According to P the resident alien and the native Israelite alike are all required to observe the regulations of the Torah, because it is the person's residence in the land that subjects him to the religiocultic ordinances. Residence in the land is deemed to be an automatic recognition of the god of the country on the part of the resident and thus also entails the obligation to worship him (cf. II Kings 17); conversely, an Israelite, who resides outside the land of YHWH is deemed to dwell in an unclean land and to be the worshiper of foreign gods (I Sam. 26:19; cf. Josh. 22:16–19 (= P)). The resident alien and the native Israelite both draw their sustenance from a common sacral source; both, consequently, are required to observe the Code of Holiness that it entails.

This is not the view of the Book of Deuteronomy. According to Deuteronomy, the laws of the Torah apply only to those who are related to the Israelite people (*ʿam*, see above) by blood and race, while the resident alien is not regarded as an Israelite and, consequently, is not required to observe the sacral laws of the congregation even though he dwells in the land and is willing to subject himself to them. He does enjoy, to be sure, the full protection of the laws and the same political and economic rights that all Israelites enjoy. As he is not a true Israelite, however, he is not required to assume the special sacral obligations imposed upon the "holy people." The Book of Deuteronomy intentionally differentiates, then, between the Israelite and the resident alien in all matters pertaining to religious obligations, the fulfillment of which it regards as exclusively binding only upon the holy people. In Deuteronomy 14:21 we read: "You shall not eat anything that has died a natural death; give it to the stranger (*ger*, גֵּר), who is within your towns, that he may eat it, or you may sell it to a foreigner (*nokhri*, נָכְרִי), for you are a people holy to YHWH your God ... " The Holiness Code (Lev. 17:15), on the other hand, ordains: "and every person that eats what dies of itself or has been torn by beasts *(nevelah u-terefah)* whether he is a native or a stranger *(ger)* shall wash his clothes and bathe himself in water ...." The two passages thus stand in open contradiction to each other. The source of the contradiction is the divergent viewpoints of the two documents. P is only concerned with the ritual problem of impurity involved: all who eat *nevelah*, whether Israelite or resident alien, carry impurity upon them. The land is unable to bear impurity no matter who the carriers of the impurity may be (cf. "lest the land vomit you out when you defile it," Lev. 18:28). The Book of Deuteronomy, on the other hand, regards the prohibition only as a matter of noblesse oblige. Israel must abstain from eating *nevelah*, because it is an act unbecoming to a holy people and not because it causes impurity from which one must purge himself by ritual bathing (Lev. 11:40; 17:15). It does not, consequently, impose this upon those who are not of the holy people.

Care of the Poor. P and D contain laws in connection with leftovers from the harvest and grape harvest for the poor (Lev. 19:9–10; 23:22; Deut. 24:19–22). The outstanding differences between the two laws are:

(a) D does not enjoin to leave "the edges" (*peʾah*, פֵּאָה) of the field or of the vineyard (cf. M. Haran, in: EM, 5 (1968), 674–5) as does P but rather commands about the gleanings from the ingathering of the crops: the fall of the wheat (*leket, leqet*, לֶקֶט) and the remainders of that which falls during the harvest of the grapes and olives.

(b) In contrast P (in fact H) does not include the law about the *ʿomer* forgotten in the field which should be left for the poor.

(c) D sets separate law for olives which are not mentioned in P. However, the vineyard also includes olives (cf. Judg. 15:5), and it may thus be possible that P is referring to olives as well. It is difficult to establish which is early and late in this instance, but here too D's formulation is more pragmatic, i.e., it presents the law in a more tangible manner and, characteristically, adds a religious moral justification (Deut. 24:22). The fact that it does not mention the leftover of the corner of the field *(peʾah)* may be explained in that the *peʾah* is a remnant of ancient magical beliefs (being intended for spirits of the field and demons) and does not conform to the specific liberal attitude of D. Perhaps for the same reason, it does not accept the taboo of the Sabbatical Year—the abandonment of the field during the seventh year, found in JE and P—but enjoins only the remission of debts during this year (see above).

(d) Laws of weights and measures are also found only in P and D (Lev. 19:35–37; Deut. 25:13–16). The law in D does not explicitly mention scales and liquid measure (the *hin*, הִין), but it is difficult to draw chronological conclusions from this. On the other hand, it is clear that D incorporates into this law idioms from wisdom literature (Prov. 11:1; 20:23; see *Deuteronomy) and the concept of "an abomination to God" which is also found only in wisdom literature (see M. Weinfeld, in: JBL, 80 (1961), 241ff.). The dependence on the law of P is evidenced in the expression "deals dishonestly" (*ʿoseh ʿavel*, עֹשֵׂה עָוֶל; Deut. 25:16) which is apparently influenced by Leviticus 19:35 (*loʾ taʿasu ʿavel ba-mishpaṭ*, לֹא תַעֲשׂוּ עָוֶל בַּמִּשְׁפָּט).

LAWS OF ASYLUM. In JE, the altar and sanctuary are the original places of asylum for the accidental manslayer (Ex. 21:13–14), while in P the temple cities in which the Levites resided (Num. 35; cf. Josh. 20–21) serve as places of refuge. The premise underlying these laws of asylum is that the accidental manslayer must atone for the shedding of innocent blood and must therefore undergo the punishment of forced residence at a sacral domicile. According to P, the homicide is compelled to reside in a city of refuge until the death of the high priest—the person who bears "the iniquity of the holy offerings of the children of Israel" (Ex. 28:38) and whose death alone might serve as the expiation of bloodguilt. The city of refuge, according to this conception, does not necessarily perform the protective function of safeguarding the accedental manslayer from the avenger but serves as the place in which he atones for his sin. The Book of Deuteronomy, however, with the abolition of provincial altars and sanctuaries, removes the institution of asylum from sacerdotal jurisdiction. It retains the numerical principle of three cities of refuge on each side of the Jordan (Deut. 4:41–43; 19:1–10), but strips it of its sacral character. The assignment of cities of refuge is no longer dependent upon sacral factors (temple cities = levitical cities) but is decided by rational and geographic considerations. The land must be measured and subdivided equally into three sections, and cities of refuge assigned at equidistant locations so that the fleeing manslayer may reach the place of asylum with the maximum speed. The asylum is not the place in which he serves his punishment, but the place which protects him from the vengeance of the blood redeemer: "Lest the avenger of blood in hot anger pursue the manslayer and overtake him . . . " (Deut. 19:6). Therefore, the Deuteronomic law does not prescribe the period of time that the homicide must reside in asylum (i.e., until the death of the high priest); he is to remain there until the rage of the avenger subsides.

Priestly Donations. P and D have preserved the laws defining the priests' portion of the well-being offering (שְׁלָמִים). According to P, the priest receives the breast and the thigh of the sacrificial animal (Lev. 7:28–34), while according to D, he receives the shoulders, the cheeks, and the stomach (Deut. 18:3). Regarding the first fruits, P defines the gifts similarly to D: "All the best of the new oil, wine, and grain" (Num. 18:12; cf. Deut. 18:4). In addition, P commands setting aside a loaf "from the first yield of your baking" (Num. 15:18–21), while D commands that the first shearing of the sheep shall be given to the priest (Deut. 18:4). JE apparently alludes to the firstfruits of grain and wine in Exodus 22:28: *mele'atkha we-dim'akha* (מְלֵאָתְךָ וְדִמְעֲךָ). P associates the rites of the firstfruits with festivals as follows: the *'omer* is waved by the farmer at the beginning of the harvest (Lev. 23:9–14) and the two loaves of bread with the addition of two lambs are given to the priest at the end of the harvest (23:15–20; see above). D also enjoins the ceremony of the bringing of the firstfruit (Deut. 26:1–10), but neither fixes a date nor defines the amount given to the priest. JE also includes the firstfruit offering which is brought to the House of God apparently during a feast (Ex. 23:19; 34:26), but its nature is not sufficiently clear. According to P, the tithe is given to the levites (Num. 18:21–24) who set aside a tithe of a tithe from it for the priests (18:25–32). According to D, the owners bring the tithes with them to the central Temple and eat them there, and every third year they leave the tithe in their towns where it is eaten by the levites as well as the stranger, the orphan, and the widow (Deut. 14:22–29; 26:12–15). An ancient law incorporated in P deals with the tithe given to the priest from the "seed from the ground," the fruit from the tree, as well as from the herds and the flocks (Lev. 27:30–32). It is not known if according to this attitude these tithes were transferred to the Temple treasury (הֶקְדֵּשׁ) or were given to the priests.

The general impression gained from the laws of gifts to the priesthood according to the various sources is that: (1) JE does not define either the firstfruit gifts or the other types of sacral donations. (2) P clearly defines the gifts but preserved two different traditions in relation to the tithe (Lev. 27:30–32; Num. 18:8ff.). (3) D defines the gifts but in its treatment they undergo a process of liberalization. The gift from the sacrifice is of far less worth than that obligated by P. The firstfruits are not associated with particular dates or with fixed quotas. The tithe (like the firstfruits) was expropriated from the levites and priests and given over to the owners who would eat it in the central Temple. This liberalization apparently originated in a reform, namely, the centralization of the cult from the time of Hezekiah-Josiah.

P and D—Comparison of Tradition and Style. The Peroration. At the end of the Holiness Code (Lev. 26), as at the end of the Deuteronomic law code (Deut. 28), there is a section comprising blessings and curses, but there is a distinct difference between these two sections. In Leviticus 26 the setting is local and agricultural in character: the threshing and vintage (26:5), the vicious beasts in the land (26:6, 22; cf. Gen. 37:33; II Kings 17:26), deserted roads (Lev. 26:30–31; cf. Amos 7:9), and the desolation of the land (Lev. 26:32ff.). There are also special literary signs which can be noted here, such as the repeated refrain: "But if you do not obey . . . and if you remain hostile to me" (26:14, 21, 23, 27), as well as the typological numbers seven (26:18, 21, 24, 28) and ten (26:26). The parallel section in D contains no material bearing a local character of the type indicated, but rather emphasizes global catastrophes alluding to an Assyrian conquest, such as: plague, pillage of property, and exile of children by a cruel nation which comes from afar (28:30–34, 48–51), a harsh siege of all the towns (28:52–57), and the king's exile (28:36). An analysis of the arrangement of cursus indeed shows that it manifests the distinct influence of seventh-century B.C.E. Assyrian treaties (see M. Weinfeld, in: *Biblica*, 46 (1965), 417ff.).

Levitical Priests. P makes a clear distinction between priests and levites while D speaks of one class: "levitical priests." As has already been indicated there is no basis to assume that P was the first code to form the distinction between the two classes, priests and levites. On the contrary, it is clear that D already recognized the two classes (cf. Deut. 18:3–5 with 6–8), but it rather deliberately identifies the status of the levite (18:6–8) and creates the single status of the "levitical priests." The levites who served in the provincial towns until the reform lost their status after the reform, and for this reason the Deuteronomic legislator displays concern for them in two ways: by giving them the opportunity to serve in the central Temple (18:6–8), and by including them in holy feasts and gifts (12:12, 18; 14:27, 29; 16:11, 14).

Stylistic and Idiomatic Differences. The two theological schools P and D each adopted its own forms of expression and linguistic usages. It is impossible to determine priority or lateness on the basis of these expressions since it is impossible to differentiate strata in the biblical language of the First Temple period. Certain differences can at least point to differences of sociological approach and attitude. The following list the main differences.

D	P
שַׁעֲרֵיכֶם	מוֹשְׁבוֹתֵיכֶם
הָאָח וְהַגֵּר	הָאֶזְרָח וְהַגֵּר
רָאשֵׁי הַשְּׁבָטִים	רָאשֵׁי הַמַּטּוֹת
קָהָל	עֵדָה
פָּדָה	גָּאַל
שָׁמַר/שָׁמַר לְ	זָכַר/זָכַר לְ
שָׁמַר וְעָשָׂה	זָכַר וְעָשָׂה
הָלַךְ בְּדַרְכֵי ה׳	הָלַךְ בְּחֻקּוֹת ה׳
הָלַךְ אַחֲרֵי (אֱלֹהִים אֲחֵרִים)	זָנָה אַחֲרֵי (אֱלִילִים)
גְּדִלִים	צִיצִת
שְׁנַת שְׁמִטָּה	שְׁנַת שַׁבָּתוֹן
הֶעֱבִיר בְּנוֹ וּבִתּוֹ בָּאֵשׁ	נָתַן מִזַּרְעוֹ לַמֹּלֶךְ
גֵּר יָתוֹם וְאַלְמָנָה	הֶעָנִי וְהַגֵּר
בִּבְלִי־דַעַת	בִּשְׁגָגָה
אָנֹכִי	אֲנִי

and the priest of *ʾEl ʿElyon*. The God of Israel is there explicitly identified with *ʾEl ʿElyon*, the local Canaanite deity of Salem (= Jerusalem). *ʾEl* and *ʿElyon* both belong to the Canaanite pantheon though they do not appear together as in Genesis 14 (see Names of *God). A similar situation is encountered among the nomadic tribes in Mesopotamia in the first half of the second millennium B.C.E., the time roughly corresponding to the period of the Patriarchs. West Semitic nomads living on the outskirts of Mesopotamian cities such as Sippar and Ur adopted the gods of these cities (cf. J. R. Kupper, *Les nomades en Mespotamie au temps des rois de Mari* (1957), 88–89). Since these various *ʾEl*'s in the mountainous region of Israel became the patrons of the Hebrew ancestors in their new settlement, they were amalgamated with their own personal gods and finally were considered as those who promised the land to their descendants. The holy sites of these gods were depicted as the scenes of the revelation to the Patriarchs at which the promises had been pledged mostly through a covenant. In later post-Mosaic times, all these *ʾEl*'s, each of them previously preserving a particular character, were identified with the God of Israel.

The last tradition (the Davidic period) is the formulation of the promise as a royal grant (see M. Weinfeld, in: JAOS, 89 (1970), 184–203). The promise of the land is an act of gratitude by God the sovereign, toward Abraham for his faithfulness (15:6; 22:16; 26:5). The promise does not relate to the territory inhabited by the Patriarchs but to the land in its imperial garb: "from the river of Egypt to the Euphrates" (15:18). That this formulation of the promise is to be linked to the Davidic period may be deduced from the fact that "the promise of the dynasty" to David is also stylized in the form of the "royal grant" given as a reward for David's faithfulness (I Kings 3:6; 9:4, 5; 14:8; 15:3). The analogy between the two covenants is strengthened by the fact that Abraham and David alike are the ideal figures in regard to the implementation of *mishpaṭ u-ẓedaqah* (מִשְׁפָּט וּצְדָקָה; "justice and righteousness"; Gen. 18:19; II Sam. 8:15; I Kings 10:9 and the relevant prophetic and psalmodic passages, see above).

The Exodus. The bare facts underlying all the Exodus stories (cf. e.g., Num. 20:15–16; Deut. 26:5–8; Josh. 24, etc.) are the enslavement of the Hebrews and their miraculous salvation. These are the constitutive elements of the Exodus theme and seem to reflect historical reality. Being the central theme in Israel's history, it gradually accumulated all kinds of religious and theological motifs. The most ancient and significant motif associated with Exodus is the Passover feast, especially the Passover sacrifice, the old spring ceremony of the nomadic Hebrews. The apotropaic rites of this ceremony (sprinkling the blood on the doorposts), originally intended to repulse the demon attacking the newborn children and animals in the spring, was reinterpreted in the light of the Exodus. The Passover sacrifice and the strange rites accompanying it were here explained as commemorating the occasion of the miraculous liberation when the demon, killing the Egyptian firstborn, spared the houses of the Israelites (Ex. 12:13, 23). Furthermore, the Passover served not only as the commemoration of the Exodus but as the commemoration of the Conquest as well. The old spring ritual of the nomads was celebrated at the time of the moving of the shepherds to their summer pastures in the settled and cultivated area. This particular feature was also dramatized in the Passover rites. The celebrants were to eat the flesh of the Paschal lamb, "their loins girded, their sandals on their feet, and the staff in their hands" (Ex. 12:11). It is indeed significant that the tradition of the entrance into the promised land after the crossing of the Jordan (Josh. 5) opens with the celebration of the Passover (the circumcision occurring there being the prerequisite for the offering of the sacrifice, cf. Ex. 12:48). The Exodus and the Conquest, the main themes of the hallowed Israelite tradition, were both dramatized with a catechetical purpose in mind. The observance of the Passover rites serves as a good opportunity to explain to the children the great miracle of Exodus (Ex. 12:25–27; 13:8), while the stones of Gilgal serve as an opportunity for extolling the wonder of the crossing of the Jordan (Josh. 4:6–7, 21–23).

Just as the old spring festival was exploited for the dramatization of the plague of the firstborn, so the old myth of the battle of God with the "sea," a fundamental motif in the cosmogonies of the Ancient Near East, was employed in the Exodus epic in order to dramatize the crossing of the Reed Sea by the Israelites. The connection between the primeval battle of God with the demonic "sea" and the victory on the Reed Sea is explicitly made in Isaiah 51:9–10, and Psalms 77:12ff. Furthermore the same myth has also been used in order to glorify the passage of the Jordan when entering Canaan. In Psalms 114 the Reed Sea and the Jordan are both mentioned as fleeing before God at the time of the Exodus. The shift of motifs from the cosmogonical sphere to the Exodus epic may also be recognized through the idea of divine kingship occurring for the first time in the Pentateuch in the Exodus tradition (Ex. 15:18). The god who defeats the sea monster is crowned as king (cf. *Enuma eliš*). In an analogous way the God of Israel is proclaimed as king after his victory on the sea (Ex. 15:18). Though some encounter at the Reed Sea between the Israelites and the Egyptians is not to be denied, the tradition as presented in the literary sources of the Pentateuch is undoubtedly an outcome of the traditional literary process indicated above.

Law and Covenant—The Sinai Theme. Tradition ascribes all the laws to Moses. Though this is a generalization—as is the ascription of the Psalms to David and wisdom literature to Solomon—the basic premise underlying this tradition, i.e., that Moses was the first legislator and, as such, responsible for the basic legislature of ancient Israel, is undoubtedly true. In spite of the differences in nature and chronological background between the various codes, a common legal lore can be discerned in them and this might be traced back to Moses. Some basic Israelite laws and restitutions are found in all of the codes. Reducing them to a minimum one may find: In the cultic domain: Sabbath, Passover, the firstlings, the three festivals, the holy donations, the destruction of idols and the ban of the Canaanites, and the prohibition of sorcery and pagan mantic practices. In the social-religious sphere: the periodical liberation of slaves, the year of release, the place of asylum, *lex talionis,* honoring parents, justice in the court, and helping the resident alien and the poor. Although not all of these laws could have been promulgated in the desert, as, for example, the festivals which presuppose an agricultural background, most of them, especially those of the religious-social sphere, had a Mosaic background.

Moses' legislative action seems to have been concerned with the cultic as well as the social aspect of Israel's life, and his main aim was the crystallization of Israel's tribal society by means of a reform. The exact nature of the reform is unclear, but in the light of social reforms in the Mesopotamian society at the end of the third millennium and the beginning of the second millennium B.C.E. (see Weinfeld, *Deuteronomy* . . ., in bibl., 150ff.), it seems that the reform included cultic regulations and social measures necessary for the new reality they were going to face. This legislation was authorized by a covenant with God (Ex. 24), a procedure found in the reform of Urukagina, the prince of Lagash revelation not mentioned in JE or D. According to P, on the eighth day of the dedication of the Tabernacle the Glory of YHWH appeared to all the people, who thereupon shouted and prostrated themselves (Lev. 9:23–24). This revelation takes place at the time when the fire comes forth from before YHWH to consume the sacrifices. This fire is understood as an expression of divine approval of the Tabernacle and of the orders of service carried on therein. Thus, in place of a description of a revelation related to the giving of laws to a nation, the author of P describes a revelation related to the dedication of the Tabernacle or to God's coming to dwell among Israel (cf. Ex. 25:8; 29:45).

(13) JE and D command "the instruction of the children" (Ex. 12:26–27; 13:8–15; Deut. 6:20–25), which bears the character of a catechism aimed at inculcating in the younger generation a religious national education by means of recounting the event of the Exodus from Egypt. However, there is a significant difference between the two sources. In JE the "instruction" is connected with the Passover ceremonies and the sacrifice of the firstborn, the ceremony serving as both educational motive and means. The child is aroused to question by the uniqueness of these ceremonies and the ceremony serves as a fitting opportunity for an educative answer. In D the "instruction" is divorced from all ceremony. The child asks not about the Passover service or the firstborn sacrifice but about the "exhortations, laws, and rules" which the Israelites were commanded to fulfill (Deut. 6:20). The question is not connected with the festival. It can be asked on any occasion.

(14) With regard to the scope of the Promised Land, D follows JE and speaks of a land which extends from "the wilderness and the sea [the Red Sea] to the Euphrates" (Gen. 15:18; Ex. 23:31 (=JE); Deut. 1:7; 11:24). P fixes the northern boundary at Lebo-Hamath (Num. 13:21; 34:8). In the historical documents of the periods of territorial expansion both types of border designations are found (II Sam. 8:3=I Chron. 18:3; I Kings 5:4 on the one hand, and I Kings 8:65 and II Kings 14:25 on the other). Under consideration here is not a historical development but rather versions which stem from different circles.

(15) In the episode of the spies' sin and the rebellion of Korah (Num. 13–17) D follows JE. According to JE, the spies reached Wadi Eshcol in the vicinity of Hebron. The faithful one among the spies was Caleb who indeed received Hebron as a reward (Num. 14:24; cf. Josh. 14:6ff.). In Deuteronomy 1:24, 36 a similar picture is portrayed. P, however, extends the reconnoitered area to Lebo-Hamath (Num. 13:21) and, accordingly, joins Joshua, conqueror of the entire land, to Caleb, thus promising both of them entry into the land (14:30). JE records the rebellion of Dathan and Abiram against Moses and their punishment: the earth swallows them up (Num. 16). D also mentions Dathan and Abiram in Deuteronomy 11:6 as well as the ground which opened up its mouth to swallow them. In contrast, P, which notes here a sacral offense and not a civil rebellion, speaks about Korah and his group who opposed the Aaronide priesthood and about their being burned by a fire from God because they sacrificed incense illegally (Num. 16:35; 17:5). This recalls the episode of Nadab and Abihu in Leviticus 10:1–2.

The Tradition Underlying the Sources—Form Criticism. In spite of differences and contradictions between the various sources of the Pentateuch a common underlying legal and historical tradition can be discerned. Scholars even applied a nomenclature to this tradition. Thus M. Noth (*Ueberlieferungsgeschichtliche . . .*, see bibl.) names it G (=*gemeinsame Grundlage*), implying an ancient written source, while E. A. Speiser (*Genesis*, see bibl.) designates it T (=tradition), considering it the living sacred history of the Israelites as had been told by them in pre-Davidic times.

There is no doubt that the themes recurring in all the sources, such as the promises to the Patriarchs, the Exodus, law and covenant at Sinai, and the Conquest, belong to the ancient sacred lore of Israel of the pre-monarchical period. It has even been suggested that these themes constituted a kind of national credo that was recited periodically in the sacred cities of ancient Israel, especially in Shechem, the northern religious center where Joshua established the covenant (Josh. 24) and where religious ceremonies of various kinds were held (Deut. 27; Josh. 8:30–35). The recapitulation of the past in Joshua 24 and in Deuteronomy 26:5–9 indeed support this thesis. The events mentioned there are: the promise of the land to the Patriarchs, the enslavement in Egypt, the liberation by means of miraculous deeds of the Lord, and finally the inheritance of the land.

These are indeed the main themes around which the pentateuchal history revolves. What is missing, however, is the Sinai tradition which is so central in the Pentateuch. This led some scholars to believe that the Sinai narrative cycle (Ex. 19–24, 32–34) is a late interpolation and that the genuine scheme of the sacred history was: Patriarchs, Exodus, and Conquest (cf. G. Von Rad, *The Problem of the Hexateuch*, in bibl.). However, this supposition is based on a misunderstanding. The recitation of the gracious deeds of God at the Shechem convocation in Joshua 24 or the credo which accompanies the offerings of the firstfruits in Deuteronomy 26 are aimed at strengthening Israel's loyalty to its God. There is no room in this context, therefore, for the demand of loyalty or observance of the law, i.e., the obligation. It is only in Nehemiah 9:13–14 that the Sinai theme, that is the imposition of the law, is considered a privilege and therefore counted among the merciful deeds. In the literature of the First Temple, however, rigid distinction is made between the description of the benevolence of God toward Israel and the demand to keep the Law. There is no place, therefore, for the motive of the Sinai covenant in those recitals and, consequently, no justification for taking out the Sinai tradition from the genuine scheme of the pentateuchal history. On the contrary, the references to Sinai in the old poems (Judg. 5:5; Ps. 68:9, etc.) seem to indicate that the Sinai theme was deeply rooted in ancient Israelite tradition. It is not easy to delineate the evolution of these themes and to trace their development systematically. However, some basic genuine elements are still traceable.

THE PATRIARCHAL THEME. The stories of the Patriarchs reflect a situation of nomadic families infiltrating the land of Canaan and living on the outskirts of the Canaanite cities such as Shechem, Beth-El, Hebron, and Beer-Sheba (cf. e.g., Gen. 23; 33:18–20). Although the Patriarchs are described as worshiping their personal familial god (cf. the terms "the God of my father" and "the God of Abraham, Isaac, and Jacob"; and see M. Haran, in: *Annual of the Swedish Theological Institute*, 4 (1965), 12ff.) which they apparently brought with them from their homeland, they gradually identified this god with that of their Canaanite neighbors, the God *'El*, the head of the pantheon in the Canaanite religion. In contrast to their personal familial god who is not related to any particular location (compare also "*'El Shaddai*—which is most probably identical with *bēl šadê*, the god of the Western Semite nomadic tribes in the Haran area—which is also not tied to any location), the divine names compounded with *El* and found only in Genesis, such as *'El 'Elyon* (14:18, 22) *'El Ro'i* (16:13) *'El 'Olam* (21:33) *'El-Bet-'El* (31:13; 35:7), *'El 'Elohei Yisra'el* (33:20), are affiliated with the old Canaanite sites: Jerusalem, Shechem, Beth-El, and Beer-Sheba. Especially instructive in this respect is the episode in Genesis 14 where Abraham gives a tithe to Melchizedek the king of Salem

Deuteronomic Code is not sold by her father as in Exodus, but like the slave, the "brother," is rather independent and sells her labor. Thus there is no difference between the law of the slave and that of the maidservant. The Deuteronomic lawgiver obligates the owner to reward the slave and maidservant who are liberated from his service with generous grants, mentioning the Israelites' liberation from Egypt in this connection. No mention of this is made in the Book of the Covenant. A significant change of a different type is the section on taking the slave, whose ear is pierced with an awl, "before God" (Ex. 21:6), which was omitted from the parallel law in D. The reason for the omission stems from the centralization of the cult which excludes the existence of "houses of God" throughout the land.

(2) The law of kidnapping found in Exodus 21:16 does not recur in Deuteronomy 24:7, but the general style of the Covenant Code has undergone a national reformulation: "kidnapping a fellow Israelite." The parenthetic phrase "you will sweep out evil from your midst," which is unique to D, is appended to the law.

(3) The casuistic laws dealing with injuries, theft, and damage to property (Ex. 21:18–22; 16) were omitted from D since they are not the concern of a religious-moral code (see *Deuteronomy). The only laws from this section which remained in D are the *lex talionis,* "punishment in kind" (Ex. 21:23–25), and the law of seducing a virgin (22:15–16). The *lex talionis* was utilized by Deuteronomy in the law of the conspiring witness (and see above) and the law of the seducer of a virgin, which in the Covenant Code embodies only a financial matter (loss of the bride-price to the father), but became in D a moral problem (Deut. 22:28–29) and was included in the code for this reason (and see above).

(4) The law of the sorceress in Exodus 22:17 was broadened and developed in Deuteronomy (18:9–13) while the ban of the idolater merited a separate chapter in Deuteronomy (ch. 13; 17:2–7).

(5) The Covenant Code forbids the Israelite to wrong or afflict the resident alien (Ex. 22:20–22; 23:9). The author of Deuteronomy, in contrast, not only enjoins the Israelite to refrain from discriminating against the resident alien, but also exhorts the Israelite to love him (10:19) and to be solicitous for his welfare.

(6) The Covenant Code commands the creditor who has taken a debtor's garment as surety to restore it to the debtor by sundown so that he may cover himself with it at night (Ex. 22:25–26). According to the Deuteronomic law, however, the creditor is also denied the right to select what article he wishes as surety (24:6, 17) and is even forbidden to enter the debtor's house to collect it (24:11).

(7) The Covenant Code ordains that that which has been torn by beasts, *ṭerefah,* which Israelites are forbidden to eat for sacral reasons, should be cast to the dogs (Ex. 22:30). The Deuteronomic law, on the other hand, ever attentive to the needs of indigent persons, enjoins the Israelite to give the carcass *(nevelah)* to the resident alien (14:21). The humanistic tendency becomes clear in the light of the juxtaposition of the resident alien and the foreigner. The author enjoins the giving of the carcass to the resident alien, but the selling of it to the foreigner, who was usually involved in trade and commerce.

(8) Exodus 23:24 ordains that a stray animal must be returned to its rightful owner. The Deuteronomic legislator, however, extends this law to garments and all types of lost articles (22:3), and exhorts the finder not to ignore the lost object but to take it home with him and keep it until it is sought by its owner (22:2–3).

(9) The laws of just judgment (Ex. 23:1–3, 6–8) were developed in Deuteronomy (16:18–20; 17:8–13; 19:15–21; 24:17–18; 25:1–3), although in Deuteronomy 16:19 there are still signs of dependence on the Covenant Code.

(10) The laws of release, festivals, and sacred gifts (Ex. 23: 10–19; cf. 34:18–26) and their connection with the codes of P and D have been discussed above. It should only be noted here that D and JE are similar as regards the absence of exact dates for the festivals (other than the Feast of Unleavened Bread in JE and the Passover in D; for חֹדֶשׁ הָאָבִיב *(ḥodesh ha-ʾaviv)*—Ex. 23:15; 34:18; Deut. 16:1–3, all of which passages stress the importance of the exact date —must surely mean "the new moon of Abib," as Ehrlich and others have observed) since both are popular sources, unlike P which represents the priestly institution and must therefore be especially concerned with calendrical and other matters pertaining to the implementation of cultic ceremonies. The same is the case with the laws concerning Rosh Ha-Shanah and the Day of Atonement which are mentioned in neither D nor JE. As has already been pointed out, these are Temple festivals in which the people do not play any active role. The laws in Exodus 23:15, 18 (=34:18, 25) connected with the Feast of Unleavened Bread and the Paschal sacrifice may be traced in Deuteronomy 16:1–4, but they are formulated here according to D's particular approach. In the Covenant Code and in P there still exists a separation between the Feast of Unleavened Bread and Passover (cf. Ex. 23:15 with 18; Ex. 34:18 with 25; in P: Ex. 12:1–14 with 15–20 and Lev. 23:5: "a Passover offering to the Lord" (פֶּסַח לה'), 23:6: "the Feast of Unleavened Bread to the Lord" (חַג הַמַּצּוֹת)). In contrast, D combines both festivals and attempts to create a single one. For this purpose it interpolates the section on the law of unleavened bread in the middle of the law of the Passover offering, which appears very artificial. The phrase "you shall not eat anything leavened with it" at the beginning of 16:3 refers to the Passover sacrifice and from the parallels in the Covenant Code it can be learned that this prohibition goes with that of leaving the flesh of the sacrifice until morning (Ex. 23:18; 34:25), repeated in Deuteronomy 16 at the end of verse 4. Indeed, if this part dealing with unleavened and leavened bread (from "seven days you shall eat unleavened bread" (שִׁבְעַת יָמִים תֹּאכַל מַצּוֹת ...) to "no leaven shall be found with you ... seven days" (וְלֹא־יֵרָאֶה לְךָ שְׂאֹר בְּכָל־גְּבֻלְךָ שִׁבְעַת יָמִים)) is taken out of verses 3–4, there remains a consecutive account of the Passover sacrifice which parallels the passages in the Covenant Code. The section on unleavened bread is taken from the Covenant Code (Ex. 23:15), while the section on leaven is from Exodus 13:7, and is perhaps influenced by Exodus 12:15, 19 (=P).

(11) D and JE both enjoin pilgrimage to the holy sites (Ex. 23:17; 34:23; Deut. 16:16), which is not found in P. This omission too can be explained by the special nature of P. This commandment is directed only toward the common people as against the priests, who dwelt in the temples all year long. Therefore, the sources intended for the common people stress this precept, while the author of P, who is concerned primarily with temple rituals and their procedures, does not speak of the pilgrimages ,which are, by their very nature, a concern of the masses. He talks instead about the ceremonies and sacrifices connected with these festivals (see Lev. 23:9–21; Num. 28–29).

(12) Another problem, which brings out the difference in the points of view of the sources under consideration is the matter of the Sinaitic revelation. JE and D speak a great deal about this, while P does not deal with it at all. Even if it is said that P regards this event as self-explanatory and even if consideration is given to the fact that he mentions laws given on Mt. Sinai, it is still difficult to explain his silence about such an important event. On the other hand, the author of P preserves for us the account of another kind of

שֵׁם ה׳	כְּבוֹד ה׳
שִׁכֵּן שְׁמוֹ	שָׁכַן
אֲרוֹן הַבְּרִית	אֲרוֹן הָעֵדֻת
לֻחוֹת הַבְּרִית	לֻחוֹת הָעֵדֻת
אֶרֶץ הַכְּנַעֲנִי וגו׳	אֶרֶץ כְּנָעַן
וּבִעַרְתָּ הָרָע מִקִּרְבֶּךָ/מִיִּשְׂרָאֵל	וְנִכְרְתָה הַנֶּפֶשׁ הַהִיא מֵעַמֶּיהָ/מִיִּשְׂרָאֵל
הָיָה בוֹ חֵטְא	נָשָׂא חֶטְאוֹ

Some of the differences can be explained on a theological basis, e.g., "Glory of God" (כְּבוֹד ה׳) in contrast to "name of God" (שֵׁם ה׳) and "[God] dwelt" (שָׁכַן) as opposed to "caused God's name to dwell" (שִׁכֵּן; see Divine *Presence). Others can be explained on a sociological basis, e.g., the use of *moshav, ʿedah, maṭṭeh, ge'ullah,* which indicate a patriarchal background, in contrast to *shaʿar, kahal (qahal), sheveṭ, pidyon,* which indicate a more socially developed background. The provincial background of P becomes evident in comparing Leviticus 26 with Deuteronomy 28 (see above). In this regard it is significant that D makes no mention of not working the land during the Sabbatical Year, which is so basic in Leviticus 25–26. In contrast, it places special emphasis on the release of debts, which is important in an urban society. Another significant fact in this connection is the role played by the foreigner (נָכְרִי), in D. As is known, foreigners acted as traders in ancient Israel and it is against the background of buying and selling that they are portrayed in D (14:21; 15:3; 23:21; 29:21; see EM, 5 (1968), 866–7).

Relation of P to JE. P shares common characteristics with JE, particularly in relation to the ancient institutions which underwent changes later on as a consequence of the reform presented by D.

(1) According to P, Moses built the Tabernacle, i.e., the Tent of Meeting, in the wilderness. Already at that time the Israelites were admonished not to perform any type of slaughter outside "the entrance of the Tent of Meeting" (Lev. 17:1–9). Thus, according to this view, the Tent of Meeting continued to exist in Palestine after the settlement and was finally transferred by Solomon to the House of God in Jerusalem (I Kings 8:4). JE also assumes the existence of the Tent of Meeting in the wilderness, but its character is different from that in P. It is not located within the camp but is outside the camp (Ex. 33:7–11; Num. 12:4; Deut. 31:14), and, in addition, it serves primarily an oracular rather than a cultic function. D makes no mention of the "Tent of Meeting" (Deut. 31:14 belongs to the JE source, and see below), and even explicitly declares that in the wilderness the Israelites acted "every man as he pleases" (Deut. 12:8) in relation to the cult, i.e., there was no organized cultic institution before they arrived at "the rest and the inheritance" (i.e., the time of David and Solomon; cf. II Sam. 7:1ff.; I Kings 3:2; 8:56).

(2) The Ark which stood within the Tent of Meeting served, according to P, as a dwelling place for God; the cherubim above it served as a kind of seat for God and the Ark was a footstool for His feet (Ex. 25:10–22; see *Ark of the Covenant; *Cherub), and in fact the commandment to build the Ark introduces the section on the building of the Sanctuary in the Priestly Source. According to JE, too, the Ark serves as God's dwelling place, and its location within the Israelite camp attests to God's presence among the Israelites (Num. 10:33–36; 14:44; cf. Josh. 3–4; 6:1ff., etc.). In contrast, D makes no mention of the cherubim and the Ark's function as God's dwelling place; its function according to D is solely to serve as a repository for the tablets and the scroll of the Law (Deut. 10:1–5; 31:25–26). Furthermore, from the material taken from JE which the Deuteronomist incorporates in his composition he omits the Ark wherever it appears in its original function as the seat of God (Deut. 1:33, 42; see also Divine *Presence).

(3) The laws of Passover in JE and P are identical (Ex. 12:1–14 (=P); 21–23 (=JE)). In both sources the Passover sacrifice is of sheep and the ceremony is performed in the house, centering around the sprinkling of the blood on the lintel and doorposts. D transforms the Passover into a public sacrifice brought from both sheep and cattle, and the domestic ceremony disappeared completely (Deut. 16:1–8).

There is a similarity in the laws of the firstborn as they appear in JE and P as well. Both sources mention three types of firstborn: the firstborn of man, of a pure animal, and of an impure animal (Ex. 13; 22:28–29; 34:19–20; Lev. 27:26–27; Num. 18:15–18). D no longer mentions the firstborn of man and of impure animals, but only the firstborn of pure animals (Deut. 15:19–23). P and JE both agree that the firstborn is to be set apart for the sacral sphere. D enjoins the eating of the firstborn by its owner in the precincts of the central Temple (Deut. 15:19–20). However, there is a difference in this matter between JE and P. According to JE, the firstborn of a pure animal is given to God (Ex. 22:28), which is explained in Exodus 13:15 as a sacrifice to God, but according to P, the firstborn is given to the priest who makes it into a sacrifice (Num. 18:15–18). JE commands that the firstborn of man be redeemed (Ex. 13:13, 15; 34:20), but does not explicitly state whether the redemption is accomplished by means of money. In contrast, P names an exact price for the purpose of redemption, namely, "five shekels" (Num. 18:15–16).

(4) JE and P are similar in regard to laws of the Sabbatical Year, both commanding that the land shall not be worked during that year and its fruits be left ownerless so that the poor and even the beasts of the field should be able to eat from them (Ex. 23:10–11; Lev. 25:1–7). A slight difference occurring in P in relation to JE is that P allows the owners too to enjoy the ownerless crop (D, as has been indicated, does not mention the law of releasing the land). On the other hand, P adds the Jubilee Year. During the Jubilee, as during the Sabbatical Year, the land is not to be worked and, according to P, this year serves as a year of freedom, i.e., of the liberation of slaves and the return of lands to their owners (Lev. 25:8ff.).

Relation of D to JE. There is a great similarity between D and JE in regard to institutions, laws, and historical traditions. Indeed, both sources have a popular character, in contrast to P which is rooted in the priestly world. The laws of D manifest a dependence on the *Book of the Covenant—the JE code (Ex. 21–23; see also *Deuteronomy). D, however, changes numerous laws in accordance with the new reality and its unique humanitarian approach. Following is a brief review of the principal changes:

(1) In the law of the slave and maidservant in Deuteronomy 15:12–18, there is a stylistic dependence on Exodus 21:1–11, though in D the law underwent a very basic revision. The casuistic section of this law in the Covenant Code (Ex 21:3–4, 8–11), which deals with the owner's rights in regard to the wife and children of the slave as well as the personal rights of the maidservant, was totally omitted from D, since D does not view the slave and maidservant as a property which is linked to the master's house, as does the Covenant Code. Their status is defined as hirelings (Deut. 15:18) who sell their labor. Their personal affairs, such as the problem of the slaves' wife or maidservant's husband, are not at all subject to negotiation with their masters. The word "master," which is mentioned six times in the Covenant Code, is not mentioned even once in the laws of the slave in Deuteronomy, which is not insignificant. The slave is here called the "brother" of his employer who, thus, cannot view himself as a "master." The maidservant in the

(2400 B.C.E.), who made a covenant with his god Ningirsu concerning his social reform.

Although the Sinai tradition occupies a central place in the pentateuchal legal traditions, one can still recognize traces of other traditions about law promulgation. Exodus 15:25 preserves information about the promulgation of law in Marah, while Genesis 14:7 (Kadesh = En-Mishpat, "the well of judgment") alludes to a tradition about the promulgation of law in Kadesh. Kadesh-Barnea has for other reasons been considered to be a tribal religious center where the Israelites spent a very long time (Deut. 1:46). Shechem, too, was considered a place of covenant and law promulgation (Josh. 24:26). Thus, it becomes clear that initially the tradition of Sinai as the place of law promulgation existed side by side with other traditions, and became the exclusive scene of revelation only in a later period, which, however, was before the United Kingdom.

There are differences in the presentation of the Sinai revelation in the various sources. JE depicts the scene of revelation in a corporeal manner. God comes down upon the mountain in sight of all the people (Ex. 19:11, 17ff.), and the people became frightened, fell back, and stood at a distance (Ex. 20:18ff.). The P source shifts the revelation to the scene of the dedication of the Tabernacle (Lev. 9) and describes the event in a way characteristic of its priestly imagery: on the day of the consecration of the Tabernacle and the ordination of the priests, the *Kavod* (see Divine *Presence) appears to all the people . . ., the people shouted and prostrated themselves (Lev. 9:6, 23–24). The D source follows JE, but frees the scene from its mythological features by having only God's fire come down on the mountain and God Himself stay in heaven (Deut. 4:36). The basic event, however, the revelation on Sinai, is taken for granted in all the sources and in all of them is linked to Moses. There is no justification therefore to deprive this tradition of its Mosaic background. [Mo.W.]

THE TRADITIONAL VIEW

The traditional view of the Pentateuch is in the most striking and most extreme contrast to the critical theories adumbrated above. Whereas the critical theory depends upon the assumption that the Pentateuch (in particular) is a composite work consisting of different documents, composed at different times and edited into a composite whole, the traditional view is fundamentally based upon the belief that the whole of the Pentateuch, the *Torah proper, is a unitary document, divinely revealed, and entirely written by Moses with the exception of the last eight verses of Deuteronomy, which record the death of Moses and, according to one opinion, were written by Joshua (BB 15a; according to the other they were written by Moses at the dictation of God "with tears" *(dema)*, but Elijah Gaon of Vilna renders the word "mixed up"). In other words, on the death of Moses the whole of the Pentateuch was complete, having been divinely revealed. Nor can any rigid doctrine be laid down as to the exact manner of communication of this revelation. Only human terms can be employed to convey the fact of revelation; that is the wider meaning of the well-known phrase, "the Torah speaks in human language" *(dibberah torah ki-leshon benei adam)* and this the only method available, is obviously inadequate to convey the mystery of *mattan torah* ("the giving of the Torah"), of the confrontation of Moses with God. The almost radical explanation of Ibn Ezra (in Ex. 20:2) as to the differences between the two versions of the Decalogue (Ex. 20 and Deut. 5), in which he maintains that the variations in wording and spelling are unimportant, is as an acceptable doctrine as the talmudic explanation of the alternative openings of the fifth commandment by saying: *zakhor ve-shamor be-dibbur eḥad ne'emru* ("remember [the Sabbath day] and keep [the Sabbath day] were uttered simultaneously"). All that can be said with certainty is that, as explicitly stated in Numbers 12:6–8, the manner of the divine communication to Moses differed from that to any other prophet. whereas the other prophets received their messages while their normal cognitive faculties were in a state of suspense, Moses alone received that communication while in full possession of all his normal cognitive faculties, "mouth to mouth, even apparently and not in dark speeches" (Num. 12:8), or, even more explicitly: "And the Lord spoke unto Moses face to face as a man speaketh to his friend" (Ex. 33:11). "Mouth to mouth" and "face to face" illustrate the inevitable anthropomorphism involved in using human terms to convey the mystery of divine communication. The unitary belief is clearly expressed by Maimonides. His formulation of the eighth of the 13 Principles (commentary to Sanh. 10 (11): 1; for the complete text see JQR, 19 (1907), 53f.) is: "That the Torah has been revealed from heaven: This implies our belief that the whole of the Torah found in our hands this day is the Torah that was handed down by Moses and that is all of divine origin. By this I mean that the whole of the Torah came to him from before God in a manner which is metaphorically called 'speaking'; but the real nature of the communication is unknown to everybody except to Moses to whom it came. In handing down the Torah, Moses was like a scribe writing from dictation the whole of it, its chronicles, its narratives, and its precepts." In his code Maimonides defines the person who denies the Torah as he "who says even of one verse or of one word that it is not of divine origin, or that Moses wrote it on his authority" (Yad, Teshuvah 3:8 based on Sanh. 99a). It is stated more succinctly in the prayer book formulation of the eighth of the 13 Principles of Faith of Maimonides: "I believe with a perfect faith that the whole Torah now in our possession is the same that was given to Moses our teacher."

Traditional Judaism rejected not only the Higher Criticism, i.e., the documentary theory, but also the Lower Criticism—textual criticism. With the sole exception of insignificant plene and defective spelling, the masoretic text is regarded as the only authoritative and authorized text of the Pentateuch. Insofar as textual criticism is concerned, one is on solid ground in maintaining the accuracy of the masoretic texts. The Sif. Deut. 356 states that "three scrolls were found in the Temple . . . In one of them they found written . . . in the other two they found written . . . the sages discarded the reading of the one and adopted that of the two: and ultimately one approved text was deposited in the Temple archives" (MK 3:4; Kelim 15:6), and a special group of readers, who were paid from the Temple funds, checked the text from time to time (TJ, Shek. 4:3, 48a). With loving care and sacred devotion the subsequent generations of scribes jealously guarded every letter of the text. Detailed regulations were laid down in order to ensure that the copying of the scrolls should be free from human error (see **Sefer Torah*). There has been nothing like it in the history of literature or religion, and in this respect the masoretic text stands indisputably in a class by itself. It could not under any circumstances be expected that those who did not accept the supreme sanctity of the revealed word of the Torah, whether they were Alexandrian Jews who had come under the influence of Greek philosophy, or the sects of the Dead Sea who rejected the *halakhah* of the Pharisees, should have the same approach of *noli me tangere* with regard to the handing down of every letter of the Torah. To them there was no harm in adding, diminishing, or amending for the sake of greater clarity or preconceived theological doctrines. In addition, the texts found in the Dead Sea Scrolls, which are a thousand years earlier than the textus receptus of *Ben Asher of 975, substantially confirm the accuracy of the present text and can be said on the whole to have demolished the ingenious emendations of two centuries of textual critics. One is therefore justified in regarding the traditional text as the most exact and authoritative. As Lieberman comments, "the sacred text of the Bible was handled by Jews, whose general reverence and awe in religious matters need not be stressed." To the sphere of the establishment of the correct text belongs the system of *keri* and *ketiv* (words written in one way but read in another), **tikkunei soferim*, dates on certain letters, and special signs (for this see Lieberman in bibl.).

With regard to the *tikkunei soferim*, Lieberman comes to the conclusion, after a close examination of the relevant sources, that they represent a later stage than that of the *keri* and the *ketiv*. This latter system modified the reading without altering the text, whereas the *tikkunei soferim* actually changed letters but only in order to remove indelicate, gross anthropomorphic, and unworthy expressions from the text, and their number is minute. It has been suggested that the very fact of the difference between the *keri* and the *ketiv* is evidence of the authenticity of the text, which was regarded as so inviolable that instead of being altered to remove difficulties, the emendations were, so to speak, relegated to the margin. The rabbis had a profound and extensive knowledge of every word, jot, and tittle of the Bible. The statement of the Talmud (Kid. 30a) that the *soferim* were so called because they counted *(soferim)* every letter of the Torah (and the passage proceeds to give the statistical results of that counting) expresses only the mechanical aspect of their intense preoccupation with the sacred text. Every word, every expression, and every deviation from the norm was made the subject of profound study. That study, however, went far beyond linguistic research; the Pentateuch was the textbook from which the whole corpus of *halakhah* had to be derived. They were therefore perfectly and acutely aware of the contradictions, real and apparent, in the text. But they resolved those contradictions by a complicated, but largely logical system of interpretations (see *Hermeneutics). Nor were differences in style unnoticed by them. The Midrash (Deut. R. 1:1) has a beautiful passage on the "healing which comes to the tongue" of the person who occupies himself with Torah, which is directly based on the unique style of Deuteronomy.

The justification on scientific and scholarly grounds of the theory of the unitary nature of the Pentateuch maintained by traditional Judaism is not nearly as satisfactory as that of the textual criticism of the text. Generally speaking, traditional scholars have not faced up to the challenge of the Documentary Hypothesis, and instead of accepting its challenge and answering it, have taken refuge in theological dogmatism. Almost the only attempt to face up to its challenge was that of David *Hoffmann in his brilliant *Die Wichtigsten Instanzen gegen die Graf-Wellhausensche Hypothese* and his biblical commentaries. He not only attempts to demolish the critical theory, but maintains, on grounds of scholarship, the doctrine of the unity of the Pentateuch. Other and more popular attempts, for example those of J. H. Hertz (see bibl.), constitute special pleading and suffer from the fact that they tend to create the false impression that the growing number of scholars who call into question the validity of the Wellhausen theory and its followers—such as J. Robertson *(The Early Religion of Israel)*, J. Orr *(The Problem of the Old Testament)*, W. L. Baxter *(Sanctuary and Sacrifice)*, Y. Kaufmann (*Toledot ha-Emunah ha-Yisre'elit*, 1937), and U. Cassuto (*The Documentary Hypothesis*, 1961; *Commentary on the Book of Genesis*, 1961–64; *A Commentary on the Book of Exodus*, 1967)—ipso facto maintain the traditional view of the unity of the Pentateuch, an assumption which is at variance with the facts.

On the other hand, the documentary theory, or at least the evidence that the Pentateuch is not a unitary document, has been so convincing to many Orthodox scholars that various attempts have been made to adopt a syncretistic view which combines an acceptance of this theory with that of the implications which derive from the belief in the unitary nature of the Pentateuch, upon which traditional Judaism is based. The most determined exponent is L. Jacobs, who quotes approvingly the following statement of J. Abelson: "The correct perspective of the matter seems to be as follows: the modern criticism of the Bible on the one hand, and faith in Judaism on the other hand, can be regarded as two distinct compartments. For criticism, even at its best, is speculative and tentative, something always liable to be modified or proved wrong and having to be replaced by something else. It is an intellectual exercise, subject to all the doubts and guesses which are inseparable from such exercises. But our accredited truths of Judaism have their foundations more deeply and strongly laid than all this. And our faith in them not only need be uninjured by our faith in criticism, but need not be affected by the latter at all. The two are quite consistent and can be held simultaneously." An even more striking attempt at such a syncretism which makes possible a complete acceptance of the critical theory with a somewhat mystic view of the belief in the unitary theory has been made by a strictly Orthodox modern scholar, M. Breuer (see bibl.). [L.I.R.]

Bibliography: General: Wellhausen, Proleg; idem, *Die Composition des Hexateuchs* (1899); J. E. Carpenter and G. Harford-Battersby, *The Hexateuch According to the Revised Version*, 2 vols. (1900); S. R. Driver, *Introduction to the Literature of the Old Testament* (1913[9]); J. Skinner, *The Divine Names in Genesis* (1914); J. Morgenstern, in: HUCA, 4 (1927), 1–138; R. Pfeiffer, in: ZAW, 48 (1930), 66–73; J. Pedersen, in: ZAW, 49 (1931), 161–81; G. von Rad, *Die Priesterschrift im Hexateuch* (1934); G. Hoelscher, *Die Anfaenge der hebraeischen Geschichtsschreibung* (1942); idem, *Geschichtsschreibung in Israel* (1952); R. North, in: H. H. Rowley (ed.), *The Old Testament and Modern Study* (1951), 48–83; A. Bentzen, *Introduction to the Old Testament* (1952[2]); Kaufmann Y., Toledot, 1 (1952); Kaufmann Y., Religion; O. Eissfeldt, *Hexateuch Synopse* (1962); idem, *The Old Testament, An Introduction* (1965); E. A. Speiser, *Genesis* (1964), introduction; M. Weinfeld, *Deuteronomy and the Deuteronomic School* (1971). Traditio-Critical Approach: L. Rost, in: ZDPV, 76 (1943), 205–16; J. Pedersen, in: ZAW, 52 (1943), 161–75; U. Cassuto, in: *Kneset*, 8 (1943/44), 121–42; Noth, Ueberlief; idem, *Ueberlieferungsgeschichte Studien* (1943); G. von Rad, *Studies in Deuteronomy* (1953); idem, *The Problem of the Hexateuch and Other Essays* (1966); G. E. Mendenhall, in: BA, 17 (1954), 26–46, 50–76; W. Beyerlin, *Herkunft und Geschichte der aeltesten Sinaitraditionen* (1961); S. E. Loewenstamm, *Masoret Yezi'at Mizrayim be-Hishtalshelutah* (1965); H. B. Huffmon, in: CBQ, 27 (1965), 100–11; M. Weinfeld, in: JAOS, 90 (1970), 184–203. Law and Institutions: Wellhausen, Proleg; Kaufmann Y., Toledot, 1 (1952); Kaufmann Y., Religion; Alt, Kl Schr, 1 (1953), 278–332; M. Haran, in: *Scripta Hierosolymitana*, 8 (1961), 272–302; H. J. Kraus, *Gottesdienst in Israel* (1962[2]). Traditional View: L. Jacobs, *We Have Reason to Believe* (1957), 58–82; S. Lieberman, *Hellenism in Jewish Palestine* (1950), 20–82; M. Breuer, in: *De'ot*, 11 (1960), 18–25; 12 (1960), 12–27; J. H. Hertz (ed.), *The Pentateuch and Haftorah* (1929–36), various "additional notes" (*Sermons, Addresses and Studies*, 3 (1938), 99–104, 157–74, 198–214); J. Abelson, in: *Jewish Review* (1913), 483ff.; L. I. Rabinowitz, in: *Tradition*, 7 no. 1 (1965), 34–40; H. Rabbinowitz, *Harofe Haivri* (1965), 190–2.

PENTATEUCH, SAMARITAN, Hebrew text of the Pentateuch used by the *Samaritans. The first copy of the Samaritan Pentateuch to reach the hands of Western Bible

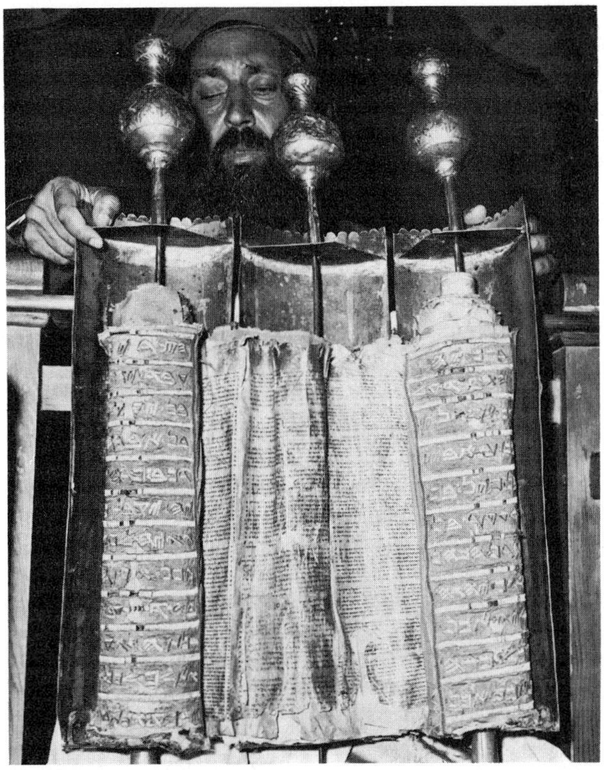

The oldest Samaritan Torah scroll. Courtesy Government Press Office, Tel Aviv.

scholars was that obtained in Damascus by Pietro della Valle in 1616. Subsequent travelers brought to Europe other copies of the Samaritan Pentateuch, Targum, and other Samaritan literature. The interest created among Bible scholars was considerable, and for a long time hopes were high that at last an older version or recension of the Hebrew Bible than that of the Masoretic Text had been recovered. The first edition of the Samaritan Pentateuch to be printed was that in the Paris Polyglot Bible of 1629–45 and the London Polyglot of 1657. These earliest editions and the improved one of Blayney (Oxford, 1790), based on several manuscripts, proved inadequate for the purpose of precise textual criticism. The edition of A. F. von Gall (Geissen, 1918, repr. 1966), based on a large number of manuscripts, made the task of careful textual study much easier. From the Polyglot editions until the time of W. *Gesenius (see below), there grew up a lively debate about the relative merits of the Samaritan Pentateuch and the Masoretic Text. Several attempts to draw conclusions from detailed comparative analysis of the two versions were made, but it was the monumental examination of them by Gesenius in 1815 *(De pentateuchi samaritani origine, indole et auctoritate commentatio philologico-critica)* that produced the most lasting effect. From then and for a century thereafter his verdict that the Masoretic Text was superior and prior held sway. Gesenius listed and analyzed the roughly 6,000 textual differences in terms of eight categories or classes: (1) grammatical revision by the Samaritan; (2) glosses and explanations introduced into the text; (3) emendation of words; (4) additional or corrected readings supplied from parallel passages; (5) larger additions and interpolations; (6) emendation of place names; (7) adjustment of forms of expression to the northern (Samaritan) dialect of Hebrew; and (8) a special category which included emendation of the verb (sing. or plur.) occurring with the Divine Name, removal of anthropomorphisms and anthropopathisms, etc. In addition he regarded the Samaritan orthography (especially the gutturals) as inadequate and due mainly to scribal carelessness. [Jo.Ma.]

The dictum of Gesenius holds true in its main points to this day. The text of the Samaritan Pentateuch always presents the *lectio facilio* against the more archaic and difficult forms of the Masoretic Text. Even a seemingly early form like *ʾatti* is in reality a late Aramaism. The Samaritan pronunciation of their Pentateuch, which is a sacred and zealously guarded tradition of the sect, shows clear affinity to the language of the Qumran Scrolls: (1) The above-mentioned personal pronoun *ʾatti,* which is the equivalent of *°at* in the Masoretic Text, is *ʾatti* also in the Scrolls; (2) The masoretic suffixes *-kem, -tem* are *-kemmah, -temmah* in the Scrolls. In the Samaritan Pentateuch they are spelled in the masoretic way but always pronounced like the longer forms found in the Scrolls; (3) The stress in the Samaritan pronunciations is penultimate (not ultimate like that denoted by the Tiberian tradition), which causes *šewa*-vowels of Masoretic Text to become full vowels like in the text of the Scrolls, e.g., Sedom (MT)=Shadem (Samaritan)=Sodom (Scrolls). From all this it can be concluded that the text of the Samaritan Pentateuch in its present form presents a later stage of development than the Masoretic Text. Its peculiarities do not reflect a special Ephraimitic dialect but represent the common Hebrew prevalent in Palestine between about the second century B.C.E. and the third century C.E. [Ay.L.]

The best-known difference of substance is the additional text regarded by the Samaritans as the tenth command of the Decalogue. After Exodus 20:14 [17] (and Deut. 5:18) the Samaritan Pentateuch has a lengthy addition which consists in the main of Deuteronomy 27:2, 3 (part), 4–7, and 11:30. This, it is generally agreed, is a deliberate Samaritan interpolation designed to provide support for their claim that Gerizim is "the chosen place." Connected with this is the Samaritan Pentateuch variant **בחר** *(baḥar)* against the Masoretic Text's **יבחר** *(yivḥar),* which occurs in all the relevant passages in Deuteronomy 12:5ff.—the claim being that Shechem had been chosen as the place of the Lord's sanctuary. On the other hand, R. H. Pfeiffer (in bibl., 102) represented the viewpoint of many students of Samaritanism when he cited the probability of a Judean attempt to minimize biblical support for the Samaritan claim for the priority and legitimacy of their temple on Gerizim. He also asserted that in their scrupulous regard for the sacred text the Samaritans left anti-Samaritan (pre-schism) additions untouched. "With utter disregard for geographical reality, the gloss in Deuteronomy 11:30 removes Gerizim and Ebal from the vicinity of Shechem (still attested in the reference to the terebinth of Moreh) to the Jordan Valley at Gilgal, near Jericho (cf. 27:12, 'when you have crossed over the Jordan'); similarly in Joshua 8:30–35 the altar was built on Gerizim [sic!] while the Israelites were still encamped at Gilgal." His explanation is that "The early account of the origin of the cult at Shechem (Deut. 11:29; 27:11–26) was thus first given a Deuteronomistic interpretation (in 11:26–28, 31–32; 27:7–10), then the scene was removed to Gilgal and connected with the famous stones there (27:1–4, 8), and finally, after the Samaritan schism, 'Gerizim' was changed to 'Ebal' in Deuteronomy 27:4 (where the Samaritan Pentateuch still reads 'Gerizim') and in Joshua 8:30." This assessment of a problematic Samaritan Pentateuch passage is supported by several scholars (e.g., O. Eissfeldt, in bibl.), who agree that both Judeans and Samaritans were forced to take defensive measures in order to maintain the supremacy of their rival claims. Another problem concerns the fact that the Septuagint often agrees with the Samaritan Pentateuch against the Masoretic Text. Some examples of this agreement are: Genesis 4:8, "Cain said to his brother Abel, 'Come, Let us go out into the field' " (the Masoretic Text lacks Cain's words); Genesis 47:21, "As for the people, he made slaves of them" (MT "As . . . he removed them to the cities"); in Exodus 12:40 the 430 years of the Israelite sojourn in Egypt include their sojourn in Canaan as well (SP-LXX add "and their fathers"). However, in most cases the Samaritan text agrees with the Masoretic against the Septuagint, as shown by B. K. Walthe. The following example of agreement between the Samaritan Pentateuch and the Septuagint introduces a type of the former's variant from the Masoretic Text that was used by Samaritan exegetes and theologians in later times as proof texts for their distinctive credal statements. Deuteronomy 32:35 contains the words "against the day [ליום] of vengeance and recompense" in contrast to the Masoretic Text's "vengeance is mine [לי] and recompense," in a difference comprising a masoretic omission or Samaritan addition of two Hebrew letters. This "proof text" is used for the Samaritan belief in the Day of Vengeance and Recompense after the Resurrection. An example of this sort of Samaritan Pentateuch variant is Genesis 3:19 (against MT); the latter reads "and to dust you shall return," while the former has "and to your dust Thou shall return," a difference of one Hebrew letter *(kaf)*. This variant is a "proof text" for the Samaritan teaching about the Resurrection. (The principal SP variants are included in BH in the *apparatus criticus*.)

Dating. Most authorities agree that the Samaritan Pentateuch, with its approximately 2,000 agreements with the Septuagint against the Masoretic Text, existed in the third century B.C.E., and it is likely that the old or proto-Palestinian text-type came to exist in three recensions, a Judean and a Samaritan soon after the time of Ezra (or a little earlier), and a Greek (LXX) in the third century. Pfeiffer (in bibl., 101) expresses a widely held view of the dating of the Samaritan Pentateuch when he writes: "We may infer . . . that the Samaritan community adopted the Pentateuch as its Bible soon after its canonization about 400 B.C. . . . " The Masoretic and Samaritan texts (in spite of their variants) were recensions of the final edition of the Pentateuch, as also the Septuagint. Evidence that the Samaritan Pentateuch existed in B.C.E. times is provided from another source. Among the Qumran discoveries from 1947 onward the text of some fragments of biblical manuscripts clearly resembles the Samaritan text-type. Here are some Samaritan-Qumran agreements occurring in the Book of Exodus: to the Divine Command in 7:16–18 the Samaritan text adds its execution by Moses and Aaron; the Qumran text has the latter statement. In 7:29 the Qumran text has the start of the Samaritan text's expansion. Similar textual traits are found in 8:19; 9:5; 9:19; and 11:2. The Samaritan and the Qumran text add "and he smote them" in 17:13. The omission of 29:21 and 30:1–10 is a feature of both texts. However, the Qumran fragment texts sometimes agree with the Samaritan, sometimes with the Septuagint against the Samaritan, and sometimes with the Masoretic against either or both the Samaritan and the Septuagint.

Manuscripts. The best-known copy of the Samaritan Pentateuch is the so-called "Abisha' (אבישע) Scroll," for which the Samaritan, since medieval times, have claimed a very ancient origin. The oldest part of this text was edited in 1959 by Pérez Castro. According to the colophon of the scroll itself the text was written by Abisha son of Phinehas, the great-grandson of Moses, in the 13th year after the Israelite conquest of Canaan. However, it is generally agreed that the scroll cannot have been written before the 12th century C.E. A fine scroll written in 1227 C.E. is a model exemplar of the best copies known. Written in gold letters, the scroll (roll) is wound around rollers of silver and has three parallel columns setting out the Hebrew, Aramaic (Targum), and Arabic versions in the one Samaritan script. The best-known manuscripts otherwise are not in roll form, but in book form, written on vellum or paper. There are no indications of vowel signs, but the text is divided into sentences and the whole into 964 paragraphs (Kiẓẓim = קצים, in other codices they number 966).

Script. On paleographic grounds, according to J. Purvis's investigation (1968), "the ancestry of the Samaritan script is to be traced ultimately to the cursive paleo-Hebrew of the sixth century B.C.E., although the direct parentage is the paleo-Hebrew of the late Hasmonean period" (in bibl., 36). There is no general accord about this, for there is a lack of evidence for the paleo-Hebrew script used in Samaria (or, for religious purposes, by the Samaritans) before the earliest-known Samaritan epigraphic materials, so that a complete history of the Samaritan script going back before Hasmonean times is not available. The Samaritan script, which is known in both uncial and cursive form, must have been in use at the time when Ezra introduced the "square" (אשורי) script for the Judean Bible. The Samaritan alphabet is the only descendant of the early Hebrew script which is still in use.

Versions. There seems to have once existed a Greek translation of the Samaritan Pentateuch (see Glaue and Rahlfs, in bibl.). Known as the *Samareitikon*, it was written after the Septuagint, by which it was influenced, but before Origen who refers to it. Its place of origin is unknown. A copy of the Samaritan Aramaic Targum was acquired for the first time by Pietro della Valle, along with the Hebrew text, in 1616. The Samaritans believe it to have been composed by Markah, i.e., in the fourth century C.E. According to J. Nutt (in bibl.), the Samaritans of his day believed it to have been the work of Nethanel (נתנאל;first century B.C.E.), but as there was a high priest of that name in the fourth century C.E., local tradition has probably confused the identification. The text is unsatisfactory in many respects, particularly in the orthography, and there are too few complete copies available for collation. The edition of Peterman-Vollers (1872) is the only complete one which is based on a number of manuscripts. The Aramaic of the Targum is similar to that of Markah's *Memar* and of the *Defter* (fourth century C.E.) of the Liturgy, and is undoubtedly Palestinian in type. The translation is literal and therefore comparable to the Targum of *Onkelos. The Arabic translation was made probably in the 13th century by Abu Said or (if he was only the reviser, as some think) by *Abu al-Ḥasan of Tyre in the 11th century (A. E. Cowley, in bibl., xxiv). This translation exists in several manuscripts. It is a fairly literal translation of the Hebrew (not the Targum), and some scholars have seen in it possible dependence on *Saadiah, but this is uncertain. The chief evaluation of the available texts was made by P. Kahle (in bibl., and subsequent articles) and L. Goldberg (in bibl.).

See also *Samaritan Language and Literature. [JO.MA.]

Bibliography: J. H. Peterman and C. Vollers, *Pentateuchus Samaritanus* (1872–91); J. Nutt, *Fragments of a Samaritan Targum* (1874); P. Kahle, *Die arabischen Bibeluebersetzungen* (1904), x–xiii; A. E. Cowley, *The Samaritan Liturgy* (1909), xxiii–xxiv; P. Glaue and A. Rahlfs, *Fragmente einer griechischen Uebersetzung des samaritanischen Pentateuchs* (1911); A. F. von Gall, *Der hebraeische Pentateuch der Samaritaner* (1914–18, 1963³); Ch. Heller, *The Samaritan Pentateuch, an Adaptation of the Massoretic Text* (1923); L. Goldberg, *Das samaritanisch Pentateuchtargum* (1935); R. H. Pfeiffer, *Introduction to the Old Testament* (1948), 101–2; P. Kahle, in: *Studia Orientalia Ioanni Pedersen* (1953), 188–92; O. Eissfeldt, *The Old Testament, an Introduction* (1965), 694–5, 782; J. Purvis, *The Samaritan Pentateuch and the Origin of the Samaritan Sect* (1968); R. Macuch, *Grammatik des samaritanischen Hebraeisch* (1969); Ẓ. Ben-Ḥayyim, *Ivrit ve-Aramit Nosaḥ Shomron*, 1 (1957), xxvii–xxviii.

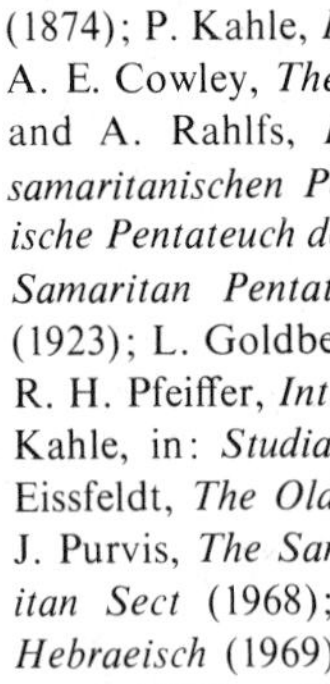

PENUEL (or **Peniel**; Heb. פְּנִיאֵל, פְּנוּאֵל), fortified city near the ford of the river Jabbok, where Jacob fought with the angel of the Lord and received the appellation Israel (Gen. 32:31). It appears with Succoth (with which it is also connected in the story of Jacob) as a city in Transjordan which refused to give food to Gideon and his men in their pursuit of the Midianites (Judg. 8:8); returning victorious, Gideon destroyed the tower of Penuel and slew the men of the city (Judg. 8:17). According to the last biblical reference to the place, it was built by Jeroboam I, king of Israel, after he built Shechem, apparently to be used as a capital for his lands beyond the Jordan (I Kings 12:25). Shishak captured Penuel in his campaign in the fifth year of Rehoboam, together with neighboring Succoth and Mahanaim (no. 53 on his list of conquered towns). It is now usually identified with the eastern mound of Tulūl al-Dhahab on the southern side of a bend in the Jabbok; the pottery on the site extends from the Late Bronze to the Byzantine periods. Some scholars suggest that both mounds of Tulūl al-Dhahab mark the site of Penuel, while others identify the western mound, on the northern side of the Jabbok, with Mahanaim (see *Mahanaim).

Bibliography: Albright, in: BASOR, 35 (1929), 12–13; Glueck, in: AASOR, 18–19 (1939), 232–4; de Vaux, in: RB, 47 (1938), 411–3; Press, Ereẓ, s.v.; Abel, Geog, 2 (1938), 406; Aharoni, Land, index.

[M.A.-Y.]

PENUELI (formerly **Pineles**), **SHEMUEL YESHAYAHU** (1904–1965), Hebrew critic and teacher. Born in Galicia, he taught at the Hebrew Teachers' Seminary in Vilna and settled in Ereẓ Israel in 1935. For 11 years he was the principal of the school at Nahalal, and later became the principal of the Givat ha-Sheloshah Teachers' Seminary. In 1954 he was appointed lecturer in literature at Tel Aviv University, subsequently becoming head of the department.

He published articles on literature and education. The literary critic's task, according to Penueli, is to uncover the author's subconscious as it is revealed in his works. Therefore, Penueli relied heavily on psychological theories, especially on Freud. His books on Hebrew literature include: *Demuyyot be-Sifrutenu ha-Ḥadashah* (1946); *Ḥayyim Hazaz* (1954); *Yeẓirato shel S. Y. Agnon* (1960); *Safrut ki-Feshutah* (1963); *Massah al ha-Yafeh she-be-Ommanut ha-Sifrut* (1965); *Brenner u-Gnessin ba-Sippur ha-Ivri shel Reshit ha-Me'ah ha-Esrim* (1965). He also co-edited the English anthology *Hebrew Short Stories,* 2 vols. (1965).

Bibliography: Kressel, Leksikon, 2 (1967), 645.

[G.K.]

PENZANCE, seaport in S.W. England. Jews trading with the fleet settled here in the mid-18th century and a small community was formed. In 1807 a synagogue was built in New Street, under the auspices of the merchant and distiller Lemon Hart (1768–1845), subsequently warden of the Great Synagogue in London. The most notable person in the intellectual life of the community was Solomon Ezekiel (1781–1867), who organized the "Penzance Hebrew Society for Promoting the Diffusion of Religious Knowledge" and carried on a vigorous running polemic against local conversionists. Toward the end of the 19th century, the community decayed. The synagogue was sold in 1906.

Bibliography: Roth, in: JC, Supplement (May and June 1933); idem, *Rise of Provincial Jewry* (1950).

[C.R.]

PE'OT (Heb. פֵּאוֹת; lit. "corners"), sidelocks grown in accordance with the prohibition of the Torah that "Ye shall not round the corners of your heads" (Lev. 19:27). The Talmud has interpreted this to mean that it is forbidden to "level the growth of hair on the temple from the back of the ears to the forehead" (Mak. 20b). The hair in this area may not be completely removed even with depilatory powder, scissors, or an electric shaver which may be used in shaving the face (see *Beard and Shaving). Although a negative precept, women are exempt from leaving *pe'ot* since the parallel prohibition against "marring the corners of the beard" (Lev. 19:27; Kid. 1:7; Kid. 35b) obviously does not extend to women. According to Maimonides a minimum of 40 hairs must be left for *pe'ot* (Yad, Avodat Kokhavim, 12:6). However, the Shulḥan Arukh (YD 181:9) rules in accordance with Rashi (Mak. 20a) that hair must be allowed to grow in front of the ears until it reaches the upper cheekbones (zygomatic arch). However, the maximum length of *pe'ot* has been determined by the custom of a particular time and place rather than by *halakhah.* The kabbalistic writings of Isaac *Luria attribute great significance to *pe'ot* because the numerical value (see **Gematria*) of *pe'ah,* 86, is the same as the numerical value of *Elohim* (i.e., God). It has become customary for Ḥasidim and Orthodox Yemenites to leave *pe'ot,* either short ones which are curled behind the ears or long ones hanging down at the sides of the head.

[ED.]

PEPPER (Heb. פִּלְפֵּל, *pilpel*), the fruit of the perennial creeping plant *Piper nigrum,* which grows in India and in the neighboring tropical regions. The Hebrew name, like its English one, is derived from the Sanskrit *pippali.* Probably it was first brought to Ereẓ Israel after the expeditions of Alexander the Great. R. Johanan notes that in former times pepper was not yet available for spicing roast meat and *roquet* was used instead (Er. 28b). Pepper was an expensive spice and sometimes the seeds of bitter vetch were used as a substitute (Eccles. R. 6:1). In the time of the Mishnah and the Talmud, people were very fond of pepper and attempts may have been made to cultivate it. The *aggadah* states that the emperor Hadrian challenged Joshua b. Hananiah to the effect that despite the Land of Israel's virtues it lacked some things, such as pepper, and in reply Joshua brought him pepper from Niẓḥana (seemingly a locality in Upper Galilee) in order to prove "that the Land of Israel lacks nothing" (Eccles. R. 2:8, no. 2; see also *Cinnamon). R. Meir uses the same phrase about pepper and adds that it is subject to the law of **orlah* just like other local trees (Ber. 36b). In addition to its use as a spice, pepper was also used to dispel halitosis and a woman was permitted to go out on the Sabbath with a peppercorn in her mouth (Shab. 6:5). A proverb had it that "Better one peppercorn than a basket full of gourds" (Meg. 7a). The term **pilpul* (Avot 6:6; Tem. 16a) is connected with *pilpel* and from it is derived the verb *palpel,* to show sharpwittedness in learning. In the Middle Ages, pepper was a medium of exchange and was called "black money." A species resembling pepper is *pilpela arikhta,* long pepper (Pes. 42b), extracted from the bunches of unripe fruit of the species *Piper longum.* In Israel today the name *pilpel* is applied to the decorative tree *Schinus molle* and also to paprika, both of which originate in America and were unknown to the ancients.

Bibliography: Krauss, Tal Arch, 1 (1910), 118f.; Loew, Flora, 3 (1924), 49–62.

[J.F.]

PEPPER, JOSEPH (1904–), British meteorologist. Born in London, Pepper began work at the Meteorological Office, then under the supervision of the Air Ministry, in 1932. During the 1930s and World War II, he served as a meteorologist and weather forecaster in the Royal Air Force and Royal Navy in various parts of the world, including the Atlantic Ocean, Cyprus, and Singapore. He published research on the winds of the North Atlantic Ocean and, while engaged in various other tasks, began writing a work on climatic conditions in various parts of the world, together with an analysis of information gathered during the 1940s and the early 1950s on the Antarctic region. One result of this work was his book, *The Meteorology of the Falkland Islands and Dependencies 1944–1950* (1954). Before his retirement from government service Pepper prepared a comprehensive work on the rules of forecasting. He subsequently taught at the Central London Polytechnic.

[D.ASH.]

PERAḤYAH, AARON BEN ḤAYYIM ABRAHAM HA-KOHEN (1627?–1697), rabbi and halakhic authority of Salonika. Peraḥyah was born in Salonika and studied there under Asher b. Ardut ha-Kohen, Ḥasdai ha-Kohen *Peraḥyah, and *Ḥayyim Shabbetai. In 1689 he succeeded Elijah *Covo as chief rabbi of Salonika. He was regarded as an important *posek* among Salonika rabbis.

His works are: *Paraḥ Matteh Aharon* (2 parts, Amsterdam, 1703), responsa which reflect the contemporary condition of Turkish Jewry in general and of Salonikan Jewry in particular; *Pirḥei Kehunnah* (*ibid.*, 1709), novellae to the tractates *Bava Kamma, Bava Meẓia, Ketubbot, Gittin, Avodah Zarah,* and *Kiddushin; Bigdei Kehunnah* (Saloniki 1753), eulogies and homilies; and *Zikhron Devarim* (*ibid.*, 1758), source references for the *Arba'ah Turim* of *Jacob b. Asher. In his *Paraḥ Matteh Aharon* he mentions another work, on *Alfasi, of which nothing is known.

Bibliography: Michael, Or, 136–7; M. Molho, *Essai d'une Monographie sur la Famille Perahia à Thessaloniki* (1938), 33–44; I. S. Emmanuel, *Maẓẓevot Saloniki,* 2 (1968), 491–4. [A.D.]

PERAḤYAH, ḤASDAI BEN SAMUEL HA-KOHEN (?1605–1678), rabbi and halakhist. Peraḥyah belonged to a well-known family in Salonika. He was one of the outstanding disciples of *Ḥayyim Shabbetai. In 1647 he was appointed one of the *dayyanim* of the old Italian community of the city. In 1671, after the death of Menahem Shullam, he was appointed chief rabbi there, and served, apparently, until his death.

Peraḥyah left behind homilies, novellae, and responsa. His collected responsa, *Torat Ḥesed,* were published in Salonika in 1722, and others appear in the works of his associates and disciples. Among his pupils were Daniel Gerasi, Jacob di Boton, and his kinsman, Aaron ha-Kohen *Peraḥyah.

Bibliography: M. Molho, *Essai d'une Monographie sur la Famille Perahia à Thessaloniki* (1938), 27–33; I. S. Emmanuel, *Maẓẓevot Saloniki,* 1 (1963), 403–6, no. 908. [A.D.]

PERAḤYAH BEN NISSIM (13th century), talmudist. No biographical details are known of him. In a document dated 1240 he is mentioned as being in Fostat, Egypt. In 1247 he wrote a commentary on the *halakhot* of Isaac *Alfasi and a manuscript of it in the tractate *Shabbat,* written in 1304, is preserved in the Bodleian Library.

Extracts from the work are cited in the novellae on Maimonides' *Mishneh Torah,* which are published at the beginning of the *Ma'aseh Roke'aḥ* of Mas'ud Roke'ah, and additional fragments were published by Assaf in *Kirjath Sepher.* Many of the quotations from Maimonides given by M. L. Sachs in his *Ḥiddushei ha-Rambam la-Talmud* (1963) were taken from this work. A section of the work on chapters five and six was published at the end of the *Siyya'ta di-Shemayya* (1970).

Bibliography: S. Assaf, in: *Sinai,* 16 (1940), 106; idem, in: KS, 23 (1946–47), 233–5; Z. Benedict, in: KS, 28 (1952/53), 211–3; Mann, Egypt, 1 (1920), 248 n. 1, 2 (1922), 297 no. 1. [S.Z.H.]

PEREFERKOVICH, NEHEMIAH (1871–1940), Russian orientalist and philologist. Born in Stavropol, Caucasus, son of a *Cantonist soldier, he studied oriental languages at the University of St. Petersburg. Beginning in 1893 he published essays, critical articles, and studies in *Voskhod* and other Russian-Jewish and Russian newspapers, under his own name or under the pseudonyms Al-Gavvas or Vostochnik.

He also wrote on Jewish history and literature for Russian encyclopedias and for the *Yevreyskaya Entsiklopediya,* of which he was an editor. His principal scientific work was a translation of the Mishnah, the Tosefta, the *Mekhilta, Sifra,* and the tractate *Berakhot* of the Babylonian Talmud into Russian (8 vols., 1898–1912), a popular work which was widely used by Jews and Christians alike. He also wrote popular books in Russian on the problems of Judaism, the Talmud, and the Shulḥan Arukh, as well as a textbook on Jewish history and religion for Jewish pupils attending Russian secondary schools. After the Revolution he settled in Riga, where he taught in local secondary and high schools and contributed articles to the Jewish and Hebrew press on public issues. He dedicated himself to research on the Yiddish language, and wrote a dictionary of Hebrew words and expressions in Yiddish (*Hebraizmen in Yidish,* 1929, 1931²).

Bibliography: Rejzen, Leksikon, 2 (1927), 944–6; LNYL, 7 (1968), 200–1. [Y.S.]

PEREIRA DE PAIVA, MOSES (17th century), Sephardi communal leader in Amsterdam. In 1686 he was head of a delegation to the Jewish community of *Cochin (India), sent to collect data on its history and way of life. He was warmly received by the leaders of the "white" Jewish community and his visit led to a close contact between the Jews of Amsterdam and Cochin, which lasted until Dutch rule over Malabar ended in 1795. On his return, he published *Notisias dos Judeos de Cochim* (Amsterdam, 1687), a comprehensive report on the origin, economic situation, traditions, and communal organizations of the "white" Jews, naming all the householders and particularly mentioning David *Rahabi. He also deals with the "black" Jews, whom he calls the Malabar Jews, though according to him they are Jews only by religion and not by race.

Bibliography: M. Pereira de Paiva, *Notisias dos Judeos de Cochim,* ed. by M. B. Amzalak (1923), introd.; *Souvenir Volume of Cochin Synagogue* ... (Cohin, 1968), 31–50); Steinscheider, Cat Bod, 2723. [W.J.F.]

PÉREIRE, ÉMILE (Jacob; 1800–1875) and **ISAAC** (1806–1880), French economists, bankers, and journalists. The Péreire brothers were the grandsons of Jacob Rodrigues

Figure 1. Émile Péreire. Jerusalem, J.N.U.L., Schwadron Collection.

*Péreire. Born and educated in Bordeaux, both became prominent disciples of Claude Henri de Rouvroy, Comte de St. Simon, and his socioeconomic system. After the dispersion of the St. Simonians, the Péreires turned to political and economic writing, and during the 1830s their articles in *Le Globe, Le Temps,* and *Le Journal des Débats* attracted much attention. Emile's emphasis on railway development led James de *Rothschild to finance the Chemin de Fer du Nord and half a dozen other railway lines. In 1848 the Péreires gave up their cooperation with the Rothschilds and joined the *Foulds. Four years later, together with the Foulds and many other leading French financiers and politicians, they formed the Crédit Mobilier, France's first modern investment bank. After spectacular initial successes the bank's fortunes sank with the Second Empire, and it was liquidated in 1867. Both Péreires were members of the French parliament and active in Jewish affairs.

In 1832 Emile edited the St. Simonian *Globe* and, from 1832 to 1835, *Le National,* the organ of the republican party. A boulevard in Paris was named after him. Isaac wrote *Leçons sur l'industrie et les finances* (1832); *Le rôle de la Banque de France* (1864); *Principe de la constitution des banques* (1865); and *La question religieuse* (1878). In the late

1870s Isaac published his own paper, *La Liberté*, in which he advanced his political and industrial views. Isaac's son EUGENE (1831–1908), a civil engineer, railway administrator, and banker, was a member of the Chamber of Deputies and active in Jewish affairs. He inherited his grandfather's interest in the education of deaf-mutes.

Figure 2. Isaac Péreire. Jerusalem, J.N.U.L., Schwadron Collection.

Bibliography: C. H. Castille, *Les Frères Péreire* (1861); M. Aycard, *Histoire du Crédit Mobilier* (1867); B. Mehrens, *Die Entstehung und Entwicklung der grossen franzoesischen Kreditinstitute* (1911); P. H. Emden, *Money Powers of Europe* (1938), index; H. Spiel, *Fanny von Arnstein, oder Die Emanzipation* (1962).

[J.O.R.]

PÉREIRE (Pereira), JACOB RODRIGUES (1715–1780), French educator of deaf-mutes and communal leader. Péreire was born into a Marrano family in Berlanga, Spain. After his father's death, Péreire was taken by his mother to France, and they returned to Judaism. Péreire's studies in anatomy and physiology helped him in his work as the first French educator of congenital deaf-mutes. He taught deaf-mutes to communicate by articulating sounds and lipreading rather than by the use of signs. He strove to educate pupils, regardless of their social class, to the maximum level of ability in relation to their probable future. His achievements brought him great distinction and a grant by King Louis XV. Other educators were inspired by Péreire's work to efforts along similar lines, the best known of them being Edouard Séguin, a pioneer in the education of deaf-mutes. Péreire also gained distinction in other fields. A mathematical invention won him an annual pension and in 1753 his proposals for increasing the speed of sailing vessels received honorable mention. Péreire was active in Jewish life. In 1749 he became the voluntary counsellor of the Sephardi community in Paris, and in 1761 was appointed officially to the position. Péreire himself wrote little, but his thought, as transmitted by Séguin, has received recognition in the educational writings of the 20th century. His works comprise a study of the articulation and vocabulary of a Tahitian native (1772) and *Observations sur les Sourds et Muets,* published by the Académie Royale des Sciences in 1778. His grandsons were Emile and Isaac *Péreire.

Bibliography: W. Boyd, *From Locke to Montessori* (1914), 36–41; J. Fynne, *Montessori and her Inspirers* (1924), 13–62; E. Séguin, *Jacob Rodrigues Péreire* ... (Fr., 1847); F. Hément, *Jacob Rodrigues Péreire* ... (Fr., 1875); F. Manuel Alves, *Os judeus no distrito de Braganca* (1925), xcviii–civ; La Rochelle, in: REJ, 4 (1882), 150ff.; L. Kahn, *Les Juifs à Paris* (1889), 52, 54, 58–59.

[W.W.B.]

PEREK SHIRAH (Heb. פֶּרֶק שִׁירָה; "chapter of song"), a short, anonymous tract containing a collection of hymnic sayings in praise of the creator placed in the mouths of His creatures. All creation, except man, is represented—the natural and supernatural orders, inanimate nature, the heavens and all their hosts, the world of plants, and the world of animals—each according to its kind. Together the hymns comprise a kind of cosmic song of praise by the whole of creation. They are set in a prose midrashic framework imparting a firm literary structure to a collection that in itself lacks textual continuity. Most of the "hymns" are in fact biblical verses, the greater part of them citations from Psalms. At the end of *Perek Shirah* there are pseudepigraphic additions, apparently of a later date, praising the one who says *Perek Shirah.* The connection between many of these texts and the creature uttering the praise in each hymn is not clear. The anthropomorphism of creation in the composition, at first sight totally foreign to the spirit of Judaism, has, from the first references in literature until the most recent, given rise to violent opposition and accusations of forgery. Consequently there have been various attempts, some apologetic, to deny the work's apparent simplicity in favor of a philosophical-allegorical, talmudic-didactic, or kabbalistic-mystical interpretation.

The text has been preserved in several manuscripts, including *genizah* fragments, the earliest dating from about the tenth century. The versions differ considerably in content and arrangement, and classification of the manuscripts reveals the existence of three distinct traditions: Oriental, Sephardi, and Ashkenazi. The first printed edition, with a commentary by Moses b. Joseph de *Trani (printed as an appendix to his *Beit ha-Elohim;* Venice, 1576), was followed by dozens of corrupt editions, generally accompanied by commentaries.

Perek Shirah is first mentioned in a polemical work of *Salmon b. Jeroham, a Jerusalem Karaite of the first half of the tenth century. References to it can be found in European sources at the end of the 12th century, and from the 13th century onward various interpretations are known, mainly kabbalistic. It would seem that from the outset *Perek Shirah* was intended as a liturgical text, as also seems apparent from the pseudepigraphic mystical additions. In the early Ashkenazi manuscripts it was included in *maḥzorim* and collections of special prayers in close proximity to prayers issuing from circles of *Ḥasidei Ashkenaz. The spread of the later custom of reciting *Perek Shirah* as a prayer and its inclusion in printed *siddurim* was mainly due to the influence of the Safed kabbalists.

Talmudic and midrashic sources contain hymns on the creation usually based on homiletic expansions of metaphorical descriptions and personifications of the created world in the Bible. The explicitly homiletic background of some of the hymns in *Perek Shirah* indicates a possible connection between the rest and tannaitic and amoraic homiletics, and suggests a hymnal index to well-known, but mostly unpreserved, homiletics. The origin of this work, the period of its composition, and its significance may be deduced from literary parallels. A tannaitic source in the tractate *Ḥagigah* of the Jerusalem (Ḥag. 2:1, 77a–b) and Babylonian Talmud (Ḥag. 12a–14b), on hymns of nature associated with apocalyptic visions and with the teaching of *ma'aseh bereshit,* serves as a key to *Perek Shirah's* close spiritual relationship with this literature. Parallels to it can be found in apocalyptic literature, in mystic layers in talmudic literature, in Jewish mystical prayers surviving in fourth-century Greek Christian compositions, in *Heikhalot* literature, and in *Merkabah mysticism. The affinity of *Perek Shirah* with *Heikhalot* literature, which abounds in hymns, can be noted in the explicitly mystic introduction to the seven crowings of the cock—the only non-hymnal text in the collection—and the striking resemblance between the language of the additions and that of **Shi'ur Komah* and other examples of this literature. In *Seder Rabbah de-Bereshit,* a *Heikhalot* tract, in conjunction with the description of *ma'aseh bereshit,* there is a clear parallel to *Perek Shirah*'s praise of creation and to the structure of its hymns. The concept reflected in this source is based on a belief in the existence of angelic archetypes of created beings who mediate between God and His creation, and express their role through singing hymns. As the first interpretations of *Perek Shirah* also bear witness to its mystic character and angelologic significance, it would appear to be an apocalyptic chapter of *Heikhalot* literature.

Some parallels to *Perek Shirah* exist outside Hebrew literature: the Testament of Adam (preserved in Syriac, Greek, and in later translations), which contains horaries of praise by the whole of creation framed in an apocalyptic angelologic vision similar to that in *Seder Rabbah de-Bereshit*, the Greek *Physiologus* of the second century, which reveals structural and formal parallels to *Perek Shirah;* and Islamic oral traditions *(Ḥadīth)* and *Ikhwān al-Ṣafā'* ("Sincere Brethren"), writings on the praise of created beings.

Bibliography: M. Steinschneider, in: HB, 13 (1875), 103–6; Ginzberg, Legends, 1 (1909), 42–46; 5 (1925), 60–62; Scholem, Mysticism, 62: M. Beit-Arié, *Perek Shirah,* critical ed., 2 vols. (Ph.D. thesis, Jerusalem, 1966).

[MA.B.-A.]

PERELMAN, CHAIM (1912–), Belgian philosopher. Perelman, who was born in Warsaw, Poland, became professor of logic and metaphysics at the Université Libre in Brussels in 1944. He was also dean of the faculty of

Chaim Perelman, Belgian philosopher. Courtesy Hebrew University, Jerusalem.

philosophy and letters and director of the Ecoles des Sciences de l'Education. Many of his early writings dealt with mathematical logic. In later years he was especially concerned with the concept of justice and with forms of discursive reasoning other than deductive reasoning.

A full statement of his theory of argument is presented in the two-volume *Traité de l'Argumentation* (1958), published jointly with Mme. L. Olbrechts-Tyteca. Some of his other major works are *De l'Arbitraire dans la Connaissance* (1933), *De la Justice* (1945), *Justice et Raison* (1963), and *Rhétorique et Philosophie* (1952). He published numerous articles in philosophical journals. Perelman was secretary-general of the Fédération Internationale des Sociétés de Philosophie, president of the Société Belge de Philosophie and of the Société Belge de Logique et Philosophie des Sciences. He was a member of the board of governors of the Hebrew University, and the secretary-general of the Belgian Friends of the Hebrew University.

[M.M.M.]

PERELMAN, SIDNEY JOSEPH (1904–), U.S. humorist. Perelman was born in Brooklyn, but grew up in Providence, Rhode Island, and studied at Brown University, where he edited a humorous magazine. He began his professional career in 1925 as a contributor to the humor magazines *Judge* and *College Humor* and began to write for the movies in 1930. From 1934 he published amusing or satirical pieces in the *New Yorker,* to which he contributed steadily for more than 30 years.

Perelman's versatility as a humorist extended to the theater. Among his better known comedies are *One Touch of Venus* (1943), written in collaboration with Ogden Nash, and *The Beauty Part* (1963). His work for the movies included scripts for the *Marx Brothers, and his screenplay for the movie *Around the World in Eighty Days* won him the New York Critics' Award as the Best Screen Writer of 1956. He also wrote two amusing travel books:

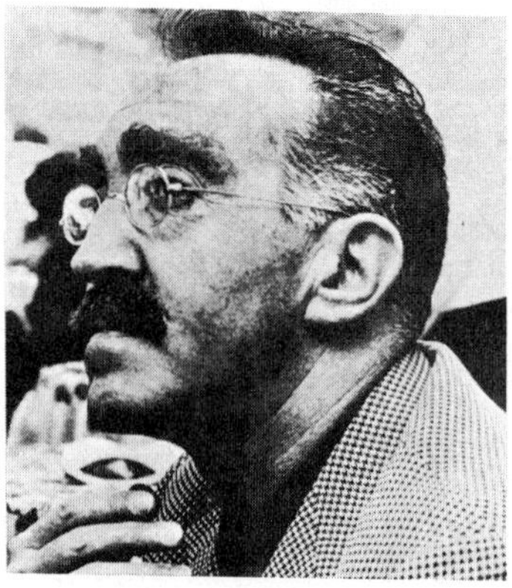

S. J. Perelman, U.S. humorist. Courtesy Simon and Schuster, New York. Photo Robert G. Edwards.

Westward Ha! (1948) and *The Swiss Family Perelman* (1950). Other works include *Dawn Ginsbergh's Revenge* (1929); *Strictly from Hunger* (1937); *Look Who's Talking* (1940); *Crazy Like a Fox* (1944); *The Best of S. J. Perelman* (1947); *Listen to the Mocking Bird* (1949); *The Road to Miltown; or, Under the Spreading Atrophy* (1957); *The Rising Gorge* (1961); and *Chicken Inspector No. 23* (1966).

The bulk of Perelman's work was made up of the relatively brief *New Yorker* pieces. A continuous sparkle of fantastic wit animates his writing, whether it be burlesque, parody, or satire. Perelman exploited all the possibilities of the English language for comic effects, especially through the devices of pun and anticlimax. With mingled compassion and mockery, he pointed up the weakness and folly of the individual as a puppet and victim of 20th-century society and its mass media.

Bibliography: N. W. Yates, *American Humorist* (1964), 331–50; Paris Review, *Writers at Work,* second series (1963), 241–56; S. J. Kunitz, *Twentieth Century Authors,* first supplement (1955), incl. bibl.

[I.J.K.]

PERELMANN, JEROHMAN JUDAH LEIB BEN SOLOMON ZALMAN (1835–1896), Lithuanian talmudist known as Ha-Gadol mi-Minsk ("the great scholar of Minsk"). Perelmann was born in Brest-Litovsk (Brisk), and in his youth he studied in Kovno at the yeshivah of Israel *Lipkin of Salant, where he was renowned as the "Brisk prodigy." In 1865 he was appointed rabbi of Seltso, in 1875 of Pruzhany, and in 1883 of Minsk, where he served until his death. He was one of the rabbis who supported the Ḥovevei Zion movement. His responsum about this matter was published in *Sinai* (6 (1940), 210–21). His *Or Gadol* (1924), consisting of responsa and studies mostly on *Even ha-Ezer,* together with a small portion on *Oraḥ Ḥayyim* and *Yoreh De'ah,* was published by his son Isaiah together with notes, glosses, and novellae. His *Or Gadol ve-Yitron ha-Or,* notes and novellae on the Mishnah, was published in the Romm Vilna edition of the Mishnah.

Bibliography: B. Eisenstadt, *Rabbanei Minsk* (1898), 34, 62f.; D. Katz, *Tenu'at ha-Musar,* 2 (1959), 449–52; *Yahadut Lita,* 1 (1960), index; 3 (1967), 80f.; Habermann, in: *Aresheth,* 3 (1961), 135.

[SH.A.H./ED.]

PEREMYSHLYANY (Pol. **Przemyslany**), town in Lvov oblast, Ukrainian S.S.R. Peremyshlyany was part of Poland until the partition of 1772 when it was annexed by Austria. Regained by independent Poland in 1919 it belonged to the province of Tarnopol. In 1945 it was incorporated into Soviet Ukraine. The Jewish community was already active during the period of the *Council of the Four Lands and became particularly famous during the 18th and 19th centuries because of its dynasty of ḥasidic leaders. These included R. Aaron Leib of Peremyshyany (d. in Ereẓ Israel, 1773) who was the son of R. Meir, of Peremyshlyany, known as "the First" or "the Great"; both were disciples of *Israel b. Eliezer Ba'al Shem Tov. The son of R. Aaron Leib was R. Meir of *Peremyshlyany, one of the most outstanding personalities among the *ẓaddikim* of Galicia. The town expanded during the 19th century. In 1865 the combined population was about 2,200 and by 1921 there were 4,093 inhabitants, including 2,051 Jews. In the 1933 elections to the Jewish community council a Zionist delegate was elected president. The interest-free loan fund and the orphanage were among the most active welfare institutions. As a result of anti-Semitic agitation, a bomb was thrown into the *bet ha-midrash* in 1935. [SH.L.K.]

Holocaust Period. The number of Jews had grown to nearly 6,000 in 1941 with the influx of refugees from the vicinity and from western Poland. The German forces arrived on July 1, 1941. Three days later they burned down the main synagogue and pushed a number of Jews into the flames. In the fall of 1941 kidnappings for labor camps in Kurowice and Jaktorow began. About 500 Jewish men were taken on Oct. 5, 1941, to Brzezina forest and murdered. In May 1942 a Gestapo official removed the inmates of the Jewish hospital and killed them. Other acts of terror continued at the end of July and in September until the end of 1942. Most of the victims were sent to *Belzec extermination camp. In August 1942 a ghetto was set up, to include Jews from *Gliňyany and Swirz as well. On May 23, 1943, the ghetto was wiped out and the city declared **judenrein*.

After the war the Jewish community was not renewed in Peremyshlyany. A number of Jews who came out of the forests or from hiding, along with a number of returnees from the Soviet Union, came to their native town, but most emigrated either to Israel via Poland or to other countries abroad. In the late 1960s there were about five Jewish families in the town. [AR.W.]

PEREMYSHLYANY, MEIR BEN AARON LEIB OF (1780?–1850), ḥasidic *ẓaddik*. He was the grandson of R. Meir of Peremyshlyany, a disciple of *Israel b. Eliezer Ba'al Shem Tov (the Besht), who, according to a later ḥasidic tradition, assisted the Ba'al Shem Tov in his struggle against the Frankists (see Jacob *Frank). R. Meir, who was born in Peremyshlyany, Galicia, was a disciple of Mordecai of Kremenets. In 1813, the year of his father's death, he became rabbi in Peremyshlyany and leader of the ḥasidic community there. As a result of a slander against him, he was compelled to leave for Lipkany, Bessarabia, where he held rabbinical office. This episode is mentioned by his Ḥasidim and in a document of the Austrian authorities of 1827. Meir lived in Lipkany for three years and became involved in a dispute with the Ḥasidim of Abraham Joshua *Heschel of Apta (Opatow). To this may be added the testimony of Abraham (Dov) Baer *Gottlober according to which Meir was always accustomed to live in the border towns, and that he changed his place of residence several times. From Lipkany he returned to Peremyshlyany and in 1843 he moved to Nikolayev, where he lived for the last seven years of his life.

In 1826 Joseph *Perl applied to the Austrian authorities for permission to reprint the *Sefer Vikku'aḥ* (of Israel *Loebl, 1798). At the end of this volume was a list of ḥasidic leaders, among whom was the name of Meir of Shebsh. Perl changed the name to Meir Shebseir, in accordance with the reading in a manuscript. The Austrian censorship wrongly identified Meir Shebseir with Meir of Peremyshlany and as a result ordered an enquiry as to whether he and the other ḥasidic rabbis were in opposition to the government, encouraging their followers to disobey the law, but the results of the investigation were negative. In 1839 the police of Lvov submitted to the government an indictment against "miracle-workers," which contained, among others, the name of Meir of Peremyshlyany. The government ordered an investigation, the results of which are unknown.

Meir was on friendly terms with Israel of *Ruzhin, whom he assisted in crossing the border when the latter was persecuted by the authorities, and Solomon b. Judah Aaron *Kluger of Brody, who eulogized Meir upon his death. In *Megalleh Temirin* by Joseph Perl some of Meir's actions are described with derision, e.g., that he engaged in the healing of the sick and childless women. Meir was accustomed to spend his money freely among the poor, as related by both his Ḥasidim and a *maskil*, Dr. Solomon Rubin, opposed to Ḥasidism. He was known for his strange behavior, which his Ḥasidim interpreted as being merely external and his opponents as insanity. He gained popularity as a *ẓaddik* and had many followers. Reports of the miracles which he performed were at first circulated orally and later in print.

Meir made no original contribution to ḥasidic doctrine, nor did he write any halakhic or homiletical works. After his death, however, his followers collected his teachings which were included in various works or handed down from hearsay; among them the following three works in Yiddish: *Ma'aseh Nora me-ha-Ẓaddik . . . R. Meir mi-Peremyshlani, Eyn Emese Mayse fun R. Meir' mi-Peremyshlany,* and *Shivḥei R. Meir.*

They were collected and published in *Divrei Me'ir* (1909), *Or ha-Me'ir* (1926), and *Margenita de-Rabbi Meir* (ed. Margalioth, 1926). A *Seder Hakkafot* ("Order of the *Hakkafot* [for Simḥat Torah]," 1891) which he composed was also published.

Bibliography: I. Layfer, *Tiferet Maharam* (1958[2]); I. Berger, *Eser Atarot* (1910), 37–56; M. H. Brawer, *Zikhronot Av u-Veno* (1966), 15–16; M. Ben-Yeḥezkel, *Sefer ha-Ma'asiyyot,* 1 (1968[3]), 108–13; 2 (1968[3]), 301–3; 4 (1968[3]), 85–87; 5 (1968[3]), 420–4; 6 (1968[3]), 269–72; A. B. Gottlober, *Zikhronot mi-Ymei Neuray,* in: *Ha-Boker Or,* 5 (1880), 310; 6 (1881), 162, 168–9, 289; Horodezky, Ḥasidut, index; R. Mahler, *Ha-Ḥasidut ve-ha-Haskalah* (1961), index; Ch. Shmeruk, in: *Zion,* 21 (1956), 94. [Z.GR.]

PERES (formerly **Persky**), **SHIMON** (1923–), Israel politician. Born in Vishneva, Belorussia, Peres settled in Palestine in 1934. He served in the Ministry of Defense from 1948 to 1959, being its director general from 1953. Elected on the *Mapai list to the Knesset in 1959, he was deputy minister of defense from 1959 to 1965, during which

Shimon Peres, Israel politician. Courtesy Government Press Office, Tel Aviv.

time he reorganized the ministry. He was instrumental in strengthening relations between Israel and France and was a special emissary on defense matters to France and other countries. In 1965 Peres left Mapai and became secretary-general of *Rafi. In 1967 he was the initiator of the negotiations that led to the formation of the united *Israel Labor Party and became its deputy general secretary. In 1969 he joined the cabinet as minister without portfolio, with special responsibility for economic development in the Israel-administered areas, and in 1970 he was appointed minister of transportation and communications. [M.L.]

PERETZ, ABRAHAM (1771–1833), one of the first *maskilim* in Russia and a leader of the Jewish community. Son of the rabbi of Lubartow, Peretz married the daughter of wealthy Joshua *Zeitlin of Shklov. He was a fellow-student of J. L. *Nevakhovich, and at the end of the 18th century he settled in St. Petersburg, where he became the protégé of Prince Potëmkin. He made his fortune in commerce and shipbuilding and earned the title of commercial adviser from Czar Paul I. Making connections with the Russian upper classes, he was on familiar terms with Minister Speranski. Peretz maintained contact with the Berlin *maskilim* and was among the subscribers of *Ha-Me'assef*. He also took part in the work of the Committee for the Drafting of Jewish Legislation (1802), presenting various memoranda to the committee. He assisted Jewish *shtadlanim* who came to the capital and encouraged Nevakhovich to write his Russian pamphlet *Vopl dshcheri yudeyskoy*. He lost his fortune as a result of unsuccessful contracts with the army during the Napoleonic invasion of Russia (1812). In 1813 he divorced his wife, converting to Christianity along with his son Gregory (Hirsch), and married a German woman.

Peretz's son GREGORY (1788–1855) received his early education in the house of his grandfather Joshua Zeitlin. In 1803 he rejoined his father in St. Petersburg and received an important position in government administration. From 1820 to 1822 he was a member of a secret society which sought to introduce reforms into the Russian government. Among other projects he also conceived of the establishment of a "Society for the Liberation of the Jews Dispersed in Russia, and even in Europe, and their Settlement in Crimea, or even in the Orient, as a Unified Nation." After the revolt of the *Decembrists (1825) he was imprisoned and banished to northern Russia. Twenty years later (1845) he received authorization to leave for Odessa. Of Abraham's other sons, mention should be made of ALEXANDER, a mining engineer who played an important role in the industrial development of the Ural Mountains. Another son, YEGOR, was a member of the National Council; his diary (publ. 1927) contains important material on the discussions of the Jewish problem in the council during the early 1800s. A great-grandson of Gregory, VLADIMIR (1870–1936), was a historian of Russian and Ukrainian literature and theater and a member of the Russian Academy of Sciences. Together with his brother LEV, Peretz wrote a monograph entitled *Dekabrist Grigori Abramovich Peretz* (1926).

Bibliography: S. L. Zitron, *Shtadlonim* (Yid., 1927), 53–67; S. Ginsburg, *Meshumodim in Tsarishn Rusland,* 9 (1946), 34–53.

[Y.S.]

PERETZ, ISAAC LEIB (1852–1915), Yiddish and Hebrew poet and author. Peretz came from a respected traditional family, and while he was privately tutored in Hebrew grammar, German, and Russian, the extreme religious outlook of his mother prevented his receiving a systematic secular education. In his youth, he had access to a large library of Polish and German books which allowed him to read voraciously. Later, his parents opposed his wish to study in a rabbinical seminary sponsored by the Russian government, and, as a result, Peretz formulated a plan, though never executed, to run away from home. At 18 his parents forced him to marry the daughter of the *maskil* and mathematician Gabriel Judah *Lichtenfeld. The marriage, however, was unhappy and three years later, in 1873, financial circumstances obliged Peretz to leave Zamosc, his native town, to earn a livelihood elsewhere. He moved to a neighboring town, but in 1875 tried his luck in Warsaw where he met and came under the influence of the writer R. A. *Braudes. This was a difficult period for Peretz. In 1876 he divorced his wife and returned to Zamosc. A year later he passed an examination permitting him to practice law, a profession in which he excelled. His financial and social position improved and in 1878 he married Helena Ringelheim, daughter of a prosperous merchant. The marriage was a happy one, and the years that followed were quiet and peaceful.

During the 1870–78 period Peretz wrote most of his works in Polish. The few poems he composed in Yiddish were not published and a number of them have been lost. He had had a negative attitude toward Yiddish before the 1881 pogroms, though he later denied this. In 1875 he started publishing in Hebrew with the poem "*Ha-Tinshemet ve-ha-Yare'aḥ*" which appeared in a book by Lichtenfeld. "*Li Omerim*" ("I am Told," in: *Ha-Shaḥar,* 1876) was his first published poem of some importance. *Sippurim be-Shir ve-Shirim Shonim me'et Shenei Ba'alei Asufot* (1877) is a joint effort of Lichtenfeld and Peretz, though most of the works in the book are by Peretz. A lull in Peretz's creativity followed.

The poet wrote little in the intervening years, until 1886, when, during a visit to Warsaw, he renewed his contacts with Jewish literary circles, and his interest in literary activity was revived. After an interval of nearly ten years, Peretz resumed writing poems and short stories. In 1888 he began to publish in Yiddish. His first poem "*Monish,*" printed in *Shalom Aleichem's *Di Yidishe Folksbibliotek* (1888), is a frivolous, sentimental, and ironic poetic work which became a milestone in the development of Yiddish literature.

In 1886 Peretz's financial condition again deteriorated and at the end of the 1880s, as a result of a false accusation, he lost his right to practice law. Depressed, with no savings and no prospects, he left Zamosc and moved to Warsaw, where in 1890 he joined a group making a statistical survey which was financed by the philanthropist Ivan (Jan) *Bloch, a Jew who had converted to Christianity. Peretz visited many small towns and villages in the province of Tomaszow, collecting information about the life of the Jewish population, not only for statistical data (which were never published) but also for raw material for his literary works. Peretz's impressions of this expedition are reflected in sketches entitled *Bilder fun a*

Isaac Leib Peretz, Yiddish and Hebrew writer. Drawing by Joseph Budko. Jerusalem, B. M. Ansbacher Collection.

Provints-Rayze ("Pictures from a Provincial Journey," 1891), where he described the poverty and pettiness of life in the *Pale of Settlement. Back in Warsaw, the unemployed Peretz plunged into various social and cultural activities, lecturing in Hebrew and publishing the Yiddish short stories *Bekante Bilder* ("Familiar Scenes," 1890, 1903). In 1891 he secured a permanent post as an official in the department in charge of burial sites of the Jewish community of Warsaw, a position he occupied until his death. In the same year, he edited the first two issues of *Di Yidishe Bibliotek* (1891; "The Jewish Library"), a periodical devoted to belles lettres and articles of general interest. The third issue appeared in 1895, and after a brief interruption, the periodical resumed publication in 1904 with popular articles on science.

In the 1870s Peretz, a typical *maskil,* had considered *Jargon* (as Yiddish was then called), as well as Hebrew, only temporary media for educating the Jewish masses until they would learn the language of their native country. After the 1881 pogroms, however, the main tendency in his writing was toward nationalism, and since he had always been concerned with the fate of the underprivileged, his attitude toward Yiddish became more positive. In *"Bildung,"* the introductory article to the first publication of *Di Yidishe Bibliotek* (1891), Peretz maintained that since three million Jews understood Yiddish, there must be a literature in Yiddish. He also wanted the people to know Hebrew as well as the language of their country of birth. It is significant that Peretz printed this article without introducing changes in it as late as 1901. (He omitted it, however, from the edition of his works published in 1908.) Three years after his first venture as an editor, Peretz launched his *Yontev Bletlekh* ("Little Pages for Festivals," 17 issues during the period of 1894 to 1896) in which he advocated enlightenment and socialism. Peretz's socialist leanings led to his arrest in 1899 when he attended an illegal meeting, and to his subsequent imprisonment for several months. He was a decisive influence on The Jewish socialist movement. In the *Yontev Bletlekh,* as well as in a collection edited by him, *Literatur un Lebn* ("Literature and Life," 1894), Peretz published in Yiddish, thus raising the prestige of *Jargon* to the status of a literary language.

Simultaneous with his Yiddish writings, Peretz also continued his literary efforts in Hebrew. In 1894 he published a volume of love poems, *Ha-Ugav* ("The Harp"), and a collection akin to the *Yontev Bletlekh, Ha-Ḥez* ("The Arrow, 1894). He also contributed to Hebrew periodicals and translated some of his own works from Yiddish into Hebrew. In his polemical writings in Yiddish and in Hebrew, he defended the Jews against anti-Semitic vilifications; on the other hand, however, he criticized the unemployment, poverty, and intolerance within the Jewish community. Notwithstanding his love for the Hebrew language, his confession that "his heart drew him to Palestine" (letter to J. *Dinesohn on Aug. 11, 1909), and his persistent fight for Jewish national revival, Peretz himself did not join the Zionist movement. He doubted whether an ancient tongue and an ancient country could be revived. He saw the future of the Jews in the Diaspora with Yiddish as their language but was not always consistent in his statements. In 1908, serving as deputy chairman of the *Czernowitz Yiddish Conference whose aim it was to promote Yiddish, Peretz in the opening address did not hesitate to state: "We have . . . our ancient Hebrew language of culture, which perhaps has a future . . ." He strongly opposed not only the resolution that "Yiddish is the only Jewish national language," but even the amended version finally adopted "Yiddish is a national language of the Jewish people." Still, in those years, Peretz wrote more in Yiddish than in Hebrew. In 1901 his collected works, both in Yiddish and in Hebrew, appeared for the first time.

Around the mid-1890s Peretz had become attracted to the new currents in Western European art, e.g., neoromanticism and symbolism. These literary schools, as well as folklore, used by neoromantics and modernists either as literary vehicles or as symbols, were a paramount influence on Peretz. Their impact can be seen in his masterpieces: the two collections of tales *Khasidish* (1908?) and *Folkstimlikhe Geshikhten* ("Folktales," 1909; Heb. *Mi-Pi ha-Am,* 1918) and in his symbolic dramas. His short stories opened new vistas for Hebrew and Yiddish belles lettres. Peretz, neither a follower of Ḥasidism nor a naïve folk poet, used ḥasidic material and folktales as a vehicle for his own beliefs and views. He imposed his own experience on the material, shaping it into a new aesthetic expression. In the midst of poverty and triviality, he discovered moral beauty and grandeur, as well as deep mystical truth in the life and faith of the poor, the ignorant, and the simple.

In 1903 Peretz published the Hebrew drama *Ḥurban Beit Ẓaddik* ("The Ruin of the Zaddik's House"). This was the first version of his Yiddish play *Di Goldene Keyt* ("The Golden Chain," 1909) whose subject is the conflict of generations. The plot revolves around a ḥasidic *rebbe*'s determination to prolong the Sabbath, and thus, by force of will, liberate the world from pettiness and anguish. In this period, Peretz was deeply interested in the promotion of the Yiddish theater. Besides several realistic one-act plays in Hebrew and in Yiddish, he published two major Yiddish dramas: *Baynakht oyfn Altn Mark* ("At Night in the Old Market," 1907) and *In Polish oyf der Keyt* ("Chained in the Vestibule," 1909). Considered his most mature aesthetic expression, *Baynakht oyfn Altn Mark* is a symbolic drama in verse in which the poet attempts to unfurl all of Polish Jewish history. Operatic and panoramic in style, the characters—from cantor to bawd—briefly appear and exit, except for the jester. Scenes from all segments of Jewish life are placed in a setting where the dividing line between the real and the unreal, the live and the dead, is blurred. Deeply pessimistic, the play has prompted much discussion, has been variedly interpreted, and severely criticized for its absence of plot and for its ambiguity. *Baynakht oyfn Altn Mark* was staged in Rumania and produced by the Moscow State Yiddish Theater in 1925 (the famed Soviet Yiddish actor S. Mikhoels played the jester). Parts of the play were also presented in Warsaw and in New York. Although Peretz is not primarily remembered as playwright, he has left his mark on the Yiddish stage; yet ironically enough it is his dramatized short stories that have been produced more widely than his plays.

One of Peretz's important, though unfinished, literary works is his memoirs *Mayne Zikhroynes* (1913–14), the main source for his biography until 1870. In the last years of his life, the poet was active in the cultural life of Polish Jews. Their sufferings in the early years of the First World War greatly depressed him. Peretz, who had always assiduously followed his literary pursuits, worked almost up to the last moment. He died of a heart attack; his funeral was an impressive demonstration of the admiration of the Jewish people for one of its greatest modern writers.

Peretz, *Mendele Mokher Seforim, and Shalom Aleichem were the founders of modern Yiddish literature; at the same time Peretz is an important figure in Hebrew literature. A prolific and versatile writer with a rich imagination and a wealth of original ideas, he always doubted and consequently experimented. Sensitive and compassionate, he championed the cause of the oppressed; his home in Warsaw was a center for Yiddish writers and aspiring authors whom he always encouraged. But first and foremost Peretz was a great artist. He introduced new literary forms and adapted genres of a previous period, e.g., the short story and the symbolic drama, into Yiddish and Hebrew literatures, enriching them also with new subject mattter—the lives of the Ḥasidim and of the common people. His literary energies encompass a number of genres, each individually securing his place both in Yiddish and in Hebrew literatures.

The best edition of Peretz's work in Yiddish is *Ale Verk fun Y. L. Peretz*, vols. 1–11 (in 8; 1947–48); and in Hebrew, *Kol Kitvei Y. L. Peretz*, vols. 1–10 (1948–60; containing also his Yiddish works translated into Hebrew). Both editions are incomplete. English translations of his works include: *The Book of Fire* (1960); *In This World and the Next* (1958); *My Memoirs* (1964); I. Howe and E. Greenberg, *A Treasury of Yiddish Stories* (1953); for bibliography of English translations see U. Weinreich, in: *The Field of Yiddish* (1954), 292–9.

Bibliography: M. Samuel, *Prince of the Ghetto* (1948); A. A. Roback, *I. L. Peretz, Psychologist of Literature* (1935); C. Madison, *Yiddish Literature* (1968), 99–133; M. Ravitch, in: *YIVO Bleter*, 36 (1952), 82–98; Jeshurun, *ibid.*, 28 (1946), 165–70; Ch. Shmeruk, in: *Scripta Hierosolymitana*, 19 (1967), 39–57; *Peretz-Bukh* (1940); N. Meisel, *Y. L. Peretz, Zayn Lebn un Shafn* (1945); idem, *Yitshok Leybush Peretz un Zayn Dor Shrayber* (1951); S. Niger, *Y. L. Peretz* (Yid. 1952); S. Meltzer, *Y. L. Peretz vi-Yẓirato*, 2 vols. (1961); idem (ed.) *Al Y. L. Peretz, Divrei Soferim Ivrim;* Shunami, Bibl., nos. 4067–95, 4721–22. [Y.A.K./Ed.]

PEREYASLAV-KHMELNITSKI (formerly **Pereyaslav**), city in Kiev oblast, Ukrainian S.S.R. A Jewish community is known to have existed in the city as early as 1620. It is also known that Jews in Pereyaslav-Khmelnitski suffered greatly during the *Chmielnicki insurrection. In 1654, on the occasion of the union of the Ukraine and Russia, Czar Alexis Mikhailovich maintained the limitation of Jewish rights of 1620. From that time until 1800, no information on Jews in Pereyaslav is available. In 1897, the city listed 5,754 Jews (40% of the total population). Pereyaslav suffered heavily from the Zielony bands; a pogrom in July 1919, which lasted four days, caused the death of 20 Jews and considerable damage to the community. The number of Jews in 1926 was 3,590 (27% of the population). At the beginning of the Soviet regime there were eight *battei-midrash*, six *shoḥatim* and 26 kosher butchers in the city. The Jewish community was destroyed during the German occupation in World War II. Pereyaslav was the birthplace of *Shalom Aleichem.

Bibliography: J. Slutsky, in: *He-Avar*, 9 (1962), 18; I. Z. Diskin, *ibid.*, 14 (1967), 220–8; E. Tcherikower, *Di Ukrainer Pogromen in 1919* (1965), index. [Ed.]

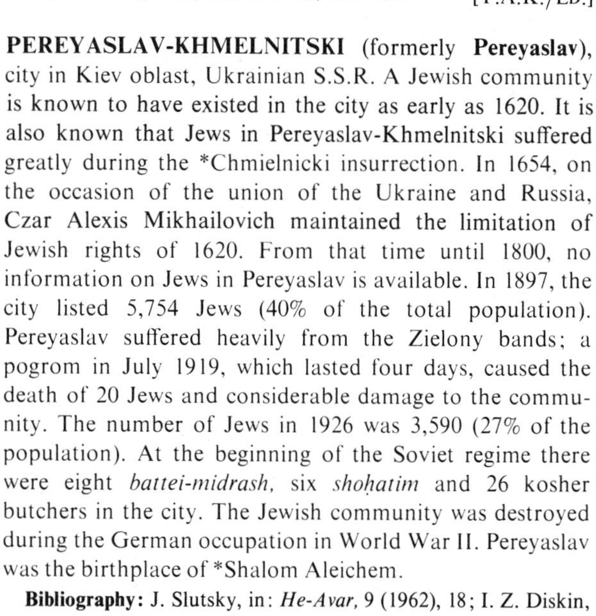

A kindergarten in Pereyaslav-Khmelnitski, Purim, 1918. Courtesy A. Raphaeli-Zenziper, Archive for Russian Zionism, Tel Aviv.

PEREZ (Heb. פֶּרֶץ; "he who breaches," "bursts forth"), one of the twins born to *Judah by *Tamar; father of Hezron and Hamul and ancestor of King David. He is said to have received his name on account of the sudden and unexpected priority of his birth to that of his twin brother Zerah, who was the first to put out a hand from their mother's womb (Gen. 38:27–29). The story of Perez' birth may well reflect a lost chapter in the tribal history of Judah when the older clan of Zerah lost its pre-eminence to the more vigorous Perezites. The Perezites are listed as an important clan in the census taken by Moses in the wilderness (Num. 26:20–21). One of them served as the first monthly chief of all the captains of David's army in the annual roster of military duty (I Chron. 27:3). Descendants of the Perezites were among the lay leaders who lived in Jerusalem after the return from the Babylonian Exile (Neh. 11:4–6). They are said to have numbered 468 "men of substance." The high station of the clan in Judah may be measured by the blessing that the men of Beth-Lehem bestowed on Boaz: "may your house be like the house of Perez whom Tamar bore to Judah" (Ruth 4:12). King David was descended from Perez through Boaz (4:18–22).

In the Aggadah. Perez, together with his brother Zerah, inherited Judah's characteristic valor and piety (Gen. R. 85:9). An indication of his virtue is seen in the fact that David's genealogy (Ruth 4:18–22), begins with his name (Zohar II 104a). The *plene* spelling of the word *toledot* ("generations") in that name is to signify that the Messiah, too would claim descent from him (Ex. R. 30:3).

Bibliography: In the Aggadah: Ginzberg, Legends, index; I. Ḥasida, *Ishei ha-Tanakh* (1964), 370. [Ed.]

PEREZ, JUDAH BEN JOSEPH (first half of 18th century), rabbi in Venice and Amsterdam.

Perez was the author of: (1) *Seder Keri'ei Mo'ed* (Venice, 1706), a kabbalistic ritual text for the festivals; (2) *Peraḥ Levanon* (Berlin, 1712), commentaries and homilies on the Torah (together with homilies by Isaac Cavallero taken from *Naḥal Eitan*); (3) *Sha'arei Raḥamim* (Venice, 1710), kabbalistic liturgies compiled from various works; (4) *Aseret ha-Devarim* (Amsterdam, 1737), containing a commentary on Exodus 19–20, poetical paraphrases in Aramaic and Arabic, and hymns in honor of *Simeon b. Yoḥai; and (5) *Fundamento Solido* (Amsterdam, 1729), a compendium of the Jewish religion in Spanish. Perez also edited *Divrei Yosef* (Venice, 1715), responsa of Joseph b. Mordecai ha-Kohen of Jerusalem.

In the Nehemiah *Ḥayon controversy he was also suspected of being a Shabbatean since he was Ḥayon's scribe for some time and possibly also his disciple. He accompanied Ḥayon on his journey to Berlin. One of Abraham Michael *Cardoso's pamphlets *Megalleh Amukkot minni Ḥoshekh*, was erroneously attributed to Perez.

Bibliography: Fuerst, Bibliotheca, 3 (1863), 77–78; Steinschneider, Cat Bod, 1366; Kayserling, Bibl, 88; I. Sonne, in: *Kobez al Jad*, 2 (1937), 193. [Ed.]

°**PEREZ BAYER, FRANCISCO** (1711–1794), Spanish ecclesiastic and orientalist; professor of Hebrew successively in Valencia and Salamanca. Francisco Perez Bayer was the most distinguished Spanish Hebraist of his day. He was the first person to study accurately the important historical inscriptions in the El Transito synagogue of Toledo (*De Toletano Hebraeorum Templo*, 1752 Ms.). His works on ancient Hebrew coinage (*De Numis hebraeo-samaritanis*, 1781), though later corrected in many details, laid the basis for the serious study of Jewish numismatics.

Bibliography: L. J. Gascía, *Pérez Bayer y Salamanca* (1918); F. Mateu y Llopis, in: *Sefarad*, 11 (1951), 37ff. [C.R.]

PEREZ BEN ELIJAH OF CORBEIL (variously referred to as **RaF**, **MaHaRaF**, **MaRaF**, **M**orenu **ha-R**av **P**erez; d. c. 1295), one of the most eminent tosafists of the 13th century. Perez was known as "Head of the French yeshivot," apparently an official title. On his mother's side he was connected with the *Kimḥi family of Provence. His teachers were *Samuel of Evreux, *Jehiel of Paris, and *Isaac of Corbeil. His brother, Joseph of Tours, was also a well-known scholar. Perez lived in Corbeil, but toward the end of his life moved elsewhere (see *Teshuvot Ḥakhmei Provence* (1967), 92). He became acquainted with *Meir b. Baruch of Rothenburg during a visit to Germany and apparently the two studied together for some time. The comments (both written and oral) and glosses of Perez on the customs of Meir contributed to their spread in France and Provence. Some of these notes were collected by one of his pupils, and a small portion published as glosses to the *Tashbeẓ* (Cremona, 1556) of *Samson b. Zadok, a pupil of Meir who collected the customs of his teacher. Perez did the same with the *Sefer Mitzvot Katan (SeMaK)* of his teacher, Isaac of Corbeil, and his glosses to it, which were more extensive and preserved in a much better state, were published in all editions of the *SeMaK* from the first 1510 editon of Constantinople onward. Better and more complete versions than those published are extant in various manuscripts. The divergence of the published work from the original is evident from the many differences in the manuscripts. Perez' glosses to the *SeMaK* differ from those to the *Tashbeẓ*, since they constitute an actual book written with the express purpose of improving his master's work (even though the form in which we have it has passed through other hands) and his own name is mentioned in the body of the work. The work on *Tashbeẓ* constitutes merely glosses on the text.

Perez' chief claim to fame in the history of rabbinic literature rests on the fact that he was one of the first to edit collections of *tosafot* to the Talmud, and that he was a prolific tosafist in his own right. However, it should be noted that many of the *tosafot* attributed to him are basically extracts from his lectures, noted down by the "pupils of Rabbenu Perez," whom Menahem *ha-Meiri extolled as illuminating and sustaining the Talmud in France. Perez' *tosafot* achieved considerable popularity, their study being widespread in Spain and Italy as early as the middle of the 14th century.

Notwithstanding his popularity, however, most of his *tosafot* are found either in manuscript or in the works of others, only a few having been published, those to *Bava Kamma* (Leghorn, 1819) and to single folios of other tractates (e.g., *Pesaḥim*, until page nine in the *Gemara Shelemah*, 1, 1960). There are many varying manuscripts of his commentary on *Bava Kamma*, apparently reflecting the editing of different pupils. In sum, it may be said fairly definitely that most of what has survived in the name of Perez is the work of his pupils, based to a very large extent upon his words. Of Perez' pupils, the most well known is *Mordecai b. Hillel. Most of them, however, including the compiler of the *Issur ve-Hetter*, attributed to *Jeroham b. Meshullam, are not known by name. Perez is cited hundreds of times in the *Orḥot Ḥayyim* of *Aaron b. Jacob ha-Kohen of Lunel, in the related work, the *Kol Bo*, and in the anonymous *Sefer ha-Neyar*, and he is often quoted by his pupil *Ḥayyim b. Samuel b. David in his *Ẓeror ha-Ḥayyim*. A list of the standard *tosafot* that were edited in the *bet midrash* of Perez is to be found in Urbach's work (see bibliography).

Bibliography: Landauer, in: ZHB, 22 (1919) 27–31; Urbach, Tosafot, index; Ḥayyim b. Samuel of Tudela, *Ẓeror ha-Ḥayyim*, ed. by S. Haggai-Yerushalmi (1966), 3–7 (introd.); I. Ta-Shema, in: *Sinai*, 64 (1969), 254–7. [I.T.-S.]

PEREZ BEN MOSES OF BRODY (18th century), rabbi and preacher. Before moving to Brody, Perez studied with Rabbi Israel, *av bet din* in Lokachi, and with R. Baruch Kahana in Ferrara. In 1769 he published *Sefer Beit Pereẓ* (Zolkiew), a homiletic work on the holidays and other religious events of the year. In addition to the classical sources, the author relies on the Zohar, *Eleazar b. Judah of Worms' *Ma'aseh Roke'aḥ*, and on *Samuel b. Meir in ascertaining both the literal and hidden and mystical meanings of the Torah. He preached with success throughout Poland and Lithuania where many communities sought him as rabbi and preacher. His second work, *Shevaḥ u-Tehillah le-Ereẓ Yisrael* (Metz, 1772), only four pages in length, deals with the holiness of the land of Israel.

Bibliography: Bruell, Jahrbuecher, 4 (1879), 96. [Ed.]

PERGAMENT, OSIP YAKOVLEVICH (1868–1909), Russian lawyer, writer, and civic leader. In 1894 he qualified as a lawyer and appeared in many important political cases. He also wrote on Bessarabian civil and commercial law. Pergament played an active part in the social life of Odessa and was a member of the municipal council. He was elected to the Second and Third Dumas, in which he took part in debates of both a political and scientific nature, as well as arguing against Jewish persecution. He wrote *Yevreyskiy vopros i narodnaya svoboda* ("The Jewish Problem and National Liberty," 1906), and *Yevreyskiy vopros i obnovleniye Rossii* ("The Jewish Problem and the Renewal of Russia," 1908).

Bibliography: S. Streich, in: YE, 12 (c.1910), 372–3. [Ed.]

PERGAMUM, ancient city (and kingdom) near the N.W. coast of Asia Minor (now Bergama, Turkey). Independent from the early third century B.C.E., Pergamum thrived primarily during the early Roman advances eastward in the first half of the second century. Following the death of the last king of Pergamum, Attalus III Philometor (133 B.C.E.), the district came under direct Roman influence as part of the province of Asia. Josephus records a "decree of the people of Pergamum" pertaining to relations with the Jewish nation (Ant., 14:247–55). The document, probably written during the reign of John Hyrcanus I (c. 113–112), refers to a decree of the Roman senate renewing its alliance with the Jews. Of particular interest are its concluding assurances of friendship between Pergamum and Hyrcanus, "remembering that in the time of Abraham, who was the father of all Hebrews, our ancestors were their friends, as we find in the public records." A similar claim, describing the common ancestry of the Jews and Spartans, is recorded elsewhere (cf. Jos., Ant., 12:226; I Macc. 12:21; cf. II Macc. 5:9), and these should be understood as an accepted mode of Greek diplomatic correspondence. Relations between Judea and Pergamum are further cited by Josephus during the reign of Herod the Great, who included the city among those to which generous donations and gifts were offered (Wars, 1:425). By the first century B.C.E. a Jewish community existed in Pergamum, as Cicero refers to the confiscation of funds in Pergamum intended for the Temple in Jerusalem (*Pro Flacco* 28:68).

Bibliography: Schuerer, Gesch, 3 (1909[4]), 13, 112 n. 45; idem, Hist, 322 n. 30; M. Stern, *Ha-Te'udot le-Mered ha-Ḥashmona'im* (1965), 151–3, 162–5; A. Schalit, *Koenig Herodes* (1969), 834 (index), s.v. *Pergamon*. [I.G.]

PERGOLA, RAPHAEL DELLA (1876–1923), Italian rabbi. Della Pergola studied at Florence and for seven years served as rabbi of Gorizia. In 1910 he was appointed head of the Jewish community of Alexandria, Egypt, retaining this post until shortly before his death which occurred in Florence. He was also of great help to the refugees from Ereẓ Israel who went to Egypt during World War I. One of the leading Zionists in Alexandria, in 1918, when the cornerstone of the Hebrew University was laid in Jerusalem, Della Pergola was invited by Weizmann to participate in the ceremony.

Bibliography: Politi, in: *Israel* (Aug. 28, 1923), 1; B. Taragan, *Les communautés israélites d'Alexandrie* (1932), 58–60; idem, *Le-Korot ha-Kehillah ha-Yehudit be-Alexandriyyah* (1947), 108–10. [Ed.]

PERI (Pflaum), HIRAM (Heinz; 1900–1962), Romance and Renaissance scholar. Born in Berlin, Peri's doctoral dissertation, published in 1926, was devoted to the Jewish Renaissance philosopher Leone Ebreo (Judah *Abrabanel).

Hiram Peri, Renaissance scholar. Photo Ricarda Schwerin, Studio Alfred Bernheim, Jerusalem.

In 1925 he emigrated to Palestine and in 1927 became assistant librarian at the Jewish National and University Library, Jerusalem. From 1928 Peri lectured on Romance languages and literature and on the history of Renaissance literature at the Hebrew University (from 1948 as professor).

Peri's scholarly interests extended to a wide range of subjects. He wrote many articles on the history of the theater, on Ladino grammar and poetry, on the relations between Church and Synagogue and religious disputations in the Middle Ages. He edited and annotated the Hebrew edition of Burkhardt's classic *Kultur der Renaissance in Italien,* with a supplement of his own (*Tarbut ha-Renaissance be-Eiropah;* 1949, 1953), and served as an editor and contributor in his field with the *Encyclopedia Hebraica.* A volume of studies was published in his memory (*Romanica et Occidentalia,* ed. by M. Lazar (1963), and contains a bibliography of works by Peri, see pp. 17–22).

Bibliography: G. Scholem and M. Lazar, *Al Professor Ḥiram Peri* (1964). [ED.]

PERI EẒ-ḤAYYIM (Heb. פְּרִי עֵץ־חַיִּים; "fruit of the tree of life"), Hebrew periodical devoted to halakhic responsa and published in Amsterdam from 1691 to 1807. *Peri Eẓ-Ḥayyim,* a forerunner of Hebrew periodical literature, was issued by the well-known yeshivah, Eẓ Ḥayyim, founded in 1616. In the 18th century the yeshivah became the largest and most important Torah center not only of Sephardi Jewry but of Ashkenazi Jewry as well. Accordingly, halakhic queries addressed to the yeshivah's outstanding talmudists reflect the entire spectrum of Jewish life in the 17th and 18th centuries and all aspects of *halakhah.* Decisions or advice were requested on such matter as inheritance laws, civil claims, social conflicts, shipping merchandise, piracy, the slave trade, the value of coinage and its fluctuations, Jewish housing difficulties in Holland, *agunot,* and marriages between those of greatly differing ages. Most of the decisions are dated and signed by the rabbis who gave them. The responsa indicate that, in the main, Dutch Jewry lived completely within the religious tradition, even though some of the inquirers, particularly among the women, no longer knew Hebrew. Halakhic inquiries came predominantly from Holland and its colonies, with some coming from the Mediterranean littoral and elsewhere. There are letters that reveal their writers to have been Marranos, whose problems are also clarified in these responsa. Although almost all the responsa are on halakhic matters, occasionally information about and reactions to other things are also recorded. Thus, there are praises for the art of printing and for science, accounts of the history of the Spanish Jews in Amsterdam, and the Hebrew poet David Franco-*Mendes' history of the yeshivah Eẓ Ḥayyim and of *Peri Eẓ-Ḥayyim.* Only a few copies of each responsa were published and as a result a complete set is no longer extant. Of the 952 responsa, 948 have been preserved and these are housed in different libraries throughout the world (e.g., the Ets Ḥayyim library in Amsterdam, the Rosenthal collection of the Amsterdam University Library, the National Library in Jerusalem, and the library of J. L. Maimon in Jerusalem). In 1936 Max Hirsch Menko published, with an introduction and indexes, a German synopsis of all the extant responsa.

Bibliography: Y. Raphael, *Rishonim va-Aḥaronim* (1957), 323–7; Y. Toury, in: *Benjamin De Vries Memorial Volume* (1968), 319–20. [G.K.]

PERIZZITES (Heb. פְּרִזִּי), pre-Israelite inhabitants of Palestine, who lived in the neighborhood of Shechem (Gen. 13:7; 34:30; Josh. 17:15; Judg. 1:4, 5), in particular in Bezek (Khirbat Ibzīq, northeast of Shechem). The Perizzites are listed among the traditional group of six (sometimes five or seven) pre-Israelite peoples of the Promised Land (Ex. 3:8, 17; Deut. 7:1; Josh. 3:10, et al.) but, unlike the others, are not included among the descendants of Canaan (Gen. 10:15–17).

The origin of the term Perizzite is still unknown. Some scholars have surmised a connection with the word *perazot,* "unwalled towns or suburbs"; others, on the basis of the element *brz* in their name, that is found in the (Sumerian) Akkadian *parzi(llu)* and the West Semitic *barzel,* meaning "iron," suggest that the Perizzites were migrating metalworkers. Others, basing themselves on the fact that *Pire/izzi* is attested as the name of an envoy sent by King Tushratta of Hurri-Mitanni to Egypt, identify the Perizzites as an Anatolian ethnic group who reached Canaan, perhaps as migrating workers or slaves, as part of the political agreement between the Hittites and Egypt during the 18th Dynasty. The sources are the *Tell el-Amarna tablets nos. 27, 28, and 29. On no. 27 there is a hieratic Egyptian note: *Pirasi.* Other forms of the same personal name in Egyptian transliterations are *Pirisija, Pirisim,* names of slaves. There is also the Nuzi-Hurrian personal name *Pirzu.* These occurrences of the name support the tentative conclusion that the Perizzites, who, in the Bible, are indeed separated from Canaanites, are of Anatolian-Hurrian origin.

Bibliography: W. F. Albright, in: JPOS, 2 (1922), 110–39; idem, *Vocalization of the Egyptian Syllable Orthography* (1934), 43; H. L. Ginsberg and B. Maisler (Mazar), in: JPOS, 14 (1934), 234–67; I. J. Gelb et al., *Nuzi Personal Names* (1943), 115; Alt, Kl Schr, 3 (1959), 38; W. Held, *Beziehungen Aegyptens mit Vorderasien* (1962), 378, nos. 17–18; P. Welten, in: ZDPV, 81 (1965), 138. [P.A./I.GRU.]

PERJURY. Witnesses are guilty of perjury if it is proved, by the evidence of at least two other competent and consistent witnesses, that they had not been present at the time and at the place where they had testified to have been when the event in issue had happened (Mak. 1:4). Such false witnesses are known as *edim zomemim* (lit. conspiring witnesses). It is not sufficient that anything to which those witnesses had testified is contradicted by new witnesses, to the effect that what they had testified was untrue (as for "contradictions," see *Witness): such contradictions are only the starting point of the evidence required to convict those witnesses of perjury (Maim. Yad, Edut 18:4), namely, that they could not possibly have witnessed the facts to which they had testified (*ibid.,* 18:2). Even though the evidence of the first set of witnesses had been accepted by the court as truthful, it is the evidence of the latter set of witnesses, testifying to the "alibi" of the first, that is to be accepted as conclusive (Mak. 5b; Yad, Edut 18:3) irrespective of the actual number of witnesses in each set. The latter set of witnesses must testify in the presence of the first set. Should this not be possible, e.g., if the first set are dead, this constitutes a "contradiction" and both testimonies will be discarded (cf. Yad, Edut 18:5). Where no evidence of perjury in the technical sense was available, but the evidence had conclusively been contradicted (e.g., where the murdered man appeared in court alive), the court would inflict disciplinary lashes (*Makkat Mardut*—see *Flogging; Yad, Edut 18:6; *Sha'arei Ẓedek* 4:7, 24 and 45; Rosh, resp., 58:4; et al.).

The punishment for perjury is laid down in the Bible: "you shall do to him as he schemed to do his fellow . . . Nor must you show pity: life for life, eye for eye, tooth for tooth, hand for hand, foot for foot" (Deut. 19:19–21). The Sadducees interpreted this law literally: the false witness would not forfeit his life, unless and until the man against whom he had testified had been executed; but the Pharisean interpretation, which is the source of the law as it was eventually established, was that the witness must be made to suffer what he had schemed to do, but not what he had actually caused to occur, to his fellow (Sif. Deut. 190; Mak. 1:6)—so that the biblical law was held to be applicable only where a man had been sentenced on the strength of false testimony, but before he was executed; the witnesses who had testified against him were then formally tried and convicted of perjury (Yad. Edut 20:2). This was a highly improbable contingency, as there was hardly an interval between sentence and execution (see *Practice and Procedure). The enunciation of this rule is followed in the Talmud by the objection that it could not be right to take the life of the witness when the life of the person he had schemed to kill had not in fact been taken; or, if the Bible really required that to be the law, then a fortiori must the life of the witness be taken after that person had been executed: if a man is liable to die because of having intended to kill, surely he must be liable to die if he had actually killed. The objection was dismissed in reliance on the rule (see *Penal Law) that no criminal offense can be created by analogy or logical deduction (Mak. 5b; and cf. Sanh. 74a and 76a; et al.).

Later commentators theorized that God's presence in the court (cf. Deut. 19:17) would sufficiently enlighten the minds of the judges to detect the falsehood of the testimony in time, before execution, for it is written, "do not bring death on the righteous and innocent, for I will not acquit the wrongdoer" (Ex. 23:7): it follows that the offense of perjury can have been committed only where the accused had not yet been executed, for a man who was executed must have been rightly convicted (Naḥmanides, commentary, Deut. 19:19).

The rule was, however, limited to capital cases only. Perjured witnesses were given the same non-capital punishments as had already been inflicted on those against whom they had testified (Yad, Edut 20:2), and where the defendant in a civil case had paid the judgment debt, the amount so paid was recovered from the witnesses (Tur, ḤM 38:2). Where the sanction imposed on the strength of their testimony could not be imposed on them (e.g., where an alleged manslayer had been banished to a *city of refuge, or where a priest had been suspended from office), they would be flogged (Yad, Edut 20:8–9; Tur, ḤM 38:3). To be convicted of perjury, no previous warning had to be given to false witnesses (Ket. 33a; Yad, Edut 18:4; Tur, ḤM 38:9). No single witness could be convicted of perjury: the conviction had always to be in respect of both (or all) the witnesses who had testified falsely together (Mak. 1:7); and when once one false witness had alone been convicted, it was said that innocent blood had been shed (Mak. 5b). As perjured witnesses are disqualified from being admitted as a witness in future, all convictions of perjury must be given wide publicity (Sanh. 89a; Maim. Yad, Edut 18:7), to fulfill the biblical command that "all others will hear and be afraid" (Deut. 19:20).

Bibliography: D. Hoffmann, in MWJ, 5 (1878), 1–14; O. Baehr, *Das Gesetz ueber falsche Zeugen nach Bibel und Talmud* (1882); J. Horovitz, in: *Festschrift . . . David Hoffmann* (1914), 139–61; idem, *Untersuchungen zur rabbinischen Lehre von den falschen Zeugen* (1914); J. S. Zuri, *Mishpat ha-Talmud*, 7 (1921), 46; Gulak, Yesodei, 4 (1922), 161–3; ET, 8 (1957), 609–23; L. Finkelstein, *The Pharisees*, 1 (1962³), 142–4; 2 (1962³), 696–8; Z. Dor, in: *Sefer ha-Shanah Bar-Ilan*, 2 (1964), 107–24; P. Daykan, in; *Sinai*, 56 (1964/65), 295–302; S. Schmida, *Li-Ve'ayat Edei Sheker* (Diss. 1965).

[H.H.C.]

PERL, JOSEPH (1773–1839), author of significant satirical works and leading figure in the Galician *Haskalah. Perl was born in Tarnopol, where he spent most of his life. In his youth he was attracted to Ḥasidism and acquired knowledge of the movement's way of life and literature. Under the influence of the *maskilim*, especially those of Brody in Galicia, Perl joined the Haskalah movement as early as the beginning of the 19th century. Perl was very active in Jewish education and public life. In 1813 he established in Tarnopol the first modern Jewish school in Galicia, whose curriculum, in the spirit of moderate Haskalah, included both general and Jewish studies. He supported and directed the school throughout his life. He sought to modernize the Jewish community of Tarnopol by attempting to enlist the aid first of the Russian government and then, after 1815, of the Austrian government. Perhaps most conspicuous was his vigorous fight against the ḥasidic movement, which had spread throughout Volhynia and Podolia as well as Galicia. Perl's literary activity began around 1814. In 1814–16, Perl published calendars which contain both scientific information and excerpts from talmudic literature in the vein of the *maskilim*. The entire body of his work has never been published, and some of his works are at present in the process of publication for the first time. Those of Perl's works in manuscript stored in his valuable library in Tarnopol were probably, for the most part, destroyed during the Holocaust; vestiges of this collection are preserved in the National Library in Jerusalem. During his lifetime some of Perl's works were circulated in manuscript, while others were published years after they had been presented to the censor for approval, e.g., *Boḥen Ẓaddik* ("The Test of the Righteous"), which was written in 1825 and published in 1838.

Perl signed his principal satirical works with the pseudonym Obadiah b. Pethahiah, which often prevented the reading public from identifying him as the author. Until recently Perl was known only as a Hebrew writer, but he wrote a polemic against Ḥasidism in German, and was also the author of works in Yiddish. His principal satirical work, *Megalleh Temirin* ("The Revealer of Secrets"; Vienna, 1819), was written in a parallel Yiddish version, which was first published only in 1937 by YIVO in Vilna. Periodical stories in the manner of Naḥman of Bratslav's *Sippurei Ma'asiyyot* were published in both their Hebrew and Yiddish versions in 1969 by the Israel Academy for Sciences and Humanities in Jerusalem. It is also known that he adapted a Yiddish version of an historical novel, *Antigonus*, and apparently translated Fielding's *Tom Jones* into Yiddish, probably from a German version.

Although Perl made an important contribution to the creation of Yiddish fiction during the first half of the 19th century he did not advocate the use of this language. Like other Haskalah authors his aim in employing Yiddish was practical—to propagate Haskalah ideas among the Yiddish-speaking masses. Yet none of Perl's Yiddish works, which in spite of his intention show an original and idiomatic use of language, appeared during his lifetime.

Both in his public activities and in his writings Perl fought Ḥasidism because he believed their doctrines and leaders to be obstacles to the modernization of Jewish life. By means of denunciatory and hostile notes and memoranda (recently discovered and published) sent incessantly to the officials, he encouraged the Austrian authorities in Galicia to intervene against the Ḥasidim. In the literary sphere he battled against the movement by means of propaganda, parody, and satire. Characteristic is his German manuscript, *Ueber das Wesen der Sekte Chassidim* (1816), in which he condemned the ḥasidic movement, its practices and beliefs, on the grounds that they jeopardized the welfare of the state and misled a multitude of innocent believers. Addressing both gentile and Jewish readers he denigrates Ḥasidism by creating a hostile, often distorted anthology of quotations lifted out of context from the ḥasidic sources. Perl wrote stories in the manner of Naḥman of Bratslav, in fact, pretending that they had been discovered after the rabbi's death by one of his Ḥasidim. Thus he published a supplement, as it were, to Naḥman's incompleted *Ma'aseh me-Avedat Bat Melekh,* claiming it to have been in the possession of a Ḥasid who was close to the rabbi toward the end of his life. Similarly, Perl wrote another story, *Ma'aseh me-Avedat Ben Melekh,* in Hebrew and Yiddish. These stories use the style and some themes and motifs of R. Naḥman only to further the Haskalah aim of criticizing and eventually eradicating Ḥasidism.

Perl's principal work, *Megalleh Temirin,* shows the influence of 18th-century satirical stories written in the form of letters, which achieved great popularity in France and Germany (especially Montesquieu's *Persian Letters* and Wieland's satirical writings). Perl integrated the structure of the secular European satirical letter not only with the style, language, and ideas of the ḥasidic letter, but with its typographical form as well. An imitation of the ḥasidic story, *Megalleh Temirin* is made up of 151 letters, a preface, and an epilogue.

The story's main character, Obadiah b. Pethahiah, who is possessed of magical powers, presents himself as a fervent Ḥasid who had miraculously obtained these letters. Here the denunciations of Ḥasidism contained in Perl's German manuscript reappear amplified by many annotations attached to the correspondence. The annotations interpret the views and facts mentioned in the letters, and they also serve as a medium for Obadiah's ironic commentary. The letters reveal a number of plots, the principal one being the search for the German "book" (Buch) which endangers Ḥasidism and undermines the authority of its leaders by revealing their innermost secrets. Therefore it must be obtained at any cost and destroyed, and revenge taken on its author. The hunt for the "book," which is actually Perl's own German manuscript, yields several subplots based on intrigues and schemes set within ḥasidic life. The search, resembling a comedy of errors, ends in complete failure. Other aspects of the plot reveal the machinations of the Ḥasidim in their struggle for influence and material gain. In Perl's satire, the ḥasidic leaders do not stop short of employing stratagems of bribery, deceit, blackmail, and intimidation against their rivals, whether rabbis or *maskilim.* In spite of his intention to demean Ḥasidism, its philosophy and practices, a number of descriptions escape Perl's satiric control, communicating vitality, naturalness, and humor. The Hebrew in which these letters are written contains Yiddishisms lending flexibility and expressiveness to the speech of the Ḥasidim. Like many *maskilim* Perl considered this ḥasidic Hebrew a ludicrous language, offensive to the Haskalah ideal of a "pure" Hebrew language written in biblical style and according to grammatical rules. In spite of these feelings Perl's ḥasidic Hebrew conveys great liveliness.

Boḥen Ẓaddik (Prague, 1838), a sequel to *Megalleh Temirin,* consists of two sections, the first, a discussion of readers' reactions to *Megalleh Temirin,* and the second, a series of letters. Obadiah b. Pethahiah reappears in this work as a man who possesses a magical device—a board on which people's conversations are secretly recorded. The board, however, can be erased only by an absolutely honest man, and the search for this ideal person brings Obadiah into contact with the diverse elements composing Jewish society, each of whose weaknesses and follies is mercilessly exposed. Thus the number of subjects coming in for satirical treatment is increased to include not only Ḥasidim, but rabbis, traders, artisans, and even *maskilim,* all of whom are found defective, each in his own way. At the end of these wanderings the honest man is discovered, paradoxically, as a Jewish pious farmer in a remote village in southern Russia, which is governed in an almost utopian fashion by Jewish farmers. Taking to heart all that he learned from his travels, Obadiah turns his back on Ḥasidism and preaches in a pathetic manner to his people.

Perl wrote also letters published in Hebrew periodicals in Austria: of special importance are his letters protesting against the collection of funds in the name of R. *Meir Ba'al ha-Nes. Ironically, there is an unpublished letter in which a Ḥasid jests at the foibles of the contributors to the periodical *Kerem Ḥemed,* who pursue honor and empty phrases and whose spiritual horizons are narrow. Perl's satire, employed to promote the aims of the Haskalah, is of interest today primarily because of its literary merit and authenticity, qualities that have outlived the author's immediate intentions.

Bibliography: N. Gordon, in: HUCA (1904), 235–42; I. Davidson, *Parody in Hebrew Literature* (1907), 61–74; Klausner, Sifrut, 2 (1937), 278–314; I. Weinles, in: *Yosef Perls Yidishe Ksovim* (1937), 7–70; R. Mahler, *Ha-Ḥasidut ve-ha-Haskalah* (1961), 155–208; Ch. Shmeruk, in: *Zion,* 21 (1957), 94–99; S. Werses, in: *Tarbiz,* 32 (1962/63), 396–401; idem, in: *Hasifrut,* 1 (1968–69), 206–27; idem and Ch. Shmeruk (eds.), *Yosef Perl, Ma'asiyyot ve-Iggerot* (1969), 11–86, Eng. summary: A. Rubinstein, in: KS, 37 (1961/62); 38 (1962/63).
[S.WE.]

PERLA, JEROHAM FISCHEL BEN ARYEH ẒEVI (1846–1934), scholar and commentator. Born in Warsaw, Perla at the age of 15 went to study under Joshua Leib Diskin in Lomza, and when Diskin left Lomza he became the pupil of Ḥayyim *Soloveichik of Brest-Litovsk. Perla was invited by many communities, including those of Cracow and Lublin to accept the position of communal rabbi. Believing that the burdens of office would interrupt his study, however, he refused all the calls extended to him and devoted himself entirely to study, supported by his wife, who kept a shop in Warsaw. Perla spent 40 years on his remarkable three-volume commentary on Saadiah's *Sefer ha-Mitzvot,* which he completed in 1917. With the appearance of this extensive and brilliant work Perla's reputation spread, reaching Ereẓ Israel long before he himself arrived there, and due to it he entered into correspondence with Ḥayyim *Sonnenfeld. They became close friends after Perla's arrival in Jerusalem in 1924, but otherwise Perla shunned people in order to spend his whole time studying. It is said that in his house there was a chest containing many manuscripts, including a commentary on Eliezer b. Nathan's *Raban,* equal in length to Perla's commentary on the *Sefer ha-Mitzvot.* Perla began to publish a commentary on *Kaftor va-Feraḥ* of Estori ha-Parḥi called *Pirḥei Ẓiyyon,* but only the first five chapters appeared (1966). The manuscript of the remainder was taken back to Europe by Perla's son and was lost in the Holocaust. Perla died in Jerusalem.

Bibliography: J. Gelis, *Mi-Gedolei Yerushalayim* (1967), 233–8; Saadiah Gaon, *Sefer ha-Mitzvot . . . im Be'ur . . . Yehudah Yeruḥam Perla* (1962), preface.
[AN.L.L.]

PERLBACH, MAX (1848–1921), German historian. Born in Danzig, Perlbach worked as a librarian at the following institutions of higher learning: Koenigsberg (1872–76),

Greifswald (1876–83), and Halle (1883–1903), and was then appointed to direct the Royal Library at Berlin. His scientific work dealt mainly with the history of the provinces of East and West Prussia during the Middle Ages.

The works he wrote or edited include: *Ueber die Ergebnisse der Lemberger Handschrift fuer die aeltere Chronik von Oliva* (1871); *Preussische Regesten bis zum Ausgang des 13. Jahrhunderts* (1876); *Simon Grunaus preussische Chronik* (1876); *Quellen-Beiträge zur Geschichte der Stadt Koenigsberg im Mittelalter* (1878), *Preussisch-polnische Studien zur Geschichte des Mittelalters* (1886), and *Prussia Scholastica: Die Ost- und Westpreussen auf den mittelalterlichen Universitaeten* (1896). Perlbach also edited some Polish medieval sources for the *Monumenta Germaniae Historica* (1888, 1893). [G.S.]

PERLE, JOSHUA (1888–c. 1943), Yiddish novelist. Born in Radom, Poland, he went as a young man to Warsaw, where he worked as a bookkeeper all his life. He came under the influence of Sholem *Asch but gradually veered to an ever more extreme realism. His book *Unter der Zun* (1920) was a collection of realistic short stories about small Polish-Jewish villages. His book *Nayn a Zeyger Inderfri* (1930), stories of Warsaw's middle-class Jews, introduced subject matter new in Yiddish literature and established his reputation. Perle then began an autobiographical trilogy under the general title *Yidn fun a Gants Yor* ("Everyday Jews," 1935), describing his own family with its complex relationships in a naturalistic style, but avoiding the extreme of brutal frankness. By obtaining forged U.S. citizenship papers, Perle was able to survive after 1939 inside and outside the Warsaw ghetto and in Bergen-Belsen, but in 1943, together with his son, he was taken from Bergen-Belsen to an unknown destination; no further trace of them has been found.

Bibliography: Rejzen, Leksikon, 2 (1927), 936–9; M. Ravitch, *Mayn Leksikon* (1945), 168–70; Finkelstein, in: J. Perle, *Yidn fun a Gants Yor* (1951), introd. [M.Rav.]

PERLES, family of scholars and writers. Joseph Perles (1835–1894), born in Baja, Hungary, studied at the Breslau Jewish Theological Seminary and at the University of Breslau. He served as preacher of the Bruedergemeinde of Posen (Poznan) during 1862–71, and then as rabbi of the Jewish community of Munich, rejecting offers to succeed A.

Joseph Perles, rabbi and scholar. Jerusalem, J.N.U.L., Schwadron Collection.

*Geiger in Berlin and to lecture at the newly founded *Landesrabbinerschule in Budapest. Perles, a faithful and outstanding pupil of the Breslau seminary, was among its first graduates, and his interests extended over a wide area of Jewish scholarship. Ancient versions of the Bible was one of his fields; his dissertation was on the Syriac version, *Meletemata Peschitthoniana* (1859), and he edited his father-in-law's (S. B. Schefftel) *Be'urei Onkelos* (1888). His work in medieval literature and Bible exegesis was extensive. Perles' main scholarly contribution was to Hebrew and Aramaic lexicography and philology, to which he devoted such studies as: *Zur rabbinischen Sprach- und Sagenkunde* (1873), which sheds light on the aggadic sources of the *Thousand and One Nights; Beitraege zur Geschichte der hebraeischen und aramaeischen Studien* (1884); and *Beitraege zur rabbinischen Sprach- und Alterthumskunde* (1893). Perles' sons were Max (1867–1894), a noted oculist, and Felix (1874–1933), rabbi and scholar. Felix was drawn into the Zionist movement in Vienna and in 1899 he became rabbi at Koenigsberg. Like his father, Felix Perles had wide scholarly interests: Bible criticism, Hebrew and Aramaic lexicography, apocryphal and pseudepigraphical literature, medieval Hebrew poetry, liturgy, Jewish dialects, and abbreviations. His best-known works are his critique of W. Bousset's *Religion des Judentums im neutestamentlichen Zeitalter* (1903), and the collection of essays, *Juedische Skizzen* (1912, 1920[2]). Joseph Perles' wife, Rosalie (1839–1932), was a writer and journalist for a number of German-Jewish papers and periodicals. She wrote a preface to a volume of her husband's sermons—edited by their son Felix (1896)—and published some lectures. Her *Aphorismen* appeared posthumously in 1932.

Bibliography: Joseph Perles: W. Bacher, in: JQR, 7 (1894/95), 1–23 (where an almost complete bibliography is given in the footnotes). Felix Perles: Hedwig Perles, in: MGWJ, 81 (1937), 369–92 (bibliography, reprinted). [Ed.]

PERLES (Perls), ISAAC MOSES (1784–1854), Hungarian rabbi. Born in Brod, Moravia, Perles studied under Meshullam Eger in Pressburg and with Joseph b. Phinehas, rabbi of Posen. He served as rabbi in several Hungarian communities: Kojetin (from 1813), Holics (1820), Eisenstadt (1822), and Bonyhad (1841). During his last years difficulties arose between him and his community. They were in the main connected with reforms in the life of the community which Perles, despite his generally liberal approach, refused to countenance. Matters reached such a stage that he was denounced to the government as "interfering with order and authority, hating light and progress," or as "robbing and wronging his congregants, making demands upon them, and taking by force . . . in excess of that to which he was entitled." The government, knowing that the charges were baseless, ignored them, but as a result of the dispute Perles left Bonyhad and returned to Brod, where he died after a few months. After his death his grandson Abraham Ẓevi published his work *Beit Ne'eman* (1907), including responsa of great interest and prefaced by Perles' biography. His son Meir (1811–1893) was born in Brod. Although a profound talmudic scholar, he did not join the Orthodox camp. He served as rabbi in Carei (Mare) from 1834. In *Beit Ne'eman* there is a letter to him from Moses *Sofer dated 1834.

Bibliography: ZHB, 12 (1908), 68–70; P. Z. Schwartz, *Shem ha-Gedolim me-Ereẓ Hagar,* 1 (1914), 51a; 2 (1914), 2b; N. Ben-Menaḥem, *Mi-Sifrut Yisrael be-Ungaryah* (1958), 170, no. 91. [N.B.-M.]

PERLES, MOSES MEIR BEN ELEAZAR (1666–1739), rabbi and author. Perles was born in Prague. About 1708 he was in Frankfort, Amsterdam, and Rotterdam, and in his work *Megillat Sefer,* he tells of the troubles which befell him in the winter of 1708, while he was in an isolated village outside Vienna: on the Sabbath of *Zakhor* and Purim he had neither *Sefer Torah* nor Scroll of Esther, and he vowed to compile a commentary on the latter if he were delivered. He reached Vienna, where he lived in the house of Samson *Wertheimer, acting as his secretary. Wertheimer supported him after he returned to Prague. Perles kept his vow and compiled his commentary entitled *Megillat Sefer* (Prague, 1710), which is based mainly on Rashi's commentary to Esther. In his introduction he also mentions his other works, which have remained in manuscript: *Penei Ḥammah* on the *aggadot* of the Talmud; *Or Olam*, sermons for the festivals; *Kiryat Arba*, sermons on the biblical portions read on the four special *Sabbaths before Passover; and *Me'ir Netivot* (which according to one view is identical with *Or Olam*). He died in Prague.

His sons included Aaron, who published the *Seder ha-Nikkur* of the *Sefer ha-Ittur* with the commentary *Tohorat Aharon* (Offenbach, 1725) containing extracts from the works of the *posekim* and the laws of porging in German, and Moses, who compiled *Mishmeret ha-Bayit* (Prague, 1739), containing in ten *mishmarot* ("vigils"), sermons and ethical admonitions.

Bibliography: Steinschneider, Cat Bod, 725, 1981; Neubauer, Cat, 792; S. Hock and D. Kaufmann, *Die Familien Prags* (1892), 280–1. [Y.Ho.]

PERLHEFTER, ISSACHAR BEHR BEN JUDAH MOSES (d. after 1701), Bohemian rabbi. Born in Prague, a member of the *Eybeschuetz family, he married Bella, the daughter of Jacob Perlhefter of Prague, whose family name he adopted. They moved to Vienna, but after the expulsion of its Jews in 1670, he went to Altdorf where he taught Hebrew to Johann *Wagenseil who was a professor there. Perlhefter's wife, a highly cultured woman, taught Wagenseil's daughter dancing and music. Perlhefter was next appointed rabbi of Mantua where his father had previously served. After six years Perlhefter was forced to leave, as a result of a dispute over Mordecai of Eisenstadt, a follower of *Shabbetai Ẓevi whom Perlhefter at first supported, but subsequently exposed when his deceptions became known. Perlhefter later returned to his native city where he was appointed *dayyan* and scribe, a position formerly held by his grandfather. Perlhefter was the author of *Ohel Yissakhar* on the laws of *sheḥitah*, with a Judeo-German translation (Wilhermsdorf, 1670); *Ma'aseh Ḥoshen u-Ketoret* (Prague, 1686), an excerpt from Abraham b. David *Portaleone's *Shiltei ha-Gibborim* (Mantua, 1619) on archaeology: and *Ba'er Heitev* (Prague, 1699) on the *Targum Jonathan* to the Pentateuch.

Bibliography: D. Kaufmann, *"Die letzte Vertreibung der Juden aus Wien und Niederoesterreich,"* in: *Jahresbericht der Landes-Rabbinerschule in Budapest 1887–88* (1889), 201f. [L.I.R.]

PERLMAN, ALFRED EDWARD (1902–), U.S. railroad executive and first Jewish president of a major American railway system. Perlman was born in St. Paul, Minnesota, and spent his early career working with the engineering and administrative departments of major United States railroad corporations. From 1952 to 1954 he was president of the New York Central System and in 1965 he became president and chief administrative officer of the Pennsylvania-New York Central Transportation Company which went bankrupt in 1970. Among Perlman's many public offices in the United States and abroad were those of an adviser to the Korean (1949) and Israel (1950) railroad systems. He was chairman of the Eastern Railroads Presidents' Conference, a member of most professional organizations connected with railroading, and a contributor to professional publications. [J.O.R.]

PERLMAN, HELEN HARRIS (1905–), U.S. social work educator. Helen Perlman, who was born in St. Paul, Minnesota, worked for family and child guidance agencies in Chicago and New York from 1927 to 1940. In 1940 she became a lecturer and a student supervisor at the School of Social Work of Columbia University. In 1945 she was appointed professor of social work at the University of Chicago's School of Social Administration. She was best known for her contributions to the theory of social casework and to training for social work practice. She wrote *Social Casework: A Problem Solving Process* (1957; 1958[2]), *So You Want to be a Social Worker* (1962), and *Persona* (1968). [J.N.]

PERLMAN, JACOB (1898–1967), U.S. economist. Perlman was born in Bialystok, Poland, and was taken to the United States in 1912. After a brief period of teaching at the University of North Dakota he entered government service, and during the 1930s worked with the Bureau of Labor Statistics and the Social Security Administration. In 1949 he became a technical expert for the United Nations and was sent as economic adviser to the governments of Colombia, Greece, Bolivia, and the Philippines. From 1956 to 1965 he was head of the Office of Economic and Manpower Studies of the National Science Foundation. In addition to his work for governmental and international institutions, Perlman also taught at various universities in the United States and abroad. He specialized in development economics and particularly in the study of the economic effects of science and technology. Perlman died while on a visit to Israel.

Bibliography: *New York Times* (April 10, 1968), 43. [J.O.R.]

PERLMAN, SAMUEL (1887–1958), editor and translator. Born in Minsk, Perlman settled in Ereẓ Israel in 1914. During World War I he was among those exiled to Alexandria; there he directed a school for refugee children. On his return he became an editor of *Haaretz*. He again left for abroad, and, in Berlin, was one of the editors of *Haolam*. Later, together with *Jabotinsky, he founded the Ha-Sefer publishing house; the two were also the joint editors of the first modern Hebrew atlas (1926). Between 1926 and 1932, Perlman was a teacher and the director of the *Boston Hebrew Teachers' College. Returning to Ereẓ Israel in 1932, he became active in the publishing field, joining Devir in 1944. While he wrote articles on literary subjects, he engaged primarily in translation; Perlman's major work was the translation into Hebrew of Heine's prose works. He also translated works by Herzl and Strindberg.

Bibliography: Kressel, Leksikon, 2 (1967), 679. [G.K.]

PERLMAN, SELIG (1888–1959), U.S. labor economist. Born in Bialystok, Poland. Perlman emigrated to the United States in 1908. After a brief period in New York, he became interested in the work of the *Bund. While studying at the University of Wisconsin, he investigated the Lawrence strike for the United States Commission on Industrial Relations (1914–15). From 1918 he taught economics at the University of Wisconsin at Madison.

Selig Perlman, U.S. labor economist. Courtesy University of Wisconsin, Madison, Wis.

Perlman's main field was the social development of the American, British, and Russian labor movements. He modified his early Marxist socialism as being too theoretical in its approach to social and economic problems and turned his attention to the labor movement and trade unionism.

These he regarded as indispensable to a stable industrial society because of their tendency to strengthen labor's bargaining position and their regard for private property. Perlman was active in secular Jewish affairs, especially in the American Jewish Labor Movement. He developed a special relationship with the garment industry unions. In his later years, he showed interest in Zionism and the State of Israel. His best-known book is *A Theory of the Labor Movement* (1928). He was a contributor to the *History of Labor in the United States* (1918–52).

Bibliography: Witte, in: *Industrial and Labor Relations Review*, 13 (1960), 335ff. [M.PE.]

PERLMANN, MOSHE (1905–), U.S. scholar in oriental studies. Born in Odessa, Russia, Perlmann studied in Odessa, Jerusalem, and London. He moved to the United States in 1940 and held positions in several U.S. universities, while maintaining a steady output of articles and studies in oriental history, literature, and thought. Perlmann taught at the New School for Social Research (1945–52), Dropsie College (1948–55), and Harvard (1955–61). In 1961 he became a professor of Arabic at the University of California in Los Angeles.

One of Perlmann's earliest projects was a compilation of all the references in the Talmud to health or medicine. This collection was published in 1926 as *Midrash ha-Refu'ah*. Perlmann translated Carl Brockelman's *History of the Islamic Peoples* (1947). His own writings include studies of early Arab manuscripts, and *Chapters of Arab-Jewish Diplomacy, 1918–22* (1944), a collection of printed materials that deal with early attempts at rapprochement. He also published letters written by Leo *Levanda to J. L. *Gordon, with an introduction in which he discusses these two literary figures and the relationship between them (in: *American Academy for Jewish Research, Proceedings* (1967), 139–85). [ED.]

PERLMUTTER, ABRAHAM ẒEVI (?1844–1926), rabbi in Poland. At the age of 18 he was nominated as rabbi in a townlet, later officiating in Leczyca, Raciaz, and other communities. Although descended from *mitnaggedim*, he sought the company of Polish *ẓaddikim* and was particularly close to the *ẓaddik* of Gostynin, *Jehiel Meir Lifschits ("Ba'al ha-Tehillim") from whom he received the authorization to study languages to assist him in his public activities. In 1886 he was appointed rabbi in *Radom, where he participated in many community activities. He was awarded a silver medal after the coronation of Czar *Nicholas II in 1894. Perlmutter was active in improving the condition of Jewish soldiers stationed in the barracks in Radom and established a *kasher* kitchen there. He was also instrumental in abolishing a severe decree against Jewish peddlers. In 1909 he was appointed rabbi in Warsaw, a position he held until his death. In 1917 he was coopted to the provisional state council of Poland, which had been organized under the German occupation. In 1919 he was elected to the first Polish parliament (Sejm) as representative of *Agudat Israel for the Warsaw district. As the doyen of the Jewish representatives he was the first to present his party's declaration on the claims of Orthodox Jews in parliament. Even in his eighties Perlmutter continued to pursue his communal activities and he participated in the Polish and world conventions of Agudat Israel. [Y.AR.]

PERLOV, YIẒḤAK (1911–), Yiddish poet, novelist, and editor. Born in Biala Podlaska, Poland, Perlov during World War I lived in Minsk, where he remained until 1939, and from 1940 to 1946 he resided in the Soviet Union. In 1947 he sailed to Ereẓ Israel on the *Exodus*, but was returned to Germany by the British. In 1949 he emigrated to Israel and lived there until 1961 when he went to New York. He began his literary career in 1928 with the publication of his poems in the *Literarishe Bleter* (Warsaw).

His works, some of which have appeared under such pseudonyms as A. Bril, Y. B. Avromarin, Itshe Matlies, and P. Itzkhakov, include: the poems *Frunza Verda* (1932), *Untergang* (1935), *Undzer Regnboygn* (1948), *Undzer Likui-Khame 1939–1946* (1947), and *Ekzodus 1947* (1948); the novels *Blandzende Kayafn* (Warsaw, 1936; on life in the theater); *Der Tsurikgekumener* (1952); *Dzebelia* (1955); *Flora Ingber* (1959); and *Mayne Zibn Gute Yor* (1959). In addition, two novels, *Di Kenign fun di Zumpn* and *Der Elnter Dor* appeared in the Yiddish daily, *Forward*. Perlov wrote many dramatic works of which *Goldene Zangen* (1938), *Abi Man Zet Zikh* (1939), and *Blinde Pasazhirn* (1939) were performed in Poland prior to World War II. In 1959 he published his Yiddish translation of Boris Pasternak's *Dr. Zhivago* (Tel Aviv). His collected works, edited by R. Ariel, appeared in Tel Aviv, 1954.

Bibliography: LNYL, 7 (1968), 185–6. [Y.SHE.]

PERLSTEIN, MEYER A. (1902–1969), U.S. pediatrician and educator. Perlstein, who was born in Chicago, practiced medicine there from 1929. A specialist in cerebral palsy and other children's neurological diseases, Perlstein was chief of the children's neurology clinic at Cook County Hospital, director of the Cerebral Palsy project at Michael Reese Hospital, and chairman of the medical advisory board of the Therapeutic Day Nursery and of the Illinois Children's Hospital School. Perlstein taught pediatrics at Northwestern University and at the postgraduate school of Cook County Hospital. A founder (1949) and president (1954) of the American Academy for Cerebral Palsy, Perlstein was a consultant and medical advisory board member of many organizations for the benefit of those affected by neurological diseases. He wrote many articles for professional journals and produced movies on medical subjects. In addition he was active on the American Physicians Fellowship Committee of the Israel Medical Association. [ED.]

PERLZWEIG, MAURICE L. (1895–), Reform rabbi and official of the World Jewish Congress. Born in Poland, Perlzweig was educated in England, where he was founder and chairman of the University Labor Federation of Great Britain and president of the World Union of Jewish Students and deputy member of the Executive of the Jewish Agency. He also officiated at the Liberal Synagogue in London. A founding member of the World Jewish Congress and the first chairman of its British section, in 1942 Perlzweig was nominated head of the World Jewish Congress Department of International Affairs in New York and represented it at the Economic and Social Council of the United Nations and subsidiary bodies. He attended numerous international conferences and meetings as a spokesman of Jewish interests and causes and drafted many documents submitted to the United Nations, particularly the Commission of Human Rights and Sub-Commission on Prevention of Discrimination, on crucial problems of Jewish communities around the world. [N.LER.]

°**PERNERSTORFER, ENGELBERT** (1850–1918), leader of the Austrian Social Democratic party. Pernerstorfer's attitude toward the Jewish question and anti-Semitism was peculiarly ambivalent: this was in part to blame for the failure of the Austrian Social Democrats to come to grips with the Jewish question in his time. Pernerstorfer was a school friend of Victor *Adler and godfather at the baptism of the then seven-year-old Friedrich *Adler. He started his public career as editor of Georg von *Schoenerer's periodical, but parted with him in 1883 because of the latter's virulent anti-Semitism. Although he was considered by his contemporaries to have anti-Semitic inclinations, Pernerstorfer vigorously opposed political anti-Semitism. His positive attitude toward Zionism stemmed from his general conception of nationality and his opposition to the cosmopolitanism professed by his Jewish colleagues in the Social Democratic leadership, among them Robert *Danneberg; Pernerstorfer averred that the left wing of the party was all Jewish. In 1916 he published an article in Martin Buber's monthly *Der *Jude,* in which he favored national autonomy for East European Jewry, and stated that the Central Powers would profit from a Jewish national home in Palestine. National Socialist propaganda later portrayed Pernerstorfer as a full-scale anti-Semite.

Bibliography: E. Silberner, *Sozialisten zur Judenfrage* (1962), 237–40, bibl. 344–7; idem, in: HJ, 13 (1951), 122–3, 129–33; 15 (1953), 15; A. Gerlach, *Der Einfluss der Juden in der oesterreichischen Sozialdemokratie* (1939, national-socialistic); J. Braunthal, *Victor und Friedrich Adler* (1965), index; idem, *In Search for the Millenium* (1945); *Neue Oesterreichische Biographie*, 2 (1925), 97–116. [M.La.]

PERPIGNAN, city in S. France, near the Spanish border. Formerly the capital of the counts of *Roussillon, in 1172 it passed to the kings of Aragon. The earliest mention of Jews in Perpignan dates from 1185; they are said to have owned real estate around this time. Toward the middle of the 13th century, King James I of Aragon offered the Jews of Perpignan land to settle which they would own in freehold. Endeavoring to attract Jews from France, he granted those of Perpignan a number of privileges and exempted them from the payment of various indirect taxes and tolls (1269). Autonomy in civil law was also granted. In 1271 the annual tax of the community amounted to 15,000 sólidos in Barcelona currency. Noteworthy among the scholars of Perpignan were R. Menahem b. Solomon *Meiri and R. Abraham *Bedersi, pupil of Joseph *Ezobi. In response to R. Abraham's petition (1274), the king granted the community a privilege to protect them against the threats of *informers. He renewed it in 1275, also forbidding the clergy to expel the Jews or summon them before the Church tribunal. At that time the community leadership consisted of 20 to 28 counsellors who were appointed for life. Infante John authorized them to convene and issue regulations, appoint procurators and other communal officials, to enforce obedience to the regulations within the community, and to punish offenders.

Some members of the community engaged in maritime commerce (in partnership with Jewish merchants of *Barcelona, *Seville, and other places); others were local merchants; an appreciable number practiced moneylending (including several of the community's trustees). Most important of the crafts was the textile industry, but there were also several silversmiths during the 14th century.

When the Kingdom of *Majorca was created after the death of James I and the seat of the monarchy established in Perpignan, the government began to oppress the local Jewish community. From the close of the century, a series of decrees were issued which sought to restrict relations between Jews and Christians; the Jews were ordered to wear special dress (1314). Restrictive decrees issued for the Kingdom of Majorca were also applied in Perpignan. A poll tax was imposed and around 1317 the king of Majorca seized the promissory notes of the Jews. There is no doubt that living conditions in Perpignan were influenced by the presence of the royal court in the town and the Jews were particularly conscious of the severity of the crown's persecution of the Jews of the kingdom. During the *Pastoureaux persecutions (1320), copies of the Talmud found in the town were burnt. Conditions improved during the reign of Pedro IV. In 1347 he appointed his physician Maestre *Crescas as a trustee of the community so as to prevent any inequalities in the financial and tax administration. At the time of the *Black Death (1348–49) several of the community's notables became converted in order to escape persecution. In 1363 Perpignan contributed toward the levy of 10,000 livres in Barcelona currency imposed to further the war against Castile. When the vessel containing the Host was stolen from a church and pledged with a Jew, the infante ordered the bailiff to conduct an inquiry in order to prevent an attack on the Jewish quarter (1367). On June 29, 1370, anti-Jewish riots broke out in Perpignan and the king appointed a procurator to investigate the damage.

During the 1360s and 1370s, Perpignan became renowned as a center of astronomers. The astronomical tables prepared by Jacob b. David Yom Tov were translated into Catalan there in 1361. In 1372 Crescas David was made physician to the king and a year later Bonet Maimon of Perpignan was appointed to the same office. The rabbis of this period included Samuel Carcossa, who was invited to Barcelona for debates with the rabbis of Aragon and Catalonia. In 1372 the king authorized the Jews of Perpignan to travel to France on business, and in 1377 protection was also granted to Jews who came to trade in Roussillon and Cerdagne from the exterior. In 1383 Pedro gave the community of Perpignan a privilege which prohibited apostates from entering the Jewish quarter in order to engage in disputes on religious questions. He also granted it permission to try informers. Anti-Jewish riots broke out on Aug. 17, 1391. During their course the Jews were given refuge in the fortress, while the inhabitants looted Jewish property. When representatives of the town demanded the conversion of the Jews, the king replied that forced conversion was prohibited. He nevertheless forbade the Jews to leave Perpignan, where refugees from other parts of Catalonia had also arrived. On September 22 John I

Page from the *Perpignan Bible*, with the colophon of the scribe Solomon bar Raphael, 1249. Paris, Bibliothèque Nationale, Ms. héb. 7, pl. 512v.

ordered the bailiff to draw up a list of property to which there were no heirs, especially that of Jews who had been martyred. On December 19 he ordered the Jews who were in the fortress to return to their homes and decreed that they were not to be molested or forced to accept baptism. The Jews of Perpignan undertook not to leave the country and in practice continued to live in the fortress until 1394.

Although the community was declining, at the beginning of the 14th century there were still 200–250 families living there, but it had lost its importance and most of the members were poor. In 1408 King Martin ratified the administrative arrangements for the election of trustees. Christians were forbidden to interfere in the affairs of the community and extensive rights were given to the trustees. In 1412 Pope *Benedict XIII wrote to the community of Perpignan on the subject of the propagation of Christianity among the Jews, writing his instructions in Hebrew so as to leave no doubt about his intentions. The community was called upon to send two delegates to a disputation to be held in Tortosa (see *Tortosa, Disputation of). At that time, Vicente *Ferrer visited the town, preaching to the Jews there. Ferdinand I prohibited the building of a new synagogue or the repair of the existing ones in 1415; he also forbade the Jews to practice medicine and pharmacy or to employ Christians in their service.

The Papal *Inquisition was active in Perpignan at the close of the 14th century. In 1346 a *Converso, Johanan David, a butcher by trade, was condemned to the stake. Many others were condemned during the 1420s and 1440s. After the Spanish Inquisition had been set up, 22 Conversos were sent to the stake in 1485. The French Army led by Louis XI and Charles VIII invaded Roussillon in 1462 and conquered Perpignan in 1475. Following the edict of expulsion from Spain (1492), a number of Jews sought refuge in Perpignan, then under Charles VIII of France; but an expulsion decree was issued against the Jews of the town in September 1493. The remnants of the large community, 39 families, sailed from Marseilles to Naples and from there to Constantinople.

At the beginning of the 20th century, there were several Jewish families living in Perpignan.

Bibliography: R. W. Emery, *Jews of Perpignan in the Thirteenth Century* (1959), includes documents: 134–95; Baer, Spain, index; Baer, Studien, 142f.; Baer, Urkunden, 1 (1929), index; I. Loeb, in: REJ, 14 (1887), 55ff.; P. Vidal, *ibid.*, 15 (1887), 19–55; 16 (1888), 1–23, 170–203; J. Miret i Sans, *Itinerari de Jaume I "El Conqueridor"* (1918); J. E. Martínez Fernando, in: *Analecta Sacra Tarraconensia*, 26 (1953), 94–95; A. López de Meneses, in: *Sefarad*, 14 (1954), 108, 275, 283, 285; J. M. Millás Vallicrosa, *ibid.*, 19 (1959), 365ff.; F. Vendrell de Millás, *ibid.*, 20 (1962), 331f.; A. Pons, in: *Hispania*, 79 (1960), 209ff. [H.B.]

°**PERREAU, PIETRO** (1827–1911), Italian philo-Semitic priest and orientalist. Perreau was born in Piacenza. In 1860 he was appointed deputy librarian of the Palatine library of *Parma (in charge of the de *Rossi collection) and in 1876 he became its director. In his *Guida Storica Antica e Monumentale della Città di Parma* (1887), Perreau describes the acquisition of Hebrew manuscripts by the Palatina library, and in his *Catalogo dei codici ebraici*... (1880) he covers the manuscripts which were not described by de Rossi. *Steinschneider published Perreau's descriptions of Hebrew manuscripts (Parma in: HB, 7–8 (1864–65); 10 (1870); 12 (1872); and in Jeshurun, 6 (1868)).

Perreau published an edition of *Immanuel of Rome's commentary to the Psalms (1879–82), Esther (1880), and Lamentations (1881). He also published various studies on biblical books such as Song of Songs (*La cantica di Solomone*... 1882); on Jewish communities in Italy (in: *Vessillo israelitico*, 27 (1879); *Corriere Israelitico*, 25, 26 (1886–8); and *Educazione e Cultura degl'Israeliti in Italia nel Medio Evo*, 1885); and on Jews in England in the 11th and 12th centuries (in: *Corriere Israelitico*, 25, 1887). Perreau wrote a lexicon of Hebrew abbreviations, *Oceano dello Abbreviature*... (1883).

Bibliography: M. Steinschneider, in: HB, 21 (1881/82), 103; idem, in: *Aresheth*, 4 (1966), 123–4 (Heb. tr. by Y. Eldad); Milano, Bibliotheca, index. [A.M.R.]

°**PERROT, JEAN** (1920–), French prehistorian. He studied in France and later in Palestine. In 1950 when Kol Zion la-Golah (overseas broadcasts from Jerusalem) was established, he headed the French department. Perrot was research director at the Centre National de la Recherche Scientifique and from 1951 was head of the French archaeological mission to Israel. He excavated the remains of Chalcolithic culture at Tell Abu Matar in Beersheba (1952–60), Mesolithic and Natufian remains at Einan (1956–62), Neve Ur (1966), and Munḥata (1962–67), a Chalcolithic cemetery at Azor, and various sites in the western Negev. He participated in the excavations of Tell al-Fāriʿa, Hazor, and Khirbat Minim. He published a series of excavation reports and studies on the early art and history of Ereẓ Israel. His work was directed toward the study of the evolution of civilizations from the fifth millennium onward that led to the rise of the great river valley cultures. He later extended his work to Persia and Turkey. [M.A.-Y.]

PERSIA (Heb. פָּרַס, *Paras*), empire whose home coincided roughly with that of the province of Fars in modern Iran. Its inhabitants, calling themselves Persians, are first mentioned in Assyrian records of approximately 640 B.C.E. According to these records, the king of "Parsuwash" acknowledged the suzerainty of the Assyrian king *Ashurbanipal. According to the Persian tradition followed by Herodotus, the Persians had submitted to the *Medes in the second quarter of the seventh century. Several central terms of political life, such as the word for king and even the name Pārsa, appear to show Median peculiarities. On the other hand, the Persians came under the cultural influence of *Elam, and it was in the Elamite language that accounts were kept in the Persian treasury at Persepolis, in the Persian homeland, as late as 459 B.C.E. The Persians' dependence on the Medes was terminated by *Cyrus II who rebelled against the last of the Median kings, Astyages. Astyages marched against him, but the Median army revolted and handed over their king to Cyrus in 550. Plundering Ecbatana (now Hamadan), the Median capital, Cyrus became ruler of Media. According to official Persian tradition, he was a maternal grandson of Astyages and was supported by Median nobles. To the outside world, his seizure of the Median crown looked like a mere change of

Figure 1. Traditional tomb of Daniel in Susa, Persia.

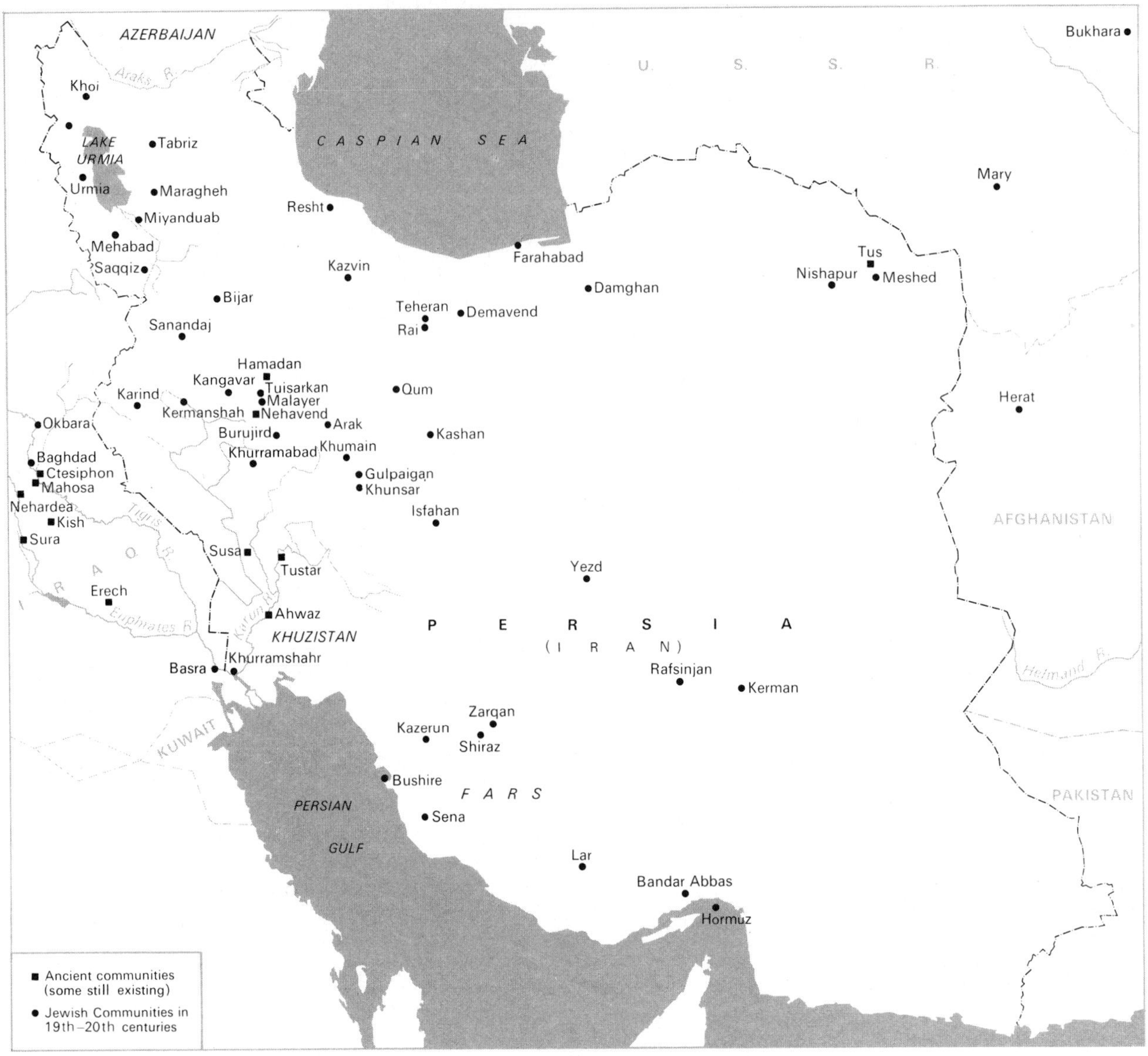

Jewish communities in Persia.

dynasty. Media, which in alliance with *Babylon had destroyed the Assyrian Empire in 612, was a great power, whereas the Persians had been unknown before Cyrus. Therefore, foreigners (e.g., Herodotus) continued to speak of "Medians" when meaning "Persians." In Daniel 8:3 the two-horned ram is a symbol of Media and Persia.

Cyrus went on to conquer the Lydian kingdom of Croesus in 547, and the Babylonian Empire of *Nabonidus in 539. His son *Cambyses II (525) added Egypt to the Persian dominions, which now extended from the Nile to the Syr-Darya (Jaxartes) and the Indus. The death of Cambyses (522) was followed by a civil war, won by *Darius I, a distant relation of Cambyses. Direct descendants of Darius I ruled the empire for six generations after him. *Darius III, from another branch of the same family, lost the empire to Alexander the Great. Kings from Cyrus to Darius III were:

Cyrus	559–530 B.C.E.
Cambyses	530–522
Darius I	522–486
Xerxes I	486–465
Artaxerxes I	465–424
Xerxes II	424–423
Darius II	423–404
Artaxerxes II	404–359
Artaxerxes III	359–338
Arses	338–336
Darius III	336–330

The paramount fact in the history of the Achaemenids was the failure of Darius I in 490 and Xerxes I in 480–479 to conquer Greece. The Athenians and their allies wrested the Aegean coast of Asia Minor and the Aegean Islands from the Persians during 479–469, and also supported the Egyptian revolt in 459–454. The Peloponnesian War between Athens and Sparta (432–404) allowed Persia to recoup its territorial losses, but economically and culturally the Greeks remained preeminent. Greek silver, and in the fourth century its imitation, was the money used in the Persian Empire; Greek merchandise, as illustrated by finds of Greek vases, dominated the foreign commerce of Persia; and Greek mercenaries became an essential part of Persian armies. For the first time in history, the monarchical, hierarchical, and priestly "East" faced the republican, egalitarian, and secular "West," and the Persian bowman following his king was always outdone by the Greek infantryman ready to die in obedience to the law of his city.

The king ruled "by the favor of Ahuramazda," the supreme god, and his power of life and death was unlimited. Nevertheless, once fixed in a certain prescribed form, his decisions could not be revoked by him, "according to the law of the Medes and the Persians" (Dan. 6:9). In practice, the king consulted his counselors (Ezra 7:14; cf. Esth. 1:13; Jonah 3:6), and could not afford to offend the Persian nobility. He could execute a wicked judge, and with his skin upholster the judge's seat, but it was a son or another relative of the judge who would be appointed to judge from the same bench (Herodotus 5:25). Though the high officials, the royal guard, and the standing army were recruited from among Persians and Medes, non-Iranians could occupy high posts. Of the 23 high royal officers *(ustarbar)* who are mentioned in the *Murashu documents, only eight have Iranian names. Though the Achaemenian king stressed that he was a "Persian, son of a Persian, Aryan of Aryan lineage," the Persians were not "nationalists." "Nationalism" in the Ancient Near East meant belonging to a city (e.g., Babylon, Jerusalem) and its deities. The Persians were tribesmen; their grandees were not citizens, or even inhabitants of a city, but lived on their estates. Being aristocrats, they did not need to be "nationalists," and used the talents of their subjects freely and easily.

Cyrus and his heirs, following the Assyrian practice, used Aramaic as the language of administration throughout the Persian Empire. As the Persian kings and their grandees were illiterate, the written language of administration was of no concern to them. Even in the ritual, the written language was Aramaic (R. A. Bowman, *Aramaic Ritual Texts from Persepolis,* 1970). The interpreters were on hand to translate the Persian orders into Elamite or Aramaic and to read aloud in Persian, an Indo-European language, the documents written in Aramaic or Elamite. The Persian script, borrowed indirectly from the Babylonians, was also cuneiform and as such inconvenient for writing on papyrus or leather. It seems to have been used only for monumental inscriptions engraved on stone or on metal.

The empire was divided into enormous administrative units known as satrapies. The satrapy "Beyond the River" (Abar-Nahara, e.g., Ezra 5:3), to which Judah belonged, extended from the *Euphrates to the Mediterranean. The satrap was the head of the administration, commander of the troops, and supreme judge and tax collector of his satrapy. Each satrapy had to pay a fixed tribute to the king, in cash and/or kind. The provinces within the satrapies had to maintain the troops, the administration of the satrapy, and the viceroy. Nehemiah, governor of the miniscule province of Judah, had to feed over 150 men daily (Neh. 5:17). There were various taxes (Ezra 4:13; 7:24), and taxation was heavy (Neh. 5:4). In addition, there was the baksheesh (Mal. 1:8). The satrap was virtually omnipotent in his satrapy, as the story of the temple of *Elephantine shows, but he had to consult his advisers and it was prudent to submit controversial questions to the king (Ezra 5:6). However, the dimensions of the satrapy made local self-administration necessary, and Nehemiah in his quarrel with the neighbors of Jerusalem does not appeal to the satrap of Abar-nahara ("trans-Euphrates"), but mobilizes the Jewish militia (Neh. 4:7ff.).

Figure 2. Part of the interior of the 16th-century synagogue at Isfahan, Persia. Courtesy Union of American Hebrew Congregations, New York.

Self-administration extended to private law, and the scribes drafting private contracts made the Aramaic common law prevalent throughout the Persian Empire.

In Ezekiel 27:10 and 38:5, the name "Persia" is probably a corruption. Deutero-Isaiah expected that Cyrus would rebuild Jerusalem (44:28; 45:1). Having conquered Babylonia, Cyrus reversed the Babylonian policy and returned captive gods and their worshipers to their homes. However, by taking care of *Marduk in Babylon and of "the God who is in Jerusalem" (Ezra 1:3), Cyrus became the legitimate successor of the kings of Babylon and of the kings of the House of David. After the restoration of the Temple and Darius I and until the revolt against Rome in 66 B.C.E., the priests of Jerusalem offered a sacrifice daily for the welfare of the heathen overlord of Zion. Written in the first half of the fourth century B.C.E., the work of the Chronicler (Chronicles, Ezra-Nehemiah) expresses this recognition of alien domination: the Temple was restored "by command of the God of Israel and by order of Cyrus and Darius and Artaxerxes, king of Persia" (Ezra 6:14). However, Jerusalem was an insignificant town in an enormous empire, and if the Persian kings took the trouble to humor the God of Jerusalem, they did it rather for the sake of the Babylonian and Persian Jewry. Knowledge of the latter is almost nil. The story of *Susanna in the Apocrypha reflects Jewish self-government in Babylonia. The story of *Tobit illustrates the family life, faith, and also the superstitions of Persian Jews. However, the society which produced *Zerubbabel, *Ezra, and Nehemiah was not that of Tobit and Susanna.

Again, almost nothing is known about contacts between the Persians and the Jews. Yet Gadal-Yama (Gadal-YHWH, Gedaliah), who in 422 was called upon to serve as a cuirassier to the royal army in a campaign at Erech (Uruk) and was the beneficiary of a fief, must have had Iranian comrades. One source indicates that a Persian magus was on friendly terms with a servant of the Lord in Elephantine (E. G. Kraeling, *Brooklyn Museum Aramaic Papyri* (1953), 4:24, 175). Because so little is known about the Iranian religions in Achaemenian Persia, it is difficult to determine the nature and extent of their influence on the Jews in the Persian period. The Jews preserved a favorable memory of the Persian kings, as their rule brought them two centuries of peace. By favoring the clergy, the Persian king laid the foundation for the later role of the high priests. For the first and last time, Jerusalem and the whole Diaspora, from the Indus to the Nile, remained under the sway of the same overlords. From Babylonia, Zerubbabel, Ezra, and Nehemiah came to the aid of Jerusalem. The Jews at Elephantine could ask Jerusalem for assistance. When, after the death of *Alexander, the unity of the political world of which the Jews were a part was destroyed, the religious and spiritual link that had been forged between Jerusalem and the Diaspora under the Achaemenids remained, and it has persisted for 23 centuries. [E.J.B.]

Pre-Islamic Persia. Traditions and legends connect the origin of the Jewish Diaspora in Persia with various events in Israel's ancient history, the starting points being regarded as the deportation of the Israelites in the time of Tiglath-pileser III (d. 727 B.C.E) from Samaria to the "cities of Media and Persia," the forced migration in the time of Sargon II of Assyria (d. 705) and of his son Sennacherib (681), or the destruction of the Temple by Nebuchadnezzar (d. 586). When the famous "Cyrus Declaration" (538 B.C.E.) allowed those Jews who were living as exiles on the "rivers of Babylon" to return to their homeland, Judea, and to rebuild their national life, some of them, who had established themselves economically and socially in their

Figure 3. Leaders of the Persian Zionist Federation, Teheran, 1911. Courtesy Central Zionist Archives, Jerusalem.

new surroundings, preferred to remain on Babylonian-Persian soil. These remaining exiles can be regarded as the nucleus of the permanent Jewish settlements which gradually expanded from the chief centers in Babylon to the interior provinces and cities of Persia, Ecbatana, Susa, and other places. The emergent group of Jewish colonies spread, in the words of the Book of Esther, "over all the provinces of the king . . . scattered among all peoples of the Persian Empire."

Favored by the tolerant attitude of the rulers toward their Jewish subjects, such dignitaries as Zerubbabel, Ezra, Nehemiah, Daniel, Mordecai, and Esther emerged from these settlements and were able to play a leading role at the royal Persian court. The gratitude of the Jews toward the Persian Achaemenid rulers found expression in subsequent generations in a mishnaic injunction that a picture of Susa, the capital of the Persian kings, should be affixed on the eastern gate of the Temple to remind the Jews of their deliverance and the tolerance of the Achaemenids (Mid. 1:3b; Men. 98a). The overthrow of the Achaemenid dynasty resulting from Alexander the Great's conquest of Persia and the rule of the Seleucids over the eastern parts of Alexander's empire does not seem to have hindered the existence and expansion of Jewish settlements in Persia.

Under the Parthian dynasty (249 B.C.E.–226 C.E.) the size and influence of well-organized Jewish communities beyond the Euphrates and Tigris was acknowledged in contemporary literature. Philo, in his *Embassy to Gaius* (245), mentions the "large number of Jews in every city" in the trans-Euphratian Diaspora. Josephus refers to Jews in Babylonia, Media, and other distant provinces, and stresses that "Jews beyond the Euphrates are an immense multitude and not estimated by numbers." Apocryphal literature, in particular the Book of the Maccabees, alludes to the existence of Jews in "the cities of Persia and Media"; and the anonymous author of the *Sibylline Oracles* refers to Jews "in every country and every sea." The New Testament makes special mention of Jewish pilgrims coming to Jerusalem from the eastern Diaspora, from Elymais, Susa, and other territories. The Book of Tobit refers to Jews in Media, in particular to the city of Rhages. The Mishnah mentions a R. Nahum of Media (Naz. 5:4; BB 5:2) and talmudic sources contain a reference to an epistle sent by Rabban Gamaliel "to our brethren in the exile of Babylon, Media, and other remote provinces" (Sanh. 11a).

Under the Sassanid dynasty (226–642) the Jewish Diaspora in Persia had grown considerably; it also increased with the voluntary movements of Jews from the Roman provinces into Persia, as well as through the forced migration of Jews from territories adjacent to Persia. According to the Armenian historian, Moses of Chorene, in 364 C.E. Shapur II (309–379) transferred a great number of Jews, some say 7,000, to the interior of Persia. The Babylonian Talmud, a product of Babylonian Jewry in the Sassanid period, though concentrating mainly on Jewish life within the boundaries of Babylon, affords glimpses into the geographical diffusion of Jewish settlements beyond the Euphrates and Tigris, and apart from the dense Jewish population in such cities as *Sura, *Pumbedita, *Nehardea, *Mahosa, *Nisibis, *Naresh, *Ctesiphon (Be-Ardashir), there were Jewish settlements remote from Babylonian centers, in the interior provinces of the Sassanid Empire, in Media, *Elam, Khuzistan, Susiana, in such cities as Hulvan, *Nehavend, *Hamadan (Ecbatana), Be Lapat (Gundashapur), *Ahwaz (Khurramshahr), *Susa, and Tustar, and up to the Persian Gulf. The spread of Jewish settlements throughout the Sassanid realm is also indicated by the express reference to them in the inscription of Karter, one of the leaders of the Mazdaan priesthood in the period following Shahpur I.

The First Six Centuries Under the Caliphate (642–1258). LEGAL STATUS. The battle at Nehavend in 642 which signaled the defeat of the Sassanid army by the invading Arab Muslims, terminated the national and political independence which Persia had enjoyed for nearly 12 centuries, from the time of Cyrus the Great until Yazdegerd III. The changes resulting from the Muslim Arab conquest of Persia affected the whole structure of the Persian Empire in its political religious, cultural and linguistic aspects. Politically, Persia ceased to be an independent entity, being incorporated as a province into the great Arab-Islamic empire. The development of Persia was henceforth controlled and shaped to a large degree by the political authorities, the Umayyad and Abbasid caliphs of Damascus and Baghdad respectively, and the viceroys appointed by them. Increasingly Arabic words infiltrated the Persian language, written from then on in Arabic script. The Islamic conquest replaced Zorastrianism with Islam as the state religion. These changes had a profound impact on the many religious minorities within Persia and in particular on the Jewish settlements within the Babylonian-Persian Diaspora, affecting first their legal and political status. The attitude of *Islam toward the non-Muslims living within an Islamic realm was regulated by a contract which deprived the **dhimmis* of social and political equality, making them in effect "second-class" citizens. At various periods in history this led to the enactment of discriminatory measures which were embodied in the so-called "Covenant of *Omar."

THE CRADLE OF JEWISH SECTARIANISM. The religious and social fermentation affecting the Persian population in the early centuries of Islamic rule also touched Jewish life, giving rise to Jewish sectarian movements, freethinkers, heretics, and pseudo-messianic claimants. The first recorded sectarian movement initiated by a Persian Jew was connected with the name of *Abu ʿĪsā, a tailor who lived in the time of the Umayyad caliph ʿAbd al-Malik ibn Marwān (d.705). Greatly influenced by the heterodox tendencies manifest within Islamic environment, he proclaimed himself a messiah, acknowledged Moses, Jesus, and Muhammad as true prophets, advocated fundamental changes in the Jewish calendar, and Jewish ritual and prayer, aimed at a reform of and a revolt against rabbinic Judaism. He seems to have gained a considerable following among the Jews of Isfahan and other places. His adherents were described as a community of simpleminded, uneducated Jews: "barbarian, ill-bred peoples, destitute of intellect and knowledge." Abu ʿĪsā's messianic claims and political ambitions brought him into open conflict with the Islamic authorities and he is said to have been killed in a battle with the troops of the caliph. After his death his movement continued under his disciple *Yudghan of Hamadan, who broke even more radically with the *halakhah.* His adherents, known as Isunians or Isfahanians, are said to have been eagerly awaiting the return of their mahdi, Abu ʿĪsā, in Isfahan until the tenth century. A certain Mushka of Qum created another movement proclaiming Muhammad as a true prophet, and calling on his adherents to wage a "holy war." In the remote region of *Khurasan in the ninth century, a Jew from the city of Balkh, known as *Ḥiwi al-Balkhi, arose among the scattered Jewish communities. Hiwi's heretical teachings are known mainly through the 200 answers which *Saadiah Gaon wrote in refutation of his beliefs.

The greatest schism in oriental Jewry in these early centuries was the rise of the *Karaite movement founded by *Anan b. David in the eighth century; some of its most distinguished leaders hailed from Persia, such as Benjamin b. Moses *Nahāwendī, Daniel b. Moses al-Qūmisi, and others. The Karaite scholar and traveler Jacob al-*Kirkisānī (tenth century) depicts the spread and distribution of Karaite communities over many Persian provinces and cities, such as Isfahan, Tustar, Jibāl, Khurasan, Fars, etc. Due to Saadiah Gaon's intervention and the activities of subsequent *geonim* and exilarchs, rabbinic-talmudic Judaism asserted its influence on the Persian communities, though Karaite communities continued to exist in many Persian cities well into the 16th century.

Relationship Between Center and Periphery. The backbone of the communal organization of Babylonian Persian Jewry was the *exilarch, the *resh galuta,* appointed by the Islamic authorities, who was responsible for the collection and prompt delivery of the annual poll tax levied on every male. He and the *gaon* of the talmudic academies in Babylonia were the recognized authorities for the widely scattered Jewish Diaspora in the East. The relationship between the Babylonian authorities, the center, and Persia, the periphery, expressed itself in subsequent centuries in a twofold way, financially and culturally. The Persian communities were expected to send financial support to Babylonia for the maintenance of the talmudic academies of Sura and Pumbedita. Available sources refer to the

Figure 4. Seventeenth-century Persian Ḥanukkah lamp decorated with Sassanian motifs, $8\frac{1}{4}\times9\frac{3}{4}$ in. (21×25 cm.). Rio de Janeiro, J. Feldman Collection.

annual contributions made by Nehavend, Fars, Hulvan, and other communities, but also indicate that some Persian communities refused or were delinquent in sending their contributions, which sometimes led to the despatch of special envoys from Babylonia to collect the revenue through the intervention of the Islamic authorities. The tenth-century chronicle of *Nathan b. Isaac ha-Kohen ha-Bavli, and a parallel version in **Seder Olam Zuta,* recount a dispute between *Kohen Zedek b. Joseph, the head of the academy in Pumbedita, and the exilarch *Ukba over the jurisdiction over the Jews of Khurasan.

The Babylonian authorities made their influence felt on the Persian communities by controlling their education and by exercising their prerogative of appointing judges, *dayyanim,* and rabbis for the Persian communities. The chief rabbi of Isfahan, in the time of *Benjamin of Tudela, was Sar Shalom and the spiritual leader of *Samarkand Obadiah ha-Nasi, both appointed by the Babylonian *gaon.* As the 12th-century *"Iggeret"* of Gaon *Samuel b. Ali indicates, vigorous efforts were made to foster talmudic education in the Persian communities culminating in the establishment of a yeshivah in Hamadan, which together with Isfahan seemed to have beeen the cultural center of the Persian Diaspora at this period. According to the *Iggeret,* the Babylonian *gaon* sent his own son-in-law, *Zechariah b. Barachel, and later dispatched a distinguished student of his, Jacob b. Eli, to Hamadan to deal with halakhic questions and advise the community. There is mention also that a young rabbinical student, David of Hamadan, arrived in Baghdad with a letter of recommendation from the *pakid,* the trustee of the Hamadan yeshivah. It is noteworthy that part of the correspondence preserved between Baghdad and Hamadan was written in Persian.

Economic Activities of the Jews. The position as *dhimmī* within Islamic society allowed the Jews complete freedom in the pursuit of economic opportunities. Scanty though the data are, a thorough examination of the available Muslim and Hebrew sources indicates that Persian Jews were engaged in many branches of artisanship and handicraft, as weavers, dyers, gold- and silversmiths, and also as merchants and shopkeepers, jewelers, wine manufacturers, and dealers in drugs, spices, and antiquities. Due to the imposition of heavy land taxes, their share in agriculture declined to a great extent. When Baghdad became the capital of the Abbasid caliphate (762), a fundamental change occurred in the economic stratification of Babylonian-Persian Jewry. With the ever-increasing urbanization of the Islamic east and the development of trade and commerce on an international scale, a wealthy class of Jewish merchants emerged in the leading centers of the Diaspora, such as Baghdad, Ahwaz, Isfahan and *Shiraz.

From the tenth century on, Jewish merchants began to participate in banking and moneylending and to play a leading role as financial experts and bankers (see *Banking) in the service of the caliphs and their viziers. Known as *Jahābidha* ("court bankers"), they carried out major financial transactions such as the administration of deposits, remittance of funds from place to place through the medium of *suftaja* ("letter of credit")—widely used instrument of the prevailing credit economy—and by supplying huge loans for the caliph, his viziers, his court, and his army. Jewish court bankers were also to be found at the courts of the Buyids, the Ghaznavids, and the Seljuk sultans. In the time of Sultan Mahmud (997–1030) of the Ghaznavid dynasty, the Jew Isaac, a resident of Ghazni, was in the sultan's service and was entrusted with the administration of his lead mines in Balkh in Khurasan. Numerous Court Jews also served the Seljuk sultans. Their celebrated vizier, Niẓām al-Mulk

Figure 5. Persian *rimmon* (Torah finial), incised silver with bells. Height 11¾ in. (30 cm.). Jerusalem, Israel Museum. Photo David Harris, Jerusalem.

(d. 1192), though in his Persian work, *Siyāsat Nameh,* he emphatically rejected the employment of *dhimmī* in governmental service, at the same time maintained close and friendly associations with Jewish officeholders, tax-farmers, bankers, and money experts who had been called upon to assist him. Many of the wealthy Jewish merchants were subjected to extortion, confiscation, and torture at various intervals, causing a wave of emigration to other parts of the Islamic world. Notable among those Persian Jews who emigrated in the 11th century were the two Jewish merchants from Tustar known as the Banu Sahl al-Tustari, who rose to great influence and position in the service of the Fatimid caliphs in Egypt.

THE GEOGRAPHICAL SETTING. The status of *dhimmī* allowed the Jews complete freedom of movement and settlement within the Islamic realm. During the first six centuries of Islamic rule over Persia, the Jewish Diaspora experienced an unprecedented expansion and remarkable geographical diffusion into all the provinces of Persia and the eastern lands of the caliphate. Muslim geographers and historians, rabbinic and geonic sources, and the account of Benjamin of Tudela and other 12th-century travelers make it possible to discern the major areas of Jewish settlement. Jewish colonies were established in all the interior provinces of Persia. These settlements seemed to have served as a springboard for further expansion into the easternmost provinces of Khurasan and *Transoxiana and even China. Jewish communites are recorded in *Nishapur, *Balkh Ghazni, Kabul, Seistan (Sistan), *Merv, Samarkand, Khiva, *Bukhara, and other regions. No clear picture emerges of the numerical strength of the Jewish Diaspora in Persia in this period. Some Persian and Arab geographers of the tenth century make comparative statements showing the relative strengths of some non-Muslim groups in various Persian provinces. Thus, the tenth-century Arab geographer, al-Muqaddasī, in comparing the various non-Muslim minorities stated, "in the province of Jibāl Jews are more numerous than Christians; in the province of Khuzistan Christians are few and Jews not numerous, while in the province of Fars the Zoroastrians are more numerous than the Jews and there are only a few Christians."

Concrete figures appear for the first time in the 12th century thanks to the travels of Benjamin of Tudela and *Pethahiah of Regensburg. According to Benjamin's account, 30,000 Jews lived in Hamadan; 15,000 in Isfahan; 10,000 in Shiraz; 25,000 in *ʿAmadiya; 4,000 in Tabaristan; 7,000 in Susa; 4,000 in Hulvan; 80,000 in Ghazni; 50,000 in Samarkand; and in the region of the Persian Gulf, 500 in Kish and 5,000 in Qatif. There is no doubt that all these figures are unreliable and exaggerated, arrived at by hearsay alone. This far-flung Diaspora in Persia and Khurasan was not just an agglomeration of immigrants without guidance and leadership; it was dependent, culturally and religiously, on the official Jewish authorities in Baghdad, the exilarchs and the *gaon,* who controlled and guided them throughout this period. Benjamin of Tudela emphasizes that the Jewish leadership in Babylonia had considerable authority over all the Jewish communities under the caliph and stresses the extent of their jurisdiction "over all the Jewish communities in Mesopotamia, Shinear, Media, Elam, Khurasan, Persia, Saba, Armenia, over the mountains of Ararat, Caucasus, Georgia, unto the borders of Tibet and India." Similarly, Pethahiah of Regensburg speaks of the power of the *gaon* "in all the lands of Assyria, Damascus, in the cities of Persia and Media, in Babylon." The extent and scope of the Jewish Diaspora in Persia must have been well known to the Persian authorities, as illustrated in the appearance of pseudo-Messiah David *Alroy in ʿAmadiya in the time of the Seljuk sultan Sanjar (d. 1156). Realizing that the messianic movement might encroach on his authority, the sultan, according to the report of Benjamin of Tudela, threatened to eliminate "all the Jews in all the parts of the Persian Empire" unless the movement was stopped.

Under the Il-Khan Dynasty (1258–1336). The invasion of Persia by Hulagu Khan, culminating in the conquest of Baghdad and the overthrow of the Abbasid caliphate in 1258, also brought about a fundamental change in the situation of the Jews in the Persian Diaspora. Under Hulagu and some of his successors of the newly established Il-Khan dynasty, the concept of the *dhimma* ("the protected people") and the division between "believers" and "nonbelievers" were abolished, and all the various religions put on equal footing. Thus Persian Jews were afforded a unique opportunity to participate actively in the affairs of the state and in the time of Arghun Khan (1284–91), a Jew by the name of *Saʿd al-Dawla al-Ṣafī ibn Hibatallah achieved an unexpected and spectacular rise to power and influence. Under subsequent Il-Khan rulers another Persian Jew, Faḍl Allah ibn Abi al-Khayribn Ali al-Hamadhānī, had a similarly meteoric rise and fall. The cultural climate which had enabled these two Jews to achieve power in the economic and political sphere also led to the genesis and growth of *Judeo-Persian literature.

Under the Safawid Dynasty (1502–1736). The fate of the Jews in Persia and Babylonia under Tamerlane (d. 1405), the greatest world conqueror Asia has produced after Genghis Khan, is shrouded in obscurity. It must be assumed that in the wake of the devastating campaigns which spread destruction and annihilation over all the lands of western Asia, the Jews did not escape the atrocities which Tamerlane and his army committed everywhere. The Jewish settlements were undoubtedly reduced and decimated through warfare, the intolerance of the authorities, and the fanaticism of the masses. But that the Jewish settlements in

Persia, although weakened and reduced in numbers, survived these troubled centuries became evident with the emergence of a new dynasty, the Safawids. Under this dynasty the Jews once again appear on the scene, and according to European travelers of that period they were living in "all the cities of Persia" and were estimated at about 30,000.

The founders of the Safawid dynasty put the country on entirely new political and religious bases. They introduced Shiʿism as the state religion and established a hierarchy of clergy with almost unlimited power and influence in every sphere of life. The concept of the "ritual uncleanliness" of nonbelievers, the principal cornerstone of their interconfessional relationship, made the life of the Jews in Persia a sequence of suffering and persecution. Under no other Persian dynasty was the hatred of the Jews more intense. They experienced a temporary improvement under Shah *Abbas I (d. 1629) who introduced reforms in order to weaken the theocratic basis of the state and free Persia from the fetters of its all-too-powerful Shiʿa clergy, and to break the political, economic, and cultural isolation of the country.

Realizing that the most urgent requirement for Persia was increased population and economic ties with the outside world, Shah Abbas fundamentally changed the policy of the state toward non-Muslims and foreigners. Far from being antagonistic, as were his predecessors, toward Europeans and nonbelievers, he encouraged the immigration of foreigners—merchants, settlers, and artisans—from neighboring countries such as Armenia, Georgia, Turkey, and also from Europe. By granting freedom of religion and special privileges and facilities to all who were prepared to come to his territory, he was able to succeed. This liberal and tolerant attitude made Persia at that time the meeting place of European envoys, emissaries, diplomats, merchant-adventurers, and missionaries—all eager to obtain commercial, political, or religious concessions and privileges. Never before in the history of Persia's relationship with the outside world were the economic and political ties between Persia and Europe closer.

For the Jews of Persia, the second part of the 17th century was a time of great suffering and persecutions. The conception of the ritual uncleanliness of the Persian Jew, which led to the introduction of a special headgear enforced on all Jews in Persia and to a crusade against Hebrew books, culminated under Shah *Abbas II (1642–66) in the forced conversion of all the Jews in Persia, a catastrophe which brought them to the very brink of destruction. This persecution, a tragic parallel to the Inquisition of Spain, was regarded as more cruel than that of the time of Ahasuerus and Haman. European sources as well as the Judeo-Persian chronicles of *Babai ibn Lutf and Babai ibn Farhad describe in great detail the sufferings of the Jews during the time of Shah Abbas II. They show how in Isfahan, the capital, and in other communities the Jews were compelled to abandon their religion, how their synagogues were closed and they were led to the mosque, where they had to proclaim a public confession of Muslim faith. After their forced conversion, they were called new Muslims; they were then, of course, freed from the payment of the poll tax and from the wearing of a special headgear or badge. Despite all the measures on the part of the Shiʿa clergy to supervise the Islamization of the Jews, most of them adhered tenaciously and heroically in secret to their religion and began to live a dual life as secret Jews, repeating the phenomenon of the *Marranos in an Islamic version. The double life of these forcibly converted Jews did not escape the attention of the Persian authorities, and led finally to an edict issued in1661 allowing the Jews to return openly to their religion.

Figure 6. Scribe's inkwell with embroidered sheath, Persia, 19th century. Jerusalem, Sir Isaac and Lady Wolfson Museum in Hechal Shlomo. Photo David Harris, Jerusalem.

When J. Fryer visited Persia a decade later (1672–81), he found the Jews "congregated on their Sabbaths, new moons, and feast days in synagogues without disturbance." Under the successors of Shah Abbas II, Shah Suleiman (d. 1694) and Shah Husein (d. 1722), the persecution and oppresssion of the Jews were, however, renewed, and it was only with the rise of a new and remarkable ruler, *Nadir Shah (1736–47), that the Jews of Persia were saved from complete annihilation.

Communal and Religious Life. The establishment of Persia as a national state under the Safawid dynasty had far-reaching repercussions on Jewish community life in Persia. During the Abbasid period, the exilarch or the *gaon*, from his central seat in Baghdad, exerted supreme authority in all religious and cultural matters over all the Jewish communities in the far-flung Diaspora of Asia, including Persia, which then formed a part of the Eastern caliphate. With the rise of the Safawids, the official bonds which the Persian Jewish communities might still have maintained formally with Jewish authorities outside the borders of the country were completely severed. The official representative of the Jews in Persia, the chief rabbi of Isfahan, was no longer appointed by the *gaon* of Baghdad as in preceding centuries, nor were Persian Jews expected or willing to support the Jewish academies in Baghdad. Persian Jews ceased to be responsible to any central Jewish leadership and their communal life was put on a purely territorial basis.

Due to their geographical proximity to the central government and their numerical strength the Jews of Isfahan, the new capital of the Safawid dynasty, assumed the religious and cultural leadership and functioned as representatives and spokesmen for all Persian Jewry. At the head of the communty of Isfahan was a *nasi*, who was assisted by the rabbi, mullah, or *dayyan*. The *nasi*, who was highly respected, was responsible for the prompt payment of taxes to the local authorities. If the taxes were not paid in due time or in the due amount requested, he could be dismissed by the authorities or even imprisoned. On the other hand, if the authorities were satisfied, the *nasi* would receive a sign of distinction and honor. It seems that in the time of the Safawids there existed in Isfahan, as part of the general administration, a special divan which regulated the financial affairs of the non-Muslims and examined petitions of protest, grievances, requests, or complaints from the Jews against officials of the administration. At the head of the divans stood a high official appointed by the grand

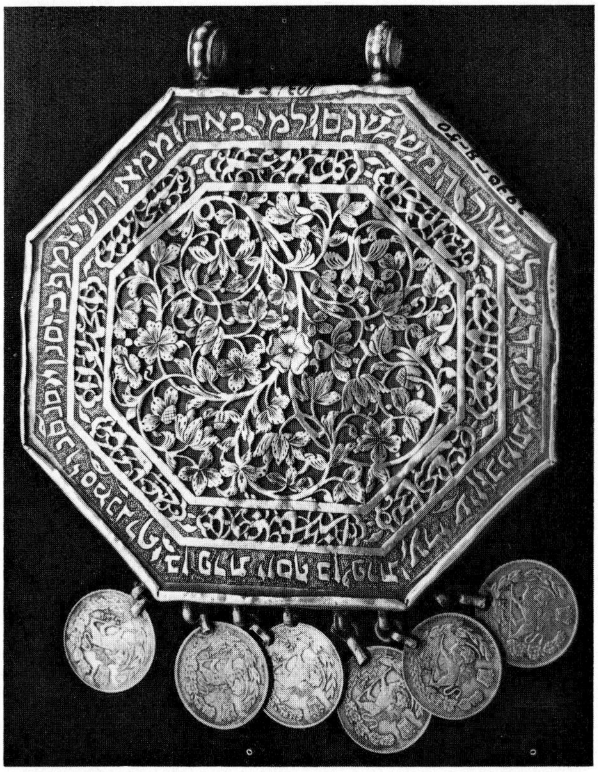

Figure 7. Silver pendant amulet with coins, Persia, 18th century. Surrounding the floral motif is a Hebrew inscription from Genesis 49:22. Jerusalem, Israel Museum. Photo David Harris, Jerusalem.

vizier, sometimes assisted by a Jewish apostate who acted as adviser or spy for the authorities.

The frequent mention of a "Jewish quarter" indicates the geographical separation of the Jews from the Christian and Muslim population. The Jewish quarter housed the residences of the Jewish population, their synagogues, and schools, the *mikveh,* and other religious institutions. In the time of the Safawids Isfahan had at least three synagogues, while *Kashan is said to have had ten; it can be assumed that at least one synagogue existed in every Jewish settlement in Persia. The religious life of the Jews in Safawid Persia was established on a rigid, rabbinical, traditional basis.There were also some Karaite communities, especially in Kazerun. A typical feature in the religious life of the Persian Jew at this, and indeed at all times, was the custom of making pilgrimages to some of the Jewish "holy places" in Persia, in particular to the mausoleum of Mordecai and Esther in Hamadan, to the tomb of the prophet Daniel in Susa, and to the burial places of other biblical heroes believed to be interred on Persian soil. At this period another "holy place" came into prominence, the alleged tomb of Sarach (Seraḥ) bat Asher in the vicinity of Isfahan at Pir Bakran.

Despite the territorial limitation, the Jews of Persia had contacts with the outside Jewish world, particularly with Ereẓ Israel through "messengers from Zion" who toured the Jewish communities in that period, fostering the love for Zion and collecting funds for the charitable institutions in the Holy Land. Among these early *sheliḥim* were R. Moses *Alshekh (c. 1593) from Safed, Baruch Gad of Jerusalem, and above all, R. Yahuda Amram Divan (d. 1752) who repeatedly visited the Jewish communities in Persia. The messianic movement of *Shabbetai Ẓevi made an impact on Persian Jewry. It was in this period that the Jews began to migrate to territories outside the border of Persia to neighboring regions such as Afghanistan, Turkestan, Samarkand, and Bukhara in the east, and to Kurdistan, the Caucasus, and Egypt in the west. Persian Jews also moved to India; most famous of them was *Sarmad, the Jew of Kashan, who became a fakir and a Sufi dervish.

Under the Kajar Dynasty (1794–1925). The political and religious foundations of the Kajar dynasty which ruled over Persia were essentially a continuation of those of the Sawafid dynasty. The Shiʿite concept of the ritual uncleanliness of the nonbelievers prevailed, with the related attitude of the Persian authorities toward their non-Muslim minorities, Christians and Jews alike. The intolerant attitude toward the Jews led to innumerable legal and political restrictions which made their daily life, throughout the 19th century, an uninterrupted sequence of persecution, oppression, and discrimination. The reports of many European missionaries and travelers to Persia describe the tragic fate of the Jews in Persia during the Kajar dynasty. Whole Jewish communities, as well as many individual Jews, were forcibly converted to Islam in many provinces of the Persian Empire, a movement which reached its peak in the forced conversion of the whole Jewish community in *Meshed in 1839 under Muhammad Shah (1835–48).

Even during the reign of Nasr-ed-Din Shah (1848–96), who realized the necessity for thorough reform of the whole Persian administration and social structure, persecution of the Jews continued, coupled with legal and social discriminations of the severest nature, including the enforcement of a special Jewish badge and Jewish headgear. The entire community was held responsible for crimes and misdemeanors committed by its individual members; the oath of a Jew was not accepted in a court of justice; and a Jew who converted to Islam could claim to be the sole inheritor of family property, to the exclusion of all relatives who had not changed their religion.

The Jewish minority in Persia had been left entirely to itself and no outside organization, Jewish or other, had taken any interest in its fate. Contact with the Jewish world at large, and particularly with the Jews in Ereẓ Israel, was occasionally maintained through the *sheliḥim* sent on behalf of the communities of Hebron, Tiberias, Safed, and Jerusalem, to the remote Jewish communities in Persia, Bukhara, and Afghanistan. In the middle of the 19th century four brothers of one Jewish family were the busiest and most popular physicians in the city of Teheran. One of them, Hak Nazar, was for some time court physician of Muhammad Shah. They had, however, just as little influence on the actual political situation of their coreligionists as did the European physicians subsequently appointed by Nasr-ed-Din and his successors, among whom figured most prominently the Austrian physician, J. E. *Polak. In the second half of the 19th century the Persian Jews acquired a powerful ally in their struggle for justice and emancipation—Western European Jewry.

THE INTERVENTION OF WESTERN JEWRY. Reports on the plight of Persian Jews moved the *Board of Deputies of British Jews and later the *Anglo-Jewish Association under Sir Moses Montefiore and the *Alliance Israélite Universelle under Adolphe Crémieux to action, urging intervention by the British and French ministers in Teheran. When news of a terrible persecution of Jews in Hamadan reached London in 1865, Sir Moses Montefiore decided to leave for Persia and to obtain from the shah an edict of safety for the persecuted Persian Jews. However, he was dissuaded by the British Foreign Office, who stated that "the journey would be perilous even to a younger man and could be undertaken by him at the risk of his life." In addition to their political plight, the Jews of Persia experienced new hardship through the outbreak of a famine in 1871, which the leaders of European Jewry tried to alleviate through a relief fund. The Jewish leaders in Paris and London were again on the point of considering sending a Jewish delegation to Persia when the news reached them in 1873 that Nasr-ed-Din Shah, anxious to appear as a tolerant and progressive monarch, had embarked on a visit to Europe. Seizing their opportunity, the leaders of the Alliance Israélite Universelle and the Anglo-Jewish Association organized a movement intended to impress the shah with the importance and influence of European Jewry, to stress their equality and emancipation in all European countries and their unanimous desire to see an improvement in the condition of their coreligionists in Persia.

In every European capital through which the shah planned to travel, committees of the most influential Jews were organized to present him personally with petitions calling for the improvement of the Persian Jews' situation. This was carried out in Berlin on May 4, 1873, in Amsterdam on June 10, in Brussels on June 17, in London on June 24, in Paris on July 12, in Vienna on August 6, and in Constantinople on August 20. In London the shah had a meeting with Disraeli and also received Sir Moses Montefiore in private audience in Buckingham Palace. In all these petitions the spirit of Cyrus the Great was recalled and the grievances of the Jews in Persia were listed. The highlight of these activities was the memorable interview in Paris between the shah and Adolphe Crémieux and his associates on July 12, 1873. Apparently impressed by the strength and unity of European Jewry, the shah promised to make the protection of his Jewish subjects his own and his grand vizier's special responsibility, to establish a special court of justice for the Jews, and above all to help in the establishment of Jewish schools in Persia as suggested by the European representatives. In order to encourage and strengthen the persecuted Persian Jews, the text of the petitions submitted to the shah in the various capitals of Europe, together with the reply of the shah and his minister, were translated into Hebrew and published as a booklet called *Mishlo'aḥ Manot* (1874), which was distributed among the Jewish communities in Persia. Despite all the well-meaning promises of the shah, the central government in Persia failed to prevent new outbreaks of hostilities against the Jews. There was, therefore, enough reason to intervene again and to remind Nasr-ed-Din during his last journey to Europe of his previous promises and assurances. On July 4, 1889, a deputation of British Jewry, led by Sir Albert Sassoon, had an interview with the shah in Buckingham Palace. The members of the deputation included Lord Rothschild, Sir J. Goldsmid, and Sebag Montefiore. The demand for the establishment of Jewish schools in Persia was again the central issue.

Under Shah Muzaffar-ed-Din (1896–1907) a definite improvement in the destiny of Persian Jews took place in connection with the constitutional movement, which had far-reaching consequences for all religious groups in Persia. Persian Jews took an active part in this constitutional movement, receiving official thanks for their efforts from the first parliament of Persia in 1906, although neither the Jews, the Armenian Christians, nor the Zoroastrian minority were yet permitted to send their own deputy to parliament and had to agree to be represented by a Muslim deputy. For Persian Jews the constitutional movement meant a step forward toward their emancipation and equality. The dualism in legislation between the religious laws, the shari'a, and the civil law, was abolished, as were the discriminatory and humiliating medieval restrictions against the Jews. Unfortunately for the country, three months after parliament convened Shah Muzaffar-ed-Din died, and under the new ruler, Shah Muhammad Ali (1907–09), the constitutional movement quickly disappointed the high hopes placed in it by the liberal elements among the Muslims and the Jews in Persia.

At this stage the Persian Jews were assisted in their struggle for survival by the intervention of the U.S. diplomatic representative in the country. Reference to Persian Jews appeared in U.S. diplomatic correspondence in 1918, in connection with the relief activities of the *American Jewish Joint Distribution Committee. The State Department, as well as U.S. diplomatic representatives abroad, helped the committee in distributing funds, food, and other necessities to the starving Jews everywhere. This intervention also continued in the period after World War I, through the U.S. representative in Persia from 1921 to 1924, namely the minister plenipotentiary, Joseph Saul *Kornfeld, a former rabbi. The dissolution of the Persian parliament; the deposition of Shah Muhammad Ali by the National Assembly; the reconvening of a second parliament in 1909 by Ahmed Shah (1909–25); the great financial crisis which brought the American experts, M. Shuster and A. C. Millspaugh, to Persia; the steady changes in the cabinet and the government; and the encroachment of Russia in the north and Great Britain in the south—all this contributed to a state of unrest and danger, so that at the outbreak of World War I, Persia stood at the very brink of dissolution.

The Establishment of Jewish Schools in Persia. For the Persian Jews the rule of Muzaffar-ed-Din was a turning point, since at this period the first Jewish schools of the Alliance Israélite Universelle were established in Persia. The idea of Jewish schools in Persia, conceived in 1866, became in 1873 the central issue in the discussions between the Jewish authorities in Europe and the Persian government; in 1889 it was still a matter of discussion alone, but finally, after ten years, it was realized. In 1898 the first school of the Alliance Israélite Universelle was opened in Teheran, followed by similar schools in Hamadan in 1900, in Isfahan in 1901, in Shiraz and Sena in 1903, and in *Kermanshah in 1904. As two main dangers threatening Jewish survival in Persia during the 19th century were Christian missionary activities and the *Bahai movement, the Jewish schools of the Alliance played an important role in the struggle for spiritual survival. The educational facilities available to Persian Jews were considerably strengthened and augmented from 1944, not only through the activities of the American Jewish Joint Distribution Committee and the establishment of vocational training schools and workshops under the auspices of the *O.R.T., but also by a new educational movement sponsored by a group of prominent U.S. and European philanthropists and generously supported by the Joint. This movement, known as "Oẓar ha-Torah" or "Gandj Danesh," which aimed at strengthening traditional Judaism and Hebrew education among the Jewish communities in Morocco, Persia, and elsewhere, succeeded in establishing, in close cooperation with the Alliance Israélite Universelle, new schools, teacher training seminars, summer camps, and other educational facilities. Under the leadership of its first director, Rabbi I. M. Levi, Oẓar ha-Torah instilled a new religious spirit into the younger generation.

Aliyah to the Holy Land. The 19th century was also characterized by a mass immigration of Persian-speaking Jews from Persia and neighboring countries to Ereẓ Israel. Almost parallel with the *Ḥibbat Zion movement in Russia, but probably without any direct contact with it, a great number of Persian-speaking Jews set out for the Holy Land. They came from Teheran and Shiraz, from Hamadan, *Yezd, and Isfahan, from Kashan and Meshed, from *Herat and Kabul, from Bukhara and Samarkand. The awakening of Persian Jews in the 20th century was also expressed in a Zionist movement which spread throughout most of the Jewish communities in Persia. This renaissance found literary expression in the establishment of a Judeo-Persian and Hebrew press in Teheran, which printed the first Persian textbook of modern Hebrew. This was followed by a history of the Zionist movement, written in Persian in Hebrew characters (1920) by Aziz b. Jonah Naim, and a Hebrew translation of Herzl's *Der Judenstaat* and his biography by A. Bein. This circle also published a Jewish newspaper in Persian, *Ha-Ge'ullah,* and another called *Ha-Ḥayyim,* which became the mouthpiece of the Jewish renaissance movement in Persia. Some of Bialik's poems were translated into Persian by Aziz b. Jonah Naim and published in these periodicals.

Under the Pahlevi Dynasty (1925–). The political and social conditions of Persian Jews were fundamentally changed with the ascent to the throne of Riza Khān Pahlevi and the establishment of the new Pahlevi dynasty in 1925. In 1921, Riza Khān Pahlevi took Teheran; in 1923 he became prime minister; and on Oct. 31, 1925 the parliament in Teheran deposed the last Kajar ruler and entrusted Riza Khān with the provisional government. On Dec. 15, 1925, he was crowned shah of Persia and became the founder of the new Pahlevi dynasty. Bent on secularization and Westernization of his country, Riza Shah, and after him his son Muhammad Riza, carried out far-reaching reforms affecting the social, cultural, and political structure of the country. By breaking the power of the Shiʿa clergy, which for centuries had stood in the way of progress, by freeing the country from the fetters of fanatical and intolerant circles, and by eliminating the Shiʿa concept of the ritual uncleanliness of the nonbelievers—once the basic foundation of the state attitude toward non-Muslims—the shah laid the foundations for a revival which had most beneficial effects on the Jewish sector of the population. No other country except Turkey went through so fundamental a change in so short a time as Persia (or, as it has since been called, Iran) under the new dynasty. This change brought about the political emancipation of the Jews in Persia, for which they, assisted by Western European Jewry, had struggled in the latter half of the 19th century. When World War II broke out, with the subsequent political upheavals and the deposition of Riza Khān Pahlevi, the whole process of the Jewish regeneration in Iran was in jeopardy. Yet under Riza Shah's successor, Muhammad Riza, a very favorable climate was provided for the continuous improvement of Jewish life in Persia.

For the modern period, see *Iran. [W.J.F.]

Bibliography: PRE-ISLAMIC PERIOD: J. Obermeyer, *Die Landschaft Babylonien* (1929); Neusner, Babylonia (incl. bibl). MUSLIM PERIOD; W. J. Fischel, *Jews in the Economic and Political Life of Medieval Islam* (1937, 1969²); idem, in: *Tarbiz,* 6 (1935), 523–6; idem, in: *Zion,* 1 (1935), 49–74; 2 (1937), 273–93; idem, in HJ, 7 (1945), 29–50; 8 (1946), 66–77; idem, in: *Alexander Marx Jubilee Volume* (1950), 203–30; idem, in: JSOS, 12 (1950), 119–60; idem, in: HTR, 45 (1952), 3–45; idem, in: *Ha-Kinnus ha-Olami le-Madda'ei ha-Yahadut 1947* (1952), 477–86; idem, in: *Joshua Starr Memorial Volume* (1953), 111–28; idem, in: PAAJR, 22 (1953), 1–21; idem, in: L. Finkelstein (ed.), *The Jews* (1960³), 1149–90; idem, in: JAOS, 85 (1865), 148–53. 19TH–20TH CENTURIES: H. Levy, *Tarikh Yahud Iran,* 3 vols. (1956–60); A. Ben-Jacob, *Yehudei Bavel* (1965); I. Ben-Zvi, *Meḥkarim u-Mekorot* (1967), 285–410.

PERSITZ, SHOSHANAH (1893–1969), Israel publisher and politician. Born in Kiev, the daughter of Hillel *Zlatopolski the banker and Zionist leader, she was educated at the universities of Moscow and Paris. From 1909 she was a leading figure in the Hebrew language movement Tarbut in Russia. In 1917, together with her husband, she established the Omanut publishing house in Moscow and in 1920, in Frankfort. When she settled in Palestine in 1925, Persitz brought her press with her and headed it until her death. For many years Omanut Press was the main publisher of Hebrew educational material and books for youth. From 1926 to 1935 Persitz was a

Shoshanah Persitz, Israel publisher and member of Knesset. Courtesy Government Press Office, Tel Aviv.

councillor of the Tel Aviv Municipality and director of its education department. From 1949 to 1961 she was a member of the *Knesset, representing the *General Zionists, and served as chairman of the Knesset's education committee. In 1968 she was awarded the Israel Prize in education. [B.J.]

PERSKI, JOEL DOV BAER (1816–1871), Hebrew author and translator. Perski, who was born in Volozhin, made major contributions to the field of translation into Hebrew.

One is *Kevod Melakhim* (Koenigsberg, 1851–53), a translation of *Telemaque* by Fénelon with Perski's own notes. The work probably interested him on account of its didactic content, since Telemachus is aided in his travels by the wise comments and interpretations of Minerva, who in the form of a mentor gives him lessons on the proper conduct of life and especially on the duties of a king and the principles of sound government. Another work is *Ḥayyei Asaf* (1858) on the life of Aesop, including morally instructive incidents from his life. The work concludes with the translations of some 35 of Aesop's fables. Perski also wrote a commentary, *Heikhal Ra'anan* and *Shemen Ra'anan,* on the *Yalkut Shimoni* on Genesis (1864); and *Battei Kehunnah,* a commentary on the *Midrash Rabbah* to Genesis and Exodus (1871). He died in Vilna.

Bibliography: *Yahadut Lita,* 3 (1967), 177. [ED.]

PERSKY, DANIEL (1887–1962), Hebraist, educator, and journalist. Born in Minsk, Persky settled in the United States in 1906 and devoted all his efforts to the Hebraist movement in that country. From 1921 until his death, with the exception of six years in Europe and in Ereẓ Israel (1927–33), he taught at the Herzliah Hebrew Teachers' College in New York. For many years he published an article in each issue of the Hebrew weekly, *Hadoar,* which enjoyed great popularity. His books are largely drawn from these articles, many of them dealing with Hebrew language and syntax. They include *Ha-Medabber Ivrit* (1921; *Spoken Hebrew,* 1921); *Ivri Anokhi* (1948); *Dabberu Ivrit* (1950; *Lashon Nekiyyah* 1962); *Matamim le-Ḥag* (1939); *Zemannim Tovim* (1944); *Kol ha-Mo'ed* (1957); *Le-Elef Yedidim* (1935); and *Ẓeḥok me-Ereẓ Yisrael* (1951).

Persky edited several children's magazines, including *Eden* (1924–25) and *Hadoar la-No'ar* (1934–46). He published posthumously works of several of his colleagues, including I. Beaber and Solomon Rabinowitz, translated the constitution of the United States into Hebrew, and wrote in Yiddish. For English translations see Goell, Bibliography, 35, 74, 89.

A leading figure in Hebrew-speaking circles in the U.S., he carried on a voluminous correspondence with Hebrew

Daniel Persky (right) on an outing in Berlin with (left to right) Meir Mohr, Saul Tchernichowsky, Zvi Wojslawski, 1927. Courtesy Mrs. Z. Wojslawski, Jerusalem.

writers all over the world and through friends gave many of them financial assistance. His visiting card bore the legend "I am a slave of Hebrew forever."

Bibliography: MacDonald, in: *The New Yorker* (Nov. 28, 1959), 57–105; Waxman, Literature, 4 (1960), 1081–82; Glenn, in: JBA, 20 (1962/63), 73–75; Kressel, Leksikon, 2 (1967), 692f. [Ei.S.]

PERSOV, SHMUEL (1890–1952), Soviet Yiddish writer. After having been active in the Jewish Labor *Bund during the Revolution of 1905, he emigrated from Russia to the United States at the age of 16. His literary career began in 1909 with articles in the New York radical periodical *Freie Arbeiter Stimme*. He returned to Russia after the 1917 Revolution filled with enthusiasm for the new regime. He worked in a Moscow cooperative and wrote articles on economics for Russian journals as well as literary sketches and short stories in Yiddish. He helped to found the Yiddish section of the Moscow Association of Proletarian Writers. His short story "*Sherblekh*" ("Derelicts," 1922) anticipated the method of socialist realism. His volume *Kornbroyt* (1928) dealt with the conflict between adherents and saboteurs of the revolutionary regime. He revealed the psychological difficulties encountered by small Jewish tradesmen in their attempt to adjust to the new Communist reality. In *Tog un Nakht* ("Day and Night," 1933), he documented his intense love for Jews; he wished them to retain their unique qualities by settling in Jewish agricultural colonies such as Birobidzhan rather than living dispersed among, and assimilating with, the non-Jewish majority. These views, tolerated at first, were later denounced as Jewish nationalist deviationism, and Persov was liquidated in 1952. Five years after his death, he was rehabilitated.

Bibliography: Rejzen, Leksikon, 2 (1927), 941ff. [S.L.]

PERTH, capital of Western Australia, founded in 1829. The first Jew arrived in the same year, but up to the 1880s only a few Jews lived in Perth. The Perth Hebrew Congregation was founded in 1892 and the synagogue opened in 1897, but the community of Fremantle, the port of Perth some nine miles (14 km.) distant, was established earlier. Most of the Jewish settlers came from Eastern Europe both before and after World War I, but a number also arrived from Palestine. A Liberal (Reform) congregation was formed in 1952. In 1970 the Jewish community, which numbered about 3,300, was the third largest in Australia. There was one Jewish day school in the city.

Bibliography: D.J. Benjamin, in: *Australian Jewish Historical Society Journal*, 2 (1946), 293–329; *ibid.*, 3 (1949), 434–6. [I.P.]

PERU.

Colonial Period. As in colonial Mexico, *Crypto-Jews were significantly involved in Spanish South America (from the Caribbean to the Plate River) from the earliest days of Spanish rule. The Judaizers attracted relatively little attention during the period of the episcopal Inquisition and during the two decades following the introduction of the formal Inquisitional structure in the viceroyalty in 1570. Judaizers began to appear in the 1580s and in large numbers during the following decades, when the authorities instituted a concentrated search for them. Ten were sentenced in 1595, 14 in 1600, and 28 in 1605. Of these, the authorities condemned a total of 15, in person or in effigy, to the stake. The general pardon granted to Judaizers in 1601 brought a lull in the activities of the Inquisition until at least 1625. During this period, considerable numbers of Portuguese New Christians, many of them Judaizers, flocked into the viceroyalty of Peru and, largely through their commercial activities, quickly rose to wealth and status. Their social conspicuousness played a definite role in the discovery of their clandestine religious deviation. An indiscretion by a Judaizing employee of a major Crypto-Jewish wholesaler in 1634 led to the arrest of 64 alleged Judaizers, nearly all of Portuguese descent, and to a general panic among New Christians and Old Christians alike. Creditors of the New Christians were especially worried, realizing that the Inquisition might well confiscate all the property of the suspects. The arrest and flight of so many New Christians brought the viceroyalty to the brink of economic ruin. The Inquisition handled the trials of these suspects with unusual dispatch, accelerating them through liberal applications of torture and completing them within three years. It convicted 63 of the suspects in this "Great Conspiracy" and sentenced them at a spectacular summer auto-da-fé, held on Jan. 23, 1639. Twelve victims were burned at the stake; 11 in person and one in effigy. They included two of the most famous Judaizers of all times. Manuel Bautista Perez, the wealthiest and most powerful merchant in Lima and the leader of the Judaizers in the capital of the viceroyalty, and the physician Francisco Maldonado de Silva.

After this auto-da-fé, the pursuit of Judaizers by the Lima Inquisition sharply declined. Some cases pending against Judaizers were even dismissed, and only a handful of those continued or subsequently started led to the stake. The infrequent cases of alleged Judaizing during the 18th century involved three extraordinary personalities. The first, in the early 1720s, was the case of Don Teodoro Candioti, a Levantine Christian arrested for his unusual practices, which he claimed were part of the customs of his land. He died in the Inquisitional prison in 1726 and was buried in one of the Inquisition's graves, but his name was

Synagogue and school building of Perth, Western Australia. From *Transactions of the Jewish Historical Society of England*, Vol. 10, 1921–23.

eventually cleared. The second was the noblewoman Dona Ana de Castra, more notable for her amatory exploits than for her religious devotion. Among her lovers was the viceroy himself. Her conviction for heresy and her death at the stake in 1736 appear to have been motivated more by official embarrassment than by religious zeal. The third involved the nobleman Don Juan de Loyola y Haro, a descendant of Ignatius of Loyola. Arrested as a suspected Judaizer on the testimony of one of his slaves, he was kept in prison even after the testimony was shown to be part of a conspiracy against him. He died in jail in 1745, but his family did not learn of his death for four years, after a change of inquisitors had led to the reopening of his case and posthumous acquittal.

A small number of Jews who cannot be classified as New Christians appear to have been present from time to time in Spanish colonial South America, mostly transients on trading missions from the West Indies. Today, many Catholic families in the lands that once formed part of the viceroyalty of Peru acknowledge their descent from New Christians and even Judaizers of the colonial epoch.

[Ma.C.]

Contemporary Period. Peru is a republic in South America with a population of 12,000,000 (Jewish population in 1968 estimated at 5,000). The majority religion is Roman Catholicism ("protected" by the state) but freedom of religion is guaranteed by the constitution (1933).

Modern Jewish history in Peru began around the middle of the 19th century with the arrival in Lima of some Central European merchants and engineers. By 1870 they were numerous enough to form a community, La Sociedad de Beneficencia Israelita de 1870, which exists to the present day. In 1875 this community acquired the land for the Jewish cemetery, which still serves the community. Most of the immigrants were males, and their Jewish ties were weak. Intermarriage and consequent conversions resulted in the fact that not one of the descendants of the founders of the Sociedad de Beneficencia of 1870 is a member of the Jewish community today. The last members of the original community survived just long enough to hand over the prayer books and the keys of the synagogue to the Central European, German-speaking Jews, who have made up a portion of the membership of the community since then.

Around 1880 Sephardi Jews, mainly from North Africa, began to arrive in the Amazon region of Peru and eventually established a community in the capital city of Iquitos. Attracted by the rubber boom, the majority became merchants and provided a great stimulus to the economic development of the region. In 1909 the Sociedad de Beneficencia Israelita was established by 38 local Jews under the leadership of Victor Israel. Difficult living conditions and adverse economic conditions, however, precluded mass settlement, and most of the immigrants were compelled to leave. A large number of those remaining intermarried, without however, foregoing the proud title of "Hijos de Hebreos" (Sons of Hebrews). Among their descendants are some prominent citizens of the Peruvian woodlands. An interesting reawakening of Jewish identification has occurred within the group since the 1950s, indicated by the establishment in Iquitos of the Instituto Peruano-Israelí for the furthering of cultural relations.

As early as World War I, some Sephardi Jews from Turkey and Syria went to Lima as merchants. The major wave, however, arrived subsequent to World War I as refugees from the war-ravished Turkish Empire and the small Rumanian border town of Novoselitsa (Nouă Sulița). The increased stringency of the U.S. immigration law, the unfortunate experience of some of the Argentine settlers, and the cotton boom on the Peruvian coast during World War I channeled the first immigrants to Peru. Letters to friends and relatives in their native countries attracted the rest. Most of the first immigrants were penniless youngsters who started out in Lima as peddlers of yard cloth and women's wear. When Lima became too small to support the growing number of Jewish peddlers, they branched out into the provinces. After they had acquired some capital, some of these settlers returned to Europe to marry. Some remained in Europe and perished in the Holocaust; others returned to Peru to found a permanent home. During the

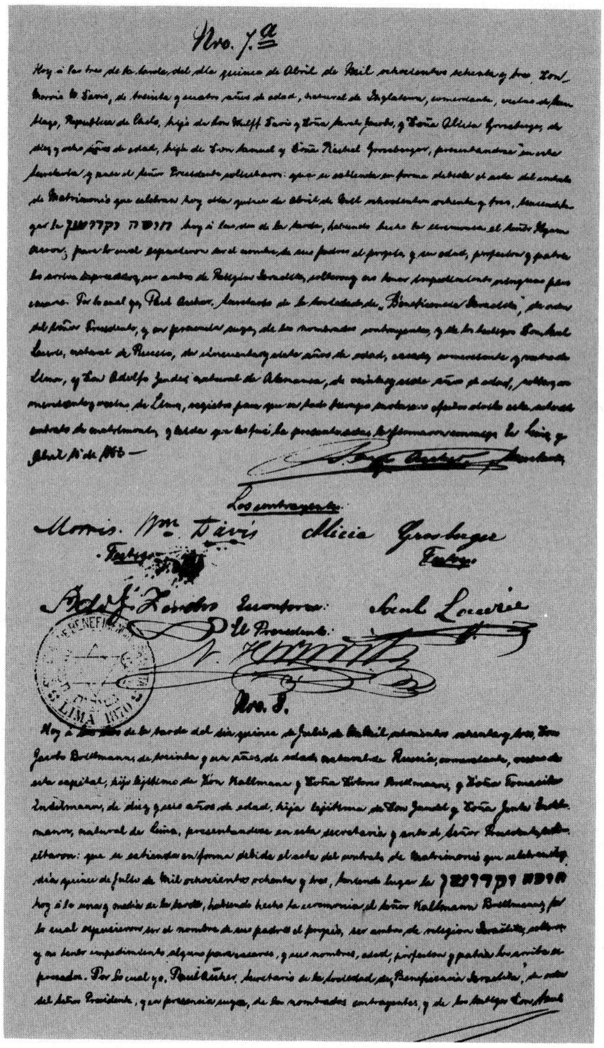

Page from the Jewish community marriage register of Lima, Peru, 1882–89. Jerusalem, C.A.H.J.P. 1030 (4).

1930s and 1940s Jews settled in many of the provincial capitals of Peru—Talara, Piura, Trujillo, and Arequipa, but only in the last two were organized Jewish communities established. There were barely ten Jewish families in the latter in 1968, but the synagogue and social center still exist and a *minyan* is assembled on the High Holidays.

General or textile merchants settled as individuals or in small groups in the Sierra—in La Oroya, a mining center, and old, picturesque little colonial towns like Huáncayo, Huancavelica, and Ayacucho, where one of the two Jews in the town served as mayor for two years. As growing children made it necessary for these settlers to seek better educational facilities and increasing prosperity made it possible to move to Lima, most of the provincial communities disintegrated.

The community of German-speaking Jews, "1870," which had gradually faded out, received an influx of new immigrants as a result of Hitler's ascent to power. Although Peruvian immigration laws were never liberal, hundreds of families managed to obtain entry visas and others, some of whom went initially to Bolivia, joined them later. Between 1933 and 1943 536 arrivals were registered by Jewish welfare organizations. Of this number 30 emigrated by January 1943.

As in other Latin American countries, large-scale settlement projects for Jews were attempted in Peru. In 1930 a group of non-Jewish, German economists inquired into the possibilities of Jewish settlement in Peru and even obtained a permit for a settlement project in the eastern part of the country, but the program never took root and was ultimately abandoned.

The earliest immigrants, who were mainly cloth peddlers, subsequently became wholesalers, importers, and industrialists. Jewish presence in all branches of the textile industry is considerable, and Jews can also be found in all other branches of commerce and light industry. Although none of the East European and few of the Central European immigrants were professionals, the number entering the professions in the second generation is steadily increasing. Dozens of doctors and engineers can now be found in the community. Contributions by Jewish artists have been made in painting, artistic photography, music, and drama.

There are three Jewish communities in Peru: the Ashkenazi, the "1870," and the Sephardi, united under the roof organization of the Asociación de Sociedades Israelitas. The 900 Ashkenazi families are grouped around the Unión Israelita; the 250 German-speaking families are organized around the Sociedad "1870"; and the 180 Sephardi families in the Sociedad de Beneficencia Israelita Sefardi. Each community has its own synagogue and rabbi, and, although each community has its own *ḥevra kaddisha,* a common cemetery is used by all. Two homes for the aged are maintained by the community: one by the Ashkenazim—Bikkur Ḥolim—and the other, primarily for members of the "1870."

The first Jewish school was established in 1946; in 1966 it had over 800 pupils, from kindergarten through secondary school, well over 80% of all the Jewish school-age children in the community and 90% of those at the kindergarten level. The Hebraica Sports and Social Club was founded by the younger generation in 1956. It participates in the Latin American and world Maccabiah events. Other institutions include *B'nai B'rith, *WIZO, and various youth organizations. All three communities are active in Zionist affairs. The Jewish community newspaper is *Nosotros,* a monthly published since 1930.

Peru-Israel Relations. Relations between Peru and Israel have been amicable since pre-State days, and in 1947 Peru was among the supporters of the UN resolution to partition Palestine. Diplomatic representation between the two countries is on an ambassadorial level. Israel has extended technical assistance to Peru, especially in the form of agricultural and water development projects. Courses on irrigation, agriculture, and cooperatives sponsored by the Israel Foreign Ministry and the Ministry of Agriculture with the help of the Organization of American States have been held in Peru since 1969. In 1966 Peru inaugurated its first agricultural settlement, patterned on the *Naḥal model and planned and directed by personnel trained in Israel. Cultural relations between the two countries are fostered by the Institute for Cultural Relations Peru-Israel. [N.L.]

Bibliography: N. Lorch, *Ha-Nahar ha-Loḥesh* (1969); Asociación Filantrópica Israelita, Buenos Aires, *Zehn Jahre Aufbauarbeit in Suedamerika* (Ger. and Span., 1943); Sociedad de Beneficencia Israelita de 1870, *25 Jahre Hilfsverein deutschsprechender Juden* (1960); J. Shatzky, *Yidishe Yishuvim in Latayn Amerike* (1952), 175–80; A. Monk and J. Isaacson, *Comunidades Judías de Latinoamérica* (1968), 109–12; J. Toribio Medina, *Historia de la Inquisicion de Lima,* 2 vols. (1956[2]); M. A. Cohen, in: *The Jewish Experience in Colonial Latin America* (1971), introd.

PERUGIA, city in Umbria, central Italy. The Perugian statute of 1279, decreeing the expulsion of the Jews from the town, is proof that a Jewish settlement had previously been in existence in Perugia. It seems, however, that this measure was never put into effect and in succeeding years there was an active Jewish group in Perugia, mostly engaged in moneylending. The artist Matteo di Ser Cambio, who acted as "procurator" of the Jews of Perugia in 1414, illuminated a Hebrew manuscript there about this time. The creation of the *Monti di Pietà (1462), in conjunction with violent anti-Jewish preaching by the Franciscans, had dire consequences for the Jews in Perugia, and they were banished in 1485. Though later readmitted to the town, they were banished again in 1569 by the bull *Hebraeorum Gens* of *Pius V. Under *Sixtus V (1587) they returned temporarily, but in 1593 were banished finally by *Clement VIII. A few Jews graduated in medicine in the University of Perugia between 1547 and 1551, including David de'*Pomis. In the 1920s and 1930s many foreigners (including some from Ereẓ Israel) studied there, receiving moral support in the home of Bernard Dessau, the professor of physics and a father of wireless telegraphy, and his wife, the artist Emma Dessau. There is again a handful of Jews living in Perugia, affiliated to the community of Rome, and services are held irregularly.

Bibliography: A. Fabretti, *Sulla condizione degli ebrei in Perugia dal XIII al XVII secolo* (1891); Scalvanti, in: *Annali della Facoltà di Giurisprudenza ... di Perugia,* 8 (1910), 93–125; RMI, 25 (1959), 151ff.; Roth, Italy, index; Milano, Italia, index; Luzzatto, in: *Vessillo Israelitico,* 45 (1897), 81ff.; Momigliano, *ibid.,* 65 (1918), 384–7; Narkiss, in: KS, 23 (1968), 285–360. [A.To.]

PERUTZ, LEO (1884–1957), Austrian novelist. Perutz, the son of a Prague industrialist, lived in Vienna as a free-lance writer after World War I, in which he served as an officer. After the *Anschluss* in 1938 he emigrated to Ereẓ Israel. In his vivid historical novels Perutz displays the visionary power and technical skill of the born storyteller.

His works, which have a fantastic and eerie quality, include one about Hernando Cortez, *Die dritte Kugel* (1915); *Zwischen neun und neun* (1918; *From Nine to Nine,* 1927), set in Prague; the prizewinning *Der Marques de Bolibar* (1920; *The Marquis de Bolivar,* 1926); *Der Meister des juengsten Tages* (1923; *The Master of the Day of Judgement,* 1929); *Turlupin* (1924), on Richelieu and his age; *Wohin rollst du, Aepfelchen?* (1928; *Where Will You Fall?,* 1930), set in postwar Vienna and Soviet Russia; and *Der schwedische Reiter* (1936). The last novel published during the author's lifetime, *Nachts unter der steinernen Bruecke* (1953), evokes the Prague of Rudolf II; *Der Judas des Leonardo,* set in the Milan of Ludovico Sforza, appeared in 1959. Perutz' short stories were collected in *Der Kosak und die Nachtigall* (1927) and *Herr, erbarme dich meiner* (1930). His plays such as *Die Reise nach Pressburg* (1930) and *Morgen ist Feiertag* (1936), were less successful. [H.Zo.]

PERUTZ, MAX FERDINAND (1914–), British biochemist and Nobel laureate physicist. Perutz was born in Vienna and went to Cambridge in 1936. In 1947 he became head of a unit of molecular biology, and in 1962 chairman of the Medical Research Council Laboratory of Molecular Biology. In 1937 he started the study of the structure of crystalline proteins by X-ray diffraction. After 30 years this enabled a complete analysis to be made of the positions of all the 2,600 atoms in the myoglobin molecule and the 10,000 atoms in the molecule of hemoglobin, the component of blood which carries oxygen to the body cells. In 1962 Perutz shared the Nobel Prize for Chemistry for "research into the structure of globular proteins." Perutz contributed to scientific periodicals, mainly in the above field. He wrote *Proteins and Nucleic Acids: Structure and Function* (1962). He was elected a Fellow of the Royal Society and member of several national academies of science, and was the recipient of other awards.

Bibliography: *Le Prix Nobel en 1962* (1963). [S.A.M.]

PERVOMAISK, city in Odessa oblast, Ukrainian S.S.R. It was formed in 1920 by the amalgamation of three neighboring localities; Bogopol, the most ancient of them (Podolia), Olviopol, and the village of Golta, in the Kherson oblast. (In 1847 there were about 1,400 Jews in Bogopol.) The number of Jews in the three communities was 8,636 (40.8% of the total population) in 1897. Most of them (about 6,000, or 82% of the population) lived in Bogopol, where a pogrom broke out in October 1905. In December 1919, when the soldiers of *Denikin retreated before the Red Army, they engaged in bloodshed and rioting. There were 9,896 Jews (31%) in Pervomaisk in 1926. When the city was occupied by the Germans in the summer of 1941, Jews who did not succeed in escaping were exterminated. According to the 1959 census, Jews numbered about 2,200 (5% of the population). There was no synagogue.

Bibliography: *Reshummot,* 3 (1923), 435–7. [Y.S.]

PESAḤIM (Heb. פְּסָחִים; "paschal lambs"), third tractate in the Mishnah, Tosefta, and two Talmuds, of the order *Mo'ed*. *Pesaḥim* deals, in ten chapters, with the laws concerning the *Passover festival.

Pesaḥ refers primarily to the paschal sacrifice, but was applied also to the festival itself. This tractate deals with both subjects, the sacrificial service (chaps. 5–9), leavened and unleavened bread (chaps. 1–4), and the *seder* (chap. 10). In geonic times the tractate was still divided correspondingly into two parts called *Pesaḥ Rishon* and *Pesaḥ Sheni*. The two parts were afterwards combined and given the name *Pesaḥim* (in the plural). In the Munich manuscript, the tenth chapter appears as the fourth, so that the "practical" chapters follow one another consecutively. There is clear evidence that the two parts of this tractate were not redacted in the same school, and there are definite differences between them. They contain conflicting topics and even those which are similar differ in details and even halakhically. The redaction of the tractate *Pesaḥim* took place relatively later than that of the other tractates and its Talmud already utilized the edited Talmud of many other tractates. The *mishnayot* of the second part are very old and refer to events from the time of the Second Temple and the early authorities. The Mishnah of the first part, though it is of later redaction, contains *halakhot* which were a subject of dispute between the latest of the **zugot* and the first of the *tannaim*, as can be proved from the parallel passages.

The following are the contents of the chapters. Chapter 1 deals with the "search" for leaven *(bedikat ḥameẓ)* and its removal. Chapter 2 continues the subject and then goes on to discuss certain aspects of the making of the *maẓẓah* and questions relating to **maror and *ḥaroset*. Chapter 3 opens with a list of various foods containing *ḥameẓ* (e.g., beer made from barley), then reverts again to problems of the search for leaven and its removal, especially in the event of the eve of Passover falling on a Sabbath. Chapter 4 opens with the ruling that abstention from work on the eve of Passover depends on local customs. It then lists various *halakhot* which depend on local customs. Chapter 5 is mainly concerned with determining the time for slaughtering the paschal lamb and other aspects of the sacrificial service. Chapter 6 deals with the sacrificial arrangement when the festival falls on a Sabbath, and with related problems. Chapter 7 deals with the roasting of the paschal lamb, and discusses problems touching on ritual impurity affecting the persons participating in the sacrifices. Chapter 8 considers the question of a person slaughtering the paschal lamb on behalf of another person, and the qualifications of the persons involved. Chapter 9 touches first on the question of Second Passover (cf. Num. 9:10–11), but then discusses a variety of other problems, such as the interchange of a paschal lamb. Chapter 10 considers the arrangement of the *seder* night.

Sacrifices being brought to the Temple, in an engraving illustrating the tractate *Pesaḥim*. From a title page of the Hebrew-Latin edition of the Mishnah, illustrated by Mich. Richey. Amsterdam, 1700–04. Jerusalem, J.N.U.L.

In the Tosefta, this tractate is also divided into ten chapters. An aggadic point of particular interest is how King Agrippa took the census of the people assembled in Jerusalem on the occasion of a Passover pilgrimage (4:3; also 63b). There is *Gemara* in the Palestinian and Babylonian Talmuds. The *Gemara* of the Babylonian Talmud contains a considerable amount of *aggadah*. The following are worthy of note: the insistence on refined language (3b); expressions of extreme antagonism between scholars and ignoramuses (49a–b); arrogance and anger make a scholar lose wisdom and a prophet his prophecy (66b); there is an advantage in the existence of a Diaspora, insofar as it makes a concentrated attack on Israel's existence impossible (87b, also 118b on the causes of Diaspora); and finally mention should be made of the story of the appointment of Hillel as *nasi* (66a). The English translation in the Soncino Talmud is by H. Friedman (1938).

Bibliography: Epstein; Tanna'im, 323–36; Ḥ. Albeck, *Shishah Sidrei Mishnah*, 2 (1958), 137–42. [A.Z.E.]

PESAḤSON, ISAAC MORDECAI (1876–1943), a pioneer of the *Bund in Russia and Poland. Pesaḥson was born in Shklov but his family settled in Warsaw, where his father, a descendant of the founder of the *Ḥabad ḥasidic movement, officiated as rabbi. As a youth Pesaḥson belonged to a group of Jewish Populist and Marxist intelligentsia. In 1893 he assisted in the publication of the first Yiddish May Day manifesto. During the 1890s, in contact with I. L. *Peretz, he instructed circles of workers in socialist studies. In 1897 he was active in bringing about the merger of Polish-born Jewish members of the Polish Socialist Party (*P.P.S.) and the Union of Jewish Workers in Warsaw led by J. *Mill, whose members came from Lithuania. After the establishment of the *Bund, he worked for it in Lodz, utilizing his familiarity with Polish ḥasidic life. Subsequently, he was alternatively imprisoned on various occasions or active for brief periods in Warsaw and Lodz. He escaped from Siberia and worked with the Bund "committee abroad." During the 1905 Revolution, he worked again in Lodz, and was a Bund delegate at the Fifth Convention of the Russian Social Democratic Labor Party (London, 1907). From 1909 until his death he lived in Bedzin, western Poland. From 1917 he was a member of the central committee of the Bund in Poland. He was employed as secretary of the Jewish community in his town and pursued his activities for the Bund until he was murdered during the Nazi occupation. Under the pen name, *An Alter Bakante*, he published reminiscences on the beginnings of the Jewish workers' movement in Warsaw and Lodz in *Der Yidisher Arbeter*, 10 (1900), 27–36; *25 Yor* (1922), 35–36; and *Royter Pinkos*, 2 (1924), 159–64.

Bibliography: A. Brandes, *Keẓ ha-Yehudim be-Ma'arav Polin* (1945); I. S. Hertz (ed.), *Doyres Bundistn*, 1 (1956), 262–9; I. S. Hertz et al. (eds.), *Geshikhte fun Bund*, 3 vols. (1960–66), index. [M.M.]

PESANTE, MOSES BEN ḤAYYIM BEN SHEM TOV (d. 1573), author and self-appointed emissary of Safed who traveled in Turkey and the Balkans between 1565 and 1573. He was murdered in Greece.

Pesante was the author of *Ner Mitzvah*, a commentary on the *azharot* of Solomon ibn *Gabirol (Constantinople, 1567; second edition with additions, Salonika, 1569); *Yesha Elohim* (Constantinople, 1567), including an exposition of the *Hoshanot* and their relevant customs together with the laws of *lulav*, and the *piyyutim* for the Rejoicing of the Law; and *Ḥukkat ha-Pesaḥ*, a commentary on the Passover *Haggadah* (Salonika, 1569). Among his unpublished works are a commentary on the order of *Zera'im* of the Jerusalem Talmud and novellae to the tractate of *Kiddushin*.

Bibliography: Yaari, Sheluḥei, 236. [Sh.A.H./Ed.]

PESARO, port on the Adriatic, central Italy. Documents attest to the existence of a Jewish community in Pesaro from 1214 onward. The Jews engaged in dyeing and later in moneylending until a public loan bank (*Monte di Pietà) was opened in 1468. In 1556, following persecutions by *Paul IV, many Marranos of *Ancona (including the famous physician *Amatus Lusitanus) fled to Pesaro where they were admitted by Duke Guidobaldo II della Rovere, in the hope of ousting Ancona from trade with the Levant. The undertaking failed, however, and in March 1558, Duke Guidobaldo banished the Marranos from his territory. The expulsion of the Jews from the Papal States in 1569 caused an influx of Jewish families into Pesaro, so that by the beginning of the 17th century the town had become the largest and most important Jewish center in the duchy of Urbino. Under papal rule, which began in 1631, the position of the Jews in Pesaro deteriorated drastically. When they were enclosed in the ghetto three years later, the Jewish population was about 500, mainly engaged in local commerce and shopkeeping. After the treaty of Campo-Formio in 1797, and the reaction following the temporary withdrawal of the French troops, the populace turned against the Jews. The ghetto of Pesaro and its two synagogues (one of Italian rite and the other, exceptionally beautiful, Sephardi) were sacked. In the 19th century, the nucleus of Jews in Pesaro was reduced. When Pesaro became part of the Kingdom of Italy in 1869, the Jewish community numbered 150 persons; at the beginning of the 20th century the total had shrunk to about 50; by 1970 they were only a few individuals.

Pesaro occupies an important position in the history of Hebrew publishing. *Abraham b. Ḥayyim "the Dyer" left there in 1477 to open one of the first Hebrew presses in Ferrara. In 1507 Gershom *Soncino opened a printing house in Pesaro and worked there with interruptions until 1520, producing, besides books in Italian and Latin, an impressive range of classical Hebrew texts: some 20 Talmud treatises, a complete Bible (1511–17), Pentateuch or Bible commentaries by Baḥya—the first Hebrew work issued in Pesaro and four times reprinted there—by Moses b. Naḥman (Naḥmanides), Levi b. Gershom, David Kimḥi, Isaac Abrabanel, as well as an edition of Nathan b. Jehiel's *Arukh* (1517). Some of these works appear as issued by the "Sons of Soncino."

Bibliography: Roth, Italy, index; idem, *The House of Nasi: Doña Gracia* (1948); Milano, Italia, index; Kaufmann, in: REJ, 16 (1888), 61–72; 31 (1895), 231–9; Servi, in: *Vessillo Israelitico,* 43 (1895), 399–401; Morpurgo, in: RI, 7 (1910), 121–4; Adler, in: REJ, 89 (1930), 98–103; Kaufmann, in: JQR, 4 (1892), 509–12; D. W. Amram, *Makers of Hebrew Books in Italy* (1909), 104ff.; Ḥ. D. Friedberg, *Ha-Defus ha-Ivri be-Italyah* (1956²), 53ff.; Freimann, in: ZHB, 8 (1904), 143f.; A. M. Haberman, *Ha-Madpisim Benei Soncino* (1933), 37–39, 50–60; M. Marx, in: HUCA, 11 (1936), 460–8. [A.To.]

PESARO, ABRAMO (1818–1882), Italian revolutionary and communal leader. Pesaro was born in Ferrara where as a young man he established a cultural and vocational training center. In 1846 he belonged to the local committee which organized a rising against the papal government and was a member of the National Assembly of Mazzini's short-lived Roman republic of 1849. After the failure of the 1848 Revolution he lived in Venice until the establishment of the kingdom of Italy in 1861. Afterward he returned to Ferrara where he was active in both Jewish and general public life. He published various monographs on Italian Jewish history, in particular what is still the only history of the Jews of Ferrara (2 pts., 1878, 1880).

Bibliography: Milano, Italia, index; Milano, Bibliotheca, nos. 1255–60. [M.E.A.]

PESHAT (Heb. פְּשָׁט), word which came to mean the plain, literal meaning of a text, as opposed mainly to *derash, the

Ark of the Law in the Sephardi synagogue of Pesaro. Built in the second half of the 16th century, it was renovated in the 18th, but has fallen into disuse. Courtesy Israel Museum. Photo Archives, Jerusalem.

homiletical interpretation, but also to any other method than the literal. According to W. Bacher (*Die exegetische Terminologie der juedischen Traditionsliteratur,* 2 (1905), 112ff.) it was *Abbaye, in the first half of the fourth century, who first made a distincion between *peshat* and *derash* as separate methods of exegesis, while Dobschuetz regards the word as the innovation of the academy of Pumbedita as a whole, including Abbaye, Joseph, and Rava. An examination of the one clear instance in which Abbaye advances two interpretations, one of *peshat* and one of *derash* (Sanh. 100b), however, does not bear out the assumption that the word indicates the literal meaning (cf. Loewe in bibliography, p. 163–4). Similarly, the frequently quoted statement, *ein mikra yoze middei peshuto,* "a text cannot be taken from the meaning of its *peshat*"—Shab. 63a; Yev. 11b, 24a—does not necessarily imply that *peshat* means the literal exegesis. In point of fact in parallel passages where one uses the verbal form *peshat,* the others use *darash,* or *shanah,* or *matne* (Heb. and Aramaic respectively for "studied," or "repeated"; Num. R. 18:22; Gen. R. 10:7 ed. Theodor Albeck p. 81, and notes), while in two interpretations given by R. Dimi to a biblical passage (Gen. 49:11–12) that which is called "the *peshat* of the verse" (*peshta de-kera*) is much further removed from the literal meaning than the other interpretation given (Ket. 111b; cf. also Kid. 80b; Er. 23b; Ar. 8b). Actually the rabbis had only two major methods of biblical exegesis, that of *halakhah* and that of *aggadah,* neither of which depended upon literal exegesis and in most instances deviated from it.

The basic meaning of the root of the word in biblical Hebrew is "to flatten out," with the secondary meaning "to extend" or "to stretch out" (hence the meaning "to make a raid"—Job. 1:17), and from this was derived the talmudic meaning of "to expatiate upon," or "to propound." In context, *peshat* in talmudic literature seems to mean not the plain meaning but "the teaching recognized by the public as obviously authoritative, since familiar and traditional"

(Loewe) or "the usual accepted traditional meaning as it was generally taught" (Rabinowitz). The present meaning of *peshat* is probably due to Rashi's biblical commentary, in which he was the first sharply to differentiate between the homiletical interpretation which he called *derash* and the literal meaning to which he gave the name *peshat*.

Bibliography: W. Bacher, *Die exegetische Terminologie der juedischen Traditionsliteratur*, 2 (1905), 173; L. Dobschuetz, *Die einfache Bibelexegese der Tannaim* (1893), 11–15; L. Rabinowitz, in: *Tradition*, 6 no. 1 (1963), 67–72; R. Loewe, in: *Annual of Jewish Studies* (1965), 140–85. [L.I.R.]

PESHER (Heb. פֵּשֶׁר), in the usage of the Qumran texts an inspired application of biblical prophecies to the circumstances of the end of days. The substantive occurs once in the Hebrew Bible, in Ecclesiastes 8:21, "who knoweth the interpretation of a thing?" The implication is that this knowledge calls for special wisdom; and this implication is confirmed by the use of the corresponding Aramaic word *peshar* which occurs 31 times in the Aramaic portion of Daniel. There it is used in Daniel's interpretation of Nebuchadnezzar's dreams and of the writing on the wall at Belshazzar's feast, and of the angelic interpretation of Daniel's night vision recorded in chapter 7. It is an interpretation which surpasses the attainment of ordinary wisdom; it comes by divine illumination. It follows that the problem which requires such interpretation is no ordinary problem; it is a divine mystery. Such a mystery is expressed by the noun of Iranian origin *raz*, which appears nine times in the Aramaic portion of Daniel. Nebuchadnezzar's dream of the great image of four metals is a *raz* which cannot be understood until the *pesher* is supplied. Both the *raz* and the *peshar* are given by divine revelation; the *raz* is the first stage of the revelation, but it remains a mystery until the second stage, the *peshar*, is forthcoming.

Raz and Pesher. Both *raz* and *pesher* are common terms in the Qumran texts. Repeatedly in the *Thanksgiving Psalms God is praised because He enabled the psalmist to understand His wonderful mysteries *(razim)*, by which His eschatological purposes seem especially to be meant. In the Qumran commentaries on various biblical books or parts of books this *pesher* pattern is particularly manifest. The first stage of divine revelation was imparted to the biblical writer, but it remained a mystery *(raz)* until the second stage, the interpretation *(pesher)*, was imparted to the Teacher of Righteousness (and by him to his disciples). Thus, in the *Habakkuk Commentary*, it says that "God commanded Habakkuk to write the things that were coming on the last generation, but the fulfillment of the epoch He did not make known to him. And as for the words, that a man may read it swiftly; their interpretation *(pesher)* concerns the Teacher of Righteousness, to whom God made known all the mysteries *(razei)* of the words of His servant the prophets" (1QpHab. 7:1–5, on Hab. 2:1ff.). This is completely in accordance with the statement at the beginning of the Damascus document, that God raised up for the righteous remnant "a Teacher of Righteousness to lead them in the way of his heart, that he might make known to the last generations what he was going to do to the last generation" (CD 1:10–12). Not until the two parts of the revelation, the *raz* and *pesher*, are brought together is its meaning made plain. The revelation, moreover, is predominantly concerned with the time of the end, the last generation of the current epoch. Three basic principles of Qumran interpretation have already shown themselves: (1) God revealed His purpose to the prophets, but did not reveal to them the time when His purpose would be fulfilled; this further revelation was first communicated to the Teacher of Righteousness. (2) All the words of the prophets had reference to the time of the end. (3) The time of the end is at hand.

Contemporary Interpretation. Much then of what the prophets had to say was believed to be in a kind of code; it could only be decoded when the Teacher of Righteousness was provided with the key. Knowledge of the context of the prophet's own day, which a modern exegete would regard as indispensable for understanding his message, was irrelevant; the historical context which made his

Part of the *Habakkuk Commentary* from the Dead Sea Scrolls with the word *pishro* (possessive form of *pesher*) appearing as the fifth word in the first line. Jerusalem, Israel Museum, The Shrine of the Book, D. Samuel and Jeane H. Gottesman Center for Biblical Manuscripts. Photo David Harris, Jerusalem.

words intelligible was the interpreter's own situation and that of the period immediately following. Isaiah might prophesy the downfall of the Assyrian, Ezekiel might foretell the rise and fall of "Gog, of the land of Magog," Habakkuk might describe the invasion of his land by the Chaldeans; but in these and other instances the reference is not to enemies of Israel in the respective prophets' days but to the great gentile power which would oppress the people of God at the end-time, regularly designated the *Kittim in the Qumran texts. For example, in a commentary on Isaiah (4QpIsa[a]), the advance and overthrow of the Assyrians in Isaiah 10:24ff., are interpreted as the eschatological "war of the Kittim." The leader of the Kittim (or so it appears, for the manuscript is badly mutilated) goes up from the plain of Acre to the approaches of Jerusalem. This is followed by the quotation of Isaiah 11:1–4 which is properly interpreted as the "shoot of David" who is to arise in the latter days to rule all the gentiles, including "Magog," but takes his directions from the priests. (This is in line with the Qumran picture of the age to come, in which the priesthood, and especially the "Messiah of Aaron," will take precedence over the Davidic Messiah, whose main function is to lead his followers to victory in battle.) In line with the interpretation of the Assyrians as the Kittim in this commentary is the quotation of Isaiah 31:8 in the *War Scroll (1QM 11:11ff.) with references to the destruction of the Kittim ("Then shall Asshur fall with the sword, not of man, and the sword, not of man, shall devour him").

The Habbakuk Commentary. The best-preserved of the Qumran commentaries is that on Habakkuk from Cave 1, and it provides the largest number of examples of this *pesher*-interpretation. The description of the Chaldeans in Habakkuk 1:6–17 is applied almost clause by clause to the Kittim, and if it is correct to identify the Kittim of the Qumran texts with the Romans, the prophet's language must have seemed especially apt. The Kittim, in their swift advance, overthrow all who stand in their way, and subdue them to their own dominion. They take possession of many lands and plunder their cities, "to possess dwelling places that are not theirs." Nor do they rely on military power alone to accomplish their ends: "With deliberate counsel all their device is to do evil, and with cunning and deceit they proceed with all the nations." "They trample the earth with their horses and their beasts; they come from afar, from the islands of the sea, to devour all the nations like vultures, and they are never satisfied . . . With wrath and anger, with hot passion and fury, they speak to all the nations," They impose heavy tribute on the nations, to be paid year by year, and thus they denude the lands of their wealth. In war they are completely ruthless; their sword regards neither age nor sex. Yet, as the prophet says, they are the agents of divine judgment against the ungodly; in particular, they are sent to punish the wicked priesthood of Jerusalem, who oppressed the godly and plundered the poor; they will deprive these priests of their ill-gotten gain and afflict them as they had afflicted others. Other parts of the Qumran commentary on Habakkuk apply the prophet's words to internal conflicts in Judea—especially to the conflict between the *Teacher of Righteousness and the *Wicked Priest, with some reference to other groups and leaders active at the same time as these. It rarely happens that the prophet's words lend themselves so literally to the commentator's purpose as do Habakkuk's words about the Chaldeans. Elsewhere the text is atomized to serve that purpose; one variant will be preferred to another on the same principle. Where other procedures fail, the text is allegorized: if in Habakkuk 2:17 mention is made of the Chaldeans' cutting down the cedars of Lebanon for military equipment and depriving the beasts there of their natural shelter, "Lebanon" is the council of the community and the "beasts" are "the simple ones of Judah, the doers of the law," while their devastator is the Wicked Priest.

Other Examples. Another example of allegorization appears in the commentary on Micah from Cave 1, where the words of Micah 1:5b ("What are the high places of Judah? Are they not Jerusalem?") are interpreted as "the Teacher of Righteousness, who teaches the law to his council and to all who offer themselves for enrollment among the elect of God." Several instances of *pesher*-interpretation are found in the Damascus document: once the actual term is used, where the *pesher* of Isaiah 24:17, "Terror *(paḥad)* and the pit *(paḥat)* and the trap *(paḥ)* are upon thee," is said to be "the three nets of Belial ... in which he catches Israel by making them look like three kinds of righteousness—namely fornication, wealth, and pollution of the sanctuary" (CD 4:12–19). The document called 4Q *Testimonia* quotes three passages from the Torah (Ex. 20:21, Samaritan text; Num. 24:15–17 and Deut. 33:8–11) with apparent reference to the eschatological prophet, prince, and priest respectively, and then quotes Joshua's curse on the rebuilder of Jericho with reference to a son of Belial and his two sons; the text, unfortunately, is so fragmentary and allusive that the identity of the "son of Belial" remains in doubt: almost every member of the Hasmonean dynasty from Mattathias to Aristobulus II has been suggested, as have also Antipater, Herod, and even Vespasian. Alongside 4Q *Testimonia* the documents called 4Q *Florilegium* and 4Q *Patriarchal Blessings* provide examples of messianic interpretation. To those who had grasped the basic principles of the *pesher* received and taught by the Teacher of Righteousness, the sacred text was luminous; those who tried to understand it otherwise still groped in darkness.

Bibliography: F. F. Bruce, *Biblical Exegesis in the Qumran Texts* (1960); Fitzmyer, in: *New Testament Studies* (1960–61), 297ff.; J. de Waard, *A Comparative Study of the OT Text in the Dead Sea Scrolls and in the NT* (1965); K. Elliger, *Studien zum Habakkuk-Kommentar vom Toten Meer* (1953); Osswald, in: ZAW, 68 (1956), 243ff.; F. Noetscher, *Zur theologischen Terminologie der Qumran-Texte* (1956); O. Betz, *Offenbarung und Schriftforschung in der Qumransekte* (1960). [F.F.B.]

PESIKTA DE-RAV KAHANA (Aram. פְּסִיקְתָּא דְרַב כָּהֲנָא), one of the oldest of the homiletic Midrashim. The word *pesikta* means "the section" or "the portion." The *Pesikta de-Rav Kahana* contains homilies on portions of the Torah and *haftarah* readings for the festivals and special *Sabbaths. There are two editions of this text which are similar in the following order of contents: Chapter 1, on Torah readings for Ḥanukkah; Chapters 2–6, on Torah readings for the special Sabbaths and *Parashat ha-Ḥodesh* (see *Sabbaths, Special); Chapters 7–12, on Torah readings for *Passover and *Shavuot; Chapters 13–22, 24, 25, on readings for the 12 *haftarot* of the three Sabbaths of "reproof" (before the Ninth of *Av) and the seven Sabbaths of "consolation" (after the Ninth of Av); and an additional two (this section is often referred to in rabbincal literature as "The Midrash דש״ח נו״ע אר״ק שד״א" an acronym consisting of the first letters of each of the **haftarot* (see Tos. Meg. 31b)). Chapters 23 to the end, on Torah readings for *Rosh Ha-Shanah and the *Day of Atonement; on *haftarah* readings for the Sabbath of Repentance, *seliḥot;* on Torah readings for *Sukkot, Shemini Aẓeret.

In 1832 L. *Zunz, in an ingenious work of scholarship, demonstrated the existence of *Pesikta de-Rav Kahana,* as distinct from the **Pesikta Rabbati* and the *Pesikta Zutarta,* although there was no text or manuscript available to him. On the basis of references and readings in the medieval *Yalkut Shimoni* and especially in the *Arukh,* Zunz even went so far as to propose an order of contents of 29 chapters. Chapter 1, on Rosh Ha-Shanah, was followed by the festivals and special Sabbaths in the normal cycle of the year. It has since been demonstrated, on the basis of its language and of rabbis and place names mentioned, that the *Pesikta* is a Palestinian text, probably of the fifth century. In 1868 Solomon Buber published an edition of the *Pesikta* based on four manuscripts. The discovery of these manuscripts represented a remarkable confirmation of Zunz's basic proposition—the existence of the *Pesikta.* However, the arrangement of chapters in Buber's edition, as indicated above, begins the cycle of the year with the chapter on Ḥanukkah.

The confirmation of the original structure of the *Pesikta* was made possible by the discovery of a new Oxford manuscript of the 16th century. It is the only one of the manuscripts which has a table of contents beginning the cycle of the year with the chapter on Rosh Ha-Shanah, almost exactly as Zunz surmised in his arrangement of the order of chapters.

The name of the work is somewhat obscure. Zunz and Buber believe that the authorship was attributed to Rav Kahana because of a reading in the 12 chapters beginning with the Sabbath after the 17th of Tammuz. The first chapter in this unit opens as follows: "'The words of Jeremiah' (Jer. 1:1) R. Abba b. Kahana opened...." An alternative theory that is suggested now is based on the opening lines in the chapter of Rosh Ha-Shanah in two manuscripts which open with a reference to Rav Kahana. If the *Pesikta* begins with Rosh Ha-Shanah, it is correct to assume that the name *Pesikta de-Rav Kahana* was based on a version which made its first reference to this *amora* in its opening lines.

There are six known manuscripts of the *Pesikta* (three from Oxford, and one each in Carmoly, Casanatense, and Safed). An analysis of their contents in terms of the Palestinian tradition of the portion of Torah which is read on a particular festival, or the reading for a second day (non-Palestinian; see *Festivals), yields the conclusion that the new Oxford manuscript, which begins with Rosh Ha-Shanah, is a consistently closer reflection of the tradition of Palestine where the *Pesikta* originated.

This manuscript, reflecting an old, original source, has many excellent readings on individual words and phrases. However, its special importance derives from the order of chapters which renders it possible to establish the original structure of the *Pesikta.* It is almost exactly the same as the remarkable prediction made by Zunz, at a time when a copy of the *Pesikta* was not available. However, in the new Oxford manuscript, an excerpt of the chapter on Shavuot and the chapter on *Simḥat Torah come at the very end of the manuscript, after the chapter for the last Sabbath of the year. This would indicate that these two chapters for the second day of a holiday, observed outside of Palestine, were not part of the original *Pesikta,* which is of Palestinian origin. In all probability, a later scribe came upon these two chapters, which are similar in style (although definitely of later origin) to the *Pesikta,* and attached them as an addendum to the manuscript. Each of the six manuscripts has such addenda within a chapter or complete chapters attached which are not to be found in the other manuscripts. This practice by scribes of adding material similar to the books which they were copying was not uncommon in ancient times.

It may therefore be concluded that the original order of the *Pesikta* chapters followed the cycle of the Jewish calendar, beginning with Rosh Ha-Shanah and concluding with the Sabbath before Rosh Ha-Shanah, as found in the new Oxford manuscript and anticipated some 130 years ago by Zunz.

Bibliography: *Pesikta de-Rav Kahana,* ed. by B. Mandelbaum (1962), introd.; Zunz, Vortraege; *Pesikta de-Rav Kahana,* ed. by S. Buber (1868), introd.; *Midrash Va-Yikra Rabbah,* ed. by M. Margulies, 5 (1960), xiii; Goldberg, in: KS, 43 (1967/68), 68–79.
[B.Ma.]

PESIKTA RABBATI (Aram. פְּסִיקְתָּא רַבָּתִי), a medieval Midrash on the festivals of the year. It has been printed several times, and a critical edition, with introduction, commentary, and indices was published by M. Friedman (Ish-Shalom) in 1880. Further fragments were published by S. A. Wertheimer (in *Battei Midrashot,* 1 (1950), 260–4), and L. Ginzberg (in *Ginzei Schechter,* 1 (1928), 172–81; all future references are to Friedman's edition). The word *pesikta* means "section," and this Midrash consists of a series of separate sections, on the pentateuchal and prophetic lessons of festivals, unlike most other *Midreshei Aggadah* (e.g., some of the *Rabbot*) which are continuous commentaries to the Bible. It is called *Rabbati* ("the greater") probably in contrast to the earlier **Pesikta (de-Rav Kahana).*

In Friedman's edition, the *Pesikta Rabbati* consists of some 47 sections, but considerably more homilies, as some sections consist of (parts of) several homilies (e.g., section 10). Seven or eight sections deal with *Ḥanukkah (2–8 or 9); sections 10 to 15 (or 16) with the Sabbaths preceding *Passover; 17–18 with Passover itself; 20–24 is a Midrash on the Ten Commandments (*Shavuot); 26–37 deals with the Sabbaths of mourning and comforting and the Ninth of *Av; while 38–48, bearing the superscription *"Midrash Harninu"* deal with *Rosh Ha-Shanah and the *Day of Atonement. Thus this Midrash spans the year from the Day of Atonement omitting only *Sukkot. Probably, in its original form, the Midrash covered the full year, but now the end has been lost.

It has five entire sections in common with the earlier *Pesikta* (15–18, 33, also part of 14), but otherwise is totally different both in style and structure. Thus, while the *Pesikta de-Rav Kahana* has no halakhic passages, no less than 28 homilies of the *Pesikta Rabbati* have halakhic exordia, many (1–14, 39–45, 47) beginning with the formula **Yelammedenu Rabbenu,* followed by proems beginning *Kakh pataḥ R. Tanḥuma.* This demonstrates clearly the *Pesikta Rabbati's* relationship to the *Tanḥuma-Yelammedenu* literature (see: **Tanḥuma Midrash*). Furthermore, it has been shown that the formula *Kakh pataḥ R. Tanḥuma* does not mean that what follows is a statement by R. Tanḥuma, but merely that this passage is taken from the *Tanḥuma (Yelammedenu).*

So far it has been discovered that two major sources are represented in the *Pesikta Rabbati:* (1) the *Pesikta de-Rav Kahana,* and (2) the *Tanḥuma-Yelammedenu.* Sections 20–24, which Ha-*Meiri calls *Midrash Mattan Torah* ("the Midrash on the giving of the Torah"), differ in style and structure from the rest of this work, and seem to form one unit. The proem in section 20 is strikingly individual in both its style and content. This work emerges, then, as a composite one, a compilation whose main body of source material is from the *Tanḥuma-Yelammedenu.*

In the first homily, one of the *Yelammedenu* sections, 845 is indicated as the date of the composition of the work. (The other date there—1219—is clearly the gloss of a later reader or copyist, perhaps *Eleazar of Worms, who made much use of this Midrash.) However, since this work is considered a composite one, possibly reflecting several periods of editing, this date is evidence only for the composition of the *Tanḥuma-Yelammedenu* stratum. The source material is all Palestinian, and though the precise date and place of compilation have not yet been fixed with certainty, modern scholarly opinion tends to view the *Pesikta Rabbati* as a Palestinian work of the sixth or seventh century.

The complete English translation of the *Pesikta Rabbati* by Braude (1968) takes into account, inter alia, the readings of Ms. Parma 1240 (completed in the year 1270) and Ms. Casanata 3324 (of the 17th century).

Bibliography: W. S. Braude, *Pesikta Rabbati* (1968), translation and introduction; L. Prys, *Die Jeremias Homilie Pesikta Rabbati* (1966); idem, in: JQR, 52 (1961/62), 264–72; idem, in: PAAJR, 30 (1962), 1–35; B. J. Bamberger, in: HUCA, 15 (1940), 427–8; V. Aptowitzer, *ibid.,* 8–9 (1931–32), 383–410; Mann, Egypt, 1 (1920), 48; Zunz-Albeck, Derashot, 117–21, 376–89. [D.S.]

PESTSZENTERZSEBET (Hung. **Pestszenterzsébet**), town, formerly a suburb of Budapest, Hungary. A Neologist congregation was founded there toward the end of the 19th century. In 1901 a synagogue was erected and in 1903 a *talmud torah* was founded. A school was opened in 1922 and existed until the Holocaust. B. Krishaber was rabbi of Pestszenterzsebet from 1900 to 1950. The Jewish population numbered 21,953 in 1910; 3,293 in 1920; 7,000 in 1929; 4,522 in 1936; and 3,978 in 1941. Most of the Jews in Pestszenterzsebet were laborers but some were occupied in commerce or were members of the liberal professions.

During World War II, after the German occupation (March 19, 1944), the 3,000 Jews in Pestszenterzsebet were among the last to be deported to Auschwitz. Very few returned, and in 1969 only six Jews were living there.

Bibliography: B. Krishaber, in: *Zsidó Évkönyv,* 1 (1927), 131–3.

[B.Y.]

PESUKEI DE-ZIMRA (Aramaic פְּסוּקֵי דְזִמְרָא; lit. "verses of song/praise"; cf. Shab. 118b; Soferim 18:1, ed. Higger), in the Ashkenazi rite, the Psalms and cognate biblical passages recited in *Shaḥarit* immediately following the morning *benedictions; the Sephardi, Yemenite, and Italian designation is *Zemirot.* The liturgical pattern requires meditation prior to formal prayer (Ber. 32a, cf. Ber. 5:1) in order to achieve the required state of mind; the recitation of the *Pesukei de-Zimra* is in place of such meditation (Tosafot ad loc.). The Ashkenazi practice is to enclose the *Pesukei de-Zimra* between the two blessings, *Barukh she-Amar* and *Yishtabbaḥ.* On weekdays, they comprise I Chronicles 16:8–36, plus a lectionary of 23 verses from Psalms; Psalm 100; another lectionary, mostly from Psalms, beginning *Yehi khevod;* Psalms 145–50; a doxology formed by the final verse of Psalms 89, 135, and 72:18–19; I Chronicles 29:10–13; Nehemiah 9:6–11; and Exodus 14:30–15:18, 19, plus three divine kingship verses. On Sabbaths and festivals, Psalm 100 is omitted while Psalms 19, 34, 90, 91, 135, 136, 33, 92, and 93 are added before *Yehi khevod.* Also the prayer **Nishmat kol ḥai* is recited before *Yishtabbaḥ.*

There is considerable variation in the other rites, especially for Sabbaths and festivals, reflecting the relatively late development of a custom not mandated by the Talmud. The expression *pesukei* ("verses") rather than *pirkei* ("chapters") suggests that "originally not whole Psalms but selections from them were prescribed" (J. Mann in HUCA, 2 (1925), 276). Liebreich distinguished two stages of evolution: before the inclusion of Psalms 145–50, and thereafter. The sages lauded "those who complete the *Hallel* [Psalms] daily" (Shab. 118b). Special merit was attached to reciting Psalm 145 *(*Ashrei).* Psalms were publicly recited in both Temples, but *Pesukei de-Zimra* did not become integral to synagogue worship until geonic times. Only a reader and two respondents are required for their public recitation (Mid. Ps. 113:3).

Bibliography: Abrahams, Companion, xxix–xxxix; Elbogen, Gottesdienst, 81–87; K. Kohler, *Studies, Addresses and Personal Papers* (1931), 141–6; Idelsohn, Liturgy, 80–84; Liebreich, in: PAAJR, 18 (1948/49), 255–67; idem, in: JQR, 41 (1951), 195–206; E. Levy, *Yesodot ha-Tefillah* (1952[2]), 132–8. [H.Kr.]

PETAḤ TIKVAH (Heb. פֶּתַח תִּקְוָה), city in Israel's Coastal Plain, 7 mi. (12 km.) E. of Tel Aviv. In the 1870s a number of observant Jews from Jerusalem decided to become farmers and establish a village called Petaḥ Tikvah

("Gateway of Hope"), after Hosea 2:17. They initially set out to purchase a tract of land near Jericho, but did not obtain the consent of the Turkish Crown to the transfer of ownership. Not abandoning their plan, in 1878 they chose an area of 3,400 dunams near the Yarkon River course, adjoining an Arab village called Mulabbis and owned by a Greek. The area looked attractive with its greenery, uncommon for the country in those days. Disregarding warnings of the danger of malaria there, the settlers acquired the land and thus laid the ground for the first Jewish village in the country, which later became known as "the mother of the moshavot." The founders, Joel Moses *Salomon, David *Gutmann, and Yehoshua *Stampfer, succeeded in mobilizing additional settlers, but soon malaria wrought havoc, the first harvests were disappointing, and quarrels broke out within the group. In 1882 Petaḥ Tikvah numbered ten houses and 66 inhabitants. As health conditions became unbearable, the settlers had to transfer to the neighborhood of the Arab village Yehud further south.

In 1883 *Bilu immigrants renewed settlement on the site of Petaḥ Tikvah itself. They again had to withstand immense difficulties caused by their own lack of farming experience and financial means, frequent raids of Arab neighbors, and the hostility of the Turkish authorities. Baron Edmond de *Rothschild soon came to their aid and enabled them to embark on the drainage of the swamps. The direction of the moshavah passed from the local committee into the hands of the Rothschild administration. This step soon became a source of tension between the officials and the settlers, until Rothschild decided (in 1900) to transfer the moshavah to the *Jewish Colonization Association (ICA). The danger of Arab attacks, causing bodily harm to settlers, damage to homes and other property, and the malicious practice of pasturing Arab flocks on Jewish fields prompted the settlers to organize a first guardsmen's group, headed by Abraham *Shapira, which succeeded in securing the village and driving off the marauders. The drainage of the swamps and planting of citrus groves led to an improvement in the economic situation and attracted more settlers and Jewish laborers.

In 1891 Petaḥ Tikvah numbered 464 inhabitants, and in 1900 there were 818. The moshavah was regarded as a center by the nascent Jewish labor movement, and in 1905 the ground was laid there for the Ha-Po'el ha-Ẓa'ir and Aḥdut ha-Avodah parties. In World War I, Petaḥ Tikvah came in between armies of the Central Powers (Turkey and Germany) and Allied lines before it was taken by the British in 1917. After the war, the moshavah absorbed many immigrants and in 1920 received municipal council status. In May 1921 an Arab attack on Petaḥ Tikvah was repulsed by a defense force consisting mainly of local youth, assisted by British troops, and four young men, among them Avshalom *Gissin, were killed. In 1930, it attained a population of 8,768. Its growth was accelerated further in the 1930s, thanks to its central location within the Jewish settlement zone, resulting in a population of 20,000 in 1938 and in the attainment of city status in 1939. Petaḥ Tikvah became the marketing center of its region's farming produce and established industries, which, initially, were based mainly on agricultural raw materials. Also in the 1930s underground Jewish defense organizations had headquarters in Petaḥ Tikvah.

Figure 1. Petaḥ Tikvah, before World War I. Courtesy Central Zionist Archives, Jerusalem.

Figure 2. Petaḥ Tikvah, 1968. Courtesy J.N.F., Jerusalem.

With the expansion of its built-up area Petaḥ Tikvah gradually absorbed adjoining workers' quarters and villages (e.g., Maḥaneh Yehudah, Ein Gannim, Kefar Gannim, Kefar Avraham, Sha'ariyyah). After 1948, the city's expansion proceeded at an even quicker pace, bringing the population to 45,000 in 1953, 54,000 in 1961, and 83,200 in 1970. Its location on the outer ring of the Tel Aviv conurbation deeply influences Petaḥ Tikvah's character. Although industry, with large enterprises in metals, rubber tires, textiles, food, and other branches, constitutes the city's main economic foundation, farming still plays a role, as the environs belong to Israel's central citrus-growing area. Two large hospitals, Beilinson and Ha-Sharon, lie within Petaḥ Tikvah's municipal limits. An important cultural institution is Yad la-Banim, which is dedicated to the fallen in all stages of Israel's defense. Efforts to restrain Petaḥ Tikvah's expansion over additional farmland of the vicinity, which counts among Israel's most productive soils, have resulted, since the 1960s, in closer and higher building in the city's zone. [S.H.]

°**PETER OF BLOIS** (c. 1135–after 1204), Christian theologian. Born in France, Peter lived in England from 1169, writing there his treatise *Contra perfidiam Judaeorum* (c. 1200). The work was composed at the request of a friend who complained that he was surrounded by heretics and Jews with whom he was often compelled to engage in argument without always being able to refute them. The treatise is divided into 34 chapters and quotes as authorities not only the Bible but also the Church Fathers, and the *Sibyl. The final passages quote both Jewish and pagan authors, and include the apocryphal text on Jesus attributed to *Josephus. The prestige enjoyed by Peter, whom several of his contemporaries designated as a "new Church

Father," while his works came to be regarded as models of style, helped to gain his treatise a wide circulation.

Bibliography: PL, 207 (1855), 825–70; J. de Ghellinck, *L'essor de la littérature latine,* 1 (1946), 132–5. [B.Bl.]

°**PETER OF CLUNY** (also named **Peter the Venerable; Petrus Venerabilis;** c. 1090–1156), abbot of Cluny, France. Peter was a contemporary of *Bernard of Clairvaux, a prolific author, and counsellor of kings and princes. On the eve of the Second Crusade, because of his advice to King *Louis VII to adopt harsh measures against the Jews, the authority of the abbot of Clairvaux had to be exerted for their protection. Peter was associated with the translation of the Koran into Latin carried out in Spain. His travels to Spain resulted in two polemical treatises against Islam, and in an anti-Jewish polemic, *Adversus Judaeorum inveteratum duritiam* (completed c. 1140). This work is set in the form of a dialogue and refers three times to oral *disputations with Jews. It is based mainly on the views of *Petrus Alfonsi, from whom Peter was the first in France to borrow criticisms alleging the "foolishness" and "insanities" of the Talmud and the midrashic texts. Peter, however, also refers to other texts not mentioned by Petrus Alfonsi. As he had no knowledge of Hebrew Peter could not have read the texts himself, but the source from which he drew them is unknown. The most important passage mentioning Jewish contemporaries is a reference to a "Jewish king" in Rouen. Thirty-four manuscripts of this work (some of them translations) have been preserved, testifying to its popularity.

Bibliography: PL, 179 (1899), 507–650; G. Constable and J. Kritzeck, *Petrus Venerabilis* (1956); S. Lieberman, *Sheki'in* (Heb., 1939). [B.Bl.]

PETHAHIAH OF REGENSBURG (12th century), traveler; son of Jacob ha-Lavan and brother of *Isaac b. Jacob ha-Lavan of Prague, both tosafists. His permanent home appears to have been in Regensburg (Ratisbon), although he was also connected with Prague. About 1175 he set out on his travels, making his way through Poland and Russia to Crimea, from there to Tartary, Khazaria, Armenia, Kurdistan, Babylonia, Syria, and Ereẓ Israel. During his journey he made notes of his experiences. However, the contents of his book of travels were not written by Pethahiah but by others according to the stories they heard directly from him. The writer does not speak in the first person but relates the events in the name of the traveler. Apparently the book was written by several people, one of whom was *Judah b. Samuel he-Hasid of Regensburg. The writers did not record the whole of Pethahiah's narrative, but a summary of what he related or those parts which they considered the most important.

The book says nothing on Pethahiah's journey to Crimea and little on Crimea and Tartary. The major part of the narrative is devoted to his travels in Babylonia, Syria, and Ereẓ Israel. Some scholars consider that his destination was Babylonia, and that he was seeking a refuge there for his persecuted brethren in Europe. There is however no basis for this. The narrative indicates that Pethahiah was a wealthy man whose principal objective was to make a pilgrimage to Palestine and to pray at the tombs of the righteous. In a letter of recommendation which he requested of the *gaon* of Babylonia, the latter wrote that "in every place where he comes, they should guide him and point out the site of the tombs of the scholars and the righteous." However in Babylonia he found, beside the holy tombs, a large and alert Jewish settlement with a flourishing spiritual life, a firmly established *exilarch, and a respected *gaon* who could implement his instructions by force. This autonomous power, and the methods of study at the great yeshivah there, left a tremendous impression on the German traveler, and he related all of this in detail. When he told of the Babylonian *gaon,* he emphasized, in addition to his erudition, his political power and princely deportment.

In contrast to Babylonia, he found only a poor and oppressed community in Ereẓ Israel. The crusaders who had conquered the country in 1099 had annihilated the Jewish settlements in Jerusalem, Hebron, and other places, and the remnants had fled to Syria and Egypt. The traveler did not therefore dwell on at length or the writer did not note down the details of the Jewish population in Palestine. Of the country's settlements, principally mentioned are Tiberias, Acre, Jerusalem, and Hebron. In Jerusalem he found only one Jew, Abraham the Dyer, whose services were needed by the crusaders. Pethahiah's main descriptions of Palestine concern the holy places and the reports and traditions about them. He does not tell anything of his return journey, and it appears that he traveled by sea, passing through Greece.

The story of Pethahiah's travels was published for the first time in Prague in 1595 under the title *Sibbuv* ("Circuit") and has been published in its original form 24 times. It has also been translated into Judeo-German, Latin, French, German, English, and Russian. The best editions are the first, and that of L. Gruenhut (1905, with German translation), which is based on manuscripts and on the first edition.

Bibliography: E. N. Adler, *Jewish Travellers* (1930), 64–91 (includes excerpts from the *Sibbuv*); A. Yaari, *Masot Ereẓ Yisrael* (1946), 48–55, 762–3. [A.Ya.]

PETIḤAH (Heb. פְּתִיחָה; "opening"), the ritual of opening the Ark in the synagogue during services to take out the Torah scroll(s) for the reading of the Law, and (particularly in Ashkenazi synagogues) to recite prayers of special importance or solemnity, especially on the High Holidays, (e.g., the prayer **Avinu Malkenu* and the entire **Ne'ilah* service on the Day of Atonement). In the Reform ritual other special prayers (e.g., for the welfare of the government) are also recited before the open Ark. The custom of the *petiḥah* may be a remnant of the ritual in the talmudic period when in times of danger and need (pestilence, drought), the Ark was carried to the town square where special penitential prayers were recited (see Ta'an 2:1, 2, etc.). Mordecai Jaffe (in his *Levush Tekhelet* to Sh. Ar., OḤ 133) explains the custom of the *petiḥah:* "The high priest entered the Holy of Holies in the Temple once a year, on the Day of Atonement, in order to stress the special sanctity of that day; therefore the most significant prayers are recited before the open Ark to stress their special importance." The congregants rise for all prayers which are recited when the Ark is open. [Ed.]

°**PETLYURA, SIMON** (1879–1926), Ukrainian nationalist leader held responsible for not having stopped the wave of pogroms which engulfed the Jews in the Ukraine in 1919 and 1920. Petlyura, who was born in Poltava, was active in the Ukrainian Social Democratic Workers' Party. During the Russian Revolution in 1917, he was one of the leaders who organized Ukrainian soldiers into nationalist battalions. When the Ukrainian puppet state, set up by the Germans, fell in November 1918, Petlyura was among those who established the "directorium" (provisional government) to protect the independent Ukraine against its many enemies. From February 1919 he was chairman of the government and also chief *atamàn* (commander) of its army. With the retreat of his forces before the Red Army in the winter of 1919, his units turned into murderous bands and perpetrated mass killings of Jews in the Ukrainian towns and townlets (*Zhitomir, *Proskurov, and elsewhere). Petlyura did little to stop the wave of mob violence which became endemic within the Ukrainian army and the gangs of rebellious peasants, connected with his government. In October 1919 the remnants of Petlyura's forces fled to Poland. The following year he made a treaty with the Poles, set up his headquarters in *Kamenets-Podolski, and joined in the Polish war against the Soviet Union. After peace was made between the U.S.S.R. and Poland, Petlyura continued to maintain his government and the remnants of his army in exile. In the summer of 1921, Vladimir *Jabotinsky conducted negotiations with Petlyura's representative for the establishment of a Jewish militia to defend the Jewish population, should Petlyura's forces return to the Soviet Ukraine (the "Jabotinsky-Slavinsky Agreement"). From 1924 Petlyura was a political émigré in Paris, where he headed Ukrainian anti-Soviet organizations. On May 26, 1926, he was assassinated in the street by a Jew, Shalom *Schwartzbard. In 1927, after a dramatic trial, in which the Jewish tragedy in the Ukraine was amply documented, Schwartzbard was acquitted by a court in Paris. Ukrainian nationalists consider Petlyura an outstanding leader and claim that he personally could not be held responsible for the pogroms, because of the anarchical conditions of the revolutionary period.

Bibliography: Committee of Jewish Delegations, *The Pogroms in the Ukraine* (1927); E. Tcherikower, *Di Ukrainer Pogromen in Yor 1919* (1965), index; J. B. Schechtman, *Rebel and Statesman,* 1 (1956), 399–415; A. Revutsky, *In di Shvere Teg oyf Ukraine* (1924); A. Shul'gin, *L'Ukraine et le cauchemar rouge* (1927); J. Reshetar, *The Ukrainian Revolution* (1952), index; Hunczak and Szajkowski, in: JSOS, 31 (1969), 163–213. [Y.S.]

PETRA (Gr. "rock," a translation of the Heb. *sela*), a ruined site in Edom, 140 mi. (224 km.) S. of Amman, 60 mi. (96 km.) N. of Elath. It is assumed that the biblical Sela was situated farther north (II Kings 14:7). In later sources (Jos., Ant., 4:161; Tosef., Shev. 4:11) it is called Rekem, after a Midianite ruler (Num. 31:8).

Petra is situated in a broad valley, which is approached from the east by a long, narrow, and winding canyon, the Sīq, also called the Wadi Mūsā, which has several confluents in the plain of the city. The valley is surrounded by steep rocks of reddish Nubian sandstone. The place is safe from attack once the Sīq and its continuation to the west, the still narrower and more difficult Sayl al-Ṣiyāgh, are barred. The earliest settlement is indicated by Edomite

Figure 1. Façade of the al-Dayr tomb at Petra, one of the city's rock-cut buildings in Roman temple style, first-second centuries C.E., Courtesy Garo's Photo Shop, Jerusalem.

Figure 2. Petra's most magnificent building, al-Khazna ("the treasury"), the façade imitating that of a Hellenistic theater, first–second centuries C.E. Courtesy Garo's Photo Shop, Jerusalem.

pottery found at the top of a rock called Umm al-Biyāra in the southwestern part of the site. This rock served mainly as a place of refuge, the last time during the attack on the Nabateans by Antigonus in 312 B.C.E. Owing to its secure position, Petra was adopted by the Nabatean kings as their capital; the caravan routes from the Syrian desert, Elath, Gaza, and the Mediterranean converged there. In 106 C.E. the city was incorporated into the Roman Empire, remaining the capital of the region—Provincia Arabia—until the time of Hadrian, who endowed it with the title of *metropolis.* Papyri discovered in the caves of the Judean Desert reveal that Petra had a senate and archives and that it was visited by the Jewish inhabitants of the province; possibly, a number of Jews lived there. When the capital of Arabia was transferred to Bosrah, the city began to decline. In the time of Diocletian (late third century), it was included in Palestine and in the fifth century became the *metropolis* of the province of Palaestina Tertia. It disappeared from history in Arab times, apart from a brief Crusader interlude when it was known as *Li Vaux Moyse* ("the valley of Moses"). Its ruins were discovered by Burckhardt in 1812. It has since been explored by a number of people, in particular by Brünnow and Domaszewski, G. Dalman, Th. Wiegand, S. and A. Horsfield, D. Kirkbride, and P. J. Par.

In the center of the plain of Petra are the remains of the town, which is partly surrounded by a wall extending from the southern suburb of al-Katūte to the tower sanctuary on ʿArqūb al-Hīsha in the east. The remains are mainly Hellenistic (Nabatean) and Roman. After 106 C.E., al-Katūte was abandoned and the town life was concentrated in the main street in the bed of the Wadi Mūsā. On the northern side of this street are, from west to east, a nymphaeum and pool near the issue of Wadi al-Matāha, a palace, and a gymnasium. On the southern side are another pool, an upper, middle, and lower agora (markets and resting places for caravans), a large temple, and a public bath. A triumphal arch (Roman) crosses the street at the bath. Beyond it are a small temple and a second-century Roman temple known as Qaṣr Bint Farʿūn ("the castle of Pharaoh's daughter"), the best-preserved building in Petra; it is a temple *in antis* on a podium with pronaos, cella, and an adytum in three parts. Another remarkable structure is the rock-cut theater in the Sīq, which was excavated in 1963. It consists of three tiers of seats with a *scenae frons* resembling that of the theater at Beth-Shean. Of princpal interest at Petra are the rock-cut facades. Some of these may belong to temples (as e.g., the famous al-Khazna in the Sīq) and dwelling houses, but above all, they belong to monumental tombs of the kings and princely merchants of the city, including that of the Roman governor, Sextus Florentinus. These facades are imitations of the *scenae frons* of the Hellenistic theater with several tiers of columns usually crowned with the type of capital known as Nabatean. The lowest tier has a doorway and mock windows and often, an inscription. The second tier is divided into round or square pavilions with broken gables and a tholos crowned by an urn in the center. There are also several "high places" and numerous rock carvings of a religious nature at and near Petra.

Bibliography: R. E. Bruennow and A. v. Domaszewski, *Die Provincia Arabia,* 1 (1904), 125–428; G. Dalman, *Petra und seine Felsheiligtuemer* (1908); idem, *Neue Petra-Forschungen* (1912); A. Kammerer, *Petra et la Nabatène* (1930); S. and A. Horsfield, in: QDAP, 7 (1938), 1ff.; 8 (1939), 87ff.; 9 (1942), 105ff.; G. L. Harding, *The Antiquities of Jordan* (1959), 114–35; D. Kirkbride, in: ADAJ, 415 (1960), 117–22; Parr, in: PEFQS, 89 (1957), 5ff.; 91 (1959), 106ff.; 92 (1960), 124–35; Wright, *ibid.,* 93 (1965), 124ff.

[M.A.-Y.]

°PETRIE, SIR WILLIAM MATTHEW FLINDERS (1853–1942), British Egyptologist. In 1880 he visited Egypt for the first time and in 1882 he was engaged in finding the exact measurements of the Giza pyramids. He excavated Tell

Sir Flinders Petrie, British archaeologist.

al-Ḥasī in 1890 on behalf of the Palestine Exploration Fund, noting the sequence of strata in the mound and the importance of pottery for dating the strata. Beginning in 1897, he worked in Egypt on behalf of the Egypt Excavation Fund. He excavated and identified, among many others, a number of pre-dynastic sites (where he applied the method of sequence dating), the early royal tombs at Abydos, cities founded by the Hyksos, the Sinai inscriptions and the greek city of Naucratis, in the process discovering many aspects of ancient Egyptian life, such as the use of papyri in mummification. From 1893 to 1935, Petrie was professor of Egyptology at University College in London. He excavated during the winter and published the results in the summer, eventually producing over 100 reports. In 1926 he founded the British School of Archaeology in Egypt, which supported several excavations in Palestine. Among the sites excavated by Petrie in southern Palestine are Tell Jamma (1926), Tell Sharuḥen (1927–29) and Tell al-ʿAjjūl (1929–31), from which he achieved valuable results, despite his mistaken identifications of the sites. He died in Jerusalem.

Petrie was the pioneer of modern archaeology and formulated many of the methods used today. He was the first to insist on the importance of everyday objects, especially pottery. His works include, in addition to numerous excavation reports, *Hyksos and Israelite Cities* (1906); *Egypt and Israel* (1906); *Methods and Aims in Archaeology* (1904); *A History of Egypt* (6 vols., 1894–1905); *The Arts and Crafts of Ancient Egypt* (1909); *Social Life in Ancient Egypt* (1923); *Religious Life in Ancient Egypt* (1924); *Seventy Years in Archaeology* (1931), an autobiography.

[M.A.-Y.]

PETROGRAD CONFERENCE, seventh national conference of the Russian Zionists and the first after the February 1917 Revolution. It opened on June 6, 1917. Five hundred and fifty-two delegates, representing 140,000 shekel holders from 680 cities and towns, took part in the conference. In the new Russia, the conference demonstrated the growing power of Zionism among Jewry and defined the Russian Zionists' attitude toward the problems of the World Zionist movement and the upbuilding of Ereẓ Israel. It discussed the specific problems of the Russian Jews under the democratic regime with the hope of expanding the movement, which up to that time had acted mainly illegally. Jehiel *Tschlenow and Menahem *Ussishkin were elected as presidents of the conference. In his programmatic address, Tschlenow said that the main task of the conference was to lay the foundations for Jewish national autonomy in Russia, as well as to emphasize the Jewish people's aspiration to return to Ereẓ Israel. Ussishkin spoke of the need to immediately mobilize Jewish capital for settlement work, especially for the purchase of land, and to train pioneer workers. Alexander *Goldstein proposed the holding of a referendum in order to prove to the world that Ereẓ Israel was the desired country of every Jew. The proposal was enthusiastically accepted. Isaac *Gruenbaum and Julius Brutzkus delivered speeches based on the *Helsingsfors Program for Zionist Diaspora activities in light of the new situation in Russia. There was a trenchant debate about the authority and character of the Jewish community as the nucleus of self-government. When the conference rejected Gruenbaum's proposal to exclude religious matters from the control of the communal boards, a 40-delegate group of his followers declared that none of them would enter the movement's executive bodies. According to one resolution a Zionist was allowed to be a member of another political party, as long as it was not Jewish and provided that it was approved by the local branch of the Zionist movement. Another resolution read that the Zionist Organization would participate in the elections as an independent party. The conference agreed that educational and cultural actions should be recognized as one of the main tasks of Zionist work, and the Tarbut society should be recognized as the only institution to do this work. This seven-day conference was the last free countrywide expression of the Russian Zionist movement before the October Revolution of the same year became the starting point of its persecution and liquidation.

Bibliography: Y. Gruenbaum, *Ha-Tenu'ah ha-Ẓiyyonit,* 4 (1954), 98–108; B. Dinaburg (Dinur), in: *Sefer Tschlenow* (1937), 46–48; J. Tschlenow, *ibid.,* 363–74; A. Raphaeli (Ẓenẓiper), *Ba-Ma'avak li-Ge'ullah* (1956), 19–24.

[Ar.R.]

PETROLEUM AND OIL PRODUCTS. In modern times Jews took part in the development of the oil industry, some in pioneering the extraction of oil and trade in its products in their respective countries, and some in financing the industry abroad.

Eastern Galicia. Oil prospecting and the development of the oilfields of eastern Galicia from the middle of the nineteenth century was due to a large measure to the initiative of Jews. In *Borislav the first attempts to find petroleum were made by a Jew, Schreiner, before the middle of the 19th century. Ozocerite, which became a substitute for the expensive beeswax in the manufacture of candles, was then discovered there. Ozocerite candles were soon extensively marketed in the region. The great demand for ozocerite led many Jews in *Drogobych to acquire plots of land in Borislav to extract it. Thousands of Jews streamed from surrounding townlets and villages to work there, in primitive conditions. The work was performed in two shifts of 12 hours each; women and children also were employed on the easier tasks. Abraham Schreiner, son of the discoverer of petroleum in Galicia, attempted to separate the petroleum from the earth admixture. After many failures, he succeeded in establishing the first petroleum refinery in Borislav in 1854. Many railway companies then ordered petroleum from him for lighting their carriages and stations. Thus he became the world's first "petroleum king" until the destruction of his refinery in a fire in 1886.

In the 1880s the enterprise, capital, and modern methods of corporations drove out the Jewish entrepreneurs with their inadequate means and primitive methods. As a result, 5,000 Jewish workers in Borislav addressed themselves to the second Zionist Congress in Basle in 1898, described their plight, and requested assistance for *aliyah* to Ereẓ Israel. Some Jews were still active in the oilfields of Galicia between the two world wars.

Czarist Russia. As the oil wells in czarist Russia were situated outside the *Pale of Settlement Jews were at first unable to participate in the industry. Later on Jewish chemists succeeded in entering the petroleum trade and subsequently also the industry. By 1910, 15% of oil extraction was carried out by Jews, as well as 44% of the manufacture of kerosene, 32% of the manufacture of lubrication oils, and 49.6% of the trade in oil products on the Baku exchange.

During the second half of the 19th century Jews were engaged in the transportation of petroleum. The Jewish petroleum company Dembo & Kagan, whose owners were A. *Dembo of Kovno and Kh. Kagan of Brest-Litovsk, laid the first oil pipeline in Russia in 1870. They set up a petroleum refinery in a suburb of Baku and established relations with shipping companies of the Caspian region which transported the oil by sea, whence it was expedited by rail throughout Russia. Because of the monopolistic position of the Nobel Company in the Caucasus, Dembo & Kagan could only operate for five years, after which it was compelled to confine itself to the marketing of oil.

The brothers Saveli and Mikhail Polyak and the engineer Arkadi Beylin, in partnership with the Rothschild Bank, founded the Mazut Company of Baku, later amalgamated with the Shell Company. The Rothschild house also financed the Batum Oil Association, founded after the construction of the Trans-Caucasian railroad and owned mainly by Jews. The *Pereire family of Paris invested considerable sums in the oil fields of the Caucasus. A. M. Feigel, one of the initiators of the petroleum trade in Baku, organized, with A. Beylin, a syndicate of oil companies to compete with the American Standard Oil. The Dembat brothers succeeded in publicizing mazut as a cheap fuel oil for ships and locomotives. They were the first Jews to be permitted by the Russian government, in appreciation of their activities, to acquire oil wells. With Baron Horace Guenzburg, they established the Volga-Caspian Petroleum Company.

Czechoslovakia. In Czechoslovakia Jews were active in oil refining, and in general branches of the trade and industry. The Kralupy refinery on the river Vltava was established by Jindřich Eisenschimel and Ludvik Heller. The refinery owned by David Fanto was prominent in the industry by 1924. The Vacuum Oil Company was headed by Charles Wachtel and Bedřich Stránsky, who transferred their affairs to New York in 1939.

England. Marcus *Samuel, Viscount Bearstead, played a central role, sometimes in cooperation with the house of Rothschild, in developing the trade and transportation of petroleum and oil on a large international scale from 1897. In 1907 he founded the Shell Royal Dutch Company together with Royal Dutch, which launched England as an oil power. He was one of the first to initiate the haulage of petroleum through the Suez Canal. During World War I, he played a role of prime importance in the supply of oil to the British Navy. Sir Robert Waley *Cohen was active in the Shell Company from 1901, and in 1905 was appointed director of the Asiatic Petroleum Company. From 1907 he served as director of the Anglo-Saxon Petroleum Company. During World War I he served as adviser on oil affairs to the Army Council.

France. In addition to the investments of the house of Rothschild of Paris and the Pereire family, Alexandre Deutsch founded the Société de Pétrole, and his sons Emile (1847–1924) and Henri (1846–1918) *Deutsch de la Meurthe succeeded him. Henri published a work on petroleum and its use and headed the petroleum industry exhibit at the Paris International Exhibition in 1889.

United States. The role of Jews in the petroleum industry in the U.S. was negligible. The petroleum industry in the U.S. was in the hands of a small number of Protestant families which did not as a rule hire Jews. The Arab boycott after 1948 strengthened this tendency not to employ Jews so as to avoid friction with the Arab oil states. An exception was the *Blaustein family, founder of the American Oil Company.

For petroleum and oil products in Israel, see *Israel, State of: Economic Section.

Bibliography: N. Shapira, in: *Gesher*, 5 (1959), 122–9; H. Landau, in: *YIVO Bleter*, 14 (1939), 269–85; I. M. Dijur, in: J. G. Frumkin et al. (eds.), *Russian Jewry; 1860–1917* (1966), 140ff.; J. C. Pick, in: *Jews of Czechoslovakia*, 1 (1968), 375; R. Mahler, *Yehudei Polin Bein Shetei Milḥamot ha-Olam* (1968), 107.

[Ed.]

°**PETRONIUS, PUBLIUS,** governor of Syria, 39–42 C.E. Petronius was ordered by Emperor Caligula to place his statue in the Temple at Jerusalem and to use force if necessary to overcome the resistance of the Jews. When they learned of the order, the Jews flocked to Petronius' headquarters at Acre to plead for annulment of this decree. Realizing that the Jews were prepared to sacrifice their lives, Petronius wrote to Caligula advancing reasons for a delay in installing the statue. The response was an impatient command to carry out the imperial order immediately. Meanwhile, as a result of Agrippa I's intercession, Caligula was prevailed upon to rescind his instructions. Unaware of this, Petronius again wrote to Caligula, who, in a rage, ordered him to commit suicide: this order reached him, however, after the news of Caligula's murder in 41 C.E. Petronius's friendship toward the Jews was demonstrated again when some Greek youths of the city of Dora set up a statue of the emperor in the local synagogue. In response to Agrippa I's remonstration Petronius ordered the magistrates of the city to send him the offenders; he enjoined them to allow everyone freely to practice his ancestral faith. Petronius' conduct is indicative not only of a desire to preserve order in the Roman provinces but also of his favorable attitude toward Judaism, which is ascribed by *Philo to his search for knowledge and to his close contact with Jews in the provinces of Syria and Asia, where he had previously been as proconsul.

Bibliography: Philo, *De Legatione ad Caium*, 31, 33; Jos., Ant., 18:261–309; 19:301f.; Pauly-Wissowa, 37 (1937), 1199–201, no. 24; Schuerer, Hist, 207–10, 219; Stern, in: *Zion*, 29 (1964), 155–67.

[L.Ro.]

°**PETRONIUS ARBITER, GAIUS,** Roman author and a companion of Nero in some of his pleasure ventures. Petronius links Jewish circumcision with the pierced ears of the Arabs and with the chalked faces of the Gauls (*Satiricon*, 102). In a poetic fragment he says that the Jews revered a porcine deity (*Fragmentum*, 97, in *Poetae Latini Minores*, ed. by Baehrens, 4 (1882), 98; = no. 24 in Loeb edition (1913), p. 354). This may be an allusion to Jewish abstinence from pork, or Petronius could be really ascribing a pig-god to Jews either out of ignorance or malice. He writes also of circumcision whereby Jews distinguish themselves from non-Jews and of the oppressive laws of the Jewish Sabbath. Some take this to refer to Sabbath observance, though most commentators regard it as an allusion to the mistaken notion, common to many Roman writers, that the Jews fasted on the Sabbath (cf. Strabo, Augustus, Trogus Pompeius, and Martial).

Bibliography: Reinach, Textes, 266. [J.P.]

PETRUS ALFONSI (Aldefonsi; b. 1062), Spanish Converso, physician, polemicist, and author, possiby born in Huesca. Known as Mosé or Moisés Sefardi before his conversion at the age of 44, he assumed the new name of Petrus Alfonsi (Aldefonsi) because his conversion took place on St. Peter's Day and his baptismal patron was King Alfonso I of Aragon. He spent the second half of his life in England, where he was physician to King Henry I. Petrus introduced the oriental apologue to western Europe through his *Disciplina Clericalis*, a collection of some 34 stories belonging to the traditional literature of the Orient (translated into English under the title *The Scholar's Guide*). He was also the author of a polemical treatise, *Dialogi . . . in quibus judaeorum opiniones . . . confutanur* (Bibliotheca Patrum, 22 (1677), 172ff.), which he wrote to defend his conversion.

These dialogues, cast in the mold of classic apologetics, take place between a Jew and a Christian, named respectively Moses and Peter, the two figurations of the author before and after his baptism. The work, divided into 12 chapters, begins with an attempt to prove that the Jews were only partially observing the Law of Moses. The author also touches upon Islam, to demonstrate its falsehoods. From chapter 6 on, he explores the concepts of the Trinity, the Immaculate Conception, the Incarnation, and the supposed fulfillment of prophecies with the birth of Jesus. Chapters 10 to 12 treat of the crucifixion, resurrection, and ascension of Jesus of Nazareth. The final arguments are that Christianity is not contrary to Mosaic Law. Additionally, Petrus was a noted astronomer and translated scientific works from the Arabic.

Bibliography: Baer, Spain, 1 (1961), 59; Ashtor, Korot, 2 (1966), 172–3; G. Díaz-Plaja, *Historia general de las literaturas hispámcas . . .*, 1 (1949), 194, 285–6; J. M. Millás Vallicrosa, *La Obra astronómica de Mosé Sefardi* (1937); idem, in: *Sefarad*, 3 (1943), 65–105; F. Ainaud de Lasarte, *ibid.*, 359–76; H. Schwarzbaum, *ibid.*, 22 (1962), 17–59, 321–44; 23 (1963), 54–73; J. J. Jones and J. E. Keller, *The Scholar's Guide* (1969). [K.R.S.]

PETSCHEK, Bohemian family of financiers and industrialists, for half a century owners of one of the leading coal mining companies in central Europe. Moses ben Israel (1822–1888), its founder, moved from his native village, Pečky (hence the family's name), to nearby Kolin, where Isidor (1854–1919), Julius (1856–1932), and Ignaz (1857–1934) were born. Moses made his fortune mainly in real estate. In 1871 he acquired stock in a lignite mining company in Most (Bruex) and in 1876 moved to Prague. The real pioneer of the Petschek family's entry into the coal industry was Ignaz, who began his career as a bank clerk. After an apprenticeship with J. E. *Weinmann in Ústí nad Labem (Aussig an der Elbe), he founded his own coal marketing agency there. In 1890 Ignaz was selling up to 7,000,000 tons of lignite a year. In 1906 he bought his first mines. The business of Isidor and Julius, conducted from Prague, became known as "Grosser Petschek" while Ignaz' firm was known as "Kleiner Petschek"; they were competitors and acquired interests in many other branches of industry and finance throughout Europe. Both groups, but mainly Ignaz', acquired coal mines during the post-World War I inflation years, and subsequently, with 50 other German mining firms, formed a syndicate, in which they themselves controlled 50% of all the output. After World War I the Prague group (Julius and Isidor) founded their own bank.

After Julius' death, the Prague group was owned by seven families, and in 1938 by 40, who transferred their property to a specially created British corporation, and as such in 1937 opened negotiations with their Nazi competitors. In May they succeeded in selling the property at a huge loss for $4,750,000 in hard currency. Subsequently they also sold the majority of their possessions in the Sudeten area, including 24 coal mines, their sales organization, and 30% of the north Bohemian coal output. All the Prague Petschek families moved to England in July 1938, and later to the U.S. The property of the Ústí branch, managed by Ignaz' son Karl, was too large to be acquired by the Germans and the family tried to withstand them. When the Nazis occupied Ústí (1938) they immediately appointed a German executor (trustee) and in spring 1939 the property was sold by the German Reich as restitution for 3000,000,-000 Reichsmark allegedly defrauded from taxes due in Germany. The Hermann *Goering Werke organized a special firm, known as Subag, to include both groups. The Petschek possessions became state-owned after World War II. Many members of the family lived in the United States.

Bibliography: F. Pinner, *Deutsche Wirtschaftsfuehrer* (1925), 305–6; J. Stoessler, in: H. Gold (ed.), *Die Juden und Judengemeinden Boehmens in Vergangenheit und Gegenwart* (1934), 22; *Jews of Czechoslovakia*, 1 (1968), index; R. Hilberg, *Destruction of the European Jews* (1967[2]), 61, 81; K. Kratochvíl, *Bankéři* (1962).

[M.La.]

PETTER BEN JOSEPH (12th century), tosafist. Petter came from Carinthia in Austria and was a pupil of *Samuel b. Meir and of his brother, Jacob *Tam. He participated in the editing of R. Tam's *Sefer ha-Yashar*, to which he made additions. Petter maintained a halakhic correspondence with R. Tam and with *Isaac b. Melchizedek of Siponto and it is probable that the quotations from the latter in the *Sefer ha-Yashar* were included by Petter. He was also an associate of *Isaac ha-Lavan, who quotes him in his *tosafot*. Most of the statements of Petter in the printed *tosafot* also appear in the *Sefer ha-Yashar*. He met a martyr's death at an early age during the Second Crusade, and Jacob of Bonn eulogized him in the highest terms.

With regard to the unusual name of Petter borne by a pupil of R. Tam, it is interesting to note that R. Tam accepts the medieval legend that Peter (Simon Caiaphas) was a devout Jew who sacrificed himself in order to effect the separation between Judaism and Christianity, and is the author of the prayer **Nishmat*, a legend whose authenticity had been rejected by R. Tam's grandfather, Rashi (see *Maḥzor Vitry*, ed. by S. Hurwitz (1923[2]), 282 n. 5, 362 n. 5).

Bibliography: Urbach, Tosafot, 191–3. [I.T.-S.]

PETUCHOWSKI, JAKOB JOSEF (1925–), U.S. rabbinic scholar and theologian. Born in Berlin, Petuchowski emigrated with his family to England before the outbreak of World War II. In 1948 he moved to the United States, where he was ordained at Hebrew Union College in Cincinnati. He served in the rabbinate in West Virginia from 1949 to 1955, and after 1956 was professor of rabbinics at Hebrew Union College. Petuchowski's thought served as a bridge linking the Reform movement to *Kelal Yisrael* and Historical Judaism. In his *Ever Since Sinai: A Modern View of Torah* (1961) he maintained a belief in the authority of revelation and *halakhah*, while interpreting both concepts in terms of the evolutionary development of Jewish tradition throughout the ages, of which Reform is simply another stage. Though severely critical of certain aspects of secular Zionism, particularly in his *Zion Reconsidered* (1966), Petuchowski's attitude toward Israel as a legitimate continuation of Jewish history became far more positive after the Six-Day War. His thought exerted great influence within the U.S. Reform movement. In 1969 he published *Prayer Book Reform in Europe: The Liturgy of European Liberal and Reform Judaism*. [L.S.K.]

"Torso (Construction)" by Antoine Pevsner, 1924–26, copper and plastic, height 75 in. (190.5 cm). New York, Museum of Modern Art, Gift of Katherine S. Dreier.

PEVSNER, ANTON (**Antoine**; 1886–1962) and **NAUM NEHEMIA** (**Gabo**; 1890–), Russian sculptors. The two brothers were born in a village near Orel, south of Moscow. Anton Pevsner studied at the academies of art in Kiev and St. Petersburg, while Gabo went to Munich to work for a civil engineering degree. From 1911 to the outbreak of World War I Anton Pevsner was in Paris, where the painter *Modigliani was among his friends. In 1917, the brothers returned to Russia and were appointed professors at the Academy of Art in Moscow. They now emerged as the leaders of Constructivism, a movement related technically and aesthetically to architecture and engineering. In 1920, they published their Realist Manifesto, which set out the theoretical foundations of Constructivism. When the Soviet State began to demand that artists apply their talent to political propaganda, the Pevsner brothers refused. In 1923 they emigrated to Paris. Here they collaborated on settings and costumes for a Diaghilev ballet and repeatedly showed their work together. In 1931 Anton Pevsner was a co-founder of the Abstraction-Creation group in Paris, and from 1946 to 1952 was an active member of the Salon des Réalités Nouvelles. In 1948 Gabo, who had settled in the United States, lectured at the Graduate School of Design, Harvard University.

The work of these two sculptors is closely related. While in their early works figurative elements still appear, their mature work is entirely nonfigurative. Anton preferred to work in metal, usually bronze, to get the solidity and permanence that are lacking in the materials—plastic and nylon—often used by his brother. The creations of both are characterized by strong rhythm, and by the movement of free forms into dynamic new shapes.

Bibliography: C. Giedion-Welcker, *Contemporary Sculpture* (1961), index; idem, *Antoine Pevsner* (Eng., 1961); A. Pevsner, *Biographical Sketch of my Brothers, Naum Gabo and Antoine Pevsner* (1964); Museum of Modern Art, New York, *Naum Gabo-Antoine Pevsner*... (Eng. 1948). [A.W.]

PEVSNER, SIR NIKOLAUS (1902–), British architectural historian. Born in Leipzig, he studied at various German universities. After working as assistant keeper at the Dresden Art Gallery (1924–28) and as lecturer in art history and architecture at the University of Goettingen (1929–33), he emigrated to England when Hitler came to power. He was professor of fine art at the University of Cambridge (1949–55) and Fellow of St. John's College, Cambridge. Books such as his classic *An Outline of European Architecture* (1942) helped to spread a knowledge of architectural history, and his *Buildings of England* series (10 vols., 1958–68) called attention to the English architectural heritage. He was knighted in 1969.

Sir Nikolaus Pevsner, British historian of architecture. Courtesy Jerusalem Municipality. Photo Yiẓḥak Amit, kibbutz Ẓorah.

Bibliography: Hughes-Santon, in: *Design*, 222 (June, 1967), 56–57. [Ed.]

PEVZNER, SAMUEL JOSEPH (1879–1930), Russian Zionist and pioneer in Palestine. Born in Propoisk, Belorussia, Pevzner was a delegate to the First Zionist

Congress (1897) and a member of the *Democratic Fraction. He contributed to *Ha-Shilo'ah* and other Hebrew papers under the pen name Shemu'el Ben-Natan. Pevzner graduated as an engineer from the Berlin Technical College and in 1905 emigrated to Ereẓ Israel. He settled in Haifa and was one of the builders and developers of the town. Together with N. *Wilbuschewitz and S. *Itzkovitz, he established the Atid factory, the first modern enterprise for the manufacture of oil and soap. He was one of the founders of Hadar ha-Carmel, the central Jewish quarter in Haifa, and head of its development committee from 1922 to 1927. Pevzner was also active in the development of the *Technion and the Reali High School in the town; a member of the community council; and a delegate to the *Asefat ha-Nivḥarim*.

Bibliography: H. Aharonovich, *Hadar ha-Karmel* (1958), 7–21; Tidhar, 1 (1947), 354; I. Klausner, *Oppoziẓyah le-Herzl* (1960), index; S. Levin, *Iggerot* (1966), index. [Y.S.]

PEWTER PLATES. Pewter vessels began to spread through Europe in the 16th century when the tin mines became more fully exploited. In the 17th century they were most commonly found in the homes of peasants, laborers, craftsmen, and middle class merchants. At that time also, pewter vessels spread to Jewish homes in Western and Eastern Europe, both among the working classes and the middle classes. Only a few of the wealthy could afford to use silver, glass, or crystal plates, and Jews in distant villages in Eastern Europe and the impoverished Jewish town dwellers continued to use pottery and wooden dishes. The smooth surface of pewter and its malleability appealed to the artist. The non-Jewish artist decorated pewter plates with subjects taken from Greek mythology, Christianity, and the Old and New Testaments; and the Jewish artist drew his inspiration from his own world, from Jewish tradition, Jewish life, and biblical stories. On the Passover *seder* plate, he depicted scenes such as members of a Jewish family reclining at the *seder* table, the Paschal sacrifice, the sages reclining at Bene-Berak, and the four sons of the *Haggadah*. A tradition of Jewish wooden plates apparently preceded the pewter, as a 15th-century plate from Germany has been discovered. The origin of the Passover *seder* plate can be traced through the dress and appearance of the reclining figures. The edge of the plate was generally decorated with Passover symbols, such as the order of the *seder* ceremony: the washing of the hands, etc., or there were designs of the zodiac and various plants and animals of symbolic significance. Most Jewish pewter plates are full of self-expression, charm, and individuality. Pewter plates were also used for the Purim gift offerings *(mishlo'aḥ manot)*. These were decorated with illustrations and quotations from the Book of Esther. Mordecai was depicted riding on the king's horse which was inscribed with the Hebrew passage, "and of sending portions one to the other" (Esth. 9:22), and the plate often bore the Pisces sign of the zodiac, the sign of the month of Adar. There were pewter plates for *Havdalah*, bearing the *Havdalah* benedictions. They often showed a Jew performing the *Havdalah* ceremony with his family. These illustrations are based on those in *minhagim* books and illuminated manuscripts. There are certainly pewter plates for *Kiddush*, showing the father of the house making the blessing over the wine, with the whole family sitting around the Sabbath table, but many of these have been lost. Though these pewter plates served their various purposes, throughout the year they decorated the Jewish home, adding to the Jewish sentiment and atmosphere. There were also plates which were mainly intended to adorn the Jewish home. The most popular subjects for these were biblical stories such as, for example the selling of Joseph, and this too was common in Persia. The Hebrew letter was also improved upon through the decorating of pewter plates as it had been neglected to a great extent after the invention of printing. In the late 18th century, pewter vessels were replaced by earthenware and glass, which began to spread through Europe. These were easier to clean, shinier and more suited to the tastes of the Rococo and later periods.

Bibliography: L. A. Mayer, *Bibliography of Jewish Art* (1967), index s.v. [Y.Ei.]

PEYREHORADE (Heb. פיגייא אורארה), town in Landes department, S.W. France. A number of Marranos established themselves in Peyrehorade, at the latest by 1597. Under the name "Portuguese merchants," they formed a community around 1628, when they acquired a plot of land for a cemetery. In 1648, when a partial expulsion was decreed, there were 42 Jewish families (about 200 persons) in the town. In about 1700 only about 15 families remained there. Subsequently the number of Jews evidently increased because in 1747 the community, which from then on is openly referred to as Jewish, acquired a second site for a cemetery. The existence of a synagogue is confirmed about 1728 (at the latest, 1747). The community, by then well organized, had its own butchery and a ritual bath *(mikveh)*, and supported three societies, the Sedaca, concerned with charitable activities, the Hebera, responsible for burial of the dead, and the Yesiba, dedicated to study. The Jews of Peyrehorade played an active role in the French Revolution. When the consistories were created, the community was at first attached to Bordeaux and later to Bayonne. In 1826 a third cemetery was acquired, which was also used by the Jews of the surroundings. (In 1970 all three cemeteries were still in existence.) From 1826 Jews began to leave the town, and the synagogue was sold in 1898, its furnishings being later removed to the synagogues of Biarritz and Bayonne. A few Jews were still living in Peyrehorade at the outbreak of World War II.

Bibliography: Gross, Gal Jud, 453; E. Ginsburger, in: REJ, 104 (1938), 35–69; G. Nahon, *Communautés judéo-portugaises du sud-ouest de la France* (mimeographed, 1969), passim. [B.Bl.]

PEZINOK (Poesing, Boesing, Bazín), town in W. Slovakia, Czechoslovakia. In 1529 Count Franz Wolf of Poesing, deeply in debt to Jewish moneylenders of Poesing and Marchegg, had a nine-year-old boy hidden by a dim-witted woman accomplice. He subsequently caused a public uproar and had his creditors and other Jews arrested and tortured; they confessed to the crime of using the boy's blood for ritual purposes, and in a variety of conflicting testimonies they admitted other crimes as well. About 30 Jews were burned at the stake and the rest were expelled from the town. When the count imprisoned the Jews of Marchegg as well, they appealed to *Ferdinand I who ordered their release and opened an inquiry. In the meanwhile the missing boy was accidentally discovered by Jewish merchants from Vienna. The Protestant reformer, Andreas *Osiander, published a booklet in about 1540 repudiating *blood libels altogether and subjecting the Pezinok blood libel affair to a minute examination, clearly incriminating the count. Osiander's booklet was viciously attacked by Johann Eck, an upholder of orthodox Catholicism, and repudiated by Martin *Luther. The booklet was republished in 1893, following the *Xanten affair; an anti-Jewish, popular version of the affair had been published in 1882, after the *Tisza Eszlar uproar.

A Jewish settlement was founded in Pezinok only in the 1850s. In 1939 the Jews were driven out of their homes and forced to set fire to their synagogues. In 1941 there were 234 Jews in Pezinok; most of them perished in the Holocaust,

Figure 1. Pewter *seder* plate from Europe, made by Leib Segal, 1773. In the center are depicted the four sons. Tel Aviv, Y. Einhorn Collection. Photo David Harris, Jerusalem.

Figure 2. Pewter Purim plate, from Frankfort on the Main, 18th century, with an engraving of Mordecai on the king's horse, being led by Haman. Formerly Wuerzburg, Mainfrankisches Museum. Photo Gundermann, Wuerzburg.

Figure 3. Pewter *Kiddush* plate from Germany, 18th century. The blessing over wine is inscribed around the edge. Tel Aviv, Y. Einhorn Collection. Photo David Harris, Jerusalem.

Figure 4. Pewter plate with a scene of the judgment of Solomon, Bavaria, 1831. Formerly Wuerzburg, Mainfrankisches Museum. Photo Gundermann, Wuerzburg.

Figure 5. Pewter dish with a scene of Joseph and Potiphar's wife. Eastern Europe, c. 1815. Prague, State Jewish Museum.

Figure 6. Pewter plate with scene of Joseph being sold into slavery. Jerusalem, 18th century. Tel Aviv, Y. Einhorn Collection. Photo David Harris, Jerusalem.

including the community's rabbi, Joshua (Leile) Sholal (b. 1885). The Jewish cemetery was almost completely destroyed.

Bibliography: M. Stern (ed.), *Andreas Osiander's Schrift ueber die Blutbeschuldigung* (1893); H. L. Strack, *The Jews and Human Sacrifice* (1909), 204–5; J. C. (May 12, 1939), 30; MHJ, 1 (1903), nos. 329, 333, 335, 336, 338; 5 (1959); 8 (1965); 9 (1966); 10 (1967), index s.v. *Bazin*. [Ed.]

PFEFFER, LEO (1910–), U.S. professor of constitutional law and constitutional lawyer. Pfeffer, who was born in Hungary, the son of an Orthodox rabbi, was taken to the U.S. in 1912. He studied law at New York University and practiced privately from 1933 to 1945, when he accepted a position on the legal staff of the Commission of Law and Social Action, the legal and political arm of the *American Jewish Congress. In 1947 he became assistant-director of the Commission and in 1957 its director, as well as general counsel of the American Jewish Congress. In 1964 Pfeffer became special counsel of the Congress. In 1965, he became professor of constitutional law and chairman of the political science department at Long Island University. He co-founded the Lawyers Constitutional Defense Committee (which later beame part of the American Civil Liberties Union), an organization formed to provide legal services in defense of civil rights.

A noted lecturer on constitutional issues, Pfeffer was recognized as a specialist in the area of church-state relations and religious liberty. He participated as counsel in numerous cases decided by the U.S. Supreme Court and other of the nation's appellate courts involving these issues. Pfeffer's writings include: *Church, State and Freedom* (1967[2]); *The Liberties of an American* (1963[2]); *Creeds in Competition* (1958; with Anson Phelps Stokes); *Church and State in the U.S.* (1964); and *This Honourable Court* (1965). [J.J.M.]

PFEFFERKORN, JOHANNES (**Joseph;** 1469–after 1521), apostate and anti-Jewish agitator. Originally from Moravia, Pfefferkorn claimed to have been educated by a relative, Meir Pfefferkorn, a *dayyan* in Prague. A butcher by profession, he was convicted of burglary and theft, but released on payment of a fine. After his release, at the age of 36, he and his wife and children were converted to Christianity in Cologne (c. 1504), where he found employment. He put himself under the protection of the *Dominicans, who were quick to make use of him in their campaign against the Jews and their literature. Between 1507 and 1509 Pfefferkorn wrote a number of anti-Jewish tracts: *Judenspiegel* ("Jews' Mirror"), in which, incidentally, he spoke out against the *blood libel; *Judenbeichte* ("Jewish Confession"); *Osterbuch* ("Passover Book"); and *Judenfeind* ("Enemy of the Jews"). All were also published almost simultaneously in Latin translation. The treatises certainly betrayed a thoroughgoing ignorance of rabbinic literature. Pfefferkorn demanded the suppression of the Talmud; prohibition of usury; forced attendance at *sermons to Jews (longstanding Dominican objectives); expulsion of the Jews from the last German cities which had sizable Jewish communities—*Frankfort, *Worms, and *Regensburg—unless such attendance took place (they were in fact expelled from Regensburg in 1519); and their employment in the most menial tasks only.

Through the influence of Emperor Maximilian's pious sister Kunigunde, and the support of the Cologne Dominicans, Pfefferkorn gained access to the emperor and in 1509 was empowered by him to confiscate any offending Jewish books, including prayer books, with the exception of the Bible. The confiscations took place on Friday, Sept. 8, 1509, in Frankfort and subsequently in Mainz, Bingen, and other German cities. When the archbishop of Mainz, the Frankfort city council, and various German princes intervened on behalf of the Jews, Pfefferkorn addressed a petition to the emperor (*Zu Lob und Ere*—"In Praise and Honor," 1510, also in Latin) in defense of his cause. Though the vacillating emperor ordered the return of the confiscated books, six weeks later, on May 23, 1510, he was apparently influenced by an alleged *Host desecration and blood libel at *Brandenburg, and under pressure from his sister, he ordered the appointment of an investigating commission.

The Pfefferkorn-Reuchlin Controversy. The commission was headed by the archbishop of Mainz, who appealed to theological faculties of Cologne, Erfurt, Heidelberg, and Mainz and sought help from *Hoogstraten, *Carben, and the famous scholar and humanist Johannes *Reuchlin, whose aid Pfefferkorn had tried in vain to enlist earlier. Pfefferkorn was to communicate the results to the emperor. When Pfefferkorn learned that Reuchlin's opinion would be favorable to the Talmud he assailed him in his *Handspiegel wider und gegen die Juden* ("Hand Mirror," 1511). Reuchlin replied in his *Augenspiegel* ("Eye-glass," 1511), strongly attacking Pfefferkorn and his backers, and thereby starting one of the great literary controversies of history, in reality a battle between the reactionary and the liberal parties within the Church. It occurred at a time when the tide of humanism was rising, and most German humanists rallied to Reuchlin's side. Erasmus, the Rotterdam humanist, though not exerting himself on Reuchlin's behalf, termed Pfefferkorn "a criminal Jew who had become a most criminal Christian." In September 1511 Pfefferkorn preached against the *Augenspiegel* outside a Frankfort church, but the main battle was now fought between Reuchlin and the Cologne theologians. When the emperor visited Cologne in 1512, Reuchlin's enemies obtained from him an interdiction against the *Augenspiegel*, and in the same year Pfefferkorn issued his *Brandspiegel* ("Burning Glass"), an even more vituperative attack on Reuchlin and the Jews. Reuchlin submitted a further defense; the emperor imposed silence on both sides in June 1513.

Title page of Johannes Pfefferkorn's *Judenfeind* ("Enemy of the Jews"), Augsburg, 1509. From Georg Liebe, *Das Judentum in der deutschen Vergangenheit*, Leipzig, 1903.

The conflict echoed in the papal court and Pope Leo X set up a special ecclesiastical tribunal at Speyer to deal with the matter (November 1513). The judgment of March 1514, favorable to Reuchlin, was torn down by Pfefferkorn in Cologne, and in the same year he published a further tract, *Die Sturmglocke* ("Alarm Bell"); however, he was taken to task for breaking the silence imposed by the emperor. A scandal connected with another apostate named *Rapp was used by Ulrich van *Hutten, Crotus Rubianus, and other supporters of Reuchlin to discredit Pfefferkorn and in 1516 they issued the *Epistolae Obscurorum Virorum* ("Letters of Obscure Men"), a virulent but effective satire on Pfefferkorn, the Dominicans, and all they stood for. In retaliation Pfefferkorn published his defense (*Beschirmung*..., 1516, also in Latin) and a further attack on Reuchlin (*Streibuech lein*—"Polemic") in the same year. In 1520 the pope finally decided against Reuchlin, though by this time the proceedings were so far removed from the original controversy against Jewish literature that the decision did not interfere with David *Bomberg's first printing of the Talmud, then in process in Venice. Pfefferkorn fired his last triumphant shot in 1521 with *Eine Mitleidige Clag* ("A Pitiful Complaint"), which Graetz describes as the most impudent and obscene of all his lampoons, and for which the printer, but not the author, was imprisoned. The outpourings from the other side were equally intemperate. Though his opponents were exaggerating somewhat when they described Pfefferkorn as a complete ignoramus, his knowledge of Jewish sources was minimal and his acquaintance with Latin nonexistent. Leading historians have come to the conclusion that Pfefferkorn received substantial help in the preparation of his treatises from his Dominican mentors. The effect of the episode was to bring about a considerable decline in the prestige of the Church. As S. Baron has pointed out, it was not merely by coincidence that Martin *Luther promulgated his thesis in 1517, at the height of the Pfefferkorn-Reuchlin controversy. The name Pfefferkorn became proverbial for unprincipled denigrators of their own origin and faith.

Bibliography: Baron, Social[2], 13 (1969), 184ff., Graetz, Gesch, 9 (1891[4]), index; Graetz, Hist, 4 (1894), 422ff.; K. H. Gerschmann, in: *Zeitschrift fuer Religions- und Geistesgeschichte*, 21 (1969), 166–71; S. A. Hirsch, *Book of Essays* (1905), 73–115; idem, *Cabbalists and Other Essays* (1922), 197–215; I. Kracauer, *Geschichte der Juden in Frankfurt*, 1 (1925), 247ff.; A. Freimann and F. Kracauer, *Frankfort* (1929), 48–59; H. L. Strack, *Das Blut* (1911[8]), 171–2; M. Spanier, in: ZGDJ, 6 (1936), 209–29; A. Kober, *Cologne* (1940), 168ff.; M. Brod, *Johannes Reuchlin und sein Kampf* (1965), index. [Ed.]

°**PFEIFFER, ROBERT HENRY** (1892–1958), U.S. Protestant Bible scholar and Assyriologist. Pfeiffer taught at Harvard University from 1922, after serving in the ministry of the Methodist Church from 1916 to 1919. He directed the Harvard-Baghdad School excavations at Nuzi, Iraq (from 1928), and from 1931 served as curator of the Harvard Semitic Museum.

Pfeiffer is mainly known for his *Introduction to the Old Testament* (1941, 1952[2]) and its sequel *History of New Testament Times, With an Introduction to the Apocrypha* (1949). These works and his *The Books of the Old Testament* (1957) show a marked influence of his major professors at Harvard, George Foot Moore and William R. Arnold. It was the influence of the latter and the writings of A. Klostermann that led him to isolate the earliest Hebrew historical source that includes II Samuel 9–20 and I Kings 1–2, published as *The Hebrew Iliad* with general and chapter introductions by William G. Pollard, and to claim that the priest Ahimaaz, the biographer of David, was "the father of history," history being defined as a narrative of past events dominated by great ideas. Pfeiffer's works in the field of Assyriology included *The Archives of Shilwateshub* (1932); *Excavations at Nuzi*, volumes 2 (1933) and 4 (with E. R. Lacheman, 1942); *One Hundred New Selected Nuzi Texts* (with E. A. *Speiser, 1936); and *State Letters of Assyria* (1935).

Pfeiffer wrote a number of papers on literary, philological, and historical critical problems of the Bible. His comments on New Testament subjects followed the methodology of his teaching, which was distinguished by a traditional Christian approach. He was editor of the *Journal of Biblical Literature*, 1943–47.

[Z.G.]

PFORZHEIM, city in Baden, W. Germany. The first reference to the presence of Jews dates from the 13th century. In 1267 the discovery of the corpse of a drowned girl gave rise to a *blood libel against the Jewish community, and their communal leaders were killed. Their martyrdom was extolled in religious verse and the day of their death (20th Tammuz) set aside as a fast day. The community was almost annihilated during the *Black Death persecutions of 1349. In the 15th century a few **Schutzjuden* lived in Pforzheim. In the early 16th century J. *Reuchlin, the renowned humanist, intervened on behalf of the Jews of Pforzheim with Margrave Philip I (1479–1533). Expelled with all the Jews of *Baden in 1614, they returned in 1670. The handful of Jewish families in Pforzheim in the 18th century dealt mainly in cattle, leather, and cloth. Prior to 1812 worship was conducted in a private home, but in that year a synagogue was built. It remained in use until 1893, when a new synagogue was built, later renovated in 1930. A cemetery was consecrated in 1846 and a school founded in 1832. The community increased from 101 in 1801 to 287 in 1875 and continued to grow, in part due to the flourishing jewelry industry; by 1900 it had reached 535, and by 1927 around 1,000. By June 1933 the Jewish population had fallen to 770 (1.1% of the total population). In the 20th century Jews were important in the financial and industrial life of the city. With the rise of Nazism, Jewish

The synagogue of Pforzheim, demolished by the Nazis on *Kristallnacht*, 1938. Courtesy Pforzheim Municipality.

enterprises were boycotted and the community was further depleted through emigration, largely to the U.S. and Ereẓ Israel. On Nov. 10, 1938, the synagogue was desecrated and partly demolished. One hundred and eighty-three Jews were deported to the *Gurs concentration camp on Oct. 22, 1940; 21 returned after the war. They were affiliated with the *Karlsruhe community and possessed a new cemetery. A memorial was erected in 1967 on the site of the synagogue.

Bibliography: Germ Jud, 2 (1968), 654–5; F. Hundsnurscher and G. Taddey, *Die juedischen Gemeinden in Baden* (1968); Salfeld, Martyrol, index; PK, Germanyah. [ED.]

PFORZHEIMER, CARL HOWARD (1879–1957), U.S. businessman, public servant, and bibliophile. Pforzheimer, who was born in New York City, established in 1901 a brokerage business that became well known for its underwriting of oil securities at a time when the U.S. financial community generally regarded such issues as a poor risk. Active in Westchester County public affairs, he served as chairman of the Westchester County Emergency Work Bureau (1931–35); the Westchester County Commission on Government, whose work subsequently led to the promulgation of Westchester's Home Rule Charter; and the Westchester County Planning Commission. Pforzheimer was a trustee of the Jewish Publication Society of America and of Montefiore Hospital, and a supporter of the Jewish Division of the New York Public Library. He was a rare-book and manuscript collector who assembled one of the finest private collections in the U.S. (including a Gutenberg Bible). Pforzheimer compiled a three-volume catalog of his collection for scholarly use. [ED.]

PHALSBOURG, little town in Moselle department, N. E. France. Between 1680 and 1691, Louis XIV's minister, Louvois, authorized two Jewish families to settle there; these increased to four in 1702, eight in 1747, and 12 in 1770; on several occasions they were threatened with expulsion. Two Jews acquired merchants' licenses in 1768 and this right was ratified by the Conseil d'Etat. The synagogue was erected in 1772 and rebuilt in 1857; the cemetery dates from 1796. From 1807 until around 1920 Phalsbourg was the seat of a rabbinate (which also served the neighboring communities of Sarrebourg, Mittelbronn, Lixheim, etc.) whose incumbents included: Mayer Heyman (1827–37), the model for the Reb-Sichel of Erckmann-Chatrian, and Lazare *Isidor (1837–47), future chief rabbi of France. From the close of the 19th century the Jewish population decreased: from 159 in 1880, to 89 in 1931, and 48 in 1970. During World War II, nine Jews of Phalsbourg died when they were being deported and two were shot.

Bibliography: D. Kahn, in: *Revue juive de Lorraine*, 8 (1932), 253–6. [G.C.]

PHARAOH. The Egyptian expression *per aʿo* ("the Great House"), transcribed and vocalized *pirʿu* in Akkadian and *parʿo* in Hebrew, did not originally designate the king of Egypt, but rather his palace, and was used in this sense in Egyptian texts until the middle of the 18th dynasty (c. 1575–1308 B.C.E.). Circumlocutions were frequently used to specify the king in the texts of the 18th dynasty, and during the reign of the great conqueror and empire-builder, Thutmosis II (c. 1490–1436 B.C.E.), *per aʿo*, i.e., the palace, began to appear as another such designation, just as in more modern times "The Sublime Porte" meant the Turkish sultan. The Egyptian texts never used this designation, however, as part of the official titulary of the king, although from the 22nd dynasty on (c. 945–730 B.C.E.), it was regularly added, in popular speech, to the king's personal name. In the non-Egyptian sources, particularly in the Bible where it occurs not infrequently, Pharaoh always means the king of Egypt, although frequently the earlier usage, without the addition of the king's personal name, is followed. Attempts have been made by modern scholarship to identify the Pharaoh of the oppression and of the Exodus with various rulers of the 19th dynasty, but unanimous consensus on the identity has not yet been reached.

[AL.R.S.]

PHARAOH AND THE EGYPTIANS IN THE AGGADAH

Influence of Jews' Experience in Roman Egypt. Rabbinic references to the biblical Egyptians are almost invariably hostile and they are probably strongly colored by the unfortunate experiences of the Jews in Roman Egypt. Ancient Alexandria was the birthplace of racial anti-Semitism and the scene of major pogroms in 38, 66, and 116–117 C.E. Egyptian Jewry outside of Alexandria was massacred toward the end of Trajan's reign. The Egyptians, even more than the Greeks, were, according to Josephus, the Jews' bitterest enemies and the originators of the worst libels against them.

The rabbis, accordingly, depicted the ancient Egyptians as uniformly evil and depraved—ugly both in appearance and character. Thus, when Abraham approached Egypt, he is said to have warned Sarah that Egypt was a center of sexual immorality (Sifra, 7:11, end; Jos., Ant., 1:162). Moreover, Abraham pointed out, they were entering "a country whose inhabitants are ugly and black" (Gen. R. 40:4), evidently a reflection of the racial contempt harbored by the relatively fair-skinned Semites for the dark-skinned Hamites.

When Pharaoh, "this wicked man" (Tanḥ. B., Gen. 33), took Sarah for himself, he was, according to the Midrash, duly informed by her that she was a married woman; but this did not deter him from trying to seduce her (Gen. R. 41:2). He was, however, whipped by an angel and stricken with leprosy.

Figure 1. Pharaoh bathing in the blood of Hebrew children in order to cure his leprosy (Ex. R. 1:34). Woodcut from the *Prague Haggadah*, 1526. Jerusalem, J.N.U.L.

Leper Motif. Leprosy figures repeatedly in the punishments inflicted or threatened on the Egyptians. The Pharaoh of the oppression became a leper and sought to cure himself by bathing in the blood of Hebrew children specially slain for this purpose (Ex. R. 1:34). Also, the Egyptian people were smitten with leprosy along with the inflammation of boils (*ibid.* 11:6). The leper motif was probably a literary vengeance for the Egyptian calumny that the Israelites of the Exodus were lepers (Jos., Apion, 1:229, 233ff., 305ff.), while the slaughter of the Hebrew children in Egypt evidently alludes to the atrocities committed in the course of the Jewish uprising and its suppression in 116–117 C.E.

Potiphar's Wife. Not surprisingly, Potiphar's wife becomes, in rabbinic literature, the seductress par excellence, a shameless, wicked woman (Ruth R. 6:1), who behaved "like an animal," was willing to murder her husband (Gen. R. 87:4–5), and went to fantastic lengths to win Joseph's love (Yoma 35b; Sot 36b).

Potiphar and Pharaoh. Even Potiphar, who according to the biblical account, bestowed many favors upon Joseph, as well as the Pharaoh who raised the Hebrew prisoner to the position of vizier and welcomed his family to Egypt, are treated by the rabbis with disdain and even outright hostility. Potiphar, "an Egyptian—a cunning man" (Gen. R. 86:3), had purchased Joseph for the purpose of sodomy, and was appropriately punished by castration (Sot. 13b). He was not even justified in having Joseph imprisoned, despite his wife's accusations, for he knew Joseph to be innocent, and, indeed, told him so (Gen. R. 87:9). When Joseph became ruler of Egypt, he sentenced his former master to lifelong imprisonment (Mid. Ps. to 105:7).

Pharaoh and Judah. Pharaoh, repeatedly consigned by the Midrash among "the wicked" (Gen. R. 89:4), was said to have been charged by Judah with making false promises and indulging in pederasty, and in his anger Judah threatened to kill both Joseph and Pharaoh and, indeed, to destroy all Egypt (*ibid.* 93:6). Judah's furious threats no doubt personify and reflect the savage fighting in Egypt and Cyrene during the Jewish rising in 116/117 C.E.

Pharaoh and Joseph. Even Joseph had scant respect for his royal benefactor. Whenever he wanted to make a false oath, he would swear in Pharaoh's name (Gen R. 91:7). When presenting some of his brothers to Pharaoh (Gen. 47:2), Joseph chose the weakest among them in order to avoid having them drafted into Egyptian military service. This Midrash seems to reflect rabbinic opposition to Jewish mercenaries who for centuries had been serving Egypt's rulers.

Oppression and Enslavement of the Hebrews. In line with the anti-Egyptian attitude of the rabbis, the Pharaoh of the oppression was depicted by some as identical with the Pharaoh of Joseph's time. He was not "new" (Ex. 1:8), only his anti-Israelite decrees were new. It was not that "he knew not Joseph" but in his ingratitude he deliberately ignored the fact that Joseph had ever existed, and he gratuitously initiated the persecution of the Hebrews (Sot. 11a). Thus, even the best of the Pharaohs who had promoted Joseph and invited the Israelites to settle in Egypt, turned out to be a wicked rogue.

According to one rabbinic view, however, the initiative to oppress and enslave the Hebrews was taken not by Pharaoh himself but by his Egyptian subjects. At first he opposed this plan on the grounds that "were it not for Joseph we would not be alive"; but the Egyptians deposed him, restoring him after three months on the express condition that he would do as they wished (Ex. R. 1:8). This interesting interpretation was probably designed to justify the severe punishment of the Egyptian people.

Having cunningly enslaved the Israelites, Pharaoh imposed on them increasingly onerous tasks, often endangering their lives, and brutally burning or immuring infants and even adults in unfinished buildings whenever the Israelites failed to complete their work quota (Sot. 11a–b; Ex. R. 1:10–11, 18:9).

Casting of Hebrew Infants into River. The decree to cast the infants into the river (Ex. 1:22) applied to the Egyptians, too, because Pharaoh was misled by his astrologers who were not sure whether the savior of Israel would be a Hebrew or an Egyptian (Sot. 12a), a legend which must have been influenced by the Egyptian stories that Moses was an Egyptian. The Hebrew girls who were to be spared were meant to be reserved to satisfy the sexual appetites of the Egyptians (Ex. R. 1:18).

Egyptian Immorality. Pharaoh is also charged with having claimed divine honors for himself (*ibid.* 8:12, Tanḥ. B., Ex. 16)—a normal practice among Egyptian rulers down to Roman times—and with an attempt to seduce the Hebrew midwives (Ex. R. 1:15).

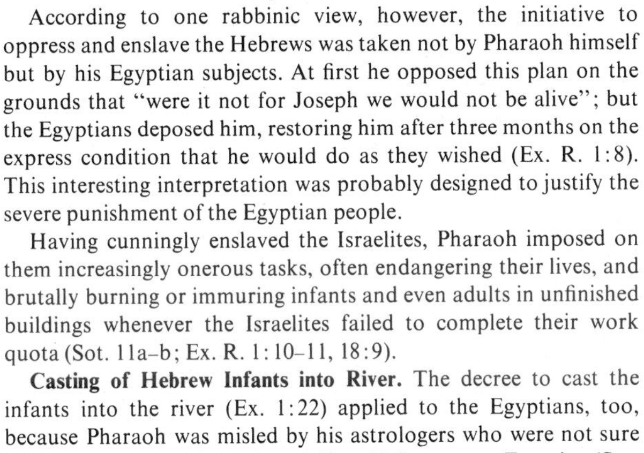

Figure 2. Pharaoh dreams of seven lean cows and seven fat cows (Gen. 41:2). Illustration from the *Cologne Bible*, Germany, 1478–80. London, Library of the British and Foreign Bible Society.

Egyptian immorality is a constantly recurring theme in rabbinic literature, due presumably to actual observation of the contemporary Egyptian scene. The killing of the Egyptian taskmaster by Moses (Ex. 2:12) was justified by the rabbis on the grounds that the Egyptian had violated the wife of the Hebrew slave and, having been detected by her husband, was on the point of beating him to death (Ex. R. 1:28; Lev. R. 32:4; cf. Targ. Ps.-Jon., Lev. 24:10). Even when the Egyptians were pursuing the Israelites into the Red Sea, they were like "inflamed stallions" driven on by expectations of sexual orgies.

Only Pharaoh's daughter who rescued Moses from the river is given favorable treatment, and her bathing in the river is interpreted as ritual immersion for the purpose of proselytization (Sot. 12b; Ex. R. 1:23). Although a firstborn, she was saved because of Moses' prayer (Ex. R. 18:3).

Legend of Moses' Taking Pharaoh's Crown. The legend of the infant Moses taking Pharaoh's crown and placing it on his own head (Ex. R. 1:26, et al.) apparently alludes, not as is commonly believed, to the plagues that Moses was to bring on Egypt, but to the messianic redemption when the kingdoms of the gentiles—including that of the Egyptians—would disappear. Significantly, an early Midrash predicts that all the plagues of Egypt would be repeated in Rome (Tanḥ. B., Ex: 15b, 22a–b).

Moses' Treatment of Pharaoh. Despite Pharaoh's overweening arrogance, Moses was commanded by God to treat him with the deference and respect due to a king (Ex. R. 7:3), a widely current political concept promoted by those rabbis who favored cooperation with the Roman authorities as being ultimately in the best interests of the Jews. Nevertheless, Pharaoh cut a sorry figure during the Exodus when he was thoroughly humbled, being compelled to look for Moses and Aaron at night, mocked and derided by the Hebrew children, and begging Moses to take the Israelites out of Egypt (Mekh., Bo, 13; Tanḥ. B., Ex. 26). This humiliation as well as the ten plagues and the drowning of the Egyptian host in the Red Sea were, however, well-deserved.

Depiction of Plague of Firstborn. The plague of the firstborn, in particular, is depicted in lurid colors. None could escape, for even the lowest classes hated the Hebrews and desired their humiliation and persecution (Mekh., Bo, 13; Tanḥ. B., Ex. 22). Only those Egyptians who joined the "mixed multitude" (Ex. 12:38), celebrated the Passover with the Israelites, and left Egypt with them, were saved from the plague (Ex. R. 18:10).

Jewish animosity toward the Egyptians found eloquent expression in the Passover *Haggadah,* where the plagues which befell the Egyptians—both in Egypt and at the Red Sea—were homiletically multiplied many times over (cf. Mekh., Amalek, 2; Ex. R. 23:9).

Conciliatory Spirit of Later Rabbis. In the light of such bitter Egyptian-Jewish enmity, it is all the more remarkable that within little more than a century after the bloodbath of Egyptian Jewry, R. Jonathan, a fervently patriotic rabbi, is reported to have said that when the ministering angels wished to chant a song of praise before God at the time when the Israelites were saved at the Red Sea, He rebuked them, saying, "The work of my hands [the Egyptians] is drowning in the sea, and you want to chant a song before me!" (Sanh. 39b; Meg. 10b). Although the parallel versions in the Palestinian Midrashim (Ex. R. 23:7; Tanḥ. B. II, 60; Mid. Ps. to 106:2) transfer God's concern from the Egyptians to Israel, it appears that R. Jonathan's statement, as preserved in the Babylonian Talmud, is the original version. Indeed one of the reasons for which, on Passover, the entire **Hallel* is recited only on the first day is that on the seventh day the Egyptians were drowned (PdRk, 189). In the same conciliatory spirit, some rabbis believed that Pharaoh was not drowned in the Red Sea, but lived to become king of Nineveh and lead the people in repentance in response to Jonah's warning (PdRE 43; Mekh., Be-shallaḥ, 6; cf. Jonah 3:4ff.). [M.A.]

IN ISLAM

Pharaoh of the Koran is the king who oppressed the people of Israel in Egypt; Musā (*Moses) and Hārūn (*Aaron) negotiated with him. In accordance with the counsel of his advisors, among them Hāmān, Pharaoh ordered that all male children be killed (Sura 2:46; 7:137). Āsiya, the wife of Pharaoh, adopted Moses, who had been found in an ark (28:9). Pharaoh believed that he was god and therefore ordered Hāmān to erect a tower which would reach the heavens, thereby enabling him to wage war against the god of

Figure 3. Joseph interpreting Pharaoh's dream. Illumination from the *Vienna Genesis,* a sixth-century Greek manuscript. Vienna, Austrian National Library, Ms. Vindobon. Theol. Gr. 31, p. 36.

Moses (28:38; 40:38). He severely penalized those who returned to God, including his righteous wife (7:111; 26:45). A description of the mission of Moses and Aaron is found in Humayya ibn Ab-Al-Ṣalt's poetry (32:13–20). Several conversations which Moses and Aaron had with Pharaoh are given in the Koran. There is a great degree of similarity in content between Humayya's description and the dialogue of Sura 20:49–56. Pharaoh conspired to kill Moses (Sura 26:33). One of the believers, who is not mentioned by name, attempted to save Moses (40:29). The unbelieving wives of the believers Noah and Lot are contrasted with Pharaoh's wife, who unlike her husband, was a believer (66:10–11). When Pharaoh saw his people drowning in the sea, he repented and believed in Allah (10:90–92). Indeed, it is not explicitly stated in the Book of Exodus that Pharaoh drowned; this can be deduced from Psalms 136:15. Therefore, there is a suggestion in the *aggadah* that Pharaoh was saved. Humayya, however, knew that Allah did not take notice of Pharaoh's prayer and that he drowned (34:19). This view also appears in Muslim legend. After Pharaoh asked to repent, Gabriel closed Pharaoh's mouth with the mud of the sea, thus making him unable to repeat the verse: "I believe that there is no god but He in whom the people of Israel believe" (10:90). Muslim legends greatly influenced later Jewish *aggadah.* Muhammad obviously was confused concerning Āsiya, since she plays the same role in the Koran as Pharaoh's daughter does in the Bible. Pharaoh was very cruel to her because she was an Israelite. Various stories are related about her death: she was cast down upon a rock; Pharaoh whipped her to death, but she did not feel the pain. [H.Z.H.]

Bibliography: A. H. Gardiner, *Egyptian Grammar* (1957³), 71–76. IN THE AGGADAH: Ginzberg, Legends, 7 (1938), 368–70 (index). IN ISLAM: Ṭabarī, *Tafsīr,* 20 (1328 A.H.), 19–22; Thaʿlabī, *Qiṣaṣ* (1356 A.H.), 140–68; Kisā'ī, *Qiṣaṣ* (1356 A.H.), 195–224; G. Weil (ed.), *The Bible, the Koran, and the Talmud* (1846); J. Horovitz, *Koranische Untersuchungen* (1926), 56; J. W. Hirschberg, *Juedische und christliche Lehren im vor- und fruehislamischen Arabien* (1939), 61–62, 129–34.

PHARISEES (Heb. פְּרוּשִׁים, *Perushim*), a Jewish religious and political party or sect during the Second Temple period which emerged as a distinct group shortly after the Hasmonean revolt, about 165–160 B.C.E. They were probably successors of the Hasideans (or *Ḥasidim), an earlier Jewish sect which promoted the observance of Jewish ritual and the study of the Torah. The Pharisees considered themselves the traditional followers of Ezra, whom they cherished, after Moses, as the founder of Judaism, maintaining the validity of the Oral Law as well as of the Torah as the source of their religion. They tried to adapt old codes to new conditions, believed in a combination of free will and predestination, in the resurrection of the dead, and in recompense for this life in the next. At first relatively small in number, the Pharisees came to represent, by the first century C.E., the religious beliefs, practices, and social attitudes of the vast majority of the Jewish people. They attempted to imbue the masses with a spirit of holiness, based on a scrupulous observance of the Torah, by spreading traditional religious teaching. So greatly did the religious values prevail over political in the Pharisaic framework that, in contrast to the *Zealots, they were willing to submit to foreign domination—so long as it did not interfere with their inner way of life—rather than support an impious government of their own.

Origin of the Name. The meaning of the word "Pharisee" is uncertain. It is generally believed that the name derives from a Hebrew stem, *parash* ("to be separated") hence "Pharisee" would mean "the separated ones" or the "separatists" (cf. Kid. 66a where this meaning is clearly implied). According to some scholars, "Pharisee" would mean "those who are set apart," i.e., avoiding contact with others for reasons of ritual purity, or those who "separated themselves" from the heathens (Gal. 2:12ff.) and from the heathenizing tendencies and forces in their own nations, such as the *Sadducees.

History of the Pharisees. The Pharisees' first bid for power was made in a period two centuries after the Babylonian exile during the struggle to remove the Temple and religious control from the sole leadership of the aristocratic Sadducees. The inception of the synagogue worship traced to this time is seen as an attempt by the Pharisees to undermine the privileged authority exercised by the Sadducees. Ceremonies originally part of the Temple cult were carried over to the home, and learned men of non-priestly descent began to play an important role in national religious affairs. While the priesthood exhausted itself in the round of Temple ritual, the Pharisees found their main function in teaching and preaching the law of God.

The conflict between the lay and priestly factions of the supreme council and tribunal, the Sanhedrin, regarding the interpretation of the Torah when decisions were required on questions arising in daily life, gave the Pharisees the opportunity to incorporate popular customs and traditions into the Temple cult and the religious life of the people. In general, the Pharisees admitted the validity of an evolutionary and non-literal approach toward the legal decisions and regarded the legal framework of the Oral Law as equally valid as the Written Law. A serious conflict eventually developed between the Pharisees and the Sadducees over the approach to these problems, and two distinct parties emerged, with theological differences entangled with politics. The antagonism between Pharisees and Sadducees extended to many spheres outside the religious domain and eventually became a fundamental and distinctive one. Under John Hyrcanus the Pharisees were expelled from membership in the Sanhedrin and branded with the name *Perushim,* "the separated ones." They took the name as their own, but used its alternate Hebrew meaning, "the exponents" of the law. Pharisaic strongholds of learning were later founded by such "exponents" as Shammai and Hillel and Ishmael and Akiva.

By the time of the Hasmonean revolt, it had become evident that the Pharasaic theological doctrines were giving utterance to the hopes of the oppressed masses and affecting the entire life of the Jews. This hope was especially seen in doctrines which included belief in the resurrection of the dead, the Day of Judgment, reward and retribution in the life after death, the coming of the Messiah, and the existence of angels, and also divine foreknowledge along with man's free choice of, and therefore responsibility for, his deeds. These beliefs touched on the theological foundations of life.

Concept of God. Based on the sayings of the prophets, the Pharisees conceived of God as an omnipotent spiritual

Being, all-wise, all-knowing, all-just, and all-merciful. They taught that God loved all His creatures and asked man to walk in His ways, to act justly, and to love kindness. Though all-knowing and omnipotent, God endowed man with the power to choose between good and evil. He created in him two impulses, a good one and a bad, advised him to do good, and gave him the Torah as a guide. Since God was transcendent, He could not be comprehended in anthropomorphic terms, nor could His totality of being be designated with a name. Several terms were used merely to describe some attributes of God. The Pharisees spoke of God as "The Creator of the World" *(Bore Olam)*, "the Place" *(Ha-Makom)*, "the Divine Presence" *(Shekhinah)*, and so forth.

Free Will and Divine Retribution. In opposition to the Sadducean belief that God took little cognizance of and little interest in human affairs, the Pharisees held that everything in the world was ordained by God, but that man had it in his power to choose between good and evil. Although "fate does not cooperate in every action," and although God could determine man's choice of conduct, He left the choice open to man himself. In talmudic reports the followers of the Pharisees declare, "Everything is in the hands of God but the fear of God" (Ber. 33b), and although "everything is foreseen, yet freedom of choice is given" (Avot 3:16). As the Talmud puts it, "If man chooses to do good the heavenly powers help him. If he chooses to do evil, they leave the way open to him" (Shab. 104a). This belief in man's responsibility for his actions led to the Pharisaic doctrine of divine retribution. For the Pharisees, man would be rewarded or punished in the next life according to his conduct. This belief in divine retribution also rests on the more basic idea that man's existence is not limited to this life alone.

Resurrection. According to the Talmud and the New Testament, the Pharisees believed in the resurrection of the dead. This belief in another world makes possible the belief in divine justice in the face of apparent injustices on earth. Ideas of immortality and resurrection are generally attributed to Greek or Persian origins, yet to the Pharisees it was a genuine Jewish belief based on passages in the Torah.

Place of the Torah. For the Pharisees, the Torah God gave to Moses consisted of the Written and the Oral Law, and both were truth. The divine revelations in the first five books of Moses were supplemented and explained by the prophets and the unwritten tradition, and were intended to guide men in the right way of life. The Torah, they felt, was the center of their teachings and sufficient for all men and all times. Their view of the law was that its commandments were to be interpreted in conformity with the standard and interpretation of the rabbis of each generation, and to be made to harmonize with advanced ideas. Therefore, when a precept was outgrown, it was to be given a more acceptable meaning, so that it would harmonize with the truth resulting from God-given reason. The law must be understood according to the interpretation of the teachers who are endowed with God-given reason to do so. When the letter of the law seemed to oppose conscience, it was to be taken, accordingly, in its spirit. The Mosaic law of "an eye for an eye," for instance, was interpreted to refer to monetary compensation and not retaliation. The Pharisees generated a ramified system of hermeneutics and found no great difficulty in harmonizing Torah teachings with their advanced ideas, or in finding their ideas implied or hinted at in the words of the Torah. It was due to this progressive tendency, therefore, that the Pharisaic interpretation of Judaism continued to develop and remain a vital force in Jewry.

For discussion of the evolution of the Oral Law and its relation to the Torah, see *Oral Law and *Talmud.

Synagogue Worship. The Pharisees believed that since God was everywhere, He could be worshiped both in and outside the Temple, and was not to be invoked by sacrifices alone. They thus fostered the synagogue as a place of worship, study, and prayer, and raised it to a central and important place in the life of the people which rivaled the Temple.

Relation to the New Testament. While the Pharisees, as a whole, set a high ethical standard for themselves, not all lived up to it. It is mistakenly held that New Testament references to them as "hypocrites" or "offspring of vipers" (Matt. 3:7; Luke 18:9ff., etc.) are applicable to the entire group. However, the leaders were well aware of the presence of the insincere among their numbers, described by the Pharisees themselves in the Talmud as "sore spots" or "plagues of the Pharisaic party" (Sot. 3:4 and 22b). The apostle Paul himself had been a Pharisee, was a son of a Pharisee, and was taught by one of the sect's most eminent scholars, Gamaliel of Jerusalem. Pharisaic doctrines have more in common with those of Christianity than is supposed, having prepared the ground for Christianity with such concepts as Messianism, the popularization of monotheism and apocalypticism, and with such beliefs as life after death, resurrection of the dead, immortality, and angels.

The active period of Pharisaism extended well into the second century C.E. and was most influential in the development of Orthodox Judaism. The Pharisees were deeply earnest in the religion of their forefathers, represented the most stable elements in their religion, and were most instrumental in preserving and transmitting Judaism. Unlike the Zealots, they rejected the appeal to force and violence, believing that God was in control of history and that every true Jew should live in accordance with the Torah. It is not surprising, therefore, that the Pharisees devoted much of their efforts to education. After the destruction of Jerusalem in 70 C.E., it was the synagogues and the schools of the Pharisees that continued to function and to promote Judaism.

See also *Sages.

Bibliography: GENERAL: J. W. Lightly, *Jewish Sects and Parties in the Time of Jesus* (1925); R. T. Herford, *Judaism in the New Testament Period* (1928); G. F. Moore, *Judaism in the First Centuries of the Christian Era,* 3 vols. (1927–30); S. Zeitlin, *History of the Second Jewish Commonwealth: Prolegomena* (1933); idem, *Rise and Fall of the Judean State,* 2 vols. (1962–67); H. Wheeler Robinson, *History of Israel* (1938); Alon, Toledot; Baron, Social[2], 1–2 (1952); N. H. Snaith, *The Jews from Cyrus to Herod* (1956); D. Daube, *New Testament and Rabbinic Judaism* (1956); Schuerer, Hist; A. Posy, *Mystic Trends in Judaism* (1966); J. L. Blau, *Modern Varieties of Judaism* (1966); R. Kaufman, *Great Sects and Schisms in Judaism* (1967). PHARISEES: Schuerer, Gesch, 2 (1907[4]), 447ff., incl. bibl.; I. Abrahams, *Studies in Pharisees and the Gospels,* 2 vols. (1917–24; repr. 1967); R. T. Herford, *Pharisaism: Its Aim and Method* (1912); idem, *Pharisees* (1924); idem, in: *Judaism and the Beginnings of Christianity* (1924); idem, *Truth about the Pharisees* (1925); H. Loewe, in: W. O. E. Oesterley (ed.), *Judaism and Christianity,* 2 (1937, repr. 1969); L. Baeck, *Pharisees* (1947); J. Z. Lauterbach, *Rabbinic Essays* (1951), 23–162; Klausner, Bayit Sheni, index, s.v. *Perushim;* R. Marcus, in: JBL, 73 (1954), 157–61; L. Finkelstein, *Pharisees,* 2 vols. (1962[3]), incl. bibl.; A. Finkel, *The Pharisees and the Teacher of Nazareth* (1964); L. Bronner, *Sects and Separatism during the Second Jewish Commonwealth* (1967); W. D. Davies, *Introduction to Pharisaism* (1967).

[M.MAN.]

PHAROS (near Alexandria), an island just over half a mile from Alexandria, on which stood the lighthouse of Pharos, regarded as one of the wonders of the ancient world. According to the "Letter of Aristeas" (par. 301), the Septuagint was translated there, and there the Jewish community of Alexandria also assembled to hear the translation and accept it (*ibid.* par. 308–11). Philo stresses the excellent qualities of Pharos which were ideal for the needs of the translators—cleanliness, peace and tranquility, solitude, and closeness to nature. Philo also relates that a festive ceremony was held annually on the island in commemoration of the translation. Both Jews and non-Jews participated in the festivity where they gave thanks and prayed to God and then spent the whole day on the shore (Philo, II Mos. 35–44).

Bibliography: *Aristeae, ad Philocratem epistula,* ed. by P. Wendland (1900), 301, 308–11; Schuerer, Gesch, 3 (1909[4]), 144, 428, 610.

[V.R.]

PHASAEL (d. 40 B.C.E.), older brother of *Herod the Great. He appears to have been more moderate than Herod. Having received from his father, *Antipater, the governorship of Jerusalem when Herod was appointed governor of Galilee, Phasael exercised firm rule coupled with discretion. Notwithstanding Josephus' generous appraisal of his character, Phasael, together with Herod, was twice accused before Mark Antony by Jewish deputations. The latter were singularly unsuccessful and on the second of these attempts Herod and Phasael were, in fact, appointed tetrarchs. Both he and Herod strove from the outset to remove the vestiges of Hasmonean domination in Judea. *Antigonus, who succeeded in gaining Parthian assistance in his efforts to reestablish his family's rule over Judea, laid siege to Phasael and Herod in Jerusalem. Phasael, accompanied by the high priest Hyrcanus II, allowed himself to be inveigled into the Parthian camp in 40 B.C.E., and both were imprisoned by the Parthians. Hyrcanus was physically disfigured to prevent his serving in the priesthood, and Phasael took his own life by dashing out his brains—this is the official Herodian account but it is more probable that he was killed in battle while trying to escape. The present-day Tower of David in Jerusalem's Old City is probably the site of the Phasael tower of Herod's palace.

Bibliography: Jos., Ant., index; Schuerer, Hist, 109, 113–5; A. H. M. Jones, *Herods of Judaea* (1938), 28, 35–36, 38–42; A. Schalit, *Hordos ha-Melekh* (1964), index.

[DA.S.]

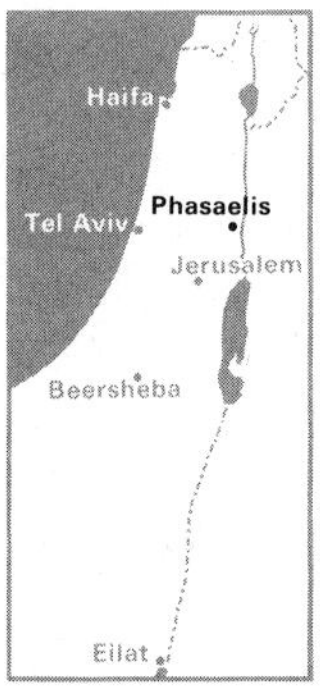

PHASAELIS, city founded by King Herod in the Jordan Valley N. of Jericho and named after his elder brother Phasael, who died in 40 B.C.E. (Jos., Wars, 1:418). The place was renowned for its dates (Pliny, *Natural History,* 13:4, 44). Herod bequeathed Phasaelis to his sister Salome; she in turn willed it to the empress Livia, the wife of Augustus; from Livia, the estate of Phasaelis passed to her son Tiberius, and remained imperial property throughout the period of the Roman and Byzantine empires. It is shown on the Madaba Map with an accompanying date palm. In Byzantine times, hermits lived there; a church of St. Cyriacus in Phasaelis is mentioned by Moschus (*Pratum spirituale,* 92) and Cyriacus of Scythopolis (*Vita Sabae,* 29). The site is identified with Khirbat Faṣṣā'il, which has remains of water channels, an aqueduct $1\frac{1}{4}$ mi. long, water mills, building foundations, and Roman roads.

Bibliography: Schuerer, Gesch, 2 (1907), 204; Abel, in: RB, 10 (1913), 235; Alt, in: PJB, 23 (1927), 31; Avi-Yonah, Geog, 120.

[M.A.-Y.]

PHEASANT, the game bird *Phasianus colchicus.* The pheasant was known in Greek as *φασιανός* and hence in mishnaic Hebrew as פַּסְיוֹנִי *(pasyoni).* It is not mentioned in the Bible, although pseudo-Jonathan identified it with the biblical שְׂלָו (*selav;* Ex. 16:13), which is however the *quail. The pheasant was originally found in Asia, from the shores of the Caspian Sea to Manchuria and Japan. It was brought to Europe and America where, acclimatized in forests, it became a notable game bird. The Romans set great store upon its flesh, and it is told that when the emperor Hadrian doubted whether there were also pheasants in Ereẓ Israel, R. Joshua b. Hananiah produced some to prove to him "that Ereẓ Israel lacks nothing" (Eccles. R. 2:8, no. 2). Whether these particular pheasants existed in a wild state in the country or were bred cannot be determined, although from other sources it is evident that they were bred together with peacocks (Tosef., Kil 1:8), this having been a sign of wealth (Eccles. R. 7:8). The pheasant is listed in the Midrash among those rare delicacies, the taste of which the manna could acquire should a person yearn for it (Num. R. 7:4). In connection with the command to honor one's father, it was said: "One may give his father pheasants as food, yet this drives him from the world, while another may make him grind in the mill, and this brings him to the world to come" (Kid. 31a). In several communities in Europe the Jews ate the pheasant, which has the characteristics of a *kasher* bird. An attempt was made in recent years to breed it in Israel, but the rabbinate cast doubt on its *kashrut* for lack of local tradition to that effect (see *Dietary Laws).

Bibliography: Lewysohn, Zool, 213f.; Feliks, in: *Teva va-Areẓ,* 8 (1965/66), 326–32.

[J.F.]

PHERORAS (d. c. 5 B.C.E.), son of Antipater and Cypros, younger brother of Herod the Great. During the war of Herod against Antigonus, Pheroras was put in command of the Roman soldiers and charged with fortifying Alexandrion, and was later appointed by Herod tetrarch of Transjordan. Pheroras was actively involved in the intrigues in the court of Herod. Together with his sister Salome, he did everything in his power to accentuate the differences between Herod and the sons of *Mariamne the Hasmonean. Herod hated Pheroras' wife and demanded that he divorce her. Unwilling to accede, Pheroras was compelled to return to his tetrarchy where he died by poisoning. After his death his wife testified that he had plotted to poison Herod.

Bibliography: Jos., Wars, 1:181, 308, 475ff.; Jos., Ant., 14:121; 15:362; Schuerer, Hist, 150, 153, 156; Klausner, Bayit Sheni, 4 (1950[2]), 58, 153, 155–7, 162f.; A. Schalit, *Koenig Herodes* (1969), index.

[E.E.]

PHILADELPHIA, fourth largest city in the United States, in the State of *Pennsylvania. The population of the metropolitan area (comprising Bucks, Chester, Delaware, Montgomery, and Philadelphia counties in Pennsylvania, and Burlington, Camden, and Gloucester counties in New Jersey) was slightly less than five million in 1970. The area's Jewish population, third largest in the nation, was estimated at 350,000–400,000, smaller than New York City and Los Angeles, but well ahead of Chicago.

Origins of the Jewish Community. Jews came from New Amsterdam to trade in the Delaware Valley area as early as the 1650s, long before William Penn founded the colony of Pennsylvania in 1682. Several individual Jews were transient in Philadelphia by 1706. Permanent Jewish settlement began in 1737 with the arrival of Nathan *Levy (1704–53) and his brother Isaac (1706–77), who were joined in 1740 by their young cousins David *Franks (1720–93) and Moses (1718–89). Nathan Levy and David Franks established a successful mercantile firm known for its shipping and import-export activity. Barnard *Gratz (1738–1801) arrived in 1754 and went to work for David Franks. Gratz, with his brother Michael *Gratz (1740–1811), the two best known Philadelphia colonial Jews, created a prosperous business

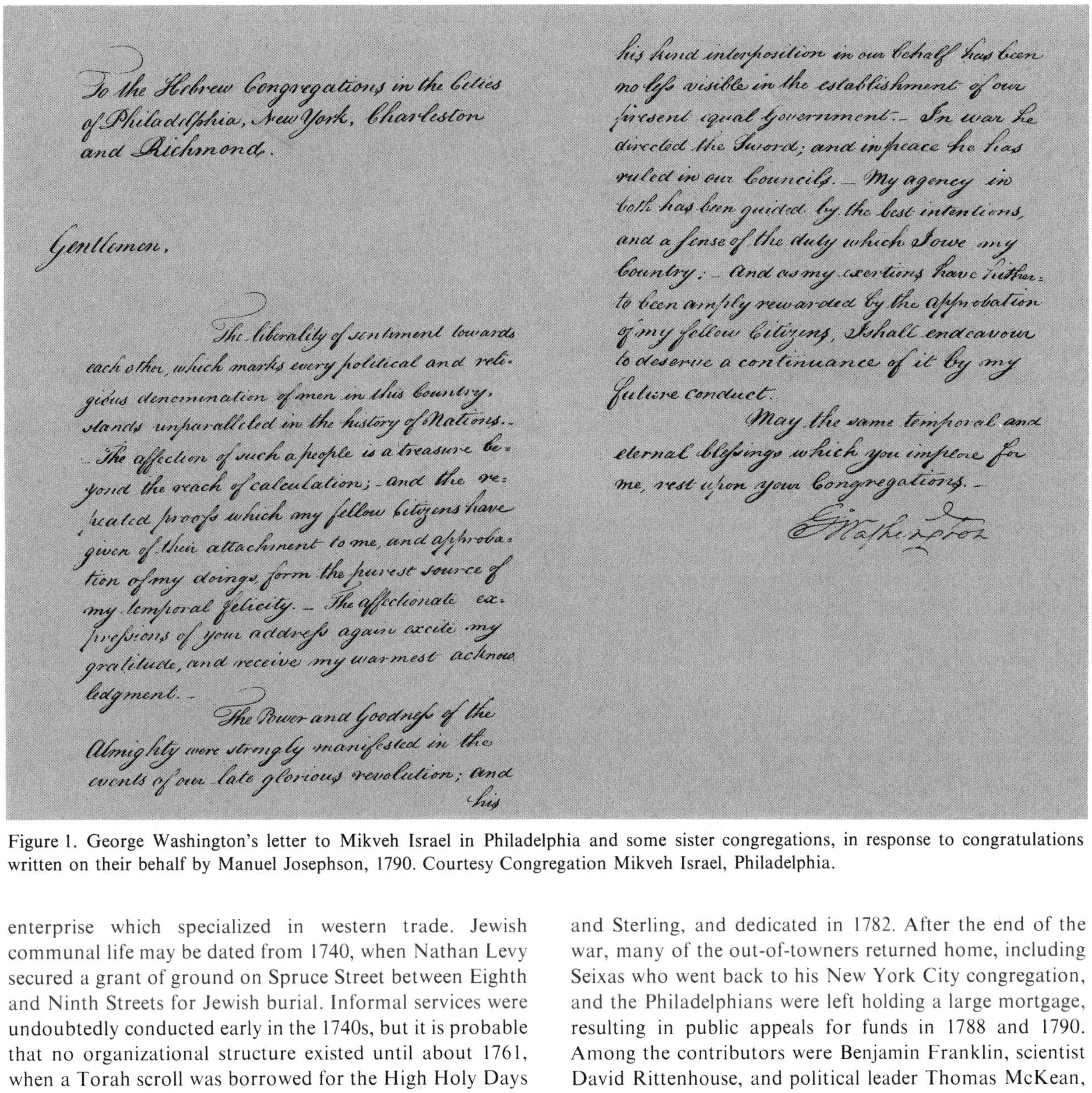
To the Hebrew Congregations in the Cities of Philadelphia, New York, Charleston and Richmond.

Gentlemen,

The liberality of sentiment towards each other, which marks every political and religious denomination of men in this Country, stands unparalleled in the history of Nations.— The affection of such a people is a treasure beyond the reach of calculation; — and the repeated proofs which my fellow Citizens have given of their attachment to me, and approbation of my doings, form the purest source of my temporal felicity. — The affectionate expressions of your address again excite my gratitude, and receive my warmest acknowledgment. —

The Power and Goodness of the Almighty were strongly manifested in the events of our late glorious revolution; and his kind interposition in our behalf has been no less visible in the establishment of our present equal government. — In war he directed the Sword; and in peace he has ruled in our Councils. — My agency in both has been guided by the best intentions, and a sense of the duty which I owe my Country: — And as my exertions have hitherto been amply rewarded by the approbation of my fellow Citizens, I shall endeavour to deserve a continuance of it by my future conduct.

May the same temporal and eternal blessings which you implore for me, rest upon your Congregations. —

G. Washington

Figure 1. George Washington's letter to Mikveh Israel in Philadelphia and some sister congregations, in response to congratulations written on their behalf by Manuel Josephson, 1790. Courtesy Congregation Mikveh Israel, Philadelphia.

enterprise which specialized in western trade. Jewish communal life may be dated from 1740, when Nathan Levy secured a grant of ground on Spruce Street between Eighth and Ninth Streets for Jewish burial. Informal services were undoubtedly conducted early in the 1740s, but it is probable that no organizational structure existed until about 1761, when a Torah scroll was borrowed for the High Holy Days from Shearith Israel Congregation of New York City. At first, services were conducted in a rented house on Sterling Alley; after 1771, in a building on Cherry Alley. The oldest extant document utilizing the name Mikveh Israel Congregation is dated 1773, although the name was probably adopted prior to that.

Revolutionary Period. Nine or ten Jewish merchants, led by the Gratz brothers, signed the Non-Importation Resolutions of Oct. 25, 1765. While a majority of Philadelphia's Jews supported the Revolutionary cause, a few were Tories, among them David Franks, who served as deputy commissary of prisoners and was expelled by the Continental authorities in 1780 for his pro-British sympathies. During the war Jews were active as suppliers to the troops, as brokers for the government (e.g., Haym *Salomon), and as military figures. The highest commissioned rank achieved by Jews was that of lieutenant colonel, held by both Solomon *Bush and David S. Franks, the latter having the misfortune of serving as aide-de-camp to Benedict Arnold at the time of his treachery, but innocent of complicity. After the evacuation of the city by the British in 1778, Philadelphia became a center for Jewish refugees from Charleston, Savannah, and New York City. Gershom Mendes *Seixas became the community's *ḥazzan* in 1780. The city's first real synagogue building, 30 × 36 feet, was erected on the north side of Cherry Street between Third and Sterling, and dedicated in 1782. After the end of the war, many of the out-of-towners returned home, including Seixas who went back to his New York City congregation, and the Philadelphians were left holding a large mortgage, resulting in public appeals for funds in 1788 and 1790. Among the contributors were Benjamin Franklin, scientist David Rittenhouse, and political leader Thomas McKean, a signatory of the Declaration of Independence.

In 1783 the leaders of Mikveh Israel Congregation unsuccessfully attempted to change the requirement in the Pennsylvania constitution of 1776 that officeholders take an oath swearing belief in both the Old and New Testaments. Another effort led by Jonas *Phillips in 1789 was successful, and the 1790 state constitution prohibited only atheists from holding state office. Phillips was also the author of a communication to the Constitutional Convention of 1787 urging the recognition of full legal equality for members of "all Religious societies," later guaranteed by the First Amendment of the U.S. Constitution. The fact that both the Declaration of Independence and the Constitution were adopted in Philadelphia gave the Jews of the community a sense of close relationship to the founding of the nation which was the first in the modern world to grant the full range of rights and prerogatives of citizenship to Jews. President George Washington, answering a letter of congratulations sent to him in 1790 by Philadelphia's Manuel *Josephson on behalf of Mikveh Israel and its sister congregations of New York City, Charleston, and Richmond, also recognized that "the liberal sentiment towards each other which marks every political and religious denomination of men in this country stands unparalleled in the history of Nations."

Early Nineteenth Century. The growth of the Jewish

Figure 2. Congregation Mikveh Israel's Cherry St. synagogue, in use 1825–60. This was the second building of Philadelphia's oldest Jewish congregation. Jerusalem, Ezra P. Gorodetsky Collection.

community of Philadelphia, like that of other major cities, was comparatively slow until about 1830. There may have been as many as 1,000 Jewish men, women, and children in the town at the time of Cornwallis' surrender, but this swollen population swiftly scattered, and so large a number was not again reached until about 1830. It is estimated that at the time of the 1820 census there were about 500 Jews in Philadelphia, of whom a little less than half were immigrants. Some of these foreign born felt uncomfortable at the Sephardi services of Mikveh Israel, and in about 1795 instituted their own Ashkenazi form of worship, under the name German Hebrew Society. In 1802 they formally organized themselves as Rodeph Shalom Congregation. Philadelphia thus became the first city in the nation with two congregations, and the first in the entire Western Hemisphere to break the unitary pattern of one *minhag* in each community. By 1825 these two congregations had spawned a handful of benevolent societies, detached from congregational control, which numbered 23 by 1860. In 1848 there were about 4,000 Jews in the city, a figure which probably doubled by 1860 when Mikveh Israel and Rodeph Shalom had been joined by five more congregations: Beth Israel (1840, merged into Beth Zion in 1964); Keneseth Israel (1847); Bene Israel (1852, disbanded 1879); Beth El Emeth (1857, dissolved about 1890); and Adath Jeshurun (1858).

National Influence of the Community During the Nineteenth Century. Beginning with the election of Isaac *Leeser to the pulpit of Mikveh Israel in 1829, and continuing until about 1906 when the *American Jewish Committee was formed in New York City in partnership with Philadelphia Jews, the Philadelphia Jewish community was innovating, pioneering, and, in many ways, the most influential Jewry in the U.S. In spite of New York City's numerical superiority—and perhaps because New York's Jewry was so immense and diverse as to be unmanageable, uncontrollable, and diffuse—it was in Philadelphia that new ideas for the shaping of U.S. Jewish communal life were tested. Such creative religious and lay leaders of Philadelphia as Leeser, Sabato *Morais, Abraham *Hart, Moses Aaron *Dropsie, Mayer *Sulzberger, and Joseph *Krauskopf were as concerned with the future and fate of Jewish life throughout the country as they were with developments on the local scene. Other factors which contributed to the achievements of Philadelphia's Jews were the city's tradition of intellectual and cultural excellence, which spurred its Jews to match the activity of their non-Jewish neighbors; the geographical location of the city and its commercial and financial links with the South and Midwest, which brought it into frequent and instructive contact with Jews in other parts of the country; and a less frenzied pace of life than New York City's, which perhaps granted the leisure and perspective necessary for intelligent assessment of current and future needs. At any rate, it was in this community that Leeser's *Occident,* prayer book, and Bible translations were published—sources of incalculable Jewish cultural and religious enrichment throughout the country. It was in Philadelphia that Leeser issued a call for an organized U.S. Jewish community in 1841. In 1845 he organized the American Jewish Publication Society in Philadelphia, and, upon its failure, and that of a New York-based successor organization, the present Jewish Publication Society was formed in 1888. Leeser's Hebrew Education Society high school, the first in the land, was founded in 1849. He also opened the first Jewish theological seminary in the country, Maimonides College, in Philadelphia in 1867. The first U.S. Jewish teachers' college, Gratz College, established under

Figure 3. Meeting of the Histadruth Ivrith of America in Philadelphia, April 1923. Members included Mordekhai Lipson (1), Zevi Scharfstein (2), Simon Bernstein (3), Daniel Persky (4), Pinkhos Churgin (5), Simon Ginzburg (6), Isaac Rivkind (7), and Reuben Brainin (8). Jerusalem, J.N.U.L. Photo Klein and Goodman, Philadelphia.

the provisions of the will of Hyman *Gratz (1776–1857), began in 1897. In Philadelphia, too, *Dropsie College (later University), the first postgraduate institution for Jewish learning in the world, was opened in 1907, bringing to Philadelphia as its president the learned Cyrus *Adler, who for several decades was the representative of U.S. Jewry. In New York the Jewish Theological Seminary was founded by a Philadelphia rabbi, Sabato Morais, who was its first president.

Mass Immigration and Communal Chaos. Philadelphia's concern for national Jewish undertakings was virtually overwhelmed by the East European immigration which began to pour into the city toward the end of the 19th century. A fairly homogenous community of approximately 12,000 in 1880 was inundated by 15 times its number within 35 years: there were upward of 200,000 Jews in the city by 1915. The process of Americanization, adjustment, and integration began all over again, accompanied by a vast proliferation of lodges, landsmanshaften, synagogues, and societies, numbering more than 150 in 1904 and twice that in 1920. Most of the community energy was channeled into social welfare and personal aid. The Jewish Foster Home (1855) and the Jewish Hospital (1866), formerly fairly modest institutions, struggled to keep pace with incessant need. Another Jewish medical institution, Mt. Sinai Hospital, was created in 1900 to serve the immense Jewish population in south Philadelphia. The Jewish Sheltering Home (1882) developed into the Home for the Jewish Aged (1899). In 1901, with Jacob *Gimbel of the department store family as its first president, the new Federation of Jewish Charities was formed through the merger of a number of societies, including the United Hebrew Charities (founded in 1869) which had been supported by the proceeds of an annual Hebrew Charity Ball since 1855.

Federation of philanthropic endeavor did not, however, connote communal unity. As wide a gulf as anywhere in the nation existed between German and East European Jews, between Reform and Orthodox, and between Zionists and anti-Zionists. Within the field of philanthropy itself, family and business associations of the German Jews, and anti-, or at least non-Zionist views continued to dominate the Federation of Jewish Charities (F.J.C.) until the end of World War II. The German Jews kept aloof from the newer immigrants in the Mercantile Club (1853) and Philmont Country Club (1906), where their social gatherings were held; only in the Locust Club (1920), beginning in the 1940s, were social distinctions overlooked and, ultimately, ignored. In religious life, hardly any common ground existed between men like Rabbi Bernard L. *Levinthal, spiritual leader of the Orthodox community, and Rabbi Joseph Krauskopf, except when they sold war bonds together during World War I, or stood for election in the American Jewish Congress campaign of 1917. Philadelphia, essentially a conservative city, preserved traditional characteristics dating back to colonial times; it also maintained social barriers which excluded Jews longer than in most other cities. In this, perhaps, lies the explanation for its Jewish community maintaining its own exclusions and distinctions longer than in most other cities. It was probably not a coincidence that the anti-Zionist American Council for Judaism (A.C.J.; 1943) was founded by Philadelphia rabbis and laymen.

Toward a United Community: Post-World War I. The anti-Zionist council was the last gasp of an outmoded view of U.S. Jewish life. Even in the 1930s under the impact of the depression, of overseas needs provoked by Hitlerism, and of the simultaneous rise of U.S. anti-Semitism, the Philadelphia Jewish community had begun to coalesce: in 1938 the first Allied Jewish Appeal campaign was conduct-

Figure 4. Class at the Samuel Netzky Adult Institute of Jewish Studies, Gratz College, Philadelphia. Photo Alan D. Hewitt, Philadelphia.

ed for funds to assist the *yishuv* and the victims of German barbarity. A council of local defense agencies was organized, resulting in the establishment of the Jewish Community Relations Council. Perceptive leaders realized that organizational divisiveness was inefficient and unproductive; that coordination of effort and expertise were essential; and that professionalization required consolidation.

Beginning in 1944 with the merger of several children's agencies into the Association for Jewish Children, there ensued in swift succession a number of steps in the gradual restructuring of the community: the three Jewish hospitals (failing to include only the Philadelphia Psychiatric Hospital) merged into the Albert Einstein Medical Center in 1951; the reorganization of the Home for the Jewish Aged and the construction of its first new building took place in 1952, followed by the erection of the York House residential centers for the healthy aged in 1960 and 1964; old hostilities and loyalties were overcome through the final merger of the Federation of Jewish Charities and the Allied Jewish Appeal into the Federation of Jewish Agencies (F.J.A.) in 1956; the insistent challenges of Jewish education were confronted through the reorganization of Gratz College, which moved into a new building in 1962, and launched a program of centralized advisory services to Jewish schools throughout the community; and the Young Men's Hebrew Association and the Neighborhood Center were united in 1965, with a projected network of leisure time agencies throughout the metropolitan area. By 1970 most of the old institutional rivalries had been forgotten. The younger leaders did not know whose grandfather had been Lithuanian, or whose great-grandfather had been German. Money for Israel was raised and bonds for Israel were sold in the very synagogues whose former rabbis had created the anti-Zionist A.C.J. Although a local Synagogue Council had failed in the 1950s, a flourishing Board of Rabbis testified to increased cooperation among Conservative, Orthodox, and Reform rabbis. Most Jewish leaders worked just as hard for the United Fund (which gave large-scale support to the health and welfare institutions of the F.J.A.) as for the Allied Jewish Appeal campaign. The F.J.A. itself had moved far beyond its conceptual origins as a fund-raising agency and was functioning vigorously in the broad areas of social planning and problem projection.

1970. The Jewish population on the Pennsylvania side of the Delaware was concentrated in the Center City, Greater Northeast, Old York Road Suburban, West Oak Lane-Mt. Airy, Wynnefield, and Main Line sections, with growing centers in Levittown and Norristown; on the New Jersey side, Jews were moving into such suburban areas as Cherry Hill in great numbers.

There are over 100 congregations in the Philadelphia area (1970), of which approximately 50 are Conservative, 45 Orthodox, and 15 Reform. These statistics are, to some degree, deceptive, because some of the Orthodox congregations are quite small, and some are served by Conservative rabbis. While two of the largest Reform congregations in the country are located in Greater Philadelphia, the dominant religious thrust of the community is Conservative. A resurgent interest in Orthodoxy has been stimulated through the work of a vigorous branch of the *Lubavich movement and by a nationally known talmudic yeshivah established in Philadelphia by students of Rabbi Aaron *Kotler. Fund-raising federations function in the greater Camden region and in Norristown and Levittown, but the dominant influence in the Jewish life of the metropolitan area is exerted by the Federation of Jewish Agencies, fulfilling most of the purposes and functions of a Jewish community council without a formal system of direct organizational representation. The three Anglo-Jewish newspapers are: *The Jewish Exponent* (1887–), official organ of the F.J.A.; *The Jewish Times* (1925–), a private and personal venture of Esther and Philip Klein; and *The Voice* (1941–), a biweekly publication of the Camden County Jewish Federation, representative of an effort to foster an independent Jewish life beyond the massive influence of Philadelphia.

Jews occupy a significant place in the political and economic life of the area. During the 1960s representative Jews were appointed to the boards of practically every bank in the city, as they had long served on the boards of the community's cultural and educational institutions. Many major corporations were actively soliciting applications for employment as executive trainees from young Jews, and almost every major law firm included a few Jews. In both law and medicine, prestigious Philadelphia professions, Jewish leaders and pioneers were numerous. Jewish cooperation and support were welcomed by the leaders of the United Fund and of practically every other civic and philanthropic activity, although Jews themselves were still rigorously and consciously excluded from most of the town and country clubs which represented the last strongholds of old Philadelphia "society."

Perhaps not since 1780 had the Philadelphia Jewish community been so thoroughly united and so optimistic about its capacity to meet the future. Indeed, the installation in 1967 of a new president of Dropsie University, Abraham I. *Katsh, and the inauguration in 1968 of the new Reconstructionist Rabbinical College in conjunction with Temple University may have portended the beginning of a new "golden age" of Philadelphia Jewish life.

Figure 5. Beth Shalom synagogue in Elkins Park, a suburb of Philadelphia. The building, designed by Frank Lloyd Wright, was completed in 1959. Photo Jacob Stelman, Philadelphia.

Bibliography: E. Wolf and M. Whiteman, *History of the Jews of Philadelphia* (1957); B. Postal and L. Koppman, *Jewish Tourist's Guide to the U.S.* (1954), 540–57; A. J. Karp, *Jewish Experience in America,* 4 vols., 1969, index; A. S. W. Rosenbach, *American Jewish Bibliography* (1926); W. Eames, in: *Studies in Jewish Bibliography—A. S. Freidus Memorial Volume* (1929), 496–502.

[B.W.K.]

PHILADELPHIA, JACOB (b. 1720 or 1735–after 1783), Colonial American physicist, mechanic, and kabbalist. Philadelphia's family name and the year when he assumed the name of his native city is unknown. He may have been educated by a Dr. Christopher Witt, a Rosicrucian mystic and anchorite survivor of the German Pietist mystic sect known as the "Women of the Wilderness." Witt was known to be a correspondent of the Duke of Cumberland, who later became Philadelphia's patron in England. After his patron's death in 1758, Philadelphia toured England, lecturing and conducting experiments to great acclaim, and later lectured throughout Europe. Considered a powerful magician by the ignorant, Philadelphia nevertheless refused to lecture at the University of Goettingen (1777) after a satirical poster campaign derided him as a miracle worker and magician. He supposedly last lectured in Switzerland in 1781. In 1783 he applied to the Prussian court for a license to form a Prussian-American trading company.

Jacob Philadelphia, American mystic. Cecil Roth Collection.

Bibliography: J. F. Sachse, in: AJHSP, 16 (1907), 73–83; J. R. Marcus, *Early American Jewry,* 2 (1953), 83–89. [Ed.]

PHILANTHROPY.

This article is arranged according to the following outline:

State Taxation for Jewish Communal Services
Voluntary Associations or Benevolent Societies in Modern Times
Fund Collectors on the Local Communal Level
France
England
Germany
Russia
United States
Canada
Argentina
Israel
Fund Raising by International Organizations
Old Type Fund Collection for Ereẓ Israel
Zionist and Modern Israel Fund Raising
The Modern Campaigns and Their Goals

At the close of the 18th century the communal system of fund raising for charity with authority vested in the charity overseers (*Gabba'ei Ẓedakah*)—to tax members of the community in order to ensure appropriate giving—was on the verge of collapse in many European communities. The situation in Rome was typical. "The enormous indebtedness of the Roman community was, in part, due to these expenses for public welfare, which in the early decades of the 18th century equaled or exceeded the total income from communal taxation" (S. Baron, Community, 2, 346–50). The financial condition deteriorated with the rise of absolute states which imposed ever harsher taxes on their subjects. The spread of secularism and individualism, and the appearance of Haskalah (Enlightenment) and Reform also tended to weaken the cohesiveness of the community and reduce its authority to exact adequate sums for their communal functions. Moreover, there were duplication and waste in fund raising and in social services due to absence of coordination between the community, the benevolent societies, and the individual donors who espoused their own favorite projects—a situation which had grown apace (see *Finances, Autonomous).

State Taxation for Jewish Communal Services. In the 19th century states altered the procedures for tax collections for communal purposes. In Russia, which then included Poland, with the dissolution in 1844 of the **kahal* (the autonomous Jewish community) a Russian government ukase forced the Jewish communities to turn over to the municipalities control of their tax collections and administration of their financial affairs and charitable institutions. A remnant of the authority left to them was the recommendation of tax collectors who frequently bade for these potentially profitable posts. The burden of caring for the needy, the poor, and the sick and for the education of the children became increasingly more difficult to bear as the number of expelled Jews and the mass emigration of breadwinners reached vast proportions in the 1880s. Revenue for charity and education became dependent primarily on the share given to the community from government taxes, of which they could never be sure and on limited income from private donations and payment for synagogue honors. Among the taxes imposed by the government one of the most oppressive was the *kasher* meat tax (**Korobka*) and the *candle tax (see *Taxation). Revenues from these taxes were divided between the state and the community to cover expenditure for social welfare, maintenance of educational institutions, and other communal activities. Frequently the share of taxes due the community was diverted by the authorities to build a road or erect a church, and often an inordinate portion of the funds collected went into the pockets of the Jewish tax collectors.

Voluntary Associations or Benevolent Societies in Modern Times. Voluntary associations or benevolent societies continued in modern times to play the important part which they had had in the Middle Ages for raising funds for specific religious, social, and educational services. Where communal charity systems were weakened or broke down completely, voluntary associations filled their place as well as they could and frequently adapted themselves to changing conditions. In England, where plans to introduce state taxation in 1795 and 1802 were withdrawn, many of the voluntary associations in the 19th century were organized on the pattern of voting societies found in the general community. An annual subscription to the association of four or five shillings entitled a subscriber to one vote which could be used to vote for himself or for someone else when benefits were to be distributed. An alternative procedure to voting was drawing the winning ticket from a box or by using a special "wheel," made for that purpose. The Bread, Meat, and Coal Society (Mashvah Nephesh, founded in 1779 and still in existence in 1970) introduced an element of self-help for the poor by arranging that subscriptions could be paid weekly at the rate of one farthing. A total annual subscription of 4s. 4d. gave the subscriber the chance to draw 12 tickets, each of which entitled him to 1s. 9d. worth of bread, meat, and coal.

The *fraternal organizations or Friendly Societies, all mutual benefit associations, were an important form of voluntary association. Many older voluntary associations ceased to exist as central welfare and fund-raising agencies took over their functions and as governments assumed responsibility for direct aid to individuals. Nevertheless, many new voluntary associations rose to provide help to those afflicted by disease, supply funds for research in medicine and other vital fields, provide care for the children of a growing number of working mothers, support programs for prevention of juvenile delinquency, ensure better facilities and more scientific treatment for the care of the aged, the chronic sick, or the convalescent, and help meet every humanitarian need which a changing world made urgent.

Fund Collectors on the Local Communal Level. In the early modern period communal collectors still made their rounds, as they had done in mishnaic and medieval times, to gather the obligatory contribution for the communal charity fund, and congregational collectors visited homes to ensure payment for synagogue honors. As in the Middle Ages, voluntary benevolent societies had collectors to collect dues or donations or the coins deposited in their boxes placed in the homes of members. Collectors for authorized societies were also permitted to use their collection boxes in front of the synagogue on Purim or the Ninth of Av. Burial societies assigned collectors at cemeteries at funeral or memorial services and this practice is continued in traditional cemeteries. Until the middle of the 19th century the majority of communal collectors appear to have served without compensation, thus fulfilling their obligation to do charity.

In the second half of the 19th century many charitable organizations employed collectors and the practice continued to grow until community leaders in the 1920s recognized its wastefulness. Though in 1970 fund collectors were still working for some local charity organizations, the number had been reduced sharply.

France. Coordination in the administration of charity and fund raising was first achieved in 1809 in the emancipated community of Paris, when seven benevolent societies in that city were amalgamated. At the direction of the Consistoire, they created the Société d'Encouragement et de Secours (from 1855 officially named the Comité de Bienfaisance Israélite de Paris). From the beginning the Comité recognized that it could not rely solely on the resources provided by the Consistoire, for although the Napoleonic regime had permitted the Consistoire to tax members of constituent congregations, it had not obligated every Jew to join a congregation and pay taxes to support the charitable and other services of the community. The offerings for the privilege of sharing in the Torah reading, the fees for other synagogue honors, and the collections from the charity boxes in the congregation, proved no adequate supplement to the limited tax revenues. Shortly after its establishment, the Comité undertook to secure annual subscriptions over a three-year period, with a minimum requirement of 18 francs payable monthly from regular members and 30 francs from those known as honorary members. After a good effort the first year, the campaign lagged, and it was only when the community began to see the benefits of coordination, substitution of preventive social techniques for palliative measures, training of the young for productive work, and building of essential institutions such as an almshouse, a hospital, and an orphanage, that an increasingly larger number of members of the community began to subscribe more generously to the appeals of the Comité. Among the many new subscribers were those in the new voluntary associations founded after the Comité had been organized. When finally given representation in the Comité, they proved to be among the most enthusiastic contributors and workers. A lottery for raising funds from the general community was instituted in 1843, but this device became less significant as fund raising began to depend on annual subscriptions, large-scale donations, trusts, endowments, and legacies. Two significant endowments were made by the Rothschilds, one for the acquisition and maintenance of a hospital in 1841 and another for an orphanage founded by the family in 1855. Other Jewish philanthropists followed their example and made large-scale donations and endowments in succeeding years. After the liberation of France in 1944, the *American Jewish Joint Distribution Committee (JDC) with the cooperation of French Jewish leaders established the Comité Juif d'Action Sociale et de Reconstruction (COJASOR); most of the resources were supplied by JDC. In 1946 the Comité de Bienfaisance resumed its full activities, including fund raising, but was still dependent in largest measure on the JDC and other foreign Jewish agencies. In 1949 the Fonds Social Juif Unifié de France was created as the national fund-raising and distributing body. Until 1964 the Fonds received additional large financial support from the Material Claims Conference and steadily diminishing aid from the JDC. In 1966, 1,600 heads of families in France contributed $1,600,000. After the Six-Day War in 1967 the Fonds Social combined with Aide à Israël (*Keren Hayesod) to form the Appel Juif Unifié, a single national fund-raising agency to help meet the budgets of both the Fonds Social and the Jewish Agency.

England. The Sephardi community was the first to coordinate its charity work in England and established its Board of Guardians in 1837. In 1966 the name was changed to the Spanish and Portuguese Synagogue Jewish Welfare Board. This board acted independently of the Ashkenazi community and relied for its funds on a portion of the Finta (a tax levied on the class of membership known as Yehidim) and on donations, trust funds, and legacies.

In 1859 the Board of Guardians for the Relief of the Jewish Poor (renamed the Jewish Welfare Board in 1963) was established in London to coordinate charity work for the immigrant poor of the three oldest Ashkenazi congregations: the *Great Synagogue (1690), the Hambro (1706), and the New Synagogue (1761). To prevent poverty the Board immediately introduced new measures by granting loans to help poor Jews become self-supporting and by providing training for young Jews to work in handicrafts and industry. Conduct of the Board was gradually placed in the hands of professionally trained workers. The Board was subsequently called upon to supervise the work of a number of institutions, which in turn made subventions to it. Aid societies, the first of which was the East End Aid Society (1902), budgeted either all or part of their income to finance the Board's operations. In 1968 there were 15 such societies. Despite its efforts to achieve coordination on a total community level, the Board had not succeeded by the end of 1969 in securing the assent of the voluntary associations and the many institutions which conducted independent campaigns, to the establishment of a fully centralized metropolitan fund-raising and distributing agency, or a fund-raising and distributing agency on a national basis, as in France.

Germany. Founded in 1869, the *Deutsch-Israelitischer Gemeindebund (Union of German-Jewish Congregations) was Germany's first federated but not all-inclusive body devoted to advancing Jewish education and performing charitable work, combined with guidance and material support to its member congregations. While its revenues were basically derived from the taxes which the government required every Jew to pay for support of his congregation's religious, educational, and social programs, it also benefited from private donations, etc. Simultaneously, Unterstuetzungsvereine (aid societies) and institutions raised funds and individual contributions for their special projects. World War I reduced the capability of the German Jewish community to give adequate aid to its members and to refugees from East European lands. Inflation wiped out the fortunes of many wealthy contributors, income from congregational taxes was reduced by 50%, and the coffers of the benevolent societies and institutions were emptied. Aid by the American Jewish Joint Distribution Committee (JDC) was forthcoming but limited by its commitments elsewhere. To meet the crisis, the Zentralwohlfahrtstelle (Central Welfare Office) was established in 1917 as a roof organization covering many but not all social welfare agencies, voluntary associations, and institutions. Substantial savings resulted nevertheless from elimination of duplication in services and competition in fund raising. Following coordination, there were larger grants from synagogue tax funds (e.g. in 1926, 52% of the total congregational budgets in Berlin was allocated to charity and education) and greater contributions from individuals, institutions, and associations.

Hitler's rise to power in 1933 altered the situation drastically. The *Reichsvertretung der deutschen Juden ("National Committee of German Jews"), formed in 1933, founded the Zentralausschuss fuer Hilfe und Aufbau ("Central Committee for Relief and Reconstruction"), as an all-embracing welfare organization, but the sharply reduced capacity of German Jewry to support its work is indicated by its revenue for 1936, namely $1,287,500 of which $737,500 came from JDC and other welfare agencies.

In 1938 the congregations which had been a primary source of funds were deprived of their privileges as public, legal corporations with authority to tax their members for upkeep of religious requirements, education, and social welfare, and were denied the tax exemption previously enjoyed by all religious institutions. Voluntary membership dues and donations were their only source of income. Moreover, with emigration of the affluent and increasingly vast requirements for relief and emigration, the congregations rapidly lost their capability to share significantly in bearing the communal burden. In 1938, both in Germany and occupied Austria, $12,000,000 was spent on relief and emigration; a large share came from foreign Jewish sources and the remainder from the sale of communal and institutional property. In 1939 the Reichsvertretung der deutschen Juden was compelled to change its name to Reichsvertretung der Juden in Deutschland and the government decree of July 4, 1939 forced upon it the responsibility, among others, for expediting emigration and providing social welfare assistance, a responsibility it bore until 1941, with the greatest difficulty despite help from JDC which was permitted to carry on its relief and emigration work during this tragic period. The relief, rehabilitation, and emigration of the remnants of German Jews in the concentration camps after World War II, and of other displaced persons, were made possible by foreign agencies.

In the late 1960s there were approximately 38,000 Jews in the Federal German Republic and West Berlin. A central welfare office in Frankfort handled the requests for help of the very few needy ones.

Russia. In August 1914, a coordinated fund-raising body, Yekopo (Yevreiski Komitet Pomoshchi Zhertvam Voiny; "Jewish Committee for the Relief of War Sufferers") was formed in St. Petersburg (Leningrad) to bring relief to Russian Jews, mainly those forcibly evacuated from the front areas to the Russian interior. In its first three years of operation it raised 32,000,000 rubles through contributions from 300 communities which taxed their members, individual donations, government subsidies, and in later years through assistance from JDC. With these funds it aided 250,000 Jews and, before ceasing its operations in 1921, had raised and spent over 50 million rubles to provide for the needs of most of Russia's charity-supported 1.5 million Jews such as health services, social and economic assistance, educational programs for children, homes for refugees, and support of institutions. Yekopo cooperated with *ORT and *OSE in many of their endeavours. Yekopo ceased to exist in Soviet Russia in 1921, but a branch office functioned in Vilna until 1924. [M.M.B.]

United States. The promise made to Peter Stuyvesant by the first boatload of 23 Jews who arrived at New Amsterdam in 1654, that they would care for their own poor, meant simply that they would act as did the other religious denominations in the village. The charitable activities of the few American Jews during the 17th, 18th, and early 19th centuries were centered in the synagogues. They consisted of the maintenance of cemeteries, aid to transients and a few needy local cases, and the freeing of Jewish redemptioners and indentured servants. The few known instances of Palestinian emissaries *(meshullaḥim)* visiting the colonies and the early republic exemplify aid to Jews overseas. The first charitable institution was the Hebrew Orphan Asylum of Charleston, South Carolina, established in 1802.

During the German Jewish immigration of the mid-19th century, the scope of Jewish charity expanded and became structurally separate from the synagogue. Almost every local community had a Hebrew Relief Society or Hebrew Benevolent Society and a feminine counterpart. Fraternal orders like B'nai B'rith, Brith Abraham, and Kesher shel Barzel provided scheduled assistance to ill or bereaved members and their families. Several institutions, such as B'nai B'rith's Jewish Orphan Asylum in Cleveland, reached beyond local boundaries, and there were occasional appeals for emergency aid in the U.S., and for overseas Jewry, especially from Sir Moses *Montefiore; but before 1900 Jewish philanthropy was local.

The great historic coincidence was the encounter of the European Jewish tradition with the American idea of voluntarism. Early observers of the American scene commented on a distinctive characteristic of Americans, that voluntary groups take into their hands the creation of voluntary organizations to meet their own needs. Jewish communal traditions of autonomy and mutual assistance found fertile soil for growth in American voluntarism.

The great underlying force which created the distinctive American Jewish philanthropy was large-scale immigration from Eastern Europe. Beginning in the 1880s the immigrants coming in the tens of thousands yearly, with their special needs and their problems of adjustment to American life, molded American Jewish philanthropy. Its institutional structure derives from the expansion of earlier charitable organizations and the establishment of new ones. Thus, the numerous local Hebrew Relief Societies raised and spent far more money than earlier, and one by one changed their name to Jewish Social Service Association (or Bureau), reflecting the greater refinement and professionalization of their operations.

The American impulse toward efficiency and the Jewish conviction of communal responsibility coalesced disparate and often rival institutions into combined effort. This began with the establishment of the first Jewish philanthropic federation in Boston in 1895. It was a strikingly simple concept: funds would be raised and disbursed jointly to the agencies to meet the needs. The agencies invariably supported by federations included services to families and children, hospitals, free loans, settlement houses, and sundry aid groups. Jewish philanthropic federations were established in most American Jewish communities; New York City's was the largest and one of the last to be established, in 1917.

The few local agencies in the first federations joined on the common platform of efficiency in fund raising and coordination of local services. But the federation idea contained seeds of future development. The early federations began rudimentary social planning for the Jewish community, designed to explore the need for new services and old ones which could be dispensed with. The founding and expansion of federations occurred during a period of professionalization of the art of helping and the emergence of social work as a new profession. Jewish social workers provided the professional skills for the expansion of services. During its existence from 1927 to 1936, the Graduate School for Jewish Social Work in New York City trained professional social workers for service in the Jewish community.

The National Conference of Jewish Social Service (later Welfare), founded in 1899, became the professional organization. Professional journals were published, beginning with *Jewish Charities* (1910) and progressing to the *Journal of Jewish Communal Service* (1956). The National Conference of Jewish Charities, established in 1900, became the Council of Jewish Federations and Welfare Funds in 1932, providing planning and statistical data and recommendations.

The "Great Depression" of the 1930s marked a watershed in American philanthropic history. The magnitude of impoverishment forced the government into granting material relief, and the voluntary agencies gave up this function. The 1920s and 1930s witnessed severe disputes between pro-Zionist advocates of higher alloca-

Table 1. Amounts Raised in Central Jewish Campaigns (except small cities without welfare funds; includes multiple gifts).

Year	Amount (in millions of $ U.S.).
1945	57.3
1946	131.7
1947	157.8
1948	205.0
1949	161.0
1950	142.1
1951	136.0
1952	121.2
1953	117.2
1954	109.3
1955	110.6
1956	131.3
1957	139.0
1958	124.1
1959	130.7
1960	127.5
1961	126.0
1962	129.4
1963	124.7
1964	126.7
1965	132.6
1966	137.3
1967 regular	146.0
Israel emergency	173.0
1968 regular	153.2
Israel emergency	83.0
1969 regular	164.9
Israel emergency	103.0

Source: *American Jewish Year Book* 71 (1970), p. 292.

tions to Palestine, and non- or anti-Zionists dominating the Joint Distribution Committee and providing most of the funds, whose views prevailed that most of the money go to European relief and to projects in Soviet Russia. Yet it was during the 1930s that the scope of organized Jewish philanthropy expanded both geographically and functionally. As the world emergency grew with the rise of Nazism, disparate agencies aiding Jews were brought together in the *United Jewish Appeal and subsequently made the desperate condition of East European Jewry the dominant cause in local campaigns of Jewish federations. After 1941, the European Holocaust and the struggle of Israel brought about ever closer agreement on the allocation of funds overseas. At the same time most federations broadened to include within organized Jewish philanthropy the support of Jewish education, community relations activities, Jewish vocational services, and national agencies that served the entire American Jewish community. New York City remained the exception and maintained a separate Federation and United Jewish Appeal. This period's expansion of the budgeting and planning activities of local federations necessitated constant assessment of priorities, and required decisions on new programs.

At the close of World War II in 1945, when the full dimensions of the European Holocaust were revealed, American Jewish philanthropy faced its greatest challenge—to provide the vast sums required to rescue the survivors and to build up the Jewish state for the redemption of the Jewish people. It responded with funds unequaled in the history of philanthropy anywhere.

In 1946 the United Jewish Appeal raised approximately $100 million, in 1948, $150 million, in addition to approximately $31,265,000 and $43.6 million in the respective years for the needs of the larger federations. Between 1939 and 1968 the United Jewish Appeal raised $2,035 billion for Israel and overseas Jewry, largely through allocations from combined campaigns in local Jewish communities throughout the United States.

The Federation's role broadened to the point where it was widely recognized as "the organized Jewish community." Philanthropy began to serve as the organizing principle for the voluntary Jewish community, especially in cities where the federations and Jewish community councils merged during the 1950s and conducted a single campaign for local, national, and overseas needs. Debate mounted during the 1960s over the proper proportion of local funds to be divided among hospitals, social services, and recreational institutions on one hand and Jewish educational and cultural services on the other. In 1968 the range of concerns stretched across the spectrum of local, national, and international Jewish needs, ranging from services to the individual and family to programs designed to insure the survival of Judaism. The dollar figures reflect the vastness of scope. In 1969 the annual campaigns of Jewish federations totaled $266 million (including $104 million in the Israel Emergency Fund). In addition approximately $40 million were raised in endowment and capital funds campaigns.

Not all of American Jewish philanthropic endeavor in 1969 was within the federation orbit. Substantial groups remained outside either from choice or tradition; in 1969 these groups raised approximately $100 million. They included institutions of higher learning, many national agencies, pro-Israel organizations and others, but not synagogues which collected and disbursed millions of dollars annually themselves.

The funds allocated by federations represented only a fraction of the money disbursed by the agencies which receive them. In addition, these agencies' expenditures derived from other sources of income: dues; tuition; fees; and various governmental bodies and third-party payments. Therefore, the Jewish gross national philanthropic product, inclusive of all of these funds, was substantially in excess of a billion dollars in 1969.

Contemporary philanthropic services under Jewish auspices utilized the highest professional skills of American society in medicine, social work, public relations, and other areas. The collection and disbursement of funds to support these services was elevated to a high art by the Jewish group in the U.S. Concepts of fund raising became sophisticated and efforts were skillfully elaborated to raise maximum sums. The result, however, was ultimately based on

Table 2. The Distribution of Federation Funds Collected in the U.S. (in thousands of $U.S.).

				National							
Year	Total Budget	United Jewish Appeal[1]	Other Overseas[2]	Community Relations[3]	Health and Welfare[4]	Cultural[7]	Religious[6]	Service Agencies[5]	Local Operating Needs	Local Refugee Care[8]	Local Capital Needs
1949	144,935,	91,078	3,491	5,426	171	351	304	1,139	22,727	4,131	16,117
1950	117,257	77,960	2,567	4,817	161	331	286	1,049	22,512	5,370	2,204
1951	110,918	72,099	2,748	2,500	225	417	527	1,188	24,085	4,560	2,561
1952	99,420	60,086	2,607	2,477	193	401	400	1,094	25,838	3,380	2,944
1953	96,882	58,197	2,448	2,553	163	424	399	1,167	27,371	2,376	1,804
1954	89,592	51,351	2,244	2,383	127	461	359	1,084	28,124	1,869	1,570
1955	88,810	51,687	2,313	2,441	114	403	354	1,109	27,473	1,486	1,423
1956	107,806	68,741	2,624	2,603	102	393	378	1,164	29,046	1,269	1,481
1957	115,658	74,986	3,005	2,641	92	388	343	1,169	30,196	1,219	1,614
1958	100,119	59,903	2,903	2,554	70	399	338	1,134	30,504	896	1,413
1959	105,382	63,168	2,940	2,687	70	417	356	1,169	32,185	807	1,581
1960	103,373	59,270	2,908	2,743	72	460	371	1,164	34,376	622	1,383
1961	102,056	57,116	2,925	2,669	60	454	341	1,161	35,285	599	1,443
1962	105,481	59,437	2,953	2,359	51	483	314	1,218	36,570	728	1,363
1963	101,402	55,618	2,743	2,343	50	461	309	1,177	36,561	708	1,430
1964	102,695	55,742	2,724	2,372	45	458	296	1,219	37,557	668	1,615
1965	107,598	58,606	2,858	2,448	46	479	287	1,231	39,411	686	1,538
1966	111,618	60,582	2,934	2,479	36	491	277	1,294	41,216	875	1,425
1967	115,832	63,026	3,075	2,529	24	508	254	1,390	42,752	686	1,586
1968	122,869	66,044	3,098	2,658	23	552	275	1,379	46,453	657	1,727

Footnotes as for Table 3.

Table 3. Receipts of National Jewish Agencies Reporting to the Council of Jewish Federations and Welfare Funds ($U.S.).

Year	UJA and Beneficiaries[1]	Other Overseas[2]	Total Overseas	Community Relations[3]	Health and Welfare[4]	National Service[5]	Religious[6]	Cultural[7]	Total Domestic	Total
1947	125,000,000	17,728,572	142,728,572	7,328,422	3,539,638	1,478,338	5,022,931	2,027,733	19,397,062	162,125,634
1948	150,000,000	22,475,548	172,475,458	7,772,570	3,230,083	1,690,785	4,965,414	3,478,201	21,137,053	193,612,511
1949	103,000,000	18,927,529	121,927,529	6,529,990	3,358,913	3,554,843	5,983,527	1,598,700	21,025,973	142,953,502
1950	93,019,734	16,879,621	109,899,355	5,909,284	3,625,981	1,478,879	6,836,345	2,499,781	20,350,270	130,249,625
1951	83,552,746	18,011,843	101,564,589	5,889,625	2,240,803	1,377,644	7,073,532	4,010,378	20,591,982	122,156,571
1952	72,334,513	17,763,765	90,098,278	5,642,016	2,434,278	1,337,955	7,316,401	3,661,664	20,392,314	110,490,592
1953	65,832,585	16,012,816	83,845,401	5,700,029	6,032,275	1,411,833	8,191,577	6,998,543	28,334,257	112,179,658
1954	51,424,801	18,212,223	69,637,024	5,665,790	6,688,511	1,425,080	8,970,749	7,966,099	30,716,229	100,353,253
1955	62,028,008	17,960,941	79,988,949	5,988,631	6,894,768	1,456,399	11,078,645	8,820,488	34,238,931	114,227,880
1956	73,897,635	18,734,827	92,632,462	6,271,358	8,813,445	1,490,096	15,005,417	10,434,681	42,014,997	134,647,459
1957	76,316,727	21,502,050	97,818,777	6,772,872	9,761,888	1,505,811	16,330,227	11,170,933	45,541,731	143,360,508
1958	59,171,932	22,786,664	81,958,596	6,915,222	9,838,873	1,521,878	21,109,621	13,167,882	52,553,476	134,512,072
1959	71,922,329	24,475,275	96,397,604	7,470,773	10,444,532	1,679,735	22,954,902	15,625,720	58,175,662	154,573,266
1960	64,054,208	24,762,251	88,816,459	7,510,730	12,378,479	1,662,065	24,040,283	17,563,600	63,155,157	151,971,616
1961	66,899,301	27,388,487	94,287,788	7,738,003	11,450,946	1,725,792	27,075,943	18,255,217	66,245,901	160,533,689
1962	68,505,849	28,107,797	96,613,646	8,442,696	12,518,525	1,756,176	33,796,041	21,856,629	78,369,967	174,983,613
1963	65,154,388	26,253,929	91,408,317	9,302,218	13,733,478	1,789,268	41,368,489	24,324,479	90,517,932	181,926,249
1964	65,787,077	26,333,641	92,120,718	10,043,750	36,672,088	1,872,405	26,614,894	31,445,012	106,648,149	198,768,867
1965	71,741,811	30,877,707	102,619,518	11,099,684	43,178,698	2,078,427	29,076,142	33,313,613	118,746,564	221,366,082
1966	69,675,850	31,492,151	101,168,001	11,918,970	48,116,964	2,199,673	23,314,580	45,093,010	130,643,197	231,811,198
1967	244,202,209	39,258,846	283,461,145	12,834,012	59,574,731	2,461,439	24,710,552	46,508,744	146,089,478	429,550,623
1968	131,082,279	42,709,976	173,792,255	14,231,993	77,265,782	2,501,311	21,646,933	53,402,826	169,048,845	342,841,100
1969	162,273,145	46,792,677	209,065,822	15,314,404	85,720,675	2,692,465	25,026,481	73,085,863	201,839,888	410,905,710

Source: *American Year Book,* 1948–1970 *passim.*
1 Beneficiaries include: Israel Education Fund, Joint Distribution Committee, New York Association for New Americans, ORT, et al.
2 Institutions of Higher Education in Israel, Hadassah, United HIAS Service, et al.
3 American Jewish Committee, Anti-Defamation League, Jewish Labor Committee, et al.
4 City of Hope, Leo N. Levi Memorial Hospital, Albert Einstein College of Medicine and Hospital, et al.
5 American Association for Jewish Education, National Jewish Welfare Board, et al.
6 Seminaries, yeshivot, national congregational associations.
7 B'nai B'rith Youth Service Appeal, Brandeis and Yeshiva universities, Jewish Publication Society, Zionist Organization of America, et al.
8 Local services of HIAS and NYANA.

fundamental Jewish commitments to philanthropy and the growing affluence and homogeneity of the Jewish population which made possible a broad consensus on the needs.

One of the distinctive Jewish contributions to philanthropy in America was the recognition that federated fund raising produced greater results for all participants. The general community also recognized this and the Community Chest movement used the Jewish Federation as its model.

Fund-raising goals were raised by the continuous education of the Jewish community to the dimensions of the needs and their responsibility to meet them. The capstone of the structure resides in the development of the responsibility of leaders. Achievements in the philanthropic campaigns have been based on the willingness of leadership to elevate the levels of giving by setting the pace through their own contributions. When this "leadership by example" takes place, matching contributions follow. In this way the Jewish group has demonstrated that it can implement its high ethical imperatives with pragmatic programs. [CH.Z.]

Canada. The first central fund-raising campaigns in Canada were conducted in 1917–18 by *Montreal's Federation of Jewish Philanthropies (renamed the Federation of Jewish Community Services and the Allied Jewish Community Services) and by *Toronto's Federation of Jewish Philanthropies (now known as the United Jewish Welfare Fund of Toronto). Funds at that time were raised exclusively for local social welfare, health, and recreational services (Jewish centers and children's camps). In 1937–38 the United Jewish Welfare Fund of Toronto began to campaign also for local Jewish education, the national work of the Canadian Jewish Congress and the Jewish Immigrant Aid Society ("HIAS"), as well as for the operations of a number of overseas agencies, including those in Ereẓ Israel.

In 1951 the United Israel Appeal and UJRA of the Canadian Jewish Congress combined their fund-raising activities in the United Jewish Appeal which then joined with the welfare funds in Toronto, Montreal, and other communities for raising funds in which they were to share. For this purpose Toronto and several other communities adopted the name of the United Jewish Appeal, and Montreal called its campaign the Combined Jewish Appeal.

Argentina. The Ashkenazi Ḥebra Kadisha ("The Holy Society"), founded strictly as a burial society in 1892, had evolved by 1949 into the Buenos Aires Kehillah, the central communal body. In 1956, it was renamed the Asociasión Mutual Israelita Argentina-Communidad de Buenos Aires (briefly AMIA) which became the community's central fund-raising and distributing agency, financing nearly all its religious, social, and cultural activities. Half its 1967 budget of $2,350,000 was devoted to support Buenos Aires' Jewish educational system, in which 60% of the pupils were children of parents who paid low dues and were not enrolled in AMIA's membership of 42,000. Its main income, however, came from the sale of burial plots in its cemetery over which it had exclusive control. While always generous in serving the needy, AMIA demanded of the wealthy what they could afford to pay and in the case of individuals who had failed in their obligation to support the community its demands were extremely high.

Israel. In the State of Israel with its state financing of religious needs (of all denominations) as well as its social services as an evolving welfare state, fund raising of the usual Jewish Diaspora type became marginal. In 1970 there was no central local or national fund-raising body in Israel, with the result that much costly overlapping and duplication occurred in fund-raising campaigns. The Tel Aviv Council of Social Agencies, a consultative body, and the Israel Fund Raisers' Association in 1969 undertook, but without success, to coordinate the separate fund-raising efforts along the lines followed in Western communities.

Fund Raising by International Organizations. The traditional concern and sense of responsibility of Jews for the well-being of their people wherever they dwell prompted them in modern times to establish organizations which devoted themselves on an international level to one or more of the following activities: (1) seeking emancipation of Jews or protecting their rights; (2) helping them to overcome their economic and social plight by building schools for educating their children and training them vocationally, and giving immediate relief in grave situations; (3) facilitating their emigration when they suffered persecution from pogroms and insurmountable poverty.

The outstanding international organizations founded in the mid-19th century were the *Alliance Israélite Universelle, the *Anglo-Jewish Association, the *Israelitische Allianz zu Wien, and the *Hilfsverein der deutschen Juden.

The Alliance Israélite Universelle organized committees in Western Europe and the United States and later in the local communities where it carried out its programs as well as in Jewish communities in other parts of the world. With the help of these committees it raised funds through dues or annual subscriptions, special appeals for donations, trusts, legacies, and endowments. For nearly four decades the principal sources of support were Baron Maurice de *Hirsch and his wife, Baroness Clara. The Alliance received from the baron 4,595 shares (at £100 per share) of the capital stock of the *Jewish Colonization Association (ICA) which entitled it to a voice in the direction of ICA's program, but these funds were used only for the work of ICA.

The *Anglo-Jewish Association (London, 1871) adopted aims similar to those of the Alliance Israélite Universelle. Its income came from dues, donations, trust funds, legacies, endowments, and earnings from an annual ball.

Four dominant organizations established in Europe set themselves one specific goal in their service to deprived, sick, or oppressed Jews. *ORT (St. Petersburg, 1880, with headquarters subsequently in Berlin, 1921, where it became the World Ort Union; Paris, 1933; and Geneva, 1943), directed its efforts initially to rehabilitating and retraining Russia's impoverished Jewish masses.

The Russo-Jewish Committee for Relief of Jewish Refugees (London, 1882) was organized to deal with the large-scale influx of immigrants after the outbreak of pogroms in 1881 and the May Day Laws of 1882. The Committee required funds for settling a number of refugees in England and making it possible for a larger number to migrate to the United States and Canada. Other funds were raised by the Russo-Jewish Committee in cooperation with the Board of Jewish Guardians to deal with immigrants who settled in London. In 1891, with the outbreak of pogroms in Russia, funds especially raised for immigrant work were virtually exhausted. Another meeting was convened at the Guildhall and $486,000 were donated to be used primarily but not exclusively for sending Jews westward, ICA provided additional resources to assist the Russo-Jewish Relief Committee, principally for the resettlement of immigrants in countries on both the North and South American continents. From 1890 to 1905 funds were raised for immigrants fleeing from famine in Galicia in 1890, economic and social restrictions in Rumania in the early 1890s, and from pogroms in Russia in 1903 and 1905, but a year later when the Alien Act of 1905 went into effect, England ceased to be a transient center for mass Jewish immigration and activity on behalf of immigrants was limited almost exclusively to help those who had reached English shores to be absorbed into the economic and cultural life of the United Kingdom.

The Jewish Health Society *OSE (St. Petersburg, 1912) moved its central committee to Berlin in 1922, where it was connected with ORT, embracing committees established in Berlin and London (1920) and in other communities in 1921 and 1922; Paris, 1934, and Geneva, 1943, and returned to Paris after World War II. It was founded to promote the health of Russian Jews by using preventive medical measures and giving instructions in hygiene, but was forced by the Soviet government in 1919 to liquidate its work in Russia. After World War I, it extended its work to Poland (where the organization was called TOZ), Lithuania, Latvia, and Rumania, and secured additional support from its branches in those countries and from supporting committees which it established in a number of countries, but the largest measure of aid came from JDC.

The *Central British Fund for German Jewry (since 1944, the Central British Fund for Jewish Rehabilitation and Relief) was organized in London in 1933 to raise funds to help German Jews meet the crisis in Nazi Germany. It engaged in operations to help them emigrate and reestablish themselves in England, Palestine, and other countries open to immigration. From 1933 to 1935 the fund campaigned under its own name; from 1936 to 1939 as the Council for German Jewry; from 1940 to 1943 as the Central Council for Jewish Refugees; and from 1939 to 1943 again under the original name of the Central British Fund for German Jewry.

In 1944, the Central British Fund became the Central British Fund for Jewish Relief and Rehabilitation extending its help to destitute Jewish communities in Italy and Greece, and made use of radio and television as well as other publicity media to bring its appeal to the community.

Organizations which devoted themselves to one specific area of service but did not conduct independent campaigns for their work included: (1) Emig-direkt (Berlin, 1921, the United Committee for Jewish Emigration) which was organized by the World Relief Conference (Carlsbad, 1920; this organization raised limited funds for relief and reconstruction work in Central, Eastern, and Southeastern Europe), and HIAS. Emig-direkt drew its major financial support from JDC, ICA, and other organizations. It was succeeded by (2) *HICEM (Paris, 1927, a name formed from the initials of the three agencies which established it, HIAS, ICA, and Emig-direkt, the last of which associated itself in 1934). HICEM gave assistance to Jews emigrating from Europe and found places for them in various countries. (3) American Joint Reconstruction Foundation (1924), a joint operation of JDC and ICA for economic rehabilitation of Jews in Central and Eastern Europe through provision of loans and other constructive measures. Also treated as an American organization is Agro-Joint (American Jewish Joint Agricultural Corporation, created by JDC in 1924 and liquidated in 1951) for resettlement of Jewish tradesmen and businessmen declassed by the Soviet government in agricultural colonies in Crimea and the Ukraine.

Old Type Fund Collection for Ereẓ Israel. On the international level, old-type emissaries and fund collectors for Ereẓ Israel were known as *meshullaḥim* (see *Sheliḥei Ereẓ Israel).

The excessive costs in the employment of *meshullaḥim* and their uneconomic use in Palestine of the funds collected by them have been reported on exhaustively (Proceedings of the U.S. National Conference of Jewish Charities, Cleveland, 1912). The costs were not less than those which had prevailed in earlier centuries. Some communities accepted responsibility for collecting the funds themselves. After the establishment of the State of Israel in 1948 the number of old-type fund-raising emissaries fell to a vanishing point. The state's program for social welfare, health, education, and social security and the supplementary services of such agencies as the Jewish Agency, Hadassah, WIZO, Histadrut, Moeẓet Ha-Poalot, Malben-JDC, and others drastically reduced the need for old-type fund raising for Ereẓ

Israel's philanthropic needs. The few *meshullaḥim* now turned their efforts chiefly to capital fund raising for new buildings and expansion of their programs. Many local committees abroad continued to collect funds for maintenance of yeshivot, *talmud torahs*, orphanages, homes for the aged, hospitals, and other institutions and sent their collections directly to the institutions in Israel. Other committees abandoned their fund raising in return for an allocation to their institutions by a community welfare fund agency. JDC, which is a partner in the *United Jewish Appeal, for some years made a sizable allocation through its Cultural Committee for Israel Institutions in Jerusalem for the support of yeshivot in Israel, refugee rabbis, scholars, and their dependents. It has also subsidized various research and publication projects on biblical and talmudic subjects. In 1969 JDC spent close to one million dollars to aid 132 yeshivot in Israel with an enrollment of over 18,000 students. The charity box (*kuppah* of mishnaic origin) and the charity plate *(ke'arah)* were still in use in modern times. It was reported that in 1900 there were more than 250,000 *ḥalukkah* boxes bearing the name of Rabbi *Meir Baal ha-Nes in homes, synagogues, and communal gathering places. From it evolved in the Zionist era the most widely used box in the Jewish world: the Jewish National Fund blue box for land purchase in Palestine (later, in Israel) which was introduced after the founding of the JNF in 1901.

Zionist and Modern Israel Fund Raising. The *Bilu, organized in the 1880s by a group of young Russian Jewish students committed to pioneer and settle on the land in Palestine, made the first modern effort to raise funds for Zionist purposes. They succeeded in establishing 25 branches with a total of 525 members, but achieved very little success in fund raising which depended on membership dues, earnings from literary and musical evenings, and meager donations.

The Ḥovevei Zion ("Lovers of Zion"; Russia, 1882), members of the *Ḥibbat Zion movement, met relatively greater but not startling success in fund raising. The Ḥovevei Zion organized societies—first in Russia and Poland and later in Germany, England, and the United States—to help existing settlements and establish new ones in Palestine. Their membership consisted of middle-class and poor Jews and was not able to provide large sums; some sold their belongings to add to the funds which would make possible their own settlement in Palestine. The Ḥovevei Zion collected dues, canvassed for donations in homes and shops, and when permitted by the few not antagonistic rabbis made appeals in the synagogues. Wherever possible they collected funds in the synagogue, on the eve of the Day of Atonement and the Ninth of Av. They established congregations of their own where they were free to propagate their ideas and raise funds but fared no better than the Bilu in their efforts to persuade wealthy Jews to support their cause. The situation improved through the intercession of Rabbi Samuel *Mohilever, founder of the first Ḥibbat Zion movement in Warsaw, and after Baron Edmund de *Rothschild began to provide funds on a munificent scale to save struggling older settlements. Some of these had been founded by Ḥovevei Zion and new ones were organized. In 1890 came another favorable turn for the Ḥibbat Zion movement when the Russian government gave its approval for the formation of a society for the support of Jewish tillers of the soil and artisans in Syria and Palestine (see *Odessa Committee), a step that made it easier to get some help from those who had been concerned about supporting the illegal movement.

It was not until the 1890s that the Ḥovevei Zion was able to win the support and leadership of men of status in England like Elim *d'Avigdor, who in 1891 joined the Ḥibbat Zion movement and became its head; his kinsman Colonel A. E. W. *Goldsmid, who succeeded him in the leadership, and others, among them Reverend Simeon *Singer, Sir Joseph *Sebag-Montefiore, and Lord *Swaythling. These men who contributed themselves were able to persuade other well-placed people to do so.

The Jewish National Fund (Keren Kayemet le-Israel), the *World Zionist Organization's first instrumentality for fund raising, was founded in Basle in 1901 by the Fifth World *Zionist Congress. It was created to raise funds for the purchase of land in Palestine and its development for settlement and agriculture. In its first decade the J.N.F. introduced the blue box for coin collections in homes, synagogues, and wherever Jews met publicly; the Golden Book in Jerusalem for inscription of the names of men and women in return for specific contributions or of individuals in whose honor contributions were given; stamps, of which there have been over 4,000 varieties, sold for use on letters, synagogue tickets, contracts documents, and even used for postage in Israel immediately before the State of Israel postal system was established in 1948; and flags, tags, and flowers which contributors received as gifts on special occasions. The "sale" of trees for planting in Israel has proved to be one of the J.N.F.'s most productive fund-raising methods. The *Keren Hayesod-*United Appeal was created in London in July 1920 at a Zionist conference convened by Chaim Weizmann to raise funds for the World Zionist Organization. The Zionist Executive and later the Jewish Agency Executive were responsible for the conduct of the activities generally performed by states, including security, until the founding of the State of Israel in 1948, when the operations of the Jewish Agency were limited chiefly to immigration, absorption, and settlement. The Keren Hayesod, which had first functioned directly under the aegis of the World Zionist Organization, became the financial arm of the Jewish Agency in 1929 with the formation of the enlarged Jewish Agency which included non-Zionists as members. At one time there were branches in 70 countries, and in 1970 owing to political changes in certain countries, there were 54, but this number did not include the U.S. where UJA campaigned independently of the Keren Hayesod.

In the years between 1920 and 1948 total Keren Hayesod UJA income in the United States amounted to $143,000,000, of which UJA raised 70% and Keren Hayesod 30%. From 1948 to 1970, both organizations raised $1,990,000,000 of which 65% came through UJA and 35% from other countries through Keren Hayesod.

Other fund raising for Israel was conducted by various organizations such as WIZO and the *Histadrut (General Federation of Labor, Israel).

Fund raising was also done in Diaspora countries by Israel schools of higher learning, yeshivot, hospitals, general health and social welfare agencies, orchestras, museums, and many other groups. The principal schools of higher learning in Israel, namely, the Hebrew University, Technion (the Israel Institute of Technology), Tel Aviv University and Bar-Ilan University, and the Weizmann Institute of Science do their fund raising through societies of friends or committees set up for this purpose.

*Magen David Adom ("Red Shield of David," Tel Aviv, 1930) is Israel's equivalent of the Red Cross. It meets its own maintenance and operating costs with income from an annual lottery and from subsidies from the government of Israel and local authorities, which together provided from 15 to 16% of its budget.

Support from societies of friends, committees, and individuals in many countries took the form of contributions in kind (ambulances, medical supplies, and equipment) and contributions in cash for Magen David Adom's building program, which envisaged completion of 17 new structures early in the 1970s.

The Modern Campaigns and Their Goals. There are various kinds of major fund-raising campaigns all of which are conducted annually, except for the biennial campaigns of the Israel United Appeal and the United Communal Fund in South Africa, which occur in alternate years. These include: (1) The independent campaign conducted by a communal federation or welfare fund for local social welfare agencies, other local institutions, and at times also certain national organizations. The goals for these campaigns are set by the local federation or welfare fund. (2) The independent campaign conducted by authorized representative local committees on behalf of national or international organizations (Keren Hayesod, Jewish National Fund, WIZO, ORT, Histadrut, and others). The goals set for an independent campaign in a community are determined by agreement between the authorized committees located in a country and the national or international organizations. The time of year to be devoted to the independent campaign is decided upon after consultation between the local federation or welfare fund and the local committee representing the national or international body. In Australian communities the Board of Jewish Deputies allots appropriate periods to various national or international campaigns. (3) The combined campaigns for local, national, Israel, and overseas needs conducted by local federations and welfare funds or through their fund-raising agencies (e.g., United Jewish Appeal in Toronto, Combined Jewish Appeal in Montreal). The principal parties to these campaigns are the local federations or welfare funds and the Keren Hayesod. Allocations to national organizations and overseas agencies are made upon application. The goal is set by the local fund-raising body in consultation with the national committee representing the Keren Hayesod acting for the Jewish Agency (in Canada the national committee is the United Israel Appeal of Canada, Inc.), after taking into account the allocations to be granted to other beneficiaries whose applications have been approved. (4) The Joint Campaign which is limited strictly to Israel's needs, conducted in Great Britain and Ireland (Joint Palestine Appeal–JPA) and in Israel (United Appeal in Israel–Ha-Magbit ha-Me'uḥedet be-Yisrael). Partners in these campaigns are the Keren Hayesod and the Jewish National Fund. In the JPA campaign, a limited number of allocations to other Zionist fund-raising agencies is made by the Keren Hayesod from its share. The campaign goal is set after consultation between the administrative committee of JPA in London and the Keren Hayesod, the Jewish Agency, and the Jewish National Fund head offices in Jerusalem. For the Israel Joint campaign the goal is set by the two partners (the Keren Hayesod and the J.N.F.) and neither makes any allocation to any other agency. [M.M.B.]

Bibliography: GENERAL: B. D. Bogen, *Jewish Philanthropy* (1917), 38–58; E. Frisch, *A Historical Survey of Jewish Philanthropy* (1924); I. Abrahams, *Jewish Life in the Middle Ages* (1932[2]), ch. xvii–xviii; Baron, Social, 3 vols. (1937), index s.v. *Charity;* Baron, Community, 2 (1942), 290–350; C. Roth, *Jewish Contribution to Civilization* (1938), ch. on "Charity" 287–315; Elbogen, Century, index s.v. *Philanthropy;* I. Chipkin, in: L. Finkelstein (ed.), *The Jews, their History, Cult and Religion,* 2 (1949), 713–44. COUNTRIES: ARGENTINE: J. X. Cohen, *Jewish Life in South America* (1941); J. Shatzky, *Communidades Judías en Latinoamerica* (1952); AJYB, 69 (1968), 394–404. CANADA: L. Rosenberg, *Two Centuries of Jewish Life in Canada 1760–1960* (=AJYB vol. 62, 1961); F. Hutner, *Fund Raising in Canada* (1969). ENGLAND: L. Wolf, *Essays on Jewish History,* ed. by C. Roth (1934); C. Roth, *The Great Synagogue London 1690–1940* (1950); V. D. Lipman, *Social History of the Jews in England 1850–1950* (1954), index; idem, *A Century of Social Service 1859–1959* (1959), index; S. D. Temkin, in: AJYB, 58 (1957), 3–63. FRANCE: L. Berman, *Histoire des Juifs de France* (1937); L. Kahn, *Histoire des écoles communales et consistoriales israélites de Paris (1809–1884)* (1884); J. Kaplan, in: AJYB, 47 (1945/46), 71–118; 49 (1947/48), 319–22; Z. Szajkowski, *Analytical Franco-Jewish Gazetteer* (1966). GERMANY: J. R. Marcus, *Rise and Destiny of the German Jew* (1934), index; A. Ruppin, *Jewish Fate and Future* (1940), index; H. Schwab, *A World in Ruins* (1946). ITALY: Vogelstein-Rieger, passim; Roth, Italy, index s.v. *Charity.* PALESTINE AND ISRAEL: H. Szold, in: *National Conference of Jewish Charities, Proceedings* (1910–12); R. Gottheil et al., *ibid.;* A. Greenbaum, *The American Joint Distribution Committee and the Yeshivot in Israel* (1964). RUSSIA: L. Greenberg, *The Jews in Russia,* ed. by M. Wischnitzer, 1 (1944); 2 (1951), index; H. L. Sahsovich et al., in: *National Conference of Jewish Charities, Proceedings* (1908). U.S.: H. L. Lurie, *A Heritage Affirmed; the Jewish Federation Movement in America* (1961); R. Morris and M. Freund (eds.), *Trends and Issues in Jewish Social Welfare in the United States* (1966); S. P. Goldberg, *Jewish Communal Services* (1969); AJYB, passim. ORGANIZATIONS: See also articles on individual organizations. ALLIANCE ISRAÉLITE UNIVERSELLE: *Les Cahiers de l'Alliance Israélite Universelle,* esp. no. 168 (Jan. 1969). ANGLO-JEWISH ASSOCIATION: *Annual Report,* 13 no. 1 (March 1969). BILU: N. Sokolow, *Hibbath Zion* (Eng., 1935), ch. 42. BOARD OF GUARDIANS (Spanish and Portuguese Synagogue Jewish Welfare Board, London): *Report* (1969). BOARD OF GUARDIANS AND TRUSTEES FOR RELIEF OF THE JEWISH POOR, LONDON (Jewish Welfare Board, London): *Annual Report* (1968) and Letter, Public Relations Officer (Oct. 8, 1969). DEUTSCH-ISRAELITISCHER GEMEINDEBUND: Wilhelm, in: YLBI, 2 (1957), 61–63; Sandler, *ibid.,* 76–84. HEBREW UNIVERSITY: B. Cherrick, *Report on Fund Raising* (1969). HICEM: M. Wischnitzer, *Visas to Freedom. The History of Hias* (1956). HILFSVEREIN DER DEUTSCHEN JUDEN: Z. Szajkowski, in: JSOS, 13 (1951), 47–70; 19 (1957), 29–50; 22 (1960), 131–58. ḤOVEVEI ZION: A. M. Hyamson, *Palestine. The Rebirth of an Ancient Nation* (1917), 5–123.

°**PHILIP,** name of six kings of France. PHILIP II or PHILIP AUGUSTUS, king of France from 1180 to 1223. All Philip's biographers agree that he detested the Jews, an attitude formed by stories he had heard in his childhood about Jews murdering Christian children. Soon after his accession, he ordered the imprisonment of all the Jews in the kingdom, and it was only in exchange for a large ransom that they were set free. Early in April 1182, in order to bolster the treasury before going to war, Philip ordered the expulsion of the Jews from his kingdom; Jewish real estate was confiscated and most of it sold on behalf of the royal treasury; synagogues were converted into churches (as was the case in *Paris and *Orleans); and debtors were absolved of their obligations to Jews on condition that they paid the treasury one-fifth of the monies owed. The king persecuted the Jews even beyond the borders of his kingdom: in 1190 he attacked in *Champagne the Jewish community of *Bray-sur-Seine (or Brie-Comte-Robert), putting to death almost 100 persons. When he authorized the return of the Jews to his kingdom in 1198, it was for purely financial reasons. At the same time as he guaranteed the Jews freedom to trade with Christians by forbidding priests to excommunicate those Christians who dealt with them, he also initiated the practice of assigning an official seal to every locality which contained an important Jewish community, for the purpose of regulating loans. An ordinance of February 1219 prohibited any loan to persons whose only source of income was their own labor. This was an attempt to put a stop to loans taken for personal consumption only; previously loans of this type were granted if paid back in three annual sums. Loans offered against pledges were not subject to compulsory registration, but the list of articles which could not be accepted in pledge was extended to cover not only church appurtenances but also agricultural tools and beasts of burden.

PHILIP III THE BOLD, king from 1270 to 1285. Shortly after his accession, Philip followed the example of his father and predecessor, *Louis IX, and in 1271 ordered his officers to enforce the wearing of the Jewish *badge. His father's policy is again reflected in an ordinance, probably issued in 1272, which prohibited the Jews from engaging in all kinds of moneylending and directed them either to pursue permitted commercial activities or to work with their hands. If there were any attempts by Jews to engage in agricultural work or handicrafts, these were in any event doomed in practice from 1280 when Christians were forbidden to enter into their service. The most disastrous of Philip's decrees from the socioeconomic point of view was that issued in 1283, forbidding the Jews to reside in smaller places.

PHILIP IV THE FAIR, king from 1285 to 1314. The various changes in Philip's policy toward the Jews were all motivated by the sole purpose of furthering the interests of the monarchy and the kingdom. Thus, asserting royal power and challenging the Church, in 1288 he reminded his officers that the number of charges for which the Jews could be tried by the ecclesiastical courts was very limited and he called upon them not to collaborate in any unjustified prosecutions. However, on February 1291 he ordered the expulsion of all the Jewish exiles who had arrived from England and *Gascony: since they had been stripped of all their belongings before they arrived, the kingdom could not derive any profit from them. On April 1 of the same year, seeking to strengthen the economic status of the large towns, he renewed the order prohibiting the Jews to live in the small localities. As a step toward legal standardization, on September 23 he dismissed all the special judges of the Jews. He took action against Jewish moneylenders on Jan. 31, 1292, but only in order to expropriate the debts owed to them. When Philip decided to protect the Jews from extortion and hindrances in their trade, his measure applied to the Jews owned by the king, for he wished to be the only one to profit from them. The practical reasons for the compulsory concentration of the Jews in special quarters put into force in 1294 were revealed in 1306. Philip's only decree that arose from religious scruples and carried no material advantage was that of 1299 directed against missionary efforts on the part of the Jews and "their blasphemies and evil spells."

The king's essentially mercenary interest in the Jews was finally manifested on June 21, 1306. An oral command called on John of Nogaret, John of Saint Just, and the seneschal of Toulouse to organize the arrest of all the Jews of the kingdom, the seizure of their belongings, and then their expulsion. A written order of the same day required all the prelates, barons, and officers of every degree to lend their assistance to these three persons in the execution of their mandate. The date had been fixed for July 22 and the secret was so well guarded that not one Jew escaped. The Jews had not even left the kingdom when Philip issued his regulations for public auction of their real estate. In the eventuality that treasures hidden by the Jews in these buildings might be discovered, such finds were reserved for the treasury. Claiming that there was a judicial distinction between the Jews of the king and those of the lords, some of the latter resisted the order to expell "their" Jews. The king easily overcame their objections by promising them the lion's share of the spoils. Immediately after the expulsion of 1306, a number of Jews were given safe-conducts to return to the kingdom in order to cooperate in the recovery of their debts. Subsequently they too were driven out in 1311. It has been said that by expelling the Jews, Philip committed not only an evil act but also made a bad bargain. The second part of this statement can hardly be substantiated: nine years later the Jews were once more to be found in France; they were again expelled in 1323, while the royal treasury continued, until 1325, to collect the debts due to the Jews which had been confiscated in 1306.

PHILIP V THE TALL, king from 1316 to 1322. Of this king's few ordinances concerning the Jews, the first (April 1317) was the most favorable: it protected them against abusive imprisonment, guaranteed their right to dispose of their own estates, and exempted them from wearing the Jewish badge outside their homes. In the course of Philip's brief reign, three major events affected the situation of the Jews. During the uprising of the *Pastoureaux in 1320, the king, together with the ecclesiastical authorities, exerted his power to the utmost to protect the Jews. In 1321 the Jews of several localities were accused of having poisoned the wells and fountains in collusion with the lepers. Philip appointed a commission of inquiry on July 21 and numerous trials ensued—as well as massacres without even the travesty of a trial. An enormous fine—at first established at 150,000 livres and consequently reduced to 120,000—was imposed on French Jewry. Finally, Philip decided on a new expulsion of the Jews from France, although this measure was not enforced until 1323, during the reign of his successor.

Bibliography: PHILIP AUGUSTUS: A. Cartellier, *Philipp II August,* 4 vols. (Ger., 1899–1922); Baron, Social², index; E. J. de Laurière et al. (eds.), *Ordonnances des Rois de France,* 1 (Paris, 1723); vol. 11, indexes; H. F. Delaborde (ed.), *Recueil des actes de Philippe Auguste,* 3 vols. (1916–66). PHILIP III THE BOLD: L. Berman, *Histoire des Juifs de France* (1937), 114ff.; *Ordonnances des Rois de France,* 1 (Paris, 1723), 312–3; vol. 12, 323. PHILIP IV THE FAIR: L. Lazard, in: REJ, 15 (1887), 233–61; I. Loeb, in: *Jubelschrift . . . H. Graetz,* 1 (1887), 39–56 (Fr.), incl. bibl. notes; L. Berman, *Histoire des Juifs de France* (1937), 116–24; G. Saige, *Juifs en Languedoc* (1881), index s.v. *Philippe le Bel; Ordonnances des Rois de France,* 1 (Paris, 1723), index. PHILIP V THE TALL: P. Lehugeur, *Histoire de Phillippe le Long,* 1 (1897), 428–35; B. Blumenkranz, in: *Archives Juives,* 6 (1969/70), 36–38; *Ordonnances des Rois de France,* 1 (Paris, 1723), index, s.v. *Philippe le Long.* [B.BL.]

PHILIP OF BATHYRA (first century C.E.), son of Jacimus and grandson of Zamaris, rulers of Bathyra in the district of Trachonitis. He was a friend of Agrippa II, who appointed him commander of the army in Bathyra. Josephus describes him as "excelling in combat and . . . possessing other virtues which could bear comparison with any other man" (Ant., 17:30). When war broke out in Jerusalem and the peace party requested for help from Agrippa, Philip was despatched at the head of 3,000 cavalry. They occupied the upper city, but with the arrival of the *Sicarii under *Menahem b. Judah, Philip's forces were driven out of the fortress of Antonia and compelled to take refuge in the palace of Herod. After a short time, they surrendered on receiving a promise that they would be permitted to leave the city in peace. Philip, fearing that he would be put to death, hid for four days in Jerusalem and by a subterfuge succeeded in escaping from the city and reaching Gamala. This saved him from the intrigues of *Varus who was plotting against him. After the dismissal of Varus, he returned with his troops to Bathyra where he was charged with the task of preventing the inhabitants from joining the revolt against the Romans. When Vespasian and Agrippa II visited Tyre, its inhabitants accused him of surrendering the palace of Herod and the Roman garrison to the Jews, and Vespasian ordered him to be sent for trial before Nero. Nothing more is known of him. Two of his brother's daughters were the only inhabitants of Gamala who escaped death by hiding from the Romans.

Bibliography: Jos., Wars, 2:421, 556; 4:81; Jos., Ant., 17:30; Jos., Life, 46ff., 59–60, 177, 179–84, 407.; Drexler, in: *Klio*, 19 (1925), 277–312; Schalit, *ibid.*, 26 (1933), 67–95. [E.E.]

PHILIPPINES, island republic off the coast of S. E. Asia. Marranos are known to have lived in Manila among the early Spanish settlers and they soon came under the surveillance of the Spanish Inquisition. The first public auto-da-fé was held in Manila in 1580, but it is not known whether there were Jews among the seven persons accused. In 1593 two Marrano brothers, Jorge and Domingo Rodriguez, old-established residents of Manila, appeared at an auto-da-fé held in Mexico City because the Inquisition did not have an independent tribunal in the Philippines. They were sentenced to imprisonment. At least eight Marranos from the Philippines are known to have been tried by the Inquisition by the end of the 17th century.

Significant Jewish immigration to the Philippines did not begin until the last quarter of the 19th century. The first Jews known to arrive on the islands were the three brothers Levy, natives of Alsace, who went to Manila in the early 1870s to establish a jewelry business and brought additional people for their store. They were joined by groups of Turkish, Syrian, Lebanese, and Egyptian Jews, by families from Russia and Central Europe (either directly or via Harbin and Shanghai), and by U.S. Jews in the first few decades of the 20th century. By the early 1930s the Jewish community numbered approximately 500. The Manila congregation, organized formally in 1922, purchased land for a synagogue and a burial plot, and in 1924 erected Temple Emil, named after a benefactor, Emil Bachrach. As a result of strenuous activity by the community, the friendliness of the then governor of the Philippine Commonwealth, Manuel Quezon y Molina (who donated some land for the purpose of refugee settlement), encouragement by the U.S. authorities, and the lack of better alternatives, the Philippines became a center for refugees from Nazi persecution. By the end of World War II the Jewish community had grown to more than 2,500. Among the refugees were a rabbi, Joseph Schwartz, and a cantor for the community. Late 1944 and the first two months of 1945 were calamitous for the Jewish community. The Japanese had used the synagogue and adjacent hall as an ammunition store, and both buildings were completely destroyed in the fighting. Ten percent of the Jews fell victim to atrocities perpetrated by the retreating Japanese or to the shelling of the advancing Americans. After the war the community reorganized, and its temple was rebuilt. In 1968 the community numbered approximately 250, about a quarter of whom were Sephardim. About 80 children attended the religious school.

The majority of Jews in the Philippines are not permanent residents of the country, but work on contract with U.S. companies, diplomatic missions, and other assignments. Only a handful live outside of Manila. U.S. military personnel stationed at bases in the islands are served by a Jewish chaplain at Clark Air Base, 50 mi. (c. 80 km.) north of Manila. [W.Z./E.E.S.]

Relations with Israel. The Republic of the Philippines was the only Asian country to vote for the partition of Palestine in 1947, and it recognized the State of Israel in 1949. Relations between the two countries have been cordial. Formal diplomatic ties developed from the exchange of honorary consuls and honorary consuls-general in the early 1950s, to nonresident ministers in the later 1950s, the establishment of an Israel legation in Manila in 1958, and finally to the appointment of resident

Philippine ambassador to Israel, Raphaelita Hilario Soriano, with President Shazar, following the presentation of her credentials in Jerusalem, June 1971. Courtesy Government Press Office, Tel Aviv.

ambassadors in Manila and Tel Aviv in 1962. An aviation agreement was signed between the two countries in 1951, a friendship treaty was contracted in 1958, several consular agreements and a technical-aid agreement were signed in 1964. Technical cooperation includes the participation of Israel experts in the establishment of a model village.

Israel has sent experts to the Philippines in the service of various UN agencies, and Philippine trainees in community development, agriculture, and cooperation studied in Israel. [SH.TU.]

Bibliography: G. A. Kohut, in: AJHSP, 12 (1904), 145–56; N. Robinson, *Jewish Communities of the World* (1963), 46; H. C. Lea, *The Inquisition in the Spanish Dependecies* (1908).

PHILIPPSON, family of prominent scholars, journalists, and financiers, originally from Germany. The first to call himself by that name was MOSES (1775–1814), who received an Orthodox upbringing and became a tutor. He was attracted to the works of Moses *Mendelssohn and German literature and was appointed teacher at the recently (1799) founded modern school at *Dessau. In order to supplement his meager income he began printing books and selling them at fairs; among them were a Hebrew reader, a short-lived periodical, *Der neue Sammler* (see **Me'assefim*), and other ventures. He died before completion of his Hebrew-German and German-Hebrew dictionary

Of his four children, LUDWIG (1811–1889) achieved renown as the founder (1837) of the **Allgemeine Zeitung des Judentums* and its editor until his death. Ludwig was an avid student of both Hebrew and classical literature. After graduation from Berlin University (1833), he took up the position of preacher in the *Magdeburg Jewish community. Though following the practice of Reform Judaism—he preached in German and introduced the organ and the rite of confirmation—he tried to steer a middle course between Reform and Orthodoxy. He was among the initiators of the Rabbinical Synods of Brunswick (1844), Frankfort (1845), and Breslau (1846), but was critical of their decisions. One of his projects was the establishment of a modern institution for training scholars, rabbis, and teachers. His newspaper was also dedicated to the struggle for emancipation in all parts of Germany and Europe and fought discrimination and anti-Semitism. Philippson published a popular translation of the Bible which went through three editions (1854, 1858, 1878) together with a revised edition illustrated by Doré (1875). Along with I. M. *Jost and A. *Jellinek he founded the Institut zur Foerderung der

Israelitischen Literatur (1854) whose main achievement was the publication of H. *Graetz's history. In 1862 he had to resign as rabbi of Magdeburg because he had become almost blind; nevertheless, he continued his journalistic and literary work in Bonn until his death. [Ed.]

Three of Ludwig Philippson's sons attained fame in their respective fields: Martin (1846–1916) was a historian and a communal leader. Born at Magdeburg, Philippson was appointed assistant professor at Bonn in 1875, and soon thereafter was designated professor of modern history. However, when Emperor William I would not sanction the appointment of a Jew, Martin took a professorship at the University of Brussels (1878), and eventually became rector there. In 1891 he was forced to resign this post in the face of agitation by anti-German and radical students, and returned to Berlin. Thereafter he devoted his energies to Jewish communal affairs and to his writing. He was chairman of the *Deutsch-Israelitischer Gemeindebund (1896–1912), chairman of the Gesellschaft zur Foerderung der Wissenschaft des Judentums (1902); and chairman of the *Verband der deutschen Juden (1904). He also headed the *Lehranstalt fuer die Wissenschaft des Judentums, which commissioned his three-volume *Neueste Geschichte des juedischen Volkes* (1907–11, 1930[2]). In all he published some 12 studies in modern history, but their scholarship has been sharply questioned by fellow historians. [H.A.S.]

Alfred (1864–1953), geographer, was born at Bonn. In the course of a distinguished career he was head of the department of geography at the universities of Berne, Halle, and Bonn. Upon his retirement his pupils and admirers published a volume of geographical essays in his honor. He continued to play a leading role in German geographical research until he was banned from the university and all other scientific bodies by the Nazi regime. In 1942 he was deported to *Theresienstadt. He managed to survive and, despite terrible suffering, returned at the age of 82 to his scientific activities, which he continued to his death. In this period he produced two of his best works, *Die Stadt Bonn: ihre Lage und raeumliche Entwicklung* (1947, 1951[12]), which is an outstanding work on urban geography, and *Die griechischen Landschaften* (1950–59). His main interest lay

1

2

3

Three members of the Philippson family. 1. Ludwig (1811–89), German scholar, educator, and journalist; 2. Martin (1846–1916), German historian and communal leader; 3. Paul (1910–), Belgian banker and communal leader. 1 and 2, Jerusalem, J.N.U.L., Schwadron Collection.

in the east Mediterranean region. Several of his many books have become classics of regional geography, among them, *Der Peloponnes* (1892), *Das fernste Italien* (1925), *Das Mittelmeergebiet* (1922[4]), *Europa* (1928[3]), and *Das byzantinische Reich als geographische Erscheinung* (1939). [M.Br.]

Franz M. (1851–1925) was a Belgian banker, financier, and communal leader. Born in Magdeburg, when still young he was sent to Brussels to work as a clerk in the *Errera banking house. In 1871 he established his own bank in Belgium and directed it until his death. Involved from the beginning in the Belgian colonization of Africa, he was an administrator of the Belgian Congo railways in 1889, becoming its president in 1924, and also was founder of the Belgian Congo Bank and its vice-president from 1911 to 1919. Philippson was president of the Brussels Jewish community and a leader of Belgian Jewry during his lifetime. He represented the Brussels community on the administrative council of the *Jewish Colonization Association (ICA) from 1896, becoming vice-president in 1901 and president in 1919. He made an important contribution to Jewish colonization efforts in Argentina and Brazil. His son, Jules (1881–1961), became head of the firm; another son, Maurice (1875–), was a zoologist. [Ed.]

Paul (1910–), son of Maurice, was a banker and Jewish leader in Belgium. Born in Brussels, he was an officer in the Belgian Forces (1940–45) and was chairman of the Central Jewish Consistory of Belgium (from 1963); he was also president of the Jewish community of Brussels (1945–63); president and founding member of the Service Social Juif (since 1945); and chairman of the Social Service Commission of the European Council of Jewish Communities.

Ludwig's brother Phoebus (1807–1870) practiced medicine and published medical studies and literary works. His granddaughter Paula (1874–1949) became one of the first woman doctors in Germany but applied herself at the age of 47 to classical studies, where she made her mark in Greek mythology. [Ma.G.]

Bibliography: J. Philippson, in: YLBI, 7 (1962), 95–118; E. G. Lowenthal, in: BLBI, 8 (1965), 89–106; J. Rosenthal, in: S. Federbush (ed.), *Ḥokhmat Yisrael be-Ma'arav Eiropah*, 1 (1958), 399–408; M. Freudenthal, in: MGWJ, 54 (1910), 103–13; 56 (1912), 104–6; 74 (1930), 315–6; *Biographie Coloniale Belge*, 3 (1952), s.v.; Wininger, Biog, s.v.; *Festschrift . . . A. Philippson* (1930); G. Kayserling, *Ludwig Philippson* (1898); J. C. Dornfeld, in: CCARY, 21 (1911).

PHILIPSON, DAVID (1862–1949), U.S. Reform rabbi. Philipson was born in Wabash, Indiana, and received his early education in Columbus, Ohio. Entering Hebrew Union College, Cincinnati, in 1875, he was one of the first group of rabbis who received their ordination in 1883. After serving as rabbi of Har Sinai Congregation, Baltimore, from 1884 to 1888, Philipson returned to Cincinnati to become rabbi of the B'nai Israel Congregation in 1888, remaining there for the rest of his life. Philipson participated in the conference which drew up the Pittsburgh Platform (1885); he was a founder of the Central Conference of American Rabbis serving as president in 1907–09; and he was an influential figure in Hebrew Union College, where he taught for many years, and in the Union of American Hebrew Congregations. Not a profound thinker, Philipson was productive in the literary field. His most important work was *The Reform Movement in Judaism* (2nd ed. 1931; repr. 1967). He also wrote *The Jew in English Fiction* (5th ed. 1927) and edited *The Letters of Rebecca Gratz* (1929). He was a member of the board of translators of the Jewish Publication Society for the translation of the Holy Scriptures (1916), an editor of *Selected Writings of Isaac M.*

Wise (1900), and translator of *Reminiscences of Isaac M. Wise* (1901, 1945). An autobiography, *My Life as an American Jew*, appeared in 1942 and a volume of occasional writings, *Centenary Papers*, in 1919. Philipson verbalized and gave a universal dimension to the optimism of the prospering Midwest Jews among whom he lived and, surviving most of its exponents, came to be regarded as a representative spokesman of "classic" Reform Judaism.

Bibliography: D. Philipson, *Reform Movement in Judaism* (1967), introd. by S. Freehof. [S.D.T.]

PHILISTINES (Heb. פְּלִשְׁתִּים), a people of Aegean origin occupying the south coast of Palestine, called Philistia (פְּלֶשֶׁת, *peleshet*) in the Bible, and often at war with the Israelites. The name Philistine is first found in the Egyptian form *prst* as one of the "Sea Peoples" who invaded Egypt in the eighth year of Ramses III (c. 1190 B.C.E.). In Assyrian sources the name occurs as both *Pilišti* and *Palaštu/Palastu* (also *Palaštaya*). The Septuagint, when not translating it as "strangers" (’Αλλόφυλοι), usually renders it as Φυλιστιίμ (i.e., in Genesis–Joshua).

In biblical tradition, the Philistines came originally from *Caphtor (Crete: Jer. 47:4; Amos 9:7; cf. Deut. 2:23). This tradition is buttressed by the fact that part of the Philistine coast was called הַנֶּגֶב הַכְּרֵתִי, "the Negeb of the Cherethites" (I Sam. 30:14), and by the occurrence of Cretans in parallelism with Philistines (Ezek. 25:16; Zeph. 2:5), but there is no direct archaeological proof for it. The Philistines participated in the second wave of the "Sea Peoples" who, according to Egyptian reports, ravaged the Hittite lands, Arzawa, the Syrian coast, Carchemish, and Cyprus, and threatened Egypt during the reigns of Merneptah and Ramses III. The excavations at Hattusas (Boghazköy) and Ugarit have shown that these cities were destroyed at the end of the Late Bronze Age (c. 1200) and tablets discovered at Ugarit and archaeological finds on Cyprus give evidence of this troubled period. Of the "Sea Peoples" only the Philistines, who settled along the Palestinian coast, and the Tjeker, who occupied Dor according to the Wen-Amon story (c. 1050), can be positively identified. The others—Shekelesh, Denyen, Sherden, and Weshesh—have only been conjecturally identified. These peoples, displaced from their original homelands, assimilated the Minoan-Mycenean culture patterns of the Aegean world.

"Philistia" or the "Land of the Philistines" is that part of the coastal plain of Palestine which lies between Tel Qasīla and the Wadi Ghazza, about 6 mi. (c. 10 km.) south of Gaza. The Philistine pentapolis consisted of Gaza, Ashkelon, Ashdod, Gath (Tell al-Ṣāfī?), and Ekron (Khirbat al-Muqanna'?). The references to Philistia and the Philistines in Genesis 21:32, 34 and Exodus 13:17; 15:14; 23:31 are anachronistic. The Greeks, familiar at first with the coastal area, gradually applied the name Palestine to the whole of the country. The Philistines depicted on the walls of the temple of Ramses III at Medinat Habu in Egypt are dressed in a kind of Aegean kilt and wear a plumed headress with chinstraps. Similar depictions from Late Bronze Age Cyprus have been found. The Philistine ship is unusual while the wagon and chariot fit well-known forms. The clearest sign of Philistine presence is "Philistine pottery," whose chief types are buff-colored craters, beer jugs with spouted strainers, cups, and stirrup vases with a white wash or slip on which are painted reddish-purple or black geometrical designs, or metope-like panels with stylized swans preening themselves. These are found from the beginning of the 12th century to the late 11th century B.C.E. in Philistia itself, in adjacent sites of the Negev (e.g., Tell al-Fāri'a) and the Shephelah ('Ayn Shams), and in cities

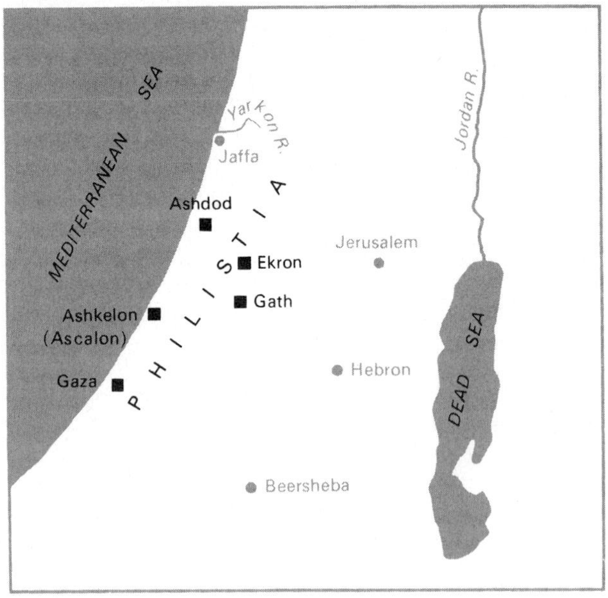

The Philistine Pentapolis.

occupied by them (e.g., *Gezer, Tell Beit Mirsim, Meggido, Afulah and Tell al-Naṣba). Similar pottery was also found at Tell Deir 'Allā in the Jordan valley. Analysis has shown that from the beginning Philistine pottery was a local product using local techniques with strong points of contact with the Mycenean IIIC1 wares discovered at Enkomi and Sinda on Cyprus and the other sub-Mycenean wares of Cyprus and Rhodes. Anthropoid clay coffins also signal Philistine presence (e.g., Tell al-Fāri'a and Beth-Shean). The Philistines had a monopoly on metal working (I Sam. 13:19–21), and smelting furnaces have been found at Ashdod, Tell Qasīla, Tel Ḥamma, and Tell Mor.

The excavations at Ashdod have uncovered as yet undeciphered seals in the Cypro-Minoan script from the 12th–11th centuries. Tablets in a related script were also found at Deir 'Allā. From the ninth century on, a variant of the Phoenician-Hebrew script was used in Philistia. Only one word of the Philistine language has been plausibly identified: *seranim* used of the five princes of the Philistine confederacy. It may be equated with the Greek *turannos*, of pre-Hellenic or Asiatic origin. Two early Philistine names have possible Asiatic connections—*Goliath with Alyattas and *Achish with Anchises (Ikausu of Ekron). The other names, from the later period, are usually Canaanite (e.g. Ahimilki, Sidqa (צדקא on a seal), Mitinti (מתת on a seal), and Hanun). Soon after coming to Palestine, the Philistines adopted a Canaanite dialect, and this in turn gave way to Aramaic. Ashdodite (Neh. 13:24) refers to such a local (Canaanite?) dialect and an ostracon from the late fifth century reading *krm zbdyh* was found at Ashdod.

The Philistines were uncircumcised and were, therefore, despised by the Israelites (Judg. 14:3; 15:18; I Sam. 17:26; 18:25), but except for certain peculiar burial practices, with Mycenean connections, we know of no other culture trait that can be attributed to them. Various ritual objects found at Ashdod and Gezer are closely related to similar objects from the Aegean but all the Philistines' known gods have Semitic names. They had temples to Dagon in Gaza and Ashdod (Judg. 16:23; I Sam. 5:1–7), to Astarte (Ashtoreth) in Ashkelon (Herodotus 1:105), and to Baal-Zebub in Ekron (II Kings 1:1–16). Some of these temples lasted into the Hellenistic period (cf. I Macc. 10:83; Diodorus Siculus 2:4). The Philistines also achieved a reputation as soothsayers (Isa. 2:6). The Philistine pentapolis, until its defeat by David, was ruled by *seranim*, "leaders," who acted in council and were able to overrule the decision of any individual *seren* (I Sam. 29:1–7). The Philistines were able to muster large, well-armed troops of foot soldiers, archers, and charioteers (I Sam. 13:5; 29:2; 31:3) and also elements of the autochthonous population and mercenaries (David—I Sam. 27–29; the Rephaim—II Sam. 21:18–22). Individual combat (Goliath—I Sam. 17:4–10) and shock troops were used by the Philistines (I Sam. 13:17–18; 14:15). In the later period they were ruled by "kings" (Jer. 25:20; Zech. 9:5).

After being repulsed by Ramses II, the Philistines first settled the coast of Palestine. Ashkelon, Ashdod, Gath, and Gaza, known from older sources, were captured by the Philistines from their Canaanite inhabitants, perhaps with the tacit permission of the Egyptians. They may also have served as part of the Egyptian garrison at Beth-Shean. The tradition concerning *Shamgar son of Anath's killing 600 Philistines may stem from this time (Judg. 3:31). Ekron may have been a newly founded Philistine city, and the excavations at the Philistine-founded Tell Qasīla and at Ashdod attest their building activity during this period. There are no reports of any opposition to the Philistines on the part of the inhabitants of the coastal cities. The Philistine expansion into adjacent areas in the Shefelah and the Negev from about 1150 on is demonstrated by the abundance of their pottery found there. The ensuing pressure upon the Danites and Judahites is reflected in the *Samson saga (Judg. 13–16), and toward the middle of the 11th century, they were able to encroach upon the hill country, destroy Shiloh, and capture the ark. They devastated part of western Palestine, occupied Gibeath-Benjamin, Megiddo, and Beth-Shean. Under Samuel (I Sam. 7:7–14) and Saul, at the beginning of the latter's reign (c. 1020), some respite from the Philistines was obtained. The Philistine return to power is highlighted by the Goliath pericope (I Sam. 17), but the freedom of David and his band as auxiliaries of Achish of Gath points up Philistine weakness (I Sam. 27). After the defeat of Saul at Gilboa, the Philistines were able to reestablish control over part of the

Figure 1. Philistine anthropoid clay coffin lid from Tell al-Fāriʿa, 13th–10th centuries B.C.E. Jerusalem, Rockefeller Museum, Israel Department of Antiquities.

land as far north as Beth-Shean, but David, after being anointed as king over all Israel, was able to use his knowledge of Philistine strategy to defeat them and to drive them back to Gezer (II Sam. 5:17–25). David subdued the city of Gath (I Chron. 18:1) and imposed vassalage upon it; Gath supplied him with faithful warriors like *Ittai the Gittite (II Sam. 15:18–22; 18:2). Mercenary troops from the other independent Philistine cities, such as the Cherethites and Pelethites (see below) under the command of Benaiah son of Jehoiada, joined the ranks of David's personal army.

Philistine history was now the history of individual cities, rather than that of a people acting in concert. It is quite possible that in the course of their battles with Saul and David, the ruling Philistine military class had been wiped out and that strong assimilation with the native Canaanite population had already taken place. Except for Achish of Gath, mentioned in I Kings 2:39–40, who is most probably the same person as the ruler of Gath under whom David served, and Ikausu of Ekron, a contemporary of Ashurbanipal of Assyria, all the known subsequent Philistine rulers have Semitic names. The typically Philistine pottery of the Early Iron Age disappears, and the pottery and other artifacts found in the following Early Iron Age III levels is the same as that found elsewhere in Palestine. The Philistines were, on the whole, limited now to their pentapolis and the immediate coastal area. Reduced to a secondary role, their hold over the sea coast was broken, and Phoenician maritime expansion became possible. The vassal status of Gath remained unchanged at the beginning of the reign of Solomon (c. 960), as can be seen by the ease with which Shimei son of Gera moved into and out of that city (I Kings 2:39–40). Toward the end of the United Monarchy and the early part of the divided Monarchy, Egyptian influence in Philistia may be surmised from the campaign of an unnamed Pharaoh of the 21st Dynasty at Gezer (I Kings 9:16–17) and the use made by Sheshonk I (biblical *Shishak) of Gaza as the starting point of his campaign in Palestine (c. 917), as reported in his itinerary. During the next 50 years *Gibbethon (Tell Malāt, near Gezer), which was held by the Israelites, was the site of border battles, involving troops of relatively large numbers, between them and the Philistines (I Kings 15:27; 16:15–17). During the reign of Jehoshaphat the Philistines paid tribute to Judah (II Chron. 17:11), but were able to make incursions into Judahite territory and raid the king's household, carrying off his son Jehoram (II Chron. 21:16–17). It is also clear, from these scant references, that Arabian tribes now occupied the territory to the south of Philistia.

During his raid into Judah in about 815, Hazael of Aram was able to capture the city of Gath (II Kings 12:18). The first definite reference to Philistia in Assyrian sources dates from the reign of Adad-nirâri III (810–783), who boasts of having collected tribute from Philistia (Palastu) in his fifth year. Uzziah successfully raided Philistine territory and, according to the biblical report, tore down the walls of some cities (as shown archaeologically at Ashdod) and set up garrisons of his own (II Chron. 26:6–7). Although no destruction of the city is reported, except in the enigmatic reference in Amos 5:2, Gath lost its former importance. Gath is not listed in the various prophetic condemnations of the Philistines (Jer. 25:20; Amos 1:6–8; Zeph. 2:4; Zech. 9:5–8), and had, in all likelihood, come under the rule of Ashdod. During the reign of Ahaz, the Philistines once again raided Judah and occupied cities in the Shefelah and the Negev (II Chron. 28:18; cf. Isa. 9:11; 14:28–32). However, Tiglath-Pileser III invaded Philistia in 734, sacked Gaza, and forced vassalage on Hanun, its king, and upon Mitinti of Ashkelon. *Sargon II stormed Gaza in 720, after Hanun had participated in the anti-Assyrian coalition, exiled Hanun, and made Gaza once again a vassal city. Tribute from various Philistine cities is recorded in Assyrian records of this period. In 713, Azuri of Ashdod was deported for treachery and was replaced by his brother, Ahimiti, but the Ashdodites placed a local usurper, Iamani, on the throne. Iamani fortified Ashdod and, by forming an alliance including Philistia, Judah, Edom, and Moab, he precipitated an attack in 712 by Sargon. This campaign is referred to in Isaiah 20:1. The capture of Ekron and Gibbethon is portrayed on wall reliefs from Dur-Sharrukin; Ashdod, Ashdod-Yam, and Gath were also captured. Excavations at Ashdod have uncovered fragments of a basalt victory stele erected by Sargon and also show that the walls of the city were destroyed at this time. Ashdod was temporarily converted into an Assyrian province. According to II Kings 18:8, Hezekiah invaded Philistia and attacked Gaza. In Ashkelon, Sidqa replaced the loyal ruler while Hezekiah was in alliance with the people of Ekron who handed over their king, Padi, to him. The Ethiopian rulers of Egypt in all likelihood planned to move into the south of Philistia. In 701, Sennacherib invaded southern Palestine and captured the cities of Beth-Dagon, Jaffa, Bene-Berak, and Azor and their capital Ashkelon; deported Sidqa and his family and imposed a new king; and punished the patriciana of Ekron, r stored Padi to his throne, and rewarded the faithful kings of Ashdod, Ekron, and Gaza with a strip of Judahite territory in the Shefelah. The traditional dislike of the Philistines, reflected in both the Prophets and the Psalms, was intensified by their participating in the Phoenician slave trade during this period (Joel 4:1–8). During the rest of Sennacherib's reign Philistia served as a buffer zone between Assyria and Egypt. During the reigns of Esarhaddon and Ashurbanipal, the kings of Gaza, Ashkelon, Ekron, and Ashdod are listed among the loyal vassals of Assyria who supplied corvée workers and troops to the Assyrian army. The constant passage of Assyrian troops through Philistia in the campaigns against Egypt guaranteed the tranquility of the area.

After the breakdown of Assyrian might, the Philistine cities, particularly Ashdod, were under strong Egyptian pressure (Herodotus 1:157). Archaeological discoveries have made it probable that Josiah annexed part of northern Philistia near Yavneh-Yam. There is also a tradition of an invasion of Scythians who destroyed the temple of Astarte in Ashkelon (Herodotus 1:105). Philistia was overrun by the Egyptians under Neco, who conquered Gaza in about 609–608 (Herodotus 1:159; cf. Jer. 47:1). The Philistines were allied with Egypt against Nebuchadnezzar of Babylon, as is now clear from the Aramaic letter found at Saqqarah from Adon (of Ashkelon?) to Pharaoh, but Ashkelon was laid waste and her king exiled in 604 by Nebuchadnezzar. Nebuchadnezzar put out any remaining sparks of Philistine independence. He deported both rulers and people, as has been shown by the mention of the kings of Gaza and Ashdod and the princes of Ashkelon in various lists from Babylon (cf. Jer. 25:20; 47:2–7; Zeph. 2:4–7; Zech. 9:5–6). The later history of the cities Ashdod (Azotus), Ashkelon (Ascalon), and Gaza is of Persian and then Hellenistic cities with a highly mixed population. Only the territorial name *Palestine connected them with their Philistine past.

The Cherethites and Pelethites (הַכְּרֵתִי וְהַפְּלֵתִי) were a section of David's personal army who joined him after he had defeated the Philistines. They were part of his retinue after he was established in Jerusalem. Their commander, *Benaiah son of Jehoiada, is listed as a member of David's administrative corps (II Sam. 8:18; 20:23). Their absolute loyalty to David was proved by their accompanying him on

Figure 2. Stirrup vase with typical Philistine decorations from Tell al-Fāriʿa, c. 12th century B.C.E. Jerusalem, Rockefeller Museum, Israel Department of Antiquities.

his flight from Jerusalem (II Sam. 20:7). Their faithfulness was again proved in their supporting the selection of Solomon as king (I Kings 1:38–44). The name Cherethite most probably meant Cretan and alluded either to the Aegean origin of part of the "Sea Peoples" who settled along the south coast of Palestine with the Philistines or to a group of Cretans settled there by the Egyptians. They probably dwelt in the area to the southeast of Philistia proper, which is once alluded to as the Cretan Negev or the Negev of the Cherethites (I Sam. 30:14). The Pelethites were, in all likelihood, recruited from the ranks of the Philistines with whom David had served during his stay in Ziklag. The form "Pelethite" *(peleti)* for "Philistine" *(pelishti)* is explicable as a formation modeled on "Cherethite" *(kereti)*. In the two passages in which the Cherethites are in parallelism with the Philistines, it is not clear from the context whether the terms are synonymous or if separate peoples are meant (Ezek. 25:16; Zeph. 2:5). The Carians were a people originating in southwest Anatolia whose services as mercenaries in Egypt and elsewhere, from the early seventh century on, is well known. Their script has not yet been deciphered, nor is their history before this period known. There may very well be a connection between them and the enigmatic Carites (הַכָּרִי) of II Kings 11:4, 19 who were considered loyal to the royal house in the story of Joash. The variant reading "Carites" (כָּרִי) for Cherethites (כְּרֵתִי) in the *ketiv* of II Samuel 20:23 is in all likelihood an error. [J.C.G.]

In the Aggadah. Most Midrashim are concerned with the alliance made of Abraham and Isaac with Abimelech, king of the Philistines (Gen. 21 and 26). Abraham is criticized for concluding an alliance with him. The Midrash tells that as a punishment for the seven sheep he sacrificed in making this covenant, the Philistines would one day slay seven righteous men—Samson, Hophni, Phinehas, and Saul with his three sons; they would destroy seven holy places; they would retain the holy Ark in their country as spoils of war for a period of seven months; and, furthermore, only the seventh generation of Abraham's descendants would be able to rejoice in the possession of the land (Gen. R. 54:4). Jacob did not stay in Philistia lest he too be compelled to make an alliance with the Philistines, thus delaying the conquest of the Holy Land (*ibid.* 68:7). David was not bound by his forefathers' covenant with Abimelech, since the Philistines' stopping of the wells which Abraham had dug constituted a breach of this agreement (Mid. Hag. to Gen. 26:28). However, they came to him with the bridle of a mule, which Isaac had given to Abimelech as a pledge of this covenant (PdRE 36). David commanded the Sanhedrin to investigate the claim carefully, but it was declared unfounded. Moreover, the Philistines of his day were not the descendants of the Philistines who had concluded the treaty; they had immigrated from Caphtor at a much later date (Mid. Ps. 60, 1).

After the capture of Samson the Philistines brought their wives to him in the Gaza prison in the hope that he might sire children who would be as strong as he (Sot. 10a). When they took the Ark, they said contemptuously: "The God of the Israelites had only ten plagues which he expended upon the Egyptians, and he no longer has it in his power to do us harm." As a result they were afflicted with a new plague consisting of mice crawling forth out of the earth and gnawing their entrails (Sif. Num. 88). [Ed.]

Bibliography: R. A. S. Macalister, *The Philistines, Their History and Civilization* (1913); B. Mazar, *The Philistines and the Rise of Israel and Tyre* (1964); B. Mazar (ed.), *World History of the Jewish People,* 3 (1971), 164–79; G. E. Wright, in: BA, 29 (1966), 70–86; H. Tadmor, in: BA, 29 (1966), 86–102; W. F. Albright, *The Amarna Letters from Palestine-Syria, The Philistines and Phoenicia* (1966); T. Dothan, *Ha-Pelishtim ve-Tarbutam* (1967); H. J. Franken, in: CAH², vol. 2 (1968), ch. 26; R. D. Barnett, in: CAH, vol. 2 (1969), ch. 28; M. Dothan, in: D. N. Freedman and J. C. Greenfield (eds.), *New Directions in Biblical Archaeology* (1969); R. Hestrin, *The Philistines and the Other Sea Peoples* (1970). In the Aggadah: Ginzberg, Legends, index.

PHILLIPS (originally **Pheibush**), early American family. The Phillips family was founded in America by Jonas Phillips (1736–1803), born in Buseck in the Rhineland, who arrived in Charleston, South Carolina, in 1756 as an indentured servant of Moses Lindo (see *Lindo family), a merchant. He became a freeman in 1759, lived in Albany, where he failed in business, and moved to New York where he was a *shoḥet.* Phillips subsequently engaged in business, and was admitted as a freeman in New York City in 1769. A patriot who subscribed to the Non-Importation Resolution,

Jonas Phillips, 18th-century U.S. merchant. Detail of a portrait attributed to Charles Wilson Peale. Nathan-Kraus Collection.

Phillips left New York when it was threatened by the British and enlisted as a private in the Philadelphia militia in 1778. After the war Phillips continued as a merchant in Philadelphia and was elected president of Mikveh Israel Congregation. He took part in signing petitions addressed both to the governments of Pennsylvania and the United States asking civil rights for Jews. Phillips had 21 children, a number of whom died in infancy; a grandson was Mordecai Manuel *Noah.

Manuel Phillips (d. 1826), son of Jonas, studied medicine at the University of Pennsylvania and served as assistant surgeon in the War of 1812. He died in Vera Cruz.

Naphtali Phillips (1773–1870), another son, was born in Philadelphia and became president of Mikveh Israel Congregation at the age of 25. He moved to New York in 1801 where he served Shearith Israel Congregation in a similar capacity for 14 terms. Naphtali Phillips was the first of a group of Jewish newspaper publishers in the United States, owner of New York City's *National Advocate.* He worked in the Customs House for 30 years. Phillips was the father of 15 children. Zalegman Phillips (1779–1839), another son of Jonas, was a graduate of the University of Pennsylvania. Admitted to the bar in 1799, he was the first Jewish lawyer in Pennsylvania.

Bibliography: Rosenbloom, Biogr Dict, s.v.; E. Wolf and M. Whiteman, *History of the Jews of Philadelphia* (1957), index; H. Simonhoff, *Jewish Notables in America* (1956) index, especially 49–52 on Jonas and 145–48 on Naphtali Phillips.

[Ab.V.G.]

PHILLIPS, LAZARUS (1895–), Canadian lawyer and senator. Phillips, who was born in Montreal, served in World War I and afterward was in the Canadian Expeditionary Force in Siberia. Called to the bar in 1920, he was named king's counsel in 1930. Phillips was a director and vice-president of the Royal Bank of Canada and sat on the boards of directors of numerous industrial, financial, and business enterprises. His involvement in Jewish community work was concentrated in Jewish education, the Jewish Theological Seminary, and the Hebrew University. Phillips was named to the Canadian Senate in 1968, the second Jewish member of this body.

[B.G.K.]

PHILLIPS, SIR LIONEL (1855–1936), South African financier and mining magnate. Born in London, he emigrated to South Africa (from England). He settled in Kimberley in 1875 and started work as a diamond sorter. In 1881 he became a director of the Griqualand West Diamond Company. He joined the leading mining house of Hermann Eckstein and Company in 1889 and succeeded Eckstein as head of the firm. In 1891 he was president of the Chamber of Mines and he played an important part in the financial organization and technical development of the gold mines. Phillips was one of the four members of the

Sir Lionel Phillips, South African mining magnate. Courtesy Fieldhill Publishing Co., Johannesburg.

Reform Committee who, after the fiasco of the Jameson Raid (1896), were sentenced to death. The sentences were commuted to a fine of £25,000 and banishment. He returned to South Africa after the Boer War, was a member of the first Union Parliament (1910–15), and was created a baronet in 1912. During the disturbances accompanying the Rand strike of 1913 he was severely wounded. Phillips' views on contemporary affairs are given in *Transvaal Problems* (1905) and *Some Reminiscences* (1924). On his retirement he settled at the Cape. Phillips and his wife Dorothea Sarah Florence Alexandra Ortlepp laid the foundations of the Johannesburg Art Gallery collection and of the Michaelis Gallery in Cape Town.

Bibliography: G. Saron and L. Hotz (eds.), *Jews in South Africa* (1955), index.

[Ed.]

PHILLIPS, PHILIP (1807–1884), U.S. congressman and jurist. The son of an immigrant from Germany, Phillips, who was born in Charleston, South Carolina, began studying law there in 1825, and was admitted to the South Carolina bar in 1828. As a delegate to the South Carolina "nullification convention" of 1832, Phillips, a unionist, strongly opposed Southern secession over the slavery issue.

Philip Phillips, U.S. congressman and jurist. Courtesy Alabama State Department of Archives and History, Montgomery, Ala.

Phillips was elected to the South Carolina state legislature in 1834 but moved the following year to Alabama, where he served in the legislature from 1844 to 1853. In 1853 he was elected as a Democrat to a two-year term in the House of Representatives in Washington, thus becoming the second U.S. Jew to sit in Congress. Phillips was admitted to the bar of the Supreme Court in 1850 and during his stay in Washington argued many cases before the Court. With the outbreak of the Civil War in 1861, he and his non-Jewish wife were placed under house arrest in Washington because of the latter's openly pro-Southern sympathies. However, later that year they were permitted to move to New Orleans. After Lee's surrender Phillips returned to Washington, where he continued to practice law. Among his published legal works was his *Statutory Jurisdiction and Practise of the Supreme Court of the United States* (1872).

Although Phillips was secretary of the Charleston Reform Society of Israelites during his residence in that city, his association with Jewish life appears to have been tenuous. He did, however, head a Jewish delegation to President Buchanan in 1857 to petition for the repeal of the anti-Jewish clauses contained in the American-Swiss treaty of 1855.

Bibliography: B. A. Elzas, *Jews of South Carolina* (1905), passim; J. R. Marcus, *Memoirs of American Jews 1775–1865*, 3 (1955), 133–96. [Ed.]

PHILO (The Elder), author of a Greek epic entitled *On Jerusalem*. He is sometimes identified with the Philo the Elder mentioned by Josephus (*Contra Apionem* 1:218) and Clemens of Alexandria (*Stromata*, 1:141, 3). If so, his presumed date can be conjectured from the fact that these list him after *Demetrius (fl. 221–204 B.C.E.) and before *Eupolemus (fl. 161–157). It is, however, by no means certain that the two are identical, since Philo was a common name. Of Philo's lengthy epic of 14 (or four) books, only three fragments consisting of a total of only 24 lines survive. About half of the lines are unintelligible, either because of faulty transmission of the text or because of the author's own obscurity. The view that the obscurity was intentional must be rejected.

Mras explains the first fragment as dealing with Abraham's circumcision and the binding of Isaac. Because the patriarch was the first to perform cicumcision according to statute, God made a covenant with him. Gutmann rejects this interpretation, as based on a too heavily emended text. But Gutmann's own interpretation of the first four lines as a statement of the Torah's antedating the creation of the world has been questioned. The remaining six lines of Fragment I, however, appear clearly to deal with the binding of Isaac, the appearance of the angel, and the slaughtering of the ram, though the details are not quite clear. Fragment II depicts the remarkable fountains that watered Jerusalem. Similar accounts, contrasting the dry parched surroundings of the city with the wealth of water in the city itself are found in the Letter of *Aristeas (88–91) and in a fragment from Timochares, the author of a *Life of Antiochus* (IV?). Philo's poem can also be compared with that of Theodotus, a Samaritan epicist, describing the marvelous streams that watered the valleys of the holy city of Shechem. Philo's poem, however, does not restrict itself to Jerusalem, but ranges widely through biblical lore. Fragment III records Joseph's rule in Egypt. If the author of the poem *On Jerusalem* is identical with the historian mentioned by Clemens, it is reasonable to assume that Philo dealt with chronology in a manner similar to Eupolemus, and that perhaps again, like Eupolemus, wrote in Jerusalem.

Bibliography: K. Mras (ed.), *Eusebius, Praeparatio Evangelica* (1954), 9:20; 24; 37; J. Gutmann, *Ha-Safrut ha-Yehudit ha-Hellenistit*, 1 (1958), 221–44. [B.-Z.W.]

PHILO (Pseudo-) or **LIBER ANTIQUITATUM BIBLICARUM,** conventional ascription and title of a Latin translation of an early Jewish chronicle. With extensive omissions, modifications, and additions, the chronicle retells biblical history from Adam to Saul's death (the archetype has lost its ending and how much followed remains uncertain). The length of the work makes it impracticable to list its chief innovations; for an outline see L. Cohn and G. Kisch (see bibl.). The period until the Exodus is briefly treated; additions and omissions are so distinct from those of *Jubilees that it has been suggested that Pseudo-Philo was correcting and supplementing that book. Especially notable are the strangely sympathetic account of Balaam, Moses' apocalyptic testament, the revisions of Joshua 22:7ff. and Judges 17–21, the novel careers of the first judge (called Kenez, as in Josephus' *Antiquities*) and his successor Zebul, Phinehas' installation of Eli, his ascension (to return as Elijah), and additional prayers, speeches, and visions, etc. throughout.

The title *Liber Antiquitatum Biblicarum* is probably a late assimilation of "Philo's" historical work to Josephus' *Antiquities*. The author (Jewish, not Christian) does not adopt any pseudepigraphical mask. He is probably from Palestine, not the Diaspora, and is totally devoid of classical allusions. The manuscript's ascription to Philo of Alexandria is impossible.

Liber Antiquitatum Biblicarum is usually dated shortly after 70 C.E., the strongest argument being Moses' prediction (19:7) that the First Temple would be destroyed on the 17th of the 4th month; it is plausible, though not inevitable, that this presupposes the cessation of the *Tamid* ("the daily offering") on that date in 70. Such a date would suit the linguistic parallels with II *Baruch and IV *Esdras, but the *Liber Antiquitatum Biblicarum* is demonstrably the source from which the other two have borrowed. Pseudo-Philo's Hebrew biblical text, furthermore, suggests an earlier date for at least much of the material. A few Septuagintal, Proto-Lucianic, and Palestinian readings have been noted by earlier scholars, but their number is far greater. That the translator, influenced by some form of Greek Bible, substituted its text for that of Pseudo-Philo is impossible, as such readings occur in passing allusions as well as in long quotations. More probably, the author himself used a notably pre-Masoretic form of Hebrew text—how late could he have done this? Further indications of date are unusable until the chronological system is explained.

Pseudo-Philo appears to be supplementing Chronicles with a history principally about Israel's cultic and national leadership from the Exodus until David. His real purpose is unclear, especially since the end is missing. The work is usually taken as a haphazard aggadic collection, with some unspecified educational or pious purpose, and the fact that many additions have parallels elsewhere suggest that not all the *aggadah* was created *de novo*. Its importance lies in the fact that it is one of the oldest substantive midrashic works extant. A. Spiro expounds it as a systematic attempt to replace the canonical history of pre-Davidic times by a version apter for anti-Tobiad and anti-Samaritan polemic. The anti-Tobiadism may be imaginary; some anti-Samaritanism is certain (there are even intriguing parallels with later Samaritan chronicles), but whether this controls the whole composition is disputable and the reason for the omissions is not yet apparent.

The affinities in Pseudo-Philo's theology and vocabulary need study; "mystical Jewish Hellenism" and "Essene Gnosis" are not too helpful characterizations. A coincidence (23:2) with Jubilees-Qumran on the date of the Feast of Weeks could be important for identifying its background and praxis; but other analogous indicators have not yet been noted.

The work survives in whole or in part only in some 20 late Latin manuscripts, but is older, having been translated (second to fourth century C.E.) via Greek from Hebrew. No clear traces of either Greek or Hebrew survive; the Hebrew form in *Chronicles of Jerahmeel* was retroverted from an important lost Latin manuscript. Strangely enough the work appears to have been unknown to the *Church Fathers. After early printings, *Liber Antiquitatum Biblicarum* was almost completely neglected until 1898. Among Jewish writers until this period it was known only to Azariah de *Rossi. The work of emendation, begun by M. R. James and L. Ginzberg (*The Biblical Antiquities of Philo*, 1970), can be systematically perfected and a critical text established. Much of the work (including chronological data and proper names presumably important for Pseudo-Philo's purposes) is as yet obscure, though it is not irremediably corrupt.

Bibliography: M. R. James (ed. and tr.), *Biblical Antiquities of Philo* (1917); L. Cohn, in: JQR, 10 (1898), 277–332; G. Kisch (ed.), *Pseudo-Philo's Liber Antiquitatum Biblicarum* (1949); Ginzberg, Legends, 7 (1938), 537–9; A. Spiro, in: PAAJR, 20 (1951), 279–355; L. H. Feldman, *Scholarship on Philo and Josephus (1937–1962)* (1963); M. Delcor, in: DBI, supplément 7 (1966), 1354–75. [J.R.S.]

PHILO JUDAEUS (Philo of Alexandria; c. 20 B.C.E.–50 C.E.), Jewish philosopher. The only known date of his life is 40 C.E., when as an elderly man he headed a delegation of the Jewish community of Alexandria to the Roman emperor Gaius Caligula. He belonged to the noblest family of Alexandrian Jewry, which had connections with the Herodian dynasty and the Roman court. Whereas his brother, the high official and rich banker Alexander, is known through Josephus, and his nephew, Alexander's son, *Tiberius Julius Alexander, is a well-known historical personality, there is only scanty information about Philo's life. His works are written in an exceedingly rich Greek, and show great erudition in classical literature and both classical and contemporary philosophy, a thorough training in the art of rhetoric, and a broad knowledge of general science. Philo must have obtained this education in Greek schools. Everything that has been inferred as to the sources of his Jewish knowledge remains highly hypothetical, since the existence of Jewish schools in the Diaspora of that time has not been proved. It is very doubtful that he had any knowledge of Hebrew, there being certain indications that he drew his Hebrew etymologies, which he used in his allegorical interpretations, from onomastica (lists of Hebrew names with Greek translations). It is clear that he grew up in a house devoted to Jewish faith and tradition. He may have acquired his very intimate familiarity with the Septuagint text of the Pentateuch (and, to a much lesser extent, his knowledge of the other parts of the Bible) through participating in Sabbath synagogue services with their ample exegetic sermons. He relates that he sometimes consulted the elders of the community about aggadic traditions. At least once in his life he undertook a pilgrimage to Jerusalem, and on that occasion he may have gathered from the priests his information about the Temple cult. His acquaintance with earlier Jewish allegorization, to which he refers, may have been acquired orally or through reading. However, he owes his most profound insights to "his own soul, which oftentimes is God-possessed and divines where it does not know" (Cher. 27).

Writings. A vast range of writings by Philo has been preserved by the Christian Church in the original Greek, others in Armenian translation. The bulk of these writings, dealing with the Pentateuch, can be divided into three series of treatises.

The first series consists of an exposition of the Pentateuch as a legal code. At the opening of the first book of the series *De opificio mundi (On the Creation)*, Philo explains that the Pentateuch, although a law code, opens with the story of creation rather than with legal material, because this story serves to demonstrate that the laws of the Pentateuch are in harmony with the laws of nature, and that through fulfilling these laws one becomes a "loyal citizen of the world." There follow biographies of the three Patriarchs (and Joseph), whom Philo interprets, in accordance with Platonic theory, as the living embodiments of the law or the archetypes on which the law was modeled by Moses. Another biography is *De Vita Mosis*, the most well written of Philo's writings, composed as a separate unit and clearly addressed to a gentile audience. Its first book gives a biographical account of Moses, based on Greek rhetorical standards, and the second deals with him as a lawgiver, a priest, and a prophet. This is followed by the small treatise *De Decalogo (On the Decalogue)*, containing the narration of the revelation on Sinai and an exposition of the Ten Commandments. The longest is the concluding treatise *De specialibus legibus (On the Special Laws)* with appendices, which categorizes all the biblical commandments under the various commandments of the Decalogue.

The second series, the *Legum allegoriarum (Allegorical Interpretation)*, is a philosophical interpretation of the Pentateuch. This series, consisting of 18 exegetic treatises (others being lost), parallels the first 17 chapters of Genesis, completely disregarding their narrative content and transposing them by way of allegorization into a set of abstract philosophical-mystical concepts, connected by a free play of associations with a wealth of other motifs, brought together from all parts of the Pentateuch. The last treatise, *De Somniis (On Dreams)*, draws its basic material from the various dream narratives of Genesis. In this whole series the thread of argument is sometimes lost and the association of ideas is comprehensible only to a reader very well versed in the text of the Bible. It has been suggested that this work is a collection of sermons that Philo delivered in the synagogue on various occasions and afterward loosely joined together.

The third series consists of *Quaestiones et solutiones in Genesin (Questions and Answers on Genesis)* and *Quaestiones et solutiones in Exodum (Questions and Answers on Exodus)*, preserved (though not completely) only in Armenian translation. This work is in the form of a Hellenistic commentary, where each paragraph is headed by an exegetic question, answered subsequently by a short literal, and a lengthy allegorical, explanation.

In addition to these three series, there is a group of treatises devoted to purely philosophical topics, that contain only occasional allusions to Jewish motifs. Some of these treatises are in dialogue form, and all are connected with the main concerns of Philo's religious outlook, such as the eternity of the world *(De aeternitate mundi)* and providence *(De providentia)*. The authenticity of some of the treatises in this group has been contested. These works may have been addressed to young Jewish intellectuals on the verge of apostasy—such as Tiberius Julius Alexander, Philo's nephew, who figures in some of them as a partner in the dialogue—people that could no longer be reached by a direct Jewish appeal. Finally, there are two books on contemporary history, *In Flaccum (Flaccus)*, on the pogroms in Alexandria (38 C.E.), and *De Legatione ad Gaium (On the Embassy to Gaius)*, which deals with Philo's mission to Rome to protest the erection of statues of the emperor in Alexandrian synagogues and later on in the Temple of Jerusalem. In addition there is *De vita contemplativa (On the Contemplative Life)*, the only source about the sect of *Therapeutae.

An edition of Philo's writings in the original Greek with English translation has been published in the Loeb Classical Library Series (F. H. Colson and G. H. Whitaker (trs.), 10 vols., 1929–62; 2 supplementary vols. containing English translations of the writings preserved in Armenian, R. Marcus (tr.), 1953). An English translation by H. Lewy of selections of Philo's writings is found in *Three Jewish Philosophers* (1960).

Philosophy. The philosophical substructure of Philo's world view may be defined as a stoicism with a strong Platonic bent and some neo-Pythagorean influences, although some scholars see him mainly as an opponent of the stoics. The Platonic element in his thought accounts for his separation of the world into a lower, material and a higher, spiritual or intelligible realm. Only in the upper, intelligible realm can ultimate truth be attained. In the concrete world of common experience there is only "opinion" or "probability," which falls between truth and lie. Thus, abstract concepts always range higher with Philo than concrete facts, and his statements about things perceived by the senses have of necessity a provisional and somewhat ambiguous character. Exoteric and esoteric sections can be distinguished in Philo's writings. The exoteric sections are concerned with the literal sense of the Bible, whereas the esoteric ones attempt to disclose the deeper philosophical-mystical meaning of Scripture through allegorical interpretation. For example, in the esoteric sections persons of the biblical narrative are interpreted as "representing" or "suggesting" abstract concepts, while the question of their historicity is left obscure. The central issues of Philo's thought are to be found not so much in the well-planned works of the above-mentioned first series, but in the diffusedly written allegorical commentaries—a point properly taken into account in H. Lewy's selections from Philo. In summarizing Philo's main ideas a distinction must be made between the realm of "opinion" and the realm of "truth."

THE REALM OF "OPINION." While the real destination and the real bliss of man consists in lifting up his soul to a contemplative life and freeing himself from bodily needs and pleasures, the right to this higher life is attained only after honestly fulfilling one's earthly duties in society. Therefore, Moses discharged the levites from their communal task only at the age of 50 (Fug. 37). It was in this spirit that Philo accepted his mission to Rome, and perhaps other political activities, although he deplored the circumstances that compelled him to do so (Spec. 3:1–6). In his historical writings he sees Providence at work in the rescue of the Jewish people, although in other works he is prone to let the concept of Israel evaporate into an allegorical designation for the "God-seeing" (apparently based on an etymology of Israel, *ro'eh el*) mystical man. The tendency to spiritualize the physical reality of Israel may account for Philo's very favorable attitude to proselytes, who, insofar as they leave their kinfolk and fleshly bonds, are considered as real imitators of Abraham (Spec. 1:52). He welcomes the widespread acceptance of Jewish religious institutions by gentiles as a proof of the superiority of the Jewish law. Philo maintained that this law was designed by Moses under divine inspiration, following the pattern of the Decalogue, which was given and promulgated by God Himself. In an appeal to the philosophically educated Jews who, because they regarded the laws as symbols, were negligent in observing them (Mig. 89–93), Philo argues against the abrogation of the law. The immanent weakness of his argument lies in his admission that the physical fulfillment of the biblical prescriptions is only the outward requirement of the law, whereas its real aim is the attaining of its symbolic meaning. Nevertheless, Philo goes to great lengths in pleading for the superior ethical, educational, and social value of Mosaic legislation on the material level as well. Philo in his exposition of Jewish law shows only scant acquaintance with the Oral Law. For example, he is not aware (Virt. 142ff.) of any halakhic extension of the prohibition against cooking a kid in its mother's milk (Ex. 23:19). The assumption of some scholars that Philo's known deviations from *halakhah* are the result of divergences of Alexandrian from Palestinian *halakhah*, and that Philo mastered the *halakhah* of his own community, is doubtful. Many more connections can be found between Philo and Palestinian *aggadah*, especially where he does not allegorize. He borrows from the Hebrew tradition not only a wealth of individual Midrashim, but also central midrashic concepts, such as the two *middot* (attributes) of God. Only in one place (Praem. 162–72) does he expound the messianic hope of Israel—so strong in his time—emphasizing its miraculous, and carefully avoiding its more military, aspects. His literary skill and rhetorical education are specially evident in his historical and political writings, where he succeeds in vivid descriptions and analyses of political situations and psychological motivation.

THE REALM OF "TRUTH." According to the inner meaning of the Holy Writ, uncovered by allegorical interpretation, Moses is a philosopher. However, Philo does not always consider philosophy the highest achievement of mind; sometimes he writes of a third stage above science and philosophy, called wisdom (Cong. 79). This is paralleled by his anthropology, i.e., his enumeration of three types of man—the man who is "earth-born," the man who is "heaven-born," and the man who is "God-born" (Gig. 60). The Platonic surge of the soul from the world of sense perception to that of intelligence is sometimes supplemented by a second soaring from the world of ideas to the Divine itself (Op. 71). Obviously, this highest sphere, which is not always distinguished from the noetic one, cannot be a relapse into the concrete, but must be an ideal realm beyond the ideas of the second stage. It is the ultimate aim of Philonic thought and striving. Philo is not interested in the traditional topics of Greek science and philosophy in themselves, but only insofar as they are ways to, or expressions for, the realm of the Divine. So, ultimately there are only two realities in Philo's world of truth: God and the soul. The timeless drama between these two poles is the content of Philo's mystical philosophy.

GOD'S ESSENCE. In discussing God's essence Philo maintains an extreme transcendentalism, surpassing even that of Plato. He describes God as "... transcending virtue, transcending knowledge, transcending the good itself and the beautiful itself" (Op. 8), and as "... better than the good, more venerable than the monad, purer than the unit ..." (Praem. 40). Whereas in lower levels of Philo's thought, God is endowed with goodness and other attributes, and activity figures as His "property" (I L.A. 5.), on the most abstract level he insists that God is "without quality" (I L.A. 36), has no name, and is unknowable. This last tenet is not meant in an agnostic way; on the contrary, man has to strive to know God and God is the only object worth knowing. But whereas it is easy to know that God is, we cannot know what He is (Spec. 1:32). Nevertheless Philo often encourages a thorough research into understanding God's essence; although this can never be successful, the research itself is utterly blissful.

God in His Relation. It has not yet been sufficiently acknowledged that the definite transcendentalist trend in Philo's discussion of God's essence is balanced by a strong immanentistic trend, based on the stoic model, in his discussion of God's relation to the world and the soul. The stoic scheme lends itself to a philosophic formulation of the working of divine powers inside things and even more inside the human soul. Since such an involvement of God in the world is in contradiction to His absolute apartness, the two aspects must be reconciled by an ontological differentiation that comes close to splitting the otherwise strongly maintained unity of God. This is the background of Philo's doctrine of the "intermediary powers." The *Logos, which for the stoics defined the Godhead, comes to be distinguished from God Himself, without being ontologically disconnected from Him. At times the Logos is identified by Philo with the mind of God, and thus it may be considered as another name for God Himself (Op. 24). At other times, however, it is symbolized by the high priest (II Som. 185ff.), and is characterized as being "midway between man and God" (II Som. 188). In a similar way, the doctrine of God's two "powers," mercy and justice, is built up into a system of intermediaries, whose activities can be referred to as God's own deeds, but sometimes are clearly meant to exonerate God from direct responsibility for severe acts of punishment (Decal. 177), which presupposes their being distinguishable from Him. Thus Abraham's three guests (Gen. 18:2) are identified (*Quaestiones et solutiones in Genesin,* 4:2) as God and His two powers. Only at a close look does Abraham discover they are one person.

These and cognate hypostases are instrumental in establishing God's relation to the world. Although Philo teaches that the world is created by God, God's direct contact with the defiling quality of matter is avoided by the interposition of the Logos or the "world-creating power" (Op. 21). In accordance with contemporary interpretation of Plato's *Timaeus,* Philo maintains that creation is carried out in two successive stages, as is illustrated in the biblical narrative; the first day of creation represents God's conceiving in His Logos the noetic world of ideas that later serves as a model for the creation of the material world, represented by the other five days. In the creation of man, the only creature capable of doing evil, God needs the cooperation of subservient powers.

Man. Man is composed of body and soul, body connecting him with matter and soul with God. Thus, he has to make a fundamental choice as to the direction of his life. The alternative is identified by Philo with the struggle of the stoic sage for the control of his passions by reason, and so the whole of stoic ethics becomes integrated into Philo's religious philosophy. However, behind the moralizing tenor of many passages lurks a religious pathos. The narration of the sin in the Garden of Eden is allegorically interpreted as the drama of man's fall. The most violent of passions, lust, is represented by the snake, who appeals not to reason (Adam) but to the senses (Eve), and succeeds with their help in subjugating reason too. Therefore (Gen. 2:24), man leaves his father (God) and his mother (wisdom) and clings to his wife (sensuality) and they are made into one flesh (II L.A. 59). It should be noted that this interpretation of the sin takes no account of the express prohibition by God, which constitutes the real issue in rabbinical exegesis.

The Soul's Ascent to God. The reconciliation between the soul and God is described by Philo in two ways: God's descent into the human soul and the soul's ascent to God. In both, the interplay of transcendence and immanence in the concept of God is of decisive importance. God the exalted, superior to every thinkable human category, comes to merge with the human soul, or the soul surpasses even the summit of Plato's ideal heaven—this is what happens in the union between God and man. The basic identity of human and divine spirit, implied in Stoic physics, here gives scientific expression to an enthusiastic mystical experience. What under stoic presuppositions was just a truism, becomes under the Philonic constellation a paradox of overwhelming power.

In order to prepare himself for God, man has to strip himself of earthly bonds, to leave "his land, his kinfolk and his father's home" (Gen. 12:1), i.e., his body, his senses, and his faculty of speech, and to segregate himself from these as much as possible for a living man (Mig. 1ff.). The sharp contrast between the self-loving and the God-loving man is symbolized by Cain and Abel, a contrast utterly foreign to the stoics who view the "self" of man as his divine part.

Unlike the moral struggle of the stoic sage, which is intended to lead to "apathy" and freedom from the passions, the entering of the Divine into man makes him jubilant and surge into a frenzy (Plant. 38). The "stream from Eden," the wine of the godly cupbearer (II Som. 254), drives the soul into ecstasy, for it fills it with an unearthly quality, called by names like "the holy spirit." Thus, the soul seeks more than intellectual knowledge, when it wants to "know what God is," although rationalistic terminology is often applied. The real aim is better indicated when Philo speaks of "reaching" God. The three Patriarchs are the archetypes of three main routes to "virtue," meaning ultimately union with God, namely, learning, nature, and training, respectively. Abraham proceeds from erudition (Hagar) to virtue (Sarah), whereas Isaac as the perfect nature reaches the mystical goal without interposing an intellectual endeavor, and Jacob is rewarded for his asceticism by the fact that the "Lord" (Justice) becomes to him "God" (Mercy; I Som. 163, alluding to Gen. 28:21), meaning that God discloses to him His higher spheres.

Here there is an additional function of the doctrine of intermediaries. These intermediaries present themselves to the ascending soul as so many stages on its way to God. Although the soul cannot advance to God Himself, it may be able to reach one of His "powers," whose number is variously given. This is developed in an allegory of the six towns of refuge (Num. 35), which are made (Fug. 86ff.) to represent a sequel of stations on the way to God, located partly on this and partly on the other side of the river, i.e., partly accessible and partly inaccessible to the soul. Schemes like this are variously adumbrated by Philo but do not harden into a fixed pattern.

In Jewish tradition man is said to relate to God in two ways—in fear and in love. Philo considers fear not only inferior to love (as do the rabbis, especially the school of R. Akiva) but sometimes as completely wrong (since fear is reckoned by the stoics as one of the passions that have to be overcome), deriving from an inadequate, vulgar idea of the Godhead (corresponding to the literal sense of Scripture). The proper attitude of the sage is love, understood as Platonic eros, but surpassing the world of ideas and directing itself to God Himself (Op. 71). This comes close to the erotic aspect of Hellenistic mysticism, and indeed, Philo indulges in sexual imagery, as for example in an allegory that he repeats a few times, always with extreme mysterious secrecy (Cher. 43ff.), on the biblical mothers, of whom it is said that "God opened their womb." He interprets this phrase as referring to the fatherhood of God and the virgin birth, it being understood that in this context the mothers themselves are to be regarded as purely allegorical figures. However, Philo usually shrinks from the idea of a full consummation of the mystical "holy marriage," so that usually the stress is shifted in Philo from the blissful union with God to the experience of eros itself, which is conceived as a state of highest bliss (e.g., Deus 138).

While Philo maintains at times that this apex of bliss is reached by elevating the soul from noetic fulfillment to a last soaring to the Divine, as symbolized in the figure of Abraham, at other times he views religious perfection as independent of philosophical perfection, as in the symbol of Isaac, or even as sharply contrasted with it: "When the light of God shines, the human light sets: when the divine light sets, the human dawns and rises" (Her. 264).

Sometimes (III L.A. 136) it is hinted that this love is a gift from God; Philo often reinterprets accomplishments ascribed to the stoic sage, such as steadfastness, peace, and kingliness, as divine gifts, by which God grants the perfect man a share in His own nature. To these virtues he adds *pistis* (meaning both "faith" and "faithfulness") that is here for the first time made into a value concept and is likewise transformed into a property of God's own essence; so, this "faith" means a blissful state of mind and not just faithful acceptance of certain creeds. Philo regards prophecy too as a divine gift. Whereas on the level of "opinion" it is praised as valuable prescience of future events (II Mos. 187ff.), in esoteric writings this popular aspect, which incorporates the biblical aspect of prophecy as a mission to the people, is abandoned. Here prophecy is an act of ecstasy, where man is overflooded with divine light. No perceptible message is connected with this experience, for in its consummation "ears are made into eyes" (I. Som. 129) and the message vanishes into flashes of light. Moses looking on from the top of Nebo into the "promised land" (Mig. 44) is the most sublime symbol for this meaning of prophecy.

Influence. Apart from Josephus, no ancient Jewish source mentions Philo, although there are traces of Philonic influence in Midrash, such as R. Oshaiah Rabbah's saying in *Genesis Rabbah*, 1:1 that is clearly modeled on Philo's *De Opificio Mundi*, 16. The medieval *Midrash Tadshe* (in: A. Jellinek, *Beit ha-Midrash*, 3 (1967), 164–93) draws largely on Philonic material, while the first medieval Jewish writer who mentions him is Azariah dei Rossi (*Me'or Einayim* (1886), 90–129), who Hebraizes his name into Jedidiah.

Philo had a much greater influence on Christianity—not on the New Testament itself but on the Church Fathers, Clement of Alexandria, Origen, Ambrose, and many others. They drew eagerly on his allegorical interpretations and adopted many of his concepts. However, owing to their different approach, many of his abstract concepts, such as wisdom, Logos, and faith, were concretized in Christianity.

Bibliography: F. H. Colson and G. H. Whitaker (tr. and eds.), *Philo* [Complete Works], 12 vols. (1953–63), introds. in each vol.; H. A. Wolfson, *Philo: Foundations of Religious Philosophy in Judaism, Christianity, and Islam*, 2 vols. (1940); E. R. Goodenough, *An Introduction to Philo Judaeus* (1940, 1962²); idem, *The Politics of Philo Judaeus* (1938), includes bibliography; J. R. Marcus, in: *Jewish Studies in Memory of George Kohut* (1935), 463–91, incl. bibl.; L. H. Feldman, *Studies in Judaica: Scholarship on Philo and Josephus (1937–1962)* (1963); S. Belkin, *Philo and the Oral Law* (1940); Pauly-Wissowa, 19 (1938), s.v.; K. Staehle, *Die Zahlenmystik bei Philon von Alexandria* (1931); J. S. Boughton, *The Idea of Progress in Philo Judaeus* (1932); G. Allon, in: *Tarbiz*, 5 (1933/34), 28–36, 241–6; P. Katy, *Philo's Bible* (1950); S. Zeitlin, in: JQR, 59 (1969), 171–214; S. Sandmel, in: CCARY, 15 (1968), 54–63, and passim.

[Y.AM.]

PHILOSOPHY. In his article on the Jewish involvement in philosophy in the *Dictionnaire des sciences philosophiques*, written over a century ago, Solomon *Munk pointed out that the Jewish mission to know God and to make Him known to the world was not basically involved with philosophy. After surveying the part played by Jews in philosophy, he concluded that "the Jews, as a nation, or as a religious society, play only a secondary role in the history of philosophy." As a nation or as a religious society this may be true, but even when Munk wrote it was not the case that Jewish participation in philosophy had been insignificant. Since his day the participation of Jews in philosophical activities has become extremely important.

It used to be said that the peculiarly Jewish role in philosophy had been that of middleman, transmitting the ideas of one culture to another, as some Jewish scholars had done in Spain, translating Arabic thought into forms available to Christian Europe. This, of course, was only part of the Jewish involvement in philosophy in the Middle Ages. Since the Renaissance many thinkers of Jewish origin have made central contributions to philosophy, and have played seminal roles in the development of modern Western thought. Some have played roles as Jews; others, who are of Jewish descent, have functioned as individual intellectuals, or sometimes as Christian thinkers.

14th to 17th Centuries. It may have been because they could not function within the Jewish nation or the Jewish religious society that many intellectuals of Jewish origin from Spain and Portugal, functioning in Iberia, Italy, France, and Holland, developed crucial philosophical views. Being spiritually dispossessed, and forced into an alien Christian intellectual world, the Marrano intellectuals may have been led into a more profound philosophical examination of their situation, and through it to a new evaluation of man's place in the cosmos. The drama of the forced conversions, the expulsion of the Jews from Spain, and the terror of the Inquisition created a class of Marrano thinkers trying to find their place in the world, trying to find meaningful values, and trying to use the intellectual tools of the Christian world they found themselves in to justify their appreciation of the nature and destiny of man. In Spain and Portugal, the efforts of many Jewish Conversos now went into explorations of theology and philosophy to find a viable and significant theory. From the time of *Paul of Santa Maria (converted in 1390), until well into the 17th century at least, Iberian intellectuals of Jewish origin were in the forefront in developing creative interpretations of the human scene, trying to define a Christian view that they could participate in. Most of the novel theories developed during Christian Spain's Golden Age were the product of this group. Spanish scholasticism, with its emphasis on universal law and natural rights, started from the views of Francisco de *Vitoria, and was developed by the humanists, Las Casas and Alonzo de la Vera Cruz. Spanish Erasmianism, with its emphasis on liberal Christianity, Christianity without theology, and a Christianity based on moral teachings rather than doctrines, was mainly a convert view. The Jesuit obedience theory was set forth by Diego Lainez, a theologian of Jewish ancestry. Christian kabbalism as a justification of the position of the New Christians was developed by Luis de *Leon, showing the role of Jewish Christians in an apocalyptic age.

Outside of Spain, exile thinkers of Jewish origin played an important role in philosophical thought. Judah *Abrabanel in Italy provided a major statement of Renaissance Platonism that was influential all over Europe. Juan Luis *Vives in the Lowlands was one of the chief exponents of humanism. It has been suggested that Montaigne's closest friend, the French humanist Etienne de la Boétie (1530–1563) was of Marrano origin. His *Discours de la servitude volontaire* (1576; Eng. *Anti-Dictator,* 1942) is a plea for human freedom and dignity against the tyranny of rulers and is the first modern statement of nonviolence as a means of protest.

The Marranos who settled in Amsterdam in the 17th century had been trained in Christian philosophy, and debated their problems in terms of European philosophical thought. *Manasseh Ben Israel, known as the Hebrew philosopher, provided the main perspective through which philosophers like Mersenne, Grotius, and Cudworth, saw Jewish ideas in philosophical terms. Within the Jewish community of Amsterdam, Marrano intellectuals like Uriel da *Costa and Juan de *Prado raised basic philosophical challenges not only to Judaism, but to the whole framework of revealed religion. Coupled with the radical biblical criticism of Isaac *La Peyrère, their criticisms led to the formulation of a new basic metaphysical ideology for a naturalistic nonreligious world in the theory of Baruch *Spinoza. Spinoza, starting from issues raised by heretical thinkers within the Jewish world in Holland, quickly developed a rationalistic, scientific metaphysics to explain the cosmos in terms of logic, psychology, and the 'new science.' Spinoza's naturalism soon became one of the fundamental presentations of the ideology of modern man, greatly affecting the materialists of the Enlightenment, the German idealists, and other movements. Spinoza has become the symbol of the pure modern philosopher, persecuted by religious orthodoxy, but preserving his philosophical ideals and mission. One of his opponents, Orobio de *Castro, tried to provide a philosophical defense of Judaism against Prado, Spinoza, Catholicism, and the liberal Christianity of Limborch and John Locke. Orobio de Castro, originally a professor of metaphysics in Spain, played a significant role in late 17th-century thought, influencing Locke, Bayle, and Fénelon.

18th to 19th Centuries. Philosophical activity in Amsterdam died out in the 18th century. The last thinker of note was Isaac de *Pinto who challenged *Voltaire's anti-Semitism, and Enlightenment atheism. His most influential work was in proposing the theory of modern capitalism against Hume and Mirabeau. He was one of the very first to understand the role of credit and circulation in the modern economic world.

The Enlightenment world, starting in Germany, led to another level of Jewish participation in philosophy. As Jewish intellectuals were emancipated and could participate in the full range of gentile society, they began to apply themselves to philosophical problems, especially of an ethical and general religious nature. The first to make his entry into the general philosophical scene in Germany was Moses *Mendelssohn. His writing on aesthetics, psychology, metaphysics, and philosophy of religion made him a central figure in Enlightenment thought, influencing his close friends, Theodor *Lessing and Immanuel *Kant. Mendelssohn sought to show that 18th-century Deism, the universal religion of reason, was the same as essential Judaism. In the spirit of the Enlightenment, he advocated religious toleration and equality for the Jews. Mendelssohn became a symbol in the general philosophical world of the enlightened and liberated Jew, who could contribute greatly to the mainstream of culture.

A Jewish doctor, Marcus *Herz, a friend of both Kant and Mendelssohn, played an important role in the development of Kant's philosophy. He was Kant's official "advocate," and discussed the latter's theories with him as they were being formed. Lazarus *Bendavid, at the end of the 18th century, became one of the major expositors of Kant's philosophy. One of the first, and most important, critics of Kant's views was the Lithuanian emigré, Solomon *Maimon, who came to Germany, learned philosophy, and offered a skeptical critique of Kant. Kant considered Maimon's views to be the most astute of any of his opponents, and some of his theories regarding the creative function of the mind became important in the development of German idealism.

People of Jewish origin only begin to play a role in the course of the development of 19th-century German thought around the middle of the century. Moses *Hess and Karl *Marx redirected German idealism into a materialistic socialist ideology. Julius *Frauenstadt became Schopenhauer's main follower, exponent, and editor of his writings. Adolf *Lasson was one of the very few advocates of Hegelianism. One of the founders of neo-Kantianism, Otto *Liebmann, attacked the various metaphysical theories after Kant, and urged a return to the master. As a result of his efforts the neo-Kantian movement developed, and one of its most important leaders was Hermann *Cohen, head of the Marburg school. Cohen emphasized a panlogistic transcendental version of Kant's thought, as opposed to some of the speculative metaphysical interpretations. Cohen stressed the objective side of Kant, and sought to justify a priori knowledge of nature and values. He also tried to identify Kantian ethics with liberal socialism. Cohen played a very significant role in the development of German philosophy. One of his students, Arthur *Liebert, edited the journal *Kantstudien,* in which many of the discussions of neo-Kantianism took place.

In the course of the 19th century, Jews were gradually able to attend the universities and hold positions in them (often only if they were converts). They began to participate in the full range of intellectual activities. Jacob *Freudenthal of Breslau became one of the foremost scholars of ancient thought, both Greek and Hebrew, as well as one of the most important Spinoza scholars. Adolphe *Franck in France, the first Jewish professor at the Collège de France, a follower of Victor Cousin, made important contributions in the history of thought, philosophy of religion, and philosophy of law. Xavier *Léon founded the *Revue de métaphysique et de morale* to combat positivism and encourage speculative philosophy. The reform rabbi, Felix *Adler, started the *Ethical Culture movement, and played an important role in formulating and advocating a humanistic nonreligious ethical view.

20th Century. By the end of the 19th century secularization and assimilation had proceeded to the point where large-scale participation by Jews in philosophy was possible since anti-Semitic barriers were gradually being removed. Jewish intellectuals could devote their energies to trying to give philosophical interpretations of man's situation and his achievements. Many of the most original theories in 20th-century philosophy are the products of thinkers of Jewish origin, who have come to play a larger and larger role in European thought.

Starting with Henri *Bergson at the end of the 19th century, some of the major speculative philosophers have been Jews. Bergson's *Creative Evolution* and Samuel *Alexander's *Space, Time and Deity* have been two of the most prominent efforts to develop metaphysical systems in terms of modern knowledge. Vladimir *Jankélévitch in Paris, starting from Bergsonism, continued to try to find metaphysical meaning in human existence. Léon *Brunschvicg devoted himself both to historical scholarship and to maintaining the idealistic tradition in France. Karl *Joel developed a system called "the new idealism" in Germany. In America Paul *Weiss has been developing an original metaphysics influenced by Whitehead, and Mortimer

*Adler has been advocating neo-Thomism. Nathan *Rotenstreich, in Jerusalem, has been setting forth a theory about human nature and the bases of values. The neo-Kantian movement in its many forms was led by Jewish thinkers, the most prominent of whom were Ernst *Cassirer and Leonhard *Nelson. Cassirer set forth a developmental Kantianism. Nelson, founder of the New Fries School, emphasized the psychological side of Kantianism. Other major figures who came out of the neo-Kantian movement were Emil *Lask, Franz *Rosenzweig, Samuel Hugo *Bergman, and Fritz *Heinemann. The phenomenological movement, which has been so important in 20th-century thought, was started by Edmund *Husserl. Seeking an unshakable foundation for human knowledge, he developed his phenomenological method and transcendental phenomenology. Max *Scheler applied the phenomenological approach to Catholic doctrines and to social psychology. Edith *Stein (who became a nun), influenced by Scheler, combined Thomism with phenomenology and existentialism. Aron *Gurwitsch has emphasized the application of phenomenology to psychology, Adolf *Reinach to the philosophy of law, and Moritz *Geiger to aesthetics. Herbert *Spiegelberg wrote the history of the phenomenological movement, and was a leading exponent of it in America along with Fritz *Kaufmann. Emanuel *Levinas, one of those who introduced phenomenology into France, played an important creative philosophical role in the contemporary European scene. Jewish thinkers, and some of Jewish origin, have played important parts in the existentialist movement. Jean *Wahl in France was a leading spokesman and theoretician. Martin *Buber was one of the most important figures in religious existentialism. The writings of Simone *Weil have played a significant role in postwar Christian existentialism. George *Simmel was one of the most important figures in the naturalistic movement, both for his biological and Darwinian interpretation of Kant, and for his theory of sociology. Wilhelm *Jerusalem followed out some of the implications of pragmatism, Darwinism, and positivism. In America, Morris Raphael *Cohen, Horace *Kallen, and Sidney *Hook have developed some of the naturalistic ideas of James and Dewey.

In radical philosophy some of the major figures have been Jewish thinkers who have developed new interpretations of Hegel and Marx. Gyorgy *Lukacs, Ernst *Bloch, and Walter *Benjamin set forth creative versions of Marxism, extending its insights into many cultural fields. Alexandre *Kojève has played a most important role in reinterpreting Hegel's thought. Herbert *Marcuse has combined *Freud's and Marx's views, including those of the early Marx, into a powerful critique of modern society that has been very influential on New Left thinkers. On the other side, two thinkers of Jewish origin have been leaders of Russian Orthodox thought in Russia. Semyon *Frank, originally a Marxist, developed a metaphysical defense of Christianity. Lev *Shestov was a leading anti-rationalist fideist. Among non-Marxist social philosophers and social critics, Jewish thinkers have also made significant contributions. Julien *Benda criticized the role of the intellectuals. Elie *Halévy wrote against the tyrannies of fascism and communism. Hannah *Arendt analyzed the bases and nature of totalitarianism, and the nature of political freedom. Chaim *Perelman has done important work on the nature of justice.

In the analytic philosophical movement, which has been important in the English-speaking world, philosophers of Jewish origin have been in the forefront. One of the first proponents of linguistic analysis was Fritz *Mauthner. Leaders of the logical positivist movement included Herbert *Feigl, Philipp *Frank, and Friedrich *Waismann. The work of the logician Alfred *Tarski has also been most important in this movement. Among the important American analytic philosophers are Max *Black, Nelson *Goodman, Arthur *Pap, and Morton *White. Thinkers of Jewish origin have played basic roles in 20th-century work in the philosophy of science and logic. Emile *Meyerson developed a philosophical view of the world based on modern science. Sir Karl *Popper has been one of the most important in evaluating the nature of science and the problems involved in gaining scientific knowledge.

In the area of historical studies and interpretations of philosophy, Jewish scholars have been in the forefront throughout this century. They have developed the best of European scholarship and have provided some of the most important ways of understanding various philosophical traditions, as well as editing some of the basic texts. Raoul *Richter wrote an important history of skepticism from antiquity onward. George *Boas wrote on Greek philosophy and on French thought. Hans *Jones, through his demythologizing method, helped in the understanding of Gnosticism. Richard *Waltzer examined the transition of Greek thought into Arabic philosophy. Shlomo *Pines wrote on Arabic and Jewish medieval philosophy. Harry Austryn *Wolfson examined the religious philosophical tradition from Philo, through the Church Fathers and medieval Islamic, Jewish, and Christian thought up to Spinoza. Raymond *Klibansky was influential in medieval and Renaissance studies. Paul O. *Kristeller was a leading figure in the many areas of Renaissance studies. One of Ernst Cassirer's contributions was a monumental study of the development of the modern problem of knowledge from the Renaissance onward. He also wrote on English Platonism and the philosophy of the Enlightenment. Alexandre *Koyré was a leading figure in the study of the history of science from the Renaissance onward, as well as an important Descartes scholar. Leon *Roth wrote important interpretations of Descartes and Spinoza and showed their relationship to Maimonides' thought. R. Ḣ. Popkin wrote on the history of skepticism from the Renaissance to the Enlightenment. David *Baumgardt did important work on the philosophy of Jeremy Bentham, and Elie Halévy wrote the basic study of British philosophical radicalism.

The historical scholarship done on German thought from Kant onward is too copious to mention in detail. Neo-Kantians, especially, have studied the development of German philosophy extensively, and much of the basic work on Kant, Fichte, Hegel, and Schelling, has been done by scholars of Jewish origin.

Participation in philosophy by Jews has grown rapidly, especially in this century. Jewish concern with fundamental issues about man and the world has, no doubt, contributed to this, as has the growing toleration in academic-intellectual circles, especially in the West. The decline of Christianity as a central factor in European philosophy has also made it more possible for Jews to play a role in this area. At the present time in America, and to a lesser extent in England and France, among younger philosophers there are many important figures of Jewish origin who will probably play a most significant role in the decades to come. In Central Europe there are few Jewish intellectuals left, and in Eastern Europe they are being driven from their positions.

Bibliography: L. Magnus, *The Jews in the Christian Era* (1929), 241–8, 330–65, and passim; C. Lehrmann, *L'élement juif dans la pensée européenne* (1947), 43–66; A. A. Roback, *Jewish Influence in Modern Thought* (1929), 333–53, 401–40, incl. bibl.; H. G. Gadamer, in: L. Reinisch (ed.), *Die Juden und die Kultur* (1961),

78–90; H. Landry, in: S. Kaznelson (ed.), *Juden im deutschen Kulturbereich* (1959), 242–77; A. Altmann, in: L. Finkelstein (ed.), *Jews, Their History, Culture, and Religion,* 2 (1960³), 954–1009.

[R.H.P.]

PHILOSOPHY, JEWISH. Jewish philosophy may be described as the explication of Jewish beliefs and practices by means of general philosophic concepts and norms. Hence it must be seen as an outgrowth of the biblical and rabbinic traditions on which Judaism rests as well as part of the history of philosophy at large. This description must, however, be expanded to include the general philosophic literature in Hebrew produced by Jews in the latter part of the Middle Ages and the various secular philosophies of Jewish existence formulated by modern Jewish thinkers. General philosophers who happened to be Jews or of Jewish extraction are not considered part of the tradition of Jewish philosophy. Whereas the biblical and rabbinic traditions were indigenous products of the Jewish community, Jewish philosophy arose and flourished as Jews participated in the philosophic speculations of the external culture. Significant religious and philosophical differences distinguish ancient and medieval from much of modern Jewish thought; nevertheless, the subject matter of Jewish philosophy may be divided into three parts. First, as interpretation of unique aspects of Jewish tradition, Jewish philosophy deals with such topics as the election of Israel; the revelation, content, and eternity of the Torah; the special character of the prophecy of *Moses; and Jewish conceptions of the Messiah and the afterlife. Second, as philosophy of religion, it investigates issues common to Judaism, Christianity, and Islam (as well as to certain kinds of metaphysics), such as the existence of God, divine attributes, the creation of the world, the phenomenon of prophecy, the human soul, and general principles of human conduct. Third, as philosophy proper, it studies topics of general philosophic interest, such as the logical categories, the structure of logical arguments, the division of being, and the nature and composition of the universe. Historically, Jewish philosophy may be divided into three periods: (1) its early development in the Diaspora community of the Hellenistic world, from the second century B.C.E. until the middle of the first century C.E.; (2) its flourishing in Islamic and Christian countries during the Middle Ages from the tenth until the early 16th century; and (3) its modern phase beginning in the 18th century and continuing to the present. Its prehistory, however, begins with the Bible.

BIBLICAL AND RABBINIC ANTECEDENTS

Although the Bible and the rabbinic literature contain definite views about God, man, and the world, these views are presented unsystematically, without a technical vocabulary, and without formal arguments in their support. Hence, it is more appropriate to speak of biblical and rabbinic theology rather than philosophy. Nevertheless, Jewish philosophers of all periods held that their opinions were rooted in the Bible and the rabbinic writings, and they quote these literatures extensively in support of their views. Interestingly, quotations from the Bible far outnumber those from the rabbinic writings, so that one may speak of a certain "Bible-centeredness" of Jewish philosophy. In quoting the Bible, Jewish philosophers often imposed a philosophic rigor on its vocabulary and thought that is not immediately apparent from the literal reading of the text. However, besides quoting the Bible, certain philosophers also had a theory concerning the nature of this document. Aware that the world view of the Bible is rather simple and unphilosophical, they found it difficult to accept that the Bible lacked philosophical sophistication. If God created man with reason, the discoveries of the human mind must be related in some fashion to the content of divine revelation. Hence, they viewed the Bible as twofold: on its literal level it was addressed to philosophers and non-philosophers alike, and thus it had to speak in a manner intelligible to all; but behind its rather simple exterior it contained a more profound meaning, which philosophers could discover by proper interpretation. This esoteric content is identical, fully or in part, with the teachings of philosophy. In assuming this methodological principle, Jewish philosophers resembled Jewish mystics, who discovered secret mystical teachings behind the literal biblical text. We may now examine some representative biblical passages which Jewish philosophers cited to support their views. (For a fuller picture the reader may refer to the indexes of biblical passages appearing in Saadiah Gaon, *The Book of Beliefs and Opinions,* tr. by S. Rosenblatt (1949); Judah Halevi, *The Kuzari,* tr. by H. Hirschfeld (1964); Moses Maimonides, *The Guide for the Perplexed,* tr. by M. Friedlaender (1904²; repr. 1956); Joseph Albo, *Sefer ha-Ikkarim,* ed. and tr. by I. Husik, 4, pt. 2, 1930).

Bible. Of verses concerning God that were cited by Jewish philosophers, perhaps the central one was "Hear, O Israel: the Lord our God, the Lord is one" (Deut. 6:4), which was held to refer to God's uniqueness as well as to His simplicity. The opening of the Decalogue—"I am the Lord thy God" (Ex. 20:2, Deut. 5:6)—was understood as a declaration of God's existence, and, by some, even as a positive commandment requiring the affirmation of the existence of God. God's omnipotence was indicated by the verse: "I know that Thou canst do all things, and that no purpose of Thine can be thwarted" (Job 42:2), and His omniscience, by the verse: "His discernment is past searching out" (Isa. 40:28). That God is incorporeal was derived from the verses: "... for ye saw no manner of form" (Deut. 4:15) and "To whom then will ye liken Me, that I should be equal?" (Isa. 40:25), and that His essence is identical with His existence, from the verse: "I am that I am" (Ex. 3:14). How God can be known was derived from a story concerning Moses. Moses had asked God to show him His ways and then he had requested that He show him His glory. God granted Moses the first of these requests, but denied him the second (Ex. 33:12ff.). This story was interpreted to mean that God's glory, that is, His essence, cannot be known by man, but His ways, that is, His actions, can be known.

Of passages and verses concerning the universe, the creation chapters (Gen. 1–2) were interpreted as stating that the world was created out of nothing and in time. The creation of the universe was also derived from the verses: "I have made the earth, and created man upon it; I, even My hands, have stretched out the heavens, and all their hosts have I commanded " (Isa. 45:12) and "It is He that hath made us, and we are His" (Ps. 100:3). That the celestial spheres are animate and rational was deduced from the verse: "The heavens declare the glory of God" (Ps. 19:2), and the verse: "The sun also arises, and the sun goes down, and hastens to his place where he arises" (Eccles. 1:5) was seen as a description of the daily motion of the uppermost celestial sphere, which produces day and night. That the heavens and the earth are finite was derived from the verses: "... from the one end of the earth even unto the other end of the earth" (Deut. 13:8) and "... from the one end of heaven unto the other ..." (Deut. 4:32). From four terms appearing in Genesis 1:2 it was deduced that the sublunar world consists of the four elements: earth *(ereẓ),* air *(ru'aḥ),* water *(mayim),* and fire (*ḥoshekh*—ordinarily darkness, but here interpreted as fire). Reference to the composition of these four elements of matter and form and to the succession of forms in matter was seen in the verses: "Then

I went down to the potter's house, and, behold, he was at his work on the wheels. And whensoever the vessel that he made of clay was marred in the hand of the potter, he made it again another vessel, as seemed good to the potter to make it" (Jer. 18:3–4). Somewhat more fancifully, Abraham and Sarah, respectively, were identified with form and matter.

Other verses provided a description of human nature. The verses: "See, I have set before thee this day life and good, and death and evil . . . therefore choose life, that thou mayest live . . ." (Deut. 30:15–19) were frequently quoted in support of the notion that man possesses freedom of choice. That man's essential nature is his reason was derived from the verse: "Let us make man in our image . . . " (Gen. 1:26), and that wisdom distinguishes him from other creatures, from the verse: "He that teaches man knowledge" (Ps. 94:10). That man has five senses is indicated by the verses "They have mouths, but they speak not; Eyes have they, but they see not; They have ears, but they hear not; Noses have they, but they smell not; They have hands, but they handle not . . . " (Ps. 115:5–7). "For the life of the flesh is in the blood . . . " (Lev. 17:11) refers to the nutritive faculty of the human soul, and "Notwithstanding thou mayest kill and eat flesh within all thy gates, after all the desire of thy soul . . . " (Deut. 12:15), to the appetitive. Some interpreted that man's ultimate goal in life is to understand God from the verses: "Know this day, and lay it to thy heart, that the Lord, He is God in heaven above and upon the earth beneath . . . " (Deut. 4:39) and "Know ye that the Lord He is God" (Ps. 100:3); but others invoked the verse "And thou shalt love the Lord thy God . . . " (Deut. 6:5) to show that man's final goal is the love of God. That man should be modest in his conduct is indicated by the verse: "The righteous eateth to the satisfying of his desire . . . " (Prov. 13:25), and that the middle way is the best is shown by the verse: " . . . and thou shalt walk in His ways" (Deut. 28:9). While many other verses and passages were cited in support of these and other teachings, Jewish philosophers were also interested in whole chapters and complete biblical books. The theophany in Isaiah 6 and the account of the divine chariot in Ezekiel 1 and 10 were used as descriptions of God and the angelic realm. Of special interest were the more philosophical books of the Bible, including Proverbs, Job, Song of Songs, and Ecclesiastes, on which numerous philosophical commentaries were written, especially in the late Middle Ages.

Rabbinic Literature. Since the Greek philosophers had appeared by the time the rabbis of the Talmud formulated their teachings, it may be asked whether the rabbinic literature reveals any Greek philosophical influence. While the rabbis had some acquaintance with Greek philosophical ideas, particularly with those of the Stoics (in popular versions), it has now been shown that the rabbis were not familiar with formal philosophy (see S. Lieberman, in: *Biblical and Other Studies,* ed. by A. Altmann (1963), 123–41). The names of the major philosophers are absent from the rabbinic writings, and the only philosophers mentioned by name are Epicurus and the obscure, second-century cynic Oenomaus of Gadara. In the tannaitic literature the term "Epicurean" *(apikoros)* is used, but it seems to refer to a heretic in general rather than someone who embraces Epicurus' doctrines. H. A. Wolfson, the modern historian of philosophy, stated that he was unable to discover a single Greek philosophic term in rabbinic literature (Wolfson, *Philo,* 1 (1947), 92). Jewish philosophers cited rabbinic sayings, as they did biblical quotations, for support of their views, once again imposing a philosophic rigor that the sources, on literal reading, lacked. To indicate that attributes describing God in human terms must be interpreted allegorically, philosophers invoked the saying: "The Torah speaks in the language of the sons of man" (Yev. 71a; BM 31b). How circumspect one must be in describing God is shown in the following story:

> Someone reading prayers in the presence of Rabbi Ḥanina said "God, the great, the valiant and the tremendous, the powerful, the strong, and the mighty." Rabbi Ḥanina said to him, "Have you finished all the praises of your Master? The three epithets 'the great, the valiant, and the tremendous,' we should not have applied to God, had Moses not mentioned them in the Law, and had not the men of the Great Synagogue followed and established their use in prayer; and you say all this. Let this be illustrated by a parable. There once was an earthly king who possessed millions of gold coins; but he was praised for owning millions of silver coins. Was this not really an insult to him?" (Ber. 33b).

To show that the substance of the heavens differs from that of sublunar beings the philosophers cited R. Eliezer's saying: "The things in the heavens have been created of the heavens, the things on earth of the earth" (Gen. R. 12:11). Similarly, that the heavens are animate beings was derived from a passage in *Genesis Rabbah* (2:2) which states in part ". . . the earth mourned and cried on account of her evil lot saying, 'I and the heavens were created together, and yet the beings above live forever, and we are mortal.'" The saying "The world follows its customary order" (Av. Zar. 54b) was taken as confirmation that a natural order exists in the world.

Other rabbinic sayings deal with human nature. The saying: "All is in the hands of heaven except the fear of heaven" (Ber. 33b; Nid. 16b) is interpreted to mean that while certain natural dispositions are fixed in man, his actions are free. That there is a correlation between what man does and the fate he suffers is supported by the sayings: "There is no death without sin, and no sufferings without transgression" (Shab. 55a) and "A man is measured with the measure he uses himself" (Sot. 1:7). The spiritual nature of the afterlife is taught in the saying of Rav: "In the World to Come, there is no eating, no drinking, no washing, no anointing, no sexual relations, but the righteous sit, their crowns on their heads, and enjoy the radiance of the *Shekhinah*" (Ber. 17a). Many other citations could be added to this list.

Of special interest are two esoteric rabbinic doctrines known respectively as "the account of creation" *(ma'aseh bereshit)* and "the account of the divine chariot" *(ma'aseh merkavah).* While it is clear that, historically speaking, these two doctrines were forms of Jewish gnosticism (see Scholem, *Mysticism,* 40ff.; idem, *Jewish Gnosticism, Merkabah Mysticism, and Talmudic Tradition,* 1960), philosophers saw in them philosophical truths. Maimonides goes so far as to identify *ma'aseh bereshit* with physics and *ma'aseh merkavah* with metaphysics, holding that the rabbis were conversant with philosophic doctrines but presented them enigmatically.

For editions and translations of philosophic works described below, the reader is referred to the entries appearing under individual philosophers' names. The modern scholarly literature concerning individual philosophers is also listed there.

HELLENISTIC JEWISH PHILOSOPHY

Jewish philosophy began, as has been noted, in the Diaspora community of the Hellenistic world during the second century B.C.E. and continued there until the middle of the first century C.E. It arose out of the confrontation between the Jewish religion and Greek philosophy (particularly the Stoic-Platonic tradition) and had as its aim the philosophic interpretation of Judaism. It also had an apologetic purpose: to show that Judaism is a kind of philosophy, whose conception of God is spiritual and whose ethics is rational. Jewish philosophers polemicized against the polytheism of other religions and against pagan practices. In spite of their philosophic interests they maintained that Judaism is superior to philosophy (see H. A. Wolfson, *Philo,* 1 (1947), 3–27). Philo of Alexandria is the only Jewish Hellenistic philosopher from whom a body of works has survived; all the other materials are either fragmentary or only allude to philosophic or theological topics. The dating of these other materials also presents considerable difficulties. The language of Hellenistic Jewish philosophy was Greek. Jewish Hellenistic culture may be said to have begun with the Septuagint, the Greek translation of the Bible. The translation of the Pentateuch dates from the third century B.C.E. Some scholars have held that this translation already manifests philosophic influences (*ibid.,* 94, n. 39).

The first Jewish philosopher appears to have been *Aristobulus of Paneas (middle of second century B.C.E.), who wrote a commentary on the Pentateuch, fragments of which have been preserved by Christian Church Fathers. He argues that Greek philosophers and poets derived their teachings from the wisdom of Moses, and he interpreted the Bible allegorically. He held, for example, that the expression "hand of God" refers to God's power. He maintained that wisdom (the Torah) existed prior to heaven and earth and that God's power extends through all things. He gives a symbolic interpretation of the Sabbath and comments on the symbolic character of the number "seven." The letter of *Aristeas, a pseudepigraphic account of the history of the Greek translation of the Bible, which incidentally polemicizes against paganism, states that God's power is manifested throughout the world, praises the mean as the best course of action, holds that the help of God is necessary for the performance of good deeds, and advocates the control of passions. The author also presents moral interpretations of the ritual laws, holding that such laws are designed to teach man righteousness, holiness, and perfection of character. II Maccabees mentions cryptically resurrection and creation out of nothing. IV Maccabees, evidently written by someone familiar with Greek philosophy, particularly with the teachings of the first-century B.C.E. Stoic Posidonius, maintains that reason can control the passions, illustrating this theme through examples from Jewish history. The author cites the Stoic definition of wisdom and identifies wisdom with the Law. The Sibylline Oracles (in their extant form a combination of Jewish and Christian teachings) denounce paganism and mention the resurrection and the messianic age. The Wisdom of Solomon, which is patterned after Hebrew Wisdom Literature, contains occasional philosophic terms and arguments. The work polemicizes against idolatry, holding that it is a source of immoral practices. H. A. Wolfson (*Philo,* 1 (1947), 287–9) maintains that the author's conception of wisdom is the same as Philo's conception of the logos (see below), although others have argued that the two conceptions are different. According to Wolfson, wisdom first existed as an attribute of God, then as an independent being created by God prior to the creation of the world, and, finally, as immanent in the world. God created the world out of formless matter. Man can love righteousness, God, and wisdom, and the love of wisdom is manifested in the observance of the Law. The attainment of wisdom also requires the help of God. The righteous are rewarded with immortality, while the wicked shall perish.

Philo of Alexandria. *Philo (c. 20 B.C.E.–c. 50 C.E.), who was well versed in Greek philosophy and poetry, presented his views in a series of commentaries on passages of the Pentateuch, works on biblical topics, and independent philosophic treatises. He was influenced largely by Platonic and Stoic ideas, and his philosophy also has a mystical streak. Because of its unsystematic presentation, his philosophy has been interpreted in several ways. Some consider Philo merely a philosophic preacher, others a philosophic eclectic, still others a mystic. H. A. Wolfson, in his *Philo* (on which what follows is based), presents him as a systematic philosopher who is the founder of religious philosophy in Judaism, Christianity, and Islam. Wolfson describes philosophy from Philo to Spinoza as essentially Philonic (*Philo,* 1 (1947), 87–115). (For a discussion of Philo's knowledge of Hebrew and of Palestinian Jewish traditions, see *Philo,* 1 (1947), 88–93.)

BIBLICAL EXEGESIS. The Bible for Philo was the revealed word of God which had an apparent and a hidden meaning: the apparent meaning was addressed to the masses, while the hidden meaning was reserved for students of philosophy. To discover these two meanings Philo used the literal and allegorical methods of interpretation. Most biblical passages lend themselves to both kinds of interpretation, but Philo insists that anthropomorphic descriptions of God must be interpreted allegorically. While he interprets certain parts of the creation story only allegorically and while he allegorizes biblical names, persons, and events, he also appears to accept biblical narrations in their literal sense. Philo's attitude toward the laws of the Pentateuch is complex and depends on one's evaluation of the nature of Alexandrian *halakhah.* In some passages he maintains that one must observe the totality of Mosaic law, but in others he states that such laws as that requiring the return of a pledge before sunset (Ex. 22:25–26) are trivial in their literal sense and must be understood allegorically.

GOD, LOGOS, AND THE WORLD. Philo's conception of the world is based on Platonic notions, particularly as interpreted and systematized by Posidonius. Characteristic of this approach is the opinion that there exist intermediary beings between God and the world. God, according to Philo, transcends the world. He is one (both in the sense of unique and simple), self-sufficient, eternal, incorporeal, and unlike His creatures. He is good, but He is not identical with the idea of the good of which Plato spoke. In His essence He is unknowable, indescribable, and unnameable; the terms used by Scripture to describe Him are properties referring to His actions. To explain creation and the structure of the world, Philo uses the Platonic notion of "ideas." These ideas, according to him, exist first as patterns in the mind of God, then as incorporeal beings between God and the world, and finally as immanent in the world. Since ideas must inhere in a mind, Philo posits a logos (also called wisdom) in which the ideas inhere. Like the ideas, the logos exists in three forms: as an attribute of God, as an incorporeal being existing between God and the world, and as immanent in the world. The ideas are patterns of things, but they are also causes producing these things; in the latter sense they are called powers. God created the world because He is good, and He created it freely and by design. He first created the incorporeal logos, also called intelligible world, and then the perceptible world. The perceptible world was created out of matter, but it is not clear whether Philo held that this matter was created or uncreated. Creation is not a temporal process, and when it is said that God is prior to His creation it is meant that He is its cause. To create the world God used the self-existent logos, but everything is said to have been created by God Himself except man's body and his irrational soul. The immanent logos, while inhering in the material world, is still immaterial. It produces the laws of nature; but since God created these laws, he can change them if he so desires, and this makes miracles possible.

SOULS. When God created the world, He created with it incorporeal rational souls of varying degrees of impurity. The souls which had greater purity remained incorporeal and became the angels which are God's messengers; the less pure souls were joined to bodies and became the souls of men. The human soul is active in sensation and cognition and it possesses free will. Upon death, the human soul may ascend to the upper realm where it may come to rest among angels, in the intelligible world, or even beyond this, close to God. Immortality is the gift of God.

KNOWLEDGE AND PROPHECY. Basing himself on Plato, Philo speaks of three kinds of knowledge: sensation or opinion, rational knowledge derived from sensation, and the knowledge of ideas. However, whereas Plato describes knowledge of ideas as recollection, Philo identifies it with prophecy. Prophecy, which is said to come from God, can come in three possible ways: through the Divine Spirit, through a specially created divine voice, or through angels. Prophecy can be accompanied by frenzy and ecstasy and it is here that Philo's mystical inclination comes to the fore. There are also three kinds of prophetic dreams which correspond to the three kinds of prophecy. Prophecy through an angel can come to a non-Jew, prophecy through the Divine Spirit can also come to a non-Jew provided he has attained moral and intellectual perfection, but prophecy through the voice of God is reserved for Jews. Prophecy has a fourfold function: prediction of the future, expiation of the sins of the people, promulgation of law, and vision of incorporeal beings.

ETHICS AND POLITICS. Philo accepts the philosophic notion that happiness comes through the acquisition of the moral and the intellectual virtues; but he holds that human laws achieve this purpose only imperfectly whereas the Law of Moses, divine in its origin, achieves it perfectly. The good life is not so much life in accordance with virtue but life in accordance with the Law. The Law contains the philosophic virtues, but adds to them additional ones of its own such as faith, humanity, piety, and holiness as well as prayer, study, and repentance. Obedience or disobedience to the Law leads to reward or punishment, respectively, which are, for Philo, individual. Philo presents Jewish law in the light of Greek political theories. The Law of Moses is the constitution of a state initiated by Moses. In this state there live citizens and noncitizens of various kinds. The state is ruled by a king, a high priest, and a council of elders. However, since this state is based on God's Law, God is the real ruler, and earthly rulers only administrate and interpret the divine Law. This state was originally only a state for the Jewish people, but it also provides the pattern for an ideal society (still composed of states) which will come to be in messianic times. Philo influenced the teachings of Church Fathers such as Clement of Alexandria, Origen, and Gregory of Nysea, but his works remained unknown to Jewish philosophers of the Middle Ages. Whatever influence he may have had on them came through the indirect transmission of his ideas. It was only in the 16th century that, through Azariah dei Rossi, his works became known once again among Jews.

MEDIEVAL PERIOD

Medieval Jewish philosophy began in the early tenth century as part of a general cultural revival in the Islamic East, and continued in Muslim countries—North Africa, Spain, and Egypt—for some 300 years. The Jews of the period spoke, read, and wrote Arabic and thus were able to participate in the general culture of their day. Although Jews produced a rich literature on biblical and rabbinic subjects and much poetry, they did not produce an extensive scientific and philosophical literature of their own. The extant literature was adequate for their needs, and their major speculative efforts were devoted to investigating how Judaism and philosophy were related. Most of their philosophic works were written in Arabic. Toward the end of the 12th century the setting of Jewish philosophy began to change. The Jewish communities in the Islamic world declined, and communities hospitable to philosophic and scientific learning developed in Christian lands, particularly Christian Spain, southern France, and Italy. As a result, Arabic was gradually forgotten, and since, with some notable exceptions, Jews had little occasion to learn Latin, Hebrew became the language of Jewish works in philosophy and the sciences. Thus, whereas in Muslim countries Jews were part of the mainstream of general culture, in Christian lands they had to foster a general culture of their own. In this period, while Jews continued to write works investigating the relation of Judaism and philosophy, they now also produced an extensive literature devoted to purely philosophic topics. As a first step they translated into Hebrew the extensive Arabic philosophical literature of the previous period. Then they commented on the newly translated works, summarized them in compendia and encyclopedias, and composed their own treatises and books. Jewish philosophy during this period was largely based on sources from the Islamic philosophic tradition, but some Jewish philosophers were also influenced by the views of Christian scholastics. The second period in medieval Jewish philosophy lasted until the early 16th century.

Sources and Translations. The philosophic literature available during the Islamic period was based on works studied in the late Hellenistic schools. As the Islamic empire expanded, these schools came under Muslim rule, and the works studied in them were soon translated into Arabic. At times these translations were made from Greek originals, but more often from intermediary Syriac translations. A number of works were translated more than once. The translators, most of whom were Nestorian and Jacobite Christians, were active from about 800 until about 1000. (For an account of these translations see R. Walzer, *Greek into Arabic*, 1962.) Of Platonic works translated, the most important were the *Timeaus*, *Republic*, and *Laws*, but Arabic translations of some other dialogues are extant. Perhaps the most important influence was exercised by the works of Aristotle, all of which were known, except for the *Dialogues* and *Politics*. Together with the works of Aristotle there were translated works by his commentators *Alexander of Aphrodisias, *Themistius, Theophrastus, Simplicius, and John Philoponus. There were also translations of works by Galen, some of which are no longer extant in the original Greek. The neoplatonic tradition was represented by the *Theology of Aristotle*, a collection of excerpts from Plotinus' *Enneads*, and the *Liber de Causis*, a collection from Proclus' *Elements of Theology*, as well as by other neoplatonic writings, some of which have been discovered only recently. There were also translations of the Hermetic writings. In addition, philosophers of the period were familiar with Epicurean, Stoic, and skeptic teachings (see *Epicurus, *Stoicism, and *Skeptics), which, however, reached them through the reports of other authors rather than through translations of original works. Jewish philosophers were similarly influenced by the works of Islamic philosophers of the period, including Al-*Kindī, Al-Rāzī, Al-*Fārābi, *Avicenna (Ibn Sīnā), Al-*Ghazālī, *Avempace (Ibn Bājja), and *Averroes (Ibn Rushd). However, Averroes influenced medieval Jewish philosophy during its second period rather than its first. Jews were familiar, also, with the collection known as the "Epistles of the *Brethren of Sincerity," and they knew the writings of Sufi mystics.

Main Schools. Paralleling Islamic philosophers, Jewish philosophers of the Islamic period may be divided into four groups: followers of the Muʿtazilite branch of the *Kalām, Neoplatonists, Aristotelians, and philosophical critics of Aristotelian rationalism. In the work of one philosopher, at times doctrines from several schools were mixed. Before expositions of the opinions of individual philosophers are given, the characteristics of each of the four groups will be briefly described.

MUʿTAZILITE KALĀM. Muʿtazilite Kalām arose in Islamic circles toward the end of the eighth century. Its views developed out of reflections on problems posed by Scripture. The two major problems were the unity of God and God's justice, and because of their concern with these problems, Muʿtazilites were also called "Men of Unity and Justice." The first problem arose from the observation that the Koran affirms that God is one, yet describes Him by many attributes; the second, from the observation that God is omnipotent and omniscient (which seems to imply that God causes everything in the world including man's actions), yet punishes man for his wrongdoing. To solve the first problem, the Muʿtazilites set out to show that God can be described by many attributes without violating His unity; to solve the second, that, although God is omnipotent and omniscient, man's freedom and hence responsibility for his actions are not precluded. These two interests were broadened to include discussions of other aspects of God and human nature. Muʿtazilites also addressed themselves to more theological problems, such as the nature of different kinds of sinners and the afterlife. Since the Muʿtazilites' speculations derived from a concern with scriptural problems, they did not formulate a systematic philosophy as the neoplatonists and later the Aristotelians did. Philosophy was for them a way of solving scriptural difficulties, and they made use of any philosophical argument that might be of help. Hence, their philosophic speculations were eclectic, and a philosopher would make use of Platonic, Aristotelian, or Epicurean arguments as the need arose. Characteristic of Muʿtazilite works is their division into sections devoted to the unity of God and His justice. Also characteristic are proofs of the existence of God based on proofs of the creation of the world and the division of scriptural commandments into rational and traditional. In reaction to the Muʿtazilites, a more orthodox kind of Kalām, known as Ashʿarite (founded by Al-Ashʿarī, d. 935), arose. While Ashʿarite Kalām was known to Jewish philosophers and is cited by them, it appears that there were no Jewish Ashʿarites. The Ashʿarites were known for their insistence on the absolute omnipotence and omniscience of God, which led them to deny the existence of laws of nature and human free will. However, to safeguard God's justice and man's responsibility they formulated the doctrine of "acquisition," according to which man, while not causing his acts, can do them willingly or unwillingly.

NEOPLATONISM. *Neoplatonism was characterized by the doctrine of emanation, which states that the world and its parts emanated from a first principle, God, in a manner analogous to the emanation of rays from the sun or streams of water from a living fountain. To safeguard the absolute unity of God, Neoplatonists posited a first emanation, identified by some with wisdom (logos) and by others with will, which was between God and the world. Drawing on an analogy between man, the microcosm, and the world, the macrocosm, Neoplatonists posited a number of spiritual substances, such as intellect, soul, and nature, between the first emanation and the world. Some Neoplatonists also held that the spiritual world, no less than the visible, is composed of matter and form. Neoplatonism is marked by the insistence that God is completely above the created order and thus can be described only by negative attributes. Some Neoplatonists held that the world proceeds by necessity from God and is contemporaneous with Him, while others, making concessions to Scripture, affirmed that the world is the product of God's will and is posterior to Him. In their conception of man, Neoplatonists subscribed to the duality of body and soul. The soul originates in the upper region and in some way is forced to join the body. It is man's purpose in life to free the soul from the body, thus making it possible for it to rejoin the upper region from which it came. This "purification" is accomplished through practice of the moral virtues and through philosophic speculation. Neoplatonic ethics generally are ascetic.

ARISTOTELIANISM. Aristotelianism (see *Aristotle) was based on the premises that the world must be known through observation and that this knowledge is gained through study of the various speculative and practical sciences. The speculative sciences, which deal with the nature of reality, are divided into physics, mathematics, and metaphysics; the practical sciences, which deal with human conduct, are divided into ethics, economics, and politics. Logic is the prerequisite instrument of all the sciences. The physics of the Aristotelians is based on an analysis of the many changes taking place in the world. These changes are explained through the four causes, the material, efficient, formal, and final causes. The world is divided into the celestial and the sublunar regions. The sublunar world is one of generation and corruption, and everything in it is ultimately reducible to the four elements, earth, water, air, and fire. Sublunar beings are divided into minerals, plants, animals, and rational beings, and all of them are composed of matter and form. By contrast, the celestial region, not subject to generation and corruption, is immaterial and the only motion occurring within it are the locomotions of the celestial spheres. The celestial region is made up of its own element—the so-called fifth element. It consists of the various celestial spheres in which are set the sun, moon, planets, and fixed stars. Each sphere consists of a body governed by an incorporeal soul and intelligence. The earth is fixed at the center of the universe and the celestial spheres revolve around it. All organic beings, plants, animals, and human beings are governed by an internal principle of motion called a soul. In man, the most complex organic being, the soul possesses nutritive, sensory, appetitive, imaginative, and rational faculties, or powers. The highest faculty is the rational, and to develop it is the purpose of human life. The rational faculty starts as the potential intellect and through exercise becomes the actual intellect and, finally, the acquired intellect. The agent in the production of human knowledge is the active intellect, which in the Islamic and Jewish traditions is identified with the lowest of the celestial intelligences. The active intellect also produces prophecy in men who have the required preparation. While there are some variations in particulars, Islamic and Jewish philosophers subscribe to this general scheme. Metaphysics is viewed as the study of being qua being, that is, of the highest categories, and also as a study of the incorporeal beings, that is, of God and the incorporeal intelligences, which are identified with the angels of Scripture. Morality is viewed as the acquisition of the moral and intellectual virtues. The moral virtues, which, generally speaking, consist of following the mean, are acquired by habituation and thereby become second nature. They are a prerequisite for the attainment of the intellectual virtues, the final goal. While in their ethics Aristotelians followed the traditions of Aristotle, in their political philosophy they followed Plato. They accepted the notion Plato set forth in the *Republic* that mankind may be divided into three classes, men of gold, men of silver, and men of bronze, and identified the first class with the philosophers, who can understand by means of demonstration, and the other two classes with those who can only follow arguments of persuasion. For Plato, the state is founded by a philosopher-king, who in the Islamic and Jewish traditions is identified with the legislative prophet.

CRITICS OF ARISTOTELIANISM. The critical reaction to philosophy was marked by the attempt to show, on philosophic grounds, that philosophers had not made good their claim to have discovered physical and metaphysical truths. The fact that philosophers could not agree on these truths was taken as evidence that they had failed. However, while the critics rejected physics and metyphysics, they accepted the principles of Aristotelian logic.

Saadiah Gaon. The first Jewish philosopher of the Middle Ages was *Saadiah Gaon (882–942), head of the rabbinical academy of Sura (near Baghdad). Influenced by the Muʿtazilites and relying on Platonic, Aristotelian, and Stoic notions, he undertook to formulate a Jewish Kalām. His major philosophic work, which, in Muʿtazilite fashion, is divided into a section on divine unity and a section on divine justice, is his *Book of Opinions and Beliefs (Emunot Ve-De'ot; Kitāb al-Amānāt wa al-Iʿtiqādāt)*, but his philosophical opinions are also found in his commentary on *Sefer Yeẓirah*, his commentary on the Bible, and in his polemics against Hiwī al-Balkhī. Saadiah wrote his *Book of Opinions and Beliefs* to rescue his contemporaries from the doubts that had befallen them and to lead them from being men whose beliefs were based on religious authority alone to becoming men whose beliefs were also confirmed by arguments of reason. Since these were his goals, he began with a methodological preface devoted to an analysis of doubt and how it may be remedied, a definition of belief (the opposite of doubt), and a description of sources of knowledge—sense perception, self-evident first principles, inference, and reliable tradition—which enable one to distinguish true from false beliefs. In typical Muʿtazilite fashion, Saadiah began the book proper (treatise 1) with four proofs for the creation of the world; from the finiteness of the world, from its composition, from accidents, and from the nature of time. Typical of these proofs is the one from finiteness. According to this argument, the finite nature of the universe requires a finite force preserving it, and everything possessing a finite force must have a beginning in time. Saadiah goes on to show that from the creation of the world it follows that it was brought into being by a creator who is distinct from it, and that this creator made it out of nothing. It was part of Saadiah's method to refute current opinions which differed from his own, and thus he adds the refutation of 12 other cosmogonic theories which he considered wrong. Saadiah next demonstrates that God is one (treatise 2). However, despite His unity, God is described by a multiplicity of attributes, such as life, power, and knowledge. According to Saadiah, these attributes only serve to explicate the divine nature and do not suggest that any multiplicity exists in God. God must be described by many attributes because human language cannot find one word describing them all. In his discussion Saadiah takes issue with dualistic and trinitarian conceptions of God. God's kindness toward His creatures requires that He provide them with a law, adherence to which will guide them to earthly happiness and to eternal bliss (treatise 3). This law, the Torah, contains commandments of two kinds: rational, such as the prohibitions against murder and theft, which reason can also discover on its own, and traditional, such as the Sabbath and dietary laws, which must be revealed through the will of God. Rational commandments are general and require particular traditional commandments for their implementation; and traditional commandments upon examination are also found to have certain reasons. The promulgation of the divine precepts requires the existence of prophets, whose mission is confirmed by the miracles they perform. However, the prophecy of Moses is confirmed not only by miracles but also by the reasonableness of the law he brought. This law is unchanging and cannot be abrogated.

Man, Saadiah held, is the goal of creation, and divine justice requires that he be free. He offers two kinds of arguments for the existence of human choice: first, man experiences himself to be free, and there is no evidence that his acts are compelled; second, holding man responsible for his acts requires that he be free. Since man is free, God justly rewards and punishes him. God's foreknowledge is compatible with human freedom, for to foreknow something is different from causing it. Invoking Muʿtazilite models again, Saadiah (treatise 5) discusses different categories of righteous and wicked men. Among them is the penitent, who accomplishes repentance in four steps: renunciation of sin, remorse, the quest for forgiveness, and the assumption of an obligation not to sin again. The sufferings of the righteous are explained as "sufferings of love" (*yissurin shel ahavah*), that is, their sufferings in this world will be compensated by the reward they will receive in the next. (Maimonides later attacked this doctrine.) Man's soul originates at the time of the formation of the body, and its place of origin is the human heart (treatise 6). The substance of the human soul is akin to that of the celestial sphere. The latter section of the *Book of Opinions and Beliefs* is devoted to eschatological issues, and Saadiah's discussion follows traditional Jewish lines. He accepts the doctrine of the resurrection of the body and offers numerous arguments in its support (treatise 7). The resurrection will occur after Israel has been redeemed. The redemption (treatise 8) may take place in two ways. If the time appointed for the Exile passes before Israel repents, God will first send the Messiah from the house of Joseph. Great calamities will befall the Jews, but in the end they will be redeemed by the Messiah from the house of David. Should Israel repent before the completion of the appointed time, the Messiah from the house of David may come right away. In the messianic era, Israel will return to its land and the Temple will be rebuilt. The Christian claims that the Messiah has already come are false. The final stage is the world to come (treatise 9), in which the righteous will be rewarded and the wicked punished. Man's body and soul will remain together in the world to come, and life in that world is eternal. Saadiah concludes his book with an appendix (treatise 10) describing how man should conduct himself in this world.

Other Rabbanite Followers of Kalām. Although Saadiah remained the major Jewish exponent of Muʿtazilite Kalām, other Jewish philosophers made use of kalamic teachings. In Rabbanite circles, kalamic influences were evident until the rise of Aristotelianism in the 13th century, while among Karaites, Kalām provided the dominant philosophy throughout the Middle Ages. David ibn Marwān *al-Mukammiṣ, probably an older contemporary of Saadiah, combined kalamic, Platonic, Aristotelian, and Neoplatonic teachings in his *ʿIshrūn Maqālāt* ("Twenty Treatises"), a work only partially preserved. His views are also cited in *Judah b. Barzillai al-Bargeloni's commentary on *Sefer Yeẓirah*. Al-Mukammiṣ cites the kalamic formula: "God is knowing, but not with knowledge; living, but not with life," interpreting it to mean that God's attributes are identical with each other and with His essence. Following the Neoplatonists, he adds that God's attributes must be understood as negations. Kalamic and Greek philosophic influences are also found in the Bible commentary (extant in fragments) of *Samuel b. Hophni (d. 1013), head of the academy of Sura. He also held that God's attributes are identical with His essence, and, again following the Muʿtazilites, he teaches that only prophets can work miracles. *Nissim b. Jacob b. Nissim ibn Shahin of Kairouan, a younger contemporary of Samuel b. Hophni, uses Muʿtazilite doctrines at the beginning of his introduction to his commentary on the Talmud. *Hai Gaon (d. 1038), last head of the academy of Pumbedita, was also acquainted with Muʿtazilite doctrines, but took issue with some of them. For example, he criticized Samuel b. Hophni for limiting miracles to prophets, holding that pious persons can also perform them.

Karaites. Karaite philosophers were stricter in their adherence to the principles of Muʿtazilite Kalām than the Rabbanite followers of that school. In the 11th century the outstanding Karaite philosophers were Joseph b. Abraham al-*Baṣīr and his disciple *Jeshua b. Judah, whose views were similar. Their rationalism goes beyond that of Saadiah, as can be seen from their opinion that rational knowledge of God must precede belief in revelation. In their view, only after it has been established that God exists, that He is wise, and that He is omnipotent is the truth of revelation guaranteed. A similar rationalism is manifest in their conception of ethics: they maintained that various specific moral principles are self-evident upon reflection, e.g., that good should be done and evil avoided, that one should be grateful, and that one should tell the truth. This awareness is independent of revelation, since even those who deny God and revelation adhere to these principles. The moral law is binding not only for man but also for God. These two philosophers argue with great subtlety for the creation of the world, but unlike Saadiah, they accept the kalamic doctrine that everything is ultimately composed of atoms. In the late Middle Ages *Aaron ben Elijah of Nicomedia, author of *Eẓ Ḥayyim* ("Tree of Life," written in 1346), is the outstanding Karaite thinker. Though his work appeared some 150 years after Maimonides' *Guide*, he was still adhering to the philosophy of the Kalām. In fact, his work is a kind of Kalām critique of the *Guide*. Aaron held that kalamic doctrines are in accord with biblical teachings, while Aristotelianism, pagan in origin, conflicts with biblical teachings on many points. Against Maimonides, Aaron argues that the Kalām proofs for the creation of the world are valid, that God can be described by positive attributes, that providence extends not only to man but also to animals, that evil is not merely a privation of good, and that the soul, not only the acquired intellect, is immortal (for Maimonides' views see below). Following Maimonides, he distinguishes the prophecy of Moses from that of other prophets. He is critical of the kalamic doctrines that God created the world by means of the "created will" and that animals will be rewarded in the hereafter, and also of kalamic conceptions of law.

Isaac Israeli. Neoplatonism in Jewish philosophy appeared at the same time that Kalām did. The first Neoplatonist was the renowned physician Isaac b. Solomon *Israeli (c. 855–c. 955), who flourished in Kairouan. Influenced by the Islamic philosopher al-Kindī and various Neoplatonic writings, he composed *Kitāb al-Ḥudūd* (*Sefer ha-Gevulim;* "Book of Definitions"), *Kitāb al-Jawāhir* ("Book of Substances"), *Sefer ha-Ru'aḥ ve-ha-Nefesh* ("Book on Spirit and Soul"), *Sha'ar ha-Yesodot* ("Chapter on the Elements"), and *Kitāb al-Ustuquṣṣāt* ("Book on the Elements"). In Latin translations some of these works influenced Christian scholastic thought. According to Israeli, God, the Creator, in His goodness and love created the world in time and out of nothing. The means of creation were His power and His will, which for Israeli are attributes of God, not separate hypostases. Two simple substances, first matter and first form, or wisdom, come directly from God. It appears that these two principles combine to form the next hypostasis, intellect; but Israeli also affirms that first matter and form have no separate existence but exist only in the intellect. Intellect is followed by three distinct hypostases of soul—rational, animal, and vegetative. The next hypostasis is nature, which Israeli identifies with the sphere or heaven. This hypostasis is the last of the simple substances and holds a position intermediate between these substances and the perceptible world. The four elements of the lower world are produced from the motion of the sphere or heavens. Israeli distinguished three stages in the creation of the world: creation proper, which produces only first matter, first form, and intellect; emanation, which produces the four spiritual substances; and causality of nature, which produces the world below the heavens. Israeli's philosophy of man is based on the Neoplatonic notion of the human soul's return to the upper world from which it came. The soul's ascent proceeds in three stages: purification, which consists of turning away from appetites and passions; illumination by the intellect, which produces wisdom defined as knowledge of eternal things; and union with, or adherence to, supernal wisdom (not God), at which stage the soul becomes spiritual. Union with supernal wisdom can be accomplished even in this life. Israeli identifies union with the religious notion of paradise, and he holds that the punishment of sinners is that their souls cannot ascend to the upper region but are caught in the fire extending below the heavens. Israeli distinguishes between philosophy, which is the quest for wisdom, and wisdom, which is the final goal. Discussing the prophet, Israeli sees no sharp distinction between him and the philosopher: both are concerned with the ascent of the soul and with guiding mankind toward truth and justice. Israeli distinguishes three kinds of prophecy, which are in ascending order: voice *(kol)*, spirit *(ru'aḥ)*, and speech *(dibbur)*. Many of Israeli's ideas are cited and developed in the commentary on *Sefer Yeẓirah* by his disciple, *Dunash ibn Tamim.

Solomon ibn Gabirol. The most important Jewish Neoplatonist was Solomon ibn *Gabirol (c. 1020–1057, possibly 1070); beginning with him the setting of Jewish philosophy shifted to Spain. Also an important Hebrew poet, Ibn Gabirol presented his philosophy in *Mekor Ḥayyim* ("The Source of Life"; *Fons Vitae*), *Tikkun Middot ha-Nefesh* ("The Improvement of the Moral Qualities"), and his Hebrew philosophical poem, *Keter Malkhut* ("The Kingly Crown"). The Arabic original of *Mekor Ḥayyim* is no longer extant, but the work was preserved in a full Latin translation and in a Hebrew paraphrase of the 13th century by Shem Tov b. Joseph *Falaquera. The Latin translation was circulated widely in Christian scholastic circles, and, possibly because the work was a pure philosophic treatise lacking biblical and rabbinic citations, its author, known as Avicebron or Avemcebrol, was considered a Muslim or an Arab Christian. Divided into five treatises, *Mekor Ḥayyim* deals mainly with different aspects of the principles of matter and form, though it also contains incidental accounts of other aspects of Ibn Gabirol's thought. It reveals influences of Neoplatonic writings as well as of the pseudo-Empedoclean writings. Ibn Gabirol's conception of God is Neoplatonic in that it emphasizes that God is beyond the world and can be known only through negations. According to *Mekor Ḥayyim*, from God, called First Substance, emanates the divine will or wisdom (logos); but, according to *Keter Malkhut*, wisdom and will as successive emanations are distinct. Next come universal matter and form. According to some passages, universal matter emanates from God, and universal form, from the will; according to others, both principles emanate from the divine will. Three spiritual substances, intellect, soul, and nature, and then the perceptible world follow. According to some interpreters, Ibn Gabirol introduced the notion of the will to give a voluntaristic complexion to the doctrine of emanation, while according to others, he subscribed to the view that emanation proceeds by necessity from God. Another characteristic doctrine of Ibn Gabirol is the notion that all beings other than God, including the spiritual substances, are composed of matter and form. Ibn Gabirol's account of matter and form is ambiguous. There are passages in which he accepts the Aristotelian notion that matter is the substratum for change, while form determines the essence; but there are other passages in which he maintains that the essence of something is determined by its matter, while the forms produce differences between substances having the same material principle. In typical Neoplatonic fashion, Ibn Gabirol presents the goal of human life as the soul's return to the upper sphere, which is accomplished through proper conduct and philosophic speculation. In his *Tikkun Middot ha-Nefesh,* he discusses 20 moral qualities (four for each of the five senses) and tries to relate them to the four humors of the human body. Ibn Gabirol's philosophic views influenced later kabbalistic thought.

Baḥya ibn Paquda. Toward the end of the 11th century, *Baḥya b. Joseph ibn Paquda wrote his *Sefer Torat Ḥovot ha-Levavot* ("Guide to the Duties of the Hearts"; *Kitāb al-Hidāya ilā Farāʾiḍ al-Qulūb*), a devotional manual which achieved great popularity among Jews. The work was influenced by Neoplatonism, Kalām, the *hermetic writings, and Sufi literature, and Baḥya readily quoted stories and sayings from Islamic, as well as Jewish, sources. Baḥya's work rests on a distinction between "duties of the limbs" *(ḥovot ha-evarim),* religious commandments that require overt actions, and "duties of the hearts" *(ḥovot ha-levavot),* those commandments which require specific beliefs and inner states (intentions). He holds that the latter are commanded by the Torah no less than the former. In the ten chapters of his work he discusses the following duties of the hearts: belief in God's unity; examination of created beings, which leads to an understanding of the divine goodness and wisdom manifest in nature; service of God; trust in God; sincerity in serving God; humility; repentance; self-examination; abstinence; and, finally, love of God. Baḥya defines and describes these traits and provides practical guidance for their attainment. Using a Kalām distinction, Baḥya divides the duties of the limbs into rational and traditional commandments, while the duties of the hearts are all rational. Although Baḥya's work is largely practical, he also insists on theoretical knowledge, holding that knowledge of God is a necessary prerequisite for practicing the other duties of the hearts. Hence, he devotes the first chapter of his work to kalamic proofs (based on Saadiah) demonstrating the creation of the world and the existence and unity of God. Of the proofs for the creation of the world, Baḥya prefers the one from composition. God's unity, he holds, is different from all other unities, and His essential attributes (existence, unity, and eternity) are to be considered as descriptions of God's actions. Similar views were later expressed by Maimonides. Of special interest is Baḥya's discussion of abstinence, one of the most extensive in Jewish philosophic literature. Baḥya acknowledges that there is a general abstinence for all mankind that is practiced to improve man's physical, moral, and political conditions, but maintains that there is also a special abstinence required of the adherents of the Torah. This special abstinence requires the rejection of everything that is not necessary for the satisfaction of man's natural desires and has as its goal the control of man's desires and the subsequent development of his intellect. However, Baḥya's asceticism is moderate. Disapproving of those who separate themselves from the world or confine themselves to their homes, Baḥya recommends that one participate in the social endeavors of his fellow men and restrict asceticism to his personal life. The final goal is the love of God, which Baḥya defines as the soul's turning to God so that it may cleave to His upper light. The soul is a simple spiritual substance, which was implanted by God in the body, but which wants to free itself from bodily desires and pain in order to attain a spiritual state.

Pseudo-Baḥya. A work written between the middle of the 11th and 12th centuries entitled *Kitāb Maʿānī al-Nafs* ("On the Nature of the Soul") was attributed to Baḥya (see *Baḥya (Pseudo-)), but it is not by him. Influenced by Neoplatonic and hermetic (Gnostic) teachings, the work describes the origin of the world by emanation and the nature of the soul. The soul is a spiritual substance, independent of the body, which comes from the upper world to which it wants to return. In its descent, the soul acquires influences from the various regions through which it passes, and they account for differences between the souls. It is also polluted by the body in which it inheres. Return to the upper world is accomplished by practicing moral virtues and acquiring knowledge. The book contains a description of the afterlife, including the punishments of various kinds of sinners.

Abraham bar Ḥiyya. *Abraham b. Ḥiyya (first half of the 12th century), who lived in Spain and was the author of works on mathematics and astronomy, was the first to write philosophical works in Hebrew. His philosophic ideas, influenced by Neoplatonism and Aristotelianism, are found in his *Hegyon ha-Nefesh ha-Aẓuvah* ("Meditation of the Sad Soul") and in his messianic treatise *Megillat ha-Megalleh* ("Scroll of the Revealer"). Central to the former work is a discussion of repentance; in general, his interests are more ethical and theological than philosophic. Abraham b. Ḥiyya subscribes to the doctrine of emanation, but, differing from earlier Neoplatonists, he interposes a world of light and a world of dominion between God and the three spiritual substances. His conception of matter and form is Aristotelian: he holds that these principles exist only in the corporeal world, not in that of the simple substances. In *Hegyon ha-Nefesh,* Abraham b. Ḥiyya divides the fates of souls after death into four categories: souls that have acquired intellectual and moral perfection will ascend to the upper world; souls that have acquired intellectual, but not moral, perfection will ascend only to the sphere below the sun, where they will be afflicted by the sun's fire; souls that have acquired moral, but not intellectual, perfection transmigrate to other bodies until they have acquired knowledge; and souls that have neither perfection will perish with their bodies. However, in *Megillat ha-Megalleh,* he denies the transmigration of the soul and makes the afterlife more dependent on moral perfection. In *Megillat ha-Megalleh* Abraham b. Ḥiyya formulates a theory of history reminiscent of Judah Halevi's theory and of Christian speculation. The history of the world can be divided into six periods corresponding to the six days of creation. There is also an analogue to the Christian notion of original sin: God created Adam with three souls, rational, appetitive, and vegetative. Before Adam sinned the rational soul existed independently of the other two souls, but afterwards it became dependent on them. After the flood, God freed the rational soul from its dependence on the vegetative soul, but not from its dependence on the appetitive soul. However, in each generation the rational soul of one man achieved independence, and this was the state of affairs until the time of Jacob. In Jacob the rational soul was so pure that all of his descendants, first his 12 sons and later all of Israel, received a rational soul independent of the lower two souls. This is Abraham bar Ḥiyya's explanation of the election of Israel, though he does not deny that there may also be righteous persons among the gentiles.

Joseph ibn Ẓaddik. Joseph ibn *Ẓaddik of Cordova (d. 1149) was the author of *Sefer ha-Olam ha-Katan* ("Book of the Microcosm"), an eclectic Neoplatonic work with Aristotelian and kalamic influences, apparently written as a handbook for beginners. In the four parts of the work he discusses the principles of the corporeal world and its constitution, the nature of man and the human soul, the existence of God (derived from the creation of the world) and His attributes, and human conduct and reward and punishment. His thought shows similarities to that of Saadiah, Israeli, Baḥya, Pseudo-Baḥya, and Ibn Gabirol, though he does not mention them, and he attempts to refute opinions of the Karaite Al-Baṣīr. With Ibn Gabirol, he affirms that spiritual beings are composed of matter and form, but he defines the matter of spiritual beings as the genus of a species rather than as a distinct principle. However, he does not mention Ibn Gabirol's universal matter and universal form. Like Ibn Gabirol, Ibn Ẓaddik mentions the divine will, but for him, it appears to be identical with the essence of God rather than a separate hypostasis. He criticizes Al-Baṣīr's notion that the divine will is a substance that God creates from time to time. For his proof of the creation of the world he selects the Kalām proof from accidents, but he describes God in Neoplatonic fashion as an absolute unity beyond the world and as incomprehensible. Yet, he also holds that God can be described by attributes that are identical with His essence. These attributes in one respect describe God's actions, and in another, His essence; as describing His essence, they must be understood as negations. The attributes of action are important for providing models for human conduct. For example, as God is good and merciful, so man should be good and merciful. A similar orientation is found in his account of human happiness. He begins by saying that the knowledge of the supernal world and God is the goal of human life; but then he seems to consider this knowledge only as preliminary to proper conduct. Ibn Ẓaddik's account of the soul's fate after death is derived from Israeli (see above).

Moses and Abraham ibn Ezra. Moses *ibn Ezra (c. 1055–after 1135) was important mainly as a poet and critic, but he presented some philosophic opinions in his *al-Maqāla bi al-Ḥadīqa fī Maʿnā al-Majāz wa al-Ḥaqīqa* (partially translated into Hebrew as *Arugat ha-Bosem*). Ibn Ezra was fond of quoting sayings (often incorrectly attributed) of such authorities as Pythagoras, Empedocles, Socrates, and Aristotle, and he preserved some Arabic quotations from Ibn Gabirol's *Mekor Ḥayyim* (see S. Pines, in *Tarbiz*, 27 (1957–58), 218–35). His orientation was Neoplatonic, and he employs the notions that man is a microcosm and everything in the upper world has its counterpart in man; the soul's knowledge of itself leads to the knowledge of the Creator; God is a unity above all unities, and, unknowable as He is in Himself, He can only be known by metaphors; the rational soul is a substance which must take care of the body; and others.

Abraham *ibn Ezra (c. 1089–1164) was important as a grammarian, as an author of works on arithmetic and astronomy (including astrology), and as a biblical commentator. He was the author of *Sefer ha-Shem* and *Yesod Mora*, on the names of God and on the commandments, but his philosophic views are scattered throughout his biblical commentaries. He often presented his opinions in enigmatic language. Ibn Ezra was profoundly influenced by Neoplatonic doctrines, which in his formulation have at times a pantheistic ring; for example "God is the One; He made all and He is all." Like Ibn Gabirol he held that everything other than God is composed of matter and form, and he alludes as well to the divine will. Speaking of creation, Ibn Ezra affirmed that the world of the intelligences and angels as well as that of the celestial spheres is coeternal with God, and only the lower world was created (through emanation). The human soul comes into being from the spiritual substance known as the universal soul, and, if worthy, it can become immortal by being reunited with that soul and being absorbed by it. Destruction is the punishment of unworthy souls. Like the Islamic Aristotelians, Ibn Ezra held that God's knowledge extends only to species, not to individuals. God's providence, also general, is transmitted through the influences of the heavenly bodies, but individuals who have developed their souls and intellects can foresee evil influences caused by the celestial spheres and avoid them.

Judah Halevi. *Judah Halevi (before 1075–1141), ranking with Ibn Gabirol as one of the two most important Hebrew poets of the Middle Ages, wrote a philosophic work whose full title is *Kitāb al-Ḥujja wa al-Dalīl fī Naṣr al-Dīn al-Dhalīl* ("The Book of Argument and Proofs in Defense of the Despised Faith"); but it is popularly known as *Sefer ha-Kuzari*. Like the Islamic philosopher al-Ghazālī, with whom he seems to have shared a common source, he is critical of Aristotelian rationalism. (By Judah Halevi's time, Aristotelianism was important in Islamic philosophy, but not yet in Jewish philosophy.) For Judah Halevi, historical experience, rather than physical and metaphysical speculations, is the source of truth, and religious practices are more important than beliefs and dogmas. Composed as a narrative, Judah Halevi's book has as its subject the conversion of the king of the Khazars to Judaism in the first half of the eighth century. Judah Halevi's views emerge in a dialogue between the king and the *ḥaver*, a Jewish scholar who acts as the author's spokesman. Judah Halevi relates that the king had a dream in which an angel appeared to him telling him that his intentions were pleasing to the Creator but not his deeds. At first the king interpreted the dream to mean that he should be more zealous in his observance of the Khazar religion; but when the angel appeared with the same message a second time, he understood that he was to look for a new way of life. He invited an Aristotelian philosopher, a Christian, and a Muslim; only after he had found their presentations unsatisfactory did he feel compelled to invite the Jew, a member of the "despised faith" (*Kuzari*, 1:10). His conversation with the *ḥaver* convinces the king to convert to Judaism (2:1). Most of the five treatises of Judah Halevi's book are devoted to the *ḥaver's* explanation of the Jewish religion.

God. Judah Halevi's point of view emerges from the *ḥaver's* opening statement that Jews believe in the God of Abraham, Isaac, and Jacob, who publicly performed many miracles for them and who gave them the Torah. When the king asks the *ḥaver* whether he should not have begun with such speculative principles as "God is the creator and governor of the world," the *ḥaver* replies that to begin with such principles bring one to a rational religion, which is subject to many doubts. Only a religion based on the experience of God's manifestation in historical events is certain and free from doubt (1:11–29).

Prophecy. Closely related to his conception of God is Judah Halevi's account of prophecy and the nature of the Jewish people. Unlike Neoplatonists and Aristotelians, who tended to describe prophecy as a natural activity of the rational faculty or of the rational and imaginative faculties combined, Judah Halevi views prophecy as the activity of a separate faculty beyond the natural faculties of man (1:31–43). God created Adam with this faculty, and it was transmitted by heredity first to individuals such as Noah, Abraham, Isaac, and Jacob; then to the 12 sons of Jacob and their descendants; and, finally, to the Jewish people as a whole (1:95). Possession of the prophetic faculty is the distinguishing feature of Israel's election, and even a convert, though equal to the born Jew in all other respects, cannot attain the prophetic gift (1:27). A sign of the inadequacy of philosophy is that no prophets were found among the philosophers (1:99). While for Judah Ḥalevi prophecy is primarily a gift of God and not the result of natural processes, he attaches two conditions to its attainment: prophecy can be attained only in Ereẓ Israel or (to account for prophets who prophesied outside Ereẓ Israel) the content of the prophecy, at least, must be about Ereẓ Israel; and only those who observe the divine commandments can be prophets (2:8–14).

PIETY. Piety is the main theme of Judah Halevi's philosophy of man. Man does not attain closeness to God, his goal in life, by pursuing philosophic speculations, but by faithfully adhering to the commandments of God. Accepting the Kalām's distinction between rational and traditional (divine) commandments, Judah Halevi holds that all men must observe the former; however, in his view they have only a preliminary function, and true guidance to human happiness is provided only by the latter (2:45–48). The servant of God is like a ruler: he apportions to each part of his body and soul its due (3:1ff.). While Judah Halevi advocates moderation in eating and drinking and control of appetites, his outlook is not ascetic. Man's joy on the Sabbath and the festivals is no less pleasing to God than his affliction on fast days (2:50). Prayer is the nourishment which sustains the soul from one prayer time to the next (3:5).

ATTITUDE TOWARD PHILOSOPHY. Judah Halevi is against philosophy as a way of life, but he is not against philosophic speculations altogether. It has already been noted that he accepts the philosophic notion of rational commandments. Philosophic distinctions appear also in his discussion of God. As YHWH, God can be known only through revelation but as *Elohim*, the ruler and guide of the universe, He can be discovered also through philosophic speculation (4:1–3). Like the philosophers, Judah Halevi holds that anthropomorphic and anthropopathic terms applied to God must be interpreted, and he states that divine attributes must be understood as negations, relations, or attributes of action (2:2). Judah Halevi holds that philosophy was known among Jews in ancient times, as can be seen from *Sefer Yeẓirah*, which tradition attributed to Abraham; but Abraham wrote this book before he received his revelation (2:66; 4:24–25). At the request of the king, the *ḥaver* explains the principles of Aristotelian philosophy and of the Kalām (treatise 5), but he points out once again the superiority of revelation. The *ḥaver* also discusses human free will (5:20), and at the end of the book (5:22ff.) he declares his intention to go to Ereẓ Israel.

Ḥibat Allah. *Ḥibat Allah Abu al-Barakāt al-Baghdādī (second half of 11th century–first half of 12th century; flourished in Baghdad), whose philosophy has only recently been studied by S. Pines, was the author of a commentary on Ecclesiastes and of a philosophic work *Kitāb al-Muʿtabar* ("The Book of What Has Been Established By Personal Reflection"). He converted to Islam at the age of 60, but the two works mentioned seem to have been written while he was still a Jew. Subjecting the doctrines of the Aristotelian philosophers to a critical review, he presents novel notions of his own on physical, psychological, and metaphysical questions.

Nethanel al-Fayyūmī. *Nethanel al-Fayyūmī (d. about 1165; flourished in Egypt or Yemen) composed a work entitled *Bustān al-ʿUqūl* ("Garden of Intellects"), which attempts to introduce doctrines of the Islamic Ismāʿīliyya sect into Jewish thought.

Abraham ibn Daud. By the middle of the 12th century Jewish philosophy entered its next phase and, under the influence of the Islamic philosophers, Al-Fārābī, Avicenna, and Avempace, turned toward Aristotelianism. Abraham b. David ha-Levi *ibn Daud (c. 1110–1180), was the first Jewish Aristotelian. He wrote his major philosophical work, *al-ʿAqīda al-Rafīʿa* ("Sublime Faith," translated into Hebrew as *Ha-Emunah ha-Ramah*, and a second time as *Ha-Emunah ha-Nissa'ah*, 1161) to explain the doctrine of free will to a friend; but, in fact, he discusses a variety of philosophical and theological topics. The work was strongly influenced by Avicenna and highly critical of Ibn Gabirol. Asserting that Judaism and philosophy are identical in their essence, Ibn Daud begins with an explanation of Aristotelian metaphysical, physical, and psychological notions (treatise 1). Having explained these notions philosophically, he cites scriptural verses that in his view allude to these notions. He proceeds to use them for an exposition of six topics: the existence of God, His unity, divine attributes, God's actions (including creation), prophecy, and the allegorical interpretation of terms comparing God to creatures (treatise 2). The work concludes with a brief discussion of ethical matters (treatise 3). To prove the existence of God, Ibn Daud uses the Aristotelian proof from motion and the Avicennian proof from necessity and contingency. According to the first proof, the analysis of motion in the world leads to a prime mover; according to the second, the contingent character of the world leads to a being necessary through itself. God, as necessary existent, is one both in the sense of being unique and of being simple. The attributes applied to God cannot have any positive meaning, but must be understood as negations or relations. Following Aristotle he holds that every change or process requires an underlying matter, but differing from Aristotle (for whom the world is eternal), he holds that God created a first matter, out of which he subsequently created the world. In a different vein, he cites aspects of the doctrine of emanation to explain the creation of the world, insisting, however, that emanation occurs not by necessity but by the free will of God. In psychology, Ibn Daud, like Avicenna, taught that the human intellect is an individual substance, not just a corporeal predisposition, as other Aristotelians believed. It is this substance as a whole that becomes immortal, not only that part known as the acquired intellect. The active intellect, the lowest of the celestial intelligences, is a cause for the actualization of the human mind, and it is also the effect of the active intellect on the mind of man that enables him to prophesy. Unlike Maimonides, who assigns to the imagination the important role in the prophetic inspiration, Ibn Daud, like Judah Halevi, restricts prophecy to the Jewish people and limits it to the land of Israel. Most difficult from the theological point of view is Ibn Daud's account of the knowledge of God: in order to safeguard man's freedom of choice, he willingly admits that God's knowledge is limited.

Maimonides. Ibn Daud was soon overshadowed by Moses *Maimonides (1135–1204), the greatest Jewish Aristotelian and the most prominent figure of medieval Jewish thought. Maimonides discusses his philosophy in popular fashion in parts of his halakhic works, his commentary on the Mishnah and *Mishneh Torah*, and in some treatises; but he reserves its technical exposition for his *Guide of the Perplexed (Dalālat al-Ḥā'irīn; Moreh Nevukhim)*. In formulating his views he drew on Aristotle and his Hellenistic commentators, and on the Muslims Al-Fārābi, Avicenna, and Avempace. Maimonides wrote his *Guide* for a faithful Jew, who, having studied philosophy, was perplexed by the literal meaning of biblical anthropomorphic and anthropopathic terms applied to God and by parables appearing in the Bible. Maimonides shows this person that his perplexities can be resolved by correct interpretation. Hence, the *Guide* is devoted in part to the philosophic interpretation of the Bible, but beyond that, to revealing the inner, i.e., philosophic, meaning of the Torah—as Maimonides puts it, to "the science of the Law in its true sense," or to the "secrets of the Law." Maimonides believed that the philosophic content of the Bible should be revealed only to an intellectual elite, not to the masses, and thus he wrote his work in an enigmatic style (*Guide,* 1: Introd.).

Divine Attributes. In accord with his exegetical program, Maimonides begins his *Guide* (1:1–49) with an interpretation of difficult biblical terms, showing that even such terms as "to sit," "to stand," and "to eat" (applied in the Bible to God) have a spiritual sense. From exegesis he proceeds to exposition, selecting as his first topic the attributes of God (1:50–60). Medieval philosophers held that attributes applied to substances are of two kinds: essential, such as existence and life, which are closely related to the essence; and accidental, such as anger and mercifulness, which are incidental to the essence. The Avicennian tradition, which Maimonides followed, maintained, in addition, that both kinds of attributes are distinct from the substances to which they are applied, and hence, introduce multiplicity into that which they describe. How, then, can attributes be applied to God, Who is one in the sense of being simple? After considering a number of possibilities of how attributes may be applied, Maimonides comes to the conclusion that essential attributes in the case of God must be understood as negations and accidental attributes as descriptions of His actions.

God. Before presenting his own views concerning the existence, unity, and incorporeality of God and the creation of the world, Maimonides offers a summary and critique of the Kalām's discussion of these four topics (1:71–76). His exposition rests on Aristotelian physical and metaphysical principles (2: Introd.), and he sets down four proofs, current in his day, for the existence of God: the proofs from motion, from the composition of elements, from necessity and contingency, and from potentiality and actuality (casuality). All of them start with some observable property of the world and conclude that a prime mover, a necessary existent, or a first cause (all of which are identified with God) must exist. These proofs for the existence of God lead in turn to proofs for His unity and incorporeality (2:1).

Creation. Maimonides next discusses the incorporeal intelligences, which he identifies with the biblical angels, the celestial spheres (2:2–12), and then the creation of the world (2:13–26). A good part of his exposition is devoted to showing that the Aristotelian arguments for the eternity of the world are not conclusive demonstrations; they only attempt to show that eternity is more plausible than creation. Maimonides' own position is that the human mind is incapable of conclusively demonstrating the eternity of the world or its creation and can only present plausible arguments for either view. An examination of these arguments reveals that those for creation are more plausible, and on this basis Maimonides accepts the doctrine of creation *ex nihilo* as his own. He finds additional support for his opinion in the teachings of Scripture. Although the world has a beginning in time, it will not have an end (2:27–29).

Prophecy. In the introduction to the *Guide* Maimonides incidentally discussed the nature of the prophetic experience, likening it to intellectual illumination; in the present section (2:32–48) he is interested in the psychology of prophecy and in its political function. Prophecy, for Maimonides, appears to be a natural phenomenon occurring when man's psychological faculties, particularly his intellect and imagination, have reached a certain perfection. God's role is limited to keeping someone who has met all the prerequisites from becoming a prophet. The prophet requires a well-developed imagination, because besides being a philosopher, he is also a statesman who brings a law, as in the case of Moses, or admonishes the people (who must be persuaded by arguments of the imagination) to adhere to a law, as in the case of the other prophets. Moses as a prophet is singular and so is his law, since through it one can attain intellectual as well as moral perfection. Maimonides concludes the portion of the *Guide* devoted to physical and metaphysical topics with an interpretation of the divine chariot *(merkavah)* described in Ezekiel chapters 1 and 10 (3:1–7).

Evil and Divine Providence. The first topic of practical philosophy is the existence of evil (3:8–12), which Maimonides defines as the absence or privation of good. There is more good than evil in the world; of the three kinds of evil—natural evil, such as earthquakes, political, such as wars, and moral, such as the various vices—the majority, i.e., political and moral evils, can be remedied by man. Closely related to the question of evil is that of divine providence (3:16–21). Maimonides rejects the opinions of the Epicureans that everything is due to chance; the Aristotelians that there is no individual providence; the Ash'arites that there is only individual providence, extending even to animals and minerals; and the Mu'tazilites that individual providence includes animals but not minerals; and he presents instead the views of the Torah. All Jews are agreed that God is just, that man is free, and that individual providence extends only to man. According to Maimonides' understanding of the Jewish view, individual providence depends on the development of the human mind, that is, the more a man develops his mind the more he is subject to the providence of God. Maimonides also holds that any suffering in this world is punishment for some prior sin, rejecting the doctrine of *yissurin shel ahavah,* according to which God may afflict man in this world in order to reward him in the next. Maimonides interprets the Book of Job in the light of his discussion of providence, showing how the characters of the book symbolize the various viewpoints about providence that he had discussed (3:22–24).

Analysis of the Torah. Rejecting the Mu'tazilite distinction between commandments produced by reason *(mitzvot sikhliyyot)* and those coming from the will of God *(mitzvot shimiyyot),* Maimonides maintains that all the commandments of the Torah are the result of the wisdom of God. Hence, all are intelligible, some *(mishpatim)* easily, others *(ḥukkim)* with difficulty. However, Maimonides adds that particular commandments which by their very nature are not subject to reason were stipulated by the will of God. The Torah has two purposes: the well-being of the soul (intellect) and the well-being of the body, by which he means man's political and moral well-being. The well-being of the soul is achieved through assent to true beliefs, such as the existence and incorporeality of God, which are true in themselves. However, there are also necessary beliefs, such as that God gets angry at those who disobey Him, whose main function is to motivate men to obey the Law. Reasons for moral laws can easily be found, but it is more difficult to explain the numerous ritual laws found in the Bible. Maimonides explains many of them, for example, the biblical prohibition against wearing garments made of wool and linen combined, as reactions to ancient pagan practices (3:25–50). He concludes his *Guide* with a supplementary section on the perfect worship of God and man's perfection (3:51–54).

THE MESSIAH. Maimonides barely refers to eschatology in the *Guide*, but he develops his views on the subject in other works. The Messiah is an earthly king descended from the House of David, who will bring the Jews back to their country, but whose main task will be to bring peace and tranquillity to the world, thereby facilitating the full observance of the Law. The Messiah will die of old age; he will be succeeded by his son, and the latter, by his son, and so on. No cataclysmic events will take place in messianic times; the world will continue in its established order. In that time the dead will be resurrected with body and soul united, but later they will die again. The central notion of Maimonides' eschatology is *olam ha-ba* ("the world to come"), where the intellect will exist without the body and contemplate God.

Hebrew Translators of the 13th Century. When, after the period of Maimonides, the setting of Jewish philosophy shifted to Christian countries and its language became Hebrew (see above), the philosophic literature produced by Jews during the preceding period was translated from Arabic into Hebrew, as were many scientific and philosophic works written by Muslims (see Steinschneider, Uebersetzungen). Among the translators of this vast literature were Judah, Samuel, and Moses ibn Tibbon, Jacob Anatoli, Jacob ben Makhir, and *Kalonymus ben Kalonymus. Maimonides' *Guide* was the most influencial work translated; next in importance were Averroes' commentaries on the works of Aristotle. Of the 38 commentaries that Averroes composed, 36 were translated into Hebrew (see H. A. Wolfson, in: *Speculum*, 38 (1963), 88–104). Under Averroes' influence, Jewish philosophy turned toward a more extreme rationalism (for details see below), and some Jewish philosophers attempted to harmonize the opinions of Maimonides and Averroes on topics on which these two philosophers differed.

Maimonidean Controversies. Maimonides' attempt to formulate a rationalistic account of Judaism produced controversies between his followers and their opponents that lasted throughout the 13th century and into the early 14th. The controversy reached such intensity that the two sides excommunicated each other, and they even went so far as to call in the Church authorities, who burned the *Guide* and *Sefer ha-Madda* in 1232. Another highlight was the ban of Solomon b. Abraham *Adret, issued in 1305, which prohibited the study of physics and metaphysics before the age of 25 (for an account of these controversies, see *Maimonidean Controversy). During the early 13th century, some philosophers were still active in the Islamic world. Joseph b. Judah ibn *Aknin (flourished in Morocco), Maimonides' younger contemporary, composed a number of talmudic and philosophic works, among them a commentary on the Song of Songs, a commentary on *Avot*, and a work on moral philosophy, *Ṭibb al-Nufūs al-Salīma wa Muʿālajat al-Nufūs al-Alīma* ("The Hygiene of the Healthy Souls and the Therapy of Ailing Souls"), which contains an interesting account of the content and order of religious and secular studies among Jews. Joseph b. Judah ibn *Sham'un (d. 1226), the disciple for whom Maimonides wrote his *Guide*, composed a small metaphysical work on the necessary existent, how all things proceed from it, and on creation. The early portion of the work follows Avicennian Aristotelianism, and the latter portion, the teachings of Kalām. It is likely that the kalamic section predated Ibn Sham'un's acquaintance with Maimonides. *Abraham b. Moses b. Maimon (1186–1237), Maimonides' only son, followed the teachings of his father and defended them against opponents. However, in his *Kitāb Kifāyat al-ʿAbidīn* ("Comprehensive Guide for the Servants of God"), he advocates a Sufi-like Jewish pietism.

SAMUEL IBN TIBBON. In southern France, Samuel ibn *Tibbon, the translator of the *Guide* and other works, composed *Perush me-ha-Millot ha-Zarot*, a philosophical glossary for the *Guide*, philosophical commentaries on Ecclesiastes and Song of Songs, and *Ma'amar Yikkavu ha-Mayim* (on Gen. 1:9), devoted to physical and metaphysical topics. He favored the allegorical interpretation of the Bible, and is said to have held that the Bible was primarily for the masses.

JACOB ANATOLI. Jacob *Anatoli (13th century), active as a translator at the court of the emperor Frederick II, wrote *Malmad ha-Talmidim*, a philosophical commentary on the Pentateuch. In this work he quotes the Christian scholar Michael Scot (he even cites the emperor) and he shows acquaintance with Christian literature and institutions. He followed the allegorical interpretation of Scripture and preached philosophical sermons publicly. This earned him the anger of the anti-Maimonists.

SHEM TOV BEN JOSEPH FALAQUERA. Shem Tov b. Joseph *Falaquera (c. 1225–c. 1295), translator and author of many works devoted largely to ethics and psychology, also wrote *Moreh ha-Moreh*, a commentary on Maimonides' *Guide*. In this commentary he corrects Ibn Tibbon's translation of the *Guide* on the basis of the Arabic original, and he cites parallel passages from the works of Islamic philosophers, particularly from Averroes. In his *Iggeret ha-Vikku'aḥ*, a dialogue between a philosopher and an opponent of philosophy, he justifies the study of philosophy. In his *Sefer ha-Nefesh* he follows Avicenna, but in his encyclopedic work *De'ot ha-Pilosofim* he follows Averroes. He translated and condensed Ibn Gabirol's *Mekor Ḥayyim* from Arabic into Hebrew.

JOSEPH IBN KASPI. Joseph ibn *Kaspi (c. 1279–c. 1340), prolific author of biblical commentaries, lexicographic works, and books on philosophy, wrote a commentary on the *Guide*, consisting of an exoteric and esoteric part entitled, respectively, *Ammudei Kesef* and *Maskiyyot Kesef*. This commentary was influenced by that of Shem Tov b. Joseph Falaquera and in turn influenced later commentaries on the *Guide*. He accepts doctrines associated with the teachings of Averroes, such as the identity of religion and philosophy, the eternity of the world, and the natural interpretation of miracles, but he tries to modify these doctrines in a way that distinguishes him from such extreme rationalists as Moses of Narbonne and Levi b. Gershom.

Hillel ben Samuel. *Hillel b. Samuel (c. 1220–1295), one of the first Jewish philosophers in Italy, translated from Latin to Hebrew the Neoplatonic work *Liber de causis* and composed *Tagmulei ha-Nefesh* ("The Rewards of the Soul"). Since he knew Latin, he was able to draw on the opinions of Christian scholastics, particularly those of Thomas Aquinas. In Aristotelian fashion, Hillel defined the soul as the entelechy of a natural organic body, but, following Avicenna and the Neoplatonists, he held that the soul is a substance that emanates from God through the intermediacy of the supernal soul. He also cites Averroes' opinion that there is only one universal soul for all men, from which individual souls emanate like rays from the sun. However, on the question of the material or potential intellect he criticizes Averroes, using arguments offered by Aquinas. Averroes had argued that there exists only one such intellect for all men, but Hillel argued that each person has his own material intellect. On the question of the active intellect, Hillel accepts the opinion of the Islamic and Jewish Aristotelians, for whom the active intellect was the lowest of the celestial intelligences; in this he differed from Aquinas, who held that each person has his own active intellect. According to Hillel, only the rational part of the soul is immortal, and its ultimate happiness consists in union with the active intellect. In its immortal state the soul retains its individuality. Hillel also composed a commentary on the 26 propositions appearing at the beginning of the second part of Maimonides' *Guide.*

Isaac Albalag. Isaac *Albalag (second half of 13th century, probably lived in Spain) translated Al-Ghazālī's *Maqāṣid al-Falāsifa* (a compendium of the teachings of Avicenna) into Hebrew and presented his own views in a commentary on the work entitled *Tikkun ha-De'ot.* A follower of Averroes, who accepted such doctrines as the eternity of the world, he has also been described as a proponent of the theory of the "double truth," advocated by Latin Averroists. Like the Latin Averroists he distinguished between two coexistent independent truths, philosophic truth and prophetic truth, and he held that the two can contradict one another. However, he does not cite in his work any instance of such contradiction (see G. Vajda, *Isaac Albalag* (1960), 251ff.). His outlook is not completely clear, but it seems that his own view on a given topic is always that of philosophy. He maintained that speculative truths are the province of philosophy, not of Scripture. The Torah has as its sole purpose the moral and political guidance of the masses and contains no speculative truths, even by implication. Nevertheless, Albalag offers philosophic interpretations of the Bible; for example, he explained the story of creation in accordance with the doctrine of the eternity of the world. In a somewhat different vein, he states that if philosophic and prophetic truths contradict each other, both should stand, and one should say that the prophetic truth is unintelligible.

Abner of Burgos and Isaac Pollegar. The first half of the 14th century saw a debate concerning the freedom of the will initiated by *Abner of Burgos. Abner, who converted to Christianity, presented his views in *Minḥat Kena'ot;* although the work was written after his conversion, it seems clear that he held the same views when he was still a Jew. Following Avicenna, whose opinions he knew through their summary in al-Ghazālī's *Maqāṣid al-Falāsifa,* he held that human acts no less than natural occurrences are causally determined. Although the will has the ability to choose between alternatives, any given choice is determined, in fact, by causes influencing the will. Causal determination of the will is also required by God's omniscience and omnipotence: were human actions undetermined until the moment of decision, God could not foreknow them, and, also, His power would be limited. Abner tried to justify the existence of divine commandments and reward and punishment: divine commandments can be among the causes affecting the will, and reward and punishment are necessary consequences of human actions. Abner viewed biblical and rabbinic statements affirming freedom of the will as concessions to the understanding of the masses. Isaac *Pollegar, who knew Abner personally, attacked his determinism in his *Ezer ha-Dat.* According to Pollegar's solution, which contains difficulties of its own, there is a correlation between the divine and human wills such that at the moment man wills to do a certain act, God also wills that it be accomplished. In willing that the act be accomplished God also knows it. Yet, although this knowledge begins in time, there is no change in God. Whatever the difficulties of this position, it is clear that Pollegar tried to defend the freedom of the will by limiting God's foreknowledge. Levi b. Gershom (see below) solved the problem in a more radical fashion. Holding that God's knowledge extends only to species and not to individuals, he excluded man's action from God's knowledge, thereby safeguarding human freedom.

Moses of Narbonne. Moses b. Joshua of Narbonne (d. after 1362) was another participant in the debate. He wrote commentaries on works by Averroes and other Muslim philosophers (including al-Ghazālī's *Maqāṣid*) and also an important commentary on Maimonides' *Guide.* Although he held Maimonides in high esteem, he criticized a number of his doctrines, which under the influence of Al-Fārābi and Avicenna had a Neoplatonic complexion; he opposes these doctrines with the more strictly Aristotelian teachings of Averroes. His critique of Abner is found in *Ha-Ma'amar bi-Veḥirah,* and he also discusses human freedom in other works. However, his position is not completely clear. In some passages he holds in agreement with Maimonides that God's knowledge extends to particular human acts without determining these acts; in others he holds that God knows only species, not individuals. The latter opinion was probably Moses' real view.

Levi ben Gershom. *Levi b. Gershom (1288–1344), also known as Gersonides, mathematician, astronomer, and biblical commentator, wrote supercommentaries on many of Averroes' commentaries on Aristotle (still unpublished) and was the author of a philosophic work, *Sefer Milḥamot Adonai* ("The Book of the Wars of the Lord"). The most important Jewish Aristotelian after Maimonides, he was influenced by Averroes, though he is also critical of some of his views (see below). In *Milḥamot* Levi discusses in great detail and with scholastic subtlety topics that in his view Maimonides had not discussed sufficiently or had solved incorrectly. In the six parts of his work he deals with immortality of the soul; foretelling the future; God's knowledge of individual contingent beings; the celestial bodies, their movers, and God; and the creation of the world. *Milḥamot* is formally devoted to these six topics, but, together with his other works, it indicates Levi's general philosophy.

IMMORTALITY. Levi begins his discussion of immortality (treatise 1) with an extensive review and critique of various theories concerning the intellect. The Aristotelian philosophers had distinguished between the material or passive intellect, the active intellect, and the acquired intellect. Rejecting Themistius' and Averroes' opinions concerning the passive intellect, Levi accepts an opinion close to that of Alexander of Aphrodisias, namely, that the passive intellect is a predisposition inhering in the sensitive soul and comes into being with each individual man. Under the influence of the active intellect, the lowest of the incorporeal intelligences, the passive intellect is actualized and becomes the acquired intellect. While the passive intellect dies with the body, the acquired intellect is immortal. Differing from Averroes, for whom immortality was collective, Levi holds that each acquired intellect retains its individuality in its immortal state.

PROPHECY. The ability to foretell the future was accepted as an established fact by the adherents of religion and philosophers alike, and Levi set out to explain this fact (treatise 2). Maintaining that there is a continuity between the celestial and terrestial world, Levi holds that terrestrial events, particularly those related to man, are caused by the celestial spheres. Since the events of human life are thus ordered, it is possible that there are certain individuals who can foretell them. However, Levi is not a complete determinist. Discussing the problem of celestial (astrological) influences from another perspective, he holds that man is free in choosing his actions and that those who understand the laws of the celestial spheres can avoid the evil influences they may have. Since the active intellect both actualizes the human intellect and is a cause in the production of sublunar substances and events, it also causes knowledge of the future. In men who have strongly developed intellects the active intellect produces prophecy; in men who have strongly developed imaginations it causes (indirectly) divination and true dreams.

PREDESTINATION AND DIVINE PROVIDENCE. Discussing God's knowledge of individuals in the sublunar world (treatise 3), Levi is critical of Maimonides. Maimonides held that God knows particulars and met the objection that this seems to introduce a change in God by holding that God's knowledge is completely different from ours. Levi took this objection seriously and denied that God knows particular individuals. God only knows the order of nature. Closely related to God's knowledge of individuals is the question of providence (treatise 4). Levi rejected the theories that God's providence extends only to the species or that it extends equally to all men; he maintained that it extends only to those individuals who have developed their intellect. Like Maimonides, he held that the more an individual develops his intellect, the more he is subject to providence.

DIVINE ATTRIBUTES. Levi's account of the celestial spheres, their movers, and God (treatise 5) need not detain us, except for one aspect of his account of God, namely divine attributes (5:2, 12; see also 3:5). Maimonides, following Avicenna, had denied that attributes applied to God can have any positive meaning. Levi, following Averroes, accepted the alternative that Maimonides had rejected. Holding that essential attributes are identical with the essence to which they belong, Levi maintained that to understand such attributes positively does not introduce a multiplicity into God. He also held that such attributes (life, knowledge, and so on) whether applied to God or man have the same meaning, though they are applied to God primarily and to creatures derivatively.

CREATION. In his account of creation (treatise 6), Levi agrees with Maimonides that Aristotle's proofs for the eternity of the world are not conclusive arguments, though Aristotle's arguments are the best offered so far. However, against Aristotle, Levi presents a number of arguments designed to show that the world is created, among them one from the finiteness of time and motion. (Levi also rejects the Neoplatonic theory of emanation.) However, Levi differs from Maimonides and most Jewish philosophers in denying creation *ex nihilo,* holding that the world was created out of a formless matter coexistent with God, though this matter is not a principle paralleling God. He concludes his *Milḥamot* with a discussion of miracles and prophets, which reflects his general rationalistic temper.

Ḥasdai Crescas. Judah Halevi and Ḥibat Allah Abu al-Barakāt al-Baghdādī had criticized the doctrines of the Aristotelians, but the most significant critique within the mainstream of Jewish philosophy was that of Ḥasdai Crescas (d. 1412?). Although Crescas was critical of certain Aristotelian notions, he was not against philosophic speculations altogether; in fact, he proposed philosophic notions of his own to replace the Aristotelian notions he rejected. Nevertheless, in his conception of Judaism he emphasized observance of commandments and love of God rather than intellectual accomplishments. His critique of Aristotle as well as his own philosophy are found in *Or Adonai* ("The Light of the Lord"); he also wrote a work in Spanish criticizing Christianity, which has been preserved in Hebrew as *Bittul Ikkarei ha-Nozerim* ("Refutation of the Dogmas of the Christians").

BASIC PRINCIPLES OF JUDAISM. Maimonides' formulation of 13 principles of Judaism sparked a lively debate in the late Middle Ages. Taking issue with Maimonides, Crescas uses his own account of such principles as the framework of his book. According to Crescas, the basic principles of all religions are the existence, unity, and incorporeality of God (treatise 1). These are followed by six principles required for a belief in the validity of the Torah: God's knowledge of existing things, providence, divine omnipotence, prophecy, human freedom, and purpose in the Torah and the world (treatise 2). Next come eight true beliefs, which every adherent of the Torah must accept, and a denial of which constitutes heresy: creation of the world, immortality of the soul, reward and punishment, resurrection of the dead, eternity of the Torah, superiority of the prophecy of Moses, efficacy of the Urim and Thummim (worn by the high priest) in predicting the future, and the coming of the Messiah (treatise 3). The book concludes with 13 questions on topics ranging from whether there exists more than one world to the existence of demons.

SPACE AND INFINITY. Crescas' critique of Aristotle is found largely in an exposition and critical evaluation of the 26 physical and metaphysical propositions with which Maimonides had begun the second part of his *Guide* (see H. A. Wolfson, *Crescas' Critique of Aristotle,* 1929). Of special interest are Crescas' conception of space and infinity. The Aristotelians had defined place (rather than space) as the inner surface of a surrounding body; they had argued that there are no empty spaces (vacuum) in the world, and that the universe is finite and unitary. They also had held that an actual infinite cannot exist. Taking issue with them, Crescas set out to show that empty space without bodies can exist (it is identical with extension), that a vacuum can and does exist, that space beyond our world exists, and that there can be more than one world. He also differed from the Aristotelians in maintaining that an actual infinite (space, quantity, magnitude, time) can exist.

EXISTENCE OF GOD. Crescas' acceptance of the existence of an actual infinite raised questions concerning the Maimonidean (Aristotelian) proofs of the existence of God. Since the proofs rested on the proposition that an actual infinite is impossible, Crescas rejected them. However, he retains the proof from necessity and contingency, which to his mind is independent of the disputed principle. In view of difficulties, he also substitutes proofs of his own for the unity and incorporeality of God. Against Maimonides, Crescas affirms the possibility of positive attributes applied to God.

PROVIDENCE AND FREEDOM. God's knowledge, according to Crescas, extends to particulars; He knows the nonexistent and He knows future contingents without removing their contingent character. Crescas also upholds individual providence and states that man's true reward or punishment, dependent on obedience or disobedience of God's will, is given in the hereafter. A similar attitude also determines Crescas' conception of prophecy. God can inspire whomever he wishes, but the one chosen for prophecy is someone who follows the Torah and loves God. Of special interest is Crescas' conception of human freedom. While Maimonides and Levi ben Gershom in different ways safeguarded the freedom of human actions, Crescas' solution is more deterministic. He holds that everything in the world is the result of prior causes and affirms that God's omniscience requires that the object of His foreknowledge come to pass. Human actions are caused by a will determined by other causes, not by an undetermined will. Crescas tried to mitigate this position by stating that commandments, training, and other factors are among the causes influencing the will and that, despite being determined, the will in its own nature is contingent. Crescas' anti-Aristotelian stance is also apparent in his doctrine of man. In place of development of the intellect as the main purpose of human life is the observance of God's commandments; not philosophic speculation but the love and fear of God bring immortality to man. It is the soul that is immortal, not the acquired intellect.

Simeon ben Ẓemaḥ Duran. After the period of Crescas, medieval Jewish philosophy declined. It became more eclectic and most philosophers accepted a more orthodox religious position. Simeon b. Ẓemaḥ *Duran, talmudist and author of a philosophic theological work *Magen Avot,* generally followed the moderate rationalism of Maimonides, though, like Crescas, he maintained that divine attributes can have a positive meaning, that immortality comes through observance of the commandments, and that divine providence extends to all men. In the introduction to his commentary on Job, entitled *Ohev Mishpat,* Duran also contributes to the discussion of dogmas. Emphasizing the centrality of a belief in revelation, Duran listed three dogmas, the existence of God, revelation, and reward and punishment, which became the foundations of Joseph Albo's philosophy.

Joseph Albo. Joseph *Albo (15th century), a student of Crescas, presented his views in *Sefer ha-Ikkarim* ("Book of Principles"), an eclectic, popular work, whose central task is the exposition of the principles of Judaism. Albo, following Duran, held that there are three basic principles *(ikkarim)* necessary for the existence of a divine law: the existence of God, revelation, and reward and punishment. From these principles follow eight derivative principles *(shorashim):* from the existence of God there follow God's unity, incorporeality, timelessness, and perfection; from revelation, God's omniscience and prophecy and authentication of the prophet; from reward and punishment, individual providence. The denial of these principles, no less than the denial of the first three, makes one a heretic *(kofer).* There are, furthermore, six branches *(anafim):* creation *ex nihilo,* the superiority of Moses as a prophet, immutability of the Torah, guarantee of immortality through the observance of any one commandment, resurrection of the dead, and the coming of the Messiah. Although it is proper that every Jew accept these branches, and although their denial makes him a sinner, it does not make him a heretic. Albo also criticizes the opinions of his predecessors concerning principles of Judaism. *Sefer ha-Ikkarim* is divided into four treatises. The first deals with the general principles of laws, the three *ikkarim,* and how a genuine divine law can be distinguished from a spurious one; each of the other three treatises is devoted to an exposition of a basic principle and of the principles derived from it. In his preliminary discussion (*Ikkarim,* 1:7ff.) Albo distinguishes three kinds of law: natural, conventional, and divine. Natural law is the same for all persons, times, and places; conventional law is ordered by a wise man in accord with reason; divine law is given by God through a prophet. It is only divine law that can lead man to true happiness and immortality. Albo's work contains explicit and implicit polemics against Christianity (for example 3:25), which are very likely the result of his participation in the debates at Tortosa and San Mateo (1413–14).

Shem Tov Family, Abraham Shalom, and Isaac Arama. The tension of the age is well illustrated by the Shem Tov family. Shem Tov b. Joseph *ibn Shem Tov (c. 1380–1441), a kabbalist and opponent of Greek philosophy, attacked in his *Sefer ha-Emunot,* not only such extreme rationalists as Albalag and Levi ben Gershom, but even more fiercely Maimonides himself. His son Joseph b. Shem Tov *ibn Shem Tov (d. c. 1480), who greatly admired Aristotle and Maimonides, tried to rehabilitate philosophy by improving its rapport with religious Orthodoxy. He attempted to show that Aristotle really believed in individual providence, and that when Aristotle stated that man's happiness comes through contemplation, he had in mind only happiness in this world, leaving room for happiness in the next dependent on the observance of the Torah. Shem Tov b. Joseph *ibn Shem Tov, who bore the same name as his grandfather, continued his father's philosophical interest in a commentary on Maimonides' *Guide* (composed 1488), in which he defends Maimonides against the attacks of Crescas. His contemporary Abraham *Shalom, in his work *Neveh Shalom,* also defended Maimonides against Crescas. Isaac b. Moses *Arama (1420–1494) wrote a philosophic-homiletical commentary on the Pentateuch, entitled *Akedat Yiẓḥak.*

Isaac and Judah Abrabanel. The last Jewish philosopher in Spain was the statesman Isaac *Abrabanel (1437–1508), who went into exile with his fellow Jews in 1492. He admired Maimonides greatly (he wrote a commentary on the *Guide*), but, nevertheless he opposed the rationalistic interpretation of Judaism. Thus he held, for example, that prophecy was caused by God Himself, not by the active intellect. His attitude also emerges in his work *Rosh Amanah,* in which he defends Maimonides' 13 principles with great subtlety against all those who had taken issue with them; but in the end he states that only the commandments of the Torah count. Abrabanel's account of history and political life was novel. In his commentary on the beginning of Genesis he held that God willed that man be satisfied with what nature provides and concentrate on cultivation of his spirit. However, men were dissatisfied and produced civilizations to gain further possessions. These civilizations distracted them from their true goal. Abrabanel had a similar attitude toward the state. Man's condition, as ordained by God, was to live in loose associations, but as man's desires increased he organized states. States are evil in themselves, since they detract man from his true goal. After the expulsion of the Jews from Spain, Jewish philosophy continued in Italy, where it had begun in the 13th century. Abrabanel, in fact, wrote his most important works in Italy. His son Judah *Abrabanel, known as Leone Ebreo (c. 1460–after 1523), under the influence of Renaissance Platonism, wrote a general philosophic work entitled *Dialoghi di Amore* ("Dialogues of Love"). Earlier, an Italian Jew, *Judah b. Jehiel (Messer Leon; 15th century), had written a work on rhetoric in Hebrew, which drew on Aristotle, Cicero, and Quintillian. He also wrote on logic.

Elijah Delmedigo. Elijah *Delmedigo (c. 1460–1497), born in Crete, lived for a time in Italy, where he exchanged views with Christian Platonists. He had lectured at the University of Padua, and at the request of Pico della *Mirandola he translated works by Averroes from Hebrew into Latin. He also wrote independent works on philosophic topics, including *Beḥinat ha-Dat* ("The Examination of Religion"), a work based on a treatise by Averroes, in which he investigated the relation of philosophy and religion. Like Averroes, he held that the masses must accept Scripture literally, while philosophers may interpret it. However, he denied philosophers the right to interpret the basic principles of Judaism. Like the Latin Averroists, he envisaged religion and philosophy as independent disciplines that may be mutually contradictory. If this should happen, the philosopher must accept the teachings of religion. He modified this position by maintaining that it is permissible to interpret philosophically doctrines which do not affect a basic principle and by affirming that, in fact, basic principles do not conflict with reason.

Joseph Delmedigo. Joseph Solomon *Delmedigo (1591–

1655), a descendant of Elijah, was influenced by the theories of Galileo; but he did not free himself completely from certain medieval notions. He accepted the heliocentric theory of the universe and also denied that there is any distinction between the celestial and terrestrial realm. He criticized the Aristotelian notion of form, holding that material substance and its qualities are adequate to explain the world. He also rejected the Aristotelian notion that incorporeal movers of the spheres exist. His conception of the soul follows the Platonic notion that the soul is a substance joined to the body, and his view of the active intellect follows Aquinas' view that it is located within the individual human soul. In addition to defending these philosophic views, Delmedigo also defended the Kabbalah, though he mocked its superstitions.

Influences on Christian Thought. Two Jewish philosophers, Gabirol and Maimonides, influenced Christian thought extensively through Latin translations of their major works. Gabirol's *Mekor Ḥayyim* was translated into Latin as *Fons Vitae* in the middle of the 12th century; Maimonides' *Guide* was translated as *Dux (Director) Neutrorum (Dubitantium, Perplexorum)* about a century later. Gabirol's *Fons Vitae,* together with the writings of Augustine and of Islamic philosophers, molded the Neoplatonic component of Christian scholastic thought. *William of Auvergne, while disagreeing with some of his views, described Gabirol as "one of the noblest of all philosophers," and he identified Gabirol's (divine) will with the Christian logos. Gabirol is also considered a proponent of the doctrine of the multiplicity of forms, according to which several substantial forms exist within a given substance. However, by far the best known of Gabirol's teachings was his notion that spiritual substances (the angels and the human soul), no less than corporeal substances, are composed of matter and form. This doctrine became the subject of a lively debate among scholastics. Among those who accepted Gabirol's view were *Alexander of Hales, Bonaventure, and *Duns Scotus; among those who rejected it were *Albertus Magnus and Thomas *Aquinas. In general the Franciscans accepted this doctrine, the Dominicans rejected it. Among Christian scholastics who were influenced by Maimonides were Alexander of Hales, William of Auvergne, Albertus Magnus, Thomas Aquinas, Meister *Eckhart, and Duns Scotus. Aquinas, for example, was influenced by Maimonides in his account of the relation of faith and reason, in his proofs for the existence of God, and in his opinion that the creation of the world in time cannot be demonstrated by philosophic arguments. However, he polemicized against Maimonides' opinion that all essential attributes applied to God must be understood as negations, against his description of the celestial movers, and against his identifying angels with the incorporeal intelligences.

Christian Scholastic Influences on Jewish Thought. Islamic philosophy and its Greek antecedents provided the foundations for medieval Jewish philosophy during its two phases. There were also Christian scholastic influences on Jewish philosophers who knew Latin: for example, Hillel b. Samuel was influenced by Aquinas and Albalag, by the Latin Averroists. But even those Jewish philosophers who did not know Latin had, in time, access to scholastic thought through Hebrew translations. As was to be expected, the works translated dealt with philosophical rather than theological topics. Among the scholastics from whose works translations were made were Albertus Magnus, Thomas Aquinas, Aegidius Romanus, Peter of Spain, and William of Ockham. Among the translators were *Judah Romano, Elijah *Habillo, and Abraham Shalom. S. Pines has advanced the view that while Jewish philosophers do not cite works by late medieval scholastics they were familiar with the problems they discussed. He has argued that physical and metaphysical notions of Duns Scotus, Buridan, Oresme, Albert of Saxony, and William of Ockham influenced Jedaiah ha-Penini Bedersi, Levi b. Gershom, Joseph ibn Kaspi and Ḥasdai Crescas (S. Pines, *Scholasticism after Thomas Aquinas and the Teachings of Hasdai Crescas and his Predecessors,* 1967).

MODERN PERIOD

Introduction. Modern Jewish philosophy shared with Hellenistic and medieval Jewish philosophy a concern for relating general philosophy to Judaism and it discussed some of the same problems that had been discussed in earlier Jewish philosophy; but, at the same time, it differed from Hellenistic and medieval Jewish philosophy in several respects. For one thing it differed in its conception of Jewish tradition. For Hellenistic and medieval Jewish philosophers, Judaism, with its Oral and Written Law, was the revealed word of God which was binding in its totality for all times. While there were modern Jewish thinkers who accepted the traditional position, most of them considered Judaism a creation of human thought, intuition, or feeling, which had developed in history and, which, while containing a perennial core, also contained parts which could be discarded in modern times. Then again, it differed in its conception of science and philosophy. Hellenistic and medieval Jewish philosophers accepted the notion of a geocentric universe with a sharp distinction between its terrestrial and celestial parts—a universe that manifests design and purpose. Modern Jewish philosophers accepted the notion of a heliocentric universe with no distinction between its terrestrial and celestial parts, a universe governed by the necessary laws of nature. Moreover, pre-modern Jewish thinkers saw no sharp distinction between science and philosophy, had strong metaphysical interests, and emphasized that the development of the human mind was the purpose of human life and morality was only a prerequisite for the fulfillment of this goal. Modern Jewish philosophers saw science as distinct from philosophy, and while those following the idealist tradition retained metaphysical interests and emphasized the primacy of intellectual cognition, there were many who denied the possibility (or at least the importance) of metaphysics, emphasizing instead the study of ethics and the centrality of proper conduct for attaining the goal of human life. It can readily be seen that it was easier to reconcile pre-modern philosophy with Jewish teachings than modern philosophy. The Enlightenment and the Emancipation also had a significant impact on modern Jewish thought. For example, the Enlightenment notion of a religion of reason which, consisting of rational beliefs and practices, was addressed to all men, was adopted by a number of Jewish philosophers of the modern period. Some, Mendelssohn for example, accepted this notion and investigated to what extent historical Judaism was identical with the religion of reason and to what extent different. Others, such as Hermann Cohen, went so far as to maintain that Judaism was the ideal embodiment of the religion of reason. The process of secularization initiated by the Enlightenment also had its impact on Jewish thought. While modern Jewish philosopny was still largely a religious philosophy, there arose Jewish thinkers who attempted to formulate secular philosophies of Judaism and for whom Judaism was a culture or a social philosophy rather than a religious tradition (see also *Haskalah).

The impact of the Emancipation was felt in Western rather than in Eastern Europe, for in the East the Jewish community retained its social (even its political) identity into the 20th century. The progressive political and social emancipation of the Jews posed special problems for Jewish thinkers, one of these being the nature of the Jewish group. While pre-modern Jewish thinkers had no difficulty in accepting the notion that the Jews were a people, many modern Jewish thinkers considered Judaism a religion and the Jews a religious society *(Religionsgemeinschaft)*, thereby emphasizing that only their religion distinguished Jews from other citizens. The Emancipation also influenced the concept of the Messiah. Whereas in classical Jewish thought the Messiah was a king from the House of David who would bring the Jews back to their own land, most modern Jewish thinkers gave up the belief in a personal Messiah, speaking instead of messianic times when all mankind would be united in justice and righteousness.

Another factor that influenced modern Jewish philosophy was the emergence of distinct religious groups within Judaism. While in former times, too, there were different groups within Judaism, e.g., Sadducees and Pharisees and Rabbanites and Karaites, Jewish philosophy for the most part moved within the mainstream of classical rabbinic tradition. However, in the 19th century there developed three distinct groups within Judaism, each of which had its philosophers. *Neo-Orthodoxy upheld the classical formulation of Judaism but attempted to make modern culture relevant to Jewish concerns. The positive-historical school (which was to become in the United States in the 20th century the *Conservative movement) was committed to classical Jewish tradition but at the same time studied Judaism from a historical-critical perspective, maintaining that Judaism was subject to evolutionary development. Liberal (*Reform) Judaism was committed to a program of change, holding that the core of Judaism was ethics (ethical monotheism) and that ritual was subject to abrogation and change.

One further factor was the rise of modern anti-Semitism. In the case of some Jewish thinkers (Hermann Cohen is a notable example) it was anti-Semitism that aroused their interest in Jewish thought. Anti-Semitism also produced in certain thinkers a despair of the promise of emancipation, which, together with the emergence of modern nationalism and classical Jewish messianic expectations, produced Zionism which advocated the reestablishment of a Jewish state, preferably in Ereẓ Israel. In its philosophic component modern Jewish thought followed the main currents of modern and contemporary Western philosophy, rationalism, Kantianism, idealism, existentialism, and pragmatism. There were also influences derived from British empiricism and positivism. Whereas medieval Jewish philosophy consisted of movements which had a certain continuity and structure, modern Jewish thought represents mainly the efforts of individual thinkers. In Western Europe the language of Jewish philosophy was the language of the country in which the philosopher lived, while in Eastern Europe its language was largely Hebrew.

Spinoza. Baruch (Benedict) *Spinoza (1632–1677) has sometimes been described as the first modern Jewish philosopher, but he cannot be considered part of the mainstream of the Jewish philosophic tradition. When in his *Theologico-Political Treatise* he set out to separate philosophy from religion (Introd., ch. 7, 14), he denied the possibility of a religious philosophy of any kind. Moreover, the pantheistic system of his *Ethics* with its identity of God and nature cannot be said to be in harmony with Jewish beliefs. Nevertheless, there are good reasons for including him in an account of Jewish philosophy: his ideas were influenced by medieval Jewish philosophers, particularly Maimonides and Crescas; he polemicized against the medieval understanding of such ideas as prophecy and miracles; modern Jewish philosophers discussed his ideas (pro and con); and his biblical criticism became one of the foundations of the liberal interpretation of Judaism to which many modern Jewish philosophers subscribed. From his medieval predecessors Spinoza accepted the distinction between a philosophic elite which can understand through reason and the masses which can understand only through imagination. Spinoza wrote his *Ethics* for philosophers, its object being to show that the good life and human happiness can be attained through reason without recourse to historical religion. (In the five parts of the *Ethics* he discusses God (1), mind (2), passions (3, 4), and human freedom (5).) Spinoza rejects the notion of a personal God who acts by will and design. Instead, God is an impersonal being who acts out of the necessity of His (Spinoza often retains theistic language) own nature and determines everything through His infinite power. God possesses an infinity of attributes, of which thought and extension are known to man; He also possesses modes. Everything that exists appears to be an aspect of God. The world and man lack any purpose other than to function in accordance with their necessary causes. Man also lacks free will. The greatest obstacle to the good life is enslavement to the passions, but man can free himself from this enslavement by understanding and controlling the passions. Philosophic understanding is the goal of human life, and Spinoza describes its highest form as "the intellectual love of the mind toward God." In his *Theologico-Political Treatise* Spinoza manifests a twofold interest in religion. He attempts, on the one hand, to show that philosophy is independent of religion, and, on the other, to show the ruler that he may enforce religious practices while granting the philosopher the freedom to philosophize. To show philosophy's freedom from religion, Spinoza develops a new method for interpreting the Bible. Holding that the Bible is a human document composed by different authors, at different times, and under different circumstances, he maintains that it must be interpreted in accordance with ordinary canons of historical and literary exegesis. The new method brings him to the conclusion that the Bible is intellectually rather naïve (a product of the imagination rather than of reason), so that one should not expect to find any philosophical profundities in it. In spite of this evaluation, Spinoza does not reject the Bible altogether. While he held that the biblical religions had sunk to the level of superstition and while he maintained that most of the biblical precepts could be discarded, he also stated that the Bible contains a viable core useful for the instruction of the masses. The Bible in its noblest core teaches "obedience to God in the singleness of heart and the practice of justice and charity." The Bible also contains seven dogmas of universal faith—God's existence, unity, omnipresence, power and will, man's obligation to worship God, salvation, and repentance—belief in which leads the masses to proper actions. While some of the dogmas reflect philosophic notions discussed in the *Ethics*, Spinoza presents them in the *Treatise* as products of the imagination. Spinoza applies his critical method primarily to the Hebrew Bible, but it can be applied to Christian Scripture as well. It appears that he considered Christianity a better embodiment than Judaism of the purified biblical religions which he favored. Jewish ceremonial law, political in its function, lost its validity with the destruction of the Jewish kingdom and hence was no longer obligatory. In passing he envisages the possibility that under the right conditions the Jews may once again establish their state.

Moses Mendelssohn. Moses *Mendelssohn (1729–1786), champion of Jewish emancipation, translator of the Pentateuch into German, and biblical commentator, is generally considered the first Jewish philosopher of the modern period. Born in Dessau where he was trained in traditional Jewish learning, he came to Berlin in 1743 and there acquired, through private study, knowledge of classical and modern languages, mathematics, and modern philosophy. His traditional training provided him with extensive familiarity with the medieval Jewish philosophers (whom he cites in his writings) and his modern training acquainted him with the thought of Locke, Leibniz, and Christian Wolff. As philosopher, Mendelssohn followed the pre-Kantian German Enlightenment, sharing with it the conviction that metaphysical knowledge is possible. He wrote on metaphysics, psychology, aesthetics, and also literary criticism. His main philosophical works were *Phaedon* (patterned after Plato's dialogue of the same name; 1767) and *Morgenstunden* (1785). In the former work he offered arguments for the immortality of the soul and in the latter he discussed proofs for the existence of God.

Mendelssohn might never have presented his views on Judaism had it not been for the challenge of the Swiss theologian Johann Kaspar Lavater. In 1769 Lavater published his German translation of Charles Bonnet's *La Palingénésie philosophique* under the title *Untersuchung der Beweise fuer das Christenthum,* and in his introduction he challenged Mendelssohn to refute Bonnet's arguments or accept Christianity. Mendelssohn, who was not given to polemics, reluctantly accepted the challenge and in his reply professed his unshakable belief in Judaism and pointed out that Judaism tolerantly held that salvation is possible for all men, while Christianity limited salvation to its adherents. Mendelssohn presented his views on religion and Judaism more fully in his *Jerusalem* (1783), a work influenced by Spinoza's *Theologico-Political Treatise.* Like Spinoza, Mendelssohn (in the first part of the work) advocated the separation of state and church, holding that, while both contribute to human happiness, the state governs man's relation to his fellow man and the church man's relation to God. Ideally, the state should govern by educating its citizens, but practically it must compel them to obey the laws. The church should not possess secular power or own property and should promote its teachings only through instruction and admonition. Religion is a personal matter, and both state and church must guarantee freedom of conscience. In the second part of *Jerusalem,* Mendelssohn discusses the nature of religion and Judaism. Religion, for him, is the Enlightenment religion of reason which consists of rational and moral truths discoverable by all men. It is inconceivable to Mendelssohn that a benevolent God should restrict salvation to the adherents of a particular historical religion; salvation must be available to all men. Judaism, then, is not a revealed religion but revealed legislation. Insofar as it is a religion it is the religion of reason. However, whereas Spinoza had held that Jewish law had lost its validity with the cessation of the Jewish kingdom, Mendelssohn maintained that it was still binding for Jews. If there were to be changes, only a new revelation from God could make them. It is the purpose of Jewish law to preserve pure religious concepts free from idolatry and it still fulfills this purpose in the modern world. It also serves to keep the Jewish community together. The Law compels man to action, but also stimulates him to contemplation. Judaism consists of three parts: religious truths about God, His rule, and His providence, addressed to man's reason (but these are not presented as compelled beliefs); historical truths disclosing the purposes of the Jew's existence; and laws, precepts, commandments, and rules of conduct, the observance of which will bring happiness to individual Jews as well as to the Jewish community as a whole.

Kant, Schelling, Hegel. The two most important general philosophic influences on 19th- and (to some extent) 20th-century Jewish thought were the critical philosophy of *Kant and the idealistic philosophies of *Schelling and *Hegel. Kant was important for his denial of speculative metaphysics; for his sharp distinction between theoretical and practical (moral) philosophy; for making God, freedom, and immortality postulates of practical reason; for his account of duty, the categorical imperative, and the autonomy of the will; and for closely connecting ethics and religion. The idealist philosophers were important for affirming the spiritual nature of all reality and for their notion that history presents the progressive self-realization of spirit. Jewish philosophers used these philosophies in varying ways and combinations, holding that Judaism is the best embodiment of the religion of reason (Kant) or the religion of spirit (idealists).

Solomon Formstecher. Solomon *Formstecher (1808–1889), rabbi and leader of the Reform movement, developed his philosophy in *Die Religion des Geistes* (1841), a work combining idealist philosophy with a special concern for ethics. From Schelling he accepted the notion of a world soul which is manifest in the phenomena of nature; but, whereas for Schelling the world soul was bound to nature, Formstecher emphasized its transcendence and identified it with God. However, there is another manifestation of the world soul and that is spirit, whose main characteristics are self-consciousness and freedom. When spirit becomes conscious of nature it produces physics; when it becomes conscious of itself it produces logic. There exists an ideal for spirit in each realm: aesthetic contemplation in nature; moral action in the realm of spirit. Corresponding to the two realms there are two forms of religion: the religion of nature which considers the world as containing divine forces or which identifies nature with God; the religion of the spirit which considers God as transcendent. There are also two corresponding goals for human life: for religion of nature it is to become one with God; for religion of the spirit it is to become like Him through moral actions. Historically, paganism embodied the religion of nature, Judaism, the religion of spirit. There exist two kinds of revelation: prehistoric revelation which consists of the ideal that spirit can attain, and historical revelation which is the gradual attainment of this ideal. Historical revelation occurs in natural religion as well as in the religion of the spirit; but in natural religion it comes to an end with the cognition of a God bound to nature, while in spiritual religion it tends toward the cognition of the transcendent God. The religion of the spirit is identical with absolute truth. (Formstecher does not succeed too well in harmonizing the idealist notion that man's final goal is understanding with his emphasis on ethics.) The religion of the spirit is the religion of the Jews, but it had a historical development. Since Judaism developed in a pagan world, the religion of the spirit had to be the religion of a specific people. However, as Judaism progressed from objectivity to subjectivity (which consisted in the spirit's becoming more and more conscious of itself) it gained greater universalism. This occurred at first through the destruction of Jewish national life. However, since the world was still hostile, Judaism had to maintain its identity, but now as a theocracy of law. Formstecher maintained that the process of becoming more and more universal was about to come to an end in the modern world which was marked by the emancipation of the Jews, and the absolute truth of spiritual religion was about to emerge.

But spiritual religion also had to penetrate natural religion and this occurred through Christianity and Islam. Since Christianity addressed itself to the pagan world, it combined the religion of the spirit with the thought of paganism. The history of Christianity is the struggle between Jewish and pagan elements. As Christianity developed historically it freed itself more and more from its pagan elements. Since Christianity, even in the modern world, has not completely freed itself from these accretions there is still room for Judaism as a separate religion. However, both religions strive toward the realization of the religion of the spirit. Judaism can prepare itself by stripping itself of its particularistic elements and its ceremonial law.

Samuel Hirsch. Samuel *Hirsch (1815–1889), rabbi and Reform leader, presented his views in *Die Religionsphilosophie der Juden* (1842), a work influenced by Hegel. Hirsch considered it the task of philosophy to transform the content of religious consciousness into the content of spirit (mind), and for him religious and philosophic truth are identical. Central to Hirsch's thought is the notion of freedom. Man by understanding himself as an "I" standing over against nature becomes aware of his freedom. However, this freedom is abstract and must be given content. One such content is natural freedom, his ability to do whatever he desires. Hegel held that abstract and natural freedom were in conflict and he held that this conflict was ingrained in man. Not so Hirsch. He tried to preserve abstract freedom for man by holding that alternate courses of action are open to him. Man may sacrifice his freedom to nature, or he may control nature by means of his freedom. These courses of action have as their concomitants two kinds of awareness of God. According to both, God is the giver of freedom, but according to the first view nature becomes the divine principle; according to the second view God transcends nature. Understanding nature as divine produces paganism; understanding God as transcendental produces Judaism. Hirsch now analyzes the history of religion in a manner reminiscent of Formstecher. But whereas for Formstecher, paganism, being the partial recognition of spirit, has some redeeming features, for Hirsch, it does not. Whatever development paganism has, it is only to show its nothingness. Judaism also had a development, but only because it originated in a pagan world (Abraham lived in that world); but once it had become free by recognizing that the true nature of religion is moral freedom, no further development was necessary. In early times Judaism required prophecy and miracles to show that God is master of nature; but once the threat of paganism had passed these were no longer necessary. The only miracle still apparent is the continuous existence of the Jewish people. There is, however, a kind of development in Judaism, for once one has discovered the truth of ethical freedom for oneself one wants to spread it to others. This Judaism attains, not by missionizing but by bearing witness to its faith. There existed, however, a tendency to bring Jewish beliefs to the pagan world in an active fashion and Jesus made this his task. Jesus still moved within the world of Judaism, but a break came with Paul. When Paul formulated a doctrine of original sin and redemption through Jesus, Christianity severed its ties with Judaism. Only when the work of Paul is undone will Christianity be able to fulfill its true mission. When Christianity reaches that stage it will be essentially identical with Judaism. However, even in messianic times, when Israel will become one with all mankind, it will retain a structure of its own.

Nachman Krochmal. Nachman *Krochmal (1785–1840), a representative of the East European Haskalah, presented his philosophy in his posthumously published (1851) Hebrew work *Moreh Nevukhei ha-Zeman* ("Guide of the Perplexed of the Time"). In this work Krochmal does not present his views in any great detail, and a good portion of the work is devoted to an analysis of Jewish history and literature, but his thought may be gathered from the introductory chapters (1–8) and from his discussion of the philosophy of Abraham ibn Ezra (ch. 17). Krochmal was influenced by German idealism, but scholars have debated whether the primary influence was Hegel or Schelling. He differed from Formstecher and Hirsch by emphasizing the speculative rather than the ethical content of religion, and he also differed from them in not accepting the distinction between nature and spirit and between the religion of nature and the religion of spirit. For Krochmal all religions are concerned with the self-realization of human consciousness and all religions accept a belief in spiritual powers. Even the idolator does not worship the physical likeness but the spiritual power it represents. All religions are religions of the spirit and they differ only in degree. Yet there is a distinction between Judaism and other religions: Judaism is concerned with infinite "absolute spirit" (Krochmal's term is "the absolute spiritual"), while other religions are only concerned with finite spiritual powers. Krochmal affirms the identity of religious and philosophical truth, the only difference between them being that religion presents this truth in the form of representation, while philosophy presents it in conceptual form. There is, however, a distinction between Judaism and the other religions: Judaism had an awareness of absolute spirit from its beginnings, while the other religions were only aware of partial spiritual powers. Judaism underwent development; but this development was only a progression from a representational understanding of the absolute spirit to a conceptual understanding of it. The world for Krochmal is a world of spirit and even inanimate nature is only a concretization of spirit. Since all existence is spirit, and since true existence can only belong to absolute spirit, i.e., God, the world is said to exist in God. This gives a decidedly pantheistic complexion to Krochmal's thought. He mitigates it somewhat by affirming that the world is descended (emanated) from God. This descent is the true meaning of the biblical account of creation. God creates the world by limiting Himself, thereby separating Himself from the world; nevertheless, His being, as has been noted, still permeates the world. The act of divine self-limitation appears to be a spontaneous act. Krochmal also interprets prophecy within the framework of his thought. Prophecy is the connecting of the human spirit with the divine and it can exist in all men; those in whom the connection exists strongly become prophets in actuality. The prophets also have the ability to predict the future, but they can only predict the future close to their own time. Thus Krochmal denies that the second part of Isaiah was written by the same prophet as the first; the author of the first was too far removed in time from the events described in the second part. He also professes a belief in miracles in the sense of direct divine intervention, but how this can be reconciled with the rest of his philosophy is not too clear.

Corresponding to his general philosophy Krochmal also develops a philosophy of history. Each of the historical nations is subject to a spiritual power which determines its history and its culture. The gods in which each nation believes are an embodiment of this spiritual principle. Each nation undergoes a three-stage development: growth, maturity, and decline. Decline sets in when desire for luxury and power increases. Once a nation has declined it ceases to exist and another nation comes to the fore. The accomplishments of the nation which has ceased to exist are often absorbed by the nation which takes its place (for example, the accomplishments of Greece by Rome), while the Jewish nation manifests the triad—growth, maturity, and decline—it is the eternal people, exempt from extinction. Once a triadic period has come to an end a new one begins. Israel is exempt from the fate of other nations, because it had a belief in absolute spirit from the beginning. This belief makes Israel the teacher of all mankind and this is Israel's mission in the world. The spirit of the Jewish people flows from absolute spirit and it is said that God dwells in Israel and that God's spirit rests on Israel. Krochmal divides Jewish history into four periods: the first extended from the period of the Patriarchs to the Babylonian Exile; the second from the Babylonian Exile to the revolt of Bar Kokhba; the third, which is not too clearly described, ended in the 17th century; and the fourth cycle was still going on in Krochmal's time.

S. D. Luzzatto. While Formstecher, Hirsch, and Krochmal attempted to harmonize idealism and Judaism, Samuel David *Luzzatto (1800–1865), translator of the Bible into Italian and biblical commentator, was an outright opponent of philosophic speculation. He agreed with Mendelssohn that Judaism possesses no dogmas, but unlike Mendelssohn he affirmed that moral action leading to righteousness is the purpose of all (even the ritual) commandments. While he does not hold that Judaism lacks beliefs altogether, he considers it the function of religious beliefs to induce moral actions. It is conceivable to him that some religious beliefs may be false. Ethical activity, according to Luzzatto, springs from the feelings of honor and pity. In his *Yesodei ha-Torah* ("Foundations of the Torah," published posthumously in 1880) he enumerates three principles of Judaism: the feeling of pity, reward and punishment, and the election of Israel. The first of these is the basic principle; the other two have only an auxiliary function. A belief in reward and punishment is necessary because without it man would be governed by the evil part of his nature; the election of Israel is important for motivating Jews to higher and higher ethical practices. Luzzatto distinguishes between Judaism which aspires to moral action and "Atticism" which has understanding as its goal. He maintains that cognition of God lies beyond the capacities of man, but he also holds that the existence of God can be demonstrated philosophically.

S. L. Steinheim. Solomon Ludwig *Steinheim (1789–1866), physician, poet, and philosopher, was also an outright opponent of philosophic rationalism. In his *Offenbarung nach dem Lehrbegriff der Synagogue* (4 vols., 1835–65) he defended the thesis that religious truth is only given through revelation. This meant to him not only that reason is inferior to revelation, but that when reason examines the contradictions contained within its content it must recognize its own insufficiency. Revelation is not the product of human consciousness but comes from without, from God. (Steinheim does not deny that religion possesses cognitive content; but this content can only come through revelation, not through rational processes.) The truth of revelation is not confirmed by external signs but by reason, which clearly recognizes the superiority of revelation and also that revelation meets human needs better than philosophy. Philosophy differs from religion in that philosophy conceives of all reality in terms of necessity, while religion understands it in terms of freedom. Corresponding to these approaches are two kinds of religion: natural religion which conceives of God as subject to the necessity of His own nature and as dependent on the matter on which he acts; revealed religion which understands God as the Creator Who, unbounded by necessity, creates the world freely and out of nothing. Creation, according to Steinheim, is the first principle of revelation; other principles are freedom, immortality of the soul, and (very likely) the unity of God. Steinheim applies the two conceptions of religion to the historical religions: paganism is the embodiment of natural (philosophical) religion; Judaism is the embodiment of revealed religion; and Christianity is a mixture of the two. As revealed religion, Judaism emphasizes, besides the cognitive principles mentioned before, human freedom and moral activity. Hence in his conclusions concerning the content of the Jewish religion, Steinheim differs little from Formstecher and Hirsch; but whereas the latter two philosophers saw Judaism grounded in reason, Steinheim sees it grounded in revelation.

Moritz Lazarus. Moritz *Lazarus (1824–1903), writer on psychology and philosophy, devoted *Die Ethik des Judentums* (*The Ethics of Judaism;* vol. I, 1898; vol. II, published posthumously, 1911) to the philosophic interpretation of Jewish ethics. The avowed purpose of the work is to use philosophy to give a structured account of Jewish ethics; but he also uses philosophic concepts to analyze its content. He derives his main notions from Kant, but he gives these notions a psychological interpretation. From Kant, Lazarus accepts the notion of the autonomy of ethics, but to Lazarus this only meant that the sphere of ethics is independent. Whereas for Kant the autonomy of ethics further implied that ethics is independent of the emotions, Lazarus maintained that ethics is grounded in the emotions of duty and obligation. Religious ethics differs from philosophical ethics in that it recognizes God as the author of ethical imperatives. However, if ethical imperatives are given by God, ethics is no longer autonomous but heteronomous. Lazarus tries to solve this difficulty by stating that God is also subject to ethical imperatives. What God commands is right, but not because He commands it: rather He commands it because it is right. Judaism is essentially religious ethics and even the ritual commandments have an ethical purpose. Jewish ethics is an ethics for the individual, but even more for society. Lazarus also interprets the idea of holiness. God is holy, not because He is mysterious or remote but because he represents moral perfection. Man becomes holy through ever increasing moral activity.

Hermann Cohen. Hermann *Cohen (1842–1918), founder of the Marburg school of neo-Kantianism, presented his views on religion in *Der Begriff der Religion im System der Philosophie* (1915) and his views on Judaism in *Die Religion der Vernunft aus den Quellen des Judentums* (published posthumously in 1919). While, in accordance with the development of his thought, Cohen's works on religion and Judaism were written only after he had retired from the University of Marburg (where from 1873–1912 he had a distinguished career) and had moved to Berlin (1912), he had strong Jewish loyalties throughout his life. As the title of Cohen's last work shows, he considered Judaism as the religion of reason, that is, in the Kantian sense, of practical reason; but, as will be seen, he tried to introduce into this conception the more personal aspects of the religious life. During the Marburg years Cohen wrote works commenting on the philosophy of Kant and also systematic works of his own. In his views on ethics he followed Kant in holding that ethics is only concerned with the general category of man as a moral being, not with individual man in his singularity. In Cohen's Marburg system there is no room for religion as an independent sphere; it is merely a primitive form of ethics which will disappear once ethics has developed sufficiently. While Cohen always maintained that Judaism should preserve its religious identity, during the early years at Marburg he found little difference between it and liberal Protestantism. While Cohen left no special place for religion in his early thought, he did speak of God. God, for him, is not a metaphysical substance but an idea bridging the gap between morality and nature. Man's moral reason tells him that his ethical task is unending, but he has no guarantee that nature is eternal, so that he can fulfill this task. The idea of God provides this guarantee. Cohen is well aware that this conception of God has little to do with the scriptural notion of a personal God, but he praises the Hebrew prophets for contributing to the progress of mankind through their non-mythological conception of God, through their concern for ethics, and through their belief in the coming of the Messiah, which for Cohen is the symbol for mankind's advance toward greater and greater moral perfection. Cohen conceived of ethics more as social ethics than personal ethics.

Cohen's conception of religion underwent a marked change. Whereas in his previous writings he had denied the independence of religion, in his *Begriff der Religion* he assigns to religion a separate domain. Ethics only knows humanity (moral man), but it does not know individual man. Yet the individual's feeling of sin and guilt possesses a reality of its own and this feeling must be removed, so that man may recapture his moral freedom. Religion accomplishes this task by teaching that man can free himself from sin through remorse and repentance and by fostering a belief in a merciful God who is ready to forgive. Cohen emphasizes that atonement is gained through human efforts and not, as in Christianity, through an act of grace on the part of God. He praises the latter prophets, primarily Ezekiel, for having formulated these religious truths. Cohen's conception of God underwent a change as well. Whereas in his early thought he had described God as an idea, he now identifies God as being. In fact only God is being; the finite changing world standing over against Him, is becoming. Though being and becoming, God and the world, always remain distinct, there exists between them a relation, described by Cohen as "correlation." The world cannot exist without God; but God also has no meaning without the world. Cohen considers God as the origin of the world and man, and he uses this thought to explain creation and revelation. Creation refers to the dependence of the world on God (Cohen does not conceive of creation in temporal terms); and revelation refers to the dependence of the human mind on God. (Redemption refers, as has already been seen, to mankind's progress toward the ethical ideal.) Cohen's notion of "correlation" is well illustrated by his understanding of the "holy spirit." He rejects the Christian belief that the holy spirit is a separate substance, describing it instead as a relation between man and God. God's holiness is the model for human action, and man becomes holy by imitating God. "Correlation" is also illustrated by the saying that man is God's partner in the work of creation. In his final work Cohen applies all these distinctions to an interpretation of Jewish beliefs and practices which combines a concern for ethics and the unity of God (ethical monotheism) with the more personal elements of religion which have been described.

Franz Rosenzweig. The first half of the 20th century saw the emergence of Jewish *existentialism, whose major proponents were Buber and Rosenzweig. Franz *Rosenzweig (1886–1929) studied the philosophy of Hegel as part of his university education, and his doctoral dissertation was a substantial scholarly work entitled *Hegel und der Staat* ("Hegel and the State"). However, even during his student days Rosenzweig became dissatisfied with the rationalism of Hegel and looked for the meaning of life in the existence of the concrete individual and in religious faith. He contemplated converting to Christianity, but resolved to remain a Jew (1913), and embarked upon the intensive study of Jewish sources which he continued throughout his life. (During the year that followed he came under the influence of Hermann Cohen.) During the first World War he fought in the German army, and during those years he sent his philosophic reflections home on postcards to his mother. These became the basis for his major work *Der Stern der Erloesung* (1921; *The Star of Redemption,* 1971). In 1921 he was struck by a disabling disease, but he continued a creative life until his death. Rosenzweig formulated his philosophy in opposition to Hegelian rationalism. According to Hegel thought preceded being, and humanity was more important than the individual man. By contrast Rosenzweig maintained that being (existence) was primary, and that the concrete individual was of supreme importance. He advocated a "new thinking" which, standing between theology and philosophy, began, not with abstract concepts, but with the suffering, anxiety, and the longing of the individual man. Philosophy, Rosenzweig states, had claimed to still man's fear of death; but death is still real and man is still afraid. Philosophy up to Hegel, according to Rosenzweig, had attempted to describe the world as a unitary whole, trying to show that the three elements given in human experience—God, the world, and man—share one essence. The various periods of philosophy differed in that ancient philosophy derived God and man from the world, medieval philosophy, the world and man from God, and modern philosophy, God and the world from man. All these attempts to unify the world, according to Rosenzweig, have failed, and the three elements of experience remain distinct. But while none of these elements is reducible to one of the others, reflection discloses that they stand in relation. God's relation to the world is creation, God's relation to man is revelation, and man's relation to the world is redemption. In creation, which for Rosenzweig is not a unique but an ongoing event, God shows that He is not a hidden God; in revelation He shows His love for man, which, in turn, leads man to a love of his fellowman; and man's love for his fellow leads to the redemption of the world. While Rosenzweig thought of redemption as occurring at the end of time, he also held that redemption may be experienced in the here and now. The three elements of experience, which so far have been discussed without reference to the historical religions, also provide the substance of these religions. In paganism God, man, and the world remain distinct, but in the scriptural religions they stand in relation. When speaking of the scriptural religions, Rosenzweig has in mind Judaism and Christianity, both of which are in his view valid. They differ, however, in that Judaism is conceived as the "eternal life," Christianity as the "eternal way." The Christian is born a pagan, who, through baptism, becomes a Christian. He is joined to other Christians through a common faith and he must go out to convert the world to his belief. The Jew is born a Jew, and it is his task to lead the "eternal life" of his people. Whereas the Christian is immersed in history, the Jew is beyond it. At present, Judaism and Christianity possess only partial truth, but God's full truth will be revealed at the end of time. While the relation between God and man is marked by love, for the Jew this relation is also governed by law. Rosenzweig advocates that the Jew must study the traditional body of law with seriousness and respect, but he does not demand blind obedience to it. He upholds the right of the individual to decide which laws to obey, maintaining that each Jew must appropriate of the Law whatever he can; however, his criterion should not be ease of life. (It is interesting to note that throughout his life Rosenzweig observed more and more of traditional Jewish law.)

Martin Buber. Martin *Buber (1878–1965) is perhaps best known for his philosophy of dialogue, a form of existentialism. In formulating his philosophic views he drew on his extensive knowledge of the Bible, Ḥasidism, and comparative religion, and he applies his philosophic findings to contemporary social and political issues. His dialogical philosophy is described in his *Ich und Du* (1923; *I and Thou*, 1937). Buber begins by holding that man has two attitudes toward the world and these two attitudes are determined by two "primary words"—I–Thou and I–It, which refer to relations, not to their component parts. An I–Thou relation is one between two subjects (persons) and is marked by reciprocity and mutuality. An I–It relation is one between a subject (person) and an object (thing) and is one in which the subject dominates and uses the object. Buber also envisages that there can be I–Thou relations between men and animals and even inanimate beings; while I–Thou relations between men often deteriorate into relations of I–It. In fact, Buber considers human life dynamic: I–Thou relations deteriorate into I–It relations, and a new effort is required to make them I–Thou relations once more. Buber also evaluates critically much of modern social and economic life; for in the modern world human relations have often sunk to the level of I–It. While human I–Thou relations cannot be sustained continually, there is one I–Thou relation that suffers no deterioration: it is the relation between man and the Eternal Thou, God. Buber does not attempt to demonstrate by philosophic proof that there is an Eternal Thou, for the Eternal Thou can only be recognized by one who is sensitive to it. God, the Eternal Thou, is not hidden but is present in every dialogic situation and speaks through it; He is not encountered in supernatural occurrences but in the events of everyday life. Buber finds this view of the Eternal Thou in Ḥasidism. The dialogue between man and God is not accomplished in isolation from life, but is best attained in the life of a community. To establish a community is a central Jewish task. Judaism is to be the community within which God dwells and it is to be the bearer of the kingdom of God. Buber's dialogic stance can also be seen in his account of revelation. He rejects the traditionalist view according to which the biblical account of revelation is literally true; but he also rejects the critical view according to which it is only symbolic. Revelation contains both history and symbol; it is the record of the meaning that the historical event had to the one experiencing and reporting it. Perhaps one of the most problematic parts of Buber's thought is his attitude toward Jewish law on which he exchanged letters with Rosenzweig. As has been seen, Rosenzweig requires the serious study of Jewish law and the appropriation of as much of it as possible. Buber sees no such necessity. Since man's existential response to any given situation is primary, he can refer to a particular commandment if it speaks to that situation; but in itself the commandment has no special claim. Buber also differs from Rosenzweig in his conception of Christianity. Whereas Rosenzweig considered Judaism and Christianity parallel, Buber cannot accept the Christian claim. That the Messiah should have come, as Christianity claims, is inconceivable to the Jew; just as the Jew's stubborn refusal to believe that the Messiah has already come is unintelligible to the Christians.

This account of Jewish philosophy has come to an end with thinkers who were active in Europe in the first part of the 20th century. (Buber is an exception since he went to Ereẓ Israel in 1938 and there produced a portion of his work.) There should be added A. I. *Kook (1865–1935), first Ashkenazi chief rabbi of Israel, who developed a mystical philosophy in a variety of works, chief among them *Orot ha-Kodesh* (3 vols., 1963–64²). Some of the main themes of Kook's thought are: God's immanence in all beings (however, he does not identify God with reality); the unity and harmony of all reality; the notion that diversity is only apparent; the notion that individual and cosmic repentance are means of bringing man and the world closer to God; and the notion that "holy" and "profane" are not antithetical concepts—the "profane" can become "holy" and, in the eyes of God, is holy. The Jewish philosophic tradition continues in the United States and Israel to the present day. Of later thinkers there should be mentioned Mordecai M. *Kaplan (1881–), Abraham J. *Heschel (1907–), and J. B. *Soleveichik (1903–). Mention must also be made of a number of outstanding historians of Jewish philosophy: I. *Husik (1876–1939), J. *Guttmann (1880–1950), H. A. *Wolfson (1887–), L. Strauss (1899–), A. *Altmann (1906–), S. *Pines (1908–), and G. *Vajda (1908–). It is probably fair to say that the current temper of Jewish philosophy is existentialist. From the 1960s, some Jewish thinkers investigated the implication of the Holocaust for Jewish thought ("post-Auschwitz" theology).

See also *Ethics; *Kabbalah; *Musar Movement.

Bibliography: For information concerning editions of texts, translations, and books, monographs, and articles dealing with topics in the thought of a particular philosopher see entry on that philosopher. Histories of Jewish and General Philosophy: A. Altmann, "Jewish Philosophy," in: S. Radhakrishnan (ed.), *History of Philosophy, Eastern and Western*, 2 (1953), 76–92; S. H. Bergman, *Faith and Reason* (1961); J. L. Blau, *The Story of Jewish Philosophy* (1962); F. Copelston, *A History of Philosophy*, 8 vols. (1950–66); T. De Boer, *The History of Islam* (1903); M. Fakhry, *A History of Islamic Philosophy* (1970); E. Gilson, *History of Christian Philosophy in the Middle Ages* (1955) incl. bibl.; Guttmann, Philosophies; Husik, Philosophy; M. Horten, *Die Philosophy des Islam* (1924); Munk, Mélanges; S. Pines, "Jewish Philosophy," in: *Encylopedia of Philosophy*, 4 (1967), 261–77; N. Rotenstreich, *Jewish Philosophy in Modern Times* (1968); M. M. Sharif (ed.), *A History of Muslim Philosophy*, 2 vols. (1963–66), incl. bibl.; B. Geyer (ed.), *Die patristische und scholastische Philosophie* (1928, repr. 1951); R. Walzer, "Islamic Philosophy," in: S. Radhakrishnan (ed.), *History of Philosophy, Eastern and Western*, 2 (1953), 120–48; repr. in: R. Walzer, *Greek into Arabic* (1962); idem, in: A. H. Armstrong (ed.), *Cambridge History of Later Greek and Early Medieval Philosophy* (1967), 643–69; W. Watt, *Islamic Philosophy and Theology* (1962); J. Weinberg, *A Short History of Medieval Philosophy* (1964); G. Vajda, *Introduction à la penseé juive du moyen âge* (1947), incl. bibl.; idem, *Juedische Philosophie* (1950); idem, in: P. Wilpert (ed.), *Die Metaphysik im Miltelalter* (1963), 126–1135 (bibliographic information on medieval Jewish philosophy between 1950 and 1960). For the current literature the reader is referred to *Kirjath Sepher*, bibliographic journal. Studies: A. Altmann, *Studies in Religious Philosophy and Mysticism* (1969); I. Efros, *The Problem of Space in Medieval Jewish Philosophy* (1917); idem, *Ha-Pilosofyah ha-Yehudit bi-Ymei ha-Beinayim: Munaḥim u-Musagim* (1969); idem, *Ha-Pilosofyah ha-Yehudit bi-Ymei ha-Beinayim: Shitot ve-Sugyot* (1965); J. Guttmann, *Das Verhaeltnis des Thomas von Aquino zum Judentum und der juedischen Litteratur* (1891); idem, *Die Scholastik des dreizehnten Jahrhunderts in ihren Beziehungen zum Judenthum und zur juedischen Literatur* (1902); J. Guttmann, *Dat u-Madda* (1955); idem, in: MGWJ, 78 (1934), 456–64; I. Heinemann, *Die Lehre von der Zweckbestimmung des Menschen im griechisch-roemischen Altertum und im juedischen Mittelalter* (1926); idem, *Ta'amei ha-Mitzvot be-Sifrut Yisrael*, 2 vols. (1954–56); S. Horovitz, *Die Psychologie bei den juedischen Religionsphilosophen des Mittelalters von Saadia bis Maimuni*, 4 vols. (1898–1912); A. Hyman and J. Walsh, *Philosophy in the Middle Ages: The Christian, Islamic, and Jewish Traditions* (1967) incl. bibl.; A. Hyman, in: *Arts libéraux et philosophie du moyen âge* (1969), 99–110; D. Kaufmann, *Geschichte der Attributenlehre in der juedischen Religionsphilosophie des Mittelalters von Saadia bis Maimuni* (1877); idem, *Die Sinne: Beitraege zur Geschichte der Physiologie und Psychologie im Mittelalter* (1884); R. Lerner and M. Mahdi, *Medieval Political Philosophy* (1963); S. Pines, *Beitraege zur islamischen Atomenlehre* (1936, 1946²); idem, *Nouvelles études sur Awhad al-Zamān Abu'l Barakāt al-Baghdādī* (1955); idem, "Translator's Introduction," in: *Guide of the Perplexed* (1963); E. Rosenthal, *Griechisches Erbe in der juedischen Religionsphilosophie des Mittelalters* (1960); Scholem, Mysticism; *On the Kabbalah and its Symbolism* (1965); idem, *Jewish Gnosticism, Merkabah Mysticism and Talmudic Tradition* (1960, 1965²); M. Schreiner, *Der Kalām in der juedischen Literatur*

(1895); C. Sirat, *Les théories des visions surnaturelles dans la penseé juive du Moyen-Âge* (1969); L. Strauss, *Philosophie und Gesetz* (1935); idem, *Persecution and the Art of Writing* (1952); idem, *Spinoza's Critique of Religion* (1965); G. Vajda, *L'amour de Dieu dans la théologie juive du Moyen Age* (1957); idem, *Recherches sur la philosophie et la Kabbale dans la pensée juive du Moyen Age* (1962); E. E. Urbach, *Ḥazal-Pirkei Emunot ve-De'ot* (1969), incl. bibl.; H. A. Wolfson, *Philo Foundations of Religious Philosophy in Judaism, Christianity and Islam* (1947); idem, *The Philosophy of the Church Fathers,* vol. 1 (1956; 1964[2]); idem, *Religious Philosophy* (1961); idem, *The Philosophy of Spinoza* (1934); *Harry Austryn Wolfson Jubilee Volume* (1965), Eng. section, 39–46. For publications in the field of Jewish philosophy by S. Pines, E. Schweid, J. Sermoneta see *Reshimat ha-Pirsumim ha-Maddaiyyim shel Ḥavrei ha-Makhon le-Madda'ei ha-Yahadut* (1957–68). [A.Hy.]

PHILO VERLAG, Jewish publishing house and booksellers; founded in Berlin in 1919 as the publishing arm of the *Central-Verein deutscher Staatsbuerger juedischen Glaubens. Philo Verlag's first manager was Ludwig *Hollaender, who was succeeded by Alfred Hirschberg. The firm was forcibly liquidated by the Nazis in 1938. From 1919 to 1932 it concentrated on books, pamphlets, and periodicals which reflected the ideology of the Central-Verein: a German-Jewish symbiosis which included a wider knowledge of Judaism by both Jews and non-Jews, and the defense against anti-Semitism by describing Jewish history and the contribution of Jews to German life and culture. The periodical *Der Morgen* (1925–38) and the *Zeitschrift fuer die Geschichte der Juden in Deutschland* (revived 1929–38) were published by the Philo Verlag. In the second, Nazi, period 1933–38, when fighting anti-Semitism became both hopeless and dangerous, the Philo Verlag concentrated on publications to strengthen Jewish morale and deepen Jewish knowledge and consciousness by works on Jewish thought, history, science, art, etc. The problems of Jewish youth and the need for preparing it for emigration called for a special type of literature. The Philo Buecherei ("Library") and such handbooks as the *Philo Lexikon* (1937[4]), the *Philo Zitaten-Lexikon* (1936), and the *Philo Atlas* (1938), a guide to Jewish emigration, served these various purposes. [E.G.L.]

PHINEHAS (Heb. פִּנְחָס), name of three biblical figures:

(1) Son of *Eleazar, son of *Aaron the priest (Ex. 6:25; cf. genealogies in Ezra 7:1–5; I Chron. 5:28–41; 6:35–38). When the Israelites suffered a plague in punishment for indulging in the orgiastic Baal-Peor cult, Phinehas slew Zimri son of Salu and Cozbi daughter of Zur, a prince of Midian, and thereby stopped the plague. By virtue of this act, Phinehas and his descendants were granted "a pact of priesthood for all time" (Num. 25:1–18). The memory of this event is reflected even in later sources (e.g., Ps. 106:30–31; Ecclus. 45:23–24; I Macc. 2:26, 53). Phinehas is encountered next in the war against the Midianites when, equipped with sacred utensils, he was sent by Moses to act as priest in the campaign (Num. 31:1–6). At the period of the Conquest, Phinehas, together with ten of the princes of the tribes that had settled west of the Jordan, formed a delegation to Reuben, Gad, and the half-tribe of Manasseh who had erected an altar on the east bank of the Jordan. There had been some suspicion that these tribes had defected from the Lord (Josh. 22:9–34). Phinehas appears to have been selected for this task because of his battle against the cult of Baal-Peor. At any rate, the issue was settled amicably. In the story of the Israelite war against the tribe of Benjamin over the incident of the concubine in Gibeah, it is stated that Phinehas served before the ark in Beth-El, and that through him the Israelites received an affirmative answer from God to their question as to whether to continue the war (Judg. 20:27–28). Many scholars believe these verses not to be part of the body of the narrative but additions by a later editor. It is related of Phinehas that he had been superintendent of the gatekeepers (I Chron 9:20). This is probably to be understood as indicating that Phinehas was considered to have been their patron. Phinehas' death and burial place are not recorded, though Joshua 24:33 does state that "Eleazar the son of Aaron died, and they buried him in the hill of his son Phinehas . . . in Mount Ephraim." This passage may have been reworked by a later editor. The formula is surprising since the usual statement about the dead is that he was buried "with his fathers." E. Auerbach believes that originally the site was known as the grave of Phinehas, and that Eleazar's name was attached to it as a result of a later tradition. Indeed, according to both Jewish and Samaritan tradition, Phinehas is also buried at this hill. Eusebius (Onom. 2:14) identified the location as being 5 mi. (8 km.) from Gophna on the way to Shechem (for genealogy of the house of Aaron, see *Aaronides). A family of priests named Gershom, directly related to Phinehas, existed as late as the time of Ezra, returning with him from the Exile (Ezra 8:2; cf. *Gershom). According to I Esdras (5:5), the priests Jeshua son of Jehozedek and Joiakim son of Jeshua were associated with the house of Phinehas.

(2) A priest, one of the sons of Eli, at Shiloh, brother of Hophni (e.g., I Sam. 2:34). See *Hophni and Phinehas.

(3) The father of Eleazar, who was one of the assistants of Meremoth son of Uriah the priest. This priest weighed the sacred vessels brought by those who returned with Ezra from the Exile (Ezra 8:33; cf. I Esd. 8:62).

The name Phinehas derives from the Egyptian *panḥśj,* meaning "the Nubian," which was also employed as a proper name in Egypt, especially for residents of Nubia. [E.Ste.]

Phinehas (1) in the Aggadah. Because of the major problems arising out of occasional cases of apostasy (TJ, Ḥag. 2:1) or fornication with pagan women (Sanh. 9:6; Sanh. 82a), Phinehas is, for the most part, highly praised in rabbinical literature for the "zeal" which he displayed in slaying Zimri and the Midianite woman whom he had caught in the act (cf. Num. 25:6ff.). While Moses, who had himself married a Midianite woman (albeit before the Sinai covenant), was humiliated and unable to cope with the situation (Sanh. 82a; Gen. R. 96:3; Num. R. 20:24, et al.), Phinehas remembered the *halakhah* that "he who cohabits with a gentile woman is struck down by zealots" (Sanh. 9:6). Seeing that even the most warlike tribes refused to punish the transgressor, Phinehas resolved to take the law into his own hands (Sif. Num. 131; TJ, Sanh. 10:2, 28d). The rabbis could not agree whether Phinehas had acted with or without Moses' permission—the issue at stake being whether a disciple could, in an emergency, decide a case without reference to his master (Sanh. 82a). In view of the unequivocal biblical approval of Phinehas' deed (Num. 25:10ff.), the legitimacy of the act could not be seriously questioned. Indeed, no less than 12 miracles were said to have been wrought in aid of Phinehas—otherwise he could not have successfully accomplished his mission (Sif. Num. 131). The rabbis, moreover, interpreted Psalms 106:30 in the sense that Phinehas had argued with God concerning the injustice of inflicting a plague on Israel which carried off 24,000 people (cf. Num. 25:9). When the angels wanted to push Phinehas away, God defended him: "Let him be; he is a zealot and the descendant of a zealot" (viz. Levi; cf. Gen. 34:25ff.). The Almighty also bestowed high praise on Phinehas when the tribes of Israel especially Simeon, tried to cast aspersions on him, taunting him with his descent from Jethro (through Putiel; cf. Ex. 6:25) who had "fattened calves for idolatry" (Sanh. 82b; Sif. *ibid.*).

There were, nevertheless, rabbis who had some legal reservations concerning the summary execution carried out by Phinehas. According to one view, Phinehas had acted "against the will of the Sages," who had therefore intended to put him under the ban but were restrained by "the holy spirit" which proclaimed "the covenant of a perpetual priesthood" (cf. Num. 25:13) for Phinehas and his descendants (TJ, Sanh. 9:9, 27b). Both Palestinian and

Babylonian rabbis stated explicitly that anyone consulting them about how to act in a similar situation would not be instructed to emulate Phinehas' example (Sanh. 82a). The implied disapproval is evident in the rabbinic speculations on hypothetical events which might have had an adverse effect on Phinehas' legal position: "If Zimri had separated (from his Midianite mistress) and Phinehas slain him, Phinehas would have incurred the death penalty, and if Zimri had turned upon Phinehas and slain him, he would not have been liable to the death penalty, since Phinehas was a pursuer [seeking to take his life]" *(ibid.)*.

Notwithstanding the legal irregularities of Phinehas' unauthorized zeal, the rabbis accorded Phinehas a prominent place in Jewish history. He was chosen to accompany the Israelites in their campaign against Midian to complete the good deed he had begun by slaying the Midianite woman (Num. R. 22:4), and also to avenge his maternal grandfather Joseph, who had been sold into slavery by the Midianites (Sif. Num. 157; Sot. 43a; cf. Gen. 37:28, 36). It was Phinehas who miraculously slew Balaam (Sanh. 106b; cf. Num. 31:8 and Targ. Ps.-Jon. ad loc.). He was also one of the two spies sent by Joshua to Jericho (cf. Josh. 21:1ff.), where he managed to make himself invisible like an angel; and he was in fact identical with the angel sent to the Israelites at Bochim (Num. R. 161:1; cf. Judg. 2:1ff.). This must probably be connected with the identification of Phinehas with Elijah (both having been distinguished for their "zeal and their peacemaking missions"; cf. Num. 25:11ff.; I Kings 19:10, 14; Mal. 3:23ff.), whose transformation into an angelic being is predicated in Malachi 3:1, 23 (PdRE 47; Targ. Ps.-Jon. to Ex. 6:18; Num. 25:12; Num. R. 21:3, et al.). He is, accordingly, the forerunner of the Messiah (Targ. Ps.-Jon. to Num. 25:12, et al.). The criticism leveled against Phinehas for failing to annul Jephthah's fatal vow, thereby causing the death of Jephthah's daughter (Gen. R. 60:3; Lev. R. 37:4, et al.), in all probability reflects the rabbinic attitude to certain priests in the talmudic age and has no bearing on Phinehas' personality even as viewed through rabbinic eyes. [M.A.]

Bibliography: North, Personennamen, 63; T. Melek, in: AJSLL, 45 (1929), 165; K. Moehlenbrink, in: ZAW, 52 (1934), 189, 217–9; C. Simpson, *The Early Traditions of Israel* (1948), 322. In the Aggadah: Ginzberg, Legends, 3 (1911), 383–9; 6 (1928), 137f.; 7 (1938), 37f. (index).

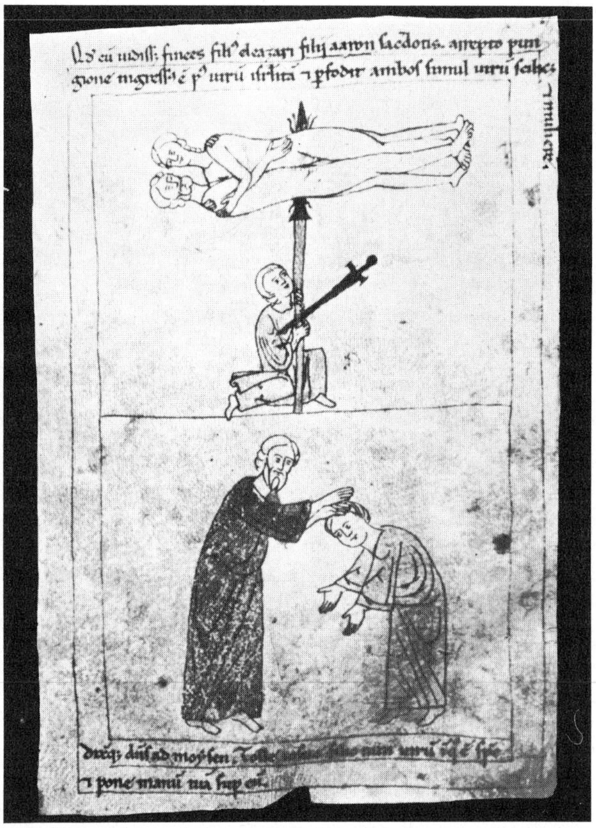

Two illustrations of the story of Phinehas in Num. 25, from a Latin Bible, León, Spain, 1197. Upper register, Phinehas slays the Israelite, Zimri, and the Midianite woman, Cozbi; lower register, Moses blesses Phinehas. Amiens, Bibliothèque Municipale, Ms. 108, fol. 64v.

PHINEHAS, guardian of the Second Temple treasury in the last days of the Temple. Josephus (Wars, 6:387–91) relates that with the seizure of Jerusalem and the Temple (70 C.E.) Phinehas, taken prisoner, "disclosed the tunics and girdles worn by the priests, an abundance of purple and scarlet kept for necessary repairs to the veil of the Temple, a mass of cinammon and cassia, and a multitude of other spices mixed and burnt daily as incense to God. Many other treasures were also delivered up by him, with numerous sacred ornaments." Phinehas was not the sole Temple custodian to disclose the sacred treasures of the Sanctuary. He was joined by one of the priests, Joshua (Jesus) son of Thebuthi. Both officials were granted pardons by the Romans in reward for their services. The mishnaic list of officials in the Temple (Shek. 5:1) includes a Pinḥas al ha-Malbush ("Phinehas, the guardian of the wardrobe"), who is probably the same person.

Bibliography: Graetz, in: MGWJ, 34 (1885), 193–205; Schuerer, Gesch, 2 (1907), 332f.; Klausner, Bayit Sheni, 5 (1951²), 272.
[I.G.]

PHINEHAS BEN ḤAMA HA-KOHEN (mid-fourth century), Palestinian *amora*. In the Jerusalem Talmud and *Genesis Rabbah* he is known as R. Phinehas, while in the later Midrashim he appears with his full name: Phinehas (ha-Kohen) b. Ḥama. Though born and brought up in Palestine, he was familiar with the genealogy of both Babylonian and Palestinian families (Kid. 71a), and showed his preference for the former *(ibid.)*. He appears to have resided in the town of Sikhnin where his brother Samuel is recorded to have died (Mid. Sam. 9:3), and he probably lived to an old age (Kid. 71a and Rashi *ibid.*).

In the *halakhah*, Phinehas was primarily a pupil of R. Jeremiah, details of whose ritual practice he records (e.g., TJ, Kil. 4:4, 29b; TJ, MK 1:2, 80b; TJ, Ket. 6:7, 31a). He was a colleague of R. Yose, with whom he often debated halakhic points (TJ, Yev. 1:2, 2d, et al.), and his main pupil in *halakhah* was Hananiah (of Sepphoris) who handed down most of his halakhic statements (see TJ, Dem. 3:1, 23b). Phinehas transmitted many aggadic aphorisms in the name of earlier *amoraim*, especially those of the previous generation—Hilkiah, Ḥanin, Reuben, and others. His own *aggadot*, both aphorisms and homiletic exegesis, are also extensive, and he often added a light anecdote to his homily to bring home the moral. In what appears to be a polemical reference to Christianity he declared, "While other laws decree that one must renounce one's parents to pledge allegiance to the king (cf. Matt. 10:35–37), the Torah says, 'Honor thy father and thy mother'" (Num. R. 8:4). His deduction from Job that "Poverty in a man's house is worse than 50 plagues" (BB 116a) may well be a bitter reflection on current economic conditions, and he laments the moral decline of the nation in its contemporary promiscuity (Lam. R. 1:11, no. 39) and gambling (Mid. Ps. to 26:7). His maxim that only one who does not leave after him a son of his own caliber is truly dead (BB 116a) is indicative of his keen concern for right education; and his best-known maxim is that "the name a person gains for himself is worth more than the one endowed him from birth" (Eccles. R. 7:1, no. 4).

Bibliography: Bacher, Pal Amor, 3; Hyman, Toledot, s.v.; Ḥ. Albeck, *Mavo la-Talmudim* (1969), 347–8.
[Be.C.]

PHINEHAS BEN JACOB HA-KOHEN (Kafra), eighth century Palestinian *paytan*. He is apparently the last in the list of the "early poets" given in *Saadiah Gaon's *Sefer ha-Agron*. As the acrostic to one of his *piyyutim* implies, he came from Kafra, near Tiberias, and his connection with Ereẓ Israel is further indicated in his *piyyutim* by the representation of a number of customs in force only in that country. His assumed identification with R. Phinehas, head of the academy, who is mentioned among the early masoretes, seems to be unfounded. A prolific poet, Phinehas wrote his works approximately in the second half of the eighth century, at least after 748. At least 59 of his compositions were found in the Cairo *Genizah*. Outstanding among those already published are *Kiddush Yeraḥim*, *piyyutim* for all the months of the year, a series of *piyyutim* concerning the 24 divisions of kohanim, and two monumental *kedushta* for Shemini Aẓeret. The *Kedushta* contains an important and colorful amount of midrashic matter; the sources of some of these Midrashim are unknown. Phinehas' style places him in the school of Eleazar *Kallir, but his expression is simpler and his poetry original.

Bibliography: A. Harkavy, *Zikkaron la-Rishonim ve-gam la-Aḥaronim*, 5 (1892), 112–5; A. Marmorstein, in: HḤY, 5 (1921), 225–8; 6 (1922), 46–47; M. Zulay, in: YMḤSI, 1 (1933), 150–62; idem, in: *Yerushalayim*, 4 (1953), 51–81; H. Yalon, in: *Ginzei Kedem*, 5 (1934), 191–2; M. Margalioth, in: BJPES, 8 (1940/41), 97–104; idem, in: *Tarbiz*, 29 (1960), 339ff.; A. Scheiber, in: JQR, 42 (1951/52), 213–4; idem, in: *Goldziher Memorial Volume*, 2 (1958), 55; E. Fleischer, in: *Sinai*, 59 (1966), 215–26; 61 (1967), 30–56; 66 (1970), 224–60.

[E.FL.]

PHINEHAS BEN JAIR (second half of second century), *tanna* renowned both for his saintliness and his ability to work miracles. He was a son-in-law of *Simeon b. Yoḥai, with whom he studied, and achieved a reputation as a keen halakhist (Shab. 33b). Nonetheless, few of his halakhic statements are recorded, and he is better known as an aggadist. Indeed his legendary saintliness made him, like his father-in-law, a prominent aggadic personality. His place of residence was "a city in the south," probably Lydda, from where he testified that he used to go down with his friends to Ashkelon (TJ, Yev. 7:3). In several passages, Phinehas is reported as traveling to redeem captives and being deflected from his mission neither by a river in flood (which he is said to have parted miraculously), nor by a pressing invitation to dine with Judah ha-Nasi (Ḥul. 7a; 7b). Phinehas was famed for his great independence, and it was said of him that from the day he grew up he would not eat from his father's table, let alone that of another. "Not that I have taken a vow to that effect," he protested wryly to Judah ha-Nasi, "Israel is a holy nation, and worthy for one to break bread with it. But one wants [to give] and has not, and another has but does not want to give. You both have and want, so with you I shall eat!" However, even here, when he saw that Judah had white mules on his estate, which were regarded as dangerous, he turned away and would not eat (Ḥul. 7b). The grandeur of the court was not for him.

Phinehas took a gloomy view of the moral and material state of Israel in his time. "Since the Temple was destroyed," he lamented, "learned and free men are put to shame, the mighty and the informers have vanquished, and none seeks Israel's welfare, and we have no one to rely upon but our Heavenly Father" (Sot. 49a). He was strict not only in his personal discipline but also in halakhic decisions for others, and would not join with Judah ha-Nasi in allowing work on the land in the Sabbatical Year (TJ, Ta'an 3:1). Even Phinehas' donkey was celebrated for its piety and the tale that it refused to eat untithed corn is developed by the Talmud into a general proposition, "If God does not bring a stumbling block through even a beast of the righteous, how much more will He not bring a stumbling block through the righteous themselves!" (Ḥul. 5b). A number of tales told about him, including the one about his donkey, are also told of his contemporary, *Ḥanina b. Dosa. *Midrash Tadshe*, a late Midrash dealing with symbolic interpretations of the vessels of the Tabernacle, was also attributed to Phinehas as it opens with one of his sayings. In the Zohar, Phinehas appears as a particularly revered member of Simeon b. Yoḥai's mystic circle, though here he is represented as Simeon's father-in-law and not his son-in-law (Zohar 3:240, 2 and 288).

Fittingly, Phinehas is the author of the famous ladder of saintliness: "Caution [against evil] leads to Eagerness [for good], Eagerness to Cleanliness, Cleanliness to Purity, Purity to Asceticism, Asceticism to Holiness, Holiness to Humility, Humility to Fear of God, Fear of God to Attainment of the Holy Spirit [divine inspiration], and Attainment of the Holy Spirit to Resurrection of the Dead" (Sot. 9:15). A millennium and a half later, this dictum was amplified as the path to holiness by Moses Ḥayyim *Luzzatto in his classic ethical work *Mesillat Yesharim*, and in this way it became the guiding principle of the *Musar movement.

Bibliography: Bacher, Tann; Hyman, Toledot; Heilprin, Dorot, 2 (1905), 313–4; A. Epstein, *Mi-Kadmoniyyot ha-Yehudim* (*Kol Kitvei*, 2) (1957), 130ff.; I. Konovitz, *Ma'arekhot Tanna'im*, pt. 4 (1969), 101–6.

[BE.C.]

PHINEHAS BEN JOSEPH HA-LEVI (13th century), Hebrew poet and *paytan* in Toledo. According to some scholars Phinehas was the brother of *Aaron ha-Levi of Barcelona to whom the *Sefer ha-Ḥinnukh* is attributed. He was one of the rivals of Todros b. Judah *Abulafia in the court of Don Caq de la Maleha. To entertain Don Caq, Todros from time to time conducted a poetic controversy with Phinehas in the course of which they exchanged with one another 35 short poems, generally filled with contempt and faultfinding. While the poems themselves have little literary value, they are of great importance for knowledge of the contemporary mode of life and society. In one of his poems, published in Abulafia's *Gan ha-Meshalim ve-ha-Ḥidot*, Phinehas addresses Don Caq and attempts to persuade him to renew his benefactions toward him; he had been driven away, in his opinion, through the effort of Todros and had fallen victim to a base charge. His *azharot for the Sabbath preceding Rosh Ha-Shanah, *Elohim Nizzav ba-Adat El* ("God stands in the divine congregation") together with their *reshut*, *Asir Tikvah le-Kez Yamim* ("Prisoner of hope for the end of days"), was published in the *maḥzor* according to the custom of Catalonia (Salonika, 1526). It is not known whether he is identical with the poet Phinehas ha-Levi also called Don Vidal Profiat, who lived in Spain in the 13th century and who forsook poetry, devoting himself to agriculture. His friend, the poet Abraham *Bedersi who regarded agriculture as degrading labor, derided him with great contempt for this in one of his poems, and even rejoiced at his misfortune when all his produce went up in flames.

Bibliography: Davidson, Oẓar, 4 (1933), 461; idem, in: *Tarbiz*, 2 (1931), 90–100; A. Neubauer, in: MGWJ, 20 (1871), 455–9; Schirmann, Sefarad, 2 (1960[2]), 449–53; idem, in: *Sefer Yovel Y. Baer* (1960), 161f.

[A.D.]

PHINEHAS BEN SAMUEL (known also as **"the man of Kefar Ḥabta"**; first century C.E.), high priest before the destruction of the Temple, 67–70 C.E. Phinehas was appointed to his office by the casting of lots. Until then the appointment was made only from among the families of distinguished birth. However, within the framework of the democratic reforms introduced by the Zealots, the selection of the high priest was made by casting lots in order to abolish the rule of these families (in this they relied on the ancient tradition in I Chron. 24:5). The lot fell on Phinehas who belonged to the watch of Jachin. Josephus censures him and says that "he scarcely knew what the high priesthood meant," for he was a farmer who tilled the earth (Wars, 4:155). This statement is to be treated with caution, however. In talmudic sources Phinehas is mentioned as a son-in-law of the house of the *nasi* (Tosef. Yoma 1:6), and the view that he was not learned in the affairs of the priesthood cannot be accepted (Klausner). This act of the Zealots gave rise to great bitterness and was the cause of civil war between them and the other parties among the people.

Bibliography: Klausner, Bayit Sheni, 5 (1951²), 208f; Jos. Ant., 4, ch. 3. [E.E.]

PHLORINA (formerly **Florina**), city in Greek Macedonia, near the Yugoslav border. In the 17th and 18th centuries there was a Jewish community in Phlorina, which was reestablished in 1912. Unsuccessful attempts to move the market day from Saturday to another day of the week had forced many of the Jews to leave. The Jews were merchants, dealers in old clothes, greengrocers, cobblers, etc. In 1940 there were 400 Jews in Phlorina; 372 of them were deported by the Nazis. In 1948 the number of Jews was 64, and in 1958 it was seven.

Bibliography: J. Angel, in: *Almanakh Izraelit* (Ladino, 1923), 79–80; Rosanes, Togarmah, 4 (1935), 267–8; M. Molho and J. Nehama (eds.), *In Memoriam,* 1 (1948), 106–7, and passim; idem, *Sho'at Yehudei Yavan 1941–1944* (1965), index. [S.MAR.]

PHOENICIA, PHOENICIANS.

Names. (a) The Greek name *Phoinike (Phoinix)* is first mentioned by Homer, and is subsequently well attested in the writings of Greek historians who consistently refer it to the eastern Mediterranean coast; in Homer, Phoenician is synonymous with Sidonian. Though the exact extent of the region called Phoenicia cannot be determined, the name is clearly the Greek equivalent of Canaan. One should also compare the Septuagint's at times mechanical translation of Canaan(ite) by Phoenicia(n) in Exodus 6:15; 16:35; Joshua 5:1, 12; and Job 40:30; as well as the parallel passages Mark 7:26 (Syro-Phoenician) and Matthew 15:22 (Canaanite); and the replacement of Canaan by Phoenicia in coins of the second century (see below). The most likely origin of the Greek name, especially in view of the Nuzi evidence, is its derivation from *phoinix,* "crimson, purple," so that *Phoinike* is "the land of purple" (see *Canaan).

(b) The name Canaan(ite) is first attested in sources from the 15th century B.C.E. down to the early 12th century B.C.E.; after that, except in the Bible or writers under its influence, it virtually vanishes. Exceptions are a Babylonian lexical text (c. 1100 B.C.E.), a final Egyptian reference (c. 900 B.C.E.), and two coins of the second century B.C.E. (in what is probably the corresponding Greek version of these coins, Phoenicia replaces Canaan; see above). These last witnesses prove that the name was not forgotten among the natives; besides, Greek writers are familiar with Χνά both as the eponymous hero of the Phoenicians and as the latter's name for their native land, and Augustine testifies that even in his day Punic peasants still called themselves *Chanani.*

Though the interpretation of the evidence is disputed, in its earliest occurrences Canaan is a region along the Levantine coast, and its borders were probably around the Nahr el-Kebir (Eleutheros River) in the north, and the area above Carmel in the south; only in northern Galilee around Hazor does it seem to have reached inland to any extent. Biblical usage, though it occasionally reflects the original restriction to the coast (Num. 13:29; Deut. 1:7; Josh. 5:1), commonly refers the name Canaan(ite) to all of Palestine and part of Syria (e.g., Gen. 10:15ff.; Num. 13:17ff.); however, this represents a later development, which was probably connected with colonization of the interior. The beginnings of this broader reference can be observed in Egyptian sources of the late 14th and 13th centuries; it is doubtful, however, whether Canaan was ever the name of an Egyptian province either embracing all of the Egyptian territory in Syria and Palestine, or, in the el-Amarna period, located in the south with its center at Gaza, though both views have their proponents (see *Canaan).

The origin of the name, a problem intimately associated with its etymology, remains a non liquet. Certainly Canaan was associated very early with one of the land's principal industries, the manufacture of purple dye from the Murex shellfish so plentiful along the coast; already in the Nuzi documents "Canaanite" is the designation of a variety of purple-dyed wool. This association is also reflected in the Greek name Phoenicia (see above). The problem is whether this connection with purple dye is primary (so W. F. Albright, hypothetical *kn'*, "Murex"; otherwise B. Mazar, "merchant" (*kn'*+Hurrian suffix), whence "merchant of purple [his staple]," etc.; S. Moscati, geographical term (origin unknown), whence derived meanings). No solution is without its difficulties; the last is best supported by parallels (cf. morocco, cordovan, etc.).

The Land. Geography played a very important role in the political and cultural history of Canaan. Lying between Egypt, Asia Minor, and Mesopotamia, and opening Asia to the Mediterranean world, Canaan was a confluence of cultures and of necessity deeply involved in the political ambitions and struggles of its neighbors. Its topography, however, led to political fragmentation; Canaan was never a state, and it was destined to centuries of vassalage under one or other of the surrounding colossuses.

To the east, most of Canaan was locked in by Lebanon, and the long, thin strip of coastal lowlands (c. 125 mi. = 200 km.) was often broken by gorges or promontories. Only at the mouth of the Eleutheros was there a plain of any size. There was one river, the Litani, besides a number of perennial streams; none of them was of use agriculturally. The climate, however, was warm (present monthly lowest median 50°F.), with ample rainfall from October to April (annually in modern times, c. 40–24 in. from north to south). The climate and soil were favorable for the cultivation of wheat, barley, olives, figs, grapes, and other fruits. The densely forested hills and mountains provided excellent timber—the famous cedars, junipers (*Juniperus excelsa,* Heb. *berosh;* cf. I Kings 5:22, 24), firs, cypresses, and oaks. Sand from the shore would be the basis of a glassmaking industry, while from the sea itself came the source of the precious dye.

People and Language. Though there is much evidence for human habitation of Canaan as far back as the Paleolithic period, fixed settlements were apparently founded only in the pottery-Neolithic period, and, therefore, relatively late in the Syro-Palestinian picture. The lag was probably due, in part at least, to the necessity of clearing this section of the coast of forests before cultivation of the land was possible. Relics of the earliest settlers are the non-Semitic place-names in early written sources, like Uzu/Ushu (Palaityros on the mainland), Ammia, and Ullaza. However, most Canaanite cities bear names which certainly, or very probably, are Semitic: Tyre (the island city), Sidon, Beirut, Byblos, Batron, Irqata, Yarimuta, Sumur. In view of the tenacity of place-names, which tend to survive despite ethnic shifts in population, Canaan must have first been settled on a large scale by Semites. They were probably an offshoot of the Semitic inhabitants of Palestine and southern Syria, whose occupation of these areas goes back to the fourth millennium, and the penetration into Canaan proper was probably not much later—roughly, around 3000 B.C.E. Racially, as far as can be judged from the meager

Figure 1. The sarcophagus of Aḥiram, king of Byblos, early tenth century B.C.E. Beirut, Musée National. From S. Moscati, *The World of the Phoenicians*, New York, 1970.

evidence, these Semites were mixed and, in this respect, indistinguishable from their predecessors; later, around 1500 B.C.E., a shift from the prevalence of a dolichocephalic to a brachycephalic type is observable, thus reflecting the more complex cultural relations of the period.

Of the language of the first settlers, except that it was Semitic, nothing is known. There is a stratum in the *Ugaritic lexicon which for a West Semitic language has an unusually close affinity with Akkadian; perhaps it is a survival of the earliest speech in the Syro-Palestinian area. The first real evidence for the language spoken in Canaan comes from the Execration Texts, shards (c. 1900 B.C.E.), or figurines (c. 1825 B.C.E.) inscribed with the names of rebellious rulers and their localities in Palestine and Canaan. These newcomers, another wave from the Syro-Arabian desert, usually called *Amorites, were also Semites and constituted another level of Semitic settlement. Their language, with dialectal differences, was identical with that of the Semites, who, in a long process of infiltration and finally invasion, seized power and set up a string of local dynasties from Babylonia to the borders of Egypt. Classification of this language in terms of the later developments which produced Canaanite and Aramaic is impossible; it is best simply called West Semitic. The question as to what happened to this language, i.e., whether it became the language of the earlier inhabitants (cf. *Aramaic), or disappeared, as in Babylonia, in favor of the established local language, unfortunately remains unanswered. The answer is crucial for the history of the Canaanite language which first emerges around 1400 B.C.E. At this time, "the language of Canaan" (Isa. 19:18) began to develop those specific features which would distinguish it from Aramaic. Their center of diffusion seems to have been Canaan itself; many of them appear only later, and then sporadically, in the north (Ugarit). The process of evolution continued—somewhat in contrast to Hebrew, a related dialect, which tended to be more conservative—and produced Phoenician. This was the language which was brought by the colonists to the western Mediterranean and became Punic.

History to 1200 B.C.E. Canaanite history falls into two periods: approximately 3000–1200 B.C.E., and approximately 1200–332 B.C.E. In the first, Canaan, by and large, was in language, religion, art, and social and political institutions indistinguishable from Palestine and a large part of Syria. With the coming of the Philistines, Arameans, and Israelites, the situation was profoundly changed, and the Canaanites, the sole direct heirs to this ancient culture, had an identity thrust upon them such as they had never known. They became, as this new situation may be conveniently designated, Phoenicians. They maintained this identity until they were submerged by Hellenism, an event that may be dated to Alexander the Great's conquest. The date of course is too exact; such a change is never effected in a single blow, and there are always survivals, especially in religion; besides, the erosion of the old order had begun before the appearance of the conqueror. However, Hellenism, best symbolized by Alexander, was new, pervasive, and a turning point.

Early in the third millennium, Canaan was already in close contact with Egypt, which was to dominate so much of its history; Byblos became the center of an intense trade in timber, and by the Sixth Dynasty (c. 2305–2140 B.C.E.) was virtually an Egyptian colony. Such it remained with little or no interruption, despite periods of Egyptian weakness, until approximately 1740 B.C.E. Though the point is controversial, the political control evident at Byblos probably extended, though somewhat loosely and with some oscillations, to the rest of Canaan and Palestine. It probably continued during the *Hyksos rule of Egypt (c. 1670–1570 B.C.E.), and then after a brief period of independence following the expulsion of the Hyksos, it was resumed again with Egyptian expansion under Thutmosis I (1525–c.1512 B.C.E.) and its consolidation under Thutmosis III (c. 1504–1450 B.C.E.). Within little more than a century, most of Canaan fell to the state of Amurru, which eventually became a Hittite vassal, and thus part of the Hittite empire (see *Tell el-Amarna). However, under Seti I (c. 1318–1301 B.C.E.) and Rameses II (c. 1301–1234 B.C.E.) it was reconquered once more, probably in its entirety. Finally, with the invasion of the Sea Peoples, in approximately 1200 B.C.E., the Egyptian yoke was broken forever.

Internal Development to 1200 B.C.E. In this long period there were other influences on Canaan besides the Egyptian. Contacts with the Aegean world are demonstrable by 2000 B.C.E., and they became particularly close in the 14th–13th century when, after the fall of Cnossus, the Myceneans conducted a vigorous trade with the entire eastern Mediterranean littoral. Relations with Mesopotamia go back even further, probably to the early third millennium, but almost certainly to around 2400 B.C.E.; and three centuries later one hears of a messenger of the "governor" of Byblos at Drehem in Babylonia (though the title should not be taken as implying the suzerainty of the Sumerian Third Dynasty of Ur). The arrival of the Amorites, already noted, added the deep cultural tie of language and religion, which commerce only strengthened; in the *Mari texts of the 18th century, Byblos is involved (along with Aleppo, Carchemish, Qatna, and Ugarit) in the movement of timber, resinous substances, wine, olive oil, and grain from Syria and Canaan to the kingdom on the Middle Euphrates.

The Amorite invasion also marks an important stage in the formation of the system of small city-states which became so characteristic of Syro-Palestine in the second millennium, and then, after the rise of the nearby national states in the Iron Age, continued in Phoenicia. The Execration Texts show the transition from a seminomadic stage—which is reflected in the earlier group—when the cities were probably not yet taken, and two or three sheikhs divided the authority over the environs, to a completely settled stage—attested in the later groups—when the cities had fallen and, with a couple of exceptions, there was a single ruler. Since the shift to monarchy is so widespread and so quick, it suggests the adoption and diffusion of an already prevailing institution. Acceptance of the institution, however, was hardly effected without important concessions, mainly in the form of land grants to the sheikhs who had helped in the conquest; at first, therefore, the king may have been only *primus inter pares*, as in early Assyria. The roots, therefore, of the city-state system probably go back to the third millennium; its feudal character began with, or was strongly reinforced by, its adoption by the Amorites.

This development may have received in Canaan, as in other parts of Syria and Palestine, further impetus in the period between approximately 1700 and 1500 B.C.E., when the Indo-Iranian chariot warriors, called *maryannu,* were introduced to the area and their services secured for the crown by grants of fiefs. At least in the following period all Canaanite kings still bear Semitic names, and never is a *maryannu* associated with the coastal cities of Canaan. However, for whatever the causes, by the 14th century B.C.E. one finds strong social unrest in Canaan as attested by the el-Amarna Letters; the half-free class who worked the land are escaping, and popular revolutions with assassination of the king are not unknown. [W.L.M.]

The Transition. With the rise of a new dynasty in Egypt (the 19th), the southern part of Phoenicia fell again under Egyptian dominion. Seti I (c. 1318–01 B.C.E.) speaks of conquering Asia, and mentions, among others, Tyre and Uzu (Ushu = Palaityros). Although Seti advanced as far as Kadesh on the Orontes, there is no evidence that Egypt could retain its hold on that vast Asian territory, for in the time of Seti's son, Rameses II (c. 1301–1234 B.C.E.), Kadesh was firmly in Hittite hands. Yet Egypt continued to rule the southern part of Phoenicia. In a famous treaty, the Egyptian and Hittite kings divided Syria and Phoenicia into two spheres of influence. The borderline may have passed north of Byblos (cf. Papyrus Anastasi I; Pritchard, Texts 475ff.). The following peace was of great importance for the cultural and material development of Phoenicia, and its overseas trade reached a peak.

1200–1000 B.C.E. In the last years of Merneptah (1234–1224 B.C.E.), there is reference to the first waves of the invasions of the Sea Peoples into the countries of the Fertile Crescent. In the days of Rameses III (1182–1151 B.C.E.), these invasions brought with them the destruction of all the coastal towns of the eastern shore of the Mediterranean Sea. The archaeological evidence shows the total destruction of Ugarit, and the Egyptian sources speak about the conflagration of Arvad. According to a Tyrian source preserved by Josephus, there were 240 years from the founding (of Tyre) until the reign of Hiram (Ant. 8:62). This date is confirmed by Justin, who says that the king of Ashkelon (= Philistines) defeated the Sidonians, who fled and founded the town of Tyre, one year before the fall of Troy (Justin, *Trogi Pompei Historiarum Philippicarum Epitoma,* 18:3, 5). These independent sources agree that Tyre was refounded at the very end of the 13th century or the very beginning of the 12th century B.C.E. Certainly there was no new foundation, but the tradition teaches us that a juncture occurred in Phoenician history. It may be suggested further that from now on the name Sidonian was applied to the Phoenicians generally.

Emergence—First Contacts with Israel. At the beginning of the 11th century, Tiglath-Pileser I (1114–1076 B.C.E.) of Assyria arrived at the Phoenician coast. He mentions Lebanon and the towns of Arvad, Byblos, and Sidon. The story of Wen-Amon (in the first quarter of the 11th century, B.C.E.; Pritchard, Texts, 25ff.) shows the low political prestige of Egypt in the coastal towns at that time, a fact which is clearly expressed by the king of Byblos. Also the comparison of Byblos with Sidon shows Sidon's political and mercantile position. The first suggestion of contact between the tribes of Israel and the Phoenicians comes from about half a century earlier. In the Song of Deborah, the tribe of Dan already lives in the north (cf. the sequence of the tribes which did not participate in the struggle, Judg. 5:16–17), and the close relationship between the tribe of

Figure 2. The Yeḥawmilk stele from Byblos, c. fifth century B.C.E. The relief shows a Persian offering a bowl to the seated goddess, while the inscription recounts the king's activities on her behalf. Paris, Louvre. From *Corpus Inscriptionum Semiticarum (C.I.S.)* No. I, Paris, 1881.

Dan and the Phoenicians can be seen from the verse: "And why did Dan remain in ships?" (Judg. 5:17), which Taeubler (*Biblische Studien . . .* (1958), 89ff.) interprets to mean that the Danites were seasonal workers in the harbors of Phoenicia. In the days of David there were already intermarriages with the Phoenicians (II Chron. 2:13). Similarly, there must have been intermingling between the tribe of Asher and the Phoenicians, for it says, "The Asherites dwelt among the Canaanites . . . for they did not drive them out" (Judg. 1:32), while the whole of the Valley of Acre and the southern Phoenician coast remained in Phoenician hands. It appears that at the end of the period of the Judges, Tyre rose to the position of the leading city on the Phoenician coast, and in the following 300 years it exercised a certain supremacy over the southern Phoenician coastal towns; W. F. Albright suggests that from this time Tyre became the capital of Phoenicia. Furthermore, Albright has propounded that it was Abibaal, the father of Hiram, who in a kind of alliance with David, destroyed the sea power of the Philistines, while David defeated them on the mainland. An alliance was formed between Hiram and Solomon (I Kings 5:15ff. = II Chron. 2:2[3]ff.). This included the supply of Phoenician lumber and technology in exchange for Israelite agricultural products, and led to a joint venture by sea to Ophir (see *Trade and Commerce).

Height and Decline—1000–750 B.C.E. From the days of *Hiram the Great (c. 969–936 B.C.E.) Phoenician history, as known, becomes the history of Tyre. The external proof is the change of title: while Hiram is still called "king of Tyre" in the Bible, Ethbaal (c. 887–856 B.C.E.), the father-in-law of Ahab, is called "king of the Sidonians" (I Kings 16:31). The reign of Hiram also saw the beginning of the Phoenician colonial mercantile empire, which culminated in the foundation of Carthage in North Africa (c. 814–813 B.C.E.). By the marriage of Ahab with Jezebel, daughter of Ethbaal, the culture and religion of Phoenicia penetrated Samaria (I Kings 16:32ff.), and later by the marriage of Athaliah with Joram of Judah they also penetrated Jerusalem (II Kings, 8:18; 11:18). On the other hand, Phoenicia proved to be a haven to Elijah (I Kings 17:10). Among the allies who banded together with Hadadezer of Damascus, Irḫuleni of Hamath, and Ahab of Israel, against Shalmaneser III of Assyria at the battle of Karkar (853 B.C.E.), were the northern Phoenician towns, Arvad, Arka, Usanata, Shian, but not Byblos, Sidon, or Tyre. It may be assumed that the king of the Sidonians, ruling over the whole coast from Byblos to Acre, was behaving exactly like his predecessors and successors and avoiding a fight on the continent; his strength was in his fleet. The poem on the "Ship Tyre" which is preserved in Ezekiel 27 is to be ascribed to about this time, for in the prophet's time Tyre had lost that firm grip upon the Phoenician towns. This poem shows Tyre at the zenith of her power both as a colonial and as a mercantile empire. From the first years of Adad-nirari III (810–783 B.C.E.), Tyre and Sidon were among the tributary countries. The question is whether Tyre and Sidon formed a single unit, or were two different states. Tyre's leading position on the Phoenician coast is shown by the fact that it is always mentioned first in all the Assyrian lists from the days of Ashurnaṣirpal II (883–859 B.C.E.), even after the Assyrians definitely set up an independent kingdom of Sidon in the third year of Sennacherib, and it is also always mentioned first in all the pre-Exilic biblical sources (cf. Isa. 23; Jer. 47:4; Zech. 9:2).

750–538 B.C.E. From the days of Tiglath-Pileser III (744–727 B.C.E.), a change in the Assyrian policy toward its neighboring states can be observed. One after another, the states were turned into Assyrian provinces (on the Phoenician coast, Sumuz became the main seat of the Assyrian governor). Only the main Phoenician city-states, such as Arvad, Byblos (the name of whose king is mentioned for the first time after a gap of 140 years), and Tyre, still remained "independent," certainly because of their commercial importance. In those days, another formidable enemy appeared—the growing colonial power of the Greek city-states in Cyprus, southern Italy, Sicily, and Sardinia. However, in the eyes of the prophets, Tyre was the "crowning city, whose merchants are princes, whose traders are the honorable of the earth" (Isa. 23:8; cf. Zech. 9:3).

While Shalmaneser V (726–722 B.C.E.) tried to break the power of Tyre by "liberating the subjugated towns (like Sidon, Acre, etc.), Sargon II (721–705 B.C.E.) came to an understanding with "the king of the Sidonians," i.e., the king of Tyre. Sennacherib separated Sidon from Tyre and set it up as an independent kingdom (in 701 B.C.E.), but after an unsuccessful revolt in the days of Esarhaddon, Sidon became an Assyrian province (in 677/76 B.C.E. for about 45 years). Again the whole struggle against the imperialistic Assyrian forces was borne by Tyre alone. After a short interlude, when the Egyptian pharaoh Neco tried to reestablish Egyptian suzerainty in Greater Syria, including Phoenicia, he was defeated by Nebuchadnezzar at Carchemish (605 B.C.E.), and thus Babylon became the overlord of the Phoenician coast. At the beginning of the sixth century B.C.E. the west again revolted, with Egypt's support. After the fall of Jerusalem (586 B.C.E.), Nebuchadnezzar turned to the Phoenician cities and laid siege to Tyre as the main city of the coast (cf. Ezek. 26ff.). This siege lasted 13 years (Jos., Apion, 1:156), and ended in a conditional surrender (cf. Ezek. 29:18). At this time, the Phoenician colonies in Spain and Sicily, looking in vain for help from the mother-city against the growing Greek colonization, turned to Carthage, and with this move the real independent history of Carthage began. The contact with Tyre still continued, but now it took only a religious form. An annual tribute was sent from the daughter colony to the mother Tyre for Melkart, the lord of Tyre.

538–64 B.C.E. According to Herodotus, the Phoenician towns opened their gates to Cyrus the Great of their own free will (*Persian Wars,* 3:91). From this time, Sidon, where the Persian king had one of his palaces, became the leading city of the Phoenician coast (cf. Ezra 3:7; I Chron. 22:4). The hegemony of Sidon is shown by the hierarchy of the command of the Persian fleet, since the king of Sidon is mentioned before the kings of Tyre and Arvad (Herod., *ibid.,* 7:96, 98). Territorial rights to parts of the coast (mostly to the south, in Palestine) were granted to the main Phoenician towns, and Sidon, Tyre, and Arvad together, founded the city of Tripolis. Here the Phoenician cities now held assemblies, and together dealt with the Persian government. The cruel suppression of the great revolt of Sidon (about 350 B.C.E.) by Artaxerxes III was not forgotten by the Sidonians, who opened their gates to Alexander the Great. Tyre, on the other hand, sustained a siege of nine months before it was conquered (332 B.C.E.) by Alexander, who built a dike from the coast to the island. Since that time, Tyre has been situated on a peninsula. During the wars of the Diadochoi, the Phoenician coast not only changed hands from the Seleucids to the Ptolemies but the main cities also exploited these quarrels to become independent and counted the years accordingly (Tyre from 274 B.C.E., and a new era from 126 B.C.E., Sidon from 111 B.C.E., Beirut from 81 B.C.E.) In 64 B.C.E. the Phoenician coast was incorporated into the Roman Empire, with certain special rights for both Sidon and Tyre. In the last years of the Second Temple in Jerusalem, the Phoenicians are called anti-Jewish by Josephus (Apion, 7:70). Still, from the time of the Maccabees until the destruction of the Temple, the Tyrian coinage because of its purity and reliability was the official standard for specific payments whose amounts were defined in the Bible (Tosef., Ket. 13:3).

Phoenician Colonization. The Phoenician colonization—which was, in fact, Tyrian colonization, for none of the other Phoenician cities established colonies—was quite different from that of the Greeks. Its main purpose was the securing of trading posts. It may be assumed that it started with the establishment of such centers in Cyprus. One of the oldest, if not the oldest, Phoenician settlement there was the town of Citium (modern Larnaka), the *Kittim of the Bible (cf. Gen. 10:4), which may have been called Utica (cf. Jos., Ant., 8:146). It is said that its inhabitants revolted against the mother-city, Tyre, and were subdued by Hiram, the contemporary of King Solomon. From Cyprus, the Phoenicians penetrated, via Rhodes, to the Aegean Sea (according to Greek mythology Cadmus of Tyre came to Boeotia and introduced a number of arts, of which the most important was writing—Herod., *Persian Wars,* 5:57–58; cf. also the Phoenician merchantmen in the poems of Homer). According to Thucydides (*Peloponnesian War,* 6:2), the Phoenicians at one time had settlements all around the island of Sicily, although later they withdrew to the southwest. From Sicily they spread out to Sardinia in the north, and by way of the islands Malta and Gozo, southward to North Africa (Utica and Carthage), and from North Africa westward to Spain. It is possible that the Phoenician merchants reached Spain as early as the tenth century during the reign of Hiram (W. F. Albright, 1961, in bibl. against B. Mazar who thinks they date from the time of Ethbaal, about the middle of the ninth century). Josephus has preserved a notice that Ethbaal founded two colonies, one on the Phoenician coast itself and one in Lybia (Ant., 8:324). This Phoenician colonization of North Africa is not only reported in the classical literature, but also reflected in the Talmud and Midrash, and much later in the early Christian historiography as "an expulsion of the Canaanites by Joshua" (cf. H. Lewy, in: MGWJ, 77 (1933), 84ff.). The climax of Phoenician colonization was the foundation of Carthage in 814/813 B.C.E. About the middle of the seventh century, the Carthaginians, the descendants of the Phoenicians, and the native populations took under their protection the Tyrian colonies, which were now endangered by the Greek colonization. Unlike the Greek colonial movement, Tyre's greatness rested on her mercantile colonies, which remained subjects of the mother-city. They paid their annual tithes to Melkart in Tyre, for Melkart, or the Tyrian Baal, now became also the chief deity in each colony.

EXPLORATION AND COMMERCE. The geographical conditions of Phoenicia dictated the pursuits and undertakings of its inhabitants: sea trade, fishing, and small industry. The Phoenicians claimed that they invented the building of ships and the art of fishing. The magnificent forest of Lebanon provided the wood for the ships, and the introduction of iron made it possible to build larger and more seaworthy ships, called "ships of Tarshish," which gave an impetus to more distant voyages. From the beginning of the tenth century, we can trace Phoenician colonization via Cyprus, to the western part of the Mediterranean—Sicily, Malta, North Africa, Sardinia, Corsica, and Spain, but it appears that the dates of the classical historians, who ascribe Phoenician colonization to the beginning of the 11th century, must be lowered by more than 100 years. Many Semitic names, however, have preserved the memory of Phoenician colonization, e.g., Cition (= Kittim) in Cyprus, Utica (= Watiga) and Carthage (qart-Ḥadasht) in North Africa, Cadez (= Gadar) and Tartessos (= Tarshish) in Spain. The Phoenicians actually founded only trading posts (this is the original meaning of Tarshish according to Albright) which engaged not only in trade, but also in a search for raw materials. The Phoenicians brought their own manufactures to the West, but to a far greater extent they acted as middlemen, transporting incense and spices from Arabia. These overseas expeditions were undertaken by guilds of merchantmen, with the king acting as representative both of the state and of the merchants (cf. *The Journey of Wen-Amon;* Pritchard, Texts, 25ff.). The trips to *Ophir undertaken by Hiram and Solomon in partnership are the most famous examples of these expeditions. Ophir was apparently on the African coast, in the general region of Somaliland (Albright, Arch Rel, 133; cf. I Kings 9:28; 10:11, and for Jehoshaphat's abortive attempt, I Kings 22:49). The daring of the Phoenicians as sailors is shown by the expedition they made at the command of Pharaoh Neco, circumnavigating Africa by sailing south from the Red Sea and home through the Pillars of Hercules. Herodotus, who writes about this (*Persian Wars,* 4:42), discounts as incredible what in fact is the proof of its truth, namely, the fact that the Phoenician sailors claimed to have seen the sun on the right, i.e., to the north. Another famous voyage was made by Hanno from Carthage to Central Africa (approximately, Ivory Coast), at the beginning of the fifth century B.C.E.

INDUSTRY AND ART. The most famous industry of the Phoenicians was the manufacture of purple dye (it is actually from this industry that the names "Canaan" and "Phoenicia" were derived, see above). Second in importance was weaving; the multicolored garments of the Phoenicians are mentioned in nearly all tribute lists of the Assyrian kings. Furthermore, the Phoenicians excelled in handicrafts: ivory objects, metalwork, metal statuettes and small stone sculptures, jewelry, and seals. Although the Phoenicians are credited with the invention of glass, it appears that they only developed the technique of its manufacture, for which they became famous in classical times. The purpose of all these handicrafts was not aesthetic but commercial. This is one of the reasons for the mixed styles, mostly borrowed from the neighboring countries and adapted to the taste of the customers. The Phoenicians were also famous as builders and architects (cf. e.g., the *Temple of Solomon).

Religion. Little is known about the Phoenician religion outside of Ugarit. It may be assumed that the Phoenicians connected their gods with the great powers in nature. The excavations at Ugarit have brought to light many religious texts, which have enriched modern knowledge. The head of the pantheon was El, and his wife was Asherat of the Sea. In the poems about Baal and his sister Anath, their war against the gods of the underworld is recorded. These Ugaritic texts confirm the short notes of Philo of Byblos, which are quoted by Eusebius (*Praeparatio Evangelica,* 1:10, 7), about the Phoenician religion. In general each city-state had its own chief deity: El in Ugarit, Dagon in Arvad, the Lady of Byblos in Byblos, Eshmun in Sidon, Melkart in Tyre, Baal (Melkert)-Hammon in Carthage. The most important goddesses were Astarte, in the east, and Tanit, in the west. B. Mazar has noted that from the first half of the tenth century, a new deity appears in the pantheon, Baalshamem. Baalshamem may be indentified with the Greek Zeus, whose temple is mentioned by Menander and Dius (Jos., Apion, 7:113, 118). Mazar suggests that this new deity should be connected with the colonial movement (cf. also the group of gods connected with navigation in the seventh-century treaty between Esarhaddon and Baal, king of Tyre: Baalshamem, Baalmadge ("Lord of Fishery"), and Baal-saphon). There is no doubt that the Phoenician temples bore similarities to the Temple of Solomon, with two main pillars in front (cf. Jos., Apion, 1:118; Herod., *Persian Wars,* 2:44; and graphically, Harden, in bibl., *The Phoenicians,* pl. 50). The Phoenicians buried their dead in coffins as a rule, but there is also some archaeological evidence that they burned them. It is known that in Carthage the custom of infant sacrifices prevailed (cf. II Kings 23:10).

Language and Literature—Later Period. The Phoenician language, which was spoken for more than 2,000 years, belongs to the northwest Semitic group. It is strongly related to Hebrew. As late as the fifth century C.E. there was to be found in North Africa a rustic dialect based on the Punic language, which is a descendant of Carthaginian, itself a descendant of the Phoenician language. The earliest Phoenician alphabetic text comes from the 11th century B.C.E.; we already find here the *alphabet of 22 consonants. Greek tradition tells us that the Phoenicians invented the alphabet, since it was from the Phoenician merchants that the

Figure 3. The sarcophagus of Eshmunezer of Sidon, thought to be either from the fifth or third century B.C.E. Paris, Louvre. From S. Moscati, *The World of the Phoenicians,* New York, 1970.

Greeks learned alphabetic writing. At the courts of the Phoenician kings, archives were kept, dealing with historical events (cf. Jos., Ant., 8:144ff., 324; 9:283ff.; Apion, 1:159ff.) and mercantile accounts (cf. *The Journey of Wen-Amon* (Pritchard, Texts, 25ff.); the correspondence between Hiram and Solomon (I Kings 5:15ff.). The Phoenician merchants were opposed to any descriptions of their voyages, with one exception. "The Periplus of Hanno," which has come down in its Greek translation *(Hannōnis Periplūs)*. The epigraphic material from Phoenicia and from its colonies is very scarce. The most famous inscriptions are the sarcophagus of Aḥiram, king of Byblos (beginning of the tenth century B.C.E.); the Yeḥawmilk stele (about the middle of the fifth century); the sarcophagi of Tabnit and of Eshmunezer of Sidon (generally dated to the middle of the fifth century, but probably from the times of the Ptolemaic kings). Yet the longest Phoenician inscription on stone was discovered not in Phoenicia itself but in Cilica at Karatepe. It is a bilingual (Hittite and Phoenician) building inscription, of 62 lines (probably mid-eighth century B.C.E.). Another Phoenician inscription comes from Zinjirli, in northwest Syria (the building inscription of Kilamuwa, king of Y'dy), and dates from the second half of the ninth century. Other Phoenician inscriptions (some of which are bilingual) have been discovered in Cyprus, Rhodes, Sicily, Sardinia (e.g., the so-called Nora stone), Malta, Egypt, and even Attica. Examples of Phoenician writings occur on the coins of the main Phoenician towns, such as Arvad, Beirut, Byblos, Marathus, Ptolemais-Acre, Sidon, and Tyre. [H.J.K.]

Bibliography: General: G. Contenau, *La civilisation phénicienne* (1949[2]); O. Eissfeldt, in: Pauly-Wissowa, Supplement, 20 (1950), 350–80; W. F. Albright, in: G. E. Wright (ed.), *The Bible and the Ancient Near East* (1961), 328–62; D. Harden, *The Phoenicians* (1962); S. Moscati, in: *Accademia Nazionale dei Lincei, Rendiconti della classe di scienze morali*, ser. 8, vol. 18 (1963), 483–506; idem, *The World of the Phoenicians* (1968); J. Gray, *The Canaanites* (1964). Names: E. A. Speiser, in: *Language*, 12 (1936), 124ff.; S. Moscati, in: AB, 12 (1959), 266–9. Land: E. de Vaumas, *Le Liban . . .*, 1–2 (1954). People and Language: G. Garbini, *Il semitico di nord-ovest* (1961); M. Noth, in: *Welt des Orients*, 1 (1947–52), 21–28; M. J. van Liere and H. Contenson, in: AASOR, 14 (1964), 125–8. History: Alt, Kl Schr; I. J. Gelb, in: JCS, 15 (1961), 27–47. Religion and Higher Culture: Albright, Arch Rel, 68–94; T. H. Gaster, *Thespis* (1950); A. S. Kapelrud, *Baal in the Ras Shamra Texts* (1952); H. Frankfort, *The Art and Architecture of the Ancient Orient* (1954); M. H. Pope, *El in the Ugaritic Texts* (1955); P. Matthiae, *Ars Syra* (1962); H. Donner and W. Roellig, *Kanaanaeische und aramaeische Inschriften*, 1–3 (1962–64); J. B. Peckham, *The Development of the Late Phoenician Scripts* (1968).

PHOENIX, capital and largest city of Arizona; in 1970 it had 14,000 Jews out of a total population of 581,000. The first known Jew in Phoenix was Dr. Herman Bendell, who arrived in 1871—a year after the town was laid out—as commissioner of Indian affairs. The first Jewish settlers came in 1872: Michael Wormser, who donated the land for the first Jewish cemetery (opened at the turn of the century); Michael and Joseph *Goldwater (Goldwasser), who founded a family dynasty on the basis of a Phoenix store that grew from a wilderness outpost to a statewide chain; and Emil Ganz, a Civil War veteran, member of the first town council, and mayor in 1917. Other early arrivers were: Hyman Goldberg, his sons Aaron and David, and his brother Isaac (1875); Adolph, Leo, and Charles Goldberg (1879); Wolf Sachs; Joe Melczer; Selig Michelson, postmaster from 1908 to 1912; Gus Hirschfield; Harry Friedman; Pincus Kalsman; I. J. Lipson; and Isaac Rosenzweig. Aaron Goldberg, who sat in the ninth and tenth territorial legislatures (1899–1901), authored the bill that made Phoenix the capital, and his brother Hyman was elected to the 19th and 20th legislatures.

Michael Goldwater of Phoenix, Arizona. Tempe, Arizona Historical Foundation, Arizona State University.

Informal Jewish worship services began in 1906 in a room over Melczer's saloon under the leadership of Barnett E. Marks, a young lawyer, who also organized the first Sunday school. Temple Beth Israel (Reform) was organized in 1921 as the Phoenix Hebrew Center. Its first synagogue, a converted church, was acquired in 1921 with funds raised by B'nai B'rith and the local section of the National Council of Jewish Women, which had been organized in 1917. Beth Israel dedicated a new building in 1949. Beth Israel and B'nai B'rith also helped impoverished Jews from the East who began coming to Phoenix for their health in about 1920. Marks later became assistant U.S. attorney for Arizona (1927–28) and his wife was elected to the state legislature (1922). The Jewish population increased 14-fold from 1940, as the city became one of the fastest-growing cities in the country, a major southwest trading center, and a haven for winter residents from all parts of the U.S. There are three other congregations: Beth El (Conservative, founded in 1926); Beth Hebrew (Conservative), and Beth Sholom (Reform), as well as two in the Scottsdale suburb in the desert—Har Zion (Conservative), and Temple Solel (Reform). There are also a Jewish Community Center, a Jewish federation, a Hebrew academy, and a Jewish family and children's service. Not far from Phoenix are Youngstown and Circle City, Jewish retirement communities, both of which have small synagogues. Jews have been active in the political and civic life of the city. Rabbi Abraham Krohn of Beth Israel was memorialized in the city in 1958 when it named a public housing development for him.

Bibliography: J. Stocker, *Jewish Roots in Arizona* (1954); F. S. Fierman, in: AJA, 16 (1964), 135–60; 18 (1966), 3–19; *Phoenix Jewish News* (1947–66); *Arizona Post* (1946–). [B.P.]

PHOENIX. The Greek legend of the phoenix, the fabulous bird that lives for ever, is mentioned in apocalyptic literature with various addenda, as for example that "its food is the manna of heaven and the dew of the earth, and from its excrement the cinnamon tree grows" (III Bar. 6:13). Some contend that the *ḥol* mentioned in Job 29:18 is the phoenix. It is so translated in the Septuagint, while the

Representation of a phoenix on the seal of the Amsterdam Portuguese Jewish Community.

Midrash explains it as referring to that bird "which lives for a thousand years. At the end of a thousand years fire comes out of its nest and consumes it, and leaving behind of itself about the size of an egg, it reproduces limbs and lives again." Another view holds that after a thousand years "its body is consumed, its wings moult," and it renews itself (Gen. R. 19:5). This idea of a bird's renewing itself after a great age is applied elsewhere to the griffon *vulture (Ps. 103:5). However, it is not definite that in Job *ḥol* refers to the phoenix, since it may mean sea sand which is "eternal."

Bibliography: Lewysohn, Zool, 352f., no. 501; N.H. Tur-Sinai, *Sefer Iyyov* (1954), 250. [J.F.]

PHOTIS, village marked on the Madaba Map between Orda and Elusa on the Gaza-Elusa road. It has been identified both with the Aphtha of Josephus (Jos., Wars, 4:155) and with the Aphta of Johannes Rufus (*Plerophoria*, 48; in *Patrologia orientalis*, vol. 8, p. 100), the more likely identification. The ancient site of Photis has been established at Khirbat Fuṭays, east of Gaza; in the nearby Wadi Fuṭays are remains of Byzantine silos. The moshav Pattish was founded on the site in 1950.

Bibliography: M. Avi-Yonah, *Madaba Mosaic Map* (1954), 73; Avi-Yonah, Geog, 169. [M.A.-Y.]

PHOTOGRAPHY. The first photographer known to be of Jewish birth was the American, Solomon Nunes *Carvalho, who in 1853–54 served as artist-photographer with John C. Frémont's expedition to the Far West. However, the 19th century did not produce many photographers with Jewish backgrounds. Jews took their place as photographers on the world scene in the 20th century. Among the inventors, the names of Leopold *Mannes and Leopold *Godowsky, the musician-scientists who in 1933 produced Kodachrome, and five years later Ektachrome, rank high. Polaroid, one of the most ingenious of all photographic devices, was invented by Edwin H. *Land. The list of distinguished Jewish photo-journalists, beginning with Erich *Salomon, who originated candid photography with the first of the miniature cameras invented in the early 1920s, through John Heartfield (1892–1968), who in montage photographs of vitriolic satire, blasted the Nazi hierarchy in various German publications until he was forced to flee for his life in the early 1930s, to the ubiquitous magazine photographers, is an extensive and impressive one.

Figure 1. "Mr. Rubin, Farmer from Metullah," photograph by Micha Bar Am, Tel Aviv.

The biggest pool of talented recorders of big world stories is to be found among the staff of *Life* magazine. Alfred *Eisenstaedt, who joined *Life* in 1936 when it was founded, had, by 1969, covered more than 2,000 assignments and more than 90 of his photographs had been used as *Life* covers. Other famous Jewish staff members included Eliot Elisofon (1911–), Fritz Goro (1901–), Dmitri Kessel, Ralph Crane, Yale Joel, Ralph Morse, David E. Scherman, and Bernard Hoffman. The equally gifted free-lance photographers whose pictures regularly appear in the pages of *Life* as well as its sister magazine, *Time*, have also included extraordinarily gifted photographers such as Cornell *Capa, Bruce Davidson (1933–), Elliot Erwitt (1928–), Burt Glinn (1926–), Philippe *Halsman, Archie Lieberman, Arnold *Newman, and Arthur Siegel (1913–). *Look Magazine* had on its staff such brilliant photographers as Arthur Rothstein (1915–), while Alex Liberman became the photographer-artist-art director for *Vogue*. Free-lance photojournalists work through photo agencies. Two of the leading ones in 1970 were Rapho-Guilumette, directed by one of the ablest administrators in the field, Charles Rado, and Magnum Photos by Inge Bondi. Among the great number of Jewish photo-journalists belonging to these two agencies have been Joe Rosenthal (1912–), of the Associated Press, who took the dramatic "Raising of the Flag on Mt. Suribachi in Iwo Jima, 1943"; Diane Arbus (1923–), whose photographs of transvestites were exhibited at the Museum of Modern Art, New York, in 1968; Morris Rosenfeld, photographer of yacht races; Robert Frank (1924–), known for his pictures of the seamy side of U.S. life; Ben *Shahn, whose photographs for the Farm Security Administration were later used as themes for his famous posters and paintings; and Arthur Rothstein, Edwin Rosskam (1903–), and Charles Rotkin (1916–), who all photographed the American dust bowl for F.S.A. during the depression years of the 1930s.

Photography has dominated fashion and product photography since the 1940s. The remarkably versatile Irving Penn (1917–) had a flair for graceful, bold compositions, and like Richard Avedon (1923–) and Eliot Elisofon was an adventurous explorer and unique stylist in fashion photography. Through unconventional lighting, exaggerated poses, startling costumes, and exotic backgrounds, fashion photographers all over the world have created eye-catching images that have more than once changed female attire everywhere. Two emerging talents in fashion photography at the end of the 1960s were Melvin Sokolsky and William Klein (1926–). Architectural photography, which requires a highly developed sense of design, and the ability to plan a series of photographs from strategic vantage points at exact moments during the day or night, found an exceptional practitioner in Ezra Stoller. Abstract images, found in objects ordinarily ignored, became the "new reality" of Aaron *Siskind, who, as head of the photography department of the Illinois Institute of Tech-

Figure 2. "Plowing the Fields at Tel Yosef in the Jezreel Valley," photograph by S. J. Schweig, Jerusalem, 1928.

nology and founder of the Society for Photographic Education, exercised considerable influence as teacher-photographer. A gifted student of Siskind's at I.I.T., Len Gittleman, became head of photography at Carpenter Center, Harvard University. Other members of the Society for Photographic Education have been Martin Dworkin of Columbia University, Bernard Freemesser of the University of Oregon; Jerome Liebling (1924–) of the University of Minnesota; Jerry Uelsmann (1934–) of the University of Florida; and Ralph Kopell of the State College of Iowa. It is not surprising that photographers of war and battle should rank as distinguished cameramen. David *Seymour (Chim; 1911–1956) was such a person—he died in the Sinai Campaign of 1956; Robert *Capa was another—he died in the 1954 Vietnam War; and among the first casualties in the Six-Day War of 1967 was Paul Schutzer (1930–1967), a staff photographer of *Life*. Combat photographers have inner discipline, and it was this same quality which caused the death in an air crash of Dan Weiner (1919–1959), who flew out in a storm to cover an assignment in the Kentucky mountains, and of Camilla Koffler (Ylla), the famous photographer of wild animals, who was killed in an accident in 1970 while photographing a wild bullock in India.

Photography, which unites art and science, was a child of the Industrial Revolution. It was the first art in history to owe its very existence to a scientific instrument. However, it would be wrong to think of science-minded Fritz Goro or Roman *Vishniac as cold and factual reporters of the modern world. They are poets who have drawn upon technology at its most advanced to reveal the poetry of an emerging world of thought and feeling. Photography was born largely as a result of the efforts of portrait painters to find some reliable means of getting an accurate likeness.

Portrait photography has been a big industry for over a century. The giants in portrait photography are few, but Arnold Newman and Philippe Halsman, two Jews, are certainly among them. So too are Eliot Elisofon, Alfred Eisenstaedt, *Izis in France, and Alfred Stieglitz. They all share the one essential quality that makes a portrait photographer, the ability to interpret a complex personality creatively, discovering something fresh and important to say. Newman is a master of symbolism that underlines and reinforces his central message. Halsman is a brilliantly inventive and witty graphic artist whose chosen medium is light.

There have been some distinguished Jewish curators, editors, journalists, and critics of photography, especially in the last three decades. Among these are Grace Mayer, curator of photography, the Edward Steichen Memorial Collection, at the Museum of Modern Art, New York, from 1962; Jacob Kainen (1909–), curator of prints and drawings, The National Collection of Fine Arts, Washington, D.C.; Eugene Ostroff, curator of photography, Smithsonian Institute, Washington, D.C.; Lewis Walton Sipley (1897–1968), director, American Museum of Photography, Philadelphia, Pennsylvania; Margaret Weiss, photography critic for the *Saturday Review;* Jacob Deschin (1900–), photography critic for the *New York Times;* David B. Eisendrath, science-oriented columnist of *Popular Photography;* Helmut Gernsheim (1913–), photography historian of London, England; and Albert Boni, who assembled and edited the comprehensive photographic bibliography published in 1962, *Photographic Literature.*

[P.P.]

In Israel. The early photographers in Ereẓ Israel included Yaakov Ben Dov, Alfred Bernheim, and Shemuel Josef Schweig. Among the contemporary photographers working

Figure 3. "The Ḥuleh," photograph by Peter Merom, kibbutz Ḥulatah.

in Israel are many doing press work and producing picture books on the Holy Land. Among them are: Werner Braun, David Rubinger, Micha Bar Am, Peter Merom, and David Harris. [Ed.]

PHRYGIA, district in central Asia Minor, part of the Roman province of Asia after the death of Attalus III (133 B.C.E.), the last king of *Pergamum. A Jewish community was established in Phrygia no later than the end of the third century B.C.E. According to Josephus, Antiochus III (the Great) transported 2,000 Jewish families from Mesopotamia and Babylonia to "the fortresses and most important places" of Phrygia and Lydia. These Jews were to serve as military settlers in support of the Seleucid monarchy, as the inhabitants of Phrygia had risen in revolt (cf. II Macc. 8:20: Babylonian Jews in the service of the Seleucid army against the Galatians). Favorable terms were granted the Jewish settlers. They were permitted to live in accordance with their own laws, and each was allotted land on which to build and cultivate. Generous exemptions from taxes were also granted, and Josephus thus considers the episode ample testimony to the friendship of Antiochus toward the Jews. The Jews of Phrygia undoubtedly had strong ties with Jerusalem and the Temple. On two occasions large sums of money which had been gathered in two cities of Phrygia, Apamea, and Laodicea, to be sent to the Temple, were confiscated in 62–61 B.C.E. by the Roman governor Flaccus on the charge of illegal export of gold (Cicero, *Pro Flacco,* 28:68). A number of Jews from Phrygia resided in Jerusalem during the first century C.E. (Acts 2:10). Several important Jewish inscriptions in Greek have been discovered in Phrygia, mostly from graves. One, dated 248–49 C.E. warns that if anyone should desecrate the tomb, "may the curses written in Deuteronomy [cf. ch. 27–29] be upon him." Nearly all the personal names are Greek, but the epithet "Joudaeos" is used several times and a *menorah* is carved on one stone. A tomb from Hierapolis, of the second or third century, states that the fee for any future additional internment is a donation to the Jewish community in Jerusalem.

Bibliography: Schuerer, Gesch, 3 (1909[4]), 6, 12, 17; V. Tcherikover, *Hellenistic Civilization and the Jews* (1959), 287f., 501; Schalit, in: JQR, 50 (1959/60), 289–318; Frey, Corpus, 2 (1952), 24–38.

[I.G]

PHYSICS.

In Medieval Philosophy. The subject matter of physics as understood by the medieval philosophers is well delineated by Aristotle, who describes it as a theoretical science dealing with natural bodies containing within themselves a source of change and rest; physics seeks the ultimate stuff of which these bodies are constituted, and the causes of the changes they undergo. The primary importance of physics in the medieval period was its use for theology. Two basic views of physics presented themselves to the medieval Jewish philosophers, the atomistic theory of Democritus and the matter and form theory of Aristotle. The former came down to them through the *Kalām philosophy of the Islamic *Mutakallimun,* who found it could be adapted more easily to their belief in God's absolute control over every event in the universe than the Aristotelian theory of matter and form, which exist eternally under unchanging natural law. The physics of Aristotle also leads to God (as is seen in Aristotle's treatise *Physics* itself), but neither to creation *ex nihilo* nor God's absolute providence. Aristotelian physical concepts were often combined with non-Aristotelian metaphysical systems such as *Neoplatonism.

Among Jewish philosophers Aristotelianism predominated and the Kalām was generally rejected, although the latter was widely accepted among Karaite thinkers. Isaac *Israeli expounds aspects of the Aristotelian system while explicitly rejecting atomism *(Book of the Elements).* *Saadiah Gaon

(Beliefs and Opinions) and *Baḥya ibn Paquda *(Duties of the Hearts)* both employ kalamistic concepts in their proofs of creation, but do not appear to accept its atomism. Joseph ibn *Ẓaddik in his survey of science *(Microcosm)* approvingly discusses various concepts of Aristotelian physics such as generation and corruption, and the four elements. Abraham *ibn Daud *(Exalted Faith)*, an avowed Aristotelian and forerunner of *Maimonides, clearly shows the significance of the Aristotelian concepts of potentiality, actuality, and motion for establishing the existence of God through natural philosophy. Maimonides *(Guide of the Perplexed)* presents a detailed critique of the Kalām and summarizes the principles of Aristotelian physics to which he subscribes and which he finds necessary for scientific theology. Maimonides rejects as unproved the Aristotelian principle of the eternity of the universe. *Levi b. Gershom *(The Wars of the Lord)* also shows a basic acceptance of Aristotelian physics, qualifying it, however, to defend his belief that the universe is not eternal, but created from eternal matter.

Two medieval thinkers stand out as opposed to the Aristotelian natural philosophy. *Judah Halevi *(Kuzari)* attacks the concept of the elements, arguing that it is nonempirical and opposed to the scriptural account of God creating natural objects as they are rather than from more basic constituents. Ḥasdai *Crescas *(Light of the Lord)* launched basic concepts as the finite universe. Crescas' work foreshadows the end of Aristotle's rule over physical science and the beginning of the modern age. [A.J.R.]

In Modern Times. The civic, political, and educational restrictions imposed on European Jewry were only effectively lifted in the mid-19th century, so there were few significant Jewish contributions to physics prior to about 1870. Some contributions were made in the early part of the 19th century, but these were to mathematics and mathematical physics rather than to physics proper. Karl Gustave Jacob *Jacobi developed elliptic functions, Herman *Minkowski developed four-dimensional space, and Tullio *Levi-Civitá made fundamental mathematical contributions to the development of the relativity theory. These men were all pure mathematicians, but theoretical physics owes them all a great debt.

The main Jewish contribution to physics began after 1870, in fact when "modern" physics was established and the stage was set for the creation of modern atomic and electron physics. As soon as they were emancipated, Jews began to contribute to physics, beginning in Germany, in Austria, in France, and then elsewhere. By 1970, no less than 15 Jews had been awarded the *Nobel Prize in physics.

Although there have been considerable advances in all branches of "classical" physics, such as optics, metals, crystals, and X-rays, perhaps the more notable developments during the 20th century can be grouped broadly under the following headings: (a) the perfection of the electromagnetic theory of radiation; (b) the emergence and development of the quantum theory and its experimental confirmation; (c) the creation of relativity concepts and their universal impact; (d) the clarification of atomic structure and with it the development of electronics; (e) the emergence of nuclear physics, application of nuclear energy, and the study of high energy particles. In each of these main branches of physics Jews have made contributions. In France, Max *Abraham extended electromagnetic theory considerably; the experiments of Albert *Michelson (with Morley), seeking the effect of the earth's movement through space on the velocity of light, proved of such significance that they sparked off the most important development in physics since Newton. They led directly to the development of *Einstein's theory of relativity, a concept which permeates the whole of modern physics. Einstein's highly original ideas were extended by Minkowski, Levi-Civitá, Summerfield, and others. The 1905 relativity theory dealt only with objects moving with steady velocity, and in 1915 Einstein took a mighty leap forward by his creation of the general relativity theory. This took into account acceleration effects and led Einstein to an entirely novel theory of gravitation which explains numerous facts inexplicable by Newtonian mechanics.

In the U.S., Isidore *Rabi carried out important studies on atomic and molecular rays, and Donald *Glaser invented the bubble chamber. In the U.S.S.R., theoretical physicists in particular have made a considerable impact. They include the distinguished theoreticians Lev *Landau, Abraham *Joffe, and Leonid *Mandelstam. In England Hertha *Ayrton had the distinction of being one of the few early women contributors to physics; Edward Neville *Andrade studied liquids and metals; and Otto Robert *Frisch played a basic part in developing the theory of nuclear fission which was to prove the basis of atomic energy. One of Italy's outstanding nuclear physicists was Emilio Gino *Segre, while Guilio *Racah, an Israeli of Italian origin, developed a special theoretical technique in connection with atomic structure. Prior to the Nazi debacle, specially valuable Jewish contributions were made in Germany. First and foremost in Germany was Einstein, who was responsible for the development of special relativity, the reformulation of a corpuscular theory of light and the invention of the photon concept, the statement of the law of photoelectricity, the theory of random movement of small particles, the quantum theory of specific heats, and, above all, the relativity theory of gravitation. A great deal of classical physics is still exploited, especially technologically. In spectroscopy A. Schuster (1851–1934), Kaplan, Kuhn, Herzberg, and S. Tolansky (1907–) have made contributions. *Simon, *Landau, *Mendelssohn, and Kurti have advanced low-temperature physics; *Andrade and Orowan contributed to metal physics; in Israel *Reiner added to rheology. Schuster developed magnetism, Tolansky exploited interferometry. T. Karman (1881–1963), S. *Brodetsky and S. *Goldstein added significantly to aerodynamics. Thus it is that Jewish physicists impinge on a very wide field of modern technologies.

Other leading German-Jewish physicists included Max *Born, who played an important part in the development of the quantum theory of solids and crystals, and James *Franck, who experimentally confirmed the predictions of Nils *Bohr as to quantum levels in atoms.

One of the notable developments in 20th-century physics has been the emergence of high energy particle physics. Not only did this lead to tapping sources of nuclear energy but, equally important, these studies have thrown new light on the extreme complexities of atomic nuclear structure and nuclear forces. Research in particle physics has produced a whole galaxy of Jewish Nobel laureates: Otto *Stern, Rabi, Felix *Bloch, Segre, and Glaser, all of whom in their different fields laid the foundations of new methods and techniques and initiated whole new schools of investigators. Lise *Meitner in Austria played a notable part in the development of radioactivity and it was she, together with her nephew Frisch, who first recognized the vast potentiality of an explosive chain through nuclear fission.

Among the Jewish physicists who have played a role in developing theories linked with high energy particles are Richard *Feynman, Murray *Gell-Mann, Lev Landau, and Sir Rudolph *Peierls. All have been concerned with the very difficult attempt to produce a consistent theoretical interpretation of the complex forces acting within atomic nuclei.

Research in Israel. Facilities for the study and research of physics were already in existence before the foundation of the State of Israel at the *Hebrew University of Jerusalem, the *Technion-Israel Institute at Haifa, and the Daniel Sieff Research Institute (later incorporated into the *Weizmann Institute of Science). These facilities were expanded after 1948. Centers created for nuclear and reactor physics are at Yavneh and Dimonah. The International Council of Scientific Unions has a national commission in Israel on pure and applied physics (see also *Israel, Scientific Research). For further information on physicists who worked in other fields see: *Aeronautics and Aviation; *Astronomy; *Chemistry; *Engineering and Inventions; *Mathematics; and *Meteorology. [S.T.]

Bibliography: C. Roth, *The Jewish Contribution to Civilization* (1945); H. Lewy et al. (eds.), *Three Jewish Philosophers* (1961); A. Altmann and S. M. Stern, *Isaac Israeli...* (Eng., 1958); Maimonides, *Guide of the Perplexed,* tr. by S. Pines (1963); Husik, Philosophy, index; H. A. Wolfson, *Crescas' Critique of Aristotle* (1929); Guttmann, Philosophies, index.

ALPHABETICAL LIST OF ENTRIES INCLUDING CAPSULE ARTICLES

The individuals whose names are marked with an asterisk in the list below form the subjects of articles in their appropriate alphabetical position in the Encylopaedia.

***ABRAHAM, MAX** (1870–1922), German theoretical electrophysicist.

***ANDRADE, EDWARD NEVILLE DA COSTA** (1887–1971), English physicist and author.

***ARONS, LEO** (1860–1919), German physicist and socialist leader.

ARTOM, ALESSANDRO (1867–1927), see *Artom family.

***AYRTON, HERTA** (1854–1923), English physicist.

BACHER, ROBERT FOX (1905–), U.S. physicist. Born in Loudonville, Ohio, Bacher joined the staff of the Massachusetts Institute of Technology in 1932. After teaching at Cornell University for a time, he returned to M.I.T. as a research associate in the radiation laboratory. During World War II he worked on the bomb project at the Los Alamos laboratory, and he became head of the bomb physics division. He was a member of the Atomic Energy Commission from 1946 to 1949. He was then appointed professor of physics at the California Institute of Technology.

***BLOCH, FELIX** (1905–), Swiss-U.S. physicist and Nobel laureate.

***BOHR, NILS HENRIK DAVID** (1885–1962), Danish nuclear physicist and Nobel laureate.

***BORN, MAX** (1882–1970), German physicist and Nobel laureate.

DEMBER, HARRY L. (1882–1943), German physicist. Born in Leimbach, Dember was at the Dresden Technische Hochschule (1905), where he was appointed professor of physics in 1914 and also director of the Physics Institute in 1923. Driven out by the Nazis, he held similar positions at the University of Istanbul from 1933 to 1941. He later emigrated to the United States and was visiting professor at Rutgers University, New Jersey, at the time of his death. His field was the photoelectricity of crystals and one aspect of his research in this area is known as the "Dember Effect."

***DE SHALIT, AMOS** (1926–1969), Israel physicist and educator.

DESSAU, BERNARDO (1863–1949), Italian experimental physicist. Born in Offenbach, Germany, Dessau became an Italian citizen. He was a member of the Italian Academy of Sciences and professor at the University of Perugia (1904). He acted as *shoḥet* for the small Perugia Jewish community. An active Zionist, he founded *Il Vessillo Israelitico,* the first Italian Zionist periodical. He wrote books on wireless telegraphy, physical and chemical properties of alloys, and physics.

***EHRENFEST, PAUL** (1880–1933), Austrian physicist.

***EINSTEIN, ALBERT** (1879–1955), German physicist and Nobel laureate.

***ESTERMAN, IMMANUEL** (1900–), U.S. physicist.

***FEYNMAN, RICHARD PHILLIPS** (1918–), U.S. atom physicist and Nobel laureate.

***FRANCK, JAMES** (1882–1964), German physicist and Nobel laureate.

***FRENKEL, JACOB ILICH** (1894–1952), Soviet physicist.

***FRISCH, OTTO ROBERT** (1904–), Austrian atom physicist.

FROHLICH, HERBERT (1905–), British physicist. Born in Rexingen, Germany, Frohlich was a lecturer at Freiburg University before emigrating to England in 1933. There he was a research physicist, lecturer, and reader in theoretical physics at the University of Bristol (1935–48), after which he became professor of theoretical physics at Liverpool. In 1951 he was elected a Fellow of the Royal Society.

***GABOR, DENNIS** (1900–), Hungarian-English physicist and Nobel laureate.

***GELL-MANN, MURRAY** (1929–), U.S. physicist and Nobel laureate.

***GINZBURG, VITALI LAZAREVICH** (1916–), Soviet physicist.

***GLASER, DONALD ARTHUR** (1926–), U.S. physicist and Nobel laureate.

***HECHT, SELIG** (1892–1947), Austrian biophysicist.

***HOFSTADTER, ROBERT** (1915–), U.S. physicist and Nobel laureate.

***INFELD, LEOPOLD** (1898–1968), Polish physicist and mathematician.

JAMMER, MOSHE (1915–), Israel physicist. Born in Berlin, Jammer settled in Palestine in 1935. In 1959 he joined the staff of Bar-Ilan University as professor of science and head of the department of physics. In 1962 he was appointed rector of the university.

***JOFFE, ABRAHAM FYODOROVICH** (1880–1960), Russian physicist.

***LANDAU, LEV DAVIDOVICH** (1908–1968), Russian physicist and Nobel laureate.

***LEVI-CIVITA, TULLIO** (1873–1942), Italian physicist and mathematician.

***LIPPMANN, GABRIEL** (1845–1921), French physicist and Nobel laureate.

***MANDELSTAM, LEONID ISAAKOVITZ** (1879–1944), Russian physicist.

***MEITNER, LISE** (1878–1968), Austrian-Swedish physicist and atom scientist.

MENDELSSOHN, KURT ALFRED GEORG (1906–), British physicist. Born in Berlin, Mendelssohn did research on low-temperature physics (1927). In 1933 he left Germany and established the first helium liquefaction plant in Britain. He was elected a Fellow of the Royal Society in 1951. He was the editor of *Cryogenics,* an international journal of low-temperature engineering and research (1961–65).

***MICHELSON, ALBERT ABRAHAM** (1852–1931), U.S. physicist and Nobel laureate.

***NE'EMAN, YUVAL** (1925–), Israel physicist.

***OPPENHEIMER, J. ROBERT** (1904–1967), U.S. physicist in charge of construction for first nuclear weapons.

***RABI, ISIDOR ISAAC** (1898–), U.S. physicist and Nobel laureate.

***RACAH, GUILIO** (1909–1965), Israel physicist.

***REINER, MARKUS** (1886–), Israel rheologist.

***SAMBURSKY, SHMUEL** (1900–), Israel science-historian.

***SCHWINGER, JULIAN SEYMOUR** (1918–), U.S. physicist and Nobel laureate.

***SIMON, SIR FRANCIS EUGENE** (1893–1956), German-English atomic physicist.

***STERN, OTTO** (1888–1969), German physicist and Nobel laureate.

***SZILARD, LEO** (1898–1964), Hungarian-U.S. nuclear physicist.

***TABOR, DAVID** (1913–), English physicist.

***TALMI, IGAL** (1925–), Israel physicist.

***TELLER, EDWARD** (1908–), U.S. physicist and leader in the development of the hydrogen bomb.

***WEISSKOPF, VICTOR** (1908–), Austrian-U.S. physicist.

***WEXLER, VLADIMIR** (1907–1966), Soviet physicist.

***ZACHARIAS, JERROLD REJNACH** (1905–), U.S. physicist and educator.

PIACENZA, city in northern Italy, formerly in the duchy of *Parma. Jewish moneylenders lived there in the 15th century and were attacked by the friars who condemned usury in their sermons. When **monti di pietà* were established here and in Parma in 1488–90, the Jews from both towns scattered throughout the country districts in order to carry on their business there. Thus, around Piacenza, the small communities (now extinct) of Monticelli d'Ongina, Fiorenzuola d'Arda, and Cortemaggiore came into being and were able to carry on even after 1570, at which date Jews were forbidden to live in Piacenza.

Bibliography: Ravà, in: *Educatore Israelita,* 18 (1870), 169–80, 212–3; Loevinson, in: RMI, 7 (1932/33), 351–8; Milano, Italia, index; Roth, Italy, index; Zoller, in: RI, 7 (1910), 87–92. [A.MIL.]

PIASECZNO, town in Warszawa province, Poland. During the 18th century there was a Jewish settlement in the town, but in 1740 King Augustus III prohibited the residence of Jews. In 1789 they were also forbidden to trade or be innkeepers in the town. After the abolition of this decree by the Russian government, the population of the town increased from 1,328 in 1865 to 5,604 in 1921. The latter figure included 2,256 Jews. An active Jewish life began after World War I and in 1932 a Zionist delegate was elected to head the community. Among the *ẓaddikim* of Piaseczno, R. Israel Jehiel Kalish (whose father R. Simḥah Bunem Kalish of Otwock died in Tiberias in 1907) was renowned at the beginning of the 20th century. [SH.L.K.]

Holocaust Period. Before the outbreak of World War II, there were about 3,000 Jews in Piaseczno. The Jewish community was liquidated on Jan. 22–27, 1941, when all the Jews were deported to *Warsaw and shared the fate of that community. After the war the Jewish community was not reconstituted. [ED.]

PIATIGORSKY, GREGOR (1903–), cellist. Born in Yekaterinoslav, Ukraine, Piatigorsky became first cellist at the Imperial Opera. He left Russia in 1921 and from 1924 he was leading cellist of the Berlin Philharmonic Orchestra.

Gregor Piatigorsky, cellist. Courtesy R.C.A., New York.

He resigned in 1928 to tour as soloist, often appearing in recitals with Serge Rachmaninoff, Arthur *Schnabel, and Vladimir *Horovitz. He also formed a trio with Nathan *Milstein and Horovitz. In 1929 he settled in the U.S. and taught at the Curtis Institute in Philadelphia and later at Boston University.

One of the leading cellists of his generation, Piatigorsky made many arrangements for the cello and commissioned cello concertos from several composers—Paul Hindemith, Mario *Castelnuovo-Tedesco, and Serge Prokofiev. He visited Israel in 1954 for concerts with the Israel Philharmonic Orchestra and returned in 1970 for concerts together with Jasha Heifetz. His autobiography, *Cellist,* was published in 1965. [U.T.]

PIATRA-NEAMT (Rum. **Piatra-Neamt,** or **Piatra**), town in Moldavia, N. E. Rumania. According to a local Jewish tradition, a synagogue existed there by the middle of the 16th century, and during the war against Turkey (1541–46), the Jews of Piatra-Neamt hid the ruler of Moldavia. The oldest tombstone dates from 1627 and the first entries in the *pinkas* (minute book) of the *ḥevra kaddisha* dates from 1771. The *ḥevra* maintained a *talmud torah* and directed various communal activities. The Jews' Guild (see *Rumania), was in charge of communal affairs. In 1819 the head of the guild was the assistant of the chief commissioner of the local police. There were 120 Jewish taxpayers in 1802. The number of Jews had risen to 3,900 (33% of the total population) in 1859 and 8,489 (c. 50% of the total) in 1907. In 1930 there were 7,595 Jews (24% of the total).

Anti-Semitism was prevalent from the 19th century on, and in 1821 the community suffered from Greek rebels who appeared in the area and robbed and murdered Jews there. The arrival of the Turkish army prevented a complete massacre of the community. In 1841, 48 Jews from the surrounding villages were arrested following a *blood libel. They were released by special order of the sultan on the intervention of Sir Moses *Montefiore.

The abolition of the **ḥakham bashi* system in 1834 and of the Jews' Guild was followed by a long period of chaos in Jewish public life; attempts to form a community failed because of quarrels among different Jewish groups and institutions which attempted to assume communal responsibility and leadership. In 1868 the police closed the *talmud torah* and the private *ḥadarim,* obliging the community to establish a modern school. A primary school was founded by the local *B'nai B'rith in 1882 and functioned until 1885 when the *talmud torah* was reopened. In 1899–1900 the *Jewish Colonization Association contributed to the building of two schools, one for boys and another for girls, which in 1910 had 810 pupils.

In addition to the "Great Synagogue" there were 16 prayer houses, some of them belonging to specific craftsmen. A *hekdesh* (hostel for travelers) was turned into an old-age home in 1898 and a Jewish hospital was established in 1905.

Most of the commerce in Piatra-Neamt was conducted by Jews: in 1891 there were 417 Jewish commercial firms. Many Jews dealt in the agricultural products of the area, such as timber, cereals, and cattle. The majority of craftsmen were also Jews and some industries were also owned by Jews.

In 1894 a branch of Ḥovevei Zion was founded in the town. After 1897 groups of supporters of Herzl's political Zionism were formed there. The Hebrew weekly *Yizre'el* was published in Piatra-Neamt from 1882, as well as a Yiddish journal *Di Hofnung* (published three times weekly). Another Hebrew magazine, *Ha-Mekiẓ,* edited by the Hebrew author and teacher M. *Braunstein-Mibashan, and A. L. *Zissu, who was born in Piatra-Neamt, was published there from 1909. Jean *Juster and the historian of Rumanian Jewry, M. A. Halevy (1900–), were also born in Piatra-Neamt.

Anti-Semitism was especially virulent in Piatra-Neamt between the two world wars. In 1925 synagogues, Jewish schools, and other institutions were looted, and in 1926 and 1928 the cemetery was desecrated. Corneliu *Codreaunu, head of the *Iron Guard, was elected to Parliament as deputy for Piatra-Neamt in 1931. In 1937, 26 out of 28 Jews practicing at the bar were dismissed. Despite these problems the community itself was more firmly organized between the two world wars. The two primary schools, serving 400 boys and girls in 1936–37, were amalgamated, and the community also supported a boarders' annex for 250 children. There were Zionist organizations of all shades.

The community of Piatra-Neamt was not destroyed in World War II. In 1947 the Jewish population numbered 8,000, declining to 5,000 in 1950. In 1969 about 300 Jewish families remained. There were two synagogues.

Bibliography: PK Romanyah 208–16; J. Kaufman, *Cronica comunităţi lor israelite din Judeţul Neamţu* (1929); *Almanahul ziarului Tribuna evreească*, 1 (1937/38), 273–4; E. Schwarzfeld, in: *Anuar pentru Israeliţi*, 7 (1884/85), 19; *Buletinul Bibliotecii Muzeului şi archivei istorice a Templului Coral, Bucureşti*, 2, no. 1 (1936), 13–15. [Th.L.]

°**PIATTOLI, SCIPIONE** (1749–1809), Italian clergyman who later became a Polish statesman. He was born in Florence and lived in Poland from 1783. In 1789, on a tour of France, he supported the political demands of the third estate and was deeply impressed by the suggestion of *Malesherbes for an improvement in the situation of the Jews in Alsace. On his return to Poland in 1790, he made contact with the reformists in the Sejm, and took an active part in the formation of the constitution of May 3, 1791. His diplomatic qualifications led to his appointment as adviser to Stanislaus Augustus, the last king of Poland. Piattoli strove to rectify the unstable legal situation of Polish Jews, combining practical suggestions on behalf of the Jews with an effort to solve the king's personal financial debts. In September 1791 he proposed that Jews be given the right to buy land and houses, and juridical autonomy and the status of a separate urban class. For these rights the Jews were to pay the king's debts (about 20,000,000 zlotys) in ten annual installments. Piattoli first addressed his proposal to the leaders of the Jewish communities, then in Warsaw, asking them for their support. He also convinced certain statesmen, H. Kollątaj, A. Linowski, J. Jeziezski, and others, to discuss his plan in the Sejm. In 1792, however, Piattoli's proposal was opposed by urban representatives and those aristocrats who inclined toward Russia. The Sejm was dissolved on May 26, 1792 with the outbreak of war between Russia and Poland, and Piattoli's proposal lapsed.

Bibliography: N. M. Gelber, in: *Nowe Życie*, no. 6 (1924), 321–3; A. D'Ancona, *S. Piattoli e la Polonia* (1915); *Encyklopedia Powszechna*, 20 (1865), 640–1. [A.Cy.]

PICA (The Palestine Jewish Colonization Association), society for Jewish settlement in Palestine, active between 1924 and 1957. In 1923, as a result of the rapid development of his settlement projects in Palestine, Baron Edmond de *Rothschild decided to establish a separate body to achieve his ideal. The new association, headed by his son James, took over from the *Jewish Colonization Association (ICA), which had managed the villages assisted by the Baron since 1900. PICA was officially recognized by the Mandatory authorities in 1924.

PICA founded and assisted Jewish settlement in the moshavot Pardes Ḥannah and Binyaminah, in moshavim such as Naḥalat Jabotinsky, Bet Ḥananyah, Shadmot Devorah, and Sedeh Eli'ezer, and in kibbutzim such as Ashdot Ya'akov, Ma'yan Ẓevi, and Kefar Glickson. It also engaged in swamp drainage (e.g., at Kabarah in 1925), afforestation (at Ḥaderah), stabilization of sand dunes, and agricultural research and modernization. It gave financial support to cultural institutions, including the Hebrew University and the Technion, and developed the industrial enterprises started by Baron de Rothschild, though it always tried in some way to link its efforts in industry with agriculture or land. After 1948 it modernized and expanded the Grands Moulins flour mill, Haifa, and the salt works at Athlit, as well as acquiring shares in Fertilizers and Chemicals, Haifa, and other enterprises. On the death of James de Rothschild in 1957, PICA wound up its operations and transferred its considerable property to the State of Israel.

Bibliography: PICA, *Memorandum and Articles of Association* (1924); idem, *Memorandum Submitted to the United Nations Special Committee on Palestine* (1947); idem, *Exchange of Letters between Mrs James A. de Rothschild... and Mr. David Ben Gurion...* (1958); *PICA: Ha-Ḥevrah le-Hityashevut ha-Yehudim be-Ereẓ-Yisrael* (1957). [Av.Le.]

°**PICARD, EDMOND** (1836–1924), Belgian lawyer and anti-Semite. Picard became an active advocate of socialism, then of anti-Semitic racialism, and attempted to forge an alliance between the two ideologies. He fought for the socialist cause between 1866 and 1907, when he left the Socialist Party, although he continued to call himself a socialist. In 1888 Picard visited Morocco on a diplomatic mission and from then on turned his talents as a writer to outright racialist propaganda. Observing Arabs and Jews there, he concluded that Semites and Aryans were irreconcilable races. In the following years he wrote *La Bible et le Coran* (1888), *Synthèse de l'antisémitisme* (1892), which was reprinted during the German occupation of Belgium in World War II, and *L'Aryano-Sémitisme* (1899), a collection of 19 articles previously published in the socialist daily *Le Peuple* under the bizarre title *L'Antisémitisme scientifique et humanitaire*. Picard abhorred any intermingling of races and urged Aryans to protect themselves from the "Semitic invasion." He presented Jesus as an Aryan and the Jews as Asians. Seeing no contradiction between anti-Semitism and socialism, he believed that brotherhood of the oppressed did not necessarily imply equality between all races. He was influenced by *Proudhon's anti-Jewish *ouvriérisme* and by *Gobineau, as well as by his Catholic education which provided a receptive ground for animosity toward the Jews. He succeeded in infecting the minds of leading socialists like Hennebicq (1871–1940) and Destrée (1863–1936); but thanks to the efforts of E. Vandervelde, L. De Brouckère, and C. Huysmans, the Socialist movement in Belgium officially proscribed anti-Semitism. Yet the Socialist Party newspaper, *Le Peuple*, never refused to print Picard's articles.

Bibliography: R. F. Byrnes, *Antisemitism in Modern France*, 1 (1950), index; Silberner, in: HJ, 14 (1952), 106–18. [Ed.]

PICARD, JACOB (1883–1967), German author and poet. Picard was born in Wangen, Wuerttemburg, and practiced law in Konstanz. He published two collections of verse, *Das Ufer* (1913), and *Erschuetterung* (1920), but turned seriously to literature when his legal career ended with the advent of the Nazi regime in 1933. He fled to New York in 1940. His lyrics expressed a traditionally religious outlook.

In 1936 he published his most important work, a collection of short stories entitled *Der Gezeichnete* (1936, reissued as *Die alte Lehre*, 1963; *The Marked One and Twelve Other Stories*, 1956), which described the folklore, piety, and traditions of Jews settled for centuries in the towns and villages of southern Germany. Some of his later poems were collected in *Der Uhrenschlag* (1960). A short autobiography, entitled "Childhood in a Village," appeared in the *Yearbook of the Leo Baeck Institute* (vol. 4 (1959), 273–93). [Ed.]

PICARD, LEO (1900–), Israel geologist and international authority on groundwater research. Born in Wangen, Germany, Picard emigrated to Palestine in 1924, entered the Hebrew University when it began in 1925, went back to Europe to continue his postgraduate studies, and returned to become lecturer in 1934. In 1936 he was appointed head of the newly created department of geology at the Hebrew University of Jerusalem. In 1939 he was promoted to associate professor and in 1941 to full professor. From 1950 to 1954 he set up the Geological Survey of Israel and served as its director. In the latter year he was chairman of UNESCO's expert committee on arid zones, and founded in 1967 the Swiss Groundwater Research Center at the Hebrew University. He was awarded the Israel Prize in natural sciences in 1958.

Leo Picard, Israel geologist and groundwater authority. Courtesy Hebrew University, Jerusalem. Photo Werner Braun, Jerusalem.

For 15 years Picard fought for his belief that underground water could be found in hard limestone formations and not only in the alluvial coastal plains. During World War II his advice was followed and deep drilling in the mountain slopes of the Jezreel Valley produced an abundant water supply. This was a decisive event in Israel's rural and urban settlement and led to successful drilling in western Galilee, the Judean hills, and the northern Negev, without which intensive settlement in these areas would have been impossible. Picard's work in Israel brought him international fame and demands for his services as an adviser on arid regions throughout the world. His surveys helped the development of numerous countries in Africa and Latin America. His wife, Ahuva, was the daughter of David *Yellin.

Bibliography: M. Avnimelech, in: *Bulletin of the Research Council of Israel,* section G, Geosciences, 10 G, no. 1–4 (July 1961), iii–ix (incl. bibl.). [Ed.]

°**PICART, BERNARD** (1673–1733), French artist and engraver. Picart settled in Amsterdam in 1710, partly to escape the restrictions to which, as a Protestant, he was subjected in Catholic France. He earned a place in the history of Jewish art by his realistic portrayal of Jewish religious rites. These constitute an invaluable record of Dutch Jewry in the early 18th century. Unlike Rembrandt and his circle, who were chiefly interested in the facial expressions of individuals, Picart sought out Jews in the synagogue and in their homes in order to acquaint himself with their ceremonies. In his picture of a Passover celebration the artist himself can be seen, hatless, participating in the meal (see illustration vol. 6, col. 1165). Picart used

"Rosh Ha-Shanah in the Synagogue," a drawing by Bernard Picart, 1724. Amsterdam, Collection Gemeentemusea.

his sketches, the originals of which are in the Stedelijk Museum, Amsterdam, to make etchings with which he illustrated the section devoted to Jews in the first volume of an 11-volume work, *Cérémonies et Coûtumes Réligieuses de tous les Peuples du Monde* (Amsterdam, 1723). The engravings were often reproduced in various editions, and served as the basis for a series of imitations published by F. Novelli in Venice in 1789. Picart also engraved the title pages for some Hebrew works, such as the Amsterdam Pentateuch of 1725.

Bibliography: A. Rubens, *A Jewish Iconography* (1954), 6, 14–22. [A.W.]

PICCIOTTO, family of merchants and community leaders from Leghorn, Italy. Of its members Hillel Ḥayyim (d. 1773) traveled to Aleppo for the first time in 1732 and settled there in 1771. His son, Hai Moses (d. 1816), author of *Va-Yehal Moshe* (Vienna, 1814), a collection of sermons and ethics, also died in Aleppo. He was the father of Raphael (d. 1827), the Austrian consul in Aleppo for about 50 years; in 1818 he emigrated to Safed, where he died. In 1806 he was honored by Austria with the title of "Ritter von Picciotto." He was also the Russian consul in Aleppo. His son, Ezra (d. 1822), was the Austrian consul from 1818 until his death in the earthquake of Aleppo. He was then replaced by his brother Elijah, who held his position until 1840. A third brother, Hillel, was Prussian consul in Aleppo from 1824. When Wolf Shorr visited the town in 1875, he found that this family provided "most of the envoys of Europe's kingdoms, such as Germany, Austria, Belgium, Sweden, Holland, and others." Moses ben Ezra (1818–1894) acted as Austrian, German, and Danish envoy in Aleppo and defended his brethren in 1875 at the time of the blood libel brought about by the Armenians.

Moses Ḥ. (1806–1879) emigrated from Aleppo to London in 1841 and died there. He played an active role in the affairs of the Sephardi Bevis Marks community and was also its president. He was also a member of the Board of Deputies over a long period. During the Spanish-Moroccan War of 1859, when a great number of Jewish refugees fled to Gibraltar and the situation of the Jews in Morocco worsened, a committee of support was formed in England and Moses Ḥ. was its emissary to report on the exact conditions of the Jews. His report was published under the title *Jews of Morocco Report* (London, 1861). His son, James (1830–1897), was a historian of English Jewry and also a hymnologist. He was for many years secretary to the Morocco Relief Fund. From 1872 onward he published in the *Jewish Chronicle* a series of discursive historical essays based to some extent on original sources. These were republished in volume form in 1877 under the title *Sketches of Anglo-Jewish History*—the earliest popular work on Anglo-Jewish history. Another member of the family, Joseph (1872–1938), was the first Jewish senator to be appointed by King Fuad of Egypt (1924). He was also a member of the Chamber of Commerce in Alexandria and a member of the Economic Council of the Egyptian government. As a Zionist, he was vice-president of the "Pro-Palestine" Society founded in Egypt in 1918. For many years he was also the vice-president of the Alexandrian Communal Board and president of the local B'nai B'rith.

Bibliography: M. Franco, *Essai sur l'histoire des israélites de l'empire ottoman* (1897), 209, 232; A. M. Hyamson, *Sephardim of England* (1951), 294, 353, 399; J. Picciotto, *Sketches of Anglo-Jewish History* (1956²), 15–22 (introd.); Hirschberg, Afrikah, 2 (1965), 306. [H.J.C.]

PICHO (or **Pichon**), **JOSEPH** (d.1379), *contador mayor* ("auditor general") of Henry II of Castile, Spain. He gradually rose in rank from being an adviser to Henry, before the latter seized power, to one of the foremost officials at court. In 1366 his signature appears on official documents, and a year later he was entrusted with an important mission, probably financial, to the king of Aragon. In 1369 Picho was appointed chief tax collector and made responsible for the crown revenues, while in 1371 he appears as chief tax farmer of Castile. In consequence of his governmental position he was vested with much authority which he abused at times. In 1379 certain Jews who were jealous of Picho's position obtained a writ issued in blank authorizing them to punish *informers. On the authority of this document Picho was convicted and executed. According to the evidence of the contemporary Spanish historian, Lopez de Ayala, the only available source for this episode, these events took place in Burgos, at the time of the coronation of Pedro III, the son of Henry. This angered the young king, and as a result the Cortes, at its session in Soria in 1380, abrogated the rights of criminal jurisdiction previously held by the Jews of Castile.

Bibliography: Baer, Spain, 1 (1961), 366f., 376, 450; Baer, Urkunden, index, s.v. *Joseph Picho;* Neuman, Spain, index; H. Beinart, *Kevuẓot Illit u-Shekhavot Manhigot* (1966), 66. [ED.]

PICK, ALOIS (1859–1945), Austrian army medical corps general, university professor, and president of the Vienna Jewish community. He was born in Karlin near Prague, studied medicine in Prague and Vienna, and graduated in 1883. After 1887 he served as army surgeon and military hospital director; in 1891 he became head of the ward for stomach and intestinal diseases in the Vienna General Hospital. He was appointed to the position of lecturer and professor at Vienna University after 1890. During World War I he was attached to the general staff, and attained the highest rank in the army medical corps. From 1920 to 1932 he headed the Vienna Jewish community assisted by two vice-presidents of the nonnationalist and Zionist groups. His respected and kind personality helped to reconcile party differences. He wrote books and numerous articles on internal medicine, among them *Vorlesungen ueber Magen und Darmkrankheiten* (1895–97) and, with Adolf Hecht, *Klinische Semiotik* (1908), both translated into English. During his service in Herzegovina he was the first to describe a form of pappataci fever. He also wrote plays and poetry.

Bibliography: Wininger, Biog, s.v.; I. Fischer, in: *Biographisches Lexikon der hervorragenden Aerzte* (1932). [HU.K.]

PICK, ERNST PETER (1872–1960), Austrian pharmacological chemist. Born in Jaromer, Bohemia, Pick worked until 1899 at the University of Strasbourg. He was head of the biochemistry department of the Serum Institute of Vienna from 1899 to 1911, and professor of pharmacology at the University of Vienna from 1911 to 1924. He was chief of the drug control department of the Austrian government from 1914 until the advent of the Nazis. In 1938 he went to the United States and was appointed professor of pharmacology at Columbia University (1939–46), as well as being attached to Mount Sinai Hospital, New York.

Pick's papers were largely concerned with serology, the breakdown of proteins, poisons, and various other fields of experimental pathology and pharmacology. He wrote *Biochemie der Antigene* (1912), *Biochemie der Antigene und Antikoerper* (1928), and co-edited *Die experimentelle Pharmakologie als Grundlage der Arzneibehandlung* (1933).

Bibliography: *Arzneimittel-Forschung,* 7 (1957), 332; *Archives internationales de pharmacodynamie et de thérapie,* 132 (1961), 205. [S.A.M.]

PICK, ḤAYYIM HERMANN (1879–1952), Assyriologist and Mizrachi leader. Born in Schildberg, Poland, Pick was a pupil of F. Delitzsch at the University of Berlin. His doctoral dissertation was entitled *Talmudische Glossen zu Delitzschs assyrischen Handwoerterbuch* (1903). He was also ordained as rabbi by David Z. Hoffmann at the Rabbinerseminar fuer das Orthodoxe Judentum. Pick joined the Zionist movement in 1898 and the Mizrachi upon its foundation, serving as a delegate to several Zionist congresses. In 1904 he joined the department of Middle Eastern studies at the Prussian State Library, and in 1918 was appointed professor and *Bibliotheksrat* (library counsellor). He was the first Jew in the Prussian civil service to be permitted not to work on the Sabbath. Concurrently he acted as headmaster of the Lippmann Taus Hebrew College in Berlin.

Pick was very active in Mizrachi affairs in Germany until 1914. In World War I, he acted as chief military censor of the Jewish press in Poland. After the war he was temporarily attached to the German Foreign Office. In 1920 he was elected a member of the Mizrachi World Executive, serving for a time as its chairman. From 1921 to 1927 he was a member of the Jerusalem Zionist Executive and was appointed to its Immigration Department. At the height of the "*Grabski *aliyah*" he kept up an impassioned fight with the British high commissioner, Sir Herbert Samuel, over the politically motivated cutbacks in the allotment of immigration certificates. Pick was among the initiators of the Mizrachi Bank. Though unable to pursue his scientific work, he was able to found, together with S. H. Bergman, **Kirjath Sepher,* the bibliographical publication of the Jewish National Library.

From 1928 to 1934, upon returning to the Prussian State Library, he was again extremely active on behalf of the Mizrachi in the Berlin Jewish Community Council. The Nazis pensioned but did not dismiss him, on account of his wartime service. After returning to Jerusalem he was again elected to the Mizrachi World Executive (1935), heading its Ereẓ Israel Fund. Later he initiated and headed the Council for Refugee Rabbis that looked after hundreds of people. Pick's last years were darkened by a crippling illness, and by the confiscation by the Germans of his unique Assyriological library, including all the cuneiform texts that were to be the basis of his life's work—an Assyrian-Aramaic-Hebrew dictionary.

Bibliography: *Ha-Ẓofeh* (Jan. 18, 1939), 3; *Deyokena'ot* (1962), 230–4. [P.A.]

°**PICO DELLA MIRANDOLA, GIOVANNI** (1463–1494), one of the most remarkable figures of the Italian Renaissance. Pico was an influential thinker, a humanist scholar of note, a pioneer of oriental studies, and the father of Christian *Kabbalah. Contemporaries with whom Pico associated include, among others, Elijah *Delmedigo, Flavius *Mithridates, Johanan *Alemanno, Marsilio *Ficino, Angelo Poliziano, and Girolamo Savonarola. Delmedigo translated several Averroist treatises for Pico. Mithridates instructed him in Arabic and Aramaic ("Chaldean"), and translated for him a considerable number of kabbalistic writings; his translations survive and are the likeliest literary sources of Pico's Christian Kabbalah. The most striking and, in the long run, most influential outcome of Pico's encounter with Jewish esoterism are his kabbalistic theses "according to his own opinion" *(Conclusiones cabalisticae secundum opinionem propriam),* which set out to confirm the truth of the Christian religion from the foundations of Jewish Kabbalah. They are included among the 900 theses derived from all branches of knowledge which he offered, in 1486, for public debate in Rome. The debate never took place, but the kabbalistic theses made a lasting impression, and may truly be considered to mark the beginning of Christian Kabbalah. What they amount to is as much a kabbalistic interpretation of Christianity as a Christian interpretation of the Kabbalah. The Kabbalah, touched upon in Pico's *Oration on the Dignity of Man*, is discussed at great length in his *Apologia* (in *Commentationes*, 1496), where he defended 13 of his theses specifically condemned by the Church, one of which was the thesis that "no science can make us more certain of Christ's divinity than magic and Kabbalah." The *Heptaplus* (1489), a sevenfold interpretation of the biblical account of Creation, also shows kabbalistic traits. Pico owned many Hebrew books, and in his writings, particularly in his refutation of astrology (*Disputationes adversus Astrologiam Divinatricem*, 1495), he mentions various Jewish authors besides the kabbalists, notably Maimonides, Ibn Ezra, and Levi b. Gershom. The precise extent of Pico's knowledge of Hebrew and of his acquaintance with the Kabbalah are still open questions.

Editions of his works are: *Opera Omnia* (Basle, 1572); *Opere*, ed. by E. Garin, vol. 1, *De hominis dignitate, Heptaplus, De ente et uno*, and *Scritti vari* (1942); vol. 2–3, *Disputationes adversus Astrologiam Divinatricem* (1946–52).

Bibliography: E. Anagnine, *Giovanni Pico della Mirandola* (It., 1937); J. L. Blau, *Christian Interpretation of the Cabala in the Renaissance* (1944); U. Cassuto, *Gli Ebrei a Firenze nell'età del Rinascimento* (1918); E. Garin, *Giovanni Pico della Mirandola* (It., 1937); idem, *La cultura filosofica del Rinascimento italiano* (1961); idem, *Giovanni Pico della Mirandola* (It., 1963); P. O. Kristeller, in: *L'Opera e il pensiero di Giovanni Pico della Mirandola nella storia dell'Umanesimo*, Convegno Internazionale, vol. 1, "Relazioni" (Florence, 1965), 35–133 (the most complete up-to-date bibliography of Pico will be found on pp. 107–33); Scholem, in: *Essays Presented to Leo Baeck* (1954), 158–93; F. Secret, *Kabbalistes chrétiens de la Renaissance* (1964), index; idem, in: *Convivium*, 25 (1957), 31–47 (It.); Wirszubski, in: *Studies in Mysticism and Religion Presented to G. Scholem* (1967), 353–62. [Ch.Wi.]

PICON, MOLLY (1898–), U.S. actress in Yiddish and English. Born in New York, she made her name playing Yiddish roles on 2nd Avenue. She was at Kessler's Theater for several years and in 1935 went touring in vaudeville with her husband, Jacob Kalich. From 1942 she managed the

Molly Picon, U.S. actress. Courtesy Lewis Sowden, Jerusalem.

Molly Picon Theater in New York. After World War II she visited the D.P. camps, went touring in Australia, South Africa, and Europe. In 1960 she was back on the English stage playing the lead in *A Majority of One* in London and appeared on TV and in films. In 1961 she scored a success on Broadway in the musical *Milk and Honey*, and in 1967 appeared in *How to be a Jewish Mother*. Her book *So Laugh a Little* (1962) was written as a family biography. [Ed.]

PIEDMONT, region in N. Italy which comprised the duchy of *Savoy (a kingdom since 1713), the duchy of Montferrat (under Savoy rule since 1709), the marquisate of *Saluzzo (under Savoy rule since 1598), and the municipalities of *Asti, *Chieri, Cuneo, and *Alessandria. The Jewish communities of Piedmont were formed or expanded following the expulsion of Jews from France in 1306, 1332, and 1394. Loan bankers were among the prominent people who settled in Piedmont. In 1430 Amadeus VIII determined the judicial status of the Jews in the duchy of Savoy, stipulating that in each city they were to live in closed quarters. The Jews were frequently subjected to special taxation: in 1551 the annual toleration tax was 500 gold crowns, increased to 14,000 in 1626, but subsequently reduced. In 1708 the Jews were ordered to file a complete inventory of their property every three years. About the middle of the 16th century there were 3,000–4,000 Jews in Savoy, somewhat less in Montferrat, and about 100 in Saluzzo. For a considerable payment, Emmanuel Philibert granted them the monopoly on *moneylending, which continued under his son Charles Emmanuel I. In 1624 there were about 100 Jewish loan-banks in Piedmont. The communities and the loan-bankers were often subjected to demands for exorbitant "gifts." Against a payment of 60,000 ducats a decree was issued in 1603 granting Jews permission to bear defensive weapons when outside the city of *Turin, in addition to the freedom to practice every profession including banking, commerce, and medicine (subject to the bishop's approval). In 1723–29 new enactments were issued, renewing the statutes of 1430 in a milder form, but extending the area to which they applied as a result of the extension of the state of Savoy. The Jews then formed a General Council of Jews (università generale degli ebrei) of Piedmont with branches in Turin, *Casale Monferrato, and Alessandria. In 1723 the Jews were forbidden to own real estate (the prohibition was slightly relaxed in 1729), and were compelled to live in the ghetto, which had been in existence in Turin since 1679. In Casale, *Vercelli, Chieri, Carmagnola, and Saluzzo, the outer walls of the ghettos were completed in 1724, while in Cherasco, *Acqui, and *Moncalvo, the walls were completed in 1730, 1731, and 1732 respectively. The dwellings in the Piedmont ghettos were generally arranged around a central courtyard (*ḥazer*), and every ghetto had a synagogue.

The constitution issued under Charles Emmanuel III in 1770 reenacted the statutes of 1430, 1723, and 1729, and during this period the voices of non-Jews, such as the publicist Giuseppe Compagnoni, were first raised in defense of Jews. In 1798 emancipation was introduced into Piedmont by French revolutionary forces, and in 1807, 13 rabbis from Italy attended the French *Sanhedrin in Paris. But after a short interval of well-being, Victor Emmanuel I restored almost *in toto* the 1770 constitution; in 1816 the re-creation of the ghetto was decreed. By then, however, attitudes had changed and men like Vincenzo Gioberti, Roberto and Massimo *d'Azeglio, Carlo *Cattaneo, and others pressed for Jewish emancipation. With the promulgation of the Piedmontese Constitution (Statuto) of 1848 by Prince Charles Albert, the Jews obtained full emancipation and began to participate more actively in political and cultural life. The rabbi of Turin, Lelio *Cantoni, started to reorganize the Jewish communities, and the Jewish publications *L'Educatore Israelita* (Vercelli, 1853–74), followed by *Il Vessillo Israelitico* (Cuneo, 1874–1922), made their appearance. In the middle of the 19th century a famous controversy arose over Rabbi Samuel Olper's project to introduce changes in Jewish religious practice. In 1840 and 1881 there were about 6,500 Jews in Piedmont; in 1911, 6,000; in 1931, 4,900; and in 1961, 6,618; and by 1970 this number dwindled to 1,820.

See also *Italy.

Bibliography: G. Volino, *Condizione giuridica degli ebrei in*

Piemonte prima dell'emancipazione (1904); M. D. Anfossi, *Gli Ebrei in Piemonte Loro condizioni giuridico-sociali dal 1430 all' emancipazione* (1914); G. Levi, in: RMI, 9 (1934), 511–34; 18 (1952), 412–37, 463–89; B. Terracini, *ibid.*, 15 (1949), 62–77; S. Foa, *ibid.*, 19 (1953), 542–51; 26 (1955), 38ff.; 27 (1961), passim; 28 (1962), 92ff.

[A.M.R.]

PIERCE, SYDNEY DAVID (1901–), Canadian government official. Pierce worked as a journalist in Montreal and New York, lectured at Dalhousie University, and was in private business until 1940. He was employed by the Canadian Department of Munitions and Supplies in Washington from 1940 to 1944 becoming its director at the end of his term of service. In 1944 he joined Canada's External Affairs Department and from 1947 to 1949 was Canada's ambassador to Mexico. In 1949–50 he was associate deputy minister of trade and commerce. Rejoining the External Affairs Department, he was Canadian ambassador to Brazil from 1953 to 1956. From 1957 to 1965 he was Canada's ambassador to Belgium, Luxemburg, and the European Common Market. Following this, he took a post as chief negotiator for Canada at the General Agreement on Tariffs and Trade (GATT) negotiations in Geneva. [B.G.K.]

PIERLEONI, ex-Jewish family who first appeared in Rome shortly after the year 1000. The founder of the family, BARUCH, lent large sums of money to church dignitaries, thereby assuring himself of their protection. He and his son, LEO, became converts to Christianity. Leo's son, PIETRO DI LEONE (hence the name Pierleoni), continued to give financial backing to successive popes. Among his numerous sons was one, also called Pietro Pierleoni, who entered the Church. Thanks to his family influence, he became a cardinal in 1120 and pope in 1130, taking the name *Anacletus II. A turreted mansion in the vicinity of what was to become the Rome ghetto still bears the name of the Pierleoni family.

Bibliography: J. Prinz, *Popes from the Ghetto* (1966), incl. bibl.; Milano, *Ghetto di Roma* (1964), index; Picotti, in: *Archivio storico italiano*, 100 (1942), 3–41 (on the supposed relationship of Gregory VII with the Pierleoni family). [A.MIL.]

PIESTANY (Slovak. **Piešt'any;** Hung. **Pöstyén**), town in W. Slovakia, Czechoslovakia. In 1756 there were 13 Jewish families in Piestany; they were originally under the guidance of the *Vrbove community. A prayer house was opened in Piestany and the number of Jews grew to 24 families by 1774 and 50 by 1795. It continued to grow in the 19th century, when Piestany became an important spa because of its thermal springs. The baths included separate compartments for upper-class, lower-class, and Jewish visitors. In the mid-19th century Jews were still restricted to special visiting hours. In October 1920 anti-Jewish riots occurred in Piestany and the president of the National Federation of Slovak Jews appealed to President T. *Masaryk. There were 1,254 Jews in the town in 1921, and 1,344 in 1930. There were two Jewish communities, one Orthodox, the other "Jeshurun," which arose from the merger of the *Neolog and *status quo ante communities. In March 1939 an anti-Jewish riot was instigated by the fascist Hlinka guards. In 1941 there were 1,539 Jews. During the Holocaust 1,500 Jews from Piestany and the neighboring towns lost their lives; many of the survivors emigrated to Israel. After World War II a new community was reorganized by about 150 Jews; the Orthodox synagogue was restored, a *mikveh* built, and a *shoḥet* employed. In 1961 only about 90 persons remained.

Bibliography: R. Iltis (ed.), *Die aussaeen unter Traenen* ... (1959), 180–4; S. Gruenwald, *Gedenkbuch der Gemeinden Piestany und Umgebung* (1969). [ED.]

PIETY AND THE PIOUS. Because of its theocentric orientation, Judaism regards piety as the supreme virtue leading to man's highest good. Moreover, according to the Mishnah, the *zaddik* ("righteous person") is credited with contributing to the preservation of the world (Avot 5:1). Although the term *zaddik gamur*, "the perfectly pious man" is found in talmudic literature (cf. RH 16b) and is contrasted with the *zaddik she-eino gamur*, "the imperfectly pious man," it is largely a theoretical designation, and on the principle that "there is none righteous upon earth who doeth only good and sinneth not" (Eccles. 7:20): no human being is regarded as the perfect paragon of piety.

In rabbinic literature a variety of terms is employed to distinguish between different types or degrees of piety. There is, however, no uniform system of ranking such terms as *yere het* ("sin-fearing"), *yere shamayim* ("God-fearing"), *zaddik* ("righteous"), and *ḥasid* ("pious"). For example, *Maimonides, explicating the term *ḥasid*, asserts that it carries overtones of excess or extremism not found in other terms describing piety (commentary to Avot 5:7; *Guide of the Perplexed*, 3:53), but in fact this is not always so. There are many instances when the term *ḥasid* describes what elsewhere would be called *zaddik* or *yere ḥet*.

Notwithstanding the wide range of definitions of piety one encounters in rabbinic literature, the emphasis on the service of God and the imitation of His ethical attributes appear to be a constant component of all the different types.

Although obedience to halakhic norms represents a necessary condition of piety, it is far from representing its perfection. It was expected that obedience to the law would inculcate such virtues as the *love and fear of God. R. Johanan, a Palestinian *amora*, attributed the destruction of Jerusalem to the failure of the Jews to observe the moral demands that extend beyond the strict requirements of the law. His contemporary, the Babylonian *amora*, Rav, indicated that even in civil litigation one must take into consideration the ethical-religious imperative of Proverbs 2:26, "to walk in the ways of the good and to keep the path of the righteous" (BM 83a). Moreover, abundant references to the special standards of piety, or the "Mishnah of the pious," are found in talmudic literature (BM 52b; Ḥul. 130b; Ter. 8:10). *Naḥmanides cites the talmudic statement "Sanctify yourself within the domain of the permissible" as evidence for his contention that even an individual who has not violated any of the specific and detailed rules set forth in the Torah may still be branded a scoundrel (commentary on Lev. 19:1).

Man's total commitment to the service of God, according to Judaism, extends over all areas of life. For example, R. Yose stated that all our actions should be performed for the sake of God (Avot 2:12). Rabbinic Judaism believed that performance of a religious act could be disciplinary, leading to higher religious sensitivity. This idea was manifested in the relatively positive attitude taken toward deeds inspired by impure motives. In contrast to Christianity's despair over the worthwhileness of human effort, resulting from the Pauline emphasis on original sin, Judaism holds an optimistic view of human nature. The individual is encouraged to perform an act even though it may originate in unworthy motives, because, ultimately, these motives may be transformed and the act performed for the sake of God (Pes. 50b).

The aim of all piety is the sanctification of life, not the withdrawal from it. There is relatively little endorsement of asceticism in rabbinic Judaism. A widely prevalent attitude is represented by the statement of the medieval philosopher, *Judah Halevi, that "contrition on a fast day does nothing to bring man nearer to God than joy on the Sabbath" (*Kuzari* 2:50). Similarly, Judaism generally recoils from tendencies designed to remove the pious from involvement with the community. Man's confrontation with God is not meant to lead to self-centeredness or a sense of isolation, but to participation in a holy community. This attitude is reflected in Hillel's maxim "Do not separate thyself from the community" (Avot 2:5). Moreover, according to a talmudic comment, the overall objective of the entire Torah was to promote peace and thus contribute to the improvement of society (Git. 59b).

Although rabbinic Judaism produced a number of extraordinary individuals endowed with special capacities for mystical union, apocalyptic visions, and saintliness, these aspects of piety were never recognized as displacing the normative component, which stressed faithful adherence to the Covenant as interpreted by the Oral Law. It was felt that the practice and, especially, the study of the Torah are not merely intrinsically valuable activities, but are also instrumental in refining man's character and lifting him to higher levels of piety. According to *Phinehas b. Jair, spiritual development reaches its climax when the individual becomes so attached to God that *Ru'ah ha-Kodesh* is conferred upon him (Av. Zar. 20b).

Maimonides held that faithful observance of the commandments is needed to inculcate the fear of God in man, while the contemplative virtues, climaxing in the intellectual apprehension of God, lead to the love of God (*Guide*, 3:52). Maimonides redefined the rabbinic notion of the *talmid ḥakham*, the scholar of the law, who, as early as the talmudic period, was regarded as the supreme religious model (see I. Twersky, in: *Jewish Medieval and Renaissance Studies* (1967), 106–18). For Maimonides, the true Torah scholar is not merely knowledgeable in *halakhah*, but is also proficient in science and philosophy. Accordingly, only he who combines obedience to the commandments with contemplative perfection can aspire to the state of true union with God.

For the medieval German ḥasid, *Judah he-Ḥasid, the love of God manifests itself in an entirely different fashion. It impels him to go beyond the legal requirements of the Torah, which makes concessions to human frailties and weaknesses. Instead, the truly pious will govern themselves by the "law of heaven," which makes far stricter demands than the "law of the Torah," addressed to the average individual.

The kabbalists' notion of piety stresses the craving for the mystical ideal of *devekut* (adherence to God), which to them represents the pinnacle of religious achievement. Unlike the complete mystical union which seeks the absorption of the self in the divine, the state of *devekut* preserves the separateness and self-identity of the individual. It is an act of communion, not a mergence, for the self is not divested of its responsibilities toward God. It is the function of the righteous individual to help bring about the *tikkun* (redemption of the world; see *Kabbalah).

In the ḥasidic movement special emphasis was placed on such personal components of piety as *kavvanah* ("intention" or "purposefulness" in prayer) and *hitlahavut* ("enthusiasm") in the attainment of the ideal of *devekut*. The charisma of the *ẓaddik*, renowned for his *devekut* rather than his knowledge of Torah, played a decisive role. It is for this reason that Gershom *Scholem observed that in the ḥasidic movement "personality takes the place of doctrine" (Mysticism, 344). The *ẓaddik*, by virtue of his special spiritual status, serves as the channel for the transmission of divine grace and plays a unique role in the redemption of the world. In the ḥasidic scheme, through attachment to the *ẓaddik*, the ordinary individual can participate in this task and achieve union with the "upper worlds."

See also *Ḥasidism.

Bibliography: J. B. Agus, *The Evolution of Jewish Thought* (1959), passim; S. Belkin, *In His Image* (1960), passim; A. Buechler, *The Ancient Pious Men: Types of Jewish Palestinian Piety* (1968); L. Jacobs, *Jewish Values* (1960), passim; S. Schechter, *Studies in Judaism*, 2 (1908), 148–81; J. B. Soloveitchik, in: *Talpioth*, 1 (1944), 651–735.

[W.S.W.]

PIG (Heb. חֲזִיר, *ḥazir*). Included in the Pentateuch among the unclean animals prohibited as food is the pig which, although cloven-footed, is a nonruminant (Lev. 11:7; Deut. 16:8). It is the sole unclean animal mentioned as possessing these characteristics. There are archaeological evidences (figurines and relics of bones) that the pig was eaten by the inhabitants of Canaan before the Israelite conquest. It was also offered as a sacrifice in idolatrous worship, provoking a protest from Isaiah (66:3), while those "eating swine's flesh, and the detestable thing, and the mouse" (66:17) apparently did so in a cultic ceremony. The pig symbolized something repulsive, and hence "as a ring of gold in a swine's snout, so is a fair woman that turneth aside from discretion" (Prov. 11:22). Other peoples, too, such as the Egyptians and the Sidonians, refrained from eating pig, which was also later prohibited to the Muslims. Abhorrence of the pig entered so deeply into the consciousness of the Jews that the expression *davar aḥer* ("another thing," i.e., something not to be mentioned by name) was used for it, at least as early as talmudic times (Ber. 43b; Shab. 129a) and in Aramaic as "that species." As early as *Antiochus Epiphanes it was decreed that the eating of swine's flesh was to be a test of the Jews' loyalty to Judaism (II Macc. 6:18). Following the incident in the days of Hyrcanus II when, instead of an animal fit for sacrifice, a pig was sent up the walls of Jerusalem during a siege, it was decreed: "Cursed be he who breeds pigs" (Sot. 49b; TJ, Ta'an. 4:8, 68c), and this prohibition was incorporated into the Mishnah (BK 7:7). Since the pig eats everything and finds its food everywhere, there arose the saying: "None is richer than a pig" (Shab. 155b). The pig suffers from various maladies: "Ten measures of diseases descended to the world, of which the swine took nine" (Kid. 49b). During a plague that afflicted pigs, R. Judah decreed a fast in Babylonia since "their intestines are like those of human beings," the fear being entertained that the plague would spread to people (Ta'an. 21b).

The domesticated pig, *Sus scropha domestica*, is descended from the wild boar, *Sus scropha*. Its domestication was a lengthy process, going back to ancient times. The pig formerly found in Ereẓ Israel differed from the present-day one whose various breeds were developed from strains brought from China about the middle of the 18th century. The wild boar (*ḥazir ha-bar*), which is found in Israel especially in Upper and western Galilee, damages plants and vegetables, and uproots the bulbs and tubers of wild flora. It is the "boar out of the wood" in Psalms (80:9–14), where reference is made to the ravages it causes to vines. The Tosefta (Kil. 1:8) states that "although the pig and the wild boar resemble each other, they are heterogeneous."

[J.F.]

In Halakhah and Aggadah. In a *baraita* mentioned three times in the Babylonian Talmud (Sot. 49b; BK 82b; Men. 64b), the prohibition against rearing pig is joined with the prohibition against studying "Greek wisdom," and some scholars have queried the trustworthiness of this tradition and tend to the opinion that the incident referred to there—when the besiegers of Jerusalem sent up a pig to the besieged in place of the two lambs for the daily sacrifices—occurred during the siege of Jerusalem by Titus, when the subsequent prohibition against rearing pigs was decreed (cf. TJ, Ber. 4:1, 7b, where a similar story occurs about sending up a pig at "the time of the wicked kingdom"). It seems, however, that the prohibition against rearing pigs was already known in the days of the early Hasmoneans; it is possible that its source is to be found in a reaction to the decrees of Antiochus Epiphanes, who ordered a pig to be offered as a sacrifice (I Macc. 1:47) and pig's flesh to be eaten (II Macc. 6:18–7:42) and that the incident in the time of the Hasmonean brothers caused the prohibition to be stressed with greater emphasis.

The phrase "Cursed be the man who rears" is worthy of attention. It would appear that, with the increase of the non-Jewish population, Jews in Ereẓ Israel apparently engaged in the business of pig rearing. Of interest is the combination "pig-breeders and usurers" (Ber. 55a, and Rashi, ad loc.) both of which were regarded as providing an easy means of livelihood. Although there are many references in the *aggadah* to a feeling of revulsion and disgust toward swine flesh, the rabbis refrained from connecting the prohibition with this feeling. Eleazar b. Azariah expounded, "Whence do we know that a man should not say, 'I have no desire to eat swine's flesh,' but rather should he say 'I would like to eat it, but what can I do seeing that my Father in Heaven has decreed against it'" (Sifra, *Kedoshim*, Perek 11:22). A substitute was even given in a fish called *shibuta* "which resembles the pig" in taste (Ḥul. 109b; Tanḥ. *Shemini*, 12).

In the Midrash the Roman kingdom is called *ḥazir* ("pig"). It is possible that the name originated in the fact that the symbol of the Roman legion in Ereẓ Israel was the boar (see ARN[1], 34:100: " 'The ... boar out of the wood doth ravage it' [Ps. 80:14], refers to the Roman kingdom"; and cf. Mid. Ps. to 80:6). The Midrashim explain the name with reference to the characteristics common to Rome and to the pig: "and the swine because he parteth the hoof'—why is [Rome] compared to a swine?—To teach that just as a swine when it lies down puts out its hooves as if to say, 'see, I am clean,' so too the kingdom of Edom [Rome] acts arrogantly, and plunders and robs under the guise of establishing a judicial tribunal" (Lev. R. 13:5). Another "etymological" explanation states: "Why is [Rome] called *ḥazir* ['pig'] ... because it will eventually restore *haḤazir* ['the kingdom'] to its rightful owner" (Eccles. R. 1:9; Lev. R. 13:5). This statement was quoted in the Middle Ages by the people with the reading, "Why is it called a pig?—Because the Holy One will restore it to Israel" (i.e., declare it clean), and in this form it became a topic in Jewish-Christian polemics.

In Israel. The raising of pigs in the Holy Land was always regarded with abhorrence not only by Jewish religious circles but also by many outside the strictly religious camp. The Jewish National Fund's leases forbade pig raising on its land. The religious parties pressed for the prohibition of pig breeding by law, but in the early years of statehood it was left to local authorities to pass their own bylaws in this matter. When the Supreme Court, in a test case, ruled that such regulations were *ultra vires*, the religious parties pressed for, and secured, the passage of a special authorization law (5717/1956) to give the local authorities the necessary authority. There was still pressure for the prohibition of pig breeding on a national basis and in 1962 a law was passed forbidding the breeding, keeping, or slaughtering of pigs, except in Nazareth and in certain other named places with a sizable Christian population. [Ed.]

Bibliography: In the Bible: Lewysohn, Zool, 146–8 (nos. 170–2); F. Blome, *Die Opfermaterie in Babylonien und Israel*, 1 (1934), 120–5, nos. 117–21; F. S. Bodenheimer, *Animal and Man in Bible Lands* (1960), 51, 103. In Halakhah and Aggadah: S. Kraus, in: REJ, 53 (1907), 15–19; Ginzberg, Legends, 5 (1925), Y. Baer, in: *Sefer Zikkaron le-Asher Gulak ve-li-Shemu'el Klein* 294; idem, *Perushim ve-Ḥiddushim ba-Yerushalmi*, 3 (1941), 35–40; (1942), 40, note by J. N. Epstein: Ḥ. Albeck, *ibid.*, 49; E. Wiesenberg, in: HUCA, 27 (1956), 233–93. In Israel: M. Elon, *Ḥakikah Datit* (1968), 20–23.

PI-HAHIROTH (Hahiroth; Heb. פִּי הַחִירֹת), town E. of Baal-Zephon, near Migdol, in the East Delta of Egypt (Num. 33:7). At the beginning of the Exodus the Israelites encamped near Pi-Hahiroth, whose site is yet to be identified. A. H. Gardiner (see bibl.) suggests that the town's name is an alteration of Pr-Ḥtḥr ("the house of Hathor"), mentioned in various Egyptian documents. The Septuagint translates Pi-Hahiroth either as "the mouth of Hiroth"—i.e., considering פִּי as the Hebrew word for "mouth" and not as part of the name—(cf. Num. 33:8, where the Hebrew text also omits פִּי), or as "the encampment" (cf. LXX, Ex. 14:2, 9), as though the Hebrew text did not use the name פִּי הַחִירֹת, but rather a word meaning encampment.

Bibliography: A. H. Gardiner, in: *Recueil d'études égyptologiques dédiées à la mémoire de Jean-François Champollion* (1922), 213; H. Gauthier, *Dictionnaire des noms géographiques contenus dans les textes hiéroglyphiques*, 2 (1925), 117; P. Montet, *La stèle du Roi Kamose* (1956), 115.
[Ed.]

PIJADE, MOŠA (1890–1957), Yugoslav revolutionary and politician. Born in Belgrade, Pijade studied painting in Munich and Paris and returned to Belgrade as an art teacher. He joined the illegal Communist Party in 1920 and was imprisoned by the authorities in the following year. On

Moša Pijade, Yugoslav revolutionary and politician.

his release he continued his revolutionary activities and in 1925 was imprisoned for a further 14 years during which time he translated Marx' *Das Kapital*. In 1940 Pijade was arrested for a third time but released shortly before the German invasion of Yugoslavia. Following the German conquest of Yugoslavia he organized the Communist partisans and set out the tasks of the People's Liberation Committee in a document known as the *Regulations of Foča*. Pijade was one of the closest assistants of the Yugoslav leader Josip Broz Tito and when the latter came to power after the liberation of Yugoslavia, Pijade was made president of the Serbian Republic, chairman of the Yugoslav National Assembly and a member of the political bureau of the party central committee.

Bibliography: S. Bosiljčić and D. Marković, *Moša Pijade* (Serbian, 1960).
[Ed.]

PIKE, LIPMAN E. (Lip; 1845–1893), U.S. baseball pioneer. Born in New York City and raised in Brooklyn, he played in numerous teams from 1858 to 1865. He became baseball's first professional in 1866 when the Philadelphia Athletics paid him a regular salary. In 1870 Pike participated in early baseball's most famous game, when his team, the

Brooklyn Atlantics, ended the 130-game winning streak of the first all-professional team, the Cincinnati Red Stockings. In 1871 Pike was player-manager of the Troy, N.Y.,

Lipman E. Pike, U.S. baseball pioneer. From B. Postal et al., *Encyclopaedia of Jews in Sports,* New York, 1965.

team of the National Association, baseball's first professional league. Pike also played with that association's teams in Baltimore, 1872–73; Hartford, Conn. (player-manager), 1874; and St. Louis in 1875 and 1876, the year when the National League replaced the National Association. In 1877 he was with Cincinnati (player-manager); in 1878 with Cincinnati and Providence; and in 1881 with Worcester, Mass., where he concluded his National League career. In 1887 he played his last professional game with the New York Metropolitans of the American Association.

An all-round player, Pike possessed great power as a batter, had a strong throwing arm, and was baseball's fastest man in his time. In 1866 he established the first home run record when he hit six in one game. [J.H.S.]

PIKKU'AḤ NEFESH (Heb. פִּקּוּחַ נֶפֶשׁ; "regard for human life"), the rabbinical term applied to the duty to save human life in a situation in which it is imperiled. The danger to life may be due to a grave state of illness or other direct peril *(sakkanat nefashot),* or indirectly, to a condition of health which, though not serious, might deteriorate and consequently imperil life *(safek sakkanat nefashot). Pikku'aḥ nefesh* is a biblical injunction derived from the verse "Neither shalt thou stand idly by the blood of thy neighbor" (Lev. 19:16), and according to the Talmud it supersedes even the Sabbath laws (*pikku'aḥ nefesh doḥeh et ha-Shabbat;* Yoma 85a). One should be more particular about matters concerning danger to health and life than about ritual observances (Ḥul 10a). The strict rules of hygiene codified in the Shulḥan Arukh center around the principle of *pikku'aḥ nefesh* (YD 116). The rabbis interpreted the verse "Ye shall therefore keep my statutes and my ordinances which if a man do he shall live by them" (Lev. 18:5), that man shall "live" by these commandments, and not die as a result of observing them (Yoma 85b; Sanh. 74a).

The Talmud (BM 62a) discusses the problem of an individual faced with the choice of saving his own life or that of his companion, and mentions the example of two men in a desert with a supply of water sufficient for one only. Although *Ben Peturah advocated that neither should attempt to save his own life at the expense of the other but that both share the water, R. *Akiva, whose opinion prevailed, ruled that one should save one's own life and not share the water. Only when faced with a choice between death and committing idolatry, unlawful sexual intercourse, or murder is martyrdom to be preferred (Sanh. 74a–b). One must also sacrifice one's life rather than submit to what may be taken for a renunciation of faith through the violation of any religious law in public (Sanh. 74a–b; Sh. Ar., YD 157). In all other cases, the rule of *pikku'aḥ nefesh* takes precedence (Sanh. 74a–b; Maim., *Iggeret ha-Shemad* 3).

The rule that one may profane one Sabbath in order to save the life of a person and enable him subsequently to observe many others (Yoma 85b) is inferred by the rabbis from the verse "The children of Israel shall keep the Sabbath to observe the Sabbath" (Ex. 31:16). Thus, on the Sabbath (or a festival), every type of medical treatment must be accorded to a dangerously ill person, to the extent of even putting out the light to help him sleep (Shab. 2:5; Sh. Ar., OḤ 278). Equal efforts must be made even where there is only a possibility of danger to life (*safek sakkanat nefashot,* Yoma 8:6; *ibid.* 84b). Only in cases of minor illnesses or physical discomforts should violations of the Sabbath be kept to the minimum; if possible a non-Jew should perform these duties (Sh. Ar., OḤ 328:17). In all other instances, the medical treatment should be administered by a Jew, and those who are assiduous in their help, comfort, and work for the sick on the Sabbath, are deemed worthy of the highest praise (*ibid.* 328:12–13). If a dangerously ill person is in need of food on the Sabbath, one should slaughter animals and prepare them according to the dietary laws, rather than feed him ritually forbidden food (*ibid.,* 328:14). If, however, it is deemed necessary for the recovery of the patient that he eat forbidden food he is allowed to do so (*ibid.* 328). A woman in confinement is considered dangerously ill for a period of three days after delivery. Should one of these days be a Sabbath, everything possible must be done to ease her pain and lessen her discomfort, including the kindling of a fire to warm her (Maim. Yad, Shabbat 2:13–14; Sh. Ar., OḤ 330:1, 4–6). A sick person is forbidden to fast on the *Day of Atonement if it is thought that this would seriously endanger his recovery. Moreover, even a healthy person seized by a fit of "ravenous hunger" which causes faintness *(bulmos),* must be fed on the Day of Atonement with whatever food is available (including ritually forbidden food (Sh. Ar., OḤ 618:9)) until he recovers (Yoma 8:6; Sh. Ar., OḤ 618).

Bibliography: Eisenstein, Dinim, 291, 342–3. [Ed.]

PILCHIK, ELY E. (1913–), U.S. Reform rabbi. Pilchik, who was born in Baranovice, Poland, was taken to the United States in 1920. He was ordained at Hebrew Union College, Cincinnati, in 1939, and after serving congregations in Baltimore, Md. (1940–41) and Tulsa, Okla. (1941–47), he was appointed rabbi of Congregaion B'nai Jeshurun, Newark, N.J., in 1947. During 1944–46 Pilchik was a chaplain in the U.S. Navy. He served as president of the Jewish Book Council of America (1954–58) and of the Association of Reform Rabbis of New York (1958–59). His publications include *Hillel* (1951); *Maimonides' Creed* (1952); *Duties of the Heart* (1953); *From the Beginning* (1956); and *Jeshurun Sermons* (1957). [S.D.T.]

PILGRIMAGE. In Hebrew the term *aliyah* (lit. "going up") has been used since ancient times for pilgrimages to Jerusalem on the three festivals known as *shalosh regalim* (see *Pilgim Festivals). The Torah prescribes that all males must go up to Jerusalem "three times a year" on the three festivals—Passover, Shavuot, and Sukkot (Ex. 23:17; 34:23; Deut. 16:16; II Chron. 8:13).

For pilgrimages in the biblical period see *Passover; *Shavuot; and *Sukkot.

Second Temple Period. Hundreds of thousands of pilgrims from within Ereẓ Israel as well as from the Diaspora streamed to the Temple at each of the three

Figure 1. Pilgrims making their way to Jerusalem. An engraving of 1581 reproduced in S. Schweigger, *Reyssbeschreibung aus Teutschland nach Jerusalem*, 1608.

festivals. The pilgrimage affected the life of every Jew, who might have to prepare for the occasion, and the journey and the accompanying sacrifices involved a not inconsiderable financial outlay. The inspiration derived from "the sojourn in the Temple courts," and from attendance at the rabbinical academies in Jerusalem, remained a powerful stimulus to the pilgrim after his return: "His heart prompts him to study Torah" (TJ, Suk. 5:1, 55a). Many of the new trends in Jewish spiritual life were ventilated in Jerusalem, and the pilgrim served as the vehicle for disseminating the ideas that were in constant ferment during the period. The pilgrimage had a considerable influence upon the life of the capital in a number of spheres; in the social sphere, from the presence there of Jews from every part of the Diaspora, and in the economic, from the vast sums spent by the thousands of pilgrims both for their own needs and on charity. It also had a national-political influence. The *aliyah* from all parts of Ereẓ Israel and the Diaspora strengthened the consciousness of national and social solidarity (Jos., Ant. 4:203–4). This national consciousness reached a new peak with the presence of the throngs of pilgrims in Jerusalem and made them even more sensitive to the humiliation entailed in their subjection to a foreign yoke. As a result of this sensitivity disorders and revolts were of frequent occurrence in Jerusalem during the festivals (Jos., Wars 5:243–4; Ant. 13:337–9).

The biblical injunction on the subject states: "Three times in the year shall all thy males appear before the Lord God" (Ex. 23:17; 34:23, Deut. 16:16). These passages were apparently not construed as mandatory, requiring *aliyah* thrice yearly, but as meaning that on these occasions it was a meritorious act to make the pilgrimage and in so doing offer up sacrifices, "and none shall appear before me empty" *(ibid.)*. The tannaitic sources speak of the obligation of *aliyah le-regel* but not of a commandment to go up on every festival (Ḥag. 1:1, 6a). In any event it is clear that not all the male population of Ereẓ Israel, and certainly not of the Diaspora, made the pilgrimage three times yearly. Although both from the Talmud (Pes. 8b) and from Josephus (Wars 2:515) one might infer that the whole population of a city would participate in the pilgrimage, it was not general that the cities, even those near to Jerusalem, would be entirely emptied as a consequence of their Jewish population going on pilgrimage. On the other hand, there can be no doubt that a considerable number went up, especially from Judea (Wars 2:43). There is ample evidence of *aliyah le-regel* from Galilee, and it may be assumed that the number who came from the Diaspora was not as great as those from Ereẓ Israel. Philo mentions that "countless multitudes from countless cities come to the Temple at every festival, some by land, and others by sea, from east and west and north and south" (Spec. 1:69). Sources in the Talmud, Josephus, and the New Testament yield a long list of places, including Babylonia, Persia, Media, Alexandria, Cyrenaica, Ethiopia, Syria, Pontus, Asia, Tarsus, Phrygia, Pamphylia, and Rome, whose residents were to be found in Jerusalem during the festivals (ARN², 27, 55; Meg. 26a; Jos., Ant. 17:26; Acts 2:9–10). Both the inscription of Theodotus found in Jerusalem and the literary sources indicate that sometimes the inhabitants of a particular city would establish synagogues in Jerusalem and hospices for the pilgrims who required such facilites (Tosef., Meg. 3:6; Acts 6:9; M. Schwabe, in *Sefer Yerushalayim*, ed. by M. Avi-Yonah, 1 (1956), 362).

The Pilgrimage. The pilgrims often traveled in caravans which mustered in the cities of Ereẓ Israel and the Diaspora. The ascent of the joyful throng of celebrants to Jerusalem is already mentioned in a number of Psalms such as Psalms 42, 84, and 122, which are songs of the pilgrim companies, and it is reflected in many rabbinic passages (cf. Lam. R. 1:17, no. 52). The procession on the occasion of the first fruits of Shavuot was particularly impresssive: "Those who lived near brought fresh figs and grapes, but those from a distance brought dried figs and raisins. An ox with horns bedecked with gold and with an olive crown on its head led the way. The flute was played before them until they were near Jerusalem" (Bik. 3:3). Josephus relates that the pilgrims from Babylonia used to assemble in *Nehardea and *Nisibis and accompany the convoys transporting the annual half-*shekel* Temple dues on the journey to Jerusalem (Ant. 18:311–2). Women also took part, the biblical passage "all thy males shall appear" being understood merely as referring only to the duty of the men who alone were obliged to bring the obligatory sacrifices (Ant. 11:109; Luke 2:41–43).

The Rituals. The pilgrims arrived in Jerusalem several days before the festival; this was especially true of those from the Diaspora who had to undergo purification for over a week from the defilement incurred in alien lands (Jos., Wars 1:229; 6:290). The essence of the pilgrimage was the entry of the individual, or the group, into the Temple to worship there on the festivals, and the offering of the obligatory sacrifices enjoined in the precept that, "None shall appear before me empty." The tannaitic tradition expounded that the celebrant was obliged to offer the pilgrim's burnt offering, the festal offering which is counted as a peace offering, and the offering of rejoicing (Ḥag. 6b). The sacrifices were offered both on the first day or during subsequent days of the festival.

The Stay in Jerusalem. According to the *halakhah*, not only did the scriptural verse, "and in the morning you shall turn and go to your tent," enjoined with regard to the Passover pilgrim, oblige him to remain overnight in Jerusalem, but "in the morning" was interpreted as the morning after the last day of the festival. The pilgrim was thus obliged to stop over for the entire Passover week, and for the eight days of Sukkot (Zev. 11:7 and 97a; Tosef. Ḥag. 1:5). The celebrants used to stay in the capital itself, or in the adjoining villages, or encamp in tents erected in the surrounding fields (Jos., Ant. 17:217; Wars 2:12). During their sojourn in Jerusalem the pilgrims engaged in study of the Torah and participated in the common festive meals at which they ate the permitted sacrificial food—the peace offering, as well as the second tithe which had to be consumed in Jerusalem (Jos., Ant. 4:205). Greater leniency was applied to the law appertaining to ritual defilement during the festival, in order that the laws of ritual purity would not prevent social intercourse. Jerusalem was regarded as the common possession of the entire Jewish people, and householders in the capital were forbidden to take rent from the pilgrims, who however left them the hides of the sacrificial animals as a token of gratitude (Tosef., Ma'as Sh. 1:12 and 13; ARN[1] 35, 103). The sources indicate that a convivial atmosphere prevailed in the capital during the days of pilgrimages: "Nobody ever had occasion to say to his neighbor 'I have been unable to find a stove for cooking the paschal meals in Jerusalem,' or 'I have been unable to find a bed to sleep in Jerusalem' " (ARN *ibid.*). [SH.S.]

Post-Temple Period. Pilgrimages to Jerusalem continued after the destruction of the Temple (cf. Ned. 23a). However, the joy that previously characterized these events was now combined with sorrow. When the pilgrims encountered the site of the ruined Sanctuary they rended their garments as a sign of mourning and recited the verse, "Our holy and our beautiful house, where our fathers praised Thee, is burned with fire and all our pleasant things are laid waste" (Isa. 64:10; MK 26a). Some even abstained from meat and wine on the day they saw Jerusalem in its destruction (Shevu. 20a). The rabbis, commenting on the verse, "These things I remember, and pour out my soul within me" (Ps. 52:5), compared the pilgrimages before and after the destruction. Previously, the Jews went up to Jerusalem along well-kept roads, the trees forming a covering over their heads, and under the protection of a government committed to God. Now they went through thorny hedges, exposed to the sun, and under the sovereignty of oppressive governments (Lam. R. 1:52). Nevertheless, the Jews continued their pilgrimages to the Temple site, and in 333 "the traveler of Bordeaux" described Jews pouring oil on a stone. In 392 Jerome related that Jews came to lament the destruction of the Temple, after paying for a permit to enter the Temple grounds (commentary on Zeph. 1:16). A fifth-century testimony reported a pilgrimage of over 100,000 Jews, made possible as a result of the sympathetic attitude of Anthenais Eudocia, wife of the emperor Theodosius II.

These pilgrimages continued throughout the Middle Ages although on many occasions the Jewish pilgrims were subject to taxes and discriminatory regulations which were enacted against them by the Christian or Muslim overlords of the holy places. The ninth-century pilgrimages of Rabbi *Ahimaaz the Elder, of Venosa, Italy, are well known. The Persian traveler Nāṣir Khosraw (1047) stated that he saw Jews from Roman lands (Byzantium) coming to visit their houses of worship. The testimony of a pilgrim from Babylonia, Phinehas ha-Kohen (c. 1030), has also survived.

Figure 2. Page from a 16th-century Hebrew "pilgrims' guide," with a description of the Mt. of Olives and pictorial representations of the house of Huldah, the Pillar of Absalom, and the grave of Zechariah. *Casale Pilgrim,* fol. 4v, Casale Monferrato, Italy, 1598. Cecil Roth Collection. Photo Werner Braun, Jerusalem.

After Ereẓ Israel was conquered by the Muslims under Saladin (1187), the Jews were once again permitted to visit their holy places freely. Numerous pilgrims came from Damascus, Babylonia, and Egypt, and they remained in Jerusalem over Passover and Shavuot. Naḥmanides, in a letter to his son, wrote: "Many men and women from Damascus, Babylon, and their vicinities come to Jerusalem to see the site of the Holy Temple and to lament its destruction." The commandment of pilgrimage was also a factor in motivating the journeys of *Benjamin of Tudela and *Pethahiah of Regensburg in the 12th century, and *Jacob b. Nethanel and Judah *al-Ḥarizi in the 13th. In his writing, Benjamin referred to the Dome of the Rock, standing "opposite the place of the holy Temple which is occupied at present by [a church called] Templum Domini . . . In front of it you see the Western Wall, one of the walls which formed the ancient Temple . . . and all Jews go there to say their prayers near the wall of the courtyard."

The number of pilgrims was greatly increased by the many exiles who settled in Turkish territory following the 1492 expulsion of the Jews from Spain. The tomb of Samuel the Prophet at Nabi Samwil (thought to be the biblical Ramah) was also a goal of their pilgrimages. Here they held annual celebrations similar to those which were instituted in Meron on *Lag Ba-Omer, a century later. In 1634, Gershom ben Eliezer Ha-Levi of Prague visited the Holy Land, and later recorded his experience in *Gelilot Ereẓ Yisrael* (Prague, 1824[4]). The most famous pilgrimage made to the Holy Land by early ḥasidic leaders was that of *Naḥman of Bratslav. His visit (1798–99) left such a profound impression upon him that when he later returned to Poland, he remarked, "Wherever I go, I am still in Ereẓ Israel."

In modern times, the pilgrimages most beneficial to the Holy Land were those of Sir Moses *Montefiore. He made his first visit in 1827, and returned in 1838, 1849, 1855, 1866, and 1875. He made his last pilgrimage when he was 91 years old, and after each visit he intensified his financial support for the new *yishuv*. With the continuing development of the Jewish resettlement in Ereẓ Israel and the improvement in the means of long-distance transportation, Jews continued in ever-increasing numbers to visit the Holy Land.

With the conclusion of the armistice agreement following the Israel War of Independence (1949), it was agreed between Jordan and Israel that talks would follow immediately to enable "free access to the holy places" in Jerusalem, and the "use of the Jewish cemetery on the Mount of Olives." However, nothing ever came of this and Jerusalem remained a divided city. This caused difficulties for pilgrims who desired to visit the shrines in both countries. While Jordan finally did make some arrangements for Christian pilgrims to enter or leave through one of the crossing points (the main one being the Mandelbaum Gate in Jerusalem), Jewish pilgrims were not allowed into Jordan at all. Most distressing to Jews was the denial of access to the Western Wall. The main goal of the pilgrims then became the traditional Tomb of David on Mount Zion from where they viewed the Old City of Jerusalem. Following the Six-Day War and the reunification of Jerusalem, the Western Wall was again reopened to Jews and became a magnet of pilgrimage. [ED.]

Christian Pilgrimages. Christian pilgrimages to Ereẓ Israel became an established institution from the fourth century on, and have continued almost uninterruptedly to the present day. The reports of the pilgrims had a wide influence, stimulating religious piety and curiosity about the Holy Land. They also provide an important source of information for the history of Ereẓ Israel, the political situation in various periods, its communities, sects, settlements, and social life. Despite its anti-Jewish bias, the pilgrim literature also gives a general picture of Jewish settlement in Ereẓ Israel, supplementing and augmenting the Jewish sources in many details.

History. Ereẓ Israel became the Holy Land to Christians as the cradle of Christianity and because of its associations with the life of Jesus and the apostles. Nevertheless the Church never aspired to make Jerusalem the center of Christianity, and its symbolic significance was in its mystic-heavenly sense (see Gal. 4:24–26 and Rev. 21). The primacy of the mystical, heavenly Jerusalem in Christian thought on the one hand, and the concrete association of the Holy Land with the life and death of Jesus on the other, resulted in an ambivalent attitude to pilgrimages (see *Jerusalem, In Christianity). While popular piety and devotion naturally tended toward a veneration of the *holy places, many writers warned against the danger of a "carnal" and material misunderstanding of essentially spiritual realities. In fact, many early Church Fathers at first discouraged pilgrimage. Jerome declared that the gates of heaven were open to believers equally in Britain as Jerusalem (Ep. 58 *Ad Paulinum*). He mentions that St. Hilarion, who lived in the Holy Land for 50 years, prided himself on the fact that he had visited the holy places only once. However the ardent wish of Christians to visit the Holy Land was eventually accepted by Jerome, who settled in a cave near Bethlehem. In practice pilgrimage was first stimulated under Constantine (306–337), with the announcement by his mother Helena of the discovery of the cross in Jerusalem, and the erection by Constantine of the magnificent rotunda and basilica at the presumed sepulcher of Jesus. Christians thereupon readily identified other places mentioned in the New Testament associated with Jesus and the apostles. The sites were immediately sanctified, and shrines or churches built near them (cf. E. Robinson, *Biblical Researches in Palestine* (1841), 371).

These attracted an increasing stream of pilgrims, interrupted only by political insecurity or pestilence, and reaching huge proportions in the Middle Ages. The *Crusades were preeminently a pilgrimage of armies, aimed at liberating the holy places from the Muslims, whatever their accompanying political motives. The duty of caring for the protection and needs of pilgrims gave rise to the influential hospitaller orders, such as the Knights Templar and the Knights of Malta. In the later Middle Ages the religious factor diminished to be replaced increasingly by commerical motives. Even in the ninth and tenth centuries the Muslim rulers had encouraged trade there, and Jerusalem became a large entrepôt between East and West. One result of the trading contacts between Europe and the East was the extension of the maritime power of the Italian republics, especially Venice and Genoa, during the Fourth Crusade (1202–04).

Character of the Pilgrimages. Jerusalem and Bethlehem remained the main centers of Christian pilgrimage, but there were others, especially in Galilee. However places in Galilee such as Nazareth, Capernaum, Magdala, or Kefar Kanna are not mentioned by early pilgrims, such as the Bordeaux pilgrim whose *Itinerarium Burdigalense* (written before 333) is the first pilgrim guide extant. This was probably because Galilee then still had a mainly Jewish population.

The chief incentive to pilgrimage remained religious. Pilgrimages were organized to gain remission of sins, as set penances, in fulfillment of vows, for atonements for crimes, for cures, and for the acquisition of relics. However they also fulfilled other purposes: the desire to see foreign lands, people and customs, love of adventure, and commercial profit. Thus, besides the thousands of the pious, the pilgrim movement attracted a bevy of adventurers, sick persons, and paupers. The journey of the pilgrim was fraught with danger. He faced local wars, attack by pirates or brigands, epidemics, bad sanitation, or arbitrary imprisonment by the local authority. In Venice in the 15th century he was given facilities to make his will before embarking. The departure of a pilgrim also posed a problem for the Church. It meant disruption of family life and the absence of a breadwinner or worker, while the conditions of the journey frequently brought a lowering of moral standards. The Church therefore insisted that pilgrims should obtain written authorizations from the bishop or abbot for their journey. If he met the Church's requirements the pilgrim received its blessing and assistance.

The Literature. Once home the pilgrim reported the glories of the holy places and the wonders he had seen and heard. These accounts circulated both by word of mouth and in written records or itineraries for the guidance of future pilgrims. Although until the end of the Middle Ages the oral accounts were predominant as the vast majority of pilgrims were uneducated, a growing number of travelers recorded their journey and impressions. Roehricht's bibliography of Palestiniana in the main European languages lists 38 authors between the years 333 and 1000, 517 up to the year 1500, and nearly 2,000 between the years 1800 and 1878. Subsequently there has been an inordinate increase of such records.

The record usually followed a set scheme providing a description of the Holy Land and the spiritual experiences of the pilgrims for those who had never been there. From the end of the 17th century much was written for the purposes of religious propaganda. The authors frequently catered to their audience and supplemented their descriptions with embellishments and imaginary adventures, where reality and legend intermingle. However, many present an accurate if limited record, often closely resembling one another. The records fall into several different categories. Some are on-the-spot accounts of events as they occurred. Many were written down after the pilgrim's return, often on the basis of notes taken on the journey, which contained details omitted from his book. A large number were written on the basis of previous works, including many passages merely copied from them or with deliberate variations. The German cleric Ludolf von Suchem (1336–41) states that he did not see all that he wrote with his own eyes, but drew on ancient history books. *The Travels of Sir John Mandeville* (in the Holy Land, 1336) is a collection of earlier sources. Some writers quote their sources, and some copy them without acknowledgment. A number, especially in the early period, related their accounts to a third person who recorded them in turn. The account of the French bishop Arculfus (670) was recorded by an abbot in Iona, off Scotland.

Educated pilgrims and scholars later made independent investigations instead of accepting everything they were told. Many, who reveal wide learning, relate the old traditions but with reservations. Fynes Moryson (16th century), although criticizing the credibility of the tales told by the monks of the Latin monastery, was still deeply impressed and moved by what he saw. The pioneer of modern researches was the U.S. theologian, philologist, and geographer Edward Robinson (1838) who voiced a much stronger and well-founded criticism of the credulity accorded by the pilgrims down the ages who had always seen the holy places through the eyes of their monastic cicerones. He considered that many sites had no historical basis and even contradicted the evidence of the New Testament. He also cast doubt on the traditions associated with Eusebius and

Jerome, from which others had originated. Robinson therefore carried out his pioneer researches independently of the Christian orders in Ereẓ Israel. [Y.GL.]

Information on the Jews. Much of the information available on Jewish life in the Holy Land in earlier periods comes from the Christian pilgrim accounts. Thus, Jacobus de Verona (1335), an Augustinian friar, speaks of Jewish guides. Ludolf von Suchem states that Jews, but not Christians, were allowed on payment to enter the cave of Machpelah in Hebron, where the Patriarchs are buried. An anonymous Englishman (1345) tells of Jews living in caves near Jerusalem. Arnold von Harff, a German nobleman from Erft, though as prejudiced against the Jews as most of the early pilgrims, showed a more intelligent interest in them. Among "the very many" Jews in Jerusalem, with some of whom he entered into learned discussion, he found several natives of Lombardy knowledgeable about Christianity, three from Germany, and also two monks who had converted to Judaism. He learned some Hebrew and his book reproduces the *alef-bet* and also a number of words and phrases in common use, from his transliterations of which it is clear that he learned them from people of Central European origin. Pierre Belon (1547), a French physician of Mans, saw in Galilee Jews engaged in fishing; and newly established villages, where, he notes, they were converting wasteland into fertile areas.

Much is reported about Safed as a flourishing Jewish center. A Franciscan from Spain (1553–55), whose name is not known, found a Jewish population of 8,000–10,000 there. William Biddulph (1600), an English priest, mentions the Hebrew that was taught there (as well as in Salonika).

John Sanderson (1601), an English merchant, traveled with a Jewish merchant who hid his money in his clothes, some 12,000 ducats, of which 3,000 was for charity and for books in the Holy Land. The Franciscan Eugenius Roger (1629–34), who estimates 15,000 Jews in the country, including 4,000 in Jerusalem, divides them into two groups: the old-established oriental Jews and the newcomers from Europe, particularly Spain, Germany, and Italy. There was little intermarriage between the two groups, the first being particularly doubtful of the authenticity of the Jewishness of those from Spain, "for they had been baptized, had for long lived as Christians and ate foods and drank drinks forbidden by the Law of Moses." Other communal troubles are reported by the Jesuit Michael Nau, who visited the land in 1665 and again in 1674. He found the Jews divided into the Rabbanites, who accepted the Talmud, and the Karaites and the Samaritans, who accepted only the Bible. Each complained to him about the other: "They hate one another with an unparalleled hatred. But there is one thing about which they must agree in Jerusalem, that is, that they must pay heavily to the Turks for the right to remain there."

A vivid description of the unhappy condition of the Jews in Jerusalem is given by Chateaubriand (1806–07): "isolated from the other inhabitants, abandoned to every kind of shame . . ., he suffers every humiliation without crying out against it, without a sound turns his cheek to him who strikes him," and Chateaubriand adds sympathetically that there is nothing more remarkable in the history of the nations than the survival of the Jews—a miracle "even in the eyes of a *philosophe*."

Another sympathetic observer is Alfonse de Lamartine (1832–33) who writes: "This land, if settled by a new Jewish people . . . is destined once again to become the Promised Land . . . if He who watches from above will return the people to it and give them the political privileges of peace and security." Robert Curzon (1834) states: "It is noteworthy that the Jews who are born in Jerusalem are completely different from those we see in Europe. Here they are of a blond race, light in movement, and, especially, refined in their conduct." At the same time John Lloyd Stephens (1835) tells of the fear under which the Jews lived in Hebron and Safed.

Edward Robinson remarks about Christian missionary activity among the Jews: "So far the efforts of the English mission have had only the most meager success." He also describes the devastation wrought by the great earthquake of 1837. Another visitor was William Bartlett (1842 and 1853) who gave exact descriptions of Jerusalem.

William Holt Yates (1843), London physician and orientalist, exemplifies an attitude toward the country radically different from the pilgrims of the earlier centuries. He thinks that Palestine (and Asia Minor and Syria) would benefit by the mingling of the "natives" with Britishers, especially Scotsmen, and with Jews: "Although the Jews as a people have never particularly distinguished themselves in literature and science they nevertheless have excellent qualities if only these were properly recognized . . ." William Francis Lynch (1848), the U.S. naval officer celebrated for his account of his voyage of discovery to the River Jordan and Dead Sea, saw the only hope for Palestine in the dissolution of the degenerate Ottoman Empire and the settlement of the Jews.

Active in assisting Jews to settle was James *Finn (1853–56), who as British consul in Jerusalem made himself their protector. His own book and his consular reports are prime sources for knowledge of conditions. Among other events he describes the blood libel raised against the Jews.

Henry Baker Tristram (1863–64), English theologian, fellow of the Royal Society, and among the founders of the Palestine Exploration Fund, finds place in his important works on the flora and fauna of Palestine for descriptions of the Jews. But the most interesting of all for that period is the diplomat and statesman Laurence *Oliphant (1883–87) who gives a first hand account of the earliest pioneers of the modern resettlement, whom he greatly assisted.

Subsequently there are accounts of historians, theologians, journalists, surveyors, and archaeologists, from all over Europe and the United States, reference to which may be found among the records of the various scientific institutions. Visitors of literary fame who wrote of their impressions include W. M. Thackeray, Mark Twain, George Moore, G. K. Chesterton, Pierre Loti, and Herman Melville.

The flood of books by pilgrims of all kinds and all intentions and pretensions in recent times is overwhelming. As with the earlier pilgrims, the accounts of many of them are colored by their preconceived opinions. Other contemporary writers convey their experiences in the form of novels, detective stories, and thrillers, experiences which are often observed more authentically than in more solemn works.

See also *Holy Places in Israel. [S.C.H.]

Bibliography: SECOND TEMPLE PERIOD: I. Elbogen, in: *Bericht der Hochschule fuer die Wissenschaft des Judentums*, 46 (1929), 27–46; S. Safrai, in: *Sefer Yerushalayim*, ed. by M. Avi-Yonah, 1 (1956), 369–91; idem, in: *Zion*, 25 (1959/60), 67–84. POST-TEMPLE PERIOD: K. Wilhelm, *Roads to Zion* (1948); S. Assaf and A. L. Mayer, *Sefer ha-Yishuv*, 2 (1944), 25–29; A. Yaari, in : KS, 18 (1941/42), 293–7, 378–80; idem, *Iggerot Ereẓ Yisrael* (1943); idem, *Masot Ereẓ Yisrael* (1946); Ya'ari, Sheluḥei, index; M. A. Shulvass, *Roma vi-Yrushalayim* (1944), passim; idem, in: *Zion*, 3 (1938), 86–7; S. A. Horodezky, *Olei Ẓiyyon* (1947); S. Assaf, *Tekufat ha-Ge'onim ve-Sifrutah* (1955), 91–7; R. Mahler, *Divrei Yemei Yisrael* (1956), 117–31; Ben-Zvi, Ereẓ Yisrael (1967[3]); S. Safrai, *Ha-Aliyyah le-Regel bi-Ymei ha-Bayit ha-Sheni* (1966); Ta-Shema, in: *Tarbiz*, 38 (1968/69), 398–9. CHRISTIAN PILGRIMAGES: R.

Roericht, *Bibliotheca Geographica Palaestina* (new ed., 1963); P. Thomsen, *Palaestina-Literatur* (1908, 1956, 1960); T. Wright (ed.), *Early Travels in Palestine* (1948); M. Ish-Shalom, *Masei ha-Nozerim le-Erez Yisrael* (1966); T. Kollek and M. Pearlman, *Pilgrims to the Holy Land* (1970).

PILGRIM FESTIVALS (Heb. שָׁלוֹשׁ רְגָלִים, "three pilgrim festivals"), collective term for the three festivals of *Passover, *Shavuot, and *Sukkot. The duty of pilgrimage on these three occasions stems from the biblical injunction, "Three times a year shall all thy males appear before the Lord thy God in the place which He shall choose, in the feast of unleavened bread, and in the feast of weeks, and in the feast of tabernacles" (Deut. 16:16; and Ex. 23:17 where the festivals are not specified). According to the Mishnah, "All are under obligation to appear, excepting a deaf-mute, an imbecile, a child, one of doubtful sex, one of double sex, women, slaves that have not been freed, a man that is lame or blind or sick or aged, and one that cannot go up [to Jerusalem] on his feet" (Ḥag 1:1). The importance of the duty is stressed by Joshua b. Levi who stated, "all who perform the duty of pilgrimage are considered as if they had received the **Shekhinah*" (TJ, Hag, 1:1, 76a). Besides the festive offerings made on these occasions (Lev. 23), it was also enjoined that "they shall not appear before the Lord empty. Every man shall give as he is able" (Deut. 16:16–17). The Mishnah ruled that the minimum value of each individual offering was to be three pieces of silver (Ḥag. 1:2).

In the times of the judges, the pilgrimages were made to Shiloh (I Sam. 1:3) and, after the construction of the Temple, to Jerusalem (I Kings 8:65; II Chron. 7:8–9). *Jeroboam, king of the northern kingdom of Israel, considered them such a threat to his authority that he established rival shrines at Dan and Beth-El (I Kings 12:26–33). After the return from Babylonia, Nehemiah reinstituted the practice of pilgrimage to Jerusalem on the festival of Sukkot (Neh. 8:15). Both Josephus (Wars 6:422–7) and the Tosefta (Pes. 4:3; also Pes. 64b) comment upon the large number of pilgrims to the Second Temple during Passover. According to the Mishnah, the fact that there was room for them all was a miracle (Avot 5:5). It seems that even Diaspora Jewry made the pilgrimage (Ta'an. 28a), and it was ruled that the prayer for rain should not be recited until 15 days after the conclusion of Sukkot in order to allow the last of the pilgrims to return to the Euphrates (Ta'an. 1:3).

In modern times, the tradition has been continued by individuals and groups from all over the country going up to Jerusalem, especially during the intermediate days of Sukkot. The center of pilgrimage is the *Western ("Wailing") Wall, but when access to it was barred pilgrims went to Mount Zion.

See *Festivals; *Passover; *Shavuot; *Sukkot.

Bibliography: S. Safrai, *Ha-Aliyyah le-Regel bi-Ymei ha-Bayit ha-Sheni* (1965).

[Ed.]

PILICHOWSKI, LEOPOLD (1869–1933), Polish painter. Pilichowski left his native village of Zadzin for nearby Lodz, where he was helped by David *Frischmann, the Hebrew writer, who made it possible for Pilichowski to study in Munich. Later, he lived in Paris for a number of years, and in 1914 he moved to London. Pilichowski became a successful portraitist. He was filled with socialist and Zionist sentiments, and struggled to give pictorial expression to both. He painted the exploited wool-dyers of Lodz, and the weary shopkeepers and artisans he met in London's Whitechapel. Many of his large pictures were crowded with pious Jews in a variety of moods and postures. His huge painting of *The Opening of the Hebrew University in Jerusalem* in 1925 has been frequently reproduced. Among the Jewish personalities he portrayed were Bialik, Einstein, Aḥad Ha-Am, Nordau, and Weizmann. [A.W.]

PILLAR (Heb. עַמּוּד; from the root *ʿmd*, "to stand"), a column that stands perpendicular to the ground and generally serves to support the beams of a roof. In this article no distinction will be made between "pillar," "column," and "post." The pillar is used in construction in three ways (see *Architecture): (1) as a functional element in construction to support a large ceiling; (2) to emphasize an ornate door at the front of a building, or to emphasize the outline of a building; and (3) sometimes to take the place of a doorpost and support a massive lintel. Another type of support performing the same functions is the pilaster which does not stand free but is attached to and stands out from the wall. There is another type of pillar that stands alone and is not connected with any other structure; this type of pillar was designed to attract attention and to serve as a place around which a crowd could gather (II Kings 11:14).

Pillars (posts) occupied an important place in the structure of the Tabernacle (Ex. 26–27). The pillars (posts) used in the Tabernacle were constructed of wood. During the period of

Leopold Pilichowski's "Opening of the Hebrew University of Jerusalem," oil on canvas, 1925, with the artist in the left foreground. Courtesy Hebrew University of Jerusalem. Photo David Harris, Jerusalem.

the monarchy, pillars were used in palaces and the Temple. Halls are mentioned which contained rows of pillars (I Kings 7:6): pillars which served to support the roof; the symbolic pillars of Jachin and Boaz (I Kings 7:21; II Chron. 3:17); and copper pillars which stood at the entrance to the Temple (II Kings 7:15, 20, 22). Pillars that were functional elements in construction are mentioned in the story of Samson, who brought down the middle pillars of the palace of Dagon and in this way destroyed the entire building (Judg. 16:29).

Pillars were introduced into the Near East with the first experiments in enlarging covered structures. In Egypt they were first used as supports for roofing in the middle of the third millennium B.C.E. As early as this, pillars served not only as supports but also as ornaments of buildings, or as ornaments in themselves. In Mesopotamia pillars began to be used in the middle of the second millennium B.C.E.

Remains of pillars uncovered in various archaeological excavations in Ereẓ Israel and the discovery of plans of various buildings have revealed much about the function of pillars in ancient architecture. In a large structure at Ai dating to the early Canaanite period a row of pillar bases was discovered in one hall, which passed through the center of a long building. The function of these pillars was to help support the beams of the roof. In general, builders saw to it that the pillars inside buildings, whether of wood or stone, should be separated from one another in order to permit free passage among them. The pillars were set up in a place where they would not hide the inside of the structure from the entrance. In most cases, only the bases of the pillars, which could have served as foundations for both stone and wooden pillars, have been found in archaeological excavations. The pillars were sometimes made from one block, but generally from several stones placed one on top of the other. The use of pillars as supports for beamed ceilings is common also in the late Canaanite period. In one of the buildings discovered at Taanach a pillar was set up in the middle of a large area that could not be beamed from wall to wall, thereby shortening the distance between walls and making it possible to place short, strong beams between the pillar and the wall in order to build a roof over this area.

The use of pillars in the construction of houses and other types of buildings was widespread in the Israelite period. Buildings from this period have been found that are divided internally into four sections: three long sections that lie side by side forming an almost perfect square, and a fourth section, of approximately the same size, running across their ends. The long rooms were sometimes divided from one another by solid walls, but generally by rows of pillars. It appears that of the long rooms, the middle one was uncovered, being a type of court lined on either side by rows of wooden or stone pillars. The roofs of the two outer rooms were supported by the outside walls and the two rows of pillars that surrounded the court. These structures are common in Tell en-Naṣbeh, Tell Qasila, and other places. Larger structures of this type were found in Hazor. Another use of pillars inside a building was discovered in the structures of the stables of Megiddo in one of the Israelite strata. In the large network of stables, stone pillars arranged in rows at equal distances from one another were discovered. In each space between the pillars a water trough was discovered, and on the pillar itself a hole for tying a horse. These pillars had a threefold function; to support the roof, to serve as a place for harnessing a horse, and to divide the building into compartments for individual horses.

Square stone columns and pillars bearing "proto-Ionian" capitals are characteristic of the elaborate structures of the Israelite period. These capitals are decorated with a bas relief of a double coil emanating from a central triangle. Discovered in strata from the beginning of the Israelite period in Jerusalem, Megiddo, Samaria, Ramat Raḥel, and Hazor, these pillars served as posts of gates. In addition to actual physical pillars, the Bible speaks of the *pillar of cloud and the pillar of fire that accompanied the Israelites during their journey through the desert (Ex. 13:22). The pillar of cloud is also described as standing at the door of the Tabernacle (Deut. 31:15). Metaphorically, in the poetic sections of the Bible, the heavens are described as standing on pillars (Job 26:11). In a poetic manner, the pillar is used metaphorically in the descriptions of the parts of the human body: "His legs are as pillars of marble set upon sockets of fine gold" (Song 5:15).

In the fifth and fourth centuries B.C.E., under the Persian rule, with the penetration of Greek influences into the Middle East generally and Ereẓ Israel in particular, many elements of classical architecture found their way into the local styles. Among these elements, the pillar holds an important place as a functional element in the structure of building or as ornamentation. Pillars appear both in private and public buildings, and also in tombs. In Ereẓ Israel pillars and capitals of different styles were in use simultaneously; for example an ancient specimen of a Doric pillar remained on a mural inside a Hellenistic tomb in Marissa. In Ereẓ Israel remains of pillars from the beginning of the Hellenistic era are rare. From the Roman period on, Hellenistic architecture spread greatly. During this period, particularly in the reign of Herod (37–4 B.C.E.), much building on the part of the king took place in Ereẓ Israel, almost all of which included elements of Roman architecture. In order to raise the level of the Temple Mount, Herod erected rows of large square pillars, remains of which exist underground southeast of the Temple Mount at the site known today as "Solomon's Stables." Examples of smooth monolithic pillars stand in the "colonnaded street" in Samaria. These pillars stand on square bases and their capitals seem to have been Corinthian. Corinthian pillars and capitals were set up by Herod in Herodium and in Masada in the northern palace. In this palace the pillars are not monolithic but are built in sections (drums) and covered with stucco intended to give the effect of marble. With the exception of the Temple and other stately buildings in Jerusalem, large pillars were not widespread in the country, as they were in other lands of the Roman Empire, large monumental structures being uncommon in Ereẓ Israel.

The use of pillars was more common in tombs of the Second Temple period. They are found in the tombs of the Sanhedrin and the tombs of the sons of Hezir in the Valley of Kidron in Jerusalem. In these places the pillars, like the whole tomb, are hewn out of rock. This style was also widespread in many other places both in the Judean Hills and Galilee, for example, in the cemetery in Bet She'arim. A different use was made of columns and pillars in "Absalom's Tomb" and in the "Tomb of Zechariah" in the Valley of Kidron, both monumental tombs from the time of the Second Temple. These monuments are partly or wholly hewn from the living rock and are cube shaped and their facades are beautified by half pillars and columns cut out of the rock. The capitals of the pillars in these two monuments are Ionic.

With the erection of synagogues in Galilee and Judea in the third and fourth centuries C.E., a mixture of styles in architecture came into use. The pillars, like the carvings and other decorations of the synagogue, were ornamented in a mixture of styles—an oriental style that was the result of Persian influence and a late Hellenistic style. This is the case with the capitals and other decorations of the synagogues of

Capernaum, Kefar Baram, Chorazin, and others. In these places there are capitals in a number of styles, chiefly Ionic and Corinthian, used together in various parts of the structure. Worthy of mention are the widespread corner pillars in these early synagogues. In cross-section the pillars are heart-shaped and their function is to emphasize the corners of the rows of pillars. The synagogue pillars had two functions—to beautify the appearance of the portico and to support the slanted roof inside. In the synagogues in Galilee there were usually two rows of pillars: those of the hall are large and stand on square bases, while those of the upper (women's) gallery on the second floor are small and narrower. These are found in Kefar Baram, Chorazin, Capernaum, and other sites. While the interiors of the synagogue were decorated with columns, the facades of the early synagogues were decorated with pillars protruding from the wall, such as those found in Capernaum, Chorazin, Kefar Baram, and other places.

This mode of decoration was a continuation of the system of building of the Herodian era and is found on the monument erected over the cave of Machpelah in Hebron. It appears that the decorations with which the cave of Machpelah was adorned are a return to the motif that decorated the Temple Mount, though that was on a much larger scale. Circular pillars, mostly with Corinthian capitals, also decorated the inside of later synagogues from the fifth and sixth centuries C.E., such as those found at Bet Alfa, Beth-Shean, on the wall of Tiberias, etc. The pillar, being a conspicous element in the architecture of magnificent buildings, also served as decoration. Thus in many places pillars are portrayed in mosaics or paintings flanking the ark of the Law in the synagogues. They were found on the murals in Dura Europos, in the mosaics of Bet Alfa, Nirim, Beth-Shean, and elsewhere. Small marble pillars with delicate ornaments usually served to support the chancel screen before the ark. Such pillars were found out of their original places in a number of synagogues in Galilee and Judea. A series of pillars symbolizing the Temple appears on the coins of Bar Kokhba. These are usually portrayed as four pillars apparently carrying the exedra in front of the facade of the Temple.

In the Jewish world it was not customary to erect a pillar as a monument in memory of a person or enterprise. Pillars were used primarily for decorating splendid houses and as functional elements in construction, chiefly in synagogue buildings. Technically, the pillars used for this purpose were either monoliths as in Samaria or Capernaum, or were built of sections, as in the synagogues in Chorazin and Kefar Baram and in the late synagogues. Apparently the pillars built of sections were to some extent an expression of the economic situation of the Jewish population in the first centuries C.E., when materials were poorer than in previous eras. When Herod built his monuments in Caesarea, Tiberias, Jerusalem, and other places, he erected huge monolithic columns whose production and also transportation were much more costly than the production and transportation of column drums.

Bibliography: E. Sellin, *Tell Ta'annek* (1904), 3; A. G. Barrois, *Manuel d'archéologie biblique, Tomb,* 1 (1939), fig. 97; See excavation reports at: *Megiddo I* (R. S. Lamon and G. M. Shipton, 1939); *Samaria I* (G. A. Reisner et al.); *Hazor I* (Aharoni); *Ramath Rahel* (Aharoni, 1964).

[Z.Y.]

PILLAR OF CLOUD AND PILLAR OF FIRE. The earliest traditions of the Exodus from Egypt refer to the pillar of cloud by day and of fire by night, which accompanied the Children of Israel on their way through the desert (Ex. 13:21–22). The visible symbol of the presence of God caused a panic among the Egyptians as it cut them off from the Israelites (Ex. 14:19b, 24a), and continued to guide and protect the latter uninterruptedly throughout their wanderings. Later generations remembered it as a special sign of divine favor (cf. Ps. 78:14), no less important than the parting of the Sea of Reeds itself. Another early tradition connected the cloud with the *Tent of Meeting. According to the view attributed by critics to the author of the Elohist account (E), the pillar of cloud served not as a regular escort marching at the head of the people, but as an intermittent presence, descending from time to time to the entrance of the Tent of Meeting when God conversed with Moses (Ex. 33:9–10; Num. 11:25; 12:5). The priestly authors, on the other hand, taught that "a cloud of the Lord" (not a pillar) with a fiery appearance by night, permanently covered the Tabernacle from the day of its completion, lifting only to signal the breaking of camp for a new journey (Ex. 40:34–38; Num. 9:15–23; 10:11–12, 34; 14:14). The Divine Presence in Solomon's Temple was similarly accompanied by the descent of the cloud (I Kings 8:10–11; cf. Ex. 16:10; Lev. 16:2) though the pillar of cloud and of fire did not accompany the Israelites into the Promised Land.

Various explantions have been sought for the origin of these traditions. Among them is the attested use of braziers filled with burning wood at the head of caravans or armies, sometimes placed before the tent of the chief or carried before him. Others derive the imagery from the *pillars before Solomon's Temple, which, they contend, were fiery cressets emitting clouds of smoke and flame by day and by night at the time of a festival. Still others point to the smoke that rose from the altar of the burnt offering as the origin of the representation. The most commonly accepted theory connects the pillar of cloud and fire with the theophany at Sinai, when the descent of the Lord was marked by a thick cloud (Ex. 19:9), by thunder, lightening, smoke, and fire. Attempts to provide a natural basis for this narrative have pointed to the possible existence of volcanic action in the vicinity of Sinai—which is highly unlikely—or to the sudden outbreak of a raging desert storm. In any event, there can be little doubt that the imagery is as old as the time of Moses, and that the cloud, and, in a lesser degree, the fire symbolism proved effective in communicating the presence of God to the people.

Post-biblical legend embellished the biblical account. Thus, not one but seven clouds descended at Sukkot to envelop and protect the Israelites, one on each of the four sides of the camp, one above and one below, and one which went before them to raise the valleys and lower the mountains. The Israelites were protected against the elements and wild beasts, even their garments did not wear out or become dirty. Eliezer maintained that the Festival of Sukkot commemorated the "clouds of glory" (Suk. 11b) which were considered among God's special creations in the "twilight" of the first six days (ARN[2] 37, 95).

Bibliography: G. B. Gray, *Numbers* (ICC, 1912), 85–86, 113, 212; Ginzberg, Legends, 2 (1910); 5 (1925); 6 (1928); S. R. Driver, *Exodus* (1953), 112–3, 147; L. Koehler, *Theologie des Alten Testaments* (1953), 8–9; R. Reymond, *L'Eau, sa Vie, et sa Signification dans l'Ancient Testament* (1958), 37ff.; M. Noth, *Exodus* (1959), 91ff.; A. Weiser, *Die Psalmen* (1959), 463; de Vaux, Anc Isr (1965[2]), 295; H. J. Kraus, *Psalmen,* 2 (1966[3]), 722; U. Cassuto, *A Commentary on the Book of Exodus* (1967), 158, 169, 336ff.; E. A. Speiser, in: J. Finkelstein and M. Greenberg (ed.), *Oriental and Biblical Studies* (1967), 106–12; T. H. Gaster, *Myth, Legend, and Custom in the Old Testament* (1969), 236–7. [D.L.L.]

PILPUL (Heb. פִּלְפּוּל), a collective term denoting various methods of talmudic study and exposition, especially by the use of subtle legal, conceptual, and casuistic differentiation. The word is derived from *pilpel* ("pepper"), indicating that these methods were employed in talmudic disputations by the more sharp-witted among the scholars (cf. *palpelan*—TJ, Hor. 3:7, 48c; *ba'al-pilpul*—BB 145b). In the talmudic period the term *pilpul* was applied to the logical distinctions through which apparent contradictions and textual difficulties were straightened out by means of reasoning *(sevarah),* leading to a more penetrating understanding and conceptual analysis. This method was distinguished from a mere cursory knowledge of the texts *(girsah)* and the oral traditions and teachings of the scholars of the past. The masters of *pilpul* would advance arguments and opinions of their own, though always based on the authority of tradition, while those strictly adhering to the texts and their traditional exegesis would reject the ways of the pilpulists, whose daring originality would sometimes lead them astray from plain reason and truth (cf. Er. 90a). Scholars hotly debated the question as to whose merits for the dissemination and advancement of Torah study were greater: *sinai,* i.e., he who faithfully preserved the established texts and traditions, or *oker harim,* i.e., he who "uproots mountains" in his intellectual struggle for clarity and logical harmony (cf. Ber. 64a). Nevertheless, it was generally agreed that *pilpul* was of vital necessity for establishing hermeneutical links between the Oral and the Written Torah thus keeping tradition from error and oblivion (cf. Kid. 66b; BM 85b; Zev. 13a; Tem. 16a). It was also valued as a didactic method to sharpen the intellect of students (Avot 6:6; Ber. 33b; Er. 13a). Members of the high court (Sanhedrin) were required to be masters of *pilpul* (cf. Sanh. 17a). Babylonian scholars were especially noted for their subtle ways of *pilpul* and their acrimonious disputations, contrasting with the moderation of the Palestinian schools (cf. Pes. 34b; BM 85a).

The talmudic *pilpul* was thus suited to meet three principal needs. The first was to safeguard the unity of the Oral and Written Torah and to harmonize between the apparently differing opinions of the sages. This was based on the religious principle that both parts of the Torah tradition flowed from one single divine revelation and that consequently what appeared to be contradictory, repetitive, or redundant, was due only to the intellectual limitations of the students. The second was to keep up the vitality and relevance of the Oral and Written Torah in its traditionally fixed form in the face of changing times and circumstances. Finally, it made Torah study a permanent challenge to the intellectual powers of masters and students and kept it safe from routine and perfunctoriness. *Pilpul* enabled the gifted student to bring new elements into Torah study, and these were themselves considered part of the divine revelation (cf. Ned. 38a; Meg. 19b; TJ, Pe'ah 2:6; 17a; for examples of talmudic *pilpul* see JE, vol. 10, p.40.).

The Babylonian scholars of the geonic period continued to employ the methods of *pilpul,* though they were chiefly occupied with arranging, editing, and explaining the text of the Talmud, as did the early school of Ashkenazi commentators up to Rashi's generation. A new wave of *pilpul* rose in the tosafist schools of France and Germany, as well as in the Spanish schools of the 13th and 14th centuries. The same methods as had previously been applied in the Talmud, now served to harmonize apparently differing talmudic passages and opinions. This new vogue gave rise to adverse criticism among the Ashkenazi Ḥasidim who deplored the over-cleverness of sharp-witted scholars who substituted originality for truth and preferred the study of *tosafot* to that of the Talmud itself (cf. *Sefer Ḥasidim* ed. by J. Wistinetzki (1924[2]), nos. 648, 1049, 1375, 1707, 1816, 1838).

The close of the tosafist era in the 14th century was followed by a short period during which scholars occupied themselves chiefly with the study and recording of the traditional laws and customs *(minhagim)* that had accumulated until then. However, the intrinsic dynamics of Torah study called for new intellectual challenges to be put to the restlessly searching minds of scholars and students. The traditional modes of study and disputation had become exhausted, and scholars strove to devise new modes in which they could distinguish themselves. In addition, yeshivah teachers became increasingly conscious of didactics and method in the education of rabbinical scholars. The prevailing spirit of humanism influenced scholars to seek intellectual independence while remaining faithful to the traditional sources. Thus the 15th and 16th centuries witnessed an unprecedented intensification of casuistic disputation. A clear distinction began to be made between lessons devoted to cursory study of the talmudic text and those given to intensive disputation. This was led by the head of the yeshivah and was of an essentially oral character, which accounts for the fact that very little of its content was recorded and preserved in manuscripts.

Some idea of the new modes of *pilpul,* which consisted mainly in the application of logical models and of increasing sharper divisions and differentiations *(ḥillukim),* may be gained from treatises on talmudic methodology such as the *Darkhei ha-Talmud* by Isaac *Canpanton. Several new modes became known by the names of communities whose yeshivot specialized in them, e.g., Nuremberg, Regensburg. These methods are characterized by a penetrating inquiry into the minutest details of halakhic discussion as recorded in the Talmud. Each and every sentence is shown to convey some novel meaning of its own and no redudancy whatsoever is allowed. A problem set by one of the sages is not an indication of any doubt or ignorance but an attempt to test the knowledge and intelligence of his colleagues and students. Since all the sages are supposed to possess knowledge and intelligence of identical width and depth, the talmudic dialogue is shown to be an interplay of diverging attitudes and opinions rather than a series of questions and answers. Furthermore, the divergences are attributed to casuistic differentiations rather than to fundamental contradictions, and thus the basic unity and conformity of the spiritual world of the Talmud is preserved and safeguarded.

In the sphere of didactics diverse pilpulistic methods were innovated by which to heighten the students' power of perception and imagination. Masters devised imaginary halakhic cases and problems and required their students to pass reasoned judgments. They also composed halakhic riddles, sometimes involving the most obstruse casuistry, which the students were required to solve. In the 16th and 17th centuries the ability to excel in pilpulistic disputation was the chief aim and mark of distinction of the yeshivah student. At a time when rabbinical learning had become widespread and rabbis as well as lay leaders were rivals for communal leadership, accomplished masters in the art of *pilpul* outshone less brilliant, if more conscientious, scholars and secured for themselves a paramount social status. In the spiritual sphere *pilpul* was reinforced by certain kabbalistic trends that glorified the contemplative, as against the pragmatic, attitude to study. The intuition of the scholars was seen as a form of divine inspiration. At the same time *pilpul* served a vital purpose in enabling rabbis to pass decisions on many new halakhic problems arising from the changing economic and political situation. Nevertheless, outstanding rabbis, such as *Judah Loew b. Bezalel (the Maharal), Isaiah *Horowitz, Ephraim *Luntschitz, and Jair Ḥayyim *Bacharach, severely criticized the universal "craze" for *pilpul* and *ḥillukim.* They had been preceded as early as the 15th century by the anonymous treatise on ethics known as *Orḥot Ẓaddikim,* which contained the first vigorous attack on the new ways of *pilpul* launched from within the circles of the Ashkenazi yeshivah. Though not opposed to *pilpul* as such, these rabbis resented the twisting of plain truth resulting out of the hairsplitting efforts of the most sharp-witted and argued that *pilpul* should serve the comprehension of the texts and not itself become an art.

They also criticized the students' passion for personal honor and aggrandizement and questioned their authority to decide on halakhic matters, since their preoccupation with *pilpul* made them wholly dependent, in matters of religious practice, on the new codes such as R. Joseph Caro's Shulḥan Arukh. Thus it is not surprising that the critics of *pilpul* often expressed concern about the publication of these codes. Criticism was much more lenient regarding the application of *pilpul* to the exposition of the Bible and homiletic literature, since this was considered irrelevant to a true understanding of *halakhah*. Consequently, popular preachers used to strain their imagination by adducing the most complicated talmudic passages and controversies in order to throw new light on a story from the Bible or the Midrash. When toward the end of the 18th century the methods of *pilpul* seemed to have been exhausted, new ways of Torah study were opened by the school of the *gaon* of Vilna, Elijah b. Solomon Zalman.

Bibliography: *Orḥot Ẓaddikim* (Prague, 1581), ch. 27 (Sha'ar ha-Torah); J. Landau, *Sefer ha-Ḥazon* (appended to his *Agur*); Z. Margaliot, *Ḥibburei Likkutim* (Venice, 1715), preface; *Alilot Devarim*, in: *Oẓar Neḥmad*, 4 (1863), 177–214; A. Jellinek, in: *Bikkurim*, 1 (1864), 1–26; 2 (1865), 1–19; M. Reines, in: *Keneset Yisrael*, 3 (1888), 137–72; J. L. Fishman, *Ha-Noten be-Yam Derekh* (1903); H. Ehrentreu, in: JJLG, 3 (1905), 206–19; M. Tosfai, in: *Ha-Shilo'aḥ*, 19 (1908), 138–46, 248–58, 329–35; Assaf, Mekorot; N. S. Grinspan, *Pilpula shel Torah* (1935); idem, *Melekhet Maḥashevet* (1955); Urbach, Tosafot; H. H. Ben-Sasson, *Hagut ve-Hanhagah* (1959), index s.v., L. Jacobs, *Studies in Talmudic Logic and Methodology* (1961); A. F. Kleinberger, *Ha-Maḥashavah ha-Pedagogit shel ha-Maharal mi-Prag* (1962); M. Breuer, in: *Sefer ha-Zikkaron le ... ha-Rav Y. Y. Weinberg* (1969). [M.Br.]

PILSEN (Czech **Plzeň**), city in W. Bohemia, Czechoslovakia; its Jewish community was one of the earliest in Bohemia. The first documentary record is a decree of 1338, signed by *Charles IV, in which the city's administrators were ordered, under penalty, to protect the Jews from molestation. In 1432 the community bought a plot from the city to be used as a cemetery. It also had a synagogue. Many transactions between Jews and Christians appear on the city records of the 15th century. In 1504 Jews were expelled from Pilsen as a result of a *Host desecration charge, and the city was granted the privilege *de non tolerandis Judaeis*. From then until 1848 Jews lived in surrounding villages and did their business in the town. Jews from all of western Bohemia and Prague attended the Pilsen markets, which became very important in Jewish life. In 1821–32 Jews were living without authorization in Pilsen, and in 1854 there were 249 Jews in the town. A Jewish cemetery was consecrated in 1856 and a synagogue in 1859. Anti-Jewish riots broke out in 1866. In 1870 the community numbered 1,207. Jews were instrumental in the development of the city into an industrial center of worldwide repute.

At the beginning of the 20th century the community was among the five largest and most affluent in Bohemia; a Moorish-style synagogue was erected in 1893. The community suffered from the conflicts between German liberal assimilationists, Czech Jews (see *Čechů-Židů, Svaz) and Zionists. In 1892 the first *B'nai B'rith Lodge of Bohemia was founded there. From 1918 the community supported two rabbis, one preaching in Czech and the other in German. **Sheḥitah* was forbidden in 1920 for "humanitarian" reasons. When the supreme court declared this prohibition illegal in 1934, the attempt to reintroduce *sheḥitah* failed because of the higher price for *kasher* meat. In 1921 there were 3,117 Jews in Pilsen and in 1930 the community numbered 2,773 (2.4% of the total population). In the fall of 1938 Pilsen became a refuge for many Jews from communities in the *Sudeten area, occupied then by

The Pilsen synagogue, built in 1893. Courtesy H. Gold, Tel Aviv.

Germany, who were supported by funds previously designated for the building of an old-age home.

After the German occupation (March 1939) there were persecutions and arrests of Jews, and the Jewish cemetery was desecrated. A plan to destroy the synagogue was given up only because it would have caused the destruction of an entire city block. In 1940 the rabbi Max Hoch and one of the community functionaries were murdered. In 1942 more than 2,000 persons from all western Bohemia were concentrated in Pilsen and deported to the Nazi extermination camps. The synagogue's ritual objects were transferred to the Central Jewish Museum in Prague.

After World War II a community was reorganized in Pilsen, numbering 293 in 1948. A memorial for the 3,200 victims of the Holocaust from Pilsen and western Bohemia was dedicated at the new cemetery in 1951. The newly established community, considerably reduced in numbers, was still active in 1970, using the old synagogue and maintaining both cemeteries. It also administered the *Ceske Budejovice congregation.

Bibliography: M. Hoch, in: H. Gold (ed.), *Die Juden und Judengemeinden Boehmens* (1934), 479–88; Bondy-Dworský, 1 (1906), nos. 213, 222, 255, 256, 258, 287, 307, 321, 322, 336, 423; R. Iltis (ed.), *Die aussaeen unter Traenen* ... (1959), 243–5. [J.Her.]

°**PILSUDSKI, JÓZEF** (1867–1935), Polish statesman, first marshal of Poland. In the early years of his political life, Pilsudski came into contact with Jews, especially Jewish workers, and the P.P.S. (Polish Socialist Party) founded by him even published a periodical in Yiddish, *Der Arbeter*, between 1898 and 1905. However, he was sharply critical of the *Bund, accusing it of "commercial and religious Jewish separation," of favoring Russification, and of opposing the

Polish independence movement. Since he was fiercely anti-Russian, he dissociated himself from the pro-Russian anti-Semite Roman *Dmowski. When Pilsudski, supported by the left, seized power in 1926, the Jews hoped for improved conditions, and indeed the prime minister, K. Bartel, proposed the abolition of several cultural, religious, and economic restrictions on the life of the Jews. However, these proposals came to nothing; on the contrary, by a law of Oct. 4, 1927 the government interfered in internal Jewish affairs and curtailed the autonomy of the Jewish communities. As a result of the pressure of the N.D. (*Endecja), in 1931 further restrictions were placed on Jewish economic and social life. Now opposed to the left, Pilsudski formed a front with the land owners and did nothing to curb the anti-Semitic right wing. In 1934 the Pilsudski government signed a pact with Hitler's Germany, with tragic results for the Jewish community in subsequent years.

Bibliography: P. Szwarc, *Józef Pilsudski* (Yid., 1936); S. Segal, *The New Poland and the Jews* (1938), index; R.L. Bruell, *Poland: Key to Europe* (1939), 297–9, 301; Y. Gruenbaum, in: EG, 1 (1953), 100–13; *Wielka Encyklopedia Powszechna,* 8 (1966), 669–71; J. Rothschild, *Pilsudski's Coup d'Etat* (1966). [Ed.]

PINA, JACOB (Manuel) DE (1616–c. 1675), Marrano poet. Born in Lisbon, Pina arrived around 1600 in Amsterdam, where he openly proclaimed himself a Jew and took the name Jacob.

The poems of his early Lisbon years were humorous in the main, for example the collection *La mayor hazaña de Carlos VI* and *Juguetes de la ninez y traversuras del ingenio* (1656). His later verse included several elegies, one dedicated to the scholar Saul (Levi) *Morteira (d. 1660), another to the martyr Isaac de Almeyda *Bernal (d. 1655), and a third to the martyred Spanish nobleman Lope de *Vera y Alarcon (d. 1644). Pina wrote in both Spanish and Portuguese.

Bibliography: M. Kayserling, *Sephardim* (Ger., 1859), 204; Kayserling, Bibl., 89. [Ed.]

PINANSKI, ABRAHAM (1887–1949), U.S. lawyer and jurist. Pinanski, who was born in Boston, Mass., worked in the legal department of the Boston Elevated Street Railway Company (1910–12), then practiced law privately from 1912 to 1930, becoming active in the Democratic Party. Appointed to the Massachusetts Superior Court in 1930, he instituted pretrial hearings to reduce case backlog and hasten court proceedings.

Pinanski, who was active in both Jewish and public affairs, was a member of the Sinking Fund Commission of Boston for five years; a trustee of the Boston Public Library; president of both the Hebrew Free Loan Society of Boston and the Jewish Child Welfare Association; and executive committee member of both the Association of Jewish Philanthropies and Beth Israel Hospital. [Ed.]

PINCUS, GREGORY GOODWIN (1903–1967), U.S. biologist. Born in Woodbine, New Jersey, he pursued his interest in the genetics of physiological characteristics. In post-doctoral studies at Cambridge and the Kaiser Wilhelm Institute he began investigations of steroid control of reproductive cycles. After teaching appointments at Harvard, Cambridge, and Clark University, he founded the Worcester Foundation for Experimental Biology in 1944 with H. Hoagland. As research director he pioneered development of the widely used oral contraceptive. Having discovered earlier that the hormone progesterone, present in increased amounts during pregnancy, prevented ovulation, Pincus tested some 200 progesterone-like compounds for their effectiveness as ovulation suppressors. In 1954 he and Dr. John Rock began clinical testing of the most promising of these. Their method proved to be virtually 100% effective in preventing conception. Its widespread adoption in the ensuing decade had great medical and sociological consequences.

Pincus was a member of the American Academy of Arts and Sciences (1939) and the National Academy of Sciences (1965). He wrote *The Control of Fertility* (1965), co-authored *Steroid Dynamics* (1966), and was editor of *Recent Progress in Hormone Research,* proceedings of the 1966 Laurentian Hormone Conference (vol. 23, 1967).

Bibliography: *Current Biography Yearbook 1966* (1967), 314–6; *New York Times* (Aug. 23, 1967), 45. [G.H.F.]

PINCUS, LOUIS ARIEH (Louis Abraham; 1912–), Zionist leader. Born in South Africa, Pincus practiced law from 1934 to 1948. He was chairman of the South African Zionist Socialist Party and co-founder of Habonim in the country. He was also vice-chairman of the Zionist Federation (1940–48). Pincus settled in Israel in 1948 and served as legal adviser and general secretary of the Ministry of Transportation until 1949. From then until 1956 he was the first managing director of *El Al. He practiced law in Israel from 1957 and was a member of the central bodies of *Mapai, the *Histadrut, and *Iḥud Olami from 1956. In 1961 he was elected a member of the *Jewish Agency Executive, and its treasurer. On the death of Moshe *Sharett in 1965, Pincus became acting chairman and at the 27th Zionist Congress (1966) was elected chairman of the executive. He was chairman of the Board of Governors of Tel Aviv University. [B.J.]

PINCZOW (Pol. **Pínczów;** Rus. **Pinchov;** Yid. **Pinchev**), town in Kielce province, S.E. Poland. During the 16th–18th centuries Pinczow was a busy market town in Sandomierz province. The date of the foundation of the Jewish community is unknown, but the fact that it sent representatives to the *Councils of the Lands testifies to its significance in the 17th century. During the attacks led by the Polish hetman S. *Czarniecki (1656), the Jews of Pinczow suffered comparatively little since they took refuge with the local margrave, and were defended by his troops. The Pinczow district *(galil)* was included in the province of *Lesser Poland. One of the most interesting relics possessed by the community is the hand-written prayer book which was completed (according to an inscription) by a scribe named Elijah b. Samuel Gronenn in January 1614 (published by S. Dubnow in *Voskhod,* 14, no. 4 (1894), 149–50). Other records of later years mention martyrs who died as a result of blood libel accusations and during the massacres in the 1640s and 1650s. In 1765 there were 2,862 Jews registered in the district, most of whom lived in the town itself; there were 2,877 Jews (70% of the total population) in the town in 1856 and 5,194 in 1897; in the latter years there were 13,716 Jews in the whole district.

Holocaust Period. At the outbreak of World War II there were about 3,500 Jews in Pinczow. In October 1942, 3,000 Jews were deported to *Treblinka death camp. During the deportation, hundreds of Jews fled into the surrounding forests. About 100 joined the two Jewish partisan units headed by Michal Majtek and Zalman Fajnsztat. These units merged and operated in the vicinity until February 1944, when they incurred heavy losses near Pawlowice. After the war the Jewish community of Pinczow was not reconstituted.

Bibliography: *Sefer Zikkaron li-Kehillat Pinchev* (1970); M. Baliński and T. Lipiński, *Starożytna Polska,* 1 (1845); M. Bersohn, *Dyplomataryusz dotyceący żydow w dawnej Polsce* (1910), s.v.; L. Lewin, *Judenverfolgungen im zweiten schwedisch-polnischen Kriege 1655–59* (1901). [Ed.]

PINE. One species of pine, the Aleppo pine *Pinus halepensis,* is indigenous to Israel. Other species of the same genus have been planted in the afforestation of modern Israel and as ornamental trees, among them the stone pine, *Pinus pinea*. The modern Hebrew name for the pine is *oren*, but this biblical name relates to a different species, the *bay tree. The Aleppo pine is one of the most beautiful forest trees of Israel. Only a few groves of it remain at the present day because it was felled for use as building material. Among the natural groves of this species is the Masrek ("comb") at Bet Meir in the Judean hills, so called because its high trunks, conspicuous on the horizon, look like a comb. The Aleppo pine was adopted as the most important forest tree of Israel, tens of thousands of acres being planted with it, because of its rapid growth, beauty, and abundant shade, as well as for its ability to grow on rocky ground. It is the *eẓ shemen* ("oil tree") of the Bible, as it is still called (in Aramaic) by the Jews of Kurdistan, and is so called because of its high turpentine content. Isaiah (41:19) mentions this tree among those that will fructify the wilderness on the path of the redeemed. In the time of Nehemiah its branches were used for covering the *sukkah* (Neh. 8:15). Ben Sira (50:10) compares the high priest to its tall evergreen flourishing top. In the Temple the cherubim and the doors were made from its wood (I Kings 6:23, 32). The pseudo-Jonathan Targum here renders *eẓ shemen* as olive tree, but it is impossible to make doors from the hollow trunk of the latter (see *Olive). Furthermore, the olive is mentioned in Nehemiah (8:15) together with the *eẓ shemen;* they cannot therefore be identical. Nor can the *eẓ shemen* be identified with the *Eleagnus angustifolia* (which in modern Hebrew is called *eẓ shemen*) since it does not fit the descriptions of *eẓ shemen* in the Bible and Mishnah. *Eẓ shemen* is enumerated among the four species of "cedar" *(erez)*, i.e., conifers (RH 23a). In mishnaic times its boughs were used for kindling the beacons that announced the appearance of the new moon (RH 2:3). They were also used as firewood for the altar (Tam. 2:3). The needle-like leaves of the pine contain fibers from which is produced "forest wool." In the Mishnah this is called *lekhesh*, and it is mentioned among the fibers whose wick may not be used for the Sabbath lamp (Shab. 2:1, 20b; TJ, *ibid.* 4d).

The stone pine, though not indigenous to Israel, is grown as an ornamental tree and for its edible and tasty nuts. These nuts are called *iẓtrubalin* in the Mishnah, which states that they may not be sold to idolators on their festivals (Av. Zar. 1:5). They are liable to tithes (TJ, Ma'as. 1:2, 48d). In the view of Saadiah Gaon the stone pine is the *tirzah* (JPS ilex; A.V. cypress) of Isaiah 44:14, mentioned as being used both for making idols and for firewood.

Aleppo pine *(Pinus halepinsis)* in a natural grove near Jerusalem. Photo Yosaif Cohain.

Bibliography: Loew, Flora, 3 (1924), 40–47; J. Feliks, *Olam ha-Ẓome'aḥ ha-Mikra'i* (1968[2]), 88–92. [J.F.]

PINEDA, JUAN DE (d. 1486), Converso martyr, commander in the Order of Santiago and the emissary of the head of the order, Juan *Pacheco, to the papal court. Born into a poor Converso family in Córdoba, in his youth, Pineda worked as a tailor and was known as Juan de Baena. Nothing is known of how he rose in Spanish society. In 1486 he was tried by the Inquisition on charges of having practiced Judaism. Among the accusations brought against him was that he had declared in 1464, when the Turks and Pope Pius II were at war, that the redemption of Israel would come through the Turks. He was burned at the stake on Aug. 16, 1486 in Toledo.

Bibliography: Baer, Spain, 2 (1966), 347ff.; Baer, Urkunden, 2 (1936), 468ff. [Ed.]

PINELES, HIRSCH MENDEL BEN SOLOMON (known as **"Shalosh"** from the last (Hebrew) letters of his name, Hir-**sch** Mende-**l** Pinele-**s;** 1806–1870), Galician scholar and writer. Pineles settled in Brody and joined the circle of young *maskilim* who gathered round Nachman *Krochmal. He perfected his German, and began to educate himself in philosophy, Greek, Latin, Arabic, and astronomy, specializing in mathematics and the calculation of the Jewish calendar. In 1853 he moved to Odessa, and in 1855 to Galati in Rumania, where he lived until his death. He was an active member of the *Alliance Israélite Universelle and involved in its program in Rumania.

Hirsch Mendel b. Solomon Pineles, Hebraic scholar. Jerusalem, J.N.U.L., Schwadron Collection.

Pineles began his literary career with a letter to Krochmal in 1836 published in *Kerem Ḥemed* (2 (1936), 108–113). He wrote the first critical article on Krochmal's *Moreh Nevukhei ha-Zeman* (in: *He-Ḥalutz*, 1 (1852), 123–4); and he published critical book reviews as well as numerous articles on a variety of subjects in *Kerem Ḥemed* (2 (1936), 125–9, 168–71), in *Ha-Maggid* (8–11 (1864–67)), *Yeshurun*, and elsewhere. For about 30 years he engaged in a fierce controversy with Ḥ. S. *Slonimsky on the method of calculating the Jewish calendar (see *Kerem Ḥemed*, 8 (1854), 27–37, 85–109).

Pineles is best known for his *Darkah shel Torah* (Vienna, 1861), a critical examination in 178 sections of the Mishnah and its interpretation, followed by a treatise on the Hebrew calendar including tables. The stated aim of the work was to justify the Oral Law and substantiate the words of the scribes where they deviate from the literal text. Pineles defended the Mishnah both against the authors of the Talmud, who honored it but distorted its plain meaning, and against the detractors of the Talmud, who attempted to find defects in it and to devalue it. He also sought to explain a number of difficult passages in the Babylonian and Jerusalem Talmuds. His work is characterized by critical acumen and boldness. Believing that some explanations given by the later *amoraim* distorted the original Mishnah, he attempted to interpret a number of *mishnayot* in a new way. His deviations from the traditional explanations of the *amoraim* were attacked by traditionalists, one of them being his brother-in-law, Moses b. Joel Waldberg, a leading banker in Bucharest (*Kakh hi Darkah shel Torah,* pt. 1, Lemberg, 1864; pt. 2, Jassy, 1868). Pineles, however, maintained that he had no heretical intent and himself attacked certain scholars for their extreme views—chiefly Abraham *Geiger for his *Urschrift und Uebersetzung der Bibel in ihrer Abhaengigkeit von der innern Entwicklung des Judenthums* (1857; a review of which is published at the end of *Darkah shel Torah*) and J. H. *Schorr—stressing his own attachment to tradition (*Darkah shel Torah,* no. 14, p. 19).

Bibliography: Fuenn, Keneset, 286–8; Lachower, Sifrut, 2 (1929), 191, 311; B. Wachstein, *Die hebraeische Publizistik in Wien,* 1 (1930), 160–1; N. M. Gelber (ed.), *Arim ve-Immahot be-Yisrael.* 6 (1955), 211; Kressel, Leksikon, 613–4. [Y.Ho.]

PINELES, SAMUEL (1843–1928), early member of Ḥovevei Zion and the Zionist Movement in Rumania. Born in Brody, Galicia, the son of Hirsch Mendel *Pineles, he moved with his family to Galati, Rumania, in 1863. Early in his youth he began his activity in the Ḥibbat Zion movement, and submitted to the central board of the Alliance Israélite Universelle in Paris periodical informa-

Samuel Pineles, early Rumanian Zionist. Jerusalem, J.N.U.L., Schwadron Collection.

tion and documents concerning Rumanian Jewry. In 1881 he was elected to the board of the Rumanian Association for the settlement of Ereẓ Israel. He took part in the conference of the settlement societies held in Focsani in January 1882 and was elected chairman of the central board, situated in Galati. Pineles did much for the Rumanian immigrants and their two settlements in Palestine, Rosh Pinnah and Zamarin (later known as Zikhron Ya'akov). As chairman of the central board, he mobilized resources from Baron Edmond de *Rothschild for the purpose of purchasing lands in the Golan to be settled by Rumanian Jews. He participated in all of the first ten congresses and was a member of the Zionist General Council. He was one of the founders of the *Jewish Colonial Trust. In 1909 he gave the *Jewish National Fund 30,000 francs, which he had received from Rothschild for the lands in the Golan acquired by Rumanian members of Ḥibbat Zion. In 1920 he took part in the Committee for Jewish refugees who went to Galati after the pogroms in the Ukraine. In 1965 his remains were reinterred in Jerusalem.

Bibliography: I. Klausner, *Ḥibbat Ẓiyyon be-Rumanyah* (1958), index; L. Jaffe (ed.), *Sefer ha-Congress* (1950[2]), 348–9. [I.K.]

PINES, MEYER ISSER (1881 or 1882–1942?), leader of the Territorialist movement in his youth, Yiddish writer, and journalist. Born in Mogilev, Russia, Pines grew up in Rozinay, Grodno district. He received his doctorate for his dissertation, *Histoire de la littérature judéo-allemande* (Paris, 1911), which was translated into Yiddish (Warsaw, 1911), Russian, and German. Israel *Zinberg and Ber *Borochov stamped the work as dilettantish, a judgment held also by later scholars. Pines is presumed to have died in a Russian deportation camp sometime after 1942.

Bibliography: LNYL, 7 (1968), 149–51. [L.P.]

PINES, NOAH (1871–1939), Hebrew educator and writer. Born in Shklov, Russia, he studied at the yeshivah of Volozhin. At an early age, he became a teacher and established a modern *ḥeder* in Lublin at the beginning of the century. After completing his pedagogic studies in German and Swiss universities, he emigrated to Palestine (1919), taught in the Levinsky Teachers' Seminary of Tel Aviv, and served as its principal from 1923 until his death.

He published study manuals, articles, and essays on educational problems. His book *Ha-Zamir* (1903), children's poems for reading and singing, was an important innovation. A volume of his poems *Ẓilẓelei Erev* (1940) and a pedagogic work, *Ketavim Pedagogiyyim* (1941), were published posthumously.

Bibliography: Kressel, Leksikon, 2 (1967), 619–20. [G.K.]

PINES, SHLOMO (**Solomon;** 1908–), historian of philosophy and science. Born in Paris, Pines taught at the Institut d'Histoire des Sciences et des Techniques de l'Universite de Paris from 1937 to 1939. He settled in Ereẓ Israel in 1940. From 1948 to 1952 he served in the Middle

Shlomo Pines, Israel historian of philosophy. Courtesy Hebrew University, Jerusalem.

East division of the Israel Ministry for Foreign Affairs. In 1952 he began teaching at the Hebrew University and in 1961 Pines became professor of general and Jewish philosophy. He was a fellow of the Israel Academy of Sciences and Humanities, and in 1968 received the Israel prize. He served as coeditor of the *Corpus Commentariorum Averrois in Aristotelem* of the Medieval Academy of America. The 20th volume of the philosophic journal *Iyyun* (1969) was dedicated to him on the occasion of his 60th birthday.

Pines wrote in the fields of Islamic philosophy and science, the Greek antecedents of Islamic philosophy and science, and Jewish philosophy. In his first book, *Beitraege zur islamischen Atomenlehre* (1936), he analyzed the atomic theories of the Muslim theologians. He wrote several detailed analyses of the thought of Abu al Barakāt ben Ali al-Baghdādī *Hibat Allah, a hitherto barely known critic of Islamic Aristotelianism. In the field of Jewish philosophy he published a new English translation of Maimonides' *Guide of the Perplexed* (1963) with an introduction tracing Maimonides' philosophic sources. In his *Scholasticism after Thomas Aquinas and the Teachings of Hasdai Crescas and his Predecessors* (1967) he proposed the thesis that late medieval Jewish philosophers, such as *Levi b. Gershom, *Jedaiah b. Abraham Bedersi (ha-Penini), and Ḥasdai *Crescas, were familiar with the philosophic and scientific doctrines of the late medieval Christian scholastics. In "Spinoza's Tractatus Theologico-Politicus, Maimonides, and Kant" (in: *Scripta Hierosolymitana,* 20 (1968), 3–54) he discusses the interrelation of Maimonides and Spinoza. He also published *A New Fragment of Xenocrates* (1961).

Bibliography: For further information on his writings between 1957 and 1968 see *Reshimat ha-Pirsumim ha-Madda'iyyim shel Ḥavrei ha-Makhon le-Madda'ei ha-Yahadut* (1969), 82–84. [Y.La./A.Hy.]

PINES, YEHIEL MICHAEL (**"Michal"**; 1843–1913), writer, early exponent of religious Zionism, and *yishuv* leader. Born in Ruzhany, Belorussia, into a family of prosperous merchants and Torah scholars, Pines was

Yeḥiel Michael Pines, Hebrew writer and early religious Zionist. Jerusalem, J.N.U.L., Schwadron Collection.

influenced in his youth by Mordecai Gimpel *Jaffe, an early leader of *Ḥovevei Zion, who headed a yeshivah maintained by Pines' family. He studied both traditional subjects and foreign languages and science, and the fusion of the two spheres of knowledge led to a romantic-religious outlook. He believed that Jewish life should be reformed, but was opposed to deliberate, religious reforms that would undermine the foundations of tradition and increase assimilation. He thought that a reformed way of life would inevitably bring about certain changes of *halakhah* without affecting the sanctity of the Jewish religion. During the 1860s Pines developed these ideas in his controversy with M. L. *Lilienblum, J. L. *Gordon, and others, mainly through his articles in *Ha-Karmel, *Ha-Meliẓ,* and **Ha-Levanon.* The articles were collected in his book, *Yaldei Ruḥi* ("Children of My Spirit," 2 vols., 1872), and his ideas were later expanded by *Aḥad Ha-Am, who restyled them in his own clear, polished language.

In 1877, while he was living at his father-in-law's home in Mogilev, Pines was asked by the Moses Montefiore Testimonial Fund in London to serve as its representative in Ereẓ Israel. He accepted eagerly, reached Jaffa a year later, and settled in Jerusalem (1878) at the home of his relative, Yosef *Rivlin, the secretary of the Va'ad Kelali (General Committee of the **ḥalukkah*), thus arousing the enmity of Rivlin's many opponents in Jerusalem (Ḥasidim and *maskilim,* Sephardim, and religious extremists; the latter, supporters of Rabbi Y. L. *Diskin persecuted Pines and proclaimed him "excommunicated").

On behalf of his London sponsors, Pines conducted investigations into the spiritual, cultural, and particularly the economic problems of the *yishuv,* proposing the founding of an agricultural settlement, the building of houses and new quarters, and the establishment of artisan and industrial projects. The Montefiore Fund concentrated on granting aid for the construction of houses and Jerusalem was thus expanded through the building of several new quarters. Pines' letters to the Fund trustees appear in volumes 2 and 3 of *Mivḥar Kitvei Y. M. Pines* ("Selected Writings of Y. M. Pines") and in his *Binyan ha-Areẓ* ("Building of the Land"), volumes 1 and 2 (1934).

Pines tried to set up artisan and industrial projects with the help of Montefiore Fund loans, and with his own money as well, but they proved a failure and brought about his dismissal in 1885. (His son-in-law, David Yellin, was appointed to the same post in 1901.) In 1882 Pines became friendly with Eliezer *Ben-Yehuda who had just arrived in Ereẓ Israel, and together they established the Teḥiyyat Israel ("Israel Renaissance") Society, whose aim was, inter alia, to introduce Hebrew as a spoken language. When the first members of *Bilu arrived at the end of the same year, Pines became their patron and established the Shivat he-Ḥarash ve-ha-Masger ("Return of the Craftsmen and the Smiths") Society for them in Jerusalem. With Ḥovevei Zion funds he bought for them the lands for the settlement of *Gederah in 1884 and was the settlement's patron for several years. In 1885 K. Z. *Wissotzky appointed him a member of the executive committee of Ḥovevei Zion in Palestine. For several months in 1886 he edited **Ha-Ẓevi,* Ben-Yehuda's newspaper, while the latter was abroad, but the friendship between the two was affected by the outbreak of the violent controversy regarding the Sabbatical Year *(shemittah),* which fell in 1888/89. Although Pines' conservative attitude to this question aroused opposition in Ḥovevei Zion circles, he was elected in 1890 to the organizations's executive committe in Jaffa, headed by Vladimir *Tiomkin. At about the same time Pines joined the *Benei Moshe Society, but its leader Aḥad Ha-Am, who wanted to prevent discussions of religious problems in the Society, advocated his departure from that group. In 1892, after a crisis in the activities of the executive committee of Ḥovevei Zion, Pines was dismissed and thereafter affiliated himself with the old *yishuv,* even becoming one of its main spokesmen. His views on nation and religion, which he then developed in his articles in **Ha-Ḥavaẓẓelet* and in special pamphlets, were shortly afterward adopted by the *Mizrachi Party. In 1893 he became a trustee of the Ashkenazi community's charitable institutions in Jerusalem, and the librarian and a teacher of Talmud in the Hebrew Teachers' college.

Pines was first and foremost a thinker, writer, and craftsman of Hebrew language and style. He displayed outstanding knowledge of biblical style and language (into which he translated various scientific books) and greatly influenced his brother-in-law and pupil, Ze'ev *Jawitz, who in turn influenced Ḥ. N. *Bialik. Pines was conversant with mishnaic style (see his *Mishnat Ereẓ Yisrael*), the medieval style rhyming prose, and the conglomerate style that he employed in his articles and his many letters to employers and to people who approached him with queries regarding settlement in Ereẓ Israel. *Yaldei Ruḥi* and some of his letters and articles appeared in the three volumes of *Kitvei Y. M. Pines* ("Writings of Y. M. Pines," 1934–39), edited by his sons-in-law, David Yellin and Yosef *Meyuḥas. His selected writings, *Mivḥar Kitvei Pines,* appeared in 1946, edited and with a preface by G. Kressel. Kefar Pines, a moshav in the Sharon Plain, is named for him.

Bibliography: N. Sokolow, *Ḥibbath Zion* (Eng., 1935), index; A. Boehm, *Die zionistische Bewegung* (1935), index; G. Raphael, *Rabbi Yeḥi'el Mikha'el Pines* (1954); M. Michaeli, *Rabbi Yeḥi'el Mikhal Pines* (1928); A. Druyanow (ed.), *Ketavim le-Toledot Ḥibbat Ẓiyyon ve-Yishuv Ereẓ Yisrael,* 1 (1919), index; 3 (1932), index; Ḥ. N. Bialik, in: *Ha-Olam,* 7 no. 13/14 (1913), 23–25; I. Yellin, *Le-Ẓe'eẓa'ai,* 2, vols. (1938–41), passim; Y. Nissenbaum, *Ha-Dat ve-ha-Teḥiyyah ha-Le'ummit* (1920), 145–51. [G.Y.]

PINHEIRO, MOSES (17th century), Shabbatean, born in Izmir. A contemporary of *Shabbetai Ẓevi, Pinheiro studied talmudic and kabbalistic literature with him in their youth (1640–50). There is no indication that he supported Shabbetai Ẓevi's messianic claims in 1648. About 1650 he left Izmir and settled in *Leghorn, where he became a highly respected scholar. When the news of the Shabbatean awakening reached Italy, he became at once one of its most ardent spokesmen, continuing to believe that Shabbetai Ẓevi was Messiah long after his *apostasy. As delegate of the Leghorn community, he went to see Shabbetai Ẓevi in the summer of 1666, at the height of the excitement, but arrived in Izmir after the apostasy. There he received communications from both Shabbetai Ẓevi and *Nathan of Gaza which strengthened his faith. In March 1667 he returned to Italy with a delegation of three other communities. Nathan stayed at his house on his visit to Italy in 1668. Pinheiro, who was the center of the Shabbatean group in

Leghorn, maintained a correspondence with Shabbetai Ẓevi over the years and also took an interest in Abraham *Cardozo. As shown by Abraham *Rovigo's notebook on Shabbatean matters (Ben-Zvi Institute, Ms. 2265), he was still considered a "believer" about 1690. When and whether he finally gave up his belief is unknown.

His daughter was the mother of the well-known kabbalist and rabbi Joseph *Ergas, who kept silent about his grandfather's Shabbatean connections. Rabbi *Malachi ha-Kohen of Leghorn, Ergas' pupil, though an outspoken foe of the Shabbatean movement, praised Pinheiro highly for his piety and ascetic life in his foreword to Ergas' responsa, *Divrei Yosef* (1742). Several of Pinheiro's recollections on Shabbetai Ẓevi have been preserved.

Bibliography: Scholem, Shabbetai Ẓevi, index; J. Sasportas, *Ẓiẓat Novel Ẓevi* (1954), index; I. Tishby, in: *Zion*, 22 (1957), 31–33; idem, in: *Sefunot*, 3–4 (1960), 93, 107; Freimann, *Inyenei Shabbetai Ẓevi* (1912), 45, 95. [G.Sch.]

PINKAS (פִּנְקָס), record book of Jewish autonomous units, used mainly in the Middle Ages. The *pinkas* contained minutes of meetings, bylaws, lists of officers elected at the annual meetings, records of disciplinary actions against recalcitrant members, of tax assessments and fines, of trials, of unusual historical events, and an endless variety of other entries reflecting the life of the local community. Each community and each **ḥevrah*, including artisan guilds, had its own *pinkas*, as did the *Councils of the Lands in Poland, Lithuania, and Moravia. *Pinkasim* of local communities and those of the Councils have been published.

See also *Autonomy.

Bibliography: Baron, Community, 2 (1942), 113, index s.v. *Minute books;* I. Levitats, *Jewish Community in Russia, 1772–1844* (1943), index s.v. *Minute book;* A. Rechtman, *Yidishe Etnografye un Folklor* (1958), 193–240. [I.L.]

PINKAS, DAVID ẒVI (1895–1952), Mizrachi leader and Israel politician. Pinkas was born in Sopron, Hungary, into a religious Zionist family, which settled in Vienna when he was a child. He became active in the Mizrachi movement and represented it as a delegate at the 13th Zionist Congress. In 1925 Pinkas settled in Palestine, became the manager of the Mizrachi bank, and, in 1932, was elected to the Tel Aviv municipal council, heading its Education Department from 1935. He was also a Mizrachi representative to the Asefat ha-Nivḥarim and the Va'ad Le'ummi, becoming treasurer and director of its department of Religious Communities and the Rabbinate. After the establishment of the State of Israel, he was elected to the First Knesset on behalf of the United Religious Front, and after the elections to the Second Knesset, in October 1951, he was appointed minister of transportation. In this capacity he regulated the austerity measures for fuel consumption and stipulated that all vehicles should not be driven two days a week, and that one of these days should be Saturday (the Sabbath). This regulation aroused sharp protest from extreme circles opposing "religious coercion."

Bibliography: Tidhar, 2 (1947), 855–6. [Ed.]

PINNER, EPHRAIM MOSES BEN ALEXANDER SUSSKIND (c. 1800–1880), talmudist. Born in Pinne (district of Poznan), Pinner studied Talmud under Rabbi *Jacob of Lissa. In 1831 he compiled an abbreviated form of the Talmud, *Kiẓẓur Talmud Yerushalmi ve-Talmud Bavli*. Pinner is best known for his ambitious scheme to translate into German the whole of the Talmud; he enlisted the moral support of some prominent rabbis, including Rabbi Moses *Sofer (Schreiber) of Pressburg, who eventually withdrew his name. It appears that Pinner maintained that Rabbi Nathan Marcus *Adler of Hanover (later of London) had undertaken to translate the difficult tractates *Eruvin* and *Yevamot* under this scheme, but Adler denied the existence of such an arrangement. In 1842 *Berakhot* was published in Hebrew with German translation. Czar Nicholas I lent his name to the project, together with other notables. The volume was dedicated to the czar, who had shown an unusual interest in the translation of the Talmud before Pinner's venture—and not with the best of intentions. No further volume appeared. Samuel David Luzzatto criticized the work somewhat adversely in *Kerem Ḥemed* (2 (1836), 174–82).

Bibliography: S. Sofer (ed.), *Iggerot Soferim* (1928), pt. 2, 73–78; R. N. N. Rabinowitz, *Ma'amar al Hadpasat ha-Talmud*, ed. by A. M. Habermann (1952), 246–8. [A.T.]

PINNER, FELIX (1880–1942), German economist and journalist. Born in Birnbaum (Posen), he engaged initially in economic and journalistic activities which also included a strong interest in the colonization of Palestine by German Zionists. In 1924 he became editor of the financial section of the *Berliner Tageblatt*, one of Germany's leading liberal dailies. He left Germany for the U.S. soon after Hilter's rise to power, but failed to integrate in his new surroundings. He took his own life, and that of his wife, in New York during a period of mental depression due to financial difficulties.

His principal publications are *Emil Rathenau und das elektrische Zeitalter* (1918); *Deutsche Wirtschaftsfuehrer* (1925, published under the pseudonym Frank Fassland); *Das Neue Palaestina* (1926); *Tannerhuette; der Roman einer Sozialisierung* (1928); and *Die grossen Weltkrisen* . . . (1937). [J.O.R.]

PINNER, MORITZ (1828–c. 1909), U.S. antislavery activist in the Civil War period. Pinner was born in Prussia. He was one of a handful of immigrant Jews who played a significant local role in the founding of the Republican Party and in the propaganda efforts against slavery which helped to bring on the Civil War. He participated in abolitionist activities in Missouri as early as 1856, served as editor of Republican antislavery papers in St. Louis and Kansas City, and was a member of state and national Republican conventions in 1860. Said to have been offered a diplomatic post by Lincoln, Pinner preferred military service, although the reports of his commissioned service are confused.

Bibliography: Kohler, in: AJHSP, 5 (1897), 152–3; Markens, *ibid.*, 17, (1909), 139–41. [B.W.K.]

PINSK, capital of Pinsk oblast, Belorussian S.S.R. The Jewish community there was established before 1506 by some 12 to 15 families (about 60–75 persons) from *Brest-Litovsk who settled in Pinsk instead of returning to Lithuania after the Jews were granted permission to return. Pinsk was then a Russian-Orthodox town and capital of a semi-independent principality. In 1506 Prince Feodor Yaroslavski granted the settlers the same rights enjoyed by the Jews of Lithuania, and the status of a community. The separate existence of the principality came to an end in 1521 and Pinsk was incorporated into Lithuania.

By 1566 the community consisted of about 55 families (approximately 275 persons; c. 7% of the total population). It numbered over 1,000 (c. 20% of the total) in 1648, and about 2,000 at the beginning of the 18th century, when they constituted the large majority of the town and controlled most of its life, there having been a severe decline in the Christian population during the second half of the 17th century. Subsequently the Jewish population numbered 13,681 in 1871 (77.7%); 21,819 in 1896 (77.3%); 28,063 in 1914 (72.5%); 17,513 in 1921 (74.6%); and 20,200 in 1939. Pinsk thus remained a "Jewish town" until the Holocaust.

Figure 1. The Great Synagogue of Pinsk, built in 1640, photographed in the 1920s. Courtesy Yad Vashem Archives, Jerusalem.

Until 1648 the Jews of Pinsk were guaranteed the legal status of citizens, complete protection of their persons and property, freedom to engage in commerce, moneylending, and crafts, and the right to organize their internal life according to the precepts of their religion. The favorable geographical position of the region of Pinsk on the junctions of roads and waterways, and colonizing activity there during the 16th century, encouraged its development. Jews engaged in varied activities including the ownership (later lease) of estates, the lease of taxes and customs duties, commerce, moneylending, and crafts. The community leaders, descendants of the founding nucleus, mainly dealt in business connected with estates and engaged in moneylending. Later they entered the wholesale trade also, as well as the leasing of tax collection and customs duties. In the middle of the 16th century, Pinsk Jews took up the then thriving export of grain and forest products. In the 1560s Nahum Pesahovich was outstanding for the scope and variety of his business activities. As in the rest of the region, the Pinsk Jews benefited from the support of the Catholic nobles against the Russian-Orthodox Belorussian townsmen. In these circumstances the status granted to the Pinsk municipality under the *Magdeburg Law in 1581 did not greatly hamper the Jews though it contained several restrictions on their trade.

The leasing and subleasing of estates by Jews resulted in an increasing periphery of Jewish inhabitants who settled in villages and new townlets established around Pinsk which came under its jurisdiction within the structure of the *Councils of the Lands. The community consolidated and developed. As one of the three original leading communities of the Lithuanian Council, Pinsk played a prominent role in the shaping of the council's policy and activity.

The period between 1648 and 1667 was one of wars and misfortunes. At the time of the *Chmielnicki massacres, Pinsk was taken on Oct. 26, 1648. Scores of Jews there were murdered in the town and on the roads, though most of them managed to escape in good time and were thus saved. A number of those who had remained in the town became converted to Christianity, but later returned to Judaism. Before the capture of Pinsk by the Russians during the Polish-Russian War (1654–67), all the Jews fled, in general managing to save much of their property. In 1660 the community suffered again from the depredations of the Muscovite armies and the Cossacks: some Jews were murdered, and property was lost. In this period of troubles, the Pinsk community showed the resilience and vital forces inherent in Jewish society and community leadership. When the numbers of the Christian townsmen were reduced they retreated to the suburbs and villages, where many of them turned to agriculture, whereas the Jews of Pinsk timed and organized their escape (in 1648 and 1655) with relative success and took measures to preserve at least part of their property. With peace they rapidly resumed their activities in the town, taking up new livelihoods if their former ones were no longer viable. The community leadership energetically restored community life, helped the refugees, aided in the ransoming of prisoners, and renewed the educational network and Torah study.

From 1667 until the beginning of the 18th century, the economic situation took a turn for the worse. Large-scale leasing disappeared, numerous Jews became impoverished and were compelled to seek new occupations, and many Jews of Pinsk turned to dealing in alcoholic beverages, most of them as retailers in the town and villages. Jewish trade diminished in scale and in part converted to retail trade; credit became difficult and many had to borrow from noblemen. Even the community administration itself had to borrow from them and from church officials, and gradually sank under a load of debt. However, the number of Jews in Pinsk increased, and the proliferation of small Jewish settlements around Pinsk proceeded. The same social circles which had led the community before 1648 continued to do so until the close of the century. In these difficult times there were many scholars in Pinsk, and renowned rabbis held office. These include Naphtali Gunzburg (officiated from 1664), Israel b. Samuel of Tarnopol (from 1667), Joel b. Isaac Eisik Heilperin (1691), and Isaac b. Jonah *Teomim Fraenkel (1693–1703). The rabbi and *maggid* Judah Leib *Pukhovitser, who lived in Pinsk during the last third of the 17th century, exerted considerable influence.

Figure 2. Ark of the Law and reader's desk of the Pinsk Great Synagogue, 1932. Courtesy YIVO, New York.

The tense situation in Poland-Lithuania during the first quarter of the 18th century, the continuing economic crisis, and the burden of taxation and debts, gave rise to internal tensions within the community and to a conflict of interests between the community of Pinsk and its subordinate communities, whose numbers continued to increase during the 18th century. In 1719, controversies broke out between the council of the communities of the province of *Volhynia and the community of Pinsk over the jurisdiction of several village communities of northern Volhynia. With the official abolition of the Council of the Lands in 1764, almost all the subordinate communities rejected Pinsk's authority, and after a prolonged struggle the weakened central community lost control.

*Ḥasidism spread to Pinsk and *Karlin during the 1760s. Aaron b. Jacob of Karlin made Karlin a center of Ḥasidism equal in importance to *Mezhirech. Until the early 1780s, Ḥasidism was the predominating influence in Pinsk and Karlin. The community leadership adopted a neutral position toward Ḥasidism. However, under severe pressure by the community leadership of Vilna and *Elijah b. Solomon Zalman, the Gaon of Vilna, the leadership of Pinsk associated itself with the ban against the Ḥasidim at the fair of *Zelva in 1781. *Levi Isaac b. Meir of Berdichev was dismissed from his position as rabbi of Pinsk in 1785, but he had apparently already completed his official ten-year term of office. At the same time Solomon of Karlin also left Karlin for *Vladimir-Volynski (Ludmir). In 1785 *Avigdor b. Joseph Ḥayyim, an avowed opponent of Ḥasidism, was elected rabbi of Pinsk and district. However, he did not succeed in imposing his authority on the community, and the ḥasidic villages in the vicinity, so that the Ḥasidim regained their strength.

Under Russian Rule. In 1793 Pinsk was incorporated into Russia and became a district capital in the province of Minsk. The Ḥasidim then gained control of the community administration and dismissed R. Avigdor from his position. Under Russian rule the Jews of Pinsk and Karlin were granted equal rights with the townsmen, and a small number of Jews belonged to the merchant sector. At the beginning of Russian rule the economic activity of the Jews was reduced and their situation apparently became precarious. A change for the better began in the 1820s. From then on Pinsk played an important role as a center for the *salt trade of Lithuania and in the exploitation of forest resources for timber export. Prominent in the economic life and community leadership of Pinsk-Karlin at that time was Saul b. Moses Levin of Karlin (1775–1834), an avowed opponent of the Ḥasidim. During the 19th century the wealthiest merchants settled in Karlin, which gradually became a stronghold of the *Mitnaggedim.*

The economic improvement in Pinsk continued during the 1830s, helped on by the government's economic policy which, among other measures, paved the way for the development of industry and the agricultural output of the Ukraine, and created opportunities for export of its agricultural surpluses. Pinsk became a transit center for trade between southwestern Russia and the Baltic ports. Members of the *Levin and *Luria families held a prominent place in this commerce. The Jewish merchant class was broadened, its capital increased, and a stratum of white-collar workers and agents from Pinsk in the service of its wealthy merchants became active throughout the Ukraine. This prosperity in Pinsk lasted until the 1870s. Much of the capital accumulated by the merchants of Pinsk was invested in the markets of the Ukraine. During the 1850s a number of Pinsk merchants put into service steamships for the transportation of goods and passengers. In the 1860s Moses Luria established a steam-powered oil

פינסקער שטימע
№ 46 Pinsker Sztyme

Figure 3. Front page of a 1937 issue of the Yiddish newspaper *Pinsker Sztyme.* From B. Hoffmann (ed.), *Toyznt Yor Pinsk,* New York, 1941.

press and mill. However after the construction in the 1860s of the Kiev-Brest-Litovsk railroad, a severe crisis struck the city.

During the 1860s there were between 750 and 950 Jewish craftsmen in Pinsk. The philanthropist Gad Asher provided training for orphans and children of the poor in crafts, and the large number of Jewish artisans at this time was a feature of the city. In 1855 a Jewish agricultural settlement was established in the village of Ivanichi near Pinsk.

At the close of the 19th century members of the Luria family established nail and plywood factories. A match factory was established in 1892. Jewish workers were employed in the factories and a Jewish proletariat formed. Of the 54 industrial enterprises in Pinsk in 1914, 49 were owned by Jews. Industrialization was accompanied by an economic recovery in both commerce and crafts, in which Jews also predominated. Stirrings of the *Haskalah movement appeared in Pinsk with the beginning of the economic prosperity of the 1830s, and its influence gradually increased. A Russian government school for the children of Jews in the first category of merchants was founded in Pinsk in 1853, and during the 1850s to 1860s, 26 to 38 pupils studied there. During the same year a Jewish school for girls was established. In 1878 a private school, in which emphasis was placed on Hebrew studies, was founded by the *Kazyonny Ravvin* Abraham Ḥayyim *Rosenberg. During the early 1860s *talmud torah* schools were founded in Pinsk and Karlin whose curricula included the study of the Hebrew and Russian languages and arithmetic in addition to religious studies. Many were still educated in the *ḥadarim.* In 1888 a vocational school was founded in Pinsk. During the 1890s modern *ḥadarim* were founded under the tutelage of the Ḥovevei Zion, whose members included the young Chaim *Weizmann. Zionist and *Bund organizations were also formed in Pinsk in this period.

In Independent Poland. During the initial period of Polish

Figure 4. Ha-Teḥiyyah Zionist Youth convention in Pinsk, 1906. Courtesy A. Rafaeli-Zenziper, Archive for Russian Zionism, Tel Aviv.

rule after World War I, on April 5, 1919, the Poles executed 35 prominent Jews following a framed-up charge against them. Between the two world wars the majority of the Jewish population in Pinsk was Zionist in orientation while a minority adhered to the Bund and other parties. Many Jews emigrated to Ereẓ Israel, among them members of *Bilu including Aharon Eliyahu *Eisenberg, the founder of Reḥovot, and Ya'akov *Shertok. The kibbutz *Gevat was founded in 1926 by pioneers from Pinsk. The Jewish educational network was widely extended. New schools were founded: the Tel Ḥai School of the *Po'alei Zion (with Hebrew and Yiddish as the languages of instruction); two *Tarbut schools, one in Pinsk and one in Karlin; and the Chechick gymnasium (Polish). The Hebrew high school Tarbut, founded in 1923, existed until the beginning of Soviet rule. [M.Na.]

Holocaust and Postwar Periods. When Pinsk was under Soviet rule from 1939 to 1941, the Jewish institutions, including political parties and schools, were closed down. Some of the Zionist and Bund leaders were arrested and many Jewish businessmen and members of the free professions were expelled from the city. A large number of Jewish refugees from western Poland found shelter in Pinsk, but were deported to the Soviet interior in 1940. Pinsk served as a stopover for many refugees trying illegally to reach Vilna. Pinsk fell to the Germans on July 4, 1941. A month later 8,000 Jewish men were rounded up and marched a few miles beyond the outskirts where they were murdered and buried in mass graves. A few individuals escaped from the mass graves. A similar *Aktion* was carried out a few days later against 3,000 Jewish men, including the elderly and children. They were executed in the nearby village of Kozlakowicze. After these executions a series of repressive economic measures were enforced. On one occasion the Jews of Pinsk were asked to hand over 20 kilograms of gold.

The first head of the *Judenrat was David Alper; he resigned after a short time and was executed in August 1941. He was succeeded by Benjamin Bokczański. A ghetto was established toward the end of April 1942. The Jews there struggled against starvation and epidemics, and some risked their lives to bring in food to the ghetto. The Judenrat established a hospital, a public kitchen, and some places of work. In July 1942 all the patients in the Jewish hospital were murdered. Soon afterward, groups of Jews secretly organized resistance. On Oct. 28, 1942, the final *Aktion* took place and all the Pinsk Jews, with the exception of 150 artisans, were killed. During this *Aktion* a desperate attempt was made by the resistance group to break through the cordon of German soldiers. Some managed to reach the forests but were caught by the local population, and a very few succeeded in joining the partisans. On Dec. 23, 1942, the remaining 150 artisans were executed at the local cemetery and the ghetto was liquidated. The swamps and forests around Pinsk sheltered many Jews. Polesie served as a base for partisan activities in which many Jews who escaped from the ghettos and from execution participated either as individuals or as Jewish units. After the war, under the Soviet regime, community life was not renewed in Pinsk, although Jewish families settled there. In 1970 the Jewish population was estimated at 1,500. There was no synagogue. The last prayerhouse had been closed down by the police in 1966. The old Karlin cemetery, desecrated by the Nazis, was converted by the Soviet authorities into a park in 1959. The Jews did not comply with the request of the authorities to remove the bones for reinterment in the Pinsk cemetery. [Ar.W.]

Bibliography: S. Dubnow, *Pinkas ha-Medinah* (1925); I. Halpern, in: *Horeb,* 2 (1935), additions to the above work; idem, in: *Zion,* 3 (1938), 51–57 (*Yehudim ve-Yahadut be-Mizrah Eiropah* (1969), 48–54); M. Nadaw, in: *Zion,* 31 (1966), 153–96; 34 (1969), 98–108; idem, *Toledot Kehillat-Pinsk, 1506–1706* (dissertation, Heb. Univ. of Jerusalem, 1964); idem, in: Israel Historical Society, *Kovez Harza'ot* (1968), 159–77; A. Shochat, *ibid.,* 12 (1965), 121–33; Meir b. Samuel of Szczebreszyn, *Ẓok ha-Ittim* (Cracow, 1650); N. N. Hannover, *Yeven Meẓullah* (Venice, 1653); N. Tamir (ed.), *Sefer Edut ve-Zikkaron li-Kehillat Pinsk-Karlin,* 2 vols. (vol. 2, 1966; vol. 1 in print); S. M. Rabinowitz, in: *Talpiyyot* (1895); M. Wilenský, *Ḥasidim u-Mitnaggedim* (1970); H. Tchemerinsky, *Ayarati Motele* (1951); Ḥ. Weizmann-Lichtenstein, *Be-Ẓel Koratenu* (1948); A. A. Feinstein, *Megillat ha-Puraniyyot* (1929); J. Eliasberg, *Be-Olam ha-Hafikhot* (1965); C. Weizmann, *Massah u-Ma'as* (1949); idem, *Letters and Papers,* 1 (1968); M. Shomer Zunser, *Yesterday* (1939); B. Hoffman (ed.), *Toyznt Yor Pinsk: Geshikhte* *fun der Shtot* (1941); A. Luria, in: *YIVO Bleter*, 13 (1938), 390–428; M. Karman, *Mayne Zikhroynes; Hundert Yor Pinsk* (stencil, Haifa, 1953); Z. Rabinowitsch, in: *He-Avar*, 17 (1970), 252–80: *Pinsker Shtodt Luekh*, 2 vols. (1903–04); K. Kontrym, *Podróż Kontryma ... odbyta wroki 1829 po Polesiu* (Poznan, 1839); S. A. Bershadski, *Russko-yevreyski arkhiv*, 1–2 (1882); idem, *Litovskiye yevrei* (1883); idem, in: *Yevreyskaya Biblioteka*, 8 (1880), 1–32 (suppl.); *Regesty i nadpisi*, 2 vols. (1899–1912); Yu. Janson, *Pinsk i yego rayon* (1869); I. Zelenski, *Materilay dlya geografii i statistiki Rossii: Minskaya guberniya*, 2 pts. (1864). HOLOCAUST AND POSTWAR PERIODS: *Sefer ha-Partizanim ha-Yehudim*, 1 (1958), index; M. Kahanovich, *Milḥemet ha-Partizanim ha-Yehudiyyim be-Mizraḥ Eiropah* (1954), index.

PINSKER, LEON (**Judah Leib**; 1821–1891), leader of the *Ḥibbat Zion movement. Born in Tomaszow, Poland, Pinsker studied at the school of his father Simḥah *Pinsker, a Hebrew writer and scholar, in Odessa. He was one of the first Jews to attend Odessa University, where he studied law. However, he discovered that being a Jew, he had no chance of becoming a lawyer and studied medicine at the University of Moscow, returning to practice in Odessa in 1849. Pinsker was one of the founders of the first Russian Jewish weekly, *Razsvet* ("Dawn"), to which he was a regular contributor. The editors attempted to acquaint the Jewish population with Russian culture and encourage them to speak Russian. These aims were more strongly expressed in the weekly Russian-language publication *Sion*, which replaced *Razsvet* and of which Pinsker was one of the editors for about half a year. He was also one of the founders of the Odessa branch of the Society for the Dissemination of Enlightenment among Jews, whose aim was similar to that of the periodical. Pinsker contributed to the Russian-language weekly *Den* ("Day"), founded by the society, which called on Jews to assimilate into Russian society. The pogroms that began in 1871 in Odessa severely shook the enlightened Jews; the weekly stopped publication, and the Odessa branch of the society closed down. Thereafter, Pinsker concentrated on medicine and published a book in German on the medicinal value of the sea and the Liman spa at Odessa (Vienna, 1881). He also became prominent in local public life. When, after an interval of six years, the Odessa Branch of the Society for the Dissemination of Enlightenment was reopened, Pinsker was elected to its committee and helped to collect documentation on the history of the Jews in Russia.

Leon Pinsker, pioneer Zionist. Courtesy Zionist Archives, New York.

The pogroms that broke out in southern Russia in 1881 and the undisguised anti-Semitism of the government had a profound effect on Pinsker and caused him to undergo a complete change of heart. He ceased to regard the spreading of Enlightenment and the Haskalah movement as the solution to the future of Russian Jewry, doubted the value of the emancipation of European Jewry, and did not believe that hatred of the Jews would be overcome by humanist ideals. He followed the debates in Jewish newspapers as to which countries were suitable for Jewish emigration. They discussed the need for an emigration organization, some demanding that Jewish emigration be channeled into one country in which a national center be created, in essence a Jewish state. Moses *Lilienblum was an advocate of the Ḥibbat Zion movement's demands that Jews emigrate to the Land of Israel. He saw anti-Semitism rooted in the fact that Jews were foreigners, a minority of strangers; Pinsker studied the problem of the fate of the Jewish people and reached similar conclusions. In his trip to Italy, to seek a cure for his heart disease (1882), he included visits to the capitals of Western Europe—Vienna, Berlin, Paris, and London—to discuss with leading personalities the need to channel Russian Jewish emigration into one country and to establish a national Jewish center. The chief rabbi of Vienna, Adolph *Jellinek, was unimpressed with the idea. In Paris, the leaders of the *Alliance Israélite Universelle rejected his suggestions; they supported emigration to the U.S., without territorial aims. The person most impressed with Pinsker's ideas was Arthur Cohen, a member of parliament and chairman of the Board of Deputies of British Jews in London. Together they emphasized the need to regard the Jewish question as an international problem and to win governments over to the idea.

It was at Cohen's suggestion that Pinsker published his famous work *"Autoemancipation." Mahnruf an seine Stammesgenossen von einem russischen Juden* (1882), in which he analyzed the psychological and social roots of anti-Semitism and called for the establishment of a Jewish national center. The book was intended to serve as a warning to his fellow Jews *(Stammesgenossen)* and was published anonymously, the author defining himself as "a Russian Jew." The book was written in a passionate style which forcefully expressed the author's deep anxiety for the fate of his people.

Pinsker first states that the reason for the old-new Jewish problem is the existence of the Jews as a separate ethnic entity among the nations, an entity which cannot be assimilated. The radical solution is the acquisition of a Jewish homeland, a country where they can live and which will be theirs, just like other nations. At best, Jews reach technical equality, but this legal change of status is not a real, social, emancipation. There are also economic reasons for anti-Semitism, because in competition, preference is given to one's own ethnic group and the foreigner is discriminated against. There is a saturation point to the number of Jews in each country, and when they exceed this point, persecution begins.

Pinsker directs his attacks against Western Jewry, the "diploma chasers" who view the dispersion of Jews throughout the world as a "mission." Moreover, the religious approach that the exile must be suffered in silence until the coming of the Messiah also weakened the desire for a Jewish homeland. He indicates that national consciousness has awakened in Russian and Rumanian Jewry, in the form of a movement to settle in Ereẓ Israel. Pinsker did not wish to decide whether Ereẓ Israel or a territory in America should be chosen as a Jewish homeland, since he felt that a national Jewish congress should decide the matter. He hoped that the worldwide process of national awakening would be of benefit to the Jewish people and that other nations would help them achieve national independence. He called on Western Jewry and on its "existing alliances" (meaning the Alliance Israélite Universelle, the *Anglo-Jewish Association, etc.) to lighten the suffering of their brethren by founding a homeland and advocated the convocation of a National Jewish Congress to organize the new exodus. In order to settle destitute emigrants, a national fund should also be established.

The book had strong repercussions, both in Russia and abroad. The Ḥovevei Zion received it enthusiastically, though it had many opponents. Lilienblum attempted to convince Pinsker not to wait for a decision by Western Jewry, but to work immediately toward the realization of the plan in Ereẓ Israel. Pinsker, however, refused to make a decision as to the location of the homeland. Nevertheless, Hermann *Schapira, who accompanied Lilienblum, managed to win him over in the summer of 1883. Discussions, also attended by Max *Mandelstamm from Kiev and several others, led to the decision to work for the establishment of a center for Jewish settlement, in Ereẓ Israel if possible, and to convene a congress, with the participation of the Ḥibbat Zion movement, to choose a central executive committee. Afterward Pinsker held a meeting of community leaders at his house, and they chose a committee to organize the movement; he was elected chairman, with Lilienblum as secretary. The committee made contact with existing groups of the Ḥibbat Zion movement, and encouraged the establishment of new groups. The Warsaw branch of the movement was also active in organizing a convention, which met at *Kattowitz on Nov. 6, 1884, and was attended by members of the Ḥibbat Zion from Russia and abroad. Pinsker was chosen chairman of the convention, and in his opening speech he indicated the need for Jews to return to working the land. He did not mention national revival or independence, since this new movement wished to attract Western Jews. At his suggestion, the convention decided to found the Montefiore Association for the dissemination of the idea of agriculture among Jews and to engage their support for Jewish settlers in Ereẓ Israel. Pinsker was elected chairman of the temporary executive committee, whose seat was in Odessa.

Attempts to establish a central bureau of the Ḥovevei Zion outside Russia failed, and Odessa thus remained the center of the movement. Pinsker invited Lilienblum to become secretary of the Odessa office. The limited activities of the committee and its small income, which did not permit any large-scale settlement activity but served to support only a very small number of settlers; the lack of legalization of the committee's activities and internal feuds; and Pinsker's ailing health caused him to resign. He called a convention in *Druskieniki (summer, 1887), at which he intended to hand in his resignation and then travel abroad to seek a cure. At the convention, relations worsened between the Orthodox and the *maskilim*. Pinsker handed in his resignation, but a majority of delegates asked him to continue at his post, and he agreed to do so. Six advisory wardens, including three rabbis, were elected to the leadership.

While abroad, Pinsker attempted to work for the movement. In Paris he met Baron Edmond de *Rothschild, who promised to help the *Petaḥ Tikvah settlement and to acquire land. Rothschild's associates told Pinsker that they would collaborate with the Ḥovevei Zion only if he headed it. As a result, Pinsker ceased to consider resigning immediately. The rabbis who were advisory wardens caused Pinsker considerable difficulty in their demands in religious matters. The declining situation in the movement and his failing health again caused Pinsker to consider resigning. He did not attend the convention held in Vilna in the summer of 1889 for he feared he would be persuaded to continue at his post. At this convention, Samuel *Mohilewer attempted to become head of the movement, but at Pinsker's suggestion in a letter to the convention, Abraham Gruenberg, a resident of Odessa, was chosen as active warden, together with Mohilever and Samuel Joseph Fuenn. The center of the movement thus remained in Odessa.

In 1890, the Ḥovevei Zion was legalized in Odessa under the name Society for the Support of Jewish Farmers and Artisans in Syria and Palestine (see *Odessa Committee) and Pinsker was again asked to be its head. He agreed, despite his grave doubts about whether the new committee would succeed any better than the old one. While the committee was carrying on its first activities, the Ḥovevei Zion movement revived in Russia, and Jews began to settle in Ereẓ Israel as a result of worsening conditions of Russian Jewry and the expulsion of Jews from Moscow (1891). Pinsker began to hope that his dream would come true in Ereẓ Israel. However, the Turkish authorities issued a prohibition on immigration, and the movement underwent a crisis. The Jaffa committee, which represented the Odessa center, ran into debt, many acquisitions of land in Ereẓ Israel were cancelled, and the contributions of associations for settling the land were lost. Pinsker, who was pessimistic by nature, began to doubt whether Ereẓ Israel would serve as the solution for saving masses of Jews from persecution. He began to believe that the activities of Baron Maurice de *Hirsch, who founded the *Jewish Colonization Association (ICA) for the settlement of Jews in Argentina, might solve the problem.

Toward his death, he reached the conclusion that Ereẓ Israel would remain only the spiritual center of the Jewish people. He expressed these opinions in an article that he read to Lilienblum 20 days before his death and which was intended to serve as a supplement to the English edition of *Autoemancipation*, shortly to be published. Despite Pinsker's wish to publicize his new attitude, the article was never published. His funeral was the occasion for a large Jewish demonstration. In his will he left the sum of 16,000 rubles to various institutions, but only 2,000 rubles to the Odessa committee. In 1934 his remains were transferred and buried in the Cave of Nicanor on Mount Scopus in Jerusalem.

Bibliography: B. Netanyahu, in: *Road to Freedom*... (1944), 7–73; N. Sokolow, *Ḥibbath Zion* (Eng., 1935), index; idem, *History of Zionism*, 2 (1919), index; A. Druyanow, *Pinsker u-Zemmano* (1953); idem, *Ketavim le-Toledot Ḥibbat Ẓiyyon ve-Yishuv Ereẓ-Yisrael*, 3 vols. (1919–32), index; Y. Klausner (ed.), *Sefer Pinsker* (1921); idem, *Ha-Tenu'ah le-Ẓiyyon be-Rusyah*, 3 vols. (1962–65); M. Yoeli, *J. L. Pinsker* (Heb., 1960); A. Hertzberg (ed.), *Zionist Idea* (1960), 178–98 and introd., passim; B. Dinur, *Mefallesei Derekh* (1946), 21–61; S. Breiman, in: *Shivat Ẓiyyon*, 3–4 (1953), 205–27.

[I.K.]

PINSKER, SIMḤAH (1801–1864), scholar. Pinsker was born in Tarnow, Galicia. Educated at home by his father, an eminent preacher *(maggid)*, he at first engaged in commerce, but lack of success induced him to move to Odessa, where he became secretary to the local rabbi. He also founded in 1826 the first successful modern Jewish school in Russia, in which he taught Hebrew language and literature. At the same time he published a series of learned papers in the periodical *Orient*, and when the famous Karaite savant Abraham *Firkovich visited Odessa, Pinsker examined and described several of the ancient Hebrew manuscripts collected by him. His work eventually earned him gold medals from the Russian government and a pension from the Jewish community of Odessa. Relieved from the daily need to earn a living, Pinsker moved to Vienna in order to devote all of his time to research, and there in 1860 he published his major work, *Likkutei Kadmoniyyot*, a history of Karaism and Karaite literature, with copious extracts from hitherto unpublished Karaite works in Hebrew and Arabic. It is these original extracts which lend his work its permanent value. His own contribution to it is now largely antiquated, particularly his exaggerated idea of the role of the early Karaite scholars, whom he erroneously regarded not only as the sole founders of the study of Hebrew grammar and lexicography, but also as the pioneers in

Simḥah Pinsker, writer on Karaism. Jerusalem, J.N.U.L., Schwadron Collection.

medieval Hebrew poetry and the precursors of the great Rabbanite poets in Spain, such as Ibn Gabirol and Judah Halevi. Some of Pinsker's misconceptions were the result of Firkovich's tendentious advice or were based on data forged by Firkovich in his zeal to magnify the otherwise very substantial contribution of Karaism to medieval Jewish learning. Pinsker subsequently returned to Odessa.

Pinsker's philological works are *Mavo el ha-Nikkud ha-Ashuri o ha-Bavli,* on the Babylonian Hebrew punctuation, with an appendix containing an annotated edition of Abraham *ibn Ezra's *Yesod Mispar* (Vienna, 1863); and *Mishlei ha-Gizrah ve-ha-Beniyyah,* on mood and inflection of the Hebrew verb, edited posthumously by S. Rubin (Vienna, 1887). The edition of Abraham ibn Ezra's *Sefer ha-Eḥad,* begun by Pinsker, was completed by M. Goldhardt and published in Odessa, 1867. His emendations to David *Kimḥi's *Mikhlol* are included in I. Rittenberg's edition of this work (Lyck, 1862). A catalog of Hebrew and Arabic manuscripts in Pinsker's library was published by J. Bardach as *Mazkir li-Venei ReSHeF* (Vienna, 1869). Pinsker was the father of Leo *Pinsker, author of *Autoemancipation.*

Bibliography: A. Druyanow, in: *Ha-Tekufah,* 12 (1922), 215ff.; Zeitlin, Bibliotheca, 269. [L.N.]

PINSKI, DAVID (1872–1959), Yiddish dramatist and novelist. Born in Mogilev on the Dnieper, Pinski grew up in Moscow and Vitebsk, studied in Vienna, and settled in Warsaw. He showed his first compositions to I. L. *Peretz in 1892, and this led to a lifelong friendship between them.

David Pinski, Yiddish dramatist and novelist. Jerusalem, J.N.U.L., Schwadron Collection.

Pinski's first short story, the satiric tale *Der Groyser Mentshenfraynd,* appeared in Mordecai *Spector's annual *Der Hoyzfraynd* (1894). In 1895 he edited the literary anthology *Literatur un Lebn,* and organized Yiddish committees in various towns to help disseminate Peretz's *Yontev Bletlekh.* In 1896, while continuing his studies in Berlin, he founded the publishing house Tsaytgayst to popularize literary and scientific works in Yiddish. He lived for a time in Switzerland and sent articles to the New York daily *Abend Blatt,* organ of the Socialist Labor Party of which he was invited to become literary editor in 1899 when he went to the U.S. With the labor leader Joseph *Schlossberg, he coedited the weekly *Der Arbeiter* from 1904 to 1911. He later edited other periodicals, notably the Labor Zionist monthly *Der Yidisher Kempfer* and the literary monthly *Zukunft.* At first Pinski had been identified with the *Bund, but after the Kishinev pogrom of 1903 he joined the Labor Zionist Movement (Po'alei Zion) of which he became a prominent leader. Participating in many Jewish cultural groups, he proclaimed the slogan of "Yiddish but also Hebrew for the Diaspora; Hebrew but also Yiddish in Ereẓ Israel." He settled in Israel in 1949, his home in Haifa becoming a center for the young Yiddish writers of Israel who looked to him for encouragement.

Pinski was talented both in drama and fiction. The subject matter of his plays ranged over most epochs of Jewish history, from biblical times to the contemporary period of martyrdom and rebirth. His drama *Der Eybiker Yid* ("The Eternal Jew," 1926) entered into the repertoire of Israel's Habimah Theater. He was among the few Yiddish playwrights whose works were performed in foreign languages, primarily English and German. *The Treasure* was a box-office success both in Berlin and in New York. The New York Theater Guild performed *The Final Balance* in 1926. Pinski's more popular plays on the Yiddish stage included *Familye Tsvi,* which deals with the Kishinev pogrom; *Ayzik Sheftl,* whose hero is the fettered workingman with a dream; *Yankl der Shmid* in which the lure of the flesh is dramatized in all its intensity; *Gabri un di Froyen ("Gabri and the Women")* in which a man of strong passions struggles for moral health and purity. Among Pinski's biblical heroes are Saul, David, and Solomon, while from post-biblical sources he drew heroes such as the apocryphal Prince Zerubbabel, R. Akiva, R. Meir and his wife, Beruryah. Pinski's longing for redemption inspired him to write plays about Solomon *Molcho, David *Reuveni, and *Shabbetai Ẓevi.

Though Pinski began as an extreme realist at a time when European Naturalism was dominant, he developed into a symbolist and romanticist. His Zionism and romanticism led him to prefer glorious moments and heroic figures of the Jewish past—messianic visions and great personalities who wanted to convert these visions to reality, heroic women capable of extreme devotion and self-sacrifice. At the height of his creativity he enriched Yiddish literature with the prose epics *Arnold Levenberg* (Eng. tr. 1928) and *Dos Hoyz fun Noyakh Edon* (1931). Both novels were written before the onset of the 1929 Depression and paint a grim picture of the morass into which assimilated U.S. Jews seemed to be sliding even after a decade of great prosperity. *Noyakh Edon* is a genealogical novel and portrays three generations of a Jewish family which emigrated to the U.S. in the 1880s from a little town in Lithuania. It ends in deepest pessimism, with the novelist pointing out the emptiness of lives divorced from ancestral cultural roots. Pinski often depicted the conflict between generations, especially between immigrant parents and Americanized children.

Pinski's tales of World War II deal with the Holocaust and emphasize heroic events in the midst of tragedy. His strength both as dramatist and storyteller lies in his depiction of antithetical forces. Though he often depicts poverty, sickness, and disappointment, he always ultimately comforts and consoles, stressing that the moments of bliss in Jewish existence made the continuing struggle for survival worthwhile. His selected works, published in Buenos Aires in 1961, include a bibliography.

Bibliography: Rejzen, Leksikon, 2 (1927), 885–98; S. Niger, *Dertseyler un Romanistn* (1946), 282–319; Z. Zylbercweig, *Leksikon fun Yidishn Teater*, 3 (1959), 1762–1806; M. Singer (ed.), *David Pinski Zikhrono li-Verakhah* (1960), contains Pinski's diary in Yiddish; S. Liptzin, *Flowering of Yiddish Literature* (1963), 118–30; Madison, *Yiddish Literature* (1968), 182–96, list of English translations, 525.

[M.S.]

PINSON, KOPPEL S. (1904–1961), U.S. historian. Born in Lithuania, Pinson was taken to the U.S. in 1907. He lectured at the New School for Social Research from 1934 to 1937, when he went to Queens College, N.Y., becoming professor of history in 1950. He was also history editor of the *Encyclopedia of the Social Sciences* (1929–35), and an editor of *Jewish Social Studies* (1938–61). In 1945–46, he was director of education and culture, Jewish Displaced Persons in Germany and Austria, United Nations Relief and Rehabilitation Association.

Pinson's principal scholarly interests embraced modern European history, with special emphasis on nationalism and modern Germany, and recent Jewish history. His contributions to general history were, *Pietism as a Factor in the Rise of German Nationalism* (1934); *A Bibliographical Introduction to Nationalism* (1935); and *Modern Germany, Its History and Civilization* (1954). In Jewish studies, he edited a number of important books: *Essays on Anti-Semitism* (1946[2]); *Yivo Annual of Jewish Social Science*, vols. 5–9 (1950–54); and notably *Nationalism and History* (1958), which made available in English Simon Dubnow's classic, *Essays on Old and New Judaism*. Pinson analyzed Dubnow's national theories and appraised his role as historian. Pinson was actively involved in the work of the *Yivo Institute for Jewish Research. He was also chairman of the modern Jewish history committee of the Jewish Publication Society of America.

[O.I.J.]

Harold Pinter, British playwright.

PINTER, HAROLD (1930–), English playwright. Born in London, he was on the stage from 1949 to 1957 under the name of David Baron, acting chiefly in repertory and with touring companies in Ireland. His first plays to become known were written for radio, a medium admirably suited to the rather sinister ambiguity of his early work. To this period belong *The Room, The Dumb Waiter*, and *The Birthday Party* (1957). The last play is symbolic of the universal guilt of man, with the central figure as a scapegoat. Pinter's subsequent plays include *The Caretaker*, produced in 1960, which is generally classed as a tragicomedy belonging to the genre of the "theater of the absurd." It shows a homeless tramp billeting himself upon two brothers, under the pretense of taking care of their home. He emerges, however, as a type of suffering humanity, making what may be felt to be excessive claims upon men's charity. *The Caretaker* was an outstanding success on stage, screen, and television. The plays Pinter wrote in the 1960s were dominated by the husband-wife relationship and several were acted by his wife, Vivien Merchant. *The Lover* (1963) depicts a marriage which can only function if both partners pretend that it is an illicit love affair. *The Homecoming* (1964) is about an English intellectual who brings a new wife back from the U.S. to meet his crude, working-class family. In this phase of his writing, Pinter was concerned with the frailty of marital relationships, with the potential violence of family life, and with the impossibility of ever knowing or possessing a woman. His other plays include *A Night Out* (1960), *The Collection* (1961), *Tea Party* (1964), and *Old Times* (1971).

Bibliography: M. Esslin, *Theater of the Absurd* (1961); idem, *The People Wound: The Work of Harold Pinter* (1970); J. R. Taylor, *Anger and After* (1960).

[P.D.H.]

PINTO, name of several families who originated in the small town of Pinto, whose Jewish community was subordinate to that of Madrid. Some Pintos arrived in Morocco from the Iberian Peninsula, particularly from Seville, in 1492 and 1496 and from the Canary Islands during the 16th century. The latter were former Marranos who settled in Agadir and Marrakesh, where they ranked among the spiritual and lay leaders of the Jewish communities of those towns. R. JACOB (d. c. 1750), a disciple of R. Abraham Azulai and a well-known kabbalist, wrote a lengthy commentary on the Zohar. His son, R. ABRAHAM (d. after 1800), was a *dayyan* in Marrakesh. The latter's commentary on the tractate *Ketubbot* is often mentioned in the work *Sefer Ḥesed ve-Emet* (Salonika, 1803). There are many manuscripts of his responsa and *haskamot*. R. ḤAYYIM (d. before 1840) was chief rabbi of Mogador, where he was revered as a saint. Pilgrimages are still made to his grave. ABRAHAM BEN REUBEN (c. 1750) was one of the leaders of the Jewish community of Agadir. A financier, he wielded considerable influence; the sultan of Morocco entrusted him with economic missions to Europe. During the 19th century the Pintos were prominent in the communities of northern Morocco, especially in Tangier and later in Casablanca, where their commercial importance was considerable down to the present day.

Bibliography: E. de Avila, *Be'er Mayim Ḥayyim* (1806), 70–71; Azulai, 67; J. M. Toledano, *Ner ha-Ma'arav* (1911), 161, 190.

[D.Co.]

PINTO, DE, family of Dutch jurists of Sephardi origin. ABRAHAM DE PINTO (1811–1878), Dutch jurist and public worker, was the elder brother of Aaron Adolf de Pinto. He graduated in law from the University of Leiden. He became editor of the law journal *Weekblad voor het recht* in 1835 and in 1840 founded the juridical review *Themis* which he edited for 36 years. De Pinto also published digests of several Dutch legal codes which served to make known the principles of Dutch law after the Codification of 1838. He was dean of the Order of Advocates in The Hague and a Hague municipal councillor from 1851 until 1878. As chairman of The Hague Sephardi congregation, De Pinto unsuccessfully favored cooperation between the Sephardi and Ashkenazi communities in contrast to many of his contemporaries. In 1850 he established the Maatschappij tot nut der Israëlieten in Nederland (Association for the Benefit of the Jews in Holland) for the promotion of educational and vocational training for poor Jews. AARON ADOLF DE PINTO (1828–1908) was a Dutch criminal lawyer. Born in The Hague, De Pinto graduated in law from the University of Leiden. As a high official at the Netherlands Ministry of Justice from 1862 to 1876, he was largely responsible for the adoption of a New Netherlands penal code which came into force in 1886, and for the Dutch East Indies Penal Code. In 1865 De Pinto initiated and drafted the law on the abolition of the death penalty. This was adopted in 1871, against the opposition of successive ministers of justice. Subsequently he drafted the law for the complete revision of the Netherlands code of civil procedure. Rejecting the offer of a professorship and the cabinet portfolio of justice, De Pinto became a member of the Supreme Court. In 1903 he was appointed vice-president. From 1878 to 1901 he was an editor of the *Weekblad voor het recht,* and a founder of the Netherlands Association of Jurists. Among De Pinto's numerous publications are several on the Dreyfus trial, showing that it was being conducted in violation of French legal procedure. In 1885, at a lawyers' conference in Rotterdam, he championed the rights of the Rumanian Jews. For many years he was chairman of the Maatschappij tot nut der Israëlieten in Nederland (founded by his brother), and in 1908 officially opened the Eighth Zionist Congress in The Hague.

Bibliography: A. A. De Pinto, *Mr. Abraham de Pinto* . . . (1879).

[H.Bo.]

PINTO, ISAAC (1720–1791), U.S. merchant and translator of prayer books. Emigrating to the U.S. from the West Indies, where one branch of the Pinto family was established, Pinto settled in Connecticut; an Isaac Pinto is listed in *Colonial Records of Connecticut* as living in Stratford during 1748. By 1751 Pinto was a resident of New York City and a member of Congregation Shearith Israel. Ezra Stiles, president of Yale College, identified him as a "learned Jew at New York." Pinto, who signed the Non-Importation Act, was a devoted patriot. The anonymous English translation in *Evening Services for Rosh-Hashanah and Yom Kippur* (New York, 1761) is attributed to Pinto; this rendering and his acknowledged translation in *Prayers for Sabbath, Rosh-Hashanah and Yom Kippur, with the Amidah and Musaph of the Moadim* of the Sephardi rite (New York, 1766) are the earliest English translations of Hebrew prayer books published in the New World. That a translation was needed indicates, in the view of Grinstein, a low level of Hebrew learning in the colonies at that time.

Bibliography: D. de S. Pool, *Portraits Etched in Stone* (1952); I. Abrahams, *By-Paths in Hebraic Bookland* (1920), 171–7; L. Huehner, in: JE, s.v.; H. Grinstein, *Rise of the Jewish Community of New York* (1945).

[L.He.]

PINTO, ISAAC DE (1717–1787), philosopher and economist of Portuguese-Jewish origin. Born perhaps in Bordeaux, Pinto lived mostly in Holland. A widely cultured man with a combative pen, he defended the Jewish people against *Voltaire's *Dictionnaire Philosophique* article *"Juifs"* in his well-known *Apologie pour la Nation Juive* (Amsterdam, 1762). He sent a copy of this work to Voltaire, who thanked him but held to his opinions. Pinto's major work on economics is the *Traité de la circulation et du crédit* (Amsterdam, 1771), one of the great documents in the history of political economy, written in refutation of the physiocrats, who advocated an economy based mainly on agriculture. Other works by Pinto are his *Essai sur le luxe* (Amsterdam, 1762), *Précis des arguments contre les matérialistes* (The Hague, 1774), and *Du jeu de cartes* (1768), a short essay on card playing which he addressed to *Diderot. For his services in arranging favorable terms for English trade in India at the Treaty of Paris, which ended the Seven Years' War (1756–63), Pinto was lavishly rewarded by the East India Company a few years later (1767).

De Pinto was, as Voltaire said, a *philosophe* and a Jew. He had a broad general 18th-century education, as evidenced by two unpublished philosophical discourses from 1742. His attack on Voltaire, whom he admired, was more a defense of the Sephardim than of Judaism. He suggested that Voltaire's anti-Semitic criticisms were justified against the Ashkenazim, but that the Sephardim were cultured and enlightened. In economics, De Pinto opposed the physiocrats, and advocated (against Hume) the economically productive role of the national debt, and modern credit and commerce. Opposed by Adam Smith, he was seen by Dugald Stewart and Sir Francis D'Ivernois as an important new economist. Marx called him "the Pindar of the Amsterdam stock exchange" for his advocacy of speculation. Werner *Sombart regarded him as the beginner of the modern age of economics, and the first to understand the growth of credit. Sée claimed he was the first to say that speculation was useful. Hertzberg saw De Pinto's economics as a covert defense of the role of Jews in 18th-century economic affairs. De Pinto was a conservative in philosophy and politics. A Deist, he opposed D'Holbach's materialistic atheism as a menace to the social order. He offered proofs of the existence of God and the immortality of the soul (borrowing from Mendelssohn among others), but not appealing to any biblical evidence. His criticisms of the American Revolution opposed popular democracy and defended the economic rights of the colonial powers, and the need for them to join together to maintain peace and social harmony.

De Pinto was a Jew of the Enlightenment (he knew Voltaire, Hume, Diderot, Marat, among others). He was a genuine innovator in economic theory, and a moderate, tolerant, pacificistic conservative in its politics and philosophy. Manuscript 48A19 of Ets Haim library (Amsterdam) contains many unpublished works of De Pinto, including two philosophical discourses.

Bibliography: M. B. Amzalak, *O economista Isaac Pinto* (1922); J. S. Wijler, *Isaac de Pinto, sa vie et ses oeuvres* (1923), incl. bibl.; A. Guenée, *Lettres de quelques juifs . . . á M. de Voltaire* (Paris, 1769), letters 2, 3, and 4; *Biographie universelle,* 34 (1823), 484–6; Sutherland, in: *English Historical Review,* 62 (1947), 189; A. Hertzberg, *French Enlightenment and the Jews* (1968), index.

[R. H. P./Ed.]

PINTO, JOSIAH BEN JOSEPH (1565–1648), talmudist and kabbalist. Born in Damascus, Pinto was for the major part of his life rabbi in Damascus, but went to Jerusalem about 1617. In 1625 he decided to settle in Safed, but when his son died in the following year, he returned to Damascus. His teacher in subjects other than Kabbalah was Jacob *Abulafia, who ordained him. In Kabbalah he adhered closely to the system of Ḥayyim *Vital whose son, Samuel, was his pupil and subsequently married his daughter.

Pinto is best known for his *Me'or Einayim* (part 1, Amsterdam, 1643; part 2, Mantua, 1743), a commentary on *Ein Ya'akov* of Jacob *ibn Ḥabib. He also wrote *Kesef Nivḥar* (Damascus, 1605), sermons on the weekly scriptural readings; part 2, entitled *Kesef Mezukkak* (Venice, 1628), sermons and explanations of unusual rabbinic comments on scriptural passages; *Kesef Ẓaruf* (*ibid.*, 1629) on the Book of Proverbs; *Nivḥar mi-Kesef* (Aleppo, 1869), responsa. Some of his responsa were in a manuscript of the responsa of his son-in-law, Samuel *Vital, which was in the possession of Ḥ. J. Michael, while others were published in the responsa of Yom Tov *Ẓahalon (Venice, 1694). Some, which he wrote in 1646, were published in the *Yad Aharon,* part 1 (Smyrna, 1735), of Aaron *Alfandari. His *Kesef Nimas,* on Lamentations, and *Kevuẓot Kesef,* on the laws of marriage and the civil laws in the Shulḥan Arukh, are in manuscript. Joseph *Delmedigo mentions a biblical commentary by Pinto entitled *Kesef To'afot.*

Bibliography: M. D. Gaon, *Yehudei ha-Mizraḥ be-Ereẓ Yisrael,* 2 (1938), 552–3, 743; Conforte, Kore, 49b; Fuenn, Keneset, 382–3; Rosanes, Togarmah, 3 (1938), 231–2; Frumkin-Rivlin, 1 (1928), 51 n. 1, 130; Benayahu, in: *Tarbiz,* 29 (1959/60), 74. [Sh.A.H./Ed.]

PINTO DELGADO, JOÃO (**Mosseh;** d. 1653), Portuguese *Marrano poet, born at Vila Nova de Portimão. His grandfather, of the same name, was in government administration in the Algarve, as was João's father, Gonçalo Delgado. On two separate occasions, João lived in Lisbon. His parents, after going to Antwerp, settled in Rouen, c. 1609, where he later joined them. In 1633 some of the Portuguese New Christians in Rouen denounced others as Judaizers, and João and his father took refuge in

Antwerp (a brother, Gonçalo, remained in Rouen). João moved to Amsterdam in 1634, followed soon after by his father. In the Dutch city he openly joined the Jewish community and was known as Mosseh Pinto (Delgado). Around 1636, 1637, and 1640, he was one of the seven *parnasim* of the *talmud torah.* João Pinto Delgado began his literary career in Lisbon, where he contributed poetry to works of a purely Catholic nature by João Baptista de Este and Luis de Tovar. In Rouen, in 1627, he published a collection of verse paraphrases of Old Testament books, *Poema de la Reyna Ester, Lamentaciones del Propheta Jeremias y Historia de Rut y varias poesías,* which he dedicated to Cardinal Richelieu. I. S. Révah has published parts of a manuscript autobiography, in prose and verse and written in Holland, in which Pinto Delgado attacked the Inquisition and Christian beliefs, and satirized those New Christians of Rouen who denounced others in 1633.

Bibliography: João Pinto Delgado, *Poema de la Reina Ester . . .,* ed. by I. S. Révah (Lisbon 1954); E. W. Wilson, in: JJS, 1 (1949), 131–42; C. Roth, in: *Modern Language Review,* 30 (1935), 19–25; idem, in: REJ, 121 (1962), 355–66; I. S. Révah, in: REJ, 119 (1961), 41–130.

[K.R.S.]

PIONEER WOMEN, worldwide labor Zionist women's organization. Pioneer Women, which was founded in New York City in 1925, aimed to provide social welfare services for women, young people, and children in Palestine, to help new immigrants become productive citizens there, and to encourage U.S. Jewish women to take a more active part in Jewish community life and U.S. civic affairs. Although its affairs were originally largely conducted in Yiddish, the organization gradually shifted to English as it became increasingly acculturated to the U.S. scene. By 1936 it had chapters in 60 U.S. cities with 10,000 members. After World War II Pioneer Women broadened its field of endeavors, while at the same time moderating its original socialist and feminist ideology on which previously much emphasis had been laid; nevertheless, it continued to cooperate with progressive and labor groups on behalf of liberal causes. In 1970, in cooperation with its sister Israel organization, Mo'eẓet ha-Po'alot, Pioneer Women maintained a large network of welfare and cultural projects in Israel. In the United States, Pioneer Women conducts Jewish educational and cultural activities, supports youth work through Habonim, and publishes a monthly journal, *The Pioneer Woman.* In 1970 the membership was about 50,000. Pioneer Women has stimulated the formation of sister organizations in other countries. The World Union of Pioneer Women's Organizations, which was formed in Tel Aviv in 1964, has member sisterhoods in the United States, Canada, Mexico, Argentina, Brazil, Chile, Peru, Uruguay, Great Britain, Belgium, and Australia. The total world membership of Pioneer Women in 1970 was 150,000. They are represented on major Zionist and Jewish bodies and, in their respective countries, on national committees dealing with family welfare and the status of women. The organization supports projects in Israel, and promotes Jewish education for adults and children, and progressive civic legislation in its own countries. [G.Hi./Sh.H.]

PIOTRKOW (Pol. **Piotrków Trybunalski,** Rus. **Petrokov,** Ger. **Petrikau**), town in Lodz province, central Poland; known from 1578 as Piotrkow-Trybunalski. Several anti-Jewish resolutions were passed at state conventions held in Piotrkow during the 14th to 16th centuries, including a series of limitations by the Sejm (Diet) of 1562. Jews settled in Piotrkow from the first half of the 16th century. In 1569 Jews were permitted by the king to settle in the suburbs of Piotrkow and trade at the fairs there on payment of 30 ducats to the Christian guild. The Jews were expelled following a *blood libel in 1590. During the greater part of the 17th century the municipality prevented Jews from entering Piotrkow, until 1679 when King John II Sobieski permitted Jews to return, to trade there, and to build a synagogue (completed in 1689). During the 1720s, under the first rabbi of Piotrkow, Eliakim Getz, a *ḥevra kaddisha* and Bikkur Ḥolim were organized. In 1744 Jewish self-defense against an attack by the mob was successfully led by Ephraim Fishel. The Jews of the community (about 800) were then compelled to leave the city and settle in the suburbs (Nowa Wiés). A *bet midrash* was founded there in 1765, and a large synagogue was built by the merchant Moses Kazin in 1781.

The Great Synagogue of Piotrkow, central Poland, 1959. Courtesy Yad Vashem Archives, Jerusalem.

After the second partition of Poland in 1793, Piotrkow passed to Prussia. In 1808 there were in Piotrkow 1,817 Jews (46% of the total population), and in 1827, 2,133 Jews (45% of the total). After the opening of the Warsaw–Vienna railway line and the development of industries in the region, Jews founded weaving mills in Piotrkow. A growing Jewish proletariat was employed in the timber and textile industries, and in services. In 1857 there were 4,166 Jews (42% of the total population). In 1861 Jews obtained electoral and elective rights on the municipal council. In 1864 a Hebrew printing press was set up in Piotrkow, which in 1900 published the Jerusalem Talmud. Moses David *Szereszewski, the Lithuanian *maskil,* introduced the Ḥibbat Zion movement into Piotrkow in 1880. There were 30 *ḥadarim,* a *talmud torah,* two *battei midrash,* and a private secular school in this period. The Jewish hospital, founded in 1836, was also extended. In 1912 a Zionist workers' party was founded in Piotrkow. The community numbered approximately 5,400 in 1865, 9,370 (33.14%) in 1897, and by 1917 had increased to 14,890.

Some of the Jews that found shelter in Piotrkow during World War I left the town during the establishment of independent Poland (1918). In 1921 there were in Piotrkow 11,630 Jews (28% of the total population). Of the 33 members of the municipal council elected in 1919, seven were Jews. In the 1928 elections their number rose to eight. Between the two world wars new educational institutions were established in Piotrkow by the *Tarbut, CYSHO, and *ORT; and sports organizations (Maccabi, Shtern, etc.) and a musical society, Zamir, were formed. From 1924 the Zionist periodical *Unzer Tsaytung* was published in Piotrkow and Zionist and other youth movements gained in strength. In the elections to the community council in 1935 six representatives of the *Bund were elected. From 1924 to 1931, Meir *Shapiro, leader of the Agudat Israel, served as rabbi of Piotrkow.

Holocaust Period. After the outbreak of World War II about 2,000 Jews, the majority of them young people, escaped from Piotrkow and attempted to find refuge in the larger towns and the Soviet-occupied zone. On Oct. 28, 1939, the Germans set up at Piotrkow the first ghetto to be established in Poland. Despite famine, disease, and terrorization, the population in the ghetto continued to increase as thousands of Jewish refugees arrived there, mostly from the regions annexed by the Germans. In April 1942 there were 16,469 Jews in the Piotrkow ghetto, of whom 8,141 had come from other localities, and by Oct. 15, 1942, there were about 25,000 Jews, including a large number of refugees from the surrounding townlets of Kamiensk, Wolborz, Serock, and others. Subsequently, in the course of one week, until Oct. 22, 1942, some 22,000 Jews of the Piotrkow ghetto were deported to the death camp of *Treblinka. About 4,000 Jews remained, half being workers in labor camps assigned to factories which worked for the German army. Some 2,000 others hid in the ghetto to escape the death transports. At the beginning of 1943 the Nazis carried out searches for those in hiding and found about 2,000 Jews, whom they murdered in the surrounding forests. In May 1943 about 500 Jews were taken from Piotrkow to the camps of *Starachowice, *Radom, and others. Among those some 40 women and children were murdered on the spot. The remainder, numbering about 1,100, were concentrated into camps near the Karo and Hortensia glassworks and the Fischer & Co. timber enterprises. In November 1944 the last few hundred Jews in the ghetto were deported to the camps of *Buchenwald, *Bergen-Belsen, and *Mauthausen.

Several attempts had been made in the ghetto to organize resistance. Between 1942 and 1944, about 500 Jews escaped from the ghetto. They found refuge in the forests and within the organizations which fought the Germans. From the middle of 1943 a group of Jewish partisans was active in the vicinity of Piotrkow. The group succeeded in escaping from the labor camp attached to the Karo glassworks and held out until the retreat of the Germans from the region in January 1945. Jewish settlement in Piotrkow was not renewed after the war.

Bibliography: A. Feldman, in: *Bleter far Geshikhte*, 1 (1938); Sz. Ashkenazy, *Ze spraw żydowskich w dobie kongresowej* (1913); M. Bersohn, *Dyplomataryusz Żydow w dawnej Polsce (1388–1752)* (1910), 179–80; *Dzieje ydów w Piotrkowie i okoliey* (1930); A. Eisenbach, in: BZIH, no. 29 (1959), 72–111; A. Rutkowski, *ibid.*, no. 15–16 (1955), 75–182. [A.Cy.]

PIOVE DI SACCO, small town in Padua province, N. Italy. Piove di Sacco was the first town to admit Jews in this region. Before 1373 a moneylending bank was founded there by a Jewish consortium. In 1455, when the Jews of Padua were forbidden to lend money, they transferred their business to nearby centers, among them Piove di Sacco—where there had never been a ghetto. Piove di Sacco is of particular interest for its Hebrew press. In 1475 Meshullam Cusi Rafa ben Moses Jacob of nearby Padua and his sons set up a Hebrew printing press and were the first to issue a *Seliḥot* prayer book in nonvocalized square type (1475). In July 1475 they printed in folio form, the first volume of the first printed edition of *Jacob b. Asher's *Arba'ah Turim*—the second dated Hebrew book in Italy (now found at Padua's Biblioteca Civica Bp 6747). Meshullam died soon after, and his widow and sons Solomon and Moses continued printing the remaining volumes. After the second and third volumes were issued, the sons were imprisoned, apparently in connection with the *Trent blood libel, and their mother completed publication of the fourth volume alone (see *Incunabula). In 1905 Leone Romanin Jacur sat in the Italian parliament as the town's deputy.

Bibliography: A. Ciscato, *Gli Ebrei in Padova* (1901), 21, 53, 158; G. B. De Rossi, in: *Annales Hebraeo-Typographici,* sect. 15, no. 2 (Parma, 1795); A. Vercesi and L. Dalla Rira, *Capitoli concessi da Francesco da Carrara... all'ebreo Abramo... in Piove di Sacco* (1900); S. Bassi, in: *Festschrift Bellini* (1959), 288–96. Hebrew Printing: D. W. Amram, *Makers of Hebrew Books in Italy* (1909), 22, 24, 26; Ḥ. D. Friedberg, *Toledot ha-Defus ha-Ivri bi-Medinot Italyah* (1956[2]), 22–25; Milano, Bibliotheca, no. 1541. [A.M.R./Ed.]

PIPERNO BEER, SERGIO (1906–), Italian judge and communal leader. Born in Rome, Piperno Beer took up a juridical career, reaching the rank of a councillor at the Court of Cassation, the highest court of Italy. During the period of racial persecutions (1938ff.) he was active in DELASEM (Delegation for Assistance to Emigrants). After the liberation he was elected councillor of the Rome Jewish community and was a member of the *Keren ha-Yesod Committee for Turin and member of the executive of the *World Jewish Congress. In June 1956 he was elected president of the Board of Italian Jewish Communities and in this office he worked for the Italian state's recognition of the rights of families who had lost members during Nazi persecutions. He was reelected as president of the Board in 1961, 1966, and 1970. [S.D.P.]

PIPES, RICHARD EDGAR (1923–), U.S. historian. Born in Cieszyn, Poland, Pipes migrated in his youth to the United States. He taught Russian history at Harvard, and was appointed professor. He also served as director of Harvard's Russian Research Center.

Pipes' principal historical studies concern both Imperial Russia and the Bolshevik period, with special attention to intellectual and national questions. His published works include *Formation of the Soviet Union* (1954), an important contribution to the study of the national question of Soviet Russia. He edited and translated *Karamzin's Memoir on Ancient and Modern Russia* (1959), and *Social-Democracy and the St. Petersburg Labor Movement 1885–97* (1963). He edited *Russian Intelligentsia* (1961) and *Revolutionary Russia* (1968). [W.K.]

PIRKEI DE-RABBI ELIEZER, eighth-century aggadic work (see *Midrash), also called *Baraita de-Rabbi Eliezer* or *Haggadah de-Rabbi Eliezer* in medieval rabbinic literature because of its opening words: "It is related of *Eliezer b. Hyrcanus."

Character and Composition. The book is not a midrash constructed on the verses of Scripture, but an aggadic narrative; the extant version is divided into 54 chapters, but this is probably not the whole book. It commences with an *aggadah* about the early days of Eliezer b. Hyrcanus, and then chronologically narrates events from the Creation until the middle of the journeys of the Children of Israel in the wilderness, concluding with *Miriam's leprosy and the *copper serpent. In the second half of the book, from Abraham onward, the narrative is related to the blessings of the **Amidah* prayer, but the last chapter terminates at the eighth blessing (for health). The book also refers to the ten occasions when God descended to earth, but in their enumeration only reaches the eighth descent. It is therefore clear that the book as it survived is incomplete; but even in manuscript the only additional portion preserved is the second half of the last chapter.

Language and Date. The book is written in Hebrew—partially artificial—reminiscent of the geonic era, and contains a few Greek words. The author made use of the tannaitic literature, the Jerusalem Talmud, the *Midreshei Aggadah of the **amoraim,* and even of the Babylonian Talmud, as well as those Aramaic *Targums to the Scripture that originated in Ereẓ Israel. The author does not quote his sources, but tends to revise them completely—shortening,

פרקי רבי אליעזר
רבי אליעזר בן הורקנוס הנקרא רבי אליעזר הגדול והיה מכת חכמי
המשנה המקבלים והיה מדור הלא בזמן הנשיא רבן גמליאל השני
בנו של רבן שמעון בן גמליאל וזה רבי אליעזר הגדול היה
בעל אחותו של רבן גמליאל הנשיא ומחכמי דורו
רבי יהושע בן חנניה · רבי אלעזר בן ערך ·
ואונקלוס הגר · ורבי יוחנן בן נורי ·
ורבי יוסי בן ברוקא ·
ושמואל הקטן :
נדפס פה סביוניטה
אשר תחת ממשלת האדון
ויספיסיאן גונזאגה קולונה יר״ה
בשם הר״ר אליעזר יצ״ו מברוינשוויג בשנת שכ״ז לפ״ק :
על יד ויצינצו קונטי וכביתו

Title page of *Pirkei de-Rabbi Eliezer*, an eighth-century aggadic work, printed in Sabbioneta, Italy, 1567. Jerusalem, J.N.U.L.

lengthening, and combining them freely. It is therefore not a collection or compilation of different sources, but a book with a unified and continuous narrative in which the personality of the author is clearly recognizable. The author was greatly influenced in both contents and form by the *Apocrypha and Pseudepigrapha of the Second Temple period, particularly the books of the *Enoch cycle. His entire manner of narration and unique method of connecting *halakhah* and *aggadah* were influenced by the Book of Jubilees. *Pirkei de-Rabbi Eliezer* has thus preserved many ancient sources. It contains almost no names of *amoraim*, but falsely attributes sayings to many *tannaim*. *Pirkei de-Rabbi Eliezer* is therefore a pseudepigraphic work par excellence; the influence of apocalyptic works of the Second Temple period is well marked in that respect, as well as in its mystical air and in the descriptions of angels. The *halakhot* of the *calendar laid down in the Byzantine period and at the beginning of the Muslim era were already known to the author. The book is filled with the halakhic customs current in Ereẓ Israel at the beginning of the geonic period. It contains Arabic legends, and remarkable descriptions of the Muslim Omayyad dynasty, and looks forward to the downfall of this (Omayyad) Caliphate as an omen of the end of the exile. All these indications prove that it was composed in Ereẓ Israel during the first half of the eighth century, just prior to the fall of the Omayyad dynasty, but before the rise of the Abbasid dynasty. Quotations from it are already found in the tractate **Soferim*, and in the work of *Pirkoi ben Baboi. The work also follows the model of the Arabic collections of biblical legends, in which narrative receives more emphasis than exegesis. *Pirkei de-Rabbi Eliezer* was first published in Constantinople (1514), and reprinted many times on the basis of the first edition. In the Warsaw edition of 1852, a valuable commentary by David *Luria was added. Many manuscripts have been preserved, and extracts from three of them were published by Higger in: *Horeb*, 8–10 (1944–48), and one of them was translated into English by G. Friedlander (1916, 1965²).

Bibliography: Zunz-Albeck, Derashot, 134–40. [M.D.H.]

PIRKOI BEN BABOI (eighth–ninth century), talmudic scholar of the geonic era and author of a polemical halakhic work. A pupil of Abba, who was a pupil of *Yehudai, a *gaon* of Sura, Pirkoi notes that it was only because of their teaching and tradition that he presumed to write to the scholars of Kairouan. His teacher Abba wrote the *Halakhot de-Rav Abba*, small fragments of which were published from the Cairo **Genizah* by S. Schechter and J. N. Epstein. Some conjecture that Abba was one of the scholars of the Pumbedita Academy and that Pirkoi also apparently studied there. It was earlier assumed that Pirkoi b. Baboi meant "the chapters of *[Pirkei]* Ben Baboi," but Epstein showed that Pirkoi was a Persian personal name. According to Epstein, Pirkoi was born in Babylon, where he studied and wrote his *Iggeret*. According to Ginzberg, however, he was a native of Ereẓ Israel who studied in Babylon, where he settled and wrote his work. Fragments of the work were scattered in various libraries—Leningrad, Oxford, Cambridge—and were published from the *Genizah*, beginning in 1903, by various scholars such as Harkavy (*Ha-Goren*, 4 (1903), 71–74) and L. Ginzberg (Geonica, 2 (1909), 50–53), neither of whom identified the author; J. Mann, who added a third fragment, succeeded in indicating Pirkoi as the author: additional fragments were published by various scholars of the period including Solomon Schechter, J. N. Epstein, B. M. Lewin, Shraga Abramson, and S. Spiegel.

Pirkoi became renowned through his work *Iggeret*, which reflects his aspiration to make the Babylonian Talmud the authoritative code for world Jewry. Echoes of the long drawn-out struggle between the two Torah centers—Ereẓ Israel and Babylon—are heard in the polemical chapters of Pirkoi which constitute, in Ginzberg's view, the earliest halakhic work extant from the geonic era. Some were of the opinion that the *Iggeret* was sent to Ereẓ Israel, but more accepted the view of Lewin and Spiegel that it was sent to the countries of North Africa (around 812), where the customs of Ereẓ Israel were followed. Pirkoi's intention was to encourage them to accept the *halakhah* of Babylon and the customs of the two academies in Babylon. It is probable that Pirkoi's words in his *Iggeret*, "God established places of learning in all localities of Africa and of Spain and He granted you the privilege of engaging in Torah study by day and by night," were directed especially to the people of Kairouan, which in the time of Pirkoi enjoyed tranquillity and economic stability. The communal leaders and scholars of Kairouan endeavored to maintain places of learning in the town as well as in various localities in Spain. Emigrants who left Kairouan for Spain founded Torah centers there. Pirkoi complains about the pupils of the Babylonian academies who "learnt the customs of Ereẓ Israel," arrived in North Africa, and were then drawn after the ignorant customs and habits of Ereẓ Israel. In his view any custom or ruling which is not in accordance with the law and *halakhah* of the Babylonian Talmud is a consequence of the apostasy decreed by the wicked kingdom of Edom upon Ereẓ Israel. As a result Torah was forgotten by the inhabitants of Ereẓ Israel, and the Ereẓ Israel customs came to be "customs of apostasy." Pirkoi, as a "pro-Babylonian," stresses the superiority of the Babylonian academies as the only source in the world for the details of the Oral Law, and says that it is fitting that from them the Torah should go forth to Jews in all countries. In the opinion of many scholars (Lewin, Mann, Aptowitzer), this polemic of Pirkoi also had an anti-Karaite purpose: to ensure that the denial of the Oral Law by Karaites should not detach the Jews from the tradition customary in the Babylonian academies.

Bibliography: S. Schechter, in: *Festschrift ... D. Hoffmann* (1914), Heb. pt. 261–6; V. Aptowitzer, in: REJ, 57 (1909), 246ff.; idem, in: HUCA, 8–9 (1931–32), 382, 415–7; idem, *Meḥkarim be-Sifrut ha-Ge'onim* (1941), 13–17; J. Mann, in: REJ, 70 (1920), 113–48; idem, in: *Tarbiz,* 6 (1935), 78f.; J. N. Epstein, in: REJ, 75 (1922), 179–86; idem, in: *Madda'ei ha-Yahadut,* 2 (1927), 149–61; idem, in: *Tarbiz,* 2 (1931), 411f.; L. Ginzberg, *Ginzei Schechter,* 2 (1929), 504–73; B. M. Lewin, in: *Tarbiz,* 2 (1931), 383–405; Ḥ. Tchernowitz, *Toledot ha-Posekim,* 1 (1946), 109–12; Baron, Social[2], index s.v.; S. Abramson, in: *Sinai,* 50 (1962), 185f.; S. Spiegel, in: *H. A. Wolfson Jubilee Volume* (1965), Heb. pt. 243–74.
[J.Ho.]

°**PIROGOV, NIKOLAI** (1810–1881), Russian physician-surgeon and civic leader. From 1856 to 1858 he was a trustee for the Odessa education district and from 1858 to 1861 he served in the same capacity for Kiev. In south and southwest Russia he came into contact with the Jewish population and became their defender. In a letter to the Ministry of Education, dated Feb. 4, 1857, he argued for compulsory general education which would, at the same time, respect the religious sensitivities of the Jews. He proposed a cadre of Jewish teachers who would have the same rights as their non-Jewish colleagues, and opposed the idea that Christian trustees should be assigned to Jewish educational institutions. In his writings Pirogov pointed out the traditional respect of Jews for education and culture, and supported O. *Rabinovich and J. *Tarnopol in their efforts to publish a Jewish periodical in Russian. He also supported A. *Zederbaum for his publication of a Hebrew periodical.

Bibliography: Morgulis, in: *Voskhod,* 5 (1881), i–iv, 1–13; Gessen, in: *Perezhitoye,* 3 (1911), 1–59; L. Greenberg, *The Jews in Russia,* 1 (1944), 102–3.
[Ed.]

PIRYATIN, city in Poltava oblast, Ukrainian S.S.R. A Jewish settlement in Piryatin was first mentioned in 1630. The community was destroyed in the massacres of 1648 and not revived until the close of the 18th century, when it became a center for *Ḥabad Ḥasidism. The community numbered 464 in 1847 and grew to 3,166 (39% of the total population) in 1897. By 1926 they numbered 3,885 (31.8%). When the Germans invaded the Soviet Union in the summer of 1941, all the Jews who had not succeeded in escaping from Piryatin were exterminated. [Y.S.]

PISA, city in Tuscany, central Italy. *Benjamin of Tudela found 20 Jewish families living there around 1165. It may be presumed that Jews had settled in the city even earlier, attracted by the possibilities offered by the close commercial ties between Pisa and countries of the Levant. Some of the Jewish tombstones embedded in the town wall, near the cathedral, date back to the middle of the 13th century. At the end of the 13th century an "Alley of the Jews" (Chiasso di Giudei) is recorded. In 1322 the Jews in Pisa were instructed to wear the distinguishing *badge but the regulation was apparently not strictly enforced. By the second half of the 14th century Pisa was in a state of political and economic decline, which culminated in its subjection to Florence in 1406. Around the same time, Vitale (Jehiel) b. Matassia of Pisa, a banker of Roman origin, began his activities in Pisa. The family he founded owned banks in Pisa and Florence, as well as branches in other towns, and for about 150 years dominated Jewish moneylending in Italy, as well as distinguishing itself in the cultural sphere (see Da *Pisa family). Some of its members had close connections with the Medici of Florence. In 1492 Jewish exiles from Spain who arrived in Pisa were assisted generously by the Da Pisa family. When a Christian loan bank (*Monte di Pietà*) was opened in Pisa in 1496, Isaac b. Jehiel subscribed over half the founding capital, so that Jews were permitted to continue their moneylending activities, although only for a short period. As a result of the struggle between the Florentine Republic, which was hostile to the Jews, and the Medici, who were favorably disposed toward them, and the war of 1494–1509 between Pisa and Florence, the Jewish community of Pisa was considerably reduced in size. It began to recover in 1547 when Cosimo I de'Medici, duke of Tuscany, urged Jews and *New Christian fugitives from Portugal to settle in Pisa and *Leghorn, and some accepted the invitation. Larger numbers were attracted by the generous terms of the proclamation issued in June 1593 by the grand duke Ferdinand I de'Medici, addressed particularly to Sephardim and Marranos wherever they happened to live. Another proclamation, issued in October 1595 to the German and Italian Jews, who had then been driven from the territories of Milan, aroused little response. The Medici wished to promote Pisa as the market capital of Tuscany, with the port of Leghorn dependent on Pisa. However, Leghorn developed more successfully and also attained greater importance as a Jewish center, and in 1614 became independent of Pisa.

Samuel *Foa (or Fua), a member of the famous printing family of Sabbioneta, established a Hebrew press at Pisa toward the end of the 18th century, and was succeeded by Samuel and Joseph Moliho (1816ff.).

There were 600 Jews living in Pisa at the beginning of the 17th century, and half that number a century later. The number remained thereafter approximately the same, totaling 365 in 1840. Most of the Jews in Pisa were governed by the liberal patents of 1593 which granted, among other privileges, Tuscan citizenship ipso jure to any person admitted as a member of the community, and semiautonomous internal jurisdiction. The Jews in Pisa lived in relative

The synagogue of Pisa, built in 1595 and remodeled in the 19th century. Photo G. Allegrini, Pisa.

tranquillity, mainly engaging in commerce. In the 18th and especially the 19th century, they played an active part in developing industries, particularly the cotton industries which attracted a certain number of Jews there. The Jewish population numbered 700 in 1881. [A.MIL.]

Holocaust and Modern Periods. In 1931 the Jewish community of Pisa numbered 535. During the Holocaust, a dozen Jews, among them Rabbi Augusto Hasdà, were sent to extermination camps. Eight more Jews were deported elsewhere. On Aug. 1, 1944, the Nazis broke into the house of the president of the community, the well-known philanthropist Pardo-Roques, and massacred him together with six Jews who had taken refuge there. After the war, the community, including the towns of Viareggio and Lucca, had a membership of 312 Jews, which declined to 210 by 1969.

[S.D.P.]

Bibliography: Cassuto, in: RI, 5 (1908), 227–38; 6 (1909), 21–30, 102–13, 160–70, 223–32; 7 (1910), 9–19, 72–86, 146–50; Toaff, in: *Scritti in memoria di Guido Bedarida* (1966), 227–62; Kaufmann, in: REJ, 26 (1893), 83–110, 220–39; 29 (1894), 142–7; 31 (1895), 62–73; 32 (1896), 130–4; C. Roth, *Jews in the Renaissance* (1959), index; Roth, Italy, index; Milano, Italia, index; Milano, Bibliotheca, index; D. W. Amram, *Makers of Hebrew Books in Italy* (1909), 396f.

PISA, DA, family of loan bankers in Italy in the Renaissance period, which ranked for many generations among the best-known Italian Jewish families. Its founder MATASSIA DI SABATO, a descendant of the Bet-El, Min-ha-Keneset, or Da Sinagoga family of Rome, settled in San Miniato, a small town in Tuscany, in 1393. His son (1) VITALE (Jehiel; d. 1422 or 1423) opened a loan bank in Pisa in 1416. Subsequently he and his descendants were known as Da Pisa (also Da San Miniato). Vitale also maintained loan banks in San Gimignano and was an associate in the banks in Prato and Colle di Val d'Elsa. A scholar and lover of letters, he became known even outside Italy: Profiat *Duran commended him to his disciple Judah Zark, who when visiting Italy received hospitality in Vitale's home. After his death his son-in-law, (2) ISAAC DI MANUELE DA RIMINI, carried on the Da Pisa family business and was himself known by the family name. At first he directed its affairs as the representative of his wife and his brother-in-law's daughters, and from 1426 as head of the enterprise. This he expanded considerably and in 1448 was among the first to receive a concession to open a loan bank in the city of Florence, in partnership with his son Vitale (3). Isaac owned a large Hebrew library and his correspondence shows that he had a wide knowledge of philosophy.

His son (3) VITALE (Jehiel; d. 1490), the most outstanding member of the family, acquired a concession to engage in loan banking in Florence, where he settled. After his father's death, he headed the family enterprise, becoming the most important of the loan bankers in Tuscany. He extended the business to Arezzo and Lucca and possibly also to Forli and Rimini. He had family connections with other important families (San Miniato and Volterra) and was friendly with notables abroad, including Abraham *Ḥayyun of Lisbon and Don Isaac *Abrabanel. In 1472 an attempt by the populace to attack his business house in Florence was prevented by the authorities. When the Franciscan *Bernardino da Feltre preached in Florence against the Jewish loan banks, Vitale led a deputation of the bankers of the city to Lorenzo de'Medici (the Magnificent) and succeeded in averting an edict of expulsion (1488). Vitale's house became known as a meeting place of scholars; among those who stayed there was Johanan *Allemanno who taught Vitale's sons. These, (4) ISAAC and (5) SIMONE (Samuel), continued the family banking enterprise, but it declined in importance after the establishment of Christian loan banks (**Monte di Pietà*) and the expulsion of Jewish moneylenders from Florence decreed in 1495. Isaac helped to establish the *Monte di Pietà* in Pisa, regarding it as an enterprise aimed at relieving the poor. He gave outstanding help to the Jewish refugees from Spain after 1492. In 1514 the Da Pisa family returned to Florence, the Medici having been restored, but in 1527, on the downfall of the Medici, they were again expelled.

Isaac's son (6) DANIEL (d. c. 1532) established connections with Rome, where he had free access to the papal court. He was entrusted with the preparation of a new code of regulations for the Rome community, to put an end to internal disputes; the code was approved in 1524. He welcomed David *Reuveni on his visit to Rome. (7) VITALE (Jehiel Nissim), son of Simone (5), a scholar, had profound knowledge of Scripture, philosophy, Kabbalah, and astronomy. He wrote *Minḥat Kena'ot* (publ. by D. Kaufmann, 1898), aimed at demonstrating the superiority of religion over philosophy, and *Ma'amar Ḥayyei Olam*, a halakhic treatise on matters of finance (publ. in 1962 by G. Rosenthal under the title *Banking and Finance among Jews in Renaissance Italy* with notes and biographical sketch). His house was open to the needy: testimony to his munificence is found in the diary of David Reuveni, who was given hospitality in his house during his stay in Italy. His son (8) SIMONE (Samuel) carried on the family tradition of learning. In 1554 he received from Pope Julius III special permission to graduate as a doctor of medicine at the University of Pisa.

Bibliography: U. Cassuto, in: RI, 5 (1908), 277–38; 10 (1913–15), 48–59; D. Kaufmann, in: REJ, 31 (1895), 62–73; Milano, Italia, index; idem, in: RMI, 10 (1935/36), 324–38, 409–26; Roth, Italy, index.

[M.E.A.]

PISGAH (Heb. פִּסְגָּה), mountain in Transjordan in the territory of the tribe of Reuben (Josh. 13:20). It lay on the border between the land of Sihon the Amorite and the territory of Reuben, northeast of the Dead Sea (Deut. 3:17; 4:49; Josh. 12:3). In the above passages, the reference is apparently to the slopes of Mt. Pisgah near the Dead Sea (Num. 21:20; 23:14; Deut. 3:27; 34:1). More precisely, they probably refer to the western slope of the mountain. The slopes of Mt. Pisgah served as an important juncture for the roads in the area of the mountain ridge of Nebo. It is probably due to the area's geographic location that biblical sources emphasized its location within the borders of Israelite settlement. The "top of Pisgah" (Deut. 34:1) is identified with Ra's al-Siyāgha, west of Mt. Nebo (supposedly the Siyaran mentioned in one version of Targum Onkelos, Num. 32:3: cf. *"Netinah la-Ger," ibid.*). This is the place from which Moses viewed the Promised Land before his death.

Bibliography: Birch, in: PEFQS, 40 (1898), 110–1; A. Musil, *Arabia Petraea*, 1 (Ger., 1907), passim; I. S. Horowitz, *Ereẓ Yisrael u-Shekhenoteha* (1923) s.v. *Ashdot ha-Pisgah;* Abel, Geog, 1 (1933), 281, 379ff.

[M.A.-Y.]

PISSARRO, CAMILLE (1830–1903), French painter. Born into a Sephardi family which had migrated from Bordeaux to the Virgin Islands, he was sent to a boarding school in Paris at the age of 12. At 17 he returned to St. Thomas to become a clerk in his father's general store, but he wanted to be an artist, and ran away to Caracas, Venezuela. After a while he obtained his father's permission to study in France, and from 1855 until his death, he remained in, or near, Paris.

With his socialist-anarchist convictions, he regarded himself a citizen of the world, with no particular religious, racial, or national ties. His wife was of Catholic peasant

Self-portrait by Camille Pissarro, French impressionist painter, 1903.

stock. He was shocked and hurt by the *Dreyfus case, but more as a man of progressive political ideals than as a Jew. Pissarro became a staunch member of a loosely organized group that came into being in 1874 under the name of "Société anonyme des artistes, peintres, sculpteurs, et graveurs" which soon became better known as the "Impressionists." He participated in all of the Impressionists' eight group shows, received his share of abuse from public and press, and held the group together until 1886, after Cézanne, Renoir, and even the prime mover, Monet, had lost interest.

He took his guidance from Corot and Courbet, blending Corot's subtlety of atmospheric effect with the strength and solidity of Courbet. In 1865 he came under the spell of Manet. By that time he had already eliminated black, and the siennas and ochers from his palette. In his mid-fifties, he was greatly influenced by Georges Seurat's pointillist technique, and for several years he experimented with the "divisionist" method of painting with little dots of primary color. Yet, he is chiefly known for his Impressionist landscapes and cityscapes. Pissarro thought he saw nature objectively but actually he rendered it just as much from feeling and knowledge as from dispassionate sight—rendered it in solidly constructed, architectural forms. Most of his canvases show a definite desire for order and organization, and a feeling for design. His work is uneven—perhaps more uneven that that of other artists, since he was forced to overproduce in his efforts to keep his family of eight from starvation.

All of Pissarro's sons—Lucien (1863–1944), Georges (1871–1961), Félix (1874–1897), Ludovic-Rudolphe (1878–1952), and Paul-Emile (1884–)—were gifted artists, but only one, LUCIEN PISSARRO, achieved a modicum of fame for his Impressionist landscapes and his woodcuts. Lucien played a major part in the introduction of Impressionist painting to England. Educated in France, he was trained by his father and in 1890 went to England, where he met William Morris, Charles Ricketts, and Charles Shannon who interested him in the art of book design. He later set up his own publishing firm, the Eragny Press, and collaborated with his wife in the production of beautifully illustrated books. Among his book productions was *The Book of Ruth and Esther*. Lucien's daughter Orovida (1893–1968) inherited his talent. She signed her work with her first name, and became known for her studies of animals.

Bibliography: J. Rewald, *Pissarro* (Eng., 1963); idem (ed.), *Camille Pissarro: Letters to his Son Lucien* (1943); A. Werner, *Pissarro* (Eng., 1963); W. S. Meadmore, *Lucien Pissarro* (Eng., 1962). [A.W.]

PISTACHIO (Heb. בָּטְנָה; *botnah*), the tree and fruit of the *Pistacia vera*, a dioecious tree. The female tree produces reddish clusters of nuts with a white shell and a greenish kernel of delicate flavor. The word occurs only once in the Bible, in the plural, בָּטְנִים *(botnim)*, among the "choice fruits of the land" sent by Jacob to the ruler of Egypt (Gen. 43:11). The Samaritan translation of the word is *biẓtekin*, i.e., pistachio. The Mishnah calls the tree *botnah* (Shev. 7:5) and its fruit *pistakin*. They were grown in Israel, and subject to tithes (TJ, Ma'as. 1:2, 48d). Two members of its genus, *Pistacia palaestina* and *Pistacia atlantica*, are indigenous to Ereẓ Israel but the fruit is hardly edible. It was customary, however, to graft the pistachio onto the branches of these species whose trees and fruit are called *botmin* (Ar. *but'm*) in the Talmud. The pistachio tree is similar to the latter, but its nuts taste like the almond, and in consequence the ancients thought it to be a hybrid of these two species (TJ, Kil. 1:4, 27a). In modern Hebrew *botnim* is used to designate peanuts. The identification is erroneous, for not only was the peanut brought from the Americas, but it is not a tree, as *botnim* definitely are, according to the Mishnah.

Bibliography: Loew, Flora, 1 (1926), 190–200; J. Feliks, *Kilei Zera'im ve-Harkavah* (1967), 106–7; idem, in: *Olam ha-Ẓome'aḥ ha-Mikra'i* (1968^{2}), 64–65; H. N. and A. L. Moldenke, *Plants of the Bible* (1952), 319 (index), s.v. Pistachio and Pistacia. [J.F.]

°**PISTORIUS (de Nida), JOHANNES** (1546–1608), German scholar. Pistorius was physician and adviser to the margrave of Baden-Durlach, whom he induced to support the Protestants; he himself later reverted to Catholicism, however, and entered the priesthood in 1591. He is mainly remembered for his *Artis Cabbalisticae, hoc est reconditae theologiae et philosophiae Scriptorum Tomus I* (Basle, 1587), a compendium of Christian mystical literature (including Johannes *Reuchlin's *De Arte Cabalistica* and Archangelus de Burgonuovo's commentaries on the "Conclusions" of Giovanni *Pico della Mirandola) which also contained a translation of Judah *Abrabanel's *Dialoghi di Amore*. A second volume, planned to contain major Jewish kabbalistic works, never appeared, probably as a result of Catholic objections to some of the material in the published compendium. The *Artis Cabbalisticae* was consulted by many later authors and is the most likely source of *Milton's knowledge of the Kabbalah.

Bibliography: F. Secret, *Les Kabbalistes chrétiens de la Renaissance* (1964), 79–80; D. Hirst, *Hidden Riches...* (1964), index. [G.E.S.]

PITHOM (Egyptian **Per Atum**, "House of the god Atum"), a city mentioned once in the Bible (Ex. 1:11) as one of the two treasury cities (see also *Ramses) which the Israelites were forced to build for Pharaoh. The identification of Pithom with the site of Tell el-Maskhutah near the eastern end of the Wadi Tumilat has been accepted for many years by a large number of scholars despite the lack of any definite evidence that the town located there, Tjeku (= biblical Succoth?), was called Pithom (Per Atum) earlier than the Egyptian 22nd Dynasty (c. 945–730 B.C.E.) or that

The cities of Pithom (above) and Ramses depicted in the illustrated edition of a printed *Haggadah,* 1527. From *Facsimile of the Prague Haggadah,* Berlin, 1926.

Ramses II, the supposed pharaoh of the bondage, had built a completely new city there (as implied in Ex. 1:11). The 19th-Dynasty Egyptian text mentioning the "pools of Per-Atum of Merneptah which are in Tjeku" (Papyrus Anastasi IV, 4:56) may or may not refer to this city. An alternative identification of the site as Tell er-Ratabeh, about 22 miles west of Ismailia, has also been proposed and has been accepted by some. The most recent and most convincing identification depends on the Egyptians' use of *Per* (literally "house") in a wider, administrative context as the large region under the control of the temple of a particular god. *Per* could then refer to a city sacred to that god, as did Per Amun to Thebes and Per Bastet to Bubastis. Since Atum was a manifestation of the sun god, Per Atum could very well have meant *Heliopolis (called On in the Bible). It is quite probable that the Beth-Shemesh of Jeremiah 43:13 is a Hebrew translation of Per Atum. Such an identification is well supported by the size, importance, and fame of Heliopolis.

Bibliography: E. P. Uphill, in: JNES, 27 (1968), 291–316; 28 (1969), 15–39. [Al.R.S.]

PITIGRILLI (pen name of **Dino Segre;** 1893–1954), Italian author and journalist. After working on the staff of *L'Epoca* in Rome, Segre was a foreign correspondent in Istanbul and later founded two popular reviews, *Le Grandi Firme* and *Il Dramma,* in his native Turin. As Pitigrilli, he wrote novels and short stories which gained considerable notoriety in France as well as Italy for their erotic, often pornographic, themes and qualities, and their analysis, superficial though it was, of moral behavior. They include *La cintura di castita* (1921), *La vergine a 18 carati* (1924), *I vegetariani dell'amore* (1932), and *Dolicocefala bionda* (1936). During the Fascist era Pitigrilli became a police informer and, between 1934 and 1938, collaborated with the O.V.R.A., Mussolini's secret police. As a result of these activities, he later had to seek refuge in Argentina. On his return to Italy after World War II, he ostentatiously embraced Catholicism and wrote anti-Jewish books such as *Mosè e il cavalier Levi* (1948).

Bibliography: D. Zucáro (ed.), *Lettere all' O.V.R.A. di Pitigrilli* (1961). [Ed.]

PITTSBURGH, a leading industrial city in western Pennsylvania; 1969 population, 600,000; estimated Jewish population, 45,000.

Early History. When the Quaker William Penn received the colonial charter for the area from Charles II in 1680 he incorporated a guarantee of religious freedom. Accordingly, many varied sects settled in Pennsylvania, including Jews. Among the early settlers were Joseph *Simon and Levy Andrew Levy.

After the Revolutionary War, the prosperous Philadelphia merchant David *Franks sent agents, among them Michael Gratz, with pack trains to Pittsburgh so often that their route was labeled Frankstown Road. They and several other Jews bought plots of land, apparently for speculation, and the map indicates a cluster of lots to the east marked "Jewstown," with another area near Sewickley marked "Gratztown." Most of the Jews, like other traders, came and went as itinerant peddlers, but a few remained, striking roots. The first known permanent resident of Pittsburgh to have Jewish ancestry was Samuel Pettigrew, son of Judith *Hart, who settled in the town in 1814 and later served as mayor.

On the whole, however, economic difficulties caused by the diversion of river traffic by the Erie Canal kept Jewish immigration down. It was not until 1842 that Jews first met in a *minyan* for worship in a home near the Point. There is a dearth of records of this period, most having been destroyed in the great fire that swept the wooden town in 1845. In that year the Beth Almon Society was formed; land for a cemetery on Troy Hill was bought in 1846. With the building of a railroad in 1849, Jewish settlement began to increase. In 1852 there were 30 Jewish families in Pittsburgh, and six years later the number doubled. By 1854 a group meeting in a room over Vigilant Fire Department organized itself as Rodef Shalom, and in 1861 a building was dedicated on Hancock Street (later Eighth Street) where a Mr. Armhold served as reader, *mohel,* and *shoḥet.* German was the language of sermons and records, but the congregants showed willingness to modify practice regarding covered heads and mixed seating, among others. This caused dissension, and a new group was created in 1864 calling itself Etz Hayim, more conservative in practice. In 1861 Rodef Shalom brought a young English Jew, Josiah Cohen, to head its religious school and preach in English. He later became a distinguished judge.

With the outbreak of the Civil War, Pittsburgh grew in importance and population. From a handful, the number of Jews in 1864 became 750, nearly all of German origin. Ten of their men were in uniform. Women served on the Sanitary Commission, forerunner of the Red Cross. The United Hebrew Relief Society assisted returning soldiers and their families. Expanding heavy industry that was to make Pittsburgh the "Workshop of the World" drew great streams of immigration from Europe. The population had outgrown the Triangle, and pushed upward with stores on Fifth Avenue and small red-brick houses on adjacent streets on the "Hill." Some moved across the river to the town of Allegheny. More affluent Jews followed them there. By 1877 there were 2,000 Jews in Pittsburgh, many of them recent immigrants from Lithuania, sharing in the ferment of the industrial growth of the city and its environs. Many peddlers moved out to the surrounding towns, but all returned to the city for the Sabbath and holidays and for *kasher* food.

Temple Sinai, a Reform synagogue in Pittsburgh, Pennsylvania.

In 1885 a national group of leading Reform rabbis led by Rabbi Isaac Mayer *Wise met in Pittsburgh and articulated a series of points that were to be known as the *Pittsburgh Platform.

East European Immigration. The Russian pogroms of 1881 set in motion the mass exodus which brought Russian Jews to America. Many thousands came to Pittsburgh, raising its Jewish population to 15,000 by 1905. The earlier residents received the penniless immigrants as their own, despite barriers of language and provincial manners. They doled out silver dollars for Sabbath meals, and helped to find lodgings and jobs. The Council of Jewish Women provided English teachers, gave guidance to homeless girls, and conducted classes in religion for children. The Gusky Orphanage was established, and various family and health services were founded. The Hebrew Free Loan Association assisted the newcomers with small sums to start them in business.

The rush of immigration brought an influx of well-educated Hebraic scholars from the yeshivot of Lithuania and Poland. In 1877 Rabbi Markowitz led the first of many Orthodox congregations. Rabbi Simon Sivitz founded the Shaare Torah Congregation and *talmud torah* in 1888. In 1901 Rabbi Aaron *Ashinsky led Beth Jacob and Beth Hamedrash Hagodol, and was a driving force in creating new agencies conducted in the Orthodox tradition, including the House of Shelter, Home for Aged, and Hebrew Institute. A variety of synagogues served Russian, Polish, Galician, and Hungarian groups. The demand for *kasher* food in a hospital and the need for professional openings for Jewish doctors inspired a group of women led by Mrs. Barnett David to inaugurate fund raising that led to the creation of Montefiore Hospital. The Irene Kaufmann Settlement was the recreation center for large numbers of immigrants. By 1912 a full complement of social agencies united in the Federation of Jewish Philanthropies with headquarters on Fernando Street, easily accessible to the Yiddish-speaking community from the Hill. In that year there were 35,000 Jews in Pittsburgh. By the close of free immigration in 1925, there were 60,000 Jews in the area, many of whom had begun spilling over the margins of the Hill to Oakland, East End, and Squirrel Hill.

A complex community was growing. The Workmen's Circle fostered socialist ideas in an agnostic framework. Largely inspired by Rabbi Ashinsky, a vibrant Zionist movement flourished. A branch of the American Jewish Committee came into being; the B'nai B'rith lodges multiplied, and the American Jewish Congress added a note of militancy. Jewish War Veterans organized a Post.

Post-World War I. A new generation of young people, native American Jews, moved with enthusiasm and talent through the public schools, heading on to colleges and eastern universities. English was spoken everywhere, and prevailing American social amenities were the norm. Attendance at worship services dropped off and religious education reached a low ebb. But the Jews were playing an appreciable role in the growth of Pittsburgh. Parallel with the vast development of the steel industry, Jewish store-keeping had blossomed into great department stores—Kaufmann's, Kaufmann and Baer's, Rosenbaum's, Frank and Seder's. These and other Jewish names appeared among those who sponsored symphony concerts, art exhibitions, and other cultural events. Although the leading social clubs still practiced exclusion, Jews had created pleasant facilities for themselves and began to emerge on the political and social scene, a number serving with distinction in the judiciary, city council, board of education, and state legislature.

With the Depression of the 1930s, the Jews were able to "take care of their own" through numerous agencies which were united in the Federation of Jewish Philanthropies. As the decade advanced and the urgency to provide help for German Jewry became evident, new service and fund-raising agencies were called into being. In 1936 the United Jewish Fund was established. Reacting to the Nazi tragedy, Pittsburgh received its share of refugees from Germany, responded with fervor to the effort to create a Jewish homeland, and raised unprecedented sums for overseas relief.

A total transfer of Jewish population had taken place from the Hill to Squirrel Hill and the suburbs. New structures housed the synagogues, old and new. Awakened by the Holocaust, a renewed zeal for Jewish education resulted in highly developed programs of the Hebrew Institute, Hillel, and the Advanced Jewish Study Program of the United Jewish Federation. Synagogues responded with emphasis on education and youth, as well as keen interest in the State of Israel.

In 1970 Pittsburgh Jewry numbered 45,000, a decrease attributable to a growing tendency to relocate in the suburbs. Leadership passed into the hands of a new generation, largely of East European origin. Rodef Shalom remained the largest and most prestigious congregation, although no longer dominated solely by the "German" families. Montefiore Hospital, with 500 beds, was a teaching arm of the University of Pittsburgh. The Symphony Orchestra included many Jews, players as well as the conductor, and many generous patrons. There were several hundred Jewish teachers and principals in the public schools, and many distinguished members of university faculties. Jewish names were outstanding in the city's history—Otto *Stern, Nobel prizewinner; Alexander Silverman, glass chemist; Joseph Slepian, electrical engineer; George S. *Kaufman, dramatist; Jonas *Salk, discoverer of polio vaccine; Solomon B. *Freehof, rabbi; Samuel Rosenberg, artist; William Steinberg, conductor; and Immanuel Estermann, physicist.

Bibliography: M. Taylor, *Jewish Community of Pittsburgh, December, 1938* (1941); A. J. Karp (ed.), *Jewish Experience in America*, 1 and 4 (1968), indexes. [L.A.F.]

PITTSBURGH PLATFORM, formulation of principles agreed upon by the Reform movement in 1885 at the Pittsburgh Conference. The conference was called together by Kaufmann *Kohler of New York and was chaired by Isaac M. *Wise of Cincinnati, the foremost figure in *Reform Judaism. The Pittsburgh Platform symbolized the reconciliation and merger of the eastern U.S. and Germanic-oriented wing of Reform Judaism—previously led by David *Einhorn, the father-in-law of Kohler—with the slightly more moderate English outlook, which was stronger in the western U.S.—led by Wise. The following points were agreed upon and became known as the Pittsburgh Platform.

First—We recognize in every religion an attempt to grasp the Infinite, and in every mode, source, or book or revelation held sacred in any religious system, the consciousness of the indwelling of God in man. We hold that Judaism presents the highest conception of the God idea as taught in our holy Scriptures and developed and spiritualized by the Jewish teachers, in accordance with the moral and philosophical progress of their respective ages. We maintain that Judaism preserved and defended, midst continual struggles and trials and under enforced isolation, this God idea as the central religious truth for the human race.

Second—We recognize in the Bible the record of the consecration of the Jewish people to its mission as priest of the one God, and value it as the most potent instrument of religious and moral instruction. We hold that the modern discoveries of scientific researches in the domains of nature and history are not antagonistic to the doctrines of Judaism, the Bible reflecting the primative ideas of its own age, and at times clothing its conception of Divine Providence and justice, dealing with man in miraculous narratives.

Third—We recognize in the Mosaic legislation a system of training the Jewish people for its mission during its national life in Palestine, and to-day we accept as binding only the moral laws, and maintain only such ceremonies as elevate and sanctify our lives, but reject all such as are not adapted to the views and habits of modern civilization.

Fourth—We hold that all such Mosaic and rabbinical laws as regulate diet, priestly purity, and dress, originated in ages and under the influence of ideas altogether foreign to our present mental and spiritual state. They fail to impress the modern Jew with a spirit of priestly holiness; their observance in our days is apt rather to obstruct than to further modern spiritual elevation.

Fifth—We recognize, in the modern era of universal culture of heart and intellect, the approaching of the realization of Israel's great messianic hope for the establishment of the kingdom of truth, justice, and peace among all men. We consider ourselves no longer a nation, but a religious community, and therefore expect neither a return to Palestine, nor a sacrificial worship under the sons of Aaron, nor the restoration of any of the laws concerning the Jewish state.

Sixth—We recognize in Judaism a progressive religion, ever striving to be in accord with the postulates of reason. We are convinced of the utmost necessity of preserving the historical identity with our great past. Christianity and Islam being daughter religions of Judaism, we appreciate their providential mission to aid in the spreading of monotheistic and moral truth. We acknowledge that the spirit of broad humanity of our age is our ally in the fulfillment of our mission, and therefore, we extend the hand of fellowship to all who operate with us in the establishment of the reign of truth and righteousness among men.

Seventh—We reassert the doctrine of Judaism, that the soul of man is immortal, grounding this belief on the divine nature of the human spirit, which forever finds bliss in righteousness and misery in wickedness. We reject as ideas not rooted in Judaism the beliefs both in bodily resurrection and in Gehenna and Eden (Hell and Paradise) as abodes for everlasting punishment or reward.

Eighth—In full accordance with the spirit of Mosaic legislation, which strives to regulate the relation between rich and poor, we deem it our duty to participate in the great task of modern times, to solve on the basis of justice and righteousness, the problems presented by the contrasts and evils of the present organization of society.

At its founding in 1889, the *Central Conference of American Rabbis (CCAR), the Reform rabbinical organization, adopted the platform in toto, and it remained the major statement of the basic tenets of Reform Judaism until its extensive revision by the CCAR in Columbus, Ohio, in 1937. [Ed.]

PITTUM HA-KETORET (Heb. פִּטּוּם הַקְּטֹרֶת; "ingredients of the incense"), the initial words of a *baraita* (Ker. 6a and TJ, Yoma 4:5, 41d) which enumerates the various species of incense offerings in the Temple service every evening and morning (see: Ex. 30:34–38). In the Ashkenazi liturgy, this talmudic passage is recited on Sabbaths and festivals at the end of the *Musaf* prayer immediately after the **Ein ke-Elohenu* hymn; in the Sephardi ritual it is recited every morning and afternoon. The custom of reciting *Pittum ha-Ketoret* is based on a quotation in the Zohar (to Num. 224a), where it is stated that a person who recites the section of incenses will be spared death (see also: Num. 17:12 and Yoma 44a). In Provence (southern France), it was customary to recite *Pittum ha-Ketoret* at the departure of the Sabbath, after the *Havdalah* service, as a good omen for wealth and prosperity (Abraham ha-Yarḥi, *Sefer ha-Manhig*, ed. Berlin (1855), Hilkhot Shabbat, 75, 35a).

See also *Incense and Perfumes.

Bibliography: G. Munk, *The World of Prayer* 1 (1961), 193; 2 (1963), 58–59; Eisenstein, Dinim, s.v. [Ed.]

°**PIUS X** (1835–1914), pope from 1903. Friendly to individual Jews and ready to acknowledge their philanthropic activities, he was, however, disdainful of Judaism and the Jewish people. On one occasion, while serving as bishop of Mantua, he prohibited the celebration of a solemn mass in honor of the king's birthday because the mayor had attended a prayer service in the synagogue on that day. The pope reacted bitterly to a festive address by Ernesto *Nathan, mayor of Rome, on Sept. 20, 1910, delivered on the occasion of the 40th anniversary of the occupation of Rome by Italian troops, and asked Catholics to pray for the Church "which was being attacked with impunity by its enemies." On Jan. 25, 1904, he received Theodor *Herzl in private audience, only to inform him that he could not support the aspirations of Zionism despite Herzl's expressed statement that Jerusalem, because of its holy places, would be extraterritorial. The pope declared: "The Jews have not recognized our Lord, therefore we cannot recognize the Jewish people," and settlement of Ereẓ Israel by the Jews, he felt, would only make it incumbent upon him to intensify missionary activities among them: "If you come to Palestine and settle your people there, we shall have churches and priests ready to baptize all of you."

Bibliography: K. Burton, *The Great Mantle. The Life of Giuseppe Melchiore Sarto, Pope Pius X* (1950); T. Herzl, *Complete Diaries*, ed. by R. Patai, 5 (1960), index. [W.P.E.]

°**PIUS XI** (1857–1939), pope from 1922. Concerned about the safety of the holy places, Pius XI had misgivings regarding the Palestine mandate. A decree of the Holy Office (March 21, 1928) proscribed the Amici Israel Association (founded two years earlier) which, though missionary in its ideology, tried to promote better understanding of Judaism. The Holy Office declared the organization contrary to the spirit of the Church, finding fault specifically with its publication *Pax super Israel*, which called upon its members to promote rapprochement with the Jews, while avoiding all offensive references and stressing the fact that the Jews continue to be the Chosen People. At the same time, however, the decree also proscribed anti-Semitism on the basis that it is contradictory to Christian doctrine.

Although Pius XI did not respond to a plea submitted to him in 1933 by a Catholic convert from Judaism, Edith *Stein, to issue an encyclical on the so-called Jewish problem, he condemned racism repeatedly. To a group of Belgian pilgrims, whom he received on Sept. 8, 1938, Pius XI declared: "It is not possible for Christians to take part in anti-Semitism. Spiritually we are Semites." His efforts to protect the Jews in Fascist Italy against anti-Semitic actions met with some success. He also helped immigrants and on Jan. 14, 1939, called upon the envoys accredited to the Holy See to provide as many immigration visas as possible "for the victims of racial persecution in Germany and Italy." It was during his pontificate that *La *Civilta Cattolica,* a Jesuit organ which had previously been anti-Jewish, protested that the periodical had been misused by the Fascists.

Bibliography: G. Lewy, *The Catholic Church and Nazi Germany* (1964); G. Schwaiger, *Geschichte der Paepste im 20. Jahrhundert* (1968); S. Friedlaender, *Pius XII and the Third Reich* (1966), index.

[W.P.E.]

°**PIUS XII** (1876–1958), pope from 1939. Born Eugenio Maria Giuseppe Giovanni Pacelli, in Rome, he entered the Secretariat of State in 1901, was professor of ecclesiastical diplomacy at the Pontifical Ecclesiastical Academy from 1909 to 1914, undersecretary of state in 1911, archbishop of Sardes and apostolic nuncio to the Bavarian court in Munich in 1917, and nuncio to Germany in 1920 but moving to Berlin only in 1925. In 1929 Pacelli concluded a concordat with the State of Prussia. He became cardinal in 1929 and secretary of state in 1930. Cardinal Pacelli was instrumental in negotiating the concordat between the Holy See and the Third Reich, which was signed on July 20, 1933, by him and Vice-Chancellor von Papen. His ambivalent stance during the Nazi period subsequently gave rise to considerable controversy (much of it engendered by Rolf *Hochhuth's play "The Deputy"; for a full analysis see *Holocaust and the Christian Churches). On April 10, 1945, he received Moshe *Sharett, director of the Political Department of the Jewish Agency, in order to discuss with him the "situation of the Jews in Europe and the future of the Jews in Palestine." His views on the situation in Ereẓ Israel found expression in the encyclicals *Auspicia quaedam* (May 1, 1948), *In multiplicibus curis* (Oct. 24, 1948), and *In redemptoris nostri* (April 15, 1949), in which he recommended that Jerusalem should be internationalized. His attitude toward the State of Israel was reserved. On June 10, 1948, the Congregation of Rites ruled that the term *perfidi Judaei* in the Good Friday liturgy be translated into the vernacular as "unbelieving" and not as "faithless" as it had been hitherto.

See also *Vatican.

Bibliography: D. Fisher, *Pope Pius XII and the Jews* (1963); E. R. Bentley (ed.), *The Storm over the Deputy* (1964); G. Lewy, *The Catholic Church and Nazi Germany* (1964); S. Friedlaender, *Pius XII and the Third Reich* (1966); L. Rothkirchen, in: *Yad Vashem Studies,* 6 (1967), 27–53; P. E. Lapide, *Three Popes and the Jews* (1967), 117–305; C. Falconi, *The Silence of Pius XII* (1970).

[W.P.E.]

PIYYUT (Heb. פִּיּוּט; plural: *piyyutim;* from the Greek ποιητής), a lyrical composition intended to embellish an obligatory prayer or any other religious ceremony, communal or private. In a wider sense, *piyyut* is the totality of compositions composed in various genres of Hebrew liturgical poetry from the first centuries of the Common Era until the beginning of the Haskalah. In ancient times, the *piyyutim* were intended to replace most of the set versions of prayer and to serve as substitutes. They ensured variety of the obligatory prayers, mainly on Sabbaths and festivals. In a later period, when the prayers became fixed, sections of *piyyut* were interspersed in certain places within the set pattern of the prayers. Naturally, most of the very extensive *piyyut* literature is devoted to the adornment of the major holy days. However, during the early oriental (eastern) period of the history of the *piyyut,* liturgical compositions were also produced in great abundance for regular Sabbaths, for simple fast days, and even for weekdays. Obligatory prayers were also embellished with special sets of *piyyutim* for private occasions, such as weddings, circumcisions, and mourning. (See below: Types of *piyyut.*)

The History of the Piyyut. *Piyyut* literature began in Ereẓ Israel while the various versions of the obligatory prayers were crystallizing. Though the evidence from this period is limited, texts of ancient *piyyutim* are to be found scattered in talmudic sources, and *piyyutim* which apparently were composed during this period were absorbed into the established versions of the various rites of prayer. These ancient segments are recognizable by their lofty style and characteristic rhythm; they do not as yet use rhyme. The ancient compositions, known in part from the Cairo *Genizah* and in part from other sources, and similarly characterized by their style and rhythm, were also apparently composed during this period, which may be called "the period of the anonymous *piyyut.*"

The earliest *paytan* known to us by name is *Yose b. Yose, who lived and worked in Ereẓ Israel in approximately the sixth century or even earlier. His works still retain the above-mentioned characteristics of the form; they do not employ rhyme, even though something similar to rhyme can be seen in his *teki'ot,* where similar words are employed as line endings. With Yose b. Yose begins the period of the *paytanim* whose names are known; the period is represented by a group of important poets from Ereẓ Israel, who all seem to have been functioning before Ereẓ Israel was conquered by the Arabs (636 C.E.). The most important of these *paytanim* are *Yannai, *Simeon b. Megas, Eleazar b. *Kallir, *Ḥaduta b. Abraham, Joshua ha-Kohen, and Joseph b. Nisan from Shaveh Kiryatayim. During their period, the structural framework of most of the classical *piyyut* types was finally crystallized. Even after Ereẓ Israel was conquered by the Arabs, all the great *paytanim* worked in the East; from then until the beginning of the 11th century this literature flourished; a great quantity of *piyyutim* was produced. For the first time *paytanim* from abroad, such as Solomon Suleiman b. ʾAmr al-Sanjari, Nissi al-Nahrawani, *Saadiah Gaon, Joseph al-Bardani, and others, begin to appear. Outstanding among the *paytanim* of Ereẓ Israel are *Phinehas b. Jacob ha-Kohen from Kafra at the beginning of the period, and Samuel ha-Shelishi b. Hoshana at its close. Toward the end of the period, creative activity spread to North Africa, which in the tenth and 11th centuries became a fruitful extension of oriental *piyyut.*

On European soil, the first blossoms of *piyyut* literature appeared in Byzantine southern Italy in the second half of the ninth century. Only a few *piyyutim* from among the

(*text continued on col. 597*)

Figure 1. *Piyyut* in an 18th-century illuminated manuscript from Italy, surrounded by a floral border. Facing the *piyyut* is a representation of the Creation. Ardmore, Pa., Sigmund Harrison Collection, *Harrison Miscellany.*

The following list contains:

1. Those *paytanim* and pre-modern poets (marked by an asterisk) who have individual entries in the Encyclopaedia—included are those who are either primarily *paytanim* or famous as such;

2. *Paytanim* and pre-modern poets who do not have individual entries and who are not included in I. Davidson's *Ozar ha-Shirah ve-ha-Piyyut* (vol. 4, pp. 347) which was completed in 1933 (Davidson's additions were published in HUCA 12–13, 1937–38);

3. *Paytanim* and pre-modern poets who are in Davidson but on whom new material has been made available in the intervening years.

The list is alphabetical according to the first names.

The abbreviations used (other than standard) are:

Bernstein, Italyah—S. Bernstein, *Mi-Shirei Yisrael be-Italyah* (1939),

Bernstein, Piyyutim—S. Bernstein, *Piyyutim u-Faytanim me-ha-Tekufah ha-Bizantinit* (1941).

Habermann, Ateret—A.M. Habermann, *Ateret Renanim* (1967).

Schirmann, Italyah—J. Schirmann, *Mivḥar ha-Shirah ha-Ivrit be-Italyah* (1934).

Schirmann, Sefarad—J. Schirmann, *Ha-Shirah ha-Ivrit bi-Sefarad u-vi-Provence,* 2 vol. (1959–60[2]).

Schirmann, Shirim Ḥadashim—J. Schirmann, *Shirim Ḥadashim min ha-Genizah* (1965).

Simonohn, Mantovah—S. Simonsohn, *Toledot ha-Yehudim be-Dukkasut Mantovah,* 2 vols. (1962–64).

YMḤSI—*Yedi'ot ha-Makhon le-Ḥeker ha-Shirah ha-Ivrit,* 7 vols. (1933–58).

Name	Place	Dates
Aaron b. Abraham of Offenbach Habermann, Ateret, 126–7, 225.	Germany	18th century
Aaron b. Isaac *Hamon		
Aaron b. Joshua ibn Alamani J. Schirmann, in: YMḤSI, 6 (1945), 265–85; S.D. Goitein, in: *Tarbiz,* 28 (1959), 343ff.; A. Scheiber in: *Sefarad,* 27 (1967), 269–81.	Alexandria	12th century
Aaron b. Mariyyon ha-Kohen M. Zulay, in: YMḤSI, 5 (1939), 178–80: idem, in *Sinai,* 23 (1948), 214–28.	Acre	11/12th century
Aaron b. Moses Malti M. Benayahu, in: *Sefunot,* 3–4 (1969), 17.	Babylonia	16/17th century
Aaron b. Samuel ha-Levi A.M. Habermann, Amarai Kaḥ (1964).	Spain	14/15th century
*Aaron Hakiman		
Abner A.M. Habermann, in: *Sefer ha-Yovel. . . S. Federbush* (1961), 173–99.	Spain	14th century
*Abraham b. Daniel		
Abraham b. Daniel Buttrio M. Benayahu, in: *Rabbi Yosef Caro,* ed. by Y. Raphael (1969), 309–12, 323–5.	Italy	b. 1510
Abraham b. Gabriel Zafrana J.L. Weinberger, in: HUCA, 39 (1968), 19–22 (Heb. part).	Corfu	16th century
Abraham b. Isaac M. Zulay, in: *Sinai,* 25 (1949), 46–47.	Babylonia?	10/11th century
Abraham b. Isaac H. Schirmann, in: *Leshonenu,* 21 (1957), 212–9; S. Abramson, *ibid.,* 25 (1961), 31–34.	Italy	11th century
Abraham b. Isaac *Bedersi		
Abraham b. Isaac Da Pisa Bernstein, Italyah, passim.	Italy	16th century
Abraham b. Isaac he-Ḥasid Tawil S. Bernstein, in: *Tarbiz,* 15 (1944), 97, 101–7; idem, in: *Ha-Tekufah,* 32–33 (1948), 780; D. Yarden, in: *Sefunot,* 8 (1964), 259, 266–72.	Lybia	
Abraham b. Jacob H. Merhaviah, in: *Tarbiz,* 39 (1970), 277–84.	Germany	11/12th century
Abraham b. Jacob Habermann, Ateret, 18–19, 225.	Germany or France	12th century
Abraham b. Jacob Gavison R.S. Sirat, in: *Fourth World Congress of Jewish Studies Papers,* 2 (1968), 66–67.	Algiers	1520–1578
Abraham b. Joseph ha-Kohen M. Zulay in: *Sinai,* 28 (1951), 162.	Ereẓ Israel	11th century
Abraham b. Mattathias Schirmann, Italyah, 78–79.	Rome	12th century
Abraham b. Mereno ha-Kohen Bernstein, Piyyutim, 27–28.	Corfu	13th century
Abraham b. Moses Doresh A.M. Habermann, in: Maḥanayim, 30 (1956), 149, 151–2.		14th century
Abraham b. Samuel Schirmann, Sefarad, 2 (1960[2]), 457–58; S. Abramson, in: *Leshonenu la-Am,* 18 (1967), 67ff.	Spain	13th century
Abraham b. Samuel ha-Levi *ibn Ḥasdai		
*Abraham b. Samuel he-Ḥasid (of Speyer)		
Abraham b. Shabbetai Kohen Schirmann, Italyah, 358.	Greece, Padua	1670–1729

Name	Place	Dates
Abraham b. Solomon ha-Levi Buqarat H.H. Ben-Sasson in: *Tarbiz*, 31 (1961), 59–71; A.M. Habermann, *ibid.*, 301.	Spain, Tunis	15/16th century
Abraham Di Medina M. Benayahu, in: KS, 35 (1960), 530.	Egypt	17th century
Abraham ha-Kohen A. Scheiber, in: *Zion*, 30 (1965), 123–7.	Babylonia	10th century
Abraham Ḥazzan Gerondi Schirmann, Sefarad, 2 (1960[2]), 291–4.	Spain	13th century
Abraham *ibn Al-Rabib		
Abraham *ibn Ezra		
Abraham Kohen N. Ben-Menahem, in: *Sinai*, 13 (1943), 363–5.	Crete	16th century
Abraham *Kurtabi (Kortabi)		
Abraham Maimin A.M. Habermann, *Toledot ha-Piyyut ve-ha-Shirah* (1970), 141. M. Benayahu, in: KS, 35 (1960), 528.	Safed	d. 1570?
Abu Ibrahim Isaac ibn Maskaran J. Schirmann, in YMḤSI, 4 (1938), 277.	Spain	12th century
Abu Isaac Abraham *Harizi		
Abu Ishaq Ibrahim *ibn Sahl		
Adonim b. Nissim ha-Levi N. Allony in: *Sinai*, 43 (1958), 393–4; Schirmann, Shirim Ḥadashim, 58–62.	Fez	10/11th century
*Ahimaaz b. Paltiel		
Ahitub b. Isaac J. Schirmann, in: YMḤSI, 1 (1933), 132–47.	Palermo	13th century
Akiva b. Jacob J.L. Bialer, *Min ha-Genazim* (1967), 69–77.	Frankfort	1520?–1597
*Ali (b. David) M. Zulay, in: *Sinai*, 23 (1948), 214–28.	Orient	12/13th century
Ali b. Ezekiel ha-Kohen A.M. Habermann, in: *Sinai*, 53 (1963), 183–4, 191–2.	Egypt	11th century
*Alvan b. Abraham		
*Amittai		
*Amnon of Mainz		
Amram b. Moses Ḥazzan S. Assaf and L.A. Mayer (eds.), *Sefer ha-Yishuv*, 2 (1944), 54; Habermann, Ateret, 149, 212, 230.	Ereẓ Israel	10th century?
*Anan b. Marinus ha-Kohen		
Anatoli J. Schirmann, in: YMḤSI, 1 (1933), 106–7, 121–4.	Italy	12th century
Anatoli (Zerahiah) b. David Cazani J. Schirmann, in: YMḤSI, 1 (1933), 107; J.L. Weinberger, in: HUCA, 39 (1968), 27–29 (Heb. part)	Greece	12th century
*Aryeh Judah Harari		
Asher b. Isaac ha-Levi S.H. Kook, *Iyyunim u-Meḥkarim*, 2 (1963), 197–201; E.E. Urbach (ed.), *Arugat ha-Bosem*, of Azriel b. Abraham, 4 (1963), 15–16.	Worms	11/12th century
Avigdor *Kara		
Avtalyon b. Mordecai	Turkey	17th century
Azriel b. Joseph Schirmann, Shirim Ḥadashim, 392–6.	Orient	13th century
*Baḥya (Baḥye) b. Joseph ibn Paquda		
Barhun (Abraham; maybe *Abraham b. Sahalan) M. Zulay, *Ha-Askolah ha-Paytanit shel Rav Sa'adyah Ga'on* (1964), 35.		
*Baruch b. Samuel of Mainz		
Benjamin b. Abraham *Anav		
*Benjamin b. Azriel		
*Benjamin b. Ḥiyya		
*Benjamin b. Samuel ha-Levi		
*Benjamin b. Zerah Habermann, Ateret, 176–7, 226.	Germany	11th century
Benjamin Peraḥyah Bernstein, Piyyutim, 36–39.	Greece?	14th century?
Benveniste b. Ḥiyya al-Dayyan J.L. Weinberger, in: HUCA, 39 (1968), 23–26 (Heb. part).	Spain	12/13th century
Ben Zion Aryeh Gerondi Habermann, Ateret, 128–9, 226.	Padua	1763–1820?
*Berechiah b. Natronai ha-Nakdan		
Caleb b. Said M. Zulay, in: *Sinai*, 25 (1949), 36–37.	Babylonia	10th century

Name	Place	Dates
Daniel b. Samuel *Rossena		
*David b. Aaron ibn Ḥassin		
David b. Gedaliah	France or Italy	12th century
Habermann, Ateret, 173–4, 226.		
David b. Huna	Italy	10th century
S. Bernstein, in: *Sefer ha-Yovel, Meir Waxman* (1966), 45–58.		
David b. Nasi	Orient	11th century
J. Ratzaby, in *Tarbiz,* 14 (1943), 204–13.		
David b. Saadiah ha-Kohen	Yemen	17th century
J. Tubi, in: *Ba-Ma'arakhah,* 11 (1971), no. 121, 18–19.		
David b. Samson	France	13th century?
H. Schirmann, in: *Kobez al-Jad,* 13 (1939), 43–44.		
David b. Yom Tov *ibn Bilia		
David ha-Kohen	Spain or Provence	13th century
Schirmann, Sefarad, 2 (1956), 463–5; Habermann, Ateret, 175, 226.		
David *ibn Paquda		
David Onkinerah	Salonika	16th century
J. Patai, in *Kobez al-Jad,* 12 (1937), 75–119.		
Dosa b. Joshua ha-Ḥazzan		
S. Abrason, in: *Tarbiz,* 15 (1944), 55–59.		
Dunash b. Judah	Kairouan	11th century
N. Allony, in: *Sinai,* 43 (1958), 90, 387, 396–400; Habermann, Ateret, 94–95.		
*Eleazar		
Eleazar b. Abun	Ereẓ Israel	
S. Spiegel, in: YMḤSI, 5 (1939), 267–91.		
*Eleazar b. Ḥalfon ha-Kohen		
Eleazar b. Phinehas	Ereẓ Israel	
M. Zulay, in YMḤSI, 5 (1939), 147–8.		
Eleazar ha-Ḥazzan	Ereẓ Israel	
M. Zulay, in: YMḤSI, 1 (1933), 155–6.		
Eleazar Hodaya	Ereẓ Israel	
E. Fleisher, in: *Tarbiz,* 36 (1967), 342 ff.		
Eleazar *Kallir		
Eleazar Kohen	Spain	
A. Scheiber, in: *Sinai,* 35 (1954), 183–6.		
Eliakim	Crimea	14/15th century
S. Bernstein, in: *Sefer Yovel li-Khevod S.K. Mirsky,* (1958), 465–6, 478–9.		
Eliakim b. Abraham	Europe	14/15th century
D. Pagis, in: *Sefer Ḥayyim Schirmann* (1970), 274–8.		
Eliashib Joshua Provençale	Italy	16th century
M. Benayahu, in: *Rabbi Yosef Caro,* ed by Y. Raphael (1969), 313, 340.		
Eliezer b. Epharaim	Germany or France	13th century
Urbach, Tosafot, 414–6.		
*Eliezer b. Samson		
Eliezer de Mordo	Corfu	17th/18th century
Bernstein, Piyyutim, 16–18; S. Simonsohn, in: PAAJR, 34 (1966), 106–8.		
Eliezer Gentili (Ḥefeẓ)	Italy	18th century
Schirmann, Italyah, 398.		
Elieẓer Leizer b. Judah Loeb	Germany	17th century
A.M. Habermann, in: *Maḥanayim,* 89 (1964), 20–23.		
Elijah b. Abraham	Greece	15th century?
Bernstein, Piyyutim, 63–65.		
Elijah b. David Mazzal Tov	Corfu	1575–1625
Bernstein, Piyyutim, 65–67.		
Elijah b. Eliezer Delmedigo	Crete	16th century
J.L. Weinberger, in: HUCA, 39 (1968), 34–37 (Heb. part).		
*Elijah b. Eliezer Philosoph		
Elijah b. Menahem ha-Zaken	Le Mans	11th century
A.M. Habermann (ed.), *Shirei ha-Yiḥud ve-ha-Kavod* (1948), 87–97.		
Elijah b. Mordecai	Italy	10th century
A. Mirsky, in: *Sinai,* 65 (1969), 179–87.		
Elijah b. Moses *Kapuzato		
Elijah b. Samuel	Macedonia	15th century
A.M. Habermann, *Sefer ha-Yovel . . .* Ḥ. Albeck (1963), 160–76.		
Elijah b. Shemaiah	Bari	11th century
Schirmann, Italyah, 41–47; Habermann, Ateret, 22–24, 225.		

Name	Place	Dates
Elijah b. Shalom, or, Samuel A.M. Habermann, in: *Haaretz* (Sept. 21, 1960).	Germany	13th century?
*Elijah Chelebi ha-Kohen of Anatolia		
Elijah of Buttrio M. Benayahu, in: *Rabbi Yosef Caro,* ed. by Y. Raphael (1969), 312–3, 326–39.	Italy	16th century
("En") Maimon *Galipapa		
*Ephraim b. Isaac of Regensburg		
Ephraim b. Joab Schirmann, Italyah, 200–2.	Modena (Italy)	14th century
Ezekiel b. Ali ha-Kohen Albasir M. Zulay, in: YMḤSI, 3 (1936), 57–58; A. Mirsky, *Yalkut ha-Piyyutim* (1958), 60–63.	Persia, Iraq, or Egypt	11th century
Ezekiel (Hezekiah) David b. Mordecai *Abulafia (Bolaffi)		
Gamaliel b. Moses Schirmann, Shirim Ḥadashim, 126–9.	Egypt	12th century
Gershom b. Solomon b. Isaac J. Schirmann, in: *Kobez al-Jad,* 3 (1939), 41–43.	France or Germany	12th century
*Ḥaduta b. Abraham ha-Efrati		
Hananel b. Amnon S.H. Kook, *Iyyunim u-Meḥkarim,* 2 (1963), 201–2.	Italy	10th century?
Hananiah S. Bernstein, in: *Sinai,* 19 (1946), 213.	Orient	12th century
Hananiah Eliakim b. Asael Raphael Rieti Simonsohn, Mantovah, 2 (1964), 544.	Bologna and Mantua	1561–1623
Ḥarizi Habermann, Ateret 113, 226	Spain	
Ḥayyim b. Machir J. Schirmann, in: *Kobez al-Jad,* 13 (1939), 58–62; A.M. Habermann, *Gezerot Ashkenaz ve-Ẓarefat* (1946), 198–202.	Regensburg	13th century
Ḥiyya b. Al-Daudi S. Bernstein, in: *Sinai,* 19 (1946), 99–104, 208–17, 313–37.	Spain	d. 1153/54
Immanuel b. David *Frances		
Immanuel Benevento I. Sonne, *Mi-Paulus ha-Revi'i ad Pius ha-Hamishi* (1954), 110–7.	Italy	16th century
Immanuel b. Joseph S. Bernstein, *Al Naharot Sefarad* (1956), 191–3, 269–70.	Spain	14th century
*Immanuel b. Solomon of Rome		
Isaac, poet of *Ezrat Nashim* Schirmann, Sefarad, 2 (1956), 87–96.	Castile	13th century
*Isaac (Isḥak)		
Isaac *Al-Avani		
Isaac Amigo M. Benayahu in: KS, 35 (1960), 528–9.	Turkey	17th century
Isaac b. Abraham G. Sed-Rajna, in: REJ, 126 (1967), 265–7.	Provence	13th century
*Isaac b. Abraham ha-Gorni		
Isaac b. Abraham ha-Parnas Bernstein, Piyyutim, 67–71.	Greece	15th century?
Isaac b. Fayun Habermann, Ateret, 120, 228.	Egypt?	early poet
*Isaac b. Ḥayyim b. Abraham		
Isaac b. Joseph ibn *Pollegar		
*Isaac b. Judah		
Isaac b. Judah *Gerondi		
*Isaac b. Judah ha-Seniri		
Isaac b. Kalo[nymus?] Habermann, Ateret, 148, 228.	Romania?	14/15th century?
Isaac b. Levi *ibn Mar Saul		
Isaac b. Moses Hezekiah ha-Levi M. Benayahu, in: *Rabbi Yosef Caro,* ed. by Y. Raphael (1969), 317, 349–51.	Italy	16th century
Isaac b. Solomon *Alḥadib I. Davidson in: *Tarbiz,* 11 (1940), 111; C. Roth, in: JQR, 47 (1956–57), 324.	Spain, Syracuse, Palermo	14th century
Isaac b. Solomon he-Ḥaver M. Zulay, in: *Sefer Assaf* (1953), 303–6.	Ereẓ Israel	10/11th century
*Isaac b. Yakar A.M. Habermann, in: *Haaretz* (Sept. 25, 1955).	Germany	12th century
Isaac b. Zerahiah ha-Levi Gerondi Schirmann, Sefarad, 2 (1956), 285–90; A.M. Habermann, in: *Haaretz* (May 28, 1963).	Spain	13th century

Name	Place	Dates
Isaac de Leon M. Wallenstein, in: *Sefer ha-Yovel, Tiferet Yisrael to I. Brody* (1966), 171–78 (Heb. part)	Egypt	17th century
Isaac ha-Ḥazzan b. Joseph M. Zulay, in: *Sinai,* 16 (1945), 39–48.	Ereẓ Israel?	10/11th century?
Isaac ha-Levi A.M. Habermann, in: *Eked,* 3 (1960), 91–98.	Orient	13th century?
Isaac Ḥandali S. Bernstein, in *Sefer Hadoar* (1957), 83–85; idem, in: *Sefer Yovel li-Khevod S.K. Mirsky* (1958), 466, 486–8.	Crimea	15th century
Isaac ibn Al-Shami J. Schirmann, in: YMḤSI, 6 (1945), 259–60.	Spain	12th century
Isaac *ibn Ezra		
Isaac *ibn Ghayyat		
Isaac ibn *Gikatilla M. Zulay, in: *Tarbiz,* 20 (1950), 161–76.	Spain	10/11th century
Isaac (Abu Ibrahim) *ibn Khalfun		
Isaac *ibn Kaprun		
Isaac *ibn Shuwayk		
Isaac Salmah J. Schirmann, in: KS, 12 (1935–36), 393.	Turkey	16th century
Isaac Samuel J.M. Matza, *Aiannistika hebraika tragoudia* (1953), 55–56.	Greece	18th century
Isaiah Ḥai b. Joseph *Carmi		
Ishmael Ḥanina b. Mordecai of Volmontono M. Benayahu, in: *Rabbi Yosef Caro* ed. by Y. Raphael (1969), 320–21, 357–58.	Bologna, Ferrara	16th century
*Israel b. Joel (Susslin)		
Israel b. Moses *Najara		
Israel Berechiah Fontanella R. Patai, *Shirei R. Yisrael Berekhyah Fontanella* (1933).	Rovigo, Reggio	d. 1763
Jacob M. Zulay, in: YMḤSI, 1 (1933), 157; Habermann, Ateret, 119–20, 228.	Ereẓ Israel	early poet
Jacob Al'ayin Habermann, Ateret, 182–228.	Babylonia?	10/11th century
Jacob Amron M. Benayahu, in: KS, 35 (1960), 529.	Turkey	
Jacob b. Abraham (Angelo d'Ascoli) Schirmann, Italyah, 193–94.	Italy	15th century
*Jacob b. Dunash b. Akiva		
*Jacob b. Eleazar		
Jacob b. Eliezer Guenzburg-Ulma J.L. Bialer, *Min ha-Genazim* (1967), 63–69.	Ulm (Germany)	16th century
Jacob b. Isaac Segre M. Benayahu, in: *Rabbi Yosef Caro,* ed. by Y. Raphael (1969), 316, 348–9.	Italy	16/17th century
Jacob b. Joab Elijah *Fano		
Jacob b. Judah H. Peri, in: *Tarbiz,* 24 (1955), 426 ff.	Germany	13th century
Jacob b. Judah ibn Ala'mani S. Abramson, in: YMḤSI, 7 (1958), 163–81.	Alexandria	12th century
*Jacob b. Naphtali		
Jacob Ḥai (Vita) Israel Schirmann, Italyah, 408–9.	Italy, Amsterdam	18th century
Jacob ibn Albene C. Roth, in JQR, 39 (1948–49), 123–50.	Toledo	14th century
Jacob Israel Bilgradi Bernstein, Italyah, 86–90, 165–6.	Ferrara	18th century
Jacob Kunat S. Bernstein, in: *Sinai,* 19 (1946), 214.	Morocco	12th/13th century
(Jacob?) Manish b. Meir J.L. Bialer, *Min ha-Genazim* (1967), 77–78.	Austria	17th century
Jacob of Castilia S. Bernstein, in: *Aresheth,* 1 (1958), 15–16, 20.	Spain, Fez	
Jacob Tarfon H. Brody, in: *Minḥah le-David* dedicated to D. Yellin (1935), 205–220.	Salonika	16th century
Jeduthun ha-Levi S. Assaf, in: *Minḥah li-Yhudah* to J.L. Zlotnik (1950), 162–9.		12th century
Jehiel b. Abraham Schirmann, Italyah, 48–54; idem, in: *Scritti in memoria*	Rome	d. before 1070

Name	Place	Dates
di E. Sereni (1970), 92–107 (Heb. part).		
Jehiel b. Asher Habermann, in: *Maḥanayim,* 82 (1963), 38–41; idem, Ateret, 191–3, 200–1, 228.	Spain	14th century
Jehiel b. Israel Luria M. Benayahu, in: *Rabbi Yosef Caro,* ed. by Y. Raphael (1969), 315–6, 345–8.	Padua	16th century
Jehiel b. Joab min ha-Anavim (Anav) N. Pavoncello, in: *Miscellanea di Studi in memoria di D. Disegni* (1969), 190–2, 195–7.	Rome	13th century
Jehiel b. Joseph Urbach, Tosafot, 317.	Germany	14th century
Jehoseph b. Hanan b. Nathan *Ezobi		
Jekuthiel J. Schirmann, YMḤSI, 6 (1945), 262.	Spain	12th century
Jekuthiel b. Isaac *ibn Ḥasan		
Jekuthiel of Vilna I. Tishbi, in: *Sefer Yovel le-Y. Baer* (1960), 385ff.	Italy	18th century
*Jerahmeel b. Solomon		
Joab S. Bernstein: *Sinai,* 19 (1946), 213–4; idem, in: *Ha-Tekufah,* 32–33 (1948), 774–5.	Syria	13th century
Joab Almagia C. Roth and C. Rabin, in: *Metsudah,* 5–6 (1948), 262–83.	Italy	18th century
Joab b. Benjamin Schirmann, Italyah, 135–6.	Rome	13/14th century
Joab b. Daniel Schirmann, Italyah, 133–4.	Rome	13th century
Joab b. Jehiel de Synagoga Bet-El Schirmann, Italyah, 170–1.	Rome	14th century
Joab b. Nathan b. Daniel de Sinagoga J.N. Pavoncello, in: *Scritti in memoria di E. Sereni* (1970), 119–32 (Heb. part).	Rome	13/14th century
*Joab the Greek		
*Johanan b. Joshua ha-Kohen		
Johanan-Judah (Angelo) Alatrino Schirmann, Italyah, 256–60.	Italy	16/17th century
Jonah ha-Kohen Rappa Schirmann, Italyah, 327–31.	Italy	17th century
Joseph (Abu ʿAmar) ibn Ḥasdai Schirmann, *Sefarad,* 1 (1959[2]), 171–5.	Saragossa	11th century
Joseph *Albaradani		
Joseph *Almanzi		
Joseph Baruch b. Jedidiah Zechariah of Urbino Schirmann, Italyah, 274–5.	Mantua, Modena and Busseto	17th century
Joseph b. Abraham Almosnino D. Yarden, in: *Sefunot,* 8 (1964), 258–60; 264–5.	Salonika?	15/16th century
*Joseph b. Asher (of Chartres)		
Joseph b. David ibn Suli S. Bernstein in: *Al Naharot Sefarad* (1956), 138–42, 144–5, 251–4; Schirmann, Sefarad, 2 (1960[2]), 485–8.	Toledo	d. after 1306
Joseph b. Isaac S. Bernstein, in: *Tarbiz,* 26 (1957), 465–8.	Orléans	12th century
Joseph b. Israel J. Ratzaby, in: *Yeda Am,* 12 (1967), 56–60.	Yemen	16th century
*Joseph b. Jacob		
Joseph b. Jacob (Abu Amr) *ibn Sahl		
Joseph b. Jacob ha-Levi N. Ben-Menahem, in: *Aresheth,* 2 (1960), 404–5.	Morocco	15/16th century
Joseph b. Jacob Kalai S. Bernstein, in: *Sinai,* 19 (1946), 214; J.L. Weinberger, in: HUCA, 39 (1968), 11–14 (Heb. part).	Crimea	13th century?
Joseph b. Joshua ibn Vives Lorki J.L. Weinberger, in: HUCA, 39 (1968), 15–18 (Heb. part).	Spain	14/15th century
*Joseph b. Kalonymus ha-Nakdan		
Joseph b. Mattathias S. Bernstein, in: *Tarbiz,* 7 (1936), 181–5.	Italy	13th century
Joseph b. Meir b. Ezra Bernstein, Piyyutim, 57–62.	Greece?	14th century?
Joseph b. Meir ibn Al-Muhadjir Schirmann, Shirim Ḥadashim, 215–6.	Andalusia	11/12th century
Joseph b. Moses *Alashkar		
Joseph b. Nathan Ḥazzan A.I. Katch, in: JQR, 58 (1967), 89–94, 60 (1968–9), 1–5; J. Schirmann, in: KS, 44 (1969), 427–8.	Germany	12th century

Name	Place	Dates
Joseph Ben-Ram M. Wallenstein, in: *Sefer Ḥayyim Schirmann* (1970), 116ff.	Egypt	17th century
Joseph b. Samuel Ẓarefati (Giuseppe Gallo) M.D. Cassuto, in: *Meḥkarim le-Zikhron R.A. Kohut* (1935), 121–28 (Heb. part).	Florence	15/16th century
*Joseph b. Sheshet ibn Latimi		
*Joseph b. Solomon of Carcassonne		
Joseph b. Solomon *Yaḥya		
*Joseph b. Tanḥum ha-Yerushalmi		
Joseph Conzio S. Olivetti, *Rassegna Mensile di Israel,* 25 (1959), 22–25.	Italy	17th century
Joseph Fiametta (Lehavah) J. Schirmann, in: *Zion,* 29 (1964), 101.	Italy	d. 1721
Joseph *Ganso		
Joseph ibn al-Shami H. Schirmann, YMḤSI, 6 (1945), 253–8.	Spain	12th century
Joseph *ibn Barzel		
Joseph *ibn Zabara		
Joseph *Kaspi		
Joseph *Kimḥi		
*Joseph Saul Abdallah		
Joseph Shalom Gallego		
Joseph Sofer S.M. Stern, in: *Zion,* 11 (1950), 141–3.	Spain	11th century
*Joshua Habermann, Ateret 158f., 227.	Ereẓ Israel	early poet
*Joshua b. Elijah ha-Levi		
Joshua b. Joseph ha-Kohen M. Zulay, in: *Haaretz* (Jan. 10, 1949); *ibid.* (Dec. 12, 1952).	Egypt	11th century
Joshua Ben-Zion Segre J. Schirmann, in: *Zion,* 29 (1964), 100.	Italy	1718–1798
Joshua ha-Kohen M. Zulay, in: *Alei Ayin* (1952), 89–90; E. Fleischer, in: *Tarbiz,* 36 (1967), 146ff., 342ff.	Ereẓ Israel	early poet
Joshua he-Ḥaver b. Nathan E. Fleischer, in: *Tarbiz,* 38 (1969), 280–2.	Ereẓ Israel	11th century
*Josiphiah (Jehosiphiah) the Proselyte		
Judah M. Zulay, *Zur Liturgie der Babylonischen Juden* (1933); Habermann, Ateret, 121ff., 226.	Egypt or Erez Israel	9th or 10th century
Judah *Abrabanel (Leone Ebreo)		
Judah *al-Ḥarizi		
Judah b. Aaron *Kilti		
Judah b. Hillel ha-Levi M. Zulay, in: *Eretz Israel,* 4 (1956), 138–44; Habermann, Ateret, 123–4, 227.	Ereẓ Israel	10/11th century
Judah b. Isaac *ibn Ghayyat		
*Judah b. Isaac ibn Shabbetai		
Judah (Leone) b. Isaac *Sommo		
Judah b. Israel Berechiah Fontanella M. Zulay, *Zur Liturgie der Babylonischen Juden* (1933); 23–24, 67–68.	Italy	b. 1719
Judah b. Jo[seph] E. Fleischer, in: *Tarbiz,* 38 (1969), 280–1.		early poet
Judah b. Joseph Segelmesi S. Bernstein, in: *Horeb,* 12 (1956), 217–33.	North Africa	14/15th century
Judah b. Kalonymus b. Moses J. Schirmann, in: *Kobez al-Jad,* 13 (1939), 38–41.	Mainz	12th century
Judah b. Menahem Schirmann, Italyah, 76–77.	Rome	12th century
*Judah b. Menahem of Rome		
Judah b. Moses Bernstein, Piyyutim, 62.		16th century
Judah b. Moses Alfaqui J. Schirmann, in: KS, 12 (1935–36), 293, 521–3.	Turkey	16th century
Judah b. Moses *Leonte		
Judah b. Moses of Saltars M. Benayahu, in: *Rabbi Yosef Caro,* ed. by Y. Raphael (1969), 313–5, 341–5.	Italy	b. 1550?
Judah b. Samuel *Abbas		
*Judah Halevi		
Judah Levi Toabah M. Attias, in: *Sefunot,* 1 (1958), 128–40.	Salonika?	17th century

Name	Place	Dates
Judah Mazli'ah Padova	Modena	d. 1728
J. Schirmann, in: *Zion*, 29 (1964), 102; G. Laras, in: *Scritti in memoria* di A. Milano (1970), 193–203.		
Judah *Zarco		
**Kalila and Dimna*		
Kalon ha-Romi	Byzantium	9th century
Schirmann, Shirim Ḥadashim, 424–6.		
*Kalonymus b. Judah the Younger		
Kalonymus b. Kalonymus (see *Kalonymus family)		
Kalonymus b. Shabbetai	Rome, Worms	1030–1096
Schirmann, Italyah, 62–67.		
Kalonymus ha-Nasi (see *Kalonymus family)	Italy	13th century
Kalonymus ha-Zaken	Italy	10th century
Leon b. Michael ha-Parnas	Greece	14th century
J.L. Weinberger, in: HUCA, 39 (1968), 30–33 (Heb. part).		
Leonte b. Abraham	Rome	12th century
Schirmann, Italyah, 70–73, 543.		
Leonte b. Moses	Rome	12th century
Schirmann, Italyah, 80–81.		
Levi b. Jacob *ibn Altabban		
Malkiel b. Meir	Greece or Italy	11th century
J.L. Weinberger, in: HUCA, 39 (1968), 45–51 (Heb. part).		
*Mattathias	Italy	13th century
Schirmann, Italyah, 179–81.		
Mazzal Tov b. David	Constantinople	15/16th century
I. D. Markon, in: *Sefer ha-Yovel . . . A. Marx* (1950), 322.		
Meir *Abulafia		
Meir b. Abraham	Bulgaria, Safed	16th century
A. Marmorstein, in: *Alim*, 3 (1937), 15–16.		
*Meir b. Baruch of Rothenburg		
*Meir b. Isaac Sheli'ah Zibbur		
Meir b. Moses	Rome	13th century
J. Schirmann, in: KS, 37 (1962), 405, no. 1140.		
Menahem b. Aaron	Germany	12th century?
S.H. Kook, *Iyyunim u-Meḥkarim*, 2 (1963), 209–10.		
*Menahem b. Jacob		
*Menahem b. Jacob ibn Saruq		
Menahem b. Mordecai ha-Parnas Corizzi	Italy	
J. Schirmann, in: YMḤSI, 1 (1933), 101–5, 109–20.		
*Meshullam b. Kalonymus		
Meshullam b. Moses	Mainz	d. 1094/5
A.N.Z. Roth, in: *Zion*, 28 (1963), 233–5; E.E. Urbach (ed.), *Arugat ha-Bosem* of Azriel b. Abraham, 4 (1963), 17, 52–54.		
Meshullam ha-Sofer	Italy	14th century
Schirmann, Italyah, 182–3.		
Mevorakh b. David	Erez Israel	early poet
A. Scheiber, in: *Tarbiz*, 22 (1951), 167–73; 36 (1966), 92–93.		
Mevorakh b. Nathan	Erez Israel	10th century?
Schirmann, Shirim Ḥadashim, 29–30.		
Mevorakh ha-Bavli	Erez Israel	11th century
A.M. Habermann, in: *Maḥanayim*, 44 (1960), 59ff.; idem, Ateret 143–4, 729.		
Meyuḥas	Italy	16th century
J. Schirmann, YMḤSI, 1 (1933), 107, 125–27.		
Michael b. Caleb	Greece	11/12th century
J.L. Weinberger, in: HUCA, 39 (1968), 52–53 (Heb. part).		
Mordecai b. Berechiah Jare	Mantua	16/17th century
Simonsohn, Mantovah, 2 (1964), 522.		
*Mordecai b. Hillel ha-Kohen		
Mordecai b. Joseph	Worms	d. 1294
Schirmann, in: *Kobez al-Jad*, 13 (1939), 52–57.		
Moses	Erez Israel	early poet
M. Zulay, in: YMḤSI, 5 (1939), 149–54; Habermann, Ateret, 140, 229.		
Moses *Abbas (ibn Abez)		
Moses b. Abraham *Dar'i		
Moses b. Adonin ha-Levi	Dara' (North Africa)	9th century
N. Allony, in: *Sinai*, 43 (1958), 394.		
Moses b. Benjamin Sofer	Rome	12th century
Schirmann, Italyah, 74–75.		
Moses b. Ḥiyya		
J.L. Weinberger, in: HUCA, 39 (1968), 41–44 (Heb. part).	Greece	12th century

Name	Place	Dates
Moses b. Isaac H. Brody, in: *Keneset,* memorial volume to Ḥ.N. Bialik, 1 (1936), 410–5.	Spain	11th century
Moses b. Isaac M. Zulay in: YMḤSI, 5 (1939), 171–4.	Tyre	early poet
Moses b. Isaac b. Jacob H. Schirmann, in: *Zion,* 19 (1954), 66.	Grenoble	13th century?
Moses b. Isaac Da*Rieti Schirmann, Italyah, 195–9.		
Moses b. Isaac *Remos		
Moses b. Israel Finzi M. Benayahu, in: *Rabbi Yosef Caro,* ed. by Y. Raphael (1969), 317–8, 351–3.	Italy	16th century
*Moses b. Jacob		
Moses b. Jacob (Abu Harūn) *ibn Ezra		
Moses b. Joseph Schirmann, Italyah, 110–5.	Rome	13th century
*Moses b. Kalonymus		
*Moses b. Levi		
Moses b. Maẓli'aḥ A. Mirsky, in: KS, 34 (1959), 363–7.		
*Moses b. Mevorakh		
Moses b. Naḥman (*Naḥmanides)		
*Moses (b. Nethanel) Nathan		
Moses b. Samuel b. Absalom S. Bernstein, in: *Tarbiz,* 10 (1939), 15–19.	France?	12th century
Moses b. Samuel ha-Kohen *Gikatilla		
Moses b. Shabbetai Schirmann, Italyah, 60–61; Bernstein, Piyyutim, 41–44, 77–78.	Rome	11th century
*Moses b. Shem Tov de Leon		
Moses b. Shem Tov *Gabbai		
Moses b. Shem Tov Ḥazzan A.M. Habermann, in *Tarbiz,* 14 (1943), 54, 67–69.	Spain, North Africa	14/15th century
Moses b. Shem Tov *ibn Ḥabib		
Moses b. Solomon d'Escola *Gerondi		
Moses b. Ẓur N. Ben-Menahem, in: *Aresheth,* 2 (1960), 383–6.	Morocco	17/18th century
Moses ha-Kohen ibn Gikatilla A. Scheiber, in: *Alexander Marx Jubilee Volume* (1950), 537–8 (Heb. part).	Spain	11th century
Moses Ḥayyim b. Abraham Catalano B.(C.) Roth in: *Kobez al-Jad,* 4 (1946), 99–101.	Padua, Montagnana	d. 1661
Moses *ibn Al-Taqana		
Moses *Kilki		
Moses Mevorakh S. Bernstein, in: *Sefer Yovel li-Khevod S.K. Mirsky* (1958), 406, 479–86.	Crimea	15/16th century
Moses *Zacuto (Zacut)		
Mubbashshir b. Ephraim he-Ḥaver A.M. Habermann, Ateret, 160–1.	Orient	11th century
Nahum Schirmann, Sefarad, 2 (1960²), 459–62.	Spain?	13th century?
Nahum b. Joseph al-Bardani A. Scheiber, in: *Zion,* 30 (1965), 123.	Babylonia	11th century
Nathan b. Isaac A.M. Habermann, in: *Haaretz* (Sept. 20, 1968).	Mainz	12/13th century
Nathan b. Samuel he-Ḥaver J. Schirmann, in: YMḤSI, 6 (1945), 291–7.	Egypt	12th century
Nehemiah S. Bernstein, in: Sinai, 19 (1946), 215.	Orient	12/13th century
Nehemiah b. Menahem Calomiti M.D. Cassuto, in: *Sefer ha-Yovel. . . S. Krauss* (1936), 211–6.	Crete	15th century
Nehemiah b. Solomon b. Heiman ha-Nasi M. Zulay, YMḤSI, 4 (1938), 197–246.	Babylonia?	10/11th century?
Nethanel b. Naaman S. Bernstein, Piyyutim, 81–83.	Corfu	16th century?
Nethanel b. Nehemiah Caspi S. Bernstein, in: *Tarbiz,* 10 (1939), 26–29.	Provence	15th century
*Nissi (Nissim) b. Berechiah al-Nahrawani		
*Ohev b. Meir ha-Nasi		
Perfet Zark Schirmann, Sefarad, 2 (1960²), 544–6.	Spain	14th century
Pesaḥ b. Abraham ha-Kohen E.E. Urbach (ed.), *Arugat ha-Bosem* of Abraham b. Azriel, 1 (1939), 281; 4 (1963), 122.	Germany	13th century

Name	Place	Dates
*Phinehas b. Jacob ha-Kohen (Kafra)		
*Phinehas b. Joseph ha-Levi		
Raḥamim Kalai	Egypt	17th century
M. Wallenstein, in: *Sefer Ḥayyim Schirmann* (1970), 111–34.		
Raphael b. Isaac de-Faenza	Florence	15th century
Schirmann, Italyah, 203–5, 573.		
Raphael Joseph b. Johanan Treves	Italy	16th century
M. Benayahu, in: *Rabbi Yosef Caro*, ed. by Y. Raphael (1969), 318–9, 353–6.		
Rehabiah b. Judah	France	11/12th century
H. Brody, in: *Emet le-Ya'akov, Sefer Yovel. . . J. Freimann* (1937), 22–26.		
Rephaiah b. Judah Kohen	Orient	12th century?
S. Bernstein, in: HUCA, 16 (1941), 150–3.		
Reuben ha-Kohen Ḥazzan		
S. Abramson, in: *Tarbiz*, 15 (1944), 51–54.		
*Saadiah b. Joseph Gaon		
*Saadiah b. Joseph ha-Levi		
Saadiah b. Maimun *ibn Danan		
Saadiah *Longo		
Sahalul	Yemen	15th century
J. Ratzaby, in: *Afikim ba-Negev*, 2 (1966), nos. 15–16.		
Sa'id b. Babshad ha-Kohen		10/11th century
Schirmann, Shirim Ḥadashim, 431–3, 482.		
Sa'id Darin (or Drin), Dinar	Yemen	17th century
J. Ratzaby, in: *Zion*, 20 (1955), 32–46.		
Salem (Salam) Abraham b. Isaac	Mantua, Venice	17th century
Simonsohn, Mantovah, 2 (1964), 529–31.		
Samson b. Samuel	Germany, Jerusalem	14th century
Habermann, Ateret 202–3, 231.		
Samson Kohen Modon	Mantua	1679–1727
Samuel	Egypt	13th century
Schirmann, Shirim Ḥadashim, 134–5.		
Samuel	Germany or France	13th century?
Habermann, Ateret, 199, 230.		
Samuel	Spain	13/14th century
Habermann, Ateret, 87–88, 109–12, 166, 194, 230.		
Samuel *Archivolti		
Samuel b. Eliasaph	Rome	16th century?
Samuel b. Hananiah	Spain	11th century
S. Abramson, in: *Sinai*, 36 (1955), 538–42.		
Samuel b. Ḥayyim	Greece	13/14th century
Bernstein, Piyyutim, 94–101.		
Samuel b. Isaac Segan Leviyyah	Germany	11th century
S.H. Kook, *Iyyunim u-Meḥkarim*, 2 (1963), 244–6.		
Samuel b. Joseph *ibn Sasson		
Samuel b. Joshua Minz Biritaro	Mantua	16th century
M. Benayahu, in: *Rabbi Yosef Caro*, ed. by Y. Raphael (1969), 319–20, 356–57.		
Samuel b. Kalonymus ha-Ḥazzan	Germany	d. 1241
E.E. Urbach (ed.), *Arugat ha-Bosem* of Abraham b. Azriel, 4 (1963), 60.		
Samuel b. Moses Anav	Bologna	16th century
Bernstein, Italyah, passim.		
Samuel b. Moses ha-Dayyan	Syria	15/16th century
A.M. Habermann, in: *Haaretz* (Sept. 27, 1964); J.L. Weinberger, in: *Tarbiz*, 38 (1969), 286–9.		
Samuel b. Moses ha-Levi	Orient	12/13th century
S. Bernstein, in: *Sinai*, 19 (1946), 216.		
Samuel b. Moses min ha-Ne'arim (Dei Fanciulli)	Italy	14th century
N. Pavoncello, in: *Miscellanea di Studi in Memoria di D. Disegni* (1969), 188–90, 192–5.		
Samuel b. Shalom	Ereẓ Israel	8th century
M. Zulay, in: YMḤSI, 3 (1936), 153–62; A.M. Habermann, *Toledot ha-Piyyut ve-ha-Shirah* (1970), 56.		
Samuel b. Simeon	Poland	17th century
A. Yaari, in KS, 16 (1939/40), 377–9.		
Samuel b. Zadok ibn Alamani	Egypt	12/13th century
A. Scheiber, in: *Sefer Ḥayyim Schirmann* (1970), 394–6.		
Samuel David *Luzzatto		
*Samuel ha-Nagid		
*Samuel ha-Shelishi b. Hoshana		
Saul *Caspi		
Shabbetai	Italy	16th century
S. Bernstein, in: *Horeb*, 5 (1939), 55.		

Name	Place	Dates
Shabbetai b. Abishai Ḥabib Bernstein, Piyyutim, 88–89.	Corfu?	15th century
Shabbetai b. Moses Schirmann, Italyah, 39–40; Bernstein, Piyyutim, 74–77.	Rome	11th century
Shabbetai Ḥayyim (Vita) *Marini		
Shalem *Shabazi		
Shape b. Said (URU?) Y. Ratzaby, in: *Ba-Ma'arakhah* (1969), no. 14–15.	Yemen	15th century?
Shealtiel b. Levi A.M. Habermann, in: *Haaretz* (April 18, 1968).	Germany?	13/14th century
*She'erit ha-Ḥazzan		
Shemariah b. Aaron ha-Kohen N. Alloni in: *Sinai*, 58 (1966), 136–7; D. Yarden, *Sefunei Shirah* (1967), 144–8; J. Tubi, in *Ba-Ma'arakhah,* 10 (1971), no. 119, 18–19.	Babylonia	12/13th century
Shemariah of Rabyuano J.L. Weinberger, in: HUCA, 39 (1968), 55–59 (Heb. part).	Greece	12th century
Shem Tov *Falaquera		
*Shephatiah b. Amittai		
Sheshet Habermann, Ateret, 96, 231.	Provence	12th century
*Silano		
*Simeon b. Isaac		
*Simeon b. Megas ha-Kohen		
Simeon b. Ẓemaḥ *Duran		
Simeon Labi A.M. Habermann, in: *Maḥanayim,* 56 (1961), 42–45.	Spain, North Africa	d. 1545
Simḥah b. Samuel A.M. Habermann, in: *Haaretz* (Aug. 19, 1963).	Germany	12/13th century
Simḥah *Issachar Schirmann, Italyah, 350–3.		
*Sindabar		
Solomon Abu Ayyuv ibn Al Muallim Schirmann, Sefarad, 1 (1959[2]), 541–3.	Seville, Morocco	11/12th century
Solomon al-Kufi Ḥazzan A.M. Habermann, *Be-Ṛon Yaḥad* (1945), 35.		10/11th century
Solomon b. David ha-Rifi N. Alloni, in: *Sinai,* 64 (1969), 22–23.	Egypt	11/12th century?
Solomon b. Elijah Sharvit ha-Zahav ha-Levi A. Ovadiah, in: *Sinai,* 6 (1940), 78–79; S.H. Kook, *Iyyunim u-Meḥkarim,* 2 (1963), 216–9; I.M. Molho, in: *Oẓar Yehudei Sefarad,* 3 (1960), 80–82.	Salonika	15th century
Solomon b. Immanuel Da Piera or De Pierrelatte M. Catane, in: KS, 42 (1966–67), 399–402; 43 (1967–68), 160.	S. France	14th century
Solomon b. Isaac Schirmann, Italyah, 186.	Italy	14th century
Solomon b. Isaac (*Rashi)		
Solomon b. Isaac b. Meir Gaon M. Zulay, in: YMḤSI, 5 (1939), 175–7.	Syria	11th century
Solomon b. Isaac *Gerondi S. Bernstein, *Al-Naharot Sefarad* (1956), 146–51, 254–6.	Spain	13th century
*Solomon b. Judah ha-Bavli		
Solomon b. Judah ibn *Gabirol		
Solomon (b. Judah?) ibn Ghiyyat J. Schirmann, in: YMḤSI, 6 (1945), 261.	Spain	12th century
Solomon b. Mazzal Tov I.D. Markon, in: *Sefer ha-Yovel . . . A. Marx* (1950), 321–49; idem, in: *Melilah,* 3/4 (1950), 260–75.	Constantinople	16th century
Solomon b. Menahem D. Goldschmidt, in: *Maḥanayim,* 60 (1961), 62–63.	Germany	13th century
Solomon b. Moses Dei Rossi Schirmann, Italyah, 105–6.	Rome	13th century
Solomon b. Reuben *Bonafed		
Solomon b. Said J. Ratzaby, in: *Oẓar Yehudei Sefarad,* 2 (1959), 85, 88.	Yemen	16th century
Solomon b. Samson A.R. Malachi, *Bitzaron,* 50 (1964), 178–80.	Germany	11th century
Solomon b. Sar Shalom J. Ratzaby, in: *Maḥanayim,* 40 (1959), 170–92.	Yemen	16th century
Solomon Ḥazzan Bernstein, Italyah, 44–45, 146; A. Yaari, *Meḥkerei Sefer* (1958), 220, 225–6.	Italy	16th century
Solomon ibn *Labi		
Solomon *ibn Zakbel		

Name	Place	Dates
Solomon Kohen Habermann, Ateret, 216–7.	Orient	
Solomon Mevorakh S. Bernstein, in: *Horeb,* 5 (1939), 61–62; J.L.Weinberger, in: HUCA, 39 (1968), 60–62 (Heb. part).	Turkey	16th century
*Solomon Suleiman b. Amar		
*Tamar b. Menahem		
Todros b. Judah ha-Levi *Abulafia		
Yaḥya b. Abraham Ḥarazi Y. Ratzaby, in: *Tagim,* 1 (1969), 54–59.	Yemen	16/17th century
Yakar b. Samuel ha-Levi Urbach, Tosafot, 452–3; C. Sirat, in: REJ, 118 (1959–60), 131–3.	Cologne and Mainz	13th century
*Yannai		
Yanon b. Ẓemaḥ M. Zulay, in: *Sinai,* 28 (1951), 167–9; J. L. Weinberger, in: HUCA, 39 (1968), 3–10 (Heb. part).	Syria	11th century
*Yo'eẓ b. Malkiel A.M. Habermann, *Gezerot Ashkenaz ve-Ẓarefat* (1946), 194, 264.	Germany	13th century
Yom Tov (Bondi), Valvason J. Schirmann, in: *Zion,* 29 (1964), 104.	Venice	1616–1660
Yom Tov b. Isaac J. Schirmann, in: *Kobez al-Jad,* 13 (1939), 35–37.	France	12th century
Yom Tov Soriano A.M. Habermann, in: YMḤSI, 3 (1936), 133–50.	Spain	15th century
*Yose b. Yose		
Yudan b. Misatya ha-Kohen *Sefer ha-Mekorot* (1970²), 128.	Greece or Italy	10th century
Zadok b. Aaron ibn Alamani S. Bernstein, in: *Sinai,* 19 (1946), 215; idem, in: *Ha-Tekufah,* 32–33 (1948), 77.	Alexandria	12th century
*Zebidah family		
*Zechariah al-Dahiri		
Ẓedakah N. Allony, in: *Oẓar Yehudei Sefarad,* 1 (1959), 54–61.	Egypt	Medieval
Zedekiah b. Benjamin min ha-Anavim (Anav) B. Dinur, in: *Sefer Zikkaron Aryeh Leon Carpi* (1967), 52–63.	Rome	13th century
Ẓemaḥ b. Yanon he-Ḥazzan M. Zulay, in: YMḤSI, 5 (1939), 132.	Syria	11th century
Zevadiah Schirmann, Shirim Ḥadashim, 422–4.	S. Italy	9th century
		[A. D.]

creations of the early Italian *paytanim,* *Silano, *Shephatiah, and his son *Amittai, are now extant, but even these testify to an extensive and consolidated literary activity, which, despite a number of interesting points of originality, reveals blatant signs of the influence of Ereẓ Israel. The creative work of the *paytanim* of southern Italy became, in the tenth century, a basis for the development of *piyyut* in central and northern Italy. The *paytanim* working there, headed by Solomon b. Judah ha-Bavli, created a precedent for Central European *piyyut,* whose major representatives henceforth worked in Italy, Ashkenaz (Germany), France, and Byzantine Greece. The most important region of Central European sacred poetry was Germany, where the *piyyut* developed impressively because of the activity of a number of great *paytanim* in the 10th–11th centuries, such as *Moses b. Kalonymus, *Meshullam b. Kalonymus (both of Italian extraction), *Simeon b. Isaac, and Meir Isaac. In the succeeding centuries, Ashkenazi *piyyut* continued to develop, and a number of important composers made major contributions to the literature.

The direct continuation of oriental *piyyut* was in Spain, where, beginning in the middle of the tenth century, several generations of great composers functioned. Outstanding among these are Joseph *ibn Abitur, Solomon ibn *Gabirol, Isaac *ibn Ghayyat, Moses *ibn Ezra, *Judah Halevi, and Abraham *ibn Ezra. These Spanish *paytanim* attained impressive peaks of perfection. Even though creativity in the realm of *piyyut* did not cease in Central Europe, Northern Africa, or the East until the beginning of the Haskalah, the 13th century marks the beginning of the decline; later *paytanim,* despite their often impressive productivity, failed to create major works. Although some of their poetry was included in local prayer rites, most of it has been excluded from accepted prayer books.

Types of Piyyut. *Piyyutim* can be divided according to their liturgical purpose into a number of categories, differing in their histories and development, their structures, and their distribution. In different periods, certain types of *piyyutim* were more prevalent than others. The earliest and most important types of *piyyut* are the *kerovah* and the *yoẓer.* The *kerovah* is designed for inclusion in the *Amidah* prayer, while the *yoẓer* belongs to the benedictions before and after the **Shema* in the **Shaḥarit* service. The *kerovot* divide into a number of secondary categories, according to the types of *Amidah* to which they are attached: the *kerovah* of the daily *Amidah* is called *kerovat Shemoneh Esreh* because of the 18 blessings in that *Amidah;* that of *Musaf* or *Ma'ariv Amidah* for Sabbaths and the holy days is called *shivata* because of the seven blessings in these *Amidot;* while that of the *Shaḥarit Amidah* of the Sabbath and holy days, which include a *kedushah,* is called *kedushata* (in ancient Ereẓ Israel, *kedushah* was said on Sabbaths and festivals only in the *Shaharit* service). Each of the types of *kerovah* has its own structural characteristics. The *kerovah*, mainly the *kedushah*, is thought of as the dominant type of ancient *piyyut*. The *yozer* is combined from several types of *piyyut*, according to the structure of the permanent prayers replaced or embellished by *piyyut*. The *yozer* enjoyed great circulation mainly in the second period of oriental *piyyut*, between the seventh and 11th centuries. Parallel to the *yozerot*, which were intended for *Shaharit*, there are also, during this period, *piyyutim* of *Ma'ariv*, intended to adorn the blessings before and after the *Shema* in the evening service. This type of *piyyut*, however, was never widely employed.

Among the *kerovot* of the major holidays, a number of special types of *piyyut* for different occasions are found. These include: *teki'ata*, which adorns the **malkhuyyot*, **zikhronot*, and **shofarot* blessings in the *Musaf Amidot* for New Year; *Seder ha-*Avodah* (which describes the sacrificial service on the Day of Atonement during the time the Temple was in existence), in the *Musaf kerovah* of the Day of Atonement; or the **azharot*, which discuss the list of 613 *mitzvot* in the Torah, in the *shivatot* of *Musaf* for Shavuot. The *kerovot* for fast days include **selihot* (penitential), while the *kerovot* for the Ninth of Av include *kinot* (dirges). In some communities these *selihot* and *kinot* were removed in later periods from the *kerovot* and placed after them. *Selihot* were also composed for the Days of Penitence during the month of Elul and between New Year and the Day of Atonement. The special processions for the days of Tabernacles (Sukkot) were embellished with *hoshana piyyutim* (see **Hoshanot*). In the early period of *piyyut*, works were not composed to adorn religious ceremonies outside of the obligatory prayers, except for the Grace after Meals, and even in that case, they were probably intended, from the start, for use at communal festive meals or at meals for religious ceremonies. Similarly, *ashkavah piyyutim* were composed in this period (*aftarot*, or *zidduk ha-din*, "funeral services").

All the classical types of *piyyut* were cultivated to some extent by the later European *paytanim*. However, the scope of the *piyyut* literature was greatly enlarged, mainly in Spain, by the creation of a number of new types of *piyyut*. The Spanish *paytanim* preceded the accepted patterns of the *yozer* with a number of *piyyut* passages which they interlaced in the prayer said on Sabbaths and festivals before the *yozer* prayers. These types are known as the *nishmat*, the *muharakh*, the *illufinu*, and the *kol azmotai*. The Spanish *paytanim* also cultivated the type known as *reshut* (pl. *reshuyyot*, "introductory *piyyutim*"), and they joined these works to the *Barukh she-Amar* prayer, to *nishmat*, to **Kaddish* after *nishmat*, to **Barekhu*, and so on. In addition to their extensive work with these types, the Spanish *paytanim* developed new types of special *piyyutim* for private religious ceremonies, such as Sabbath songs and *havdalot* (see **Havdalah*), as well as types of religious poetry intended to satisfy the spiritual needs of the individual. To a certain extent, the Ashkenazi *paytanim* followed them in these areas.

A considerable part of the creative efforts of the European *paytanim* was dedicated to the type known as *selihot* for fast days and days of penitence. Because of the great creative activity in this area, a number of secondary types within the category have been distinguished, some partly because of thematic distinctions and some because of formal distinctions. The early oriental *selihah* recognized only the category *hatanu* (*selihot* of confession), and the *tokhahah* ("rebuke") as a secondary type. In a later period, the **Akedah* type was added to them, in which God's mercy is requested for Israel because of the merit of the binding of Isaac. According to structural distinctions, a number of secondary types of *selihot* are distinguishable, of which the important ones are: the *pizmon* (a *selihah* with an opening refrain and a strophe), and the *mustagib* (a *selihah* in which a biblical passage appears as a refrain at the end of every verse). In specific sources, especially Ashkenazi, the *selihot* are distinguished by special names according to their place

Figure 2. *Piyyut* decorated with animal grotesques and towers, from a *Haggadah* of unknown origin. Manchester, John Rylands Library, Ms. Heb. 29, fol. 10v–11r.

in the calendar, their composers, the way they are said, or the number of lines in their poetic phrases.

Language and Style. The style and the vocabulary of the *paytanim* vary in the different periods and different poetic schools. In the anonymous period of *piyyut*, the style followed the stylistic and lexical paths of the permanent prayers; the vocabulary is mostly biblical, even though some later linguistic bases—midrashic and talmudic—may be found in it. The style of the *piyyutim* is lucid and clear and contains little wordplay or rhetorical embellishment. With the work of Yannai, Hebrew sacral poetry becomes more and more expansive in its vocabulary and increasingly vague and flowery in its style. During the whole oriental period of the *piyyut*, the composers used not only the whole Hebrew lexicon, with all its various layers and strata (to a certain extent, in the early *piyyut* creations, ancient Hebrew words with no mention in the sources are preserved) but they also adorned the *piyyut* with idioms and words of their own creation. The poetic novelties of language and form, which do not always fit the classical rules of Hebrew grammar, gave a singular stylistic character to the poetic creations, and frequently aroused harsh criticism. These *paytanim* (who are included among those of the Kallir school, so called after its major representative, the *paytan* Eleazar b. Kallir), often used a complicated set of terms, flavoring their works with an abundance of talmudic and midrashic material, or with (sometimes vague) allusions to this material. Thus, some of their works became enigmatic, constituting difficult exegetical problems. From a linguistic point of view, *piyyut* reached its peak in the works of Saadiah Gaon and his pupils, during the tenth and 11th centuries. The *paytanim* of the "Saadiah school" were the most radical in establishing novel uses of language in their *piyyutim*.

As a reaction to the Saadianic style of exaggerated innovations, Hebrew sacred poetry in Spain crystallized within clearly biblical frameworks of language and style. The first of the Spanish *paytanim* composed their works according to the example of the later oriental *paytanim*. In addition to the works written in this style, there exists a parallel group of works, written in the Spanish model in a language which strives to recognize only a biblical vocabulary and in a style which strives to free itself of talmudic and midrashic material and allusions to the teachings of the rabbis. The style of the Spanish *piyyutim* is impressively lucid and flexible, approaching the style of secular poetry; in this period, sacred poetry was notably influenced by secular poetry both in form and in lyrical means of expression. Solomon ibn Gabirol was instrumental in the process by which the *piyyut* was increasingly purified of the linguistic-stylistic exaggerations of eastern *piyyut;* the earliest of the Spanish *paytanim* whose work appears to be entirely within the new stylistic framework is Isaac ibn Ghayyat. During this period, the style of writing of the Spanish *paytanim* greatly influenced the *paytanim* of other lands, such as North Africa, Yemen, Ereẓ Israel, Babylonia, and Provence. Certain traces of Spanish influence are found also in later Ashkenazi *piyyut*. In general, Central European *piyyut* remained faithful to the Kallir model in language and style. Even so, Italian and Ashkenazi poets were more restrained and moderate in their use of language and style. In the creations of the greatest of them, the poetic language reaches impressive heights of beauty and flexibility.

Rhyme and Meter. The ancient anonymous *piyyut* did not employ rhyme. The *piyyutim* composed during this period with the characteristic method of dividing each poetic line into four feet, each one having two or three stresses, are limited. With the beginning of the use of rhyme, or more specifically, with the period of the literary activity of Yannai, the *paytanim* concentrate much more on rhyme than on rhythm. Those of the Kallir school attained great virtuosity in their methods of rhyming and playing with rhyme, and this lowered the level and content of the creations, especially in the works of mediocre *paytanim*. A number of eastern *paytanim* wrote their works in a peculiar rhythmic system (known as *mishkal ha-tevot*), by establishing an identical number of words or stresses in every poetic line, but this method is found in only a few works, and was used more widely in the works of the first Central European *paytanim*, who also continued and developed the traditions of rhyme of the early Kallir school. It was the Spanish *paytanim* who introduced a precise method of rhythm in their *piyyutim*. Many of their works, mainly in the specific types of *piyyut* which originated in Spain, are subject to the quantitative method of meter—Arabic in its source—of secular poetry, but the major part of their work is in a unique meter created in Spain for sacred poetry. This is mainly syllabic, meting out to each line of poetry a specific fixed number of grammatical syllables. In Spain, however, the *paytanim* also continued to compose *piyyutim* without meter, particularly in the classical types of *piyyut*. Rhyme also developed impressively in Spain, particularly in the short types of *piyyut*, under the influence of the *ezor* (Muwassaha) type of secular poems. Many *piyyutim*, some metered precisely according to the example of the *ezor* type, some metered according to the special method of Spanish *piyyut*, have a variegated and rich rhyme, which competes successfully with the best achievements of Hebrew secular poetry in Spain.

Signatures. The first *paytanim* signed their *piyyutim* only with their own names. Later, they added patronymics and the places where they wrote; and, after a while, they added blessings and the like. At times, the *paytanim* also added the names of relatives.

Collections of Piyyutim. The extent to which *piyyutim* were incorporated into the prayer service differs in time and locality. In ancient times, there was fierce opposition to the *piyyut* literature, mainly from the great academy in Babylonia. Nevertheless, it appears that there was a wide use of *piyyutim* in most of the early eastern communities. During this period there were still no fixed collections of *piyyutim* for the use of various communities. Rather, each cantor recited *piyyutim* according to his taste and choice. Only in later periods, when the congregations took greater part in prayer services, was the set recitation of certain *piyyutim* for various liturgical occasions practiced. These fixed prayers, which multiplied, led to the collections of *piyyutim* (*maḥzorim*, books of *seliḥot*, and *kinot*) which established for every occasion passages of *piyyut*, whose recitation was repeated year after year. At first, each community established its own collection, usually by choosing *piyyut* passages and adding the works of local composers. In a later period, the distinctions between the collections of *piyyutim* of the various communities became increasingly blurred and, with the invention of printing, unified collections of *piyyutim* crystallized for different rites of prayer.

See also *Liturgy; *Poetry; *Prosody.

Bibliography: Waxman, Literature, 1 (1960), ch. 9; 2 (1960²), ch. 3; Zunz, Poesie; Zunz, Ritus; Zunz, Lit Poesie; Elbogen, Gottesdienst, 206–31, 280–353; Zulay, in: YMḤSI, 5 (1939), 107–80; Mirsky, *ibid.*, 7 (1958), 1–129; A. Mirsky, *Reshit ha-Piyyut* (1965); S. Abramson, *Bi-Leshon Kodemim* (1965); Davidson, Oẓar, index s.v. names of *paytanim*. [E.Fl.]

PIZMON (pl. *pizmonim;* Heb. פִּזְמוֹן, pl. פִּזְמוֹנִים), a term transferred to Hebrew from Greek by way of Aramaic, meaning "adoration and praise," i.e., a poem praising God. It was first applied to the refrain in *piyyutim* in which either the first or the last line of the first stanza was repeated at the end of each stanza. Subsequently, the *piyyutim* themselves in which these refrains occur were called *pizmonim*.

Pizmonim can be inserted almost anywhere in the liturgy; the Sephardi *paytanim* inserted them in the *kerovot* (the groups of *piyyutim* in the *Amidah*). In Spain the one who sang or read the *pizmon* before the congregation was called *pizmanana*. In a later period editors used the word *pizmonim* for poems and songs in general. The name often appears on the title page of collections of poems, particularly those printed in oriental countries. In modern Israel the word is used to mean a popular song.

Bibliography: Zunz, Poesie, 88–89, 367–8; Elbogen, Gottesdienst, 208; Schirmann, Sefarad, 2 (1956), 714.

[A.M.H.]

PLACZEK, ABRAHAM (1799–1884), **Landesrabbiner* of Moravia. In 1827 he became rabbi in his birthplace, Přerov (Prerau, Moravia), and in 1832 in *Hranice (Maehrisch Weisskirchen). From 1840 until his death he was rabbi in *Boskovice. When Samson Raphael *Hirsch left the *Landesrabbinat* of Moravia in 1851, the provincial authorities appointed Placzek acting *Landesrabbiner*, declaring the election regulations of 1754 obsolete. He held the post until his death. By this act the *Landesrabbinat* was removed from *Mikulov after more than 200 years. Placzek was considered an outstanding talmudic scholar and was strictly Orthodox, supporting Solomon *Spitzer in his struggle against liturgical reform in Vienna (1872). Nevertheless he attempted to avoid open conflicts between the factions, both in Boskovice and in Moravia.

His son, BARUCH JACOB (1835–1922), succeeded him and became the last *Landesrabbiner* of Moravia. He taught at Jewish secondary schools in Germany for some years and was called as rabbi to *Brno (Bruenn) in 1860. He established a teachers' seminary offering a course in *ḥazzanut*, a project favored by his father, and was an adherent of moderate religious reform. Baruch published, partly under the pseudonym Benno Planek, various works on Jewish themes: *Im Eruw* (1867), poems, and *Der Takkif* (1895), a short novel documenting a Moravian Jewish quarter before 1848. He also published articles on natural science, mainly zoology.

Bibliography: H. Gold (ed.), *Die Juden und Judengemeinden Maehrens*... (1929), 52 (a list of Baruch's works), and index; D. Feuchtwang, in: *Gedenkbuch... D. Kaufmann* (1900), 384; A. Frankl-Gruen, *Geschichte der Juden in Kremsier*, 2 (1898), 138–43, 174–6; *Dr. Blochs Oesterreichische Wochenschrift*, 28 (1911), 11–12.

[M.LA.]

PLAGUES OF EGYPT. The Bible has three accounts of the plagues (*maggefot*, Ex. 9:14; *negaʿim*, cf. Ex. 11:1, *makkot*, cf. I Sam. 4:8; cf. LXX, Targ.) that struck Egypt prior to the Exodus: a full, prose account is given in Exodus 7:14–11:10; 12:29–33, and brief, poetic ones in Psalms 78:43–51 and 105:27–36. The variations are set out in the table below listing the plagues and their effects. While the ten items of the Exodus narrative are distinctly separate, some of the items in Psalms are but synonyms or components of plagues. Thus Psalm 105 lists ten items, but refers to seven

The Plagues

EXODUS	PSALM 78:44–51	PSALM 105:28–36
1. Blood Nile; all water; fish died	1. Blood Nile; liquids	1. Darkness
2. Frogs nuisance to men	2. Swarms[1] "consumed them"	2. Blood water; fish died
3. Lice nuisance to men and beats	Frogs "ruined them"	3. Frogs nuisance
4. Swarms[1] nuisance to men; ruined land	3. *Ḥasil*[2] ate produce	4. Swarms[1] } nuisance
5. Pestilence killed livestock	Locusts ate "toil"	Lice } nuisance
6. Boils pained men and beasts	4. Hail destroyed vines	5. Hail } destroyed vines, figs, trees
7. Hail and fire destroyed plants, men and beasts	*Ḥanamel*[3] destroyed sycamores	Fire } destroyed vines, figs, trees
8. Locusts destroyed plants	5. Hail[4] destroyed beasts	6. Locusts } destroyed all vegetation
9. Darkness immobilized men	*Reshafim*[5] destroyed livestock	*Yeleq*[2] } destroyed all vegetation
10. Firstborn death	6. Death } killed men[6]	7. Firstborn death
	Pestilence } killed men[6]	
	7.[7] Firstborn death	

1 Heb. *ʿarov*; LXX: "dogflies"; R. Nehemiah (Ex. R.) "gnats and mosquitoes"; NJPS "swarms of insects." But Josephus (Ant. 2: 303), R. Judah (Ex. R.), and Targ. "mixture of birds and beasts."

2 A kind (or stage of development) of locusts.

3 Meaning obscure; LXX: "frost"; medieval conjectures: "locust," "stones".

4 Symmachus: "pestilence" (*dever* for MT *barad*).

5 Traditionally "fiery bolts", but *Reshef* is a Canaanite plague-god, and *reshef* in Deuteronomy 32:24 (|| *qetev*) and Habakkuk 3:5 (|| *dever*) means "pestilence" (cf. note 4).

6 *Ḥayyatam* = *nafsham*, "their life" (Ibn Ezra; cf. Rashi); LXX, Targ. misconstrue as "their beasts"

7 Ibn Ezra joins to the preceding.

Figure 1. The ninth and tenth plagues, depicted in the *Sarajevo Haggadah,* Spain, 14th century (fol. 26). Upper register, right, Moses pleads with Pharaoh as darkness appears; left, Israelites in their lighted home. Lower register, right, rats attack the corpses of the firstborn; left, Pharaoh entreats Moses and Aaron to take the Israelites out of Egypt. Sarajevo, National Museum.

plagues only. Psalm 78 lists 11 items, but only seven (or six) plagues. The climactic order in Psalm 78 is most satisfactory: nuisances, destruction of plant life, of animals, and of human beings. The order of Psalm 105 is similar, while in the Exodus account the ascending line is not consistently realized. The Psalms' divergence from Exodus has been ascribed to poetic license; the likelihood is, however, that it attests to independent, variant traditions (see further below).

Their Function. The leading motif of the plague series in the Exodus account is introduced in 7:5: "The Egyptians shall know that I am YHWH when I stretch my hand over Egypt . . ." Repeated variously (7:17; 8:6, 18; 9:14, 16, 29), it shows the plagues to be the answer to Pharaoh's challenge in 5:2: "Who is YHWH . . .? I do not know YHWH, nor will I release Israel." Intended, thus, as revelations of the nature and power of Israel's God, the plagues are distinguished from both magic and natural calamities. The magicians' failure to produce lice elicits from them the confession that "it is the finger of God" (8:15). The plagues' onset after an announcement or at a signal, and their removal by order, links them to YHWH, whose agents, Moses and Aaron, announced, signaled, and removed them in His name. The accumulation of disasters, their discriminating between Israel and the Egyptians (starting from 8:18), and the unprecedentedness of the last four plagues succeed in eliciting from Pharaoh's court increasingly frequent acknowledgments of God's authority (8:4, 21, 24; 9:20, 27–28; 10:7–8, 16–17, 24), ending with the release of Israel to worship Him (12:31–32). As 9:14–16 and 10:1–2 make clear, the reason for prolonging the series is not to secure Israel's release (which might have been achieved by one crushing blow), but to establish for all time the fame of YHWH and the folly of defying Him.

The Structure of the Narrative. The narrative evidences a deliberate, if imperfectly realized design:

(1) The plagues gradually intensify, beginning with nuisances, passing through destruction of livestock and crops, and ending with the death of human beings. The intensification sometimes falters (e.g., boils after pestilence), and sometimes the effects of a plague transgress its proper limits (e.g., the death of men and beasts in the hail). These appear to result, on the one hand, from the combination of variant traditions, and, on the other, from a desire to aggrandize God (see further below). A comparison with the strategy of reducing a rebellious population is found in the Midrash: God used the tactics of kings against the Egyptians. First He cut off their water supply (blood), then He raised a clamor around them (frogs), then shot arrows at them (lice), then arrayed legions against them (swarms), then caused a pestilence, then threw burning naphtha at them (fever boils), then sent hosts against them (locusts), then incarcerated them in dungeons (darkness), then put to death their chiefs (firstborn; Tanḥ. *Bo.* 4). Levi b. Gershom perceives cycles of increasing severity: God began with a harmless wonder (Ex. 7:8–13); when that failed, He spoiled their water—but not totally; next He sent the frogs, which caused discomfort; but that was less than the distress caused by the lice. A second round began with the swarms that attacked livestock and food; then pestilence that killed off the livestock; then boils that afflicted the body. A third round followed, starting with hail and locusts, wiping out the food supply, followed by darkness—a bodily affliction just short of death. The death of the firstborn climaxed the series.

(2) These rounds correspond to the formal division of the story into three sets of three plagues, capped by a tenth, in a pattern determined by an invariably recurring order of introductory clauses. Plagues one, four, and seven begin with God commanding Moses to stand before Pharaoh in the morning (at the Nile) to warn him; two, five, and eight begin with a command to enter Pharaoh's residence to warn him there; three, six, and nine begin with a command to bring on the plague without warning. Early perception of this pattern is reflected in R. Judah's mnemonic, cited in the *Haggadah*, דצ״ך עד״ש באח״ב (cf. also Rashbam to 7:26; Baḥya to 10:1).

(3) A certain design can also be discerned in the various agents who induce the plagues. In the first triplet Moses warns, but Aaron signals the coming of the plague; in each case the Egyptian magicians respond. The triplet continues, on an intensified level, the contest begun with the accredition episode (7:10–12) between the very same characters. It is decided only in the third plague, when the magicians, unable to produce lice, confess it is the work of a higher power. In this contest, the principles—Moses and Pharaoh—are each represented by their seconds; when the magicians retire from the fray, Aaron does too (and when Aaron reappears in a subsidiary role in the sixth plague, the magicians momentarily reappear with him). In the last triplet Moses both announces and induces the plagues, thus enhancing his prestige as God's plenipotentiary in the negotiations that mark this climactic triplet (cf. 11:3). God directly brings on two plagues of the middle triplet—the third (boils), induced by Moses and Aaron, is asymmetrical—and the final firstborn plague. The reason emerges from an examination of the distinctive motif of each triplet.

(4) A purpose clause in the first member of each triplet adumbrates its distinctive motif. As the aim of the first

triplet is to dispel the courtiers' notion that the power of the Hebrew envoys is magical, God fittingly admonishes Pharaoh before the blood plague: "By this you shall know that I am YHWH" (7:17). Two plagues of the second triplet explicitly (and the third implicitly) discriminate the Israelites from the Egyptians (8:18–19; 9:4, 6, 11). Such discrimination realizes the purpose stated in 8:18, "That you may know that I, YHWH, am in the midst of the land," for the presence of God—His overseeing providence (cf. Ex. 17:7; 33:5; Num. 14:42; Deut. 6:15; 31:17)—is typically manifest in the separation between the fates of the innocent and the guilty. The opening speech of the third triplet asserts that its aim is to let Pharoah know "that there is none like Me in all the earth" (Ex. 9:14). The words are echoed four times in phrases expressing the unparalleled intensity of the first two plagues of the triplet (the last member (darkness) again is asymmetrical). There is a notable accumulation of motifs in the last plagues. Thus the last triplet twice refers to discrimination (in different words; 9:26; 10:23) besides its own motif, while the warning of the last plague mentions the last two motifs (11:6–7) and alludes to an intensified form of the first (11:8; the court will bow to Moses). That God directly brings on plagues of the second triplet suits its stated purpose of demonstrating God's presence in the land. The presence-discrimination motif is linked again to God's direct action in the last plague (11:4, 7; 12:12, 29). Where God's presence is to be felt, mediators are out of place.

(5) Design (without strict systematization) is also evident in the characterization of Pharaoh and Moses. Pharaoh's reactions oscillate erratically during the first two triplets between impassivity (7:23; 8:15; 9:7, 12) and insincere concessions (8:4, 21, 24). In the first plague of the third triplet he confesses guilt (9:27), and in the last two he negotiates seriously over Israel's release, as is indicated by his measured concessions at each stage (10:8, 11, 24). Moses' manner changes from a certain sportiveness (8:5) to pained rebuke (8:25), to disbelief (9:30), and finally, in negotiation, to provocative baiting that enrages Pharaoh (10:25–26).

Figure 2. Hail, the seventh plague, in an illumination from a *Haggadah*, Spain, 14th century. Moses stretches his hand toward heaven, and hailstones fall on man, beast, and tree. London, British Museum, Ms. Or. 2737, fol. 76b.

Hardening Pharaoh's Heart. This drama is embedded in (and manages to overcome the stultifying potential of) a deterministic framework. God's policy of hardening Pharaoh's heart is announced in advance (7:3), and notice of its operation is repeatedly given (9:12; 10:1, 20, 27; 11:10). Some mitigation of it is probably to be seen in the fact that during the first five plagues Pharaoh's stubbornness is consistently represented as self-motivated (7:22; 8:11, 15, 28; 9:7; cf. Ex. R. 13:3: God hardened Pharaoh's heart from the sixth plague in order to punish him for his voluntary defiance during the first five; cf. further Maimonides, introduction to Avot, ch. 8; Yad, Teshuvah, 6). But this still makes the last, worst plagues—an infliction of suffering on an involuntary sinner—paradoxical, since precisely in the last plagues Pharaoh's reactions are adequately motivated, perhaps even justifiable in view of Moses' provocations. There is here the parade example of the "two-level" view of history characteristic of biblical narrative. Human events are shaped by the will of God, yet they unfold in accord with the motives of actors who do God's will without realizing it (Gen. 45:5, 8; Judg. 14:4; I Kings 12:15). Thus God determined for His own purposes that Pharoah should resist the plagues; indeed He saw to it. But Pharaoh conducted himself throughout conformably with his own motives and his own godless arrogance. God made it so, but Pharaoh had only to be himself to do God's will.

Interpretations of the Plagues. Attempts have been made to interpret the plagues in terms of ancient Egyptian beliefs or the natural conditions of Egypt. A Middle Kingdom description of anarchy speaks of the Nile's turning into blood (The Admonitions of Ipuwer; Pritchard, Texts, 441); a New Kingdom prophecy of the darkening of the sun (Nefer-rohu; Pritchard, Texts, 445). Philo and the Midrash understand the blood plague as an attack on the deified Nile (I Mos. 98; Ex. R. 9:9), and this clue has been followed by some moderns who look for the humiliation of Egyptian deities in the course of the plagues (e.g., Hapi, the Nile god; Ḥekt, a frog-headed goddess; Re, the sun god), though no hint of this is to be found in the biblical plague narrative. On the other hand, most of the plagues can be linked with local or seasonal phenomena. During its annual rise, in the summer, the Nile is reddened by organisms carried in it; swarms of frogs and insects follow the inundation (insects normally abound in Egypt); Egyptian boils were proverbial (Deut. 28:27); hail, though uncommon, has been known to fall in January—the time indicated by the agricultural data of Exodus 9:31–32; locusts may be blown across the country in winter or spring; three-day, palpable darkness conforms with the heavy sandstorms raised by the *ḥamsin* winds that blow in the early spring. Thus the plagues have been viewed as a miraculous intensification and concentration of local phenomena, crowded into a single year (Moses was 80 years old when they began (7:7), lived 40 years more, and died at the age of 120 (Deut. 34:7); cf. also Eduy. 2:10).

The Variant Versions. The narrative appears to combine two major versions of the plague series. Hence arose such inconsistencies as are found in the depiction of the agent, the signal, and the extent of the blood plague in Exodus 7:17–21 (cf. the dispute between R. Judah and R. Nehemiah in Ex. R. 9:11); such inconsequence as the skipping of the boils in the backward glance of 9:15, or the unmotivated reappearance of Aaron and the boils-afflicted magicians after the lapse of two plagues; and such asymmetry and stylistic differences as set lice, boils, and darkness apart from the rest of the plagues. (1) One version began with the accreditation sign given by God to Aaron and Moses: Moses orders Aaron to turn his staff into a serpent; the magicians imitate the sign (7:8–13). The plagues proper follow; (2) Moses orders Aaron to turn all the waters of Egypt to blood; this is imitated by the magicians (7:19–20*aa*, 21b–22); (3) Moses orders Aaron to induce frogs; this is again imitated by the magicians (8:1–3, 11b (fragmentary)); (4) Moses orders Aaron to produce lice; the magicians fail and confess God's power (8:12–15); (5) Moses, aided by Aaron, induces boils; the magicians are themselves afflicted and retire routed (9:8–12); (6) Moses alone induces

Figure 3. Page from the *Golden Haggadah*, Spain, 13th century, illustrating four of the plagues. Upper right, frogs; upper left, lice. Lower right, beasts; lower left, murrain. London, British Museum, Add. Ms. 27210, fol. 12v.

darkness, immobilizing everyone for three days (10:21–23, 27a (fragmentary)); (7) God strikes the firstborn (cf. 12:12, belonging to this version). In this conjecturally restored version (which, with the exception of item 6, agrees with conventional criticism's P) the agents of the plagues ascend climactically, the effects intensify steadily, and all before the last are designed to outdo and overwhelm rather than destroy. They are tokens of God's might rather than punishments.

The second version ran thus: (1) After a morning warning, Moses turned the Nile into blood, which killed its fish; Pharaoh was unmoved (7:14–17, 20a*b*–21a, 23–25); (2) After a warning in the palace . . . (there follows the other version of frogs); negotiation with Pharaoh (7:26–29 (gap), 8:4–11a (fragmentary)); (3) After a morning warning by Moses, God sends swarms of insects, separating the Israelites; negotiations (8:16–28); (4) After a warning in the palace by Moses, God strikes Egypt's livestock with a pestilence, separating the Israelites (9:1–7); (5) After a morning warning, heeded by some courtiers, Moses signals the onslaught of an unprecedented hail mixed with fire; negotiations (9:13–35); (6) After a warning in the palace, followed by fruitless negotiation, Moses signals the coming of an unprecedentedly severe locust plague; Pharaoh asks relief just this once; further negotiations end in Moses' expulsion (10:1–19, 24–29); (7) Moses announces the death of the firstborn (11:4–8), which comes that night (12:29–33).

This conjectured version (roughly consisting of the conventional JE) represents the plagues as increasingly severe injuries to Egyptian property and life, as blows designed to afflict the land. The story seems to have been expanded at times by reflective comment (9:15–16; 10:1b–2), or to broaden the scope of a plague (e.g., 9:19–21 includes men and beasts among the victims of the hail). The redactorial interweaving of the two accounts was relatively smooth once the first triplet was constituted on the basis of the overlapping of the two versions and the lice plague's deciding the issue posed in the accreditation sign The formal pattern of that triplet determined the rest of the interweaving, the genial device of three triplets plus one (an expansion of the 3.3.1 pattern of Gen. 1:1–2:3) nicely accommodating the total of ten separate plagues. Since both versions were climactic, their fusion was on the whole reasonable, although it impaired thematic symmetry, stylistic unity, and strict progress of the narrative. The variant Psalms passages may attest to independent traditions of the plagues. The affinity of the listing in Psalm 78 to the reconstructed second version is particularly striking: both lack the three distinctive plagues of the first—lice, boils, darkness. The present Exodus narrative presumably represents an effort to create a standard account of the plagues, embodying maximally the data of the various traditions known to the author-redactor.

Midrashic Embellishment. The local color of a number of the plagues makes it plausible to assume that the traditions concerning them rose out of events that happened in Egypt. In time, the events were added to, embellished, and reflected upon, most likely in connection with the religious celebrations of the Exodus. The Passover laws of Exodus 12:26–27; 13:8 and the firstborn redemption rite in 13:11–16 suggest occasions for use of a liturgical formulation of the pre-Exodus events. Various statements of the plague series may have originated in and for such occasions, just as, in post-biblical times, the standard Exodus listing was taken up into the *Haggadah*. The tendency to enlarge the scope of the plagues—formally legitimized in the Midrash cited in the *Haggadah* ("How can you prove from Scripture that each plague was really four [or five]

Figure 4. Woodcuts of the ten plagues, made by Jakob Steinhardt in 1921 for his *Haggadah*, published in a limited edition. Berlin, 1923. Jerusalem, B. M. Ansbacher Collection.

plagues . . .?")—shows itself already in the components of the Exodus narrative, e.g., while in one version the blood plague affects the Nile only, in the other it spreads to all the waters of Egypt. Similarly, just as the Exodus version of hail has already made it deadly to man and beast, so does Philo raise blood (I Mos. 98) and Josephus raise lice, swarms (of beasts), ulcers, and darkness to the level of death-dealing scourges (Ant., 2:293ff.). The Midrash gives free rein to the imagination in this direction: the Egyptians' spittle and fruit juice turned to blood; their wood and stone household objects oozed blood (Ex. R. 9:11; Mid. Hag. to 7:19); the frogs castrated them (Ex. R. 10:4); deadly pestilence accompanied all the plagues (Ex. R. 10:2); the darkness lasted six days, and at its worst was so thick that no one could move a muscle (Ex. R. 14:3). The Midrash also enlarges upon the brief biblical reflections on the rationale of the plagues. The "measure for measure" interpretation is typical: Blood—because they kept Israel's women from their post-menstrual immersion, to stop their childbearing (another view—because they cast the male infants into the Nile); frogs—because they made Israel clean and repair streets; lice—because they made them sweep homes and markets; mixture of beasts—because they made them catch wild beasts; pestilence—because they made them tend flocks; fever boils—because they made them tend baths; hail—because they made them tend fields; locusts—because they made them plant trees; darkness—so that they could not witness the burial of wicked Israelites; firstborn—because they enslaved Israel, whom God called "my firstborn son" (Ex. 4:22; Mid. Hag. to 10:2). Thus the plagues grew ever more marvelous "to spread the fame of God's great power . . . that Israel might realize that He is the Lord, and teach it to their descendants, so that this true belief might live on in Israel forever" (Ralbag, Comment., end of *Va-Era* and *Bo*).

Bibliography: A. Macalister, in: DB, s.v.; J. C. Mihelic and G. E. Wright, in: IDB, 3 (1962), 822ff.; G. Hort, in: ZAW, 69 (1957), 84ff.; 70 (1958), 48ff.; H. Eising, in: *Lex tua veritas* (*Junker*

Festschrift, 1961), 75ff.; G. Fohrer, *Ueberlieferung und Geschichte des Exodus* (1964), 60ff.; S. E. Loewenstamm, *Masoret Yezi'at Mizrayim be-Hishtalshelutah* (1965), 25ff.; M. Greenberg, *Understanding Exodus* (1969), 151ff.; Ginzberg, Legends, 2 (1910), 341ff. [Mo.G.]

PLANE TREE (Heb. עַרְמוֹן ; *armon*). The oriental plane, *Platanus orientalis,* is indigenous to Israel and grows on the banks of rivers, especially in the north. It is one of the most beautiful of Israel's trees and is recognizable by its lofty trunk, spreading crest, and large leaves. Its Hebrew name is connected with the fact that its bark peels so that the trunk is left bare *(arom).* It grows also in Syria and Babylon; while sojourning with Laban in Mesopotamia, Jacob peeled "white streaks" off rods from the tree (Gen. 30:37). Ezekiel, who prophesied in Babylon, mentions it among the beautiful trees in "the garden of God" (Ezek. 31:8). The Targum (Gen. 31:37) rightly renders the word *doleva* ("the plane") and the Septuagint similarly has *platanos.* Rashi, however, identifies the *armon* with the chestnut, an identification which was accepted by European rabbis and by the biblical commentators, and it has been adopted in modern Hebrew. However, this identification is erroneous since the chestnut does not grow in Israel or in Mesopotamia. Beautiful plane trees are found especially on the banks of the River Dan and the River Senir, the sources of the Jordan. Particularly well known is the great plane tree at the Banias Falls which divides the falls in two.

Bibliography: Loew, Flora, 3 (1924), 65–67; B. Cizik, *Ozar ha-Zemaḥim* (1943), 224ff.; J. Feliks, *Olam ha-Zome'aḥ ha-Mikra'i* (1968²), 120–1; H. N. and A. L. Moldenke, *Plants of the Bible* (1952), 391 (index), s.v. [J.F.]

°**PLANTAVIT DE LA PAUSE, JEAN** (**Plantavitius;** 1576–1651), French Hebraist. Born into an aristocratic Protestant family, Plantavit was brought up in Nîmes and became pastor of Béziers. In 1604 he converted to Catholicism and later became bishop of Lodève. He left a detailed account of his Hebrew teachers, who included the erudite and prolific convert Philippe d'Aquin (born Mordecai Cresque de Carpentras, c. 1575–1650), Leone *Modena, Abraham Jedidiah Shalit of Ferrara, Elisha Mazzal-Tov of Modena, Jacob b. Moses Senior of Pisa, and Solomon b. Judah Ezobi of Carpentras. One of the outstanding Christian Hebraists of the age, Plantavit spent 30 years preparing his monumental *Thesaurus synonymicus Hebraico-Chaldaico-Rabbinicus* (Lodève, 1644–45), which gave the Latin equivalent of Hebrew and Aramaic terms, appropriate biblical references, and a wealth of synonyms. He also published *Florilegium Biblicum* and *Florilegium Rabbinicum* (both Lodève, 1645), in the latter of which he records his gift of a copy of the Zohar to his master, Philippe d'Aquin.

Bibliography: F. Secret, *Les kabbalistes chrétiens de la Renaissance* (1964), 336–7. [G.E.S.]

°**PLANTIN, CHRISTOPHE** (c. 1520–1589), French humanist printer and publisher. Plantin, who was born near Tours, learned the book trade in Normandy and Paris. His Protestant sympathies led him in 1549 to the more congenial atmosphere of Antwerp in the Spanish Netherlands, where he devoted himself to fine printing from about 1555 onward. Plantin was, after Daniel *Bomberg, the outstanding 16th-century Christian printer of Hebrew books. By 1576 he operated 22 presses and was the leading printer-publisher of northern Europe. Following the "Spanish Fury" of 1576, he spent some years in France and Holland, eventually returning to Antwerp, where he died.

Plantin's greatest publishing achievement was the eight-volume "Antwerp Polyglot," *Biblia Sacra hebraice, chaldaice, graece et latine...* (1568–72), an improved and expanded version of the first Complutensian Bible (Alcalà de Henares, 1514–17). The undertaking received the Vatican's approval in 1568 owing to fears of a rival project by Immanuel *Tremellius, a Jewish convert to Protestantism. The four volumes devoted to the Old Testament included revised texts of the Targums, and a Latin translation; the fifth covered the New Testament; and the last three volumes constituted the *Apparatus Sacer,* which included pioneering lexicons of Syriac and Aramaic. The introduction to the first volume, inspired by the prefaces to Daniel Bomberg's second Rabbinic Bible (1525), contains interesting Hebrew panegyrics by Benito *Arias Montano, Guy *Le Fèvre de la Boderie, and Gilbert *Génébrard (one of the Polyglot's obliging censors). From every aspect, the work was a masterpiece of Bible scholarship, typography, and illustration. Hebrew punches were either especially cut by Guillaume *Le Bé or provided by the Bombergs. Of the 1,200 copies printed, 12 sets on vellum were prepared for Philip II of Spain, who made Plantin his Architypographer Royal, but never furnished the sum promised for naming the Bible in his honor. The "Antwerp Polyglot" was speedily denounced by Spanish obscurantists, who objected to its philological, rabbinic, and kabbalistic preoccupations, but it was cleared of suspicion in 1580. Plantin also printed Hebrew Bibles for export to Jewish communities in North Africa (1567) and may have issued the anonymous Hebrew prayer book which appeared in Antwerp c. 1577. His descendants maintained the press until 1875, when the Antwerp municipality transformed it into the present-day Plantin-Moretus Museum—a unique monument to Renaissance printing and publishing.

Bibliography: C. Clair, *Christopher Plantin* (Eng., 1960); M. Rooses, *Christophe Plantin, imprimeur anversois* (1882); idem, *Correspondance de Christophe Plantin* (1883–84); S. H. Steinberg, *Five Hundred Years of Printing* (1955), index; *Gedenkboek der Plantin-Dagen 1555–1955* (1956); F. Secret, in: *Sefarad,* 18 (1958), 121–8; G. E. Silverman, in: JC (Jan. 8, 1960); B. Rekers, *Benito Arias Montano 1527–1598...* (1961); I. S. Revah, in: REJ, 2 (1963), 123–47. [G.E.S.]

PLANTS. Research into the flora mentioned in the ancient Hebrew literature is grounded on the basic assumption that within historical times no fundamental changes have taken place in the country's climate (see *Agriculture). This assumption, which allows conclusions to be drawn from present-day plants about the floral landscape of bygone days, is particularly important for identifying the flora of the Bible and of talmudic literature. The overwhelming majority of them can be identified with those of today, but, as with all the terms of biblical and talmudic realia, many and varied identifications and interpretations have been suggested for them. Modern botanical and philological studies have, however, helped greatly in arriving at a correct identification.

In the Bible. The Bible mentions about 100 names of plants, the bulk of them of Ereẓ Israel, the others being trees of Lebanon and tropical plants that yield an aromatic substance or were used in incense. These names refer to specific plants, but some are generic names, such as *koẓ ve-dardar* ("thorns and thistles") and *shamir va-shayit* ("briars and thorns"). Although the biblical plants are chiefly those which were economically important, they are to a large extent mentioned fortuitously. The carob, for example, although undoubtedly grown at that time, is not mentioned in the Bible, while specific vegetables are mentioned in one verse only of the Bible; and these are the vegetables of Egypt for which the children of Israel longed during their wandering in the wilderness (Num. 11:5).

In Talmudic Literature. The Mishnah, the Talmuds, and

Plants and Products of Plants Mentioned in the Bible and Mishnah

English Name	Scientific Name	Hebrew Name	Description of Plant	Reference
Acacia	Acacia albida	שִׁטָּה, שִׁטִּים	thorn tree	Ex. 26:15; Isa. 41:19, et al.
Alga	Chlorophyta	יְרוֹקָה	seaweed	Shab. 2:1
Almond	Prunus amygdalus (Amygdalus communis)	לוּז	fruit tree	Gen. 30:37
		שָׁקֵד		Num. 17:23; Jer. 1:11, et al.
Aloe	Aquilaria agallocha	אֲהָלִים	fragrant tropical tree	Num. 24:6; Prov. 7:17
		אֲהָלוֹת		Ps. 45:9; Song 4:14;
		אַלְמֻגִּים		I Kings 10:11–12
		אַלְגֻּמִּים		II Chron. 2:7; 9:10–11
Amaranth	Amaranthus retroflexus	יַרְבּוּז	vegetable (herb)	Shev. 9:1
Amomum	Amomum cardamomum	חָמָם	tropical spice plant	Uk. 3:5
Apple	Pyrus malus	תַּפּוּחַ	fruit tree	Joel 1:12; Song 2:3, et al.
Artichoke	Cynara scolymus	קִנְרֵס	garden vegetable	Kil. 5:8; Uk. 1:6
Asafetida, Fennel	Ferula assafoetida	חִלְתִּית	herb whose gum is used in spices and medicine	Shab. 20:3; Av. Zar. 2:7, et al.
Balm, Balsam	Commiphora opobalsamum	בֹּשֶׂם	the balsam shrub whose resin yields an aromatic substance	Song 5:1
		נָטָף		Ex. 30:34
		צְרִי, צֳרִי		Gen. 37:25; 43:11, et al.
		קֶטָף		Shev. 7:6
Barley	Hordeum sativum	שְׂעוֹרָה	cereal grass	Ex. 9:31; Deut. 8:8, et al.
Barley, two-rowed	Hordeum distichum	שׂוֹרָה,	cereal grass	Isa. 28:25
		שִׁבּוֹלֶת שׁוּעָל		Kil. 1:1; Pes. 2:5, et al.
Bdellium	Commiphora africana	בְּדוֹלַח	tropical tree whose resin yields an aromatic substance	Gen. 2:12; Num. 11:7
Bean, broad	Vicia faba	פּוֹל	legume	II Sam. 17:28; Ezek. 4:9, et al.
Bean, hyacinth	Dolichos lablab	פּוֹל הַלָּבָן	legume	Kil. 1:1; Ma'as. 4:7, et al.
Bean, yard-long (asparagus bean)	Vigna sesquipedalis	פּוֹל הֶחָרוּב	legume	Kil. 1:2
Beet spinach	Beta vulgaris var. cicla	תְּרֶד	garden vegetable	Kil. 1:3; Ter. 10:11, et al.
Bermuda grass	Cynodon dactylon	יַבְּלִית	weed	Kelim 3:6
Box	Buxus sempervirens	אֶשְׁכְּרוֹעַ	hardwood shrub	Yoma 3:9; Kelim 12:8; Neg. 2:1
Boxthorn	Lycium europaeum	אָטָד	thorny shrub	Gen. 50:10–11; Judg. 9:14–15, et al.
Broom plant	Retama roetam	רֹתֶם	desert shrub	I Kings 19:4–5; Job 30:4, et al.
Cabbage, garden	Brassica oleracea var. capitata	תְּרוֹבְתוֹר	garden vegetable	Kil. 1:3
Cabbage, kale	Brassica oleracea var. acephala	כְּרוּב	hardy cabbage	Kil. 1:3; Ter. 10:11, et al.
Calamus, Indian sweet	Cymbopogon martini	קָנֶה הַטּוֹב	tropical aromatic plant	Jer. 6:20
		קְנֵה־בֹּשֶׂם		Ex. 30:23
		קָנֶה		Isa. 43:24; Song. 4:14, et al.
Cane, biflorate	Saccharum biflorum	אַגְמוֹן	reed that grows near water	Isa. 9:13, 58:5, et al.
Caper	Capparis spinosa	צָלָף, קַפְרֵס	thorny plant whose buds and fruit are used as spices	Ma'as. 4:6
		אֲבִיּוֹנָה	Caperberry	Eccles. 12:5; Ma'as. 4:6

English Name	Scientific Name	Hebrew Name	Description of Plant	Reference
Caraway	Carum carvi	קַרְבּוֹס (קַנְבּוֹס)	vegetable used as a spice	Kil. 2:5
Carob	Ceratonia siliqua	חָרוּב	fruit tree	Pe'ah. 1:5; Dem.2:1, et al.
Castor-oil plant	Ricinus communis	קִיקָיוֹן	shrub whose seed yields oil	Jonah 4:6, 7, 9, 10
Cattail	Typha angustata	סוּף	marsh and water plant	Ex. 2:3; Isa. 19:6, et al.
Cedar	Cedrus libani	אֶרֶז	forest tree of Lebanon	Isa. 2:13; Amos 2:9, et al.
Celery	Apium graveolens	כַּרְפַּס	garden vegetable	Shev. 9:1
Chick-pea	Cicer arietinum	חָמִיץ אֲפוּנִים	legume	Isa. 30:24 Pe'ah 3:3; Kil. 3:2
Chicory	Cichorium intybus	עוֹלְשִׁין	garden vegetable	Shev. 7:1; Pes. 2:6
Chicory, wild	Cichorium pumilum	עוֹלְשֵׁי־שָׂדֶה	wild vegetable	Kil. 1:2
Cinnamon, Ceylonese	Cinnamonum zeylanicum	קִנָּמוֹן	aromatic tropical spice tree	Ex. 30:23; Prov. 7:17, et al.
Cinnamon, Chinese	Cinnamonum cassia	קִדָּה	aromatic tropical spice tree	Ex. 30:24; Ezek. 27:19
Cinnamon, Indo-Chinese	Cinnamonum laurei	קְצִיעָה	aromatic tropical spice tree	Ps. 45:9
Citron	Citrus medica	עֵץ הָדָר אֶתְרוֹג	fruit tree	Lev. 23:40 Ma'as. 1:4; Bik. 2:6, et al.
Colocasia	Colocasia antiquorum	קַרְקָס	vegetable with edible bulb	Ma'as. 5:8
Coriander	Coriandrum sativum	גַּד כֻּסְבָּר	herb whose seed is used as a spice	Ex. 16:31; Num. 11:7 Kil. 1:2; Ma'as. 3:9, et al.
Cotton	Gossypium herbraceum	כַּרְפַּס	plant with fibrous fruit	Esth. 1:6
	Gossypium arboreum	צֶמֶר־גֶּפֶן		Kil. 7:2
Cowpea	Vigna sinensis	פּוֹל הַמִּצְרִי	legume	Kil. 1:2; Shev. 2:9, et al.
Cowpea, Nile	Vigna nilotica	שְׁעוּעִית	legume	Kil. 1:1
Cress	Lepidium latifolium	עֲדָל	garden vegetable	Uk. 3:4
Cress, garden	Lepidium sativum	שַׁחֲלַיִם	garden vegetable	Ma'as. 4:5
Crocus, saffron	Crocus sativus	כַּרְכּוֹם	plant used as a spice and for coloring	Song 4:14; Nid. 2:6
Cucumber, bitter	Citrullus colocynthis	פַּקּוּעוֹת	wild desert plant	II Kings 4:39; Shab. 2:2
Cucumber, squirting	Ecballium elaterium	יְרוֹקַת הַחֲמוֹר	wild herb	Oho. 8:1
Cumin	Cuminum cyminum	כַּמּוֹן	herb whose seeds are used as a spice	Isa. 2:25, 27; Dem. 2:1
Cypress	Cupressus sempervirens	גֹּפֶר תְּאַשּׁוּר	forest evergreen tree	Gen. 6:14 Isa. 41:19; 60:13, et al.
Daffodil, sea	Pancratium maritimum	חֲבַצֶּלֶת	fragrant wild flower	Isa. 35:1; Song 2:1
Darnel	Lolium temulentum	זוּן	weed grass	Kil. 1:1; Ter. 2:6
Dill	Anethum graveolens	שֶׁבֶת	plant used as a spice	Pe'ah 3:2; Ma'as. 4:5; Uk. 3:4
Durra	Sorghum cernuum	דֹּחַן	summer cereal	Ezek. 4:9; Shev. 2:7
Ebony	Diospyros ebenum	הָבְנִים	tropical hard-wood	Ezek. 27:15
Emmer	Triticum dicoccum	כֻּסֶּמֶת	winter cereal	Ex. 9:32; Isa. 28:25, et al.
Eryngo	Eryngium creticum	חַרְחֲבִינָא	edible wild herb	Pes. 2:6

English Name	Scientific Name	Hebrew Name	Description of Plant	Reference
Fennel	Foeniculum vulgare	גְּפְנִין	herb used as a spice	Dem. 1:1
Fennel flower	Nigella sativa	קֶצַח	herb whose seeds are used as a spice	Isa. 28:25, 27; Eduy. 5:3
Fenugreek	Trigonella foenum-Graecum	תִּלְתָּן	cultivated legume used as forage or medicine	Kil. 2:5; Ter. 10:5
Fern, ceterach	Ceterach officinarum	דַּנְדַּנָּה	medicinal fern	Shev. 7:1–2
Fern, maiden-hair	Adiantum capillus veneris	יוֹעֶזֶר	medicinal fern	Shab. 14:3
Fig	Ficus carica	תְּאֵנָה	fruit tree	Num. 20:5; Deut. 8:8, et al.
Fig, sycamore	Ficus sycomorus	שִׁקְמָה	fruit tree	I Kings 10:27; Isa. 9:9, et al.
Flax	Linum usitatissimum	פִּשְׁתָּן פִּשְׁתָּה	herb whose stem yields fiber and from whose seed oil is extracted	Josh. 2:6; Hos. 2:7; et al. Pe'ah 6:5
Frankincense	Boswellia carteri	לְבוֹנָה	tree yielding aromatic resin used in incense	Ex. 30:34; Isa. 60:6, et al.
Galbanum	Ferula galbaniflua	חֶלְבְּנָה	herb whose resin was used in incense	Ex. 30:34
Garlic	Allium sativum	שׁוּם	vegetable used as spice	Num. 11:5
Ginger, wild	Arum dioscoridis	לוּף שׁוֹטֶה	wild vegetable	Shev. 7:1, 2, et al.
Gourd, Calabash	Lagenaria vulgaris	דְּלַעַת	vegetable with edible fruit	Kil. 1:2; Ma'as. 1:5, et al.
Grape vine	Vitis vinifera	גֶּפֶן עֲנָבִים	fruit shrub	Gen. 40:9; Num. 20:5, et al.
Graspea	Lathyrus sativus	טֹפַח	legume	Pe'ah 5:3; Kil. 1:1, et al.
Hawthorn	Crataegus azarolus	עֻזְרָר	wild fruit tree	Dem. 1:1; Kil. 1:4, et al.
Heliotrope	Heliotropium europaeum	עַקְרַבָּנִין	medicinal wild herb	Shev. 7:2; Er. 2:7
Hemlock, poison	Conium maculatum	רוֹשׁ,רֹאשׁ	poisonous herb	Deut. 29:17; Hos. 10:4, et al.
Hemp	Cannabis sativa	קַנְבּוֹס	herb whose stem yields fiber	Kil. 5:8; 9:1, 7
Henna	Lawsonia alba	כֹּפֶר	shrub which yields a dye	Song. 1:14; 4:13, et al.
Hyssop (v. marjoram)	Hyssopus officinalis	אֱזוֹב כּוֹחֲל	aromatic herb	Neg. 14:6; Par. 11:7
Iris	Iris germanica Iris pallida	אִירוּס	plant whose bulb yields an aromatic substance	Kil. 5:8; Oho. 8:1
Ivy	Hedera helix	קִיסוֹס	climbing ever-green vine	Kil. 5:8; Suk. 1:4, et al.
Jujube	Zizyphus vulgaris	שֵׁיזָפִין	fruit tree	Kil. 1:4
Jujube, wild	Zizyphus spina-christi	צֶאֱלִים	wild tree with edible fruit	Job 40:21–22
		רִימִין		Dem. 1:1; Kil. 1:6
Juniper (savin high)	Juniperus exelsa	בְּרוֹשׁ בְּרוֹת	coniferous tree of Lebanon	Isa. 14:8; 37:24, et al. Song. 1:17
Knotweed	Polygonum aviculare	אֲבוּב־רוֹעֶה	medicinal wild herb	Shab. 14:3

English Name	Scientific Name	Hebrew Name	Description of Plant	Reference
Laudanum	Cistus ladanum	לֹט	shrub yielding aromatic resin	Gen. 37:25; 43:11
Laurel	Laurus nobilis	אֹרֶן	forest tree with aromatic leaves	Isa. 44:14
Lavender, Lavandula	Lavandula officinalis	אֵזוֹבְיוֹן	aromatic shrub	Shab. 14:3; Neg. 14:6, et al.
Leek	Allium porrum	חָצִיר כְּרֵישָׁה כַּרְתִּי	garden herb	Num. 11:5 Kil. 1:2; Shev. 7:1 Ber. 1:2; Suk. 3:6
Leek, wild	Allium ampeloprasum	כְּרֵישֵׁי שָׂדֶה	wild herb	Kil. 1:2; Uk. 3:2
Lentil	Lens esculenta	עֲדָשִׁים	legume	Gen. 25:34; II Sam. 17:28, et al.
Lettuce	Lactuca sativa	חֲזֶרֶת	garden vegetable	Kil. 1:2; Pes. 2:6, et al.
Lettuce, wild	Lactuca scariola	חֲזֶרֶת גַּלִּים	wild vegetable	Kil. 1:2
Lily, madonna	Lilium candidum	שׁוֹשָׁן, שׁוֹשַׁנָּה	aromatic flower	Hos. 14:6; Song. 6:2–3, et al.
Lily, Solomon's (black calla)	Arum palaestinum	לוּף	wild vegetable with edible bulb	Pe'ah, 6:10; Kil. 2:5
Love grass	Eragrostis bipinnata	חִילָף	weed used for making baskets	Kelim 17:17
Lupine	Lupinus termis	תֻּרְמוֹס	legume	Kil. 1:3; Shab. 18:1, et al.
Lupine, yellow	Lupinus luteus	פַּלְסְלוּס	legume	Kil. 1:3
Madder	Rubia tinctorim	פּוּאָה	climbing plant whose roots are used for dyeing	Shev. 5:4; 7:2, et al.
Mandrake	Mandragora officinarum	דּוּדָאִים	wild herb with aromatic fruit	Gen. 30:14–16; Song. 7:14
Marjoram, Syrian	Majorana syriaca	אֵזוֹב	aromatic wild plant	Ex. 12:22; Lev. 14:4, et al.
Mastic	Pistacia lentiscus	בָּכָא, בְּכָאִים	wild shrub	II Sam. 5:23–24; Ps. 84:7
Melon	Cucumis melo	מְלָפְפוֹן	garden vegetable	Kil. 1:2; Ter. 2:6, et al.
Melon, chate	Cucumis melo var. chate	קִשּׁוּת, קִשֻּׁאִים	garden vegetable	Num. 11:5; Kil. 1:2, et al.
Millet	Panicum miliaceum	פְּרָגִים	summer cereal	Ḥal. 1:4; Shev. 2:7
Mint	Mentha piperita	מִינְתָּא	herb used as spice	Uk. 1:2
Mudar	Calotropis procera	פְּתִילַת הַמִּדְבָּר	wild shrub with fibrous fruit	Shab. 2:1
Mulberry	Morus nigra	תּוּת	fruit tree	Ma'as. 1:2
Mushroom	Boletus, etc.	פִּטְרִיָּה	generic name for the mushroom species	Uk. 3:2
Mustard, black	Brassica nigra	חַרְדָּל	wild herb whose seeds are used as a condiment	Kil. 1:2
Mustard, field	Sinapis arvensis	לִפְסָן	wild herb	Kil. 1:5
Mustard, white	Sinapis alba	חַרְדָּל מִצְרִי	wild herb whose seeds are used as a condiment	Kil. 1:2
Myrrh	Commiphora schimperi Commiphora abyssinica	מוֹר	tropical aromatic tree	Ex. 30:23; Song 1:13, et al.
Myrtle	Myrtus communis	הֲדַס עֵץ עָבֹת	aromatic shrub	Isa. 41:19; 55:13, et al. Lev. 23:40; Neh. 8:15, et al.

English Name	Scientific Name	Hebrew Name	Description of Plant	Reference
Narcissus	Narcissus tazetta	שׁוֹשַׁנַּת הָעֲמָקִים(?)	wild flower	Song 2:1
Nard (Spikenard)	Nardostachys jatamansi	נֵרְדְּ, נְרָדִים	aromatic plant	Song 1:12; 4:13–14, et al.
Nettle	Urtica sp.	סִרְפָּד	stinging wild weed	Isa. 55:13
Oak	Quercus ithaburensis Quercus calliprinos	אַלּוֹן	forest tree	Gen. 35:8; Isa. 2:13, et al.
Oak, gall	Quercus infectoria (Boissieri)	מֵילָה	forest tree	Mid. 3:7
Oleander	Nerium oleander	הַרְדוּפְנֵי	river bank evergreen shrub	Ḥul. 3:5
Olive	Olea europaea	זַיִת	fruit tree	Deut. 6:11; 8:8, et al.
Onion	Allium cepa	בָּצָל	garden vegetable	Num. 11:5
Orange, trifoliate	Poncirus trifoliata	קִדָּה לְבָנָה	tropical fruit tree	Kil. 1:8
Orchid	Orchis sp.	חַלְבְּצִין נֵץ־הֶחָלָב	flower with edible bulb	Shev. 7:2 Shev. 7:1
Palm, date	Phoenix dactylifera	תָּמָר דֶּקֶל	fruit tree	Ex. 15:27; Num. 33:9, et al. Pe'ah 4:1; Shab. 14:3, et al.
Papyrus	Cyperus papyrus	גֹּמֶא	aquatic plant	Ex. 2:3; Isa. 18:2, et al.
Peach	Persica vulgaris	אֲפַרְסֵק	fruit tree	Kil. 1:4; Ma'as. 1:2
Pear	Pyrus communis	אַגָּס קְרִיסְטוֹמֵלִין	fruit tree	Kil. 1:4; Uk. 1:6, et al.
Pear, Syrian	Pyrus syriaca	חִזְרָר	forest tree with edible fruit	Kil. 1:4
Pepper	Piper nigrum	פִּלְפֵּל	tropical aromatic plant used as a condiment	Shab. 6:5; Beẓah 2:8
Pine	Pinus sp.	תִּדְהָר(?)	coniferous tree	Isa. 41:19; 60:13
Pine, aleppo	Pinus halepensis	עֵץ שֶׁמֶן	coniferous forest tree	I Kings 6:23; Isa. 41:19, et al.
Pine, stone	Pinus pinea	תִּרְזָה	coniferous tree with edible kernels	Isa. 44:14
Pistachio	Pistacia vera	בָּטְנָה, בָּטְנִים	fruit tree	Gen. 43:11; Shev. 7:5
Plane	Platanus orientalis	עַרְמוֹן	river bank tree	Gen. 30:37; Ezek. 31:8
Pomegranate	Punica granatum	רִמּוֹן	fruit tree	Num. 20:5; Deut. 8:8, et al.
Poplar	Populus euphratica	צַפְצָפָה	river bank tree	Ezek. 17:5
Purslane	Portulaca oleracea	חֲלַגְלוֹגָה רְגֵלָה	wild herb used as a vegetable	Shev. 9:1 Shev. 7:1, 9:5, et al.
Quince	Cydonia oblonga	פָּרִישׁ	fruit tree	Kil. 1:4; Ma'as. 1:3, et al.
Radish	Raphanus sativus	צְנוֹן	garden vegetable	Kil. 1:5; Ma'as. 5:2, et al.
Rape	Brassica napus	נָפוּץ, נָפוּס	garden vegetable used as forage	Kil. 1:3; 1:5, et al.
Raspberry, wild	Rubus sanctus	סְנֶה	thorny climbing shrub	Ex. 3:2–4; Deut. 33:16
Reed, ditch	Phragmites communis	קָנֶה	river bank weed	Isa. 19:6, 35:7, et al.
Rice	Oryza sativa	אֹרֶז	annual summer cereal grass	Dem. 2:1; Shev. 2:7, et al.
Rocket, dyer's	Reseda luteola	רִכְפָּה	herb whose leaves and stem yield a dye	Ma'as. 5:8; Shev. 7:2
Rocket, garden	Eruca sativa	אֹרֹת	medicinal herb	II Kings 4:39
Rose	Rosa, sp.	וֶרֶד	shrub with fragrant flowers	Shev. 7:6; Ma'as. 2:5, et al.

English Name	Scientific Name	Hebrew Name	Description of Plant	Reference
Rue	Ruta graveolens	פֵּיגָם	shrub used as a spice	Kil. 1:8; Shev. 9:1
Safflower	Carthamus tinctorius	חָרִיעַ קוֹצָה	herb used as a spice and for dyeing	Kil. 2:8; Uk. 3:5; Shev. 7:1
Saltbush	Atriplex halimus	מַלּוּחַ	desert shrub	Job 30:4
Savory	Satureja thymbra	סִיאָה	aromatic wild plant	Shev. 8:1; Ma'as. 3:9
Sesame	Sesamum orientalis	שֻׁמְשֹׁם	plant used as a spice and yielding oil	Shev. 2:7; Ḥal. 1:4, et al.
Shallot	Allium ascalonicum	בְּצַלְצוּל	garden vegetable used for seasoning	Kil. 1:3
Sorrel, garden	Rumex acetosa	לְעוּנִים	garden vegetable	Kil. 1:3
Spanish cherry	Mimusops balata	פַּרְסָאָה	tropical fruit tree	Shev. 5:1
Spelt	Triticum spelta	שִׁפּוֹן	cereal	Kil. 1:1; Ḥal. 1:1, et al.
Squill	Urginea maritima	חֲצוּב	wild toxic onion	Kil. 1:8
Storax	Styrax officinalis	לִבְנֶה	forest tree	Gen. 30:37; Hos. 4:13
Sumac	Rhus coriaria	אוֹג	forest tree with edible fruit	Pe'ah 1:5; Dem. 1:1, et al.
Tamarisk	Tamarix, sp.	אֶשֶׁל עַרְעָר	desert and saline tree	Gen. 21:33; I Sam. 22:6, et al. Jer. 17:6; Ps. 102:18
Terebinth	Pistacia palaestina Pistacia atlantica	אֵלָה	forest tree	Gen. 35:4; Hos. 4:13, et al.
Thistle	Centaurea, sp.	דַּרְדַּר	prickly herb	Gen. 3:18; Hos. 10:8
Thistle, golden	Scolymus maculatus	חוֹחַ	prickly herb	Hos. 9:6; Prov. 26:9, et al.
Thistle, silybum	Silybum marianum	קִמּוֹשׂ	prickly herb	Isa. 34:13; Hos. 9:6, et al.
Thistle, sow	Sonchus oleraceus	מָרוֹר	bitter herb	Ex. 12:8; Lam. 3:15, et al.
Thorn	Calycotome villosa	חָרוּל	prickly shrub	Zeph. 2:9; Job 30:7, et al.
Thorn, camel	Alhagi maurorum	נַעֲצוּץ	prickly dwarf shrub	Isa. 7:19; 55:13
Thorn, gundelia	Gundelia tournefortii	גַּלְגַּל	prickly herb	Isa. 17:13; Ps. 83:14
Thorn, poterium	Poterium spinosum	סִירִים סִירָה	prickly dwarf shrub	Isa. 34:13; Hos. 2:8, et al. Ps. 58:10
Thorn, prosopis	Prosopis farcata	נַהֲלֹל	prickly dwarf shrub	Isa. 7:19
Thyme	Thymus capitatus	קוֹרָנִית	aromatic dwarf shrub	Shev. 8:1; Ma'as. 3:9
Tragacanth	Astragalus gummifer Astragalus tragacantha	נְכֹאת	dwarf shrub yielding a fragrant resin	Gen. 37:25; 43:11
Truffle	Ascomycetes-Tuberaceae	שְׁמַרְקָעִים	edible subterranean fungus	Uk. 3:2
Turnip	Brassica rapa	לֶפֶת	garden vegetable	Kil. 1:3, 9, et al.
Vetch, bitter	Vicia ervilia	כַּרְשִׁינָה	legume	Ter. 11:9; Shab. 1:5, et al.
Vetch, French	Vicia narbonensis	סַפִּיר	legume	Kil. 1:1
Walnut	Juglans regia	אֱגוֹז	fruit tree	Song 6:11
Watermelon	Citrullus vulgaris	אֲבַטִּיחַ	garden vegetable	Num. 11:5
Weed, ridolfia	Ridololfia segetum	בָּאְשָׁה	weed	Job 31:40
Wheat	Triticum durum Triticum vulgare Triticum turgidum	חִטָּה	cereal	Ex. 9:32; Deut. 8:8; et al.
Willow	Salix, sp.	עֲרָבָה	river bank tree	Lev. 23:40; Ps. 137:2, et al.
Woad, isatis	Isatis tinctoria	אִסְטִיס	herb which yields a dye	Kil. 2:5; Shev. 7:1, et al.
Wormwood	Artemisia, sp.	לַעֲנָה	desert dwarf shrub	Deut. 29:17; Jer. 9:14, et al.

the Midrashim add hundreds of names of plants to those mentioned in the Bible. They are particularly numerous in the Mishnah of *Zera'im* which treats of laws connected with agriculture. In the aggadic Midrashim, too, many plants are mentioned in simile and parable. In all, the ancient literature on Ereẓ Israel mentions close to 500 names of flora. The Babylonian Talmud refers to scores of plants of Babylonia and its neighborhood. In the above list of the plants of the Bible and Mishnah, only one identification is given. Alternative suggestions of identification will be found in the individual articles.

See also *Israel, Flora and Fauna.

Bibliography: H. B. Tristram, *Natural History of the Bible* (1877[5]); J. Schwarz, *Tevu'ot ha-Areẓ* (1900); Loew, Flora; G. Dalman, *Arbeit und Sitte in Palaestina*, 7 vols. in 8 (1928–42); H. N. and A. L. Moldenke, *Plants of the Bible* (1952); J. Feliks, *Ha-Ḥakla'ut be-Ereẓ Yisrael bi-Tekufat ha-Mishnah ve-ha-Talmud* (1963); idem, *Kilei Zera'im ve-Harkavah* (1967); idem, *Olam ha-Ẓome'aḥ ha-Mikra'i* (1968[2]), contains additional bibliography.

[J.F.]

PLASENCIA, city in the Estremadura region of Spain, near the Portuguese border. The Jewish quarter was in the suburb of Jaraíz, and in the 13th century ranked with the flourishing communities in Castile. From the beginning of the 14th century, restrictions issued against the Jews in Castile by the various *cortes*, or legislative assemblies, were also applied in Plasencia; for instance, those of the *cortes* of *Medina del Campo (1305) stipulating that no Jew was to farm taxes or acquire real estate from Christians. In 1313 Queen Dona María and the infante Pedro ratified the decisions of the *cortes* of Plasencia which prohibited the Jews from holding public office; furthermore, suits in which one of the parties was not Jewish were to be tried according to local and not Jewish law, and Hebrew documents would not be accepted as proof. Toward the end of the 14th century, there were 50 Jewish heads of families in Plasencia who paid the annual tax. The decline which overtook the Castile communities after the persecutions of 1391 was also felt in Plasencia.

In the mid-15th century several Jewish names appear among the tax farmers of Plasencia and the kingdom. Various documents give further details on the life of the community during the final period of Jewish residence in Spain. In 1490 a sum of 501,183 maravedis was levied on the community for the redemption of the Jewish captives of *Málaga. The monarchs were dissatisfied with the incomplete residential segregation of the Jews in Plasencia and in 1491 they ordered that the decisions of the *cortes* of 1480 be stringently fulfilled. Even after the edict of expulsion of March 1492, the crown continued to collect money in payment of the debts which the Jews had left in the hands of various Christians. One of the collectors was Gernando Perez Coronel (formerly Meir *Melamed). The exiles from Plasencia, about 50 heads of families, left for Portugal; the synagogue was converted into the Santa Isabel Church in honor of the queen; and the cemetery was sold to the local church. There was also a *Converso community in Plasencia, but little is known of it. An *auto-da-fé was held in the town in 1489 and Conversos from nearby *Trujillo were then burnt at the stake.

Bibliography: V. Paredes, in: *Revista de Extremadura*, 9 (1907), 499f., 556f.; Baer, Urkunden, 2 (1936), index; B. Netanyahu, *Don Isaac Abravanel* (Eng., 1953), 280, 285; F. Cantera y Burgos, *Sinagogas españolas* (1955), 266f.; Suárez Fernández, Documentos, index.

[H.B.]

PLASZOW (Pol. **Płaszow**), Nazi forced-labor camp on the outskirts of *Cracow, functioning from June 1942 until January 1945. Plaszow became an assembly point for all the able-bodied Jews who survived the deportations from the various ghettos in the Cracow district. About 6,000 Jews were brought to Plaszow from Cracow proper in April 1943, after the ghetto was liquidated. In September 1943, 2,000 Jews from *Tarnow ghetto were brought there. In January 1944, 1,300 women and a small number of men were brought in from *Hungary. At certain periods the total number of inmates exceeded 20,000.

The prisoners were employed in glass- and metalwork, clothing, and brush making. Orders were placed by various German firms. The camp regime caused rapid decimation of the inmates, apart from the frequent executions which took place on the slightest pretext. In January 1944 the conditions further deteriorated with the introduction of the *Strafkommando*, which forced prisoners to perform inhuman work in the stone quarries.

In March 1944 some of the prisoners were deported to the extermination camp at *Auschwitz and others to *Mauthausen, *Stutthof, and Flossenbuerg. In the last stage of Plaszow's existence, the Nazis tried to obliterate all traces of their crimes: a group of Jewish workers was forced to exhume some 9,000 bodies from 11 mass graves and burn them in heaps. The work lasted several weeks. The Nazis made sure that all teeth were removed from the skulls. By the end of 1944 only 600 prisoners were still alive and a few weeks later the camp was liquidated.

The commander of the camp and its chief hangman was an *S.S. officer, Amon Goeth. He was sentenced to death by the Supreme Tribunal in Cracow in 1946.

Bibliography: United Nations War Crimes Commission, *Law Reports of Trials of War Criminals*, 7 (1948), 1–10; Nirensztajn, in: *Bleter far Geshikhte*, 5, nos. 1–2 (1952), 226–63, passim; N. Blumental (ed.), *Dokumenty i materialy*, 1, *Obozy* (1946), 267–76, and index; *Proces ludobójcy Amona Leopolda Goetha* . . . (1947); Podhorizer-Sandel, in: BZIH, no. 30 (1959), passim.

[De.D.]

°**PLATO AND PLATONISM.** The influence exercised by the Greek philosopher Plato on posterity both directly and through his interpreters was enormous and has been detailed in a vast literature. The direct influence of Plato on Jewish circles is much less pervasive. It seems quite clear that Greek philosophical writings in general had little or no influence on biblical and rabbinic literature, though current popular philosophic notions evidently became known also in the Jewish world. In Alexandria, one of the great centers of *Hellenistic civilization, Philo in the first century C.E. was faced with the necessity of effecting a reconciliation between Greek philosophy and scripture. This he did by reading the principles of the Platonism of his day into the Pentateuch by interpreting the latter in an allegorical manner. Philo did not leave any direct impression on later Jewish literature until reintroduced by Azariah de' *Rossi in the 16th century. After the Hellenistic period Plato did not have a great influence on Jewish thought until the period of the Arabic translations from the Greek, at which time Jews shared in general humanistic culture.

Among the dialogues reported to have been translated into Arabic were the *Republic*, the *Timaeus*, and the *Crito*. Quotations in Arabic from the *Republic*, *Timaeus*, *Laws*, and *Symposium*, among others, have been identified. Another source was the synopses of certain of the Platonic dialogues by *Galen. *Maimonides quotes from Galen's "commentary" on the *Laws* (*Galeni Compendium Timaei Platonis*, ed. by P. Kraus and R. Walzer (1951), 101), and his contemporary and friend Joseph ibn *Aknin quotes from Galen's *Summary of the Republic* (*ibid.*, 100; and A. Halkin, "Classical and Arabic Material in Aknin's 'Hygiene of the Soul'" in: PAAJR, 14 (1944), 135). However, it was mainly through the works of his later interpreters and followers that the doctrines of Plato had an effect on Jewish intellectuals in the Islamic cultural sphere, first of all through quotations and interpretation of Platonic doctrine occurring in the body of Aristotle's writings, and secondly through neoplatonic interpreters of Plato, mainly Plotinus and Proclus. The doctrines of Plotinus became known through the medium of the pseudepigraphical *Theology of Aristotle*, which consists of excerpts from the fourth, fifth, and sixth *Enneads* of Plotinus, as well as other works. The longer version of the *Theology of Aristotle* includes extracts from an as yet unknown neoplatonic work cited in the works of Isaac *Israeli and translated partially into Hebrew by Abraham *ibn Ḥasdai in **Ben ha-Melekh ve-ha-Nazir* ("The Prince and the Ascetic"), which itself is a translation of an Arabic work which goes back to the legend of Buddha. Also interpolated in the longer version are texts relating to the doctrine of the Divine Will, which are not Plotinian and had an influence, along with the whole *Theology*, on Ibn *Gabirol in his *Fons Vitae*. The longer version is extant in Leningrad in three fragmentary manuscripts, all Arabic in Hebrew script, which testify to its influence on Jewish circles. In the early 16th century, Moses Arovas made a Hebrew as well as an Italian translation of the longer version. The Italian version was then translated into Latin and published in Rome in 1519.

*Avicenna utilized neoplatonic sources in the construction of his philosophic system and had a vast influence on philosophic circles, Jewish as well as non-Jewish. The influence of neoplatonism on Jewish mystical (kabbalistic) thought is also very great. A third major source of Platonic doctrine was through the works of al-*Fārābī, who seems to have been dependent on a tradition of Platonic interpretation which emphasized the political aspect of his thought. The influence of the *Republic* and the *Laws* as well as the *Statesman* are apparent in his political works. In his *Philosophy of Plato and Aristotle*, he summarizes briefly all of the dialogues and considers them from a political point of view. Extensive excerpts from this work were translated into Hebrew by the polymath 13th-century historian of philosophy, Shem Tov ibn *Falaquera. Maimonides in his *Guide* leans heavily on al-Fārābī in his attempt to explain the relationship which should obtain between philosophy and religion. Plato indirectly thus influenced the whole course of later Jewish medieval philosophy, which was mainly a reaction to the position taken by Maimonides in his *Guide*. Maimonides' esotericism in the *Guide* may also have been influenced by the tradition of Platonic esotericism common in Arabic philosophic literature.

The *Politics* of Aristotle was not known in the Arabic west, where Plato was the major classic of political philosophy. *Averroes composed an *Epitome of the Republic* in which he expresses interesting personal views, more openly than he would in works addressed to a more religious audience, on the relation between philosophy and politics. This work, along with Averroes' *Middle Commentary on the Nichomachean Ethics*, was translated by *Samuel b. Judah of Marseilles into Hebrew in the 14th century, and marks the first time that a classical work of political philosophy was translated into Hebrew. The work was soon summarized by Joseph ibn *Kaspi, Samuel's contemporary, and exercised some influence on the course of later Jewish philosophy. In the 16th century the Jewish physician Jacob *Mantino translated it from Hebrew into Latin and it appears in the standard Latin editions of Averroes' works.

Another source of Platonic sentiments were the collections of the sayings of the philosophers, notably that of Ḥunayn ibn Isḥāq, which was translated into Hebrew by Judah *al-Ḥarizi in the 13th century. Joseph ibn Aknin includes a number of Platonic dicta in his "Hygiene of the Soul" (see Halkin, as above in: PAAJR, 14 (1944), 69ff.).

Finally, Judah *Abrabanel or Leone Ebreo, the son of Isaac Abrabanel, utilizes the basic ideas of Platonic philosophy in his *Dialoghi di amore*. Moses *Mendelssohn wrote on the immortality of the soul in his *Phaedon* (1767) and follows the Platonic dialogue of the same name.

Bibliography: A. H. Armstrong (ed.), *Cambridge History of Later Greek and Early Medieval Philosophy* (1967); Walzer, in: EI², s.v. *Aflāṭūn;* Guttmann, Philosophies, index; H. A. Wolfson, *Philo, Foundations of Religious Philosophy...*, 2 vols. (1947), index; Plessner, in: *Tarbiz*, 24 (1954/55), 60–72; C. Roth, *Jews in the Renaissance* (1959), 128–36; Stern, in: *Oriens*, 13–14 (1961), 58–120; Maimonides, *Guide of the Perplexed*, tr. by S. Pines (1963), ixxvff. (introd.); E. I. J. Rosenthal (ed.), *Averroes' Commentary on Plato's Republic* (1966²). [L.V.B.]

PLAUT (Flaut), HEZEKIAH FEIVEL (1818–1895), Hungarian rabbi. Born in Kolin, Plaut studied under Moses *Sofer of Pressburg, whom he venerated exceedingly, paying particular attention to every detail of his way of life so that he could emulate him. A profound talmudic scholar, Plaut was renowned for his piety. He engaged in halakhic correspondence with Hillel Lichtenstein, rabbi of Kolommya, Galicia, with whom he had studied. In 1849 he was appointed rabbi of Nagysurany and remained there until his death. Students from every part of Hungary came to study at the large yeshivah he established there. As rabbi of Nagysurany he was also rabbi for the whole region, which included the community of Nove Zamky (Ersekujvar). He spent a number of Sabbaths there every year and preached there despite the fact that the leaders of the synagogue had, against accepted custom, moved the reading desk from the center of the synagogue to the front of the ark. When a ban was eventually issued by the Orthodox Hungarian rabbis against even entering such a synagogue, he established a separate synagogue in the old style. Plaut had no children but brought up orphans as his own children.

He was the author of *Likkutei Ḥaver Ben Ḥayyim*, in 11 parts (1878–93), containing talmudic novellae, glosses on the four parts of the Shulḥan Arukh, a number of his responsa, eulogies, the glosses of the Ḥatam Sofer (Moses Sofer) on the Shulḥan Arukh, *Yoreh De'ah*, and the customs of Ḥatam Sofer and the latter's biography, as well as Plaut's correspondence with Hillel Lichtenstein.

Bibliography: H. F. Plaut (Flaut), *Likkutei Ḥaver Ben Ḥayyim*, 1 (1878), introd.; P. Z. Schwartz, *Shem ha-Gedolim me-Erez Hagar*, 2 (1914), 26b, no. 5; 3 (1915), 21bf., no. 13; A. Stern, *Melizei Esh*, 3 (1962), 27th Kislev, no. 219. [Sh.W.-H.]

PLAUT, HUGO CARL (1858–1928), German bacteriologist. Born in Leipzig, Plaut settled in Hamburg in 1913 and became director of the Institute for Fungus Research. In

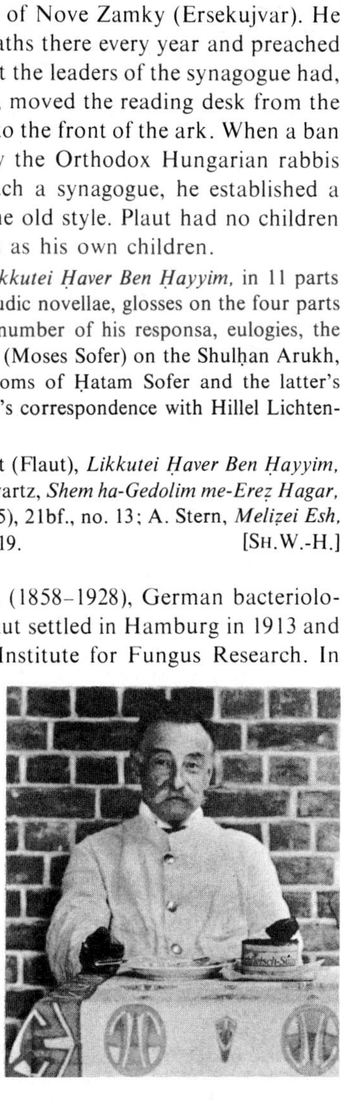

Hugo Carl Plaut, German bacteriologist. Jerusalem, J.N.U.L., Schwadron Collection.

1918 he was appointed titular professor. He made his greatest contribution to medicine in 1896, when he described the etiology of trench mouth. Two years later H.

Vincent of the Pasteur Institute described the same condition and it became known as the Plaut-Vincent disease or angina ulcero membranosa caused by fusiform spirochaeta. Of significance also were Plaut's works on streptococcus mocosus, streptothrix, and actinomyces. His publications include *Die Hyphenpilze oder Eumyceten* (1903, 1913[2]), *Dermatomykosen* (1909), and *Mykosen* (1919). He also carried out fundamental work in veterinary medicine.

[S.M.]

PLAUT, W. GUNTHER (1912–), U.S. and Canadian rabbi. Born in Muenster, Germany, Plaut went to the U.S. in 1935, and was ordained a rabbi at the Hebrew Union College in 1939. Plaut served congregations in Chicago (1939–43, 1946–48), St. Paul (1948–61), and Toronto, Canada (from 1961). He served as a U.S. Army chaplain in 1943–46, earning the bronze star. Plaut served on many Jewish and civic commissions. He was chairman of the Zionist Emergency Council (1953–61) and the Governor's Commission on Ethics in Government (1958–61) in St. Paul.

His writings include: *Mount Zion, The First Hundred Years* (1956); *The Jews in Minnesota* (1959); *The Rise of Reform Judaism* (1963) and its sequel, *The Growth of Reform Judaism* (1965), documentary histories; and *The Book of Proverbs—A Commentary* (1961).

His brother, WALTER H. PLAUT (1919–1964), was a rabbi in the U.S. Born near Berlin, Germany, Plaut went to the U.S. in 1937, and received his rabbinical ordination at the Hebrew Union College in 1947. He was an active Zionist and was also among the first clergymen to join the Freedom Ride to the South in 1961 on behalf of civil rights for Negroes. From 1955 until his death he was rabbi of Temple Emanuel in Great Neck, New York, where he was chairman of the Jewish Community Council and a member of the Nassau County Commission on Human Rights.

[E.GR.]

PLEAS.

Nature of Pleas. Talmudic law developed certain well-defined forms of pleading in civil cases (not unlike the *actio, formula,* and *exceptio* in Roman law). These forms of pleading constitute a catalog of causes of actions and defenses which could be applied in, and adapted to, all kinds of civil litigations. Unlike Roman law, pleas were not reduced to abstract terms, but expressed in direct language: for instance, the action of debt is rendered as the plea of "I have money in your hands"; the defense of payment is rendered as the plea of "I have paid." The law of pleas thus comprises the catalog of the various pleas and the provisions governing the applicability and effect of each particular one. However, in the sources there is no systematic differentiation between the two, and they will be considered together below. It often happens that not only the burden of proof (see *Evidence) or of taking the *oath will depend on the pleas chosen by the party but also the immediate outcome of the action, where in the circumstances a given plea is considered conclusive.

Pleas of the Plaintiff. Plaintiff's pleas, or causes of action, can be roughly divided into three classes: debt—"I have money in your hands"; or "I have a loan in your hands"; or "I have wages with you"; chattels—"I have a deposit in your hands"; or "I have deposited this or that chattel with you"; or "you have stolen this chattel from me"; and oath—where the cause of action depends on accounts to be rendered and the defendant (e.g., an agent, executor, or guardian) is sued to verify his accounts on oath.

In order to be valid and to require a plea (or an oath) in reply, the plaintiff's plea must be such as to disclose a legally valid cause of action. Where a plaintiff would not be entitled to judgment, even though his plea be proved or admitted, no defense is called for. Thus, the plea "you promised to lend me money"—which is a promise unenforceable in law—or the plea "you insulted me"—which, if proved or admitted, could not bear weight in a case of damages—would be rejected as irrelevant from the outset.

Pleas of the Defendant. Whenever a cause of action has been pleaded by the plaintiff, "it is not a proper reply for the defendant to say, I owe you nothing, or you have nothing in my hands, or you are lying; but the court will tell the defendant to reply specifically to the plaintiff's plea and be as explicit in his defense as the plaintiff was in his claim: have you or have you not taken a loan from him?; has he or has he not made this deposit with you?; have you or have you not stolen his chattel?; have you or have you not hired him?; and in the same way with all other pleas. The reason is that a defendant may err [in law] ... and believe that he is not liable to the plaintiff; therefore he is told: how can you say 'I owe him nothing'? maybe the law renders you liable to him and you do not know; you must submit to the judges explicit statements of fact, and they will advise you whether you are or are not liable. Even a great scholar is told: you do not lose anything by replying to his plea and explaining to us how it is that you are not liable to him; is it because 'the thing has never happened' or although 'it happened, it is because you already made restitution to him'" (Yad, To'en 6:1).

Defendant's pleas may roughly be divided into admissions and denials.

*Admissions are of three kinds:

(1) full and express admission of the whole claim—such an admission establishes the claim "like a hundred witnesses";

(2) partial admission and partial denial, with the result that the oath will be administered to the defendant;

(3) implied admission—plea of "I have not borrowed" is, on proof of the loan, taken as an admission that the defendant has not repaid the loan; or, a plea of "I have repaid" is, on proof of non-repayment, taken as an admission that a loan had been made (BB 6a; Shevu. 41b; Yad, To'en 6:3). For pleas of "feigning" or "satiation" to revoke out-of-court admissions, and for the effect of admissions in general, see *Admission.

Denials are also of three kinds: "no such thing has ever happened"—i.e., a total denial of the fact (the loan, the contract, the tort) underlying the cause of action; "I have paid"—i.e., an assertion that any liability which may have existed has already been fully satisfied; and "you have renounced the debt," or "the money you gave me was in repayment of a debt which you owed me, or was a gift" (Yad, To'en 6:2)—i.e., in the nature of a plea of confession and avoidance.

The general rules that the burden of proving his case rests upon the plaintiff (see *Evidence) and that, in the absence of such proof, the defendant has to take the oath to verify his denial, apply to all these pleas of denial. The presumption that a debtor will not lie in the face of his creditor was in the course of time superseded by the presumption that the plaintiff will not lodge a claim unless he has a cause of action. While by virtue of the former presumption the defendant would be believed on his oath, by virtue of the latter he was required to take the oath to disprove the plaintiff's claim (Shevu. 40b).

Plea of Repayment. In the case of the plea of repayment, the following special provisions should be noted:

Where the defendant pleaded repayment, it was not sufficient for the plaintiff to prove that he had given the defendant a loan, because a loan given before witnesses need not necessarily be repaid before witnesses (Shevu. 41b), and the claim would be dismissed on the defendant's oath verifying his plea. The same rule applied to claims on bills: where the signature of the defendant on the bill was proved or admitted, his defense of repayment would be accepted on his taking the oath (BB 176a; Yad, Malveh 11:3; Sh. Ar., ḤM 69:2); but some later jurists held that the plea of repayment was not available against a bill which was in the hands of the plaintiff, as it would normally have been returned or destroyed on payment (*Rema,* ḤM 69:2 and the references given there). The matter appears to be left to the discretion of the court in each particular case (Resp. Ribash, no. 454; *Siftei Kohen,* ḤM 69, n.14). Where the plea of repayment is inadmissible in law, e.g., where the loan or bill was made with formal *kinyan* (see *Acquisition, Modes of; ḤM 39, 3), the plaintiff will recover on the bill on taking the oath that it is still unpaid (Shevu. 41a; Yad, Malveh 14:2). Where a debt is repayable at a certain date, the defendant will not be heard to plead that he repaid it before that date because of the presumption that no debtor pays a debt before it matures (see *Evidence). The plaintiff will be entitled to recover without oath, on proof of the debt and of the time stipulated for repayment (BB 5a–b; ḤM 78:1).

In order to forestall pleas of repayment and their all too easy verification by oath, it became customary to stipulate beforehand either that repayment must be made in the presence of witnesses—in which case the plaintiff could recover without oath unless the defendant produced witnesses of repayment (Shevu. 6:2; Yad, Malveh 15:1; ḤM 70:3)—or that the plea of repayment should not be available to the defendant, and that the plaintiff should be entitled to recover on his assertion that he had not been paid (Yad, Malveh 15:3; ḤM 71:1).

Plea of Insolvency. Originally the law was that a debtor who pleaded that he was unable to pay was not required to take the oath, but the burden was on the creditor to discover property of the debtor on which execution could be levied (Yad, Malveh 2:1). However, when "defrauders increased and borrowers found lenders' doors closed," it was laid down that the debtor should take the oath that he possessed nothing and concealed nothing and that he would disclose any property coming into his hands (Yad, Malveh 2:2; ḤM 99:1). There are two noteworthy exceptions to this rule: a man reputed to be poor and honest will not be required to take the oath if the court suspects the creditor of desiring to annoy or embarrass him; and a man reputed to be a cheat and swindler will not be allowed to verify his plea on oath even though he volunteers to do so (Yad, Malveh 2:4; ḤM 99:4–5; see also *Execution, Civil).

Plea of Counterclaim. Where a plaintiff sues on a bill, it is no defense for the defendant to plead that the plaintiff is indebted to him on another bill: each sues and recovers on his own bill separately (Ket. 13:9; Yad, Malveh 24:10; Sh. Ar., ḤM 85:3). But where the defendant denies the bill sued upon by the plaintiff, his plea prevails that the plaintiff would not have made a later bill in favor of the defendant had he really been indebted to him (Sh. Ar. loc. cit.; but see Yad, loc. cit. and *Siftei Kohen* to Sh. Ar., ḤM 85, n.7). Where the defendant pleads that the plaintiff already "has mine in his hands," the plaintiff is entitled to have his claim judged first, and the defendant's claim for restitution or to have one claim offset by the other will be adjudicated separately (BK 46b; Rashi and Tosef. thereto; Tur, ḤM 24:1; *Rema,* ḤM 24:1).

Identical Pleas. Where, in respect of a certain sum of money or of a chattel, both parties plead "this is mine," and both are in possession of it (i.e., each holds it with his hand), and none can prove previous or present title, both will have to take the oath that they are entitled to at least one-half of it, and then one-half will be judged to belong to each (BM 1:1; Yad, To'en 9:7; ḤM 138:1). Where the mutual "this is mine" is pleaded in respect of land, or in respect of a chattel not in the possession of either, the party who first succeeds in taking possession, even by force, cannot be ousted unless the other can prove that he has a better title to it (BB 34b–35a; Yad, To'en 15:4; ḤM 139:4). For this rule, which in effect legitimizes seizing by force, the Solomonic reason was given that it would only be the true owner who would go to the length of using force and facing the ensuing lawsuit (Resp. Rosh 77:1; *Beit Yosef,* ḤM 139, n.1; see also *Extraordinary Remedies).

Pleas of Law. As a general rule, pleas are assertions or denials of fact only; but there are some exceptions to the rule, two of which are noteworthy: (1) the plea of "I do not want this legal privilege." Wherever the law confers a benefit on the class of persons to which the pleader belongs, he will be heard if he waives that benefit (Ket. 83a). Thus, the rule that a husband must maintain his wife in consideration of her handiwork for him was established in favor of his wife, and she may plead, "I will not claim *maintenance and I will not work" (Ket. 58b). Or, where a plaintiff is allowed by law to recover on taking the oath, he may plead, "I do not want the privilege of taking the oath," and have the oath shifted to the defendant (Yad, To'en 1:4; ḤM 87:12); and (2) the plea of "I rely on the other view." Where the authorities are divided on a given question of law the defendant is entitled to plead that the opinion most favorable to him should be adopted (*Keneset ha-Gedolah,* ḤM 25, *Beit Yosef*). This post-talmudic rule is based on the premise that the benefit of any possible doubt on what the law is must accrue to the defendant, the burden of establishing his case always being on the plaintiff (see also *Codification of the Law).

Weight of Pleas. Even where no evidence is available or forthcoming to substantiate a plea and even before such evidence is called for, the court will accept a plea as valid and conclusive in the following cases:

(1) Where the plea is fortified by a legal presumption (see *Evidence) or by generally recognized standards or patterns of conduct. For instance, the plea, "I have not been paid" is accepted as conclusive if fortified by the presumption that no debtor pays a debt before maturity (BB 5b).

(2) Where the plea is eminently reasonable *(sevarah).* The reasonableness cannot generally be determined from the particular circumstances of the case at issue, but rather from legal rules evolved for this purpose. Thus, a man's plea is not believed if by that plea he accuses himself of wrongdoing (Ket. 22a, 23b), unless he can adduce a good reason *(amtala)* for so doing. Where, by his own mouth, a man has taken upon himself a certain status or obligation which could not otherwise be proved against him, he is believed on his plea that that status has come to an end or that obligation has been performed, for "the mouth that obligated is the mouth that discharged" (Ket. 2:5). For instance, a woman who cannot otherwise be proved to have been married is believed on her plea that her marriage has been dissolved (Ket. 2:5; Yad, Gerushin 12:1; Sh. Ar., EH 152:6).

Witnesses whose attestation to a deed cannot be proved other than by their own testimony are believed on their plea that they were incompetent or coerced to attest (Ket. 2:3; Ket. 18b; Yad, Edut 3:6; ḤM 46:37), provided they did not plead that their incompetency was due to criminal conduct (Yad, Edut 3:7; ḤM 46:37). Opinions are divided on whether a defendant who admitted that a bill, which could not otherwise be proved, had been authorized by him, would be believed on his plea that he had paid the bill (BM

7a; Ket. 19a; BB 154b); the better opinion seems to be that as long as the bill is in the hands of the plaintiff it is presumed to be unpaid (Tur, ḤM 82:3), and the defendant's unsworn plea of repayment is not sufficient to discharge him (see above; and Rashi, Ket. 19a, s.v. *Ein ha-Malveh*). Similarly, a plea is believed if it was "in the hands" of the pleader to execute it by his own act (Sanh. 30a; ḤM 255:8).

(3) A particular brand of reasonableness is known as *miggo*, meaning something like "inasmuch": inasmuch as you could have succeeded by some other more far-reaching plea, the lesser plea, by which you likewise succeed, can be accepted as credible. "If A makes a certain statement which does not appear probable on the face of it, this fact will not tend to weaken his case, if he could have made another statement which would have appeared probable. If that other statement would have been acceptable to the court, the one that he actually makes must also be accepted, for had he wished to tell an untruth he would have rather made that other statement" (Herzog, Instit, 1 (1936), 250ff.). In the much shorter and clearer words of *Shabbetai b. Meir ha-Kohen (Shakh) in his "Rules of *Miggo*" (appended to his commentary *Siftei Kohen* to ḤM 82, hereinafter referred to as Rules), "he is known to speak the truth, for if he had wanted to lie, a better plea would have been open to him" (Rule 26). *Miggo* is the amoraic version and elaboration of the mishnaic "the mouth that obligated is the mouth that discharged" (cf. Ket. 2:2, 16a; the different problems of *miggo* are dealt with in the Shakh at the end of ḤM 82).

Miggo is, generally speaking, available in respect of pleas of defendants only (Rules 1, 14, 15); *miggo* is of no use against witnesses (Rules 5, 12); *miggo* is of use against a written deed (Rule 11); where the taking of an oath is prescribed (other than the post-mishnaic oath), *miggo* is not available in lieu of it, nor will it be allowed where the more far-reaching plea could have resulted in a Pentateuchal or mishnaic oath being imposed, for the the actual plea may have been put forward only for the purpose of evading the oath (Rules 25, 28); *miggo* does not apply where it would contradict local custom in matters of commerce (Rule 2); both the more far-reaching and the actual plea must relate to the same subject matter (Rule 13); *miggo* does not operate retroactively (Rule 8); where the more far-reaching plea would obviously have been a lie, it cannot operate as *miggo* on the actual plea; nor will *miggo* be of any avail to strengthen a plea which is manifestly false (Rule 9); whether the *miggo* is of avail against presumptions of fact is discussed (Rules 10, 16); *miggo* is of no avail against any possessory title *(ibid.)*; *miggo* is not allowed where the more far-reaching plea would have been "I do not know" (Rule 3); *miggo* is allowed only in respect of pleas which are outspoken and unambiguous (Rule 7); there are differences of opinion on whether *miggo* would be allowed where the pleader could have remained silent instead of pleading, and by remaining silent would have attained the same or a better result (Rules 19, 21); whether *miggo* is available where the more far-reaching plea would have been unreasonable or unusual, or would have been an affront or an impertinence to the creditor is discussed (Rules 6, 22); *miggo* is not available where the more far-reaching plea would have incriminated the pleader (Rule 24); *miggo* is applied only to the plea of a single pleader: where the same plea is put foward by more than one, none can avail himself of *miggo* (Rule 4); *miggo* is allowed in respect of pleas of fact only, and not in respect of pleas of law (Rule 31); and where there recommends itself to the court a reasoning *(sevarah)* which appears (however slightly) better than *miggo* in the particular case before it, *miggo* may be discarded at the discretion of the court (Rule 32).

Rejection of Pleas. UNTRUSTWORTHINESS. Once a defendant has denied having taken a loan and the fact that he has is proved by witnesses, he will not be allowed to plead that he has repaid the loan (BM 17a; Yad, To'en 6:1; ḤM 79:5), provided the denial has been made in court (Yad, To'en 6:2; ḤM 79:9). The denial which proved untrue renders the pleader, insofar as the same subject matter is concerned, a "potential denier," *huhzak*, whose pleas will no longer be accepted as trustworthy. The same rule applies where a debtor had admitted the debt and, when sued in court, denied it (ḤM 79, 10), provided the previous admission could not be explained away as unintentional (Sanh. 29b; Yad, To'en 6:6).

INCONSISTENCY. No alternative or inconsistent pleas are allowed (BB 31a; ḤM 80:1). While pleading in court, however, the pleader may rectify his plea and explain it or even substitute another plea for it, as long as his original plea has not been proved or disproved by evidence (Yad, To'en 7:7–8; Tur, ḤM 80:4). Statements made out of court are not regarded as "pleas" and may freely be contradicted by pleas in court (ḤM 79:9, 80:1).

PUBLIC POLICY. Pleas which may otherwise be perfectly legitimate may sometimes be rejected because their acceptance might lead to undesirable results from a moral, humanitarian, or economic point of view. Examples of purposes for which pleas might be rejected are: that a wrongdoer should not reap a reward (Ket. 11a, 39b; et al.); that the lenders' doors not be closed in the face of borrowers (Ket. 88a; Git. 49b–50a; BK 7b–8a; et al.); for the protection of open markets (BK 115a); that it be not too easy for a husband to divorce his wife (Ket. 39b); and that equity and generosity may prevail over strict law (BM 51b–52a; 83a; 108a; Ket. 97a; et al.).

Suggestion of Pleas. Where the defendant (or, in exceptional cases such as widows and orphans, the plaintiff) appears unable or unfit to formulate the plea which is open to him in the circumstances, the court will "open the mouth of the dumb for him" (Prov. 31:8) and enter the plea for the defendant of its own accord (Ket. 36a; Git. 37b; BB 41a; *Piskei ha-Rosh;* BK 1:3). The court will not, however, of its own accord enter for the defendant a plea to the effect that any admission made by him out of court was false or unintended (Yad, To'en 6:8; ḤM 81:21; but see *Rema*, ḤM 81:14).

Bibliography: Gulak, Yesodei, 4 (1922), passim; Herzog, Instit, 1 (1936), 57f., 241, 250–5, 268; 2 (1939), 108, 117f.; ET, 1 (1951[3]), 140, 224–6, 253f., 255–7, 263–6, 267f.; 2 (1949), 52–55, 70f.; 3 (1951), 106–10; 4 (1952), 199–208; 5 (1953), 524–7; 6 (1954), 200; 7 (1956), 290–5, 321–8, 733–8; 8 (1957), 404–35, 722–43; 9(1959), 451–9, 722–46; B. de Vries, in : *Tarbiz*, 36 (1966/67), 229–38; Z. Frankel, *Der gerichtliche Beweis nach mosaisch-talmudischen Rechte* (1846); H. B. Fassel, *Das mosaisch-rabbinische Gerichtsverfahren in civilrechtlichen Sachen* (1859); Z. Freudenthal, in: MGWJ, 9 (1860), 161–75; M. Bloch, *Die Civilprocess-Ordnung nach mosaisch-rabbinischen Rechte* (1882); D. Fink, *Miggo als Rechtsbeweis im babylonischen Talmud* (1891); T. S. Zuri, *Mishpat ha-Talmud*, 7 (1921); Elon, Mafte'aḥ, 84–88; idem, in: ILR, 3 (1968), 437f.

[H.H.C.]

PLEDGE.

The Concept. In Jewish law, in addition to the personal right of action against the debtor, the creditor also has a right of *lien on the latter's property. This lien automatically comes into being when the debt is created and is termed *aḥarayut* or *shi'bud nekhasim*. Sometimes the operation of the lien may be limited by the parties to a specified asset or part of the debtor's property, in one of two possible ways: either this distinct asset remains in the debtor's possession, in which case the lien is termed *apoteke*, or possession of the asset is surrendered to the creditor, which is termed *mashkon* ("pledge"). In both cases limitation of the lien to a distinct asset may be effected either so that it operates over and above the general lien on all the debtor's property, or so as to free all but the distinct asset from its operation; in the case of pledge, these two forms are referred to repectively as *mashkon stam* ("unconditional") and *mashkon meforash* ("express pledge"; Tur, ḤM 117:1).

Jewish law distinguishes between three types of pledge: a pledge taken when the debt is due for repayment, not in payment of it but as a security for its repayment; a pledge taken when the debt is established with the consent of both debtor and creditor, as security for repayment of the debt on the due date; and a pledge given by the debtor to the creditor for the latter's use and enjoyment of its fruits.

Taking a Pledge After Establishment of the Debt. There are various biblical enjoinders concerning taking a pledge from the debtor: "If thou lend money to any of My people, even to the poor with thee, thou shalt not be to him as a creditor; neither shall ye lay upon him interest. If thou at all take thy neighbor's garment to pledge, thou shalt restore it unto him by that the sun goeth down; for that is his only covering, it is his garment for his skin; wherein shall he sleep?" (Ex. 22:24–26); similarly, "When thou dost lend thy neighbor any manner of loan, thou shalt not go into his house to fetch his pledge. Thou shalt stand without, and the man to whom thou dost lend shall bring forth the pledge without unto thee. And if he be a poor man, thou shalt not sleep with his pledge; thou shalt surely restore to him the pledge when the sun goeth down, that he may sleep in his garment, and bless thee; and it shall be righteousness unto thee before the Lord thy God" (Deut. 24:10–13); and, "No man shall take the mill or the upper millstone to pledge, for he taketh a man's life to pledge" (Deut. 24:6). In their plain meaning, these passages refer to a debtor from whom a pledge is taken as such. These passages (which also lay down general principles concerning the creditor-debtor relationship; see *Execution, Civil) are the source of a threefold direction in matters of pledge and relate to articles which may never be taken in pledge; which may be taken in pledge but must be returned to a poor debtor when he needs them; and the prohibition against taking a pledge from a widow.

From the biblical prohibition on taking "the mill or upper millstone to pledge," the scholars deduced that it is forbidden to take in pledge "aught wherewith is prepared necessary food" (BM 9:13). They generally agree that the prohibition applies to utensils which are used in the actual preparation of "necessary food," such as a grain mill, certain cooking pots, an oven, and a sieve (Tur, ḤM 97:17), as well as water, wine, or oil jugs, "since this involves taking from a man a utensil which was fashioned for the actual preparation of necessary food for himself and his family, and this the Torah has forbidden, to save him hurt" (ḤM 97:11). In the case of things which do not meet this exact requirement but are used by a man to earn his livelihood, such as oxen for plowing and the like, some scholars hold that these may be taken in pledge, except for the essentials of his sustenance which must be left with the debtor, in terms of the rule of making an "arrangement" or assessment for the debtor (*Rema,* ḤM 98:8); other scholars hold that these things too fall into the category of "necessary food" and, therefore, may not be taken in pledge (Tur, ḤM 97:17; BM 113b; this opinion also conforms with the ordinary meaning of the statements in Tosef., BM 10:11 and those surrounding the discussion about a yoke of oxen and a pair of barber's shears, in BM 116a). With regard to articles which may be taken in pledge but must be returned to a needy debtor, Maimonides states "when a person takes a pledge from his neighbor [when the debt is due for payment]—whether through a court, or forcibly of his own accord, or with the debtor's consent—then if the debtor is poor it is a *mitzvah* to return the pledge to him if and when he be in need thereof; he must return to him the pillow at night to sleep thereon, and the plow by day to work therewith" (Yad, Malveh 3:15). Anyone who does not return a poor man's pledge when he needs it transgresses two prohibitions of the Torah and one positive precept.

It is in the interest of the creditor to take a pledge—notwithstanding his obligation to return it to the debtor when the latter is in need of it—in order that the debt shall not be wiped out in the Jubilee Year, just as a debt established against a pledge is not wiped out in order to recover payment of it on the death of the debtor, so that it should not be like movable property in the hands of orphans, which is not charged in the creditor's favor (Tosef., BM 10:9; BM 115a, Yad and Sh. Ar., loc. cit.). "Why then does he continue each day to take the pledge after he has returned it to the debtor whenever necessary? So that the debtor shall hurry to repay the debt because he is ashamed of having his pledge returned by the creditor day after day" (Tos. to BM 115a). In a dispute with R. Simeon b. Gamaliel, the scholars held that the creditor must return the debtor's pledge in this way as long as the debtor is alive; Gamaliel's opinion was that the creditor need only return the pledge during a period not exceeding 30 days; thereafter it must be sold through the court. All the scholars agree that if the creditor takes in pledge articles which are not essential to the debtor and therefore need not be returned to him from time to time, the creditor will be entitled to have the pledge sold through court, in similar manner to a pledge taken at the time of the establishment of the debt.

In the case of a widow, R. Judah held that the prohibition applies to all widows, rich or poor, giving to the word "widow" its ordinary meaning, since "he did not seek the reason for the scriptural law." R. Simeon, because "he sought the reason for the scriptural law," was of the opinion that the prohibition only applied to a poor widow, since the creditor would have to return her pledge if she needed it, and by entering and leaving her house from time to time would bring her into disrepute. The *halakhah* was decided according to R. Judah's opinion. Maimonides' opinion that the prohibition extends also to a pledge taken from a widow at the time the debt is established (Yad 3:1) is disputed in most of the codes on the grounds that the Torah deals solely with the question of a pledge taken when the debt is due for payment and that this is also to be deduced from the statements in the Talmud, even when the debtor is a widow (*Hassagot Rabad* and *Maggid Mishneh,* ad loc.).

The laws concerning a pledge of the debtor's property which the creditor takes after the debt is due as security for but not in payment of a debt are set out in detail in Scripture; although these laws were also dealt with in the Talmud and in the codes, by then they had become of less practical importance in daily life. The result was that the relevant laws came to be interpreted as applying also to the matter of actually satisfying a debt out of the debtor's property. (Maimonides, for instance, incorporates a number of matters pertaining to the *siddur le-va'al-ḥov* in his treatment of the above laws (Yad, Malveh 3:6) and this is done by other commentators also.) This process is particularly noticeable in the treatment of the prohibition against entering the debtor's home; the prohibition was interpreted in talmudic discussions and until the 12th century as applying also to the case of the creditor seeking to recover his debt, and only R. Tam interpreted the prohibition as applying solely to the case of entry for the purpose of taking a pledge.

In talmudic times, when the creditor came to take any of the debtor's assets after the debt was due, he generally did not do so in order to take a pledge, but rather as a means of recovering his debt. For this purpose too the scholars specified a number of articles which a debtor needed for the sustenance of himself and his family which might not be taken from him. From talmudic times onward it became most common for the pledge to be delivered by the debtor to the creditor at the time the debt was established.

Pledge Taken When the Debt is Established. The distinction drawn in Hebrew legal parlance in the State of Israel between the terms *mashkon* and *mashkanta,* pertaining to movables and to immovable property respectively, does not appear in the sources, where the term *mashkanta* is simply the Aramaic form of *mashkon* (although the distinction is already hinted at in earlier periods—see, e.g., Elon, Mafte'aḥ, note on p. 152).

Modes of Establishing a Pledge. The ancient form of pledge was apparently executed in the following manner: the debtor would sell one of his assets—land or movable property—to the creditor on the condition: "whenever I so desire I shall return the money and take it back." On receipt of the property the creditor would hand over the money; if, in the course of time, the money was returned by the debtor, the transaction constituted a loan and the property a pledge, otherwise the property would be forfeited to the creditor, presumably upon determination and expiry of a maximum period allowed the debtor for redemption of the property. This form of pledge also existed in other legal systems (Tosef., BM 4:4; Gulak, *Toledot ha-Mishpat be-Yisrael bi-Tekufot ha-Talmud,* 1 *(Ha-Ḥiyyuv ve-Shi'budav),* 62–65). A variation of this form of pledge was one in which the sale only came into effect upon the debtor's failure to make repayment on the date due (BM 63a). In the first case the creditor was entitled to sell the property after it had been delivered to him, although the debtor retained the right to redeem the property from a third party—i.e., within the period determined for this purpose; since the property had already been sold to the creditor, his usufruct thereof was not in conflict with the prohibition against *interest (see below). In the second case, however, it was forbidden for the creditor to sell the property before the agreed date of repayment and, therefore, according to some scholars, the fruits of the property were forbidden to the creditor, as amounting to interest, since the property had not yet been effectively sold to the latter. Common to both the above forms of sale was forfeiture of the property to the creditor upon the debtor's failure to return the money within the determined period (Gulak, 65–66). Forfeiture of this kind, although likely to have resulted in the creditor gaining property whose value exceeded the amount of the debt, was not regarded by the scholars as prejudicial to the debtor since the latter retained the option of selling the pledged property to a third party before the due date for repayment of the debt and then paying the creditor the exact amount only (Tos. to BM 65b).

In the later form of the pledge that was customary in talmudic times, the creditor was only entitled to recover out of the pledge—when the debt matured—the exact amount owing to him, and the remainder belonged to the debtor; conversely, if the value of the pledge was less than the amount of the debt, the creditor was entitled to recover the shortfall from the debtor. (Nevertheless, from a number of *halakhot* it is discernible that later, as early as amoraic times, forfeiture of the whole of the pledge continued to be practiced; see Gulak, 69–71.) It was customary for the parties to stipulate that the whole of the pledge be forfeited to the creditor upon the debtor's failure to repay the debt within a prescribed period, even if the value of the pledge exceeded the amount of the debt. Some scholars upheld the validity of such express conditions, but R. Judah held a contrary opinion: "In what manner shall this party become entitled to that which is not his!" (Tosef. BM 1:17). For part of the amoraic period some scholars maintained that the above condition was valid, but later the *halakhah* was decided to the effect that this condition was invalid because of the defect of **asmakhta* (BM 66a–b). A similar decision was made in the codes; namely, that this condition was invalid unless imposed in a special manner so as to obviate the defect of *asmakhta* (Yad, Malveh 6:4; Sh. Ar., ḤM 73:17).

Ownership and Responsibility for the Pledge. Property pledged by the debtor remains in his ownership, but cannot be alienated by him to another since it is not in his possession (Rashi, Pes. 30b). The debtor may, however, alienate the pledge to another in such manner that the *kinyan,* i.e., transfer of ownership, shall take effect after he has redeemed the pledge from the creditor, and then retroactively to the time of alienation; in addition, the debtor may immediately alienate that portion of the pledge which is in excess of the amount of the debt (Ket. 59a–b, Tos. to BM 73b; s.v. *hashata;* s.v. *hakhi ka-amar; Rema,* YD 258:7).

The creditor acquires a limited proprietary interest in the pledge (Pes. 31b; et al.), hence a marriage contracted by him through the means of a pledge he holds is valid (according to Maimonides, the creditor has *mikẓat kinyan,* "a measure of *kinyan,*" in the pledge: Yad, Ishut 5:23). The creditor may assign to another the charge which he has on pledged property. According to the *posekim,* the creditor only has *mikẓat kinyan* in a pledge that is taken after the debt is established, and no *kinyan* whatever in a pledge taken at the time of establishment of the debt, so that a marriage contracted by the debtor through the means of pledged property of the latter kind will be invalid (Tos. to BM 82b, s.v. *emor; Rema; Siftei Kohen* ḤM 72, n. 9; R. Isaac's above statement is also based on a passage dealing with a pledge taken after establishment of the debt).

Opinions were divided on the question of the creditor's responsibility for the pledge in his possession, some holding him liable as a bailee for reward and others regarding him as an unpaid bailee (BM 6:7). The majority of the *posekim* decided according to the first view: "hence if the pledge was lost or stolen, he will be liable for its value; if the value of the pledge equaled the amount of the debt, the one party will have no claim against the other; if the debt exceeded the value of the pledge, the debtor must pay the difference; but if the value of the pledge exceeded the debt, the creditor must refund the difference to the debtor; if the loss of the pledge was due to **ones,* the creditor must swear that this was the case, whereupon the pledger must repay the debt to the last penny" (Yad, Sekhirut 10:1; *Hassagot Rabad,* ad loc.; *Rema,* ḤM 72:2).

Use of the Pledge. The use of the pledge is forbidden to the creditor, since this is tantamount to taking interest on the loan. In the case of a poor debtor, if the nature of the pledge is such that it suffers only slight deterioration upon use and the return for its hire is great—for instance a plowshare or spade—the creditor will be entitled to hire the pledge to others and to apply the proceeds in reduction of the debt, since this is assumed to be convenient for the debtor. It is precisely to others and not to himself that the creditor may hire the pledge in this manner, lest he be suspected of using the pledge without reducing the debt accordingly. If originally, however, the parties stipulate with each other that the creditor might use the pledge and apply the hire in reduction of the debt, then he will be entitled to use the pledge himself, since anyone who knows that he holds a pledge will also know what he stipulated with the debtor. When the pledge consists of books, the use of the pledge is permitted by some scholars because it is a *mitzvah* to lend books for study, but other scholars include books in the general prohibition against the use of the pledged property (*Rema,* ḤM 72:1; and YD 172:1).

Recovering Payment out of the Pledge. When the debt matures the creditor must notify the debtor, before two witnesses, that the debt must be repaid and the pledge redeemed or else he will seek leave from the court to sell the pledge in satisfaction of the amount owing to him. The debtor, according to some of the *posekim*, has 30 days in which to make payment, failing which the value of the pledge is assessed by three knowledgeable assessors and "he [the creditor] shall sell it at the assessment price allowed by the above three and he is given the advice to sell it before witnesses, lest the debtor say that it was sold for more than the assessment price" (Yad, Malveh 13:3; Sh. Ar., ḤM 73:12–15). The creditor himself may not purchase the pledge, but some scholars aver that he may do so if the pledge is sold through a court of experts.

Pledge (Mortgage) with a Right of Usufruct in the Creditor's Favor. Usufruct and the Prohibition Against Interest. In the case of a long-term debt in a large amount, land was generally given in pledge, to remain in possession of the creditor until the debt matured; this practice is illustrated in Nehemiah 5:3–5. According to the Jewish laws of interest, any benefit derived by the lender over and above repayment of the original amount of the loan is regarded as interest and prohibited (BM 5:9). Strict observance of the minutiae of the prohibition posed no particular economic hardship in the case of small short-term loans, but when large credits were involved it was difficult to deny the creditor the right to derive any benefit from the mortgaged land in his possession. In other legal systems it was customary for the creditor to enjoy the fruits of the mortgaged property by way of interest and the existence of this phenomenon in Greco-Roman laws was mentioned in the Talmud (TJ, BM 6:5). In order to ensure the availability of credit, the halakhic scholars sought to evolve special ways for the creation of a mortgage in a manner enabling the creditor to derive some usufructuary benefit from it without transgressing the prohibition against interest.

As already noted, the use and enjoyment of the pledge was permitted the creditor in case of a sale for return and—in the opinion of R. Judah—even in the case where the sale only came into effect upon the debtor's failure to make payment on the due date. This was because the property was regarded as sold to the creditor whereas the question of interest could only arise in the case of loan. The Babylonian *amoraim* regarded even the above cases as involving prohibited interest, since upon repayment of the debt the land would return to the debtor and the sale become voided retroactively (see BM 67a and Rif, *Halakhot;* Sh. Ar., ḤM 182:12; and *Ha-Gra*). A way of permitting the creditor a usufruct of the pledged property was found by the latter scholars on the principle of a reduction of the debt, at times until full liquidation thereof, by virtue of and in return for the usufruct. Even if such reduction bore no proportion to the actual value of the usufruct enjoyed by the creditor, yet this method—unlike the case of a sale of the body of the land—involved some real and not fictitious consideration for the usufruct. An important consideration for the Babylonian *amoraim* in treating the permissibility of such usufruct was the distinction between a mortgage "in a place where it is customary to make the creditor give up possession" and a mortgage "in a place where it is not the custom . . ." In the former case the debtor could repay the debt at any time and recover possession of his land from the creditor and therewith regain the usufruct of his land; in the latter case the creditor could not be made to give up possession within a fixed period and thus the mortgage was akin to a sale for a specified period, whereby the suspicion of prohibited interest was reduced. In certain places it was laid down that, unless expressly stipulated between the parties, the debtor might not recover possession of the land from the creditor during the first year at least (BM 67a–b).

Three forms of usufruct of the mortgaged land were customarily recognized by the Babylonian *amoraim*.

Mortgage with a Fixed Deduction. With a mortgage of this kind the practice was to make a deduction from the amount of the debt against the creditor's enjoyment of the usufruct, as if the fruits were sold for the amount deducted. The rate of the deduction was fixed and amounted to far less than the value of the usufruct enjoyed, hence a *talmid ḥakham* was forbidden from enjoying the usufruct of the mortgaged property, even with the deduction (BM 67b).

Mortgage with a Stipulated Time Limit. The practice in this case was for the creditor to enjoy the usufruct of the mortgaged land against a deduction for the first five years—i.e., with a minimal reduction of the debt (and none at all according to another opinion)—and thereafter enjoyment of the usufruct would be assessed at its full value for purposes of repayment of the debt. Some of the scholars held this form of mortgage to be permissible also to a *talmid ḥakham* (BM 67b). During the first five years the creditor apparently could not be made to surrender possession of the land, the mortgage being akin to a sale and the suspicion of prohibited interest therefore reduced.

Mortgage "as Arranged in Sura." In this form of mortgage the parties would insert into the bond the condition: "on the expiry of so-and-so-many years, this estate reverts [to the debtor] without any payment." Here the creditor would enjoy the usufruct for a period stipulated in advance, at the end of which the land reverted to the debtor and the debt was considered as fully repaid. In this case too the value of the usufruct may have exceeded the amount of the debt, but this method was preferable to the "time limit" mortgage as regards the interest prohibition. In the "Sura" mortgage the creditor, as against his profits, also had to face a possible loss, since the land would revert to the debtor at the end of the stipulated period even though the creditor may not have enjoyed any profits during one or more years; on the other hand, in the "time limit" mortgage, repayment of the debt, after the first five years, would take place according to the measure of the profits enjoyed, and during the first five years the profits could be enjoyed without any risk of loss. With the "Sura" mortgage the suspicion of prohibited interest was entirely eliminated, since it in no way resembled a loan transaction, but rather one of "purchasing the fruits of these particular years against this particular payment" (Rashi, BM 67b). Hence all the scholars agreed that a "Sura" mortgage was permissible even to a *talmid ḥakham* (BM, loc. cit.).

In permitting a usufruct of the mortgaged property, both with reference to the ancient forms of mortgage and those sanctioned by the Babylonian *amoraim*, the scholars relied on the law of the redemption of dwellings in walled cities and fields of possession (Lev. 25:16, 27, 29; Tosef., BM 4:2; TJ, BM 5:3, 10b; BM 67b).

Disputing Opinions in the Codes. The problem of the creditor's enjoyment of a usufruct of the mortgaged property continued to engage halakhic scholars in post-talmudic times and became a subject of much controversial discussion in the codes (*Ha-Gra*, YD 172, n.1, enumerates six different methods entertained by the *posekim*). The main points of dispute may be briefly summarized as follows:

It was generally agreed that a "Sura" mortgage was permissible. As regards a mortgage "with deduction," Alfasi's opinion (to BM 67b) was that although enjoyment of the fruits is initially prohibited to the creditor, nevertheless the *post facto* value of this cannot be reclaimed from him, since no fixed or direct interest is involved, but only *avak ribbit* or indirect interest. The distinction between the two forms of interest, even as regards mortgage, was already discussed in the Talmud (BM 67b). In this case Maimonides permitted enjoyment of the usufruct from the start, but only with reference to a field, "since in the case of a field, the profits are not yet in existence at the time of the loan, and it is possible that the creditor may either derive fruits and profits therefrom or suffer loss in the sowing and cultivation of the field." In the case of a courtyard or a dwelling, Maimonides held the profits to be available at the time of loan and enjoyment of them, although prohibited initially, became permissible, *ex post facto*—because this entailed no more than *avak ribbit* ("dust of interest"; see *Usury) by virtue of the reduction (Yad, 6:7). Rabad held that a mortgage "with deduction" is only permissible from the start where the local custom is not to make the creditor give up possession of the mortgaged property (against repayment of the debt) and that for this purpose no distinction should be made between a dwelling and a field (*Hassagot Rabad* to Malveh 6:7). Rashba, on the other hand, held all mortgages "with deduction" to be permissible from the start, whether relating to a field or dwelling and regardless of local custom on the question of the debtor regaining possession of the mortgaged property.

A great deal of difference of opinion is also expressed in the codes concerning a mortgage with no deduction at all in return for the usufruct. Alfasi (to BM 67b) regarded this as amounting to fixed interest which could be reclaimed by action. Maimonides (Yad, Malveh 6:7) regarded this form of mortgage as entailing direct interest when relating to a courtyard or dwelling, and "dust of interest" when relating to a field or vineyard, and Rabad's view *(ibid.)* was that such a mortgage entailed direct interest or "dust of interest" depending respectively on whether it was local custom to make the creditor give up possession of the mortgaged property (against repayment of the debt) or not. Rashi (on BM 62a, 67a) was of the opinion that in the case of a field a mortgage, even without deduction, was permissible from the start wherever it was the custom not to make the creditor give up possession of the property, since by virtue of the latter fact, "all agree that all these years he holds the field as if purchased by him" (see also Tur, YD 172). However, in the case of a dwelling, such a mortgage (i.e., a usufruct without further deduction of the debt) entailed direct interest (see *Leḥem Mishneh* to Malveh 6:7). Although extremely liberal as regards the permissibility of a mortgage with deduction, Ibn Adret nevertheless held that where it was customary to make the creditor give up possession of the property, a mortgage without deduction entailed direct interest, and where it was customary not to make the creditor give up possession, it was "dust of interest" (*Nimmukei Yosef*, BM 67b; *Leḥem Mishneh*, loc. cit.).

The diversity of opinions made it difficult to decide the law in practice: " how shall we enter into the scholarly discussions . . . we have no power to decide the issue, but the court must act in accordance with its own understanding" (Resp. Abraham b. Isaac of Narbonne, no. 173). In one of his responsa Naḥmanides similarly expressed regret at the diversity of opinion, which left the *halakhah* on the subject uncertain and lacking in binding force. Therefore it had to be left for every community to act in this matter according to local custom. The opinions of the *posekim* were summarized by Isserles in a similar fashion: "Local custom is to be followed in this matter and in these countries the custom is to permit [enjoyment of usufruct] in the case of a mortgage with deduction, even when the debtor may reclaim possession [of the property from the creditor] and in this regard no distinction is drawn between a field and a dwelling or the different kinds of movables, since in all cases a mortgage with deduction is permissible" (*Rema*, YD 172:1).

In the State of Israel. The laws of pledge are ordered in two laws of the Knesset: the Pledge Law, 1967, and the Land Law, 1969. Sections 85–91 of the second law deal with a pledge of land, termed *mashkanta*, i.e., mortgage (sec. 4), to which all the provisions of the Pledge Law are applicable save as otherwise provided in the Land Law itself (sec. 91). The provisions of the Pledge Law are partially in accord with the attitude of Jewish law on the subject. The bill originally submitted to the Knesset (in 1964) included a provision entitling the creditor to enjoy the income of the pledge, with the debtor's consent and in return for an appropriate consideration to the latter, his waiver thereof to be of no validity (sec. 23). In the final version passed by the Knesset, the law provides that the creditor shall pay the debtor appropriate remuneration "unless otherwise agreed." This in effect means that upon the debtor's waiver of consideration the creditor becomes entitled to use and enjoy the income of the pledged property without making any reduction of the debt, which is contrary to Jewish law, where this amounts to prohibited interest.

Bibliography: F. Goldmann, in: *Zeitschrift fuer vergleichende Rechtswissenschaft,* 21 (1908), 197–241; N. A. Nobel, in: *Judaica . . . H. Cohen* (1912), 659–68; J. S. Zuri, *Mishpat ha-Talmud,* 4 (1921), 67–71; T. Ostersetzer, in: *Tarbiz,* 8 (1936/37), 301–15; 9 (1937/38), 395–7; J. N. Epstein, *ibid.*, 316–8; Herzog, Instit, 1 (1936), 339–44, 361–3; 2 (1939), 196; ET, 1 (1951[3]), 128f.; 2 (1949), 19f.; 11 (1965), 100–12; T. Be'eri, in: *Mazkeret . . . Herzog* (1962), 113–9; M. Elon, *Ḥerut ha-Perat be-Darkhei Geviyyat Ḥov* (1964), 1f., 59–7; Elon, Mafte'aḥ, 152–60. [M.E.]

°**PLEHVE, VYACHESLAV KONSTANTINOVICH VON** (1846–1904), Russian statesman, a leader of Russian reactionary circles during the reigns of Alexander III and Nicholas II. In 1881 he was appointed director of the police department of the Ministry of the Interior and from 1884 to 1894 he was deputy minister. He adopted a systematic anti-Jewish policy in interpreting the restrictive laws against Jews. In 1902 Plehve was appointed minister of the interior, in which capacity he took strong measures to subdue the revolutionary movement. When riots broke out in *Kishinev on Passover 1903, liberal and Jewish circles declared that Plehve was responsible for them and the London *Times* published an order which he had sent to the provincial governor of Bessarabia not to open fire on the rioters, although the authenticity of this order was not definitely proved. In June 1903 Plehve called for strict measures to be taken against the Zionist movement which, according to information available to the secret police, had become a powerful political movement encouraging youth to organize self-defense and take up a struggle against the anti-Jewish regime. These measures impelled Herzl to request a meeting with the rulers of Russia. In August 1903 Herzl met with Plehve, Finance Minister *Witte, and other high officials, asking for the support of the Russian government in establishing a Jewish state to absorb the persecuted Jews of Russia. The reply was that as long as the Zionists encouraged emigration of Jews from Russia the authorities would not disturb them; any political activity in Russia, however, would be crushed. On July 15, 1904, Plehve was assassinated by a member of the socialist revolutionaries, E. S. Sazonov. His successor, Svyatopolk-Mirski, adopted a more liberal policy.

Bibliography: Dubnow, Hist Russ, index; T. Herzl, *Complete Diaries,* ed. by R. Patai (1960), index; E. Feldman, in: *He-Avar,* 17 (1970). [Y.S.]

PLESSNER, MARTIN (**Meir;** 1900–), orientalist. Plessner, born in Breslau, was the great-grandson of Solomon Plessner (1797–1883), a prominent German Orthodox preacher and scholar. The classical heritage in Islam and its influence on medieval Judaism was Martin Plessner's main scholarly interest. An assistant to H. Ritter in Hamburg, he edited a comprehensive work on magic which was wrongly attributed to Maslama al-Majrīṭī (Spain, d. 1004) but written about 50 years later (1933; Ger. tr. 1962). Plessner worked as assistant to J. Ruska at the Berlin Forschungsingstitut fuer Geschichte der Naturwissenschaften (1927–29), and in 1933 became lecturer in Semitics at Frankfort University, leaving Germany for Palestine in 1933 to teach at the Reali secondary school in Haifa. There he wrote an Arabic grammar, the first in modern Hebrew. From 1945 he taught at the Ma'aleh school in Jerusalem, also working (from 1949) at the Jewish National and University Library, and later as librarian of the School of Oriental Studies of the Hebrew University, where he became an external teacher in 1952 and professor in 1955.

Among Plessner's other published work was his Hebrew edition (with J. J. Rivlin) of I. Goldziher's lectures on Islam (*Harẓa'ot al ha-Islam,* 1951). One of his main achievements was the discovery that the alchemical "parliament," *Turba Philosophorum,* is based on the doxographical tradition about the pre-Socratic philosophers, thus establishing a new chronology and evaluation of early Arabic alchemy. [ED.]

PLETTEN (Yid. פּלעטען; "meal tickets"), an arrangement begun at the end of the 15th century which ensured meals for the itinerant needy. In many communities in Germany, Poland, and other countries, the itinerant poor person—usually either a yeshivah student or a beggar—received a slip of paper bearing the name of the house owner who would provide food, drink, and lodging for him for at least three days. It was obligatory to provide for someone who had one of these *pletten* and householders who refused were fined; in many communal registers the rates of such fines were recorded. Eventually those who refused were publicly denounced in the synagogue, and in some synagogues the names of such offenders were recorded on a special board.

See also *Hospitality, **Hekdesh.*

Bibliography: Baron, Community, 3 (1942), index; I. Levitats, *Jewish Community in Russia* (1943), 250–1. [N.E.]

PLEVEN (Plevna), city in N. Bulgaria. During Byzantine rule, there was a Jewish community in Pleven. This community later included Hungarian Jewish refugees, who had been expelled in 1376, Walachian refugees who fled during the revolt of Vlad V in 1461 against Sultan Mehmed II, Jews of Bavaria who were expelled in 1470, Spanish refugees, and again Hungarian refugees, who came after the conquest of Hungary by Suleiman the Magnificent in 1526. During the 16th century, there were Ashkenazi, Hungarian, and Sephardi communities in Pleven which united into one general community. After the great fire of 1582, a single synagogue was built, but apart from the Sephardi ritual the different communities partly kept their customs. In 1593 Michael of Wallachia rebelled against Sultan Murad III and burned the town, taking many Jews prisoner. The Jews of Pleven traded in hides and copper and also wove cloths. During the invasion of the city by the adventurer Ottoman Pazvanoglu in 1799, the Jews took up arms in self-defense. In 1877, they fled to Sofia before the Russian invasion, but after a time, the community was reorganized. In 1910 there were 623 Jews in Pleven and in 1928, 550. After the establishment of the State of Israel, the Jews of Pleven, like almost all Bulgarian Jewry, immigrated there.

Bibliography: Rosanes, Togarmah, 7 (1930[2]), 62, 115, 221, 252–3, and passim; idem, in: *Yevreyska Tribuna* (1928), 120–33, 172–80. [S.MAR.]

°**PLINY THE ELDER** (23–79 C.E.), Roman historian, naturalist, and administrator. Pliny's voluminous *Naturalis Historia,* the only work of his extant, contains a number of references to Jews and Judaism. Some of these references relate to the physical characteristics of Judea and its natural resources, in particular the Dead Sea and the bitumen found there. Pliny notes the excellence of balsam (a monopoly of Judea), describes the tree, and praises the date palms of Jericho. The sections on Judea (*Naturalis Historia,* 5:66–73) in the geographical volumes include a survey of the administrative division of Judea into toparchies, which differs slightly from that given by *Josephus. Pliny describes the *Essenes, discussing their settlement by the Dead Sea, their separation from women, and their renunciation of money. Jerusalem, he observes, is the most illustrious city in the East (*"longe clarissima urbium Orientis non Iudaeae modo"*). The sources which Pliny used in his description of Judea cannot be ascertained, but he evidently relied on material dating from the period of Herod, which he adjusted to the situation of his time. Thus, he mentions the destruction of Jerusalem and the establishment of new Roman colonies in Palestine by *Vespasian. However, in addition, he must have used earlier sources. The theory that Pliny was present at the siege of Jerusalem as an officer in the army of Titus is hardly tenable.

Bibliography: Reinach, Textes, 267–83; H. G. Pflaum, *Les carrières procuratoriennes équestres sous le Haut-Empire romain,* 1 (1960), 106ff. [M.ST.]

PLISETSKAYA, MAYA (1925–), Russian dancer, prima ballerina of the Bolshoi Ballet. Plisetskaya, who was born in Moscow, entered the Bolshoi School in 1934 and was recognized as a gifted dancer by the time she graduated and

Maya Plisetskaya, prima ballerina of the Bolshoi Ballet. From A. Chujoy and P. W. Manchester (eds.), *The Dance Encyclopedia,* New York, 1967.

joined the company in 1943. Her first great success came in 1947, when she danced Odette-Odile in *Swan Lake,* subsequently regarded as her greatest role, allowing her to combine brilliant technique with fiery temperament. She also excelled in other classical roles, such as the ballerina in *Raymonda,* Aurora in *Sleeping Beauty,* and Kitri in *Don Quixote;* and in contemporary Soviet ballets such as *Stone Flower, Spartacus, Romeo and Juliet,* and *Ballet School.* Plisetskaya, who married the Soviet composer Rodion Shchedrin, was awarded the Lenin Prize in 1964, and also received the title People's Artist of the U.S.S.R.

[M.B.S.]

PLOCK (Pol. **Płock;** Rus. **Plotsk**), city in Warszawa province, central Poland. As Jews settled there before 1237, when the city was the capital of Masovia, the Plock Jewish community is one of the oldest in Poland. In the first 200 years of their residence there, the Jews usually engaged in moneylending, sometimes accepting landed estates and other immovable property as security. Before the 16th century, however, they began to earn their living from trade and crafts. At the beginning of that century legal and municipal documents record the names of 28 Plock Jews who traded in wool, leather, spices, horses, and grain. About the middle of the century the burghers made a stubborn attempt to limit Jewish trade, but in 1555 King *Sigismund II Augustus granted the Jews economic rights equal to those of the other citizens, and in 1576 King Stephen Báthory forbade the city authorities to hinder the Jews in their business pursuits. However, at the beginning of the 17th century the burghers succeeded in limiting the activities of the Jewish traders and artisans for some time. From the middle of the 17th century many Plock Jews engaged in weaving, glasswork, arms manufacture, and tailoring and some were accepted in the local Christian guilds, but the struggle of the Christian bakers, butchers, and harness makers against Jewish artisans continued. In the 16th century there were six Jewish physicians in Plock.

The Jewish quarter was first mentioned in 1532; in 1616 there were 25 houses in the town owned by Jews in which probably around 400 members of the Jewish community lived. The synagogue was opened in 1534, and a cemetery was consecrated in a suburb in 1570. In 1577 the *parnasim* of Plock—the physician Lewek and "Black Jacob"—appeared as prosecutors in the trial of the men who had hastily passed sentence in the *Sochaczew blood libel. In riots against the Jews in 1534, 1570, 1579, 1590, and 1656, the men of the Plock community took up arms in self-defense. After the depredations of the Great Northern War in 1705, the Jewish community suffered further economic loss through the hostile attitude of the nobility and the Church. In 1754 their situation deteriorated even further when a *blood libel caused an uproar in the city. About the middle of the 18th century the Jewish tailors organized their own guild in order to protect their livelihood (see E. Ringelblum, in: *Miesiecznik żydowski,* 2 no. 2 (1932), 46–47). The spiritual leaders of Plock Jewry in the 17th century included R. Ẓevi Hirsch Munk (in the 1680s), R. Menahem Nahum b. Israel (d. 1691), and Zelig Isaac Margolioth, author of *Kesef Nivḥar* (Amsterdam, 1712). Rabbis in the 18th century included Samuel b. Israel, Ḥayyim Ginzburg, and Judah Loeb *Margolioth (1747–1811), one of the supporters of moderate *Haskalah.

In the first years of the 19th century, under Prussian rule, the Jewish population of Plock grew from 731 in 1800 to 1,932 in 1808 (49% of the total population). As a result of the great fire in 1810, the synagogue and a considerable part of the Jewish quarter were destroyed. A year later the government of the grand duchy of Warsaw confined the Jews to a separate quarter which contained only eight streets, a restriction which remained in force until 1862.

The *mikveh* in Plock. From A. Eisenberg (ed.), *Plock, Toledot Kehillah Attikat Yamim be-Polin,* 1967.

In the middle of the 19th century the Jews of Plock earned their living from trade and transportation and Jewish entrepreneurs established textile factories in the city. In 1827 there were 3,412 Jews in Plock (35% of the population). In 1841–44, on the initiative of the industrialist Solomon Zalman *Posner, farming villages (Kuchary, Ickowiec) were founded near Plock in which 170 Jewish families had settled by 1850. In 1897 the Jewish population of the city numbered 1,480 (33% of the total). At the beginning of the 20th century about 5% of the Jews of Plock were engaged in commerce, 31% in crafts and industry (clothing, food, metals, printing), and about 12% earned their living as hired laborers. From 1865 to 1871 the town contained a government school where Jewish children were taught in Hebrew and Russian, and in 1888, on the initiative of the writer Abraham Jacob *Paperna, a Jewish school sponsored by the government was founded. In the *talmud torah,* founded in 1868, secular studies were introduced at the end of the 1880s on the initiative of the noted educator Aharon *Kahnstam. In 1872 the first Jewish hospital was built.

At the beginning of the 20th century, branches of the *Bund, the Zionist Socialists, and *Po'alei Zion began to operate in Plock. A yeshivah was opened in 1912 under the direction of Michael Rubinstein and Mendel Mendelson; in 1916 a Jewish high school was founded. In 1921, 7,352 Jews (29% of the total population) lived in Plock. In the period between the two world wars there were three Jewish cooperative banks and Jewish trade unions for the garment industry, transport workers, clerks, and salesmen. In the 1930s a *Tarbut school was founded and in 1938 an *ORT school. During this period the monthly *Dos Plotsker Vort* was published. The authors Jakir *Warszawski and Sholem *Asch, the painters Nathan Korzeń, Fishl Zilberberg (1909–1942), and Jehiel Meir (Max) Eljowicz, and the miniaturist David Tysziński lived in the city, as did the Zionist leaders Nahum Sokolow and Yizḥak Gruenbaum. [A.Cy.]

Holocaust Period. At the outbreak of World War II, Plock had nearly 10,000 Jews, around one-third of the total population. When the Germans entered on Sept. 9, 1939, the majority of Jews had fled to nearby Gabin, but they gradually returned. Immediately, men were hunted down for forced labor. In December 1939 a *Judenrat was established. It created an *Arbeitsamt* ("labor bureau") to supply the Germans with manpower. It also maintained a clinic, an old-age home, and a soup kitchen subsidized by the *American Jewish Joint Distribution Committee and by 10% of the wages Jews received from the Germans. In November 1939 a ghetto was created. Jews could not leave the ghetto without permission, but Poles entered without difficulty and supplied food at high prices. Although private workshops and stores were liquidated, some of the cooperatives, such as those of cobblers and tailors, continued.

The German police carried out night raids involving searches and plundering, accompanied by beating and sometimes killing. Before the establishment of the ghetto the authorities requested that the Judenrat supply a list of the elderly invalids and chronically ill. Some days later all the inmates of the old-age home and all the others on this list were rounded up and deported. After one of the night raids some Jews lodged a complaint before the German authorities. In retaliation, the Germans arrested and executed 180 Jews. The Plock community was liquidated in two deportations on Feb. 20 and 28, 1941. During the first deportation, the main street was surrounded; all the Jews were driven outdoors. More than half were sent to the concentration camp in Dzialdowo. During the next deportation the remaining Jews were sent to the same camp, where they were tortured and sent on to Radom District. During February and March 1941 six transports of Jews from Plock arrived in Radom District (5,000–7,000 Jews). They were dispersed in small localities—barefoot, in rags, and exhausted. Most of the deportees died in camps.

About 100 survivors (most of whom returned from the U.S.S.R. and a few of whom were saved on the "Aryan" side of the city) reconstituted the community and reestablished public and mutual-welfare institutions. In October 1949 the community erected a monument in memory of the victims of the Holocaust. Organizations of the former residents of Plock exist in many countries. [De.D.]

Bibliography: A. Nowowiejski, *Płock* (1931); Y. Trunk, *Geshikhte fun Yidn in Plotsk* (1939); S. Grinshpon, *Yidn in Plotsk* (1960); A. Eisenberg (ed.), *Plock, Toledot Kehillah Attikat Yamim be-Polin* (1967); S. Dubnow, in: *Voskhod*, no. 9 (1894), 119–24; R. Rybarski, *Handel i polityka handlowa Polski w XVI stuleciu*, 2 (1928), 141–3, 151–9; Z. Rubashov (Shazar), in: *YIVO Historishe Shriftn*, 1 (1929), 153–4; B. Wasiutyński, *Ludność żydowska w Polsce w wiekach XIX i XX* (1930), 7, 10, 18, 22, 41, 45–46, 70, 176, 180, 184, 209; S. B. Weinryb, *Neueste Wirtschaftsgeschichte der Juden in Russland und Polen* (1934), 42, 44–45; I. Schiper, *Dzieje handlu żydowskiego na ziemiach polskich* (1937), index; Halpern, Pinkas, index; Warsaw, Archiwum Glówne Akt Dawnych, *Komisja rządowa spraw wewnętrznych i duchownych*, no. 4584 (= C.A.H.J.P., HM 3598); Lodz, W.A.P., *Rząd gubernski, wydział administratywny*, no. 8206 (= C.A.H.J.P., HM 6351); BZIH, no. 52 (1964), 71–77.

PLOESTI (Rum. **Ploeşti**), city in Walachia, S. central Rumania. The first Jews settled in Ploesti in the second half of the 17th century. There were so few, however, that they continued to bury their dead at the cemetery at *Buzau. At the end of the same century they purchased ground for a cemetery, far from the city, where tombstones have been found dating back to 1719–40. A second cemetery was confiscated by a landowner to enlarge his estate. A third, established on ground acquired in 1818 by the "Jews' Guild" (see *Rumania), was also closed, being too near the city. Consequently, a fourth cemetery was established outside the city. In the early 18th century the synagogue was demolished by order of the ruler, and the Jews had to move two kilometers out of the city. However, their commercial importance was so valued that the cattle market and general market of the city were established in their neighborhood. The road linking the Jewish quarter with the city became known as the "Jews' street" till 1882. At the beginning of the 19th century, Sephardi Jews migrated to Ploesti from the Balkan states; their neighborhood was called "the Spanish street." In 1830 the Sephardim requested the *ḥakham bashi* to approve the establishment of their own community, but the request was refused. Thus Ploesti became the only Rumanian locality whose *kahal* combined Ashkenazim and Sephardim in communal activities (although distinctions persisted in regard to separate synagogues and *ḥevra kaddisha*).

From 280 Jews listed as taxpayers in 1831, the number reached 2,478 in 1899 (5.5% of the total population) and 3,843 (3.3%) in 1930. Five synagogues were eventually established, including one for artisans and another for Sephardim. The boys' school, built in 1875, was named after Luca Moise who granted funds for its building and maintenance. A girls' school was built in 1896. Among noted rabbis who served Ploesti were those of the Brezis family, Judah Aryeh Brezis (1869–1908) and Dr. Joseph Ḥayyim *Brezis (1911–22). Menahem Safran officiated as rabbi from 1939 to 1956. Rabbi David *Friedman, a ḥasidic *ẓaddik* of the *Ruzhin dynasty, lived in Ploesti until his murder by the *Iron Guard in 1940.

The Jews did much to develop the city by organizing the export of agricultural produce, leather, and other goods to Hungary and on to Vienna. From the middle of the 19th century many dealt in oil, developing Ploesti into a center for that commodity. After the emancipation of the Jews in Rumania, Jews officiated as representatives on the city council and for a time a Jew served as vice-mayor.

Holocaust Period. Immediately after the outbreak of World War II, Ploesti became a center of German interest because of its oil resources. Units of the German army appeared in the city as early as the autumn of 1940. After Antonescu assumed power (September 1940), Cojocaru, a member of the Iron Guard, was appointed commander of the local police. Immediately upon taking over the post he introduced serious measures against the Jews, i.e., confiscation of their businesses and wide-scale arrests of merchants and community leaders. On the night of Nov. 27/28, 1940, 11 of the Jewish prisoners were executed in a nearby forest. Among those killed was Rabbi David Friedman. During the same period members of the Iron Guard destroyed three synagogues and the Luca Moise school; they burned the Scrolls of the Law taken from the synagogues and transferred the furniture to churches, while the school equipment was taken to Rumanian educational institutions.

A number of Jews were sent to the Tirgu-jiu concentration camp. After the outbreak of war with the U.S.S.R. (June 1941), all the Jewish men from ages 18 to 60 were arrested and sent to the Teiş concentration camp. Youth from the ages of 13 to 18 remained in Ploesti and were mobilized into different forms of forced labor. In January 1942 men over the age of 50 were released from Teiş and returned to the city. The rest were scattered throughout various cities in Rumania but were forbidden to leave their new locations. Later on they were sent to do forced labor in various places in Bessarabia and Moldavia. After the war, practically all of Ploesti's Jews returned to the city.

In 1947 the Jewish population numbered about 3,000, decreasing to 2,000 in 1950. By 1969 about 120 Jewish families remained. They had one synagogue.

Bibliography: PK, Romanyah, 218–24; I. Sapira, in: *Analele Societălii istorice Juliu Barasch*, 3 pt. 1–2 (1889); A. D. Rosen (ed.), *Istoricul Comunitătii cultului israelit din Ploeşti* (1906); *Almanachul evreesc ilustrat* . . . (1932), 37–38; *Almanachul ziarului Tribuna evreească*, 1 (1937/38), 251–5. [Th.L.]

PLONSK, town in Warszawa province, E. central Poland. A Jewish settlement existed in Plonsk from 1446. The princes of Masovia encouraged the settlement of Jews to help develop the economy of the town, although this aroused the jealousy of the Polish merchants, and conse-

The Great Synagogue of Plonsk, dating from the early 17th century. From *Sefer Plonsk ve-ha-Sevivah,* Tel Aviv, 1963.

quently, Jewish activity was later restricted by various decrees. In 1677 King John III Sobieski prohibited all Jewish commerce on market days, with the exception of the sale of kosher meat. In spite of the restrictions, the number of Jews increased, as did their importance in the town. In 1887 Jews owned most of the houses and the shops; they dealt in the wholesale trade of cereals and owned brandy distilleries, beer breweries, underwear factories, etc. They were also engaged in tailoring and the fur trade, exporting goods to the interior of Russia. Jews numbered 2,801 in 1808; in 1910 they numbered 7,665 (64% of the population), and in 1939 there were 8,200 Jews in the town of Plonsk. World War I and the advent of an independent Poland restricted Jews to business transactions in the local Polish market where they engaged primarily in the trade of inexpensive ready-made clothing. The economic crisis of the late 1920s and the economic boycott brought on by Polish anti-Semitism in the 1930s struck a severe blow at Jewish economic life.

During the 15th century the Jewish community was under the guardianship of Plock, the leading community of Masovia. With the organization of the Council of the Four Lands it was subordinated to the community of Ciechanow, but due to its expansion it eventually became an independent community. During the 19th century the community administration was under the influence of the *mitnaggedim,* even though the courts of the *zaddikim* (especially that of Gur) exerted considerable influence on the Jews of the town. In the 20th century the influence of the *maskilim* and the Zionists rose. The community supervised the activities of the relief and educational institutions. The rabbinical positions of the community were held by R. Abraham Jekuthiel *Lichtenstein during the second half of the 18th century and by R. Ẓevi Ezekiel *Michaelsohn at the close of the century. On the eve of the Holocaust, the rabbinical post of the town was held by R. Abraham Ḥayyim Horowitz. A synagogue was erected at the beginning of the 17th century and its Ark was a work of art. The Jews of Plonsk participated in the Polish Revolt of 1863. Solomon Posner, one of the commanders of the Plonsk company, was killed in battle.

Jews were elected to both the provincial and the municipal councils. At the municipal council elections of 1927, out of the 23 delegates 13 were Jews. In addition to the religious, educational, and cultural institutions of the town, there were also societies for the propagation of Jewish and general education. In 1865 a society named Doreshei ha-Torah ve-ha-Ḥokhmah was founded by the *maskilim,* offering lectures on Jewish subjects. In 1910 the Ha-Or society was established, having been authorized by the Russian authorities to propagate Jewish and general education. Zionist societies were also active in promoting Hebrew language and culture. The Zionist Organization wielded considerable influence. It was quite evident in daily life, and especially apparent at the time of the elections to the Zionist Congresses. The author Shelomo *Ẓemaḥ and David *Ben-Gurion originally came from Plonsk. [SH.L.K.]

Holocaust Period. At the outbreak of World War II there were about 6,000 Jews in Plonsk. The German army occupied the town on Sept. 5, 1939. Some Jewish men were sent to the forced-labor camp in Nosarzewo and Jewish women to the forced-labor camp in *Sierpc. Few of them survived. A closed ghetto was established in May 1941. The Jewish community was liquidated when 12,000 Jews from Plonsk and the vicinity were sent to *Auschwitz in four transports between Nov. 1 and Dec. 5, 1942. After the war, the Jewish community of Plonsk was not reconstituted. Organizations of former residents of Plonsk are active in Israel, the United States, and Argentina. [ED.]

Bibliography: *Sefer Plonsk ve-ha-Sevivah* (1963; Heb. and partly Yid.).

PLOTZKI, MEIR DAN OF OSTROVA (1867–1928), Polish rabbi. Plotzki studied under R. Israel Joshua of Kutno, R. Ḥayyim Eleazar Wax of Piotrkow, and R. Abraham of Sochaczew. In 1891, he was elected rabbi of Warta. The publication of the first part of his *Ḥemdat Yisrael* in 1903 made him famous throughout Poland, and in 1908 he was appointed rabbi of the large town of Ostrow. In 1926 he resigned from the rabbinate and was appointed *rosh yeshivah* of the "Metivta" in Warsaw. This institution, founded by the Ḥasidim of *Gur (Gora Kalwarja), of whom he was a fervent adherent, was the most important yeshivah in Poland. In 1912 Plotzki visited Ereẓ Israel and instituted many improvements in the administration of the Polish *kolel.* One of the leaders of *Agudat Israel, he spent a year as its emissary in Belgium, England, and the United States. He was chairman of the executive committee of the Agudat ha-Rabbanim in Poland.

In addition to his *Ḥemdat Yisrael* (1903–24), partly on Maimonides' *Sefer ha-Mitzvot,* he wrote *Keli Ḥemdah,* a commentary on the Pentateuch, in six parts (1906–38); *Sha'alu Shelom Yerushalayim* (1910), to expose the forgery of the purported Jerusalem Talmud on the order of *Kodashim* published by Solomon *Friedlander (1907–09); and *Niẓoẓei Or,* novellae on the *Or ha-Ḥayyim* by R. Ḥayyim b. *Attar, printed together with the *Toledot Rabbenu Ḥayyim ibn Atar* (1925) by Reuben *Margolioth. Many of his other works have remained in manuscript.

Bibliography: *Diglenu,* 8 (1928), nos. 8, 10, 11; *Ha-Derekh,* (1943), no. 35; I. Frankel, *Yeḥidei Segullah* (1964[4]), 161–5. [Y.AL.]

PLOVDIV (ancient **Philippopolis**), city in the S. central part of Bulgaria. During the Byzantine rule, the Jews lived in a special quarter. Under the Turks, their quarter was known as *Orta Mezar.* During the 16th century, there were some Sephardi Jews in the town: they engaged in commerce. During the 18th century, the rabbi was Judah *Sid (d. 1815), the author of *Ot Emet* (Salonika, 1799) and *Ner Mitzvah* (*ibid.,* 1810–11). He was succeeded by R. Abraham ibn Aroiio (1750–1819), the author of the responsa *Mayim ha-Ḥayyim* (*ibid.,* 1846–64). Plovdiv was the seat of the regional assembly of Eastern Rumelia, an entity established in 1878 by the Congress of Berlin; some Jews played a role in the assembly's proceedings. In 1912, there were 3,000 Jews in Plovdiv and in 1938, 6,000. In 1895 a Yishuv Ereẓ Yisrael society was founded. At that time Joseph Marco (Marcou) *Baruch published there, in French, *Carmel,* which was the foremost Jewish-national newspaper of Bulgaria. From 1901 *Ha-Shofar,* the bulletin of the Zionist Organization, was published in Plovdiv, and from 1924 the Zionist headquarters was situated there. The

Inscription from the Yeshurun synagogue of Plovdiv, Bulgaria, dated 1786. Courtesy C.A.H.J.P., Inv./1494(1), Jerusalem.

Jews of Plovdiv were engaged in commerce and crafts. Later they opened some factories. During World War II, in 1943, an expulsion decree ordering all the Plovdiv Jews to leave Bulgaria was issued, but it was not carried out. In 1967 there were 1,000 Jews in the town.

Bibliography: Ubicini, in: *Revue de Géographie,* 3 (1880), 6; J. Nitzani, in: *Reshumot,* 5 (1953), 25–50. [S.MAR.]

PLUM, the *Prunus domestica,* of which there are many different varieties. In modern Hebrew, the name *shezif* is applied to the plum, but erroneously, since the ancient name *shezaf* is the *jujube. A species of plum, *Prunus ursina,* grows wild in the groves of Upper Galilee and in Lebanon. It is a shrub or tree, somewhat prickly, producing small yellow tasty fruits. In Syriac it is called *ḥuha* and in Arabic *ḥoḥ*. Some identify it with the "*ḥo'aḥ* in Lebanon," which in the parable of Jehoash is contrasted with the cedar of Lebanon, but the parable concludes that the wild beasts of Lebanon trod it down (II Kings 14:9). It would therefore seem that a prickly weed is intended and not a tree, which is, in fact, the meaning of *ḥo'aḥ* in other passages in the Bible (see *Thistles and Thorns). In Greek and Roman literature a choice plum is referred to as *damascena* (*δαμασκηνά* which is also its name in modern Greek and in modern Arabic) because it originated from Damascus. In rabbinic literature it is found under the names *dormaskin, dormaskenin, dormaskeniyyot,* and is mentioned as a fruit which was mainly imported (Tosef., Dem. 1:9). It was regarded as good for sick people (BK 116b) and was served to important visitors (Ber. 39a). The parallel passage in the Jerusalem Talmud (Ber. 6:2, 10b end) has *aḥvanita* which is the Arabic for the plum.

Bibliography: Loew, Flora, 3 (1924), 163–9; Krauss, Tal Arch, 1 (1910), 488. [J.F.]

PLUNGE (Lith. **Plungė;** Rus. **Plungyany**), city in W. Lithuania. The 15th-century tombstones in the Jewish cemetery indicate that there was a Jewish settlement in Plunge at that time. In 1847 there were 2,197 Jews living there; 2,502 (55% of the population) are recorded in 1897. Most Jews engaged in commerce with eastern Prussia and the surrounding villages as well as in crafts and agriculture. During the period of Lithuanian independence, Jewish commercial enterprises were repressed and a period of intensified emigration followed. The number of Jewish residents in Plunge decreased to 1,815 (44% of the population) in 1933 and 1,700 in 1939. There were six synagogues and a yeshivah with 50 pupils in the town, as well as a *Tarbut and Yiddish school, a Hebrew secondary school, two libraries, and a Jewish bank. Political and communal organizations of every kind and relief institutions were also active. For a time, the office of mayor was held by a member of the Jewish community. When the Germans entered Plunge on June 25, 1941, they murdered a number of Jewish youths who had participated in its defense. A few weeks later they massacred all the remaining Jews. [D.LE.]

The Great Synagogue of Plunge, Lithuania, photo 1937/8. Courtesy Yad Vashem Archives, Y. Kamson Collection, Jerusalem.

PLUNGIAN (Plungiansky), MORDECAI (1814–1883), Hebrew writer. Born in Plunge, Lithuania, he became learned in talmudic and rabbinical literature; later, he was attracted to the Haskalah and studied foreign languages. In his biography of R. *Manasseh b. Joseph of Ilya, *Ben Porat* (1858), Plungian dissociated himself from extremist Haskalah ideology as well as from unenlightened Orthodoxy. This work angered the religious elements, and Plungian backed down and destroyed the manuscript of the second part.

He wrote for the journals **Kerem Ḥemed,* **Ha-Maggid, Ha-Karmel,* and **Ha-Shaḥar* and also wrote poetry. His writings include: *Kerem Shelomo,* a commentary in two parts on Ecclesiastes (1857) and the Song of Songs (1877); *Tel-Piyyot* (on the Mishnah, 1849); *Shevet Eloha* (on blood libels, 1862); and *Or Boker* (part of a large work on the reading of the Torah, 1868).

Bibliography: N. Z. Golomb, in: *Ha-Ẓefirah,* no. 46 (1883); P. Smolenskin, in: *Ha-Shaḥar,* 11 (1883), 635–6; N. Nathansohn, *Sefat Emet* (1887). [Y.S.]

°**PLUTARCH** (c. 46–120 C.E.), Greek biographer and antiquarian. He discusses whether the Jews abstain from the use of swine's flesh out of reverence for the animal or because of aversion to it (*Quaestiones Conviviales,* 4). In a symposium (*ibid.*) "Who is the God of the Jews," Bacchus is identified with the God of the Jews and the Bacchanalian celebrations with the Festival of Tabernacles. "They set up tables laden with all kinds of fruit and live in tents and in huts made of vine branches and ivy intertwined. The first day of this Festival is called the Festival of Tabernacles" (Gr. *skēnē,* "tent"). This identification is refuted by his contemporary *Tacitus (*Historiae,* 5:5). Plutarch also mentions the widespread anti-Jewish slander (cf. *Apion and Tacitus) that the Jews worshiped the head of an ass because that animal helped them discover wells of water in the wilderness. In his essay on superstition, Plutarch states that the Jews did not defend their city on Sabbath, but remained "clothed in their superstition, as if in a great net." Plutarch's treatment of Judaism is prompted by neither hatred nor respect. The Jewish religion was considered by cultured pagans a pious superstition, in common with other oriental cults.

Bibliography: Reinach, Textes, 136–50. [S.R.]

PLYMOUTH, port and naval base in Devon, S.W. England. One of the earliest provincial Jewish communities after the Resettlement was established here and the beautiful synagogue, dating from 1761, is the oldest in England outside London. In the 18th century, Plymouth's Jewish inhabitants, mainly Ashkenazim from Poland and Germany, included silversmiths, merchants, petty traders, old-clothes men, opticians, and pen cutters. Jews were also active as suppliers of stores and clothing for the navy and a subsidiary congregation was formed at Plymouth Dock (Devonport). By the end of the Napoleonic Wars there were about 30 Jewish licensed navy agents. The community was one of the four most prominent in Britain until 1815, when its importance declined. In the early 20th century the Jewish population numbered 300, and in 1969 225 (out of a total population of 212,000).

Bibliography: D. Black, *The Plymouth Synagogue* (1961); C. Roth, *The Rise of Provincial Jewry* (1950), 91–93; Roth, England 230–1, 241; JYB.

[V.D.L.]

PO'ALEI AGUDAT ISRAEL (P.A.I.), an Orthodox religious party in Israel, affiliated to the World Union of Po'alei Agudat Israel, founded in Lodz, Poland, in 1922 as an affiliate of *Agudat Israel. Its central ideal was the application in daily life of the social principles contained in the Torah. In its struggle for social progress, P.A.I. clashed with the Orthodox industrialists in Poland, from whom it demanded a better treatment of the workers, and eventually with Agudat Israel over this same issue.

In Ereẓ Israel, P.A.I. was first established in 1925 by newly arrived young Orthodox settlers, but it broke up after a short period and was reestablished in Tel Aviv in 1933, under the leadership of Binyamin Mintz of Poland and Ya'akov Landau of Germany. The Histadrut ha-Po'alim ha-Ḥaredit ("Federation of Orthodox Workers"), which had been formed shortly before at Petaḥ Tikvah, joined the new party. It fought for the upbuilding of the country as its central ideal, within Agudat Israel. At the Third Kenesiyyah Gedolah ("Great Synod") of Agudat Israel (Marienbad, Czechoslovakia, 1937), P.A.I. advocated support for a Jewish state according to the Peel Commission's plan and the setting up of kibbutzim with the assistance of Zionist funds. In spite of the Great Synod's rejection of its policy, P.A.I. groups from Kefar Sava and Gederah settled on Jewish National Fund land in May 1944 and established the Kibbutz Ḥafeẓ Ḥayyim. P.A.I. continued to go its own way after the national convention at Kefar Sava the following year, at which Binyamin Mintz was elected to the leadership, and in 1946 the World Union of Po'alei Agudat Israel was founded at a convention in Antwerp. This step was regarded as secession from World Agudat Israel, although no formal severance took place. P.A.I. members next joined the *Haganah, and Binyamin Mintz became a member of the *yishuv*'s security committee.

Shortly after the establishment of the state, P.A.I., under a special arrangement, joined the trade union department of the *Histadrut without joining the Labor Federation as such. On the other hand, it did not dissociate itself completely from Agudat Israel; in particular, it continued to accept the authority of its Mo'eẓet Gedolei ha-Torah ("Council of Torah Sages"). In the elections to the third, fourth, and fifth Knessets, the two parties appeared on joint lists, and both left the government coalition in 1952 over the issue of the drafting of girls to national service. In 1960, however, P.A.I. contravened a decision of the Mo'eẓet Gedolei ha-Torah by joining the government, and as a result the formal ties with Agudat Israel finally came to an end. In the elections to the sixth Knesset, P.A.I. appeared independently (as it had done in the second), and polled 1.8% of the votes, with two seats in the House. After the death of Binyamin Mintz in 1961, R. Kalman Kahana was the party's leader. P.A.I. does not frown upon secular education and both boys and girls are members of its youth movement. It has two kibbutzim, Ḥafeẓ Ḥayyim and Shaalbim, as well as several moshavim. In 1948 the Israel Youth Movement, Ezra, affiliated to the P.A.I. [M.Fr.]

In the U.S. Po'alei Agudath Israel of America is an Orthodox organization founded in the U.S. in 1948 for the purpose of educating and preparing young people for *aliyah* to Israel as *ḥalutzim*, and supporting the institutions of the parent movement in Israel. In 1970 P.A.I. consisted of five branches located in Brooklyn, New York. Membership figures were unavailable, but were known to be small, possibly stemming from a lack of approval by the heads of yeshivot in the U.S. which rendered P.A.I. incapable of providing an effective alternative to the anti-Zionist Agudath Israel in the U.S. P.A.I.'s women's division, N'shei Po'alei Agudath Israel (founded in 1948), concerned itself in 1970 with supporting six Israel children's homes and villages with a population of more than 2,000 children. P.A.I. also supported a summer camp program for U.S. children in Israel, and aided its membership in securing employment. In 1969 P.A.I. published the periodicals *Achdut, PAI-Views,* and *Yedi'ot PAI.* On issues affecting Israel, P.A.I. generally followed the Israel parent party line. Domestically, P.A.I. was one of the few Jewish organizations to support the Elementary and Secondary Education Act of 1965, which authorized the provision of federal funds to aid students in private schools. [Ed.]

Bibliography: H. Seidman, *History of a Movement and a Man* (1963); Y. L. Orlean, *La-Seve'im ve-la-Re'evim* (1955[2]); Po'alei Agudat Israel, *Yedi'ot* (weekly bulletin stencil, 1935–37); idem, *She'arim* (weekly, later daily, 1945–); idem, *She'arim, Gilyon ha-Elef* (1955); I. Breuer, *Le-Khivvun ha-Tenu'ah* (1936). In the U.S.: AJYB, index; *Achdut; PAI-Views; Yedi'ot PAI.*

PO'ALEI ZION, movement that tried to base itself upon the Jewish proletariat whose ideology consisted of a combination of Zionism and socialism. Attempts to combine Jewish nationalism and Zionism with socialism were made by *Zhitlovsky and *Syrkin in the 1890s, but a movement came into existence in Russia toward the end of the 19th century and at first consisted of local groups and regional associations. Later, countrywide Po'alei Zion parties were established in Russia, the Austrian Empire, the United States, England, Argentina, Rumania, and Ereẓ Israel. In 1907 a World Union of Po'alei Zion was founded. In 1920 the movement split over the attitude toward the Socialist and Communist Internationals, the Zionist Organization, and the place to be accorded to the movement's activities in Ereẓ Israel. One faction (the Left Po'alei Zion) sought unconditional affiliation with the Third International (the Comintern); by 1924 it had abandoned this attempt and reorganized itself on an independent basis. The other faction, the Right Po'alei Zion, merged in 1925 with the Zionist Socialists (Z.S.) and in 1932 joined with Hitaḥadut in founding the Iḥud Olami (see *World Labor Zionist Movement).

In Russia. At the turn of the century, societies bearing the name Po'alei Zion were founded in various places in the *Pale of Settlement, largely independent of one another. Some of these societies were made up of Jewish workers affiliated with the general Zionist movement, while others were composed of Zionists who seceded from the Russian Social Democratic Party or from the *Bund, particularly when the latter adopted (1901) a resolution declaring membership in the Zionist Organization incompatible with membership in the Bund. The Zionist workers and wage earners who were thus compelled to leave the Bund also had to renounce membership in the trade unions sponsored by it and, as a result, had to establish their own trade unions.

In the years 1901–03, many Po'alei Zion societies were founded in the northwestern part of the Pale of Settlement (e.g., in Vilna, Dvinsk, and Vitebsk) and in southern Russia (Yekaterinoslav, Odessa, Poltava) and one was founded in Warsaw. All these societies shared the view that the economic problem of the Jews in general and the Jewish workers in particular was of a special nature and could be solved only by means of their territorial concentration in Ereẓ Israel. Only there could a Jewish socialist society be established. They differed, however, on the immediate program for action on the local scene. Thus, the leading Po'alei Zion group of that time, the Minsk group, advocated the restriction of local activities to the economic interests of the workers and confined its political and ideological struggle to the World Zionist Organization, where it posed special demands on behalf of the Jewish workers. Other societies called for active participation in the revolutionary struggle in Russia and cooperation with the non-Jewish revolutionary parties. The latter trend was strengthened by the 1903 Kishinev pogrom, in the wake of which Po'alei Zion societies also organized for Jewish self-defense. Another difference among the various societies emerged in the period 1903–05 over the question of *Territorialism. By the end of 1904 the Territorialists had achieved a measure of consolidation (they were later joined by the Minsk group), and at the Seventh Zionist Congress in 1905 they appeared as an independent faction, separate from the "Palestine-oriented" Po'alei Zion. Assuming the name of Zionist-Socialist Workers' Party (for short S.S., according to their Russian name, "Sionisty-Sotsialisty"), they wielded considerable influence on the Jewish population during the 1905 Russian revolution.

Another split occurred in the remaining Palestine-oriented faction of Po'alei Zion at the Seventh Congress, when a new party arose in its midst, advocating emphasis on the development of Jewish life in the Diaspora within an autonomous framework. The faction had its origin in an ideological group founded in 1903 called Vozrozdheniye (Renascence); as a party, it took on the name Jewish Socialist Workers' Party. In 1906, under the leadership of Ber *Borochov, the Jewish Social Democratic Workers' Party Po'alei Zion came into being; it continued to adhere to the idea of the territorial concentration of the Jewish people in Ereẓ Israel. Borochov's approach was based upon an analysis of objective processes in the economic condition of Jewish life that pressed for mass emigration and territorial concentration; it was also founded upon the principle of the class struggle, for which a sound basis could be established only in Ereẓ Israel. Two trends existed within this group of Po'alei Zion: one regarding settlement in Ereẓ Israel only as the outcome of an objective historical process (the "Prognosticists"), the other supporting concentrated mass settlement in Ereẓ Israel and nowhere else as a matter of principle (the "Principlers"). Within the latter group a small movement of *ḥalutzim* for Ereẓ Israel developed.

Po'alei Zion in Russia advocated boycotting the elections to the First Duma. Later it changed its attitude and actively participated in the elections to the Second Duma. The laws regulating the election to the Second Duma were less favorable, however, than those for the first, and Po'alei Zion nominees reached only the stage of electors. The political reaction in Russia after 1906 resulted in the almost complete dissolution of Po'alei Zion. Like other movements, it was outlawed, and its leaders were either arrested and exiled or emigrated from the country. Out of a membership of about 25,000 in 1905, only 300 were left, who were organized in clandestine groups. The movement took a turn to the left and in 1909 decided to secede from the Zionist Organization and the Zionist Congress. In the last prewar years, its activities were confined to modest efforts in trade unionism and propaganda.

In the Austro-Hungarian Empire. At the end of the 19th century, various groups made up of Jewish workers and employees who were members of the Zionist movement came into being. They resulted from the efforts of the Zionist Organization to recruit Jewish workers to its cause, as well as the feeling among Jewish workers that the Austrian Social Democratic Party showed no understanding for their special needs. The spokesman for this group was S. R. *Landau. At the Second Zionist Congress he demanded that Jewish workers be allowed the right to organize into groups of their own and of separate representation in the Zionist bodies; he also became the editor of *Der juedische Arbeiter.* This scheme of independent organization met with fierce opposition on the part of the Austrian and German Social Democratic parties. In June 1903 the Galician groups established a Federation of Zionist Employees' and Workers' Groups in Galicia. The federation was influenced by the Zionist Socialist groups led by Nachman *Syrkin and by the Zionist Workers' Groups of Vienna and their publication, *Der juedische Arbeiter.*

Led by Shlomo *Kaplansky and Nathan *Gross, the Vienna groups initiated the establishment of a Po'alei Zion Federation in Austria. As its name indicated, the federation was to be composed of workers who were Zionists, without, however, committing itself to any detailed ideology. The first conference took place in May 1904 and was attended by 37 delegates, representing 2,000 members. It decided to form an organization that was to function as both a political party and a trade union. At its second conference (June 1905) the new party decided to accept the discipline of the Zionist Organization in all Zionist matters, while retaining its independence in labor matters. Zionism and the class struggle were to be regarded as being of equal importance; membership in the party was to be incompatible with membership in any other party or trade union. The conference also adopted the party's own program for activities within the Zionist Organization; it called for cooperative settlement in Ereẓ Israel (along the lines proposed by Franz *Oppenheimer) as a means of expressing the special interests of the workers in the Zionist movement.

It was not until the third conference (October 1906) that the Austrian Po'alei Zion adopted a clearly defined socialist program and assumed the name of Jewish Socialist Workers' Party Po'alei Zion. The conference also decided to secede from the Austrian Zionist Organization and demand that Po'alei Zion be accorded the status of an autonomous federation in the World Zionist Organization. This move resulted in several groups of Zionist intellectuals leaving the party. The Austrian Po'alei Zion did not, however, emulate the Russian party of that name when the latter decided to secede from the World Zionist Organization in 1909. In 1910 the party ran into difficulties in maintaining its function as a trade union, when the Congress of the International in Copenhagen decided that there was to be a single trade union for each country. When the Jewish National Party was founded in Austria in 1907 as a pro-Zionist list for the elections to parliament, Po'alei Zion did not join; in the parliamentary elections, however, it recommended that its members give preference to candidates of the Jewish National Party over Social Democratic candidates. In the 1910 census, Po'alei Zion urged Jews to list Yiddish as their national language (although it was not included in the census questionnaire). It also developed a program for the Jewish community councils from 1908 onward and presented its own lists for the council elections.

In the United States. Po'alei Zion came into being in the United States in 1903 as an offshoot of the Russian groups. It differed from the existing Jewish socialist organizations by emphasizing the need for Jewish national activities and by supporting the Zionist *Basle Program. There were two influences at work among the U.S. Po'alei Zion: the ideas imported by the continued immigration from Russia and the ideologically more relaxed atmosphere prevailing in the United States, much less doctrinaire in its approach than that in Europe. The first conference of Po'alei Zion groups in the U.S. took place in 1905. It brought about no concrete results, in view of a split between the Territorialists (who were in the majority) and the supporters of Ereẓ Israel. At the end of 1905, however, a Jewish Socialist Party Po'alei Zion came into being in the U.S. and Canada, and the following year the party founded its own newspaper, *Der Yidisher Kemfer*. The failure of the efforts to find a territory other than Ereẓ Israel, as well as the revolution of the Young Turks in Constantinople, persuaded the Territorialists to join the party, led by Syrkin and Baruch *Zuckerman (1909). This move was preceded by a slight change in the party's platform to include "neighboring countries," in addition to Ereẓ Israel itself, as possible areas of settlement.

The U.S. Po'alei Zion, like its Austrian counterpart, stood for cooperation with non-labor Zionists. They founded Aḥavah, a society for the creation of cooperative settlements and garden towns in Ereẓ Israel; contributed to the Zionist funds; and supported labor enterprises in Ereẓ Israel, including the periodicals **Ha-Aḥdut* and **Ha-Shomer*. On the local scene, Po'alei Zion engaged in a variety of activities, founding the Yidisher Natsionaler Arbeter Farband (a mutual aid society) and a network of "national-radical" schools. During World War I, the U.S. Po'alei Zion became the center of activities for the entire movement. Upon the initiative of Syrkin and Borochov, it sponsored the movement for the establishment of a Jewish Congress and the creation of the *He-Ḥalutz movement and supported the drive for volunteers to the *Jewish Legion battalions, led by Yizhak *Ben-Zvi and David *Ben-Gurion.

In Ereẓ Israel. The Po'alei Zion Party in Ereẓ Israel came into being from various Po'alei Zion groups composed of immigrants who had come from Russia starting with the Second *Aliyah. There were differences among them in the wording of their ideological approach to Ereẓ Israel and the Hebrew language. The party was founded in 1906 and consolidated in 1907 under the leadership of Ben-Zvi. It advocated the class struggle and organized trade unions and strikes (one at the Rishon le-Zion wine cellars in 1907 and another in the Jerusalem printing trade in 1909). Its first newspaper, *Onfang*, was published in Yiddish. After the Young Turks came to power in 1908, the party became interested in political activities in the Ottoman Empire and among its Jewish communities and supported the nonpartisan organization of Jewish agricultural workers and the cooperative enterprises sponsored by the Zionist Organization. In 1910 it founded a Hebrew newspaper, *Aḥdut*, and at its sixth conference made a significant change in its platform by renouncing the postulate that the class struggle is the sole means of creating the national center of the Jewish people in Ereẓ Israel. Po'alei Zion in Ereẓ Israel grew away from the mother party in Russia and from the Bolshevist ideology. It no longer relied on the spontaneous uprising of the proletariat and the spontaneous creation of a cooperative economy which would provide the proletariat with work. It began to support the constructive activities of the Zionist Organization and to demand practical activity on the part of the World Union. A sharp debate was caused by the decision of the World Union of Po'alei Zion to establish an Ereẓ Israel Workers' Fund and an Ereẓ Israel Labor Office, centering on the question of who should have the authority over the two institutions. Po'alei Zion in Ereẓ Israel also encouraged the arming of the Jewish settlers and took the *Ha-Shomer organization under its wing. The party in Ereẓ Israel did not want the institutions to be directed by the World Union, and the Association of Agricultural Workers and Ha-Po'el ha-Ẓa'ir Party rejected the idea of intervention by a party factor. Po'alei Zion was forced to take into consideration the position of a large portion of the workers and to reduce the scope of the fund and the labor bureau's activities.

The World Union. The World Socialist Union of Jewish workers–Po'alei Zion was founded in 1907 in The Hague, where its first conference was held, following the Eighth Zionist Congress. It was recognized by the Zionist Organization as a "special federation," a step which ensured the status of the Po'alei Zion parties in various countries that were not affiliated with the local Zionist bodies. The World Union wished to conduct its own work in Ereẓ Israel, and at its second conference, held in Cracow in 1909, it decided to establish an Ereẓ Israel Workers' Fund (Kuppat Po'alei Ereẓ Israel—for short Kappai) "to further the emigration of Jewish workers and their settlement in Ereẓ Israel." At its third conference (Vienna, July 1911), the World Union decided to establish its own information office in Ereẓ Israel to be financed by the Workers' Fund. The World Union also defined the party's political attitude toward the Ottoman Empire and the direction of its activities among the Ottoman proletariat. It dealt with problems of Jewish workers in the Diaspora, especially in connection with emigration and finding employment (productivization) and supported the public protest against the methods employed by the *Jewish Colonization Association (ICA) in the Jewish agricultural settlements in Argentina.

The World Union also took up the struggle of the Russian, Austrian, and American Po'alei Zion parties, begun in 1907, toward achieving independent representation in the Socialist International. It called for national Jewish representation on a worldwide basis, independent of the national socialist parties. In 1910 it was joined in this demand by the Russian Zionist Socialists (S.S.) and the Sejmists (see *Jewish Socialist Workers' Party) and together they addressed a memorandum on this subject to the International (1911), which did not elicit a favorable reply. The Po'alei Zion World Union abstained from participating in the work of the Zionist Executive, and at the Zionist congresses stressed the need for practical work in Ereẓ Israel, with special emphasis on cooperative enterprises. It supported the idea of creating national farming estates, opposed the use of the means of the *Jewish National Fund (JNF) for private noncooperative settlement, and criticized the proposals for the establishment of a university in Ereẓ Israel.

The fourth conference (1913) was marked by ideological differences between a leftist group, led by Borochov, and the Austrian and U.S. parties (with which the Ereẓ Israel party also associated itself). The former called for organization on a class basis and a determined class struggle, as well as dissociation from the Zionist Organization, while the latter supported active partnership with the Zionist Organization in the creation of cooperative enterprises in Ereẓ Israel.

During World War I. The World Union of Po'alei Zion maintained its headquarters in The Hague (1915–16) and Stockholm (1917–19) during World War I. By that time it was accorded representation on the Socialist International, although technically it represented the Ereẓ Israel party. Its main activity was explaining the special situation of the Jews in the war and formulating Jewish demands for the postwar peace conference. Thus, as a result of the World Union's efforts, the Netherlands-Scandinavian socialist peace committee included in 1917 in its proposals a demand for international responsibility for the Jewish problem, the personal autonomy of Jews in the areas where they were settled in large numbers (Russia, Austria, Rumania, and Poland), and protection of Jewish settlement in Ereẓ Israel. After the war the World Union became a full-fledged member of the Socialist Conferences (Berne, 1919). The steering committee of the Socialist International at Amsterdam adopted in April 1919 a Po'alei Zion-sponsored resolution affirming the right of the Jewish people to a national life of its own in Ereẓ Israel under League of Nations auspices and with the safeguarding of the interests of the non-Jewish population. It also demanded the protection of civil rights and national minority rights for the Jews in the Diaspora, the freedom to emigrate, and Jewish representation at the League of Nations.

Po'alei Zion also stood in the forefront of the Jewish Congress movement in the U.S. during World War I to formulate Jewish demands for autonomous rights in the Diaspora, and organized assemblies of Jewish workers to draft the demands concerning Ereẓ Israel. Following the war, the membership of the parties in the World Union began to grow. Before the war there were approximately 600 members in Russia, 1,000 in Austria, 1,200 in the United States, 100 in England, and 200 in Ereẓ Israel. After the war it was estimated that there were 15,000 members in Poland, 1,000 in Lithuania, 800 in German Austria, 2,000 in Czechoslovakia, 4,000 in east Galicia, 4,500 in the United States, 1,200 in Argentina, 500 in Germany, 1,000 in England, and 2,200 in Aḥdut ha-Avodah in Ereẓ Israel. In addition there were a number of small parties in Estonia, Belgium, South Africa, Egypt, and Siberia. In total, there were 30,000 members outside Russia, and the number inside Russia was estimated between 10,000 and 20,000. The splits around 1920, however, weakened the movement and reduced the number of its members. The momentous events that took place during the war sharpened the differences in outlook that had existed before it inside the movement. The Po'alei Zion party in each country was confronted by questions of principle and had to find its own answers. Thus the Ereẓ Israel party had to deal with the question of political orientation—between loyalty to the Ottoman regime and support for the Allies—and enlistment in the Jewish Legion; its vast majority abandoned internationalism and advocated enlistment in the Legion. For the Russian party, at first, it was the attitude toward the war that was at stake, and, later on, the attitude toward the two revolutions of 1917. The October Revolution caused a split in the Russian Po'alei Zion; on local questions it was close to Bolshevik ideology, whereas on the issue of Ereẓ Israel it supported the idea of "class Zionism." At the end of 1917, a faction calling itself Radical Po'alei Zion, centered in Odessa, split from the party and advocated cooperation with the Zionist Organization and the fostering of Hebrew. Another faction emerged in 1919, demanding total identification with the Bolsheviks and advocating postponement of the Zionist program until after the socialist revolution had been accomplished; it called itself the Jewish Communist Party-Po'alei Zion (JCP). The majority of the party in Russia (Po'alei Zion-Social Democrats) regarded the revolution as a long drawn-out process and rejected the postponement of Zionism.

Postwar Developments. In Ereẓ Israel, the Po'alei Zion party merged after the war with the nonparty Independents, which included most of the membership of the Federation of Agricultural Workers, and formed the Zionist-Socialist Union of Ereẓ Israel Workers—*Aḥdut ha-Avodah. This was both a political and economic organization. It regarded the creation of a national economy in Ereẓ Israel, based on labor economy, as its main task and did not put the emphasis on the class struggle. A small faction, which opposed the merger and did not agree to the abandonment of the class struggle and of Yiddish, established its own party, the Socialist Workers' Party (Mifleget Po'alim Soẓyalistim—MPS), which became the first nucleus of the Palestine Communist Party. In the course of time, the radicalization of this party along Communist lines and its abandonment of the ideals of Zionism proved to be intolerable for a group of its members. This group was headed by Abraham *Revusky, who proceeded to establish a preparatory committee for the reestablishment of a Po'alei Zion Party in Ereẓ Israel.

The World Union of Po'alei Zion resumed its activities in the Zionist Organization in 1919. A council meeting held in Stockholm in August 1919 elected a commission to visit Ereẓ Israel and draw up a plan to develop the country along socialist lines. The commission, which spent some time in Ereẓ Israel at the beginning of 1920 was unable to arrive at an agreed report; its differences reflected the range of opinions among the various parties in the World Union. The fifth conference of the World Union, which met in Vienna in July 1920, was to consider the differences among the various member parties. It split over the issue of joining the Third (Communist) International, 178 delegates voting in favor and 179 abstaining. All efforts of the abstaining delegates to heal the breach were unsuccessful. They claimed that the Third International was liable to prevent the independent development of Ereẓ Israel and ties with the Zionist organization and the Jewish people. Some of them objected to the exclusive nature of the Russian approach to Communism and demanded the unification of all the revolutionary parties (an attitude near to that of the "Two and a Half International"); they held that only the speedy initiation of the Jewish people in Ereẓ Israel would ensure the survival of Zionism after the expected world revolution was achieved. The left World Union was composed of leftist parties only, which opposed any connection with the Zionist Organization and held that only by cooperation with the world revolution would Zionism stand a chance of realization. The parties which supported this stand were those of Russia, Czechoslovakia, Austria, and Poland (the last being the largest). The right wing held the majority in the U.S., Argentine, British, and Ereẓ Israel parties. It decided to engage in practical work in the upbuilding of Ereẓ Israel on a cooperative basis, which would ensure the growth and development of the Jewish working class. It became the mainstream of the Zionist labor movement, whereas the World Union gradually dwindled due to Communist secession. The right-wing leaders abroad were Shelomo *Kaplansky, Marc *Yarblum, Zalman Rubashov (*Shazar), and Berl *Locker; in Ereẓ Israel they were Ben-Gurion, Ben-Zvi, and Yiẓhak *Tabenkin. The left-wing leaders in Ereẓ Israel were Nahum *Nir (Rafalkes) and Jacob *Zerubavel.

The right wing, which opposed joining the Third International, also left the Second International. It joined the Viennese "Two-and-a-half" International and in 1923 returned to the Socialist International, together with the latter. It also participated actively in the Zionist Organization, despite the reservations of a number of its member parties. It engaged in political activities in the International and within the British Labor Party, to which Po'alei Zion in Britain belonged from 1920. In its activities on behalf of Ereẓ Israel, the right wing succeeded in obtaining the cooperation of other Zionist labor parties, and in August 1923 it convened a conference for Ereẓ Israel labor and established a league for practical activities. The common sphere of Zionist activities led to a convergence between the World Union of Po'alei Zion and the Zionist-Socialist Union, and after difficult negotiations, especially over the question of the status of the Yiddish language, the two unions merged in August 1925, adopting the name the Socialist World Jewish Workers' Party Po'alei Zion (united with the Zionist Socialist Union). Following the merger between Ha-Po'el ha-Ẓa'ir and Aḥdut ha-Avodah in Ereẓ Israel in 1930, a united world movement, called Ha-Iḥud ha-Olami, was founded in Danzig in 1932; it was composed of the Union of Socialist Jewish Workers'–Po'alei Zion (united with Z.S.) and the World Zionist Labor Party—Hitaḥdut.

The second congress of the Third International, which was attended by a representative of the Ereẓ Israel leftist Po'alei Zion (appearing on behalf of MPS), adopted not only the famous 21 rules which had to be accepted by any party seeking admission to the Comintern but also an anti-Zionist resolution. The bureau of the left-wing World Union of Po'alei Zion decided to accept the 21 rules, adopted the name of Jewish Communist Union Po'alei Zion, and applied for admission to the Third International. The Comintern, however, rejected the application out of opposition to the principle of a world union and of territorial concentration in Ereẓ Israel, and demanded that members of the Jewish Communist Union join individually the respective Communist parties in various countries. Nevertheless, it sought to make use of the union in order to gain influence among Jewish workers and prolonged the negotiations with it.

The sixth conference of the World Union, held in Danzig in June 1922, rejected the Comintern demands and insisted upon its right to independent organization and to maintain its Ereẓ Israel program, but declared itself an integral part of the World Communist Movement. As a result, the Social Democratic Po'alei Zion in Russia and the Revusky group in Ereẓ Israel left the World Union and in 1923 formed the Organizing Committee of the Left Po'alei Zion in Berlin. In the following two years most of the remaining parties in the World Union disintegrated, joining local Communist parties. The Russian "Jewish Communist Party Po'alei Zion" was liquidated, whereas the Social Democratic faction of Po'alei Zion there changed its name to the Jewish Communist Workers' Party Po'alei Zion and had a technically legal existence until 1928. In Austria and Czechoslovakia the left Po'alei Zion joined the local Communist parties. Thus only the Polish party was left as a major party in the World Union. A renewal of the left World Union took place in Paris in 1926 (the seventh conference), and it included the Revusky group. It adopted the name World Communist Union of Jewish Workers Po'alei Zion, continued to oppose association with the Zionist Organization and the He-Ḥalutz movement, and maintained the belief that in the course of time it would be able to join the Comintern.

The left Po'alei Zion Party in Ereẓ Israel had been renewed in 1923 and was based on the Revusky group and former members of the Social Democratic Po'alei Zion in Russia. Within the *Histadrut they opposed the exclusion of Arab workers from the general framework and demanded separation of trade-union from cooperative activities. In 1923 the Polish party also began to establish a Po'alei Zion Party in Ereẓ Israel. Israel Washer was sent to organize it. The two groups merged in 1924. Four years later another split occurred in the Ereẓ Israel left Po'alei Zion when a group led by Yiẓḥak and Ze'ev Abramovitz seceded from the majority group led by Nir (Rafalkes) and Moshe Erem over the issue of Hebrew versus Yiddish (opposing the Yiddishist attitude prevailing in the World Union). They were reunited in 1931, only to split again in 1934 over the question of *aliyah,* pioneering youth movements, and He-Ḥalutz. In the same year, however, the ninth world conference adopted a more positive stand on He-Ḥalutz; but only the tenth conference, held in 1937, decided to rejoin the Zionist Congress. Further differences in the party arose over the attitude toward World War II, and they were settled only when the Soviet Union entered the war in 1941. In 1944 the left Po'alei Zion in Ereẓ Israel joined with *Ha-Shomer ha-Ẓa'ir in the Left Front in the elections to the *yishuv* institutions (Asefat ha-Nivḥarim and Va'ad Le'ummi). Then, in 1946, it united with the opposition group of *Mapai, Si'ah Bet, which seceded from Mapai in 1944 and formed an independent party, Ha-Tenu'ah le-Aḥadut ha-Avodah. The united party was called Ha-Tenu'ah le-Aḥadut ha-Avodah–Po'alei Zion. This party joined *Mapam in 1948 and remerged in 1954 with the split in Mapam. In 1968 it joined Mapai and *Rafi to form the Israel Labor Party. Its Diaspora groups joined the World Zionist Labor movement, which was largely based on the Iḥud Olami previously centered on Mapai.

Bibliography: Po'alei Zion, America, *The Aims of Jewish Labor* (1918); B. Sherman, *Labor Zionism in America* (1957); B. Zuckerman et al., *Geshikhte fun der Tsionistisher Arbeter Bavegung,* 2 vols. (1955); M. Braslavsky, *Tenu'at ha-Po'alim ha-Ereẓ Yisre'elit,* 4 vols. (1955–63); Z. Even-Shoshan, *Toledot Tenu'at ha-Po'alim be-Ereẓ Yisrael* (1955); S. Eisenstadt, *Perakim be-Toledot Tenu'at ha-Po'alim ha-Yehudit,* 1970; A. Tartakower, *Toledot Tenu'at ha-Ovedim ha-Yehudit,* 3 vols. (1929–31); I. Ben-Zvi, *Po'alei-Ẓiyyon ba-Aliyyah ha-Sheniyyah* (1950); idem, *Ketavim,* 1 (1936); L. Shpeizman, *Geshikhte fun der Tsiyonistisher Arbeter Bavegung in Tsfon Amerike* (1955); N. M. Gelber, *Toledot ha-Tenu'ah ha-Ẓiyyonit be-Galiẓyah* (1958); Z. Abramowitsch, *Be-Sherut ha-Tenu'ah* (1965); N. Nir (Rafalkes), *Pirkei Ḥayyim 1884–1918* (1958); R. Yannait-Ben Zvi, *Coming Home* (1963); Z. Shazar, *Kokhevei Boker* (1961[6]); idem, *Or Ishim* (1963[2]); N. Syrkin, in: *Ketavim,* 1 (1939); B. Borochow, in: *Ketavim,* 1–3 (1955–66); S. Kaplansky, *Ḥazon ve-Hagshamah* (1950); Z. Abramowitsch et al. (eds.), *Yalkut Po'alei Zion* (1947). [I.Ko.]

°**POBEDONOSTSEV, KONSTANTIN PETROVICH** (1827–1907), Russian statesman and jurist. From 1860 until 1865 he was professor of civil law at the university of Moscow. During the years 1880 to 1905, Pobedonostsev acted as "Supreme Prosecutor of the Holy Synod," a function which resembled that of minister of religious affairs, except that his behind-the-scenes influence on the czar and the government greatly surpassed his official responsibilities. Pobedonostsev fostered the idea of maintaining a regime of absolute power, with the support of the police and the Church, and strove for the Russification of all the peoples of Russia. Under his influence the Synod intensified its persecutions of the sects that had broken away from the official Church as well as other religions. In 1905, with the partial victories of the revolutionary movement and the limitations on the czar's absolute power, Pobedonostsev resigned from his duties. His hatred of the Jews stemmed from the belief that, because the Jews were a more talented people than the Russians, it was likely that in time they would dominate the latter both materially and intellectually.

Pobedonostsev supported the anti-Jewish legislation ("*May Laws") of 1882, and the law of 1887 limiting the percentage of Jews in schools, and he rejected decisions of the Pahlen Commission of 1887 which might be considered favorable to Jews. In 1891 he supported the program of Baron *Hirsch for the emigration of 3,000,000 Jews from Russia within 25 years. He objected to the idea that the *Jewish Colonization Association (I.C.A.) be granted authorization to settle Jews on land within the Russian Empire. The famous remark concerning the fate of the Jews of Russia, i.e., "One-third will die, one-third will leave the country, and the last third will be completely assimilated within the Russian people" has been attributed to Pobedonostsev. Collections of his letters and other writings which reveal much of his thought have been published (e.g., *K. P. Pobedonostsev i yego korrespondenty*; 1923). In addition, *Reflections of a Russian Statesman* (1898) was also published.

Bibliography: A. V. Amfiteatrov, *Pobedonostsev* (Rus., 1907). [Y.S.]

POBEZOVICE NA SUMAVE (Czech **Pobežovice na Šumavě**; Ger. **Ronsperg**), village in W. Bohemia. The Jewish community there apparently existed in the 16th century, although the first documentary mention is not until 1664. Until the beginning of the 19th century it was the seat of the district rabbi for *Pilsen and *Klatovy, an office held by Falk Kohner, Samuel Kohn-Kostelhore, and Eleasar *Loew (1810–12). In 1724 there were 17 Jewish families in Pobezovice. The synagogue—the third in Pobezovice—was built in 1816 on the initiative of R. Joel, father of R. Bezalel *Ranshburg. Great interest was aroused in 1927 by the discovery, in the *mikveh*, of a stone bearing a Hebrew inscription reporting that *Israel b. Eliezer Ba'al Shem Tov had bathed there and pronounced the waters salutary. Consequently, Ḥasidim went there to seek cures. An extract from the confiscated *pinkas* (1773) records a tradition about the community's destruction in 1096, describes *Shabbatean and *Frankist activities, and mentions the visit of the Ba'al Shem Tov in 1744. Pobezovice was the birthplace of R. Moses Loeb Bloch and the pharmacologist Emil *Starkenstein, and the residence of Heinrich *Coudenhove-Kalergi, whose library of Judaica was deposited in the synagogue. The Jewish population declined from 212 persons in 1848 to 193 in 1893, 63 in 1921, and 41 (2% of the total population) in 1930. With the annexation of the Sudeten area by Germany in 1938, almost the entire community fled, the remaining few being expelled to no-man's-land. The synagogue was burnt down on Nov. 10, 1938, and the cemetery was destroyed.

Bibliography: M. Gold, *Die Juden und Judengemeinden Boehmens in Vergangenheit und Gegenwart* (1934), 575–6; B'nai B'rith, *Monatsblaetter ... des čechoslowakischen Staats*, 6 (1927), 320–8; 7 (1928), 40–48; *Selbstwehr* (Sept. 9, 1927). [M.La.]

POCHEP, city in Bryansk oblast, Russian S.F.S.R. Before the 1917 Revolution, Pochep was in the province of Chernigov in the *Pale of Settlement. There were 3,172 Jews (about 33% of the total population) living in Pochep in 1897. The *Ḥabad yeshivah in the town was headed by the local rabbi Joshua Nathan Gnessin. Among the yeshivah students were his son Uri Nissan *Gnessin and J. Ḥ. *Brenner. Jews numbered 3,616 (27.1% of the population) in 1926. When the Germans invaded Russia in the summer of 1941, those Jews who did not succeed in escaping from Pochep were murdered. [Y.S.]

°**POCOCKE, EDWARD** (1604–1691), English orientalist and Hebraist. In 1630–36, as Anglican chaplain to the English merchants in Aleppo, Syria, Pococke was able to perfect his knowledge of Arabic, Syriac, and Ethiopic, to translate Arab historical works, and to collect the Greek and oriental manuscripts (bought with funds provided by Archbishop William Laud) which now constitute the Pococke collection in the Bodleian Library at Oxford. On his return to England in 1636 Pococke was appointed to a chair of Arabic at Oxford especially created for him by Laud. In 1640 Pococke found himself almost dispossessed because of his royalist sympathies and friendship with the unpopular archbishop. However, the eminent Puritan Hebraist John *Selden befriended Pococke, who was reappointed to the chair of Arabic at Oxford in 1647; in the following year he was also made regius professor of Hebrew and canon of Christ Church.

Pococke was an outstanding English Hebraist and one of the leading orientalists of the age. His share in the preparation of Bryan *Walton's London Polyglot Bible (1657) was unmatched by any other editor: he prepared the Arabic text of the Pentateuch; provided manuscript texts of the Syriac Old Testament, the Ethiopic version of Psalms, and two Syriac manuscripts of Psalms; and also prepared parts of the Syriac New Testament with annotations and a Latin translation. Pococke's biblical scholarship may also be gauged from other works, such as his English commentaries on some of the Minor Prophets (Micah and Malachi, 1677; Hosea, 1685; Joel, 1691), which display familiarity with rabbinic exegesis and wide knowledge of Christian commentators (*Calvin, *Muenster, *Pellicanus). Among his other notable works are two translations of *Maimonides: *Porta Mosis* (Oxford, 1655), an annotated edition of six sections of the Mishnah commentary with the Arabic text in Hebrew characters and a Latin translation (this was the first Hebrew book printed in Oxford and at the university's expense); and a Latin version of Maimonides' preface to the Mishnah (Oxford, 1690). Pococke also cultivated friendly relations with Jews in the East (he studied with Judah Romano in Constantinople).

Of his two sons, the elder, Edward Pococke (b. 1647), was also an orientalist; the younger, Thomas Pococke, issued an English translation of *Manasseh Ben Israel's treatise *De termino vitae* on free will and predestination, entitled *Of the Term of Life ... with the Sense of the Jewish Doctors* (London, 1699).

Bibliography: L. Twells, in: E. Pococke, *Theological Works* (1740); G. H. Box, in: E. R. Bevan and C. Singer (eds.), *Legacy of Israel* (1927), 353–5; DNB, 16 (repr. 1921–22), 7–12; C. Roth, in: *Bodleian Library Record*, 2 no. 27 (1948), 215–9; I. Abrahams, in: JHSET, 8 (1915–17), 105. [G.E.S.]

°**POCOCKE, RICHARD** (1704–1765), British ecclesiastic and traveler. From 1735 to 1742 he traveled extensively in the Near East, visiting Ereẓ Israel in 1738. He spent some time in Jerusalem, visited the Dead Sea in order to check Pliny's account of it, and journeyed along the Mediterranean coast to Galilee, from there going to the Lebanon, Baalbek, and Cyprus. These travels resulted in the *Description of the East and some other Countries* (2 vols., London, 1743–45), with numerous copperplate engravings. He was a good observer and the plans he made of the various sites are numerous, although not very reliable. He had a preference for less-traveled routes, which enhances the value of his journeys. He was appointed archdeacon of Dublin in 1745 and bishop of Ossory in 1756. [M.A.-Y.]

PODGAITSY (Pol. **Podhajce**), city, W. Tarnopol oblast, Ukrainian S.S.R. A Jewish community existed in Podgaitsy during the 16th century. At the beginning of the 17th century the rabbinical seat was held by Benjamin Aaron b. Abraham Solnik, who died in 1610. He published a collection of 112 responsa and legal novellae in his work *Masat Binyamin*. After the invasion of the town by the Tatars in 1667 and the massacre which they perpetrated among the Jews, R. Ze'ev b. Judah Leib wrote an elegy in memory of the victims. According to the census of 1764 there were 1,079 Jews. During the 19th century, under Austrian rule, the Jewish population increased, and by 1910 numbered about 6,000. However, Podgaitsy's importance subsequently declined and according to the census of 1931 only 2,872 Jews were left. [Sh.L.K.]

Holocaust Period. When war broke out between Germany and the U.S.S.R. (June 22, 1941), Podgaitsy was occupied by the Germans, and the Jews immediately became victims of attacks by the Ukrainian population. They were forced to pay fines, their movement was restricted outside the city, and they were subjected to forced labor.

L. Lilenfeld headed the *Judenrat. In the winter of 1941/42 many died from hunger and disease. On Sept. 21, 1942, over 1,000 Jews were sent to the *Belzec death camp, and on October 30, 1,500 people were sent there. Survivors of the community tried to find shelter in neighboring forests; due to informers, however, many fell into German hands and were executed. On June 6, 1943, the community was completely liquidated and the ghetto and the city were declared *judenrein*. After the war the community was not reconstituted. [Ar.W.]

PODHORETZ, NORMAN (1930–), U.S. editor and author. Born in Brooklyn, Podhoretz was educated at Columbia, the Jewish Theological Seminary, and Cambridge University, England. In 1960 he became editor of **Commentary*, which, under his direction, is one of the chief intellectual forums in the United States. A distinguished literary critic, Podhoretz published *Doings and Undoings: The Fifties and After in American Writing* (1964); *The Commentary Reader* (1968); and the autobiographical *Making It* (1968). The last book describes the New York literary scene after World War II, as well as the psychological drives that brought Podhoretz to his important position in American literary life at a relatively youthful age.

Bibliography: *Current Biography Yearbook 1968* (1969), 319–22.

[M.H.H.]

PODKAMEN, town in Lvov oblast, Ukrainian S.S.R. A Jewish community existed in Podkamen in the 17th century at the time of the Council of the Four Lands, when the town was within the province of "Russia." During the 18th century its rabbinical seat was held by Ḥayyim Segal Landa, who also played a role in the Council of the Four Lands. In 1765 there were 922 Jews living in the town. During the 19th century its Jewish population increased. By 1910 it numbered 2,000 persons. As a result of World War I, it decreased to 822 (or about 27.4% of the population) in 1921. In spite of this decline, the Jewish community maintained an active public life. In the elections to the communal organization in 1932, the delegate of the Zionists was elected to the presidency. There was a Hebrew school in the town and a home for Jewish orphans. [Sh.L.K.]

Holocaust Period. At the outbreak of World War II there were about 1,000 Jews in Podkamen. The first *Aktion* took place in August 1942, and the second at the end of September. The Jewish community was liquidated on Dec. 3, 1942, when the remaining Jews were deported to *Brody and shared the fate of that community. After the war the Jewish community of Podkamen was not reconstituted.

[Ed.]

PODOLIA, region in S. W. Ukrainian S.S.R.; formerly a region of S.E. Poland, passed to Russia in 1793. The history of the Jews in the region was largely dominated by its position as a border territory between Poland-Lithuania and the Ottoman Empire. *Medzibozh, the most ancient community in Podolia, is first mentioned in 1518. On the eve of the Union of Lublin between Lithuania and Poland (1569), there were at least 750 Jews living in nine communities of Podolia, about half of them in Medzibezh. Under Polish rule Jews took part in the settlement of Podolia, though not at the same pace and extent as in neighboring regions. In many places the settlement of Jews met with opposition on the ground that their presence as a foreign element was undesirable within the vicinity of the Ottoman Empire (see *Kamenets-Podolski). In 1639 Jews of Podolia were granted the right to have lawsuits with Christians tried before the provincial governor *(wojewoda)*. There were then 18 communities in the region, of which the most important were *Nemirov, *Tulchin, *Bar, and Medzibozh. Yom Tov Lippmann *Heller was rabbi in Nemirov.

On the eve of the *Chmielnicki uprising of 1648 there were 4,000 Jews in Podolia. During this period numbers of Jews there were massacred in Nemirov, Tulchin, Bar, and other communities. Thousands of Jews from Podolia and other regions of Ukraine took refuge in the fortified city of Kamenets-Podolski, where in ordinary times Jewish residence was forbidden.

Under Ottoman rule in Podolia (1672–99) the Jews enjoyed the same rights and protection as the rest of the Jews in the empire. With the return of Polish rule in Podolia, their situation again deteriorated, and it was only in 1713 that they regained the right to bring lawsuits before the provincial governor. In 1765 the Jews of Podolia numbered 38,365. Some communities of northern and eastern Podolia suffered severely at the hands of the *Haidamacks.

With the first partition of Poland in 1772, the region of "Red Russia," where about one-third of Podolian Jewry lived, was annexed by Austria and became an integral part of *Galicia. In 1787 there were 25,438 Jews in the rest of Podolia living in about 60 towns and 853 villages. The Jews there at the time earned their livelihood by trading, as innkeepers, and especially by **arenda*, which was almost entirely in Jewish hands. The proximity of Podolia to the territories dominated by Turkey, and the commercial relations between the Jews and their coreligionists in the Balkans and Turkey, resulted in the spread of kabbalistic teachings in Podolia during the 16th century, and subsequently in the success of the movement of *Shabbetai Ẓevi and its aftermath. The Frankist movement (see Jacob *Frank) originated in Podolia. The disputation with the Frankists forced on the rabbis of Podolia by the Frankist leaders in 1757 resulted in the burning of the books of the Talmud (see *Talmud, Burning of), seized from the communities throughout Podolia, in Kamenets-Podolski. Podolia was also the cradle of Ḥasidism. *Israel Ba'al Shem Tov lived and died in Medzibozh. Many ḥasidic leaders, including *Naḥman of Bratslav, set up their "courts" in its towns.

When Podolia passed to Russia in 1793 the administrative province of Podolia was established, which at first had a Jewish population of 16,687. The Jews formed the majority of merchants and townsmen in the province throughout the 19th century. There were 165,000 Jews in Podolia in 1847 and an estimated 418,458 in 1881. During Passover of 1882, *pogroms broke out in *Balta and the surrounding villages, accompanied by murder and rape. Subsequently the number of Jews in Podolia declined, mainly due to the legislation of May 1882 (see *May Laws) which restricted Jewish economic activity in the villages, and to the retardation of industry and commerce in Podolia. Thousands of Jews emigrated to the provinces of "New Russia" and Bessarabia, as well as overseas. In 1897 Podolia was the only province whose Jewish population had decreased in comparison with the figures for 1881. The Jews then numbered 370,612 (12.3% of the total population), with a proportion of 100 men to 106 women (compared with 101 women in the neighboring province of *Kherson and 102.8 in Bessarabia). There were 88 communities with over 1,000 Jews in Podolia, including Kamenets-Podolski, Balta, *Mogilev, *Vinnitsa, *Proskurov, Tulchin, *Bershad, Medzibozh, *Chmielnik, Bar, Bogopol, *Krivoye Ozero, and Nemirov. About 55,000 Jews lived in villages. Approximately 47% of Podolia Jewry was engaged in commerce (compared with 38.6% of the Jews in the whole of Russia) and 30% in crafts and industry (35.4% in the whole of Russia). About 7,000 Jews (2%) were engaged in agriculture in Podolia, almost half of them in 16 Jewish settlements.

During the civil war in Russia (1918–21) Podolia was among the regions which suffered most severely. Pogroms began with the retreat of the Ukrainian army through Podolia before the advancing Red Army, fomented by Ukrainian army units, bands of peasants who rebelled against the Soviet regime, and units of the "White Army" commanded by A. I. *Denikin. Massacres took place in Proskurov and Felshtin (Gvardeyskoye) in February 1919. Up to the end of 1921, 162 pogroms had occurred in 52 localities of Podolia, of these 125 by the Ukrainians, 28 by the "White Army," and nine by the Poles. The total number of victims has been estimated at about 3,700. The most sinister pogroms (after Proskurov and Felshtin) took place in Trostyanets (with 342 dead), *Bratslav (where pogroms occurred 11 times), and *Litin. The small Jewish settlements in the villages were destroyed and completely abandoned. Refugees from the villages and the townlets streamed into the larger towns of the region and *Odessa. Many crossed the borders into Bessarabia and Poland. Typhus and famine also devastated the Jewish population. In many settlements (Orinin, Chmielnik, Kamenets-Podolski, etc.), Jewish *self-defense units were organized against the pogroms. They withstood the rioters but could not resist the regular army units. Many Jewish youths joined the ranks of the Red Army, within whose framework Jewish units were occasionally formed. These were specially sent on punitive expeditions against rebellious villages.

Under Communist rule Jewish communal life ceased and the position of the Jews of Podolia was the same as that of the rest of Russian Jewry. In the 1920s Jews in Podolia organized cells of *He-Ḥalutz and other secret Zionist youth movements. In 1925 a petition for the right to study Hebrew, signed by thousands of Jewish children in Podolian towns and townlets, was presented to the authorities. The Jewish population in 1926 numbered 347,481 in the seven regions which comprised the former province of Podolia (and some smaller areas outside it).

Holocaust and Contemporary Periods. During World War II, after the Germans invaded the Soviet Union, they ceded the greater part of Podolia to the Rumanians. The whole of the area between the Dniester and Bug rivers extending to the Black Sea (including Odessa) became known as *Transnistria. The northwestern part of Podolia (including Kamenets-Podolski) was taken over by the German military government which systematically murdered the Jews who did not succeed in escaping eastward, in a series of massacres which continued until the end of 1942. The region of Transnistria became a center for the concentration of the 120,000 Jews expelled from *Bessarabia, *Bukovina, and other parts of Rumania, who were segregated in the ghettos set up in Mogilev, *Shargorod, Bershad, Tulchin, Balta, and other towns.

At the time of the liberation of Transnistria by the Red Army in the spring of 1944, there were some 60,000 Jews in the region, of whom 15,000 had lived there before the German occupation while the remainder were from Rumania. In 1970 there were still many thousands of Jews living in Podolia but their exact number is unknown. There was apparently no Jewish communal life except for small groups of worshipers connected with local synagogues.

Bibliography: M. N. Litinski, *Sefer Korot Podolya ve-Kadmoniyyot ha-Yehudim* (1895); Ettinger, in: *Zion*, 21 (1956), 107–42; *Pogrom Korbones in Podolia Gubernie 1918–1921*, 4 (1929), 290; A. D. Rosenthal, *Megillat ha-Tevaḥ*, 3 vols. (1927–31); *Reshumot*, 3 (1923), 60–131, 157–214; 264–310, 356–446; A. Gumener, *A Kapitl Ukraine* (1921); M. Carp, *Transnistria* (Yid., 1950); M. Carp, *Cartea Neagră*, 3 (1947) [Transnistria (Rum.)]; M. Osherovitch, *Geshikhtes fun Mayn Lebn* (1945); R. Feigenberg, *Na va-Nad* (1942); A. Friman, *1919* (Heb., 1968). [Y.S.]

PODVOLOCHISK (Pol. **Podwołoczyska**), town in Ternopol oblast, Ukrainian S.S.R. Before World War II Podvolochisk was within the Tarnopol district in Poland, and was a grain and milling center. Between the two world wars the town included a customs station between Poland and the Soviet Union. In 1865 there were 2,200 inhabitants in the town, the majority of whom were Jews; in 1921 the Jews numbered 2,275 (62% of the total population). After World War I, in independent Poland, the economic situation of the Jews became precarious because the town was isolated from its previous markets; trade was reduced and the Jews could not earn their livelihood. The organization of Jewish merchants attempted to alleviate the situation but could not find a solution because of the hostile attitude of the Polish authorities who sought to strengthen the Polish element of this border town. The situation became so bad that, by 1925, the tradesmen required communal assistance. Jewish life was vibrant in Podvolochisk and community elections were held in 1924 and 1928. Jews also participated in the municipal elections in 1933. Among the rabbis of the community were members of the *Babad family, including Joshua Heshel and his son Judah Leibush who was rabbi on the eve of the Holocaust. [Sh.L.K.]

Holocaust Period. With the outbreak of the German-Soviet war, the city was captured by the Germans (July 1941) and about 70 Jews were immediately killed. Economic restrictions were decreed, and seizure of Jews for forced-labor camps began. The Ukrainian population also attacked the Jews. An extension of the Kamionki labor camp was established in the city, a number of streets were marked off by barbed wire, and young Jews were put there. Many died of overwork, disease, and torture. In September 1942 a part of the camp population was transferred to Zbaraz and Kamionki. The labor camp in the city was liquidated on June 29, 1943. Those who worked in the Kamionki camp perished later. After the war, the Jewish community was not reconstituted in the city. [Ar.W.]

POETRY.

This article is arranged according to the following outline.

Biblical Poetry
- The Hebrew Language and Poetry
- History of Interpretation
- Parallelismus Membrorum
  - Synonymous Parallelism
  - Antithetic Parallelism
  - Synthetic Parallelism
  - Other Types
- Strophe
- Meter
- Genre
  - Cultic Speech
  - Hymn
  - Royal Psalm
  - Lament
  - The Song of Thanksgiving
  - Liturgy
  - Other Genres
- Style
  - Assonance
  - Rhyme
  - Alliteration
  - Paronomasia
  - Onomatopoeia
  - Imagery

Medieval Hebrew Secular Poetry
Spain and Provence
Secular Poetry in Andalusian Spain
Language
Philology and Poetry
Forms
Rhetorics and General Poetics
Genres
Trends in Secular Poetry in Andalusian Spain
Secular Poetry in Christian Spain
Trends in Secular Poetry in Christian Spain
Italy
France and Germany
England

BIBLICAL POETRY

The origins of poetry in ancient Israel, as among other peoples, were closely related to *music. The words were not simply recited but chanted to the accompaniment of stringed instruments (Gen. 31:27; Isa. 23:16; 30:29; Amos 6:5; see Finesinger and Werner in bibl.). The songs were in all probability sung antiphonally, which may explain the source of the parallelistic structure of Hebrew and Ancient Near Eastern poetry (see below). The early *nevi'im* (see *Prophets) sometimes prophesied ecstatically to the sounding of musical instruments (I Sam. 10:5–6), and possibly rhythmic speech was commonly associated with prophetic inspiration. Ancient Israel was profoundly influenced by the poetic style and metrical forms of the Canaanites (see bibl., Albright, Arch Rel; idem, in: CBQ; Gordon) who appear to have been preeminent among the peoples of the Near East in the art of music. From early times singing was indispensable to all cultic celebrations (Ex. 32:18; Judg. 21:21; II Sam. 6:5). The Bible contains a number of early cultic songs, notably Miriam's paean of praise (Ex. 15:21), the Song of the *Sea (Ex. 15:1–18), and the Song of *Deborah (Judg. 5). The Book of Psalms has numerous musical references of different kinds. Various genres of song are mentioned, among them the *mizmor* and *shir* ("song"), the *tehillah* ("hymn"), the *tefillah* ("prayer," of lament or petition), and perhaps the **maskil* ("artistic song"). The superscriptions and notes give the titles of the tunes, musical directions, and the occasions for which the song was designed. Such superscriptions and directions are also to be found in Sumerian and Akkadian hymns and prayers.

The Hebrew Language and Poetry. The Hebrew language is eminently suited for poetic expression. It is relatively poor in abstractions, but rich in concreteness, which is frequently obscured by modern translations. Nouns and verbs perform a primary function in the Hebrew sentence. Pronouns are generally attached to the verb and pronominal modifiers to the noun, frequently resulting in the assonance of the lines. Adjectives and adverbs are employed only sparingly. The conjunction "and" appears with great frequency in contexts where a subordinate conjunction should be used. Hebrew biblical poetry conforms to Milton's familiar dictum that good poetry should be "simple, sensuous, and passionate." The lines are short; each line has an identity of its own and elicits a corresponding effect. Speech is concentrated to the barest minimum, and prolixity is rare. Repetitions, on the other hand, are common, but these usually have a special function in the composition of the poem. Verbs play a primary and strategic role and account in large part for the style and the ordering of the words. The most characteristic features of biblical poetry are action, imagery, simplicity, vigor, and concreteness.

History of Interpretation. While the understanding of the characteristic features of biblical poetry is an achievement of relatively modern times, the recognition of its presence goes back to an early period (for detailed discussion, see Gray, in bibl.). The earliest discussions of Hebrew poetry go back to Philo of Alexandria and Josephus, but their observations are governed by Greek canons of meter, as are those of Origen, Eusebius, and Jerome. Among Jewish scholars, David Kimḥi, Levi b. Gershom, and Abraham ibn Ezra pay attention to the features of Hebrew poetry and anticipate to a degree the work of R. Lowth (see below). However, it remained for Azariah dei *Rossi, in his work *Me'or Einayim* (1573), to break decisively with the application of classical norms by stressing the rhythm of meaning and "the logical parts of propositions." Rhythm is to be discerned, not in the number of syllables, but in the number of substantial ideas.

The true beginning of the modern understanding of the nature of biblical poetry is to be recognized in the work of R. Lowth, professor of poetry at Oxford University, where he delivered a course of 34 lectures, which were published in 1753 under the title *De sacra poesi Hebraeorum praelectiones academicae* (*Lectures on the Sacred Poetry of the Hebrews,* 1835). Lowth saw that poetry has its own techniques: its cadences and rhythms, its structures and patterns, its styles and fields of imagery. But the best-known feature of his work is his insight into the major feature of biblical poetry, the parallelism of its lines, the relationship they bear to each other, and the various modes of this relationship. Only the 19th lecture of his work bears on the subject, but it is developed at length and with ample illustrations in his *Isaiah, a New Translation with a Preliminary Dissertation* (1787, 1834[10]). Here his theory of parallelism is succinctly stated: "The correspondence of one verse or line with another, I call parallelism. When a proposition is delivered, and a second is subjoined under it, equivalent, or contrasted with it in sense, or similar to it in the form of grammatical construction, these I call parallel lines; and the words or phrases, answering one to another in the corresponding lines, parallel terms" (p. ix).

Lowth identified three major kinds of parallelism: synonymous, in which the second line repeats the first; antithetic, in which the second line contrasts with the first; and synthetic, in which the second line develops or expands upon the first. That this is an inadequate or incomplete rendering of the poetic situation is true, and it is not surprising that it has required restatement and reformulation (see Gray in bibl.; Albright, *Yahweh* . . .). Nevertheless the basic position of Lowth is still maintained by all scholars, and it has been eloquently confirmed by the poetic formulations of the literatures of the Ancient Near East.

Parallelismus Membrorum. One of the major sources for confusion in the study of biblical poetry has been the absence of generally recognized scientific nomenclature for describing its stylistic phenomena. Lowth offered no clearly defined terminology for the structural elements in parallelism, and since his time, there has been no general agreement on the terms employed. Perhaps the most common designation for the line or half-line has been the stich (στίχος), but it is not always clear whether the one or the other is meant. It is better to follow W. F. Albright in designating each member of the line as the unit, each line as the colon, each pair of lines as the bi-colon, and each triad as the tri-colon. Parallelism is said to be complete when all the units of the colon are paralleled by all the units of the others. It is incomplete when only some of the units are parallel. The most elemental and purest form appears when the terms or members of one correspond successively to those of the other, as in the elegy of David:

Tell-it-not-in-Gath,
  publish-it-not in-the-streets of-Ashkelon . . .
From-the-blood of-the-slain,

from-the-fat of-the-mighty,
the-bow of-Jonathan
turned-not-back,
and-the-sword of-Saul
returned-not empty (II Sam. 1:20, 22).

The parallel scheme here may be represented by the symbols

a b / a' b'

The units may appear chiastically:

a b / b' a'

They-stirred-him-to-jealousy with-strange-gods,
with-abominable-practices they-provoked-him-to-anger (Deut. 32:26).

Similarly there are many instances of

abc/b'c'a'

Praise-him with-the-sound of-the-trumpet,
praise-him with-lute and-harp!
Praise-him with-timbrel and-dance,
praise-him with-strings and-pipe!
Praise-him with-sounding cymbals
praise-him with-loud-clashing cymbals (Ps. 150:3–5).

Again the units may appear chiastically:

a b c / c' b' a'

The-heavens are-telling the-glory-of-God,
and-his-handiwork proclaims the-firmament (Ps. 19:1 [2]).

The sequence of units within the successive cola shows great diversity, as in

a b c / b' c' a'

Therefore shall-slay-them a-lion out-of-the-forest
a-wolf from-the-desert shall-destroy-them (Jer. 5:6).

Here the first word is to be taken as anacrusis and is not to be reckoned within the parallelism. The foregoing examples illustrate complete parallelism and the great variety of its stylistic formulations. Incomplete parallelism exists in two forms: without compensation, when the second line has a smaller number of units than the first; with compensation, when the second line contains the same number of units, but only some of them are parallel. The following are instances of incomplete parallelism without compensation:

(1) Zebulun is-a-people that-jeopardized its-life to-death
Naphtali on-the-heights of-the-field (Judg. 5:18).

abcd/a'ef

(2) Psalm 114 is entirely composed of incomplete parallel bi-cola and is a superb illustration of the stylistic diversities the form could assume:

At-the-presence of-Yahweh, tremble, O earth,
at-the-presence of-the-god of-Jacob (Ps. 114:7).

abcd/a'b'e

The following are examples of incomplete parallelism with compensation:

(1) Came the-kings and-fought
then-fought the-kings of-Canaan

a b c / c' b' d

(2) It-is-good to-give-thanks to-Yahweh,
to-sing-praises to-thy-name, O-Most-High (Ps. 92:1 [2]).

a b c / b' d c'

Synonymous Parallelism. Synonymous parallelism occurs when the second line repeats or paraphrases the first, the sense of the units of the one balancing the sense of the units of the other in whole or in part. Not a few of the citations cited above fall into this classification. It will be readily seen, however, that the correspondence is seldom perfect. Rather, the second line not merely repeats or paraphrases the first but enriches, or expands upon it, adding fresh nuances or shades of meaning. It is precisely this versatility of formulation that makes biblical poetry the artistic and stylistic creation that it is. This iterative propensity is much more pronounced in the poetry of the other Near Eastern peoples, where the same line is repeated frequently with little or no change at all (Falkenstein and von Soden, in bibl., pp. 81–83, 129–30, 222–5). But synonymous parallelism is frequent, as in Ugaritic:

I've a word I fain would tell thee,
a speech I would utter to thee:
Speech of tree and whisper of stone,
converse of heaven with earth,
e'en of the deeps with the stars (VAB, C, 18ff.; Pritchard, Texts, 136).

That Hebrew poetry has been influenced by Canaanite poetry is further demonstrated by the fact that the same pairs of parallel terms are to be found in both (Gevirtz, in bibl., 7ff.):

Glaze will be poured on my *head,*
Plaster (?) upon my *pate.*

The same pairs appear in other Ugaritic texts as they do in the Old Testament (Gen. 49:26; Deut. 33:16; Ps. 7:17; 68:22). Synonymous parallelism appears in many different forms and guises in all biblical poetry:

O YHWH, who shall sojourn in the tent?
Who shall dwell on thy holy hill? (Ps. 15:1).
God from Teman came,
the Holy One from Mount Paran (Hab. 3:3).
Because I have called, and you refused to listen,
I have stretched out my hand and no one heeded.
And you have ignored all my counsel,
and my reproof you would have none of (Prov. 1:24–25).

Antithetic Parallelism. In antithetic parallelism the cola are set over against each other; the second colon is contrasted with the first, sometimes in specific words or expressions, sometimes only in sense. It is profusely illustrated in the Book of Proverbs as a didactic device:

A wise son makes a glad father,
but a foolish son is a sorrow to his mother (Prov. 10:1).
Some boast of chariots, and some of horses;
but we boast in the name of YHWH our God.
They will collapse and fall;
but we shall rise and stand upright (Ps. 20:7–8 [8–9]).
For a brief moment I forsook you
but with everlasting life I will have compassion on you (Isa. 54:7).

Synthetic parallelism. Synthetic parallelism was described by Lowth as parallelism which "consists only in the similar form of construction; in which word does not answer to word, and sentence to sentence, as equivalent or opposite; but there is a correspondence and equality between different propositions, in respect of the shape and turn of the whole sentence, and all the constructive parts" (*Isaiah* . . ., in bibl., p. xvii). Perhaps the majority of scholars today reject this as being parallelism in any true sense. Some prefer to speak of emblematic ("token") parallelism as in Psalm 42:1 [2]:

As a hart longs
for flowing streams,
so longs my soul,
for thee, O God.

Others include another form of parallelism, namely, stairlike or climatic parallelism, which occurs frequently in the "Psalms of Ascent" (Ps. 120–134):

YHWH is your guard:
YHWH is your shade [i.e., shield, shelter]
on your right hand . . .
YHWH will guard you from all evil;
he will guard your life.
YHWH will guard your going out and your coming in
from this time forth and for evermore (Ps. 121:5, 7–8).

Other Types. In recent years attention has been directed to various types of repetitive parallelism in Hebrew poetry, i.e., the repetition of the same words or phrases in successive cola, bi-cola, or tri-cola. As early as 1918, C. F. Burney in his commentary on the Book of Judges recognized this stylistic phenomenon in his treatment of the

Song of Deborah, where there is a profusion of repetitive devices of different kinds. Burney was followed in 1922 by a study by W. F. Albright on "The Earliest Forms of Hebrew Poetry" (in JPOS, 2 (1922), 69–86) and somewhat later by a stylistic analysis of Habakkuk 3 (in H. H. Rowley (ed.), *Studies in Old Testament Prophecy* (1950), 1–18). Meanwhile H. L. Ginsberg had discovered the presence of the repetitive tri-colon in Canaanite and adduced numerous parallels to the Old Testament (in *Orientalia*, 5 (1936), 171ff.). The stock example is as follows:

Behold, thine enemies, O Baal,
behold, thine enemies shalt thou crush,
behold, thou shalt crush thy foes (IIIAB A, 8–9).

The lines are very similar to those of Psalm 92:9 [10]:

For, behold, thine enemies, O YHWH,
for, behold, thine enemies shall perish;
all evil-doers shall be scattered.

It is to be found in the ancient hymn, which teems with Canaanite affinities.

Ascribe to YHWH,
you sons of gods,
Ascribe to YHWH
glory and strength.
the glory of his name.
Worship YHWH in holy array (Ps. 29:1–2; see also Ps. 92:96; Hab. 3;and Ps. 68).

Repetitions of other kinds abound in Hebrew poetry, for example:

O mighty mountain,
mountain of Bashan!
O many-peaked mountain,
mountain of Bashan!
Why look you with envy,
O many-peaked mountain,
at the mount which God desired for his abode,
yea, where YHWH will dwell for ever? (Ps. 68:15–16 [16–17]).

A poem of quite a different order, but equally impressive in its impact, is Jeremiah's sublime contemplation:

I looked on the earth, and lo, it was waste and void;
and to the heavens, and they had no light.
I looked on the mountains, and lo, they were quaking,
and all the hills moved to and fro.
I looked, and lo, here was no man,
and all the birds of the air had fled.
I looked, and lo, the fruitful land was a desert,
and all its cities were laid in ruins
before YHWH, before his fierce anger (Jer. 4:23–26).

Strophe. A second major feature of Hebrew and Ancient Near Eastern poetic compositions is intimately related to parallelism. The bi-cola or tri-cola tend to fall into clusters, groups, or stylistic units, which are usually designated strophes. The strophe has most frequently been described as a metrical unit, i.e., as following pervasive metrical regularity. There is considerable force to this characterization, but exceptions are too numerous to insist upon absolute uniformity. It is better to speak of prevailing metrical consistency. The poet intentionally breaks the metrical pattern, particularly at the close of the strophe or poem, to give it stress. Other stylistic features are also to be taken into account, such as syntax, ordering of the units, and diversity of rhetoric within a poem. While many strophes have the same number of bi-cola or tri-cola, there are too many exceptions for this pattern to be a criterion for determining the length of a strophe. A strophe, then, may be defined as a series of bi-cola or tri-cola with a particular beginning and a particular close, possessing unity of thought, structure, and style. In general the prosody group coincides with the sense or meaning.

But how are the limits of a strophe to be determined and its beginning and ending defined? In a number of poems there are refrains, which make strophic structure clear. Among these are Psalms 42–43 (42:5 [6], 11 [12]; 43:5); Psalm 46 (7 [8], 11 [12] and originally after 3); Psalm 80 (3 [4], 7 [8], 14 [15], 19 [20]); and Psalm 107 (8, 15, 21). The prophets also employ refrains upon occasion (Isa. 9:8–21 [8–20] and 5:24–25; Amos 4:6–11). The strophic structure is also apparent in the alphabetic acrostic, as in Psalms 9–10; 25; 119; and in Lamentations 1–3. However, there are also numerous other rhetorical features which may serve as guides, for example, the change of speaker or of the addressee in successive strophes, as in many psalms, but also in the prophets. The strophe may open with an exclamation like "Behold" or "How long?"; with an urgent imperative, "Praise," "Hear," "Bless," "Give thanks"; with a rhetorical question; or with a vocative, most impressively and frequently, "O YHWH." Conclusions may be of the same kind, but they are also formulated by citations, figures of speech, summary lines, and, above all, by motivations. More important than the external devices is the shift of thought that takes place from strophe to strophe. Form and thought are related. It is the coalescence of the two that provides an important clue for the interpretation of the poem and for the articulation of the poet's thought.

Meter. The foundations for a scientific and inductive approach to Hebrew meter were first laid by a number of scholars during the 19th century, chief among whom were J. Ley, K. Budde, and E. Sievers (see bibl.). While they differed on many important issues, they agreed that Hebrew meter is neither syllabic nor quantitive but accentual. Each colon contains a fixed number of accents or stresses, and there is no ratio between the length of the stressed and unstressed syllables. (Sievers and others, however, argued for the presence of anapestic meter.) Some scholars maintain that in certain periods of Israel's history the successive cola contained the same number of syllables, as in Syriac and late Hebrew.

The poetic texts from the Ancient Near East confirm the foregoing analysis. The same structural phenomena are encountered in the poetic materials from Egypt (in spite of the absence of vowel signs), Mesopotamia, and Canaan as in Hebrew poetry. In an ancient Akkadian poem on the creation, the text of which is accompanied by musical signs and notes, there is at least one, but usually two or three, unstressed units between each two stresses. Akkadian poetry has a prevailing 2'2' meter, but some of the bi-cola have a 3'3' meter, a metrical fluidity characteristic of biblical poetry as well. As in biblical poetry, tri-cola often appear in 2'2'2'. More revealing are the disclosures from Ugaritic poetry. It is clear that the same principles governed Canaanite and Hebrew prosody. The most common meter of the former is 3'3', as it is in the Old Testament, but 2'2' is by no means uncommon.

There are two main types of bi-cola or tri-cola: those in which the parallel cola are equal in length and those in which they are unequal. In the former there may be the 2'2', the 3'3', or even, upon occasion, the 4'4' meter; in the latter the most characteristic and impressive is 3'2' meter; the so-called *kinah* or dirge, first discovered by K. Budde in his study of the Hebrew lament. It is not an altogether happy designation because the meter appears frequently in literary genres other than the lament, and the lament often assumes meters other than the 3'2'.

Among the numerous instances of 2'2' are the whole of Psalm 29, David's elegy over Saul and Jonathan (II Sam. 1:19–27), and parts of the Song of Deborah (Judg. 5). The 3'3' meter is by far the most common, and is profusely illustrated by the Books of Job, Proverbs, Deutero-Isaiah, and Psalms. Examples of *kinah* meter are frequent in Lamentations 1–3, but also in the Prophets, and Psalms.

Genre. Biblical poetry conforms to conventional modes or types of speech. Form criticism has identified many of these literary genres, calling attention to the features which characterize each: its structure, terminology, style, and linguistic articulation. Each type has its own life situation, the occasion which evoked or inspired this manner and form of utterance, whether the vicissitudes of human life—birth, death, marriage, or events of communal life—war, famine, coronation of the king, and so on. Accompanying the prose narration of the Pentateuch and the historical books are a number of poems elicited by the particular occasion recounted. The Song of the Well accompanied the opening of a well and was doubtless often employed upon similar occasions (Num. 21:17–18). Jotham's fable is a superbly fashioned piece, containing numerous Canaanite stylistic features (cf. "Baal and Anath," in Pritchard, Texts, 134–5, 140). It contains summons to battle and war shouts (Ex. 15:3; Josh. 10:12–14; II Sam. 20:1b; I Kings 12:16), and salutations on return of the hero from battle (I Sam. 18:7; Judg. 11:34). Love poetry is strikingly rare, with the notable exception of the *Song of Songs, a collection of impassioned love lyrics with affinities to the other literatures of the Ancient Near East, e.g., Sumerian lovesongs, the Tammuz fertility-cult songs, and Egyptian poems.

As could be expected, poetry of a sacral nature is much more abundant. Two ecstatic shouts are preserved in connection with the ark: its setting forth and its return to camp (Num. 10:35–36). Miriam's song on the occasion of the crossing of the Sea of Reeds preserves an authentic memory in its exultant shout (Ex. 15:21). The quatrain was later expanded into a litany of YHWH's victory over the sea (Ex. 15:1–18; see Muilenburg, 1966, in bibl.). Deborah's ode (Judg. 5) belongs to the same genre. Such songs are paralleled by a number of representative specimens of the genre among the peoples of the Ancient Near East. Closely paralleling the hymn of victory are the oracles of Balaam (Num. 22–24), delivered by the seer before engagement in battle (W. F. Albright, in: JBL, 63 (1944), 207–34). Another early genre, but one that persists throughout the Old Testament, appears in a number of different formulations and guises, not least of all in those contexts which witness to Israel's sense of familial or tribal solidarity, namely, the blessing (Gen. 14:19–20; 27:27–29; 48:15–16; 49:1–27; Deut. 33).

There were ballad singers in Ancient Israel (Num. 21:27), and their songs were doubtless chanted by the people. Many of them were committed to writing in two anthologies to which occasional reference is made: the *Book of the Wars of the Lord (Num. 21:14) and the *Book of Jashar (Josh. 10:13; II Sam. 1:18). They are in all probability the earliest books recorded in the Bible. To the former belongs the taunt song of Heshbon (Num. 21:27–30), to the latter, David's elegy over Saul and Jonathan (II Sam. 1:19–27) and Solomon's dedicatory quatrain (I Kings 8:12–13; cf. LXX).

Cultic Speech. In the sphere of worship, Israel when it entered the precincts of the Temple and the sphere of holiness gave expression in manifold ways and forms to the aspirations and petitions of the worshipping community and of the individual suppliant. Every holiday, every festival, every occasion of national celebration or mourning had its own form of cultic expression (see also *Psalms).

Hymn. The hymn has its own characteristic structural and rhetorical features. It opens with a summons to praise, usually followed by an address to the congregation. This, in turn, is often followed by a motivating bi-colon, introduced by the article *ki*, "because," giving the reasons why Israel should extol its God. The conclusion brings the hymn to its culmination, often by returning to the opening words or motif, sometimes by another motivation. Most numerous of the hymns are those in the Book of Psalms (Ps. 19; 29; 33; 96; 98; 100; 103; 105; 145–150), but the form and style has penetrated many other formulations.

Royal Psalm. A genre intimately related to the hymn is the royal psalm. In it the king plays a central role. The major vicissitudes of his reign are celebrated in the Temple; his anointing or enthronement (Ps. 2; 101; 110), the celebration of the founding of the Davidic monarchy and the royal sanctuary on Mount Zion (Ps. 132), his wedding (Ps. 45), his setting out for battle (Ps. 20), and his victorious return (Ps. 21). The style is often that of the royal courts of the Ancient Near East, as, for example, the oracular words, probably spoken by the court prophet (Ps. 2:7–9; 132:11–18). Closely associated with the royal psalm is the hymn of the divine enthronement (Ps. 47; 93; 96–99). It has been contended that this took place on New Year's Day and that the king played the role of YHWH. Its most conspicuous feature is the acclamation, "YHWH reigns" or "YHWH has become king" (Ps. 93:1; 96:10; 97:1; 99:1; see Mowinckel, 1961, in bibl.).

Lament. The lament appears in two forms: the personal and the communal lament. The occasions for the former are times of personal distress or adversity, whether sickness, unjust accusation, persecution, ostracism, or the shattering sense of the absence of God. This type appears more frequently than any other (Ps. 3; 5; 13; 22; 42–43; 54; 55; 56; 57; et al.; and the penitential psalms 6; 32; 38; 51; 102; 130; 143). The confessions of Jeremiah also conform to this genre (Jer. 15:10–21; 17:14–18; 18:18–23; 20:7–18). The communal laments are represented not only in the Book of Psalms (e.g., Ps. 44; 74; 79; 80; 125) but also in the Prophets (Jer. 14:2–9; Hos. 6:1–3; Micah 7:7–17). Such outpourings of grief were occasioned by some disaster threatening the community as a whole, times of national crisis such as foreign invasion, defeat in war, famine or drought, exile, or the death of the king. The parallels with the cognate literatures are especially striking. The Sumerian "Lamentation over the Destruction of Ur" (Pritchard, Texts, 455–63) contains numerous interesting parallels. A characteristic feature of the lament is that it sometimes closes with an expression of certainty that God has heard the supplicant's cry (Ps. 5:12 [13]; 7:10–11 [11–12]; 13:6; 52:9 [11]; 22:22–31 [23–32]). Such expressions are sometimes accompanied by a vow, as in the Akkadian laments (Ps. 54:6 [8]; 56:12 [13]; 61:8 [9]). Closely associated with the personal lament is the psalm of trust (Ps. 4; 11; 16; 23; 62; 131).

The Song of Thanksgiving. The song of thanksgiving is in the same general category as the hymn, and its affinities with the hymn are very close. It is represented by relatively few exemplars (Ps. 30; 32; 34; 41; 66; 92; et al.; Isa. 38:10–20, et al.). It is the reverse of the lament in that it expresses gratitude for deliverance from death or destruction or some other adversity.

Liturgy. Two examples connected with entrance to the sanctuary have been preserved in the Book of Psalms (Ps. 15 and 24). Psalms 75, 85, and 126 are also liturgies, while a number of specimens are found in the prophetic books (Isa. 33; 63:7–64:12 [11]; Micah 7:7–20). It has been held by some scholars that Joel 1:1–2:27, the Book of Habakkuk, and the Book of Nahum also belong to this type.

Other Genres. While the prophets often borrow and imitate secular forms, such as the vintage song (Isa. 5:1–7), the taunt song (Isa. 37:22–29; 46), the lament (Ezek. 19:2–14; Amos 5:2), and the judicial proceedings at the city's gate (Isa. 3:13–15; 43:8–13), they also employ genres more characteristically their own, such as the messenger's report opening with "Thus YHWH is saying," the judgment speech with its indictment and verdict (Amos 1:3–2:16) and the related oracle of woe (Isa. 5:8–17, 18–25; Amos 5:18–20; Hab. 2:9–17), the lawsuit (Isa. 1:2ff.; Jer. 2:1–13; Micah 6:1–8), and the oracle of salvation (Isa. 41:8–13; 42:5–17; 43:1–7). The literature of wisdom is rich in the variety of its formulations and ranges from the simplicity of the individual proverb, maxim, or apothegm to the more extended essay-like reflections of Ecclesiastes. There are the prohibitions (Prov. 3:25–32), the similitudes (Prov. 9:1–6), and the autobiographical vignettes (Prov. 4:3–9). In the late seventh century B.C.E. biblical poetry tends to become more expansive and artistically fashioned, as in Jeremiah (e.g., 3:1–4:4), but even more in the two supreme literary classics Deutero-*Isaiah and *Job. The old conventional forms are still employed, but with greater freedom, versatility, and independence. The structural forms are transformed and artistically expanded, and the rhetorical features more skillfully wrought. In contrast to his predecessors, Deutero-Isaiah employs invective seldom; instead he uses the oracle of salvation, which is sometimes accompanied by hymnic effusions. Job employs the form of the legal controversy, but in a more artistic manner than the prophets. Equally notable are the piercing laments which are developed at great length. His poetry rises to the heights of sublimity in the hymnic rhetoric of the speeches from the whirlwind (Job 38–41).

Style. Style is concerned with the appropriate choice of words, with their ordering or sequence, and with the ways in which they are to be employed in a given context. It is not merely an aesthetic device or instrument; it is also a reflection of the writer's cast of mind, expression of the modes whereby he articulates meaning into language.

ASSONANCE. The biblical poets were very sensitive to sound. It is characteristic of them to make the meaning conform to the sound. Thus in Psalm 29, immediately following the majestic invocation, is heard the sevenfold peal of thunder, *qol YHWH,* each accompanied by the sounds or words appropriate to its content. Related to this hymn are many lines in the enthronement songs (see, e.g., Ps. 93:4). Elsewhere is heard the dying shriek of the prostitute in her agonizing birthpangs (see Jer. 4:31). The assonance of the laments is especially noteworthy. In the confessions of Jeremiah the "ee" sound tends to prevail (e.g., Jer. 15:10), but elsewhere and more often the "oo" sound of weeping is prevalent, as in the Song of the Suffering Servant (Isa. 52:13–53:12), where the pronominal suffixes *hu* ("he") and *nu* ("us") are contrasted most impressively in 53:4–7.

RHYME. While rhyme cannot be said to be characteristic of biblical poetry, as it is in many other languages, notably in Arabic metrical verse, it appears often enough to merit attention. It is sometimes to be explained by the pronominal suffixes at the close of successive cola or bi-cola. Lamech's Song (Gen. 4:23–24) and the four bi-cola of Isaiah 41:11–13 are typical examples. But it is present in other texts also (see Isa. 53:6; Ps. 8:4[5]; 23:2; cf. Ps. 6:1[2]; 55:6[7]; 75:6–7[7–8]).

ALLITERATION. Alliteration often appears in pairs of words, as in *sason we-simḥah,* "joy and gladness" (Isa. 22:13a; 35:10b; Jer. 7:34, et al.), *ʿanan wa-ʿarafel,* "clouds and thick darkness" (Ezek. 34:12; Joel 2:2; Zeph. 1:15; Ps. 97:2, et al.), or *hod we-hadar,* "splendor and majesty" (Ps. 21:6; 99:6; 104:1, et al.). A striking example is found in Isaiah 62:10. In this verse the repetitions accentuate the sound, but each verse has the same consonant repeated four times (cf. also Isa. 16:9–11; 22:5; 40:6; 43:24; 45:9; 47:1; Jer. 5:30; Nah. 2:10[11]).

PARONOMASIA. Paronomasia refers to the use of the same word in different senses or of words of similar sound to produce a particular effect. Following are some of the most familiar instances. The first is the finale of Isaiah's "Song of the Vineyard":

He looked for justice *[mishpaṭ],*
but behold bloodshed *[mispaḥ];*
for righteousness *[ẓedaqah];*
but behold, a cry */ẓeʿaqah/* (Isa. 5:7cd).

An equally striking finale produces a similar effect:

If you will not have faith *[taʾaminu];*
you will not be stayed *[teʾamenu]* (Isa. 7:9c).

Here the crucial issue for Isaiah is expressed in the play upon the central word. Micah preserves one of the most notable instances of paronomasia:

be-Gat ʾal taggidu,	Tell it not in Gath
bakho ʾal tivku,	weep not at all;
be-Veit le-ʿAfrah	in Beth-Le-Aphrah
ʿafar hitpallashiti,	roll yourselves in the dust.
ʿivri lakhem	Pass on your way,
yoshevet Shafir	inhabitants of Shaphir,
ʿeryah-voshet loʾ yaẓeʾah	in nakedness and shame;
yoshevet Ẓaʾanan.	the inhabitant of Zaanan
	does not come forth
	(Micah 1:10–11d).

In these verses there are wordplays involving the names of cities and verbs accentuating their destruction by the Assyrian foe. Among numerous other examples, the following may be noted: Isaiah 34:6; 40:11; 41:5a; 43:24a; 54:6ab; Jeremiah 6:1; Hosea 10:10; Amos 5:5.

ONOMATOPOEIA. Onomatopoeia is the use of words whose sounds imitate or suggest the meaning they seek to portray. Through onomatopoeia the sense becomes acoustically perceptible. It has already been mentioned that Psalm 29 reproduces the rolling thunder of the storm. The Song of Deborah is rich in assonance, nowhere more strikingly than in the "galloping, galloping" of the stallions: *daharot daharot ʾabbiraw* (Judg. 5:22). The inimitable proem to the poems of Deutero-Isaiah sounds the major motif of comfort:

naḥamu naḥamu ʿammi
yoʾmar ʾElohekhem.
dabberu ʿal lev Yerushalayim
we-qireʾu ʾeleha (Isa. 40:1–2).

Sibilants are all but absent; the soft breathing of the repeated imperative at the opening and the prevailing "oo" sound of the first words of the cola are in themselves consoling, and this is reinforced by the repetitions and assonance of the bi-cola which follow. In Jeremiah's poem on the return of primeval chaos the turbulence of the earthquake is superbly described by the concluding words of each colon in 4:24: *roʿashim, hitqalqalu.* Perhaps the best example is the description of the roar of the surging billows and the loud crashing of the booming seas:

hoi hamon ʿammim rabbim
ka-hamot yammim yehemayun
u-sheʾon leʾummim ki-sheʾon
mayim kabbirim yishaʾun
leʾummin ki-sheʾon mayim rabbim yishaʾun
we-gaʿar bo we-nas mi-merḥaq
we-ruddaf ke-moẓ harim lifnei ruʾaḥ
u-khe-galgal lifnei sufah.

Ah, the thunder of many peoples,
they thunder like the thundering of the sea!
Ah, the roar of nations,
they roar like the roaring of the mighty waters!
The nations roar like the roaring of many waters,
but he will rebuke them, and they will flee far away,
chased like chaff on the mountains before the wind
and whirling dust before the storm (Isa. 17:12–13).

IMAGERY. The most striking characteristic of biblical poetry, the feature which more than any other makes it the supreme lyrical literature that it is, are the images and figures which the poet employs to embody his feelings and thoughts. There is scarcely a poem within the entire corpus of Old Testament literature which does not bear witness to

Israel's genius for imagery. The poet scales the loftiest heights and plumbs the lowest depths for his images. He enlists every aspect of nature, every human emotion and experience, every fragment drawn from daily life to translate his thoughts into living reality. The Book of Psalms has for that reason often been said to be the supreme lyrical literature of the world. Such books as Hosea and Jeremiah are monuments to the imagination of Israel, excelled only by the sublime poetry of Job and the superlative lyrical sequences of Deutero-Isaiah. The supremacy of Israel's poetry has but one explanation: its poets addressed themselves to the loftiest themes that ever inspired the mind and heart of man, the themes that concern men ultimately, kindle their highest aspirations, and demand their deepest devotion. [JA.MU.]

Hebrew Poetry in the Second Temple period is to be found in the *Apocrypha and the *Dead Sea Scrolls. It sprang up again as a religious expression in the geonic period, as described in the entry **Piyyut*. See also *Literature, Jewish.

MEDIEVAL HEBREW SECULAR POETRY

Spain and Provence. Hebrew secular poetry flourished in Muslim Spain (Andalusia) from the middle of the 10th century to the middle of the 12th and in Christian Spain and Provence from the middle of the 12th century to the end of the 15th (shortly before the expulsion). During these two eras, particularly the former, Spanish Jewry developed a versatile poetry of far-ranging scope which was rooted in the revival of the biblical tradition. At the same time it also evolved in the light of Muslim, and later of Christian, culture and poetry and in the spirit of contemporary rationalistic trends.

SECULAR POETRY IN ANDALUSIAN SPAIN (C. 950–1150). A "golden era" was reached by the Hebrew poetry of Andalusia whose principal exponents, including *Samuel ha-Nagid, Solomon ibn *Gabirol, Moses *ibn Ezra, and *Judah Halevi, attained artistic excellence both in secular and in devotional poetry, i.e., liturgical poetry incorporated in the prayer service (see **Piyyut*). The most remarkable innovation of this period, however, was the creation of secular poetry which became a vehicle through which the poet could express his personal thoughts and feelings and his relation to man and society. The style and motifs of secular poetry came to influence devotional poetry, which, however, developed separately and was considered a distinct genre.

Prior to the rise of secular poetry in Spain, Hebrew poetry in the various centers (Ereẓ Israel, Babylon, Byzantine Italy, etc.) had been liturgical only, except for a few early texts. The earliest non-liturgical poems (works by *Saadiah Gaon (tenth century) and his contemporaries), dealing with public matters, stem from Babylonia; however, the firm religious tradition of the Babylonian Jewish community precluded any far-reaching innovations. Congenial conditions for secular poetry evolved in the new Jewish community in Muslim Spain, a community not bound by tradition and prospering in an environment of religious tolerance and great cultural and ethnic diversity. It absorbed the culture of its environment and developed rapidly under the Cordoba caliphate and the petty kingdoms that were formed after the caliphate disintegrated.

The patronage of the Jewish courtier, who was either a government official, a financier, or a landowner, created favorable conditions for the development of secular Hebrew poetry. The most eminent Jewish courtiers attracted scholars, artists, and poets to their courts as did their Muslim counterparts. *Menahem b. Jacob ibn Saruq and *Dunash b. Labrat, the earliest Hebrew poets in Spain, were the court poets of *Ḥisdai ibn Shaprut who was himself a courtier of Abd-al-Raḥman III, caliph of Cordoba. Most of the later poets of the Andalusian period were also court poets; a few poets, however, made their living as physicians and *dayyanim*, etc. The institution of patronage in Muslim Spain began to decline in the middle of the 12th century but continued in Christian Spain for a long time though not as prominently.

The court poet depended on his patron's favor and was closely connected with the latter's fate at the royal court. (Some patrons, such as Ibn Gabirol's Jekuthiel, were executed as a result of court intrigues.) From the literary point of view the main drawback of court poetry was the conventionality in creativity that necessarily prevailed in the most commonly used poetic genres. One of the poet's main social functions was to compose panegyrics for his patron and dirges on the death of the latter's relatives. Thus the same motifs, images, and conventional formulations constantly recurred.

On the other hand the status of the court poet had many advantages. Poetry was part of the cultural life at the court and added to the prestige of the patron since it was the far-reaching dissemination of the poetry written at his court and the popularity it gained which spread his fame. Poetry was also a weapon in the hand of the poet, mainly in the guise of satiric poems. The poet enjoyed economic security, respectability, and sometimes even friendship since many patrons were erudite, and true lovers of poetry. Cultural life at the court also afforded the means for the extensive development of different poetic genres: wine and love songs for feasts, as well as other genres which did not have an immediate social function, e.g., universal wisdom poems and personal poetic complaints. The evolvement of a cultured and refined reading public at the numerous courts developed a keen critical sense both in the public and in the poet and stimulated the development of poetry into a highly refined art. The dependence of the court poet on his patron was considered natural, and the decline of the institution of patronage at the end of the Andalusian period was seen by poets as a direct cause of the decline of poetry.

Poetry was a very popular art. The works of Samuel ha-Nagid, for example, were already known during his lifetime, as testified to by Moses ibn Ezra in his poetics, "In all the regions of East and West . . . Babylon . . . Ereẓ Israel . . . Egypt . . . Ifriqiya (Tunis, etc.) . . . and Spain." Evidence from the Cairo *Genizah* shows that manuscripts of Spanish poems were brought from Spain to Egypt and thence to Yemen. The fact that after the decline of the Spanish center its poetry was preserved and copied in remote countries testifies to its wide distribution. In Spain itself there were many centers of poetry: Lucena, Seville, and other towns were called "cities of poetry."

Language. The language of the Bible had a glorious renascence in secular poetry and superseded other linguistic layers which had developed since the end of the biblical period, i.e,. talmudic and especially paytanic Hebrew which in Spain were considered arbitrary and chaotic. The opposition to these latter developments was at times extreme, as Abraham ibn Ezra's criticism (in his commentary on Eccles. 5:1) of the style and language of Eleazar *Kallir, the greatest of the early poets, who lived in Ereẓ Israel.

This return to the ancient source of the language was a great innovation. Biblical Hebrew, considered the only accurate form of Hebrew, was seen as a clear, precise, beautiful, and divine tongue, which was superior to all other languages. The view reflected the spiritual contest with the Arabs who set up the style of the Koran as a theological and aesthetic model and developed linguistic and poetic tools for its interpretation. An answer to this challenge could only be in the adoption of a biblical style which, because of its antiquity, diversity, poetry, and accuracy preserved by the masorah, was a formidable opponent. In his *Poetics* (c. 1135) Moses ibn Ezra illustrates each rhetorical figure by using both contemporary Arabic and Hebrew poetry but he primarily refers to the Bible "so that the Arabs will not discredit it and think . . . that the Hebrew tongue (i.e., biblical Hebrew) lacks aesthetic rules." He also mentions the work *Kitāb la-Badīʿ* (around 900) which discusses rhetorical figures in the Koran, but insists that though contemporary poetry applies the Arabic poetic form and style, it is mainly rooted in the language of the Bible.

Philology and Poetry. The new approach not only developed out of internal apologetics and external rivalry, but was fostered by the spirit of rationalism expressed in the flourishing of sciences, including philology and philological exegesis—a prerequisite to a biblical renascence and to the development of a new poetic style. Already the earliest poets, Menahem ibn Saruq, Dunash b. Labrat, and Samuel ha-Nagid were also philologists, while all poets had a distinct inclination for philology.

An important innovation in form was the introduction into Hebrew of an exact quantitative poetic meter, as found in Arabic poetry. The metric system (establishing a new symmetry of sound which aroused admiration) was based on a grammatical (morphological) principle: the distinction between short and long metrical units according to the exact biblical vocalization of the words.

Since quantitative meter had from its inception in Hebrew poetry been accepted as an immutable law, a preoccupation with biblical grammar and a mastery of biblical style in general was a natural outcome. Hebrew poetry used not only biblical vocabulary but also biblical idioms or verses which were interwoven into the fabric of the poem among other ornaments of style. This style, called *mussiv*, was not a mechanical mosaic of quotations, but a peculiar and original combination in a new context, which often led to a surprising change in meaning whose effect sometimes was humorous. Readers brought up on the Bible studied these new effects, examined the poems in the light of the new linguistic and poetic norms, criticized them, and even corrected them.

In time, though poetry tended toward extreme biblical purism, both in vocabulary and in form (for later changes see below), semantic and syntactical changes were nevertheless introduced into biblical Hebrew. Syntax was at times determined by meter and biblical words consequently acquired a new meaning either through the influence of similar Arabic words or through motifs drawn from Arabic poetry. The fusion of the biblical background with the new elements of stylized poetry followed clear aesthetic principles.

The poetics of the time, though formulated for Hebrew poetry by Moses ibn Ezra at the end of the Andalusian period (c. 1135), is found already in the early poetry of the period and reflects Arabic critical works and poetry. Normative and neo-classic in character, it considers secular poetry (it does not deal with devotional poetry) as an art which demands education and training even for the naturally talented. It calls for clear, formal, rhetorical, and thematic requirements.

Forms. Spanish Hebrew poetics thus demands that each poem be carefully rhymed and its meter be meticulous. Most of secular Hebrew poetry was written in the Arabic *qaṣīda* form (or in its abbreviated form, *qit'a*), i.e., it had to have one unchangeable rhyme throughout the poem and one quantitative meter dividing each verse *(bayit)* into two hemistichs. Poems in which homonyms replace the rhymes are a variation of this type of poem. The other type of secular poem was the "girdle poem" (the *muwashshaḥ*) whose strophic pattern Andalusian Arabs had inherited from ancient Spanish folk poetry. While the monotony of the classical form was relieved in the "girdle poem," allowing for virtuosity in metrical schemes and rhyme patterns, it was based on a unique principle of form. The "girdle poem" combines fixed and variable rhyme elements. Each stanza has a different rhyme and is followed by a section of a varying number of verses which have the same rhyme. This rhyme recurs only in each of these sections.

In their imitation of complex and intricate forms of Arabic "girdle poems" (or of Hebrew ones by their predecessors), the Hebrew poets showed great skill in techniques of poetry. Some concluded their poems with an Arabic or Hispano-Roman *jarya* which was taken literally from a popular folk song. The *muwashshaḥ* form was mainly a vehicle for entertaining and encomiastic poetry; but in Hebrew it was also assimilated into devotional poetry.

Rhetorics and General Poetics. Poetry was mainly regarded as "ornamented speech" and the creative process as a conscious art. The poet chooses the subject and themes which he then "embellishes" with figures and tropes. This view which separates form and content is foreign to the modern conception of poetry. The approach, basic to the rationalistic exegesis of metaphorical language in the Koran and the Bible (in order to refute an anthropomorphic interpretation of descriptions of God), was adopted by the theory of poetry and was also used by poets.

The poet's art is revealed in the rhetorical weave of the poem and in the details of poetic diction. It, too, is bound by tradition: conventional phrases and images recur in new combinations, as in a colorful kaleidoscope of style which changes the patterns of its permanent elements. Originality is praised but its scope is limited and is usually expressed by subtle, though sometimes surprising, variations on conventional elements rather than by daring individualistic vent and outburst, or by a new sensibility.

The choice of themes is circumscribed and conventionally fixed. Many subjects were considered unsuitable for poetry, others were only conventionally treated. Some poetic genres employ the neo-classical style which is beyond the individual and the specific. In wine songs, for example, the scenery is conventional, reinforced by traditional images: the feast par excellence or the ideal qualities of wine. Similarly, love poetry usually centers around a beautiful but harsh mistress of the type of *la belle dame sans merci.* The unhappy rejected lover humiliates himself before the beloved (in front of others who watch him, or in front of a moralizer); but he draws supreme pleasure from his torment.

In general, this poetry posits an ideal world of opposites (absolute beauty or absolute ugliness, heights of joy and delight or abysses of grief, etc.). The imagery is also often based on real or fictitious antitheses (pearls of wisdom as against the mire of folly; flames of anguish as against rivers of weeping, etc.).

Genres. Secular poetry includes panegyrics, dirges, poems of self-praise, satire, wine songs, love poems, wisdom poems, complaints, etc. Genres were considered to be defined mostly by theme and to some extent by tone. This type of division, however, is not exhaustive since each genre also has in addition to theme a specific pattern reflected in many ways, e.g., in the attitude of the speaker (personal or universal), the specific use of motifs, imagery, and even recurring formula.

The autonomy of the genres is most striking in the long poems which are not one unit. Traditionally, these have an "introduction" (on any subject, e.g., a feast), the "body" of the poem (treating the actual theme, e.g., panegyrics), and between these a "transition verse." In these poems the division is also not exhaustive. There is often a further subdivision into many diverse secondary sections, each belonging to a different genre. Many of the long poems therefore resemble a series of short poems of different genres. Though the elements of stylization in secular poetry were highly conventionalized, poetry was not stifled; it is richer in themes than is usually thought; variations in rhetorical and descriptive usages or in combination of genres, etc., are exceedingly numerous; some important poems do not even belong to any of the set genres. The basic principles of theoretical and practical poetics, however, differed from the modern and appealed to a different type of sensibility.

Trends in Secular Poetry in Andalusian Spain. The development of secular poetry testifies to a conscious and directed aim toward a continuous improvement of vehicles of expression and the increase of genres and themes within a normative framework. The character of secular poetry became defined in a relatively short period of time. Its inception was around 950 in Cordoba, under the patronage of Isaac ibn Shaprut and particularly at the court of his son *Ḥisdai ibn Shaprut. The earliest secular poet was apparently Menahem ibn Saruq; the novelty of his poems (of which only fragments are extant or merely the names) lay in their purpose and theme, but not as yet in the synthetic Hebrew-Arabic style which was to mark the school. That style was introduced as a deliberate novelty by Dunash b. Labrat, Menahem's rival at Ḥisdai's court. Dunash adapted the principle of the Arabic quantitative meter to Hebrew poetry and changed its whole outlook through the integration of images, figures of speech, motifs, and genres taken from Arabic poetry. His innovation in meter aroused a sharp controversy between his and Menahem's disciples who claimed that he corrupted the Hebrew language (see Isaac *ibn Kapron, Isaac ibn *Gikatilla). While Dunash's views prevailed and greatly influenced Spanish Hebrew poetry, he seems to have been unable to realize them in his own poetry—encomiastic and polemical poems and a quasi wine song which remain poor in style. His innovations were developed and extended in the following generation by Isaac b. Levi *ibn Mar Saul and particularly by Isaac *ibn Khalfun who was the first professional poet to write secular poetry.

Secular poetry expanded with the appearance of Samuel ha-Nagid, who introduced (or fully developed for the first time) universal wisdom poems, encomiastic and derogatory poems, official and personal dirges, wine and love poems, ornamental epigrams, and most of the other genres of secular poetry, including a genre which was not taken up by his followers, i.e., war poems. Samuel ha-Nagid's achievement is spectacular not only in the diversity of genres and themes he used, but in the flexibility of his style, his glittering descriptiveness, and in some aspects of his poetic diction. His high status as Jewish leader, minister, military commander of the Muslim armies, halakhist, and philologist undoubtedly also contributed toward establishing secular poetry (which greatly developed in his generation) as a branch of literature. As stated by Abraham *ibn Daud "In the days of Ḥisdai they started chirping and in the days of Samuel ha-Nagid they gave voice" (see Moses b. Samuel ha-Kohen *Gikatilla, and Judah b. Samuel *ibn Balam).

His younger contemporary, Solomon ibn Gabirol, famous as a philosopher and poet, added to secular poetry a dimension of introspective depth and complexity, particularly in his personal poems which express the poet's struggle against fate and his yearning for love. The paradox, which had served his predecessors as a rhetorical device, became in Gabirol's poems a means through which the poet expresses his divided soul. The change of mood from despair to joy, to boasting, in his secular poetry contrasts sharply with the tone of his excellent devotional poetry, which was written in a different style (see **Piyyut*). Gabirol not only wrote personal secular poems which depart from conventions but modified existing genres by refining the diverse aspects of their conventions.

At the end of the 11th century the Spanish style had already become defined and even minor poets, whose range was limited, produced commendable works and enriched the extensive background from which the great talents emerged. Literary activity in secular and devotional poetry increased greatly; "these groups of poets are as water, at first it flows slowly and then it gushes forth" (Moses ibn Ezra; see **Piyyut* in Spain, Isaac ibn Ghayyat, Levi b. Jacob *ibn Altabban, *Baḥya b. Joseph ibn Paquda, *Joseph b. Sheshet ibn Latimi, and Joseph b. Jacob *ibn Sahl). The characteristics were defined and expressed in theory and in practice in the works of Moses ibn Ezra (c. 1055 to 1135) who to some extent represents the school. In *Kitāb al-Muḥāḍara wa al-Mudhākara,* his work on poetics, he states the school's views on poetry: its essence, function, sources, and its practical theory of ornamentation. In another essay *Maqāla bi al-Hadīqa fī ma'anī al-majāz wa al-haqīqa,* he introduces a theory of metaphor as related to biblical exegesis and to contemporary poetry. Among his diverse secular poems some are written in a very ornamental style, showing a preference for the metaphor over the simile and combining it with various figures of speech. He was the first to develop homonymic poems which he collected in his *Sefer ha-Anak.*

Secular poetry attained its classical peak with the works of the greatest Hebrew poet of the period, Judah Halevi. He gained fame not just through his personality and nationalistic sentiments, expressed in his poems and in his book *Sefer ha-Kuzari,* but for the quality of his poetry which aroused the admiration of his contemporaries. His talent found scope both in his extensive and excellent devotional poetry and in his secular poetry, expressed in its range, versatility, and perhaps most of all in its pleasing style which the poet achieved by a very flexible use of rhetorical devices, surprising twists, and a personal tone accompanying well-known themes. Judah Halevi infused new life into the literary tradition of his time even to the extent of deviating from convention which he did with the freedom of the master. Through new combinations he modified and changed most of the poetic genres of his time. In dirges, for example, he not only used the classic form but innovated the genre with the strophic form to which he gave a ballad-like quality by introducing a dialogue with the deceased. His poems are also marked by a change of tone and his love poems range from lightness and humoristic brilliance to sensuality. Judah Halevi also created new genres: poems about Zion and sea poems. He developed the new possibilities that secular poetry afforded, yet none of the later poets reached his poetic excellence or versatility.

The Andalusian period of Hebrew poetry came to an end in Judah Halevi's generation (see *Solomon ibn al-Mu'alem, *Joseph b. Ẓaddik, and Judah b. Isaac *ibn Ghayyat)—a very short time after his death in Egypt (1141) and that of Moses ibn Ezra in northern Spain (1138?). The Almohads invaded Andalusia (1145) and wrought havoc among the Jewish communities which were completely destroyed.

Secular Poetry in Christian Spain. From the mid-12th century (during the Reconquista), as Jews emigrated to the north and the Christians advanced southward, secular Hebrew poetry (and Hebrew poetry in general) passed into Christian Spain. Although the cultural environment was no longer Muslim and the Arabic language and poetry were superseded by the Spanish language and literature, and to some extent by troubadour poetry, secular poetry deliberately and consciously carried on the tradition of the Andalusian period. The Hebrew poets of Christian Spain at times declared themselves to be the guardians of the Andalusian tradition or merely its epigones (e.g., Judah *al-Ḥarizi in *Taḥkemoni*). Sometimes they might evince an affinity for a particular Andalusian poet and his fate (e.g., Solomon b. Reuben *Bonafed for Solomon ibn Gabirol who had lived about 400 years earlier). In reality, however, important changes occurred in secular Hebrew poetry in Christian Spain due both to external influence and to internal development, one of which was in the sphere of language. In theory the ideal of biblical Hebrew still prevailed. Many poets who wrote and translated *maqāmāt* stressed their intention to glorify biblical Hebrew and to prove its vigor. Al-Ḥarizi (in his introduction to *Taḥkemoni*) even presented an allegorical personification of biblical Hebrew as his muse. In practice, however, poetry by the middle of the 13th century no longer adhered to biblical purism and used more and more rabbinic (talmudic and midrashic) language, and even the contemporary scientific and philosophical language which had evolved in the late 12th century. At the same time translated literature developed in order to bring scientific and philosophic writings to the Jews of Christian Spain who could not understand the original Arabic. Speculative literature written in Hebrew also began to flourish during this period.

Though the vocabulary was expanded, poetic diction tended to a prose-like sparseness or conversely to a baroque-like elaborateness and to manneristic forms, i.e., the use of certain letters only, poems composed in a geometrical form, poems which could be read backward, vertically, etc. Such devices appeared in some poetry only, but rarely allowed for genuine poetic expression. Humor and satire as poetic vehicles were already comparatively prominent in the 12th century. Parody was a popular device (e.g., parody of the marriage contract, the Mishnah, the prayer for the dead, etc.), especially in *maqāmāt* (*Judah b. Isaac ibn Shabbetai, Vidal Benveniste; see **Maqāma* and *Parody), for entertainment and, even more, for pungent social satire.

In the sphere of genres, the most prominent innovation in the Christian period was the development of the *maqāma* which was primarily an amusing story, written in rhymed prose with special emphasis on stylistic brilliance (sometimes at the expense of the plot), interlaced with poems that had both rhyme and meter. The plot at times was only a pretext for their introduction. The *maqāma* therefore may be classified as poetry, but it also contains prose narrative elements. Al-Ḥarizi's *maqāmāt* were patterned on the Arabic works of Al-Hamdani and Al-Ḥariri in which the hero, a likable scoundrel, appears in many independent stories, and the narrator relates his adventures. Most of the other rhymed stories—some by authors earlier than Al-Ḥarizi, e.g., Judah ibn Shabbetai and Joseph b. Meir *ibn Zabara, while others were later, e.g., *Jacob b. Eleazar and Isaac b. Solomon ibn *Sahula—adopted a different technique to unravel the plot and to present the characters and their function. They thus deviated from the *maqāma* genre. Some also show Christian influence, both in subject and in motif. In the 13th century, and perhaps somewhat earlier, the *maqāma* acquired a didactic-moralistic and satiric chatacter and was strongly influenced by philosophy (e.g., Shem Tov *Falaquera) and by the *Kabbalah (e.g., Isaac ibn Sahula).

Non-narrative metrical secular poetry also had a much wider range of subjects than in the Andalusian period. It broached topical matters, the most important of which was the major 13th-century controversy on the character and teaching of Maimonides (see Meshullam b. Solomon *da Piera, Meir *Abulafia, and the *Maimonidean Controversy). In the 14th and 15th centuries forced conversion and resistance to it was a foremost topic. While these polemical poems were not always of great artistic value, they were typical of the adherence to reality found in secular poetry and the avoidance of ideal classicist generalizations of the Andalusian period. This trend also found expression in other poetic genres, seen in the explicit mention of places, dates, etc., in the ready acceptance of new specific concrete themes, and in the realistic description of objects (e.g., a prison cell, a chess game, or a poor man's torn coat). Other themes testify to Christian influence, particularly troubadour poetry (through Provençal and related dialects, such as Catalan) and to a much lesser extent Spanish poetry which was then in its beginning (though some Hebrew poets also wrote in Spanish, e.g., *Santob de Carrion Shem Tov Ardutiel). Such themes were spiritual love (for a woman; e.g., Todros *Abulafia), a debate between abstract ideas (Abraham *ibn Ezra and others), the wanderings of a Hebrew troubadour (*Isaac b. Abraham ha-Gorni), mutual invectives between poets written in the form of a troubadour tenson (Todros Abulafia and *Phinehas b. Joseph ha-Levi), nature described pastorally (Meshullam da Piera), and other subjects (as well as some manneristic effects).

Secular poetry in the Christian period through its expansion of themes and forms was more variegated than the secular poetry of the Andalusian period. At the same time, however, it usually was inferior in literary merit. There were some talented poets and some groups of poets but there was no pleiad centering around great poets as in the Andalusian period.

Trends in Secular Poetry in Christian Spain. The beginning of the period of secular poetry in Christian Spain (during and shortly after the destruction of the Jewish communities of Andalusia) is represented by the versatile Abraham ibn Ezra, poet, commentator, philologist, and scientist, who disseminated the Hebrew-Spanish style and culture in Christian Spain. His extensive poetry already reveals the particular blend of Andalusian tradition and the beginning of the new trends in its humor, satire, realistic approach and description—mentioning places, etc., the use of new genres (e.g., poems of debate in which the proponents are abstract ideas), and in some manneristic effects. From the 12th to the 15th centuries, the fusion of Andalusian tradition with the various new elements (humor in parody, satire, concreteness, etc.) was differently effected in *maqāmāt,* rhymed stories (similar to the *maqāma* in form), and the poems interlaced in these stories which sometimes appear in a special section, e.g., at the end of *Taḥkemoni* by Al-Ḥarizi (see Joseph ibn Zabara; Isaac, author of *Mishlei Arav;* Judah ibn Shabbetai; Isaac, author of *Ezrat Nashim;* Judah al-Ḥarizi; Jacob b. Eleazar; Abraham b. Samuel ha-Levi *ibn Ḥasdai; Shem Tov Falaquera; Isaac ibn Sahula; *Kalonymus b. Kalonymus; Isaac b. Joseph ibn *Pulgar; Shem Tov Ardutiel; Maimon *Galipapa; and Vidal Benveniste for the development of this literature; see also **Maqāma*).

The principal innovations are first fully developed in the highly original poetry of Meshullam da Piera (early 13th century). He extensively resorts to rabbinic language and even to the language of the translators using unusual syntactic links between verses, but also sudden conceptual transitions and at times an obscure style which bears affinity to the troubadour *trobar clus*. He reduces the laudations in the panegyrics to a closing dedication (a type of troubadour *envoi*), etc.

The poet Todros Abulafia (late 13th century), whose patron was Don Isaac de la Maleha (courtier of Alfonso X, "the Wise"), also introduced novel themes into secular poetry such as spiritual love and love poems about Arab and Christian women, description of the court and of the prison in which the poet was incarcerated, and comments in his poems on hackneyed poetic conventions. He created new genres—a panegyric for the king patterned on a troubadour poem, panegyrics in which he used bold erotic imagery, and poems of controversy with another poet. To some extent he was also an innovator in clever manneristic forms (letter combination, echo rhymes, etc.). His poetry, however, shows him to be also an epigone of the Andalusian school (particularly of Moses ibn Ezra). Todros Abulafia was still bound to the Arabic language and poetry 150 years after his city Toledo had been conquered by the Christians.

During the 13th century secular poetry also developed in countries which had not been under Muslim rule, particularly Provence, which was under Spanish influence and received the Andalusian tradition through Hebrew only. Abraham b. Isaac *Bedersi (Habadrashi; of Beziers, Perpignan) tends to verbosity and flowery playfulness, employing strange images and even conspicuous mannerism in form. He seems to have been particularly fond of literary controversy with the poets of his time. His view on tradition and innovation is found in a fragment of a long and tedious poem in which he reviews early Hebrew poets, contemporary poets, and even Christian troubadours. His contemporary, Isaac ha-Gorni with whom he disputed, was a kind of Jewish troubadour who made the round of the communities with his musical instruments, as he himself states in some of his poems.

The poems by *Jedaiah (ha-Penini), son of Abraham Bedersi, are manneristic like his father's, but show more talent and poetic restraint. Jedaiah is perhaps the best-known Provencal Hebrew poet by virtue of his philosophical satiric work, *Beḥinat Olam*, which imitates the biblical style (division into verses, etc.). *Even Boḥan* (1322), by Kalonymus b. Kalonymus (the greatest translator of Provence), a similar work but of greater literary merit, is rich in talmudic expressions. It is characterized by despair about the Jewish condition, by biting satire, and by humor.

During the last 200 years (the 14th and 15th centuries) in which secular poetry flourished, Spanish Jewry lay under the shadow of persecutions and had to contend with forced conversion. The theme, however, is expressed in Spanish Hebrew literature as early as the 13th century. Among these is the controversy on religion between Isaac Pulgar and the apostate *Abner of Burgos carried on in polemical poetry and in *maqāmāt*.

The tendency in secular poetry toward formal mannerism and the use of linguistic and stylistic trick devices for their own sake is partly found in the poems of Ibn Soli, Joseph b. Sheshet ibn Latimi, and Samuel b. Joseph *ibn Sasson, Isaac Pulgar's friend. While there was also a number of good single poems there was an increase of uninspired versification of the books of the Bible and of philosophy. Some secular poems attained a high degree of excellence, e.g., the amusing *maqāmāt* of Shem Tov Ardutiel, of Maimon Galipapa, and to some extent the works of the last group of poets, Adat Nogenim, that toward the end of the 13th and the beginning of the 14th century centered around the Lavi family—Solomon da Piera (a descendant of the poet Meshullam da Piera), Joseph b. Lavi, Vidal Joseph Benveniste (b. Lavi), Astruc *Rimoch, Solomon Bonafed, and others. While most of them converted to Christianity after the *Tortosa Disputation in 1414, some continued to write in Hebrew.

The last prominent Hebrew poet in Christian Spain, Solomon Bonafed, one of the younger members of the Adat Nogenim group (which had disintegrated), did not convert to Christianity. He launched a biting satirical attack against his enemies and attended to problems of immediate import; at the same time he also wrote personal poetry, e.g., love poems to various women. (For other poets of the time see Solomon ha-Levi, Profiat *Duran (ha-Efodi), Moses b. Isaac *Remos, Simeon b. Ẓemaḥ *Duran (the Rashbaẓ), and *Mattathias.) Saadiah b. Maimun *ibn Dannan, one of the last Hebrew poets of Spain, lived in Granada, the last Muslim stronghold, which had been a center of Hebrew poetry hundreds of years earlier. After the conquest of Granada and the expulsion of all Jews from Spain in 1492, Ibn Dannan moved to North Africa. Among the Jews expelled from Spain were a number of poets who continued writing in other countries, e.g., Judah b. Isaac *Abrabanel who gained some fame for his book on love written in Italian.

The Jews expelled from Spain and their descendants continued to foster the Spanish style in their countries of refuge. The influence of the Hebrew-Spanish style had, however, extended beyond the Spanish borders long before—at the time secular poetry flourished in Spain. From the 12th century onward it was taken up by Jewish communities throughout the Muslim world (Egypt, Babylonia, Yemen, etc.) but it also influenced Jews in the Christian world (Italy, to some extent Germany, northern France, and especially Provence). The expulsion from Spain led to a new flourishing of the Hebrew-Spanish style in such widely dispersed Jewish communities as in Turkey, Greece, North Africa, Ereẓ Israel, and Holland. The period extended from the 16th to the 18th centuries.

Echoes of secular and devotional poetry, particularly of the great Andalusian poets, are found in modern Hebrew poetry at the end of the 19th century and in the 20th century. This harking back, however, is only sporadic. [D.Pa.]

Italy. Italy was the first European country, other than Spain, in which Hebrew poetry, both sacred and secular, was developed. Although the Jewish population there was never large, the Hebrew poets in Italy made a notable contribution to Hebrew poetry. In prayer the Jews in Italy originally used the *piyyutim* of Ereẓ Israel, but, beginning in the ninth century, Italian *paytanim* arose who, for all their dependence upon the Ereẓ Israel *piyyut*, made their poems express something of their own time and place. Secular Hebrew poems written in Italy during the earliest period have not survived, and only one *paytan*, *Silano, who lived in the ninth century in Venosa, is known to have composed humorous verse. The best-known early *paytanim* in Italy were members of the Ahimaaz family: *Shephatiah b. Amittai and *Amittai b. Shephatiah, and later, members of the *Kalonymus family, and *Elijah b. Shemaiah. Ahimaaz b. Paltiel's family chronicle, *Megillat Yuḥasin (Megillat Aḥima aẓ)*, written in rhymed prose, dates from the middle of the 11th century. Undoubtedly there was communication between the Jews of Spain and Provence and those of Italy, and Hebrew poetry written in Spain was known in Italy. From the beginning of the 12th century metrical poems were already being composed by Italian poets, e.g., *Jerahmeel b. Solomon (in southern Italy) and *Isaiah b. Mali di Trani. In the 13th century Benjamin delli Mansi composed a satire on his contemporaries in rhymed prose entitled

Massa Gei-Ḥizzayon. The greatest secular Hebrew poet of Italy, *Immanuel b. Solomon of Rome (Manoello Giudeo), lived during the 13th and 14th centuries. His *Maḥberot Immanu'el* (Brescia, 1492; critical ed., Jerusalem, 1957), containing all his prose and poems, was influenced by the poetry of Italy and Provence and the writings of Judah al-Ḥarizi, an influence Immanuel himself admitted. Immanuel was one of the first to compose sonnets in Italian and the first to compose Hebrew sonnets. His works comprise 28 compositions *(maḥberot),* the last being *Maḥberet ha-Tofet ve-ha-Eden* ("Hell and Paradise") in which the influence of Dante's *Divine Comedy* is recognizable. It has been suggested that since Dante's work is called *The Divine Comedy,* Immanuel's be called "The Human Comedy."

Immanuel's work inspired a diversification in secular poetry. Similarly, sacred poetry also began to acquire a new character; the poets of Italy, after the manner of the poets of Spain, composed metrical *piyyutim.* In the 15th century Italian Hebrew poets began to emancipate themselves from their servitude to Spanish meter, utilizing instead a new (syllabic) meter which did not differentiate between the long and the short syllable.

Translating works from Arabic into Hebrew became a major literary activity in 13th- and 14th-century Italy, as it had been earlier in Provence. One of the great Hebrew translators, Kalonymus b. Kalonymus b. Meir (Maestro Calo), who lived several years in Italy, became the friend of Immanuel of Rome and others of the "group of the poets" in Rome.

The first Hebrew play *Zaḥut Bediḥuta de-Kiddushin,* by Judah Leone b. Isaac *Sommo of Mantua (c. 1527–1592), was written in Italy and may have been performed during the author's lifetime. Sommo stated that he wrote the comedy to demonstrate that the Hebrew language was not dead and that it was capable of expressing contemporary concerns. Apart from this play, and apparently others, Sommo also wrote poetry and was known for his "Dialogues on Stagecraft," a discussion in Italian of the history and nature of the theater. However, Sommo's original work was preceded by the Hebrew translation made by Joseph b. Samuel Zarfati (b. in Rome, Giuseppe Gallo; d. 1527) of the Marrano Fernando de *Rojas' important Spanish play, *Tragicomedia de Calisto y Malibea (La Celestina).* The play, which first appeared in Burgos in 1499, had considerable influence on the development of drama. Although the translation itself has been lost, the translator's prologue is extant (see *Drama).

Leone *Modena, a man of great learning, composed poetry and prose in Hebrew and Italian and also a play in Italian. Moses b. Mordecai *Zacuto, the 17th-century kabbalist and poet, composed two Hebrew plays: *Yesod Olam* (Berlin, 1875), on the patriarch Abraham, and *Tofteh Arukh* (Venice, 1715), on punishment after death. *Tofteh Arukh* ("Prepared Hell"), a play which reflects the influence of Immanuel of Rome, was at one time read as a *musar* book. Scholars who had read the play at communal gatherings requested the poet Jacob Daniel b. Abraham *Olmo (Ferrara, 1690–1757) to compose a play about the Garden of Eden. Complying with this request Olmo wrote *Eden Arukh* ("Eden Prepared"), which was published together with *Tofteh Arukh* in Venice in 1744. In the 17th century the brothers Jacob and Immanuel *Frances wrote poetry, satire, and polemic. Although subsequently a great deal of Hebrew poetry was composed in Italy, few innovations were introduced until the appearance in the 18th century of Moses Ḥayyim *Luzzatto, who began a new chapter in Hebrew poetry.

France and Germany. In the Middle Ages the Jewish inhabitants of France and Germany constituted a single cultural entity. Although it is probable that secular poetry in the vernacular was composed by Jews living in this area, none of it is extant. The Hebrew poetry of the Jews of France and Germany was initially liturgical (for a further treatment see **Piyyut*). In their synagogues the Jews of these countries initially used the *piyyutim* of Italian Jewry, and those Ereẓ Israel *piyyutim* which had been adopted in Italy. The first *paytanim* in France and Germany, who appeared at the beginning of the tenth century, were members of the Kalonymus family (Moses and Meshullam) originating from Italy. In the mid-tenth century *Simeon b. Isaac and *Gershom b. Judah ("the light of the exile") lived there. With the increase in the number of French and German *paytanim,* two of the greatest medieval *paytanim,* *Ephraim b. Isaac of Regensburg and *Ephraim b. Jacob of Bonn, made their appearance in the 12th century. Ephraim b. Isaac was the first to use Spanish meter in his *piyyutim,* and Ephraim b. Jacob integrated short *piyyutim* into his *Sefer Zekhirah,* a chronicle of the persecutions suffered by Jews of his time. Although in his *Tefillah Tikkaḥ Teḥinna Tivḥar* (Oẓar, 473) the 11th-century *paytan,* *Meir b. Isaac, anticipated Ephraim b. Isaac in the use of the Spanish meter in *piyyut,* this innovation was not followed up until much later. In the 12th and 13th centuries, *Judah b. Kalonymus and his son, *Eleazar b. Judah of Worms, author of the *Sefer Roke'ah,* reflected in their *piyyutim* the sufferings endured by the Jews of their era. In medieval times every rabbi composed *piyyutim,* since the people wished to hear not only the traditional *piyyutim* but also new ones expressive of their time and place, and composed by a *paytan* whom they knew. Although these *piyyutim* are important from an historical point of view, poetically they contain little originality.

A parody, *Leil Shikkorim Hu Zeh ha-Laylah* (Oẓar, 721), attributed to *Menahem b. Aaron ibn Zeraḥ, was inserted into the *Maḥzor Vitry* apparently as a joke. Also extant are the satirical poems *Golim Holekhei Derekh* (Oẓar 119) of Gomplin, the song, *Yom mi-Ẓarefat Yaẓati* ("The Day I Left France"), by Isaac, and the jocose poems in Hebrew and Yiddish of Menahem Oldendorf (15th–16th centuries). From the 16th to 18th centuries *paytanim* and rhymesters, whose poetry is of little value, appeared in France and Germany and in countries to which French and German Jews immigrated, e.g., Bohemia, Russia, and Poland.

England. Before the expulsion in 1290, *paytanim* in England such as *Joseph b. Asher of Chartres, who lamented the pogrom in York (1191) and *Meir b. Elijah of Norwich (13th century) were influenced by the French *paytanim.* Meir of Norwich, in addition to *piyyutim,* composed metrical rhymes of four lines in which the first two and last two letters of the line are identical. Secular poetry, some of which was inspired by Spanish poetry, was also written. Indebted to the French fabulist, Marie de France, is the secular poetry found in *Mishlei Shu'alim* ("Fox Fables," latest edition, Jerusalem, 1946) by *Berechiah b. Natronai ha-Nakdan, who lived in the 13th century in Normandy and also in England. The work is written in rhymed prose and the fables end with metrical poems.

For the modern period see *Hebrew Literature, Modern. See also **Piyyut* (includes a list of *paytanim* and poets); *Prosody. For a general review, see *Literature, Jewish. Hebrew poetry. [A.M.H.]

Bibliography: BIBLICAL, GENERAL: T. H. Robinson, *The Poetry of the Old Testament* (1947); idem, in: VT Supplement, 1 (1953), 128–49; N. K. Gottwald, in: IDB, 4 (1962), 829–38. EARLY POETRY: G. A. Smith, *The Early Poetry of Israel* . . . (1910); E. G. King,

Early Religious Poetry of the Hebrews (1911); A. Causse, *Les plus vieux chants*... (1926); Finesinger, in: HUCA, 3 (1926), 21–77; Albright, Arch Rel, 14–16; F. M. Cross, *Studies in Ancient Yahwistic Poetry* (1950); E. Werner, in: IDB, 3 (1962), 457–76; S. Gevirtz, *Patterns in the Early Poetry of Israel* (1963). PARALLELISM: R. Lowth, *Lectures on the Sacred Poetry of the Hebrews* (1835); idem, *Isaiah, a New Translation*... (1834[10]); G. B. Gray, *The Forms of Hebrew Poetry* (1915); C.F. Burney, *The Poetry of Our Land* (1925); W. F. Albright, *Yahweh and the Gods of Canaan* (1968), 1–46. STROPHE: D. H. Mueller, *Strophenbau und Responsien* (1898); A. Condamin, *Poèmes de la Bible avec une introduction sur la strophe hébraïque* (1933); C. F. Kraft, *The Strophic Structure of Hebrew Poetry* (1938); idem, in: E. C. Hobbs (ed.), *A Stubborn Faith* (1956), 62–89. METER: J. Ley, *Die metrischen Formen der hebraeischen Poesie* (1866); idem, *Grundzuege des Rhythmus, des Vers- und Strophenbaues in der hebraeischen Poesie* (1875); K. Budde, in: ZAW, 2 (1882), 1–52; idem, in: DB, 4 (1902), 3–13; E. Sievers, *Metrische Studien*, 1–2 (1901–05); S. Mowinckel, in: *A. Bertholet Festschrift* (1950), 379–94; Robinson, in: ZAW, 54 (1936), 28–34. GENRE: S. Mowinckel, *Psalmenstudien*, 2 (1961); H. Gunkel and J. Begrich, *Einleitung in die Psalmen* (1933); O. Eissfeldt, *The Old Testament*... (1965), 57ff.; J. Muilenburg, in: *Studia Biblica et Semitica t. Ch. Vrieren Dedicata* (1966), 233–57; G. Fohrer, *Introduction to the Old Testament* (1968); A. R. Johnson, in: H. H. Rowley (ed.), *The Old Testament and Modern Study* (1951), 162–209; A. Bentzen, *Introduction to the Old Testament*, 1 (1956). STYLE: I. M. Casanowicz, *Paronomasia in the Old Testament* (1894); E. Koenig, *Stilistik, Rhetorik, Poetik* (1900); Rankin, in: JTS, 21 (1930), 285–91; J. Muilenburg, in: VTS, 1 (1953), 97–111. COMPARATIVE LITERATURE: C. G. Cumming, *Assyrian and Hebrew Hymns of Praise* (1934); G. Widengren, *The Accadian and Hebrew Psalms of Lamentations*... (1937); J. H. Patton, *Canaanite Parallels in the Book of Psalms* (1944); Albright, in: CBQ, 7 (1945), 5–31; C. H. Gordon, *Ugaritic Handbook* (1947), 94–113; A. Falkenstein and W. von Soden, *Sumerische und akkadische Hymnen und Gebete* (1953). MEDIEVAL HEBREW SECULAR: SPAIN AND PROVENCE: For editions and studies of individual authors see the individual articles. Davidson, Oẓar, 4 vols. (1924–33); second enlarged edition with general introduction by Ḥ. Schirmann (1970); Ḥ. Schirmann, in: KS, 26 onward (from 1950 onward), annual bibliography of research in secular and sacred poetry; Schirmann, Sefarad (1961[2]), an anthology of poetry in Spain and Provence, with an introduction on each poet, and a bibliography; idem, *La poésie hebraique du Moyen Age en Espagne*, in: *Mélanges de Philosophie et de Littérature juives* (1962), 171–210; idem, *Shirim Ḥadashim min ha-Genizah* (1965); idem, *Problems in the Study of Post-Biblical Hebrew Poetry*, in: *Proceedings of the Israel Academy of Sciences and Humanities*, 2 (1967), 228–36; A. M. Habermann, *Toledot ha-Piyyut ve-ha-Shirah* (1970); B. Halper, *The Scansion of Mediaeval Hebrew Poetry*, in: JQR, 4 (1913/14), 153–224; J. Schirmann, *La métrique quantitative dans la poesie hébraïque du Moyen Age*, in: *Sefarad*, 8 (1948), 323–32; D. Yellin, *Torat ha-Shirah ha-Sefaradit* (1939); S. Abramson, *Bi-Leshon Kodemim* (1965); D. Pagis, *Shirat ha-Ḥol ve-Torat ha-Shir le-Moshe ibn Ezra u-Venei Zemanno* (1970); J. Schirmann, *The Function of the Hebrew Poet in Medieval Spain*, in: JSOS, 16 (1954), 235–52; J. Weiss, *Tarbut Ḥazranit ve-Shirah Ḥazranit* (1948); S. D. Goitein, *Ha-Makamah ve-ha-Maḥberet—Perek be-Toledot ha-Sifrut ve-ha-Ḥevrah be-Mizraḥ*, in: *Maḥbarot le-Sifrut*, 5 (1951), 25–40; I. Goldziher, *Bemerkungen zur neuhebraeischen Trauerpoesie*, in: JQR, 14 (1901/02), 719–36; J. Schirmann, "The Ephebe in Medieval Hebrew Poetry," in: *Sefarad*, 15 (1955), 58–68; I. Levin, *Zeman ve-Tevel be-Shirat ha-Ḥol ha-Ivrit be-Sefarad bi-Ymei ha-Beinayim*, in: *Oẓar Yehudei Sefarad*, 5 (1962), 68–79; J. Schirmann, *Der Neger und die Negerin; Zur Bildersprache und Stottwahl der Spanisch-Hebraeischen Dichtung*, in: MGWJ, 83 (1939), 481–92. ITALY: B. Klar (ed.), *Megillat Aḥima'aẓ* (1945); Schirmann, Italy; idem (ed.), *Ẓaḥut Bediḥuta de-Kiddushin* (1946); P. Naveh (ed.), *Kol Shirei Ya'akov Frances* (1969); S. Bernstein (ed.), *Divan le-Rabbi Immanu'el ben David Frances* (1932); C. Roth, *The Jews in the Renaissance* (1959). FRANCE AND GERMANY: I. Elbogen et al., *Germania Judaica* (1934); A. M. Habermann, *Piyyutei Rabbi Shimon bar Yiẓḥak* (1938); idem, *Gezerot Ashkenaz ve-Ẓarefat* (1966); idem, *Hebrew Poems of Meir of Norwich* (1966); idem, in YMḤSI, 2 (1936), 92–115; idem, in: *Sinai*, 15 (1945), 288–98; S. Spiegel, in: L. Finkelstein (ed.), *The Jews, their History, Culture, and Religion*, 1 (1960[3]), 854–92.

POGREBISHCHENSKI (known as **Pogrebishche** up to 1945, referred to by the Jews as **Pohorbishch** and in Polish documents as **Bohybryszcze**), town in Vinnitsa oblast, Ukrainian S.S.R. Jews settled in Pogrebishchenski at the beginning of the 17th century, and it is listed among the communities destroyed during the *Chmielnicki massacres of 1648. The community, restored at the end of the 17th century, suffered severely from the uprisings of the *Haidamacks in 1736 and 1768. There were 664 Jews in Pogrebishchenski in 1765 and 1,726 in 1847; the census of 1897 showed 2,494 Jews (39.5% of the total population). The 17th-century wooden synagogue, whose construction and appurtenances were renowned for their original artistic execution, attracted the attention of researchers of Jewish art. During the years of the civil war (1918–19), a Jewish *self-defense group was maintained, which prevented bands of peasants of the region from attacking Jews. In the summer of 1919 troops of *Petlyura conquered the locality and ordered the self-defense group to be disarmed. A few days later (on Aug. 22, 1919) an armed band of peasants entered and gained control of the town, carrying out a massacre of the Jews which lasted several hours. About 400 people were murdered, many were wounded, and property was looted. There were 2,881 Jews (30% of the total) in the town in 1926. The Jewish community was destroyed during the German occupation in 1941.

Drawing of the synagogue of Pogrebishchenski, built during the 17th century. From M. and K. Piechotka, *Wooden Synagogues*, Warsaw, 1959.

Bibliography: Committee of Jewish Delegations, *The Pogroms in the Ukraine* (1927), 231–3; E. Tcherikower, *Di Ukrainer Pogromen in Yor 1919* (1965), 261–3. [Y.S.]

POGROMS. Pogrom is a Russian word designating an attack, accompanied by destruction, the looting of property, murder, and rape, perpetrated by one section of the population against another. In modern Russian history pogroms have been perpetrated against other nations (Armenians, Tatars) or groups of inhabitants (intelligentsia). However, as an international term, the word "pogrom" is employed in many languages to describe specifically the attacks accompanied by looting and bloodshed against the Jews in Russia. The word designates more particularly the attacks carried out by the Christian population against the Jews between 1881 and 1921 while the civil and military authorities remained neutral and occasionally provided their secret or open support. The pogroms occurred during periods of severe political crises in the country and were outbreaks linked to social upheavals and nationalist incitement in Eastern Europe.

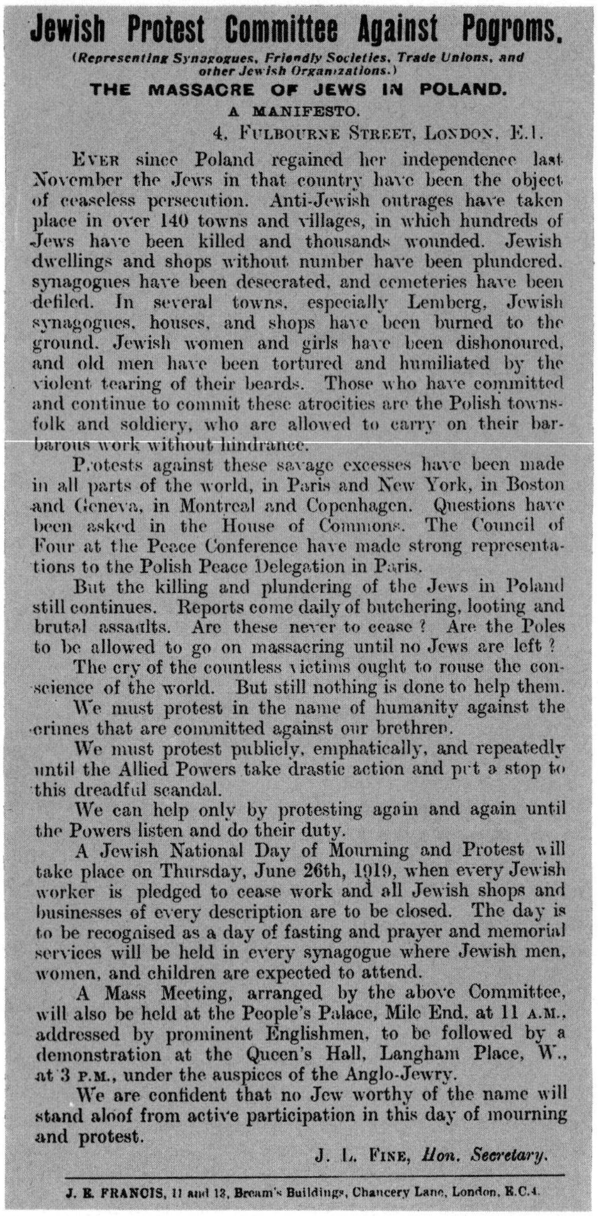

Jewish Protest Committee Against Pogroms.

(Representing Synagogues, Friendly Societies, Trade Unions, and other Jewish Organizations.)

THE MASSACRE OF JEWS IN POLAND.

A MANIFESTO.

4, FULBOURNE STREET, LONDON, E.1.

EVER since Poland regained her independence last November the Jews in that country have been the object of ceaseless persecution. Anti-Jewish outrages have taken place in over 140 towns and villages, in which hundreds of Jews have been killed and thousands wounded. Jewish dwellings and shops without number have been plundered, synagogues have been desecrated, and cemeteries have been defiled. In several towns, especially Lemberg, Jewish synagogues, houses, and shops have been burned to the ground. Jewish women and girls have been dishonoured, and old men have been tortured and humiliated by the violent tearing of their beards. Those who have committed and continue to commit these atrocities are the Polish townsfolk and soldiery, who are allowed to carry on their barbarous work without hindrance.

Protests against these savage excesses have been made in all parts of the world, in Paris and New York, in Boston and Geneva, in Montreal and Copenhagen. Questions have been asked in the House of Commons. The Council of Four at the Peace Conference have made strong representations to the Polish Peace Delegation in Paris.

But the killing and plundering of the Jews in Poland still continues. Reports come daily of butchering, looting and brutal assaults. Are these never to cease? Are the Poles to be allowed to go on massacring until no Jews are left?

The cry of the countless victims ought to rouse the conscience of the world. But still nothing is done to help them.

We must protest in the name of humanity against the crimes that are committed against our brethren.

We must protest publicly, emphatically, and repeatedly until the Allied Powers take drastic action and put a stop to this dreadful scandal.

We can help only by protesting again and again until the Powers listen and do their duty.

A Jewish National Day of Mourning and Protest will take place on Thursday, June 26th, 1919, when every Jewish worker is pledged to cease work and all Jewish shops and businesses of every description are to be closed. The day is to be recognised as a day of fasting and prayer and memorial services will be held in every synagogue where Jewish men, women, and children are expected to attend.

A Mass Meeting, arranged by the above Committee, will also be held at the People's Palace, Mile End, at 11 A.M., addressed by prominent Englishmen, to be followed by a demonstration at the Queen's Hall, Langham Place, W., at 3 P.M., under the auspices of the Anglo-Jewry.

We are confident that no Jew worthy of the name will stand aloof from active participation in this day of mourning and protest.

J. L. FINE, *Hon. Secretary.*

J. E. FRANCIS, 11 and 13, Bream's Buildings, Chancery Lane, London, E.C.4.

Figure 1. Announcement of a general strike as a demonstration against pogroms in Poland, by the Jewish Protest Committee Against Pogroms, London, June 1919. Courtesy J. Fraenkel, London.

(Similar events also occurred during that period, though on a more limited scale, in the context of the anti-Semitic movements in Germany, Austria, Rumania, and the Balkan countries, and of nationalist and religious fanaticism in *Morocco, *Algeria, and *Persia.)

The Jews of Russia were the victims of three large-scale waves of pogroms, each of which surpassed the preceding in scope and savagery. These occurred between the years 1881 and 1884, 1903 and 1906, and 1917 and 1921. There were outbreaks in Poland after it regained independence in 1918, and in Rumania from 1921.

In the 1880s. The pogroms of the 1880s took place during the period of confusion which prevailed in Russia after the assassination of Czar Alexander II by members of the revolutionary organization *Narodnaya Volya on March 13, 1881. Anti-Jewish circles spread a rumor that the czar had been assassinated by Jews and that the government authorized attacks on them. The pogroms at first also received the support of some revolutionary circles, who regarded this action as a preliminary awakening of the masses which would lead to the elimination of the existing regime. The first pogrom occurred in the town of Yelizavetgrad (*Kirovograd), in Ukraine, at the end of April 1881. From there, the pogrom wave spread to the surrounding villages and townlets—about 30 in number. At the beginning of May, the pogroms spread to the provinces of *Kherson, Taurida, Yekaterinoslav (*Dnepropetrovsk), *Kiev, *Poltava, and *Chernigov. The most severe attack was perpetrated in Kiev over three days before the eyes of the governor-general and his staff of officials and police force while no attempt was made to restrain the rioters. The pogroms in *Odessa were of more limited scope. During the months of July and August there was again a series of pogroms in the provinces of Chernigov and Poltava. During this period, the pogroms were mainly restricted to destruction, the looting of property, and beatings. The number of dead was small. The attackers came from among the rabble of the towns, the peasants, and the workers in industrial enterprises and the railroads. At the end of this period, the government forces reacted against the rioters and in several places even opened fire on them, leaving a number of dead and injured. The pogroms occurred in a restricted geographical region—southern and eastern Ukraine. Here there was a combination of aggravating circumstances: the traditional rebelliousness among the masses, a tradition of anti-Jewish hatred and persecutions from the 17th and 18th centuries (the massacres perpetrated by *Chmielnicki and the *Haidamacks), together with the presence there of homeless seasonal workers in the factories, railways, and ports, the rise of a rural bourgeoisie and local intelligentsia, who regarded the Jews as most dangerous rivals, and an extremist revolutionary movement which was unscrupulous in the methods it adopted.

After the pogroms in the spring and summer of 1881, there was a remission, although occasional pogroms broke out in various parts of the country. Among these was a severe pogrom in *Warsaw on the Catholic Christmas Day and an Easter pogrom in *Balta, in which two Jews were killed, 120 injured, and many cases of rape occurred. In *Belorussia and *Lithuania, where the local authorities adopted a firm attitude against the rioters, large fires broke out in many towns and townlets; a considerable number of these were started by the enemies of the Jews. The murder of individual Jews and even whole families also became a common occurrence during this period. On June 21, 1882, the new minister of the interior, Count D. Tolstoy, published an order which placed the blame for the pogroms on the governors of the provinces and declared that "every attitude of negligence on the part of the administration and the police would entail the dismissal from their position of those who were guilty." Isolated pogroms nevertheless occurred during the following two years or so. In the spring of 1883, a sudden wave of pogroms broke out in the towns of *Rostov and Yekaterinoslav and their surroundings. On this occasion, the authorities reacted with vigor against the rioters and there were several victims among them. The last great outburst occurred in June 1884 in Nizhni Novgorod (see *Gorki), where the mob attacked the Jews of the Kanavino quarter, killing nine of them and looting much property. The authorities tried over 70 of the rioters and severe penalties of imprisonment were imposed on them. This marked the end of the first wave of pogroms in Russia.

The pogroms of the 1880s greatly influenced the history of Russian Jewry. In their wake, the Russian government adopted a systematic policy of discrimination with the object of removing the Jews from their economic and public positions. This was achieved either by restrictive laws (the *May Laws of 1882, the percentage norm of admission (*numerus clausus) to secondary schools, higher institutions of learning, etc.) or by administrative pressure, which reached its climax with the expulsion of the Jews from

*Moscow in 1891–92. A mass Jewish emigration began from Russia to the United States and other countries. One reaction to the pogroms was the birth of a nationalist and Zionist movement among the Jews of Russia, while many of the Jewish youth joined the revolutionary movement. The year 1881, the first year of the pogroms, was a turning point not only for Russian Jewry but also for the whole of the Jewish people.

1903 to 1906. The second wave of pogroms was connected with the revolutionary agitation in Russia and the first Russian revolution of 1905. In its struggle against the revolutionary movement, the Russian government gave the reactionary press a free hand to engage in unbridled anti-Jewish incitement in an attempt to divert the anger of the masses against the Jews and to represent the revolutionary movement as the result of "Jewish machinations." Monarchist societies, such as the *Union of Russian People, the Double-headed Eagle Society, and others, which were referred to by the general name of the *Black Hundreds, played a prominent role in the organization of the pogroms. The first results of this incitement were pogroms which occurred in Kishinev during Passover 1903, in the wake of the wild agitation propagated by the anti-Semitic local newspaper *Bessarabets,* edited by P. *Krushevan. This pogrom was accompanied by savage murders (45 dead and hundreds of injured) and mutilations of the injured and dead. About 1,500 Jewish houses and shops were looted. The pogrom angered public opinion throughout the world. Subsequently, a *self-defense movement was organized among the Jewish youth. Its organizers were mainly drawn from the Zionist socialist parties and the *Bund. In a pogrom which broke out in *Gomel in September 1903, the self-defense group played a prominent part in saving Jewish lives and property. In the fall of 1904, a series of pogroms was perpetrated in *Smela, *Rovno, *Aleksandriya and other places by army recruits about to be sent to the war against Japan and by the local rabble. In 1905, when the revolutionary movement gained strength, reactionary circles, with the support of the government, intensified the anti-Jewish propaganda, and an atmosphere of terror reigned in many towns of the *Pale of Settlement and beyond it. Occasionally pogroms occurred in reaction to revolutionary demonstrations, which the opponents of the revolution condemned as Jewish demonstrations. In February 1905 a pogrom took place in *Feodosiya, and in April of the same year in *Melitopol. A pogrom which took place in the provincial capital of *Zhitomir surpassed all these in scope (May 1905). However, the severest pogroms of this period took place during the first week of November 1905, immediately after the publication of the manifesto of the czar (October 1905), which promised the inhabitants of Russia civic liberties and the establishment of a state *Duma (Parliament). On publication of the manifesto, spontaneous manifestations of joy broke out throughout Russia. The celebrants came from the liberal and radical elements of Russian society, while the Jews, who hoped to obtain rapid *emancipation, prominently participated in this rejoicing. In response to these manifestations, the reactionary circles organized popular processions of elements loyal to the regime; these were headed by the local civil and ecclesiastical leaders. In many places these processions developed into pogroms against the Jews (on some occasions, the non-Jewish intelligentsia was also attacked).

The most serious pogrom occurred in Odessa (with over 300 dead and thousands of wounded); another severe pogrom took place in Yekaterinoslav, where 120 Jews lost their lives. Altogether, pogroms were perpetrated in 64 towns (including, in addition to Odessa and Yekaterinoslav, Kiev, Kishinev, *Simferopol, *Romny, *Kremenchug, *Nikolayev, Chernigov, *Kamenets-Podolski, and Yelizavetgrad), and 626 townlets and villages. About 660 of the pogroms took place in the Ukraine and Bessarabia, 24 outside the Pale of Settlement, and only seven in Belorussia. There were no pogroms in Poland and Lithuania. The total number of dead in these pogroms was estimated at over 800. The pogroms lasted only a few days. The most prominent participants were railway workers, small shopkeepers and craftsmen, and industrial workers. The peasants mainly joined in to loot property.

From the outset, these pogroms were inspired by government circles. The local authorities received instructions to give the pogromists a free hand and to protect them from the Jewish self-defense. Commissions of inquiry were appointed after the pogroms which explicitly pointed out the criminal inactivity of the police and military forces. After a while, it became known that pamphlets calling for the pogroms had been printed on the press of the governmental secret police.

Two further pogroms occurred in 1906. The first took place in *Bialystok in June. About 80 Jews lost their lives and the mob looted and murdered under the protection of the military and police forces, who systematically opened fire on the Jews. This pogrom occurred during the session of the first Duma, which sent a commission of inquiry to Bialystok. It also held a debate, in which direct responsibility for the pogrom was placed on the authorities. The second took place in *Siedlce in August and was directly perpetrated by the police and military forces. About 30 Jews were killed and 180 wounded. With the suppression of the first Russian revolution, the pogroms were brought to a halt until the downfall of the old regime in 1917.

The pogroms of 1903–06 stimulated a great nationalist awakening among the Jews of Europe, they encouraged the development of organized self-defense movements among Jews, and accelerated Jewish emigration for the Second *Aliyah and the formation of the *Hashomer society in Ereẓ Israel.

1917 to 1921. The third wave of pogroms occurred during the years 1917–21, in scope and gravity far surpassing the two previous outbreaks. These attacks on the Jews were connected with the revolutions and the civil war which took place in Eastern Europe during this period. At the end of 1917, pogroms had already occurred in the townlets and towns within proximity of the war front. The riot was headed by groups of soldiers from the disintegrating czarist army, and consisted of unruly acts against Jews by drunkards and of looting. Many pogroms of this type occurred in the Ukraine after the declaration of its independence in 1918. The first pogroms to be accompanied by slaughter of Jews were, however, perpetrated by units of

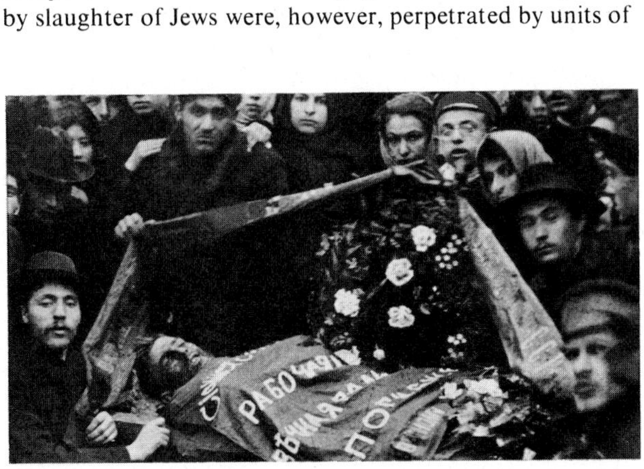

Figure 2. Funeral for a member of the Socialist Zionist Party of Odessa, killed in the pogrom of 1905. Courtesy A. Raphaeli-Zenziper, Archive for Russian Zionism, Tel Aviv.

Figure 3. "After the Pogrom," an oil painting by S. Fabjanski. The painting was exhibited in Munich in 1910. Courtesy Z. Efron, En Harod.

the Red Army which retreated from the Ukraine in the spring of 1918 before the German army. These pogroms took place under the slogan of "Strike at the bourgeoisie and the Jews." The communities of *Novgorod-Severski and Glukhov in northern Ukraine were the most severely affected. After a short period of confusion, the Soviets adopted stringent measures against pogromists found in the ranks of the Red Army. In addition to a fundamental and comprehensive information campaign, severe penalities were imposed not only on guilty individuals who were executed but also on complete army units which were disbanded after their men had attacked Jews. Even though pogroms were still perpetrated after this, mainly by Ukrainian units of the Red Army at the time of its retreat from Poland (1920), in general, the Jews regarded the units of the Red Army as the only force which was able and willing to defend them.

In the spring of 1919, at the time of the retreat of the Ukrainian Army before the Red Army which occupied Kiev, units of the Ukrainian Army carried out organized military pogroms in *Berdichev, Zhitomir, and other towns. These pogroms reached their climax in the massacre at *Proskurov on Feb. 15, 1919, when 1,700 Jews were done to death within a few hours. On the following day, a further 600 victims fell in the neighboring townlet of Felshtin (Gvardeiskoye). Those responsible for these pogroms went unpunished, and henceforward the Ukrainian soldiers considered themselves free to spill Jewish blood. The Jews regarded Simon *Petlyura, the prime minister of the Ukraine and commander of its forces, as responsible for these pogroms (in 1926 he was assassinated while in exile in Paris by Shalom *Schwarzbard). The general chaos which reigned in the Ukraine in 1919 resulted in the formation of large and small bands of peasants who fought against the Red Army. The commanders of these bands (atamans) occasionally gained control of whole regions. The Jews in the villages, townlets, and towns there were constantly terrorized by the peasants, who extorted money ("contributions") and supplies from them or robbed and murdered them. These atamans included Angell, Kazakov, Kozyr-Zyrko, Struk, Volynets, Zeleny, Tutunik, and Shepel. The ataman Grigoryev, who in May 1919 seceded from the Red Army with his men, was responsible for pogroms in 40 communities and the deaths of about 6,000 Jews in the summer of 1919. He was killed by ataman Makhno, who led a peasant rebellion in eastern Ukraine and endeavored to restrain his men from attacking the Jews. One of the most notorious pogroms carried out by the peasant bands was that in Trostyanets in May 1919, when over 400 people lost their lives.

In the fall of 1919, there was a wave of pogroms in the wake of the counterrevolutionary "White Army," under the command of General A. I. *Denikin, in its advance from northern Caucasus into the heart of Russia. This army, which sought to restore the ancient regime, proclaimed the slogan: "Strike at the Jews and save Russia." Its officers and soldiers made savage attacks on the Jews in every place which they occupied. The most sinister of these pogroms was in Fastov at the beginning of September 1919, in which about 1,500 Jewish men, women, and children were massacred. The soldiers of the "White Army" also perpetrated similar pogroms in other regions of Russia: in Siberia, where they were led by Admiral Kolchak and where the Cossack battalions of Baron R. Ungern-Sternberg gained notoriety for the systematic destruction of many communities in eastern Siberia and Mongolia; and in Belorussia, where Bulak-Balachowicz was in command in 1920. During 1920–21, when the Red Army gained control of Ukraine, the armed anti-Soviet bands still retained their full strength and the pogroms and brutalities against the Jews assumed a character of revenge, such as the massacre in Tetiev, in which about 4,000 Jews were put to death and the whole townlet was set on fire. The anti-Jewish movement set the total annihilation of the Jews as its objective and destroyed whole townlets. Only the military weakness of the attackers prevented a holocaust of Ukrainian Jewry.

During this period of pogroms, Jewish self-defense organizations were formed in many places throughout the Ukraine. The "Jewish Militia for War against Pogroms" of Odessa was renowned; it prevented pogroms in the largest community of Ukraine. Such groups were created in many towns and townlets but they were not always capable of withstanding military units or large armed bands. It was only after the consolidation of the Soviet regime that they received its support and played an important role in the suppression of the armed bands movement.

It is difficult to assess the scope of the pogroms during the civil war years and the number of victims they claimed. Partial data are available for 530 communities in which 887 major pogroms and 349 minor pogroms occurred; there were 60,000 dead and several times that number of wounded (according to S. Dubnow). The pogroms of 1917–21 shocked East European Jewry, as well as world Jewry. On the one hand, they rallied many Jews to the Red Army and the Soviet regime; on the other, they strengthened the desire for the creation of a homeland for the Jewish people and a powerful and independent Jewish force. This aspiration found its expression in the Zionist movement, the *He-Ḥalutz movement, and the *Haganah in Ereẓ Israel.

Bibliography: Zionist Organization, *Die Judenpogrome in Russland,* 2 vols. (1909); Dubnow, Hist Russ, 3 (1920), index; Yevreyskoye istoriko-etnograficheskoye obshchestvo, *Materialy dlya istorii anti-yevreyskikh pogromov v Rossii,* 2 vols. (1919–23); I. Halpern, *Sefer ha-Gevurah,* 2 (1944), 104–58; 3 (1951), 1–229; E. Heifetz, *The Slaughter of the Jews in the Ukraine in 1919* (1921); Committee of Jewish Delegations, *The Pogroms in the Ukraine* (1927); L. Khazanovich, *Der Idisher Khurbn in Ukraine* (1920); E. Tcherikower, *Antisemitizm un Pogromen in Ukraine 1917–1918* (1923); idem, *Di Ukrainer Pogromen in Yor 1919* (1965); J. Schechtman, *Pogromy dobrovolcheskoy armii na Ukraine* (1932); N. Gergel, *Di Pogromen in Ukraine* (1928); A. D. Rosenthal, *Megillat ha-Tevah,* 3 vols. (1927–31); A. Druyanow (ed.), *Reshumot,* 3 (1923); R. Feigenberg, *A Pinkas fun a Toyter Shtot* (1926); *Yevreyskiye pogromy 1918–1921—album* (1926); *He-Avar,* 9 (1962), 3–81; 10 (1963), 5–149; 17 (1970), 3–136. [Y.S.]

°**POHL, OSWALD** (1896–1951), *S.S. officer, formerly a naval paymaster. In 1934 he became head of the administrative office of the S.S. which dealt with all its financial and administrative matters. In 1939 he was appointed head of the construction office of the S.S., including the concentration camps. On Feb. 1, 1942, the officers under his charge were brought into the Economic and Administrative Main Office (WVHA). In the spring of 1942 the Inspection Authority of the concentration camps was added to his responsibilities. Pohl aimed at financing all S.S. activities, including the Waffen S.S., from the profits of S.S.-owned enterprises for which he utilized the slave labor of concentration camp prisoners and expropriated Jewish property. Another source of income was gained from the belongings of murdered Jews, including their gold teeth. Pohl always urged longer working hours, less respite, and stricter supervision over the camp inmates. He enslaved prisoners of war contrary to international conventions. Always pressed for manpower, he even opposed the *RSHA policy for the total destruction of the Jews and advocated sparing able-bodied Jews from immediate extermination to be worked to death. Pohl was sentenced to death by the U.S. Military Tribunal in 1947 and hanged in Landsberg in 1951.

Bibliography: IMT, Trial of the Major War Criminals (1949), index; *Trial of the War Criminals before the Nurenberg Military Tribunals,* 5 (1950), Case 4, against Pohl et al.; R. Hilberg, *Destruction of the European Jews* (1961), index; R. M. W. Kempner, *SS im Kreuzverhoer* (1964), 130–46; G. Reitlinger, *Final Solution* (1968[2]), index. [Y.RE.]

POHORELICE (Czech **Pohořelice;** Ger. **Pohrlitz**), village in S. Moravia, Czechoslovakia. It had one of the most ancient Jewish communities in Moravia, and according to legend, the oldest. Although the earliest known documentary evidence for the existence of a Jewish settlement in Pohorelice dates from 1490, a Jewish community apparently already existed there at the beginning of the tenth century. At the close of the 18th century about 500 Jews lived in Pohorelice. From 1849 (officially from 1862) until the dissolution of the Austrian Empire in 1918, a local Jewish political authority also existed. From 1847 to 1918 the community supported a Jewish elementary school whose language of instruction was German. In 1930 the community numbered 277. The majority perished in the Holocaust. After World War II, the Jewish community was not renewed. Berthold *Feiwel was born in Pohorelice.

Bibliography: T. Haas, *Die Juden in Maehren* (1908); H. Gold (ed.), *Die Juden und Judengemeinden Maehrens* (1929), index.
[CH.Y.]

POISON (Heb. חֵמָה , לַעֲנָה , מְרֵרָה , רֹאשׁ [רוֹשׁ], רַעַל , תַּרְעֵלָה; Akk. *imtu, martu;* Ug. *ḥmt*). The biblical terms for poison are derived mainly from two sources: types of poisonous plants and the poisonous venom of snakes and other reptiles. Many attempts have been made to identify the specific plants involved based on the translations of these terms in the Septuagint and the other ancient versions, but any conclusions based on this evidence must be considered extremely uncertain. The Bible itself offers no evidence whatsoever, since its usage of these terms is generally metaphorical, offering no identifying characteristics. Therefore, when discussing these various terms, this article will deal with the biblical usage and its Ancient Near Eastern parallels rather than attempting to arrive at specific identifications.

La'anah, Rosh. The terms *rosh* ("gall") and *la'anah* ("wormwood") are often found in synonymous parallelism (Jer. 9:14; 23:15; Amos 6:12) or in hendiadys (Deut. 29:17; Lam. 3:19). They are most often used metaphorically to represent the concepts of poison and bitterness. As her punishment for disobeying the Lord, Israel is forced to consume bitter food and drink (Jer. 8:14; 9:14; 23:15; Lam. 3:15), while a psalmist contends that his enemies are giving him such a hard time that he feels that he is being given bitter food (Ps. 69:22). Another common theme for which these terms are employed is the turning of justice into bitterness (Hos. 10:4; Amos 5:7; 6:12). The especially general nature of the term *rosh,* "gall," in the bible may be demonstrated by its usage in contexts referring to snake venom (Deut. 32:33; Job 20:16) and grapes (Deut. 32:32).

Ḥemah. The biblical term most commonly employed for the venom of snakes and other reptiles is *ḥemah.* In the Song of Moses, the calamity which befalls Israel as a result of God's judgment takes the metaphorical form of *ḥamat zoḥalei 'afar,* "the venom of snakes" (Deut. 32:24; for the meaning of *zoḥalei 'afar* cf. Micah 7:17), while later in the same chapter, *rosh* and *ḥemah,* which are parallels, are again used metaphorically: "the venom *(ḥamat)* of serpents is their wine, and the poison *(rosh)* of vipers . . ." (Deut. 32:33). Elsewhere *ḥemah* is used for snake poison in Psalm 58:5 and for the venom of an unknown reptile *('akhshuv)* in Psalm 140:4.

Both Akkadian *(imtu)* and Ugaritic *(ḥmt)* utilize an etymological and semantic equivalent of חמה as one of their regular words for "poison." The usage of Akkadian *imtu* is very close to the usage of biblical *ḥemah.* The following two passages illustrate the usage of *imtu* as "snake venom":

1. *azzūzâ izarri imta ana sursurru*
izarri imta
imat ṣēri imassu
imat zuqaqīpi imassu
She [Lamaštu] spits venom now and then,
she spits venom suddenly,
her venom is snake venom,
her venom is scorpion venom (A. Falkenstein, *Literarische Keilschrifttexte aus Uruk* (1931), 33:21ff.).

2. *patûni šapti šinnašunu našâ imta*
[Their] lips are open, their fangs carry venom
(*Enūma eliš,* 4:53; Ps. 140:4).

Two Ugaritic texts (*Ugaritica,* 5 (1969), nos. 7, 8), which appear to be "serpent charms" contain, for the first time in Ugaritic, the substantive *ḥmt,* "poison, snake venom." This substantive is found more than 25 times in these two texts whose provenance has already been compared to such biblical passages as Jeremiah 8:17; Psalms 58:5; and Ecclesiastes 10:11. In the first of these two texts, an incantation formula consisting of six lines is repeated 11 times, each time invoking a different deity. While the translation of all the lines of this incantation is far from certain, the lines containing the noun *ḫmt*, while not without their difficulties, are relatively clear:

lnh mlḫš/ ʾabd
lnh ydy ḫmt
From him [the serpent], the conjurer shall destroy,
from him, he shall remove the venom (*Ugaritica*, 5 (1969), 7: 5–6, 10–11, 16–17, 21–22, 27–28, 32–33, 37–38, 42–43, 47–48, 53–54, 59–60).

There are many biblical passages (e.g., Isa. 51:17, 22; Jer. 25:15; Job 21:20) where the substantive *ḥemah* is employed to evoke a double entendre based on its most regular meaning of "wrath" (e.g., Gen. 27:44–45; Deut. 29:22, 27; Isa. 63:3, 6; Jer. 21:5; *ʾaf*, "anger") and its less common denotation of "poison, venom" (see above). This usage is further demonstrated by the occurrence of such idioms as the "pouring out of God's wrath/poison" (e.g., Isa. 42:25; Jer. 10:25; Ezek. 7:8; Ps. 79:6) and "full of God's poison/wrath" (e.g., Isa. 51:20; Jer. 6:11). While there are no Akkadian passages where *imtu* could be translated "wrath," *The Assyrian Dictionary of the Oriental Institute of the University of Chicago* (7 (1960), 139) defines *imtu* in one of its meanings as "poisonous foam, slaver produced from the mouth of angry gods, demons, humans, and animals." (For a full discussion of the semantic range of words for "anger, wrath" in Semitic languages, see H. Cohen, in bibl.)

Mererah. The substantive *mererah* ("poison, venom, gall") is obviously connected with the root *mrr*, "to be bitter," and is generally used in the same way as *ḥemah* (see above). This is demonstrated by the Akkadian lexical equation *imtum = martum* (*malku = šarru*, 8:124; where *martum* is the Akkadian etymological and semantic equivalent of Hebrew *mererah*) as well as by the following biblical passages:

Their grapes are grapes of poison *(rosh)*, Their clusters are venomous *(merorot)* (Deut. 32:32; cf. Deut. 32:33 quoted above); The venom serpents *(merorat petanim)* is within him (Job 20:40; cf. all examples for *ḥemah*, "snake venom" quoted above); He pours out my gall *(mererati)* upon the ground (Job 16:13; cf. the idiom לשפך חמת יהוה quoted above); He has filled me with poison *(merorim)*, sated me with wormwood *(laʿanah)* (Lam. 3:15; cf. the idiom "the pouring out of God's wrath/poison" quoted above).

The Akkadian substantive *martu*, "gall," is used in the same way as *imtu*, *ḥemah*, and *mererah*, as may be seen from the following proverb which is somewhat parallel to Deuteronomy 32:32 (see above):

ina nāri tabbaššīma mūka daddaru
appūnāma ina kirî tabšīma suluppaka martum
When you are in a canal, the water around you is foul-smelling;
Furthermore, when you are in a palm grove, your dates are gall (W. G. Lambert, *Babylonian Wisdom Literature* (1959), p. 244, lines 19–24).

Thus, the biblical *ḥemah* (in its meaning of "poison, venom") and *mererah* must be considered poetic synonyms like the Akkadian *imtu* and *martu*.

Raʿal, Tarʿelah. The exact meaning of *raʿal* and *tarʿelah* is unknown. That it must refer to some kind of poison is clear from Isaiah 51:17, 22, where *tarʿelah* parallels *ḥemah*. The occurrence with *yayin* ("wine") in Psalm 60:5 *(yayin tarʿelah)* also fits in well with the usage of *ḥemah* and *mererah* as stated above. The other few passages (Isa. 3:19; Nah. 2:4; Hab. 2:16 [read והרעל, as in 1QpHab]; Zech. 12:2) in which this substantive or its denominative verb occurs are far from clear, however, and offer nothing in the way of identification. What is clear from the little evidence is that the biblical *raʿal* cannot be derived from Aramaic *rʿl* ("to reel, tremble") because its usage is identical with that of two known biblical words for poison, *ḥemah* and *mererah*. While the etymology of the Modern Hebrew *raʿal* ("poison") is unclear (*raʿal* "poison" is almost nonexistent in the Talmud and Midrash), because its usage in modern Hebrew appears consistent with biblical usage, it is more likely that it is derived from the biblical term than from the Aramaic *rʿl*.

Bibliography: Loew, Flora, passim; N. H. Tur-Sinai, *The Book of Job* (1957), 114–7; R. H. Harrison, *Healing Herbs of the Bible* (1966); A. L. Oppenheim, et al. (eds.), *The Assyrian Dictionary of the Oriental Institute of the University of Chicago*, 7 (1960), 139–41; W. G. Lambert, *Babylonian Wisdom Literature* (1960); M. C. Astour, in: JNES, 27 (1968), 13–36; C. Cohen, in: *Journal of the Ancient Near Eastern Society of Columbia University*, 2 (1969), 25–29.

[H.Co.]

POITIERS, capital of Vienne department, W. France. The history of the Jewish community of Poitiers is almost entirely interwoven with that of *Poitou. During the 13th century, Nathan b. Joseph *Official was involved in a religious disputation with the bishop of Poitiers. An expulsion order against the Jews of Poitiers had already been issued in 1291 but it was canceled in exchange for a large sum of money. The community ceased to exist in 1306. The Rue de la Juiverie, the modern Rue Arsène-Orillard, was closed off by ogival gates which still existed during the 19th century. The cemetery was situated in the present suburb of Montbernage. According to local tradition, treasures buried by the Jews lay hidden there. On the eve of World War II, there were a few hundred Jews in Poitiers. Their numbers increased with the arrival of Jewish refugees from Alsace and Lorraine and later with the internees detained in several camps within the vicinity of the town. In 1970 the community consisted of about 100 persons.

Bibliography: Gross, Gal Jud, 452f.; *Intermédiaire des chercheurs et curieux*, 39 (1899), 20; 40 (1899), 1104; J. Gueriniere, *Essai sur l'ancien Poitou*, 1 (1836), 491; R. Brothier de Rolliere, *Poitiers—Histoire des rues* (1930), 293; Z. Szajkowski, *Analytical Franco-Jewish Gazetteer* (1966), 284.

[B.Bl.]

POITOU, region and former province of W. France, now included in the departments of Vendée, Deux-Sèvres, and Vienne. In the Middle Ages Jews lived in at least 20 localities in Poitou, the most important of which were *Poitiers, Niort, Vitré, Moncontour, Loudun, Bressuire, Lusignan, Montmorillon, and Thouars. Their presence is also remembered by a large number of sites named La Juderie, La Judrie, Les Judes, etc. The earliest evidence of Jewish settlement in Poitou dates from 1134 to 1143, with arrivals from Narbonne. After 1160 Jewish scholars from Poitou took part in the synod of Troyes convened by *Samuel b. Meir and Jacob b. Meir *Tam. One *takkanah* with which the scholars of Poitou were also associated referred to the custom of Narbonne Jewry connected with the dowry. When Poitou passed to English rule, the kings of England provided both individuals and groups of Jews (Niort, 1221) with letters of protection. Under French rule (1224) the Jews of Poitou (like those of Anjou, etc.) were attacked by the crusaders in 1236 (see *Crusades). Soon after he received Poitou in appanage, *Alphonse of Poitiers threatened the Jews with expulsion, but this was not carried out. In 1268, in order to finance his joining a crusade, Alphonse had all the Jews of Poitou, as well as all those in his other territories, imprisoned and their belongings seized, extorting a ransom of 8,000 livres for their release. In 1269, following the example of *Louis IX, he imposed the wearing of the distinctive Jewish *badge. Although Poitou was incorporated into the kingdom of France in 1270, the Jews there were subjected to special decrees and were finally expelled in 1291, 15 years before their coreligionists in other parts of France. A few of them who returned in 1315 were among the first to be accused (1321) of collusion with the lepers (see *France). An even smaller number of Jews returned after 1359 (or more exactly after 1372 when Poitou was liberated by the English). Some Jews from Comtat Venaissin traded in Poitou during the 18th century.

Bibliography: Gross, Gal Jud, 451; Finkelstein, Middle Ages, index; Dr. Vincent, in: *Revue d'histoire économique et sociale*, 18 (1930), 265–313; G. Nahon, in: REJ, 125 (1966), 167–211.

[B.Bl.]

POKI, JUDAH BEN ELIEZER CHELEBI (16th century), Karaite scholar of Constantinople, a nephew of Elijah *Bashyazi. He traveled widely in order to study Karaite writings. In 1571 he was living at the house of the Karaite *nasi* in Cairo. In his *Sha'ar Yehudah*, on forbidden marriages (published by his son Isaac in Constantinople, 1581), he opposed the modifications introduced in this subject by Joseph ha-Ro'eh and Jeshua b. Judah. Poki is the only Karaite scholar of the period to uphold the *rikkuv* ("catenary") theory of forbidden marriages. He mentions also a second work, *Ve-Zot li-Yhudah*, on the determination of the new moon. Jedidiah Solomon of Troki refers in his *Appiryon* to a prayer book compiled by Poki, as well as works on poetry and grammar.

Bibliography: A. Neubauer, *Aus der Petersburger Bibliothek* (1866), 65; I. D. B. Markon, *Texte und Untersuchungen* (1908), xvii.

[I.M./Ed.]

POLACCO, VITTORIO (1859–1926), Italian jurist. Born in Padua, Polacco was professor of civil law at the University of Padua from 1885 to 1918 and at the University of Rome from 1918 until his death. He was renowned as a jurist and was invited to teach law and the history of religions to Prince Umberto of Savoy. Polacco was a member of the Italian Senate from 1910 and played an important part in the drafting of the Senate's legislation. He kept aloof from politics and aroused great interest when, in 1925, he delivered the only political speech he ever made in parliament, his subject being freedom of conscience and the protection of religious minorities. He wrote a number of legal works, including *Le Obbligazioni nel Diritto Civile Italiano* (1898); and *Delle Successioni* (2 vols., 1902), both of which ran into many editions, and *Contro il divorzio* (2 vols., 1892) in which he set out his opposition to divorce. Rome's Jewish elementary school was named after him.

[G.R.]

POLÁČEK, KAREL (1892–1944), Czech author and probably the outstanding Czech humorist after Hašek. He began his career as a reporter in the law courts, where he gained insight into the ordinary people about whom he wrote in his short stories and novels. In these Poláček introduced many Jewish characters, mainly traders, salesmen, and commercial travelers, recording their way of life and mode of speech with accuracy and understanding. A number of these novels and stories were screen successes.

One of Poláček's major works was the tetralogy, *Okresní město* ("District Town," 1936), which presents the panorama of a small Czech township. His volumes of short stories include *Povídky pana Kočkodána* ("Mr. Kočkodán's Tales," 1922), *Maryáš a jiné živnosti* ("Cardplaying and Other Professions," 1924), *Povídky israelského vyznání* ("Stories of the Mosaic Persuasion," 1926), and *Život ve filmu* ("Life in the Movies," 1927). Two humorous novels are *Muži v offsidu* ("Men at Offside," 1931) and *Michelup a motocykl* ("Michelup and the Motorbike," 1935). Poláček wrote two comedies, one of which, *Pásky na vousy* ("The Beard-binders," 1926), was produced by the Prague National Theater. During the Nazi occupation, Poláček was deported, first to Theresienstadt and later to Auschwitz, where he died.

Bibliography: O. Donath, *Židé a židovství v české literatuře* (1930); J. Kunc, *Slovník českých spisovatelů beletristů* (1957); Frýd, in: *Terezín* (1965), 206–18 (publ. by the Council of Jewish Communities in the Czech Lands).

[Av.D.]

POLACHEK, SOLOMON (1877–1928), talmudic scholar and teacher. Polachek was early recognized as a precocious youngster and became widely known as the *illui* ("prodigy") of Meitshet where he studied. He entered the Volozhin yeshivah at the unusually early age of 12 and his bar-mitzvah was celebrated at the home of the head of the yeshivah, Naphtali Ẓevi Judah *Berlin. After the yeshivah was closed by the czarist government in 1892, Polachek studied with Ḥayyim *Soloveitchik in Brest-Litovsk and became "R. Ḥayyim's" most beloved pupil. Polachek also studied in the Slobodka yeshivah and at the "kibbutz" of Ḥayyim Ozer *Grodzenski in Vilna. Polachek mastered secular studies and modern Hebrew on his own and acquainted himself with the literature and problems of his time. In 1905, J. J. *Reines appointed him head of the Talmud department in the newly organized Lida yeshivah where the curriculum also included secular studies. After Reines' death in 1915 the entire burden of the yeshivah fell on Polachek. Shortly afterward, as a result of World War I, Polachek and the yeshivah were compelled to move to central Russia, where the school continued for five more years. During the war Polachek lost the notes he had amassed on over 1,500 different talmudic topics. After the war and the Bolshevik revolution, Polachek succeeded in escaping to Poland, where he became head of the Talmud department of the Taḥkemoni Rabbinical Seminary in Bialystok. In 1922 Polachek emigrated to America and accepted the position of senior *rosh yeshivah* in the Rabbi Isaac Elchanan Theological Seminary (the forerunner of *Yeshiva University). He was enthusiastically received by American Orthodoxy since he was the first renowned European talmudist who agreed to remain in the U.S. for the purpose of teaching Talmud in an advanced yeshivah. While in the U.S., he was a member of the *Union of Orthodox Rabbis and was active in the *Mizrachi movement. Polachek's *Ḥiddushei ha-Illui me-Meitshet* was published posthumouly in 1947.

Bibliography: A. Rothkoff, in: *Jewish Life*, Nov.–Dec. 1967, 29–35; O. Feuchtwanger, *Righteous Lives* (1965), 119–21; O. Z. Rand (ed.), *Toledot Anshei Shem* (1950), 94; *Yahadut Lita*, 1 (1960), index s.v., 3 (1967), 75f.

[A.Ro.]

POLACK, JOEL SAMUEL (1807–1882), adventurer. Born in London, he was the son of the artist Solomon Polack (1757–1839). Before his arrival at Hokianga, New Zealand, in 1831, he had been an artist, Californian gold miner, South African ordinance officer, and Australian ship's chandler. His dominant personality enabled him to survive among the rough whalers and semi-cannibalistic Maoris of Hokianga and Kororareka, where he opened a store in 1833. He learned to speak Maori fluently, and won the confidence of the Maoris. In 1838 his Kororareka store containing military and naval explosives blew up and he returned temporarily to London. There he urged the

Engraving of Kororareka Bay by Joel Samuel Polack with his store in the foreground, 1836. Wellington, New Zealand, Alexander Turnbull Library.

colonization of New Zealand in evidence before a select committee of the House of Lords. *The Times* attacked Polack's New Zealand dealings, describing him as "a worthy and wandering offshoot of the seed of Abraham." Suing *The Times* for libel, he was awarded £100 damages.

In 1838 Polack wrote *New Zealand,* being a narrative of travels and adventures in that country betweeen 1831 and 1937, and *Manners and Customs of New Zealanders* in 1840. Both books, especially the second which is profusely illustrated by Polack himself, are valuable documentaries of New Zealand's precolonization history. Polack returned to New Zealand after the proclamation of British sovereignty in 1840, but soon left for the Californian goldfields. He died in San Francisco.

Bibliography: *Journal and Proceedings of the Australian Jewish Historical Society,* 3 (1949–53), 142–51; Rubens, in: JHSET, 14 (1940), 108–12. [M.S.P.]

POLAK, family of Dutch lawyers. MORITZ (1865–1938), son-in-law of Jacques *Oppenheim, was born in Veendam and passed through the various ranks of the Dutch judicature, becoming a supreme court judge in 1926. He was the author of several works on Dutch law including a manual on commercial and bankruptcy law which became a standard work. He was an active figure in the Jewish community.

Polak's three sons also achieved distinction in the legal profession. NICO J. (1904–) became vice-president of the district court in Leewarden in 1957 and a supreme court judge in 1968. JACQUES A. (1908–) was vice-president of The Hague District Court from 1957 to 1964 when he became a judge of the Higher District Court. CAREL H. F. (1909–) was professor of public law at Wageningen College from 1949 to 1951 and was appointed to a chair at the University of Leiden. A representative of the Liberal Party, he was minister of justice from 1967 to 1971. [H.Bo.]

POLAK, GABRIEL ISAAC (1803–1869), Dutch scholar, Hebrew author, and bibliographer. Born in Amsterdam, Polak served as head of a school there. He provided Dutch Jewry with accurate liturgical texts translated into Dutch.

Among these were a Pentateuch with *haftarot* and Rashi (1828; his *le'azim* translated into German), Sabbath prayers (1828), and *piyyutim* (*Torat Emet–Tikkun Soferim,* 1827, repr. 1937); *Amarot Tehorot* (biblical books with Dutch translation, 1862/63; also Job, with M. S. Polak, 1844); a *maḥzor* (1857[2]), with commentary in Hebrew and Judeo-German and another edition with Dutch translation (with M. L. van Ameringen, 1850[2]); *Areshet Sefatayim* (1960[23]), a *siddur;* a Passover *Haggadah* (1930[9]); *Ezrat ha-Sofer* (1866), a *tikkun;* and *Sefer Ḥayyim la-Nefesh* (1867). He also edited orders of service for Purim (1857), circumcision (1878), and the seventh of Adar (death of Moses; 1851), *Kinot* (1868) and *Seliḥot* (1869). Polak published a small Hebrew-Dutch dictionary, *Divrei Kodesh,* with S. E. Heigmans, in 1857[2]. Among his other works were: *Ḥukkei Ha-Elohim* (1841, 1883), on the 613 commandments; a translation with commentary of *Josippon (1868, with van Ameringen); an edition of a manuscript he discovered of Judah ibn Balam's *Sha'ar Ta'amei Sefarim Emet* on the accents of Psalms, Proverbs, and Job (1858); and an enlarged edition of Abraham Bedersi's (Bedarshi's) dictionary of Hebrew synonyms (1865). Polak completed H. A. Wagenaar's biography of Jacob Emden (1868), and annotated Menahem Mann b. Solomon's *She'erit Yisrael* (with L. Goudsmit, 1855), with notes on the history of Dutch Jewry. He also wrote Hebrew poetry and translated Dutch works into Hebrew (*Ha-Poret,* 1836; *Halikhot Kedem,* 1847; *Ben Gorni,* 1851). In addition, he wrote a biography of the Dutch Hebrew poet D. Franco-Mendes and published letters and essays by S. *Dubno, J. S. Reggio, S. L. Rapoport, and S. D. Luzzatto, maintaining contact with some of them. Among his bibliographical work is *Me'ir Einayim* (1864) a catalog of the M. L. Jacobson and M. B. Rubens collections in Amsterdam *Ḥok Shelomo* (1857) and catalogs of S. B. Rubens' collections in Amsterdam (1864).

Bibliography: J. H. Gurland, in: *Ha-Maggid,* 12 (1869), no. 22, 175; no. 23, 181–2. [J.H.C.]

POLAK, HENRI (1868–1943), Dutch trade unionist and socialist politician. Born in Amsterdam, Polak worked as a diamond polisher in London from 1887 to 1890 and became acquainted with the Fabian Society and the Trade Union movement. In 1895 he founded the Dutch General Diamond Workers Guild (A.N.D.B.) which he made exemplary both for its organization and for the cultural education of its members, many of whom were Jewish. For over 40 years Polak was chairman of the A.N.D.B. and editor of its weekly and chairman of the World Federation of Diamond Workers. Polak was one of the founders of the Dutch Labor Federation and was a member of the Second Chamber of Parliament from 1913 to 1922 and of the Senate, 1923–37. He wrote several books on the Dutch diamond industry and translated Sidney and Beatrice Webb's *History of the Trade Unions* and *Theory and Practice of the Trade Unions.*

Though not a Zionist, Polak served on the executive of the *Keren Hayesod in Holland. Arrested by the Nazis in 1940, he spent two years in solitary detention, and died shortly after his release.

Bibliography: O. Montange and J. Winkler, *Doctor Henri Polak. Van het vuur dat in hem brandde* (1948). [H.Bo.]

POLAK, JACOB EDUARD (1820–1891), physician and writer. Born in Bohemia, he studied medicine and science in Prague and Vienna and in 1851 was invited to Teheran by the Persian government to serve as professor of anatomy

Drawing of Jacob Eduard Polak, as court physician to Shah Nasr-el-Din. Courtesy Israel Medical Association, Jerusalem.

and surgery at the military college. In 1856 he was appointed court physician to Shah Nasr-el-Din. Polak returned to Vienna in 1860 and was associated with the general hospital there while acting as lecturer in Persian at the University of Vienna. When Nasr-el-Din toured Europe in 1872 he visited Polak, who is mentioned in the shah's "Diary" as his "good old friend." Polak wrote a number of important treatises in Persian on anatomy, surgery, ophthalmology, and military medicine, some of which became standard works. He also compiled a medical dictionary in Persian, Arabic, and Latin in order to provide the Persian language with a system of medical terminology, and composed a much-used dictionary, *Deutsch-persiches Konversationswoerterbuch* (1914).

A faithful and devoted Jew, Polak used his prestige and influence at the court of the shah in favor of his coreligionists. He drew the attention of European Jewry to the plight of the Jews in Persia at the time and proposed that the Alliance Israélite Universelle should send a Jewish representative to Teheran or establish a Jewish school there, as was ultimately done. Polak wrote extensively on various aspects of Jewish life in Persia; *Persien, das Land und seine Bewohner* (1865) and other publications contain important information about the Jews.

Bibliography: P. Goldberg, *Dr. J. E. Polak: eine biographische Skizze* (1856); Fischel, in: JSOS, 12 (1950), 119–60. [W.J.F.]

POLAK, LEONARD (1880–1941), Dutch philosopher. Born in Steenwijk, Polak graduated in law, in 1925 became assistant professor at the University of Leiden, and in 1929 was appointed to the chair in philosophy at the University of Groningen. A rationalist and agnostic, Polak played an important part in the free-thought movement in the Netherlands. He followed the Marburg neo-Kantian school of philosophy holding that mechanical causality reigns in nature while freedom reigns in the realm of the spirit.

Polak wrote on important social questions such as the philosophy of war, the philosophy of punishment, sexual ethics, and religious divisions. His principal works include: *Kennisleer contra materie-realisme* (1912); *De zin der vergelding* (1921); *Hegel's leer der straf* (1925); and *Noodlot en vrije wil* (1937). After World War II, Polak's works were collected in *Verzamelde werken* (4 vols, 1947).

Bibliography: P. Spigt, *Leo Polak, een erflater van onze beschaving* (1946); L. van der Wal, *Herdenking van Leo Polak* (1946); F. Sassen, *Wijsgerig leven in Nederland in de twintigste eeuw* (1948[2]). [R.H.P.]

POLAND, republic in E. Central Europe; the kingdom of Poland and the grand duchy of Lithuania united formally (Poland-Lithuania) in 1569 (see map 1). This article is arranged according to the following outline:

- The Early Settlements
- Jewish Legal Status
- Economic Activity
- Cultural and Social Life
- 1569–1648: Colonization of the Ukraine
- Internal Jewish Life
- From Chmielnicki to the First Partition
- After Partition
- Independent Poland
- Holocaust Period
  - Reichsgau Wartheland
    - Ghettoization
    - Physical Annihilation
  - Reichsgau Danzig-Westpreussen
  - Regierungsbezirk Zichenau
  - Regierungsbezirk Kattowitz
  - General Government
    - Warsaw District
    - Lublin District
    - Cracow District
    - Radom District
    - Galicia District
  - Bezirk Bialystok
  - Generalbezirk Litauen und Weissrussland
  - Generalbezirk Wolhynien-Podolien
  - Demographic Total
  - Jewish Resistance
    - Partisans
  - Jewish-Polish Relations during the War
- After World War II
  - Rescue of Jewish Children
  - Renewal of Jewish Life
  - Cultural, Religious, and Economic Life
  - The Flight from Poland
  - Anti-Jewish Excesses
  - The Soviet Example
  - 1956–1967
  - Final Liquidation
- Relations with Israel
  - The Change of 1950
  - Improved Relations in 1956
  - The Six-Day War
  - Emigration to Israel
  - Trade Relations

THE EARLY SETTLEMENTS

While Jews had visited the kingdom of Poland and been economically active there at an early stage of the country's consolidation, from the tenth century approximately, they had no conctact with the grand duchy of Lithuania until King Gedimin conquered the regions of Volhynia and Galicia (as it was later called) in 1321.

Jews came to Poland mainly from the west and southwest and from the very beginning were of *Ashkenazi culture. Those in the regions conquered by Gedimin had come there from the south and the southeast, chiefly from *Kiev, and were thus influenced to a large degree by Byzantine Jewish culture patterns; some think that they could have had traces of *Khazar ethnic descent and culture patterns. Jews in the region of *Lvov and its environs were of the same provenance to a large extent. In the end the western Ashkenazi culture became dominant.

Polish-Jewish legendary tradition tells about a Jewish merchant, Abraham Prochownik (unlikely to mean "the gun-powder man," which would be completely anachronistic, but probably, "the dust-covered," an epithet found in the early Middle Ages in relation to merchants), who was offered the Polish crown around the middle of the ninth century, before Piast, the first, legendary, Polish king, ascended to the throne. According to another legend, at the end of the ninth century a Jewish delegation in Germany appealed to Prince Leszek to admit them to Poland. The request was granted after prolonged questioning, and later on privileges were granted to the immigrants. Although almost certainly formulated in their present version in the 16th–17th centuries—at a time of fierce struggle between Jewish and Christian townsmen (see below)—the legends do transmit meaningful historic elements. Jews did first come to Poland as transient, dust-covered merchants, and they did come there to escape the suffering and pressure brought to bear on them in the lands of the German Empire. The theories of some historians, that place-names like Żydowo, Żydatycze, Żydowska Wola, and Kozarzów indicate the presence of Jewish villages and peasants and even the presence of Khazar settlements in the regions where they are found, have been thoroughly disproved. The first Jews that the Poles encountered must certainly have been traders, probably slave traders, of the type called in 12th-century Jewish sources *Holekhei Rusyah* (travelers to Russia). Some of them may have stayed for years in Poland, giving rise to the legends and fixing their dates. The chronicler Cosmas of Prague relates that the persecutions of the First Crusade caused Jews to move from *Bohemia to Poland in 1098. From this point undisputed and datable information on Jews in Poland begins to appear. According to the chronicler Vincent Kadlubek, under Boleslav III heavy penalties were laid on those who harmed Jews bodily.

The first sizable groups and fixed communities of Jews settled and established themselves in the region of Silesia, then part of Polish society and culture but later Germanized. A large part of Jewish settlement in what was later consolidated as the kingdom of Poland came from Silesia, and a great proportion of the immigration from further west and from the southwest passed through it. As late as the 15th century Silesian Jewry kept its ties with Poland. Jewish settlement grew steadily, though at first slowly, in Polish principalities to the east of Silesia. Excavations in *Great Poland and near *Wloclawek have unearthed coins with Hebrew inscriptions issued under the princes Mieczyslaw III (1173–1209), Casimir II the Just (1177–94), Boleslav the Curly (1201), and Leszek the White (1205). Some inscriptions directly concern the ruler, like the Hebrew legend "Mieszko King of Poland" (משקא קרל פולסקי) or "Mieszko Duke" (משקא דוכוס); others include the names and titles of the Jewish *mintmasters, one of them even with its honorific title of **nagid;* "of the [coining] house of Abraham the son of Isaac Nagid" (דבי אברהם בר יצחק נגיד); another showing that the Jewish mintmaster was settled in Poland: "Joseph [of] Kalisz (יוסף קאליש). Minting money was an important social and economic function, and as some of the inscriptions indicate, these finds are evidence of a circle of rich and enterprising Jewish merchants in the principalities of great Poland and Mazovia in the 12th century, some of them in close contact with the princely courts, some priding themselves on their descent from old Jewish families or on their own role in Jewish leadership. Rulers were quick to realize what they could gain from such immigrants: in 1262 Prince Boleslav the Shy forbade a monastery in *Lesser Poland to take Jews under its sovereignty.

By that time, however, a new era had already begun in the history of the colonization of Poland in general and of the settlement of Jews in it in particular. From 1241 onward the Mongol invasions caused heavy losses in life and destruction to property in Poland. Subsequently, the princes of Poland eagerly sought immigrants from the west, mainly from Germany, and gave them energetic assistance to settle in the villages and towns. Various organized groups settled in the cities that were granted the privilege of living according to German *Magdeburg Law; thus Polish towns became prevailingly German in origin and way of life. Though the children of the immigrants became gradually Polonized, the traditions and social attitudes of the German town remained an active force and basic framework of town life in Poland of the 15th to 17th centuries. From the Jewish point of view the most important, and harmful, result of this basic attitude of the Polish towns was the tradition of the *guilds against competition and against new initiative in individual commercial enterprise and the activities of craftsmen. The townsmen also inherited a direct and bitter legacy of hatred of the Jews and the baleful and deeply rooted German *image of the Jew.

Jews did not only come to Poland in the wake of the German *Drang nach Osten*, traces of which are found in the 13th-century *Sefer Ḥasidim*, for instance, in the description of the creation of a new settlement in a primeval forest by Jews (*Sefer Ḥasidim*, ed. J. Wistinetzki (1924), 113, no. 371). For them the move was a continuation of and linking with earlier Jewish settlement in Poland. They also had compelling reasons stemming from the circumstances of their life in Western and Central Europe to leave their homes there and go to Poland-Lithuania. Their insecure position in this region was a compound of the atmosphere of fear and danger generated by the *Crusades, the insecurity of settlement caused by the *expulsions, the wave of massacres in Germany in particular between 1298 and 1348 (see *Rindfleisch; *Armleder; *Blood Libel; *Black Death; *Host, Desecration of), the insecurity and popular hatred in Germany and German-Bohemian-Moravian towns in the second half of the 14th century and the first half of the 15th, the tensions and dangers created by the *Hussite revolution and wars in Bohemia-Moravia and southern Germany in the early 15th century, and the worsening situation of Jews in the kingdoms of Christian Spain after the massacres of 1391. All these factors, combined with the success of the settlers in Poland-Lithuania, induced large and variegated groups of Jewish immigrants from various countries—Bohemia-Moravia, Germany, Italy, Spain, from colonies in the Crimea—to go to Poland-Lithuania long after the original German drive had died out. As Moses b. Israel *Isserles put it in the 16th century, "it is preferable to live on dry bread and in peace in Poland" than to remain in better conditions in lands more dangerous for Jews (Responsa, no. 73). He even coined a pun on the Hebrew form of Poland (Polin), explaining it as deriving from two Hebrew words, *poh lin* ("here he shall rest").

The results of this immigration were evident almost immediately. In 1237 Jews are mentioned in Plock. The Jewish community of *Kalisz bought a cemetery in 1283, so it must have been organized some time before, as the fact that the first writ of privileges for Jews was issued in 1264 by the prince of Kalisz also tends to show (see below). A *Judengasse* (*Jewish Quarter) is mentioned in *Cracow in 1304, lying between the town market and the town walls, but there must have been a community in Cracow long before then for about 1234 "Rabbi Jacob Savra of Cracow that sits in Poland, a great scholar and fluent in the entire Talmud" put forward his own opinion against that of the greatest contemporary scholars of Germany and Bohemia. In 1356 there is a record of the Jewish community at *Lvov; in 1367 at *Sandomierz; in 1379 at *Poznan; in 1387 at Pyzdry; and about 1382 at *Lyuboml. In the grand duchy of Lithuania Jewish communities are found in the 14th century at *Brest-Litovsk (1388), *Grodno (1389), and *Troki (1398). The volume of immigration grew continuously. By the end of the 15th century more than 60 Jewish communities are known of in united Poland-Lithuania. They were dispersed from Wroclaw (*Breslau) and *Gdansk in the west to *Kiev and *Kamenets Podolski in the east. The number of Jews living in Poland by that date is greatly disputed: at the end of the 15th century there were between 20,000 and 30,000.

JEWISH LEGAL STATUS

The foundations of the legal position of the Jews in Poland were laid down in the 13th to 15th centuries. The basic "general charters" of Jews in Poland have their origin in the writ issued by Prince *Boleslav V the Pious of Kalisz in 1264. This "statute of Kalisz" (Pol. *Statut kaliski*)—as it is called in literature—was also an "immigrant" from the countries which Jews left to come to Poland, being based on the statute of Duke *Frederick II of Austria and on derivative statutes issued in Bohemia and Hungary. The Jews are seen, accepted, and defended as a group whose main business is *moneylending against pledges. With the unification of Poland into a kingdom, King *Casimir III the Great strongly favored the Jewish element in the cities of Poland, the German element having proved untrustworthy under his father, the unifier of Poland, Ladislaus I Lokietek. Casimir broadened the statute of Kalisz while ratifying it for the Jews of his kingdom (in 1334, 1364, and 1367). Yet basically the same conception of the Jews as **servi camerae regis* and as protected moneylenders remains throughout. The legal status of the Jews changed considerably in Poland, but not through any central reinterpretation of their rights and standing, which remained in theory based on and conceived of in terms of the Boleslavian-Casimirian statutes, codified and ratified by King *Casimir IV Jagello in 1453. Throughout the 14th century, there was opposition to Jews accepting landed property as security for loans; while throughout the 15th century town and church tried to insist that Jews should wear the distinctive *badge.

On several occasions these undercurrents broke out in sharp and violent decisions and action. During the Black Death "All Jews... almost throughout Poland were massacred" (*omnes judaei... fere in tota Polonia deleti sunt;* Stanislas of Olivia in his *Chronica Olivska*, for the year 1349). The martyrs were defined by German Jews as "the communities and kingdom of Cracow, its scholars and population" (S. Salfeld, *Das Martyrologium des Nuernberger Memorbuches* (1898), 82). By that time hatred of the Jews was also widespread among the nobility. In the statute of Lesser Poland of 1347, paragraph 26 claims that "the aim of the perfidious Jews is not so much to take their faith away from the Christians as to take away their wealth and property." In 1407 the Cracow populace was diverted by the spectacle of a Jewish moneylender being led through the streets adorned with a crown set with forged coins—he was accused of forging currency—to be horribly tortured and burned in public. The citizens of Cracow claimed as early as 1369 that the Jews were "dominating" the town and complained of their cruelty and perfidy. In the main King Ladislaus II Jagello was hostile to Jews, though some of

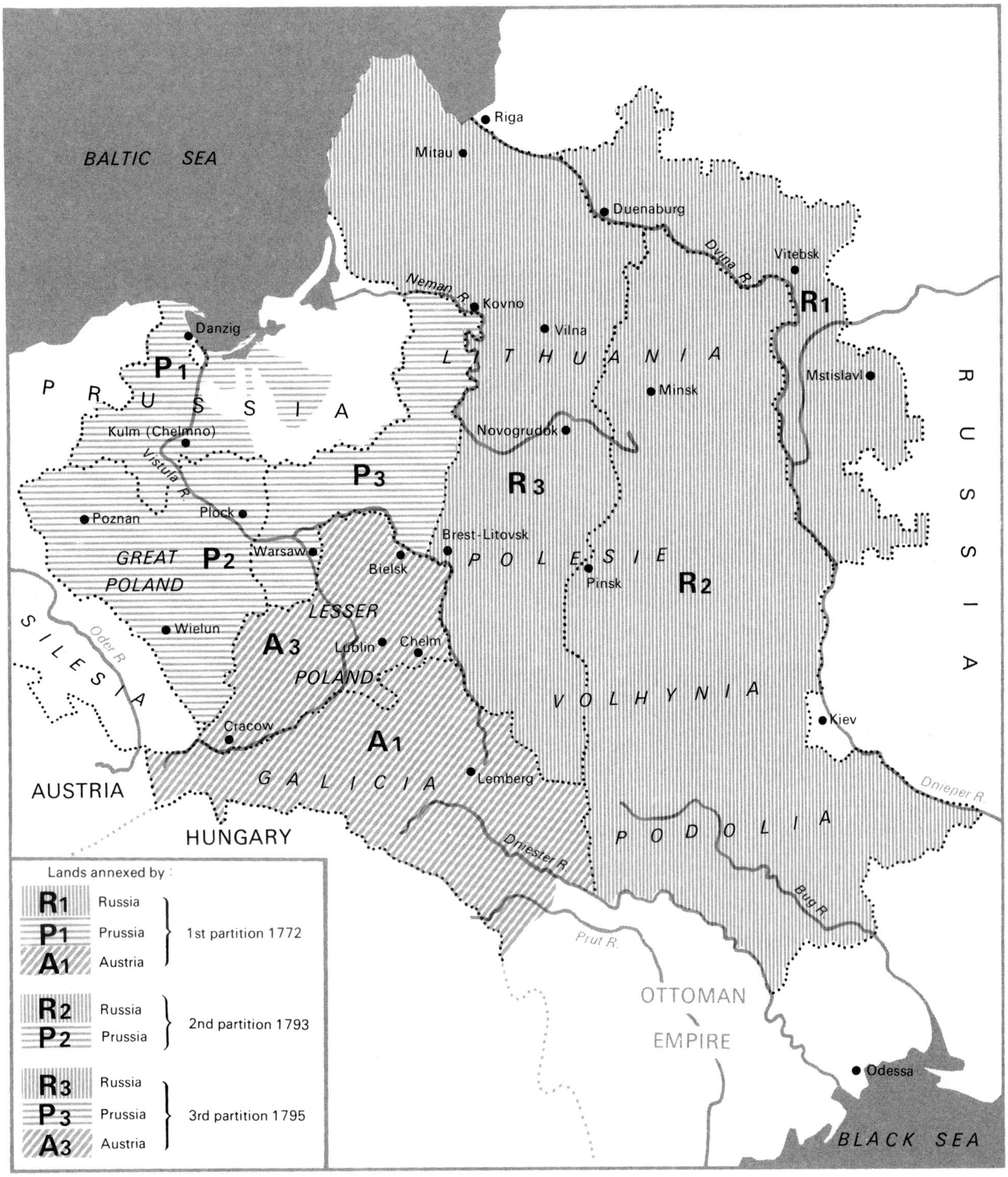

Map 1. The partitions of Poland.

them were numbered among his financial and business agents, like Volchko, whom the king hoped in vain to bring over to Christianity.

Church circles were very active in their opposition to the Jews. Many priests and directors of monasteries, who had originally come from Germany, brought to Poland the hostile traditions concerning the city-dwelling accursed Jew. As early as 1267 the Polish Church Council of Wroclaw (Breslau) outlined its anti-Jewish policy; its main aim was to isolate the Jews as far as possible from the Christians, not only from the communion of friendship and table but also to separate them in quarters surrounded by a wall or a ditch: "for as up to now the land of Poland is newly grafted on to the Christian body, it is to be feared that the Christian people will more easily be misled by the superstitions and evil habits of the Jews that live among them" (*quum adhuc Terra Polonica sit in corpore christianitatis nova plantatio, ne forte eo facilius populus christianus a cohabitantium Iudeorum superstitionibus et pravis moribus inficiatur;* Aronius, Regesten, 302 no. 724). With various modifications, this was restated in subsequent Church councils. In the 15th century this ecclesiastical attitude found new and influential expression. Cardinal Zbigniew *Oleśnicki and the chronicler Jan *Długosz were the main leaders of the anti-Jewish faction. When Jewish representatives came to King Casimir IV Jagello to obtain the ratification of their charters, Oleśnicki opposed it vehemently. He invited to Poland "the scourge of the Jews," John of *Capistrano, fresh from his "success" in engineering a *Host desecration libel which resulted in the burning of many Jews and expulsion of the community of Wroclaw. In vain Capistrano tried to influence the king not to ratify the Jewish charters. Oleśnicki himself wrote to the king in support of his effort: "Do not imagine that in matters touching the Christian religion you are at liberty to pass any law you please. No one is great and strong enough to put down all opposition to himself when the interests of the faith are at stake. I therefore beseech and implore your royal majesty to revoke the aforementioned privileges and liberties. Prove that you are a Catholic sovereign, and remove all occasion for disgracing your name and for worse offenses that are likely to follow" (*Monumenta Mediaevi*, ed. Szugski, Codex Epistolaris s. XV, T. II past posterior p. 147). As a result of this pressure the Nieszawa statute of 1454 decreed the repeal of all Jewish charters, but the repeal was short-lived. Perhaps central to the definition of the status of the Jews was the decision of King Sigismund I in 1534 that the Jews need not carry any distinguishing mark on their clothing. Despite the contrary resolution of the Sejm (Diet) of *Piotrkow in 1538, the king's decision remained.

Major changes in the status of the Jews occurred throughout the 16th and 17th centuries, but they came about either through the issuance of particular writs of rights by kings for towns and communities—both in favor of Jews as well as to their detriment (e.g., the *privilegia de non tolerandis judaeis* given to many towns in Poland)—or through the action of various magnates, whose power was continuously growing in Poland in these centuries. Some of the latter, nicknamed *Krolewięta* ("kinglets"), granted Jews many and costly rights in the new municipal settlements they were erecting on their expansive estates—the "private townships" of Poland, so-called in distinction to the old "royal townships." To a slight degree, change resulted from the new economic activity of the Jews, mainly in the east and southeast of Poland-Lithuania, and their move toward colonization there.

The foundations of the legal status of the Jews in the grand duchy of Lithuania were laid by Grand Duke Vitold in writs of law granted to the Jews of Brest-Litovsk in 1388 and to the Jews of Grodno in 1389. Though formally based on the rights of the Jews of Lvov in Poland, in letter and spirit these charters reveal an entirely different conception of the place of Jews in society. The writ for the Grodno community states that "from the above-mentioned cemetery—in its present location as well as on ground that might be bought later—and also from the ground of their Jewish synagogue, no taxes whatsoever will have to be given to our

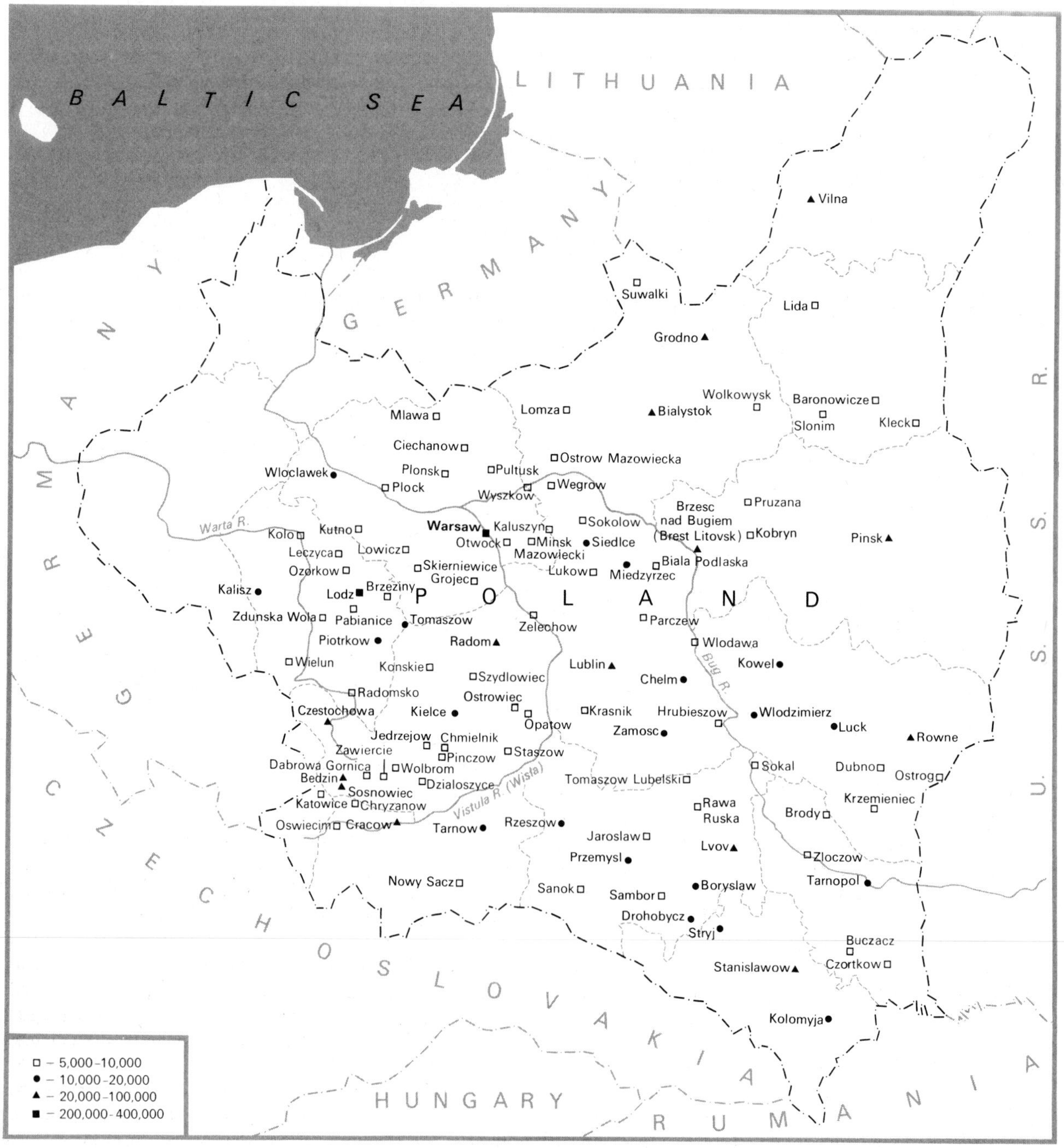

Map 2. Major Jewish communities in Poland in 1931.

treasury." Not only are the Jewish place of worship and cemetery tax free—a concession that indicates interest in having Jewish settlers in the town—but also "what is more, we permit them to hold whatever views they please in their homes and to prepare at their homes any kind of drink and to serve drinks brought from elsewhere on the condition that they pay to our treasury a yearly tax. They may trade and buy at the market, in shops and on the streets in full equality with the citizens; they may engage in any kind of craft." Thus, in granting the Jews complete freedom to trade and engage in any craft, the grand duke gave them economic equality with the Christian citizens. He also envisaged their having agricultural or partially agricultural occupations: "As to the arable lands as well as grazing lands, those that they have now, as well as those that they will buy later, they may use in full equality with the townspeople, paying like them to our treasury." The Jews are here considered as merchants, craftsmen, and desirable settlers in the developing city. As the grand duchy merged with Poland to an ever increasing degree, in particular in the formal, legal, and social spheres, the basic concepts of the *servi camerae* also influenced the status of Lithuanian Jews (as was already hinted at in the formal reference to the rights and status of the Jews of Lvov). In spite of this, the general trend in Lithuanian towns and townships remained the same as that expressed in the late 16th-century charters. In 1495 the Jews were expelled from Lithuania. They were brought back in 1503: all their property was returned and opportunities for economic activity were restored.

Thus, on the threshold of the 16th century, the gradually merging grand duchy of Lithuania and kingdom of Poland had both a fully worked out legal concept of the status of the Jews. In Poland, the whole conception was medieval to the core: legally and formally the attitude to the Jews remained unchanged from their first arrival from the west and southwest. In Lithuania, on the other hand, from the start the formal expressions reveal a conception of a Jewish "third estate," equal in economic opportunity to the Christian townspeople. Particular legal enactments in Poland took cognizance of the change in the economic role of the Jews in Polish society. In Lithuania the formal enactments were always suited to their economic role, and to a large extent the dynamics of 16th- and 17th-century development could be accommodated in the old legal framework.

ECONOMIC ACTIVITY

From the very first the Jews of Poland developed their economic activities through moneylending toward a greater variety of occupations and economic structures. Thus, by the very dynamics of its economic and social development, Polish Jewry constitutes a flat existential denial and factual contradiction of the anti-Semitic myth of "the Jewish spirit of usury." On the extreme west of their settlement in Poland, in Silesia, although they were mainly engaged in moneylending, Jews were also employed in agriculture. When the Kalisz community in 1287 bought a cemetery it undertook to pay for it in pepper and other oriental wares, indicating an old connection with the trade in spices. As noted above, the Jewish mintmasters of the 12th century must undoubtedly have been large-scale traders. In 1327 Jews were an important element among the participants at the *Nowy Sacz fair. Throughout the 14th and 15th centuries Jews were occupied to a growing degree in almost every branch of trade pursued at that time. Jews from both the grand duchy of Lithuania and Poland traded in cloth, dyes, horses, and cattle (and on a fairly large scale). At the end of the 15th century they engaged in trade with Venice, Italy, with Kaffa (Feodosiya), and with other Genoese colonies in the Crimea, and with Constantinople. Lvov Jews played a central role in this trade, which in the late 15th and early 16th centuries developed into a large-scale land-transit trade between the Ottoman Empire and Christian Europe. Through their participation in this trade and their contacts with their brethren in the Ottoman Empire, many Jewish communities became vital links in a trade chain that was important to both the various Christian kingdoms and the Ottoman Empire. Lithuanian Jews participated to the full and on a considerable scale in all these activities, basing themselves both on their above-mentioned recognized role in Lithuanian civic society and on their particular opportunities for trade with the grand principality of *Moscow and their evident specialization in dyes and dyeing. Obviously, in all these activities, all links with Jewish communities in Central and Western Europe were beneficial.

During all this period Jews were engaged in moneylending, some of them (e.g., *Lewko Jordanis, his son Canaan, and Volchko) on a large scale. They made loans not only to private citizens but also to magnates, kings, and cities, on several occasions beyond the borders of Poland. The scope of their monetary operations at their peak may be judged by the fact that in 1428 King Ladislaus II Jagello accused one of the Cracow city counsellors of appropriating the fabulous sum of 500,000 zlotys which the Jews had supplied to the royal treasury.

To an increasing extent many of the Jewish moneylenders became involved in trade. They were considered by their lords as specialists in economic adminstration. In 1425 King Ladislaus II Jagello charged Volchko—who by this time already held the Lvov customs lease—with the colonization of a large tract of land: "As we have great confidence in the wisdom, carefulness, and foresight of our Lvov customs-holder, the Jew Volchko . . . after the above-mentioned Jew Volchko has turned the above-mentioned wilderness into a human settlement in the village, it shall remain in his hands till his death." King Casimir Jagello entrusted to the Jew Natko both the salt mines of Drohobycz (*Drogobych) and the customs station of Grejdek, stating in 1452 that he granted it to him on account of his "industry and wisdom so that thanks to his ability and industry we shall bring in more income to our treasury." The same phenomenon is found in Lithuania. By the end of the 15th century, at both ends of the economic scale Jews in Poland were becoming increasingly what they had been from the beginning in Lithuania: a "third estate" in the cities. The German-Polish citizenry quickly became aware of this. By the end of the 15th century, accusations against the Jews centered around unfair competition in trade and crafts more than around harsh usury. Not only merchants but also Jewish craftsmen are mentioned in Polish cities from 1460 onward. In 1485 tension in Cracow was so high that the Jewish community was compelled to renounce formally its rights to most trades and crafts. Though this was done "voluntarily," Jews continued to pursue their living in every decent way possible. This was one of the reasons for their expulsion from Cracow to Kazimierz in 1495. However, the end of Jewish settlement in Cracow was far from the end of Jewish trade there; it continued to flourish and aggravate the Christian townspeople, as was the case with many cities (like *Lublin and *Warsaw) which had exercised their right *de non tolerandis Judaeis* and yet had to see Jewish economic activity flourishing at their fairs and in their streets.

CULTURAL AND SOCIAL LIFE

In Poland and Lithuania from the 13th century onward Jewish culture and society was much richer and more

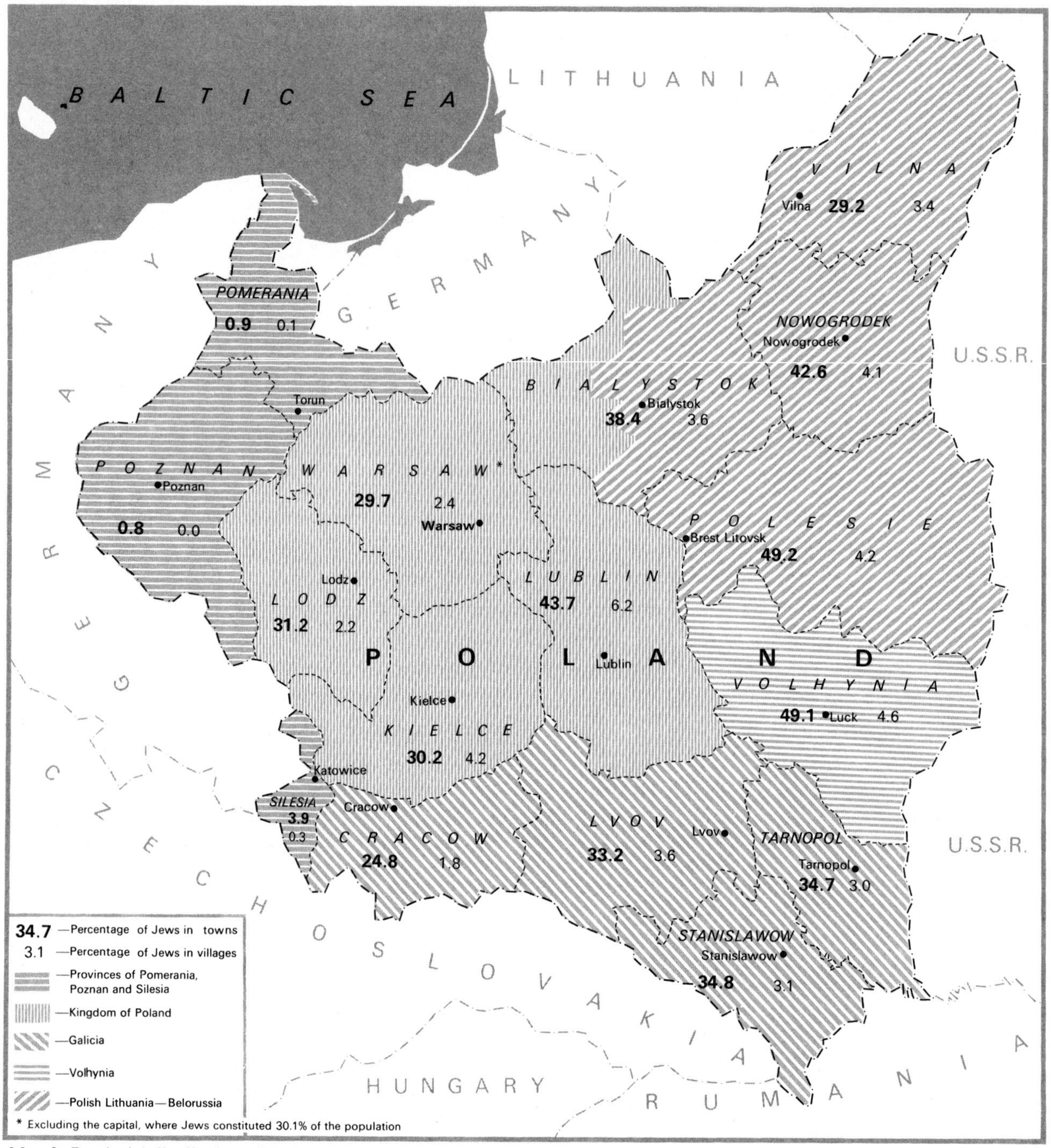

Map 3. Provincial distribution of Polish Jewry in towns and villages (1931). Based on data from R. Mahler, *Yehudei Polin bein Shetei Milhamot Olam,* 1968.

variegated than has been commonly accepted. Even before that, the inscriptions on the bracteate coins of the 12th century indicate talmudic culture and leadership traditions by the expressions used (*rabbi,* רַבִּי, *nagid,* נָגִיד). About 1234, as mentioned, Jacob Savra of Cracow was able to contradict the greatest talmudic authorities of his day in Germany and Bohemia. In defense of his case he "sent responsa to the far ends of the west and the south" (E. E. Urbach (ed.), in *Sefer Arugat ha-Bosem,* 4 (1963), 120–1). The author of *Sefer Arugat ha-Bosem* also quotes an interpretation and emendation that "I have heard in the name of Rabbi Jacob from Poland" (*ibid.,* 3 (1962), 126). Moses Zaltman, the son of *Judah b. Samuel he-Ḥasid, states: "Thus I have been told by R. Isaac from Poland in the name of my father . . . thus I have been told by R. Isaac from Russia . . . R. Mordecai from Poland told me that my father said" (Ms. Cambridge 669. 2, fol. 69 and 74). This manuscript evidence proves conclusively that men from Poland and from southern Russia (which in the 13th century was part of the grand duchy of Lithuania) were close disciples of the leader of the *Ḥasidei Ashkenaz. The names of Polish Jews in the 14th century show curious traces of cultural influence; besides ordinary Hebrew names and names taken from the German and French—brought by the immigrants from the countries of their origin—there are clearly Slavonic names like Lewko, Jeleń, and Pychacz and women's names like Czarnula, Krasa, and even Witosława. Even more remarkable are the names of Lewko's father, Jordan, and Lewko's son, Canaan or Chanaan, which indicate a special devotion to Ereẓ Israel.

By the 15th century, relatively numerous traces of social and cultural life in the Polish communities can be found. In a document from April 4, 1435, that perhaps preserves the early *Yiddish of the Polish Jews, the writer, a Jew of Breslau, addresses "the Lord King of Poland my Lord." The closing phrases of the letter indicate his Jewish culture: "To certify this, have I, the above mentioned Jekuthiel, appended my Jewish seal to this letter with full knowledge. Given in Breslau, on the first Monday of the month Nisan, in Jewish reckoning five thousand years and a hundred years and to that hundred the ninety-fifth year after the beginning and creation of all creatures except God Himself" (M. Brann, *Geschichte der Juden in Schlesien*, 3 (1901), Anhang 4, p. lviii).

(דש צו בקינטניש האבע איך אֵי גנבטר יקותיאל מיין יודיש זיגל אנ דיזן בריבֿא מיט רעכטר ווישן גהאנגן. גגעבן צו ברייסלא אנדעמא אירשטן מאנטאג דש מאנדש ניׄסן איין יידישר צאל בֿונץ טאוזנט יאר אינ הונדרט יאר אונ דר צו אין צעמא בֿינווא אונ׳ נויינציקשטן יאר נאך אנבגינן אונ׳ שיפֿפונגא אללר קריאטייר זונצו גוטא אליין)

Though Israel b. Ḥayyim *Bruna said of the Jews of Cracow, "they are not well versed in Torah" (Responsa, no. 55, fol. 23b), giving this as his reason for not adducing lengthy talmudic arguments in his correspondence with them, he was writing to one of his pupils who claimed sole rabbinical authority and income in the community of Poznan (*ibid.*, no. 254, fol. 103b). Israel b. Pethahiah *Isserlein of Austria writes, "my beloved, the holy community of Poznan." Two parties in this community—the leadership, whom Isserlein calls "you, the holy community," and an individual—were quarreling about taxation and Isserlein records that both sides submitted legal arguments in support of their cases (*Terumat ha-Deshen, Pesakim u-Khetavim*, no. 144). Great scholars like Yom Tov Lipmann *Muelhausen, who came to Cracow at the end of the 14th century, and Moses b. Isaac Segal *Mintz, who lived at Poznan in 1475, must certainly have left traces of their cultural influence there. Some of the responsa literature contains graphic descriptions of social life. "A rich man from Russia"—either the environs of Lvov in Poland or of Kiev in Lithuania—asked Israel Bruna, "If it is permissible to have a prayer shawl of silk in red or green color for Sabbath and the holidays" (Responsa, no. 73, fol. 32b), a desire fitting a personality of the type of Volchko. Something of the way of life of "the holy company of Lvov" can be seen from the fact that their problem was the murder of one Jew by another in the Ukrainian city of *Pereyaslav-Khmelnitski. As the victim lay wounded on the ground, a third Jew, Naḥman, called out to the murderer, Simḥah: "Hit Nisan till death" and so he was killed by being beaten on his head as he lay there wounded. The victim was a totally ignorant man, "he couldn't recognize a single [Hebrew] letter and has never in his life put on *tefillin*." The murderer was drunk at the time and the victim had started the quarrel; they were all in a large company of Jews (*ibid.*, no. 265, fol. 110a–b). The rough social and cultural climate of Jewish traders in the Ukraine in the middle of the 15th century is here in evidence. Moses Mintz describes from his own experience divorce customs in the region of Poznan (Responsa (Salonika, 1802), no. 113, fol. 129b). He also describes interesting wedding customs in Poland which differed in many details from those of Germany: "when they accompany the bride and bridegroom to the *ḥuppah* they sing on the way . . . they give the bridegroom the cup and he throws it down, puts his foot on it and breaks it, but they pour out the wine from the cup before they give it to the bridegroom. They have also the custom of throwing a cock and also a hen over the head of the bride and bridegroom above the canopy after the pronouncing of the wedding blessings" (*ibid.*, no. 109, fol. 127a). Thus, in the western and central parts of Poland there is evidence of an established and well developed culture and some learning, contrasting sharply with the rough and haphazard existence of Jews living southwards from Lvov to Pereyaslav-Khmelnitski.

Jewish culture in Poland and in Lithuania seems to have had a certain rationalist, "Sephardi" tinge, as evidenced both by outside reports and by certain tensions appearing in the second half of the 16th century. At the beginning of the 16th century the Polish chronicler Maciej Miechowicz relates that in Lithuania, "the Jews use Hebrew books and study sciences and arts, astronomy and medicine" (*Tractatus de duabus Sarmatiis* (1517), II:1,3). The cardinal legate Lemendone also notes that Lithuanian Jews of the 16th century devote time to the study of "literature and science, in particular astronomy and medicine." At the end of the 15th century, Lithuanian Jews took part in the movement of the *Judaizers in Muscovite Russia, whose literature shows a marked influence of rationalistic Jewish works and anti-Christian arguments. The Jewish community of Kiev—in the 15th and early 16th centuries within the grand duchy of Lithuania—was praised by a Crimean Karaite in 1481 for its culture and learning. In about 1484 another Karaite, Joseph b. Mordecai of Troki, wrote a letter to Elijah b. Moses *Bashyazi (Mann, Texts, 2 (1935), 1149–59) telling about a disputation on calendar problems between him and "the Rabbanites who live here in Troki, Jacob Suchy of Kaffa (Feodosiya) and Ozer the physician of Cracow" (*ibid.*, 1150). He closes his letter with ideas showing a decided rationalist tendency, "The quality of the sermon will be through the quality of the subject, therefore as we have none such more important than the Torah, for in it there is this teaching that brings man straight to his scientific and social success and the chief of its considerations is that man should achieve his utmost perfection, which is spiritual success; and this will happen when he attains such rational concepts as the soul, the active reason, can attain, for the relation between a phenomenon and its causes is a necessary relation, i.e., the relation of the separate reason to the material reason is like the relation of light to sight" (*ibid.*, 1159).

In Poland a dispute between two great scholars of the 16th century—Solomon *Luria and Moses *Isserles—brings to the surface elements of an earlier rationalist culture. Luria accuses yeshivah students of using "the prayer of Aristotle" and accuses Isserles of "mixing him with words of the living God . . . [considering] that the words of this unclean one are precious and perfume to Jewish sages" (Isserles, Responsa, no. 6). Isserles replies: "All this is still a poisonous root in existence, the legacy from their parents from those that tended to follow the philosophers and tread in their steps. But I myself have never seen nor heard up till now such a thing, and, but for your evidence, I could not have believed that there was still a trace of these conceptions among us" (*ibid.*, no. 7). Writing around the middle of the 16th century, Isserles tells unwittingly of a philosophizing trend prevalent in Poland many years before. A remarkable case of how extreme rationalist conceptions gave way to more mystic ones can be seen in Isserles' pupil, Abraham b. Shabbetai *Horowitz. Around 1539 he sharply rebuked the rabbi of Poznan, who believed in demons and opposed *Maimonides: "As to what this ass said, that it is permissible to study Torah only, this is truly against what the Torah says, 'Ye shall keep and do for it is your wisdom and understanding in the eyes of the gentiles.' For even if we shall be well versed in all the arcana of the Talmud, the gentiles will still not consider us scholars; on the contrary, all the ideas of the Talmud, its methods and sermons, are funny and derisible in the eyes of the gentiles. If we know no more than the Talmud we shall not be able to explain the ideas and exegetical methods of the Talmud in a way that the gentiles will like—this stands to reason" (See MGWJ, 47 (1903), 263). Yet this same man rewrote his rationalistic commentary on a work by Maimonides to make it more amenable to traditionalistic and mystic thought, declaring in the second version, "The first uproots, the last roots." Later trends and struggles in Jewish culture in Poland and Lithuania are partly traceable to this early and obliterated rationalistic layer (see below).

Polish victories over the Teutonic Order in the west and against Muscovite and Ottoman armies in the east and southeast led to a great expansion of Poland-Lithuania from the second half of the 16th century. In this way Poland-Lithuania gained a vast steppeland in the southeast, in the Ukraine, fertile but unpacified and unreclaimed, and great stretches of arable land and virgin forest in the east, in Belorussia. The agricultural resources in the east were linked to the center through the river and canal systems and to the sea outlet in the west through land routes. These successes forged a stronger link between the various strata of the nobility (Pol. *szlachta*) as well as between the Polish and Lithuanian nobility. In 1569 the Union of Lublin cemented and formalized the unity of Poland-Lithuania, although the crown of Poland and the grand duchy of Lithuania kept a certain distinctness of character and law, which was also apparent in the *Councils of the Lands and in the culture of the Jews (see below). With the union, Volhynia and the Ukraine passed from the grand duchy to the crown. The combined might of Poland-Lithuania brought about a growing pacification of these southeastern districts, offering a possibility of their colonization which was eagerly seized upon by both nobility and peasants.

1569–1648: COLONIZATION OF THE UKRAINE

The Polish nobility, which became the dominant element in the state, was at that time a civilized and civilizing factor. Fermenting with religious thought and unrest which embraced even the most extreme anti-trinitarians; warlike and at the same time giving rise to small groups of extreme anarchists and pacifists; more and more attracted by luxury, yet for most of the period developing rational—even if often harsh—methods of land and peasant exploitation; despising merchandise yet very knowledgeable about money and gain—this was the nobility that, taking over the helm of state and society, developed its own estates in the old lands of Poland-Lithuania and the vast new lands in the east and southeast. Jews soon became the active and valued partners of this nobility in many enterprises. In the old "royal cities"—even in central places like Cracow, which expelled the Jews in 1495, and *Warsaw, which had possessed a *privilegium de non tolerandis Judaeis* since 1527—Jews were among the great merchants of clothing, dyes, and luxury products, in short, everything the nobility desired. Complaints from Christian merchants as early as the beginning of the 16th century, attacks by urban anti-Semites like Sebastian *Miczyński and Przecław *Mojecki in the 17th century, and above all internal Jewish evidence all point to the success of the Jewish merchant. The Jew prospered in trade even in places where he could not settle, thanks to his initiative, unfettered by guilds, conventions, and preconceived notions. The *kesherim*, the council of former office holders in the Poznan community, complain about the excessive activity of Jewish intermediaries, "who cannot stay quiet; they wait at every corner, in every place, at every shop where silk and cloth is sold, and they cause competition through influencing the buyers by their speech and leading them to other shops and other merchants." The same council complains about "those unemployed" people who sit all day long from morning till evening before the shops of gentiles—of spice merchants, clothes merchants, and various other shops—"and the Christian merchants complain and threaten." There was even a technical term for such men, *tsuvayzer*, those who point the way to a prospective seller (*Pinkas Hekhsherim shel Kehillat Pozna*, ed. D. Avron (1966), 187–8 no. 1105, 250 no. 1473, 51 no. 1476). Miczyński gives a bitter description of the same phenomenon in Cracow in 1618. Large-scale Jewish trade benefited greatly from the trader's connections with their brethren both in the Ottoman Empire and in Germany and Western Europe. It was also linked to a considerable extent with the *arenda system and its resulting great trade in the export of agricultural products.

Through the arenda system Jewish settlements spread over the country, especially in the southeast. Between 1503 and 1648 there were 114 Jewish communities in the Ukraine, some on the eastern side of the River Dnieper (see map and list by S. Ettinger, in *Zion*, 21 (1956), 114–8); many of these were tiny. Table 1 shows the main outlines of the dynamics of Jewish settlement in these regions of colonization (*ibid.*, p. 124):

Table 1. Growth of Jewish Settlement by Places and Numbers in the Colonization Period

Województwo	Before 1569		c. 1648		
(district)	Places	Numbers	Places	Numbers	
Volhynia	13	3,000	46	15,000	
Podolia	9	750	18	4,000	
Kiev	—	—	33	13,500	32,325
Bratslav	2	?	18	18,825	
Total	24	c. 4,000	115	51,325	

The further the move east and southward, the greater the relative growth in numbers and population. The Jewish arenda holders, traders, and peddlers traveled and settled wherever space and opportunity offered.

Life in these districts was strenuous and often harsh. The manner of Jewish life in the Ukraine, which as we have already seen was uncouth, was both influenced and channeled through Jewish participation in the defense of newly pacified land. Meir b. Gedaliah of Lublin relates "what happened to a luckless man, ill, and tortured by pain and suffering from epilepsy . . . When there was an alarm in Volhynia because of the Tatars—as is usual in the towns of that district—when each one is obliged to be prepared, with weapon in hand, to go to war and battle against them at the command of the duke and the lords; and it came to pass that when the present man shot with his weapon, called in German *Buechse*, from his house through the window to a point marked for him on a rope in his courtyard to try the weapon as sharpshooters are wont to do, then a man came from the market to the above mentioned courtyard . . . and he was killed [by mistake]." The rabbi goes on to tell that a Christian, the instructor and commander of this Jew, was standing in front of the courtyard to warn people not to enter. The Jew was "living among the gentiles in a village" with many children (Meir b. Gedaliah of Lublin, Responsa, no. 43). There is reference to an enterprising group of Jews who went to Moscow with the armies of the Polish king during war, selling liquor (one of them had two cartloads) and other merchandise to the soldiers (*ibid.*, no. 128). Among the Cossack units there was a Jew about whom his Cossack colleagues "complained to God . . . suddenly there jumped out from amongst our ranks a Jew who was called Berakhah, the son of the martyr Aaron of Cieszewiec." This Jew was not the only one in the ranks of the Cossacks, for—to allow his wife to marry—one of the witnesses says that "he knew well that in this unit there was not another Jewish fighter who was called Berakhah" (*ibid.*, no. 137). Life in general was apt to be much more violent than is usually supposed: even at Brest-Litovsk, when the *rebbe* of the community saw a litigant nearing his door, he seized a heavy box and barricaded himself in for fear of harm (*ibid.*, no. 44).

Arenda did more than give a new basis to the existence of many Jewish families; it brought the Jews into contact with village life and often combined with aspects of their internal organizational structure. Thus, the Jew Nahum b. Moses, as well as renting the mills, the tavern, and the right of preparing beer and brandy, also rented for one year all milk produce of the livestock on the manors and villages. Elaborate and complicated arrangements were made for payment and collection of these milk products (S. Inglot, in: *Studja z historji społecznej i gospodarczej poświęcone prof. Franciszkowi Bujakowi* (1931), 179–82; cf. 205, 208–9). In contact with village life, the Jew sometimes formed a sentimental attachment to his neighbors and his surroundings. In 1602 a council of leaders of Jewish communities in Volhynia tried to convince Jewish arendars to let the peasants rest on Saturday though the Polish nobleman would certainly have given them the right to compel them to work: "If the villagers are obliged to work all the week through, he should let them rest on Sabbath and the Holy Days throughout. See, while living in exile and under the Egyptian yoke, our parents chose this Saturday for a day of rest while they were not yet commanded about it, and heaven helped them to make it a day of rest for ever. Therefore, where gentiles are under their authority they are obliged to fulfill the commandment of the Torah and the order of the sages not to come, God forbid, to be ungrateful [*livot* לִבְעֹט] to the One who has given them plenty of good by means of the very plenty he has given them. Let God's name be sanctified by them and not defiled" (H. H. Ben-Sasson, in *Zion,* 21 (1956), 205).

The interests of the Jews and Polish magnates coincided and complemented each other in one most important aspect of the economic and social activity of the Polish-Lithuanian nobility. On their huge estates the nobles began to establish and encourage the development of new townships, creating a network of "private towns." Because of the nature of their relationship with their own peasant population they were keen to attract settlers from afar, and Jews well suited their plans. The tempo and scale of expansion were great; in the grand duchy of Lithuania alone in the first half of the 17th century between 770 and 900 such townships *(miasteczki)* existed (S. Aleksandrowicz, in: *Roczniki dziejów społecznych i gospodarczych,* 27 (1965), 35–65). For their part, the Jews, who were hard pressed by the enmity of the populace in the old royal cities, gladly moved to places where they sometimes became the majority, in some cases even the whole, of the population. Since these were situated near the hinterland of agricultural produce and potential customers, Jewish initiative and innovation found a new outlet. Through charters granted by kings and magnates to communities and settlers in these new towns, the real legal status of the Jews gradually changed very much for the better. By the second half of the 17th century everywhere in Poland Jews had become part of "the third estate" and in some places and in some respects the only one.

Jews continued to hold customs stations openly in Lithuania, in defiance of the wishes of their leaders in Poland (see Councils of the Lands). Many custom station ledgers were written in Hebrew script and contained Hebrew terms (see R. Mahler, in *YIVO Historishe Shriftn,* 2 (1937), 180–205). Sometimes a Jew is found with a "sleeping partner," a Pole or Armenian in whose name the customs lease has been taken out. That some customs stations were in Jewish hands was also of assistance to Jewish trade.

This complex structure of large-scale export and import trade, the active and sometimes adventurous participation in the colonization of the Ukraine and in the shaping of the "private cities," in the fulfilling of what today we would call state economic functions, created for the first time in the history of Ashkenazi Jewry a broad base of population, settlement distribution, and means of livelihood, which provided changed conditions for the cultural and religious life of Jews. Even after the destruction wrought by the *Chmielnicki massacres enough remained to form the nucleus of later Ashkenazi Jewry. The later style of life in the Jewish **shtetl* was based on achievements and progress made at this time.

INTERNAL JEWISH LIFE

The Councils of the Lands, the great superstructure of Jewish *autonomy, were an outgrowth of such dynamics of economy and settlement. Beginning with attempts at centralized leaderships imposed from above, appointed by the king, they ended with a central elected Jewish leadership. The aims, methods, and institutions of this leadership were intertwined with the new economic structure. Great fairs—notably those of Lublin and Jaroslaw—since they attracted the richest and most active element of the Jewish population, also served as the meeting place of the councils. Throughout its existence the Council of the Province of Lithuania cooperated with its three (later five) leading communities through a continuous correspondence with them and between each of them and the smaller communities under its authority. Here the council was adapting the organizational methods of large-scale trade to the leadership structure. The concern of the councils with the new economic phenomena, like arenda, is well known. They also concerned themselves with matters of security and morals which arose from the thin spread of Jewish families in Christian townships and villages. On the whole, up to 1648 a sense of achievement and creativity pervades their enterprises and thought. A preacher of that time, Jedidiah b. Israel *Gottlieb, inveighed against a man's gathering up riches for his children, using the argument of the self-made man: "The land is wide open, let them be mighty in it, settle and trade in it, then they will not be sluggards, lazy workers, children relying on their father's inheritance, but they themselves will try . . . to bring income to their homes, in particular because every kind of riches coming through inheritance does not stay in their hands . . . easy come, easy go . . . through their laziness . . . they have to be admonished . . . to be mighty in the land through their trading: their strength and might shall bring them riches" (*Shir Yedidut* (Cracow, 1644), *Ẓeidah la-Derekh,* fol. 24a).

This buoyancy was based on a continuous growth of population throughout the 16th and the first half of the 17th centuries, due both to a steady natural increase thanks to improving conditions of life and to immigration from abroad resulting from persecution and expulsions (e.g., that from Bohemia-Moravia for a short period in 1542). As noted, the growth was most intensive in the eastern and southeastern areas of Poland-Lithuania, and it was distributed through the growing dispersion of Jews in the "private cities" and in the villages. At the end of the 16th century, Great Poland and Masovia (Mazowsze) contained 52 communities, Lesser Poland 41, and the Ukraine, Volhynia, and Podolia about 80; around 1648, the latter region had 115 communities. From about 100,000 persons in 1578 the Jewish population had grown to approximately 300,000 around 1648. It is estimated that the Jews formed about 2.5–3% of the entire population of Poland, but they constituted between 10% and 15% of the urban population in Poland and 20% of the same in Lithuania.

The dynamics of Jewish economic life are evident not only in the variety and success of their activities, but also in certain specific institutions and problems that reveal the tension behind their strain for economic goals which tended to entail risks. By the end of the 16th century, Jews were

Figure 1. Examples of Polish coins minted by Jews in the 13th century. These coins, many of which have Hebrew inscriptions, were engraved on one side only. Jerusalem, C.A.H.J.P.

Figure 2. Drawing of the Jewish quarter and mid-17th-century synagogue of Chodorow, Poland, by George Lukomski.

Figure 3. The fortress-type synagogue of Lyuboml, built in the 17th century.

Figure 4. Engraving of a Jew from Warsaw and his wife. From L. Hollaenderski, *Les Israélites de Pologne,* Paris, 1846. Jerusalem, Israel Museum. Photo David Harris, Jerusalem.

Figure 5. Engraving of a Polish Jew, 1703. Jerusalem, Israel Museum. Photo David Harris, Jerusalem.

borrowers rather than lenders. Seventeenth-century anti-Semites—Miczyński and Mojecki—accused Jews of borrowing beyond their means and deceiving Christian lenders. From their accusations it is clear that much of this credit was not in ready cash but in goods given to Jewish merchants on credit. Borrowing was a real problem with which the Jewish leadership was much concerned. Many ordinances of the Councils of the Lands, of the provincial councils, and of single communities are preoccupied with preventing and punishing bankruptcy. Great efforts were devoted to prevent non-payment of debts to Christians in particular. Young men who were building up a family were especially suspected of reaching beyond their means. These ordinances tell in their own way the story of a burgeoning economy which is strained to dangerous limits, inciting in particular the young and the daring. A good name for credit was then a matter of life and death for the Jewish merchant. The great halakhist Solomon Luria was prepared to waive an ancient talmudic law in favor of the lender because "now most of the living of the Jews is based on credit; whereas most of those called merchants have little of their own and what they have in their hands is really taken from gentiles on credit for a fixed period—for they take merchandise [on credit] till a certain date—it is not seemly for a judge to sequester the property of a merchant, for news of this may spread and he will lose the source of his living and all his gentile creditors will come on him together and he will be lost, God forbid, and merchants will never trust him again. I myself have seen and heard about many merchants—circumcised and uncircumcised—to whom, because people said about them that they are a risk, much harm was caused and they never again could stand at their posts" (*Yam shel Shelomo, Bava Kamma,* ch. 1, para. 20). Because of the importance of credit the practice of a Jew lending on interest to another Jew became widespread in Poland-Lithuania despite the fact that it was contrary to Jewish law (see *usury). This necessitated the creation there of the legal fiction of *hetter iskah,* formulated by a synod of rabbis and leaders under the chairmanship of Joshua b. Alexander ha-Kohen *Falk in 1607. Widespread credit also led to the use of letters of credit specific to the Jews of Poland, the so-called **mamram* (Pol. *membrana, membran;* Heb. ממרנ״י, ממרם״א, ממרים, in initials: ממ״א, מ״מ): the Jew would sign on one side of the paper and write on the other side "this letter of credit obliges the signed overleaf for amount *x* to be paid on date *y*."

Jewish cultural and social life flourished hand in hand with the economic and demographic growth. In the 16th and early 17th centuries Poland-Lithuania became the main center of Ashkenazi culture. Its *yeshivot were already famous at the beginning of the 16th century; scholars like *Ḥayyim b. Bezalel of Germany and David b. Solomon *Gans of Prague were the pupils of *Shalom Shakhna of Lublin and Moses Isserles of Cracow, respectively. Mordecai b. Abraham *Jaffe; Abraham, Isaiah, and Jacob b. Abraham *Horowitz; Eliezer b. Elijah *Ashkenazi; *Ephraim Solomon b. Aaron Luntshits; and Solomon Luria were only a few of the great luminaries of talmudic scholarship and moralistic preaching in Poland-Lithuania of that time. Councils of the Lands and community ordinances show in great detail if not the reality at least the ideal of widespread Torah study supported by the people in general. This culture was fraught with great social and moral tensions. Old Ashkenazi ascetic ideas did not sit too well on the affluent and economically activist Polish-Lithuanian Jewish society. Meetings with representatives of the Polish *Reformation movement, in particular with groups and representatives of the anti-trinitarian wing like Marcin Czechowic or Szymon *Budny, led to disputations and reciprocal influence. Outstanding in these contacts on the Jewish side was the Karaite Isaac b. Abraham *Troki, whose *Ḥizzuk Emunah* sums up the tensions in Jewish thought in the divided Christian religious world of Poland-Lithuania. It was Moses Isserles who formulated the Ashkenazi modifications and additions to the code of the Sephardi Joseph Caro. Isaiah b. Abraham ha-Levi *Horowitz summed up in his *Shenei Luḥot ha-Berit* the moral and mystic teaching of the upper circles of Ashkenazi Jewry. Yet his writings, and even more so the writings of Isserles, give expression to the tensions and compromises between rationalism and mysticism, between rich and poor, between leadership and individual rights. To all these tensions, Ephraim Solomon Luntshits gave sharp voice in his eloquent sermons, standing always on the side of the poor against the rich and warning consistently against the danger of hypocrisy and self-righteousness. Fortified and wooden synagogues expressed the needs and the aesthetic sense of Jewish society of that time. In the old "royal cities" magnificent synagogue buildings were erected as early as the 16th century (e.g.,the Rema synagogue at Cracow and the Great Synagogue of Lvov). Hebrew manuscripts were brought from abroad and some of them illuminated in Poland. Jewish printing developed early and many beautiful works were published. Various sources describe carnival-like Purim celebrations, and the fun, irony, and joy of life expressed in now lost folk songs and popular games and dramas.

FROM CHMIELNICKI TO THE FIRST PARTITION

The *Chmielnicki revolt and massacres of 1648–49, the Tatar incursions from Crimea, and the subsequent war with Moscow combined with the Swedish War to bring on the Jews of Poland-Lithuania approximately 30 years of bloodshed, destruction, and suffering. Thousands were killed, thousands forced to adopt Christianity. At the end of these convulsions, Poland-Lithuania had lost much territory in the east which of course was also lost for Jewish life and settlement. Thousands of refugees thronged westward, bringing heavy pressure to bear on charity and the very structure of Jewish society. The arrangements of the Councils of the Lands to prevent competition for arenda had to stand the severe test of diminished opportunities and increasing demand. Contemporary figures like Nathan Nata *Hannover saw in this catastrophe a fissure in Jewish life and institutions, as indicated by the tenor of his chronicle, *Yeven Meẓulah.* In reality, Jewish cultural and social life in the second half of the 17th century and in the 18th continued to a considerable extent along the lines developed in the great era of the 16th and first half of the 17th centuries. Recent research has shown that *Pinsk, a community in the east of Lithuania, recovered from its troubles more completely and at greater speed than had been known before. But the dynamism had gone out of institutions and activities; inertia set in. Much that had been full of imminent promise of development and change before the disasters tended now to be petrified. Tensions that had been submerged in the buoyant pre-Chmielnicki times became more open, causing dissension and revolt. The councils and communities were burdened with the growing debts incurred mostly to meet unexpected demands for defense against multiplying libels and massacres, but at the same time the oligarchic structure within the community and the councils and the dominating attitude adopted by the larger communities toward the smaller ones—in Lithuania in particular—caused the lower strata of the population and the members of the smaller communities to suspect their intentions and greatly resent the increasingly heavy tax burden. Jewish economic activity continued to develop, though Jews in the "private towns" and on arenda in the villages came to feel more and more the heavy and capricious hand of the Polish nobles, who by that period had lost the vigor of earlier times and become tyrannical, petty lords.

Despite the loss of territory and the worsening of conditions, the Jewish population in Poland-Lithuania continued to grow both absolutely and, from many aspects, in its relative strength in the country. With the abolition of the Councils of the Lands in 1764, a census of the Jewish population was taken. Jews tried to evade being counted by any means available for they were certain that the purpose of the census was to impose heavier taxation on them, as they had every reason to suspect the intentions of the authorities. For this reason at least 20% should be added to the official figures. Accordingly in 1764 there were 749,968 Jews over a year old in Poland-Lithuania: 548,777 of them in Poland and 201,191 in Lithuania; 16.5% of the Jewish population of Poland lived in western Poland, 23.5% in Lesser Poland, and 60% in the Ukraine and neighboring districts; in Lithuania 77% lived in the western part and only 23% in the eastern, Belorussian districts. Taking into account the overall population of Poland, it can be seen that the concentration of Jewish population had shifted eastward in the 18th century to an even greater extent that in the early and successful 17th century. The census also shows that Jews lived mostly in small communities:

Table 2. Distribution of Jews According to Size of Communities

Region	Percentage of communities of less than 500	Percentage of communities of more than 500
Great Poland	91.7	8.3
Masovia	93.5	6.5
Lesser Poland	76.5	23.5
Lvov	61.7	38.3
Ukraine	85.0	15.0

As the entire Christian urban population of Poland-Lithuania was estimated at that time to be about half a million, and as the Jews were concentrated mainly in the townships and "private towns," there emerges a clear picture of a predominantly Jewish population in the smaller Polish-Lithuanian urban centers, at least 70% to 90% in many of these places.

The economic structure of the Jewish population at this time is shown in Table 3:

Table 3. Economic Structure of Jewish Population in Poland-Lithuania in the 18th century

Region	Arenda and Alcoholic Beverages	Trade	Transportation	Crafts	Professions	Unspec.
Great Poland	1.8	6.1	—	41.8	12.4	38.0
Masovia	15.2	0.7	—	19.0	13.0	52.0
Lesser Poland	3.1	4.8	1.0	24.0	11.0	56.0
Lvov	2.8	3.0	3.2	20.6	12.5	58.0
Ukraine	28.0	3.6	2.0	26.5	14.5	23.5

Although the predominance of unspecified professions does indicate the impoverishment of the Jews, it is largely an aspect of the evasive attitude toward the census. As this table does not include the village Jews, among whom the occupations of arenda and the production and sale of alcoholic beverages certainly predominated, only the following economic conclusions can be drawn with certainty: a considerable proportion of the Jews were engaged in crafts; and arenda and alcoholic beverages became more important as sources of livelihood as the Jews moved eastward and into villages (according to R. Mahler, *Yidn in Amolikn Poyln in Likht fun Tsifern,* 1958).

The Jewish population of Poland-Lithuania was still seething with creativity and movement in the 18th century. The messianic claims of *Shabbetai Ẓevi not only stirred the masses of Jews in 1665–66 but also left a deep impression on later generations. This is evident in the suspicion expressed about itinerant **maggidim* (it was also demanded that they be supervised), who were suspected of disseminating heretical and critical ideas. The personality and movement of Jacob *Frank made the greatest impact on the distressed population of Podolia, in the extreme southeast. From the same region too arose *Israel b. Eliezer Ba'al Shem Tov and the movement of *Ḥasidism he originated. Talmudic scholarship and traditional ways of life, which continued to flourish throughout the period, found a supreme exemplar in the vigorous personality and influence of *Elijah b. Solomon Zalman, the Gaon of Vilna, and in the way of life and culture originated by him and his circle in the Mitnaggedic Lithuanian yeshivot. At that time too the first influences of *Haskalah and *assimilation began to appear in Poland-Lithuania.

With the partitions of Poland (beginning in 1772), the history of ancient Jewish Poland-Lithuania comes to an end. During the agony of the Polish state, several of its more enlightened leaders—e.g., H. Kołłątaj and T. *Czacki—tried to "improve the Jews," i.e., improve their legal and social status in the spirit of western and European enlightened absolutism. With the dismemberment of Poland-Lithuania, their belated efforts remained suspended. Even when broken up and dispersed, Polish-Lithuanian Jewry was not only the majority and the cultural source of Jewish society in czarist Russia, but those elements of it which came under Prussia and Austria also served later as the reservoir of Jewish spirit and manpower which resisted the ravages of assimilation and apostasy in the German and Austrian communities in the late 18th and 19th centuries.
[H.H.B.-S.]

AFTER PARTITION

The geographic entity "Poland" in this part of the article refers to that area of the Polish commonwealth which, by 1795, had been divided between Austria and Prussia and which subsequently constituted the basis of the grand duchy of Warsaw, created in 1807. Following the Congress of *Vienna in 1815 much of this area was annexed to the Russian Empire as the semi-autonomous Kingdom of Poland, also known as Congress Poland. The kingdom constituted the core of ethnic Poland, the center of Polish politics and culture, and an economic area of great importance. It is to be distinguished from Austrian Poland (Galicia), Prussian Poland (Poznan, Silesia, and Pomerania), and the Russian northwestern region also known as Lithuania-Belorussia.

During and after the partitions the special legal status enjoyed by the Jews in Poland-Lithuania came under attack—while disabilities remained, efforts were made to break down the Jews' separateness and transform them into "useful" citizens. This new notion, brought to Poland from the west and championed by Polish progressives with the support of the tiny number of progressive Jews, advocates of the Haskalah, was clearly expressed during the debates on the Jewish question at the Four-Year Sejm (1788–92). The writings of H. Kołłątaj and M. *Butrymowicz demanded the reform of Jewish life, meaning an end to

Figure 6. Nineteenth-century caricature of Jews in the Polish militia. The text reads: "'You Jews listen to my command: Attention, present arms!' 'What did he say? What did he say?' Herschel thereupon asked the corporal." Tel Aviv, I. Einhorn Collection.

Figure 7. Caricature and music entitled, "March of the Jewish National Guard in Warsaw," 1831. Tel Aviv, I. Einhorn Collection.

special institutions and customs (from the *kahal* to the Jewish beard), sentiments to be expressed later on by S. Staszic and A. J. *Czartoryski. The attack on *"l'état dans l'état,"* as Czartoryski put it in 1815, was accompanied by an attack against Jewish economic practices in the village, which, it was claimed, oppressed and corrupted the peasantry. From Butrymowicz, writing in 1789, to the writings of Polish liberals and Jewish assimilationists in the inter-war period, there runs a common assumption: the Jews suffer because they persist in their separateness—let them become like Poles and both they and Poland will prosper. This assumption was also shared by many anti-Semites of the non-racist variety.

Some effort was made during the 19th century to implement this belief. For example, the *kahal,* symbol of Jewish self-government, was abolished in 1822, and a special tax on Jewish liquor dealers forced many to abandon their once lucrative profession. On the other hand Jews were encouraged to become agriculturalists and were granted, in 1826, a modern rabbinical seminary which was supposed to produce enlightened spiritual leaders. Moreover, in 1862 the Jews of Poland were "emancipated," meaning that special Jewish taxes were abolished and, above all, that restrictions on residence (Jewish ghettos and *privilegium de non tolerandis Judaeis*) were removed. Nonetheless, the legal anti-Semitism of Russia's last czars was also introduced into Poland: in 1891 aspects of N. *Ignatiev's *May Laws were extended to Congress Poland, resulting in the expulsion of many Jews from the villages, and in 1908 school quotas *(*numerus clausus)* were officially implemented. In sum, during the 19th and early 20th centuries the policy of the carrot and the stick was employed. By the end of the pre-World War I era the stick had prevailed, making the legal status of Polish Jewry nearly identical to that of Russian Jewry. The efforts to assimilate Polish Jewry by legislation aimed at making it more productive and less separatist had virtually no impact on the Jewish masses.

The "Jewish question" in Poland and the legal efforts to deal with it were to a certain extent the result of the Jews' special demographic and economic structure. From the demographic point of view two striking tendencies may be observed. First, the natural increase of Polish Jews was greater than that of non-Jews, at least during most of the 19th century, leading to an increasing proportion of Jews within the population as a whole. In 1816 Jews constituted 8.7% of the population of the kingdom; in 1865, 13.5%. In 1897, despite the effects of large-scale Jewish emigration, 14 out of every 100 Polish citizens were Jews. This increase, attributable in part to the low Jewish death rate, was accompanied by the rapid urbanization of Polish Jewry. A few examples may suffice to illustrate this important process. Table 4 demonstrates the growth of Warsaw Jewry, where restrictions on residence were not entirely lifted until 1862:

Table 4. Growth of Warsaw Jewry

Year	Number of Jews	Percentage
1781	3,532	4.5
1810	14,061	18.1
1856	44,149	24.3
1882	127,917	33.4
1897	219,141	33.9

A similar trend is found in Lodz, the kingdom's second city (see Table 5):

Table 5. Lodz Jewry

Year	Number of Jews	Percentage
1793	11	5.7
1856	2,775	12.2
1897	98,677	31.8
1910	166,628	40.7

This remarkable urbanization—the result of government pressure, a crisis in the traditional Jewish village professions, and the economic attractions of the growing commercial and industrial centers—had the following impact on the Jewish population: in 1827, according to the research of A. Eisenbach, 80.4% of the Jews lived in cities and the rest in villages, while in 1865 fully 91.5% of Polish Jewry lived in cities. In the same year 83.6% of the non-Jewish population lived in the countryside. As early as 1855 Jews constituted approximately 43% of the entire urban population of the kingdom, and in those cities where there were no restrictions on Jewish settlement the figure reached 57.2%. The Jews, traditionally scattered, could claim with some justification that, by the end of the century, the cities were their "territory."

This demographic tendency meant that the traditional Jewish economic structure also underwent certain changes. Jews, of course, had always predominated in trade; in 1815, for example, 1,657 Polish Jews participated at the Leipzig fair compared with 143 Polish gentiles. During the course of the century, as the Jews became more and more dominant in the cities, their role in urban commercial ventures became more pronounced. Thus, in Warsaw, at the end of the century, 18 out of 26 major private banks were owned by Jews or Jewish converts to Christianity. A wealthy Jewish merchant and financial class emerged, led by such great capitalists as Ivan *Bliokh and Leopold *Kronenberg, who played a role in the urbanization and industrialization of Poland. On the other hand, the vast majority of Jews engaged in commerce very clearly belonged to the petty bourgeoisie of shopkeepers (of whom, in Warsaw in 1862, nearly 90% were Jews) and the like. In the same year, according to the calculations of the economic historian I. *Schiper, more than two-thirds of all Jewish merchants were without substantial capital.

Two tendencies must be emphasized with regard to the Jewish economic situation in the kingdom. First, it became apparent by the end of the century that the Jews were gradually losing ground to non-Jews in trade. Thus, for every 100 Jews in Warsaw in 1862, 72 lived from commerce, while in 1897 the figure had dropped to 62. For non-Jews, on the other hand, the percentage rose from 27.9 in 1862 to 37.9 in 1897. The rise of a non-Jewish middle class, with the resulting increase in competition between Jew and gentile, marks the beginning of a process which, as we shall see, gained impetus during the interwar years. Second, there was a marked tendency toward the "productivization" of Polish Jewry, that is, a rise of Jews engaged in crafts and industry. The following figures, which relate to the whole of Congress Poland, are most revealing: in 1857 44.7% of all Jews lived from commerce and 25.1% from crafts and industry, while in 1897 42.6% were engaged in commerce and 34.3% in crafts and industry. In this area, as in trade, the typical Jew was far from wealthy. For every wealthy Jew like Israel Poznański, the textile tycoon from Lodz, there were thousands of Jewish artisans (some 119,000, according to the survey of the *Jewish Colonization Association (ICA) in 1898) who worked in tiny shops with rarely more than one hired hand. It is noteworthy that for various reasons—the problems of Sabbath work, the anti-Semitism of non-Jewish factory owners, fear of the Jewish workers' revolutionary potential—a Jewish factory proletariat failed to develop. Even in Lodz and Bialystok the typical Jewish weaver worked in a small shop or at home, not in a large factory. One further development should be mentioned. By the end of the century a numerically small but highly influential Jewish professional class had made its appearance, particularly in Warsaw. This class was to provide the various political and cultural movements of the day, Jewish and non-Jewish, with many recruits, as well as to provide new leadership for the Jewish community.

The Jews, therefore, constituted an urban, middle class and proletarian element within the great mass of the Polish peasantry. There existed in Poland a long tradition of what might be called a "Polish orientation" among Jews, dating back to the Jewish legion which fought with T. *Kościuszko in 1794 and continuing up to the enthusiastic participation of a number of Jews in J.*Piłsudski's legions. The Polish-Jewish fraternization and cooperation during the Polish uprising of 1863 is perhaps the best example of this orientation, which held that Polish independence would also lead to the disappearance of anti-Semitism. The idea of Jewish-Polish cultural assimilation took root among the Jews of the kingdom far earlier than in Galicia, not to mention multi-national Lithuania-Belorussia. **Izraelita*, the Polish-Jewish periodical advocating assimilation, began publication in 1866, and a number of Jewish intellectuals like Alexander Kraushar hoped for the eventual merging of the Jews into the Polish nation. Such men took comfort from the views of a few Polish intellectuals, notably the poet Adam *Mickiewicz, who hoped and worked for the same event. The slogan "for our and your freedom" had considerable influence within the Polish-Jewish intelligentsia by the century's end.

The Jewish masses, however, had nothing to do with such views, knew nothing of Mickiewicz, knew little if any Polish, and remained (as the assimilationists put it) enclosed within their own special world. Here, too, as was the case regarding the economic stratification of Polish Jewry, a thin stratum separated itself from the mass. It was usually the offspring of the wealthy (Kraushar's father, for example, was a banker) who championed the Polish orientation, while the typical Jewish shopkeeper or artisan remained Yiddish-speaking and Orthodox. On the Polish side, too, Mickiewicz was a voice crying in the wilderness. It is true that the great wave of *pogroms in the Russian Empire was concentrated in the Ukraine and Bessarabia (although Russian Poland was not wholly spared); nor was there anything in Poland resembling the expulsion of the Jews from Moscow in 1891. Indeed, Russian anti-Semitism led to the influx of so-called "Litvaks" into the kingdom. But the rise of Polish national fervor, accompanied by the development of a Polish middle class, naturally exacerbated Polish-Jewish relations. The founding of the National Democratic Party (*Endecja) in 1897 was symptomatic of the growing anti-Semitism of the period. The economic and political roots of this anti-Semitism (not to mention the traditional religious factor) were clearly expressed in 1912, when the Jews' active support of a Socialist candidate in elections to the *Duma resulted in an announced boycott of Jewish businesses by the National Democrats. On the eve of World War I relations between Poles and Jews were strained to the utmost, a state of affairs which led to a decline in the influence of the assimilationists and a rise in that of Jewish national doctrines.

In comparison with Russia, specifically Jewish political movements had a late start in the kingdom. The Haskalah, progenitor of modern Jewish political movements, was far less influential in Poland than in Galicia or Russia. Warsaw, unlike *Vilna, Lvov, and other great Jewish cities, did not become a center of the Enlightenment; its Jewish elite, like the elite in Germany, tended toward assimilation. True, the city of *Zamosc was, for a time, a thriving Haskalah center, but Zamosc was part of Galicia from 1772 to 1815 and followed the Galician rather than the Polish pattern. Later on, the pioneers of Jewish nationalism and Jewish Socialism came from the northwest region (Belorussia-Lithuania) or the Ukraine. While in Lithuania the Jewish intelligentsia, though Russianized, remained close to the masses, in Poland the intelligentsia was thoroughly Polonized. Its members tended, therefore, to enter Polish movements, such as the Polish Socialist Party (*PPS). Thus the *Bund, although it succeeded in spreading into Poland in the early 20th century, remained very much a Lithuanian movement. It is striking that the so-called "Litvaks" played a major role in spreading the ideas of Jewish nationalism to Poland; it was they, for example, who led the Warsaw Ḥovevei Zion (*Ḥibbat Zion) movement, the precursor of modern Zionism. On the eve of World War I, however, Jewish political life in Poland was well developed. The Bund had developed roots in such worker centers as Warsaw and Lodz, while the Zionists felt strong enough to challenge, albeit unsuccessfully, the entrenched assimilationist leadership of the Warsaw Jewish community.

INDEPENDENT POLAND

As a result of World War I and the unexpected collapse of the three partitioning powers, Poland was reconstituted as a sovereign state. The final boundaries, not determined until 1921, represented something of a compromise between the federalist dreams of Pilsudski and the more ethnic Polish conception of R. *Dmowski. To Congress Poland, purely Polish save for its large Jewish minority, were added Galicia, Poznania, Pomerania, parts of Silesia, areas formerly part of the Russian northwestern region, and the Ukrainian province of Volhynia. The new state was approximately one-third non-Polish, the important minorities being the Ukrainians, Jews, Belorussians, and Germans.

The heritage of the war years was a particularly tragic one for Polish Jewry. The rebirth of Poland, which many Jews had hoped for, was accompanied by a campaign of terror directed by the Poles (as by the invading Russian army in the early years of the war) against them. The Jews too often found themselves caught between opposing armies—between the Poles and the Lithuanians in Vilna, between the Poles and the Ukrainians in Lvov, and between the Poles and the Bolsheviks during the war of 1920. And it is probably no accident that the two major pogroms of this period, in Lvov in 1918 and in Vilna in 1919, occurred in multi-national areas where national feelings reached their greatest heights. The triumph of Polish nationalism, far from leading to a rapprochement between Jews and Poles, created a legacy of bitterness which cast its shadow over the entire interwar period. For the Poles the war years proved that the Jews were "anti-Polish," "pro-Ukrainian," "pro-Bolshevik," etc. For the Jews the independence of Poland was associated with pogroms. The legal situation of the Jews in independent Poland was, on the surface, excellent. The Treaty of Versailles, concluded between the victorious powers and the new states, included provisions protecting the national rights of minorities; in the Polish treaty Jews were specifically promised their own schools and the Polish state promised to respect the Jewish Sabbath. The Polish constitution, too, delared that non-Poles would be allowed to foster their national traditions, and formally abolished all discrimination due to religious, racial, or national differences. The Jews were recognized by the state as a nationality, something the Zionists and other Jewish nationalists had long fought for. There were great hopes that the Jews would be allowed to develop their own national institutions on the basis of national autonomy.

These hopes were not fulfilled. The two cornerstones of Jewish autonomy—the school and the *kehillah* (see *Community)—were not allowed to develop freely. The state steadfastly refused to support Jewish schools, save for a relatively small number of elementary schools closed on Saturday which possessed little Jewish content. The Hebrew-language *Tarbut schools, along with the Yiddish-language CYSHO (see *Education) network, were entirely dependent on Jewish support, and the diplomas issued by the Jewish high schools were not recognized by the Ministry of Education. The Jewish schools were successful as pedagogical institutions, but the absence of state support made it impossible for them to lay the foundation for a thriving Jewish national cultural life in Poland. As for the *kehillah*, projected by Jewish nationalists as the organ of Jewish national autonomy on the local level, it was kept in tight check by the government. While elections to the *kehillah* were made democratic, enabling all Jewish parties to participate on a basis of equality, the government constantly intervened to support its own candidates, usually those of the orthodox *Agudat Israel. By the same token the government controlled the budgets of the *kehillot*. These institutions remained essentially what they had been in the preceding century, concerned above all with the religious life of the community.

Far from barring discrimination against non-Poles, the policy of the interwar Polish state was to promote the ethnic Polish element at the expense of the national minorities, and above all at the expense of the Jews, who were more vulnerable than the essentially peasant Slav groups. The tradition of *numerus clausus* was continued at the secondary school and university level, efforts were made to deprive the "Litvaks" of Polish citizenship, local authorities attempted to curb the use of Yiddish and Hebrew at public meetings, and the Polish electoral system clearly discriminated against all the minorities. All Jewish activities leading toward the advancement of Jewish national life in Poland were combatted; the government favored Zionism only insofar as it preached emigration to Ereẓ Israel, and in domestic politics tended to support the traditional Orthodoxy of Agudat Israel. Worst of all was the economic policy of the state.

According to official statistics, most likely too low, Jews made up 10.5% of the Polish population in 1921. The density of their urban settlement was related to the general development of the area. In less developed regions, such as East Galicia, Lithuania, and Volhynia, the Jewish percentage in the cities was very high, while in more developed areas, such as Central Poland (the old Congress Poland), the existence of a strong native bourgeoisie caused the Jewish percentage to be lower. As for the Jewish village population, it too was higher in backward areas, since the number of cities was naturally less. There were, therefore, substantial Jewish village populations in Galicia and Lithuania but not in the old Congress Poland (with the exception of Lublin province, economically backward in comparison with the other provinces of the region). The most striking development in the demography of Polish Jewry between the wars is the marked loss of ground in the cities. Table 6 illustrates this point.

Among the factors contributing to this decline was the Polish government's "colonization" policy in non-Polish areas, its changing of city lines to diminish the Jewish proportion, and Jewish emigration (though with America's gates shut this last factor was not very significant). Another

Table 6. Decrease in the Percentage of the Jews in the Total Population in the Cities of Poland in the Interwar Period.

City	Percentage of Jews in 1921	in 1931
Warsaw	33.1	30.1
Lvov	35.0	31.9
Vilna	36.1	28.2
Bialystok	51.6	43.0
Grodno	53.9	42.6
Brest-Litovsk	53.1	44.3
Pinsk	74.7	63.4

major cause would appear to be the low Jewish natural increase, caused by a low birth rate. Table 7 presents the natural increase of four major religious groups in interwar Poland:

Table 7. The Natural Increase of Four Major Religious Groups in Poland in the Interwar Period

Religion	Natural increase
Roman Catholic	13.1
Greek Catholic	12.5
Greek Orthodox	16.7
Jewish	9.5

Thus the process of Jewish population expansion in Poland ended, itself the victim of urbanization (which led, in turn, to a low birth rate). If the cities were Judaized during the 19th century, they were Polonized in the 1920s and 1930s.

The demographic decline of Polish Jewry was paralleled by a more serious economic decline. On the whole, Polish Jews between the wars continued to work at the same trades as their 19th-century predecessors and the tendency toward "productivization" also continued. The vast majority of those engaged in industry were artisans, among whom tailors predominated; those working in commerce were, above all, shopkeepers. What distinguished the interwar years from the prewar era was the anti-Semitic policy of the Polish state, which Jewish leaders accused of leading to the economic "extermination" of Polish Jewry. Jews were not employed in the civil service, there were very few Jewish teachers in the public schools, practically no Jewish railroad workers, no Jews employed in state-controlled banks, and no Jewish workers in state-run monopolies (such as the tobacco industry). In a period characterized by economic *étatisme*, when the state took a commanding role in economic life, such official discrimination became disastrous. There was no branch of the economy where the state did not reach; it licensed artisans, controlled the banking system, and controlled foreign trade, all to the detriment of the Jewish element. Its tax system discriminated against the urban population, and its support of peasant cooperatives struck at the Jewish middleman. Such specific legislation as the law compelling all citizens to rest on Sunday helped to ruin Jewish commerce by forcing the shopkeeper to rest for two days and to lose the traditionally lucrative Sunday trade.

More natural forces were also at work in the decline of the Jews' economic condition, e.g., the continued development of a native middle class, sponsored by the government but not created by it. According to research carried out by the *YIVO in 113 Polish cities between 1937 and 1938, the number of Jewish-owned stores declined by one, while the number of stores owned by Christians increased by 591. In the western Bialystok province, to cite another example, the number of the Jewish-owned stores declined between 1932 and 1937 from 663 to 563, while

Figure 8. Open-air gathering of the Bundist Youth Organization, Warsaw, June 1932. Courtesy Bund Archives of the Jewish Labor Movement, New York.

Figure 9. *Ḥeder* c. 1930. Courtesy YIVO, New York.

Figures 10–16. Jewish types in Poland between World War I and World War II. Courtesy YIVO, New York.

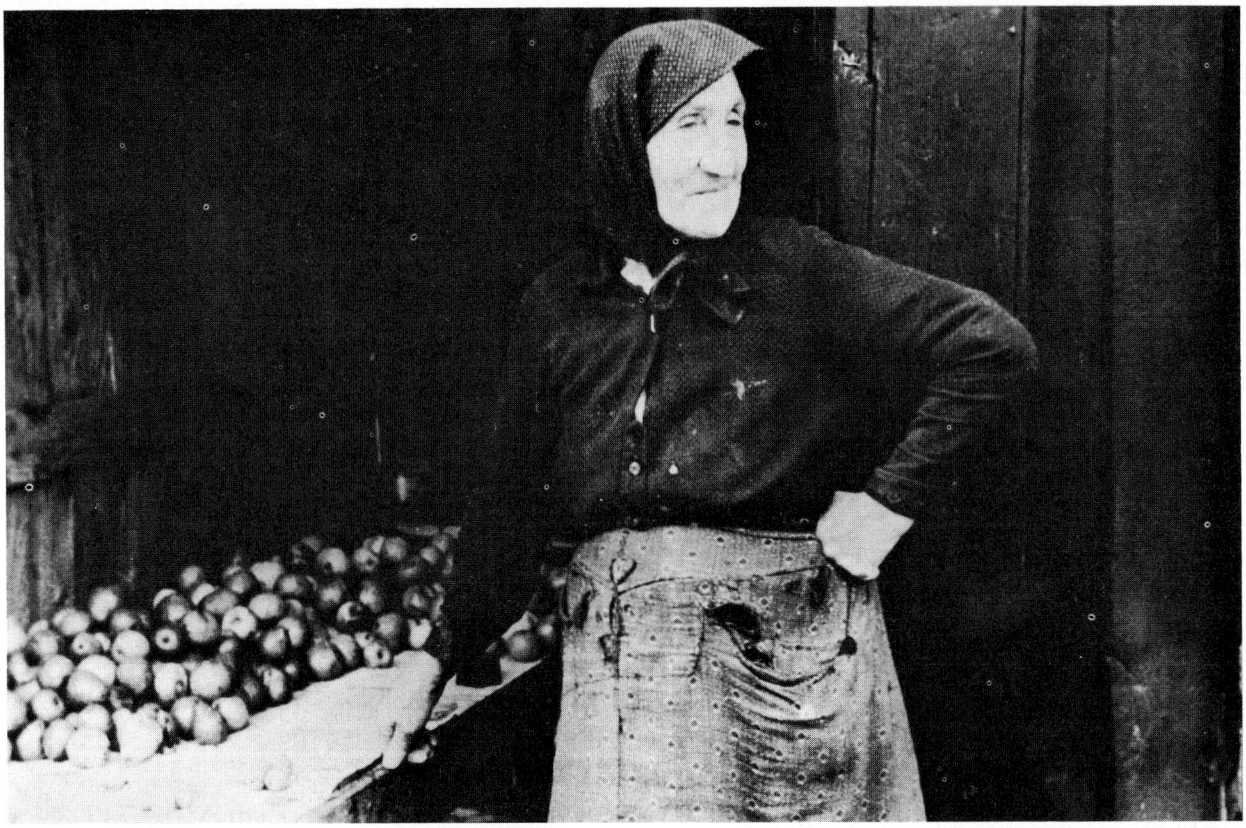

10

11

12

13

14

15

16

Figure 17. Summer camp, 1925. Courtesy Joint Distribution Committee, New York.

Figure 18. Training farm of He-Ḥalutz, Grodno, c. 1930. Courtesy Central Zionist Archives, Jerusalem.

the number of Christian-owned stores rose from 58 to 310. These figures reflect both the impact of anti-Semitism (in the late 1930s the anti-Jewish boycott became effective) and the impact of the developing Polish (and Ukrainian) middle class.

The Jews' economic collapse in the interwar period bears witness to the disaster, from the Jewish point of view, inherent in the rise of exclusive nation-states on the ruins of the old multinational empires. Jews were employed in the old Austrian public schools of Galicia, but not in the Polish state-operated schools. They worked as clerks in the railroad offices of Austrian Galicia, but not in Poland. Thousands of Jewish cigarette factory workers in the old Russian Empire were dismissed when the Polish state took over the tobacco monopoly. It also demonstrates the extremely vulnerable position of the Jews vis-à-vis the other Polish minorities, largely peasant nations which did not compete with the Polish element. The urban Jewish population found itself in a situation in which the traditional small businessman was being squeezed out, while the policy of the state also ruined the wealthy Jewish merchant and industrialist. This was then the end of a process already discernible in the late 19th century, immeasurably speeded up by a state which wanted to see all key economic positions in the hands of "loyal" elements, i.e., Poles.

What was the Jews' political response to this situation? In the beginning of the interwar period the *General Zionists emerged as the strongest force within the Jewish community, thus reflecting the general trend in Eastern Europe toward nationalism and, in the Jewish context, reflecting the impact of the terrible war years. In the 1919 Sejm elections the list of the Temporary Jewish National Council, dominated by General Zionists, received more than 50% of those votes cast for Jewish parties. In 1922, when Jewish representation in the Sejm reached its peak, the percentage of General Zionists (together with the *Mizrachi) among the Jewish deputies was again over 50% (28 out of 46). The Jewish Club (Koło) in the Sejm, which claimed to speak for all Polish Jewry, was naturally dominated by General Zionists, who with considerable justice regarded themselves as the legitimate spokesmen of the community. General Zionism in Poland was divided into two schools, that of "Warsaw-St. Petersburg" and that of "Lvov-Cracow-Vienna." The former came of age in the revolutionary atmosphere of the czarist regime and consequently tended to be more extreme in its demands than the Galicians, who had learned their politics in the Austrian Reichsrat. The clash between Yiẓhak *Gruenbaum, leader of the Warsaw faction, and Leon *Reich of Lvov was well expressed in the negotiations carried on between the Jewish Sejm Club and the Polish government in 1925. Gruenbaum, rejecting negotiations with anti-Semites and offering instead the idea of a national minorities bloc, found himself outnumbered in the club by adherents of Reich's position, namely that negotiations should be carried on in order to halt the deterioration of the Jewish position. In the end neither Gruenbaum's minorities bloc nor Reich's negotiations caused any improvements; the tragedy of Jewish politics in Poland was that the government would not make concessions to the Jews so long as it was not forced to do so, and the Jews, representing only 10% of the population, could find no allies.

All General Zionists agreed on the importance of "work in the Diaspora," though Gruenbaum, the central figure in this work, was castigated by Palestinian pioneers as the apostle of "Sejm-Zionismus." They did not agree, however, on various aspects of Zionist policy; the efforts to broaden the *Jewish Agency and the nature of the Fourth *Aliyah caused a split within the Warsaw Zionists, Gruenbaum leading the attack on Chaim *Weizmann and upholding the young pioneering emigration while his opponents defended the "bourgeois" *aliyah* and Weizmann's conciliatory tactics toward non-Zionist Jewry. Gruenbaum's faction, Al ha-Mishmar ("On Guard"), remained in the minority throughout the 1920s, but the so-called "radical Zionists" returned to power in the 1930s following the failure of the Agency reform, the crisis in the Fourth Aliyah, and the stiffening of the British line in Palestine. The General Zionists, of course, did not monopolize Jewish political life in interwar Poland. On the right, non-Zionist Orthodoxy was represented by the Agudat Israel, which succeeded in dominating the Jewish *kehillot,* but its generally good relations with the government did not stem the anti-Semitic tide. On the left the dominant Jewish party was the Bund, which had disappeared in Russia but survived to play its last historic role as the most important representative of the Jewish proletariat in Poland. The Bund, like Gruenbaum's Zionist faction, also recognized the need for allies in the struggle for a just society in which, its leaders hoped, Jews would be able to promote their Yiddish-based culture. Such allies were sought on the Polish left rather than among the disaffected minorities, but the Polish Socialist Party (PPS), for reasons of its own, had no desire to be branded pro-Jewish. Unable to create a bloc with the Polish proletariat, the Bund devoted itself to promoting the interests of the Jewish working class and took a great interest in the development of Yiddish culture. Despite the fact that this party, too, was split into factions (the split turned chiefly on different attitudes toward the international Socialist movement), it was to grow in influence. Sharing the left with the Bund, though overshadowed by it in terms of worker allegiance, were the various Socialist Zionist parties, ranging from the non-Marxist *Hitaḥadut to the leftist *Po'alei Zion (the Po'alei Zion movement had split into right and left factions in 1920; in Poland the left was dominant, at least in the 1920s). The moderate Socialist Zionists were concerned mainly with the pioneering emigration to Ereẓ Israel, while the Left Po'alei Zion steered a perilous course of non-affiliation either with the Zionist organization or with the Socialist International. Its ideological difficulties with the competition of the anti-Zionist Bund (which went so far as to brand Zionism as an ally of Polish anti-Semitism) sentenced the Left Po'alei Zion to a relatively minor role among the Jewish proletariat, though its influence among the intelligentsia was by no means negligible.

Two other Jewish parties deserve mention. The Polish Mizrachi, representing the Zionist Orthodox population, enjoyed a very large following (eight of its representatives sat in the Sejm in 1922). The Mizrachi usually cooperated with the General Zionists, though its particular mission was to safeguard the religious interests of its followers in Ereẓ Israel and in the Diaspora. The *Folkspartei, on the other hand, never managed tō make an impression on political life in Poland, though its intellectual leadership was extremely influential on the cultural scene. Both anti-Zionist and anti-Socialist, it could never attain a mass following.

The economic collapse of Polish Jewry, together with the rise of virulent anti-Semitism, led to the radicalization of Jewish politics in Poland. Extreme solutions to the Jewish question gained more adherents as the parliamentary approach clearly failed to lead anywhere; hence the growth of the pioneering Zionist movements—*He-Ḥaluẓ, He-Ḥaluẓ ha-Ẓa'ir, *Ha-Shomer ha-Ẓa'ir, and others—resulting in the large-scale emigration to Ereẓ Israel in the mid-1930s, and also the inroads of Communism among the Jewish youth. Another symptom of this radicalization was the great success of the Bund in the 1930s; by the late 1930s the Bund had "conquered" a number of major *kehillot* and was probably justified in considering itself the strongest of all Jewish parties. This spectacular success did not occur as a result of any apparent party success, since the efforts to improve the lot of the Jewish proletariat and to forge a bloc with the Polish left had failed. Rather, the Bund's success may be attributed to the rising protest vote against attempts to mollify the regime and in favor of an honorable defense, no matter how unavailing, of Jewish interests. Within the Zionist movement the process of radicalization was very clearly illustrated by the decline of the General Zionists and the rise of the Socialists and the Revisionists. In the elections to the 18th *Zionist Congress, held in 1933, the labor Zionists of Central Poland received 38 mandates and the General Zionists only 12. The same congress seated 20 Polish Revisionists, whose growing strength faithfully reflected the mood of Polish Jewry. In short, a transformation may be discerned of what might be called the politics of hope into the politics of despair. The slogans of *ḥaluẓiyyut* ("pioneering"), evacuation, and Communist ideology became more and more palatable as the old hopes for Jewish autonomy and the peaceful advancement of Jewish life in a democratic Poland disappeared.

By the late 1930s the handwriting was clearly on the wall for Polish Jewry, though no one could foresee the horrors to come. The rise of Hitler in Germany was paralleled by the appearance of Fascist and semi-Fascist regimes in Eastern Europe, not excepting Poland. A new wave of pogroms erupted along with a renewed anti-Jewish boycott, condoned by the authorities. The Jewish parties were helpless in the face of this onslaught, especially as the disturbances in Ereẓ Israel resulted in a drastic decline in *aliyah*. The political dilemma of Polish Jewry remained unresolved; finding no allies, Jewish parties could do little to influence the course of events. It should be recalled, however, that the role of these parties was greater than the narrow word "political" implies. Their work in raising the educational standards of Polish Jewry was remarkable, and the Jewish youth movements were able to supply to the new generation of Polish Jews a sense of purpose and a certain vision of a brighter future.

Polish Jewish history, from 1772 to 1939, reveals an obvious continuity. The Jews remained a basically urban element in a largely peasant country, a distinct economic group, a minority whose faith, language, and customs differed sharply from those of the majority. All attempts to break down this distinctiveness failed, and the Jews naturally suffered for their obvious strangeness. A thin layer of assimilated, or quasi-assimilated, Jews subsisted throughout the entire period, but the masses were relatively unaffected by the Polish orientation. In the end all suffered equally from Polish anti-Semitism. There were also several basic discontinuities. The rise of an exclusively national Polish state in 1918 was a turning point in the deterioration of the Jews' position, though the signs of this deterioration were already visible in the late 19th century. The rise of a native middle class, encouraged by state policy, put an end to the Jews' domination of trade and forced them into crafts and industry, resulting in the emergence of a large Jewish proletariat. Politically speaking perhaps the greatest change was the triumph within the community of Jewish nationalism, whether Zionist, Bundist, or Folkist, at the expense of the traditional assimilationist or Orthodox leadership. In this sense Polish Jewry followed the same course of development as the other peoples of Eastern Europe. It was a tragic paradox that these nationalist parties, which extolled the principle of activism and denounced the passivity of the Jewish past, also depended for their effectiveness on outside forces. Neither the Polish government nor the Polish left proved to be possible allies in the struggle for survival. [E.ME.]

HOLOCAUST PERIOD

The outbreak of the war (Sept. 1, 1939) and the invasion of Poland by German troops were marked by immediate heavy loss of civilian (especially Jewish) life and material damage. Military operations caused the death of 20,000 Jews, while bombing destroyed some 50,000 Jewish-owned houses, factories, workshops, and stores in about 120 Jewish communities, in some of which 90–95% of the houses went up in flames. In Warsaw alone, in the first month of the war, 30% of the Jewish buildings were destroyed when entire Jewish neighborhoods burned down. A tremendous stream of refugees sought shelter in the large cities, particularly in Warsaw. Subsequently, tens of thousands of Jewish enterprises not destroyed in the bombing were now lost in liquidation measures, bringing the total amount of Jewish property and business concerns lost or destroyed to an estimated 100,000. Jewish losses on the battlefield totaled 32,216 dead (officers and enlisted men) and another 61,000 taken prisoner, the majority of whom died in captivity.

Military operations were still going on when the German army and SD Einsatzkommandos undertook a campaign of bloody repression (see *Holocaust, General Survey). They usually arrested a group of Jews or Poles, who were kept as hostages and eventually shot. Sometimes mock executions were staged, in which the victims stood for hours in suspense anticipating execution. Pious Jews had their beards removed by blunt instruments, which tore their skin, or had their beards burned off. Swastikas were branded on the scalps of some victims; others were subjected to "gymnastics," such as "riding" on other victims' backs, crawling on all fours, singing and dancing, or staging fights with one another. The Nazis took a special sadistic pleasure in violating religious feelings, deliberately choosing Jewish religious holidays on which to carry out their assaults.

They instituted a special campaign of burning down synagogues, or, after destroying their interiors, turned them into stables, warehouses, bathhouses, or even public latrines (see *Synagogues, Desecration and Destruction of). At *Bedzin the synagogue at the old market place was set on fire on Sept. 9, 1939. The flames spread to the neighboring Jewish houses, and as the area was cordoned off by soldiers and SS-men who did not permit anyone to escape or to fight the fire, 56 houses were burned down, and several hundred persons were burned to death. In some places, e.g., *Wloclawek and *Brzeziny, the president or rabbi of the community was forced to sign a "confession" that the Jews themselves started the fire and to pay heavy fines as punishment for the "arson." The tenants of the houses burned down were brought before a military court. Any Jew who tried to enter a burning synagogue in order to save the Torah scrolls was either shot or thrown into the flames. In many places the military staged autos-da-fé of Torah scrolls, Hebrew books, and other religious articles, and forced the Jews to sing and dance around the flames and shout that the Jews were to blame for the war. The Jewish communities were also compelled to bear the cost of tearing down the remaining walls of the houses and clearing the rubble. It is estimated that several hundred synagogues were destroyed in the first two months of the occupation.

At the same time, mass arrests of Jews were carried out in which thousands of men, women, and children were interned in "civilian prison camps" set up in synagogues, churches, movie houses, and the like, or put behind barbed-wire fences on open lots and exposed to the soldiers' cruelty and torture. Afterward the prisoners were sent on foot to larger centers (such as *Wegrow, *Lomza, *Sieradz, *Tomaszow Mazowiecki), where some were set free and others put on forced labor or deported to Germany. In the latter instance their transport to Germany was used for propaganda purposes, as in the case of groups of Jews from Kalisz and Wieruszow who were borne around German towns in trucks bearing the inscription: "These are the Jewish swine who shot at German soliders."

Precise instructions issued by the High Command of the Wehrmacht on July 24, 1939, for the internment of civilian prisoners provided for the arrest of Jews and Poles of military age at the outset of the invasion. In practice, however, a wild huntdown of Jews was made, without regard to age. In the campaign of terror that followed, hundreds of civilians, Poles, and Jews (in *Czestochowa, *Przemysl, *Bydgoszcz, and Dynow) were slaughtered outright or imprisoned in buildings which were sealed and then set on fire or blown up, the imprisoned dying a horrible death (in Dynow, Lipsk-Kielecki, Mszczonow). No precise figures are available on the number of victims in this period of terror. In the rampage of persecution throughout Poland, people were taken off the streets or dragged from their homes and put on forced labor. They were tortured and beaten, and deprived of their human dignity when forced to perform such acts as cleaning latrines with their bare hands or, in the case of women, washing the floor with their own underwear. Normal life was paralyzed by the arbitrary arrests for forced labor even at a later stage, when forced labor was "regulated" and the still-existing communities or the Judenraete (see *Judenrat) had to provide labor contingents on the basis of an understanding reached with the various German offices or commands.

The systematic robbery of Jewish property involved the closing of all the Jewish shops in many towns, or enforced sale of the wares at nominal prices or against worthless receipts. To facilitate the identification of Jewish property, the chief of the civilian administration attached to the army, Hans *Frank, issued an order (Sept. 8, 1939) for all Jewish stores to display a Star of David or other appropriate inscriptions on their stores by the following day. Practically all Jewish communities were also forced to make large "contributions" of money, gold, silver, and jewelry. In many towns compulsory contributions were paid several times over. Large sums were extorted from wealthy individuals under threat of imprisonment. Whenever a Nazi "visit" to the offices of the communities took place, all the money in their safes was confiscated, e.g., in Warsaw on Oct. 5, 1939, when 100,000 zlotys ($20,000) were taken in this manner. "Legal" forms of robbery were also instituted. The civilian administrators attached to the occupation forces issued orders restricting the sums Jews could hold in their bank accounts, while the accounts themselves were blocked. Restrictions were also placed on the amount of cash a Jew could keep in his home. Jewish-owned property was frozen, Jews were prohibited from engaging in the textile and leather business, and their inventories were registered with the Nazi authorities. Any infringement entailed heavy punishment, including death.

Two decrees by Hitler (Oct. 8 and 12, 1939) provided for the division of the occupied areas of Poland into the following administrative units: (a) Reichsgau Wartheland, which included the entire Poznan province, most of the Lodz province, five Pomeranian districts, and one county of the Warsaw province; (b) the remaining area of Pomerania, which was incorporated into the Rechsgau Danzig-Westpreussen; (c) Regierungsbezirk Zichenau (Ciechanow) consisting of the five northern counties of Warsaw province (*Plock, *Plonsk, Sterpe, *Ciechanow, *Mlawa), which became a part of East Prussia; (d) Regierungsbezirk Kattowitz—or unofficially Ost-Oberschlesien (East Upper Silesia)—which included *Sosnowiec, Bedzin, *Chryzanow, and *Zawiercie counties and parts of *Olkusz and *Zywiec counties: (e) the General Government of Poland, which included the central Polish provinces and was subdivided into four districts, Warsaw, Lublin, *Radom, and Cracow.

The areas listed under (a)–(d) were incorporated into the Reich. After the outbreak of the Soviet-German War, the Polish territories previously occupied by the Russians were organized as follows: (f) Bezirk Bialystok, which included the Bialystok, *Bielsk Podlaski, *Grajewo, Lomza, *Sokolka, *Volkovysk, and Grodno counties and was "attached" (not incorporated) to East Prussia; (g) Bezirke Litauen und Weissrussland—the Polish part of White Russia (today western Belorussia), including the Vilna province, which was incorporated into the Reichskommissariat Ostland; (h) Bezirk Wolhynien-Podolien—the Polish province of Volhynia, which was incorporated into the Reichskommissariat Ukraine; and (i) East Galicia, which was incorporated into the General-Government and became its fifth district.

The Jewish population of this entire area was 3,351,000, of whom 2,042,000 came under Nazi rule and 1,309,000 under Soviet occupation in September 1939. The ultimate fate of the Jewish population under Nazi rule was the same in all the areas, though the various administrative areas differed in the degree and pace of persecution, depending on local leadership (a Nazi principle of administration).

Reichsgau Wartheland. The area was subdivided into three *Regierungsbezirke* ("administrative districts")—Poznan, *Inowroclaw, and Lodz. On Sept. 1, 1939, it had 390,000 Jews (including 4,500 in Poznan, 54,090 in Inowroclaw, and 326,000 in the Lodz district—233,000 in the city of Lodz). Like all Polish areas incorporated into the Reich, Wartheland was from the beginning designated to become *"judenrein"* (*Heydrich's *"Schnellbrief"* of Sept. 21, 1939). In a secret order to the *RSHA (Reichssicherheitshauptamt—Reich Security Main Office) and the high *SS and police officials, issued on Oct. 30, 1939, *Himmler fixed the period of November 1939–February 1940 for clearing the incorporated areas of their entire Jewish population and the majority of their Polish population as well. A similar decree was issued on Nov. 4, 1939, by Wartheland's Gauleiter Arthur Greiser.

Arrangements were made for the transfer of 100,000 Jews from its territory during this period. In fact, more than 50 Jewish communities were deported wholly or in part to the Lublin district between the fall of 1939 and May 1940; the larger communities among those deported were Poznan, Kalisz, Ciechocinek, *Gniezno, Inowroclaw, Nieszawa, and *Konin. In some towns the deportation was carried out in stages, with a small number of Jews remaining, engaged in work for the Nazi authorities. In some instances, the regime of terror drove the Jews to desperation, so that they chose "voluntary" exile. This happened in *Lipno and in Kalisz, where many Jews, unable to withstand the persecution, fled from the city in October and November 1939. In Lodz, over ten thousand Jews, including most of the Jewish intelligentsia, were deported in December 1939. For weeks the deportees were kept at assembly points, and had to supply their own means of subsistence, though they had been deprived of all their valuables. Large assembly points were located at Kalisz, Sieradz, and Lodz. There, the *Selektion* ("selection") took place in which able-bodied men, aged 14 and over, were sent to labor camps which had been established in the meantime, while women, children, and old men were deported in sealed freight cars to the

Lublin and *Kielce areas. This occurred in the severe winter of 1939–1940, and upon arrival at their destination, some of the deportees were dead, others nearly frozen, or otherwise seriously ill. The survivors were bereft of clothing, food, and money. A few found refuge with relatives or friends, but most of them had to find places in the crowded synagogues and poorhouses. For the Jewish communities of the Lublin and Radom districts, the influx of deportees was a very heavy burden. Most of the deportees perished before mass deportation began.

GHETTOIZATION. At this time, a second campaign was launched to concentrate the Jewish population in ghettos. The first ghetto in Wartheland was established at Lodz, on orders given by *Polizeipraesident* (Chief of Police) Johannes Schaefer (Feb. 8, 1940). By the latter half of 1940, all the Jewish communities that had survived the mass deportations were sealed off in ghettos. Lodz ghetto had a population of 162,000 on the day of its establishment (May 1, 1940). The larger ghettos in Wartheland included *Pabianice (with about 8,500 persons), *Kutno (7,000), *Belchatow (5,500), *Ozorkow (4,700), *Zelow (4,500), *Zdunska Wola (10,000), Wloclawek (where 4,000 were left after the deportations), and *Wielun (4,000). Lodz became a central ghetto *(Gaughetto)* for the entire province, absorbing Jews sent from ghettos that were liquidated or reduced in size, as well as from the Reich, *Vienna, and *Prague. Between Sept. 26 and Oct. 9, 1941, 3,082 Jews from Wloclawek and the vicinity arrived at Lodz Ghetto, and between Oct. 17 and Nov. 4, 1941, approximately 20,000 arrived from Vienna, Prague, Berlin, Frankfort, Hamburg, Cologne, Emden, Duesseldorf, and Luxembourg. From May to August 1942, 14,440 "selected" Jews from liquidated ghettos arrived at Lodz.

From the end of 1942 until its liquidation in August 1944, Lodz was the only remaining ghetto in Wartheland. Its comparatively long existence was due to the fact that it became one of the largest industrial plants working for the Wehrmacht or private contractors. In August 1943, some 76,000 workers (about 85% of the entire ghetto population) were employed in 117 warehouses. According to the Nazi *Ghettoverwaltung* ("ghetto adminstration"), the total wages and production in 1942 reached a value of 27,862,200 RM ($5,572,440). Large tailor shops also existed at Pabianice, Belchatow, Ozorkow, and other ghettos in the Lodz district. Lodz Ghetto bore the imprint of its *Judenaeltester* ("Jewish elder") Mordecai *Rumkowski, who at an early stage imposed his rule over the ghetto. The ghetto was administered by division of the population into various socio-economic groups, each with a different status, in accordance with their status in the ghetto hierarchy or their usefulness for the war industry. In those areas of ghetto life in which the Nazis allowed the Jews autonomy, Rumkowski held absolute power.

PHYSICAL ANNIHILATION. Partial liquidation actions affecting certain categories of Jews, such as the sick and the old, began in Wartheland as early as the fall of 1940 (in Kalisz). In September or October 1941, experiments in the murder of Jews were carried out in Konin county, where Jews were forced into ditches and covered over with wet quicklime. On Dec. 8, 1941, the murder camp at *Chelmno began operation. On Jan. 2, 1942, Greiser's *Erlass, die Entjudung des Warthelands betreffend* ("Decree on Clearing all Jews from the Wartheland") was issued. In December 1941, the remaining Jews from *Kolo and Dabie were deported to Chelmno, followed in January 1942 by the inmates of the ghettos of Izbica Kujawska and other places. From Jan. 16 until mid-May 1942, numerous transports of Jews were dispatched from Lodz Ghetto to Chelmno. By May some 55,000 were murdered there. Between March and September 1942, all the remaining ghettos, with the exception of Lodz, were evacuated. Lodz ghetto was the scene of a bloody "action" against children under ten years of age, the old, and the sick, resulting in the murder of 16,500 persons.

In mid-1943, Himmler and Albert Speer (Reich Minister for Armament and War Production) entered a long-drawn-out contest over the disposition of Lodz Ghetto. Himmler sought to incorporate the ghetto industries into the SS camp combine in the Lublin district, while Speer tried to retain a monopoly over this important industrial center. Their rivalry prolonged the existence of Lodz Ghetto until the summer of 1944, by which time Germany's strategic situation had deteriorated to such an extent that the evacuation of Poland was imminent. In August 1944, Lodz, the only ghetto still left in Europe, was liquidated and all its inmates, some 68,500 Jews, were deported to *Auschwitz.

Reichsgau Danzig-Westpreussen. This area, with a total Jewish population of 23,000, had few and small Jewish communities; e.g., *Danzig, *Torun, and *Bydgoszcz. The province became *"judenrein"* at a comparatively early stage. The Jews and Poles were exposed to a campaign of terror from the very beginning, which resulted in the massacre of part of the Jewish inhabitants. Others fled from the area, and the rest were deported to the General Government. The last transport of Jews (some 2,000 persons) from Danzig and Bydogszcz, including the surviving Jews of *Koenigsberg, arrived at the Warsaw Ghetto on March 10, 1941.

Regierungsbezirk Zichenau (Ciechanow). According to the 1931 census, there was a Jewish population of 80,000 in the area of this newly-created administrative district. In the first weeks of the occupation, a large number of Jews from the towns near the German-Soviet demarcation line, e.g., *Ostrow Mazowiecka, Przasnysz, *Ostroleka, and *Pultusk, were forced to cross over to the Soviet zone. Their expulsion was accompanied by acts of terror, such as forcing the Jews to cross the Bug or the Narew rivers and opening fire on them, so that some people drowned or were shot to death. This group shared the fate of all the other Polish refugees in the Soviet Union. At the end of February 1941, about 10,000 Jews from Plock and Plock county were driven out, first passing through the Dzialdowo transit camp, where they were tortured and robbed, and from there to various towns in the Radom district, where within a year most of them died of starvation and disease. In Ciechanow, Mlawa, Plonsk, Strzegowo, and Sierpc, the Jews were segregated into ghettos, along with the few Jews left in towns whose Jewish populations had largely been expelled to the Soviet Union in the fall of 1939. These ghettos situated in the administrative area of East Prussia, ruled by the notorious Erich Koch, endured particularly harsh and bloodthirsty treatment, and the murder of members of the Judenrat and ghetto police was a frequent occurrence. In the fall of 1942 the ghettos were liquidated and the Jews dispatched to *Treblinka.

Regierungsbezirk Kattowitz (East Upper Silesia). According to statistics published by the "Central Office of the Councils of Elders of the Jewish Communities in East Upper Silesia," comprising 32 communities, a Jewish population of 93,628 existed in these communities in March 1941. The largest among these were Bedzin (25,171), Sosnowiec (24,149), Chrzanow (8,229), Zawiercie (5,472), *Dabrowa Gornicza (5,564), and *Oswiecim (6,454). Jews played an important role in the life of this highly industrialized region (in mining, metallurgy, and textiles), and were heavily hit by the early-instituted "Aryanization" process.

A special office, the Dienststelle des Sonderbeauftragten

Figure 19. Boy from the Warsaw Ghetto after its subjugation. Courtesy Yad Vashem Archives, Jerusalem.

Figure 20. Jews branded with a *magen David* on their foreheads. From Polish Ministry of National Defense, *Męczeństwo walka zagłada żydow w Polsce 1939–1945,* Warsaw, 1960.

Figure 21. Jews forced to ride each other for the amusement of the Nazis, Minsk Mazowiecki, 1941. Courtesy Leib Rochman, Jerusalem.

Figure 22. Jewish women in Poland forced to undress prior to being shot.

(TRANSLATION)

The Vatican, November 25, 1942

It is reported from Warsaw:

"The struggle continues throughout the country. Numerous arrests are being made. The Germans have fired on the crowds: Many Poles have been executed by hanging. The families of the persons executed have often been forced to witness the executions which, in large part, are carried out in public, often along the railway where the bodies remain for long periods exposed so that they can be seen from passing trains. (Poznań, Cracow).

Wheat is taken away, without thought being given either to the need for seed or to the food requirements of the country. Villages, where requisitioning has not given the results hoped for by the Germans, have been razed, and their inhabitants (men, women and children) massacred. The villages located in the areas where parachutists landed were subjected to the same treatment.

Prisons are filled and emptied regularly. Every time they are emptied, it is for the purpose of filling them again with new prisoners. The others are sent to die in concentration camps. The prisons at Warsaw, Radom, Cracow, Przemyśl, Rzeszow and Lublin are notorious for the torture inflicted on those held.

There are many concentration camps. The death of those interned is brought about by undernourishment and overwork. The families of the dead are notified of the demise of their near relations by means of cards on which are entered the date and the name of the victim above the printed notice: "Died in the concentration camp". The cards arrive at all the localities every day often in batches of tens and hundreds.

The "manhunt", engaged in by detachments specially trained for the purpose, continues so as to provide labor for forced work in Germany. Young people especially, men and women, are taken away. Trains, packed with deportees, pass through Warsaw every day. (The number of Poles deported to Germany for forced labor is estimated by the Reichsarbeitsblatt, a German official publication, to have amounted to 744,500 men and 262,700 women, that is to say more than one million Poles in a total of 2,139,500 foreign workers working in Germany; the figure

740.00116 EUROPEAN WAR 1939/726 PS/DLB

FILED JAN 12 1943

- 2 -

figure has become considerably greater since then).

The Germans are endeavoring to decrease the demographic strength of the Polish nation, so as not to have to fear an increase in the number of Poles after the war. Farms for the breeding of human beings are being organized to which women and girls are brought for the purpose of being made mothers of children who are then taken from them to be raised in Nazi establishments. Many women and men, who are sent to Germany, are subjected to sterilization.

Mass execution of Jews continues. At Warsaw, Lwow, Wilno, Lublin, Przemyśl, Przeworsk, Tarnow - the number of Jews killed is numbered by the tens of thousands in the case of each of the towns in question, without mentioning all the others. They are killed by poison gas in chambers especially prepared for that purpose (often in railway cars) and by machine gun fire, following which the dead and the dying are both covered with earth. There are frequent cases of collective suicide by Jewish families: Jewish mothers jump from high windows with their children. At Lublin, the Germans themselves threw Jewish children onto the pavement. At Przeworsk, a crowd of hard pressed Jews assembled around a cross and invoked the pity of Christ. Convoys of Jews being led to their death are seen everywhere. Reports are being circulated to the effect that the Germans are making use of their corpses in plants manufacturing chemical products (soap-making factories).

An early end to the extermination of Jews in Poland is forseen, as well as the urgent need by the special detachments, trained for such work and incapable of interrupting the daily shedding of blood, for new victims. Already in Eastern Poland, the beggars, both men and women, have been hunted down and killed. It is feared that the general extermination of old people will be ordered in the near future. All these measures are taken with a view to reducing the number of persons who need to be fed.

The witnessing of these acts is having a tremendous effect on the mind of the Poles; feelings of hatred continue to grow. The opinion is gaining ground according to which only immediate retaliation against the towns of the occupying forces could induce their rulers to modify the measures applied to the Polish population

---

TR:CA:DVA

Figure 23. The English translation of a document (in French) describing conditions in Poland, which was received by the U.S. Department of State from an undisclosed source in the Vatican in January 1943. Washington, D.C., National Archives of the United States (740.00116 EW 1939/726).

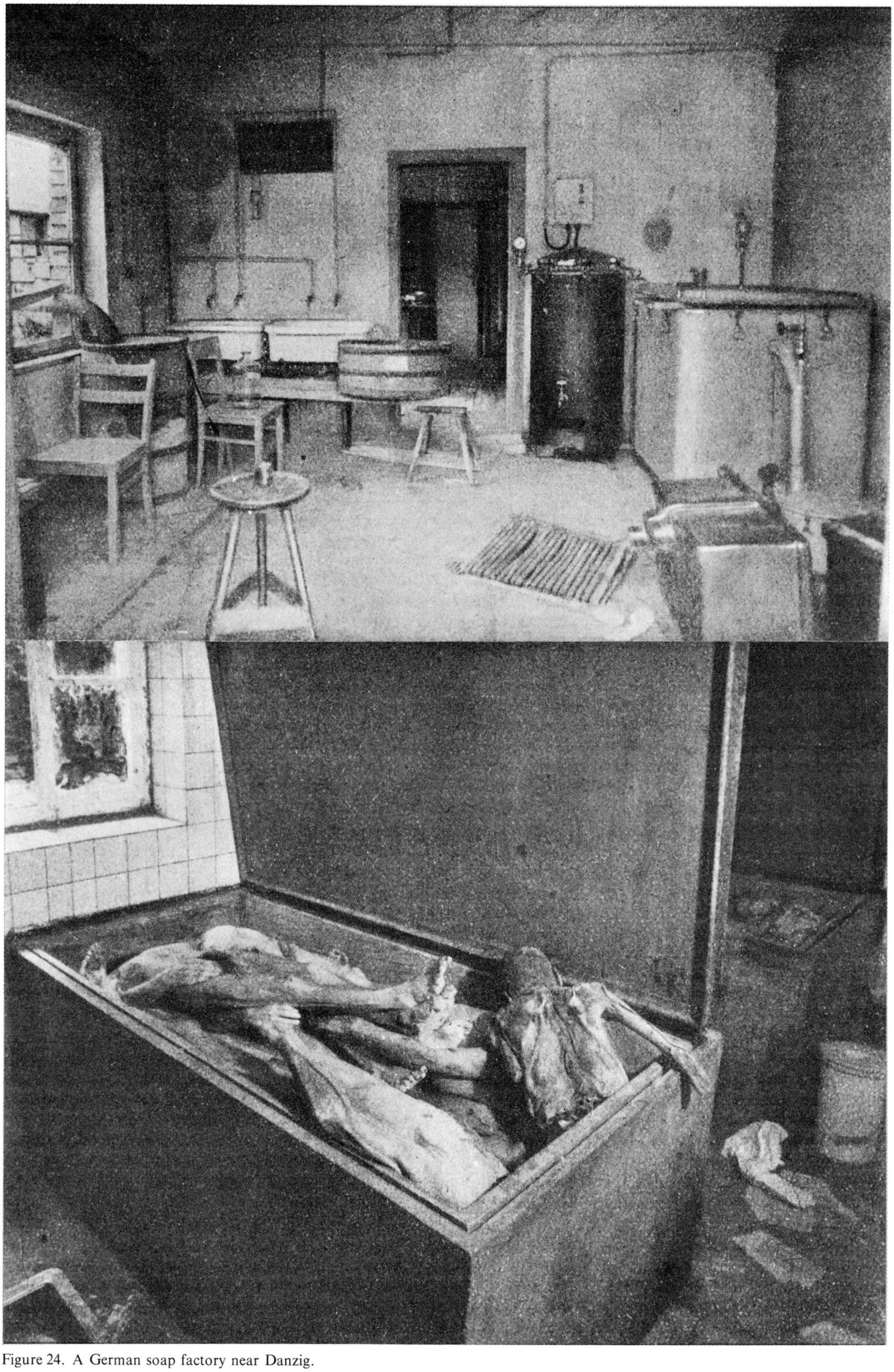

Figure 24. A German soap factory near Danzig.

der R.R.S.S. und Chefs der deutschen Polizei fuer fremdvoelkischen Einsatz in Oberschlesien, headed by Gen. Albrecht Schmelt (and commonly referred to as the Schmelt Organization), was in charge of sending the comparatively large number of skilled Jewish workers to German firms in Silesia and the Reich. No German firm was permitted to employ Jewish workers without the consent of the Schmelt Organization, and the latter maintained complete control over the Jewish "work effort." The German firms paid the Jewish workers at the normal rate (in this the Katowice (Kattowitz) area differed from the other occupied areas), but the workers received only a part of their wages and the firms had to submit the remainder to the Dienststelle. In 1942 the Schmelt Organization controlled 50,570 Jewish workers. When the evacuation of Jews from East Upper Silesia took place (starting May–June 1942), the Jewish workers were deported to Auschwitz, which was the major concentration camp as well as the largest industrial combine in Silesia.

The chairman of the Central Office of the Councils of Elders in Sosnowiec, Moshe Merin, exercised a decisive influence on the internal affairs of the Jewish communities and had considerable authority over the Judenraete (the Jewish councils). The formal ghettoization of East Upper Silesia did not take place until a comparatively late date. In Bedzin and Sosnowiec, for example, a closed ghetto was not established until May 1943, but it was liquidated by August 1943. These ghettos also absorbed the Jews left over from previous *Aussiedlungen* ("evacuation actions"). Merin was a consistent protagonist of the strategy of "rescuing" Jews by voluntarily providing the Nazi Moloch with contingents of victims to give others the chance of survival. He carried out this policy to its extreme, lending his own active cooperation, as well as that of the ghetto police, to the *Aussiedlungsaktionen.*

General Government. Originally, the General Government consisted of four districts, Warsaw, Lublin, Radom, and Cracow. When the district of Galicia was added, the Jewish population reached 2,110,000. The transfer of the administration from military to civilian authorities, which took place at the end of October 1939, did not alleviate the harsh conditions, for the uncontrolled terror of the first period was then replaced by "legally" imposed restrictions and persecution. The first proclamation, issued by General Governor Hans *Frank on Oct. 26, 1939, stated that "there will be no room in the General Government for Jewish exploiters," and from the very first day of his rule, Frank inundated the Jewish population with a flood of anti-Jewish measures. The personal rights of Jews were severely curtailed in all spheres of private and social life. Jews were deprived of freedom of movement, the right to dispose of their property, exercise their professions, and benefit from their labor. They were denied social and medical insurance benefits (which the anti-Semitic regime in Poland had granted them), religious observance (ritual slaughter and public worship), and a normal school education for their children. Finally, they lost the right to dispose of their own persons. Jews could no longer associate freely and Jewish societies, institutions, and organizations were disbanded and their property confiscated. The Judenrat, a quasi-representative body of the Jews, was established in their place by the Nazi authorities.

Warsaw District. This district was divided into ten counties, Warsaw, Garwolin, *Grojec, *Lowicz, *Skierniewice, *Sochaczew, Blonie, Ostrow Mazowiecki, *Minsk Mazowiecki, *Siedlce, and *Sokolow Podlaski. In the first half of 1940 the total Jewish population of this district was 600,000, of whom 400,000 lived in Warsaw. Its Jews were concentrated into ghettos in the western counties in 1940, and in the eastern counties in the fall of 1941. The Warsaw Ghetto was established on Nov. 15, 1940. The ghettos in the western part were of short duration. From the end of January to the beginning of April 1942, 72,000 Jews from this area were brought into the Warsaw Ghetto, where they lacked even the most rudimentary means for existence. With their arrival, the total number of refugees in the ghetto rose to 150,000, but the population was being constantly decimated by starvation and disease.

In the fall of 1941, the Jews in each of the eastern counties were concentrated into between five and seven ghettos. This step was in fact in preparation for *Aussiedlungsaktionen* which began with the Warsaw Ghetto on July 22, 1942, and continued until Oct. 4–6, 1942. In the General Government these actions, under the code name of "Einsatz Reinhard," were always carried out by special commando units (see Reinhard *Heydrich and *Holocaust, General Survey), headed by the SS and police chief of the Lublin district, Odilo *Globocnik. A decree issued by Frank on June 3, 1942, transferred the civilian authority's jurisdiction over the Jewish population in the General Government to Wilhelm Krueger, its chief of SS and police.

On the eve of its destruction, the Warsaw Ghetto contained 450,000 Jews, of whom approximately 300,000 were deported to Treblinka by Sept. 21, 1942. Officially, 35,639 Jews remained in Warsaw as workers in German factories, employees of the Judenrat, or policemen. In fact, some 60,000 were left, including those in hiding. It is to be noted that Himmler's order to Krueger of July 19, 1942, formally fixed the date of Dec. 31, 1942, as the final date for "cleansing" the General Government of the Jews. Between July 19 and 24, 1942, the Jews of *Otwock, Minsk Mazowiecki, and Siedlce were deported. Between September 22 and 27, most of the ghettos in the Sokolow Podlaski, Wegrow, and Minsk Mazowiecki counties were liquidated, followed, in the last days of October, by the remaining ghettos in the Warsaw district. Small groups of Jews tried to hide out on the "Aryan" side or in the countryside. In order to lull the intended victims into a false sense of security, Krueger issued a decree (Oct. 28, 1942) when the annihilation of the Jewish population in the district had been almost completed, providing for "residential quarters" in Warsaw and Siedlce. His aim was to influence the Jews in hiding to believe that these "newly established ghettos" which had already passed through a partial liquidation would now be a safe haven for the survivors. In this he was largely successful. The intolerable conditions in which the Jews found themselves, hiding out in the forests amid a hostile population, induced them to seek out and settle in the new "residential quarters." Only a short while later they were deported. The "new" Siedlce Ghetto, for example, did not last a month, and by November 25, Siedlce was *judenrein.* In November, too, the liquidation of most of the Jewish labor camps was begun and after "selections" the workers were deported to the Warsaw Ghetto. In the course of the *Aktion* on Jan. 18–19, 1943, the SS men met with armed resistance from the Jewish Fighting Organization and were forced to cease action for the time being. The Warsaw Ghetto, according to Himmler's decree (Feb. 16, 1943), was to be liquidated at the earliest possible date, and the workers and machinery were to be transferred to the Lublin SS camps.

Lublin District. The ten counties in the Lublin district—Lublin, *Biala Podlaska, *Bilgoraj, *Chelm, *Hrubieszow, *Janow Lubelski, *Krasnystaw, *Pulawy, *Radzyn, and *Zamosc—had a Jewish population of 250,000 in March–April 1941, including 55,000 refugees and deportees. In the beginning, the eastern part of the Lublin district was regarded as a "Jewish reservation" and

Jews from parts of Poland that had been incorporated into the Reich, as well as from the Reich itself, from the Czech Protectorate of Bohemia-Moravia, and from *Austria were deported there on a systematic basis. Jozefow, Izbica Lubelska, Krasnystaw, and Zamosc were some of the towns which served as concentration points for these deportees. The local population was also displaced, generally in order to make room for the new arrivals. Even after this plan for the "Jewish reservation" had been given up, tens of thousands of Jews deported from Germany, Czechoslovakia, and Austria continued to stream into the district, to be "evacuated" to the *Belzec death camp, whose murder installations began functioning in March 1942.

The Nazi ideologists also regarded Lublin as a reservoir of "World Jewry," which presumably maintained secret links with Jewish communities everywhere (see *Hitler). As a result, the Lublin district was turned into an experimental station for various Nazi schemes for the annihilation of Polish Jewry. It was the headquarters of "Einsatz Reinhard" from where its "action groups" began their destructive march through the General Government. The first ghetto in the district was set up in the city of Lublin in April 1941. Since the area designated for the ghetto was too small to hold the approximately 45,000 Jews who were in Lublin at the time, the Nazi authorities forced over 10,000 to leave the city "voluntarily" and move to other towns in the district. The restricted area of the ghetto and its dense population caused epidemics and a high rate of mortality. In November and December 1941 there were 1,227 cases of typhus and the mortality rate that year was three times that of a year before the war (40.8 per 1,000).

In the second half of 1940, about 50 forced labor camps for Jews were established in the Lublin district for local Jews and Jews from other districts. In the winter of 1940–41, there were over 12,000 Jews in these camps. Many succumbed to the intolerable living and working conditions—starvation; wretched accommodation (usually in decrepit old barracks, stables, and barns); lack of hygiene; strenuous work (regulating rivers, draining swamps, and digging canals); and inhuman treatment by the camp commanders. In Osowa camp, 47 inmates were shot in July 1941 after two or three of them had contracted typhus. The Judenraete in ghettos from which the workers had come organized aid for them. The Warsaw Judenrat, for example, spent 520,000 zlotys ($104,000) in aid to the camps in 1940, and the Lublin Judenrat, 150,000 zlotys ($30,000). The "evacuation" campaign in this district preceded those in other parts of the General Government. In the period from March 17 to April 20,1942, 30,000 Jews from Lublin Ghetto were deported to Belzec and murdered there, while 4,000 others were deported to the Majdan Tatarski Ghetto close to Lublin, which existed until Nov. 9, 1942. In the same period, 3,400 Jews from Piaski and 2,200 from Izbica were dispatched to Belzec, preceded by about 17,000 Jews from Pulawy county (May 6–12). The ghettos which had thus been made *judenrein* became temporary collection points for Jews deported from the Reich, the Protectorate, and Vienna, and after a short stay there they were sent on to Belzec to be murdered.

Krueger's decree of Oct. 28, 1942, set up eight ghettos in the Lublin district, and like the ghettos in the Warsaw district, their existence was of short duration. By Dec. 1, 1942, five ghettos were left (Piaski, Wlodawa, Izbica, *Lukow Lubelski, and Miedzyrzec Podlaski) and the last of these was liquidated in July 1943. The Jewish workers remained in the concentration and labor camps until November 1943. On Nov. 3–7, 1943, 18,000 Jews were murdered in *Maidanek concentration camp, over 13,000 in the Poniatowa camp and approximately 10,000 in the Trawniki camp, to which several thousands of Jews had been deported from Warsaw after the ghetto revolt in April 1943.

CRACOW DISTRICT. The Cracow district, consisting of 12 counties (Cracow, Debica, *Jaroslaw, *Jaslo, *Krosno, Miechow, *Nowy Sacz, Nowy Targ, *Przemysl, *Sanok, and *Tarnow), had a prewar Jewish population of over 250,000. By May 1941 this number dwindled to 200,000, in spite of the additional influx of 20,000 refugees and deportees from the incorporated areas, including Silesia, Lodz, and Kalisz, in the fall of 1939 and spring of 1940. The expulsion of Jews from the Cracow district, where the General Government capital was situated, was accelerated. In the first few months, Jews living in the border towns along the San River were expelled to the Soviet zone. From the spring of 1940 to November 1941, Jews living in the spas and summer resorts in Nowy Sacz and Nowy Targ counties were expelled, and from May 1940 to April 1941, 55,000 Jews left Cracow voluntarily or were driven out. The Jewish population thus became concentrated in an ever-decreasing number of places—in Cracow county, in seven townships and ten villages, in Nowy Sacz in five places, and in the Nowy Targ county in seven.

The first ghetto was established in March 1941 in the Podgorze quarter of Cracow. A wall sealed it off from the rest of the city and the gates of the wall had the form of tombstones. The first "evacuations" took place in Cracow Ghetto, which underwent three such actions, on May 30–31, October 28, 1942, and March 13–14, 1943. In the final evacuation, 2,000 Jews were murdered on the spot, about 2,000 were deported to Auschwitz, and approximately 6,000 were sent to the nearby camp in *Plaszow, located on the site of two Jewish cemeteries. The first *Aktion* in Tarnow took place on June 11–13, 1942, involving 11,000 Jews. The Jews of Przemysl county were murdered on July 27–August 3 (after 10,000 Jews from the county had been concentrated in the city). At the beginning of August, the Jews from Jaroslaw were deported to Belzec, followed at the end of that month by deportation of the Jews from Cracow county, where at an earlier date the Jews from the ghettos in *Bochnia, *Wieliczka, and Skawina had been concentrated. In September 1942 approximately 11,000 Jews from Sanok county (earlier concentrated at a camp at *Izyaslav (Zaslav) were deported to Belzec or shot in the surrounding forests. That month the ghettos in Tarnow county were finally liquidated.

Krueger's decree of Oct. 28, 1942, setting up six ghettos in the Cracow district (Cracow, Bochnia, Tarnow, Rzeszow, Debica, and Przemysl), was immediately followed by murder "actions" there. From June to November 1942, a total of over 100,000 Jews were murdered, and by Jan. 1, 1943, according to official figures, 37,000 destitute Jews were left in "residual ghettos" and a number of camps. There were over 20 labor camps in the Cracow district, the largest at *Mielec (with 3,000 Jewish inmates on the day of its liquidation, Aug. 24, 1944)—and others in Pustkow (1,500), Rozwadow (1,200), Szebnie (2,000–2,500), and in Plaszow with two branches in Prokocim and Biezanow. Plaszow, a collection point for the Jews who survived the liquidation of ghettos and camps in the entire district, had 20,000 imprisoned there in the fall of 1943. In March 1944, large transports were sent from Plaszow to Auschwitz, Stutthof, Flossenburg, and *Mauthausen, while the 567 Jews left were liquidated in January 1945 together with the rest of the Jewish survivors from the Cracow district.

RADOM DISTRICT. The newly created Radom district, comprising the larger part of the Kielce province and parts of the Lodz and Warsaw provinces, had a Jewish population of about 360,000 on Sept. 1, 1939. In this district too the evacuation of the Jews proceeded at a rapid pace. First of all, the district had been heavily bombarded, and there were cities and towns in which up to 80% of the Jewish population had lost their homes and sought refuge elsewhere. Secondly, the deportations from the incorporated areas, the Protectorate (an undetermined number from Prague), and Vienna brought into the district large numbers of homeless Jews—4,000 from Wartheland, about 10,000 from the Plock county, and 4,000 from Vienna. In 1941, the total number of refugees and deportees reached 70–75,000 (over 20% of the local Jewish population). In 1940–41, a kind of internal expulsion process went on in the district, e.g., in December 1940, when 2,000 Jews were expelled from Radom, and in October 1941, when several thousand were driven out from Tomaszow Mazowiecki.

The ghettos in this district were created at an earlier stage than in other parts of the General Government—in *Piotrkow at the end of October 1939, and in *Radomsko at the end of December that year. Ghettos were set up in March–April 1941 in the three large cities of the Radom district—in Radom (which in January 1941 had 28,000 Jews), Czestochowa (36,000), and Kielce (20,000). At the end of 1940 the ghetto of Tomaszow Mazowiecki was established (this town had 16,500 Jews in June 1940), divided into three different sections (the Radom Ghetto also consisted of two sections in two different quarters of the city). Many places were in ruins, causing severe overcrowding in the ghettos, and in some of the smaller ghettos there were as many as 12–30 persons to a room. In order to prepare for the *Aussiedlungen* the Nazis concentrated the Jews in a few ghettos. In the first stage, the Jews who were still living in villages were expelled to the neighboring towns. In the second stage, the Jewish population from the smaller towns was concentrated in the large ghettos, and each of the ten counties had several concentration points assigned to it. At the end of this stage, over 20,000 Jews were living in a few large, heavily guarded ghettos.

The first deportation, to Treblinka, took place on Aug. 5, 1942, in Radom. The Kielce Ghetto inhabitants were deported on August 20–24, and the Czestochowa Ghetto inhabitants, between Sept. 2 and Oct. 5, 1942. By Nov. 7, 1942, most of the Jews had been deported to Treblinka. On Jan. 1, 1943, according to a German source, there were only 29,400 Jews left in the four ghettos ("residential districts") in Radomsko, Sandomierz, *Szydlowiec, and Ujazd, provided for in Krueger's second decree (Nov. 10, 1942). These ghettos came to an end in January 1943. Only the Jewish slave laborers in the labor camps were left, mainly near the industrial concerns of Radom, Kielce, Czestochowa, Ostrowiec-Swietokrzyski, Skarzysko-Kamienna, Blizyn, Piotrkow, Tomaszow Mazowiecki, and other towns. These were in fact concentration camps run by the district SS and police chiefs, to whom the German factory owners directly paid the fees for exploitation of Jewish manpower (as was the case in the other districts also). Some of these camps went through a series of transfers and "selections," but continued to exist until the second half of 1944. The German *Hasag* factories in Czestochowa were still functioning as late as January 1945.

Galicia District. The district of Galicia, established in August 1941, comprised the *Stanislav and *Tarnopol provinces and the eastern part of the Lvov province, and consisted of 16 counties. The 1931 census report indicated a Jewish population in this area of 500,000. As a result of the great influx of refugees from Nazi-occupied Poland in the fall of 1939, the number of Jews had considerably increased, and it is estimated that at the outbreak of German-Soviet hostilities, there were 600,000–650,000 Jews in the area, taking into account the natural increase from 1931 to 1941. The German invasion was accompanied from the very beginning by the mass murder of Jews, initiated and perpetrated by local Ukrainians with the support and participation of the Einsatzkommandos and the German army. Pogroms took place in Lvov (on the "Petlyura Days," July 25 and 27), in Tarnopol, *Zolochev, and *Borislav. Many of the Jews living in the countryside, about 25% of the total Jewish population, were murdered in this period.

In the part of Galicia temporarily occupied by the Hungarian army (Kolomyya, Borshchev, and *Gorodenka), the situation was quite different, the Hungarian commanders taking the Jews under their protection and preventing murders from taking place. During the short period of German military occupation, until Aug. 1, 1941, when its civilian administration took over, several tens of thousands of Jews were killed. The civilian administration immediately introduced the anti-Jewish legislation applying to the General Government. In fact, some of the provisions of this legislation were applied even before a "legal" framework was created. The first ghettos were set up in the beginning of October at Stanislav (for about 30,000 Jews) and Tarnopol (18,000). These were followed in the spring of 1942 by ghettos in Kolomyya and Kolomyya county, and at *Chortkov. By the second half of 1942, ghettos existed in all the cities and towns, and a large part of their population had already been deported to Belzec. The last ghetto to be established was the one at Lvov, in August–September 1942, after several postponements. This came after the great *Aussiedlung* action, 36,000 surviving out of a population of about 150,000. Krueger's decree of Nov. 10, 1942, provided for 32 ghettos in the Galicia district, in Lvov, Stanislav, Tarnopol, Chortkov, *Stry, *Drogobych, *Sambor, Borshchev, *Zholkva, *Brody, Rava-Russkaya, *Rogatin, and *Skalat.

Large-scale physical extermination campaigns began in the second half of 1941 and were initially directed mainly against Jews in the professions and intellectuals. During the High Holiday period, on Oct. 12, 1941, about 10,000 Jews were shot to death at the Jewish cemetery of Stanislav. In November numerous executions took place in Lvov, when the first attempt was made to organize a ghetto there, and mass shootings occurred in Kolomyya county in December of that year. This is only a partial listing and it is estimated that some 100,000 Jews were murdered in July 1941–March 1942. In the latter month, the extermination camp at Belzec went into operation and from then until the end of 1942, about 300,000 Jews—50% of the Jewish population of the district—were deported to Belzec or shot on the spot, or taken away for execution in the forests. The others remained for a short while in the ghettos and labor camps, and by June 1943 they were all liquidated. According to *SS-Gruppenfuehrer* Fritz *Katzmann's report on the "Final Solution" in Galicia, only 21,000 Jews were left in Galicia, distributed in over 21 camps, the largest of which was the Janowska Street camp in Lvov. Selected workers from liquidated ghettos were transferred to this camp in Lvov, while those who were no longer fit for work were executed in the vicinity. In the second half of 1943, nearly all the Jewish labor camps were liquidated and their inmates murdered. In this period, several thousand Jews who had been engaged in agricultural work were also murdered.

Bezirk Bialystok. This district, created in July 1941, was attached to but not incorporated in East Prussia. The chief of the East-Prussian provincial government was also appointed head of the civilian administration of the Bialystok district and the central provincial organs at Koenigsberg were responsible for all district affairs. The area of the district, practically identical with Bialystok province, was divided into seven counties: Bialystok, Grodno, Bielsk Podlaski, Grajewo, Lomza, Sokolka, and Volkovysk. The Bialystok district suffered two eruptions of war, on Sept. 1, 1939, and June 22, 1941. The first German occupation was restricted to the western part of the district and lasted only a fortnight, after which the area was turned over to the Soviets. The Soviet occupying forces imposed far-reaching changes in the economic, social, and political life of the Jews. The Jewish population of the district in September 1939 was estimated at 240,000–250,000. Later on, the district was flooded by a stream of refugees from the western and central part of Poland. Among the officials and specialists brought in from the Soviet Union, there were also a considerable number of Jews, and the total increase in population is estimated at 100,000. It may therefore be assumed that in June 1941 the district had a Jewish population of about 350,000.

The second German invasion was accompanied by mass murders, carried out by the *Einsatzkommandos* comprising Tilsit police battalions. These operated in the rear of the army and caused the destruction of entire communities (Jedwabne, *Kolno, Stawiski, *Tykocin, and others). In Bialystok, over 6,000 Jews were murdered between June 27 and July 13, 1941. The great synagogue was burnt down and at least 1,000 Jews who had been forced into it perished in the flames. Special murder campaigns were instituted against Jewish intellectuals. Anti-Semitic elements within the local Polish and Belorussian population, as well as among the Polish police which continued to serve under the occupying power, took an active part in the mass murder of Jews. (Even before the war, the influence of the Polish anti-Semitic parties had been especially strong in this area.) Most of the ghettos were established in August 1941. The larger among these were Bialystok (over 50,000), Grodno (25,000), *Pruzhany (12,000), Lomza (10,000), *Sokolka (8,000), and Bielsk Podlaski (7,000). Grodno Ghetto consisted of two parts, one inhabited by artisans and skilled workers and their families, and the other by the rest of the Jewish population. Each had its own Judenrat and ghetto police, but the chairman of the Judenrat of the artisans' ghetto had the title of *Generalobmann* ("chief chairman") and represented both parts vis-à-vis the authorities.

While the ghettos were in the process of formation, "selections" and mass slaughter of Jews often took place. In Szczuczyn, for example, the ghetto was inhabited almost entirely by women and children, most of the men having been killed. The overcrowding in the ghettos was phenomenal. In Czyzow, for example, 200 persons were squeezed into seven tiny houses. Systematic mass annihilation began on Nov. 2, 1942. In a single day, most of the ghettos were wiped out (except for Bialystok, Pruzhany, the first part of the Grodno Ghetto, *Krynki, and Sokolka). Before reaching their final destination at the extermination camp of Treblinka, the deportees were kept in assembly camps for a period of three to ten weeks, during which many of them succumbed to the inhuman conditions. In November, 120,000–130,000 Jews were killed in the murder campaign. The *Aktionen* were renewed in February 1943, after the liquidation of the Pruzhany, Sokolka, and Krynki ghettos. In Bialystok Ghetto, the first "action" took place on Feb. 5–12, 1943, resulting in the death of 13,000 Jews, of whom 1,000 were killed on the spot. Over 40,000 persons were killed in the third phase of the extermination campaign. Bialystok Ghetto was the last in the district to be liquidated (Aug. 16, 1943). Armed resistance, organized by the Jewish Fighting Organization (see Mordekhai *Tenenbaum), was suppressed by German military forces, including tanks. Over 30,000 Jews were deported to Treblinka, Majdanek, and Auschwitz.

Generalbezirk Litauen und Weissrussland (Lithuania and Belorussia). The Polish parts of these districts, which belonged to Reichkommissariat Ostland, consisted of almost the entire Vilna and Novogrudok provinces and of the northern portion of Polesie province. In 1931 this area was inhabited by over 230,000 Jews. From September to December 1939, a large number of refugees arrived in the area, especially in Vilna. For nearly 11 months (from Oct. 10, 1939, until the end of August 1940), Vilna and its environs formed a part of Lithuania. In August, the entire country was absorbed by the Soviet Union. Under Soviet occupation, thousands of Jews were arrested and deported to distant parts of the Soviet Union, but several thousand escaped to the United States, Palestine (see *Beriḥah), and *Shanghai. It is therefore impossible to determine the size of the Jewish population in June 1941. The larger communities in the Lithuania district were Vilna, Vileika, *Oshmyany, Svienciany, and Trakai (*Troki); in the Belorussian district they were *Novogrudok, *Baranovichi, *Lida, *Slonim, *Molodechno, and *Stolbtsy. Like everywhere else in "Ostland," the military invasion brought in its wake large-scale murder by the *Einsatzkommandos,* in this case Einsatzgruppe 'A'. In many places they had the assistance of locally recruited "Hiwis" (*Hilfswillige*—local volunteer units). On July 11–Dec. 24, 1941, 45,000 Jews were killed in Vilna (which in 1931 had a total Jewish population of 55,000). At approximately the same time, 9,000 Jews were slaughtered in Slonim; 5,000 in Vileika; 4,000 in Molodechno; 2,500 in Novogrudok; 1,800 in *Volozhin, and other places. During the murder campaign, or a short while later, ghettos were established where further mass executions took place (Vilna Ghetto was set up on Sept. 6, 1941). Many small communities were completely wiped out.

Ghettos continued to exist in Vilna, Vileika, Oshmyany, Novogrudok, Lida, *Glubokoye, Slonim, and Baranovichi, and in a few smaller communities from which Jews were dispatched to larger ghettos in the summer of 1942, in preparation for the second phase of the annihilation program. Vilna Ghetto was also used for this purpose. Jacob Gens, chief of the Vilna Ghetto and of the ghetto police, had some measure of jurisdiction over the smaller ghettos in "Wilnaland," and the Vilna ghetto police participated in the *Aktion* that took place in Oshmyany at the end of October 1942. In Belorussia the same procedure was initiated of concentrating the Jewish population of a certain area in one of the larger ghettos in preparation for murder "actions." Here there was an almost continuous murder campaign, with breathing spells only between one "action" and the next. The longest such period of respite was granted to Vilna Ghetto, lasting from early 1942 until September 1943.

The final phase extended from August 1942, when the ghetto in Slonim was destroyed, until September 1943, when the Jews of Vilna, Novogrudok, and Lida were sent to their death. In the course of August and September 1943, about 10,000 Jews were deported from Vilna Ghetto to concentration camps in Estonia. Six thousand were murdered on September 23, and the ghetto was liquidated. Several thousand Jewish workers employed outside the ghetto were exterminated later (July 1944). Specialists and skilled workers were sometimes concentrated in certain houses in the liquidated ghetto or sent to labor camps. Such camps, containing the pitiful remnants of the liquidated ghettos of Belorussia, were located at *Koldychevo (near Baranovichi) and Kelbasin. They too ceased to exist at the end of 1943.

Generalbezirk Wolhynien-Podolien. Of the Polish territories, this district, which formed part of the "Reichskommissariat Ukraine," contained the larger part of the Polesie province and the entire Wolyn (Volhynia) province belonging to prewar Poland. The 1931 census of the population in this area indicated about 300,000 Jews. The larger communities were Pinsk, Brest, *Kobrin, *Kovel, *Dubno, *Rovno, *Lutsk, *Ostrog, *Kremenets, and *Vladimir-Volynski. Here too, a large influx of refugees came from Poland shortly after the outbreak of the war, while a certain number of Jews were moved by the Soviets to other parts of the U.S.S.R., so that it was impossible to determine the size of the population in June 1941. A mass slaughter in this district was carried out mainly by Einsatzgruppe 'C', commencing with the German invasion. The murder action at *Rovno was carried out on Nov. 5–6, 1941, when 15,000 Jews were shot. In general the local Ukrainian population cooperated in the annihilation campaign against the Jews.

Only a few communities escaped in the initial phase (one of these was Kovel). As was the case elsewhere, the surviving Jews were herded into temporary ghettos. Dubno Ghetto was among the first to be liquidated (May 27 1942), and 5,000–7,000 Jews were killed. The first *Aktion* took place on May 10, 1942, and the handful of Jewish workers who survived it were shot on May 23, 1942. In Kovel the "city" ghetto was destroyed on June 2, 1942, with 8,000–9,000 victims, while the "workers'" ghetto in the city was liquidated on Sept. 18, 1942. Lutsk Ghetto came to an end on Aug. 20, 1942 (17,000 people murdered). In Kremenets, the ghetto's agony lasted for two weeks, starting on Aug. 10, 1942, in the course of which 19,000 Jews went to their death. In September, it was Vladimir-Volynski's turn (18,000 victims) and from October 28 to 31, the Jews of Pinsk Ghetto were murdered. As in "Ostland," the mass executions took place in the vicinity of the ghettos, in front of prepared mass graves, and were marked by extraordinary manifestations of sadism. The Ukrainian police displayed a murderous zeal in their cooperation with the Nazis. In the course of December 1942, the Jewish workers who had survived the mass executions were also liquidated. In a report on a trip in the Ukraine in June 1943, Hans Joachim Kausch of the Propaganda Ministry stated that the Jews of that area had been "completely" liquidated and throughout his entire stay there he had found only four Jews, working as tailors in an SD camp.

Demographic Total. Up to September 1939 Poland had a Jewish population of 3,351,000. Exact figures on the number killed between September 1939 and 1944 are not available, but the following account is a relatively well-founded estimate. Shortly after the end of the war, the Central Committee of Polish Jews began registering all surviving Polish Jews and by June 15, 1945, 55,509 had registered. Since some people registered several times with different local committees a round figure of 55,000 is assumed, which included a certain number of Jews who succeeded in returning to Poland from the Soviet Union. To this must be added 13,000 Jews in the Polish army formed in the U.S.S.R. in 1941, and approximately 1,000 Jews (out of 2,000) who had saved themselves by posing as "Aryans" and had not registered with the Jewish committees, bringing the total to 69,000. The number of Polish Jews who were saved by fleeing in September 1939 to the Soviet Union, to certain European countries, to Palestine, or to North and South America, or who survived the camps in Germany, is estimated at a maximum of 300,000 (250,000 of whom had fled to the U.S.S.R.). The sum total of surviving Polish Jews is therefore about 369,000, i.e., 11% of the prewar population, while 2,982,000 Jews were killed.

Jewish Resistance. Nazi plans called for a campaign of repression utilizing legal and economic restrictions and hard labor to bring about a rapid reduction of the Jewish population by pauperization, starvation, and epidemics. The Jews developed a system of self-defense to thwart the rapid achievement of the plans for their destruction, or at least succeeded in slowing down the realization of the Nazi program. Jewish resistance applied to all spheres of life—economic and spiritual; on an individual as well as on a collective basis; and in the final stage, when the Nazis resorted to the "Final Solution" (physical annihilation) of the Jews, it took the form of armed insurrections. In the economic sphere, the Jews succeeded in circumventing the regulations designed to isolate them from the gentile society, due to the fact that large numbers of Jews were put to work outside the ghetto. They established secret industries in the ghetto itself, by which they staved off rapid starvation and carried on business with the "Aryan" market. Foodstuffs were also smuggled into the ghetto by various means, often displaying astounding inventiveness. Jewish industrialists and artisans managed to obtain substitutes for all kinds of raw materials. In Warsaw Ghetto, for example, the export of wares produced in the ghetto workshops under orders of the German "Transferstelle" was in no proportion to that of articles produced in secret and exported without the knowledge of the official German office. The considerable gap between legal and illegal economic activities became characteristic of the economic situation in all the occupied areas. Officially the Jews were given the opportunity of working for the German economy only, military as well as civilian, for as long as this served the German war effort. In practice, many of the Jews, inured by a long tradition of existence under harsh conditions of persecution, and fortified by a powerful will to live, were able to break out of the economic straitjacket into which the Nazis had forced them and to surmount the dangers of the ghetto walls.

The Nazis were disappointed by the ability of the ghettoized Jews to adapt themselves to the abnormal conditions of their existence, and surprised that "so few" Jews were dying from "natural" causes and that there were no mass suicides. At a meeting of Nazi officials, held in Cracow on Aug. 24, 1942, General Governor Frank openly admitted: "By the way, I wish to state that we have sentenced 1,200,000 Jews to death by starvation; the fact that the Jews are not dying from hunger will only serve to speed up enactment of further anti-Jewish decrees." Thus, the Jews' vitality served to frustrate partially the biological war that the Nazis waged against them and was one of the causes for the Nazis' decision to resort to the "Final Solution."

Jewish aid organizations which existed before the war, such as the *American Jewish Joint Distribution Committee (JDC), *TOZ, and *CENTOS, the Yidishe Sotsiale Alaynhilf (YISA) founded in May 1940, and, after liquidation of the last in Oct. 1942, the Juedische Unterstuetzungsstelle (JUS), established formally in March 1943, were permitted by the General Government to carry on their activities in its area. The YISA set up a highly diversified system of social and medical assistance. Almost every ghetto provided some form of public assistance, such as soup kitchens and accommodation for deportees and refugees. As early as May 1940, according to an incomplete list, some 200 welfare committees were sponsored by the Judenraete, and their budgets were provided mainly by the JDC. These committees also collected funds, clothing, and other articles among local Jews. By the end of 1941 the YISA organization was active in over 400 localities in the General Government, maintaining 1,500 social and medical institutions and serving 300,000 adults and 30,000 children.

This of course was not enough to cope with the demands posed by the constantly growing pauperization of the Jewish population and the continual influx of new arrivals (in some ghettos, 60% of the population was dependent on public assistance). The constant lack of nourishment and hygiene in the ghettos, which the Nazis set up in the most dilapidated parts of the towns, resulted in diseases and epidemics to which the entire Jewish population might have easily succumbed. However, health and sanitary departments were set up and maintained by the Judenraete and TOZ which in turn subsidized 117 hospitals and 123 out-patient clinics and sanitary posts. To prevent the spread of the epidemics to the "Aryan" city quarters, the Nazi authorities used police measures, the results of which were even worse than the epidemics. In fact the ghetto population was so weakened that a large loss of life could not be avoided. In Warsaw, Lodz, Lublin, and Kutno, 15–20% of the Jewish population died in the two or three years of the ghettos' existence.

The Jews also displayed moral resistance to the starvation and debilitating forced labor, whereby the Nazis hoped to divest the Jews of all interest in spiritual life and dehumanize them. Moral resistance took varied forms. Pious Jews convened in secret for prayers, disregarding the dangers thus incurred; yeshivah students continued their studies and held clandestine *minyanim* to which they took the orphans to recite *kaddish* for their deceased parents. They also abstained from using the public soup kitchens which under ghetto conditions were not kept *kasher,* despite the greater suffering this entailed for them. Nonobservant Jews had their own means of moral resistance. Teachers established clandestine student groups and conducted classes in private homes. Persons who had been active before the war in cultural societies established secret libraries, choirs, orchestras, and dramatic groups, and held lectures and celebrations of important historical anniversaries. The Judenraete also established schools, wherever the Nazi authorities did not put obstacles in their way. (According to a decree issued by Frank on Aug. 31, 1940, the Judenraete were to be permitted to run elementary and vocational schools, but with few exceptions were prevented from actually doing so by the local Nazi authorities.)

Intensive cultural and educational activities were carried on in the Warsaw ghetto by the Yidishe Kultur-Organizatsye and the CENTOS, and in Vilna Ghetto by the cultural department of the Judenrat. Lodz Ghetto also maintained a large network of schools until the summer of 1941 (45 schools with 500 teachers and an average monthly attendance of 10,300 children). In most ghetto schools the emphasis was placed on Jewish studies. The teaching of history and geography was prohibited. Cultural activities fulfilled the dual purpose of protecting the inhabitants of the ghetto, especially the youth, against the demoralizing atmosphere of the ghetto created by the Nazis, and of strengthening their resistance to Nazi attempts to deprive them of their human dignity.

Organized physical and armed resistance was closely linked to political activities in a number of ghettos, and took various forms. Illegal publications, including pamphlets, were issued periodically or singly, and were either handwritten or duplicated. (In Warsaw Ghetto, for example, incomplete reports indicate that from mid-1940 to April 1943, 40 illegal periodicals were issued by various illegal movements representing every shade of political opinion.) Organized secret listening-in to foreign broadcasts, to reduce the Jews' isolation from the outer world, provided information on the political and military situation, and served as a source of hope and encouragement. In some ghettos, political parties—particularly workers' parties, e.g., the Bund, Po'alei Zion, and the communists—actively opposed the Jewish ghetto administration, i.e., the Judenraete and the ghetto police. (In Lodz Ghetto, opposition to Rumkowski's regime took the form of street demonstrations and strikes in the ghetto workshops.) Opposition to the Judenraete was also voiced in the underground press. The parties' youth movements conducted a cultural education campaign among their secret membership.

At a later stage, when the mass deportations began, the movements made preparations for armed resistance to the deportation "action." It was on the basis of organizing armed resistance that the political parties began to cooperate. Thus, in Warsaw Ghetto, a Jewish Coordinating Committee was set up in October 1942, composed of representatives of all the Zionist parties (with the exception of the Revisionists)—who were united in the Jewish National Committee—and of representatives of the Bund. On Oct. 27, 1942, the Jewish Fighting Organization (ZOB) was established which united the above-mentioned Jewish parties and the communists under one command. The heroic revolt of Warsaw Ghetto (which lasted from April 19 until the end of May 1943) was the result of the collective, self-sacrificing efforts of the youth of almost all political parties. The Revisionist Jewish Military Organization took an active part in the fighting. Similarly, in Bialystok Ghetto, a united fighting organization was set up on the eve of the revolt that broke out on Aug. 16, 1943.

In Czestochowa, the planned revolt was frustrated when an unexpected deportation "action" (on Sept. 21, 1942) barred access to the bunkers where the arms were hidden. During the liquidation of Bedzin Ghetto, underground fighters of the Zionist youth movements fought against vastly superior Nazi armed forces from fortified bunkers until they all fell. In Cracow Ghetto, the fighting organization, consisting of Zionist and Communist youth, carried out acts of sabotage and direct attacks on the Germans (such as the armed attack against German officers in the Cyganeria Café on Dec. 23, 1942). In Vilna Ghetto, a United Partisans Organization was founded in January 1942, comprising in later stages members of all the political movements. Following the Gestapo demand for the surrender of the Vilna underground commander, Yiẓḥak *Wittenberg, in July 1943, the leadership of the organization was forced to give up the struggle inside the ghetto, and smuggled its members into the forests, where they set up a partisans' group under the name of *Nekamah* ("Revenge").

Revolts broke out in the extermination camps of Treblinka (on Aug. 2, 1943) and Sobibor (Oct. 14, 1943) in which large numbers of prisoners managed to escape (most of whom were later killed). These insurrections later brought the murder installations in those camps to a halt. An armed revolt of the Jews in the "Sonderkommando" in Auschwitz took place on Oct. 7, 1944. [I.TR.]

PARTISANS. The guerilla warfare in Poland (i.e., within the area designated by post-World War II boundaries) was confined to the territories of the so-called General-Government and the province of Bialystok. The first Jewish attempts to organize partisan units were undertaken by the resistance movement of the *Warsaw Ghetto in spring 1942, but these, as well as some other early attempts, failed due to lack of experience and the lack of support from the local population. In July 1942, the Germans began to implement the so-called "Operation Reinhard." At that time, mainly in the provinces of Lublin and Kielce, there began a spontaneous movement of thousands of Jews fleeing the townlets to the forests to escape deportation. Many of them formed groups that offered active resistance to the Nazis. Although numerically strong, they had very few arms and no supply bases at all. Those who managed to hold out through the winter of 1942/43 came in contact with the Polish underground, as in the course of spring and summer 1943 a number of Polish partisan units began to operate from the forests.

The attitude of the Polish partisans toward the Jews depended upon the political framework to which they belonged and the goodwill of local commanders. The closest relations were between the Jewish partisans and the Communist-dominated People's Guard (Gwardia Ludowa). About a dozen Jewish partisan units were subordinated to the command of that organization and later acted as its units. Among them were: partisan detachment "Chil" (known also as the Second Company of the "Holod" battalion), under the command of Yehiel Grynszpan, which operated in the eastern part of the Lublin province; detachment "Emilia Plater," under the command of Samuel Jegier, and detachment "Kozietulski," under the command of Mietek Gruber, in the northern parts of the Lublin province; detachment "Berek Joselewicz," under the command of Forst, in the southern part of the Lublin province; detachment "Lwy" ("Lions"), under the command of Julian Ajzenman (Kaniewski), in the northern part of the Kielce province; detachment "Zygmunt," under the command of Zalman Fajnsztat, in the southwestern part of the Kielce province; detachment "Iskra" ("Spark"), under the command of Lejb Birman, in Rzeszow province; and detachment "Mordecai Anielewicz" commanded by Adam Szwarcfus, Mordecai Growas, and Ingac Podolski, in the forests near Wyszkow (northeast of Warsaw) which was organized after the Warsaw Ghetto uprising by remnants of the Jewish Fighting Organization. Jews also constituted a significant percentage in a number of other units of the People's Guard.

Remnants of the fighters in the *Bialystok Ghetto uprising formed the partisan unit "Forwards" ("Foroys"), which was later part of a Soviet partisan brigade under the command of General Kapusta. The attitude of the Armia Krajowa (Home Army), sponsored by the Polish government-in-exile residing in London, and of the Peasants' Battalions ("Bataliony Chłopskie") were different. These organizations did not accept Jewish units, but some of them accepted individual Jewish fighters, while others often took part in the murder of Jews. The extreme right-wing National Armed Forces ("Narodowe Siły Zbrojne") were strongly hostile toward Jews, organized attacks against Jewish partisans, and murdered all Jews they found hiding in the forests. Some Jewish units managed to operate independently of any Polish underground organization. The greatest of them was the unit in the Doleza forests under the command of Abraham Amsterdam.

A number of Jews won great fame in various Polish partisan units, mainly in those belonging to the People's Guard. Among the best known are: Colonel Ignacy Robb-Rosenfarb (Narbutt), commander of the People's Guard in the Kielce region; Colonel Robert Satanowski, commander of a partisan brigade; Colonel Niebrzydowski, commander of the Peasants' Battalions in the Miechow region; Major Menashe Matywiecki, member of the general staff of the People's Guard; Alexander Skotnicki, commander of the "Holod" battalion; Yehiel Brawerman, commander of the detachment "Bartosz Glowacki," and Captain Lucyna Herz, the only Polish woman officer parachuted into the woods for partisan activity. Jews also played a significant role in the Special Attack Battalion, which organized parachute units for guerilla warfare in the rear of the German army. The commander of that unit was the Jewish officer Lieutenant Colonel Henryk Toruńczyk. Four of the 12 units parachuted into the forests during the summer and autumn of 1944 were commanded by Jewish officers: Robert Satanowski, Julian Komar, Joseph Krakowski, and Zygmunt Gutman (later known as one of the best partisan commanders in the Kielce province). The significant feature of the Jewish partisan movement in Poland was that almost all Jewish partisans started their guerilla activity at a very early period (second half of 1942), when the Polish partisan movement hardly existed; thus Jews constituted in the early period a high proportion of the partisans and guerilla fighters. Among the first nine partisan detachments organized at the beginning of 1943 in the Kielce province, four were Jewish units, with a number of Jews present in all other units. Later in spring 1944, when the partisan movement in Poland grew rapidly, thanks to the great flow of arms from England (for the Armia Krajowa) and from the Soviet Union (for the left-wing guerillas), the Jewish communities were already destroyed and there were no more Jewish youth who could fill the partisan ranks. (See also: *Partisans.) [S.Kr.]

Jewish-Polish Relations During the War. Relations between Jews and Poles in occupied Poland were complicated in nature, especially in the Polish underground movements. The entire Polish population was vehemently anti-German, but the vast majority of people were also violently anti-Semitic. In the first month of the war, anti-Semitism seemed to have completely disappeared out of hatred for the Nazis, but it reemerged soon afterwards.

The Polish political parties' attitude to the Jews before the war generally remained much the same during the entire period of occupation. The right-wing parties, led by the Narodowa Demokracja (Endecja) officially denounced Hitler's barbaric methods, but in fact remained anti-Semitic and regarded the Nazi "solution of the Jewish problem" in Poland with quiet satisfaction. The extreme right-wing radicals, the Obóz Narodowo-Radykalny (ONR) and the Falanga, rejoiced over Hitlerism and approved of the Nazi murders. They contended that the victims were no better than murderers, and deserved their fate. The Polish Socialist Party (PPS), on the other hand, and especially its left wing (RPPS) and the reorganized Communist Party (PPR) condemned the murder of the Jews in their illegal publications, took part in campaigns to aid Jews, and appealed to the Polish people to assist. A similar stand was taken by the Democratic Party and the People's Party, although the latter, formerly an important party, did not have a uniform approach. In general it identified itself with the stand taken by the Polish government-in-exile represented inside Poland by the Delegatura. The Delegatura also maintained contact with the Jewish National Committee and the Jewish Coordinating Commission. Through the Delegatura these Jewish bodies were able to keep in touch with Jewish political movements and organizations abroad.

Relations between the Jews and the Delegatura, initially quite friendly, deteriorated in the course of time. This was due to the Delegatura's negative attitude in regard to supplying the Jewish Fighting Organization with sufficient quantities of arms. It was not until the resistance of the Jewish Fighting Organization in Warsaw in January 1943 that the fighters at last received a small quantity of arms from the Delegatura. The strained relations with the Delegatura were partly the result of the reactionary and anti-Semitic groups' influence within the Polish underground, which grew in strength as the German front moved back toward Poland and a general anti-Soviet attitude came to the fore. (Anti-Soviet feelings among the Poles were also heightened by the story of the Katyn massacre, and the resulting break in Soviet-Polish diplomatic relations in the summer of 1943.) Anti-Jewish agitation among the Polish population was also fed by the reports of the situation of the Jews in Eastern Poland under the Soviet occupation, when Jews were appointed to official positions. The Delegatura also adopted a negative attitude to the Jewish partisan movement, refusing to support it or even to recognize its existence.

As the Soviet army drew near the Polish frontier, a rapprochement took place between the Sanacja (the ruling party of Piłsudski's successors) and the Endecja and between the Sanacja and such outright Fascist organizations as the ONR, whose military arm, the National Armed Forces (NSZ), was recognized in March 1944 as a component of the Delegatura's underground army, the Armia Krajowa. The NSZ went so far as to murder Jewish partisans and Jews who had succeeded in escaping from the slaughter taking place in the ghettos. More and more, an anti-Jewish tendency made itself felt in the official underground publications issued by the Delegatura.

The Nazi propaganda machine cleverly exploited the anti-Semitism existing among the Polish population. Reviving the old Polish slogan of "Żydo-Komuna," they identified Jews with Communism and succeeded in further poisoning the prevailing anti-Jewish feelings among the Poles. As a result, Jews who had been in hiding on the "Aryan" side were denounced to the Nazis. In many places Poles not only assisted in the search for Jews, but joined the Nazis in torturing and killing them as well. The Polish police, with hardly any exception, took part in the "actions" and on several occasions were themselves in charge of rounding up the Jews and dispatching them to the death camps.

There were, however, some social groups and individuals, from all segments of the population, who helped Jews at the risk of their own lives. The activities of the "Council for Aid to Jews," which provided "Aryan" documents and shelter in Polish houses, rescued children, and extended financial aid, helped some 50,000 Jews. There were more than a few individual Poles who had the moral strength to overcome the fear of death (the punishment for giving refuge to Jews) and the pressure exerted on them by the prevailing anti-Jewish climate of opinion, to stretch out a helping hand to the persecuted Jews. Some of these Poles, along with their families, had to pay with their lives for the courage they displayed in aiding Jews.

It may be concluded that the attitude of the Poles to the Jews was marked by both active participation in the murder of Jews and rescue efforts at great risk. The motives for these attitudes also varied from religious, humanitarian, or simply materialistic considerations, to a "biological" hatred of Jews. Of all the occupied countries, the percentage of Jews saved in Poland was the smallest, since the predominant attitude was hostile, while rescue was an exception to the rule. [I.TR.]

AFTER WORLD WAR II

Rescue of Jewish Children. When Poland was liberated in 1945, thousands of orphaned and abandoned Jewish children were wandering through villages and in the streets of the towns. Many were found in Polish homes and in convents. Some had been baptized, and some had been exploited by the peasants as a source of cheap labor. The official Jewish committees *(komitety)* established institutions for homeless children. Jewish parents applied to the Jewish organizations for help in finding children, who had been entrusted to non-Jewish families in order to save their lives but later disappeared without trace. Some Poles refused to return Jewish children, either because they had become attached to them or because they demanded financial remuneration for maintaining the child and for the risk they had incurred in hiding Jews from the Germans. There were a few cases of Jewish children living under conditions of starvation and terror. With the mass repatriations from the Soviet Union, 31,700 children under 14 years of age returned to Poland, including many hundreds of orphans, who also needed immediate care. Three separate bodies worked to save Jewish children. The first of these, the official Jewish committees, acting under the auspices of the authorities, maintained 11 boarding schools with a total of 1,135 orphans, and day schools and nurseries which cared for about 20,000 children. The youth department of the committees cared for about 7,700 boys and girls. Material conditions were good, but education was oriented toward Polish assimilation. The second, the Jewish Religious Council (Kongregacja), sent people to redeem children from Polish homes, particularly at the request of religious relatives. These children were delivered to their relatives abroad, or sent to be adopted by Jewish families in the United States, Great Britain, and other countries. The third organization was established by the Zionist movement, and given the abbreviated name of the "Coordination" (Koordynacja). Its emissaries wandered through Poland to rescue children, very often risking their lives in doing so. The Koordynacja established four children's homes, which housed hundreds of children aged between two and 12. The older children were sent to "children's kibbutzim" of the youth movements. Funds were supplied mainly by the *American Jewish Joint Distribution Committee (JDC). The special psychological problems of the Holocaust period, such as fear and hatred of Jews, necessitated the establishment of a special seminary for educators at Lodz. The Koordynacja systematically sent children abroad, with the intention of finally enabling them to reach Palestine. By the end of 1947, more than 500 children had been taken out of Poland. Together with their teachers and educators they entered *Youth Aliyah institutions in Germany, Austria, and France, most of them settling later in the State of Israel. Scores of Jewish children are believed to have remained in Poland, mainly in Catholic institutions and convents. [S.N.]

Renewal of Jewish Life. The first attempts to renew Jewish life took place in Lublin, the seat of the Polish Committee of National Liberation. In a manifesto issued on July 20, 1944, this committee published a solemn declaration assuring equal rights and full rehabilitation to the survivors of Polish Jewry. The Jewish Committee was formed to extend emergency aid to Jews converging on Lublin from the liberated parts of Poland. This group included adults who returned from the forests and other hiding places or who miraculously survived the concentration camps, and children who found refuge in convents or with individual Polish families. In October 1944 the Jewish Committee was renamed the Central Committee of the Jews in Poland and moved to Warsaw when the Polish capital was liberated. The committee was composed of representatives of the various Jewish parties and was presided over by the Zionist Emil *Sommerstein. At first it was primarily concerned with providing material assistance to the Jewish survivors and facilitating their return to a productive life. Before long, however, the committee extended the range of its activities to social and cultural spheres.

By 1945 it comprised ten districts *(województwa),* two subdistricts, and about 200 local committees. Several dozen Jewish cooperatives, in a variety of trades, and 34 Jewish farms run by several hundreds of Jewish agricultural laborers were founded. A considerable number of Jewish weeklies and bi-weeklies, representing every shade of Jewish political opinion, made their appearance. Among them was the organ of the Central Committee, *Dos Naye Lebn.* An elementary school having Yiddish as the language of instruction with Hebrew as a compulsory subject was established in Lodz. There was also a society of Jewish writers, journalists, and actors in that city, while in Lower Silesia the Jewish Society for Art and Culture was formed. After the Zionist pioneering youth movements were reorganized, they established hundreds of training farms, children's homes, etc., and prepared their members for *aliyah.* In July 1945 the American Jewish Joint Distribution Committee (JDC) entered the Jewish scene in Poland. Through the Central Committee, it subsidized a variety of social welfare agencies, emphasizing the care of children, the aged, and the sick. In addition the JDC provided food, clothing, and medicine to educational and cultural institutions, and supported a variety of plans to help able-bodied men and women become productive again. The following year, *ORT began its work in Poland, creating a network of vocational schools. In the medical field TOZ provided the assistance. At the beginning of 1946, this organization was running eight mobile clinics, seven hospitals, and medical aid stations in all major cities.

In addition to the 80,000 Jews already in Poland, over 154,000 Polish Jews were repatriated from the U.S.S.R. in the summer of 1946, bringing the total Jewish population of Poland close to 250,000. The Polish government and the Communist-dominated ruling party (the Polish Workers' Party—PPR) encouraged the Central Committee in its social and cultural activities and lent support to the Jewish efforts to establish new economic foundations and restore communal life. At the same time, the government placed no obstacles in the path of Jews who wished to emigrate. It permitted the Zionist movement to exist and displayed a friendly attitude to the aspirations of the *yishuv* in Palestine and later to the State of Israel. Polish government support (or at least tolerance), aid from world Jewry, and, especially, the growth of the community by mass repatriation from U.S.S.R., led many Polish Jews in the immediate postwar period to believe that the conditions being created in the "new" Poland would enable them to live a free and full Jewish life.

Cultural, Religious, and Economic Life. At first these hopes had some basis in fact. In 1946–47 two Yiddish theaters were founded—in Lodz and Wroclaw—and employed some 80 actors. In 1950 they joined forces as the Jewish State Theater with a government subsidy under the direction of Ida *Kaminska. The theater discontinued its activities after 1968, when most of the Jews emigrated from Poland. A publishing house and a literary monthly came into being. The Society for Art and Culture founded Jewish libraries, promoted amateur societies in various cultural fields, and arranged public lectures. The *Jewish Historical Institute embarked upon a program of collecting and publishing historical material on the Holocaust. According to figures published in the anniversary edition of *Dos Naye Lebn* (1945–47), the Central Committee's Board of Education served 34 Jewish schools staffed by 179 teachers and attended by 2,874 children. Jewish religious life was renewed in every town where Jews resettled. In prewar Poland there had been 2,000 rabbis, 8,000 ritual slaughterers and religious teachers, and 10,000 yeshivah students. Of these, only a few dozen rabbis, slaughterers, and about 100 yeshivah students survived the war, mainly in the U.S.S.R., but only a few of them refrained from emigrating and remained in postwar Poland. Nevertheless, the Union of Religious Communities was established, comprising some 30 communities. The Union attended to Jewish religious needs by refurbishing and using two synagogues which had not been destroyed—one in Warsaw and the other in Wroclaw—establishing prayer-houses in all the communities, providing *mazzot* for Passover, arranging for the supply of *kasher* meat, and founding *kasher* public kitchens. In cooperation with the Central Committee, the Union rededicated Jewish cemeteries and reburied according to Jewish rite the victims of Nazism buried in mass graves.

In mid-1948, the Union of Religious Communities formally joined the Central Committee of Jews in Poland. The cooperation between the two bodies, however, lasted only into the early 1950s, when the Stalinization taking place in the country also affected Jewish life and made the cooperation of secular and religious bodies impossible. By the end of 1960, there were 23 member communities in the Union, and by 1966 the number was reduced to 18. The number of individual members varied greatly from one community to another; thus, in Warsaw, there were only 20 registered members, while in Katowice there were 1,200 and in Wroclaw 2,000. The Union of Religious Communities was still in existence in 1969, but the mass emigration of 1968–69 reduced its membership severely. At the end of 1947, there were 200 Jewish cooperative societies, with a membership of 6,000. About 15,000 Jews were employed in communal institutions, coal mines, heavy industry, textile factories, and a variety of government and private factories; 124 Jewish families were employed on farms. By the end of 1946, ORT was conducting 49 different vocational courses staffed by 81 instructors and attended by over 1,100 pupils. Contact with Jewish communities outside of Poland was maintained by both the Central Committee and by the various Zionist groups which were active in the early postwar years. In the beginning of 1948, the Central Committee joined the *World Jewish Congress and participated in its meetings and conferences.

The Flight from Poland. The revival of a sound Jewish community life in Poland was the declared aim of those Jews who had been Communists before the war. They believed that the conditions were now ideal for the renewal of Jewish life and argued that a revived Jewish community would both demonstrate the vitality of the Jewish people and the failure of Nazism and other forms of anti-Semitism. The majority of Polish Jews, however, including those who were being repatriated from the Soviet Union, did not want to reestablish their lives in Poland, where the Nazis had found thousands of collaborators among the local population eager to cooperate in the extermination of the Jews. Moreover, pogroms continued even after the Nazi occupation ended. To most Polish Jews it was unthinkable to renew their life on the Polish soil soaked with the blood of millions of Jews. Thus tens of thousands of Polish Jews who fled from the U.S.S.R. and Poland made their way to Rumania and Germany in the hope of reaching Palestine. After the *Kielce pogrom this exodus took on an organized and semi-legal character. A coordinating committee for *aliyah* was formed from representatives of all Zionist groups to make arrangements for up to a thousand persons a day to cross the Polish border at three points in Lower Silesia near Kudowa. The operation lasted about six months, until the end of 1946 (see **Beriḥah*). Thereafter, Jews encountered difficulties in leaving Poland, but emigration did not come to a stop. In 1949, when the Zionist parties were disbanded, all former Zionists were permitted to leave for Israel, and some 30,000 people took advantage of this opportunity. Thus, mass emigration continually depleted Polish Jewry from 1944 to 1950. The Central Committee, which did all in its power to combat this movement, was forced to accept the reality of a drastic decrease in the Jewish population.

Anti-Jewish Excesses. Jewish emigration from Poland

Figure 25. Israel Barzilai (center on balcony), first Israel envoy to Poland, at the Israel consulate building, Warsaw, 1948.

Figure 26. Jewish shoemakers' cooperative, in the early 1960s assisted by the JDC. Courtesy Joint Distribution Committee.

Figure 27. Communal *seder* in Warsaw, 1960, with Israel Consul-General Rehavam Amir second from right.

Figure 28. Official visit to Auschwitz by Israel Foreign Minister Abba Eban and members of the Israel diplomatic corps, as part of a convention of Israel ambassadors to Eastern Europe, Warsaw, May 1966.

Figure 29. Desecrated tombstone in the Warsaw Jewish cemetery following the Six-Day War of June 1967.

was motivated not only by the recent tragic past and by prewar Zionist education, but also by the continuation of a clear and present danger to the Jews. There were murderous attacks upon Jews on Polish roads, railroads, buses, and in the towns and cities. The murders were committed by members of Polish reactionary organizations, such as the NSZ (Narodowe Siły Zbrojne). In cruelty and inhumanity, their crimes often equaled those committed by the Nazis. Beginning in 1945 the assaults upon Jews swiftly assumed mass proportions. In two pogroms—one in Cracow on Aug. 11, 1945, and the other in Kielce on July 4, 1946—thousands of Polish men, women, and children ran amock in the Jewish quarters, killing in Kielce 42 Jews and wounding 50 others. The attacks spread throughout the country, and in 1945 alone 353 Jews were reported murdered. The wave of anti-Jewish excesses continued well into 1946 and reached its climax in the Kielce pogrom. The government and the ruling party issued declarations designed to placate the Jews and there were public protests against anti-Semitism by intellectuals and large parts of the working class. Above all, the Jewish Communists and the Central Committee of Jews in Poland tried to reassure the Jews that the government would stamp out the anti-Semitic underground. The Jews, however, did not heed the exhortations and raced for the borders. By the end of 1947, only 100,000 Jews remained in Poland.

The Soviet Example. A second factor discouraging any hope for a viable Jewish community in Poland was the rising tide of anti-Semitism in the U.S.S.R. Soviet anti-Semitism was at first disguised as a campaign against "rootless cosmopolitans." This was followed by the judicial murder of leading Jewish writers and artists and the total liquidation of Jewish cultural life in the Soviet Union. The campaign culminated in the so-called *Doctor's Plot (see *Anti-Semitism, In the Soviet Bloc). These Soviet developments had an immediate effect on the Polish scene. In 1948 the central committee of the ruling party, the PPR, on Moscow's initiative, accused its first secretary, Wladyslaw Gomulka, and his associates of rightist-nationalist deviation, and Poland became, more than ever, a Soviet satellite. The entire country was overrun by the Soviet secret police. Under these circumstances Poland's attitude toward its Jews could not be substantially different from the Soviet model.

Nevertheless, Stalinist anti-Semitism was effected in Poland without bloodshed and mass arrests. It was the cultural activities of Polish Jewry that were immediately affected, reduced in their scope, and adapted in their content to the new spirit. The Stalinization of Poland was carried out by a variety of measures. The existing workers' parties were merged into a single party, and all other parties were liquidated. The Soviet Union was glorified and its policies in internal and foreign affairs were slavishly copied. In all creative activities "socialist realism" became the rule. In the Jewish sphere, "unifications" and liquidations were carried out. The first to be liquidated were the Zionist parties and the Bund in November 1949. This was followed by a ban on the operation of the JDC and ORT, in spite of the assurance given by the Polish Committee of National Liberation in its manifesto of July 20, 1944, and the appeal in December 1945 by the Polish provisional government for foreign aid to be extended to Polish Jews. Similarly, the recognition of the JDC's work expressed in November 1946, when JDC director, Joseph *Schwartz, was awarded a high decoration by the government, no longer had any meaning.

An act of liquidation by "unification" affected the Union of Jewish Cooperative Societies, representing 200 societies, 15,000 workers, and substantial assets (originally financed by the JDC) which was forced to merge with the general Polish Union of Cooperatives. On May 16, 1949, a "recommendation" was made to the Central Committee of the Jews in Poland to secede from the World Jewish Congress. Finally, the Central Committee itself, whose continued existence as a seemingly independent representative body was not in harmony with the new trend, was ordered to merge with the Jewish Society for Art and Culture. The new organization bore the name Cultural-Social Association of the Jews in Poland (Kultur-Gezelshaft-lekher Farband fun di Yidn in Poyln). All Jewish schools were nationalized in the 1948–49 school year, resulting in the further reduction of Jewish studies. Yiddish as the language of instruction and the teaching of Hebrew had already been eliminated. Such organizations as the Jewish Agency came to be regarded as "agents of imperialism," and any contact with them was highly suspect. The spiritual life of Polish Jews was now restricted to preoccupation with the "progressive" tradition. The mass emigration had resulted in a radical reduction in the number of district and local Jewish committees. Their total number dropped to 30. The largest concentrations of Jews were in Warsaw (about 8,000), Wroclaw (about 6,000), Lodz (about 5,000) and Szczeczin, Katowice, Cracow, Legnica, and Walbrzych.

In spite of these far-reaching quantitative and qualitative changes, the leaders of the Cultural-Social Association and the other Jewish establishments (such as the Historical Institute, the theater, the publishing house, the literary journal, and the newspaper *Folksshtime*), both in Warsaw and the provinces, did all in their power to maintain at least a modest level of Jewish activity. In fact, in the period 1950 to 1957, Jewish life in Poland was relatively stable. Even so, there were those in the association who, encouraged by the ruling party, sought to promote assimilation and achieve results.

1956–1967. Stalin's death in 1953 resulted in an easing of tension, but Gomulka's assumption of power, in 1956, completely transformed the Jewish scene in Poland. Revelation of the innumerable crimes committed in the U.S.S.R. during the period of Stalin's rule enabled the Jewish newspaper *Folksshtime* to publish a passionate protest against Soviet anti-Semitism and its destruction of Yiddish literature and culture. In Poland it was once more possible to foster Jewish literature and to reestablish contact with Jewish organizations abroad. The JDC and ORT returned to devote themselves primarily to the approximately 25,000 Polish Jews who were being repatriated from the U.S.S.R., under an agreement between Gomulka's government and the Soviet Union (along with hundreds of thousands of people who had been Polish citizens in 1939 but for some reason had not been repatriated after the war). Once again the JDC extended aid to the sick, the aged, and children. It also assisted various cultural institutions, including schools. ORT, for its part, reestablished its network of vocational training schools.

The great majority of Jews repatriated from the U.S.S.R. did not, however, have any intention of staying in Poland. Even before their departure from the Soviet Union, most of them resolved to move on from Poland, primarily to Israel. Similarly, thousands of long-established Jews now decided to leave Poland for good. Their decision was influenced by the anti-Semitic incidents that occurred soon after Gomulka's rise to power. Poland again allowed Jews to emigrate, and some 50,000 people left the country in 1958–59. In some cases, whole towns were emptied of their Jewish population, and the Jewish community in Poland was now reduced to about 30,000 people. Of those who remained some 3,000 were too old or too sick to earn their livelihood and were supported by the JDC, as were various children's homes, camps, and clubs. In addition, the JDC financed the Historical Institute, the Cracow Jewish Museum, cultural enterprises, the reestablishment of Jewish cooperatives, and the construction of a Jewish home for the aged.

The Jewish cooperative movement, revived after 1957 with help from the government and the JDC, was soon able to stand on its own feet and to transfer 20% of its yearly profits—ranging from one to two million zlotys—to the Jewish Cultural-Social Association. This situation prevailed until 1967.

Final Liquidation. In 1968–69, a fourth mass emigration of Jews from Poland took place, resulting in the virtual dissolution of the Jewish community as an identifiable and creative group. It also spelled the final disillusionment of those Jews who hoped the Gomulka regime would differ from the Soviet Union in its approach to the Jews. The Six-Day War (1967) and the March 1968 student riots in Polish university towns were seized by the Polish government as the opportunity to utilize popular anti-Semitism for its own political purposes. When the party faction called the Partisan Group, led by Minister of Interior Mieczysław Moczar, initiated anti-Semitic action in an attempt to oust Gomulka from power, the Polish Communist leader adopted a clearly defined anti-Jewish policy. In March 1968 Gomulka publicly declared those Jews whose loyalty wavered between Poland and Israel to be "rootless cosmopolitans" unworthy of holding public office. He reiterated, however, the principle that Israel-oriented Jews should be allowed to emigrate to the Jewish state. In the course of 1968, Jewish youth camps, schools, and clubs were disbanded. Jews were dismissed from whatever public positions they still held, and the Cultural-Social Association was reduced to a mere paper existence. Restrictions were placed even on the status of Yiddish, a language which had been used in Poland almost as long as Polish itself. Yiddish was declared a foreign language, with the result that any publication in Yiddish had first to be translated into Polish before it could be released for distribution. In practice this signified the end of the Yiddish publishing house "Yidish Bukh" and of *Yidishe Shriften,* the literary journal. The Yiddish newspaper *Folksshtime,* which formerly appeared four times a week, was now restricted to a weekly appearance. The JDC and ORT were again forbidden to operate in Poland, and the Jewish cooperatives were again handed over to the general Cooperative Union. The Jewish home for the aged, financed by the JDC, was turned into a general institution.

The liquidation of all organized forms of Jewish life was accompanied by a relentless anti-Semitic campaign carried through the press, radio, and television. The majority of Polish Jews, the tragic remnant of a community that had once numbered over 3,250,000 people, reacted to these events by choosing to emigrate. Since the Polish authorities allowed Jewish emigration only to Israel, and then only upon renunciation of Polish citizenship, many Jews who intended to emigrate to other countries (Canada, Australia, Scandinavia) ostensibly applied for papers and visas to Israel. Efforts to assure the continued existence of Jewish life in Poland were in vain. Young Jews, most of whom left the country, were especially shocked by the anti-Semitism displayed by leading Polish Communists. The few Jewish institutions still in existence in 1971 were devoid of all creative content and had been stripped of all authority. (See also *Cooperatives; *American Jewish Joint Distribution Committee; *ORT; *OZE; **Beriḥah*.) [D.Sf.]

RELATIONS WITH ISRAEL

Poland was among the first countries to recognize Israel (May 18, 1948). During the period preceding the establishment of Israel, Poland was unstinting in its support for the *yishuv*. At a convention of Soviet-bloc foreign ministers, the Polish foreign minister introduced a resolution congratulating Israel and condemning Arab agression. Polish public opinion also strongly supported Israel and its struggle, as evidenced by resolutions passed by various public institutions, including the National Conference of Polish writers. Israel also received practical aid. In 1948, before the declaration of independence, a Haganah camp was set up in Poland, where 1,500 young Jews underwent preparatory military training before leaving for Israel. During the actual fighting, shipments of wheat were brought to Israel by a Polish boat. In August 1948 an Israel legation was established in Poland, one of Israel's first diplomatic missions.

The Change of 1950. The cooling of U.S.S.R.-Israel relations from 1950 affected relations between Poland and Israel. A certain ambivalence characterized Poland's attitude toward Israel, for, together with criticism of Israel on the international scene, particularly at the UN, there was also understanding and sympathy for Israel's problems and a courteous attitude in official relations, in contrast to the attitude of other member states of the Eastern bloc, even in 1950–55, which were particularly difficult years for Israel relations with Eastern Europe. The change, which started to make itself felt at the beginning of 1950, was reflected in a decrease in the number of exit permits issued, although emigration from Poland never ceased altogether. Polish authorities began to display animosity toward the Israel legation, with a view to minimizing its contacts with Polish Jewry. During this period there were mass arrests and staged trials in a number of Eastern European countries, and, while the situation did not reach such proportions in Poland, police measures were intensified there and the Israel legation was put under police surveillance. A sharp turn of events occurred in 1953, when the Israel minister in Warsaw, A. L. Kubovy, who was stationed in Prague, was declared *persona non grata* as a result of a similar action taken against him by the Czechoslovak government after the *Slánský trial. Thereafter two other Israel diplomats were expelled.

Improved Relations in 1956. Wladyslaw Gomulka's ascension to power as secretary of the Communist Party in the fall of 1956 ushered in a liberalization in Poland's internal regime and a more independent foreign policy. Relations toward Israel improved primarily through an open emigration policy. Israel's problems were given more objective treatment in the press. In 1956 Israel again appointed a resident minister in Warsaw after a three-year period during which a chargé d'affaires headed the Israel legation. In 1963 the mission was elevated to the level of an embassy. After 1956 there was also a broadening of cultural and scientific relations in the form of reciprocal visits by individuals and delegations. Nevertheless, the Polish government maintained a constant reserve and did not respond to all of Israel's initiatives, sometimes even failing to implement plans they themselves had suggested. Thus, for example, cultural and scientific relations were not established on a formal basis, although such a step would have been justified by the extent of these activities. Nor was a Polish-Israel Friendship League set up in Poland, although an Israel-Polish Friendship League functioned in Israel.

Nevertheless, Poland was undoubtedly foremost among the East European countries in fostering relations with Israel, especially in the areas of culture, science, and information. Israel artists participated regularly in international music festivals in Poland, and many Polish performers appeared in Israel. Radio musical programs were exchanged. Exhibitions of Hebrew books were held in

Poland, and Polish books were distributed in Israel. Regular exchanges of scientific publications took place, and individuals and figures in public life paid reciprocal visits. Exhibitions of graphic art were organized in Poland and in Israel. Of special note during the period between 1956 and 1967 were the tour of a Polish medical delegation in Israel; the visit to Israel of the chairman of the Polish Academy of Sciences; and the visit of the Israel ministers of health and welfare to Poland. After 1956 Israel participated regularly in the International Fair in Poznan. An information bulletin distributed by the Israel embassy influenced public opinion, and the Polish press often drew upon it.

In the political arena (for example in voting at the UN), Poland continued to identify with the U.S.S.R. but nevertheless was willing to support the election of Israelis for various functions in international agencies. Its spokesmen would point out that Poland's guiding principle was to foster relations both with Israel and with the Arab states, but neither at the expense of the other. An event in May 1966 seemed to herald a marked improvement in Polish-Israel relations and a development in Israel's relations with the entire Communist bloc: a convention of Israel diplomatic representatives in Eastern Europe was held in Warsaw with the participation of Foreign Minister Abba Eban. It was the first time that such a convention was held in a capital of the Eastern bloc, and Warsaw was willing to serve as its venue; it was also the first visit in an East European capital by an Israel foreign minister. Eban held discussions with the Polish foreign minister, Adam Rapacki, who displayed the attitude usually accorded an official foreign visitor.

The Six-Day War. Fairly normal relations were maintained between the two countries when the U.S.S.R. began escalating the Middle East crisis, which resulted in the Six-Day War. Significantly, a visit to Poland at the end of April by the Israel minister of welfare, heading a delegation for the establishment of the Auschwitz memorial, was handled in a way that reflected a change for the worse in Poland's attitude. The fact that the visit was not mentioned in the press was interpreted as one expression of the attempt to minimize the Jewish character of the Holocaust. In the first half of May, Polish newspapers and communications media were still presenting a balanced view of the Middle East crisis. A sharp change occurred, however, during the second half of the month. The press began to give unilateral coverage to the Arab-Soviet position. Grotesque accusations with anti-Semitic overtones were leveled against Israel and its leaders. On May 28 the president of Poland sent a message to Nasser expressing "full support for the struggle of the Arab nations." After that time, Poland's statements were characterized by an animosity toward Israel even more venomous than in other Eastern European countries.

According to all indications, Polish public opinion generally supported Israel in its struggle for survival, but in the hands of groups competing for power in the party and in the Polish government, the Middle East crisis became a weapon for infighting, with the declared intent of displacing Jews from public positions. On June 12, 1967, following the Soviet Union's example, Poland notified Israel that diplomatic relations between the two countries were being severed, and inimical demonstrations against the Israel diplomats initiated by the authorities took place in sight of the diplomatic staff that came to take leave of the Israelis at the Warsaw airport. The Dutch embassy, which represented Israel's interests in Poland from that time, strongly protested against this behavior.

Emigration to Israel. In 1948 there were approximately 70,000–80,000 Jews in Poland. This number was swollen by thousands of Jews who returned from the U.S.S.R. in 1956–57 under the Polish-Soviet repatriation agreement. One of the major tasks of the Israel legation in Poland was the struggle on behalf of the majority of Jews who wished to migrate to Israel. Despite accusations leveled periodically by Polish authorities at the Israel legation and its staff for propagandizing and organizing the Jews for migration to Israel, there was continuous emigration. Between 1948 and 1949 the Polish authorities were issuing several hundred passports a month to Jews wishing to emigrate, especially to the aged, handicapped, and women left alone. Between 1949 and 1956 the number of passports issued decreased to a few dozen per month. The major years of Polish Jewish immigration to Israel were 1956–60 with their numbers reaching around 52,000. The peak year was 1957, during which some 31,000 Jews migrated to Israel. Despite the breakdown in diplomatic relations in June 1967, the Polish government continued to issue exit permits for emigration to Israel, but the motivation for this policy became more and more an anti-Semitic intent to "purge" Poland of its Jewish population.

Trade Relations. A trade agreement signed between Poland and Israel in 1954 was renewed annually until 1968. The numerous industrial and agricultural products traded were valued at approximately $4,000,000 in both directions. Major Israel exports were citrus fruit and tires, with Poland exporting frozen meat, sugar, iron and steel products, and chemicals. Two Israel exports added in the later years were potash and cotton, which then exceded the citrus export. During 14 years the scope of the agreement had doubled, in effect, and in certain years it had tripled. A shift in the trade balance in Israel's favor occurred in the first months of 1966 and continued thereafter due to a steep increase in the export of potash. Upon the severance of diplomatic relations, Poland was in debt to Israel for over $5,000,000, but despite its hostile attitude toward Israel it did not revoke the trade agreement of 1954, and it was automatically renewed in 1968. By then, however, the agreement was meaningless, with Israel having discontinued its exports to Poland to avoid increasing the Polish debt, which was, in effect, a credit extended to Poland without interest. In June 1968 the Israel government informed the Polish government of the revocation of the trade agreement. Poland's debt to Israel, then $2,700,000 was repaid thereafter. [M.Avi.]

Bibliography: Poland (until Partition): Dubnow, Hist Russ, 1 (1916), 13–305; R. Mahler, *Toledot ha-Yehudim be-Polin* (1946); I. Halpern (ed.), *Beit Yisrael be-Polin,* 2 vols. (1948–54); *Istoriya yevreyskogo naroda: Istoriya yevreyev v Rossii,* 11 (1914); I. Schiper, *Studya nad stosunkami gospodarczymi Żydów w Polsce podczas średniowiecza* (1911); idem, *Kultur-Geshikhte fun di Yidn in Poyln beysn Mitlalter* (1926); idem, *Dzieje handlu żydowskiego na ziemiach polskich* (1937); T. B. Heilikman, *Istoriya obshchestvennago dvizheniya yevreyev v Polshe i Rossii* (1930; rev. ed. of *Geshikhte fun der Gezelshaftlekher Bavegung fun di Yidn in Poyln un Rusland,* 1926); H. H. Ben-Sasson, *Hagut ve-Hanhagah* (1959). After Partition: Dubnow, Hist Russ; S. Segal, *The New Poland and the Jews* (1938); B. Johnpoll, *The Politics of Futility* (1967); W. Gliksman, *A Kehilah in Poland during the Inter-War Years* (1970); J. Shatzky, in: YIVOA, 7 (1962), 146–74; M. Mishkinsky, *ibid.,* 14 (1969), 27–52; Y. Gruenbaum, *Milḥamot Yehudei Polin* (1941); idem (ed.), EG, 1 (1953); idem, *Ne'umim ba-Sejm ha-Polani* (1963); J. Lestschinsky, *Oyfn Rand fun Opgrunt* (1947); idem, in: *Yidishe Ekonomik,* 1 (1937); 2 (1938); M. Linder, *ibid.,* 1 (1937); J. Shatzky, *Geshikhte fun Yidn in Varshe,* 3 vols. (1947–53); idem, in: *YIVO Bleter,* 36 (1952), 24–62; I. Halpern (ed.), *Beit Yisrael be-Polin,* 2 vols. (1948–54); N. M. Gelber (ed.), *Ha-Yehudim ve-ha-Mered ha-Polani* (1953); R. Mahler, *Ha-Ḥasidut ve-ha-Haskalah* (1961); idem, *Yehudei Polin bein Shetei Milḥamot ha-Olam* (1968); idem, *Divrei Yemei Yisrael, Dorot Aḥaronim,* vol. 2 bk. 1 (1970); A. Tartakower, in: Velt-Federatsye fun Poylishe Yidn, *Yorbukh,* 3 (1970); *Sbornik materialov ob ekonomicheskom* *polozhenii yevreyev v Rossii,* 2 vols. (1904); M. Wischnitzer, *Perezhitoye,* 1 (1908), 164–221; J. Kirszrot, *Prawa Żydów w Królestwie polskiem* (1917); I. Schiper, *Żydzi Królestwa polskiego w dobie powstania listopadowego* (1932); idem, *Dzieje handlu żydowskiego na ziemiach polskich* (1937); idem, in: *Miesięcznik Żydowski,* 1 (1931), 513–29; 2 no. 4 (1932), 311–27; idem et al. (eds.), *Żydzi w Polsce odrodzonej,* 2 vols. (1932–33); L. Halpern, *Polityka żydowska w Sejmie i Senacie Rzeczypospolitej Polskiej* (1933); P. Friedman, *Dzieje Zydów w Łodzi od początków osadnictwa do roku 1863* (1935); E. Ringelblum, *Żydzi w powstaniu kościuszkowskiem* (1938); S. Bronsztejn, *Ludność żydowska w Polsce* (1963); A. Eisenbach et al. (eds.), *Żydzi a powstanie styczniowe* (1963); idem, in: *Społeczeństwo Królestwa polskiego,* 2 (1966), 177–316. Holocaust Period: Bernstein, in: *Algemeyne Entsiklopedye: Yidn,* 6 (1963), 165–242; Brustin-Bernstein, in: *Bleter far Geshikhte,* 1, nos. 3–4 (1948), 125–64; 3, no. 2 (1950), 51–78; 4, no. 2 (1951), 103–22; 6 no. 3 (1953), 45–153; Rutkowski, *ibid.:* 12 (1959), 75–118; Rutkowski and Brustin-Bernstein, in: BZIH, 38 (1961), 28–38; Winkler, in: *Bleter far Geshikhte,* 1 nos. 3–4 (1948), 3–40; Trunk, *ibid.,* 1 no. 1 (1948), 114–69; 1, no. 2 (1948), 14–45; 2 (1949), 64–166; idem, in: YIVO *Bleter,* 37 (1953), 58–100; idem, *Geshtalten un Geshenishn* (1962), 127–261; idem, *Lodzer Geto . . .* (1962), preface, conclusion, and list of documents in English; Żydowski Instytut Historyczny, *Dokumenty i Materiały,* 3 vols. (1946); P. Friedman, *Zagłada Zydów polskich w okresie okupacji hitlerowskiej 1939–1945* (1947); Podhorizer-Sandler, in: BZIH, no. 30 (1959), 37–108; Datner, *ibid.,* no. 60 (1966), 3–29; J. Kermisz, *Akcje i wysiedlenia* (1946); A. Eisenbach, *Hitlerowska polityka zagłady Żydów* (1961); idem, *Di Hitleristishe Politik fun Yidn-Farnikhtung,* 2 vols. (1955); T. Berenstein et al. (eds.), *Eksterminacja Żydów na ziemiach polskich w okresie okupacji hitlerowskiej* (1957). For Further Reading in English: G. Reitlinger, *The Final Solution* (1962²), 143–53, 260–319 and passim, includes bibliography; R. Hilberg, *Destruction of European Jews* (1961), index; American Federation for Polish Jews, *Black Book of Polish Jewry* (1943); American Jewish Black Book Committee, *Black Book* (1945); Central Commission for War Crimes, Warsaw, *German Crimes in Poland,* 2 vols. (1946–47); M. Muszkat, *Polish Charges against War Criminals* (1948); A. Melezin, *Demographic Processes among the Jewish Population of Poland 1939–1945* (1948); J. Tenenbaum, *In Search of a Lost People* (1949); idem, *Underground, the Story of a People* (1952). Partisans: *Sefer Milḥamot ha-Geta'ot* (1954² = *The Fighting Ghettos,* partial trans. by M. Barkai, 1962); J. Tenenbaum, *Underground* (1952); Y. Suhl (ed.), *They Fought Back* (1968). Rescue of Jewish Children in Poland: N. Orelovitch-Reznik, *Imma, ha-Muttar Kevar Livkot?* (1965); L. Kuchler-Silberman, *One Hundred Children* (1961); E. Mahler, *Yad Vashem Bulletin,* no. 12 (Dec. 1962), 49–56; J. Goldman, *Rabbi Herzog's First Rescue Journey* (1964), passim; S. Nishmit, *Dappim le-Ḥeker ha-Sho'ah ve-ha-Mered,* 2 (1952); *Tetikeyts-Baricht fun Tsentral-Komitet fun di Yiden in Poyln* (1947); *Farn Yidishn Kind* (1946); After World War II; P. Lendvai, *Communism without Jews* (1971), 89–239.

POLÁNYI, KARL (1886–1964), economist and anthropologist. His scientific work was based on the place of economics in society, and the relation between production and distribution of goods. He also made a study of kinship and religion. Born in Vienna and educated in Budapest, Polányi was the foreign editor of the *Der Oesterreichische Volkswirt,* Austria's leading economic journal. Later he moved to England and in 1940 to America where he taught at Bennington College (Vermont) and New York. He was a socialist and in his later years the maintenance of peace became his major concern.

Polányi's writings include *The Great Transformation* (1945); jointly with A. Rothstein, *Dahomey and the Slave Trade* (1966); and *The Plough and the Pen-Writings from Hungary 1930–1956* (1963, jointly edited with Ilona Duczynszka).

Bibliography: J. Helm (ed.), *Essays in Economic Anthropology Dedicated to the Memory of Karl Polanyi* (1965), includes biographies. [J.O.R.]

POLANYI, MICHAEL (1891–), British physical chemist and economist. Polanyi was born in Budapest. In 1923 he joined the Technische Hochschule in Berlin, and was professor of physical chemistry from 1926 until the advent of the Nazi regime. He also worked under Fritz *Haber at the Kaiser Wilhelm Institute of Physical Chemistry (1923–33). In 1933 he went to England and became professor of physical chemistry at Manchester University.

Polanyi published his book *Atomic Reactions* in 1932 and contributed papers to scientific journals on crystal structure, kinetics, polymerization, and other subjects. However, he devoted an increasing proportion of his scientific perceptiveness and logic to political economy. From 1935, when his *U.S.S.R. Economics* appeared, he published many works in this field, and in 1948 switched chairs at Manchester, becoming professor of social studies. After his retirement he was, from 1959 to 1961, a senior research fellow at Merton College, Oxford. Polanyi was elected to fellowship of the Royal Society in 1944 and received many other honors.

His books include *The Contempt of Freedom* (1940), *Patent Reform* (1944), *Full Employment and Free Trade* (1945), *The Logic of Liberty* (1951), *The Study of Man* (1959), and *The Tacit of Dimension* (1966). [S.A.M.]

POLEMICS AND POLEMICAL LITERATURE. There were internal polemics with Jewish sectarians in the talmudic and post-talmudic periods, and a rich Jewish polemical literature in the Middle Ages. It does not include the continuous and sustained controversies which characterize rabbinical literature throughout the ages on the interpretation of the Oral Law. For this see *Conflict of Opinion. Polemics with non-Jews in the Bible, Talmud, and Middle Ages is discussed under *Disputation and Polemics and *Islam.

Talmudic Period. The talmudic literature is replete with details of polemics between the upholders of normative Judaism, the Pharisees and their successors, and the numerous sects which flourished at the time. Insofar as they are referred to by name, these are the *Samaritans, the *Sadducees, and those who are referred to under the generic name of **minim* (sectarians). Confusion exists as to the exact nomenclature and identification of the last two. As a result of *censorship, the original word in the Talmud had to be changed. Reference to the manuscripts as well as internal evidence provided by the context, show that the word *Ẓeduki,* Sadducee, which appears in the printed text refers to other sects. In addition, the word *min* applied to a wide range of sectarians, Judeo-Christians, Gnostics, Manicheans, Magi, etc. Thus whereas in the Sifra (Lev. 2) in the phrase "from here is provided an opening to the *minim*" the word refers to Gnostics who believed in dualism, the identical phrase in Exodus Rabbah 13:4 refers to those sectarians who denied the doctrine of free will. Jacob of Kefar Sakhnayya "of the disciples of Jesus of Nazareth" (these words, which are in the Mss., have been omitted from the printed text; Av. Zar. 17a) is referred to as a *min* in 27b. The Talmud states in the name of R. Naḥman "there are no *minim* among the gentiles" (Ḥul. 13b). The *minim* were all Jewish sectarians, and the Christian *minim,* Judeo-Christians.

There are a few polemics which can be definitely ascribed to Sadducees and Samaritans. With regard to the former, the Mishnah records a number of polemics between the Sadducees and the Pharisees in one of which Rabban Johanan b. Zakkai was the spokesman of the Pharisees. "The Sadducees said 'We cry out against you, O ye Pharisees' for they say 'the Scriptures render the hands unclean' [a typical rabbinic enactment]. Yet the writings of Hamiram [Homer?] do not render the hands unclean." In typical polemic vein Rabban Johanan carried the war into the enemy camp: "They say that the bones of the ass are clean, and the bones of Johanan the High Priest are clean" and the argument continues with the victory of the Pharisees (Yad. 4:6–8).

R. Eleazar b. Yose polemicized against the Samaritans by pointing out to them that the identification of Mt. Gerizim, the holy mountain, overlooking Shechem depends entirely upon the application of the *gezerah shavah*, an inference from analogy which was one of the 13 *hermeneutical rules evolved by the rabbis which the Samaritans rejected (Sot. 33b). Whereas this, like so many of the polemics in the Talmud, was a literary and academic controversy, the Midrash gives one with a Samaritan which belongs to a less refined sphere. R. Ishmael b. Yose, on a pilgrimage from Galilee to Jerusalem, came to Mt. Gerizim. There he met a Samaritan who asked him where he was bound. When he answered "Jerusalem," the Samaritan said "Is it not better for you to pray on this blessed mountain than that accursed one?" To which Ishmael retorted, "You are like a dog which digs up a buried carcass. It is because you know that there are idols buried here, which Jacob hid away [Gen. 35:4] that you are so full of fervor for this mountain" (Gen. R. 81:3; TJ, A.Z. 5:4, 44c). The polemics with the *minim* are legion in the rabbinical literature. They cover every biblical and theological topic including: monotheism, dualism (Sanh. 38a), that "he who created the wind did not create the mountains" (Ḥul. 87a), freedom of will, and predetermination (see above); the validity of the principles of rabbinic exegesis (Ber. 10a); that the destruction of the Temple was a sign that God had rejected the Jewish people (obviously a Judeo-Christian, though the printed text has a Sadducee; Yoma 57a); and other topics.

One fact seems to emerge clearly from a consideration of the many polemics in the Talmud, namely that they were rarely if ever sought out by the rabbis. Almost invariably the challenge came from the setarians. The sectarian who "used to annoy Joshua b. Levi greatly with his biblical texts" (Ber. 7a) represents the general attitude of challenge by them and only response by the rabbis.

In the Geonic Period. As was the case in the talmudic period, the rise of the various sects was the cause of various polemics. To a special category belongs *Saadiah Gaon's *Kitab al-Amanat* in which he answers the heretical opinions expressed by Hiwi al-Balkhi who lived in Persia in the last quarter of the ninth century. The fact that Saadiah found teachers in Babylonia teaching children from books based on Hiwi's biblical criticism makes it a contemporary polemic. The greatest polemic, however, in which Saadiah took a leading part, but which extended over at least three centuries, was against the *Karaite schism. [ED.]

Polemical Literature of the Middle Ages. The literature of the period reflects this preoccupation with disputation, polemical works being composed in almost every literary form then used by Jews: e.g., poetry, homiletics, ethical literature, fiction, and halakhic writing. In addition, the polemic—a genre whose main purpose was to express the views of the conflicting parties—was developed.

Purely halakhic and rabbinic disputes were usually dealt with in the literature of *she'elot u-teshuvot* (rabbinic responsa) and other halakhic literary forms. Medieval halakhists followed the literary style and legal precedents found in the vast body of talmudic literature, in which almost every point of law was contested, clarified, and usually determined. Even in controversies touching basic beliefs and carried on with intense emotion, medieval Jewry accepted opposing views as at least worthy of consideration. For example in his *Hassagot*, *Abraham b. David, the leading rabbi of Provence, contested many of the legal decisions in Maimonides' *Mishneh Torah*. Yet when the celebrated code of laws was printed, the *Hassagot* were included, as if they were a commentary on Maimonides' text. Opposing views, therefore, were regarded as important and worthy of being studied by all rabbinical scholars. Sometimes halakhic controversies originated from political differences rather than legal ones; thus the contentions between the leading rabbis in Palestine and Babylonia in the time of Saadiah Gaon, carried on in the traditional halakhic literary forms, were in fact struggles for recognition as the supreme religious authority in the Jewish world.

Halakhic literary forms, however, were both inadequate and inappropriate for the resolution of basic ideological problems and new literary forms were used. One of the earliest literary documents recording a fierce ideological controversy is *Milḥamot ha-Shem* ("The Lord's Fight," 1830), a small tenth-century book by the Karaite writer, Solomon b. Jeroham. Part of the polemical literature of the Rabbanite-Karaite dispute, the work is a Hebrew reply to Saadiah Gaon's attack against the Karaites, though Arabic was usually the language in which this controversy was sustained. *Milḥamot ha-Shem*, like most medieval polemical works, is written in the literary form of a letter (see *Letters and Letter Writing). But whereas only the opening and concluding portions of such a letter were usually written in rhymed prose, this work is written entirely in that manner. The most striking characteristic of Solomon's book is its satirical nature; he quotes (and rhymes) passages from the Talmud and from the literature attributed to talmudic sages, including the **Shi'ur Komah*, to show how far these rabbinic sayings had strayed from the biblical text and from the accepted theological ideas of the times—even those accepted in Saadiah's philosophical works. The three elements—the epistolary form, the rhymed prose, and the satirical statement of the main thesis—became the common feature in medieval Hebrew polemical literature.

Polemical literature in the form of a literary epistle served as the main vehicle of expression in one of the greatest controversies in medieval Jewry—the controversy over the writings of Maimonides, which began in the last year of Maimonide's life and continued throughout the 13th and the beginning of the 14th century, and especially during the years 1232–35 and 1304–05. The subjects of the controversy—the meaning of the anthropomorphic passages in the Bible and the talmudic literature, the reasons behind the commandments *(ta'amei ha-mitzvot)*, the question of the resurrection and the nature of the afterlife, the existence of angels and demons, the problem of the creation *ex nihilo*, the allegorical interpretation of the biblical stories—were discussed in letters exchanged between the leading disputants. Most of the letters are written partly in rhymed prose, with some written completely so.

The use of the literary epistle resulted from the fact that the disputants usually did not intend to clarify the ideological, theological, or even exegetical problems over which the controversy arose. Their main aim was to disqualify the opponent as a competent judge in the issue, to prove that he does not have the requisite knowledge or awareness of the problems which would entitle him to be heard in the controversy. Thus, early in the 13th century, when *Aaron b. Meshullam of Lunel answered Meir b. Todros Abulafia ha-Levi's letters concerning Maimonides' alleged disbelief in the resurrection, he dedicated the bulk of his letter to a discussion of Abulafia's character, knowledge, and understanding, and a review of his own feelings about Maimonides and his critics. The small portion of the letter that actually deals with the problem of the resurrection says nothing more than that Maimonides' views do not differ from those of the Talmud and the *geonim*, especially Saadiah Gaon. The letter is entirely written in rhymed prose and makes extensive use of biblical and talmudic phrases, leaving no doubt that the writer intended to win the public over to his views mainly by the beauty with which he expressed his feelings. This form of polemic, therefore, encouraged not so much the clarification of the issues as the demonstration of the writer's personal qualities and literary ability, and the enumeration of his opponent's faults. Another example of the evasive character of the polemical epistle is *Naḥmanides' reply to the rabbis of northern France in the same controversy over Maimonides' *Guide of the Perplexed.* Naḥmanides did not address himself to the issues raised by the French rabbis, rather he concentrated on proving that the rabbis, being far removed from the culture of the Jews in Spain and the Provence, were not qualified to judge Maimonides. In addition, he said that the *Guide* was not written for them, but for the perplexed Jewish scholars in Spain who could not avoid contact with Greek and Arabic philosophy. In this letter, Naḥmanides did not reveal his own kabbalistic ideas nor make known his stand on the problems themselves. Neither his duties as a responsible rabbi, nor the conventions of the polemical letter required Naḥmanides to express his own opinions about the issues involved. Although other letters exchanged in this controversy deal more closely with the ideological problems, they never do so fully or exhaustively. Abraham Maimon, for example, in his letters collected as *Milḥamot ha-Shem* ("The Wars of the Lord," a very common name for a polemical work), treated some problems, especially the allegorical interpretation of biblical and talmudic passages, as did Abraham b. Samuel in his defense of Maimonides against the criticism of the French rabbis. But even in these cases the personal allusions and the flow of rhymed phraseology make up a great part of the letters. These conventions persist in the letters exchanged during the controversy in 1305, when Abba Mari *Astruc again raised the issue of the dangers stemming from allegorical interpretation and the study of philosophy. Astruc tried to organize a movement, to be headed by Solomon b. Abraham *Adret, to oppose these practices.

Ashkenazi Ḥasidism, which flourished during the Middle Ages among the Jews in Germany and northern France, also gave rise to controversy. An extant fragment of Moses b. Ḥisdai *Taku's detailed polemical work, *Ketav Tamim* ("Book of Righteousness," published by R. Kirchheim, in: *Oẓar Neḥmad,* 3 (1960), 54–99), indicates that the work pays almost no attention to literary form, the issues themselves being the writer's major concern, although inflamed accusatory language is sometimes used. Moses did not hesitate to declare that his opponents, who included *Judah he-Ḥasid, Saadiah Gaon, Maimonides, and Abraham *ibn Ezra, were followers of the Karaites and the Christians who were destroying Judaism from within.

*Kabbalah, probably the most innovating Jewish ideology during the Middle Ages, aroused surprisingly little controversy when it began to flourish in Provence in the 12th century and in Christian Spain during the 13th century. From this period only one letter in clear opposition to the Kabbalah is extant. It is known that there was some disagreement among the kabbalists themselves over whether the Kabbalah should be discussed openly and brought to the attention of the Jewish community, or kept a secret known only to the selected few, the mystically inspired elect. Like most medieval disputes, these discussions were carried on in the form of letters.

During the 16th and 17th centuries both Jewish philosophy and Kabbalah again became objects of controversies, but with a larger part of the discussions now carried on in the form of special polemical books. Thus Joseph *Jabez, who wrote in Italy after the expulsion of Jews from Spain, termed the teachings of the Jewish philosophers as the cause of the conversion of thousands of Jews to Christianity during the 15th century in Spain. Isaac b. Judah *Abrabanel held somewhat similar views. Accusations and polemics against the philosophers are found in the works of many scholars up to and including Jacob *Emden and *Naḥman of Bratslav. Many polemical letters were written concerning the 16th-century controversy over whether the Zohar, the major work of the Kabbalah, should be printed. The opponents of publication comprised two groups: the devout kabbalists, who thought that a work of kabbalistic mysticism should be kept secret in order to prevent the uninitiated from reading it; and the opponents of the Kabbalah in general, who opposed its printing in order to reduce the influence of the Kabbalah which they regarded as false. A few anti-kabbalistic works were written in Italy, the most notable being *Ari Nohem* by Leone *Modena who systematically sought to prove that kabbalistic beliefs were invalid and that the kabbalists' claim that their theory and literature are ancient, transmitted from the time of the *tannaim,* is historically untrue. Modena was one of the first to use methods of literary and historical criticism in polemics against the Kabbalah. Two other 16th-century controversies deserve mention. The first was initiated by Azariah de' *Rossi's *Me'or Einayim,* a critical study of Jewish history and tradition which claims that the accepted system of chronology, i.e., counting from the creation, has neither a historically nor a traditionally sound basis. For this view he was criticized both by Renaissance scholars and by traditional Jewish scholars like *Judah Loew b. Bezalel of Prague. Azariah answered his more learned critics in a special book, *Maẓref la-Kesef.*

During the 1530s dozens of polemical letters were written by supporters and opponents of the *semikhah,* the ordination of rabbis, after the rabbis of Safed tried to reinstate the tradition that had been broken early in the Middle Ages. The rabbis of Jerusalem, however, opposed this; participation in the controversy increased, engaging the attention of many rabbis from various countries. The participants tried to treat the controversy as a purely halakhic one and the language of the polemical letters exchanged on this problem is clearly halakhic. But there is no doubt that beyond the halakhic references lay the true question: Should the rabbis take upon themselves activities concerned with messianic times (the reestablishment of the *semikhah* was regarded as one of the events connected with the redemption) or should they wait patiently until the coming of the Messiah who will reinstitute the *semikhah* himself? A similar consideration probably lay behind the dispute over the printing of the Zohar, for it was believed that wide acceptance of the Zohar and its teachings was one of the signs indicating the approach of messianic times.

The fiercest controversies in Jewish history were those arising over Shabbateanism and *Ḥasidism. Although there was some 17th-century criticism of *Shabbetai Ẓevi and his prophet, Nathan of Gaza, even before the former was converted to Islam, it was neither intense nor widespread. After the conversion, however, the critics knew no bounds in their accusations against the Shabbateans, and for 150 years thereafter the persecution of believers in Shabbetai Ẓevi and those influenced by his teachings was carried out relentlessly by some of the greatest rabbis. Jacob b. Aaron *Sasportas, among the first to oppose Shabbateanism, published his collection of anti-Shabbatean epistles under the title *Ẓiẓat Novel Ẓevi* (though it was proven recently that he re-edited some of his early letters to make them more anti-Shabbatean than they originally were). Later, anti-Shabbateans concentrated their efforts on discovering scholars with Shabbatean sympathies and bringing about their excommunication (*ḥerem*). Thus, Moses *Ḥagiz accused Moses Ḥayyim *Luzzatto of Shabbateanism, the same charge Jacob Emden leveled against Jonathan *Eybeschuetz. Both Luzzatto and Eybeschuetz were defended against the accusation by a number of supporters, and the controversies raged for decades.

In the second half of the 18th century, the newly founded ḥasidic movement was also suspected of heretical and Shabbatean tendencies. This suspicion, one of the causes for the unflaggingly intense opposition to the movement, led to the *ḥerem* brought against the Ḥasidim in 1772, a ban which was renewed many times in the next 40 years. The Ḥasidim were mainly accused of disregarding the importance of traditional Talmud study and of abusing the traditional scholars. Rarely did Ḥasidism's opponents clearly express their real suspicion—that the ḥasidic movement was a new version of the Shabbatean and Frankist movements—a suspicion which was the underlying reason for the vehemence of the various *ḥerem* declarations, in the anti-ḥasidic epistles, and in the collections of letters and special polemical works written by the *Mitnaggedim*. It is to be noted that very little material in the vast anti-ḥasidic literature is concerned with the basic ideas of Ḥasidism. The *Mitnaggedim* attacked the Ḥasidim because of the way they behaved, or the way they believed they behaved, almost totally disregarding the ideology of the new movement. In this omission the *Mitnaggedim* followed the tradition of epistolary polemical literature since the early Middle Ages.

For Polemics in the modern period see *Haskalah, *Reform, *Zionism. [Y.D.]

Bibliography: I. Davidson (ed.), Solomon ben Jeroham, *Milḥamot ha-Shem* (1934); D. J. Silver, *Maimonidean Criticism and the Maimonidean Controversy* (1965), incl. bibl.; A. Halkin, in: *Tarbiz*, 25 (1955/56), 413–28; J. Sarachek, *Faith and Reason, the Conflict over Rationalism of Maimonides* (1935); Baron, Social[2], 5 (1969), 82ff.; J. Shatzmiller, in: *Zion*, 34 (1969), 126–44; Baer, Toledot, passim; S. Z. Ḥ. Halberstam, *Kevuẓat ha-Mikhtavim* (1875); G. Scholem, in: *Sefer Bialik* (1934), 141–62; I. Tishby, in: *Perakim*, 1 (1967), 131–82; J. Katz, in: *Zion*, 16 (1951), 28–45; S. Ginzburg, *Rabbi Moshe Ḥayyim Luzzatto u-Venei Doro* (1937); I. Tishby (ed.), Jacob Sasportas, *Sefer Ẓiẓat Novel Ẓevi* (1954); M. A. Perlmutter, *Rabbi Yonatan Eybeschuetz* (1947); M. Wilensky, *Ḥasidim u-Mitnaggedim* (1970).

POLEMON II (d. 74 C.E.), king of Cilicia. The Judean princess, *Berenice, widow of *Herod of Chalcis, induced Polemon to undergo circumcision and marry her in an attempt to suppress rumors detrimental to her reputation. Polemon, with an eye to her wealth, accepted the proposal, but the marriage did not last long. Berenice deserted her husband, and the king, according to Josephus, "was relieved simultaneously of his marriage and of further adherence to the Jewish way of life" (Ant., 20:145–6). Polemon of Cilicia has been confused with Julius Polemon, king of Pontus from 37–63 C.E., who vistited *Agrippa I at Tiberias.

Bibliography: D. Magie, *Roman Rule in Asia Minor*, 2 (1950), 1407. [I.G.]

POLGAR, ALFRED (1873–1955), Austrian essayist and critic. One of Austria's foremost prose stylists and drama critics, Polgar was the son of a Viennese musician. Until 1925 he worked as a reporter and as drama critic for the Vienna *Montagsblatt*, but then moved to Berlin, where he contributed to such eminent periodicals as *Die Weltbuehne*. He returned to Vienna upon the Nazis' accession to power in Germany, but later fled to Paris. In 1940 he settled in the U.S. After 1949 he spent much of his time in Europe and died while on a visit to Zurich.

A prolific and subtle writer, Polgar produced many brilliant *feuilletons*, impressionistic sketches, reviews, parodies, satires, and elegant short essays and vignettes in the style of Peter *Altenberg. Polgar collaborated with Egon *Friedell on the witty satirical plays *Goethe im Examen* (1908) and *Soldatenleben im Frieden* (1910). One of several collections of his short stories appeared in 1912 under the title *Hiob*. Polgar's collected critical writings appeared as *Ja und Nein* (4 vols., 1926–27), followed in 1938 by *Handbuch des Kritikers*. In his years of exile and after the war Polgar was active as a translator, adapter, and cultural mediator.

Bibliography: K. Schuemann, *Im Bannkreis von Gesicht und Wirken* (1959), 133–70; F. Lennartz, *Deutsche Dichter und Schriftsteller unserer Zeit* (1959[8]), 591–3; H. Kesten, *Meine Freunde die Poeten* (1959), 79–84; H. Zohn, *Wiener Juden in der deutschen Literatur* (1964), 57–60. [H.Zo.]

POLIAKOV, LÉON (1910–), historian. Born in Saint Petersburg, Russia, Poliakov went to France in 1920. He was on the staff of the *Pariser Tageblatt* until 1939. During World War II he served with the French army. Participating in the establishment of the Centre de Documentation Juive Contemporaine, he became head of its research department after the war. In 1952 he was appointed research fellow at the Centre National de la Recherche Scientifique and in 1954 joined the Ecole Pratique des Hautes Etudes. Poliakov wrote extensively on the Holocaust and on anti-Semitism.

Two of his books have been translated into English—*Harvest of Hate* (1954) and volume I of his three-volume *History of Anti-Semitism* (1965). His other works include *Auschwitz* (1964), *Les banchieri Juifs et le Saint-Siège du xiii au xvii siècle* (1965), and *De l'antisionisme à l'antisemitisme* (1969). Poliakov also edited a number of works, including *La condition des Juifs en France sous l'occupation italienne* (1946) and, with Josef Wulf, *Das Dritte Reich und seine Diener; Dokumente* (1956) and *Das Dritte Reich und die Juden; Dokumente und Aufsaetze* (1955). [Ed.]

POLICE OFFENSES, offenses arising in connection with the prevention of public mischief and for the maintenance of public security, as laid down in the Bible, that have formed the basis for elaborate regulations in later periods of Jewish law. Thus, the biblical injunction against false weights and measures (Deut. 25:13–15) led to the appointment of special inspectors who were authorized not only to enter shops and ascertain the accuracy of weights and measures in use, but also to impose penalties, e.g., *floggings or *fines. Similarly, the biblical injunction against *fraud (Lev. 25:14, 17) and *oppression (Lev. 19:13) led to the prohibition of profiteering and to the appointment of special officers charged with the supervision of prices (cf. Yoma 9a); and profiteers too were liable to be flogged. *Gambling and betting were prohibited as if they were species of larceny, and so were such potentially injurious acts as hunting in populated areas or taking animals already captured in the trap of another (Yad, Gezelah 6:8–12). The biblical injunctions for the protection of animals (Deut. 22:4, 6–7; Ex. 23:5) gave rise to the prohibition against hurting any living creature (BM 32a, b), and led to the elaboration of rules for the prevention of collisions between loaded animals in the street and hence also between ships and vehicles (Yad, Roẓe'aḥ 13:11–12).

The injunction that you shall not bring bloodguilt on your house (Deut. 22:8) was interpreted as not limited to the traditional requirement of providing a *parapet for the roof lest anyone should fall from it, but as extending to any act or omission likely to endanger human life (Yad. loc. cit.). It is no excuse for a man to say that his conduct endangers himself too; even if he chooses to disregard his own safety, he cannot disregard that of others—and he is liable to be flogged if he does. Thus the supply or consumption of unclean or noxious food or water is prohibited (*ibid.*, 11:7–16) and so is the creation of any danger to the public (BK 27a–30a). There are also express provisions for the annual inspection of streets and thoroughfares by officers of the court to make sure they are not damaged by rain and are safe for traffic (Tosef. Shek 1:1). Where particular roads or journeys were dangerous, the court would appoint officers to accompany travelers and guard their safety; if they failed in watchfulness, the officers were regarded as if they had shed innocent blood (Yad. Evel 14:3). Where there were dangers of overcrowding or public licentiousness, court officers would mingle among the crowds to maintain law and order (Yad, Yom Tov 6:21).

The biblical prohibition against a woman putting on a man's clothing and vice versa (Deut. 22:5) may have served as the authority and pattern for later regulations governing dress and appearance. As dressing in the clothing of the opposite sex was regarded as conduct conducive to sexual perversion, so was dressing in the gentile fashion regarded as a first step toward assimilation. Sumptuary laws against extravagance and luxury became increasingly frequent, not only to prevent the following of the practices of gentiles (cf. Lev. 20:23), but also to ensure humility in walking before God (cf. Micah 6:8). Penalties were imposed mostly as fines, but we find also public denunciations (see *ḥerem*). In some places, regulations were also laid down to make certain dresses or robes obligatory, e.g., for judges and notables (*Takkanot Mehrin,* 530). Generally, the biblical injunction to appoint executive officers in addition to judges (Deut. 16:18) was interpreted as imposing a duty to attach to each court "men with sticks and rods, standing at the service of the judges, to patrol markets and streets, inspect shops, rectify prices and measures, and redress all injury: they act only on the orders of the court, and when they detect a breach of law, they bring it before the court for adjudication" (Yad, Sanhedrin 1:1). It appears that until the destruction of the Temple, petty offenses were not, in Jerusalem, brought before the ordinary criminal courts, but before two or three police courts (*dayyanei gezerot,* Ket. 13:1), who were sitting full time and therefore (in contradistinction to judges) entitled to remuneration (Ket. 105a).

Bibliography: M. Block, *Das mosaisch-talmudische Polizeirecht* (1879); Frankel, Mishnah; C. Roth, in: JQR, 18 (1927/28), 357–83; ET, 3 (1951), 163f.; J. R. Marcus, *The Jew in the Medieval World* (1960), 193–7. [H.H.C.]

POLISH, DAVID (1910–), U.S. Reform rabbi and Zionist leader. Polish, who was born in Cleveland, Ohio, was ordained by Hebrew Union College in 1934. From 1934 to 1939 he held a pulpit in Cedar Rapids, Iowa, where he organized a state-wide Zionist movement. Throughout the 1940s he was active in a variety of positions in the American Zionist movement. In 1950 Polish founded the Beth Emet Free Synagogue in Evanston, Illinois. There he introduced the *Seliḥot* services that are now used in many Reform congregations. He also helped found the Chicago Board of Rabbis, of which he became the first president. In 1969 he was chosen vice-president of the Central Conference of American Rabbis. His books include: *A Guide for Reform Jews* (1957), written with Frederic Doppelt, and *The Higher Freedom* (1965). [E.Gr.]

POLISH LITERATURE.

Biblical and Hebraic Influences. Translations of the Bible played an important part in the development of Polish as a literary language. Fron the early 14th century onward, the Old Testament—particularly the Psalms—provided a major source of poetical inspiration in Polish literature and culture. Some of the best-known of these Polish versions of the Scriptures were the 15th-century Queen Sophia Bible; the 14th-century Floriański Psalter; the Calvinist Brześć (Radziwill) Bible (1562); Szymon Budny's Nieświez Bible (1572); and Fr. Jakub Wujek's classic Catholic Bible (1593–99), which injected the greatest concentration of biblical imagery and expression into the Polish language. Polish Bibles from the 16th century onward were mainly the work of Protestants, who also produced many paraphrases of biblical books such as the Psalms. New translations have been produced in the 20th century, and there have also been a few Polish Jewish versions of Old Testament texts, notably Song of Songs (1922) by Juliusz Feldhorn (1901–1943), who was murdered by the Nazis; and complete Old Testaments by F. Aszkenazy (1927–30) and S. Spitzer (1937). In Polish literature proper, the influence of the Bible may be detected during and after the Renaissance era in works such as *Żywot Józefa z pokolenia żydowskiego* ("The Life of Joseph," 1545), a biblical interlude by Mikolaj Rej, the Calvinist "father of Polish literature" who also published a verse translation of Psalms (1546); and the *Kazania sejmowe* ("Parliamentary Sermons," 1597) of the Jesuit Piotr Skarga. The impact of the Old Testament was most evident in the outstanding Polish poet of the Renaissance, Jan Kochanowski, whose works include *Pieśń o potopie* ("The Song of the Flood," 1558), *Zuzanna* (1562), and *Treny* ("Lamentations," 1580; English selections, 1920). Kochanowski's sensitive and beautiful version of Psalms, *Psałterz Dawidów* (1578), was the finest poetical work of its time and served as a literary model until the 19th-century romantic period. Some later Psalters by his followers and imitators were Maciej Rybiński's *Psalmy monarchy i proroka św. Dawida* ("The Psalms of David, King and Prophet," 1598) and the paraphrase by Mikolaj Sęp-Szarzyński in *Rytmy* (1601). Some Polish writers were also interested in other books of the Bible, which they either translated or used as stylistic models. The staunchly Catholic poet and historian Wespazjan Kochowski celebrated the tenth anniversary of the battle of Vienna (in which King Jan III Sobieski defeated the Turks) with his *Psalmodia polska* ("Polish Psalmody," 1693), written in the form of biblical prose. There were also scores of dramatic works and interludes on biblical subjects belonging to the theatrical repertory of the Polish court from the 16th and 17th centuries onward.

Later Biblical Writing. Scriptural phraseology, syntax, and imagery constantly recur in the works of Poland's greatest writers, particularly in the romantic era. Some notable examples are Adam *Mickiewicz's *Księgi narodu polskiego i pielgrzymstwa polskiego* ("The Books of the Polish Nation and Pilgrimage," 1832), Juliusz Slowacki's *Anhelli* (1838), and Zygmunt Krasinski's *Psalmy przyszłości* ("Psalms of the Future," 1845). Cyprian Kamil Norwid ranks next with his *Żydowie Polscy* ("Polish Jews"), which summarizes the history of the Jews from the time of Moses until the era of the struggle of the Poles and Jews ("Maccabees") against their common oppressors. Biblical books such as Isaiah, Jeremiah, and Job; figures such as Cain and Abel, Moses, Samson, Saul, David, Judith, and Daniel; historic sites such as Mount Ararat and Babylon; and even objects such as Samson's pillar or the prophet's staff were, for centuries, the poetical stock-in-trade of many Polish writers. These include Kazimierz Brodziński, Stefan Witwicki, Kornel Ujejski, Maria Konopnicka, Wladislaw Belza, Kazimierz Przerwa-Tetmajer, Stanislaw Wyspiański, Jan Kasprowicz, Leopold Staff, and Jan Dobraczyński. After Poland lost her independence, writers used biblical themes to discuss the present in the guise of an ancient historical setting, this being the only means of presenting the slavery into which the Poles had been forced, without exposing the authors to the wrath of foreign oppressors. Polish poets found in the Bible the moral values required by a people condemned to slavery, contempt, and humiliation. Biblical and other Jewish figures had the same function as those drawn from Greek and Roman mythology in the dramas of Stanislaw Wyspiański (*Daniel*, 1907) and Karol Hubert Rostworowski; *Opowiesci biblijne* ("Biblical Tales," 1963) of Kosidowski had a vast sale even in post-World War II Communist Poland.

The Image of the Jew. Evidence of an unfriendly attitude toward the Jews may be found in Polish literature of the 16th and 17th centuries, as well as in Catholic polemical literature of the Reformation period. This was also the case with epigrams and satires of the so-called bourgeois literature, in the satirical *Worek Judaszów* ("Judas' Sack," 1600) by Sebastian Fabjan Klonowicz, who was mayor of Lublin, and in *Wyprawa żydowska na wojne* ("The Jewish War Expedition," 1606), a comedy by an anonymous author. In writings of this type there are sometimes echoes of anti-Jewish riots, as in *Taniec Rzeczypospolitej Polskiej* ("The Dance of the Polish Republic," 1647), a rhymed chronicle by Gabriel Krasiński which describes part of the student riots at Kazimierz, the Jewish district of Cracow.

Favorable Portrayals. A markedly different attitude governs works about Jews during the period of the so-called Four-Year Sejm (1788–92) and at the beginning of the 19th century, which appealed for tolerance toward the Jews (see *Poland). This also characterized the first Polish social novel about Jews, *Lejbe i Sióra* ("Leib and Sarah," 1821), by Julian Ursyn Niemcewicz. Polish folk poetry also mentions Jewish participation in the Kościuszko revolt, one instance being the song about Berek *Joselewicz, the commander of a squadron of Polish lancers who died a hero's death near Kock in 1809. The figure of the Jew and the Jewish problem both appear in the works of the great Polish romantic poets (Mickiewicz, Słowacki, and Z. Krasiński) and their imitators. Juliusz Słowacki portrayed the fate of the Jew as a human being—hated, alien, and condemned to shame, contempt, and death—in Judith, a character in his drama *Ksiądz Marek* ("Father Marek," 1843). Proud and conscious of her fate, she seeks revenge on her anti-Semitic persecutors. The third of the great romantics, Zygmunt Krasiński, symbolized the role of Jewish converts in the revolutionary movements of Europe in his historical drama *Nieboska Komedia* ("The Ungodly Comedy," 1835). The events preceding the outbreak of the November insurrection (1830) and its collapse inspired a rich political and polemical literature dealing with the problem of the Jews. Works of this type were *Au People d'Israël* (1832), a French appeal by the historian Joachim Lelewel, who also wrote the booklet *Sprawa żydowska w roku 1859* ("The Jewish Question in 1859," 1860), defending the Jews against anti-Semitic attack; and papers by the Jew Ludwik Ozeas Lubliner author of *Des Juifs en Pologne* (1839), *Obrona Żydów* ("The Defense of the Jews," 1858), and *Do Polaków Izraelitów w Polsce* ("To Polish Israelites in Poland," 1862). Pro-Jewish works were also written by other romantics, such as Cyprian Norwid, Wladislaw Syrokomla, Mieczyslaw Romanowski, Aleksander Teofil Lenartowicz, and Wlodzimierz Wolski. Their sympathetic references to the Jews were often interwoven with others about Polish suffering under the foreign oppressor. In 1883 the poet Wladislaw Belza published poems of this kind about the Jews in his anthology *Żydzi w poezyi polskiej—głosy poetów o Żydach* ("Jews in Polish Poetry—Voices of the Poets on the Jews," 1906²), a work inspired by the Jewish assimilationist Agudas Achim society. The short-lived rapprochement between Poles and Jews before and after the outbreak of the January Revolution (1861–63) was reflected in poems by some Poles, such as Ludwik Mieroslawski, a nationalist politician and general, and in the verse of Jews like Henryk Merzbach and M. Epstein, who also participated in the uprising; but these were phenomena of minor literary importance.

The Jews as a Social Phenomenon. The deep changes in political outlook after the defeat of 1863 and the attitude adopted by literature of the so-called Positivist period toward everyday contemporary themes made Polish poets increasingly aware of the Jews and the Jewish problem, not only from the Polish point of view, but also as a specific, characteristic feature of contemporary society. The role of Jews in science, industry, commerce, and banking was reflected in Polish literature of the period. The radical development of Polish socialism on the one hand and of Polish nationalism on the other made the Jew a stock character—artisan, merchant, scholar, politician, journalist, or yeshivah student—and writers portrayed him according to their specific outlook. Polish poets, far from despising the Jews, pitied and defended them in their works. This was especially true of the Warsaw urban poet Wiktor Gomulicki, although such writers tended to overlook the Jewish world discovered by playwrights and prose writers. However, sympathetic insight was evident in the works of Poland's greatest poetess, Maria Konopnicka, who condemned anti-Semitic outrages in one of her novellas, and in *Żydzi* (1843), a play by Józef Korzeniowski. Much space was also devoted to the Jewish problem by prose writers such as Eliza, *Orzeskowa, Klemens *Junosza, Józef Rogosz, and Ignacy Maciejowski (Sewer). Another leading writer, Boleslaw Prus, introduced two Jewish figures in *Lalka* (3 vols., 1887–89), the first important Polish realistic novel. Szlangbaum, a Jewish stereotype, is avaricious, ruthless, self-abasing before the rich, and self-confident with the poor, sacrificing everything for the sake of business; but the second Jew, Dr. Szuman, partly resembles the romantic hero of the novel. In his great historical novel *Faraon* ("The Pharaoh," 3 vols., 1895–96), set in ancient Egypt, Prus also alludes to the Jewish situation in contemporary Poland. In his weekly column in a Warsaw newspaper, Prus displayed a contradictory attitude, either attacking the Jews for their financial skill and resourcefulness or praising them for the same abilities, through which the Jews, unlike Polish Christians, served the interests of society in general. The Jew as a revolutionary social innovator was a figure created by the great radical prose writer Stefan Żeromski. In his novel *Ludzie bezdomni* ("The Homeless," 2 vols., 1900) he depicted the role of a Jewish physician in initiating the fight for reforms in stagnant Polish society. Żeromski's last novel, *Przedwiośnie* ("Early Spring," 1925), aimed against the right-wing Pilsudski regime, assigned a much more important task to the Jews as the co-authors of the Polish Communist movement. In Communism Żeromski saw a force capable of redeeming Poland's disinherited youth.

Negative Portrayals. A different tendency also made its appearance from the late 19th century, some writers setting out to prove the destructive role of the Jews in the social, political, economic, and cultural life of Poland. Wladislaw Stanislaw Reymont (1867–1925) drew an unfavorable picture of the Jews in his novel *Ziemia obiecana* ("The Promised Land," 1899), where he showed the different cross sections of industrial life in Lodz during the period of czarist occupation. Both Jewish and German capitalists exploit the Polish working classes, which are thus denied the benefits of a native capitalism. Other hostile assessments were presented by Teodor Jeske-Choiński, a mediocre novelist and critic who expressed reactionary, clericalist opinions, and Roman Dmowski, the ideologist of Polish nationalism and a leader of the National Democratic movement, who played a major role in the propagation of anti-Semitism. Aleksander Świętochowski, once broad-minded and progressive, joined the conservative, anti-Semitic groups of writers, as did the poet Andrzej Niemojewski, who edited *Myśl niepodległa.* In his youth Niemojewski had been a revolutionary democrat, but in his later years he joined the extreme reactionary, nationalist circles frequented by Adolf Nowaczyński (Neuwert), a playwright and pamphleteer of Jewish birth. Many anti-Semites were active as essayists and literary critics, although scarcely anyone of major importance campaigned against the Jews.

LATER TENDENCIES. After Poland attained independence and national sovereignty in 1918, new forms of social and artistic life came into being. At the same time the whole basis of political thought underwent a change under the impact of the new conflicts in a society liberated from foreign oppression. Polish poetry, which was revitalized during the years 1918–39, also echoed the voice of Polish Jewry. Some poets dedicated works to the Jews, whom they considered to be fellow citizens sharing common ideals determined by the same political program. In two pre-World War II poems, *"Księżyc ulicy Pawiej"* ("The Moon of Pawia Street") and *"Na śmierć rewolucjonisty"* ("On the Death of a Revolutionary"), Wladislaw Broniewski, a communist, sympathetically portrayed the life of the Jewish poor and the struggle of the Jewish revolutionaries who died in the cause of the Polish working classes. In his moving *Ballady i romanse*, written after a pogrom organized by the Nazis, Broniewski expressed his admiration for the Jews, while his *"Pamięci Szmula Zygielbojma"* commemorated Samuel *Zygelbojm who committed suicide in London in order to draw world attention to the destruction of the Jewish people by the Nazis. Artur Oppman (Or-Ot), a Warsaw poet, eulogized a certain Rabbi Jawor who chose to remain within the walls of the embattled Polish capital. Among its citizens he enjoyed "the credit of the ancient sons of Judah, the servants of Jehovah, and of the bards and knights." On the other hand, another outstanding poet, Konstanty Ildefons Galczynski, sometimes described the Jews in a satirical manner in poems such as his *"Sonata księżycowa rodziny Kon"* ("The Moonlight Sonata of the Kon Family"), *"Ballada o Aronku"* ("The Ballad of Little Aaron"), and *"Wilno, ulica Niemecka"* ("Vilna, the German Street"). Wanda Melcer's *Czarny ląd* ("The Black Land," 1896), a series of reportages written after a visit to the Jewish section of Warsaw, stressed the exoticism of Jewish customs, clothing, speech, behavior, and way of life. This account was not written for the sake of cheap sensation, but indicated the many aspects of a social problem.

PROTESTS AGAINST FASCISM. The upsurge of Polish anti-Semitism immediately before the outbreak of World War II found reflection in the satirical poetry of Antoni *Slonimski, whose *Dwa końce świata* ("Two Ends of the Earth," 1937) attacked racism and Fascism. Many leading Polish writers dealt with issues involving the Jews and fought anti-Semitic manifestations. They included members of the *Przedmieście* group founded in 1933: Jerzy Kornacki, Helena Boguszewska, Pola Gojawiczyńska, and Halina Górska. Allied with them were other writers and journalists who worked for weeklies such as *Oblicze Dnia, Epoka, Czarno na białym, Sygnały, Poprostu, Lewar,* and *Dziennik Popularny.* Weeklies ranged on the opposing side included *Prosto z mostu* and *Merkurjusz Ordynaryny.* In the battle against Fascism and anti-Semitism during the years preceding World War II many satirical poets took an active part. Among them were Jewish writers such as Antoni Slonimski, Juljan *Tuwim, Leon Pasternak (1910–1969), Stanislaw Jerzy *Lec, Jan Brzechwa, Wlodzimierz Slobodnik (1900–), Lucian *Szenwald, Jerzy Jurandot, and Jerzy Kamil Weintraub (1916–1943); and non-Jewish writers such as Artur Marya Swinarski, and Eduard Szymański. After the defeat of the Nazi invaders, many Polish writers—Jews and non-Jews—devoted books to the "Final Solution" of the Jewish problem, as put into effect during the German occupation. Events in Poland two decades later, after the Israel-Arab Six-Day War of 1967, were reflected in "Israel" (1968), an outstanding poem by the émigré Polish writer Kazimierz Wierzyński, a member of the old *Skamander* literary group, and Czeslaw Milosz, émigré Polish writer.

The Jewish Contribution. Since Polish Jewry was almost entirely Yiddish-speaking until the early part of the 20th century, Jews who wrote in Polish were at first comparatively few. The pioneer of Jewish literary activity in Polish was the converted essayist Juljan *Klaczko. Two writers who followed his lead later in the 19th century were Wladislaw Ordon (Wladislaw Szancer, 1848–1914), a tragic figure of humble origin whose poems were once highly regarded, and the poet and historian Alkar (Aleksander Kraushar, 1843–1931), who translated works by *Heine. By the beginning of the 20th century, Jews had become more active in Polish literature, their participation being reflected in the symbolic figure of the Jewess Rachel in Stanislaw Wyspiański's drama *Wesele* ("The Wedding" 1901). The Jewish share in Poland's cultural life gained momentum during the first two decades of the 20th century, and particularly after the achievement of national independence following World War I. Those representing this trend include the poets Franciszka Arnsteinowa (1865–1942), Henryk Balk (1901–1941), Mieczysaw Braun, Julia Dickstein-Wielczynska (1880?–1943), Juliusz Feldheim (1901–1943), Zuzanna Ginczanka (1917–1944), Bruno *Jasieński, Cezary Jellenta (Napoleon Hirszband, 1861–1935), Boleslaw *Leśmian, Stefan Napierski (Stefan Marek Eiger, 1899–1949), Artur Prędski (Artur Pfeffer, 1900–1941), S. R. Stande, Jan Stur (Hersz Feingold, 1895–1923), L. Szenwald, and J. K. Weintraub. Among the novelists were Leo Belmont (Leopold Blumenfeld, 1865–1940), Henryk Drzewiecki, Halina Górska, Gustawa Jarecka (1908–1942), Alfred Aleksander Konar (Aleksander Kinderfreund, 1862–1940?), Bruno *Schulz, and Bruno Winawer. The last also wrote plays, as did Jasieński. Three early Jewish literary critics and historians were Samuel *Adalberg, Henryk *Biegeleisen, and Wilhelm *Feldman. Many of these writers died during the Nazi occupation of Poland, and among them also the famous children's writer and educator Janusz *Korczak. Both between the world wars and after 1945 Jews, or men and women of Jewish origin, continued to make an important contribution as poets, playwrights, novelists, short story writers, and literary historians and critics. Some who were active before World War II resumed their careers in Poland after the German defeat. Leading poets in this category were Jan Brzechwa, Mieczyslaw *Jastrun, Stanislaw Jerzy Lec, Tadeusz *Peiper, Tadeusz Różewicz, Antoni *Slonimski, Arnold Slucki, Juljan Tuwim, Aleksander *Wat, Adam Ważyk, Józef *Wittlin, Wiktor Woroszylski, and Stanislaw *Wygodzki. Of these, Slonimski maintained his independence of the Communist Party line on Zionism, while Wygodzki left Poland for Israel after the Six-Day War of 1967. Other poets included Stefania Grodzieńska (1914–), Leon Pasternak, Józef Prutkowski (Józef Nacht, 1915–), Wlodimierz Slobodnik, and Irena Tuwim (1900–), Juljan Tuwim's sister. Two major playwrights were the émigré satirist Marjan *Hemar and the ex-Zionist convert Roman *Brandstaetter; others included Benedykt Hertz and Jerzy Lutowski (1923–). Kazimierz *Brandys, Adolf *Rudnicki, and Julian *Stryjkowski were leading novelists, the last specializing in stories of pre-World War I Jewish life; and others included Michal Maksymilian Borwicz (Maksymilian Boruchowicz, 1911–), whose anthology, *Pieśń ujdzie cało* ("The Song Will Prevail," 1947), contained Jewish songs of the occupation era, as well as Irena Krzywicka (1904–) and Stanislaw Lem (1921–). Hanna Mortkowicz-Olczakowa (1905–1967), who in 1936 published *W Palestynie: obrazy i zagadnienia* ("In Palestine: Pictures and Problems") on the situation of Palestinian Jewry, later wrote the biographical *Janusz Korczak* (1949; *Mister Doctor,* 1965). Some Jewish authors in other genres were the screenwriter Józef Hen (1923–), the émigré author and actor Henryk Grynberg, the satirist Karol Szpalski (1908–1963), and Krystyna Żywulska (1918–), author of *Przeżyłam Oświęcim* ("I Survived Auschwitz," 1946).

Polish Jews were also prominent as literary historians and critics and as editors and publishers of important literary reviews which influenced cultural life, notably *Wiadomości Literackie* (edited by M. Grydzewski). Juljusz Kleiner (1866–1957), who wrote many literary monographs and standard textbooks on Polish literature, trained a whole generation of literary critics, including scholars such as Henryk Balk and Henryk Szyper (1900–1949). Some later writers of eminence in this field were Jan Kott (1914–), whose works on Shakespeare were translated into many languages; Henryk Markiewicz (1922–), a leading Marxist literary theorist; Maria Renata Mayenowa (1910–); Henryk Wolpe (1899–1967); and Wiktor Weintraub (1908–), who became professor of Polish literature at Harvard University, U.S. Other authorities on Polish literary history and criticism included Rafal Marcel Blueth (1891–1939), Emil Breiter (1886–1943), Wilhelm Fallek (1888–1941), Ludwik Fryde (1912–1942), Dawid Jakub Hopensztand (1904–1943), Roman Karst (1911–), Jerzy Pomianowski (1921–), Artur Sandauer (1913–), and Henryk Vogler (1911–). A number of major writers and critics were also distinguished translators.

Bibliography: *Udział żydów w kulturze,* 2 vols. (1938); J. Feldhorn, *Literatura polska wieku XVI a Żydzi* (1929); K. Bartosiewicz, *Antysemityzm w literaturze polskiej XVI i XVII wieków* (1940); T. Jeske-Choiński, *Żyd w powieści polskiej* (1914); W. Fallek, in: *Pamiętnik zjazda naukowego im. Jana Kochanowsskiego...* (1931), 383–471; K. Dresdner, in: *Miesięcznik Żydowski,* 2 pt. 1 (1932), 399–426.

[Ed.]

Alphabetical List of Entries including Capsule Articles. The individuals whose names are marked with an asterisk in the list below form the subjects of articles in their appropriate alphabetical position in the Encyclopaedia.

***ADALBERG, SAMUEL** (1868–1939), literary historian and folklorist.

***BIEGELEISEN, HENRYK** (1855–1934), literary historian and ethnographer.

***BRANDSTAETTER, ROMAN** (1906–), poet and playwright.

***BRANDYS, KAZIMIERZ** (1916–), novelist and author.

BRAUN (Braunstein), MIECZYSLAW (1900–1941), poet. Braun published verse collections, some of which reflect the industrial society in his native Lodz: *Rzemiosła* ("Craftsmanship," 1926), *Przemysły* ("Industry," 1928), *Zywe stronice* ("Living Pages," 1936), *Sonety* (1937), and *Poezja pracy, Wiersze wybrane* ("Poetry of Toil, Selected Verse," 1938). He died of typhus in the Warsaw Ghetto.

BRZECHWA, JAN (Jan Wiktor Leśman; 1900–), poet. A lawyer by profession, Brzechwa wrote satirical works and poems for children and adults in the style of the folk song or fairy tale. His works include *Oblicza zmyślone* (1926), *Talizmany* (1929), and *Wiersze wybrane* (1955), collected verse, and *Poszla w las nauka* (1956), a fairy tale.

DRZEWIECKI, HENRYK (Hercel Rosenbaum, 1902–1937), novelist and critic. An avowed Communist, Drzewiecki wrote essays and reviews advocating revolution in order to abolish Poland's economic misery. His controversial novel *Kwaśniacy* (1934) greatly influenced Polish proletarian literature and the writer only escaped imprisonment by fleeing first to Paris and then to the U.S.S.R. He was executed during the Stalinist purges of the late 1930s. He was rehabilitated in 1956.

***FELDMAN, WILHELM** (1866–1919), author and literary critic.

GÓRSKA (Endelman), HALINA (1898–1942), novelist and social worker. Active in the League for the Defense of the Rights of Man, Halina Górska fought anti-Semitism and helped to found the Socialist periodical *Sygnały.* Her four major novels were *Nad czarną wodą* ("Over the Black Water," 1931), *Chłopcy z ulic miasta* ("Boys from the Streets," 1934), *Druga brama* ("The Other Gate," 1935), and the two-part *Barak płonie* ("The Burning Hut," 1937–39). She was arrested and shot by the Gestapo.

GRYDZEWSKI (Grytzhendler), MIECZYSLAW (1894–1970), literary editor. Grydzewski played an important part in Polish literary and intellectual life between the world wars as editor of the weekly *Wiadomości Literackie* (1924–39) and of the monthly *Skamander* (1935–39). He also ran the French-language monthly *La Pologne littéraire* (1926–). An exile after 1939, he edited (in London) the Polish émigré weekly *Wiadomości* and published literary essays such as *Henryk Dąbrowski* (1945).

GRYNBERG, HENRYK (1936–), author and actor. World War II memories and the European Holocaust dominate his *Ekipa "Antygona"* ("The Crew of the *Antigone,*" 1963), collected stories, and the haunting *Żydowska wojna* (1965; *Child of the Shadows,* 1969). Grynberg's novella *Buszujący po drogach* ("The Catcher on the Roads," 1967) denounced officially inspired postwar anti-Semitism. A member of the Warsaw State Jewish Theater, he remained in the West after the company's 1967 season in New York.

***HEMAR (Hescheles), MARIAN** (1901–), a playwright and satirist.

HERTZ, BENEDYKT (1872–1952), author. Transposing social and political themes into the animal kingdom, Hertz published allegorical works that display keen observation and a gift for comedy. These include *Bajki* (1903), *Bajki i satyry* (1911), and *Bajki minionych dni* (1919), collections of fables; and plays such as *Szkice dramatyczne* (1910).

***JASIEŃSKI (Zyskind), BRUNO** (1901–1939), poet, novelist, and playwright.

***JASTRUN (Agatstein), MIECZYSLAW** (1903–), poet, essayist, and translator.

***KLACZKO, JULJAN** (1825–1906), literary historian, essayist, and Hebrew poet.

***KORCZAK, JANUSZ (Henryk Goldszmidt,** 1878–1942), author, educator, and physician.

***LEC, STANISLAW JERZY (Stainslaw Jerzy de Tusch-Letz;** 1909–1966), poet.

***LEŚMIAN (Leśman), BOLESLAW** (1878–1937), poet.

NOWACZYNSKI, ADOLF (1876–1944), playwright and satirist. The son of a Catholic aristocrat and of a Jewess, Nowaczyński (who used the pen name Neuwert) joined the right-wing, anti-Semitic pamphleteers and wrote many satirical attacks on the Jews and the Polish bourgeoisie. His historical dramas include *Wielki Fryderyk* ("Frederick the Great," 1910), *Pułaski w Ameryce* ("Pułaski in America," 1917), and *Cezar i Człowiek* ("Cesare Borgia and Copernicus," 1937). Nowaczyński was killed during the anti-German Warsaw Uprising.

***PEIPER, TADEUSZ** (1891–), poet and literary theorist.

RÓŻEWICZ, TADEUSZ (1921–), poet. The terrors of the Nazi occupation dominate Różewicz' earlier verse collections, such as *Niepokój* ("Anxiety," 1947). An outstanding representative of his generation, he published more than 20 books of poetry, plays, stories, and satires, including *Czas który idzie* ("The Coming Time," 1951) and *Głos anonima* ("The Anonymous Voice," 1961), poems, and *Kartoteka* ("The File,"1961), a play influenced by Beckett and Ionesco.

***RUDNICKI, ADOLF** (1912–), novelist and author.

***SCHULZ, BRUNO** (1892–1942), novelist.

***SLONIMSKI, ANTONI** (1895–), poet.

STANDE, STANISLAW RYSZARD (1897–1939), poet and translator. Stande's numerous verse collections were political salvoes for Communism and range from *Młoty* ("Hammers," 1921) to *Nasz krok* ("Our Step," 1937). From 1931 he was an exile in the U.S.S.R., where he joined the editorial board of the monthly

Internatsionalnaya Literatura. During the Stalinist purges of the late 1930s Stande died in prison.
***STERN, ANATOL** (1899–1968), poet.
***STRYJKOWSKI (Stark), JULJAN** (1905–), novelist and journalist.
SZENWALD, LUCJAN (1909–1944), poet and translator. Szenwald wrote revolutionary verse on themes such as the Nazi peril and the Spanish Civil War, outstanding for its cultural breadth and technical virtuosity. He also translated many works by leading foreign authors. *Z ziemi gościnnej do Polski* ("From the Friendly Land to Poland," 1944) appeared in the year of Szenwald's death in action with the Red Army. A posthumous selection of his works was *Pisma wybrane* (1955).
***TUWIM, JULJAN** (1894–1953), poet.
***WAT, ALEKSANDER (Szymon Chwat,** 1900–1967), poet, author, and translator.
WAŻYK (Wagman), ADAM (1905–), poet and novelist. A member of the *Awangarda* group, he published poems and prose and coedited the "New Art" *Almanach Nowej Sztuki* (1924–25). After World War II, Ważyk coedited *Kuźnica* and *Twórczość* and wrote many verse collections, plays, novels, and essays. His *Poemat dla dorosłych* ("Poem for Adults," 1956) heralded Poland's anti-Stalinist campaign.
WINAWER, BRUNO (1883–1944), playwright and novelist. A Warsaw physicist, Winawer wrote many successful comedies in the style of G. B. Shaw. His belief that technical progress was the basis for social and political change found expression in his novels and in plays such as *Roztwór profesora Pytla* ("Professor Pytel's Chemical Solution," 1919) and *R. H. Inżynier* ("R. H. the Engineer," 1923).
***WITTLIN, JÓZEF** (1896–), poet, author, and translator.
WOROSZYLSKI, WIKTOR (1927–), poet editor, and translator. Born in Grodno, Woroszylski began writing in 1945 and was chief editor of the literary weekly *Nowa Kultura* (1956–57). His works include the verse collections *Ojczyzna* ("Fatherland," 1953) and *Wiersze i poematy wybrane* (1955); *Noc komunarda* ("Night of the Communards," 1949); and a comprehensive study of the Soviet poet Mayakovski (1965). He also published translations from Russian literature.
***WYGODZKI, STANISLAW** (1907–), poet and author.

POLITICS. Introduction. Jewish involvement in national politics in the various countries in which they settled dates from the period of Jewish emancipation at the end of the 18th and the first half of the 19th century. In fact, personalities such as Joseph *Nasi, duke of Naxos, and Solomon *Ashkenazi held powerful positions in Ottoman politics in the late Middle Ages; Jewish ministers held office in medieval Spain; and Jews served as court advisers to various rulers in Holland, Germany, and Sweden. Nevertheless, professing Jews entered representative institutions of modern states only at a much later date. Until the Emancipation, Jews who were eager to hold political office were generally obliged to content themselves with participation in local government (as in Russia) or to convert to Christianity. The political emancipation of the Jews came in the U.S. from the late 18th century and in parts of Western Europe it was effected soon after the outbreak of the French Revolution. Thus, in Holland, Moses *Asser and Jonas Daniel *Meyer were appointed in 1797 to the legislative council and state council and, in Venice, following the overthrow of the oligarchy, the elected municipal council contained three Jewish members. In France and Germany, Jews were still generally excluded from political office but, even after the onset of reaction at the end of the Napoleonic Wars, it was clear that Jewish emancipation could not be long delayed. Soon after the 1848 revolutions in Europe, Jews were permitted to become members of representative institutions in nearly all major European states, outside the Russian Empire.

In English-speaking countries other than Britain and Canada, Jewish entry into political life developed more rapidly than elsewhere. The small Jewish community in the United States enthusiastically supported the revolutionary cause, and in 1775 Francis *Salvador was elected to the South Carolina Provincial Congress, probably the first Jew to be elected to a representative assembly in modern times. The Declaration of Independence, issued the following year, affirmed the principle of equality and Jews were freely admitted into all American legislative bodies from that time onward. No restrictions ever existed on Jewish political activities in Australia and South Africa, and Jewish pioneers in these territories were prominent in public affairs, as mayors of cities, legislators, and, in the case of Sir Julius *Vogel and Vabian Solomon (see *Solomon family), as prime ministers. On the other hand, in Canada and Great Britain, where Jews received the right to serve as representatives in parliament in 1832 and 1851, respectively, they had previously been refused this right because they could not swear "on the true faith of a Christian," as the oath required.

Once admitted to parliament, Jews rapidly achieved top government posts in the democracies outside America and rose to ministerial rank in France in the 1850s (Achille *Fould), Holland in the 1860s (Michael *Godefroy), Australia in the 1870s (Sir Julius Vogel), Britain in the 1880s (Henry de *Worms), and Italy at the turn of the 20th century (Luigi *Luzzatti). On the other hand, professing Jews were generally deprived of ministerial status in Germany and Austria, but there was no discrimination against converts, and Franz Klein, Austrian minister of justice, was the only unconverted Jew to become a minister in a Central European national government before 1918. In America, on the other hand, Jews were not victims of discrimination, but neither were they as a rule sufficiently integrated into American society to participate in national politics.

One important reason why Jews did not hold ministerial posts in many states, especially before World War I, was that Jewish politicians were generally numbered among the opposition radical parties of the center and left. This was particularly true of Germany and Austria where, following the upheavals after World War I, a number of Jews who had been prominent in the Socialist parties assumed senior government positions. The same situation proved true of France and Britain, where Socialist administrations brought Jews into cabinets, but conservative governments rarely included any Jewish members. Thus, in France all three Jewish prime ministers professed varying shades of socialism, and in England, of ten professing Jews to become members of British cabinets (up to 1970), only Sir Keith *Joseph was a Conservative. A similar trend was noticeable elsewhere.

A number of reasons have been advanced for the Jewish tendency toward radical parties. One of the most obvious is that liberal and left-wing political groups have generally been far less hostile to underprivileged newcomers (as Jews generally were) than conservative parties. The Right associated itself with the Church, the establishment, and social tradition—three concepts with which Jews had no connection—and was frequently anti-Semitic, while the radical groups, committed to challenge the establishment and alter tradition, were obviously more attractive to Jewish voters and prospective politicians alike. This reason also explains why Jews found advancement in left-wing parties much easier than in rightist ones (e.g., Ferdinand *Lassalle, Eduard *Bernstein, Leon *Blum, and others). Even in 1970 it was as true as at the beginning of the 20th century, that Jews in Western Europe were found mainly in the Socialist and Liberal parties and in the United States in the Democratic Party.

In pre-revolutionary Russia Jews were officially discriminated against and deprived of the opportunity to air their grievances democratically. Many of them, particularly young intellectuals who did not choose to emigrate overseas or join the Zionist movement, were impelled toward revolution. The Socialist revolutionaries and both Menshevik and Bolshevik factions of the Social Democrats seemed to be the only real alternative to the autocracy of the czars, which openly professed anti-Semitism. Many middle-class Jews in Russia did vote for the liberal Constitutional Democratic (Kadet) Party, but many more supported political groups which sought not to reform, but to destroy the existing regime. As a result, a significant proportion of the Social Democratic party consisted of the Jewish *Bund, and among the leaders of the general revolutionary parties the number of Jews was also disproportionately high.

Undoubtedly, Socialist doctrine, with its emphasis on equality and the destruction of the ruling classes, had a considerable appeal to Jewish intellectuals fighting against discrimination. This proved true not only in Russia, but in other European countries amid the convulsions at the end of World War I. Jews practically dominated the short-lived Communist regimes in Hungary (Béla Kun) and Bavaria (Kurt *Eisner), and it is reasonable to assume that this fact contributed to their quick downfall, since they lacked support in the general population. They were murdered or forced into exile when the counterrevolutionaries took control. After World War II Jews were again prominent at the head of East European Communist regimes (*Rakosi became the party leader in Hungary, *Minc and *Berman leading members of the Polish Communist regime under Bierut, and a number of Jews held key ministries in Czechoslovakia). This was largely a result of the fact that during the Stalin period Moscow could rely more on Soviet-trained old Communists of the satellite countries, among whom Jews played a prominent part. These Jews, however, did not reflect the general political attitude of the Jewish population in those countries and ultimately, when the Stalinist regimes crumbled there, they mostly disappeared or were openly attacked, frequently with anti-Semitic allusions (particularly in Poland and Czechoslovakia). In the Soviet Union the number of Jews in the top leadership sharply declined from the great Stalinist purges of the 1930s onward. In contrast to the prominent position of individual Jews in the Communist movement, Jews were never active in other totalitarian regimes and hardly any right-wing dictatorships included Jewish ministers. Clearly, Jews could not be expected to support regimes whose policy was specifically anti-Semitic, and in other dictatorships not characterized by anti-Semitism, the authorities were nonetheless reluctant to number Jews in their party in order not to cause offense to anti-Semitic elements.

An important issue connected with the involvement of Jews in politics is the degree to which Jewish and national interests have clashed. In Germany most leading Jews generally accepted the principle that German national interests were of paramount importance (e.g., Levin *Goldschmidt), and were anxious to prove their loyalty to the state in the face of attacks by anti-Semites. Furthermore, Jewish politicians, with very few exceptions—mostly Zionists—were assimilationists and had no interest in Jewish affairs. Most Jewish Socialist politicians in Germany as well as Austria rejected Judaism and, either by converting to Christianity or professing atheism, demonstrated their detachment from any Jewish interests. On the other hand, in English-speaking countries, where Jews were less subject to anti-Semitic pressures and were not required to prove their social integration by assimilation, Jewish politicians were frequently prepared to oppose government policies even in face of accusations of "dual loyalty." In the United States and Great Britain Jewish political leaders repeatedly pressed their governments to take steps to stop anti-Semitic excesses in Central and Eastern Europe and help Jewish immigration and settlement in Palestine. Later, in the United States, Jews were also in the forefront of demands upon the government to increase its assistance to Israel in the face of Arab threats. In supporting Israel, Jewish politicians in English-speaking countries often clashed openly not only with the government of their country but also with their parties as, e.g., Labor MPs in Britain during the Sinai Campaign (1956) or Jewish supporters of De Gaulle in France after the Six-Day War of 1967. Jewish politicians in South Africa generally accepted Israel's clear stand at the U.N. against their government's apartheid policy. However, the degree to which Jewish politicians canvassed Jewish issues often tended to reflect the political advantage to be gained by it. Jewish politicians in New York City have an interest in the large Jewish vote; those in most parts of Europe are more conscious of the anti-Semites. Nevertheless, though Jewish interests have been pressed hard on occasion, Jews rarely organized themselves for solely political purposes and have in most instances denied the existence of a Jewish political interest. In some East European countries, before World War II, many Jews were elected to parliament as Jews, i.e., as representatives of the Jewish community or of Jewish parties, and in such cases there was no question of conflicting loyalties. In Hapsburg Austria-Hungary Jews had the choice of voting for the assimilationist Socialists, many of whose leaders were Jewish, or the Jewish, i.e., Zionist Party, while before and after World War I Jews from different political parties united to defend the Jews from state persecution. Although these groups never had substantial influence in general politics, they played an important part in maintaining the unity of the Jewish communities and providing a forum for airing Jewish grievances. [Ed.]

Australia. No discrimination existed against Jews in Australia and they played an important part in the early development of the Australian colonies. As a result, Jews were identified with Australian political life from the first years of self-government. The first Jew to be elected to an Australian legislative body was Sir Saul *Samuel, who became a member of the New South Wales legislative council in 1854. He was joined by Jacob Montefiore, who was elected in 1856 while the first Jewish members of the Victoria legislative assembly were Nathaniel Levi who was elected in 1860, Charles Dyte who represented Ballarat East from 1864 to 1871 and championed miners rights on the Ballarat goldfields, and J. F. Levien, who was a member of the Victoria parliament for over 30 years. Other prominent figures included Judah Moss Solomon (see *Solomon family) who represented Adelaide in the South Australian parliament from 1858 to 1874, Edward Cohen (1822–1877) who represented East Melbourne from 1864 until his death, and Ephraim Zox (1837–1897) who succeeded him as member for East Melbourne. Jewish representation in the 19th-century Australian parliament was out of proportion to their total number and in Adelaide where the Jewish population was only 500 there were four Jewish members of the legislative assembly (Judah Moss Solomon, Emanuel Solomon, Vabian Solomon, and Lewis Cohen). Four Jews also held ministerial posts in Australian colonial governments: Sir Saul Samuel was minister of finance and trade, Edward Cohen served as commissioner of customs, Sir Julian *Salomons became vice-president of the New South Wales executive council, while Vabian Solomon was premier of South Australia for a short time in 1899.

When the first Australian federal parliament met in Melbourne in 1901 there were three Jewish members, Vabian and Elias Solomon, and Pharez Phillips. However, few Jews were subsequently elected to the Australian federal parliament, prominent exceptions being Senator Sam *Cohen, who was deputy leader of the Australian Labor Party, and Max Falstein. Many Jews played an important part in the various state parliaments, however, particularly in Victoria where several rose to the rank of minister, among them Theodore *Fink, minister without portfolio, Henry

Isaac Cohen who held several ministerial appointments, Harold Edward Cohen who was minister of public instruction and solicitor general, and in New South Wales Abram *Landa who was successively minister of labor, housing, and cooperative societies. In addition, Matthew Moss was a minister in the government of Western Australia and Sir Asher Joel was a member of the New South Wales Legislative Council. Two Jews also acquired distinction as speakers of parliaments, Sir Daniel Levy being speaker of the New South Wales parliament and Sir Archie Michaelis was speaker of the Victorian parliament. Most distinguished of all was Sir Isaac *Isaacs, chief justice of Australia, who was governor-general of Australia from 1931 to 1936, the first Australian-born governor-general and the first Jewish governor-general of any British Dominion territory. [I.SOL.]

Austria. Although a few Jews were prominent in Austrian political society in the 17th and 18th centuries as court advisors to Hapsburg monarchs, Jews were not generally allowed to hold political posts until after the reforms which followed the outbreak of the 1848 Revolution. Five Jews were elected to the first revolutionary parliament of that year: Adolph *Fischhof, Joseph Goldmark, Abraham Halpern, Isaac Noah *Mannheimer, and Rabbi Dov Ber *Meisels. The suppression of the revolutionary movement, however, led to the renewal of restrictions on Jews and they were denied the right to hold government or municipal offices. These rights were restored in 1860 when liberal legislation allowed the Jews various civil liberties and two Jews, Ignaz *Kuranda and Simon Winterstein, were elected to the Reichsrat. In the same year Baron Anselm von *Rothschild was made a member of the Austrian upper house. The constitution of 1867 abolished all discrimination on the basis of religion, and for over half a century Jews suffered no legal restrictions on their entry into public life though anti-Jewish prejudice frequently acted as an equally effective bar. Except for Franz Klein who was twice minister of justice, no professing Jews held ministerial posts in the Hapsburg Empire until October 1918. In the half century between the promulgation of the constitution of 1867 and the collapse of the Hapsburg Empire, a number of Jews became prominent figures in Austrian politics. They included successful industrialists and bankers such as Simon Winterstein, Baron Anselm von Rothschild, Moritz von *Koenigswarter, and Rudolph *Auspitz. Most Jews were members of the German Liberal Party but toward the end of the century many turned to the new Social Democratic Party under Victor *Adler which acquired wide support among the Jews of Austria and rapidly became the target of anti-Semitic attacks. Among the leaders of the party were Wilhelm *Ellenbogen, Friedrich Austerlitz, and Otto *Bauer, all of whom pledged their sole allegiance to the Socialist cause, supported Jewish assimilation, and opposed all forms of Jewish nationalism, believing that this was an effective way of combating growing anti-Semitism. By contrast, Rabbi Joseph Samuel *Bloch formed the Union Oesterreichischer Juden to defend Austrian Jewry against the anti-Semites and on the two occasions he was elected to the Reichsrat fought strenuously against anti-Jewish discrimination. Following the granting of universal suffrage at the end of 1906 four Jews were elected to parliament as members of the newly formed Jewish National Party (*Volkspartei, Juedische) which advocated an independent Jewish policy and was pro-Zionist. Its members were Heinrich Gabel, Arthur Mahler, and Adolf Stand, all from Galicia, and Benno Straucher from Bukovina. During World War I many Jewish Socialists opposed the war and for most of the war were an ineffective minority, but the pro-Western liberal politician Joseph *Redlich became increasingly more important and was briefly minister of finance at the end of the war. With the creation of the Austrian Republic in November 1918, a Socialist government took office with the Socialist leader Otto Bauer as foreign minister. Bauer and Friedrich *Adler were among the party leaders to combat the threat of a Communist revolution which became a serious possibility as long as the short-lived Bolshevik regime of Béla Kun held power in Hungary. But though the Socialists retained their respectability as an anti-Communist party, the fact that a large number of their leaders were of Jewish origin, among whom were Julius *Braunthal, Robert Danneberg, and Hugo *Breitner, was a continual source of embarrassment to the party. Many Vienna Jews voted for the Socialist Party but many also supported the Zionist candidates of whom Robert *Stricker was elected to the Austrian National Assembly and three others were elected to the Vienna city council. The Zionist candidates were not subsequently successful, however, largely because the Jewish refugees from the eastern part of the old Hapsburg Empire, who were the least assimilated and the most pro-Zionist, were denied the right to vote at all. However, toward the end of the 1920s the Zionist parties gained strength in the Jewish communal elections while the Jewish Socialists declined in importance in both communal and national politics following the resurgence of the nationalist and later fascist parties. When Chancellor *Dollfuss assumed rule by executive decree, Jewish Socialist leaders like Braunthal and Breitner were among those temporarily imprisoned as part of the policy of destruction of the Social Democratic Party, but for a time Jews were allowed to become members of the Vaterlaendische Front. However, following the *Anschluss* with Germany in March 1938 Austrian Jews were deprived of all their political and civil rights and many fled the country to avoid arrest, among them Otto Bauer, Friedrich Adler, and Hugo Breitner. After World War II few Jews were active in politics in Austria, a notable exception being Bruno *Kreisky who became successively foreign minister, chairman of the Social Democratic Party, and in 1970, chancellor of the Austrian Republic. [ED.]

Canada. Prior to the British conquest in 1759, Canada was a French colony. Only Roman Catholics were allowed to settle in the country, thus excluding Protestants and Jews. But when France ceded Canada to Great Britain at the Treaty of Paris in 1763, the common law of England became the law of the new British colony. Nevertheless, Ezekiel *Hart was prevented from taking his seat in the Legislative Assembly of Canada, first in 1808, and again in 1809. The Jews of Montreal petitioned the Legislature of Lower Canada for the recognition of a Jewish religious corporation. A "Jewish Magna Carta" of 1831–32 was passed in which it was declared that Jews were to be "entitled to the full rights and privileges of other subjects of His Majesty ... and capable of taking, having, or enjoying any office or place of trust within this Province." Nevertheless, long before the passage of the 1832 Bill of Rights, a tradition of public service among the early Jews of Canada had already existed—as early as Aaron *Hart, who was postmaster in Three Rivers in 1763, and John Frank, who was chief of the fire brigade of Quebec in 1790.

The theoretical question of whether Jews possessed equal rights of citizenship had long before been resolved by parliament in England. Ironically, almost a full century before such rights had been accorded them in the mother country by an act of parliament in 1740, Jews in the British colonies of North America were granted naturalization as citizens. In Canada the problem was complicated at first by the absence of an oath-taking procedure appropriate to Jews on their assumption of public office. And even later, after the Law of 1832, it took royal intervention to smooth the way. Thereafter, however, Jews held political office without any of the former impediments.

The political development of Canada's Jews, like the community itself, is very much a 20th-century phenomenon. More particularly, it is only since World War II that the Jewish community has come to be represented widely on all levels of government, local, provincial and federal, in the judiciary, and in the higher echelons of the Civil Service. As early as 1871, Henry *Nathan from Victoria, British Columbia, was a member of parliament in Ottawa. Almost a half-century would pass before another Jew would be sent to Ottawa as an elected member, Samuel Jacobs in 1917. After World War I, seats in the House of Commons were held by Peter *Bercovitch, Maurice Hartt, A. A. Heaps, David *Lewis, Leon *Crestohl, and David A. *Croll, with representation in the 1960s including Barnett Danson, Marvin Gelber, Philip *Givens, Herbert *Gray, Robert Kaplan, Milton Klein, Jack Marshall, David *Orlikow, and Max Saltsman. In the senate, there were two Jewish members, David A. Croll and Lazarus *Phillips. The following Jewish citizens were leaders of provincial parties in Canada in the early 1970s: David Barrett, leader of the New Democratic Party in British Columbia (1969–); Stephen Lewis, leader of the New Democratic Party in Ontario (1970–); I. H. Asper of Winnipeg, leader of the Liberal Party in Manitoba (1970–); Sidney Spivak of Winnipeg, who, as leader of the Manitoba Progressive-Conservative Party, also served as the official leader of the opposition (1971–). When the New Democratic Party came to power in Manitoba in 1969, three Jews became ministers of the crown. Saul Cherniack was installed as deputy-premier in addition to his cabinet post as minister of finance. Saul Miller became minister of youth and education; Sydney Green, minister of health and social service. David Lewis, deputy leader of the New Democratic Party, became the first Jew in the history of Canadian politics to be elected leader of a national political party (1971). In an earlier Progressive-Conservative government in Manitoba, Sidney Spivak had been minister of trade, and Maitland Steinkopf was secretary of state.

Percy Gaum was first elected to Nova Scotia's Legislative Assembly in 1956, later reelected in 1960, 1963, and 1967. A Progressive-Conservative, he was appointed minister of public welfare in 1968.

In Ontario, beginning with 1934, David Croll had served as minister of labor, public welfare, and municipal affairs, resigning in 1937. Allen Grossman had served in Progressive-Conservative cabinets in Ontario in various positions from 1960. Joseph *Salsberg, a leading member of the Canadian Communist Party, was a member of the Ontario Legislature from 1942 to 1955, when Grossman ran against him and unseated him. There have been many Jewish mayors in Canada, particularly in the smaller towns of Ontario, and in the West. The first Jewish mayor elected in the Province of Quebec since William Hyman of Gaspé in 1858 was Jules Loeb of South Hull.

In Toronto Nathan Phillips served as mayor for eight years, the longest on record (1952–60), and Philip Givens was mayor of Toronto from 1963 until 1966. In the Province of Quebec, history was made in 1970 when Victor Goldbloom of Montreal, a member of the Provincial Liberal Party, became the first Jew in the history of Quebec to be appointed to the cabinet. He was first minister without portfolio; then in 1971 he became minister responsible for the quality of the environment. In previous years Peter Bercovitch, Louis Fitch, and Maurice Hartt were also members of the Quebec Provincial Legislature. The first member of a federal cabinet of Jewish faith was Herbert Gray who was first appointed to the Liberal Cabinet in 1969 as minister without portfolio and later, in 1970, became minister of revenue. [St.E.R.]

England. After the resettlement of the Jews in England in 1656, they enjoyed social freedom, but did not achieve full political emancipation until 1858. For a century and a half their exclusion from national and local government was shared by nonconformists and Roman Catholics, although these minorities were emancipated in 1818 and 1819, respectively. The insistence of the House of Lords on retaining the words "on the true faith of a Christian" in the parliamentary oath prevented Jews from sitting in parliament for almost 30 more years. Thus, before 1858 only converts or the descendants of converts were able to enter parliament or hold any state or municipal post. Nevertheless, the very fact that such men were permitted to sit in parliament testified to the fact that the bar was purely religious and not racial. Benjamin *Disraeli, for example, who was an active supporter of Jewish emancipation, was regarded as a Jew by many of his contemporaries and was the victim of social discrimination but not of any legal bars. In 1845 the Jewish Disabilities Removal Act allowed Jews to hold office in municipal government and two years later David *Salomons became an alderman of the City of London. In the same year Lionel de *Rothschild became the first Jew to be elected to parliament but was not allowed to take his seat. In 1851 Sir David Salomons was elected to parliament but was forcibly removed from the Commons Chamber after he had voted three times and even made a speech to explain his position. Eventually, a bill was passed in 1858 allowing each House to fix its own oath to be administered to a Jew; Lionel de Rothschild became the first Jewish member (but, incidentally, never made a speech). Lionel de Rothschild was one of eight Jewish MPs in the Liberal Party during the 19th century; the others were Sir David Salomons, Sir Francis Goldsmid, Sir Frederick Goldsmid, Sir Julian Goldsmid (who sat for 30 years and became speaker of the House of Commons; see *Goldsmid family), Sir John *Simon, Sir George *Jessel, who, as solicitor general in 1871, became the first Jewish minister in a British government, and Arthur *Cohen. The first Jewish Conservative member was Saul Isaac, elected in 1874, who was followed by Lionel Louis Cohen (see *Cohen family) and Henry de *Worms, who as Lord Pirbright was made parliamentary secretary to the board of trade and undersecretary of state for the colonies. Jews at first found the road to political advancement easier in the more progressive Liberal Party, but after Disraeli became prime minister, the Conservatives became the party of reform. Nevertheless, most Jewish politicians were to be found in the ranks of the Liberal Party, among them Herbert *Samuel who became Chancellor of the Duchy of Lancaster, postmaster general, home secretary, and the first Jewish cabinet minister in Britain. Others included Rufus Isaacs, Lord *Reading, who was Lord Chief Justice of England and later viceroy of India, and Edwin *Montagu who was Chancellor of the Duchy of Lancaster, minister of munitions, and secretary of state for India. The decline of the Liberal Party in the 1920s led many Jews to switch their allegiance to the growing Labor Party and a number of Jews sat in parliament, first in the Liberal cause and later as Labor members. Among them were Harry *Nathan, who was minister of civil aviation in the Labor government after World War II, George Spero (1894–), and Barnett *Janner. Few Jews held important positions in the national governments of the 1930s, though a prominent exception was Leslie *Hore-Belisha, who was minister of war from 1937 to 1940. In the general election immediately after World War II the number of Jewish Labor members of parliament rose from 4 to 26. Considerable influence was also wielded by Harold *Laski who was chairman of the Labor Party. Jewish MPs from other parties were virtually eliminated, a notable exception being Phil Piratin, the only Jewish Communist in parliament in Britain. Jewish liberals were gradually eliminated by the failure of the party at elections while Jewish Conservative candidates tended to be passed over by the constituency associations, though Henry d'Avigdor Goldsmid (see *Goldsmid family) sat for many years in the Conservative interest and Sir Keith *Joseph became the first Jewish Conservative cabinet minister. Lord Reading had served in 1931 as foreign secretary in a national government and Leslie Hore-Belisha as a National Liberal in Conservative-dominated conditions. Several Jews became cabinet ministers in the Labor governments of 1945–51 and 1964–70. In the former Labor government under Clement *Attlee, Lewis *Silkin was minister of town and country planning; Emanuel *Shinwell was minister of fuel and power and secretary of state for war; Harry Nathan was minister of civil aviation; and George *Strauss was minister of supply. In the Labor government of 1964–70 there were more than 30 Jewish Labor MPs and Jewish ministers included John *Diamond and Harold *Lever, who held senior posts at the Treasury, and John Silkin (see Lewis *Silkin), who was minister of public building and works. In addition, several Jewish members who never held ministerial posts had considerable influence on Labor policy, in particular Sydney *Silverman and Ian Mikardo (1908–). Nevertheless, Jews played little part as Jews in the formation of government policy and there was never a "Jewish vote" even on the Palestine question during the last days of the British Mandate. A few Jewish women played a part in Jewish parliamentary life. Marion Phillips (1881–1932) was the first Jewish woman member, while Barbara *Ayrton Gould (c. 1890–1950) was chairman of the Labor Party (1939–40). Two Jewish women were returned to parliament in 1970, Renée Short (1919–) for the Labor Party and Sally Oppenheim (1930–) for the Conservatives. Four women were among the first ten Jews to be made life peers: Dora Gaitskell (1909–), Beatrice Serota (1919–), Alma Birk (1917–), and Beatrice Plummer (1903–).

Ireland. Robert *Briscoe, who represented the Fianna Fail party, was the only Jewish member of the Irish parliament from 1927. On his retirement in 1965 he was succeeded by his son, Benjamin. [V.D.L.]

France. Before the French Revolution of 1789 Jews had neither civil nor political rights and very few took part in French public affairs. They were granted civil rights in 1791 and from then onward no formal bars remained before their advancement in politics, though for many years they were not active in public affairs largely because of the exclusiveness of French society. One of the first Jews in politics in France was Benjamin David (1796–1879), who was elected deputy for the department of Deux-Sèvres in 1834 and became mayor of his native city of Niort in 1846. The first Jewish minister was the banker Michel *Goudchaux who led the opposition to King Louis Phillipe's economic policy and himself became minister of finance in 1848, shortly before the revolution of that year. The famous advocate, Isaac *Crémieux, was another prominent opponent of the regime who participated in the revolution and was briefly minister of justice. After the revolution Achille *Fould served as minister of finance until 1852 when he became a senator and then minister of state, the first Jew in France to hold these positions. His three sons,

Ernest Adolphe, Edouard Mathurin, and Gustave Eugène, and his grandson Achille Charles (see *Fould family) were subsequently elected to the chamber of deputies. During the Franco-Prussian War of 1870 two Jews came to the fore. Camille Sée (see *Sée family) became secretary general of the Ministry of Interior in the government of National Defense and Leo *Frankel, a Hungarian émigré, was minister of labor in the Paris Commune. Subsequently, Jewish politicians tended to support socialist or radical parties largely because the royalist and clerical groups tended to be anti-Semitic. Thus Camille Sée was a member of the Republican Party as was David *Raynal, who was minister of public works in Gambetta's ministry in 1881 and later minister of the interior. Nevertheless, Jews were not particularly prominent in French politics at the end of the 19th century and the anti-Semitic attacks during the *Dreyfus case were directed more against Jews in the professions generally than against Jews in public affairs. Following the turn of the century, however, an increasing number of Jews served in Clemenceau's war cabinet from 1917 to 1919: Georges *Mandel, who was *chef de cabinet,* Edouard Ignace (1864–1924), and Louis *Klotz, the latter serving as minister of finance. After the war Klotz was raised to the senate, Abraham *Schrameck, formerly governor of Madagascar, became minister of the interior and minister of justice, and Maurice Bokanowsky was minister of commerce and industry from 1926 to 1927. Thereafter, however, most Jewish politicians tended to represent socialist parties, a notable exception being Mandel who served in several non-socialist cabinets before the outbreak of World War II and was minister of the interior until the fall of France. Salomon *Grumbach was a member of the Socialist Party central committee, Leon *Meyer was a Socialist minister of mercantile marine, and in 1936 Léon Blum became prime minister of France, the first Jew and the first Socialist to hold this post. Blum's cabinet included Jules *Moch as minister of public works and Jean Zay as minister of education. Blum was briefly prime minister of France after World War II as were the Radical Socialist René *Mayer and the Radical leader Pierre *Mendès France. France was thereby the only European state in which three Jews held the post of prime minister, each representing a different shade of socialist policy. In addition, Moch, René Mayer, and the Socialist Party leader Daniel Mayer all held posts in postwar French coalition cabinets until the end of the Fourth Republic in 1958 and the return to power of General de Gaulle. Few Jews held positions of influence during De Gaulle's term of presidency from 1958 to 1969 but following the election of Georges Pompidou as president in June 1969 two Jews were appointed to ministerial posts, Maurice *Schumann, as minister of foreign affairs, and Leo *Hamon as secretary of state to the prime minister.

Germany. Although individual Jews acted as *Hoffaktoren* and *Hofjuden* (*Court Jews) to monarchs in a number of German states during the 17th and 18th centuries, acting both as advisers and financial agents, Jews played no part in German national politics until the middle of the 19th century, and almost no part in government until the 20th. Jews who converted to Christianity, however, enjoyed full political rights and rose to high office. Thus, Friedrich Julius *Stahl became leader of the reactionary Conservative Party and a firm opponent of political emancipation for his former coreligionists. Other converted Jews who rose to high office included Martin Eduard von *Simson, president of the Reichstag, Heinrich von Friedberg (1813–1895), Prussian minister of justice, and Karl Rudolf Friedenthal (1827–1890), Prussian minister of agriculture under the Empire. The first professing Jew to hold a public position in Germany was David *Friedlaender who was elected to the Berlin municipal council in 1809. Not until the 1840s, however, did the Jews gain electoral rights, including the right to vote for the German National Assembly and to be elected to the Assembly or to state parliaments. Jews participated in the liberal revolution in 1848, and among the Jewish representatives to the National Assembly held in Frankfort after the revolution were Moritz *Veit and Gabriel *Riesser, who was vice-president of the Assembly. Both were staunch champions of Jewish emancipation as were Fischel *Arnheim, the only Jewish member of the Bavarian Diet and Johann *Jacoby, an early leader of the liberal movement. The German states finally removed all political restrictions from the Jews during the 1860s and after the unification of Germany (1871) they were granted legal equality in most spheres. Nevertheless, they were still effectively excluded from holding government office and with the exception of Moritz *Elstaetter, minister of finance in Baden from 1888 to 1893, no unbaptized Jew held ministerial office. On the other hand, Jews were very active in political life, being among the leaders of the progressive political parties. They were particularly well represented among the liberals, whom the Jews tended to favor. Thus Eduard *Lasker was one of the founders of the National Liberal Party and was influential in framing the social legislation of his regime while his colleague Ludwig *Bamberger helped organize the state finances. Other Jewish politicians included Max Hirsch, the trade unionist and advocate of popular education, Leopold *Sonnemann, a leader of the Democratic Party, Ludwig *Loewe, a founder of the Progressive Party in North Germany, and Wolf *Frankenburger, leader of the Liberal Party in Bavaria.

Toward the end of the 19th century Jewish politicans became increasingly prominent in left-wing parties. At the same time the political allegiance of German Jewry was itself undergoing a process of radicalization, moving from moderate to progressive liberalism, and eventually to Socialism, with the upper strata of Jewish society retaining a traditional allegiance to liberalism. Thus Jews were very prominent in the leadership of the Socialist Party though they formed but a fraction of the electorate. The party itself was founded by Ferdinand *Lasalle who adopted the ideology of Karl *Marx and formed the General German Workers Association (ADAV) which was the forerunner of the German Social Democratic Party. The Social Democratic Party was later much influenced by Eduard *Bernstein, who called for a fundamental revision of Marxist doctrine arguing that the party should work for social reform rather than revolution, and by Rosa *Luxemburg, who advocated workers' control by revolution and led the abortive Communist rising at the end of 1918. After the outbreak of World War I the German Social Democratic Party split into two factions, the majority supporting the war while the minority opposing the war included a number of Jews, among them, Hugo *Haase, president of the German Social Democratic Party in the Reichstag, Bernstein, and Luxemburg.

The prominence of Jewish left-wing intellectuals in German political life was successfully exploited by the anti-Semites and right-wing parties and revolutionary socialism became identified with Jewry especially since the Soviet and Hungarian revolutions after World War I were led by Jews. In Germany, too, Jews rose to high office in the revolutionary ferment that followed the collapse of the German Empire at the end of 1918. Paul Hirsch (1868–1938) was briefly prime minister of Prussia, Kurt *Eisner headed the revolutionary government of Bavaria and Hugo Haase and Otto *Landsberg were two of the six people's commissars in the first postwar government. In addition Paul *Levi succeeded Rosa Luxemburg as head of the Communist Party and the Communists included many Jewish members, among them Ruth *Fischer and Gerhart *Eisler. During this period of the Weimar Republic there were no restrictions on Jews holding political posts and four Jews held high ministerial office. Hugo *Preuss, one of the drafters of the Weimar Constitution, became minister of the interior, Otto Landsberg was minister of justice, Walther *Rathenau was foreign minister, and Rudolf *Hilferding minister of finance. The Nazis deliberately overstated the importance of Jews in German politics, however, and condemned the Weimar Republic as being the hated *Judenrepublik* dominated by Jews.

Soon after the Nazis came to power in 1933 all political parties were banned except the Nazi Party from which Jews were excluded. Jewish politicians were either arrested or forced to leave the country. After World War II a small number of Jews took part in German political life, among them Herbert *Weichmann who was president of the Bundesrat and Joseph Neuberger (1902–) who was minister of justice in North-Rhine-Westphalia. In East Germany the only figure of importance was Gerhart Eisler who was for a time minister of information.

Holland. The first Jewish politicians in Holland represented William III of Orange in international diplomatic negotiations. Thus Samuel Palecke was made representative of the king of Morocco in Holland, Isaac Belmonte (see *Belmonte Family) was agent-general of the king of Spain to the Netherlands, and several Jews were involved in his negotiations to secure the British crown. Jews were not active in Dutch internal politics, however, until after their emancipation in 1795, following the conquest by France and the formation of the Batavian republic. In 1798 Jews were given the right to vote and be elected to state offices and two Jews were elected to the national assembly. Subsequently, two Jewish lawyers held high government posts, Moses Salomon Asser who became a member of the legislative council and Jonas Daniel *Meyer who was appointed to the state council during the reign of Louis Napoleon. Nevertheless, Jews played very little part in Dutch politics until the second half of the 19th century when Michael *Godefroi became minister of justice and Samuel *Sarphati became a leading campaigner for social reform. Jews elected to the second chamber of parliament included Abraham Hartogh (1844–1901), Samuel van den *Bergh, Abraham *Wertheim and Joseph Limburg (1866–1940), all of whom were members of the Liberal Party. In the 20th century two Jewish women were prominent in Dutch politics: Aletta Jacobs (1854–1929) and Betsy Bakker-Nort (1874–1946), both of whom championed the rights of women. Several Jewish socialists sat in Parliament, among them A. B. *Kleerekoper, Henri *Polak, Ben Sajet, and the Communist Party chairman, David *Wijnkoop. However, only two Jews were appointed to ministerial posts before World War II: Eduard van *Raalte, minister of justice at the beginning of the 20th century and Salomon Rodrigues de *Miranda who was socialist minister of housing in the 1930s. After World War II two more Jewish ministers of justice held office, Ivo *Samkalden being appointed in 1956 and 1965 and Carel *Polak taking office in 1968. Samkalden also served as mayor of Amsterdam, the only Jew to be mayor of an important municipality in Holland.

Italy. In 1778 Jews were given the right to become members of municipal councils in Tuscany and this right was extended to other parts of Italy at the end of the century following the French invasion of Italy under Napoleon. Thus in 1796 the venerable oligarchic government of Venice was overthrown and a new municipality was elected that included three Jews: Moses *Luzzatto, Vita Vivante, and Isaac Grego. After the defeat of Napoleon at the hands of the Holy Alliance, Jews were deprived of their newly acquired civic equality and as a result actively supported the secret revolutionary forces, such as the *Carbonari* and Young Italy movements. In this respect Italy was the only 19th-century European state in which substantial elements of the Jewish population took up a political cause.

Following the outbreak of the 1848 Revolution, Jewish rights were restored in most parts of Italy and two Jews became ministers in the Venetian Republic, headed by the half-Jew Daniel *Manin: Leone Pincherle, minister of agriculture and commerce, and Isaac Maurogonato (1817–1892), minister of finance. In 1858 Isaac *Artom became private secretary to the Piedmontese prime minister Count Cavour and in the following year Sansone d'*Ancona became director of finance and public works in the government of Tuscany. When the reunification of Italy was completed in 1870, a number of Jews were members of the Italian parliament and by 1894 their numbers had increased to 15, representing a wide variety of political views. The number of Jewish deputies and senators never became large in proportion to the size of the Italian parliament but a number of Jews held important posts at the turn of the century. Luigi *Luzzatti served as minister of finance on several occasions and later became prime minister, the first Jew in modern times to achieve this distinction; Leone *Wollemborg was minister of finance for a short period in 1901, Guiseppe *Ottolenghi was minister of war from 1902 to 1903, and Ernesto *Nathan became mayor of Rome. The rise of Fascism after World War I virtually brought to an end Jewish involvement in Italian politics. Many Jews did support Mussolini at first but with the exceptions of Guido Jung, minister of finance (1932–35), and Aldo Finzi, who was assistant minister of the interior, none held important posts in his party or government and Jewish politicians of the left such as the socialist leaders Guiseppe *Modigliani and Claudio Treves (1869–1944; see *Treves) and the Communist Umberto *Terracini were systematically persecuted or forced into exile. When the Fascists became anti-Semitic in the late 1930s Jews were expelled from the Fascist Party, by then the only legal political party in Italy, and effectively excluded from all political activity. Political rights were restored to the Jews after World War II but only Terracini, who became a leading Communist figure in the Italian senate, played a significant part in Italian politics.

Muslim States. TURKEY. Jews played an important part in Turkish politics in the 16th century, a few Jews acting as ministers and financial advisers, among them Joseph *Nasi, Duke of Naxos, Solomon *Ashkenazi, and Esther *Kiera. The decline in the status of Turkish Jewry from the beginning of the 17th century led to the exclusion of Jews from public affairs, and civil rights were not granted to Turkish Jews until the middle of the 19th century. Exceptional were the *Picciotto family of merchants, five of whom, Hillel, Raphael, Ezra, Elijah, and Moses ben Ezra, were consuls for European powers in Aleppo. In 1876, Daniel Carmona (see *Carmona family) became the first Jew to serve in the Turkish Parliament and in 1899 Behor *Ashkenazi became the representative of Turkish Jewry in the Ottoman Parliament, later becoming vice-prefect of Istanbul and a member of the senate. A few Jews joined the Young Turk movement at the beginning of the century, among them Haim *Nahoum who was appointed chief rabbi of Egypt when the Young Turks came to power. After World War II Solomon Adato was the sole representative of Turkish Jewry in Parliament and after his death in 1953 he was succeeded by Henry Soviano.

EGYPT. Jews took little part in Egyptian affairs during the centuries that Egypt was under Turkish rule. One of the first Jews active in Egyptian politics in modern times was Joseph Aslan Cattaui (see *Cattaui family) who worked with Sir Ernest *Cassel on engineering projects and was made pasha in 1912 and a member of the legislative assembly. He was appointed minister of finance and transport and later became a member of the senate. Other prominent Jews in Egyptian politics who were elected to the senate were Joseph Picciotto (see *Picciotto family), a leader of the Egyptian Zionist movement, and Cattaui's elder son, Cattaui Bey. Following full Egyptian independence after World War II, Jews were made to suffer for the government's anti-Zionist policy and no Jews held positions in the government or parliament.

IRAQ. Few Jews were prominent in politics in Iraq either during Turkish rule or after independence but a few were elected to the Iraqi parliament where at one time seats were specifically reserved for candidates elected by the Jewish community. The first Jewish representative from Iraq in the Turkish parliament was Menahem ben Salaḥ Daniel (see *Daniel family) who was appointed in 1876. *Sasson ben Ezekiel ben Solomon David was the first Iraqi delegate to the Turkish Parliament after the Young Turk revolution and from 1920 to 1923 was Iraqi minister of finance during the British protectorate.

Following Iraqi independence in 1924, three Jews were elected to the Iraqi lower house and Menahem ben Salaḥ Daniel, at the age of nearly 80, was appointed to the senate. On his retirement in 1935 he was succeeded by his son Ezra. The number of Jews representing Iraqi Jewry was raised to six and many prominent Jewish businessmen were active in politics. The anti-Zionist campaign after World War II led to a change in government policy toward Iraqi Jewry. The right of separate Jewish representation in parliament was abolished and Jews were deprived of civil rights. Following the death of Ezra Daniel in 1952 no Jews sat in the Iraqi parliament.

MOROCCO. Jews were prominent in Moroccan state affairs during the reign of the Marinids (1269–1465). Two members of the Roggasa (or Waqqasa) family were influential ministers and toward the end of the dynasty *Aaron ben Batash was prime minister. In the 17th century Abraham Maimaran and Moses Attar (see *Atar) were ministers and advisors to King Mulay Ishmael. In the 18th century Samuel *Sumbal was advisor to the sultan on foreign affairs and his son Joseph Hayyim was Moroccan ambassador to London. Several members of the *Corcos family were advisors on financial and foreign affairs to five successive sultans during the 19th century, and Meir Macnin was ambassador to London. However, wealthy Jews no longer held a prominent place in state affairs during the period of the French Protectorate (1912–56). Following Moroccan independence in March 1956, Leon *Benzaquen was made minister of posts and David Benazeraf became a member of the advisory council. Growing Muslim nationalism acted as a brake on Jewish political activity from July 1957 to 1961 but after the accession of King Hassan II Jews once again held representative posts, David Amar as a senator and Meyer Obadia and Jacob Banon as members of the National Assembly.

TUNISIA. Although Jews held powerful economic and political positions in Tunisia in the Middle Ages, Jews were deprived of all their rights in the 16th century. Nevertheless, members of the Cohen-Tanudji family were advisors on foreign affairs to the bey and in the 19th century Abraham Belaish and Nessim *Samama were finance ministers. Several members of the *Valensi family were statesmen and one was Tunisian minister of war. In the 20th century Jews tended to support the French administration and many fought in the French army in World War I. Later many Jews joined the Zionist movement and some were active in the nationalist Destour Party, among them Albert *Bessis who was made minister of public works in the Tunisian cabinet upon independence and André Barrouch who was appointed to the cabinet on Bessis' resignation. The anti-Zionist campaign at the end of the 1950s led to Barrouch's resignation and a sudden decline in Jewish involvement in politics. Following the mass emigration from Tunisia in the 1960s, Jews ceased to take any part in Tunisian politics.

Poland. Until the end of the 18th century Jews played no part in public life in Poland. Their interests were bound up with those of the Polish Jewish community as a whole and in any case they were granted no civil rights in Polish society. The decline in the cohesion of the Jewish community, however, led to increasing involvement of the Jews in the large cities in Polish affairs and after the partition of Poland and the outbreak of the French Revolution a number of Jews joined the insurrection against the Russians in 1794, among them Berek *Joselewicz who commanded a force of 500 Jews in the defense of Warsaw. Nevertheless, though Jews fought in the army of Napoleon, they were not granted political rights in the Grand Duchy of Warsaw, nor, after 1815, when the Russians regained control over most of Poland. During the Polish insurrections of 1830 and 1831 Jews were again prominent as supporters of the revolutionary cause and following the suppression of the insurrection, Stanislaus Hernisz Ludwig Lubliner and Leon Hollandaerski were leaders of the group of émigré Polish leaders agitating abroad for Polish independence. In the 1860s Rabbi Dov Ber *Meisels, chief rabbi of Warsaw, organized the Jewish community's support for the Polish nationalist movement. He was arrested by the czarist authorities for closing the Warsaw synagogues as an act of solidarity with the Catholic leaders who closed the churches in defiance of the authorities. Meisel's funeral in 1870 was the occasion for a mass demonstration of Polish national feeling. Other Jewish revolutionary leaders were Henryk *Wohl who became head of a department in the insurgent government of 1863 and was later arrested and imprisoned and Bernhard *Goldman. Toward the end of the century a number of Jewish intellectuals joined the Social-Democratic Party of Poland and Lithuania, one of whose founders was Rosa *Luxemburg. The party's leaders included Herman *Diamand, Feliks *Kon, Herman *Lieberman, Adolf *Warski-Warszawski, and Boleslaw *Drobner, the last being among the many Jews to take part in the anti-czarist uprisings between 1905 and 1907. Following the granting of universal suffrage in the Austro-Hungarian Empire and the establishment of the Duma in Russia, Polish Jews were allowed to vote for and to be elected to the Austro-Hungarian Reichsrat and the Russian Duma. Herman Lieberman and Herman Diamond were elected to the Reichsrat in 1917 as representatives from Galicia and several Jews stood as candidates for the Duma. None was successful, however, largely because they attracted the Jewish vote only and also because they were officially opposed by the authorities. Furthermore in the elections to the fourth Duma, the Jews supported the Polish Socialist Party candidate en masse and this led to an organized boycott of Jewish traders in protest. After the outbreak of World War I, Jews ceased to play any part in politics in Russian Poland even after the Central Powers occupied the territory. Nevertheless Jewish representatives from Galicia sat in the Austro-Hungarian Reichsrat.

Following the declaration of Polish independence at the end of World War I the Polish government concluded a minorities treaty granting full equality to the Jews and other minorities and the provisions of the treaty were incorporated in the Polish constitution. In the first Sejm of 1922 45 Jews were elected, six of them being elected to the senate. Jews represented Zionist parties, the non-Zionist Agudat Israel and the Polish Socialist Party, the last being the only non-Jewish political party which was not anti-Semitic. Most of the Jewish members of the chamber of deputies joined together to form a Jewish parliamentary club ("Koło") headed initially by the Zionist leader Yitzḥak *Gruenbaum and were mainly concerned with attempting to improve the social and political condition of the Jews in the face of government-inspired anti-Semitism. Jewish Socialists, of whom Herman Lieberman and Boleslaw Drobner were among the leaders of the party, were more concerned with general Polish politics. In 1925 the Jewish club agreed to support the government on condition that the government acted to improve the condition of the Jews. However, when it became clear that the government had no intention of fulfilling its side of the bargain, most of the Jewish members rejoined the Socialists in opposition. Government policy became increasingly anti-Semitic and during the 1930s the number of Jews in the Sejm dwindled to seven and many of the Jewish Socialist leaders were imprisoned or exiled, among them Herman Lieberman who led the opposition to the government, Isaac *Schwarzbart and the Polish communist leaders Roman *Zambrowski and Adolf Warski-Warszawski.

The destruction of Poland on the outbreak of World War II and the Nazi Holocaust did not result in the end of political activity among Polish Jews. Adolf *Berman cooperated with left-wing political groups in Warsaw and fought in the Warsaw uprising of 1944. Herman Lieberman was briefly a member of the Polish government in exile in London and a number of Polish Jews who fled to the Soviet Union in 1939 held important position in the Soviet-sponsored Union of Polish Patriots and the Polish army in the U.S.S.R., among them Eugeniusz *Szyr, Stefan Wierblowski, Roman Zambrowski, Hilary *Minc, Jacob *Berman, and Drobner. On the formation of the Polish Committee of National Liberation in 1944, Drobner was made minister of labor and social care, the first Jew to hold a portfolio in a Polish government.

The liberation of Poland at the end of World War I led to the formation of a Provisional Government of National Unity in which the Communist Party with its prominent Jewish members played a key part. All discrimination against Jewish politicians ceased and when the pro-Communist Socialists merged with the Communists into the Polish United Workers Party, Boleslav Bierut became head of the party with two Jews, Jacob Berman and Hilary Minc, as close colleagues, the latter serving as minister of commerce and later as vice-premier. Berman and Minc were, like Bierut, loyal supporters of Stalin and included several other Jewish Stalinists in the government and party, among them Szyr, Starewicz, and Wierblowski, and Julius *Katz-Suchy. Following the death of Bierut, however, and the rise to power of Wladyslaw Gomulka, Berman and later Minc were forced to resign. In the 1960s Zambrowski and Szyr held important party posts but the former was dismissed during the government-inspired anti-Semitic campaign of 1968 in which a number of Jews holding lesser positions were also forced to resign. By 1971, two Jews were left in the goverment—Szyr as deputy prime minister and Edward Sznajder, minister for home trade.

Russia. As early as 1783 Jews were given the right to hold municipal office in Belorussia. The right was extended to all parts of Russia in 1835 but was later limited to western Russia, where most Jews lived, so that Jews could not be elected as mayors or municipal chairmen, nor could they constitute more than a third of the number of municipal councillors even in areas where Jews constituted a majority of the inhabitants. Jews were thus prevented from playing an influential part in municipal affairs while they were completely excluded from national politics by the very nature of the autocratic and anti-Semitic czarist rule. As a result, many Jews, particularly among the secularly educated, joined or supported the illegal revolutionary organizations that sprung up in the 1870s. Their number included Pavel *Axelrod, Aaron Zundelevich, and O. Aptekman (see *Socialism). The abolition in 1882 of the right to vote for local councils or to be elected to them added impetus to the Jewish opposition to the regime. Several Jews were founders of the Narodniki (Populists) and of the Social Democratic Party (among them Axelrod and Lev Deutsch), both of which groups received wide support in Jewish assimilationist or semi-assimilationist circles. Most Jews, however, remained in purely Jewish frameworks; they were Orthodox, Zionists, or joined the *Bund. The failure of Nicholas II to make any substantial reforms brought about a resumption of revolutionary activity at the turn of the century. Jews held leading positions in the Social Democratic Workers Party but when the party split in 1903, most of the Jewish members, among them members of the Bund, joined the Menshevik group under Julius *Martov, among them Fyodor *Dan, Raphael *Abramowitz, and Grinevich, who from 1905 to 1917 was chairman of the All-Russian Council of Trade Unions. Jews were also prominent in two other political parties, the

Socialist Revolutionary Party, which continued the heritage of the Populists, and the liberal Union of Liberation. The Socialist Revolutionary Party, formed in 1902, appealed mainly to the peasants as the Social Democrats appealed to the industrial workers. Its leaders included Chaim *Zhitlovsky, Grigori *Gershuni, and Mikhail Gots. The Union of Liberation was a radical liberal group who drew their support from the urban professional classes and attracted Jewish professionals such as the lawyers Maxim *Vinaver and Henry *Sliosberg. When the abortive 1905 revolution led to the setting up of the first *Duma, the Union of Liberation, called Kadet (short name for the Constitutional Democratic Party), formed the largest single political group, their 179 members including nine Jews. However, owing to changes in electoral law during the period of reaction, the party's strength in the later Dumas declined, and there was also a decline in representation of the small Jewish parties (Zionists, Folkspartei, Jewish People's Group, and Jewish Democratic Group), whereas Jewish socialists were not elected at all. The outbreak of revolution in February 1917 brought the immediate abolition of all restrictions against Jews, and four Jews from the Kadet and Menshevik groups were offered posts in Kerensky's provisional government, M. *Vinaver, L. M. Bramson, Fyodor Dan, and M. I. Liber. All refused on the grounds that the time was not yet ripe for Jews to enter a Russian government. On the other hand, A. Galperin was secretary of the provisional government and later Mark Vishniak became secretary of the Constituent Assembly, which was dispersed by force by the Bolshevik Soviet government [Ed.]

U.S.S.R. In Lenin's first Soviet government Jews were prominently represented, not only among the Bolsheviks (e.g., *Trotsky, *Zinoviev, *Kamenev, *Sverdlov) but also among their left Socialist-Revolutionary partners in the short-lived coalition (e.g., the people's commissar for justice, Isaac *Steinberg). Jews were also strongly represented in republican and local soviets and in all echelons of the ruling party hierarchy. Some Jewish politicians in areas densely populated by Jews, and during the first stages of the *Birobidzhan experiment particularly those engaged in *Yevsektsiya work, could be regarded Jewish representatives, since they communicated mainly with the Jewish population or represented its interests. This situation changed quickly in the 1930s. The Yevsektsiya itself was closed down in 1930 and with the purges of the later 1930s most leading Jewish Bolsheviks were imprisoned and liquidated, together with other members of the Old Guard. Simultaneously, the last shreds of Jewish regional and cultural autonomy disappeared and the Birobidzhan experiment, as a "nascent Jewish republic," was practically abandoned. Prominent exceptions were Lazar *Kaganovich, a close associate of Stalin, and Maxim *Litvinoff, people's commissar for foreign affairs. During and after World War II, very few Jews remained in the Soviet top leadership. Under Stalin only Kaganovich was a member of the ruling circle and when Khrushchev assumed personal leadership in 1957 Kaganovich was declared a member of a subversive "anti-party group" and disappeared. No other Jew ever became a member of the policy-making bodies of the party, particularly the Politburo, which is the real government of the country. In 1962 the Jewish economist Venyamin *Dymshyts was appointed one of the six deputies of Soviet prime minister Khrushchev and put at the head of the central planning body *Gosplan,* but the post was without much political significance. Jews also practically disappeared from the middle and lower party hierarchy and the number of Jews in the representative organs of central and local government (both houses of the Supreme Soviet of the U.S.S.R. as well as the republican, regional, and local soviets) declined rapidly. By 1970 it was much below the percentage of the Jews in the total population, not only of the cities (where 95% of the Jews live) but even of the population at large. [B.E.]

South Africa. Although Jews first settled in South Africa in the beginning of the 19th century, for many years they played little part in South African politics. An exception was Benjamin *Norden, one of five brothers who emigrated from England in 1820 and became a municipal commissioner (city councillor) in Cape Town in 1840. Norden was narrowly defeated in the elections to the Cape parliament. Saul *Solomon was elected to the Cape parliament in 1854, 20 years after he and his brother Henry had converted to Christianity. He and Simeon *Jacobs, who was elected in 1866, campaigned for the separation of Church and State in Cape Colony. Four other Jews were elected to the parliament of Cape Colony, Julius and Joseph Mosenthal, Ludwig Henry Goldenschmidt, and Ludwig Wiener. Jews were also among the pioneers of some of the other South African colonies. One of the first settlers in Natal was Nathaniel *Isaacs who unsuccessfully canvassed a treaty between the Zulu monarch and the British crown as the basis for the European settlement of Natal. Another was Jonas Bergtheil, who emigrated to South Africa in 1834 and became the first Jewish member of the Natal legislative council. In the Orange Free State, Isaac Baumann, who arrived in South Africa from Germany in 1840, became chairman of the municipal board of Bloemfontein, and Adolphe Coqui, an immigrant from Belgium, negotiated the establishment of republican government for the Orange Free State after Britain announced that she was terminating her sovereignty over the territory. A third Jewish personality in the early days of the Orange Free State was Moritz Leviseur, who was elected to the provincial parliament in 1905 and became mayor of Bloemfontein in 1906. Leviseur was elected to the Union of South Africa parliament in 1921.

The discovery of diamonds and gold brought a number of Jews to prominence in South African politics. Barney *Barnato became a member of the Transvaal parliament and a personal friend of President Paul Kruger. Barnato did not commit himself in the Anglo-Boer dispute but his nephew Solly *Joel became a member of the reform committee which organized the Jameson raid. Barnato's cousin, Sir David *Harris, took Barnato's seat in the Cape parliament after the latter's death. He was one of six Jews elected to the first Union parliament in 1910, the others being Morris *Alexander, who was a member for over 30 years, Emile Nathan, Sir Lionel Phillips, C. P. Robinson, and Sammy *Marks, a member of the senate. Subsequent Jewish members of the Union parliament included Morris *Kentridge, the first Jewish Labor member of parliament, who sat continously from 1924 to 1958, Leopold *Lovell, Hyman Davidoff, Sam Kahn—the first Jewish communist MP, who was unseated in 1952 following the Suppression of Communism Act—Abe Bloomberg, and Charles Barnett. Jewish senators included: Franz Ginsberg, Fritz Baumann Adler, Alfred Friedlander, Hyman Basner, and Leslie Rubin. Two Jewish women also became prominent in the Union parliament: Bertha *Solomon, who advocated the cause of women's rights in parliament and initiated the Matrimonial Affairs Act of 1953, and Helen *Suzman who formed the Progressive Party to fight against apartheid and was the sole Progressive elected in the elections of 1961, 1966, and 1970. One Jew only was made a minister, Henry *Gluckman, who served as minister of health in the *Smuts cabinet from 1945 to 1948, and no Jew has ever been a member of the Nationalist Party in the House of Assembly. [Ed.]

South America. Before World War II Jews were not generally active in politics in South America, although in most South American states there were no legal bars to their entering parliament. They were handicapped by the fact that most were immigrants from Central and Eastern Europe and by deep-rooted anti-Semitism in many of the Catholic states. Nevertheless, a few Jews did achieve considerable prominence in political life. One of the first was Horacio *Lafer who was appointed Brazilian delegate to the League of Nations in 1928. He was a member of the Federal Chamber of Deputies from 1934 to 1964 and served as minister of finance and foreign minister in postwar Brazilian governments. Another important figure was Angel *Faivovich Hitzcovich who was elected to the Santiago municipal council in 1935. During a 30-year political career he was president of the Chilean Radical Party and vice-president of the senate. The number of Jews in politics gradually increased after World War II, particularly in Argentina where the Jewish population was at one time over half a million. Several Jews represented the Argentine Radical Party (Union Civica Radical Intransigente) in the Chamber of Deputies, among them Santiago Nudelman, David *Blejer, who was undersecretary to the ministers of the interior and of labor, Isaac Breyter, David *Schapira, and Naum Jaroslavsky. Enrique Dickman and Adolfo Dickman were prominent socialist deputies. Few Jews were prominent in Argentine politics during the rule of the dictator Domingo Peron but an exception was Jose Alexenicer (1903–) who was head of Peron's "Justice" Party in Cordoba and a member of the provincial parliament. In Chile, Miguel *Schweitzer, was minister of labor, and several other Jews were elected to the Chamber of Deputies. Among them were Jacobo *Schaulson Numhauser who was president of the Chamber of Deputies, and Daniel *Schweitzer, both of whom served as Chilean delegates to the United Nations. There were also two Jewish communist deputies in Chile, Adolfo Berman and Volodia Teitelbaum. Jews were also elected to parliament in Brazil where Marcos Melzer and Aarao Steinbruch sat in the Chamber of Deputies, while in Uruguay Jacobo *Guelman was a member of the senate as was Benazar *Serfaty in Venezuela. In Panama Max *Delvalle became first vice-president of Panama and was president for two months in 1968 following a controversial decision of the National Assembly to remove the constitutional president. He thus became the only Jew ever to become president of a state (outside of Israel).

In South America in general, both the Foreign Office and the army remain almost closed to Jews, and the few Jewish ambassadors who have served owe their appointment to personal friendships with the president in office. [P.Li./Ed.]

United States. Three facts stand out in connection with Jews in American politics. First, Jews have not been prominent as political office holders, political appointees, or party leaders. Perhaps the only time Jews held a disproportionately high number of political offices was during the 19th century in those areas of the country where they constituted a very small proportion of the population. Second, support for liberal and left of center parties and candidates is proportionately higher among Jews than among any other group in the United States. Third, Jews have never expressly organized themselves for solely political purposes and have not pressed expressly Jewish demands except where they perceived an acute danger to Jews outside the United States. They have been at pains to deny the existence of a Jewish political interest.

In the first half of the 19th century the small Jewish community in the United States tended to support the party of Jefferson. A disproportionate number of Jews, then largely of German origin, switched to the party of Lincoln, the Republican Party, by the end of the Civil War, paralleling a similar trend among other German immigrants. Jews continued to support the Republican Party even when its candidate for president was Ulysses S. Grant, who as a general in the Union army ordered the expulsion of all Jewish traders from an area under his command. (Lincoln canceled the order when he heard of it.) Grant later apologized, offered the post of secretary of the treasury to Joseph *Seligman, one of the most prominent Jews of his day, and appointed Benjamin *Peixotto as consul general to Rumania in the expectation that he would help Jews who were persecuted there. Republicans controlled the presidency from 1860 to 1912 except for Cleveland's two terms. They solidified their Jewish support through efforts on behalf of Jews in Eastern Europe. Among the Jews elected to Congress in the period were Lucius *Littauer from New York State and Michael Hahn from Louisiana. Abe *Ruef was "boss" of San Francisco and Simon *Wolf, president of B'nai B'rith and the leading Jewish public figure of this time, was appointed consul general to Egypt. Not all Jews were Republicans. In New York City Henry *Morgenthau and the *Straus brothers, Oscar, Isador, and Nathan, enlisted in the Democratic Party though they remained independent of Tammany Hall. Isador was elected to Congress but later broke with the party. Oscar was appointed minister to Turkey by Cleveland. He was not the first Jew to serve in that post. Earlier, Solomon *Hirsch had been appointed by Harrison. Indeed, the position became known as a Jewish preserve and when Woodrow *Wilson offered it to Henry Morgenthau, many Jews urged Morgenthau to decline for precisely that reason.

The Republican hold over the Jews was shaken in 1912. The Republican candidate, President Taft, had been unsympathetic to Jewish petitions to denounce the discriminatory Russian-American Passport Treaty and while Louis Marshall supported him, others, like Jacob *Schiff, switched to Theodore *Roosevelt. Jews were also attracted by the idealism and professorial background of Taft's Democratic opponent, Woodrow Wilson. Henry Morgenthau became chairman of the Democratic Finance Committee while Oscar Straus ran for governor of New York on Roosevelt's ticket. The Socialists also ran well among the immigrant Jews. Jewish candidates tended to come from Democratic or third-party ranks during this period. Immigrant Jewish voters in New York City sent Meyer *London to Congress on the Socialist ticket while Chicago voters elected Adolph *Sabath as a Democrat. In 1922 Sol *Bloom and Emanuel *Celler were first elected to Congress as Democrats from New York City. The most significant Jewish appointment in American history came with Wilson's nomination of Louis D. *Brandeis to the Supreme Court. Prominent Jewish Republicans included Murray *Seasongood, long-time mayor of Cincinnati, and Samuel Koenig, Republican leader of Manhattan. Judge Julian *Mack was appointed to the Circuit Court of Appeals by President Taft.

In the absence of voting studies it is difficult to estimate the distribution of the Jewish vote at this time. Socialist candidates did well among the immigrant Jews who comprised the vast majority of American Jewry. Outside New York City, the Socialists were less organized, Jewish trade union leaders less influential, Jewish workers less class conscious, and the most influential Yiddish newspaper, the Socialist *Daily Forward,* less available. One may presume that support for the Socialists was accordingly lower. However, even in New York, an attractive Democratic candidate with a liberal image such as Alfred E. Smith cut heavily into the Socialists' Jewish vote.

From 1930 Jews turned in ever larger numbers to the Democratic Party and three Jewish governors were elected in that year, including Henry *Horner of Illinois. In New York, Herbert *Lehman, running together with Franklin D. Roosevelt, was elected lieutenant governor and polled the highest plurality on the ticket. Lehman succeeded Roosevelt as governor in 1932. With the restoration of Democratic control at the national level after 1932, Jewish support for candidates whom they perceived as liberal in domestic politics and internationalist in foreign politics reached proportions of 80% and more. Since these candidates generally ran on the Democratic ticket, Jews became the most solidly Democratic voting group in the United States (with the possible exception of Negroes in later elections). Jewish support for Democratic candidates solidified during the presidency of Roosevelt whom Jews perceived as especially sympathetic to the plight of European Jewry. Roosevelt appointed a number of Jews to important positions: Henry *Morgenthau Jr. was secretary of the treasury, Felix *Frankfurter was an adviser and later an appointee to the Supreme Court, and men such as Samuel *Rosenman, David *Lilienthal, Bernard *Baruch, and Sidney *Hillman held his confidence and served him in various official and unofficial capacities.

Unlike other minority groups, Jews continued to support Democratic candidates after Roosevelt's death. However, third-party candidate Henry Wallace drew a heavily disproportionate share of the Jewish vote in 1948, indicating that Jews were more attracted by a candidate's ideology or personality than by party orientation. An estimated 75% of American Jews voted for Adlai Stevenson against the very popular military hero Dwight Eisenhower in 1952. Jews continued to support Stevenson in his 1956 campaign despite his lukewarm sympathies for Israel; after initial suspicions, they were also attracted to John Kennedy. A Connecticut Senator, Abraham *Ribicoff, was an intimate political ally of Kennedy both before and during the time he held office, and Arthur *Goldberg was a Kennedy nominee as secretary of labor and later to the Supreme Court. In 1964 distrust of Barry Goldwater as much as enthusiasm for Lyndon Johnson brought Jewish support for the Democratic candidate up to 90%. In the 1968 presidential election. Hubert Humphrey, the Democratic candidate, received an estimated 81% of the Jewish vote, compared to 17% for the victor, Richard Nixon, and 1% for the right-wing third-party candidate, George Wallace. Among the very few prominent Jews associated with Nixon was UJA leader Max *Fisher. (Nixon's foreign policy adviser, Henry Kissinger, a Jew, was rather distant from the Jewish community.) In 1970 there was no Jew in the cabinet or the Supreme Court and no leader of the Jewish community especially close to Nixon. The leading Jewish figure in the Republican Party during the 1960s was New York Senator Jacob *Javits. The leading Democrat was Arthur Goldberg, who served as secretary of labor, Supreme Court justice, ambassador to the United Nations, and unsuccessful candidate for governor of New York in 1970. There were numerous cases of political candidates detached from the Jewish community who fervently sought to re-identify themselves before an election. On the other hand, Jews tended to be repelled by excessive appeals to them as Jews by Jewish candidates, as in the case of contests for the New York City mayoralty in 1945 and 1965. Jewish political figures holding elective office, particularly where a high proportion of their constituents were Jews, usually fulfilled expectations that they would support Jewish causes, particularly Israel. In large cities the Jewish community and other ethnic groups seemed to expect political "recognition" by the political parties in the form of nominees and major appointments from their ranks. In general, Jewish candidates have not been put at a disadvantage by their religion. A 1969 national survey found that only 8% of the voters would oppose a candidate because he was a Jew whereas in 1937 the figure was 46%. A disproportionately large number of Jews go to the polls; they are better informed about politics than most other American groups and are among the large contributors to the funds of both main parties. Nevertheless, they have not been very prominent in the number of elective or appointive positions they have held. Only among left-wing parties and pressure groups were Jews particularly prominent in leading posts, but even here their numbers were not disproportionately great in relation to the number of Jews who were members of these groups. Jews were prominent in the Reform clubs that developed after 1945 in New York, Chicago, and California as efforts to reorganize and reform the parties, especially the Democratic Party. They have always been prominent in mildly leftist organizations such as the Americans for Democratic Action while Jewish labor leaders were among the most militant in demanding the partisan political mobilization of American workers. They were founders and chief supporters of the New York State American Labor Party (A.L.P.) in 1936 and the anti-communist Liberal Party which split off from the A.L.P. In 1944 Jews were also prominent in the Communist supported Progressive Party whose candidate, Henry Wallace, ran for president in 1948 and among the supporters, activists, and leaders of the radical left ("old left" perhaps more so than "new left"). At one time Jews comprised an estimated 50% of the U.S. Communist Party.

Jewish propensity for the radical left is a fascinating and important subject. In the light of the anti-Israel and even anti-Semitic orientation of the far left, its continued attraction for many intelligent, idealistic young Jews is a subject of much concern within the Jewish community. But the fact remains that both the old left and the new left attract only a small number of Jews. The more significant question which has received relatively little attention is why Jews so overwhelmingly support liberal and moderate leftist candidates. This support is all the more striking and dramatic, given the very high socioeconomic position of the Jews. Among other ethnic and religious groups, high socioeconomic position has resulted in support for the Republican Party and center, or right of center, candidates. One study found that Jews voted 45% more Democratic than would be expected from their social and demographic characteristics. This compares to Catholics who were 3% more Democratic or non-Southern Negroes who were 12% more Democratic than was to be anticipated. But, as was indicated, it is not the Democratic Party which Jews support but rather political liberalism. There are at least four theories which purport to explain Jewish orientation to left of center ideologies and parties. One theory explains Jewish liberalism on the basis of traditional Jewish values. Three values have been suggested as particularly relevant politically: the value of study and learning, which is translated into support for social planning; the value of communal responsibility for the welfare of others which is translated into support for social justice and welfare policies; and a worldly, non-ascetic orientation which is translated politically into a stress on creation of a better life in the present rather than awaiting a heavenly reward. All these values presumably result in support for liberal rather than conservative candidates.

There are a number of difficulties with this theory. (1) Jewish religious values are not unambiguously liberal. There are elements within the religious tradition which are folk-oriented, ethnocentric, and even hostile to non-Jews and to secular education, rather than universalistic, cosmopolitan, and positive toward knowledge of all kinds. While Jewish liberals may find their source of values in the religious traditions, conservatives may do so as well. At the least, each group is choosing selectively. (2) It is not at all clear that theological values or beliefs are readily transferable to the arena of politics. Indeed, the evidence suggests that political behavior is not a direct consequence of a diffuse ideology, particularly an ideology derived from theology. (3) If the source of Jewish liberalism is the religious tradition, one would expect that the more religious a Jew was, the more liberal he would be. In fact, it would seem that Orthodox Jews are the least liberal politically. Certainly, Orthodox rabbinical organizations have been less liberal politically in their public posture than have Conservative rabbis, and the latter less liberal than the Reform. One study, confined to members of a Conservative synagogue, found that those who were most religiously involved in Jewish life were no more likely to be politically liberal than those who were least religiously involved.

A second theory for Jewish liberalism is based on the purported status inferiority of Jews. According to this argument, Jews enjoy a social status far below what they might anticipate from their economic attainments. Consequently they are attracted to political ideologies which challenge the establishment and culture that disadvantage them. Among the difficulties with this theory are that it accounts for Jewish radicalism rather than liberalism. Secondly, it leaves unanswered the question why Jews should respond to society's image of them rather than to their own self-image. Thirdly, it faces the difficulty that after World War II Jews in America—certainly young American Jews—do not perceive of themselves as suffering from status inferiority. Finally, while there is no empirical evidence in support of the theory, there is some to the contrary. A study of a small sample of Jews found an inverse relationship between political liberalism and feelings of ethnic subordination. Ethnic subordination was defined as insecurity and defensiveness in social situations with gentiles or concern about recriminations for conspicuous Jewish behavior and thus seems very close to status inferiority.

A third theory accounts for Jewish liberalism by historical factors. Following the French Revolution it was the left which adopted the view that citizenship should be extended to everyone, that the national state was secular, and that religious affiliation was irrelevant to political equality. The right associated citizenship with the nation's Christian traditions. Jews, therefore, were attracted to parties of the left, particularly the moderate left which was anti-conservative but also upheld law and order against plebian attacks and revolutionary capriciousness that often included anti-Semitic sentiments. Furthermore, the extreme left's political ideology, unlike that of the moderate left, comprised a total *Weltanschauung* which left no room at all for Jewish allegiances. Among the problems with the historical theory is that it posits too much for events that occurred so many generations ago in an environment totally foreign to the American political tradition. American Jews after the Civil War were predominantly Republican. Even among the immigrants at the turn of the century, the Orthodox Yiddish press was Republican, not Democratic and not Socialistic. The historical theory accounts for Jewish orientation to parties of the left rather than to leftist ideologies and fails to explain why, in the American context, Jews should have left the Republican Party. The final theory suggests that Jewish liberalism, rather than stemming from the Jewish tradition, finds its source in the values of modern, estranged, partially assimilated Jews who seek a universalistic ethic to which they can adhere. Liberalism, they believe, will help integrate them into the broader community by destroying the barriers of cultural, religious, and political traditions separating them from non-Jews. The effect of liberalism, unlike radicalism, is that it leaves room for Judaism as a purely religious, narrowly defined aspect of life. Liberalism makes one's religio-ethnic-cultural identity politically irrelevant, and this is precisely what the emancipated and partially assimilated Jew desires. Indeed, the basic Jewish commitment according to this theory is less to liberalism than to "enlightenment," the optimistic faith that the application of human intellect can create a constantly progressing, universal, cosmopolitan society. Internationalism, civil libertarianism, and welfarism are merely consequences of this basic commitment. But it is the image of the "enlightened" society and the "enlightenment" liberal that holds greatest resonance for the Jew. To this extent political style may be more important than policy content. It is difficult to cite examples where Jews had to choose between an "enlightenment" candidate and one who was more liberal. One case may be the contest between Woodrow Wilson and Theodore Roosevelt for the 1912 presidency, and another between Adlai Stevenson and Estes Kefauver for the 1956 Democratic nomination. In both cases Jews supported the "enlightenment"-style candidates, Wilson and Stevenson, over their opponents who were more liberal politically. Generally, however, the "enlightenment" candidate is the more liberal candidate. The liberal-enlightenment ideology satisfies the basic desire of most American Jews to be accepted in the society as individuals with their Judaism a matter of irrelevance, but on the other hand to be free to live as the kind of Jews they wish to be. The principal difficulties which arise in connection with this theory are that it seems to rest on a particular interpretation of Jewish behavior and identity since the emancipation and that there is no direct empirical evidence to support it.

[C.S.L.]

Bibliography: C. Roth, *Jewish Contribution to Civilization* (1956[3]), 230ff.; V. D. Lipman (ed.), *Three Centuries of Anglo-Jewish History* (1961), index; L. H. Fuchs, *Political Behaviour of American Jews* (1956); W. Cohn, in: M. Sklare (ed.), *The Jews* (1958), 614–26; N. Glazer and D. P. Moynihan, *Beyond the Melting Pot* (1964); C. S. Liebman, in: D. Cutler (ed.), *Religious Situation 1969* (1969), 1034–61.

Noted Jewish Politicians. The individuals whose names are marked with an asterisk in the list below form the subjects of articles in their appropriate alphabetical position in the Encyclopaedia.

***ADLER, FRIEDRICH** (1879–1960), Austrian Socialist politician and secretary of the Socialist International.

***ADLER, VICTOR** (1852–1918), Austrian Socialist leader.

***ALEXANDER, MORRIS** (1877–1946), South African lawyer and politician.

***ALEXANDER, MOSES** (1853–1932), Democratic governor of Idaho.

***ARDITI, ALBERT** (1891–1942), Greek Socialist leader.

***ARNHEIM, FISCHEL** (1812–1864), German politician.

***ARVEY, JACOB M.** (1893–), U.S. politician.

***ASHENHEIM, SIR NEVILLE** (1900–), Jamaican minister of state for France.

***ASHKENAZI, BEHOR** (1840–1909), Turkish senator.

***BAERWALD, MORITZ** (1860–1919), German politician.

BAKKER-NORT, BETSY (1874–1946), Dutch parliamentarian and feminist. Betsy Bakker-Nort was one of the first woman lawyers in Holland. Elected to the second chamber as a liberal democrat in 1922, she advocated rights for women and fought for women's suffrage. She continued in parliament until the German invasion in 1940. Deported to Theresienstadt in 1944, she died a year after her release.

***BAMBERGER, EDOUARD-ADRIEN** (1825–1910), French Republican deputy.

***BAMBERGER, LUDWIG** (1823–1899), German banker and liberal politician.

***BAMBERGER, SIMON** (1846–1926), U.S. industrialist and first Democratic governor of Utah.

***BARZILAI, SALVATORE** (1860–1939), Italian senator.

***BAUER, OTTO** (1881–1938), Austrian Socialist foreign minister.

BENJAMIN, BARUCH BENZION (1904–), Indian govern-
BENSANCHI, MENTESH (Mordecai; 1882–1943), Greek
ment official. Born in Bombay, Benjamin joined the Indian government service following independence in 1947 and was made deputy chief controller of imports and exports in 1953. From 1955 until his retirement in 1959 he was an undersecretary in the Indian Ministry of Finance. Active in Jewish affairs, Benjamin was a vice-president of the World Council of Synagogues and president of the Delhi Jewish Welfare Association.
journalist and member of parliament. Born in Salonika, he became editor of several Salonika newspapers, including *El Imparcial* and *L'Indépendant.* A liberal Zionist and an outstanding orator, he was sent by Salonika Jewry as its representative to the Greek parliament. When the Nazis invaded Greece, he fled to Crete where he was seized and tortured to death by the Germans.

***BERGH, GEORGE VAN DEN** (1890–1966), Dutch lawyer, Socialist politician, and writer.

***BERGH, SAMUEL VAN DEN** (1864–1942), Dutch liberal politician.

***BERMAN, ADOLPH** (1906–), Polish Socialist and Zionist leader.

***BERMAN, JACOB** (1901–), Polish Communist leader and deputy premier.

***BESSIS, ALBERT** (1883–), Tunisian minister of public works.

***BLEJER, DAVID** (1913–), Argentine statesman.

***BLOCH, PIERRE** (1905–), French Socialist leader.

***BLOOM, SOL** (1870–1949), U.S. Democratic politician.

***BLUM, LEON** (1872–1950), French Socialist prime minister.

***BOKANOWSKI, MAURICE** (1879–1928), French minister of commerce and industry.

***BRANDES, CARL** (1847–1931), Danish minister of finance.

***BRAUN, ADOLF** (1861–1929), leader of the German Social Democratic Party.

***BREITNER, HUGO** (1873–1946), German Socialist politician.

***BRISCOE, ROBERT** (1894–1968), Irish politician and lord mayor of Dublin.

***CARASSO, EMMANUEL** (1862–1934), a leader of the Young Turk movement.

***CELLER, EMANUEL** (1888–), U.S. Democratic congressman.

***COHEN, SAMUEL** (1918–1969), Australian labor senator.

***CREMIEUX, ISAAC-ADOLPHE** (1796–1880), French lawyer, politician, and minister of defense.

***CRESTOHL, LEON** (1900–1963), Canadian liberal politician.

***CROLL, DAVID ARNOLD** (1900–), Ontario minister of labor, public welfare, and municipal affairs.

***CZECH, LUDWIG** (1870–1942), Czechoslovak Socialist minister of works.

***DAN, FYODOR ILYICH** (1871–1947), Russian Socialist.

DANIEL, EZRA (1876–1952), Iraqi senator and communal leader (see *Daniel, Menahem).

***DANIEL, MENAHEM** (1846–1940), Iraqi senator and philanthropist.

DELLA SETA, UGO (1879–1958), Italian politician and philosopher. Della Seta taught philosophy in Italian nonconformist high schools and universities and was dismissed and persecuted by the Fascist regime after refusing to take the oath. After World War II he was elected member of the Constituent Assembly and was a senator in the first two Republican parliaments. He was active on behalf of religious minorities in Italy. He wrote works on philosophy and *La Legge fondamentale sui culti ammessi* (1937).

***DELVALLE, MAX** (1911–), vice-president of Panama.

***DIAMAND, HERMAN** (1860–1930), Polish Socialist politician.

***DIAMOND, JOHN, BARON** (1907–), English Labor politician.

***DISRAELI, BENJAMIN (Lord Beaconfield;** 1804–1881), British prime minister.

***DROBNER, BOLESLAW** (1883–1968), Polish Socialist leader.

***DYMSHYTS, VENYAMIN** (1910–), deputy premier of the Soviet Union.

***EISNER, KURT** (1867–1919), German Socialist and premier of the Bavarian Democratic Republic.

***ELLENBOGEN, WILHELM** (1863–1951), Austrian Socialist politician.

***ENNERY, JONAS** (1801–1863), French politician.

***FAIVOVICH HITZCOVICH, ANGEL** (1900–), Chilean professor of law and Radical Party leader.

***FISCHER, RUTH** (1895–1961), German Communist leader.

***FOULD, ACHILLE** (1800–1867), French minister of finance.

***FRANKEL, LEO** (1844–1896), Socialist leader and minister of labor in the Paris Commune.

FRANKLIN, LUMLEY (1812–1873), mayor of Victoria, British Columbia (see *Franklin, Selim).

***FRANKLIN, SELIM** (1814–1883), Canadian politician.

***FRIEDMAN, NAPHTALI MARKOWITZ** (1863–1921), Russian Kadet politician.

GASTON-MARIN (Grossman), GHEORGHE (1919–), Rumanian politician and engineer. Born in Petrosani, Transylvania, Gaston-Marin was active in Zionist circles in his youth. He went to Paris where he qualified as an electrical engineer and was a member of the French Resistance during World War II. After the war he returned to Rumania, joined the Communist Party, and was made minister of electrical energy in 1949. In 1954 he became first vice-chairman of the State Planning Commission and from 1962 to 1969 was head of the Rumanian industrialization program with the rank of deputy-premier.

***GHELERTER, LITMAN** (1873–1946), Rumanian Socialist.

***GLUCKMAN, HENRY** (1893–), South African minister of health.

***GODEFROI, MICHAEL** (1813–1883), first Jewish minister of justice in Holland.

GOETSCHEL, JULES (1908–), Swiss politician and communal leader. Goetschel was the Social Democratic member of the cantonal parliament of Basle (1949–68) and its president for

1967–68. He was active in the affairs of the Basle Jewish community.

*GOLDBERG, ARTHUR (1908–), U.S. ambassador to the United Nations and Supreme Court Justice.

*GOLDSTEIN, ANGELO (1889–1947), Jewish Party leader in the Czechoslovak parliament.

*GOUDCHAUX, MICHEL (1797–1861), French banker and minister of finance.

GRANDVAL (Hirsch-Ollendorf), GILBERT YVES EDMOND (1904–), French statesman. Born in Paris, Grandval was director of a chemical production concern from 1917 to 1940 and after the fall of France joined the French Resistance, becoming one of its leaders. He was appointed military governor of the Saar region in 1945 and from 1948 to 1952 was French High Commissioner for the Saar. Grandval was later resident-general in Morocco (1953), secretary of state for foreign trade (1962), and from 1962 to 1966 was minister of labor.

*GRAY, HERBERT (1931–), Canadian liberal politician and the first Jewish federal minister.

*GRAY, MORRIS (1889–1966), Canadian Socialist politician and Zionist figure.

*GRUENBAUM, HENRY (1911–), Danish Socialist minister of finance.

*GRUENING, ERNEST (1887–), U.S. Democratic senator.

*GRUMBACH, SALOMON (1884–1952), French Socialist leader.

*GUELMAN, JACOBO (1900–), Uruguayan liberal senator.

*GUTT, CAMILLE (1884–1971), Belgian liberal minister of finance.

*HAAS, LUDWIG (1875–1930), German politician.

*HAASE, HUGO (1863–1919), German Socialist leader.

HAHN, MICHAEL (1830–1886), governor of the state of Louisiana. Born in Bavaria, Germany, Hahn was brought to New Orleans, La., as a child and was admitted to the bar in 1851. During the Civil War he supported the Unionist cause and was elected to Congress in 1863. He became governor of Louisiana in the following year, the first Jewish governor in the U.S. Hahn resigned the governorship in 1865 following his election to the Senate but never took his seat. He returned to Congress as a Republican in 1884 and served until his death.

*HAMON, LEO (1908–), French Gaullist politician.

HARRIS, SIR PERCY (1876–1952), English statesman. Born in London, Harris was admitted to the bar in 1899. He traveled around the world three times and lived in New Zealand for three years. From 1907 to 1934 and from 1946 until his death he was a member of the London County Council and served as its deputy chairman from 1915 to 1916. In that year he returned to parliament as Liberal member for Harborough. Harris was elected for a second time in 1922 and sat continously until 1945 when he retired. He was made a baronet in 1932 and from 1940 to 1945 was deputy leader of the Liberal Party in the House of Commons. His publications include *London and Its Government* (1931[2]).

*HART, DANIEL (1800–1852), Jamaica judge and politician.

*HART, SAMUEL (c. 1747–1810), merchant and Nova Scotia politician.

*HASSAN, SIR JOSHUA (1915–), chief minister of Gibraltar.

*HILFERDING, RUDOLF (1877–1942), German Socialist minister of finance.

*HORE-BELISHA, LESLIE, LORD (1898–1957), British minister of war.

*HORNER, HENRY (1878–1940), governor of Illinois.

*HYMANS, PAUL (1865–1941), Belgian liberal politician and four times foreign minister.

JACOBS, ALETTA (1854–1929), Dutch physician, feminist, and pacifist. She was the first woman to study at a Dutch university, and became the first Dutch woman to practice as a doctor. She championed women's emancipation and advocated neo-Malthusianism for the working class. As a pacifist she sponsored the International Peace Congress at The Hague in 1915 which led to the foundation of the Women's International League for Peace and Freedom.

JAKOBSON, MAX (1923–), Finnish journalist and diplomat. Born in Viborg, Jakobson worked in the Finnish News Agency and later in the Finnish department of the B.B.C. He was also the correspondent for *Helsingin Sanomat* and *Uusi Suomi.* He was press attaché at the Finnish embassy in Washington (1953–59) and chief of the press department of the Finnish foreign ministry (1962–65). In 1965 he was made permanent representative of Finland at the United Nations.

*JAVITS, JACOB (1904–), attorney general of New York state and New York Republican senator.

*JOGICHES, LEON (1867–1919), Polish Socialist leader.

JOSEPH, SIR KEITH (1918–), British Conservative politician and cabinet minister (see *Joseph family).

*KAGANOVICH, LAZAR (1893–), Soviet Communist leader.

*KAHN, JULIUS (1861–1924), U.S. Republican congressman.

*KAMENEV, LEO BORISOVICH (1883–1936), Soviet Communist Party leader.

*KENTRIDGE, MORRIS (1881–1964), South African Labor politician.

*KLEEREKOPER, ASSER (1880–1943), Dutch Socialist politician.

*KLOTZ, LOUIS-LUCIEN (1868–1930), French minister of finance.

*KREISKY, BRUNO (1911–), Socialist chancellor of Austria.

KRIEGEL-VALRIMONT, MAURICE (1914–), French Communist politician. Born in Strasbourg, he became in World War II, under the assumed name of Valrimont, one of the three members of the Action Committee of the French Resistance. After the liberation of France, he was a member of the Communist Party's Central Committee. He sat in the National Assembly from 1944 to 1958, when he was expelled from the party as a revisionist. His wife, Annie Besse, at one time an active Communist, later wrote several books criticizing the evolution of Marxism.

*KUN, BELA (1886–1939), Hungarian Communist who was briefly dictator of Hungary.

*KUNFI, ZSIGMOND (1879–1929), Hungarian Socialist.

*LAFER, HORACIO (1893–1965), Brazilian statesman, industrialist, and minister of finance and foreign affairs.

*LANDA, ABRAM (1902–), New South Wales cabinet minister.

*LANDAUER, GUSTAV (1870–1919), German Anarchist-Socialist and minister of information in the Bavarian revolutionary government.

*LANDSBERG, OTTO (1869–1957), German Socialist leader and minister of justice.

*LASKER, EDUARD (1829–1883), leader of the German National Liberal Party.

*LEHMAN, HERBERT HENRY (1878–1963), four times Democratic governor of New York.

*LEVER, NORMAN HAROLD (1914–), British politician and financial expert.

*LEVI, PAUL (1883–1930), German lawyer and Communist Party leader.

*LEVINE, EUGENE (1883–1919), head of the short-lived Bavarian People's Republic.

*LEWIS, DAVID (1909–), leader of the Canadian New Democratic Party.

*LIEBERMAN, HERMAN (1870–1941), Polish advocate and Socialist leader.

LIMBURG, JOSEPH (1866–1940), Dutch politician. One of the founders of the Liberal Democratic Party, Limburg was a member of the second chamber of parliament (1905–17). The education act adopted in 1917 bears his name. He was a member of the Netherlands delegation to the League of Nations in 1920. In 1926 he was entrusted with the formation of a cabinet, but failed and left politics. He was a member of the Council of State until 1940, when, on the Netherlands' surrender to Germany, he committed suicide.

*LONDON, ARTHUR (1915–), Czechoslovak statesman and Communist leader.

*LONDON, MEYER (1871–1926), U.S. lawyer and Socialist congressman.

*LOVELL, LEOPOLD (1905–), South African Labor Party politician and Swaziland minister of finance.

*LOVESTONE, JAY (1898–), U.S. Communist labor leader.

*LOZOVSKI, SOLOMON ABRAMOVICH (1878–1952), Soviet statesman and trade union leader.

*LUZZATTI, LUIGI (1841–1927), Italian lawyer and economist and first prime minister of Italy.

*MANCROFT, LORD (**Sir Arthur Mancroft**; 1877–1942), British Conservative politician and minister for the Department of Overseas Trade.

*MANCROFT, LORD (Sir Stormont Mancroft; 1914–), British Conservative minister.
*MANDEL, GEORGES (1885–1944), French cabinet minister.
*MANDEL, MARVIN (1920–), Democratic governor of Maryland.
*MARSHALL, DAVID (1908–), chief minister of Singapore.
*MARTOV, JULIUS (1873–1923), Russian revolutionary and Menshevik leader.
*MAYER, DANIEL (1909–), secretary-general of the French Socialist Party.
*SCHWEITZER, MIGUEL (1908–), Chilean lawyer and premier.
*MEIER, JULIUS L. (1874–1937), U.S. statesman and governor of Oregon.
MENDELS, MAURITS (1868–1944), Dutch Socialist politician. A son of a Hague *shamash,* Mendels worked as a journalist, and from 1909 practiced as a lawyer in Amsterdam. A member of the Dutch Socialist Party, he was a member of the second chamber of parliament (1913–19) and a member of the senate (1919–37), where he specialized in legal affairs. He was also a municipal councillor and a member of the Provincial Council of North Holland. He died in Theresienstadt in 1944.
*MENDES-FRANCE, PIERRE (1907–), Radical Socialist politician and premier of France.
*MEYER, LEON (1868–1957), French Radical Socialist minister of mercantile marine.
*MINC, HILARY (1905–), Polish Communist leader.
*MIRANDA, SALOMON RODRIGUES DE (1878–1941), Dutch Socialist minister of housing and public works.
*MOCH, JULES (1893–), French Socialist politician who held numerous cabinet appointments.
*MODIGLIANI, VITTORIO (1872–1947), Italian Socialist politician.
*MONTAGU, EDWIN (1879–1924), British liberal politician and cabinet minister.
*MYERS, SIR ARTHUR (1867–1926), mayor of Auckland and New Zealand cabinet minister.
*NAQUET, ALFRED JOSEPH (1834–1916), French chemist and Republican politician.
*NATHAN, ERNESTO (1845–1921), Italian statesman and first Jewish mayor of Rome.
*NATHAN, HENRY (1842–1914), first Jew to sit in the Canadian federal parliament.
*NILES, DAVID (1890–1952), U.S. Democratic politician and presidential aide.
NUDELMAN, SANTIAGO I. (1904–), Argentine politician. Born in the colony of Medanos in the province of Buenos Aires, Nudelman graduated in both medicine (1930) and law (1936) from the University of Buenos Aires. He was a member of the Federal Chamber of Deputies (1946–55) and championed the cause of civil liberties in parliament. In 1958 he became director of the daily newspaper *Critica.*
*ORLIKOW, DAVID (1918–), Canadian politician.
*PAUKER, ANA (1890–1958), Rumanian Communist leader and minister of foreign affairs.
PHILLIPS, NATHAN (1892–), Canadian lawyer and politician. Born in Brockville, Ontario, Phillips was made a king's counsel in 1929. He was counsel for the successful plaintiff in the case of *Applebaum v. Gilchrist* (1946) which established legal rights for Canadian women. A member of the Toronto city council for 36 years, he was the first Jewish mayor (1954–62). The area surrounding the new city hall was named Nathan Phillips Square in his honor. He was president of the Toronto *B'nai Brith in 1932. His autobiography, *Mayor of All the People,* appeared in 1967.
*PIJADE, MOŠA (1890–1957), Yugoslav Communist leader.
*POLAK, CAREL (1909–), Dutch minister of justice.
*POLAK, HENRI (1863–1943), Dutch Socialist senator.
*RADEK, KARL (1885–1939), Soviet Communist leader.
*RÁKOSI, MÁTYÁS (1892–1971), Hungarian Communist dictator.
*RATHENAU, WALTER (1867–1922), German industrialist, liberal politician, and foreign minister of Germany.
*RAUH, JOSEPH (1911–) U.S. lawyer and politician.
*RAYNAL, DAVID (1841–1903), French cabinet minister.
*READING, LORD (Rufus Isaacs; 1860–1935), English attorney general, lord chief justice, viceroy of India, and foreign secretary.
*READING, LORD (Gerald Isaacs; 1889–1960), English lawyer and Conservative statesman.
*REDLICH, JOSEF (1869–1936), Austrian jurist and minister of finance.
*REINACH, JOSEPH (1856–1921), French statesman and historian.
*RIBICOFF, ABRAHAM (1910–), U.S. Democratic secretary of health, education, and welfare.
*ROMANIN JACUR, LEONE (1847–1928), Italian senator.
*ROSE, ALEX (1898–), leader of the U.S. Labor and Liberal parties.
*ROSENBERG, ARTHUR (1889–1943), German Communist and historian.
*SABATH, ADOLF (1866–1952), U.S. Democratic congressman.
*SALOMONS, SIR JULIAN (1836–1909), Australian lawyer and politician, New South Wales solicitor general and agent-general in London.
*SALSBERG, JOSEPH (1902–), Canadian Communist leader.
SALVADOR, FRANCIS (1747–1776), first Jewish member of a legislative body in the U.S. (see *Salvador).
*SAMKALDEN, IVO (1912–), Dutch minster of justice and mayor of Amsterdam.
*SAMUEL, HERBERT LOUIS, VISCOUNT (1870–1963), British statesman, cabinet minister, philosopher, and first high commissioner of Palestine.
*SAMUEL, SIR SAUL (1820–1900), Australian politician, member of the New South Wales government.
SCHANZER, CARLO (1865–?), Italian statesman. Born in Vienna, Schanzer emigrated to Italy with his family and qualified as a lawyer. He joined the Italian government service and in 1901 he was made director general of civil administration in the Italian Ministry of the Interior. He was elected to the National Assembly in 1906 and was made minister of posts soon afterwards. After World War I Schanzer became a senator, and served as minister of finance (1919–20) and foreign minister (1922), but retired from political affairs following Mussolini's seizure of power.
SCHAPIRA, DAVID (1901–), Argentine politician. Born in Carlos Casares at one of the agricultural settlements established by Baron *Hirsch, Schapira practiced medicine, and in 1958 was elected senator for the province of Buenos Aires. He was chairman of the Senate Public Health Committee and from 1963 to 1966 sat in the National Chamber of Deputies until the military regime of General Ongania closed the parliament.
*SCHAULSON NUMHAUSER, JACOBO (1917–), Chilean lawyer and Radical Party leader.
*SCHRAMECK, ABRAHAM (1867–1948), French cabinet minister.
*SCHWARZ, SOLOMON (1883–), Russian Menshevik leader and historian.
*SCHWARZBART, ISAAC IGNACY (1888–1961), Polish statesman, leader of the World Jewish Congress in the U.S.
*MAYER, RENÉ (1895–1972), French Radical Socialist and politician.
SERFATY BENAZAR, RAFAEL (1919–), Venezuelan politician. Born in Los Teques, Serfaty was first director and later vice-president of the National Telephone Company. He was elected senator of the Republic in 1963 in the federal elections.
SERUYA, SOLOMON (1926–), Gibraltar politician (see *Seruya).
*SHAPP, MILTON J. (1912–), Democratic governor of Pennsylvania.
SHINAH, SELMAN (1898–), Iraqi lawyer, politician, and Hebrew writer. An officer in the Turkish army in World War I, Shinah was captured and exiled to India until 1919. He was elected the Jewish representative in the Iraqi parliament in 1947 and 1949. He founded the Hebrew Writers' Union in 1920, and published a Zionist weekly in Arabic, *Al-Mazaret* ("The Menorah"), which lasted until 1929. He settled in Israel in 1951. His autobiography, *Mi-Bavel le-Ẓiyyon* ("From Babylon to Zion"), appeared in 1955.
*SHINWELL, LORD (Emanuel Shinwell; 1884–), British Socialist politician and cabinet minister.
*SILKIN, LORD (Lewis Silkin; 1889–1972), British Socialist politician and minister of town and country planning.
SILKIN, JOHN (1923–), British Socialist cabinet minister; see *Silkin, Lewis.

***SILVERMAN, SAMUEL SIDNEY** (1895–1968), British Socialist politician.
***SIMON, JOSEPH** (1851–1935), U.S. Republican senator.
***SINGER, PAUL** (1844–1911), leader of the German Social Democratic Party.
***SOLOMON, BERTHA** (1891–1969), South African lawyer and politician.
SOLOMON, VABIAN (1859–1908), prime minister of South Australia; see *Solomon.
SOMEN, ISRAEL (1903–), public figure in Kenya. Born in London, Somen was taken to South Africa when he was a child, and in 1923 went to Kenya where he joined the colonial service. Somen was mayor of Nairobi from 1955 to 1957 and honorary consul for Israel before Kenya's independence. He was also president of the Nairobi Hebrew congregation.
***SONNINO, SIDNEY** (1847–1922), prime minister of Italy.
***STAHL, FRIEDRICH JULIUS** (1801–1861), German Conservative leader.
***STEINBERG, ISAAC NACHMAN** (1888–1957), Russian revolutionary, Zionist, and Soviet minister of justice.
***STEINBRUCH, AARÃO** (1915–), Brazilian senator and president of the Labor Party.
STEINGUT, IRWIN (1893–1952), U.S. lawyer and Democratic politician (see *Steingut).
***STERN, JACQUES** (1881–1949), French cabinet minister.
***STERN, PHILIP** (1847–1933), Jamaica lawyer and politician.
***STRAUSS, GEORGE** (1901–), British Socialist politician and minister of supply.
***SUZMAN, HELEN** (1917–), South African politician and representative of the Progressive Party in parliament.
***SVERDLOV, YAKOV MIKHAILOVICH** (1885–1919), Soviet revolutionary and Communist leader.
***SZENDE, PÁL** (1879–1930), Hungarian minister of finance.
***SZYR, EUGENIUSZ** (1915–), Polish Communist leader and deputy prime minister.
***TEITELBOIM, VOLODIA VALENTIN** (1916–), Chilean Communist leader.
***TERRACINI, UMBERTO** (1895–), Italian Communist senator.
***TROTSKY, LEV DAVIDOVICH** (1879–1940), Russian revolutionary and organizer of the Red Army.
***VADÁSZ, LIPÓT** (1861–1924), Hungarian lawyer and politician.
***VÁZSONYI, VILMOS** (1868–1926), Hungarian minister of justice.
***VLADECK, BARUCH** (1886–1938), leader of the U.S. Labor Party.
VOS, ISIDOR H. J. (1887–1942), Dutch physician and liberal politician. Vos was head of the hygiene department of the Netherlands army headquarters (1914–18), and later an Amsterdam councillor and alderman. From 1928 to 1940 he was a member of the second chamber of the Dutch parliament. Given the opportunity to leave Holland after the German invasion in World War II, he sent his family away but he stayed, and died in a concentration camp.
***WARSKI-WARSZAWSKI, ADOLF** (1868–1937), founder of the Polish Communist Party.
***WEICHMANN, HERBERT** (1896–), German Social Democrat, president of the upper house of the German parliament.
***WELENSKY, SIR ROY** (1907–), prime minister of the federation of Rhodesia and Nyasaland.
***WIJNKOOP, DAVID** (1876–1941), chairman of the Dutch Communist Party.
***WOLLEMBORG, LEONE** (1859–1932), Italian minister of finance.
***WORMS, HENRY DE (Lord Pirbright;** 1840–1903), English liberal politician and undersecretary of state for the colonies.
***YAROSLAVSKY, YEMELYAN** (1878–1943), Soviet Communist leader, publicist, and historian.
***YULEE, DAVID** (1810–1886), first Jewish senator in the United States.
***ZAMBROWSKI, ROMAN** (1909–), Polish Communist leader.
ZAY, JEAN (1904–1944), French socialist politician. Born in Orleans, Zay joined the Radical Socialist Party in his youth and was elected a deputy in 1932. He became undersecretary of state in 1936 and was appointed minister of national education in Léon *Blum's Popular Front government in the same year. He held this position in successive governments until 1940, despite bitter criticism of his support for the republican cause in Spain. Following the fall of France Zay was arrested and held in prison, and was summarily executed on June 20, 1944.
***ZINOVIEV, GRIGORY EVSEEVICH** (1883–1936), Soviet Communist leader and head of the Communist International.

POLITISCHE GEMEINDE ("political community"), political group right conferred on Jewish communities in *Moravia. In Moravia Jews had for centuries been permitted to reside in a restricted number of locations only (52 according to the patent issued by Francis II on Feb. 15, 1798). These, and other restrictions, were abolished on March 4, 1849. On March 17, however, the *provisorisches Gemeindegesetz* ("provisional communities law") created 25 "political communities" (out of the 52 Jewish communities); the remainder were either placed under the jurisdiction of the local city or town authorities or merged with them (two additional political communities, Boskowitz (*Boskovice), and Holleschau (*Holešov), were created later, raising the total number to 27). The political communities were constituted as autonomous territorial units within the towns, having their own mayor and functionaries, municipal services, and right of taxation. Membership of the political community was hereditary. However as Jews tended to move out of the area of their former quarters while Czechs moved there instead, an anomalous situation was created, as for instance in Trebitsch (*Třebič), where of 1,342 persons living in 194 houses in 1921, only 178 were Jews. All the same, electoral rights for the political community were retained by Jews living elsewhere, either in the same town or in other localities.

The existence of the political communities was a factor in helping the Germans maintain an electoral majority in the country, since the political communities were represented in the municipal *curia* out of proportion to their numerical importance, and Jews, who tended to adopt German culture, generally supported Austro-German policies against the rising Czech national movement. The Czech parties tried to exclude the Jews from the assembly of municipal *curia* and to diminish their influence in the representation of the country (Landgemeindenkurie). It was indicated that in many cases there was no basis for the existence of a political community and that their existence was illegal because they were not territorial units. The political Jewish communities increasingly concentrated on political functions and ceased to be suitable for dealing with religious needs.

In 1880 the Austrian Ministry of the Interior ordered the amalgamation of the political communities with the local authorities, but this was not implemented because of the opposition of both Jews and Germans, which was given support by the courts. Ten years later a type of purely religious community, the *Kultusgemeinde,* was established by law. About 50 *Kultusgemeinden* were established in Moravia and they took over the religious functions of the political communities there. The political community, however, continued to exist until the dissolution of the Hapsburg Empire after World War I; 25 were liquidated by the Czechoslovak authorities in 1919–20, and the last two, Trebitsch and Misslitz (*Miroslav), in 1921. The institution of the political community was unique in retaining the features of the old Jewish communal autonomy within the modern political framework.

For map see *Moravia. [A.M.Rab.]

POLITZER, ADAM (1835–1920), founder of modern otology. Politzer, who was born in Alberti, Hungary, studied at Vienna University where from 1870 to 1907 he was professor of otology. During his tenure Vienna became the center for study in otology for students from all over the world. His *Lehrbuch der Ohrenheilkunde,* published in 1878 was translated into many languages and his *Geschichte der Ohrenheilkunde* (2 vols., 1907–13) was the authoritative book in that field.

Adam Politzer, Viennese physician, founder of modern otology. Jerusalem, J.N.U.L., Schwadron Collection.

Politzer devised many new methods for diagnosing and treating ear diseases. He invented a method of opening a blocked eustachian tube (a method which bears his name all over the world), a method for illuminating the eardrum, an ear speculum, and a bag for inflating the middle ear. He also showed how to test for deafness in one ear. Politzer founded the Otologic Clinic at Vienna University and the Austrian Otologic Society as well as the journal *Archiv fuer Ohrenheilkunde.*

Bibliography: S. R. Kagan, *Jewish Medicine* (1952), 493; *Biographisches Lexikon der hervorragenden Aerzte,* 4 (1932).

[S.M.]

POLLACK, JACOB BEN JOSEPH (1460/70–after 1522), rabbi and first Polish halakhic authority. His name has given rise to the conjecture that he was born in Poland, but it appears that he was born in Bavaria. Pollack studied under Jacob Margolis in Regensburg, and was already known in his youth as a profound talmudist. He married Esther, the daughter of Moses and Rachel Fischel of Cracow, who acted as government tax farmers and were on intimate terms with the Polish royal court, upon whom they were able to exercise some influence. Pollack was appointed rabbi in Prague and was a member of the *bet din* together with Isaac Margolis, the son of his teacher. In 1492 an incident took place which roused a violent controversy. His wife's sister, Sara had been married while a minor to David Zehner of Buda, Hungary. Before she reached her majority she exercised her right of *me'un* (see *Child Marriage) to free herself from her husband and Pollack permitted her to remarry, in accordance with talmudic law, despite the fact that *Menahem of Merseburg had 50 years earlier enacted a *takkanah* abolishing *me'un.* This permission roused against him all the great contemporary scholars and he was laid under a ban. The only one to support him was Meir Pfefferkorn because Jacob Pollack's mother-in-law had used her influence to obtain the release from prison of his wife and children.

Pollack left Prague and went to Cracow where he opened the first yeshivah in Poland and transferred there the method of *ḥillukim* ("fine distinctions") that he had learnt from his teachers. At that time knowledge of the Talmud in Poland was generally at a low ebb, and the talmudists were not conversant with this method of study. He was given the sobriquet of *avi ha-ḥillukim.* In Cracow he was highly admired and immediately became one of the communal leaders. When in 1494 the king of Poland imprisoned the dignitaries of Cracow, Pollack and his father- and mother-in-law were among them. After his release he moved together with the whole of the Cracow community to Kazimierz, a suburb of the town. In 1503 he was appointed by King Alexander as rabbi of the whole of Poland, or Lesser Poland—the letter of appointment is not clear. But Pollack was to find no tranquility in this position either. The friction and quarrels between the two local communities of Polish and Bohemian Jews embittered his life. Under pressure from the king, separate rabbis were finally chosen for the two communities, R. Perez for the Bohemians and Asher Lemel, Pollack's brother-in-law, for the Polish. Pollack retained only the conduct of his yeshivah. In 1520 a dispute which broke out in Italy on a financial matter between Emanuel of Ferrara and Abraham Raphael of Bologna was brought before Abraham Mintz of Padua. One of the parties turned to Pollack and as a result Pollack excommunicated Mintz. Some two years later, Pollack became involved in a libel against Samuel, the court physician of Cracow, as a result of which he was compelled to flee. From this time all traces of him disappeared. However in the *Birkat Avraham* of Abraham b. Solomon Trebitsch-Ẓarefati of Constantinople, written in 1524, there is a commendation, without a date, which concludes with the words "I have signed here, says the 'quiet' and 'smooth' [the words are applied to Jacob in the Bible (Gen. 25:27) and are applied here to mean "innocent" and "free of sin"] Jacob b. Joseph Ashkenazi Pollack of Jerusalem." If the signature is indeed that of Jacob Pollack and was written in the same year as the commendation of Israel Dayana to the same work in 1532, then Pollack must have been in Constantinople that year on his way to Jerusalem. It is even possible that he settled in Ereẓ Israel before 1532, since he signs "of Jerusalem." The year of his death and his place of burial are not known. (Some think a tombstone found in Lublin with the inscription: "The *gaon* Koppelman named Jacob ha-Levi . . ., the *gaon* Jacob b. Joseph died 23rd of Sivan 301" (1541) is his, however, it is doubtful, whether Pollack was called Koppelman and nowhere is there mention of his being a levite.) No works by Pollack are known.

Bibliography: Halberstamm, in: *Jeschurun* (ed. by Kobak), 5 (1865), Heb. pt. 153; Bruell, Jahrbuecher, 7 (1885), 31–37; M. Balaban, in: MGWJ, 57 (1913), 59–73, 196–210; idem, *Historja żydow w Krakowie,* 2 (1936), 105–18; J. L. Ritmann, *Ma'aneh* (1878), 20; Ḥ. N. Dembitzer, *Kelilat Yofi,* 1 (1888), introd. 2; Wetstein, in: *Ha-Maggid,* 5 (1896), nos. 17, 20–21; idem, in: *Sefer ha-Yovel . . . N. Sokolow* (1904), 278; idem, in: *Ha-Eshkol,* 6 (1909), 218–22; S. J. Fuenn, *Kiryah Ne'emanah* (1915[2]), 56; M. Straschun, *Mivḥar Ketavim* (1968), 168.

[Sh.T.]

POLLAK, MIKSA (1868–1944), Hungarian rabbi and historian; born in Beled, Hungary. He was a rabbi in Sopron from 1894 until he was killed in Auschwitz.

His main works are *Die Juden in Wiener-Neustadt* (1927, earlier in Hung., 1892) and *Die Geschichte der Juden in Oedenburg* (1929, in Hung., 1896). Despite new sources, Pollak's works are still considered valid in their major conclusions. His other scholarly activities were centered on exploring biblical influences on great Hungarian poets—Arany János (1904), Tompa Mihály (1912), and Madách Imre (in IMIT, 1935–39). He also published a Hungarian translation of the prayer book. Pollak was an outstanding preacher; a volume of his collected sermons was published in 1938.

Bibliography: A. Scheiber, in: MHJ, 11 (1968), 5–15.

[Al.Sch.]

POLLAK, MOSES HA-LEVI (1845–1888), Hungarian rabbi. Born in Szerdahely, Pollak studied under Judah Aszod and Abraham Samuel Sofer. In 1872 he was appointed rabbi of Bonyhad, where he established a yeshivah which attracted pupils from all parts of Hungary. He was one of the founders of the Orthodox community of Bonyhad, which he developed to a considerable extent.

Pollak was the author of *Va-Yedabber Moshe* (1894–95; photo-print New York, 1943), in five parts, on the Pentateuch and various talmudic themes; *Tikkun Moshe* (1894–99), in five parts, sermons and discussions on talmudic topics; and *Birkat Moshe* (1911) on tractate *Ḥullin*.

Bibliography: P. Z. Schwartz, *Shem ha-Gedolim me-Ereẓ Hagar*, 2 (1914), 11b, no. 165; A. Stern, *Meliẓei Esh*, Marḥeshvan (1933), 122f., no. 287.

[N.B.-M.]

POLLAK, WALTER HEILPRIN (1887–1940), U.S. attorney. Born in New Jersey, Pollak was admitted to the New York bar in 1911 and entered private practice in New York City. During World War I he worked on the legal staff of the War Industries Board. He was a special assistant attorney general for the Arnstein bond theft case (1923–1924) and was counsel, consultant, and chairman of a number of important federal and state commissions. One of the most prominent lawyers at the U.S. bar, Pollak rendered services for the defense of those who were persecuted for unpopular views and causes, and inspired his younger associates to follow this same path. He helped in the drafting of the brief of Arthur Garfield Hays in the Scopes evolution case. He argued the Whitney and Gitlow free speech cases in the U.S. Supreme Court and in 1932 and 1935 was counsel before the Supreme Court in the Scottsboro case involving the issue of a fair trial for Negroes in the South.

[M.H.C.]

POLLEGAR (Pulgar, Policar), ISAAC BEN JOSEPH IBN (first half of 14th century), Spanish scholar and philosopher. Pollegar's chief literary work was the *Ezer ha-Dat* ("Support of Faith"), consisting of five sections, which was published with an English summary by G. Belasco in 1906, while a variant text of the second section was published by E. Ashkenazi in *Ta'am Zekenim* (1854), 12–19. The purpose of the work was to answer the criticisms of certain schools of thought against Judaism. In the first and main section, the author sets forth the chief principles of Judaism, such as the superiority of Moses and the Torah, the world to come and the Messiah, and rejects despair over the sufferings of Israel. Combatting the apostate *Abner of Burgos, whom he had befriended in his youth, he refutes the latter's christological interpretation of the *aggadah* by claiming that the *aggadot* are not binding and need not be taken literally. The second section consists in large part of a dialogue between an opponent of philosophical studies and someone who believes that philosophical studies should be pursued, and concludes with the author's reconciliation of Judaism and philosophy along Averroistic lines. In the third section, Pollegar opposes the view, usual in medieval Judaism, that human affairs are guided by the influence of the heavenly bodies, and attacks determinist views such as those expounded by Abner of Burgos. Pollegar attempts to solve the problem posed by Abner of the alleged contradiction between human freedom and divine foreknowledge by his theory of the mutual cooperation of the divine and human wills. The source of all action is the divine will. All of man's actions are founded upon the imitation of the divine will by the human. At the moment when human actions are realized, their completion is ordained by the divine will, and at the very same moment they become objects of the human will, which thus imitates the divine will. Since God's foreknowledge and the decision of His will exist within His essence at the same moment, neither precedes man's actions. God's knowledge, however, does not change, since knowledge of particulars originates in His all-embracing knowledge identical with his essence. The fourth section consists of an attack on various kinds of pseudosciences which conflict with true philosophy. This section includes a four-part critique of (a) the philosophizers who do not really know philosophy yet mock religion, (b) the kabbalists, criticized for their language, their belief in their tradition and its authority, and their alleged non-monotheism, (c) those who see nature as an independent force, and (d) believers in sorcery. In the fifth section Pollegar praises pure intellectual activity which, he states, can only be fully developed in the next world.

Pollegar also composed at least one treatise against astrology, a translation of the third book of Al-Ghazālī's *Maqāṣid al-Falāsifa*, and a reply to Abner of Burgos known as the *Iggeret ha-Ḥarifot* ("Epistle of Blasphemies"). He refers to commentaries on Genesis, Psalms, and Ecclesiastes, and also to a work called *Musar Banim* ("Discipline of Sons"); none of these is extant.

Bibliography: Baer, Spain, index s.v. *Isaac Policar;* idem, in: *Tarbiz*, 27 (1958), 278ff.; Guttman, Philosophies, 205–6; I. Loeb, in: REJ, 18 (1889), 63–70; G. Belasco, in: JQR, 17 (1905), 26–56; Zinberg, Sifrut, 2 (1956), 101ff.; Schirmann, Sefarad, 2 (1956), 520–3.

[F.T.]

POLNA (Czech **Polná**), town in S.E. Bohemia, Czechoslovakia. Jews are mentioned in the vicinity in 1415 and two Jewish families in Polna itself in 1570. The town's law-manual of 1582 also contains a Jewish *oath formula. A cemetery was established in 1619. In 1681 Jewish and town representatives signed an agreement to build a Jewish quarter of 16 houses (one of its gates was still extant in 1970). The synagogue was built in 1684 and renovated for the first time in the 18th century. The register of synagogue seats was kept in the town archives. In a conflagration in 1863 the synagogue and 32 houses were destroyed. There were 27 Jewish families in Polna in 1724, and 541 Jews lived in the town in 1847. The synagogue was renovated for a second time in 1861. In 1869 there were 430 Jews in Polna, and 238 in 1890. Polna acquired a dubious notoriety through the *Hilsner blood libel case in 1899. In 1930 the community numbered 51 (1.2% of the total population). In 1942 the Jews remaining in Polna were deported to Nazi death camps. The synagogue equipment was sent to the Central Jewish Museum in Prague. Although no congregation was reorganized after the Holocaust, the synagogue and the Jewish cemetery were still extant in 1970.

Bibliography: H. Gold (ed.), *Juden und Judengemeinden Boehmens* . . . (1934), 508–11.

[J.Her./M.La.]

POLONNOYE, town in the Kamenets-Podolski oblast, Ukrainian S.S.R. It is not known when the Jewish community was established there, but in 1648, the time of the *Chmielnicki massacres, it was regarded as one of the most important in *Volhynia. When the Cossack armies approached the town about 12,000 Jews found refuge in its fortress, defending themselves, together with Poles, against the enemy. When the Cossacks overran the town about 300 Jews gathered in the *bet ha-midrash* and, led by the kabbalist R. Samson *Ostropoler, they wrapped themselves in their *tallitot* and met death with a prayer on their lips. The number of dead in the town was estimated at 10,000. In 1684 the owner of the town, Countess Lyubomirskaya, granted Jews letters-patent which authorized them to build houses in one of the town's quarters. They were also exempted from military service in exchange for a special payment in favor of the Christian inhabitants, ". . . with the exception of a general mobilization in the event of an attack by the enemy."

Polonnoye rapidly became an important commercial and spiritual center. During the second half of the 18th century, two of the pillars of Ḥasidism (and disciples of the Ba'al Shem Tov), *Aryeh Judah Leib ("The 'Mokhiaḥ' of Polonnoye," d. 1770) and after him, *Jacob Joseph ha-Kohen (d. 1782), held the rabbinical positions of the town.

Hebrew printers were active in Polonnoye between 1782 and 1820. Among them was Samuel b. Issachar Ber, who also printed in *Korets and *Shklov, and who transferred the press to *Ostrog in 1794. Another was Joseph b. Ẓevi ha-Kohen, active from 1800 to 1820, who founded another press in *Medzibezh, in 1815. Altogether some 90 works, mostly kabbalistic, ḥasidic, and ethical, were issued, some of the latter in Yiddish.

In 1847 there were 2,647 Jews in Polonnoye and, according to the census, there were 7,910 Jews (48.5% of the population) in 1897. In 1919 the town was at the center of the battle area between the Red and Ukrainian armies, and consequently, during Passover of that year, most of the inhabitants fled to nearby towns. In September cavalry units of Budenny rioted, robbing and killing about 40 Jews. In 1926 there were 5,337 Jews (32.5% of the population) in Polonnoye. During the German occupation in the summer of 1941 the Jews were exterminated. There was no information available on the existence of Jews in Polonnoye after World War II.

Bibliography: N. N. Hannover, *Yeven Meẓulah; Sefer Zwihl [Novograd-Volynskiy]* (1962), 253–5 (Heb. part); Ḥ. D. Friedberg, *Toledot ha-Defus ha-Ivri be-Polanyah* (1950²), 102–3. [Y.S.]

POLOTSK, city in Polotsk oblast, Belorussian S.S.R., one of the oldest Jewish communities in Lithuania. There is evidence that Jews settled in Polotsk toward the end of the 15th century. In 1551 the Jews of the city were exempted from paying a special tax known as the *srebrzczyzna.* When Ivan the Terrible captured Polotsk in 1563, he ordered that all the Jews who refused to be baptized (around 300), should be drowned in the Dvina River. (Memorial prayers for these martyrs were recited in Polotsk each year on the 25th of Kislev.) The Jewish community was revived soon after, but in 1580, when the town adopted the *Magdeburg law, it forbade Jewish commerce and purchase of real estate within the city. Jews lived on six landholdings outside municipal jurisdiction. The Jewish community was destroyed in 1654 by Cossack rebels, but was rebuilt shortly after. When local residents complained in 1681 that the Jews were purchasing land within the city without paying municipal taxes, King John III Sobieski ordered them to pay. In 1765 there were 1,003 poll-tax paying Jews in Polotsk. The city was one of the earliest centers of Ḥasidism in Belorussia and *Israel of Polotsk was a leader of ḥasidic immigration to Ereẓ Israel in 1777. Polotsk had 2,600 Jews in 1815 (56.3% of the total population). The figure rose to 7,275 by 1847 and to 12,481 in 1897 (61% of the total). In the late 19th century the city became a center of anti-Jewish agitation, largely because several Russian Orthodox monasteries and an officers' training school were located there. When pogroms broke out in October 1905, the authorities prohibited Jewish self-defense activities in the city. There were 19,252 Jews living in Polotsk in 1910. The *kehillah* (Jewish community organization) was abolished under Soviet rule in 1918, along with many other Jewish public institutions. In 1926 the number of Jews had fallen to 8,186 (32% of the total). With the German conquest in World War II, the 8,000 Jews remaining in Polotsk were herded into a brick factory near the city, and in December 1941 all were murdered. In 1970 the Jewish population of Polotsk was estimated at about 500. There was no synagogue.

Bibliography: A. Arnin, in: B. Karu (ed.), *Sefer Vitebsk* (1957), 209–12; S. Ogurski (ed.), *1905 in Vaysrusland* (1925), 164–71; *Prestupleniya nemetsko-fashistskikh okkupantov v Belorussii* (1963), 285–6. [Y.S.]

POLOTSKY, HANS JACOB (1905–), orientalist and linguist. Born in Zurich to Russian parents, Polotsky attended the universities of Berlin and Goettingen, studying Egyptology and Semitics. While at Goettingen he was employed at the "Septuaginta Unternehmen," in connection with Greek, Coptic, Syriac and Arabic material. In Berlin he edited Manichaean texts in Coptic. These texts brought him into contact with Turkish (and Iranian) dialects. His interest in Ethiopic languages (Ge'ez, Amharic, Gouragé, Tigrina etc.) widened when he began teaching at the Hebrew University in 1934, as professor from 1948. He received the Israel Prize in humanities (1965). In Jerusalem he discovered native speakers of Eastern Neo-Aramaic (modern Syriac) dialects, and thus became acquainted with this long neglected subject. Being familiar with Russian besides many other European languages, he was able to use important Russian contributions in this field. The discovery of Greek Papyri in Israel (Naḥal Ḥever) provided him with the opportunity of returning to Hellenistic Greek. Polotsky is the rare, if not the last of a type of linguist whose achievements are outstanding in several language families. This enabled him to obtain remarkable results in such studies as his *Etudes de syntax Copte* where he solved problems that had been vexing generations of Coptologists, such as the use of the so-called "second tenses," which he approached through the comparison of Coptic texts with their Greek "Vorlage" and by adducing Arabic on French and English constructions of the type "it is who . . ." (cleft sentence). This type of work, using parallels from different language families, relied less upon dictionaries and grammars of the languages concerned than upon his own material which he collected himself. As an Egyptologist he made his mark with several important studies, e.g., *Egyptian Tenses* (the Israel Academy of Science and Humanities, Proceedings no. 5; 1965). Polotsky proceeds along the lines of synchronic description, following the Saussure school. Only after achieving his aim does he take recourse to comparative material, sometimes nailing down his results by employing diachrocical proofs. Since he never published an article on general linguistics, his approach to languages can be pieced together only by studying carefully all his articles, dealing with different languages. In his *Études de grammaire Gouragé*, he reconstructed a form that (he thought) had disappeared from Ethiopian dialects and had the satisfaction to learn that the "reconstructed" form does indeed exist in one of them. In his studies in modern Syriac he showed his firsthand knowledge of the different Neo-Aramaic dialects spoken near the sea of Urmia (in Iran and Iraq), and proved that synchronic problems of certain dialects can be solved by comparative dialectology plus the diachronic approach. In his article *Syntaxe Amharique et syntaxe Turque* (1960), a study of two languages which belong to two entirely different language families (Semitic and Uralo-Altaic), he showed how close they are in the field of syntax, without having had any contact with each other.

Hans Jacob Polotsky, orientalist. Courtesy Hebrew University, Jerusalem. Photo Werner Braun, Jerusalem.

While conversant with recent linguistic trends, including that of N. Chomsky, Polotsky tended toward the school of de Saussure. His *Collected Papers* have been published by the Magnes Press of the Hebrew University (1971). A bibliography of his writings appeared in H. B. Rosén (ed.), *Studies in Egyptology and Linguistics in Honour of H.J. Polotsky* (1964), ix–xi. Quite a few languages, never dealt with by Polotsky in his articles are even more familiar to him than those mentioned, e.g., Latin (Classical and Middle) and, of course, Hebrew, biblical, mishnaic, that of the prayer book and of Israel Hebrew. Polotsky is the linguists' linguist. [E.Y.K.]

POLTAVA, capital of Poltava oblast, Ukrainian S.S.R. Jews began to settle there at the close of the 18th century. In 1801 there were 18 Jewish merchants in Poltava and 292 Jews classed as townsmen (about one-fifth of the total number of inhabitants). The community in Poltava and its environs numbered 2,073 in 1847. The number of Jews in the town doubled by the 1870s, and in 1897 reached 11,046 (20.5% of the total population), of whom a considerable number were from Lithuania and Belorussia. The Poltava community was one of the best organized and most progressive in Russia. It had ten synagogues. At the close of the 19th century the *talmud torah* was converted into a modern elementary school, when it was attended by 300 children who studied both religious and general subjects; its teaching staff included Alexander Siskind *Rabinovitz and M. Haezraḥi. There were also a girls' vocational school supported by the *Jewish Colonization Association, a yeshivah, and 20 *ḥadarim*. The community's hospital and clinic provided free services, and there were an old age home and a loan bank. The Jewish library contained 8,000 volumes. The influence of the Russian intelligentsia, led by the author V. Korolenko, prevented the outbreak of pogroms in Poltava during both periods of revolutions in Russia in 1905 and 1917. There was a strong Zionist movement in Poltava which was one of the foremost centers of the *Po'alei Zion movement in Russia; several founders of this party were born in Poltava and began their activities there: B. *Borochov, I. *Ben-Zvi, and Y. *Zerubavel. The ideological organ of the party, *Yevreyskaya Rabochaya Khronika* (founded in 1906), was published in Poltava, and the founding conference of Po'alei Zion was held there. Rabbi of Poltava from 1893 to 1917 was E. A. *Rabinowich, a leader of the extreme Orthodox and a strong opponent of the Zionists. He published the religious monthly *Ha-Peles* (1903–06) and the weekly *Ha-Modi'a* (1910–15) in Poltava. The historian Elias *Tcherikower was born in Poltava.

Under the Soviet regime the fate of the community was the same as that of the rest of Russian Jewry. Until 1927 Poltava remained a center for printing of Jewish religious books (particularly *siddurim* and calendars). The Jewish population numbered 18,476 (20.1% of the total) in 1926. There is no information available on Jewish life in Poltava from the 1930s to the 1940s.

When the Germans entered the city in 1941 those Jews who did not succeed in escaping were put to death. In the late 1960s the Jewish population was estimated at 5,000. There was no synagogue, the remaining one having been closed down in 1959 by the militia who broke in, confiscated all religious articles, dispersed the congregation, and prohibited the holding of further gatherings. Subsequently Jews have prayed in private. There is a Jewish cemetery in Poltava. There are also two mass graves of Jewish martyrs murdered by the Nazis; one in which 13,000 bodies were buried, and in the other 7,000. The monuments there do not specify that all the victims were Jews.

Region of "Poltavshchina." Jews began to settle in the region during the early 17th century in the process of Jewish participation in the colonization of Ukraine. By 1610 there was a Jewish community in Berezan (to the north of Pereyaslav), and within a few decades about a dozen Jewish

The Poltava Zionist Committee, 1918. Courtesy A. Raphaeli-Zenziper, Archive for Russian Zionism, Tel Aviv.

communities were established in the districts of *Pereyaslav and Mirgorod, of which the largest were in Pereyaslav and *Lubny. Jews engaged in commerce and the leasing of estates, flour mills, liquor distilleries, breweries, and inns. There was strong competition from Christian townsmen, and during the *Chmielnicki massacres of 1648 these communities were among the first to be destroyed. After the region came under Russian rule Jews were not permitted to live there until the first partition of Poland in 1772. Individual Jewish families, however, settled in various estates under the protection of their owners despite frequent expulsions by the authorities.

After the first partition of Poland in 1772, Jewish settlement on the eastern bank of the river Dnieper was renewed, and by 1792 there were over 700 Jews in the region, most of whom lived on estates or in villages. In 1794 this region, which then formed part of the province of Yekaterinoslav, was incorporated within the *Pale of Settlement. In 1803 there were 82 Jewish merchants and 2,030 Jews classed as townsmen living in the province of Poltava, which was formed in 1802. The community of *Kremenchug was the largest in the district, and developed in particular owing to its position on the Dnieper, the main waterway from Lithuania to the south. It accounted in 1897 for 30% of the Jews in the province. In 1847, 15,572 Jews were enumerated in the 18 communities of the province (which also included the Jews in the small settlements and their environs). Their numbers increased as a result of large emigration from Lithuania and Belorussia, and were estimated at 84,000 in 1881. The census of 1897 recorded 111,417 Jews (4% of the total population) in Poltava province (the lowest percentage of Jews in all the provinces of the Pale). The Russian-Ukrainian majority had a strong assimilationist influence on the Jews in the province who were a minority in all the towns; it was only in Kremenchug that their numbers approached half the population. On the other hand, *Ḥabad Ḥasidism, which penetrated from the north, was an important spiritual influence (the tomb of *Shneur Zalman of Lyady, the founder of Ḥabad Ḥasidism, is in *Gadyach in Poltava province).

About one-half of the Jews of the province of Poltava earned their livelihood from commerce (in contrast to 38.5% in the whole of Russia), and about 30% were engaged in crafts and industry. Commerce was principally conducted in grain and other agricultural produce. Although some Jews owned saw mills, brick-kilns, flour mills, alcohol distilleries, and other enterprises, the overwhelming majority of the workers in them were non-Jews. During the spring of 1881 pogroms occurred in the north of the province of Poltava. In 1905 a wave of pogroms swept across 52 settlements of the province. The most severely affected were Gadyach, Kremenchug, *Romny, and *Zolotonosha.

During World War I thousands of refugees and Jews

expelled from the battle zone arrived in the province of Poltava and found refuge in the Jewish communities. During the Civil War, the communities of the western section of the province suffered especially from pogroms by bands of Ukrainians and the "volunteer army" of A. I. *Denikin. In 1926 there were approximately 93,000 Jews in the five districts (Kremenchug, Lubny, Poltava, *Priluki, Romny) of the former territory of the province of Poltava.

Bibliography: S. Ettinger, in: *Zion*, 21 (1956), 107–42; Zionist Organization, *Die Judenpogrome in Russland* (1909); *Reshumot*, 3 (Berlin, 1923), 157–71; Y. Zerubavel, *Alei Ḥayyim* (1960), 14–124 passim, 233–5; B. Ḥaikin, in: J. Erez (ed.), *Sefer Ẓ-S.* (1963), 120–1. [Y.S.]

POLYAKOV, family of railroad constructors and bankers in Russia, headed by the brothers Jacob, Samuel, and Eliezer. They originated in Dubrovno, Belorussia. Jacob (1832–1909) began his economic career as a liquor excise farmer and later went on to railroad construction. He participated in the founding of the Don-Azov and other Russian banks and also acted as the vice-chairman of the *Jewish Colonization Association in Russia. He received a Russian title of nobility. Samuel (1837–1888) was one of the most important railroad constructors in Russia. He was responsible for laying over 1,600 mi. (2,500 kms.) of railroads, including the Kozlov (Michurinsk)-Rostov and the Kursk-Kharkov-Azov lines and strategic railroads in Rumania during the Russo-Turkish War of 1877–78. He also founded the "South Russian Coal Mining Society" and several important banks (Moscow estate bank, Don estate bank, etc.). He contributed generously to Russian educational and cultural institutions and showed a special concern for technical education (he founded the first technical school for railroad construction in Yelets in 1867 and the first school for mining in Korsun). He was unpopular among Jews because of his refusal to employ Jewish workers in his enterprises, but toward the end of his life played a role in Jewish public life. He initiated the foundation of the *ORT organization, participated in negotiations with the minister of the interior P. N. *Ignatyev in 1881–82 and contributed to the construction of the synagogue of St. Petersburg. He received a Russian title of nobility. Eliezer (1842–1914) constructed railroads in partnership with his brother Samuel and was one of the leading bankers in Moscow. He was president of the Moscow estate bank and in 1873 founded the Polyakov bank. He invested large sums in the development of industries in Russia and Persia. Eliezer was president of the Jewish community of Moscow and received a Russian title of nobility. In 1908, after a crisis befell his enterprises, he was removed from the majority of them by the government.

Bibliography: Y. Mazeh, *Zikhronot*, 2 (1936), 10–20. [Y.S.]

POMEGRANATE (Heb. רִמּוֹן, *rimmon*), the tree, *Punica granatum*, and its fruit. It is one of the seven choice fruits of Ereẓ Israel (Deut. 8:8), and among the fruits brought by the spies sent by Moses, as proof of the land's fertility (Num. 13:23). After the devastation of the land "the vine, the fig tree, and the pomegranate and olive tree" ceased producing their fruit (Hag. 2:19). The pomegranate, with its beautiful red flowers, decorative fruit, and its delicate flavor, was especially beloved by the poet of the Song of Songs, who mentions it six times. The loved one is compared to "a park of pomegranates" (4:13); her cheek *(rakkah)* to a "pomegranate split open" (4:3, 6:7), the reference being to a divided pomegranate, as the cheeks are called "the *rimmon* of the face" in the Talmud (Av. Zar. 30b). In the spring its large flowers are conspicuous in their beauty (Songs 6:11). The juice of pomegranates is a delicious drink (8:2). Adornments in the shape of the fruit embellished the hem of the robe of the high priest Aaron (Ex. 28:33–34) and the capitals of the pillars of the Temple (I Kings 7:18, 42). Three joined pomegranates also appear on the Hasmonean coins, and it also appears upon the one *lirah* coin of modern Israel. A number of localities in Israel have its name: Ein Rimmon, Gat Rimmon, Sela ha-Rimmon, etc.

In the time of the Mishnah and Talmud, the pomegranate was one of the important plants, and details about it abound. It grew in nearly every region of the country, but the best were the pomegranates of the valleys (Tosef., Bik. 1:5). Those from Badan, apparently in the Wadi Badan near Shechem, won particular praise (Or. 3:7). Various species of it were grown (Tosef., Ter. 2:4) and there were both sweet and sour varieties (*ibid.* 5:10). Pomegranates were of different sizes (Kel. 17:5), but the average size was less than that of the average *etrog* (TJ, Naz. 1:4, 51c). It is noted that the pomegranate's "fruit is beautiful but not its tree" (TJ, Suk. 3:5, 53d). Unlike the seeds, the peel is very bitter, hence the pomegranate was used metaphorically for a pupil who selected only the good: "he found a pomegranate, ate the fruit and discarded the peel" (Ḥag. 15b). Schoolchildren sitting in their rows and learning Torah were compared to the compact kernels of the pomegranate (Song R. 6:11), and the Talmud interprets the Song of Songs 4:3 homiletically to the effect that "even the most empty of Jews is as full of good deeds as the pomegranate" (is of kernels, Ber. 57a). The delicate beauty of pomegranate kernels found poetic expression in the description of the beauty of Johanan of whom it was said that anyone wishing to see it: "Let him bring a silver cup from the smelter, fill it with the kernels of a red pomegranate, surround it with a crown of red roses, and put it between the sun and the shade, he will then sense in its brilliance the beauty of Johanan" (BM 84a). The kernels were eaten fresh, or pressed into juice or they were dried and a sort of raisin made from them (Tosef. Shev. 6:29).

The peel of the pomegranate contains a dark brown dye that was used for dyeing (Shev. 7:3) and also as a test for invisible ink (Git. 19b; *narah* there being the Persian for pomegranate). Pomegranate trees are cultivated in Israel and are frequently to be seen near the houses of Arabs. In the valley of Beth-Shean extensive pomegranate orchards were planted but with doubtful success, since the promegranate was attacked by pests.

Bibliography: Loew, Flora, 3 (1924), 80–113; J. Feliks, *Olam ha-Ẓome'aḥ ha-Mikra'i* (1968[2]), 48–51; H. N. and A. L. Moldenke, *Plants of the Bible* (1952), 319, index, s.v. [J.F.]

POMERANIA, former duchy, subsequently Prussian territory; divided between Poland and East Germany since 1945. The earliest references to Jewish settlement in Pomerania date from the 13th century, when (in 1261) Duke Barnim I decreed that the clauses of the *Magdeburg Law concerning the Jews would apply to Stettin (*Szczecin) and the rest of Pomerania. It is recorded that in 1320 the Jews of Templin, Prenzlau, and Pasewalk enjoyed civic equality; indeed, until the *Black Death persecutions (1350) the position of Pomeranian Jewry was relatively favorable. Originally the Jews made their living as traders, later turning to moneylending. Nevertheless, in spite of the privileges of 1481 and a grant of residence to 22 Jewish families, Boguslaw X expelled them in 1492/3. On the other hand, Frederick William, the "Great Elector" (1640–88), extended an invitation to Jewish merchants who had been expelled from Vienna in 1670 to settle in his domains, and by 1682 at least four Jewish families were living in the part of Pomerania that was under Prussian rule. However, numerous complaints against Jewish business practices caused him to threaten Jewish expulsion in 1687/8. By then 15 families had been licensed to reside in Pomerania, the gentry frequently interceding on their behalf. Polish Jewry continued to emigrate to Pomerania in spite of obstructive regulations. In 1706 a rabbi was elected by an assembly of Pomeranian Jewry (46 licensed families), but the king appointed his own nominee to the position.

In the western half of Pomerania, intermittently under Swedish rule, harsher regulations against Jews were in force. From 1728, however, all laws of Prussia applied to the Jews of Pomerania, who at that time totaled about 325 persons. During that period the Jews were mainly engaged in the wool, wheat, and amber trades, and in peddling.

The communities grew after 1812 (c. 1,700 Jews) until 1880 (13,886), after which date they began to decline. In 1932 there were 7,760 Jews (0.4% of the total population) in 50 communities, 28% of whom lived in the modern industrial city of Stettin. During World War II the majority of Pomeranian Jews were deported and annihilated. After the war a community was renewed in Stettin.

Bibliography: H. Loewe, in: *Zeitschrift fuer Demographie und Statistik der Juden*, 7 (1911), 146–9; L. Hiller et al., in: *Der Jugendbund* (Jan. 1931), 1–3; *Fuehrer durch die juedische Gemeindeverwaltung und Wohlfahrtspflege in Deutschland* (1932/33), 69–81; U. Grotefend, *Geschichte und rechtliche Stellung der Juden in Pommern von den Anfaengen bis zum Tode Friedrich des Grossen* (1931); B. Brilling, in: *Gemeindeblatt der Synagogen Gemeinde zu Stettin* (1932), no. 9; AJYB, 63 (1962), 376–7; Germ Jud, 2 (1968), 658; S. Stern, *Der preussische Staat und die Juden* (1962), 1 Akten, 125–48, 385–414, 536; 2 Akten, 713–804. [H.W.]

POMERANTZ, BERL (1900–1942), Hebrew poet. Pomerantz was born in the Polish village of Udrzyn. He studied in Vilna and later settled in Warsaw, where he unsuccessfully applied to the British authorities for an entrance visa to Ereẓ Israel. In December 1942, while hiding with a group of fellow Jewish escapees in the forest near the townlet of Janow, he was killed by German soldiers.

Berl Pomerantz, Hebrew poet. From B. Pomerantz, *Shirim*, Tel Aviv, 1966.

His work constitutes one of the most significant achievements in Hebrew poetry written in Poland between the two world wars. As distinct from the poetry of Bialik and his followers, Pomerantz's poems are in the modern manner. Composed in rhymeless *vers libre*, they are daringly figurative and evince a close affinity with the Yiddish poetry of the day which had been affected by German expressionism. His themes and preoccupations—nostalgic reminiscences of his native village with contrasting urban tableaux suggested by Warsaw (seen as the epitome of the city)—are in keeping with the spirit of his age. He is at his best when rendering visual impressions which are figuratively elaborated until they acquire the status of symbols of an uprooted, humiliated, poverty-ridden humanity. Although emotionally intense and figuratively hyperbolic, Pomerantz's language is also characterized by the concrete detail in its natural contours. His facility in perceiving metaphoric relationships never interfered with his ability to delineate what was actually observed and genuinely felt.

Pomerantz's poetry is closest to that of Ḥayyim *Lensky and Abraham *Shlonsky, but Pomerantz's work is more concrete than the latter's, as well as more intimate in tone. His longest poem, *Me-al ha-Hadom* ("From Above the Footstool"), is dedicated to the memory of his father, "whose grace lasted longer than his meal," as the poet puts it. This is an impressive work, moving in its simple sincerity, which has been compared with Bialik's *Yatmut* ("Orphanhood") cycle. *Bi-Sefatayim el ha-Sela* ("With Lips to the Rock"), his first book of poems, appeared in Warsaw in 1935. His second book, *Ḥallon ba-Ya'ar* ("A Window in the Forest"), the last to come out during his lifetime, was published in 1939 by the Stybel Publishing House in Warsaw. In Ereẓ Israel, his poems were regularly printed in the literary journal, *Gilyonot*. However, to make a living Pomerantz engaged in teaching, translation from Yiddish and Polish, and various forms of literary hackwork. Despite his trials, his poetry is never devoid of gentle and compassionate humanity nor does it ever become embittered or aggressive. His last poems, written in occupied Poland, were never recovered and were probably buried with him in the forest. Other works were published in 1966 under the title, *Shirim* ("Poems").

Bibliography: S. Y. Penueli, in: *Gilyonot*, 26 (1951–52), 308–10; Y. Lamdan, *ibid.*, 28 (1953), 110f.; N. Peniel, in: B. Pomerantz, *Shirim* (1966), 7–26. [N.Z.]

POMI(S), DE' (Heb. מִן הַתַּפּוּחִים, *Min ha-Tappuḥim*), one of the four distinguished Roman families which, according to an ancient tradition, were brought by Titus from Ereẓ Israel to Italy (see title page of David de' Pomis, *Ẓemaḥ David*).

Elijah de' Pomi(s) (d. 1298), rabbi and possibly also head of the community in Rome, was martyred on the 20th Tammuz 5058. The Inquisition sought to strike at the richer Jews since it considered them supporters of the Patrician Colonna family, who opposed Pope Boniface VIII (1294–1303). While denying that there was any basis for the allegation, Elijah allowed all suspicion to fall on him alone. He was burned at the stake and his family sought refuge in Spoleto. Two anonymous elegies on his death have been preserved.

David de' Pomis (1525–1593) was linguist, physician, and philosopher. Son of the learned R. Isaac, he was born in Spoleto. He received his early education from his father and later, at Todi, from his uncles Rabbi Jehiel (Vitale) and Moses *Alatino, both physicians who were well versed in philosophy. For six years David studied medicine and philosophy in Perugia, where he received his doctorate in medicine in 1551. He was rabbi and physician at Magliano near Rome, but on account of the edict of Pope *Paul IV forbidding Jewish physicians to attend Christians (1555), he moved from town to town in Italy before he settled in 1569 in Venice, where he published the greater part of his works. Pius IV (1559–65) gave him permission to attend Christians, a concession revoked by Pius V (1565–72) and later restored by Pope Sixtus V (1585–90). In his booklet *De Medico Hebraeo Enarratio Apologica* (Venice, 1588) David de' Pomis refutes the charges brought against Jews and Jewish physicians in particular by a bull of 1581 by Gregory XIII (1572–85). He stresses that according to the Bible and Talmud a Jewish physician must give help to every sufferer, and cites numerous instances of Jewish doctors who had distinguished themselves by their work and their loyalty.

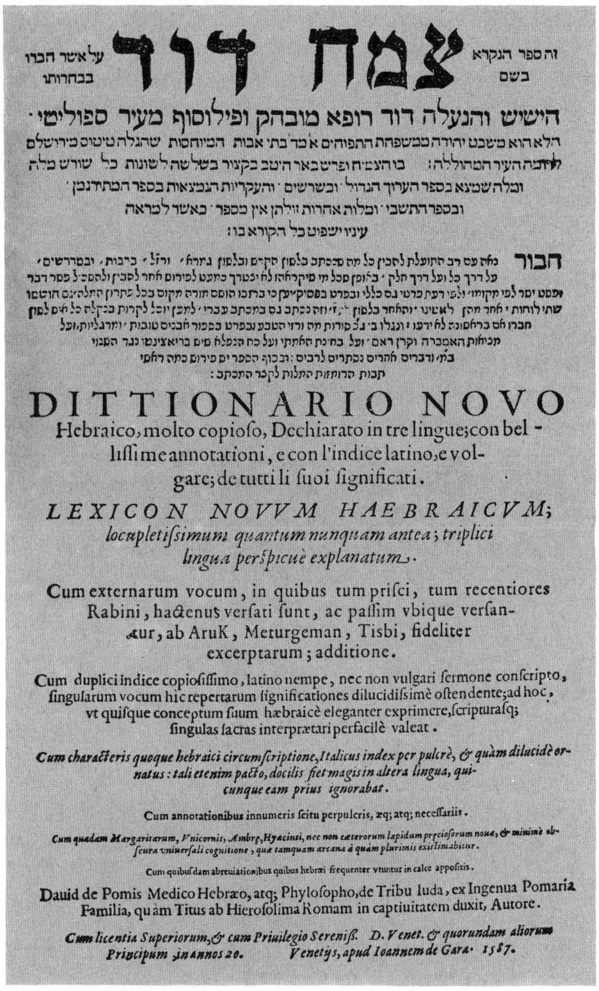
וזה ספר הנקרא בשם צמח דוד על אשר חברו בבחרותו

הישיש והנעלה דוד רופא מובהק ופילוסוף מעיר ספולייטי·

DITTIONARIO NOVO
Hebraico, molto copioso, Dechiarato in tre lingue; con bellissime annotationi, e con l'indice latino, e volgare; de tutti li suoi significati.

LEXICON NOVVM HAEBRAICVM;
locupletissimum quantum nunquam antea; triplici lingua perspicuè explanatum.

Cum externarum vocum, in quibus tum prisci, tum recentiores Rabini, hactenus versati sunt, ac passim vbique versantur, ab AruK, Meturgeman, Tisbi, fideliter excerptarum; additione.

Cum duplici indice copiosissimo, latino nempe, nec non vulgari sermone conscripto, singularum vocum hic repertarum significationes dilucidissimè ostendente; ad hoc, vt quisque conceptum suum hæbraicè eleganter exprimere, scripturasq; singulas sacras interpretari perfacilè valeat.

Cum characteris quoque hebraici circumscriptione, Italicus index per pulcrè, & quàm dilucidè ornatus: tali etenim pacto, docilis fiet magis in altera lingua, quicunque eam prius ignorabat.

Cum annotationibus innumeris scitu perpulcris, æq; atq; necessariis.

Cum quadam Margaritarum, Vnicornis, Ambre, Hyacinti, nec non cæterorum lapidum preciosorum noua, & minimè obscura vniuersali cognitione, quæ tamquam arcana à quàm plurimis existimabitur.

Cum quibusdam abreuiationibus quibus hebræi frequenter vtuntur in calce appositis.

Dauid de Pomis Medico Hebræo, atq; Phylosopho, de Tribu Iuda, ex Ingenua Pomaria Familia, quàm Titus ab Hierosolima Romam in captiuitatem duxit, Autore.

Cum licentia Superiorum, & cum Priuilegio Serenis. D. Venet. & quorundam aliorum Principum, in annos 20. Venetijs, apud Ioannem de Gara. 1587.

Title page of *Ẓemaḥ David,* the Hebrew-Latin-Italian dictionary by David de' Pomis, Venice, 1587. Cecil Roth Collection.

The volume ends with a selection of talmudic rules translated into Latin in order to prove that the Talmud should not be despised.

David de' Pomis is famous above all for the *Ẓemaḥ David,* a trilingual Hebrew, Latin, and Italian dictionary (Venice, 1587). The work, which is dedicated to Pope Sixtus V, contains numerous discourses of a scientific and historical nature; the preface embodies the author's genealogy and autobiography. Among his other works are a translation into Italian of Ecclesiastes with explanatory notes (Venice, 1571) dedicated to Cardinal G. Grimani; *Discorso intorno a l'humana miseria e sopra il modo di fuggirla* ("A Discourse on Human Suffering and How to Escape It"; Venice 1572), dedicated to Margaret of Savoy, was published as an appendix to this work. His medical works include a treatise on the plague (Venice, 1577) and another on maladies of old age (Venice, 1588) dedicated to the doge and senate of Venice; in the latter, he mentions a work on the divine origin of the Venetian Republic which has not been preserved; also lost were *Sukkat David* and *Migdal David* (mentioned in the preface to *Ẓemaḥ David*) and a treatise on the battering ram (mentioned under the name of תותח). His translations of Daniel and Job have never been published.

Bibliography: Vogelstein-Rieger, 1 (1896), 255–7; 2 (1895), 259–60; H. Friedenwald, in: JQR, 32 (1941/42), 228–30; 407–8; idem, *Jews and Medicine* (1944), index s.v. *Pomis, David de;* C. Roth, *Venice* (1930), 95, 186–8; idem, *Jews in the Renaissance* (1959), 223–5; L. Muenster, in: *Revue d'Histoire de la Médicine Hebraique,* 7 (1954), 7–16, 125–36; Milano, Italia, 82, 633, 662; idem, *Il ghetto di Roma* (1964), 418, 422. [A.M.R.]

°**POMPEIUS TROGUS** (c. first century B.C.E.), Roman historian of the Augustan age. His comprehensive *Historiae Philippicae* (perhaps completed in 9 C.E.), concentrating on the Macedonian-Hellenistic empires, is not extant. However, an abstract made by Justin in the third or fourth century C.E., and the prefaces to all 44 books, remain. The Jews are first discussed in Book 36 in the context of events in the reign of *Antiochus Sidetes. The account falls into three sections: antiquities (archaeology); a geographical description of Judea; and the history of the Jewish nation from the Persian period. The first section is a combination of the biblical account, a Damascene account, and the hostile Greek-Egyptian tradition. Pompeius Trogus emphasizes the close connection existing between the priesthood and the monarchy in Jewish affairs, and his work reflects the conditions prevailing under the Hasmonean monarchy. He undoubtedly had access to Greek sources, evidently among them Timagenes. The preface to Book 39 shows that he also extended his history to later developments in Hasmonean Judea.

Bibliography: Reinach, Textes, 250–8; I. Heinemann, *Poseidonios' metaphysische Schriften,* 2 (1928), 80–81; L. Ferrero, *Struttura e metodo dell' Epitome di Giustino* (1957), 120–3. [M.St.]

°**POMPEY** (**Gnaeus Pompeius Magnus;** 106–48 B.C.E.), Roman general and one-time triumvir with *Julius Caesar and *Crassus. In 64–63 B.C.E. Pompey effectively established Roman rule throughout Syria and Palestine. He ostensibly attempted to arbitrate between the Hasmonean factions, represented by the brothers *Hyrcanus II and *Aristobulus II, contending for supremacy in Judea. A third party, according to Diodorus (4:2; cf. Jos., Ant., 14:41), expressed preference for Roman domination which would allow for Jewish religious autonomy. Pompey, though receiving costly gifts from both the brothers, was only biding his time, and when the moment was opportune made his way to Jerusalem. The pro-Hyrcanus party opened the city gates to him. Aristobulus' faction (though he himself was now a prisoner of Pompey) resisted a siege of several months' duration. Both Jewish (Jos., *ibid.,* 64ff.) and pagan sources (Dio Cassius, 37:16) confirm that Pompey took advantage of the Sabbath day, on which Jews refrained from taking the offensive, to accelerate siege operations. The Temple appears to have been stormed in midsummer 63 B.C.E. According to Josephus Pompey entered the Holy of Holies on a "fast-day" but left it intact. There is evidence by Dio Cassius, however, that the Temple treasury was robbed by Pompey. Wholesale slaughter of the defenders took place and the country became tributary to Rome. With this, Jewish independence came to an end, save for the few fitful years of the Jewish War (66–70) and the Bar Kokhba War (132–135). A telling blow was the severance from Judean control of the vital coastal towns of Gaza, Jaffa, Straton's Tower (later Caesarea), among others, as well as Samaria (Ḥag. 25a) and large areas of Transjordan. This act was the prelude to *Gabinius' later subdivision of the country. Aristobulus was carried off to Rome in chains together with the members of his family, including his two sons, Alexander and Antigonus, the former escaping en route. Hyrcanus was rewarded by being granted the high priesthood and leadership of the nation.

The noncanonical Psalms of Solomon are generally attributed to the period of Pompey's capture of the city where this event is described. Pompey is regarded as the "alien to our race" and rod of God's wrath against Hasmonean usurpation of the Davidic throne (Ps. of Sol. 7–9). According to some scholars his era may also be the background of the first century C.E. *Pesher Habakkuk* of the Dead Sea Scrolls.

Bibliography: Jos., Loeb (ed.), vol. 9, p. 762; Schuerer, Hist, index s.v.; T. Mommsen, *Roemische Geschichte,* 3 (1922[13]), 143ff.; A. Schalit, *Ha-Mishtar ha-Roma'i be-Erez Yisrael* (1937), index; Klausner, Bayit Sheni, 5 (1951[2]), 315; A. Schalit, *Koenig Herodes* (1969), 7ff., 678f., 757f. [Da.S.]

PONARY (Lithuanian, **Paneriai**), a resort area about 5 mi. (8 km.) from Vilna, where from July 1941 to July 1944, about 100,000 people were executed by the Nazis, with the aid of special Lithuanian units. The decisive majority of the victims were Jewish men, women, and children from Vilna and the surrounding area, as well as from other countries. In addition, a few thousand non-Jewish Soviet prisoners of war and civilians were killed there. In spite of the deceit that the Nazis staged to mislead the victims brought to Ponary, the nature of the place was known in the Vilna ghetto, as early as the fall of 1941, from reports of the few people who managed to escape during the executions. A frequently sung lullaby in the Vilna ghetto, *"Shtiler, Shtiler"* ("Quieter, Quieter"), by Shmerle *Kaczerginsky, included the line: "Many roads lead to Ponary, but no road leads back."

It is known from Nazi documents and other sources that there were instances of resistance on the part of the Jewish victims at Ponary when they were taken out to be executed. At the end of 1943 the Nazis, in order to cover up the traces of their crime, began to burn the corpses. The work was carried out by a group of 70 Jews and ten Soviet prisoners of war, bound in chains. A secret group was organized among them and, during a period of about three months, its members dug a tunnel about 30 meters long with spoons and with their bare hands. On the night of April 15, 1944, this group carried out its escape. Only 13 managed to get away alive, and of these 11 reached the Rudniki forests, where they joined partisan units.

After the war a monument was erected to the memory of the victims and a museum was opened containing remains discovered at the place. An information bulletin entitled *Der Muzey in Ponar* was published for Jewish visitors (1966), who come in large numbers from throughout the world. In 1969 the singer Neḥamah *Lifshitz brought remains of Ponary victims to Israel, and they were placed in the Memorial Hall of Yad Vashem in Jerusalem. [D.Le.]

PONTECORVO, BRUNO (1913–), Italian nuclear physicist. Born in Italy, Pontecorvo studied at Pisa University and at Rome University, where he taught from 1933 to 1936. He then served with scientific institutions in France and in 1940 moved to the U.S., where he worked as an expert in radiographic prospecting for oil. In 1943 he became a member of the Anglo-Canadian atomic energy team in Montreal and worked under the Nobel prizewinner Enrico Fermi in the Chalk River atomic project, participating in research leading to the development of neutron physics. From 1948 he was in England as an associate in the Harwell Atomic Research Laboratory. In 1950 Pontecorvo defected to the Soviet Union, where he was put in charge of a team at the Joint Nuclear Research Institute. He became a member of the U.S.S.R. Academy of Sciences and won the Lenin Prize and Order of Lenin (both in 1963).

His main fields of research were neutron physics (1943–48), the production of pi°-mesons from neutrons (1950–55), and the interaction of pi-mesons with nucleons. Among his publications are: "Artificial Radioactivity Produced by Neutron Bombardment" (in *Proceeding of the Royal Society of London*, 1935); "Isomérie nucléaire produite par les rayons x du spectre continu" (with A. Lazard, in *Comptes rendus des séances de l'Académie des Sciences, Paris*, 1939); *O protsessakh obrazovaniya tyazholykh mezonov i chastits* ("Production Processes of Heavy Mesons and Particles," 1955); and *Slabye vzaimodeystviya elementarnykh chastits i neytrinov* ("Weak Interactions of Elementary Particles and Neutrinos," 1963).

Bibliography: A. M. Moorehead, *The Traitors: the Double Life of Fuchs, Pontecorvo and Nunn May* (1952); *Prominent Personalities in the U.S.S.R.* (1968), s.v. [Ed.]

°**PONTIUS PILATE,** Roman procurator of Judea from 26 to 36 C.E. Pilate held office at the time of Jesus' crucifixion. At the outset of his rule, he incurred the resentment of the Jews when his army, in Jerusalem for its winter encampment, brought into the city its standards bearing the imperial image (Philo, *De Legatione ad Gaium*, 38). This act

Coin issued by Pontius Pilate, with the representation of a *lituus*, his symbol of office. Courtesy Israel Department of Antiquities, Jerusalem.

utterly disregarded the religious sensibilities of the Jews, who staged a mass protest before Pilate in Caesarea. Pilate, who realized that his threats of force would not deter the Jews, yielded to their demands and had the standards removed from Jerusalem to Caesarea. He caused even greater bitterness by his appropriation of Temple funds in order to build an aqueduct. When angry crowds demanded the abandonment of the project, Pilate planted Roman soldiers among them. At a signal from him, the soldiers fell upon the demonstrators, killed and injured many of them, and crushed the resistance. The situation worsened when Pilate ordered his soldiers to attack the Samaritans who had gathered on Mount Gerizim for a religious ceremony. Many, including several of their leaders, were killed. The Samaritans sent a delegation to protest to Vitellius, governor of Syria. Vitellius ordered Pilate to Rome to account for his conduct to Emperor Tiberius and appointed Marcellus in Pilate's place. Before Pilate reached Rome, however, the emperor died and Pilate never returned to Judea.

Bloody riots in the time of Pilate are also hinted at in the New Testament, though there is no clear statement of the circumstances. Pilate is best known with regard to the crucifixion of *Jesus. According to the Evangelists, Pilate considered Jesus innocent of any crime. Jewish pressure alone is supposed to have caused Pilate to have him tried and executed. Christian sources, presumably motivated by a desire to place complete responsibility for the crucifixion on the Jews, are generally sympathetic to Pilate. This is in contrast to the account given in the epistle of Agrippa I (Philo, *ibid.*) which depicts Pilate as corrupt, cruel, and bloodthirsty. In Christian tradition, Pilate's death is attributed either to suicide or to execution by the emperor. An inscription mentioning the emperor Tiberius and Pilate was discovered at Caesarea in 1961.

Bibliography: G. A. Mueller, *Pontius Pilatus...* (Ger., 1888) contains earlier bibliography; Schuerer, Hist, index; M. Radin, *Jews among the Greeks and Romans* (1915), 280ff.; G. Lippert, *Pilatus als Richter* (1923); D. R. Fotheringham, *Suffered under Pontius Pilate...* (1930); Pauly-Wissowa, 40 (1950), 1322–23; J. Blinzler, *Der Prozess Jesu* (1951, 1955[2]); P. Winter, *On the Trial of Jesus* (1961); R. Caillois, *Pontius Pilate* (Eng., 1963); Doyle, in: JTS, 42 (1941), 190–3; Vardaman, *ibid.*, 81 (1962). For further literature see: *Jesus (biblography). [L.Ro.]

PONTOISE, town in the department of Seine-et-Oise, France. Toward the close of the 12th century, the Jews of Pontoise were accused of having murdered a Christian child named Richard. In 1204 there was already an established Jewish community supervised by a Christian provost. Proof of the considerable financial activities transacted by the Jews of Pontoise was the introduction of a special royal seal which was to be affixed to all documents. Notable among the scholars of Pontoise was *Moses b. Abraham of Pontoise, the *paytan,* tosafist, and commentator on the Pentateuch and Talmud. Until World War II, there were about 30 Jewish families in Pontoise, but no community was established after the war.

Royal seal (reversed) for documents of Jews of Pontoise. Paris, Archive Nationale.

Bibliography: Gross, Gal Jud, 443ff.; J. Depoin, in: *Mémoires de la societé historique de Pontoise et du Vexin,* 36 (1921), 120f.; Z. Szajkowski, *Analytical Franco-Jewish Gazetteer* (1966), 274.

[B.Bl.]

POOL, DAVID DE SOLA (1885–1970), U.S. rabbi, civic and communal leader, and historian. Pool, who was born in London, pursued his rabbinic studies, first at Jews' College, London, and then at the Hildesheimer Rabbinical Seminary in Berlin. Pool went to the U.S. in 1907 to become minister of the Sephardi Congregation Shearith Israel in New York City, the oldest synagogue in the U.S. He served there until his retirement in 1956.

Pool's other posts and activities included: president of the New York Board of Rabbis (1916–17); member of Herbert Hoover's food conservation staff (1917); field organizer and director of army camp work of the Jewish Welfare Board during World War I (1917–18); U.S. representative of the Zionist Commission in Jerusalem to help implement the Balfour Declaration (1919–21); regional director for Palestine and Syria of the Joint Distribution Committee (1920–21); founder and director (1922) of the Jewish Education Committee of New York; president of the Union of Sephardic Congregations from 1928; president of the Synagogue Council of America (1938–40); chairman of the Committee of Army and Navy Religious Activities of the National Jewish Welfare Board (1940–47); vice-president (1951–55) and president (1955–56) of the American Jewish Historical Society; and U.S. delegate to the NATO Atlantic Congress in London (1959).

Pool wrote several significant works and monographs in the fields of American Jewish history, religion, education, and Zionism, and edited and translated Sephardi and Ashkenazi Hebrew liturgical works. His works include: *The Kaddish* (1909; 1964³); *Hebrew Learning Among the Puritans of New England Prior to 1700* (1911); *Capital Punishment Among the Jews* (1916); *Portraits Etched in Stone: Early Jewish Settlers, 1682–1831* (1952); *An Old Faith in the New World: Portrait of Shearith Israel, 1654–1954* (1955); *Why I Am a Jew* (1957); and *Is There an Answer?: An Inquiry in Some Human Dilemmas* (1966), the last three with his wife, Tamar de Sola Pool (1893–). Mrs. Pool was national president of Hadassah from 1939 to 1943 and held executive positions with several other national and world Jewish organizations, among them the American Jewish Committee, the World Zionist Organization, and Youth Aliyah.

Bibliography: D. de Sola Pool, in: AJHSP, 52 (1962), 3–7; idem, in: Jewish Theological Seminary of America, *Thirteen Americans: Their Spiritual Autobiographies* (1953), 201–17.

[Ed.]

POONA, city 75 mi. S.E. of Bombay, India, formerly seasonal headquarters of the British government of Bombay. Poona's Jewish community, which was established in the middle of the 19th century, consisted of Arabic-speaking Jews who made Poona their summer residence and of *Bene Israel from Bombay. David *Sassoon built the synagogue Ohel David, and the Sassoon family endowed a hospital, infirmary, and leper asylum. The Bene Israel synagogue, known as Sukkath Shlomoh, was founded later. Since 1870 Poona had a Hebrew printing press, publishing many works in Hebrew with Arabic translations for the Baghdadi Jews, and the Bene Israel published several liturgical works there. Once prosperous and numerous, the Jewish population has declined in recent years as a result of emigration to Israel.

Bibliography: A. Yaari, *Ha-Defus ha-Ivri be-Arẓot ha-Mizraḥ* 2 (1940), 83–89.

[W.J.F.]

POOR, PROVISION FOR THE. The Bible makes frequent references to the obligation to help the poor, to render them material assistance, and to give them gifts. This obligation is mentioned in the Prophets (Isa. 58:7, 10; Ezek. 18:7, 16) and especially in the Wisdom Literature (Prov. 31:20; Job 22:5–9; 29:12–13; 31:16–20; cf. Ps. 112:9). The Wisdom Literature also urges consideration of the destitute, i.e., by making loans to them (Prov. 14:21, 31; 19:17; 28:8; cf. Ps. 37:21, 26; 112:5). Concern for the poor and hungry is one of the qualities of God Himself (Ps. 132:15; 146:7, etc.); Deuteronomy says that "He loves the sojourner, in giving him food and raiment" (10:18—sojourners (Heb. *gerim*) were among the poor).

In post-Exilic times it was customary to give gifts to the poor on holidays (Esth. 9:22; Neh. 8:10). This obligation gained in importance in post-biblical times, and in the language of the rabbis, *ẓedakah* (originally "righteousness") came to mean giving to the poor. This meaning of *ẓedakah* appears already in Ben Sira (3:30; 7:10; 29:12; Tob. 4:7–11; 12:8–9), as well as in Syriac, *ẓedketa,* and in Arabic, *ṣadaqa.* In biblical usage, however, this meaning is not yet attached to *ẓedakah.*

Several gifts are mentioned in the Pentateuchal laws; some are to be given to the poor along with other people, while others are intended solely for the poor. Exodus 23:11 says of the produce of the seventh year: "... let the needy among your people eat of it, and what they leave let the wild beasts eat." According to Leviticus 25:6, these crops are eaten by masters and their slaves, and also by hired servants, sojourners, and strangers, i.e., the poor of the people. In Deuteronomy, the seventh year is a year for the release of debts (Deut. 15:1–2); a warning is given against withholding loans from the poor because of the proximity of the year of release (15:7–11; see *Sabbatical and Jubilee Year). Deuteronomy also commands that the poor be included in the celebration of the pilgrimage feasts (16:11, 14), which means that they must be allowed to partake of the eating of the sacrifices. Similarly, the poor are the recipients of the tithe of the third year, which, according to Deuteronomy, is not brought to the chosen city but is eaten in the local settlements hence the name of the year "the year of the tithe" (14:28–29; 26:12–15) and the rabbinic name of the tithe "the tithe of the poor" (see *Tithe). The gifts which are specifically intended for the poor are mentioned in Leviticus (19:9–10; again briefly, 23:22 in conjunction with Shavuot, the festival of wheat harvesting) and in the laws of Deuteronomy (24:19–22). The rabbis derived from these passages four gifts from the vineyard—*pereṭ* ("individual grapes [fallen off during cutting]"), *shikhḥah* ("what is forgotten"), *pe'ah* ("[unharvested] edge"), and *'olelot* ("small single bunch [of grapes]"); three gifts from grainfields—*leqet* ("gleanings [of what is dropped by harvesters]"), *shikhḥah*, and *pe'ah*; and two from orchards—*shikhḥah*, and *pe'ah* (Tosef., Pe'ah 2:13).

According to the plain sense, Leviticus 19:9–10 designated two types of gift, both given from field and vineyard. The first gift consists of part of the produce which is to be left for the poor. The farmer is enjoined not to reap his entire crop, but to leave part of it unharvested for the poor: "And when you reap the harvest of your land, you shall not reap all the way to the edges of your field"; and the owner of a vineyard is commanded: "you shall not strip your vineyard bare" (Lev. 19:9–10). The *pe'ah* which is left in the field parallels the *'olelot* of the vineyard. The second gift consists of what falls to the ground during the harvesting: it is to be left there for the poor: as is written: "neither shall you gather the gleanings *[leqet]* of your harvest . . . neither shall you gather the fallen grapes *[peret]* of your vineyard" (*peret* in the vineyard is the same as *leqet* of the harvest, as the rabbis have explained).

Deuteronomy 24:19–22 refers to the second type of gift, exemplified, in the rhetorical manner peculiar to Deuteronomy, by produce of the field, olive grove, and vineyard. The prohibition against returning to gather the sheaf forgotten in the field is another version of the prohibition of total harvest in Leviticus. Similarly, the prohibition of beating the boughs of olive trees again and picking the vineyard again is the equivalent of Leviticus' ban on gathering up grapes fallen during the harvest.

Ruth's gleaning the *leqet* after the harvesters (Ruth 2), and the common reference to gleanings after the grape harvest (Judg. 8:2; Isa. 24:13; Micah 7:1, etc.) indicate that these laws were grounded in current practices. Various customs of other peoples have been compared: leaving the last sheaf in the field after the harvest in the superstitious fear that it contained the grain-demon and should therefore be left for strangers; or burial of a "corn baby," shaped out of a sheaf, in the field in order to assure the renewal of the crop the next year. Such conceptions, however, are alien to the Bible; its injunctions on behalf of the poor are given explicitly moral grounds. Permitting the widow to glean unhindered and giving gifts of oil to the poor are commended in Egyptian wisdom literature as approved by the gods ("The instruction of Amen-em-opet," 28; in Pritchard, Texts, 424).

For Talmudic Period see **Leket, Shikhḥah*, and *Pe'ah* **Terumot u-Ma'aserot;* *Sabbatical Year and Jubilee. See also *Charity, **Hekdesh*.

Bibliography: W. Nowack, *Die sozialen Probleme in Israel* (1896), 12–16; F. Buhl, *Die sozialen Verhaeltnisse der Israeliten* (1899), 102–5; D. Hoffmann, *Das Buch Leviticus*, 2 (1906), 36–38, 240–1 (= *Sefer va-Yikra*, 2 (1954), 31–32, 168); P. J. Baldensperger, in: PEFQS (1907), 19; G. Beer, in: ZAW, 31 (1911), 152; J. G. Frazer, *The Golden Bough*, 2 (1911, 1932), 171ff., 232ff.; G. A. Smith, *Deuteronomy* (1918, 1950), 284; I. Schur, in: ZAW, 32 (1921), 154; M. Lurje, in: BZAW, 45 (1927), 61–62; P. Joueon, in: *Biblica*, 15 (1934), 406–10; N. Peters, *Die soziale Fuersorge im Alten Testament* (1936), 66–72; J. Hempel, in: BZAW, 67 (1938), index, s.v. *Armer;* H. Bolkestein, *Wohltaetigkeit und Armenpflege im vorchristlichen Altertum* (1936), 38–40, 53–54, 56ff.; C. van Leeuwen, *Le développement du sens social en Israel avant l'ère chrétienne* (1955), 173ff.; E. Kutsch, in: RGG, 1 (1957[3]), 617–8.

[M.HA.]

POPES. The earliest, semi-legendary popes, Peter and his immediate successors, were of Jewish birth, yet nothing specific is known of their relations with the Jews. The first pope reported historically to have entered into direct relations with Jews was SYLVESTER I (314–335), who is said to have discussed religious matters with a Jew named Noah and to have conducted a triumphant disputation with a number of Jews, headed by Zambri the magician, in the presence of Emperor Constantine. LEO I (the Great; 440–461) composed some polemical sermons nominally (though not really) directed against Jews. Nothing further is known of papal-Jewish relations until the time of *Gelasius I (492–496), who had in his service, perhaps as physician, a Jew named Telesinus, whom he called *vir clarissimus*, recommending one of his relatives, Antonius, in a letter to Bishop Quingesius. He also ordered an inquiry (496) into the complaint of a Christian slave who claimed he had been circumcised by his Jewish master.

By far the most important medieval pope as regards relations with Jews, as in other respects, was *Gregory I (the Great; 590–604), whose letters are replete with information on the subject. He may be regarded as the founder of the accepted papal Jewish policy in both its positive and its negative aspects. On the one hand Pope Gregory ordered that the Jews should not be molested, that they should be protected from violence and permitted the free exercise of their religion, and on the other hand he said the Jews should be restrained from exercising any semblance of authority over Christians, or from enjoying equal status with Christians, or any privileges beyond those guaranteed them by existing law (i.e., the laws of the Roman Empire after the triumph of Christianity). A letter he wrote to the bishop of Palermo opened, "In the same way as the Jews should not have license to practice in their synagogues anything more than is allowed them by the law, so they should not suffer any disability in that which is conceded to them." This position summed up papal policy and set the example for all later papal legislation on the matter. The statement was reproduced as a fixed rubric, *Sicut Judaeis*, in bulls of protection issued by popes of the later Middle Ages on at least 22 occasions. It is with Gregory I, moreover, that the papacy came to be recognized as the supreme authority of the Western Church and accordingly Jews outside *Rome, and even outside Italy, began to address appeals for protection to the various popes, primarily through the mediation of the Jews of Rome.

Succeeding popes carried out the policy laid down by Gregory I without, however, extending it. At times of danger to the Church and consequent internal reformation, the tendency was to emphasize the negative rather than the positive side of that policy. Thus STEPHEN III (768–772), protested against the privileged position of the Jews of *Narbonne, their possession of landed property, and their mingling with their Christian neighbors on equal terms. NICHOLAS I (858–867) prohibited the wearing of "Jewish vestments" (i.e., those based on Old Testament prescriptions) by Christian priests. *Leo VII (936–939), departing from the tolerant policy of his immediate predecessors, authorized the archbishop of *Mainz to offer the Jews of his diocese the alternatives of expulsion or apostasy. So far as is known, in the persecutions which took place throughout most of Europe early in the 11th century (in the wake of a report that the Jews had persuaded the Muslims to destroy the Church of the Holy Sepulcher in Jerusalem) the popes took no part. Although a spurious document connected with the event is ascribed to SERGIUS IV (1009–12) a very old Hebrew account tells how on the occasion of a persecution at Rouen the Jews appealed to the pope for protection. If the extant report is reliable, Pope *Benedict VIII (1012–24) must have condoned the persecution of the Jews of Rome (1020–21) on a charge of blasphemy which was supposed to have brought about an earthquake. On the other hand, *Alexander II (1061–73) admonished the Christian warriors setting out to fight the Muslims in Spain (1063) not to molest Jews, and in 1065 he reproved the ruler of *Benevento, in Italy, for forcibly converting the Jews of that city to Christianity. The reformist popes who succeeded Alexander, and who reverted to strict Church discipline, inevitably emphasized the repressive aspect of papal policy. In 1078 GREGORY VII (1073–85) renewed the canon laws against placing Jews in positions of trust, with a particular view to their employment as taxfarmers or mintmasters; he renewed the prohibition in a brief to *Alfonso VI of Castile in 1081. (The suggestion that this pope and his kinsman Gregory VI (1045–46) were of Jewish extraction is based on error: see G. B. Picotti, in *Archivio Storico Italiano,* 1942.)

The popes were not implicated in the persecutions in Europe at the time of the early Crusades, although URBAN II (1088–99) berated Emperor *Henry IV for permitting those Jews who had been baptized by force to return to their faith. Urban's position was based on the doctrine that although compulsion could not properly be used in the baptismal act, once performed the sacrament of baptism was irrevocable, however it had been carried out. In 1120 *Calixtus II (1119–24) issued the protective bull, or *Constitutio pro Judaeis,* beginning with Gregory the Great's words *Sicut Judaeis,* in which any sort of persecution of the Jews was condemned in unqualified terms. Henceforth, for generations, this bull was often renewed by popes shortly after their accession, on the petition of the Jewish communities and presumably accompanied by gifts. In the next three centuries, the bull was reissued 21 times. Although his authority was not recognized elsewhere, ANACLETUS II, who was of immediate Jewish extraction and who for this reason was inveighed against by his opponents, maintained himself as pope in Rome between 1130 and 1138. It is possible that his career was the source of the medieval Jewish legend of the Jewish pope, Elhanan. Although his enemies lost no opportunity of calling attention to his Jewish origin, this had no lasting ill effects upon the Jews.

On his visit to Rome (c. 1165) Benjamin of Tudela found the Jews enjoying a favorable status. R. Jehiel, grandson of the author of the *Arukh* Nathan b. Jehiel, was then in the service of the reigning pope, *Alexander III (1159–81), who on his state entry into Rome (1165) had been greeted by the Jews, headed by their rabbis and bearing embroidered banners. However, this same pope presided over the Third *Lateran Council of 1179, which renewed the conventional canonical restrictions against Jews, forbidding them to exercise any authority over Christians or to live in close associations with them. The council marked the beginning of reform forced on the Church by the danger inherent in the development of the Albigensian movement (see *Albigenses) of southern France, in which Jewish influences were wrongly suspected.

The reform reached its climax with the Fourth Lateran Council of 1215–16, convened under the auspices of Pope *Innocent III (1198–1216), who may be recognized as at least the systematizer, if not the founder, of medieval clerical anti-Semitism. He is also the most important figure in the history of relations between the papacy and the Jews after Gregory I. The anti-Jewish canons of the Fourth Lateran Council, while not necessarily enforced or obeyed forthwith, set a standard of policy which afterwards was kept constantly before the eyes of Christian rulers, especially by the *Dominicans, who established their order at about this time to combat heterodoxy and heresy. Even Innocent, however, did not overlook the other aspect of the traditional papal policy and confirmed the *Constitutio pro Judaeis* in 1199, which protected Jews against violence from the French crusaders. At the same time he contested the claims of the Holy Roman emperor, as the successor to their conquerer, Vespasian, to suzerainty over the Jews throughout Europe.

Although all, or almost all, Innocent's successors confirmed the *Constitutio pro Judaeis,* they usually attempted to secure the enforcement of the anti-Jewish canons of the Lateran Council. *Honorius III (1216–27) was, however, forced by circumstances to permit the king of Castile to suspend the obligation of wearing the Jewish *badge as prescribed by this council, so as to prevent the Jews from migrating to Muslim realms. Under *Gregory IX (1227–41), who attempted to enforce the wearing of the badge in Navarre (1234), the papal offensive against the Jews was extended to Jewish literature, for it was with his authorization that the attack upon Jewish books and the Talmud was launched. Copies of the latter were sequestered pending an inquiry into its contents (1239; see Nicholas *Donin; *Jehiel b. Joseph of Paris). This was followed by its condemnation and sentence to burning, which apparently took place not only in France but also (under the pope's specific authority) in Rome (see *Talmud, Burning of). *Innocent IV (1243–54) repeated the condemnation of the Talmud in his bull *Impia judaeorum perfidia* of 1244. In 1253 he approved the archbishop's expulsion of the Jews from *Vienne in France for not obeying the Lateran decrees, and in 1250 he intervened to prevent the erection of a new synagogue in *Córdoba. On the other hand, in two bulls of 1246 he condemned in unqualified terms *blood libels which had begun to arise, and embodied his condemnation in the *Constitutio pro Judaeis,* which he issued for the second time that year. This condemnation remained an integral part of the text of the *Constitutio* whenever it was subsequently reissued by his successors. Although *Alexander IV (1254–61) attempted to enforce the Jewish badge and incited further attacks on the Talmud, he recognized also the value of the Jewish merchants for his treasury, and in 1255 relieved a number of them of all tolls throughout the papal possessions.

In the course of his brief papacy (1265–68) *Clement IV professed anxiety over the conversion of Christians to Judaism and authorized the *Inquisition to take measures against it, thus bringing Jews and the Inquisition into official contact for the first time (1267). A further extension of the Dominican offensive against Jews was approved by *Nicholas III (1277–80); in his bull *Vineam Soreth* (1279) he ordered that the Jews be compelled to listen to conversionist sermons. (There is, however, no evidence that this was enforced in Rome until much later.) This was the pope from whom the mystic Abraham b. Samuel *Abulafia sought to demand in person the release of the Jews from captivity, and was saved from the stake, according to his own account, only by the death of the pope at his summer residence at Soriano on the very night before Abraham entered the city to interview him. *Boniface VIII (1294–1303) was the first pope recorded to have treated disdainfully the Jewish deputation who regularly came to congratulate the pope on his accession; he returned over his left shoulder the Torah Scroll presented to him with the scornful remark that they could not comprehend it. Under his pontificate, moreover, R. Elijah de *Pomis was put to death by the Holy Office in Rome, apparently for allegedly having helped the Colonna family in their rebellion. This instance opened up serious possibilities of blackmail, and in 1299 a bull was procured which excluded the Jews, regardless of their material means, from the category of "powerful persons" who could be denounced anonymously to the inquisitors. On the other hand, it was at this time, notwithstanding the canonical prohibition, that popes are first recorded as having Jews regularly in their employment as personal physicians. The first known case is that of the philosopher and translator, Isaac b. Mordecai ("Master

Gaio"), who was in the service either of Boniface or his predecessor, Nicholas IV.

On the death of Boniface, there began the "Babylonian Exile" of the papacy at *Avignon (1309–77) which, along with the adjacent *Comtat Venaissin, had at that time finally become a papal possession by purchase. From this time onward, these papal territories in France were treated in much the same way as those in Italy, and Jews were consequently permitted to remain there when they were expelled from the rest of Provence. Not much is recorded about the policy toward the Jews of the first Avignonese pope, CLEMENT V (1305–14). His successor, *John XXII (1316–34), however, adopted a singularly antagonistic attitude toward Jews, although he did attempt to protect them at the time of the *Pastoureaux disturbances in 1320. John expelled Jews from certain places in the French papal dominions and temporarily (1321) from Rome itself. He converted former synagogues into churches, enforced the wearing of the Jewish badge (1317), encouraged conversion by permitting apostates to retain their property (1320), instituted special surveillance over converts to prevent backsliding (1317), and once more stirred up the French bishops against the Talmud (1320). John's successors proved themselves more favorably disposed toward the Jews. With them, there are records of Jews acting as tailors and parchment makers to the papal court in Avignon. *Benedict XII (1334–42) actively protected the Jews of Germany from a wave of massacres which broke out after a charge of the desecration of the *Host, by refusing to give credence to the charge without proper inquiry. *Clement VI (1342–52) was among the most benevolent of all medieval popes. Besides reconfirming the *Constitutio pro Judaeis* (as almost all other popes of the period had done), he condemned forcible baptism, and in 1348 he issued a benevolent edict protecting Jews in the widest terms from the fantastic accusations and brutal massacres which followed the *Black Death.

During the period of the great schism (1378–1417) the papacy was so absorbed in its own problems that it had little opportunity to occupy itself with the Jews. Hoping to score an impressive victory by having the Jews acknowledge the truth of Christianity, thereby to reinforce his personal status, the Spanish antipope *Benedict XIII established an almost frenetic anti-Jewish policy. It was he who was responsible for and presided over the disputation of *Tortosa (1413–14) and who instigated the persecutory movement, including condemning the Talmud and imposing wide-sweeping restrictions upon the Jews, which followed also in the Spanish Peninsula.

The Italian popes, however, influenced by the spirit of the Renaissance, reverted (with some exceptions) to a more tolerant policy. *Boniface IX (1389–1403), for example, had a succession of Jews in his employ as physicians and was responsible for a number of protective edicts, including one in 1402 which recognized the citizen rights of the Roman Jews. *Martin V (1417–31), with whose election the great schism ended, followed the example of Boniface, owing in part possibly to the influence of his Jewish physician, *Elijah b. Shabbetai Be'er. Martin greatly favored the Jews of Rome, prohibited forcible baptism, and even abolished the clerical prohibition on employing Jewish physicians. There is extant a drawing showing him greeting a deputation of Jews from Constance who came to welcome him to that city. This, however, was the period of intensified agitation against the Jews by the friars, led by John of *Capistrano, which could not fail to influence the papacy. In 1422 the alarmed Jews obtained a further edict of protection from the pope, and the friars were warned not to continue to incite the populace against them. (The edict was actually withdrawn a year later on the grounds that it had been obtained by fraud.) In 1427, as a result of reports that the Franciscan chapel on Mount Zion had been seized, the pope forbade Italian vessels to convey Jews to Palestine. A number of other unfavorable edicts led the Jews of Italy to organize countermeasures, backed by appropriately bestowed monetary gifts. This resulted in a very sweeping edict from the pope in 1429 protecting the Jews from the propaganda of the friars. The two conflicting currents, favorable and unfavorable, appear also in the policy of *Eugenius IV (1431–47) who, though at first renewing the privileges and safeguards of the Jews, was later forced to issue a bull putting into effect the severe decisions of the Council of Basle against Jews, forbidding them to practice handicrafts and moneylending, to engage in intercourse with Christians in any capacity, and even to study the Talmud. Once again there was a conference of Italian Jews and countermeasures (no doubt including bribery) were taken until the pope, persuaded that his policy was economically ruinous, withdrew the prohibitions. Restrictions were, however, renewed though apparently not enforced under the successors to Eugenius, *Nicholas V (1447–55) and *Calixtus III (1455–58), under whose rule the influence of Capistrano and the Observantine *Franciscans reached its climax. The humanist PIUS II (1458–64), who maintained the poet Moses da *Rieti in his service as his physician, was bent on a crusade against the Turks and therefore heavily increased taxation on the Jews.

With *Sixtus IV (1471–84) the Renaissance spirit triumphed in Rome, and for the next three quarters of a century relations between the popes and Jews were particularly close and cordial. Formally, of course, the popes had to conform with the external demands of unbending Christian orthodoxy. Thus Sixtus was nominally responsible for the introduction of the *Inquisition into Spain by his bull of 1478. On the other hand he had close personal relationships with Jews, as did his immediate successors down through the middle of the 16th century. Sixtus was interested to some extent in Hebrew literature and employed Hebrew copyists at the Vatican library. He also employed Jewish physicians, one of whom is said to have attempted a blood transfusion to save him in his last illness. In 1475 Sixtus initially refused to countenance a blood libel associated with the name of Simon of *Trent. The notorious *Alexander VI (1492–1503) permitted refugees from Spain to settle in Rome and had as his body physician Bonet de *Lattes, who dedicated his *Annuli . . . super Astrologiae utilitate* to him in 1493. JULIUS II (1503–13) extended his favor in the same manner to Samuel Sarfatti.

The climax in the favorable relations between the Jews and the Holy See was, however, reached with the popes of the house of Medici. *Leo X (1513–21) was so well disposed in fact that it was said that the Roman Jews considered his pontificate a presage of messianic times. Leo issued a notably benevolent edict in favor of the Jews in 1519, in which he repealed the obligation of wearing the Jewish badge in the papal dominions in France and allowed it to fall into disuse in Italy. He employed the converted Jewish musician, *Giovanni Maria, took a lively interest in Jewish literature, and permitted the printing of the Talmud. It is significant at this time that when Johann *Reuchlin made his appeal to the pope from the sentence of the Dominicans of Cologne, he requested the papal physician Bonet de Lattes, a Jew, to support him, such was the influence and esteem the latter enjoyed at the papal court. A kinsman and successor to Leo, *Clement VII (1523–34), showed even greater benevolence toward the Jews, so much so in fact that he was called "the favorer of Israel." He was especially noted for his close and friendly relations with David *Reuveni and Solomon *Molcho. His outstandingly favorable attitude was continued by his successor, PAUL III (1534–49), who invited refugee Marranos from Portugal to settle in Ancona and who employed Jacob *Mantino as his physician. The reluctance of the Medici popes to authorize the Inquisition in Portugal or to permit it to go into effect, although ultimately defeated, typifies the general tolerance of their approach to the Jews.

By now the spirit of the Counter-Reformation was beginning to make itself felt. *Julius III (1550–55) was personally friendly enough; he employed *Amatus Lusitanus as his physician, confirmed the rights of the Marranos of Ancona, condemned the blood libel, and prohibited the baptism of Jewish children without the consent of their parents. But the reactionary party led by Cardinal Caraffa, the embodiment of the Counter-Reformation, ultimately gained the upper hand. Before long this resulted in the establishment in 1553 of the House of *Catechumens *(Casa dei Neofiti)* in Rome at the expense of the local Jewish communities, the confiscation and burning of the Talmud (1553), the institution of the Congregation of the Holy Office with the surveillance of the Jews as one of its functions (1553), and the institution of a regular censorship of Hebrew books (1554). After the brief papacy (April 1555) of MARCELLUS II, Cardinal Caraffa himself became pope as Paul IV (1555–59), and the spirit of the Counter-Reformation triumphed with him and through his personal influence. The reaction against the Jews (especially in Rome and the Papal States, where he was able to carry his policy into effect) began immediately after his accession with the fanatical bull *Cum nimis absurdum* of 1555, which in effect drove the Jews out of civilized life and began the age of the *ghetto in Italy with all its horrors. Pope Paul IV was, moreover, personally responsible for the treacherous and faithless onslaught on the Marranos of Ancona, as a result of which some 25 were burned at the stake in the spring and summer of 1556. When he died on Aug. 18, 1559, there was a general reaction against his severity and a story is told that his overthrown statue was surmounted by a yellow hat such as he had imposed on the Jews of his dominions.

PIUS IV (1559–65), Paul's successor, brought a brief respite, and in 1562 he modified the severity of the enactments of his predecessor, even permitting the printing of the Talmud with certain omissions or, without them, under a different name (1564). He also induced the Holy Roman emperor to withdraw an edict of expulsion against the Jews of Bohemia, and eased living conditions in the newly established Roman ghetto by prohibiting the increase of rentals there. He was succeeded by PIUS V (1566–72), who, as Cardinal Ghislieri, had formerly been at the head of the Roman Inquisition, in which capacity he led the assault on Jewish literature during the preceding decade. With him the policy of repression triumphed again; the regulations of 1555 were renewed and the concessions made by his predecessor revoked. In 1567/68 he forbade Jews of the Papal States to lend money at interest, and his bull *Hebraeorum gens* of 1569 expelled Jews from the smaller places in the papal dominions, with the exception of Rome and Ancona in Italy, and Avignon, Carpentras, and two other places in France. His personal zeal, moreover, was responsible for the introduction of the ghetto system into the duchies of Urbino and Tuscany (1570–71).

There were some slight ameliorations under *Gregory XIII (1572–85), but he was responsible for the renewal of the institution of the conversionist sermons which Jews were compelled to attend, and for the stringent prohibition of the practice of medicine by the Jews among Christians. The latter marked the end of the tradition of Jewish medical practitioners in the service of the Vatican, which had been commonplace since the 13th century.

There was again a brief favorable interlude under SIXTUS V (1585–90), who made a determined attempt to restore the economic prosperity of the papal states and for that reason reversed the anti-Jewish policy of former popes, although before his election he had shown great severity against the Marranos when he was inquisitor in Venice. He had in his service as his majordomo Joao Lopes, a Marrano who had reverted to Judaism. He also granted Meir *Magino a monopoly for an improved method of silk manufacture, accepted the dedication to himself in David de' Pomis' dictionary, *Ẓemaḥ David,* and protected the Jews of the Papal States physically on more than one occasion. His bull *Christiana pietas* of 1586 revoked the persecutory edicts of his predecessors and permitted the Jews to return to the Papal States, to employ Christian servants as before, and to practice medicine. Moreover, he reversed the policy of former popes in regard to the practice of usury, permitting the opening of loan banks in the Papal States and issuing licenses or "absolutions" for Jewish moneylenders in various parts of Italy, which for the next 100 years provided a considerable income to the papal treasury. This favorable interlude was short-lived, ending soon after the death of Sixtus V. *Clement VIII (1592–1605) must at one time have been on friendly terms with Jews, for a Ḥannukkah lamp bearing his coat of arms as cardinal is preserved in the Victoria and Albert Museum, London. Nevertheless, in the year after his accession he issued the bull *Caeca et obdurata* (1593), which reinforced once more the persecutory policy of Paul IV and Pius V, except for the prohibition on moneylending, which remained permissible for some time longer.

From this period on, for between 200 and 300 years, there was no intermission or change in the policy of the popes who, absorbed with fears for the position of Roman Catholicism in Europe, considered that the repression of the Jewish communities under their control was an essential part of Catholic orthodoxy. Still, they preserved something of traditional balance in protecting the Jews of their dominions from the physical violence and the more fantastic anti-Semitic allegations common elsewhere. Occasionally, they were successfully appealed to by the Jewish communities of other countries for protection against such violence and allegations. With the extension of the area of Italy politically subject to the pope, the Roman policy was extended to the Jewish communities of the duchy of Ferrara (in 1625) and to Urbino (in 1634) by URBAN VIII (1623–44), who was responsible also for prohibiting tombstones in Jewish cemeteries. He also legalized forced baptisms in certain circumstances, declaring that the baptism of the head of a family could include, if he so desire, that of all his household who were under age or dependent on him. Popes *Innocent X (1644–55), ALEXANDER VII (1655–67), and CLEMENT IX (1667–69) enforced the policy somewhat less severely, the last named in his brief pontificate abolishing (in 1668) the humiliating race run by the Jews at carnival time. In 1674 *Clement X (1670–76) suspended the activities of the Portuguese Inquisition which were, however, renewed in 1681 by INNOCENT XI (1676–89). Innocent again (and this time finally) prohibited the practice of moneylending by the Jews of the papal possessions and suppressed their loan banks, a measure so harsh that its execution had to be twice postponed, eventually bringing the Jewish communities to the edge of ruin. At the same time this pope discouraged forced baptisms (which decreased somewhat under his rule) and in 1685 secured the release by the republic of Venice of the Jewish prisoners captured in the Morea.

With the 18th century conditions deteriorated still further. Renewed severity began under *Benedict XIII (1724–30) and *Clement XII (1730–40). The latter commissioned Cardinal Petra in 1733 to draw up a new anti-Jewish code, which introduced various new degradations, e.g., that the Jewish badge was to be worn even while traveling and that rabbis were not to be permitted to have any distinguishing costume. In 1766 this code was renewed and rigorously enforced by *Benedict XIV (1740–58) and the condition of the Jews of the papal dominions reached its nadir. The pope reinstituted rigorous measures against Hebrew literature, and in 1747 he ruled that a Jewish child once baptized, even against Church law, had to be brought up as a Christian. This ruling gave impetus to the scandal of forced baptisms, which from then on assumed tragic prominence in the history of Roman Jewry. Yet even this pontiff did not forget the nobler papal traditions. When in 1758 the Jewish communities of Poland appealed to him, through Jacob Selek, for protection against the wave of blood libels which were becoming a perpetual menace to their lives, he sympathetically referred the matter to the Holy Office of the Inquisition, an act which resulted in the famous report of Cardinal Ganganelli condemning the libel. In 1759 this report was presented to and approved by the next pope, *Clement XIII (1758–69), who communicated the findings to the papal nuncio in Warsaw and instructed him to protect the Jews from violence in this matter. Ten years later, Ganganelli himself became pope, as CLEMENT XIV (1769–74). Profoundly moved by the misery into which the Jewish communities of the Papal States had fallen, he wanted to improve their economic condition. Among other reforms, he accorded Jews some freedom of occupation and released them from the immediate jurisdiction of the Inquisition. He showed marked favor to the Roman Jewish leader, Ezekiel *Ambron. This proved to be only a brief interlude, however, for with his successor, PIUS VI (1775–98), a complete reaction set in. The *Editto sopra gli ebrei* (1775) of Pius codified, reinforced, and intensified the whole of former, degrading anti-Jewish legislation, however barbarous it was, and went so far even as to forbid Jews from passing the night outside the ghetto, under pain of death. These were the conditions under which the Jews of the Papal States continued until the armies of the French Revolution overthrew the temporal power of the popes in 1797–98 and as a matter of course abolished all discriminatory legislation. After the overthrow of Napoleon, PIUS VII (1800–23) led the way in the reaction which followed throughout Italy. (The papal possessions in the south of France, with control over the Jewish communities of that region, were by now lost.) To an antiquated religious obscurantism was now added the more cogent consideration that Jews were correctly suspected of sympathy with the liberal movement in Italian politics. From this time down to the overthrow of the temporal power of the papacy, the old policy of repression was renewed, from this point of view the Papal States now being the most reactionary area in Europe. Pope Pius VII returned from his long exile determined to reestablish the pre-revolutionary ecclesiastical regime down to the last detail, including the ghetto, conversionist sermons, and so on. Only the wearing of the Jewish badge, though nominally prescribed, was not actually enforced. Pius VII was, however, almost moderate as compared with his successor, LEO XII (1823–29), who revived the most fierce anti-Jewish prejudices, even to the point of having the gates of the ghettos restored and reenacting the *Editto sopra gli ebrei* of 1775. Pope PIUS VIII (1829–30) found time in the course of his brief pontificate to forbid the Jews to enter into personal relations with Christians for any purpose except in the course of business. His successor, Gregory XVI (1831–46), even reimposed the carnival tax, which had replaced the old abuse of the Jewish carnival race, with all its degrading associations. In 1836 he expelled the few Jews who had settled "illegally" in Bologna. PIUS IX (1846–78) began his pontificate as the hope of the liberal movement, introducing several measures for the amelioration of the position of the Jews of the Papal States. Later, however, he too turned to reaction, and though his personal attitude remained not unfriendly he kept to all of his predecessors' restrictions with an unabated vigor. Under him even the abusive forced baptism of children prevailed, the most notorious (but not the only or the last) instance being the infamous *Mortara case of 1858, in which the pope maintained an absolutely unyielding attitude.

After the fall of Rome and the end of the Church's temporal power in 1870, up to which time the policy of repression had continued in force almost unmodified, the relationship of the papacy with the Jews inevitably changed. It was no longer a question of political treatment in an area subject to direct papal rule, but of a general attitude toward them on the intellectual and theological plane, political influence being therefore indirect. The papal attitude was inevitably influenced to some extent by the natural sympathy of the Jews in Catholic countries with the secular and anti-clerical party and their natural antagonism to Church influence in education. Although LEO XIII (1878–1903) was guilty in 1895 of the blunder of sending his blessing to the clerical-anti-Semitic coalition in Austria, he did, on the other hand, try to some extent to moderate passions in France. In 1892 he called on all right-thinking persons in that country, including Protestants and Jews, to unite against the "enemies of religion and society," i.e., the Freemasons and secularists. *Pius X (1903–14), though no less opposed to modernism, was not as interested in political matters as his predecessor. Early in 1904 he received Theodor *Herzl in audience, his secretary of state subsequently expressing mild sympathy with the humanitarian, though not the political objectives of Zionism. BENEDICT XV (1914–22), on the other hand, though he vaguely endorsed the *Balfour Declaration in an interview with Nahum *Sokolow, afterward expressed grave concern over the control of the holy places in Palestine. *Pius XI (1922–39) was confronted with the problems which arose with the triumph of the Nazi movement in Germany and anti-Semitism in Italy, and expressed his disapproval of racism in the most outspoken fashion, declaring that "spiritually we are all Semites." In 1935, at the time of the revival of the blood libel in Germany, he formally accepted from Cecil Roth a copy of his new edition of Pope Clement XIV's report condemning the libel, thereby confirming in effect the declaration of his predecessor. His successor, *Pius XII (1939–58), though less outspoken at a period of greater danger and failing even to condemn publicly the deportations and annihilation of European Jewry, nevertheless, on the occupation of Rome by Germans in 1943, received many refugees in the Vatican, and thus set the example for, even if he did not inspire, the protection of the Jews of Italy by the Catholic population. His reaction to the establishment of a Jewish state was unfavorable, since this falsified the Catholic interpretation of prophecy. The personal relations of *John XXIII (1958–63) with individual Jews were cordial both before and after his elevation to the papacy, and as cardinal he showed active sympathy with the victims of Nazi persecution. Jews moreover shared in the atmosphere of tolerance toward non-Catholics which became manifest during his pontificate. Under his successor Paul VI (1963–), the Second Vatican Council adopted a schema deploring anti-Semitism and stating that the blame for Jesus' death must be attributed to some of his contemporaries and not to the Jewish people as a whole. The declaration was less forthright than had been advocated by John XXIII but its spirit led to important modifications in Catholic textbooks. In 1964 Paul visited Christian holy places in Israel for a day.

See entries on individual popes. See also *Church; *Church Councils; *Vatican.

Bibliography: E. A. Synan, *Popes and the Jews in the Middle Ages* (1965); S. Grayzel, *Church and the Jews in the XIIIth Century* (1933); idem, in: HJ, 2 (1940), 1–12; J. Parkes, *Conflict of the Church and the Synagogue* (1934); idem, *Jews in the Medieval Community* (1938); E. Rodocanachi, *Le Saint-Siège et les Juifs* (1891); I. Loeb, in: REJ, 1 (1880), 114–8, 293–8; M. Stern, *Urkundliche Beitraege ueber die Stellung der Paepste zu den Juden*, 2 vols. (1893–95); idem, *Die paepstlichen Bullen ueber die Blutbeschuldigung* (1893); P. Browe, *Judenmission in Mittelalter und die Paepste* (1942); K. Eubel, in: *Roemische Quartalschrift*, 7 (1903), 183–7. [C.R.]

POPLAR (Heb. צַפְצָפָה), tree. The *Populus euphratica* grows wild on the banks of the Jordan. Its leaves are usually broad though some are long and narrow, resembling those of the willow. In Israel the white poplar, *Populus alba*, is grown as an ornamental tree. It is a tall tree with a white bark, and the underside of its leaves are silvery white. This species, which flourishes on the banks of rivers, is one of the two that Ezekiel refers to as a tree growing by the side of water (Ezek. 17:5). It is possible that the white poplar was the *livneh* peeled by Jacob to place in front of the sheep (Gen. 30:37; but see *Storax). When stating that it was not permitted to use the poplar for the *willow branch, one of the *Four Species, the Talmud indicates its characteristics: "The poplar has a white stem, a round leaf, and an edge serrated like a sickle" (Suk. 34a), and notes that whereas the serrations of the leaf edges of the willow are small and dense, those of the poplar are like the teeth of a saw (Maim. Yad, Lulav 7:3–4). The warning against confusing the poplar with the willow was due to the fact that their names were interchanged.

Bibliography: Loew, Flora, 3 (1924), 325–7, 338–9; J. Feliks, *Olam ha-Ẓome'aḥ ha-Mikra'i* (1968²), 116–7. [J.F.]

°**POPPAEA, SABINA,** second wife of Nero (62–65 C.E.). Josephus describes her as being sympathetic toward Judaism, even terming her a "god-fearing" woman (Ant. 20, 189–96). She twice interceded successfully on behalf of the Jews. When Josephus went to Rome in 64 C.E. to plead for the priests imprisoned by Felix, he was introduced to Poppaea by the Jewish actor *Aliturus. With her assistance the priests were freed and she bestowed many gifts on Josephus himself (Life, 16). On the second occasion she interceded on behalf of a delegation headed by the high priest *Ishmael b. Phabi, sent by the priests to Rome to appeal against a decision of the procurator *Festus, who had, at the request of *Agrippa II, ordered the demolition of a wall erected by the priests to prevent the king from viewing the proceedings in the Temple. Poppaea influenced Nero to uphold the appeal and the wall was allowed to stand. Tacitus, who makes no mention of her attitude toward the Jews, pictures Poppaea as a corrupt and cruel woman.

Bibliography: Schuerer, Gesch, 1 (1901³ and ⁴), 579, 585, 591; 3 (1909⁴), 64; Klausner, Bayit Sheni, 5 (1951²), 26, 39, 167. [L.Ro.]

POPPER, family of entrepreneurs and communal leaders in Bohemia. Members of the Popper family from Breznice, Bohemia, attended the Leipzig fairs from the late 17th century. WOLF POPPER, the "Primate of Bohemian Jewry," was in charge of the collection of taxes for 18 years (1749–67). His son ḤAYYIM (Joachim; 1720–1795) moved to Prague and was a successful merchant (woolens, potash, whalebone), banker, manufacturer, and co-lessee of the profitable tobacco monopoly. In 1775 he is mentioned as holding his father's position in perpetuity. Joachim Popper was a patron of literature and also donated large sums to philanthropy, maintaining a balance between Christian and Jewish causes. In 1790 he was ennobled as Edler von Popper in recognition of his contributions to the welfare of the state. On the day he received his patent of nobility he presented a petition to Leopold II requesting the introduction in Bohemia of the more liberal *Judenpatent* of Galicia, which included obligatory military service for Jews. However, a group of Prague Jews presented a counterproposal arguing against conscription. He suggested reform of the system of taxation in 1792, the same year he resigned from office. On his death he bequeathed large sums to charity, and provided for the creation of a synagogue in his home in which prayer and study were to be subsidized perpetually. He also stipulated that his firm continue to bear his name.

Bibliography: S. Krauss, *Joachim Edler von Popper* (1926); idem, in: *Zeitschrift fuer die Geschichte der Juden in der Tschechoslovakei*, 4 (1934), 40–44, 69–84; R. Kestenberg-Gladstein, *Neuere Geschichte der Juden in den boehmischen Laendern* (1969), index. [ED.]

POPPER, JOSEF (pseudonym, **Lynkeus;** 1838–1921), Austrian social philosopher, engineer, and inventor. Born in Kolin, Bohemia, Popper studied at Prague University. As a Jew, he was refused a teaching post at the university and worked for a while with the national railroads in Hungary. He then went to Vienna where, after a series of fairly humble jobs, he invented, at the age of 30, a device to prevent fur from accumulating on engine boilers. The meager profits from this and other inventions enabled him to devote his later years to writing on social reform. His pseudonym, Lynkeus, is the name of the keen-sighted, mythological, Argonaut helmsman.

As a scientist Popper was far ahead of his time. In 1862 he proposed a system for the electrical transmission of energy, but sent the monograph to the Vienna Academy of Sciences in a sealed letter to be opened 20 years later. He discussed the possible existence of quanta of energy before Max Planck enunciated the quantum theory; in 1884 he tried to relate matter and energy, 20 years before *Einstein's theory of relativity; and in 1888 discussed the possibility of lightweight steam engines for flying machines in a treatise, *Flugtechnik* (1889). In *Phantasien eines Realisten* (2 vols., 1899), suppressed by the Austrian government as "immoral," he anticipated, as Freud himself acknowledged, the fundamental basis from which the latter elaborated his theory of dreams.

Popper was best known, however, for his writings on social reform.

In his first work of this nature, *Das Recht zu Leben und die Pflicht zu Sterben*... (1878), he contrasted man's natural right to live with the alleged obligation to sacrifice himself when required to do so by the state. He denied that man has a duty to let himself be killed when ordered and, in *Die allgemeine Naehrpflicht als Loesung der sozialen Frage* (1912), advocated the right of the individual to live in freedom and dignity within the framework of a social system created for the benefit of its members. Popper's solution to social problems was the formation of a labor force *(Naehrarmee)* whose purpose was "producing or procuring all that physiology and hygiene show to be absolutely indispensable." This was to be regarded as a minimum contribution by every member of society. Popper's philosophy differed from Marxism, in that it was based on simple humanitarianism and common sense and endeavored to eliminate class hatred by a synthesis of socialism and realism. In trying to revive Voltaire's philosophy, he advocated a policy which in fact became crystallized in the modern welfare state.

Popper regarded metaphysics, theology, and traditional religion as harmful, and to be eliminated from an economically and socially reformed state. He saw religion, especially Christianity, as opposed to genuine individual human values, and believed that education, especially about the history of religions, could lead to a superstition-free culture.

Josef Popper, Austrian social philosopher and inventor. Jerusalem, J.N.U.L., Schwadron Collection.

Although he suffered considerable humiliation as a Jew, Popper refused to convert, and accused the German chancellor, Bismarck, of anti-Semitism in *Fuerst Bismarck und der Antisemitismus* (1886). He believed that only a Jewish State would eliminate anti- Semitism, and although he never took an active part in the Ziònist movement he bequeathed his substantial collection of books to the National Library in Jerusalem.

Popper was a close friend of Albert Einstein, who described him as a "prophetic and saintly person" who had forecast that "the continued existence of mankind without organized planning is inconceivable." He was widely regarded as a genius, and a bust of him was erected in the Rathauspark in Vienna. It was destroyed by the Nazis in 1938. Popper's writings include: *Die technischen Fortschritte nach ihrer aesthetischen und kulturellen Bedeutung* (1886), *Friedensvorschlaege, Schiedsgerichte, Voelkerbund* (1910), and *Krieg, Wehrpflicht und Staatsverfassung* (1921).

Bibliography: J. Popper-Lynkeus, *Selbstbiographie* (1917); H. I. Wachtel, *Security for All and Free Enterprise: A Summary of the Social Philosophy of Josef Popper-Lynkeus* (1955), incl. bibl.; A. Gelber, *Joseph Popper-Lynkeus, sein Leben und sein Wirken* (1922); F. Wittels, *An End to Poverty* (1925); P. Edwards (ed.), *Encyclopedia of Philosophy*, 6 (1967), 401–7 (incl. bibl.); E. Relgis, *Der Humanitarismus und die "Allgemeine Naehrpflicht"* (1931).

[J.J.L.]

POPPER, JULIUS (1857–1893), Rumanian explorer. Popper's father was the principal of the first Jewish school in Bucharest. After studying engineering in Paris, he went on a world trip during which he heard about gold deposits on Tierra del Fuego. His exploration of the island proved the stories to be true, and he accordingly designed a machine for extracting the gold. Establishing himself as ruler over the island, Popper gave it a code of laws and defended it against other adventurers. [Ed.]

POPPER, SIR KARL RAIMUND (1902–), philosopher. Popper was born in Vienna of Jewish parents who had converted to Christianity. In the early 1920s he worked with juvenile delinquents in Alfred *Adler's clinic in Vienna. In 1930 he became a secondary school teacher of mathematics and science. The rise of Fascism led to his leaving Austria in 1937, and until 1945 he taught philosophy at Canterbury University College, New Zealand. He then moved to the University of London, and in 1949 became professor of logic and scientific method at the London School of Economics. He was knighted in 1964. Popper's philosophical views were profoundly influenced by the Einsteinian revolution in physics.

As early as 1919 Popper began to draw the philosophical consequences of this revolution. He saw that the "inductive method," hitherto supposed to be the distinguishing mark of science, was a myth. Empirical evidence was used in science, not to establish cautious hypotheses, which is impossible, but to refute bold ones. The mark of a scientific theory was its refutability, and the scientific pretensions of those other contemporary revolutions in thought, the theories of *Marx, *Freud, and Adler, were suspect on this count. Popper's revolutionary philosophy of science was eventually published in *Die Logik der Forschung* (1934; *The Logic of Scientific Discovery,* 1959). He had close contact in these early years with the logical positivist movement. He criticized the postivists' inductivism, and their attempt to dismiss all metaphysics as meaningless. This, he argued, ignored the suggestive value of many metaphysical ideas for science. Popper wrote *The Open Society and Its Enemies* (2 vols., 1945, 1965), which criticized the authoritarian political philosophies then in vogue. He attacked their belief in the inexorable laws of history, and the idea that the task of the social sciences was to discern these laws and to prophesy the future development of society. His elaboration of these criticisms, and his positive views on the method of the social sciences, later appeared in his book *The Poverty of Historicism* (1957). From the time Popper began working in England a stream of articles issued forth, witnessing to his new, more metaphysical interests in such things as indeterminism and emergent evolutionism. A collection of these, entitled *Conjectures and Refutations: The Growth of Scientific Knowledge,* appeared in 1963. Popper's influence, through his fertile and original contributions to a wide variety of problems, has been great: his concept of *critical fallibilism* is an important trend in contemporary philosophy.

Bibliography: M. A. Bunge (ed.), *Critical Approach to Science and Philosophy* (1964), incl. his bibl.; K. Popper, in: C. A. Mace (ed.), *British Philosophy in the Mid-Century* (1957), 155–91 (philosophical autobiography); P. Edwards (ed.), *Encyclopedia of Philosophy* (1967), index. [A.Mu.]

POPPER, WILLIAM (1874–1963), U.S. orientalist and biblical scholar. Born in St. Louis, Missouri, Popper served from 1902 to 1905 as an associate editor of the *Jewish Encyclopedia* and acting head of the Oriental Department of the New York Public Library. During this period and again in 1919/20, he also lectured on Semitic languages at Columbia University. From 1905 onward he taught at the University of California, Berkeley, becoming a full professor and head of the Semitic department in 1922. He retired in 1945.

Popper's biblical research centered on the literary and stylistic aspects of Isaiah (*Parallelism in Isaiah,* 1923), whose text he tried to reconstruct, publishing with an English translation of his own (*The Prophetic Poetry of Isaiah,* 1931). In the field of Arabic studies his critical editions and translations of Arabic historical texts of the 15th century have made this period accessible to non-Arabist historians. Among his works are: parts of the critical edition of Yūsuf ibn Taghrī-Birdī's *Al-Nujūm Al-Zâhira fī Mulûk Miṣr waal-Kâhirâ* (History of Egypt; 1909) and part of his *Hawādith al-Duhūr* (4 vols., 1930–42). *History of Egypt* (8 vols., 1954–63) is the English translation to Taghrī-Birdī's Arabic Annals. *The Cairo Nilometer* (1951) presents studies in Ibn Taghrī-Birdī's "Chronicles of Egypt." *Egypt and Syria under the Circassian Sultans 1382–1468* (2 vols., 1955–57) offers systematic notes to Ibn Taghrī-Birdī's chronicles. In the field of Jewish scholarship he wrote *The Censorship of Hebrew Books* (1899, reprinted with introduction by M. Carmilly-Weinberger, 1969). On the occasion of his 75th birthday, Popper was presented with a Jubilee Volume (*Semitic and Oriental Studies,* ed. by W. J. Fischel, 1951).

Bibliography: W. J. Fischel, in: JAOS, 84 (1964), 213–220.

[W.J.F.]

POPPER BOZIAN, WOLF (d. 1625), merchant and banker in Cracow. His father, Israel Gershon ha-Kohen, was from *Checiny; and his wife, Cyrl, was the daughter of Judah Lewek *Landau, one of the heads of the Jewish community in Kazimierz. Popper Bozian engaged in import, especially of cloth from *Cologne, and in financial transactions in a number of fairs which took place in several towns in Poland and Schleswig, from which businesses he became very rich. His will revealed that his financial transactions, which amounted to many thousands of zlotys, were often carried out with use of special promissory notes (*mamram). His success in business was used as an excuse for blaming the Jews for a period of commercial strife in Cracow in the second decade of the 17th century. In a pamphlet entitled *Zwierciadło korony polskiej* ("The Mirror of the Polish Kingdom," Cracow, 1618), the anti-Semite Sebastian *Miczyński describes Popper Bozian as a businessman who owned seven stores in Cracow and whose transactions extended to many towns and amounted to more than 300,000 zlotys. In order to incite mob hatred, Miczynski also implicated him in a blood libel. In 1620 Popper Bozian financed the construction of a synagogue (Popper Shul, destroyed by the Nazis) and a *bet midrash*.

Bibliography: M. Balaban, *Historja żydów w Krakowie i na Kazimierzu*, 1 (1931), 75, 199, 238, 270–6. [A.Cy.]

POPPERS (POPERS), JACOB BEN BENJAMIN HA-KOHEN (d. 1740), German rabbi. Born in Prague, Poppers studied under his father and in various yeshivot. He was subsequently appointed rabbi of Coblenz and of Trier, in the Rhineland. He declined an invitation to Halberstadt in 1718 but accepted the rabbinate of Frankfort where he headed a large yeshivah. His disciples included Jacob Berlin, Joseph *Steinhardt, and Joseph Wassertrilling. Poppers corresponded with the great scholars of his time on halakhic and contemporary problems. He was among those who imposed a ban on Moses Ḥayyim *Luzzatto in 1725 for teaching Kabbalah and on suspicion that he adhered to the Shabbatean doctrine. Compelled to leave Italy, Luzzatto arrived in Frankfort, where he was summoned before the *bet din* of Poppers and, after much discussion, was obliged again to promise not to teach Kabbalah nor to engage in its study until he was 40 years old. Poppers was the author of *Shav Ya'akov* (Frankfort, 1741–42), responsa in two parts. Some of his novellae are included in *Minḥat Kohen* (Fuerth, 1741) by Shabbetai b. Moses. Poppers died in Frankfort.

Bibliography: M. Horovitz, *Frankfurter Rabbinen* (1969[2]), 117–24. [Y.Ro.]

POPPERS, MEIR BEN JUDAH LOEB HA-KOHEN (d. 1662), kabbalist of Ashkenazi descent who was active in Jerusalem after 1640. A pupil of Jacob Ẓemaḥ, he became the last editor of the Lurianic writings. He divided the mass of Vital's different versions of Luria's teachings into three parts, *Derekh Ez Ḥayyim*, *Peri Ez Ḥayyim*, and *Nof Ez Ḥayyim*. Poppers' version became the one in most widespread use in Poland and Germany. After 1640 he composed a large number of his own kabbalistical writings in the vein of Lurianic Kabbalah. They are said to have comprised 39 books, each of which contained the word *or* ("light") in its title, the entire corpus being called *Kokhevei Or*.

Several parts have been preserved (Ms. Jerusalem no. 101, Ms. R. Alter of Gur (no. 170). They included commentaries on *Sefer Bahir*, on Naḥmanides' Torah commentary, on the Zohar, and on Luria's writings according to his own edition (Ms. Jerusalem no. 102). In the latter manuscript Poppers reports that he had studied Luria's writings for 17 years. Only two of these books have been published: *Or Ẓaddikim* (Hamburg, 1690), written in Jerusalem in 1643, and later incorporated in Moses *Katz's compilation, *Or ha-Yashar* (Amsterdam, 1709); and *Me'orei Or*, a dictionary of kabbalistic symbolism, published with copious notes by Jacob Vilna and Nathan Neta Mannheim under the title *Me'orot Natan* (Frankfort, 1709). In addition, *Mesillot Ḥokhmah*, a booklet summarizing Lurianic metaphysics in 32 paragraphs, later published under Poppers' name (Shklov, 1785), was first printed anonymously (Wandsbeck, c. 1700). Poppers is credited with the authorship of a graphic description and summary of the Lurianic system, in the form of a scroll, published under the title *Ilan ha-Gadol* (1864). This tree, however, shows the distinct influence of Israel *Sarug's version of Lurianism, which is not to be found in Poppers' other writings. Part of his homilies on the Torah were published as *Tal Orot* (1911).

He mentions as his teachers one R. Israel Ashkenazi and his father-in-law, Azariah Ze'evi (probably from Hebron). During the 1650s Poppers spent about two years in Constantinople. He died in Jerusalem.

Bibliograpy: Azulai, 1 (1852), 120 no. 27; Frumkin-Rivlin, 2 (1928), 38–39; G. Scholem, *Kitvei Yad be-Kabbalah* (1930), 146–9. [G.Sch.]

POPULATION. Methodological Uncertainties. Because of the great difficulties in ascertaining human population data in general, and Jewish data in particular, especially in ancient and medieval times, a word of caution is even more necessary here than in most other areas of historical and sociological research. Even the size of the world Jewish population today is questionable because the two largest countries of Jewish settlement, the United Sates and the Soviet Union, are supplying only inadequate estimates, rather than scientifically verifiable facts (see below). The same holds true for many other countries embracing substantial numbers of Jews.

In their report to the International Congress of Historical Sciences in 1950 Carlo Cippola and his associates reported on behalf of their Committee that "in the eyes of demographers bent on scientific precision and certainty all demographic research undertaken for any period before the 18th century runs the risk of appearing as a mere fantasy." Nevertheless, the Committee felt impelled to present some results of their investigations, as have many other scholars dealing with population statistics of past ages. They have felt that the rise or fall of populations, and the concomitant facts relating to natality and mortality rates, sex and age distribution, marriages and divorces, and so forth, are too vital for the understanding of all other socioeconomic, political, and even intellectual developments for scholarship to be satisfied with a resigned *ignoramus et ignorabimus*. Many demographers and historians are, indeed, convinced, to cite the Spanish sociologist Javier Ruiz Almanza's pithy epigram, that "history without demography is an enigma, just as is demography without history."

Population *censuses were not completely absent in the ancient and medieval worlds. As a matter of fact, an Egyptian record of about 3000 B.C.E., preserved on the so-called Palermo Stone, gives us a fair idea of how the population was counted at that early age. Egyptian censuses were rather frequently conducted during the Middle Kingdom; they went into such details as naming all members of the respective families. In ancient Israel, too, the censuses attributed to Moses and David have a high degree of probability as to fact, if not with respect to the actual results. However, these counts were much too sporadic to serve as reliable guides. Even modern censuses become truly dependable only when they are periodically repeated and employ the same basic methods. If their final results are not absolutely accurate, they at least reveal some fundamental trends in growth or decline and other variations during the intervening periods. Ancient and medieval censuses, even when recorded, were taken too far apart, and used unknown or, at least, variable statistical methods. Hence they furnish almost no guidance for the prevailing trends. The resultant figures, moreover, are frequently available to us only in texts reproduced by successive copyists over many generations, or even centuries. It is a well-known fact that copyists are more likely to err with respect to numbers than in regard to almost any other words, because such changes, as a rule, do not make the meaning of the entire phrase or sentence incomprehensible. It is enough, for example, for a Hebrew copyist to omit a *lamed* in *shalosh* to produce the word *shesh* which immediately doubles the figure. In its abbreviated form a change from a *dalet* (representing four) to a *resh* (two hundred), or vice versa, can play havoc with any number intended by the author. Nor does any proofreader or ordinary reader, unless well-informed about the particular situation, notice such changes which, by constant repetition, sometimes assume the appearance of dependability.

Even informed students, moreover, often approach the recorded figures with set presuppositions. Until the 18th century Jewish, as well as general, European opinion believed that ancient times were in all aspects more glorious than the Middle Ages or the modern period. They assumed that ancient populations were far larger than those familiar to them from observation or readings of more recent events. Even so critical a thinker as Montesquieu was convinced that the world population of his day did not total more than one-tenth of what it had been in antiquity. The first scholar to question these assumptions was David Hume. Subsequently, the pendulum swung to the other extreme. As in other areas of life, most scholars were convinced of mankind's gradual progress, despite occasional relapses, and believed that the size of human populations, too, as a rule showed an upward curve. In time, however, more careful studies revealed that there were constant ups and downs, with periods of growth followed by those of decline, and the other way around. Another drawback of the recorded censuses and other population records consisted in their underlying purposes. Ancient and medieval governments rarely, if ever, undertook counting population out of general scientific curiosity. They did it principally in order to secure lists of prospective taxpayers, soldiers, or both. Understandably, since they often served as instruments of greater fiscal oppression and more effective military levies, censuses were heartily disliked by the masses of the population. Thus readily grew the widespread superstition that censuses caused divine wrath and retribution. Even King David's census provoked the biblical writer to observe: "And again the anger of the Lord was kindled against Israel, and He moved David against them, saying: 'Go, number Israel and Judah'" (II Sam. 24:1). In fact, it is related, the king later repented his irreligious act. As a result of this popular resentment many persons undoubtedly succeeded in evading the count, thus greatly reducing its value. A remarkable talmudic anecdote states that when Persian tax collectors arrived in a city to number the Jews subject to the capitation tax, the latter were forewarned by their leaders to go into hiding until the collectors departed. The community at large had a self-interest in reducing the figures thus obtained because it afterwards had to negotiate with the government for some lump-sum payment to cover the total tax due.

Bearing all these deficiencies in mind, scholarship must nevertheless make concerted efforts to come to grips with the demographic facts of life in both the past and the present. Wherever possible a number of convergent hypotheses, even if by themselves none too reliable, may offer at least some more or less acceptable approximations. Yet in the summary here presented its often extremely tentative nature must never be lost sight of.

Ancient Israel. There are only a few direct pieces of information about the population of ancient Israel. Some of it is quite dubious. The well-known figure of 600,000 adult male Israelites (601,730 men aged 20 or over in addition to 23,000 male levites, including minors, according to Num. 26:51 and 62), who are said to have been counted by Moses after the Exodus from Egypt, has long been discounted by critical scholars. Including the women and minors, this number would have represented a population of about 2,500,000, much too large for the small province of Goshen in northeastern Egypt where the majority of Israelites had lived before their departure. The addition of some non-Israelites of the "mixed multitude" (Ex. 12:37–38) who joined the Exodus was undoubtedly more or less balanced by those Israelites who refused to leave the "fleshpots" of Egypt and remained behind. It is to them and their descendants that some Egyptian papyri of the 12th century B.C.E. refer when they speak of some "Hebrew" *(apiru)* still living in Egypt at the time. Moreover, a mass of 2,500,000 persons crossing the "Red Sea" and migrating through the desert for 40 years staggers the imagination. Even if we accept the extreme emendation by some scholars which reduces the figure to 6,000 adult males, it would still leave a considerable number of 25,000 or more persons finally entering Canaan, where they may have joined some descendants of the ancient Ḥabiru ("Hebrews") who had never left Palestine for Egypt but had slowly been occupying Canaanite territory from the days of the El-Amarna Letters in the 15th and 14th centuries B.C.E.

Much more informative are the figures yielded by the census conducted by Joab at the behest of King David. Here there is a major difficulty in having two apparently contradictory records. The figures given in II Samuel 24:9, namely that "there were in Israel eight hundred thousand valiant men that drew the sword; and the men of Judah were five hundred thousand men," seem to be controverted by the report in I Chronicles (21:5) that "all they of Israel were a thousand thousand and a hundred thousand men that drew sword; and Judah was four hundred three-score and ten thousand men that drew sword." Whichever figure is taken—and with some difficulty they can be harmonized—it indicates a population of well over 5,000,000, which is possible, if at all, only if Joab counted the population, including the subject peoples, of the entire Davidic empire from parts of Syria to the border of Egypt. In that case, the Israelite population doubtless formed but a minority of those counted. If, in the following generations, Israel rapidly assimilated some of the subject tribes in its midst, the area under its control had shrunk considerably under Solomon and his successors. Another figure of great interest is given in the Assyrian king Sennacherib's boast that at the time of his siege of Jerusalem in 701 B.C.E. he had deported 200,150 men, women, and children from the Judean kingdom, all of which except the capital had been occupied by the Assyrian troops. This number too, has been subjected to much carping by modern critics. One of them, Karl Ungnad, suggested that it be reduced to 2,150 persons—a number which would have rendered the royal boast entirely meaningless. While Sennacherib's grandiloquent inscription may indeed have exaggerated considerably the number of prisoners taken back to Assyria, it must to some extent have approximated reality.

Some of the figures here quoted are partially supported by the existence in the country of a large number of "cities." As early as the 15th century B.C.E. the famous Egyptian inscription by Thutmoses III named more than 100 Palestinian cities conquered in an area covering only about one-fourth of what was later to become the land of Israel and Judah, which bears out the development of some 400 "municipalities" under the Israelitic regime indicated by both the ancient *Onomastica* and modern geographic research. These cities were for the most part very small. Even in Israel's heyday their vast majority embraced only 1,000 inhabitants or less, but from Canaanite times on they had served the purpose of protecting the farming population against raids from hostile outsiders. Most farmers seem indeed to have lived within walled cities while cultivating their soil by "going out" to their fields or vineyards in the morning and returning in the evening. (This is, therefore, the sequence of the well-known biblical phrase.) Incidentally, this situation explains why ancient Palestine did not have any such major cleavage between the urban and rural populations as has characterized the medieval and modern West.

Finally, there is also some interesting data concerning the kingdom of Judah during the Babylonian conquests and its aftermath in the years 597–582 B.C.E. One source reports that 3,023 Judeans had been deported in the seventh year of Nebuchadnezzar, 832 Jerusalemites in the 18th year, 745 Judeans in the 23rd year, together "all the persons were four thousand and six hundred" (Jer. 52:28–30). In contrast, II Kings (24:14–16) states that the Babylonians "carried away all Jerusalem, and all the princes, and all the mighty men of valor, even ten thousand captives, and all the craftsmen and the smiths." Somewhat differently, the figure of 7,000 is mentioned in the same context. These contradictory data have been subjected to a variety of interpretations, but with some effort and ingenuity they can be harmonized. In any case, both sets of figures evidently refer only to a small elite of landowners, priests, and craftsmen whose absence would deprive the subject population of leadership and the supply of arms, but the Babylonians must have simultaneously deported a great mass of captives from the lower classes. Archaeological discoveries have confirmed the fact that after 586 B.C.E. the Judean countryside was quite deserted, although the conquerors may have brought in some replacements in addition to maintaining their own garrisons on the spot. This exchange of populations had long been practiced by the Assyrians in order to stem irredentist movements and, a century and a quarter before the fall of Jerusalem, they had deported a great many Northern Israelites before and after the fall of Samaria in 733–719 B.C.E.

In short, on the basis of these and numerous other scattered data, supported by a number of demographic considerations, the present writer ventured to propose the following highly tentative table for the approximate population of ancient Israel and Judah between 1000 and 586 B.C.E.:

Table 1.

	1000	733/701	586
Judah	450,000	300,000–350,000	150,000
Israel	1,350,000	800,000–1,000,000	—
Total Israelite Judean population	1,800,000	1,100,000–1,350,000	150,000
Per square mile	40	28–32	24

The decline in the population, here assumed, may well be explained by the general deterioration in the political and economic strength of the two kingdoms in the intervening four centuries. It did not seriously affect, however, the number of "cities" (about 300–400 in the whole country and about 60–70 in Judah alone), the population of which may have been greatly reduced, but which continued to function as more or less autonomous municipalities. These avowedly extremely tentative "guesstimates," made more than 40 years ago, still seen to offer the most acceptable approximations. The enormous amount of additional archaeological and other source material and interpretation which have since been brought forth by biblical scholars has, if anything, helped to support them.

Second Commonwealth. During the restoration period the recovery of Palestine's Jewish population was very slow. At first the Second Commonwealth embraced only an area of some 1,200 square miles in and around Jerusalem. According to Ezra (2:64–65), "the whole congregation [of returning exiles] together was forty and two thousand three hundred and threescore, besides their manservants and their maidservants, of whom there were seven thousand three hundred thirty and seven; and they had two hundred singing men and singing women." Even adding to these figures a number of survivors from the pre-Exilic period, the population of the Commonwealth could not have amounted to much more than 60,000–70,000. In time, this population must have increased considerably so that, writing in the third century B.C.E., Pseudo-Hecataeus could estimate the number of Jerusalem's inhabitants alone at 120,000 (Jos., Apion, 1:197). There also were growing Jewish settlements outside the boundaries of the autonomous Jewish province, particularly in Galilee (still called the Gelil Ha-Goyim; "the district of gentiles"), along the coast, and in Transjordan. Yet at the outbreak of the Hasmonean Revolt in 165 B.C.E. the total Jewish population in the country still was very small. It grew by leaps and bounds, however, after the establishment of the sovereign Judean state by Simeon Maccabee in 140 B.C.E. and particularly after the annexation of large territories conquered by his successors, John *Hyrcanus and Alexander *Yannai. It now included a considerable number of Idumeans and others forcibly converted to Judaism by these conquerors, whose amalgamation with the older Jewish inhabitants proceeded apace with great speed. In the days of Jesus and the *tannaim* Galilee was as Jewish as the environs of Jerusalem. This growth was not stemmed by the occupation of the country by the Romans under Pompey in 63 B.C.E. and the conversion of Judea into a sub-province of the Roman Empire. Only some cities, organized along the lines of a Hellenistic polis along the coast and in Transjordan, were now under the control of their "Greek" city councils, with the Jews often constituting but a tolerated minority.

During the two centuries of Hasmonean and Herodian rule over Palestine the Jewish people expanded numerically to an unprecedented degree not only in Palestine but also in other lands, in part by active proselytization. Curiously, the Phoenician-Carthaginian Diaspora, long a major factor throughout the Mediterranean world, suddenly vanished at the beginning of the Common Era. It has been suggested that, with their ancient kinship to the Canaanite-Hebrew civilization, these offshoots of enterprising Tyre and Sidon were now submerged within the Jewish Dispersion. Be this as it may, unquestionably, many new communities now sprang up as far west as Italy and Tunisia and possibly even Spain and Morocco. Few reliable figures, however, are available for either the total Jewish population of any Roman province or that of individual communities. Not even Palestine has left behind records from which one could derive dependable statistics. Babylonian Jewry fell almost totally silent from the days of Ezra and Nehemiah to the second century C.E., although the presence there of great masses of Jews is not subject to doubt. Josephus' attempt to justify his behavior during the great Roman-Jewish War of 66–70 by first writing his history of that war in Aramaic is definite proof of the importance of those communities outside the Roman Empire. But numerically there are only such vague assertions as Josephus' statement that "myriads upon myriads" of Jews lived in the Euphrates Valley, while admitting that their "number could not be ascertained" (Ant., 11:133). Egypt, next to Palestine harboring the most culturally creative Jewish community of the time, embraced about a million Jews in the first century C.E., according to a casual remark by the well-informed Philo Judaeus. Other sources show that Jews probably predominated in two of the five quarters of Alexandria, that great emporium of trade and cultural activity, the population of which is variously estimated at 500,000 to 1,000,000. They may, indeed, have formed almost 40% of the population, in which case the Alexandrine community may well have exceeded in size that of Jerusalem in its heyday. There are also glimpses of such lesser Egyptian communities as the *Elephantine Jewish colony under the Achaemenids and Apollinopolis Magna or Edfu under the Ptolemies and Romans.

To be sure, certain data reported by the rabbis seem vastly exaggerated. For instance, the figures given for the attendance at the Passover sacrifices at the Temple of Jerusalem shortly before its destruction (Tosef., Pes. 4:3; Pes. 64b) cannot be taken at their face value. The Temple could not possibly have accommodated at any time a bare fraction of that number even if the Jews offered their sacrifices in frequent relays. A little more informative are the reports of the casualties in deaths and prisoners sustained by Jerusalem during the Roman siege. The figures transmitted by such distinguished historians as Josephus and Tacitus ranging between 600,000 fatalities and 1,197,000 dead and captured (Jos., Wars, 6:420; Tacitus, *Historiae,* 5:13) are not quite so out of line as they appear at first glance. Jerusalem's population before the siege had been swelled by countless numbers of pilgrims from all over the Dispersion and refugees from the provinces previously occupied by the Roman legions.

A new factor was injected into the discussion by the report of Gregory bar Hebraeus, a 12th-century Syrian chronicler of Jewish descent, about a census of the Jewish population taken by Emperor Claudius in 48 C.E. (*Historia compendiosa dynastiarum,* ed. by E. Pococke, 75, 116; ed. by A. Salhani, 115). According to this report, first brought to the attention of students of ancient Jewish history by Jean Juster, Claudius found no less than 6,944,000 Jews within the confines of the empire. To be sure, some scholars denied the authenticity of this report, or attributed the census to one of Roman citizens, rather than of Jews. However, the weight of evidence still favors the acceptance of that figure as the most likely approximation of the number of Jews living within the empire. To them must be added the numerous Jews of Babylonia, the Iranian Plateau, the Yemen, and Ethiopia. It stands to reason, therefore, that shortly before the fall of Jerusalem the world Jewish population exceeded 8,000,000, of whom probably not more than 2,350,000–2,500,000 lived in Palestine. Other major countries of Jewish settlement included Egypt, Syria, Asia Minor, and Babylonia, each probably embracing more than 1,000,000 Jews. Even Rome, the capital of the empire, seems to have included a Jewish community of about 40,000 in a total population of some 800,000, if we accept the figure of 8,000 Roman Jews accompanying a Palestinian delegation in the year 4 B.C.E., and 4,000 Jewish youths reputedly deported by Tiberius to the salt mines of Sardinia, as reported by Josephus (Ant., 17:300; 18:84) and Tacitus (*Annales,* 2, 85). This numerical strength of the Jewish population was important not only for the subsequent destinies of the Jewish people but also for the rise and expansion of Christianity. No less an authority than Adolf Harnack developed the theory that only where Jewish communities existed in the first century were there substantial Christian congregations before Constantine the Great in the early fourth century.

Unfortunately, after the fall of Jerusalem the demographic sources relating to Jews almost completely dry up. Unquestionably, the total number of Jews rapidly declined. As a result of the war ravages in 66–70, during the uprisings against Trajan in 115–117 and the *Bar Kokhba War in 132–35 the population of Palestine, Egypt, Cyprus, and other areas diminished sharply. Jerusalem for a while ceased to be a Jewish city altogether. After Trajan, Egyptian Jewry, though not completely suppressed, became almost totally silent for nearly a century; it never recovered from that mortal blow until centuries after the Muslim conquest. The conversion of some Jews to the new Christian religion was further aggravated by the more or less continuous Roman oppression culminating in the anti-Jewish legislation of the Christian Roman emperors from the fourth to the sixth centuries. Nor could the Jews entirely escape the impact of the biological decline of the empire as a whole from the third century on. Ultimately, in 632 Emperor Heraclius outlawed Judaism altogether. At the same time, through both immigration and natural growth, the Jewish population in Babylonia and elsewhere throughout the resurgent Persian Empire under the Sassanid dynasty (after 226) grew rapidly and, by the fourth century, may have equaled in size that of Rome and Byzantium. But no estimates of any kind, nor even informed guesses, can be made for the actual numbers of Jews inhabiting either empire.

Characteristically, however, the Jewish dispersion continued to expand in all directions. During those centuries some Jews seem to have penetrated India, as well as parts of Africa outside of Rome's control, while, if tradition is to be believed, some individuals even reached China. In the West there is some documentary and epigraphic evidence about Jewish settlements in Gaul, Germany, Hungary (Pannonia), Rumania (Dacia), and perhaps even Britain. But these outlying Jewries were, for the most part, very small, and influenced the size of the world Jewish population to but a minor extent.

Medieval Islam and Byzantium. Curiously, for the long medieval period (from 313 or 476 C.E. to 1492) there is no global figure for the Jewish population of any year even comparable to the reconstruction, however uncertain, of the Claudian census in the mid-first century. There are only stray records pertaining to individual communities in different areas and periods which rarely lend themselves to any overall "guesstimates." The following medieval data are, therefore, even more tentative than those for the Ancient period. Palestine Jewry, though greatly decimated by the wars and Roman persecutions, seems nevertheless to have recovered sufficiently to be able to stage several revolts against their oppressive masters. According to one Christian chronicler even 4,000 Jews living in neighboring Tyre were able to start a revolt in 610, with the aid of 20,000 Jewish soldiers assembled from Palestine, Damascus, and Cyprus (Eutychius ibn Baṭrīq, *Annales,* in J. P. Migne's *Patrologia graeca,* 111:1084f.; and in Arabic text, ed. by L. Cheikho et al., 1:216). Another large-scale uprising, supported by an invading Persian army, was so successful that for three years the Jews seem to have exercised control over large parts of the country including Jerusalem and Tiberias (614–617). The repression in 629–632, however, was sharp and swift. Yet the total outlawry of Judaism in 632 hardly began to be implemented when five years later the Arab armies overran the country.

Jerusalem, which since the days of Bar Kokhba's defeat had only a sporadic and largely surreptitious Jewish settlement, was gradually reopened to Jewish residents under the Muslim domination. At first, Caliph Omar I admitted only 70 Jewish families. But this number increased considerably in the following generations owing to both Rabbanite and Karaite immigration. Similarly Caesarea, which in the Byzantine period had served as the administrative capital of the province, continued to harbor a substantial Jewish population, although the figures given by Balādhurī (200,000 Jews, 30,000 Samaritans, 700,000 Byzantine soldiers) and Yāqūt (100,000 Jews, 80,000 Samaritans, 100,000 soldiers) are fantastically exaggerated. This evolution was cut short by the bloodbath perpetrated by the conquering Crusaders in 1099 from which the Jewish community but slowly recovered. Some 70 years later the traveler Benjamin of Tudela found in Jerusalem a small community of perhaps 1,000 persons (the extant manuscripts differ between 4 and 200 families), while in 1218 Judah Al-Ḥarizi noted the presence there of three Jewish congregations. A similar divergence may be observed between Benjamin's estimate of 3,000 Jews in Damascus and the 10,000 Jews quoted, a decade later, by another visitor, Pethahiah of Regensburg.

The other great center of Jewish life, Babylonia, seems more successfully to have conserved its biological strength. Despite the numerous sufferings inflicted upon the Jews by the Mazdakite movement during the chaotic fifth century, the figure of 90,000 Jews welcoming the arrival of the Arab general Ali (*Iggeret Sherira Ga'on,* ed. by B. M. Lewin (1921), 101) is not out of the range of historical probability. Under the Muslim administration the Jews of Babylonia and the neighboring Iranian Plateau continued to expand. The city of Sura, for example, the seat of a famous rabbinic academy, was found by a tenth-century Muslim investigating committee to have a large Jewish majority (Ibn abī Uṣaybiʿa, *Ṭabaqāt al-aṭibbāʾ,* ed. by A. Mueller, 1:221). The original Aramaic name of Mosul, Ḥesna Ebraya ("Hebrew Castle": the Jews themselves called it Ashshur) was undoubtedly deserved before the city grew into a major administrative and economic center. These old communities were speedily overshadowed by Baghdad after 762 when it became the capital of the vast Caliphate. In spite of the empire's dissolution and the chaotic conditions which prevailed there in the tenth century, Benjamin still found in the Baghdad of the 1160s a flourishing Jewish community of perhaps 40,000 persons. According to the Arab writer, Ibn al-Naqqāsh, the Mongolian invaders of Baghdad in 1258 counted there no less than 36,000 Jewish taxpayers—doubtless an exaggeration. In any case Jews constituted but a small segment of a population which at times may have ranged from 1,000,000 to 2,000,000 in size.

Egyptian Jewry, too, seems to have gradually recovered from its sharp decline of the second century. Although the glorious community of Alexandria had never recovered its former size and intellectual eminence and, in 414, had suffered from a serious, if unauthorized, expulsion, the conquering Arabs exaggeratingly claimed to have found there in 640 no less than "400,000 poll-tax paying Jews" (Eutychius, *Annales,* in: PG 111:1107; in the Arabic text, ed. by Cheikho, 2:26). Here, too, the recovery proceeded apace under the Muslim rule, particularly the friendly Fatimid and Seljuk regimes of the 11th and 12th centuries. In the newly developed capital of Fostat (Old Cairo) Benjamin found 7,000, and in Alexandria, 3,000 Jewish families. He also saw or heard of numerous other Jewish communities throughout the land. Taking these figures as representing persons, rather than families, some careful historians calculated that all of Egypt had a Jewish population of no more than 20,000–40,000, which is probably too conservative a ratio in the country's general population of perhaps 7,000,000–8,000,000. While Benjamin's estimates do not quite tally with the evidence of local sources, particularly those preserved in the Cairo **Genizah,* they all give the impression of populous and often flourishing Jewish settlements.

To the west of Egypt there were growing Jewish communities in Kairouan (Tunisia), Morocco, and particularly Muslim Spain. However, no precise data are available on the demographic situation in most of these communities. Only here and there are there some figures, as a rule none too reliable, in the writings of Arab chroniclers and geographers or in rabbinic sources. The famous Moroccan community of Fez, for example, is said to have sustained 6,000 Jewish fatalities during the massacre of 1032–33. In Spain, al-Idrīsī calls the frontier town of Tarragona a "city of Jews" (*Description de l'Afrique,* ed. and trans. by R. Dozy and M. J. de Goeje, 191 (Ar.) and 231 (Fr.). In addressing the Jewish leaders of Lucena the ninth-century Babylonian *gaon,* Natronai b. Hilai, casually mentions that "there are no gentiles living among you at all" (Responsum, reproduced in B. M. Lewin's *Oẓar ha-Ge'onim,* vol. 3, 1, 24f. no. 64). Even the celebrated city of Granada is, doubtless for good reason, called by al-Ḥimyarī *Ighranāṭat-al-Yahūd* ("Jewish Granada"; in *La Peninsule Ibérique,* ed. by E. Lévi-Provençal, 23, 42f. (Ar.), 29ff., 53ff. (Fr.)). Córdoba, the metropolis of Muslim Spain, also included a very sizable Jewish community. Although these stray data do not allow for any comprehensive estimate of the Jewish population of the whole country, it appears that here, too, Ely Ashtor's estimate of but 50,000–55,000 Jews in the whole Iberian Peninsula around 1050 (in a general population of some 7,000,000–9,000,000) is the result of excessive caution. Even under the intolerant Almohad domination of the 12th century many, perhaps most, Jews continued secretly to profess Judaism. They "rolled with the waves" until the 13th-century reconquest by the Christian Spaniards, when they could once again overtly profess Judaism and resume their demographic as well as socioeconomic and cultural expansion.

Similar uncertainties beset the demographic historian trying to ascertain the size of the Jewish population in the Byzantine Empire. It is a remarkable testimony to the enormous vitality of the Jewish people that, despite four successive total outlawries of Judaism in 632, 722–3, 873–4, and 930, it survived and resumed its historic evolution, without noticeable breaks in its continuity. At any rate, when around 1160 Benjamin of Tudela visited Constantinople, he found there no less than 2,000 Rabbanite and 500 Karaite families. For that time this was an impressive estimate of 12,000–15,000 Jews, although they evidently constituted but a small minority of the capital's population which, ranging between 50,000 and 100,000 persons, by far exceeded that of any Christian city of the period. Some ten to fifteen years later, Pethahiah of Regensburg, on arriving in Byzantium, was so overawed by the number and size of its Jewish communities, which sharply contrasted with the underpopulated cities and Jewish settlements of his German homeland, that he exclaimed: "There are there [in the Byzantine Empire] so many congregations that the land of Israel could not contain them, were they to be settled therein." Nonetheless, there is no way of closely estimating the total Jewish population of the empire, both before or after the Arab expansion of the 630s.

Here, too, much of the demographic information depends on data supplied by Benjamin of Tudela. Regrettably, different manuscript of his travelogue quote figures with considerable variants. The question whether he had in mind persons, taxpayers, or families still is largely unresolved. It is quite possible that some of his figures represented different entities and that he merely reported numbers as they were given to him by local informants in the towns he happened to visit. Though displaying unusual interest in Jewish demography and probably quite accurately transmitting the information he received, he was, needless to say, unable to check it. With all these weaknesses, Benjamin is relatively the most reliable guide. It has been shown that the sum total of his figures was 512,532. Since he did not visit all communities and did not record figures even in many of those he had seen, these numbers must at least be doubled. In short, at the end of the 12th century the world Jewish population may well have embraced 1,000,000, perhaps even close to 2,000,000 persons, the large majority of whom still resided in countries under the domination of Islam. This situation began changing rapidly in the 13th century, when the center of gravity of the Jewish people shifted to the Western lands. With the rest of the population, the Eastern Jewries declined sharply, to be revitalized only under the Ottoman Empire of the late 15th and the 16th centuries.

Medieval West. Despite the availability of much more ample and better-investigated source materials, population studies of medieval Western Jewry are likewise affected by great uncertainties. Apart from the general decline of population during the Barbarian invasions, many Jewish settlements were totally destroyed during the wave of intolerance which, in the seventh century, swept through Visigothic Spain, Merovingian France, and Langobard Italy. Thereafter the total number of Jews in Western Europe, including Germany, must have been very small indeed. The only continuous major settlements carried over from Antiquity were in the Papal States, southern Italy, parts of Spain, and southern France. However, here, too, the general population decline is well illustrated by the city of Rome which, from a metropolis embracing some 1,000,000 inhabitants at the end of the second century, was reduced to but 35,000 eight centuries later. Nonetheless, in the 1160s Benjamin could find substantial Jewish communities in Rome, Naples, Messina, and particularly in Palermo, whose 1,500 Jewish families undoubtedly formed the largest Jewish community under Roman Catholic Christianity. Rome itself may also have embraced at that time about 1,000 Jews.

Relatively, the best information deals with the conditions in medieval England. Owing to the comparatively small number of Jews, the availability of large and well-preserved source material, and untiring research by scholars, Christian and Jewish, over several decades, the evolution of the medieval Anglo-Jewish community has been fairly well elucidated. Its demographic aspects, however, have left many questions open. It appears that, beginning with the Norman Conquest of 1066, the number of Jewish settlers gradually reached about 2,500 persons before the massacres of 1190–91 and the ensuing flight of numerous Jews to the Continent. Within a few years English Jewry recovered its strength, however, and resumed its growth in the first half of the 13th century. Yet the endless fiscal exactions of Henry III and the general hostility of the population, which found expression in a number of cities securing privileges *de non tolerandis Judaeis,* before long began taking their toll. Even at the expulsion of 1290 there were probably no more than about 10,000 Jews in a total population of about 3,500,000 in the country. This is avowedly a compromise figure between the decided underestimate by George Caro of no more than 3,000 Jewish residents and the records of contemporary chroniclers, whose reports about the Jews effected by the decree of expulsion of 1290 ranged from 15,000 to 17,500. Even that relatively small number was scattered over 91 cities, of which 21 (at their heyday, 27) were sufficiently important to contain royal *archae* where records of all Jewish loans were officially kept. In addition, there were more than 100 other localities in which individual Jews were mentioned in the sources. A few individuals seem also to have penetrated Wales, Scotland, and Ireland, though no organized community existed in any of these areas in the Middle Ages.

On the Continent Jewish demography depends for the most part on sporadically preserved tax records. In the case of capitation taxes it is relatively easy to multiply the number of taxpayers by whatever quotient is derived from our knowledge, otherwise obtained, of their ratio to minors, indigents, and other non-paying groups. Of course, here, too, it was in the best interest of the Jewish communities to underestimate the number of taxpayers whereas the government authorities sought to exaggerate them. In addition, there were sporadic censuses of population, including Jews, such as was instituted in Aix-en-Provence in 1341 on orders of King Robert of Anjou. It revealed that, at that time, 1,205 Jews occupied 203 houses and constituted some 10% of the city's population. A Jewish taxpaying "hearth" averaged 5.9 members, while individual households included a membership of up to 30 persons. In contrast, a similar census in Carpentras in 1471 revealed a Jewish average of only 4.3 per "hearth," as against 5.2 persons per Christian "hearth." The latter discrepancy is explainable only by the intervening trials and tribulations of Carpentras Jewry which was always treated more harshly by both the populace and the city council than that of its larger neighbor, Avignon. Here no less than 210 Jewish heads of households were called upon in 1358 to take an oath of allegiance to the pope, which indicates the presence of a Jewish community of well over 1,000 persons. In general, the Jewish population of Provence and the papal possessions in France exceeded the general ratio of Jews in the rest of France and for that matter anywhere in Europe north of the Alps and Pyrenees. Already in the days of Benjamin the community of Arles, with its 200 families, seems to have formed some 20% of the city's population. The smaller town of Tarascon embraced 125 Jewish families in 1442, 183 families in 1487. On the other hand, Narbonne, once the leading southern French community and, in Carolingian times, the seat of a "Jewish king," steadily declined and, shortly before the 1306 expulsion, numbered no more than 1,000 Jews among the city's 15,000 inhabitants. Similarly, Toulouse in 1391 had only 15 Jewish families in a population of 25,000–30,000. All of Gascony under English domination apparently never exceeded that total of 1,000 Jews before their banishment in 1288. More remarkably, the "great city" of Paris (Benjamin), where, before the expulsion of 1182, some chroniclers spoke exaggeratingly of Jews forming half the city's population and owning half its real estate, in fact embraced at no time before the final expulsion of 1394 many more than the 124 taxpayers (in 86 households) among the 15,200 taxpayers recorded in 1292 in a total population of 80,000 or more counted in 1328.

No house-to-house canvasses are recorded in the Holy Roman Empire. There we depend principally on tax records which, however, are almost invariably incomplete. Even the very significant list of taxpaying Jewish communities in 1241 omits such large Jewish settlements as that of Nuremberg. On the other hand, Germany has preserved a number of examples of the *memorbuch* which, by recording victims of persecutions by name, are the most dependable, if partial, sources of demographic information. In Nuremberg, for example, 628 such fatalities are recorded as a result of the *Rindfleisch massacres of 1298; despite the community's subsequent recovery, 570 more Jews lost their lives in the massacre of 1349. Wuerzburg sustained in 1298 no less than 900 casualties, of whom 100 are specifically mentioned as nonresidents. Even smaller communities like Weissensee or Ueberlingen could lose 125 and over 300 Jews respectively, in massacres resulting from local *blood libels in 1303 and 1332. However, such incidental records give us but a remote approximation of the total Jewish population in the respective periods. The only conclusion one may draw from these stray references is that, especially after 1350, most German Jewish communities were very small.

In Jewish, as in general West and Central European life, the 14th century was a period of great crisis, both economically and biologically. The recurrent famines (1315–17, etc.) and pestilences—the greatest of the epidemics, the *Black Death of 1348–49, was but one of a series of destructive diseases—resulted in a long-lasting decline in population. During many decades an annual birthrate of 39 per 1,000 population was exceeded by a mortality rate of 41 per 1,000. Hence life expectancy of newly born children in many areas sank as low as 17–20 years. Jews not only fell victim to these widely spreading contaminations, but were often massacred in advance of the plague by their panic-stricken Christian neighbors, as alleged "poisoners of the wells" responsible for the contagion. Not surprisingly, their numbers declined frightfully even in a city like Vienna, which was restrained by its rulers from attacking Jews, despite its daily losses of 500 (occasionally up to 1,200) dead to the plague. Its Jewry, considered by some informed contemporaries the largest Jewish community in the empire, 70 years later had only 92 male and 122 female martyrs during the persecution (the so-called *Gezerah*) of 1421. The celebrated Jewish community of Augsburg listed only 17 and 21 Jewish taxpayers in 1401 and 1437, and in the following year banished the whole community of 300 persons. Erfurt, which a short time before possessed four or five synagogues and four slaughterhouses for the supply of ritually permissible meat, dwindled to a total of only 50–86 taxpayers in 1357–89. Similarly Frankfort, which was destined to play so great a role in German Jewish history in the following centuries, embraced only a few Jewish families in the 1360s, and as late as 1462, when its new ghetto was formally established, it counted no more than about 200 inhabitants. If during that period many German Jews found shelter in the neighboring lands of Poland, Lithuania, and Hungary (each destined to occupy an imposing place in the modern history of the Jewish people), before 1500 C.E. their total numbers, even when augmented by the earlier settlers in part stemming from territories further east, still were quite small before the end of the Middle Ages.

The largest agglomerations of Jews under medieval Christendom were to be found on the Iberian and Apennine peninsulas together with the adjacent Balearic Islands and Sicily. Spain, the largest and most influential focus of medieval Judaism, has preserved a great many demographically relevant records, some of which are yet to be explored. However, their evaluation by modern scholars has diverged very greatly. While the first careful investigator of the subject, Isidore Loeb, estimated the Jewish population of Castile at 160,000 around 1300 C.E., Yitzḥak Baer, the outstanding student of Spanish Jewish history, attributes to that kingdom only some 3,600 Jewish families at that time. Together with Navarre and Aragon, he believes, the combined Jewish population did not exceed 40,000. Once again the truth seems to be somewhere in between, and a total of 150,000 would seem to offer a much closer approximation. Remarkably, neither the Jewish nor the general population suffered permanently irretrievable losses as a result of the Black Death of 1348–49, or the subsequent major plagues of 1394–96 and 1490. Despite various setbacks, especially after 1391, the Iberian Jewish population continued to grow, particularly in Castile, and there is somewhat more agreement about the number of Jews affected by the expulsion of 1492. The best approximation was given by Meir Melammed, son-in-law of "Chief Rabbi" Abraham Senior, and another Jew (both of whom preferred conversion to exile) who estimated the number of Jewish families affected by the decree of expulsion at 35,000 in Castile and 6,000 in Aragon (Andrés Bernaldez, *Historia de los Reyes Catolicos*, cxff.). Not very much higher is the figure of 300,000 Jewish inhabitants of Spain, cited by Isaac Abrabanel, the leader of the departing exiles (*Ma'yenei ha-yeshu'ah*, introd.). If it be true that some 120,000 of these expatriates proceeded to neighboring Portugal (Abraham Zacuto, *Sefer Yuḥasin*, 277a), the total Jewish population of the smaller country may have reached 200,000 to be affected by the forced conversion of 1496–97. These large figures lent themselves to easy exaggeration and even such a well-informed and careful 16th-century historian and political theorist as Juan Mariana glibly speaks of 800,000

Table 2

Country	1300 C.E.		1490 C.E.	
	Jews	General population	Jews	General population
France (including Avignon)	100,000	14,000,000	20,000	20,000,000
Holy Roman Empire (including Switzerland and the Low Countries)	100,000	12,000,000	80,000	12,000,000
Italy	50,000	11,000,000	120,000	12,000,000
Spain (Castile, Aragon, and Navarre)	150,000	5,500,000	250,000	7,000,000
Portugal	40,000	600,000	80,000	1,000,000
Poland-Lithuania	5,000	500,000	30,000	1,000,000
Hungary	5,000	400,000	20,000	800,000
Total	450,000	44,000,000	600,000	53,800,000

Spanish Jews affected by the expulsion (*Historia general de España*, ed. by J. M. Gutiérrez, vol. 5, 440). In the Iberian case, moreover, there is a major problem of estimating the number of Conversos (including numerous secret Judaizers) who lived under the reign of Ferdinand and Isabella and whose number was greatly increased by those Jews who in 1492 preferred baptism to exile. These Conversos were to furnish a considerable number of members to the growing Marrano dispersion in the West, while others found ways of speedily returning to Judaism by settling in Muslim lands.

Somewhat less controversial is the size of the large Jewish population of Sicily and the kingdom of Naples. Sicily alone doubtless had a Jewish population of more than 50,000 in the 15th century, many of whom departed in 1492 for Naples, Rome, and other localities. Combined with refugees from Spain, the Sicilian exiles may well have temporarily doubled the Jewish population of the kingdom of Naples before the expulsion of Jews in 1511 and 1541. At the same time, the resettlement of Jewish communities in Italy north of the Papal States was proceeding rather slowly and the glorious Renaissance republics of Florence, Ferrara, Venice, and others became really important areas of Jewish settlement only in the early modern period.

In short, after considering these and many other complicated factors and in full realization of the perilous nature of any computation, S. Baron has submitted the above table (Table 2) for Jewish population in Western and Central Europe during the last centuries of the Middle Ages.

1500–1800. The three centuries of the early modern period were at first marked by a simultaneous expansion and contraction of Jewish settlement, which of course had an important bearing on Jewish demography as well. On the one hand, the wave of expulsions from England, France, the Iberian Peninsula, and many Italian and German territories of the period from 1290 to 1500 now continued unabated. Jews were ousted permanently from the kingdom of Naples in 1511 and 1541; from the duchy of Milan in 1597; and from the Papal States (except Rome and Ancona) on a more temporary basis, in 1569 and 1593. The banishment of the Jews from Regensburg in 1519 and Rothenburg in 1520 was followed during the early Reformation period by expulsion from Saxony in 1536, Brandenburg (after their readmission in 1540) in 1571, and many other German principalities, bishoprics, and free cities. The result was a greater diffusion of Jews into smaller localities, even villages, in both Italy and Germany—a trend which was reversed only during the Thirty Years' War. At the same time there was not only a great expansion of the Jewish people into Poland-Lithuania, the Ottoman Empire, and other Muslim countries, but through the Marrano dispersion there was the incipient resettlement of Jews, first secret and later overt, in Western Europe. There was also the beginning of Jewish participation in the colonization of the New World, as well as of the Far East and some African territories by the great colonial powers.

If, on balance, the Jewish settlement in the middle of the 17th century extended over a much larger area than that of 1500 C.E., the growth of Jewish population did not keep pace with that geographic expansion. Certainly those New Christians, who by 1660 had formally returned to Judaism, were but a small fraction of the descendants of the original Conversos on the Iberian Peninsula. The small size of the Jewish or Marrano settlements did not prevent, however, unfriendly observers from magnifying the Jewish presence beyond measure. Even a great scholar like Erasmus of Rotterdam, who had had hardly any contacts with living Jews, could exclaim with abandon: "Jews are very numerous in Italy; in Spain there are hardly any Christians. I am afraid that when the occasion arises that pest, formerly suppressed, will raise its head again" (*Opus epistolarum*, 3:253; 4:114). More recklessly, temperamental Martin Luther once contended that Italy was so full of Jews that, for instance, Cremona had no more than 28 Christians among its inhabitants (*Tischreden*, 3:369f.; 4:619f.). These comments were made at a time when Italy's most populous areas of Naples and Sicily no longer had any professing Jews. After 1569, moreover, the Papal States, too, but grudgingly admitted Jews outside Rome and Ancona but never in sufficient numbers to justify the maintenance of some 115 synagogues such as had existed before the 1569 expulsion. Similarly, the Jews readmitted to Brandenburg in 1540 formed but tiny communities of eight to ten families in Berlin, Stendal, and Frankfort on the Oder when they were once again banished 31 years later. It was only in the 17th and particularly the 18th century that the German-speaking Jewry of the Holy Roman Empire, aided by immigration from Eastern Europe and later by the inclusion in Prussia and Austria of formerly Polish territories through the partitions of Poland in 1772–95, started rising significantly throughout the country.

At the same time, the "Golden Age" of both Polish Jewry and Poland as a whole in the 16th and early 17th centuries was largely terminated in the era of the Chmelnicki uprising (1648–49) and the Swedish-Muscovite wars of 1648–56. Not only did Polish Jewry sustain very severe losses in human lives but, combined with the general economic decline of the country, these disturbances set in motion a Jewish mass emigration which kept the growth of the population at a relatively low rate. Nevertheless the Jewish numerical strength continued gaining and the area of what was Poland-Lithuania in 1648 may well have embraced a Jewish population twice as large in 1800. The majority was now included in the Russian Empire which, after many centuries of refusing to admit Jews—as late as 1740 the whole Jewish population of 292 men and 281 women, scattered through 130 manorial estates in the Ukraine and Belorussia, was expelled—thus suddenly became the largest country of Jewish settlement.

Unfortunately, dependable demographic data on Jews are available only in very few areas. Italy, to be sure, often conducted population censuses, and information concerning Jews in various Italian communities of the early modern period is quite illuminating. The emergent Jewish communities in France, England, and particularly Holland can also be estimated with close approximation to the truth. On the other hand, the Holy Roman Empire, until its dissolution in 1806, offers only sporadic insights into the number of its Jewish inhabitants. In Poland-Lithuania the Jewish population in certain cities can be estimated with a fair degree of accuracy, while vast areas in the country are subject to more or less questionable estimates based on the yield of the capitation tax which in 1560 amounted to only 6,186 florins (on an assessment of 1.50 florins per family), but rose to 80,000 florins in 1634 and to 220,000 florins in 1714 (both representing collections of 3 florins per person). Interveningly, there were also a number of regional censuses (so-called *lustracje*), but only those of 1764–65 shortly before the partitions of Poland have left behind more comprehensive and reliable records; they have also been subjected to closer scrutiny by modern scholars.

In contrast, the enormously important Jewish settlement of the Ottoman Empire, with its western Asiatic and North African provinces, offers an almost hopeless problem to the demographic historian. It stands to reason that, since the empire had seen its glory progressively dimmed from 1600 on and its Jewish subjects suffered serious setbacks several decades later in the era of the Shabbatean movement, the forward motion of both the Jewish and the general populations also greatly slowed down. Yet it appears that, as in Poland, such retardation did not completely halt the numerical expansion of the Jewish masses. However, this assumption cannot be supported by precise statistical data despite the fact that the Ottoman archives have preserved many records of detailed censuses, some of which go back to the 15th century. These records are in many ways far superior to what is preserved in most Western countries of that period. Yet even with the aid of so-called *defters*, or brief summaries kept in the archival registries, these sources have thus far been scrutinized only to a very slight extent. The few Jewish studies heretofore published relate almost exclusively to Palestine's population under the early Ottoman regime. They have opened up new vistas and whetted the appetite for more information but they have supplied only disjointed fragments which do not add up to a total picture. Equally unsatisfactory is knowledge of Jewish demography in the North-African countries. Only here and there do the sources, often derived from casual observation by foreign visitors, mention figures pertaining to the size of Jewish communities. Yet with some effort and ingenuity Maurice Eisenbeth succeeded in compiling, on the basis of such reports, approximate statistics of Jewish inhabitants in the city of Algiers. His estimates for the 16th century range from 1,000 to 5,000 Jews. About 1600 their number rises to 8,000 or 9,000 persons, while about 1700 it reaches a peak of 10,000–12,000. In the course of the 18th century the Jewish population declines to some 7,000 and is further reduced to but 5,000 by 1818 (M. Eisenbeth, *Les Juifs en Algerie et en Tunisie à l'epoque turque (1576–1830)*, 147ff.).

In the following we can refer, therefore, only to a number of illustrations of Jewish communities which have undergone extraordinary expansion, while others have lagged behind. In Italy the papal capital under the Renaissance popes allowed its Jewry to grow, so that it may have reached the number of 2,500–3,000 Jews before the expulsion from the rest of the Papal States in 1569. Although locked in a formal ghetto since 1555, the Rome community continued to grow because after 1569 it had to absorb a great many refugees from the provinces. It is estimated that in 1592 it embraced 3,500 persons in a total population of 97,000. A century later the Jewish population is said to have reached a peak of 10,000–12,000 persons which was never exceeded thereafter even in the 20th century. In the 18th century the Jewish population dropped back to a median of 3,076 persons, according to the official records of 1775–1800. Venice, after the expulsion of Jews in the Middle Ages, did not tolerate them at all until 1509 and in 1516 shut them off in a ghetto, the first to bear that name. But subsequently it allowed the Jewish community to grow rather speedily so that by the middle of the 17th century it may have reached a total of 5,000 persons. Even more remarkably, Leghorn, which had few Jews before 1593, embraced 114 in 1601, 711 in 1622, and 1,175 in 1642. It continued to grow in the following decades; the official censuses refer to a Jewish population of 3,476 in 1738, 4,327 in 1784, and 4,697 in 1806. Leghorn thus competed with Rome and Venice for the designation of the largest Jewish community in Italy. Even a medium-sized community, such as that of Verona, grew to 400 persons in 1600 and over 1,000 in 1751. In contrast, many cities, including Genoa, never admitted more than a handful of Jews. The constant ups and downs in the size of respective communities are well illustrated by the following estimates for the three neighboring Jewish centers in the duchy of Urbino. In 1628 Pesaro had 610 Jewish inhabitants, Urbino 370, Senigallia 200. By 1700 the respective figures were about 600, 200, 600, Senigallia assuming the cultural, as well as numerical, leadership. Historically, the relatively small Jewish communities of Piedmont (its capital Turin first reached a Jewish population of 500 in 1563) were to play an important role in the 19th century when their country marched in the vanguard of Italian unification. All of Italy embraced some 25,000 Jews in 1638, according to the well-informed apologist Simone Luzzatto (*Discorso circa il stato degl' hebrei*, 91). At this level Italian Jewry remained more or less stabilized during the following two centuries while the general Italian population grew from about 11,000,000 in the 17th century to 18,125,000 in 1800, and 23,000,000 in 1850.

In Germany, too, some startling increases contrasted with declines or, at best, demographic stagnation. In Frankfort, which had only 110 Jews at the time when the community moved into its assigned quarter in 1462, the number grew to 250 in 1520, 900 in 1569, 2,200 in 1600. By 1613 the assailants of Jews led by Vincent Fettmilch complained that the 454 Jewish families in the city engaged in too sharp a competition with the Christian artisans and traders. The concentration of about 3,000 Jews within the original quarter throughout the 17th and 18th centuries caused that tremendous overcrowding which made the Frankfort ghetto a byword in Jewish literature. Hamburg admitted a few New Christians in the 16th century but did not legally recognize the presence of a Jewish community until 1612. Its Jewry, both Sephardi and Ashkenazi, grew rapidly (together with the sister communities of Altona and Wandsbeck which jointly formed the single tri-community of Altona-Hamburg-Wandsbeck, abbreviated into AHU according to its Hebrew initials) during the following two centuries, reaching in 1810 the number of 6,299 Jews, according to the official census. It thus was second only to the community of Prague among the Jewish settlements in the empire. The Bohemian capital, a much older community, which had maintained its historic continuity despite several decrees of expulsion in the 16th century and again in 1744 (often not seriously implemented), was throughout the early modern period a major center of Central European Jewish life and learning. By 1729 it embraced, according to an official census, 10,507 persons.

At the same time a great many German Jews of the 16th and early 17th centuries lived scattered through countless hamlets and villages. An investigation conducted in 1541 in the Memmingen district revealed the presence of but 40 Jewish families living in 11 localities. Throughout Germany there were such small Jewish settlements with but one to ten families trying to eke out a meager livelihood and yet instilling in their children a pride in, and knowledge of their Jewish heritage. This great dispersal was largely the result of the preceding wave of expulsions of Jews from the major cities, including their famous medieval settlements of Mainz, Speyer, Cologne, and Regensburg, and their finding shelter, however precariously, under the domination of the petty lords. This trend was reversed, however, during the Thirty Years' War (1618–48) when Jews fleeing before the marching armies and pillaging marauders often had to be admitted to the larger cities, which in turn found that they often benefited greatly from Jewish trade and taxation. Thus was ushered in the era of progressive urbanization of German Jewry, which was to make tremendous strides in the 19th and early 20th centuries. An example of such growing concentration in German metropolitan areas is offered by Prussia of the days of Frederick the Great. While no reliable data for Jews in that rapidly expanding state are available, a well-informed student, Friedrich Wilhelm August Bratring, estimated that in 1750 Berlin had 2,188 Jews (in a population of 133,520), while the rest of the Kurmark accommodated only 1,685 of their coreligionists. Twenty years later the Berlin Jewish community embraced

3,842 persons (an increase of nearly 80%), whereas the provincial communities together totaled only 1,996 persons (an increase of but 20%). In the subsequent three decades, to be sure, Berlin's Jewish inhabitants numerically declined in contrast to both the city's general population and the provincial Jewries, but this was a mere temporary interruption in the process of rapid growth which brought the size of Berlin Jewry up to 172,672 in 1925.

The Netherlands, emerging from the War of Liberation as a forward-looking and relatively liberal state, embraced but a few New Christians in the late 16th century. But, beginning in 1593, the country witnessed a tremendous expansion in the number and size of Jewish settlements which, two centuries later, embraced a population of well over 50,000. Amsterdam alone accommodated in 1795 no less than 21,000 Ashkenazi and 2,400 Sephardi Jews. Its community, often styled the "New Jerusalem," exceeded in size any contemporary or earlier European Jewish community, except perhaps those of ancient Rome and early modern Constantinople.

France's total Jewish population at the outbreak of the Revolution in 1789 amounted to less than 40,000. Their majority was concentrated in Alsace—which at the time of its annexation by France after 1648 included a number of older Jewish communities. Lorraine's Metz speedily developed into a major center of some 3,000 Jews, whereas Strasbourg, the metropolis of the area, saw its privilege *de non tolerandis Judaeis* breached only in the 1780s. A governmental census of 1784, probably incomplete, enumerated 182 Alsatian localities embracing a Jewish population of 3,913 families and 19,707 persons (9,945 males and 9,762 females). The actual figures were a bit higher; Z. Szajkowski estimates the total at between 22,570 and 23,800 persons. It may also be noted that, in contrast to the German areas, Alsace under French domination witnessed a continued dispersal of Jewish settlements from 95 in 1689, to 129 in 1716, and 182 in 1784. Simultaneously, southern France, particularly Bordeaux and Saint Esprit, a suburb of Bayonne, in the 18th century accommodated a total of some 4,500 Jews. Characteristically, Paris, the very heart of French life and culture, barely tolerated 500–800 Jews at the outbreak of the French Revolution.

England's Jewish population, too, still was very small, as was that of the New World. It is estimated that English Jewry embraced some 6,000 persons in 1730, and 12,000 in 1791. Other contemporary estimates raise this figure to 20,000 and more at the end of the 18th century. The large majority was concentrated in London (R. D. Barnett, in: V. D. Lipman (ed.), *Three Centuries of Anglo-Jewish History* (1961), 60f.). In contrast, the six known communities in the United States during the American Revolution counted among them only little more than 2,000 Jews. Possibly the same number was scattered through the Caribbean Islands and Surinam; the largest community among them, that of Kingston, Jamaica, numbered some 500 Jews, and thus rivaled New York in continental North America. On the other hand, the community of French Martinique, which was allegedly reinforced by 400 Jewish refugees from Brazil in 1654, was wiped out by the French decree of expulsion of 1683. In Latin America, under its intolerant Spanish and Portuguese regimes, only New Christians were sometimes grudgingly allowed to settle. In some areas they were quite numerous. Out of them subsequently emerged groups of professing Jews who helped populate the Western Hemisphere. The largest of these groups lived in Recife, Brazil; more than 1,000 of them publicly professed Judaism during the short-lived Dutch domination (1630–54). Upon the return of the Portuguese, the majority found refuge in Surinam, the Caribbean Islands, New Amsterdam (later New York, where 23 of them in 1654 laid the foundations for the largest Jewish community in history), as well as Holland.

1800–1939. A new phase of Jewish demography began with the 19th century. More and more countries now conducted regular censuses; many included a column relating to religious faith. The vast majority of Jews unhesitatingly indicated their Jewish allegiance to the census takers. In the early 1800s, to be sure, when censuses were still taken primarily for fiscal and military purposes, numerous Jews hesitated to appear before the enumerators. Their fears of discriminatory treatment were enhanced by the old folkloristic apprehensions, nurtured by the biblical references to the effects of David's census. According to Gustav Adolf Schimmer, one of the early pioneers in Jewish population studies (1873), there were many localities in Eastern Europe, where upon the advent of the census takers the entire Jewish youth vanished from the scene, to reappear only after the enumerators' departure. In time, however, as the censuses became more purely administrative and scholarly undertakings and were periodically repeated, their accuracy usually improved by the use of more refined techniques. Apart from supplying definite figures of the Jewish population and such other relevant information as that of the Jewish birth and mortality rates, sex and age distribution, marriages and divorces, they offered periodic data revealing the prevailing trends.

Regrettably, this practice was not universal. Czarist Russia, where before 1914 almost half of the world Jewry resided, had no such dependable investigations until 1897 when the government and the Alliance Israélite Universelle from its Paris headquarters collaborated in the attempt to obtain more detailed statistical information about the Russian Jews who, because of recurrent pogroms and discriminatory legislation, had attracted world-wide attention. This endeavor was not repeated, however, except for a valiant but incomplete effort by the ORT in 1921, until 1926 when the Soviet Union took a comprehensive census of its own. Here the Jews were listed as a national, rather than religious group; however, removing some elements of comparison with the earlier accounts. Even worse was the situation in the Ottoman Empire and the other Muslim lands, where before World War I all population statistics were in a deplorable state.

Not much better was the situation in the United States, the burgeoning world center of the Jewish people, which after World War I became the largest country of Jewish settlement. Because of the constitutional separation of state and church, the governmental censuses conducted every ten years since 1790 did not include a question on the person's religious allegiance. For a time the government collected data on the number of congregations affiliated with each denomination, their membership, and other pertinent factors. After 1890, however, the combination of these inquiries with the official decennial censuses was abandoned and a special "census of religious bodies" was instituted in the middle of each decade following the general census of 1900. The first such specific survey was made in 1906; it was followed by others in 1916, 1926, and 1936. However, the preparation of replies was left to the respective denominations themseves, many of which used different criteria for counting their members. In the case of Jews the religious censuses of 1906 and 1916 by definition counted only Jews who were members of congregations. In 1926 and 1936 a new definition was employed. The instructions given to the agent in charge read: "The Jews . . . now consider as members all persons of the Jewish faith living in communities in which local congregations are situated" (U.S. Census Bureau, *Religious Bodies Summary*, 1 (1926), 16).

This definition greatly increased the totals from 357,135 in 1906 to 4,081,242 in 1916 and thereby removed the most important element for comparing the new results with the earlier accounts. The census itself admitted it by deleting any reference to Jews in the column recording the membership growth over the preceding two decades. Since the Jewish communites were unable to undertake a house-to-house enumeration, they had to rely upon information supplied by more or less informed local leaders whose estimates, frequently mere "guesstimates," often widely differed. The result was that the compilers of the census had to reach median numbers of such diverse estimates. The general result was that many figures, including the total membership of 4,641,184 in 1936, tended toward exaggeration. When almost simultaneously with the census of 1936 a more detailed canvass of ten important communities was conducted by local leaders under the sponsorship of the Conference on Jewish Relations, it turned out that the resulting more accurate figures ran between 8% and 20% below those suggested in the census. Of course, no one could be sure that the experience of these ten cities was typical of the whole country, particularly of the New York metropolitan area which apparently embraced some 40% of American Jewry.

Even in those Western European countries, such as France, Belgium, the Netherlands, Switzerland, or Italy, where the governmental censuses included a query concerning the inhabitants' religious preference, the returns are not completely reassuring. In the first place, all census bureaus (including that of the United States which uses highly refined statistical techniques) count with a margin of error of at least 1–1.5%. In the case of Jewish respondents the difficulty is aggravated by the uncertainty of "who is a Jew." Many persons who considered themselves Jews refused to give the enumerator straight answers about their religious preference, either because they felt that religion should be treated as a "private" concern which no government had any right to probe, or because, for a variety of reasons, they personally tried to hide their Jewishness. There is also the problem of children of mixed marriages who, according to rabbinic law, are automatically considered Jews if their mother is Jewish—a distinction which in practice is often disregarded, positively as well as negatively. Baron has suggested, therefore, that for practical reasons everyone be regarded as a Jew "who (1) is born of Jewish parents and has never been converted to another faith; (2) is born of mixed parentage but declares himself a Jew and is so considered by the majority of his neighbors; and (3) one who by conscious will has adopted Judaism." In view of these largely subjective criteria it has been found doubly imperative to supplement the official census data, wherever such exist, by more searching sample studies.

Another complication has arisen in various countries as a result of the new Jewish national movement. Some Jews, professing no religion, nevertheless counted themselves as belonging to the Jewish "nationality," while others, even if staunchly Orthodox, regarded themselves as members of a different "nationality." Still other Jews who neither professed Judaism nor regarded themselves as nationally Jewish nonetheless thought of themselves as Jews and were thus regarded by their neighbors, Jewish and non-Jewish. The confusion arising from these varying definitions was well illustrated in 1921 in the first Czechoslovakian census. "The official figures showed that there were 336,520 Czechoslovak nationals [in addition to 17,822 foreigners] professing the 'Israelite' religion. Their majority, 180,616, declared themselves to be members of the Jewish nationality (this majority was larger in Slovakia and Carpathian Ruthenia but it turned into a minority in the main provinces of Moravia, Bohemia, and Silesia). Of the rest, 73,371 signed up as members of the Czech nationality, 49,123 as Germans, 29,473 as Magyars, 3,751 as Russians, 74 as Poles, and 112 as belonging to other nationalities. In addition, there were 100 persons who professed no religion but were members of the Jewish nationality. More astonishingly, there also were some members of the Jewish nationality who professed the Roman Catholic faith (74), Greek Catholicism (23), Greek Orthodoxy (12), Protestantism (19), and one woman, who was an adherent of the new Czechoslovak national faith. Thus the 180,616 members of the Jewish nationality who also professed the Jewish faith were joined by 229 co-nationals who professed other religions or none. There probably were many more thousands of Jews who never signed up as Jews by either nationality or religion and thus did not appear as such in the census" (S. W. Baron, "Who Is a Jew?" in *History and Jewish Historians*, 16f.).

The matter is far more serious in the Soviet Union. With its anti-religious bias the government eliminated all references to religious preference from the census, leaving only the Jewish nationality as a criterion. While most Jews delared themselves Jews by nationality, in each case the decision depended on the nationality entered in the passports of the respective heads of households. For one example, Leon Trotsky always signed up as a Russian by nationality, whereas Maxim Litvinov, even while serving as Soviet ambassador to the United States or as a Soviet foreign minister, always carried with him a passport marking his membership in the Jewish nationality. There is no way of telling how many Jews thus escaped being counted in the censuses of 1926, 1939, and again, in 1959. If the first Soviet census, even with respect to the territories which had formerly been part of Czarist Russia, was not quite comparable to the 1897 enumeration, the one of 1939 came on the eve of World War II and the German invasion of Russia. It has been subjected, therefore, to little detailed scrutiny and its Jewish aspects in particular have been inadequately explored.

Nonetheless, the situation is not hopeless. Many countries such as Austria-Hungary and its successor states, Germany, interwar Poland, the Baltic states, Rumania, the emergent settlement in Palestine under the Mandate, and others had regular censuses which yielded relatively reliable information also on all aspects of Jewish demography. From these data one may deduce much also concerning the conditions in countries lacking satisfactory official census records. At any rate, quite apart from the accuracy of specific figures, certain major trends in the rise or decline of the Jewish population clearly manifested themselves throughout the Jewish world in the course of the 19th and the first third of the 20th centuries. This period was characterized by a "population explosion" of the Western world. In the relatively peaceful period of 1815–1914 Europe's population more than doubled (from some 190,000,000 to over 400,000,000), while European émigrés helped populate the Western Hemisphere and other continents. The United States alone increased its population from 7,240,000 in 1810 to 91,972,000 in 1910. Growth of this rapidity was owing less to increase in natality than to a sharp decrease in the death rate—a result of the great progress of medical science and the spread of more hygienic ways of life among the European and American masses.

In the Jewish case these factors operated with redoubled intensity. Like their neighbors in Eastern Europe, Jews still married quite early, definitely earlier than the average couples in Central and Western Europe. Marriages of boys aged between 15 and 18 with 14–16-year-old girls were quite common. An 18th-century Polish census mentions a Jewish wife aged eight. (Even in the West the burgomaster of Amsterdam had to prohibit in 1712 a marriage of a Jewish couple under the age of 12.) These conditions prevailed through most of the 19th century. As late as 1891, Arnold White, an English visitor to the Jewish agricultural colonies in the Ukrainian province of Kherson, was told by some Russian landowners who employed Jews that "they have no vice, unless early, improvident, and fruitful marriages can be deemed a vice" (*New Review*, 5, 98). Moreover, more than their neighbors, East European Jews (and many West Europeans as well) took the rabbinic interpretation of the blessing in Genesis (1:28) "Be fruitful, and multiply, and replenish the earth" as the first commandment in the Bible, rather than a blessing. A great many did not even consider the "moral restraint," propagated by Thomas Robert Malthus, as truly moral and hence shunned any form of birth control. More importantly, while their natality may more or less have equaled that of their equally fruitful East European neighbors, mortality, particularly the most decisive one of infants under one year of age and of children between two and five, was decidedly lower. In Czarist Russia's European provinces, for example, where general mortality per 1,000 inhabitants had declined from 37.1 to 31.2 between 1861–70 and 1895–1904, respectively, of 1,000 newly born children no less than 268 died before reaching their first birthday—a figure practically unchanged for several decades. Suffice it to mention that by 1967 the United States reduced its infant mortality to 22.1 per 1,000 and the U.S.S.R. to 26.3. Nor can these two superpowers boast of leading the world in this respect; they lag far behind Sweden, the Netherlands, New Zealand, Australia, and Japan. The Jewish population of Israel had in 1966 an infant mortality of only 21.6 per 1,000. Among the reasons for the long-term Jewish record of keeping newly born children alive was the extreme rarity of illegitimate births among Jews. As late as 1929 and 1930 among 100 Jewish children born in Vilna only 0.5 and 0.9 were illegitimate, whereas the ratio among the Catholics was 14%. More generally, even in the crowded East European ghettos medical help was much more readily available, while better hygienic conditions prevailed owing to the numerous requirements for religious ablutions and ritual food controls. There also was relatively greater family cohesiveness and devotion of Jewish parents to their children. Moreover, because of the strong sense of responsibility for each member by the community at large and the presence of numerous charitable societies specifically devoted to help the indigent sick, even the destitute groups were rarely deprived of basic nourishment and medical care. The result was that even in New York City, where the gap between Jews and non-Jews was constantly narrowing, Jewish infant mortality in 1915 was only 78 for each 1,000 births, whereas that for the rest of the population amounted to 105.

Similarly favorable, at least between 1800 and 1914, was the Jewish ratio in deaths occasioned by violence, particularly wars. It so happened that even most of the great Napoleonic battles took place outside territories densely inhabited by Jews. The same held true for the rest of the century until World War I. Jewish fatalities among combatants were relatively small because the two large centers of Jewish population, Czarist Russia and the Ottoman Empire, did not begin drafting Jews into the army until 1827 (in Congress Poland, 1845) and 1908, respectively. While in previous centuries Jews had suffered numerous casualties as a result of uprisings and massacres, the period of 1800 to 1914 was relatively quiescent in this respect. The Russian pogroms of 1881, 1891, 1903, and 1905, though highly significant in their psychological impact upon Jews and non-Jews, did not cause enough fatalities significantly to retard the growth of the Russian Jewish population. The situation changed abruptly during World War I when Poland, Galicia, Lithuania, Rumania, as well as Salonika, Palestine, and other areas with large Jewish concentrations, were turned into theaters of war. Jewish combatants in the various armies also were quite numerous, probably exceeding 500,000 in the Russian, Austrian, German, and the Western Allied armies. Their high ratio of fatalities was exemplified by the death in battle of about 12,000 German Jewish soldiers. The aftermath of the war, particularly during the Communist Revolution and the civil war in Russia, and the following massacres of Ukrainian Jews, likewise caused much destruction of Jewish lives. However, the biological vitality of the people was still so great that losses thus sustained were quickly made up by the continuous natural increase in the world's Jewish population.

Incipient signs of retardation became noticeable in the Western countries toward the end of the 19th century, however. As is well known, the French population during the first decades of the 20th century had become practically stationary. Germany, England, and the United States also had declining birthrates which progressively narrowed down the surplus of births over deaths. Because of their increased concentration in urban, even metropolitan areas, which revealed these tendencies most pronouncedly, Jews were ahead of their neighbors in reducing their birthrate. At the same time their death rate, which had long declined, began to be stabilized owing to the relatively larger segment of old persons in the Jewish population, the result of the previous decline in Jewish mortality. Even in Polish Lodz, in 1919–29, where Jewish infant mortality of 134–54 contrasted favorably with the corresponding non-Jewish mortality of 171–203 per 1,000 births, the ratios were reversed in the case of persons over 70. At the beginning of the 20th century these trends had become so manifest that in 1908 Felix A. Theilhaber (in *Der Untergang der deutschen Juden*) warned his German coreligionists that, if these demographic weaknesses were to continue unabated, German Jewry, without the aid of immigration from the outside, would decline rapidly and ultimately die out.

These tendencies became more pronounced during and after World War I. In the years 1911–24 the general Prussian population still had an excess of births over deaths of 3,019,100 persons, but the Jewish population, on the contrary, had an excess mortality of 18,252. In 1925–28 Prussia's general population gained 1,182,056 persons, while the Prussian Jews lost 5,090 through natural causes (H. Silbergleit, *Bevoelkerungs*..., p. 39). These losses were made up only by the continued influx of Jews from Eastern Europe, as well as from the province of Posen (Poznan), which was allotted by the peace treaties to Poland. These adverse factors gradually unfolded also among the Jews of Western Europe and the United States. For example, a Jewish census taken in Buffalo in 1938 testified to a marked decline of the Jewish birthrate, much larger than that of non-Jews. While in the total population the age group under 15 amounted to 26.4% (1930), in the Jewish population it amounted to only 23.2%. The ratios of children under five were more unfavorable: 8.3 versus 6.3% (U. Z. Engelman, in: S. Robinson's *Jewish Population Studies*, 40). Most remarkably, these trends began affecting also the main reservoir of Jewish manpower in East-Central Europe. In 1926 the Soviet Jews had a birthrate of only 24.6 per 1,000 (as against 35.9 30 years before, and 43.3 of the 1926 Soviet population as a whole), the lowest of all major nationalities in the Union. Such large cities as Vienna and Budapest actually had an excess of Jewish mortality over natality (2,709 deaths vs. 1,343 births in Vienna in 1929 and a still larger surplus of 1,588 deaths in Budapest in 1932). Even in Warsaw in 1925–29 the Jewish ratio of 15.5 births vs. 11.1 deaths per 1,000 contrasted with that of 22.4:15.4 among the city's Christians. On a world scale these retarding tendencies still were partially made up by an increasing growth of the Jewish population in North Africa and some other Oriental communities. There the introduction of improved sanitary conditions and health services by the colonial powers before and after World War I created conditions similar to those of the European nations in the preceding century. With the speedily declining death rate, particularly among infants and children, and continued high birthrate, the surplus of births over deaths constantly increased. Nonetheless, the disquieting demographic trends in the much larger Ashkenazi communities were so great that in the 1930s sociologists began to warn the Jewish people that, before very long, their world population would become stationary and begin declining at an accelerated pace thereafter.

Other socioreligious factors, especially conversions and mixed marriages, further aggravated the decline in the rate of increase in Jewish population. In the history of the Jewish dispersion both in the East and the West there always existed converts out of Judaism to Christianity and Islam. For the most part this was a one-way street, since conversions from the dominant faiths to Judaism were outlawed, often under the sanction of capital punishment. Such prohibitions continued throughout the 19th century in Czarist Russia and the Ottoman Empire. Elsewhere, too, social and economic pressures led many more Jews to adopt Christianity than vice versa. Even in Russia, with its staunchly Orthodox Jewish majority, strong conversionist impulses were generated by the *Rekrutchina* (forcible draft for long-term military service, often involving young children) over the three decades of 1827–56 (see *Cantonists). Under these and other pressures the number of baptized Jews increased substantially during the 19th century. According to the Berlin missionary, Johannes de la Roi, a biased but informed student of the missionary movements, no less than 84,500 Russian Jews found their way to the baptismal front in the 1800s ("*Judentaufen im neunzehnten Jahrhundert, ein statistischer Versuch,*" in *Nathanael,* vol. 15, 65–118). The ratio was understandably higher in such a Western country as Prussia, where the number of Jewish converts to Christianity seems to have reached a peak of 3,771 in the years 1812–14, according to A. Menes' computation.

Elsewhere the statistics are not too good but the number of Jews who left their community often increased threateningly. In Austria-Hungary, before World War I the second-largest center of the Jewish population, most of those who took that step were not necessarily converts. Many of them simply declared themselves persons without religion *(konfessionslos).* In Vienna alone the number of such losses to the community often amounted to 1,000 annually in the period after World War I. In Prussia, on the other hand, as a result of the Jewish Community Law of 1876 many Jews severed their ties with the existing communities because of real or alleged "religious scruples." While some of these Jews merely wished to separate themselves from the middle-of-the-road communities and to join special Orthodox groupings (the so-called *Trennungsorthodoxie*), most others did it for financial or other secularist reasons. In other countries, too, conversions to Judaism were relatively rare; they were far outweighed by conversions of Jews to other faiths, or their simple disappearance within the majority without formal action. Many of the *konfessionslos* persons, particularly in Austria, adopted this status in order to marry out of the faith, since until the interwar period the marriage of a Catholic to a Jew was legally invalid. In Germany, France, and Italy, too, mixed marriages were quite frequent. In one year (1927) 52% of marriages entered into by the Jews of Trieste had a non-Jewish partner. Demographically, intermarriage interfered with the growth of Jewish population in two ways. Unlike in the United States in recent years, European couples, when denominationally divided, as a rule raised their children as Christians rather than as Jews. Secondly, perhaps to avoid further complications, many intermarried couples refrained from having children altogether or were satisfied with but a single child. The end result was a further diminution of the Jewish numbers.

Table 3.

	1820–25		1900		1939	
	Jewish population	Total population	Jewish population (in thousands)	Total population	Jewish population	Total population
Europe						
Russia (including Congress Poland)	1,600	46,000	5,190 (1897)	126,368		
U.S.S.R. (including Asiatic parts)	—	—	—	—	2,825	132,519
Poland (including Galicia, Posen, etc.)	—	—	—	—	3,250	32,183
Lithuania (1923)	—	—	—	—	155	2,029
Latvia (1935)	—	—	—	—	95	1,951
Estonia (1934)	—	—	—	—	4.56	1,126
Rumania (enlarged after 1918)	80	3,335	267	5,956	850	18,053
Austria-Hungary (before 1918)	568	26,000	2,069	44,400	—	—
Austria (1934)	—	—	—	—	191	6,760
Czechoslovakia (1930)	—	—	—	—	357	14,730
Hungary (1930)	—	—	—	—	445	8,688
Yugoslavia (1931)	—	—	5.1	2,494	68	13,934
Greece	—	—	5.8	2,434 (1896)	73 (1928)	6,205
Turkey (European, 1935)	—	—	—	—	50	1,266
Germany	223	26,624	520	56,367	504 (1933)	65,988

Table 3 (cont.)

	1820–25		1900		1939	
	Jewish population	Total population	Jewish population	Total population	Jewish population	Total population
			(in thousands)			
Switzerland	2	2,190 (1837)	12.5	3,315	18 (1930)	4,066
Italy	25	19,000	35	32,449	48 (1936)	42,528
Great Britain and Northern Ireland	20	21,130	200	41,457	300 (1931)	46,190
France (including Alsace-Lorraine)	50	30,000	115 (A.-L.) 35	38,961	260 (1936)	41,906
Netherlands	45	2,460	104	5,179	112 (1930)	7,936
Belgium	2	3,500	20	6,693	60 (1930)	8,092
Europe (as a whole)	2,730	190,000	8,690	423,000	9,480	512,849
The Americas						
United States	8	5,308	1,000	75,995	4,975 (1940)	131,669
Canada	—	—	16	4,833	155.7 (1931)	10,377
Mexico	—	—	1	13,600	9 (1930)	16,523
Argentina	—	—	30	4,900	275 (1935)	12,958
Brazil	—	—	2	17,300	35 (1930)	40,273
Uruguay	—	—	0.9	840	12 (1931)	1,903
The Americas (as a whole)	10	—	1,175	144,000	5,537	261,985
Asia						
Palestine	45	—	78	650	475	1,467
Asiatic Turkey	—	—	300	16,134	30	14,935
Iraq	—	—	—	—	91 (1935)	3,560
Syria and Lebanon	—	—	—	—	26 (1935)	3,630
Yemen and Arabia	—	—	30	7,000	50 (1935)	1,000
Iran	—	—	35	9,000	50 (1935)	15,000
India	—	—	18.2	232,000	24 (1931)	352,838
China	—	—	2	402,680	10 (1936)	457,835
Japan	—	—	—	43,760	2	72,876
Asia (as a whole)	300	—	420	857,000	1,047	1,094,524
Africa						
Egypt	—	—	30.7	9,734	70 (1937)	15,905
Morocco	—	—	103.7 (1904)	5,000	162 (1936)	7,096
Algeria	20,000 (1851)	—	51	4,729	110 (1931)	7,235
Tunisia	—	—	62.5	1,500	59.5 (1936)	2,608
Ethiopia	—	—	50	5,000	51 (1935)	10,000
Union of South Africa	—	—	40	1,100	90.7 (1936)	9,590
Africa (as a whole)	240	—	300	120,000	627.5	157,650
Oceania						
Australia	—	—	15	3,036	23.6 (1933)	6,630
New Zealand	—	—	1.6	773	2.7 (1936)	1,574
Oceania (as a whole)	1	—	17	4,730	33	—
World total	3,281	1,171,000	10,602.5	1,608,000	16,724	2,296,000

Under these circumstances only tentative estimates can be given for many figures in Table 3 (above). They relate to the three periods of 1820–25 (rather than 1800, because after the rapid changes during the Napoleonic Wars the frontiers of the countries of Jewish settlement essentially stable until (World War I), 1900 (before World War I), and 1939 (on the eve of World II).

From the above figures, however unreliable in detail, one may obtain an approximation of both the growth and the shifts of the Jewish population over the 120 years from 1820 to 1939. They are largely cited here from the works of Jacob Lestschinsky, notwithstanding serious reservations as to the accuracy of all such computations. The most startling evolution was, of course, that of the Jewish population in the Western Hemisphere which was owing more to Jewish migrations than to natural increase. The United States, in particular, in the half-century preceding World War I became the great magnet for immigrants from Eastern Europe, as well as from almost all other European and Middle Eastern countries. Suffice it to say that in the course of merely 24 years, from 1890 to 1914, some 30% of all East European Jews changed their residence to some overseas country, particularly the United States. In addition, there were major migratory movements of Jews within their countries of settlement. Many Russian Jews moved into the newly annexed neo-Russian territories in the south, including a number of agricultural colonies established for them on the initiative of the Czarist regime. They also spoke in the 1830s of the Jewish "discovery of Volhynia" which brought many new Jewish settlers from the western provinces into that area which had made noteworthy contributions to Jewish culture already in pre-partition Poland. On the other hand, a great many Russian Jews, often simply called Litvaks, settled in Congress Poland in the years before World War I. After the removal of the *Pale of Settlement as a result of that war and the Communist Revolution, there was a great exodus of Jews from the original Pale into the interior of Russia, particularly the two metropolises of Moscow and Leningrad, as well as such newly founded industrial centers as Magnitogorsk in the Urals. There also was a small Jewish movement to Far Eastern *Birobidzhan, more significant ideologically than numerically. Similarly, there was a constant transplantation of Jews from Galicia to other parts of Austria-Hungary, particularly to neighboring Bukovina and Slovakia and the two capitals of Vienna and Budapest. The same holds true for the formerly Polish possessions incorporated into Prussia in the years 1772–95 but subsequently lost to resurrected Poland in 1919. The majority of Jewish residents of that area had been leaving it for other parts of Germany, England, and the United States throughout the 19th century, but their departure was accelerated after 1918.

These migratory movements gave additional stimuli to the process of Jewish urbanization which had long been under way. The settlement of Jews in many major cities and metropolitan areas far exceeded their ratio in the respective populations. Table 5 below well illustrates the climactic urban and metropolitan concentration of Jews in the course of the 20th century.

1940–1971. These three decades belong to the most portentous periods of human history, general and demographic. They also were of decisive historic importance in the destinies of the Jewish people. Begun with the great Holocaust, which destroyed thousands of European Jewish communities and ended eight centuries of European Jewish hegemony, the decade of the 1940s ended with the rise of the State of Israel. This ushered in an entirely new period of Jewish history which has already had demographic effects of enormous importance.

Despite the ever-growing literature on the Holocaust, certain aspects have not yet been sufficiently explored. Among the questions still incompletely resolved is the precise number of victims of the Nazi extermination squads. The accepted figure of 6,000,000 Jews, along with many more millions of non-Jews slain by the Nazis, has often been challenged, especially by some German writers. One of the major difficulties in obtaining definitive and

Table 4.

Country	1948		1967	
	Jewish population	Total population	Jewish population	Total population
	(in thousands)			
Europe				
U.S.S.R. (including Asiatic parts)	2,000	187,581	2,650 (1959)	237,914
Poland	88	23,930	21	32,207
Rumania	380	16,472	100	19,285
Austria	31	6,945	12.5	7,233
Czechoslovakia	42	12,170	15	14,305
Hungary	174	9,333	80	10,217
Yugoslavia	10	14,800	7	20,186
Bulgaria	45	7,048	7	8,310
Greece	8.5	7,450	6.5	8,716
Turkey (including Asiatic provinces)	80	21,274	39	29,920
Germany (West and East)	153[1]	41,000	30	73,700
Italy	53[1]	45,486	35	52,354
Great Britain	345	49,478	410	55,068
Ireland	4.5	2,972	5.4	2,899
France	235	41,000	535	49,866
Netherlands	28	9,636	30	12,743
Belgium	45	8,289	40.5	9,581
Switzerland	35	4,543	20	6,071
Sweden	15.5	6,803	13	7,908
Denmark	5.5	4,146	6	4,839
Spain	3	27,503	7	32,140
Portugal	4	8,312	0.6	9,505
Europe (as a whole)	3,780	589,781	4,070.5	721,240

Table 4. cont.

Country	1948		1967	
	Jewish population	Total population	Jewish population	Total population
	(in thousands)			
The Americas				
United States	5,000	144,000	5,870	201,166
Canada	180	12,582	280	20,772
Mexico	25	23,425	30	47,267
Argentina	360	16,108	500	23,607
Brazil	111	46,726	140	88,209
Uruguay	37	2,281	54	2,818
Chile	25	5,522	35	9,351
Venezuela	3	4,300	12	9,686
Colombia	6	10,545	10	19,191
The Americas (as a whole)	5,778	303,202	6,952	482,290
Asia				
Israel (Palestine)	750	1,000	2,436	2,841[2]
Iraq	90	4,803	2.5	8,440
Syria	20	3,006	4	5,570
Lebanon			3	2,520
Yemen	45	3,500	——	5,000
Iran	50	17,000	80	26,284
India	30	411,500	15	523,893
Pakistan			0.3	109,520
China (Mainland)	15	461,000	——	720,000
Taiwan				13,142
Japan	2	78,000	1	101,091
Asia (as a whole) without U.S.S.R. and Turkey	1,030	1,142,115	2,544	1,907,481
Africa				
Egypt (U.A.R.)	75	19,090	1	30,907
Morocco	286	8,100	50	14,580
Algeria	130	7,600	1.5	12,943
Tunisia	71.5 (1946)	2,730	10	4,560
Ethiopia	51	9,500	12	23,667
South Africa	100	11,600	115	18,733
Rhodesia	3.5	1,448	5.5	4,530
Africa (as a whole)	745.5	61,000	196	142,606
Oceania				
Australia	37	7,344	70	12,031
New Zealand	3.5	1,802	5	2,751
Oceania (as a whole)	40.5	9,146	75	18,127
World				
Total	11,373	2,516,000 (1950)	13,837.5	3,419,420

[1] Including displaced persons.
[2] 3,767 including territories occupied in 1967.

precise figures consists in the fact that, in pursuing their "final solution" of the Jewish question, the Nazi authorities were quite careful in simultaneously destroying human lives and the records pertaining to them. In his oft-quoted Posen speech of Oct. 4, 1943, Heinrich Himmler alluded to the "very grave matter" of exterminating Jews and declared: "Among ourselves it should be mentioned quite frankly, and yet we shall never speak about it publicly . . . I mean . . . the extirpation of the Jewish race. This is a page of glory in our history which has never been written and is never to be written."

Yet not only does the partial evidence from various localities confirm the 6,000,000 estimate, but it also emerges as the most likely figure from the demographic changes in European and world Jewish population during the war and postwar periods (see *Holocaust). If on the eve of World War II the Jewish people numbered some 16,750,000, by 1945 this number was reduced to about 11,000,000. True, in addition to their victimization at the hands of Nazi extermination squads, Jews suffered considerable losses in manpower as combatants in the Soviet, U.S., and other armies, as well as from the numerous other adverse by-products of the great war. But these losses should easily have been made up by the natural growth of the Jewish population during the six wars years, especially in the Western Hemisphere and other continents where the war touched only the periphery of Jewish life. Moreover, even the defeated nations of Germany, Italy, and Japan quickly recovered their biological strength and in the two decades of 1940–60 increased their populations by 25–33%. But the Jewish people which, if allowed to continue its population growth of the preceding two decades, by 1960 should have reached a total of 19,000,000–20,000,000 persons, counted instead no more than 12,800,000 persons. Even today, another decade later, it still is very far from returning to its populousness of 1939. As a result of the Holocaust and World War II there was a complete shift of the center of gravity of the Jewish people from the Old to the New

World. With Russian Jewry not only weakened, but subject to a severe anti-Semitic onslaught especially during the declining years of Stalin's regime in 1948–52, its isolation from the rest of Jewry became even tighter than before. Its influence on the historic progress of the entire people, particularly in the cultural sphere, declined rapidly. The demographic picture, too, of the entire European Continent was affected adversely, although Western Europe, particularly France, has staged a steady recovery in the postwar era: in the French case because of the growing immigration of North African Jews. During the prolonged Algerian uprising the Jewish communities of that country reaching back to antiquity and glorying in a great historic tradition were nearly emptied; their majority found shelter in either France or Israel. So did many refugees from other Arab countries.

In reaction to the rise of the State of Israel in 1948 anti-Jewish pressures on the declining Jewries in all Arab countries became unbearable. With the exception of Morocco and Tunisia where substantial remnants of the Jewish inhabitants have carried on against tremendous odds, the other Arab countries almost totally lost their long-established Jewish populations (see Table above). On the other hand, the very rise of Israel opened untold new possibilities for the concentration of Jews in that country. By absorbing the majority of Jewish émigrés from the Arab lands, as well as most of the surviving remnants of victims of Nazi persecution in continental Europe located in the displaced persons camps, together with migrants from many other countries, Israel's unparalleled population growth more than redressed the balance as far as the continent of Asia was concerned. But Africa continued to be in the losing column also in many of the newly arisen black republics, where the small Jewish communities were further reduced in size by emigration.

Regrettably, during the last three decades the demographic facts relating to Jews have become less rather than more thoroughly investigated. To begin with, such leading European countries as Poland, Czechoslovakia, Austria, Germany, and Holland, which before World War II offered, through their governmental censuses, excellent source material for Jewish demography, have become so depopulated of Jews that between them they accommodate but little more than 1% of world Jewry. Their place was taken only by Israel, whose excellent censuses and annual statistical estimates have in many ways become a mainstay of Jewish demographic research. Israel scholarship has even helped to stimulate such investigation in other lands. In the largest country of Jewish settlement, the United States, the situation has likewise improved somewhat. Although the governmental censuses still fail to supply adequate information, the awareness of U.S. Jewry of the need to be acquainted with the demographic facts of life has been sufficiently aroused to call forth a number of local surveys in the 1950s and the 1960s. While these have not been consistently enough pursued so as to furnish successive data from decade to decade, nor have they been conducted with the same methods so as to make them fully comparable with one another, they have by now assembled a substantial body of material from which statistical conclusions of a sort can be derived with somewhat greater assurance. All this is merely a beginning, but it appears, at least, to be a step in the right direction. Similar hesitant steps have also been made in Western Europe, Argentina, and most successfully, in Canada, where the governmental censuses help to supply many vital statistics relating to Jews.

At the same time figures for the second-largest Jewish community, that of the Soviet Union, are still almost exclusively dependent on foreign Jews analyzing the results of the official censuses. That of 1959 was published by the government in 16 volumes, together with some additional data periodically supplied by the official census bureau in regular bulletins. One of the most puzzling problems concerning that census was the question of the extent to which the figures given for Jewish "nationality" really covered Soviet Jewry. Though every Soviet citizen has to carry a "passport" indicating his "nationality" many Jews could escape registering as members of that nationality in the presence of enumerators, since the census takers were instructed to register only the indications made orally by the inhabitants without checking their documents. A good case has been made, therefore, for raising the results of the 1959 census which gave the total number of Jews as 2,267,814 and to postulate that their total really came close to 3,000,000.

On April 17, 1971 the Soviet press published the first summaries of the population census taken on Jan. 15, 1970. According to the figures quoted, the Jewish population fell from 11th to 12th in size among 100 nationalities in the Soviet Union, and the overall number of Jews declined from 2,267,814 (January 1959) to 2,151,000.

Despite all the obscurities and uncertainties, one may perhaps venture to propose the following table, largely based (with all due reservations) upon the estimates annually published in the *American Jewish Year Book* and the United Nations' *Statistical Yearbook*.

Regrettably, some of the above data refer to censuses or estimates of populations in the cities proper, while others cover metropolitan districts of a wider area. In the same 1969 edition of *The World Almanac* (pp. 578f., 604ff., and 651), for example, the number of inhabitants in New York City, according to the census of 1960, is given as 7,781,984, and in Greater New York (embracing an additional 8 New Jersey and 5 New York counties) as 14,114,927. In Los Angeles the respective 1960 figures are 2,479,015 and 6,488,791; in Chicago: 3,550,404 and 6,488,791; in Buenos Aires: 2,966,816 and 6,762,629; in Paris: 2,811,171 and 7,369,387 (1962 census) or 9,811,171 (1968 estimate), and so forth. (Incidentally, the same issue of the *Almanac*, p. 602, offers somewhat different estimates of the Jewish population by counties and cities, as prepared by Dr. S. H. Linfield.) Jews had fully participated in that postwar movement, some call it flight, from the core cities to the suburbs, making estimates between official censuses or several years after the completion of communal surveys quite hazardous. Nevertheless, the tentative lists (Tables 4 and 5) suggest several significant general conclusions. In the first place, it is quite evident that at the present time about one-half of world Jewry lives in the Western Hemisphere, the United States embracing far more Jews than any other country. The second- and third-largest concentrations are to be found in the U.S.S.R. and Israel, although the respective positions of these two countries may soon change and Israel assume the second place. This would rather speedily be the case, it appears, if the Soviet Union were to open her gates to Jewish mass emigration. At any rate, the United States, the U.S.S.R., and Israel between them embrace more than 80% of world Jewry.

Secondly, as may be seen from Table 5 the progress of Jewish settlement in major cities during the period of 1900–69 proceeded apace at a tempo even more rapid than that of the general population. Already before 1939 about one quarter of the entire Jewish people lived in metropolitan areas of over 1,000,000 each. Another quarter lived in cities with populations of between 100,000 and 1,000,000 inhabitants. Thirty years later the latter ratio still is approximately correct. But the percentage of "metropolitan" Jews has risen to about 40% of the whole people, leaving barely a third for localities, urban and rural, with

Table 5.

Cities	1900		1939		1948		1967	
	Jewish population	Total population	Jewish population	Total population (in thousands)	Jewish population	Total population	Jewish population	Total population
United States			(1937)			(1950)		(1960)
New York Metropolitan area	600	3,437	2,035	7,380	2,000	7,892	2,520	7,882
Los Angeles	2.5	102.5	82	1,496.7	225	1,970.3		2,479
Metropolitan area							500	
Philadelphia Metropolitan area	75	1,294	293	1,951	246	2,071.6	330	2,002
Chicago Metropolitan area	60	1,699	363	3,384.5	300	3,620	269	3,550
Boston	40	561	118	781	137	801.4	176	697
Miami				172	40	249.2	140	291
Baltimore	25	509	73	854	75	949.7	100	939
Newark (With Essex County)	15	246	73	428	56.8	438.8	100	405
Washington, D.C.,		278.7		663				
Greater					30	802.2	100	764
Cleveland	20	382	90	878	80	914.8	85	876
Detroit	10	286	90	1,618.5	90	1,850	84.5	1,670
San Francisco	17	343	40.9	629.5	50	775	73	740
St. Louis	34	575	51	813.7	44	856.8	57.5	750
Pittsburg	20	322	52	670	54	676.8	45	604
Cincinnati	15	326	21.8	453	22	504	28	502
Hartford		80	23.4	166	26	177.4	26	162
Milwaukee	8	285.3	29.6	587.5	30	637.4	23.9	483
Kansas City, Mo.		163.7	25	399	20	456.6	22	475
Denver		133.8	18.4	322.5	16	415.8	24	494
Rochester		162.6	23.4	325	20.5	332.5	21.5	318
Minneapolis		202.7	20.7	492	21	521.2	20.5	483
Dallas		42.6	10.4	295	10	434.5	22	680
New Haven		108	24.7	160.6	20	164.5	20	152
Houston		44.6	13.5	384.5	14	596.2	20	938
Providence		175.6	23.8	253.5	25	248.7	19.6	207
Elizabeth (with East Union County)		52	11.7	110	10	113	16.5	107
Atlanta		90	12	302	10.2	331.3	16.5	487
There were 22 other cities with a Jewish population of 10–15,000 in 1967.								
Canada								
Montreal	10	267	48.7	818.5	55		105	
Metropolitan area			(1831)			1,140		2,321
Toronto	3.5	208	45.3	631	65		88	
Metropolitan area						942.5		2,106
Winnipeg			17.2	280		222	21	508
South America								
Buenos Aires	10	836	120	2,364	165	3,150	360	2,967
Rio de Janeiro				1,802	40	1,781.5	55	4,076
Saō Paulo				1,168	30	1,380	60	4,098
U.S.S.R.								
Moscow	8.5	989	400	3,663		4,137	285	6,422
Kiev	31.8	247	175	846		846	220	1,457
Leningrad		1,133	275	3,191		3,191	165	3,341
Odessa	139	405	180	604		604		797
Kharkov	11	175	150	833		33.5		1,148
Lvov	44.3	160	105	317.7		317.7		
Vilna	64	155	55 (1931)	208		209		
Other East European Cities								
Bucharest	43.3	282	50	650	160	984.6		1,247
Jassy	30.4	78	45	104.5	27.5	95		
Prague	20	202	35.5	849	10	924		1,023
Budapest	169	732	180	1,586	110	1,162.8	65	1,928
Warsaw	219	638	365	1,265.7	4.4	557.7	5	1,261
Lodz	98.7	315	220	665	14	497		745
Cracow	25.7	66	46	219				
Central European Cities								
Berlin (Greater)	106	1,889	82.8	4,332	8	4,332	6.4	3,270
Hamburg	18	706	17	1,682	1.4	1,384		1,847
Frankfort	22	289	26	547	1.6	546.6		684
Vienna	147	1,675	91.5	1,918.5	11.2	1,930	9.2	1,640

Table 5 (cont.)

Cities	1900 Jewish population	1900 Total population	1939 Jewish population	1939 Total population	1948 Jewish population	1948 Total population	1967 Jewish population	1967 Total population
	(in thousands)							
Rome	7.8	663	11	1,348	12	1,551.5	13	2,560
Leghorn	4	98	2.5	112.5				
Milan				713	5	1,264	9	675
Venice	3.8	152		286		302.5		
Zurich			5.7	312.6		674.5	6.2	432.5
The Balkans								
Istanbul	44		47	883.6		845	38	1,751
Salonika	60		55	236.5	1.6		1.3	309
Athens				657	3.7	652	2.8	1,853
Belgrade			9	238.8	1.9	405	1.4	585
Zagreb			9.5	185.5	1.7		1.4	431
West European Cities								
London	150	6,581	250	8,655	234	8,700	280	7,881
Manchester	28	544	37.5	736.5	36 (1952)	684.6	28	616
Leeds	20	429	25	458	29 (1952)	493	18	507
Amsterdam	60	520	65.5	793.5	14	769	12	865
Antwerp	4.5	285	22	274.5		256	13	661
Paris	58	2,660	200	2,830	125	2,725	300	2,811
Marseilles	5.5	495	2	914		636	65	850
Lyons				570.6		570.6	25	543
Strasbourg			7	181.5			14	233
Nice						211	20	295
Toulouse				213.2		264.5	20	330
Israel								
Jerusalem			77	126	95		187.5	195
Tel Aviv			140	140	250	250	389.7	389.7
Haifa			58	100	80		200	207
Asia								
Teheran				540	25	699	30	2,317
Damascus				318.9	2.5	286		600
Beirut				160.7		234		700
Shanghai			5.5	3,490	9	6,000		6,900
Africa								
Cairo	14	570	38	1,307.5	36	1,312		
Metropolitan area								4,197
Alexandria	12.5	320	27	682	28	686		
Metropolitan area								1,801
Casablanca				453	100	453	40	1,085
Tunis				202.4	30	220		662
Algiers			23.5	252	30	252		943
Johannesburg	10		26 (1931)	257.7	30	324	57.7	1,244
Capetown			11	173.4		214		836
Oceania								
Melbourne Metropolitan area				1,046		1,193	35	2,228
Sydney Metropolitan area				1,305		1,398	28	2,540

less than 100,000 inhabitants. In many countries, moreover, the metropolitan ratios were considerably exceeded; for instance, in England, France, and Argentina, the majority of Jews have long lived in the capitals, while in the United States such a majority may be found in a radius of 100 miles from Times Square in New York. This evolution would not have been surprising even under more normal circumstances, since this is indeed a world-wide trend. Even the Soviet Union, which half a century ago started as an overwhelmingly rural country, now has an urban majority. The Holocaust, however, has greatly accelerated that trend, inasmuch as it put an end to most of the agricultural colonies and other rural Jewish settlements in Russia, Carpathian Ruthenia (where originally more than one quarter of the Jewish population engaged in agriculture), and elsewhere. It also eliminated most of the hamlets which still accommodated a large segment of the East European Jewish population. Even in the United States recent developments were not favorable to Jewish agricultural colonization. The same holds true for Israel, where the mass immigration of the last 20 years has strengthened the trend toward urban concentration.

Thirdly, the increase in Jewish population during the last two decades has lagged far behind that of the world population as well as that of most environmental peoples. Mankind as a whole increased by around 36% between 1948 and 1968, but world Jewry has added less than 20% to its numbers. This is clearly not the result of increased mortality, but rather of a relatively smaller birthrate. The phenomenon of the declining Jewish birthrate so manifest in the Western countries in the interwar period has given way to a growing natality in the 1940s and the 1950s. However, this trend seems not to have lasted to the same extent into the 1960s. While conversions to other religions have greatly diminished, the relative demographic ravages caused by intermarriage have increased, particularly in the U.S.S.R. and Western Europe, where the offspring of mixed marriages is more likely permanently to sever its ties with the Jewish community. Under these circumstances, it will evidently take many more years before the Jewish people recovers its population strength of 1939.

See also *Demography; *Vital Statistics.

Bibliography: J. Jacobs, *Studies in Jewish Statistics* (1890); A. Nossig, *Juedische Statistik* (1903), incl. extensive bibl.; U. O. Schmelz (comp.), *Jewish Demography and Statistics: Bibliography for 1920–1960* (1961), Heb. and Eng., with R. Shebath, addenda and index of names (1961); *Zeitschrift fuer Demographie und Statistik der Juden* (1905–1919); AJYB, index; JSOS, index; JJS; Baron, Social and Social²; idem, in: L. Feldman (ed.), *Ancient and Medieval Essays;* E. Ashtor, in: JJS, vols. 18–19 (1967–68); idem, in: *Zion,* 28 (1963); I. S. Revah, in: REJ, 122 (1963); R. Bachi, in: RMI, 12 (1938); idem, in: JJS, 4 (1962); G. Kleczyński and Z. Kluczycki, *Licba głów żydowskich w koronie, z taryf roku 1765* (1898); R. Mahler, in: *Lodzer Visenshaftlekhe Shriftn,* 1 (1938); B. Wasiutyński, *Ludność żydowska w Polsce w wiekach XIX i XX* (1930); J. Unna, *Statistik der Frankfurter Juden bis zum Jahre 1866* (1931); A. Ruppin, *Soziologie der Juden,* 2 vols. (1931–32); idem, *Jewish Fate and Future* (1940); L. Livi, *Ebrei alla luce della statistica* (1920); J. Lestschinsky, in: *Historishe Shriftn,* 1 (1928); idem, in: UJE, 10 (1943), s.v. *Statistics;* idem, *Tefuẓot Yisrael Aḥarei ha-Milḥamah* (1948); I. Cohen, *Contemporary Jewry* (1950); A. Tartakower, in: HUCA, 23 (1950–51); idem, *Ha-Ḥevrah ha-Yehudit* (1957); *Annual of the Institute of Jewish Affairs* (1956), 315–44; S. Shaul (ed.), *Am Yisrael be-Dorenu* (1964); idem, *La vie juive dans l'Europe contemporaine* (1967, also in Heb.); U. Z. Engelman, in: JSOS, 9 (1947); H. S. Linfield, *Jews in the United States 1927* (1929); S. M. Robinson, *Jewish Population Studies* (1943), with J. Starr; I. Rosenberg, *Canada's Jews* (1939); I. Rosenwaite, in: JSOS, 22 (1960); M. Friedman (ed.), *A Minority in Britain* (1955); F. Bosse, *Die Verbreitung der Juden im Deutschen Reich ... 1880* (1885); H. Silbergleit, *Bevoelkerungs—und Berufsverhaeltnisse der Juden im Deutschen Reich,* 1 (1930); G. A. Schimmer, *Statistik des Judenthums der im Reichsrate vertretenen Koenigreiche und Laender* (1873); L. Goldhammer, *Die Juden Wiens* (1927); B. Blau, in: *Yidishe Ekonomik,* 3 (1939); I. Schiper, *Żydzi w Polsce odrodzonej,* 2 vols. (n.d.), with a demographic study by A. Tartakower; I. Canter, *Di Yidishe Bafolkerung in Ukraine* (Kharkov, 1929); L. Zinger, *Dos Banayte Folk* (Moscow, 1941); M. Altschuler, in: *Gesher,* nos. 47–48 (1966); J. Rothenberg, in: JSOS, 29 (1967), 234–40; 31 (1969), 37–39; Palestine, Department of Statistics, *Vital Statistics, Tables 1929–1945* (1947); Israel, Central Bureau of Statistics, *Statistical Abstract of Israel;* United Nations, Statistical Office, *Statistical Yearbook;* U. O. Schmelz and P. Glikson (ed.), *Jewish Population Studies 1961–1968* (1970). [S.W.B.]

°**PORCHETUS SALVAGUS (Victor Porchetto de Salvatici;** d. c. 1315), Italian Carthusian of Genoa. Porchetus wrote an anti-Jewish work entitled *Victoria adversus impios Hebraeos, in qua tum ex sacris litteris tum ex dictis Talmud ac cabbilistarum et aliorum omnium authorum quos hebraei recipiunt monstratur veritas catholicae fidei.*

The first part (24 chapters) enumerates proofs to demonstrate the truth of Christianity from the Holy Scriptures, and the second part (16 chapters) similarly instances proofs from the Kabbalah and rabbinic sources, Porchetus' material was not original, being copied mostly from the *Pugio fidei* of Raymond *Martini. His book in turn was copied by later writers such as Pietro *Galatinus Columna and others. The book by Porchetus appeared in Paris in 1520. Its introduction *(prologus)* was reprinted by J. C. Wolf in his *Bibliotheca Hebraea* (vol. 2, 1124–27).

Bibliography: P. Browe, *Die Judenmission im Mittelalter und die Juden* (1942), 104, 108; A. Posnanski, *Schilo* (1904), 370–8; H. Merhavia, *Ha-Talmud bi-Re'i ha-Naẓrut* (1970), index. [J.M.R.]

PORGES, MOSES BEN ISRAEL NAPHTALI (17th century), rabbi and emissary of the Ashkenazi community of Jerusalem. Born in Prague, he was a relative of Isaiah ha-Levi *Horowitz, whom he followed to Ereẓ Israel, settling in Jerusalem, where he became a scribe. When, after the *Chmielnicki massacres of 1648–49, the contributions from Poland to Jerusalem ceased, and the Ashkenazi community in Jerusalem was overwhelmed with debt, Porges was sent as their emissary to Germany. During this mission he published, in Prague or in Frankfort, his small work *Darkhei Ẓiyyon* designed to arouse sympathy and obtain support for the Jewish community in Ereẓ Israel.

This work, one of the best examples of this type of literature, is divided into four sections: the virtue of living in Ereẓ Israel, prayer, study, memorial prayers. The first section is a kind of guidebook for new immigrants to Israel, in which Moses draws upon his personal experiences and advises them on what to take for the journey, the easiest routes, how to conduct themselves on the way and the like. In this section he also gives practical details on prices and currency, describes the foods available in Ereẓ Israel, recounts in detail how much is needed for living, rent, and taxes, and lists customs of dress and conduct in everyday life. In the second section he describes in detail the liturgical customs of Jerusalem, in the third section, the methods of study there, including various details about the holy places, and in the fourth, customs then practiced in Jerusalem, among them those of reciting memorial prayers for the departed and of obtaining contributions from generous individuals outside of Ereẓ Israel, in whose honor lights were kindled in the synagogues on Sabbaths and festivals and for whom blessings were invoked. The book was directed to the masses, and therefore was written in the language they knew best—Yiddish. It succeeded admirably in its aim of presenting an attractive picture of Israel. *Darkhei Ẓiyyon* has only been published once and is very rare.

Bibliography: A. Yaari, *Masot Ereẓ Yisrael* (1946), 267–304, 770f.; Yaari, Sheluḥei, 275–6. [A.Ya./Ed]

PORGES, NATHAN (1848–1924), rabbi, scholar, and bibliographer. Born in Prossnitz, Moravia, Porges received his rabbinical diploma at the Breslau seminary, in 1874. He served as rabbi in Nakel, Mannheim, Pilsen, and Karlsbad (Karlovy Vary), and from 1888 to 1917 in Leipzig, where he was awarded the title of professor in 1913. His important library contained many incunabula and rare books, which were dispersed and sold through book dealers (cf. Shunami, Bibl, index s.v.).

He wrote articles on Hebrew bibliography which appeared in the *Revue des Etudes Juives,* the *Zeitschrift fuer hebraeische Bibliographie,* and other periodicals. Porges was an expert in medieval Hebrew philology and literature, publishing essays on Dunash ibn *Labrat, Judah *Ḥayyuj, and Joseph *Bekhor Shor, as well as *Bibelkunde und Babelfunde* (1903) and some sermons.

Bibliography: M. Brann, in: *Breslau Festschrift zum 50-jaehrigen Jubilaeum der Anstalt* (1904), 188 (includes bibliography). [Ed.]

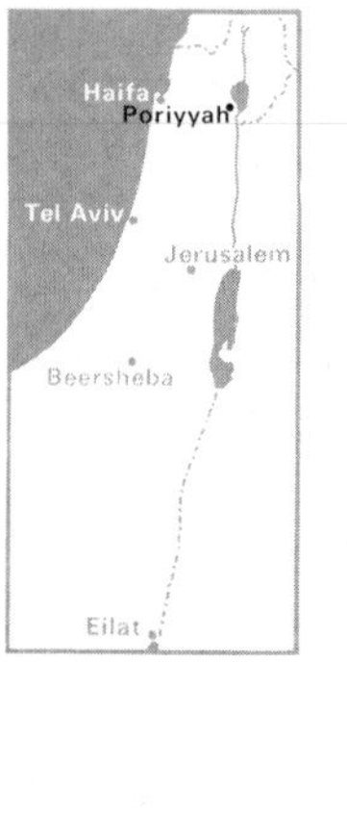

PORIYYAH (Heb. פּוֹרִיָּה), two urban quarters and a village in northern Israel, on the Poriyyah Ridge, just S. of *Tiberias. Poriyyah was founded in 1912 as a fruit farm, mainly based on almond plantations, by a group of American Zionists. A few of these Zionists went to settle on the site which was worked by Jewish laborers. The place was abandoned in World War I. In 1940 kibbutz *Alummot temporarily settled on the site. In 1949 a work village *(kefar*

avodah was established there by immigrants from Yemen. In 1952 it became an affiliate of Tenu'at ha-Moshavim but later left the association and remained unaffiliated. A government regional hospital was built further north in 1949, as well as housing projects of Upper Tiberias. A youth hostel, named after the veteran Tiberias inhabitant, Y. Taiber, was opened at Poriyyah. In 1968 the village had 180 inhabitants, the Poriyyah Illit quarter had 790, and the Neveh Oved quarter, 750. [E.O.]

°**PORPHYRY** (233–305 C.E.), Greek philosopher, disciple of Plotinus, and one of the most versatile thinkers of his day. Porphyry displayed considerable interest in Judaism, both as one of the ancient religions of the Orient and as the source of Christianity, to which he was hostile. His attitude to Judaism is sympathetic. In his *De Abstinentia* he cites Josephus (the only pagan writer to do so), drawing upon his description of the Essenes and he describes with commiseration the misfortunes suffered by the Jews during the reign of *Antiochus Epiphanes and under Roman rule. In his life of Pythagoras, he features him as a disciple of the Hebrews. In his lost polemic against Christianity, Porphyry did not confine himself to criticism of the books of the Bible and of the New Testament, but conducted an empirical investigation which revealed a knowledge of biblical sources even greater than that of *Celsus, his predecessor in this field. Porphyry devoted an entire book to discussion of the Book of Daniel (referred to in Jerome's commentary), concluding that it was written by a Jewish contemporary of Antiochus Epiphanes, and that it can, therefore, only be regarded as "prophecy after the event."

Bibliography: J. Bidez, *Vie de Porphyre* (1913); A. B. Hulen, *Porhyry's Work against the Christians* (1933); Schroeder, in: *Welt als Geschichte,* 17 (1957), 196–202; Reinach, Textes, 203–6. [M.St.]

PORTAL. The design of a single or double doorway, with flanking columns, appeared early in Jewish funerary art, synagogue mosaics and paintings, and on glass, lamps, and later in textiles and manuscripts. At first it signified a physical symbol of the concept of the heavenly abode and, later, came to represent the Torah Shrine and the destroyed Temple of Jerusalem. Together with the **menorah,* snuff shovel, **etrog,* **lulav,* and **shofar,* the portal is one of the most common Jewish symbols found from the first centuries of the Common Era. The meaning of the design goes back to the ancient oriental symbol for the residence of the gods on high. The doorway represented and signified the entrance to the heavenly precincts. Gods were portrayed standing or sitting in the doorway while the sun god Shamash from the second millennium B.C.E. Akkadian art was frequently shown rising in the eastern mountains from between open double doors. These were the "portals of the sky" from which he called out to the world. In Egypt, too, gods made their appearance standing between pillars that symbolized the heavenly sky. Later, in pagan art the portal was formed into a cult niche (*aedicula* or *naos*) holding the god and indicating his divinity. The early Jews conceived of a portal of heaven opening onto the house of God (Gen. 28:17). The Temple of Solomon is spoken of as the earthly residence of the Divine; the "glory of the Lord" enters, as did the image of Shamash in the Mesopotamian world, through its East Gate (Ezek. 43:4–7). The twin pillars that flanked the Temple, called *Jachin and Boaz, are also found in pagan temples of the Palestinian period. Probably the visual device of the portal was adopted into Jewish art from the neighboring Canaanites and Phoenicians, among whom the portal enclosed and sanctified the cult image. The Jews, having no cult idol, substituted Jewish symbols between the columns of the doorway. This is seen in the Jewish catacombs in Rome on the Via Torlonia where the portal was made in the form of a miniature Roman temple. It is shown with open doors, exposing the ends of scrolls, thus indicating the holy nature of the Torah. Painted directly above the Torah niche on the wall of the third-century C.E. synagogue at *Dura Europos is a classicized portal probably symbolizing Solomon's Temple. Two columns

Portal enclosing the Ark of the Law in the center of a floor mosaic from the synagogue of Beth Shean, early sixth century C.E. On either side are a *menorah,* a *shofar,* and a shovel. Jerusalem, Israel Museum, Israel Department of Antiquities Collection.

supporting an arched lintel on a lead coffin from the first—and second—century necropolis at *Bet She'arim in Israel enclosed the *menorah*, thereby signifying the sacred aspect of the candelabrum. Other sepulchers are ornamented with elaborate portals and stone doors that probably retain some of the symbolic value of the heavenly portal. The sixth-century C.E. synagogues at Bet Alfa and Tiberias have mosaic representations of the pedimented portals surrounded by other Jewish symbols. When the portal was used in Jewish funerary art it probably represented not only the holiness of the tomb, but also the gates of heaven through which the deceased had passed.

Bibliography: B. Goldman, *The Sacred Portal* (1966), includes bibliography. [B.Go.]

PORTALEONE, family in N. Italy which originated in the Portaleone quarter of Rome; the *Sommo (or Sommi) family also belonged to it. From the last half of the 14th century the family produced rabbis, physicians, authors, and poets. Among the first important members was ELHANAN BEN MENAHEM (14th and 15th centuries), rabbi of Fano. He is mentioned in 1399 in connection with a bill of divorce (Responsa of Isaac b. Sheshet, no. 127, New Responsa no. 27; Responsa of Simeon b. Zemaḥ Duran, no. 1). In 1416 he represented the town of Ferrara at a synod held in *Bologna, and he is last mentioned in Fano in 1428. His son BENJAMIN PORTALEONE and his grandson JUDAH PORTALEONE were both physicians. Elhanan's brother, MORDECAI (Angelo), is mentioned in Ferrara in 1420. The latter's son, BENJAMIN (Guglielmo Mizolo; d. before 1432), lived in Ferrara, and his grandson, MORDECAI (Angelo) was mentioned there in 1432. BENJAMIN (Guglielmo Mizolo; c. 1420–c. 1500), Mordecai's son, was born in Mantua and was a renowned physician, well thought of by his Christian colleagues. He completed his studies in Sienna and served as physician to a number of princes; in Naples he served Ferdinand I who knighted him (thereafter he was often referred to as the Jewish knight), and in Milan, Galleazzo Maria Sforza. By 1446 Benjamin returned to his native town, where he served as the physician of the dukes of Mantua: Ludovico Gonzaga, Federico, and Francesco.

Benjamin's son, ABRAHAM, was the physician of the duke of Urbino, Guida Baedo, later returning to Mantua, where he served as the physician of the noble Federico and other nobles. He was regarded as one of the best physicians of his generation and also won the esteem of Pope Clement VII. His other son, ELEAZAR, also engaged in medicine in Mantua. In 1499 he received a permit to practice from Pope Alexander VI, and he, too, became physician to a number of noblemen, among them Prince Carlo Giovanni Sassatelli, commander of the army of the Venetian Republic. In 1530, when David *Reuveni visited Italy, he met Eleazar in Sabbioneta and some time later was entertained by Abraham in Mantua. Eleazar had two sons, DAVID and ABRAHAM. In 1518 both were authorized to practice medicine by Pope Leo X, the former in Mantua and the latter in Sermide. The sons of Abraham were JUDAH, MEIR, and SOLOMON. The first two practiced as physicians in Sermide and served the princes of the house of Gonzaga. Despite an injunction forbidding Jewish physicians to attend Christians, they received special permits from the pope and the rulers to do so. (Meir received such permits in 1593 and 1598.) David's son was the well-known physician, Abraham *Portaleone, author of *Shiltei ha-Gibborim*. Abraham had three sons, ELIEZER, JUDAH, and DAVID; the last was also a physician authorized by popes Clement VIII and Gregory XV to attend Christians. In 1596 David was in Padua but later he returned to Mantua. David's son, BENJAMIN (d. c. 1683), studied medicine at the University of Sienna, receiving his diploma in 1639, with the special authorization of Pope Urban VIII. His brother's son-in-law, SOLOMON, was a well-known surgeon (though without a degree in medicine) serving until 1727. The author of the first Hebrew play, Judah Leone *Sommo, also belonged to this family.

Bibliography: M. Steinschneider, in: HB, 6 (1863), 48–49; M. Mortara, in: REJ, 12 (1886), 113–6; L. Luzzatto, in: *Vessillo Israelitico*, 43 (1895), 154–5; D. Kaufmann, in: JQR, 10 (1898), 445–56; idem, *Gesammelte Schriften*, 3 (1915), 303–14; I. Abrahams, JQR, 5 (1893) 505–515; W. Colorni, in: *Annuario di Studi Ebraici*, 1 (1934), 176–82; idem, in: *Scritti in Memoria di Sally Mayer* (1956), 38ff.; H. Friedenwald, *The Jews and Medicine*, 2 (1944), 597–9; S. Simonsohn, *Toledot ha-Yehudim be-Dukkasut Mantovah*, 2 vols. (1962–64), index; Roth, Italy, index. [A.D.]

PORTALEONE, ABRAHAM BEN DAVID II (1542–1612), Italian physician and author. After graduating in philosophy and medicine at the University of Pavia in 1563, he was admitted to the College of Physicians in Mantua in 1566, and was authorized to practice in his father's place; in 1573 he was appointed body physician to the ducal house. Three years later he escaped from an assassination attempt. In 1591, he received papal authorization to attend Christian patients not withstanding the current restrictions. He built up a considerable practice both among Jews and non-Jews and enjoyed a great reputation. At the duke's request he composed a Latin work containing medical guidance *(consilia medica)* as well as *Dialoghi tres de duro* (Venice, 1584) on the application of gold in medicine. He also mentions his volume of selected remedies. When in 1605 he had a stroke and was half-paralyzed, he composed for the use of his children his great work *Shiltei ha-Gibborim* ("Shields of the Mighty"; Mantua, 1612), the first Hebrew book using European punctuation. In this, he attempted to

Gold and copper seal assumed to have belonged to David Portaleone (d. 1655), son of Abraham ben David II. The seal depicts a gateway *(porta)* with a lion *(leone)* crouching on it. The handle depicts the *Akedah* scene. Height 3 in. (8 cm.). The seal was discovered in 1970 by Yitzḥak Einhorn, the Tel Aviv collector. Photo David Harris, Jerusalem.

elucidate the details of the Temple, its service, and everything pertaining to it, in order to make the prescribed daily recitals of the relevant passages more intelligible. His treatment is so discursive as to make the work a compendium of all branches of science known in his day, in which all of the ten languages which he knew were amply used.

He begins by describing the architecture of the Temple, this serving as the basis for discussing the architectural measurements and scales and the relationships of parts of a building and their proportions. In discussing the songs of the Levites in the Temple service and the musical instruments they used, he treats of music in general and instrumental music in particular, as well as poetic meter. The division into priests, Levites, and Israelites offers him the opportunity to discuss the social order and general structure of an ordered society or "political unit." Returning to a discussion of Temple sacrifices, he touches upon the cubic measurements of solids and liquids, their weights and the relationship between the two, and attempts to clarify it through his own experiments. For example, he determines the specific gravities of liquids such as wine, oil, and honey, and solids such as wheat, sifted wheat flour, and barley flour (e.g., the *omer*). The salting of the sacrificial meat gives him an opportunity to give a lengthy description of salts in general, which, together with precious stones and medicinal herbs, were his favorite topics. Salts interested him also as ingredients of explosives, and he therefore describes in detail how saltpeter was produced, and also how to prepare gold salts and silver salts and their use in medicine, and the use of other salts in medicine. The chapter on salts thus becomes a kind of pharmacopeia.

Having completed his scientific excurses, Portaleone returns to his main topic . . . urging his children to be sure to recite the account of the sacrificial service and the incense burning included in the daily prayers, and he gives in three of the "shields" the order of sacrifices for each day, the passages for evening study of the Torah for each day in the year, arranged according to the days of the week and according to the weekly Scriptural portions, as well as a complete list of the chapters from Pentateuch, Prophets, Hagiographa, Mishnah, Talmud, Midrash, and Zohar. Finally, as a kind of introduction to the list of errata, Portaleone discusses reading, writing, and all aspects of the art of printing, and alphabets, Hebrew as well as others. His method of linking different subjects resulted in confusing the important with the trivial in the light of the goal he set himself, but this very confusion increases the importance of his book as a cultural-historical document, both Jewish and general, in addition to its value as a biographical document. He combines the faith of his forefathers and the traditional Jewish intellectual preoccupations with the theories and accomplishments of the technology and science of the Renaissance and the Italian humanism of his time.

Bibliography: C. Roth, *Jews in the Renaissance* (1959), 315–9; D. Kaufmann, in: JQR, 4 (1892), 333–41; 10 (1898), 455; *Ozar Neḥmad,* 3 (1860), 140–1; N. Shapiro, in: *Ha-Rofe ha-Ivri,* 33 (1960), 137ff. [M.H.B-S.]

PORT ELIZABETH, city in Cape Province, Republic of South Africa. Jewish families were among the founding British settlers of 1820. A congregation was formed in 1861 (or 1862) and the first synagogue building (a converted Lutheran church) was acquired in 1862. Port Elizabeth became an important center of the wool trade, in the development of which Jewish merchants, notably the *Mosenthal brothers, played a leading part. Hyman Henry Salomon was mayor in 1873–75 and Max Gumpert in 1900. Ministers of Port Elizabeth were: Samuel Rapoport 1873–94, Jacob Philips 1897–1912, and Abraham Levy 1912–54 (with a short break). In 1923 Adolph Schauder, merchant and industrialist, was elected to the city council and remained a member for more than 40 years. He served as mayor in 1940–42; a township for colored people was named after him in recognition of his work for nonwhites. He was also president of the Orthodox Hebrew Congregation for some years. The United Hebrew Institutions include a Hebrew school, a *ḥevra kaddisha,* and a benevolent society. The United Synagogue and Raleigh Street Synagogue are under joint control. The Summerstrand Orthodox Hebrew Congregation was founded in 1947, and a Progressive Congregation (Temple Israel) in 1949. There is a Jewish day school. The headquarters of both the Eastern Province Committee of the Jewish Board of Deputies and the Eastern Province Zionist Council are in Port Elizabeth. In 1969 the Jewish population of Port Elizabeth numbered 2,811 (1.1% of the population). [L.S.]

Western Road Synagogue, Port Elizabeth, built 1877, one of the oldest synagogues in South Africa. From G. Saron and L. Hotz (eds.), *The Jews in South Africa,* Capetown, 1955.

PORTELLA, DE, a family of courtiers in the kingdom of Aragon, Spain, who flourished at the close of the 13th century, at the time the Jews were removed from the royal administration. Its most distinguished members were the brothers Muça and Ishmael. MUÇA (d. 1286) was the royal *baiulus* ("baliff") and *merino* in *Tarazona. He first held these functions during the last years of James I (1213–76), who granted him and his family the privilege of not having to pay more than a fifth of the tax which was imposed on the Jewish community of Tarazona (1267). Even though he was considered the private official of the king, he was recognized as the chief administrator of the state's incomes during the reign of Pedro III (1276–85), who also entrusted him with the repair and maintenance of the fortifications of the border regions. In November 1286 he was assassinated in unknown circumstances. His property was at first confiscated by *Alfonso III (1285–91) but after negotiations his family succeeded in redeeming both property and status and settled in Albatar, near Borja.

His brother ISHMAEL (d. c. 1312) also participated in the administration of the state incomes, especially after the death of Muça. Until 1289 he acted as dispensator (administrator of the household) of the infante Pedro. In appreciation of his numerous services James II (1291–1327), who entrusted him with various diplomatic missions, granted him many privileges and favors, such as exemption from the payment of taxes. He appointed him rabbi of all the Jewish communities of Aragon. After Ishmael's death, his family settled in Navarre. Its decline marked the end of the presence of Jews in the royal administration of Aragon during the period of the Christian reconquest.

Bibliography: Baer, Spain, index; Baer, Urkunden, index; Neuman, Spain, index; D. Romano *Los funcionarios Judíos de Pedro el grande de Aragón* (1970), 19-20. [ED.]

PORTLAND, city and port in N. W. Oregon on the West Coast of U.S.; Jewish population (1970) approximately 8,000. The earliest Jewish settlers in the Oregon Territory arrived at the beginning of its development in the 1850s.

While initially their arrival coincided with German immigration to the U.S., they came successively from Germany, Poland, and Russia. Others moved to Oregon after settling for some years in the East of the U.S. The early arrivals included peddlers, doctors, soldiers, farmers, bricklayers, musicians, telegraph operators, as well as rabbis. Portland quickly became the major Jewish community and remained the only Oregon city with any numerically significant Jewish population. The earliest formal Jewish worship and study seems to have taken place in Jacksonville, Oregon, in 1856 in the Oddfellows Hall; a small cemetery attached to the town still exists. The first congregation established for the worship of the "one and only and everlasting God according to the ancient ritual of the Jewish faith" was Temple Beth Israel, May 2, 1858. Its present structure was completed in 1928 and its rabbis included Stephen S. *Wise, Jonah B. *Wise, and Emanuel Rose.

As immigration from Europe increased, the Jewish population rose to some 6,000 in 1904. Congregation Ahavai Shalom was founded by Southern and Eastern European Jews in 1869. In 1883 a group of Jews, formerly of North Dakota, established the Neveh Zedek Talmud Torah, which then formally became a congregation in 1889. Ahavai Shalom and Neveh Zedek merged in 1962 to form Congregation Neveh Shalom, and their synagogue was completed in 1964; its rabbi was Joshua Stampfer (1971). In 1905 a group of Russian Jews established Congregation Shaarei Torah; a new synagogue was constructed in 1964 and in 1971 the rabbi of this Orthodox congregation was Yonah H. Geller. In 1911 a group of Sephardi Jews from the island of Rhodes founded Congregation Ahavat Achim, and in 1916 Kesser Israel and then Linath Hazedek and Tiphereth Israel were founded.

From the early years of their settlement in Portland and the State of Oregon, many Jews served in important political and judicial, as well as civic, business, and cultural positions. The Jewish community founded a vocational training school free to all races and creeds as early as 1866. In the field of music, Jacques Gershkovitz founded the Portland Junior Symphony, and was succeeded by Jacob Avshalomov. Ernest *Bloch, who made Oregon his home, wrote his famous "Sacred Service" on the Oregon coast. Jacques Singer was the conductor of the Oregon Symphony Orchestra. Oregon has been the home of many prominent Jewish authors, artists, and physicians. Solomon *Hirsch was a state assemblyman and senator (1872–82) and U.S. minister to Turkey (1889–92), while Joseph *Simon was U.S. senator (1898–1903). Julius L. *Meier, who served as governor of Oregon (1931–35), was also president of Congregation Beth Israel. Jewish state legislators, mayors,

Beth Israel Synagogue, Portland, Oregon, erected 1861. Courtesy Oregon Historical Society, Portland.

and judges were numerous in proportion to the Jewish population of Oregon. Richard L. *Neuberger served in the U.S. Senate, Gus. J. Solomon was a Federal judge, and Herbert M. Schwab was chief judge of the Oregon State Court of Appeals.

The Jewish community of Oregon is organized in regard to Jewish service, defense, and educational organizations, headed by the Jewish Welfare Federation with all its affiliates. The executive director (1971) was Morris Stein. The Portland community maintains the Robison Home for Jewish aged and a joint community Hebrew school, the Jewish Education Association. The Jewish Community Center of Portland was built in 1914 by the local B'nai B'rith Lodge (founded 1879) and serves the Jewish and gentile communities.

Bibliography: S. M. Suwol, *Jewish History of Oregon* (1958); J. J. Nodel, *Ties Between* (1959); *The "Oregonian"* (1866). [EM.R.]

PORTNOY, JEKUTHIEL (**Noah; Yuzef;** 1872–1941), one of the pioneers of the *Bund. Portnoy joined a revolutionary circle at the Jewish teachers seminary in Vilna (1888–92). As a teacher in Kovno (Kaunas), he was active among the Jewish workers and in contact with Polish and Lithuanian socialists. Sent to Siberia for revolutionary activities, he managed to escape in 1899 and shortly thereafter joined the central committee of the Bund. He edited its paper, *Arbeter Shtime,* and directed its organizational matters, settling internal differences of the Bund and

Jekuthiel Portnoy opening the celebrations of the 30th anniversary of the founding of the Bund, Warsaw, October 1927. Courtesy Bund Archives of the Jewish Labor Movement, New York.

lending direction to its program. After 1908 he lived permanently in Warsaw. During World War I he worked for cooperation of the Bund with the Polish socialist parties, but was imprisoned by the Germans. After World War I, in independent Poland, he headed the central committee of the Bund, and in 1925 and 1930 was sent as an emissary to the United States. When the Nazis occupied Poland, he succeeded in escaping to the United States and served as head of the U.S. delegation of the Bund of Poland.

Bibliography: J. S. Hertz (ed.), *Doyres Bundistn,* 1 (1956), 68–122. [M.M.]

PORTO, Italian family prominent during the 16th and 17th centuries. Its members were scattered in various Italian towns, notably Mantua, Venice, Verona, and Rome. The family originated in Germany, from the Rafa (Rabe, "raven") family, which settled in the town of Porto in the province of Verona, and from which the noted *Rapoport family was descended. Its members include Abraham Menahem ben Jacob ha-Kohen *Porto, one of the heads of the family. ABRAHAM (d. 1593) was a rabbi of Mantua, and author of *Ammudei ha-Golah* (in manuscript). His sons were Jehiel (1532–1577), a pupil of Meir *Katzenellenbogen of Padua, and Gershon (1538–after 1593), also a scholar of Mantua. Gershon's son, Simḥah, was a pupil of Samuel Judah Katzenellenbogen in Venice, where he worked as a proofreader until 1589. In 1602 he left for the Moravian town Prossnitz (Prostejov), where he published *Kol Simḥah* (1603), a rhymed work on the Sabbath laws. From there he went on to Vienna.

Other members of the family include Menahem Zion (Emanuel) Porto (d. c. 1600), rabbi and mathematician. Born in Trieste, he held rabbinical office in Padua, and wrote a number of works on mathematics and astronomy in Italian, and one in Hebrew entitled *Over la-Soḥer* on various mathematical subjects (Venice, 1627). Zechariah ben Ephraim Mahalalel (d. 1672) lived in Urbino, Rome, and Florence. He was a wealthy philanthropist and many Italian communities benefited from his generosity. He wrote *Asaf ha-Mazkir,* a reference book of sayings and legends of the Talmud (Venice, 1675). Isaac ben David (d. c. 1577) was rabbi in Mantua. Toward the end of his life he was imprisoned, having been slandered by his opponent R. Abraham Jagel Gallico. Ẓemaḥ ben Isaac (d. c. 1666) was appointed rabbi in Mantua in 1637. (See also *Rapoport family.)

Bibliography: E. Carmoly, *Ha-Orevim u-Venei Yonah* (1861), 1–13; A. Berliner, *Hebraeische Grabschriften in Italien* (1881), 10, 26; Mortara, Indice, 51; I. T. Eisenstadt and S. Wiener, *Da'at Kedoshim* (1897–98), 144ff.; S. Simonsohn, *Toledot ha-Yehudim be-Dukkasut Mantovah,* 2 vols. (1962–64), index; A. Yaari, in: KS, 20 (1933–34), 48/50; idem, in: *Meḥkerei Sefer* (1958), 303–6.

[A.D.]

PORTO (Rafa-Rapaport), ABRAHAM MENAHEM BEN JACOB HA-KOHEN (1520–after 1594), one of the important rabbis of Verona. In his youth he studied in Venice where he became acquainted with Elijah *Levita and where he was a proofreader in the printing press of *Bragadini. Porto witnessed the burning of the Talmud in Venice on the 13th and 14th of Marḥeshvan 1553, and appointed these days annually as days of mourning and fasting. In 1555 he published his *Ẓafenat Pane'aḥ,* containing a cypher-code of his own invention. He left Venice not later than 1574 and may have gone to Cremona where he is known to have been in 1574 and where he stayed until at least 1582. From 1584 to 1592 he was rabbi of Verona. The period of his rabbinate in Verona was that of its crowning glory, and the yeshivah which he conducted there became famous. In 1593 he was in Cologne (Germany).

He was the author of *Minḥah Belulah* (Verona, 1594), a commentary on the Pentateuch based upon the Midrashim. It was reprinted together with the text of the Pentateuch (Hamburg, 1795). He compiled similar commentaries on several other books of the Bible and on *Avot* which have never been published, although they have been preserved in manuscript with some of his writings (the Ms. is in Hekhal Shelomo, Jerusalem). Some of his responsa and rulings are scattered in the works of contemporary scholars; additional responsa are extant in manuscript (H. Hirschfeld, *Descriptive Catalogue of the Hebrew Mss. of the Montefiore Library* (1904) nos. 480/1).

Abraham Menahem Porto was among those who forbade the reading of Azariah de *Rossi's work, *Me'or Einayim,* which had been published in Mantua in 1573 (his letter to Menahem Azariah *Fano). However, after the rabbis of Mantua David b. Abraham *Provencal and Judah b. Joseph *Moscato allowed it to be read, he retracted and joined them in permitting this (his letter to Azariah de Rossi). His signature appears on *takkanot* forbidding gambling (1573) and the infringement of moneylending franchises held by fellow-Jews.

Bibliography: E. Carmoly, *Ha-Orevim u-Venei Yonah* (1861), 1, 5–8; J. Reifmann, in: *Ha-Shaḥar,* 3 (1872), 353–76; S. Z. H. Halberstam, in: *Tehillah le-Moshe* dedicated to M. Steinschneider (1896), 1–3 (Heb. part); A. Kahane, *Sifrut ha-Historyah ha-Yisre'elit,* 2 (1923), 252–5; D. Kaufmann, *Gesammelte Schriften* 3 (1915), 86ff; I. T. Eisenstadt and S. Wiener, *Da'at Kedoshim* (1897–98), 144; I. Sonne, in: *Kobez al Jad,* 3 (1940), 147, 169–78; S. Simonsohn, in: KS, 35 (1960), 265.

[T.P./A.D.]

PÔRTO ALEGRE, capital of the State of Rio Grande do Sul, Brazil; population: 617,625 (1960); Jewish population estimated at 12,000 (1969). The first Jews went to Pôrto Alegre at the end of the 19th century, but the first organized congregation was formed only in 1910, when settlers from the Jewish agricultural colonies in other provinces began to drift into the city. In 1915 the first Jewish newspaper to appear in Brazil, *Di Menshhayt,* was published in Pôrto Alegre. As the number of immigrants who settled in Pôrto Alegre increased, cultural, religious, and social institutions were established. German Jews arrived during the 1930s, and after 1956, scores of refugees from Egypt and Hungary, as well as emigrants from Israel joined the community. Located in a region with considerable economic development and large ethnic minorities (Germans, Italians, Poles, etc.), the Jewish community of Pôrto Alegre flourished and developed its institutions. Most of its public buildings and synagogues were rebuilt in the 1960s.

The Federação das Sociedades Israelitas do Rio Grande do Sul was founded in 1950 as an umbrella organization and includes all the groups and institutions of Pôrto Alegre's Jewish community. The most important among these are: the Círculo Social Israelita (founded 1930) — a recreational and cultural club with 2,000 members; the Centro Israelita Pôrto Alegrense (founded 1917) and União Israelita Pôrto Alegrense (founded 1910) which are Ashkenazi religious organizations; and the Centro Hebraico Rio Grandense (founded 1922) and Sociedade Israelita Brasileira de Cultura e Beneficiência (founded 1936), which are the communal organizations of the Sephardim and German Jews respectively. The Cooperativa de Crédito Popular, which emerged as an important financial institution from a small fraternal loan society founded in 1922, provides its 2,000 members with credit and banking services. The community's day school, the Colégio Israelita Brasileiro also founded in 1922, has 1,300 students in kindergarten through high school. A modern country club (founded 1958) and a big Jewish sports club (inaugurated 1966) furnish the community with modern recreational facilities.

Several efforts to publish local newspapers or periodicals were short-lived. However, two radio programs are broadcast for the Jewish community. There are many Jews from Pôrto Alegre who have distinguished themselves in the public life of the city and the country: the first Jewish general of the Brazilian army, first chief of police, a Jewish senator, two professors at the local university, and dozens of renowned physicians, lawyers, and engineers. In the late 1960s there was no rabbi in Pôrto Alegre. [S.Go.]

PORTO-RAFA (Rapaport), MOSES BEN JEHIEL HA-KOHEN (d. 1624), Italian scholar. Moses was a member of the German family Rafa that settled in the town of Porto in the vicinity of Verona and became the progenitors of the renowned *Rapaport family. In 1602 Moses served as rabbi of Badia Polesine in Piedmont. Subsequently he became rabbi of Rovigo. While he was there a great controversy broke out about the validity of its **mikveh.* He was among those, headed by his relative Avtalyon b. Solomon of *Consiglio, who prohibited its use. Moses collected, edited, and published all the rulings of those who took a stringent view in the dispute in a work entitled *Palgei Mayim* (Venice, 1608), appending to it a criticism of the *Mashbit Milḥamot*, which gave all the rulings of those who permitted the use of the *mikveh*. Moses was on friendly terms with Leone *Modena. He died in Venice.

His brother, Abraham Menahem Porto (1569), studied in his youth under members of his family in Cremona and Mantua. He appears to have been one of the rabbis of Verona.

He was the author of *Ḥavvot Ya'ir* (Venice, 1628), giving epigrams and other witty deductions of rabbinic sayings in alphabetic order. He corrected and published the *Minḥah Belulah* (Verona, 1594), a commentary on the Pentateuch by his relative Abraham Menahem b. Jacob Ha-Kohen *Porto (Rafa-Rapaport). The following works by him have remained in manuscript: *Gat Rimmon*, a collection of poems; *Shimmush Avraham*, a commentary on the Pentateuch; and *Ḥasdei David*, a commentary on the Psalms. A few of his responsa have been published in the works of his contemporaries.

Bibliography: Ghirondi-Neppi, 35; E. Carmoly, *Ha-Orevim u-Venei Yonah* (1861), 9–11; I. T. Eisenstadt and S. Wiener, *Da'at Kedoshim* (1897–98), 145; L. Blau (ed.), *Leo Modenas Briefe und Schriftstuecke* (1905), Heb. part, 87f.; A. Yaari, *Meḥkerei Sefer* (1958), 420–9. [A.D.]

PORTO-RICHE, GEORGES DE (1849–1930), French playwright. Born in Bordeaux into an assimilated family of Italian origin, Porto-Riche began his literary career with some collections of poetry: *Prima Verba* (1872), *Pommes d'Eve* (1874), and *Tout n'est pas rose* (1877). After writing two plays in verse—*Le Vertige* (1873) and *Un Drame sous Philippe II* (1875)—he turned his dramatic talent to plays dealing with the psychology of love. The most successful of these witty and well-constructed dramas were *La chance de*

Georges de Porto-Riche, French playwright. Jerusalem, J.N.U.L., Schwadron Collection.

Françoise (1888), *Amoureuse* (1891), *Le passé* (1898), *Le vieil homme* (1911), and *Le marchand d'estampes* (1918). Collected as *Théâtre d'amour* (1928), his plays fill four volumes.

Porto-Riche's view of love was the 17th-century classical concept of a tyrannical and destructive passion. His success was due largely to what was, at the time, a daring novelty: the presentation on the stage of the most intimate problems of people in love. This won him great popularity with many critics as well as with the public, but it also earned biting criticism from some of the more conservative. This, in the case of the extreme reactionaries of the "Action française," often took an anti-Semitic turn.

In 1906 Porto-Riche was appointed director of the Bibliothèque Mazarine. He was elected to the Académie francaise.

Bibliography: E. Sée, *Porto-Riche* (Fr., 1932), includes bibliography; W. Mueller, *Georges de Porto-Riche, 1849–1930* (Fr., 1934). [M.C.]

PORTRAITS OF JEWS. Portraits were known among the Jews in the classical period: Josephus (Ant. 17:6) records that *Alexandra sent portraits of her sons to Mark Antony

Figure 1. Portraits of Daniel da Norsa and his family at the foot of a 15th-century painting of the Madonna executed for the Basilica di Sant' Andrea in Mantua, Italy, which was built on land confiscated from the Norsa family. Courtesy Alinari, Florence.

in order to rouse his sympathy. The Jewish "zoographos" Eudoxios who lived in Rome was presumably a portrait painter. No such portraits have survived, though an extant statue of the classical period has been said to represent *Josephus. In the Middle Ages there are numerous representations of Jews in biblical (especially New Testament) scenes, but none that can be identified with any specific living person. What has been described as the earliest Jewish portrait is the Scharfzandt window of the Church of Our Lady in Munich but it is no more than a vivid representation of a Jewish type. The earliest actual representations of identifiable Jews are presumably the medieval Anglo-Jewish caricatures of *Isaac of Norwich (1233) and of Aaron 'fiz Diaboli' of Colchester (1277). In a late 14th-century Spanish prayer book in the Vatican library (Ms. Vat. ebr. 324) there are a number of crude sketches of various members of the community, similarly caricatures rather than portraits.

Figure 2. Portrait of Leone Modena, from his book, *Riti Ebraici*, Paris, 1637.

The earliest identifiable portraits of Jews in the full sense are those of Daniel da *Norsa and his family at the foot of the painting of the Madonna made for the Basilica di Sant' Andrea in Mantua in 1495, built on land confiscated from him. Somewhat later is the portrait of *Joseph of Rosheim in a contemporary German document. It is somewhat curious that the earliest known specially commissioned portraits of Jews are three medals of the Renaissance period, for the religious prohibition was considered to apply more strictly to plastic art than to a plane surface. Leone *Modena stated that in his day Jews had portraits in their homes, but his own portrait, prefixed to his *Riti Ebraici,* was made as an exercise by a gentile acquaintance.

From about this time portraits of prominent Jews, including rabbis, became commonplace in the northern European Sephardi communties, where presumably the former traditions to which they had become accustomed as *Marranos had become deeply engrained. On occasion the Jews went to the most eminent artists of their time for the purpose: while *Rembrandt's portraits of *Manasseh Ben Israel may have been executed as an act of friendship, there is every reason to believe that his Dr. Bueno was commissioned. In 18th-century England, artists of the caliber of Reynolds and Gainsborough carried out portrait commissions for the wealthy Anglo-Jewish families. Sculptured portraits begin to emerge in the Jewish communities only in the late 18th century. To this day some of the extreme Orthodox object to having their portraits taken even by photography, because of their stern interpretation of the biblical prohibition. On the other hand, portraits of the dead person in high relief are to be found in the Jewish cemetery of Curaçao, and in some parts of the U.S. photographs are incorporated into tombstones. In recent times, eminent Jewish portraitists include, P. de *Laszlo and S. J. *Solomon, and the sculptor Jacob *Epstein.

Bibliography: A. Rubens, *A Jewish Iconography* (1954); *Anglo-Jewish Portraits* (1935); Frankel, in: HJ, 5 (1943) 155–64; Friedman, in: HUCA, 23 pt 2 (1950–51), 433–48; Mayer, Art, index, s.v. *Medals, Portraits.*

[C.R.]

Figure 3. Portrait of Dr. Ephraim Hezekiah Bueno, known as "The Jewish Doctor," by Rembrandt van Rijn, oil on wood. Amsterdam, Rijksmuseum.

Figure 4. Portrait of Dr. Isaac Henrique Sequeira by Gainsborough (1727–1788). Madrid, Prado.

PORT SAID, city N. E. of Cairo on the Mediterranean, at the entrance to the Suez Canal. With the construction of the Port Said harbor in 1856 Jews began to settle there. The Anglo-Jewish traveler S. Samuel found about 20 families (70 souls) in the town in 1879, earning their livelihood as tailors, retail traders, and moneylenders. In 1882 there was a blood libel against the Jews of Port Said, but the local governor protected them. In April 1892 there again was a blood libel which resulted in the death of a Jewish merchant and an attack on the synagogue. Some Jews then left the city. Nevertheless, a census of 1897 showed that the Jewish population had increased to 400 (out of a total of 42,972 inhabitants). In 1901, 1903, and 1930, there were further blood libels. The census of 1907 found 378 Jews in Port Said; the majority were of Aden and Yemenite origin and a minority of Egyptian origin, Ashkenazi and Sephardi Jews. During World War I, the Jewish population temporarily increased. At that time, there were also some Zionist activities in the town. During the 1920s, the community had two synagogues and a school built by the Binyan family of Aden. It closed down in the 1930s. In 1956 the number of Jews in the town was estimated at 300, most of whom were compelled to leave as a result of the Suez Campaign in 1956. There are now no Jews in Port Said.

Bibliography: J. M. Landau, *Ha-Yehudim be-Miẓrayim ba-Me'ah ha-Tesha-Esreh* (1967), 38–41. [H.Y.C.]

PORTSMOUTH, seaport and naval base in Hampshire, S. England. The Jewish community, perhaps the oldest in continuous existence in England outside London, was founded in 1746 and a cemetery was acquired in 1749. Among early settlers were a family of engravers, a jeweler, navy agents, and small tradesmen. In a boat disaster in 1758 11 Jews were drowned, the only survivor being Samuel Emanuel, ancestor of a family later prominent in civic life. A communal split occurred in 1766 over the recognition of the rabbi of the Great Synagogue or the rabbi of the Hambro' Synagogue as spiritual leader. A reconciliation in 1771 led to reunion of the two groups in 1789. In 1780, the original synagogue was reconstructed and was still in use until 1936, when it was replaced by a new building in Southsea, the residential suburb. Portsmouth's prosperity as a naval and garrison town during the Napoleonic Wars attracted large numbers of Jews, but with the decline of the town after 1815 the community also decreased. In 1969 the Jewish population numbered 600 (out of a total of 215,000). The only communal institutions apart from the synagogue were the benevolent institution and a Board of Guardians for the poor.

Bibliography: C. Roth in: JHSET, 13 (1936), 157–87; idem, *Rise of Provincial Jewry* (1950), 94–95; Newman, in: JHSET, 17 (1953), 251–68; JYB. [V.D.L.]

PORTUGAL, southwesternmost country of continental Europe, in the Iberian Peninsula. Jewish settlement in the area began prior to Portugal's emergence as a nation. The existence of a significant Jewish settlement on the peninsula by 300 C.E. is apparent from the edicts of *Elvira which proscribe "taking food with the Jews" and single out the Jewish group in a number of dicta. A tradition among the Sephardi Jews ascribes their arrival in Iberia to Roman times, in the wake of the destruction of the Temple in 70 C.E. and subsequent dispersion toward Europe. James *Finn endeavored to make a case for dating the initial Jewish involvement in the area as early as 900 B.C.E., based on reports of two ancient Hebrew inscriptions, one mentioning *Amaziah, king of Judah, and a second marking the grave of King Solomon's treasurer, *Adoniram.

When Portugal emerged as a distinct national entity under Affonso (Henriques) I (1139–85), a number of wholly Jewish districts existed, including communities in *Lisbon, *Oporto, *Santarém, and *Beja. Affonso employed as his treasurer Yaḥya ibn Ya'ish, thereby initiating the pattern of Portuguese rulers enlisting Jewish talent in the management of affairs of state. Under King Affonso III (1248–79) Portugal attained total independence and fixed its historic geographic boundaries, and during his reign the classic Portuguese model of Jewish communal life emerged. The crown recognized the Jewish community as a distinct legal entity, headed by the royally appointed **arraby mor*. The *arraby mor*, in turn, named seven **dayyanim*, one for each of seven regional centers; Santarém, Oporto, *Moncorvo, *Viseu, *Faro, *Evora, and *Covilhã, each with his own administrative staff to adjudicate both civil and criminal cases. Their decisions were subject to appeal before the *arraby mor*, who visited the district courts annually for this purpose, accompanied by an **av bet din* ("chief justice") and an executive staff. The vast power of the *arraby mor* was balanced by the right of the people to select the local rabbis—who, however, were paid by the crown and required its confirmation—and to elect the *tovei ha-ir* (see *Community, *Elders) who directed the daily functions of the community. In the larger towns Jews generally lived together in a *juderia* (see *Jewish Quarter) such as Oporto's Jews' Hill or Loulé's Jews' Vale.

Portuguese Jewry prospered under these separatist conditions, continuing the attentiveness to learning that marked the peninsula's formative years. The community's autonomy amid officialness was the crucible in which the proud, enduring Portuguese Sephardi heritage was shaped. By the 15th century the Jews were playing a major role in the country's monarchical capitalism, as that economic system has been characterized. The concentration of Jews in Lisbon and other population centers rendered obvious the group's business success and—as a result of their access to royalty—their disproportionate prominence in society. At the same time, Portuguese Jews were fastidious in loyalty to

Places of Jewish settlement in Portugal, 1200–1497. Names in boldface indicate Jewish communities also existing in 1971.

their faith and reciprocated the distant posture assumed by their devout Catholic neighbors, making way for the suspicions that feed on envy. Furthermore, the independence enjoyed by the Jewish community, in the otherwise Christian state, aroused the ire of the clergy. Their efforts to erode Jewish civil rights were resisted by the cultured King Diniz (1279–1325), who retained the *arraby mor* Don Judah as his treasurer and reasserted that the Jews need not pay tithes to the church. In any event the Jews were heavily taxed as the price of remaining unmolested, including a special Jews' tax intended to redeem the "accursed state of the race," and a tax based on the number of cattle and fowl slaughtered by the *shoḥatim*. The unsympathetic Affonso IV (1325–57) increased the direct tax load to bring him an annual state income of about 50,000 livres. He also reinstituted the dormant requirement that Jews wear an identifying yellow *badge, and restricted their freedom to emigrate. The emboldened clergy accused the Jews of spreading the *Black Death in 1350, inciting the populace to action. During the short rule of Pedro I (1357–67)—who employed as his physician the famed Moses *Navarro—the deterioration of the Jewish position was halted. The situation then fluctuated from ruler to ruler until the reign of Affonso V (1438–81), who gave the Jews his conscientious protection, affording them a last peaceful span of existence in Portugal. The general populace was seething with envy and religious hate. In 1449 there occurred a riot against the Jews of Lisbon; many homes were sacked and a number of persons were murdered. Local assemblies in 1451, 1455, 1473, and 1481 demanded that steps be taken to reduce the national prominence of the Jew.

Somehow the Jews of Portugal never considered their predicament as hopeless, and when *Spain expelled its Jews in 1492, some 150,000 fled to nearby Portugal, where both the general and Jewish culture approximated their own (see *Spanish and Portuguese Literature). King John II (1481–95), eager to augment his treasury, approved their admission. Wealthy families were charged 100 cruzados for the right of permanent residence; craftsmen were admitted with an eye to their potential in military production. R. Isaac *Aboab was permitted to settle with a group of 30 important families at Oporto. The vast majority, however, paid eight cruzados per head for the right to remain in Portugal for up to eight months. When this unhappy group found that a dearth of sailings made their scheduled exit impossible, John II proclaimed them automatically his slaves. Children were torn from their parents, 700 youths being shipped to the African island of Saõ Tomé (Saint Thomas) in an unsuccessful scheme to populate this wild territory.

With the accession of Emanuel I the Fortunate (1495–1521), the harsh distinctions between the displaced Spanish and the native Portuguese Jews began to be erased, and hopes for a tranquil period were raised. Instead, Emanuel's reign signaled the end of normative Jewish life in Portugal, for within a year of his accession he contracted a marriage with the Spanish princess Isabella—hoping thereby to bring the entire peninsula under a single monarch—and Spanish royalty made its consent dependent on his ridding Portugal of all Jews. Consenting reluctantly, on Dec. 4, 1496, Emanuel ordered that by November of the following year no Jew or Moor should remain in the country. Forthright action was not taken against the Moors, if only because Christians in Moorish lands would then be subject to reprisals. As the departures proceeded Emanuel reconsidered the loss of the Jewish citizenry and the attendant economic losses. He resolved to keep them in the country by turning the Jews into legal Christians. He tried persuasion and torture, but with little success, and the chief rabbi, Simon *Maimi, died resisting conversion. Accordingly on March 19, 1497, all Jewish minors were forcibly baptized and detained, a move that tended to prevent their parents from attempting to flee. The order then went out for all who were still intent on embarkation to assemble at Lisbon. Some 20,000 gathered there, but instead of being evacuated they were ceremonially baptized and declared equal citizens of the realm. Bewildered, these *Conversos cautiously began to emigrate, prompting Emanuel to respond on April 21, 1499, by withholding the right of emigration from the *New Christians, as this new class was officially designated, but technicalities aside, the Portuguese majority continued to regard them as Jews. In the spring of 1506, over 2,000 New Christians were massacred during a Lisbon riot. If the Conversos had had any thoughts of finding solace in the religion thrust upon them, such riots dissuaded them. Consequently even those who were otherwise weak of spirit tended to cling to their God, with the resultant emergence of *Crypto-Judaism, or Marranoism. While attending church and conducting themselves outwardly as Catholics, in secret they maintained Jewish observances, to whatever extent was possible.

As early as 1516 King Emanuel, suspecting that such a situation existed, proposed to Pope *Leo X that an *Inquisition—on the Spanish model—be authorized to ferret out backsliding New Christians. John III (1521–57) enlisted Enrique *Nuñez, an apostate from the Canary Islands, to mingle with the Marranos and report on their practices. In 1527 Nuñez presented King John with an exposé of Marrano life, appending a list of Crypto-Jews. Popular support for a Portuguese Inquisition surfaced in 1531, when the populace attributed the earthquake of that year to divine retribution for New Christian duplicity. Unable to resist these pressures, Pope Clement VII authorized the Inquisition, with King John's confessor Diogo da Silva as the first inquisitor general. Attempting to counter this, the Marranos dispatched Duarte de *Paz to Rome. Armed with unlimited funds, Paz was to attempt, at the very least, to deny the Inquisition the right to confiscate the property of those condemned, recognizing that this would be an incitement to prosecution. The ensuing diplomatic fray lasted half a century. On April 5, 1533 the Marranos won a suspension of the Inquisition, but on May

Figure 1. Portrait of the *arraby mor*, judicial head of Portuguese Jewry (holding book), in a panel from the painting "Poliptico de San Vincente" attributed to Nuño Gonçalves, 1460. Lisbon, Museu Nacional de Arte Antiga. Photo Oronoz, Lisbon.

23, 1536 it was reauthorized, to be effective three years hence. A first *auto-da-fé took place in Lisbon on Sept. 20, 1540, but in 1544 the Inquisition was again suspended. Finally Emperor *Charles V brought his influence to bear and King John offered the bribe of Viseu's total tax revenue; irrevocable papal consent was given on July 16, 1547. Permanent tribunals were established at Lisbon, Evora, *Coimbra, and in Portugal's Far East outpost *Goa. Ultimately, in 1579, the right to confiscate the culprit's property also accrued to the inquisitors, so that

Figure 2. Decorated page of the *Hispanic Society Bible*, Portugal, late 15th century. New York. Hispanic Society, Ms. B. 241.

every wealthy Portuguese not certified as pure-blooded (**limpieza de sangre*) lived in terror. The Portuguese Inquisition became inspired more by greed than by piety, as Padre Antonio *Vieira charged. Soon the tribunal authorities were able to construct lavish palaces, to proffer large sums to receive condemnatory testimony, and to produce spectacular autos-da-fé, which competed with the bullfights in drawing crowds of tens of thousands. Accused Marranos could escape death by repentantly admitting to Judaizing, but in such an event they would be forced into implicating family and friends, thus providing a spiraling supply of victims. Occasionally even a genuine Christian was martyred for Judaizing, young Don Lope de *Vera y Alarcon (1620–1644) being the most notable example. Crypto-Jews sought precarious safety among the ruling classes and clergy; in time this tendency resulted in a significant percentage of Marrano blood being found within Portugal's ruling circles—as bitterly documented by Mario Saa.

The surest method of evading the Inquisition was to abandon the peninsula, and a constant flow of Conversos escaped—some with daring (see Samuel *Nunez), some with luck—to the communities of the *Marrano Diaspora, where many of them quickly reverted to normative Judaism. Some ex-Marranos, however, such as Spinoza's teacher Juan de *Prado, were not found acceptable by congregational leaders, giving rise to a responsa literature debating the status of the New Christians and ex-Marranos in Jewish law. The leading city of the Portuguese Diaspora was *Amsterdam, with *Salonika ranking first in the Ottoman East, but the former Marranos became ubiquitous in all the Old and New World centers of trade, to the extent that "Portuguese" became synonymous with "Jewish"—much to the consternation of gentile Portuguese travelers. The stream of refugees continued until the end of the inquisitional period. As late as 1795, immigrants to London cited flight from the Inquisition on their aliens' certificates. In 1791 Isaac Lopes Simões fled Lisbon to enter the covenant of Abraham at Bordeaux, France.

The Inquisition was brought to an end during the reign of Joseph Emanuel I (1750–77) through the initiative of Sebastião José de Carvalho ê Mello, Marques de Pombal (1699–1782), who was the power behind the titular monarch. In a series of acts from 1751 to 1774 Pombal deprived the Holy Office of real power, placing it under secular control, and restored the civil rights of the New Christian class, even bullying certified Old Christian families into contracting marriages with New Christians. A last auto-da-fé took place in 1791; on March 31, 1821, the Inquisition was abolished in Portugal. During the nightmare centuries of Portugal's Inquisition, over 40,000 persons were implicated, of whom 30,000 were sentenced at autos-da-fé. A total of 750 of these were staged, at which 29,000 persons were reconciled to the Church, 600 persons burned in effigy, and 1,200 persons burned at the stake. The majority of the victims were accused of Judaizing. The terror that weighed on the Marranos who managed to avoid detection cannot be measured.

Historians writing at the beginning of the 20th century supposed that the last Marranos had by then disappeared. In 1917, however, a mining engineer named Samuel *Schwarz discovered a community of Marranos in the remote northern region near *Belmonte. Apparently they had succeeded in maintaining their identity in the remote mountain areas, marrying among themselves, harboring memories of Jewish observances, being called Jews by their neighbors, and holding to the belief in a single, personal Deity who would redeem His people at the end of days. While Schwarz was publicizing his discovery, a Portuguese hero of Marrano descent, Captain Arturo Carlos de *Barros Basto, openly espoused Judaism and undertook to revitalize the spiritual life of the Marranos. World Jewry took a warm interest in the Barros Basto enterprise, with British Jews taking the lead in a plan to forge a link between the Marranos and the Jewish community that had sprung up in Portugal since the end of the Inquisition. In 1970 Portugal's Jewish population approximated 1,000, apart from the Marrano community which perhaps still numbered several thousand. [A.Li.]

Resettlement. Jewish settlement in Portugal was renewed around 1800: a corner of the British cemetery in Lisbon contains Hebrew tombstones dating from 1804. The first settlers, who held British nationality, had been buried in a separate plot allotted to them in the English cemetery. Later, in March of 1833, a Portuguese nobleman by the name of António de Castro let to Abraham de José Pariente, at an annual rent of 4,000 reis, a plot of land to serve "as a cemetery for the tenant, Abraham de José Pariente, his descendants, and relatives." It was used as a

Figure 3. Cornerstone ceremony for the Kadoorie synagogue of former Marranos in Oporto, 1929.

Figure 4. Synagogue in Ponta Delgada in the Azores, a Portuguese possession. Courtesy Mathilde Bensaude, Oeiras, Portugal.

general Jewish cemetery. By a decree published in 1868, the Jews of Lisbon were permitted to "construct a cemetery for the burial of their coreligionists." Official recognition was not accorded to the Jewish community until 1892, when a decree was published entitling it "to hold religious services, maintain a cemetery for the burial of Jews resident in or in transit through Portugal, to establish funds for the assistance of the poor, and to keep registers of births, deaths, and marriages." After the establishment of the republic by the revolution of Oct. 5, 1910, the government of Portugal approved the community's statute presented to it in 1912. In accordance with the approved statute, the community was authorized to maintain places of worship, a cemetery, and a *ḥevra kaddisha,* to slaughter in accordance with the Jewish law, to keep registers of births, deaths, and marriages, and to establish charity funds. Beginning in the 1920s, cases of conversion to Catholicism were not infrequent and several families were split into Jewish and Catholic branches. However, after 1950, this tendency declined to a great extent. [Re.N.]

Holocaust Period. At the outbreak of World War II, Portugal had an organized Jewish community of about 380 Portuguese nationals, in addition to another 650 Jews, many of whom were refugees from Central Europe, who were granted "resident" status. The Jewish community was headed by Moses *Amzalak, a personal friend and associate of President Salazar. After the fall of France, Portugal adopted a most liberal visa policy under which thousands of refugees, including a large proportion of Jews, were allowed to enter the country as immigrants. This policy, however, excluded those of Russian origin or birth. Starting late in 1940, and particularly from the Spring of 1941, Portuguese immigration policy became increasingly stringent as a result of the limited sailings from Portuguese ports. During the second half of the war, Portugal agreed to grant entry visas as part of various rescue operations, on the condition that its territory be used only for transit purposes. For reasons outside Portugal's control, these plans were never realized. During this period, however, Portugal saved all of its 245 Jewish citizens and those Jews in occupied countries to whom it granted consular protection, forcing the Germans to return part of their confiscated property. Portugal joined the other neutral countries in saving Hungarian Jews (see *Hungary, Holocaust) in late 1944, by granting them her protection. Throughout the war Lisbon served as a base for the operations of Jewish organizations in and beyond the Iberian Peninsula. [H.A.]

Contemporary Period. In 1971 the Jewish community of Portugal consisted of 650 persons, about half of them Sephardim and the others Ashkenazim. Of these, 630 lived in Lisbon, 15 in Oporto, and five in Algarve. Most of the Ashkenazim (mainly of German and Polish origin), with such notable exceptions as Kurt Jacobsohn, the vice-rector and the interim rector of Lisbon University, who settled in Portugal in the late 1920s, took up residence in Portugal after World War II. The majority of the Jews were in the liberal professions, or engaged in business, real estate, construction, and private employment. Several occupied high positions in the academic and medical fields. There were four synagogues in Portugal, one in Lisbon opened in 1902, one in Oporto, built with the assistance of the Portuguese communities in London and Holland and the generous donation of the Kadoorie family, and two private synagogues in Faro, one belonging to Semtob Sequerra and the other to the Amram family. Apart from the Lisbon synagogue, these were seldom frequented. The former community center in Lisbon was used as a prayerhouse by the Ashkenazim. [Re. N.]

Relations with Israel. Diplomatic relations were not established between Portugal and Israel. In 1958, after diplomatic contacts had been made in other European capitals, Israel established a consulate general in Lisbon on the understanding that this step would be followed by the establishment of full diplomatic relations. The expectation did not materialize, however, probably due to Portugal's fear of Arab reactions. In 1959 an agreement was signed between the Bank of Israel and the Bank of Portugal, and trade relations developed in the 1960s. In 1969 Israel's exports to Portugal amounted to $1,542,000, mainly in cotton and diamonds, and imported commodities reached $297,000, mainly copra and wood. In the United Nations, Portugal usually abstained on issues related to Israel or supported the Arab viewpoint. Israel voted against Portugal several times on questions of colonialism. [Shi.A.]

Bibliography: A. Herculano de Carvalho e Araujo, *History of the Origin and Establishment of the Inquisition in Portugal,* tr. by J. C. Branner (1926); I. M. Ford (ed.), *Letters of John III, King of Portugal, 1521–1557* (1931), introd. in Eng., letters in Portuguese; H. V. Livermore, *A History of Portugal* (1947), index s.v. *Jews;* M. A. Cohen, *Samuel Usque's Consolation for the Tribulations of Israel* (1965), introd.; C. R. Boxer, *Four Centuries of Portuguese Expansion, 1415–1825* (1969), 47f. 52; Baron, Social, 13 (1969), 44–158; Graetz, Hist, index; E. N. Adler, in: JQR, 15 (1902/03), 413–39; *The American Sephardi,* 4, no. 1–2 (Autumn 1970); J. Mendes dos Remedios, *Os Judeus em Portugal,* 2 vols. (1895); A. Novinsky and A. Paulo, in: *Commentary* (May 1967), 76–81; M. Kayserling, *Geschichte der Juden in Portugal* (1867); A. Baião, *Episodios dramáticos da inquisação portuguesa,* 2 vols. (1919–24); J. Lucio d'Azevedo, *Historia dos Christaos Novos Portugueses* (1921); S. Schwarz, *Inscrições hebraicas em Portugal* (1923); idem, *Os Cristãos-novos em Portugal no seculo XX* (1925); A. C. de Barros Basto, *Os Judeus no velho Porto* (1929); N. Slouschz, *Ha-Anusim be-Portugal* (1932); E. H. Lindo, *History of the Jews of Spain and Portugal* (1970).

PORTUGALOV, BENJAMIN OSIPOVICH (1835–1896), Russian physician and publicist. He was imprisoned for his activities in the *Narodnaya Volya* movement in 1860 in the fortress of St. Peter and Paul. After his release he qualified as a physician but was arrested again in 1874 and exiled to the Urals. Later he settled in Samara (Kuibyshev). Portugalov devoted a great deal of his time to philanthropic work and to combating drunkenness. He was the first physician in Russia to advocate social medicine. A fanatic assimilationist, Portugalov was opposed to the rituals of **sheḥitah* and *circumcision and even asked the authorities to forbid them. He took an active part in the Jewish-Christian movement initiated by Jews in southern Russia in the 1880s. He considered the pogroms in the 1880s as a social movement against the injustice perpetrated by leading classes. Portugalov was also opposed to Zionism, seeing the solution of the Jewish problem in social religious reform, based on a general humanistic religion free of ritual ceremonies.

Bibliography: E. Tcherikower, in: *Historishe Shriftn,* 3 (1939), 81–82; S. Ginsburg, *Meshumodim in Tsarishn Rusland* (1946), 256.

[ED.]

PORUMBACU (Schwefelberg), VERONICA (1921–), Rumanian poet and novelist. Born in Bucharest, Veronica Porumbacu grew up in an intellectual circle, and studied psychology and sociology. A member of the anti-Fascist underground during World War II, she began her literary career under the postwar Communist regime, first publishing children's books in 1946.

Like many of her subsequent publications, her first collection of verse *Visele Babei Dochia* ("The Dreams of Baba Dochia," 1947) dealt with contemporary political questions. She also wrote lyrical works, notably *Intoarcerea din Cythera* ("Return from Cythera," 1966). Her volumes of poetry include *Generația mea* ("My Generation," 1955), *Lirice* ("Lyrics," 1957), *Diminețele simple* ("Simple Mornings," 1961), *Memoria cuvintelor* ("Recollections of Worlds," 1963), and *Histriana* (1968). Many of her poems have been translated into other languages. In 1968 she published a much-praised autobiographical novel, *Porțile* ("Gates"). Set in the period of the pre-Nazi Antonescu regime, the book tells of her reaction to anti-Semitism and of the exclusion of Jewish children from the Rumanian educational system. Despite her assimilated upbringing, Veronica Porumbacu became aware of her Jewish heritage and was impressed by the traditional loyalties of her ancestors, whom she decribes sympathetically. She has also published translations from Hebrew poetry (N. Alterman, A. Shlonsky, and Y. Amichai) and from English the 19th-century U.S. author E. Dickinson.

Bibliography: G. Călinescu, in: *Națiunea* (1945) no. 1; O. Crohmălniceanu, in: *Contemporanul* (1961), no. 12; P. Georgescu, in: *Viața Romînească* (1964), no. 10; Perpessicius, in: *Gazeta Literară* (Dec. 1, 1966).

[D.L.]

POSEKIM, a Hebrew term for scholars whose intellectual efforts were concentrated on determining the *halakhah* in practice (for whom the word "decisors" is sometimes used) in contrast to those commentators who applied themselves to study for its own sake, and in order to facilitate the understanding of the subject under discussion and who are called *mefarshim* (expositors or commentators). This distinction was already recognized by early authorities who stressed, for instance, that *halakhah* should not be derived from *Rashi's commentary on the Talmud—since Rashi did not introduce into his commentary various ancillary considerations without which no practical decision can be arrived at, except perhaps for those few instances where Rashi explicitly states that the *halakhah* is in accordance with his exposition.

In the early period, especially in Germany, the term *posekim* was identical with the teachers and leaders of the generation in every locality. It included the heads of the yeshivot, *avot battei din,* rabbis and talmudic scholars generally, on condition that their statements were made "by way of *pesak,*" on actual cases which arose. The ruling of the *posek* was binding only upon those subject to his authority, since he laid down the *halakhah* in accordance with local tradition and for the people who accepted his authority. A ruling was never successfully imposed upon communities outside the area of the jurisdiction of the *posek.* The authority of the *posek* during this period depended on his being a competent talmudic scholar, possessing a comprehensive knowledge in every field on his subject, and on the fact that he continued the tradition of his locality and of his teachers transmitted to him while he studied under them. In the course of time this situation gradually changed, as a result of the dissemination of the codes, which afforded easy access to sources necessary for deciding the *halakhah.* From the second half of the 16th century with the beginning of the spread of the Shulḥan Arukh, the character of the works by the *posekim* changed fundamentally. Henceforth the outstanding *posekim* hardly engaged at all in theoretical exposition, and to the extent that they did do so their commentaries were generally forgotten and ignored. The *posek* during this period won general recognition by virtue of the extensive practical experience he accumulated and by gaining the approbation of contemporary scholars, by devoting the whole of his intellectual and physical energy to this goal, and by virtue of "divine aid," the charisma with which he was endowed. For a survey of the **posekim* and their development see *Codification of Law.

Bibliography: C. Tchernowitz, *Toledot ha-Posekim* (1947); Waxman, Literature, 2 (1960²), ch. 4; H. Z. Benedikt, in: KS, 25 (1950), 164, 76; I. Z. Kahana, in: *Sinai,* 34 (1954), 311–24; idem in: *Bar-Ilan Sefer ha-Shanah,* 1 (1963), 270–81; A. Goldrat, in: *Tagim,* 1 (1969), 22–31; Friedberg, Eked, 4 (1956²), nos. 1212–14, 1222–26; Shunami, Bibl. 181–3.

[ED.]

POSENER, GEORGES HENRI (1906–), French Egyptologist. Born and educated in Paris, Posener was a member of the Institut Française d'Archéologie Orientale in Cairo from 1931 to 1935. In 1945 he was named directeur d'études of the Ecole Pratique des Hautes Etudes (4th section). From 1961, he held the chair of Egyptian philology and archaeology of the Collège de France. He was elected president of the Société Française d'Egyptologie in 1963.

Posener's work concentrated on ancient texts. He published for the French Institute in Cairo the *Catalogue des ostraca hiératiques littéraires de Deir el Medineh* (2 vols, 1934–52). His *La première domination Perse en Egypte* (1936) collected the hieroglyphic inscriptions relating to the Persians in Egypt. In *Princes et pays d'Asie et de Nubie* (1940) he studied the hieratic texts written on figurines, believed to have magic properties. *Littérature et politique dans l'Egypte de la XIIe dynastie* (1956) continued his interest in the use of literature in historical studies. He also wrote *De la divinité du pharaon* (1960), but is probably best known for the *Dictionnaire de la civilisation egyptienne* (1959; A Dictionary of Egyptian Civilization, 1962).

[IR.M.]

POSENER (Pozner), SOLOMON (1876–1946), social historian and writer. Born in Minsk, Posener began to write for the Russian-Jewish press under the name of Stellin.

He contributed to the report prepared by *ICA on the economic position of Russian Jewry (1904). He also wrote a study on "Jews in government schools in Russia" for *Novy Voskhod* (printed separately in 1913). In Paris from 1903, he contributed to the French press on conditions in Russia and on Russian Jewry, as well as editing *La Correspondence Russe* and *La Tribune Juive.* He published articles in French on the history of Jews in France in various journals. His most important work is a biography of Adolphe *Cremieux (French, 1933/34; 1939; English, 1940).

[Y.S.]

°**POSIDONIUS** (c. 135–c. 51/50 B.C.E.), Greek philosopher, ethnologist, scientist, and historian from Apamea in Syria, one of *Cicero's teachers. He lived on the island of Rhodes. No book of his survives, though his influence was great. His voluminous writings included a history and ethnology of the Jews, who were treated also in his book on Pompey. The anti-Semitic accusations he retailed in his writing (on Jewish asocial behavior, misanthropy, impiety, inhumane religion and rites) reflected common Hellenistic opinions and attitudes, and later found wide echoes, e.g., in Apion (according to Jos., *Apion,* 2:79). His anti-Semitic remarks can be reconstructed from the more or less close paraphrase of Posidonius by Diodorus Siculus (as quoted in Photius, *Bibliotheca,* 244; 379), including the story that Antiochus Epiphanes found a statue of a bearded man seated on an ass in the Holy of Holies. However, if, as is likely, the respectful appraisal of Moses and his beliefs found in Strabo 16:2, 35ff. also derives from Posidonius, it is probable that the latter did not concur fully in the slanders he related.

Bibliography: Reinach, Textes, 56–59; F. Jacoby, *Fragmente der griechischen Historiker* 2A (text, 1926), 222–317, no. 87; 2A (1926), 154–220 no. 87. [D.E.G.]

POSNANSKI (Poznański), family of scholars. ADOLF POSNANSKI (1854–1920) was a rabbi and a scholar. Born in Lubraniec, Poland, Posnanski served as rabbi at Reichenberg (Liperec) and Pilsen, Bohemia, and from before World War I as teacher of religion in high schools in Vienna.

Samuel Abraham Poznański, rabbi and scholar. Jerusalem, J.N.U.L., Schwadron Collection.

Posnanski's scholarly work was mainly concerned with the messianic idea in Judaism and Christianity; his major contribution in this field was *Schilo, ein Beitrag zur Geschichte der Messiaslehre* (1904). He also published an edition of Profiat *Duran's anti-Christian work, *Kelimat ha-Goyim* (in HḤY, vols. 3–4, 1914–15), and prepared *Abraham b. Ḥiyya's *Megillat ha-Megalleh,* for publication (1924). Posnanski's study of the *Tortosa Disputation also appeared posthumously (in REJ, vols. 74–76, 1922–23); other editions of polemical literature which Posnanski was working on at the time of his death remained unpublished.

SAMUEL ABRAHAM POZNAŃSKI (1864–1921), rabbi, scholar, and bibliographer, was the younger brother of Adolf Posnanski. Born in Lubraniec, Poland, he studied at Berlin University and at the *Lehranstalt (Hochschule) fuer die Wissenschaft des Judentums, where he came under the influence of M. *Steinschneider. In Poland he served as spiritual leader of the Tlomacka "choir" synagogue in Warsaw. There he took great interest in Hebrew education and culture, founding a government-supported training college for Jewish teachers. He was an early and ardent Zionist, and was a delegate to the First Zionist Congress.

Poznański's scholarly interests and achievements were catholic and were greatly helped by his linguistic propensities. His interests covered the history of Hebrew grammar and philology in the Middle Ages, the cognate field of Bible exegesis in the geonic, Spanish, and French periods, the Palestinian and Babylonian *geonim,* the North African communities, Jewish-Arabic literature, and others. [ED.]

As a Karaitologist. Poznański's interest in early geonic literature led him as a young man to the study of Karaite history and literature, first of the geonic period, and subsequently as a whole, from the earliest times to the modern period. The result of this lifelong attention was a vast amount of published material, mostly in the form of papers contributed to learned journals (for the most part the *Jewish Quarterly Review,* the *Revue des Études Juives,* and the *Zeitschrift fuer Hebraeische Bibliographie*), jubilee and memorial volumes, and similar publications. Some of these were also issued separately, as reprints. As a Karaitologist Poznański ranks with Abraham *Harkavy, and indeed surpasses him in the overall range of his interest. His erudition in rabbinic literature, his command of Arabic philology, his extensive use of original manuscript sources, and his accuracy and industry have endowed his works in this field with a value which has not succumbed to the passage of time. They include, among others, studies of *Anan and his immediate successors, of the various writers of the golden age of Karaite learning (10–12th cent.), and of Saadiah's Karaite opponents (from Saadiah's time to the 19th cent.); a pioneering survey of Karaite printing and book production; a genealogy of the eminent Karaite family Firuz; an annotated list of copyists and owners of Karaite manuscripts; and an edition of the *Zekher Ẓaddikim* by the 19th-century Karaite historian Mordecai Sultansky. As a frequent reviewer of Karaitological publications by other scholars, Poznański often enriched his reviews with extensive and valuable corrections and annotations. His long article on Karaism in Hasting's *Encyclopedia of Religion and Ethics* (1915) is still the best available general sketch of Karaite history and literature. For many years Poznański assembled material for his major work in this field, a comprehensive bio-bibliographical dictionary of Karaite writers, of which a file of some 8,000 cards had been prepared by the time of his death. [L.N.]

The extensive bibliography of his works, prepared by his son Edward Poznański (see below) and A. Marx (see bibl.), runs into many hundreds of items. His countless book reviews are an indispensable commentary on modern Jewish scholarship. In 1908 Poznański, together with D. J. Simonsen and A. Freimann, reorganized the *Mekiẓei Nirdamim society and continuously stimulated its activities. His excellent relations with scholars and directors of libraries the world over made his vast knowledge and generous advice and assistance in all scholarly matters invaluable assets for all concerned. A memorial volume in his honor was published in 1927 (repr. 1970). EDWARD (Isaac Jacob) POZNAŃSKI (1901–), the son of Samuel Abraham Poznański, was a bibliographer and lecturer in philosophy at the Hebrew University, of which he was academic secretary from 1947 to 1964. [ED.]

Bibliography: A. POSNANSKI: J. Rosenthal, in: S. Mirsky (ed.), *Ishim u-Demuyyot be-Ḥokhmat Yisrael* (1959), 275ff. S. A. POZNAŃSKI: A. Marx, in: *Festschrift . . . S. Poznański* (1927), 7ff. (= REJ, 74 (1922), 169ff.); idem and E. Poznański, *ibid.,* xxixff. (= REJ, *ibid.,* 184ff.); M. Balaban, *ibid.,* ixff. (separately publ. in Polish as *S. Poznański,* 1922).

POSNER, AKIVA BARUKH (Arthur; 1890–1962), rabbi, scholar, librarian, and bibliographer. Born in Samter (Szamotuly), Poznan, Posner taught at Mainz, Halle, and Vienna, and he served as rabbi at Kiel, Schleswig-Holstein, from 1924 to 1934. He was an outspoken and courageous critic of Nazism. After being forced to leave Germany, he settled in Jerusalem where he worked as a librarian, first of the E.L. Prinz Library of the Mizrachi Teachers' Seminary (until 1954), and then of the central rabbinical library at Heikhal Shelomo in Jerusalem.

While still in Germany, Posner published *Das Buch des Propheten Micha* (1924); *Die Psalmen, das Religionsbuch der Menschheit* (1925); *Prophetisches und Rabbinisches Judentum* (1925); and *Die Freitag-Abendgebete* ("Friday Night Prayers," 1929), with translation and commentary. He later prepared similar editions in Hebrew of the Sanctification of the Moon and Sanctification of the New Moon liturgies (1945, 1948), as well as a *siddur* of domestic prayers (*Le-Veit Yisrael,* 1957). Posner wrote communal histories on Czarnkow (Heb. and Eng., 1957), Gniezno (Heb. and Eng., 1958), and Rawicz (with Eng. abstract, 1962)—all towns in his native Poznan. His literary legacy included 35 such histories in manuscript. Among his bibliographical studies were a biography of the book collector E. L. Prinz (*E. L. Prinz, Ḥayyav ve-Avodato ha-Sifrutit,* 1939); a bibliography of E. M. *Lipschuetz (*E. M. Lipschitz, Reshimah Bibliografit,* 1941); a monograph on the Hebrew printer Monasch of Krotoszyn (in *Aresheth,* 1 (1958), 260–78); and a supplement to the index of the first 75 volumes of the MGWJ, which is extant in manuscript. A memorial brochure, *Zikkaron ba-Sefer la-Rav A.B. Posner,* published by Heikhal Shelomo and edited by A. Piczenik (1964), contains a biography of Posner by A.Z. Givon and a bibliography by Rachel Posner. [ED.]

POSNER, DAVID BEN NAPHTALI (mid-17th cent.), talmudist. David lived in Posen and then in Krotoschin. He was the author of *Yalkut David* (Dyhernfurth, 1691), a collection of Midrashim serving as a kind of supplement to the *Yalkut Shimoni.* The material, edited by his father, Naphtali Hirsch Shpitz, is arranged in the order of the weekly Torah portions. Fuenn holds that David Posner is to be identified with David Tevele Posner, author of the *Sha'arei Ẓiyyon* (Hamburg, 1615).

Bibliography: Steinschneider, Cat Bod, 863; Fuenn, Keneset, 248; Braun, in: MGWJ, 40 (1896), 524f. [Ed.]

POSNER, SOLOMON ZALMAN BEN JOSEPH (c. 1778–1863), rabbi and author. Posner studied under his father, the rabbi of Poznan (Posen), and under Akiva *Eger, Solomon Zalman of Warsaw, and his own uncle, Zeeb Wolf Kalafri. He occupied himself mainly with commerce in the city of Lubraniec and amassed great wealth, but nevertheless found time for extensive study. He wrote many works, some of which have remained in manuscript.

Among his unpublished workers are *Zemir Ariẓim,* against those who regarded the study of Talmud as unnecessary; *Gal-Ed,* 33 (the numerical equivalent of "*Gal*") letters on educational topics addressed to his children when they left home to study in yeshivot; *Tal Yaldut,* a letter to his young children; *Nir Rash,* on the Torah, containing in particular explanations of obscure allusions in Rashi's commentary; and *Dodo Yigalenu,* on the Book of Esther. His *To'ar Penei Shelomo* (1870) is a valuable and unique book describing his own life and the lives of his forebears as far back as the 17th century, and contains many interesting details of the civilization of the period. This book also includes educational directives to his children. His testament is appended to it. It has been claimed that this book is not his own, but that of his son, Moses, who was also rabbi of Poznan and that Solomon gave his name to it. Of his other sons, Aryeh Leib became rabbi of Pniewy, and Elijah, rabbi of Wodzislaw.

Bibliography: *Ha-Meliẓ* (1887), 906. [I.Al.]

POSQUIÈRES, ancient name of the present town of Vauvert, S. France. The earliest record of the presence of Jews in Posquières is from 1121: the dowry that Ermensinde, daughter of the viscount of Béziers and Nîmes, brought to her husband, the lord of Posquières, included a Jew of Béziers, Benjamin. According to *Benjamin of Tudela, there were 40 Jews (or 40 heads of families) in the town in about 1165. It appears that the lords of the town employed the Jews in public office: after an admonition of Pope *Innocent III in 1209, the lord of Posquières solemnly swore not to entrust such offices to Jews. The Jews lived in a quarter known as *Carrière des Juifs.* Wealthy Jews who possessed more than 100 sols paid an annual tenure of one gold florin to the lord. After the expulsion of 1306 the Jews of Posquières migrated to *Provence, *Comtat-Venaissin, and *Perpignan. Of the scholars of the town named by Benjamin of Tudela, the only one known from other sources was the renowned *Abraham b. David, head of the yeshivah of Posquières.

Bibliography: Gross, Gal Jud, 446–50; P. Palgairolle, *Histoire de la ville de Vauvert* (1918); S. Kahn, in: *Mémoires de l'Académie de Nîmes,* 35 (1912), 1–23; G. Scholem, *Ursprung und Anfaenge der Kabbala* (1962), index; I. Twersky, *Rabad of Posquières* (1962).
[B.Bl.]

POSTAN, MICHAEL MOISSEY (1899–), British economic historian. Postan, who was born in Tighina, Bessarabia, began his teaching career in 1927 at University College, London. He was a lecturer on economic history at the London School of Economics from 1931 to 1935, when he became a lecturer at Cambridge University. From 1938 to 1965 he held the professorship of economic history at Cambridge.

Postan's lucid style, searching enquiries and comprehensive analyses of economic problems of the past made him one of the world's leading historians in his field. His major contribution, in addition to many publications, was the coeditorship of the *Cambridge Economic History of Europe* from 1952 onward. [J.O.R.]

°**POSTEL, GUILLAUME** (1510–1581), French orientalist and philosopher, and an outstanding exponent of the Christian *Kabbalah. A self-taught prodigy, Postel was appointed in 1538 professor of mathematics and philology at the College of the Three Languages in Paris and thereafter produced an enormous output of books, tracts, and pamphlets. Four years later he abandoned his post following the first of several mystical visions. His first major work, *De orbis terrae concordia* (1544), made room for Islam in its universal scheme and Postel thereafter exploited rabbinic and kabbalistic literature in support of his pretensions, notably his "immutation" as Elijah and Balaam and as the "Angel-Pope." Postel traveled constantly in search of rare manuscripts and prophetic writings. In Venice he met Elijah *Levita and Daniel *Bomberg, the Christian pioneer of Hebrew printing, whose Jewish publications he was engaged to censor during his second visit to Venice in 1546–49. Here he began his first translation of the *Zohar and published an extraordinary mystical treatise on the significance of the **menorah* ("candelabrum"), first in a Hebrew broadsheet entitled *Or Nerot ha-Menorah* (undated; 1547?) and then in a modified Latin version, *Candelabri typici in Mosis Tabernaculo . . . interpretatio* (1548). A Latin-Hebrew copy made by Conrad *Pellicanus has been preserved in Zurich, and unpublished versions in French and Italian are also extant. During the next few years, Postel's millenarianism reached frenzied heights. He visited Ereẓ Israel (1549–50), accepted the emperor's invitation to teach in Vienna (1554–55), and multiplied his publications in anticipation of the messianic year 1556. In his Hebrew

Illustration of a kabbalistic *menorah* from Guillaume Postel's *Candelabri typici in Mosis Tabernaculo . . . interpretatio,* Venice, 1548. Newton, Mass., Andover Newton Theological School.

Candelabrum, Postel had styled himself *Ish Kefar Sekhanya u-Shemo Eliyyahu Kol-Maskalyah she-Nitgayyer le-Ḥibbato shel Yisrael*... ("A man of Kefar Sekania, named Elijah Kol-Maskalyah, who converted [to Judaism] out of love for Israel..."), which suggests that he had then become some kind of Judeo-Christian (cf. Av. Zar. 27b; and see *Jacob of Kefar Sakhnayya). During his imprisonment by the Inquisition at Ripetta (1555–59), he was said by a Jewish fellow-captive to have prayed in Hebrew. Postel returned to Paris in 1562 and spent the rest of his life in protective custody. However, he continued his voluminous writing and correspondence, and also influenced such younger scholars as G. *Génébrard, A. *Maes, and the French poet Guy *Le Fèvre de la Boderie, through whose agency Postel's approach even penetrated the "Catholic" Antwerp Polyglot Bible printed by Christophe *Plantin (*Biblia Regia*, 1568–72). His published works include many of Jewish interest—grammatical and philological compendia, a guide to the Holy Land (1562), and a Latin version of the *Sefer* **Yeẓirah* (1552), with his own mystical comments. Postel's unpublished Latin translations of the Zohar on Genesis and of other Jewish classics have in recent years been discovered and discussed by François Secret. Long derided as a heretic or madman, Postel has emerged as one of the impressive and influential personalities of the Renaissance.

Bibliography: W. J. Bouwsma, *Concordia Mundi: the Career and Thought of Guillaume Postel* (1957); S. K. Stahlmann, *Guillaume Postel* (Ger., 1956); C. Clair, *Christopher Plantin* (1960), 34–35, 247; I. Zaneh, *Mi-Paulo ha-Revi'i ad Pius ha-Ḥamishi* (1954), 71ff.; F. Secret, *Guillaume Postel (1510–1581) et son Interprétation du Candélabre de Moyse* (1966); idem, in: *Archivio di Filosofia*, 3 (1963), 91–118; idem, *Kabbalistes Chrétiens de la Renaissance* (1964), 171ff.; idem, in: REJ, 124 (1965) 174–6; Baron, Social², 13 (1969), 177–8, 394, 398, 403–4; G. E. Silverman, in: JC (Jan. 8, 1960); idem, in: JC (Oct. 23, 1964).

[G.E.S.]

POTIPHAR (Heb. פּוֹטִיפַר), Egyptian royal official who purchased *Joseph (Gen. 37:36; 39:1). His wife attempted unsuccessfully to seduce Joseph and then brought false charges against him, as a result of which Potiphar had him incarcerated. The name reflects an underlying Egyptian prototype *Pa-diu-pa-Re*, "The one whom the sun god Re has given." The Egyptian name occurs on a stele from the Late Period (c. 1087–664 B.C.E.), during which time the near variant *pa-di* followed by the name of a god is most commonly found. Potiphar's titles, "servant of Pharaoh" and "chief [or "master"] of the cooks," while not Egyptian in themselves, may well be Hebrew translations of two Egyptian titles. The former could have been a general term for almost any servant, official, or courtier, and the latter appears to be a translation of the Egyptian *wpdw nsw* or *wbꜣ nsw* ("butler/cook of the king"). In any event, the title did not imply that its bearer was a lowly servant, but rather a very high official. It first comes to prominence very late in the Twentieth Dynasty, and its bearers are attested as leading military expeditions, heading royal commissions, and exercising high administrative functions. Both Potiphar's name and his title strongly suggest that the writing down of the Joseph story should be dated no earlier than the later Twentieth Dynasty (and possibly even to the Twenty-First to Twenty-Second dynasties), a suggestion substantially supported by other Egyptian elements occurring in it, particularly the Egyptian names. Further support for this dating is given by the parallel between the attempted seduction of Joseph by Potiphar's wife and the opening portion of an Egyptian literary text, "The Tale of the Two Brothers" which is dated, on paleographic grounds, to about 1225 B.C.E. [Al.R.S.]

In the Aggadah. Potiphar is regarded as identical with *Poti-Phera (Gen. 41:45), indicating different aspects of his idola-

Potiphar's wife tempting Joseph (upper register), an illumination from the sixth-century Byzantine *Vienna Genesis*. Vienna, Austrian National Library, Ms. Vindobon, Theol. Gr. 31, p. 31.

trous behavior. "Potiphar" refers to his practice of rearing bullocks, *mefattem parim*, for idolatrous sacrifices; and "Poti-Phera" to his habit of indecently exposing himself *(pore'a)* in honor of his gods. He purchased Joseph in order to perform sodomy with him, but was castrated by God (or by the angel Gabriel; Sot. 13b.), in order to prevent him fulfilling his desire and for this reason is called the "eunuch of Pharaoh" (Gen. 37:36). From the fact that the light-skinned Joseph was offered for sale by the negroid Midianites, he realized that Joseph had been kidnapped. The conflicting scriptural account of the purchase indicates that Potiphar insisted that the Midianites prove prior purchase, in order that he should not be party to a theft (Gen. R. 86:3). Two of Potiphar's actions are favorably commented on. He saw that "the Lord was with [Joseph]" (Gen. 39:3), although he personally was a sun worshiper. Secondly, he was extremely skeptical of his wife's account of Joseph's attempted seduction; had he believed it he would have put Joseph to death instead of imprisoning him. He apologized to Joseph for his action, explaining that his purpose was to prevent a stigma upon his children (Gen. R. 87:9). [S.A.C.]

In Islam. Qitfīr (also Qutayfar) of Muslim legend is the biblical Potiphar, who bought Joseph from the Midianites or the Ishmaelites (Gen. 37:36; 39:1). Although his name is not mentioned in the tale of Joseph in the Koran, there is no doubt as to his identity, in spite of the error in the first letter of the source, which is due to the Arabic script. Tabarī calls him Aṭfīr. Thaʿlabī counts Qitfīr among the three valiant ("afras"): al-ʿAzīz, i.e., Qiṭfīr, for his defense of Joseph; the woman who brought Moses to her father; and the caliph Abu-Bakr, when he appointed Omar.

[H.Z.H.]

Bibliography: Janssen, in: *Jaarbericht van het Vooraziatisch-Egyptisch Gezelschap "Ex Oriente Lux,"* 14 (1955–56), 67–68; J. Vergote, *Joseph en Egypte* (1959). In the Aggadah: Ginzberg, Legends, 2 (1946), 13, 38, 56–58; 5 (1947), 338–39, 341, 369; I. Ḥasida, *Ishei ha-Tanakh* (1964), 360. In Islam: *Ta'rikh*, 1 (1357 A.H.), 236–7; Thaʿlabī, *Qiṣaṣ* (1356 A.H.), 98–99 and passim in the story of *Yūsuf*; Kisāʾī, *Qiṣaṣ* (1356 A.H.), 161–2 (Quṭayfar).

POTI-PHERA (Heb. פּוֹטִי פֶרַע), father-in-law of *Joseph. According to Genesis 41:45, 50, and 46:20, Joseph was married to *Asenath the daughter of Poti-Phera, "the priest of On." Since On, the city of *Heliopolis, was the center of the Egyptian solar cult, the "priest of On" could hardly have been any other than the high priest of the sun god Re. The name Poti-Phera contains the same underlying elements as that of Joseph's former master, *Potiphar, but in a transcription more fully and more accurately reflecting the original Egyptian form. [Al.R.S.]

POTOCKI, VALENTINE (Abraham ben Abraham; d. 1749), Polish count martyred as a proselyte. According to legend, Potocki, a gifted scion of the celebrated Potocki family, while studying in Paris became friendly with

Zaremba, another young Polish aristocrat. Once, while in a tavern, they noticed the owner, an old Jew, immersed in the study of the Talmud, and expressed a desire to be instructed in the principles of Judaism. The two vowed that they would become Jews if convinced of the error of Christianity. Zaremba married and forgot both his vow and his friend. Potocki, however, after spending some time at the papal academy in Rome, went to Amsterdam and became a Jew. When Zaremba heard the report, which had spread throughout Lithuania, of Potocki's disappearance from Rome, he recalled his vow, and, taking his family with him to Amsterdam, also became a Jew there, and subsequently settled in Ereẓ Israel. Potocki went to Lithuania and settled as a Jew in *Ilya, near Vilna.

Once Potocki scolded a boy for disturbing the prayers in synagogue. The boy's father, a coarse tailor, took umbrage and reported the existence of the proselyte to the authorities, thus leading to his arrest. Potocki was put on trial, and despite the pleas of fellow aristocrats refused to recant. On the second day of Shavuot, 5509 (1749), he was burned at the stake at the foot of the fortress of Vilna, on his lips the prayer, "Blessed art Thou, O Lord, . . . who sanctifiest Thy name before multitudes." A local Jew, Eliezer Ziskes, pretending to be a Christian, succeeded through bribery in collecting some of the ashes and a finger from the corpse, and these were eventually buried in the Jewish cemetery. From the soil over the grave of Potocki, who was called by them the *Ger Ẓedek* ("the righteous proselyte"), there grew a big tree which drew vast pilgrimages of Jews. The grave was demolished by Polish vandals. The first to publish the story of the *Ger Ẓedek* was the Polish writer J. Kraszewski in 1841. He claimed to have found it in a Hebrew manuscript. Later it was published by I. M. *Dick in Hebrew (1862) and in Yiddish (n.d.) under the title *Gerei ha-Ẓedek* (see *YIVO-Bleter,* 1 (1931), 331–3). So far no historical evidence for the story has been discovered, although it is generally believed to have been true. The story served as a theme for a drama in Yiddish, called *Dukus* ("Prince"), by Alter *Kacyzne and for some novels. The Jews of Vilna celebrated the anniversary of Potocki's death by reciting the *Kaddish* and by making pilgrimages to his purported grave on the Ninth of Av and on the High Holy Days.

Bibliography: I. Cohen, *Vilna* (1943), 73–74, 416, 484–6; M. Balaban, in: *Nayer Haynt* (1925), nos. 68, 80, 81, 94, 99, 113, 119, 134; *Yevreyskaya Biblioteka,* 3 (1873), 229–37; A. Litvin, *Yidishe Neshomes,* 1 (1916), 1–8; *Gerei ha-Ẓedek* (Vilna, 1862); *Gerei Ẓedek* (Berlin, 1921). [A.Cy.]

POTOFSKY, JACOB SAMUEL (1894–), U.S. labor leader. Potofsky, who was born in the Ukraine, went to Chicago in 1908. His trade union career began almost immediately. From 1916 to 1946 he held a succession of important posts in the Amalgamated Clothing Workers Union and during these years worked closely with union leader Sidney *Hillman. Upon Hillman's death in 1946, Potofsky was elected as the president of the union and continued the major programs developed under Hillman's leadership. Thus, the Amalgamated Clothing Workers continued the policy of avoiding strikes and substituting arbitration wherever possible, a policy over which it clashed with such militant labor unions as John L. Lewis' United Mine Workers. It expanded its insurance programs, increased the number of its group health centers, maintained two banks, and led in sponsoring cooperative housing. Potofsky headed the United Housing Foundation, a combine of his and other trade unions and organizations, which erected large cooperative housing developments.

Under Potofsky's leadership, the Amalgamated continued to play an active political role in national, state, and municipal elections, normally in support of the candidates of the Democratic Party. As a member of the CIO Political Action Committee after 1947 and a vice-president of the AFL-CIO after 1955, as well as a leading figure in New York State's Liberal Party, he was one of the prominent, most influential U.S. labor leaders. Potofsky was a supporter of the State of Israel, and the Amalgamated has established a close relationship with the Histadrut. He was also a delegate to many international labor conferences. A vigorous opponent of all forms of prejudice, Potofsky was closely associated with the efforts of the American Jewish Committee and the Anti-Defamation League of B'nai B'rith. He served on a number of public bodies, including the New York Temporary State Commission on Economic Expansion (1959–1960) and the New York City Temporary Commission on City Finances (1965). In both cases, he dissented freely from recommendations that seemed to compromise the interests of wage earners.

Jacob Samuel Potofsky, U.S. labor leader. From M. U. Schappes, *A Pictorial History of the Jews in the United States,* New York, 1958.

Bibliography: Finkelstein (ed.), *American Spiritual Autobiographies, Fifteen Self-portraits* (1948), 226–242. [I.Y.]

POTTERY. Pottery appears for the first time in the Neolithic period, toward the end of the sixth millennium B.C.E. For two reasons, it serves as a major tool for the study of the material culture of ancient man: first because of its extensive use in everyday life and second because of its durability; for although the vessels break easily, the material survives as potsherds. Pottery is of great value for acquiring the knowledge of the technological progress of various periods, the trends in the development of early plastic art, and international cultural and commercial relations which form the basis of the comparative chronology of different cultures in the Ancient Near East. On the basis of stratigraphic finds at archaeological excavations, pottery is seen to have undergone changes in different periods as well as in different phases of the same period—changes in form, decoration, technique of working the clay, and firing. As a result, pottery serves as a major index of the relative chronological framework of a culture. For cultures and periods containing few or no written remains, which are the primary source of absolute chronology, the relative chronology constructed on pottery sequence serves as a substitute. Once the absolute date of a potsherd is established, the stratum in which it was found can be dated, and thus it also becomes an aid in fixing the absolute chronology.

POTTERY MANUFACTURE

The clay from which pottery is produced is an aluminum silicate mixed with various additions such as iron oxides, alkalies, quartz, and lime. Two kinds of clay have been differentiated: clean clay, of pure aluminum silicate, which is not found in Ereẓ Israel, and a rich clay, consisting of aluminum silicate mixed with iron ozides, carbon compounds, etc. The material was prepared for use by sifting and removing foreign matter, mixing it with water and levigating it. If the clay was too rich and not sufficiently plastic, it was tempered by the addition of substances such as sand and quartz grit. The wet sifted clay was then wedged by hand or treaded; after it was well mixed it was ready for shaping. The earliest pottery was handmade. In the Neolithic period, pottery was made by joining together coils of clay, smoothing the junction line by hand. The pottery was shaped on a base or stand of wood, stone, or matting. A technical innovation was shaping pottery from a ball of clay. In the Chalcolithic and Early Bronze periods primitive potter's wheels consisting of a turning board (tournette) were used. Examples of the next stage in the development of the potter's wheel have been found in excavations in Palestine. It consists of two horizontal stone disks placed one on top of the other, the lower one with a conical depression and the upper with a conical projection which could be turned by hand. Several types of pottery were thrown on the wheel in the Early Bronze Age but it was used extensively only in the Middle Bronze Age. After the pot was shaped it was removed from its stand and set aside to dry until its water content was not more than 15%. The pot was then of a leather hard consistency and handles, base, spout, projecting decorations, etc. were applied and various types of ornamentation were added: slips and burnishing, paint, incisions, reliefs, and impressions. When the pot was completely fashioned it was dried a second time until it retained only about 3% of its water content. Afterward it was fired in an open or closed kiln at a temperature of 450°–950° C. The best wares were produced at the highest temperatures. The earliest pottery was fired in open pits, in which combustible material was laid over the pottery. At a later stage the pottery was separated from the fuel by a perforated clay partition built above the fuel compartment. With the invention of the closed kiln it was possible to use an oxidizing fire, which produced pottery of a red color, or a reducing fire, without oxygen, which turned the pottery black.

NEOLITHIC PERIOD

The pottery of the Neolithic period is handmade, coarse, and badly fired. The pottery types include bowls and storage jars decorated with a red-burnished slip or painted triangular and zigzag lines, and with incised and painted herringbone designs. The main finds of this period come from the Jordan Valley, Sha'ar ha-Golan, Jericho, etc.

CHALCOLITHIC PERIOD (FOURTH MILLENNIUM B.C.E.)

In the Chalcolithic period several new forms are added to the pottery repertoire of the previous period. The pottery is handmade and decorated with a rope ornament and occasionally painted. Tiny lug handles are characteristic of the period, and the shapes include cornets, V-shaped bowls, goblets, jugs, and kraters. Mat impressions are found on the bases of the storage jars. A bird-shaped pot with a lug handle at each end has been named "churn" since it apparently served for making butter. The largest assortment of Chalcolithic pottery was found in the Ghasulian and Beer-Sheba cultures. At the end of this period the gray burnished work appears.

EARLY BRONZE AGE (THIRD MILLENNIUM B.C.E.)

The Early Bronze Age may be subdivided into three or four secondary phases: (1) Early Bronze I—the typical pottery of the period is gray burnished ware, band-slip (grain-wash) ware, and burnished red-slip ware. (2) Early Bronze II—the most distinctive pottery type is the so-called "Abydos (Egyptian) ware," a group of pitchers and storage jars with burnished red-slips on the lower half and triangles and dots painted brown-black on the upper half. This pottery is named after the site where it was first found—the royal tombs of the First Dynasty at Abydos in Upper Egypt. It is of great value for correlating the chronology of Egypt and Palestine. Another important pottery group consists of storage jars with two loop handles and surfaces decorated with pattern combing. (3) Early Bronze III—the characteristic pottery of this phase is called Khirbat Karak ware (named after Bet Yeraḥ (Khirbat Karak) where it was first found). The pottery types include kraters, bowls, pitchers, and stands. The ware is made of a poor-quality clay and is covered throughout with a highly burnished slip. Occasionally it has a red slip all over but often the rim and interior are red and the exterior is black. The decoration consists of incised lines or groups of lines in relief. This ware apparently originated in eastern Anatolia. (4) Early Bronze IV—an additional phase, probably a continuation of the ceramic tradition of the previous period.

MIDDLE BRONZE AGE (c. 2000–1550 B.C.E.)

Middle Bronze I. The Middle Bronze I period constitutes a transitional stage between the Early Bronze Age and the Middle Bronze II period. This culture was apparently introduced by invading nomadic tribes who overran and destroyed the Early Bronze Age culture. Their material remains have been discovered mainly in tombs. The pottery of the period is globular or cylindrical in shape, with wide flat bases, and lacks shoulders and handles. The handles which do occur—enveloped ledge handles and lug handles between the neck and the body—are apparently a continuation of the Early Bronze ceramic tradition. The body of this type of vessel is handmade while the neck, which flares outward, is formed on the wheel; the line where the two are joined together is decorated with combing or with single incised grooves. A group by itself is an assortment from the Megiddo tombs, which consists of "teapots" and goblets made on the wheel of black clay decorated with yellow bands and also jugs with red slips. There are no distinctive cooking pots; hole-mouth jars were apparently used for cooking. The typical lamp of the period is a small bowl with four pinched corners.

Middle Bronze II (Patriarchal Period). With the reestablishment of an urban civilization in Palestine based on a sedentary population, a significant change occurred in the material culture, which is evident also in its pottery. All the pottery is now produced on the wheel, which allowed for great artistic development. The period is subdivided generally into Middle Bronze IIA (the pre-Hyksos phase) and Middle Bronze IIB (the period of Hyksos rule in Palestine).

MIDDLE BRONZE IIA. In the Middle Bronze IIA period a red slip burnished with a shell appears on many vessels such as small and closed carinated bowls with disk bases (imitations of metal prototypes); open bowls with flat or disk bases; jugs and juglets with double or triple handles, often set on the shoulder, and dipper juglets. The storage jars are elliptical with a flattened base and often have two loop handles in the center of the body. The cooking pot has straight sides with a thumb-indented projecting band surrounding the body and some are perforated above the band. An interesting group are the storage jars, jugs, and juglets decorated on the upper part of the body with black and red bands, triangles, or circles on a white slip. This ware is similar in ornamentation to that found in the Khabur region and in Byblos.

MIDDLE BRONZE IIB. The red burnished slip ceases to be dominant in the Middle Bronze IIB period and many vessels are undecorated. The technique of manufacture is highly developed and many vessels are produced with thin walls and complicated shapes, such as open carinated bowls with disk or trumpet bases, made of a well-fired, levigated clay. The storage jars have elongated elliptical bodies with two to four loop handles. A special group consists of pear-shaped (pyriform) juglets with a button base and red, brown, or black burnished slips. In the final phase of the period, the characteristic juglet is cylindrical with a flat base. The lamps are small pinched bowls with one wick hole. The cooking pots are shallow with rounded bases and rounded flaring rims. An unusual group of pyriform juglets are known as Tell al-Yahūdiyya ware—named after the site where they were first found in the Nile Delta. They are attributed to the beginning of the Middle Bronze IIB period. The juglets have black, gray, or red burnished slips and a white puncture-filled decoration on the surface made with a pointed tool.

LATE BRONZE AGE (c. 1550–1200 B.C.E.)

The Late Bronze Age extends from the conquest of Palestine by the first pharaohs of the 18th Dynasty to the Israelite Conquest. Palestine in this period was under Egyptian rule, and its culture was influenced both by Egypt as well as by extensive trade connections with the Aegean and East Mediterranean civilizations. It is possible to subdivide the period into three phases (according to Egyptian chronology): Late Bronze I (c. 1550–1400 B.C.E.), the beginning of the 18th Dynasty; Late Bronze IIA (c. 1400–1300 B.C.E), mainly the Tell el-Amarna period; Late Bronze IIB (c. 1300–1200 B.C.E.), 19th Dynasty.

Late Bronze I. The pottery types and technique of manufacture of the Middle Bronze IIB period persist partly in the Late Bronze I period. The pottery repertoire includes carinated bowls with ring bases or high ring bases; kraters with two loop handles and a ring base, often with a rope decoration as in the previous period; storage jars with elongated bodies, rounded bases, and flaring rims. The ceramic tradition of the Middle Bronze IIB period is also seen in the jugs, juglets, cooking pots, and lamps. Two new groups of ware appear in this period: pilgrim flasks and the so-called "biconical" vessels. The latter have one loop handle. The upper part is decorated with metopes painted red, black, or brown. A new class of vessels first appearing in the transition period between the Middle and Late Bronze Age and continuing into the Late Bronze I is the Bichrome Ware. Made of finely levigated and well-fired clay it is slipped and burnished. The group includes jugs, kraters, and bowls decorated with metopes formed by bands painted red and black. The metopes contain animal decoration—birds, fishes, oxen—and geometric patterns. The character of the ware, which contains a number of unique forms, the decoration, and the uniform method of production indicate that this pottery may have been created by a group of artists in a single center, possibly Tell al-ʿAjūl, south of Gaza.

Late Bronze II. In the Late Bronze II period the previous pottery tradition continues on the whole but shows a certain degeneration in form and quality. The workmanship of the carinated bowls is cruder. The bowls are mainly simple flat vessels with flat or disk bases. The storage jar now shows a sharp shoulder and thickened button base (this type of storage jar was exported from Ereẓ Israel and has been found, together with imitations, in countries in the Aegean Sea and Egypt). The typical jug has a prominent neck with the handle from the rim to the shoulder, and the most common juglet is a dipper juglet generally with trefoil mouth. A new style of painted pottery develops in this period. The ornamented ware—biconical vessels, jugs, kraters—are painted in a single color, red, black, or brown, and a typical decoration has two gazelles facing each other with a palm tree between them. This style degenerates in the second half of the period, Late Bronze IIB, and becomes more schematic and cruder. The pilgrim flasks are flattened and generally decorated with painted concentric circles. In the Late Bronze IIA the neck is attached to the handles of the flask like a flower among leaves while in the second half of the period the flasks are lentoid shaped and the attachment of the neck to the handles is effaced. The lamps have an enlongated sharply pinched rim; the cooking pots are shallow with a rounded base and have an ax rim and no handles

There is an abundance of imported pottery in this period, mostly of Mycenean and Cypriot origin. All the Cypriot pottery occurs in Palestine parallel with its appearance in Cyprus. The most distinctive feature of this pottery is the technique of manufacture—it is all handmade and the handles are inserted inside the body of the vessels. This pottery falls into two main groups—White Slip Ware, which includes the "milk bowls, " half-globular bowls with wishbone handles and a white-slip and ladder decoration painted brown or black. The second type is called Base Ring Ware and is characterized by a high ring base. This ware is made of well-fired clay and has a metallic ring when struck; it is covered with a reddish brown slip. Its most common types are bowls with wishbone handles and jugs with high tilted necks called *bilbil.* Groups of Monochrome Ware are also found in Palestine as well as the knife-pared type—usually dipper juglets—and other groups. The bulk of the Mycenean pottery appears in Late Bronze II. It is wheel-made of a light-colored, finely levigated clay, and well fired. The vessels are covered with a light slip and painted with bands of geometric patterns and floral and animal motifs. Aside from a number of shards and a cup decorated with an ivy-leaf design which are attributed to the Late Bronze I (Mycenaean II), the entire assortment belongs to the Mycenaean IIIA–B period. The vessels include cups, pear-shaped amphoriskoi, stirrup-jars, pilgrim flasks, juglets, bowls, pyxides, etc. A small amount of pottery imported from Syria and Egypt is also found in this period.

IRON AGE (c. 1200–587/6 B.C.E.)

The Iron or Israelite period extends from the Conquest and Settlement of Palestine by the Israelite tribes to the destruction of the Kingdom of Judah in 587/6 B.C.E. The history of this period encompasses many phases—the periods of Settlement, Judges, United Monarchy, and the Kingdoms of Israel and Judah. Several archaeological divisions have been proposed for this period; W. F. Albright's division is still generally accepted and will be followed here: Iron I (1200–925 B.C.E.), from the settlement to the breakup of the Monarchy; Iron II (925–587/6), from the divided kingdoms to the destruction of Jerusalem.

Iron I. In the areas not settled by the Israelites, the Late Bronze pottery tradition seems to continue in the first phase of the period. At the same time a new type of pottery appeared in the areas of Israelite settlement which is cruder and more primitive—the pottery of the Settlement period. The pottery types which continue the Late Bronze tradition include kraters with two loop handles and painted metope decoration, cooking pots which continue the ax-shaped rim and are without handles, lentoid flasks which are decorated with painted concentric circles, and lamps. The pottery attributed to the area of Israelite settlement, mostly coarse in shape and carelessly made, includes simple, crude bowls, storage jars mostly with a collar rim, many-handled kraters (up to eight) with a rope or incised decoration. The cooking pot shows numerous variations of the ax-shaped rim. During this period there also appear carinated bowls, especially in the south of the country, often with a pair of degenerated horizontal handles. Toward the end of the period new pottery features develop—two loop handles are added to the cooking pot which also has a ridge beneath the rim on the outside; tiny juglets appear with a black or red burnished slip; red-slipped vessels are also common with irregular hand burnishing which is the hallmark of the period. A very distinctive pottery assortment occurs in the 12th–11th centuries B.C.E., called Philistine Ware; it is found mainly in the area inhabited by the Philistines. The shapes and decorative motifs of the pottery are derived from the Mycenean pottery tradition, mainly Mycenean IIIC 1. The typical Philistine shapes include kraters with two horizontal loop handles; stirrup jars; jugs with long narrow necks, loop handles, and strainer spouts, which are known as "beer jugs"; long-necked jugs influenced by Egyptian pottery; elongated pyxides; and horn-shaped vessels. Some vessels are covered with a whitewash on which metopes are painted in red and black and ornamented with geometric designs. With the assimilation of the Philistines into the material culture of Palestine in the late 11th century B.C.E., the typical animal motifs become debased and their pottery is no longer differentiated from the Israelite pottery of the period.

Iron II. Although many differences are found in the pottery of the north and south of the country in various periods, a sharper differentiation occurs with the division of the Monarchy. In Judah the red-slip and wheel-burnished vessels are most common; the bowls are carinated with enveloped rims toward the end of the period; the kraters have from two to four handles, are covered with a red slip, and are wheel-burnished on the inside, and on the rim of the outside; the rims of the cooking pots are ridged on the outside, and toward the end of the period a special type of cooking pot with a high ridged rim appears; the typical storage jar has four ridged loop handles, often stamped with *la-melekh* ("of the king") seal impressions, an elliptical body, and a rounded base; the hole-mouth jars have a round bottom and a wide enveloped or ridged rim; the jugs have bulging bodies and thick necks; at the end of the period the lamps have high bases. In Israel not only the red-slip burnished ware is dominant but red- and black-slip pottery is also very common. The typical storage jar has an elongated globular body, prominent shoulder, and pointed base; bowls and kraters are often decorated with bar handles under the rim. A distinctive northern group is known as Samaria Ware, appearing in two groups—thick-walled and thin-walled ware. This pottery is characterized by a very high standard of workmanship. The walls of the thin ware are of eggshell thinness; it is slipped and burnished throughout in red or in alternating concentric circles of red and yellow. The thick ware, made of a creamy clay, has thick walls and either ring, high ring, or stepped bases. The bowls are covered with a red, yellow, or black burnished slip.The pottery common to both Israel and Judah includes water decanters, spouted jugs, carinated bowls, dipper juglets, etc. Several types of imported pottery also occur in this period—the most prominent is known as Cypro-Phoenician Ware which first appears in Palestine toward the end of the Iron I period and continues until the eighth century B.C.E. This pottery includes bowls with two degenerated horizontal handles and juglets with a flat base and one or two handles. The vessels are decorated with black stripes and concentric circles on a lustrous red slip ("Black on Red"). Some imports from Assyria are also found.

PERSIAN PERIOD (586–330 B.C.E.)

This period is identical with the post-Exilic period, and covers the half century of Babylonian rule after the destruction of the Temple as well as the subsequent two centuries of Persian rule. The pottery in this period deteriorates and the clay and firing are of inferior quality. In addition to degenerated pottery types which continue from the pre-Exilic period, vessels are also found which are common to the entire Near East in this period. These include coarse bowls with a high ring base and ribbed sides; storage jars with an elongated stump base and two loop handles rising above the shoulders; carrot-shaped juglets; storage jars with two deformed loop handles, elongated pointed base, straight shoulders, and slightly projecting rim. The lamps have flat bases with one elongated wick hole and a wide rim around the bowl. A number of pottery types imported from Greece are found in Palestine.

HELLENISTIC PERIOD (330–63 B.C.E.)

Palestine in the Hellenistic period was for most of the time part of an empire and under its cultural influence. The local pottery made for ordinary domestic use was on the whole coarse and clumsy, but two groups of imported ware are found: fine luxury ware and amphorae for storing imported goods, especially wine. The most characteristic of the local ware are bowls with inverted or outward flaring rims and ring or flat bases; spindle-shaped juglets; cooking pots with two handles and a low erect neck which are reminiscent of the Iron Age pots. There is also a group of open pinched lamps with one wick hole. Both classes of imported ware are widely distributed in this period, the most widespread being the Rhodian wine amphora. The luxury ware included Megarian bowls which were cast in molds; various types of black-glazed bowls ("fish plates") with impressed or roulette decoration. At the end of the period appears the terra sigillata ware—fine red-glazed pottery with impressed and roulette decoration.

ROMAN PERIOD (63 B.C.E.–325 C.E.)

Of the pottery of the Roman period, only the Herodian phase may be connected with the pottery of the biblical period. The typical local pottery of the Herodian period includes pilgrim flasks with twisted handles; bottles with high necks and thick bodies; juglets with flaring rims; closed lamps cast in molds with flaring nozzles. The cooking pots follow the tradition of the previous period. An increasingly prominent feature is the ribbing of the surface of vessels, mostly on large jars but also on small pots, such as cooking pots. Of the imported ware the most common type is the terra sigillata ware, mainly platters and flat bowls with ring bases; they are covered with a red glaze and have a roulette and impressed decoration. Both eastern and western sigillata appear in Palestine. The western, Arretine style (30 B.C.E–30 C.E.) is outstanding in workmanship and finish. Nabatean Ware also appears in this period—eggshell-thin bowls decorated with red floral patterns on an orange background. In the Late Roman period these shapes continue to develop—the lamps are round and closed, cast in a mould, with a handle or a knob; the bowls are often decorated with a roulette on the outside. Ribbing is very common on large jars and becomes increasingly so on small vessels.

THE BYZANTINE PERIOD (325–640)

Pottery types of the previous period continue into the Byzantine period, the ribbing of the surface of the vessels remaining the distinguishing mark of the period. From the beginning of the period, "pseudo-sigillata" vessels, consisting mainly of red-glazed bowls, make their appearance. Toward the end of the period this type of pottery degenerates and disappears entirely. Closed cooking pots with two ear-like handles give way to shallow cooking pots with two horizontal handles and a lid. There are also clay pans with only one horizontal handle. The lamps are closed, cast in molds, and elongated in form. Most of them are decorated with relief ornamentation. At the end of the period a wave-like engraved ornamentation appears on the upper portion of large jars and bowls: this form of ornamentation carries over into the following period, the early Arabic period.

For chart of pottery types, see the entry *Archaeology, vol. 3, cols. 307–10 and also supplementary lists.

IN THE BIBLE

The collective term for pottery in the Bible is *kelei ḥeres* (כְּלֵי חֶרֶשׂ, Lev. 6:21; Num. 5:17; Jer. 32:14), while pottery sherds are called *ḥeres* (חֶרֶשׂ, Job. 2:8). Pottery vessels were used for cooking (Lev. 6:21), as containers for liquids (Num. 5:17), and containers for scrolls (Jer. 32:14). There are references in the Bible to some of the methods that the potter used in his work—"the potter treads clay" (Isa. 41:25) and "I went down to the potter's house, and there he was working at his wheel. And the vessel he was making of clay was spoiled in the potter's hand, and he reworked it into another vessel, as it seemed good to the potter to do" (Jer. 18:3–4). Only two types of vessels in the Bible are designated as pottery. They are: "earthen pots" (*nivlei ḥeres;* Lam. 4:2) and "earthen flasks" (*baqbuq yoẓer ḥeres;* Jer. 19:1). Other vessels that presumably were made of clay are: e.g., *aggan, agganot,* "bowl, cup" (Song 7:3 [2]; Isa. 22:24); *asukh,* "jar" (II Kings 4:2); *gaviʿa,* "pitcher" (Jer. 35:5); *kad,* "jar" for water (Gen. 24:14) or flour (I Kings 17:14); *kos,* "cup" (Jer. 35:5); *sir,* "pot" (Ex. 16:3); *sefel,* "bowl" (Judg. 6:38); *pakh,* "vial" (of oil; Jer. 25:28; I Sam. 10:1); *ẓappaḥat,* "cruse" (I Kings 17:14); *qubbaʿat,* "cup" (Isa. 51:17, 22); *qeʿarah,* "bowl" (Num. 7:85).

Bibliography: R. Amiran, *The Ancient Pottery of Palestine* (1970); EM, 4 (1962), 120–84. [I.M.]

°**POUND, EZRA LOOMIS** (1885–1972), U.S. poet and critic. Born in Idaho, Pound left the United States in 1907 and lived in London and in Paris before settling in Rapallo, Italy, in 1925. By then he had already won international acclaim as a modern poet. A prolific writer, he published over 40 volumes of poetry, verse translations, and literary criticism whose influence on 20th-century poetic style has been enormous. In Italy, Pound became an admirer of Mussolini and came to adopt an increasingly pro-Fascist, anti-British, and anti-Semitic tone. He developed an ardent, if amateur, interest in economics and became an advocate of the Canadian C.H. Douglas' social credit doctrine, which vocalized agrarian discontent and blamed human misery on the financial manipulations of a small capitalistic class, largely Jewish in composition and inspiration. Pound's *Money Pamphlets* (6 vols., 1950–52), published in Italy in the 1930s, spoke repeatedly of the "Jewish poison," and in 1939 he wrote an article for the Italian press entitled "The Jew, Disease Incarnate." Many of his poems are also violently anti-Jewish. During World War II Pound broadcast pro-Axis propaganda over the Italian radio.

He was arrested by the American army in 1945 and returned to the United States to face an indictment of treason, but was judged mentally unfit to stand trial and was committed to a mental hospital in Washington, D. C., in 1946. In 1958, following the intervention of many noted poets, he was released, and returned to Italy.

Bibliography: M. Reck, *Ezra Pound* (1967); C. Norman, *Case of Ezra Pound* (1969), includes bibliography; N. Stock, *Poet in Exile* (1964), includes bibliography; N. Stock, *Life of Ezra Pound* (1970); J. Cornell (ed.), *Trial of Ezra Pound* (1966). [CH.R.]

POUPKO, BERNARD (1918–), U.S. Orthodox rabbi. Poupko, who was born in Russia, was ordained by the Rabbi Isaac Elchanan Theological Seminary in 1941 and was appointed rabbi of Pittsburgh's Sha'are Torah Congregation in 1942. He was a founder of the Hillel Academy in Pittsburgh. Poupko visited the U.S.S.R. several times after 1964. A collection of his articles based on his Russian visits was published as *In the Shadow of the Kremlin* (1969). In 1970 he became president of Mizrachi in the U.S [L.BE.]

POVERTY. Distinctions between rich and poor predate recorded history. In Israel, however, these differences do not seem to have become pronounced until the eighth century B.C.E., following the social revolution produced by the monarchy and the dissolution of the earlier tribal solidarity. The expansion of trade and foreign conquest brought an influx of wealth into the land, while urbanization and the rise of favored classes resulted in the amassing of fortunes (Isa. 2:7; Hos. 12:9; Amos 3:15) and the cruel impoverishment of many families (Amos 8:5; Micah 2:2).

The gross social injustice drew stinging rebukes from the prophets (e.g., Isa. 1:23; 3:14; Amos 4:1; 5:11), who called for obedience to the divine command for righteous living (Isa. 1:16–17; Amos 5:14–15) and loyalty to His covenant (Hos. 12:7ff.). Unlike the authors of the wisdom literature, the prophets did not condemn the poor for having brought poverty on themselves through sloth (Prov. 6:6–7; 10:4) and irresponsibility (13:18; 23:21). At the same time, they did not idealize the poor, recognizing that they, too, were often guilty of ignoring God's commands (Isa. 9:12–16; Jer. 5:3–5; 6:13).

Those who were in a better economic position were expected to treat the poor with compassion in order to avoid the further aggravation of their wretchedness (Ex. 22:24–26). Indeed, God Himself was their protector and His blessing to Israel was contingent upon the generous treatment they received (Deut. 15:7–11). Accordingly, Israel's laws—for example, those concerning the prompt payment of wages (Deut. 24:14–15), the prohibition of usury (Ex. 22:24; Lev. 25:36; Deut. 23:20), allotments from vintage and harvests (Lev. 19:9–10), the right to enjoy the Sabbatical fruits (Ex. 23:11) and third-year tithes (Deut. 14:28–29; 26:12–13), and the privilege of eating one's fill from a neighboring vineyard or field (Deut. 23:25–26)—provided for the amelioration of their conditions. It was the duty of the judge to protect the rights of the lowly (Ex. 23:6ff.; Lev. 19:15), as it was that of the more fortunate citizen to enable them to participate in the festivals (Deut. 16:11, 14). The king could assure the stability of his rule by concerning himself with the just treatment of the humble (Prov. 29:14).

The Torah recognized that poverty as such could not be eliminated (Deut. 15:11). At the same time, it sought to avoid the evils of pauperism by providing for periodic remission of debts during the Sabbatical Year (Deut. 15:1ff.), and the return of ancestral landed properties in the Jubilee Year as well as the manumission of Israelite slaves (Lev. 25:8ff.). In this way, it was hoped, the ancient covenant fellowship of Israel could retain its original force, as the tribal solidarity was reaffirmed and restored to the social conditions of pre-monarchical times.

Social oppression, however, did persist, and a "spiritual transposition of vocabulary" is apparent in the later literature, with *ʿani* (עני) and *ʿanaw* (ענו) becoming functionally equivalent to "God-fearing" and "pious" (Zeph. 2:3; 3:12–13), the opposite of *rasha*ᶜ. By this time, though, the term had lost its sociological significance. In any event, neither before nor after the Exile did the poor constitute a religious party or social class.

See also *Poor, Provision for. [D.L.L.]

In the Talmud. The Talmud reveals a distinctly ambivalent attitude toward poverty. It would appear that poverty was so widespread and was regarded as so irremediable that it was raised to the level of a virtue which had its positive value. Poverty appears to have been particularly endemic in Babylonia. "Of ten measures of poverty which descended to the world, Babylonia took nine" (Kid. 49b) and it was stated that the poverty of the Jews there was the reason that the festivals were celebrated with special joy (Shab. 145b). Both the negative and positive aspects are equally stressed. The former finds its expression in such statements as that "grinding poverty deprives a man of his mental balance" (Er. 41b) and it is the worst of all sufferings in the world (Ex. R. 31:12). "Poverty in a man's house is worse than 50 plagues" (BB 116a). The statement in the Talmud (Ned. 64b) that the "poor man" is one of the four who are regarded as dead has to be amended, as the context shows, to "he who has lost his property," i.e., the man who was once wealthy and is reduced to poverty. Rav's daily prayer, which included "a life of wealth and honor" (Ber. 16b), is only one of a host of statements which extol the contrary desirable ideal of wealth, or at least the absence of poverty.

On the other hand poverty is extolled as having a positive value, from the point of view of its salutary effect both upon the character of the poor and upon the sense of generosity which it engenders in those who relieve it. All the various statements in the Talmud which emphasize both aspects are collated in one statement in a late Midrash, "the Holy One Blessed be He considered all the boons which He could confer upon Israel, and selected poverty, since as a result of poverty they fear the Lord. Righteousness derives only from poverty; **gemilut ḥasadim* derives only from poverty; a man becomes godfearing only through poverty; a man studies Torah only through poverty" (EHZ 24). For the last, compare "take special care of the children of the poor; from them comes Torah" (Ned. 81a). Indeed "Poverty is as becoming to Israel as red trappings on a white horse" (Ḥag. 9b). The parallel passage (Lev. R. 35:6) which has "the daughters of Israel" is ascribed to R. Akiva and it is he who answers the other aspect of the positive value of charity. "If your God loves the poor why does he not support them?" asked *Tinneius Rufus, and Akiva answered, "so that through them [i.e., by relieving their wants] we may be delivered from Gehinnom" (BB 10a). A particular aspect of the virtue of poverty is found in the statement "the men of the Great Synagogue fasted 24 fasts that scribes of Torah scrolls, **tefillin*, and **mezuzah* should not become prosperous" (Pes. 50b). The Midrash enumerates eight names for the poor man in the Bible. The comprehensive one is *ani;* the *evyon,* as the root of the word conveys, is the needy man in the literal sense ("he who is in need of something"); while the *misken* is "the most despised of all" (Lev. R. 34:6). The poor man who was entitled to receive food from the public soup kitchen *(tamḥui)* was one who did not have sufficient for two meals a day (Shab. 118a).

Poverty was almost predetermined and was regarded as independent of man's efforts. "R. Meir said: one should always pray to Him to whom all wealth and property belong, for there is not a craft in which are not [the potentialities] of poverty and of wealth, for neither poverty nor wealth is due to the craft, but all depends upon one's [spiritual] merit" (Kid. 4:14).

The relief of the poor had to be effected with the utmost delicacy and consideration. "God stands together with the poor man at the door, and one should therefore consider whom one is confronting" (Lev. R. 34:9). One of the earliest talmudic authorities, Yose b. Johanan of Jerusalem, made as his maxim: "Let the poor be members of thy household" (Avot 1:5); "he who is openhanded to the poor will be vouchsafed male children" (BB 10b). The previous circumstances of the poor man were taken into consideration, and the story is told of Hillel who, when a poor man who had once been in prosperous circumstances came to him for help, provided him with a horse and a "servant to run before him" since that was the minimum to which he was accustomed, and when he could not find (or afford) a servant he acted himself in that capacity (Ket. 67b). Applicants for food were examined as to the genuineness of their needs, but not applicants for clothes, but the contrary view also has its advocates (BB 9a). In the dispensation of charity the local poor took precedence over those from other towns (BM 71a). A peripatetic mendicant was provided with a minimum of a loaf of bread of a certain value, and lodging for the night (BB 9a). It was stated that most poor are descendants of the tribe of Simeon; this being the effect of Jacob's curse "I will scatter them in Israel" (Gen. 4, 9:7; Gen. R. 98:5).

See also *Begging; *Leket, Shikhḥah, and Pe'ah; *Hekdesh; *Charity; *Poor, Provisions for. [L.I.R.]

Bibliography: A. Kuschke, in: ZAW, 57 (1939), 31–57; de Vaux, Anc Isr, 72–74; H. J. Muller, *Freedom in the Ancient World* (1961), 34; S. N. Kramer, *The Sumerians* (1963), 77; Baron, Social², index, 234; M. Lazarus, *The Ethics of Judaism* (1900).

POZNAN (Ger. **Posen**), city in historical *Great Poland; in Prussia 1793–1807 and 1815–1919; now in Poznan province, W. Poland. One of the most ancient and leading Jewish communities of Poland-Lithuania, it was probably one of those for whom the charter of rights granted by Prince Boleslav the Pious (1264) was intended. Jews are known to have lived in Poznan in 1379; a *blood libel is mentioned in 1399. The development of the community was interrupted in 1447 when a fire ravaged the town, impoverishing the Jews. The first signs of economic recovery appeared during the second decade of the 16th century, inaugurating a period of progress and spiritual efflorescence which lasted until approximately the close of the century. Then one of the largest communities in Poland-Lithuania, with 3,000 persons (about 10% of the city's population) and 137 wooden and stone houses, Poznan became the Jewish center of Great Poland. Its rabbis, among the most prominent authorities of the generation, were recognized throughout the country and the "sages of Poznan" were renowned. Nevertheless this period of prosperity was marked by a severe struggle with the local townspeople and the monks. The townsmen repeatedly (1521, 1523, 1554, 1556) endeavored to hinder the retail trade of the Jews, to restrict the number of houses in the Jewish quarter and beyond it (1532, 1537, 1545), and to expel new Jewish settlers (1549). Students of the Jesuit seminary organized bloody attacks (*Schuelergelaeuf,* 1575) on the Jewish quarter. During riots in 1577, 20 Jews lost their lives and after a fire in 1590 the Jewish quarter was abandoned for two years.

Through further misfortunes the community began to decline. Jesuit persecutions were renewed in 1607, and in the wake of another fire (1613) the Jews temporarily settled on the outskirts of the town, from where they were expelled in 1620. The plague known as St. Anthony's Fire claimed a number of victims and those who fled at this time did not return. Signs of decline became apparent in the middle of the 17th century with a one-third decrease in the population, although the proportion of Jews within the general population rose to 15%. The burden of taxation became severe and attempts to raise funds by new lease methods did not alleviate the financial plight. There was constant recourse to loans but these were insufficient for the growing needs and settlement of former debts (not finally settled until the middle of the 19th century). As German merchants from Silesia penetrated the region, trade rivalry grew. Jewish traders at the fairs (*Brandenburg, *Gniezno, *Frankfort on the Oder) met with difficulties that reduced their sources of livelihood. In riots in 1639 some lost their lives and property was destroyed. Famine and plagues following the Swedish War (1655–60) and renewed riots (1687) brought economic ruin and accelerated the depletion of the community. A call for assistance to the communities of Germany and Bohemia (1674) failed to raise sufficient funds for charity or for redemption of the *Sifrei Torah*, mortgaged in payment of debts (which amounted to 60,000 zlotys to the nobility alone). Economic distress was accompanied by social and cultural decline: tension prevailed and quarrels became endemic; even education was neglected.

Deterioration continued during the 18th century. In 1709 there was a renewed outbreak of St. Anthony's Fire, and an attack by the army of the so-called Tarnogrod Confederation (1716–17) further depleted the community. A severe fire (1717), the flooding of the Warta River, and a blood libel (1736) had disastrous consequences, and rehabilitation of the community became beyond its means. Growing numbers of Jews left the city, some for Swarzęc, a subsidiary community of Poznan. Those who remained could not halt the process of disintegration in all aspects of Jewish communal, social, and economic life. In 1759 the conquering Prussian army imposed an enormous fine of 2,676 guilders. Another fire in 1764 destroyed 76 houses and claimed many victims. The debts of the community increased to unprecedented figures (686,081 guilders, with 27,800 guilders annual interest). A royal commission failed to solve the problem of the debts. The majority of the members of the community, which numbered 3,000 persons (about 40% of the population) at the end of the 18th century, were poor recent arrivals, unable to bear the burden of taxation and payment of debts.

When Poznan was under Prussian rule (1793–1807), *Prussia's legislation relating to the Jews and its general legislation affected Jewish life in Poznan in many new spheres, e.g., it restricted communal jurisdiction in favor of the local Prussian tribunal. General elementary and secondary schools were opened to Jews. Haskalah and Germanization received considerable impetus. The municipality attempted to induce the new rulers to restrict the numbers and activities of Jews in the city, and seized the opportunity after the fire of 1803, in which the Jewish quarter was severely damaged, to submit proposals for the confinement of the Jews to their original quarter. For hygienic reasons, however, the Prussian government decided not to rebuild the Jewish quarter and to allow the Jews to settle in any part of the town, with the sole reservation that they should have no more houses than they had previously owned. The purchase of houses from Christians was permitted. This decision could not take effect because of the outbreak of the Napoleonic War, and so the Jews of Poznan returned to their quarter and rebuilt a number of houses. A minority, presumably *maskilim*, settled outside the Jewish quarter.

The situation of Poznan's Jews was certainly not improved during the period of the Grand Duchy of Warsaw (1807–13); the *maskilim* were disillusioned by the abrogation of emancipation (1808), while the general Jewish population was burdened by new taxes (the recruits' tax and the kosher meat tax). The community viewed with suspicion the activities of David *Caro. A member of the Berlin Haskalah and contributor to *Ha-Me'assef*, he called for reforms in education and Divine Worship and disseminated Haskalah literature. When Prussian rule was reestablished (1815), a conflict broke out within the community over the election of the rabbi. The *maskilim* were opposed to the candidacy of Jacob Moses Eger, whose scholarly authority and social influence worked against their plans for the closure of the *ḥadarim* in favor of public schools and the opening of a teachers' seminary. Toward the end of his life (1833), these questions were again raised by the Prussian government in the form of "temporary directives," aimed at achieving a Germanic assimilation to counter the Polish element in the city. The resistance of the community prevented their implementation and the *ḥadarim* were not replaced until 40 years later. Another article of the "temporary directives" granted equality to that tiny section of the community whose education (knowledge of the German language), length of residence (from 1815), or act of Prussian patriotism entitled them to state citizenship. The overwhelming majority of the Jewish population (85%) was merely "tolerated," a status which was not changed until 20 years later. Germanization of the Jewish community was partially achieved during the 1850s, under the pressure of the Prussian authorities, who forced the German settlers to consent, and in the face of growing hostility of the Poles. When delegates of the Jews were elected to municipal institutions in 1853, Poles for the first time were in the minority. Relations between Germans and Jews improved and, as a result, Germanization was intensified. The ties between the community of Poznan and those of Prussia and central Germany were strengthened while those with communities to the east weakened. The Jewish population increased (about 6,000 in the 1860s) and its economic situation improved. Communal authority confined itself to religious and philanthropic spheres: a magnificent synagogue was built and rabbinical conventions were held there in 1876, 1877, 1897, and 1914.

The defeat of Germany in World War I and the annexation of Poznan by Poland came as a severe blow to the Jews, who had supported Germany in the struggle (1918–19). The renewal of Polish rule was marked by riots and clashes and the community rapidly declined. By the late 1930s, about 2,000 Jews remained in the city.

The Organization of the Community (16th–18th Centuries). The records of the Poznan community (the memorial volumes and the lists of *kesherim* ("eligibles")) provide a detailed picture of its organization and of the activities of its institutions (1611–1833). Communal officials were chosen by means of eligible arbitrators or by the community council (there were about 100 delegates every year). The eligible arbitrators were elected by the outgoing community council from among the members of the community and they in turn elected the higher officials by secret ballot and majority vote: the *parnasim*, the elders, the council, the *dayyanim*, and the treasurers (about 35 people). The new community council selected the lower officials: the city representatives, the initiators of regulations, various functionaries, the superintendents of the guilds, assessors, the council of the *bardan* (a specific tax levied partly on food consumption and partly on trade turnover), accountants, and those responsible for relief work (about 65 people). Election procedures followed very elaborate rules, designed to fulfill certain halakhic requirements while embodying various methods designed to ensure a moderate oligarchical regime in the community. The salaried community officials—rabbis, preachers, *shtadlanim*, *ḥazzanim*, and beadles—were selected by 32 men (13 from the council and 19 from the three classes: the wealthy, the middle class, and the poor) and their term of office was from one to three years, fixed by letter of appointment. As the rabbi of Poznan also acted as rabbi of the province of Great Poland, the arbiters of the province assisted at his election; an inhabitant of Poznan was disqualified from holding this office. Later, after obstruction by the province, the election of the rabbi was entrusted to 32 men. The *kesherim* also had legislative power, formally in pursuance of their electoral power. Their ordinances were intended as guidance for the higher and lower officials. The overt legislation (the regulations) and the hidden legislation ("secret letters") were decreed by the *kesherim* themselves at their meetings (these constituted about 85% of the whole legislation), sometimes on the initiative of the "initiators of the regulations." The *kesherim* advised and passed regulations in the spheres of economy, jurisdiction, relief, and education. Sumptuary regulations were also included. The *kesherim* also undertook the supervision of the community's institutions. It was considered their task to ensure that the regulations were executed to the full, in letter and spirit. Thus the *kesherim* became one of the most distinctive and firmest institutions of the Poznan community, but because they were selected annually and about 50% were newcomers every year, they did not become a closed ruling group. Through them the members of the community felt that their leadership was under permanent control and that their selection was a responsible public act.

The community determined the number of permanent and temporary residents, as well as the number of dwelling houses in the community. In general they acted according to principles accepted in Jewish society (see **Ḥerem ha-Yishuv*) but there were special considerations prevailing in the Poznan community. Acceptance of new settlers was dependent on the agreement of the 32-member committee or a commission acting in its name. Their decision was based on two considerations: the quota of Jewish inhabitants permitted by the municipal council and the number of poor members, which could not be increased. Community membership was granted to a new settler after three years' residence and after payment of special fees. Those living "outside the community" as a result of wars, floods, plagues, and fires became once more full-fledged members when they had equipped themselves with a letter of residence granting its bearer the right to trade in Poznan in exchange for his sharing the burden of taxation. The optimum number of houses in the Jewish quarter was fixed. In 1641 there were 80 wooden houses (40 housing one family, 39 two families, and one three families) and another 57 stone houses (48 housing two families and nine three families). In 1710 the number of houses decreased to 98, but in 1714 it increased to 109. The ownership of many dwellings by the wealthy during the community's period of prosperity and their refusal to rebuild after various calamities resulted in a shortage of houses, a rise in rents, and the demand that rents be paid in advance. Because of the opposition of the municipal authorities it was difficult to find temporary lodging—especially after wars, plagues, and fires—beyond the Jewish quarter. Specialized community institutions dealt with fiscal problems, with the collection and assessment of taxes. The collection of "gifts for the authorities" (to the *wojewoda*, the ministers, the municipal council, and the monks) was borne by the communal institutions. To achieve greater efficiency in the collection of charity donations and payments for *mitzvot*, a list of the needy was drawn up and collection methods and procedures for the distribution of allocations were established.

The community intervened in the regulation of trade competition. The *kesherim* supported the merchants against the craftsmen (butchers, tailors, hatters, furriers, buttonhole makers), the brokers, and the moneylenders. The attitude of the *kesherim* toward the middleman, i.e., the itinerant broker in the town or at the fair, was based on the extent of his usefulness or the damage caused by his economic activities to commerce and moneylending. The merchant class waged a fierce struggle against the permanent brokers to non-Jews, against the middleman between one non-Jew and another, and against the brokers who acted as messengers or attracted customers from one trader to another. Loans for consumption were not encouraged, but a loan for trading purposes was viewed favorably. A loan which surpassed the means of the borrower was condemned and invalidated. Guarantees for loans were defined (*pledge, agreement by handing over an object (*kinyan sudar*), mortgage, and **mamram*) and a rate of interest was fixed (in towns 22%; at fairs 33%; for squires 15%; for monks 8%). In the legal and judicial field, special and detailed attention was given to procedures, such as summons to court, the actual trial, and the execution of the sentence. The community tried to impose sumptuary laws based on the principles of: "everyone according to his wealth and prevailing conditions"; "a man is only authorized to spend according to his status"; and "the Torah took pity on the money of Israel." These restrictions were applied to clothes and religious celebrations in accordance with financial means (middle class, lower class, and religious officials). The poor were supported by various funds, most important being the charity fund for the poor, and assistance funds for poor brides, the needy aged, guests, youth, the sick, and paupers. The youth of Poznan attended two educational institutions: the *bet midrash* (or the synagogue) and the yeshivah. In the *bet midrash* they studied in three classes and the teachers were supervised by the community. In the yeshivah the number of students was predetermined and limited. Adults also studied in these institutions under the guidance of the *av bet din*, the preacher, the *dayyan*, and learned laymen. Public religious life was centered around the numerous synagogues. The larger synagogues enjoyed more extensive rights with regard to the status of their treasurers, the selection of *ḥazzanim*, the distribution of *etrogim*, and the determination of the seat of the *gaon* or preacher. [D.Av.]

Holocaust Period. At the outbreak of World War II there were about 1,500 Jews in Poznan. Many of them escaped before the entry of the Germans or in the first weeks of the occupation. Poznan became the capital of the Reichsgau Wartheland under the Nazi occupation. The Jewish community in occupied Poznan existed for only three months. In that time the synagogue was transformed into a stable, Jewish property was systematically plundered, and the Jews were driven out of the better residences. On Nov. 12, 1939, the S.S. and police chief of Warthegau, Wilhelm Koppe, ordered that Poznan be made *"judenrein"* within three months. On Dec. 11–12, 1939, the Jews were deported to Ostrow Lubelski and other towns of the General Government. Some of the refugees reached Wloszczowa; others went to Grodzisk Mazowiecki, Zyrardow, Wiskitki, and Blonie. On April 15, 1940, the Nazi paper *Ostdeutscher Beobachter* reported the solemn, symbolic, ceremonial removal of the Star of David from the last synagogue in Poznan. From November 1939 until August 1943 Jewish forced labor camps existed in the town and vicinity. The inmates, who came from various towns in Warthegau, worked on road building, land estates, and other work sites. [De.D.]

Postwar Period. A report issued in 1947 by the Central Committee of the Jews of Poland (set up immediately after the liberation of the country) showed that 224 Jews were living in Poznan in January 1946 (148 men, and 76 women), and 343 in June of the same year (208 men, and 135 women).

No data are available for the period 1947–1971 on the Jews in Poznan. [Ed.]

Bibliography: M. M. Zarchin, *Jews in the Province of Posen* (1939), incl. bibl.; B. D. Weinryb, *Texts and Studies in the Communal History of Polish Jewry* (1950); J. Lukaszewicz, *Historisch-statistisches Bild der Stadt Posen* (1878); A. Heppner and J. Herzberg, *Aus Vergangenheit und Gegenwart der Juden und der juedischen Gemeinden in den Posener Landen* (1909); T. Ereciński, *Prawo przemysłowe miasta Poznania w XVIII wieku* (1934); D. Avron, *Pinkas ha-Kesherim shel Kehillat Pozna* (1966); J. Perles, in: MGWJ, 13–14 (1864–65); Berliner, *ibid.*, 17 (1868), 174–8; D. Kaufmann, *ibid.*, 38 (1894), 184–92; 39 (1895), 38–46, 91–96; P. Bloch, *ibid.*, 47 (1903), 153–69, 263–79, 346–56; J. Jacobsohn, *ibid.*, 64–65 (1920–21); T. Nożyński, in: *Kronika miasta Poznania*, vol.10; W. Feilchenfeld, in: *Zeitschrift der historischen Gesellschaft fuer die Provinz Posen*, 10–11 (1895–96); J. Landesberger, in: *Festschrift . . . Dr. Wolf Feilchenfeld* (1907), 40–46; idem, in: JJLG, 10 (1912), 361–71; J. Jacobsohn, in: *Menorah—juedisches Familienblatt*, 7 (1929); F. Kupfer, in: BZIH, no. 2–3 (1953), 56–121. Ḥ. D. Friedberg, *Ha-Defus ha-Ivri be-Polanyah* (1950[2]), 61; L. Lewin, in: *Soncino-Blaetter*, 1 (1925/26), 171ff. Holocaust:

Megillat Polin, 5 pt. 1 (1961), 158, 160; I. Trunk, in: *Bleter far Geshikhte,* 2 no. 1–4 (1949), 78; D. Dabrowska, in: BŻIH, no. 13–14 (1955), 122–84, passim.

POZNANSKY, MENAḤEM (1887–1956), Hebrew writer. Born in Kamenets-Podolski (Russia), Poznansky emigrated to Palestine as a result of his close friendship with J. H. *Brenner, who was one of the main influences in his life. Besides teaching, Poznansky wrote stories, which were posthumously collected together with his sketches in *Demuyyot Melavvot* (1958). After Brenner was killed, Poznansky devoted himself to Brenner's literary estate, and published the first complete edition of his works (8 vols., in 9 books, 1924–30). This was followed by an abridged edition (3 vols., 1946–51), and a revised complete edition (1961), of which Poznansky succeeded in preparing only the first volume. All these editions included introductions and notes by Poznansky. He also published an annotated collection of Brenner's letters (vols. 1–2, 1941). Poznansky translated into Hebrew works by Turgenev, Goncharov, and Gogol. One of his stories appears in English translation (Goell, Bibliography, 74, no. 2349).

Bibliography: Kressel, Leksikon, 2 (1967), 575–6. [G.K.]

P.P.S. (**Polska Partia Socjalistyczna**), Polish Socialist Party. Founded in Paris in 1892, the P.P.S. began activities in Poland despite Russian political restrictions. While in Galicia, then under Austrian control, the movement formed a legally recognized popular party, the P.P.S.D. (Polish Socialist Democrat Party). In Congress Poland, as a result of czarist oppression, the P.P.S. became an underground movement. The P.P.S. also was in conflict with the general Social Democratic movement in Poland and Lithuania, which on cosmopolitan principles opposed the nationalist tendency among the leaders of the P.P.S. During World War I the right wing of the P.P.S. organized its own military units (the "legions") to act for the liberation of Poland. With the attainment of Polish independence, the P.P.S. organized a national convention in April 1919 which brought about the establishment of the party throughout the country.

From the outset many Jews were active in the P.P.S. However, in the wake of ideological conflicts during and after the war a considerable number of Jewish activists left the party to join the extreme left. Three Jews became prominent in the party in the interwar years. (1) Feliks Perl (1871–1927), a native of Warsaw, who influenced the program of the united movement by his adherence to the party's socialist views as opposed to its rightist nationalist tendencies; (2) Herman *Diamand (1860–1931) of Lvov, lawyer and economist, who was a P.P.S. member in the Austrian parliament between 1907 and 1914, and the party's economic expert in the Polish *Sejm (parliament); and (3) Herman *Lieberman (1870–1941), lawyer, journalist and outstanding speaker, member of the Austrian parliament and the Polish Sejm, and later (1940) minister of justice in the Polish government-in-exile in London. All three considered that the solution to the Jewish problem lay in Polish patriotism and eventual assimilation; they were opposed to the principles of Zionism and the efforts of Jewish leaders to preserve Jewish cultural identity.

The P.P.S. made efforts to approach the mass of Jewish workers through Yiddish publications. It tended to regard the Jewish socialist parties, such as the *Bund and the leftist *Po'alei Zion, as potential competitors for voters, accusing them of separatism and nationalism. In its attitude to actual discrimination against Jews, the P.P.S. showed a willingness to assist them in principle. However it was cautious in the extent of its support so as not to be suspected of "serving Jewish interests." In the trade unions the P.P.S. showed a tendency to make difficulties in the admission of Jewish workers to industrial enterprises, even where the owners themselves were Jews.

It was only in the late 1930s that the P.P.S. showed more courage in the struggle against anti-Semitism, then being overtly exploited by the reactionary successors of *Pilsudski, as a means of hitting at the opposition.

Bibliography: H. M. Rabinowicz, *The Legacy of Polish Jewry* (1965), 55; I. Schiper et al. (eds.), *Żydzi w Polsce odrodzonej,* 1 (1932), 531–41. [M.LAN.]

PRAAG, SIEGFRIED EMANUEL VAN (1899–), Dutch novelist and critic. Born in Amsterdam, he was for some time a schoolteacher and settled in Brussels before World War II. Several of Van Praag's novels have Jewish or biblical themes. Among them are two of his historical novels, *Maria Nunes* (1928) and *La Judith* (1930; in the latter the central character is the actress Sarah *Bernhardt). He also wrote *Het Ghetto* (1930), *Saul* (1947), and *Jezus en de Menacheem* (1951). He excelled in studies of women, as in his historical novels *Julie de l'Espinasse* (1934) and *Madame de Pompadour* (1936). During World War II, Van Praag escaped to London, where he worked for the BBC.

Some of his later books nostalgically recall the Jewish life of Amsterdam which vanished with the Nazi invasion. These include *Een vrouw van tact* ("A Tactful Woman," 1947), *De weg van het heimwee* ("The Road of Nostalgia," 1947), *De Hebreeuwse lichtekooi* ("The Hebrew Prostitute," 1954), and *Seizoenen* ("Seasons," 1957). Best known is *Jeruzalem van het Westen* ("Jerusalem of the West," 1961), in which Van Praag recreates the life and death of the Amsterdam Ghetto, showing how its spirit survived in some of those who escaped to Ereẓ Israel. Van Praag's major critical essays include *De westjoden en hun letterkunde sinds 1860* ("Western Jews and their Literature after 1860," 1926), an important source of information on Western European Jewish writers; *Wij en de dieren* ("We and the Animals," 1932); and *Wereldburgers* ("World Citizens," 1933). In 1969, on the occasion of his 70th birthday, Van Praag was offered a selection of his works including a complete bibliography: R. Bulthuis (ed.), *Siegfried E. Van Praag, Een schrijver en zijn werk.*

Bibliography: H. Boas, in: *JC, Supplement* (Dec. 24, 1965). [G.A.-T.]

PRACTICE AND PROCEDURE.

Civil. COURT SESSIONS. The courts of three (judges) exercising jurisdiction in civil matters (see *bet din*) held their sessions during the day, but—following Jethro's advice to Moses that judges should be available "at all times" (Ex. 18:22)—they would continue sitting at night to complete any proceedings commenced during the day (Sanh. 4:1). The session started early in the morning, with the judges robing themselves—they had special robes "wrapped around them," so that they would not look around too much (*Sma,* ḤM 5 n. 16)—and usually continued for six hours until mealtime (Shab. 10a). While originally the session was not interrupted even for prayers, the law was later revised so that in this case it may be interrupted (ḤM 5:4). No court was held on the Sabbath or holidays, lest any writing was done. On the eves of the Sabbath or holidays the courts would sit only in exceptionally urgent cases (*Rema,* ḤM 5:2), but a party summoned was not punished for failing to appear on such a day (ḤM 5:2). The court may sit on the intermediate days of a festival (*Ḥol ha-Mo'ed,* MK 14b).

PARTIES. Any person, male or female (Sif. Deut. 190), may sue and be sued, except minors, deaf-mutes, and lunatics (see *Legal capacity). Actions brought by or against guardians on behalf of such incapacitated persons may be heard by the court, but any judgment rendered is binding only if in their favor (Git. 52a). Non-Jews who sue or are sued in a Jewish court may demand that their own non-Jewish law be applied to them (Yad, Melakhim 10:12); a Jew litigating with a non-Jew was originally entitled to claim any benefit of non-Jewish law, but this discrimination was later abolished (cf. *Beit ha-Beḥirah* thereto).

The rule is that parties must litigate in person and may not be represented; and even when and where representation is allowed, the parties are required to attend in person so as to enable the court to form a direct opinion of them (*Sma,* ḤM 13 n. 12, 17 n. 14). An exception was made in favor of women defendants: if such women were accustomed to stay at home and not to be seen in public they were allowed to make their statements to a scribe of the court in their own homes (Tos. to Shevu. 30a). When suing for his own usufruct in his wife's property, a husband may also sue for the principal without special authorization, but not otherwise (Git. 48b; ḤM 122:8).

Joint claimants may sue jointly or separately (Ket. 94a; ḤM 77:9, 122:9), but in an action by one of them, the others will normally be included by order of the court. In cases of joint liabilities each defendant can be sued only for his share of the debt, unless he expressly or by implication guaranteed the whole debt (ḤM 77:1); such a guarantee is implied in the debts of partners, joint contractors, and joint tort-feasors *(ibid.)*.

Venue. The plaintiff "follows the defendant," i.e., the claim has to be lodged in the court of the place where the defendant resides (*Rema,* ḤM 14:1); but if the plaintiff finds the defendant at a place where there is a court in session, he may sue him there and then (Resp. Maharik no. 14). The ancient rule that a party had the right to insist on trial by the Great Court at Jerusalem (Yad, Sanh. 6:7), though obsolete (*ibid.* 9), has been interpreted in many countries as enabling the plaintiff to compel the defendant to stand trial outside his place of residence in a court of higher repute or authority (Sanh. 31b; Tur ḤM 14; ḤM 14:1 and *Rema* thereto). The debtor's property may be attached by order of the court sitting at the place where the property is situated (*Rema,* ḤM 73:10).

Summonses. On the plaintiff's application a summons is issued to the defendant to appear in court on a day named in the summons (MK 16a; ḤM 11:1). A plaintiff need not disclose particulars of his claim before the defendant stands in court to answer the summons (BB 31a), and, if he does, he is not bound by any such summons unless he repeats them in court (ḤM 80:1). This rule was devised in order that the defendant should not have time, before coming into court, to fabricate a defense (*Rashbam,* BB 31a); but later jurists held this purpose to be outweghed by the more desirable opportunity of an out-of-court settlement if the claim was disclosed in advance (*Siftei Kohen,* ḤM 11, n.1).

The issue of a summons requires an order of the full court (Sanh. 8a), but one judge may make the order if the others are present in court. The summons is delivered by the officer of the court, either orally or by a written notice endorsed by the court (ḤM 11:6). It must specify not only the exact time the defendant is required to appear in court, but also the name of the plaintiff suing him (Nov. Ritba thereto). It may specify alternative dates of hearing (MK 16a), so that if the defendant fails to appear at one date, he must appear at the next specified date (*Rashi* thereto). Originally, such alternative summonses were issued for the next following Monday, Thursday, and Monday (Yad. Sanh. 25:8), these being the fixed court days in talmudic times (Ket. 3a). If not drawn up as alternative summonses, they could be issued subsequently one after the other in case of nonappearance (*Rashi,* BK 113a).

The court has discretion on whether or not to issue a summons; it may refuse to summon scholars of great eminence (Kid. 70a), practicing rabbis, and women who live in seclusion (ḤM 124). Each summons contained a warning that, failing his appearance in court on the date (or one of the dates) specified, the defendant was liable to be declared under a ban (see *Rashba,* BK 113a). A defendant who had to go on a journey or was otherwise prevented from attending court had to send an apology and request an adjournment (ḤM 11:1 and *Rema* thereto). Failing both appearance and apology, the court would issue a bill of attainder *(petiḥah)* to be served on the defaulter, and a ban would be imposed on him, unless he appeared in court within one week, paid the expenses of the *petiḥah,* and produced it to be torn up (BK 112b–113a). A less rigorous mode of enforcing court summonses was the attachment of the defaulter's property (Resp. Rosh 73:1, 97:4).

Default Procedure. It is forbidden to adjudicate the plaintiff's case in the absence of the defendant (though duly summoned) except where the plaintiff's claim is prima facie valid, e.g., where it is based on a bill signed by the defendant and confirmed by witnesses (BK 112b; Tur ḤM 106 and *Beit Yosef* thereto), or where the defendant is abroad more than 30 days' journey away (Yad, Malveh 13:1; ḤM 106). The reason for this deviation from the general rule that there shall be no adjudication unless both parties stand before the court (cf. Deut. 19:17), is said by Maimonides to be "that not everybody should take the money of other people and then go and settle abroad, with the result that borrowers will find all doors closed to them" (Yad, Malveh 13:1). Judgments in civil cases may always be given in the absence of the parties (ḤM 18:6).

Cause List. Hearing "out high and low alike," and fearing no man (Deut. 1:17) was interpreted as prohibiting any preference of major over minor cases (Sanh. 8a; Yad, Sanh. 20:10): the case that came in first must be heard first, whatever its relative importance (Rashi, Sanh. 8a; ḤM 15:1). There are several exceptions to this rule: the case of a scholar is given preference, so that he should not be kept too long from his studies (Ned. 62a); orphans and widows are given preference even over scholars, for it is by judging them that justice is done (Isa. 1:17); and cases in which one of the parties is a woman are advanced so as not to keep her waiting in court (Yev. 100a).

Subject Matter. The court will not entertain a claim for anything of less than minimal value (BM 55a; Yad, Sanh. 20:11). Opinions were divided on whether the court, once seized of a claim for *shaveh perutah,* could proceed to deal with other (ideal and non-valuable) matters between the same parties; the leading view is that it could (BM 55b; Yad, loc. cit.; ḤM 6:1).

Settlement. When the parties stand before the court, they must first be advised to settle their dispute by a friendly *compromise (Sanh. 6b), which is the "judgment of peace" alluded to by the prophet (Zech. 8:16). Failing such compromise, the court will ask them whether they insist on adjudication according to law, or whether they would not rather empower the court to adjudicate between them by way of fair compromise (Yad, Sanh. 22:4; ḤM 12:2); and courts were admonished to do everything in their power to dissuade parties from insisting on adjudication according to law (ḤM 12:20). However, so long as a compromise had not actually been implemented by *kinyan* (see *Acquisition) or by performance, the parties might go back on their agreement and resort to law (ḤM 12:7, 19).

Court Decorum. The parties are required to stand up before the court (cf. Deut. 19:17), and so are the witnesses (Shev. 30a), and they may not sit down except with the court's permission (Yad, Sanhedrin 21:3; ḤM 17:1). Maimonides comments sadly upon the fact that the post-talmudic courts always allow parties and witnesses to be seated—there being no longer sufficient strength in us to conduct ourselves according to the law (loc. cit. 21:5; ḤM 17:3). Permission to be seated may not be given to one party unless it is also given to the other (Tosef., Sanh. 6:2; TJ, Sanh. 3:10, 21c). Even where a scholar is permitted to be seated out of respect for him, his opponent must be given the same permission, and it is up to him whether he avails himself of it or not (Shev. 30b; Yad, Sanh. 21:4; ḤM 17:2).

There is no rule requiring parties (or attorneys) to be dressed in any particular manner; but where one party is more richly dressed than the other, he will be ordered to dress in the same manner as the other before being allowed to address the court (Shev. 31a). This rule has been said to be now obsolete, because differences in dress are no longer so ostentatious (*Siftei Kohen,* ḤM 17 n. 2); others have held that instead of ordering the party to change his dress, the court should rather assure the other party that his adversary's showy appearance makes no impression on it (Maharshal, quoted in *Baḥ.,* ḤM 17:1 and in *Be'er ha-Golah,* ḤM 17, n. 4).

EQUALITY OF PARTIES. The injunction: "Judge your neighbor fairly" (Lev. 19:15) was interpreted as prescribing equal treatment by the court for all parties before it (Shev. 30a; Yad, Sanh. 21:1; ḤM 17:1). In particular, the parties must all be given the same opportunity and the same time of audience *(ibid.);* no party may be heard in the absence of the other (Shevu. 31a; Sanh. 7b; Yad, loc. cit. 21:7; ḤM 17:5). Where one party desires to be represented or to be accompanied by friends, relatives, or partners, the other party may be so represented or accompanied too, and will be heard to oppose such representation or escort through lack of equal facilities (ḤM 17:4 and *Pitḥei Teshuvah,* ḤM 17 n. 7). Where there are several plaintiffs and one defendant (or vice versa), they will be asked to choose one of them to argue for all, so as to keep the proportions even (*Sma,* ḤM 17 n. 8).

The injunction not to favor the poor or to show deference to the rich (Lev. 19:15; cf. Ex. 23:3) was elaborated as follows:

> No judge should have compassion for the poor and say, this man is destitute and his adversary is rich—why should he not support him? I will give judgment for the poor man and thus cause him to be honorably provided for; nor should a judge favor the rich: when there are before him a wealthy notable and a poor ignorant man, he should not greet the notable and show him any respect, lest the other may be embarrassed; nor should he say to himself, how can I decide against him and cause him disgrace? I will rather send him away now and tell him in private later that he ought to satisfy the other party—but he must give true judgment forthwith. And when there are before him two men, one good and one evil, he may not say, the one is a criminal and probably lies, and the other is virtuous and will stick to the truth—but he must regard both as if they were potential evildoers who might lie in order to strengthen their own case, and he must judge them according to his best conscience; and, having so judged them, he should then regard them both as perfectly in order (ḤM 17:10).

PLEADINGS. The rule is that the parties must plead for themselves (see *Attorney), orally, but if both so agree, they may be allowed to put their arguments into writing, either by dictating them to the scribe of the court or by filing written briefs (*Rema,* ḤM 13:3); in the latter case, they cannot be allowed to go back on anything they have written *(ibid.),* and it appears that the courts have resorted to written pleading so as to prevent parties from changing their positions every now and then (cf. *Rema,* ḤM 80, n. 2). The costs of all such written records are borne equally by both parties (BB 10:4; 168a).

The court may not put any argument in a party's mouth or teach him how to argue his case (Avot 1:8; Yad, Sanh. 21:10; ḤM 17:8), nor may the court express an opinion presupposing a hypothetical argument ("if A would plead this way, judgment might be given for him"; *Rema,* ḤM 17:5). On the other hand, the court is admonished to open the mouth of the dumb for him (Prov. 31:8), i.e., to help a litigant who is intellectually or emotionally unable to express himself to formulate his argument (Yad, Sanh. 21:11; ḤM 17:9). This rule applies especially to orphans and imbeciles (cf. *Baḥ.,* ḤM 17, n. 12).

The plaintiff pleads his case first (BK 46b; ḤM 24), but he may be allowed by the court to postpone his pleading in whole or in part if he so desires (*Rema,* ḤM 24). There is a curious exception to the rule: if by hearing the plaintiff first, the property of the defendant may depreciate (e.g., by rumors in the market that the title is disputed), the defendant is heard first (ḤM 24 and *Siftei Kohen* thereto, n. 1). When the plaintiff has stated his case, the defendant is bound to reply forthwith, but the court may, in a suitable case, give him time to think and prepare his defense (*Rema,* ḤM 16:2). For the various pleadings open to litigants and their respective effects, see *Pleas.

EVIDENCE. Where a case cannot be disposed of on the pleadings and has to be proved by *evidence, the parties must be ready with their witnesses and documents on the day of the pleading, but the court may allow them up to 30 days' grace to produce their witnesses or documents (Sanh. 3:8; BK 112b; ḤM 16:1). Opinions were divided on what should happen if they failed to do so within this time limit (Sanh. 3:8), and the law was eventually settled to the effect that while the court would not extend the time limit (except where the witnesses are known to reside at a distance of more than 30 days' journey; ḤM 16:1), any judgment given on the pleadings was subject to review, and could be annulled, if and when warranted by any further evidence being adduced (ḤM 20:1). Where a party had declared in court that there were no witnesses or documents available to prove his case, he would not afterward be allowed to adduce such evidence, the suspicion being that it would be fabricated (Yad, Sanh. 7:7–8; ḤM 20:1); but where a party declared that there were witnesses or documents in existence but he could not trace them, the court would make a public announcement threatening a *ḥerem* on any person who withheld evidence (ḤM 16:3); such an announcement would even be initiated by the court where evidence was lacking to prove claims or defenses by representatives of estates (ḤM 71:8). Before testifying, witnesses were warned by the court of the consequences of perjury and the moral turpitude this involved (Yad, Edut 17:2; ḤM 28:7).

For the burden of adducing evidence, and presumptions in lieu of evidence, see *Evidence.

DELIBERATIONS. Having heard the parties and their witnesses, the judges confer with each other. According to ancient Jerusalem custom, the conference is conducted in private (Yad, Sanhedrin 22:9; ḤM 18:1); but while the parties always had to be excluded, primarily because they ought not to know how each judge voted (Maim. *Comm. to Mishnah,* Sanh. 3:7), it appears that some courts allowed the general public to be present while they conferred (*Baḥ.,* ḤM 18:1); and there is a talmudic tradition that the judges' students were allowed not only to be present but also to participate in the discussions (Sanh. 33b, and *Rashi* thereto). Witnesses who testified in the case could express their opinion on the merits of the case while giving testimony, but could not be heard during the judges' conference, because "no witness is made a judge" (Yad, Edut 5:8).

The conference starts with the oldest (or presiding) judge stating his opinion (Sanh. 4:2, Yad, Sanhedrin 11:6); but the view was expressed that, as in criminal cases, it should rather be the youngest member of the court who states his opinion first, the same reasons applying in civil cases as well (*Rema*, ḤM 18:1; see also below). Any judge may, in the course of deliberations, change any opinion he previously expressed (Sanh. 4:1). If a judge cannot make up his mind, he must say so, and need not apologize or give reasons for saying so (Yad, Sanhedrin 8:3). Two more judges will then be added to the court (Sanh. 3:6), as the judge unable to form an opinion is regarded as being absent and the remaining two judges, even if of one mind, are not regarded as a court (*Rashi*, Sanh. 29a). The augmented court (of five) will start deliberations anew, but need not hear the case once more (ḤM 18:1).

JUDGMENT. At the close of the deliberations, the parties are called back into court and asked to stand up (Shevu. 30b; Yad, Sanh. 21:3; ḤM 17:1); the presiding judge announces the decision, without disclosing whether or not the judgment is unanimous, or how each judge voted. If the judgment is unanimous, so much the better; if not, the majority prevails (Sanh. 3:6, Sanh. 3b; et al.). If (owing to the judges being unable to form an opinion) the court has been increased time and again up to the maximum of 71 members and is still almost equally divided, judgment will be given for the defendant as the plaintiff has not established his case to the satisfaction of a clear majority (Yad, loc. cit. 8:2; ḤM 18:2).

Any party may ask the court for a record of the judgment in writing (Sanh. 30a; Yad, loc. cit. 22:8, ḤM 19:2) and for a written statement of the reasons behind it (BM 69b and Tos. thereto; Sanh. 31b; Tur ḤM 14 and *Beit Yosef* thereto), if only for the purposes of appeal to the Great Court (Yad, Sanhedrin 6:6). The written judgment (and the reasons for it) must be signed by all the judges, including the dissenter (R. Johanan in TJ, Sanh. 3:1, 21d). While judgment is given on the day the case was heard (Sanh. 4:1; Maim. *Comm. to Mishnah*, Avot. 5:8; ḤM 17:11), and any delay of justice is regarded as a violation of "Ye shall do no unrighteousness in judgment" (Lev. 19:15), the written record of the judgment and the reasons for it may be given whenever a party applies for it, without any time limit (*Rema*, ḤM 14:4). Where the judgment has not been put into writing, the fitness of the judges to say what judgment they gave ceases when the parties no longer stand before them (Kid. 74a; ḤM 23:1), i.e., when they are no longer associated with the case (Tosef., BM 1:12). This rule apparently caused great hardship and was later restricted, first to discretionary judgments given without pleadings and without evidence, and then to judgments given by a single judge (ḤM 23:1; Resp. *Rosh* 6:15, 56:4; *Mordekhai* Kid. 541), and was thus virtually abolished.

The judgment may not exceed the amount of the claim (*Rema* ḤM 17:12); but where the court is satisfied that the plaintiff was genuinely ignorant of the real extent of his rights, it may impose fines and other sanctions on the defendant to compel him to satisfy the plaintiff even beyond his claim (*Sma*, ḤM 17:26; *Baḥ* ḤM 17).

For the effect of judgments *inter partes* and *inter alios*, see **Ma'aseh*.

REVISION. A judgment is always subject to revision, normally by the court that made it in the first place, if new evidence has come to light disproving the facts which the judgment was based on, provided the party seeking to adduce such new evidence is not debarred from so doing (see above; Sanh. 3:8; Yad, Sanhedrin 7:6; ḤM 20, 1). Every judgment is also subject to revision for errors of law. Originally the rule appears to have been general and to have applied in all civil cases, whatever the quality of the error (Sanh. 4:1); later it was confined to erroneous judgments of nonprofessional and non-expert judges (Bek. 4:4); finally, the rule was confined to errors of mishnaic (i.e., clear and undisputed) law, as distinguished from "errors of discretion" (Sanh. 6a, 33a; Ket. 84b, 100a). While "discretion" was originally understood in its wide literal sense (cf. Sanh. 29b; TJ, Sanh. 1:1, 18a), it was eventually confined to matters on which there were different views in the Talmud and the *halakhah* had not been decided; whatever view the judge followed, his judgment would not (for that reason alone) be subject to revision. It might otherwise be where the court followed one opinion in ignorance or disregard of the fact that another opinion had been accepted and put into practice "throughout the world" (Yad, Sanh. 6:2; ḤM 25:2). The revisable error could (in certain well-defined circumstances) be of great moment to the judge personally, as he might find himself saddled with the obligation to pay out of his own pocket any irrecoverable damage caused by his error (Yad, loc. cit. 6:3; ḤM 25:3).

Apart from revisable error, unwarranted assumption of judicial authority (whether it resulted in error or not) is a cause for having the judgment set aside, but it stands until set aside (Yad, loc. cit. 6:4; ḤM 25:4). The finding of unwarranted assumption of judicial authority is tantamount to a finding of a trespass, and counts in damages (*ibid.*). In many countries, the revision of judgments of errors of law was reserved to courts of appeal, i.e., mostly courts presided over by the leading scholars of the community.

MODERN LAW. While the procedure in Israel civil courts is mainly based on English law, the procedure in the rabbinical courts is governed by the *Takkanot ha-Diyyun* which were enacted by the chief rabbinate of Israel in 1960 (revising earlier *takkanot* of 1943). They purport to reflect talmudic and post-talmudic law, but actually deviate from it and follow modern procedural concepts in many important particulars; for example, the requirement of written statements of claim, representation by attorneys, cross-examination of parties (in addition to witnesses), reduction of judgments into writing before delivery, and discretion in the matter of costs.

Penal. For the composition of courts competent to adjudicate in criminal cases, see **Bet din*. The composition of the court and certain matters of procedure differ in capital and non-capital cases. While the following account deals with capital cases (unless otherwise indicated), practice and procedure were modeled on them as far as possible (cf. Maim., Yad, Sanh. 16:1–4).

COURT SESSIONS. In criminal cases, the court sits only during the day and adjourns at sunset (Sanh. 4:1; Yad, Sanh. 11:1). If the proceedings have been concluded during the day, a judgment of acquittal will be announced forthwith, but a judgment of conviction and sentence may not be announced until the following day (Sanh., loc. cit.; Yad, loc. cit.), since there is a chance that the judges may change their minds during the night (*Rashi*, Sanh. 32a). No criminal sessions may therefore be held on the eves of the Sabbath and holidays (Sanh. 4:1; Yad, Sanhedrin 11:2); and either because a trial is regarded as potentially a first step in an execution, which may not take place on a Sabbath (TJ, Sanh. 4:7, 22b), or because the trial involves writing prohibited on the Sabbath (Tos. to Beẓeh 36b and Sanh. 35a), no criminal trials may be held on the Sabbath or holidays.

In the Temple precincts (see **Bet din*), criminal sessions started after the morning sacrifices and ended with the late afternoon sacrifice (Sanh. 88b); otherwise the time of court sessions is the same in criminal as in civil cases. The following is a mishnaic account of the manner in which courts of 23 held criminal trials:

The court sat in the form of a half-circle, so that the judges could all see one another. The two court scribes stood before them, one at the right and one at the left, and recorded the words of the judges—one the words of those in favor of conviction, and the other the words of those in favor of acquittal. Three rows of learned disciples sat before them, each knowing his place; when the seat of a judge became vacant, his place would be filled with the first sitting in the first row (Sanh. 4:3–4—According to Maim., Yad, Sanhedrin 1:9; but Rashi (to Mishnah, Sanh. 36b) states that the two scribes write the words both of those in favor and those against, so that if one scribe errs the other can correct him).

The public and the disciples would be already in court when the judges entered—the presiding judge last—and everyone present would rise and remain standing until the presiding judge gave them leave to sit down (Tosef., Sanh. 7:8).

Duplicity of Trials. Only one capital case may be tried on any one day in any one court (Sanh. 6:4; Tosef., Sanh. 7:2). An exception was made where there were several participants in one crime, provided they were all liable to the same penalty (Sanh. 46a). However, where participants in one crime were liable to execution by different methods, as, e.g., in *adultery where the male adulterer was liable to strangulation and the female adulteress, if a priest's daughter, to burning, they had to be tried separately on different days (Yad, Sanh. 14:10).

Arrest. The arrest and detention of persons awaiting trial is reported in the Bible (Lev. 24:12; Num. 15:34), and the appointment of judges presupposed the concomitant appointment of police officers (*shoterim:* Deut. 16:18). Maimonides describes *shoterim* as officers equipped with sticks and whips who would patrol streets and market-places, and bring any criminals they caught before the court; these officers would also be dispatched by the court to arrest any person against whom a complaint had been brought ("they act upon the judges' orders in every matter": Yad, Sanhedrin 1:1). In capital cases the accused would be detained pending trial (Sif. Num. 114; Yad, Sanhedrin 11:2), if he was caught *in flagranti delicto* or there was at least some *prima facie* evidence against him (TJ, Sanh. 7:8). However, the fact that the available evidence was as yet insufficient to put a man on trial was no reason not to detain him until sufficient evidence was available (Sanh. 81b). Or, where death had not yet ensued but the victim was dangerously wounded, the assailant would be detained until the degree of his offense could be determined (Sanh. 78b; Ket. 33b). The accused would always be held in custody (Yad, Sanhedrin 12:3). Opinions were divided on whether an arrest could be made on the Sabbath.

Bail. The release of an accused person on bail pending trial is already mentioned in early sources (Mekh. Nezikin 6). The rule evolved that in capital cases no bail should be allowed (*ibid.;* and Resp. Ribash no. 236, quoted in *Beit Yosef,* ḤM 388, n. 5), from which it may be inferred that in non-capital cases bail would be granted as a matter of course.

Default Proceedings. No criminal proceeding may be conducted in the absence of the accused (Sanh. 79b; Yad, Roẓe'ah 4:7, Sanh. 14:7).

Prosecution. There is good authority for the proposition that in cases of *homicide the *blood-avenger acted as prosecutor (Nov. Ran; Sanh. 45a). Where no blood-avenger was forthcoming, the court would appoint one for this purpose (Sanh. 45b). By analogy, it may be assumed that in cases other than homicide the victim of the offense acted as complainant and prosecutor. In offenses of a public nature, the court initiated the proceedings and dispensed with prosecutors. Such proceedings were normally prompted by witnesses who came forward and notified the court that an offense had been committed; if they could identify and name the accused and satisfy the court that a *prima facie* case could be made out against him, the court would take action (Yad, Sanh. 12:1).

Defense. In criminal matters, any person who wished to plead in favor of the accused was allowed and even encouraged to do so (Sanh. 4:1). If a disciple of the judges wished to plead for the accused, he was raised to the bench and allowed to stay there until the end of the day (Sanh. 5:4), clearly a potent encouragement. There are records in post-talmudic times of defense attorneys having been appointed by the court (e.g., Ribash Resp. no. 235).

Evidence. Unlike civil trials, criminal trials started with the interrogation of the witnesses. Before this, each witness had to be warned separately by the court in the following terms:

> If you are going to tell us anything which you only believe or opine, or anything you may have heard from any other person, however trustworthy he may seem to you, or anything you know from rumors—or if you are not aware that this court is going to examine you by a probing cross-examination—you had better know that a criminal trial is not like a civil trial; in a civil case, a false witness pays money to the man he has wronged and will then be discharged; but in a criminal case, his blood and the blood of his children will be on him until the end of the world. Man was created single in this world, to show you that whoever causes one single soul to perish from this world is regarded as if he had caused the whole world to perish; and he who keeps one single soul alive in this world is regarded as having kept the whole world alive. Are not all men created in the form of Adam, the first man, and still the form of each man is different from that of anybody else? Therefore can each and everybody say, it is for me that the world was created. And do not say, why should we bring this calamity upon ourselves? for it is written, whoever is able to testify from what he has seen or known, and does not do so, will be punished [Lev. 5:1]; nor may you say, it is more convenient for us to incur punishment for our silence, than to bring upon ourselves the blood of that criminal; for it is written, there is rejoicing when the wicked perish (Sanh. 4:5; Yad, Sanh. 12:3).

The evidence of at least two witnesses (Deut. 17:6) is required to prove not only that the accused was seen to have committed the act constituting the offense (Ket. 26b; Sanh. 30a; Git. 33b), but also that, immediately before committing it, he had been warned of its unlawfulness and of the exact penalty he would incur (Sanh. 12:2). No circumstantial evidence is ever sufficient to support a conviction (Sanh. 37b; Tosef., Sanh. 8:3; see *Evidence; *Penal law). The accused must be present during the examination of the witnesses, but opinions are divided on whether he must stand up or may be seated. The judges, are of course, seated when hearing evidence (ḤM 28:6), while the witnesses stand (Shevu. 30a; ḤM 28:5).

For the methods of examination of witness, see *Witness.

Deliberations. It is only if and when the evidence of all the witnesses heard is first found consistent, i.e., if it is established to the satisfaction of the court that the witnesses do not contradict themselves or each other in any material particular, that the deliberations (in the technical sense) start (Sanh. 5:4; Yad, Sanh. 12:3). If the evidence is found to be inconsistent, the accused is acquitted and discharged there and then. The rule is that the youngest member of the court has the first say in the deliberations (Sanh. 4:2; Yad, Sanh. 11:6), in case the junior members be unduly impressed and influenced by what their elders have to say (Yad, Sanh. 10:6; Rashi to Ex. 23:2 and to Sanh. 36a); but this rule yields to another that the deliberations must always start with a view propounded in favor of the accused (Sanh. 4:1, 5:4; Yad, Sanh. 11:1, 12:3). Talmudic scholars wondered how anything could be said in favor of the accused once the evidence against him had been found to be consistent, and they solved the problem by suggesting that "opening in favor of the accused" really meant asking the accused whether he could adduce any evidence in rebuttal (Sanh. 32b; TJ, Sanh. 4:1), or reassuring the accused that if he was innocent he had nothing to fear from the evidence adduced against him (*ibid.;* Yad, Sanh. 10:7). Deliberations were thus held in the presence of the accused, and it would appear that at this stage he was given the opportunity of saying anything he wished in his defense: "If he says, I wish to plead in favor of myself, he is heard, provided there is some substance in his words" (Sanh. 5:4). According to Maimonides, he is even raised to the bench for this purpose (Yad, Sanh. 10:8). However, he is not allowed to say anything to his detriment, and as soon as he opens his mouth to admit his guilt or otherwise prejudice himself, he is silenced and reprimanded by the court (Tosef., Sanh. 9:4). Where the accused is not capable of speaking for himself, the court or a judge will do so for him (Sanh. 29a).

It appears that the credibility and weight of the evidence, even though it was found consistent (and hence admissible), was an open issue for the deliberation of the judges, as was the legal question whether the act committed by the accused constituted a punishable offense (Yad, Sanh. 10:9). Having once expressed his view in favor of an acquittal, a judge is not allowed to change his view during the deliberations (Sanh. 4:1, 5:5, 34a; Yad, Sanh. 10:2); but having expressed his opinion condemning the accused, a judge may change his mind even during the deliberations (*ibid.;* Yad, Sanh. 11:1). Judges ought not to follow the opinion of other, greater judges, especially in criminal cases, but must decide solely according to their own knowledge and personal conviction (Tosef., Sanh. 3:8; Yad, Sanh. 10:1).

If, at the end of the day, a majority for an acquittal has been reached, the accused is acquitted forthwith; if no such majority has emerged, the case is adjourned to the next day (see above), the judges conferring, in groups of two, throughout the night, abstaining from too much food and from all alcohol. The next morning, back in court, the scribes checked the judges' views with those they had expressed the day before, so that the number of those arguing in favor of an acquittal could meanwhile only have increased (Sanh. 5:5, Yad, Sanh. 12:3). If a clear majority for conviction has eventually been reached, judgment will be pronounced accordingly; but a "clear majority" presupposes some minority and accordingly, where the whole court is unanimous that the accused be convicted, proceedings are adjourned and deliberations continued until at least one judge changes his view and votes for an acquittal (Sanh. 17a; Yad, Sanh. 9:1). It is believed that this rule applied only to the Great Sanhedrin of 71 (Maim., Yad, *ibid.,* speaks of the "Sanhedrin" as distinguished from the "Small Sanhedrin" in the immediately following paragraph), while in courts of 23 and of three unanimity was as good as, or even better than, a majority.

JUDGMENT. The sentence pronounces the accused guilty and specifies the punishment to be inflicted on him; it is not reasoned. Unlike in civil cases (see above), the accused knows which of the judges were in the majority and which in the minority, and what were the reasons which prompted each judge in his voting, since he had been present at their deliberations.

Once a capital sentence is pronounced, the accused is in law deemed to be dead (Sanh. 71b), and a person killing him would not be guilty of homicide (Yad, Mamrim 7, 9), nor would a person wounding him be guilty of any offense or liable for damages (Tosef., BK 9:15). The theory was propounded that it is this legal fiction which enables the court and the executioners to execute capital sentences without incurring liability as murderers.

On the other hand, as long as the sentence has not been carried out, the judgment is subject to revision: on the way from the court to the place of execution, a herald announces that *A* son of *B* is going to be executed for having committed the offense *C*, and witness *D* and *E* have testified against him; whoever has anything to say in his defense should come forward to say it (Sanh. 6:1). The case is returned to court for a retrial not only if any such person is forthcoming but even if the accused himself wishes to plead again in his own defense—provided there is some substance in what he says *(ibid.)*. In order to find out whether or not there is some substance in what the accused wishes to say, two men learned in the law are seconded to accompany him on his way to the place of execution (Yad, Sanh. 13:1), and if they are satisfied that there is some such substance, they will have him brought back into court even two and three times *(ibid.)*. If, on retrial or redeliberation, the accused is acquitted, the sentence is deemed to be annulled *ex tunc,* as if it had never been passed.

Where the accused escapes after sentence and before execution and then is caught and brought before the court which had sentenced him, his trial is not reopened, but the sentence stands (Mak. 1:10). It might be different if he were brought before a court in Ereẓ Israel, and the court which had sentenced him had sat outside Ereẓ Israel (Yad, Sanh. 13:8). For the purpose of establishing that sentence had duly been pronounced against him, two witnesses must testify that in their presence sentence had been passed on this particular accused and they had also heard the evidence given against him by two named witnesses (Mak. 1:10; Yad, Sanh. 13:7). Before the sentence is finally executed, the accused is asked to confess in order that he may have a share in the world to come (Sanh. 6:2). If he does not know how to make confession, he is asked to repeat the words, "may my death expiate all my sins" *(ibid.)*.

For the various modes of execution, see *Capital Punishment.

Bibliography: CIVIL: H. B. Fassel, *Das mosaisch-rabbinische Gerichts-Verfahren in civilrechtlichen Sachen* (1859); M. Bloch, *Die Civilprocess-Ordnung nach mosaisch-rabbinischem Rechte* (1882); J. Kohler, in: *Zeitschrift fuer vergleichende Rechtswissenschaft,* 20 (1907), 247–64; Juster, Juifs, 2 (1914), 93–126; T. S. Zuri, *Mishpat ha-Talmud,* 7 (1921); Gulak, Yesodei, 4 (1922); S. Assaf, *Battei ha-Din ve-Sidreihem Aḥarei Ḥatimat ha-Talmud* (1924); idem, in: *Ha-Mishpat ha-Ivri,* 1 (1925/26), 105–20; M. Frank, *Kehillot Ashkenaz u-Vattei Dineihem* (1937); N. Kirsch, in: *Yavneh,* 3 (1948/49), 128–36; B. M. Rakover, in: *Sinai,* 38 (1955/56), 312–20; A. Weiss, *Seder ha-Diyyun* (1957); Elon, Mafte'aḥ, 190–9; idem, in: ILR, 3 (1968), 426–8, 437f.; 4 (1969), 103f. PENAL: H. B. Fassel, *Das mosaisch-rabbinische Strafgesetz und strafrechtliche Gerichts-Verfahren* (1870); J. Fuerst, *Das peinliche Rechtsverfahren im juedischen Alterthume* (1870); M. Bloch, *Das mosaisch-talmudische Strafgerichtverfahren* (1901), Juster, Juifs, 2 (1914), 127–214; T. S. Zuri, *Mishpat ha-Talmud,* 7 (1921); H. E. Goldin, *Hebrew Criminal Law and Procedure* (1952); A. Weiss, *Seder ha-Diyyun* (1957); J. Ostrow, in: JQR, 48 (1957/58), 352–70; N. Rakover, in: *Ha-Peraklit,* 18 (1961/62), 264–72, 306–30; Elon, Mafte'aḥ, 190–9; Mendelsohn, *The Criminal Jurisprudence of the Ancient Hebrews* (1968[2]); H. E. Baker, *Legal System of Israel* (1968), 197–231.

[H.H.C.]

PRADO, JUAN (Daniel) DE (c. 1615–c.1670), *Marrano physician. Born in Spain, probably at Alcalá de Henares, Prado studied at the university there and then at the University of Toledo, where he received a medical diploma in 1638. Outspoken by nature, Prado felt impelled to leave inquisitorial Spain and made his way to Picardy, in northern France. By 1655 he had moved to Holland, where he proclaimed himself a Jew and took the name of Daniel. A dozen contemporaneous documents reveal how upon settling in Amsterdam, Prado formed a circle of young intellectuals and led them in the development of unorthodox philosophical ideas. One of the group was Baruch *Spinoza, then 22. As early as 1656, Prado was charged with being publicly critical of the Bible, derogating the distinctiveness of Jewish people, denying the authority of rabbinic tradition, and preaching the supremacy of Natural Law. To avoid being condemned, Prado read the required statement of regret for heresy. Nevertheless, he was excommunicated in 1657. Unlike Spinoza, however, he strove to have the ban (*ḥerem*) lifted. A full review of Prado's expulsion in 1657 resulted in a reaffirmation of the ban. Inquisition arrest warrants for the "tall, black-bearded" Prado and for Spinoza were circulated twice during 1659. The Inquisition had been an indirect factor in their excommunications, for the congregation had feared that their liberal pronouncements would offend the Church and would serve as pretexts to force the Dutch authorities into restricting the freedom of Amsterdam Jewry. After 1659 there was no apparent contact between Prado and Spinoza. Spinoza, content in the *ḥerem*, went on to develop his pantheistic philosophy, in which Prado had no share; Prado continued to grapple with the problems of universalism versus Jewish identity, still seeking reentry into the Jewish fold.

Three letters attacking Prado were written around 1665 by Isaac *Orobio de Castro. Legalistically thorough and longest is the *Epistola Invectiva Contra Prado, un Philosopho Medico, que Dubitava, o no Creya la Verdad de la Divina Escritura, y Pretendió Encubrir su Malicia con la Affecta Confaesion de Dios y Ley de Natureza* ("Epistle against Prado, philosopher/physician who doubted or disbelieved the truth of Divine Writ, maliciously hiding behind affectations of faith in God and natural law"). Another Spanish Marrano, the poet Daniel Levi de *Barrios, took Prado as his subject, condemning him in three poems composed during 1665–72. The most ironic was occasioned by Prado's death, with Barrios bidding good riddance "to that master of false dogmas."

Bibliography: C. Gebhardt, in: *Chronicon Spinozanum*, 3 (1923), 269–91; I. S. Revah, *Spinoza et le Dr. Juan de Prado* (1959); Roth, Marranos, 300; JE, s.v. *Castro, Balthasar (Isaac) Orobio de*. [ED.]

PRAEFECTUS JUDAEORUM (Hebraeorum supremus, Obrister der Judischkait, prince des juifs, etc.), office of the leader of Jews in Hungary during the Middle Ages. It may be assumed that the position of *Praefectus Judaeorum* was established by the Hungarian king, Matthias Corvinus, at the suggestion of János Ernuszt, a treasurer of Jewish origin, at the time of the financial reforms (1467–76). The principal function of the *Praefectus* was the collection of taxes for the royal treasury. In exchange for this he enjoyed royal privileges and could effectively defend the rights of the Jews against any attack. On festive occasions, he was authorized to accompany the king with much splendor at the head of a battalion. The *Praefectus* governed the Jews of the country and was exempted from wearing distinctive signs. Until its abolition in 1539, this position was held by members of the *Mendel family.

Bibliography: S. Kohn, *A zsidók története Magyarországon*, 1 (1884), 212–22; S. Buechler, *A zsidók története Budapesten a legrégibb időktől 1867-ig* (1901), 48–51; S. Balog, *A magyarországi zsidók kamaraszolgasága és igazságszolgáltatása a középkorban* (1907), 68–72; J. Hajnik, in: *Akadémiai Értesitő*, 5 (1866), 203–49; S. Scheiber, in: *Mult és Jövő*, 33 (1943), 107–8; L. Zolnay, *Buda középkori zsidósága* (1968), 23–26; *Magyar Zsidó Lexikon* (1929), s.v. *Zsidó prefektura;* P. Gruenwald, in: *Sefer ha-Yovel . . . N. M. Gelber* (1963), xiii–xx (Ger.). [A.KU.]

PRAGER, RICHARD (1883–1945), German astronomer. Prager was born in Hanover. In 1908 he joined the Berlin Academy of Sciences; and in 1909 was appointed head of a department in the National Observatory in Santiago, Chile. From 1913 onward he worked as scientific collaborator, and from 1924 as observer at the Berlin University Observatory at Babelsberg. He made an important contribution to photoelectric stellar photometry, and also extended, by several volumes, the large enterprise of a complete history and bibliography of the light variations of variable stars. He was imprisoned in Potsdam by the Nazis in 1938, an experience from which he never recovered. His friends in Britain and the United States were able to free him and brought him to England and America, where he applied his talents to pure astronomy and war work for the U.S. Navy.

Bibliography: A. Beer, in: *The Observatory*, 66 (1945), 186–7; J. C. Poggendorff, *Biographisch-literarisches Handwoerterbuch*, 7A (1961), s.v. [A.BE.]

PRAGUE (Czech **Praha**), capital of *Czechoslovakia; it has the oldest Jewish community in *Bohemia and one of the oldest communities in Europe, for some time the largest and most revered. Jews may have arrived in Prague in late Roman times, but the first document mentioning them is a report by *Ibrahim ibn Ya'qūb from about 970. This may be interpreted as showing that Jews had either settled in Prague or carried on business there without necessarily settling permanently. The first definite evidence for the existence of a Jewish community in Prague dates to 1091. From an analysis of medieval commerce in Prague it is reasonable to assume that its beginnings date from about the middle of the tenth century. Jews arrived in Prague from both the East and West around the same time. It is probably for this reason that two Jewish districts came into being there right at the beginning, one in the suburb of the Prague castle (*Suburbium Pragense*) and the other close to the second castle, Wissegrad (*Vicus Wissegradensis*).

The relatively favorable conditions in which the Jews at first lived in Prague were disrupted at the time of the First Crusade in 1096. The Crusaders murdered many of the Jews of Prague, looted Jewish property, and forced many to accept baptism. During the siege of Prague castle in 1142, the oldest synagogue in Prague and the Jewish quarter below the castle were burned down and the Jews moved to the right bank of the river Moldau (Vltava), which was to become the future Jewish quarter, and founded the "Altschul" ("Old Synagogue") there.

The importance of Jewish culture in Prague is evidenced by the works of the halakhists there in the 11th to 13th centuries. The most celebrated was *Isaac b. Moses of Vienna (d. c. 1250) author of *Or Zaru'a*, a native of Bohemia, who spent part of his life in Prague. Since the Czech language was spoken by the Jews of Prague in the early Middle Ages, the halakhic writings of that period also contain annotations in Czech. From the 13th to 16th centuries the Jews of Prague increasingly spoke German. At the time of persecutions which began at the end of the 11th century, the Jews of Prague, together with all the other Jews in Europe, lost their status as free people. From the 13th century on, the Jews of Bohemia were considered servants of the Royal Chamber (**servi camerae regis*). Their residence in Prague was subject to the most humiliating conditions (the wearing of special dress, segregation in the ghetto, etc.). The only occupation that Jews were allowed to adopt was moneylending, since this was forbidden to Christians and considered dishonest. Socially the Jews were in an inferior position, but economically many of them were relatively well off. Against payment of high taxes they were protected by the king by means of special privileges (e.g., the privilege issued by *Přemysl Ottokar II in 1254).

Protection by the kings made it possible for larger

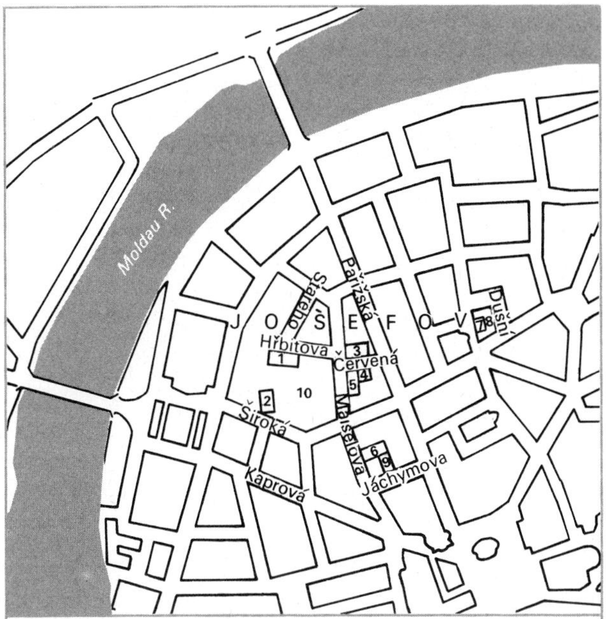

1. Klaus Synagogue, built 1680.
2. Pinkas Synagogue, built 1535.
3. Altneuschul Synagogue, built 1270, still in use today.
4. High (Town Hall) Synagogue, built second half of 16th century.
5. Jewish Town Hall, residence of the Prague Jewish community today, last reconstruction 1765.
6. Maisel Synagogue, reconstructed 1885–1913.
7. Dušní Synagogue, formerly Altschul Synagogue; built 1605 and reconstructed 1866.
8. State Jewish Museum, formerly the Sephardi Synagogue.
9. State Jewish Museum, formerly Bet Sefer ha-Torah.
10. Jewish Cemetery.

The Jewish quarter in Prague.

numbers of Jews to settle there, particularly from Germany. In the 13th century a new Jewish settlement was founded in Prague, in the vicinity of the Altneuschul (the "Old-New Synagogue"), construction of which was completed in 1270. The synagogue, which still exists, is the oldest remaining in Europe. By the 13th century the Jewish community of Prague owned a cemetery which as then situated outside the city walls (in the present Vladislav street), and also served other Jewish communities in Bohemia. It was sold, under pressure, to the citizens of Prague as a building plot in the 15th century.

The community suffered from persecutions accompanied by bloodshed in the 13th and 14th centuries, particularly in 1298 and 1338. Charles IV (1346–78) protected the Jews, but after his death the worst attack occurred in 1389, when nearly all the Jews of Prague fell victims. The rabbi of Prague and noted kabbalist Avigdor *Kara, who witnessed and survived the outbreak, described it in a *seliḥah: Et Kol ha-Tela'ah.* It was also described in a Christian work *Passio Judaeorum Pragensium secundum Joannem rusticum quadratum.* Under *Wenceslaus IV the Jews of Prague suffered heavy material losses following an order by the king in 1411 canceling all debts owed to Jews.

At the beginning of the 15th century the Jews of Prague found themselves at the center of the Hussite wars (1419–36; see *Hussites). An analysis of Hussite biblical interpretation shows possible Jewish influence. The attitude of German Jews toward the Hussites reveals a certain sympathy on the part of the Jewish communities for this movement (as expressed, e.g., by Jacob b. Moses *Moellin, the "Maharil" of Cologne). The attitude of the Hussites to the Jews was not entirely friendly. Some Hussite ideologists (e.g., Jacobellus of Stříbro (Mies) in the treatise *De usura*) demanded that Jewish moneylending be prohibited. However, no such prohibition was ever issued in Prague during the time of the Hussites. The Jews of Prague also suffered from mob violence (1422) in this period. The unstable conditions in Prague compelled many Jews to emigrate. Nevertheless, the Jewish community continued to exist there throughout the Hussite period and this in itself may be considered proof of the relatively tolerant attitude of the Hussites toward the Jews.

The position of the Jews in Prague in the second half of the 15th century remained insecure. There were also attacks in that period (as in 1448 and 1483). Following the legalization, at the end of the 15th century, of moneylending by non-Jews in Prague, the Jews of Prague lost the economic significance which they had held in the medieval city, and had to look for other occupations in commerce and crafts. Thus the Jews began to compete economically with the citizens, at a time when the traditional crafts were in a state of crisis.

The tension between the Jews and the citizens brought about a considerable change in the position of the Jews in Prague. From the beginning of the 16th century the citizens repeatedly attempted to obtain the expulsion of the Jews from the city. Their demands to this effect, in 1501, 1507, 1517, etc., were unsuccessful, however. Despite the growing tension between the Jews and the citizens of Prague, the position of the Jews began to improve at the beginning of the 16th century, mainly owing to the assistance of the king and the nobility. The Jews found greater opportunities in trading commodities and monetary transactions with the nobility. As a consequence, their economic position improved. The number of Jews in Prague increased from the beginning of the 16th century. In 1522 there were about 600 Jews in Prague, but by 1541 they numbered about 1,200. At the same time the Jewish quarters were extended. At the end of the 15th century the Jews of Prague founded new communities in the New Town and on the *"Kleinseite."* At the beginning of the 16th century they left these districts and concentrated on extending the Jewish quarter in the Old Town. At the turn of the 15th and early in the 16th centuries they rebuilt the devastated Altschul and built the Pinkas Synagogue (the construction of which was completed in 1535).

Under pressure of the citizens, King *Ferdinand I was compelled in 1541 to approve the expulsion of the Jews. The elegy *Anna Elohei Avraham,* composed by *Abraham b. Avigdor, is related to that expulsion. The Jews had to leave Prague by 1543, but were allowed to return in 1545. Following the defeat of the first anti-Hapsburg rebellion in Bohemia in 1547, in which the towns played an important part, the latter lost a great deal of their political importance in the country and were no longer able to threaten the Jews of Prague seriously. However, in 1557 Ferdinand I once again, this time upon his own initiative, ordered the expulsion of the Jews from Prague. They had to leave the

Figure 1. The Altneuschul of Prague, the oldest extant synagogue in Europe, with the Jewish town hall behind it on the right, c. 1930.

city by 1559. Only after the retirement of Ferdinand I from the government of Bohemia were the Jews allowed to return to Prague in 1562.

The progress of the Jewish community of Prague had been noticeable also in the cultural sphere even before their expulsion when the Gersonides (successors of Gershom Kohen) founded a Hebrew printing establishment before 1512 (see Hebrew printing in Prague, below). During the reign of Rudolf II (1576–1611), who transferred his court to Prague, and of his successor Matthias (1611–19), the position of the Jews was particularly favorable. L. *Zunz called that period the golden age of Prague Jewry. Some Jews attained fabulous wealth and became the patrons of the Jewish community, notable among them Marcus Mordecai *Meisel (1528–1601), the Gersonide Mordecai Ẓemaḥ Kohen (d. 1592), and Jacob *Bassevi von Treuenberg (d. 1634).

The favorable position of the Jewish community of Prague during the reign of Rudolf II is reflected also in the flourishing Jewish culture. Among illustrious rabbis who taught in Prague at that time were *Judah Loew b. Bezalel (the "Maharal"); *Ephraim Solomon b. Aaron of Luntschitz; Isaiah b. Abraham ha-Levi *Horowitz, who taught in Prague from 1614 to 1621; and Yom Tov Lipmann *Heller, who became chief rabbi in 1627 but was forced to leave in 1631. The chronicler and astronomer David *Gans also lived there in this period. At the beginning of the 17th century about 6,000 Jews were living in Prague. To extend the Jewish quarter the community acquired in 1627 the so-called Lichtenstein houses, thus almost doubling the area.

In 1648 the Jews of Prague distinguished themselves in the defense of the city against the invading Swedes. In recognition of their acts of heroism the emperor presented them with a special flag which is still preserved in the Altneuschul. Its design with a Swedish cap in the center of the shield of David became the official emblem of the Prague Jewish community.

After the Thirty Years' War, government policy was influenced by the Church Counter-Reformation, and measures were taken to separate the Jews from the

Figure 2. Etching of the interior of the Altneuschul in Prague. In the center is the banner presented to the Jewish community by the Emperor Ferdinand III in 1648.

Figure 3. "The Expulsion of the Jews from Prague, 1745," a contemporary etching. Nuremberg, Germanisches Museum.

Christian population, to reduce the number of Jews and segregate them in ghettos, to limit their means of earning a livelihood, and to extort larger contributions and higher taxes from them. The ultimate aim of this "anti-Semitism of the authorities" was to reduce the importance of the Jews in Prague. A number of resolutions and decrees were promulgated; among them the resolution of the provincial diet of Bohemia passed in 1650, and the *Familiants Law of 1727 were particularly oppressive. According to the latter only the eldest son of every family was allowed to marry and found a family, the others having to remain single or leave Bohemia.

In 1680, more than 3,000 Jews in Prague died of the plague. Shortly afterward, in 1689, the Jewish quarter burned down, and over 300 Jewish houses and 11 synagogues were destroyed. The authorities initiated and partially implemented a project to transfer all the surviving Jews to the village of Lieben (Libén) north of Prague, later a suburb of the capital. The clergy fanned anti-Jewish feelings. Great excitement was aroused in 1694 by the murder trial of the father of Simon Abeles, a 12-year-old boy, who, it was alleged, had desired to be baptized and had been killed by his father. Simon was buried in the Tyn (Thein) church, the greatest and most celebrated cathedral of the Old Town of Prague. Concurrently with the religious incitement against the Jews an economic struggle was waged against them.

The anti-Jewish official policy reached its climax after the accession to the throne of *Maria Theresa (1740–80), who in 1744 issued an order expelling the Jews from Bohemia and Moravia. This was actually carried out against the Jews of Prague, who were banished (1745–48) but were subsequently allowed to return as a result of influential intervention on their behalf, and after they promised to pay high taxes. In 1754 a great part of the Jewish quarter burned down. Despite all these persecutions Jewish culture continued to flourish in Prague. In the Baroque period noted rabbis were Simon Spira; Elias Spira; David *Oppenheim; and Ezekiel *Landau, chief rabbi and *rosh yeshivah* (1755–93).

The position of the Jews greatly improved under *Joseph II (1780–90), who issued the **Toleranzpatent* of 1782 and other decrees connected with it. The new policy in regard to the Jews aimed at gradual abolition of the limitations imposed upon them, so that they could become more useful to the state in a modernized economic system. At the same time, the new regulations were part of the systematic policy of Germanization pursued by Joseph II. Jews were compelled to adopt family names and to establish schools for secular studies; they became subject to military service, and were required to cease using Hebrew and Yiddish in business transactions. Wealthy and enterprising Jews made good use of the advantages of Joseph's reforms. Jews who founded manufacturing enterprises were allowed to settle outside the Jewish quarter in Prague. Among the first Jewish industrialists of Prague, who were engaged particularly in the textile industry, were the Porges (later Porges of Portheim), Dormitze, and Epstein families.

Subsequently the limitations imposed upon Jews were gradually removed. In 1841 the prohibition on Jews owning land was rescinded. In 1846 the Jewish tax was abolished. In 1848 Jews were granted equal rights, and by 1867 the process of legal *emancipation had been completed. In 1852 the ghetto of Prague was abolished and united with four other "cities" as the fifth district of Prague, called Josefov (Ger., Josefstadt). Because of the unhygienic conditions in the former Jewish quarter the Prague municipality decided in 1896 to pull down the old quarter, with the exception of important historic sites. Thus the Altneuschul, the Pinkas and Klaus, Meisel and Hoch synagogues, the famous "Radnice" or "Rathaus" (Jewish town hall), erected by Mordecai Meisel, the larger part of the old cemetery, and some other places of historical and artistic interest remained intact. Many Jews moved out of the old quarter and dispersed through the city. Whereas in 1870 over half of Prague Jewry still lived in the old quarter, in 1900 less than one-quarter remained.

In 1848 the community of Prague, numbering over 10,000, was still one of the largest Jewish communities in Europe (Vienna then numbered only 4,000 Jews). In the following period of the emancipation and the post-emancipation era the Prague community increased considerably in numbers, but did not keep pace with the rapidly expanding new Jewish metropolitan centers in Western, Central, and Eastern Europe. While an increasing proportion of Bohemian Jewry concentrated in Prague, the importance and size of Bohemian Jewry within world Jewry began to dwindle. In the period 1880 to 1900 Jewish natural increase reached its peak in the world, whereas the number of Jews in Bohemia reached its maximum in 1880 and subsequently decreased. The following table shows the numerical development of the Jewish population of Prague (including the suburbs incorporated in the city, some only after World War I):

Figure 4. The clock tower of the 16th-century Jewish town hall of Prague. The main clock, with Roman numerals, functions in the conventional manner. The lower one, with Hebrew numerals, added in 1754, works anti-clockwise. Courtesy State Jewish Museum, Prague.

Table 1.

Year	No. of Jews	% of Jewish population of Bohemia	% of total population of Prague
1880	20,508	21.7	6.52
1890	23,473	24.8	5.91
1900	27,289	29.4	5.31
1910	29,107	33.9	4.72
1921	31,751	39.8	4.69
1930	35,463	46.4	4.17

During the revolutionary period of 1848 there were violent anti-Jewish outbreaks in Prague. In consequence the emigration of Bohemian Jews to America and Western Europe that had begun in the 1840s increased and gained momentum.

After emancipation had been achieved in 1867, emigration from Prague abroad ceased as a mass phenomenon; movement to Vienna, Germany, and Western Europe continued, but in Prague the loss had been offset by the influx of Jews from the smaller provincial communities. Jews contributed to the economic progress of the city. They were now represented in industry, especially the textile, clothing, leather, shoe, and food industries, in wholesale and retail trade, and in increasing numbers in the professions and as white-collar employees. Some Jewish bankers, industrialists, and merchants achieved considerable wealth. The majority of Jews in Prague belonged to the middle class, but there also remained a substantial number of poor Jews.

Emancipation brought in its wake a quiet process of secularization and assimilation. In the first decades of the 19th century Prague Jewry, which then still led its traditionalist orthodox way of life, had been disturbed by the activities of the followers of Jacob *Frank. The situation changed in the second half of the century. The chief rabbinate was still occupied by outstanding scholars, like Solomon Judah *Rapaport (Shir; officiated from 1840 to his death in 1867), the leader of the Haskalah movement; Markus *Hirsch (officiated 1880–89); Nathan *Ehrenfeld (1890–1912); and Heinrich (Ḥayyim) *Brody (1912–30), but the mainstream of Jewish life was no longer dominated by the rabbinate. Many synagogues introduced modernized services, a shortened liturgy, the organ and mixed choir, but did not necessarily embrace the principles of the *Reform movement.

Jews availed themseves eagerly of the opportunities to give their children a secular higher education. Table 2 below shows the participation of Jewish university students at Prague (the famous Charles University, founded in 1348, was split in 1882 into a German and a Czech university).

Emancipation was accompanied by a strong tendency to adopt the German language, and by assimilation to German culture and national consciousness. Jews formed a considerable part of the German minority in Prague, and the majority adhered to liberal movements. David *Kuh founded the German Liberal Party of Bohemia and

Table 2.

Year	% of Jews among university students	
1852	7.2	
1862	11.2	
	German University	Czech University
1890	44.6	0.67
1900	46.5	1.6
1925	29.8	9.7

represented it in the Bohemian Diet (1862–73). Despite strong Germanizing factors, many Jews adhered to the Czech language, and in the last two decades of the 19th century a Czech assimilationist movement (see Čechů-židů, Svaz) developed which gained support from the continuing influx of Jews from the rural areas. Through the influence of German nationalists from the Sudeten districts anti-Semitism developed within the German population and opposed Jewish assimilation. At the end of the 19th century Zionism struck roots among the Jews of Bohemia, especially in Prague. The following table, showing the national affiliation of the Jews of Prague, indicates the extent of assimilation there (Jews were entitled to declare their nationality as Jewish from 1920):

Table 3.

Year	% of the Jews of Prague who declared themselves to be:		
	Czechs	Germans	Jews
1900	55.3	44.4	—
1921	53.5	25.3	20.1
1930	54.8	18.1	27.0

Growing secularization and assimilation led to an increase of *mixed marriages and abandonment of Judaism. Whereas under Austrian rule cases of baptism were not very frequent, at the time of the Czechoslovak Republic, established in 1918, many more people registered their dissociation of affiliation to the Jewish faith without adopting another. The proportion of mixed marriages in Bohemia was one of the highest in Europe, amounting to 24.3% in 1927 and 30.73% in 1933 of the marriages of all Jewish males and 22.1% and 25.25% respectively of Jewish females. The proportion in some small communities may have been higher than in Prague, but the difference could not change the overall picture substantially, since almost half of Bohemian Jewry resided in Prague. The consequences of this development are clearly demonstrated in the census of 1939, conducted under the German occupation. Of those classified as Jews in Prague according to the Nazi racial laws, 12.1% did not profess the Jewish faith.

After the establishment of the Czechoslovak Republic, when the suburbs were incorporated in the municipality of Prague, the Jewish communities did not similarly affiliate. The paradoxical situation therefore developed that there were seven Jewish communities in Prague, one covering the inner city (districts I–VII) with approximately one-half of the Jewish population of Prague, and the other six in the various suburbs. These seven communities were federated in the Union of Jewish Religious Communities of Greater Prague, cooperated on many issues, and also established joint institutions; among these the most important was the Institute for Social Welfare, established in 1935. There were many Jewish associations, organizations, and institutions in Prague. Among associations of a religious character the most important was the *ḥevra kaddisha* existing from the early 16th century. The *Afike Jehuda Society for the Advancement of Jewish Studies was founded in 1869. There were also the Jewish Museum and the Jewish Historical Society of Czechoslovakia. A five-grade elementary school was established with Czech as language of instruction. The many philanthropic institutions and associations included the Jewish Care for the Sick, the Center for Social Welfare, the Aid Committee for Refugees, the Aid Committee for Jews from Carpatho-Russia, orphanages, hostels for apprentices, old-age homes, a home for abandoned children, free-meal associations, associations for children's vacation centers, and funds to aid students. Zionist organizations were well represented. There were three *B'nai B'rith lodges, several other fraternities, women's organizations, youth movements, student clubs, sports organizations, and a community center. Four Jewish weeklies were published in Prague (three Zionist; one Czecho-assimilationist), and several monthlies and quarterlies. Most Jewish organizations in Czechoslovakia had their national headquarters in Prague.

Jews first became politically active, and some of them prominent, within the German orbit. David Kuh and the president of the Jewish community, Arnold Rosenbacher, were among the leaders of the German Liberal Party in the 19th century. Bruno *Kafka and Ludwig *Spiegel represented its successor in the Czechoslovak Republic—the German Democratic Party—in the chamber of deputies and the senate respectively. Many Jews also joined the German Social Democratic Party and some rose to leadership; Emil Strauss represented that party in the 1930s on the Prague municipal council and in the Bohemian Diet. From the end of the 19th century an increasing number of Jews joined Czech parties, especially T. G. *Masaryk's Realists and the Social Democratic Party. In the latter party Alfred Meissner, Lev Winter, and Robert Klein rose to prominence, the first two as ministers of justice and social welfare respectively. Klein, leader of the white-collar employees, participated in the founding of the World Jewish Congress; he was tortured to death in a concentration camp. Meissner (d. 1952) was a member of the last Council of Elders in *Theresienstadt, and survived the Holocaust.

The Zionists, though a minority, soon became the most active element among the Jews of Prague. Before World War I the students' organization *Bar Kochba, under the leadership of Samuel Hugo *Bergman, became one of the centers of cultural Zionism. At the same time Zionism also spurred Jewish political activity. The Prague Zionist Arthur *Mahler was elected to the Austrian Parliament in 1907, though as representative of an electoral district in Galicia. Under the leadership of Ludvik *Singer the Jewish National Council was formed in 1918. Singer was elected in 1929 to the Czechoslovak Parliament, and was succeeded after his death in 1931 by Angelo *Goldstein. Singer, Goldstein, František Friedmann, and Jacob Reiss represented the Zionists on the Prague municipal council also. Some important Zionist conferences took place in Prague, among them the founding conference of *Hitaḥadut in 1920, and the 18th Zionist Congress in 1933.

Jews were prominent in the cultural life of Prague. Their contribution to German literature was most significant. Of the older generation Salomon *Kohn dealt mainly with Bohemian Jewish topics, Friedrich *Adler, Auguste Hauschner, and Hugo *Salus were among the most prominent authors; Heinrich Teweles was important as an author, editor, and director of the theater. The group of Prague German-Jewish authors which emerged in the 1880s, known as the "Prague circle" *(Der Prager Kreis)*, achieved international recognition and included Franz *Kafka, Max *Brod, Franz *Werfel, Oskar *Baum, Ludwig Winder, Leo *Perutz, Egon

Erwin *Kisch, Otto Klepetar, and Willy *Haas. Among Jews who contributed to Czech literature a pioneer was the poet Siegfried *Kapper; he was later considered the herald of Czech-Jewish assimilation. To this group also belonged at a later time Eduard *Lederer (Leda), Vojtěch *Rakous, celebrated for his novels about Jewish life in the Czech countryside, and Jindřich *Kohn, the philosopher and ideologist of assimilation. Other important authors were Otakar *Fischer, Richard *Weiner, František *Langer, his brother Mordecai Jiří *Langer, Jiří *Weil, František *Gottlieb, and Egon *Hostovský. Important scientists teaching at Prague universities included Arnold Piek, Max Saenger, and Edmund Weil (medicine), Samuel *Steinherz (history), Ludwig *Spiegel (constitutional law), Moritz *Winternitz (Sanskrit), Otakar Fischer (German literature), Oskar Engländer (economics) and Guido *Adler (musicology). Albert *Einstein taught in Prague in 1911–12, and Hans *Kelsen, a native of Prague, taught there in 1936–38. The composer Jaromir *Weinberger was born in Prague and lived there until his emigration in 1937; Gustav *Mahler, a native of Bohemia, spent several years in Prague as a conductor. Among many other noted Jewish conductors and musicians from Prague were Walter Suesskind, Frank *Pelleg, George Singer, and Karel Ančerl. The German theater in Prague knew its most glorious period under the directorships of Angelo Neumann, Heinrich Teweles, and Leopold Kramer. Ernst *Deutsch and Franz Lederer were among the most celebrated actors on the German stage, and Hugo Haas and Jiří Voskovec on the Czech stage. Emil *Orlik and Hugo Steiner-Prag were outstanding artists.

Jewish topics, and particularly the history and legends of Prague Jewry, were a frequent theme in the work of non-Jewish authors and artists, more so in the Czech cultural sphere than in the German. Retrospectively, the Jewish ghetto has been considered part and parcel of Prague's history. The statue of Judah Loew b. Bezalel at the entrance to the new City Hall, and a statue of Moses near the Altneuschul, both works of Czech sculptors commissioned by the Prague municipality, are monuments to this attitude. The Jews of Prague responded with gratitude and pride in their history; but latterly only a minority was still capable of living a meaningful Jewish life, much less of forging a creative Jewish future.

[J.HER./CH.Y.]

Holocaust Period. From 1935, two years after Hitler's seizure of power in Germany, a constant influx of refugees arrived in Prague from Germany, followed in 1938 by refugees from Austria and the German-speaking occupied parts of Czechoslovakia. As a result the number of Jews in Prague on March 15, 1939, the day of the Nazi occupation, amounted to about 56,000. On July 22, 1939, *Reichsprotektor* Constantin von Neurath ordered the establishment of a Zentralstelle fuer juedische Auswanderung in Boehmen und Maehren ("Central Office for Jewish Emigration in Bohemia and Moravia"). Its director in fact was Adolf *Eichmann. Initially the office dealt only with Prague's Jews but as of Feb. 16, 1940, it affected all the Jews in the protectorate.

Figure 5. Exhibition of Jewish ritual objects in the Klaus Synagogue, now part of the State Jewish Museum of Prague.

At the outbreak of the war (Sept. 1, 1939), prominent Prague Jews were arrested and deported as hostages to *Buchenwald concentration camp. Various anti-Jewish measures, e.g., deprivation of property rights, prohibition against religious, cultural, or any other form of public activity, expulsion from the professions and from schools, a ban on the use of public transportation and the telephone, affected Prague Jews much more than those still living in the provinces. Jewish organizations provided social welfare and clandestinely continued the education of the youth and the training in languages and new vocations—in preparation for emigration. The *Palestine Office in Prague, directed by Jacob *Edelstein, enabled about 19,000 Jews to emigrate legally or otherwise until the end of 1939. In March 1940, the Prague Zentralstelle extended the area of its jurisdiction to include all of Bohemia and Moravia. In an attempt to avert the deportation of the Jews to "the east," Jewish leaders, headed by Jacob Edelstein, proposed to the Zentralstelle the establishment of a self-administered concentrated Jewish communal body; the Nazis eventually exploited this proposal in the establishment of the ghetto at *Theresienstadt (Terezin). The Prague Jewish community was forced to provide the Nazis with lists of candidates for deportation and to ensure that they showed up at the assembly point and boarded deportation trains. In the period from Oct. 6, 1941, to March 16, 1945, 46,067 Jews were deported from Prague to "the east" or to Theresienstadt. Two leading officials of the Jewish community, H. Bonn and Emil Kafka (a former president of the community) were dispatched to *Mauthausen concentration camp and put to death after trying to slow down the pace of the deportations. The Nazis set up a Treuhandstelle ("Trustee Office") over evacuated Jewish apartments, furnishings, and possessions. This office sold these goods and forwarded the proceeds to the German *Winterhilfe* ("Winter Aid"). The Treuhandstelle ran as many as 54 warehouses, including 11 synagogues (as a result, none of the synagogues was destroyed). The Zentralstelle brought Jewish religious articles from 153 Jewish communities to Prague on a proposal by Jewish scholars. This collection, including 5,400 religious objects, 24,500 prayer books, and 6,070 items of historical value the Nazis intended to utilize for a "Central Museum of the defunct Jewish Race." Jewish historians engaged in the creation of the museum were deported to extermination camps just before the end of the war. Thus the Jewish Museum had acquired at the end of the war one of the richest collections of Judaica in the world. The Pinkas Synagogue, which is included in the museum complex, contains inscriptions of the names of 77,297 Jewish victims of the Nazi extermination campaign in Bohemia and Moravia.

In April 1945 the Prague representative of the International Red Cross (IRC), Paul Dunant, negotiated with *Reichsprotektor* Karl Hermann Frank for the transfer of Theresienstadt ghetto to IRC auspices. When the Czechoslovak government-in-exile in London returned to Prague, a Jewish member of the State Council, Arnošt Frischer, also

Figure 6. Clocks looted from Jews in the Nazi "Trustee Office," in Prague, 1942–43. From H. Volavkova, *Story of the Jewish Museum in Prague*, Prague, 1968.

came back, and under his leadership the Prague Jewish community was reconstituted and a council of Jewish communities in Czechoslovakia established. According to the monthly *Věstník*, the official Jewish community publication, Prague had a Jewish population of 10,338 in 1946, of whom 1,396 Jews had not been deported (mostly of mixed Jewish-Christian parentage); 227 Jews had gone underground; 4,986 returned from prisons, concentration camps, or Theresienstadt; 883 returned from Czechoslovak army units abroad; 613 were Czechoslovak Jewish emigrés who returned; and 2,233 were Jews from Ruthenia (Carpatho-Ukraine), which had been ceded to the U.S.S.R., who decided to move to Czechoslovakia.

Contemporary Period. In the three years following the end of the war, the Jewish population of Prague rose to 11,000, after the return of Prague Jews and the settlement of other survivors of the Holocaust. Thus a basis for Jewish life again existed in the city, and Chief Rabbi Gustav Sicher, who had returned from Palestine, sought to establish firm foundations for the further development of Jewish activities. The Communist takeover of 1948, however, put an end to these endeavors and marked the beginning of a period of stagnation. By 1950 about half of the Jewish population had gone to Israel or emigrated to other countries. The Slánský Trials and the officially promoted anti-Semitism had a destructive effect upon Jewish life. Nazi racism of the previous era was replaced by political and social discrimination. Most of the Jews of Prague were branded as "class enemies of the working people" and suffered from various forms of persecution, including imprisonment, exile, forced labor, and, in some cases, execution. During this period (1951–64) there was also no possibility of Jewish emigration from the country. The assets belonging to the Jewish community—estimated at 100 million Czech crowns—had to be relinquished to the state, the charitable organizations were disbanded, and the budget of the community, provided by the state, was drastically reduced. The general anti-religious policy of the regime resulted in the cessation, for all practical purposes, of such Jewish religious activities as bar mitzvah religious instruction, and wedding ceremonies. Two Prague rabbis—E. Davidovič and E. Farkas—left the country, and in 1964 the office of the chief rabbi also became vacant; only two cantors and two ritual slaughterers were left. Services were held in only two of Prague's nine synagogues, while the other seven were used as exhibition halls and warehouses for the State Jewish Museum. The Hebrew inscription on the wall of the Talmud Torah Synagogue was removed by the museum director. The museum's collection of Jewish art and religious articles were used by the Czechoslovak Travel Bureau as a tourist attraction. Officials of the Jewish communal organizations achieved their positions by manipulated elections.

The liberalization of the regime during 1965–68 held out new hope for a renewal of Jewish life in Prague. At the end of March 1967 the president of the *World Jewish Congress, Nahum *Goldmann, was able to visit Prague and give a lecture in the Jewish Town Hall. Among the Jewish youth many tended to identify with Judaism. In August 1968, however, the Soviet invasion of Czechoslovakia put an end to this trend. The festivities that were to mark the millennium of Jewish life in Prague were canceled four times. A new wave of emigration began, and the Jewish population of Prague was further reduced to about 2,000. [E.Ku.]

Hebrew Printing in Prague. Prague was the first city north of the Alps where Hebrew books were printed. The earliest, printed in 1512, was a book of miscellaneous prayers. Of the early printers Gershom *Kohen emerged as the leading figure; from 1526 he and his sons carried on the printing business which for several generations remained one of the outstanding Hebrew presses in Europe. Gershom Kohen, with his brother Gronim (Jerome), produced independently in 1526 the famous illustrated Passover *Haggadah* (facsimile edition, 1926). In the following year (under the name of Herman) he obtained from King Ferdinand of Bohemia a printing privilege, which at his death in 1545 was reissued to his son Moses and in 1598 to his great-grandson Gershom b. Bezalel. He and his brother Moses after him were active until the middle of the 17th century. The Gersonides printed mainly liturgical items in this period, but also such important works as Jacob b. Asher's *Turim* (1540) and Moses Isserles' *Torat ha-Olah* (1569). Another printing press was founded by Jacob Bak who was printing in Prague by 1605. Jacob died in 1618, and after him eight generations of Baks printed Hebrew books in Prague up to the threshold of the 19th century. Their productions were mostly liturgical and for local use, and they, like other Hebrew printers, suffered much under the Jesuit censorship (from 1528) and occasional book burnings (1715, 1731). Jonathan *Eybeschuetz obtained permission to print the Talmud at Bak's (1728–41).

Figure 7. Wall in the Pinkas Synagogue, Prague, with the names of 77,297 Jews of Bohemia and Moravia murdered by the Nazis from 1939 to 1945. From A. Reith, *To the Victims of Tyranny*, Tubingen, 1968.

Besides Kohen and Bak, other Hebrew printers of note in Prague included Abraham Heide-Lemberger and his sons (1610–41). From 1828 Moses Landau printed independently, in particular a Talmud edition (8°, 1830–35). [Ed.]

Bibliography: The standard guide is O. Muneles, *Bibliographical Survey of Jewish Prague* (Ger. and Czech, 1952); M. Kreutzberger (ed.), *Bibliothek und Archiv,* 1 (1970), and the bibliographies appended to the *Yearbook of the Leo Baeck Institute* (1956–) offer additional information. New material on Prague appears mainly in the communal journal *Věstník,* the scholarly *Judaica Bohemiae* (since 1965), and in works commissioned by the Jewish State Museum of Prague. General Works: S. Steinherz, *Die Juden in Prag* (1927); G. Klemperer, in: HJ, 12 (1950), 33–66; 13 (1951), 55–82; G. Kisch, *Die Prager Universitaet und die Juden* (1969); L. Schnitzler, *Prager Judendeutsch* (1966); *Gesher,* no.2–3, 15 (1969); *The Jews of Czechoslovakia* (1968); *Jewish Studies. Essays in Honor of Dr. Gustav Sicher* (1955). Middle Ages: Germ Jud, 1 (1963); 2 (1968); S. Steinherz, in: *B'nai B'rith Monatsblaetter* 6 (1927), 433–8; idem, in: JGGJČ, 1 (1929), 1–37; J. Prokeš, *ibid.,* 41–224; R. Kestenberg, *ibid.,* 8 (1936), 1–25; V. Rynes, in: *Judaica Bohemiae,* 1 (1965), 9–25; P. Trost, *ibid.,* 4 (1968), 138f. Renaissance: M. Wischnitzer, in: JSOS, 16 (1955), 335–50; idem, *Jewish Crafts and Guilds* (1965), index; O. Muneles (ed.), *Prague Ghetto in the Renaissance Period* (1965); F. Thieberger, *The Great Rabbi Loew of Prague* (1954). Prague Expulsion: B. Brilling, in: *Zeitschrift fuer die Geschichte der Juden,* 1 (1964), 37–42; A. Newman, in: JHSET, 22 (1968), 30–42; B. Mevorah, in: *Meḥkarim be-Toledot Am-Yisrael ve-Ereẓ Yisrael* (1970), 187–232; idem, in: *Zion,* 28 (1963), 125–64. Modern Era: F. Weltsch (ed.), *Prag vi-Yrushalayim* (1954); H. Tramer, in: YLBI, 9 (1964), 305–39; F. Meissner, *German Jews of Prague* (1961; = AJHSP, 50 (1960/61), 98–120); R. Kestenberg-Gladstein, *Neuere Geschichte der Juden in den boehmischen Laendern* (1969); idem, in: YLBI, 9 (1964), 295–304; M. Brod, *Der Prager Kreis* (1966); W. Benda, in: *Zeitschrift fuer die Geschichte der Juden,* 2–3 (1966), 85–94; J. Urzidil, in: BLBI, 10 (1967), 276–97; G. Kisch, in: *Judaica Bohemiae,* 3 (1967), 87–100; J. Vyskočil, *ibid.,* 36–55; K. Baum, in: MGWJ, 73 (1929), 349–65. Hebrew Printing: Zunz, Gesch, 261–303; S. H. Lieben, in: *Die Juden in Prag...* (1927); A. Freimann, in: *Soncino-Blaetter,* 3 (1929–30), 113–43 (189–219); Ḥ. D. Friedberg, *Toledot ha-Defus ha-Ivri ba-Arim she-be-Eiropah ha-Tikhonah* (1935), 1–29; [see also KS, index to vols. 1–40 (1967), nos. 126, 176, 213]. Holocaust Period: M. Moskowitz, in: JSOS, 4 (1942), 17–44; M. Y. Ben-Gavriel, *Bayit bi-Prag* (1945); O. Kraus and E. Kulka, *The Death Factory* (1966), index; *Juedisches Nachrichtenblatt* (Prague, 1939–44); Juedische Kultusgemeinde Prag, *Wochen-, Monats- und Vierteljahresberichte,* 10 vols. (1933–42); H. G. Adler, *Theresienstadt 1941–45* (Ger., 1960), passim. Contemporary Jewry: A. Charim, *Die toten Gemeinden* (1966), 13–21; R. Iltis (ed.), *Die aussaeen unter Traenen mit Jubel werden sie ernten* (1959). Museum, Ghetto and Cemetery: *Historica Hebraica* (1965); H. Volavková, *Story of the Jewish Museum in Prague* (1968); idem, *The Pinkas Synagogue* (1955); J. Lion and J. Lukas, *The Prague Ghetto* (1960); idem, *The Old Prague Jewish Cemetery* (1960); I. Herrmann, J. Tege and Z. Winter, *Das Prager Ghetto* (1903); S. Muenzer, in: JGGJČ, 4 (1932), 63–105; A. Deutsch, *Die Zigeuner-Grossenhof- und Neusynagoge in Prag* (1907); S. Hock and D. Kaufmann, *Die Familien Prags* (1892); B. Wachstein, in: *Jewish Studies... G. A. Kohut* (1935), 25–40.

PRATO, DAVID (1882–1951), rabbi and Zionist leader. Born in Leghorn, Prato was chief cantor in Florence, rabbi of Alexandria (Egypt) from 1927 to 1936, and chief rabbi of Rome from 1936 to 1938. Conditions became impossible for him when the Fascist regime began its anti-Semitic policy, and Prato moved to Ereẓ Israel. He resumed his post in Rome in 1945. An ardent Zionist, Prato played a prominent part in the administration of the *Jewish National Fund and *Keren Hayesod in Italy. In 1929 he founded in Alexandria the French-Hebrew review *L'Illustration Juive,* which was followed by *Cahiers Juifs* in 1933. He published two collections of sermons, *Cinque anni di Rabbinato* (1933), and *Dal pergamo della Comunità di Roma* (1950), covering his activities in Rome.

Bibliography: *Ha-Rav David Prato* (1940). [G.R.]

PRAWER, JOSHUA (1917–), Israel historian. Born in Bedzin, Poland, Prawer settled in Palestine in 1936. He began teaching at the Hebrew University of Jerusalem in 1947 and was promoted to the chair of medieval history in 1958. During the years 1962–66 he was dean of the faculty of humanities. Prawer also served the Israel Ministry of Education as chairman of the pedagogical council for the planning of national education (1957–59) and headed the committee that recommended reforms in secondary education, which constituted the basis of the reform law adopted by the Knesset in 1968. He was also a co-founder and first dean of the Haifa University College, whose academic chairman he was from 1966 to 1968. Prawer's scholarly interests centered mainly on the Crusades. He wrote *Mamlekhet Yerushalayim ha-Ẓalbanit* ("The Crusader Kingdom of Jerusalem," 1946–47) and *Toledot Mamlekhet ha-Ẓalbanim be-Ereẓ-Israel* ("A History of the Latin Kingdom of Jerusalem," 2 vols., 1963). He was a member of the Israel Academy of Sciences and Humanities and from 1967 chief editor of the *Encyclopaedia Hebraica.* In 1969 he was awarded the Israel Prize for Humanities. [G.S.]

PRAYER, the offering of petition, confession, adoration or thanksgiving to God.

In the Bible. The concept of prayer is based on the conviction that God exists, hears, and answers (Ps. 65:3; cf. 115:3–7)—that He is a personal deity. In a sense it is a corollary of the biblical concept that man was created "in the image of God" (Gen. 1:26–27), which implies, inter alia, fellowship with God (see *Man, Nature of). Although prayer has an intellectual base, it is essentially emotional in character. It is an expression of man's quest for the Divine and his longing to unburden his soul before God (Ps. 42:2–3 [1–2]; 62:9[8]). Hence prayer takes many forms: petition, expostulation, confession, meditation, recollection (anamnesis), thanksgiving, praise, adoration, and intercession. For the purpose of classification, "praise" is distinguished from "prayer" in the narrower, supplicatory sense, and "ejaculatory" from formal, "liturgical" prayer. But the source is the same; in its irresistable outpouring, the human heart merges all categories in an indivisible "I–Thou" relationship. Thus prayer and praise may intermingle (I Sam. 2:1–10) and supplication and thanksgiving follow in close succession (Ps. 13:1–5, 6). Indeed many scriptural passages might be called "para-prayers"—they seem to hover between discourse and entreaty (Ex. 3:1–12), meditation and petition (Jer. 20:7ff.), or expostulation and entreaty (Job, passim). It has been estimated (Koehler-Baumgartner) that there are 85 prayers in the Bible, apart from 60 complete psalms and 14 parts of psalms that can be so termed; five psalms are specifically called prayers (Ps. 17, 86, 90, 102, 142). But such liturgical statistics depend on the definition given to prayer.

Terminology. The variegated character of biblical prayer has given rise to a rich nomenclature for praying. The rabbis already noted that "prayer is called by ten different expressions" (Sif. Deut. 26), but on closer examination even more can be found. The most common word for prayer is *tefillah* (Isa. 1:15); the corresponding verb is *hitpallel* (I Kings 8:42). The stem, *pll,* has been explained to mean "to cut oneself" and to refer to the primitive pagan custom of slashing oneself in a frenzy during worship. This etymology is not only hypothetical, but is wholly irrelevant to the biblical situation. It was the idol-worshipers who cut themselves (I Kings 18:28) and the verb used is *wa-yitgodedu;* the Torah forbids such practices (Deut. 14:1). In Scripture the stem *pll* signifies "to interpose, judge, hope." These meanings are eminently suited to the biblical conception of prayer as intercession and self-scrutiny leading to hope. Other terms are: *qara'* ("to call" on the name of the Deity, i.e., worship—Gen. 4:26); *za'aq* ("to cry out" for redress of wrongs—Judg. 3:9); *shiwwa'* ("to cry aloud" for help—Ps. 72:12); *rinnah* ("ringing cry" of joy or sorrow—Ps. 17:1); *darash* ("to seek" God—Amos 5:4); *biqqesh penei* ("to seek the face of" God—Hos. 5:15); *sha'al* ("to inquire"—Ps. 105:40); *nasa'* ("to lift up"—Jer. 7:16); *paga'* ("to encounter," i.e., to appease, gain favor—Jer. 7:16); *hithannen* ("to seek favor," i.e., beseech—Deut. 3:23); *shafakh lev* ("to pour out heart"—Ps. 62:9[8]); and *si'aḥ* ("complaint"—Ps. 142:3[2]).

The Character of Prayer. Despite its multifaceted character, biblical prayer is essentially a simple human reaction. The rabbis called it "the service in the heart" (Ta'an. 2a); the expression has its roots in biblical thought (Hos. 7:14; Ps. 108:2; 111:1). But the needs of man are so numerous and complex that prayer inevitably came to reflect the vast range of human moods, fears, hopes, feelings, desires, and aspirations. In early times—in the patriarchal age—a simple invocation, a calling upon the name of the Lord (Gen. 12:8; 21:33), would suffice. The approach to God at this stage was marked by spontaneity, directness, and familiarity—God was near. Yet the future was veiled by mystery; man was often undecided how to act. Hence the request for a sign or oracle addressed directly to God (Gen. 24:12–14), or indirectly through a priest (I Sam. 14:36–37) or prophet (II Kings 19:2ff.). From this stratum grew the magnificent prayers for understanding and guidance (Num. 6:24–26; I Kings 3:6ff.; Ps. 119:33ff.).

But in emergency man does not merely want to know the future; he seeks to determine it by entreating God's help. Thus Jacob (in a votive supplication) prayed for essential material needs (Gen. 28:20ff.); Eliezer for the success of his mission (Gen. 24:12–14); Abraham for the salvation of Sodom (Gen. 18:23–33); Moses for erring Israel (Ex. 32:31–32); Joshua for divine help in the hour of defeat (Josh. 7:6–9); Hezekiah for deliverance from Sennacherib (II Kings 19:15–19); the prophets on behalf of their people (Jer. 14:1ff.; 15:1ff.; Amos 7:2ff.); Daniel for Israel's restoration (Dan. 9:3–19); Ezra for the sins of his people (Ezra 9:6–15); and Nehemiah for the distress of his people (Neh. 1:4–11). Solomon's noble dedication prayer at the consecration of the Temple (I Kings 8:12–53) includes almost every type of prayer—adoration, thanksgiving, petition, and confession. It also strikes a universal note (8:41ff.) so often echoed by the prophets. The spectrum of biblical prayer thus ranges from the simplest material needs to the highest spiritual yearnings (Ps. 51:1ff.; 119:1ff.), transcending, like prophecy, the horizon of history and reaching to the realm of eschatology (Isa. 66:22–23).

There was an early relationship between *sacrifice and prayer (Gen. 13:4; 26:25), which persisted until the destruction of the Second Temple. The sacrifice suggested man's submission to the will of God; the prayer often provided a commentary on the offering. But the two are not necessarily linked. It is noteworthy that the sacrificial regulations make no liturgical provisions (except for the Day of Atonement, Lev. 16:21); but actually the offerings were themselves a dramatic form of prayer. Contrariwise, prayer could replace sacrifice (Ps. 141:2). In the synagogue, prayer, accompanied by Scripture reading and exposition, entirely took the place of altar offerings.

Examples of prayers of intercession have already been cited. The intercessor, whether prophet, priest, king, or national leader, does not point to the need for an intermediary in worship: "The Lord is near to all who call upon Him in truth" (Ps. 145:18). The intercessor is one who, by his innate spiritual attributes, lends weight to the entreaty. The ultimate criterion still remains not the worthiness of the pleader but of those for whom he is pleading (Ezek. 14:14, 20).

The Accessories of Prayer. Prayer, unlike sacrifice, could be offered up anywhere (Gen. 24:26; Dan. 6:11 in the upper chamber; Ezra 9:5ff.), but there was a natural tendency to prefer a sacred site (e.g., Shiloh or Gibeon). Eventually the Temple at Jerusalem became the major place of prayer (Isa. 56:7); those who could not be there physically at least turned toward it when worshiping (Dan. 6:11; cf. Ps. 5:8 [7]). In time to come the Temple would be a house of prayer for all nations (Isa. 56:7). The synagogue had its origin during the Babylonian exile; originally a place of assembly, it became in due course a house of prayer and study. The emphasis on congregational prayer began to grow but private prayer was never abolished. The heart and not the hour dictated the occasion for prayer. Day and night the Heavenly Father could be entreated (e.g., I Sam. 15:11; Ps. 86:3; 88:2[1]). But the need for regularity brought about a synchronization of the times of prayer and of sacrifice: morning worship corresponded to the morning oblation (Ps. 5:4[3]), afternoon orisons to the late afternoon sacrifice (I Kings 18:36; Ezra 9:5). Nightfall provided yet another occasion for worship, so that prayers came to be offered thrice daily (Ps. 55:18; Dan. 6:11; though twice in I Chron. 23:30). The seven times mentioned in Psalms 119:164 mean "often" or "constantly."

In the Bible no particular gestures are prescribed in connection with prayer. But certain postures developed naturally to lend emphasis to the content of the prayer: standing, which is normal (I Sam. 1:26; I Kings 8:22); kneeling (Dan. 6:11; Ezra 9:5); prostration (Josh. 7:6); head bowed (Gen. 24:26; Neh. 8:6); hands stretched out or uplifted (I Kings 8:22; Ps. 28:2); face between knees (I Kings 18:42); and even sitting (II Sam. 7:18). More important accompaniments of prayer were fasting, mourning, and weeping (Isa. 58:2–5; Joel 2:12); but the ultimate criterion remained earnestness of heart (Joel 2:13).

Originally prayer was undoubtedly spontaneous and personal; but the need to organize religion gave rise to liturgical patterns and musical renderings (Ezra 2:65; I Chron. 16). Prayer formulas are found already in the Pentateuch (Deut. 21:7ff.; 26:5–15). The Psalms provide examples of fuller liturgical development, including choral and instrumental features (see *Psalms). The response "Amen" occurs in Numbers 5:22, Psalms 41:14, etc.; a prayer before the reading of the Torah in Nehemiah 8:6; a doxology in Nehemiah 9:5, 32; a typical review of God's dealings with Israel leading to a confession and a pledge in Nehemiah 9:6–10:1 (9:38).

Answer to Prayer. That prayer is answered is an accepted biblical verity (e.g., Gen. 19:17–23; Num. 12:9ff.); but Scripture is no less emphatic that not all prayers are answered (Gen. 18:17ff.; Isa. 29:13ff.). Ritual is not enough, while hypocritical worship is an abomination (Isa. 1:15; Amos 4:4ff.); and there are occasions when intercession is forbidden (Jer. 7:16; 11:14). It is at this point that the biblical concept of prayer is seen in its true inwardness. Paganism regarded worship as a form of magic, whereby the deity could be compelled to fulfill the worshiper's wishes; the moral element was wholly absent. In biblical faith the divine response is essentially linked to ethical and spiritual values. Man, as it were, answers his own prayer (Gen. 4:7), and fundamentally the answer is a significant change of spirit and outlook. Abraham learned the lesson of faith (Gen. 15:1–6); Moses became his people's deliverer (Ex. 3:2–4:18); Isaiah was transformed into a prophet (Isa. 6:5–8). Prayer and prophecy were probably closely correlated, the former providing spiritual soil in which the revelatory seed took root (Jer. 1:6ff.; Hab. 1:13–2:3). In many instances prayer assumes a tempestuous character (Jer. 12; Ps. 22; Job, passim [cf. 16:17]), but the storm always ends in newfound faith and peace. At times, moreover, God answers before He is appealed to (Isa. 65:24; cf. Dan. 9:20ff.), for man not only beseeches God, but God also seeks man (Isa. 50:2; 65:12). The "I–Thou" relationship is reciprocal.

In sum, the Bible conceives prayer as a spiritual bridge between man and God. It is a great instrument of human regeneration and salvation, worthy even of martyrdom (Dan. 6:11). Rooted in faith (Ps. 121) and moral integrity (Ps. 15), it banishes fear (Ps. 23) and asks, in its noblest formulations, only the blessing of divine favor (Num. 6:24–26). Clothed in language of simple but matchless beauty, it is imbued with religious love and a sense of sweet fellowship with God. Both the Christian and Muslim liturgies have been profoundly influenced by the spirit, thought, and forms of biblical prayer. [I.ABR.]

In the Apocryphal Literature. There are a number of references to prayer in the apocryphal books, including the idea of the living offering up prayers on behalf of the dead (II Mac. 12:44–45). The apocryphal work, The Prayer of Manasseh, is a penitential prayer. The biblical concept that God is near to those who suffer is also developed (Ecclus. 35:13–17). Prayer is associated with the giving of alms (Ecclus. 7:10), and there is a national prayer for deliverance from an enemy (Ecclus. 36:1–17).

In Rabbinic Thought. On the biblical verse "And serve Him with all your heart" (Deut. 11:13), the rabbis commented "What is service of the heart? This is prayer" (Ta'an. 2a). "Service" *(avodah)* in this context is connected with the Temple and its worship, for which prayer is seen as a substitute. On the other hand, the saying of R. Eleazar that prayer is dearer to God than good works and sacrifices (Ber. 32b), though hyperbolic, may nonetheless be intended to express the real superiority of prayer. Possibly, the tension in this matter is to be perceived in the two reasons given for the statutory prayers of the day. According to one opinion, these were ordained by the patriarchs, while another view has it that they correspond to the perpetual offerings in Temple times (Ber. 26b).

The obligation of offering up prayer, though supported by a scriptural verse, is considered to be rabbinic, not biblical (Ber. 21a). Prayers are to be recited three times a day: morning, afternoon, and night (Ber. 4:1). In addition to the statutory prayers and private prayers of various kinds, public prayers were offered in times of distress; prayers for rain, for instance, in times of drought (Ta'an. 2:1–5).

THE VALUE OF PRAYER AND CONCENTRATION IN PRAYER. Prayer stands high in the world of values (Ber. 6b). God Himself prays, His prayer being that His mercy might overcome His judgment (Ber. 7a). Nevertheless, the study of the Torah occupies a higher rung than prayer, and some scholars, whose main occupation was study, only prayed periodically (Shab. 11a; RH 35a). A rabbi who spent too much time on his prayers was rebuked by his colleague for neglecting eternal life to engage in temporal existence (Shab. 10a). Communal prayer is of greater significance than private prayer (Ber. 8a; Deut. R. 2:12). Too much reflection on one's prayers in the expectation that these will be answered was discouraged (Ber. 32b). Prayer should be offered with proper concentration *(kavvanah)* on the words uttered in God's presence (Ber. 31a). R. Eliezer said: "He that makes his prayer a fixed task, his prayer is not supplication" (Ber. 4:4). R. Simeon b. Nethanel said: "... and when thou prayest make not thy prayer a fixed form, but [a plea for] mercies and supplications before God" (Avot 2:13). One way of avoiding the deadening familiarity of a "fixed form" was to recite a new prayer each day (TJ, Ber. 4:3, 8a). When R. Eliezer was asked by his disciples to teach them the ways of life that they might learn them and by following attain the life of the world to come, part of his reply was: "When you pray, know before Whom you stand" (Ber. 28b). A person who has just returned from a journey and is consequently unable to concentrate properly, should not pray until three days have elapsed (Er. 65a).

PROPER FORMS OF PRAYER. Not every prayer is valid. A prayer for God to change the past, for instance, is a "vain prayer" (Ber. 9:3). The impossibility of God answering every prayer addressed to Him is acknowledged in the account of the prayer of the high priest on the Day of Atonement who used to pray before the rainy season that the prayers of the travelers who required fair weather should not be allowed to enter God's presence (Yoma 53b). A man should not only pray for himself but should also think of others, using the plural form "grant us" rather than the singular "grant me" (Ber. 29b–30a). If a man needs something for himself but prays to God to grant that very thing to his neighbor who needs it, such an unselfish prayer causes God to grant him his wish first (BK 92a). Man should never despair of offering supplication to God "even if a sharp sword rests upon his neck" (Ber. 10a). In praising God, man should be circumspect, using only the standard forms of praise found in Scripture and established for use in prayer (Ber. 33b). Prayers of thanksgiving, particularly in the form of the benediction *(berakhah),* are repeatedly enjoined by the rabbis (Ber. 6:1–3), as well as praise of God for His wondrous works and the marvelous beings He has created (Ber. 9:1–2; Ber. 58b).

THE ADDRESSING OF PRAYERS DIRECTLY TO GOD. R. Judah said that if a human being is in trouble and wishes to invoke the aid of his patron he must first stand at the door and call out to a servant or a member of the patron's family and he may or may not be allowed to enter. But it is otherwise with God. God says, "When a man is in trouble, do not cry out to the angel Michael or to the angel Gabriel but to Me and I will answer immediately" (TJ, Ber. 9:1, 13a). On the other hand, R. Johanan said: "When one petitions for his needs in Aramaic, the ministering angels do not heed him, for they do not understand Aramaic" (Shab. 12b). Possibly a distinction is to be made between the angels bringing man's prayers to God and direct intercession, with the angels as intermediaries between man and God (cf. Tob., 12:12, 15). Some men were renowned for their capacity to pray and to have their prayers answered, so that great scholars, less gifted in this direction, would ask these saints to pray on their behalf (Ber. 34b). A number of miracle tales are told to illustrate the immediacy of God's response to the prayers of such men (Ta'an. 3:8; Ta'an. 23a–b).

In Medieval Thought. Although medieval Jewish thinkers profoundly considered major theological problems, there is surprisingly little discussion in their writings of the intellectual difficulties involved in prayer. One of the few discussions as to why prayer should be necessary, since God knows man's needs, is that of Joseph *Albo (Ikkarim 4:18). Albo replies that the act of turning to God in prayer is itself one of the conditions upon which God's help depends, just as it depends on other forms of human effort.

MAIMONIDES. True to his doctrine of theological negation, *Maimonides in the standard liturgy only permits the use of those divine attributes in prayer which have been ordained by the "prophets," and he is opposed to the indiscriminate writing of hymns (Guide, 1:59; cf. Ibn Ezra to Eccles. 5:1). In spite of the talmudic statement that the obligation to pray is of rabbinic origin *(mi-de-rabbanan),*

Maimonides observes that this only applies to the number, form, and times of prayer, and that it is a biblical duty for the Jew to pray daily (Yad, Tefillah, 1:1). The need for adequate concentration in prayer *(kavvanah)* is particularly stressed in the Middle Ages and formed part of the general tendency prevalent among medieval Jewish thinkers who stressed greater inwardness in religious life. *Baḥya ibn Paquda (*Ḥovot ha-Levavot,* 8:3, 9) remarks that prayer without concentration is like a body without a soul or a husk without a kernel. Maimonides' definition of *kavvanah* reads: "*Kavvanah* means that a man should empty his mind of all other thoughts and regard himself as if he were standing before the Divine Presence" (Yad, Tefillah, 4:16; cf. H. G. Enelow, in: *Studies in Jewish Literature Issued in Honor of Prof. Kaufmann Kohler* (1913), 82–107).

The Kabbalists. The kabbalists stress the difficulty of petitionary prayer to a God who is unchanging. They advance the view that prayer cannot, in fact, be offered to God as He is in Himself *(Ein Sof),* but only to God as He is manifested in the ten divine potencies (the *Sefirot*). God Himself is, therefore, not entreated directly to show mercy, for example, but prayer is directed to God as He is manifested in the *Sefirah* of loving-kindness. As a result of the power of man's prayer, this potency might function on earth. The magical nature of kabbalistic prayer and the dangers of setting up the *Sefirot* as divine intermediaries were the topic of much subsequent debate (Ribash, Resp. no. 157). The kabbalists, in fact, substituted for the older doctrine of *kavvanah* the concept of special intentions *(kavvanot)* i.e., meditations on the realm of *Sefirot.* Instead of concentrating on the plain meaning of the prayers, the kabbalist dwells on the realm of divine potencies and directs his mind, when reciting the words, to the supernal mysteries which govern and are controlled by them (see I. Tishby, *Mishnat ha-Zohar,* 2 (1961), 247–306).

The Ḥasidim. In Ḥasidism, the kabbalistic type of *kavvanot* yields to a far more emotional involvement and attachment *(devekut)* to God. "The metamorphosis which took place in the meaning of *kavvanot* at the advent of Ḥasidism, and more explicitly after the Great Maggid [*Dov Baer of Mezhirech], consists in this—that an originally intellectual effort of meditation and contemplation had become an intensely emotional and highly enthusiastic act" (Weiss, in: JJS, 9 (1958), 163–92). In Ḥasidism, prayer is a mystical encounter with the Divine, the heart leaping in ecstasy to its Source. Violent movements in prayer were not unusual; some of the ḥasidic groups even encouraged their followers to turn somersaults during their prayers (Dubnow, *Ḥasidut,* 112–5).

Prayer is frequently seen in Ḥasidism as man's most important religious activity. R. Shneur Zalman of Lyady, the founder of the intellectual *Ḥabad sect in Ḥasidism, writes: "For although the forms of the prayers and the duty of praying three times a day are rabbinic, the idea of prayer is the foundation of the whole Torah. This means that man knows God, recognizing His greatness and His splendor with a serene and whole mind, and an understanding heart. Man should reflect on these ideas until his rational soul is awakened to love God, to cleave to Him and to His Torah, and to desire His commandments" (M. Teitelbaum, *Ha-Rav mi-Ladi u-Mifleget Ḥabad,* 2 (1914), 219).

In Ḥabad Ḥasidism, the true meaning of prayer is contemplation on the kabbalistic scheme whereby God's infinite light proceeds through the whole chain of being, from the highest to the lowest. Man should reflect on this until his heart is moved in rapture, but he should not engage in prayer for the sake of the pleasure such rapture will bring him; he must take care not to confuse authentic ecstasy with artificial spiritual titivation (Dov Baer of Lubavich, *Kunteres ha-Hitpa'alut*). Many ḥasidic groups, otherwise strictly conformist, disregarded the laws governing prayer at fixed times on the grounds that these interfere with the need for adequate preparation and with the spontaneity which is part of the prayer's essence.

The Practice of Swaying in Prayer. During the Middle Ages, the practice of swaying during prayer is mentioned. The Zohar (3:218b–219a) refers to the difference between Israel and the nations. It states that the soul of the Jew is attached to the Torah as a candle is attached to a great flame, and hence Jews sway to and fro while studying the Torah. *Judah Halevi (*Kuzari* 2:79–80) also refers to the custom as practiced during the study of the Torah, but makes no mention of prayer. Isserles, however, quoting earlier authorities, also mentions the custom for prayer, while other authorities disagree (see Sh. Ar., OḤ, 48:1 and *Magen Avraham,* ad loc.). The explanation given by Simeon Brainin (quoted by Judah David Eisenstein in JE 11 (1907), 607), that swaying during study and prayer was intended to afford the body with exercise, is incredibly banal. Bodily movements during prayer are, of course, not unusual among the adherents of most religions.

In Modern Thought. The early reformers were much concerned about such questions as prayers for the restoration of sacrifices or the return to Zion, and whether prayer might be recited in the vernacular. Very few challenges, however, were presented to the idea of prayer as such in its traditional understanding. In the 20th century, Jewish thinkers began to consider the basic philosophical problems surrounding prayer. Petitionary prayer was felt to be especially difficult in the light of scientific views regarding cause and effect. A definite move away from the idea of prayer as a means of influencing God and toward its function as a way to affect man's attitudes can be observed. "Self-expression before God in prayer has thus a double effect; it strengthens faith in God's love and kindness, as well as in His all-wise and all-bountiful prescience. But it also chastens the desires and feelings of man, teaching him to banish from his heart all thoughts of self-seeking and sin, and to raise himself toward the purity and the freedom of the divine will and demand" (K. Kohler, *Jewish Theology* (1918), 275).

The tendency in some circles to reinterpret the God-idea itself in impersonal terms has cast prayer into a different light. It is seen as an attempt by man to attune himself to those powers in the universe which make for human self-fulfillment and as a reaching out to the highest within his own soul. Defenders of the traditional view of God and of prayer to Him have, however, not been lacking. (See *Proceedings of the Rabbinical Assembly of America,* 17 (1953), 151–238, for these two opinions). [L.J.]

Bibliography: K. Kohler, *The Psalms and Their Place in the Liturgy* (1897); A. Greiff, *Das Gebet im Alten Testament* (1915); F. Heiler, *Das Gebet* (1923); A. Wendel, *Das freie Laiengebet im vorexilischen Israel* (1932); Idelsohn, Liturgy; P. A. H. de Boer, in: OTS, 3 (1943); S. H. Blank, in: HUCA, 21 (1948), 331–54; 32 (1961), 75–90; idem, *Jeremiah, Man and Prophet* (1961), 92–93, 105ff., 234ff.; F. Hesse, *Die Fuerbitte im Alten Testament* (1951); M. D. Goldmann, in: *Australian Biblical Review,* 3 (1953), 1ff.; D. R. Ap-Thomas, in: *Scottish Journal of Theology,* 9 (1956), 422–9; idem, in: VT, 3 (1956), 225–41; J. Scharbert, in: *Theologie und Glaube,* 50 (1960), 321–38; J. Has-Paecker, in: *Bibel und Leben,* 2 (1961), 81–92, 157–70; E. A. Speiser, in: JBL, 82 (1963), 300–6; H. Ḥamiel (ed.), *Ma'yanot* (1964); H. A. Broncers, in: ZAW, 77 (1965), 1–20; L. Krinetzki, *Israels Gebet im Alten Testament* (1905); A. Gonzáles, *La oración en la Biblia* (1968); M. Kadushin, *Worship and Ethics: A Study in Rabbinic Judaism* (1964); R. Schatz-Uffenheimer, in: *Studies in . . . Gershom G. Scholem* (1967), 317–36.

PRAYER BOOKS. Books containing the texts of the customary daily prayers did not exist in ancient times. Sources of tannaitic and amoraic times take it as understood that prayer is by heart (e.g., Ber. 5:3–5; RH 4:5–6; Ta'an. 2:2). In public prayer the reader prayed aloud before the congregation, which responded *"amen"* to the blessings. The writing down of the text of blessings and prayers was considered forbidden ("writers of blessings are [like] those who burn the Torah," Tosef. to Shab. 13:4; Shab. 115b; TJ, Shab. 16:1, 15c). After the completion of the Talmud, however, this prohibition was disregarded, and in the geonic era written prayer books undoubtedly existed already (L. Ginzberg, *Geonica,* 1 (1909), 119ff.). In Babylon it was permitted, at first, to use them only on the Day of Atonement, and on other fast days, but later they were permitted generally. This development was complete at the beginning of the eighth century. The Cairo *Genizah* has preserved fragments of prayer books both from Ereẓ Israel and the countries bordering it from this period (see *Liturgy).

Siddur and Maḥzor. The book that included the regular prayers for the whole year was called *seder (siddur) tefillah*—a name fixed by the *geonim* themselves—or, according to the cycle of the year, *maḥzor* (i.e., the cycle of prayers). At first there was no difference between the two names, and in the early period (in certain communities, until the present time) they were used indiscriminately. In the course of time the additions for special days (i.e., the *piyyutim*) were also included. However, the present Ashkenazi custom (and, through their influence, that of certain Sephardi communities as well) to differentiate between the *siddur* (pl. *siddurim*)—containing only the regular prayers—and the *maḥzor* (pl. *maḥzorim*)—containing also the *piyyutim,* in most cases only those of the festivals—came into being at a very late period, and is without foundation. The (Arabic-speaking) Jews of Yemen call the comprehensive *siddur, Tikhlal.* All the *siddurim* that have been preserved are designed for a particular rite. In the manuscripts there are a greater number of rites than those of the countries or the cities which finally came to be established or which later reached publication.

Early Siddurim. The beginnings of the order of prayer are found in the second part of tractate *Soferim,* which is a compilation from the period of the first *geonim.*

Seder Rav Amram Gaon. The first true prayer book, however, is the *Seder Rav Amram Gaon* from the ninth century. This prayer book (compiled at the request of the Jews of Spain) contains the regular prayers, according to the order of the whole year—weekdays, Sabbath, New Moon, fast days, Ḥanukkah, Purim, and all the festivals—together with the relevant *halakhot* preceding each section. At the end are the *benedictions and special prayers for occasions such as marriage, circumcision, redemption of the firstborn, and the burial service. Unfortunately this text of the prayers cannot serve as an authentic source for the custom of the *geonim* since all the extant manuscripts of this *seder* differ greatly from one another, in accordance with the rite of the copyist (ed. by N. N. Coronel, 1865, A. L. Frumkin in 1912, partially by D. Hedegård, 1951).

Siddur Saadiah Gaon. The *Siddur Saadiah Gaon,* which was written 100 years later, and which also contains the relevant *halakhot* along with the text of the prayers—the former written in Arabic for the benefit of the Jews of Egypt—is apparently, in the sole extant manuscript (ed. by I. Davidson, S. Assaf, and B. I. Joel, 1941), the rite of the Babylonian *geonim* (with some influence of the rite of Egypt). In contrast the *Genizah* fragments of the *siddur* contain the text of the prayers in a different and adapted version. The logical, methodical order of this prayer book, however, which differs from the ordinary calendar order, was not generally accepted (except by Maimonides); its order possibly explains as well the limited circulation of this *siddur.* Another prayer book compiled in the 11th century by *Hai b. Sherira Gaon, has been lost except for some quotations from it in halakhic literature.

The work entitled *Siddur Rashi,* which emerged in the 11th/12th centuries from the school of *Rashi (ed. by S. Buber, 1911), does not contain the text of the prayers at all, but only the halakhic material, with full talmudic treatment. Also the *Seder ha-Tefillot* that *Maimonides (12th century) attached to his *Mishneh Torah* is not a true prayer book but a collection of versions of prayers from which it is possible to compile a *siddur;* his rite is apparently that current in Egypt in his time, very different from that of the Spanish Jews; it was also adopted in Yemen.

Maḥzor Vitry. In contrast to these works, the **Maḥzor Vitry,* compiled in the 11th century by *Simḥah b. Samuel of Vitry, a pupil of Rashi, is a prayer book in the full sense of the word. It contains the text of all the regular prayers, in accordance with the rite of northern France, which is close to that of Germany. The laws of prayer precede each section in great detail. In the halakhic part, which is mainly consistent with the *Siddur Rashi,* large sections have been copied from the *Seder Rav Amram Gaon,* but later *geonim* are also cited. The edition of S. Hurwitz, published in 1889–93, is based on a London manuscript, amplified by additions of the 13th and 14th centuries. Besides the regular prayers, the *Maḥzor Vitry* includes only a limited number of *piyyutim,* namely *ma'arivim* and *hoshanot;* added to it are the Passover *Haggadah* and the prayers for Simḥat Torah; it lacks all the *kerovot* (which were, however, already in use at that time), and thus cannot be regarded as a complete *maḥzor.* It seems, however, that this format came about through a certain logic; beginning with the Middle Ages, prayer books were copied mostly in a small format for individual use, and it was usual among Germans and French to include in them *ma'arivim* and *hoshanot,* while the *maḥzorim* including the *kerovot,* mainly in large format (folio), were designed for the cantors. The prayer books themselves, apart from a few differences in text, do not differ from one another in their scope. The sole difference is in the laws of the prayers, which are sometimes brought at length and sometimes briefly. In place of the full talmudic explanation of the themes and the discussion of the various opions found in the *Seder Rav Amram Gaon* and the *Maḥzor Vitry,* the final ruling alone came to be given.

Manuscripts from Other Rites. From this period prayer books of other rites have also been preserved (see *Liturgy) in manuscript: those of the Jews of Italy *(Roman Maḥzor)* mainly in small folio format, and also of the Jews of the Balkans, and of the Jews of Spain, mostly in quarto. Among the Jews of Yemen (where there was no printing press at all) the writing of prayer books continued (mostly *Tikhlalim* in small folio) until the beginning of the 20th century. This wealth of manuscripts, most of which are in the large libraries, has not yet been fully exploited for scientific editions and for research into the history of the text. There is still no critical text of any of the well-known rites constructed out of the actual texts in the manuscripts.

Commentaries on the text of the prayers began simultaneously with the composition of the ancient prayer books. In the prayer books of the *geonim* there is as yet no explanation of the texts of the prayers but the *Maḥzor Vitry* contains explanations of a number of prayers, such as *Kaddish,* **Nishmat Kol Ḥai, hoshanot,* and the Passover *Haggadah.* The greatest rabbinic authorities, such as Rashi, Joseph *Caro, *Eliezer b. Nathan of Mainz (Raban),

*Ephraim b. Jacob of Bonn, Baruch the father of *Meir of Rothenburg, Judah he-Ḥasid of Regensburg, *Eleazar b. Judah of Worms, author of *Ha-Roke'aḥ* (see Abraham b. Azriel, *Arugat ha-Bosem*, ed. by E. E. Urbach, 4 (1963), introd., passim), participated in the exposition of the prayer books. Their comments were transmitted anonymously from place to place and passed into the customary manuscript expositions, and then into print in the margins of the *siddurim* and *maḥzorim*.

Printed Prayer Books. With the advent of printing, prayer books for different customs, both *maḥzorim* for the whole year as well as *siddurim* in small format for use of the individual, were printed. Among the *incunabula there are already many prayer books (see A. Freimann, *Thesaurus Typographiae Hebraicae Saecue; XV*, Suppl. to pt. 1, 1967–69; list of incunabula). Prayer books of the Roman rite were published first (*Maḥzor Roma*, Soncino-Casalimaggiore 1485/86; *Siddur Katan* called "Sidorello," 1486), then those of the Spanish rite (*Seder Tefillot*, 1490). Printed Spanish and Portuguese books have come down only in fragments. In the 16th century, German and Polish prayer books were published (*maḥzorim*, beginning with 1521, 1522, and *siddurim*, about 1508), and those of the Romaniot custom (*maḥzorim*, from 1510, *siddurim*, later still). Prayer books for the communities of southern France were not printed until the 18th century (*Maḥzor* Avignon 1765–66, Carpentras 1739–62), while the *Tikhlal* of the Yemenite Jews was published only at the end of the 19th century (Jerusalem, 1894–98). Certain categories of prayers such as *seliḥot* and *kinot* for the Ninth of *Av were printed long ago in special editions (e.g., *seliḥot* according to the German custom, Soncino 1496; *kinot* for the Ninth of Av according to the Polish custom, Cracow 1584), although in the main they were also incorporated in the *maḥzorim*.

Types of Prayer Books. In the course of time the following types of prayer book became established among Ashkenazi Jews: (1) *Ha-Maḥzor ha-Gadol* in folio (also called *Kol Bo*), containing, according to the ancient custom, all the prayers of the year—weekday, Sabbath, festivals, and special days; (2) the so-called *Maḥzor*, which included only the festival prayers, usually a separate volume for each festival; (3) the small *siddur*, containing only the regular prayers; (4) *Ha-Siddur ha-Shalem*, completed by the addition of the *yoẓerot* for the special Sabbaths, the *hoshanot*, *seliḥot* for fast days, *ma'arivim* for the nights of the festivals, and supplemented at times by the Book of Psalms and *ma'amarot*. The Sephardi Jews, on the other hand, arrived at the following subdivision: (1) *Tefillat ha-Ḥodesh*, comprising the prayers for weekdays, Sabbath, the New Moon, Ḥanukkah, and Purim; (2) *Mo'adim*, consisting of the prayers for the three pilgrim festivals; (3) *Rosh Ha-Shanah*, for the New Year; (4) *Kippur* for the Day of Atonement; (5) *Ta'aniyyot*, which also included the Ninth of Av and its *kinot*. Only the Jews of Italy and Yemen maintained the original form of the *Maḥzor ha-Shanah*, which contained all the prayers in cyclical order; small *siddurim* were, however, also published by them.

Textual Editions. As to the text of the regular prayers, the *siddur* of the Sephardi Jews was edited in the 16th century in accordance with the "intentions" (**kavvanah*) of Isaac *Luria; as a result hardly any pre-Lurianic prayer books are extant. In many editions they made the divine names conform with the Lurianic "intentions" by a different pointing or by interlacing the ineffable name with various forms of the word *Adonai*. The text of the Ashkenazi *siddur* occupied several scholars, particularly in the 17th to 19th centuries, who published the prayer book in new editions or wrote books in which they justified substantiation or amendment of the text: Naḥman Lieballer (Dyhrenfurth, 1690); Azriel and his son, Elijah of Vilna (*Derekh Si'aḥ ha-Sadeh*, Frankfort on the Main, 1704); Solomon Zalman Katz Hanau (*Kunteres Sha'arei Tefillah* and the ed. *Beit Tefillah*, Jesnitz, 1725); Jacob Emden (Yaveẓ; *Lu'aḥ Eresh*, an appendix to his prayer book, Altona, 1769); Mordecai Duesseldorf (*Kunteres Hassagot al Siddur Sha'arei Tefillah*, published after his death, at Prague in 1784); Isaac Satanow (*Va-Ye'etar Yiẓḥak*, Berlin 1785, who polemicizes with all his predecessors); Judah Leib Ben Ze'ev (*Tikkunei ha-Tefillah*, published after his death with the edition *Tefillah Zakkah*, Vienna, 1816); Wolf Heidenheim (*Siddur Safah Berurah* with notes at several points, Roedelheim, 1806). In the course of time Heidenheim's text was accepted as a sort of standard text. All disputes about the text, however, turn on such grammatical niceties as the insertion of a *dagesh* or *meteg* and matters of pointing, and only very rarely on establishing the text. In the case of Heidenheim, particularly, and those following him, it should be pointed out that they preferred, to too great an extent, the language of the Bible to "the language of the scholars."

Critical Editions. Critical treatment of the prayer book begins with the activity of E. L. Landshuth who contributed to the *Siddur Hegyon Lev* (published by Z. H. Edelmann, 1845) the commentary *Mekor Berakhah*, in which he consistently gathered the sources of the prayers and tried to establish the date of their compilation and composition. This method was continued by W. Jawitz (*Mekor ha-Berakhot*, 1910), A. Berliner (*Randbemerkungen zum taeglichen Gebetbuch*, 2 vols., 1909–12), and S. Elbogen (*Der juedische Gottesdienst*, 1913, 1931^3).

Commentaries. Commentaries to the prayer book appeared in fairly large numbers, and it is impossible to mention here even an appropriate part of them. The old commentaries, based upon manuscript commentaries, were printed in the folio editions of *maḥzorim* (e.g., *Hadrat Kodesh*, Venice, 1554, et al.; *Ma'gelei Ẓedek*, Venice 1588, et al.; to the *maḥzor* of Rome, *Kimḥa de-Avshuna*, Bologna 1540). There are commentaries with a kabbalistic approach (like that of Lipmann *Muehlhausen, in *Siddur Dikduk Tefillah*, Thiengen 1560; the *Sha'ar ha-Shamayim* of Isaiah *Horowitz, Amsterdam 1717; *Beit Tefillah*, with the commentary of Isaac Luria and Moses *Zacuto to the Sephardi *siddur*, Amsterdam 1712, et al.; and the *siddur Ha-Gra* of *Elijah b. Solomon, the Gaon of Vilna, Jerusalem 1895). Other commentaries deal more with explanations of the words and themes, such as *Beit-El Sha'ar ha-Shamayim* (Altona, 1745/47) of Jacob Emden, though here too comments of an esoteric nature are intermingled; *Iyyun Tefillah* (1857) of Jacob Ẓevi Meklenburg; *Avodat Yisrael* (1868) of Isaac Seligman *Baer, containing sources of the prayers, many notes on grammatical topics, and comparisons of the texts of different rites, as well as a short exposition of the *seliḥot* and *yoẓerot*; *Ishei Yisrael* (c. 1900) following the rite of Elijah b. Solomon, with two commentaries—*Avnei Eliyahu* of Elijah Landau, and *Si'aḥ Yiẓḥak* of Isaac Malzan; *Oẓar ha-Tefillot* (1915, et al.) with the commentaries of A. L. Gordon and Enoch Zondel b. Joseph, to the sections of *piyyut*, too, and with a special section, "*Tikkun Tefillah*," on the textual variations—apparently the most complete prayer book; *Siddur Tefillah* (1912) with the commentaries "*Magen ha-Elef*" and "*Mekor ha-Berakhot*" of A. L. Frumkin (in his edition of the *Seder Rav Amram Gaon*); *Avodat ha-Levavot* (1922) with the commentary of Wolf Jawitz, dealing mainly with the dependence of the language of the prayer book upon that of the Bible; *Olat Re'iyyah* (1939–49), with the commentary of Abraham Isaac Kook; *Ẓelota de-Avraham* (1957–62), in accordance with the usage of Abraham Landau, rabbi of Czechanow (d. 1875), with the commentary of his grandson

M. M. H. Landau, and with additional exposition by Jacob Werdiger, the latter's grandson, containing important studies of the sources of the prayers and of the various rites. To these should be added the commentary *"Eẓ Ḥayyim"* of Yaḥya b. Joseph Ẓelaḥ to the Yemenite *Tikhlal* (1894–98). The ancient connection between the text of the prayers and their laws was renewed in the 19th century when the *Derekh ha-Ḥayyim* (1828) of Jacob *Lorberbaum of Lissa and the *Nehora ha-Shalem* (1827) of Jehiel Michael of Michailishki (Vilna region), author of the *Korban Aharon* on the *maḥzor*, were accepted into the prayer books; both have been published innumerable times. The Sephardi Jews created similar editions for the use of their congregations, when they added to their prayer books the *Kesher Godel* (Leghorn, 1802) of Ḥ. J. D. Azulai, dealing with the laws of the prayers, and the *Shelemut ha-Lev* of an anonymous author.

Ḥasidic Siddurim. In the 18th century the Sephardi tradition with certain modifications was adopted by the ḥasidic communities of Poland and Russia. From that time on ḥasidic prayer books were published, i.e., Ashkenazi prayer books with the regular prayers adapted to the needs of the Ḥasidim. A careful editing of this version was executed by the founder of the Ḥabad ḥasidic sect, *Shneur Zalman of Lyady—he called this version specifically the Lurianic version *(Nosaḥ ha-Ari)*. It was published and disseminated in many editions, in part enlarged by commentaries in the form of lectures to the Ḥasidim (Kapust, 1816, reprinted New York, 1965, with full printing history). [D.G.]

Modern Prayer Books (English Editions). Mention should be made of some of the better known translations of the prayer books in English. The *Authorized Daily Prayer Book* (1890) by S. *Singer has been a standard for the English speaking world for many years. It went through many editions and by 1970 had sold nearly 500,000 copies (a revised edition was published in 1962). A companion to this prayer book was published by I. *Abrahams (1914) and an annotated edition by J. H. Hertz (1941) with the addition of occasional prayers. In the U.S. another version with notes was edited by P. *Birnbaum (*Daily Prayer Book* (1949, and many editions)), and the *High Holyday Prayerbook* (1951, and many editions). The best-known modern Sephardi prayer book and *maḥzor* were the ones edited by David de Sola *Pool. [Ed.]

Reform Prayer Books. Liturgical reform began in the practical sphere, with most of the attention being given to the external aspects of worship. During the initial stages the aesthetics of the synagogue service occupied the minds of the early Reformers more than the doctrinal content of the prayer book. The major emphasis as exemplified by the efforts of Israel *Jacobson, I. S. *Fraenkel, and M. I. *Bresselau, was placed on the form of worship rather than on serious grappling with theological issues. In 1810 Jacobson, a financier and philanthropist, provided a simplified, decorous service for boarding-school children in Seesen, and in 1815, opened a synagogue in Berlin in which he installed an organ and instituted the confirmation ceremony (see *Bar Mitzvah), while the editorial labors of Fraenkel and Bresselau created the Hamburg *Gebetbuch* (*Sefer ha-Avodah, Ordnung der oeffentilichen Andacht*, first ed. 1819). However, the more scholarly contributions of Wolf *Heidenheim's *"Mendelssohn des Gebetbuches"* (Elbogen) were not ignored by the early Reformers. The closing pages of the Hamburg volume contain learned notes citing dissenting views in older sources that might lend support to Reform. Yet the emphases of the first Reformers were practical, and it was not until later that the burgeoning *Wissenschaft des Judentums*, as well as recent developments in Jewish theology, left their influence on the reformulated *siddur*. While the German Reform Rabbinical Conferences (1844–46) were in session, lending shape and direction to the amorphous variety of liturgical changes then in the making, the founders of the Berlin Reform community broke company and began to devise its own radical, predominantly German rite which limited the Hebrew to a few selected biblical verses. When the congregation secured Samuel *Holdheim as its spiritual leader, he was authorized to revamp its liturgical manuals. While keeping much of their dissentient character, Holdheim brought classical and traditional forms and recent liturgical research into greater play, thus moderating the excesses of the Reform community's ritual. D. W. Marks, a remarkably well-versed layman, edited *Seder ha-Tefillot—Forms of Prayer*, published in 1841–43. A spiritual offspring of the Hamburg *Gebetbuch*, the prayer book was used in the West London Synagogue of British Jews of which Marks was the spiritual leader. Although in the introduction the editor admits his debt to the scholarship of *Zunz, *Rapoport, and others, in actuality, he relied very little upon the content of their works. Rather Marks derived from these learned men the encouragement and inspiration for his own original endeavors. Unlike its continental counterparts, *Forms of Prayer* evinces an almost Karaitic scriptural fundamentalism. Marks imitates his Hamburg predecessors, however, in some choices of Hebrew prayers to be read in the vernacular, in shunning repetitions, in the offhand treatment of the *haftarah*, in slight abbreviations of the standard text, and in the partiality toward Sephardi *piyyutim*. Apart from occasional pseudo-Karaizing, *Forms of Prayers* may be said to stand in the Orthodox tradition. Only infrequently did Marks contribute original Hebrew compositions. These works were often written in a felicitous classical style, as in his unique *Birkat ha-Mo'adim* which replaces the festival additional service. The prayer books of the aforementioned Reform community were probably the first to pay particular attention to the theological principles underlying the prayer text and to make emendations accordingly. In line with his evolutionary view of Judaism, Abraham *Geiger was the first consistently to introduce Reform principles into the body of the traditional Hebrew text. Historical consciousness and theological integrity are the hallmarks of Geiger's liturgical works (the first edition of his prayer book was published in 1854) that became the major characteristics of the moderate Reform (Liberal) liturgy in Germany for nearly a century.

During the middle of the 19th century, German Jewish immigrants to the U.S. brought with them the liturgical reforms that were then emerging in Central Europe. The single formative influence to dominate all others was the Hamburg *Gebetbuch*. The principal U.S. prayer books of the day, Leo *Merzbacher's *Seder Tefillah—The Order of Prayer for Divine Service* (1855), David *Einhorn's *Olat Tamid—Book of Prayers for Israelitish Congregations* (1856), and Isaac M. *Wise's *Minhag Amerikah—The Daily Prayers for American Israelites* (1857), which varied in degree of reform, revealed the tastes and talents of their authors, and reflected the demands of their respective congregations, nevertheless, bore the stamp of the Hamburg *Gebetbuch*, the parent Reform prayer book. *Seder Tefillah, Olat Tamid*, and *Minhag Amerikah* contain similar treatments of *Ausheben (Hoẓa'at ha-Torah)* and have either the expanded Hamburg Mourner's Kaddish and/or an elaborate *Todtenfeier (Hazkarat Neshamot)* for the Day of Atonement, rendered almost entirely in the vernacular. (For sentiment's sake, Wise kept his German version even in his English translation). All of the prayer books have recourse to hymns from the Hamburg *Gesangbuch*. Each carries the Sephardi *hashkavah,* usually replacing *El Male Raḥamim* of Ashkenazi tradition, and all delete *Kol Nidrei* in favor of Leopold Stein's *O Tag des Herrn* ("O Day of God") or some other appropriate substitute. *Piyyutim* of Spanish-Portuguese origin take precedence over the more recondite and allusive Ashkenazi *piyyutim.* Influenced by a process already begun in the Hamburg rite, Einhorn progressed further than his German-American counterparts by making his ritual bilingual, although German predominated, especially in the new, protracted pieces recited by the rabbi in oratorical style. Merzbacher pared his Hebrew service to mishnaic simplicity and occasionally recast phrases or whole sections in unexceptionable Hebrew, saving the vernacular for extra-liturgical, non-statutory prayers and hymns. Both Merzbacher and Einhorn dropped the **Musaf,* the former, however, reserving it for the day-long worship on the *Day of Atonement. Wise, however, kept the order intact, concentrating chiefly on revising the text in accordance with Reform doctrine. (On rare occasions he permits himself such liberties as replacing the **Pesukei de-Zimra* on the festivals with the *Hallel* psalms and creating an unusual private service for *yahrzeit.*) All of these rites were incorporated in the most important Reform work of the following century, *The Union Prayer Book for Jewish Worship—Seder Tefilot Yisrael* (first ed. 1894–95). Of particular importance in the compilation of *The Union Prayer Book* were the transitional works of Adolph *Huebsch (e.g., his prayer book for Congregation Ahawath Chesed (1889) in New York, translated by A. Kohut) and Isaac S. *Moses. Huebsch combined Holdheim's work with Wise's *Minhag Amerikah;* while Moses combined *Seder Tefillah, Olat Tamid,* and later, Huebsch's synthesis as well. The end of the 19th century witnessed the writing of many new vernacular compositions. Some from predominantly English formularies, beginning with Joseph *Krauskopf's *The Service Ritual* (1888) and *The Service Manual* (1892), Gustav *Gottheil's *Morning Prayer* (1889), and Kaufmann *Kohler's *Sabbath Eve Service* (1891), found their way into the *Union Prayer Book.* After much weighing and harmonizing of texts, the result was an abbreviated and simplified liturgy with both languages kept in balance, interspersed with prayers and responses in the language of the country. The *Union Prayer Book* represents the cumulative efforts of the American Reform movement to achieve a uniform rite that would meet the needs of diverse congregations throughout the nation. The remarkable durability of the prayer book in its various editions testifies to the success of those efforts. Each edition mirrors changes in theological views and reflects the vicissitudes of the Jewish community both in the U.S. and abroad. The second edition (1922), for example, shows an increased interest in ceremonial life which hitherto had been substantially eliminated. Neither Merzbacher's volume nor Einhorn's contains the ritual *berakhot* for the blowing of the *shofar* or the kindling of the Ḥanukkah candles, whereas the second edition of the *Union Prayer Book* readmits them. The greater quality of the Hebrew in the revised 1940 edition attests to a heightened ethnic consciousness. Jewish group solidarity is expressed by the inclusion of Hebrew prayers from all eras and places, which enhance the diminished rabbinic *stammgebete* (regular prayers). This last edition is distinguished by variety and richness.

Outside U.S. in 20th Century. Reform in the U.S. was generally dependent upon Central European prototypes for doctrinal reformulations until the early 20th century, when American Reformers took the lead in liturgical renewal. Two cases in point, Caesar *Seligmann's *Israelitisches Gebetbuch* (1910) and the French Union Libérale Israélite's *Tefillot Kol ha-Shanah—Rituel des Prières Journalières* (1925), which take considerable liberties with the historical text and the directions for the performance of the ritual, were inspired by American models. While there is no slavish imitation—distinctively European requirements having been given attention—the desire to forestall monotony during the service by introducing variety and meaningful alternation of languages was substantially derived from the U.S. *The Liberal Jewish Prayer Book* (1923–26) by Israel I. *Mattuck, former U.S. Reform rabbi and a founder of English Liberal Judaism, displays unique and wide-ranging literariness. (The same disposition toward variety is maintained in *Avodat ha-Lev—Service of the Heart* (1967).) Largely influenced by the *Union Prayer Book,* the emended West London Synagogue's *Seder ha-Tefillot—Forms of Prayer* (1931) exhibits renewed appreciation for both traditional rabbinic arrangement and religious liberalism in being shorn of its eccentric and ostensibly fundamentalist character. This is seen in the selection of benedictions for the weekday *Amidah,* in the choice of the *Aleinu* text, and in the reinstitution of *berakhot* for rabbinic ordinances. The *Einheitsgebetbuch* (edited by C. Seligmann, I. Elbogen, and H. Vogelstein, 1929) deserves special mention not only because it appropriated a variety of texts from the *Union Prayer Book,* but, more significantly, because it succeeded in achieving unity among the Liberal congregations of Germany before World War II. This major accomplishment serves as a becoming *Memorbuch* to a decimated German Jewry.

Conservative and Reconstructionist Prayer Books. The Conservative and Reconstructionist manuals adhere to the classical outlines, although also constituting a departure from traditional Judaism, representing what J. J. *Petuchowski calls "Reform from within." *Maḥzor le-Shalosh Regalim—The Festival Prayer Book* (United Synagogue of America, 1927), a Conservative publication, is closer to the enlightened Orthodoxy of Hermann *Adler and Joseph H. *Hertz, former chief rabbis of Great Britain, than to any publication of the moderate Reform or proto-Conservative movement such as Benjamin *Szold's and Marcus *Jastrow's *Avodat Yisrael—Israelitish Prayer Book* (first ed. 1865), or Aaron Wise's *Shalhevet Yah—The Temple Service* (1891). A reason for this may lie in the Conservative movement's loyalty to Solomon *Schechter's motto "catholic Israel." Dependence upon the official British books can be seen in the use of the festival *piyyutim* and of the introductory memorial prayer at *Hazkarat Neshamot.* This anglophile penchant gave way approximately 20 years later to a more independent *Seder Tefillot Yisrael le-Shabbat u-le-Shalosh Regalim—Sabbath and Festival Prayer Book* (Rabbinical Assembly of America and United Synagogue of America, 1946), wherein a minimum of textual reforms are permitted as in some of the preliminary benedictions of the morning service and in the middle benediction of the additional service where *sham na'aseh ve-nakriv* is altered to *sham asu ve-hikrivu.* With unity of Conservative congregations their overriding aim, the editors were determined not to add unnecessarily to the plethora of variations on controverted texts. Among the more innovative features of the *Sabbath and Festival Prayer Book* are the supplementary readings and explanatory notes at the end of the volume. The most far-reaching of the Conservative liturgical publications in hard-cover is the *Siddur li-Ymot ha-Ḥol—Weekday Prayer Book* (1961). The editors introduce significant changes in wording to bring the prayers into closer harmony with the consensus of Conservative belief. Apart from obvious Zionist sentiment, the rewritten *Musaf* for the festivals and for Rosh Ḥodesh reads materially as a 19th-century German Liberal reconstruction. The Reconstructionist *siddurim* (*Seder Tefillot le-Shabbat—Sabbath*

Prayer Book, 1945; *Maḥzor le-Yamim Nora'im—High Holy Day Prayer Book*, 1948; *Festival Prayer Book*, 1958; and *Seder Tefillot li-Ymot ha-Ḥol—Daily Prayer Book*, 1963) also make extensive use of supplementary readings. Reconstructionist tenets, such as the denial of the idea of the Chosen People, and the diminution or deletion of supernatural and anthropomorphic references, set them apart from the Conservative prayer books.

Prayers for Contemporary Events. It has taken time for the events of World War II, the Holocaust, and the rebirth of the State of Israel to be fully comprehended and treated in adequate liturgical form, but none of the official prayer books of American Jewry alludes to any of these momentous happenings except the Reconstructionist *Daily Prayer Book*, and the Conservative *Siddur li-Ymot ha-Ḥol—Weekday Prayer Book* (1961), which includes a newly composed *Al ha-Nissim* for Israel Independence Day. That these events have not been forgotten is proven by the fact that individual congregations and communities mark these occasions by circulating mimeographed prayers, privately or locally printed. Because Europe was the battleground, the remnant of Progressive Jewish communities in Europe have already responded to this chain of circumstances. Virtually all of the latest European Liberal and Reform prayer books include at least an entreaty on behalf of the State of Israel. Within the last two decades, as the shock of the Holocaust has been absorbed and its implications assimilated, a number of new prayer books have been compiled both in Europe and in Israel that give proper weight to the twin experiences touching world Jewry. The majority of these prayer books show an awareness of the scope of tradition and clearly enunciate principles of 20th-century Reform (e.g., Zionism is obviously no longer the taboo it once was). A modern and uniform liturgy is beginning to emerge in which the mishnaic nucleus of the *Stammgebete* is preserved and the *Musaf* dismissed. Differences consist mainly in wording, in selections from the opening sections of the prayer book, i.e., *Birkhot ha-Shaḥar* and *Pesukei de-Zimra*, and in the length of individual prayers. Variety is emphasized even within this simplified and relatively fixed framework. Novel and unexpected developments have been taking place in the U.S., including experimentation with jazz, rock, and multi-media in the performance of the liturgy. [E.L.Fr.]

There have been many innovations by the Rabbinate in Israel with regard to certain events. The most extensive of these new prayers concerns Israel Independence Day (see Prayers for *Independence Day). In addition the Israel rabbinate has composed special prayers for Holocaust Remembrance day (Nisan 27) and for the day of general *yahrzeit* for victims of the Holocaust (Tevet 10). They have also produced special *El Male Raḥamim* prayers for victims of the Holocaust and for those who fell in the defense of the State of Israel, and special prayers on behalf of Soviet and Arab Jewry. The Israel Army Rabbinate composed a special *Tefillat ha-Derekh* for paratroopers (written by the Chief Chaplain Rabbi Shelomo *Goren). After the Six-Day War the religious kibbutz movement Ha-Kibbutz ha-Dati issued a new version of the *naḥem* prayer (which mourns the destruction of Jerusalem) recited on the Ninth of Av, emphasizing the opportunity to rebuild Jerusalem. [Ed.]

Bibliography: General: Zunz, Ritus; Elbogen, Gottesdienst; Benjacob, Oẓar and Friedberg, Eked, s.v. titles of prayer books; JE, 10 (1907), 174 (list of principal prayer books); J. J. Cohen, in: S. D. Luzzatto, *Mavo le-Maḥzor Benei Roma*, ed. by E. D. Goldschmidt (1966), 105–36; Goldschmidt, in: *Sefunot*, 8 (1964), 207–36 (Romaniot rite). Reform: Abrahams, Companion; S. S. Cohon, in: CCARY, 38 (1928), 246–70; M. Davis, *Emergence of Conservative Judaism* (1963); Elbogen, Gottesdienst; S. B. Freehof, in: *Reform Judaism: Essays*...(1949); E. L. Friedland, *Historical and Theological Development of Non-Orthodox Jewish Prayerbooks in the United States* (1967); E. D. Goldschmidt, in: YLBI, 2 (1957), 119–35; J. Heinemann, *Ha-Tefillah bi-Tekufat ha-Tanna'im ve-ha-Amora'im* (1966²); Idelsohn, Liturgy; B. Italiener, in: HUCA, 26 (1955), 413–24; J. J. Petuchowski, *Prayerbook Reform in Europe* (1968); D. Philipson, *Reform Movement in Judaism;* G. W. Plaut, *Growth of Reform Judaism* (1931); idem, *Rise of Reform Judaism* (1963); M. Silverman, in: *Proceedings of the Rabbinical Assembly of America*, 4 (1933), 322–43.

PREACHING. In the Talmudic Period. Nature and Purpose of the Sermon. The sermon, delivered in the synagogue or in the house of study, mainly on Sabbaths and festivals, is a very ancient institution. Nothing is known of its beginnings. It may have originated in the *Targum, i.e., the translation of the lections from Scripture into the Aramaic vernacular for the benefit of those who could not follow the Hebrew reading. The Targum in days of old was paraphrastic and the biblical texts were embellished with much aggadic material. Eventually, the Targum was curtailed and additions to the text were no longer allowed (Tosef., Meg. 4:41). Its former function of instruction and edification was then taken over by the sermon. By the end of the Second Temple period, sermons were a well-established custom both in Palestine and in the Diaspora.

The importance of the sermon can hardly be overestimated. Not only did it serve as the chief means of instructing all the people—peasants, women, and children—and imparting to all and sundry at least an elementary knowledge of the Torah and its teachings, but it also provided the sages with a means of guiding the people, strengthening their faith, and refuting heretical views.

By using at times daring methods of interpretation, the preachers succeeded in making the Bible an unceasing source of ever-new meaning and inspiration in which answers to the problems of every generation could be found. Thus when the unquestionable biblical faith in the rewards of the righteous in this life could no longer satisfy the people in times of disasters and persecutions, the rabbis would unhesitatingly substitute for it the belief of reward in the world to come: "He has given food unto them that fear Him, He will ever be mindful of His covenant" (Ps. 111:5) became—by means of a play on the words *teref* "food," and *teruf*, "confusion"—"He has given confusion to those who fear Him in this world; but in the future to come He will ever be mindful of His covenant" (Gen. R. 40:2). To the outcry of those who witnessed the destruction of the Temple, and who, on reading such a verse as "Who is like unto Thee O Lord, among the mighty?" (Ex. 15:11) would ask: "Where then is His might, if he looks on while His Temple is destroyed and keeps silent?" The rabbis answered: "Who is like unto Thee among the mute ones" (a play on the words אֵלִים, *elim*, "the mighty ones," and אִלֵּם, *illem*, "mute"). The explanation was: "His very restraint and silence is the proof of His strength and power: for who is mighty? He who conquers his passions!" (TJ, Ber. 7:4, 11c; Mekh., Shira, 8; Yoma 69b; Avot 4:1).

The Sermon and the Audience. Through their reinterpretations of the Bible, their bold use of the biblical material to give expression to the burning issues of their own times, and the application of ancient traditions to new circumstances, the rabbis succeeded in keeping the Bible alive and meaningful for their own generations.

Entertaining Devices Used in Sermons. In addition to the use of exegesis, the preachers would amplify and recreate stories, would enliven their preaching by ample use of folktales and parables, and employ dramatization and various rhetorical means to make their sermons attractive and challenging. They would modulate their voices in presenting dialogues and imitate the different characters represented. The "entertainment value" of the sermon was often not less important than its educational and edifying aspects. Some critics indeed compared the Jewish preachers to actors whose "performance" was too "theatrical" for their liking. Small wonder then that the people would come in masses to hear sermons, especially of well-known preachers (TJ, Hor. 3:7, 48b). They would come even from outlying villages, and would make special arrangements beforehand to permit them to exceed the "Sabbath-limit" of 2,000 cubits (Er. 3:5).

The rabbis contrasted the synagogues and the houses of study and their sermons with the attractions of the circus and of the theater of the Roman-Hellenistic world. Remarkably enough, they succeeded in making the bulk of the people prefer the former: "They that sit in the gate talk of me" (Ps. 69:13) was given two different interpretations: "... those are the gentiles who sit in their theaters and circuses ... scoffing me ... ; and ... those are Israel who sit in the synagogues and houses of study ... reading dirges and lamentations and *Eikhah*" (Lam. R., Proem 17). However, the well-to-do would, at times, stay away from such "vulgar" gatherings (Git. 38b). The audience expressed their approval and enjoyment; at times, they reacted with laughter, or, when the preacher did not succeed in arousing them, with indifference. The preachers would adapt their interpretations and examples to the level of the audience; and when addressing simple people they would not refrain from using very telling, even ribald, phrases or illustrations (Lev. R. 18:1; S. Lieberman, *Greek in Jewish Palestine* (1942), 161–2). The popularity of the aggadic sermon emerges clearly from the following statement: "In times of old when the *perutah* [a small coin] was easy to come by, a man would desire to hear words of Mishnah and of Talmud; but now when the *perutah* is no longer easily found, and moreover we are suffering from the kingdom [i.e., Roman rule], a man desires to hear words of Scripture and words of *aggadah*" (PdRK 101b).

Time of Delivery of Sermon. Sermons were delivered, whenever possible, on every Sabbath and on other special occasions including fast days, especially on the Ninth of *Av. They would be based mostly on the Torah section read on the day when it was delivered, i.e., the *sidra* of the so-called *triennial cycle on an ordinary Sabbath and the special lections on festivals. On special Sabbaths (e.g., before and after the Ninth of Av), the prophetic reading might provide the text for the homily. The exact time of the sermon varied. It is known that there were sermons delivered on Friday night (TJ, Sot. 1:4, 16d), on Sabbath morning after the reading from Scripture (Luke 4:16ff.), or on Sabbath afternoon (Yal. Prov. 964). It appears that many sermons were given before the scriptural reading, serving as an introduction to, and preparation for, the latter (see below). Probably, such sermons were rather brief.

The Preacher. If one of the great sages delivered the sermon, he would make his appearance only after the whole audience had assembled; in the meantime, younger rabbis, acting as auxiliary preachers, would keep the people occupied (TJ, Suk. 5:1, 55a; Gen. R. 98:11; but also Deut. R. 7:8). The preacher made use of a *turgeman* ("translator"), or of several of them whose task it was to broadcast the words of the preacher in a loud voice which could be heard by all sections of the audience. This served not so much a practical purpose, for some of the preachers at least must have had voices powerful enough to make themselves heard, but was a token of respect (I. M. Kosowsky, in *Sinai*, 45 (1959), 233–43). The preacher would take care to prepare his sermon properly; but in some places, at least, it was customary for members of the audience to address questions to him which he was expected to answer on the spot. Some inexperienced preachers found this custom disconcerting and were unable to reply (Gen. R. 81:2).

The Openings of Sermons. The sections opening with a halakhic question, preceded by the formula *yelammedenu rabbenu* ("may our master teach us"), or the like, which appear at the beginning of homilies, especially in the **Tanḥuma* Midrashim, reflect the custom of introducing a sermon by a question posed by a member of the audience. The challenge to the preacher was not so much in finding the answer—for mostly the questions referred to well-known *halakhot*—but to improvise a way of linking up both the question and the answer with the real subject matter of his sermon, concerned usually with an aggadic interpretation of the Bible reading for the day. It is, however, quite possible that often the question posed to the preacher had been prompted and was known to him beforehand.

Forms of the Sermon. Though the "classical" Midrashim undoubtedly drew the bulk of their material from the tens of thousands of sermons which had actually been preached in the synagogues of Palestine during the first four or five centuries C.E., they have hardly ever preserved these sermons in their original form. In many cases, they present mere outlines of actual sermons or of parts of them, while, on the other hand, they take sections from many separate sermons and weld them into new and larger units.

The Proem Type. One of the rhetorical forms, found frequently in practically all of the old Midrashim, the proem (*petiḥta*), undoubtedly had its origin in the live sermon. It opened with a quotation from Scripture, not taken from the text read on that day, but mostly from the Hagiographa. Through a series of aggadic interpretations and stories, the quotation was gradually linked up with the first verse of the pericope (or the prophetic lesson) of the day. Often, the preacher intentionally chose a verse which seemed completely unconnected with the weekly portion so as to arouse the curiosity of the audience and increase their interest. Sometimes the connection would be established by means of a play on words or similar rhetorical devices. Nearly always, the opening verse chosen expressed a general idea which was subsequently illustrated by the specific example provided by the contents of the pericope. Such proems served originally either as opening sections of a complete sermon (according to Maybaum, Bacher) or, more likely, were sermons complete in themselves (according to Bloch, Baeck) and were preached, presumably, immediately before the reading from Scripture, serving as an introduction to the latter (Heinemann).

Other Types. But the proem type was by no means the only kind of sermon in vogue. Apart from the *yelammedenu* form, mentioned already, there were sermons opening with a form of benediction, praising God for giving Torah to Israel, and proceeding from this to the specific theme to be developed (J. Heinemann, *Ha-Tefillah bi-Tekufat ha-Tanna'im ve-ha-Amora'im* (1964), 160–2). Undoubtedly, other sermons took for their point of departure the first verse of the weekly portion itself; the section in *Mekhilta*, beginning with "And Moses took the bones of Joseph with him" (Ex. 13:19) may serve as an example of this type. Another type of opening of the sermon has been preserved in passages where the first verse of the pericope is immediately followed by a reference to a verse elsewhere, in the light of which the former is interpreted, e.g., "'Then came Amalek' ... This verse is to be ... explained in connection with the passage in Job where it is said 'Can the rush shoot up without mire ...'" (Mekh., Amalek, 1 beginning).

Conclusions of Sermons. The concluding section of homilies in the Midrashim mostly sounds the messianic theme, contrasting the suffering and the troubles of "this world" with the joys of "the world to come." It stands to reason that also these sections represent perorations of actual sermons. Other sermons appear to have ended in a prayer which either expressed thanks to God for the giving of the Torah or a request for the speedy coming of redemption or both (Heinemann, loc. cit.). One example of such a concluding prayer is the **Kaddish*.

Example of a Complete Sermon. One of the few sermons whose entire structure appears to have been preserved (though probably only in outline) is the one by R. *Tanḥum of Nevay (Shab. 30a–b): It starts with the halakhic question whether one may extinguish a light on the Sabbath for the sake of a person dangerously ill. It then proceeds to discuss the relation of life and death on the basis of scriptural quotations, illustrating its argument with poignant stories from the lives of David and Solomon and making, among others, the point that even one day in the lives of the righteous is of supreme value in the eyes of God. It concludes by answering the question posed at the beginning that man's soul "is the lamp of the Lord" (Prov. 20:27) and it is better that a lamp made by man be extinguished (on the Sabbath) rather than the soul (life), the lamp made by God. In form, this sermon is unique, for, in spite of its affinities with the *yelammedenu* type, it differs from it by placing the answer to the halakhic question at the conclusion of the entire sermon.

Homilies in the Midrashim. It follows that in different times and places sermons exhibited a variety of structures and patterns. Against this, in the so-called homiletic Midrashim all homilies are constructed more or less in a uniform pattern; after a series of proems there follows the "body of the sermon" (whose structure is not clearly defined) and finally, the messianic peroration (Lev. R.; PdRK). In Midrashim of the *Tanḥuma-yelammedenu* type, the parts mentioned are preceded by the section opening with a halakhic question. Such homilies do not represent single, actual sermons as preached in public. Even if the proems are considered to be mere opening sections, no preacher would have used a whole series of such introductions, independent of one another, consecutively, in order to arrive again and again at the same point which he had already reached with the first one, i.e., the first verse of the pericope. Hence these homilies must be taken as creations of the editors of the Midrashim who made use of a number of sections, especially proems, taken from different sermons, and combined them into a new form, the "literary homily," which must not be confused with the actual live sermon as preached in the synagogue (in a variety of forms).

J. Mann developed a highly ingenious theory that both the halakhic question (in the *yelammedenu* type of homily) and the Bible verses with which the proems open, were chosen for the sake of verbal tallies to the prophetic reading *(haftarah)* for the day. Thus a system of associations with the *haftarah* provides the hidden links between the various sections of the sermon (even though the *haftarah* itself is not quoted as a rule). Pertinent objections to this theory have been raised by S. Lieberman (*Kovez̤ Madda'i le-Zekher M. Schorr* (1944), 186) and by Ḥ. Albeck (Zunz-Albeck, Derashot, 473–4, n. 180). Among the weaknesses of Mann's hypothesis is the fact that associations consisting of a mere verbal link—provided often by very common words—could presumably be discovered in practically all cases, even if they had not been intended. What is more, where the required tally with the known *haftarah* cannot be found, Mann unhesitatingly stipulates a different one. Even the actual *yelammedenu* sermons, to the analysis of which Mann's book (see bibliography) is devoted, are frequently not the ones found in fact in the Midrashim, but sermons reconstructed by Mann himself by combining parts taken from different sources. Moreover, Mann assumes that such homilies were invariably composed of a good many parts: the halakhic opening, a series of proems, the body of the sermon, and the peroration. Although he occasionally states that some of these parts (e.g., the proems) may be more ancient than others, he remains ambiguous as regards the all-important question whether such complex structures represent live sermons actually preached, or are mere literary creations of the editors of the Midrashim. [J.Hei.]

Medieval Period. Through the *derashah,* or homily, the medieval synagogue pulpit could respond to and influence communal life on the pressing issues of the day and reinforce the traditions and ethics of the Torah. It served, too, as a vehicle for social criticism and reform, arousing concern and giving encouragement in times of trial and gloom. The sermon also provided scholars with the opportunity to show their worth, erudition, and acuteness. The *derashah,* while always based on biblical verses and rabbinic sayings, and utilizing the approach of the traditional commentary, aims, nevertheless, to interpret its subject matter according to contemporary needs and concepts. For the most part, the preacher also attempts to attune his homilies to the level and tastes of his listeners.

The Preacher. Over the generations, especially at times of crisis, scholars arose who regarded the sermon as their chief interest and duty. Many of them served as peripatetic preachers among the various communities and lands. Preachers appointed by a particular community received a fixed salary, while itinerant preachers usually had to rely on irregular contributions and, on occasion, congregational allotments for their support. The majority of homilies have survived in the form in which they were composed and written down by the preachers themselves, which is undoubtedly different from the form in which they were originally delivered. The *darshan* ("preacher") organized the written text and made it more scholarly than the original oral version. The language, also, was different, since the homily as preached in the tongue spoken by the Jews of the locale, while it was written down in Hebrew.

Contents. Because the sermon was directed at the congregation as a whole, the *darshan* was frequently faced with the problem of reconciling the different levels of education within his audience, being caught between the use of a simple, clear approach, on the one hand, and his desire for an original, innovative, and profound manner of preaching, on the other. At times the focus on nuances of interpretation would far outweigh the ethically instructive and socially beneficial aspects of the homily, which while pleasing the learned members of the community, worked to the detriment of the simple folk, as well as impairing the effectiveness of the sermon itself. Midrashim from the early Middle Ages indicate that ethical teachings and commentaries touching on matters of communal interest were also at this time closely related to Torah reading in the synagogue. During that period anthologies of such material were prepared specifically for preachers. Their purpose was "to broaden the scope of Scripture and interpret it in terms of the world scene, thereby showing that God has from the very beginning of time foretold the end of days, and that we may learn many things about the commandments from the conversations of the Patriarchs" *(Midrash Lekaḥ Tov, Va-Yez̤e).* The chronicle of *Ahimaaz relates that a certain learned preacher from Erez̤ Israel had a number of prepared sermons written in rhymed Hebrew. The exegetical method as well as the socio-religious function of the *darshan* was already well established and defined for the Mediterranean Jewish communities from the time of Isaac *Alfasi and *Maimonides (11th and 12th centuries). The latter even ruled that "each Jewish congregation must arrange to have a respected and wise elder who has been known for his piety from his youth and is beloved by the people, who will publicly admonish the community and cause them to repent" (Yad, Teshuvah 4:2; cf. also Tefillah 11:3; Maim. Responsa, ed. by J. Blau, 1 (1957), no. 67). Judah *Hadassi in his *Eshkol ha-Kofer* records that by the 12th century the *Karaites had recognized the importance of the homily and accepted it as a standard practice: "The learned preacher would expound and comment upon the current Scriptural reading and Psalm before the people, who piously sought his presence and interpretation on Sabbaths, festivals, fast days, in the house of mourning, at weddings, and at circumcisions . . . and turns many away from transgression" (para. 18).

The homily likewise had become an accepted part of Jewish life in Germany by the first half of the 12th century. Accounts of Jews martyred in 1096 include an actual *derashah* publicly delivered to "the first to be slain" and urging them to accept martyrdom. A substantial number of the stories and ethical teachings in *Sefer Ḥasidim* appear to have been passages from sermons, parables, and the like. R. *Eleazar b. Judah b. Kalonymus of Worms ruled that "one must preach in words more precious than gold on the Sabbath . . . one must assemble the people at that time and preach to them" (Comment. to Prayers, Mss. Bodleian, Opp. 110; see also A. M. Habermann, *Gezerot Ashkenaz ve-Ẓarefat* (1945), 166). After the holocaust during the *Black Death, the homily in Germany in the late 14th and early 15th centuries became mainly a means to exhort the people to remain observant, as well as to teach laws and commandments as they should be practiced. In the second half of the 13th century, *Moses b. Jacob of Coucy, France, personally described a journey which he made throughout Spain giving sermons of admonition. His purpose was to strengthen the ritual practices of *tefillin, mezuzot,* and *ẓiẓit;* to persuade the men to give up their non-Jewish wives and to prevent them from profaning the name of God through abusing the gentile (*Sefer Mitzvot ha-Gadol,* 1, 2, 112; 11, introd.). He also records a complete sermon in a style very similar to the manner in which it was delivered, obviously directed to a group particularly in need of spiritual awakening. For this he used the system of explaining biblical verses, raising the threat of divine punishment as well as the promise of a heavenly reward. This wandering halakhist and *darshan* is the first known preacher in the Middle Ages to appear as a moral and ethical preceptor of the masses. Most of the ethical works of *Jonah Gerondi appear to be the literary residue of fiery preaching. The homilies of *Naḥmanides which have been preserved (as, e.g., for Rosh Ha-Shanah and in the debate with the king of Aragon in the synagogue on the Sabbath) are in reality profound, comprehensive essays on ethical theory, an indication of the high level of his Spanish audience. The rationalist followers of Maimonides in 14th-century Provence also publicly delivered philosophical-allegorical homilies (compare Jacob *Anatoli in his *Malmad ha-Talmidim*).

In Spain, by the 14th century, the *derashah* had attained a well-developed methodology and compact structure. To the halakhic and philosophical content of the *derashah* were now added mystic elements (e.g., cf. the *Kad ha-Kemaḥ* of R. *Baḥya b. Asher). One of the most renowned preachers of this period was *Nissim b. Reuben Gerondi. The 15th-century sermon reflects the struggle with Christianity and points up the social crises which arose at a time of persecution. The homilies of the most illustrious *darshan* of the generation of the Expulsion, R. Isaac *Arama, show that periods of vigorous anti-Jewish Christian preaching have called forth an equally strong reaction from contemporary Jewish preaching (introd. to *Akedat Yiẓḥak*). Arama's sermons in *Akedat Yiẓḥak* combine a more difficult speculative analysis with popular appeal in order to strengthen the faith, be alert against Christian slanders, and safeguard the character of his hearers during the calamities threatening them.

STRUCTURE AND STYLE. Joel *ibn Shuaib, a *darshan* who taught the transposition of laws from theory to practice, summed up the architectural and aesthetic tradition of the *derashah* in Spain around the time of the Expulsion. The preacher, he counseled, should "concern himself with two essentials in his sermons: (1) the integrity of the subject matter, and (2) the perfecting of his manner of expression . . . . Regarding the first, he must be careful . . . that, whatever he will say, his listeners will derive benefit. Though his sermons be very profound, he must make them clear enough for the masses of the people to gain something from them on their level. Yet no less must he have regard for the special interests of the more intellectually inclined who may be present when his subject is mostly directed to the simple folk. On the second principal concern, the form of the sermon, three considerations are paramount: (1) the length—it should not be the least bit longer than is absolutely necessary to convey the intended *derashah;* (2) the structure—the sermon should be well organized, not lacking in proper order, now in the streets, now in the broad places (Prov. 7:12); (3) his phrases and words should possess grace and dignity, and they ought to be delivered in a pleasing and proper way according to the following conditions: along with an attractive style and an inherent order within the sermon, the preacher must also make proper use of his voice in addressing the people so that they should understand even from his external manner of speaking that his words have value for them" (Introd. to *Olat Shabbat,* Venice, 1577). An interesting illustration of the actual style of the *derashah* as it was preached has been preserved in the homily delivered by Isaac *Aboab, the last principal of the yeshivah of Lisbon, in 1492–93, to the exiles from Spain:

> "How can I endure so much suffering? A man can exist in this world for one of two reasons: either because he is in his own land, or because the Lord is watching over him. About the first reason, Cain said: 'Behold, Thou hast driven me out this day from the face of the land' (Gen. 4:14). Regarding the second, he added, 'whosoever findeth me will slay me' *(ibid.),* meaning, whatever may befall me, whether through the air or from some other part of the world, may be a reason for Him to kill me. The Holy One will have mercy on us. . . . There is a parable of a father and son walking together. Tired and feeling weak, the son asks the father if they are far from the city . . . and the father explains to him how he may know: once you see a cemetery, then you will be near the city . . . . When we see many misfortunes at hand, it signals the coming of the Messiah" (*Nahar Pishon,* Constantinople, 1538, 11a).

This homily is an immediate, live reaction to the expulsion from Spain.

The *derashah* developed further in the 16th and 17th centuries among the exiles, and Jews in Italy influenced by them, who were all nourished to some extent by Renaissance culture. The sermons of the most prominent 16th-century preacher in Italy, Judah *Moscato, intersperse references to music and astronomy and Italian phrases with rabbinic aphorisms. Within this milieu, Leone *Modena compared the preacher to "a stone engraver carving out a fine statue" (*Midbar Yehudah,* Venice, 1602, 5a). To the Venetian Jewish community the homily was a work of art valued for the perfection of its form.

Homiletics underwent a more turbulent development in Poland and Lithuania, reflecting communal dissension and social problems. A number of Polish-Jewish preachers openly declared that they had the right to interpret Scripture freely in order to admonish and instruct their congregants. Yet some scholars complained about the preachers who would take liberties with biblical verses not in order to reprove their communities but to prove their own dialectical subtlety and to satisfy the eagerness of their listeners for novel and clever interpretations. This tendency led to confusion and awkwardness in the *derashah.* From the same period there are many *midreshei-peli'ah* ("wonder tales") invented by preachers who attributed them to early Midrashim. *David b. Manasseh, an itinerant often-persecuted preacher, wrote *Ketav Hitnaẓẓelut la-Darshanim* ("Writ of Apology for Preachers") in 1574 in which he argues for homiletic license to interpret and use various rhetorical devices to influence listeners. The *darshan* *Berechiah (Berakh) b. Isaac Eisik of Cracow testifies (in his *Zera Berakh*) that the homily provided the learned with a means of persuading the leaders of the community to their point of view.

Social Impact. Some preachers battled openly and vigorously in communal affairs. Outstanding among these was *Ephraim Solomon of Luntshits, whose sermonic works (*Ir Gibborim, Olelot Efrayim, Ammudei Shesh,* and *Oraḥ le-Ḥayyim*) influenced his own as well as later periods. R. Ephraim forcefully attacked egotism, the avaricious pursuit of wealth, the haughtiness of the rich, and their self-righteous hyprocrisy. Formerly a wandering *darshan,* frequently derided and little known, by his dynamic preaching Luntschitz achieved such recognition that he was invited to deliver a homily before the Council of Four Lands (see *Councils of the Lands) in session at Lublin. He later served as rabbi of Prague, succeeding *Judah Loew b. Bezalel, who was himself an eminent preacher.

The pervasive influence of the *derashah* is apparent, too, from regulations and communal actions in Poland-Lithuania. In 1638 and 1648 the salary of the preacher appointed by the Poznan community was set as second only to that of the *av bet din,* and the difference between the two was negligible. In 1717, the Jews of Cracow defined the ideal preacher as one who "in his pleasant utterances gives joy to both God and man, and quenches the spiritual thirst of every class of people according to the depth and breadth of their understanding. Sometimes he teaches the Law in depth, explaining the words of our rabbis, distilling the strong waters of *Gemara,* codes, and *tosafot.* Yet he can still clarify, instill his hearers with a sense of reverence, sweeten the bitterness of life through his pleasant manner of speaking with straightforwardness . . . , in sermons open and understood by all, including those whose minds cannot fathom the depth of his words" (D. Weinryb, *Te'udot le-Toledot ha-Kehillot ha-Yehudiyyot be-Polin* (1950), 185).

The regulations issued by the Council of Lithuania indicate that the communal leadership was apprehensive of the potential force of the *derashah* which they could not control. In 1628, they instituted supervision over all sermons in reaction to the freedom which the itinerant preachers had assumed. In 1667, during the agitation which followed the appearance of *Shabbetai Ẓevi, they again protested that "a number of men go around in this region, preaching publicly in synagogues and other places, pompously delivering open reproofs. However, their preaching appears in some part for their own self-glorification." The Council placed supervision of the sermons under "the local rabbi and seven city elders. If a man attempts to preach without their express permission, they may say to him: 'Step down from the pulpit,' aside from imposing additional penalties" (S. Dubnow (ed.), *Pinkas ha-Medinah* (1925), no. 596). In Moravia, too, the governing body issued regulations regarding "the acceptability of preachers who station themselves at houses of learning," and in 1701 they felt it necessary to warn the local leaders not to allow such *maggidim* ("wandering preachers") to deliver sermons without the approval of the local *av bet din* (I. Halpern, *Takkanot Medinat Mehrin* (1951), 100, 168).

18th- to Early 19th-Century. The changes which occurred in Jewish life as a result of the partitions of Poland, the rise of *Ḥasidism, the development of *Haskalah, and *Emancipation, brought a modification of the character and status of the homily. Significantly, even in the 18th century, preaching in the medieval style still retained its importance. Just as the Jewish leaders in Poland had epitomized their concept of the ideal preacher of the past in 1717, *Elijah b. Solomon ha-Kohen of Izmir in his homiletic work *Shevet Musar* (Constantinople, 1712) summed up the method of admonition which invokes the fear of Gehinnom and sufferings in the afterlife. His work was widely read, and translated into Yiddish. Jonathan *Eybeschuetz achieved fame in his lifetime as well as posthumously for his homilies (*Ya'arot Devash*). In the 18th century, Jacob *Kranz, the Dubno *Maggid,* exerted a profound effect upon his listeners through the effective use of parables. Some scholars believe that in 18th-century Poland these itinerant *maggidim* made up an intelligensia opposed to the existing intellectual establishment, who indirectly aided the rise of Ḥasidism. Yet the ḥasidic movement gradually substituted "the saying of Torah" by the ḥasidic rabbis for the standard *derashah,* thereby eventually replacing the wandering preachers.

Within the cultural sphere of the **Mitnaggedim* the homily continued to play a role. Itinerant *darshanim* like *Moses b. Isaac ha-Darshan of Kelmy, and Ḥayyim Zadok, the *Maggid* of Rumschischki, were influential in Jewish society. Their chief concern focused on the struggle against Ḥasidism and Haskalah, as well as the founding of charitable institutions in the small towns of Lithuania and White Russia. They often intoned their sermons using a special plaintive melodic mode, and the parable was one of their most essential homiletic tools. For the *derashah* given by the boy who had become bar mitzvah see *bar mitzvah. Also there was a custom that the bridegroom or the scholar give a *derashah* under the wedding canopy or at the festivities following. [EH/Ed.]

In Modern Times (From the Beginning of the 19th Century). The Modern Sermon. Part of the aim of Zunz's most famous work, *Gottesdienstliche Vortraege der Juden* (1832), was to demonstrate, when this was challenged by the Prussian government (under the influence of Orthodox groups who saw the sermon in the vernacular as the beginnings of Reform), that preaching is not an innovation but an ancient Jewish institution. While this is true, the traditional *derashah* was, in fact, replaced in the 19th century by a new type of Jewish sermon, the *Predigt,* as it was called in Germany. There were a number of important changes in language, style, and content which, first in Germany and then in other European countries, gave a completely new cast to the sermon. This new type of sermon was delivered in the vernacular and unlike the occasional *derashah,* it was a regular feature of the service. It sought to express Jewish values in a contemporary idiom and in the thought-patterns of the day. Woven around one central theme, the modern sermon developed in orderly fashion, without academic digressions on the texts quoted, emphasizing edification rather than pure instruction. Although the early 19th-century preachers in Germany were not rabbis, preaching, instead of being delegated to a special functionary, eventually became the preserve of the rabbi and one of his most important duties in Western countries. Among the well-known preachers in 19th-century Germany were: Eduard *Kley, Gotthold *Salomon, Abraham *Geiger, Samuel *Holdheim, Jehiel Michael *Sachs, Samson Raphael *Hirsch, and David *Einhorn; and in the 20th century: Siegmund *Maybaum, Nehemia Anton *Nobel, and Leo *Baeck.

A. Altmann (see bibl.) has demonstrated the influence of the Protestant pulpit on the development of the modern Jewish sermon. The early German preachers consciously modeled their sermons on the patterns of Christian homiletics and used Christian guides to the art of preaching. Even Isaac Noah *Mannheimer, the most outstanding 19th-century preacher, who pleaded for a closer link with the Jewish homiletical tradition, admitted "that we as pupils and disciples, as novices in the art of preaching which we have been practicing only a little while, can learn a great deal from the masters of the art, and we have gratefully to accept every guidance and instruction offered to us in their schools." Zunz, in his brief career as a preacher at the New Synagogue in Berlin (1820–22), was influenced by *Schleiermacher. It is even on record that the most popular Christian preachers of the time, such as Ritschl and Schleiermacher, used to hear the young preachers at Israel *Jacobson's temple in Berlin and give them, after the sevice, "manifold hints and directives."

A reaction soon set in. There was a persistent demand for a truly Jewish homiletic, arguing, in Mannheimer's words, that "it is always better to feed on one's own resources than to live from alms." But, generally speaking, the reaction in the 19th century only amounted to a greater use of rabbinic, especially midrashic, material as exemplified in the sermons of the illustrious preacher Adolf *Jellinek in Vienna. Jellinek's preaching attracted many of the intellectuals of his day who, in their quest for Jewish identity, needed his reassurance that Judaism was supremely worthwhile and still capable of making important contributions. Jellinek was fond of preaching that too many were saying: "Now Israel's eyes were dim with age; he could not see" (Gen. 48:10), whereas the truth was that Moses still spoke and God still answered him in thunder (Ex. 19:19). Jellinek's methods and strong Jewish emphasis influenced Jewish preaching everywhere. A later occupant of Jellinek's pulpit, Hirsch (Ẓevi) Perez *Chajes, for example, preached to a bar mitzvah the story of the woman whose vessels were miraculously replenished by the oil (II Kings 4:1–7). The never-ending power of Judaism is always available if only Jews will provide the vessels with which to contain it. No matter how great the Jew's spiritual demands, Judaism is capable of satisfying them (*Ne'umim ve-Harẓa'ot* (1953), 400).

Tobias *Goodman is credited with being the first Jew to preach in the English language. Two of his printed sermons are: *A Sermon on the Universally Regretted Death of the Most Illustrious Princess Charlotte,* preached on Wednesday, Nov. 19, 1817, at the synagogue, Denmark Court, London (the first sermon to be both delivered and printed in English), and *A Sermon Occasioned by the Demise of Our Late Venerable Sovereign, King George the Third,* preached on Wednesday, Feb. 16, 1820, at the same synagogue (A. Barnett, *The Western Synagogue Through Two Centuries* (1961), 48–51). In December, 1828 a Committee of Elders was appointed at the Bevis Marks Sephardi Synagogue in London, to inquire into the best means of elevating the tone of public services. Among their recommendations was that an English sermon based on a text taken from Scripture should be delivered every Saturday afternoon. Before delivery every sermon should be examined by a committee of three elders for statements contrary to Jewish doctrines or hostile to the institutions of the country (J. Picciotto, *Sketches of Anglo-Jewish History* (1956[2]), 318–20). In the U.S., preaching in the English language was introduced much later. Some preachers, like the Reform Rabbi David Einhorn, preferred to give sermons in their native German. Einhorn declared that "Where the German sermon is banned, there the reform of Judaism is nothing more than a brilliant gloss, a decorated doll, without heart, without soul, which the proudest temples and the most splendid theories cannot succeed in infusing with life." The Jewish sermon in English was developed to a fine art by such preachers as Simeon *Singer, Morris *Joseph, Joseph Herman *Hertz, Israel *Mattuck, A.A. Green, Abraham *Cohen, and Ephraim Levine in England; Stephen S. *Wise, Israel Herbert *Levinthal, Abba Hillel *Silver, Solomon *Goldman, and Solomon Bennett *Freehof in the U.S. Two annual collections of sermons in English are those published by the Rabbinical Council of America (Orthodox) since 1943; and since 1954, the collection by rabbis from all three groups in *Best Jewish Sermons,* edited by Saul I. Teplitz.

In Eastern Europe the older type of *derashah* delivered in Yiddish by the *maggid* still predominated, but certain new features manifested themselves even here. The winds of change in the Jewish world moved the *maggidim* to find a rather more sophisticated approach. Preaching in Yiddish became directed to the needs of the individual as well as the community. The Haskalah movement was frequently fought by the *maggidim* with the weapons of pulpit oratory. With the rise of Zionism, many of its opponents used the same weapons to combat it, while others sympathetic to Zionism preached the love of the Holy Land and the legitimacy of Jewish nationalistic aspirations with new fervor. In fact, a new type of nationalistic preacher emerged and was given the name *mattif* ("speaker"; Micah 2:11), to distinguish him from the old-type *maggid.* Under the influence of the Lithuanian Musar movement, with its strong moralistic concern, the *derashah* began to place greater emphasis on ethical matters. The hellfire preaching of *Moses Isaac, the Kelmer *Maggid* (1828–1900), the most popular of the folk preachers, was directed largely against dishonesty in business and general unethical conduct (D. Katz, *Tenu'at ha-Musar,* 2 (c. 1958), 395–407). Many of the *maggidim* went to the U.S., England, and South Africa where their preaching was directed against the widespread desecration of the Sabbath and neglect of the dietary laws, abuses unknown in their native countries. *Maggidim* still flourish in the State of Israel, but there has been little development of the sermon in Hebrew and the rabbi-preacher is virtually unknown there as a regular and respected synagogue functionary. Among the Yiddish preachers of renown were: Ḥayyim Zundel, H. Z. *Maccoby (the Kamenitzer *Maggid*), J. L. Lazarov, Ẓ. H. *Masliansky, Isaac *Nissenbaum, M. A. *Amiel, Zalman *Sorotzkin, and Ze'ev *Gold.

Preaching Techniques. Simeon Singer in "Where the Clergy Fail," an address delivered to young preachers on Jan. 17, 1904 (*Lectures and Addresses* (1908), 203–25), describes the aim of the Jewish preacher thus: "to teach the word of God to their brethren, young and old; to help them to the perception of the highest truths of religion; to uplift their souls out of the rut of the common, the sordid, the selfish, in life; to speak a message of comfort to the sorrowing, of hope to the despondent, of counsel to the perplexed, of courage to the struggling and aspiring." In the belief that the art of preaching can be taught, the major rabbinical seminaries have departments of homiletics. Sigmund Maybaum taught homiletics at the Hochschule in

Berlin, Israel *Bettan at Hebrew Union College, Mordecai Menahem *Kaplan at the Jewish Theological Seminary, and Abraham Cohen at Jews' College.

The modern Jewish sermon is usually based on a text chosen from the portion (the *sidra* or *haftarah*) read in the synagogue on the day the sermon is delivered. Books of the Bible which are not read in public, like Job, rarely furnish texts for sermons, though they may be quoted in support of a position the preacher adopts. Normally the sermon is delivered toward the end of the service. While the note of exhortation is never entirely absent from the sermon, many preachers nowadays prefer to use the sermon chiefly as a means of instruction, imparting information about Jewish faith, history, and teachings. The length of the sermon varies from preacher to preacher but on the average is about 20 minutes. Preaching from a prepared manuscript is the rule for some preachers while others prefer to speak extemporaneously. Adequate preparation is counselled by the best preachers. In the preface to his *Faith of a Jewish Preacher* (1935), Ephraim Levine compares the preacher who waits for Providence to put words into his mouth to Balaam who said the very opposite of what he intended to say. Oratory has now generally yielded to an easier conversational tone. Few preachers would today follow the example of Leo Baeck of whom it was said that he never used the personal pronoun "I" in the pulpit.

Sermon illustrations are taken from the personal experience of the preacher, Jewish history, the Midrash, natural science and psychology, and, latterly, ḥasidic lore. L. I. Newman's *Hasidic Anthology* (1934) and M. Buber's *Tales of the Hasidim* (1947–48) have come to serve as sources for sermon illustrations. Quotations from secular literature are used to develop themes. In a typical sermon outline on *Kol Nidrei* by Milton *Steinberg (*Sermons*, B. Mandelbaum, ed. (1954), 58–63) there are references to the *geonim*, Walter Pater, Tennyson, Leibnitz, Omar Khayyam, and W. L. Phelps. Louis I. *Rabinowitz (*Out of the Depths* (1951), 332–5) builds a *Kol Nidrei* sermon around a poem by the modern Hebrew writer Zalman *Shneur. In a Day of Atonement sermon by Israel H. Levinthal (*Steering or Drifting—Which?* (1928), 128–35), there are quotations from *Judah Halevi, the Talmud, the prayer book, a Christian legend, folk language, the Bible, and the Midrash. Preachers in the U.S. frequently take for their sermon theme a book, movie, or play that has received much attention for its treatment of some moral or religious question. Some sermons conclude with a prayer. This and other pulpit pretensions, however, were severely criticized by Franz *Rosenzweig in his scathing attack on preaching in *Sermonic Judaism* (N. N. Glatzer, *Franz Rosenzweig* (1953), 247–50). The chosen text and the way it is treated depend on the individual bent of the preacher but, judging by published sermons, certain themes are constant. Each of the festivals, for example, has its particular message so far as the preacher is concerned. The theme of Passover is freedom; of Shavuot Jewish education (in Orthodox pulpits the immutability of the Torah); of Sukkot trust in God and thankfulness for His bounty; of Ḥanukkah spiritual light; of Purim Jewish peoplehood; of Rosh Ha-Shanah the need for renewal; and on the Day of Atonement sin and atonement. In addition to the weekly Sabbath sermon the rabbi preaches on the special occasions in the life of his congregation; anniversaries, weddings, funerals, installation of officers, at a bar mitzvah, and at his own induction. A number of rabbinic manuals contain sermonic material in capsule form for the rabbi's use on special occasions (e.g., H. E. Goldin, *Ha-Madrikh*, 1939).

Issues of the Day in Preaching. The modern Jewish sermon frequently addresses itself to particular problems which agitate the Jewish community as well as to wider issues of universal import. There is much discussion on the extent to which politics should be introduced, but few Jewish preachers accept a total ban on political questions. There are numerous instances of preachers seeking to influence their congregants either when a topic is a source of controversy in the community or when they feel that widely held views are contrary to Jewish teaching. Themes treated in the contemporary pulpit are: the controversy between religion and science, the role of the State of Israel, the permissive society, intermarriage, Jewish education, war and peace, social injustice, racial discrimination, the use and abuse of wealth, and Judaism and its relation to other faiths. The 1968 edition of *Best Jewish Sermons* contains sermons against the taking of drugs; on the "death of God" movement; fair housing; the estrangement of the Jewish intellectual from Judaism; recreation; and the need to care for the hungry of the world. Rabbis have fought to free the pulpit from control by the lay leaders of the congregation. When Stephen Wise was being considered for the influential post of rabbi of Temple Emanu-El in New York, Louis *Marshall, the president, held that in controversial matters the pulpit must remain under the control of the trustees. Wise refused to consider the post under such conditions and eventually founded the Free Synagogue to uphold the principle of pulpit liberty.

In 19th-century America the slavery issue was echoed from the Jewish pulpit. Morris J. *Raphall preached that slavery was a divinely ordained institution since it is sanctioned in the Bible. David Einhorn, however, attacked slavery from the pulpit as "the greatest crime against God." As a result, his life was placed in jeopardy and on April 22, 1861, Einhorn and his family were secretly escorted out of Baltimore.

With the rise of the *Reform movement the issue of Reform was hotly debated from the pulpit. A favorite text for the Reform sermon, used by Geiger and others, was: "One generation passeth away, and another generation cometh; but the earth abideth for ever" (Eccles. 1:4). The "earth" represents the essential, unchanging spirit of Judaism, which must be interpreted by each generation in the light of its own needs and insights. Often the same set of texts would be used by both Orthodox and Reform preachers in support of their positions. The "wicked son" of the Passover *Haggadah* was, for the Orthodox preacher, the Reform Jew who asks "What is this service to you?" For the Reform Jew the son who represented their point of view was the "wise son" who was ready to ask the intelligent questions demanded by the new age. Chief Rabbi N. M. *Adler preached in London, on the second day of Passover in 1868, a sermon against the abolition of the second day of festivals in the Diaspora, a matter which at that time had begun to be an issue in the struggle betweeen Orthodoxy and Reform. His son and successor, Hermann *Adler, at the beginning of the 20th century, refused to permit a synagogue under his jurisdiction to appoint Morris *Joseph as preacher because the latter had published views "at variance with traditional Judaism." Solomon *Schechter, living at that time in Cambridge, pointed out that if doctrines were to become the test of a minister, then the greatest names in Jewish learning—Zunz, Graetz, Herzfeld, Joel, Gotthold Salomon, Rapoport and others—would never have been permitted to preach in a United Synagogue (R. Apple, *The Hampstead Synagogue* (1967), 23–27). Chief Rabbi J. H. *Hertz preached a series of sermons, *Affirmations of Judaism* (1927), attacking the new Liberal movement founded by Claude Goldsmid *Montefiore and others.

See also *Homiletic Literature. [L.J.]

Bibliography: GENERAL: Zunz-Albeck, Derashot; N. R. Rabinowitz, *Deyokena'ot shel Darshanim* (1967). TALMUDIC PERIOD: Aptowitzer, in: MGWJ, 76 (1932), 558–75; Ḥ Albeck, *Mavo u-Mafteḥot le-Midrash Bereshit Rabba*, 1 (1965²), 11–19 (in *Midrash Bereshit Rabba* ed., by J. Theodor and Ḥ. Albeck, 3 (1965²)); L. Baeck, *Aus drei Jahrtausenden* (1958²), 158; W. Bacher, *Die Prooemien der alten juedischen Homilie* (1913); Bloch, in: MGWJ, 34 (1885), 166–84, 210–24, 257–69, 385–404; 35 (1886), 165–87, 389–405; J. Heinemann, *Derashot be-Ẓibbur bi-Tekufat ha-Talmud* (1970); idem, in: *Divrei ha-Kongress ha-Olami ha-Revi'i i le-Madda'ei ha-Yahadut*, 2 (1960), 3–47; idem, in: JJS, 19 (1968), 41–48; J. Mann, *The Bible as Read and Preached in the Old Synagogue*, 1 (1940); J. Mann and I. Sonne, *The Bible as Read and Preached in the Old Synagogue*, 2 (1966); S. Maybaum, *Die aeltesten Phasen in der Entwicklung der juedischen Predigt*, 1 (1901); M. Kadushin, *The Rabbinic Mind* (1965²), 59ff.; Stein, in: *Sefer ha-Yovel... Schorr* (1935), 85–112; H. L. Strack, *Introduction to the Talmud and Midrash* (1945), 210ff.; Theodor, in: MGWJ, 28 (1879), 97–112, 164–75, 271–8, 337–50, 408–18, 455–62; 29 (1880), 19–23; 30 (1881), 500–10. MEDIEVAL PERIOD: I. Bettan, *Studies in Jewish Preaching* (1939); S. Y. Glicksberg, *Ha-Derashah be-Yisrael* (1940); S. B. Freehof, *Modern Jewish Preaching* (1941); Baron, Community, index, s.v. *Preaching;* A. Steinman, *Kitvei ha-Maggid mi-Dubno* (recast in modern style), 2 vols. (1952); H. H. Ben-Sasson, *Hagut ve-Hanhagah* (1959), 34–54; J. Katz, *Tradition and Crisis* (1961), 173–5. MODERN TIMES: A. Altmann, in: YLBI, 6 (1961), 3–59; idem (ed.), *Studies in Nineteenth-Century Jewish Intellectual History* (1964), 65–116; A. Cohen, *Jewish Homiletics* (1937); New York Board of Jewish Ministers, *Problems of the Jewish Ministry* (1927), 1–43; The Rabbinical Assembly of America, *Proceedings*, 10 (1946), 85–102; L. Treifel, in: *Festschrift zum 75 Jaehrigen Bestehen des Juedisch-Theologischen Seminars Breslau*, 2 (1929), 373–6.

PRECIOUS STONES AND JEWELRY. In The Bible. Precious stones are mentioned in various contexts in the Bible, the most comprehensive list appearing in the description of the breastpiece worn by the high priest. The breastpiece was set with 12 precious stones arranged in four rows with three stones in each row to represent the 12 tribes: "set in it mounted stones, in four rows of stones. The first row shall be a row of *ʾodem, piṭdah,* and *bareqet;* the second, of *nofekh, sappir,* and *yahalom;* the third of *leshem, shevo,* and *ʾaḥlamah;* and the fourth, of *tarshish, shoham,* and *yashfeh...*" (Ex. 28:17–20). Most of these stones are mentioned again as present in the Garden of Eden where the king of Tyre originally abode (Ezek. 28:13).

From the talmudic period onward, biblical translators and commentators have attempted to determine the mineralogical nature of these stones and to identify them in terms of the names of modern minerals. However, the identity of the stones of the breastpiece cannot be established by a mineralogical study, since there is no statement even about their colors except in the late Midrash (in Midrash Rabbah). Philological research is of assistance only in a few cases. Archaeological excavations can help somewhat by establishing which minerals were utilized as precious or semiprecious stones in pre-Exilic times. The chart presented here summarizes a few of the different identifications of the stones of the breastpiece found in ancient and modern Bible translations, and advanced by the modern scholars N. Shalem and R. Sverdlov. There is also disagreement between the Palestine Targum (followed by Maimonides and Baḥya) and the Targum Jonathan (followed by Rashi) as to the order of the names of the tribes on the stones. According to the Palestine Targum, the six sons of Leah appear first, then the sons of the maidservants, and lastly the sons of Rachel. Targum Jonathan, on the other hand, claims that they followed the order of their birth, i.e., the sons of the maidservants preceded Issachar and Zebulun. The only source specifying a mineralogical property is the description found in Midrash Rabbah (Num. R. 2:7):

> There were distinguishing signs for each prince; each had a flag and a different color for every flag, corresponding to the precious stones on the breast of Aaron... Reuben's stone was *ʾodem* and the color of his flag was red; and embroidered thereon were mandrakes. Simeon's was *piṭdah* and his flag was of a yellow (or green) color... Levi's was *bareqet* and the color of his flag was a third white, a third black, and a third red... Judah's was *nofekh* and the color of his flag was like that of the sky... Issachar's was *sappir* and the color of his flag was black like stibium... Zebulun's was *yahalom* and the color of his flag was white... Dan's

The Precious Stones in the High Priest's Breastplate in the Hebrew Bible and Its Versions

Hebrew Bible	Onkelos	Targum Jonathan	Palestine Targum	Ex. Rabbah 38, 10	LXX	J.P.S.A.	New English Bible
אֹדֶם	סַמְקָן	סִימוּקְתָא	סַמְקָתָא	שרדנגין (שדרנבין)	σάρδιον	carnelian	sardin
פִּטְדָה	יַרְקָן	יַרְקְתָא	יַרְקָתָא	טומפזין (שומפזין)	τοπάζιον	chrysolite (topaz)	chrysolite
בָּרֶקֶת	בַּרְקָן	בַּרְקְתָא	בַּרְקָתָא	דיקינתון	σμάραγδος	emerald (smaragd)	green felspar
נֹפֶךְ	אִזְמַרַגְדִּין	אִיזְמוֹרַד	כַּדְכְּדָנָא	ברדינין	ἄνθραξ	turquoise (carbuncle)	purple garnet
סַפִּיר	שַׁבְזִיז	סַפִּירִינוֹן	סִמְפּוֹרְיָנָא	סאפירינון	σάρφείρος	sapphire	lapis lazuli
יַהֲלֹם	סִבְהֲלוֹם	כַּדְכּוֹדִי	עֵין עִיגְלָא	אזמרגדין	ἴαστις	amethyst (emerald)	jade
לֶשֶׁם	קַנְכֵּרֵי	קַנְכִּרִינוֹן	זוֹזִין	כוכלין (בוחלין).	λιγύριον	jacinth	turquoise
שְׁבוֹ	טַרְקְיָא	טַרְקִין (ערקין)	בִּירְזְלִין	אכאטיס	ἀχάτης	agate	agate
אַחְלָמָה	עֵין עֶגְלָא	עֵין עֵיגֶל	זְמַרְגַּדִּין	הימוסיון (המטוסיון)	ἀμέθυστος	crystal (amethyst)	jasper
תַּרְשִׁישׁ	כְּרוּם יַמָּא	כְּרוּם יַמָּא רַבָּא	כְּרוּם יַמָּא	קרומטסין	χρυσόλιθος	beryl	topaz
שֹׁהַם	בּוּרְלָא	בֵּירְלֵיַת חַלָּא	בְּדוּלְחָא	פראלוקין	βήρύλλιον	lapis lazuli (onyx)	cornelian
יָשְׁפֶה	פַּנְטֵירֵי	מַרְגְּנִיַּת אַפַּנְטוֹרִין	מַרְגָּלִיתָא	מרגליטים	ὀνύχιον	jasper	green jasper

was *leshem* and the color of his flag was similar to *sappir* . . . Gad's *ʾaḥlamah* and the color of his flag was neither white nor black but a blend of black and white . . . Asher's was *tarshish* and the color of his flag was like the precious stone with which women adorn themselves . . . Joseph's was *shoham* and the color of his flag was jet black . . . Benjamin's was *yashfeh* and the color of his flag was a combination of all the 12 colors . . .

If this ancient Midrash is accepted, it appears that the color of the stones was the most accurate mark of identification that popular Jewish tradition could preserve. Ibn Ezra (Ex. 28:9), on the other hand, sharply criticizes the translations of Saadiah Gaon: "and we have no way of clearly knowing the 'stones for setting' because the Gaon rendered them as he wished, and he has no tradition which he can rely on . . ."

Through a comparison of the various translations and commentaries, reasonable identification may be advanced for some of the stones; with others, an identification is impossible. Some of the stones may be identified mineralogically, but because they are different in color they were called by different names.

ʾODEM (אֹדֶם; Ex. 28:17; 39:10; Ezek. 28:13), a red stone. *ʾOdem* is rendered as *samqan* (סַמְקָן), i.e., "red," in Aramaic translations; as *sardion* in the Greek versions; and *aḥmar* in Arabic. This stone is probably carnelian sard, one of the red cryptocrystalline varieties of quartz (SiO_2). It is found in excavations. Some regard it as the opaque red jasper found in Egypt and in the vicinity of Eilat.

PIṬDAH (פִּטְדָה; Ex. 28:17; 39:10; Ezek. 28:13), according to the commentators, a green stone, and generally identified in the versions as the green-yellow topaz. According to Pliny, however, what was known as the topaz in antiquity was not identical with the modern stone called topaz $Al_2F_2SiO_4$, but with the modern chrysolite or peridot belonging to the olivine group. This mineral is usually green in color and is used as a gem. The identification of topaz or chrysolite with *piṭdah* is rejected by N. Shalem who proposed plasma, a green variety of cryptocrystalline quartz. *Piṭdah* is also mentioned in Job 28:19 as *piṭdah* of Ethiopia, which is used as a symbol of the value of wisdom. This is apparently a reference to *piṭdah* imported from Ethiopia.

BAREQET (בָּרֶקֶת; Ex. 28:17; 39:10; Ezek. 28:13), a similar term in Akkadian, *barraqtu,* also means a precious stone. Both words may share a common etymology in the Semitic root *brq* or may be borrowed from the Sanskrit *marakata* which means smaragd. Most Greek versions explain *bareqet* as smaragd, which is a variety of beryl $Al_2Be_3Si_6O_{18}$ with small additions of other elements, i.e., the emerald. Emerald-smaragd mines were located in ancient times in Kosseir in Egypt. Smaragd was considered the most valuable green stone, and it has been found in the form of gems in the tombs of the pharaohs. U. Cassuto and others identify *bareqet* with malachite, which is similar in color to smaragd and was easier to work in ancient times. According to these explanations, *bareqet* is green and thus does not fit the description in the Midrash which states that *bareqet* is found in three colors. N. Shalem therefore proposed to identify *bareqet* with jasper (SiO_2).

NOFEKH (נֹפֶךְ; Ex. 28:18; 39:11; Ezek. 27:16; 28:13). *Nofekh* is mentioned as one of the stones on the breastpiece, in the description of the precious stones belonging to the king of Tyre in the Garden of Eden, and also among the valuable goods brought to Tyre by the Arameans. *Nofekh* has been identified by some scholars as the red mineral pyrope $Mg_3Al_2(SiO_4)_3$ of the garnet group. According to the Midrash, it was sky blue in color and N. Shalem, therefore, proposed to identify it with turquoise ($Cu_3Al_2O_3 \cdot 2P_2O_5 \cdot 9H_2O$) which was well known in Sinai as early as the time of the first pharaohs.

SAPPIR (סַפִּיר). This stone appears in the Bible as the second stone in the second row of the breastpiece (Ex. 28:18; 39:11) and also in other passages as a very costly gem. It is included among the precious stones brought to Tyre by the Arameans (Ezek. 28:13); the firmament is said to have the appearance of the *sappir* stone (Ezek. 1:26); it is used as a symbol of beauty (Song 5:14; Lam. 4:7) and of value—"It cannot be valued in the gold of Ophir, in precious onyx, or *sappir*" (Job 28:16). The Midrash describes the *sappir* as "black, like stibium." Most translations identify the *sappir* with the present-day blue sapphire (Al_2O_3); this stone, however, was apparently unknown in antiquity. In contrast to the Midrash, which regards the *sappir* as blue, Saadiah Gaon calls it white, on the basis of the verse "the likeness of *livnat ha-sappir*" (Ex. 24:10), where he interprets *livnat* as "whiteness." Ibn Ezra disagreed with Saadiah, explaining that the *sappir* is red on the basis of the verse "their bodies were more ruddy than coral, the beauty of their form was like *sappir*" (Lam. 4:7). Despite these sources, most scholars identify *sappir* with lapis lazuli, a translucent blue mineral of the lazulite group, which was used as a decorative stone in antiquity. Lapis lazuli was known in Cyprus as a natural stone and in ancient Egypt also as an artificial gem.

YAHALOM (יַהֲלֹם), the third stone in the second row of the breastpiece (Ex. 28:18; 39:11), also mentioned in Ezekiel 28:13 as one of the precious stones found in the Garden of Eden. The *yahalom* was a white stone according to the Midrash, and Ibn Ezra rendered it as diamond "which breaks all stones and precious *bedolaḥ*" (on Ex. 28:9). Although in modern Hebrew *yahalom* means diamond, the hardest mineral found in nature, it is not likely that the Bible refers to this stone, which was apparently unknown in biblical times. N. Shalem has proposed chalcedony, a variety of quartz (SiO_2), which is a relatively hard white mineral which fits the midrashic description.

LESHEM (לֶשֶׁם), the first stone in the third row of the breastpiece (Ex. 28:19; 39:12). Scholars disagree as to the identity of this stone: Sverdlov attributed it to the zircon family, whereas Shalem identifies it with aventurine; others regard it as amber. The name Leshem and the tribe of Dan are connected by means of the *leshem* stone on the breastpiece as well as by means of the city Leshem, also called Laish, which was settled by the tribe of Dan in the north of Israel (Josh. 19:47).

SHEVO (שְׁבוֹ), the second stone in the third row of the breastpiece (Ex. 28:19; 39:12). According to the Midrash, it is neither white nor black but of a mixed color. *Midrash Rabbah* renders it as *achatis,* as does the Septuagint. This corresponds to the agate, a variety of chalcedony (SiO_2) which has variegated colors as a result of impurities—sometimes in the form of stripes and sometimes in other forms. Agate, a very common mineral, was known in Near Eastern countries in biblical times.

ʾAḤLAMAH (אַחְלָמָה), the third stone in the third row of the breastpiece (Ex. 28:19; 39:12). Most translators and commentators identify it with amethyst, a transparent purple stone of the SiO_2 group. The Septuagint, Vulgate, and most other versions render it as amethyst. It was believed in antiquity that wine drunk from an amethyst cup would not intoxicate, since the word amethyst in Greek apparently means "not drunken." Ibn Ezra connects the word,*aḥlamah* with *ḥalom,* "dream": "whoever wears this stone on his finger never fears dreams," and goes on to say that the,*aḥlamah* possesses a magic power which influences dreams, just as there is "a stone which attracts iron" (magnet) and "a stone which flees from vinegar" (the influence of acid on certain minerals). The identification of,*aḥlamah* with amethyst, which was well known in antiquity, is generally accepted by most scholars.

TARSHISH (תַּרְשִׁישׁ), the first stone in the fourth row of the breastpiece (Ex. 28:20; 39:13). The *tarshish* apparently had an unusual luster and brilliance and is thus mentioned several times in the Bible: "the appearance of the wheels . . . was like the gleaming of a *tarshish*" (Ezek. 1:16; 10:9); "his arms are rounded gold set with *tarshish*" (Song 5:14); "his body was like *tarshish,* his face like the appearance of lightning" (Dan. 10:6). The Targums Onkelos and Jonathan translate *tarshish* as "color of the sea." In all probability, the reference is to the mineral known today as aquamarine, a transparent, bluish green variety of beryl which was considered a very beautiful and costly stone. The aquamarine stone was apparently known in southern Egypt and Spain. This explanation also seems to agree with the Midrash which states that its color resembles a precious stone, since aquamarine was known from earliest times as a precious stone. N. Shalem, in 1931, identified *tarshish* with opal, but later suggested it was mother-of-pearl, perhaps because of the connection between the "color of the sea" and the "sea stone" of Targum Onkelos, which can refer only to pearls. No connection should apparently be sought between the *tarshish* stone and the country or island of the same name to which boats were sent to bring back metals (I Kings 10:22) and to which Jonah fled. It seems that aquamarine is the most correct suggestion.

SHOHAM (שֹׁהַם), the second stone in the fourth row of the

breastpiece (Ex. 28:20; 39:13). *Shoham* is mentioned as one of the stones of the land of Havilah in the Garden of Eden (Gen. 2:12). The translations are not agreed on any one definition: the Septuagint renders it as beryl, as apparently does Onkelos ("burla"); the Palestine Targum translates it as *bedolaḥ* and Josephus, in *The Jewish Wars,* as onyx. According to the Midrash, it was very black in color, whereas Ibn Ezra calls it white (on Ex. 28:9). Onyx is also a variety of silica and usually has different shades and colors. There is no evidence to substantiate the ancient translation of beryl. There is no doubt that *shoham* was considered one of the precious stones of the Garden of Eden (Ezek. 28:13), and it also appears in Job as a symbol of wealth and importance: "wisdom ... cannot be valued ... in precious *shoham*" (Job 28:16). It was apparently a very costly, hard, and rare stone, but as yet no well-founded identificaton has been proposed.

Y.ASHFEH (יָשְׁפֵה), the third stone in the fourth row of the breastpiece (Ex. 28:20; 39:13) and one of the precious stones of the Garden of Eden (Ezek. 28:13). This stone appears with the same name in many ancient documents, including the Tell el-Amarna letters, and is apparently identical with the mineral jasper. This is the only case where one of the stones of the breastpiece is identified with a modern mineral through a similarity of names (that is, if we accept the above theory that the biblical *sappir* is not the modern sapphire). *Yashfeh* was translated as jaspir or jasper from very early times, although the Targums Onkelos and Jonathan do not mention them. Jasper is also a variety of silica.

ʾELGAVISH (אֶלְגָּבִישׁ) appears in the Bible in connection with heavy rains: "there will be a deluge of rain, great *ʾelgavish* stones will fall" (Ezek. 13:11; 38:22). The Septuagint translates *ʾelgavish* stones both as hail and as slingstones. It is very likely that hail was seen as the slingstones of God, and for this reason the term was used in both senses. Some scholars read it as *ʾel gavish, gavish,* as in Job 28:18, probably meaning crystal as in modern Hebrew. The common crystal is quartz, also known as rock crystal. Hail was called *ʾelgavish* since it was similar in form to real crystal, but as it was only water it could not be called *gavish* but only *ʾelgavish.*

ʾEQDAḤ (אֶקְדָּח), mentioned only once in the Bible: "I will make your pinnacles of *kadkod,* your gates of *ʾeqdaḥ*" (Isa. 54:12). It has not been identified. Some commentators associate the word *ʾeqdaḥ* with a sparkling, lustrous stone, on the basis of the verse: "you are all kindlers of fire *(qodḥe ʾesh),* who set brands alight" (Isa. 50:11). According to Rashi, *ʾeqdaḥ* is not a mineral but a gate constucted from a large stone in which an opening was made by drilling *(qiddu'aḥ).*

KADKOD (כַּדְכֹּד), a term that appears twice in the Bible: "I will make your pinnacles of *kadkod*" (Isa. 54:12) and in the list of precious goods brought to Tyre by the Arameans (Ezek. 27:16). *Kadkod* apparently denotes a shiny, sparkling stone, and it is possible that it does not refer to one specific mineral but is a name based on the expression *kiddode ʾesh,* "sparks of fire" (Job 41:11). The Septuagint substituted the letter *resh* for *dalet* which makes the word closer to *karkond,* the Arabic name for spinel, a red precious stone. Some identify *kadkod* with the hyacinth, a transparent orange, red, or brown precious stone which is a variety of zircon.

BAHAṬ, SHESH, DAR, SOḤARET (בַּהַט, שֵׁשׁ, דַּר, סֹחָרֶת), four terms appearing in the description of the floor of Ahasuerus' palace (Esth. 1:6). This floor was apparently a mosaic pavement containing these four stones. *Bahaṭ* is possibly a type of marble. Alabaster, which was very common in all Near Eastern countries, is sometimes called *bahaṭ* in modern Hebrew. *Shesh* is marble. *Dar,* which means "pearl" in Arabic, may designate stones with a pearl-like luster. The identity of the last term, *soḥaret,* is unknown. These four terms denote decorative building stones which could be polished, but apparently not precious stones.

RAʾMOT (רָאמוֹת), mentioned in the Bible in various contexts. It is listed among the precious goods brought by the Arameans to Tyre (Ezek. 27:16); as a precious stone which is compared to wisdom in the eyes of a fool: "Wisdom is for a fool as *raʾmot*" (Prov. 24:7); and again as a very costly stone whose value is nevertheless surpassed by wisdom (Job 28:18). *Raʾmot* is clearly a precious stone; its identity, however, is unknown. [U.S.W.]

In Rabbinical Literature. Talmud, Midrash, Aramaic and other versions as well as the medieval commentators give translations or interpretations of the two *shoham* (onyx?) stones on the high priest's Ephod and of the 12 precious stones that make up the "Breastplate of Judgment" (Ex.

28:6–12; 15–30). Rav Assi (Meg. 12a) endeavored to explain "stones of a crown, glittering over His land" (Zech. 9:16) and the *bahaṭ* of Esther 1:6 by אבנים שמחוטטות על בעליהן ("stones that flash back at their owner," but see Rashi and He-Arukh s.v. חט). Another explanation given *(ibid.)* reads המחיטטות לעינים במקומן ("which dazzle the eyes in the place where they are found" (see Jastrow, Dict, s.v. חטט). The precious stones mentioned in Job 28:18 are translated in the Targum by סנדלכון (corrupted from Greek σαρδόνυχ) and בירולין or בירוצין (beryl), the former also being used in the Talmud as a generic term for precious stones (Sanh. 59b; ARN¹ 1, 5 and 38, 114). The onyx stone (אנך) is mentioned (Av. Zar. 8b, 11b and Tosef. Kel. BM 1:3).

Under the influence of beliefs prevalent among other peoples and cultures, Talmud and Midrash attach magical, in particular medical but also psychological influences to precious stones, ideas which continued to prevail among medieval Jewish Bible commentators like Abraham ibn Ezra, David Kimḥi, Baḥya b. Asher and also in the Zohar (see *Astrology). Simeon b. Ẓemaḥ Duran (14th–15th centuries) in his *Magen Avot* 2, 1 refers to the more than 400 precious stones and their qualities mentioned by Aristotle, and Abraham b. David Portaleone (16th century) devoted a special chapter to this subject in his *Shiltei ha-Gibborim* (1612). Abraham wore a precious stone, hanging from his neck, which healed all those who looked at it (BB 16b); cf. the pearl-bag worn by animals (Sanh. 68a and Rashi ad loc.). Josephus mentions that the Essenes used precious stones for healing purposes (Wars 2:136). Many legends have been woven round the *Shamir* stone (or worm?) which was said to have been used to cut stones for Solomon's Temple and to engrave the Ephod and breastpiece stones (Avot 5:6; Sot. 48a–b; Git. 68a). Similar qualities were ascribed to the sapphire (PdRK 135b) which was believed to be indestructible and out of which the Two Tablets of the Law (the Ten Commandments) were said to have been made (Tanḥ. Ki Tissa 26; Song. R. 5:14, 3). Precious stones almost invariably occur together with gold and silver as signs of wealth throughout rabbinic literature, and are the subjects of numerous legends (see Ginzberg, Legends, index s.v. Stone (Stones), Precious). Precious stones were also used for *seals and signet rings.

The expression תכשיט (esp. תכשיטי נשים) = finery, covers not only jewelry but also *cosmetics. Women's finery as a means of seduction was said to have been the invention of the daughters of Cain (see Krauss, TA. I. 198), yet women were entitled to possess and wear it (Ket. 65a). Jewelry formed part of the marriage settlement (Song R. 4:12; TJ, Ket. 6:3, 30d), and was sometimes given in lieu of betrothal money (Kid. 48a); cf. certain restrictions on Sabbath wear and some purity regulations (Shab. 6:1; Tanḥ. Gen. 34, 1; Kel. 11:8, 9; cf. Shab. 62b; Tosef. Kid. 1:11). A bride in particular, was to adorn herself lavishly (Song R. 4:10, 1; Tanḥ. Ex. 31, 18). Jewelry was of gold, silver, precious stones, pearls, and sometimes coral. There are full details of the treatment of pearls, their size, color, and shape and the manner in which they were pierced. They were strung together into necklaces sometimes consisting of several rows. Pearls were also set in diadems, together with precious stones; they were also inset in them or vice versa. In general pearls rated above jewels as the most precious objects, and served as presents between royalty (Artaban of Persia to Judah ha-Nasi, TJ, Pe'ah 1:1, 15d). Not only men wore these but even animals were sometimes adorned with precious stones as amulets as can be seen from the story of the ass bought by Simeon b. Shetaḥ (TJ, BM 2:5, 8c).

The main types of jewelry mentioned are signets (see *seals) usually worn as finger rings; women generally wore no signet rings, only ordinary rings (Shab. 6:1, 3; 62a; Kel. 11:8). Metal rings with a seal made of sandalwood or vice versa are mentioned. Rings, probably as other jewelry, were acceptable as loan-pledges (TJ, Shev. 10:9, 39d). They could also contain poison (Deut. R. 2:24). Women, brides in particular, wore as diadems a "City of Gold" (representing Jerusalem, Shab. 6:1; Kel. 11:8; Sot. 49b) such as Akiva once gave to his wife (Shab. *ibid.;* TJ, Shab. 6:1, 7d; ARN[2] 12:30). Above all, women wore necklaces *(catella)*, some of the "choker" type which were made of precious metal or stones, pearls, glass beads or sandalwood. Ear- and nose rings were very common among women and also children of both sexes. An amulet-text was inserted in a capsule worn round the neck; children wore also small tablets or scrolls containing a Bible verse. Officials and tradesmen wore the insignia of their office or trade as adornments. Other ornaments included anklets, bracelets, and also strings of coins, worn, by children in particular, on the forehead, as a necklace or on the upper part of the dress. Women also wore bells around the neck or attached to their dress. [Ed.]

Bibliography: Eisenstein, Yisrael, 1 (1907), 71–74 (with bibliography); I. Loew, *Fauna und Mineralien der Juden* (1969); N. Shalem, in: *Leshonenu* 3 (1931), 291–9; idem, in: *Kovez ha-Ḥevrah ha-Ivrit la-Ḥakirat Erez Yisrael va-Attikoteha,* 2 (1935), 197–214; U. Cassuto, *A Commentary on the Book of Exodus* (1967); S. Tolansky, *The History and Use of Diamond* (1962); E. S. Dana, *A Textbook of Mineralogy,* ed. by W. E. Ford (1966[4]); S. Shefer (ed.), Abraham b. David Portaleone, *Bigdei Kehunnah* (1964); R. Z. Sverdlov, *Yesodot ha-Minerologyah . . .* (1948), 177–87; A. Rosenzweig, *Kleidung und Schmuck in Bibel und talmudischen Schriften* (1905).

PREGER, JACOB (1887–1942), Yiddish playwright and poet. Born in Kobrin (Belorussia), Preger grew up in Drogichin and Warsaw.

His reputation is based largely upon two highly successful plays, *Der Nisoye* (1925) and *"Simkhe Plakhte,"* a comedy which Maurice Schwartz produced in the U.S. under the title *Der Vasertreger.* His published verse includes *Oyf di Vegn* (1914), *Oyfn Veg* (1919), and *Shlomo Hameylekh* (1932), a "dramatic poem in three acts." Preger's art is rooted in folklore and the popular imagination. He is reported to have been killed by the Germans in Otwock.

Bibliography: LNYL, 7 (1968), 227–8; Z. Zylbercweig, *Leksikon fun Yidishn Teater,* 3 (1959), 1888–94. [L.P.]

PREIL, GABRIEL JOSHUA (1911–), U.S. Hebrew poet. Born in Dorpat, Estonia, Preil was taken to the United States in 1922. Though he published essays from time to time, wrote in Yiddish and English, and translated from Hebrew into English and from English into Hebrew, he was mainly a modernist Hebrew poet who introduced new themes and cadences into Hebrew literature in America. His lyrical pieces, which form the bulk of his collected poems, usually move in subtle, unrhymed rhythms on the boundary of prose and poetry. He is a poet of things and facts: a map, a mailbox, Lincoln Center in New York City, a Chinese sketch, a picture of Vincent van Gogh serve as foci for poetical aperçus and reflective moods. Though influenced by Whitman, Frost, and Sandburg, whose "Prairie" he translated into Hebrew, he was mainly an introspective lyricist. The New Hampshire and Vermont landscapes fascinated him: the cool sobriety of the north corresponded to his temperament which never ventured into flights of pathos.

Preil's poetry appeared in the following volumes: *Nof Shemesh u-Kefor* (1944); *Ner Mul Kokhavim* (1954); *Mappat Erev* (1961); and *Ha-Esh ve-ha-Demamah* (1968). A volume of his Yiddish poems, *Lider,* including his translations of his Hebrew poems, appeared in 1966, a monograph in English on *Israeli Poetry in Peace and War,* in 1959.

Bibliography: A. Epstein, *Soferim Ivrim ba-Amerikah,* 1 (1952), 229–36; A. Shabtay, *Gavri'el Preil* (Heb., 1965); A. Marthon, in: *Bitzaron,* 43 (1961), 49–53; 54 (1966), 163–7. [Ei.S.]

PREMINGER, OTTO LUDWIG (1906–), U.S. film and stage director and producer. Born in Vienna, Preminger worked at Max *Reinhardt's Josefstadt Theater in Vienna in 1923, and in 1928 was engaged by him as director. He went to the U.S. in 1935 and gained prominence in the theater with productions which included the anti-Nazi play *Margin for Error* (1943). Taking up film work he became one of the most controversial and important directors.

His successes include *Laura* (1944); *The Moon is Blue* (1953), which led to a Supreme Court decision that prohibited local censors from stopping distribution; *The Man with the Golden Arm* (1956); *Exodus* (1960), based on Leon *Uris' novel which dealt with the pre-1948 migration of European refugees to Israel; *Advise and Consent* (1962); and *Bunny Lake is Missing* (1965), all of which he produced and directed. Preminger also directed *Porgy and Bess* (1959). Despite condemnation of several of his films by the Roman Catholic Legion of Decency, Preminger was later decorated by the Vatican for his film *The Cardinal* (1963).

Bibliography: A. Sarris (ed.), *Interviews with Film Directors* (1967), 339–49; *Current Biography Yearbook 1959* (1960), 369–71. [H.C.]

°**PŘEMYSL OTTOKAR II** (c. 1230–1278), margrave of Moravia in 1247, duke of Austria in 1251, and king of Bohemia in 1253. Following his general policy of developing the cities, Přemysl protected the Jews in his dominions. The city privilege of *Jihlava (Iglau), which he signed in 1249, contained clauses concerning Jews. In 1254 he issued a charter, based on the 1244 declaration of *Frederick II of Babenberg and even more liberal than the earlier proclamation. It was valid for all his dominions. Among other provisions, it added sacred vestments to the articles forbidden as pledges, but it left the adjustment of the rate of interest to the contracting parties. Though omitting the provisions about capital punishment for desecration of cemeteries, it laid down that the Jews were not to be disturbed on their holidays with the return of pledges. Another provision was that an oath taken by a Jew was itself sufficient to absolve him of responsibility in the case of a pawn that was accidentally destroyed. Moreover, Přemysl included the bulls of *Innocent IV against the blood libel. He employed two Jewish *comes camerae,* and Jewish tax collectors and mintmasters. His favorable treatment of the Jews was opposed by the clergy. In 1268, apparently as a reaction to the Vienna Church Council of 1267, he renewed the Jewish rights "of his youth"; since the Jews belonged to his chamber, he indicated, they came under his protection. Between 1273 and 1278 he exempted the *Brno (Bruenn) community from all taxes for one year.

Bibliography: J. E. Scherer, *Die Rechtsverhaeltnisse der Juden in den deutsch-oesterreichischen Laendern,* 1 (1901), 336–8; B. Bretholz, *Quellen zur Geschichte der Juden in Maehren* (1935), 2–10; idem, *Geschichte der Juden in Maehren im Mittelalter,* 1 (1934), index s.v. *Přemysl Otakar II;* Bondy-Dworský, 1 (1906), 17–32; M. Grunwald, *Vienna* (1936), index, s.v. *Ottakar II;* H. Tietxe, *Die Juden Wiens* (1935), index, s.v. *Przemysl Ottokar von Boehmen.* [M.La.]

PRESBYTER JUDAEORUM (arch-presbyter, or *le prestre* in Norman French), secular head of the exchequer of the Jews in 13th century England who supervised the collection of taxes and fees for the crown. He has been variously identified by historians as chief rabbi, high priest, bishop, or judge. As one of the most prominent Jews in England, he was often called upon by the king to advise on a variety of matters affecting his people, and was sworn "to look after the administration of justice on behalf of the king and to explain the king's laws," largely, presumably, on administrative matters. Six such arch-presbyters are known, all of them wealthy. Jacob of London, appointed in 1199, was followed in 1207 by Josce fil' Isaac, who was succeeded by *Aaron of York in 1236. *Elias le Eveske assumed the position in 1243. After protesting against the onerous taxes and fines, he was deposed in 1257 and eventually became an apostate. The king then offering the Jews the right to select a successor, they chose Hagin (Ḥayyim), son of Master Moses of Lincoln, in 1258. The last arch-presbyter, who held office from 1281 till the expulsion of the Jews from England a decade later, was Cok Hagin, son of Deulecresse of London.

Bibliography: H. P. Stokes, *Studies in Anglo-Jewish History* (1913), 23–43; Roth, England, 112n., 30–31, 79–80; A. M. Hyamson, *History of the Jews in England* (1928²). [I.L.]

PRESENCE, DIVINE. The notion of the Divine Presence is expressed in the Bible in two different senses: 1) in the corporeal sense, i.e., the actual dwelling (*shakhan,* שָׁכַן) of God in His abode; 2) in the abstract sense, i.e., symbolic representation by means of calling or establishing His name (*shikken shem,* שִׁכֵּן שֵׁם) upon the Sanctuary or the people.

The Corporeal Notion. God's presence, according to the ancient view, is confined to the Tabernacle/Sanctuary and to other visible phenomena serving as the vehicles of God, such as the Ark and the *cherubim or the cloud enveloping the Godhead in its movements. That the Tabernacle was considered an indicator for God's presence in ancient Israel may be learned from the words of Nathan the prophet to David: "... I have been moving about *[mithalekh]* in a Tabernacle and tent *[be-ohel u-ve-mishkan]* ... All the time I was moving about among the Israelites ..." (II Sam. 7:6–7). The same concept is given expression in the Priestly source of the Pentateuch: "I will establish My abode *[mishkani]* in your midst ... and I will be moving about [i.e, be present] in your midst: I will be your God and you shall be my people" (Lev. 26:11–12). Similar statements are found in other parts of the Priestly literature, where *shakhan,* "dwelling," is used instead of *hithalekh,* "moving about," as in Exodus 25:8: "Let them make me a Sanctuary that I may dwell *[we-shakhanti]* among them," and at the end of the inauguration of the Tabernacle in Exodus 29:45–46: "And I will dwell among the Israelites and I will be their God." The rabbinic term **Shekhinah* is actually an abstraction of this concept of "dwelling," which in the sources just quoted is understood literally. Indeed the Tabernacle, as depicted in the Priestly tradition, represents a royal house with all its necessary facilities.

Within the inner recesses of the Tabernacle, removed and veiled from the human eye sits the Deity ensconced between the two cherubim and the entire conception of the service is anthropomorphic (see below). It is performed "before the Lord" (לפני ה׳) that is, in His presence.

The presence of the Deity in the Sanctuary demands a rigorous observance of all rules concerning holiness and purity; any laxity might incur the wrath of the Deity and thus invite disaster. The divine seclusion must be respected. Thus in an adjoining chamber, the high priest, the most intimate of God's ministrants, attends to His essential needs. Only the priest who ministers to the Lord may approach the divine sanctum; the "stranger" who draws near must die (Num. 17:28 etc.). Drawing near to the Deity here signifies entrance into the actual sphere of the Divine Presence and for this reason is fraught with great physical danger (cf. Lev. 10:1–2; Num. 16:35).

This anthropomorphic theology derives from early sacral conceptions. The Ark was conceived as the footstool of the Deity and God as sitting enthroned upon the cherubim (I Sam. 4:4; Ps. 80:2; 99:5, etc.) The shewbread (לחם הפנים) laid out before the Lord by the high priest, the lamp kindled before Him to furnish light, the sweet incense burned mornings and evenings for His pleasure, the offerings consumed by the Divine fire, and the danger that accrues from approaching the Divinity are all alluded to in the early historiographic narratives.

In the ancient Israelite traditions God's presence is manifested mainly by the Ark and the pillar of cloud (see below). The Ark guided the people in the desert (Num. 10:33–34) and preceded the Israelites in the crossing of the Jordan before entering the Holy Land (Josh. 3:3ff.). The Ark also accompanied the people in their battles with their enemies (Num. 10:35–36) a fact which is well exemplified in the story of the critical encounter between the Israelites and the Philistines in Aphek (I Sam. 4). When the Ark was brought into the camp, the Israelites shouted with a great shout so that the whole earth stirred (4:5), and the Philistines, hearing the shout, became terrified, saying that "God has come into the camp" (4:7). The most common expression for the manifestation of God's presence is *Kevod YHWH.*

The Kavod of the Lord. The Godhead and its appearance are associated with the term *kavod,* a term underlying the imagery of the Divine Presence in the Bible and paralleling the term *Shekhinah* in rabbinic literature. The Tabernacle is said to be sanctified by the "*Kavod* of the Lord" (Ex. 29:43) and indeed when God enters the Tabernacle after its inauguration the Tabernacle is said to be filled with the *kavod* (Ex. 40:34–35). The dedication of the Jerusalem Temple is described in similar terms in I Kings 8:11. In both cases the *kavod* enters the holy abode, accompanied by the cloud, up to the Holy of Holies during which time Moses, on the one hand, and the Jerusalem priests, on the other, could not come in to minister. Only after the cloud departed and the *kavod* arrived at its place between the cherubim could Moses or the Jerusalem priests reenter the holy House.

The cloud serves as an envelope which screens the Deity from mortal view. Only Moses, who converses with God face to face, may enter into the cloud (Ex. 24:18). To the Israelites, however, God manifests Himself only when covered by a cloud. Unlike Moses they see only flames flashing forth from the cloud (Ex. 24:17). Only once does God manifest Himself to Israel without His screen of cloud—on the day of the inauguration of the Tabernacle (Lev. 9:23), an event whose importance parallels the Sinaitic revelation. The cloud departs from the Deity only when He assumes another mode of concealment, namely the Tent of Meeting or the Sanctuary. When the *kavod* enters the Tabernacle, the cloud remains outside and covers the tent. When the Tabernacle is dismantled, the *kavod* leaves the tent which is enveloped once again by the cloud which awaits Him and rises upward (Num. 9:15ff.).

The Nature of the Kavod. Knowledge of the underlying imagery of the concept of *kavod,* which is embedded in Priestly tradition, is provided by Ezekiel whose ideology and divine imagery is grounded on Priestly doctrine. In Ezekiel 1, the *kavod* is described as an envelope of fire and brightness conveyed on a chariot. From afar, the apparition is like a blazing fire upon a great cloud swept by a storm wind (1:4). It is this radiance and brightness of the *kavod* which made Moses' face radiant after he spoke with God (Ex. 34:29–35).

This characteristic feature of God, i.e., His being surrounded by an aureole or nimbus, is salient in the description of gods in Mesopotamia. The terms denoting the halo of the gods in Mesopotamia, *pulḫu-melammu,* actually correspond to the Hebrew *kavod-yir'ah* and indeed refer to the flame and fire enveloping the Godhead. Like the Tabernacle and Temple in Israel, the Mesopotamian shrines and chapels were clad with the *melammu*, i.e., the divine splendor. The *kavod* is said to cover (cf. Hab. 3:3, *ksh*) and fill (Num. 14:21; Isa. 6:3, *ml'*) heaven and earth. The same idea occurs in connection with the *pulḫu-melammu* in Akkadian expressed by the verbs *katāmu* and *malû* which are identical with the Hebrew *ksh* and *ml'*. The Akkadian *pulḫu-melammu* is often employed in connection with overwhelming the enemy and terrifying him. This is in fact expressed in Isaiah 2 where on the "day of the Lord" God appears in "terror" and "majestic glory" *(paḥad YHWH ve-hadar ge'ono)* a pair of concepts which can now be better understood on the basis of the Mesopotamian parallels.

The correspondence of *pulḫu-melammu* to *kavod-yir'ah* may be discerned in some other biblical descriptions. The Mesopotamian god imparts his *melammu* to the king who is the god's representative and thus endows him with divine power. When the god rejects the king and deprives him of the *melammu*, the king no longer continues to reign by divine grace. Reflections of these beliefs may also be discerned in biblical literature. Though the Priestly document describes only Moses as being endowed with the divine radiance, biblical wisdom and psalmodic literature describe man in general, in contexts in which he is likened to a king, as being endowed with the divine *kavod* and splendor: "Thou hast made him little less than God, and dost crown him with *kavod* and splendor" (Ps. 8:6). If man becomes unworthy then God deprives him of the divine *kavod:* "He has stripped me of my *kavod* and taken the crown from my head" (Job 19:9).

Ezekiel in his divine chariot vision describes the divine animals as endowed with terror (*yir'ah;* 1:18). The passage appears to employ the term in the sense of a dazzling and awe-inspiring covering or dress of heavenly and divine beings as does its Akkadian counterpart in Babylonian and Assyrian literature (see Oppenheim, in bibl.). The obscure expression in the Song of the Sea *nora' tehillot* (Ex. 15:11a) is also best rendered in this sense. The word *tehillot* in this verse does not mean "praises" but "radiance" (cf. Job 29:3; 31:26, 41:10) as it does in Habakkuk 3:3: "His splendor covered the heavens and the earth was full of his *tehillah*." The *tehillah* of God fills the universe as does His *kavod* (cf. Num. 14:21; Isa. 6:3). The terms *yir'ah* and *kavod*, then, are used synonymously in biblical literature as are their Akkadian counterparts *pulḫu* and *melammu* in Babylonian literature.

The Abstract Notion. In contradiction to this corporeal representation of the *kavod*, Deuteronomy promulgates the doctrine of the "Name." The Deity cannot be likened to any form whatever, and He cannot therefore be conceived as dwelling in a Temple. God has caused the Temple to be called by His name or has caused His name to dwell therein, but He Himself does not dwell in it. The Deuteronomic school used the word *shem*, "name," to indicate the incorporeal aspect of God in a very consistent manner and never made the slightest digression from it. There is not one example in the Deuteronomic literature of God's dwelling in the Temple or the building of a house for God. The Temple is always the dwelling of His "name." This consistency is seen most clearly when a Deuteronomic text is interwoven with an earlier text which does not know the "name theology." Thus the account of the building of the Temple and the ancient story of its dedication speak plainly about building a house for God (I Kings 6:1, 2; 8:13), while the Deuteronomist whenever he mentions the building, describes it as being for the "name" of God (I Kings 3:2; 5:17, 19; 8:17, 18, 19, 20, 44, 48).

The most definitive expression of this theology is to be found in the prayer of Solomon in I Kings 8. The Temple is not God's place of habitation but serves only as a house of worship in which Israelites and foreigners alike may deliver their prayers to the Lord Who dwells in heaven. The idea that God's habitation is in heaven is here articulated most emphatically in order to eradicate the belief that the Deity sat enthroned between the cherubim in the Temple. Whenever the expression "Thy dwelling place" *(mekhon shivtekha)* is employed it is invariably accompanied by the word "in heaven" (8:39, 43, 49). The Deuteronomic editor is here disputing the older view implied by the ancient song that opens the prayer (8:12–13) and that designates the Temple as God's "exalted house and dwelling place [or pedestal] forever." The word *ba-shamayim*, "in heaven," is consistently appended to the expression *mekhon shivtekha* to show that it is heaven which is meant and not the Temple as the ancient song implies.

In actual fact, however, the term "thy dwelling place" in the early sources as well as in Solomon's song (8:12–13) denotes the Sanctuary; it is the editor who is here attempting to alter this meaning and thereby wrest the song from its natural sense. This may be apprehended from the Song of the Sea (Ex. 15) in which the poet declares: "Thou wilt bring them in, and plant them on Thy own mountain, the foundation, O Lord, which Thou hast made for Thy abode *[makhon le-shivtekha]* the Sanctuary, O Lord, which Thy hands have established" (15:17). The Israelites can only be planted in YHWH's own mountain. The latter denotes not the Temple mount alone but the entire Holy Land (cf. Isa. 11:9; 14:25; 25:6, 7, 10; see *Isaiah), but "the place for You to dwell in" and "the Sanctuary" means naturally the Temple, and one suspects an adaptation of Solomon's dedication with "you made" substituted for an original "I made" and "Your hands" for an original "my [i.e., Solomon's] hands" (cf. *Eretz-Israel*, 9 (1969), 45 n. 4). Indeed, Isaiah who visualizes God as seated upon a throne in the Temple (chapter 6), designates the Temple as the "foundation *[mekhon]* of Mount Zion" (4:5) and elsewhere explicitly describes the Lord as dwelling on Mount Zion (*ha-shokhen be-har Ẓiyyon;* 8:18; cf. 31:9). The expression "a place to dwell in," or rather the concept of a permanent abode for the Deity, goes back to the period of the United Monarchy when the House of the Lord was first erected, and constitutes an innovation in the Israelite conception of the Divinity. The psalms which extol Zion and Jerusalem, most of which are rooted in the court theology of the United Monarchy, consistently stress the idea that Jerusalem and its house of worship are the place of God's domicile (Ps. 46:5; 48:9; 50:2; 76:3, etc.). Thus, Psalms 132, which describes the transfer of the Ark to Jerusalem, expressly declares that "the Lord has chosen Zion, for He has desired it for His habitation *[moshav]*" (132:13). It is in the Temple of Jerusalem that God found, in a sense, His true place of rest, hence the Psalmist declares in the name of the Lord: "This is My resting place for ever, here will I dwell, for I have desired it" (132:14).

This conception appears to have been first contested during the period of the Hezekian-Josianic reforms, in all probability by the circle which was then engaged in the final crystallization of Deuteronomy. It is interesting that the very book which elevates the chosen place to the highest rank of importance in the Israelite cult should at the same time divest it of all sacral content and import. With remarkable consistency it resorts again and again to the phrase "the place where He shall choose to cause His name to dwell" *(le-shakken/la-sum shemo)* so as to emphasize that it is God's name and not God Himself who dwells within the Sanctuary, as against the Priestly tradition which speaks of God's dwelling in the midst of the children of Israel (Ex. 25:8; 29:45; Num. 16:3).

It appears then that it was the Deuteronomic school that first initiated the polemic against the anthropomorphic and corporeal conceptions of the Deity and that it was afterward taken up by the prophets Jeremiah and Deutero-Isaiah. It is by no means coincidental that the only passages which reflect a quasi-abstract conception of the Deity and negation of His corporeality are to be found in Deuteronomy and Deutero-Isaiah: Deuteronomy 4:12: "You heard the sound of words, but saw no form *[temunah]*" (cf. 4:15) and Isaiah 40:18: "To whom will you liken God or what likeness compare Him," and similarly in Isaiah 40:19 and 46:5.

These later conceptions, then, are diametrically opposed to the earlier views articulated in the JE and P documents and in the prophetic books antedating Deuteronomy. Thus Exodus 24:9–11 refers to the leaders, elders, and so on seeing God; in Exodus 33:23 Moses is said to have beheld God's back, and Numbers 12:8 speaks even more strikingly of Moses as gazing upon "the form *[temunah]* of the Lord." Amos similarly sees the Lord "standing beside the altar" (9:1), and Isaiah beholds God sitting upon a throne with His train filling the Temple (6:1; cf. I Kings 22:19–20).

Revelation and the Ark in Deuteronomic Literature. In contrast to the account in Exodus 19 of God's descent upon Mt. Sinai (19:11, 20), Deuteronomy 4:36 says: "Out of heaven He let you hear His voice, that He might discipline you; and on earth He let you see His great fire and you heard His words out of the midst of the fire." In other words, the commandments were heard from out of the midst of the fire that was upon the mount, but they were uttered by the Deity from heaven. Deuteronomy has, furthermore, taken care to shift the center of gravity of the theophany from the visual to the aural plane. In Exodus 19, the principal danger confronting the people was the likelihood that they might "break through to the Lord to gaze" (19:21); it was to prevent this that there was need to "set bounds for the people round about" (19:12) and to caution them not to ascend the mountain. Indeed, the pre-Deuteronomic texts always invariably speak of the danger of seeing the Deity: "For man shall not see Me and live" (Ex. 33:20), and similarly in Genesis 32:30: "For I have seen God face to face, and yet my life is preserved" (cf. Judg. 13:22; Isa. 6:5). Deuteronomy, on the other hand, cannot conceive of the possibility of seeing the Divinity. The Israelites saw only "His great fire" which symbolizes His essence and qualities (Deut. 4:24: "For the Lord your God is a devouring fire, a jealous God"; cf. 9:3), whereas God Himself remains in His heavenly abode. In Deuteronomy the danger threatening the people and the greatness of the miracle is that of hearing the voice of the Deity: "Did any people ever hear the voice of a god speaking out of the midst of the fire as you have heard, and survived" (4:33; cf. 5:23).

This attempt to eliminate the inherent corporeality of the traditional imagery also finds expression in Deuteronomy's conception of the Ark. The specific and exclusive function of the Ark, according to Deuteronomy, is to house the tables of the covenant (10:1–5); no mention is made of the Ark cover, *kapporet*, and the cherubim which endows the Ark with the semblance of a divine chariot or throne (cf. Ex. 25:10–22 [P]). The holiest vessel of the Israelite cult performs, in the Deuteronomic view, nothing more than an educational function: it houses the tablets upon which the words of God are engraved, and at its side the Book of the Torah is laid from which one reads to the people so that they may learn to fear the Lord (Deut. 31:26; cf. 31:12, 13). The Ark does not serve as God's seat upon which He journeys forth to disperse His enemies (Num. 10:33–36), but only as the vessel in which the tables of the covenant are deposited. This becomes quite clear when Deuteronomy 1:42–43 is compared with Numbers 14:42–44, a tradition on which the Deuteronomic account is based. Numbers 14:44 states that after the incident of the spies "the Ark of the Covenant of the Lord departed not out of the camp" and that this was the reason for the Israelites' defeat in their subsequent battle with the Amalekites and Canaanites. The Deuteronomic account, on the other hand, completely omits the detail of the Ark and ascribes the Israelite defeat to the fact that God was not in their midst, without referring to the whereabouts of the Ark.

The author of Deuteronomy similarly relates that it was God who went before the people to seek out new resting places (1:33), whereas the earlier source, upon which Deuteronomy was dependent, relates that it was the Ark which journeyed forth before the people to seek out new resting places for them (Num. 10:33). The absence of the Ark is especially striking in the Deuteronomic law of warfare (23:15). One would expect a passage which speaks of the presence of the Divinity within the military encampment to make some mention of the Ark which accompanied the warriors on their expeditions, as in I Samuel 4:6–7 (see above). The Deuteronomic law, however, speaks of the Lord as moving about the camp but does not make any allusion to the Ark or the holy vessels.

A similar conception is encountered in Jeremiah, for example, in 3:16–17: "They shall say no more, 'The Ark of the Covenant of the Lord.' It shall not come to mind . . . At that time Jerusalem shall be called the throne of the Lord." In other words, the Ark of the Covenant shall no longer serve as God's seat, as the people were previously accustomed to believe, but all of Jerusalem shall be "the seat of YHWH," that is in a symbolic sense. In another passage the prophet declares: "Do I not fill heaven and earth, says the Lord" (23:24), recalling the words of Deutero- (or Trito-) Isaiah when he expressly repudiates the notion of the Sanctuary as the place of God's habitation: "Heaven is My throne and the earth is My footstool, what is the house which you build for Me, and what is the place of My rest" (66:1). This view is also encountered in the Deuteronomic prayer of Solomon: "Behold, heaven and the highest heaven cannot contain Thee; how much less this house which I have built" (I Kings 8:27). The Sanctuary is here conceived as a house of prayer and not as a cultic center.

Although the abstract notion of the Divine Presence associated with the so-called "Name" theology found its full expression in Deuteronomy and in the Deuteronomic school, it should be pointed out that traces of it are already found in some of the earlier sources, especially in E (see *Pentateuch). The latter source does not contain theophanies in which God appears visibly in human form but revelations through various media, such as the dream or the angel. In one particular case, the angel, representing God, is said to contain God's "name" in himself (Ex. 23:21), which is at least an anticipation of the Deuteronomic "Name" theology.

See also *God; **Shekhinah*.

Bibliography: A. L. Oppenheim, in: JAOS, 63 (1943), 31–34; G. E. Wright et al., in: BA, 7 (1944), 158–84; 10 (1947), 45–68; G. von Rad, *Studies in Deuteronomy* (1953), 37–44; M. Haran, in: IEJ, 9 (1959), 30–38, 89–98; idem, in: *Scripta Hierosolymitana*, 8 (1961), 272–302; R. E. Clements, *God and Temple* (1965); M. Weinfeld, in: *Tarbiz*, 37 (1968), 116–20, 131–2; idem, *Deuteronomy and the Deuteronomic School* (1971); J. Milgrom, *Studies in Levitical Terminology*, 1 (1970).

[Mo.W.]

PRESIDENT OF ISRAEL, the official head of the State of Israel, resembling a constitutional monarch in function and powers, bears the ancient Hebrew title of *"*nasi.*" According to the Basic Law: President of the State, passed by the Knesset on June 16, 1964, any citizen of Israel resident in the country is eligible for the office and may hold it for no more than two consecutive terms. The seat of the president is Jerusalem. With the exception of these two provisions, the Basic Law does not differ substantially from the Presidency of the State Law, 1951, which provides that the president must be elected by a majority of all members of the Knesset (i.e., by at least 61 votes) for a five-year term beginning on the day when he makes and signs the declaration of allegiance before the Knesset. He cannot be called to account before any court but he may be deposed by the Knesset for unbecoming behavior or in the case of ill-health, which makes it impossible for him to carry out his duties.

The president signs all laws (other than those concerned with his own powers) and treaties ratified by the Knesset. He appoints (upon the recommendation of the foreign minister) the diplomatic representatives of the state, and accepts the credentials of diplomatic representatives of foreign states accredited to Israel. Upon the recommendation of the appropriate governmental authorities, he appoints the state comptroller, the governor of the Bank of Israel, the members of the civil judiciary, and the judges of the religious courts. The president receives the resignation of the government and sets in motion the process of forming a new government by consultng representatives of all the political parties in the Knesset and then entrusting a member of the Knesset with the task of setting up a government. He is also given reports of government meetings. The president is empowered to pardon offenders and to mitigate sentences.

The first president of the state, Chaim *Weizmann, was elected on Feb. 16, 1949, at the opening session of the First Knesset—held with symbolic significance in Jerusalem, though the seat of the Knesset and government was still in Tel Aviv. He brought to the presidency his extraordinary experience in Zionist leadership and diplomatic negotiation, but illness restricted his activities to the formal duties of the office. Weizmann died on Nov. 9, 1952, and was succeeded by Izhak *Ben-Zvi. Under President Ben-Zvi, the official residence and office of the president were established in Jerusalem. There for two full terms and part of a third, until his death on April 23, 1963, Ben-Zvi filled the office with rich human, spiritual, and scholarly content. He and his wife Raḥel made the residence a meeting place for the diverse "tribes of Israel," aiding notably in the process of national amalgamation during those years of mass immigration from Europe and the Islamic countries. The monthly "New Moon" meetings of groups from particular countries and the "Open House" held annually during Sukkot week were typical of the direct contact established with the masses of Israel's citizens, including the Muslim, Druze, Christian, Bahai, and Samaritan communities. President Ben-Zvi paid state visits to Belgium and Holland, to Burma, and to Congo Brazzaville, the Central African Republic, and Liberia.

When Zalman *Shazar was elected president on May 21, 1963, he brought with him the qualities of a historian, Israel and Zionist leader, and orator, who had devoted himself to the world Jewish community, its educational problems, and its literature in Hebrew, Yiddish, and other languages. All these interests were expressed in the activities of the president's residence. The Bible Study Circle, originally led by the Prime Minister, David *Ben-Gurion, met there regularly, as did the Circle for the Study of the Diaspora under the aegis of the Hebrew University's Institute of Contemporary Jewry. The president instituted a special fund for the encouragement of literature and scholarship and invited outstanding writers, artists, and thinkers from abroad to visit Israel as his guests. He and his wife Raḥel, a writer and women's leader, paid state visits to Nepal, Uruguay, Chile, and Brazil in 1966, and Canada in 1967.

[S.NA.]

PRESOV (Slovak. **Prešov;** Hung. **Eperjes**), town in E. Slovakia, Czechoslovakia. In the 15th century Matthias Corvinus granted Presov the privilege of excluding the Jews. Later, immigrants escaping the harsh *Familiants Laws and the Orkuta *blood libel (1764) settled in the vicinity of the city and attended its annual fairs. The communities of the district eventually united under the vigorous leadership of Marcus Hollaender (1760–1849), originally of Tarnopol, who in 1790 received citizen rights in Presov. Becoming a prosperous merchant and collector of the toleration tax, he founded a synagogue outside the city gates. Jews began settling within the town in the early 19th century and services were held in Hollaender's home. In 1843 a community was founded under the leadership of Leo Hollaender, Marcus' son, and subsequently a synagogue and school were built. In 1848 some Presov Jews served as officers of the revolutionary Hungarian army. Prominent among them was the rabbi Solomon *Schiller-Szinessy, who was forced to emigrate and went to England. During the revolution the Christian craftsmen vehemently demanded the expulsion of the Jews, particularly those who had recently arrived from Poland. Mayer *Austerlitz served as rabbi for half a century (1860–1913). In 1871 the Orthodox founded their own community, which soon grew to include more than half of Presov's Jews. Most of their institutions were founded in the late 19th and early 20th century. In 1930 an impressive Orthodox synagogue was built. The two communities led parallel, separate, and unconnected lives; there was also a ḥasidic community. A yeshivah, founded by Rabbi M.C. Law, had 100 students in 1927. A Jewish museum was founded in 1928; during the war it was confiscated by the Fascists and subsequently moved to

The synagogue of Presov, Slovakia, after its restoration in 1957. From R. Iltis (ed.), *Die Juedischen Gemeinden in der Tschechoslowakischen Republik nach dem Zweiten Weltkrieg,* Prague, 1959.

Prague. Zionism was established in Presov at an early date by Karl Ferbstein, one of the Zionist leaders of Czechoslovakia and delegate to Zionist congresses. In 1930 there were 3,965 Jews in Presov and in 1940 about 4,000 (about 40% of the total population), supplemented by about 2,000 refugees from the countryside. All were deported to various camps during World War II. After the war a new community was established. The synagogue, desecrated during the war, was restored in 1957.

Bibliography: M. Atlas, in: *Zeitschrift fuer die Geschichte der Juden,* 4 (1967), 17–32, incl. bibl. [Ed.]

PRESS. This article is arranged according to the following outline:

Introduction
In Australia and New Zealand
In Belgium
In Canada
In Czechoslovakia
In England
In France
In Germany and Austria
In Holland
In Hungary
In India
In Italy
Ladino Press
Latin America
In the Middle East and North Africa
In Poland
In Rumania
In Russia
In the U.S.S.R. (1917–70)
In Scandinavia
In South Africa
In Switzerland
In the United States

Introduction. The first Jewish newspaper is generally considered to be the *Gazeta de Amsterdam,* which appeared in 1675. Holland had by then become an important Jewish center, having attracted many Spanish-Portuguese and Polish Jews seeking a refuge from persecution, and some years earlier *Manasseh Ben Israel had set up the first Hebrew *printing press there. The appearance of the *Gazeta* was no accident. It was issued by a Sephardi printer, was written in Judeo-Spanish or Ladino, the language of the exiles, and carried dispatches from other countries. The next notable publication, *Dinstagishe un Fraytagishe Kurant* in Yiddish, appeared twice a week and then once a week as the *Dinstagishe Kurant* in 1686 and 1687. The first Jewish periodical was *Peri Ez Ḥayyim,* also of Amsterdam, a monthly bulletin containing rabbinical decisions of the Sephardi community. It appeared from 1728 to 1761.

As Emancipation and Haskalah gained ground among European Jewry in the middle of the 18th century, Jewish journals appeared in Germany and other countries. Their numbers increased with the revival of Hebrew, the growth of Yiddish literature, and the continued flight of Jews from Eastern Europe. The rise of modern Zionism and the emergence of political parties among the Jews stimulated printing and publishing, and by 1882 Isidore Singer of Vienna, in the brochure *Presse und Judenthum,* was able to list 103 extant Jewish newspapers and journals. Thirty of them were in German, 19 in Hebrew (three of them appearing in Jerusalem), 15 in English, 14 in Yiddish, six in Ladino, five in French, and the rest in eight other languages.

The first successful Jewish newspaper in the modern sense was the **Allgemeine Zeitung des Judentums,* launched in Leipzig in 1837 and surviving until 1922. The *Jewish Chronicle,* founded in London in 1841, was to prove even more successful and flourishes as the oldest Jewish newspaper in the world. On Jan. 17, 1896, it published the first Zionist article by Theodor *Herzl. Herzl himself launched *Die *Welt* in 1897. These two weeklies published the latest Jewish and Zionist news and served as sources for other newspapers before the Zionist Organization established its own press bureau to supply the Jewish press with the latest news from Ereẓ Israel and the Diaspora. The first Jewish news agency was the Neue Juedische Korrespondenz, which was founded in Berlin in 1907 and served the Jewish press until shortly after the outbreak of World War I. In order to keep in touch under war conditions with communities in other parts of the world, some Jewish organizations established offices in neutral countries. The World Zionist Organization, with headquarters in Berlin, opened offices in Copenhagen where an information bulletin appeared under its auspices in English, French, and German, and reached (sometimes in reprint) the countries of both the Allied and Central powers. Another well-organized agency was the Juedische Presse Zentrale in Zurich. The main function of these agencies was to scan the world press for information of Jewish interest and pass it on to the newspapers. They were mostly short-lived; but the *Jewish Telegraphic Agency, established in The Hague in 1914 by Jacob *Landau and reestablished in London in 1919 by Landau and Meir *Grossman, proved more permanent. In 1922 its headquarters were transferred to New York. It had correspondents and bureaus in many countries, and it issued a *Jewish Daily Bulletin* in English and other languages; in 1962 it began a weekly bulletin, *Community News.*

Until World War II, Europe had the largest number of Jewish periodicals. There were Yiddish dailies in Warsaw,

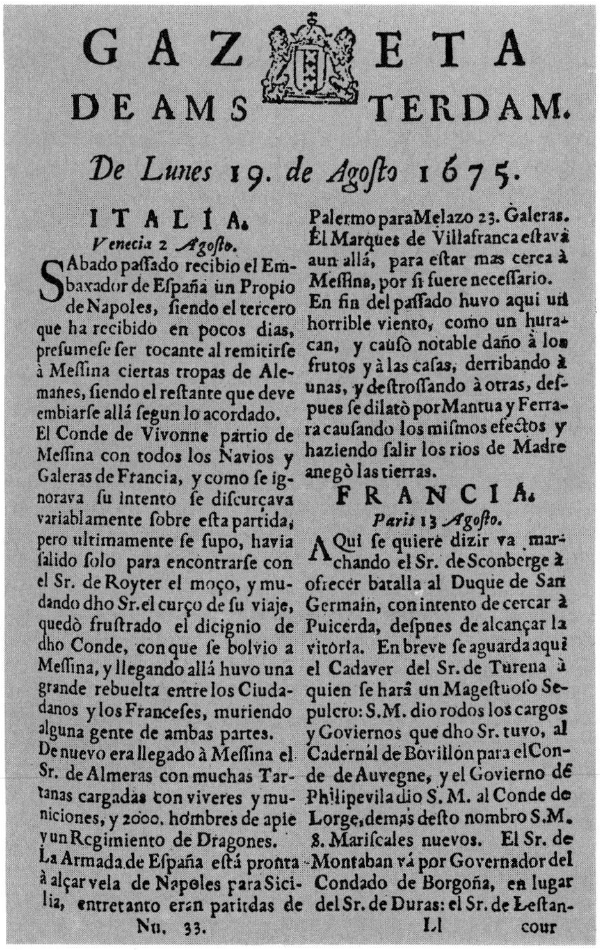

GAZETA DE AMSTERDAM.

De Lunes 19. de Agoſto 1675.

ITALIA.

Venecia 2 Agoſto.

SAbado paſſado recibio el Embaxador de Eſpaña un Propio de Napoles, ſiendo el tercero que ha recibido en pocos dias, preſumeſe ſer tocante al remitirſe à Meſſina ciertas tropas de Alemanes, ſiendo el reſtante que deve embiarſe allá ſegun lo acordado.
El Conde de Vivonne partio de Meſſina con todos los Navios y Galeras de Francia, y como ſe ignorava ſu intento ſe diſcurçava variablamente ſobre eſta partida, pero ultimamente ſe ſupo, havia ſalido ſolo para encontrarſe con el Sr. de Royter el moço, y mudando dho Sr. el curço de ſu viaje, quedò fruſtrado el dicignio de dho Conde, con que ſe bolvio a Meſſina, y llegando allá huvo una grande rebuelta entre los Ciudadanos y los Franceſes, muriendo alguna gente de ambas partes.
De nuevo era llegado à Meſſina el Sr. de Almeras con muchas Tartanas cargadas con viveres y municiones, y 2000. hombres de apie y un Regimiento de Dragones.
La Armada de Eſpaña eſtá pronta à alçar vela de Napoles para Sicilia, entretanto eran partidas de Palermo para Melazo 23. Galeras.
El Marques de Villafranca eſtavà aun allá, para eſtar mas cerca à Meſſina, por ſi fuere neceſſario.
En fin del paſſado huvo aqui un horrible viento, como un huracan, y cauſò notable daño à los frutos y à las caſas, derribando à unas, y deſtroſſando à otras, deſpues ſe dilatò por Mantua y Ferrara cauſando los miſmos efectos y haziendo ſalir los rios de Madre anegò las tierras.

FRANCIA.

Paris 13 Agoſto.

AQui ſe quiere dizir va marchando el Sr. de Sconberge à ofrecer batalla al Duque de San Germain, con intento de cercar à Puicerda, deſpues de alcançar la vitoria. En breve ſe aguarda aqui el Cadaver del Sr. de Turena à quien ſe harâ un Mageſtuoſo Sepulcro: S.M. dio rodos los cargos y Goviernos que dho Sr. tuvo, al Cadernàl de Bovillon para el Conde de Auvegne, y el Govierno de Philipevila dio S. M. al Conde de Lorge, demas deſto nombro S.M. 8. Mariſcales nuevos. El Sr. de Montaban và por Governador del Condado de Borgoña, en lugar del Sr. de Duras: el Sr. de Leſtan-

Nu. 33. Ll cour

Figure 1. Issue of the *Gazeta de Amsterdam,* written in Ladino (Judeo-Spanish), the first Jewish newspaper, Amsterdam, August 19, 1675. From J. Fraenkel, *The Jewish Press of the World,* London, 1967.

Lvov, Cracow, Lodz, Bialystok, Vilna, Riga, Kovno, and other large East European towns, including Soviet Yiddish newspapers in Moscow, Kharkov, and Minsk. There were also Jewish Polish dailies, more than two dozen weeklies in Yiddish, Hebrew, and Polish, and nearly 100 monthlies. There were more than 100 Jewish German-language weeklies, fortnightlies, and monthlies in Germany and Austria. A Jewish German-language daily appeared in Vienna, 1919–27. The rise of Nazi power brought most of these papers to an end. When the Nazi forces overran any country, one of their first acts was to close down the Jewish publications. "Underground" newspapers also appeared in the ghettos, among the partisans in the forests, and even, if rarely, in the concentration camps.

In 1967 there were 580 Jewish newspapers and periodicals in the world, outside Israel: 178 in Europe, 245 in the U.S., 82 in Central and South America, 29 in Africa, 21 in Canada, 19 in Australia and New Zealand, several in Asia, and two in the Soviet Union. English was the language of the largest number (300), with Yiddish coming second (112). The position of the Yiddish language presented a paradox. Though Yiddish was regarded as generally losing ground, all the Jewish daily papers outside Israel, ten in number, were in Yiddish. Efforts to establish a Spanish Jewish daily in Argentina were without success, and an English Jewish daily in London proved unsuccessful.

[L.S./Jo.Fr.]

In Australia and New Zealand. *The Voice of Jacob,* founded in Sydney in 1842, was the first Jewish newspaper in Australia, and before the end of the century several others, all in English, had run their brief careers and ceased publication. A few, however, became firmly established, notably the *Australian Jewish Herald* (1879), the *Australian Jewish Times* (1893), and *Hebrew Standard* (1894). There was no significant growth in the Jewish press until the middle decades of the 20th century, when the Jewish population rose from about 27,000 in 1938 to 67,000 in 1960. The *Australian Jewish News,* founded in Melbourne in 1933 as a bilingual English and Yiddish weekly, published a Sydney edition under the name of *The Sydney Jewish News.* In 1967 the two editions had a combined circulation of 20,000.

The Jewish press attained a high standard under the guidance of Newman Rosenthal, O. Rubinstein, and Reuben Havin, its leading editors during the 1930s and 1940s. They made it an important factor in molding opinion both in the Jewish community and among prominent non-Jews. Leading political figures gained their knowledge of Zionism, the Holocaust, and Israel from pages of the *Australian Jewish Herald* and the *Australian Jewish News.* This bore fruit in the pro-Jewish stand taken by Dr. C. Evatt of Australia, as chairman of the UN Advisory Committee on Palestine in 1947. Within the community, the press exercised a strong influence on the development of representative bodies, particularly the state Boards of Deputies and the Executive Council of Australian Jewry. It also influenced the decision in favor of establishing the Melbourne day school, Mount Scopus College, and later the Jewish day-school movement generally.

The strong support which the Jewish press gave to Zionism influenced the outlook of the Jewish community, eventually winning over old-established families who had opposed political Zionism in the pre-State era. The pro-Israel opinion thus formed eventually led to the downfall of the *Australian Jewish Herald* and its Yiddish subsidiary, the *Australian Jewish Post.* In 1968 the *Australian Jewish Herald,* the oldest existing Jewish paper in Australia, published an article with an anti-Israel bias. During the controversy that followed, David Lederman, publisher of the *Herald* and the *Post,* also attacked the Victoria Jewish Board of Deputies. Pressure by the board and the immediate loss of popularity compelled both papers, with a total circulation of 12,500 weekly, to cease publication. Among the other publications which appeared in Australia were *The Bridge,* a literary quarterly, and Yiddish periodicals, *Der Landsmann* and *Unzer Gedank.*

In New Zealand, the *Jewish Times,* a monthly, appeared in Wellington in 1931, and was succeeded by the *New Zealand Jewish Chronicle,* a bimonthly, in 1944. A monthly, *Hashofar,* was founded in 1959.

[L.S]

In Belgium. The small size of the Jewish community of Belgium for long limited the publication of Jewish periodicals. The first, *Revue Orientale,* edited from 1841 to 1846 by Eliakim *Carmoly, did not have enough local interest to last. No others were published until shortly before World War I, when several publications were sponsored by Jews of East European origin.

By 1959, however, no fewer than 225 Jewish periodicals had appeared in Belgium, reflecting the vitality of the community in the 20th century. Of these, 46 were in a mimeographed or lithographed form; 97 were in Yiddish, four in Hebrew, 80 in French, two in German, one in Russian, one in English, and 27 in more than one language. Four were published between 1900 and 1918, 137 from 1919 until the German occupation of Belgium in 1940, seven illegally during the German occupation of 1940–44, and 70 after the liberation of Belgium. Most of these were intended for the membership of an organization, rather than for the public at large.

In 1970 there were five Jewish journals in Belgium: the weekly *Belgisch Israelietisch Weekblad,* founded in 1954; the bimonthly *Tribune Sioniste,* founded in 1951 and having a circulation of 5,500; three monthlies, *Centrale* (circulation 8,000), *Regards (Cahiers du Centre Communautaire Laic Juif),* and *Kehilatenou;* and a quarterly, *Central,* in Flemish and Yiddish.

[Ed.]

In Canada. The earliest Jewish newspaper to appear in Canada was the *Jewish Times,* a weekly first, published in 1897. In 1909 its name was changed to *Canadian Jewish Times,* and in 1915 it merged with the weekly *Canadian Jewish Chronicle* of Montreal, which had been founded in 1914. The *Chronicle* amalgamated with the *Canadian Jewish Reiew* and appeared as the *Canadian Jewish Chronicle Review* from 1966 in both Toronto and Montreal, becoming a monthly in 1970. There was no Yiddish press until 1907, when *Der *Kanader Adler* ("The Canadian (Jewish) Eagle") began publication in Montreal as a daily. In Canada, where despite a relatively small Jewish population the position of Yiddish had been strengthened by national patterns of ethnic and linguistic separatism, three other Yiddish weeklies were being published in 1970: the *Canadian Jewish Weekly* (1941–), and the *Daily Hebrew Journal* (1911–) in Toronto, and the *Yiddish Press* (1910–) in Manitoba. Side by side with these journals, others appeared both in Yiddish and English, and by the 1960s there were more than 20 Jewish periodicals published in Montreal, Toronto, Winnipeg, Ottawa, Vancouver, and other cities. In 1967, the *Canadian Jewish News, Dos Yiddishe Vort-Israelite Press* (Yiddish-English), and *Vokhenblat* of Toronto, had a wide circulation.

Among the monthlies were the *Congress Bulletin,* published by the Canadian Jewish Congress from 1943; the *Canadian Zionist,* in English and Hebrew, published by the Zionist Organization (1931–); *The View-Dos Vort* in English and Yiddish, of the Labor Zionist movement (1940–); and *Orah* of the Canadian Hadassah Organization.

A French monthly, *Bulletin du Cercle Juif,* published by the Canadian Jewish Congress from 1954, and a quarterly in English and Spanish, *Newsletter,* founded by the International Council of Jewish Women, were both widely distributed.

[L.S.]

In Czechoslovakia. Jewish journalists worked in papers of all political parties in Czechoslovakia. There were Conservatives like Josef Penížek, Liberals like Josef Kodícek, Karel Poláček, and Richard Weiner; Social Democrats like Gustav Winter; and Communists like Rudolf Slánský. There were also baptized Jewish editors on the Catholic press, among them Alfred Fuchs and Pavel Tigrid. Adolf Stránský founded the daily *Lidové Noviny.* The *Prager Tagblatt* had many Jews on its staff (Max *Brod among them) and a large Jewish readership.

The Jewish press itself was characterized by vehement public discussion between the Zionists and the organized assimilationist movement, which created its first paper, *Českožidovské Listy,* in 1894. In 1907 it amalgamated with a similar periodical published by Viktor Vohryzek and appeared then as a weekly under the name *Rozvoj* until 1939. The first Zionist organ was the German weekly for youth, *Jung Juda,* which was established in 1899 by Filip Lebenhart and survived until late in the 1930s. Another weekly, *Selbstwehr,* edited from 1918 by Felix *Weltsch, assisted later by Hans Lichtwitz (Uri Naor), became one of the outstanding Zionist

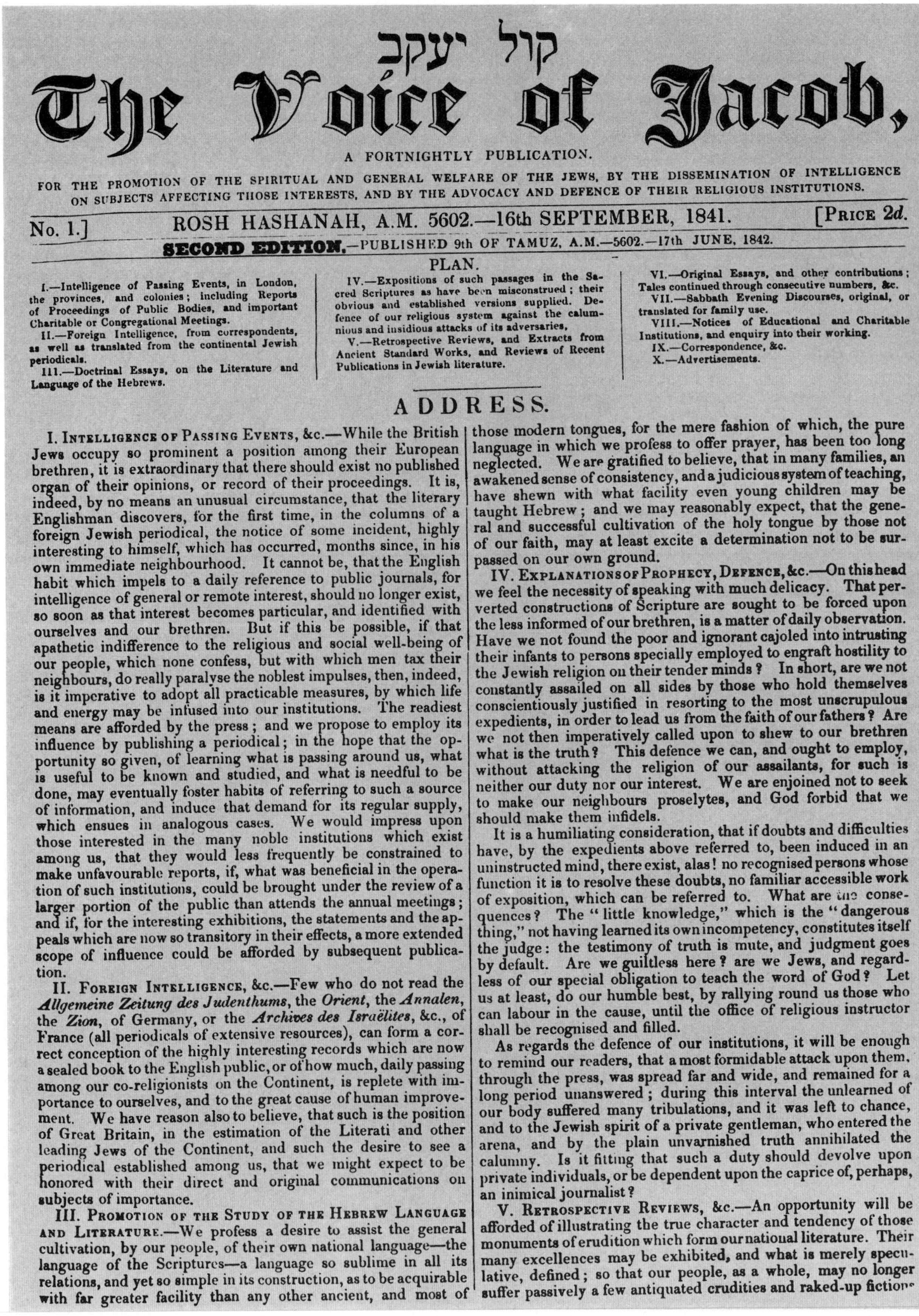

קול יעקב

The Voice of Jacob,

A FORTNIGHTLY PUBLICATION.

FOR THE PROMOTION OF THE SPIRITUAL AND GENERAL WELFARE OF THE JEWS, BY THE DISSEMINATION OF INTELLIGENCE ON SUBJECTS AFFECTING THOSE INTERESTS, AND BY THE ADVOCACY AND DEFENCE OF THEIR RELIGIOUS INSTITUTIONS.

No. 1.] ROSH HASHANAH, A.M. 5602.—16th SEPTEMBER, 1841. [Price 2*d*.

SECOND EDITION.—PUBLISHED 9th OF TAMUZ, A.M.—5602.—17th JUNE, 1842.

PLAN.

I.—Intelligence of Passing Events, in London, the provinces, and colonies; including Reports of Proceedings of Public Bodies, and important Charitable or Congregational Meetings.

II.—Foreign Intelligence, from correspondents, as well as translated from the continental Jewish periodicals.

III.—Doctrinal Essays, on the Literature and Language of the Hebrews.

IV.—Expositions of such passages in the Sacred Scriptures as have been misconstrued; their obvious and established versions supplied. Defence of our religious system against the calumnious and insidious attacks of its adversaries.

V.—Retrospective Reviews, and Extracts from Ancient Standard Works, and Reviews of Recent Publications in Jewish literature.

VI.—Original Essays, and other contributions; Tales continued through consecutive numbers, &c.

VII.—Sabbath Evening Discourses, original, or translated for family use.

VIII.—Notices of Educational and Charitable Institutions, and enquiry into their working.

IX.—Correspondence, &c.

X.—Advertisements.

ADDRESS.

I. Intelligence of Passing Events, &c.—While the British Jews occupy so prominent a position among their European brethren, it is extraordinary that there should exist no published organ of their opinions, or record of their proceedings. It is, indeed, by no means an unusual circumstance, that the literary Englishman discovers, for the first time, in the columns of a foreign Jewish periodical, the notice of some incident, highly interesting to himself, which has occurred, months since, in his own immediate neighbourhood. It cannot be, that the English habit which impels to a daily reference to public journals, for intelligence of general or remote interest, should no longer exist, so soon as that interest becomes particular, and identified with ourselves and our brethren. But if this be possible, if that apathetic indifference to the religious and social well-being of our people, which none confess, but with which men tax their neighbours, do really paralyse the noblest impulses, then, indeed, is it imperative to adopt all practicable measures, by which life and energy may be infused into our institutions. The readiest means are afforded by the press; and we propose to employ its influence by publishing a periodical; in the hope that the opportunity so given, of learning what is passing around us, what is useful to be known and studied, and what is needful to be done, may eventually foster habits of referring to such a source of information, and induce that demand for its regular supply, which ensues in analogous cases. We would impress upon those interested in the many noble institutions which exist among us, that they would less frequently be constrained to make unfavourable reports, if, what was beneficial in the operation of such institutions, could be brought under the review of a larger portion of the public than attends the annual meetings; and if, for the interesting exhibitions, the statements and the appeals which are now so transitory in their effects, a more extended scope of influence could be afforded by subsequent publication.

II. Foreign Intelligence, &c.—Few who do not read the *Allgemeine Zeitung des Judenthums*, the *Orient*, the *Annalen*, the *Zion*, of Germany, or the *Archives des Israëlites*, &c., of France (all periodicals of extensive resources), can form a correct conception of the highly interesting records which are now a sealed book to the English public, or of how much, daily passing among our co-religionists on the Continent, is replete with importance to ourselves, and to the great cause of human improvement. We have reason also to believe, that such is the position of Great Britain, in the estimation of the Literati and other leading Jews of the Continent, and such the desire to see a periodical established among us, that we might expect to be honored with their direct and original communications on subjects of importance.

III. Promotion of the Study of the Hebrew Language and Literature.—We profess a desire to assist the general cultivation, by our people, of their own national language—the language of the Scriptures—a language so sublime in all its relations, and yet so simple in its construction, as to be acquirable with far greater facility than any other ancient, and most of those modern tongues, for the mere fashion of which, the pure language in which we profess to offer prayer, has been too long neglected. We are gratified to believe, that in many families, an awakened sense of consistency, and a judicious system of teaching, have shewn with what facility even young children may be taught Hebrew; and we may reasonably expect, that the general and successful cultivation of the holy tongue by those not of our faith, may at least excite a determination not to be surpassed on our own ground.

IV. Explanations of Prophecy, Defence, &c.—On this head we feel the necessity of speaking with much delicacy. That perverted constructions of Scripture are sought to be forced upon the less informed of our brethren, is a matter of daily observation. Have we not found the poor and ignorant cajoled into intrusting their infants to persons specially employed to engraft hostility to the Jewish religion on their tender minds? In short, are we not constantly assailed on all sides by those who hold themselves conscientiously justified in resorting to the most unscrupulous expedients, in order to lead us from the faith of our fathers? Are we not then imperatively called upon to shew to our brethren what is the truth? This defence we can, and ought to employ, without attacking the religion of our assailants, for such is neither our duty nor our interest. We are enjoined not to seek to make our neighbours proselytes, and God forbid that we should make them infidels.

It is a humiliating consideration, that if doubts and difficulties have, by the expedients above referred to, been induced in an uninstructed mind, there exist, alas! no recognised persons whose function it is to resolve these doubts, no familiar accessible work of exposition, which can be referred to. What are the consequences? The "little knowledge," which is the "dangerous thing," not having learned its own incompetency, constitutes itself the judge: the testimony of truth is mute, and judgment goes by default. Are we guiltless here? are we Jews, and regardless of our special obligation to teach the word of God? Let us at least, do our humble best, by rallying round us those who can labour in the cause, until the office of religious instructor shall be recognised and filled.

As regards the defence of our institutions, it will be enough to remind our readers, that a most formidable attack upon them, through the press, was spread far and wide, and remained for a long period unanswered; during this interval the unlearned of our body suffered many tribulations, and it was left to chance, and to the Jewish spirit of a private gentleman, who entered the arena, and by the plain unvarnished truth annihilated the calumny. Is it fitting that such a duty should devolve upon private individuals, or be dependent upon the caprice of, perhaps, an inimical journalist?

V. Retrospective Reviews, &c.—An opportunity will be afforded of illustrating the true character and tendency of those monuments of erudition which form our national literature. Their many excellences may be exhibited, and what is merely speculative, defined; so that our people, as a whole, may no longer suffer passively a few antiquated crudities and raked-up fiction-

Figure 2. Issue of *The Voice of Jacob*, edited by Jacob Franklin, London, September 16, 1841. Jerusalem, J.N.U.L.

periodicals in Europe, and from the 1920s issued a woman's supplement edited by Hanna Steiner. Another Zionist weekly, *Juedische Volksstimme*, edited by its founder Max Hickl and later by Hugo *Gold, appeared in Brno. The paper was established in 1901 and appeared until 1939.

The first Zionist organ in Czech, *Židovské Listy pro Čechy, Moravu a Slezsko*, appeared in 1913, but was suspended during World War I and replaced in 1918 by the weekly *Židovské zpravy*, edited by Emil Waldstein, František Friedman, Gustav Fleischmann, Zdeněk Landes, and Viktor Fischl (Avigdor *Dagan). In Slovakia and Carpathorussia the Jewish press included Orthodox organs and papers in Hungarian and Yiddish. In Slovakia were the Zionist weekly *Juedische Volkszeitung* (with a Slovak supplement), edited by Oskar Neumann, and the Mizrachi organ *Juedisches Familienblatt*; in Carpathorussia the Zionist weekly *Juedische Stimme*, the Revisionist *Zsidó Néplap*, and the journal of the rabbi of Munkacz, *Yidishe Tsaytung,* had the largest circulation. Of the many other Jewish periodicals the following were notable: the historical review *Zeitschrift fuer die Geschichte der Juden in Boehmen und Maehren* (editor Hugo Gold); *B'nai B'rith Blaetter* (editor Friedrich Thieberger); the Revisionist *Medina Iwrit-Judenstaat,* edited by Oskar K. *Rabinowicz (1934–39); the *Po'alei Zion paper *Der Neue Weg* (editor Karl Baum); and the sports monthly *Hagibor-Hamakabi.* The Jewish youth and student movements also published periodicals of varying duration in the different languages of the country. The *Juedische Revue* was issued by emigrants from Germany in the late 1930s. Between 1945 and the Communist take-over in 1948, attempts were made to revive some Jewish periodicals, but eventually all that remained of the extensive Jewish press in Czechoslovakia was the organ of the Prague congregation; *Věstník židovské náboženské obce v Praze,* edited by R. Iltis, who also edited the almanac *Zidovská ročenka.*

[Av.D.]

In England. The Anglo-Jewish press had its beginnings in the first half of the 19th century. During the next 100 years and more,

The Jewish Standard
דגל ישורון

Vol. I. No. 1. LONDON :—FRIDAY, ADAR 22, 5648—MARCH 2, 1888 Price Two Pence

I. B. WECHSLER,
13, CLIFTON STREET, E.C.
Cellars - - DUKE STREET, ALDGATE,
BEGS to recommend to the Jewish Public his selected stock of
כשר WINES FOR פסח
at very moderate prices.

MUSCAT from	... ...	30/- per doz.
CLARET „	... ...	20/- „
HOCK „	... ...	24/- „

Country Orders promptly executed.

GROCERY FOR PASSOVER USE,
(Especially recommended by the Ecclesiastical Authorities.)
SPICES, Selected, especially prepared.
LUMP SUGAR, manufactured under especial supervision.
BEST OILS, FRYING, &c., analysed pure.
DRIED FRUIT, POTATO-FLOWER, VINEGAR ESSENCE, etc., etc., with special הכשר
Wholesale and Retail,
To be had at—
M. LANDAU'S,
96, Leman Street, E.

STRICTLY KOSHER WORK.
P. SILVERSTONE & SON,
PRACTICAL TAILORS AND CUTTERS.
FIT, STYLE AND WORKMANSHIP GUARANTEED.
Orders by Post Promptly Attended to.
87, BRICK LANE, SPITALFIELDS, E.

E. BARNETT,
42, Middlesex Street, Aldgate.
Caterer to the élite of the community by special authority of the Chief Rabbi.
Specialities :—
TINNED MEATS, TONGUES, SOUPS, & POULTRY
Of the finest quality.
Try the Montefiore Brand Beef.
All kinds of Provisions kept in stock.

BRIGHTON.
PRIVATE BOARDING HOUSE.
12, ORIENT PLACE,
Facing the Sea.
Conducted by Mrs. Moss Heilbron. Conveniently situated midway between the West Pier and the New Parade. Every home comfort with moderate charges.
Early application for Passover will oblige.—Terms moderate.

J. KOTLIAREVSKY,
Manufacturer of
TURKISH TOBACCO
And all kinds of
CIGARETTES.
Also manufacturer of the
ROYAL CHESS CIGARETTE
Placed in Novelty Registered Boxes
TRADE MARK
of Tens, at the lowest prices.
Price List on Application.
13, MANSELL STREET, ALDGATE, E.

D. GOLDSTEIN'S
RESTAURANT & CAFE,
5, BLOMFIELD ST., CITY.
Dinners from 12 till 10 o'clock

CIRCUMCISIONS—ברית מילות
REV. A. TERTIS, 8, PRINCES STREET, Spitalfields, (who was taught and certified by the late Rev. S. Levy, in the year 1874) is well known in London and the Provinces to be the most practical and skilful in this special operatfon at the present time. שאל רעך ויגדך. Ask your friends who have witnessed Rev. Tertis's circumsicions, and they will tell you.
N.B.—The Rev. A. Tertis is certified by surgeons and physicians to be an excellent Surgeon-Mohel. Testimonials of eminent surgeons are too numerous to specify, but can be seen on application. Letters, &c., will receive prompt attention, irrespective of age or distance, as heretofore.

TO MEN AND WOMEN.
THREE times the value of a house is usually paid away in rent in the course of a lifetime. If you pay a premium to insure your life, why not also purchase your house if you can do so without additional expenditure?
For particulars apply to
M. I. BECKER,
Superintendent,
82, New Road. E.

JEWS' REFUGE.
THE Public are respectfully requested to attend a Meeting to be held on Saturday, March the 3rd, at 7 o'clock, at the Princes' Street Synagogue, with a view to taking steps to open a House of Refuge for destitute Jews.
By Order,
J. BERLINER,
Hon. Sec.

GENUINE VARSOWER WURST AND SMOKED BEEF,
LEAN AND FAT OF BEST QUALITY.
EVERY piece bears the stamp of maker with the הכשר of בית דין of Warsaw.
To be had about 8 days before Passover at
J. LOEVENSTEIN,
138, Brick Lane,
Bethnal Green, E.

HOUSE & ESTATE AGENT
ASHER LEVY
47, Coborn Koad, Bow.
Begs to inform the general Public that he has taken over part of the old establishment and well conducted business of his father, Mr. Lawrence Levy, as a house and estate agent and respectfully solicits commissions of all kinds. Rents collected from 2½ per cent.

PASSOVER FOOD.
I BEG to inform my customers that I have reduced my rate for Boarders for the 8 days of Passover from 30s. to 20s. The character of my cuisine is guaranteed, and is well known to be of the best quality.
Dinners and suppers à la carte at all times.
M. TUCHBAND,
6, Great Elic Street,
Aldgate, E.
(Opposite Jewish Workmen's Club.)

על פסח הבע״ל
ברשות בית דין לונדון והמדינה
PRINS' PURE COCOA POWDER
In tins from 6d. and upwards.
THE only unadultered Pure Cocoa in existence. Contains no fatty matter; fit for milk and meat dishes. Authorised by the chief Rabbis of Amsterdam, London, Kovna (Russia), Frankfort-on-the-Maine, etc.
LOUIS PRINS, Amsterdam,
Manufacturer of Kosher and Pure Cocoa and Chocolate.
Order of your Grocer. Every tin is labelled and stamped.

Figure 3. First issue of *The Jewish Standard,* London, March 2, 1888. Jerusalem, J.N.U.L.

numerous publications appeared both in London and the provinces. Many of them were short-lived, but some had long and influential careers, and in 1968 the Jewish press in Britain comprised about 60 publications.

The first periodical was *The Hebrew Intelligencer*, printed and published by J. Wertheimer in London. Intended as a monthly, it first saw light in January 1823, but published only three issues. More successful was *The Hebrew Review and Magazine of Rabbinical Literature*, also a monthly, which lasted from 1834 to 1837, under the editorship of Morris Jacob *Raphall. Persecution of Jews abroad demonstrated the need for a channel of expression in England and brought about the first effective enterprise in Anglo-Jewish journalism. *The Voice of Jacob*, edited by Jacob *Franklin, was initiated in September 1841 as a fortnightly, and was followed two months later by the *Jewish Chronicle*. The two papers were in competition until 1848, when the *Jewish Chronicle* gained the field for itself and was destined to become the most long-lived of Jewish newspapers. Among other papers that appeared in the ensuing years were *Sabbath Leaves* (1845) sponsored by Haim *Guedalla; *The Cup of Salvation* (Liverpool, 1846–47); *The Hebrew Observer* (1853), which merged with the *Jewish Chronicle* in the following year; *The Jewish Sabbath Journal* (1855); and the *Hebrew National* (1867).

The first Jewish penny paper, *The Jewish Record*, was a weekly that ran for four years (from 1868). *The Jewish World*, established in 1873, was edited by the novelist S. L. *Bensusan in 1897, when its circulation rose to 2,000. In 1931 it was acquired by the *Jewish Chronicle* and was amalgamated with it in 1934. Other papers were *The Jewish Times*, a penny weekly of 1876; *The Jewish Standard*, also a penny (1888–91); and *Jewish Society* (1888–91), under the nominal editorship of Frank Danby (the novelist Julia *Frankau). Provincial Jewry had periodicals such as *Jewish Topics* (Cardiff, 1886), *The Jewish Record* (Manchester, 1887), and *The South Wales Review* (1904). A Hebrew weekly *Ha-Yehudi* appeared in London 1897–1913 issued by Isaac *Suwalski.

The period after World War I produced *The Jewish Woman* (1925–26); *The Jewish Family* (1927); *The Jewish Graphic* (1926–28); *The Jewish Echo* (Glasgow, 1928–); *The Jewish Gazette* (Manchester, 1928–); *The Jewish Weekly* (1932–36); *World Jewry* (1934–36); and *The Jewish Guardian* (1920–36), which was founded under the editorship of Laurie *Magnus by a group of anti-Zionists. In 1968 the Jewish press of Great Britain included a branch of the Jewish Telegraphic Agency; the *Press Survey* of the World Jewish Congress, founded in 1945; the Jewish World News Agency (Yiddish), founded in 1940; and the *Jewish Chronicle* Feature and News Service, founded in 1948. There were weeklies in Glasgow, Manchester, Leeds, and Newcastle. In London, another weekly, *The Jewish Observer and Middle East Review*, was founded in 1952, as a successor to the *Zionist Review*, and in 1970 had a circulation of 16,000. The fortnightlies included the Mizrachi *Jewish Review*, the Po'alei Zion's *Jewish Vanguard*, and *The Jewish Tribune* in English and Yiddish. The others varied widely from monthly trade journals to learned quarterlies and annuals.

Yiddish Press. Attempts to establish Yiddish newspapers in England preceded the mass immigration from Eastern Europe in the 1880s. The *Londoner Yiddish-Deitche Zeitung* was started in 1867 and the socialist *Londoner Israelit* in 1878, but both were short-lived. Later enterprises were more successful. The weekly *Peilisher Yidel* (later *Die Zukunft*) was founded in 1884 and lasted for two years. As the immigrant communities increased in numbers in London, Leeds, and Manchester, they were served by dailies and weeklies, mostly socialist in outlook—*Der Arbeter*, *Arbeter Fraynd* (1886–91), *Germinal* (anarchist fortnightly), *Der Veker* (anti-anarchist), *Di Naye Velt* (1900–01), and humorous periodicals such as *Pipifax*, *Der Bluffer*, and *Der Ligner*. It was not until the 20th century that Yiddish newspapers like the *Advertiser* and the *Yidisher Telefon* began to flourish. The *Advertiser* was absorbed by the *Yidisher Zhurnal*, founded in 1907, which was itself absorbed in 1914 by the *Yiddisher Ekspres*. The *Ekspres* began publication in Leeds in 1895 and became a London daily in 1899. The *Yidisher Tageblat* appeared from 1901 to 1910, and *Di *Zeit*, a daily founded in 1913, survived until 1950. A Yiddish fortnightly, *Yidishe Shtime*, founded in 1951, was edited in 1970 by I. A. Lisky. There was also a Yiddish literary journal *Loshn un Lebn*.

[L.S.]

In France. There was no Jewish press in France before the French Revolution. The first Jewish publication was the *Caitung*, a weekly in Alsatian Yiddish issued by a Metz printer for five months from November 1789. Several later journals were also short-lived, and it was not until the early 1840s that a monthly, *Les Archives Israélites de France*, showed any capacity for survival. It was founded by S. Cahen and advocated reform. This stimulated J. *Bloch to launch a rival conservative monthly, *L'Univers Israélite*, in 1844. For nearly 100 years both periodicals exercised considerable influence on Jewish life, *Les Archives* surviving until 1935 and *L'Univers* continuing as a weekly until 1940. This 100-year period, however, saw the birth and demise of more than 300 other publications. A total of 374 appeared from 1789 to 1940. Only 38 of these saw the light before 1881; the largest number, 203, came into being after 1923. Of the total, 134 were in French, 180 in Yiddish, and nine in Hebrew; 56 of them (21 in Yiddish) were Zionist, and 28 (all in Yiddish) were communist. Many of them were stable and influential. Two of them were Yiddish dailies. During World War II a few underground papers were published in Yiddish and French. After the war, the Jewish press recovered its prewar character. In 1957 the illustrated *L'Arche*, edited by Joseph Samuel and published by the Fonds Social Juif Unifié, the leading Jewish welfare and fund-raising organization in France, began to appear. *L'Arhe* was intended to express the revival of French Jewry after World War II by reflecting its religious, intellectual, and artistic life. In 1967 there were three Yiddish dailies, among them *Unzer Vort* (Po'alei Zion) and *Unzer Shtime* (*Bund), and a large number of weeklies and monthlies in French and Yiddish.

[Ed.]

In Germany and Austria. Jewish periodicals appeared in Germany from the middle of the 18th century, when they became an expression of the era and its movements—Enlightenment, Reform, and Emancipation. One of them, the *Dyhernfurther Privilegierte Zeitung*, published in 1771–72 in the Lower Silesian town famous for its Hebrew printing presses, was a German-language journal written in Hebrew script. A few years later *Ha-*Me'assef* (Berlin, 1784–1811), was founded by Moses *Mendelssohn and used Hebrew as its medium. The first periodical intended for Jews published in the German language and script was *Sulamith*, which appeared in Dessau from 1806 to 1833. Apart from this, the only periodical before 1850 that lasted for any significant length of time was the *Wissenschaftliche Zeitschrift fuer Juedische Theologie*, which Abraham *Geiger edited in Frankfort from 1835 to 1847. The longest-lived journal in German Jewish press history—85 years—was the religiously liberal weekly *Allgemeine Zeitung des Judentums*, founded in 1837 by R. Ludwig Philippson of Magdeburg, and edited by him for 50 years.

Of the 75 Jewish newspapers and periodicals that came into existence during the 60 years before World War I, only 16 of those appearing at least once a month held out for more than 12 years. They were: (1) the **Monatsschrift fuer Geschichte und Wissenschaft des Judentums* (1851–1939); (2) **Jeschurun* (Frankfort, 1854–70), founded by Samson Raphael *Hirsch; (3) the Hebrew **Ha-Maggid* (Lyck, 1857–92); (4) the Orthodox **Israelit* (Mainz and Frankfort, 1860–1938); (5) the *Juedische Zeitschrift fuer Wissenschaft und Leben* (Breslau, 1862–75); (6) the **Juedische Presse* (Berlin, 1869–1923), edited by Hirsch *Hildesheimer; (7) the Conservative *Israelitische Wochenschrift fuer die religioesen und sozialen Interessen des Judenthums* (Breslau and Magdeburg, 1870–94); (8) the *Monatsblaetter zur Belehrung ueber das Judentum* (Frankfort, 1881–1908); (9) the liberal *Allgemeine Israelitische Wochenschrift* (Berlin, 1891–1906); (10) *Im deutschen Reich* (Berlin, 1895–1921), the organ of the Central Union of German Citizens of Jewish Faith; (11) the independent *Juedisches Volksblatt* (Breslau, 1896–1923); (12) the Zionist **Juedische Rundschau* (Berlin, 1896–1938, see below); (13) the Mizrachi *Israelitisches Familienblatt* (Frankfort, from 1900) called after 1920 *Neue Juedische Presse;* (14) the arts periodical *Ost und West* (Berlin, 1901–22); (15) the *Zeitschrift fuer Demographie und Statistik der Juden* (Berlin, 1904–22; (16) the *Israelitisches Familienblatt* (Hamburg, 1898–1938).

Between the Two World Wars. The Jewish political press was at its most flourishing after World War I, when German Jewry enjoyed a cultural revival. This political press consisted mainly of weeklies such as: (1) the Zionist *Juedische Rundschau;* (2) the **C. V. Zeitung* (Berlin, 1922–38) edited by Ludwig Hollaender, Alfred *Weiner, Alfred Hirschberg, and others, founded in Berlin in 1922 as an outgrowth of the Central Union's monthly *Im*

Deutschen Reich; (3) the *Israelitisches Familienblatt,* established in Hamburg in 1898 by Max and Leo Lessmann; (4) the **Israelit;* and (5) *Der Schild,* founded in 1921 by the Jewish ex-servicemen's association.

Of more than three dozen community papers that appeared at various periods, most of them neutral in their handling of Jewish politics, the most prominent ones were those appearing in Berlin from 1911, Frankfort from 1922, and Munich (serving the Bavarian region) from 1924. A considerable number of papers served the special interests of youth, women, teachers, cantors, social workers, and other groups. In addition to these, a large number of periodicals—published, practically without exception, in German—dealt with religious, scientific, and politico-cultural affairs. Among these was *Der Morgen* (Darmstadt, later Berlin, 1925–38), which had a "German-Jewish" or assimilationist policy. *Der *Jude* was the name given to a periodical published by Gabriel *Riesser during his campaign for Jewish Emancipation (Altona, 1832–35). The same name was used some 75 years later for another periodical, directed by Martin *Buber in Berlin from 1916 to 1924 and supporting Jewish nationalism. The title *Zion* was given first to a religious fortnightly (Berlin, 1833–35), then to a Reformist monthly (Frankfort, 1840–43), later still to a Zionist monthly (Berlin, 1895–99), and finally to a Mizrachi periodical (Berlin, 1929). In this connection J. *Ettlinger's monthly *Der Zionswaechter* (Altona, 1845–55) should be mentioned.

Until *Kristallnacht* (Nov. 10, 1938), as a direct result of which the entire Jewish daily and periodical press of the Reich was wiped out, there were about 12 regular publications in Berlin and nearly three dozen more outside the capital. The *Juedisches Nachrichtenblatt* established on the orders of the Nazi authorities shortly after the general ban on Jewish publications, first appeared on Nov. 23, 1938. It was restricted to announcements of official decrees, bulletins of the Nazi-enforced organization of the Jews in Germany (Reichsvereinigung der Juden in Deutschland), and of the larger Jewish communities, and the issue of important notices about emigration and welfare matters. This paper, which had none of the characteristics of a Jewish publication, appeared until 1943.

After World War II. The Jewish press revived in West Germany after World War II was little more than a shadow of what had existed in pre-Nazi days. The first journal to appear, in 1946, was the Duesseldorf *Mitteilungsblatt fuer die juedischen Gemeinden der Nordrheinprovinz.* In the following year the *Juedisches Gemeindeblatt fuer die britische Zone* was published in the same city. The German journalist Karl Marx founded the popular *Allgemeine Unabhaengige Juedische Wochenzeitung* in 1946. In 1951 two pro-Israel weeklies were founded: the *Muenchner Juedische Nachrichten* and the Yiddish *Naye Yidishe Tsaytung.* By 1970 these three were the only three Jewish newspapers in the whole of the German Federal Republic, including West Berlin. Apart from occasional publications, a monthly bulletin published by the *Juedischer Pressedienst* of Duesseldorf (the JPD) has appeared from 1965. In the German Democratic Republic one newspaper, the *Nachrichtenblatt,* has been issued since 1961 by an editorial board divided between East Berlin, Dresden, Erfurt, and Schwerin, its full title being *Nachrichtenblatt der juedischen Gemeinde von Gross-Berlin und des Verbandes der juedischen Gemeinden in der Deutschen Demokratischen Republik.*

In Vienna. The German language was also predominant in the Jewish papers of Austria, all of which were published in Vienna. The first weekly came into existence in the second half of the 19th century. It was the politically liberal *Neuzeit* (1861–1904), a paper well disposed to religious reform, founded by Leopold *Kompert and Simon Szánto and vigorously promoted by Adolf *Jellinek. The *Oesterreichische Wochenschrift,* founded in 1884 by R. Joseph Samuel *Bloch, several times a member of the Austrian parliament, lasted for 37 years. This was for a time the organ of the Vienna Jewish community, and as such it actively opposed both the anti-Semitic Christian Social movement and early Zionism. *Die Wahrheit,* the weekly organ of the Union of Austrian Jews, which first appeared in 1885, was emphatically assimilationist and anti-Zionist; its last editor was Oscar Hirschfeld. *Die Welt* (1897–1914), founded by Theodor Herzl, which appeared in Cologne and Berlin as well as in Vienna, was the weekly organ of the Austrian Zionist movement; in 1918–19 Robert *Weltsch edited the Zionist *Juedische Zeitung* (1907–21). He was also associated with the only Jewish daily ever to appear in Vienna, the *Wiener Morgenzeitung* (1919–27). The weekly *Die Neue Welt* (1928–38) was directed by Robert *Stricker, the founder of the Jewish People's Party. The weekly *Juedische Presse* (1915–34) represented the interests of the Agudat Israel; and the *Juedische Welt,* founded in 1929, was close to the Austrian Mizrachi movement. *Die juedische Front* (1931–38) was the organ of the Jewish ex-servicemen.

On Nov. 10, 1938, all Jewish newspapers and periodicals in Austria were forced to close down. A Vienna edition of the official Nazi *Juedisches Nachrichtenblatt* appeared from the end of 1938. After World War II the Austrian Jewish press was confined to monthlies. By the end of the 1960s there were a half dozen in existence, the two leading ones being *Neue Welt,* founded in 1948 and directed by Georg Kuenstlinger (1892–1969), and *Die Gemeinde,* founded by the Vienna Jewish community in 1958 and edited by Wilhelm Krell. [E.G.L.]

In Holland. The *Gazeta de Amsterdam,* which was issued in 1675, is generally regarded as the first Jewish newspaper. It was printed by David de Castro Tartas, a Sephardi Jew, and though its contents were not specifically Jewish, its language, Judeo-Spanish, shows that it was intended for the Spanish-Portuguese or Marrano community. The first Yiddish paper was the *Dinstagishe un Fraytagishe Kurant,* which appeared first as a semiweekly from Dec. 5, 1680, and then as a weekly, *Dinstagishe Kurant,* in 1686–87. It was issued by the Amsterdam Jewish printer Uri Phoebus Halevi. In 1797–98 the secession of a number of Amsterdam Jews from the *alte kehile* ("the old congregation") and their formation of the new congregation called Adath Yeshurun led to the publication of a polemical Yiddish weekly *Diskursen fun di Naye Kehile,* which appeared for 24 issues (November 1797–March 1798). Its rival, *Diskursen fun di Alte Kehile,* appeared for 13 issues.

During the next 50 years, several yearbooks or almanacs appeared for short periods, but there was no regular Jewish press until about 1850, when a number of Jewish weeklies made their appearance under various titles. The first was the *Nederlands*

Figure 4. Issue of *Dinstagishe Kurant,* an Amsterdam Yiddish weekly, August 27, 1687. From J. Fraenkel, *The Jewish Press of the World,* London, 1967.

Israëlitisch Nieuws- en Advertentieblad (1849–50), started by A. M. Chumaceiro (1813–1883), who became chief rabbi of Curaçao in the Dutch West Indies in 1855. It then continued as *Israëlitisch Weekblad,* under a new editorial committee. The original editors established the *Weekblad voor Israëlieten* (1855–84), which was continued as *Nieuwsblad voor Israëlieten* (1884–94). As the *Weekblad voor Israëlieten* it defended Reform Judaism, while a rival Orthodox weekly, the *Nieuw Israëlitisch Weekblad (N.I.W.)* was started in 1865 "to advocate the real love of truth." Its founder and first editor was the bibliographer M. M. *Roest. During the last quarter of the 19th century, it was one of several Jewish weeklies in Holland and had a circulation of 3,000. By 1914 its circulation had risen to 13,000 and in 1935 to 15,000 among a Jewish population of about 120,000. Publication was interrupted by the Nazi occupation of Holland but was resumed in 1945, when its policy, formerly anti-Zionist, became pro-Israel, while its approach remained Orthodox. By 1970 it was the only Jewish weekly in Holland and had a circulation of about 4,500 among a Jewish population of about 20,000.

Contemporary with the *N.I.W.* until 1940 were the *Weekblad voor Israëlietische Huisgezinnen* (1870–1940), edited by the firm of Haagens in Rotterdam, and the *Centraal Blad voor Israëlieten in Nederland* (1885–1940), published by Van Creveld in Amsterdam. These three publications carried detailed reports of local Jewish events, and readers' letters, with foreign Jewish news usually in a subordinate place. Different was the approach of the weekly, later a bimonthly, *De Joodse Wachter,* established in 1905, which became the official publication of the Netherlands Zionist Federation. Its editors, always unpaid honorary officers of the federation, included Fritz (later Peretz) *Bernstein in the 1920s. From 1967 until 1969 it existed only as a one-page supplement to the *N.I.W.,* appearing once every two or three weeks, but has since become independent again as a monthly. Other Zionist periodicals were *Tikvath Israel* (1917–40), the official monthly of the Zionist Youth Federation; the Zionist youth leaders' *Baderech* (1925–38) which continued as *Ḥerutenu* (1938–40); the woman's monthly *Ha Ischa* (1929–40), and *Het beloofde Land* (1922–40), later called *Palestine,* and issued by the Keren Hayesod. An important cultural journal, opening horizons far beyond the confines of Holland, was *De Vrijdagavond* (1924–32), established by Izak M. Prins, J. S. da Silva Rosa, librarian of Ẹẓ Ḥayyim, and Justus Tal, then chief rabbi of Utrecht.

By order of the Germans, most Jewish journals had to cease publication in October 1940. Only one Jewish weekly was allowed, the obscure *Joods Weekblad,* which first appeared in August 1940 and which, from April 1941 until September 1943, was issued under the auspices of the Joodse Raad ("Jewish Council"). It published official announcements. After the liberation of the southern part of the Netherlands in the autumn of 1944, Jews who had survived there, mostly from Amsterdam, started publishing *Le-Ezrat ha-Am.* Postwar publications of a more than ephemeral nature include *Ha-binjan* (1947–), the monthly of the Sephardi Congregation of Amsterdam; *Hakehillah* (1955–), the monthly of the Ashkenazi Congregation of Amsterdam; and *Levend Joods Geloof* (1955–), the monthly of the Liberal Jewish Congregation (all of them printed). *Studia Rosenthaliana,* (1966–) in a scientific biannual, devoted to Dutch Jewish history and related subjects, published by the Bibliotheca Rosenthaliana of the Amsterdam University Library. [H.Bo.]

In Hungary. The beginning of a Jewish press in Hungary dates back to the 1840s. A few issues of a Hungarian-language quarterly, *Magyar Zsinagóga,* appeared in Papa in 1846–47, and a German-language weekly, *Der Ungarische Israelit,* appeared in 1848. The first journal of any importance was **Ben Chananja,* a German-language quarterly which had originated in Leipzig but from 1858 was published in Szeged, Hungary, by R. Leopold Loew, who used it in the struggle for Jewish Emancipation; in 1861 it became a weekly in reduced format. There had hitherto been little demand for Jewish newspapers in Hungary, where capable Jewish journalists usually found employment in the general press. But now the position underwent a change. Several short-lived papers appeared in the 1860s, and in 1869 a Yiddish paper, *Pester Juedische Zeitung,* was founded in Budapest. It appeared five times weekly and continued publication until 1887, when it was converted into a German-language weekly, *Allgemeine Juedische Zeitung* (in Hebrew characters), which lasted until 1919. More significant was the Hungarian-language weekly **Egyenlôség* (1881–1938), which, during the *Tiszaeszlár blood libel case of 1882–83, appeared daily with reports of the proceedings. An important contemporary was the monthly **Magyar Zsidó Szemle* ("Hungarian Jewish Review"), which was founded in 1884 and appeared until 1948. It was produced by members of the Budapest rabbinical seminary and also joined in the struggle for Jewish Emancipation and religious equality. The same personnel simultaneously published a review in Hebrew, which was at first entitled *Ha-Ẓofeh le-Ḥokhmat Yisrael* ("Judaic Studies Observer"), later *Ha-Ẓofeh me-Ereẓ Hagar* ("Hungarian Observer"), and finally *Ha-Soker* ("The Observer"). This review provided a forum for Hebrew writers at a time when almost all Jewish publications in Central Europe were in German.

Between 1846 and World War I, many periodicals appeared for short periods, most of them weeklies and most of them in German or Hungarian. During the early years of Zionism, the authorities refused permission for the publication of a Zionist paper. This was largely the result of the attitude of Jewish organizations which were opposed to the development of Hungarian Zionism. The first Zionist weekly was the German-language *Ungarlaendische Juedische Zeitung* which appeared from 1908 to 1914. A Zionist periodical in Hungarian, *Zsidó Néplap,* appeared from 1903 to 1905 and reappeared in 1908 as *Zsidó Élet* ("Jewish Life"). In 1909 the Hungarian Zionist Federation founded its own organ, *Zsidó Szemle* ("Jewish Review"), which was banned in 1938. The poet J. *Patai published a literary monthly **Mult és Jövő* from 1912 to 1939 and opened its columns to Zionist discussion.

Between the two world wars, there were only about 12 effective weeklies and monthlies in Hungary. The Jewish press practically came to an end in 1938, after which time the Hungarian totalitarian regime (whether Nazi or Communist) authorized only one Jewish periodical. The periodical *Új Élet* ("New Life") was founded in November 1945 by the Central Board of Hungarian Jews, and from 1948 reflected the policies of the Communist rulers, giving no space to the subject of Israel. Its circulation in 1967 was 10,000. [B.Y.]

In India. The first Jewish periodicals of India were in Judeo-Arabic. *Doresh Tov le-Ammo,* edited by David ben-Ḥayyim had a short life around 1870 and was followed by the Calcutta weeklies, *Mevasser; the Jewish Gazette* (1873–77), edited by Ezekiel Solomon; and *Maggid Meisharim* (1889–1900) edited by Solomon Abed Twena. *The Bene Israelite* appeared in English and Marathi (the mother tongue of the *Bene Israel) from 1896, and reported the rejection by the Bene Israel leaders in Bombay of Theodor Herzl's invitation to send two delegates to the First Zionist Congress in 1897. It gave as the main reason the community's support for the "**Protestrabbiner*" of Germany and the extremely Orthodox section of Anglo-Jewry.

The first national periodical to appear in India was *The Jewish Advocate,* an independent monthly published by the Bombay Zionist Association from 1923 to 1951. Another Zionist paper, *The Jewish Tribune,* appeared in Bombay from 1933 to 1939. *India and Israel* was owned and edited from 1949 to 1953 by F. W. Pollack, who in 1952 became Israel trade commissioner and consul in Bombay. In 1968 there were three regular Jewish periodicals. The fortnightly *News from Israel, founded in 1954 and published in Bombay by the Israel consulate,* had a circulation of 2,000. The *Maccabi* monthly, founded in 1947, was published in both English and Marathi. Other organizations published house journals from time to time.

[P.S.G.]

In Italy. The Italian Jewish press dates from the middle of the 19th century. The first newspaper, *La Rivista israelitica,* edited by Cesare Rovighi, appeared in Parma in 1845 and continued until 1848. Jewish journalism in the 19th century gave rise to such short-lived publications as Leghorn's *L'Israelita* in 1866, and Pitigliano's *Il romanziere israelitico* in 1895. It also produced two important reviews, *L'educatore israelita* and *Il Corriere israelitico.* The first, founded in Vercelli in 1853 by the rabbis Giuseppe Levi (1814–1874) and Esdra Pontremoli (1818–1888), published articles on religious affairs and news from the Jewish communities abroad. Among its contributors were Elijah *Benamozegh, S. D. *Luzzatto, and Lelio *della Torre. In 1874 *L'educatore israelita* became *Il Vessillo israelitico,* which appeared at Casale Monferrato under the editorship of Flaminio *Servi and lasted until 1922. *Il Corriere*

Figure 5. Issue of *Gemeindeblatt*, organ of the Berlin Jewish community, October 1932. Jerusalem, B. M. Ansbacher Collection.

israelitico, founded in Trieste by A. V. *Morpurgo in 1862 and later edited by A. Curiel and then by Dante *Lattes, was a publication sensitive to the pressing problems of Jewish life. This newspaper staunchly supported the Zionist movement when it came into being.

In 1901 the rabbinical college at Leghorn launched the short-lived review, *L'Antologia ebraica*. *L'Idea sionista* appeared in Modena from 1901 to 1910. In 1904 the journal *Lux*, edited by Arrigo Lattes and Alfredo *Toaff, appeared in Leghorn, but ceased publication after ten numbers. *La Rivista israelitica*, published in Florence from 1904 to 1915, was edited by the chief rabbi S. H. *Margulies and became a source of great interest for Italian studies. Umberto *Cassuto, P. H. *Chajes, Ismar *Elbogen, S. *Colombo, and E. S. *Artom were among the contributors. In 1910 Rabbi Margulies also founded *La Settimana israelitica*, a weekly in the style of the Florentine cultural weeklies, which appeared until 1915, edited by Alfonso *Pacifici, Carlo A. *Viterbo, Q. Sinigaglia, and G. *Ottolenghi. In 1916 the *Corriere israelitico* and *La Settimana israelitica* were amalgamated in Florence under the title *Israel* and was edited by Carlo A. Viterbo. Offshoots of *Israel* were *Israel dei ragazzi* (1919–39) and *La *Rassegna mensile di Israel* (from 1925).

Other publications with considerable circulation in 1970 were *Bollettino della Comunità israelitica di Milano*, founded in 1945 and edited by Raoul Elia; *Shalom*, a monthly of Roman Jewry since 1952; *Ha-Tikvah*, the monthly organ of the Federation of Jewish Youth (1953); *Karnenu*, the semimonthly publication of the Jewish National Fund (1948); and *Hed ha-Ḥinnukh*, an educational monthly. [Y.C.]

Ladino Press. One of the reasons for the growth of a Ladino press was the reluctance or inability of the exiles from Spain to learn the languages of the countries in which they found themselves. Before World War II—during which the Sephardi communities of the Balkan countries were either entirely or partly destroyed—a considerable number of Sephardi Jews, mainly of the older generation and especially women, spoke Ladino. They had only an elementary knowledge of the local language—enough for local business and social intercourse with the surrounding population. There was, therefore, a growing need for some kind of Ladino reading material.

As mentioned above, the first Jewish newspaper appeared in 1675 in Amsterdam and it was *Gazeta de Amsterdam*, printed in Ladino. It lasted less than a year and had no Ladino successors until the beginning of the 19th century. The main reason for this delayed development of the Ladino press, in spite of its early start, is to be found in the social environment of the Ladino-speaking Jews, the bulk of whom lived in the countries of the Balkans and the Middle East. During the 18th century these countries were socially and culturally retarded, and their newspapers were neither many nor widespread. Like the population around them, the Jews, even the educated exiles from Spain among them, felt little need for the stimulus or enlightenment that newspapers could give. All this changed gradually in the 19th century and when in 1882 Isidore Singer of Vienna listed 103 extant Jewish newspapers, six of them were in Ladino.

Newspapers in Judeo-Spanish, transcribed in *Rashi type, had appeared in Jerusalem, Smyrna, Constantinople, Salonika, Belgrade, Paris, Cairo, and Vienna. One of them was the Smyrna journal, *La Puerta del Oriente* ("Gateway of the Orient"), which first appeared in 1846 under the Hebrew name *Sha'arei Mizraḥ*. Edited by Rafael Uziel, it contained material of general interest, commercial notices, and literary articles. It lasted just one year. *El Luzero de la Paciencia* ("The Light of Patience"), the first Judeo-Spanish newspaper to appear in Latin characters, was started in 1885 by Elia M. Crespin, in the Rumanian city of Turnu Severin. It was a bimonthly and continued publication until 1889. The reason for publishing in Latin characters, according to the editor, was that the writing of Spanish had become greatly corrupted because Rashi often spelled words of different meaning in the same way. The corruption of Ladino by the violation of the rules of Spanish, from which it derived, was a subject often discussed in the Ladino press. Thus *El Tiempo* ("The Times") of June 28, 1907, ridiculed the Ladino used by a Bulgarian Ladino paper. *El Tiempo*, a literary, political, and financial paper, was first published in Constantinople in 1871 under the editorship of Isaac Carmona, and continued to appear until 1930. Its last editor was David *Fresco, one of the best-known Ladino writers of his time. Fresco was also the editor of *El Sol* ("The Sun") of Constantinople (1879), a scientific and literary bimonthly. It seems to have lasted for about two years. He also edited *El Amigo de la Familia* ("The Friend of the Family"), an illustrated periodical, which was published in Constantinople in 1889.

There were journals which were published partly in Ladino and partly in other languages. *Salonik* ("Salonika"), which appeared from 1869 to 1870, was published in Ladino, Turkish, Greek, and Bulgarian, the Bulgarian part being edited in Sofia. It seems to have been the official newspaper of the Turkish authorities in Salonika under the editorship of Rabbi Jacob Uziel. *Djeridie y Lesan* ("The Journal of the Language") appeared in Constantinople in 1899 in Ladino and Turkish. Its purpose was to make Turkish a living language among the Jews.

Ladino found considerable support among the Jewish socialists of the Balkans, who claimed that it was the language of the Sephardi masses and should be preserved and encouraged. They insisted, therefore, that it should be the medium of instruction in Jewish schools. A number of Ladino newspapers were exponents of the socialist idea. Among them the best known was *Avante* ("Forward"), which began publication in 1911 in Salonika under the name *La Solidaridad Ouvradera* ("Workers' Solidarity"). It may be said that the history of this journal, which began as a biweekly and during the Balkan Wars (1912–13) became a daily, is the history of socialism among the Jewish workers of Salonika. Its first editor was Abraham ben Aroya, who was succeeded by Alberto Arditi. In 1923 the paper became the mouthpiece of the Jewish Communists with its editor Jack Ventura, for some time one of the Communist representatives in the Greek Parliament. *Avante* ceased publication in 1935. *El Azno* ("The Donkey"), a satirical journal which appeared as a weekly for three months in 1923, was apparently designed to counter *Avante* when the latter became communistic. Another important Ladino journal published in Salonika was *La Epoca*, edited by Bezalel Sadi Halevi. It appeared from November 1875, first as a weekly, then twice a week, and finally as a daily, until 1912.

In Bulgaria, where a number of Ladino newspapers and

periodicals appeared under the auspices of the community and the rabbinate *(El Eco Judaico, La Luz)* the best-known Zionist journal was *El Judio* ("The Jew"), whose editor was David Elnecave, one of the most prominent Zionist leaders in the Balkans. It first appeared in 1909 in Galata, and was later published in Varna and Sofia. It ceased publication in 1931, when Elnecave emigrated to Buenos Aires where he launched *La Luz.* On his death, the editorship was taken over by his son, Nissim.

ZIONISM. With the rise of Zionism, Hebrew was revived as a spoken language among the Jews of the Balkans, and newspapers made their appearance in both Hebrew and Ladino. *Yosef ha-Da'at* or *El Progresso,* a bimonthly, was published in Adrianople in 1888 in Hebrew and Ladino under the editorship of Abraham *Danon. Devoted mainly to historical research among the Jews of Turkey, it was published for about a year. Another Adrianople periodical was *Karmi Shelli* ("My Vineyard"), a literary and national monthly (1881), published under the editorship of David Mitrani. Among the better-known Zionist Ladino journals was *El Avenir* ("The Future"), started in 1897. It existed for 20 years under the editorship of David Florentin. The organ of the Zionist Federation of Greece, the weekly *La Esperansa* ("The Hope"), appeared in Salonika from 1916 to 1920. A Zionist weekly which was predominantly French but also contained articles in Ladino was *Lema'an Yisrael—Pro Israel,* founded in Salonika in 1917 and edited from 1923 to 1929 by Abraham Recanati, who eventually settled in Israel.

A number of satirical Ladino journals also appeared. At the beginning of the 20th century, *El Kirbatj*—the Turkish word for "whip" that found its way into Ladino—appeared in Salonika as a "liberal, humorous, independent weekly journal" under the editorship of Moise Levy. It was followed in 1918 by *El Nuevo Kirbatj* ("The New Whip") under the editorship of Josef Karaso, which ceased publication in 1923.

Altogether, about 43 satirical and humorous journals were published among the Balkan communities at various times. Among them were *El Burlon* ("The Joker"), of Constantinople, edited by Nisim Behar; and *La Gata* ("The Cat"), a satirical journal established in Salonika in 1923 with M. Matarasco as editor.

At no time were the incentives for the creation or maintenance of Ladino newspapers in any sense great or compelling. The Sephardi Jews found themselves mostly in countries of little cultural development and they long retained the desire for knowledge inherited from Jewish life in Spain. This enabled them to resist for some time the primitive influences of their surroundings, to which in time, however, they succumbed. The intellectual classes of Sephardi Jews, educated in the cities of Central Europe, spoke the vernacular and other languages such as French and German. They, therefore, did not feel the need for Ladino newspapers. Finally, to most of the Sephardim in the Balkans the study of the Holy Scriptures, the Talmud and the Codes, and above all the daily recitals of prayers, were not merely religious duties: they also provided almost all their educational and cultural needs. The Bible, the prayer books, and certain rabbinical works were available in Spanish or Ladino. Textbooks were also available for the learning of Hebrew. Aspirations for a wider world outlook did not exist among the Sephardim, largely because the countries in which they lived were on the whole cut off from the mainstream of European intellectual life. There was, therefore, little scope for newspaper activity. According to Moshe David Gaon in his *Ha-Ittonut be-Ladino* (1965) there were 296 publications in Ladino between 1845 and World War II, most of them in the Balkans and the Middle East, with Salonika as the greatest center. In 1968 there was hardly any regular Ladino press, except for two weeklies in Israel and one, partly in Ladino, in Turkey.

IN THE U.S. Although Sephardim were the first Jews to settle in the New World and founded the first Jewish congregation there in 1654, Ladino newspapers did not appear in the United States until the beginning of the 20th century, when the second wave of Sephardi immigrants began to arrive, mainly from the Balkan countries. The daily *La Aguila* ("The Eagle") and the weekly *La America* appeared under the editorship of Moshe Gadol between 1911 and 1925. Moshe Gadol, a native of Bulgaria, and his partners Jacob Farhi, Asher Benveniste, Eliyahu Hananya, and Josef Abulafia, acquired their own printing press in New York. In 1926 *El Luzero* ("The Dawn"), an illustrated monthly, was launched by the Sephardic Publishing Company, its editors being Albert Levy and Moise Sulam. Only 12 issues appeared. The weekly *La Vara* ("The Stock") existed from 1928 until 1948, advertised as "the only Spanish Jewish newspaper in America"; the editors were the same as those of *El Luzero.* A weekly journal edited by Nisim and Alfred Mizrahi appeared from 1915 under the name *El Progresso* and later took the name *La Boz del Pueblo* ("The Voice of the People"). In 1919 it became *La Epoca de New York* but survived for only one more year.

For all practical purposes the Ladino press in the United States had come to an end by 1948. A new English-speaking generation was taking the place of the older people, and even when the young Sephardim knew Ladino, their use of it approximated to modern Spanish.

ISRAEL. Before World War II there was a constant *aliyah* of Sehardim from the Balkan countries and the Middle East. Many of these immigrants had acquired a good knowledge of Hebrew in their native countries and when they settled in the Holy Land it required no special effort for them to use Hebrew in their daily life, while preserving Ladino in their family circles and among friends. For this reason there was a real need for Ladino papers, which were usually concerned with the preservation of Sephardi culture, customs, and literature. *Ḥavaẓẓelet-Mevasseret Yerushalayim* was published in 1870, its editor being Ezra Benveniste. During the year of its existence 25 issues appeared.

After the establishment of the State of Israel, a number of Ladino journals appeared, mostly sponsored by political parties. In 1968 there were two weeklies, *El Tiempo* (affiliated to Mapai) and *La Verdad.* [So.G.]

In Latin America. The Jewish press plays an important part in the life of Latin American Jewry. Though it started almost exclusively in Yiddish, it has been going over to Spanish, although in 1970 Yiddish still held a predominant position. The first Jewish papers appeared in Argentina in 1898; one of them, *Folks Shtime,* lasted for 16 years. There were many other short-lived publications, but in 1914 the first daily, *Di Yidishe Tsaytung,* came into being, and was followed in 1918 by *Di Prese.* They continued to appear into the 1970s. Until the 1920s *Di Prese* was inclined toward the left, but both papers supported Zionism, and after the establishment of the State of Israel the ideological differences between them diminished. Although exercising political and social importance, neither paper ever achieved a circulation of more than 10,000. The only Jewish daily in Spanish, *Amanecer,* appeared in 1957. It was supported by most Jewish writers in the Spanish language, but lasted only until the following year.

Besides the Yiddish dailies, Argentine Jewry produced also a variety of weeklies and other publications. Their contents ranged from popular medicine to humor, literary criticism, and philosophical essays in quarterly reviews. Some of them, like *Ilustrirte Literaishe Bleter,* a monthly which started in 1953, and *Davke,* a philosophical quarterly founded in 1949, were in publication in 1970. Jewish weeklies and monthlies in Spanish, *Juventud* and *Vida Nuestra,* made their first appearance before or during World War I. The monthly *Israel* was established in 1917, serving especially Jews of Sephardi or Near Eastern origin, among whom it found lasting support. Other enduring weeklies were *Mundo Israelita* ("Israel World"), founded in 1923; *La Luz,* which started as a fortnightly in 1930; *Davar,* issued from 1945 by Sociedad Hebraica; and the literary quarterly *Comentario,* founded in 1953. Although closely identifying itself with Zionism and Israel, Argentine Jewry has produced few periodicals in Hebrew. *Ha-Bimah ha-Ivrit* ("Hebrew Forum"; 1921–30), *Atidenu* ("Our Future"; 1926), and *Darom* ("South"), founded 1938 and amalgamated with *Ẓohar* ("Window") in 1964, were the most important. Only the last mentioned survives. By 1970 the circulation of the popular press had declined considerably, but two dailies, about seven weeklies, 20 monthlies, and a dozen other periodicals, most of them representing political parties, were still flourishing in Argentina (see also *Argentina).

In Brazil, Jewish newspapers date from the period of World War I. Subsequently there were Yiddish and Portuguese weeklies and biweeklies of varying duration. Attempts at establishing a Yiddish daily were only partly successful, but the others were more enduring. In 1970 *Der Nayer Moment* (Yiddish) appeared three times a week, the *Yidishe Prese* appeared as a weekly, and a paper in Portuguese appeared biweekly. São Paulo and Rio de Janeiro were the main centers of publication (see also *Brazil). There was practically no Jewish press in Mexico until the *Meksikaner Yidish Lebn* appeared in 1927. In 1970 *Der Veg* appeared weekly and *Di*

Shtime (1939–) biweekly, both in Yiddish. There was also a Zionist Spanish-language weekly, *Prensa Israelita* (1948), and several fortnightlies (see also *Mexico). A daily, *Yidishe Tsaytung*, appeared in Uruguay shortly after World War I, but was short-lived. The weekly *Unzer Lebn* was initiated in 1926, but a Jewish press was not firmly established in Uruguay until the daily *Unzer Fraynd* was launched in 1935. *Haynt*, a daily with Zionist affiliations, began publication in 1957. Several weeklies were also flourishing in 1970 (see also *Uruguay). [Ed.]

In the Middle East and North Africa. Oriental Jewish newspapers emerged only during the first half of the 19th century, but they soon acquired importance among the communities they served. Some of them were published in two or more languages; Hebrew, which was rarely used, was sometimes employed not because there were many Hebrew readers, but with the aim of reviving the language. The Hebrew press in the Middle East was in fact preceded by Jewish papers in Ladino, from 1841, and papers in the colloquial Arabic of the Baghdadi Jewish dialect, such as *Doresh Tov le-Ammo*, from 1855. The first Hebrew paper to appear in Baghdad was *Ha-Dover* (1863), which was published by Moses Baruch Mizraḥi. At a rough estimate, the circulation of Jewish papers in the Middle East, even though these served communities beyond the city or land in which they appeared, never exceeded 5,000. Many papers were short-lived, surviving for no more than a year or two, with only a few appearing regularly for more than five years. Jewish papers appeared in Turkey, Tunisia, Algeria, Ereẓ Israel, Egypt, Syria, Lebanon, Iraq, and Persia. The languages used were literary Arabic, colloquial Arabic, Jewish dialects (i.e., local languages written in Hebrew characters), Hebrew, French, English, Ladino, Spanish, Turkish, and Persian.

In Turkey, only a few papers appeared in languages other than Ladino, such as Hebrew or French, and these had a Zionist orientation, first making their appearance after 1910. In North Africa, Egypt, and Lebanon many Jewish papers appeared in French, some examples being *La Renaissance Juive* (Cairo, 1912), the fortnightly *L'Israélite algérien* (Oran, 1900), and the religious *Gazette de Jérusalem* (Jerusalem, 1882). Another Jewish newspaper which had a long career was the Zionist weekly *L'Aurore*, founded by Lucien Sciuto in 1908. It appeared in Istanbul until 1919, but from 1924 to 1931 was published in Cairo. It then came under the control of Jacob Elmaleh, who, with the support of the B'nai B'rith, transformed it after the rise of Hitler into the organ of the League for War on anti-Semitism, based in Egypt.

Among the longer-lived oriental Jewish newspapers was the weekly *Israel*, which first appeared in French, Hebrew, and Arabic (Cairo, 1920). Although the Hebrew section was soon dropped, the Arabic section survived with some interruption for 14 years. In 1939 the paper was amalgamated with *La Tribune Juive*, which had been established at Alexandria in 1936. In Tunisia most Jewish papers appeared in French (e.g., *La Justice*, 1917–), and in Turkey a B'nai B'rith monthly, *Ha-Menorah*, appeared in Turkish and French. The English-language press was mainly confined to India (see above), but in Baghdad there was also the *Iraq Times*.

After the papers appearing in Hebrew, the largest number of Jewish newspapers appearing in Arab countries were published in Arabic. The origins of this press may be traced to Yaʿqūb *Ṣanūʿ, who issued an Egyptian Jewish paper in Arabic in the 1870s. These papers were both religious and secular and were irregular and short-lived. Most of them were ardent supporters of the Zionist cause and defended Zionism and the idea of a Jewish national home against the attacks of the general Arabic press. Papers that survived for some years included the monthly (later weekly) *al-ʿĀʾila* ("The Family"), founded by Esther *Moyal in 1898; the weekly, *al-Miṣbāḥ* (Baghdad, 1924–29); the literary and cultural weekly *al-Ḥāṣid* (Baghdad, 1924–39); the Lebanese *ʾĀlam al-Isrāʾīlī* (*L'Univers Israélite*, Beirut, 1921–46); the Egyptian Karaite paper *al-Ittiḥād al-Isrāʾīlī* (Cairo, 1924–30); and *al-Shams* ("The Sun," Cairo, 1934–48), published in literary Arabic.

Christiane Souriau's research on the Tunisian and Algerian press brought to light a large number of Jewish papers that had appeared in colloquial Arabic and in Arabic characters from the year 1878, when the dual-language (Judeo-Arabic and French) *al-ʿAmāla al-Tūnisiyya* first appeared. From then until 1900, as many as 22 papers were established, most of them lasting no more than a year or two. The Zionist *al-Bustān* ("The Garden," 1888–97) was exceptional. During the years 1901–19, a further 37 Jewish newspapers and periodicals in colloquial Arabic were published in Tunisia, only two of which lasted for more than four years: *al-Ṣabāḥ* ("The Morning," 1904–29) and *al-Sion* ("The Voice of Zion," 1913–20). The number of papers declined from 1920, although the life-span of those that remained became longer, e.g., *al-Najma* ("The Star," 1920?–38). Souriau mentions 37 Jewish papers in colloquial Arabic appearing in Tunisia. After the establishment of the State of Israel, the Arabic Jewish press in the Arab lands ceased to exist. Instead, the number of papers appearing in Arabic in Israel increased as a result of the immigration of Jews from the Arab countries. [Sh.M.]

In Poland. For the period up to World War I, see below: In Russia. The great development of the Jewish press in Poland that took place in the years immediately after the war reflected the vigorous life of the Jewish population. More than 200 newspapers and periodicals appeared in the 1920s, and many of them were still flourishing when the Nazi armies overran Poland in September 1939. The papers represented all shades of opinion; most of them were in Yiddish, but a few were in Hebrew and some in Polish. During this period, about 20 daily papers appeared, three in Vilna—*Letste Nayes* (1915), which became *Der Tog* (in 1920), *Avend-Kurier* (from 1924, and *Tsayt* (1924); two in Bialystok—*Dos Naye Lebn* (1919), and *Bialystoker Telegraf;* three in Lodz—*Lodzer Tageblat* (1908, under J. Unger, having a circulation of 20,000); *Dos Morgenblat* from 1912, and *Naye Folksblat* (1923); in Lublin the *Lubliner Tageblat* (1918); and in Grodno, the *Grodne Moment* (1924). Lvov had two, one in Polish, *Chwila* (1919), and one in Yiddish, *Der Morgen* (1926); and Cracow had two, one in Polish, *Nowy Dziennik* (1918), first under Wilhelm Berkelhammer and from 1921 to 1924 under Isaac *Schwarzbart.

The others were published in Warsaw, where *Haynt* and *Der Moment* had the largest circulations and were in close competition. Other Warsaw dailies were *Der Yid* (later, *Dos Yidishe Vort*, from 1917), *Varshever Ekspres* (1926), *Naye Folkstzaytung* (1926), and *Unzer Ekspres* (1927). The daily *Nowy Czas* (1929) was in Polish, as was the Zionist daily *Nasz Pzeglad* (1923). Besides these publications there were literary weeklies like *Literarishe Bleter*

היהודים במצרים
מצרים
MISRAIM
Direction et Administration
Isaac Harmona
עיד אל גלום אל סעיד

Figure 6. Issue of *Misraim*, a paper written in Arabic with Hebrew characters, Cairo, January 12, 1904. From J. M. Landau, *Ha-Yehudim be-Miẓrayim*, Jerusalem, 1967.

(Warsaw, from 1924), *Kino-Teater-Radio* (1926), *Veltshpigl* ("World Mirror," 1927), and the Yiddish *P.E.N. Klub Nayes of Vilna* (1928). The scientific *Land un Lebn* (1927) appeared monthly; a popular science fortnightly, *Der Doktor,* appeared in Warsaw from 1929; and another, *Folksgesunt,* in Vilna from 1923. A humorous weekly, *Der Blufer,* was prominent in Warsaw journalism from 1926. This body of newspapers and periodicals, employing thousands of people, was closed by the Germans in 1939, and its editors, contributors, and printers fled or perished as the Nazi terror fastened on the country. [A.Fi.]

After World War II. The first Jewish newspaper in postwar Poland, *Dos Ňaye Lebn,* appeared in Lodz on April 10, 1945. At first it was published weekly, then semiweekly and on March 1, 1947, at the conference of the Jewish regional committees, it was decided to make *Dos Naye Lebn* a daily paper and the official organ of the Central Committee of Polish Jews, which comprised all existing Jewish parties. Between 1945 and 1949 there were also weekly and semiweekly publications of various Jewish parties, e.g., the *Arbeter Tsaytung* of the Po'alei Zion, the *Iḥud* of the Liberal Zionists, *Di Folkshtime* connected with the Communist Polish Labor Party (P.P.R.), the *"Głas Młodzieży,"* of the Ha-Shomer ha-Ẓa'ir, and *Yidishe Shriftn,* a publication of the Jewish Writers' Association. After the liquidation of the Jewish political parties in November 1949, most of the Jewish press was gradually closed down by the authorities (see *Poland). The literary monthly *Di Yidishe Shriftn* continued to be published by the Jewish Cultural Society as an organ of the Jewish writers, who elected its editorial board. *Di Folkshtime* alone remained as a newspaper appearing four times a week and serving officially as the Yiddish organ of the ruling party, controlled to a large degree by the Jewish Cultural Society. By 1968 *Di Folkshtime* became a weekly, publishing a Polish section once in two weeks, and *Di Yidishe Shriftn* ceased its publication after its 25th issue. [D.Sf.]

In Rumania. The Jewish press in Rumania developed with the social and intellectual life of the Rumanian Jews. Two short-lived publications made their appearance in the middle of the 19th century and were followed in 1857 by the weekly *Israelitul Român* ("Rumanian Israelite") of Bucharest and in 1874 by the review *Revista Israelită* of Jassy. In 1890 Moses *Schwarzfeld, publicist and historian, founded the weekly *Egalitatea* ("Equality"), which lasted until the rise of the Fascist regime. Other publications of that period were the weekly *Ha-Yo'eẓ* ("The Adviser"), which leaned toward the Ḥovevei Zion, appearing from 1876 to 1920, and the review *Likht* ("Light," 1914), both in Yiddish. In 1906, Horia *Carp founded the weekly *Curierul Israelit* ("Israelite Messenger"), which became the official organ of the group Uniunea Evreilor Pământeni (Union of Native Jews; after 1918, Uniunea Evreilor Romani—Union of Rumanian Jews) and continued until 1941.

After World War I most of the Jewish newspapers in Rumania had Zionist leanings. Major influences in forming a Zionist outlook among the Jewish population were two weeklies: *Mântuirea* ("The Deliverance"), founded by A. L. *Zissu in 1922 and republished, after a long break, from 1945 to 1949; and *Renaşterea Noastră* ("Our Revival"), founded by S. Stern, publicist and Zionist, in 1928. The weekly *Viata Evrească* ("Jewish Life," 1944–49) had a Zionist Socialist tendency. In addition to these weekly publications, there were literary and political reviews. The monthly *Hasmonaea,* founded in 1915, was the official organ of the association of Zionist students. The review *Adam* (1929–39) founded by I. O. Ludo, attracted to its pages Jewish writers in the Rumanian language.

Except for a brief period in 1877, there was never a daily Jewish press in Rumania because there was no autonomous national Jewish life. The information published by the Jewish weekly and monthly papers in Yiddish, German, and Rumanian, was limited to Jewish international and local life. Political outlook was centered on events of specific Jewish interest, and the Jewish press had a rather polemic character. The weekly Zionist paper *Renaşterea Noastră* resumed publication in 1944. Five more papers that appeared in 1945 were similarly oriented. In the years that followed, various attempts were made to maintain other Jewish papers, several in Yiddish and one in Hebrew, but by the end of 1953 all had ceased publication. From 1956 the Jewish population in Rumania was served by a review published by the Jewish community in Bucharest, **Revista Cultului Mozaic* ("The Mosaic Cult's Review"), edited by Moses *Rosen, the chief rabbi. [I.Be.]

In Russia. The history of the Jewish press in Russia before the Bolshevik Revolution falls into two periods: the mid-19th century to the 1905 Revolution—years during which severe restrictions and censorship were in force; and 1906 to 1917—a period during which restrictions were partially relaxed. Jewish newspapers in czarist Russia appeared in four languages: Hebrew, Yiddish, Russian, and (in Warsaw) Polish. During the first period, the publication of Jewish periodicals was beset with obstacles. A license to publish was obtained only with great difficulty, and when granted, the official censor controlled the paper's contents. This situation accounted for the strange practice of publishing journals intended primarily for Russian Jews in places outside the country, mainly in Prussia and Austria. Even these newspapers had to pass the Warsaw censor, who deleted any item he did not approve. In spite of its distance from the centers of Jewish population, many newspapers were published in St. Petersburg because the censor there held more liberal attitudes.

Efforts at establishing a Jewish press in the early decades of the 19th century resulted in such short-lived publications as **Beobachter an der Weichsel,* a Yiddish weekly issued in Warsaw in 1823, and *Pirḥei Ẓafon,* an annual that published two volumes in Vilna in the 1840s. The first enduring Hebrew periodical intended for Russian Jewry was *Ha-Maggid,* published from 1856 to 1891 in Lyck (later Elk), a Prussian border town. It contained news and essays, whose prominent tone was a moderate approach to the Haskalah. In 1860, Alexander *Zederbaum, who became a leading figure in the Jewish press, founded a Hebrew weekly, *Ha-Meliẓ,* which was published until 1871 in Odessa and then for another three years in St. Petersburg. Its stated purpose was to be "the mediator *(ha-meliẓ)* between the Jews and government and between faith and Haskalah." Zederbaum also published the first weekly in Yiddish, *Kol Mevasser* (1862–71), which grew to become very popular. In Vilna S. J. *Fuenn issued *Ha-Karmel,* intended mainly for local consumption, which ran as a weekly from 1860 to 1870 and as a monthly until 1880. In Warsaw, **Ha-Ẓefirah,* edited by Ḥ. S. *Slonimski, began as a weekly in 1862 but was published for only six months. In Odessa, Russian-speaking members of the Jewish intelligentsia published Russian-language weeklies, such as *Razsvet,* renamed *Sion* (1860–61), and later *Den* (1869–71). These

№ 1.

דער עלטסטער פון די יידן אין ליצמאנשטאט

געטא=צייטונג

Litzmannstadt-Getto, den 7. März 1941.

פראגראם פון דער געטא=צייטונג

1) ארבעט
2) ברויט
3) זארג פאר קראנקע
4) השגחה איבערן קינד און
5) רו אין געטא.

Figure 7. First issue of the *Geto Tsaytung,* published in the Nazi-controlled Lodz Ghetto, March 7, 1941. Jerusalem, Yad Vashem Archives.

papers had the dual purpose of serving as a forum for the discussion of Jewish themes and for presenting Jewish problems to the general Russian public in order to combat anti-Semitism. In 1871 Zederbaum launched a Russian-language weekly in St. Petersburg, *Vestnik russkikh yevreyev* ("Russian Jewish Herald") which, however, was boycotted by the Jewish intelligentsia and ceased publication in 1873. The first Jewish weekly in Polish, *Jutrzeńka,* was published in Warsaw in 1861–63; it had a pronounced assimilationist tendency and was eventually replaced by *Izraelita,* which appeared from 1866 to 1906. A Hebrew monthly, *Ha-Boker Or,* was published by Abraham *Gottlober in Lemberg and later in Warsaw (1876–86). Eight volumes of a Russian annual, containing a variety of literary works and named *Yevreyskaya Biblioteka,* edited by Adolph *Landau, appeared in the period 1871–80.

Ha-Ẓefirah resumed publication in 1874, first in Berlin and from 1875 in Warsaw. In addition, *Ha-Meliẓ* was revived in 1878. The Balkan Wars of 1877–78, the pogroms of the early 1880s, and the anti-Jewish restrictions that followed aroused greater interest in newspapers among the Jewish public. In 1879 two Russian-language weeklies made their appearance in St. Petersburg: **Razsvet* (1883), which pioneered in awaking the national consciousness of Russian Jewish youth, and *Russkiy yevrey* (1884). Another weekly, **Voskhod* (1881–1906), edited by Adolph Landau until 1899, served as the major forum for Russian Jewish intellectuals. Because of the oppressive restrictions placed on them, Yiddish publications were constantly in difficulties, and only the indefatigable Zederbaum succeeded in issuing a Yiddish weekly in St. Petersburg, *Yidishes Folksblat* (1881–90). A revolutionary development in Hebrew journalism took place in 1886, when the first Hebrew daily, *Ha-Yom,* edited by Judah Leib *Kantor, made its appearance in St. Petersburg. Although its career was short (two years), *Ha-Yom* exerted a profound influence on the style employed by the Hebrew press, hastening the transition from florid phraseology to practical prose. The two competing weeklies, *Ha-Meliẓ* and *Ha-Ẓefirah,* were forced to become dailies. The spread of the *Ḥibbat Zion movement in the 1880s resulted in the publication of a considerable number of annuals which served as a forum for the movement's ideology. Among the annuals were *Ha-Asif,* edited by Nahum *Sokolow (1884–88, 1893); *Keneset Yisrael,* edited by Saul Phinehas *Rabbinowitz (Warsaw, 1886–88); and *Ha-Pardes* in Odessa (1892–96, three vols.). They were followed by *Ha-Shilo'aḥ* (1896–1905 in Berlin and Cracow, 1902–19 in Odessa, and until 1926 in Jerusalem). Under the editorship of *Aḥad Ha-Am, and later J. Klausner, *Ha-Shilo'aḥ* became the leading Hebrew monthly, printing articles of a literary and general nature. Attempts which were made by D. Frischmann to publish the intellectual literary weekly *Ha-Dor* (1901, 1904) were unsuccessful as the readership required for this kind of publication was as yet too small.

The need for Yiddish reading matter was met by such annuals as *Hoysfraynd,* edited by Mordecai *Spector (Warsaw, 1888–96); *Yidishe Folks-Bibliothek,* edited by *Shalom Aleichem (Kiev, 1888–89); and *Yidishe Bibliotek,* edited by I. L. *Peretz (3 vols., Warsaw, 1891–95). A Zionist weekly, *Der Yid,* directed at the educated reader, was published in Cracow from 1899 to 1902, and a popular weekly (vocalized for easy reading), *Yidishe Folkstsaytung,* also in Cracow (1902–03), had a women's supplement, *Di Yidishe Froyen Velt.* These weeklies paved the way for the first Yiddish daily to appear in Russia—*Der Fraynd* (1903–08 in St. Petersburg, 1909–13 in Warsaw), which gained immediate acceptance by the Jewish masses and had a circulation of tens of thousands.

In the beginning of the 20th century, the older Hebrew dailies ceased publication (*Ha-Meliẓ* in 1904 and *Ha-Ẓefirah* in 1906) and were replaced by more modern newspapers, *Ha-Ẓofeh* (Warsaw, 1903–05) and *Ha-Zeman,* the latter founded by Benzion *Katz (St. Petersburg, 1903–04; Vilna, 1905–15), which tried to keep pace with the general Russian press in reporting the latest news and commenting upon it. At the end of the 19th century, the Bund undertook the publication of underground newspapers such as ***Arbeter Shtime, Der Yidishe Arbeter,*** and *Posledniye Izvestia,* which were printed in the West and smuggled into Russia.

At the end of 1905 censorship was abolished and the press enjoyed a short period of freedom. It soon turned out, however, that the authorities still retained means of controlling the press by administrative measures, ranging from economic reprisals (such as prohibiting advertising, stopping the sale of single copies, closing down the printing press) to temporary or permanent suspension of publication. The immediate result of the short interval of freedom was the appearance of party newspapers. The Bund published *Der Veker,* and, when this was closed down, *Folks Tsaytung* and other newspapers. The Zionist Socialists issued *Der Yidisher Proletarier, Der Nayer Veg,* and *Dos Vort.* Another workers' party, the *Sejmists, sponsored the *Folks Shtime.* *Po'alei Zion had a Yiddish weekly, *Der Proletarisher Gedank,* and a Russian periodical, *Yevreyskaya Rabochaya Khronika.* All these party publications disappeared in 1907, when the revolutionary movement was suppressed. The Zionist press, nevertheless, continued to flourish. There were Zionist newspapers in Yiddish (*Dos Yidishe Folk,* Vilna, 1906–08); in Hebrew (*Ha-Olam,* Cologne, 1907; Vilna, 1908; Odessa, 1912–14), and in Russian. The first Zionist Russian-language monthly was *Yevreyskaya Zhizn* (1904–06), followed by *Razsvet,* which became the most popular Russian Jewish weekly with a circulation of tens of thousands. Attempts were made to revive the Hebrew press in Warsaw with the dailies *Ha-Yom* (1906–07) and *Ha-Boker* (1909). In 1910, *Ha-Ẓefirah* also reappeared as a daily, and, with the support of the Zionist Organization, attained a circulation of 15,000.

The most significant development of this period, however, was the growth of a popular Yiddish press centered in Warsaw. At the end of 1905, a Yiddish daily, *Der Veg,* edited by Ẓevi *Prylucki, was founded in the Polish capital and became the forerunner of the popular Yiddish press in Poland. It was succeeded by *Haynt* (1908–39) and *Der Moment* (1910–39), two Yiddish dailies which catered to popular taste and reduced the price of the papers. Along with the news and literary articles they printed sensational items and fostered the cheap novel. The papers enjoyed a circulation of many thousands and acquired great influence. Politically they supported Jewish nationalism and Zionism. Yiddish periodicals also appeared in the large provincial cities (Odessa, Lodz, Vilna, Kiev) but were of local character. An extreme Orthodox weekly, *Ha-Modi'a,* made its appearance in Poltava from 1909.

The non-Zionist Russian Jewish intelligentsia issued its own weeklies, such as *Yevreyskiy Mir* (1910–12) and *Novy Voshkod* (1910–17), both published in St. Petersburg. There were also magazines devoted to special subjects, such as the educational magazines *Yevreyskaya Shkola* (1904–05) and *Vestnik,* the latter

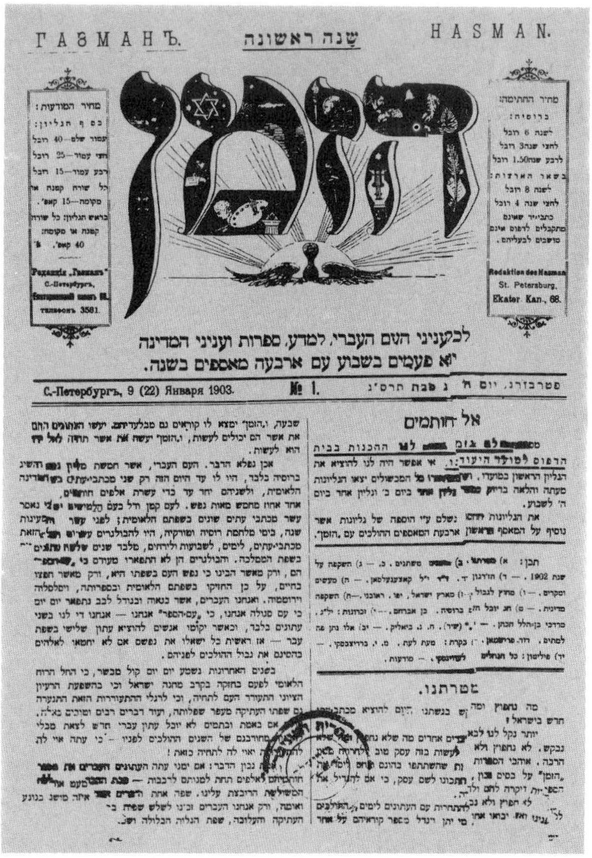
ГАЗМАНЪ.
שנה ראשונה
HASMAN.
מחיר המודעות:
מחיר החתימה:
Редакція „Гасманъ" С.-Петербургъ, Екатерининскій каналъ 68. телефонъ 3581.
Redaktion des Hasman St. Petersburg. Ekater. Kan., 68.
לכעניני העם העברי, למדע, ספרות ועניני המדינה
יוצא פעמים בשבוע עם ארבעה מאספים בשנה.
С.-Петербургъ, 9 (22) Января 1903. № 1. פטרבורג, יום ה׳ ג טבת תרס״ג

Figure 8. First issue of the Hebrew newspaper, *Ha-Zeman,* founded by Benzion Katz and edited by David Frischmann, St. Petersburg, 1903.

founded in 1910 by the Society for the Spread of Enlightenment; *Yevreyskiy Meditsinskiy Golos,* a medical quarterly founded in Odessa in 1908; *Perezhitoye,* a history annual; *Yevreyskaya Starina,* a scientific quarterly (1909–30); and *Vestnik Yevreyskoy Obshchini* (1913–14), which dealt with community administration. There were children's magazines in Hebrew, Russian, and Yiddish (see *Children's Literature). In 1913 a literary magazine *Di Yidishe Velt,* edited by S. *Niger and maintaining high standards, was founded in Vilna.

The outbreak of World War I caused a crisis in the Jewish press: the price of paper and printing rose sharply, and military censorship restricted freedom of expression. The advance of the Central Powers into Poland and Lithuania also separated the masses of readers from the sources of their newspapers. In July 1915 a government decree ordered all Hebrew and Yiddish journals to cease publication. Jewish papers in the Russian language, especially the Zionist-oriented *Razsvet,* did their best to fill the void. The ban was lifted with the outbreak of the February 1917 Revolution.

IN THE U.S.S.R. (1917–1970). The February 1917 Revolution ushered in a short period of freedom of the press which lasted until the Bolshevik Revolution in October. Newspapers independent of the Communist Party continued to appear until September–October 1918 and in some regions (such as the Ukraine and Belorussia) until Soviet rule was established there in 1920. This brief period proved to be the golden era of the Jewish press in the U.S.S.R. The leading newspapers were the Zionist Hebrew daily *Ha-Am* in Moscow (July 1917–June 1918), which had a circulation of 15,000 at its height, and the Zionist Yiddish daily *Tagblat* in Petrograd (May 1917–August 1918). Kiev had no less than four papers: the Bundist *Folks Tsaytung* (August 1917–May 1919), the United Socialists' *Naye Tsayt* (September 1917–May 1919), the Po'alei Zion's *Dos Naye Lebn* (December 1917–March 1919), and the Zionist *Der Telegraf* (November 1917–January 1918). Minsk had *Der Yid* (December 1917–July 1918) and *Far'n Folk* (September 1919–January 1920), which were both Zionist in outlook, and the Bundist *Der Veker* (first published in May 1917, and becoming a Communist paper in April 1921).

Hebrew periodicals were also revived after a two-year lapse. In Odessa, *Ha-Shilo'aḥ* resumed publication in June 1917 and continued until banned by the Soviet authorities in April 1919. In the same city, *Barkai,* the last of the Hebrew weeklies, appeared until the beginning of 1920. There were educational magazines such as *Ha-Ginnah* in Odessa, *Ha-Moreh* in Kiev, and *Ha-Makkabbi,* dealing with physical education. A children's magazine in Hebrew, *Shetilim,* was published in Petrograd. A number of annuals served as the forum for literary and scientific work, such as *Keneset, Massu'ot,* and *Ereẓ* in Odessa and *Olamenu* in Petrograd. Outstanding for size and quality was the quarterly *Ha-Tekufah,* the first three issues of which appeared in Moscow in 1918. Collections were devoted to history and ethnography: *He-Avar* (2 vols., Petrograd), *Reshumot* (1 vol., Odessa), and *Sefatenu* (Odessa). Publication of Hebrew periodicals ended with the ban on the use of Hebrew in the Soviet Union.

Before long, the Jewish press in the Russian language also ceased to exist. *Raszvet* was closed down in September 1918 and *Khronika Yevreyskoy Zhizni* in July 1919. In the period 1924–26, when *He-Ḥalutz was a legal organization, it published the central organ of the movement, *He-Ḥalutz,* in Moscow. The left Po'alei Zion was permitted to publish its central organ, *Yevreyskaya Proletarskaya Mysl,* until 1926 (with a Yiddish edition appearing until 1927). A group of writers and scholars, members of the long-established *Society for the Promotion of Culture and the Historical Ethnographical Society, published several collections of literary and historical pieces in the 1920s, including *Yevreyskaya Starina* (vols. 9–13, 1924–30), *Yevreyskaya Letopis* (4 vols., 1923–26), and *Yevreyskaya Mysl* (2 vols., 1922–26). One official publication in Russian, *Tribuna* (Moscow, 1927–37), the central organ of OZET (see *Yevsektsiya), was directed at the Jews.

When Yiddish was recognized as the national language of the Jews in the 1920s, the Yiddish press (like Yiddish literature and the Yiddish theater) became part of the official apparatus for mass propaganda and indoctrination. It was controlled by the authorities, but its writers and correspondents enjoyed the substantial material advantages accorded to all writers who were loyal supporters of the regime. A widespread network of newspapers, entirely dependent upon the regime for its existence and policy, was created. In the 1920s and 1930s, these newspapers had considerable achievements to their credit. There were three central dailies: in Moscow, *Der Emes* was first published in 1918 as *Di Varhayt* and ceased publication in 1938; in Kharkov, *Der Shtern* (1925–41); and in Minsk, *Oktyaber* (1925–41). In addition, there were numerous local papers, such as *Der Odeser Arbeter* (1927–37) and *Proletarisher Fon* (Kiev, 1928–35).

A newspaper, *Biro-Bidzhaner Shtern,* began to appear in *Birobidzhan in 1930; it continued into the 1970s, appearing three or four times weekly. Important literary periodicals included *Prolet* (1928–32), *Farmest* (1932–37), and *Sovietish Literatur* (1938–41), all published in the Ukraine; *Shtern* (1925–41), in Belorussia; and a literary annual, *Sovietish* (12 vols., 1934–41). Specialized publications, such as *Oyf dem Veg tsu der Nayer Shul* (Moscow, 1924–28) and *Ratebildung* (Kharkov, 1928–37) dealt with educational problems. Children found reading matter in *Oktyaber* (Kiev, 1930–39), *Zey Greyt* (Kharkov-Kiev, Kiev, 1928–41), and *Yunger Leninetz* (Minsk, 1929–37). The Jewish scientific institutes in Minsk and Kiev published periodicals on scientific and literary subjects and on the Yiddish language: *Tsaytshrift* (5 vols., Minsk, 1926–31); *Oyf'n Visnshaftlikn Front* (Minsk, 1932–35); *Lingvistisher Zamlbukh* (3 vols., Minsk, 1933–36); *Die Yidishe Shprakh* (Kiev, 1927–30), and *Oyf'n Shprakh Front* (Kiev, 1931–39).

In 1939–40, when eastern Poland and Lithuania were incorporated into the Soviet Union, local Yiddish newspapers were established to serve the Yiddish-speaking population in Vilna, Bialystok, Kovno, and Riga. With the Nazi occupation of large parts of the U.S.S.R. in the summer of 1941, the Yiddish press ceased publication. In 1942, to rally the Jews to the war against the Nazis, the Jewish *Anti-Fascist Committee established **Eynikeyt* in Kuibyshev. After the war, the paper moved to Moscow and continued to appear there. In the immediate postwar period, several literary journals also made their appearance: *Heymland* (7 vols., Moscow, 1947–48), *Der Shtern* (7 vols., Kiev, 1947–48), and *Biro-Bidzhan* (3 vols., 1946–48).

In November 1948, all Yiddish literary publications and the entire Yiddish press in the Soviet Union were liquidated. The "thaw" that set in after Stalin's death brought no revival. In the summer of 1961, in response to pressure exerted by Jewish public opinion in the West, a bimonthly, **Sovetish Heymland,* was founded, and subsequently published the works of the remaining Yiddish writers in the U.S.S.R. In 1965 *Sovetish Heymland* became a monthly publication, claiming a circulation of 25,000 in 1967.

[Y.S.]

In Scandinavia. Jewish newspapers in Sweden before World War II included: the Yiddish fortnightly *Volkshilf* (1916–1923); and the monthly *Israeliten,* founded in 1914, as well as two monthlies, *Judisk Tidskrift* (1928–) and *Juediska Kroenika* (1932–). The Jewish community of Stockholm issued its own quarterly, *Försammlingsblad,* from 1941 under the editorship of David Kőpnivski. A later arrival was the *Center Bladet,* which was founded as a family journal in Stockholm in 1966. It appears about five times a year in Swedish, deals with Jewish communal life, youth clubs, and the problems of Israel, and reaches about 1,400 Jewish homes. Two Jewish publications existed in Norway before World War II: the Zionist monthly *Ha-Tikvah,* founded in 1929, which did not survive the war, and the quarterly *SJUF-Bladet* of the Scandinavian Jewish Youth Organization. Founded in 1917, the organization revived its periodical after World War II and issued it in Norwegian, Swedish, and Danish. The magazine also circulates among the Jewish communities of Finland, where a knowledge of Swedish is widespread. This magazine also supports the maintenance of Jewish tradition. In Finland, *Den Finski Juden* (1918) of Viborg was short-lived, but the *Judisk Krönika,* a monthly founded in Helsinki in 1923, had a longer career. The first attempt at publishing a Jewish journal in Denmark was made at the beginning of the 19th century. It was called *Nordlyset* and was an answer to current anti-Semitic literature. When the Jewish community achieved full civil rights in 1814, the publication was no longer considered necessary. In 1857 and 1865 new publishing attempts were made, but the *Israelitisk Ugeblad for Norden* and *Israelitisk Tidende* appeared only for a few issues. In 1907 two periodicals were started. The Zionist leader Louis Fraenkel was the editor of *Jødisk Tidsskrift,* a fortnightly of literary standard which survived for only a year and a half. The other was *Mosaisk Samfund,* which survived until the German occupation of Denmark in 1940. With the influx of immigrants from Eastern Europe, the need arose for a Yiddish press and in 1911 *Dos Yidishe Vokhenblat* appeared, edited by Joseph Litischevsky. The paper flourished until 1921. Other Yiddish papers were *Di Yugendshtime* and *Yidishe Folkstsaytung*, the latter as a daily from 1917 to 1925. From 1920 to 1923 the Scandinavian Jewish youth organization produced the Copenhagen *Israeliten* edited by Max Goldschmidt. In 1929 Goldschmidt founded *Jødisk Familieblad* which, after two changes of name (*Jødisk Samfund* and *Jødisk Orientering*), is now in its fifth decade. Among its editors was Chief Rabbi Marcus Melchior, and from 1947 it was edited by Torben Meyer. In 1947 the Zionist Federation issued *Palestine Telegram Service* as a weekly, which in 1950 turned into a periodical called *Israel*. [L.S.]

In South Africa. The bulk of Jewish journalism in South Africa has been in English in the form of weeklies, which have enjoyed wide readership and considerable advertising support. The earliest attempts at establishing a Jewish press, however, were in Yiddish. They date from 1890 when N. D. Hoffman imported Hebrew type and started *Der Afrikaner Israelit* in Johannesburg; it lasted for six months. Since then there has been an almost continuous, if tenuous, line of Yiddish publications, including *Der Kriegstaphet*, a daily run by David Goldblatt in Cape Town from 1899. Hoffman also started a fortnightly Hebrew journal, *Kinneret*, which ran for 12 issues in 1905. The first Jewish newspaper in English was *The South African Jewish Chronicle*, started as a fortnightly in Cape Town by Lionel L. Goldsmid (1867–1952). In 1970 the most prominent journals were: in English, *The Zionist Record* and *The South African Jewish Chronicle* (1908–), *The South African Jewish Times* (1936–), and *Jewish Herald* (1937–), all weeklies; *Jewish Affairs* (1941–) and the *Federation Chronicle* (1954–), monthlies; in Yiddish, *Afrikaner Yidishe Tsaytung* (1930–), a weekly; *Dorem Afrike* (1948–), literary journal; and in Hebrew, *Barkai* (1932–bi-monthly). All were published in Johannesburg. [L.S.]

In Switzerland. Apart from a monthly periodical of the 1830s, the first attempt to establish a regular medium of Jewish news was made by Alexander *Kisch, who in 1878–80 issued in Zurich a German-language fortnightly *Neue Israelitische Zeitung*. The first journalistic effort to meet with any success was the *Juedische Volkszeitung*, later the *Israelitisches Wochenblatt Zentralorgan fuer die Israeliten in der Schweiz, Baden und Elsass-Lothringen*, which appeared from 1895 to 1898 under the editorship of H. Berliner.

The first newspaper to prove of enduring influence was the German-French *Israelitisches Wochenblatt fuer die Schweiz/Revue Juive*, which was founded in Zurich in 1901 by Martin Littman (d. 1925) and David Strauss (d. 1921). Ownership and editorship passed in 1916 to David Weinbaum and in 1921 to Erich-Marx Weinbaum, whose son, Manfred Marx, took over in 1966. Hans Klee directed the weekly from 1953 to his death in 1959, with Leon Wohlmann as main contributor for more than 20 years. Kurt Roschewski became editor in 1958. In its earlier years, the ***Israelitisches Wochenblatt*** was a journal on communal life that contained religious and other reading matter. Later it widened its field of interest and published reports on Zionism, Palestine, and world Jewry. After the creation of the State of Israel, the paper added comprehensive reports on events in Israel and acquired a wide readership in Switzerland, Alsace, and other German-speaking Jewish districts of Europe. A Zionist weekly, *Juedische Pressezentrale*, appeared from 1917 to 1940 in Zurich under the editorship of Oscar Gruen, and numbering Hermann Witzhum and Benjamin Segalowitz (d. 1970) among its contributors. The Zionist fortnightly *Das Juedische Heim* had a short career from 1927. In Basle the *Juedische Rundschau-Maccabi*, a Zionist weekly, appears from 1940 as an independent organ in German with Adrien Blum as editor. The establishment of the State of Israel in 1948 stimulated further enterprises. *Das Neue Israel* was founded in June of that year as the monthly organ of the Swiss Zionist Organization, with the additional aim of furthering relations between Switzerland and Israel. Containing both German and French contributions, it has appeared under the editorship of Veit Wyler since its inception. Another monthly, *Liaison*, with Daniel Halperin, Emanuel Haymann and Michael Wyler as editors, was initiated in Geneva in 1967 as a magazine of news, politics, and the arts. [V.W.]

In the United States. In addition to English, four other languages have served as the vehicle for a Jewish press in the United States. A flourishing German Jewish press came into being as a result of Jewish immigration from Central Europe in the mid-19th century and thrived for over 50 years. Of considerably more importance, far exceeding even the Anglo-Jewish press in size and vitality, was the Yiddish press, the product of the great Eastern European immigration to the U.S. in the late 19th and early 20th centuries. This same immigration also led to the establishment of a modest Hebrew press. Finally, early in the 20th century, Jewish immigrants from the Balkans founded a number of periodicals in Ladino (see above: Ladino Press). By 1970, however, the Anglo-Jewish press alone continued to be read regularly by significant numbers of American Jews. Of the foreign-language Jewish publications still appearing, many were being published partly in English, while most had dwindling readerships. [ED.]

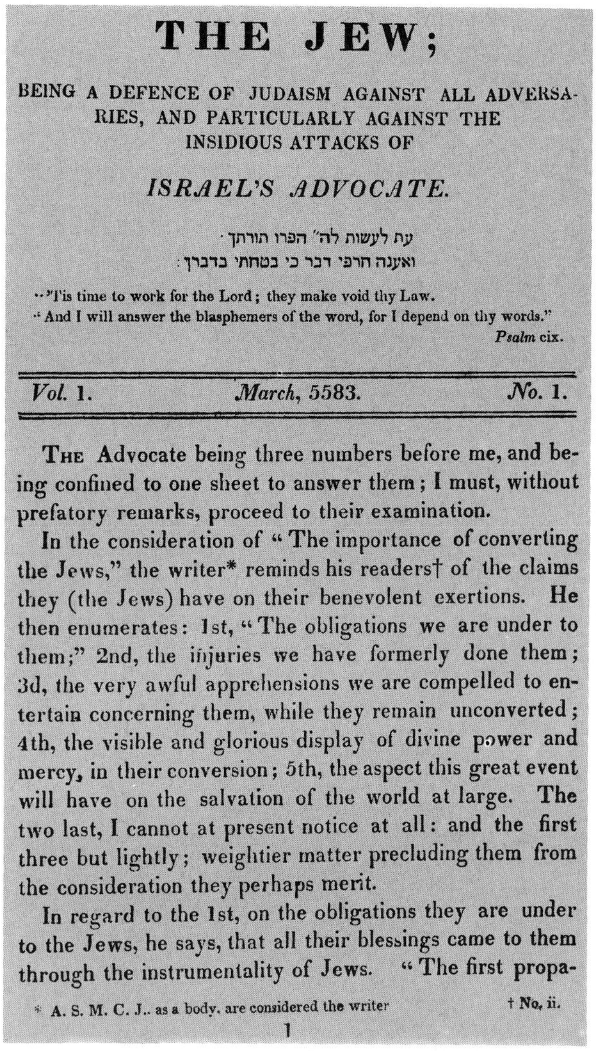

THE JEW;

BEING A DEFENCE OF JUDAISM AGAINST ALL ADVERSARIES, AND PARTICULARLY AGAINST THE INSIDIOUS ATTACKS OF

ISRAEL'S ADVOCATE.

עת לעשות לה׳ הפרו תורתך ·
ואענה חרפי דבר כי בטחתי בדברך׃

"'Tis time to work for the Lord; they make void thy Law.
" And I will answer the blasphemers of the word, for I depend on thy words."
Psalm cix.

Vol. 1. *March*, 5583. *No.* 1.

THE Advocate being three numbers before me, and being confined to one sheet to answer them; I must, without prefatory remarks, proceed to their examination.

In the consideration of "The importance of converting the Jews," the writer* reminds his readers† of the claims they (the Jews) have on their benevolent exertions. He then enumerates: 1st, "The obligations we are under to them;" 2nd, the injuries we have formerly done them; 3d, the very awful apprehensions we are compelled to entertain concerning them, while they remain unconverted; 4th, the visible and glorious display of divine power and mercy, in their conversion; 5th, the aspect this great event will have on the salvation of the world at large. The two last, I cannot at present notice at all: and the first three but lightly; weightier matter precluding them from the consideration they perhaps merit.

In regard to the 1st, on the obligations they are under to the Jews, he says, that all their blessings came to them through the instrumentality of Jews. "The first propa-

* A. S. M. C. J.. as a body, are considered the writer † No. ii.

1

Figure 9. First issue of *The Jew*, the first American-Jewish newspaper, founded to combat missionary activity, New York, March 1823. Cincinnati, Ohio, American Jewish Archives.

ANGLO-JEWISH PRESS. According to the 1970 *American Jewish Year Book*, there were about 51 Anglo-Jewish weeklies in the United States, 17 biweeklies, 36 monthlies, and 28 quarterlies, besides one daily news bulletin and a number of established publications appearing at less regular intervals. This activity can be traced back to 1823, when S. H. Jackson, a New York printer, started *The Jew* with the intention of combating missionary influence. Twenty years later Isaac *Leeser founded *The Occident*, a monthly devoted mainly to religious articles from a traditionalist standpoint but containing news items as well. The first Anglo-Jewish weekly in the U.S. was *The Asmonean*, started in New York by Robert Lyon in 1849 as a "family journal of commerce, politics, religion, and literature." Apparently successful, *The Asmonean* ceased publication after Lyon's death in 1858. It was followed by *The Hebrew Leader* (1856–82), but more important, it formed the model for *The Israelite* (later known as *The *American Israelite*), which I. M. *Wise launched when he settled in Cincinnati in 1854. The *Asmonean* was thus the overall prototype for what became the characteristic element of the Anglo-Jewish press: the privately owned weekly covering local, national, and overseas news, and carrying serialized fiction, feature articles, and editorial comments. Among early examples of this type of publication were the New York *Jewish Messenger* (1857–1902), founded by the Orthodox S. M. *Isaacs, and the *San Francisco Gleaner* (1855) of Julius *Eckman. *The American Hebrew,* established by a group of five young men in 1879, traditional in its religious views, represents perhaps the best level to which this class of journal attained.

Unlike *The Asmonean,* many of these weeklies, *The Israelite* most obviously, had as their primary object the projection of their editors' opinions, a characteristic they shared with much of the general U.S. press at the time. (A surviving example of such personal journalism is *The Jewish Spectator,* put out by Trude *Weiss-Rosmarin from 1935.) When this impulse waned after 1900 approximately, such papers became dependent for their survival on commercial considerations, and as none of them had developed into a national organ, concentration on local news seemed most advantageous. Moreover, as the daily press, especially in the New York area, began to give more space to Jewish news, Jewish weeklies lacking resources or stimulus to cover the same news in greater depth were again led to concentrate on local items. Thus they tended to become increasingly parochial. Many Jewish weeklies, such as the Philadelphia *Jewish Exponent* (est. 1887), have become community property outright, while in other cases advertising or block purchase of copies has made Jewish papers dependent on local institutions. In recent times the influence of community institutions has been further enhanced by the fact that the Jewish Telegraphic Agency (est. 1918), from which the Anglo-Jewish press obtains the bulk of its extra-local news, is supported by the Council of Jewish Federations and Welfare Funds.

A parallel development has been the growth of periodicals directly sponsored by Jewish organizations. One of the first of these was the B'nai B'rith *Menorah* (1886–1907), which was followed by the *B'nai B'rith News,* whose name was later changed to the *B'nai B'rith Magazine* (1924) and the *National Jewish Monthly* (1939). This example has been followed in one way or another by most of the major organizations in U.S. Jewry. A prominent example is the monthly *Hadassah Magazine,* with an organizational circulation exceeding 300,000. Also to be mentioned are the American Jewish Congress' *Congress Weekly* (est. 1934, biweekly since 1958), *The Reconstructionist* (est. 1930), the Labor Zionist *Jewish Frontier* (est. 1934), and **Midstream.* Probably the most intellectually influential periodical of this sort is the American Jewish Committee's **Commentary.* In 1952 the American Jewish Congress began to publish *Judaism,* a quarterly largely devoted to Jewish thought. In the field of religion and theology there are *Conservative Judaism* (est. 1954), the Reform *Dimensions in American Judaism,* (est. 1966), and the Orthodox *Tradition* (est. 1958), all quarterlies. During the late 1960s an autonomous "radical" Jewish student press emerged on campuses and in metropolitan areas in the United States and Canada, with a common editorial philosophy that was critical of the established American Jewish community, politically leftist, yet pro-Israel. Its prime concerns were the reordering of the priorities of organized Jewry, with an emphasis on Jewish education, the establishment of a just and equitable peace in the Middle East, the plight of Soviet Jewry, and general problems of students and of society. [S.D.T.]

German Jewish Press. The large German Jewish immigration to the United States in the middle of the 19th century gave a pronounced German quality to U.S. Jewry, and led naturally to the creation of a Jewish German-language press of considerable dimensions. German remained the language of U.S. Jewish congregations and organizations for a relatively long time. From about 1850, German Jewish periodicals appeared in many of the major and some of the less important cities in the United States, such as New York, Baltimore, Boston, Cincinnati, Memphis, Milwaukee, Philadelphia, San Francisco, St. Louis, and Syracuse. Some were exclusively German, others both German and English, and yet others were supplements to English publications. Practically all were weeklies or monthlies, many passing from the one status to the other, and then on to more irregular intervals, on their way to extinction. The total number of such publica-

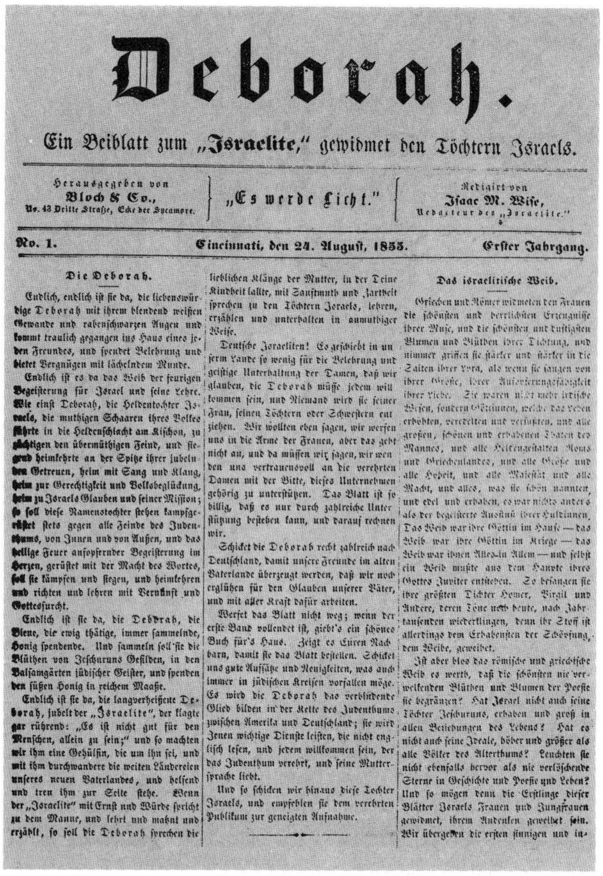

Deborah.

Ein Beiblatt zum „Israelite," gewidmet den Töchtern Israels.

Herausgegeben von Bloch & Co., No. 43 Dritte Straße, Ecke der Sycamore. | „Es werde Licht." | Redigirt von Isaac M. Wise, Redakteur des „Israelite."

No. 1. Cincinnati, den 24. August, 1855. Erster Jahrgang.

Die Deborah.

Endlich, endlich ist sie da, die liebenswürdige Deborah mit ihrem blendend weißen Gewande und rabenschwarzen Augen und kommt traulich gegangen ins Haus eines jeden Freundes, und spendet Belehrung und bietet Vergnügen mit lächelndem Munde.

Endlich ist es da das Weib der feurigen Begeisterung für Israel und seine Lehre. Wie einst Deborah, die Heldentochter Israels, die muthigen Schaaren ihres Volkes führte in die Heldenschlacht am Kischon, zu züchtigen den übermüthigen Feind, und siegend heimkehrte an der Spitze ihrer jubelnden Getreuen, heim mit Sang und Klang, heim zur Gerechtigkeit und Volksbeglückung, heim zu Israels Glauben und seiner Mission; so soll diese Namenstochter stehen kampfgerüstet stets gegen alle Feinde des Judenthums, von Innen und von Außen, und das heilige Feuer aufopfernder Begeisterung im Herzen, gerüstet mit der Macht des Wortes, soll sie kämpfen und siegen, und heimkehren und richten und lehren mit Vernunft und Gottesfurcht.

Endlich ist sie da, die Debdrah, die Biene, die ewig thätige, immer sammelnde, Honig spendende. Und sammeln soll sie die Blüthen von Jeschuruns Gefilden, in den Balsamgärten jüdischer Geister, und spenden den süßen Honig in reichem Maaße.

Endlich ist sie da, die langverheißene Deborah, jubelt der „Israelite", der klagte gar rührend: „Es ist nicht gut für den Menschen, allein zu sein;" und so machten wir ihm eine Gehülfin, die um ihn sei, und mit ihm durchwandere die weiten Ländereien unseres neuen Vaterlandes, und helfend und treu ihm zur Seite stehe. Wenn der „Israelite" mit Ernst und Würde spricht zu dem Manne, und lehrt und mahnt und erzählt, so soll die Deborah sprechen die lieblichen Klänge der Mutter, in der Deine Kindheit lallte, mit Sanftmuth und Zartheit sprechen zu den Töchtern Israels, lehren, erzählen und unterhalten in anmuthiger Weise.

Deutsche Israeliten! Es geschieht in unserm Lande so wenig für die Belehrung und geistige Unterhaltung der Damen, daß wir glauben, die Deborah müsse jedem willkommen sein, und Niemand wird sie seiner Frau, seinen Töchtern oder Schwestern entziehen. Wir wollten eben sagen, wir werfen uns in die Arme der Frauen, aber das geht nicht an, und da müssen wir sagen, wir wenden uns vertrauensvoll an die verehrten Damen mit der Bitte, dieses Unternehmen gehörig zu unterstützen. Das Blatt ist so billig, daß es nur durch zahlreiche Unterstützung bestehen kann, und darauf rechnen wir.

Schicket die Deborah recht zahlreich nach Deutschland, damit unsere Freunde im alten Vaterlande überzeugt werden, daß wir noch erglühen für den Glauben unserer Väter, und mit aller Kraft dafür arbeiten.

Werfet das Blatt nicht weg; wenn der erste Band vollendet ist, giebt's ein schönes Buch für's Haus. Zeigt es Euren Nachbarn, damit sie das Blatt bestellen. Schicket uns gute Aufsätze und Neuigkeiten, was auch immer in jüdischen Kreisen vorfallen möge. Es wird die Deborah das verbindende Glied bilden in der Kette des Judenthums zwischen Amerika und Deutschland; sie wird Jenen wichtige Dienste leisten, die nicht englisch lesen, und jedem willkommen sein, der das Judenthum verehrt, und seine Muttersprache liebt.

Und so schicken wir hinaus diese Tochter Israels, und empfehlen sie dem verehrten Publikum zur geneigten Aufnahme.

Das israelitische Weib.

Griechen und Römer widmeten den Frauen die schönsten und herrlichsten Erzeugnisse ihrer Muse, und die schönsten und duftigsten Blumen und Blüthen ihrer Dichtung, und nimmer griffen sie stärker und stärker in die Saiten ihrer Lyra, als wenn sie sangen von ihrer Größe, ihrer Aufopferungsfähigkeit ihrer Liebe. Sie waren nicht mehr irdische Wesen, sondern Göttinnen, welche das Leben erhöhten, veredelten und versüßten, und alle großen, schönen und erhabenen Thaten des Mannes, und alle Heldengestalten Roms und Griechenlandes, und alle Größe und alle Hoheit, und alle Majestät und alle Macht, und alles, was sie schön nannten, und edel und erhaben, es war nichts anders als der begeisterte Ausfluß ihrer Huldinnen. Das Weib war ihre Göttin im Hause — das Weib war ihre Göttin im Kriege — das Weib war ihnen Alles in Allem — und selbst ein Weib mußte aus dem Haupte ihres Gottes Jupiter entstehen. So besangen sie ihre größten Dichter Homer, Virgil und Andere, deren Töne noch heute, nach Jahrtausenden wiederklingen, denn ihr Stoff ist allerdings dem Erhabensten der Schöpfung, dem Weibe, geweihet.

Ist aber blos das römische und griechische Weib es werth, daß die schönsten nie verwelkenden Blüthen und Blumen der Poesie sie begränzen? Hat Israel nicht auch seine Töchter Jeschuruns, erhaben und groß in allen Beziehungen des Lebens? Hat es nicht auch seine Ideale, höher und größer als alle Völker des Alterthums? Leuchten sie nicht ebenfalls hervor als nie verlöschende Sterne in Geschichte und Poesie und Leben? Und so mögen denn die Erstlinge dieser Blätter Israels Frauen und Jungfrauen gewidmet, ihrem Andenken geweihet sein. Wir übergeben die ersten sinnigen und in-

Figure 10. First issue of *Deborah,* a German-language American Jewish newspaper founded by Isaac Mayer Wise, Cincinnati, Ohio, August 24, 1855. Cincinnati, Ohio, American Jewish Archives.

tions, including some that appeared for one issue only, was nearly 100.

The first German Jewish weekly in the United States and the first Jewish weekly to be published in any language in New York was *Israels Herald,* which appeared briefly in 1849. Its editor was Isidor *Bush, who had previously been the publisher in Vienna of the *Kalender und Jahrbuch fuer Israeliten.* Among his contributors were a number who had written for the *Kalender,* among them Leopold *Zunz. Although the *Herald* received financial help from B'nai B'rith, it failed after three months and 12 issues. In 1854 Isaac Mayer Wise founded *The Israelite* in Cincinnati (after 1874 *The American Israelite*), which one year later added a German-language supplement called *Deborah.* The most important German Jewish publication of its time, *Deborah* appeared until 1903, first as a weekly and subsequently as a monthly. The shifting nature of its contents during this period can be read in the changing subtitle on its masthead: originally *Gewidmet den Toechtern Israels* ("Dedicated to the Daughters of Israel"), it next became *Juedisch-Amerikanische Familien Zeitung* ("Jewish American Family Paper"), then *Allgemeine Zeitung des amerikanischen Judentums* ("General Newspaper of American Jewry"), and finally *Eine deutsch-amerikanische Monatsschrift zur Foerderung juedischer Interessen in Gemeinde, Schule und Haus* ("A German-American Monthly Magazine for the Advancement of Jewish Interests in the Community, School and Home").

Sinai (1856–63), an English and German monthly published by Rabbi David *Einhorn was noteworthy on account of its radical Reform and vigorous abolitionism. The English and German weekly *The Hebrew Observer* existed in San Francisco for over 30 years (1856–88), while Cincinnati's *The Sabbath Visitor* (1874–95) had a German supplement for much of its career. Two notable German Jewish publications survived into the 20th century, the monthly *Der Freund Israels* ("The Friend of Israel," 1880–1907), edited by P. Weber in Baltimore, and the one-page German supplement of *The Hebrew* in San Francisco (1863–1912).

The contents of the German Jewish press in the U.S. reveal that besides such topics of general Jewish interest as education, religion, and charity, its readers were concerned with the problem of identity: the first generation of immigrants tended to think of itself as part of the larger German-speaking colony in the United States, while the second generation identified strongly with native America. Both young and old preserved a definite sense of their Jewishness, especially from the 1870s on, when anti-Semitic attitudes on the part of newly rich gentiles toward newly rich Jews began to be felt. Toward the end of the century some small German Jewish papers committed to Zionism, as well as others of a socialist or anarchist persuasion, appeared and disappeared quickly.

The large German Jewish immigration to the United States during the Nazi period led to the founding in New York in 1934 of the weekly *Aufbau* ("Reconstruction"), which began as a newsletter of the German Jewish Club. Under the editorship of Manfred *George, the *Aufbau* developed into a paper of high journalistic standards with an emphasis on the analysis of political and cultural events in the U.S. and elsewhere from a Jewish point of view. After George's death in 1965 the *Aufbau* was edited by Hans Steinitz. Its circulation in 1970 was 25,000. [F.R.L.]

YIDDISH PRESS. The history of the rise, golden age, and decline of the Yiddish press in the U.S. parallels that of the arrival and absorption of the great Eastern European Jewish immigration that flowed to the United States in the last quarter of the 19th and first quarter of the 20th centuries. It took place largely in New York City, whose preeminence as a center of Jewish immigration and Yiddish culture in the New World was never challenged elsewhere.

The first attempt at a Yiddish newspaper in New York appeared as early as 1870 when J. K. Buchner, an immigrant from Prussia, published his *Juedische Zeitung,* which ambitiously aspired to keep the reader abreast of all aspects of "politics, religion, history, science, and art"—a foreshadowing of the broad scope and sense of acculturating mission that was to characterize the Yiddish press in the U.S. in years to come. With the help of a political subsidy from Tammany Hall, the paper appeared irregularly until at least 1876, longer than Ẓevi Hirsch Bernstein's and Henry Gershoni's *Juedische Post* (1870–71) and the *New Yorker Yidishe Tsaytung* (1872) of Kasriel *Sarasohn, who justly deserves to be called the father of the U.S. Yiddish press. Sarasohn's next publication, the weekly *Yidishe Gazeten* (1874–85, thereafter the weekly magazine of the *Tageblat*), proved more successful and gradually absorbed or outlived such competitors as the *New Yorker Israelite* (1875), the *Yidishe Folkstsaytung* (1878–80), and Abraham *Goldfaden's *Yidishe Illustrierte Tsaytung* (1884–88). Meanwhile, the first Yiddish weekly outside of New York, the *Israelitische Press* (1877–84), was founded in Chicago but moved to New York three years later. In 1881 Sarasohn launched the first Yiddish daily in the U.S. and indeed in the world, the *Teglikhe Gazeten,* but within two months financial troubles forced the paper to return to a weekly status, while a second attempt to publish it daily failed again in 1883. All of these early efforts were traditionalist in outlook and written in a formal, Germanized Yiddish far removed from the speech of the immigrant masses.

In 1885 Sarasohn established a successful Yiddish daily at last, the politically and religiously conservative *Yidishes Tageblat* (1885–1928). Meanwhile, the rise of political activism among Jewish immigrants in the late 1880s and 1890s led to the founding of a number of Yiddish periodicals with a more radical and ideological content and a more popular style. These included the socialist *Naye Tsayt* (1886), edited by Abraham *Cahan, the *New Yorker Yidisher Folkstsaytung* (1886–89), United Hebrew Trades' *Arbayter Tsaytung* (1890–1902), and the **Zukunft* (1892–), edited by Phillip *Krantz; the anarchist *Warheit* (1889), *Fraye Geselshaft* (1895–1914), and *Fraye Arbayter Shtime* (1890–93, 1899–) of S. *Janovsky; and Zionist publications such as Joseph *Bluestone's *Shulamis* (1890–91) and Menahem *Dolitzky's *Di Tsayt* (1897–98). Of the independent weeklies, the most prominent was the *Folksadvokat* (1888–1925). The *Tageblat* was followed by a second New York daily, Michael Mintz's *Teglikher Herald* (1891–1905), while in 1894, on the heels of the great cloakmakers' strike, the first socialist daily, the *Abendblatt* (1894–1902), made its appearance under the editorship of Phillip Krantz. In 1897 the ideological quarrel that had split the American Socialist Labor Party into left-wing and right-wing factions flared up in the *Abendblatt* as well, and the more moderate staff, led by Abraham Cahan and Louis *Miller (Bandes), left to found the **Jewish Daily Forward.* By the turn of the century the daily Yiddish press alone spanned nearly the entire spectrum of opinion in the immigrant community and had a circulation of close to 75,000, the equivalent of several hundreds of thousands of readers, concentrated largely on New York's Lower East Side, for whom it served as an indispensable source of news, entertainment, guidance, and political orientation in their adopted homeland.

With the founding of the *Forward* a new era can be said to have been ushered in, and the history of the Yiddish press in the U.S. ceased to be parochial and sectional and strove on a firmly professional basis to compete with its English counterpart in size, numbers of readers, and quality of reportage. Even in their period of greatest prosperity large Yiddish papers like the *Forward* kept few reporters in the field and tended to rely for all but local news on the national and international wire services; at the same time, however, they devoted much of their pages to serious fiction, belles lettres, and articles of all sorts on economics, politics, history, and sociology, of a kind rarely seen in daily English newspapers. The *Forward* was soon followed by several equally ambitious ventures. The Orthodox publisher Jacob Saphirstein was the first to enter the field with the afternoon *Abendpost* (1899–1903), and two years later, with the **Jewish Morning Journal* (1901–). The following year witnessed the founding under the editorship of Zvi Hirsch *Masliansky of the short-lived *Jewish World* (1902–04), which was sponsored by the Educational Alliance and had the financial backing of an impressive array of wealthy "uptown" Jews led by Louis *Marshall, who hoped to wean the Yiddish reader away from the political and religious extremism of the immigrant ghetto and hasten the process of his Americanization. More successful was Louis Miller's social-democratic *Warheit* (1905–19). Bitter competition between these rivals made them seek to outdo each other in illustrated weekend magazines, popular romances or *shundenromanen,* and human-interest features and "scoops" of all kinds, to attack each other politically, to raid each other for talent, and to aggressively hawk each day's edition on the streets by means of newsboys and often sensational headlines.

The first decade of the 20th century witnessed several attempts to establish Yiddish dailies in other American cities where immigrants had settled in large numbers, such as Boston, Baltimore,

די נויאָרקער
יידישעטשע צייטונג
Hebrew Times.
ערשיינט
יעדע וואָכע פרייטאַג מאָרגענס
№ 1, פרייז זעכס צענט פער נוממער

Figure 11. First issue of the *New Yorker Yidishe Tsaytung,* the first Yiddish paper published in the U.S., New York, March 1, 1870. Jerusalem, J.N.U.L.

and Philadelphia, where Yiddish weeklies had been in existence since the early 1890s. The most notable were the *Chicago Daily Courier* (1887–1944, daily after 1892) and the *Cleveland Jewish World* (1908–43). None of these endeavors was able to compete for long with the Yiddish papers that were trucked in from New York every day.

Another feature of these years was the proliferation of topical Yiddish periodicals in New York. Among these weeklies and monthlies were humor magazines like *Der Groyser Kibitser* (1908–14) and Jacob *Marinoff's *Der Groyser Kundes* (1909–27), literary publications like Abraham *Reisin's *Naye Land* (1910–11) and David *Pinski's *Yidishe Vokhenshrift* (1912), journals of opinion like Chaim *Zhitlowsky's *Naye Lebn* (1909–13) and the **Yidisher Kemfer* (1905–), and theatrical reviews like Jacob *Gordin's *Theater Journal and Familienblatt* (1901–02). In addition there were local Yiddish trade journals, papers catering to specific immigrant groups from Hungary, Rumania, and Galicia, and even neighborhood papers such as the *Brownsviller Post* (1910–c. 1920) and the *Bronx-Harlem Presse* (1913–14). Most of these were started on a shoestring and many failed to survive the first few issues.

World War I marked a high point for the Yiddish press in the U.S. The new flood of immigrants in the prewar years and anxiety in the immigrant community over the fate of relatives and Jewish life in Eastern Europe sent the readership of Yiddish dailies soaring to new heights. Two or more editions a day were frequently the rule and in the peak year of 1915–16 the circulation of the daily Yiddish press reached 500,000 in New York City and 600,000 nationally. Reflecting the anti-Russian sentiments that were widely prevalent at the time in the Jewish community, most Yiddish papers took a pro-German position until American entry into the war, at which times they were forced to do an embarrassing about-face; only the newly founded **Jewish Day* (1914–) supported the Allies from the outset. The *Forward*, on the other hand, was editorially alone in refusing to condemn the Bolshevik Revolution in 1917, though before long it too took a hostile stand against Russian communism.

The years after World War I marked the beginning of the U.S. Yiddish press' long decline. The restrictive Immigration Act of 1924 cut off the flow of Yiddish-speaking immigrants to the United States, while the inevitable processes of aging and acculturation began to take their toll of the existing generation of readers, whose Americanized children preferred to read the news in English. Several older papers merged—the *Day* and the *Warheit* in 1919, the *Morning Journal* and the *Tageblat* in 1928—while attempts to establish new ones such as *Haynt* (1919), *Di Tsayt* (1920–22), *Dos Yidishe Likht* (1926–27), and the Chicago *Yidishe Arbayter Velt* (1917), soon foundered financially. The one permanent addition to the daily Yiddish press was the pro-communist **Morning Freiheit* (1922–), which owed its continued existence largely to support from the American Communist Party. Apart from it, however, ideological differences in the Yiddish press grew smaller, reflecting a similar closing of ranks in the immigrant community and U.S. Jewry as a whole. Both the *Forward* and *Morning Journal* abandoned their opposition to Zionism, while as the former grew politically more conservative, the latter became religiously less so. From a literary point of view, the Yiddish press enjoyed its most outstanding array of talent during these years: in addition to such older novelists, poets, and essayists who regularly contributed to its pages such as Aaron *Glanz, Joel *Entin, Joseph *Opatoshu, H. *Leivick, Moshe Leib *Halpern, Zisho *Landau, David *Ignatoff, Sholem *Asch, Abraham *Reisin, and Zalman *Shneur, there was an influx of new writers like Shmuel Niger, Jacob *Glatstein, Jonah *Rosenfeld, I. J. *Singer, and Melech *Ravitch. The early 1940s brought with them such additional talents as Isaac *Bashevis Singer, Aaron *Zeitlin, and Chaim *Grade. Yet throughout the 1920s and the 1930s falling circulations forced the Yiddish dailies to cut back on the size of their staffs and editions. By 1939 their combined circulation had fallen to about 400,000, while a study in 1945 showed a further reduction to 300,000 readers whose average age was 55.

Despite the modest Yiddish-speaking immigration that came to the United States in the wake of World War II, the Yiddish press continued to lose its long war of attrition, which was further aggravated by rapidly rising production costs and the competition of radio and television. The *Day* and *Morning Journal* merged in 1953, leaving but three Yiddish dailies in the entire United States, and after 1967, in the whole of North America. As of 1970 their combined circulation was about 100,000. Apart from the Chicago quarterly *Unzer Veg* (1945–), all Yiddish periodicals in the United States were published in New York, many with organizational support. The more prominent of these included the weekly *Yidishe Kemfer* (1905–); the monthlies *Zukunft* (Congress for Jewish Culture, 1892–), *Der Veker* (Jewish Socialist Verband, 1921–), *Unzer Veg* (United Labor Zionist Party, 1925–), *Yidishe Kultur* (Yiddisher Kultur Farband, 1938–), and *Unzer Tsayt* (International Jewish Labor Bund, 1941–); and the bimonthlies *Fraye Arbayter Shtime* (1890–) and *Kultur un Lebn* (Workmen's Circle, 1967–).

For Hebrew press in the U.S., see *Newspapers, Hebrew. [H.H.]

Bibliography: J. Fraenkel, *Jewish Press of the World* (1967). CANADA: L. Lakson, in: *Yidisher Almanak* (1923), 262–4; A. Rhinewine, *Der Yid in Kanade* (1925), 210–20. BELGIUM: Z. Szajkowski, in: *Studies in Bibliography and Booklore*, 4 (1959/60), 103–22. CZECHOSLOVAKIA: O. Donath, *Židé a židovství v české literatuře 19. a 20. století*, 2 vols. (1923–30); M. Enten, *Zsidó sajtó jelene Csehszlovákiában* (1933); A. Dagan, in: *Jews of Czechoslovakia*, 1 (1968), 523–31. ENGLAND: C. Roth, *Jewish Chronicle 1841–1941* (1949); V. D. Lipman, *Social History of the Jews in England 1850–1950* (1954), 131. FRANCE: Z. Szajkowski, in: E. Tcherikower (ed.), *Yidn in Frankraykh*, 1 (1942), 236–308. GERMANY AND AUSTRIA: JL, 4 (1930), 1102–10, iv–vi; xxii–xxiv; M. T. Edelheim-Muehsam, in: YLBI, 1 (1956), 163–76; *Juedische Presse im 19 Jahrhundert; Aus dem Internationalen Zeitungsmuseum der Stadt Aachen* (1967), 7–86. HOLLAND: I. Lipschits, *Honderd jaar N.I.W. 1865–1965* (1966); *Catalogue: De Joodse Pers in de Nederlanden en in Duitsland, 1674–1940* (1969; also in German). HUNGARY: Ẓ. Spirn, in: *Zukunft*, 28 (1923), 309–12 (Yid.); N. Katzburg, in: *Aresheth*, 1 (1958), 279–98; S. Scheiber, in: KS, 32 (1956/57), 481–94; N. Ben-Menahem, *Mi-Sifrut Yisrael be-Ungaryah* (1958), 224–35, 379. ITALY: E. Zolli, in: *Ost und West*, 6 (1906), 823–8; idem, *Il giornalismo israelitico in Italia* (1924); A. Milano, in: RMI, 12 nos. 7–9 (1938), 96–136. LADINO PRESS: M. D. Gaon, *Ha-Ittonut be-Ladino* (1965). MIDDLE EAST AND NORTH AFRICA: C. Souriau, in: *Annuaire de L'Afrique du Nord*, 6 (1967); A. Yaari, *Ha-Defus ha-Ivri be-Arẓot ha-Mizraḥ*, 2 vols. (1936–40); Y. Ben-Hananya, in: *Al-Yawn* (June 13, 1958); idem, in: *Yad la-Kore*, 4 (1956/57), 14–21, 119–28; S. Moreh, in: *Middle Eastern Studies*, 3 (1966/67), 283–94; A. Ben-Jacob, *Yehudei Bavel* (1965), index s.v. *Ittonim*. RUSSIA: A. Kirzhnitz, *Di Yidishe Prese in Rotnfarband 1917–1927* (1928); idem, *Di Yidishe Prese in der Gevezener Rusisher Imperiyeh 1823–1916* (1930); *Fun Noentn Over*, 2 (1959); S. L. Citron, *Di Geshikhte fun der Yidisher Prese 1863–1889* (1923); J. Slutzky, in: *He-Avar*, 11 (1964), 37–52; idem, *Ha-Ittonut ha-Yehudit-Russit ba-Me'ah ha-19* (1970). U.S.S.R.: Ch. Shmeruk (ed.), *Pirsumim Yehudiyyim bi-Verit ha-Mo'aẓot 1917–1960* (1961); M. Altschuler (ed.), *Pirsumim Rusiyyim bi-Verit ha-Mo'aẓot Al Yehudim ve-Yahadut 1917–1967* (1970; bibl. in Russian; introd. in Eng. and Heb.). SOUTH AFRICA: J. A. Poliva, *A Short History of the Jewish Press and Literature of South Africa* (1961). UNITED STATES. ANGLO-JEWISH PRESS: C. Angoff, in: *Jewish Spectator* (Nov. 1957), 24–26; J. Neusner, in: *Congress Bi-Weekly*, 29 no. 5 (1962), 9–11; *National Jewish Monthly*, 61 (1946), 94–95, 108f.; B. Postal, in: *Dimensions in American Judaism*, 4 (Fall, 1969), 30. GERMAN JEWISH PRESS: R. Glanz, *German Jew in America; an Annotated Bibliography . . .* (1969). YIDDISH PRESS: H. Hapgood, *Spirit of the Ghetto* (1902), ed. by H. Golden (1965), 176–98; M. Rischin, *Promised City: New York's Jews 1870–1914* (1962), 115–27; R. Sanders, *Downtown Jews: Portraits of an Immigrant Generation* (1969), index, s.v. *Yiddish newspapers;* M. Soltes, *Yiddish Press—An Americanizing Agency* (1950); J. L. Teller, *Strangers and Natives* (1968), 27–36; J. Shatzky (ed.), *Zaml-Bukh tsu der Geshikhte fun der Yidisher Prese in Amerike* (1934), esp. 13–21; idem, in: *Algemeyne Entsiklopedye: Yidn*, 3 (1942), 256–75; M. Starkmann, in: J. Shatzky (ed.), *Zamlbukh Likhvod dem Tsvey Hundert un Fuftsiksten Yovel fun der Yidisher Prese* (1937), 115–35; idem, in: *Zukunft*, 67 (1962), 471–80 (Yid.); idem, in: S. Rawidowicz (ed.), *Pinkas Chicago* (1952), 69–78 (Yid.).

PRESS, FRANK (1924–), U. S. geophysicist. Born in Brooklyn, Press was a pupil of Beno *Gutenburg and joined the staff of Columbia University in 1946. In 1955 he was appointed professor of geophysics at the California Institute of Technology, where he headed the seismology laboratory. In 1965 he transferred to the Massachusetts Institute of Technology as head of the department of geology and geophysics. Press served on the President's Scientific Advisory Committee from 1961 to 1964 and was a consultant to the Department of Defense. He earned the reputation of being the leading seismologist in the U.S. and his research included submarine geology and geophysics, crystal and mantle structure as well as lunar seismology and pulse propagation in the atmosphere. He published *Elastic Waves in Layered Media* (with Ewing and Jardetzky, 1957). [Ed.]

PRESS, YESHAYAHU (1874–1955), Israel historian and topographer of Ereẓ Israel. Press was born in the Old City of Jerusalem. He was a teacher and headmaster of the Laemel School until his retirement and was active in the civic life of Jerusalem for almost 50 years. His scholarly work was devoted to the history of Ereẓ Israel, and especially of its Jewish communities. His main work is *Ereẓ Yisrael Enẓiklopedyah Topografit-Historit—A Topographical-Historical Encyclopedia of Palestine* (4 vols., 1946–55). His memoirs *Me'ah Shanah bi-Yrushalayim*, published posthumously (1964), are a vivid description of life in the Old City.

Bibliography: M. Ish-Shalom et al. (eds.), *Yerushalayim*, 4 (1953), 7–11. [M.A.-Y.]

PRESSER, JACOB (1899–1970), Dutch historian and writer. Presser was born in Amsterdam. He studied history at the University of Amsterdam and wrote a thesis about *Das Buch "De Tribus Impostoribus"* (1926). He became professor of modern history at the University of Amsterdam (1948), and was best known for his history of the deportation and extermination of Dutch Jewry (*Ondergang: de vervolging en verdelging van het Nederlandse Jodendom 1940–45*, 1965; *The Destruction of Dutch Jews*, 1969).

During the Nazi occupation, when he was in hiding, Presser wrote may poems, most of them in memory of his wife, Deborah Appel, who had been deported. These poems were published after World War II in various volumes, notably *Orpheus en Ahasverus* (1945), which appeared under the pseudonym of J. van Wageningen. Presser's short story, "De nacht der Girondijnen" (1957; "Breaking Point," 1958) was a poignant account of the Dutch Jewish transport camp of Westerbork. Presser also wrote detective stories. His historical works include studies of Dutch history (*De tachtuig-jarige Oorlog*, 1941), Napoleon (1946), and U.S. writing (*Amerika, Van Kolonie tot Wereldmacht*, 1949). [L.D.J.]

PRESSMAN, LEE (1906–1969), U.S. lawyer. He left his law practice in order to accept a position in Roosevelt's New Deal administration. In 1934, while assistant general counsel in the Agricultural Adjustment Administration, Pressman gravitated within the Communist Party orbit. Although he severed formal affiliation with the party after leaving government service a year later, he did not break ideologically with Stalinism until 1950. In 1937 Pressman became counsel for the Steel Workers Organizing Committee, and soon thereafter general counsel for the CIO. Brilliant and quickwitted, Pressman won the confidence of John L. Lewis, and later, CIO president, Philip Murray. He came to be considered "indispensable" in CIO administrative matters. While holding his position in the CIO, Pressman continued to consult with Communist Party leaders. However, he was actually forced to act more as a check on, rather than agent of, the Stalinist interests in the CIO. Pressman resigned from the CIO in 1948 to back the Progressive Party standard-bearer Henry Wallace's unsuccessful attempt for the presidency. He retired to the practice of law during the Korean War.

Bibliography: M. Kempton, *Part of Our Time* (1955), 37–81; U.S. House of Representatives: Committee on Un-American Activities, *Hearings Regarding Communism in the United States Government*, 81 Congress 2 Session (1950), 2844–901. [K.W.]

PRETORIA, administrative capital of the Republic of South Africa. The earliest Jewish settlers after the foundation of Pretoria in 1855 were among the officials whom the Boer government brought from Holland. One such was M. de Vries, and although the laws of the Transvaal Republic placed civil disabilities upon non-Protestants, he became state prosecutor in 1868 and a member of the Volksraad (Legislative Assembly) in 1871. Jewish communal life dates from 1876, when *minyanim* were held in the home of Daniel M. Kisch, a photographer, and a Jewish wedding was celebrated in 1878. The first meeting of the congregation was held there in 1890, and the first synagogue building was consecrated in 1898. The first minister, the Rev. E. Jaffe, was appointed the following year. Jewish institutions include the United Hebrew Congregation (with two

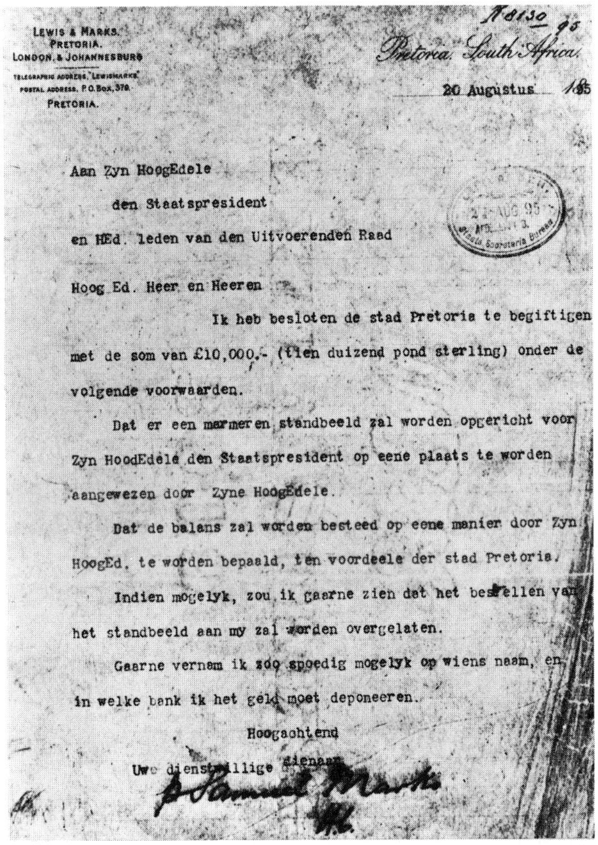

LEWIS & MARKS.
PRETORIA.
LONDON, & JOHANNESBURG
TELEGRAPHIC ADDRESS, "LEWISMARKS"
POSTAL ADDRESS, P.O. BOX, 370.
PRETORIA.

N 8130 95

Pretoria, South Africa,
20 Augustus 1895

Aan Zyn HoogEdele
den Staatspresident
en HEd. leden van den Uitvoerenden Raad

Hoog Ed. Heer en Heeren

Ik heb besloten de stad Pretoria te begiftigen met de som van £10,000.- (tien duizend pond sterling) onder de volgende voorwaarden.

Dat er een marmeren standbeeld zal worden opgericht voor Zyn HoodEdele den Staatspresident op eene plaats te worden aangewezen door Zyne HoogEdele.

Dat de balans zal worden besteed op eene manier door Zyn HoogEd. te worden bepaald, ten voordeele der stad Pretoria.

Indien mogelyk, zou ik gaarne zien dat het bestellen van het standbeeld aan my zal worden overgelaten.

Gaarne vernam ik zoo spoedig mogelyk op wiens naam, en in welke bank ik het geld moet deponeeren.

Hoogachtend
Uwe dienstwillige dienaar
Samuel Marks

Letter from Samuel Marks, Pretoria financier, to President Paul Kruger and the Pretoria Municipal Council, informing them of his decision to donate £10,000 to the town of Pretoria for the purpose of erecting a statue of the president, 1895. Courtesy South African Jewish Board of Deputies, Johannesburg. Photo centenary album of Pretoria.

synagogues) and the Progressive Jewish Congregation, a Jewish day school (Carmel College, up to matriculation standard), a *ḥevra kaddisha* and other philanthropic bodies, a branch of the Union of Jewish Women, a Zionist Council, and a community council which acts as a coordinating body. The Jewish population numbered 3,553 in 1969 (1.2% of the total population).

Bibliography: G. Saron and L. Hotz (eds.), *The Jews in South Africa* (1955). [Ed.]

PREUSS, HUGO (1860–1925), German jurist and politician, creator of the Weimar constitution. Born in Berlin, Preuss was elected to the Berlin city council where he advocated a new system of decentralized government based on strong, independent municipal councils. Preuss was an authority on German constitutional law and lectured at the University of Berlin but was refused a professorship because of his Jewish origins and liberal view. In 1906 he became professor of public law at the Berlin Handelshochschule and later rector. At the end of World War I Preuss became minister of the interior of the new

Hugo Preuss, creator of the Weimar constitution. Jerusalem, J.N.U.L., Schwadron Collection.

German republic and headed the committee drafting the so-called Weimar constitution. It was hailed as the epitome of democracy in liberal circles but was attacked by right-wing circles as being "Un-German." Preuss opposed the signing of the Versailles Peace Treaty and resigned from the government. Though not active in Jewish affairs and an opponent of Zionism, Preuss was highly regarded in Jewish circles.

Bibliography: E. Feder, *Hugo Preuss* (Ger., 1926); W. Simons, *Hugo Preuss* (Ger., 1930); S. Grossmann, *Hugo Preuss* (Ger., 1965); T. Heuss, *Profile* (Ger., 1964), 255–67; H. Preuss, *Staat, Recht und Freiheit* (1926), preface by T. Heuss, incl. bibl. [Ed.]

PREUSS, JULIUS (1861–1913), German physician and medical historian. Born in Gross-Schoenebeck (Saxonia), Preuss settled in Berlin as a practitioner and became an important writer on medicine in Jewish sources. He also took an active part in Orthodox community life. Preuss scientifically researched the problems of biblical and talmudic medicine, and his writings on the subject have remained a reliable guide.

His series on Hebrew medicine and Jewish medical men began with his *Der Arzt in Bibel und Talmud* (separate publication of *Virchow's Archiv*, 138 (1894), 261ff.). It was followed by a large number of essays on various aspects of biblical and talmudic medicine in scientific and literary journals. These were later collected in *Biblisch-talmudische Medizin* (1911, repr. 1921, 1923, 1969). The book is a model of scholarly research and presentation and has become a classic reference work.

Bibliography: *Korot*, 2 (1961), nos. 9–10 (incl. bibl. and Eng. summaries); S. R. Kagan, *Jewish Medicine* (1952), 562; J. Carlebach, *Zur Erinnerungen an Sanitaetsrat Dr. Julius Preuss...* (1913). [S.M.]

°**PREZIOSI, GIOVANNI** (1881–1945), Fascist journalist and leading theorist of racial anti-Semitism in Italy. Even before World War I, Preziosi, a former priest, began a crusade to preserve "Italianness" from "foreign intrigue," chiefly through the review he founded in 1913, *La Vita Italiana all' Estero* (later renamed *La Vita Italiana*). In 1917 Preziosi formed one of the first *Fasci*. In August 1920, with an article in *La Vita Italiana* entitled "The Jewish International," he initiated a campaign of hatred and slander against Jews and Judaism, with the avowed purpose of "inoculating anti-Semitism into the blood of the Italians." Preziosi was an anomaly on the Italian scene, even among Fascist hotheads, and more than anyone else he was responsible for preparing the Italian people for the psychological acceptance of racism. The anti-Semitism of *Farinacci and even *Mussolini was chiefly political and opportunistic, while Preziosi, inspired by his own phobias, saw the Jews, both foreign and Italian, as objective enemies who had "infiltrated" Italy at all levels. In 1921 he was the first to publish the Italian version of the *Protocols of the Elders of Zion*, which he reissued in 1937. Preziosi's ideas were the main inspiration for the July 1938 *Manifesto della Razza*, which served as a basis for the subsequent racial legislation and discrimination. In 1941 he became minister of state, ever in quest of "integral racism" and complete friendship with Germany. Under German pressure Mussolini appointed Preziosi head of the Inspectorate for Racial Affairs (Ufficio della Razza) in March 1944, during the last and most brutal phase of Italian Fascism. In April 1945 he committed suicide.

Bibliography: R. de Felice, *Storia degli ebrei italiani sotto il fascismo* (1961), index; J. Starr, in: JSOS, 1 (1939), 105–24; G. Bedarida, *Ebrei d'Italia* (1950), index. [E.B.]

PRIBRAM, ALFRED FRANCIS (1859–1942), historian and political publicist. Pribram, who was born and died in London, was professor of history at the University of Vienna from 1894 to 1930.

He wrote copiously on 17th-century Austrian history and published scholarly editions of documents on international relations, including the dispatches of Venetian ambassadors to the Court of Vienna. He edited the final volume of Heinrich Friedjung's *Das Zeitalter des Imperialismus* (3 vols., 1919–22) and, after 1918, contributed to the study of the "war guilt" problem, notably the role of Austria-Hungary, with his *Austrian Foreign Policy 1908–1918* (1923). His lectures at Oxford University were published in 1931 as *England and the International Policy of the European Great Powers, 1871–1914*. His work on the relations between Austria and Britain before World War I appeared in an English translation in 1951 as *Austria-Hungary and Great Britain 1908–1914*. In 1938 he published *Materialien zur Geschichte der Preise und Loehne in Oesterreich*. Pribram's contribution to Jewish history was *Urkunden und Akten zur Geschichte der Juden in Wien* (2 vols., 1918). [H.A.S.]

PRIBRAM, KARL (b. 1877), economist. Born in Prague, he obtained his professional training in Prague, Berlin, and Vienna. From 1907 to 1914 he taught at the University of Vienna, and in 1911 he entered the Austrian civil service. During 1921–28 he served as head of the statistical office of the International Labor Office in Geneva, and in 1928 he became professor of economics at the University of Frankfort. After moving to the United States in 1934, he was successively connected with the Brookings Institution, in Washington, D.C., the Social Security Administration, and the United States Tariff Commission. After his retirement in 1951, he taught at the American University in Washington and in Frankfort.

Pribram was an authority in the field of the history of economic thought and of international commercial policy. His main publications include *Cartel Problems* (1935); *Conflicting Patterns of Thought* (1949); and *Prolegomena to a History of Economic Reasoning* (in *Journal of Economics*, 65, 1951). [J.O.R.]

PRIESTLY BLESSING (Heb. בִּרְכַּת כֹּהֲנִים), the formula in Numbers 6:24–26 ordained by God and transmitted to the priests by Moses for the blessing of Israel. Verse 27, "They shall invoke My name on behalf of the Israelites and I will bless them," makes explicit the intent of the ordained formula: to invoke the power of the Lord, who alone dispenses blessing. The threefold arrangement of the benediction may reflect an older incantation form; the three verses probably represent synonymous rather than climactic parallelism.

The blessing has been customarily translated "The Lord bless you and keep you; the Lord make His face to shine upon you and be gracious to you; the Lord lift up His countenance upon you and grant you peace." The literalness of this translation obscures the

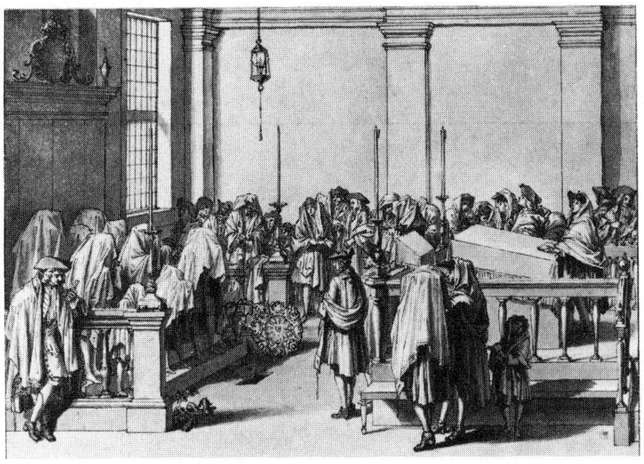

Figure 1. The Priestly Blessing given in the Portuguese synagogue of the Hague, drawing by Bernard Picart, early 18th century. Amsterdam, Stedelijk Museum.

force of the Hebrew and fails to convey the court imagery of the biblical idiom. In biblical idiom the king shows favor (the verb *ḥanan*) to his subjects by giving them audience, access to "the light of his face," whereas his disfavor is expressed by "hiding" his face from them. The third verse of the benediction presents a problem, for the king never "lifts up his face upon" his subjects as a token of favor: "to lift one's own face" means "to look up" (II Kings 9:32), and it is rather the recipient of favor whose "face is lifted up" (who is *nesu panim* by the one who shows favor, see II Kings 3:14; Job 42:8, 9). In the blessing, however, the idea seems to be that of raising the features in a smile, the opposite of dropping them in a frown (cf. *lo appil panai ba-khem;* lit. "I will not drop my face against you," Jer. 3:12; cf. Gen. 4:5–6; Job 29:24). Finally, favor is a good deal more than the mere absence of hostility; consequently not just "peace" but friendship is what *shalom* means here, as in Judges 4:17 and in *beriti shalom* (Num. 25:12), and *berit shelomi* (Isa. 54:10), both of which mean "my covenant/promise of friendship." If one further assumes that a ו *(vav)* has been omitted at the end of שָׁלוֹם before the ו *(vav)* at the beginning of וְיָשֵׂם לְךָ, וְשָׂמוּ שְׁלוֹמוֹ will mean the exact opposite of אָסַפְתִּי אֶת שְׁלוֹמִי מֵאֵת הָעָם הַזֶּה ("I have withdrawn my friendship from that people"; Jer. 16:5). With this small change, the rendering of Numbers 6:24–26 in the Jewish Publication Society's translation of the Pentateuch (1962) is reproduced below in order to bring out the synonymity of the verses:

The Lord bless you and keep you!
The Lord deal kindly and graciously with you!
The Lord bestow His favor upon you and grant you His friendship!

The structure of this threefold blessing is interesting to note: the first sentence contains three words, the second five words, and the third seven words. The name of the Deity (*Tetragrammaton) is found in the second word of each sentence. [H.Br.]

In the Halakhah. This priestly blessing was part of the Temple cult. Every morning and evening at the *Tamid offering, the priests ascended a special platform called **dukhan* (the Yiddish expression *dukhenen,* i.e., "to deliver the priestly blessing," is derived from this), and pronounced the blessing with their hands uplifted (Mid. 2:6; Tam. 5:1; 7:2; Sot. 7:6; Meg. 18a, etc.). In rabbinic literature the Priestly Blessing is also known as *nesi'at kappayim* ("raising of the hands"). On Sabbaths and festivals the Priestly Blessing was pronounced also at the *Musaf* service and on certain public fast days during the *Minḥah* service, too (Maim. Yad, Tefillah, 14:1–2). In the Temple the priests uttered the *Tetragrammaton whereas in the synagogues *Adonai* was substituted (Sot. 38a). The congregation then responded "Blessed be the Lord God, the God of Israel, to all eternity" (Sot. 40b).

During the time of the Second Temple the Priestly Blessing was pronounced outside the Temple in the synagogues; after the destruction of the Temple and the cessation of the sacrificial cult it became the main remnant of priestly ritual. It was also inserted into the last benediction of the *Amidah.* Every adult kohen is enjoined to perform this function unless disqualified by certain physical and other defects. Thus a kohen may not participate in the ritual if he has killed a person, committed idolatry, married a woman forbidden to him, or is intoxicated. He is also disqualified if he suffers from certain physical deformities or is unable to articulate the words properly (Ber. 32b; Meg. 24b; Ta'an. 26b; Maim. Yad, Tefillah, 15:1–6; Sh. Ar., OḤ 128:30–41). It was argued, in explanations of these rules, that physical defects might distract the attention of the congregants, or that bodily perfection was a symbol for a perfect soul (Philo, *De Monarchia,* 2:5)

The Priestly Blessing is pronounced only at a public synagogue service with the required quorum of ten male adults (Sh.Ar., OḤ 128:1). If all worshipers are priests, some of them ascend to say the blessing while the rest listen to it as "congregants" (Sot. 38b). Priests in mourning are exempted from participating in the ritual, but should leave the synagogue before the *ḥazzan* invites the priests to ascend the platform. Originally the Priestly Blessing was part of the morning service each weekday, but as the daily business of the people did not allow them to concentrate with proper devotion, it was reserved, in the Diaspora, for Sabbaths and holidays. Local customs differ as to the place (**Shaharit* or **Musaf*) and time of the recital of the Priestly Blessing. The general *Ashkenazi custom is to recite it only on the High Holidays and three *pilgrim festivals. In Ereẓ Israel, it is customary to recite it every Sabbath both at *Shaḥarit* and *Musaf* and in Jerusalem, every day. If the Priestly Blessing is not performed for some reason, its text is recited by the *ḥazzan* at the end of his repetition of the *Amidah* before the last benediction.

The general procedure of the Priestly Blessing is: After **Kedushah* the priests prepare themselves, removing their shoes and washing their hands with the assistance of the levites, whereafter they ascend the platform before the Ark. The *ḥazzan* then recites the prayer: "Our God and God of our fathers, bless us with the threefold blessing of the Law, written by the hand of Moses Thy servant, which was spoken by Aaron and his sons the priests . . . " At this last word, the priests turn toward the congregation and pronounce the benediction for the *mitzvah* of the Priestly Blessing. In Israel, however, it is customary for a member of the congregation to call out *"kohanim"* immediately after the 17th blessing of the *Amidah* at which the priests begin their benediction. The *ḥazzan* says each word of the Priestly Blessing which is then repeated aloud by the priests.

The kohanim recite the blessing with their prayer shawls drawn forward to cover their heads and their hands stretched out at shoulder height with the palms facing forward. The hands are held touching at the thumbs with the first two fingers of each hand separated from the other two, thus forming a sort of fan. This figure became the device of the kohanim and is often inscribed on their tombstones. It has become the custom not to look at the kohanim while they are performing the Priestly Blessing. In many communities the father draws his children to himself and covers them with his *tallit.* Originally the congregants listened silently to the Priestly Blessing, but in the course of time they began to accompany it with the silent recital of appropriate biblical quotations (Sot. 40a). There is a widespread custom to respond "Amen" after each of the three sections of the Priestly Blessing, when said by kohanim but "so may it be Thy will" when the *ḥazzan* recites it. In the course of time considerable magical power came to be ascribed to the Priestly Blessing, especially the power to neutralize bad dreams, which were considered to be evil omens for the future. Thus, a special prayer to God

Figure 2. Priestly Blessing at the Western Wall, Jerusalem, 1971. Photo K. Weiss, Jerusalem.

to turn bad dreams into blessings was inserted in some rites, and said by the congregants at the end of both the first and the second verse (Ber. 55b). Later, other prayers of kabbalistic origin were added to those recited by the congregation. They necessitated the prolonging of the Priestly Blessing, and this was accomplished by the insertion of a chant by the priests before the final word of each section. This custom impinged on the solemn character of the Priestly Blessing, but although opposed by some rabbis (e.g., Moses of Przemysl, *Matteh Moshe,* 1 (1591), 193) it became widely accepted.

In Conservative Judaism the recital of the Priestly Blessing by the priests is optional. *Reform Judaism discarded the notion of special priestly privileges in modern times; the Priestly Blessing is read by the rabbi as a closing benediction at the end of the service. The Priestly Blessing is also used as a formula of blessing at other ceremonies such as circumcisions or weddings (**ḥuppah*) where it is recited by the officiating rabbi. See also *Blessing of Children.

Bibliography: S. Abramson, in: *Turei Yeshurun,* 16 (1970), 15–17; Maim., Yad, Tefillah; Sh. Ar., OḤ 128f.; Elbogen, Gottesdienst, 67ff.; Eisenstein, Yisrael, s.v. *Nesi'at Kappayim,* Eisenstein, Dinim, 58, 276f.; JE, 3 (1902), 244–7; H. D. Halevy, in: *"Shevilin,"* 18–19 (1967), 114–28. [ED.]

PRIESTLY VESTMENTS, the special garments that were worn by the priests during divine worship, as was customary in cultic services in the Ancient Near East and elsewhere (see e.g., II Kings 10:22). The priests are commanded to leave their priestly garments in the holy chambers after the service (Ezek. 42:14; 44:19), and to refrain from carrying them into the outer court (Lev. 6:4). It is likewise stated: "He shall then take off his garments and put on other garments," the latter apparently referring to garments worn by the people, as in Ezekiel 42:14. (The talmudic sages (Yoma 23b) disputed whether these were priestly garments inferior to the former ones or profane garments.) In the Bible, the priestly garments are described only in the Priestly Code. Several of them are briefly referred to in Ezekiel 44:17–18; the ephod, the sole exception, is also mentioned in non-Priestly sources. Many scholars maintain that with respect to the garments, the Priestly Code reflects post-Exilic times, for, according to the prevalent view, this source was not committed to writing until this period. The ephod mentioned in sources other than the Priestly Code is held by these scholars to be either an image, not a garment, a garment of divine images, or the earliest priestly garment. However, it actually appears that all the garments described in the Priestly Code are from the pre-Exilic period, and it is only this source which had need to describe them, since it is a priestly work whose contents called for such a description.

Several features characterize the priestly vestments. Some of them are made "for splendor and for beauty" (Ex. 28:40); others, as is usual with cultic apparel, undoubtedly preserve vestiges of an old style, while some reflect acts of cultic significance. The breeches were for modesty (see below). Bearing as they do the hallmark of holiness, the priestly garments as a whole are frequently referred to as holy garments (see below). A total of eight garments, the number also prescribed by the sages (Yoma 7:5), are enumerated in the Priestly Code, but only Aaron attired himself in all eight. Of these, the four undergarments are to be worn by the common priests too, but those of Aaron are somewhat more embellished. Mentioned as a special group in connection with Aaron as well as with the common priests are four other garments of simple linen, which were worn when acts of extraordinary holiness were performed.

The four undergarments are to be made of fine twined linen *(shesh moshzar),* that is, a superior quality of linen; an exception within this group is Aaron's girdle made of a mixture *(kilayim)* of fine linen and wool. The four undergarments consist of:

(1) A coat. Of Aaron's coat it is said: "And you shall weave the coat in checkerwork of fine linen" (Ex. 28:39), and hence it is called "a coat of checkerwork" (28:4; cf. the ornamented coat mentioned in connection with Joseph in Gen. 37:3ff., and Tamar in II Sam. 13:18–19). No mention is made of checkerwork with respect to the coats of the

HIGH PRIEST

COMMON PRIEST

Model of the high priest and common priest wearing their vestments. The models were prepared by Moshe Levin for his book *Melekhet Hammishkan,* Tel Aviv, 1968. High priest: 1. blue band, פְּתִיל תְּכֵלֶת; 2. miter, מִצְנֶפֶת; 3. gold plate, נֵזֶר; 4. onyx stones with names of the tribes (6 on each stone), אַבְנֵי הַמִּלּוּאִים; 5. robe of the ephod, מְעִיל הָאֵפוֹד; 6. breastplate, חֹשֶׁן; 7. blue band, פְּתִיל תְּכֵלֶת; 8. band of the ephod, חֵשֶׁב אֵפוֹד; 9. ephod, אֵפוֹד; 10. bells of gold and pomegranates of dyed wool and linen, פַּעֲמוֹנִים וְרִמּוֹנִים; 11. coat, כְּתֹנֶת; 12. girdle, אַבְנֵט. Common priests: 1. headdress, מִגְבַּעַת; 2. coat, כְּתֹנֶת; 3. girdle, אַבְנֵט.

common priests (Ex. 28:39–40; cf. Ibn Ezra's comment). In Second Temple times, the priests' coats descended apparently to the ankles and had sleeves reaching to the palms (Jos., Ant., 3:153; cf. Yoma 72b; Maim., Yad, Kelei ha-Mikdash, 8:17).

(2) A girdle. The girdle, bound around the coat, is also regarded as a vestment of distinction (cf. Isa. 22:21). Whereas the girdles of the common priests were made exclusively of fine twined linen (Ex. 28:39), Aaron's was of fine linen and dyed wools and was of embroidered work, *ma'aseh rokem* (Ex. 28:39; 39:29).

(3) A headdress. For the common priests turbans or "decorated turbans," *pa'are migba'ot*, are prescribed, while for Aaron there is a miter, *miẓnefet* (Ex. 28:39–40; 39:28; cf. Ezek. 44:18). The "decorated turban" is considered an attire of beauty and distinction (cf. *pe'er* in Isa. 3:20; 61:3, 10; Ezek. 24:17), but more imposing is the miter, which is mentioned as synonym for crown (Ezek. 21:31; cf. Isa. 62:3).

(4) Breeches. The breeches are worn "to cover the flesh of their nakedness; from the hips to the thighs" (Ex. 28:42; 39:28; Ezek. 44:18).

The four outer garments, which pertain specifically to the high priest, are of greater richness and splendor than the undergarments. They consist of a mixture of dyed wool and fine linen, and display "skillful workmanship," *ma'aseh ḥoshev*. Some also contain threads of pure gold, while others are woven of gold filaments and yarn of a mixture of wool and linen. In conformity with the system of the Priestly Code, these costly substances allude to a high degree of holiness, as is also attested by the mixture of wool and linen. Such a mixture was generally prohibited in profane garments as it was conducive to holiness (Lev. 19:19; Deut. 22:9–11). Precisely for this reason, however, it was preserved among the priests. In this respect, the priestly garments correspond to the curtains and the veil of the Tabernacle, which are also said to have been made of a mixture of wool and linen, and have displayed "skillful workmanship" (Ex. 26:1, 31, et al.).

The very wearing of the four outer garments is regarded as an act of worship and is connected with the other acts performed by the high priest inside the Temple. True, nowhere is it specifically stated that the high priest has to wear the four outer garments when he enters to officiate inside the Temple, that is, to perform the daily cultic act in the morning and in the afternoon. Furthermore, from Second Temple times there are evidences that the high priest actually appeared in court dressed in garments of gold and a mixture of wool and linen (Ecclus. 45:7ff.; Jos., Wars, 5:239). However, this custom seems to have come into being in Second Temple times, whereas in the pre-Exilic period the high priest wore the outer garments only when he officiated inside the Temple. Proof of this is the fact that in composition as well as mode of workmanship these garments resemble the curtains and the inner vessels of gold, while the undergarments resemble the hangings and screens in the court. Moreover, the outer garments are too heavy, cumbersome, and splendid for the tasks performed at the outer altar.

The four outer garments have several features characteristic of royalty (the gold, the blue, and the purple, as well as the crown) and when combined with the miter and with the anointing oil poured on the high priest (Ex. 29:7, et al.) they give him a regal appearance. In Ezekiel's constitution there is no mention of these garments; of the priestly vestments, Ezekiel knows only those of ordinary linen (Ezek. 44:17–8), just as there is no hint in Ezekiel of the existence of the high priesthood itself.

The four outer garments are the following:

(5) The ephod, made of gold and a mixture of wool and linen, displaying "skillful workmanship" (Ex. 28:6–12; 39:2–7). This is the most distinguished of the priestly garments; hence it alone is mentioned in the Former and the Latter Prophets (Judg. 8:27; 17:5; Hos. 3:4, et al.). A garment by this name is mentioned in Ugaritic writings (*ipd;* C. H. Gordon, *Ugaritic Textbook* (1965), 67, 1:5) and in the Assyrian documents from Cappadocia (*epattu*).

(6) The breastplate, measuring a span by a span, attached to the ephod. It is either a square tablet or a pouch. In it are set 12 precious stones on which are engraved the names of the tribes of Israel, and on the breastplate are placed the *Urim and the Thummim. The breastplate is made in the same manner as the ephod—that is, of gold and a mixture of wool and linen, and displayed "skillful workmanship" (Ex. 28:15–30; 29:8–21).

(7) The robe of the ephod, that is worn under the ephod. The robe is probably longer than the ephod, and extends below it. It is made of woolen threads only, all of blue. On its hem hang bells of gold and pomegranates of a mixture of dyed wool and fine linen (Ex. 28:31–35; 39:22–26). The number of bells and pomegranates, not specified in the text, was a subject of controversy among the sages, who disputed over whether there were 72 or 36 (Zev. 88b), while still other numbers were given by Church Fathers. In Second Temple times the robe, like the tunic, apparently reached the high priest's heels (Jos. Ant., 3:159; Jos. Wars, 5:231; cf. Philo, II Mos. 118–21).

(8) The plate also called a crown, *nezer*, hangs on a blue thread in front of the miter. Made of pure gold the plate has two words engraved on it: *qodesh le-YHWH*, "Holy to the Lord" (Ex. 28:36–38; 39:30–31), as stated by the sages (Shab. 63b, et al.). However, in Second Temple times, apparently only the Tetragrammaton was inscribed on it (Jos., Ant., 3:178; cf. Jos., Wars, 5:235; Philo, II Mos. 115, 132; Arist. 98).

Shoes are not included among the priestly vestments and the priests evidently ministered barefoot, as was obligatory in a holy place (cf. Ex. 3:5; Josh. 5:15; cf. also the remark in Ex. R. 2:6 end).

In four passages (Ex. 31:10; 35:19; 39:1, 41) all the priestly garments of Aaron and of his sons, are referred to by the special designation "the garments of *serad*," the etymology of which has not as yet been adequately explained. The talmudic sages assumed that this designation applies to the high priest's eight garments (Yoma 72 a–b). According to the literal meaning of the text, however, it seems that Aaron's eight garments, i.e., his four undergarments and the four outer ones that were specifically for him, are referred to not as "the garments of *serad*" but as "the holy garments for Aaron the priest" (see the references above, and also Ex. 28:4; 29:29; 40:13), while the four garments of the common priests are called "the garments of his sons, for their service as priests."

A third group of priestly garments consists of those made of ordinary, not fine, linen, which are used for officiating in the holiest of places. On the Day of Atonement, Aaron enters the inner sanctum clothed in four garments of ordinary linen: a coat, breeches, a girdle, and a miter (Lev. 16:4), which, as the sages correctly stated, were of white linen (Yoma 3:6, et al.). However, garments, including breeches, of ordinary linen are also worn by the common priest when he ascends the outer altar to remove the ashes (Lev. 6:3), and these are assumed to be similar to the former four garments. The simple garments of ordinary linen bear a holiness still greater than that of the vestments of gold and a mixture of wool and linen, and the text finds it necessary to emphasize that "they are the holy garments" (Lev. 16:4). In the Egyptian priesthood, too, garments of simple linen were regarded as holy. In the Bible, angels of the heavenly entourage are represented as clothed in simple linen (Ezek. 9:2–3, 11; 10:2; Dan. 10:5; 12:6–7). Because of their extraordinary holiness, the custom was instituted that the inner sanctum should be entered and the altar ascended in these garments only.

Bibliography: W. Nowack, *Lehrbuch der hebraeischen Archeologie* (1894), 116ff.; E. Nestle, in: ZAW, 25 (1905), 205; 32 (1912), 74; F. C. Burkitt, in: JTS, 26 (1925), 180; J. E. Hogg, *ibid.*, 72–75; 28 (1927), 287ff.; J. Gabriel, *Untersuchungen ueber das alttestamentliche Hohepriestertum* (1933), 25–90; Galling, Reallexikon, 429–32; G. Beer and K. Galling, *Exodus* (Ger., 1939), 139–43, 151; K. Elliger, in: VT, 8 (1958), 19–35; M. Haran, in: *Scripta Hierosolymitana*, 8 (1961), 279–85, 298; idem, in: HUCA, 36 (1965), 191ff. [M.HA.]

PRIESTS AND PRIESTHOOD.

Definition of Priesthood. The priests are the principal functionaries in divine services, their special task being to engage in cultic ceremonies which they conducted mainly in the Temple. In general the priests' post is authorized by hereditary right and they constitute a distinct class separate from the rest of the people. In extrabiblical sources the title *kohen* ("priest") is found in Canaanite inscriptions and in Ugaritic documents. Apparently the Aramaic form *kahana* is borrowed from the Hebrew, just as the Ethiopian *kahen* is found in the sense of seer or soothsayer, and on the basis of this term various scholars attempted to explain the primal nature of the priesthood in Israel (see below). It seems, however, that the Arabic term too was borrowed from the Canaanite, and that by way of the Aramaic. The etymology of the title is not sufficiently clear.

The institution of priesthood in its typical crystallization as a social class is encountered in many different religions, both primitive and advanced, in the Ancient Near East and elsewhere—but not in all religions. Thus, priesthood, at least in its cultic manifestations, did not exist among the early Arabs or among other nomadic-tribal religions. At the same time, any given priesthood with its procedures and customs tends to be shaped by the specific style and religious attitudes characterizing the particular culture. Even the Canaanite priesthood differed from that of the Israelites, although the Canaanite term for priest is identical with the biblical one. For example, among the Canaanites one finds a priestess and even a female "high priestess" *(rb khnt)* paralleling the male "high priest" *(rb khnm)*. In Israel, in contrast, the priesthood is restricted to males; there are no priestesses in their own right (i.e., other than the female members of a priest's family, such as his wife or daughter).

The priests' involvement in the cult was conceived of essentially as service of the deity. This concept is rooted in the primary nature of the temple, which was regarded literally as a "house of the god," i.e., the special abode of the deity-king, his dwelling place. In this abode there are servants who attend on him and fulfill his wants, the whole cult being designed essentially to provide for the needs of the deity. This conception of the nature of the priesthood was accepted throughout the ancient world and found its expression in images and even in technical terms connected with the priesthood. For example, the Egyptian name designating priest, *hom-neter*, literally means "servant of the god." In Israel this conception lost its actual, concrete meaning as it became fossilized in linguistic usage; but it still echoes throughout the biblical sources. The priests are called ministrants of God (Isa. 61:6; Jer. 33:21–22; Joel 1:9, 13; 2:17, et al.) and their function in the temple is called service—holy service (Ex. 28:43; 29:30, et al.); they stand before God to minister to Him (Deut. 10:8; cf. 17:12; 18:5, 7, et al.), they approach Him to minister to Him (Ezek. 40:46; 43:19; 44:15), draw near to His table to serve Him (Ezek. 44:16), and the like.

Right to Serve in the Priesthood. The question of who is entitled to serve in the priesthood—whether the whole levite tribe, only part of it, or every male Israelite—is one of the basic questions necessary for a comprehension of the character of the Israelite priesthood. On this point the biblical laws appear contradictory, and this too seems to be the case with testimony provided by the historical books.

THE CONCEPTIONS OF P AND D. According to P, the right to priesthood is maintained exclusively for one family of the levite tribe, the family of Aaron. Therefore Aaron and his sons are dressed in special garments (Ex. 28:1ff.) and are also anointed with the anointing oil, in exactly the same manner as are the holy vessels (Ex. 30:26–30; 40:9–15). The ceremony of their consecration for the priesthood follows the construction of the Tabernacle (Ex. 29: Lev. 8). The other members of the levitical tribe have other functions connected with the service in the Tabernacle (Num. 3–4; cf. below), but they play no role in the cultic ceremonies themselves. Moreover, they are forbidden to approach the altar and the other holy vessels.

According to the point of view of Deuteronomy (10:8–9), also formulated in the blessing of Moses (Deut. 33:8–10), the entire levitical tribe is appointed to serve in the priesthood. To put it more precisely, those levites serve in the priesthood who reside in the chosen city, which is the only place where cultic service is permitted. Hence the characteristic terminology of this book—"priests, sons of Levi," and levitical priests" (17:18; 18:1; 21:5; 31:9, et al.). Levites who reside in provincial towns do not participate in the cult. However, it maintains that every levite has the right to come to the chosen city and to serve before God there (18:6–7). This means that at least de jure each member of the levitical tribe may join the priesthood if he so desires.

THE ALLEGED CONCEPTION OF JE. The conception of JE is a little more obscure. At first glance it appears that these sources permit every man in Israel to offer sacrifices on the altar himself (see Ex. 20:24 [21]), and indeed they relate that the Patriarchs not only used to build altars but also used to offer sacrifices on them (e.g., Gen. 22:9; 31:54; 46:1). In the same way, Moses erects altars in Rephidim and at the foot of Mt. Sinai and offers sacrifices with the aid of the "young men of the Israelites" and together with Jethro and the elders (Ex. 17:15; 18:12; 24:4). This same attitude is characteristic of the authors of the narratives in the Former Prophets. Moreover, it appears that this was even the historical reality. *Gideon, for example, offers sacrifices himself on the altar at Ophrah (Judg. 6:20–28), as does *Manoah at Mahaneh-Dan (13:15–23), the people of Beth-Shemesh on the large stone in the field (I Sam. 6:14–15), *Adonijah on the stone of Zoheleth near Jerusalem (I Kings 1:9), and many other biblical personalities who have no connection with the priesthood. Thus Elijah the prophet rebuilds the ruined altar on the Carmel and makes an offering on it (I Kings 18:30–38).

These facts served as the decisive starting point for the description advanced by many scholars of the evolution of the priesthood in Israel. According to this description—which was formulated in a crystallized form by J. Wellhausen and W. Robertson-Smith—in the early stages of Israelite history there was no difference between priests and laymen. Every citizen was entitled to participate in cultic ceremonies, and there was no special priestly class in existence. Eli at the temple of Shiloh or Ahimelech at the temple of Nob are viewed merely as gatekeepers, like similar functionaries among the ancient Arabs, called *ḥājib* or *sādin*, whose function, which was hereditary, was limited to guarding the temple. The temple guards in the early period of Israel also used to engage in soothsaying, as did the ancient Arab *kāhin,* but they did not as yet constitute a true priesthood since they had no special cultic functions. Only after the establishment of the monarchy, with the growth of ceremony in public life, were special people appointed to serve in the priesthood. These people were assigned to serve in the royal temples and were regarded as officials of the monarchy, which had granted them their positions. Their tribal origin was not necessarily levitical. Thus the Bible attests that the sons of David were priests (II Sam. 8:18) and that Ira the Jairite was a priest of David (20:26). Zadok, whose descendants continued to officiate in the Temple of Jerusalem, also did not belong to the levite tribe, according to this theory. A member of Solomon's entourage who served as priest was Zabud son of Nathan, the king's friend (I Kings 4:5), while Jeroboam also appointed priests from among all the people (12:31; 13:33). In the course of time the appointed royal priests and their descendants became a consolidated and closed class. This theory generally regards the ancient levite tribe as an ordinary secular tribe. The conception of Deuteronomy and particularly of P according to which Levi is a sacred tribe having a special connection with the priesthood, in fact, refers, according to this theory, only to a late class of rejected priests, a class which was created as a result of the cultic innovations of Josiah and was fictitiously attached to the levitical tribe which by that time had already disappeared.

Various scholars, both before and after Wellhausen, tended to acknowledge the antiquity of the Israelite priesthood and its actual existence as early as the time of the Judges (thus H. Ewald, F. Delitzsch, A. Dillmann, and esp. W. W. Baudissin; more recently, Y. Kaufmann). However, in relation to the right to perform cultic ceremonies and to offer sacrifices on the altar, most of these scholars too adhered to the theory that originally this right was not reserved necessarily for the priests. As for the tribal descent, most of these scholars were inclined to admit at times that the first priests were not necessarily from the levite tribe, though several dynasties of priests did descend from this tribe. This is, then, the reality underlying the narratives of the Former Prophets and reflected in JE, which explicitly mention the offering of sacrifices by laymen, without considering this objectionable. Among those who rejected the antiquity of the Israelite priesthood there were some who went so far as to say that in J, or in the early strata of JE, there is no mention of priests. To the extent that Aaron is mentioned there by name, he is not regarded as a priest but as one of the elders of Israel.

CRITICISM. Both the above-mentioned conceptions, that which denies the antiquity of the Israelite priesthood and that which acknowledges it, overlook the difference between altar and temple, and, therefore, are incapable of explaining with adequate precision the early history of the Israelite priesthood and even the conceptions of JE themselves. Altars consisted of any type of structure, even merely large stones, and were placed outside. In contrast, temples were primarily closed structures, i.e., "houses of God." Every temple had an altar in an adjoining courtyard, but not every altar was necessarily joined to a temple. Many altars stood by themselves in inhabited places or far from them. The difference between these two institutions is also reflected in the scope and nature of cultic activity. Furthermore, the altars were extremely numerous and were found in every corner of the land, which was not the case with the temples whose number was fairly limited. It should be emphasized that the high place *(bamah)* was of the category of an altar; it is a specific type of large altar (not a "house of God"). Now, the place of the priests, whether in Israel or elsewhere, was only in the temples. While every man of Israel was entitled to offer sacrifices on individual altars without the intermediation of authorized personnel, the cultic service associated with the altars attached to the temples, like the service in the temples themselves (in Israel and everywhere in the Ancient Near East), was always reserved for regular priestly families.

Moreover, it can be seen that the families which officiated regularly in the priesthood of the Israelite temples, as far as is known, were related to the levitical tribe. The family of Eli which served in the temples of Shiloh and Nob (I Sam. 14:3; 21:1–10; 22:9, 12) is presented as being of ancient lineage going back to the period of bondage in Egypt and as being chosen from among all the tribes of Israel (2:27–28). There should be no doubt that these statements are based on the assumption that the family belonged to a chosen tribe and it may be even deduced that this family was considered to be what is called in P Aaronide. The priestly dynasty which served in the temple of Dan (Judg. 18:30) originated with the young levite. Zadok, who was the founder of the dynasty of Jerusalem's priests, was apparently also of the levite stock. When the ark is being carried from the city of David, he appears within a group of levites (II Sam. 15:24; there is no justification for assuming the words "and all the levites with him" to be a later addition). In any case, Ezekiel refers to the Zadokites (following the style of Deuteronomy) as "priests, sons of Levi," or "levitical priests" (Ezek. 40:46; 43:19; 44:15). It may be assumed that the priests of the Beth-El temple, too, were related to a fixed dynasty, of which Amaziah, a contemporary of Amos (Amos 7:10–17), was a member. In a small and provincial temple such as that of Micah, the son of the owner could serve in the capacity of priest, but even here it was preferred that a levite fulfill that function (Judg. 17:13). There is no information extant regarding the priests of other Israelite temples in the biblical period, but there is no justification for assuming that those who officiated in those temples undertook their functions only by chance and that their origin was precisely from the other tribes of Israel.

It thus cannot be proven that in the houses of God (as distinguished from the high places) the priesthood was likely to be granted to people from any family in Israel. The bearers of the ark for David were Abiathar and Zadok, the legitimate priests, while David's sons (II Sam. 8:18) and Ira the Jairite (20:26) apparently served as priests only in connection with the sacrifices of the king which took place in the high places and at private altars, not in the temples of God. It should not be forgotten that David did not yet have his own temple. Similarly, Zabud son of Nathan (I Kings 4:5) was probably engaged by Solomon in high-place sacrifices, and he is included in a list of officials of the time preceding the building of the Temple in Jerusalem. Jeroboam appointed priests from among all the people, but the text explicitly states that these were priests of high places (I Kings 12:31–32; 13:33), i.e., their cultic function was outside the framework of the temples. The altars at Beth-El were numerous (cf. Amos 3:14; Hos. 10:8), and not all were attached to the temple of that town, in which Jeroboam even built a special "house of high places" (I Kings 12:31). The Deuteronomistic editor naturally regards even these actions as sinful.

Thus, the historical reality was that at individual altars every man of Israel was entitled to perform cultic activities, whereas in the temples the right to officiate as priests was reserved for specific families which generally traced their lineage to the tribe of Levi. Now, this same reality is reflected in JE. The narrative content of these sources often concerns altars of the popular type, i.e., altars which are not attached to any temple and which can be found even outside settled areas. However, houses of God are also mentioned in these sources both in the legal sections (Ex. 23:19; 34:26) and as projections of the future (Gen. 28:22; see also Ex. 22:7–8; Josh. 6:19, 24; 9:23). The dearth of references to the temples in these sources stems not only from their specifically popular nature but also from their assumption that temples emerged in Israel only after the settlement of the land (in contrast, according to P a temple was built immediately after the theophany at Sinai, which is the *Tabernacle described in it). Anachronistically, priests are mentioned incidentally in JE's accounts (Ex. 19:6 (paralleling a "holy people"), 22–24 (it is difficult to consider this an addition); see also Josh. 6:4–16, et al.). It is clear that their natural place is only in a house of God. Aaron is mentioned in these sources and there should be no doubt that he is considered a priest, in fact, the head of the priests, although this facet of his figure cannot be actualized in Egypt or against the wanderings in the wilderness, when the Israelites do not yet have temples. In Exodus 4:14, Aaron is called "the levite," on the assumption that Levi is the tribe that usually serves as priests, so that membership in it turns into a synonym of priesthood. Moreover, it is explicitly stated in a JE account that after the levites had proven their loyalty to the God of Israel when the people sinned with the golden calf, Moses said to them: "Fill your hands today for God" (Ex. 32:29). This is the usual phraseology designating an ordination for the priesthood.

CONCLUSION. To summarize, all parts of the Pentateuch indicate that in the temple cult only families of priests officiated. According to P, this was only one family from the levite tribe, the family of Aaron. According to D, every levite family is entitled to serve in the priesthood in the temple. According to ancient historical reality (which conforms to the conceptions of JE), various families from the tribe of Levi regularly officiated as priests in various temples (e.g., the various branches of the family of Eli in the temples of Shiloh and Nob, the family of Jonathan son of Gershom in the temple of Dan, the family of Zadok in the Temple of Jerusalem). There are thus no great divergences among the conceptions, since all the sources indicate at least that the priesthood was not granted to common Israelites but only to the tribe of Levi, and, in fact, was limited to special families within this tribe. If it is assumed that in historical reality several levitical families were descended from Aaron (according to Josh. 21:8–19, the descendants of Aaron received 13 towns), the actual divergence between the conceptions is still further reduced.

To put it differently, the disagreements among the sources concern only the altars which were distant from the temples. JE permits every Israelite to sacrifice at such altars at will (this indeed corresponds to the ancient historical reality, hence the impression that common Israelites served in the priesthood). D demands the demolition of such altars, while P assumes a priori that they did not exist. (For this question, which is connected with the centralization of the cult, see *Deuteronomy and *Pentateuch.)

Levels Within the Priesthood. Cultic service in the temple, being generally multifaceted and complex, tended to be crystallized in a complex and graded organizational framework. Thus the priesthood was not composed of a single group but rather several groups can be discerned within it which were of various levels, according to the various functions devolving upon them and their degree of importance. This was the case with all the priesthoods of the Ancient Near East as well as with the biblical priesthood.

THE GRADATION OF PRIESTHOOD ACCORDING TO P. In the P sections the classification of the priests is a fairly simple one into just two levels: the high priest and the ordinary priests. The epithet "high priest" *(ha-kohen ha-gadol)* occurs only once in the Pentateuch (Num. 35:25, 28, hence also in Josh. 20:6; cf. Lev. 21:10 "the priest who is exalted above his fellows"). In several places he is called the anointed priest (Lev. 4:3, 5, 16; 6:15). To be sure, all the priests were anointed with the holy oil (Ex. 28:41; 30:30; 40:13–15; Lev. 7:36) and even the ordinary priests were called anointed priests (Num. 3:3), but there are differences in the method of anointing at the consecration ceremony: all the priests, including Aaron, are anointed with oil sprinkled on their vestments (Ex. 29:21; Lev. 8:30), whereas in Aaron's case it is also poured on his head before the bringing of sacrifices for that ceremony (Ex. 29:7; Lev. 8:12; 21:10). Thus the anointing with holy oil refers primarily to him (Ex. 29:29; Lev. 6:13; 16:32; Num. 35:25).

According to P, the high priest was granted several special privileges, especially in the area of the cult, insofar as his degree of holiness also exceeded that of the ordinary priests. He alone is allowed to go behind the veil on the Day of Atonement (Lev. 16:2ff.) and he deals with the sin offerings whose blood is brought into the sanctuary (4:3–21). In general, all the cultic activities which take place inside the Temple are performed solely by him (see below). The cultic activity of the ordinary priests is actually limited to offering regular sacrifices on the outer altar. The high priest must take more care than the ordinary priests with the restrictions concerning impurity and marriage (see below). His eldest son serves as the head chieftain of the levites (Num. 3:32). The high priest's death terminates the sojourn of manslayers in *cities of refuge (Num. 35:25–28; Josh. 20:6). Moreover, the high priest bears certain signs of royalty. In addition to his anointment, which is performed in the manner of that of a king, i.e., with the pouring of oil on his head (cf. I Sam. 10:1; II Kings 9:6), his garments contain gold and purple. He wears a miter *(miẓnefet)* on which is placed the plate (*ẓiẓ*, Ex. 28:36–39), which is also called *nezer* (Ex. 29:6; 39:30; Lev. 8:9). The miter is considered a sign of distinction being a form of headdress worn by kings, and in poetic parallelism is synonymous with *aṭarah* (Ezek. 21:31; cf. Isa. 62:3). The plate (*ẓiẓ*, perhaps "rosette") is also mentioned in relation to the *aṭarah* (Isa. 28:1, 3–4), while the *nezer* is considered the distinguishing mark of kings (II Sam. 1:10; II Kings 11:12; Ps. 89:40; 132:18). According to P, only the line of eldest sons of the descendants of Aaron can serve as high priests (cf. Lev. 21:10). An ordinary priest cannot become a high priest, in the same way that a levite cannot be made a priest. A man's position in the hierarchy of holiness and cult is determined from the time of his birth, and he is not free to liberate himself from his position. In Numbers 25:10–13 the descendants of Phinehas are promised a "covenant of eternal priesthood," and apparently this refers particularly to the right to the high priesthood.

Most scholars who hold that P was committed to writing at the beginning of the Second Temple period assume that this type of high priesthood existed in Israel only during that period. The high priests of the First Temple, according to this view, were only the first among equals, and their degree of cultic holiness was no greater than that of ordinary priests. Other scholars, especially those who recognize the antiquity of Israelite priesthood in general (see above), also ackowledge the existence of this type of high priesthood in Israel as early as the time of the Judges. According to this view, Eli in the temple of Shiloh might already have been a type of high priest, as that described in P.

W. F. Albright, in particular, points to the fact that among all the peoples of the Ancient Near East there was a head of the priestly hierarchy. In Ugarit too (and in Phoenician inscriptions) such a person is mentioned and is called *rb khnm*. However, it turns out that the antiquity of the Israelite priesthood can be proven not necessarily by analogy with the nations of the Ancient Near East, but especially by an analysis of its cultic and mantic functions (for this matter see below). In the code of Ezekiel 40–48 there is no mention of the high priest. It is possible that the reason for this is not that the high priest did not yet exist, as is maintained by those who reject the antiquity of the high priesthood but, on the contrary, because by this time this type of high priesthood had already vanished; and during the Second Temple attempts were made to reinstate it following the canonization of the Torah (which now included the Priestly Code). A high priest is not mentioned in Deuteronomy either, but this may be because it does not deal with priestly matters and has no need to describe them. Deuteronomy 20:2 mentions a priest who encourages the people before the battle, and it is possible that the high priest is intended here. But the rabbis interpreted this as a priest anointed for war who was appointed specifically for that purpose (Sot. 42a).

Priestly Gradation in the First Temple. During the First Temple period there was actually a slightly more complex group of priests than that described in the Pentateuch. High priests are mentioned, some of them even by name, and possibly they are all descendants of Zadok. Some of these high priests of First Temple times are explicitly called high priest *(kohen gadol)*, while others are called the head priest *(kohen ha-rosh)*, and sometimes one of them might be called simply priest. The following are specified by name: *Jehoiada, a contemporary of Joash (II Kings 11:4–12:11; cf. Jer. 29:26); Urijah (Uriah), a contemporary of Ahaz (II Kings 16:10–16; Isa. 8:2); *Hilkiah, a contemporary of Josiah (II Kings 22:4–14; 23:4, 24); Seraiah, a contemporary of Zedekiah (25:18). Chronicles also mentions Amariah, a contemporary of Jehoshaphat (II Chron. 19:11); Azariah, a contemporary of Uzziah (26:17–20); and another Azariah, a contemporary of Hezekiah (31:10). It is difficult to determine to what extent these conform to the image of the high priest as it is described in P, since there is no real information regarding their character and functions. Several other functionaries should be added to these. The nature of the secondary priests *(kohen mishneh)* is unclear, and apparently there could be several secondary priests simultaneously (II Kings 23:4). At the time of the Destruction, however, there was only one, named Zephaniah (II Kings 25:18). Perhaps the deputy *(segan)* priest of the Second Temple was merely a continuation of the secondary priest of the First. In the First Temple there were also several priests who served as gatekeepers (II Kings 12:10; 22:4; 23:4), and there were three of these during the Destruction (25:18). From the time of Jehoiakim, one is known by name, Maaseiah son of Shallum, who had a special chamber in the Temple court (Jer. 35:4). Jehoiada the priest commanded watchmen in the Temple (II Kings 11:18), i.e., small groups of priests whose function it was to supervise the decorum at the gates and in the courts of the Temple (cf. Ezek. 44:11). The members of these groups were called *pekidim* (officers) and they were authorized to apprehend those who appeared to them to be riotous and to put them in prison and in stocks (Jer. 29:26). One of these *pekidim* was Pashhur son of Immer the priest who was a "chief officer" in the sanctuary, i.e., one of the overseers of the officers, and it was he who struck Jeremiah and put him in prison (Jer. 20:1–3). It is possible that Irijah son of Shelemiah, an officer who while on guard at one of the gates apprehended Jeremiah and brought him to the ministers, also belonged to these groups (37:13–14). The senior priests (lit. "elders of the priests") are also mentioned (II Kings 19:2; Isa. 37:2; Jer. 19:1), and it is not known whether they had some kind of definite function. Perhaps the function of keeper of the wardrobe (II Kings 22:14) was also given to one of the priests.

The Priests' Servants. Together with the priests there is mention of another group which, while its place is outside the cult, is nevertheless related to it; this is the group of priests' servants. They are mentioned in the Temple of Shiloh (I Sam. 2:13–17), and Samuel was one of them (2:11, 18; 3:1). Possibly some of those included among the priests of Nob (22:11) were in fact nothing more than "priests' servants." Their function was to help the priests in their work, but they had no contact with the cultic ceremonies proper. The priest himself would burn the fats on the altar, sprinkle the blood, light the candles, and so on, and the servant would only help him by bringing the portion of meat belonging to the priest, lying down within the house of God (I Sam. 3:3), opening the doors of the house (3:15), and engaging in other similar activities. Thus, these were mere servants, like the servants that every citizen of Israel used to have. Some of them, being close to the sphere of holiness, were permitted to put on a linen ephod (I Sam. 2:18; 22:18). They were members of all the tribes of Israel, like Samuel who was brought from the tribe of Ephraim.

Functions of the Priests. The functions of the priests, although mainly concerned with the cult, were not solely limited to it. In general four types can be distinguished among them: specifically cultic functions; mantic functions, i.e., functions concerned with the solution of mysteries of the future or the past and the making of decisions in uncertain cases through the revelation of divine will; treatment of impurities and diseases, with the special ceremonies involved; and judging and teaching the people.

Cultic Functions. The primary and outstanding cultic function of the priests was the offering of the sacrifices on the altar which stood in the Temple court. The priests' activities in this ceremony are described in detail at the beginning of Leviticus, and they can be classified into two major roles: sprinkling the blood and burning portions of sacrifices (see *Sacrifice). This function was generally performed by the ordinary priests. Aaron did not engage in this function except when the sacrifice was brought by all the priests (such as the sacrifices of the eighth day, Lev. 9; the daily offering sacrificed from the day of consecration on, 6:12–15). However, public sacrifices are not necessarily performed by the high priest. Aaron is not mentioned in connection with the daily offerings and the additional offerings of Sabbaths and festivals (Num. 28–29). Similarly, in the description of the Temple of Shiloh, it was the sons of Eli who dealt with sacrifices (I Sam. 1:3; 2:12–17). However, those sacrifices (sin offerings) whose blood is brought into the inner temple are offered by Aaron himself (Lev. 4:3 –21; 16:3–25; the burnt offering that acompanies the sin offerings of the Day of Atonement is also made by Aaron).

The priests blessed the people in the name of God (Deut. 10:8; 21:5). Numbers 6:22–26 includes a version of the *priestly blessing that comprises three verses in each of which the name of God is mentioned. Later it is stated (6:27) "Thus they shall link My name with the people of Israel, and I will bless them." The blessing priest would raise his hands and would sometimes proclaim his blessing to the people from above the altar (Lev. 9:22); Melchizedek king of Salem, who was a priest, blessed Abraham (Gen. 14:18–20); the priests also proclaimed blessings and curses to the people in a special ceremony held between Mt. Gerizim and Mt. Ebal (Deut. 27:12–26; Josh. 8:33–34).

On various occasions the ordinary priests sounded trumpets, e.g., on festivals and New Moons, when the offerings and sacrifices for these days were brought, and this served as a reminder of the sacrifices of Israel before God (Num. 10:10). On the Day of Atonement in a *Jubilee year it was obligatory to blow a *shofar* (ram's horn) throughout the land (Lev. 25:9) and on the first day of the seventh month it was obligatory to carry out a "memorial blowing" (Lev. 23:24; Num. 29:1) probably of the *shofar,* but it cannot be known if this was a function of the priests.

A distinct function of the priests was to carry the ark. Deuteronomy mentions this as one of the distinguishing features of priesthood (10:8; 31:9, 25), and in all the transportations of the ark during the period of the Conquest it is told that the "priests, sons of Levi," were its bearers (Josh. 3:3–17; 4:3, 9–10, 16–18; 8:33). This is also the view of the sources marked by the characteristics of JE (Josh. 6:6, 12), and this was actually the case in historical reality whenever the ark was carried out to the battlefield. When it was brought to the camp near Eben-Ezer, *Hophni and Phinehas sons of Eli accompanied it (I Sam. 4:4, 11). When it was returned from the field of the Philistines to Beth-Shemesh it was carried by the levites (who according to the point of view of these sources are the ones who serve in the priesthood; cf. Ex. 33:29; and see above) from the cart to the large stone (I Sam. 6:15). When the ark was in the war camp of Saul, *Ahijah the priest is mentioned near it (14:18; according to MT). When an attempt was made to remove it from the City of David, during Absalom's rebellion, it was carried by Zadok and all the levites (i.e., insofar as they are considered priests, as above; II Sam. 15:24). Solomon testified regarding Abiathar the priest that he was among the bearers of the ark (I Kings 2:26; there is no reason to emend the text here). Again, when it was brought to the temple which Solomon had built and into the Holy of Holies, this was done by the priests (8:3, 6, 10). Where it is not explicitly stated who the bearers of the ark were (such as when it was brought up from the house of *Obed-Edom to the City of David, II Sam. 6:13; as distinct from the way from the house of *Abinadab to the house of Obed-Edom, where it was transported on a cart; 6:3–7), there is no need to assume that they were not priests.

P contains a complete description of several cultic activities inside the Temple, all performed daily at fixed times, in the morning and at sunset, and according to the plain sense of the text these are all done by the high priests alone (but the talmudic sages permitted them to be done by an ordinary priest). These activites included the burning of frankincense on the inner altar (Ex. 30:7–9), the care of the lamps (Ex. 27:20–21 = Lev. 24:1–4; Num. 8:1–3), and setting out the shewbread on the table (Lev. 24:5–9). Some trace has been preserved of a libation which was put in some of the vessels on the table (Ex. 25:29; 37:16; Num. 4:7), but possibly in biblical times this special libation had already been abolished. In addition to these four activities there are three others which stem from the cultic functions of the high priests' vestments: the stones of the ephod and breastplate serve as reminders of the names of the Israelite tribes before God (Ex. 28:12, 29): the bells at the hem of the ephod coat resound at the times of the daily offerings, i.e., in the morning and at sunset, when Aaron enters and leaves the sanctuary (28:35); and the plate on Aaron's head bears "any guilt incurred in the holy offerings" of Israel so that they will be accepted favorably by God (28:38). These activities, simultaneously performed by the high priest inside the temple, complement one another and constitute a uniform and comprehensive system. They provide, as it were, food (bread), drink (the libation on the table), aroma (frankincense), light (candles), sound (bells), and arouse the memory (the stones of the ephod and breastplate), and the will (plate). Thus they encompass all the human senses and should be discussed as a single and self-contained cultic phenomenon. This inner system of ceremonies is rooted in the primal conception of the Temple as God's dwelling place, in which He, as it were, "lives" His life, and in which all His needs are to be satisfied (cf. above). The Israelite religion inherited the system of ceremonies as a fixed and crystallized pattern of divine worship.

Mantic Functions. According to the viewpoint of P, the high priest consults the *Urim and Thummim (Num. 27:21), which are located on the breastpiece attached to the ephod (Ex. 28:30; Lev. 8:8). In order to obtain a reply, the high priest must enter with the Urim and Thummim "before God," i.e., into the sanctum. The use of Urim and Thummim was common in the ancient Israelite priesthood. However, it may be deduced from Ezra 2:63 (= Neh. 7:65) that by the Second Temple the Urim and Thummim had been entirely forgotten and the returnees to Zion did not know how to reinstate them despite the fact that they had found them mentioned in the Torah (see *Urim and Thummim). The Urim and Thummim were consulted when it was necessary to decide between two contradictory possibilities, and a yes or no answer was received. Solution by lots was needed in more complex situations, such as the division of allocated areas. The Bible mentions two kinds of lots. The one was a popular lot used by the masses in daily life, to which the Prophets (Isa. 34:17; Ezek. 24:6; Micah 2:5, et al.) and the Hagiographia (Ps. 22:19; Prov. 1:14; 16:33) frequently refer and which was also common among foreign peoples (Joel 4:3; Obad. 11; Jonah 1:7; Neh. 3:10, et al.). The other was a formal priestly lot which took place in the temple court, "before God," and was used for decisions of public, national significance, such as the following cases related by biblical tradition: the division of the land west of the Jordan (Num. 26:55–56; Josh. 14:21; Judg. 1:3), the separation from the rest of the people of a man who has taken from the *ḥerem* (Josh. 7:13–18), choosing the fighters with Benjamin (Judg. 20:9–10), Saul's election as king (I Sam. 10:17–21), and others. In all these cases it is written that the lot was cast "before God," i.e., in the temple court. The lots for the scapegoats of the Day of Atonement are cast by Aaron (Lev. 16:7–10). In connection with the division of the land it is stated that next to *Joshua stood Eleazer the priest (Num. 34:17; Josh. 14:1–2; although later (Josh. 18:6–10) it is stated that it is as if Joshua alone casts the lot before God). It is possible, therefore, that while this action was attributed to the national leader it was actually performed by the high priest.

Priests would conduct ordeals to resolve doubtful cases. Such a ceremony, held by the priest in the court of the sanctuary, was conducted in the case of a suspected adulteress (Num. 5:11–31) and it appears that this was not the only ceremony of its kind.

Treatment of Impurity; Purification and Apotropaic Rites. Disease and plague were not viewed in the Ancient Near East simply as an organic-physiological phenomenon, but as an external-tangible embodiment of an impure spirit which came to rest within the body of the afflicted person or object. Healing was thus performed by waiting until the impurity left the body or by purification activities aimed at hastening its exit. These attitudes prevalent in the Ancient Near East also found expression in the actions of the Israelite priesthood, although they were stamped with the special mark of biblical religion.

It is generally agreed in the Bible that it is the function of the priests to deal with impurities or diseases. True, the prophet too could heal leprosy, but this was performed by the prophet as a miraculous action (Num. 12:13; II Kings 5:1–15; cf. Ex. 4:6–8), while the regular and systematic care was in the hands of the priests. Deuteronomy admonishes the people to follow carefully the instructions of the priests pertaining to these matters (Deut. 24:8; cf. 21:5). According to the code of Ezekiel, too, the priests must guide the people in matters of impurity and purity (Ezek. 44:23).

This aspect of priestly activity is described especially in P in the sections dealing with impurities of animals and carcasses (Lev. 11), leprosy (Lev. 13–14), emissions (Lev. 15), and laws concerning impurity of the dead (Num. 19). The ceremonies described in these sections are aimed at expelling impurity from the body undergoing purification. A special role is played in these ceremonies by, among other things, blood—blood of the slaughtered bird (Lev. 14:5–6), or the blood of the red heifer (Num. 19:4). In other circumstances the priests could use the blood of sacrifices for purification, especially for the purification of the altar or temple. The essence of the sin offering is the purifying action of the victim's blood, some of the blood being applied to the corners of the altar (Lev. 4:25, et al.). The great sin offerings whose blood was brought into the sanctuary would purify not only the altar but the temple as well (Lev. 4:3–21). The decisive ceremony of temple purification was conducted on the *Day of Atonement. The temple purification ceremony described in the code of Ezekiel is already much more general and diluted, and contains no mention of the scapegoat (Ezek. 45:18–20). Another ceremony of purification, performed by Aaron on the levites during their consecration rites, was accompanied by the sprinkling of "sin waters," the shaving of all the hair, and the washing of clothes (Num. 8:7). Purification by means of sprinkling "pure waters" is also mentioned in Ezekiel 36:25 (cf. Zech. 13:1).

The process of purification is not completely ended until the priests offer the sacrifices for the person who is being purified, usually sin and burnt offerings. However, a leper who is being purified also brings a guilt offering and a *log* of oil. Some of the blood of the guilt offering and the oil is used by the priest, in this case, for various ceremonial activities (Lev. 14:11–18), which apparently had an apotropaic significance, i.e., were intended to place a barrier before the forces of impurity so that they could not return to the purified body. A similar ceremony was also held during the consecration of priests (Ex. 29:20–21; Lev. 8:23–24, 30). Frankincense could also serve as a defense against impurity (Num. 17:11–13), and parallels to this are found in the customs of the Ancient Near East.

JUDGING AND INSTRUCTING THE PEOPLE. The priests also participated in judging. Although this was generally a function of the elders and heads of families, in temple towns where there were priests, they would participate in judging together with the elders. This is made sufficiently clear in Deuteronomy. In a difficult case requiring fuller investigation Deuteronomy enjoins the litigants to go up to the chosen city and be judged there (17:8–13), although the assumption is that judging there is not only in the hands of the priests since they are mentioned in the Bible together with judges (Deut. 17:9; cf. 19:17). Deuteronomy requires that "every law suit" be decided by the priests (21:5), but this seems to be a somewhat generalized mode of speech, referring as it does to "every" lawsuit. Apparently the description contained in Deuteronomy, if the point of the centralization of the cult is removed from it, essentially reflects actual historical reality according to which the priests participated in judicial authority. In P there is no mention of this priestly function; and indeed this source—which views the priests as detached from the people and endowed with supreme holiness—would not be likely to attribute the function of judging to the priests, since this would generally have necessitated direct contact with the public in judging. However, in historical reality Eli the priest could have achieved the status of a great judge of Israel (I Sam. 4:18). Ezekiel as well says of the priests that "in controversy they shall act as judges" (Ezek. 44:24).

The priests also served as teachers of *"torah"* to the people. This function is mentioned as early as the blessing of Moses (Deut. 33:10). The priests' instruction of the people did not exist as a special institution but was generally a by-product of their other activities. Thus *torah* followed from the legal discussions held before the priests (Deut. 17:11; 33:10). *Torah* was also taught by way of guidance given by the priests to the people in matters of impurities and diseases (Deut. 24:8; Haggai 2:11ff.). Indeed, the various types of laws of impurity were called *torah* (Lev. 11:46; 13:59, et al.) and were to be learned by the public (Lev. 10:10–1). The various cultic customs were also called *torah* (Lev. 6:2, 7, et al.), and many of the sections dealing with laws and rebukes interspersed throughout the Pentateuch actually constitute scrolls of *torah*. Books of law were preserved mainly by the priests (see *Pentateuch).

Holiness of the Priesthood. The priests, being essentially servants of God, enjoy greater holiness than the rest of the people. This is a basic notion common to every culture of the Ancient Near East, although there were differences in its actual formulation from place to place. The priests did not function as emissaries of the public, since the right to priesthood itself is not in the hands of the public. This right is seen in the Bible basically as divine grace extended to a chosen tribe, or part of it. The holiness of the priests is agreed upon in all biblical sources, and is expressed in various ways. The servants of Saul, for example, refuse to harm the priests of God, despite the king's explicit command (I Sam. 22:17). Solomon refrains from killing Abiathar since he has the merit of being a priest and bearer of God's ark, though as a traitor to the monarchy he is subject to death (I Kings 2:26). In Exodus 19:6 a kingdom of priests and a holy nation are mentioned as synonymous terms. However, the holiness of the priesthood is most explicitly pronounced in P, as well as in its extension, that is, the code of Ezekiel 40–48.

According to the conceptions of P (and the code of Ezekiel 40–48), the holiness of the priests equals the holiness of the house of God itself. Both are on the same level of holiness which is the level also of the sacrifices of the highest rank of sanctity. This is the most extreme holiness, the most palpable, which can be transferred by contact from one body to another. In the Former Prophets this type of holiness is attributed to the ark alone, while P and the code of Ezekiel 40–48 extend it to include the temple with all its appurtenances. Several external signs affirm the identification of the priests with the holiness of the house of God.

In order to maintain this holiness, especially during their cultic service, the priests are subject to special obligations and restrictions. A blemished priest cannot approach the altar or enter the temple in order to serve there (Lev. 21:17–23), in the same way that a sacrifice has to be "whole," i.e., without taint (Lev. 22:18–25; cf. 1:3; 3:1; 4:3, et al.). Before the priests approach the altar or enter the temple in order to serve, they must wash their hands and feet in the laver in the court (Ex. 30:18–21). Though not required to abstain from wine at all times, they are forbidden to drink wine and other intoxicants during the performance of their cultic or didactic duties (Lev. 10:9; Ezek. 44:21).

They were even forbidden to defile themselves for the dead, except in cases of the closest family blood ties (Lev. 21:1–14; Ezek. 44:25). The priest's wife is not included in the list of such relatives (Lev. 21:2b–3; Ezek. 25b), and Leviticus 21:4 apparently specifically excludes her. In the latter verse, however, *baʿal* is to be omitted as a mutilated dittography (or an abbreviation?) of *be-ʿamaw le-heḥallo*. The rabbis permitted the priest to defile himself for his legal wife (Yev. 22b and parallels). In no case were priests permitted to perform certain mourning rites such as shaving the head smooth, shaving the corners of the beard, and making gashes in the flesh (Lev. 21:5). These mourning rites were introduced into Israel from foreign sources, and in the pentateuchal law were also forbidden to the people (Lev. 19:27–28; Deut. 14:1–2), but in the case of priests the text found it necessary to add a special admonition for them. Mourning rites which would normally be practiced both by the priest Ezekiel and by Israelite laymen are mentioned in Ezekiel 24:15–23, and it may be inferred from these verses that priests in general normally observed them no less than Ezekiel.

The rigors of priestly purity become even more severe during the seven days of consecration. The high priest is admonished that while he is being consecrated and the anointing oil is poured on his head, he is forbidden to bare his head, rend his clothes, be defiled even for the limited circle of his relatives, or even go out of the temple (Lev. 21:10–12; according to the plain sense the text is speaking here only of the days of consecration; cf. Ibn Ezra). Actually the ordinary priests were subject to the same restrictions. During the entire seven days of consecration Moses forbade Aaron and his sons to go out of the entrance of the Tent of Meeting (8:33–35), and when Nadab and Abihu, Aaron's sons, died before the days of consecration were over, Moses forbade the others to bare their heads, rend their clothes, or go out of the entrance of the Tent of Meeting (10:6–7). Those defiled for Nadab and Abihu were levites, relatives of Aaron (10:4–5). Thus the admonitions in Leviticus 21:10–12 are merely an added warning to the high priest and not intended to separate him in this matter from the ordinary priests. On the other hand, the restrictions mentioned in Ezekiel 44:20 refer not to the days of consecration or to mourning rites but to the priests' custom throughout the year. Ezekiel enjoins the priests to cut their hair elegantly (Heb. *kasom yikhsemu*, on the basis of the Akkadian *kasāmu;* the Heb. root *gzm* is close to it). That is, in their daily lives the priests were commanded to care for their hair—neither to shave it entirely nor to neglect it entirely, but to comb it decoratively. The rabbis for their part said that a high priest cuts his hair once a week and an ordinary priest once every 30 days (Sanh. 22b).

The holiness of the priesthood is also expressed in restrictions concerning marriage. The priests were forbidden to marry a woman degraded by harlotry or a divorced woman (Lev. 21:7). The high priest is also forbidden a widow, and the text admonishes him to marry only a virgin "from among his people," i.e., of Israel (21:13–15). Aaron married Elisheba daughter of Amminadab from the tribe of Judah (Ex. 6:23). Ezekiel warns the priests to marry virgins of Israelite origin, but permits them a priest's widow (Ezek. 44:22). At the same time, it is difficult to attribute legal precision to these distinctions. They are aimed primarily at removing any suspicion of prostitution from the priestly families, for otherwise the holiness of the priestly seed is profaned (Lev. 21:1–9). Divorcees and widows are subject to a certain suspicion of prostitution, since they are removed from any familial framework and are independent. In contrast, a priest's daughter who was widowed or divorced returns to her father's house and eats of the holy meat (22:13), and it does not stand to reason that she could be forbidden to marry a priest a second time. Indeed, care was exercised in priestly families to allow no deviation from modesty. Every Israelite citizen was admonished not to profane his daughter through prostitution (19:29), but such a sin perpetrated by a priest's daughter was extremely grave and she was sentenced to be put to the fire (21:9).

Outlines of the History of the Israelite Priesthood. From the Patriarchal Period Until After the Settlement. During the patriarchal period, the Hebrew tribes had no temples, as was commonly the case in nomadic communities, and thus there was also no priestly class. The locus of cultic service was the open altar and the priestly functions could be performed by every head of a household. A trace of this situation has been preserved in the expression "a father and a priest," which was fossilized in linguistic usage (Judg. 17:10; 18:19). The period of temples in Israel began after the conquest of Canaan. Thus the main crystallization of the Israelite priesthood began with the settlement, although to a certain extent it already had existed in the period which preceded the settlement. Its real activity began with the message of Moses, which brought Yahwism to the world and laid the foundations for the history of Israel. From that time the priesthood became one of the faithful bearers of this religion and the preserver of its cultic rites. The rites themselves were generally taken over from the pagan culture which preceded Moses, but the Israelite priesthood used them as raw material to actualize by their means the new message and to give it an expression by way of symbolic concretization.

From earliest times the priesthood was exclusively in the hands of the levite tribe. In the period which preceded the religious innovation it was a secular tribe, and something of its secular character probably remained for a long time afterward, but in the context of Yahwistic religion it appears in all the sources as a sanctified tribe, all, or at least part, of which was destined to serve in the priesthood. This tribe, from which Moses himself originated, was the first to be attracted by his religious announcement and when necessary even made conquests by force for the new faith. In the episode of the golden calf it is related that the levites supported the prophet and gained control of the unruly camp by means of the sword, as a reward for which they were authorized for the priesthood (Ex. 32:26–29; cf. Deut. 10:8–9). Such upheavals apparently occurred more than once. The blessing of Moses, in which Levi is described as a tribe of priests, mentions the tribe's "foes and enemies" and prays for their discomfiture (Deut. 33:11). The distribution of the levites among the other Israelite tribes is already mentioned in the blessing of Jacob, where it is stated as a curse (Gen. 49:7). Possibly this distribution preceded their sanctification and stemmed from other motives. However, in any case, the fact that they remained without allotted land increased their connections with cultic activities and made them dependent on the holy gifts.

At the same time, the sources contain vague echoes of tension between the house of Aaron and the tribe of Levi. In the sin of the golden calf, Aaron is mentioned as the head of rioters whose behavior compelled Moses and the levites to take warlike steps. According to P, on the other hand, the levites are not permitted to serve in the priesthood, although the source admits that they have a certain measure of holiness and that they were given to God in place of the firstborn (Num. 3:40–45). In the polemic of *Korah it is related that some of the levites rebelled against Moses and Aaron seeking the priesthood for themselves, but they paid with their lives (Num. 16). Likewise, there are several allusions here to opposition to the priesthood of Aaron on the part of all the tribes. Korah's rebellious group also contained Israelites, or at least gained the support of the public (Num. 16:2–3, 19). After Korah and his group were burned in the ordeal of the frankincense, all the people gathered to complain that Moses and Aaron had killed "the people of God," as a result of which a great plague broke out (17:6–15). Later another ordeal was conducted, this time involving the staffs of the tribal heads, in order to confirm that it was indeed Aaron who had been chosen for the priesthood of all the people (17:16–26).

It appears that the family of Aaron was the first to join the new religion, preceding the whole of the levite tribe. It is told of Aaron that he was the first to meet Moses when the latter returned from Mt. Horeb and believed in him (Ex. 4:14–16, 27–30). He serves as a "mouth" for Moses (4:16), or a kind of "prophet" for him to others (7:1–2), and Moses and Aaron participated together in most of the signs and miracles in Pharaoh's court. Of the family of Eli, which was probably considered to be descended from Aaron, it is also said that even in Egypt and in the house of Pharaoh it had been chosen "from all the tribes of Israel" to serve in the priesthood (I Sam. 2:27–28). Many scholars have assumed that originally Aaron's family was not even included in the tribe of Levi. The names bearing an Egyptian coloring that appear in it (Phinehas, Putiel father-in-law of Eleazar (Ex. 6:25), Hophni, Hananiel, a relative of Jeremiah (Jer. 32:7ff.); some say Aaron's own name as well) indicate its alien origin and genealogical distinctness. However, it is clear that in the course of time it became assimilated into the levite tribe. In all the biblical sources Aaron is already considered a member of the tribe and a brother of Moses, despite the fact that his name bears Egyptian characteristics.

The history of the Israelite priesthood from the Conquest on is connected with the history of the temples. These were erected in the course of time throughout the area of settlement, from Dan to Beer-Sheba, and various families from the levite tribe served as priests in them. At the beginning, the family of Aaron apparently officiated near the ark (see also Judg. 20:27–28), and when the ark was established at Shiloh this family held the priesthood of that temple. According to the tradition of P, Shiloh was the last location of the Tabernacle (Josh. 18:1). There is no doubt that in the period preceding the monarchy, the Temple of Shiloh was elevated above most of the other temples and became a kind of national-religious center for the Israelite tribes. Eli, the high priest at Shiloh, reached the status of one of the judges of Israel, and the figure of Samuel also evolved within the walls of this temple.

During the Period of the Monarchy. The connection between the monarchy and the priesthood in the Ancient Near East was expressed in two ways: in several places the kings themselves are considered high priests, and this identification appears also in the case of Melchizedek, king of the town of Salem and priest of *ʾEl ʿElyon,* who blesses Abraham and takes a tithe from him (Gen. 14:18–20). In other places the priesthood was separate from the monarchy and entrusted to special dynasties. This arrangement was the custom in Israel; however, even when this was the case the monarch could still perform several typical priestly functions. The monarchs were permitted to ascend the altar in the court of the house of God, to sprinkle blood upon it, and to offer sacrifices (I Sam. 13:9; I Kings 12:33; 13:4; II Kings 16:12–13). David allowed himself to wear a linen ephod (II Sam. 6:14; yet this is not a regular priest's ephod). David also blesses the people, apparently from the altar (6:18), and Solomon does likewise (I Kings 8:14–21, 54–61).

On the other hand, during the period of the monarchy several families of priests who served in the royal temples attained economic and social advancement. These priests were henceforth considered as royal ministers and were included in the lists of bearers of high positions.

A notable change in the important priestly houses occurred at the beginning of the monarchical period. The family of Eli lost its importance and its place was taken by the family of Zadok, which from then on served in the priesthood of the central Temple in Jerusalem. This family, too, like that of Eli, originated from the levites who were scattered in the towns of Judah and Benjamin; according to Joshua 21:9–19, they lived in 13 towns and all were descended from Aaron. (For the division of functions among the priests of the temple in Jerusalem, see above.) The great influence of the Jerusalem priesthood was revealed in the time of Jehoiada, who rebelled against Athaliah and in her place crowned Joash in the house of God, and served as the young king's teacher throughout his life (II Kings 11:3–12:3). He himself was related by marriage to the royal household (II Chron. 22:11).

A notable change in the situation of the priesthood took place in the time of Josiah, following the cultic reforms introduced by this king. His reforms, too, were made doubtless under the influence of the Jerusalem priesthood and the final impetus for their implementation was the book found in the Temple. In addition to purging idolatry, these reforms included the destroying of the high places and the altars outside the temple, even those that were in Jerusalem itself. All the priests in the towns of Judah were brought to Jerusalem (II Kings 23:8). Most biblical scholars (since W. M. L. de Wette) assert that these reforms were made in accordance with the conceptions of Deuteronomy, which was the book found at the time in the Temple. Several scholars, however, maintain that there are a number of contradictions between the requirements of Deuteronomy and the reforms instituted in the time of Josiah. One of their main arguments (held by K. Budde, G. Hoelscher, and others) is that the priests of the high places who were gathered together in Jerusalem were not permitted to ascend the altar (II Kings 23:9), while Deuteronomy permits every levite to come and serve as a priest in the chosen place (Deut. 18:6–8). This, however, is a seeming contradiction since the text speaks of "priests of high places," i.e., priests who served in the altars distant from the houses of God, and these priests were never considered as belonging to the levite tribe (cf. above). It is not surprising, therefore, that after they had been transferred to Jerusalem they were not permitted to serve in the priesthood. The reforms of Josiah necessarily involved also the abolishment of the temples outside Jerusalem (as distinct from the high places), and possibly their priests were added to the Jerusalem priesthood. However, the temples in Judah outside Jerusalem were few, and the one to which there are allusions, the temple at Hebron, may already have declined by the beginning of the monarchy. The temples of Israel probably stood desolate after the destruction of Samaria. Thus, the number of priests eligible to serve in the priesthood who were brought to Jerusalem was not significant.

After the Babylonian Exile. In the Babylonian Exile the prophet-priest Ezekiel rose, and in his visions of redemption demanded that basic changes in the organization and order of service of the priesthood be introduced. His visionary code (Ezek. 40–48) is merely a later and diluted extension of that earlier school that finds expression in P. They share basic conceptions of cultic holiness and nature of priesthood as well as a common technical style. And yet, they differ in concrete details. Many priestly customs described in P are restricted in *Ezekiel to simple and schematic activities, like vague shadows of distant models, or are entirely absent. There is no proof that the demands of this prophet were implemented in his time or wrought any change in the priesthood.

The decisive change took place with *Ezra, who brought with him from Babylon those old scrolls which constitute the Priestly source, and these were integrated into the Book of the Torah, which then became a determining force in the life of all Israel. Henceforth, the ancient priestly concepts and customs of P were revived and attempts were made to realize them in life. It was a kind of rebirth of the semi-utopian world of the Israelite priesthood, but even now it was not fully realized. True, during the Second Temple only those who were considered descendants of Aaron served in priesthood, and levites served beside them as a lower clergy. However, several basic elements from the priestly contents of P were not realized even now. The ark as well as the cherubs of the holy of holies were missing. Also missing were the anointing oil (and with it the concept of tangible holiness, transferrable by contact from one body to another), the Urim and Thummim, various customs connected with matters of impurity, and other things. Several of the demands and principles of P were not actualized in reality because of objective obstacles. On the other hand, much of the content of this source was given a secondary significance through the interpretation of the Torah and by comparison and coordination with the other parts of the Torah.

The economic and social position of the priests in this period also changed. Their number reached several thousand, about a tenth of the total population of Judah. Most of them lived in the towns outside Jerusalem, like all the inhabitants of the country (Ezra 2:70 [=Neh. 7:72]; 11:3, 20), and they made their living from the soil. The priestly gifts were not sufficient for their livelihood, and besides the people were not punctilious about bringing them. While the obligation to bring the gifts was included in the covenant (*ʾamanah),* and was accepted by all the signatories (Neh. 10:33–40), apparently the declaration itself did not have sufficient coercive power and Nehemiah had to prod the people periodically to fulfill their obligation (Neh. 12:44–47; 13:10–13; and see 13:31). It is told of the levites and singers that when they did not receive their portions they fled "every man to his field" and the house of God was deserted (Neh. 13:10–11), and there is no doubt that this alternative was also sometimes available to the priests. Many of them became economically independent of the temple service, and in Nehemiah's time many of them volunteered to build the wall, together with other well-to-do citizens, and some of them participated in bringing the wood sacrifice to the Temple (10:35).

These new conditions of total cultic centralization, the increased number of priests, and their decreased dependence on the priestly gifts led to a regulation of the temple service among all the priests (and the levites), which took on the form of a system of divisions, or courses, *mishmarot.* Every *mishmar* would work during its assigned week until the round was completed and was then begun anew. The sources mention 24 divisions, and every priestly division was allotted a period of only two weeks per year. The service for these limited periods of time was regarded partly as a privilege, with the enjoyment of the material benefit entailed, partly as a duty, that the house of God should not be emptied of its servants. The divisions are mentioned in sources from the Second Temple on, but apparently this system is rooted in the reality of the end of the First Temple period, after the cultic reforms of Josiah. The Chronicler dates the establishment of the divisions earlier, to the time of David (I Chron. 24:3–19), but in this he is merely adhering to his method of attributing all the arrangements of the temple to King David. Josephus states that the 24 divisions persisted in his time (Ant. 7:366; Life 1–2; cf. Luke 1:5). The rabbis stated that every priestly division was composed of several households each of which had a fixed day of the week for its work (Tosef., Ta'an. 2:2, et al.). According to one tradition, the rabbis ruled that each division should be divided into six households, one for each weekday, and the entire division would officiate on the Sabbath (cf. Men. 107b). During the pilgrim festivals all the divisions served together (Suk. 55b–56a). The splitting of the divisions into daily households apparently reflects the reality of the end of the Second Temple period, when the number of priests became still larger.

For the garments of the priests see *Priestly Vestments; see also *High Priest; *Levi; *Levitical Cities; for the income of the priests see *Tithe; *Sacrifices; **Ḥerem.*

[M.HA.]

From the Beginning of the Hellenistic Era Until the Destruction of the Temple. During the whole of the Hellenistic era the priesthood was the class with the highest status among the people. From it came the administrators of Judea. In practice the high priest was head of independent Judea, and most of the other responsible people in politics and in administration were also priests. It appears that until the time of the Hasmoneans the outstanding spiritual leaders, such as *Yose b. Joezer and others, were also from their midst. The temple overshadowed all other institutions and even foreign writers like *Hecataeus regarded the Jews as a nation of priests, and at all events designated them as a nation dominated by priests. When Antiochus III granted rights to Jerusalem he freed the priests from a series of taxes. Hecataeus estimated their number in his time at 1,500 but it is possible that he was only referring to Jerusalem, since many of them were settled in the country towns and villages of Judea and southern Samaria and only went up to Jerusalem in accordance with their duty in the system of priestly watches.

The high priests belonged to the family of Zadok and to the watch of Jedaiah, and were descendants of Joshua b. Jehozadak. The office passed from father to son, and if this was not possible, a member of the family was appointed. The high priest served until his death, but Antiochus Epiphanes brought about the cessation of this custom. The high priest, together with the elders, represented the nation to the monarchy. He supervised the temple service, cared for the security of the capital and the water supply, and was responsible for the collection of taxes. Spiritual cultural activities were also placed upon him. A high priest with personality, such as Simeon son of Onias II—who was apparently *Simeon the Just—exercised great influence upon the religious and spiritual development of the nation. The high priests had close connections with institutions outside of the country; the sister of *Onias II was married to the *Tobiad family in Transjordan. Foreigners, too, regarded the high priest as the head of the Jewish people and the Spartans turned to him in negotiations they conducted with Judea (I Macc. 12). The high priestly house was not uniform and unequivocal in its national religious view. Simeon II and *Onias III continued in practice the activity of Ezra and Nehemiah, while *Jason was one of the leaders of the Hellenists and it was he who turned Jerusalem into a polis. Besides the dynasty of the high priest the dynasties of other priests were conspicuous like those of the sons of Hakkoz who already played an important role in financial administration in the Persian era. One of them, Johanan, obtained its privileges for Jerusalem from Antiochus III. His son Eupolemus headed on behalf of Judah the Maccabee the delegation which made the first pact with Rome. Although this family was influenced by Hellenism, its members placed themselves at the service of the Hasmonean dynasty who were themselves priests of the watches of Jehoiarib. The members of another priestly house, of the watch of Bilgah, were converted—in partnership with the sons of Tobiah—into the mainstay of the Hellenistic movement; Simeon fought against Onias II and *Menelaus was appointed high priest by Antiochus IV after he had removed Jason. A Hellenistic high priest from another house was *Alcimus. The connections of some of the priests with the policy of Antiochus brought about a diminution in in the prestige of the class, but when the government passed to the Hasmoneans the priesthood seemed to reach its highest peak among the Jewish people. For the Hasmonean high priest became also the leader, and the king, of an independent nation. At that time, however, began the rise of the *Pharisee scholars, the students of the Torah, and these began to supplant the priests as spiritual leaders. This fact is particularly important in view of the fact that the priests stood out in general as the leaders of the *Sadducee sect whose central sector was composed of the upper grades among the priests, and these were an important element in the Sanhedrin. Among the separatist sects (the Essenes, the sect of the Damascus covenant, the Judean desert sect), too, the priests retained an honorable status as is evident in their writings. With the ascent of Herod to the monarchy, the political leadership of Judah passed—for the first time in the Second Temple era—to a non-priestly element. After the extermination of the Hasmonean dynasty, Herod appointed the high priest at his will from among the priests. He loosened the linking of the high priesthood with a particular family and also abolished finally the custom for the high priest to serve the whole of his life. His status remained exalted and hallowed but his role was chiefly limited to the service of the Day of Atonement, which could be performed by him alone. After the death of Herod and the removal of Archelaus, the appointment of the high priest passed to the Roman governors. In the final generation of the temple this authority was restored to the dynasty of Herod (*Agrippa I, *Herod of Chalcis, and *Agrippa II). During that period a group of wellborn wealthy priestly families became established from among whom most of the high priests were appointed; such were the *Boethus family, the Phiabi family, and the family of Anan. According to the Talmud (Yoma 18a; Yev. 61a), these high priests bought the office from the government, and they were changed each year. Since an ex-high priest kept his additional rights as to dignity and status, there came into being a kind of oligarchy of high priests and of their families, some of whom were related by family ties; some of these were inordinately wealthy. This aristocracy of distinguished and wealthy noble families tyrannized the people, though at times there were struggles between the high priests and fisticuffs between their followers, from which the dwellers of Jerusalem and the villages suffered. The attitude of most of the people of the Pharisee leadership to this Sadducean oligarchy was given pungent expression (Pes. 57a; Tosef. Men. 13:21): "Woe is me because of the house of Boethus! Woe is me because of their staves! Woe is me because of the house of Hanim! Woe is me because of their whispering! Woe is me because of the house of Kathros! Woe is me because of their pens! Woe is me because of the house of Ishmael son of Phiabi! Woe is me because of their fists!; for they are high priests, their sons treasurers, their sons-in-law trustees, and their slaves beat the people with staves." These aristocrats were also regarded as loyalists and protected persons of the Roman government. However, there were individual priests whom the sages mention with praise because of their piety and good deeds, among them being *Joshua b. Gamala to whom is attributed the important regulation to erect a school for children in every town. There was a great contrast, ideological and material, between the upper class high priesthood and the mass of ordinary priests, many of whom did not live in Jerusalem but in the towns and villages of Judea, and also in Galilee, in Transjordan and in the lands of the dispersion. Many of them could not exist on the priestly perquisites, and some of them engaged in work and in commerce. The whole of the priestly class did not belong to the Sadducees. Among the Pharisees, too, were many priests and also among the leaders of the Jerusalem zealots (*Eleazar b. Hananiah, *Eleazar b. Simeon, *Zechariah b. Avkilus). In the defense of the Temple Mount in the time of Pompey, and at the time of the destruction of the Temple, the priests of the Temple displayed wonderful self-sacrifice.

The hatred of the people for the aristocratic high priesthood found expression at the time of the great revolt. When the zealots dominated Jerusalem they expelled all of them, slew a number of them, and chose a high priest from the ordinary priests, viz. *Phinehas b. Samuel a stonemason by profession, a relative by marriage of the family of Hillel. He was the last Jewish high priest. [M.St.]

In the Halakhah. The main function of the priests during the Second Temple period was the offering of sacrifices in the Temple, while the levites served as choristers, musicians, and gatekeepers. Their biblical role as teachers and judges was preserved in the expectation that the Sanhedrin contain priests and levites (Sif. Deut. 153), but the destruction of the Temple completed the process by which they were replaced by the sages and their students. The sacrificial service, from the receiving of the victim's blood on, must be performed by a priest (Zev. 2:1, 3:1). He must wear four sacred vestments (tunic, drawers, turban, and girdle; the high priest wore eight sacred vestments) and be free of physical blemish or defect. The rabbis further declared that a priest who contracts an improper marriage (see below) is declared unfit to perform the Temple service until he severs all connection with his wife (Bek. 7:7). A priest must himself be of proven pedigree to serve in the Temple (Mid. 5:4; Kid. 4:5). Those currently designated "priests" are "presumed priests," inasmuch as there is no legally sufficient proof testifying to their descent from ancient priestly families (see Maim., Yad, Issurei Bi'ah 20:1–2; *Magen Avraham* to OḤ 457:2).

Priests received "twenty-four priestly donations" (BK 10b). Twelve of these referred to parts of the animal- and meal-offerings in the Temple. The others were: firstlings of animals; firstfruits; a share of the agricultural produce *(terumah)*, often given at the rate of 2%; a share of the tithe given to the levites; a share of baked products *(ḥallah)*; the redemption price—five shekels—for firstborn male children; the sheep given as redemption for the firstlings of asses; the first fleece sheared; the shoulder, two cheeks, and maw of slaughtered animals; fields donated to the Temple and sold revert to the priests at the Jubilee year; fields declared *ḥerem* by their owners; and property stolen from a proselyte who dies leaving no issue. With the destruction of the Temple, the tendering of some of those "gifts" became impossible, while the bestowal of others fell into a gradual decline. Currently, the redemption of the firstborn *(pidyon bekhor)* is widely practiced, though the law continues to require that—in Ereẓ Israel at least—firstlings be given to a priest as well as the first fleece and the shoulder, cheeks, and maw of slaughtered animals (Sh. Ar., YD 61:21, 333:1, 305, 360:1).

The priest may not marry a divorced woman or a harlot (Lev. 21:7)—the latter being defined as a woman who has had sexual relations with a man forbidden to her in marriage, or with a profaned priest (see below), or with a convert to Judaism (Sh. Ar., EH 6:8)—and the rabbis added the woman who had been rejected by her levir (Yev. 2:4). In addition to these, the high priest may not marry a widow. The child born of most of these unions is "profaned" *(halal)* and, if female, may not be married to a priest. Finally, the priest ought not to marry a woman both of whose parents were proselytes, but he need not divorce her if he does so (Sh. Ar., EH 7:21). The motive for these restrictions is that the holiness of the priest demands that he marry an unblemished wife.

The priest is forbidden any direct contact with the dead; he may not enter into or step above an enclosure in which a dead body, or its constituents, is lying, nor may he touch anyone or anything that is impure through contact with the dead. He must, however, defile himself for his mother, father, son, daughter, brother, and unmarried sister (Lev. 21:2–3), and for his wife (Yev. 22b; see Sifra to Lev. 21:2). He must also bury the abandoned dead *(met mitzvah).* The priest is assigned priority as an expression of his sanctity: he speaks first, makes the first benediction, and receives first choice; he is also called to the Torah first (Git. 59b). Furthermore, one is not to be served by a priest unless he has waived his prerogatives (Isserles to Sh. Ar., OḤ 128:45).

The tithe (one-tenth of agricultural produce) was assigned by the Torah to the levite. His main distinction in modern times is to be called up to the Torah immediately after the priest, whose hands he washes for the *priestly blessing.

See also *City of Refuge; *Levitical Cities; **Mishmarot* and *Ma'amadot.* [G.J.B.]

In Modern Times. Although, as stated above, the prevailing halakhic opinion is that the claim to be an Aaronide, of priestly descent, is mainly a presumptive one, which, in the absence of pedigree registers, cannot be proved, all the rights and privileges of the kohen, as well as the prohibitions, apply among Orthodox Jews today in full force where they are applicable. These privileges are, the right to be called up first to the reading of the Law (see "Reading of the *Torah"), invoking the Priestly Blessing in the Synagogue, and the redemption of the first born, both of humans and of animals. The only reservation is that in view of the fact that Aaronide descent is mainly presumptive, some authorities suggest that the redemption money should be returned after the ceremony to the father of the child or the owner of the animal (Sh. Ar. YD, 305:8 and 306).

The provision that the kohen has the privilege of reading the Grace after Meals (Sh. Ar. OḤ 201:2) is largely disregarded at the present time, though in some places the custom exists, where a kohen is present, for the person leading the grace to say *bi-reshut kohen* ("with the permission of the kohen").

The laws prohibiting contact with the dead are in full force. As a result, it is the custom to bury kohanim at the end of a row and arrange for the paths to be at least eight cubits wide, so that his priestly relations may visit the grave and be able to stand four cubits from the grave. The fact that a kohen is forbidden to be under the same roof with a corpse, unless there is a permanent partition between the place in which he is standing and the location of the corpse would render it impossible for a kohen to visit a hospital if the mortuary is under the same roof as the hospital proper. Special arrangements have been made in the Hadassah hospital in Jerusalem: double doors, one of which is always closed, or swinging doors which always "seal" the entrance are used to enable kohanim to visit the sick.

Similarly, the fact that the main highway from Jerusalem to Jericho was built by the Jordanians over a portion of the Mt. of Olives cemetery has resulted in a halakhic prohibition against kohanim using that road, and signposts have been erected in Jerusalem and its outskirts indicating an alternative possible route for kohanim.

Similarly the question whether a kohen may practice medicine, since he must come into contact with the dead, is discussed in the *halakhah.*

The laws of the marriages prohibited to the kohen, an unchaste woman, a proselyte, a divorcee, a widow who has received *ḥaliẓah* (see *Levirate Marriage) are still operative. In view of the fact that, unlike other prohibited marriages, such a marriage, if it is celebrated is valid, and the children are legitimate except that they are *ḥalalim* (non-kohanim) considerable pressure is being exercised in Israel today to permit such a marriage, though the rabbinical authorities remain adamant in their refusal. Some Conservative rabbis agree to marry a kohen and a divorcee.

There is a difference of opinion as to whether a kohen may marry the daughter of proselytes (Sh. Ar. EH 7:21). It is referred to as a "blemish" and not a prohibition and though the tendency is toward stringency, it is permitted by some.

Since a kohen is forbidden to remarry even his own divorced wife, it is the custom to delay the execution of his *get* as long as possible.

Reform Judaism disregards all the laws applying to a kohen. [ED.]

Bibliography: E. Ewald, *Die Alterthuemer des Volkes Israel* (1866[3]), 345ff.; S. I. Curtiss, *The Levitical Priests* (1877); H. Oort, in: *Theologisch Tijdschrift,* 18 (1884), 289–335; H. Vogelstein, *Der Kampf zwischen Priestern und Leviten seit den Tagen Ezechiels* (1889); A. Kuenen, *Gesammelte Abhandlungen zur biblischen Wissenschaft* (1894), 465–500; Wellhausen, Proleg, 115–53; idem, *Reste arabischen Heidentums* (1927), 130–40, 143; W. W. Baudissin, *Die Geschichte des alttestamentlichen Priesterthums* (1889); E. Sellin, *Beitraege zur israelitischen und juedischen Religionsgeschichte,* 2 (1887), 109–21; D. Hoffmann, *Die wichtigsten Instanzen gegen die Graf-Wellhausensche Hypothese,* 1 (1904), 112–48; V. T. Budde, in: ZAW, 22 (1904), 42–50, 160; R. H. Kennett, in: *Journal of Theological Studies,* 6 (1905), 161–86; G. Westphal, in: ZAW, 26 (1908), 201ff.; E. Meyer, *Die Israeliten und ihre Nachbarstaemme* (1906), passim; Kittel, Gesch, passim; H. Gressman, *Mose und seine Zeit* (1913), passim; Pedersen, *Israel, 3–4* (1940), 150–97; G. R. Berry, in: JBL, 42 (1923), 227–38; T. J. Meek, in: AJSLL, 45 (1929), 149–66; idem, *Hebrew Origins* (1950), 119–47; A. Bentzen, in: ZAW, 51 (1933), 173–6; K. Moehlenbrink, *ibid.,* 52 (1934), 187ff.; G. von Rad, *Die Priesterschrift im Hexateuch* (1934), passim; J. Begrich, in: BZAW, 66 (1936), 63–88; S. H. Hooke, *Prophets and Priests* (1938); J. Morgenstern, in: AJSLL, 55 (1938), 1–24, 183–97, 360–77; O. Eissfeldt, in: ZAW, 57 (1939), 6; H. H. Rowley, in: JBL, 58 (1939), 113–41; idem, in: JNES, 3 (1944), 73ff.; L. Waterman, in: AJSLL, 58 (1941), 50ff.; R. Brinker, *The Influence of Sanctuaries in Early Israel* (1948), 65–88; Albright, Stone, 18–19; Albright, Arch Rel, 107–10; O. Ploeger, in: ZAW, 63 (1951), 157–92; I. W. Bailey, in: JBL, 70 (1951), 217–25; A. C. Welch, *Prophet and Priest in Old Israel* (1953); E. O. James, *The Nature and Function of Priesthood* (1955); M. Noth, *Geschichte Israels* (1950), passim; A. Cody, *A History of the Old Testament Priesthood* (1969). FROM THE BEGINNING OF THE HELLENISTIC ERA UNTIL THE DESTRUCTION OF THE TEMPLE: A. Buechler, *Die Priester und der Cultus im letzten Jahrzehnt des Jerusalemischen Tempels (= II. Jahresbericht der Israelitisch-Theologischen Lehranstalt in Wien fuer das Schuljahr 1894/95)* (1895); Schuerer, Gesch, 2 (1907[4]), 277ff.; S. Klein, *Meḥkarim Arẓiyisre'eliyyim,* 1 no. 2 (1924), 2, 1–29; idem, *Ereẓ ha-Galil* (1946), 64–70, 187–202; A. C. Welch, *The Work of the Chronicler* (1939), 81–96; G. Hoelscher, *Die Hohenpriesterliste bei Josephus und die evangelische Chronologie* (1940); Kaufmann, Toledot, 4 (1956), 358ff.; E. Bammel, in: ZDPV, 70 (1954), 147–53; W. Rudolph, *Chronikbuecher* (1955), 152–79; S. Talmon, in:

Iyyunim bi-Meggilot Midbar Yehudah (1957), 24–39; idem, in: *Scripta Hierosolymitana*, 4 (1958), 162–99; Allon, Meḥkarim, 1 (1957), 48–76; M. J. Gevaryahu, in: *Sefer Tur Sinai* (1960); E. M. Smallwood, in: JTS, 13 (1962), 14–34; J. Jeremias, *Jerusalem in the Time of Jesus* (1969), 147–221; E. E. Urbach, in: *Ma'amad ve-Hanhagah be-Olamam shel Hakhmei Erez Yisrael (Divrei ha-Akademyah ha-Le'ummit ha-Yisre'elit le-Madda'im 2/4)* (1965); M. Stern, in: *Tarbiz*, 35 (1966), 235-53; J. Lives, *Perakim be-Toledot ha-Kehunnah ve-ha Leviyyah* (1969). IN MODERN TIMES: Eisenstein, Dinim, s.v. *Kohen;* JE, s.v. *Priest, Blemish* (d); JL, s.v. *Priester.*

PRIJS, JOSEPH (1889–1956), bibliographer and historian. Born in Wuerzburg, Bavaria, Prijs served as rabbi and teacher at Breslau (1918–21), became rabbi and head of the *talmud torah* at Munich, and in 1927 lecturer in Jewish subjects at Munich University. When the Nazis came to power (1933), he went to live in Switzerland, where he devoted himself to research in Swiss university libraries and cataloged the Jewish holdings in several Swiss university libraries.

Prijs wrote on the Hebrew book collections in Bavaria (1927) and on Hebrew printing in *Sulzbach (JTLG, 21, 1930, 319) *Mitteilungen der Soncinogesellschaft*, no. 7 (1931), 26–33) and in Fuerth (*Nachtraege zu L. Loewensteins Bibliographie*... etc., 1938). His great achievement is the monumental work *Die basler hebraeischen Drucke* (1964), published posthumously by his son Bernard. Since Basle was a great center of learning in the 16th century, Prijs's book is an important contribution not only to the history of Jewish printing but also to history of the culture of the early Reformation. Prijs also published some genealogical studies: *Familie Hirsch auf Gereuth* (1931); *Stamboom der Familie Goldsmidt-Cassel te Amsterdam* (1936).

Prijs's son, LEO (1920–) was research fellow at Yeshiva University, New York, and at the Institutum Judaicum, Muenster (Westphalia), Germany. From 1957 to 1960 he was lecturer in Bible at Bar Ilan University and from 1968 professor at Munich University.

Among his published works are: *Juedische Tradition in der Septuaginta* (1948); *Die grammatische Terminologie des Abraham ibn Esra* (1950); and *Die Jeremia Homilie, Pesikta Rabbati XXVI* (1966), a critical edition with German translation and commentary. [W.BA.]

PRILUKI, town in Chernigov oblast, Ukrainian S.S.R. A Jewish settlement in Priluki is mentioned for the first time in 1648 in connection with its destruction during the *Chmielnicki massacres. The community was restored at the beginning of the 19th century. There were 2,007 Jews in Priluki in 1847, 5,722 (31% of the total population) in 1897, and 9,001 (31.4%) in 1926. When the Germans invaded Russia in the summer of 1941, those Jews who did not succeed in escaping from Priluki were exterminated. There were about 2,200 Jews (about 5% of the population) in Priluki in 1959. The last remaining synagogue was closed down by the authorities in 1961. [Y.S.]

PRIMO, SAMUEL (c. 1635–1708), talmudist and Shabbatean leader. Probably born in Cairo, where he studied under Judah Sharaf, Primo later settled in Jerusalem and in 1662 represented the Jewish community there in its quarrel with the heirs of the late David *Habillo, the kabbalist. Primo was considered an outstanding talmudist and kabbalist. Meeting *Shabbetai Ẓevi during his stay in Jerusalem, he joined the first group of fervent "believers" at the outbreak of the messianic movement (1665), and was present at the height of the messianic excitement in Gaza during May and June 1665. Later he left, joining Shabbetai Ẓevi in Constantinople, becoming a member of his most intimate circle. While Shabbetai was imprisoned in the fortress of Gallipoli, Primo served as his "scribe" and secretary and held court for the masses of his followers. It was he who composed the circular letters and pronouncements of the "Messiah," written in a highflown and majestic style, and received the delegations visiting Shabbetai Ẓevi. In the absence of *Nathan of Gaza, he and Abraham *Yakhini were the outstanding spokesmen for the movement at that time. In a famous letter (summer, 1666) he encouraged messianic terrorism against those who spoke disparagingly of Shabbetai Ẓevi. When catastrophe befell the movement with Shabbetai's apostasy, Primo remained faithful, but refrained from any public display of his belief and participation in Shabbatean activities. He stayed for many years in Sofia, making frequent visits to Shabbetai Ẓevi in Adrianople and later in Dulcigno, and maintaining close contact with Nathan of Gaza and other Shabbatean leaders. Shabbetai Ẓevi initiated him into his later kabbalistic teaching concerning the "mystery of the Godhead." In later years Primo divulged this teaching, under the greatest secrecy, only to those whom he deemed trustworthy. He embraced Shabbetai Ẓevi's theory of divine apotheosis and other teachings of the radical wing, while outwardly returning to his occupation of orthodox talmudic scholar and acquiring a great reputation as such. Sometime after 1680 he moved to Adrianople where, after several years of study on behalf of the community, he became rabbi of the Apulian synagogue and later its *av bet din,* enjoying the highest esteem until his death. For a long time he suffered from severe rheumatism in his legs, and after a serious illness he added Judah to his name, signing all documents Judah Samuel Primo. He did not join the *Doenmeh sect, strongly opposing every public demonstration of Shabbatean faith, but he is known to have said to confidants that the *amoraim* did not really understand the secrets of the faith and that in some respects their wisdom was obsolete. When Abraham *Cardozo publicly preached his brand of Shabbatean theology and tried to settle in Adrianople, in 1693 and in 1697, Primo repudiated his teachings and caused him to be expelled. In his last years Cardozo wrote several papers against Primo's secret teachings without, however, suggesting that Primo had abandoned his belief in Shabbetai Ẓevi. Primo's equivocal stand on Shabbateanism resembles that of many of the scholars of his day.

In addition to being an outstanding preacher, Primo wrote many responsa and halakhic decisions, but almost all his writings were destroyed by the great fire in Adrianople in 1704. His son-in-law, R. Moses Kohen, included his remaining responsa in his own collection, *Kehunnat Olam* (Constantinople, 1740), and Primo's pupil, David ibn Shanji, added his edition of his extant sermons under the title *Imrei Shefer* to the end of this volume. Summaries of his secret teachings are preserved in several Shabbatean manuscripts (for instance, Ben Zvi Institute 2262). Among his chief pupils and followers were Ḥayyim *Malakh, who stayed with him for two or three years (1694–96), and Ḥayyim Alfandari, (see *Alfandari family) originally of Brusa and later one of the leading rabbis of Constantinople, whom, according to Cardozo, Primo believed for some time (between 1696 and 1700 if not earlier) to be the man destined to take Shabbetai Ẓevi's place after his apotheosis. It is not clear how he reconciled the appointment of a possible successor to Shabbetai Ẓevi with his consistent aloofness from Shabbatean activities on other than strictly esoteric levels. Primo died in Adrianople.

Bibliography: Scholem, Shabbetai Ẓevi, index; A. Danon, in: REJ, 37 (1898), 104–7; Z. Rubaschow (Shazar), *Sofero shel Mashi'aḥ* (1970=*Ha-Shiloaḥ*, 29 (1913), 36–47; Rosanes, Togarmah, 4 (1934–35), 234–9; G. Scholem, in: *Abhandlungen... H. P. Chajes* (1933), Heb. pt. 330–3; idem, in: *Zion*, 7 (1942), 20–21; *Sefunot*, 3–4 (1960), index s.v.; A. Amarillo, *ibid.*, 5 (1961), 270–4 (incl. facsimile of an autograph letter). [G.SCH.]

1

2

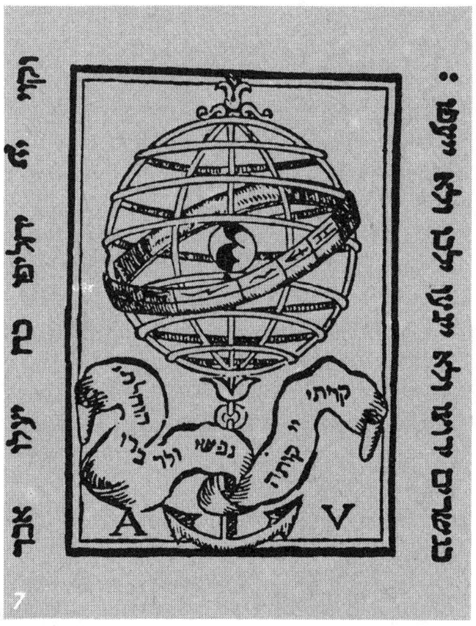

3

4

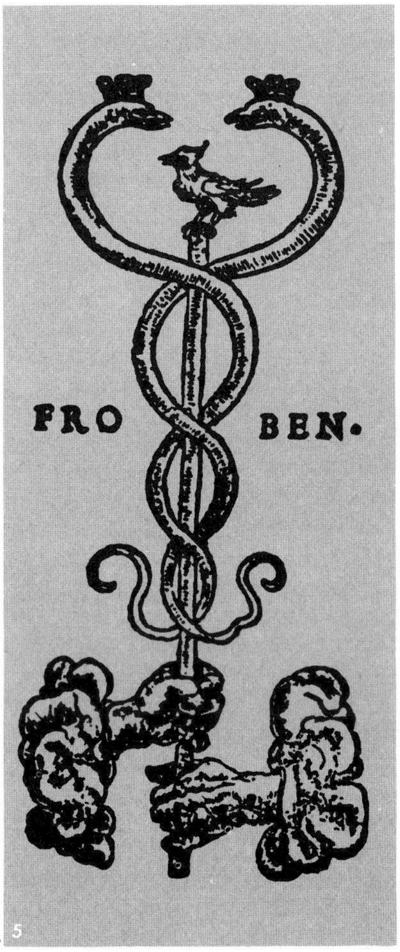

5

6

7

8

9

1. Eliezer Alantansi, Hijar, 1885 and after. 2. Giustiniani press, Venice, 1545–52. 3. Abraham Usque, Ferrara, 1553–58. 4. The Basevi family, Verona, 1594–1605. 5. Hieronymus Froben, Basle, 1531–64. 6. Immanuel Benveniste, Amsterdam, 1641–49. 7. Manasseh Ben Israel, Amsterdam, 1635–50. 8. Alvise Bragadini, Venice, 1550–54 and 1564–74. 9. Paulus Fagius, Isny, 1541–42. All printer's marks are from A. Yaari, *Hebrew Printers' Marks from the Beginnings of Hebrew Printing to the End of the 19th Century,* Jerusalem, 1943.

PRINS, ABRAHAM (1769–1851), scholar. Born at Alkmaar, Holland, Prins was one of the founders of "Pekidim and Amarkalim of the Holy Land" (1809), an organization for collecting money for Ereẓ Israel.

In that same year, along with the widow of Joseph *Proops, he edited some liturgical works, among them *Likkutei Ẓevi* and a chapter from the unpublished commentary on the Tosefta by Isaac Lemgo. He also issued with H. Lehren a collection of letters of European rabbis (*Torat ha-Kena'ot,* 2 vols., 1845) and of the rabbis of Ereẓ Israel (*Kinat Ẓiyyon,* 1846), as well as *Hartelijke toespraak aan al zijn Israelitische broeders* (1845). Both the collections of letters and his work spoke out against the Reform movements.

Bibliography: R. Kisch-Spitz, *Herinneringen* (1952). [F.J.H.]

PRINS, LIEPMAN PHILIP (1835–1915), merchant and scholar of Arnhem, Holland. Until 1876 Prins was privately tutored after which time he continued his studies in Amsterdam and moved to Frankfort in 1887.

He was the publisher of the previously unedited part of the work of David Abudarham, *Tashlum-Abudraham* for *Mekizei Nirdamim (1900). He also wrote the introduction to a second edition of *Seder Berakhot* by Michael Moravsky. His own writings include annotations on the tractate *Hullin* (204b), and on the *siddur* (in *Oẓar Ha-Tefillot,* 1915), as well as numerous articles in Jewish weeklies and journals.

Bibliography: A. B. Posner, *R. Eliezer, Liepman P. Prins, Ḥayyav va-Avodato ha-Sifrutit* (1939). [F.J.H.]

PRINTERS' MARKS, the devices or badges used by early printers to distinguish their productions. The first known printers' mark in Hebrew printing is the lion rampant within a red shield, which was used by Eliezer Alantansi at Híjar in and after 1485. The *Soncino family of printers, both in Italy and in other countries, used a tower, probably the badge of the city of Soncino in Lombardy; this was subsequently adopted by the Soncino Gesellschaft in Germany and by the 20th-century Soncino Press in London. Later, various printers of the Kohen family, especially the Proops' of Amsterdam, used a printers' mark of the hands spread in priestly benediction. The Giustiniani Press in Venice employed a conventional representation of the Temple in Jerusalem—subsequently much copied—and the Bragadini used three crowns symbolizing the diadem of royalty, priesthood, and Torah (cf. Avot 4:13). At a later time Italian printers often employed their family badges as printers' marks. Thus, the productions of the Foa family, from the middle of the 16th century down to the 18th, were distinguished by a badge showing two lions rampant against a palm tree supporting the shield of David, with various permutations. Abraham Usque of Ferrara adopted the Portuguese royal badge of a sphere, losing the significance of the punning motto *spera in dominum* by translating it back into the Hebrew original *kavveh el Adonai* (Ps. 27:14). The Basevi brothers of Verona used their family badge, subsequently incorporated into their coat of arms, of a white lion back to back with a black eagle, both crowned. The badge of Manasseh Ben Israel was memorable, with the words *emet me-ereẓ tiẓmaḥ* ("Truth springeth out of the earth," Ps. 85:12) shown as a rebus, or in his non-Hebrew productions, a pilgrim with the motto *Apercebido como hu romeiro.* The Benveniste family of Amsterdam used a lion rampant against a tower, surmounted by a star, which presumably was their coat of arms. The symbols of fertility, fish, were common throughout the 17th and 18th centuries in various countries. Monograms in Latin characters were sometimes used. The Eastern European printers' marks were for the most part unoriginal and often poorly printed and designed. Among the Christian printers of Hebrew books, Froben used intertwined serpents, and *Fagius, a leafy tree. From the 18th century, the use of printers' marks became less common and their designs less distinctive.

Bibliography: A. Yaari, *Hebrew Printers' Marks from the Beginnings of Hebrew Printing to the End of the 19th Century* (Heb. and Eng., 1943), with 208 reproductions. [C.R.]

PRINTING, HEBREW.

PRE-MODERN PERIOD

The first mention of Jews in connection with printing is found in Avignon c. 1444 (before Gutenberg) when a Jew, Davin de Caderousse, studied the new craft. The first Hebrew books were printed at least within 35 years after the invention of printing—the first dated ones being Rashi's commentary on the Pentateuch and Jacob b. Asher's *Arba'ah Turim* of 1475 (see *Incunabula). This new and wonderful invention was called the "crown of all science," and its practice, like that of writing of sacred books, *melekhet shamayim* ("a divine craft," see Er. 13a) or *melekhet ha-kodesh* ("a sacred craft," Ex. 36:4). It was regarded as a means to realize Isaiah's prediction (11:9) that "the earth shall be full of the knowledge of the Lord." There were, on the other hand, interested parties such as the copyists, who feared for their livelihood and who opposed the innovation, as did those monk-copyists who described it as the "work of the devil." Printing raised halakhic problems as shown by contemporary responsa: the question arose whether the *halakhah* concerning the writing of sacred books and the care and respect due to them was applicable to printed books as well and whether, in particular, *Sifrei Torah, tefillin, mezuzot,* bills of divorce, etc., could be printed. Despite difficulties, the production of Hebrew books grew: David Kimḥi's *Sefer ha-Shorashim* saw three editions within a decade.

Figure 1. Opening page of *Leviticus Rabbah* with an initial word made up of individual blocks framed by an elaborate engraving, from the *Midrash Rabbah* on the Pentateuch printed by Daniel Bomberg, Venice, 1545. At bottom left is the printer's signature in Hebrew alphabetical and Arabic numbers. Jerusalem, J.N.U.L.

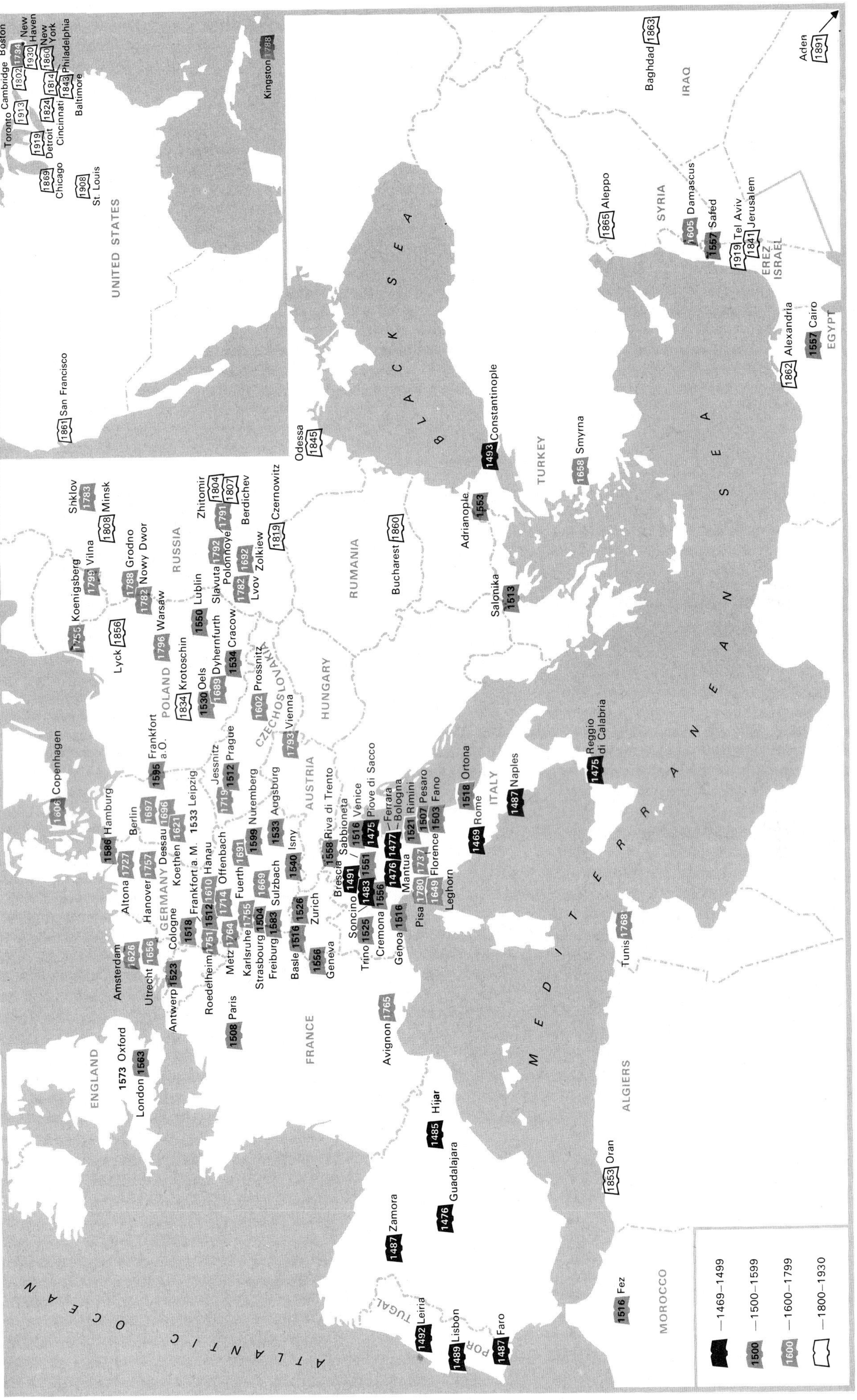

Main locations of Hebrew printing, 15th–20th centuries.

Printing had a revolutionary influence on the religious and cultural life of Jewish communities everywhere: on books and their distribution, on learning and education, on synagogal rites, etc. The order and division of the books of the *Bible, which today differ from both the talmudic and masoretic traditions, and the division into chapters in particular, are the result of printing. The printing of the Bible popularized it, while dictionaries and grammars, now easily obtainable, contributed greatly to the understanding of the Bible. The same is true for the Talmud, with its standard pagination originating in the first complete Bomberg edition (1520–23). The study of the Talmud became easier and far more widespread, and the printing alongside of the text, in addition to Rashi's commentary, of the *Tosafot* of Touques gave talmudic learning a new direction which led to the development of the novellae literature and of *pilpul.* The widespread use of printed prayer books reduced the importance and relative freedom of the reader; minor rites were eliminated in favor of the major ones, which in turn became fixed and standardized by the printed text. Purely local variations of rite have survived in manuscripts only. Earlier (1477) the word *defus* (talmudic: frame, mold) was used as a noun for printing, alliterating to the Latin *typus.* To describe the activity, the same word as for writing *(katav)* or engraving *(ḥakak)* was chosen, from which was derived *meḥokek* for the printer; but also *ha'atek* (to copy) which led to the noun *he'etek* for the copy of a printed book. Occasionally one finds such strange circumscriptions as "writing with many pens" (cf. Yoma 38b) or "writing without a pen." By the 16th century the derivatives from *defus* in the verb-forms of *hidpis* and *nidpas*—and *madpis* for the printer—were in common use, though some of the early terminology such as *meḥokek* survived in Germany and Eastern Europe for a considerable time. (For Hebrew printing in the 15th century, see *Incunabula.)

SIGNATURE AND PAGINATION

The early book productions had no signature, a device which was introduced by Joshua *Soncino in 1483. Usually, the signature is found on the left side of the bottom of the page in Hebrew alphabetical numbers, but some Augsburg, Constantinople, and Salonika issues of the early 16th century have them on the top left or bottom right corner. Up to about 1515 only Hebrew letters were used, but Daniel *Bomberg introduced Arabic figures as well. In rare cases the alphabet took the place of numbers (*Kol Bo,* Rimini, 1525, Rome, 1545). Pagination was introduced later than the signature. No incunabulum appears to have had it. The first to have had numbered folios, though not very consistently so, is Maimonides' *Mishneh Torah,* printed in Constantinople in 1509. Soncino did not number his pages to the end. Of Bomberg's productions those prepared by Adelkind—with the exception of Bibles and prayer books—have numbered folios; from 1525 this is the case with all Bomberg's work, and most other Italian printers followed his example. The Hebrew number appears on the upper left of the first page in Bomberg's works; other printers added Arabic figures. One work printed in Sabbioneta and one in Cremona repeat the number on the upper right of the second page of the leaf. Pagination of pages is rather rare at first, exceptions being the works of Stephanus at Paris, Plantin at Antwerp, and Zanetti at Rome in the 16th century. The Cremona Zohar of 1559 has two columns to each page and numbers opposite every tenth line.

TITLE PAGES AND DECORATION

Title pages, too, make their first appearance in the 16th century. In the incunabula the text begins at first on the first page, but from 1483 the first page or folio is empty. The early title pages were very simple, with only a title, *colophon, place, and year. Whatever ornaments would appear on the first page of the text were then transferred to the title page. Such decorations—woodcuts of initials and border ornaments—were introduced by the Soncinos. Printers in Naples (Joseph b. Jacob *Gunzenhauser), as well as in Spain and Portugal, also used framed initials. Bomberg, following the general trend in book production, discarded the border ornaments and introduced the title page portal.

1500–1550

The first half of the 16th century was in many ways the golden age of Hebrew printing, with Italy and the house of *Soncino (until 1526) in a leading position. Gershon Soncino published mainly the Bible and its commentators, prayer books, and single Talmud tractates. His great competitor was Daniel Bomberg, the Christian printer from Antwerp, who from 1516 (or perhaps a few years earlier) to 1549 systematically issued the basic texts of Judaism in hitherto unequaled typographical perfection. With Bomberg Venice became the capital of Hebrew printing until well into the 18th century: in the above period the names of *Giustiniani and *Bragadini were outstanding. Elsewhere in Italy Samuel Latif printed in Mantua (1513–15). In 1518 the sons of Avigdor of Padua were active in Rome, where Samuel Ẓarefati printed in 1540–45 and Antonio Blado in 1545–46; another son of Avigdor used German square type in a *siddur* issued in Trino in 1525. More important were the productions of the Jewish silk-makers in Bologna (1537–40), mainly beautifully finished prayer books of the Italian rite of which many copies printed on parchment have survived.

Constantinople, Salonika, and Fez. Next to Italy in importance were Constantinople (1493) and Salonika (1513) where Hebrew printing was introduced by exiles from Spain and Portugal; the Soncinos began their activity in Salonika in 1527/28 and in Constantinople in 1530. Iberian refugees also brought printing to North Africa. Hebrew books were printed in Fez with Lisbon type, 1516–22.

Northern Europe. Hebrew printing in northern Europe began in Prague in 1512 with a group of printers who were later joined by Gershom b. Solomon Kohen, founder of a long and famous line of printers (the "Gersonides"; see *Kohen family). He used German square and a new cursive rabbinic type and many ornaments: angels, birds, lions, municipal coats of arms, and outspread hands, the priestly symbol of the family. To this group also belonged Ḥayyim *Shaḥor, who left Prague in 1526 to print at Oels (1530), Augsburg (1533–44), Ichenhausen, and Heddernheim (1546). Apart from continuing in the Prague style of type and decoration, Shaḥor also used the smaller Italian type. In Poland, Cracow and Lublin became important centers of Hebrew printing.

Hebrew Printing by and for Non-Jews. This was a special feature of the first half of the 16th century though it continued long afterward. The age was that of the Reformation and humanism, when enlightened Christian scholars became interested in the Hebrew Bible, its language, and grammar. This demand was filled by such men as Stephanus in Paris (1508–?), who used his own rabbinic and square types which bore a resemblance to the Spanish ones. Only after 1542 did he go over to the Italian type. In Basle Hebrew printing began in 1516—and continued through the century; here the German square type, but somewhat slanting, was used. Psalms, Hebrew grammars, and some Christian liturgical pieces in Hebrew, Latin, and Greek were printed in Lyons from 1520 by Gryphius, who utilized the same type. German cities in which Hebrew printing took place were Tuebingen (1511), Augsburg (1514), Cologne (1518), Wittenberg (1521), Leipzig (1533), Solingen (1538), and Mainz (1542). A special position was occupied by the Hebrew press, set up in 1540 by the Christian Hebraist Paulus *Fagius in conjunction with Elijah *Levita at Isny, Wuerttemberg, and later at Konstanz on the German-Swiss border, where some books were printed in separate editions for Jews and Christians (e.g., Levita's *Tishbi* of 1541–42). They used the German type for their meticulous productions.

1550–1627

The single most influential event in the history of Hebrew

printing in this period was the papal prohibition and subsequent burning of the Talmud in 1553. The virtual monopoly of Venice on Talmud printing came to an end, resulting in complete or partial Talmud editions in Lublin (1559), Salonika (1563), and Basle (1578). In Cracow and Constantinople, too, single tractates were printed at this time. In Italy itself two different periods are distinguishable: (1) the decentralization of Hebrew printing over many small presses in different places during 1550–68; (2) the reemergence of Venice as the center of Hebrew printing and the predominance of certain presses in the town from 1569 onward.

Ferrara, Sabbioneta, Mantua, Cremona, and Riva di Trento. In 1551 Samuel Ẓarefati, who had worked as a Hebrew printer in Rome, set up a press at Ferrara, which was taken over two years later by the Marrano Abraham *Usque. Simultaneously, Tobias *Foa established a Hebrew press at Sabbioneta, near Mantua, with Joseph Shalit of Padua, Jacob b. Naphtali, and later Cornelio *Adelkind (1553–55) as printers. The last-mentioned printed the last Talmud tractate *(Kiddushin)* before the prohibition, as well as an exemplary edition of Alfasi, the study of which was now substituted for that of the Talmud. In Sabbioneta, too, Salonika's influence was paramount, and the two types were so similar as to lead to confusion. The very small type used found its way to Mantua and later to Venice (De Gara, 1572; Bragadini, 1616). Sabbioneta productions are more lavishly decorated than those of Ferrara. Joseph Shalit and Jacob b. Naphtali continued printing at Mantua from 1556 at Rufinelli's, 1557–63. After a rather quiescent period (1563–90), of which only Azariah dei Rossi's *Me'or Einayim* of 1574 was noteworthy, more active printing was resumed at the press of Tomaso Ruffinelli. A new one was set up in 1612 by Eliezer d'Italia where besides smaller liturgical items such larger works as Abraham Portaleone's *Shiltei ha-Gibborim* appeared. In 1622 the Perugia family took over this press which remained active for another 50 years. Mantua productions show little originality in their decorations. Jacob ha-Kohen first introduced a title page with

Figure 2. Page from the 1526 edition of the *Prague Haggadah*, printed in German square typeface and published by Gershom b. Solomon Kohen and his brother Gronem (Geronim), with art work apparently by Ḥayyim Shaḥor (Schwarz). Jerusalem, J.N.U.L.

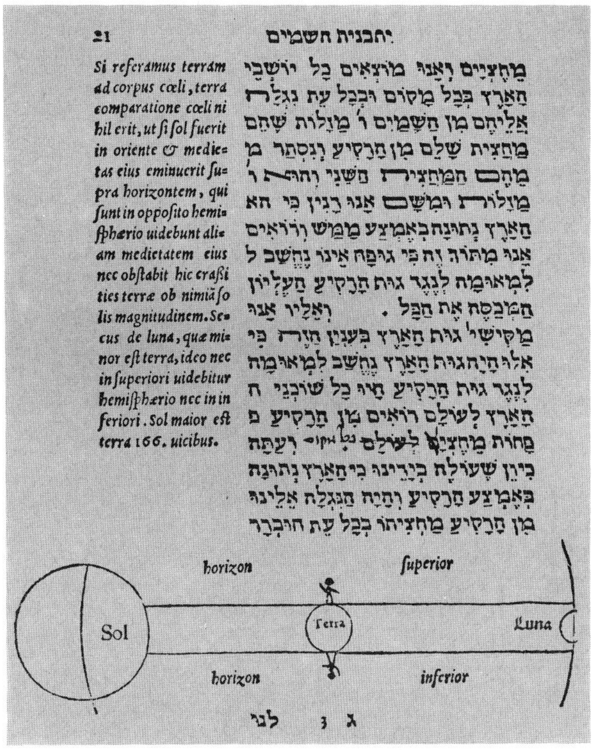

Figure 3. Page from an edition of a Hebrew work on astronomy, with Latin translation and notes on difficult Hebrew words, *Sefer Ẓurat ha-Areẓ* by Abraham b. Ḥiyya. Printed by a non-Jew, Hericus Petrus, in Basle, 1546. Jerusalem, J.N.U.L.

a decorative border and the outspread hands of the priesthood. When he entered into partnership with Meir Sofer, the typical Mantua title portal with winding pillars made its appearance. They also used the various vignettes of Bragadini and De Farri and those of Sabbioneta. The Mantua illustrated *Haggadot* with the big German type have become famous. In Cremona Vincenzo Conti printed, between 1556 and 1566, some 40 books, of which the most important was the Zohar of 1559. His assistants were Samuel Boehm, Zanvil Pescarol, and Vittorio Eliano. From 1558 works display the *cum licencia* of the Inquisition. Conti extended his activities to Sabbioneta, where Israel Zifroni printed several books for him in 1567. The last book printed in Cremona was *Yosef Lekaḥ* by Eliezer Ashkenazi, issued by Solomon Bueno at Draconi's in 1576. Riva di Trento received its Hebrew press in 1558 when the physician Jacob Marcaria obtained a license from Cardinal Madruzzi. With the help of R. Joseph *Ottolenghi he first issued a reasonably priced edition of Alfasi for Ottolenghi's yeshivah students. This was followed by some philosophical and rabbinic works. The last of these, *Me'ir Iyyov* by Meir Arama, of 1562, had to be completed by Cavalli in Venice in 1566. Marcaria used mainly square types, among them a small one. His decorations are similar to those of Mantua in their title portals and decorated initials. Books of 1562 have their own vignette, later copied in Cracow.

Venice. When in 1563 the printing of Hebrew books in Venice was once more permitted, most of the printers mentioned before moved or moved back there and found employment with the houses of Gryphio (1564–67), Cavalli (1565–67), and Zanetti (1565–67), each using his own printer's mark. At that time mostly *Turim* with Caro's commentary and his Shulḥan Arukh came off the presses, taking the place of the prohibited Talmud. Eventually Di Gara and Bragadini emerged as the leading presses. Di Gara, whom some of the best printers had joined, aspired to continue the Bomberg tradition. He succeeded as far as externals were concerned until 1585, when new title pages, borders, and decorated letters gave the productions a different character. In the choice of books Di Gara followed in the footsteps of Bomberg. Di Gara also printed many homiletical works, mostly by oriental authors, such as Alshekh, Alkabeẓ, and Almosnino. He was assisted in this by Isaac Gershon of Safed, as corrector. Bragadini resumed printing immediately after the repeal of the prohibition, with Meir Parenzo and, after the latter's death, his brother Asher as his managing printers. They published the first (1565) and two further editions of

Caro's Shulḥan Arukh and a new edition of Maimonides' *Mishneh Torah* with Caro's commentary *Kesef Mishneh* (1574–75). From 1579 to 1600 Bragadini and Di Gara worked together. After a period of recession, there was a revival under Giovanni Cajon's management (c. 1615) which produced a new Bible (1617/18) under Leone *Modena's supervision. From 1625, under Caleoni, several *maḥzor* editions and other liturgical items were printed, but with the rise of the Amsterdam and German presses, Bragadini's lost its impetus. A short-lived revival took place in 1710–15 as shown by the two-volume folio German *maḥzor,* printed with new, large types. Another press active at Venice at the time was that of Zanetti, with Isaac *Gershon as supervisor (1593–1608). Outside Venice, apart from Mantua, there was Padua, where Samuel Boehm printed at Lorenzo Pasquato in 1562–67, and Crivellari's press with two works, 1622–23. Some Hebrew and Judeo-German books were issued at Verona by Francesco della Donne (1594–95).

Cracow and Lublin. Italian influence made itself felt in Cracow when Isaac b. Aaron *Prostitz with the aid of Samuel Boehm set up his press in 1569. They had brought type and decorations with them from Italy and imitated the ornaments of most Italian presses. They printed, largely for local needs, the works of German and Polish authors as well as ethical and liturgical items in Hebrew and Yiddish. From 1595 onward larger works were published. With Isaac b. Aaron's return to Prossnitz (*Prostejov) some Hebrew printing, such as an *Ein Ya'akov,* took place there (1603–05). In Lublin, where Kalonymus Jaffe was active from 1562, the influence of both Prague and Venice were at work. Jaffe printed, besides local authors, the Talmud and Zohar as well as some philosophical (or anti-philosophical) works. In Bistrowicz he prepared in 1592 a *Haggadah* with Abrabanel's commentary. His printer's mark was the Temple, which was also used in Prague and by Giustiniani.

Prague, Basle, and Hanau. The Kohen family in Prague continued to be active from 1562; in 1605 another printing family, the *Baks, established themselves. They both continued the Prague tradition, Italian influence making itself felt only occasionally. The Prague productions were mainly in the liturgical and ethical field, both in Hebrew and Judeo-German. Israel Zifroni guided the Hebrew press of Frobenius in Basle, which hitherto had worked mainly for the Christian market, in a different direction by printing several rabbinic works, including an edition—censored—of the Talmud (1578–88) and without the "objectionable" tractate *Avodah Zarah,* which was, however, supplemented in Cracow (1580). Zifroni-Froben printed a couple of works in Freiburg-im-Breisgau as well (1583–84). The original Basle type had to give way to the Italian one. Another Basle Hebrew press at the time was that of Konrad Waldkirch who, with the assistance of printers from Poland, issued among others a Bible (1618–19) and Joseph Solomon Delmedigo's *Ta'alumot Ḥokhmah* (1629–31). About this time Hebrew printing took place in Hanau (Hesse), where from 1610 to 1630 several important kabbalistic and Judeo-German works were issued. Both sides of their title pages showed the figures of Moses and Aaron—which set a fashion among later printers—and above was a representation of the **Akedah.*

Figure 4. Title page of Abraham b. Isaac Averbuch's *Seliḥot,* with a representation of the reunion of Joseph (the printer's namesake) with his father. Printed in Amsterdam, 1677, by Joseph Athias. From A. Ya'ari, *Hebrew Printers' Marks from the Beginnings of Hebrew Printing to the End of the 19th Century,* Jerusalem, 1943.

Turkey, Egypt, and Palestine. In Constantinople and Salonika in the second half of the 16th century, the *Jabez brothers took the place of the older printers. After a short stay in Adrianople, they arrived in the two cities in 1559 and produced up to 1586 a series of rabbinic, philosophical, anti-Christian, and Karaite works, among them two Talmud editions based on Bomberg's edition with elements from Giustiniani (Salonika, 1563–65; Constantinople, 1580–82). The printers used the Italian type but not the decorations, their only ornament being the trefoil. Between 1578 and 1600 Joseph Nasi's widow Doña Reyna had Hebrew presses at her palace of Belvedere and in other places near Constantinople. Her husband had been a patron of Hebrew printing. About 1590 members of the Italian Bat-Sheva family settled in Salonika and set up a press, using Italian type and decorations. In Cairo a fourth-generation Soncino printed two Hebrew books in 1557 and 1562. The aforementioned Eliezer b. Isaac printed several works in Safed during 1577–87, and the same type was used a generation later to print Josiah Pinto's *Kesef Nivḥar* in Damascus (1605).

THE 17TH AND 18TH CENTURIES

Amsterdam. Hebrew printing followed the wanderings of the Jews. Fugitives from the Inquisition established the new Portuguese community in Amsterdam at the turn of the 16th century. Ignorant of Hebrew, they recited their prayers in Spanish, and prayer books in that language were printed in Amsterdam by 1604. When Hebrew became more familiar, Venice supplied prayer books in Hebrew, with or without translation. In 1626 *Manasseh Ben Israel set up the first Hebrew press in Amsterdam—a turning point in the history of Hebrew printing. He discarded Italian type, making himself independent of Venice, and had his own type cast which was destined to become dominant all over Europe, including Venice. Amsterdam productions were much sought after as those of Venice had been earlier and they found imitators among Hebrew printers elsewhere. Amsterdam was at the time a great center of general printing, and in format, composition, and decoration Manasseh followed the Dutch style; thus he added the author's portrait to some works. Manasseh's press changed owners several times, though he remained connected with it. Simultaneous with this press another was set up by Daniel de *Fonseca but only two works were issued: Meir Aldabi's *Shevilei Emunah* and Abraham de Fonseca's *Einei Avraham* (1627). Manasseh found successors among his fellow Sephardim, among them Joseph *Athias (1658–98) and his son (d. 1709). In externals such as vignettes and diagrams they adopted in some way the style of the famous Dutch printer Elsevier. Athias first used Manasseh's title pages, but later had one designed for himself depicting Joseph (his namesake) meeting his father Jacob. This was later adopted by Jablonski in Berlin. He also added a neatly executed copperplate engraving to some of his productions, which found a number of imitators; one of them (*Shenei Luḥot ha-Berit,* 1698) was by the proselyte Abraham b. Jacob, who illustrated the famous *Amsterdam Haggadah* of 1695, produced by the German-Jewish printer Kosmann Emmerich. Another member of the Athias family, Abraham b. Raphael Hezekiah, printed some handsomely produced books during 1728–40. To the same Sephardi group belongs David de *Castro Tartas, who learned the craft at Manasseh's press and often used Manasseh's borders. His frontispieces show scenes from the life of David. Of particular interest are his small-format liturgical items of 1666, dated year one of the new Shabbatean era and with an engraving of Shabbetai Ẓevi as king-messiah. Smaller entrepreneurs were Moses b. Abraham Mendes Coutinho (see *Coutinho family), for whom Solomon Proops (see *Proops family) worked for some time; Isaac de Cordova (1688–1710), later in Hamburg; Moses b. Isaac Dias (1706–13); Isaac Templo (1714–34), who printed Nehemiah Ḥayon's *Ha-Ẓad Ẓevi* (1744) but otherwise mainly liturgical items of the Sephardi rite; and Nethanel Foà (1700–15) who displayed as printer's mark the coat of arms of this well-known family. In addition to these printers, who produced mainly for their own community, there were those who endeavored to meet the needs of the German community established in Amsterdam in the course of the 17th century. There was Manuel (Immanuel) Benveniste, whose productions lack the finish of those of Manasseh, though his title page with the initials CVS has been imitated by German, Italian, and even Salonika printers. Benveniste was succeeded by his former employee *Uri Phoebus b. Aaron ha-Levi (1658–89), who worked even more for the German and also for the newly established Polish communities. From Manasseh he borrowed the title border and the vignettes. The frontispieces in his Bibles and prayer books have engravings with motifs borrowed from Prague, Augsburg, and Hanau, showing Moses and Aaron on each side. This engraving has been much copied by German presses. In 1612 he founded a Hebrew press at Zolkiew, thus bringing the Amsterdam type to Poland. Less important Ashkenazi printers in Amsterdam were Samuel b. Moses ha-Levi, who was active from 1650 to 1655, having for assistants Reuben b. Eliakim and Judah b. Mordecai; and Asher Anshel Shoḥet, who had worked with Uri Phoebus from 1663 to 1665 and printed some liturgical and popular items. The two Ashkenazi *dayyanim* Joseph Dayyan and Moses Frankfurter printed some Talmud tractates, the latter in particular a large, four-volume Bible, *Kehillat Moshe* (1724–27). Of greater importance was the physician Naphtali Herz of Emden (1721–42, to 1768 with his son-in-law) who printed some fine books. Some Christians too engaged in the Hebrew printing in Amsterdam—employing Polish refugees—such as Kaspar Steen. Albertus Magnus brought out a handsome *Seder Berakhot* with Spanish translation in 1687; G. Surenhuys printed a famous and impressive edition of the Mishnah with Latin translation and notes (1698–1703). In the 18th century the dominant figure in Amsterdam Hebrew printing became Samuel Proops (1702–34). He printed mainly *siddurim* and *maḥzorim* of the various rites. From 1715 a list of his publications is advertised at the end of every copy. He was also the first to bring out a sales catalog of Hebrew books (*Appiryon Shelomo,* 1730). The press remained in the family until 1849 and was as important to Amsterdam as Bragadini was to Venice.

Germany. The unsettled conditions in Central and Eastern Europe—wars, frequent expulsions, sack, and fire, and, above all, the Chmielnicki pogroms in Poland with thousands of refugees fleeing westward and leaving behind everything including their books and libraries—had a profound influence on Hebrew book production. There was in particular an urgent need for Talmud copies and rabbinic literature in a period of unabated, passionate interest in these disciplines. This need was met by Amsterdam and the many Hebrew presses springing up in Germany. During the 18th century the Talmud was printed ten times, each edition in several thousand copies. Catastrophic events produced a desire among the less learned and the womenfolk for works of solace and edification, which accounts for the great increase in the publication of Yiddish literature. Printing became a profitable business besides being a pious enterprise, and large sums were being invested, loaned, or donated for these diverse reasons. In Central and Eastern Europe, Jews found it difficult to obtain the necessary printing licenses from feudal lords, and therefore had to associate with Christians as their nominal printers. On the other hand, economic considerations such as the needs of local papermills and fiscal expectations led many small princes or authorities to grant licenses, at the same time protecting the new industry and their country's balance of payments by prohibiting the importation of Hebrew books. Large sums were involved: in about 1780 it was calculated that the Jews of Vienna spent 290,000 florins annually on books. Typographically the new Hebrew printers in Germany were at first dependent on Prague whence most of the personnel came. Gradually the influence of Amsterdam made itself felt, even in Prague itself. The German square type was increasingly

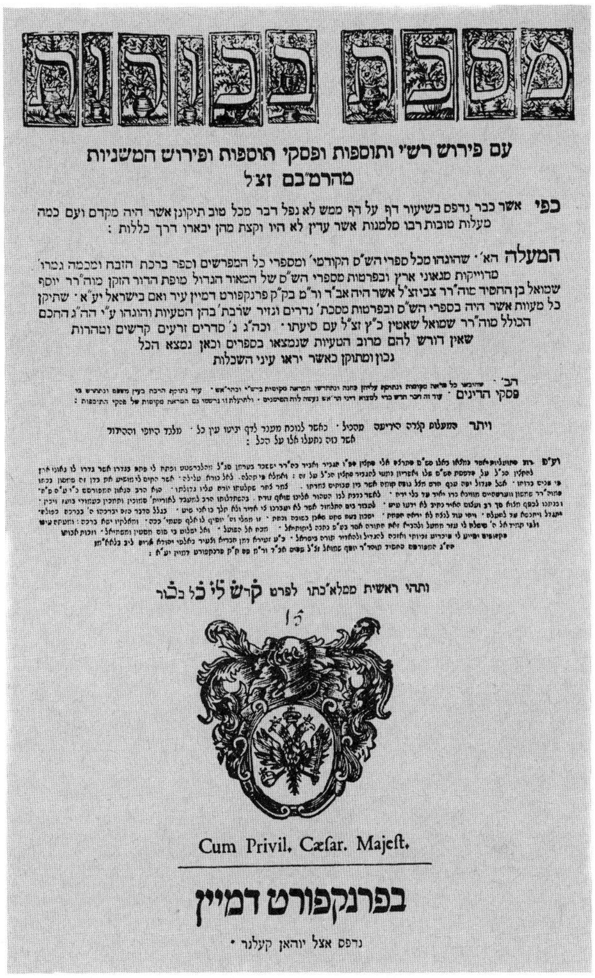

Figure 5. Title page of the tractate *Bekhorot* from the Babylonian Talmud, bearing the double-headed eagle of the Hapsburgs in an escutcheon, printed by the non-Jew Johann Koelner in Frankfort, 1720. Jerusalem, J.N.U.L.

discarded. The Hebrew presses of Germany consisted of two groups: those with the Prague connection, such as Sulzbach, Wilhermsdorf, and Fuerth; and those originating with the Ashkenazi printers of Amsterdam, such as Dyhernfurth, Dessau, Halle. Apart from Christian presses which issued Hebrew books sporadically only, and small, ephemeral Jewish printers, Germany produced a considerable number of important Hebrew presses. One of the most prominent Jewish agglomerations was the triple community of Altona, Hamburg, and Wandsbeck (AHW), which was reflected in printing as well. S. Poppert was active in Hamburg and Altona (1715–36); Ephraim Heckscher and his partner Aaron b. Elijah Kohen (1732–75); Abraham b. Israel of Halle, son of the printer at Offenbach, Homburg and Neuwied (1743–47). In 1745 Jacob *Emden, the great rabbinic scholar and polemicist, set up his own press which printed mainly his own works, such as the three-volume *siddur Ammudei Shamayim* (1745–48) and his polemics against Jonathan *Eybeschuetz.

The Two Frankforts, Berlin, etc. In the ancient and influential community of Frankfort on the Main no Jew could obtain a printing license from the guild-dominated city authorities, but Christians owned Hebrew presses: Johannes West (1677–1707), Blasius Ilsner (1682–?), the Andreas (1707–?), Nikolas Weinmann, and Anton Heinscheit. Of special importance was Johann Koelner (1708–28) from whose printing office came a five-volume *Arba'ah Turim* with J. Sirkes' commentary (1712–16) and an excellent edition of the Talmud (1720–23) which became the basis for later editions. Aryeh Loeb, son of the Frankfort rabbi Joseph Samuel of Cracow, and later rabbi in Mattersdorf, was responsible for this enterprise. Aryeh Loeb had also prepared the second Amsterdam Talmud of 1714–17, the unacknowledged master copy for the later Berlin-Frankfort on the Oder edition. The Frankfort on the Oder Christian presses had issued Hebrew books before the end of the 16th century, but widespread printing began in 1695 with J. C. Beckmann and Michael Gottschalk, whose successors, F. Grillo, his widow, his daughter, and J. T. Elsner continued Hebrew printing until 1818. Gottschalk prepared the first Talmud edition in Germany (1697–99) which Behrend *Lehmann of Halberstadt financed, with 50,000 taler. A second edition, which Lehmann first wanted to divert to the other Frankfort, was eventually printed (1715–22) in both Frankfort on the Oder and Berlin. Midrashim *(Rabba, Tanḥuma, Yalkut)* were also issued there. Gottschalk employed setters from Prague and Venice; his type and vignettes were of Amsterdam origin. In Berlin, the court preacher D. E. Jablonski established a Hebrew press with Judah Loeb Neumark as manager. From 1708 to 1717 Baruch Buchbinder of Radow printed, among others, the *Ein Ya'akov* (1709) and several works of the Shabbatean writer Nehemiah Ḥayon. Neumark's son Nathan had his own press from 1719 to 1727 on which he printed some Talmud tractates from 1723. His brother-in-law Aaron b. Moses Rofe was active for three decades from 1733. He printed the Talmud (1734–39) with the backing of Jablonski, whose type was used, and Grillo of Frankfort on the Oder; it was thus an undertaking of both cities. Aaron's press continued under his grandson Moses and his great-grandson Mordecai Landsberg. There was also Hebrew printing in Dessau (1694–), Jessnitz (1718–), and Koethen (1717–) in the duchy of Anhalt. In Halle, the proselyte Moses b. Abraham of Nikolsburg (Mikulov) and Prague was active from 1709 to 1714, after having worked with Hebrew printers in Amsterdam, Dessau, Berlin, and Frankfort on the Oder. In Dyhernfurth (Silesia), Shabbetai Bass of Prague, who had learned the trade with Uri Phoebus at Amsterdam, founded a press in 1689; his son Joseph took over in 1712 (till 1739). While his newly cast type and decorations were mostly of Amsterdam origin, Bass's employees came from Poland, among them Ẓevi Hirsch b. Ḥayyim. Neuwied (Rhineland) had Hebrew presses (Grat and J. B. Haupt), run by Israel b. Moses. Another printer there was Benjamin Solomon Kroneburg.

Southern Germany. In southern Germany and the environs of Frankfort in particular, Hebrew printing had already taken place early in the 17th century in Hanau and was resumed from 1709, partly by Christian printers such as H. J. Bashuysen and J. C. Beausang. Among Jewish printers there was Seligman Reis (1710–30), who also had been active in Frankfort on the Main, Offenbach, and Homburg v.d.H. (1711–12). Aaron Dessau and partners set up a press in Homburg in 1736 (to 1757). In Offenbach, Seligmann Reis and his son Herz printed from 1714 to 1721. Bonaventura de Nannoy worked with the Jewish printer Israel b. Moses, who was also active in Neuwied and Homburg. In 1724 Israel acquired the press and worked it until 1733 and on his return from Neuwied in 1737 finished a Mishnah edition begun there in 1736.

Sulzbach, Wilhermsdorf, and Fuerth. In Sulzbach (Bavaria) an interesting and successful experiment in Christian and Jewish cooperation in the production of Hebrew books began in 1667, when Abraham Lichtenthaler, a Lutheran, set up a Hebrew press. He was assisted by Isaac b. Judah Loeb Yuedels, a Prague-trained printer, who had a license but no capital, and who was soon after in Wilhermsdorf. The patron of the project was Duke Christian August, an enthusiast of theosophy. Most early Sulzbach title pages have no decorations; only later did there appear simple border lines or illustrations engraved or on woodblocks. Some show a serpent winding round a tree (the Tree of Knowledge); others show crabs and fishes, or Moses and David on the right and Aaron and Solomon on the left. Some of these title pages were used in Fuerth and Dyhernfurth as well. The type was at first that of Prague, but for certain works the type of Amsterdam was used. Moses Bloch was succeeded by his widow and sons (1694–99) who printed some tractates as part of a plan to print the entire Talmud. Then Bloch's son-in-law Aaron Frankl took over, his first production being a two-volume folio *maḥzor,* attractively printed with decorated initials and a convenient arrangement of the prayers. Aaron was followed by his son Meshullam Zalman (1721–64), who printed a Talmud edition, 1755–63. His competitor, Proops of Amsterdam, obtained from the rabbinical assembly at the Four Council meeting at Staro-Konstantinov (1755) an injunction, which was countermanded by the decision of a ten-member rabbinical court presided over by the rabbi of Fuerth, David Stanss. A similar controversy arose in the next century over the Talmud editions of Vilna and Slavuta. Meshullam Zalman's sons and grandsons continued the business into the middle of the 19th century, when it was carried on under the name of S. Arnstein and Sons (1818–51); their publisher's catalogs appeared from 1830. The firm founded by Moses Bloch had been active for 160 years, issuing about 600 works, among them many cheaply printed but popular liturgical items. Another center of Hebrew printing in Bavaria was Wilhermsdorf, where Isaac b. Judah Loeb Yuedels (see before under Sulzbach) set up a press in 1669 with staff recruited from Prague, among them his daughters as setters and a son-in-law as proofreader. Another Prague printer, Israel Meir, set up a press in 1712 but sold it the same year to Hirsch b. Ḥayyim of Fuerth, whose son worked later in Fuerth, printing until 1739. Hirsch cultivated book decorations: his printer's mark was the tree with the serpent and a crab and a lion on each side; the title page showed Moses and Aaron and angels hovering above them and the last page a flower basket as vignette. Nearby Fuerth, a center of talmudic learning, had its first Hebrew presses by 1691. One was established by Solomon Shne'ur and his son Joseph with the help of the Cracow printer Moses Menahem Katz, and later continued under another son (Abraham) and a son-in-law Isaac Bing, and their sons or successors to 1730. This press printed some important rabbinic and Yiddish works. The other enterprise was that of Hirsch Frankfurter (till 1701), who had the backing of his brother-in-law, the Court Jew Mordecai Model of Ansbach; the latter had a license to print the Talmud. Another press was founded in Fuerth in 1737 by Ḥayyim b. Ẓevi Hirsch, son of the Dyhernfurth printer (see above), and it continued under him and his widow until 1774.

Italy, Prague, and Poland. In Venice, bereft of its former glory, Bragadini was still dominant at this period with Vendramini (de Zara) as his main competitor (from 1631) until they joined forces. Their activities were soon limited to *siddurim* and similar items. In Mantua, too, Hebrew printing continued, first under J. S. Perugia and his descendants, and from 1724 under the physician Raphael Ḥayyim d'Italia and his successor Eliezer Solomon d'Italia. From 1718 to 1723 Isaac Jare b. David and Jacob Ḥaver-Tov also printed

Figure 6. Title page of the fourth volume of Jacob Culi's Bible commentary in Ladino, *Me-Am Lo'ez.* Printed by Reuben and Nissim Ashkenazi, sons of the printer Jonah b. Jacob of Zalocze in Constantinople, 1764. Jerusalem, J.N.U.L.

Figure 7. Title page of *Sefer Ḥikrei Lev*, responsa on a section of the Shulḥan Arukh by Joseph Ḥazzan. Printed by Saadiah ha-Levi Ashkenazi, son of Bezalel, in Salonika, 1806. Jerusalem, J.N.U.L.

in Mantua. A new center was to arise in Leghorn, where Abraham Ḥaver-Tov, one of Bragadini's best proofreaders, printed some important works in partnership with Jedidiah Gabbai. They used as printer's mark the three crowns—borrowed from Bragadini—with the addition of the coat of arms of the Medicis. Some Hebrew printing took place at Rossi's press in Verona during 1645–52, with the Amsterdam influence predominating. Such was the case in Venice from 1700 and, in particular, in Leghorn, where Israel da Paz, who had worked with Isaac Templo at Amsterdam, was active from 1740. In Prague Hebrew printing resumed, after an interval of two decades, at Jacob Bak's press. During the 17th century Prague preserved its own style, but in the 18th century the old German square type disappeared from the superscriptions and much was borrowed from Amsterdam. In 1746 the archbishop's press issued the Gospels in Hebrew, Yiddish, German, and Latin for missionary purposes. In Cracow Menahem N. Meisels established his press in 1631 and returned to the Prague style which replaced the Italian introduced by Isaac b. Aaron of Prossnitz. Meisel's manager was Judah Kohen of Prague, and there is a great similarity between their productions and those of Prague. Lublin too, where Hebrew printing took place with interruptions until 1683, remained under the Prague influence. Only when Uri Phoebus went to Zolkiew in 1692 did the Amsterdam style find a home in Poland.

Turkey. Constantinople too experienced an almost complete break in Hebrew printing from 1585 to 1638. In the latter year Solomon Franco set up his press, which his son Abraham continued until 1683 and where several refugees from the Chmielnicki massacres were employed. Jonah b. Jacob of Zalocze in Galicia set up a press in 1710 and printed mostly in the Amsterdam style, but Italian influence was also present. When his press burned down in 1741, the Constantinople rabbi Abraham Rosanes helped him to reestablish himself, and his sons continued to print from 1743. Both Franco and Jonah modified the old decorations in the oriental style, as can be seen by comparing the Temple as printer's mark used in Venice, Prague, and Lublin with that of Constantinople, e.g., Joshua Benveniste's *Sedeh Yehoshu'a* of 1749. In Salonika too, after a long interval, Hebrew printing was resumed in 1650 on a modest scale. A revival began in 1709 under Abraham b. David and Yomtov Canpillas, the latter printing alone from 1729 and with partners from 1732. They printed mainly rabbinic novellae, responsa, and homiletics. Salonika preserved in type, decorations, and even paper its own easily recognizable style. Jedidiah Gabbai's Leghorn press was transferred to Smyrna by his son Abraham in 1657. Jonah b. Jacob (see above) also printed there in 1729–41. In Chufut-Kale, Afda and Shabbetai Jeraka with other partners set up the first Karaite press in 1734 (until 1741), working with types similar to that of Constantinople.

MODERN PERIOD

CENTRAL AND EASTERN EUROPE: 1760–1900

From the middle of the 18th century the center of Hebrew printing shifted more and more to Central and Eastern Europe. States, large and small, in these regions wanted to prevent the importation of Hebrew books and the resulting drain on their capital resources. In addition, the increasing severity of the church-state censorship—severer than it ever was in other parts of Europe, in a region that had not known such censorship before—made it desirable to them to have Hebrew presses under their immediate supervision. For both these reasons the setting up of local Hebrew presses was encouraged. A more positive cause of the rise of these presses was the efflorescence of Talmud study in the growing number of yeshivot in Lithuania and Poland as well as of Ḥasidism and its literature, creating an ever larger demand for Hebrew books. The beginnings of Haskalah should also be mentioned in this context. This shift to Eastern Europe admittedly meant a lowering of the standards of printing and book production.

Austria. The Hapsburg Empire occupied a middle position between East and West, and its capital, Vienna, a leading position in Hebrew printing in this period. Presses established in the last decade of the 18th century by the court printers Joseph Hrazchansky and Anton Schmidt succeeded the great Hebrew printing houses of Venice and Amsterdam. By 1850 they had issued five editions of the Talmud. Schmidt, who acquired a great part of the Bomberg and Proops presses, printed most of the classical texts, including Bibles and prayer books of all the rites. Later in the century and well into the 20th century Joseph Schlesinger was the leading publisher-printer of such liturgical items with translations into the main European languages. In what is now Czechoslovakia and what were, up to 1914, provinces of the Austro-Hungarian monarchy, the old center in Prague, the capital of Bohemia, never regained its former prominence. An attempt at revival by the Bak press from 1762 was stifled by the severity of the censorship. A certain revival took place under Moses *Landau (1820–50), who produced two Talmud editions and a good deal of Enlightenment literature emanating from the Mendelssohn school. In Bruenn (Brno), capital of Moravia, a Hebrew press had been founded in 1754 on the initiative of the Moravian chamber by Joseph Neumann which until 1802 produced mainly liturgical items, works of edification in Yiddish for the local market and those of local authors. Another Bruenn Hebrew printer at the time was Bezalel (Gottlieb) Jeiteles (see *Jeiteles family). In Pressburg (Bratislava), capital of Slovakia, where some Hebrew printing had taken place in 1789–90, Schmidt of Vienna set up a press in 1838 from which important items were issued. Joseph Schlesinger, too, printed there in the 1860s. In the Austrian-dominated parts of Poland (Galicia), Cracow retained its importance, with Naphtali Herz Shapiro and his sons active in 1802–22; Karl Budweiser (1863–74), who is found later in Lemberg (Lvov); and, in particular Joseph Fischer (1878–1914). The several small presses of Zolkiew were forced to transfer to Lvov in 1782, which led to the rise of that city as a center of Hebrew printing in the next century, with the presses of Mann (Grossmann-) Rosanes, Letteris, and, above all, Madfes, and some as yet unsurpassed editions of the Shulḥan Arukh were produced there. In Zolkiew itself a new press was founded in 1791 by a certain Meyerhofer, where works of the local rabbi Z. H. Chajes appeared in 1840–50. In Czernowitz Hebrew printing took place from 1819; in 1835 a Talmud edition was issued. In the Rumanian capital of Bucharest the *Sifra* with the commentary by M. L. Malbim, then rabbi at Bucharest, came out in a fine edition.

Poland and Russia. In Russia proper the first Hebrew book is said to have been printed in 1760 in Oleksinets (Y. L. Heller's *Berit Melaḥ*), where printing continued until 1770. The press of Slavuta (Ukraine), founded in 1792, issued three Talmud editions between 1800 and 1820; and one each (1816–28) in Kopys (Belorussia, founded 1807) and Grodno-Vilna (1835–54). The Shapira family of Slavuta continued in Zhitomir, printing fine editions of both Talmuds and the Zohar. Toward the middle of the 19th century Vilna became a great printing center—the Talmud editions of Romm (see *Romm family), who also issued other standard rabbinic texts, being recognized universally as the best editions. They continued to be reproduced to modern times. Romm's competitors in this field were printers like Samuel *Orgelbrand and Rosenkranz-Schriftsetzer in Warsaw, where the first Hebrew book was issued in 1796, and which eventually became an important center of Hebrew printing. Following is a list of places in Poland and Russia where Hebrew printing took place in this period:

Berdichev	Ukr.	1807	Nowy Dwor	Pol.	1782
Boguslav	Ukr.	1819	Odessa	Ukr.	1845
Bratslav	Ukr.	1821	Oleksinets	Ukr.	1760
Dubno	Ukr.	1794	Ostrog	Ukr.	1793
Dubrovno	Bel.	1802	Piotrkow	Pol.	1876
Grodno	Bel.	1788	Polonnoye	Ukr.	1791
Hrubieszow	Pol.	1817	Poritsk	Ukr.	1786
Jozefow	Pol.	1825	Radziwillow	Ukr.	1814
Kopys	Bel.	1807	Shklov	Bel.	1783
Korets (Korzec)	Ukr.	1778	Slavuta	Ukr.	1792
Lutsk	Ukr.	1787?	Sudilkov	Ukr.	1817
Medzhibozh	Ukr.	1817	Ternopol	Ukr.	1813
Mezkorov	Ukr.	1789	Vilna	Lith	1799
Minkovtsy	Ukr.	1796	Warsaw	Pol.	1796
Minsk	Bel.	1808	Zaslavl	Ukr.	1807
Mogilev	Bel.	1825	Zhitomir	Ukr.	1804
Mogilev-Podolski	Ukr.	1809			

Ukr. = Ukraine Lith. = Lithuania
Pol. = Poland Bel. = Belorussia

The Russian Karaites too resumed printing in Chufut-Kale, 1804–06, and in Goslov-Yevpatoriya, Crimea, 1833–36, issuing prayer books and works of Karaite literature.

WESTERN EUROPE

It should not be assumed that in Germany Hebrew presses had ceased working. In Berlin the *Orientalische Buchdruckerei* was founded in 1760. The apostate Julius Sittenfeld was active in the middle of the 19th century, producing a fine Talmud, 1862–68, for which N. A. Goldberg was responsible. Another Berlin printer from the second half of the century onward was H. Itzkowski. In Koenigsberg, where there had been sporadic printing during the 18th century, Gruebe and Longrien printed some fine rabbinic texts from 1858. To this group belongs Johannisberg, also in East Prussia, in the 1850s; Stettin, from 1859, where parts of the Talmud and a fine Mishnah were printed; Danzig (Mishnah with *Tiferet Yisrael* commentary, 1843); Hanover, at Telgeners, from 1828; Halberstadt from 1859 (Jeruham Fishel b. Ẓevi Hirsch); Leipzig; Breslau, from 1790; Lyck, east Prussia, where the weekly *Ha-Maggid* was printed, 1856–91, and the Mekiẓe Nirdamim Society brought out its early editions; Krotoszy, from 1834, with a fine Jerusalem Talmud; and in Posen from 1802. Of special importance is the press founded by Wolf *Heidenheim in Roedelheim, near Frankfort on the Main, about 1800, where he issued his famous Pentateuch, *maḥzor,* and other liturgical texts. This tradition was continued by his successor, M. Lehrberger, later in Frankfort, who printed Seligman Isaac *Baer's well-known liturgical texts. Karlsruhe had a Hebrew press both in the 18th and the 19th centuries. In France Hebrew presses were established in Metz (c. 1760), Strasbourg (1770), and later in Paris (1806). Here the house of Durlacher has been active from the 19th century. In England, where Hebrew had been printed—in London and Oxford—in earlier centuries, London, as well as Edinburgh in Scotland, had their Hebrew presses in the 19th century. In Italy, Venice continued to decline, with Leghorn becoming from 1740 the center of liturgical work for the Mediterranean area. First Sadun and then Solomon *Belforte were the leading printers in Leghorn. Venice printers branched out to Pisa in 1779, printing for the oriental market, and in Constantinople (so it was stated) books exclusively printed by Jews were preferred. Reggio Emilia had a small press from 1805 to 1820. Salonika and Smyrna continued in this period to turn out large amounts of rabbinical literature but no copies of the Talmud.

UNITED STATES

Hebrew printing in the United States at first took the form of Christian printers inserting isolated Hebrew words or phrases into their English publications, for which the type was brought over from England. Thus, in the first book printed in the U.S., an English version of Psalms

Figure 8. Title page of the Karaite work *Emunah Omen,* written in 1712 by Abraham b. Josiah Yerushalmi. Printed by Mordecai Tirishkan in Goslov-Yevpatoriya, Crimea, 1846. Jerusalem, J.N.U.L.

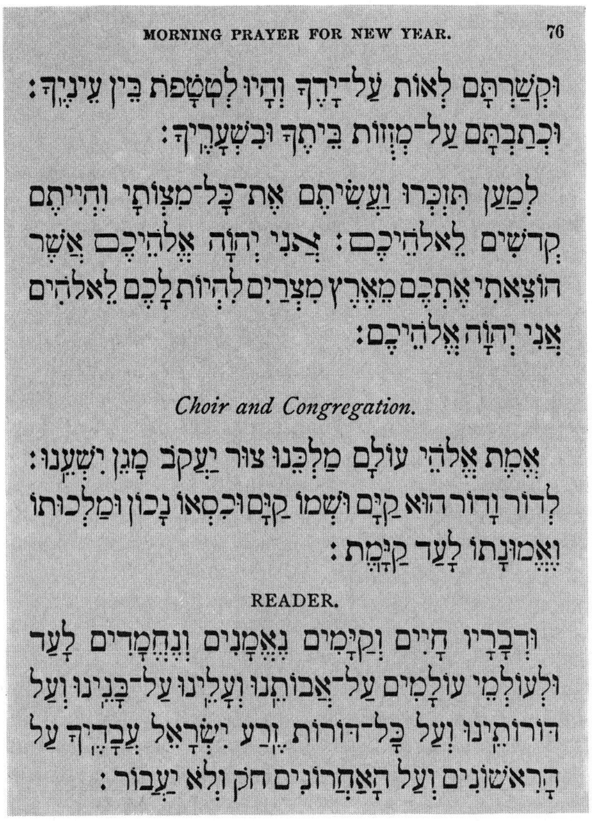

וּקְשַׁרְתָּם לְאוֹת עַל־יָדֶךָ וְהָיוּ לְטֹטָפֹת בֵּין עֵינֶיךָ:

וּכְתַבְתָּם עַל־מְזוּזֹת בֵּיתֶךָ וּבִשְׁעָרֶיךָ:

לְמַעַן תִּזְכְּרוּ וַעֲשִׂיתֶם אֶת־כָּל־מִצְוֹתָי וִהְיִיתֶם

קְדֹשִׁים לֵאלֹהֵיכֶם: אֲנִי יְהֹוָה אֱלֹהֵיכֶם אֲשֶׁר

הוֹצֵאתִי אֶתְכֶם מֵאֶרֶץ מִצְרַיִם לִהְיוֹת לָכֶם לֵאלֹהִים

אֲנִי יְהֹוָה אֱלֹהֵיכֶם:

Choir and Congregation.

אֱמֶת אֱלֹהֵי עוֹלָם מַלְכֵּנוּ צוּר יַעֲקֹב מָגֵן יִשְׁעֵנוּ:

לְדֹר וָדֹר הוּא קַיָּם וּשְׁמוֹ קַיָּם וְכִסְאוֹ נָכוֹן וּמַלְכוּתוֹ

וֶאֱמוּנָתוֹ לָעַד קַיֶּמֶת:

READER.

וּדְבָרָיו חָיִים וְקַיָּמִים נֶאֱמָנִים וְנֶחֱמָדִים לָעַד

וּלְעוֹלְמֵי עוֹלָמִים עַל־אֲבוֹתֵנוּ וְעָלֵינוּ עַל־בָּנֵינוּ וְעַל

דוֹרוֹתֵינוּ וְעַל כָּל־דּוֹרוֹת זֶרַע יִשְׂרָאֵל עֲבָדֶיךָ עַל

הָרִאשׁוֹנִים וְעַל הָאַחֲרוֹנִים חֹק וְלֹא יַעֲבוֹר:

Figure 9. Page from a U.S. Reform prayer book compiled by Adolph Huebsch for Congregation Ahawath Chesed, New York, 1889.

(Cambridge, Massachusetts, 1640), the Hebrew alphabet accompanied Psalm 119 and Hebrew words were used six times in the preface. In the two centuries following, many works containing some Hebrew were printed in Cambridge, Andover, Boston, New Haven, New York, and Philadelphia, comprising mainly Hebrew lexica, grammars, primers, and single books of the Bible. Hebrew was also used in printed rules and regulations of Jewish communities and religious societies, or in special orders of services. From the middle of the 18th century onward complete prayer books (*maḥzorim* with English translations) began to appear. In the 19th century Hebrew printing of sorts is found also in Baltimore (1843), Charleston, South Carolina (1842), Cincinnati (1824), New Orleans (1850), San Francisco (1850), and Kingston, Jamaica (1842). Jewish printers began to be active from 1825 (Solomon Henry *Jackson, Henry Frank, both in New York). With rising immigration from Eastern Europe, Hebrew and Yiddish newspapers began to appear from 1874 onward. By 1926 there were Hebrew presses, apart from those in the cities already mentioned, in Chicago, Cleveland, Detroit, Los Angeles, Minneapolis, Pittsburgh, St. Louis, and Toronto (Canada).

NEW TRENDS

While no new trends developed in Hebrew printing up to World War I and even World War II, the Russian Revolution and the debacle of European Jewry in the Holocaust terminated almost all Hebrew printing in Central and Eastern Europe. With the establishment of the Jewish National Home in Palestine (1918–47) and the State of Israel (1948), Jerusalem and Tel Aviv have become the centers of Hebrew printing and publishing. New York too, as well as other cities in the U.S., produce a good deal of Hebrew, particularly rabbinic literature. England, France, and Switzerland play a minor part. The invention of new

processes of photomechanical printing have been applied to a great number of the best editions of the 19th century as well as incunabula and rare early prints to satisfy—if not the bibliophiles—the growing demand for rabbinic and other scholarly literature. On the other hand, the phenomenal growth of modern Hebrew (and Yiddish) literature is reflected in the work of the Hebrew printers and publishers in Israel, some of whom began their activities in Russia, Poland, or Germany before or after 1900. Yiddish literature too is being printed in the U.S. and to a very small extent in Soviet Russia.

See also the individual articles on most of the places where Hebrew printing took place and on the most important printers.   [EJ/ED.]

IN EREẒ ISRAEL

Before Statehood. SAFED. About 120 years after the invention of printing, in 1577, Rabbi Eliezer *Ashkenazi of Lublin attempted to set up a printing press in Safed. The press lasted for only ten years and printed ten books, including *Lekaḥ Tov* by Rabbi Yom Tov Ẓahalon, considered to be the first book ever printed in Ereẓ Israel and the Near East. Two and a half centuries later, in 1831, a fresh start was made in Safed by Israel *Bak, who had brought with him from Berdichev, Russia, type-founding equipment and two wooden presses. His printing house was destroyed by the earthquake that struck the town in 1837, after he had printed only six books.

JERUSALEM. Four years later, in 1841, he opened a printing house in Jerusalem. This was the first step toward developing the craft of printing, which later became one of the city's main industries. A second printing house was opened in 1862 and ten years later others were established and employed many yeshivah students who had hitherto lived only on the charity of the *ḥalukkah*. In 1882 Bak's printing house was liquidated and his equipment was sold, but his name remained a symbol as the pioneer of printing in Ereẓ Israel. The iron printing press presented to him as a gift in 1835 by Sir Moses Montefiore is still on show at the Lewin-Epstein Press at Bat Yam.

For many years Jerusalem continued to be the printing center of Ereẓ Israel. The industry's chief clients were at first the weekly newspapers *Ha-Ḥavaẓẓelet* and *Ha-Levanon* and the many religious institutions in the city. Jerusalem printing was distinguished for its own peculiarly decorative style in calendars, greeting cards, and *mizraḥs,* which were sent to all parts of the Diaspora. The Printing Workers' Association, established in 1897, was the first trade union in the country.

After World War I Zionist and communal institutions began to give out considerable printing orders, and the first process engraving works were established in Jerusalem to facilitate the printing of Jewish National Fund stamps, pictures, and illustrated publicity material for public bodies. Non-Jewish printing houses were to be found mainly in monasteries; there was one in the Schneller orphanage, which specialized in printing school exercise books. In the 1920s the new town of Tel Aviv began to replace Jerusalem as the printing and publishing center.

TEL AVIV. The first Jewish printing works in the area was opened in Jaffa in 1906, where most of them were to be found until the 1920s. Sa'adyah Shoshani, nephew of the owner, Aaron Eitan, was a pioneer in the organization of the industry and became president of the Organization of Printing Presses in Israel. Many printing workers arrived from Poland in the 1920s with the Third and Fourth Aliyah. Some of them established the Ha-Po'el ha-Ẓa'ir cooperative; others joined the Aḥdut cooperative, which had been set up in Jerusalem in 1909 and subsequently transferred to

Tel Aviv. The daily press that grew up in Tel Aviv was an important factor in the industrialization of printing and modern equipment was purchased to meet its needs. When the canning industry started in the 1930s, Eliezer Lewin-Epstein, of the famous Warsaw printing family, set up a tin-can printing enterprise which became the first offset press in the country and was particularly noted for the printing of postage stamps and posters. Other offset presses were soon established and supplied Israel industry with advertising material and printed packing materials.

In the State of Israel. The establishment of the Government Printer—at first in Tel Aviv and soon with a branch in Jerusalem—gave an impetus to the development of printing. It did photogravure work, which had previously to be sent to Britain, and printed postage stamps and banknotes for various African and Asian countries. In 1966 it was transferred to Jerusalem. It is the largest printing establishment in the country, with some 300 workers, and is also a channel for handing out government orders to other printers in Jerusalem and elsewhere.

Since 1966 modern machinery for cold type composition, including IBM, Monophoto, and Photon equipment, has been installed by several firms, including Isratypeset and the *Israel Program for Scientific Translations (IPST) in Jerusalem, enabling high-quality bookwork to be done for local and foreign publishers. Offset notary presses for printing illustrated weeklies have also been imported; in 1970 there were over 30 offset presses in Israel that were capable, inter alia, of producing good-quality color work. Printing presses have also been opened in Haifa, in many development towns, and in three kibbutzim. There are three Arabic presses in Nazareth and several in Jerusalem.

In 1969 there were some 900 printing and publishing enterprises in Israel, with 9,500 persons employed (about two-thirds of the employees working in Tel Aviv). Aggregate output was IL262,000,000 (about $75,000,000) and exports totaled about $5,000,000 (about half of which went to the U.S.), compared with $2,900,000 in 1966 and $400,000 in 1956. About 80% of the enterprises employed a little more than a quarter of the workers, while two-fifths of the personnel were employed by 3.5% of the enterprises, as shown in Table 1.

Table 1. Printing and Publishing Establishments and Employed Persons, by Size-group (percentages)

Number of employees	Establishments	Employed persons
1–10	79	26.4
11–20	9.5	11.9
21–50	8	21.2
51–100	1.9	11.5
Over 100	1.6	29.0

VOCATIONAL TRAINING. The first school of printing was established in 1946 by the *Hadassah Women's Organization in Jerusalem as part of the Brandeis Center. Additional schools were set up in Tel Aviv (the Amal School), Jerusalem (Boys' Town), and Kefar Ḥabad. In 1968 these schools had over 300 pupils, and another 600 apprentices in printing houses were taking part-time courses there. [G.Z.]

Bibliography: Major bibliographical periodicals: HB (1858–82); ZHB (1896–1921); KS (1924–); *Soncino-Blaetter* (1924–30); *Journal of Jewish Bibliography* (1938–43); JBA (1942–); *Aresheth* (1958–); Shunami, Bibl, 2679–997, 4689–96a; M. Steinschneider and D. Cassel, *Juedische Typographie* (1851; repr. 1938); A. Berliner, *Ueber den Einfluss des ersten hebraeischen Buchdrucks auf den Cultus und die Cultur der Juden* (1896); D. W. Amram, *Makers of Hebrew Books in Italy* (1909; repr. 1963); E. N. Adler, *Gazetteer of Hebrew Printing* (1917); A. S. W. Rosenbach, *American Jewish Bibliography* (1926); E. Deinard, *Kohelet Amerikah* (1926); W. Eames, in: *Studies in Jewish Bibliography* (1929); Ḥ. D. Friedberg, *Toledot ha-Defus ha-Ivri . . . be-Eiropah ha-Tikhonah* (1935); idem, *Toledot ha-Defus ha-Ivri . . . be-Eiropah* (1937); idem, *Toledot ha-Defus ha-Ivri be-Polanyah* (1950²); idem, *Toledot ha-Defus ha-Ivri ba-Medinot Italyah, Aspamyah-Portugalyah, Togarmah ve-Arẓot ha-Kedem* (1956²); A. Ya'ari, *Ha-Defus ha-Ivri be-Arẓot ha-Mizraḥ*, 2 vols. (1936–40); idem, *Meḥkerei Sefer* (1958); Y. Z. Cahana, in: *Sinai*, 16 (1945), 49–61, 139–59; A. Freimann, *Gazetteer of Hebrew Printing* (1946); A. M. Habermann, *Ha-Sefer ha-Ivri be-Hitpatteḥuto* (1968); G. Zilberg, *Ha-Ot ha-Mudpeset be-Yisrael* (1961).

PRINZ, JOACHIM (1902–), U.S. rabbi and communal leader. Prinz, who was born in Burchartsdorf, Germany, was ordained by the Breslau Jewish Theological Seminary in 1925. In 1926 he became the rabbi of the Berlin Jewish community. His adherence to the Zionist movement brought him into conflict with Berlin Jewish community leaders. Prinz continually attacked Nazism from his pulpit, even after Hitler came to power, and was arrested several times by the Gestapo. In 1937 he held his last meeting with his congregation before emigrating to the U.S. The meeting was spied on by Adolf *Eichmann, who reported to the Gestapo that Prinz's plan to emigrate proved that an international Jewish conspiracy had New York headquarters. Prinz was subsequently arrested by the Gestapo and expelled from Germany. In 1939 he was appointed rabbi at Temple B'nai Abraham, Newark, New Jersey.

After a long association with the Zionist movement, Prinz left it in 1948, contending that the establishment of Israel made it obsolete. He suggested a new movement based on what he called "Jewish peoplehood," be created to strengthen further ties and community of interest between Israel and U.S. Jews. Prinz was a leader in the fight against anti-Semitism and a staunch civil libertarian. He opposed government aid to religious and private schools and advocated that state governments permit exceptions to their Sunday closing laws to non-Christians.

Extremely active in Jewish organizational affairs, his posts included: president of the Jewish Educational Association of Essex County (1944); chairman of the Essex County United Jewish Appeal (1945); member of the executive board of the World Jewish Congress (1946); vice-president (1952–58), and president (1958–66) of the American Jewish Congress; director of the Conference on Jewish Material Claims Against Germany (1956); and chairman of the Conference of Presidents of Major Jewish Organizations (1965–67).

Prinz's writings include: *Juedische Geschichte* (1931), in which he contended that Jews, despite their emancipation, still existed in the ghetto's shadow; *Illustrierte juedische Geschichte* (1933); *Die Geschichten der Bibel* (1934); *Wir Juden* (1934), urging Jews to be proud of their patrimony and to leave Germany; *Das Leben im Ghetto* (1937); *The Dilemma of the Modern Jew* (1962); and *Popes from the Ghetto* (1966). [ED.]

PRISCUS, a Jewish agent of the Frankish king Chilperic I (561–584). In 581 Chilperic engaged Priscus in a religious debate in the presence of Bishop *Gregory of Tours. Courageously rejecting the arguments of the king, Priscus stated that "God does not need to share Himself, and He does not divide His power with others." Priscus asked "Can God be made a man, be born of a woman, be struck with rods, and condemned to death?" The king did not reply but Gregory, who brought all his oratorical talent to bear, quoted a great number of christological passages from the Bible and Apocrypha as evidence for the Christian truth. Nevertheless, all his arguments were of no avail as Priscus stood his ground.

When all the Jews of Paris were ordered to accept

Christianity, Priscus, who was imprisoned, but later released, withstood the king's attempts to baptize him by force. On a Saturday, while on his way to the synagogue together with several men of his household, Priscus was assassinated by the convert Phatir and a band of his henchmen. Priscus was avenged by his relatives who killed Phatir.

Bibliography: Gross, Gal Jud, 497; A. Temko, in: *Commentary*, 15 (1953), 166–71; B. Blumenkranz, *Les Auteurs chrétiens latins du Moyen Age* (1963), 70–71; idem, *Juifs et Chrétiens*... (1960), index; Baron, Social, 3 (1957), 52; 5 (1957), 114. [J.M.R.]

PROBST, MENAHEM MENDEL (1881–1941), Hebrew bibliographer. Born in Galicia, he settled in Ereẓ Israel in 1928 and joined the staff of the National Library in Jerusalem, devoting himself to bibliography of Hebrew and Palestinian journalism.

Among his works are *Ha-Ittonut ha-Ivrit be-Hitpatteḥutah ha-Keronologit* (*Lu'aḥ Aḥi'asaf* (1923), 239–87); *Ḥomer Mispari le-Toledot Hitpatteḥutah shel ha-Ittonut ha-Yisre'elit le-Arẓoteha... 1667–1920* ("Statistical Material to the History of the Jewish Press... 1667–1920"; KS, 2 (1925–26), 212–4); *Yalkut Sefarim* (1929), a complete and detailed listing of modern Hebrew literature according to subjects. He also published articles on bibliographical subjects in the daily press. [G.K.]

PROCURATOR, title of the governors (first over Judea, later over most of Palestine) appointed by Rome during the years 6–41 and 44–66 C.E. From a recently discovered inscription in which *Pontius Pilate is mentioned, it appears that the title of the governors of Judea was also *praefectus*. Procuratorial rule came into force with the banishment of *Herod's son *Archelaus in the year 6 and was interrupted for three years during the reign of *Agrippa I (41–44). The Judean-Palestinian procurator held the power of jurisdiction with regard to capital punishment *(jus gladii)*. Roman citizens had the privilege of *provocatio*, i.e., the right to transfer the trial from the provincial governor to the emperor (cf. the case of *Paul, Acts 25:10–12; cf. 22:25ff.). The procurator was subject to the Roman legate in Syria, an illustration of this being the deportation of Pontius Pilate (26–36 C.E.) by *Vitellius. Josephus also states (Wars, 2:280–1) that formal charges would have been preferred by the Jews against the last procurator Gessius *Florus (64–66 C.E.; see below) but that they refrained from taking their case to *Gallus in Syria from fear of reprisals. The Sanhedrin was allowed to exercise jurisdiction in civil matters, although the procurators could exercise control in this sphere as well. As a rule, the procurators maintained supervision over the country from their official residence at Caesarea. On Jewish festivals, their seat was temporarily transferred to Jerusalem in order to control the thousands who flocked to the Temple and on these occasions they sometimes gave physical expression to their hatred of Rome.

It is fair to assert that the procurators were either openly hostile or, at best, indifferent to the needs of the Jewish populace. They were notorious for their rapacity. Their relatively short tenure, coupled with hostility toward Jews as a whole, may have impelled them to amass quick profits. Whatever the case, the last two procurators before the Jewish War (66 C.E.), *Albinus and Gessius Florus, as a consequence of their monetary extortions and generally provocative acts, were indubitably instrumental in hastening the outbreak of hostilities. The only exception appears to have been Porcius *Festus (60–62 C.E.) who made vain attempts to improve conditions. The procuratorial administration made an unfortunate beginning when the very first procurator, *Coponius, was dispatched to govern Judea, while the Syrian legate *Quirinius carried out a census (Jos., Ant. 18:1). The political consequences of this act were not delayed, as it led to the establishment of the Fourth Philosophy (*Sicarii) by *Judah the Galilean and the Pharisee Zadok. *Valerius Gratus (15–26) went so far as to depose high priests at will, an outrage on popular feeling hitherto perpetrated only by Herod. The outraged feelings of the populace were not calmed with the appointment of Gratus' successor, Pontius Pilate, during whose term of office Jesus was crucified. Pilate's decision to introduce into the city military standards bearing the emperor's likeness may have been inspired by Rome. Incontrovertible, however, are his own acts of cruelty and his miscarriages of justice, such as the execution of Galilean patriots without trial and his violence toward the Samaritans (35 C.E.). The latter act caused his recall to Rome and deposition by Vitellius in the spring of 36. So serious were the possible consequences of his misrule in the eyes of Rome that Vitellius was specially charged with the task of regaining Jewish favor by granting minor concessions.

While the "second series" of procurators, after the interlude of semi-independence under Herod Agrippa I, were deprived of the power of appointing the high priest, the very first of them, Cuspius *Fadus, gained custody of the priestly vestments. Although appointed by Claudius to counteract the Syrian legate's antipathy toward the Jews, Fadus adopted violent means in suppressing the followers of the pseudo-Messiah *Theudas. Tiberius *Alexander ordered the execution of Jacob and Simeon, sons of Judah the Galilean. Ventidius *Cumanus, next in office, not only let his troops cause a panic in the overcrowded Temple area on Passover, resulting in the death of 20,000 Jews (Jos., Ant., 20:105–12) but in addition armed the Samaritans against them. Whether the measure was actually considered necessary in order to maintain order is unclear. Cumanus was, however, subsequently removed by the Syrian legate. The last of the Judean procurators, Gessius Florus (see above), is reported by Josephus to have sparked off the Jewish War with his demand for 17 talents from the Temple funds, which caused rioting leading up to the outbreak of hostilities on a large scale. After 70 C.E. the office of procurator sometimes alternated with that of legate and was subordinate to the governor of the region, eventually being disbanded altogether.

LIST OF PROCURATORS

Coponius 6–9 C.E.
Marcus Ambibulus 9–12 C.E.
Rufus Tineus 12–15 C.E.
Valerius Gratus 15–26 C.E.
Pontius Pilate 26–36 C.E.
Marcellus 36–37 C.E.
Marullus 37–41 C.E.
Cuspius Fadus 44–46 C.E.
Tiberius Julius Alexander 46–48 C.E.
Ventidius Cumanus 48–52 C.E.
Antonius Felix 52–60 C.E.
Porcius Festus 60–62 C.E.
Albinus 62–64 C.E.
Gessius Florus 64–66 C.E.

Bibliography: T. Mommsen, *The Provinces of the Roman Empire*, 2 (1909), 188–206; A. Schalit, *Ha-Mishtar ha-Roma'i be-Ereẓ Yisrael* (1937); H. G. Pflaum, *Les Procurateurs Equestres*... (1950), 146ff.; Klausner, Bayit Sheni, 4 (1950²), 196ff., and passim; Schuerer, Hist, index; Smallwood, in: *History Today*, 15 (1965), 232–9, 313–9; S. Krauss, in: REJ, 46 (1903), 219–36; A. Reitenberg, *Israel's History in Coins* (1953), 12–13 (with illustrations); A. H. M. Jones, *Herods of Judea* (1938). [DA.S.]

PROFANITY. Judaism has always stressed the importance of the spoken word and hence cleanliness in speech was inculcated in addition to strict prohibition of certain forms of speech such as lying, slander, calumny, or insults. Not only was outright indecent speech to be avoided, but even gross expression was to be shunned. According to the Talmud the Torah uses eight additional letters rather than utter a graceless expression in order to illustrate this principle, for it is written "and of the beasts that are not clean" (Gen. 7:2), instead of "unclean" (Pes. 3a). Likewise, the single word "unclean" would have saved nine letters in the Hebrew text in the verse, "If there be among you any man that is not clean by reason of that which chanceth by night" (Deut. 23:11; Pes. 3a). The Talmud relates that two disciples sat before Rav. One said: "This discussion has made us as tired as an exhausted swine"; the other said: "This discussion had made us as tired as an exhausted kid." Rav would not speak to the former. Similarly, there were three priests; one said, I received as much as a bean of the shewbread: the second said, I received as much as an olive; while the third said, I received as much as a lizard's tail. They investigated the third priest and found that his genealogy was impure and that he was unfit to serve in the Temple (Pes. 3b).

The Talmud considered obscene speech a grievous sin. Many calamities befalling the community were considered by the sages to be punishments for this offense. R. Ḥanan b. Rabbah remarked that even though all know for what purpose a bride enters the bridal chamber, yet God would punish him who say it *expressis verbis.* *Gehinnom is deepened for the individual who puts his mouth to folly, and punishment is meted out also to one who hears obscenities and does not protest (Shab. 3a). The Rabbis explained that fingers are jointed like pegs so that if a man hears an unworthy statement he should be able to plug them into his ears. The whole ear is hard and the earlobe soft so that if a man hears an unworthy thought he should be able to bend the earlobe into the ear (Ket. 5a–b). Proper language at times of warfare was particularly stressed; the interdiction that "thy camp be holy; that He see no unseemly thing in thee, and turn away from thee" (Deut. 23:15) is interpreted to mean that God shall hear no improper language in the military camp (Lev. R. 24:7).

See also *Euphemisms. [A.Ro.]

PROHOVNIK, ABRAHAM (in Polish *prochownik* is a dealer either in powder or gunpowder), legendary Jewish figure in the pre-political period of the Polish tribes. After the death of the legendary prince Popiel (attributed to the middle of the ninth century) in the town of Kruszwica, a public meeting *(wiec)* was called to elect a new ruler. Conflicting opinions, however, prevented the nomination of a candidate acceptable to all the assembled. It was therefore decided to choose the first man to enter the town on the next day. This happened to be a Jew named Abraham Prohovnik. When brought to the assembly to be crowned Abraham refused. After some discussion, he was given three days in which to reflect, being warned that he would forfeit his life if still unwilling. After the delay, a crowd, led by a Pole named Piast, approached Abraham's lodgings to crown him. The latter remained adamant, and pointed to Piast as suitable to wear the princely crown. His suggestion was accepted, thus inaugurating the reign of the equally legendary founder of the Polish Piast dynasty. The origin of the legend and the period of its appearance are unknown. A number of Jewish historians consider it to be a transmutation of the Saul *Wahl legend, which arose during the golden era of Polish Jewry at the end of the 16th and early 17th centuries. Other scholars regard it as an echo of the Jewish presence and influence in Poland at the beginning of its political existence and connect the person of Abraham Prohovnik with the arrival of Jews in Poland from the southeast. The Polish Piast legend (first formulated in 1112) contains no mention of Jewish elements. The story undoubtedly is merely an expression in legendary form of the Jewish sense of deep-rootedness in Poland.

Bibliography: W. Zamoyski, *Wspomnienia domowe* (1837); J. Lelewel, *Polska wieków średnich,* 2 (1846), 417: A. Kraushar, *Historya Żydów w Polsce,* 1 (1865), 41–44; M. Gumplowicz, *Poczatki religií żydowskiej w Polsce* (1903), 22–23; I. Schiper, in: *Almanach żydowski* (1918), 236–65; B. Mark, *Di Geshikhte fun Yidn in Poyln* (1957), 168–74.

[A.Cy.]

PRONUNCIATIONS OF HEBREW. This article is arranged according to the following outline:

I. The Transmission of Hebrew as a Liturgical Language.
II. Classification of the Traditional Pronunciations of Hebrew
- A. The Yemenite Pronunciation
- B. The Sephardi Pronunciation
  - a. Phonological Features
  - b. Morphological Features
- C. The Ashkenazi Pronunciation

III. The Realizations of the Consonants and Vowels and the Stress Patterns in the Various Pronunciations
- A. The Consonants
  - a. בגדכפ"ת
  - b. The Gutturals
  - c. The Emphatics
  - d. The Sibilants
  - e. ר (R)
  - f. The Semivowels
  - g. Gemination
- B. The Vowels
  - a. Šureq-Qibbuṣ
  - b. Ḥolem
  - c. Qameṣ and Pathaḥ
  - d. Ṣere and Segol
  - e. Ḥireq
  - f. The Šewa
  - g. The Ḥaṭefs
  - h. Vowel Quantity
- C. Stress

Specimen Texts

I. THE TRANSMISSION OF HEBREW AS A LITURGICAL LANGUAGE

Before its revival at the end of the 19th century, Hebrew existed, for a period of about 1700 years, mainly as a literary and liturgical language. This period in the history of Hebrew probably began around the third century C.E. There is evidence that Hebrew was spoken, at least in some parts of Palestine, in the second century C.E. This is clear from the story in the Talmud about the maid of Rabbi Judah ha-Nasi who knew the meanings of some Hebrew words with which the scholars of that time were not acquainted (RH 26b; Meg. 18a; TJ, Meg. 2:2, 73a). Evidence that Hebrew was spoken in the first half of the second century C.E. is also borne out by the Hebrew letters of Bar-Kokhba, some of the grammatical forms of which show that Hebrew was still a living language at that time (c. 135 C.E.). It should be mentioned, however, that at that period, and for centuries before, other languages were spoken concomitantly by the Jewish communities of Palestine, mainly Aramaic and Greek. The use of Hebrew as a spoken language became more and more limited, and finally it was superseded by Aramaic and Greek. Although the exact time when Hebrew ceased to be spoken is not known, there is no unequivocal evidence for the use of Hebrew as the ordinary spoken language of any Jewish community in a period later than the second century. It may be assumed, therefore, that the period in which the use of Hebrew was limited to literature and liturgy only began about the third century C.E.

As a liturgical language Hebrew has been transmitted during this long period, and in fact up to the present day, in a number of forms which are known as the "traditional pronunciations" of Hebrew. This term denotes those pronunciations which have been used by the various Jewish communities in reading the Bible and the post-biblical literature and in prayers. Another term used for "traditional pronunciation" is "reading tradition," or "liturgical reading tradition." A few words explaining these terms are in order here. A "reading tradition" may be defined as a corpus of linguistic information, transmitted orally, upon which the correct reading of a text is based; a "liturgical reading tradition" is a reading tradition that is used in the transmission of those parts of the literature which have particular religious importance. The traditional pronunciations of Hebrew have been transmitted in the various communities over a long period. They still exist in Israel and in various Jewish communities of the Diaspora. In Israel, however, the traditional pronunciations are disappearing at a fast rate, as a result of the mutual contact among the various communities, and of the influence of the current pronunciation of Hebrew.

The traditional pronunciations of Hebrew extant with most communities are of two major categories: (a) the pronunciations used in the reading of the Bible; (b) the pronunciations used in the reading of the post-biblical literature, primarily the Mishnah. In the pronunciations pertaining to the first category, the reading is based upon the vocalized text of the Bible, whereas in the second it is based, in many communities, upon an unvocalized text. This results from the fact that for the Mishnah no authorized vocalization exists that could be compared to the Tiberian vocalization of the Bible (which was accepted by all Jewish communities, except for the Samaritan, as the authoritative vocalization according to which the Bible should be read). Therefore, the reading of the Mishnah in most communities is based upon a text which does not possess vocalization signs and which, for many words, represents only their consonantal skeleton. The reader supplements those phonological entities that are not represented in the orthography according to the oral tradition of his community. In other words, in reading the Bible the reader gives each grapheme (that is, the letters and the vocalization signs) the phonetic value it has in the traditional pronunciation of the community. In reading the Mishnah, on the other hand, in addition to giving each grapheme the phonetic value it has in the traditional pronunciation of the community, the reader also supplements, according to the oral tradition of his community, those phonological entities which are not represented by the orthography. Since the oral traditions of the various communities differ from each other, it follows that the various reading traditions of the Mishnah disclose different forms of the same word. To illustrate the difference between the traditional pronunciation of the Bible and that of the Mishnah, the word *qereaḥ* (קרח) "bald" may be taken. This word appears both in the Bible and in the Mishnah. In the Bible this word is spelled קרח and vocalized *qereaḥ*, and the communities differ from each other in the phonetic values they give to the consonants and the vowels. Thus ק is pronounced as */g/* or */q/* by the Yemenite (the exact pronunciation depending on the district from which the individual reader comes; for further details, see below), as */q/* by the Iraqi readers, and as */k/* by the Ashkenazi and some of the Sephardi readers; the ֵ (the vowel sign *ṣere*) is pronounced as */e/* by the Yemenite and Sephardi readers, and as */ey/* or */ay/* by the Ashkenazi; the ח is pronounced as */ḥ/*, an unvoiced pharyngeal fricative, by the Yemenite and some of the Sephardi readers, but as */x/* by the Ashkenazi. The situation is utterly different in the reading of the Mishnah. Here the word is spelled קרח, as it is in the Bible, but no vocalization signs appear in the text which would make a certain form of the word binding for a specific community. Therefore, there are differences among the communities as to the very form of the word—the Iraqi reading it as */qareyaḥ/*, the Yemenite as */qereḥ/*, all other communities as *qereaḥ* (that is, a form identical to the biblical)—and not only in the phonetic values given to the consonants and the vowels.

II. CLASSIFICATION OF THE TRADITIONAL PRONUNCIATIONS OF HEBREW

1. First, a differentiation must be made between the Samaritan pronunciation and all other pronunciations. Due to its specific features, the Samaritan pronunciation occupies a unique position within the bulk of the traditional pronunciations, and is of particular importance. We shall mention a number of the features typical of the Samaritan pronunciation: (a) the total disappearance of ח and in many cases also of ע; (b) the realization of the letter ו as */b/*; (c) the existence of four degrees of length in the realization of the vowels, two of which are phonemic; (d) the realization of historical */i:/* as */ə/* (for example, the word הַבַּדִּים—Ex. 25:13—is pronounced as *abbaddəm*—Z. Ben-Ḥayyim, *The Literary and Oral Tradition of Hebrew and Aramaic Amongst the Samaritans*, vol. III pt. 1, p. 40); (e) the distinction between the counterparts of the historical vowels ū, u and those of ō, o disappeared; in most cases, the realization of these vowels as either */o/* or */u/* depends on their position in the word. Thus Tiberian סוּס, "horse," is */sos/* in the Samaritan pronunciation (Ben-Ḥayyim, *ibid.*, p. 37), whereas Tiberian שְׁמוֹ, "his name" is */se:mu/* in Samaritan *(ibid.)*. These features, and a number of others make the Samaritan pronunciation unintelligible to the members of all other Jewish communities. In this connection it should also be mentioned that the Samaritan reading tradition of the Pentateuch is not based on vocalized texts. Such texts have not been used by the Samaritan community in the teaching of the traditional pronunciation, and in the reading of the Pentateuch. The Samaritan reader supplements the Pentateuch with the missing phonological entities according to the oral tradition transmitted in the community. In this respect the Samaritan traditional pronunciation differs from the traditional pronunciation of the Bible extant in all other Jewish communities, which use the Tiberian vocalization for the reading of the Bible.

2. The traditional pronunciations of the communities except the Samaritan are to be classified into three major groups: the Yemenite, the Sephardi, and the Ashkenazi.

A. The Yemenite Pronunciation. Geographically isolated for generations, the Yemenite community has preserved a traditional pronunciation possessing a number of peculiar features. Some of these features, it is true, resulted from the influence of the pronunciation of the Yemenite Arabic vernaculars on the pronunciation of Hebrew. This influence is disclosed, e.g., in the realizations of גּ (when having a *dageš*) by members of the community who originally came from various regions of Yemen as an affricate */ǧ/*, a velar */g/*, or a palatalized */g'/*. These realizations correspond to the realizations of the Arabic phoneme */g/* in the respective regions of Yemen (for which see below). Other features of the Yemenite pronunciation—particularly as regards the vowels—reflect, however, the traditional pronunciation of the Jewish community of geonic Babylonia. The correspondence between the present-day Yemenite pronunciation and the Babylonian pronunciation may best be proven by two phonetic phenomena: (a) the identity of the realizations of *pathaḥ* and *segol;* (b) the realization of *ḥolem* as *ṣere* by members of the communities of southwestern Yemen and of Aden. Both these phenomena are attested by the Babylonian vocalization, that is, the vocalization which reflects the pronunciation of Hebrew in Jewish communities of geonic Babylonia. However, whereas the former phenomenon is a regular feature of the Babylonian system of vocalization, which has only one vowel as the counterpart of both Tiberian *pathaḥ* and *segol,* this is not the case with the latter. The Babylonian system has signs for both *ḥolem* and *ṣere;* but in certain Babylonian manuscripts the signs for these two vowels interchange freely, and this indicates that in the pronunciation of the vocalizers of these manuscripts the two vowels were identical. Evidence for the identity of the realizations of *ḥolem* and *ṣere* by the Jewish communities of some provinces of Babylonia in the first half of the tenth century C.E. is borne also by a literary source, mainly al-Qirqisānī's *Kitāb al'anwār walmarāqib.* It is, therefore, clear that the identity of the realizations of *ḥolem* and *ṣere* by members of some Yemenite communities reflects a feature of the pronunciation of Hebrew in geonic Babylonia, and the Yemenite community is the only community to have preserved the Babylonian pronunciation of Hebrew. In fact, Yemenite Jewry has been the recipient of the legacy of geonic Babylonia in other fields as well: for centuries the Yemenites have used the Babylonian vocalization, in periods when it has been completely unknown to other Jewish communities; the Yemenites have used the Babylonian recension of the Bible at least until the beginning of the 13th century C.E.; the Yemenite reading tradition of post-biblical Hebrew resembles in many of its morphophonemic and morphological features the Babylonian tradition of post-biblical Hebrew, which is reflected by manuscripts of the Mishnah and Midrashim possessing Babylonian vocalization. The Yemenites have preserved a stable tradition of the vocalization of Targum Onkelos and Targum Jonathan, a tradition which most probably received its final shape in geonic Babylonia.

The fact that Yemenite Jewry has been the recipient of the Babylonian traditions in a number of fields is to be seen in the light of the close relations that existed between the Jewish community of Yemen and that of Babylonia in the geonic period. Historical evidence for these relations is found in some Genizah documents.

The Yemenite tradition of biblical Hebrew is to be clearly differentiated from that of post-biblical Hebrew. In reading the Bible, the Yemenites use the Tiberian vocalization and masorah; however, they give the Tiberian vocalization signs the values they had in the traditional Babylonian pronunciation. Thus, no distinction is made in the Yemenite pronunciation between Tiberian *pathaḥ* and *segol* since in the Babylonian pronunciation of Hebrew these two vowels were identical. In other words, the Yemenite pronunciation of biblical Hebrew discloses phonological features of the Babylonian tradition, but the morphology of biblical Hebrew in this tradition is Tiberian. Hence it follows that in their pronunciation of biblical Hebrew the Yemenites differ from other communities in aspects which are purely phonetic, but not in the morphology.

The situation is, however, different in the pronunciation of post-biblical Hebrew. The Yemenite reading of post-biblical Hebrew is not based upon vocalized texts, but upon an oral tradition of the vocalization. Therefore, the reading of these texts discloses in the morphology, and not only in the phonology, a number of specific features. Many of those morphological features are originally Babylonian. This is readily proved by comparing the morphology of post-biblical Hebrew as reflected by the Yemenite pronunciation with the morphology of Hebrew as represented by manuscripts of Mishnah and Midrashim possessing Babylonian vocalization. Thus, for example, both the Yemenite pronunciation and the manuscripts have הֶם for "they" (versus הֵם in biblical Hebrew and זוֹג for "pair" (versus זוּג in other pronunciations).

It should be noted that the Yemenite pronunciation is not homogeneous. Within what is usually called "Yemenite pronunciation of Hebrew" five major groups may be distinguished, each group representing a different geographical zone of Yemen. These groups are: (a) central Yemen, around the capital Ṣanʿa; (b) northern Yemen, the region of Ḥaydān ashshām—Ṣaʿda (c) southwestern Yemen, the region of Sharʿab; (d) Eastern Yemen, consisting of the communities of Ḥabbān and Ḥāḏina; (e) the city of Aden. The differences existing among these groups in the consonantal aspects of the pronunciation of Hebrew mostly correspond to the differences which exist among the Arabic dialects of the respective geographical zones. This is not the case, however, as regards a number of variations in the pronunciation of the vowels, which do not reflect the influence of the Arabic dialects on the pronunciation of Hebrew. These variations probably disclose inner varieties of the Babylonian pronunciation, which, as seen above, is to be considered as the source of the Yemenite pronunciation of Hebrew. Of these features we shall mention the following: 1. the realization of *ḥolem* as *ṣere* by groups (c) and (e); 2. the realization of *ḥireq* as a central vowel in group (d); 3. the realization of *qameṣ* as a back low unrounded vowel /ɒ/ in group (d).

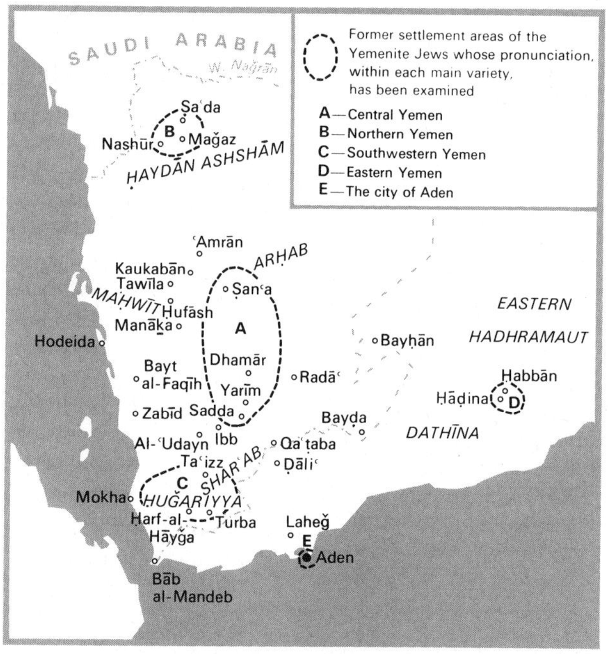

Map 1. Major varieties of the traditional pronunciation of Hebrew in Yemen. After S. Morag, *The Hebrew Language Tradition of the Yemenite Jews,* Jerusalem, 1963.

B. The Sephardi Pronunciation. This term denotes a rather large variety of pronunciations used by the Jewish communities of the Orient (except the Yemenite community, whose pronunciation as observed above, differs basically from that of the other communities of the Orient) and of North Africa, as well as by the Sephardi communities of Europe (such as the Dutch-Portuguese, the Sephardi communities of Greece, Bulgaria, Yugoslavia, and Italy). Among these pronunciations there are considerable differences, which are mostly due to the influence of the vernaculars of the respective communities on the pronunciation of Hebrew. Two features, however, are common to all the pronunciations known as "Sephardi" or Oriental (but non-Yemenite): lack of distinction between *pathaḥ* and *qameṣ* on the one hand (except a *qameṣ* is a closed unstressed syllable; see below), and *ṣere* and *segol* on the other. These two features are characteristic of certain manuscripts possessing 'Palestinian' vocalization. A certain variety of the 'Palestinian' pronunciation is, therefore, to be regarded as the source of the Sephardi pronunciation. By the term "Palestinian pronunciation" we denote the pronunciation reflected in manuscripts (mostly of *piyyutim* and of biblical texts) whose vocalization is called Palestinian, which was used by some communities of Palestine in a period approximately lasting from the sixth to the ninth century C.E. The Palestinian vocalization was apparently used in Palestine concomitantly with the Tiberian vocalization, but most probably not by the same communities. Each of these two vocalizations was based upon a different reading tradition, and in a general way it may be said that the Tiberian vocalization reflects a more classical and more pure reading tradition than the one reflected by the Palestinian. The latter vocalization is apparently based upon a more popular, or rather "vulgar," reading tradition. It may be added here that the Palestinian vocalization and pronunciation disclose a number of affinities with the vocalization and pronunciation of Samaritan Hebrew. The Palestinian pronunciation was adopted by many communities, far beyond the boundaries of Palestine, as the standard pronunciation of Hebrew, the pronunciation to be used in the liturgy and the teaching of the language. The Tiberian pronunciation, on the other hand, had, for some time at least, a classical standing. However, in spite of this classical standing of the Tiberian pronunciation, the Sephardi communities, some of which, particularly those of Spain and North Africa, may have used the Babylonian pronunciation during a certain period, finally adopted the Palestinian pronunciation. This may have resulted from the fact that the use of the Tiberian pronunciation was current only in a rather small group of Masoretes, whereas that of the Palestinian was far more common. The Palestinian pronunciation was probably first transplanted from Palestine to Italy, and later, when the influence of Italian Jewry on the Jewish communities of Spain became prominent, it was transplanted from Italy to Spain (this transplantation possibly took place in the time of Rabbi Moses ben Ḥanokh, in the second half of the tenth century C.E.

After the expulsion of the Jews from Spain, the Palestinian pronunciation, known by then as the Sephardi pronunciation, was transferred by the emigrants to the many communities in which they settled. These communities include the Dutch-Portuguese community of Amsterdam, the Sephardi communities in the Mediterranean countries (Italy, Yugoslavia, Bulgaria, Greece, Turkey, North Africa). The communities of the East (Syria, Palestine, Egypt, Persia) apparently used the Palestinian pronunciation for generations prior to the expulsion of the Jews from Spain.

The term "Sephardi" (or "Palestinian-Sephardi") pronunciation comprises in fact a number of pronunciations which differ from each other in a number of details, such as the pronunciation of the gutturals (for which see below). The features common to all varieties of pronunciations which are called "Sephardi" are, as stated above, lack of distinction between *pathaḥ* and *qameṣ* on the one hand, and between *ṣere* and *segol* on the other. The term "Sephardi" reading tradition when applied to the post-biblical literature (primarily the Mishnah) is a general term, covering a number of reading traditions, such as the Iraqi, the Aleppo, the Moroccan, etc. As yet the Sephardi reading traditions of the Mishnah have not been sufficiently studied, and an exhaustive description of their features is not possible. We shall therefore present here only a few phonological and morphological features of the "Sephardi" reading traditions of the Mishnah.

A. PHONOLOGICAL FEATURES. A number of Sephardi reading traditions of the Mishnah have a *quiescent šewa* in forms which in the reading of the Bible have a *mobile šewa*. This occurs when a medial *šewa* follows a *qameṣ* or a *ḥolem*, in forms like שׁוֹמְרִים, שָׁמְרָה. In such forms all the "Sephardi" pronunciations have in the reading of the Bible a *mobile šewa* (with primary stress on the last syllable, and secondary stress on the syllable preceding the *šewa*), that is, *ˌšame'ra ˌšome'rim*. In the reading of the Mishnah a number of "Sephardi" communities have in these forms a *quiescent šewa* (with primary stress on the syllable preceding the *šewa*), that is, *'šamra, 'šomrim*. Another phonological (or, to be more precise, morphophonemic) feature in which the "Sephardi" reading traditions of the Mishnah differ from the "Sephardi" reading traditions of the Bible is disclosed by the distribution rules of the hard and soft realizations of those consonants of the בגדכפ״ת series for which the traditional pronunciations of the respective community have a double realization, hard and soft (for the realization of בגדכפ״ת consonants, see below). In the reading of the Bible the distribution rules of those */bgdkpt/* consonants for which the Sephardi communities have a double realization agree with the distribution rules of the Tiberian vocalization. This is not, however, the case in the reading of the Mishnah. Thus, for example, a number of Sephardi reading traditions of the Mishnah have a hard realization of a בגדכפ״ת consonant when this consonant follows an initial preposition whose vowel is a *šewa*. Such a realization—e.g., in the form *bekerem*, "in a vineyard"—stands in contradiction to that extant in the reading of the Bible, which is, in the form given here, *bek̲erem*.

B. MORPHOLOGICAL FEATURES. Morphologically, the Sephardi reading tradition of post-biblical Hebrew is not homogeneous, that is to say, there are differences in the forms of words in the various traditions, e.g., in the Iraqi tradition as compared with that of Aleppo, Morocco, and other traditions. There is lacking, for the time being, sufficient information as to the morphological structure of post-biblical Hebrew in the various Sephardi traditions; therefore, we shall mention here only two features which are shared by many of those traditions. (1) The use of the pausal forms of the third person, fem. sing. and masc. plur., in the *hofʿal* stem (e.g., *huqama*, "she was raised," *huqamu*, "they were raised") as the usual forms, that is, the forms which appear both in pausal and contextual positions. (2) The appearance of *-ak̲* as the pronominal suffix for the second person masc. sing., as in e.g., *kevodak̲* "your (masc. sing.) honor" (sometimes, in some traditions side by side with *kevodek̲a*).

C. The Ashkenazi Pronunciation. The term "Ashkenazi" pronunciation is used to denote a variety of pronunciations used by the communities of Eastern and Central Europe and by immigrants from these communities who settled down in other parts of the world. We shall first survey briefly the salient features of the Ashkenazi pronunciation in the consonantal and vowel system. As regards the former system, the Ashkenazi pronunciation possesses two main features, which are shared by all its varieties, namely: (a) the realization of ע as א that is, as "zero" (in some varieties of the Ashkenazi pronunciation */n/* appears sporadically as the reflex of ע ; this */n/* may appear also as the reflex of historical א, e.g., *kanšer*, "when" (Heb. כַּאֲשֶׁר)). (b) the realization of the soft ת as */s/*, e.g., *'bayis*, "house."

The vowel system of the Ashkenazi pronunciation is far

from being homogeneous. Thus the *ḥolem* is pronounced as *[ey]*, and its realization is identical to that of the *ṣere*, in the northeastern variety of the Ashkenazi pronunciation (this variety is more commonly called the "Lithuanian"): as *[oy]* in the southeastern and central variety; as *[aw]* in many of the subtypes of the western varieties; as *[ow]* in those varieties of the Ashkenazi pronunciation used in the last generations in English-speaking countries. By and large the geographical distribution of the main varieties of the Ashkenazi pronunciation agrees with that of the dialects of Yiddish (see Map 2).

To quote another illustration of the heterogeneity extant in the Ashkenazi pronunciation as to the realizations of the vowels: the *qameṣ* is realized, in different varieties of the Ashkenazi pronunciation as *[o]* or *[u]*. Of all the three major groups into which the traditional non-Samaritan pronunciations of Hebrew are divided, the Ashkenazi pronunciation is the only one to possess distinct phonetic realizations for all seven vowel graphemes of the Tiberian vocalization system: *šureq-qibbuṣ* (the *qibbuṣ* in the Tiberian vocalization is an allograph of the *šureq* and does not denote a different vowel phoneme), *ḥolem, qameṣ, ḥireq, ṣere, segol,* and *pathaḥ*. In the Yemenite pronunciation, which reflects the Babylonian, there is no distinction between *pathaḥ* and *segol* (see above); in the Sephardi, which continues the Palestinian, there is no distinction between *qameṣ* and *pathaḥ* on the one hand and between *ṣere* and *segol* on the other. In the course of time, however, some varieties of the Ashkenazi pronunciation developed a leveling of the realizations of two of the seven Tiberian vowels. In the northeastern ("Lithuanian") variety the realization of the *ḥolem* had been equaled with that of the *ṣere*, both becoming consequently *[ey]*; in most, if not all, subtypes of the southwestern and central varieties the realization of the *šureq-qibbuṣ* had been equaled with that of the *ḥireq*, both becoming consequently *[i]* or rounded *[i]*. These developments within the Ashkenazi pronunciation resulted from parallel developments in the Yiddish dialects of the regions in which the above varieties of the Ashkenazi pronunciation were used. The fact that the Ashkenazi pronunciation had originally possessed distinct phonetic realizations for all seven vowels of the Tiberian vocalization system led some scholars to surmise that the Ashkenazi pronunciation constitutes, in its vowel system, a direct continuation of the Tiberian pronunciation. This opinion, however, cannot be accepted since there is evidence that until the 13th century C.E. the Sephardi pronunciation was used by the Ashkenazi communities. The above evidence is borne out by various sources (vocalized texts, transcriptions of Hebrew words in Latin character, notes in grammatical treatises), which show that in Ashkenazi communities until the 13th century C.E. the *qameṣ* was realized as *pathaḥ* and the *ṣere* as *segol,* and these two features are typical of the Sephardi pronunciation. The evidence is reinforced by certain Hebrew loanwords in Yiddish in which historical *qameṣ* is reflected by *pathaḥ* and historical *ṣere* by *segol*.

How can the fact be explained that until the 13th century C.E. there prevailed in the Ashkenazi communities (or, at least, in a number of them) the Sephardi pronunciation, making no distinction between *qameṣ* and *pathaḥ* on the one hand and between *ṣere* and *segol* on the other, and later these communities developed the Ashkenazi pronunciation, which differenciates between the above vowels? Max *Weinreich suggested that the pronunciation which is known as Ashkenazi was formed, in its main features, in Central Europe approximately in the 13th century; until that period the pronunciation used by the Ashkenazi communities was rather close to the Sephardi. The formation of the Ashkenazi pronunciation at that time in

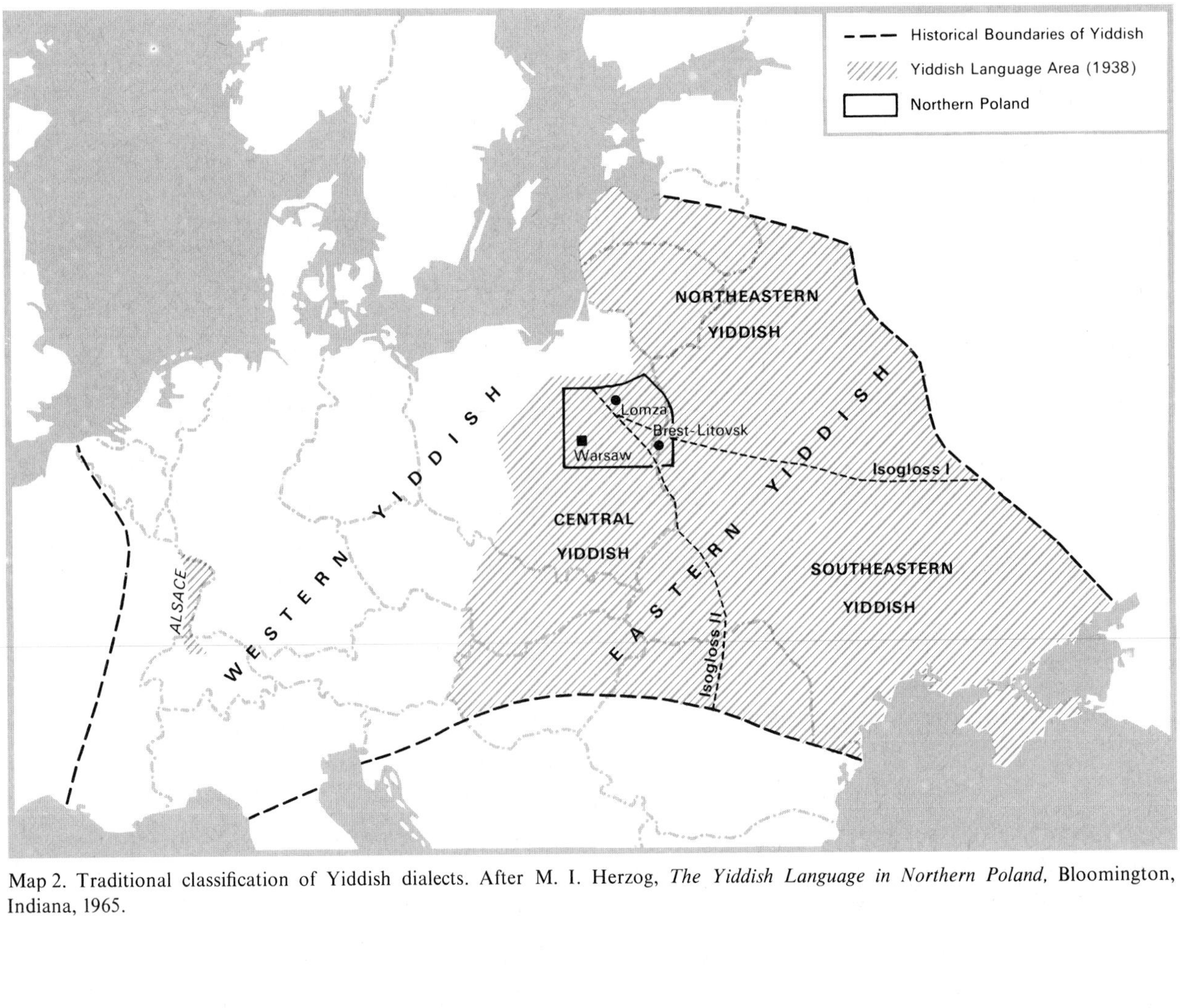

Map 2. Traditional classification of Yiddish dialects. After M. I. Herzog, *The Yiddish Language in Northern Poland,* Bloomington, Indiana, 1965.

Europe resulted from the introduction of the Tiberian pronunciation (mainly as concerns the vowel system) into the Ashkenazi communities, this introduction being made by "Babylonian" scholars and teachers who immigrated to Central Europe from Babylonia (Iraq). By that time, and in fact for generations before, the original Babylonian pronunciation (for which see above) had been superseded in the Babylonian communities by the Tiberian. The Babylonian teachers and scholars were the carriers of the Tiberian pronunciation, and its transplantation into the Ashkenazi communities is due to their activity in these communities. The introduction of the Tiberian pronunciation into the Ashkenazi communities, which, according to Weinreich, played a major role in the formation of the Ashkenazi pronunciation, is a part of a more general process that took place at that time in Ashkenaz, and which Weinreich calls "The Babylonian Renaissance." Weinreich's theory is weak in that there is not sufficient historical evidence for the transplantation of the Tiberian pronunciation into the Ashkenazi communities through the medium of "Babylonian" scholars and teachers. The explanation offered by Yalon, with whom Weinreich agrees as to the very existence of a Sephardi pronunciation (or a pronunciation close to the Sephardi) in the Ashkenazi communities prior to the 13th century is more plausible. Yalon's opinion is that the development of the distinction between *qameṣ* and *pathaḥ*, as well as between *ṣere* and *segol*—that is, of the main features in the vowel system in which the Ashkenazi pronunciation differs from the Sephardi—is due to the influence of the vowel system of Yiddish of that period (the Judeo-German dialects of the 13th century) on the pronunciation of Hebrew current in the Ashkenazi communities. In these dialects there was a sound shift *a* > *o* (cf. e.g., German *das*, Yiddish *dos*, "this"), and this sound shift brought over the realization of the *qameṣ* (which had been realized before as a *pathaḥ*, that is, as */a/*) as */o/* in the Ashkenazi pronunciation of Hebrew. The rise of the differentiation between *ṣere* and *segol* followed a similar course.

Table 1. Historical classification

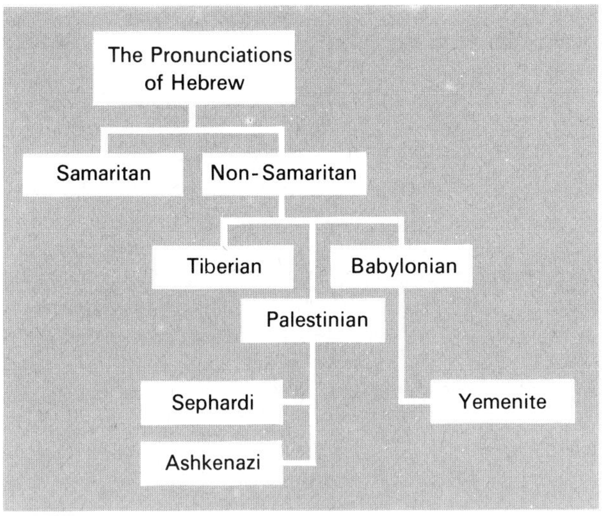

Classification of the Pronunciations of Hebrew. The classification of the pronunciations of Hebrew is here presented in two tables, the first showing the historical aspects of the classification, the second indicating the present-day ramifications (or, to be more precise, the ramifications that existed, especially as to the varieties of the Ashkenazi pronunciation, until the extermination of the Jewish population of central Europe during the Second World War).

Table 1 shows that whereas the Babylonian pronunciation was continued by the Yemenite and the Palestinian by the Sephardi and (indirectly—see above) by the Ashkenazi, there is no direct continuation of the Tiberian pronunciation in any of the pronunciations that were adopted by the Jewish communities.

Table 2. Present-day classification

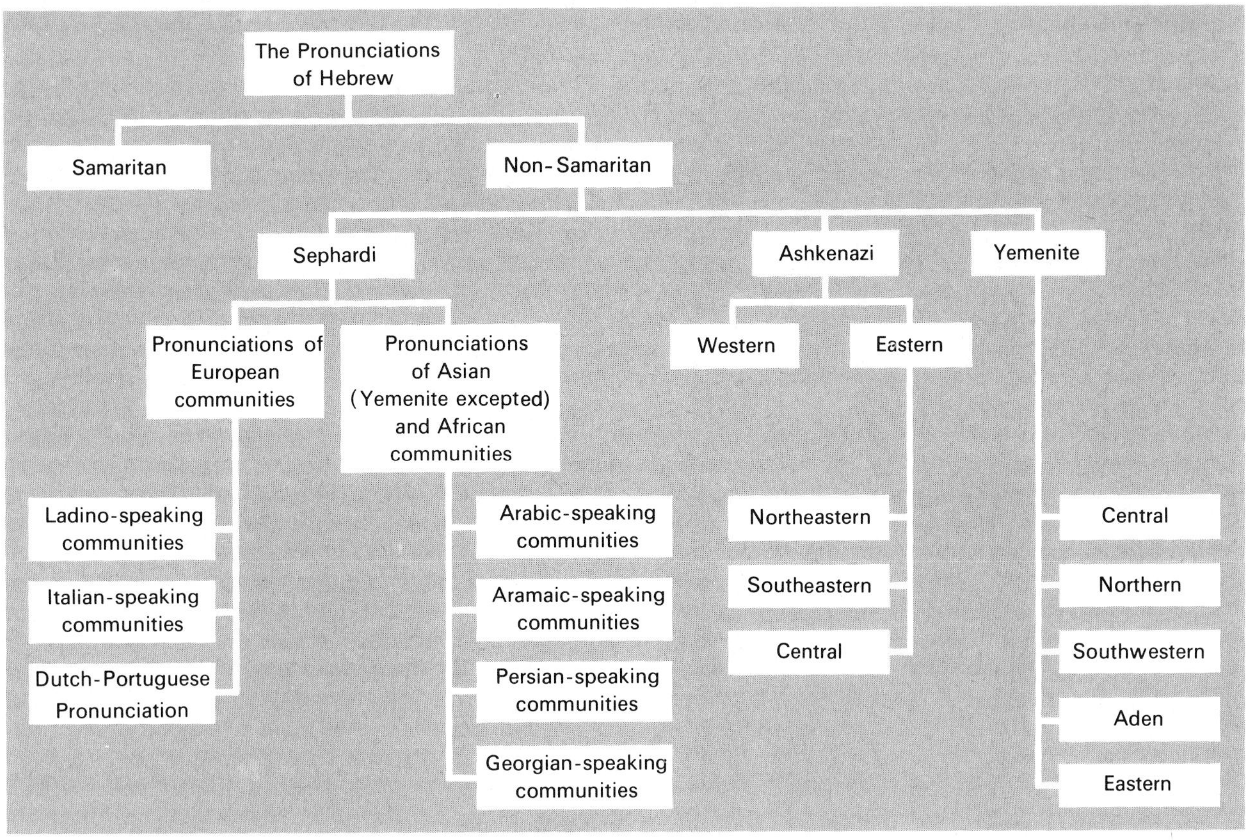

III. THE REALIZATIONS OF THE CONSONANTS AND THE VOWELS AND THE STRESS PATTERNS IN THE VARIOUS PRONUNCIATIONS

First, a word of comment on the term "realization." In describing the sounds extant in the traditional pronunciations of Hebrew we have to deal with a pronunciation of a literary language transmitted from generation to generation through a reading tradition. In each of these reading traditions specific phonetic values are given to the letters that represent consonants and vowels, as well as to the vocalization signs which represent vowels and some other phonological entities. These phonetic values are called the realizations of the letters and the vocalization signs.

A. The Consonants. A. בגדכפ״ת. The realization of these letters as plosives */bgdkpt/* in initial position and medially after a consonant and as fricatives */vḡḏḵfṯ/* is attested in the Middle Ages in all Arabic-speaking communities, including Spain, and in France (I. Garbell, in: *Bulletin de la Société de Linguistique de Paris,* 50 (1954), 232). Of the pronunciations of Hebrew extant today, only the Yemenite pronunciation, and that of the Aramaic-speaking communities of Zakho (near Mosul, in Iraqi Kurdistan) differentiate the plosive series from the fricative series in the realizations of all the six letters. Other communities have fricative counterparts for the plosive realizations of some of the letters only, and the details will be given here. The realization of each of the בגדכפ״ת letters in the various communities will be presented according to the phonetic order of these letters (that is, in the order, פ, ב, ת, ד, כ, and ג).

For the letter פ, there exist in all communities, but for the Georgian-speaking community of the Caucasus, a plosive, */p/*, and a fricative, */f/*, realization for the hard and the soft *p* respectively. The Georgian-speaking community has only the plosive realization */p/* for both hard פ and soft פ. Members of Arabic-speaking communities tend to replace */p/* by */f/* as the realization of hard פ, but all these communities have both */p/* and */f/* as the realizations of hard and soft פ respectively.

The letter ב is constantly, whether hard or soft, realized as the plosive */b/* by many Arabic-speaking communities (those of Iraq, Syria, Egypt, Libya, North Tunisia, and Algeria), as well as by the Dutch-Portuguese community of Amsterdam and by some Italian communities, such as the community of Leghorn. In the Yemenite community, the learned members distinguish between the plosive realization, */b/*, for hard ב and the fricative realization, */v/*, for soft ב; other members of the community have */b/*, or both */b/* and the bilabial fricative */β/*, as the realizations of the letter ב, hard or soft. Such a free variation between */b/* and */β/* is found also in other communities, namely those of eastern Kurdistan, the island of Djerba, southern Algeria and some of the provinces of Morocco. In the Persian-speaking communities, hard ב is realized as */b/*, soft ב as either */β/* or */v/*, and, in the vicinity of a back vowel, as the semivowel */w/*. This realization of soft ב as */w/* also occurs, when it comes at the end of a syllable, in some communities in the northwestern part of Italy. The Georgian-speaking community has only */b/* as the realization of both soft and hard ב. All the communities not mentioned here have */b/* and */v/* as the realization of hard and soft ב, repectively.

The letter ת, when hard, is realized as voiceless (or fortis) dental (or alveolar) plosive by all communities but not a few exceptions: in some communities of Yemen, affricate */ t^s /* occurs (mostly as a free variant of */t/*). When it is soft, it is realized as */s/* by the Ashkenazi communities, as interdental voiceless */ṯ/* by the Yemenite community, the Arabic-speaking Iraqi community, and the Aramaic-speaking community of Zakho in northern Iraq; as */d/* by the communities of Italy (but for the Sephardi communities of this country); and as voiced interdental or postdental */ḏ/* by the Cochin community of India. All other communities have */t/* as the realization of both hard and soft ת, but for some communities of Morocco which have the affricate */t^s/* for both hard and soft ת.

Only relatively few communities differentiate the realization of soft ד from that of hard ד. Soft ד is realized as an interdental */ḏ/*, whereas hard ד is */d/*, by the Yemenite community, by the Aramaic-speaking Zakho community of northern Iraq (where */z/* appears as a free variant), and by a number of communities in the Balkan countries. The Arabic-speaking community of Iraq has */ḏ/* as the realization of soft ד only in a few words: in the divine name */ʾaḏonay/* and in the word */ʾeḥaḏ/*, "one," but only when occurring in the first verse of *Qeriat Shema.* In all other words */d/* is the realization of both hard and soft ד in the Iraqi community.

כ is realized as a voiceless velar stop, */k/*, when hard, and as a voiceless velar fricative */ḵ/*, when soft, by all communities but for the Samaritan, who has */k/* for both hard and soft כ.

ג, when soft, is realized as a voiced velar fricative, */ḡ/*, by most Arabic-speaking communities, as well as by some communities of the Balkan. The Dutch-Portuguese community has a voiceless velar fricative, */ḵ/*, as the realization of soft ג. All communities not mentioned here have only one realization, */g/*, for both hard and soft ג. This is also the realization of hard ג in the above communities who do maintain this differentiation, except for certain Yemenite communities. The communities of central Yemen have a voiced prepalatal affricate, */ǧ/*, as the realization of hard ג; those of extreme eastern Yemen, and some of those of northern Yemen—a voiced prepalatal plosive, */g'/*.

B. The Gutturals. (aa) *The Laryngeals.* The letter א is realized as a glottal stop, */ʾ/*, in most pronunciations. It should be noted, however, that in the Ashkenazi pronunciation, and occasionally, but much less frequently, also in some Sephardi (including the Italian) and Yemenite pronunciations, it may be realized as zero, that is, it is not represented by any sound. In some Ashkenazi pronunciations the contact between two vowels caused by the elision of א in medial intervocalic position gives birth to a glide. In the Georgian-speaking community as well as in some North African communities, and in the community of Cochin (India), */h/* appears as free variant of א.

The letter ה is realized as a glottal fricative [voiced or voiceless] by most communities. In the Italian-speaking communities its realization is, however, zero, as that of א. In some Ashkenazi communities, as well as in some communities of the Balkan countries, and in a great number of communities located in the area stretching from Libya to southeast Morocco, it varies freely with the realizations of א, that is also with zero.

Final consonatal ה (הּ with a *mappiq*) is realized as */h/* in the Yemenite pronunciation and in those of some other Arabic-speaking communities. In the Ashkenazi communities and in most Sephardi communities of Europe it is generally realized as zero. In the Dutch-Portuguese community it is realized as */aha/.*

(bb) The Pharyngeals. The realizations of the letters ח and ע as voiceless and voiced pharyngeal fricatives, */ḥ/* and */ʿ/*, respectively, are found in all Arabic-speaking communities and in most Aramaic-speaking communities. Most of the Persian-speaking communities, however, have */h/* as the realization of ח, and zero as that of ע. ח is realized as a

voiceless velar fricative, */ḵ/*, by all European communities, both Ashkenazi and Sephardi, and by the Georgian-speaking community. ע is realized as */ʾ/* or zero by all of the European communities, with the exception of those of Italy and the Dutch-Portuguese of Amsterdam. The latter communities have a voiced velar nasal, */ŋ/*—the sound of *ng* in the English word "king"—as the realization of ע. The Georgian-speaking community has for this letter a voiceless glottalized uvular plosive, */qʾ/*, in initial and final position; intervocally it is realized as a voiced laryngealized uvular fricative.

C. THE EMPHATICS. ט is realized identically to its non-emphatic counterpart, ת in the pronunciations of the Ashkenazi, Italian, Dutch-Portuguese, and Sephardi communities of Europe, as well as in the pronunciation of the communities of Persia and eastern Kurdistan (in the pronunciation of the Kurdish communities, however, a historical ט is reflected in the quality of the phones of the word, which became emphatic). In the Arabic-speaking communities, the Aramaic-speaking community of Iraqi Kurdistan and in the Georgian-speaking community the realization of ט differs from that of ת: it is a velarized dental (or alveolar) voiceless (or fortis) plosive, */ṭ/*, in most Arabic-speaking communities and in the aforementioned Aramaic-speaking community; either */ṭ/* or */ḍ/*, the voiced (or lenis) counterpart of voiceless (or fortis) */ṭ/*, in the Yemenite community, and */tʾ/*, a voiceless glottalized dental plosive in the Georgian-speaking community.

צ is realized as a voiceless dental affricate */ts/* by the Ashkenazi, Italian, and Dutch-Portuguese communities; as */ṣ/*, a velarized hissing sound, in the Arabic-speaking communities and the Aramaic-speaking community of Iraqi Kurdistan; as a non-emphatic */s/*—its realization being identical to that of ס—in the Persian-speaking communities, in the Aramaic-speaking communities of eastern Kurdistan and Azarbaijan, in the Georgian-speaking community, in the community of Cochin (India), and in some communities of the Balkan countries.

ק is realized identically to its non-emphatic counterpart, כ, in the Ashkenazi, the Italian, the Dutch-Portuguese and the other Sephardi communities of Europe, in some Algerian and east Moroccan communities, and a number of Persian-speaking communities. In the following communities ק is realized in a way different from כ : in the communities of central, northern and eastern Yemen it is realized as a voiced velar or uvular plosive */g/* or */g̣/*. In the communities of southwest Yemen and Aden it is realized as a voiceless uvular plosive, */q/*, which has, particularly in the community of Aden, a voiced uvular fricative, */ʁ/*, as its variant in certain positions. In some Persian-speaking communities ק is realized as a voiced uvular stop, */q/*, which has as its variant a voiced uvular fricative */ʁ/*; other Persian-speaking communities realize ק as */k/*. Many Arabic-speaking communities and those speaking Aramaic have a voiceless uvular plosive, */q/*, as the realization of ק. In the community of Aleppo, as well as in some communities of Algeria and Morocco, ק is realized as a glottal stop, */ʾ/*; in these communities, however, this realization of */ʾ/* exists alongside with */q/*. In the communities of southern Algeria and Cochin, ק has a velar, or uvular, voiceless fricative, */ḵ/*, as its realization (along with the realization */q/*). In the Georgian-speaking community ק is realized as a glottalized velar plosive, */kʾ/*.

D. THE SIBILANTS. (aa) No community maintains the distinction that existed in biblical Hebrew between the phonemes represented by the letters ס, שׁ, and שׂ. In the Samaritan community the realization of שׂ is identical to that of שׁ; in all other communities the realization of שׂ is equal to that of ס.

(bb) Most communities realize שׁ as an unvoiced hushing sound, */š/*, and ס (as well as שׂ) as an unvoiced hissing sound, */s/*. Exceptions are the following:

(1) In the northeastern ("Lithuanian") Ashkenazi communities, no distinction was made between the realization of שׁ on the one hand and that of ס (and שׂ) on the other, the exact articulation of the sound representing both שׁ and ס (and שׂ)—whether */š/* or a sound intermediary between */š/* and */s/*—varying locally. This pronunciation, which corresponds to dialectal features of northeastern Yiddish, tended to disappear after about 1930. A similar phenomenon occurs in some Moroccan communities in which both שׁ and ס (and שׂ) are realized as a sound intermediary between */š/* and */s/*, or as */s/*.

(2) In some communities of Greece the realization of שׁ as */š/* has a variant */s/*.

(3) In the communities of northwest Italy, and to a lesser extent in the communities of northeast Italy, שׁ is realized as */s/*.

ז is realized by most communities as a voiced hissing sound, */z/*. In some Italian-speaking communities it is realized as a voiceless hissing sound, */s/*; in other communities as an affricate, voiced, */dz/*, or voiceless, */ts/*. In both categories of these communities, the exact realization of ז depends on the position of the letter in the word. In some communities of Morocco it is realized as a sound intermediary between */z/* and */ž/*.

E. ר. The letter is realized as an apical flap or trill, */r/*, by most of the Arabic-speaking, Aramaic-speaking, and Persian-speaking communities as well as by the Sephardi communities of Europe. Most of the Ashkenazi communities, on the other hand, realize it as a voiced velar fricative */g/*, or a velar frictionless continuant; some Ashkenazi communities, however, realize ר as an apical flap or trill, */r/*.

F. THE SEMIVOWELS. (aa) The letter ו is realized by most Arabic-speaking communities as the semivowel */w/*; in some communities of Syria and Egypt, as well as in northwest Morocco, it is realized as a labiodental voiced fricative, */v/*; in the communities of northeast Morocco the realization */w/* has the variant */v/*; in some communities of Algeria */w/* is realized as a bilabial voiced stop, */b/*. In the Aramaic-speaking communities ו is realized as */w/*; this realization, however, has a bilabial voiced fricative, */β/*, as its variant. In the Persian-speaking communities the realization of ו is identical to that of soft ב: it is either a bilabial voiced fricative, */β/*, or a labiodental voiced fricative, */v/*; in the environment of a back vowel it has as its variant the semivowel */w/*. Some Italian-speaking communities realize as */v/* when it comes in initial and medial position, but as */w/* in final position.

All Ashkenazi communities have */v/* as the realization of ו.

ו (bb) The letter י is realized by the great majority of the communities as the palatal semivowel */y/*. Some communities have for this realization the variants */i/* or */ʾi/*, the particular positions in which these variants occur differing for the various communities. In some communities in northeast Italy, י, when occurring at the beginning of a syllable, is realized as the voiced prepalatal affricate, */ğ/*. According to the medieval grammarians Profiat Duran and Abraham de Balmes, such was the realization of geminated י in Provence and Italy.

G. GEMINATION. The *dageš forte* is realized by doubling the consonant in the Arabic-speaking communities and the Aramaic-speaking communities of eastern Kurdistan. However, a single consonant occurs in some of these communities as the realization of a letter which has a *dageš forte*, particularly in an unstressed syllable. Most of the Italian-speaking communities also have a doubling of the consonant as realization of the *dageš forte;* the communities of northeast and northwest Italy, however, tend to realize a letter with a *dageš forte* in a way identical to that of a letter not possessing a *dageš forte.*

All the Ashkenazi communities, as well as the Persian-speaking communities, disregard the *dageš forte* in their traditional pronunciations.

B. The Vowels. The basic features of the vowel systems of the three major groups of the traditional pronunciations, in their relation to the Tiberian system of vocalization, were described above. We shall now present the realizations of the vowels in the various pronunciations.

A. ŠUREQ-QIBBUṢ וּ , ֻ. The Ashkenazi communities of the regions in which southeastern and central Yiddish was spoken—that is the Ukraine, Poland, Western Hungary, Western Slovakia, etc.—realize the *šureq* and the *qibbuṣ* as */i/,* or, some of them, as */ü/* (rounded */i/*). A realization of the *šureq* and the *qibbuṣ* as */ü/,* or as a centralized variant of this vowel, */ʉ/,* also exists in a number of other communities—in some communities of Yemen, in Shiraz (Persia), Azarbaijan, in western Kurdistan, in some communities of northwestern Morocco, in northwestern Italy—but in most of these communities the realizations in question, rounded */i/* and */ʉ/,* are in fact variants of */u/.* Since *qibbuṣ* appears in the vocalization of the Bible mostly in closed unstressed syllable, some scholars stated that in these communities a realization of the *qibbuṣ* is found—rounded */i/* or */ʉ/*—which differs from that of the *šureq,* which is */u/.* But the situation is not so. Today a consistent and regular differentiation between the realization of the *šureq* and that of the *qibbuṣ* does not exist in any community.

For communities in which the difference between the realizations of the *šureq* (and the *qibbuṣ*) and that of the *ḥolem* was neutralized, see below, b.

B. ḤOLEM וֹ ,ֹ. In two groups of communities, which were geographically located quite apart, the realization of the *ḥolem* was identical with that of the *ṣere:* in the communities of the regions in which northeastern ("Lithuanian") Yiddish was spoken, and in the communities of southwest Yemen (as well as in the community of Aden): in the former group both the *ḥolem* and the *ṣere* were realized as */ey/,* in the latter as */e/.* From a historical point of view, however, there is no relation between the realization of *ḥolem* as *ṣere* in these two groups of communities. In the "Lithuanian" communities this realization apparently resulted from an interference of Yiddish in the traditional pronunciation of Hebrew. In the pronunciation of the aforementioned Yemenite communities, the realization of *ḥolem* as *ṣere* constitutes a feature of the pronunciation that prevailed in some Babylonian communities of the geonic period (see above).

The communities of the regions in which central and southeastern Yiddish was spoken realized the *ḥolem* as */oy/,* some German-speaking communities as */au/,* English-speaking communities as */ou/.* In the communities of central, northern, and eastern Yemen—that is, in all Yemenite communities but for these in which *ḥolem* is realized as *ṣere* (see above)—the *ḥolem* is realized as a lower-mid rounded central vowel, */ö/* (quite similar to the realization of *eu* in French *peur*). A similar realization of the *ḥolem* is attested in the Aramaic-speaking communities of Persian *Azerbaijan.

C. QAMEṢ AND PATHAḤ ָ , ַ. All the Sephardi communities of Europe, the Italian communities, the Dutch-Portuguese communities of Amsterdam, and all the Asian and African communities—but for the Yemenite and the Persian (to some extent—see below)—do not differentiate between the realization of *qameṣ gadol* (that is, a *qameṣ* not occurring in a closed unstressed syllable) and that of a *pathaḥ:* they are both realized as a low front (or, in some communities, low central) vowel, */a/.* This is a feature typical of the Sephardi pronunciation. In the Aramaic-speaking communities of eastern Kurdistan and Persian Azerbaijan a historical *qameṣ gadol* (which is realized as */a/*) is reflected by the emphaticization of the phones of the word in which it occurs. All the above-mentioned communities realize *qameṣ qaṭan,* i.e., *qameṣ* which comes in a closed unstressed syllable (and which historically reflects the phoneme */u/*) *as /o/,* that is as a *ḥolem.* It should be noted, however, that the communities in question make two exceptions to the realization as */o/* of *qameṣ* which historically reflects the phoneme */u/,* namely:

(1) A *qameṣ* preceding a *ḥatef-qameṣ,* e.g., in נָעֳמִי, is consistently regarded by these communities as a *qameṣ gadol,* and is realized as */a/.* This realization of the *qameṣ* originated in the fact that these communities regard the *metheg* that follows a *qameṣ* preceding a *ḥatef-qameṣ* as indicating that the *qameṣ* is a *qameṣ gadol* (whereas in fact it indicates that the syllable is open and that it has secondary stress).

(2) In the word כָּל, but only in two instances in the Bible (Ps. 35:10; Prov. 19:7) the *qameṣ* is realized as */a/,* that is, this word is pronounced */kal/.* The reason for this lies in the fact that in these two instances the word כָּל has an accent, and this has been taken by the communities whose pronunciation is Sephardi to indicate that the *qameṣ* is a *qameṣ gadol,* which is realized as a *pathaḥ,* namely */a/* (see Z. Ben-Hayyim, *Studies in the Traditions of the Hebrew Language* (1954), 71–72.

The Ashkenazi, the Yemenite, and some Persian communities differentiate between the realizations of *qameṣ* (*qameṣ gadol* as well as *qameṣ qaṭan:* no distinction is made in these communities between these entities) and that of *pathaḥ.* In the Ashkenazi communities the *qameṣ* is realized as */o/* or */u/* (the latter realization prevailing in communities of the region in which central and southeastern Yiddish is spoken). Most of the Yemenite communities realize the *qameṣ* as a rounded lower-mid back vowel, */å/;* the communities of Ḥabbān and Ḥādina in Ḥadramaut realize the *qameṣ* as an unrounded low back vowel, */ɒ/.* Some Persian-speaking communities realize the *qameṣ* as a rounded lower-mid back vowel, */å/.*

D. ṢERE AND SEGOL ֵ , ֶ. All the communities which follow the Sephardi pronunciation have one realization for both *ṣere* and *segol* (see above). This realization is a front higher-mid or lower-mid vowel, */e/* or */ɛ/.* In some North African communities no distinction is made between the realizations of *ṣere* (and *segol*) and that of *hireq.* This applies also, to some extent, to the Iraqi community. In the Yemenite pronunciation the realization of the *segol* is identical with that of the *pathaḥ.* The Ashkenazi pronunciations are divided into two major groups as to the realizations of *ṣere* and *segol:*

(1) The communities of the area of northeastern Yiddish (the "Lithuanian" communities), as well as some other Ashkenazi communities, realized the *segol* (in a stressed syllabe) as a front unrounded higher-mid vowel, */e/;* the *ṣere* is realized as the diphthong */ey/.*

(2) Many communities of the areas of central and southeastern Yiddish realize the *segol* in a stressed syllable as */ey/* and the *ṣere* as */ay/.* No community makes any distinction between the realization of a defective *ṣere* and that of full ("plene") *ṣere,* as well as between the realization of a defective *segol* and that of a full ("plene") *segol.*

E. Ḥɪʀᴇǫ ִ . All communities realize the *ḥireq* as a high front vowel, */i/,* with some positional variants. In eastern Yemen and *hireq* is realized as a central vowel, */ə/.*

F. Tʜᴇ Šᴇᴡᴀ . In presenting the realizations of the *šewa* two points should be considered: the principles that guide the various communities in differentiating a *mobile šewa* from a *quiescent šewa;* the realizations of the *mobile šewa* in the various communities.

(aa) *Mobile Šewa and Quiescent Šewa in the Various Communities.* The Yemenite community and the communities that adhere to the Sephardi pronunciation, including the Italian community, regard the *šewa* sign as denoting *mobile šewa* when it belongs to one of the following categories: (1) when it appears in the beginning of a word; (2) when it follows another *šewa;* (3) when it comes with a letter that has a *dageš forte;* (4) when it comes with the second of two identical letters, as in the word הִנְנִי (to this rule, however, there are exceptions); (5) when it follows, in medial position, *qameṣ, ṣere, ḥolem, šureq,* or *ḥireq* which do not come in a syllable that has a primary stress, but may have a secondary stress (the reading traditions of many communities regard the *metheg* as a sign denoting secondary stress), and after which a *dageš forte* does not come (this applies mostly to the *ḥireq*). It should be noted that there is no general consistency as to the realizations of the *šewa* of this category as a *mobile šewa.* In Hebrew grammar this *mobile šewa* is known as "a *šewa* following a 'long vowel'"; in the traditional pronunciation of these communities, however, there is no consistent differentiation between "long" and "short" vowels in accordance with the opposition between these two categories of vowels in Hebrew medieval grammatical theory (primarily, in the grammatical theory of the school of the Kimḥis). Therefore, for the actual pronunciation of the communities in question this kind of *mobile šewa* cannot be defined in terms of "a *šewa* following a 'long vowel.'"

In some Yemenite pronunciations the second of two final *šewas* is regarded as *mobile.*

In the reading of the post-biblical literature the communities who adhere to the Sephardi tradition disclose some deviations from the ways they follow in differentiating the *mobile šewa* from the *quiescent šewa* in the reading of the Bible. The most prominent among these deviations is the realization as a *quiescent šewa* of the *šewa* in forms of the *qatĕla, qatĕlu, qotĕlim,* and *qotĕlot* patterns.

In the pronunciations of the Ashkenazi communities a *šewa* which historically should be regarded *mobile* is in fact *quiescent* in many cases. This is always the case with a *šewa* coming with a letter that has a *dageš forte* (see above, category (3)); these communities do not geminate the consonants) and with a *šewa* that follows a so-called "long vowel" (above, category (5)). As to an initial *šewa* (above, category (1)), its realization either as a vowel (that is, as a *mobile šewa*) or as zero (that is, as a *quiescent šewa*) depends on the phonological rules according to which initial clusters may or may not exist in the vernaculars of the various communities.

(bb) *The Realizations of the Mobile Šewa.* In the Yemenite community there exist three categories in the realizations of the *mobile šewa:* (1) when it comes with a letter which is not followed by י or by a guttural (that is, a laryngeal—א, ה, or a phryngeal—ח, ע), the *šewa* is realized like an ultrashort *pathaḥ,* namely, */ă/;* (2) when it comes with a letter which is followed by י, the *šewa* is realized as an ultrashort *ḥireq,* namely */ĭ/.;* (3) when it comes with a letter which is followed by a guttural (but is not itself a guttural), the *šewa* is realized as an ultrashort vowel, whose quality is identical to that of the vowel of the following guttural. Thus, when the vowel of the following guttural is a *qameṣ,* the *šewa* is realized as an ultrashort *qameṣ* namely, */ŏ/;* when it is a *šureq,* the *šewa* is realized as an ultrashort *šureq,* namely */ŭ/;* when it is a *holem* the *šewa* is realized as an ultrashort *ḥolem,* namely */ŏ/.*

A *šewa* followed by a *gaʿya* ("*šewa-gaʿya*") is realized by the Yemenite community as a short (not an ultrashort) vowel, its quality being determined by the nature of the following consonant as stated above, in categories (1), (2), (3). The realizations of the *mobile šewa* in the traditional pronunciation of the Yemenite community disclose complete agreement with the realizations of the *mobile šewa* in the pronunciation that prevailed in the Tiberian school. To these latter realizations a number of medieval grammatical treatises bear evidence. Very few communities except the Yemenite have preserved the above realizations that the *mobile šewa* had in the Tiberian school: they exist—but much less consistently than in the Yemenite community—in the Aramaic-speaking communities of western Kurdistan. Some Persian-speaking communities, as well as the Aramaic-speaking communities of Persian Azerbaijan (see above) have the realization */a/,* or */ʌ/,* a lower-mid unrounded back bowel, for the *mobile sewa.* This realization is identical, in quality, to category (1) of the realizations of the *sewa* in the Yemenite community; but whereas in the Yemenite community this realization occurs when the *sewa* comes in certain positions only (see above), in the above-mentioned communities it is the regular realization of the *mobile šewa.* The Dutch-Portuguese community realizes the *sewa-gaʿya* as */a/* and a *sewa* preceding י as */i/,* an ordinary *mobile šewa* as */e/.* All the communities that follow the Sephardi tradition—except the Dutch-Portuguese community and the above-mentioned Aramaic- and Persian-speaking communities, which can be regarded as following the Sephardi tradition in as much as they realize the *qameṣ* as *pathaḥ* and the *ṣere* as *segol*—realize the *sewa* as a phone which is qualitatively identical to the realization of the *sere* and the *segol.* Quantitatively, the *sere* and the *segol,* when they come in stressed syllables, may be realized as long vowels, whereas the *sewa,* which does not come in a stressed syllable, is always realized as a short vowel.

In the Ashkenazi communities, the *šewa,* in those instances in which it is realized as a vowel (see above) is realized as */e/* or */ə/.* The Samaritan community has usually a vowel as the counterpart of a *mobile šewa* of the Tiberian vocalization.

G. Tʜᴇ Ḥᴀᴛᴇғs. The Yemenite community is the only one to have preserved the quantitative difference between the realization of a *ḥatef* and that of a vowel which is its counterpart, that is between *ḥatef-pathaḥ* and *pathaḥ,* between *ḥatef-segol* and *segol,* between *ḥatef-qameṣ* and *qameṣ:* the *ḥatefs* are realized as ultrashort vowels which are qualitatively identical with the vowels which are their counterparts—*ḥatef-pathaḥ* and *ḥatef-segol* as */ă/, ḥatef-qameṣ* as */ǎ̊/.* The reason for the identity of the realizations of the *ḥatef-pathaḥ* and the *ḥatef-segol* is that in the Yemenite pronunciation the realizations of the *pathaḥ* and *segol* are identical.

In the Sephardi and Ashkenazi pronunciations the *ḥatefs* are realized as the vowels which are their counterparts: *ḥatef-pathaḥ* is realized as */a/, ḥatef-segol* as */e/* (or as a variant of this phone, in accordance with the variants of the realizations of the segol in the various communities), *ḥatef-qameṣ* as */o/.*

H. Vᴏᴡᴇʟ Qᴜᴀɴᴛɪᴛʏ. No community maintains, in the realizations of the vowels, the distinction between a "long" and a "short" vowel (*"tenuʿah gedolah"* and *"tenuʿah qeṭanah"*), a distinction prevalent in later medieval grammatical theory. In most communities long realizations of the vowels occur in stressed syllables. The Yemenite

Table 3. The realizations of Hebrew graphemes (letters, vowel-signs, gemination signs) in the traditional pronunciations

Hebrew grapheme	Samaritan pronunciation	Yemenite pronunciation: Central	Yemenite: Northern	Yemenite: South-western	Yemenite: Aden	Yemenite: Eastern	Sephardi pronunciation, European communities: Ladino speaking	Sephardi, European: Italian speaking	Sephardi, European: Dutch-Portuguese	Sephardi, Asian (Yemenite excepted) and African communities: Arabic speaking	Sephardi, Asian/African: Aramaic speaking	Sephardi, Asian/African: Persian speaking	Sephardi, Asian/African: Georgian speaking	Ashkenazi pronunciation: North-eastern	Ashkenazi: South-eastern	Ashkenazi: Central
א	ɔ, "zero"	ɔ,"zero"	ɔ	ɔ	ɔ	ɔ	"zero"	"zero"	"zero"	ɔ, "zero"	ɔ, "zero"	ɔ,"zero"	ɔ, h	"zero"	"zero",(h)	"zero"
בּ	b, (β)	b	b	b	b	b	b	b	b	b, β	b, β	b	b	b	b	b
ב̄		v	v, b	v, b	v, b	v, b	v	v			b, β, v	β, v, w	v	v	v	v
גּ	g	ğ	g'	g	g	g'	g	g	g	g	g	g	g	g	g	g
ג̄		ḡ, q^x	ḡ	ḡ	ḡ	ḡ, q^x			x	ḡ	ḡ	ḡ				
דּ	d	d	d	d	d	d	d	d	d	d	d	d	d	d	d	d
ד̄		d̲	d̲	d̲	d̲	d̲					d̲[1]					
ה	ɔ,"zero"	h	h	h	h	h	h, "zero"	h, "zero"	h	h	h	h	"zero"	h	"zero", h	"zero", h
ה̄	"zero"								ha	h, "zero"	h, "zero"	h, "zero"		"zero"	"zero"	"zero"
ו	b, (w)	w	w	w	w	w	v	v, w	v	w, v[1]	w, β	β, v, w	v	v	v	v
ז	z	z	z	z	z	z	z	z, s, dz, ts	z	z[2]	z	z	z	z	z	z
ח	ɔ, "zero"	ḥ	ḥ	ḥ	ḥ	h	x	x	x	ḥ	ḥ	ḥ, h	x	x	x	x
ט	ṭ, t	ṭ, ḍ	ṭ, d	ṭ, ḍ	ṭ, ḍ	ṭ, ḍ	t	t	t	ṭ	ṭ, t	t	tʾ	t	t	t
י	y	y	y	y	y	y	y	y, (ğ)	y	y	y	y	y	y	y	y
כּ	k	k	k	k	k	k	k	k	k	k	k	k	k	k	k	k
כ̄		k̲	k̲	k̲	k̲	k̲	k̲	k̲	k̲	k̲	k̲	k̲	k̲	k̲	k̲	k̲
ל	l, (ḷ)	l	l	l	l	l	l	l	l	l	l	l	l	l	l	l
מ	m	m	m	m	m	m	m	m	m	m	m	m	m	m	m	m
נ	n	n	n	n	n	n	n	n	n	n	n	n	n	n	n	n
ס	s, (ṣ)	s	s	s	s	s	s	s	s	s[3]	s	s	s	š[4]	s	s
ע	ɔ,"zero", c	c	c	c	c	c	"zero"	ŋ	ŋ	c	c	c, ɔ,"zero"	qʾ	"zero"	"zero"	"zero"
פּ	b, f	p	p	p	p, f	f	p	p	p	p, f	p, f	p	p	p	p	p
פ̄		f	f	f	f		f	f	f	f	f	f		f	f	f

צ	ṣ, s	ṣ	ṣ	ṣ	ṣ	ṣ	ts	ts	ts	ṣ	ṣ, s	s	s	ts	ts	ts
ק	q, ɔ	g, ǥ	g, ǥ	q	q, ʁ	g, ǥ	k	k	k	q, ɔ	q	ǥ, ʁ, (k)	kʾ	k	k	k
ר	r	r	r	r	r	r	r	r	r	r	r	r	r	r, ḡ	r, ḡ	r, ḡ
שׁ	š	š	š	š	š	š	š	š, s	š	š[5]	š	š	š	see ס	š	š
שׂ		s	s	s	s	s	s	s	s	s[5]	s	s	s		s	s
תּ	t	t	t	t	t	t	t	t	t	t, (tˢ)	t	t	t	t	t	t
ת		ṯ	ṯ	ṯ	ṯ	ṯ		d		t, (tˢ), ṯ[6]	t, ṯ[1]			s	s	s
dageš forte	CC	CC	CC	CC	CC	C	C	CC	C	CC	CC, C	C	C	C	C	C
šureq-qibbuṣ	u, o[7]	u, (ü), (ʉ)	u	u	u	u	u	u	u	u	u, (ü)	u, (ü), (ʉ)	u	u	i, (ü), (ʉ)	i, (ü), (ʉ)
ḥolem		ö	ö	e	e	ö	o	o	o	o[8]	o	o	o	ey	y	oy[9]
qameṣ	a, å	å	å	å	å	ɒ	qameṣ (except when coming in closed unstressed syllable: "qameṣ qaṭan") is identical to pathaḥ, both being realized as a. "qameṣ qaṭan" is realized as o. Exception: some Persian speaking communities realize the qameṣ as å.							o	u	u
pathaḥ		a, ä	a, ä	a, ä	a, ä	a, ä								a	a	a
ṣere	ε[10]	e	e	e	e	e	In all varieties ṣere and segol are realized alike, as e ∼ ε							ey	ay	ay
segol		realization is identical to that of pathaḥ												ε	ey, e	ey, e
ḥireq	i	i	i	i	i	ə	i	i	i	i	i	i	i	i	i, ə	i, ə
mobile šewa		basic realization = ă; when preceding y = ĭ; when preceding ʾ, h, ḥ or ʿ = ultrashort vowel, identical in quality to the vowel of the following consonant					e∼ε	e∼ε	e∼ε[11]	e∼ε	e∼ε[12]	a, (ʌ)	e	e, ə	e, ə	e, ə
ḥatef-pathaḥ		ă	ă	ă	ă	ă	a	a	a	a	a	a	a	a	a	a
ḥatef-segol							e∼ε	e∼ε	e∼ε	e∼ε	e∼ε	e∼ε	e	ε	ey, e	ey, e
ḥatef-qameṣ	å̆	å̆	å̆	å̆	å̆	å̆	o	o	o	o	o	o	o	o	u	u

1. In some communities.
2. In some North African communities a sound intermediate between z and ž.
3. In some North African communities a sound intermediate between š and s (for these communities see also footnote 4).
4. No distinction between ס (and שׂ) and שׁ; both realized as š or as a sound intermediate between š and s.
5. For North African communities see ס.
6. In Iraq.
7. Merger of šureq-qibbuṣ and ḥolem into one phoneme, whose allophones are o, u.
8. In North African communities merger of ḥolem and šureq-qibbuṣ into one phoneme, whose allophones are o, u.
9. In German-speaking communities: aw.
10. Merger of these phonemes into one phoneme: ε; allophones: e, ə.
11. Šewa ga'ya = a; šewa preceding y = i.
12. In some communities as in the Yemenite pronunciation, but less consistently.

community maintains the distinction between ultrashort and ordinary vowels, the *mobile šewa* and the *ḥatefs* being realized as ultrashort vowels.

C. Stress. The communities who follow the Sephardi tradition follow, in reading the Bible, the Tiberian rules of stress distribution, as regards both primary and secondary stress. In reading the post-biblical literature there are, in these communities, quite a few cases of deviations from these rules (detailed studies as to the stress distribution in the reading traditions of post-biblical literature in the Sephardi communities are, as yet, missing).

The Yemenite community generally maintains in reading the Bible the Tiberian rules of stress distribution in words which have disjunctive accents; words which have conjunctive accents, on the other hand, quite frequently have stress patterns differing from those of the Tiberian tradition. This latter phenomenon is manifest in the fact that words which in the Tiberian tradition have an ultimate stress *("millera^c")*, have in the Yemenite pronunciation the stress on the penultimate syllable *("mille^cl")*, and occasionally on the antepenultimate, when they come with a disjunctive accent. In the reading of post-biblical literature the number of the words having a penultimate or an antepenultimate stress, and which according to the Tiberian rules of stress distribution should have an ultimate stress, is greater than in the reading of the Bible.

The Ashkenazi communities do not adhere to the Tiberian rules of stress distribution. Quite frequent is the occurrence of penultimate (or, in some communities, antepenultimate) stress where the Tiberian tradition has ultimate stress.

Samaritan Hebrew has as a rule, penultimate primary stress (with concomitant secondary stress on the second syllable preceding the one which has the primary stress; secondary stress may fall on the syllable directly preceding the syllable which has the primary stress— this is the case when the former syllable has a long vowel). It may be, however, proven that the actual stress patterns of Samaritan Hebrew are rather late, and that the stress patterns that Samaritan Hebrew formerly possessed were identical with those of Tiberian Hebrew (Z. Ben-Hayyim, *Sefer Ḥanokh Yalon* (1963), 149–160).

Notes to Table 3 (*see columns 1139–1142*):

1. Two or more phonetic signs are given as the realizations of any letter (or of a vowel sign) in a specific community, when the letter has two or more realizations, the relationship between them being that of "free" or "positional" allophones (that is, sounds whose articulation depends on their position in the word, the preceding and the following sounds, the structure of the syllable etc.). One of the phonetic signs that represent the realizations of a letter comes in brackets when it is less common than the other realizations, or when it is used only by a part of the community in question.
2. C stands for "consonant." CC = a geminated, double, consonant.
3. The sign ˘ above a letter representing a vowel, denotes that the vowel is ultrashort, e. g. [ă] = ultrashort [a].
4. A long vowel is denoted by a line above it, e.g. [ā] = long [a].

SPECIMEN TEXTS

The text of Genesis 47:28–31 is given here in the traditional pronunciations of several communities.

Notes on the Phonetic Transcription

1. ʹ = primary stress; ͵ = secondary stress. Both signs appear before the stressed syllable. When a word has no stressed syllable, no space is left in the transcription between this word and either the preceding or the following word. Since in the Samaritan pronciation, stress usually falls on the penultimate syllable, it is not marked in specimen text no. 1, unless it occurs in the last syllable.
2. A colon that follows a letter representing a vowel denotes that the vowel is ultralong, e.g. [ā:] = ultralong [a].

1. THE SAMARITAN COMMUNITY
(transcription kindly provided by
Professor Z. Ben-Ḥayyim)

Gen. 47:28: wyī yå̄:qob bå̄rəṣ miṣrəm šå̄ba ʿå̄šå̄rå šēna wyå̄yyu yå̄mi yå̄:qob šēni ʿayyo šå̄ba šēnəm warʹbīm wmå̄t šēna.

29: wyiqrābu yå̄mi yišrå̄ʾəl almot wyiqra albēno alyūsəf wyå̄ʾūmər lū am nā må̄ṣå̄tti ån bīnək šim nā yēdåk tēt yirki waššītå nā immå̄di ēsəd wå̄mət al nā tiqbå̄rinni bå̄miṣrəm.

30: wšå̄kåbti am å̄būti wnå̄šå̄ttå̄ni mimmiṣrəm wqå̄bårtå̄ni afqēbirrå̄timma wyå̄'ūmər å̄nå̄ki ēšši kå̄dēbå̄rək.

31: wyå̄ʾūmər iššāba li wyiššāba lū wyištabbi yišrå̄ʾəl ʿal rēʾoš ammēṭå.

2. THE YEMENITE COMMUNITY (Ṣanʿa)

28: wayhʹḥi ͵yaʿaʹgöv băʹʾāraṣ miṣʹrāyim šăʹvaʿ ʿasʹre šåʹnå wayʹhi yăʹme ͵yaʿăʹgöv šă͵ne ḥayʹyow ʹšāvaʿ šåʹnim wăʹʾarbåʿim ʾumʹʾaṯ ͵šåʹnå.

29. Wayyigrăʹvu yăʹme yisråʹʾel låʹmūṯ wayyigʹrå livʹnö lĭyöʹsef wayʹyömar ʹlȫ ʾimʹnå måʹṣå̄ṯi ʹḥen beʿeʹnāḵå ʹsimnå ͵yåḏăʹḵå ʹtāḥaṯ yăreʹḵi wå̆ʿåʹsīṯå ʹʿimmåḏi ʹḥāsaḏ waʾăʹmaṯ ʹʾalnå ṯigbăʹrēni bamiṣʹrå̄yim.

30: wašåḵavʹti ʿim ʾavöʹṯay ʾunsåʹṯāni mimmiṣʹrāyim ʾugvarʹtāni big͵vūråʹṯåm wayʹyömar ͵ʾånöʹḵi ʹʾaʿăsa ḵiḏʹvåʹrāḵå.

31: wayʹyömar hiš͵šåvå̆ʹʿå li way͵yiššåʹvaʿ ʹlö wayyišʹtaḥu yisråʹʾēl ʹʿalröš ͵hammīʹṭṭå̄.

3. THE IRAQI COMMUNITY (Baghdad)

28: wayʹḥi ʹyāʿaʹqob beʹʾēreṣ məṣʹrāyəm šəʹbaʿ ʿəsʹre šaʹna wayʹhi yeʹme ͵yāʿaʹqob šeʹne ḥayʹyaw ʹšēbaʿ šaʹnim weʾarbaʹʿim ʾumʹʾaṯ šāʹnā.

29: wayyiqreʹbu yeʹme yisraʹʾēl laʹmūṯ wayyəqʹrā ləbʹno leyoʹsef wayʹyomer ʹlo ʹʾimna maʹṣāṯi ʹḥen beʿeʹnēḵa simʹna yadeʹḵa ʹtaḥaṯ yereʹḵi weʿaʹsiṯa ʹʿəmmadi ʹḥesed weʾeʹmēṯ ʾalʹna ṯəgbeʹrēni beməṣʹrāyəm.

30: we͵šāḵabʹti ʿimʾaboʹṯay wunsaʹṯāni məmməṣʹrāyəm wuqbarʹtani biq͵buraʹṯam wayyo'mar ʹʾanoʹḵi ʾeʿʹse ͵kədbaʹrēḵa.

31: wayʹyōmer həš͵šābeʹʿa ʹlī way͵yiššaʹbāʿ ʹlō wayyišʹtaḥu yisråʹʾēl ʹʿalrös ͵hammīʹṭṭā.

4. THE ALEPPO (Syria) COMMUNITY

28: wayʹḥi[1] ͵yaʿaʹqob beʹʾereṣ məṣʹrāyim ši͵vaʿesʹre šaʹna wayʹhi ye͵me yaʿaʹqov šeʹne ḥaʹyav ʹševaʿ šaʹnim weʾarbaʹʿim umʹat šaʹnā.

29: wayiqrəʹvu ye͵me yisraʹʾēl laʹmut wayəqʹrā lĭbʹno leyoʹsēf waʹyomer ʹlo ʾəmʹna maʹṣati ʹḥen ͵beʿeʹnēḵa ͵simʹna ͵yadeʹḵa ʹtaḥat yereʹḵi veʿaʹsita ʿəmmaʹdi ʹḥesed ͵veʾeʹmet ʾalʹna təqbeʹrēni beməṣʹrāyim.

30: we͵šaḵavʹti ʿəmʾavoʹtay wunsaʹtāni məməṣʹrāyim wuqbarʹtani bəq͵būraʹtam wayoʹmar ͵ʾanoʹḵi ʾeʿʹse ͵kədbaʹrēḵa.

31: waʹyomer hiš͵šaveʿalʹli wayiš͵šaʹvāʿlo wayišʹtaḥu yisraʹʾel ʿalʹroš hamməṭʹṭā.

[1] Var.: vayhi . [v] and [w] both appear in the pronunciation of the Aleppo community as the realizations of Heb. ו .

5. THE COMMUNITY OF LITHUANIA

28: vay'ḵi 'yankev be ʸeḡets mits'ḡaim 'švaesrey 'šono va'yi yemey'yankev šney 'ḵayov 'ševa 'šonim veaḡ'boim u'meas 'šono.

29: va'yikḡvu yemey yis'ḡoel lo'mus va'yikḡo liv'ney le'yeyeʸ seyf va'yeymaḡley im'no mo'tsosi 'ḵeyn bey'nēḵo 'simno 'yodḵo 'taḵas ye'ḡeyḵi veʸ o'siso i'modi 'ḵesed ve'ʸemes 'alno tigbe'ḡeyni bemitsḡaim.

30: vešo'kavti ima'veysay unso'sani mimits'ḡaim ukvaḡ'tani bikvu'ḡosom va'yeymaḡ o'neyḵi ee'se kidvo'ḡēḵo.

31: va'yeymeḡ i'šovoli vayi'šovaley vayiš'taḵu yis'ḡoel al'ḡeyš a'mito.

Bibliography: I. General (includes works dealing with the pronunciations of more than one community): J. Cantineanu, *Essai d'une phonologie de l'hébreu biblique*, in: BSL, 46 (1950), 82–133; I. Garbell, *Quelques observations sur les phonèmes de l'hébreu biblique et traditionnel, ibid.*, 50 (1954), 231–43; idem, *Mesorot ha-Mivta ha-Ivri shel Yehudei Asya ve-Afrika la-Ḥativotei-hen*, in: *Fourth World Congress of Jewish Studies, Papers*, 2 (1968), 453–4 (Eng. summ., 212); G. Garbini, *Il Consonantismo dell' Ebraico attraverso il Tempo*, in: *Annali dell' Istituto Universitario Orientale di Napoli*, 14 (1964), 165–90; S. Morag, *Ha-Ivrit Shebbefi Yehudei Teiman* (1963); idem, *Oral Tradition as a Source of Linguistic Information*, in: *Substance and Structure of Language*, ed. by J. Puhvel (1969), 127–46; G. M. Schramm, *The Graphemes of Tiberian Hebrew* (1964); S. Morag, Review of *Schramm, The Graphemes*, in: KS, 42 (1967/68), 78–86; M. Ẓ. Segal, Yesodei ha-Fonetika ha-Ivrit (1918); M. Sister, *Probleme der Aussprache des Hebraeischen* (1937). II. Specific Communities: (1). The Samaritan: Z. Ben-Ḥayyim, *Ivrit va-Aramit Nosaḥ Shomron*, 1–2 (1957); 3 pt. 1 (1961), for the pronunciation see particularly pp. 13–27; idem, Some Problems of a Grammar of Samaritan Hebrew, *Biblica*, 52 (1971), 229–52; R. Macuch, *Grammatik des samaritanischen Hebraeisch* (1969). (2). The Yemenite: S. Morag, *Ha-Ivrit* (see I; Bibliography pp. 295–305); I. Garbell, Review of Morag, Haivrit in: KS, 40 (1964/65), 323–30; E. Y. Kutscher, *Yemenite Hebrew and Ancient Pronunciations*, in: JSS, 11 (1966), 217–25. (3). Sephardi, Italian, and Oriental Communities (except the Yemenite); I. Garbell, *Mesorot ha-Mivta* (see I); M. J. Premsela (Perat), in: *Ha-Olam* (Sept. 11, 1941), on the pronunciation of the Dutch-Portuguese community; A. S. Corré, *The Anglo-Sephardic Pronunciation of Hebrew*, in: JJS, 7 (1956), 85–90; E. S. Artom, *Mivta ha-Ivrit eẓel Yehudei Italia, in: Lešonenu*, 15 (1946/47), 52–61; idem, *La pronuncia dell'ebraico presso gli Ebrei della Tripolitania*, in: *Vessillo Israelitico*, 70 (1922), 5; H. Zafrani, *La lecture traditionelle de l'hébreu chez les Juifs arabophones de Tiznit (Maroc)*, in: GLECS, 10 (1964), 29–31; I. Garbell, *Mivta ha-Izzurim ha-Ivriyyim befi Yehudei Iran*, in: *Lešonenu*, 15 (1946/47), 62–74. (4) The Ashkenazi: M. Altbauer, *Meḥkar ha-Masoret ha-Ivrit ha-Ashkenazit ve-Zikato la-Dialektologyah shel ha-Yidish*, in: *Fourth World Congress of Jewish Studies, Papers*, 2 (1968), 455; D. Leibel, *On Ashkenazic Stress*, in: *The Field of Yiddish*, ed. by U. Weinreich, 2 (The Hague, 1965), 63–72; M. Weinreich, *Prehistory and Early History of Yiddish, ibid.*, 1 (New York, 1954), 73–101; idem, *Reshit ha-Havara ha-Ashkenazit be-Zikatah li-Veayot Kerovot shel ha-Yidish ve-shel ha-Ivrit ha-Ashkenazit*, in: *Lešonenu*, 27–28 (1966/67), 131–47, 230–51, 318–39. III. Historical Problems (in addition to the bibliography given in I): I. Garbell, *The Pronunciation of Hebrew in Medieval Spain*, in: *Homenaje a Millás-Vallicrosa*, 1 (1954), 647–96; Y. G. Gumperz, *Mivta'ei Sefatenu* (1952/53); S. Morag, *Sheva Kefulot BGD KPRT*, in: *Sefer Tur-Sinai* (1959/60), 207–42; H. Yalon, *Shevilei Mivta'im*, in: *Kuntresim le-Inyenei ha-Lashon ha-Ivrit*, 1 (1937), 62–78; 2 (1938), 70–76; idem, *Hagiya Sefaradit be-Ẓarefat ha-Ẓefonit*, in: *Inyenei Lashon* (1941/42), 16–31; *Al Hagiyat ha-Kameẓ ve-ha-Kameẓ he-Ḥatuf be-Ashkenaz, ibid.*, 31–36; idem, *Le-Toledot Hagiyat ha-Ivrit be-Ashkenaz*, in: *Inyenei Lashon* (1942/43), 52–58.

[Sh.Mo.]

PROOPS, see Supplementary Entries.

PROPERTY. Classification. Property may be divided into different classes in accordance with the various legal principles applicable thereto. One common division is between immovable property and movables, distinguished from each other in the following respects among others: in their different modes of *acquisition, since there cannot be a "lifting" *(hagbahah)* or "pulling" *(meshikhah)* etc., of land; the law of overreaching (see **Ona'ah*) applies to the sale of movables but not land, apparently because land is always distinctive by virtue of its quality and situation and frequently it is of varying value for different people (see *Sefer ha-Ḥinnukh*, no. 340); in the case of land a rival claim to ownership may be resisted upon proof of three-year possession (see **Ḥazakah*), whereas movables which are in a person's possession for any period of time are presumed to belong to him; litigants are only required to swear an *oath if the dispute concerns movables and not land; unlike movables, land can never be stolen (see *Theft and Robbery) since it cannot be removed or carried away—and it is for this reason that originally only the debtor's land and not his movables became subjected to the creditor's *lien (although later, as a result of changed economic circumstances, the lien was extended by the Babylonian *geonim* to both categories, probably because the majority of Jews had ceased to be landowners at that time). The laws relating to slaves resemble those applicable to land in some respects—for instance as regards overreaching—and in other respects resemble the laws applicable to movables—for instance as regards incidental acquisition (*kinyan aggav*, Tos. to BK 12a).

For the purposes of debt recovery, land is divided into best, median, and poorest quality (*iddit, beinonit,* and *zibburit*, respectively). A claim arising from tort is recovered from land of the best quality, the creditor's claim from the median, and the wife's *ketubbah* from the poorest (Git. 5; see also *Execution). In biblical times land was further classified according to location, thus, "a dwelling house in a walled city," "land of one's holding," "land that is purchased" (Lev. 25:25ff.; 27:16ff.).

Movables may be classified by a number of criteria: (1) *perot* ("fruits" or "produce") and *kelim* ("vessels" or "utensils"), the one for consumption and the other for use respectively; the latter serve for the purpose of acquiring by barter by way of *kinyan sudar*, the former not (see *Acquisition, Modes of); (2) animals and other movables, the former requiring three-year possession for establishment of title whereas *ḥazakah* of the latter is immediately acquired (Sh. Ar., ḤM 133–5); (3) coins which are legal tender constitute a special category of movables which cannot be acquired or alienated by barter and can only be given as a loan for consumption but not for use and return (i.e., the borrower need not return the very coins of the loan); (4) deeds are another separate category of movables since these are not in themselves property but only serve as evidence of their contents, and they differ from other movables in their modes of acquisition (see **Shetar*; *Assignment).

A criterion unrelated to physical differences is one between property that is owned and ownerless property *(hefker)*, for which there are different modes of acquisition. Owned property is further subdivisible into public property (see Meg. 26; BB 23a and *Tosafot*) and private property (including joint ownership (see *Partnership); and into consecrated property *(*hekdesh)* as distinct from property of the common man *(nikhsei hedyot)*. It is forbidden for the common man to derive a benefit from consecrated property as long as it retains its sanctity of which there are different categories (see **Hekdesh*).

Consecrated property if further distinguished from property of the common man as regards the modes of acquisition and the applicable laws of overreaching, tort, etc. Land which is owned may be classified into free, unencumbered property *(nekhasim benei ḥorin)* and encumbered and mortgaged property *(nekhasim meshu'badim),* the latter being land sold by the debtor to others but remaining charged in favor of his creditors for the repayment of debts which cannot be recovered out of his free property (see *Lien).

Another separate category is property from which no enjoyment may be derived, such as **ḥamez* ("leaven") on Passover, the ox that is condemned to death by stoning, fruit of the *orlah* (i.e., the first three years), etc. Such property is not considered to be in the possession of its owner, nor apparently does the latter have a full proprietary right thereto since it not only cannot be enjoyed but may not even be purchased or sold (see *Lien).

Property is further divisible into capital, fruits or profits, and improvements (*keren, perot,* and *shevaḥ,* respectively). The capital is the property as it is at any given time; the fruits are the profits derived therefrom; and the improvement is the increase in market value of the property—whether deriving from actual improvement, natural or effected, or from increase in market price without such.

Proprietary Rights. OWNERSHIP. This is the most common proprietary right and is closely connected with possession. A person is the owner of property if he has possession thereof for an unlimited period, or if it is out of his possession for a limited period only and thereafter is due to be restored to him for an unlimited period—for instance when it had been let, lent, or even when it has been lost or stolen or robbed from the owner in circumstances where it may be surmised that he will regain possession of the property; if not, his ownership of the property will likewise terminate. Since the same property may be in the possession of different people—for instance, one in possession of a dwelling and another of its upper floor—it follows that ownership may be shared by different people with each owning a defined part of the property. The owner does not have unrestricted freedom to deal as he pleases with his property. In biblical times for instance it was not possible to sell a field in perpetuity, but only until the Jubilee Year. Other restrictions have applied at all times, including the following: a person may not use his land in such a manner as to disturb his neighbors in the normal use of their land (see *Nuisance); in certain special circumstances a person is obligated to allow others the use of his land (BK 81a).

RIGHTS IN THE PROPERTY OF OTHERS. Short of ownership, a person may have proprietary rights in the property of others *(jura in re aliena).* Such rights are not exhausted by the recognized legal categories thereof, but may be freely created by the parties thereto in a form and on conditions suited to their needs, without restriction. Broadly, however, these rights may be classified as falling into one of the following three categories: a right to the use of another's property along with its possession as in the case of hire (see *Lease and Hire), loan, and bailment; a right to the enjoyment of another's property without its possession—such as the right to project a bracket into the space of the neighboring courtyard; a right in the form of a charge on another's property, such as a mortgage, and the abutter's rights (see **Mazranut;* *Execution). All the above proprietary rights have in common the fact that they avail against the whole world, including the owner of the property concerned, continue to attach to the property even if it be sold to a third party, and cannot be cancelled without the rightholder's consent. Hence these rights are like a form of limited or partial ownership for a specific purpose—their acquisition being a "transfer of the body for its fruits," such as transfer of a tree for its fruit, a dovecote for the fledglings, or land for a road or thoroughfare (see *Servitude). Similarly, hire is like a sale for a limited period and loan like a gift for a limited period (Yad, She'elah 1:5; Sekhirut 7:1). However, this does not really amount to full, nor even limited ownership (*Nimmukei Yosef,* BM 56b, in the name of Ran), but only to a real right in the property, available against the whole world.

The most common of the first of the above-mentioned categories of *jura in re aliena,* i.e., with possession, is hire or *lease. The lessor, like the lender or bailor, may not withdraw during the subsistence of the contract and the lessee's rights are protected against all comers, including the lessor. A contract of lease may take various forms and, in the case of land, may be for monetary remuneration or the right to work the land for a proportional part of the produce (Yad, Sekhirut 8:1)—the latter right either for a fixed period or passing on inheritance; the lease may even take the form of a sale of the land for return after a number of years. The "sale for the fruit" is so close to the transfer of ownership that the *amoraim* disputed whether acquisition for the fruits was an acquisition of the land itself (*kinyan ha-guf;* Git. 47b), i.e., whether the sale of a field for its fruits involved transfer of the field's ownership or not. When the law of Jubilee Year was observed, any sale of a field was in fact no more than a sale for its fruits.

The proprietary rights attaching to the above relationships carry also corresponding personal rights or obligations. Thus in the case of movables it is the duty of the hirer to take care of the hired property and he assumes liability for damage arising from his negligence, or from the loss or theft of the property, and—in the case of loan—even from inevitable accident. These obligations are separate from the proprietary right in question and the two may even come into effect at different times (see Tos. to BM 99a). Thus an unpaid bailee who has mere custody or detention, but not possession, of the deposit—since it may be removed by the owner at any time—apparently has not proprietary right in the deposit but only the obligation to take proper care thereof and to compensate for his neglect to do so. Other similar obligations may be circumscribed by agreement in the same way as are the terms of the real rights, since both may be created by the parties in a manner they think fit.

The second of the above-mentioned categories of proprietary rights are those which allow a person the enjoyment of another's property without its possession. These include a man's right to cause a nuisance to his neighbor or to project an abuttment into the airspace of his neighbor's court (see *Servitude). Similarly, a man buying a tree has the right of having it stand in the land of the seller (BB 81b), or the owner of a vine or shrub to have it cling to the tree of his neighbor (BM 116b). These too are proprietary rights which are transferable to others and available against purchasers of or heirs to the servient property, the owner whereof may not withdraw from or cancel the said rights.

Acquisition and Transfer of Proprietary Rights. The usual transfer of proprietary rights is by the parties' will. There are two categories of voluntary acquisition of ownership, the first involving the acquisition of ownerless property, and the second acquisition of property from its former owner. For acquisition of the former, i.e., original acquisition, it is necessarily required that the person becoming entitled thereto have possession of the property together with the intention of acquiring its ownership. Hence in this case the formality of acquisition is satisfied by way of a "lifting" or "pulling" of the property, or by its presence within his "premises which are guarded for him" or his "four cubits" *(arba ammot),* or, in the case of land, by acts revealing his control thereover (i.e., *ḥazakah*).

For the acquisition of property from its former owner, it is not necessary that the acquirer have possession of the property, which may be at any place whatever. In this case acquisition takes place by consent of the parties and their making up their minds to the transaction so as to exclude withdrawal therefrom. Here too it is not sufficient that the parties make up their minds, but this fact must also be revealed in a manner that is recognized by all. In general it is customary for the parties to make up their minds and complete the formal acquisition by the same modes as those applicable to the acquisition of ownerless property; additional modes of acquisition in this case are those which naturally reveal that the parties have made up their minds—including by way of money, deed, delivery *(mesirah)*, barter, or by way of an act or formality which for historical reasons had become recognized as an act of acquisition, such as *kinyan sudar* (acquisition by means of the "kerchief") and *kinyan aggav* (incidental acquisition). These acts are not symbolic of anything else, but are acts bringing about the making up of the parties' minds and its revelation. Hence if in a particular locality some other act is equal legal validity (as, e.g., in the case of *kinyan* customary in the closing of a transaction, it will be of *sitomta*, i.e., affixing of a mark).
For details, see *Acquisition, Modes of.

Extinction of Ownership. A person's ownership of property is extinguished when he is reconciled (makes up his mind) to the fact that he no longer has permanent possession of the property or that it will no more return to his permanent possession. Here too his state of mind must be revealed and recognizable to all, save that no formal act is required and it may be indicated by speech or conduct alone. Thus ownership terminates upon: (1) **ye'ush* ("despair"), i.e., when the owner abandons hope of recovering possession of property of which he has been deprived, for example through loss or theft; (2) abandonment or reunification, whereby the owner reveals his intention to terminate his ownership, whether or not the property be in his possession (see **Hefker*); (3) transfer or alienation of property to another, whereby the owner reveals his intention to terminate ownership thereof but only through its acquisition by a specific person and only from the moment of such acquisition. Transfer of ownership other than by the will of the parties concerned, takes place on a person's death (see *Succession), or upon forfeiture by order of the court, or by the operation of law (see *Confiscation, Expropriation, Forfeiture). Ownership is also extinguished upon the destruction of property or its transmutation *(shunnui, specificatio)*.

In the State of Israel. Property law in the State of Israel is governed mainly by Knesset laws, such as the Water Law, 5719-1959; the Pledges Law, 5727-1967; the Bailee's Law, 5727-1967; the Sale Law, 5728-1968; the Gift Law, 5728-1968, the Land Law, 5729-1969; etc. Some of the provisions of the above laws are in accordance with Jewish law on the particular subject.

Bibliography: T. S. Zuri, *Mishpat ha-Talmud*, 4 (1921); Gulak, Yesodei, 2 (1922), 172–6; idem, *Le-Ḥeker Toledot ha-Mishpat ha-Ivri bi-Tekufat ha-Talmud*, 1 (*Dinei Karka'ot*, 1929); G. Webber, in: *Journal of Comparative Legislation*, 10 (1928), 82–93; Herzog, Instit, 1 (1936); Elon, in: ILR, 4 (1969), 84f., 90–98, 104f. [SH.A.]

PROPHETS, LIVES OF THE, name given to one of the few examples of ancient Jewish hagiographic writings (another example being the "Martyrdom of Isaiah"). Although in its present form the book contains some Christian elements, there is a general consensus among scholars as to the antiquity and the basic Jewish character of the work. Many of the traditions, such as that of Isaiah's death at the hands of Manasseh, find echoes in Jewish apocryphal and rabbinic literature (see also Martyrdom of *Isaiah).

The primary text is preserved in Greek. The Greek version falls into four recensions, two attributed to Epiphanius of Cyprus (hence the title "Pseudo-Epiphanius" sometimes given to this work), one to Dorotheus, and one anonymous. The anonymous recension is to be found in Codex Morchalianus (Codex Q of the Septuagint). It is generally considered to be the oldest extant form of the work. Certain of the other recensions, especially that attributed to Dorotheus, are much expanded, containing the lives of various New Testament figures, apostles, and so forth. The "Lives of the Prophets" is also known in a number of the Oriental Churches in translation. There are various Syriac forms of the book which all appear to be developments of a single original translation from Greek. Although it is attributed to Epiphanius, Nestle and Schermann were of the opinion that the form of the Syriac "Lives" contained in the Syrohexaplar Code represents a different translation, but this is denied by Torrey. The "Lives" are also extant in Armenian, in a number of forms, but little is known of this version. Most scholars consider the Greek to be original, although Torrey posited a Hebrew original for the book.

The recension of Q contains the lives of Isaiah, Jeremiah, Ezekiel, and Daniel, followed by the lives of the Twelve Minor Prophets. These are followed by the lives of Nathan, Ahijah, Joed (identified with the anonymous prophet who is mentioned in I Kings 13), Azariah (son of Oded—II Chron. 15:1ff.), Zechariah b. Jehoiada (II Chron. 24:20–22; cf. Matt. 23:35; Luke 11:51), Elijah, and Elisha. Some of these "Lives" are quite extensive, containing many traditions of extra-biblical character touching on the circumstances of birth, acts, or death of the prophet concerned. Others seem to be limited to the very barest of details of place of birth and death. The traditions contained in these brief narratives are of considerable interest. Some of them are found in other sources, others are extant only in the "Lives." It is plausible that the "Lives" preserve references to lost apocryphal documents or at least traditions in common with them. The popular character of many of the traditions also adds to their interest. The "Lives" abound with geographical names, not all of which can be identified.

Bibliography: E. Nestle, *Marginalien und Materialien* (1893), 1–64, 2nd pagination; T. Schermann, *Propheten- und Apostellegenden* (1907); idem, *Prophetarum Vitae Fabulosae* . . . (1907); C. C. Torrey, *The Lives of the Prophets* (Gr. and Eng. 1946). [M.E.S.]

PROPHETS AND PROPHECY. This article is arranged according to the following outline:

- In the Bible
  - Classifications
  - Nature of Prophecy
    - Origin and Function
    - Dreams
    - Divination
  - Preclassical Prophets
    - Terminology
    - Group Prophecy
    - Ecstasy
    - Group Life of Prophets
    - Role in Society
      - Politics
    - Clairvoyance and Prediction
    - Symbolic Acts
    - Miracles
    - Extra-Biblical Prophecy: Mari
  - Comparison of Preclassical and Classical Prophets
    - Ritual versus Morality
    - Nationalism versus Universalism
    - Mantics versus Reprovers
    - Group versus Individuals
    - Ecstatics versus Non-Ecstatics
    - Role in Society
    - Symbolic Acts

Signs and Wonders
Visions
Classical Prophecy
Historical Scope
Dedication and Commissioning of the Prophet
His Reluctance and God's Reassurance
Life of the Prophet
Reproaching God
False Prophets
The Prophet as Intercessor
History
Universalism and Election
Supremacy of Morality
Attitude Toward Ritual
Morality and Destiny
Repentance
Suspension of Freedom and God's Inaccessibility
New Covenant
Future of Israel
In the Talmud
In Jewish Philosophy
Medieval Jewish Philosophy
Saadiah
Judah Halevi
Maimonides
Joseph Albo
Modern Jewish Thought

IN THE BIBLE

Classifications. The second division of the Hebrew Canonical Scriptures is today subdivided into "The Former Prophets," i.e., the books of Joshua, Judges, Samuel, and Kings, and "The Latter Prophets," i.e., the books of Isaiah, Jeremiah, Ezekiel, and the Twelve Minor Prophets.

This division is basically a chronological one. A preferable nomenclature would be the preclassical, or popular, prophets and the classical, or literary, prophets. The latter terminology is reserved for those prophets whose oracles were preserved in writings either by themselves, their disciples, or their scribes (e.g., Jer. 36:4, 18). The primary literary remains of the preclassical, or popular, prophets, on the other hand, are the stories and accounts of their lives transmitted at first, no doubt, orally by followers and admirers. Though several third-person biographical accounts of the classical prophets have also been preserved in their respective books (e.g., Isa. 36–39; Jer. 26ff.; Amos 7:10–17), these stories are secondary to their prophetic pronouncements. The terminological division, however, is merely a formal external criterion for distinguishing between the two. Of far greater significance are the essential internal differences which decisively mark off the literary prophets from their forebears.

Nature of Prophecy. The institution of prophecy is founded on the basic premise that God makes his will known to chosen individuals in successive generations. A prophet is a charismatic individual endowed with the divine gift of both receiving and imparting the message of revelation. As the spokesman for the deity, he does not choose his profession but is chosen, often against his own will, to convey the work of God to his people regardless of whether or not they wish to hear it (Ezek. 3:11). A prophet does not elect to prophesy, nor does he become a prophet by dint of a native or an acquired faculty on his part. Prophecy is not a science to be learned or mastered. There is no striving to be one with God, no *unio mystica,* no indwelling of God within the spirit of the prophet through rapture, trances, or even spiritual contemplation. The prophet is selected by God and is irresistibly compelled to deliver His message and impart His will, even if he personally disagrees with it. He is consecrated to be set apart from his fellowmen and is destined to bear the responsibility and burden of being chosen. The prophet stands in the presence of God (Jer. 15:1, 19) and is privy to the divine council (Isa. 6; Jer. 23:18; Amos 3:7). He speaks when commanded, but once commanded, must speak (Amos 3:8). Appointed messenger, he must translate his revelatory experience into the idiom of his people. For though the prophet is overwhelmed by the divine word and becomes "word possessed," he does not lose his identity nor does he suffer from any effacement of personality. The "word of YHWH" and not His "spirit" is the primary source of prophecy. The "spirit" may prepare the prophet to receive divine revelation, may evoke the revelatory state of mind, but the "word" is the revelation itself. What makes him a prophet is not the spirit which envelops or moves him—for this spirit also motivated elders, judges, Nazirites, and kings—but the word which he has heard and which he transmits to others. In fact, the "spirit" or the "hand" of God (see below) is mentioned only occasionally in the writings of the classical prophets (a major exception being Ezekiel), and then it constitutes the stimulus, not the content, of revelation. The prophet, although conscious of being overwhelmed by the divine word and of being involved in an encounter with God, is still capable of reacting and responding and may even engage God in a dialogue. The divine constraint does not exclude the prophet's personal freedom; his individuality is maintained, and the divine message is accented by his own tones.

The prophetic experience is one of confrontation. The prophet is both a recipient and a participant. Armed solely with the divine word and as conveyor of the divine will, he becomes a radical iconoclast who views the world *sub specie dei.* He is concerned not with the being of God but with the designs of God. He has knowledge not about God but from God concerning His actions in history. The prophet is neither a philosopher nor a systematic theologian, but a covenantal mediator who delivers the word of God to his people in order to shape their future by reforming their present. He is not the ultimate source of the message nor its final addressee; he is the middleman who has the overpowering experience of hearing the divine word, and who must perform the onerous task of bearing it to a usually indifferent if not hostile audience.

The individuality of the prophet is never curtailed. No two prophets prophesied in the same style. Their unique literary styles, whether expressed in prayers, hymns, parables, indictments, sermons, dirges, letters, mocking and drinking songs, or legal pronouncements, bear the mark of independent creativity. The divine message is refracted through the human prism. This is dramatically brought out by the striking image of the prophets' receiving, literally eating, God's word, and then bringing it forth (Jer. 15:16ff.; Ezek. 3:1ff.). God speaks to the prophet and the prophet speaks out. The divine revelation is delivered by a human agent.

ORIGIN AND FUNCTION. The Hebrew term for a prophet, *navi'*, cognate of the Akkadian verb *nabû*, "to call," i.e., "one who has been called," is first applied to Abraham. He merits this title because of his role as intercessor (see below): "But you [Abimelech] must restore the man's wife [Sarah]—since he is a prophet, he will intercede for you—to save your life" (Gen. 20:7). The origin of the office of prophecy, according to Deuteronomy, is rooted in the event at Sinai. Since the people were afraid of receiving God's word directly in a public theophany, they requested Moses to "go closer and hear all that our Lord our God tells you . . . and we will willingly do it" (Deut. 5:24). This is corroborated by the personal description of Moses: "I stood between the Lord and you at that time to convey the Lord's word to you, for you were afraid of the fire and did not go up the mountain" (Deut. 5:5; cf. Ex. 19:19). Thus Moses became the spokesman for God to the people.

The term *navi'*, translated in the Septuagint by the Greek word προφήτησ, *prophētēs* ("prophet"), which means "one who speaks on behalf of" or "to speak for" (rather than "before"), is a "forthteller" and spokesman more than a "foreteller" and prognosticator. He is God's mouthpiece (Jer. 15:19); the one to whom God speaks, and who, in turn, speaks forth for God to the people. This, indeed, is the very definition of the prophet's role as found in several places in the Bible. In Exodus 4:15–16 the roles that Moses and Aaron are to assume before Pharaoh are delineated: "You [Moses] shall speak to him [Aaron] and put the words in his mouth ... and he shall speak for you to the people. Thus he shall be your spokesman and you shall be an oracle *['elohim]*." In Exodus 7:1, "The Lord replied to Moses, 'See I make you an oracle *['elohim]* to Pharaoh, and your brother Aaron shall be your spokesman' *[navi']*." So, too, in Deuteronomy 18:18, "I will raise up a prophet for them among their own people, like yourself. I will put My words in his mouth, and he will speak to them all that I command him."

DREAMS. Moses, though he is called a *navi'* for the first time only in Deuteronomy (18:15; 34:10), is cast as the prophet par excellence. He is distinguished by God's revealing Himself directly to him, "mouth to mouth, plainly and not in riddles," while to other prophets, God revealed Himself only in visions or dreams (Num. 12:6–8). This distinction between *dreams and prophecy is made because of the universal belief that gods communicate their will to man through the medium of dreams. Several instances of divine revelation through dreams are attested in the Bible, e.g., the dreams of Abimelech (Gen. 20:3; cf. Gen. 31:10–13); Solomon (I Kings 3:5–14); Joel (3:1); and Job (33:14–18).

In Deuteronomy 13:2ff. dreams are directly linked to prophecy. It is no wonder, then, that they are considered a possible means for determining the will of God, e.g., I Samuel 28:6 (cf. 28:15). Nevertheless, this means for revealing the will of God is frowned upon by later prophets (see Jer. 23:28; 27:9; Zech. 10:2; cf. Jer. 29:8). Furthermore, with the exception of Joseph and Daniel, both of whom served in foreign courts, but, nevertheless, related their knowledge of dream interpretations directly to God, there existed in Israel no science of dream interpretation such as that prevalent in Egypt and Mesopotamia.

DIVINATION. In the aforementioned quotations from the books of Jeremiah and Zechariah, the medium of dream communication is coupled with that of divination, a science that was well known and widely spread throughout the entire Ancient Near East. It was a highly specialized skill, which enabled the expert practitioner to peer into the world of the future by fathoming the inexplicable will of the gods. The art of divination was extremely elaborate and encompassed many different fields, including hepatoscopy, extispicy, lecanomancy, libanomancy, necromancy, belomancy, reading entrails, bird omens, astrology, and so on. Against these common practices of Israel's neighbors the Bible inveighs, "You shall not practice divination or soothsaying" (Lev. 19:26); "Do not turn to ghosts and do not inquire of familiar spirits" (Lev. 19:31; cf., also, 20:6, 27). The most comprehensive prohibition is found in Deuteronomy 18:10–11: "Let no one be found among you who consigns his son or daughter to the fire, or who is an augur, a soothsayer, a diviner, a sorcerer, or one who casts spells, or who consults ghosts or familiar spirits, or who inquires of the dead." All of these injunctions are leveled against the divinatory practices of the Canaanites. But the Bible is well aware of its occurrence in other nations as well, e.g., Philistines (I Sam. 6:2; Isa. 2:6); Babylonians (Isa. 47:9, 12–13; Jer. 10:2; 50:35; Ezek. 21:26–28), and Egyptians (Isa. 19:3).

Though there are several biblical analogues to various forms of divination, e.g., hydromancy or oleomancy (Gen. 44:5, 15), communication through dead spirits (I Sam. 28), and tree oracles (II Sam. 5:24), the biblical injunctions cited above categorically ban their practice—even in time of dire stress as Isaiah mockingly comments (9:18)—since they are all assumed to be illegal means of discovering the will of God (cf. also I Sam. 28:3, 9; II Kings 23:24; Isa. 2:6; 8:19; 44:25; Ezek. 13:17ff.). They all imply an art or a science and rely on human skill to penetrate divine mysteries. Divination is pagan in origin, and its practitioners are linked with the false prophets (Micah 3:6–7; Jer. 27:9; 29:8; Ezek. 13:9, 23). For through technical expertise man attempts to initiate the action. In prophecy, on the other hand, the initiative is taken entirely by God, who communicates His intentions through visions and auditions, and who cannot be coerced by any humanly devised means to reveal His designs.

There are, nevertheless, several biblically sanctioned, legitimate means through which God discloses His will other than prophecy: dreams (I Sam. 28:6; see above), the *Urim and Thummim placed in the priest's breastplate (Ex. 28:30; Lev. 8:8; Num. 27:21; I Sam. 14:41; Ezra 2:63), and the *ephod (I Sam. 23:9ff.). In fact, it seems that the earlier prophets may have, at times, fulfilled the same function as the last two. This is suggested by the manner of framing questions in the simple form of alternatives in I Samuel 14:37, 42 (cf. Greek version); 23:11, and I Kings 22:6. Lots (Num. 26:55–56) and the ordeal (Num. 5) were also occasionally resorted to. All of these, however, are not heard of again after the time of David. From then on, the only legitimate form of revelation was the one which came from God through His chosen prophets: "For God does not do anything unless He has first revealed his plans to His prophets" (Amos 3:7).

Preclassical Prophets. TERMINOLOGY. The preclassical prophets are referred to by four different names: *ḥozeh*, *ro'eh*, both meaning "seer"; *'ish ha-'Elohim*, "man of God" (I Kings 13:1; Elijah, I Kings 17:18, 24; II Kings 1:10; Elisha, II Kings 4:7, 9, 21; 8:4, 8, 11; 13:19; cf. Moses, Deut. 33:1; Josh. 14:6; Ps. 90:1; Ezra 3:2; I Chron. 23:14; II Chron. 30:16); and *navi'*, "prophet." (The last is also the standard term for the classical prophets.) The seer was one who possessed the ability to reveal that which was concealed from ordinary mortals; he was able to foretell the future. The term *ro'eh* is first applied to Samuel in I Samuel 9, when Saul, in search of his father's asses, seeks the aid of the seer Samuel and is prepared to pay a fee of one-quarter of a shekel. Samuel, who in this narrative (9:6) is also called *'ish ha-'Elohim*, and who had been previously informed by the Lord of Saul's arrival, provides the necessary information and, in addition, anoints Saul king of Israel (I Sam. 10). He then informs Saul of the events which are about to befall him on his way home. It is within this account that the editor of the narrative adds an important historical-chronological footnote (9:9): "He who now is called *navi'* was formerly called *ro'eh*." The title *ro'eh* is later applied to Samuel in I Chronicles 9:22; 26:28; and 29:29. The only other one clearly designated by this title is Hanani (II Chron. 16:7, 10; some also attribute it to the priest Zadok (II Sam. 15:27), but this is highly dubious). In I Chronicles 29:29 the three diversely titled prophets of the period of David, Samuel the *ro'eh*, Nathan the *navi'*, and Gad the *ḥozeh*, are named together.

The title *ḥozeh* is first applied to Gad in II Samuel 24:11, where he is called the *ḥozeh* of David (so, also, in I Chron.

21:9), where he once again is distinguished by protocol from Nathan the *navi*ʾ. (On the interchangeability of these two terms, however, one may note that Gad is also called *navi*ʾ in I Sam. 22:5, and in II Sam. 24:11 he is accorded the dual title *navi*ʾ and *ḥozeh.*) According to Chronicles, several other kings kept in their courts men who bore the title *ḥozeh:* I Chronicles 25:5, Heman is mentioned as a *ḥozeh* for David; II Chronicles 9:29, Jedo (Iddo) for Jeroboam (in II Chron. 12:15, he is distinguished from Shemaiah the *navi*ʾ); II Chronicles 19:2, Jehu son of Hanani, for Jehoshaphat; II Chronicles 33:18, anonymous men for Manasseh; and II Chronicles 35:15, Jeduthun, Heman, and Asaph for Josiah. Since only the term *ḥozeh* (and not *ro*ʾ*eh* or *navi*ʾ) is found when reference is made to a king *(ḥozeh ha-melekh),* it most probably indicates that the seers who bore this title were officially attached to the court, the so-called court prophets.

The term *ḥozeh* was at times also connected with *navi*ʾ: positively, in II Samuel 24:11 and II Kings 17:13, and negatively, in Isaiah 29:10 (cf. 28:7); Amos 7:12; and Micah 3:7. That this technical term was not confined to Israel, but was a common West Semitic title for such seers is attested by the inscription of King Zakir of Hamath (early eighth century B.C.E.), who states "I lifted up my hands to Baʿalsha[may]n and Baʿalshamayn answered me [and spoke] to me through seers [חזין] and diviners" (lines 11–12; Pritchard, Texts³, 655).

Group Prophecy. The first story in the Bible which makes reference to a seer also mentions bands of prophets. When Saul consults the seer Samuel as to the whereabouts of his father's lost asses, he is told that he is to become "prince over his people Israel" (I Sam. 10:1). To substantiate the authenticity of this prediction, he is informed that upon arriving at Gibeah he will meet "a band of prophets coming down from the high place with harp, tambourine, and lyre before them." And when he did subsequently meet them, a "spirit of God came mightily upon him and he spoke in ecstasy among them." This encounter became the source for the proverbial question "Is Saul also among the prophets?" (I Sam. 10:12). I Samuel 19:18–24 relates this proverb to another instance of the contagious nature of group prophecy: Saul sends men to capture David, who was then in the company of Samuel. However, when the men "saw the company of prophets with Samuel standing as head over them, the spirit of God came upon the messengers of Saul and they also prophesied." This incident is repeated two more times as subsequent messengers are overcome by their contact with the band of prophets. Finally, Saul himself goes to capture David, but the spirit of God comes upon him and he, too, prophesies before Samuel, strips off his clothes, and lies naked all that day and night. Hence, it is said, "Is Saul also among the prophets?"

Ecstasy. The ecstatic nature of these groups of prophets is foreshadowed in Numbers 11:16ff., a narrative whose purpose may have been the legitimization of the phenomenon of ecstatic prophecy. Moses gathered 70 of the people's elders and stationed them around the Tent of Meeting. "Then the Lord came down in a cloud and spoke to him. He drew upon the spirit that was on him and put it upon the 70 elders. And when the spirit rested upon them they spoke in ecstasy" (11:25; cf. 11:16–27).

Another instance of group ecstasy is found in I Kings 22, where some 400 prophets rage in ecstasy before kings Jehoshaphat and Ahaz on the eve of their attack against Ramoth-Gilead. This feature of collective dionysiac frenzy is not confined to early Israelite prophets. In I Kings 18 it is recorded that 450 Canaanite prophets of Baal (and 400 prophets of Asherah, verse 19) "cried aloud and cut themselves after their manner with swords and lances till the blood gushed out upon them. And it was so, when midday was past, that they prophesied in ecstasy until the time of the evening offering..." (18:28–29). Ecstatic seizures, moreover, were not limited to groups; individuals, too, could have them. Thus, the seizure of Elijah: "The hand of the Lord was upon Elijah ... and he ran before Ahab['s chariots]" (I Kings 18:46; see also *Ecstasy).

An extra-biblical ecstatic prophet is attested in the 11th-century tale of the Egyptian Wen-Amon, which takes place in Byblos. It relates that "while he [Zakar-Baal, king of Byblos] was making offering to his gods, the god seized one of his youths and made him possessed. And he said to him, 'Bring up [the] god! Bring the messenger who is carrying him! Amon is the one who sent him out! He is the one who made him come!' And while the possessed [youth] was having his frenzy on this night..." (Pritchard, Texts, 26). Additional examples of this phenomenon are to be found among the Hittite *šiunianza* and the pre-Islamic *kāhins.*

In such a state one turns, as Saul did, into "another man" (I Sam. 10:6) and may behave madly, as witnessed by Saul's attempt to take the life of David in I Samuel 18:10ff. The irrational and ecstatic behavior of such possessed individuals makes them appear to be madmen. Thus, when Elisha goes to Ramoth-Gilead to anoint Jehu king of Israel, Jehu was asked, "Is all well? Why did this madman come to you?" (II Kings 9:11). A juxtaposition of "madman" and "ecstatic prophet" is found in Jeremiah 29:26; and in Hosea 9:7 the parallel to "prophet" is "madman." (The Hebrew term for madman, *meshuggaʿ* in these verses may very well be a *terminus technicus,* related to the Akkadian *muḫḫûm,* "crazy/frenzy," found in Mari; see below.)

In Israel an ecstatic seizure might be induced by external means, e.g., music. In II Kings 3:15 Elisha requests a musician, "and when the musician played, the power of the Lord came upon him." Specific mention of various musical instruments of the band of prophets is found in I Samuel 10:5 and II Chronicles 35:15. (Dancing in order to induce a prophetic frenzy is mentioned only in connection with the Canaanite prophets of Baal, I Kings 18:26.) Nevertheless, this seizure is always conceived of as dependent on God. It is ascribed directly to Him and is caused either by "the hand *[yad]* of YHWH," "the spirit *[ru'aḥ]* of YHWH" or "the spirit *[ru'aḥ]* of God." The term "the hand of YHWH" to indicate divine inspiration is employed when Elisha resorts to music to help induce this state (II Kings 3:15). It is also found in I Kings 18:46 in the description of Elijah in an ecstatic fit running before Ahab's chariot (cf. Jer. 15:17). The term "the spirit of God" appears in both I Samuel 10:6, 10 and 19:20, 23, where the spirit "came mightily" upon Saul and his messengers (cf. I Sam. 18:10). In I Kings 22:21–24 the "spirit" is responsible for the inducing of false prophecy. Azariah son of Oded in II Chronicles 15:1 and Jahaziel son of Zechariah in II Chronicles 20:14 are both inspired by "the spirit of God/YHWH," which comes upon them (cf. Neh. 9:30). It is important to note, moreover, that the "spirit" is not conceived of as the divine revelation itself but only as the psychological precondition for the reception of revelation.

Group Life of Prophets. The prophets as a group were distinguished by several prominent personalities, e.g., Samuel, Nathan, Elijah, and Elisha, and by their number, at times in the hundreds. They were often banded together in groups of "disciples of the prophets" (Heb. *benei ha-nevi*ʾ*im*) who may or may not have been located at a shrine. Such groups first appear when Saul encounters a "band of prophets" (I Sam. 10:5, 10) and reappear in the Elijah and Elisha cycles. Though in II Kings 4:38 it is stated that they have their meals in common, some of their members are married and have families. Elisha performed a miracle for the widow of one of the members of this order (II Kings 4:1–7). Some of them owned their own houses (I Kings 13:15ff.). One group was found at Beth-El, and another at Jericho, the latter consisting of 50 members (II Kings 2:3, 5, 7, 15). Elisha performed miracles on behalf of his coterie at Gilgal (II Kings 4:38–44, where 100 are mentioned), and sent one of them to anoint Jehu (II Kings 9:1ff.). He is also called their master (lit., "father," II Kings 6:21). Obadiah, the chief steward of Ahab, saved 100 of them, during the siege of Jezebel (I Kings 18:3–4, 13), and kings Ahab and Jehoshaphat consulted some 400 prophets prior to their attack against Ramoth-Gilead (I Kings 22:6). There is also one possible, but far from certain, indication that heredity may have played some role in such circles, for Jehu, the *ḥozeh*, was a son of Hanani, presumably the same Hanani who was himself a *ro'eh* (II Chron. 16:7; 19:2; I Kings 16:1, 7).

Some of these prophets had attendants in their service. Elisha ministered to Elijah (I Kings 19:21), and Elisha had an attendant *(mesharet)* himself (II Kings 4:43; 6:15). A synonymous term, *na'ar* is also employed for the servants of Elijah (I Kings 18:43; 19:3), of Elisha (II Kings 4:38; 9:4), who was also attended by Gehazi (II Kings 4:12, 25; 5:20; 8:4), and of the attendant of the "man of God" in II Kings 6:15.

Role in Society. These early prophets played a prominent role in communal affairs and were often sought out and consulted for advice and asked to deliver oracles in the name of God. In I Kings 14:5, the wife of Jeroboam turns to Ahijah; in I Kings 22:8, Jehoshaphat and Ahab to Micaiah (cf. verses 5ff.); in II Kings 3:4ff., Jehoshaphat and Jeroboam to Elisha; in II Kings 8:8, Ben-Hadad (king of Aram!) to Elisha; and in II Kings 22:13, Josiah to Huldah. There are several references to remunerations for such services, sometimes amounting to as little as one quarter of a shekel (I Sam. 9:8) or ten loaves of bread, some cakes, and a jar of honey (I Kings 14:3); or as much as 40 camels bearing the treasures of Aram (II Kings 8:9). Prophets delivered their oracles whether asked to or not. In II Kings 1:3ff. Elijah stops Ahaziah's messengers on their way to inquire of Baal-Zebub; Ahijah the Shilonite tears his new garment when he confronts Jeroboam and announces the division of the United Kingdom (I Kings 11:29ff.); and Shemaiah announces to that same king that he should not go to war against his kinsmen of Israel (I Kings 12:22ff.).

Politics. These early prophets greatly influenced the political destiny of Israel. Samuel chose both Saul (I Sam. 9) and David (I Sam. 16) to be kings over Israel. Nathan castigated David for his conduct with Bath-Sheba and Uriah, her husband (II Sam. 12:7ff.), and later instigated the scheme to have David recognize her son, Solomon, as the next king (I Kings 1:8ff.). Ahijah announced both the selection and the rejection of Jeroboam as king of Israel (I Kings 11:29–39; 14:1–18; 15:29). Another "man of God" declared to Jeroboam the future birth of Josiah, who would destroy the idolatrous priests of the high places (I Kings 13:1–2). Shemaiah, mentioned above, forbade that king to attempt to regain the ten tribes of the North (I Kings 12:22–24; II Chron. 11:2–4). Azariah son of Oded influenced King Asa to institute a reform in Judah and to rely on God (II Chron. 15:1ff.), but the seer Hanani reprimanded Asa for requesting Ben-Hadad's aid against the blockade set up by Baasha, king of Israel (II Chron. 16:1ff.). Jehu denounced Jehoshaphat, king of Judah, for allying himself with Ahab (II Chron. 19:2–3). (He also chronicled that king's career, II Chron. 20:34.) In I Kings 22 both Ahab and Jehoshaphat turn to the prophets for an oracle to instruct them whether or not to go to war, and they receive an answer from Micaiah. ("Shall I go to battle against Ramoth-Gilead, or shall I forbear"; the alternative form of this question is reminiscent of the type formerly addressed to the Urim and Thummim.) Elisha foretells the defeat of Moab at the hands of Jehoshaphat and Jehoram (II Kings 3:16ff.). Elisha has one of his colleagues anoint Jehu king of Israel, inspires the latter's rebellion against Jehoram (II Kings 9), and later (II Kings 13:14ff.) by means of a symbolic act (see below) helps insure the victory of Joash over the Arameans.

Prophets were so important to the crown that several kings had their own court prophets. Both Nathan (II Sam. 7; I Kings 1:8ff.) and Gad (I Sam. 22:5; II Sam. 24:11; I Chron. 21:9; 29:29; II Chron. 29:25) served with David. Also in David's court were the sons of Asaph, Heman, and Jeduthun "who could prophesy with lyres, harps, and cymbals" (I Chron. 25:1ff.; II Chron. 29:30; 35:15—the interesting connection between the prophets and musical guilds may be noted). According to the Chronicler, both Nathan and Ahijah wrote accounts of Solomon's career (II Chron. 9:29); Jedo (Iddo) wrote of either Solomon or Jeroboam (II Chron. 9:29); Iddo and Shemaiah recorded Rehoboam's acts (II Chron. 12:15); and Iddo did the same for Abijah, Rehoboam's successor (II Chron. 13:22).

Clairvoyance and Prediction. These early prophets were both clairvoyant and capable of predicting future events. For example, Ahijah predicted the overthrow of Jeroboam's house and the death of his son (I Kings 14:6ff.); Elijah predicted a drought (I Kings 17:1), and the death of Ahaziah (II Kings 1:4); and Elisha predicted a famine for seven years (II Kings 8:1), and many other events. The prophetic groups in Beth-El and Jericho knew that the Lord would take Elijah away that very day to die (II Kings 2:3ff.). Elisha was aware that Gehazi had accepted a remuneration, for "did I not go with you in spirit when the man turned from his chariots to meet you? Is it a time to receive money ...?" (II Kings 5:26). He also knew where the Arameans were encamping (II Kings 6:9) and hears their very words (6:12). Only in exceptional cases does he not foresee events, e.g., when the Shunamite's son died and he declared, "the Lord has hid it from me, and not told me" (II Kings 4:27). Elisha even falls into a trance and foretells the future harm that Hazael, king of Aram, is going to cause Israel (II Kings 8:11ff.). Even if some of these events are *vaticinium ex eventu*, "prophecy after the events," the narratives make it abundantly clear that the people believed in the prophet's ability to foresee the future. Some prophets are also visionaries, e.g., in I Kings 22:19ff., Micaiah sees God enthroned on high; in II Kings 6:17, Elisha sees a mountain full of horses and chariots.

Symbolic Acts. The prophets did not merely predict the future, however. They often performed symbolic acts, which dramatized and concretized the spoken word. Though the dynamism of the spoken word is considered to have a creative effect in and of itself, it is given further confirmation by this act, which is efficacious and actually plays the role of prime mover in creating and causing the coming into being of the event. Ahijah rends his garment into 12 pieces and bids Jeroboam take ten of them for "thus says the Lord of Israel: 'Behold I will rend this kingdom out of the hand of Solomon and will give you ten tribes, but he shall take one tribe for my servant David's sake ...'" (I Kings 11:29ff.). Elisha, in turn, orders Joash to take bow and arrows, open the window eastward, and shoot: "The Lord's arrow of victory, the arrow of victory over Aram! For you shall fight the Arameans in Aphek until you have made an end of them" (II Kings 13:14ff.).

Miracles. These prophets were also miracle workers.

The two most famous are Elijah and Elisha. Elijah causes the jar of meal and the cruse of oil not to fail the widow of Zarephath, "according to the word of the Lord which he spoke" (I Kings 17:8ff.); later, he brought her son back to life (17:17–24). He succeeded in bringing fire down from heaven in his famous contest with the Canaanite prophets (I Kings 18); split the Jordan River by striking it with his mantle (II Kings 2:8); and was swept up on high into heaven by a whirlwind (II Kings 2:11). His successor, Elisha, was no less successful in performing miracles. He, too, split the waters of the Jordan into two with Elijah's mantle (II Kings 2:13–14), made a small jug of oil fill many large vessels (4:1–7), and brought back to life a child who had died (4:8ff.). When the inhabitants of Jericho complained that "the water is bad and the land is unfruitful," he requested a new bowl and salt, which he then threw into the water and said, "Thus says the Lord: 'I have healed these waters; henceforth neither death nor miscarriage shall come from it.' And so the waters were healed" (II Kings 2:19–22). Once in Gilgal during a famine, the prophetic guild complained that the pottage they were eating had the taste of death. By pouring some flour into the pottage, he effected a miracle and made the food edible (II Kings 4:38–41). Another miracle made a small allotment of food suffice for 100 men, "For thus says the Lord, 'They shall eat and leave some'" (4:42–44). His potency for producing miracles continued even after his death. A dead man was reported to have come back to life when his corpse was thrown into Elisha's grave and touched his bones (II Kings 13:20–21).

It is of the utmost significance to realize that most, though not all, of these interventions into public affairs, feats of clairvoyance, predictions of the future, symbolic acts, and miraculous signs and deeds are related to the will of God and are ascribed to Him. There are no supernatural or impersonal powers invoked to accomplish the desired results. No native abilities or faculties aid the prophet. Only the will of God is operative in both their words and deeds. There is no magical or occult art which they must master; revelation proceeds directly from God. God stands behind the prophet and it is to God alone to whom the prophet prays and asks for intercession, e.g., when Jeroboam's hand is restored (I Kings 13:4ff.); when the sons of the wives of Zarephath and Shunem are restored to life (I Kings 17:20ff.; II Kings 4:32ff.), and when fire comes from heaven as answer to Elijah's prayer to God (I Kings 18:36).

These prophets did not always enjoy the security and immunity that their prophetic position should have assured them. Ahab persecuted or permitted Jezebel to persecute Elijah (I Kings 17ff.); Micaiah was put into prison because he foretold the defeat of Israel and the death of Ahab (I Kings 22:27); and Asa, king of Judah, put Hanani, the seer, in the stocks, because the prophet reprimanded him for not relying on God but accepting the help of the king of Aram (II Chron. 16:7–10).

Extra-Biblical Prophecy: Mari. Seers are attested by name outside of Israel (cf. above, the Zakir inscription). In the neo-Assyrian period favorable oracles are delivered personally to King Esarhaddon by individuals, mostly women, who address him in the name of Ishtar. But of much greater significance for the understanding of early prophecy are the cuneiform documents from *Mari, which refer to charismatic individuals who spontaneously appear before the king to deliver an oral message at the command of their deity: Dagan, god of Terqa and Tutul; Adad, god of Kallassu and Aleppo; or Anunitu of Mari. These god-inspired individuals are called by the Akkadian terms *muḫḫüm* (fem., *muḫḫūtum*), "frenzied, mad, ecstatic" (cf. Heb. *meshugga*ʿ, II Kings 9:11; Jer. 29:26; Hos. 9:7), and *āpilum* (fem., *āpiltum*), "answerer." The latter appear to be somewhat similar to the court prophets, such as Gad and Nathan. There is also mention of a group of *āpilum*, who might correspond to the groups of prophets mentioned in the Bible. Females in Mari also bear these same titles; they may be compared to the female prophetesses in the Bible: Huldah (II Kings 22:14), Noadiah (Neh. 6:14), and Miriam (Ex. 15:20).

The established introductory formula of their prophetic announcements (excluding pronouncements in a temple) is the well-known "messenger formula": "Thus he spoke to me; The God [personal name] sent me." The Bible frequently uses similar expressions, e.g., "Thus says YHWH"; "YHWH the God of the Hebrews sent me" (Ex. 7:16); and "YHWH has sent me" (Jer. 26:12). The prophet at Mari delivers the word of his god, which is sometimes revealed to him in a dream (cf. Num. 12:6; Deut. 13:2; I Sam. 28:6, 15; Jer. 23:25ff.; 29:8; Zech. 10:2), to the king and demands that he fulfill the will of the god. In one tablet (*Archives royales de Mari* (= ARM), 13 (1964), no. 23) there is even an example of a prophecy to a foreign nation, Babylonia.

Though the Mari documents contain by far the closest parallels to biblical prophecy, there are several major points of difference: (1) Unlike Israelite prophecy, the prophet at Mari does not come with any social or ethical demands but concerns himself with cultic and political affairs of limited significance. (2) His message is primarily to the king and is usually intended to gain the king's favorable attention to the cult of the god who sent him. He does not address himself to the people. (3) No religious ideology like that of the Israelite prophets characterizes his activity, nor is there any proclamation of divine involvement in the course of human history. (4) In the Mari documents there are at least two instances (ARM, 2 (1950), no. 90; 3 (1950), no. 40) in which the final decision is left to the discretion of the king; the prophet's word is not absolute. (5) The practice at Mari of sending a lock of hair or the fringe of the prophet's tunic in order to identify the prophet and to guarantee his veracity is completely unattested in the Bible, where the prophet's word is his sole and absolute attestation. (6) Even with these signs of verification, the prophet's word at Mari is occasionally submitted to omens for authentification; unlike the words of the prophets of the Bible, those of the Mari prophets do not command unqualified acceptance. (7) There is, in addition, no analogy to the Israelite chain of prophecy (cf. Isa. 30:10; Jer. 7:25; 25:4; 29:19; Hos. 6:5; 12:11; Amos 2:11–12; 3:7), which produced a successive line of prophets spanning several centuries who guided and taught the people, reproved and censured them for their sins, and threatened impending destruction or promised future restoration. Nevertheless, the prophets at Mari may still be favorably compared with the early Israelite court and cult prophets who primarily addressed themselves to the reigning monarch. Herein lies the common Near Eastern background of this institution.

Comparison of Preclassical and Classical Prophets. The preclassical prophets, after having been compared to their predecessors at Mari, should also be viewed in the light of their successors, the classical prophets. A broad consensus of scholarship draws the following main distinctions between the two: (1) The classical prophets rejected the cult and ritual and called for ethical monotheism. (2) They rejected the nationalistic outlook of the popular prophets and replaced it with their concept of universalism. (3) The preclassical prophets were originally mantic; their main function was predicting the future. The classical prophets, on the other hand, were interested in reproving their people in order to save them. (4) Whereas the popular prophets functioned as part of guilds, the classical prophets always appear alone (e.g., Amos 7:14). (5) The popular prophets were ecstatics, given to intoxication of the senses (I Sam. 19:20–24), and they employed musical accompaniment to induce or heighten their frenzy (II Kings 3:15). The classical prophets, however, for the most part pronounced their oracles soberly in clear control of their senses.

It was thought that there was an unbridgeable gap between the two, and with *Amos, the first of the literary prophets, the watershed was reached. True, there is an element of greater or lesser truth in all the above-mentioned criteria. However, it will be seen that the break was not total, and that there are many points of contact and continuation in the lives and writings of the classical prophets. Classical prophecy, like every other institution in ancient Israel, did not exist in a vacuum but came into being bearing clouds of ancestral glory behind it. The classical prophets were indebted in many ways to the heritage of their predecessors. The technical title *navi'* is applied to both. Both speak solely in the name of the God of Israel, who reveals His will directly to them. They are both sent by God, hear the divine word, and are admitted into His council; their messages are rooted in the Covenant. These and the following considerations lead to the conclusion that there was one continuous religious tradition.

Ritual versus Morality. A clear-cut dichotomy between the preclassical and the classical prophets on this issue should not be made. The prophet Nathan rebukes King David for his breach of the moral law in his conduct with Bath-Sheba, and Elijah takes Ahab to task for the Naboth incident, in which Ahab was an accessory to murder. True, both indictments concern a primary breach of the moral law, adultery and murder, and are leveled against kings; but they are still an integral part of the ethical-moral dimension. Here, too, may be added Samuel's rebuke of Saul "Has the Lord as great delight in burnt offerings and sacrifices, as in obeying the voice of the Lord? Behold to obey is better than sacrifice, and to hearken than the fat of rams" (I Sam. 15:22). The classical prophets, on the other hand, do not reject the cult per se any more than they absolutely reject prayer or any other type of worship. To them, as will be seen, the cultic obligations are secondary to, and dependent upon, the fulfillment of the moral code of behavior. There is a decided change in the degree of emphasis but not in the principle. Moreover, the words of castigation leveled against the cult are found in the writings of the pre-Exilic prophets; in the books of the Exilic and post-Exilic prophets, on the other hand, the ritual is often highly accented and favorably viewed (see below).

Nationalism versus Universalism. Nationalistic as well as universalistic tendencies are present in greater or lesser degree in the writing of both. This can be seen in Elijah's command that Elisha anoint Hazael king of Aram (I Kings 19:15), for YHWH is considered equally the God of Aram as of Israel. Other universalistic themes in the early prophets are exemplified in I Kings 20:28, in which a man of God says to the king of Israel, "Thus says the Lord, 'Because the Arameans have said, "the Lord is a god of the hills but he is not a god of the valleys," therefore I will deliver all of this great multitude into your hand, and you shall know that I am the Lord'," and in I Kings 5:15 in which Naaman, the commander of the Aramean army, after being cured by immersing himself in the Jordan River as prescribed by Elisha, confesses, "Behold, I know that there is no God in all the world but in Israel." The universalistic prophecies of the classical prophets on the other hand, do not preclude, of course, their predominate number of nationalistic oracles.

Mantics versus Reprovers. Mantic behavior was not restricted to the popular prophets. For example, Isaiah foretells the future for Hezekiah (Isa. 37:1ff.; 38:1ff.), and Jeremiah, for Zedekiah (Jer. 32:4–5, and see below). The latter also predicts the death of his prophetic rival, Hananiah (Jer. 28:16–17). On the other hand, the early prophets Nathan, Elijah, and Elisha do not restrict their activity to merely predicting the future and the answering of queries, but are themselves messengers, apostles, reprovers, and chasteners who deliver the word of God.

Group versus Individuals. Although Samuel, Elijah, and Elisha are followed by bands of prophets, when they fulfill their missions, they do it alone as individuals just as the later prophets did. The latter, too, may have had their followers (e.g., the controversial verse, Isa. 8:16), for it is most likely that it was the disciples of these prophets who recorded their masters' words (e.g., Jer. 36:4).

Ecstatics versus Non-Ecstatics. Ecstasy, too, is not limited to the preclassical prophets. The classical prophets had visions and unnatural experiences during their prophetic "seizures." Ezekiel, in particular, was prone to various ecstatic fits; Hosea is called a "madman" (Hos. 9:7) and so too, by direct implication, is Jeremiah (Jer. 29:26).

Role in Society. The classical prophets played an extremely important role in the Israelite society, as is well known. Like the earlier prophets, they were consulted by those who wanted information from God. Jeremiah is requested by King Zedekiah's messengers to "inquire of the Lord for us, for Nebuchadnezzar, king of Babylon, is making war against us..." (Jer. 21:1–2; cf. similar requests in Jer. 37:7ff.; 42:1ff, and the advice given in Jer. 23:33ff.; Ezek. 8:1ff.; 14:1ff.; 33:30ff.; and contrarily, Isa. 30:1–2).

Symbolic Acts. The classical prophets, too, performed significant symbolic acts which not only presaged future events but were efficacious in initiating their process of realization. These acts, its should be stressed, are different from magic in that they do not depend on any occult art or science but derive directly from God's will and always serve to fulfill His plans and purposes. In this category may be included the symbolic names which Isaiah gave his children: "a remnant shall turn back" (Isa. 7:3), and "pillage hastens, looting speeds" (Isa. 8:3), and most probably his own name (Isa. 8:18; cf. the child's name, "God is with us," Isa. 7:14). Isaiah walked about naked and barefoot for three years as a sign that the king of Assyria would lead the Egyptians and Ethiopians naked into exile (Isa. 20:2ff.). Jeremiah (16:1ff.) refrained from marrying and having children as a portent that both the parents and children of Israel would perish by the sword and famine. He buys a linen waistcloth, wears it, and then buries it in a cleft of the rock, and later upon recovering it, he finds that it has become spoiled, "good for nothing": "Thus will the Lord spoil the pride of Judah and Jerusalem who were made to cling to God but would not obey" (Jer. 13:1ff.). He buys a potter's earthen flask and promptly smashes it to signify that the Lord "will break this people and this city, as one breaks a potter's vessel so that it can never be mended" (Jer. 19:1ff.). He is commanded by the Lord to make thongs and yoke bars and put them on his neck as a portent that any nation or kingdom which does not put its neck under the yoke of Nebuchadnezzar, king of Babylon, will be punished, and only those who submit will be left alone to till their own land (Jer. 27:2ff.; cf. the same act performed by Zedekiah, I Kings 22:11).

The "false" prophet Hananiah, as a symbolic act of his own, breaks these very bars and says, "Thus says the Lord: 'Even so will I make the yoke of Nebuchadnezzar king of Babylon break from the neck of all the nations within two years.'" Jeremiah subsequently replaces his wooden yoke with one of iron and repeats the same message (Jer. 28). During the very last months of the siege of Jerusalem, he purchases a field from his uncle as a sign that "houses and fields and vineyards shall again be bought in this land" (Jer. 32:6ff.). In Jeremiah 43:8ff. he is commanded to take large stones and hide them in the mortar in the pavement which is at the entrance to Pharaoh's palace in Tahpanhes as a sign that the Lord will set the throne of Nebuchadnezzar over these stones. In Jeremiah 51:61–64, when Seraiah comes to Babylon, Jeremiah commands him to read the book he has written concerning all the evil that would befall Babylon. He is then to bind a stone to it and cast it into the Euphrates and say, "Thus shall Babylon sink, to rise no more, because of the evil I am bringing upon her." Both the recitation of curses and the sinking of the scroll portend the final downfall of Babylon. Ezekiel (4:1ff.) takes a brick, portrays upon it the city of Jerusalem, puts siege works against it, builds a siege wall, casts a mound, sets camps against it, and plants battering rams round about. He then takes an iron plate and places it as an iron wall between himself and the city and presses the siege against the city, "a sign for the house of Israel." He also lies alternately on his left and right sides for an extended period of time, presaging the oncoming days of punishment of Israel and Judah. He eats and drinks during those days only a very small amount of food including barley cake baked on human dung to indicate that the people of Israel and Jerusalem "shall eat their bread unclean among the nations" and "shall eat bread by weight . . . and water by measure" (Ezek. 4:9ff.). In chapter 5 he takes a sharp knife, uses it as a barber's razor to cut the hair of his head and beard, takes balances and weights, and divides the hair for impending judgement. And in chapter 12 he conspicuously prepares for exile in full sight of his people.

In sum, though the sole power of the classical prophet, his "weapon of war," resides in the creative force of the spoken word, this word is occasionally reinforced dramatically, as it was by the preclassical prophets, by the self-fulfilling power of the symbolic act.

Signs and Wonders. The literary prophets, following their predecessors, also resorted to the use of signs and wonders to authenticate their prediction of impending events. Isaiah tells King Ahaz that since the latter did not put his complete confidence in the Lord in order to withstand the Syro-Ephramite coalition, "The Lord Himself will give you a sign: Behold a young woman is with child and shall bear a son and shall call his name, Immanuel." Before this lad reaches maturity, the kingdoms of Aram and Ephraim would be destroyed (Isa. 7:10–25). The same prophet gives a sign to King Hezekiah in order to prove to him that the Lord has heard his prayer; 15 years would be added to his life, and he would be delivered from the hand of the king of Assyria: "This is the sign to you from the Lord, that the Lord will do this thing that he has promised: Behold I will make the shadow cast by the declining sun on the dial of Ahaz turn back ten steps" (Isa. 38:5–8). He also cures the king by rubbing a cake of figs over his inflammation (38:21–22; II Kings 20:7). In the previous chapter he gives the following sign to that same king: "And this shall be the sign for you: This year eat what grows of itself, and in the second year what springs of the same; then in the third year sow and reap, and plant vineyards" (Isa. 37:30). This is a sign that the surviving remnant of Judah would take root and bear fruit.

Jeremiah, in an embarrassing confrontation with the "false" prophet Hananiah, who later smashed the wooden yoke bars of Jeremiah and subsequently replaced them with bars of iron, says, "Thus says the Lord . . . 'This very year you shall die, because you have uttered rebellion against the Lord'." The next verse tells that in that very year Hananiah died (Jer. 28:15–17). In one instance Ezekiel himself becomes a sign to the people, when God predicts and then executes the death of the prophet's wife and forbids him to mourn for her as an omen of what the people are about to experience (Ezek. 24:15ff.).

Visions. Both the preclassical and classical prophets share the common oracular terminology "Thus says YHWH." Though the latter are more "hearers" than "seers," they, too, often report visions, e.g., those of Amos (7:8); Isaiah (6); Jeremiah (1:11ff.; 24:1ff.), and the extraordinary visions of Ezekiel (particularly in chapters 1–3, 8–10); and Zechariah (5–6). Indeed, visions play an important role in the classical prophetic writings, as the following quotations further attest:

> I spoke to the Prophets;
> It was I who multiplied visions (Hos. 12:11).

> And it shall come to pass in the future
> that I will pour out my spirit in all flesh;
> your sons and daughters shall prophesy,
> your old men shall dream dreams, and your young
> men shall see visions (Joel 3:1).

> For they are a rebellious people, lying sons,
> sons who will not hear the instruction of the Lord;
> who say to the seers, 'See not!' and to the prophets,
> 'Prophesy not to us what is right' (Isa. 30:9–10; cf. Isa. 29:10; Amos 7:12 in negative contexts).

Like their preclassical forerunners, the literary prophets occasionally employ the terms "the hand of YHWH" (Isa. 48:16; 59:21; 61:1; Joel 3:1; Micah 3:8; Zech. 7:12; cf. Isa. 11:2; Hos. 9:7) and "the spirit of YHWH" to describe the power that activates and evokes their revelatory state of mind. The ecstatic character of literary prophecy is exceptionally documented in the various trances of Ezekiel. Finally, classical prophets also, at times, bore the consequence of their dire predictions. Just as Ahab persecuted Elijah (I Kings 17ff.) and had Micaiah imprisoned, because he foretold the destruction of Israel and the death of the king (I Kings 22:27), so too Jeremiah was put into the stocks (Jer. 20:2) as well as in prison (Jer. 32ff.), and Uriah was put to death (Jer. 26:20–23).

Classical Prophecy. The classical prophets, thus, cannot be fully understood without a knowledge of their antecedents. They developed within the framework of Israelite monotheism. They considered themselves successive links in the chain of divine messengers extending back to Moses. Some prophets were greatly influenced by the literature of the Torah, e.g., Jeremiah by Deuteronomy and Ezekiel by the Priestly Code, and were indebted to many of the earlier traditions concerning Exodus, David, and Zion. Nevertheless, they cannot be entirely explained by their predecessors or by earlier traditions. For in the middle of the eighth century B.C.E., a new dimension was added to Israelite religion which definitively shaped the character of the nation. Commencing with Amos, a herdsman from Tekoa, there arose a series of great religious teachers and thinkers, inspired spokesmen who became the passionate bearers of the word of God.

Historical Scope. Their appearance was engendered by specific historical and political events. The temporal limits of the classical apostolic prophets can be placed within a historical framework extending over some 300 years and highlighted by two cataclysmic events. The first prophets appeared a few decades before the fall of Northern Israel (722 B.C.E.), after the conclusion of the 100-year war with the Arameans—a war which produced a vast societal cleavage between the impoverished masses and the wealthy minority, and they disappeared approximately a century following the destruction of Jerusalem (587/6 B.C.E.). Within this period three major empires successively dominated the world scene: Assyria, Babylonia, and Persia.

The prophets, however, always addressed their message to the contemporary situation. Amos, living in the time of Jeroboam II before the rise of Tiglath-Pileser (745 B.C.E.) and the neo-Assyrian empire, foretold exile and destruction for Israel, but he never indicated that it would be executed by Assyria. Second *Hosea (chs. 4–14), a somewhat later contemporary, also foresaw destruction, but although he was aware of both pro-Egyptian and pro-Assyrian factions, he did not designate Assyria as the enemy par excellence. Isaiah's call, on the other hand, came at the time of the peak of Assyrian ascendancy. He called that nation the rod of God's wrath and considered it the last of the world powers. Simultaneous with the fall of Assyria would come the demise of arrogance, the root of man's idolatrous behavior. Micah and *Zephaniah, too, knew of the Assyrian menace, but except for one late interpolation in the former (Micah 4:10), they, like Isaiah, did not include Babylonia within their historical purview. *Nahum, coming a bit later, rejoiced over the fall of Assyria, but was silent about Babylonia. The Book of *Habakkuk reflects the transition period between Assyrian and Babylonian hegemony. Jeremiah, who received his call to prophecy in 627 B.C.E., identified the enemy described as the "nation from the north" with Babylonia only after the battle of Carchemish in 605 B.C.E. When he portrays the eventual defeat of Babylonia, however, he once again resorts to his initial image of a "nation from the north." Persia is never mentioned as the successor to Babylonia in Jeremiah. Ezekiel, living in the time of Nebuchadnezzar, prophesied the fall of Babylonia but never specified Persia as the conqueror. (Persia is mentioned only once in this connection and then incidentally, 38:5.)

Only with the advent of the anonymous prophet of the Exile who is called Deutero-Isaiah (Isa. 40ff.), was Cyrus, king of Persia, specifically mentioned and then favorably so (Isa. 44:28; 45:1). The three last prophets of Israel, *Haggai, *Zechariah, and *Malachi, were active during the post-Exilic period under the Persian rule and were not aware of the future ascendancy of the Greek Empire. (For the dating of all these prophets as well as *Jonah, *Joel, and *Obadiah, see the individual articles under their names.) Except for an occasional later supplement or interpolation, the oracles of the prophets are oriented to their own contemporary situation.

Thus, classical prophecy arose and reached its zenith during the rise and fall of world empires. In the period of the preclassical prophets, the political-historical horizon was of limited local significance. The enemies of those days—Ammonites, Moabites, Edomites, Philistines, and Arameans—did not strive for world dominion. The age that witnessed the emergence of great empires bore witness to the unique religious phenomenon of classical prophecy, which interpreted these world-significant events in the light of its own theological viewpoint. The Lord of Israel was seen as the director of the drama of world history. His ever-changing cast included the leading historical figures of those days—Sargon, Sennacherib, Nebuchadnezzar, Cyrus—but his attention was continually focused on Israel; her destiny within the divinely controlled arena of world politics was his main concern. The prophets provided an answer to the "why" of destruction and the "how" of future restoration.

DEDICATION AND COMMISSIONING OF THE PROPHET. The dedication and commissioning of a prophet created a new literary genre, the account of his being called. Such commissioning or recommissioning accounts are found in Isaiah 6 (which does not describe the prophet's original call to prophecy, but rather his recommissioning, so Kaufmann); Jeremiah 1:4ff. and 15:19–21 (the latter, too, being a re-dedication; see below); Ezekiel 1–3; and perhaps Deutero-Isaiah 40:6–8.

The first description of a prophetic dedication, that of Moses, foreshadows several motifs which recur from time to time in the descriptions of the dedication of other prophets: (1) the humble occupation of the prophet (so, too, Amos, who was taken from his flocks to become a prophet, Amos 7:14); (2) the human response; (3) a protest of inadequacy for the mission; and (4) the divine reassurance. Moses made several attempts to dissuade God from selecting him, since he felt that he did not possess sufficient credentials for his mission. He pleaded inadequacy: "Who am I that I should go to Pharaoh and free the Israelites from Egypt" (Ex. 3:11) and "Please, O Lord, I have never been a man of words . . . I am slow of speech and slow of tongue" (Ex. 4:10).

Isaiah, in chapter 6, which describes his re-dedication to the prophetic office, after complaining of "unclean lips," first has his mouth sanctified, and then upon hearing God's question, "Whom shall I send?" volunteers his services, "I am ready, send me." (In an augural vision, the prophet would most likely not be asked to volunteer but would be compelled to go willy-nilly.) Jeremiah, who was prenatally designated and consecrated for his calling, recounts how God touched his mouth, too, and put His words into his mouth (Jer. 1:9). Ezekiel describes his consecration as the devouring of a scroll written by God (Ezek. 3:1ff.). The organ of speech is specifically mentioned in all of these prophetic accounts, because the prophet becomes, upon dedication, God's "mouthpiece." Not only the lips, however, but the prophet's whole being becomes dedicated to the service of God.

His Reluctance and God's Reassurance. The prophets, however, were often reluctant to accept their calling. The most dramatic example by far is the unsuccessful flight of Jonah. The unwillingness of Moses, Isaiah, and Jeremiah to accept the divine call is also concentrated on their organ of speech: "I have never been a man of words" (Ex. 4:10); "Woe is me, for I am lost; for I am a man of unclean lips" (Isa. 6:5); "Alas, Lord God, I do not know how to speak, for I am inexperienced" (Jer. 1:6). God, in turn, responds with encouraging assurances, for Moses (Ex. 4:11), for Isaiah (Isa. 6:7), and, in particular, for Jeremiah, "Gird up your loins . . . Do not be dismayed . . . They will fight against you; but they shall not prevail against you, for I am with you, says the Lord, to deliver you" (Jer. 1:17–19; cf. 15:19–21).

LIFE OF THE PROPHET. Why such initial opposition? Why, too, such an outpouring of divine encouragement? The prophet's distinction of being chosen by God was matched only by his frustration and rejection on the part of his fellowman. The prophetic office was not easy to bear. The description of the prophet's emotional experience upon receiving a "stern vision" is at times overwhelmingly frightening: his loins are filled with anguish; his pain is comparable to birth pangs; he is tortured, anguished, terror-stricken; he reels, and he is filled with the wrath of God (Isa. 21:3–4; Jer. 4:19; 6:11; 15:17; Hab. 3:16).

Of far greater significance, however, is the fact that such a selected messenger becomes a solitary individual, whose life is marked by loneliness and bitterness: "I sat not in the company of merrymakers, nor did I rejoice; I sat alone because Your Hand was upon me" (Jer. 15:17); "Oh that I had a lodge in the wilderness that I might leave my people and go away from them, for they are all adulterers, a troop of treacherous men" (Jer. 9:1). Jeremiah, whose personal tribulations and confessions are better known than those of any other prophet, became the paradigm of one who suffers for his mission. It is no wonder that he was not euphoric about being selected for such a task. Rejected and spurned, he bemoans his fate, "Woe unto me, my mother, that you bore me, a man of strife and contention to the whole land. I have neither a lender nor borrower been, yet everyone belittles me" (15:10). Even his own kinsmen and family are counted among his chief antagonists (12:6; cf. 20:10). Enemies were continually plotting against his life (11:19). Eventually, he even cursed his fate, "Cursed be the day on which I was born. Let the day my mother bore me not be blessed... Why did I come forth from the womb to experience trouble and grief and to waste my days in chagrin" (20:14–18).

The prophets were fated to become harbingers of their nation's downfall. Messengers of doom, they were doomed to suffer from their very message: "Lord, how long!" (Isa. 6:11); "Let me weep bitterly. Seek not to comfort me for the destruction of the daughter of my people" (Isa. 22:4); "For this I will lament and wail. I will go stripped and naked... For incurable are her blows, for it has come to Judah, has reached the gate of my people, to Jerusalem" (Micah 1:8–9); "O that my head were water and my eyes a fountain of tears, that I might weep day and night for the slain of the daughter of my people" (Jer. 8:23). The prophet bemoans their imminent tragedy and weeps over their tragic rejection of his words: "But if you will not listen, I will weep in secret for your pride; my eyes will weep bitterly and run down with tears because the Lord's flock has been taken captive" (Jer. 13:17; cf. 10:19ff.; 14:17–18).

The life story of a prophet is liable to be one of anguish, fear, rejection, ridicule, and even imprisonment (Isa. 28:9–10; Jer. 11:18–23; 12:1ff.; 15:10, 15; 17:14–18; 18:18–23; 20:7–18; 37:12–21; Ezek. 21:11–12; Hos. 9:8; Amos 7:12–13; Micah 2:6). Some did not escape their assassins (Jer. 26:20–23; Uriah). Though the prophet weeps with his destined victims and takes up the cry of his compatriots, he is not understood by them. Great yet unbearable is the fate of one who claims that he was seduced, even forced into his role: "O Lord you have seduced me, and I was seduced; you have overpowered me, and have prevailed" (Jer. 20:7). Nevertheless he cannot cease from being a prophet: "If I say, 'I will not mention Him or speak any more His name,' there is in my heart as it were a burning fire shut up in my bones, and I am not able to hold it in" (Jer. 20:9). Yet paradoxically when he does prophesy, he may be silenced by God (Jer. 7:16; 11:14; 14:11) or mocked and spurned by man. Jeremiah is eventually led to curse his people and demand vengeance against his adversaries (11:20b; 12:3b; 15:15a; 18:21–23).

Reproaching God. He is even driven in extremis to reproach God Himself: "Why are you like a man dumbfounded, like a mighty man who cannot save?" (Jer. 14:9); "You are to me like a deceitful stream, like waters that fail!" (15:18). With this last outburst the prophetic protest reached its ultimate, as is indicated by the response of God, "If you return, I will restore you, and you shall stand before me" (15:19). Paradoxically, he who dedicated his life to persuading the people to return must now "return" himself. And why? So that he can once again perform the role of God's emissary, "You shall be my spokesman" (15:19). Thus, it seems that for a short period of time Jeremiah had actually lost prophetic office. This "demotion" is further substantiated by the remainder of God's response, where He repeats in almost exactly the same words the original encouragement at the time of the prophet's initial call, "I will make you before this people an impregnable wall of bronze; They will attack you, but they will not prevail over you, for I am with you to save you and deliver you, says the Lord" (15:20). Jeremiah, after his defiant outcry of reproach, was recommissioned to deliver the word of God.

False Prophets. The problem of how to distinguish a prophet who was truly commissioned by God from a "false" prophet is perplexing. There is no term for a false prophet in the Bible. The distinction, which is found in rabbinic literature, was introduced by the Greek translation of the Bible into some verses in the books of Jeremiah (6:13:26 (=Greek 33); 7, 8, 11, 16; 27 (=Greek 34):9; 28 (= Greek 35):1) and Zechariah (13:2), as *pseudoprophētēs*. In the Hebrew Bible, however, both "false" and "true" prophets are called *navi'*, and both claim inspiration and a mission.

In Deuteronomy there are several, not too successful, attempts to provide infallible criteria for distinguishing between them. Deuteronomy 18:20–22 states "Any prophet who presumes to speak in My name an oracle which I did not command him to utter, or who speaks in the name of other gods—that prophet shall die. And should you ask yourselves, 'How can we know that the oracle was not spoken by the Lord?'—if the prophet speaks in the name of the Lord and the word does not come true, that word was not spoken by the Lord; the prophet has uttered it presumptuously: do not stand in dread of him." Deuteronomy 13:2ff. goes one step further: even if the prophet gives oracles which are subsequently confirmed by signs, should his message be to worship other gods, that prophet, too, is not to be heeded, since his appearance is only a test to determine whether the people really love and revere the Lord alone.

However, examples of an Israelite prophet delivering his message in the name of another god (Jer. 2:8; 23:13) are rare and not one demands that an alien god be worshiped. Most of them spoke, apparently with sincerity and conviction, in the name of God. As for the chronological criterion of the fulfillment of the oracle, this was of no value whatever at the moment the prophecy was uttered. How could the people suspend judgment if Hananiah told them not to submit to the king of Babylon and foretold the release from Babylonian captivity within two years, while Jeremiah declared that it was God's plan that Israel surrender and remain in exile for 70 years (Jer. 27–28)? Jeremiah, himself, was completely perplexed and left the scene of confrontation without further contradicting Hananiah (28:11). Furthermore, several occasions are specifically recorded in which an oracle delivered by an acknowledged true prophet did not materialize in the manner in which he predicted—even within his own lifetime! Only a few examples of unfulfilled prophecies need be cited: Jeremiah predicted an ignominious end for King Jehoiakim (Jer. 22:19); yet II Kings 24:6 clearly belies this oracle. Ezekiel predicted the destruction of Tyre by Nebuchadnezzar (26:7–14), but later he acknowledged that the king's siege of the city was unsuccessful (29:17–20). Both Haggai's (2:21–23) and Zechariah's (4:6–7) glorious anticipations and designs for Zerubbabel never materialized.

Jeremiah sought another objective criterion for distinguishing between a true and false prophet when he was dramatically confronted and confuted by Hananiah son of Azzur (Jer. 28). Hananiah declared in the name of YHWH that the Lord was going to break the yoke of Babylon, and that within two years the exiled community in Babylon and their king Jehoiachin would return to Israel. Jeremiah sincerely wished that Hananiah's words were true. He did not question his sincerity nor did he call him a false prophet, but he merely pointed out that "the prophets who were of old, before my time and yours, prophesied against many countries and great kingdoms of war, disaster, and plague." Only the future would vindicate the prediction of a prophet who foresaw peace; "As for the prophet who prophesies of well-being, when that prophet's word comes to pass, then it can be acknowledged that he is the prophet whom YHWH really sent." But then again how could one suspend judgment until history decided?

Jeremiah, more than any other prophet, was in constant combat with these prophets. He attacks three different types of "false" prophets (Jer. 23): (1) those who have dreams and report them as though they were the word of God and thus mislead the people, "The prophet who has a dream, let him tell his dream"; (2) those who are plagiarists "who keep stealing My words from one another" and pretend that they have had direct revelation; and (3) those "who using their own speech" concoct their own oracles and pass them off as prophecy. Nevertheless, when prophet clashed with prophet not only were the people confounded, but Jeremiah himself, in the case of Hananiah, was left speechless, and was unable to point to any irrefutable objective standard by which to verify or disqualify his opponent (Jer. 28).

To confound matters even more, a true prophet might be misled by a "false" prophet (I Kings 13), and false prophecy might even be inspired by God in order to deceive and entice Israel (I Kings 22:21ff.). According to Ezekiel 14:9–11, moreover, God might actually seduce a bonafide prophet to deliver a false message!

If the individual prophet had a questionable moral character—if he was a drunkard (Isa. 28:7), an adulterer, or a liar (Jer. 23:14); if he used his office to make a living by telling the people what they wanted to hear and not what they ought to hear (Micah 3:11); or if he was a "professional" prophet attached to the staff of temple personnel (the joint denunciation of priest and prophet may be noted in Isa. 28:7; Jer. 23:11, 34; Micah 3:11; Zech. 7:2–3), his veracity obviously would be highly dubious. But what of the others? If there was no difference in the technical form of the prophecy, what of the contents? Apparently the only, and by no means infallible, criterion would be the nature of the message, whether it was one of weal or woe. Proclamations of national-religious salvation were suspect for over 250 years (cf. I Kings 22:11ff.; Jer. 6:14; 8:11; 14:13; 23:17; 28:2ff.; Ezek. 13:16; Micah 3:5ff.). It is also possible that such prophecies were related to the national interests of the crown and the cult—Hananiah predicted the early return of the cult vessels (Jer. 28:3).

But this, too, was not an absolute definition, for both pre-Exilic, e.g., Nahum 2:1, Jeremiah 30–33 (if these chapters stem from the early part of his career), and Exilic, e.g., Deutero-Isaiah, as well as post-Exilic prophets, Haggai, Zechariah, and Malachi, brought messages of comfort, and some also took a positive view of the cult (see below). Hence, the falsity or veracity of prophecies could not be determined on the external basis of form or content. They could only be judged by the person who had true insight into the intentions of God at that historical moment. A prophet "who has My word, let him faithfully speak My word. What has straw to do with wheat? . . . Is not My word like fire . . . like the hammer that shatters the rock" (Jer. 23:28–29).

The Prophet as Intercessor. The irresistible character that such a religious experience has on a "God-intoxicated" individual (Jer. 23:9), "who has stood in YHWH's council and seen and heard His word . . ." (Jer. 23:18), not only constrains him to deliver the divine message but compels him, at times, to intercede on behalf of his people. Herein lies one possible means of distinguishing between the two kinds of prophets: the function of the prophet as an intercessor. In this role, as distinct from his role as a messenger, the prophet attempts through prayer to offset the impending doom. The first individual in the Bible to be designated a prophet, Abraham, does not merit this title because he delivered oracles in the name of God, but because he was ready to intercede: "Since he is a prophet, he will intercede for you to save your life" (Gen. 20:7). Abraham also valiantly attempted to save the twin cities of Sodom and Gomorrah, and with unbridled daring challenged God: "Shall not the judge of all the earth deal justly" (18:25).

The paragon of prophets, Moses, paradigmatically and eloquently exemplifies this aspect of his prophetic mission several times: (1) After the incident of the golden calf, "Let not Your anger, O Lord, blaze forth against Your people, whom You delivered from the land of Egypt with great power and with a mighty hand . . . Turn from Your blazing anger, and renounce the plan to punish Your people. Remember Your servants, Abraham, Isaac, and Jacob, how You swore to them by Your Self and said to them: 'I will make your offspring as numerous as the stars of heaven, and I will give to your offspring this whole land of which I spoke, to possess for ever' " (Ex. 32:11–13). Moses' plea was successful. "And the Lord renounced the punishment He had planned to bring upon His people" (Ex. 32:14). (2) At Taberah, "The people cried out to Moses. Moses prayed to the Lord and the fire died down" (Num. 11:2). (3) After the incident of the spies, Moses prayed, "Therefore, I pray, let my Lord's forbearance be great . . . Pardon, I pray, the iniquity of this people according to Your great kindness, as You have forgiven this people ever since Egypt" (Num. 14:13ff.). Once again he met with success, "And the Lord said, 'I pardon, as you have asked'" (Num. 14:20). (For Moses' personal intervention on behalf of Miriam and Aaron, see Num. 12:13 and Deut. 9:20, respectively.)

Next in line in the tradition of prophetic intercession stands Samuel, who prayed on behalf of his people after their defeat at the hands of the Philistines (I Sam. 7:5–9), on their behalf after their request for a king, which so embittered God (I Sam. 12:19, 23), and on behalf of Saul after God rejected his election as king of Israel (I Sam. 15:11).

In the Book of Jeremiah, both Moses and Samuel are singled out as the exemplars of great intercessors on behalf of their people (Jer. 15:1; cf. Ps. 99:6). Jeremiah proved a worthy, though unsuccessful, successor to these two. That he prayed to God on behalf of his nation is explicitly stated several times, e.g., in a time of drought, when he was driven by the enormity of his task to defy God, "Why are You like a man confused, like a mighty man who cannot save" (Jer. 14:1ff.; cf. his words in 4:10; 15:11; and his confession in 18:20, "Remember how I stood in Your presence speaking good on their behalf so as to avert Your anger from them"). Even more impressive are God's express commands to Jeremiah not to intercede! "Do not pray for this people, or lift up cry or prayer for them, and do not intercede with Me, for I do not hear you" (Jer. 7:16; cf. 11:14). When God attempts to silence Jeremiah in 14:11–12, the prophet, nevertheless, blurts out a plea on their behalf (verse 13). The die, however, was cast; the nation was doomed. Even Moses and Samuel (Jer. 15:1) would be helpless in such a situation. Intercession would no longer avail, or more properly stated, God would not permit any further intercession, because it just might have been successful in diverting Him from His self-prescribed course.

The passages cited above and the pleas of Amos (Amos 7:1–3, 4–6) make it patently clear that a prime function of the prophet was to defend his people and to act as mediator on behalf of his nation. Kings Hezekiah and Zedekiah also requested Isaiah (Isa. 37:2ff.=II Kings 19) and Jeremiah (Jer. 37:3; cf. 42:2, 20) respectively, to intercede on behalf of Israel in the face of an enemy onslaught.

Intercession, thus, is an integral component of the true prophet's mission. To be a prophet means to speak for the people to God, represent their case, and take up their cause. Should one shirk from such a duty by refusing to engage God in polemics and confine himself to merely speaking to the people for God, he would be belying his prophetic call. He would then be a "false" prophet. This interpretation finds confirmation in Ezekiel, who himself carries on the tradition of intercession (cf. 9:8; 11:13). In Ezekiel 13:4–5, God declares, "Your prophets have been like foxes among ruins, O Israel. You have not gone up into the breaches to prepare the broken wall around the Israelites, that it may stand firm in battle on the day of the Lord." The prophet's mission was to stand in the breach of the nation's wall, a breach caused by the sin of his people. He was to prevent God from entering; for entrance spelled doom and destruction. This is explicitly stated in Ezekiel 22:30–31, "I looked for a man among them who could build up a barricade, who could stand in the breach before Me to defend the land from ruin; but I found none. Thus I poured out my indignation upon them and utterly destroyed them in the fire of My wrath . . ." It is of interest to note that the very same imagery is employed in Psalms 106:23 (Y. Muffs).

In sum, though some of the "false" prophets did have revelations and visions, performed symbolic actions (Jer. 28:10ff.), imparted oracles (23:31), and prophesied in YHWH's name (14:14; 29:9), since they promised good fortune and prosperity and thereby lulled the people into false security (6:14; 8:11; 14:13; 23:17; 28:2ff.), they were accused by Jeremiah of not having been sent by God (14:14–15; 23:21, 32; 28:15; 29:9), of not having been admitted to the divine council (23:18), and of not interceding with God on behalf of the people (27:18). However, after all, the final verdict could only be given by a true prophet, and even he was not always completely certain.

HISTORY

Universalism and Election. To the prophets, events of history disclosed the finger of God. God revealed Himself in the language of history. It is true that other nations in the Ancient Near East also regarded their gods as being active in history on significant occasions, but none of them conceived of a panoramic world outlook in which all of history was seen to be governed by the will of one God, nor did they interpret the history of their nation as a unified sequence governed by one, all-encompassing divine plan. Though the God of Israel addressed Himself to all men (see, e.g., Isa. 13:23; Jer. 27:2ff.; 28:8; 46–51; Ezek. 25–32; Amos 1:3–2:3; 9:7; Obad.; Nah. 3), the concept of covenantal election was unique to Israel: "Only you have I chosen from amongst the nations; therefore I shall punish you for all your sins" (Amos 3:2). Election was not a bonafide guarantee for special protection. Some prophets actually fought against this popular conception of inviolability (e.g., Isa. 28:15; Jer. 5:12; Amos 5:14). The consequence of being chosen was not immunity but heightened responsibility.

Whereas the nations of the world were held culpable solely for gross violations of the established order, Israel alone was taken to task for any and every infringement of the moral and ethical code of behavior. Indeed, one of the distinctive characteristics of the writings of the classical prophets is their insistent and adamant denunciation of corruption in the moral, ethical, and social fields. No one was impervious to their attack: not kings, priests, prophets, judges, women, creditors, wealthy landowners, or even the poorer classes. They leveled severe criticisms against murder, juridical corruption, violence, cruelty, dishonesty, greed, oppression, exploitation, bribery, harlotry, degeneracy, debauchery, arrogance, luxury, callousness, apathy, lust for power, and militarism. Each and every one of these vices exemplifies a "forgetting of God," which leads to the disintegration and the eventual condemnation of the nation (e.g., Isa. 3:14–15, 16–24; 5:8, 11–12, 18–19, 20–23; 9:8–9, 16; 31:1; Jer. 5:26; 7:9; Ezek. 22; Hos. 1:7; 4:2, 6, 11–13; 6:8–10; 7:1–7; 8:14; 10:13; 12:8–9; 13:6; Amos 2:6–8; 3:10–11; 4:1; 5:7; 6:1–7, 13; Micah 3:1–3, 11; Zeph. 1:12). Idolatry, too, was subjected to its usual severe criticism (e.g., Isa. 65:3–4; Jer. 7:18, 30–31; 19:4–5; Ezek. 8; Hos. 2:15; Amos 8:14; Zeph. 1:4–6).

Supremacy of Morality. Special attention should be given to the prophets' new concept of the cult and their novel idea of the supremacy of morality. The problem of the relationship of the prophets to cultic worship has gone through several stages of interpretation. One of the basic axioms of biblical scholarship was the notion that the priest and prophet were fundamentally opposed to one another. The major contribution of the prophets was considered to be the de-ritualization of religion. The basic message of the prophets was "ethical monotheism," with the stress on morality rather than ritual. Thus, it was thought that the independent spirit of the prophet conflicted head-on with the priest, the professional officiant of organized religion. The former was interested in right; the latter in rites. The prophet was "word-possessed"—he brought the word of God to man. The priest was "cult-possessed"—he raised man's sacrifice to God.

The development of form-critical studies brought a partial scholarly reversal, and the attempt was made to demonstrate the positive attitude of the prophets toward the cult. Their utterance of divinely inspired oracles was supposed to be an integral component of Israelite worship. The time, and later even the content, of these oracles were understood to be liturgically fixed. The prophets were identified as members of the cultic personnel.

Both views, especially the latter, are extreme and are constantly being debated. What can be said with certainty is that the prophetic attacks on the cult did introduce a new principle into the religion of Israel: The essence of God's demand is not to be found in the cult but in the moral and ethical spheres of life. In the Torah and preclassical prophetic literature there is no sharp distinction between cultic and moral prescriptions. Both are equally important, and both are essential to the continued existence of the nation. With the words of the classical prophets, however, a new aspect was introduced. While Samuel argued for the primacy of obedience over sacrifice (I Sam. 15:22), Amos and his fellow prophets stressed the primacy of morality (Isa. 1:11–17; 66:1ff.; Jer. 6:20; 7:21–23; 14:12; Hos. 6:6; Amos 5:21–25; Micah 6:6–8). The prophets were no more unequivocably opposed to the cult than they were to song and psalm (Amos 5:23) or prayer, festival, and Sabbath (Isa. 1:13–15), all of which they mentioned in their attacks. On the contrary, Isaiah's call came apparently while he was in the Temple (Isa. 6). The Exilic (Isa. 44:28; 52:11; 66:20–24; Jer. 33:11, 18; Ezek. 20:40–44; 22:8, 26; 40–48), as well as the post-Exilic prophets Haggai and Zechariah, had a very positive attitude toward the Temple and its cult. They advocated the rebuilding of the sanctuary, with the restoration of sacrificial worship, and stressed ceremonial law. The prophets did not denounce the practice of sacrifice per se, but they did adamantly oppose the absolutization of the cult.

Attitude Toward Ritual. In Israel, ritual is conceived of as God's gift to man, an act of grace intended for the good of man. It affords man a means by which he can draw closer to God. Worship and ritual are means, justice and righteousness are ends. "God requires devotion, not devotions" (S. Spiegel, *Amos versus Amaziah* (1957), 43), right not rite. When cult becomes a substitute for moral behavior, it is to be condemned. Religion is not to be equated with formal worship, nor is it to be restricted to certain specified times during the calendar year; it is to encompass the whole life of man. Hence, any cultic act performed by a worshiper whose moral or ethical character is not beyond reproach is considered an abomination to God. It is no wonder that, after disparaging independent importance of the cult, the prophets clashed with the acknowledged heads of established religion, the priests. Clashes such as of Amos with Amaziah (Amos 7:10ff.), Jeremiah with Pashhur (Jer. 20), or with Zephaniah son of Maaseiah (Jer. 29:25ff.), are unheard of in preclassical times. In the dramatic, near tragic confrontation of Jeremiah with his antagonists (Jer. 26) the priests are among the forefront in demanding the death sentence for the prophet, who was accused of "blasphemy" for repudiating the inviolability of the Temple (Jer. 7).

Moreover, it should be recalled that in all other religions of the Ancient Near East the correct observance of the cult was of paramount importance, since it was thought that the welfare of the gods was dependent on both the maintenance of their temples and the daily upkeep of their sacrifices. The prophets, however, devaluated the intrinsic significance of ritual, and stressed God's ultimate concern with correct behavior. Justice, righteousness, kindness, integrity, and faithfulness were among God's chief demands (e.g., Jer. 9:22–23; 22:15–16; Hos. 6:6; Amos 5:15, 24; Micah 6:8).

Morality and Destiny. The prophets took yet another step. Not only was morality of ultimate importance but it became the decisive factor in determining the national destiny of Israel. This was a shift from the older tradition expressed in the Torah literature and in the Former Prophets, according to which the sin of idolatry was the primary transgression. Not only were the cardinal sins of murder and incest denounced as before but the everyday immoral acts of society were condemned as well. With the emergence of the classical prophets a new criterion became operative—moral rectitude. The destiny of the nation was bound up with it, and unrighteousness would spell the end of Israel.

Repentance. The prophets consistently pleaded with Israel to seek God that they might live (Amos 5:4, 14). They demanded piety and faithfulness to the covenant between God and Israel, and threatened punishment and fulfillment of the covenant's curses for those who were disloyal to it. Yet all of their denunciations and frightful maledictions were not meant as ends in themselves. They were, rather, a vain attempt to arouse man from his lethargic status quo; they were didactic means to achieve the desired end—repentance. The objective of the prophetic threat of dire punishment was that it should not take place. Paradoxically, the prophets wished to make their own calling self-defeating by persuading man to return to God. They censured, warned, and admonished man to forsake his immoral ways in order to avoid imminent destruction. They addressed man who had been granted the supreme blessing of the freedom and the ability to repent.

The prophets were not always ready to accept the finality of divine judgment (for Amos and Jeremiah, see above). They prayed that repentance would have the desired effect: "Who knows, God may yet have a change of heart and turn from His fierce anger so that we shall not perish" (Jonah 3:9, the words of the king of Nineveh expressing the prophetic sentiment; cf. the "perhaps" of the sailors in 1:6). There are other examples: "Who knows whether He will not turn and change His decision and leave a blessing behind Him" (Joel 2:14). "It may be that the Lord, the God of hosts, will be gracious to the remnant of Joseph" (Amos 5:15). "Perhaps you may find shelter on the day of the Lord's anger" (Zeph. 2:3). Divine plans are not unchangeable; man's actions tip the scales of justice and mercy: "If at any time I declare concerning a nation or a kingdom, that I will pluck up and pull it down and destroy it, and if that nation, concerning which I have spoken, turns from its evil, I will repent of the evil that I intended to do it. And if at any time I declare concerning a nation or a kingdom that I will build and plant it, and if it does evil in My sight, not listening to My voice, then I will repent of the good which I intended to do to it" (Jer. 18:7–10; cf. Ezek. 3:17–21; 33:7–20). Even the possibility of a "divine turning" not predicated upon the prior repentance of the people was contemplated, "How can I give you up, Ephraim! [How can I] hand you over, Israel! How can I treat you like Admah or make you like Zeboim! My heart is changed within Me; My compassion grows warm and tender, I will not execute My fierce anger, I will not again destroy Ephraim ..." (Hos. 11:8–9). Compassion may overcome wrath (cf. Jer. 33:8; Micah 7:18–19).

Suspension of Freedom and God's Inaccessibility. Yet the prophets were not often so optimistic. They knew very well the futility of chastisement (e.g., Amos 4:6–11; Isa. 1:5ff.; 9:12; Jer. 2:30; 5:3). This incurable stubbornness and hardheartedness of the people (Jer. 5:21; Isa. 42:18–20; 43:8; 46:12; 6:10, 17; 9:25; Ezek. 2:4; 12:2) led one prophet to take the most radical step of all: the suspension of freedom. Isaiah was commissioned to "make the heart of this people fat, their ears heavy, and their eyes dim, lest they see with their eyes, and hear with their ears, and understand with their hearts, and turn and be healed" (Isa. 6:10). The prophet became God's messenger to harden their hearts and thereby to prevent the people from repenting! Since Israel had so often spurned the words of God and since they had not returned to Him, the privilege of repentance was to be denied them (until only one-tenth of the population remained). The only "cure" for obdurate hardness was to intensify it.

At other times God would make Himself inaccessible to the people as a punishment (e.g., Hos. 5:6; Amos 8:11–12), or to the prophet himself. Jeremiah had no immediate answer for Hananiah (Jer. 28:11) and had to wait once for ten days for the word of God (Jer. 42:7).

New Covenant. The frustration of waiting for man's response and the realization that man by his own efforts could not effect a total return to God led to the development of an entirely new idea. If man would not initiate the process, God would. He would not only initiate it but finalize it as well. This is the thought implicit in the concept of a "new covenant." Since the old covenant was broken, God despairing of further futile warnings and punishments, would implant His will directly into man's heart, thereby changing the nature of man by a divine "grafting." Man's heart of stone would be turned into a heart of flesh. His whole being would be filled with the "knowledge of God," and thus he could not but obey God; he would no longer be capable of rejecting God's teachings. This new covenant would be unbreakable and would presage final redemption (Isa. 55:3; Jer. 24:7; 31:30–33; 32:38–41; Ezek. 16:60; 34:25ff.; 36:26ff.; 37:26ff.; cf. Deut. 30:6; Isa. 11:9; 54:13).

Future of Israel. With the covenant renewed, the future community of Israel, constituted by the *remnant (e.g., Isa. 4:3–4; 8:16–17; 10:20–21; Jer. 31:31ff.; Amos 9:8ff.; Micah 7:8; Zeph. 2:3, 9), which will have survived the

"*Day of the Lord" (see also *Eschatology), would live in peace, no longer troubled by oppression, injustice, or war (e.g., Isa. 2:1–5; 10:27; 11:1–9; 60:5–16; 61:4–9; Hos. 2:21ff.; Micah 4:3–4). It would be an age in which God's glory would be manifested to all mankind (Isa. 40:5), and so all the nations would come to reject idolatry and recognize and revere the God of Israel alone (Isa. 19:18–25; 45:22ff.; Jer. 3:17; 12:16; Ezek. 17:24; Micah 7:16ff.; Hab. 2:14; Zeph. 2:11; Zech. 2:15; 8:20–23; 14:16–21). Jerusalem would become the spiritual center of the world (Isa. 2:2), from which would flow God's instruction to all mankind (Isa. 2:3; 51:4ff.). Israel, would, according to Deutero-Isaiah, become a prophet nation (49:2–3; 51:16; 59:21), spreading the teaching of God to all humanity (42:1–4) and recounting His glory (43:21). It would become "a light to the nations" (42:6; 49:6) and bring God's blessing and beneficence to the ends of the earth (45:22–24). [Sh.M.P.]

IN THE TALMUD

Despite the many aggadic elements in the references to prophecy or the prophets in rabbinical literature, there emerges a clear picture of the rabbinic view of the prophets. Substantially it is based upon two main principles. The first is that Moses was the "master of the prophets" and no prophet after him succeeded as did Moses in penetrating into the nature of the Divine, communing with Him, and receiving His message while in full possession of his normal cognitive faculties. This is of course clearly expressed in the Bible (Num. 12:6–8) but it is extended to apply to all future prophecy. This concept is expressed in various ways, the most striking being that whereas Moses beheld the Divine as through a clear mirror, the other prophets did so through a distorted mirror ("a mirror which does not shine," Yev. 49b; cf. "through a glass darkly," I Cor. 13:12).

However, there is noticeable a definite tendency to give Isaiah precedence over all other prophets. Although it is stated that of the four near-contemporary prophets, Isaiah, Amos, Micah, and Hosea, the last was first both in time and in importance (Pes. 87a), it is stated that of all the prophets only Moses and Isaiah "knew what they were prophesying" (Mid. Ps. 90:1, no. 4). Both are referred to together as "the greatest of the prophets" (Deut. R. 2:4). Isaiah is responsible for more prophecies than any other prophet and he prophesied not only to Israel but to mankind as a whole (PR 34:158a); he received revelation direct from God and his prophecies were "doubled" (PdRK 125b). If Ezekiel was vouchsafed a revelation of the Divine Essence equal to that of Isaiah, he saw Him as "a villager sees the person of the king," while Isaiah saw Him as an "inhabitant of a metropolis *[kerakh]* who sees the person of the king" (Ḥag. 13b).

The second principle is a corollary of the first. It is to the effect that the prophets were not responsible for any religious innovations or novel doctrines, their function being confined to expounding and clarifiying the teachings of the Pentateuch. The Talmud interprets the verse (Lev. 27:34) "these are the commandments which the Lord commanded Moses for the children of Israel in Mount Sinai," to mean that "henceforth a prophet may make no innovations" (Shab. 104a). "The prophets neither took away from, nor added to, aught that is written in the Torah, save only the commandment to read the *megillah*" and even for that they sought biblical sanction (Meg. 14a). In conformity with this view, in the chain of tradition with which tractate *Avot* opens, the prophets appear merely as the tradents of the Torah of Moses, the successors to the elders after Joshua, and the predecessors of the men of the Great Synagogue. It is highly probable that this view was influenced by the contrary Christian view of progressive revelation through the ages, culminating in Jesus, though one need not go so far as does Weiss (Dor, 2 (1904[4]), 8) in seeing in it a polemic against the antinomianism of Paul. Consequently statements of the prophets which have no pentateuchal confirmation or support cannot normally be made the basis of the *halakhah*.

According to the rabbis the number of prophets was innumerable ("double the number of the children of Israel who went forth from Egypt") and every tribe produced them (Suk. 27b). However only the prophecies of those which contained a lesson (lit. "were required for") future generations were recorded. They amount to 48 prophets and seven prophetesses: to Miriam (cf. Ex. 15:20 and Num. 12:2), Deborah, and Huldah, the rabbis add Sarah, Hannah, Abigail, and Esther (Meg. 14a). There were also seven gentile prophets: Balaam, his father Beor (Sanh. 105a), Job and his three companions, and Elisha the son of Barachel (BB 15b), but of them Balaam was incomparably the greatest. He was even regarded as the equal of Moses (see *Balaam in Aggadah) and the gentile nations cannot therefore claim that they were not vouchsafed prophecy (Yalk 966; Num. R. 14:34). Nevertheless prophecy came to them only by night and in "half words" and from "behind the curtain" (Gen. R. 52:5). All the prophets prophesied only concerning the messianic age (i.e., the present world in its ideal state) but were not vouchsafed to see the celestial world to come (Ber. 34b). The statement "the same message [*signon*, lit. "sign"] is given to a number of prophets but no two prophets prophesy in the same *signon*" (Sanh. 89a) is probably to be taken to refer to the fact that although they all reveal the word of God, each one has his own particular message or doctrine. The daring use of anthropomorphisms by the prophets is regarded as a sign of their "greatness" (Num. R. 19:4). With the exception of Jeremiah, all the prophets conclude their prophecies on a note of hope and comfort (TJ, Ber. 5:1, 8d). Where the patronymic of the prophet is given, it is to show that his father was also a prophet; when his place of origin is not given he was a Jerusalemite (Meg. 15a).

The prophets are divided into the Early and Later Prophets, but the former encompass all those of the period of the First Temple, only the post-Exilic—Haggai, Zechariah, and Malachi—constituting the latter (Sot. 48b). All the prophets were wealthy. An interesting proof is given with regard to Amos. Since he was both a herdsman of Tekoa (Amos 1:1) and a dresser of sycamore trees (7:14), and sycamores grow only in the Shephelah but not in the hilly country of Tekoa, he must have been a wealthy landowner with flocks in Judea and plantations in the Shephelah (Ned. 38a). When prophecy came to an end, the **Shekhinah* departed from Israel and the **Bat Kol* became a partial substitute (Yoma 9b).

For the order of the prophets according to the Talmud (BB 14b) see *Bible Canon. [L.I.R.]

IN JEWISH PHILOSOPHY

Philo. The teaching of *Philo concerning prophecy has to be reconstructed from discussions scattered throughout his writings. Philo conceives of the prophet as priest, seer, and lawgiver all in one. Prophetic understanding is the highest form, transcending reason, which is based on sense perception. When the divine prophetic spirit rests on a man, he is "possessed" by it in a kind of frenzy or "sober intoxication." All prophecy is by grace of God, but prophecy through the divine spirit, in contrast to communication through angels or the divine voice, demands preparation in the recipient, be he Jew or non-Jew: he must be refined, wise, and just, and emancipated from bodily concerns.

Medieval Jewish Philosophy. That prophets and prophecy should be a major theme in medieval Jewish philosophy is hardly surprising. Where a religious community defines itself by a divinely revealed law, the character of that law, the manner of its transmission, and the qualities of the human promulgator are all problems of importance. It would be overly simple, but not wrong, to say: no prophet, no Torah; no Torah, no Israel.

The more prominent medieval philosophic writings regard this theme as highly significant, and for none is this judgment more true than the most prominent of such writings, the *Guide of the Perplexed* of *Maimonides (see below). Through his elaborate analysis Maimonides provides a new vantage point by which to take and understand the phenomenon of prophecy. By superimposing on earlier rabbinic discussions the analyses of the *falāsifa,* Muslim students of Plato and Aristotle, he changed the way in which the Jewish prophets, and especially the greatest one, Moses, could be viewed. To fully measure the distance between Maimonides' view of prophecy and the traditional views would entail close examination of his selective, critical use of the philosophic teachings of al-*Fārābi and *Avicenna. For Maimonides as for these *falāsifa,* the study of prophets and prophecy is part of political science. Their corresponding emphasis upon the prophet's political function is at most only faintly present in pre-Maimonidean Jewish writings.

Saadiah. The tenth-century Babylonian *gaon* *Saadiah in his *Book of Beliefs and Opinions* (ch. 3) sees a necessity for prophecy with respect both to rational and revealed commandments (see Reasons for Divine *Commandments). In the latter case, the prophet is God's instrument for apprising men of His will. In the former, the prophet's revelation supplements, corrects, and reinforces human reason. Instead of being left to their own devices to produce a rational moral code, men are given commandments that anticipate the eventual conclusions of reason, while being specific rather than indeterminate, as the conclusions of reason would be. The prophet's authenticity is confirmed by the miracles he works, but such confirmation can apply only to teaching that accords with reason. Miracles alone do not confirm a prophet whose message is absurd or rationally impossible.

Judah Halevi. The view of prophecy presented by *Judah Halevi in the *Kuzari* stresses the singularity of the children of Israel and the land of Israel. All the chosen people in their chosen land sought to attain the level of prophecy, and many or most of them did in fact attain it (1:103, 109; 2:14; 4:17). The least among the adherents of the divine law is greater than the noblest of the heathens. We know of no prophecy among the other nations or the philosophers (5:20; 1:4, 99 end). Prophecy appears to be a gift. The means of achieving or deserving prophetic inspirations are variously stated in the *Kuzari,* but perfection of the intellect is not explicitly mentioned. Emphasis is rather on the prolonged performance of pious acts, a concern with sanctity and purity. In this way men approach as near to God as is humanly possible, in the highest case coming to know "the meaning of *Adonai.*" This knowledge of the Lord is grasped through prophetic intuition, and its possessor is raised to the rank of angels. In contrast, "the meaning of *Elohim,* the presence of a superintending God, is accessible to unassisted human reason, but this God of Aristotle is not the God of Abraham" (2:14; 5:20; 4th principle; 1:103; 4:15–16). Those who through prophetic inspiration "taste and see that the Lord is good" are able to draw the multitude after them. When the Jews formed a body politic, the priests and prophets were the people's councillors, their head. An adherent of the divine law finds satisfaction in the prophets' teachings; their artless speeches are more attractive than the philosophers' eloquent arguments (2:28; 4:17). Not least of the prophet's strengths is his ability to speak to the children of man.

Maimonides. Maimonides' analysis of the psychology and political function of prophecy circumspectly avoids quick and easy resorts to the miraculous and the suprarational. Prophecy is natural, an intelligible device by which divine wisdom secures the existence and perfection of the human species. Prophecy's preconditions are understood in the light of its purposes: in its highest form, the promulgation of a divine law; in its lower forms, popular instruction or the urging of men to adhere to the divine law. By grasping the distinctive character of the law, one comes closer to comprehending the nature of the bringer of the law.

As law the Torah is prospective, general, and indifferent to the exceptional case. All laws seek to conceal and overcome the natural diversity of men through multiple points of conventional accord, such harmony being a prerequisite to domestic tranquillity. Where the Torah differs from a merely human law is seen in their respective ends. A human law is directed solely to the well-being and happiness of the body politic, however defined by that community or lawgiver, without regard to the soundness of the populace's beliefs or opinions beyond their bearing on civil order. Its promulgator is no prophet. Divine law, on the other hand, does all that conventional law seeks to do and, further, concerns itself with the well-being of the soul, inculcating true opinions about God and the whole of existence in every man to the limit of his capacity. What sets the Torah apart from ordinary laws also sets the genuine prophet apart from ordinary lawgivers: a grasp of speculative truths combined with the ability to reach and teach the multitude.

The vulgar opinion concerning prophecy, that God may take any moral man, be he wise or ignorant, and turn him into a prophet, deserves rejection. The philosopher's opinion, that a certain human perfection leads naturally to prophecy, needs correction. "The opinion of our Law and the foundation of our doctrine" is that prophecy is the natural result of a fit natural disposition, perfected through training and study, yet subject to the divine will. A man may be fit for prophecy, having perfected his moral and rational qualities, and yet miraculously not become a prophet.

Maimonides defines prophecy as an overflow coming from God, through the Active Intellect, toward the individual's rational faculty and then toward his imaginative faculty. For a man to prophesy, both of these faculties must be perfect, over and above the moral perfection that frees a man from a concern for physical pleasure and domination and allows him to be utterly preoccupied with divine things. Men of science engaged in speculation have only a rational faculty capable of receiving the divine overflow. Those who govern cities, such as legislators and soothsayers, have only a perfected imagination, their rational faculty being defective or insufficiently trained. The measure of the divine overflow reaching both prophets and men of science determines whether these men alone are perfected or, as in the superior cases, they also are driven by an overpowering desire to perfect others. By reason of their involvement, be it with a disobedient and unbelieving people or in defense of the nation against a royal oppressor, true prophets also need highly developed faculties of courage and divination. As teachers and leaders of the people in the way of the divine law, true prophets surpass both the men of science and the rulers of cities. All the more is this true of the greatest prophet, Moses. His direct knowledge of the upper world, his grasp of speculative truths about God without recourse to premises and inferences, qualifies him to be a teacher even of philosophers. His perfect imagination, by which he is able to present these truths metaphorically to the benefit of all men, qualifies him to be a leader even of political rulers. Only the greatest prophet legislates. Through his perfect law, the Torah, cast in language meaningful to all, a perfect community is formed, dedicated to knowing and worshiping God.

Joseph Albo. The broad features of Maimonides' view of prophecy are reaffirmed by the 14th–15th-century Spanish rabbi Joseph *Albo in his *Sefer ha-Ikkarim* ("Book of Roots"). The absence of prophecy among the philosophers suggests to Albo that prophecy is not merely a natural consequence of investigative knowledge. Though the divine overflow goes to the individual's rational faculty, his preparedness is less critical than the divine will to so favor a man (1:21, 1; 3:8, 6). Neither divination of the future nor working of miracles most distinguishes prophets (1:18, 13; 3:10, 16). Prophecy is emphatically a means by which the greatest number may realize the human end. In prophecy's highest stage, a man is informed of the rules and governance by which he may lead a nation or nations or the entire human species to human perfection (3:8, 9; 3:10, 11; 3:12, 1). According to Albo "there is no one among us who has reached this stage except Moses our teacher" (3:10, 11).

[R.Le.]

Modern Jewish Thought. Depending on their attitude toward *revelation, modern Jewish philosophers treat prophecy either as a subjective experience or as a supernatural phenomenon. Those philosophers who regard prophecy as a subjective experience account for the phenomenon in a variety of ways. Some dismiss it as a form of psychological delusion; others view it as a mystical experience or an "inspired" insight, deriving from excellence of moral, intellectual, or imaginative faculties. Those who treat prophecy as a supernatural phenomenon differ over the nature of the prophetic experience. Of those philosophers who accept the notion that revelation constitutes a supernatural communication of content, some regard prophecy as the authentic disclosure of a message received word by word from God, a view referred to as "the doctrine of verbal inspiration," and others regard it as the record of a human response to a divine revelation of content. According to the latter view, human and divine elements are intermingled in prophecy. Other philosophers, while accepting supernatural revelation, deprive it of any ideational or instructive content and restrict it to the manifestation of the Divine Presence; they look upon the words of the prophet as a personal response to a revelatory experience.

As a dogmatic rationalist, Moses *Mendelssohn maintained that reason could supply man with all the theoretical insights needed for salvation. Therefore, he restricted the function of prophecy to the practical sphere, to the divine communication of instruction for human action (*Jerusalem* (1852), pt. 2, ch. 3).

The idealistic philosophers, emphasizing the cognitive aspects of prophecy, viewed it as a special aptitude for moral and religious insight. Hermann *Cohen regarded the prophets as pioneering thinkers who removed the mythical elements from religion and developed Judaism from a tribal religion into a universal ethical monotheism. The essence of the universal ethical monotheism is belief in God and adherence to the moral law (*Juedische Schriften,* 1 (1924), 310–6). Kaufmann *Kohler, like many other exponents of the doctrine of "progressive revelation," viewed the "inspired" moral and religious insights of the prophets as important milestones in the evolution of the human spirit toward higher ethical and metaphysical truths.

Sharply reacting to idealistic theories that reduce prophecy to a function of the human spirit, Solomon Ludwig *Steinheim insisted that revelation cannot be explained solely in terms of rational or spiritual insight. The central religious affirmations of Judaism could not have originated within our own cognitive faculties because of their inherent limitations. The primary function of prophecy is to disclose religious truths that can be known only through supernatural revelation (*Die Offenbarung nach dem Lehrbegriffe der Synagoge,* 5ff.). However, Steinheim assigned reason an important function in determining which parts of Scripture represent the revelation of eternal truth.

Samson Raphael *Hirsch and other Orthodox thinkers subscribed to the doctrine of verbal inspiration of the Scriptures. Bitterly objecting to any form of biblical criticism, Hirsch insisted that one must look upon the Scripture as a basic datum in the same manner scientists look upon natural phenomena as given (*Nineteen Letters* (1960), note to letter 18). As a staunch exponent of the traditional view, he rejected the evolutionary theory, according to which the contributions of later prophets are an advance over earlier formulations (*Horeb* (1962), 7).

Naturalist thinkers, such as *Aḥad Ha-Am and Mordecai *Kaplan, ruled out all supernatural elements in prophecy. However, because of their positive attitude toward Jewish nationalism, they could not follow Hermann Cohen in treating the prophet merely as an exponent of ethical universalism. According to Aḥad Ha-Am, who regarded the nation as the bearer of true ethical universalism, the prophet personifies the finest manifestation of the Jewish national spirit.

Jewish existentialist thinkers characterize prophecy as a dialogic relationship between man and God, rather than as the disclosure of a message. Martin *Buber in his book *The Prophetic Faith* (1949) maintained that the prophet is involved in a divine-human encounter. The prophet's message reflects the prophet's personal subjective response to his encounter with God. In the view of Franz *Rosenzweig, although revelation is a supernatural event occurring at specific times to particular individuals, the words of the prophet are nonetheless a purely human "interpretation" of a revelatory experience in which God reveals His love to man. Abraham J. *Heschel contends that the prophet experiences not merely the presence or the love of God, but a revelation of the "divine pathos." However, although prophecy is a revelatory experience in which God's concerns and designs for man are apprehended (*The Prophets* (1962), 307–23), the expression of this experience is affected by the cultural background as well as the personal style of the prophet (*God in Search of Man* (1965), 258–62).

Of the most recent Orthodox thinkers, Joseph B. *Soloveitchik, maintains in his article "The Lonely Man of Faith" (*Tradition,* summer 1965) that the prophetic encounter, a dialogue initiated by God, makes possible the establishment of a "covenantal community" between God and man. Unlike the mystical experience, however, prophecy cannot be limited to religious feelings or intuitions, but entails a normative content. Abraham Isaac *Kook's treatment of prophecy, in his work *Orot ha-Kodesh* (pt. 1 (1963), 267–72), reflects his mystical orientation. Genuine metaphysical insights, according to Kook, cannot be obtained by reason alone. When properly cultivated by a life of piety and holiness, man's imaginative faculties enable him to attach himself to the Divine Source and apprehend reality in the light of the **Shekhinah,* or "Divine Presence."

Illumination derived from union with the Divine reaches its highest level in prophecy. Thus, Kook regarded prophecy as the ultimate religious goal.

See also *Revelation. [W.S.W.]

Bibliography: G. Hoelscher, *Die Profeten* (1914); T. H. Robinson, *Prophecy and the Prophets in Ancient Israel* (1932); R. B. Y. Scott, *The Relevance of the Prophets* (1944); S. Mowinckel, *Prophecy and Tradition* (1946); M. Buber, *The Prophetic Faith* (1949); Y. A. Seligmann, in: *Eretz Israel*, 3 (1954), 125–32 (Heb.); A. Malamat, *ibid.*, 4 (1956), 74–84 (Heb.); 5 (1958), 67–73 (Heb.); 8 (1967), 231–40 (Heb.); idem, in: VT *Supplement*, 15 (1965), 207–27; Kaufmann Y., Religion, 87–101, 343–446; A. J. Heschel, *The Prophets* (1962); J. Lindblom, *Prophecy in Ancient Israel* (1962); O. Eissfeldt, *The Old Testament, An Introduction* (1965), 76–81, 146–52, 301–443 (incl. bibl.); G. von Rad, *Old Testament Theology*, 2 (1965), 3–300; H. M. Orlinsky, in: *Oriens Antiquus*, 4 (1965), 153–74. IN MEDIEVAL JEWISH PHILOSOPHY: S. Pines, introduction to M. Maimonides, *Guide of the Perplexed* (1963), lvii–cxxxiv; L. Strauss, *Philosophie und Gesetz* (1935), 87–122; idem, in: REJ, 100 (1936), 1–37; Husik, Philosophy, 224–6 and index s.v. *Prophecy;* Guttmann, Philosophies, 216–8 and index s.v. *Prophecy* and *Prophets;* H. A. Wolfson, *Philo*, 2 (1947), 11–72; B. Netanyahu, *Don Isaac Abravanel* (1968²), 121–3; Reines, in: HUCA, 31 (1960), 107–35; 33 (1962), 221–53; 38 (1967), 159–211; idem, *Maimonides and Abrabanel on Prophecy* (1970). MODERN JEWISH PHILOSOPHY: Guttman, Philosophies, index s.v. *Prophecy* and *Prophets;* S. Noveck (ed.), *Great Thinkers of the Twentieth Century* (1963), index; N. Rotenstreich, *Jewish Philosophers in Modern Times: From Mendelssohn to Rosenzweig* (1968), index.

PROSBUL (Heb. פרוזבול or פרוסבול), a legal formula whereby a creditor could still claim his debts after the *Sabbatical Year despite the biblical injunction against doing so (Deut. 15:2). The text of the prosbul reads, "I declare before you, so-and-so, the judges in such-and-such a place, that regarding any debt due to me, I may be able to recover any money owing to me from so-and-so at any time I shall desire." The prosbul was signed by witnesses or by the judges of the court before whom the declaration was made (Shev. 10:4, Git. 36a). The principle underlying the prosbul was based on the passage "and this is the manner of the release: every creditor shall release that which he hath lent unto his neighbor; he shall not exact it of his neighbor and his brother ... Of a foreigner thou mayest exact it; but whatsoever of thine is with thy brother thy hand shall release" (Deut. 15:2, 3). From this the law was deduced that the operation of the year of release did not affect debts of which the bonds had been delivered to the court *(bet din)* before the intervention of the Sabbatical Year (Shev. 10:2), since the Court was regarded as a corporate body to which the words "thy brother," suggesting an individual, did not apply. The court would therefore collect its debts after the Sabbatical Year (Yad, Shemittah ve-Yovel 9:15). Through a slight extension of this precedent, the prosbul was instituted, which in effect amounted to entrusting the court with the collection of the debt. Without actually handing over the bond to the court as previously required, the creditor could secure his debt against forfeiture by making the prescribed declaration.

The prosbul was instituted by Hillel. The Mishnah states that when he saw that the people refrained from giving loans one to another before the Sabbatical Year, thereby transgressing "Beware that there be not a base thought in thy heart," etc. (Deut. 15:9), he instituted the prosbul (Shev. 9:3). The Talmud therefore explained prosbul as *pruz buli u-buti*, meaning an advantage for both the rich and poor. It benefited the rich since it secured their loans, and the poor since it enabled them to borrow (Git. 37a). The word seems, however, to be an abbreviation of the Greek expression πρὸς βουλῇ βουλευτῶν meaning "before the assembly of counselors" (cf. *Boule). The rabbis later

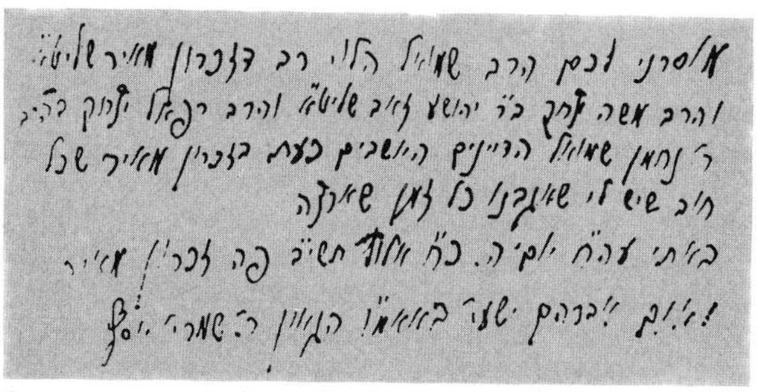

Prosbul written by Abraham Yeshayahu Karelitz ("Ḥazon Ish") in 1952, a year before his death. From S. Cohen, *Pe'er ha-Dor: Ḥayyei Ḥazon Ish*, Bene-Berak, 1969.

explained that Hillel only abrogated the Mosaic institution of the release of all debts every seventh year since the law of release itself was only of rabbinic authority during the Second Temple period when the Jubilee was not operative because the land was not fully occupied by Israel (Git. 36a–b). It was only permitted to write a prosbul when the debtor possessed some real property from which the debt could be collected. The rabbis were very lenient with this rule, however, and permitted the writing of a prosbul even when the debtor possessed a minute amount of land such as a flowerpot or the trunk of a tree. The creditor was also permitted temporarily to transfer to the debtor a small parcel of land so that the prosbul could be written (Shev. 10:6, 7; Git. 37a). An antedated prosbul was considered valid, but a postdated one was void (Shev. 10:5).

During the Hadrianic persecutions, all religious practices were forbidden on the penalty of death and it was hazardous to preserve a prosbul. The rabbis therefore ruled that a creditor could collect his debt even if he did not produce a prosbul since it was assumed that he previously wrote one, but had destroyed it out of fear (Ket. 9:9). This temporary provision later became the established law, and the creditor was believed when he alleged that he had lost his prosbul (Git. 37b; Sh. Ar., ḤM 67:33). Orphans were not required to execute one since they were considered wards of the court. Money owed to them was therefore automatically considered as being owed to the court (Git. 37a). The *amoraim* debated the virtue of Hillel's institution. Samuel declared that if he had the power he would abolish it, while R. Naḥman held that even if no prosbul was actually written it should have been regarded as written. Samuel also maintained that only the leading courts of each generation could supervise the writing of a prosbul. Subsequent practice, however, entrusted all courts with this responsibility (Git. 36b; Isserles to Sh. Ar., ḤM 67:18). During the Middle Ages, the writing of prosbuls was widely disregarded since there was an opinion that the laws of the Sabbatical Years were no longer operative (Rema to Sh. Ar., ḤM 67:1 and commentaries). Nevertheless, meticulous individuals continued to write prosbuls even in modern times (e.g., *Pe'er ha-Dor: Ḥayyei Ḥazon Ish*, 2:245; see also **Takkanot;* *Usury). [A.Ro.]

PROSELYTES. There is ample evidence of a widespread conversion to Judaism during the period of the Second Temple, especially the latter part of the period, and the word *ger*, which in biblical times meant a stranger, or an alien, became synonymous with a proselyte (see "Strangers and Gentiles").

Among the notable converts to Judaism may be mentioned the royal family of *Adiabene, *Aquila and/or *Onkelos, *Flavius Clemens, the nephew of Vespasian, and Fulvia, wife of Saturninus, a Roman senator. Unique, as the only case of forced conversion in Judaism, was the mass conversion of the Edomites by John *Hyrcanus.

In addition to those outstanding figures, however, it is obvious that proselytism was widespread among the ordinary people. The statement of the New Testament that the Pharisees "compass sea and land to make one proselyte" (Matt. 23:15), suggesting a vigorous and active proselytization may possibly be an exaggeration, but on the other hand, the near pride which the rabbis took in the claim that some of their greatest figures were descended from proselytes (see below) point to an openhanded policy toward their acceptance. Such incidents as the different approach of Shammai and Hillel to the request to be taught the principles of Judaism by a potential proselyte (Shabb. 31a) and the incidental mention of "Judah the Ammonite proselyte" (Ber. 28a) point to the fact that the movement was not confined to the upper classes. In fact Josephus states explicitly that in his day the inhabitants of both Greek and barbarian cities evinced a great zeal for Judaism (Contra Ap. 2. 39).

It was during this period that the detailed laws governing the acceptance of proselytes were discussed and codified, and they have remained standard in Orthodox Judaism. [Ed.]

Laws of Conversion. The procedure, established by the *tannaim,* according to which a non-Jew may be accepted into the Jewish faith, was elucidated as follows: "In our days, when a proselyte comes to be converted, we say to him: 'What is your objective? Is it not known to you that today the people of Israel are wretched, driven about, exiled, and in constant suffering?' If he says: 'I know of this and I do not have the merit,' we accept him immediately and we inform him of some of the lighter precepts and of some of the severer ones . . . we inform him of the chastisements for the transgression of these precepts . . . and we also inform him of the reward for observing these precepts . . . we should not overburden him nor be meticulous with him . . ." (Yev. 47a; cf. Ger. 1, in: M. Higger, *Sheva Massekhtot Ketannot* (1930), 68–69). This text refers to a person who converted through conviction. The *halakhah* also accepts a posteriori, proselytes who had converted in order to marry, to advance themselves, or out of fear (Yev. 24b, in the name of Rav, see TJ, Kid. 4:1, 65b–d; Maim. Yad, Issurei Bi'ah 13:17; Sh. Ar., YD 268:12). The acceptance of a proselyte "under the wings of the Divine Presence" is equivalent to Israel's entry into the covenant, i.e., with circumcision, immersion, and offering a sacrifice (Ger. 2:4, in: M. Higger; loc. cit. 72).

A proselyte had to sacrifice a burnt offering either of cattle or two young pigeons. R. Johanan b. Zakkai instituted that in those times when sacrifice was no longer possible, a proselyte was not obliged to set aside money for the sacrifice (Ker. 9a). Therefore, only circumcision and immersion remained. R. Eliezer and R. Joshua disagreed as to whether someone who immersed himself but was not circumcised or vice versa could be considered a proselyte. According to R. Eliezer, he is a proselyte, even if he performed only one of these commandments. R. Joshua, however, maintained that immersion was indispensable. The halakhic conclusion is that "he is not a proselyte unless he has both been circumcised and has immersed himself" (Yev. 46). The act of conversion must take place before a *bet din,* consisting of three members; a conversion carried out by the proselyte when alone is invalid (Yev. 46b–47a). There is a suggestion that the three members of the *bet din* must be witnesses only to his acceptance of the precepts but not to the immersion. Maimonides, however, decided (Yad, Issurei Bi'ah 13:7), that a proselyte who immersed himself in the presence of two members only is not a proselyte. The schools of Shammai and Hillel differed on the issue of a proselyte who had already been circumcised at the time of his conversion: "Bet Shammai states: 'One must draw from him the blood of circumcision'; Bet Hillel states: 'One need not draw the blood of circumcision from him'" (Tosef., Shab. 15:9; TB, Shab. 135a). Most of the rabbinic authorities decide in favor of Bet Shammai (Tos. to Shab. 135a; Maim. Yad, Issurei Bi'ah 14:5; Sh. Ar., YD 268:1), and "who hast sanctified us with Thy commandments and hast commanded us to circumcise proselytes and to draw from them the blood of the covenant" (Shab. 137b) is said in the circumcision benediction of proselytes.

A proselyte must observe all the precepts that bind Jews. The statement: "There shall be one law for the citizen and for the stranger that dwelleth amongst you" (Ex. 12:49), which refers to the paschal lamb, the sages interpreted to mean that the stranger (proselyte) was the equal of the citizen concerning all the precepts of the Torah (Mekh. Pisḥa, 15). They tried to equalize the status of the proselyte and that of the Jew; certain differences stemming from the origin of the convert, however, remained. According to an anonymous Mishnah, a proselyte may not confess himself after taking out the tithes since the statement occurs in the confession "the land which Thou hast given to us"; nor does he read the section on the first fruits, where the statement is: "which the Lord hath sworn unto our fathers to give unto us." The proselyte, praying by himself must say: "the God of the Fathers of Israel"; in the synagogue he says: "the God of your Fathers" (Ma'as. Sh. 5:14; Bik. 1:4). According to one tradition, R. Judah permitted a proselyte to read the section on the first fruits, claiming that Abraham was the father of the whole world (TJ, Bik. 1:4, 64a; but in Tosef., Bik. 1:2 this permission is only extended to the Kenites). The Palestinian *amoraim,* R. Joshua b. Levi and R. Avihu, agreed with R. Judah. The authorities (particularly R. Samson in his commentary to *Bikkurim (ibid.),* and Maimonides in his letter to Obadiah the Proselyte, below) in permitting a proselyte to say "the God of our Fathers" in the prayers based themselves on the same rationale.

A proselyte terminates all former family ties upon conversion and "is considered a newly born child." His Jewish name is not associated with that of his father and he is referred to as "the son of Abraham (our father)." Later, it became the custom to name the proselyte himself after the first Jew who knew his Creator "Abraham the son of Abraham." According to the letter of the law, a proselyte may marry his relatives. The sages, however, decreed against this "So that they should not say: 'We have come from a greater sanctity to a lesser sanctity'" (Yev. 22a, Yad, Issurei Bi'ah 14:12). The disqualifications pertaining to testimony of relatives in judicial cases of family members do not apply to the proselyte; his relatives also may not inherit from him. If no heirs were born to him after his conversion, his property and his possessions are considered not to belong to anyone, and whoever takes hold of them becomes their owner (BB 3:3, 4:9; Git. 39a; Yad, Zekhi'ah u-Mattanah 1:6).

A proselyte may marry a Jewish woman, even the daughter of a *priest (Kid. 73a; Yad, Issurei Bi'ah 19:11; Sh. Ar., EH 7:22). A female proselyte, however, cannot marry a kohen, unless she was converted during childhood, not later than the age of three years and one day (Yev. 60b; Kid. 78a). R. Yose permits the marriage of the daughter of a male or female proselyte to a kohen; R. Eliezer b. Jacob, however, disputes the matter. The statement "From the day of the destruction of the Temple, the kohanim have preserved their dignity and followed the opinion of R. Eliezer b. Jacob" shows that tradition tended toward the latter's opinion. The *amoraim,* however, decided that he be followed only in those cases where the marriage has not yet taken place. If a female proselyte is already married to a kohen, she is not bound to leave him (Kid. 4:7; TB, Kid. 78b; Yad, Issurei Bi'ah 19:12). A proselyte may also marry a **mamzer* ("bastard"). According to some opinions, the permission may extend over ten generations, while others claim it should be only until his heathen origin is forgotten (Kid. 72b, 75a).

A proselyte cannot be appointed to any public office. The rabbis based their decision on the verse: "Thou shalt appoint over thee a king from among thy brothers—appointments shall be only from among thy brothers." This injunction does not apply to a proselyte whose mother or father are of Jewish origin (Yev. 45b; Kid. 76b; Tos. Sot. 41b, Yad, Melakhim 1:4). A proselyte may not hold the office of judge in a criminal court; he may act as such in a civil court (Sanh. 36b) and also judge a fellow proselyte, even in a criminal law case (Rashi to Yev. 102a). Unless one of his parents was born Jewish, most authorities bar a proselyte from acting as judge even in a civil court (Alfasi on Sanh. 4:2, Yad, Sanh. 2:9, 11:11). Others are of the opinion that even in a civil court he can only judge a fellow proselyte (Tos. Yev. 45b; RaShBA on Yev. 102a).

Appreciation of the Proselyte. In the Talmud and the Midrashim, as well as in other contemporary literature, the accepted attitude toward proselytes is usually positive. There is, however, strong evidence in rabbinic sources that some authorities were opposed to the concept of conversion and proselytes. Those scholars who ignore or obliterate such evidence cannot be justified. The differences in outlook found in rabbinic sources can partly be explained by disparities in character and temperament. However, the deciding factors were usually contemporary conditions and the personal experiences of the rabbis. R. Eliezer b. Hyrcanus, who was under ban, objected to the acceptance of proselytes (Eccles. R. 1:8). When *Aquila the Proselyte wondered and asked: "Is this all the love which the Lord hath given unto the proselyte, as it is written 'and He loveth the stranger to give him bread and clothing?'" R. Eliezer was angry with him, but R. Joshua comforted him, saying: "Bread means Torah . . . clothing means the *tallit:* the man who is worthy to have the Torah, will also acquire its precepts; his daughters may marry into the priesthood and their grandsons will sacrifice burnt offerings on the altar." (Gen. R. 70:5). It is possible that R. Eliezer's negative attitude may have been influenced by his contacts with the first Christians. He may have seen that many of the new heretics were proselytes who had relapsed and it is only concerning these that he said, "They revert to their evil ways" (BM 59b). The same R. Eliezer also states: "When a person comes to you in sincerity to be converted, do not reject him, but on the contrary encourage him" (Mekh. Amalek 3). From his time, proselytes out of conviction were mentioned in the benediction for the righteous and the pious in the *Amidah* (Meg. 17b). The bitter experience of Jews with proselytes in times of war and revolt influenced the negative attitude to conversion. Proselytes and their offspring became renegades, often slandering their new religion and denouncing the Jewish community and its leaders to the foreign rulers. In Josephus there is a description of Hellenist proselytes who apostatized and returned to their evil ways (Jos., Apion 2:123). Reference to the situation which existed after the destruction of the Temple and the abortive revolt which followed it is made in the *baraita* statement: "Insincere proselytes who wear *tefillin* on the heads and on their arms, *ẓiẓit* in their clothes, and who fix *mezuzot* on their doors—when the war of Gog and Magog will come. . . each one of them will remove the precepts from himself and go on his way. . . " (Av. Zar. 3b). At the time of the revolt of Bar Kokhba the expression "they impede the arrival of the Messiah" (Nid. 13b), referred to such proselytes. At the same epoch, R. Nehemiah taught: a proselyte who converted in order to marry or converted to enjoy the royal table or to become a servant of Solomon, proselytes who converted from fear of the lions (see: II Kings 17:24–28), proselytes who converted because of a dream, or the proselytes of Mordecai and Esther, are not acceptable as proselytes, unless they convert themselves (as) at the present time (Yev. 24b), i.e., by conviction in times of political decline, oppressions, persecutions, and lack of any material benefit. R. Simeon b. Yoḥai, upon seeing Judah b. Gerim ("a son of proselytes"), who was responsible for the rabbi's criticism of the Romans reaching the ears of the rulers, said: "Is this one still in the world!" and set his eyes upon him, turning him into a heap of bones (Shab. 33b–34a). This experience throws light on the commentary of R. Simeon: "Those who feared the Lord were a hindrance to Israel . . . the best of the gentiles, you should put to death . . ." (Mekh. Va-Yeḥi 2). His real opinions, however, found expression in the commentary (Mekh. Nezikim (Mishpatim) 18): "It is said—'And those that are beloved by Him are compared to the sun when it rises in all its strength'; Now who is greater—he who loves the king or he whom the king loves? One must say—he whom the king loves, as the verse says: 'and He loves the stranger [proselyte]'"; the statement of R. Ḥiyya: "Do not have any faith in a proselyte until 24 generations have passed because the inherent evil is still within him" (Mid. Ruth Zuta on 1:12); and other statements of *amoraim* who despised proselytes: "Proselytes are as hard for Israel [to endure] as a sore" (Yev. 47b) were prompted by the bad experiences Jews had with proselytes who had turned national or religious recreants. To these the rabbis referred: "The proselytes who left Egypt with Moses, made it [the Golden Calf] and said to Israel: These are your gods" (Ex. R. 42:6). The rabbis distinguished between three categories of proselytes: "Proselytes are of three types: There are some like Abraham our Father, some like Hamor, and some that are like heathens in all respects" (SER 27). In the teachings of the *amoraim* the basic tone is that of the tannaitic statement: "Proselytes are beloved; in every place He considers them as part of Israel" (Mekh. *ibid.*). They too made efforts "not to close the door before the proselytes who may come" *(ibid).* In the third century, R. Johanan and R. Eleazar separately deduced from different verses that "the Holy One, Blessed be He, exiled Israel among the nations only in order to increase their numbers with the addition of proselytes" (Pes. 87b). R. Eleazar also said: "Whoever befriends a proselyte is considered as if he created him" (Gen. R. 84:4). There are numerous other statements which praise proselytes (e.g., Tanḥ. Lekh Lekha 6; Num. R. 8:9; Mid. Ps. 146:8). A tendency to increase the honor of the proselytes and to glorify conversion can perhaps be found in the tradition which traces the origins of such great personalities as R. Meir, R. Akiva, Shemaiah, and Avtalyon to proselytes. They were descendants of such wicked men as Sisera, Sennacherib, Haman, and Nero (Git. 56a, 57b; Sanh. 96b). The name of R. Akiva's father does not appear explicitly in the Talmud, but *Dikdukei Soferim, ibid.*, 9 (1878), 283 and also Maimonides' introduction to *Mishneh Torah* relate that Joseph, the father of R. Akiva, was a proselyte by conviction. The last of the Babylonian *amoraim,* R. Ashi, said that the destiny of the proselytes had also been determined at Mount Sinai (Shab. 146a). Most of the rabbis of the Talmud observed the tradition: "When a proselyte comes to be converted, one receives him with an open hand so as to bring him under the wings of the Divine Presence" (SER 7; Lev. R. 2:9).

Post Talmudic. During the following era the proponents of the two ruling monotheistic religions—in contrast to polytheism—regarded abandonment of their faith and transfer to another religion as a capital offense. The canons of the Church forbade proselytism and Christian rulers fiercely opposed any tendency to adopt Jewish religious customs. The number of proselytes diminished in Christian countries, and those who endangered their lives by adherence to Israel were generally compelled to flee to lands beyond the bounds of the rule of the Church.

At the commencement of this period, however, during the period of transition from polytheism to belief in One God, Judaism also succeeded in winning the hearts of the upper classes of two peoples, as formerly occurred with the kingdom of *Adiabene. In the fifth century the kings of *Himyar in southern Arabia adopted Judaism, and in the first half of the eighth century the upper classes of the *Khazars. There is no information about Muslim proselytes, but the adoption of Judaism by Christians in Muslim countries was not forbidden, and even common. The sources chiefly mention Christian male and female slaves in the houses of Jews whose owners were enjoined by Jewish law to circumcise them and have them undergo ritual immersion. The *geonim* *Sar Shalom and *Ẓemaḥ Ẓedek b. Isaac were asked about a "gentile woman slave who was conversant with the idolatry of the Christians and was compelled to undergo ritual immersion by her owner," and about "a slave woman who says I am a Jewess, but acts in all respects like a gentile" (*Oẓar ha-Ge'onim,* Yev. 114). They also mention that there are some slaves "who become proselytes immediately and some eventually. Some of these do not want to convert at all; most are such and do not convert but there are some who say: 'Wait until we see your laws and learn them, and we shall convert . . .'" (*ibid.,* 199). It may be assumed that many of these slaves became assimilated into the Jewish community. Sometimes Jews became over-intimate with women slaves and had them undergo ritual immersion for the purpose of proselytism; their children were regarded as full-fledged proselytes. The best known of these cases concerns the Exilarch *Bustanai b. Ḥaninai (*ibid.,* 39–43, 173).

Besides such converts, there were also proselytes from conviction in Christian countries who voluntarily adopted Judaism out of love for Jewish law and about whom only fragmentary information has been preserved. Such proselytes were mainly members of the Christian clergy, whom theological study, and especially comparison of the New Testament with its roots in the Old, brought to Judaism. After becoming proselytes some even attempted to win over souls for their new religion. *Bodo-Eleazar, court deacon of Louis the Pious in the ninth century, escaped to Muslim Spain and wrote sharp polemics attacking Christianity (B. Blumenkranz, in: RHPR, 34 (1954), 401–13). In 1012 the priest Vicilinus in Mainz became a proselyte, and he, too, wrote works to prove from the Bible the correctness of his course and the truth of the religion of Israel. Some scholars consider that his action was the cause of the expulsion of the Jews from Mainz by Emperor Henry II (Aronius, Regesten, nos. 144, 147). From about the same period record has been preserved about a wealthy Christian woman of distinguished family who became a proselyte, settled in Narbonne, and married R. David, a member of the family of the *nasi* *Todros.

One remarkable case of proselytism in the Middle Ages concerns the Norman proselyte *Obadiah (c. 1100), a member of a noble family of Oppido in Lucano, southern Italy. The events that befell him are known from a number of fragments preserved in the Cairo *Genizah.* This proselyte left notes in which he introduces himself by his gentile name Johannes and relates first concerning "the archbishop Andreas, chief priest of the province of Bari . . . in [whose] heart God placed love of the Torah of Moses. He left his land and priesthood, and all his glory, went to the province of Castantinia and circumcised himself. Troubles and evils befell him. He arose and fled for his life because the uncircumcised sought to kill him, and God delivered him from their hands. . . strangers arose after him, saw his deeds, and acted as he had done, and they too entered the covenant of the Living God. This man then went to Egypt and dwelt there until his death. The name of the king of Egypt at that time was Al-Mustanzir . . ." News of the action of Andreas, bishop of Bari from 1062 to 1078, spread throughout Greece and Italy and reached the ears of Johannes while he was a youth. In the first year of his entering the priesthood he had a dream which influenced him to follow in the path of Andreas. In 1102 he was circumcised and began to observe the Sabbath and the festivals, and even wrote pamphlets calling upon all religious people to return to the religion of Israel. The authorities, however, imprisoned him and threatened to kill him unless he repented of his deeds. He succeeded in escaping, arrived in Baghdad, and dwelt in "the home of Isaac b. Moses, head of the Academy." He also visited Jewish communities in Syria, Ereẓ Israel, and Egypt, and wrote the events of his life.

There were also proselytes who remained in Christian countries and apparently succeeded in concealing themselves from the vigilance of the Church by roaming from one country to another. There is also mention of a proselyte family at the time of Jacob *Tam which originated in Hungary and was living in northern France or Germany. The father, Abraham the proselyte, interpreted the rabbinic dictum "Proselytes are as hard for Israel [to endure] as a sore" (Yev. 47b) in favor of proselytes: because they are meticulous in observing the precepts they are hard for the Jews since they recall their iniquities. He and his two sons Isaac and Joseph, engaged in biblical interpretation, taking issue with Christian exegesis, and also criticizing the Gospels and the Christian prayers. A pupil of Jacob Tam, *Moses b. Abraham of Pontoise, tells of a proselyte who used to study "Bible and Mishnah day and night." Six *piyyutim* composed by the *paytan* Josephiah the proselyte who lived in France in the 12th century are known (Zunz, Lit Poesie, 469). Toward the end of the 12th century a proselyte living in Wuerzburg who knew "the language of the priests" (i.e., Latin) but not Hebrew made a copy of the Pentateuch for his own use from "a rejected book belonging to priests." R. Joel permitted this proselyte to act as reader for the congregation.

A talmudist who was a proselyte by conviction sent halakhic queries to *Maimonides, who addressed him in respectful terms: "Master and teacher, the intelligent and enlightened Obadiah, the righteous proselyte," and wrote to him, "You are a great scholar and possess an understanding mind, for you have understood the issues and known the right way." In his letters to this proselyte, Maimonides expresses high appreciation of proselytism and the proselyte: he permits him to pray:

> . . . as every native Israelite prays and recites blessings . . . anyone who becomes a proselyte throughout the generations and anyone who unifies the Name of the Holy One as it is written in the Torah is a pupil of our father Abraham and all of them are members of his household . . . hence you may say, Our God, and the God of our fathers; for Abraham, peace be upon him, is your father . . . for since you have entered beneath the wings of the Divine Presence and attached yourself to Him, there is no difference between us and you. . . . You certainly recite the blessings: Who has chosen us; Who has given us; Who has caused us to inherit; and Who has separated us. For the Creator has already chosen you and has separated

> you from the nations and has given you the Torah, as the Torah was given to us and to proselytes.... Further, do not belittle your lineage: if we trace our descent to Abraham, Isaac, and Jacob, your connection is with Him by Whose word the universe came into being.

(Resp. Rambam (ed. Freimann), no. 42). Concerning the vexations and humiliating words violently addressed to this proselyte by certain Jews, Maimonides writes to him:

> Toward father and mother we are commanded honor and reverence, toward the prophets to obey them, but toward proselytes we are commanded to have great love in our inmost hearts.... God, in His glory, loves proselytes.... A man who left his father and birthplace and the realm of his people at a time when they are powerful, who understood with his insight, and who attached himself to this nation which today is a despised people, the slave of rulers, and recognized and knew that their religion is true and righteous ... and pursued God ... and entered beneath the wings of the Divine Presence ... the Lord does not call you fool [Heb. *kesil*], but intelligent *[maskil]* and understanding, wise and walking correctly, a pupil of Abraham our father ...

(*ibid.*, no. 369). There were proselytes who suffered martyrdom *(*Kiddush ha-Shem)* and even those who became proselytes with this intention. Among those who suffered martyrdom during the massacres of the First Crusade in 1096 was a man whose "mother was not Jewish"; before his martyrdom he said: "hitherto you have scorned me." In 1264 the burning took place at Augsburg of "Abraham, son of Abraham our Father, of Ishpurk, who rejected the gods of the nations, broke the heads of the idols ... and was tormented with severe tortures." This proselyte had conducted a campaign for Judaism among the Christians and attacked the symbols of Christianity. Elegies on his death were written by the great scholars of the generation; *Mordecai b. Hillel ha-Kohen described how the man became a proselyte: "And Abraham journeyed, reaching the Hebrew religion, attached himself to the house of Jacob and cut his foreskin," and related that the words spoken by the proselyte in public against his former religion were the cause of his being burned at the stake: "when he proclaimed his ideas ... in the town, he was taken to the stake." Another elegist spoke of his courage during his life and at his death: "He walked in purity and broke images ... he revealed the glory of the Creator to the nations, denying belief in the crucified one; to martyrdom he walked like a bridegroom to the bride." In 1270 Abraham b. Abraham of France was burned in Wiesenburg. He was a respected monk and fled from his country after he became a proselyte: "he rejected images and came to take refuge in the shadow of the wings of the Living God." In 1275 it was noted that a monk, Robert of Reading, became a proselyte in England.

It is difficult to ascertain with certainty the extent of proselytism in the Middle Ages. The historical sources mention isolated cases only. However, the fact that such cases recurred in every generation, as well as the preachings and admonitions by the heads of Church against *Judaizing and the many regulations and decrees they issued to prevent this danger, testifies to the persistence of the phenomenon, at least to a limited extent. Some scholars regard proselytism as being of quantitative significance also during the Middle Ages and explain the marked anthropological differences between the various Jewish communities, and the resemblance of every community to the ethnic type of its environment, as being due in great measure to the inflow of external ethnic elements which continued at least throughout the first half of the Middle Ages.

With the decline in the number of proselytes by conviction, the fundamental attitude of the medieval Jewish scholars toward proselytism as a phenomenon of profound religious significance did not change, and some of them continued to consider that the purpose of Israel's dispersion among the nations was to gain proselytes. *Moses b. Jacob of Coucy (mid-13th century) explains to his contemporaries that they must act uprightly toward gentiles since "so long as they [i.e., Jews] act deceitfully toward them, who will attach themselves to them?" (*Semag,* Asayin 74). *Isaiah b. Mali di Trani the Younger permits the teaching of the books of the Prophets and the Hagiographa to gentiles, because he regards them as consolation spoken to Israel, "and as a result he [the gentile] may mend his ways" (*Shiltei Gibborim,* Av. Zar., ch. 1).

In Modern Times. The Jewish attitude to proselytism at the beginning of the modern period was inclined to be negative; aspirations to win over people of other faiths to Judaism dwindled. However, the **bet din* has no authority to repudiate proselytes wishing to convert despite the admonitions concerning the gravity of such a step; the *Shulḥan Arukh and the other *posekim* of the period left the laws concerning proselytism in force, but examination of the texts reveals, and at times it is even expressly stated, that it was only a formal duty to accept proselytes, and, indeed, attempts at active conversion were infrequent. However, isolated cases of conversion continued to occur. Proselytes were associated with the Hebrew press in *Amsterdam, in various cities in Germany, in *Constantinople and *Salonika (see A. Yaari, in: KS, 13 (1936/37), 243–8). A Christian who visited Jerusalem in 1494–96 relates that he found there two monks "who had three years before gone over from the Christian faith to the Jewish religion" (*Die Pilgerfahrt des Ritters Arnold von Harft* (ed. by E. V. Groote (1860), 187). On the other hand, there is no real evidence to indicate attempts at actual conversion or proselytizing activity in the "Jewish heresy" (see *Judaizers) that was reported in the Orthodox Church in the principality of Moscow at the end of the 15th and beginning of the 16th century.

R. Solomon *Luria warned against receiving proselytes, and the Jewish councils of Lithuania and Moravia even threatened to impose severe penalties on anyone who began to proselytize or gave protection to converts. The reason for this in part stemmed from the fear of the consequences and dangers this activity entailed, since it was severely prohibited by the authorities. The Jewish communities in Poland and Lithuania were more than once obliged to clear themselves of the charge of proselytizing, and it is not always clear whether this was the result of a false accusation by agitators or of the prevalent public opinion in regard to actual occurrences.

When Lutheranism began to spread in Poland in the 16th century, many who inclined to "reforms" were accused by the Catholics of "Judaizing." In 1539 an old woman of 80, Catherine *Weigel, the wife of a citizen of Cracow, was burned at the stake for having embraced Judaism; the clarification of her case took ten years. Before she perished she said: "God had neither wife nor son ... we are His children and all who walk in His ways are His children." Jews were falsely accused of smuggling proselytes into Turkey, and an official investigation of this matter took place in Lithuania causing great harm to the Jews of that country. Nevertheless, it appears that most Jews not only refrained outwardly from engaging in proselytizing activities as the result of external pressures and penalties, but the attitude of Judaism itself in that period formed an important factor. The Jews increasingly withdrew from the outside world; the difference between Judaism and the other faiths was regarded as an inherent, radical distinction between two unbridgeable worlds with scarcely any points of contact. The general tendency of that entire period is expressed in the words of Solomon Luria: "Would that the seed of Israel continue to stand fast and hold its own among the nations throughout the days of our exile and no stranger be added to us who is not of our nation."

With the relative toleration that began to prevail in the ruling circles and among intellectuals in the 17th century, especially in Western Europe, the negative attitude to Christianity among Jews diminished. There was a growing tendency not to regard Christianity as an idolatrous religion but to look upon its adherents as Noachides (see *Noachide Laws) who are absolved from the belief in absolute monotheism. Such a view left no room for conversion efforts to bring Christians under the wings of the *Shekhinah*. This abandonment of conversionary activity on the part of Jews was thus given a theoretical, intellectual basis. However, individual proselytes continued to find their way to Judaism by their own inner conviction. At the end of the 16th century a pious Christian who embraced Judaism on his own initiative is known (see Germanus, Moses). In 1716 two Christian women were put to death in *Dubno because they became Jews; in 1738 the naval officer Alexander *Voznitsyn was publicly burned to death in Russia for having become a Jew, together with the Jew, Baruch b. Leib, who persuaded him to take this step. The memory of the "*Ger Ẓedek* of Vilna," Count Valentine *Potocki, who was allegedly burned in Vilna in 1746, is preserved in popular folklore. Another notable 18th-century proselyte was the English politician Lord George *Gordon.

The Enlightenment strengthened this inclination to religious contraction. The slogan of religious toleration discouraged propaganda activities among the different faiths. The *maskilim* pointed with pride to the resemblance between the principles of Enlightenment and the aims of Judaism—which, in their opinion, were tolerance. Emphasis on Jewish tolerance and abandonment of all active proselytizing became a fixed principle in modern Jewish *apologetics. This apologetical attitude even influenced study of the past, and historical accounts tended to ignore that active Jewish proselytizing had occurred, as if Judaism had never desired to make converts. There was no change from the psychological point of view in the self-defensive attitude of Judaism even after it had been granted a status of juridical equality with the other religions of the state. Even though no legal obstacles now prevent proselytizing little attempt has been made to propagate conversion.

A certain number of proselytes came from the sects of the Sabbath Observers in Russia (see *Judaizers; *Somrei Sabat), who adopted a number of Jewish customs and finally went over to Judaism completely. Others embraced Judaism because of an experience or religious conviction, but chiefly it was the result of unhampered social contacts that ended with intermarriage (see also *San Nicandro).

[EH/ED.]

Recent Trends. Whereas in some countries of the Diaspora, particularly England and South Africa, there was a distinct tendency to adopt more stringent regulations for the acceptance of proselytes in the Orthodox community, it was generally appreciated that a greater leniency could be permitted in the State of Israel, since the prospective proselytes, most of whom were either partners in, or the children of, mixed marriages, would become much more integrated in the Jewish people than would be likely in the Diaspora. Despite this the rabbinical authorities were slow to alleviate the difficulties in the way of applicants for proselytization. They normally insisted on a year's postponement of consideration after making application, and on the ability and undertaking of the candidate to adhere to the requirements of Orthodox Judaism. From 1948 to 1968, 2,288 proselytes were accepted by the rabbinical courts of Israel, out of a total of 4,010 who applied. A tendency toward leniency became more pronounced at the beginning of the 1970s as a result of two factors. One was the expectation of an increased immigration from Soviet Russia where, owing to prevailing circumstances, intermarriage had taken place on an unprecedented scale; and the other was the situation created by the amendment to the Law of Return adopted by the Knesset in 1970. Two provisions made the need for an acceleration of proselytization urgent. The first was that the law was extended to include the partners, children, and grandchildren of mixed marriages who were not Jews according to *halakhah*, and the second that, whereas in Israel only those converted in accordance with *halakhah* were registered as Jews, in the case of immigrants, conversion by Reform and Conservative rabbis was accepted by the civil authorities for these immigrants to be registered as Jews. The resulting anomaly, that these non-Orthodox proselytes were regarded as Jews by the civil authorities while their conversion was not accepted by the Orthodox rabbinate, which was the only legal body determining personal status, had to be reduced as much as possible. In 1971 the Ministry for Religious Affairs, for the first time, established schools for prospective proselytes in Israel, at the Orthodox kibbutzim of *Sa'ad and *Lavi, where candidates may undergo an intensive course in Judaism.

There have also been a number of instances of the conversion of Muslims to Judaism (see A. Rotem, in: *Maḥanayim*, no. 92 (1964), 159).

In 1955 a World Union for the Propagation of Judaism was established in the belief that the time had come for Jews to undertake conversionist activity, and it published a brochure, *Jedion*. There was, however, little response to this suggestion from the public, and some of the steps taken in that direction, particularly among the *Chuetas, proved abortive.

See also *Jew. [L.I.R.]

In the U.S. In 17th-century colonial America Jewish slaveholders, following ancient custom, converted their slaves to Judaism. A number of Negro Jewish congregations in the United States are made up, in part, of the descendants of these early proselytes. During the first quarter of the 18th century a community of German Baptists, in what is now Schaefferstown, Pennsylvania, voluntarily "Judaized." They observed dietary laws and the Sabbath, built a "schul" and a home for their *ḥazzan* from rough logs, and in 1732 laid out a cemetery. The community lasted from about 1720 to 1745. The cemetery—now destroyed—was still intact in 1885; the home of the *ḥazzan* still stood in 1926 but was destroyed later.Whether or not these "Judaizers" actually became Jewish proselytes is uncertain.

The earliest well-known U.S. proselyte was a Quaker, Warder *Cresson, who became U.S. consul in Jerusalem in 1844. There, in 1848, he converted and assumed the name of Michael Cresson Boaz Israel. His American wife divorced him and he then married a Palestinian Jewess. He was a prominent member of the Jerusalem Sephardi community and is buried on the Mount of Olives.

The first incorporated Jewish missionary society in modern times, the United Israel World Union (U.I.W.U.), was established in New York City in 1944 by the journalist David Horowitz. Groups of U.I.W.U. proselytes have their own congregations in Wilbur, West Virginia, and West Olive, Michigan. Another such missionary society, the Jewish Information Society of America, was founded in Chicago in 1962. U.S. Reform Judaism has maintained that Jews have an obligation to teach their religion to all mankind and to attract like-minded non-Jews into the Jewish community. This theoretical determination was followed by the establishment in 1951 of a Committee on the Unaffiliated, by the Central Conference of American Rabbis, to develop "practical means for extending the influence and acceptance of the Jewish religion." The Conservative rabbinate declined to undertake such efforts, although it accepted prospective converts. The Orthodox remained extremely reluctant to accept converts, making stringent demands of all prospective candidates.

Reports from 785 U.S. congregational rabbis in 1954 regarding conversions to Judaism in the United States showed that approximately 3,000 persons were then being converted annually to Judaism. The number increased yearly. In 95% of the conversions, an impending or existing marriage to a Jew was involved; female proselytes outnumbered males five to one. [D.M.E.]

Non-Orthodox Views. Reform rabbis have insisted upon a training in Judaism and the reading of books as prerequisites for conversion. However, in conflict with the traditional Jewish attitude they have stressed the importance of the declaration of faith by the convert, disregarding the ritual aspects of conversion to Judaism (*tevilah,* and in the case of male converts, circumcision). In 1892 the Central Conference of American Rabbis (C.C.A.R.) decided that any Reform rabbi in conjunction with two colleagues could accept as a convert any person without any initiatory rite, and also published manuals for guiding their rabbis in regard to conversion. Nor did Reform follow the *halakhah* with regard to children—children of converted parents born prior to their conversion are considered Jews if the parents declare they will raise them as Jews. With regard to children of school age their confirmation at the end of their schooling is considered the ceremony of their official entry into Judaism. Children past confirmation age are considered adults, and have to undergo instruction prior to conversion.

The Conservative movement has always officially upheld the *halakhah* as regards the ceremonies of conversion. They demand that three rabbis be present, but they emphasize the preparation of the proselyte in Jewish sources and texts on Jewish history and customs. In 1970 the Rabbinical Assembly committee on Jewish Law and standards reaffirmed that its members "may not conduct a conversion *ab initio* without *tevilah.*" [Ed.]

Bibliography: B. J. Bamberger, *Proselytism in the Talmudic Period* (1968²); W. G. Braude, *Jewish Proselyting in the First Five Centuries* (1940); and D. M. Eichhorn (ed.), *Conversion to Judaism: A History and Analysis* (1965); JSOS, 16 (1954), 299–318. H. Graetz, *Die juedischen Proselyten im Roemerreiche*... (1884); A. Bertholet, *Die Stellung der Israeliten und der Juden zu den Fremden* (1896); I. Lévy, in: REJ, 50 (1905), 1–9; 51 (1906), 1–31; Juster, Juifs, 1 (1914), 253–90; A. S. Herschberg, in: *Ha-Tekufah,* 12 (1920/21), 129–48; 13 (1921/22), 189–210; I. Lévy, in: *Ha-Goren,* 9 (1922), 5–30; G. Rosen, *Juden und Phoenizier*... (1926); M. Guttmann, *Das Judentum und seine Umwelt,* 1 (1927), 43–97; S. Bialoblocki, *Die Beziehungen des Judentums zu Proselyten und Proselytentum* (1930); Ẓ. Kasdai, *Ha-Mityahadim* (1930²); A. Ẓ. Markus, *Le-Toledot Dat Naẓerat* (1937, 1950²), pt. 1: *Gerin;* G. Alon, in: KS, 23 (1946/47), 37–42; A. M. Habermann, *Sefer Gezerot Ashkenaz ve-Ẓarefat* (1945), 186–90; S. Assaf, *Mekorot u-Meḥkarim be-Toledot Yisrael* (1946), 143–54; I. A. Seligmann, in: EM, 2 (1954), 546–9; ET, 6 (1954), 21–32, 253–304, 426–49; A. Scheiber, in: KS, 30 (1954/55), 93–98; E. E. Urbach, *Ba'alei ha-Tosafot* (1955), 112, 180, 193f., 265, 388; J. Katz, *Exclusiveness and Tolerance* (1961, repr. 1969).

PROSKAUER, JOSEPH MEYER (1877–1971), U.S. lawyer and community leader. Proskauer, who was born in Mobile, Alabama, was a partner in the law firm Elkus, Gleason, and Proskauer from 1903 to 1923, then served as judge in the Appelate Division of the First Department of the Supreme Court of New York (1923–30). A close associate of Alfred E. Smith, whom he first met through his political activities for the Citizens Union in New York, Proskauer served with Belle *Moskowitz and Robert *Moses on the non-Tammany faction of the "War Board" which helped Smith plan his gubernatorial campaigns, and later worked closely with Smith in his 1928 presidential campaign. In 1935 Proskauer served on the New York City Charter Revision Commission.

Early in the Nazi regime, he joined the *American Jewish Committee. He became its president in 1943 on the platform "Statement of Views with Respect to the Present Situation in Jewish Life," prepared by him, Irving *Lehman, Samuel I. *Rosenman, and George Z. *Medalie, which proposed free Jewish immigration into Palestine and an international trusteeship status but opposed a Jewish state. From October 1947, however, the committee publicly supported creation of a Jewish state in the form proposed by the UN Special Commission on Palestine. Proskauer led it in the thrust for a Jewish state. Elected essentially as an anti-Zionist, his 1948 presidential address, "Our Duty as Americans—Our Responsibility as Jews," marked his complete commitment to political Zionism. The desire to find a common Jewish front on settlement of the Palestine question and the need for continued support from the U.S. Jewish community for the committee's primary interest in Jewish defense probably contributed to Proskauer's change of direction. In his *Segment of My Times* (1950), he describes his pre-1943 anti-Zionist stand as based on instinctive opposition to a state identified with a religion; once he began to study the problem as committee president, he found that the U.S. form of national allegiance he was committed to could not apply in Eastern Europe, where Jews were accorded only partial rights. He thus came to believe that a state in which they could be free was essential. Proskauer remained committee president until 1949. He had served as consultant to the U.S. delegation to the 1945 UN Conference in San Francisco. Proskauer returned to private law practice as senior member of Proskauer, Rose, Goetz, and Mendelsohn. He was chairman of the New York State Crime Commission in 1951–53 and also served as director of the National Refugee Service.

Bibliography: S. Halperin, *Political World of American Zionism* (1961), index. [Ed.]

PROSKUROV (today **Khmelnitzki**), city in Kamenets-Podolski oblast, Ukrainian S.S.R. In 1765 there were 750 Jews in the city who paid poll tax; by 1847 the number had risen to 3,107. With the expansion of the city toward the end of the 19th century, the Jewish population increased, reaching 11,411 (50% of the total population) in 1897. With the retreat of Ukrainian troops before the Red Army in February 1919, Proskurov suffered one of the most vicious pogroms of the civil war period. Units of local Communist forces, both Ukrainians and Jews, rebelled and attempted to gain control of the railroad station. On the failure of the attempt, Semosenko, hetman of the Ukrainian troops stationed in the city, gave orders to slaughter all the Jews. On February 15th Semosenko's forces marched into the city, methodically killing every Jew they could find. A local priest who begged the soldiers to stop was killed at the door of his own church. Three and a half hours after the soldiers had entered the city, a telegraphed order came from headquarters, calling a halt to the slaughter, but by then 1,500 people had been murdered and thousands injured. Despite the demands made by representatives of the Jewish community to the *Petlyura government, Semosenko was never punished. There were 13,408 Jews (42% of the population) in Proskurov in 1926, but Jewish communal life has declined under Soviet rule. With the German invasion of Russia in the summer of 1941, Proskurov's Jews were herded into a ghetto and murdered; the last on Nov. 30, 1942. The 1959 census recorded 6,200 Jews (10% of the total population). In 1970 there was no synagogue but kosher poultry was available.

Bibliography: *The Pogroms in the Ukraine* (1927), 58–61, 176–95; E. Tcherikower, *Di Ukrainer Pogromen in Yor 1919* (1965), 118–60; B. West, *Be-Ḥevlei Kelayah* (1963), 124. [Y.S.]

PROSODY, HEBREW. This article is a survey of the history of Hebrew poetic forms from the Bible to the present time. The entry is arranged according to the following outline:

Introduction
- The Variety of Formal Systems
- The Specific Nature of Hebrew Literary History
- The Major Periods of Hebrew Prosody
  - Post-Biblical Poetry
  - The Rhymed Piyyut
  - The Spanish Tradition
  - Italy
  - The Area of Ashkenazi Jewry
  - The East
  - Haskalah
  - The Period of "Revival"
  - "Classical" Verse in Israel
  - Free Verse

Some Principles of Biblical Verse
- Parallelism
- Rhythm
- Sound

The Classical Piyyut
- The Formal Period
- The Structure of One Cycle
- Forms of Composition
  - An Undivided Poem
  - Regular Strophic Structure
  - Pattern Poems
  - Free Strophic Forms
- Rhyme
  - The Origins of Rhyme in European Poetry
  - The Major Norm: The Discontinuous Rhyme
  - Language and Rhyme
  - The History of Kallirian Rhyme
  - Other Kinds of Rhyme
- Rhythm

Medieval Hebrew Poetry in Spain
- Kinds of Verse
- The Hebrew Quantitative Meter
  - The Basis of Hebrew Quantitative Meters
  - Regular Meters
  - Variegated Meters
    - Alternating Meters
    - Changing Meters
  - The Meters Used in Hebrew Poetry
  - Verse Endings
  - Rhythm
- Girdle Poems
- Other Metrical Principles Used in Strophic Poems
- Rhymed Prose
- Rhyme in Medieval Poetry
  - Terminal Rhyme
  - The Rule of Maximum
  - "Feminine" Rhyme
- The Dispersion of the Hebrew Terminal Rhyme

Hebrew Poetry in Italy

Haskalah
- The Syllabic System of Versification in Hebrew

The Modern Period
- The Historical Setting
- The Two Dialects of Modern Hebrew
- Accentual Syllabic Meter in Hebrew
  - Types of Meters
  - Definition of Meter
  - Rhythmic Variation
- Limited Free Verse: the "Ternary Net"
- Free Verse
- Rhyme in Modern Poetry
  - The Basic Norm of the Exact Rhyme
  - Secondary Norms
    - The Numeric Norm
    - The Historical Factor
    - The Morphological Norm
    - Three Criteria of the Rhyming Norm
  - The Relativity of the Morphological Norm
  - Minimum and Maximum
  - A Comparative Perspective
  - Rhyme in the Ashkenazi Pronunciation
  - "Modernistic" Rhyme
  - The "Inexact" Rhyme

Summary
- A Pan-Historic Synopsis of Hebrew Prosodic Systems
- The Major Systems of Hebrew Rhyme

INTRODUCTION

Hebrew poetry throughout the ages has used many forms of verse, rhyme, sound patterns, and strophic structure which changed from period to period, often from country to country, and from genre to genre. Since the close of the Bible, an enormous number of Hebrew poems have been written in Palestine and throughout the Diaspora, most of them following strict forms which were often quite complex and elaborate. To date no history of these forms has been published and while for the major periods some central concepts are known, they are usually framed in normative terms. The following survey should therefore be considered merely as a tentative outline.

The term "form," used here in a limited sense, refers to all poetic patterns which employ sound elements for the organization of the language material of a poem, such as rhyme, acrostic, meter, stanza, and other principles of composition. The term "poem" here refers to any text composed in such forms and does not necessarily imply aesthetic values in a modern sense. In the Middle Ages thousands of Hebrew texts, written as liturgy, chronicles, rhymed letters, dedications, etc., used the same formal norms employed in works which could be classified from a modern or aesthetic point of view as "poetic."

Of the few ancient literatures that have continued uninterruptedly throughout the ages, Hebrew poetry is the most variegated and versatile in its forms, due to its permanent creativity and to its interaction with different systems of language and poetry: Arabic, Italian, German, Russian, Yiddish, English, and others. The pronunciation of Hebrew, as well as the norms of writing, have undergone considerable changes during the wanderings of the centers of this literature. On the other hand, there were strong tendencies of continuity and conservatism in Hebrew forms and poetic genres, as well as in the language itself.

Unlike other languages, Hebrew, as a semi-"dead" tongue, has never changed the core of its vocabulary, or the written form of its words, its basic morphology, certain patterns of syntax and of idiomatic formulations, or the fundamental framework of its historical, semantic, and mythological allusions. Hebrew poems separated by a time span of a thousand years are from the point of view of their language comparable, and may be intelligible to the same reader. The major changes in the language (insofar as this survey) occurred in the field of pronunciation, but even these did not alter the basic form of the written word. However, due to its interaction with a variety of foreign prosodic and aesthetic norms, most known systems of verse have been created in Hebrew over the past two thousand years.

The Variety of Formal Systems. The following prosodic systems are found in Hebrew poetry: (1) a purely *accentual* poetry with a free variation of the verse units (primarily in the Bible); (2) a meter based on a regular *number of accents* (in post-biblical poetry); (3) a meter based on the *number of words* (in the major tradition of liturgy); (4) a *quantitative* meter based on the opposition of short and long syllables (especially in medieval Spain and Italy); (5) a *syllabic* meter (in Italy since the Renaissance and in Central and Eastern Europe in the 19th century); (6) an *accentual-syllabic* system (in modern poetry in Eastern Europe, Israel, and the U.S.); (7) an *accentual meter with restricted syllabic freedom,* influenced by the verse of Russian modernism (in Israel poetry since World War I); (8) a variety of *free verse* forms, based largely on a rhythm of phrase groups (which evolved in Europe in the 1920s during the vogue of Expressionism and in Israel since the 1950s under the impact of English imagism).

The earliest known systematic use of rhyme in poetry was invented in Hebrew sometime between the fourth and the sixth centuries C.E. It grew out of a cluster of principles of repetition, based on semantic, morphological, and sound elements. During its long history, Hebrew verse passed through a gamut of rhyme norms: terminal or accentual, continuous or discontinuous, grammatical or sound-autonomous, based on suffixes or on the lexical morpheme, using word repetition or excluding it. The same kind of variety runs through the rhyme patterns, strophic forms, and through the principles of composition of a poem.

The Specific Nature of Hebrew Literary History. A study of the changes in the forms of Hebrew verse should take into account the peculiar nature of its history. A Hebrew poet, regardless of his time, was at the crossroads of three lines of development. (1) There was the historical factor common to all literatures: the tension between synchrony and diachrony, i.e., trends of the poet's generation as juxtaposed to norms of the immediate past as well as classical works. The other two factors are specific to the geographic and sociological situation of the Hebrew writer: (2) the influence of Hebrew poetry written in other countries; (3) the impact of non-Hebrew poetry of his own time and place.

The tension between the three systems, of which the Hebrew poet was aware, was of primary importance to the history of Hebrew poetic forms. Quite often cardinal differences existed between the three. Thus the 13th-century Hebrew poets in Rome wrote in the strophic forms of Byzantine Ereẓ Israel (canonized long before any Italian language existed) in which words rather than syllables were counted and in which each rhyme had multiple members but did not alternate with other rhymes. But they were confronted with two other poetic systems as well: contemporary Italian poets used stanzas with alternating rhymes and syllabic meters; the Hebrew poets in Spain used a purely quantitative versification mostly without any strophic forms. It took time until Hebrew poets in Italy changed their poetic system and, typically enough, they adapted quantitative meters (developed in Spain in genres of Hebrew secular poetry) to write Hebrew strophic poetry in the Italian sonnet form. Similar dilemmas faced Jewish poets in other generations and countries.

A Jewish poet was closer to each of the three traditions than poets usually are when experiencing influences of a foreign literature. Thus, the impact of Hebrew poetry written in other countries was enhanced by the closeness of the language and the mobility of men of letters and of written and printed texts. The influence of aesthetic norms dominant in other languages was particularly strong, in spite of traditional Hebrew conservatism, because most Hebrew poets did not speak primarily Hebrew, but were intimately acquainted with other languages which they read and used in everyday life. In many cases they knew at least one more Jewish language and one or two foreign languages, e.g., Arabic and Spanish (in Christian Spain), or Yiddish and Italian (in 16th-century Venice), or Yiddish and Russian (in 19th-century Eastern Europe), or Yiddish, Russian, and English (in America since the late 19th century). Shifts in the forms of Hebrew poetry, whether gradual or drastic, were wrought by such factors as the influence of literary authorities, changes in the relationship to another culture, or changes in the system of genres of Hebrew writing itself. Such changes were usually accompanied by a sudden leap from one way of writing to another, brought about by a realization of a potential influence from one of the three above-mentioned directions.

The influences, however, were implemented neither automatically nor immediately. There was a strong awareness of the peculiar Hebrew tradition and there usually was neither eclecticism nor chaos of forms. Forms created under the influence of one culture were transposed by Hebrew poetry into the domain of quite a different foreign culture; e.g., (1) quantitative meters, developed in Spain under Arabic influence, were used for centuries in Christian Europe where no such meters had been employed; (2) syllabic versification, developed in Italy, dominated 19th-century Hebrew poetry in Germany and Russia where such meters were no longer used. Even adaptations of poetic elements and themes from other literatures were not automatically introduced in their original forms.

Moreover, there was not necessarily an acceptance of a whole system of forms from the influencing source, but quite often a reconciliation, or a readjustment, of several traditions. Thus (1) *Immanuel (b. Solomon) of Rome combined the form of the Italian sonnet with the Hebrew-Spanish quantitative meter which was of Arabic origin; (2) Italian strophic forms were used for several centuries with their original rhyme patterns but without the requirement of stress accord, which is compulsory in Italian rhyme.

Foreign influences on Hebrew poetry were not necessarily contemporaneous, e.g., while accentual-syllabic versification was introduced into Hebrew under Russian influence, it occurred only toward the end of the 19th century when this metrical system began to fall into disuse in Russian poetry. These influences should also not be considered as organic transplantations or imitations of a literary trend or poetic school. Belated as such an impact may have been, it was not necessarily accepted in all its aspects. Thus, Judah Leib *Gordon, though influenced by his Russian contemporary Nekrasov as to theme, genre, and even tone of language, did not accept the Russian verse system; the poetry of Abraham *Shlonsky of the 1920s and 1930s was strongly influenced by the imagery of Russian futurism, but in meter it was as classical as the verse of Pushkin. On the other hand, many Hebrew poets were very much aware of the relativity of prosodic systems. They knew how to use diverse, and sometimes even opposing, systems for different genres (such as religious and secular poetry) or for different languages (especially in the case of bilingual poets, such as Elijah Baḥur *Levita and J. L. *Gordon). Despite these complex circumstances and the great body of rhymed and versified Hebrew texts, the varying norms of Hebrew poetry can be described exactly, since in most ages these norms were conventional rather than individual and constituted a firm part of the language of Hebrew verse. The history of these forms epitomizes the worldwide scope of Hebrew poetry; the tensions between tradition and openness which were basic to its evolution; and the symbiotic, but autonomous, nature of Hebrew culture throughout the ages.

The Major Periods of Hebrew Prosody. The peculiar nature of Jewish history does not permit the development of Hebrew poetic forms to be divided into pure historical "periods," but rather into "areas," determined by a combination of historical, geographic, and generic factors. Since the close of the Bible, the following major areas of Hebrew poetic traditions may be distinguished:

(1) Post-Biblical Poetry. This is a rather amorphous area consisting of several distinct trends: *Wisdom poetry (*Ben Sira), the poetry of religious sects, the formulation of the basic prayers, and the beginnings of liturgy. A variety of rhythmic formulae, occasional rhyme, patterns of sound, and parallelism were widely used, but no established formal system of any kind can be discerned.

(2) The Rhymed Piyyut. Created in Byzantine Ereẓ Israel sometime between the fourth and the sixth centuries C.E., the rhymed *piyyut* comprehends some clearly defined poetic genres which have specific functions in Jewish liturgy. Fundamental to it are large poetic cycles of a complex structure in which the poems use strophic patterns and obligatory rhyme. This kind of *piyyut* spread to the East (Babylonia and Egypt) and to Italy and Ashkenaz (the German Rhine area). A vigorous strain in this tradition, which used the difficult "Kallirian" rhyme, flourished in the tenth century and determined the formation of the Italian and Ashkenazi **maḥzor*. The rhythm crystallized in this evolution was based on a strict number of words.

(3) The Spanish Tradition. It is based on quantitative meters (under Arabic influence), which were used mainly in secular poetry but also in religious genres. Developed in Islamic Spain since the tenth century, it flourished in Christian Spain and Provence until the 15th century and dominated Hebrew poetry in Italy and throughout the Islamic East almost until the present time. Beside the long metrical poems which use one single rhyme, a peculiar strophic tradition evolved in Spain ("girdle" poems), as well as a major genre of rhymed prose *(maqāmat)*.

(4) Italy. Created from the ninth to the 20th century, Hebrew poetry in Italy passed through all possible stages of Hebrew poetic forms: several periods of forms stemming from the Palestinian *piyyut;* Italian strophic patterns; Spanish quantitative meters, which in time were transformed into Italian-like syllabic verse; and even onsets of accentual-syllabic iambs.

(5) The Area of Ashkenazi Jewry. Hebrew poetry was written throughout the Middle Ages by Ashkenazi Jews, at first in Germany and France, then in the Slavic countries. The Palestinian-Italian tradition formed its early stages (10th to 12th centuries). A "weaker" line descending from the Palestinian *piyyut,* followed and continued until modern times, especially in several shorter genres (notably the **seliḥah* and the **kinah*). The forms of this tradition influenced other genres too, such as the Hebrew verse chronicle and some Yiddish poems.

(6) The East. Babylonia, North Africa, and other countries under Islamic rule passed easily from the old *piyyut* forms to the Spanish tradition (similar to Arabic forms). In the 16th century, however, the influence of Turkish song forms may be discerned in the writings of Hebrew poets in the Ottoman Empire (including Ereẓ Israel itself).

(7) Haskalah. Toward the end of the 18th century in Central and Eastern Europe purely syllabic versification was introduced. It continued to be the medium of Hebrew verse until the end of the 19th century.

(8) The Period of "Revival." Since the early 1890s Hebrew poetry in Russia, using the Ashkenazi pronunciation, accepted accentual-syllabic meters and became receptive to all forms of modern European poetry. The system spread immediately from its Russian center to all countries of Hebrew creativity: Germany, Ereẓ Israel, the U.S., etc.

(9) "Classical" Verse in Israel. Accentual-syllabic meters, transferred to the Israel (basically "Sephardi") pronunciation, appeared at the beginning of the 20th century, but started to dominate Hebrew poetry only since the late 1920s. The system spread from its center in Israel to other countries where Hebrew literature was being written (Poland, U.S.S.R., U.S.).

(10) Free Verse. There are two varieties: (1) the Russian influenced strophic and rhymed free verse which is close to regular meters (the so-called Russian "Dolnik"); (2) free irregular verse beginning with some poems by H. N. Bialik (written in period 8), developed in Europe in the 1920s and in Israel and the U.S. especially since the 1950s. These forms followed both foreign examples (English, German) and Hebrew antecedents (notably some of the so-called "biblical" verse of the Period of "Revival").

Approaching the present day, the periods become shorter; different forms, traditions, and influences become more intermingled, frequently coexisting in time, in place, often in one literary journal, and even in the writings of one poet.

SOME PRINCIPLES OF BIBLICAL VERSE

The forms of biblical poetry constitute a world of their own, at the same time, however, a discussion of post-biblical verse must consider the Bible which had an overpowering influence on Hebrew poetry of all periods. The language of the Bible has dominated the language of Hebrew poetry, more often than it did prose, in a variety of poetic conceptions, at least since *Saadiah Gaon (10th century) and almost to the present. Despite this fact, however, post-biblical Hebrew poetry has not relied on biblical rhythm and verse forms. With few exceptions, post-biblical Hebrew prosody at every stage of its development was based on highly formal conventions and it could not have been satisfied with the fluid, though rich orchestration of biblical verse. Nevertheless the patterns of biblical poetry, its syntactic-rhythmical tendencies, its typical word groups, its alliterations, loomed large behind the language of the Hebrew poets in subsequent generations. These patterns did not prevail or mold the new forms, but embellished and imbued Hebrew poems with the power of internal rhythm. The strength of the biblical example was not merely in its sanctified status, but in the very "weakness" of "impurity" which its rhythm had from any normative or classicistic point of view: the intimate, almost inseparable relationship between the semantic, syntactic, and accentual aspects of its rhymic patterns of language.

Though including writings which range nearly over a millennium, the Bible has been viewed by later ages as primarily a unified work with basically a common language. Whatever may have been the developments in phonetics and prosody during the time of its creation, the Bible for post-biblical readers was the canonized text with its system of stresses, intonation marks, and vocalization. In this survey of post-biblical poetry the major principles of biblical verse, as seen from the point of view of a reader of later times, shall merely be mentioned and illustrated.

Parallelism. The foremost principle dominating biblical poetry is parallelism. Usually two versets (sometimes three or even four) are parallel to each other in one or several aspects. The parallelism may be either complete or partial; either of the verset as a whole or of each word in it; of words in the same order or reversed. It may be a parallelism of semantic, syntactic, prosodic, morphological, or sound elements, or of a combination of such elements. In most cases there is an overlapping of several such heterogeneous parallelisms with a mutual reinforcement so that no single element—meaning, syntax, or stress—may be considered as competely dominant or as purely concomitant. The parts of the parallelism may be equal or unequal in their size or form; they may be related to each other in a variety of ways: synonymous, antithetic, hierarchic, belonging to a category of some kind, etc. The principles of the parallelism used may change from verse to verse. The basis of this type of rhythm may be described as semantic-syntactic-accentual. It is basically a free rhythm, i.e., a rhythm based on a cluster of changing principles. Its freedom, however, is clearly confined within the limits of its poetics. The following is an example of a rather ordered type:

הַאֲזִינוּ הַשָּׁמַיִם וַאֲדַבֵּרָה   וְתִשְׁמַע הָאָרֶץ אִמְרֵי־פִי.
יַעֲרֹף כַּמָּטָר לִקְחִי   תִּזַּל כַּטַּל אִמְרָתִי,
כִּשְׂעִירִם עֲלֵי־דֶשֶׁא   וְכִרְבִיבִים עֲלֵי־עֵשֶׂב.

Give ear, o, ye heavens, and I will speak;
  And hear, O earth, the words of my mouth.
My doctrine shall drop as the rain,
  My speech shall distil as the dew,
As the small rain upon the tender herb,
  And as the showers upon the grass
(Deut. 32:1–4).

There are 3:3 stresses in the first two pairs of versets, and 2:2 stresses in the last pair. But syntactically the last two pairs are linked. The words הַאֲזִינוּ ("give ear"), and וְתִשְׁמַע ("hear") are synonymous in meaning though not in morphology; "I will speak" and "the words of my mouth" are not synonyms, but their meanings are parallel. "Heavens" and "earth" are parallel by opposition. "Rain" and "dew" both express fruition by water, but one is strong and the other is subtle, these are two poles of one scale. There is also a concatenation of the three parts: versets 3 and 4 unfold the theme of the first pair ("the words of my mouth"); versets 5 and 6 develop the images of 3 and 4. But the versets of the last pair are parallel only to one member of the previous pair ("the rain" or "the dew").

The parallelism of meaning in the last four versets is chiastic: the water is strong (3)—weak (4)—weak (5)—strong (6). In the last pair דֶשֶׁא and עֵשֶׂב are on one level, but שְׂעִירִים and רְבִיבִים, though morphologically alike, are quite different in degree. Some additional devices of rhythm and sound reinforce the effect of this passage.

Rhythm. If the equivalent meaning or syntactic pattern of parallel versets draws the reader's attention to the parallelism and its reinforcing quality, it is the rhythmical structure proper which embodies it. The major rhythmic element is stress. The rhythm is accentual, but the number of stresses in each verset is not necessarily fixed or permanent. There may be an exact repetition: 3:3 stresses, or a freer relationship: 3:4, as well as changing numbers throughout the poem. The specific numerical relationship is however important. The numbers are quite often equal or similar. Moreover, whenever there is freedom it is confined within fixed boundaries. Each verset is usually a phrase, a basic syntactic and logical unit, consisting of 2, 3, or 4 stressed words. The smallness and compactness of the verset lends each stress conspicuous force. The condensed, laconic nature of biblical Hebrew also contributes to the prominence of each word within the line, the more so when it is reinforced by the parallel verset. The versets are static, independent units, well balanced against each other. This is supported by the nature of biblical syntax which favors parataxis to the subordination of clauses and phrases.

Is stress the only sound element determining biblical rhythm? For many generations scholars have argued over the "secrets" of biblical prosody; there have been attempts to correct or rewrite the text so that it might conform with pseudoclassic ideas of rhythm which require strict numbers of some kind: regularized "feet," equalized hemistichs, or stanzas of recurring numbers of lines. Such attempts seem pointless today since no exact regularity of any kind has been found and since rhythm need not be based on strict numerical regularity. Considering the rhythm to be based on free variation, it is clear, however, that stress is not enough to describe the effects of biblical rhythm. The number of unstressed syllables between two stressed ones, though not fixed in the sense of modern accentual-syllabic versification, is certainly limited: by rule no two stresses are permitted to follow each other, on the other hand long words have secondary stresses. Thus each stress dominates a group of 2, 3, or 4 syllables; there are 2, 3, or 4 such groups in a verset; and 2, 3, or 4 parallel versets in a sentence. It is a three-stage hierarchy of simple, indivisible, though flexible groups. Within this free framework there are clearly functional specific patterns, such as the so-called "rhythm of elegy" based on an opposition of 3:2 stresses. The rhythm of major stresses is so strong that sometimes it may be the only supporter of the parallelism of two versets, without any actual repetition of meaning or syntax.

Sound. Within this framework of rhythmical parallelism there is a whole gamut of sound repetition and sound patterns, freely distributed, but clearly embellishing the text. Whatever the origins of Hebrew rhyme and puns or sound patterns in later poetry, the later poets were able to draw on a variety of such devices in the Bible. There is: (1) simple alliteration: הוֹד וְהָדָר, חֵן וָחֶסֶד; (2) a chain of one repeated sound: צַדִּיק מִצָּרָה נֶחֱלָץ; (Prov. 11:8); (3) a repetition of the same root which is syntactically justified: אָחוּדָה־נָּא לָכֶם חִידָה ("I will riddle you a riddle," Jud. 14:12), חוּדָה חִידָתְךָ וְנִשְׁמָעֶנָּה ("riddle your riddle and we will hear," *ibid.* 14:13); (4) puns on similar sounding roots: פַּחַד־פַּחַת פָּח ; אִישׁ־אֵשׁ־אֵשֶׁת; אַל תַּחֲרשׁ עַל רֵעֲךָ רָעָה (Prov. 3:29); (5) root rhyming בָּבֶל – בָּלַל (cf. Gen. 11:9), צְדָקָה – צְעָקָה (cf. Isa. 5:7); (6) occasional rhymes in modern sense יֵינָהּ – שֻׁלְחָנָהּ (cf. Prov. 9:4), צֶמַח – קֶמַח (cf. Hos. 8:9), etc.

Rhyme is sometimes obviously linked to the parallel structure, e.g.,

פֶּן־תִּתֵּן לַאֲחֵרִים הוֹדֶךָ/   וּשְׁנוֹתֶךָ לְאַכְזָרִי
פֶּן־יִשְׂבְּעוּ זָרִים כֹּחֶךָ/   וַעֲצָבֶיךָ בְּבֵית־נָכְרִי

Lest thou give thy vigor unto others,
  And thy years unto the cruel;
Lest strangers be filled with thy strength,
  And thy labors be in the house of an alien;
(Prov. 5:9–10).

The two sentences are similar in rhythm (3:2 stresses) and are linked by an anaphora, as well as by parallel syntax, meaning, morphology, and rhyme. Though the symmetry is pervasive and multiple, it is however neither regular nor permanent: the first versets of each line are parallel in meaning as a whole but not in each word; אחרים ("others") and זרים ("strangers") are parallel in morphology and rhyme but not in their syntactical function; וּשְׁנוֹתֶךָ ("thy years") and וַעֲצָבֶיךָ ("thy labors") are not parallel in the same sense as אחרים ("others") and זרים ("strangers"); אכזרי ("the cruel") and בית־נכרי ("the house of an alien") are not synonymous in the language but become so when enforced by this context. In the same way all parallel words rhyme with each other, except for the second word.

This is an extreme example of order; usually the patterns are less symmetrical and the sentence that follows may not have any of the above devices. Rhyme, as it is known at present, i.e., as a regular organizing principle of a poem which is not an internal ornament of a line but links lines together, was created as concomitant to an unequivocal strophic structure and a formalization of poetic patterns.

This occurred centuries later in the Palestinian *piyyut* of *Yannai and Eleazar *Kallir.

THE CLASSICAL PIYYUT

Piyyut (from *paytan* (poet) from the Greek Ποιητής) is the common term applied to a variety of genres of Hebrew liturgical poetry which originated in Ereẓ Israel under Byzantine rule. Some scholars distinguish between *piyyut* and *seliḥah* (a penitential prayer), including under the former all kinds of hymns and under the latter several types of elegies, supplicating or exhortative religious poems. For the purposes of this survey it is convenient to include the entire range of Hebrew religious poetry of the Middle Ages under the general term *piyyut*. The chronological division of the earlier periods of the *piyyut* from a formal point of view is as follows: (1) the so-called beginnings of the *piyyut,* primarily in Ereẓ Israel and in Babylonia from the close of the Bible until the creation of the formal rhymed *piyyut;* (2) the formal period, employing formalized, strophic, and rhymed poems patterned in highly complex *piyyut* cycles, apparently originating in their complete form in Byzantine Ereẓ Israel somewhere between the fourth and sixth centuries C.E. Only the latter will be discussed here.

The Formal Period. Various forms of rhythm, sound patterns, sporadic rhyme, acrostic, and strophic patterns have been developed in biblical literature and during the first centuries of the *piyyut*. But only by an act of formalization were the new complex structures created. Even if it were possible to trace every single device of the formal *piyyut* to earlier examples, there is no precedent to any of the complex structures as a whole. Rhyme, refrain, stanza, etc., whatever had been sporadic, was now formalized and organized in complex cycles of poems, governed by strict rules which set the formal conventions of all poems belonging to a given genre.

In the same way as the period is characterized by the introduction of unequivocal rules of formal structure, differences in genres are marked by differences in form. Moreover, some diversities between poets, or successive generations, or local traditions are marked by minor or major changes both in the complex structures, as well as in the use of particular devices or genres of the *piyyut*.

The large variety of genres, formal differences, and historical changes in these structures does not permit a complete, even schematic, description here. Since the complex structures are determined by the genre, it is preferable to describe the formal structure together with the thematic aspect of each genre, its liturgical function and the particular way of its inclusion in the basic text of the prayer book. The difficulty of such a detailed description is underlined by the present limited knowledge of the history of the *piyyut*. While there are many scattered studies and insights, there is no detailed up-to-date historical description of the whole field. The objective circumstances were a contributing factor to this state of scholarship: tens of thousands of poems and fragments, found in the Cairo *Genizah,* are in the process of being deciphered. These poems, written over many centuries, are by and large undated, often fragmentized or written in a cryptic language, and are either anonymous or only have the first name of the poet who in most cases is unknown from other historical sources. Most of this material is as yet unpublished. On the other hand a considerable number of *piyyutim* was known for centuries because they were included in the prayer book. More and more of them have been published in recent years. Below only the principles of some basic patterns employed in the complex structures will be outlined and only schematic examples of major formal principles will be given.

The Structure of One Cycle. The widespread forms of the older formal *piyyut,* especially the **kerovah* with its varieties and the **yoẓer,* are cycles of a complex nature, e.g., a *kerovah* by Yannai is a superstructure of 9 parts with a permanent set of rules for each. Yannai wrote hundreds of *kerovot*—a different cycle for each week of the triennial cycle of the Torah reading. The structure of each of these poems is governed to the smallest detail by one set of rules. Other poets wrote cycles of poems for the Sabbath, the festivals, and often several different sets of poems for the same purpose, apparently written for the services of different years or different synagogues.

Yannai's *kerovot* are mostly of the *kedushta* type. The *kedushta* is a poetic cycle incorporated in the prayer in which the *Kedushah* is recited. The *kedushta* has a fixed theme for every week based on the weekly biblical portion. The theme and its language are integrated into the poems of the cycle. It consists of the following parts:

(1) A poem to the first benediction of the *Amidah* composed of 3 stanzas of 4 versets each. Every stanza has a separate fourfold end rhyme, linking all its versets. Every verset begins with a separate letter following the order of the Hebrew alphabet; the poem is thus linked by an unfinished acrostic from the letters א to ל. The concluding verset alludes to the first sentence of the weekly portion which follows and introduces a series of biblical sentences in their original form, having neither rhyme nor meter. The biblical passage gives, as it were, authoritative support to the content of the poem. This chain of biblical sentences is linked to a closing stanza of 3 or 4 versets, with the last word of the chain of sentences repeated at the beginning of the closing stanza. The last verset of this stanza is again linked to what follows, alluding to the *Magen Avot* benediction (the second) recited after this poem.

(2) A poem to the second benediction which is similar in its strophic structure to the first poem. It continues the interrupted acrostic (from the letter מ to ת) and uses the last two letters twice in order to fit the 22-letter Hebrew alphabet into a framework of a series of four-verset stanzas (all together 24 versets). This poem too is linked to the weekly portion with the final verset alluding to its second sentence. A chain of explanatory sentences also lead toward a closing stanza in which the final verset anticipates the following benediction, *Meḥayyeh ha-Metim*.

(3) A short poem of 4 stanzas, each starts with a letter which is part of an acrostic of the poet's name ינאי. Every stanza consists of 4 short cola of 2 or 3 words each, rhymed either with a fourfold rhyme or with a twofold rhyme. The poem ends with an allusion to the first word of the *haftarah* which follows, together with an explanatory passage.

(4) A poem of a rather free structure, having no fixed rules for its rhyming though usually consisting of 3 fourfold stanzas. Concluding the first part of the *piyyut,* the poem is marked by the obligatory use of the final word—*Kadosh*.

(5) A poem traditionally called *asiriyyah* because it is composed of 10 stanzas which are linked by an acrostic of the first ten letters of the Hebrew alphabet. The stanzas are rhymed couplets having quite often a large variety of internal rhymes.

(6) A poem consisting of 11 stanzas, each using a separate fourfold rhyme. Every couple of versets is linked to a complete alphabetical acrostic. The poem introduces a group of poems and is preceded by the biblical statement which it discusses. Frequently, the biblical statement or parts of it are interwoven into the poem either as beginnings of the first lines of the poem or of its stanzas.

(7) This part consists of 1 to 3 pattern poems *(rehitim),* each of which has an individual structure, usually of a complex form, which permeates the text in every detail. Variegated and individual in their composition, they follow

a fixed set of rules (described below). Only in this category is the poet allowed to use strictly organized poems without rhyme.

(8) The *silluk*, a kind of free verse poem that introduces the *kedushah*. It has a free structure which varies from *kerovah* to *kerovah* and is richly rhymed in an unrestricted manner. In the poetry of Yannai's follower (or disciple), Eleazar Kallir, the *silluk* developed into a very long, exuberant, richly orchestrated, yet unrestricted poem. Yannai's *silluk*, however, is rather short.

(9) The *Kedushah;* it has neither rhyme, nor strophic structure. In the period of Yannai there was no fixed version as yet, and the poet was free to formulate his *Kedushah* in every cycle anew. It was based on an exegesis and elaboration of the formula *Kadosh, Kadosh, Kadosh (Holy, Holy, Holy).*

The above is a simplified account of a poetic cycle, as described by M. *Zulay. It is impossible to delineate here in detail the forms of other cycles, their liturgical functions, and their development throughout the ages. Each cycle is determined by a combination of certain thematic, verbal, and formal elements. Though the intricate rules for each cycle changed from genre to genre, there was no free combination in each new creation: the basic forms used in these compositions were quite restricted. Some of these basic forms are discussed below:

Forms of Composition. Within a given cycle the form and length of each poem was restricted, depending on its place in the cycle, its use of acrostic, and its strophic form. The following strophic forms existed in the *piyyut:*

(1) AN UNDIVIDED POEM. One single end-rhyme runs throughout the poem *(ḥaruz mavri'aḥ).* At the beginnings of the lines there is a compulsory acrostic which covers the whole Hebrew alphabet, each letter is repeated one or several times; the number of versets being either 22, 44, or 88.

(2) REGULAR STROPHIC STRUCTURE. Each poem is composed of a number of stanzas of a permanent form and length. Every stanza has its own independent rhyme both differing from and not interfering with members of other rhymes: *aaaa bbbb cccc*, etc. The length of stanzas may vary from 2 to 10 versets. A stanza of 4 versets became the major form of the *seliḥah,* especially in the variety created throughout the ages in Ashkenazi Europe. The multiple (fourfold or eightfold) repetition of each rhyme and the lack of rhyme alternation in the rhyming *piyyut* create an effect quite distinct from standard European strophic poetry which uses its rhymes in alternation.

Stanzas may have an additional internal structure and may be molded by means additional to rhyme, primarily meter, acrostic, and the refrain. Thus, in Kallir's *kerovah* to the *Musaf* prayer of the Day of Atonement (in the Ashkenazi prayer book), one of the poem *Essa De'i le-Meraḥok* is based on a stanza of 9 versets. The following is one stanza of the poem:

יַשְׁלְגוּ אָדְמֵי שָׁנִים/ שֶׁל כָּל־יְמוֹת הַשָּׁנִים/ חֲדָשִׁים וְגַם יְשָׁנִים
יַלְבִּנוּ כִּתְמֵי שׁוֹשַׁנִּים/ וְיוּשְׁבוּ לְתַעֲרָם שְׁנוּנִים/ בִּפְלוּל אֲשֶׁר מְשַׁנְּנִים
רַחֲצוּ וְהִזַּכּוּ מֵעִשּׁוּנִים/ לְאִוֶּלֶת מִהְיוֹת שׁוֹנִים/ וְעַל מִבְטָחֵימוֹ שְׁעוּנִים

Each verset has 3 words, 3 versets form a line, each line begins with a letter from the acrostic (in this case it is the end of the poet's name קליר, the י repeated twice) 3 lines form a stanza by means of the particular rhyme which is repeated 9 times.

This particular poem belongs to the *kiklar* (from the Greek κύκλος, cycle) genre, in which there is a refrain like shorter stanza of 3 versets after each regular stanza. There are 3 different refrains in the above poem, alternating between the 7 regular stanzas. In the following general scheme of the poem each verset of the regular stanzas shall be represented by letters from *a* to *g*, according to the rhyme patterns; the refrains by letters *p* to *r;* capital letters represent versets linked by an acrostic:

Aaa	Ddd	Ggg
Aaa	Ddd	Ggg
Aaa	Ddd	Ggg
ppp	ppp	ppp
Bbb	Eee	
Bbb	Eee	
Bbb	Eee	
qqq	qqq	
Ccc	Fff	
Ccc	Fff	
Ccc	Fff	
rrr	rrr	

The poem is organized, as it were, both vertically and horizontally. The triadic principle is dominant throughout: 3 words make a verset, 3 versets a line, 3 lines a stanza, 3 stanzas complete a refrain cycle. The third refrain cycle is however not completed since there are 7 stanzas.

(3) PATTERN POEMS. An unusual kind of formal poem—the pattern poem—was developed in the *piyyut,* especially by Yannai. A pattern of a line elaborated in all its details—syntactic, semantic, morphological, and sound devices—was established in the poem and was then repeated throughout its 22 lines (the number being determined by the acrostic). A great variety of such patterns appear in Yannai's poetry, all in the seventh part of the *kerovah* cycle. The following is an example of a very simple kind:

If you loved who would hate?	אִם אָהַבְתָּה מִי יְשַׂנֵּיא
If you blessed who would curse?	אִם בֵּירַכְתָּה מִי יְאָרֵר
If you fenced who would break out?	אִם גִּדַּרְתָּה מִי יִפְרוֹץ
If you joined who would separate?	אִם דִּבַּקְתָּה מִי יַפְרִיד

Every line is a rhetorical pattern with two fixed and two free words. The initial letter of the first free word depends on the place of the word in the alphabetically arranged poem; this word is a verb in the second person past, and its meaning has a positive connotation. The second free word is opposite in meaning, it has a strongly negative connotation, and is a verb in the third person future.

There are more complex patterns, such as this:

תּוֹלְדוֹת אָהוּב וְשָׂנוּאוּי אָהוּב (ל...) חס וְשָׂנוּאוּי לְמַאֵס
תּוֹלְדוֹת בָּחוּר וּבָזוּי בָּחוּר לְסֶגֶל וּבָזוּי לְסֶגֶר
תּוֹלְדוֹת גְּדִי וְנָמֵר גְּדִי לְרִצּוּי וְנָמֵר לְנִיצּוּי

The story of a loved one and a hated one/loved for respect and hated for neglect
The story of a chosen one and despised one/chosen for virtue and despised for rejection
The story of a lamb and a tiger/a lamb for pleasing and a tiger for strife

Every line consists of two parts, of 3 and 4 words respectively. The first part refers to a story of two personae: one positive, the other negative. The second part elaborates on the first, repeating the two personae and modifying the description of each. The first word is permanent, creating an anaphoric chain ("the story of . . ."); the second word is positive in meaning and is strung on an acrostic; the third word is either a direct or indirect opposite of the second. The other hemistich repeats words (2) and (3) and qualifies them, explaining the reason for the opposition: in what perspective are the personae to be cast. The modifiers do not provide a full explanation, but allude to a biblical text. Both modifiers—words (5) and (7)—are introduced by a preposition of purpose (-ל) and are linked to each other by some kind of rhyme, though the rhyming principle changes throughout the poem. It may be:

a terminal sound rhyme — רְצוּי – נִיצּוּי
or an initial rhyme — עזוז – לעזאזל, סגל – סגר
or a semantic rhyme — זכות – חובה, חיים מות

Since the morphology of most words of the pattern is fixed, in all cases where suffixes are used the rhyme is inevitable, e.g.,

וירא אהובים ויאמל ואבה לאררם
וירא באים ויבעת וביקש לבלעם
וירא גרים ויגר וגמר לגרשם

The meaning of the pattern is: "He saw ("positive personae") and he was frightened (or shocked, or worried, etc.) and he wished (or planned, or hurried, etc.) to curse them (or swallow them, or uproot them, etc.)." All four changing words are linked to the acrostic, the second and the fifth, using plural suffixes, create each a chain of rhymes. In the rhyming chain of the second words there are, however, two exceptions: המון, רבבה —words which designate plurality but do not have the grammatical plural form. Indeed, rhyme is concomitant to grammatical parallelism but is not an absolute necessity. It is possibly the only structured poem in a Yannai cycle which may have no rhyme, if rhyme does not appear with the grammatical form. In most cases there is rhyme, but of a peculiar variety; a morphological rhyme based on a suffix.

The form of the pattern poem is derived from biblical parallelism, but two new principles were applied: (a) the symmetry of two versets was turned into a chain of synonymous sentences; (b) there was a rigorous formalization of the pattern, and all deviations are excluded.

(4) Free Strophic Forms. These are of two kinds: (a) the unrhymed *piyyut,* an exceptional form, fulfilling strict liturgical functions and employing phrases of a formulaic nature; (b) the rhymed free poem, especially the *silluk,* developed by Kallir into a long chain of rhymed versets, with changing rhymes and shifting rhyme principles and without any strophic structure or measure of length. Each rhyme usually has many members (e.g., 25 LAKH+20 MU +18 ŠEV+13 MEM etc.—in Kallir's *silluk* to *Parashat Zakhor*). Besides sound rhyme there may be in the rhyming position semantic rhymes (names of rivers or of time periods), word repetition, words of one root, etc.

Rhyme. The Origins of Rhyme in European Poetry. Rhyme, the great innovation of the *piyyut,* had impact on the history of world poetry. Since not many *piyyutim* were known before the recent studies of the *Genizah* (where thousands of liturgical poems were discovered), and also since the external circumstances of the *piyyut* were obscure and its language almost puzzling, it was not until recently that scholars have become aware of this original contribution of Hebrew poetry. All its aspects however have not yet been fully explored.

It is clear by now that rhyme grew out of the internal development of Hebrew poetry and became in Hebrew a permanent, even obligatory, feature of poetry earlier than in any other language. It is assumed that the principle of rhyme was then transferred to the poetry of the Syriac Church, written in Aramaic (a language closely related to Hebrew, spoken *inter alia* by Jews and written in the same area; i.e., in the Middle East) and through this mediation introduced into Latin poetry and then into all other languages of Europe.

The Major Norm: The Discontinuous Rhyme. Not one, but several kinds of rhyme existed in the *piyyut,* each associated with different strophic forms. The most important was the rhyme of the strophic poems. The basic norm of this rhyme is unknown in the poetry of other languages. Each rhyme of a strophic *piyyut* had to meet two requirements: (1) parallelism of all the sounds of the last syllable, beginning with the consonant preceding the last vowel; (2) parallelism of two consonants belonging to the root of each rhyming word, e.g., in Eleazar Kallir's stanza quoted above (from the *piyyut Essa De'i le-Meraḥok*), the rhyming words are: ŠaNIM — ha-ŠaNIM — ye-ŠaNIM — Šo-ŠaNIM — ŠenuNIM — meŠaneNIM — meiŠuNIM — So-ŠaNIM — ŠenuNIM — meŠaneNIM — meiŠuNIM — Šo-NIM — ŠeuNIM. For the sake of identification capital letters represent the rhyme (all the sounds repeated in all members of one rhyme).

The rhymeme in this system is both terminal and discontinuous. The principle of terminality implies that the rhymeme covers the final syllable of each rhyming member whereas in European or in modern Hebrew poetry its basis is the stressed syllable rather than the final one. In most cases in Hebrew, though, the two overlap, but in instances of discrepancy, stress in the rhyme of the *piyyut* is disregarded. The principle of discontinuity of the rhymeme is unique in rhyming systems and is based on the nature of the Hebrew lexical morpheme, which is discontinuous, consisting merely of consonants. Thus the changes of vowels in such Hebrew words as ŠaVar—ŠeVeR—ŠoVeR cause morphological differences only (Š+V+R is a root meaning "break," the vowels in the example creating: past, noun, present), whereas in English the differences between, e.g., "lever—liver—lover" are lexical.

Though rhyme may have had, as one of its sources the puns on words of one root, rhyme became an autonomous pattern, independent of grammar or word repetition. The discontinuous rhyme is merely similar in structure to the Hebrew root, but is not necessarily based on words of one root. In the above case the rhyme is S+NIM. Between the discontinuous sounds of the rhymeme there appeared changing vowels and even consonants, though usually consonants of the kinds found in the rhymeme (as in our case).

Thus rhyme was based on sound parallelism of the roots of words as well as of their endings. Since a Hebrew root can have no more than three sounding consonants, only one (at most) is given to variation. In stanzas with many rhyme members, it is extremely difficult to find enough words which may meet such requirements, especially when the rhyming words are at short distances from each other. Such rhyming was possible in the *piyyut* due to the difficult "Kallirian" style which allowed, on the one hand, for an almost unlimited number of neologisms and, on the other hand, was abundant in allusions and ellipses which permitted the bringing together of words from quite distant semantic areas.

There are in this system five major forms of rhyme, dependent upon the morphological structure of the rhyming words: (1) if the final syllable is open (e.g., LA), an additional preceding consonant was necessary, e.g., in Kallir's rhyme: GoLA—GeuLA—beGiLA—niGLA—GiLA—veeGLA—aGuLA—meGiLA—veGoLA (the rhymeme is G+LA); (2) if the final syllable is closed (e.g., NIM) and one consonant belongs to a suffix, a root consonant has to be preceded as in the above case with plural endings: ŠaNIM—haŠaNIM—ŠenuNIM, etc. The rhymeme is Š+NIM; (3 and 4) if the final syllable has no root consonants, two discontinuous root consonants are added, e.g., צוּרֵינוּ – נַעֲצְרֶנוּ – יוֹצְרֵינוּ – מְצָרָתֵינוּ —ẒuReNU—naaẒReNU—yoẒReNU—ẒaRateNU (the rhymeme is Ẓ+R+NU). The same holds for a suffix in a closed syllable (e.g., M+R +HEM); (5) if the final syllable is closed and includes no suffix, then it meets in itself both requirements. There is no discontinuity, but the difficulty in finding or inventing rhyme words remains, e.g., the famous stanza which served as a symbol of Kallir's unintelligible (or even cacophonous) style: אץ קוצץ בן־קוצץ / קצוצי לקצץ / בדבור מפוצץ / רצוצי לרצץ / לץ בבוא ללוצץ / פלץ ונתלוצץ / כעץ מחצצים לחצץ / כנץ על צפור לנצץ.

Due to the neologisms, allusions, and the elliptic syntax, this passage is almost unintelligilbe without a commentary. On the other hand, the richness of rhyme and sound effects is obvious.

Using the symbols N — the norm; R — a root consonant; C — a morphological consonant; V — a vowel; +—a possible discontinuity in the sound string, the above five forms of the Kallirian rhyme may be summarized as follows:

$$N_1 = R + RV$$
$$N_2 = R + RVC$$
$$N_3 = R + R + CV$$
$$N_4 = R + R + CVC$$
$$N_5 = RVR$$

A typical case of discontinuous rhyme can be found in the *Hoshanot* read on the first and second days of Sukkot where the poet rhymes 22 times שׁ + עִי (in the poem אֶעֱרוֹךְ שַׁוְעִי) or 22 times שׁ + עוֹת (in the poem אֵל לְמוֹשָׁעוֹת) מוֹשָׁעוֹת – שְׁבוּעוֹת – בְּשַׁוְעוֹת שׁוּעוֹת – שַׁעְשְׁעוֹת etc.

In Yannai's poetry, repetitions of four equivalent or similar words are often found in rhyme (such as–פָּנִים – פָּנִים לְפָנִים–לִיפְנִים). A repeated word obviously meets both requirements of the rhyme norm. But Yannai's pupil Kallir excluded word repetition as a substitute for a strophic rhyme, thus enforcing his difficult norm. Word repetitions remained a device of rhyming, but in a distinct kind of rhyme chain.

Language and Rhyme. The rhyme norm described above was primarily based on sound. Sound was not identical with letter or with the later canonized vocalization. For the sake of rhyme the *qameš* (ָ) and the *pattaḥ* (ַ were equivalent *(a);* also the *ṣere* (ֵ) and *segol* (ֶ) *(e).* The letters ע, ח, ה, א lost their consonantal qualities and in the rhyme of the *piyyut* they are interchangeable and may be either disregarded or counted as consonants. Kallir rhymes אֱלוֹהַּ – לְשְׁלוֹחַ, טְמֵאָה – קִמְעָה, etc., ב and ו seem to be equivalent מַחֲשָׁבָה – שָׁוֶה, אֵבָה – גַּאֲוָה etc. On the other hand, however, consonants with or without a *dageš* rhyme freely with each other, thus פּ פ, e.g., נֶפֶשׁ – טִפֵּשׁ and בּ ב, e.g., מַרְבֵּץ – רוֹבֵץ – מַשְׁבֵּץ – קוֹבֵץ. The equivalence of בּ ב, according to the graphic principle, and that of ב ו, according to the sound principle, established a new equivalence for the sake of rhyme: בּ ו, e.g., Kallir rhymes דְּבָרִים – שְׁוָרִים – גִּבּוֹרִים or רְבִיד – מַעֲבִיד – לְהַאֲבִיד – הִרְבִּיד – דָּוִד

This tradition of equivalents for the sake of rhyme was carried with the *piyyut* into Italy and Franco-Germany. Thus *Meshullam b. Kalonymus of the tenth century (born in Italy, lived in Mainz) rhymes freely בּבו; הַרְבָּה – רָוָה – מְרִיבָה, etc.; Rabbi *Meir b. Baruch of Rothenberg in the 13th century rhymes: טְבוּעִים – מְצֻבִּיעִים – מְשֻׁוּעִים etc.

The History of Kallirian Rhyme. The forms of "Kallirian" *piyyut* spread throughout the Diaspora to the East and to the West. In the East they were superseded in the 10th and 11th centuries by the forms of Arabic versification, especially as adapted by the Hebrew poetry of Spain. In Italy and Franco-Germany they dominated the basic form of the *maḥzor* and do so to the present day. With time, the difficult rhyme norm was simplified: poets dropped the requirement to include two root consonants; rhyme was based on a repetition of the final syllables and became *terminal,* i.e., the standard Hebrew rhyme of the Middle Ages. The process of simplification apparently originated in Ereẓ Israel. (Thus in the ninth century the Palestinian-influenced *piyyut* of southern Italy was based on final syllables only.) But the "strong" norm prevailed again in the 10th century in Babylonia, Italy, and Franco-Germany to be dropped finally toward the end of the 11th century.

Other Kinds of Rhyme. In Yannai's poetry the discontinuous rhyme of the strophic poem is not the only rhyme form. All aspects of the Hebrew word were employed in one form or another for the sake of rhyme: the root, the suffix, the meaning, the sound. In pattern poems it is obvious: not only the final sounds of the parallel words are repeated, but also their meaning and morphological structure. In this genre, however, rhymes, as other kinds of repetition, are tied: they serve the composition of the poem not independently but as a whole cluster. For the later development the untied free rhyme is of primary interest.

The following kinds of rhyme may be discerned: (1) *Sound Rhyme,* a rhyme based on parallelism of sounds especially in the discontinous terminal form described above. (2) *Morphological Rhyme.* This rhyme is based on a suffix. It appears sporadically in the Bible and was used several times at considerable length in the Dead Sea Scrolls and in Ben Sira. It became a legitimate variety of rhyme in non-strophic *piyyutim,* especially in the pattern poems. (3) *Semantic Rhyme.* The relations of the rhyming members are in parallelism of meaning rather than in sound: זמר – רנן אכילה – שתיה etc. Even in a strophic poem, in a chain of sound rhymes, Yannai writes suddenly: סוס – סוס – חמור – חמור rhyming horse with donkey! (4) *Root Rhyme.* Found in the rhyming of words of one root, they do not necessarily have similar sound endings. e.g., צֶדֶק – צַדִּיק – יִצְדַּק – תּוּצְדַּק, or גֵּאִים – גַּאֲוָה – גָּאָה – גֵּאָה . Semantic rhyme and root rhyme are used only occasionally, especially in free strophic forms, such as the *silluk,* or as an additional device within the line. They are of particular interest for the understanding of the origins of sound rhyme which grew in an environment of repetition of any possible aspect of the language. (5) *Word Rhyme.* This rhyme is based on the repetition of one word, usually a key word (life, death, night, war, etc.), throughout a poem. It is older than systematic rhyme and is often employed in *piyyutim*—either in poems of 22 lines or in free strophic patterns.

A distinct kind of *piyyut* uses a word rhyme together with sound rhymes in one single rhyme chain of a long poem, such as Kallir's rhyme of the word טל ("dew"), (in his "prayer for dew" "תפלת טל"), repeated endlessly and interwoven with words ending with same sounds: נטל, טלטל etc.

Rhythm. Biblical rhythm was accentual but with free variation of the numbers of stresses in parallel versets. It seems that later developments led in two directions: (1) The rhythm as found in the poetry of Ben Sira where there are usually 2 versets to a line, with 4 metrical stresses being the optimal limit of a verset. A four-stress pattern is achieved if long words are seen as having two metrical stresses (in a way quite similar to our reading of iambs in modern Hebrew poetry), e.g.,

אחרי תאותיך אל תלך ומחמדותיך המנע
אם תעשה רצון נפשך תשיגך שמחת שונא

This was apparently a tradition of a poetry which sensed an inherent semi-regular meter, approaching syllabic regularity. (The syllabic principle is said to be underlying Syriac poetry of the early Christian centuries.) (2) The tradition of early liturgical poetry which was based on the number of major stresses. Here, too, 4 stresses were a common optimal frame, but these were major stresses, each dominating a word or a group of words. Thus *Yose b. Yose, in his famous *Avodah le-Yom Kippur* has regular stanzas of 4 lines each (determined by a fourfold repetition of each letter in the alphabetical acrostic). Each line consists of two versets (or hemistichs), each verset having 4 major stresses:

אתה כוננת עולם ברוב־חסד / ובו יתנהג עד קץ הימים,
אשר לא ימוט מעון יצורים / ולא ימעד מכבד פשעים וחטאים

in Ben Sira there are often two stresses on one long word; in Yose b. Yose two smaller words are linked by one stress. The number of stresses is similar, but the interpretation of the rhythm in the language is quite different.

Yannai usually has no regular rhythm, except for pattern poems in which the number of words is fixed by the pattern. Neither is any syllabic regularity, similar to the one which is supposed to govern Syriac meters, discernible. But in Kallir's poetry there are already *piyyutim* (beyond the pattern poems) which have a fixed meter, based on the number of words, such as the meter of the *kiklar* analyzed above. In Italy, this meter became obligatory from the ninth century. While this meter may have grown out of earlier stress regularity, it was now strictly based on the graphic division of words, requiring a permanent number of words in each verset. It became the dominant form of the Ashkenazi *piyyut* in the Middle Ages. Some genres had norms peculiar to them, e.g., the *seliḥah* was usually written in Italy and in Franco-Germany in 5-word lines and 4-line rhymed stanzas.

MEDIEVAL HEBREW POETRY IN SPAIN

Hebrew poetry entered a new era with its emergence in Islamic Spain, in the tenth century. The Arabic rules of versification were adopted by the Hebrew verse; quantitative meter became the dominant system in Hebrew poetry in Spain from its beginnings, through the "Golden Age," until the destruction of Jewish life in Spain at the end of the 15th century. Due to the authority and the achievements of Hebrew culture and poetry in Spain, its poetic language and metrical system spread to other countries. It dominated Hebrew poetry throughout the Islamic world—Egypt, Babylonia, Yemen, North Africa, the Ottoman Empire—until recent times. It ruled Hebrew poetry in Provence, spread throughout Europe, and reigned in Italy until the 19th century.

Hebrew literature in the East in the first centuries of Arabic rule, though flourishing in the very heart of Islamic culture and strongly influenced by Arabic science and literature, shows no trace of having come under the sway of the forms of Arabic poetry. Saadiah Gaon of Babylonia (tenth century), a distinguished philosopher and linguist in Arabic, followed the norms of the pre-Islamic *piyyut* in his Hebrew poetry. He used the strophic structure of the *piyyut* in fourfold or manifold rhymes which change from stanza to stanza and there was no trace of any syllable-counting meter. However, Saadiah Gaon's pupil, *Dunash b. Labrat, a native of Fez, who was educated in Baghdad and went to Cordoba, Spain, introduced there in the middle of the tenth century the Arabic quantitative metrical system into Hebrew poetry. Ben Labrat's innovation, which became the subject of a fierce polemic, was seen as violating the nature and grammar of the Hebrew language. But even Ben Labrat's opponents used quantitative meters in their caustic polemical poems against this very same system. Arguments against quantitative metrics, raised time and again, especially emphasized the biblical tradition and the accentual nature of the Hebrew language. The opponents themselves, however, notably *Judah Halevi, seldom strayed from this metrical system in their secular poetry.

Kinds of Verse. Hebrew literature in Spain was written in a variety of genres, secular as well as liturgical. Generic properties included theme, forms of composition, attitude of the speaker, use of language. But hardly any thematic genre had its own peculiar meter or rhyme scheme. On the other hand, there was a strong distinction between several kinds of literature, based on principles of meter, rhyme, and strophic structure. The following major types may be discerned: (1) Non-strophic poems using one single rhyme throughout, linking all the lines of the poem. In this type quantitative meter in one of the classical regular forms was obligatory (used in most of Spanish Hebrew poetry, especially secular poetry). (2) Strophic poetry of the type of the "girdle" poem, employing a quantitative metrical pattern which may be irregular in itself but permanent throughout the poem. (3) Poems with a plain syllabic meter, primarily in strophic forms. (4) Strophic poetry in "free" verse, i.e., without syllable counting, used primarily in liturgical genres. (5) Rhymed prose, used primarily in genres of oriental storytelling.

The Hebrew Quantitative Meter. A quantitative meter is based on a regular pattern of short and long (rather than stressed and unstressed) syllables. Hebrew quantitative meters though derived from Arabic versification were quite different from their prototypes as well as from Greek quantitative patterns. This was basically due to the different properties of the Hebrew language.

Traditional descriptions of Hebrew verse in Spain did not distinguish between problems of diachrony and synchrony. The derivation of a particular meter from this or that Arabic prototype seemed to be more relevant than the assessment of its place in the synchronic system of Hebrew verse. The existing classification of medieval Hebrew meters, basically unchanged for the last 800 years, relies on medieval Arabic cataloguing. One finds usually long taxonomic lists of patterns rather than structural rules to explain the nature of the Hebrew quantitative meters.

Twelve of the 16 basic meters codified in the theories of classical Arabic versification were adopted by Hebrew poets (the other being impossible to imitate in Hebrew). With their many derivations, the number of particular regular meters runs into several dozens (Yellin's list has 67), whereas the irregular patterns of the "girdle" poems may account for several hundred forms. No explanation is usually given why no other meters existed.

The traditionally identified meters will not be enumerated here but rather an attempt will be made to explain the basic rules and tendencies. One reason for the large number of metrical types is that each is used as a label for a pattern of a whole line which has not been analyzed into its distinctive features. Three such features should be considered: (a) the basic metrical units, or recurring groups of syllables ("feet"); (b) the number and order of such groups (i.e., the length of the line); (c) the form of the final group—whether complete, short, or changed (cf., in accentual-syllabic poetry an analytical term such as "iambic pentameter"—one word signifies the basic foot, the other the length of the line, whereas the nature of the end of the line is described in terms of rhyme gender: "feminine" or "masculine"). Thus the difference between the two traditionally distinct meters *ha-merubbeh* (/∪ - - -/∪ - - -/∪ - -/) and *ha-marnin* (∪ - - -/∪ - - -) (∪ stands for a short syllable, - for a long, the direction of the symbols here is from left to right) is one of length of line only; whereas for a parallel difference between (- ∪ - -/- ∪ - -/- ∪ - -) and (- ∪ - -/- ∪ - -) only one term (*ha-kalu'a* a' and b') has been used. While a difference in the length of a line may be an important rhythmic factor, it should not justify the use of unanalyzed terms.

THE BASIS OF HEBREW QUANTITATIVE METERS. The Hebrew poets in Spain did not resort to the distinction between short and long vowels of the biblical vocalization. Only the mobile *sewa*, the *ḥataf*, and the conjunction ו (when pronounced *u*) were considered short vowels. All full vowels were considered long, e.g., in Ibn *Gabirol's poem (from right to left):

מְלִיצָתִי בְּדַאֲגָתִי הֲדוּפָה, / וְשִׂמְחָתִי בְּאַנְחָתִי דְּחוּפָה

In comparison with Arabic or Greek quantitative meters, the number of short syllables in Hebrew is conspicuously small. Moreover, whereas in Greek verse a long (i.e., a strong) syllable constitutes the distinguishing element of a foot, in Hebrew it is a short (i.e., a weaker) element. It is hard to conceive how such a weaker element could provide a rhythmic basis for a foot. Indeed, there was a different way of describing this kind of meter, through use of another kind of contrast, namely that of cord (C=-) (*tenu'ah,* i.e., vowel) and peg (P= /◡ -/) *(yated).* A short followed by a long was called a peg. (In traditional Hebrew grammar a peg is considered one syllable.) All other syllables are cords. The above quoted line from Ibn Gabirol can be rewritten (from left to right): PCC PCC PC/PCC PCC PC, the basic foot consisting of one peg and two cords (rather than one short and 3 longs). Besides the rhythmic factor considered above, this system of description is justified because in Hebrew there is practically no short "syllable" which is not followed by a long one, i.e. a short is not an independent unit (even though modern pronunciation may create such an illusion). Except for experimental poems, there are no meters of pegs only. Thus a quantitative meter may be described as based on a regulated opposition of pegs and cords.

The basic group of syllables recurring several times in a line is called a foot. A foot may consist of either 2 or 3 syllables. The basic feet are:

Number of Syllables	Place of the Peg
Binary:	PC (initial)
	CP (final)
	CC (neutral)
Ternary:	PCC (initial)
	CPC (medial)
	CCP (final)

No foot has more than one peg. (In some meters there may be a substitute of 2 pegs: PP, but not as a regular recurring unit.) In Hebrew, as opposed to Arabic, there was a meter without pegs, the so-called *mishkal ha-tenu'ot* (meter of cords) of 8 long syllables, but it retained the quantitative opposition, since the text avoids all pegs in the language (i.e., all the mobile *šewa'im* and the like). No ternary foot without pegs may constitute a regular metrical scheme (though CCC may occur as a substitute within a meter with pegs).

The verse form of classical poetry is a distich *(bayit)* consisting of 2 lines identical or differing slightly at the end: the first line is called *délet,* the second *soger.* At the end of the *soger* there is a rhyme member linking it to the whole poem, which has one rhyme with a long chain of members, connecting the ends of the distichs as a string. A poem often consists of several dozens of distichs repeating again and again the same rhyme, with the typical effect of emphasis and monotony. In the first distich usually both lines are rhymed.

Any meter in this system is based on the principle of rhythmic impulses of recurring groups of pegs and cords, combined with a tendency to repeat each group at least twice, but an exact repetition of the same group more than twice in each line is avoided in most meters. The variations are codified within the metrical pattern of a line. This pattern, however, is in all its details permanent throughout the poem.

In each line the basic foot is repeated several times, but the last foot may be incomplete. The feet of a line may be of one kind only (as in the accentual-syllabic system of modern poetry), or of two kinds, unknown in modern poetry. If the first two feet are identical, the meter is *regular;* if they are different, the meter is *variegated.*

The length of a line is not as varied as in Hebrew or European poetry of modern times. There is a strong interrelation between the nature of the feet and their number. The rules governing the length of a line are the following: (a) if one of the first two feet is binary, there are 4 feet in a line; (b) if both first feet are ternary, there are 2 or 3 feet in a line, and the third may be either complete, shortened, or changed.

The last foot of a line can be described separately; if it is the third foot, it is either complete, shortened, changed, or avoided. But for this element, the length of a line can be seen as automatic. Indeed there are 5 basic regular meters. These can be illustrated by using the list of all meters and variants which appear in J. Schirmann's famous anthology of Hebrew poetry in Spain and Provence:

REGULAR METERS.

PC binary initial	PC PC PC PC	המתקרב	*ha-mitkarev*
CC binary neutral	CC CC CC CC	משקל התנועות	*mishkal ha-tenu'ot*
PCC ternary initial	PCC PCC PC	המרובה	*ha-merubbeh*
	PCC PCC	המרנין	*ha-marnin*
CPC ternary medial	CPC CPC CP	הקלוע א׳	*ha-kalu'a* (a)
	CPC CPC	הקלוע ב׳	" (b)
CCP ternary final	CCP CCP CCP	השלם א׳	*ha-shalem* (a)
	CCP CCP CC$\frac{P}{C}$	השלם ב׳	" (b)
	CCP CCP CCC	השלם ג׳	" (c)
	CCP CCP CPC	השלם ז׳	" (g)
	CCP CCP CPCC	השלם ח׳	" (h)
	CCP CCP CP	המהיר א׳	*ha-mahir* (a)
	CCP CCP CC	המהיר ב׳	" (b)
	CCP CCP C	השלם ד׳	*ha-shalem*
	CCP CCP $\frac{-}{C}$	השלם ה׳	"
	CCP CCP C	השלם ו׳	"

(The symbol $\frac{P}{C}$ shows two differing endings of the two lines in a distich.) In spite of the different labels, all the variations are in the third foot and can be described separately. Binary meters have practically no variations (due to rule a) and there is practically no binary final meter. Only the rule of length (a) can explain why the meter of cords (binary neutral) uses 8 syllables. There is no regular ternary meter of cords. Moreover, the ternary medial meter is rare in Hebrew. No other regular meters are possible. In the ternary meters the third foot may be complete only if the peg is at the very end. But this weak position of the last peg calls for a great variety of substitutes.

VARIEGATED METERS. From the rules of length follows also the structure of the variegated meters of which there are two kinds:

(1) Alternating meters: if one of the first two feet is binary and one is ternary there are 4 feet in a line (according to rule a); the whole pattern is repeated twice (e.g., PC PCC PC PCC in the meter *ha-arokh*).

(2) Changing meters: if both first feet are ternary (and different) there cannot be 4 feet (according to rule b), i.e., there can be no repetition of the whole group within each line. In this case, if there is a third foot it either repeats the first or is changed (as the last foot of a line).

Alternating Meters. In alternating meters the following rules hold for the basic patterns: (1) there are 4 feet in a line; (2) the meter is based on a regular alternation between ternary and binary feet; (3) both kinds of feet are either initial or final; (4) in each hemistich, if there are 2 pegs they are removed from each other by only one cord. From rules (3) and (4) follows that there may be only 2 basic meters:

alternating initial	PC PCC PC PCC	הארוך	*ha-arokh*
alternating final	CCP CP CCP CP	המתפשט	*ha-mitpashet*

There can be no medial feet since there must be a common rhythmical denominator; if it is not the foot, it is its direction. Since each line has two symmetrical hemistichs, variations of the scheme may be accepted at the end of the line as well as in the second foot, e.g., the alternating falling meter has a variant PC CCC PC CCC (the meter of Dunash b. Labrat). The variants shall not be listed here.

Changing Meters. If the first two feet are different but ternary, the whole group cannot be repeated twice. Only two ternary feet combine: the medial and the final. Hence the two basic metrical schemes are:

medial and changing	CPC CCP CPC	הקל א׳	*ha-kal (a)*
final and changing	CCP CPC	הקטוע	*ha-katu'a*

Variations occur in the third foot (the end of the line) and in the second (the end of the basic group). These meters are however rare and shall not be enumerated here.

The Meters Used in Hebrew Poetry. All the basic meters practically used in Hebrew poetry may be summed up in the following diagram:

Meter / Feet	Regular		Variegated	
	binary	ternary	alternating	changing
Initial	PC	PCC	PC PCC	—
Medial		CPC	—	CPC CCP
Final	—	CCP	CCP CP	CCP CPC
Neutral	CC	—		

The structural symmetry is obvious. There are practically no meters beginning with a binary final foot; no medial foot in the alternating patterns, and no initial foot in the changing meters (rare exceptions may be found).

In actual poetry the situation is even simpler. Indeed, some poets liked experimenting. As Yellin has shown, *Samuel ha-Nagid used 57 different metrical schemes. The bulk of Hebrew poetry in Spain, however, employed only a small number of basic meters, with some variations, of which the most widespread are (in this order): initial and final ternary meters and the meter of cords. More precisely:

(1) ternary initial, esp.	PCC PCC PC	הַמְרֻבֶּה	*ha-merubbeh*
but also	PCC PCC	הַמַּרְנִין	*ha-marnin*
(2) ternary final, esp.	CCP CCP CC $\frac{P}{C}$	השלם ב׳	*ha-shalem* (b)
also	CCP CCP CC	המהיר ב׳	*ha-mahir* (b)
(3) cords (binary neutral)	CC CC CC CC	התנועות	*ha-tenu'ot*

These three groups, with a few variations, account for 94% of Moses *ibn Ezra's meters in his secular poetry. The major meter, *ha-merubbeh,* found in about half of the Hebrew poems in Spain, later gave way to *ha-shalem* (b).

Following these three groups, though far behind, are the alternating meters, initial (PC PCC PC PCC—*ha-arokh*), and final (CCP CP CCP CP—*ha-mitpashet*). The preference of initial over final meters is due to the structure of the Hebrew word; the majority of vocal *šewa'im* are at the beginnings of words and a *šewa* may easily be added before a word with a preposition or conjunction (ו, ל, כ, ב). Medial or changing meters are quite rare.

The bulk of the poetry uses ternary meters, with 3 (incomplete) feet in a line. Since the length of the line is regulated, it varies only within narrow limits. There are only lines of 6 to 10 syllables. If the short syllables are also counted (as they were later, in Hebrew poetry in Italy) the limits are 8–14. Since in contemporary Israel poetry about half of the *sewa'im* are considered syllables, those limits are comparable with 7 to 12 syllables today. If the special effect of the *ha-marnin,* which has the typical rhythm of a short line, is excluded, all other meters compare well with the variations given in modern poetry between 4 iambics and 4 anapests. Thus the length of a line in Spanish Hebrew poetry as well as its rhythmic-syntactical form are similar to the length of typical lines in modern poetry. The optimal line has 8 to 9 long syllables (or 11, counting the short ones), which is similar to a line of 4 or 5 iambs.

Verse Endings. There are many variations of verse endings in the last foot of the basic metrical schemes. Any such variant creates a permanent pattern, repeated in all the lines of a poem. As opposed to modern poetry or to Greek and Arabic quantitative meters, Hebrew poets allowed very rarely for changes from line to line (feet-substitutes) or deviations from a given metrical scheme (i.e., changes occurring only in some lines, e.g., in Hebrew in the changing meter CPC CCP CPC the second foot may be substituted by PP). The variations in Hebrew in the third foot are felt not against the pattern of the poem but against the rhythmic impulse of the first 2 feet of the same line.

Variations of feet in verse endings are of several kinds: (1) the last foot is short (catalectic), PCC→PC, CPC→CP; CCP→CC; this change occurs almost only in ternary meters where it is the usual case (unless it is the last peg which is shortened, as in the final *ha-shalem*); (2) hypercatalectic: CCP→C which is very rare; (3) a peg is substituted by a cord: CCP→CCC; CP→CC, which occurs quite often since short syllables are scarce in Hebrew; (4) two cords are substituted by a peg, CCP→PP; PPC→PP; a rare variation, occuring in changing meters, especially in the second foot; (5) a peg is advanced, CCP→CPC (or: CP), e.g., in *ha-shalem* (g) CCP CCP CPC. The most widespread changes are: a catalectic foot (1) or a substitute by a cord (3) (cf., instances in the list of regular ternary meters).

Rhythm. The quantitative opposition provides the Hebrew poet with a metrical framework rather than with a pervasive rhythmic movement. The role of short syllables in the Hebrew language is much less than in Arabic. Thus the two major meters in Arabic, *tawil* and *basīt* (equivalent to our alternating final and initial meters) are far from being major meters in Hebrew. Moreover, every possible substitution of longs for shorts is resorted to in Hebrew. Thus the scheme of the Arabic *basīt* is: (from left to right):

/ ∪–∪–/ ∪∪–/ ∪̄–∪–/ ∪̄∪–/
its Hebrew derivation: /––∪–/–∪–/––∪–/–∪–/
CCP CP CCP CP

Instead of 8 shorts to 6 longs, the proportion became 4:10. A common variation of this meter has even less shorts:

/ C̄C̄ P̆ ¯ / C̄C̄ / C̄C̄ P̆ ¯ / C̄C̄ /

No two consecutive short syllables are possible in Hebrew, therefore some Arabic meters could not be reproduced. There is also the favorite Hebrew innovation: the meter of cords in which all short syllables are avoided.

On the other hand, in many Hebrew poems can be distinguished a strong tendency of regulating stress order and word boundaries. Although no permanent laws hold in this area, the tendencies are clearly felt, e.g., in the poem by Solomon ibn *Gabirol:

נחר/בק ראי גרוני/דבק לח/כי לשוני
היה לב בי סחרחר מרב כא בי ואוני

The formal division of the quantitative meter in this poem, though consistent, seems artificial. The language of the poem follows quite clearly a different pattern:

נחר/בקראי/גרוני/דבק/לחכי/לשוני

The accents are clearly regulated, and so are the word boundaries. Though it is not an absolute rule in this poem, in 85% of the cases there are word boundaries in marked places (whereas only 36% observe the formal foot boundaries of the meter). This kind of regularity in stress order and word boundaries is partly due to the correlation between the following factors: (1) short syllables cannot be stressed in Hebrew; (2) short syllables are most common at the beginning of a word, therefore, a boundary usually precedes them. It seems however that the major force behind this tendency is the subconscious rhythmical sense for stress order felt especially in the works of the great poets, Ibn Gabirol and Judah Halevi.

Relative regularity in stress order may be felt as a rhythmic substitute in meters without the peg/cord alternation. Thus in the meter of cords there are lines which are clearly "iambic" in the modern sense:

כתנות פסים לבש הגן/וכסות רקמה מדי דשאו

Girdle Poems. Though the bulk of Hebrew poetry in Spain used regular meters and one rhyme running throughout the poem (with as many as 60 or 80 rhyming members—distichs), several kinds of strophic forms also flourished.

The *muwaššaḥ*, or "girdle" poem (שִׁיר אֵזוֹר, *shir ezor*), an original development of Arabic Andalusian poetry, was represented in Hebrew poetry almost from its beginnings (11th century) and was the form of some of the best Hebrew lyrical poems in the 12th century. Though originally used in love poetry, it was employed widely for religious poems. The girdle poem combines in its composition both the strophic principle of changing rhymes and the principle of the "running" rhyme, which runs through all parts of the poem in a refrain-like manner. There are two kinds of stanzas: (1) the changing stanzas with changing rhymes. Every stanza has one or several distinct rhymes, different from the rhymes of other stanzas; (2) the girdle stanza, a strophic pattern recurring after every changing stanza, with the same rhyme or rhymes repeated in all girdle stanzas throughout the poem. A girdle stanza often appears at the beginning of the poem, it is the "guiding" stanza. In many poems the final girdle, the so-called *ḫarğa*, is written not in Hebrew but in popular Arabic or in the old Romance language of Spain. Usually it is a quotation of a love conversation. The *ḫarğa* thus determines the meter and rhyme of the girdle, as well as the melody (most girdle poems were apparently created as songs).

The meter of the changing stanzas and of the girdle may be identical, but often is not. Each line may consist of 1, 2, or 3 parts, rhymed or unrhymed. The metrical pattern may either be regular or highly irregular: within the line there is a free combination of all kinds of feet, which seems often to be a kind of "free verse." But the same irregular pattern is repeated throughout the poem, in the stanzas of each kind separately. The two metrical schemes are often related to each other, in a variety of ways, e.g., one may include a partial repetition of the other. A simple example, in Judah Halevi's song "בִּי הַצְּבִי בִּי אֲדוֹנִי" (*"Bi ha-Ẓevi, Bi Adoni"*)

the meter of the changing stanza is CCP CPC
and that of the girdle: CC CPC/CCP CPC

The stanza has a simple but irregular scheme. The metrical pattern of the girdle repeats the meter of the stanza in its second part, but the first part of the girdle is different (in this case a slight variation).

An example of a complex rhyme scheme can be found in a poem by Joseph ibn Jacob ibn *Ẓaddik (1075–1149), which begins with a guiding girdle,

נומי, אהה, נגזל – / ברח, אהה, גוחל / מאהלי!
דמעי, אהה, יזל – / עפרי אהה, אזל – / מי גואלי?

בוגן! שלח אצבע / לעות חלילך / טוב מענה,
אלם – אבל יבע / צחות, כקולך / כן יענה.
שלש וגם ארבע / על פי נבליך / בשמאל מנה.

שירים נצר על דל / שפה, ואל יחדל מפי כלי־
שיר – קול אשר יגדל עתים ,ועת ידל – לא מחלי!

The rhyme pattern is as follows (capital letters represent the girdle rhymes):

PPR	abc	def	ghi	jkl	mno
PPR	abc	def	ghi	jkl	mno
	abc	def	ghi	jkl	mno
	PPR	PPR	PPR	PPR	PPR
	PPR	PPR	PPR	PPR	PPR

The principles of the girdle poem were widely used in Hebrew religious poetry, especially by the great poets Judah Halevi and Abraham ibn Ezra.

Other Metrical Principles Used in Strophic Poems. In the genres of religious poetry the metrical principles varied: (1) the quantitative principle, using regular or irregular patterns of pegs and cords; (2) patterns using free numbers of cords where no pegs appeared; (3) syllabic meter where the opposition P/C was disregarded (i.e., the short syllables *šewa* and *ḥataf* appeared irregularly, but were not counted); (4) a free verse in the vein of older Hebrew liturgy, though usually tending toward a syllabic semi-regularity.

Rhymed Prose. The *maqāma* is a genre of rhymed prose, usually written as a chain of stories in the oriental manner, and interwoven with anecdotes, fables, and metrical poems. Many books in this genre were written during the Middle Ages or translated and adapted from Arabic (notably by Judah b. Solomon *al-Ḥarizi and *Immanuel of Rome). Usually the prose text of the *maqāma* rhymes throughout, though it has no meter. The number of members of each rhyme is not fixed; the distance between the rhyming members constantly changes and the sound patterns of such rhymes also vary: from a mere minimum to near-homonyms. On the other hand, the poems, which are frequently introduced into this rhymed prose, are clearly marked by their strict adherence to classical meters and rhyming.

A typical case of a different kind of rhymed prose is the religious philosophical poem *"Keter Malkhut"* by Ibn Gabirol. Though rhyme and rhythm play an important role in this work, their use is neither permanent nor regular; it may be considered a kind of richly adorned free verse, changing its rhythmical tone from a densely rhymed sound-orchestration to mere prose employing parallelism.

Rhyme in Medieval Poetry. Terminal Rhyme. Rhyme in Hebrew poetry in Spain, and throughout the Diaspora in the Middle Ages, was terminal. It disregarded stress or morphology. The rhymeme included all sounds from the consonant preceding the last vowel to the end of the line:

DO	להגידו – הודו – נודו
DOT	חידות – חמודות – חרדות
DOD	כידוד – מדוד – ונדוד

The norm is: N = CV(C). The number of sounds (2 or 3) depends on the language: whether the final syllable is open or closed. The principle was obviously derived from the rhyme of the Palestinian *piyyut*, after it dropped the requirement of including two root consonants in the rhymeme.

In order to make rhyming easier, the poets made wide use of rhymemes with open syllables or with suffixes (as in the first two of the above examples), thus having to change only one root consonant. This tendency was motivated by other principles of medieval poetics. Since there was no requirement for individuality in imagery or theme, the poets could widely use the Hebrew plural suffixes throughout their long poems. The same holds for possessive particles, such as ־ךְ (yours, when addressed to God) אַרְךְ (to Zion), etc.

The obligatory requirement that a consonant precede the final vowel, similar to the French *consonne d'appui,* was peculiar to medieval Hebrew poetry and was not required in other languages. It was, as it were, a compensation for the missing stress principle required in modern Hebrew poetry. A typical example:

Medieval Hebrew				Modern Hebrew	
REG	סוֹרֵג	LEG	מְדַלֵּג	סוֹרֵג – מְדַלֵּג	ÉG
	דֶּרֶג		שֶׁלֶג	שֶׁלֶג – פֶּלֶג	ÉLEG

In modern Hebrew ÉG is a perfectly sufficient rhymeme, in medieval poetry an additional preceding consonant had to be included in the rhyme. On the other hand, in penultimately stressed (feminine) rhymes in modern poetry the inclusion of one syllable is not enough. The principles changed, but the overall proportion between the vocabulary of the language and the rhyming patterns remained similar.

This relationship between modern and medieval Hebrew rhyme may be compared to the difference between English and French rhyme. Whereas in French *rime riche* (using *consonne d'appui*) was highly welcome, in English it was often excluded from rhyme. The situation is similar: French rhymemes are based practically on the last syllable, the words are longer, and an addition to the minimal rhymeme is welcome in order to avoid trite rhyming. Only in Hebrew however was the use of the *consonne d'appui* obligatory, hence it may be called: the Hebrew terminal rhyme. Its peculiar impact was felt especially against the background of Italian, German, Yiddish, or Russian rhyme, where such enrichments were discouraged.

THE RULE OF MAXIMUM. If the final syllable was based on a suffix, the poets often strove to enrich the rhymeme, adding to it at least some part of the root. Though this was not a necessary rule (there appeared rhymemes of pure suffixes too), it was a strong tendency.

But rich rhyming was limited by unwritten rules: (1) if the normally required final syllable (N) had two root consonants, no sound could be added to N; rhymemes such as מִיד, דוֹד, בָּל are both minimal and maximal; (2) if the final syllable (N) included one root consonant, a preceding vowel could be added; thus there are rhymemes, such as: לִי, כִי, לִים, רִים; but also ־ָלִי, ־ָרִים, etc.; (3) if the final syllable (N) included no root consonant, one root consonant could also be added; thus, beside rhymemes such as ־הֶם, נוּ, ־יךָ there are: ־ֵינוּ, ־יהֶם, ־ֵינוּ and בֵינוּ, לֵיהֶם, רַיךְ.

"FEMININE" RHYME. Though stress was disregarded, in meter as well as in rhyme, a secondary tradition developed a "feminine" rhyme, which is based on penultimately stressed endings (which are a small minority in the language, but are represented in several suffixes and in word endings with ע, ח (־ֶעַ, וֹעַ, ־ֶחַ, וּחַ).

Feminine rhyme became obligatory on one kind of meter composed of unequal hemistichs in which the final foot had a cord instead of a peg appearing in the first hemistich, e.g., the *ha-shalem* (b): CCP CCP CCP/CCP CCP CCC. The end presents a change in the regularity of the meter —where a P was expected a C appeared instead. As a compensation for this frustrated expectation, the poet used in this case feminine rhyme.

Feminine rhyme appeared occasionally in other meters too. But with the meter *ha-shalem* (b) it became prominent in Romance-speaking countries, especially in Italy, where feminine rhymes were the dominant rhyming form.

Elsewhere, i.e., in the majority of Hebrew medieval poems, stress was disregarded, words ultimately and penultimately stressed rhymed freely with each other.

The Dispersion of the Hebrew Terminal Rhyme. The Hebrew terminal rhyme originated in the Palestinian liturgy as an alleviated form of its "difficult" rhyme. It may be found both in Ereẓ Isael after Kallir and in ninth-century Byzantine in Southern Italy. It developed again, as a simplification of the "Kallirian" rhyme in tenth-century Babylonia (Saadiah Gaon) and in 11th-century Germany. It was strengthened by the comparison with the Arabic rhyming norm (basically requiring a consonant and the vowel following it) and later with European terminal rhyme which knew no discontinuous rhymeme.

This norm persisted in Hebrew throughout the world until the end of the 18th century, except for Italy, where stress was accepted in rhyme since the 17th century (but in Italy, too, no violation of the Hebrew norm could be found). The norm also remained obligatory throughout the Ashkenazi domain (Germany, Poland), though Hebrew had become a penultimately stressed language there. The penultimate stress caused a neutralization of all final vowels. Nevertheless rhyme remained exclusively in the final syllable. Thus Meir b. Samuel of Sczebrzeszyn in his historical chronicle rhymes in 8-line stanzas words such as: פָּקִיד־נִפְקַד־עוֹקֵד, apparently pronounced: *pokəd - nifkəd - oykəd.* Though the original *i, o, ey* (or *i, a, e*) were blurred in an unstressed position, rhyme remained terminal: a repetition of final sounds. This Hebrew conservatism is even more astounding in bilingual poems, such as the *Megillat Vinẓ* (1616), with regularly alternating Hebrew and Yiddish stanzas. In the Yiddish stanzas all rhymes are stress-bound (feminine and masculine), according to the standard European norm; even Hebrew words follow this rule. But in the Hebrew stanzas the same Hebrew words disregard stress: terminal rhyme is preserved.

Only in some cases under the influence of foreign poetry did Hebrew rhyme relinquish the requirement of the *consonne d'appui* (in closed syllables only), rhyming N=VC. Such was the case in some of the girdle poems (patterned on rhymes in a foreign language), e.g., Judah Halevi rhymes: צַח־פַּח־נֶאֱנָח. (AḤ). The same holds for the bilingual Hebrew-Arabic strophic poems of the Yemenite classical poet Shalom *Shabazi and for the strophic songs the 16th-century kabbalist poet of Safed, Israel b. Moses *Najara, who was apparently influenced by Turkish songs.

HEBREW POETRY IN ITALY

The Jewish community in Italy was probably the oldest in Europe; though small in number, it was an important center throughout the Middle Ages. Located in a central position, between Israel, Yemen, and Babylonia in the East and Spain in the West, between North Africa in the South and Germany and France in the North, Italy was on the crossroads of the major cultural trends in Jewish history. Hebrew poetry in Italy, the first examples of which are from the ninth century, continued to flourish uninterruptedly until the 20th century. The changes of poetic systems in Italy may be representative of the shifts in Hebrew prosody throughout the centuries. The major formal periods in Italy will be briefly listed below:

(1) The poetry of Byzantine Southern Italy in the

ninth century consisted of strophic *piyyutim,* from 2 to 10 lines in a stanza, each stanza having one separate rhyme. The rhymes were simple (terminal norm). Usually an acrostic was required and sometimes a permanent refrain was used to close all stanzas of a poem. Contrary to the "Kallirian" *piyyut,* the early Italian *piyyut* required a compulsory meter, based on a constant number of words in a line.

Though strophic poems were known in Latin and in Greek-Byzantine poetry of the period, in these languages rhyme was not yet a required, regular, or permanent device. Only in Hebrew did rhyme serve as a criterion for strophic structure and was obligatory.

(2) In the tenth and beginning of the 11th centuries Italy accepted again the "difficult" "Kallirian" rhyme. It was, as it were, a "reversed evolution." But strict meters were required too. *Solomon b. Judah ha-Bavli and other poets of this period composed in this vein. Their followers who moved to the Rhine area introduced this norm into the Hebrew *piyyut* of Franco-Germany. These circles edited the *maḥzor* and apparently included in it only such rhymed strophic poems which were written by Kallir or followed his rhyming norm. A number of *yoẓerot* and a large number of *seliḥot* were created in this style.

(3) In the 11th and 12th centuries the norms of the ninth century were again revived: the *piyyut* used strophic poems with changing but separate rhymes, written in exact meters, based on the number of words. The simplification of rhyme was apparently due to a variety of factors, the foremost being: (a) The influence of the Hebrew rhyme of Spain and Provence (though neither the pattern of one running rhyme nor the quantitative meter was accepted). The Spanish scholar and poet Abraham *ibn Ezra propagated the simpler rhyme in Rome in the 11th century. (b) The decline of the difficult enigmatic style of Ha-Bavli, which occurred in Franco-Germany too. Without this style "Kallirian" rhyming was almost impossible.

In the 13th century Italian poetry in the vernacular emerged and flourished. Hebrew poets living in Rome could not have been unaware of the differences in the respective prosodic systems: (a) Hebrew strophic poems used changing but separate rhymes (*aaaa bbbb cccc,* etc.), whereas Italian rhymes were usually alternating (*abba; aba bcb,* etc.); (b) Hebrew meter was based on the number of words, Italian—on the number of syllables; (c) Hebrew rhyme was terminal but required a *consonne d'appui:* N=CV(C), whereas Italian rhyme was stressed, usually feminine: N=V́CV. Thus Hebrew rhyme was based on one syllable, Italian on two. Hebrew leaned primarily on consonants, Italian on vowels. In these three respects Hebrew poetry in Italy adopted the Italian norms, but it was done over a period of centuries, primarily through the transformation of forms existent in some Hebrew tradition.

(4) Alternating rhyme was introduced into Roman Hebrew poetry in the 13th century. The major poet who initiated this change was Benjamin b. Abraham *Anav. But Benjamin Anav did not directly imitate Italian forms; he switched to alternating rhymes, meeting thus an Italian aesthetic norm by adopting the patterns of the girdle poem which had been developed in Hebrew poetry in Spain and Provence. However the poets of this generation did not transfer the system of quantitative meters from Spain; only a semi-regular syllabic meter, as in many a strophic *piyyut* of Judah Halevi or Isaac *ibn Ghayyat, was employed. Many such poems, both of Italian and Spanish origin, were by that time absorbed into the Italian *maḥzor.*

(5) *Immanuel of Rome (end of 13th–beginning of the 14th century) was the major Hebrew poet who shifted to the use of both quantitative syllabic meters as well as of Italian strophic forms, primarily the sonnet. In both techniques he had predecessors, but the major achievement was his. With him Hebrew poetry in Italy switched from liturgy to secular poetry. It seems that in order to find an equivalent for Italian poetic forms, Immanuel had to seek a language for secular poetry in Hebrew; this he found in the Spanish tradition, which he accepted with its rhymed prose *(maqāma),* quantitative meters, oriental storytelling, and imagery. Suddenly Hebrew poetry discovered exact syllabic meters, required by the Italian aesthetic taste, in its own language and tradition. Though the distinction between long and short syllables, a vestige of Arabic influence, was apparently disregarded in the Italian Hebrew pronunciation, its patterns persisted until the 20th century: Isaac Ḥayyim (Vittorio) *Castiglioni wrote his poem on the death of Theodor Herzl in 1904 in a quantitative meter.

Moreover, Hebrew poets in Italy found in the Spanish tradition meters which fitted the lengths of line favored in Italian poetry. The major meter, especially in the sonnets, was the endecasyllabic line for which a Hebrew poet was able to use either *ha-merubbeh* or *ha-shalem* (b), counting both "long" and "short" as whole syllables. *Ha-shalem* (b): /- - ∪ -/- - ∪ -/- - -/ became the major meter of Hebrew poetry in Italy, due to its compulsory feminine rhyme which fitted both Hebrew-Spanish and Italian taste. Immanuel accepted it for his sonnets, breaking each distich into two lines, with a rhyme for each; lines with an even number of syllables had a masculine rhyme, and those with uneven numbers—a feminine rhyme.

But Immanuel introduced stressed rhyme and alternating rhyming only for his Italian strophic forms. In other parts of his book he completely accepted the Spanish Hebrew tradition, employed widely the running rhyme, rhymed prose, disregarded stress, etc. His was a combination of two systems with a common denominator: the quantitative metrical system.

(6) After Immanuel of Rome, Hebrew poetry adopted a variety of other Italian strophic forms (besides the sonnet which became the most popular), the *ottava rima,* Dante's *terza rima,* the *sestina,* the *canzonetta,* and some others. Nevertheless, strophic forms of the *piyyut* on the one hand and the Spanish running rhyme on the other lived on for centuries.

(7) Despite the domination of the quantitative meter, a new syllabic meter evolved. Its first major poet was Moses b. Isaac *Rieti (beginning of the 15th century) called "Il Dante Ebreo" for his book *Mikdash Me'at* written in the form of Dante's *terza rima.* Rieti understood that Hebrew had to rhyme primarily in the ultimately stressed form (masculine rhymes) and accordingly reduced his line to 10 syllables.

Whereas previous Italian attempts at syllabic meters (13th century) disregarded short syllables altogether, according to their Spanish prototypes, Rieti counted short syllables as completely equivalent to long ones. Hence he abolished the limitation of short syllables to particular spots in the metrical scheme. But Rieti's innovation, i.e., syllabic meters without quantitative distinctions, did not become prominent in Italian Hebrew verse until the 18th century.

(8) For several centuries Hebrew poets proceeded to retain in their rhyme forms the distinction between Italian strophic patterns and the Spanish or the liturgical tradition. On the whole, rhyme was terminal, stressed rhyme being reserved for the sonnet and other Italian patterns. Thus *Joseph ha-Zarefati (12th century) writes his octaves in masculine rhymes but still follows the Hebrew rule of a required *consonne d'appui* (thus פֵּר and בֵּר are for him two different rhymemes). Only in the 17th century was the

change completed; stressed rhyme according to the European norm became compulsory. Despite the nature of the Hebrew language, which favored masculine rhymes, under Italian impact feminine rhyme became dominant. Since the 18th century feminine rhyme was almost exclusive. It was employed primarily in the *ha-shalem* meter, or in derivations of it: either dropping one or both short syllables, or shortening the line, e.g., in Moses Ḥayyim *Luzzatto's *La-Yesharim Tehillah* there are two kinds of verse line: (a) the 11-syllabic - - ∪ -/- - - -/- - -, and (b) the 7-syllabic: - - ∪ -/- - -, each retaining merely one short syllable. Some of his followers in Italy and in Amsterdam dropped this last vestige of quantitative metrics, thus paving the way for the forms of the new era, the Haskalah.

(9) Another Italian development of great interest should be noted: the earliest invention of accentual iambs in Europe was accomplished in Yiddish rhymed romances by the Venetian poet Elijah Baḥur Levita, about 1508/09. Northern Italy was at that time a center of Yiddish literature. Elijah Levita, a grammarian, a versatile scholar, and a poet was fluent in several languages. He wrote Hebrew verse both in the Sephardi pronunciation, using quantitative meters, and in the Ashkenazi vein, using free accentual verse. When adapting long Italian strophic romances, such as *Buovo d'Antona* (the *Bove Bukh*) and *Paris un Viene,* and creating stanzas in pure *ottava rima* in a quite modern Yiddish, he merged the Italian syllabic principle with the Germanic accentual principle (which ruled Yiddish poetry until his time) and developed his iambic tetrameter. The process of this invention is of major interest to comparative prosody, but with the decay of the Italian center, it did not last in Yiddish poetry. Accentual-syllabic meters reappeared in Yiddish and in Hebrew under Russian influence only as late as around 1890 (with the one exception discussed below).

(10) In the later centuries of Italian Hebrew poetry iambic pentameters began to appear.

The combination of principles from three metric systems in one verse line—the Hebrew quantitative, the Italian syllabic, and the biblical accentual—did not hamper but encouraged the creation of a fourth system in the same verse: the accentual-syllabic meter, in its iambic form. How did it come about? The major quantitative meter used in Italy was: - - ∪ -/- - ∪ -/- - -. Since short syllables cannot be stressed in Hebrew, the third and seventh syllables were unstressed. Italian poetry opposed a stress on the fifth syllable. On the other hand, the tenth syllable was stressed by the rule of rhyme. Since the biblical rule precluded two adjacent syllables from being stressed (if it happens, the first stress would move backward) and the ninth and eleventh were also excluded from stress, the following pattern emerged (x marking unstressed positions): $- - \overset{\times}{\cup} - \overset{\times}{-} - \overset{\times}{\cup} - \overset{\times}{-}\overset{|}{-}\overset{\times}{-}$. Thus only even syllables were allowed to receive a stress and a perfect iambic pentameter evolved. (The first foot only was free for variation, but this is the case in English or German iambics too.) Only when the Italian requirement for not stressing the fifth syllable was disregarded did these iambs not materialize.

Hebrew stress was apparently strong and this tendency was felt and spread to other meters too (primarily meters without fixed short syllables). Despite this obvious iambic tendency, it was never formulated as such, being rather an automatic, unintentional result of rules of quite a different nature. The 19th-century Haskalah poets were strongly influenced by late Italian Hebrew poetry, but having a different pronunciation (Ashkenazi as opposed to the Italian "Sephardi"), they could not feel this underlying iambic meter. Though they dropped entirely all distinctions of a quantitative nature, they interpreted this verse as purely syllabic. Only poets in Erez Israel of the 1930–40s, such as J. *Fichmann writing again in a "Sephardi" dialect, rediscovered the iambs of their Italian predecessors.

HASKALAH

The modern age of Hebrew literature began with the revival of Hebrew poetry in Germany in the second half of the 18th century. It is regarded as a "secular" period (though many of the poets were religious and some of their themes were of a religious nature) since there was a conscious creation of poetry and prose written in the genres of contemporary European literature which were conspicuously different from the genres of liturgy. Haskalah poetry was a direct descendant of Hebrew poetry in Italy and Holland. However since this poetry emerged with a new social and cultural trend, the Enlightenment movement, and flourished closer to the center of the Jewish population in Eastern Europe, it expressed a reorientation of Hebrew literature and may rightly be considered a new period.

Haskalah literature was written and published by small groups of writers and their followers in Germany, Austria, Hungary, and Russia (including Poland) throughout the 19th century. Though their ideas were, to some extent, typical of the European Enlightenment of the 18th century, Haskalah poetry cannot be considered of a monolithic nature, but rather as an eclectic body of verse. This new poetry was indeed, from its beginnings, influenced primarily by 18th-century German literature, especially in the typical genres of epic and fable. It embraced, however, also genres developed previously in Hebrew, in Italy, such as allegorical drama, and absorbed themes and motifs from 19th-century European lyrical and social poetry.

It seems that Hebrew literature lagged considerably behind the evolution of European poetry, going into the stages of the development of neighboring literatures only after those had been established as "classical." Thus one of the major Hebrew writers of the Haskalah in Russia, Judah Leib *Gordon, who knew Russian well and lived for many years in the capital of Russia, wrote poetry in the vein of the Haskalah in the 1860s and 1870s, i.e., in the time of Tolstoy and Dostoevski and after Pushkin, Lermontov, and Tyutchev. But though Haskalah verse seemed to be a fossilized remnant of the 18th century, untouched by the poetics of Russian classical poetry, Gordon also absorbed some influences from the social and "civic" poetry of his Russian contemporary Nekrasov. On the other hand, he continued to use forms which antedated the Haskalah.

The meter of Hebrew poetry throughout the Haskalah was syllabic. Thus the poets continued the basic form of Hebrew versification in Italy in spite of the fact that their prototypes in German and Russian were written in accentual-syllabic meters. Even translations from German poetry were transposed in Hebrew into syllabic meters, regardless of the German prototype, e.g., Schiller's *Glocke* (written in accentual-syllabic meters) was translated into Hebrew in syllabic meters, without stress regularity, and into Yiddish in accentual meters, without syllable counting. Stress, strangely enough, played no role in the Hebrew meters of this period, despite the fact that it was prominent in the speech of these writers and even dominant in the meter of folk song in their spoken language, Yiddish, as well as in the small amount of Yiddish poetry which they wrote, and despite the fact that it ruled the versification of German and Russian poetry which they strove to imitate. There was no traditional Hebrew poetic authority to back up this choice of syllabic versification—the venerated poetry of the Bible was accentual and relatively free in its verse forms. The only explanation could be the sense of continuity and the typical conservatism of Hebrew verse.

A few attempts were made in the second half of the 19th century to introduce accentual-syllabic meters (notably by A. B. *Gottlober). But only S. *Frug, well-known as a Russian poet, transferred the Russian system of versification into Yiddish when he started writing in this language. Ḥ. N. *Bialik in the 1890s, strongly influenced by Frug, was among the first to use predominantly accentual-syllabic versification in his Hebrew poetry.

The new meter, influenced by the Russian prototype, swept Hebrew and Yiddish poetry in the 1890s, paradoxically enough at the same time when the symbolist movement, which tried to break away from meter altogether, emerged in Russia.

The Syllabic System of Versification in Hebrew. Haskalah poetry used the pure syllabic system, which had developed in Hebrew literature in Italy, after the last vestiges of quantitative versification have been dropped. Every poem had its own meter, i.e., a permanent number of syllables in each line, with a stress on the penultimate syllable. Otherwise stress was not regulated. A permanent caesura was rarely implemented.

Apart from marginal uses of quantitative meters, inherited from medieval Spanish Hebrew poetry, the poetry of the Haskalah did not apply the distinction between short and long syllables. The traditionally short syllables, *ševa* and *ḥataf,* confused the poets and were considered sometimes as syllables and sometimes as non-syllables. Naphtali Hirz *Wessely, who introduced this system, used the *ḥataf* at the beginning of words as a syllable and in the middle of words as a non-syllable; the mobile *ševa* as a syllable in the middle of a word and as a non-syllable at the beginning. It seems that Wessely tried to avoid the mobile *ševa* at the beginning of words in order to eschew the problem. With time, however, it became impossible to refrain from using a whole group of words (beginning with the mobile *ševa*) in Hebrew poetry.

Shirei Tiferet, Wessely's epic, was the classical prototype of all the poetry of the Haskalah. The prologues to each of the 18 parts of his epic were written in 11-syllabic rhymed stanzas, but the epic itself was composed in 13-syllabic unrhymed verse. Wessely used feminine endings exclusively both in his rhymed and unrhymed poetry. Unrhymed feminine endings in his poem conformed with the Hebrew tradition inherited from Italy (where the penultimate syllable was stressed) and with Wessely's German prototype, Friedrich Gottlieb Klopstock's *Der Messias.* Wessely, however, in accordance with his Italian prototypes, resorted only to words which were penultimately stressed in the Sephardi pronunciation; these constitute a small and very specific part of the Hebrew vocabulary.

The firm grip of tradition led to the exclusive use of penultimately stressed *(mille'eil)* endings in the Sephardi pronunciation in much of Haskalah poetry; it was an absolute rule in the higher genres of poetry, especially poetic drama and epic verse, and in the "higher" circles of the Haskalah, such as the centers of Germany and Vilna, though not in Galicia or Hungary. The paradox of this use of *mille'eil* in the Sephardi pronunciation is underscored by the fact that in other respects Hebrew was obviously pronounced according to the Ashkenazi dialect, even in specific Ashkenazi subdialects. Thus in the poetry of Lithuania (a major center of Haskalah literature in the second half of the 19th century) the rhymes often betray the poet's pronunciation: חֹפֶשׁ - נֶפֶשׁ (both *ḥolam* and *segol* being pronounced as *ei*), רַעַשׁ - כַּעַס (שׂ and ס being equal to *s*). Though Lithuanian Ashkenazi pronunciation is evident in their poetry and the penultimate stress was the general rule of the Hebrew words in all varieties of the Ashkenazi dialect, the Haskalah poets did not dare use Hebrew in their own pronunciation as a natural resource for the compulsory use of feminine rhymes. Consequently most of the vocabulary of their language was excluded from final verse positions.

When the young poet, Mikhal (Micah Joseph *Lebensohn) was negligent in this respect and rhymed words which were perfectly equivalent in his own dialect, but appeared as a mixture of *millera* and *mille'eil* (masculine and feminine) to a distant Sephardi ear, he was scolded by the Italian scholar S. D. *Luzzatto. Both Mikhal and J. L. Gordon, in his later period, broke the rule and on and off used words which are feminine only according to the Ashkenazi pronunciation. But even then the majority of rhymes was still based on words which are considered *mille'eil* in the Sephardi pronunciation: what used to be a compulsory rule became a habit, or a matter of merit in poetic style.

This phenomenon had a strong effect on the style of Haskalah poetry. Words of the *mille'eil* form exist only in several specific groups: (1) a small group of nouns penultimately stressed (אֶרֶץ–פֶּרֶץ–קֶרֶץ) which recurred endlessly in the rhymes of the Haskalah and became trite symptoms of this poetry; (2) a variety of archaic forms (אֱחֱלוֹמָה, בָּמוֹ, לָמוֹ, מֶנְהוּ); (3) several forms of the verb (הפריעה, אמרתי,), notably in the biblical end-stop pronunciation (יִנְהָרוּ, יִבְעָרוּ); (4) a group of feminine endings (אוֹמֶרֶת, תְּבִינִי). Since other sources were limited, the penultimately stressed forms of the verb became prominent in the rhymes of Haskalah poetry. As a further result, the rules of rhyme caused sentence inversion, since the verb was closing a verse line, and enjambement was excluded; all complements of the verb, similes, etc., preceded the verb rather than followed it (as the usual word-order would require). The following is a typical stanza of this kind:

וּבֵין כֹּה וָכֹה הַדְּמָמָה הִפְרִיעוּ
תּוֹפְשֵׂי הַמָּשׁוֹט בַּמַּיִם יַחְתּוֹרוּ;
גַּם קוֹל עַל הַמַּיִם עַם רָב הִשְׁמִיעוּ,
גַּם דָּוִד גַּם רֵעוֹ מִשְּׁנָת נֵעוֹרוּ.

Meantime the silence they interrupted,
The crew who in the water rowed;
A voice on the water a multitude emitted,
And David and his friend from their sleep awoke

Thus, in spite of the accepted Ashkenazi pronunciation in the later poetry of J. L. Gordon, most of the words in his poetry were excluded from rhyme position: a group of words constituting 8% of the normal language continuum was used in 90% of his rhymes. With the abolition of the restriction to the Sephardi stress, no revolutionary change occurred in the rhymes of the Haskalah since the typical rhymes became part of poetic style as such. Only a fundamental change in poetic style and in the very conception of poetic language, introduced by Ḥ. N. Bialik and his generation, was to alter radically the resources of Hebrew rhyme, making available for rhyme practically the whole range of the Hebrew language. During the Haskalah, this freedom was enjoyed only sometimes in minor genres and by poets on the geographical "periphery" (poets from Galicia or Hungary).

Though the tradition of epic poetry in the Haskalah began with Wessely's blank verse, in time rhyme became dominant in this domain too, especially in the Lithuanian center. The poets of the Haskalah used a variety of strophic forms very often of more than 4 lines, notably the stanza developed by Wessely consisting of 6 lines and rhyming *aabccb,* the *ottava rima* inherited from Italy, and other strophic patterns, especially of 6 or 8 lines. The 4-line stanza was also widespread, primarily in the form of *abab,* but it was not as predominant as in the poetry of later generations.

The strophic forms in all their variety usually used alternating rhymes, the members of one rhyme alternating with the members of another rhyme. Rarely did a Haskalah poet systematically use one rhyme more than twice without alternating. In this respect Hebrew poetry conformed to the prevalent European sense of rhyme variation. On the other hand, there was no alternation whatsoever or rhymes insofar as their rhythmical properties. Though Russian poetry alternated, as a rule, not only the rhymes, but also their rhythmic patterns, i.e., combining throughout a poem feminine and masculine, or masculine and dactylic rhymes, Hebrew poetry of this period did not accept this norm. Feminine rhymes were the absolute rule, except for sporadic, non-systematic uses of masculine-rhyming words.

In Italy such a restriction of the language could be understood as influenced by a taste formed through the reading of Italian poetry in which predominantly feminine rhymes are used; this is a concomitant of the structure of the Italian language. In Russia, however, the restriction made no sense and can only be explained through the compulsion exerted by the internal Hebrew tradition. Paradoxically enough, this requirement continued to obtain even at a time when feminine rhymes were drawn merely from the words regarded as feminine according to the Sephardi pronunciation, i.e., when the bulk of the language could have been used for the purpose of masculine rhymes. It was only the generation of Bialik that, again paradoxically enough, attempted to alternate between feminine and masculine rhymes, in spite of the scarcity of the latter in the Ashkenazi dialect, which became in this generation the accepted language of Hebrew verse.

Nevertheless, though stress was disregarded by the syllabic system, it may subconsciously have played a role in forming the rhythmic nature of Hebrew verse in the Haskalah period. The most widespread meters were 13 and 11 syllables. Such a length of lines conformed very well with the structure of 4 major accents, or 4 words, grouped mostly in 2 pairs. This condition may have played a role in the acceptance of Haskalah poetry, for there was, to the ear, as it were, an underlying quasi-biblical meter, felt even more because of the biblical language used in this poetry. A line of 11 or 13 syllables, using 4 major stresses, in a language in which the average number of syllables to each stress is about 3, can easily be brought to approximate an amphibrachic tetrameter, e.g., the first stanza of A. D. *Lebensohn's poem לַבֹּקֶר רִנָּה in the Ashkenazi pronunciation can be read:

קוֹל תִּשְׁמַע נַפְשִׁי // הֲמוֹן צִבְאוֹת חַיִל
רִנַּת כּוֹכָבִים // וּבְרֹאשָׁם יָרֵחַ;
עַל מִשְׁמֶרֶת אֶרֶץ // עָמְדוּ בַּלָּיִל,
עַתָּה כִּי בָא שַׁחַר // לִבָּם שָׂמֵחַ;
גַּם נֶגַע זֶה // עַל עֵינַי וַיְעוֹרוּ,
וּמְלֹא כָל הָאָרֶץ // אֶרְאֶה כִּי אוֹרוּ.

This is a typical Haskalah stanza *(aba bcc)*, rhyming Sephardi *mille'eil*. But an Ashkenazi reading reveals the underlying dactylic-amphibrachic meter, sidestepped only in the first hemistichs of lines 3, 4, and in the second hemistich of line 5.

Toward the end of this period the unregulated stresses within the line became more and more often "ordered," many lines approximating 4 amphibrachs (such were, for example, the poems of S. L. *Gordon in the early 1890s).

Thus, for the second time in its history, Hebrew syllabic verse developed again toward an accentual-syllabic meter, dominated however by the amphibrach rather than the iamb, prevalent in Italy, and it followed the Ashkenazi rather than the Sephardi pronunciation.

Such is the story of the transformations of a major Hebrew metrical form: the quantitative meter of Spanish Hebrew poetry, originating in Arabic versification, was reinterpreted in Italy as syllabic, under the influence of Italian versification. Hebrew syllabic poetry stretched over a period of centuries (from the 12th to the 19th), adopting Italian strophic forms without relinquishing the quantitative patterns of the Arabic heritage, but shifting time and again into accentual-syllabic iambs. The Haskalah took up the same syllabic verse forms, continued to use them in spite of a literary environment which accepted exclusively accentual-syllabic meters and imbued them with an underlying semi-biblical (that is accentual) rhythm. It finally brought Hebrew poetry again to the verge of accentual-syllabic meters.

The development of Hebrew poetry should be considered as a chain in transformation rather than a series of totally opposed and separate periods. As regards sentence structure and syntactical rhythm, there was no fundamental change: similar groups of words could constitute a verse line, since a line of 11 syllables was the most frequent length in all these periods.

THE MODERN PERIOD

The Historical Setting. Though echoes of European literature and of European poetics of the modern age had reverberated in Hebrew poetry since the days of Dante in Italy, and throughout the literature of the Haskalah, Hebrew poetry had not accepted fully, until the very end of the 19th century, the consequences of the lyrical revolution accomplished by Goethe, Pushkin, or the English romantics.

From the limited point of view of this survey, one can observe the striking fact that Hebrew meter was based, until the end of the 19th century, on syllable-counting rather than on the subtle and complex instrument developed in other languages with "free" stress in the form of accentual-syllabic (or tonic-syllabic) versification. English poetry since the 16th century, German poetry since Opitz (17th century), Russian poetry since the middle of the 18th century—the whole modern period of these poetries—cannot be imagined without the metrical system. It is an instrument whose exact structures made possible the clear-cut distinction of a large variety of forms and also provided the background for clearly pronounced effects of particular rhythmical variations. These two assets were of primary importance for a poetry characterized by the individuality of the writer, the individuality of the poem, the reliance on a living language, and the immediate appeal in concrete sensuous images to the imagination of the reader. Even free verse was rich and effective when playing on this background. Such a poetics was accepted and absorbed by the Hebrew poets who, through an externist's secondary education, came to know the classical Russian heritage of Pushkin, Lermontov, and their followers. The first poet to write consistently in accentual-syllabic meters was Ḥ. N. Bialik whose first poem *"El ha-Ẓippor"* ("To the Bird") was published in 1894, in the very year when Russian symbolism emerged, i.e., a movement which strove to break away from the regularities of this very same metrical system.

In Odessa before World War I where Hebrew poets wrote some of the best of Hebrew poetry in the poetic mode of Russian literature of the 1830s, young Jewish poets, writing in Russian, launched modernistic journals such as "The Flying Omnibus." The beginning and end of the major cycle of modern Russian poetry seemed to meet at one time and in one place. Obviously, Hebrew poetry could not for long be excluded from the general developments, the more so because Yiddish poetry was sometimes written by the same poets in a language more alive and actual and therefore absorbed the waves of modernism more rapidly. Thus in one generation Hebrew poetry not only caught up with the European classical heritage as conceived by the early 19th century, but at the same time landed, in one grand leap, into the European 20th century. The struggle and interaction between a variety of poetic trends—evolution turned into contemporaneity—make it one of the most panoramic and interesting periods of Hebrew poetry. But, as regards this survey, it is a handicap: it is difficult to keep apart the "generations" of poetry in which unequivocal norms persist. Free verse was developed almost contemporaneously with exact meters or Greek verse forms. Modernistic rhymes were intermingled with exact "classical" rhyming and with blank verse. Hence it is advisable to discuss forms and formal systems—"regular" or "modernistic"—rather than periods of poetry.

A second objective difficulty in discussing the rhythms of Hebrew poetry in the 20th century is due to the revolution in the pronunciation of the Hebrew language which undermined its whole prosodic foundation. The rhythm and sound orchestration, so essential to the concept of poetry of the classics of the last generation—H. N. Bialik, S. *Tchernichowsky, J. *Fichmann, J. *Steinberg, Z. *Shneour—is lost to the ears of Israeli readers. The poetry of the Hebrew revival in Russia at the end of the 19th century, which is concrete and sensuous and employed the Russian sensibility for subtleties of rhythm and sound, unfolded the sound values of the language in the Ashkenazi dialects. But almost at the same time there was in Israel a revival of Hebrew as a spoken language, which used the "Sephardi" or "Israel" pronunciation. The clash between the two dialects was sometimes fierce. The changing laws of language will be discussed below. Here one example may suffice. The two words עֹז־רֶתֶת were a perfect rhyme in the Lithuanian Ashkenazi Hebrew of U. N. *Gnessin EYS-rsEYS (both *ḥolam* and *ẓere* being pronounced *ey;* ת sounding like *s;* and *z*=*s* in rhyme, according to the Russian convention of neutralizing voiced consonants in an end position); but the same rhyming pair lost all sound identities to the ears of an Israeli who reads it: *oz-retét.* The Sephardi pronunciation was also employed in Hebrew meters in this period, as early as 1900 (not to count some experiments during the Haskalah period as well as the unintentional iambs of Hebrew poetry in Italy). The Ashkenazi pronunciation was still dominant in the 1920s and was alive with some poets until the 1960s. This coexistence again complicates our discussion.

The shift of dialects was a revolution in the sound system of a language, which did not occur elsewhere in such an abrupt manner. In this process most of the poetry of the period of Revival was lost from the point of view of its musicality and rhythm. But the poets who moved from one Hebrew tongue to quite a different one, despite the pangs of readjustment, remained the same, and so did the poetic ideals and norms. These had no time to change. It was simply a matter of readjusting to the new sound system, of regaining a *modus vivendi* with the spoken language. Therefore it is possible, despite the crucial shift, to discuss the prosodic norms, using at first illustrations from Hebrew poems in the contemporary Israel pronunciation.

The Two Dialects of Modern Hebrew. When Hebrew became a spoken language in Ereẓ Israel, it adopted the principles of the "Sephardi" pronunciation in which the location of stress is based on the accentuation marks of the Bible. The majority of words in this Israel pronunciation have a stress on their final syllable. Only a small group of words are penultimately stressed; these are of two varieties; the so-called *segoliyyim* having two *e* vowels, patterned like *dégel,* and words with the furtive *pattaḥ* ending in an originally guttural consonant, like תַּפּוּחַ *(tappú'aḥ),* רֵיחַ *(rei'aḥ)* לָנוּעַ *(lanu'a).* A larger group of penultimately stressed words is provided by several suffixes, such as the feminine forms אוֹמֶרֶת (*omeret*—versus the masculine *omer*), verbs in some perfect forms: אָמַרְתִּי, אָמַרְתָּ, אָמַרְנוּ *(amarti, amarta, amarnu),* or nouns in the plural with some possessive pronouns (דְּבָרֶיךָ, דְּבָרַיִךְ—*devarekha, devarayikh*). A new group of penultimately stressed words consists of foreign borrowings: *akadémya, gemnázya,* etc. On the other hand, several distinctions in the quality of sounds marked in the biblical vocalization system, are blurred in the Sephardi dialect. Thus both *pattaḥ* and *qameṣ* are pronounced *a; ṣere* and *segol* are pronounced *e;* תּ and ת are both *t.*

The Ashkenazi pronunciation of Hebrew, developed in Europe since the 14th century, is based primarily on the penultimate stress. With a few exceptions, a penultimate stress is absent only when it is impossible to implement it: (a) in monosyllabic words (a small group in Hebrew); (b) in bisyllabic words, if the first syllable is a short one (*ḥataf* or *šewa*), e.g., אֲנִי, בְּנִי; (c) in longer words where the penultimate syllable is a short one, the stress moves to the third-to-last syllable, e.g. הַמְּחוֹנְנִים *(ha-meḥónenim),* נַעֲרָה *(ná'arah).* In (b) and (c) there are exceptions, based on the fact that historically short syllables became normal and may be stressed, like in Hebrew words in Yiddish (e.g., חָלוֹם should be *khalóym,* but it is often pronounced as in Yiddish: *khólem*). On the other hand, there is in Ashkenazi a wider range of vowel qualities: *qameṣ* is distinguished from *pattaḥ; ḥolam* and *ṣere* are diphthongs. The weak ת is pronounced *s* (rather than the Israel *t*). Within the Ashkenazi domain there were several dialects, on the whole resembling the dialects of Yiddish. In poetry these subdialects are felt not in the meter but in the rhyme.

Ashkenazi Hebrew with its diphthongs and penultimate stress was felt by the poets to be "softer" and more "musical" than the "harsh" Israel Hebrew which is ultimately stressed and in which *a* makes up fifty percent of its vowels. Until the late 1930s some tried to keep poetry in the traditional Ashkenazi dialect, but finally they had to give in to the spoken language of Israel. Several poets attempted "translating" their poetry into the new dialect. On the whole they succeeded in making a mechanical meter, but in most cases the poem was severely harmed in the process. A variety of interesting transitional forms developed. Thus U. Z. Greenberg, though still writing in Ashkenazi Hebrew, let the Israel workers in his poems speak in their authentic Israel pronunciation.

Accentual Syllabic Meter in Hebrew. The dominant system of Hebrew prosody since the 1890s was accentual-syllabic, though throughout the period other forms also existed. Accentual-syllabic versification came to Hebrew poetry under the influence and in the forms of the Russian tradition of the 19th century. However, some rhythmical characteristics of these meters are due to the structural properties of the Hebrew language. Accentual-syllabic meters are based on the ordering both of the number of syllables and of the location of stresses in a verse line. But it is rare, especially in Hebrew poetry, that the actual stresses in the language of a line constitute a neatly ordered pattern, copying exactly the metrical scheme. There is a discrepancy between the units of the language and the units of meter: stress and word boundaries on the one hand

and metrical accents and feet on the other. A meter exists in a poem if its actual stresses and word boundaries meet certain rules of correlation with the underlying metrical scheme.

TYPES OF METERS. A meter is a permanent order of accented and unaccented syllables, underlying all lines of a poem (or part of it). The sign (–) represents a metrically accented syllable, the sign (ᴗ) an unaccented one. The elementary recurrent group of syllables is called a "foot." Thus in a line of the type: ᴗᴗ-ᴗᴗ-ᴗᴗ-there are three feet /ᴗᴗ-/. A foot is not a rhythmical unit; its boundaries do not mark any stop in reading; it is a mere abstraction of the basic principle underlying the pattern of a line. Each foot has one accented and one or two unaccented syllables.

There are two binary feet: iamb /ᴗ–/
trochee /–ᴗ/

and three ternary feet: anapest /ᴗᴗ–/
amphibrach /ᴗ–ᴗ/
dactyl /–ᴗᴗ/

A meter of a line is determined by the kind of feet and their number, e.g., an iambic pentameter is a line of five iambs. The number of feet is determined by the number of accents; the last foot may be incomplete and may vary throughout a poem. Thus, in an iambic pentameter there may be either 10 or 11 syllables: ᴗ-ᴗ-ᴗ-ᴗ-ᴗ-(ᴗ) (depending on the gender of rhyme or on the line ending). Usually in Hebrew poetry there is only one kind of foot in a poem, i.e., one form of alternating accented and unaccented syllables (binary or ternary).

DEFINITION OF METER. A poem has a certain meter, when it can be read according to a metrical pattern without contradicting its language. The general rule of correlation is: if a word receives metrical accents, at least one of them must fall on the stressed syllable. This rule implies that a word (1) may be unaccented; or (2) may have an accent on its stressed syllable; or (3) may have several accents, one of them falling on the stressed syllable, e.g., *Nŏshẻv, ērĕ̆v ăfŏ̇r vĕ̆-ŏ̆r*[(e)]*vim ă̆l t* [(e)]*r̆ănạ̇v*. This is a line of four anapests (by Alterman) in which the stress (marked) of the first word is disregarded by the meter, the stresses of other words are employed by the meter as regular accents. The following is an example of a Hebrew stanza meter of 4 iambs (by Alterman):

Ăz ḥivvărŏ̇n gădŏ̇l hē'ir̊
Ĕt ha-r[(e)]*hŏvŏ̇t vĕ̆-hā-sh*[(e)]*vă̆kĭ̊m*
Ămă̇d nătŭ̇i ă̆l p[(e)]*nẻi*
Năḥshŏ̇l shămă̊yĭm yērŭ̆kĭ̊m

The first word of the first line is unaccented by the meter, the second word has 2 accents (one of them on the stressed syllable). The second line provides only two stresses in its language, etc.

RHYTHMIC VARIATION. Obviously, an expressive reading of a poem will consider language stress and word boundaries rather than the mechanical pattern of the metrical accents. Thus rhythmical variation is created primarily by the fact that not all accents of the meter are realized in the language, the division of actual stresses and word boundaries may vary from line to line, e.g., a trochaic stanza (*Alterman):

Dumiyyáh la-merḥavím shoreket
Bóhak ha-sakkín be-éin ha-ḥatulím
Láylah, kámmah láylah! Ba-shamáyim shéket
Kokhavím be-ḥittulím.

It has 5-6-6-4 trochees, but the number of stresses is 3-4-5-2, irregularly dispersed. When read according to its language, every line seems to be rhythmically different (every box represents a word, x denotes a syllable, x́ an accented syllable):

x x x́	x x x x́	x x́ x		
x́ x	x x x́	x́ x́	x x x x́	
x́ x	x́ x	x́ x	x x x́ x	x́ x
x x x́	x x x x́			

In modern Hebrew there is, on the average, one stress to each three syllables. In binary meters, which constitute the bulk of modern Hebrew metrical verse, rhythmical variation is based primarily on avoiding stresses in accented positions. This tendency usually follows the Russian symmetrical pattern of variation. Thus in a meter of four iambs or trochees, the fourth and the second accents are almost always stressed, the third and the first are quite often unstressed. (This is obviously different from English binary meters where variation is largely based on the opposite possibility: stressing unaccented syllables.) In short, Hebrew iambs and trochees are not based on a regular number of stresses to each line, but on changing deviations from a regular abstract scheme.

Limited Free Verse: the "Ternary Net." Whereas in binary meters variation is built into the system (a 3:2 relationship between accent and stress), in ternary meters almost all accents coincide with stresses. In the Israel pronunciation where in most words stress coincides also with word boundary, the effect becomes tedious, especially in the anapestic meters where almost every foot is a word and every accent a stress. Poets did their best to create variation here too, but the solution came in the form of a kind of free verse adapted from Russian modernist poetry (Blok, Akhmatova, Yessenin). In this system, the number of accents in a line remains regular, but the number of syllables is free to a certain extent. Usually an impulse of a ternary meter is created, to be disturbed on and off; instead of two unaccented there are occasionally one or none (and in some poets also three). The abstract pattern looks like a "net": a ternary scheme with "holes" in it which appear without any regularity, but rarely enough, so as not to destroy the underlying ternary pattern. Beginnings of lines are usually free too, thus abolishing any distinction between anapest, amphibrach, or dactyl, e.g., two stanzas by the poetess Raḥel:

Hen damáh be-dami zorém	ᴗᴗ–ᴗᴗ–Oᴗ–
Hen koláh bi rán—	ᴗᴗ–Oᴗ–
Rahél, ha-ro'áh ẓón laván	Oᴗ–ᴗᴗ–ᴗᴗ–
Rahél—em ha-ém	Oᴗ–ᴗᴗ–
Ve-al kén ha-bayit li ẓar	ᴗᴗ–Oᴗ–ᴗᴗ–
Ve-ha-ir zarah	ᴗᴗ–Oᴗ–
Ki hayah mitnoféf, sudaráh	ᴗᴗ–ᴗᴗ–ᴗᴗ–
Le-ruḥot ha-mid-bár	ᴗᴗ–ᴗᴗ–

The conversational tone is achieved here by breaking the anapestic flow. But the same principle may be used for a variety of rhythmic tendencies and poetic themes and tones. It became a major form of Hebrew poetry since the 1920s, developed by *Raḥel, Alterman, *Zusman, Lea *Goldberg, *Bat-Miriam, and other poets of the Russian tradition.

Free Verse. Since the beginnings of Hebrew accentual-syllabic meters, varieties of freedom from their strictures were sought. Thus Tchernichowsky used widely the dactylic hexameter, varying often two or one unaccented syllables. The effect was similar to the ternary net, but the "excuse" was an interpretation of the Greek meter followed by German poets, which varied the dactyls by using trochees (instead of the Greek spondee). Bialik developed his so-called "biblical" rhythms; but, unlike in the Bible, the number of accents was fixed and the number of unaccented syllables varied in a limited way: 1 or 2 (and occasionally 3) syllables in each interstress interval. About ten years after the initiation of the accentual-syllabic meters, a Hebrew poet appeared who wrote purely free verse: Avraham *Ben Yiẓḥak. This trend, based on the balancing of small word groups and phrases, was enhanced by the influence of German expressionism (exerted on such poets as David Vogel). It was renewed in some of the young poets of the Palmaḥ generation (1948) and in the 1950s, under the influence of English modernism. The forms of free verse are too varied to be discussed here. Basically they lean on syntactic patterns, strengthened by parallelism and sound orchestration. At present the whole scale from strict meters to prose-like free verse is productive in Hebrew poetry.

Rhyme in Modern Poetry. Though rhyme in Hebrew was older than in any of the surrounding languages, and though its forms changed throughout the centuries, it was not before the 1890s that Hebrew rhyme accepted fully the European rhyme system. (As has been seen, the principle of stressed rhyme was adopted already in Hebrew poetry in Italy in the 17th century, but it actually applied to feminine rhymes only and did not involve the whole language until the end of the 19th century.)

In modern Hebrew poetry it is convenient to distinguish "exact" from "inexact" rhymes. In "exact" rhymes the rhymeme always extends to the very end of the rhyming members (*x*=*ḥ* or *kh; c*=*ẓ*): *sma MA-eyMA, novÉYAX-KerÉYAX;* in "inexact" rhymes some of the final sounds are not identical, i.e., the rhymeme does not always reach the end of the verse line: *mesoRÉGEt-baRÉGEv; la ḥaDSÍ - kiDuŠIn; ba-xÓFEn - ha-OFEk,* etc. The inexact rhyme, a symptom of modernism, should be discussed after the basic "exact" norm from which it deviated.

The Basic Norm of the Exact Rhyme. The rhymeme is the basic norm in modern Hebrew poetry, as it is in most European languages; it includes all sounds from the last stressed vowel to the end of the line: N=V́ ( ). (The parentheses represent all sounds, which may come after the stressed vowel.) As opposed to the terminal Hebrew rhyme of the Middle Ages, this is an accentual-terminal rhyme norm, e.g., *šovÁX - heÁX; šenavÓXA - kamÓXA; dÁY LA - LÁYLA; lirKOŠET - xarOSET.* The rhyme in these cases includes 2, 3, or 4 sounds (V́C, VCV, V́CCV, VCVC). All of these are minimal rhymemes: they may be enlarged, but deducting one sound destroys the rhyme. Thus, the basic norm is not determined by the number of sounds but by their position. The number of sounds following the stressed vowel depends on the structure of the words, it is a matter of language rather than of rhyming norm. In this system, a *rime riche* is based not on the number of sounds in the rhymeme, but on the employment of sounds additional to the required norm. Thus *ticNAX - aNAX* (תִּצְנַח – אֲנָךְ) is a rich rhyme, though its rhymeme *NAX* has only 3 sounds, since *AX would be good enough; whereas ESET* in *IESET - nogÉSET* (לֶסֶת־נוֹגֶסֶת) is not rich, though it has 4 sounds, since it is the minimal sound group in such feminine rhymes.

Secondary Norms. In addition to the basic norm, several secondary norms are at work, some are more general, others less obligatory or more restricted to certain poets or trends.

The Numeric Norm. Hebrew poetry in the Israel pronunciation requires a minimum of 2 sounds in the rhymeme. In English, German, or Yiddish poetry, one stressed vowel is enough, if it comes at the end of the word: *free - tranquility - sea, be - we, go - snow* are perfect rhymes in English. But in Israel Hebrew, as in Russian, in such cases, a consonant has to precede the final vowel: *bitfiLÁ - leoLÁ* is a minimal rhyme (N_2=CV). Two sounds are enough, even when there is no consonant: *ligvÓA - elÓA.*

Hebrew poetry in the Ashkenazi pronunciation did not require this numeric norm. Bialik rhymed *lÍ - bnÍ* (לִי – בְּנִי), *hazE - hapE* (הַזֶּה־הַפֶּה), etc. The reason is obvious: there are in the Ashkenazi pronunciation very few ultimately stressed words (primarily monosyllables, a rather small group in Hebrew) and even less such words with open syllables. With the additional rule it would be almost impossible to rhyme these words. On the other hand, in the Israel pronunciation most of the words are ultimately stressed, the number of vowels has been reduced to 5, and there is an enormous amount of words which terminate in *á* (resulting both from the historical *pattaḥ* and *qameṣ*). The use of such an á as a rhyme would be too easy and trite to be effective.

The Historical Factor. There was a historical factor to this development, too. Bialik and many of his contemporary "Ashkenazi" poets at the end of the 19th and the beginning of the 20th century (Z. Shneour, I. *Katzenelson, Jacob Steinberg, J. Fichmann) wrote Yiddish as well as Hebrew poetry. Yiddish, as other Germanic languages, does not require the numeric norm. But the Israel poets of the next generation (Raḥel, A. Shlonsky, Lea Goldberg) were overwhelmingly influenced by Russian poetry where this norm is required.

The historical factor is felt again in the "young" Israel poetry of the 1950s. Hebrew poetry now moved from the Russian to the English sphere of influence and away from rich "colorful" rhyming to a rather "prose-like" poetics. Here again rhymes appeared, based on a single stressed vowel: *kÍ - civonÍ; lezokhrÓ - be-motÓ,* etc.

The Morphological Norm. In the Israel pronunciation *sIR - kabIR, niM - allM* (נִים־אֲלִים) are perfect rhymes, but *mexusIM - allM* (מְכוּסִים־עָלִים) is not, since *IM* in this case is a morphological ending: the non-feminine plural suffix of nouns, verbs, and adjectives. This secondary norm requires the participation of at least one stem consonant in a rhyme: *mesuSIM - ma'aSIM* or *aLIM - keLIM* are minimal rhymes in this case.

Three Criteria of the Rhyming Norm. The basic norm with the secondary norms may now be combined: "exact" rhyme in modern Hebrew poetry in the Israel pronunciation requires in its rhymeme all the sounds from the last stressed syllable to the end of the verse line, provided that there are at least two sounds and at least one is part of the root of the rhyming word. This complex rule makes three kinds of demands: (a) a norm for the *place* of the rhymeme; (b) a norm for its minimal *size;* (c) a norm concerning its *morphological* structure.

The Relativity of the Morphological Norm. The three heterogeneous norms have different degrees of validity in different poets or generations. The morphological subnorm seems to be the most flexible. Some suffixes are less susceptible to this norm. Thus, Raḥel, a poetess of the 1920s who preceded the "young" generation in the use of "prosaic" language in her lyrical poetry (influenced not by English Imagism but by the Russian Acmeists, especially the poetry of Akhmatova), strictly applies the morphological norm to the non-feminine plural suffix *IM* (e.g., *raVIM-asaVIM*), but disregards this requirement for the feminine plural *OT (kallOT - netivOT)* and other suffixes. Some "young" poets of the 1950s use even obvious grammatical rhymes, with the plural suffix *IM* as a rhymeme.

On the whole, the more widespread the use of a suffix in a language, the stronger is the tendency not to rely upon that suffix alone. The opposition to grammatical rhyme, inherited from Russian poetry, was strongest in the plural

IM. On the other hand, the requirement to add a root consonant is entirely weak in two-syllabic suffixes, which are penultimately stressed, such as the dual: *áyim*.

The "mistrust" of grammatical rhyme is often expressed in poetry far beyond the required norm. Thus Shlonsky uses rich rhymes especially when a suffix occurs, as if to compensate for the very use of a suffix in rhyme: *DIRIM - aDIRIM, MeDuROT - MiDoROT* (where *RIM* or *ROT* would be sufficient), etc.

Minimum and Maximum. The norm described above concerns the minimal group of sounds required in a rhymeme. In Hebrew poetry in the Israel pronunciation there is a wide discrepancy between the minimum sounds required and the maximum actually used. Some poets, such as A. Shlonsky or N. Alterman, influenced by the poetics of Russian modernism, employ rhymes as rich as possible: *tiKTEFÉNU - KTEFENU, AKuMÓT - hAKOMÓT*, etc. The words in modern Hebrew, having no secondary stress, are usually long (3 syllables and more). Most of the sounds in the rhyming words of the poets under discussion are employed in the rhymeme. This tendency is doubly connected with the poetics of Hebrew "imagistic" poetry: (a) It is part of the general "colorful" aesthetics which abounds in striking imagery, rich sound patterns, "strong" themes, etc. There is a strongly expressed "set toward the message," a high "density" of the poetic language. (b) Since many sounds are involved in each rhyme, it is quite difficult to find words rhyming with each other; only a poetic language with a high degree of flexibility in imagery and elliptic combination could enable such freedom in connecting rhyming words drawn from distant spheres of meaning.

The maximal limit for a rhymeme consists in leaving a minimal difference between the rhyming members. In such rhymes as Yehudah *Karni's *K'ILU MAT - KIL'UMAT* (כְּאִלּוּ־מַת – כִּלְעוּמַת) or *YIF'AM - YIF AM* (יִפְעָם – יִיף עָם), the difference may only be in a junction between words. In Alterman's rhyme בְּגוּמַת לְחָיַיִךְ – אֶת יֵינָן הַלּוֹהֵט לְחַיַּיִךְ *(LEXAYAYIX)*, the difference lies merely in the different morphological structure: in the first case ("your cheeks") the *l* is part of the root לחי, in the second case ("for your life") the *l* is a separate morpheme ("for") connected only graphically with the word חיים.

A Comparative Perspective. Rich rhyme in Israel Hebrew can be explained not merely by the influence of one kind of modernist poetics. The properties of the language also encourage this trend. Most of the words in this pronunciation are stressed ultimately and most of the words are multisyllabic. Rhyming merely one syllable time and again would be tedious. Moreover, since most of the words are stressed ultimately, there is a multitude of words available for each rhyme ending. It may be compared to other languages. In Russian, where many words are also multisyllabic, stresses may occur on any syllable of a word, therefore the number of words rhyming ultimately is relatively smaller, and multisyllabic rhyme is usual. In Yiddish, too, the amount of feminine and dactylic rhymes is incomparably higher.

In English the number of monosyllables is so high that masculine rhymes are usual, as in Hebrew. But the "neutral" sounds of each number are not felt strongly, since they are few. In a usual Hebrew word one or three syllables do not participate in a minimal rhymeme: cf., the English pARTS - mARTS (though the rhymeme is monosyllabic most sounds of each member are covered by it) with the Hebrew *mešuxrÁR - veaxzÁR* where the nonparticipating, "neutral," sounds of each member are conspicuous. Moreover, English has some 13 different rhyming vowels (as compared to the mere 5 of Israel Hebrew) and many consonant clusters, preceding and following the vowel, which make the number of possible rhyme endings incomparably higher and the number of words available for each relatively much smaller. Since there are very few possible rhyme endings in Israel Hebrew, it is much easier to meet the minimal rhyme requirements and also easier, and more necessary, to add sounds and "enrich" the rhymeme. French with its ultimate stress, though it is more abundant in rhyme endings than Hebrew, also tends to prefer *rime riche*.

Rhyme in the Ashkenazi Pronunciation. The basic norm of the accentual-terminal rhyme is identical in the poetry of the "Sephardi" pronunciation (in Italy since the Renaissance) or in the Israeli, as well as in the Ashkenazi pronunciation, which was accepted in European Hebrew from the 14th century, but entered rhyme only in the 19th century. But the realization of the norm differed strongly due to the difference in the rhythmic structure of the Hebrew word.

Since the Ashkenazi stress falls on the second or third syllable from the end, most rhymes were automatically polysyllabic and most sounds of a word were included in the rhymeme. Thus, *mÍDBOR - nÍDBOR* is a very usual rhyme in Bialik's poetry, but the same pair makes a very rich rhyme in the Israel pronunciation: *mIDBÁR - nIDBÁR* (since *AR* would be enough). Therefore, rich rhymes are few in Ashkenazi but may abound in Israel Hebrew (at least in the practice of some poets). Moreover, the necessity to include in most cases at least two syllables in the rhymeme leads the poets to search for alleviating devices. Thus Bialik in his early poetry tends to use grammatic rhymes which have already one syllable given in the morphological suffix, and the poet has to find words which differ in one syllable only. This necessity also leads to the use of archaic endings, feminine forms, etc. In short: any *manqué* form of a word, e.g., the Israel rhyme צוֹהֵל – נוֹזֵל is not a rhyme in Ashkenazi *(cohel-nozel)*, but the feminine form, with an added syllable, is: צוֹהֶלֶת – נוֹזֶלֶת *(coheles-nozeles)*. Therefore Bialik uses not אוֹר נוֹזֵל ("running light") but a more archaic form, which is feminine אוֹרָה נוֹזֶלֶת. Feminine verbs or adjectives in rhyme position obviously bring about feminine nouns in the middle of the line. The same holds for plurals and archaic forms.

"Modernistic" Rhyme. The "Inexact" Rhyme. Modernistic Hebrew poetry uses a large amoung of inexact rhymes, such as Alterman's *ŠKuFÁ hI - miŠKaFAyIM: KoS HaMÁyIM - KSuMÁ hI*, etc. In such rhymes at least one member ends with a "neutral" sound not participating in the rhymeme. But the effect is strong, since such rhymes usually have many sounds. There is a great variety of concrete forms, but in all cases the stressed vowel is constant, i.e., it is an accentual rhyme. In most cases the rhymeme is discontinued and the system may be called: *accentual-discontinuous*. The rhymeme, in addition to the fixed-stressed vowel, is based primarily on consonants. This phenomenon of the discontinuous rhymeme, particular to Hebrew poetry, is based on the nature of the Hebrew lexical morpheme, which is discontinuous and purely consonantal.

This system, representing a strong break from the standard European norm where rhyme is *accentual-terminal* and is usually continuous, had its forerunner in the earliest system of rhyme, in old Hebrew liturgy (the *piyyut*). But the concrete immediate influence which created this norm in Hebrew modernism came from the poetry of Mayakovsky and Pasternak, where rhymemes were also inexact in their endings and moved deeper into the middle of the line. While discontinuity in Russian rhyme was an occasional form of deviation rather than the rule, for Alterman and his contemporaries it became the norm, based on the characteristics of the Hebrew language. Alterman uses both exact and inexact rhymes in the same poems. The minimal requirement for a rhymeme now is: two sounds, at least one of which is the last stressed vowel. But only rarely was the minimal rhymeme employed (e.g., an exact rhyme: *zahÁV* - *yadÁV;* an inexact rhyme: *koXÓ* - *harXÓv*). Most of the rhymes are very rich. The sound contrast between the rhyming members was strongly emphasized through the introduction of neutral sounds in between the sounds of the (discontinuous!) rhymeme, e.g., *SiPuNÉXA* - *kaSE PaNÉXA, LEORÉR* - *LEOR nER;* or by changing the order of the parallel sounds, e.g., *miTPARECet* - *TRAPECioT (TPAR* TRAP*)*.

In short, modernist rhyme cannot be described merely in negative terms, as a deviation from a "classical norm." The norm of the *accentual-discontinuous* rhyme creates a system as consistent and as effective as the *accentual-terminal* one, though the range of variation given to particular poets may be considerably wider now.

SUMMARY

A Pan-Historic Synopsis of Hebrew Prosodic Systems. The preceding historical survey, though simplified as much as possible, presented a long chain of changes. When pan-historical comparisons are made, one finds logical relationships; similarities and contrasts between systems which are distant in time and place, but created in the forms of one language and culture. The diagram below may present the basis of such a comparison. The major systems of Hebrew verse are arranged in this diagram clockwise, in the order of their emergence in the history of Hebrew poetry. Except for a meter based on pitch, all known verse systems were productive in Hebrew. As can be seen from the diagram, there is a logical pattern, a kind of cyclic movement in this history. The major basis of the meter moved from *phrase* to *word* to *syllable* and vice versa.

The earliest and the latest verse systems were based on a free rhythm of phrase groups, though in the Bible there was a strong symmetricity of parallelism, whereas in modernist free verse there is a typical flow of continuity and lengths of lines may be highly varied. On the other hand, in modernist free verse poets often employ changing segments of accentual-syllabic meters as well as effects of irregular rhyme. It is not the freedom of "primitive" poetry, preceding any system, but the freedom of a "late" post-classical period, which is also free to employ any device developed in the "classical" rules of previous periods.

From biblical rhythm, based on semantic-syntactic-accentual free parallelism of phrases, the development of Hebrew verse moved toward basing its meters on more and more exact measures, i.e., ordering smaller elements of the language from phrases to the number of stresses, through the exact number of words, to the number of syllables, to a distinction of syllables according to their prosodic features.

Meters based on syllable counting ruled Hebrew poetry from about 950 almost to 1950.These were the most exact and variegated systems of Hebrew versification. Within this tradition, the change in the internal organization of the verse line from a quantitative principle to an accentual principle represented the general development of European poetry, but marked also the shift from the artificial "high" style of reading poetry to the intrusion of the cadences of the spoken language. (In religious poetry of Franco-Germany throughout the Middle Ages, a system based on the number of words persisted, i.e., a rhythm which, though numerically rigorous, was closer to representing some phrase patterns and clearly resembled the rhythm of medieval Yiddish and German poetry.)

In modernist poetry the movement of the early centuries of the Christian era was reversed: from strict syllable counting through a semi-regular meter, relying almost exactly on the number of major word stresses (though with a still limited freedom of syllable numbers VII), to a free verse system, based primarily on a rhythm of phrase groups, relying on the tension between the verse line and syntactic units. But in this period, even within the domain of free verse (VIII), the previous regular norms (VI accentual-syllabic and VII, accentual net) were still widely employed. On the other hand, the essential difference between the major systems of Hebrew verse should not lead to the overlooking of some basic consistent trends which cut across several systems. Within each system not all possibilities were equally employed. In any system, a rather small number of all possible forms were prevalent in poetry. Observing the syntactic possibilities of Hebrew verse in different periods, one finds a predilection for a certain optimal length of line, persistent throughout the ages: 3 or 4 major stresses in the Bible, 4 or 5 graphic words, 11 or 13 syllables (including short ones), 3 or 4 amphibrachs, and 5 iambs which are very similar in length of line and conveniently accommodate similar groups of words and phrases.

The Major Systems of Hebrew Rhyme. A similar pattern can be discerned in the history of Hebrew rhyme norms. Here, again, Hebrew poetry completed a whole cycle in its development. But rhyme was not as obligatory as meter. The earliest and the latest periods have no regular rhyme, i.e., no rhyme in the strict sense of a sound device used

The Major Systems of Hebrew Verse (In their logical and chronological order)

Length of a line	Free	Fixed		
Major Basis of the Meter	Phrase	Word		Syllable
Antiquity and Middle Ages (From phrase to syllable)	I. *Bible : free accentual* Phrase-parallelism (group of stresses)	II. *Early Piyyut: accentual* Number of major stresses	III. *Rhymed Piyyut: word meter* Number of words	IV. *Spain: quantitative* Number of syllables + + order of long/short
				V. *(Italy) Haskalah: syllabic* Number of syllables
Modern Age (From syllable to phrase)	VIII. *Modernist: Free Verse* Changing balance of phrase groups	VII. *Modernist ("Russian") accentual net* Number of major stresses (+ limited freedom of syllables)		VI. *Modern: accental = syllabic* Number of syllables + + order of stressed/ unstressed

Regular rhyme

No Regular Rhyme	Form of Rhymeme / Decisive Vowel	Discontinuous		Continuous	
I. *Bible* Free sound orchestation	final	II. *Kallirian Piyyut: terminal-discontinuous* RVR R+RV R+RVC R+R+CV(C)	 ריק מ + רי מ + ריס מ + ר + הם (תִי)	III. *Medieval: terminal* CVC CV CVC CV(C)	 ריק רי רים הֵם (תִי)
VI. *Modernist* ("Free") Scattered rhymes	stressed	V. *Modernist ("Russian"): accentual-discontinous* CV́+ V́C (V)+ CV́C (V) C+C+CV́+(V)+ (KoS ha Malm-KSuMAhl)	 מַבְרִיק רי + מוֹרִי דְבָרִים וֹר + (אֹרַת עוֹרֶק) דֶר + (דֶרֶך - קוֹדֵר-אַץ) ק + ס + מָ + :	IV. *(Italy, Haskalah) Modern: accentual-terminal* V́C CV́ RV́C V́CVC	 יק רי רים וֹרֶק

regularly for the strophic composition of a whole poem. The diagram (above) represents typical rhymemes, using the following symbols: V — vowel, C — consonant, R — root consonant (only where relevant), V́ — stressed vowel, ł — discontinuity in the rhymeme. When read clockwise, the diagram represents the history of Hebrew rhyme.

Disregarding some secondary developments, there were 4 major rhyme systems. The similarities and the differences between these systems are related to the form and location of the rhymeme. The upper part of the diagram is opposed to the lower part from the point of view of the decisive vowel: in the Middle Ages the rhymeme relied on the final vowel, in the modern age on the stressed vowel. On the left hand (the extremes of this history) the rhymeme could be discontinuous, whereas on the right hand (in the "classical" periods) the rhymeme had to be a continuous and a terminal chain of sounds.

There is also a correlation (though not overlapping) between the corresponding major systems of meter and rhyme, as may be seen from a comparison of both diagrams. At the extreme ends of this cycle, when rhythm was based primarily on phrases, i.e., was dominated by a balancing of syntactic and semantic patterns, no regular rhyme was necessary. In the "classical" periods, when meter was based on the number of syllables, rhyme, too, was syllabic: the medieval rhymeme was based on one (terminal) syllable; modern rhyme based its major distinction of rhyme gender (masculine-feminine) on the number of syllables. Typically enough, in verse systems in which the prominence of the word was basic, discontinuous rhyme developed, i.e., rhyme based on the nature of the Hebrew word. However, this parallelism, essential as it was, was by no means automatic, e.g., word meter continued a long time after the suppression of the early discontinuous rhyme.

Bibliography: GENERAL: (There is no general history or survey of Hebrew versification). On rhyme: B. Hrushovski, *Ha-Shitot ha-Rashiyyot shel he-Ḥaruz ha-Ivri min ha-Piyyut ad Yameinu,* in: *Hasifrut,* 4 (1971), 721–49. BIBLE: W. H. Cabb, *A Criticism of Hebrew Metre* (1905); J. Begrich, *Zur hebraeischen Metrik,* in: *Theologische Rundschau,* 4 (1932), 67–89; I. Gabor, *Der hebraeische Urrythmus* (1929); B. Levin, *Zivvug ha-Millin ba-Tanakh* (1926). PIYYUT: J. Schirmann, *Hebrew Liturgical Poetry and Christian Hymnology,* in: JQR, 44 (1953/54), Zunz, Lit Poesie; A. Mirsky, *Mahzavtan shel Ẓurot ha-Piyyut,* in: YMḤSI, 7 (1958), 1–129; M. Zulay, *ibid.,* 2 (1936), 213; idem, *Piyyutei Yannai* (1938); E. Fleischer, *Le-Ḥeker Tavniyyot ha-Keva be-Fiyyutei ha-Kedushta,* in: *Sinai,* 65 (1969), 21–47; idem, *Iyyunim bi-Ve'ayot Tafkidam ha-Liturgi shel Sugei ha-Piyyut ha-Kadum,* in: *Tarbiz,* 40 (1971), 41–63; idem, *Mivnim Strofiyyim Me'ein-Ezoriyyim ba-Piyyut ha-Kadum,* in: *Hasifrut,* 2 (1970), 194–240; B. Hrushovski, *Ẓurot ha-Piyyut ha-Kadum ve-Reshit ha-Ḥarizah ha-Ivrit,* in: *Hasifrut,* 3 (1971). SPAIN: Schirmann, Sefarad; idem, *La métrique quantitative dans la poesie hebraique du Moyen-Age,* in: *Sefarad,* 8 (1948), 323–32; B. Halper, *The Scansion of Mediaeval Hebrew Poetry,* in: JQR, 4 (1913/14), 153–224; D. Yellin, *Torat ha-Shirah ha-Sefaradit* (1940); idem, *Ha-Mishkalim be-Shirat Shemu'el ha-Nagid,* in: YMḤSI, 5 (1939); I. Davidson, in: JQR, 30 (1939/40), 299–398; N. Aloni, *Torat ha-Mishkalim* (1951); S. Almoli, *Shekel ha-Kodesh* (1965); K. Heger, *Die . . . Ḫarǧas . . .* (1950); A. Mirsky, *Mashma-ut he-Ḥaruz be-Shirat Sefarad,* in: *Leshonenu,* 33 (1969). ITALY: A. Mirsky, *Mishkal ha-Tenu'ot ha-Italky,* in: *Sefer Ḥanokh Yalon* (1963), 221–7; B. Hrushovski, *The Creation of Accented Iambs in European Poetry and their First Employment in a Yiddish Romance in Italy (1508–09),* in: *For Max Weinreich, on his Seventieth Birthday* (1964), 108–46. YIDDISH POETRY. U. Weinreich, *On the Cultural History of Yiddish Rime,* in: *Essays on Jewish Life and Thought* (1959), 423–42; B. Hrushovski, *On Free Rhythms in Modern Yiddish Poetry,* in: U. Weinreich (ed.), *The Field of Yiddish* (1954), 219–66. THE MODERN AGE: B. Benshalom, *Mishkalav shel H. N. Bialik* (1945), idem, *Keri'at Deror la-Ḥaruz ha-Monosilabi,* in: *Hasifrut* (1968–69), 161–75; S. Span, *Massot u-Meḥkarim* (1964); B. Hrushovski, *"Ritmus ha-Raḥvut" Halakhah u-Ma'aseh be-Shirato ha-Ekspresyonistit shel U. Z. Greenberg, ibid.,* 176–205. [B.HR.]

PROSSNITZ, JUDAH LEIB BEN JACOB HOLLESCHAU (c. 1670–1730), Shabbatean prophet. Born in Uhersky Brod, he settled in Prossnitz (Prostejov) after his marriage. An uneducated man, he made his living as a peddler. About 1696 he underwent a spiritual awakening and began to study the Mishnah, and later the Zohar and kabbalistic writings. Believing that he was visited by the souls of deceased, he claimed that he studied Kabbalah with Isaac *Luria and *Shabbetai Ẓevi. Whether his Shabbatean awakening was connected with the movement in Moravia around *Judah Ḥasid, Heshel *Ẓoref, and Ḥayyim *Malakh is still a matter of conjecture. Possibly he was won over by Ẓevi Hirsch b. Jerahmeel *Chotsh, who spent some time in Prossnitz in 1696. Judah Leib first turned to teaching children but later his followers in Prossnitz provided for him and his family. Taking up residence in the *bet midrash* of Prossnitz, he led a strictly ascetic life; he became generally known as Leibele Prossnitz. Before long he started to divulge kabbalistic and Shabbatean mysteries and to preach in public in the manner of a revivalist preacher *(mokhi'aḥ)*. He found many adherents, his most important supporter for some years being Meir Eisenstadt, a famous rabbinic authority who served as rabbi of Prossnitz from 1702. At the same time his Shabbatean propaganda, especially since it came from an uneducated lay mystic, aroused strong hostility in many critics. Between 1703 and 1705 he traveled through Moravia and Silesia, causing considerable agitation in the communities. Along with other Shabbatean leaders of this period, he prophesied the return of Shabbetai Ẓevi in 1706. His open Shabbatean propaganda led to clashes in Glogau and Breslau, where the rabbis threatened him with excommunication unless he returned to Prossnitz and stayed there. As 1706 approached his agitation reached a pitch. He assembled a group of ten followers who studied with him and practiced extravagant mortifications.

Judah Leib was widely credited with magical practices connected with his attempts to bring to an end the dominion of *Samael and is reported to have sacrificed a chicken as a kind of bribe to the unclean powers. The facts concerning this and his promise to reveal the *Shekhinah* to some of his followers, including Meir Eisenstadt, are shrouded in legend, but they contain some kernel of historical truth. Since by then he was widely considered by his foes to be a sorcerer, Meir Eisenstadt left him and Prossnitz was put under a ban by the rabbinical court and sentenced to exile for three years; however, he was allowed to return after several months. He persisted at the head of a secret Shabbatean group in Prossnitz, again working as a children's teacher. Maintaining connections with other Shabbateans, in 1724 he tried to obtain the appointment of one of his closest followers, R. Sender, to the rabbinate of Mannheim (L. Loewenstein, *Geschichte der Juden in der Kurpfalz* (1895), 198–9). Jonathan *Eybeschuetz, a pupil of Meir Eisenstadt in Prostejov (Prossnitz) for several years, is said to have studied secretly with Judah Leib, who was then propagating teachings close to the radical wing of Shabbateanism. Along with others in this group, he supported heretical teachings regarding divine providence. When Leib b. Ozer wrote his memoir on the state of Shabbateanism in 1717, Judah Leib was refraining from public manifestations of Shabbatean faith and was said to be working on a kabbalistic commentary on the Book of Ruth. With the resurgence of Shabbatean activities in 1724, in the wake of the emissaries from Salonika, Judah Leib again appeared publicly on the scene, claiming to be the Messiah ben Joseph, the precursor of the Messiah ben David. Once more, he found many followers in Moravia and even in Vienna and Prague. Some of his letters to Jonathan Eybeschuetz and Isaiah Mokhi'aḥ in Mannheim were found among the papers confiscated from Shabbatean emissaries. In the summer of 1725 Judah Leib was again excommunicated by the rabbis of Moravia in Nikolsburg (Mikulov) and after that led a vagrant life. When he came to Frankfort on the Main in early 1726 he was not allowed to enter the Jewish quarter, but he was given material assistance by one of his secret supporters. His last years were reportedly spent in Hungary. Whereas the friendly contact between Judah Leib and Eybeschuetz is well established, there is no conclusive proof of Jacob *Emden's claim that Judah Leib saw Eybeschuetz as the future leader of the Shabbateans (J. Emden, *Beit Yonatan ha-Sofer* (Altona, 1762(?), 1b), or that he would even be the Messiah after Shabbetai Ẓevi's apotheosis (*Shevirat Luḥot ha-Aven* (Zolkiew, 1755), 18b). After Judah Leib's death a strong group of Shabbateans survived in Prossnitz during the 18th century.

Bibliography: J. Emden, *Torat ha-Kena'ot* (Amsterdam, 1752), 34bf., 41a–42a; A. Neubauer, in: MGWJ, 36 (1887), 207–12; D. Kahana, *Toledot ha-Mekubbalim ve-ha-Shabbeta'im,* 2 (1914), 168–75, 184; M. A. Perlmutter (Anat), *R. Yehonatan Eybeschuetz, Yaḥaso el ha-Shabbeta'ut* (1947), 43–47; Chr. P. Loewe, *Speculum Religionis Judaicae* (1732), 80–82.

[G.Sch.]

PROSSTITZ (Prossnitz), DANIEL (Steinschneider; 1759–1846), Hungarian rabbi. Born in Tobitschau near Prossnitz (Prostejov), Daniel studied first in Moravia and later in Pressburg under the rabbi of the town Meir b. Saul *Barby and was later appointed by Meshullam *Igra to his *bet din* there. Eventually he succeeded Rabbi M. Toska, the head of the *bet din.* In addition he was appointed rabbi to a society for the study of the Talmud *(Ḥevrah Shas)* established in Pressburg. He served the Pressburg community in these capacities for 50 years. Prosstitz recommended Moses *Sofer for the vacant position of rabbi of Pressburg and it was largely due to his conduct of the negotiations that Sofer was appointed. Prosstitz also occupied himself with Kabbalah and used to fast frequently, especially after a dream.

He published the *Sefer ha-Yashar* of Jacob Tam, and left responsa and novellae to the Talmud in manuscript. Responsa addressed to him are found in the Resp. Ḥatam Sofer, in Ezekiel *Landau's *Noda bi-Yhudah,* and in the responsa of his other great contemporaries.

Bibliography: D. Prosstitz Steinschneider, *Dan mi-Daniel,* 1 (1881), introd.; I. Weiss, *Avnei Beit ha-Yoẓer* (1900), nos. 1:11, 2:11; S. Sofer, *Iggerot Soferim,* pt. 2 (1928), 5; H. Gold, *Die Juden und die Judengemeinde Bratislava in Vergangenheit und Gegenwart* (1932).

[Sh.W.-H.]

PROSTEJOV (Czech **Prostějov,** Ger. **Prossnitz,** Heb. פרוסטיץ), city in central Moravia, Czechoslovakia. From the Middle Ages Prostejov was a center for the textile and ready-made clothing industries, in which Jews played an important part. A Jew is mentioned in a document of 1445. The Jewish community, founded by people expelled from nearby *Olomouc (Olmuetz) in 1454, was, from the 17th to the 19th century, second only to *Mikulov (Nikolsburg) among the communities of Moravia. The Jews dealt in luxury goods and locally made textiles. In 1584 the Jews' right of residence was confirmed but the branches of trade open to them were restricted. The community then numbered 31 families. A minute book *(pinkas)* opened in 1587 began with the *takkanot* of *Judah Loew b. Bezalel regulating synagogal arrangements. A compendium of Sabbath hymns, *Kol Simḥah,* was printed in 1602 by a short-lived local printing house.

The Jewish community and its importance in local industry increased after the Protestant inhabitants had left when the town became Roman Catholic under duress. In 1639 there were 143 Jewish men in Prostejov and 64 houses in the town were owned by Jews. Prostejov absorbed many refugees after the *Chmielnicki massacres in 1648 and the Vienna expulsion in 1670. The community numbered 64 families in 1669. The synagogue was dedicated in 1676. The first known rabbi was Isaac Ḥayyut b. Abraham (d. 1639); among his successors were Meir b. Isaac Ashkenazi and Wolf Boskowitz. The Prostejov rabbinate was a stepping-stone to the office of **Landrabbiner* for Menahem *Krochmal and Nahum *Trebitsch. A compromise reached in 1677 (and supplemented in 1688) concerning the extent of trade between Jews and gentiles testifies to the importance of Jewish participation in the textile and clothing trades. The community numbered 318 families in 1713, 1,393 persons in 1787, and 1,495 in 1798. The number of families allotted under the *Familiants Law was 328. The Prostejov community was strongly influenced by the Shabbatean movement, and one of its leaders, Judah Leib *Prossnitz, lived in the town. The community was also affected by Frankism (see Jacob *Frank and the Frankists) and was one of the first to absorb the ideas of the *Haskalah. The first sermon in German in the Hapsburg dominions was preached there by Loew *Schwab (1835). In 1843 a Jew founded a private elementary school for Jewish and Christian children. In 1831 Feith *Ehrenstamm founded a factory, the beginning of Jewish enterprise in modern textile industry. By 1842 there were 135 Jewish textile merchants in Prostejov. The first factory for ready-made clothes on the European continent was founded by Mayer and Isaac Mandel in 1859. The 200 Jews in the National Guard units were lauded for their conduct in fighting during the anti-Jewish riots in 1848. Prostejov became a political community *(*Politische Gemeinde)* in 1849. In 1880 there were 1,804 Jews in Prostejov. The community absorbed many World War I refugees from Eastern Europe. Between the two world wars the community was one of the most active in Czechoslovakia and the first to arrange modern Hebrew courses. The clothing industry, represented mainly by the Sborowitz firm, which had 108 sales establishments throughout Czechoslovakia and a vast export business, brought affluence to the community which attracted many new members from *Sub-Carpathian Ruthenia (Carpatho-Russia). In 1930 the community numbered 1,442 (4.3% of the total). Among the natives of the town were Menahem Katz, rabbi of the *Deutschkreutz community and leader of Hungarian *Orthodoxy, Gideon Brecher, physician and author of a booklet on circumcision, his son Adolph, author and physician, and the bibliographer Moritz *Steinschneider. Jonathan *Eybeschuetz and Adolf and Hermann *Jellinek were among the pupils of the Prostejov yeshivah.

Many refugees from the Sudeten area arrived in Prostejov in autumn 1938. After the German invasion (March 1939) Jews suffered from Gestapo raids, mainly in July when the synagogue also was closed. Many Jews left Prostejov during 1940. Those who remained were deported to the Nazi extermination camps in 1942. The synagogue appurtenances were transferred to the Jewish Central Museum in Prague. In 1945 a small congregation administered by the Olomouc community was reestablished, mostly by Jews from Sub-Carpathian Ruthenia. A memorial to the victims of the Holocaust was consecrated in 1950. The congregation was still active in 1969.

Bibliography: J. Freimann, in: JJLG, 15 (1923), 26–58; B. Wachstein, *ibid.*, 16 (1924), 163–76; L. Goldschmied, in: H. Gold (ed.), *Juden und Judengemeinden Maehrens* (1929), 491–504; B. Heilig, in: JGGJČ, 3 (1931), 307–448, incl. bibl.; idem, in: BLBI, 3 (1960), 101–22; R. Iltis (ed.), *Die aussaeen unter Traenen...* (1959), 71–76; *The Jews of Czechoslovakia*, 1 (1968), 417–8; R. Kestenberg-Gladstein, *Neuere Geschichte der Juden in den boehmischen Laendern*, 1 (1969), index; Y. Toury, *Mehumah u-Mevukhah be-Mahpekhat 1848* (1968), index.

[M.LA.]

PROSTITUTION (Heb. זְנוּת, *zenut*), the practice of indiscriminate sexual intercourse for payment or for religious purposes. Prostitution was practiced by male and female prostitutes. The word *zenut*, applied to both common and sacred prostitution, is also often used metaphorically.

The prostitute was an accepted though deprecated member of the Israelite society, both in urban and rural life (Gen. 38:14; Josh. 2:1ff.; I Kings 3:16–27). The Bible refers to Tamar's temporary harlotry and to the professional harlotry of Rahab without passing any moral judgment. The visits of Samson to the harlot of Gaza (Judg. 16:1) are not condemned, but conform with his picaresque life. Harlots had access to the king's tribunal, as other people (I Kings 3:16ff.). Nevertheless, harlotry was a shameful profession, and to treat an Israelite girl like a prostitute was considered a grave offense (Gen. 34:31). The Israelites were warned against prostituting their daughters (Lev. 19:29), and priests were not allowed to marry prostitutes (21:7). The punishment of a priest's daughter who became a prostitute, thus degrading her father, was death through fire (Lev. 21:9). According to the talmudic sages, however, this law applies only to the priest's daughter who is married or at least betrothed (Sanh. 50b–51a). Prostitutes might be encountered in the streets and squares, and on street corners, calling out to passersby (Prov. 7:10–23); they sang and played the harp (Isa. 23:16), and bathed in public pools (I Kings 22:38). Their glances and smooth talk were dangers against which the immature were warned (Jer. 3:3, Prov. 2:16; 5:3, 6:24–25, 7:5, et al.).

In the Ancient Near East, temple women, of whom one class was called *qadištu*, probably served as sacred prostitutes. Sometimes dedicated by their fathers to the deity, they had special statutes, and provisions were made for them by law (Code of Hammurapi, 178–82). Customs connected with them are likely to underlie Herodotus' lurid and misleading statement that in Babylon every woman was to serve once as a sacred prostitute before getting married, thus sacrificing her virginity to the goddess Mylitta (Ishtar; 1:199). In Israel the sacred prostitutes were condemned for their connection with idolatry. Deuteronomy 23:18–19 forbids Israelites, men and women alike, to become sacred prostitutes, and states that their wages must not be used for paying vows.

It has been supposed that "the women who performed tasks at the entrance to the Tent of Meeting," mentioned in I Samuel 2:22, were sacred prostitutes—though this hardly suits their other occurrence in Exodus 38:8. There were male and female prostitutes in Israel and Judah during the monarchy, and in Judah they were, from time to time, the object of royal decrees of expulsion (cf. I Kings 14:24; 15:12; 22:47; II Kings 23:7; Hos. 4:14). Sacred prostitution, because of its association with idolatry, was the object of numerous attacks in the Bible, especially in the historical and prophetic books (cf., e.g., II Kings 23:4–14; Jer. 2:20; Ezek. 23:37ff.). Terms connected with harlotry are used figuratively to characterize unfaithfulness toward the Lord (Num. 25:1–2; Judg. 2:17; 8:27, 33; Jer. 3:6; Ezek. 6:9; Hos. 4:12; et al.). [L.J.A.]

Post-Biblical. The many warnings of Ben Sira against prostitution is evidence that it was widespread in the Hellenistic period. According to II Maccabees 6:4, Antiochus Epiphanes introduced sacred prostitutes into the Temple. Throughout the whole of the apocryphal and pseudepigraphical literature, in the Damascus Document, in the documents of the Dead Sea sects (Seraḥ ha-Yaḥad 1:6), in Josephus (Ant. 4:206), and by Philo (Jos. 43, Spec. 3:51), prostitution is vigorously denounced. [ED.]

In Talmud and Halakhah. Different opinions are expressed in the Talmud with regard to the prostitute of the Bible, both concerning her hire and her marriage to a priest. Some were of the opinion that these references apply only to a professional prostitute, but there were also other opinions. With regard to her hire (Deut. 23:19) the *halakhah* was decided in accordance with the opinion of R. Judah ha-Nasi that it was not forbidden except to those for whom "cohabitation is a transgression" (Tosef., Tem. 4:8; see Prohibited *Marriage). With regard to the unmarried woman who engages in prostitution, however, "her wage is permitted" (i.e., for use in the Temple; Maim. Yad, Issurei ha-Mizbe'aḥ 4:8). Some were of the opinion that her wage is forbidden only with regard to such reward "the like of which can be offered on the altar," but not to money (Tem. 6:4; but Philo refers explicitly to a prohibition on money). The term *be'ilat zenut* ("intercourse of prostitution") was, however, applied not only to those relations forbidden in the strict legal sense (see also Yev. 8:5) but also to any intercourse not expressly for the purpose of marriage (TJ, Git. 7:448d; Git. 81b), and even to a marriage not celebrated in accordance with the *halakhah.*

The *halakhah* imposed a general prohibition on the professional prostitute, and the term came to include any woman who abandoned herself to any man even if not for pay, and states that "Whoever hands his unmarried daughter [to a man] not for the purposes of matrimony," as well as the woman who delivers herself not for the purposes of matrimony, could lead to the whole world being filled with **mamzerim* since "from his consorting with many women and not knowing with whom, or if she has had intercourse with many men and does not know with whom—he could marry his own daughter, or marry her to his son" (see **Mamzer;* Sifra, Kedoshim 7, 1–5). The ruling is based on the verse "Profane not thy daughter, to make her a harlot" (Lev. 19:29), as well as the verse "There shall be no harlot of the daughters of Israel" (Deut. 23:18; *kedeshah* being taken as referring to every prostitute (Sanh. 82a)). The penalty for both parties is flogging (Maim. Yad, Ishut 1:4; Na'arah Betulah 2:17). *Abraham b. David of Posquières in his gloss *(ibid.)* stressed that this law applies only to the woman "who is ready to prostitute herself to every man," and he makes an express exception in the case of a woman "who gives herself solely to one man without benefit of marriage." The rabbis were eloquent in their condemnation of the prostitute and her like, but in most cases their strictures apply to every kind of licentiousness. They warned particularly against approaching a harlot's door (Ber. 32a; Av. Zar. 17a) and passing through a "harlots' market" (ARN[1] 2, 14; ARN[2] 3, 13), such as were to be found in large cities (Pes. 113b; Ket. 64b), especially in Ereẓ Israel, where the Romans "built marketplaces in which to set harlots" (Shab. 33b). Even the inns served as brothels—sometimes the Targum gives *pundekita* ("woman innkeeper") as the translation of the "harlot" of the Bible. After the destruction of the Temple and during the Hadrianic persecutions, the Romans placed Jewesses in a brothel (ARN[1] 8, 37; Av. Zar. 17–18), and even men were taken captive for shameful purposes (Lam. R. 1:16, no. 45; cf. Or. Sibyll. 3:184–6, and 5:387–9). Some succeeded in maintaining their virtue and were ransomed; others committed suicide to avoid being forced into prostitution. But there were also Jewesses who willingly engaged in prostitution (TJ, Ta'an. 4, 8, 69a) and Jews who were pimps *(ibid.* 1:4). There are even stories in the *aggadah* about sons of scholars who were very dissolute (BM 85a). The *halakhot* of ritual purity and impurity mention several garments which were peculiar to prostitutes: a "net" for the hair and a harlot's shift made like network (Kel. 24:16, 28:9). The sages, who realized that the urge to prostitution is greater than that to *idolatry (Song R. 7:8), considered it one of the important causes of the destruction of the Temple, and its spread as a sign of the advent of the Messiah (Sot. 9:13, 15). But there are also stories about prostitutes who repented completely (Av. Zar. 17a; SEZ 22), as well as about a gentile prostitute who converted to Judaism out of conviction (Sif. Num. 115; Men. 44a). [M.D.H.]

Post-Talmudic. The sex life of Jews was generally distinguished by modesty, and in those places and times where Jewish life was conducted in the framework of a community under the domination of tradition and the *halakhah,* extra-marital sexual relations were rarer among Jews than among other peoples. As stated above, every sexual act between a man and woman outside marital relations was considered as coming within the definition of prostitution *(be'ilat zenut),* and the rabbis strongly condemned every manifestation of sexual license in the Jewish community. Many regulations were issued by the various communities to fight prostitution in all its forms. Relations between Jews and gentiles were regarded as especially heinous, because in most places they were against the laws of the land and the church, and were therefore apt to evoke an undesirable reaction by non-Jews and involve the whole community. Even with the Jews' isolation in the Middle Ages and until the beginning of modern times, it was impossible to prevent completely the influence of their surroundings from penetrating their lives. Immorality was naturally rife in those countries where sexual morality was weak, such as Spain, Italy, the countries of North Africa, etc., where the Jewish communities sometimes felt the need to unite in taking steps in this area.

Jewish communities were never reconciled to the existence of prostitution among them, especially organized prostitution on a commercial basis. They reacted energetically to every attempt to maintain a brothel in the Jewish quarter. There is mention of brothels actually being closed down by order of the communities in various German and French cities in the 17th and 18th centuries. Heavy fines were imposed on landlords who rented their houses for the purpose of prostitution. Anybody who knew of such a case was obliged to report it to the community. The Jews did not always manage to prevent brothels being opened within their neighborhoods, although protests against their establishment sometimes brought about their removal. In many places the laws of the country forbade their being maintained in the cities, so that they were relegated to the outskirts. Sometimes they were located in the vicinity of the Jewish quarter merely by chance, but in some cases they were established there deliberately, out of contempt for the Jews. At times the rabbis closed their eyes to the visits of unmarried men of the community to the brothels, in order to prevent other forms of lewdness.

There is some evidence in the responsa literature that Jewish girls engaged in prostitution, and no doubt there were also Jews who lived on pimping, but there is no data to the extent. The *halakhah* literature in the Middle Ages mentions several regulations against Jewish prostitutes and against Jews who frequented gentile prostitutes, but the prostitute was entitled to claim her fee (Rema). At the end of the Middle Ages it was laid down that a married man who frequented prostitutes was obliged to give his wife a divorce.

Modern Period. After the period of emancipation, when many Jews discarded the traditional way of life, assimilation to their surroundings brought about a change in the area of sexual morality, particularly in the first wave of mass emigration from Eastern Europe overseas, when many were suddenly uprooted from their previous social and spiritual way of life, and failed to be integrated into their new surroundings. This phenomenon was exploited by anti-Semitic propaganda through generalization and exaggeration (see *Argentina). It recurred among the displaced persons, refugees, and survivors of the concentration camps after World War II and the European Holocaust. Until World War II the Jewish community in Ereẓ Israel was almost free of prostitution. After the establishment of the State, however, it began to emerge in urban centers, but there are no authoritative data on its dimensions. Mass immigration and the disintegration of traditional family life are given as contributory factors in its spread. [M.Wu.]

Bibliography: M. G. May, in: AJSLL, 48 (1931–32), 73–98; B. A. Brooks, in: JBL, 60 (1941), 227–53; R. Patai, *Sex and Family in the Bible and the Middle East* (1959), 145–52; J. Lévi, in: REJ, 38 (1899), 111, 120–2; I. Abrahams, *Jewish Life in the Middle Ages* (1932), 109–11; Baron, Community, 2 (1942), 311–5; Kaufmann, Y., Toledot, index s.v. *Zenut* in vols. 1, 2, and 3; L. M. Epstein, *Sex Laws and Customs in Judaism* (1948), 152–78; Ḥ. Albeck, *Shishah Sidrei Mishnah, Kodashim* (1959), 413f.

PROSTITZ, ISAAC BEN AARON (d. 1612), Hebrew printer. Isaac was born in Prossnitz, Moravia, and learned the printing trade in Italy, working with G. Cavalli and G. Grypho in *Venice. There he met the proofreader Samuel Boehm (d. 1588), who later joined Isaac in *Cracow, where he printed from 1569. From Italy they had brought with them typographical material, decorations etc., and in the privilege issued in 1567 to Isaac by King Sigmund August II of Poland for 50 years he is called an "Italian" Jew. In spite of initial intrigues by the Jesuits, Isaac and later his sons—Aaron and Issachar—and grandsons were able to print for nearly 60 years some 200 works of which 73 were in Yiddish, using fish and a ram (symbol for the offering of Isaac) as printer's mark. The productions covered a wide field: rabbinics, Bible, Kabbalah, philosophy, history, and even mathematics. The Babylonian Talmud was printed twice (1602–08; 1616–20); these were poor editions after an earlier and more auspicious beginning in 1579. The Jerusalem Talmud of 1609 has become standard in the form it was reissued in Krotoschin in 1886. Isaac was printer to the great scholars of the time: Moses *Isserles of Cracow, Solomon *Luria of Lublin, and Mordecai *Jaffe of Prague and Poznan. In 1602 he returned to his native Prossnitz, where he printed some works until 1605, while his son Aaron remained active in Cracow to 1628 printing apart from the Talmuds, the Zohar (1603), and the Shulḥan Arukh (1607, 1618–20), Turim with Joseph Caro's commentary (1614–15), and *Ein Ya'akov* (1614, 1619). Isaac's descendants were working as printer's assistants until nearly the end of the 17th century.

Bibliography: Steinschneider, Cat Bod, 2901–02; idem, *Juedische Typographie* (1938), 34–35; Ḥ. D. Friedberg, *Toledot ha-Defus ha-Ivri be-Polanyah* (1950[2]), 5–25; M. Balaban, in: *Soncino Blaetter*, 3 (1929/30), 9–11, 47–48; R. N. N. Rabbinovicz, *Ma-'amar al Hadpasat ha-Talmud* (1877), 70–75. [ED.]

PROTESTANTS.

Up to World War II. Seen in perspective, the attitude of the Protestant movement toward Jews and Judaism was ambivalent and unstable. For the earlier periods see *Luther, *Calvin, and *Reformation. By the beginning of the 18th century the Protestant churches had amassed a vast amount of material on the Jews and on Judaism. The traditional hostility of more than a millennium was fully recorded in books such as *Entdecktes Judentum* (1700), an immense storehouse of learning and abuse collected by Johannes Andreas *Eisenmenger. The Jewish response in polemic and apologetic was equally comprehensively dealt with in *Tela Ignea Satanae* (1681) by Johann Christoph *Wagenseil. Of more interest was the appearance of material of a different kind—material which for the first time described Jews, Jewish customs, and Judaism sympathetically and objectively, and without either a controversial or theological bias.

In the historical field the most important work was *L'Histoire et la Religion des Juifs depuis Jésus Christ jusqu'à Présent*, by the Huguenot diplomat and scholar Jacques *Basnage. It appeared at the beginning of the century, and was immediately plagiarized by the Jesuits, who altered or omitted all his references to Christian responsibility for Jewish sufferings. The increase of travel led to an interest in Jewish customs, social, domestic, and religious; and books describing these customs in Europe, Africa, and the Middle East became part of the stock of any well-equipped library. But the most attractive field for Protestant study was rabbinic, and almost every university claimed a chair in Hebrew. Leiden and Franeker in Holland, Cambridge in England, and Jena in Germany were among the most distinguished. While the Christian Hebraists wrote much that was of little value, their studies of the Talmud removed the atmosphere of mystery and even blasphemy which medieval scholars had imparted to it. John *Selden in *De Synedriis et Praefecturis Juridicis veterum Hebraeorum* (1650–55) laid the foundation for the serious study of Jewish legal procedures. At the beginning of the 18th century, Wilhelm *Surenhuys of Amsterdam, in his introduction to a Latin edition of the Mishnah and in other writings, was the first to speak of rabbinic Judaism as the natural and proper development of the Judaism of the Bible.

Side by side with this interest in rabbinic Judaism was the concern of some of the Protestant sects with biblical Judaism as an ideal expression of natural law. John *Toland in *Nazarenus* (1718) made the first study of Judaic Christianity as something distinct from its gentile brother, and more valuable in that it retained the laws of Moses. But as the century progressed, this attitude of the free-thinking sects changed to violent hostility which saw "Jehovah" as the model of all tyranny. Hermann Samuel Reimarus (1694–1768) subjected the Scriptures to so detailed a critical examination that he can be regarded as the father of much of 19th-century biblical scholarship.

Missionary Activities. While these various developments helped to maintain a general interest in the Jews, it was not until the very end of the century that any organized approach to them evolved. Protestantism had been slow to develop missions in any field, and still slower to create organized missions to Jews. But individual authors, some of them converts from Judaism, exhorted the Jews to recognize the truth of Christianity. Traditionally such writings were filled with mockery and hatred; but in the 18th century, although there was a good deal of writing in the old style, a new approach of friendliness and respect appeared. This contradiction was also manifested in the 18th-century view as to the general status of the Jews in a Christian society. In 1753 a bill was passed through the British Parliament to facilitate the naturalization of Jews. It provoked an immense flow of pamphleteering; of those pamphlets written from a Christian standpoint some were hostile and others favorable. When full political emancipation became an issue a hundred years later, the archbishop of Canterbury opposed it, while the archbishop of Dublin supported it. Even with individual Jewish converts to Protestantism the same contradiction was apparent, and in many cases they were received with scarcely veiled hostility and suspicion.

The leading figure in the emergence of organized Protestant missionary activity was Lewis *Way. He had unexpectedly inherited an enormous fortune upon the sole condition that he used it for the glory of God; and events led him to fulfill this condition in work for the conversion of the Jews. In 1809 the London Society for Promoting Christianity among the Jews had been founded, largely through the enthusiasm of a German Jewish convert, J. S. C. F. Frey. Way wished to increase his understanding of the whole question, and traveled extensively. He was horrified by the treatment that Jews received in Christian countries, and came to the conclusion that full emancipation was the fundamental preliminary to a missionary approach. He visited St. Petersburg and so impressed Czar Alexander I that he was invited to the Congress of Aix-la-Chapelle by the emperor, and succeeded in getting a resolution passed commending the idea of emancipation to the governments of Europe. Emancipation came slowly, but Way's influence brought into existence throughout the Protestant world societies which devoted themselves to sending missions to the Jews. Jewish life at that period was at a low ebb; and while actual conversions were few, many communities in eastern Europe, as well as in Palestine and North Africa, profited from the schools and hospitals established by the missions.

In 1910 an International Missionary Council was formed, and it included a special committee on missions to the Jews. (In 1961 the Council was incorporated in the World Council of Churches; and under its new name of "Committee on the Church and the Jewish People" it to some extent disavowed its proselytizing activity.)

Converts' Participation in Academic Life. Alfred Edersheim (1825–1889), the son of Viennese Jewish parents, first served the Scottish mission in Jassy, and then had a distinguished academic career at Edinburgh and Oxford. His *Life and Times of Jesus the Messiah* was the first scholarly picture of the Jewish environment of the Gospels. Even more distinguished was the son of a Jewish peddler of Goettingen by the name of Emmanuel Mendel, who on his baptism took the name of Neander (new man). As August Johann Wilhelm *Neander, he became a prolific historian of the Christian Church and professor of theology at Berlin University. More interesting than individual scholars was the group of distinguished converts who published a short book absolutely denying the authenticity of the ritual murder accusation at the time of the Damascus Affair in 1840. The accusation had first originated with a converted Jew of Cambridge in the 12th century, but this was the first time that a group of Jewish converts turned to defend their old religion. The most valuable contribution to the scholarly work of the missions was made by social institutes for Judaic studies (1650 in Strasbourg and 1702 in Halle) and chiefly by Franz *Delitzsch, who wrote extensively on post-biblical Judaism; in 1880 the Institutum Delitzschianum was founded in his honor, and it continued to produce scholarly works until the time of the Nazis.

While the leadership in missionary work was largely British, in the field of scholarship it was unquestionably German. Freedom of criticism was inevitably more possible in the Protestant than in the Catholic universities, and from the end of the 18th century onward Protestant German scholars made great contributions to the understanding of the literature, history, and religion of the people of Israel. The list begins with Johann Gottfried *Eichhorn, professor at Jena, and continues down to the present day. Among many famous names those of Karl Heinrich *Graf and Julius *Wellhausen are conspicuous; and their theory of how different sources were combined in the Pentateuch held the field until the emergence of the contemporary "form-critical school" pioneered by Herman *Gunkel. While German scholarship often tends to extremes which others find unnecessary and unacceptable, it has immensely enriched knowledge by its research, even for those who reject its conclusions.

At the very end of the 19th century, the work of *Selden and Surenhuys in recognizing and defining the spiritual validity of Judaism was taken up by two scholars—George Foot *Moore in America, who published his two volumes on *Judaism in the First Centuries of the Christian Era* in 1927, and R. Travers *Herford, an English Unitarian, whose first work *Pharisaism* appeared in 1912, and was, during the next 30 years, followed by a whole series on talmudic Judaism.

Jewish Return to the Land of Israel. The 19th century witnessed a new understanding between Jews and Protestants in another field. As far back as the millenarians of the 17th century there had been a fluctuating interest in a Jewish return. John Toland predicted that this would lead to the creation of a society of unparalleled power and prosperity. Many other 18th- and 19th-century writers did so too. In 1839, under the influence of the deeply religious Earl of Shaftesbury, Lord Palmerston set up a British consulate in Jerusalem with a special mandate to protect Jews who had no other source of defense. From then onward until the Balfour Declaration in 1917, there were always some members and even whole sects of the Protestant churches who, motivated partly by eschatological beliefs, gave their support to Zionism.

To all this varied work there was a reverse side. The Protestant Church in Germany produced powerful support for the new *anti-Semitism in the Christian Socialist Workingmen's Union, founded and led by a court chaplain, Adolf *Stoecker; and its failure to speak and act against Nazi anti-Semitism was a lasting disgrace. [J.W.P.]

From 1945. (For the 1939–45 period, see *Holocaust and the Christian Churches.) A new era in the development of relations between Protestantism and the Jewish people opened in 1945, and had four major causes: (1) the influence of the Holocaust, which led many Christians to question the responsibility of the Church's "teaching of contempt" (Jules *Isaac's phrase) which had nurtured anti-Semitism; (2) the establishment of the State of Israel; (3) the general reconciliation between different churches and religions and the rise of ecumenism; and (4) the consolidation of pluralism in Western culture.

Declarations Against Anti-Semitism. The foundations of the new attitude toward Jews were laid at the International Emergency Conference of Jews and Christians which was held in 1947 in Seelisberg in Switzerland and was attended by 64 theologians, educators, and thinkers, Jewish, Catholic, and Protestant. They deliberated on methods of fighting anti-Semitism through educational, political, religious, and social channels. At the conclusion of the conference, the "Ten Points of Seelisberg" were drafted and adopted. These were principles to assist the Churches "to show their members how to prevent any animosity toward the Jews which might arise from false, inadequate or mistaken presentations or conceptions of the teaching and preaching of the Christian doctrine, and how on the other hand to promote brotherly love toward the sorely-tried people of the old covenant." The conference thus established the lines for the new process of reconciliation between Jews and Christians, which was to be developed in two spheres: the struggle against anti-Semitism and a new form of dialogue.

At its foundation conference in Amsterdam in 1948, the World Council of Churches (WCC; the roof organization of the majority of larger Protestant, Anglican, and Orthodox churches) moved a resolution strongly condemning anti-Semitism. The organization again passed this resolution at its third world conference in New Delhi (1961), with the additional recommendation that Christians should repudiate the idea of the collective guilt of the Jews for the crucifixion of Jesus. However, the texts of both these resolutions are ambiguous, because there is an evangelist-missionary undertone in their attitude toward the Jews.

In 1964, further declarations condemning anti-Semitism were issued by several important Protestant organizations: the roof organization of the Protestant churches in the United States (National Council of the Churches of Christ in the United States) passed a "Resolution on Jewish-Christian Relations," calling among other things for the fostering of a dialogue between Jews and Christians. The Lutheran World Federation also made a declaration, following an international consultation in Denmark on the subject of "The Church and the Jews"; and the House of Bishops of the Protestant Episcopal Church in the United States drafted a statement of condemnation of anti-Semitism in extremely strong terms. The Lutheran and Episcopalian declarations also contained expressions of regret for past persecutions of the Jews fomented by the churches.

Liquidation of Theological Anti-Semitism. As seen above, the Churches recognized that some of the roots of anti-Semitism were implanted in their religious literature and that it was their duty to uproot them. In a number of countries, a fundamental examination of religious literature, teaching manuals of the Church, prayers, and so on was carried out in order to assist the Church in purifying this material from all versions or commentaries which were liable to create hatred of Judaism or prejudices about it. The Protestants' most comprehensive research was carried out at Yale University under the direction of the sociologist B. E. Olson, who published his findings in *Faith and Prejudice* (1963). This work brings to light the various aspects of the "teaching of contempt" in the curriculum of the Fundamentalist, the Conservative, the Neo-Orthodox, and the Liberal Protestants in the United States. Further research into the religious roots of anti-Semitism, especially within Protestantism, was carried out by the sociologists Ch. Y. Glock and R. Stark of the University of California at Berkeley and published in their work *Christian Beliefs and Antisemitism* (1966).

Church Committees for the Fostering of Relations with the Jews. The interest shown by Protestantism in a dialogue with the Jews led to the establishment of new Church bodies for this specific purpose. A special committee to the Jews known as the Committee on the Christian Approach already existed in 1932 as part of the International Missionary Council (IMC; the world roof organization of Protestant missions). In 1961, the IMC amalgamated with the WCC, and the committee for Jews became an integral part of the WCC, its name being changed to CCJP (Committee on the Church and the Jewish People). This committee, which considers that its aim is "to further the Church witness to the Jewish people by study and other appropriate means," has in fact principally taken upon itself the duty "to study the Jewish world in its various aspects in order to develop an effective program to combat anti-Semitism and arouse Christian responsibility toward the Jews." The CCJP has convened a number of international conferences (usually held at the Ecumenical Institute of the WCC at the Château de Bossey, near Geneva) which have been attended by theologians of many countries, in order to lay down a new theological standpoint toward Judaism and the State of Israel. However, to the regret of the promoters, the recommendations agreed upon at the end of these deliberations have never become official decisions of the WCC and are therefore not binding upon the member Churches. It should also be noted that Protestant institutions have always shown reticence in adopting a clear theological stance toward the existence of the State of Israel. The declaration made in 1956 by the WCC is characteristic. It states: "We cannot say a plain yes, nor can we say a plain no, because the Church does not stand for a vague cosmopolitanism."

Special committees for the fostering of relations with the Jews have also been formed within the Protestant churches of a number of Western European countries, independently of the framework of the world organization. An outstanding example is that of the Reformed Churches of the Netherlands, which have concentrated their efforts for the strengthening of contacts with the Jews by means of a joint coordination committee ("Interchurch Contact for Israel"), which publishes its own bulletin. The Reformed Church of the Netherlands was also the first to mold a more positive theological approach to Judaism, in one of its publications, *Israel and the Church* (1960), and to advocate the adoption of a dialogue in place of missionary activities.

The Evangelical Church of Germany has also worked intensively toward a Jewish-Protestant reconciliation. During the national conferences of the Church (Evangelische Kirchentage) in 1961 (Berlin), 1963 (Dortmund), and 1965 (Cologne), study days were dedicated to the "Jewish-Christian problem" under the direction of joint working groups of Protestant delegates and specially invited Jews. The lectures and discussions were published by the German Church in two volumes which contain extensive documentation and an exhaustive bibliography on the Protestants' attitude toward the Jews since 1945 (*Der ungekuendigte Bund*, 1962; *Das gespaltene Gottesvolk*, 1966).

In comparison with the situation in Europe, organized Protestantism in the United States and Canada has shown less interest and initiative in furthering relations with the Jews; and activity in this field is led by a small group of "concerned Christians." Although their numbers include theologians and members of the clergy, they are not generally representative of the churches (see below).

The Protestant Mission. Most of the Protestant Churches view the "Christian witness to the Jewish people" as a fundamental religious obligation. However, as a result of a recommendation of the WCC that it was preferable for the mission to the Jews to engage in its activity "as a normal part of parish work, rather than by special agencies, and with avoidance of all 'unworthy pressures'" the majority of the member Churches, especially those of the United States, decided to abolish all organizations devoted especially to the evangelization of the Jews. The Lutheran, Reformed, and Anglican Churches of Europe continue to maintain separate missionary agencies in many countries, including Israel, for activities among the Jews. Even within these Churches, however, there is growing opposition to the antiquated methods of conversion, although Evangelicals and Fundamentalist Protestants still continue to attach the utmost importance to the evangelization of the Jews. These denominations, as well as many organizations of converted Jews (Hebrew Christians), carry on intensive and sometimes even aggressive missionary activities.

In recent years a new conception has been evolved repudiating the theological value of the missions; but it has been expressed by only a limited number of Protestant thinkers, the most notable among them being Reinhold *Niebuhr, Roy *Eckhardt and James *Parkes. These theologians believe in the Jewish religion's right to independent existence as a road to Redemption, and they deny validity to all forms of evangelization of the Jews.

Development of the Interfaith Movement. The dialogue between Jews and Christians is also conducted independently of the organizational framework of the churches. In the British Isles, most European countries, in the United States, Canada, and Australia, as well as in Israel, councils composed of Jews and Christians have been formed for the advancement of understanding and for holding a dialogue between the two religions. These bodies function in many countries under various names and employ different methods. Some of them publish bulletins dedicated to the aims of their activities. In 1961, a roof organization of all these councils, the International Consultative Committee of Organizations for Christian-Jewish Cooperation, was established. A number of Jewish organizations, such as the World Jewish Congress, the Anti-Defamation League of

B'nai B'rith, and the American Jewish Committee, have created special departments for the advancement of interfaith activities. Reform and Conservative Jews, especially in the United States, attach especial importance to the achievement of a deeper understanding between Jews and Christians and have set up their own organizational frameworks to this end.

Since 1950, there has been a growing tendency among the promoters of interfaith contacts to change the character of their interreligious relationships and to translate such expressions as "good will" and "brotherhood" into an honest and fruitful dialogue adjusted to the requirements of a pluralistic society. Upon the initiative of interested Jews and Christians, interfaith dialogues have been held in academic and theological institutions, with important religious and intellectual personalities of both faiths taking part. As a result of these numerous encounters, there has emerged a ramified literature on the question of dialogues in general and Jewish-Protestant relations in particular. Within Orthodox Judaism there are many reservations toward the movement, considered on principle unacceptable. Some other Jewish circles have also expressed their suspicions that these dialogues may become a means of disguised missionary activity on the part of some churches. Moreover, despite the extensive activity carried on by the promoters of the dialogues, the interfaith movement has only succeeded in winning over to its cause a limited elite among Protestant believers. This was no doubt one of the reasons for the crisis in Jewish-Protestant relations which broke out in 1967 after the Six-Day War. The silence of the Churches which had preceded the war and the unfriendly, even hostile, declarations of the Protestant leadership concerning Israel and her postwar policies proved that the dialogue, as conducted previously, was a disappointment. It also became evident that Christians who had participated in these dialogues, due to their ignorance of the true essence of Judaism as a synthesis of a people and a religion bound to the Land of Israel and the Holy City of Jerusalem, had no understanding of the way in which Diaspora Jews identified themselves with the Jews of Israel. Those Jews and Christians who despite all these setbacks insisted on continuing the dialogue arrived at the conclusion, expounded by Rabbi Marc Tanenbaum, one of the leaders of interfaith in the United States, that "no future dialogue will take place without Jews insisting upon the confrontation on the part of Christians on the profound historical, religious, and liturgical meaning of the Land of Israel and of Jerusalem to the Jewish people."

[Yo.M.]

In the U.S. Throughout its history the vast but decreasing majority of the inhabitants of the United States was classed as Protestant (about 98% in 1776 and 66% in 1965), in contrast to the very small Jewish minority. Despite a strong evangelical and missionary outlook in American Protestantism, the two groups have maintained a relatively harmonious relationship. The reasons for this are embedded in the social and religious history of the U.S. Since U.S. independence (1776) was achieved in an age of religious laxity and suspicion of ecclesiastical authority, Jews were from the very first accorded a measure of hospitality. Constitutional guarantees of religious freedom and the separation of church and state assured U.S. Jews a legal security unprecedented in Western history. Concentrated in urban areas, Jews also possessed a regional influence disproportionate to their actual numbers. Creedal and denominational diversity within U.S. Protestantism also meant that this majority group could rarely approach U.S. Jewry, and Catholics, with a single voice.

Cognizant of their organizational weaknesses, spokesmen for U.S. Protestantism periodically made great efforts to strengthen and unify their position. Prior to the 20th century many Protestants believed that the U.S. was "chosen" to be a Christian light to the world; and because of the lack of official public support they were determined to lean upon their own resources to Christianize the U.S.

As long as Protestant efforts were aimed to "convert" the West, U.S. Jews, sparse in that region, were not seriously touched by their efforts. After 1870, however, when Protestant revivalism turned toward the more Eastern cities, its impact was felt more sharply. Protestant Christianizing programs included street corner preaching, distribution of Bibles and Christian tracts, efforts to inject Christian teaching into public education, the erection of Young Men's and Young Women's Christian Associations, institutional churches, and Christian-oriented settlement houses. In part to counteract the possible influence of these efforts, U.S. Jews created their own settlement houses, YMHAs, Hebrew schools, and Jewish centers. Increasingly, U.S. Protestants began to associate social reform with the conversion of the U.S.

The years 1880–1914 witnessed the most intense involvement of the Church in social and economic problems. Protestantism also adopted during these years a new theological outlook, which emphasized the goodness of man rather than his depravity, a new view of God as an Immanent Deity directly involved in human history, and stressed the moral and ethical aspects of theology. A rising interest in comparative religious studies and Higher Criticism motivated Protestants to examine more critically ancient Jewish life. This period, referred to as the Social Gospel, elicited considerable interest, especially among Reform Jews, who believed that the Jewish tradition shared many similar social and theological beliefs. An ecumenical outlook, which first manifested itself in the World Parliament of Religions, held in Chicago in 1893, facilitated a dialogue between Protestants and Jews. During the early years of the 20th century some liberal spokesmen of both camps exchanged pulpits and joined in worship. Nevertheless, despite such outbursts of friendship, an undercurrent of suspicion persisted within both religious groups; and even the most liberal Protestants, be they Unitarians, Transcendentalists, Social Gospelers, or mid-Twentieth Century ecumenicists, continued to view Judaism as merely a bridge from paganism to Christianity.

Recent decades have witnessed the creation of new Protestant-Jewish bonds which, however, were periodically severed. Both have joined in opposing Communism, the outspoken enemy of all organized religions. Involvement in the 1960s in the Civil Rights movement and in the Viet Nam debate forged ties between rabbis and ministers of all denominations. Among the leading voices of Protestantism, Paul Tillich and Reinhold Niebuhr evinced an abiding respect for Judaism. Yet Protestant silence in the face of Nazi destruction of Europe's Jews was disturbing. Anti-Semitism persists among U.S. Protestants and continues to be disseminated in religious literature. As mentioned above, the response of Protestants to the Six-Day War was disappointing and disillusioning to U.S. Jews and seriously threatened the dialogue between the two faiths. On the theological level, Jews and Protestants have also parted roads. The "God-is-dead" theological movement among liberal Protestants—a group which in the past significantly influenced Jewish thought—to secularize theology, was completely rejected by virtually all Jewish religious thinkers. [Eg.F.]

Bibliography: J. F. A. de Le Roi, *Geschichte der evangelischen Judenmission,* 2 vols. (1899); H. J. Schonfield, *History of Jewish Christianity* (1936); D. McDougall, *In Search of Israel* (1941); J.

Parkes, *Judaism and Christianity* (1948); idem, *Antisemitism* (1963); P. W. Massing, *Rehearsal for Destruction* (1949, 1967); G. Hedenquist (ed.), *Church and the Jewish People* (1954); S. S. Schwarzschild, in: *Judaism,* 13 (1964), 259–73; *Conservative Judaism,* 19 (1964/65), no. 3, 1–56; G. A. F. Knight (ed.), *Jews and Christians* (1965); JBR, 33 (1965), 101–65; H. J. Schoeps, *The Jewish-Christian Argument* (1965); P. Schneider, *Sweeter than Honey* (1966); U. Tal, *Yahadut ve-Naẓerut ba-Reich ha-Sheni* (1970); C. Y. Glock and R. Stark, *Christian Beliefs and Antisemitism* (1966); A. R. Eckardt, *Elder and Younger Brothers* (1967); A. Gilbert, in: *Journal of Ecumenical Studies,* 4 (1967), 280–9; M. H. Vogel, *ibid.,* 684–99; Y. Malachy, in: WLB, 23 (1969); *Lutheran Quarterly,* 20 (1968), 219–89; F. Heer, *God's First Love* (1970). In the U.S.: A. P. Stokes, *Church and State in the United States,* 3 (1950); B. H. Levy, *Reform Judaism in America* (1933); C. H. Hopkins, *The Rise of the Social Gospel in American Protestantism, 1865–1915* (1940); E. Feldman, in: *Journal of Church and State,* 9 (1967), 180–9; M. Davis, in: L. Finkelstein (ed.), *The Jews,* 1 (1949), 488–587, incl. bibl.; W. Herberg, *Protestant, Catholic, Jew* (1955); W. S. Hudson, *American Protestantism* (1961); J. Hershcopf Banki, *Christian Reactions to the Middle East Crisis* (1968); B. E. Olson, *Faith and Prejudice* (1962).

PROTESTRABBINER ("Protest Rabbis"), phrase coined by Herzl (in an article in *Die *Welt,* 1, no. 7 (July 16, 1897)), as a designation for the five German rabbis who had signed a trenchant protest letter against Zionism and the Zionist Congress in the name of the German Rabbinical Association. This association comprised two opposing wings—Orthodox and Reform (liberal)—united in their opposition to Zionism. Their attitude as formulated in the protest letter contained three postulates: the intention to establish a Jewish state in Palestine contradicts the messianic destiny of Judaism; Judaism obligates all her believers to be faithful to their native land, serving it as best they can; philanthropic support for agricultural settlers in Palestine is permissible, since it is not connected with the establishment of a Jewish national state. The letter closes with the assertion that love for one's country obligates all those who care for Judaism to shun Zionism and in particular the Zionist Congress.

It was mainly because of this letter that the first Zionist Congress was held in Basle rather than in Munich, as was originally planned. The letter also aroused an unusual amount of agitation because of its hints about the Zionists' unfaithfulness to Germany. Herzl severely criticized the signatories (two Orthodox rabbis—M. Horowitz of Frankfort and A. Auerbach of Halberstadt—and three liberals—S. Maybaum of Berlin, J. Gutmann of Breslau, and K. Werner of Munich), and a great number of Zionist rabbis, Orthodox, and liberal, wrote letters and articles condemning the "protest rabbis." The protest letter was endorsed, however, by the general assembly of the Rabbinical Association, convened in Berlin a year later (July 1–2, 1898), with only one rabbi—Selig Gronemann (Samuel *Gronemann's father)—voting against it. Seventy years after the publication of the protest letter, a survey discovered that almost all the children, grandchildren, and great-grandchildren of the "protest rabbis" had settled in Israel.

Bibliography: *Zionistisches A-B-C-Buch* (1908), 227–30; *Ma'ariv* (July 16, 1968). [G.K.]

°**PROUDHON, PIERRE JOSEPH** (1809–1865), French Socialist and anti-Jewish theorist. For Proudhon, the Jew was the "source of evil," as "incarnated in the race of Shem" (*Césarisme et christianisme,* 1 (1883[2]), 139). He accused the Jews of "having rendered the bourgeoisie, high or low, similar to them, all over Europe" (*De la justice dans la Révolution et dans l'Eglise* (1858), 458). In his "diary," published posthumously, he called them an "unsociable race, obstinate, infernal . . . the enemy of mankind. We should send this race back to Asia, or exterminate it" (*Carnets,* 2 (1961), 23, 337). Proudhon's unremitting hatred of the Jews was probably influenced by *Bonald and by *Fourier, but above all by his own xenophobic passion for France, which he saw as "invaded by the English, Germans, Belgians, Jews," and other foreigners (*France et Rhin* (1867[2]), 258). In the France of the first half of the 19th century, Proudhon was the mainstay of a grass-roots socialism, which has been seen as an early version of National-Socialism.

Bibliography: L. Poliakov, *Histoire de l'antisémitisme,* 3 (1968), index; R. F. Byrnes, *Antisemitism in Modern France,* 1 (1950), index; E. Silberner, *Sozialisten zur Judenfrage* (1962), index. [Ed.]

PROUST, MARCEL (1871–1922), French novelist. Proust was born in Paris to Adrien Proust, a successful non-Jewish physician, and Jeanne (née Weil), a member of an old Alsatian-Jewish family. Through his mother, Proust was related to the eminent statesman Adolphe *Crémieux and to the wife of Henri *Bergson. By 1893 it became obvious that Proust's delicate health would not allow him to follow any profession, and he thereafter devoted himself to writing and to the pursuit of social advancement. His wealth and personal qualities gave him an entrée into the high society that was to form the background to his literary works. He became a contributor to literary reviews, helped to found the short-lived *Le Banquet* (1892) and in 1896 published two books—*Portraits de peintres,* a volume of poems, and *Les Plaisirs et les jours,* a collection of poems, stories, and sketches. Proust's outstanding work, *A la Recherche du temps perdu* (15 vols., 1913–27), consists of seven parts: *Du côté de chez Swann* (1913); *A l'Ombre des jeunes filles en fleurs* (1918); *Le Côté de Guermantes* (1920); *Sodome et Gomorrhe* (1921); *La Prisonnière* (1923); *Albertine disparue* (1925); and *Le Temps retrouvé* (1927). Though not strictly autobiographical, the novel cycle contains much material based on personal recollections and encounters. During the last 17 years of his life he was an invalid, and spent most of his time locked up in his Paris apartment, feverishly working on his manuscripts and revising his published work. Raised as a Catholic, Proust alludes to his Jewish ancestry in his writings, describing his mother and maternal grandparents, and mentioning his grandfather's practice of placing a pebble on his parents' grave. In *Du côte de chez Swann,* his grandfather admits a preference for his Jewish friends and Proust himself remained on the closest terms with Jews such as Léon *Brunschvicg, and

Stamp commemorating Marcel Proust, issued by the French postal service in 1966. Jerusalem, B. M. Ansbacher Collection.

the convert Daniel *Halévy. He always retained some Jewish sympathies, and it was he who persuaded Anatole France to intervene in the *Dreyfus Affair. *A la recherche du temps perdu* contains three major Jewish characters: the actress *Rachel; the aggressive unsympathetic intellectual Albert Bloch; and the assimilated Charles Swann, a member of the exclusive Jockey Club, who has been seen as Proust's own alter ego. The snobbishness of Proust's Jewish characters masks their basic insecurity and, like his creator, Swann finally discovers his identity when he sides with Dreyfus and detaches himself from high society. The contrasting titles of *Du Côté de chez Swann* ("the Side of Swann") and *Le Côté de Guermantes* ("the Side of Guermantes") reflect the conflicting Jewish and non-Jewish sides of Proust's own heritage. Other works published after his death include the fragmentary novel, *Jean Santeuil* (3 vols., 1952), and the critical study *Contre Sainte-Beuve* (1954).

Bibliography: A. Spire, *Quelques juifs et demi-juifs* (1928), 45–61; Quenell, in: H. Bolitho (ed.), *Twelve Jews* (1934), 177–99; L. Pierre-Quint, *Marcel Proust, sa vie, son oeuvre* (1936); Van Praag, in: *Revue juive de Genève*, 5 (May–July, 1937); A. Maurois, *The Quest for Proust* (1950); Mesnil, in: E. J. Finbert (ed.), *Aspects du Génie d'Israël* (1950), 297–300; G. Cattavi, *Marcel Proust* (Fr., 1958); C. Lehrmann, *L'Elément juif dans la littérature française*, 2 (1961), 134–41; G. D. Painter, *Marcel Proust, a Biography*, 2 vols. (1965); C. Mauriac, *Proust par lui-même* (1953); de Silva Ramos, in: *Les cahiers Marcel Proust*, 6 (1932), 13–86 (incl. bibl.) [GE.C.]

PROVENÇAL, ABRAHAM BEN DAVID (16th century), scholar of Mantua. He was the son of David b. Abraham *Provençal. Abraham was the teacher of Azariah dei Rossi and Abraham Portaleone, who refer to him in terms of the highest praise and make mention of his extensive knowledge of Torah and Talmud, Latin, philosophy, and medicine. The titles of doctor of philosophy and doctor of medicine were conferred upon him, and from 1563 he started to become widely known as an outstanding physician. At the same time he served as rabbi in various Italian towns, including Ferrara and Mantua. With his father, he planned, in 1564, the founding of a university for the study of Judaism and the general sciences. Both David and Abraham Provençal belonged to a group of Italian scholars who aspired toward a beneficial merger between the curricula of Jewish religious studies and of general knowledge in order to strengthen religious education among Jews and to minimize the influences of general education.

Bibliography: M. Guedemann, in: *Festschrift . . . A. Berliner* (1903), 164–75; J. R. Marcus, *Jews in the Medieval World* (1938), 381–8; H. Friedenwald, *Jews and Medicine* (1944), 221f.; C. Roth, *Jews in the Renaissance* (1959), 42f., 247f., 254, 331; S. Simonsohn, in: KS, 37 (1962), 106, 115, 118f.; M. A. Shulvass, *Ḥayyei ha-Yehudim be-Italyah bi-Tekufat ha-Renaissance* (1955), 239f. [Y.Ho.]

PROVENÇAL, DAVID BEN ABRAHAM (b. 1506), rabbi of Mantua, preacher, and linguist. He was the brother of Moses *Provençal. Provençal had the idea of establishing a Jewish university in Mantua because he feared a decline in the study of Torah in Italy after the burning of the Talmud. In 1564 he addressed an appeal on this subject to the Italian communities (later published in *Ha-Levanon*, 5 (1868), 418f., 434f., 450f.). According to his plan the curriculum was to include the written and oral law, philosophy, Hebrew grammar, Hebrew poetry, Latin and Italian, grammar, medicine, and astronomy. There are differences of opinion as to the extent to which the proposed program was carried out. The traditional view is that many of the fundamental points were implemented, even though the atmosphere of intolerance on the part of the Catholic Church toward the Jews of Italy undoubtedly served to hinder the fulfillment of the university program.

Provençal was the author of *Ir David*, a commentary on the Pentateuch, and a commentary on the Song of Songs; *Dor Haflagah*, on the Hebrew words adopted in foreign languages; and *Migdal David*, on Hebrew grammar. All three books have been lost, though they were seen by Azariah dei Rossi. Provençal's defense of Philo against Azariah dei Rossi's criticisms is not extant either. His commentary to *Avot* has been preserved in manuscript (N. Weisz, *Kataloge . . . D. Kaufmann* (1906), no. 131). He also proofread the Venice 1565 edition of the *Paḥad Yizḥak*.

Bibliography: M. Guedemann, in: *Festschrift . . . A. Berliner* (1903), 164–75; S. Assaf, *Mekorot le-Toledot ha-Ḥinnukh be-Yisrael*, 2 (1930), 115–20; J. R. Marcus, *Jews in the Medieval World* (1938), 381–8; M. A. Shulvass, *Ḥayyei ha-Yehudim be-Italyah bi-Tekufat ha-Renaissance* (1955), index; C. Roth, *Jews in the Renaissance* (1959), 42f., 247f., 331; S. Simonsohn, *Toledot ha-Yehudim be-Dukkasut Mantovah*, 2 (1964), 422f., 450, 458, 533f. [D.TA.]

PROVENÇAL, JACOB BEN DAVID (15th century), scholar of France and Italy. It is probable that Jacob was the ancestor of the Provençal (Provenzale) family that settled in Mantua in the 16th century. He resided first in Marseilles, where he engaged in maritime trade, but subsequently went to Naples, where he is mentioned in c. 1480 as one of its rabbis.

It was from Naples that he wrote a letter to Messer David b. Judah *Leon of Mantua, in which he expressed his opinion on the value of secular studies, particularly medicine (see *Divrei Ḥakhamim* (1849) edited by Eliezer Ashkenazi). He gave an approbation for the *Agur* of Jacob Baruch b. Judah *Landau which appears in the Rimini edition of 1526. He also seems to have written a commentary on the Song of Songs which was published together with the commentaries of Saadiah Gaon and Joseph ibn Kaspi in about 1577.

Bibliography: Ghirondi-Neppi, 215; Gross, Gal Jud, 383f.; M. A. Shulvass, *Ḥayyei ha-Yehudim be-Italyah bi-Tekufat ha-Renaissance* (1955), 75, 142, 238; C. Roth, *Jews in the Renaissance* (1959), 43n. [Y.Ho.]

PROVENÇAL, MOSES BEN ABRAHAM (1503–1575), rabbi. He is sometimes referred to as Moses da Rosa from the town near Vicenza in which he was apparently born. Brother of David *Provençal, Moses was considered one of the greatest talmudists and one of the most illustrious scholars of Italian Jewry in the Renaissance period. For many decades he was rabbi of the Italian community of Mantua, which therefore became a center of talmudic study. Rabbis turned to him from all over Italy and beyond with halakhic problems. With the Catholic Counter-Reformation a sociocultural ferment was set off in Italy, which spread even to the ghettos, with the result that zealous rabbis began to persecute such liberally minded scholars as Moses. Matters reached a head when Moses introduced a new formula for the **Havdalah* when a festival immediately followed the Sabbath. The innovation so aroused the wrath of Meir *Katzenellenbogen of Padua and Moses *Basilea that they secured his expulsion from office, although for some unknown reason they later repealed the ban. Another ruling, in which he invalidated Samuel Venturozzo's divorce of his wife, the daughter of Joseph Tamari, on the grounds of its having been given under duress — brought down upon him the censure of many Italian rabbis. He appealed with the help of the Court impresario Judah Leone *Sommo to Duke Guglielmo who granted him a hearing before an impartial rabbinical tribunal. In 1566 he was banned by the rabbis of Venice from holding office for three years. Rabbis in Turkey and Greece also associated themselves with the ban, and even the scholars of Safed entered into the controversy. Moses *Trani supported the excommunication, but many of the outstanding rabbis of Safed, including almost certainly Joseph *Caro, supported Provençal. This was apparently the reason that his second dismissal also was not implemented, since he continued to act as rabbi of Mantua until his death. In 1560 he was asked to decide on the permissibility of playing tennis on the Sabbath. In his reply, which sheds much valuable information on the development of the game, he permitted tennis on the Sabbath provided that there was no betting, that rackets were not used, and it was not played at the time of the sermon. The approbation he gave to the Mantua (1558–60) edition of the Zohar shows him to have been in favor of the publication of kabbalistic works, which was the subject of a dispute in Italy at the time.

Moses' works include: *Be'ur Inyan Shenei Kavvim*, a dissertation on the Theorem of Apollonius, on two straight lines which never meet, which is discussed by Maimonides and published in the Sabionetta (1553) edition of Maimonides' *Guide of the Perplexed*. His commentary on this dissertation was translated into Italian by Joseph Shalit (Mantua, 1550) and from Italian into Latin with a commentary by F. Barocius (Venice, 1586); *Elleh ha-Devarim*, and a commentary, *Be'ur Zeh Yaza Rishonah* (Mantua, 1566), on the Tamari-Venturozzo divorce; *Hassagot* ("notes") to *Me'or Einayim* (Mantua, 1573) of Azariah dei Rossi, published at the end of the book; *Be-Shem Kadmon* (Venice, 1596), abridged rules of Hebrew grammar in poetic form; responsa published in various works. Moses' major literary legacy, responsa, and commentaries on various tractates of the Talmud, and a commentary to Maimonides' *Guide of the Perplexed* are almost entirely unpublished.

Bibliography: Rivkind, in: *Tarbiz*, 4 (1933), 366–76; C. Roth, *Jews in the Renaissance* (1959), 28–29, 236, 266; R. W. Henderson in: JQR, 26 (1935/36), 1–6; Benayahu, in: *Rabbi Yosef Caro*, ed. by Y. Raphael (1969), 304–5; S. Simonsohn, in: *Tarbiz*, 28 (1958), 381–92; idem, *Toledot ha-Yehudim be-Dukkasut Mantovah*, 2 vols. (1962–64), index; I. Tishby, in: *Perakim*, 1 (1967–68), 140: E. Kupfer, in: *Sinai*, 63 (1968), 137–60; idem, in: *Tarbiz*, 38 (1969), 54–60.

[A.D.]

PROVENCE (Heb. פרווינצא), region and former province of S.E. France corresponding to the present departments of Bouches-du-Rhône, Var, Basses-Alpes, and parts of Vaucluse and Drôme. In rabbinical literature the name of Provence is frequently applied simultaneously to a part of Languedoc, a practice also adopted by some modern scholars which has given rise to numerous confusions. *Comtat Venaissin and the county of *Nice were detached from Provence from the administrative point of view at an early date and are therefore mainly excluded from this survey. Recent archaeological discoveries prove that the settlement of Jews in Provence is of ancient date and goes back to at least the end of the first century C.E. The earliest documentary evidence for the presence of Jews dates from the middle of the fifth century in *Arles. They were to be found in large numbers in *Marseilles at the close of the sixth century. It was not until the 13th and especially the 14th century that Jews were to be found in numerous localities of Provence, between 80 and 100, more particularly in *Aix-en-Provence, *Apt, Aubagne, Berre, Cadenet, Castellane, Chateaurenard, Cotignac, *Digne, *Draguignan, Forcalquiers, Fréjus, Grasse, *Hyères, Istres, Lambesc, *Manosque, Moustiers-Sainte-Marie, Pertuis, Peyrolles-en-Provence, Maximin, *Saint-Rémy, Salon, *Tarascon, *Toulon, and Trets. The Jewish population reached a peak on the eve of 1348, when it probably numbered about 15,000.

Regulations governing the activity and administration of the communities in Provence are known from 1215 on, as evidenced from the community of Arles. Later the first sumptuary regulations appear in Provence, as well as charitable confraternities and the introduction of compulsory education. From at least the end of the 13th century an inter-community organization existed, though imposed by the government to facilitate the collection of the tax rendered by Jews to the sovereign of Provence. From the beginning of the 15th century, a special official, the "Conservateur des Juifs," was responsible for their protection and adjudication; the office was coveted by the leading families of Provence, because of the considerable revenue it brought in.

The principal occupation of the Jews in Provence was *moneylending; the rate of interest charged was very low for that period, from 10 to 25%. However they only lent small sums destined for expenses and did not possess the capital required for commercial loans on a large scale; the latter was furnished by Christians of Provence and Languedoc, Italians, and Catalans. Hence, not a single Jew is found among the creditors of King René of Provence (1434–80) although members of the Forbin family of Provence and of the Doria family of Genoa are frequently recorded. Jewish participation in commerce was also dependent on this factor. Jews did not have the capital required to engage in large business upon their own initiative but often acted as brokers. They were therefore involved in most transactions of wheat and wine. They also traded in spices and textiles and the sale or lease of houses. The number of Jewish physicians in Provence was particularly great and in some towns they formed 5% of the Jewish working population; this would have amounted to one physician for every 100 persons if their services had been restricted to the Jewish community, but they also treated Christians, often holding the official function of municipal physician, and were particularly in demand when epidemics broke out. Their fees were nevertheless far lower than those of their Christian colleagues. In agriculture, Jews in Provence often cultivated vineyards. They also owned and worked fields, as well as market gardens, especially in the vicinity of Digne.

From having been subject to the direct authority of local lords, particularly the bishops, the Jews were placed under the jurisdiction of the count from the time of Charles of Anjou's suzerainty (1246–85). In 1276 he limited the jurisdiction over the Jews which had been assumed by the Inquisition. In contrast, his successor Charles II (1285–1309) issued a regulation in 1294 which reintroduced several anti-Jewish measures of ecclesiastical origin: the employment of Christians by Jews was forbidden; the Jews were barred from public functions; they were compelled to wear the distinctive *badge. At the time of the expulsion of the Jews from France in 1306, those of Provence were exposed to vexations of a fiscal nature. In 1310 King Robert (1309–1345) ordered his officers to assist the Jews to collect the debts which were due them. He refused to consider a request of several ecclesiastics to expel the Jews, but stringently applied the separationist measures which had been issued against them. Jewish quarters had developed in various towns spontaneously, but from 1341 at the latest, Jewish residence was confined to a separate quarter in the towns of Provence. The first anti-Jewish disturbances on a large scale broke out in Provence in 1331. In 1340 other disturbances occurred in Moustiers and Forcalquiers. The severest anti-Jewish riots of the 14th century took place in 1348, at the time of the *Black Death; in Toulon, the community was almost completely annihilated; there were also attacks in Apt and throughout Provence. The loss of life and property suffered by the Jews was so considerable that Queen Jeanne (1343–82) reduced the tax of the Jews of Provence to one-half of its usual rate for ten years. Before the end of this reprieve, new persecutions broke out in several towns in 1355.

The 15th century on the whole was an extremely

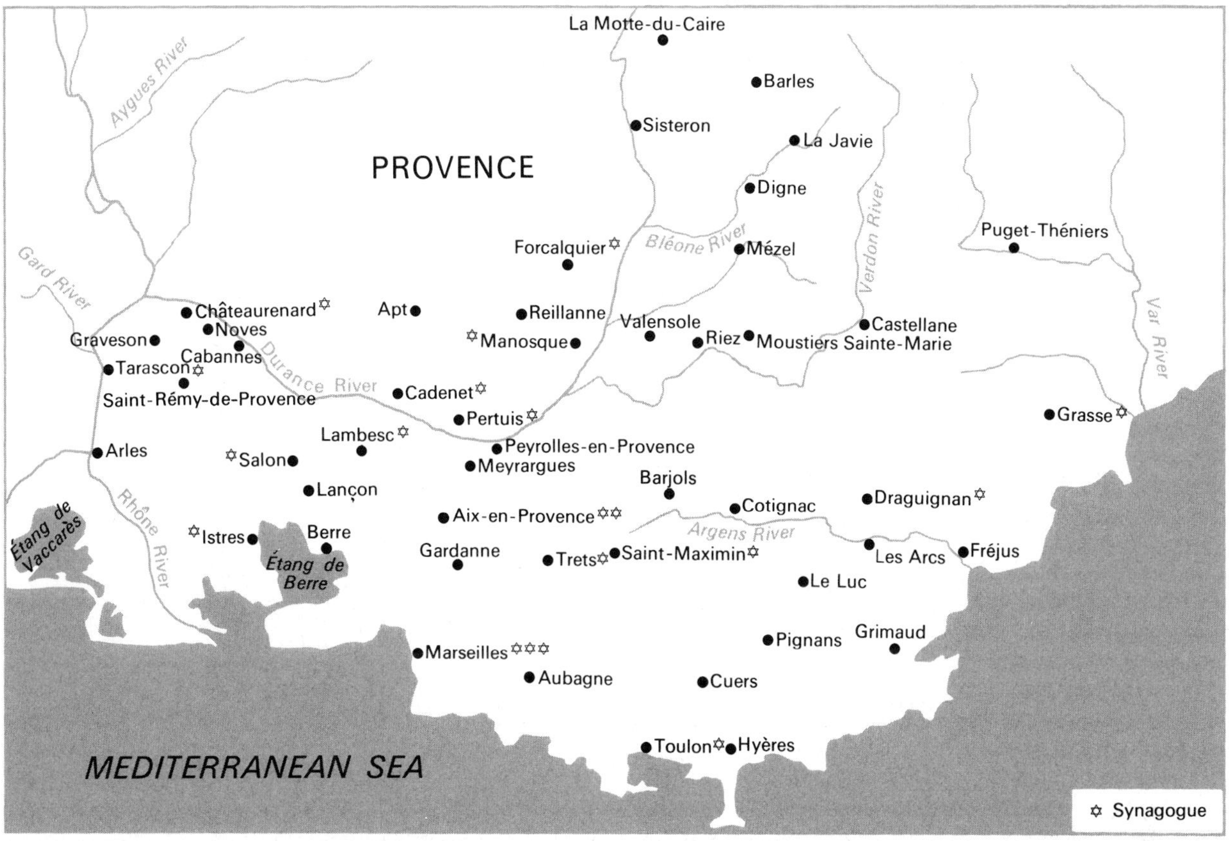

Principal Jewish settlements in medieval Provence.

favorable period for the Jews of Provence. In an edict of 1423, Queen Yolande extended protection to the Jews from arbitrary arrest if there were no reliable witnesses; every accuser of a Jew was required to identify himself by name and provide a surety; a Jew was not to be imprisoned if he could provide bail, unless for crime liable to corporal punishment. King René was known as "the good king," a sobriquet which applied to his treatment of the Jews as well. In 1443 he renewed the edicts of Queen Yolande which had been so favorable to the Jews. In 1454 he authorized the admission of Jews to every category of commerce, trade, and craft, as well as to certain public functions of a fiscal nature. He reduced the size of the Jewish badge and exempted the Jews from wearing it while traveling. He expressed his opposition to instances of forced baptism and even penalized those who had perpetrated such acts.

Within France. In 1481, after the death of René, Provence became united with the Kingdom of France, from which the Jews had been "definitively" expelled in 1394. The privileges of the Jews of Provence were nevertheless renewed in 1482. However, from 1484, anti-Jewish disturbances broke out in Arles, Aix, and Marseilles. This looting and violence was perpetrated by bands of laborers hired for the harvest season from Dauphiné, Auvergne, and the mountain regions of Provence. In Tarascon, where they threatened the Jews, the latter were effectively protected by the officials of the town. Charles VIII, who, although aged only 14, already nominally governed France, took the Jews under his protection. However, a voluntary exodus began and was accelerated when similar disorders were repeated in 1485. On this occasion, the bands of seasonal workers were reinforced by the inhabitants of the town who took part in looting the Jewish quarter. The Jews once more took refuge in the castle. From 1484, one town after another called for their expulsion. In Marseilles, which had also demanded their expulsion, a veritable gang had been organized to rob the Jews, although protests were voiced against their departure. New anti-Jewish disorders broke out in Tarascon in 1489, in Arles before July 1493, and in Manosque in 1495, led by the Carmelites and Franciscans. Louis XII finally issued a general expulsion order against the Jews of Provence in 1498. Not enforced at the time, the order was renewed in 1500 and again at the end of July 1501. On this occasion, it was definitively implemented.

The only alternative to exile offered to the Jews of Provence was conversion to Christianity and a number chose such a solution. However, after a short while—if only to compensate partially for the loss of revenues caused by the departure of the Jews—the king imposed a special tax on them, referred to as "the tax of the neophytes." A roster dating from 1512 enumerates 122 to 164 persons (probably heads of families) subjected to this tax living in 16 important localities of Provence. These converts and their descendants soon became the objects of social discrimination, a situation against which the parliament of Provence reacted in 1542. The campaign of discrimination was nevertheless maintained. A pamphlet published in 1611 attributed the miserable condition of the parliament of Provence to the neophytes. Around the beginning of the 18th century a lampoon entitled *"Critique du nobiliare de Provence,"* which accused a large number of aristocratic families of being of Jewish origin, gained notoriety. To this campaign must also be attributed the adaptation to Provençal of a forgery of Spanish origin: this was a mere literary farce in the form of an exchange of letters between the Jews of Arles and those of Constantinople. The correspondence was supposedly conducted at the close of the 15th century, when the Jews of Provence asked how they were to act in order to avoid expulsion. The Jews of Constantinople, according to this, counseled them to accept baptism while inwardly remaining Jews, stating that once they had attained the powerful positions to which the Christian religion admitted them, they would be able to avenge all the former miseries which they had endured.

During the second half of the 17th century a number of Jews attempted to reestablish themselves in Provence, following the edict issued by the minister Colbert in March 1669 which granted Marseilles the status of a "tax-free port." However, on complaints of the chamber of commerce of that town the parliament of Provence renewed the prohibitions against the residence of Jews there. Although the parliament authorized their temporary residence during the 18th century to enable them to trade at the fairs, a further attempt by a number of Jews to settle permanently, on this occasion in Aix, was prevented. Before the French Revolution abolished the administrative entity of Provence, the first community outside the southwest, Alsace-Lorraine and Comtat Venaissin, was formed in Marseilles.

For later history see *France. [B.BL.]

Cultural life. The fortuitous geographical circumstance in which Provence was situated between three great intellectual centers—Spain, Italy, and Franco-Germany—had a decisive effect on the development of Provence as a major center for Jewish learning and literature. The incorporation of Provence into the Christian Carolingian Empire severed it from contact with Jews in Muslim lands until the 12th century. As a result the early cultural life of Provence was closely allied with that of the Franco-German center. Unlike their contemporaries in Spain, Provençal scholars focused entirely on the Talmud in the development of their cultural life. Their achievements were of some importance. While scholars in Arles at one time turned to those in Lucca, Italy, for guidance, Torah centers in France, Germany, and Italy often looked to Provence for the solution of halakhic difficulties and exchanged responsa with Provençal scholars. Provençal halakhic traditions were expressed largely in oral rather than in written form. Provence had an important influence on the development of Midrash, both in their creation of new *midrashim* and the editing of older ones; of equal importance were its *minhagim*, some merging Babylonian and Palestinian influences.

At the beginning of the 12th century a large part of Provence was incorporated into Catalonia, bringing Provençal scholars into contact with those of *Barcelona. The result was a greater spirit of enlightenment in Provence and the broadening of its intellectual horizon to include interest in the sciences and language. That development was speeded up considerably with the invasion of Spain by the *Almohads in the middle of the 12th century and the consequent flight of many Spanish thinkers to Provence when Jewish centers in Spain were destroyed. The cultural life of Provence was considerably enriched as a result. Major changes took place in biblical exegesis; scholars increasingly engaged in the natural sciences; there was a flowering of interest in poetry, lexicography, grammar, and philosophy. Major effort was expended on the translation of literature from Arabic to Hebrew. Nevertheless, the halakhic knowledge of Provençal scholars was not lost, Ashkenazi influences remained, and the contact with Ashkenazi scholarship was deepened. Through the work of Spanish scholars the influences of Isaac *Alfasi and the Babylonian *geonim* were deeply felt in Provence; Ashkenazi and Spanish approaches to the *halakhah* found a new synthesis in the work of Provençal halakhists. Unlike Spain it was in Provence that the philosophers and grammarians also wrote works on *halakhah*. Great interest was kindled in mysticism, also, and philosophical knowledge was profound enough to make Provence a major focus of the *Maimonidean controversy. Into the 14th century Provence remained the meeting point of different intellectual systems and an area of considerable intellectual ferment.

Prominent among the scholars of Provence were R. Moses of Arles, a correspondent of Kalonymus of Rome; R. Judah b. Moses of Arles, his son, mentioned by Rashi in *Sefer ha-Pardes;* *Gershon b. Solomon of Arles, author of the metaphysical work, *Sha'ar ha-Shamayim;* *Kalonymus b. Kalonymus (1281–after 1328), translator and author of *Even-Boḥan;* Kalonymus b. David b. Todros, 14th-century Bible commentator; *Isaac b. Abba Mari of Marseilles (12th century), author of a commentary to the Code of Alfasi as well as *Sefer ha-Ittur;* Joseph of Marseilles, Bible commentator mentioned by Judah Messer Leon; Aaron b. Abraham b. Isaac and Shem Tov Falcon, the correspondents of Solomon b. Abraham *Adret; Samuel b. Judah, 14th-century scientist and translator of the commentary of Averroes on Aristotle's *Ethics;* Moses de Salon, philosopher and teacher of Kalonymus b. Kalonymus; Bonjudas Nathan Crescas, physician, noted through the medical work, *Sod ha-Sodot;* and *Nissim b. Moses of Marseilles, 14th-century author of a commentary on the Pentateuch entitled *Ma'aseh Nissim.* [A.SHA.]

Bibliography: Gross, Gal Jud, 489ff.; R. Busquet, in: *Mélanges Institut Historique de Provence,* 4 (1927), 68–86; A. Kober, in: JSOS, 6 (1944), 351–74; Z. Szajkowski, *ibid.,* 31–54; idem, *Franco-Judaica* (1962), index; Schirmann, Sefarad, passim; E. Camau, in: *La Provence à travers les âges* (1928), 249–367; A. Z. Aeskoly, in: *Zion,* 10 (1945), 102–39; B. Blumenkranz, in: *Evidences,* 12 (March–April 1961), 29–33; idem, in: *Bulletin Philologique et historique* (1965), 611–22; B. Benedict, in: *Tarbiẓ,* 22 (1951), 85–109.

PROVERB (Heb. מָשָׁל, *mashal;* pl. מְשָׁלִים, *meshalim*). The term "proverb" as a translation of the biblical Hebrew word *mashal* denotes certain specific literary forms, particularly of wisdom literature. Several of these forms are also referred to by the words *pitgam* and *mikhtam* in post-biblical Hebrew (although in the Bible these two terms have other connotations). The literary forms referred to in the Bible by the term *mashal* are of different types, and scholars are divided on the question of the connection between these forms, as well as on the basic meaning of the biblical term *mashal.* In post-biblical Hebrew, *mashal* signifies several poetic forms, i.e., figures of speech or types of ornate style. The nature of these poetic forms, which are found particularly in classical literature, has been elucidated in Western thought. Parallels to these poetic forms are found in the Bible, although its authors were not conscious of them. Discussions of the term *mashal,* therefore, may fall into two sections: the first, devoted to *mashal* in its broader post-biblical sense, i.e., as referring to poetic forms in general, and the second, to *mashal* in its more limited sense, i.e., in its specific use in the Bible as a concept associated principally with wisdom literature.

Poetic Forms. Many examples of basic figures of speech, such as similes and metaphors, occur in the Bible. These are common in every language, and occur even in daily conversation. The complex literary forms known as *meshalim* in post-biblical Hebrew are structured on these basic figures of speech.

ALLEGORY. An allegory is a metaphor expanded to the dimensions of a narrative in which all the details reflect the actual subject of the metaphor. Examples of allegory in the Bible are to be found, in particular, in Ezekiel's account of the great eagle and the top of the cedar (17:3–12), of the lioness and her whelps (19:2–9), of the vine that was uprooted and withered (19:10–14), of the pot set on fire (24:3–5), of the cedar in Lebanon that was cut down (31:3–17), and of the shepherds who neglected the sheep (34:2–31), as well as others. The description of old age at the end of Ecclesiastes (12:2–6) is not allegorical, but consists rather of a series of metaphors which do not combine to form a narrative. On the other hand, there are expressions which, while they are not allegories, contain the elements of allegory, being extended metaphors which do not reach the proportions of an actual narrative, for example, Balaam's comparison of Israel to a lion (Num. 24:8–9).

PARABLE. A parable is an independent narrative in which a particular detail contains a moral that is applicable beyond the content of the narrative itself. Examples of parables in the Bible are Nathan's tale of the poor man's ewe lamb (II Sam. 12:1–4), and, to some extent, Jehoash's story of the thistle and the cedar in Lebanon (II Kings 14:9). Isaiah's song of the vineyard (5:1–6) may be either an allegory or a parable.

FABLE. A fable is a story whose figures are taken from the animal or vegetable realm and are endowed with human characteristics; it has a moral which is applicable beyond the content of the narrative itself. Examples of fables in the Bible are Jotham's tale of the trees that sought a king for themselves (Judg. 9:8–15), and, to a certain extent, Jehoash's account of the thistle and the cedar in Lebanon (II Kings 14:9). The sayings drawn from the animal realm in Proverbs (6:6–8; 30:24–31) and the descriptions of animals in God's reply to Job (38:39–39:30; 40:15–41:26) cannot be considered fables because they do not contain personification; they are rather didactic statements based on observation of natural phenomena.

Mashal in the Bible. The term *mashal* in the Bible can be elucidated either by means of etymological investigation or by examining its actual usage and combining the features common to all the literary forms to which it refers. These two methods have been accompanied by conjecture and differences of opinion among scholars, and neither has as yet produced any definitive results.

Etymology. The root *mšl*, from which the word *mashal* is derived, has two etymologies, both of which have been used to explain the nature of the biblical *mashal*. Some scholars base their interpretation of *mashal* on one meaning of the root *mšl*, which is "resemblance" or "the equating of one thing to another," found in the Arabic *mithl*, and the Aramaic *mtl*. While some scholars maintain that this meaning indicates the primary tendency of the *mashal* which is to compare and allegorize (Koenig, Eissfeldt, Johnson, et al.), others find it an allusion to the element of sympathetic magic prevalent in the ancient proverb (Godbey). This meaning of the root *mšl* does not occur in Canaanite, but a trace of it is to be found in the Bible: "Upon earth there is not his like" (Job 41:25[33]), although the absolute state of the noun here is *moshel* (מֹשֶׁל), not *mashal* (מָשָׁל). The Bible contains examples of *meshalim* that are not allegorical in character but simply songs (see below). Another meaning of the root *mšl* implies government and rule; equivalents are found in Canaanite inscriptions, and in the Bible *mšl* commonly has this meaning. On the basis of this meaning of the root, some scholars seek to explain the primary significance of the *mashal* as the statement of an influential man who is endowed with authority (Pedersen, Bostroem, Bentzen). However, this explanation, too, is forced and cannot be completely reconciled with the examples of *meshalim* in the Bible.

Literary Forms. The following are the literary forms called *mashal* in the Bible:

The Folk Saying. The characteristic features of the folk saying are its widespread use and its pithy, concentrated formulation, which gives pointed expression to popular experience and wisdom. In the Bible, such sayings are prefaced by expressions attesting to their popular character. At times the identical saying occurs in two different passages, further evidence of its widespread use. The saying, "Is Saul also among the prophets?" is quoted in two narratives and is introduced by the statements: "Therefore it became a *mashal*" and "wherefore they say" (I Sam. 10:12; 19:24). A folk saying of the period of the Babylonian Exile, "The fathers have eaten sour grapes, and the children's teeth are set on edge," is mentioned in two prophetic books (Jer. 31:29; Ezek. 18:2–3). Another contemporary saying current in Palestine is quoted by Ezekiel (12:22–23), while David repeats to Saul the *mashal* of the Kedemites, "Out of the wicked comes forth wickedness" (I Sam. 24:13). There are introductory expressions hinting at other folk sayings quoted in the Bible which, by analogy, may presumably also be regarded as *meshalim*, although they are not called such in the Bible, for example: "Like Nimrod a mighty hunter before the Lord" (Gen. 10:9). There are other statements which have the characteristics of folk sayings even though they are not prefaced by introductory expressions, for example, "For as the man is, so is his strength" (Judg. 8:21) and "Let not him that girds on his armor boast himself as he that puts it off" (I Kings 20:11).

The Literary Saying. The literary saying does not differ in form from the folk saying, except that it is not in common use, being coined by a wisdom writer who uses a fixed formula in which to cast conventional thoughts of his school. Compilations of literary sayings are extant in the second and fifth collections of the Book of Proverbs (10:1–22:16; chs. 25–29) and segments of them are embodied in other collections of that book (see *Proverbs). These sayings inculcate the particular outlook of wisdom literature. Groups of literary sayings have also been incorporated in Ecclesiastes as quotations from its author's wisdom compositions, their conventional contents frequently contradicting Ecclesiastes' essentially pessimistic reflections. One passage attests that Koheleth "also taught the people knowledge, weighing, and studying, and arranging proverbs */meshalim/* with great care" (12:9), that is, he redacted and composed many *meshalim* that are not included in this book. At times it is impossible to know whether a saying is literary or popular, such as the following statement by Ezekiel concerning Jerusalem: "Everyone who uses proverbs will use this proverb about you saying, 'Like mother, like daughter'" (Ezek. 16:44), and Jeremiah's remark, "What has straw in common with wheat?" (Jer. 23:28). It cannot be determined whether in these passages the prophets are quoting current sayings or coining new ones. Sometimes a literary saying may be adopted and widely used by the people, as is the case with many biblical verses which in the course of time became popular sayings.

The Poetic Utterance. The poetic utterance is also called *mashal* in the Bible. Sometimes such an utterance contains obvious metaphorical and allegorical features, as in Ezekiel's statements about the great eagle and the top of the cedar (17:2–10), the forest of the South (21:1–5), and the pot set on the fire (24:3–11), all of which he calls *meshalim*. Sometimes, although the poetic utterance lacks these features it is still termed a *mashal*. It may have been popular—a sort of folk saying, like the song which the ballad singers uttered on the overthrow of Heshbon by Sihon king of the Amorites (Num. 21:27–30). In some cases the poetic utterance may not even have been popular and yet been called a *mashal*. The first collection in Proverbs (1–9) contains about a dozen poetical-rhetorical units, all of them literary compositions bearing the imprint of the wisdom school; most of these have no allegorical features; their contents are evident and explicit, yet all are called *meshalim* (Prov. 1:1). Two psalms that are referred to as *meshalim* have neither a folk character nor employ allegory—the one speaks of the fate of the wicked (Ps. 49), the other reviews the history of Israel from the Exodus until the building of the Temple in Jerusalem (Ps. 78). Job's last two monologues are similarly called *meshalim*, and from their superscriptions: "And Job took up his *mashal*, and said" (Job 27:1; 29:1), it seems that his earlier utterances during the discussion are also regarded as *meshalim*. At the same time, several poetic utterances that are called *meshalim* do not even seem to belong to wisdom literature, e.g., Balaam's songs (Num. 23:7–10, 18–24; 24:3–9, 15–24); the derisive elegy on the fall of the king of Babylon (Isa. 14:4–22); and the song of the ballad singers on the overthrow of Heshbon, referred to above.

Conclusion. To understand more fully the meaning of *mashal* in the Bible, the features common to all the above-mentioned literary forms may be combined and in this way the essential characteristics of the concept determined. The first, and indispensable, characteristic of the *mashal* is its poetic form. All the *meshalim* quoted or alluded to in the Bible take the form of a song, while the *mashal* and the song *(shir)* are mentioned as analogous concepts in I Kings 5:12. Folk sayings of a few words (see above) must thus be understood as versets of poetry. Prose statements are never termed *meshalim* in the Bible. Thus the story of Jotham in Judges 9:8–15 and that of Nathan in II Samuel 12:1–4 are not called *meshalim*. The difference between a *mashal* and a song *(shir)* apparently lies in the fact that the song was set to a tune and its recitation accompanied by musical instruments, whereas the *mashal* may have been associated with some melody, but was generally simply declaimed. The wisdom psalm is an exception, however, insofar as it has the form of a *mashal* and yet is at the same time a psalm (Ps. 49:5). Another characteristic of the *mashal* is its rhetorical aspect. It is intended for oral recitation only. Every *mashal* quoted in the Bible is accompanied by a statement indicating that it was, or was supposed to be, uttered aloud. Frequently it is prefaced by the phrase "to take up a *mashal*" (Num. 23:7, 18; 24:3; Isa. 14:4; Micah 2:4; Hab. 2:6; Job 27:1; 29:1). In Ezekiel, the usual phrase employed is "to use [or speak] a *mashal*" (Ezek. 12:23; 16:44; 17:2; 18:2–3, et al.). The Bible says that Solomon "spoke three thousand *mashal*" (I Kings 5:12). Of the literary compositions assembled in Proverbs and called *meshalim*—the poetic units in the first collection (Prov. 1–9) and the literary sayings in the second and the fifth (10:1–22:16; chs. 25–29)—some bear a clear rhetorical stamp, and all were apparently intended to be declaimed and memorized in the wisdom schools (see *Proverbs). Also characteristic of the *mashal* is its essentially secular nature. It is not the word of God but specifically the product of human "wisdom." A prophetic statement in the name of God, even if in the form of a poem, is never called a *mashal,* unless the prophet is commanded to compose *meshalim,* as in Isaiah 14:4 and in Ezekiel. In such instances, the prophet employs, as it were, his own wisdom and creative talents to proclaim the word of God specifically in the form of a *mashal.* Balaam's *meshalim* are similarly to be understood as the product of his occult science, as the expression of his skill in cursing and blessing (cf. Num. 22:6; Josh. 13:22; see *Balaam). These characteristics lend probability to the view that the *mashal* originated either in wisdom circles, or in those close to it, or in ancient folk wisdom (as distinct from artistocratic wisdom whose compositions have been assembled in the Book of Proverbs), the occurrence of the *mashal* in the prophetic books being explained as the use by the prophets of ready-made formulas. The figures of Balaam and of the ballad singers who on important occasions expressed themselves in *mashal* (Num. 21:27) point to pre-Solomonic times. The figure of Balaam also suggests that the ancient *mashal* was connected with sorcery and magic, those who practiced them being likewise included in the category of wise men (cf. Gen. 41:8; Ex. 7:11; Isa. 44:25; Ps. 58:6; cf. Isa. 3:3: "the skillful enchanter"). In the course of time the *mashal* apparently developed in several directions. Mention has been made above of the pithy saying and the poetic utterance. Other changes of nuance in the character of the *mashal* are expressed in the Bible by combining *mashal* with another word thus producing hendiadys or parallelism. The words *mashal* and *ḥidah* ("riddle") in parallelism allude to a *mashal* whose contents are somewhat obscure and for whose comprehension some knowledge and ability are necessary (Ezek. 17:2; Hab. 2:6; Ps. 49:5; 78:2; Prov. 1:6). Accordingly, it may be inferred that the *ḥidah,* too, in particular one which is in the form of a poem and whose solution takes a poetic form (cf. Judg. 14:14, 18), is in essence close to the *mashal.* The combination of *mashal* and *sheninah* ("byword"; Deut. 28:37; I Kings 9:7; Jer. 24:9; II Chron. 7:20; and in elliptic form in Ps. 69:12) refers to a *mashal* marked by derision and irony. This characteristic is also alluded to in the combination of *ʾot,* "sign," and *meshalim* (Ezek. 14:8) and of *mashal* and *menod rosh* ("shaking of the head"; Ps. 44:15). An example of the derisive *mashal* occurs in Isaiah 14:4–23. Another term used in the Bible to express irony is *meliẓah,* "taunt," and hence the combination of *mashal* and *meliẓah* (Hab. 2:6; Prov. 1:6). Some maintain that the *moshelim,* mentioned by the prophet in Isaiah 28:14, refer to composers of *meshalim.* According to this interpretation, they composed taunting *meshalim,* as is also evident from the verses that follow. The parallelism of *mashal* and *nehi,* "lamentation" (Micah 2:4), alludes to a *mashal* which has the characteristics of an elegy. An example of this type of *mashal* occurs in Isaiah 14:4–23, and to some extent in Numbers 21:27–30. Another possible tendency in the development of the *mashal* is the emphasis on metaphorical and allegorical features, which are the determining characteristics of Ezekiel's *meshalim* and are found, to a certain extent, in other *meshalim* as well. The verse which says of Solomon that "he spoke of trees, from the cedar that is in Lebanon to the hyssop that grows out of the wall; he spoke also of beasts, and of birds, and of reptiles, and of fish" (I Kings 5:13 [4:33]) may refer to *meshalim* of an allegorical and fabulous nature. On the other hand, it may simply refer to didactic sayings and poems. It is difficult to assume that originally the allegorical aspect determined the essential character of *meshalim.*

Bibliography: E. Koenig, *Stylistik, Rhetorik, Poetik in Bezug auf die biblische Literatur* (1900), 77–110; A. Wuensche, *Die Schoenheit der Bibel* (1906); O. Eissfeldt, *Der Maschal im Alten Testament* (=BZAW, 24 (1913)); idem, in: *Einleitung in das Alten Testament* (1964), 89, 109–13, 123–6, 166–70; J. Pedersen, *Der Eid bei den Semiten* (1914), 12; A. H. Godbey, in: AJSLL, 39 (1922–23), 89–108; G. Bostroem, *Paronomasi i den aeldre Hebreiska Maschalliteraturen* (1928); M. Hermaniuk, *La parabolé évangélique* (1947), 62–189; J. Pirot, in: *Recherches de science réligieuse,* 37 (1950), 565–80; A. Bentzen, *Introduction to the Old Testament* (1952), 167–77. [M.HA.]

PROVERBS, BOOK OF (Heb. סֵפֶר מִשְׁלֵי, *Sefer Mishle(i)*), one of the three "wisdom books" of the Hagiographa, representing the affirmative and didactic element in wisdom *(ḥokhmah)* in contrast to the radical questioning of Job and Ecclesiastes. In its present form the book appears to have served as a manual for the moral and religious instruction of the young. Comprising materials of various kinds gleaned from the long tradition of wisdom, the book was used in schools by professional sages (cf. Eccles. 12:9–12; Ecclus. 6:23–28). The teacher's objectives and methods are outlined in Proverbs 1:2–6, namely, cultivation of the mind and training in ethical principles by the use of *proverbs *(mashal),* warnings *(meliẓah),* sayings of the sages, and riddles *(ḥidah)* or puzzling questions. The teacher's basic theme is summed up in the motto with which he begins and ends the introduction to the older materials—"The fear of the Lord is the beginning [or first requirement, chief part] of knowledge [wisdom]" (1:7; 9:10).

Title. In the Masoretic Text the title *Mishle Shelomo ben David Melekh Yisrael* is usually abbreviated *Mishle* (so LXX, Vulg.). Solomon is here named as the traditionally supreme sage and patron of wisdom; this neither proves nor necessarily implies a claim of authorship. According to I Kings 5:12–13, the subject matter of Solomon's proverbs was not human character and behavior as in the Book of Proverbs, but nonhuman creatures. Statements such as Proverbs 20:2, 8, 26 are not such as would come from a king's own lips. Two divisions of the book are each headed *Mishle Shelomo,* which would be redundant if the title in 1:1 were intended to be comprehensive. Other authors are named in 22:17, 24:23; 30:1; and 31:1. It is therefore probable that the title of the book was taken over and adapted from 10:1 when chapters 1–9 were prefixed to the previously existing materials. The word *mashal,* literally "likeness, comparison," or "powerful word," is used elsewhere of prophetic oracles (Num. 23:7; Ezek. 17:2) and of a solemn oath (Job 27:1), as well as of such traditional wise sayings as "Like mother, like daughter" (Ezek. 16:44). By the use of such comparisons, or by setting a *mashal* alongside a phenomenon or experience, the inner meaning of the latter was brought to light. In Parts 2 and 4 of Proverbs the heading *Mishle Shelomo* may have designated the literary form characteristic of these sections, namely, a

Illuminated miniature at the opening of Proverbs from a 15th-century Hebrew manuscript from Italy. Shown is the judgment of Solomon. Jerusalem, Israel Museum, 180/55, fol. 186v. Photo David Harris, Jerusalem.

single-line proverb in poetic parallelism, as distinguished from the half-line or prosaic form of colloquial sayings (cf. I Sam. 10:12; 24:14).

The Wisdom Tradition. The cultivation of wisdom as an understanding of the good and satisfactory life had a long history in ancient Israel. Originally the term had no ethical content, but meant simply a special skill or superior ability. The moral and religious element, broadly speaking, is a later enlargement of its meaning. In Job 38:36 and 39:17 it denotes simply intelligence. The "wisdom" of Bezalel was his expertness as a craftsman (Ex. 35:30–35). The word is used even of the disgraceful cunning of Jonadab (II Sam. 13:3). In I Kings it refers successively to Solomon's cleverness (2:6), his moral discernment (3:12), his encyclopedic knowledge (5:9), and his special ability as a king (5:21). Royal counselors and local sages were consulted for their intelligence and good judgment (II Sam. 16:20–23; 20:15–22). The "wise" with whom Isaiah and Jeremiah disputed were powerful courtiers (Isa. 29:13–16; Jer. 9:22). However, "wisdom" as embracing ethical qualities in personal and social life was rooted in the ethos of family and tribe, and found expression in the divinely given moral obligations of the covenant people (Deut. 4:5–6), and in the prophetic picture of the ideal king (Isa. 11:1–2). It finally took literary form in the piety of "wisdom" psalms, e.g., Psalms 1 and 34, of the author of Proverbs 1–9 and of Ben Sira, and in the dogmatism against which the writers of Job and Ecclesiastes revolted (see also *Wisdom).

International Wisdom. Hebrew wisdom was distinctive but not unique, as is recognized in the Bible itself. Solomon's wisdom is compared to his advantage with that of Egypt and of the people of the East. Edom was famous for its sages (Jer. 49:7; Obad. 8), as was Tyre (Ezek. 28:2ff., 12ff.). Surviving "wisdom" literature from Egypt and Mesopotamia exhibits the same kind of divergence as between Proverbs and Ben Sira on the one hand, and Job and Ecclesiastes on the other—the first conservative, affirmative, didactic, and practical, the second skeptical of traditional values and radically speculative. The lengthy "instruction" addressed by a pharaoh or high official to his son and expected successor is a well attested genre from Egypt. The influence of this form has been traced in the admonitory discourses in Proverbs 1–8, and more certainly in 22:17–24:22. The latter has a demonstrable literary connection with the Egyptian *Instruction of Amen-em-ope.* A late example of the "instruction," ascribed to *Onchsheshonqy,* contains many sayings and proverbs of which some recall those of Proverbs, including examples of antithetical parallelism.

Precepts and Proverbs. Inherent in the biblical idea of wisdom was that it could be taught to those capable of learning (Ex. 35:34). The *peti* in Proverbs 1:4 is "simple," "untutored"; he is not a "fool" *('evil)* unless he despises learning (1:7). There were two methods of education—the authoritative *musar* ("training, precept") of parent and of the teacher in a parent's role, and *ʿezah,* the "counsel" of the sage and of the teacher as sage. *Musar* is found in Proverbs in peremptory "do's and don'ts" (e.g., 3:25–32; 22:22ff.), and in longer discourses in chapters 1–9 and 30:1–9. *ʿEzah* is expressed in the sentence-long sayings about how life is lived well or badly, which form the substance of the "Solomonic" proverbs in 10:1–22:16 and chapters 25–19. The precept speaks in the imperative mood, the proverb in the indicative, with the occasional variant of a rhetorical question. The one seeks to impose the teacher's will and knowledge on the student; the other to elicit from him a free and positive response. They have the same objectives of forming the mind, building the moral character, and training the judgment of the pupils (1:2–4). The form of extended instruction differs from that of the shorter precept by including a motive clause indicating the welcome or unwelcome results that would follow from obedience or disobedience respectively. In this it resembles many proverbs describing the character and behavior of men, and thus serving as indirect precepts encouraging virtue and holding up vice to contempt. "A little sleep, a little slumber, a little folding of the hands to rest—and poverty will come upon you like a robber" (24:33–34) has the same effect as "Love not sleep lest you come to poverty" (20:13). The precept in 25:16 is the equivalent of the saying in 25:27a. Precepts reflect the imperatives of social order and religious values. Proverbs were rules of another kind, pointing to a right order in life which exists or should exist, expressed in the stylistic pattern: "this is like that," "this is better than that," "this results in that." Happy or unhappy consequences of actions occur in accordance with an unseen order of justice. The observations and counsels of the proverbs in 10–22:16 and chapters 25–29 are on two levels of moral and religious understanding. On one level they are exhortations to personal piety and probity, and the affirmations that the Lord is master in human affairs and guarantor of the moral order (e.g., 10:3; 11:1; 12:2; 16:1). With these are associated the encomiums on wisdom and wise men, and the identification of the latter with "the righteous" and of fools with "the wicked" (e.g., 10:6–8; 12:1, 15; 13:20; 16:22). On the second level are the more secular sayings, caustic comments on anti-social behavior, and pathetic reflections on "the way things are" (e.g., 13:7; 14:13; 20:14; 26:6–16). Some short colloquial sayings seem to have been recast in verse form, as when an identical saying in 10:15a and 18:11a has been differently supplemented in the second half of the line. In 15:33 and 18:12, what looks like a simple parental admonition has been given different parallel lines. Other sayings possibly of popular origin are 11:2a; 12:4a; 17:14a; 22:8a; 27:7b, 10c. A special type of proverb compares phenomena in a culminating numerical series. "Three things are never satisfied, four never say, 'Enough!': Sheol, the barren womb, the earth ever thirsty for water, and the fire which never say 'Enough'!" (30:15b–16; cf. 30:18–19, 21–31). Since a whole number cannot have an exact synonym, it is paired with the number next lower when used in synonymous parallelism (see *Poetry). The form originated in the effort of early wisdom thinkers to classify phenomena by common characteristics. It is a kind of riddle: "What do such similarities mean for man's understanding of the world about him?"

Structural Outline of the Book. PART 1. Chapters 1–9. Didactic discourses and "wisdom poems."

Title, preface and motto—1:1–7.

Ten instructional discourses—1:8–19; 2:1–22; 3:1–12; 3:21–26 + 31–35; 4:1–9; 4:10–19; 4:20–27 + 5:21–23; 5:1–14; 6:20–21 + 23–35; 7:1–27.

Five poems:

(a) the rewards of wisdom—3:13–20;

(b) personified Wisdom addresses men in rebuke, appeal and self-affirmation—1:20–33; 8:1–36; 9:1–6 (+ Folly, 13–18).

Precepts, direct or implied—3:27–30; 5:15–20; 6:1–19, 22; 9:7–12.

PART 2. Chapters 10–22:16. First Collection of "Solomonic Proverbs."

PART 3. (A): Chapters 22:17–24:22. The "Thirty Precepts" of the Sages; an "Instruction" modeled on the Egyptian *Instruction of Amen-em-ope.*

(B): Chapter 24:23–34. Other Sayings of the Sages; an appendix to (A).

PART 4: Chapters 25–29. Second Collection of "Solomonic proverbs," transmitted by Hezekiah's scribes.

Appendixes to the book:

(1) Chapter 30:1–9. The skepticism of Agur, and a believer's reply.

(2) Chapter 30:10–13. Warnings and numerical proverbs.

(3) Chapter 31:1–9. A queen mother's diatribe.

(4) Chapter 31:10–31. Acrostic poem on the capable housewife.

Subject Matter. Since none of the main divisions of the book is entirely homogeneous in spite of their clear distinction from one another, some further comments are called for.

In Part 1 the points where each of the ten discourses begins are clearly marked, but their extent and possible expansions are less certain. Each opens with an exhortation to learn wisdom because of its value for living. All except no. 2 have as their pivotal point a specific precept, with corresponding promises or threats. In no. 2 the casuist form ("if you . . . then") replaces the imperative. In nos. 3, 5, and 7 the counsel is positive and general: "learn wisdom, and keep to the right path." In nos. 1, 4, and 6 the pupil is sternly warned against casting his lot with evildoers, and in 2, 8, 9, and 10 against the seductions of adultery. The latter evidently has here both a literal meaning and a metaphorical reference to religious unfaithfulness. A notable feature in nos. 1, 6, 8–10 is the vividness of the descriptions of temptation and the fateful consequences of yielding to it. The poems in 1:20–33, 8:1–36, and 9:1–6 not only conceptualize Wisdom but personify her in striking fashion. Chapter 8, arranged in three strophes and an epilogue, is one of the most remarkable passages in the wisdom literature, picturing Wisdom as YHWH's associate in the creation of the world. This poem appears to be based on the shorter one in 3:13–20, which, however, speaks of Wisdom in the third person. The short poem on Folly in 9:13–18 is a companion piece to that on Wisdom in 9:1–6. Following the eighth discourse, four short warnings against particular vices are inserted, together with a numerical list of hateful sins (4:15–20; 6:1–19). Again in 9:7–9 three proverbs intrude into the context.

Part 2 brings together about 375 single-line metrical proverbs or "wisdom sayings," haphazardly arranged except for one or two small groups on related topics (16:1–15). Some formal differences can be noted between chapters 10–15 and 16–22:16, though the point of division is indefinite and the teaching of both halves of the collection is essentially the same. In 10–15 there is a much higher incidence of antithetical parallels than later; "righteous" and "wicked" are contrasted most frequently in chapters 10–12, and "wise man" and "fool" most often in 12–15. After chapter 15 synonymous and extended parallelism predominates, together with scornful descriptions of the fool. References to YHWH's over-ruling providence and to divine sanctions on man's conduct are most frequent in 15 and 16. These may have been inserted by the teacher who prefaced 1–9 to the earlier collection of proverbs.

The literary relationship of Part 3 (A) to Amen-em-ope is clear, but difficult to spell out in detail. The structure of the two is the same: a summons to hear "thirty" (*sheloshim,* for MT vocalization *shalishim*) admonitions, a series of extended negative precepts. The first six and the ninth of these have topical and some verbal echoes of their Egyptian counterparts, but in a different order. The most striking verbal correspondence is the counsel against avarice in Proverbs 28:4–5: for wealth "grows wings, like an eagle it flies away into the sky." Amen-em-ope gives the same counsel but uses the simile "geese" rather than an "eagle." Because the order of corresponding sections is different, and 21 of the Egyptian precepts have no counterparts in the Hebrew work, it seems that the Hebrew scribe was depending on what he remembered from an earlier acquaintance with the Egyptian work. Part 3 (B) is a brief miscellaneous section attributed like 3 (A) to "the wise men," that is, to tradition. The first seven verses have enough points of contact with (A) to raise the possibility that they were left over from an earlier or alternative form of (A).

Part 4, the second collection of "Solomonic proverbs," resembles the first in some particulars and differs in others. It also falls into two parts unmarked in the text, 25–27 and 28–29. Chapter 25 opens with a series of precepts of double length, and chapter 26 has groups of sayings that pillory the fool and the sluggard. Throughout 25–27 precepts and similes predominate, rather than the declaratory sentences common in the first collection. The tone also is more secular and less moralizing; the name YHWH occurs only once, and then in a supplementary line. In 28–29 the resemblance to 10–22:16 is greater both in form and content. Parts 2 and 4 have six proverbs in common, seven others are nearly identical, and four more have identical half-lines. The virtues extolled and the vices held up to scorn are much the same. The four appendixes differ markedly from each other and from the rest of the book. In 30:1–9 the challenge of Agur the agnostic is answered (either in dialogue or as a later addendum) by a believer who affirms his faith and adds a humble prayer. In 30:10–33 there are five numerical sayings or riddles, a numbered list of sinners like 6:16–19, and some miscellaneous proverbs. In 31:1–9 the mother of an unknown king Lemuel harangues her son for his dissolute behavior and neglect of his duties to his people. The fourth appendix is an acrostic poem on the capable housewife; it is remarkable for the light it throws on domestic activities in well-to-do homes and on the managerial responsibilities undertaken by the woman.

Text and Dating. The questions of the text and its dating are interrelated. The Hebrew text is relatively well preserved. The Septuagint seem to have worked from essentially the same text, in spite of the idiosyncracies of that version. The only significant difference is in the order of some sections, indicating that the text was still not finally fixed in the first century B.C.E. One problem of dating is that an atomistic work, which so much of Proverbs represents, was peculiarly susceptible to minor expansions. Hence the rare occurrence of Aramaic words may be meaningless for dating. There are no Persian or Greek words, and it is no longer necessary to posit the Greek period on philosophical or theological grounds. The customary post-Exilic dating of the book may have been influenced, more than is realized, by its association with Ben Sira. The book is composed throughout in classical Hebrew, with the exception of some Phoenicianisms, chiefly in chapter 8, which may have resulted from the use of older sources. Material as early as the time of Solomon may be included in the numerical proverbs of 30:15–31 and many of the more secular sayings. If reliable, 25:1 indicates that older materials were assembled in Hezekiah's reign. The activity of Wisdom teachers in the eighth century B.C.E. is evident in Isaiah (cf. Prov. 19:11–12; 21:2), in the prophet's adoption of a "wisdom" form for his oracle in Isaiah 28:23–29, and in apparent references to schools (Isa. 28:9–10; cf. 6:9–10). The literary influence of the Egyptian "instructions" and the optimistic serenity of tone point to a time when concern for individual conduct and education were not crowded out by alarm over national security. However, both older and later materials undoubtedly are included. Although the evidence is inconclusive, the late monarchical period seems as likely as any for the completion of the work in substantially its present form.

Ethical and Religious Teachings. The contents of Proverbs range from purely intellectual observations about natural phenomena, to "secular" comments on how men behave and life's occurrences, to a final positive association of right conduct with true wisdom and religious faith. The teacher's introduction in chapters 1–9 emphasizes the spirit in which the older wisdom materials are to be approached. Virtues and vices which had been discerned in the long experience of the community and by its older sages were still valid. The principal new emphasis is on resisting the temptation to fall into the ways of hardened evildoers and adulterous women. The "wise" and the "fools" have become the "righteous" and the "wicked" in newly composed moralistic couplets, inserted in the "Solomonic" collections. Whereas in the older wisdom it was asserted on grounds of experience that good conduct generally led to prosperity and its opposite to ruin, the reason for each now is seen to be "the eyes of the Lord are in every place, keeping watch on the evil and the good " (15:3). In the older parts of the book, "wisdom" means simply the state of being wise. Its conceptualization begins with the idea in the "Solomonic sayings" that wisdom is an inner fountain of life (13:14). The teacher in 1–9 further develops both ideas: the state of being wise is attained by training, but it is also a gift of divine grace (2:1–6), and will act as a personal guide through life. This personification of Wisdom is dramatically enhanced in 1:20–33 and 8:1–31, yet still within the limits of poetic imagery (cf. Ps. 85:11–12). Wisdom here addresses men in her own name and in the guise of a goddess; she is a living power in the order of the world and has been YHWH's associate in its creation. Scholars differ as to whether in 8:22ff. Wisdom has become a full-blown hypostasis of YHWH, or whether it is an imaginative image of what is said in 3:19: "YHWH by [His] wisdom founded the world." The structure of the whole passage 8:12–31, when compared to 3:13–20, favors the latter alternative, though the picture may be colored to some degree by mythic language.

Bibliography: R. Gordis, in: HUCA, 18 (1843–44), 77–118; C. I. K. Story, in: JBL, 64 (1945), 319–37; Kaufmann, Y., Toledot, 2 (1960), 631–46; C. T. Fritsch, and R. W. Schloerb, in: *Interpreter's Bible*, 4 (1955), 767–957; Pritchard, Texts, (1955²), 405–52; W. G. Plaut, *Book of Proverbs* (1961); B. Gemser, *Sprueche Salomos* (1963); M. Haran, in: *Tarbiz*, 39 (1969/70), 116–18, 130–32; W. McKane, *Proverbs* (1970), incl. bibl. [R.B.Y.S.]

PROVERBS, TALMUDIC. The Talmud abounds in proverbs of all kinds. Important sources are the tractates *Avot, Avot de-Rabbi Nathan, Derekh Ereẓ Rabbah,* and *Derekh Ereẓ Zuta,* and numbers of proverbs occur together in several smaller collections (BK 92a–b; Bek. 17a; et al.), although they are scattered through all rabbinical literature.

Scholarly and Popular Proverbs. The proverbs of scholars are usually introduced with the words, "it was customary for A to say" or "he used to say," and their popular ones by "as the rabbis say." In most cases these proverbs have an ethical and didactic character. The Talmud also contains many popular proverbs which are quoted with the opening words "the proverb says" (in Hebrew and in Aramaic), "they say," "as people say," "the proverb says," "the common proverb says," and in "the language of the people." These popular proverbs are mainly expressed in Aramaic. In many cases there is no clear distinction between scholarly and popular proverbs, and it is then difficult to determine their source. For example, the saying of Rabban Simeon b. Gamaliel, "One who gives bread to a child must inform its mother" (Shab. 10b), is also cited in the Midrash (Num. R. 19:33) as "a popular proverb." The word "he used to say" merely indicate that a particular scholar quoted it frequently. Thus the saying of Samuel the Younger, "Rejoice not when thine enemy falleth, and let not thine heart be glad when he stumbleth" (Avot 4:19), is a verse from Proverbs (24:17). The dictum of Shammai, "receive all men with a cheerful countenance" (Avot 1:15), is quoted with a slight variation by Ishmael (3:13). The dictum of Hillel on the Feast of Water Drawing, "Whither I desire to go thither my feet lead me" (Tosef., Suk. 4:2), was originally a popular saying which Hillel applied to God (S. Lieberman, *Tosefta ki-Feshutah,* ad loc.). This is probably why Rashi quotes "walls have ears" as a popular proverb (Ber. 8b), although it is given in the Midrash in the name of R. Levi (Lev R. 32:2; Eccles. R. 10:21). Sometimes contradictory proverbs appear to be directed at one another. An example is found in the ethical dictum, "Be rather a tail to lions than a head to foxes" (Avot. 4:15), which contradicts the popular saying, "The proverb says: Be a head to foxes rather than a tail to lions" (TJ, Sanh. 4:10, 22b), and indeed parallels to this popular version are found in Hellenistic literature.

The rabbis spared no effort to introduce beautiful popular proverbs into the world of scholarship. They sought authority for them in early sources, in the Bible and in the tannaitic literature (BK 92a–b), and also derived proverbs from the interpretation of biblical verses, although in these cases it is also possible that the proverb anticipated the interpretation (cf. "From here we see that the ignorant person pushes himself to the front" (Meg. 12b); "When wine enters, counsel departs" (Er. 65a; Sanh. 38a); "Woe is me because of my Creator *[yoẓer]*, woe is me because of my [evil] inclination" (*yeẓer;* Ber. 61a)).

Proverbs and Halakhah. The sages did not hesitate to utilize the wordly wisdom in the proverbs for halakhic ruling. "Once a man borrowed a cat to deal with mice, but the mice killed the cat. The case came before Ashi for judgment. Thereupon a certain Mordecai, who was present, intervened, quoting Rava: A man killed by women gets neither judgment nor judge," i.e., the cat was itself responsible and the owner can have no claim (BM 97a). They applied the proverb "It is not the mouse that is the thief, but the hole" (Git. 45a) in halakhic discussions. From the ancient, pointed proverb, "An olive's bulk of the paschal offering, yet the rejoicing splits the roof," expressing the popular attitude toward an inflated ceremony, Ḥiyya inferred a *halakhah* in connection with ritual uncleanness (TJ, Pes. 7:10, 35b). The reverse also occurred, namely that the proverb was created through the halakhic ruling, as in the case of a ruling of Akiva expressed in a proverbial form: "You have dived into the depths and brought up only a potsherd" (BK 91a). The rabbis utilized the dictum: "That which made you unclean, did not make me unclean, yet you have made me unclean" as a mnemotechnic chain connecting a collection of *mishnayot* on the laws of ritual defilement (Par. 8:2–7).

Rabbinic Study of Proverbs. The sages engaged in the study of proverbs. Mention has been made of a series of dialogues in which *amoraim* searched for the classical source of popular sayings, and it is worth noting that for one of them (BK 92b) they discovered five possible sources. They also compared the dicta of Ereẓ Israel and Babylon: "Here [in Babylon] they say, 'Tobias sinned and Ziggas was flogged.' There [in Ereẓ Israel] they say, 'Shechem married and Mabgai was circumcised' " (Mak. 11a; i.e., because Shechem—Gen. 34—wished to marry Jacob's daughter the whole population had to undergo circumcision).

Ereẓ Israel and Babylon. Undoubtedly much use was made of proverbs in Ereẓ Israel; but for some reason the number of them in the Jerusalem Talmud is relatively meager in comparison with those in the Babylonian, and most of those quoted in the Jerusalem Talmud are also found in the Babylonian Talmud.

Translations from Aramaic to Hebrew. In the late Midrashim there occur translations into Hebrew of the Aramaic proverbs in the Babylonian Talmud. At times the translation is inferior to the original. Thus the dictum (BK 92b), "Into the well from which you have drunk water do not throw clods," becomes in the Midrash (Num. R. 22:4), "Into the well . . . do not throw stones." The Aramaic word for "clod" is more suitable, since it suggests the defiling of the water.

Comparison with Biblical Proverbs. Talmudic proverbs surpass the biblical ones in pungency and appositeness but are inferior in sophistication and poetry. Thus the biblical (Eccles. 10:8), "He that diggeth a pit shall fall into it," parallels, "If a man spits into the air, it will fall on his face" (Eccl. R. 7:9, no. 1), and the verse (Prov. 17:10), "A rebuke entereth deeper into a man of understanding than a hundred stripes into a fool," parallels, "A hint is sufficient for a wise man but a fool needs the fist" (Mid. Prov. 22:15).

Animal Proverbs. The sages made extensive use of the animal world for their proverbs. The miser is compared to "a mouse lying upon the coins" (Sanh. 29b). Of a coward who treats harshly those subservient to him, it says: "One who cannot hit the donkey [lest it kick], hits the saddle" (Tanḥ. Pekudei 4). A warning against women occurs in the saying: "If the dog barks—enter; if a bitch,—leave" (Er. 86a; from which Rav exemplified a *halakhah* in the laws of *Eruvin* based upon the difference in a man's relationship to his son-in-law and to his daughter-in-law). Of a weak character it says, "He never controlled two flies" (Deut. R. 1:5).

Stylistic Characteristics. Alliteration occurs in several dicta, such as "A man's character can be recognized in his cup, his purse, and his anger" (Heb. *koso, kiso, ka'aso*—Er. 65b). In some instances the alliteration is somewhat rhymed such as, "He who eats the fat tail *[allita]* must hide in the loft *[alita]*, but he who eats cress *[kakule]* may lie by the dunghill *[kikle]* of the town" (Pes. 114a); and "When a Jew must eat carobs *[ḥaruva]*, he repents *[tetuva]*" (Lev. R. 13:4). Ingenious homiletical interpretations of words occur: "Why are some coins called *zuzim?* Because they are removed *[zazim]* from one and given to another. Why are other coins called *ma'ot*, because they signify *mah la-et* [what of the future time?]" (Num. R. 22:8).

Eulogistic Dicta. The Talmud cites dicta uttered by professional mourners. Thus, "if the flame has fallen upon the cedars [the great] what avails the hyssop on the wall!" (the lowly; MK 25b); "Many have drunk the cup of death; many shall drink" (Ket. 8b). Tawiow noted that the Bible and the Talmud contain no derogatory proverbs about deformed persons such as occur in abundance in the sayings of other peoples.

Rabbinic Proverbs in Popular Parlance. Hundreds of rabbinic dicta have found their way into popular usage. In many of them changes have occurred which are worth noting. Very many others originally quoted in a halakhic or theoretical framework have become popular sayings with a meaning different from the original. Thus, "A man may see any leprous signs except his own" (Neg. 2:5), taught originally as a law that a leprous priest must be examined by some other priest, received the popular psychological meaning that no man is objective with reference to himself. The expression *dikdukei aniyyut* ("the minutiae of poverty"; Er. 41b), first used of the sufferings of poverty, is used already by Ibn Ezra (Eccles. 12:5) with reference to a forced explanation, i.e., the writer is lacking imagination. *"Damim tarte mashma,"* in the original means "the word *damim* [blood] applies to two kinds of blood" and is popularly used to express both "blood" and "money." Hundreds of rabbinic sayings found their way into the spoken language in the form in which they occur in more popular works, such as Rashi's commentary, *piyyutim*, etc. The expression, "The Omnipresent has many agents of death" (Ta'an. 18b), is current among people in the form it occurs in Rashi (to Ex. 16:32): "The Omnipresent has many agents." The dictum, "Four count as if dead: a poor man, a blind man . . ." (Ned. 64b), is better known in the abridged form of Rashi (to Ex. 4:19): "A poor man is regarded as dead." Akiva's dictum, "No pity may be shown in a lawsuit" (Ket. 9:2), is popularly known by the form in which it occurs in a **silluk* (type of *piyyut*) for the first day of the New Year: "[The Supreme King preserves the world through justice, for] there is no pity in judgment." The changes popularly introduced did not result from ignorance but from didactic grounds whether consciously or unconsciously. These changes gave greater clarity and accuracy to the dicta, furnished a general and abstract form to dicta that needed it, and also added interpretation where necessary. The talmudic dictum, "In the place where penitents stand, the wholly righteous do not stand" (Ber. 34a) was popularly revised into the clearer dictum, "In the place where penitents stand, the wholly righteous are unable to stand," stressing the superiority of the penitent more clearly than in the original. The statement of Rava (Meg. 16a) that the help given Mordecai was given "not because of the love for Mordecai but because of the hatred for Haman" received a general abstracted meaning in the mouth of the people: "not from love of Mordecai but from hatred of Haman" (a version already found in the *Massekhet Purim* attributed to *Kalonymus b. Kalonymus, ed. by J. Willheimer (1871), 43). The expression "R. Yose always has his reason" (Git. 67a) became through the influence of Rashi, "his justification and reason are with him," i.e., he always has good reason. During recent years many works have appeared comparing talmudic sayings with those of other peoples (see bibliography) which prove that among cultures and languages far from Ereẓ Israel and Babylonia, such as the Far East, independent proverbs similar to those in the Talmud were common.

Bibliography: I. H. Tawiow, *Oẓar ha-Meshalim ve-ha-Pitgamim* (1922), 10–25; L. Taubes, *Talmudishe Elementn inem Yidishn Shprikhvort* (1928), 9–16; M. Waxman, *Mishlei Yisrael* (1933), 23–31; I. Davidson, *Oẓar ha-Meshalim ve-ha-Pitgamim* (1957); M. Glueck, in: *Hadoar*, 36)1957), 484–6 (=*Leshonenu la-Am*, 8 (1957), 260–6; 9 (1958), 20–27; S. Ashkenazi, in: *Leshonenu la-Am*, 11 (1960), 261–65; 12 (1961), 99–105; E. Blankenstein, *Mishlei Yisrael ve-Ummot ha-Olam* (1964); I. Davidson, in: *Jivobleter*, 13 (1938), 354–72 (bibl.); Y. L. Zlotnik, in: *Barkai*, no. 66 (1940), 14f. (additions to bibl.). [AR.ST.]

PROVIDENCE, capital and largest city of the state of Rhode Island, United States, located at the head of Narragansett Bay. The population of Providence alone in 1963 totaled approximately 177,000 persons, of which the estimated Jewish population was 9,100; 4,800 for Cranston;

2,300 for Warwick-East Greenwich; 2,250 for Pawtucket. Slightly more than two-thirds of the Jews lived in the urban center of the metropolitan area, and the rest lived primarily in the suburban towns of Cranston, Warwick, and Barrington.

Although there was a Jewish community in Newport, Rhode Island as early as the mid-17th century, Jews did not settle in Providence until 1838, when Solomon Pareira, a merchant, arrived with his family. Other settlers were attracted after the state's adoption of a liberal constitution in 1841. During this period the European revolutions of 1840 produced a stream of immigrants, including the early Jewish settlers of Providence. Largely shopkeepers, they found Providence a busy seaport with a growing population. In 1854 they founded the city's first congregation, Congregation Sons of Israel. By 1880 about 150 Jewish families lived in the area. Most of the early arrivals came from the countries of Western Europe, particularly Germany. The significant growth of the Jewish community began after 1880, as immigrants from Eastern Europe poured into the city. As the community grew, so did its formal organizations and institutions. As early as 1870 a lodge of B'nai B'rith was organized, and subsequently, scores of mutual-aid societies were organized, including the Rhode Island Shoe Makers Association and the Ladies Hebrew Benevolent Association. Other services were provided by such groups as the Ladies Friendship Lodge (sick benefit), Rhode Island Home for Jewish Orphans, Gemilath Chesed Association, and United Hebrew Citizens Association of Rhode Island. The first synagogue building was erected in 1890 by Congregation Sons of Israel and David. By then four other congregations had been formed and were meeting in rented quarters. These early synagogues were all Orthodox; in 1922 the first Conservative congregation, Temple Beth Israel, was chartered.

Population Growth and Demographic Changes. The curbs on immigration in the 1920s eliminated a major source of growth for the Jewish community; since World War II its size has remained stable, having changed only one percent between 1951 and 1963. As a result, the Jewish population has become increasingly American-born and further from its European origins. Although in 1910 the community was comprised largely of immigrants, in 1963 only 17 percent was foreign born; and of the 83 percent who were native born, almost half were third-generation Americans.

As usual in American Jewish communities, there have been sharp alterations in the distribution of the population within the metropolitan area. The immigrants arriving in Providence were concentrated in selected older areas of the city; in 1951, 45 percent of the Jewish population was still living in these areas, and another 43 percent resided in the newer urban areas. By 1963 the older urban ghetto had virtually disappeared; only 18 percent of the total Jewish population still lived there, while over half of all the Jews in Greater Providence lived in the newer urban areas. The Jewish population of the suburbs rose from 13 percent of the total Jewish community in 1951 to 31 percent in 1963.

Occupations and Public Office. The earliest Jewish arrivals in Providence were employed in the clothing trade, either as merchants or tailors. With increasing numbers came greater occupational diversity. In 1963 over 85 percent of the Jews were in the white-collar occupations, and of these almost half were managers or proprietors. The Jews of Greater Providence were exceptionally well educated: one-fourth of the adults had completed college, and an additional 16 percent had at least some college training.

From the late 19th century Jews served on city councils, boards of education, district courts as well as Superior and Supreme courts, and in both houses of the state legislature.

The first synagogue of Providence, erected by Congregation Sons of Israel and David in 1890. From *Rhode Island Jewish Historical Notes*, Vol. 3, no. 1. November 1958.

Frank Licht, a Superior Court justice, was elected governor of Rhode Island in 1968 and reelected in 1970. Alfred H. Joselin was an associate justice of the Rhode Island Supreme Court, and after serving as vice-chancellor of Brown University was elected a member of its Board of Fellows. Other Jews of Providence have also served on the boards of trustees of both private and public colleges and universities in the state and have been leaders in the annual United Fund campaigns. They include Joseph W. Ress, who was president of the Rhode Island United Fund and the Jewish Federation of Rhode Island; a member of the board of trustees of Brown University, he was elected treasurer of the university in 1970. Jews have also been active in promoting the cultural life of the community by serving on the state's Fine Arts Council, on the board of the Rhode Island Philharmonic, and by sponsoring concerts by noted musical artists. Jewish painters are also active participants in Providence's lively art group.

Synagogues and Religious Education. The Jewish community has 18 synagogues, seven Orthodox, eight Conservative, and three Reform. The largest Reform congregation, Temple Beth El, traces its origin to Congregation Sons of Israel and David. Its rabbi from 1932 was William G. *Braude. In 1968 the largest Conservative congregation was Temple Emanu-El, whose rabbi was Eli A. Bohnen. The most recent congregations are those serving the growing suburban populations. More than three-fourths of the Jewish population of Greater Providence report membership in a synagogue, a high level of affiliation; 57 percent were Conservative; slightly over one-fourth Reform, and 17 percent Orthodox. Most religious schools are combined Hebrew-Sunday schools and are affiliated with the Greater Providence Bureau of Jewish Education, supported by the Jewish Federation of Rhode Island. The Bureau sponsors a community-wide Hebrew high school as well as adult-education programs, and the community supports a Hebrew day school for primary grades and high school. Three-fourths of all children between 5 and 14 years of age are enrolled in a program of Jewish education.

Organizations. There is a wide range of formal organizations and services, including various fraternal and Zionist groups. Among them are the Jewish Community Center, which provides year-round activities and a summer day camp; home for the aged; Jewish Family and Children's Service; and Hebrew Free Loan Society. The Miriam Hospital of Providence is under Jewish auspices and is associated with Brown University. General coordination of community activities is provided by the Jewish Federation of Rhode Island, which also conducts the major annual fund drive. Merrill L. Hassenfeld, a past president of the General Jewish Committee of Greater Providence and past campaign chairman of the United Fund, served as a national chairman of the United Jewish Appeal and on the board of directors of the Council of Jewish Federations and Welfare Funds. The *Rhode Island Herald,* a weekly newspaper, caters primarily to the Jews of Greater Providence. Research into the history of the Jewish community is sponsored by the Rhode Island Jewish Historical Association, which also publishes a journal, *Rhode Island Historical Notes,* founded in 1954.

Bibliography: S. Goldstein, *Greater Providence Jewish Community: A Population Survey* (1964); S. Goldstein and C. Goldscheider, *Jewish Americans: Three Generations in a Jewish Community* (1968). [Si.G.]

PROVIDENCE, in religion and philosophy, God's guidance or care of His creatures, emanating from His constant concern for them and for the achievement of His purposes. Providence includes both supervision of the acts of men and the guidance of the actors in specific directions. Its object is also to deal out fitting retribution—in order to establish justice in the world, retribution itself often serving as a means of guidance (see below). Hence there is a connection between providence and the principle of *reward and punishment. The origin of the term providence is Greek (*πρόνοια*, lit. "perceiving beforehand") and first appears in Jewish literature in the Wisdom of Solomon, 14:3; 17:2.

In the Bible. The basis of the belief in a constant and eternal divine providence is the biblical conception of God. In polytheism there is generally a belief in a fixed "order" of nature, which is above the gods. This "order" serves to some extent as a guarantee that right prevails in the world (this is the Greek Θέμις or *μοῖρα*; the Egyptian *ma'at;* and the Iranian-Persian *artha,* "truth"). However, in this type of belief the right is, as it were, a product of action (this is also the Buddhist belief in "karma") and is not dependent on a divine providence with a universal moral purpose. On the contrary, through the use of certain magical acts, man can even overcome the will of the god. In any case, there is a basic belief in fate and necessity. By contrast, the belief in providence is in the first instance a belief in a God who has cognition and will, and who has unlimited control over nature and a personal relationship with all men—a relationship which is determined solely by their moral or immoral behavior. Biblical belief does not deny the existence of a fixed natural order—"the ordinances" of heaven and earth, of day and night (Jer. 31:35–36; 33:25)—but since God is the creator of nature and is not subject to its laws (e.g. Jer. 18:6ff.), He can guide man and reward him according to his merit, even through the supernatural means of miracles. Such guidance may be direct (through divine *revelation) or indirect—through a prophet or other animate or inanimate intermediaries ("Who maketh His angels spirits; His ministers a flaming fire," Ps. 104:4; cf. Joel 2:1ff.; Amos 3:7; Ps. 103:20–22). God's providence is both individual—extending to each and every person (Adam, Abel, Cain, etc.), and general—over peoples and groups, especially Israel, His chosen people. The guarding and guidance of the Patriarchs (Abraham, Isaac, and Jacob) and their families (Sarah in the house of Pharaoh, Hagar in the desert, Joseph in Egypt, etc.) aimed at the ultimate purpose of creating an exemplary people exalted above all other nations (Deut. 26:18). The whole history of the Israelites, beginning with the Exodus from Egypt, is, according to the biblical conception, a continuous unfolding of divine providence's guidance of the people as a whole as well as of its individual members in the way marked out for them. Even the sufferings undergone by the people belong to the mysteries of divine providence (cf. e.g., the doctrinal introductions in Judg. 2:11–23; 3:1–8; 6:7–10, 13–17; 10:6–15; II Kings 14:26–27; 17:7ff.).

It can be said that the entire Bible is a record of divine providence, whether general or individual. While the Pentateuch and the Prophets emphasize general, national providence, Psalms and Proverbs are based on the belief that God is concerned with the individual, hears the cry of the wretched, desires the well-being of the righteous, and directs man, even against his will, to the destiny which He has determined for him ("The lot is cast into the lap, but the whole disposing thereof is of the Lord," Prov. 16:33; "The king's heart is in the hand of the Lord, as the rivers of water; He turneth it whithersoever He will," Prov. 21:1; etc.). Prophets (Jeremiah, Ezekiel, Habakkuk) and psalmists (Ps. 9; 71; 77; 88) sometimes question the ways of providence and divine justice, but they ultimately affirm the traditional belief in providence. In the last analysis, this position is also maintained by the author of Ecclesiastes, who otherwise expresses the gravest doubts regarding providence ("But know that for all these things God will bring thee to judgment," Eccles. 11:9). This is true also of Job, but his doubts and misgivings are confined to the question of a divine providence which rules the universe, and particularly mankind.

The unlimited belief in providence would seem to conflict with the doctrine that man can freely choose good and evil (for which God rewards or punishes him), which is also integral to the biblical world view. This issue was grappled with only in later times, with the development of religious philosophy in the Middle Ages.

In the Apocrypha. In the Apocrypha, too, the belief is widespread that God watches over the deeds of mortals in order to requite the wicked and the righteous according to their deserts. The suffering of the righteous is but a temporary trial in order that they be well rewarded in the end. Tobit, for instance, for dealing kindly with the living and with the dead is persecuted by the authorities. It appears as if the hand of God, too, was turned against him but his righteousness is rewarded. In the end he is vindicated and is vouchsafed the victory of righteousness. The same applies to the community of Israel—the enemy invariably receives his punishment and the righteous nation is saved, almost unexpectedly. According to I Maccabees (9:46), Judah Maccabee urged the people to pray because he knew that God pays attention to prayer ("Now therefore cry unto Heaven that you may be delivered out of the hand of your enemies"). Similarly, the inhabitants of Jerusalem were convinced that their prayer saved them in time of trouble (II Macc. 1:8). As in ancient times, so too in the time of the Hasmoneans, God continued to save His people by means of angels sent by Him (Heliodorus, who went to desecrate the Temple, fell into a faint at the hand of angels: II Macc. 3; angels in heaven hastened to the assistance of Judah Maccabee: *ibid.* 10:29–30). Lysias also realized that the Hebrews were invincible because God helped them (*ibid.* 11:13).

In the concept of providence in the apocalyptic works, particularly in the writings of the *Dead Sea sect, one can detect a tendency toward an important innovation. In these works the idea is expressed that God, who has preknowledge of everything, also decrees everything in advance; both the wicked and the righteous are formed at their creation ("all the sons of light each one to his fortune according to the counsel of the Lord . . .; all the sons of darkness each one to his guilt according to the vengeance of the Lord,"—Manual of Discipline 1:9–10; "From the Lord of Knowledge, all is and was . . . and before they came into being he prepared all their thought . . . and it is unchangeable,"—*ibid.* 3:15–16; "and unto Israel and the angel of his truth [Michael?] [they] are a help to all the sons of light," while "the angel of darkness" rules over "all the dominion of the sons of wickedness,"—*ibid.* 20–24; and see Jub. 1:20 and 2:2). According to Jubilees everything is also written beforehand in the "tablets of the heavens" (3:10). Josephus, too (Ant., 13:171–3, 18:11f.; Wars, 2:119f.), distinguishes between the different sects that arose in the time of the Second Temple, primarily on the basis of the difference between them in the concept of providence. According to him, "the Pharisees say that some things but not all depend on fate, but some depend upon us as to whether they occur or not" (Ant., 13:172). "The Essenes hold that fate rules everything and nothing happens to man without it; while the Sadducees abolish fate, holding that it does not exist at all, that human actions do not occur through its power, and that everything is dependent upon man himself who alone is the cause of the good, and evil results from man's folly" (*ibid.;* see also *Essenes; *Sadducees; *Boethusians; *Pharisees). If the definitions of Josephus are accurate, one may say that the Sadducees deviated from the biblical concept and believed in providence in general but not in detail; something of the same can be said of the Essenes in what pertains to their belief in predestination, but judging from the writings found in Qumran, this belief was not without qualifications and exceptions.

In the Talmud. The outlook of the scholars of the Mishnah and Talmud on the nature and purport of divine providence is summarized in the dictum of Akiva (Avot 3:15): "All is foreseen, but freedom of choice is given; and the world is judged with goodness, and all is in accordance with the works." It is apparent that the first part of this dictum expresses an attempt to reconcile the principle of providence on the one hand with freedom of choice on the other; but it is possible that the idea here expressed is identical with that contained in the dictum: "Everything is in the hand of heaven except for the fear of heaven" (Ber. 33b), which is intended to build a bridge between freedom of choice and the idea of predestination. From various dicta in the Talmud it is possible to infer that the idea of providence during this era embraced not only all men but even all creatures. For the gazelle that is wont to cast its seed at parturition from the top of the mountain, the Holy One prepares "an eagle that catches it in its wings and places it before her, and were it to come a moment earlier or a moment later [the offspring] would die at once" (BB 16a–b); in similar vein is: "The Holy One sits and nourishes both the horns of the wild ox and the ova of lice" (Shab. 107b). Of man it was said: "No man bruises his finger on earth unless it is decreed in heaven" (Ḥul. 7b); and all is revealed and known before God: "even the small talk of a man's conversation with his wife" (Lev. R. 26:7). Similarly: "The Holy One sits and pairs couples—the daughter of so-and-so to so-and-so" (Lev. R. 8:1; Gen. R. 68:4; and cf. MK 18b), or: "He is occupied in making ladders, casting down the one and elevating the other" (Gen. R. 68:4).

The continuation of Akiva's dictum ("and the world is judged with goodness") accords apparently with the traditional outlook of the Talmud. Thus, for example, it was said that even if man has 999 angels declaring him guilty and only one speaking in his favor, God assesses him mercifully (TJ, Kid. 1:10, 61d; Shab. 32a); that God is distressed at the distress of the righteous and does not rejoice at the downfall of the wicked (Sanh. 39b; Tanḥ., be-Shallaḥ 10) and does not deal tyrannically with His creatures (Av. Zar. 3a); and he sits and waits for man and does not punish him until his measure is full (Sot. 9a).

[Y.M.G.]

In Medieval Jewish Philosophy. The treatment of providence *(hashgaḥah)* in medieval Jewish philosophy reflects the discussion of this subject in late Greek philosophy, particularly in the writings of the second-century C.E. Aristotelian commentator Alexander of Aphrodisias, and in the theological schools of Islam. The Hebrew term *hashgaḥah* itself was apparently first coined by Samuel ibn Tibbon as a translation of the Arabic word *ʿanāʾyah.* In his *Guide of the Perplexed* (trans. by S. Pines, 1963), Maimonides uses the latter synonymously with *tadbīr,* the Hebrew equivalent of which is *hanhagah* (i.e., governance of the world). In most Hebrew philosophical works, however, *hanhagah* designates the universal providence which determines the natural order of the world as a whole, while *hashgaḥah* is generally used to designate individual providence. For the latter, Judah *al-Ḥarizi also used the Hebrew term *shemirah* ("safekeeping"), and it should be noted that originally Ibn Tibbon, too, preferred this, as is shown in a manuscript copy of a letter to Maimonides (see below).

*Saadiah Gaon deals with the problem of providence in treatise 5 of his *Emunot ve-De'ot* (*Book of Beliefs and Opinions,* trans. by S. Rosenblatt, 1948), whose subject is "Merits and Demerits." In chapter 1, he identifies providence with the reward and punishment meted out by God to the individual in this world, which is "the world of action"; though, ultimately, reward and punishment are reserved for the world to come. Echoes of the philosophical debate on the problem of providence may be found in other parts of Saadiah's book. Thus, he asks how it is possible that God's knowledge can encompass both the past and the future and "that he knows both equally" in a single, eternal, and immutable act of knowing (*ibid.,* 2:13). His reply is that it is impossible to compare man's knowledge, which is acquired through the medium of the senses, with God's, which "is not acquired by any intermediate cause" and is not derived from temporal facts, but rather flows from His essence. This linking of the problem of providence with that of the nature of God's knowledge originated with Alexander of Aphrodisias, as did the question of the reconciliation of God's foreknowledge with man's freedom of the will. Saadiah's solution to the latter problem is to point out that the Creator's knowledge of events is not the cause of their occurrence. If that were the case, all events would be eternal, inasmuch as God's knowledge of them is eternal (*ibid.,* 4:4). Abraham *ibn Daud devotes an entire chapter of his book *Emunah Ramah* (6:2; ed. by S. Weil (1852), 93ff.) to the problems involved in the concept of providence. Ibn Daud, too, was considerably influenced by Alexander of Aphrodisias, who upheld "the nature of the possible," thereby allowing for human choice, in opposition to the absolute determinism of the *Stoics. Like Alexander, he limits God's knowledge to that which stems from the necessary laws of nature through natural causes, to the exclusion of the effects of accident or free will which are only possible. He argues that God's ignorance of things that come to be as a result of accident or free will does not imply an imperfection in His nature, for whatever is "possible" is also only possible for God, and hence He knows possible things only as possible, not as necessary.

Maimonides deals with the question of providence in light of the philosophic teachings on "governance" *(hanhagah, tadbīr),* which identify it with the action of the forces of nature (*Guide,* 2:10). He fully discusses *hashgaḥah* (*ʿanāʾyah;*

ibid., 3:16–24), listing five main views on the matter: those of *Epicurus, *Aristotle, the Ash'arites, the Mu'tazilites (see *Kalām), and, lastly, of the Torah, which affirms both freedom of the human will and divine justice. The good and evil that befall man are the result of this justice, "for all His ways are judgment," and there exists a perfect correspondence between the achievements of the individual and his fate. This is determined by the level of man's intellect, however, rather than by his deeds, so that it follows that only he whose perfected intellect adheres to God is protected from all evil (*Guide*, 3:51). Such a man realizes that governance, providence, and purpose cannot be attributed to God in a human sense, and he will, therefore, "bear every misfortune lightly, nor will misfortunes multiply doubts concerning God . . . but will rather increase his love of God." Maimonides argues against Alexander of Aphrodisias and Ibn Daud that God's knowledge instantaneously encompasses the numerous things subject to change without any change in His essence; that God foresees all things that will come to be without any addition to His knowledge; and that He therefore knows both the possible ("privation," i.e., that which does not yet exist but is about to be) and the infinite (i.e., individuals and particulars which are unlimited in number). The philosophers, he states, arbitrarily asserted that it is impossible to know the possible or the infinite, but they overlooked the difference between God's knowledge and human knowledge. Just as man's intellect is inadequate to apprehend God's essence, so it cannot apprehend His knowledge (*ibid.*, 2:20).

In his letter to Maimonides (published by Z. Diesendruck in: HUCA, 11 (1936), 341–66), Samuel ibn Tibbon calls attention to a contradiction between Maimonides' treatment of providence in *Guide*, 3:17ff., and his discussion at the end of the *Guide* in chapter 51, where, departing from the philosophical approach that providence is relevant only to the welfare of the soul, Maimonides expresses the conviction that the devout man will never be allowed to suffer any harm. Shem Tov ibn *Falaquera (*Moreh ha-Moreh*, 145–8), Moses ibn *Tibbon, in a note to his father's letter (ed. Diesendruck, *op. cit.*), *Moses of Narbonne, in his commentary on the *Guide* (3:51), and Efodi (Profiat *Duran), in his commentary on the same chapter, all dwell on this point. Shem Tov b. Joseph *Ibn Shem Tov, in his book *Emunot* (Ferrara, 1556, 8b–10a) and Isaac *Arama, in his *Akedat Yiẓḥak*, take Maimonides to task for having made the degree of providence exercised over man dependent on perfection of the intellect rather than on performance of the commandments. The Karaite *Aaron b. Elijah devotes several chapters of his book *Eẓ Ḥayyim* (ed. by F. Delitzsch (1841), 82–90) to the subject of providence, and he, too, criticizes Maimonides. Once the position has been taken that God's knowledge cannot be restricted, the activity of providence likewise cannot be made to depend only upon the degree of development of man's intellect. Just as God knows everything, so He watches over all things (ch. 88).

Isaac *Albalag, in his *Tikkun De'ot*, discusses providence in the course of his critique of the opinions of *Avicenna and al-*Ghazālī. It is impossible, he contends, to comprehend God's mode of cognition, but it is possible to attribute to Him a knowledge of things which are outside the realm of natural causation, i.e., free will and chance. God's knowledge and providence also provide the subject of a penetrating analysis in the *Milḥamot Adonai* of *Levi b. Gershom (treatises 2 and 3), who returns to the Aristotelian position as understood in the light of Alexander of Aphrodisias' commentary. It is inadmissible, he states, that God should know the possible and the numerically infinite, that is, the particulars qua particulars, but He does know all things through the order embracing them all.

In contrast to this view, Ḥasdai *Crescas argues in his *Or Adonai* (2:1–2) that the belief in individual providence is a fundamental principle of the Mosaic Law, according to which God's knowledge "encompasses the infinite" (i.e., the particular) and "the non-existent" (i.e., the possible) "without any change in the nature of the possible" (i.e., without His knowledge nullifying the reality of free will). Crescas maintains that the biblical and talmudic faith in providence is based on a belief in individual providence. His disciple, Joseph *Albo, also deals extensively with God's knowledge and providence in his *Sefer ha-Ikkarim* (4:1–15), during the course of his discussion concerning reward and punishment. [A.ALT.]

In the Kabbalah. The question of divine providence almost never appears in the Kabbalah as a separate problem, and therefore few detailed and specific discussions were devoted to it. The idea of providence is identified in the Kabbalah with the assumption that there exists an orderly and continuous system of government of the cosmos, carried out by the Divine Potencies—the *Sefirot*—which are revealed in this government. The Kabbalah does no more than explain the way in which this system operates, while its actual existence is never questioned. The world is not governed by chance, but by unceasing divine providence, which is the secret meaning of the hidden order of all the planes of creation, and especially in the world of man. He who understands the mode of action of the *Sefirot* also understands the principles of divine providence which are manifested through this action. The idea of divine providence is interwoven in a mysterious way with the limitation of the area of action of causality in the world. For although most events which happen to living creatures, and especially to men, appear as if they occur in a natural way which is that of cause and effect, in reality these events contain individual manifestations of divine providence, which is responsible for everything that happens to man, down to the last detail. In this sense, the rule of divine providence is, in the opinion of *Naḥmanides, one of the "hidden wonders" of creation. The workings of nature ("I will give you your rains in their season," Lev. 26:4 and the like) are coordinated in hidden ways with the moral causality determined by the good and evil in men's actions.

In their discussions of divine providence, the early kabbalists stressed the activity of the tenth *Sefirah*, since the rule of the lower world is principally in its hands. This *Sefirah* is the *Shekhinah*, the presence of the divine potency in the world at all times. This presence is responsible for God's providence for His creatures; but according to some opinions the origin of divine providence is actually in the upper *Sefirot*. Symbolic expression is given to this idea, particularly in the *Zohar, in the description of the eyes in the image of **Adam Kadmon* ("Primordial Man"), in his two manifestations, as the *Arikh Anpin* (lit. "The Long Face" but meaning "The Long Suffering") or *Attikah Kaddishah* ("the Holy Ancient One"), and as the *Ze'eir Anpin* ("The Short Face," indicating the "Impatient"). In the description of the organs in the head of *Attikah Kaddishah*, the eye which is always open is taken as a supernal symbol for the existence of divine providence, whose origin is in the first *Sefirah*. This upper providence consists solely of mercy, with no intermixture of harsh judgment. Only in the second manifestation, which is that of God in the image of the *Ze'eir Anpin*, is the working of judgment also found in the divine providence. For " . . . the eyes of the Lord . . . range through the whole earth" (Zech. 4:10), and they convey his providence to every place, both for judgment and for mercy. The pictorial image, "the eye of providence," is here understood as a symbolic expression which suggests a certain element in the divine order itself. The author of the Zohar is refuting those who deny divine providence and substitute chance as an important cause in the events of the cosmos. He considers them to be fools who are not fit to contemplate the depths of the wisdom of divine providence and who lower themselves to the level of animals (Zohar 3:157b). The author of the Zohar does not distinguish between general providence (of all creatures) and individual providence (of individual human beings). The latter is, of course, more important to him. Through the activity of divine providence, an abundance of blessing descends on the creatures, but this awakening of the power of providence is dependent on the deeds of created beings, on "awakening from below." A detailed consideration of the question of providence is set forth by Moses *Cordovero in *Shi'ur Komah* ("Measurement of the Body"). He, too, agrees with the philosophers that individual providence exists only in relation to man, while in relation to the rest of the created world, providence is only directed toward the generic essences. But he enlarges the category of individual providence and establishes that "divine providence applies to the lower creatures, even animals, for their well-being and their death, and this is not for the sake of the animals themselves, but for the sake of men," that is to say, to the extent to which the lives of animals are bound up with the lives of men, individual providence applies to them as well. "Individual providence does not apply to any ox or any lamb, but to the entire species together . . . but if divine providence applies to a man, it will encompass even his pitcher, should it break, and his dish, should it crack, and all his possessions—if he should be chastized or not" (p. 113). Cordovero distinguishes ten types of providence, from which it is possible to understand the various modes of action of individual providence among the gentiles and Israel. These modes of action are bound up with the various roles of the *Sefirot* and their channels which convey the abundance (of blessing) to all the worlds, in accordance with the special awakening of the lower creatures. He includes among them two types of providence which indicate the possibility of the limitation of divine providence in certain instances, or even its complete negation. Also, in his opinion, things may happen to a man without the guidance of providence, and it may even happen that a man's sins cause him to be left "to nature and to chance," which is the aspect of God's hiding his face from man. In fact, it is uncertain from moment to moment whether a particular event in an individual's life is of this latter type, or whether it is a result of divine providence: "And he cannot be sure—for who will tell him if he is among those of whom it is said: 'The righteous man is as sure as a lion'—perhaps God has hidden His face from him, because of some transgression, and he is left to chance" (p. 120).

Only in the Shabbatean Kabbalah is divine providence seen once again as a serious problem. Among *Shabbetai Ẓevi's disciples was handed down his oral teaching that the Cause of Causes, or the *Ein-Sof* ("the Infinite") "does not influence and does not oversee the lower world, and he caused the *Sefirah Keter* to come into being to be God and *Tiferet* to be King" (see Scholem, Shabbetai Ẓevi, p. 784). This denial of the providence of *Ein-Sof* was considered a deep secret among the believers, and the Shabbatean Abraham *Cardozo, who was opposed to this doctrine, wrote that the emphasis on the secret nature of this teaching arose from the Shabbateans' knowledge that this was the opinion of Epicurus the Greek. The "taking" *(netilah)* of providence from *Ein-Sof* (which is designated in these circles by other terms as well) is found in several Shabbatean schools of thought, such as the Kabbalah of Baruchiah of Salonika, in *Va-Avo ha-Yom el ha-Ayin,* which was severely attacked for the prominence it gave to this opinion, and in *Shem Olam* (Vienna, 1891) by Jonathan *Eybeschuetz. The latter work devoted several pages of casuistry to this question in order to prove that providence does not actually originate in the First Cause, but in the God of Israel, who is emanated from it, and who is called, by Eybeschuetz, the "image of the ten *Sefirot.*" This "heretical" assumption, that the First Cause (or the highest element of the Godhead) does not guide the lower world at all, was among the principle innovations of Shabbatean doctrine which angered the sages of that period. The Orthodox kabbalists saw in this assumption proof that the Shabbateans had left the faith in the absolute unity of the Godhead, which does not permit, in matters pertaining to divine providence, differentiation between the emanating *Ein-Sof* and the emanated *Sefirot.* Even though the *Ein-Sof* carries out the activity of divine providence through the *Sefirot,* the *Ein-Sof* itself is the author of true providence. In the teachings of the Shabbateans, however, this quality of the First Cause or the *Ein-Sof* is blurred or put in doubt. [G.Sch.]

Bibliography: In the Bible: E. Koenig, *Theologie des Alten Testaments* (1923), 208ff.; K. Kohler, *Jewish Theology* (1928²), 167ff.; W. Eichrodt, *Theologie des Alten Testaments,* 2 (1935), 177ff.; M. Pohlenz, *Die Stoa* (1948), passim; O. Procksch, *Theologie des Alten Testaments* (1950), 503ff.; E. E. Urbach, in: *Sefer ha-Yovel le Y. Kaufmann* (1960), 122–48; idem, *Ḥazal-Pirkei Emunot ve-De'ot* (1969). In Kabbalah: I. Tishby, *Mishnat ha-Zohar,* 1 (1957²), 265–8; M. Cordovero, *Shi'ur Komah* (1883), 113–20; Scholem, Shabbetai Ẓevi, 779, 784; M. A. Perlmutter, *R. Yehonatan Eybeschuetz ve-Yaḥaso el ha-Shabbeta'ut* (1947), 133–41, 190–1. In Medieval Jewish Philosophy: Strauss, in: MGWJ, 45 (1937), 93–105; Pines, in: PAAJR, 24 (1955), 123–31; Moses Maimonides, *The Guide of the Perplexed* (1963), introd. by Pines, lxv–lxxviii, lxxvi–lxxvii; idem, *Le guide des égarés,* ed. and trans. by S. Munk, 3 (1866), 111, 116ff.; J. Guttmann, *Dat u-Madda* (1955), 149–68; S. Heller-Wilensky, *R. Yiẓḥak Arama u-Mishnato* (1956), 132–6; G. Vajda, *Isaac Albalag, Averroïste juif, traducteur et annotateur d'Al-Ghazali* (1960), 15–17, 64–71, 144–7, 121–3; Guttmann, Philosophies, index; Husik, Philosophy, index.

PROVINS, town in the department of Seine-et-Marne, France. The earliest evidence of the presence of Jews in Provins dates from 1201. Concentrated in two streets, Rue de la Vieille-Juiverie and the Rue des Juifs, the Jews rapidly increased in number. They owned at least two synagogues and a cemetery. The importance of the market of the Provins Jewish community is described in the polemic work of Joseph "the Zealot" *(le Zélateur).* The extent of Jewish financial activity in Provins is apparent from the use of a special seal for ratifying documents in business transactions which involved Jews. The town itself, as well as the Jewish community—which disappeared entirely after the expulsion of 1306—began to decline with the reign of *Philip the Fair and the transfer of the town (which had formerly belonged to *Champagne) to royal authority.

In the early 13th century, the yeshivah of Provins was under the direction of Jacob b. Meir author of a biblical commentary (not preserved) sometimes erroneously attributed to a certain Jacob of Provence. Some medieval remains have been found in a modern house on the Rue des Juifs; these include a hall with ogive vaults, which local tradition claims is the remains of a medieval synagogue.

Bibliography: Gross, Gal Jud, 493ff.; F. Bourquelot, *Histoire de Provins* (1840); M. Veissière, *Une communauté . . . à Provins* (1961), 116f. [B.Bl.]

PRUSSIA (Ger. **Preussen**), former dukedom and kingdom, the nucleus and dominant part of modern united *Germany (1870). The name came to signify a conglomerate of territories whose core was the electorate of *Brandenburg, ruled by the Hohenzollern dynast from the capital, *Berlin.

1300–1740. The order of Teutonic Knights, who ruled East Prussia from the 13th century, in 1309 expressly prohibited Jews from entering their territory. From the 15th century East Prussia was dominated by Poland and became economically dependent on it. As Jews constituted an important section of the merchant class in Poland, East Prussia acquiesced to the presence of Jewish merchants (exporters of furs, leathers, wax, and honey) although prohibiting them from settling and repeatedly threatening them with expulsions, which were rarely enforced. It was only with the complete secularization of the Teutonic order under Duke Albert I of Prussia (1522–77) that two Jewish physicians were allowed to settle temporarily in *Koenigsberg (1538–41). From the 17th century Jews came in ever increasing numbers to the then staunchly Protestant region, where they were welcomed by the ruling circles. In 1664 Moses Jacobson de Jonge of Amsterdam received very favorable commercial privileges (subsequently renewed) in *Memel, where he became the most important merchant, paying more customs dues than any of his Christian counterparts. He became a *Court Jew in 1685 and his sons inherited the function. In Koenigsberg, capital of East Prussia, Jews were permitted to graduate in medicine from the university in 1658, and Jewish merchants were encouraged to settle soon after. A synagogue was built there in 1680 and a cemetery opened in 1703. The community grew during the 18th and 19th centuries, remaining the economic, social, and religious center of the region. In the latter half of the 18th century Jewish communities were founded in *Elblag, Marienwerder, *Lyck, and elsewhere.

Jews were expelled from Brandenburg in 1573 by Elector Joachim II. The great elector, Frederick William (1640–88), who became absolute master of East Prussia, inherited principalities in Western Germany where Jews had already settled (see *Cleves, Behrend *Levi); subsequently he acquired *Halberstadt and *Minden (1648), and at a later date *Magdeburg and *Halle (1680) where Jews were granted rights of residence soon after the annexation. Frederick William, anxious to repair the havoc wrought by the Thirty Years' War and influenced by mercantilistic and tolerant ideas, encouraged foreigners to settle on his lands. In 1650 he permitted Polish Jews to trade in Brandenburg for seven years but not to settle there; this privilege was renewed in 1660. Israel Aron, a military contractor and purveyor to the mint (see *Mintmasters) received permission to settle in Berlin in 1663 and became Frederick William's Court Jew.

The basis for a Jewish settlement, however, was created by the expulsion from Vienna (1670). Through his resident agent in Vienna, Andreas Neumann, the elector, declared that he was not opposed to receiving 40–50 "rich and wealthy persons, prepared to bring and invest their means here"; on May 21, 1671, he permitted 50 families to settle, buy houses and shops, and engage in trade almost unrestrictedly. They could not, however, open a synagogue. The leaders of the small and interrelated group, Benedict Veit and Abraham Ries, and the richer Jews were encouraged to remain in Berlin. Other families settled in the cities of *Brandenburg, *Frankfort on the Oder, and Landsberg (*Gorzow Wielkopolski) where the first **Landrabbiner*, Solomon Kajjem Kaddish, and his successor had their seat. The elector disregarded his subjects' objections to Jewish settlement, being concerned with the economic benefits he derived from direct taxation of the **Schutzjuden* and indirect taxation through customs, tolls, and excise, which the Jews paid at a higher rate. During his reign the Berlin Jewish community grew to 40 families, that of Halberstadt to 86, that of Frankfort to 43, while 15 families had settled in Pomerania.

His son Frederick I (1688–1713; crowned king of Prussia in 1701) confirmed existing Jewish privileges on his succession; new communities were founded and existing ones grew. A noted collector of gems, Frederick patronized

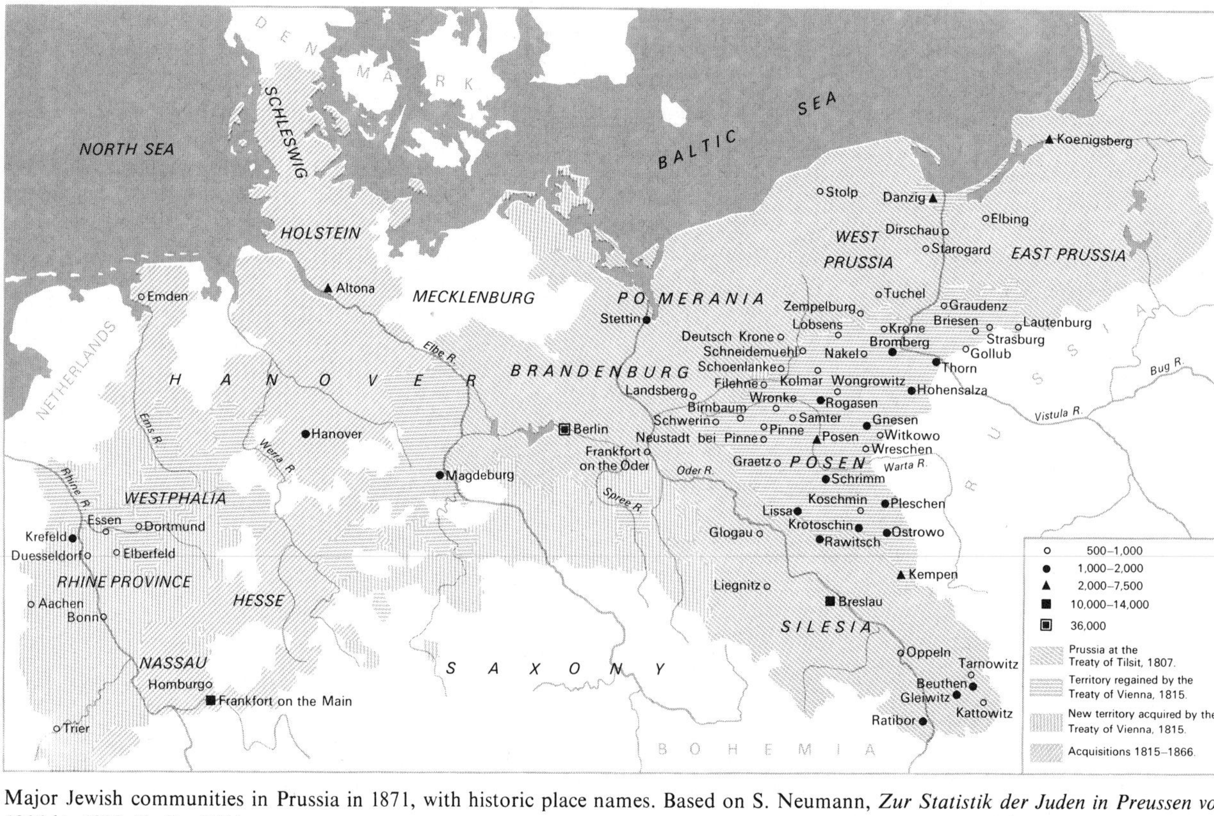

Major Jewish communities in Prussia in 1871, with historic place names. Based on S. Neumann, *Zur Statistik der Juden in Preussen von 1816 bis 1880,* Berlin, 1884.

jewel purveyors such as Jost and Esther *Liebmann and Marcus *Magnus. Under his son Frederick William I (1713–40), a generally harsh regime was introduced. On his accession he ordered a thorough inquiry into Jewish affairs, the outcome of which was the law of 1714 restricting to one the number of sons who could inherit their father's right of residence *(Schutzbrief);* to be granted this right the second son had to possess 1,000 taler and pay 50, and the third son twice these amounts. Thus a dominant theme in Prussian-Jewish relations, the attempt to restrict and even to reduce the number of Jews, was formally introduced. In 1717 the king appointed Moses Levin Gumpertz (see *Gomperz family) as *Oberaeltester* ("chief elder," *parnas*) of Berlin and Prussian Jewry, an appointment probably connected with the supervision of the just distribution of the tax load, conducted by representatives of communities and *Landjudenschaften. In 1728 the sum was fixed at 15,000 taler annually, to be reapportioned every five years. In 1730 a new Jewry law was promulgated: the eldest son was now obliged to own 1,000 and pay 50 taler and the second twice these amounts; all were subject to the condition that the number of protected Jews *(Schutzjuden)* in any given locality should not increase. Foreign Jews in possession of at least 10,000 taler were allowed to settle in Prussia. The law also prohibited Jews from engaging in all crafts (except seal engraving) competing with Christian guilds; it prohibited them from dealing in a large number of goods (mainly local produce). *Peddling, in particular, was suppressed. Commerce in luxury wares (expensive textiles, spices, etc.) was permitted, as was moneylending and dealing in old clothes. The law applied not only to Brandenburg but to all Prussian territories, creating uniform conditions for the Jews and defining (in article 24) their juridical relationship to the state. The regular tax load was raised, in addition to extraordinary exactions. Jewish merchants were encouraged to become entrepreneurs and invest in manufacture, particularly of textiles (silk, ribbons, satin, lace, etc.). These businessmen were granted highly favorable conditions. Thus the king passed on to his son a basically contradictory policy, at the same time mercantilist and anti-Jewish; needing and encouraging Jews for their economic contribution he attempted to restrict their rights and numbers.

From Frederick II to Emancipation. *Frederick II, the Great, enforced his father's policies even more rigorously. By his conquest of Silesia (1742) his rule extended over a sizable Jewish population; appreciating their economic importance he exempted them from his otherwise obnoxious Jewish legislation. In 1750 Frederick promulgated his *Revidiertes Generalprivilegium und Reglement,* prompted by the results of an inquiry which showed the number of privileged Jewish families in Prussia (excluding Silesia) in 1749 at 2,093, almost double the 1728 figure. The preamble stated that the law was intended to help both Christians and Jews, whose livelihood was being threatened by the increasing number of Jews. It created two types of *Schutzjuden:* an unrestricted number of "extraordinary" ones whose rights could not be inherited, and a restricted number of "ordinary" *Schutzjuden* who could pass on their rights to one son only. As in 1730, Jews were excluded from almost all professions and expressly prohibited from brewing, innkeeping, and farming. Trade in livestock, wool, leather, and most local produce was prohibited; the permitted occupations were moneylending and dealing in luxury wares and old clothes. The strictures against peddling were made more severe, as were those against beggars. During the Seven Years' War (1756–63) Frederick relied on monetary manipulations effected by Daniel *Itzig, V. H. *Ephraim, and other purveyors to the mint. His armies were provisioned by Jewish military *contractors (supplying horses, grain, fodder, wine, etc). After the war he encouraged a newly created, sparse layer of very wealthy Jews to invest their capital in industry and manufacture. Frederick levied onerous and distasteful taxes. In 1766 he introduced the *Silberlieferung:* 12,000 silver marks to be delivered annually at below face value to the royal mint; the 15,000 marks annual tax (from 1728) was increased to 25,000 in 1768. In 1769 he ordered every Jew to purchase and export a certain quantity of local porcelain (expensive, inferior wares produced by the royal factory) whenever he needed a royal concession or privilege (e.g., for marriage).

During Frederick's reign the Berlin community gradually became preponderant in Prussian Jewry. The *Landrabbinat* was occupied by such leading authorities as David Fraenkel (1742–62), Aaron Mosessohn (1762–71), and Hirschel *Levin. The dual office of *Oberlandes-Aeltester* was successively occupied by elders of the Berlin community, V. H. Ephraim (1750–75), Daniel Itzig (1775–99), and Jacob Moses (1775–92). In Berlin, Breslau, and Koenigsberg the upper strata of the Jews, who were rich and influential, took the first steps toward assimilation, acquiring the *General-Privilegium,* which granted them the rights of Christian merchants (such as freedom of movement and settlement). Through the First Partition of Poland (1772) Prussia's Jewish population had almost doubled, and Frederick feared above all an influx of Jews from the newly annexed province of West Prussia.

Frederick's nephew, Frederick William II (1786–1797), inaugurated a period of liberalization and reform in Prussia. As crown prince he had borrowed large sums from Berlin's Jewish financiers. An admirer of *Mendelssohn and *Mirabeau, in the first years of his reign he abolished the porcelain law and repealed the **Leibzoll* for foreign Jews. On May 2, 1791, Daniel Itzig and his family received the first *Naturalisationspatent,* which granted them full citizenship. A year later the *solidarische Haftung* (collective responsibility and liability of the Jewish community for non-payment of taxes and crimes of theft) was abolished. The king nominated a commission to draft a new and liberal Jewry law but due to the procrastination of his counselors, his own hesitations, and his increasing preoccupation with foreign affairs this was never carried out. New problems were created by the Second (1793) and Third (1795) Partitions of Poland, which respectively added about 53,000 and 75,000 Jews to the Prussian realm. New legislation became urgent. Shortly before his death Frederick William II passed a Jewry law for the new territories, which was in some respects more progressive than previous laws. His early death and the conservative nature of his son, *Frederick William III, disrupted all reformatory activity until Napoleon's defeat of Prussia at Jena (1806), when far-reaching reforms were carried out under the leadership of Karl August von *Hardenberg and Wilhelm von *Humboldt. In 1808 municipal citizenship and offices were opened to all, irrespective of religion.

The decisive step was taken with the promulgation in March 11, 1812, of an edict concerning the civil status of the Jews. The first article declared all legally resident Jews to be full citizens. All occupations were declared open to Jews, as were academic positions. Article 9, however, postponed the question of Jewish eligibility to state offices; the *oath *more Judaico* also remained in force. Marriage to a Prussian Jewess did not bestow citizenship and foreign Jews were prohibited from becoming communal employees. The edict was received with thanksgiving by the elders of the main Jewish communities, Berlin, Breslau, and Koenigsberg. A year later, during the War of Liberation, Prussian Jews expressed their patriotism by volunteering in large numbers (see *Military service). The high expectations of Prussian

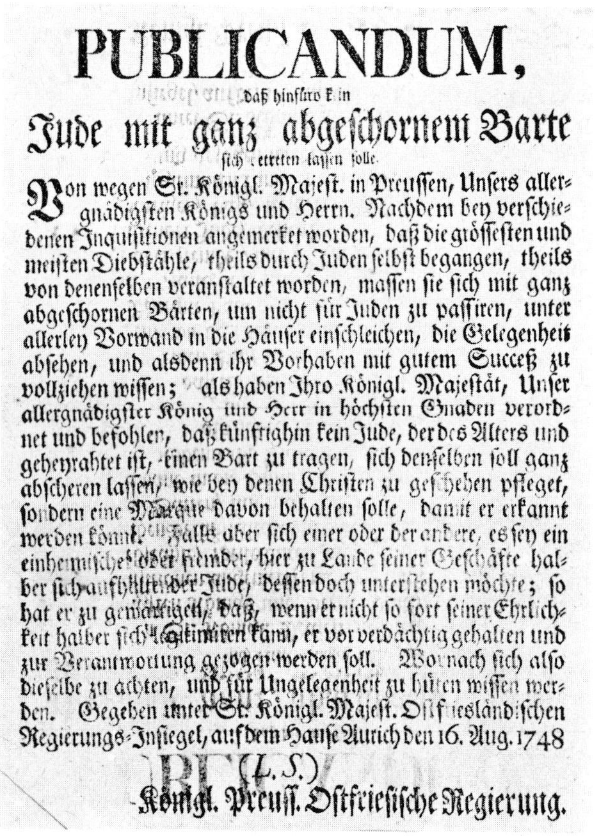
PUBLICANDUM,
daß hinführo kein
Jude mit ganz abgeschornem Barte
sich betreten lassen solle.

Von wegen Sr. Königl. Majest. in Preussen, Unsers allergnädigsten Königs und Herrn. Nachdem bey verschiedenen Inquisitionen angemerket worden, daß die grössesten und meisten Diebstähle, theils durch Juden selbst begangen, theils von denenselben veranstaltet worden, massen sie sich mit ganz abgeschornen Bärten, um nicht für Juden zu passiren, unter allerley Vorwand in die Häuser einschleichen, die Gelegenheit absehen, und alsdenn ihr Vorhaben mit gutem Succeß zu vollziehen wissen; als haben Ihro Königl. Majestät, Unser allergnädigster König und Herr in höchsten Gnaden verordnet und befohlen, daß künftighin kein Jude, der des Alters und geheyrahtet ist, einen Bart zu tragen, sich denselben soll ganz abscheren lassen, wie bey denen Christen zu geschehen pfleget, sondern eine Marque davon behalten solle, damit er erkannt werden könne. Falls aber sich einer oder der andere, es sey ein einheimischer oder fremder, hier zu Lande seiner Geschäfte halber sich aufhaltender Jude, dessen doch unterstehen möchte; so hat er zu gewärtigen, daß, wenn er nicht so fort seiner Ehrlichkeit halber sich legitimiren kann, er vor verdächtig gehalten und zur Verantwortung gezogen werden soll. Wornach sich also dieselbe zu achten, und für Ungelegenheit zu hüten wissen werden. Gegeben unter Sr. Königl. Majest. Ostfriesländischen Regierungs-Insiegel, auf dem Hause Aurich den 16. Aug. 1748

(L. S.)

Königl. Preuss. Ostfriesische Regierung.

Royal decree of Frederick II of Prussia prohibiting Jews from cutting off their beards, so that they might be distinguished easily. Jerusalem, C.A.H.J.P., Inv. 1628.

Jewry were not put to the test until after the Congress of *Vienna, at which Prussia was given back the province of Posen (*Poznan) and received the Rhineland and part of *Westphalia (where Jews had been fully emancipated).

As King Frederick William III had no intention of carrying out the 1812 edict, he repudiated his express promise that volunteers, irrespective of their religion, would be eligible for state offices. On Sept. 18, 1818, Jews were excluded from all academic positions (causing Heinrich *Heine, Eduard *Gans, and others to apostatize); the following January Jewish officials in Westphalia and the Rhineland were dismissed (including Heinrich Marx, father of Karl *Marx). The benefits of the 1812 edict had not been applied to Posen (where the laws of 1750 and 1797 remained in force), while its restrictions were applied to the western territories. Thus the Napoleonic "infamous decree," which by then had lapsed in France, was renewed by Prussia in 1818 to cover the Rhineland for an indefinite period. Prussian Jewry's legal position was encumbered by the coexistence of 22 different legislative systems with the various provinces. The king actively encouraged conversion to Christianity and prohibited conversion to Judaism; between 1812 and 1846, 3,171 Jews in Prussia converted. In addition he closed down Israel *Jacobson's private Reform prayer room in Berlin; on Sept. 12, 1823, he made the minister of the interior responsible for ensuring that "no sects among the Jewries *(Judenschaften)* of my lands be tolerated." The king's policy toward the Jews of Posen province—the historical *Great Poland (where they were 6.4% of the population and 42% of all Prussian Jews in 1816)—was even more restrictive. Severe steps were taken to keep them within the boundaries of the province. In 1833 a new Jewry law was promulgated for Posen; its main feature was the division of the province's Jews into naturalized citizens, whose rights were conditional on their economic, moral, and educational achievements (command and use of German), and the remainder, who remained deprived of basic rights. By 1846, 80% of Posen Jews were still not citizens and one-third of Prussian Jews had not attained that status.

The accession of *Frederick William IV (1840) was accompanied by rising hopes, which were soon dashed when he took steps to implement his medieval conception of a corporationist "Christian state." In this crisis Prussian Jewry, led by Moritz *Veit and Ludwig *Philippson, was supported by the liberal majorities in the provincial estates. Nevertheless, with the aid of the upper house and Friedrich Julius *Stahl, the king succeeded in passing the 1847 Jewry constitution which recognized the corporate status of individual Jewish communities. It permitted Jews to occupy "offices not carrying executive, juridical, or law enforcement powers"; at universities all chairs in the humanities were closed to them, as were the senate and rectorate: Jews owning landed estates could not enjoy the rights accorded the gentry. The law, introduced for the benefit of the Jews the king declared, was not applicable to Posen. It had barely been introduced when the 1848 revolution proclaimed the principles of religious freedom and equality for all, reconfirmed in 1869 for the whole North-German Confederation. In practice, however, discrimination in the army, bureaucracy, and university remained the rule.

During the 19th century the geographic, demographic, social, and economic makeup of Prussian Jewry underwent great changes. Their number increased from 123,823 in 1816 to 194,558 in 1840. In 1840 about two-fifths of Prussian Jewry were concentrated in Posen province (where they formed about 6% of the population), and another two-fifths in Silesia, the Rhineland, and West Prussia (where they constituted about 1% of the population). Posen had the largest Jewish community (6,748), with Berlin (6,458), and Breslau (5,714) following. The majority of Prussian Jewry lived in rural and semi-rural conditions; peddling, shop- and innkeeping, commerce, and the livestock trade were the main occupations. In 1816 Prussia contained 48.2% of German Jewry; in 1871, 325,000 Jews were natives of Prussia (69.2% of German Jewry), including the Jews of the recently (1866) annexed territories of *Hanover, *Schleswig-Holstein, *Hesse-Nassau, and *Frankfort on the Main. Due to internal migration the percentage of Posen Jews had declined proportionately, to 22.8% in 1871, and also absolutely, so that by 1910 only 26,512 remained (about 7.7% of Prussian Jewry). A similar process of depletion occurred in West Prussia. As a result of industrialization and urbanization, Brandenburg (Berlin) attracted a greater proportion of Prussian Jewry, increasing from 6.5% in 1816, to 17.5% in 1871, and 43.9% (151,356) in 1910. In the other provinces, Westphalia, Rhineland, and Silesia, the number of Jews remained proportionately stable while increasing at a regular rate. Demographically, Prussian Jewry reached its peak around 1870–80. The process of urbanization continued, causing small-town communities to remain stable or decline while village communities gradually vanished. By 1925, 60% of Prussian Jewry (342,765) was to be found in the four largest communities and another 15% in communities with more than 1,000 persons.

Prussia Within the German Empire. In spite of the noteworthy cultural, economic, and social achievements of Prussian Jews within the new German Empire, Prussia retained a specific conservative, anti-Jewish, social and political attitude, which found expression in the influence of the Prussian mentality within the empire and in its political parties (see *Bismarck, E. *Lasker, I. D. *Bamberger, and *Central-Verein). Until World War I the majority of Prussian communities were organized within the

*Deutsch-Israelitischer Gemeindebund (D.I.G.B.). The organization's main difficulties were caused by differences between the numerous small, rural, and needy communities and the large wealthy ones, primarily Berlin. Thus, when a common communal organization did not immediately emerge after the war the Berlin community entrusted Ismar *Freund with organizing the Preussischer Landesverband juedischer Gemeinden. Its opening session (1921) was attended by 110 communities, who soon numbered 656 (96% of Prussian Jewry), making it the largest regional communal organization in Germany. Its charter and activities were modeled on the defunct D.I.G.B.; although a Prussian official was present at its founding and it received state subsidies, it was not officially recognized by the government of Prussia.

Throughout the late 19th and 20th centuries the Prussian reactionary mentality found a persuasive anti-Jewish argument in the *"Masseneinwanderung,"* the alleged mass immigration of unwanted East European Jews *(Ostjuden)* into Prussia, particularly into Berlin and the major cities. Their number was greatly magnified by anti-Semitic propaganda which eventually caused the expulsion of 30,000 Russian Jews, mainly refugees from the 1883 pogroms. In fact, the number of Prussian Jews was decreasing, due to a low birth rate and emigration. After World War I the problem of the unwanted East European Jews again became a political issue; in fact, the majority of these were Jews from Posen, then once more in Poland, who had preferred to be repatriated to Prussia (one-third of c. 45,000 Jews). When the Nazis seized power, H. *Goering was appointed prime minister of Prussia, where he enforced the Nazi anti-Jewish measures (see *Germany).

Bibliography: Wiener Library, *German Jewry* (1958), 62–66 (bibl.); BJCE (bibl.); LBI, *Bibliothek und Archiv,* 1 (1970), index (bibl); *Gesamtregister zur MGWJ* (1966), index; I. Freund, *Die Emanzipation der Juden in Preussen,* 2 vols. (1912); S. Stern, *Der preussische Staat und die Juden,* 2 vols. (1925, repr. 1962); H. D. Schmidt, in: YLBI, 1 (1956), 28–47; H. Strauss, *ibid.,* 11 (1966), 107–36; H. Fischer, *Judentum, Staat und Heer im fruehen 19. Jahrhundert* (1968); H. Schnee, *Die Hoffinanz und der moderne Staat,* 1 (1953), 5 (1965), 15–53; M. Aschkewitz, *Zur Geschichte der Juden in Westpreussen* (1967); H. Neubach, *Die Ausweisungen von Polen und Juden aus Preussen 1885/86* (1967); S. Wenzel, *Juedische Buerger und kommunale Selbstverwaltung in preussischen Staedten 1808–1848* (1967); A. Sandler, in: YLBI, 2 (1957), index, H. Strauss, *ibid.,* 11 (1966), 107–38; E. Hamburger, *Juden im oeffentlichen Leben Deutschlands* (1968). [H.W.]

PRUZHANY (Pol. **Pružana**), city in Brest oblast, Belorussian S.S.R. Situated on the road which leads from Brest-Litovsk to Moscow, it was under Polish rule until 1795; in the third partition of Poland it was incorporated into Russia, and in 1919 regained by Poland until 1939. Jews lived in Pruzhany during the middle of the 15th century and around 1450 there was a *ḥevra kaddisha* which noted its activities in a register. In 1463 the first synagogue (destroyed by fire in 1863) was erected near the center of the Jewish quarter. In 1495 the Jews of Pruzhany were included in the general expulsion of Jews from Lithuania, but they returned after a few years. In 1563 there were 11 Jewish families and 276 Christian families. Both Christians and Jews earned their livelihood primarily from agriculture and livestock, although there were some engaged in commerce and crafts. In 1588 the town was granted autonomous rights according to the *Magdeburg Law. The rights of the Jews were formally drawn up and ratified by Ladislaus IV in 1644 and subsequently, on several occasions, by his successors. According to these rights Jews were authorized to reside in Pruzhany, to practice their religion and freely engage in their occupations. At the close of the 17th century there were 571 Jews (42% of the population); in 1868, during the period of Russian rule, there were 2,575 Jews (61% of the total). By the close of the 19th century the Jewish community enjoyed a vigorous social and cultural life in which all trends and parties were active. In 1921 the Jewish population was 4,152 (about 57% of the total). With the establishment of independent Poland, Jews also participated in the municipal government. In 1927, 16 of the 24 delegates elected to the administration were Jews. In the elections of the Jewish community in 1928, M. Goldfein, a delegate of the merchants, was elected president.

Distinguished rabbis served in the town. At the close of the 16th century, R. Joel *Sirkes, the renowned author of the *Baḥ (Bayit Ḥadash),* officiated as rabbi and *rosh yeshivah* for some time. R. *David b. Samuel ha-Levi, author of the *Turei Zahav (Taz)* also held the rabbinical office for a brief period. Among the last rabbis of the town, one of the most prominent was R. Elijah Feinstein (1842–1929) who was appointed in 1884. Active in the affairs of Polish Jewry, he wrote *Sefer Halikhot Eliyahu* ("Book of the Demeanors of Elijah," 1932), and a novella on Maimonides which was published in 1929. He was succeeded by his son-in-law R. David Feigenbaum, who perished in the Holocaust. [Sh.L.K.]

Holocaust Period and After. Under Soviet rule (1934–41) the Jewish communal bodies were disbanded. Private enterprise was gradually liquidated as merchandise was sold and no new stock made available. Cooperatives were set up for the skilled craftsmen. Educational institutions were reorganized, and a Yiddish-language school set up. The Jewish orphanage was combined with its Christian-run counterpart and placed under the municipality.

On June 27, 1941, after war broke out between Germany and the U.S.S.R., the Germans entered Pruzhany. They immediately exacted a fine from the Jewish community of 500,000 rubles, 2 kg. gold, and 10 kg. silver, to be paid within 24 hours. A Judenrat was set up, first chaired by Welwel Schreibman and later by Yiẓhak Janowicz, which tried to cope with the emergency. The Germans set up a ghetto on Sept. 22, 1941. Workshops were created in the hope that the economic utility of the Jews to the Germans would forestall deportations. The Judenrat combated the decrees against the Jewish inhabitants, gaining the confidence of members of the community. The ghetto swelled when four thousand Jews were brought in, 2,000 from Bialystok, and 2,000 from towns in the vicinity. In the latter half of 1942 an underground resistance organization was formed in the ghetto. Cells were established, arms acquired, and contacts sought with the partisans on the outside. On Jan. 27, 1943, two Jewish partisans approached the Judenrat to strengthen contact with the underground. Germans caught them there by surprise, but with the help of some of the Judenrat members the partisans escaped. The Judenrat was then charged with collaborating with the partisans. The following day the Germans began the deportation of the 10,000 inmates of the ghetto, 2,500 being dispatched daily to *Auschwitz. Within four days the community was destroyed. Some groups of Jews fled to the forests and joined the Jewish partisans who operated in the vicinity. In the late 1960s there was a Jewish population of about 60 (12 families). The former Great Synagogue was turned into an electric power plant. A mass grave of Jewish victims massacred by the Nazis was repeatedly desecrated and a road was built through its site. [Ar.W.]

Bibliography: *Pinkes fun Funf Fartilikte Kehiles: Pruzhana, Bereza . . .* (1958), 3–323, 599–690.

PRYLUCKI, NOAH (1882–1941), Yiddish philologist and journalist, and Polish political leader. Born in Berdichev, Ukraine, he grew up in Kremenets and in Warsaw, and practiced as a lawyer after 1909. Having published a collection of erotic lyrics, *Farn Mizbeakh* (1908), he gave up poetry and devoted himself to journalism and Yiddish philology. He was a pioneer of research into the Yiddish

Caricature of Noah Prylucki, Polish Yiddishist and politician. Jerusalem, J.N.U.L., Schwadron Collection.

language and helped to classify the various dialects of Eastern, Central, and Western Yiddish. His closest collaborators were the linguist M. *Weinreich, the literary historian Z. *Rejzen, and the folklorist Shmuel Lehman. At the Czernowitz Language Conference of 1908, he fought unsuccessfully for an extreme resolution declaring Yiddish as the national Jewish language. In 1905, together with his father, Ẓevi *Prylucki, he founded the Warsaw Yiddish daily *Der *Moment,* which existed until the German occupation of Warsaw in 1939. Active in politics from 1916, he was the defender of the impoverished Jews and of the middle-class artisans. He founded the Folkspartei, which fought for Jewish autonomous rights in Poland. In 1918 he was elected as the party's representative in the Polish Sejm. Besides publishing philological studies, he influenced the modernization of Yiddish orthography, helped to found the *YIVO Institute for Jewish Research, edited YIVO's organ *Yidish far Ale* (1838–1939), and published articles and reviews in *YIVO Bleter.* When World War II began, he fled to Vilna, where he lectured on Yiddish philology until 1941. When the Germans marched into Vilna he was arrested, compelled to classify YIVO's treasures for the Gestapo, and tortured to death.

Bibliography: Rejzen, Leksikon, 2 (1927), 954–66; M. Ravitch, *Mayn Leksikon* (1945), 174–6. [M.RAV.]

PRYLUCKI, ẒEVI HIRSCH (1862–1942), Hebrew and Yiddish journalist, one of the first members of Ḥovevei Zion. Born in Kremenets, Ukraine, Prylucki began his journalistic career with a series of critical essays in Hebrew criticizing *Aḥad Ha-Am's "Truth from Ereẓ Israel." From then on he wrote for Hebrew, Yiddish, and Russian-Jewish journals. In 1905 he moved to Warsaw, establishing the first Yiddish daily there, as well as a Hebrew daily, *Ha-Yom.* Both newspapers were of a Zionist and literary character. After several failures, at the end of 1910 Prylucki began to publish the daily *Der Moment,* whose circulation amounted to more than 60,000 copies on the eve of World War I. Prylucki, the editor, wrote the weekly political review. The newspaper was Jewish nationalist in a general sense, giving expression to non-Zionist opinions as well (Folkism, Yiddishim). Prylucki died in the Warsaw ghetto during the German occupation.

Bibliography: J. Heftman, in: A. S. Stein et al. (eds.), *Pinkas Kremenets* (1954), 189–90; S. L. Zitron, *Leksikon Ẓiyyoni* (1924), 544–8. [Y.S.]

°**PRYNNE, WILLIAM** (1600–1669), Puritan barrister and pamphleteer. Prynne first came to notice through his vehement opposition to the theater. A fierce tirade against the stage coincided, unfortunately for him, with Queen Henrietta Maria's appearance in a court play. After he had been imprisoned in the tower for one year, his ears were struck off.

While in the tower Prynne wrote an essay, published in 1654, entitled *A Briefe Polemical Dissertation,* concerning the "true time of the Inchoation and determination of the Lordsday—Sabbath ... that the Lordsday begins and ends in evenings and ought to be solemnized from evening to evening: against the novel errors of such who groundlessly assert that it begins and ends at midnight or daybreaking ..." At that time the question of the observance of Sunday was a highly controversial issue between Catholics and Protestants. The Church of England inclined toward the Catholic view, maintaining that Sunday, being essentially the commemoration of the resurrection of Jesus, had no connection with the Jewish Sabbath. This infuriated the Puritans, who insisted that Sunday had taken over the characteristics of the Jewish Sabbath. Prynne contended that all days in Scripture begin and end at evening, the Sabbath being no exception. Furthermore, the beginning and termination of days is perpetual and was not altered by the resurrection of Jesus in the morning. These points were proved by a wealth of citations from the Bible, the Church Fathers, and subsequent medieval writers, among whom was the Franciscan *Nicholas of Lyra, whom Prynne declared to be a convert from Judaism, possibly because of his knowledge of Hebrew and his use of Rashi. But, as Prynne amply demonstrates, Puritans could admire Judaism while still hating Jews. At the time the sabbatical pamphlet was published, the question of the official readmission of the Jews into England was being discussed, and during the following year Prynne produced yet another pamphlet entitled *A Short Demurrer to the Jewes Long Discontinued Remitter into England, Comprising an Exact Chronological Relation of Their First Admission into, Their Ill Deportment, Misdemeanours, Condition, Sufferings, Oppressions, Slaughters, Plunders ... With a Brief Collection of Such English Laws, Scriptures, as seem strongly to plead and conclude against their Readmission into England, especially at this Season.* The *Demurrer* is an important source for the study of medieval Anglo-Jewish history.

Bibliography: A. Saltman, in: *Jewish Academy,* 4 (1947), 35–39; Roth, Mag Bibl, index; D. Bush, *English Literature in the Earlier Seventeenth Century 1600–1660* (1962[2]), index. [ED.]

°**PRYSTOR, JANINA,** deputy in the Polish Sejm; wife of Alexander Prystor (1874–1941), premier of Poland from 1931 to 1933.With the growing influence of the reactionary anti-Jewish elements in leading circles after the death of Marshal Piłsudski (1935), Janina Prystor proposed in 1936 that *sheḥitah* should be prohibited, claiming that it contradicted Christian moral and religious principles. The proposal had an obvious economic aim for it would have broken the Jewish monopoly on trade in cattle destined for slaughtering. After a struggle in which the Jews boycotted buying meat and strong objections were voiced by all Jewish circles, the proposal, which would have prevented Jews from eating *kasher* meat, was rejected. After prolonged discussions the government adopted a compromise, allowing limited *sheḥitah* in areas of dense Jewish population and prohibiting it in districts where the Jewish population was less than 3% of the total. Although intended to reduce political tension, the compromise succeeded in breaking the Jewish livestock monopoly.

Bibliography: H. M. Rabinowicz, *The Legacy of Polish Jewry* (1965), 179–82; Y. Gruenbaum (ed.), EG, 1 (1953), 116. [M. LAN.]

PRZEDBORZ (Pol. **Przedbórz**), town in Kielce province, S. central Poland. Jews lived in Przedborz from the time of the town's earliest development. At the beginning of the 15th century, urban population increased when King Ladislaw II Jagello granted the merchants of the town privileges according to the *Magdeburg Law. In the years 1550 and 1570 King Sigismund II Augustus further aided the town's Jews by exempting them from customs duties and certain other payments. In 1595 King Sigismund III

The synagogue of Przedborz, presumed to have been reconstructed in 1760. From M. and K. Piechotka, *Wooden Synagogues*, Warsaw, 1959.

restricted their rights to own houses. The restriction was lifted, however, in 1638 when a fire destroyed the town and it had to be rebuilt. A second fire destroyed Przedborz in 1834. The Jewish population increased during the 19th century when Jews established trade relations with markets of the Russian empire. In 1865 about 75% of the town's population were Jews; in 1921 Jews numbered 3,749 (63.6% of the total population). [Sh.L.K.]

Holocaust Period. Before the outbreak of World War II, there were about 4,500 Jews in Przedborz. The Jewish community was liquidated on Oct. 9–12, 1942 when all Jews were deported to *Treblinka death camp. After the war, the Jewish community of Przedborz was not reconstituted. [Ed.]

PRZEDBORZ, ḥasidic dynasty founded by Isaiah of Przedborz (d. 1830). He was one of the closest disciples of *Jacob Isaac, Ha-Ḥozeh ("the Seer") of Lublin, and a companion of Jacob Isaac, the *Yehudi ha-Kadosh* ("Holy Jew") of *Przysucha (Pshiska), with whom he studied at the renowned yeshivah of *David Tevele b. Nathan of Lissa (*Leszno). Rabbi in Przedborz from 1788, in 1815 Isaiah became a ḥasidic *zaddik*. His son, Immanuel Weltfreid (1802–1865), officiated as rabbi in Przedborz from 1850, and was famed as a miracle worker. He married the granddaughter of Jacob Isaac Ha-Ḥozeh of Lublin, and was a disciple of Dov Baer of Radoshits. His son, Abraham Moses of Rozprze (d. 1918), became leader of the ḥasidic community after his father's death. He had three sons, Emmanuel of Lodz, Isaiah of Kalish (Kalisz; both d. 1939), and Solomon of Tomaszow who perished in the Holocaust.

Bibliography: M. Friedensohn, in: *Elleh Ezkerah*, ed. by I. Levin, 5 (1963), 229–33; Z. M. Rabinowitz, *Ya'akov Yizḥak mi-Pshiskhah* (1960), 10, 29, 57, 125–6; M. Buber, *Gog u-Magog* (1967²), 28, 80–83; L. H. Grossmann, *Shem u-She'erit* (1943), 81. [E.Z.]

PRZEMYSL (Pol. **Przemyśl**), city in Rzeszow province, S. E. Poland; after the partition of Poland, it passed to Austria (1772–1919), subsequently reverting to independent Poland. In 1939–40 the German-Soviet borderline ran through Przemysl. A Jewish community existed in the city by 1367. In 1542 some 18 Jewish families were living there. The community numbered 1,558 by 1775. A Jew of Przemysl, Moses (Moshko) Shmuhler, was sentenced to death in 1630 following a *Host desecration libel. In 1638 the communities in the vicinity were ordered to pay their taxes through the Przemysl community, and from 1670 Przemysl became a leading community for the region of "Red Russia" within the framework of the *Councils of the Lands. Przemysl Jewry was granted detailed charters of rights by King Sigismund II Augustus (March 29, 1559) and King Stephen Báthory (June 27, 1576) enabling the Jews to trade despite opposition from the municipality. The economic position of Przemysl Jewry declined in the 18th century and the community fell heavily into debt. When in 1772 the community passed to Austrian rule its autonomy was curtailed, and the Jews in Przemysl, like the rest of the Jews in the territories incorporated into Austria, came under the Austrian system of supervision limiting their numbers and marriages (see *Familiants Laws). On the other hand they also benefited from the more favorable Austrian attitudes toward the Jews and legislation concerning them. The Austrian authorities gave support to the *Haskalah movement, directed Jews to attend government schools, and were inimical to *Ḥasidism. Half of the members of the Przemysl city council were Jews. Among the heads of the Jewish community the most influential was Moshe Sheinbah, an active member of both the municipal and community councils before World War I. The Jewish population numbered c. 5,692 in 1870; 16,062 in 1910 (29.6% of the total population); 18,360 (38.3%) in 1921; and 17,300 (34.0%) in 1931. Wealthy Jews of Przemysl engaged in the wholesale commerce of wheat and timber; some were purveyors to the Austrian army garrison in the town. Jews also engaged in banking, small- and large-scale industry, and agriculture. A large section of the Jewish population was impoverished.

Among rabbis of Przemysl in the 19th century Samuel Heller and Isaac Judah *Schmelkes were prominent. In 1875 the Yishuv Ereẓ Israel organization was founded, and from 1897 many Jews in Przemysl joined Zionist organizations, prominent among them Aguddat Herzl. The *Bund, *Agudat Israel, and the *Folkspartei were also active in Przemysl. H. *Lieberman was active in organizing the Polish Socialist Party (*P.P.S.). In World War I Przemysl was occupied for a short time in 1915 by the Russians. Many Jews then left the city and some were expelled by the Russians.

After the war Przemysl was incorporated in independent Poland. In the municipal elections of 1928 the Jewish National bloc in coalition with the Polish Sanacja party won 18 seats out of 40; a Jew was elected deputy mayor. In the communal elections of 1928 Agudat Israel gained the majority. In the 1936 elections it was defeated by the Zionists whose representative, Jacob Rebhan, was elected president of the community organization. [Sh.L.K.]

Holocaust Period. There were approximately 20,000 Jews living in Przemysl in 1939. When war broke out that year

The Sheinbah Synagogue of Przemysl, used as a warehouse after World War II. Courtesy C.A.H.J.P., Jerusalem.

many Jews from areas further west took refuge in the city. On Sept. 14, 1939 Przemysl fell to the Germans and within a few days some 500 Jews, about half of them refugees, were murdered on a trumped-up charge that 12 Germans had been shot by Jews. On September 18 Przemysl was handed over to the Soviet Union; two days prior to this, the Jews of Zasanie, which remained under German occupation, were expelled to the eastern sector of the city. Under Soviet rule all Jewish communal activities ceased. Jewish artisans were organized in cooperatives; Jews in the professions (except physicians) faced difficulties in finding employment. In April and May 1940, 7,000 Jews were deported to Russia. Most of them were refugees from the western parts of Poland.

Following the German attack on the Soviet Union in June 1941, Przemysl fell to the Germans on June 28, 1941. Subsequently a Judenrat was set up, headed by Ignacy Duldig. In June 1942 the Germans shot 45 of the Jews from Zasanie. This was followed by the expulsion of 1,000 Jews to the camp of Janowska in *Lvov and the transfer, by Aug. 3, 1942, of 12,500 Jews to *Belzec extermination camp. On Nov. 18, 1942 a further 4,000 Jews were sent to the same camp. Some ten months later, on Sept. 2–3, 1943, 3,500 Jews were sent to *Auschwitz. In subsequent months the remaining Jews in Przemysl —some 2,000 persons—about half of whom had been in hiding, were murdered by the Nazis.

The Jews made an attempt at armed resistance. In April 1943 a group of young Jews went to the nearby forests with the intention of joining the partisans. They were all captured and murdered.

The Soviet army reentered the city on July 27, 1944, and a few days later some 250 Jewish survivors gathered in Przemysl. A Jewish council was established under the leadership of Mordechai Schatner and later of Ẓevi Rubinfeld to assist the survivors; in 1947 its activities were limited to religious needs only. Przemysl Landsmannschaften had been established in Israel and in New York. A memorial book on the Jewish community of Przemysl has been published (*Sefer Przemysl,* Heb. and Yid., 1964).

[AR.W.]

Bibliography: M. Schorr, *Żydzi w Przemyślu do końca XVIII wieku: opracowanie . . . materyału archiwalnego* (1903).

PRZEWORSK, town in Rzeszow province, S.E. Poland. The town was overrun by the Turks in 1498, it endured the invasion of the Swedes in 1656 during the reign of John Casimir, and recovered after 1677 when the Polish *Sejm decided to lend its assistance in its development. From then on it enjoyed economic prosperity. In 1865 its total population was 4,000 and in 1921 it was 3,371 of which 1,457 were Jews. Moses *Sofer (d. 1805), a rabbi of the community, achieved fame in his lifetime and was regarded as a saint after his death. After World War I its library played a prominent role in the cultural life of the Jewish population. After the great fire of 1930 many of the town's Jews were left homeless and dependent on support from charitable institutions. With the increase of anti-Semitism during the 1930s the community organized a protest campaign and a self-defense group. Elections to the community were held in 1934. No information is available on later years. [SH.L.K.]

PRZYSUCHA, city in Kielce province, S. E. central Poland. The Jewish population of the city increased during the 19th century. In 1865 there were 2,907 inhabitants; this number grew and in 1921, 3,238 inhabitants, including 2,153 Jews (66%) lived in Przysucha. The ancient synagogue, which stood in the town until the Holocaust, testified to the antiquity of the Jewish community. The Jewish settlement became renowned through its *ẓaddikim.* One such prominent ḥasidic leader, R. Jacob Isaac b. Asher *Przysucha (*ha-Yehudi ha-Kadosh;* see next entry), acquired a world reputation among Jews. Another renowned ḥasidic leader of Przysucha was R. *Simḥah Bunem, the disciple of the *Yehudi ha-Kadosh.* After World War I there was a considerable amount of communal activity. Upon the eve of World War II the Jewish community was headed by Joseph Meisels. Its rabbi was R. Elhanan Fuks. [SH.L.K.]

Holocaust Period. On the outbreak of World War II there were about 2,500 Jews in Przysucha. The Jewish community was liquidated on Oct. 27–31, 1942, when 4,000 Jews from Przysucha and its vicinity were deported to *Treblinka death camp. After the war the Jewish community of Przysucha was not reconstituted. [ED.]

PRZYSUCHA (Pshiskhah), JACOB ISAAC BEN ASHER (ha-Yehudi ha-Kadosh, "the holy Jew"; 1766–1814), *ẓaddik* and founder of Pshiskhah Ḥasidism in Poland. He was born in *Przedborz, where his father R. Asher, scion of a distinguished rabbinic family, was a preacher. Jacob Isaac studied there under Aryeh Leib Ḥarif whom he followed to *Opatow (Apta) and at the yeshivah of *Leszno, under *David Tevele b. Nathan of Lissa. Though as a youth Jacob Isaac excelled in physical strength, he was weakened as a result of his withdrawal from worldly matters, prolonged fasts, and ecstatic supplications. At first he attempted to conceal his spiritual qualities and his charitable deeds, but when the *ẓaddik* *Moses Leib of Sasov settled in Apta he influenced Jacob Isaac to join the Ḥasidim. He was particularly influenced by the *ẓaddik* David of *Lelov from whom he gained an insight into the obligation of loving one's fellow Jew. Jacob Isaac became famous as a Torah savant and man of intense devotions. He would say: "If a sword were stuck into the body of a praying man and he felt pain, then his prayer is not authentic." He performed charitable deeds dispensing his money among the poor, although his own fortune deteriorated and he was obliged to work as a village schoolmaster *(melammed).*

A turning point in his life came when he met *Jacob Isaac Horowitz "the Seer" *(Ha-Ḥozeh)* of Lublin and became his closest disciple. Because his name was the same as that of his master, and possibly for other reasons, the Ḥasidim called him "the Jew" (Heb. *ha-Yehudi*) or "the holy Jew" *(ha-Yehudi ha-Kadosh).* The Seer of Lublin admired his disciple and appointed him spiritual counsellor of the young scholars. In this capacity he advised his pupils to cast off pride and, above all, sentiments of one's own worth. He maintained that a *ẓaddik* always sees his friends' virtues and his own lowliness. According to Jacob Isaac, there are three kinds of *ẓaddikim.* One who acknowledges that he is a *ẓaddik* is the least worthy. One who recognizes the fact that he is not a *ẓaddik* of high order is more worthy. Better than both is the true *ẓaddik* who holds that he is yet to achieve perfection. He stressed the imperative of striving for self-perfection—the absence of endeavor implying deterioration—through the honest performance of the *mitzvot,* untarnished by any interest in honor or material gain. Indeed, Jacob Isaac's own integrity earned him the nickname *Shibbolet Zahav* ("golden ear of corn"), which he was said to resemble in that he, too, was golden to the very kernel.

Pshiskhah Ḥasidism. Jacob Isaac initiated (in the words of Uri *Strelisk) "a new path in Ḥasidism"—the service of God through Torah study together with prayer. He thus founded a Polish version of *Ḥabad Ḥasidism, which assigned a greater importance to Torah study and the role of scholars, and started to campaign against the superficiality and ignorance which had developed within Ḥasidism. Jacob Isaac opposed wonder-workers and the *ẓaddikim* who occupied themselves with material matters. He pointed out that anyone who had attained a certain spiritual level could perform wonders; a more difficult task is simply to fulfill one's obligations honestly as a Jew. "The good is sufficient even if it is only a hairsbreadth, provided it be offered in truth and wholeheartedly." Because of this the Pshiskhah Ḥasidim were not meticulous in fixing the time of prayer according to the law as set out in the Shulḥan Arukh, preferring to wait until spiritual preparation produced the requisite devout frame of mind. Pshiskhah Ḥasidism was thus a combination of emotional attitude with rational scholarship.

The Schism. Jacob Isaac's new path, especially the delay in the set time of prayer, aroused the opposition of all contemporary *ẓaddikim* who were the disciples of the Seer of Lublin. A split was created between Pshiskhah Ḥasidim and the popular Ḥasidim. The disciples faithful to the Seer regarded Jacob Isaac as a competitor of their master and began to harass him and his disciples. The Seer himself was harsh on Jacob Isaac who, unwanted at Lublin, set about to lead a community of his own. This further aggravated the controversy between the master and his disciple. Eager for peace, Jacob Isaac requested Mendel of *Rymanow to intervene but he did not succeed. During Jacob Isaac's last years, world happenings in the wake of the Napoleonic wars, which some of the *ẓaddikim* regarded as the war of *Gog and Magog, created among Jews new expectations for redemption. Accordingly, on the Passover *seder* night of 1814 they sought to bring the Messiah through mystical means, but Jacob Isaac refused to take part in this undertaking.

In the same year, before he reached the age of fifty, he died in Przysucha. Though he was succeeded by his son Jerahmeel, most of the Ḥasidim accepted the leadership of his outstanding disciple, *Simḥah Bunem of Przysucha. Jacob Isaac's important disciples included Menahem Mendel of *Kotsk, *Ḥanokh of Aleksandrow, Isaac of Worky (*Warka), and Issachar Baer of *Radoshits, all of whom were ḥasidic leaders of influence among Polish Jews.

Jacob Isaac's works were published in *Nifla'ot ha-Yehudi* ("The Wonders of the Jew," 1909), *Tiferet ha-Yehudi* ("The Splendor of the Jew," 1912), and *Torat ha-Yehudi* ("The Teachings of the Jew," 1911).

Bibliography: W. Z. Rabinowitsch, *R. Ya'akov Yiẓḥak mi-Pshiskha* (1932); Y. K. K. Rakacz, *Nifla'ot ha-Yehudi* (1909); idem: *Tiferet ha-Yehudi* (1910); A. Marcus, *Der Chassidismus* (1901), 158–9; M. Buber, *Tales of the Hasidim*, 2 (1966³), 224–36; Dubnow, Ḥasidut, index; A. Z. Aescoly, in: *Beit Yisrael be-Polin* (1954), 98–110; R. Mahler, *Ha-Ḥasidut ve ha-Haskalah* (1961), 311–3.

[Z.M.R.]

PRZYTYK, town near Radom, E. central Poland. In 1936, 90% of its 3,000 inhabitants were Jews. Przytyk became notorious because of the pogrom which occurred there in 1936 and aroused sharp reaction from Jewish public opinion throughout the world. After the death of Marshal *Pilsudski in May 1935, his followers in the government were weakened, and unable to check the virulent anti-Semitism which erupted as a result of reactionary and nationalist pressure from the *Endecja party. A series of bloody riots broke out against Jewish students in metropolitan universities and against small Jewish shopkeepers, who were regarded as competitors by impoverished peasants who had been driven to seek a livelihood in the cities. Anti-Jewish *boycott propaganda was followed by several attacks on Jews, which the authorities took no measures to prevent. Against this background of tension, a pogrom broke out in Przytyk. In March 9, 1936, when the peasants came to the seasonal fair, they were incited to attack Jewish stallkeepers and even break into Jewish homes; three Jews were killed and 60 wounded. The Jews organized a self-defense group, and in the ensuing clashes one Pole was shot and killed. In the subsequent trial no attempt was made to distinguish between attackers and defenders. The Jew accused of the shooting was found guilty and given a harsh sentence. As a mark of Jewish protest the Bund announced a general strike starting on March 18, 1936; the majority of Jews in Poland, as well as many Polish workers, joined in the strike. [M.LAN.]

Holocaust Period. On the outbreak of World War II there were about 2,500 Jews living in Przytyk (about 70% of the total population). The German army entered the town on Sept. 4, 1939, and initiated persecution of the Jews. A decree of March 5, 1941 ordered the immediate evacuation of the Jewish population from Przytyk and about 160 surrounding villages. Their passive resistance prolonged the deportation action for over a month's time. The Jewish refugees settled in about 30 different places in the Kielce province, but within a short time were again ordered to concentrate in two towns only—Przysucha and Szydlowiec. All of them were afterward deported to Treblinka death camp and exterminated, in part together with the Jewish population of Przysucha (Oct. 31, 1942), and partly with those of Szydlowiec (Jan. 13, 1943). The community was not reestablished after the war. [S.KR.]

Bibliography: H. M. Rabinowicz, *The Legacy of Polish Jewry* (1965), 57–58; Y. Gruenbaum (ed.), EG, 1 (1953), 116.

PSALMS, APOCRYPHAL. Syrian manuscripts have preserved a group of five apocryphal Psalms, one of which is also contained in the Septuagint version of the canonical Book of Psalms. This Psalm, which occurs as a "supernumerary" in the Septuagint, found its way into the *Vetus Latina* and the *Syrohexapla* (see *Bible, Versions) as well. It was not known whether the five apocryphal Psalms were a translation from an original Hebrew version or whether they were originally composed in some other language in imitation of the Hebrew Psalms.

An answer to this problem came in 1962 with the publication of the Psalms Scroll found among the *Dead Sea Scrolls in Qumran Cave 11 (11QPs^a), which included, among the canonical Psalms, three of the five apocryphal Syrian Psalms. This unexpectedly confirmed the supposition, of M. Noth, of the Hebrew origin of (at least some of) the Syrian Psalms. Moreover, the fact that the apocryphal Psalms were included in 11QPs^a among the canonical Psalms raised the possibility that the members of the Qumran sect regarded them as part of the Canon. This assumption, if correct, would imply that shortly before the beginning of the Common Era—when 11QPs^a was written—a great flexibility existed in the books of Psalms in circulation in Ereẓ Israel both as regards the Psalms they included and as regards the internal arrangement of the biblical Psalms themselves. This is a further indication that the final crystallization of the Book of Psalms, in its present form, is comparatively late. Thus the boundary line between canonical and apocryphal materials—at least as far as the Book of Psalms is concerned—becomes rather blurred. Some scholars however maintain that 11QPs^a does not represent the Book of Psalms, as generally understood, but rather a liturgical compilation used in religious services. This "liturgical theory" removes two major difficulties for those scholars rejecting such a late date for the final canonization of the Biblical Psalter: (1) a compilation of this nature would naturally contain various non-biblical excerpts without any intention of ascribing to them a canonical status; (2) the biblical chapters quoted in such a liturgical compilation would not necessarily follow the order in which they occur in the Bible. Hence the Qumran Psalms Scroll cannot, at this stage, confirm the canonicity of the apocryphal Psalms even among certain Jewish circles at the turn of the Common Era. It can however prove the existence of an original Hebrew text from which (some of) the Syrian Psalms were translated.

Date and Place of Origin. The content of these Psalms do not provide a clear solution for the problem of their date and place of origin, since they too exhibit those nontemporal features characteristic of the canonical Psalms. The attemps to find in them traces of "an Orphic influence" or indications of "an Essene origin" cannot be conclusively proved. Linguistic criteria, although insufficient for fixing any definite dating, at least furnish grounds for stating that in their present form the apocryphal Psalms (including the Septuagint Psalm 151, apparently the earliest of them) were possibly composed in Hellenistic times and certainly not before the Persian period. This is borne out by the use not only of characteristically postclassical Hebrew idioms and phraseology but also of terms and epithets typical of rabbinic and post-biblical literature: "sons of the covenant"; "a faithful judge" (*dayyan emet*); "the Lord of all" (but this reading is disputed). The apocryphal Psalms also display significant parallels to the Wisdom of Ben Sira and to Qumran post-biblical writings, as do other "Psalms" contained in other scrolls.

If it should be proved that the apocryphal Psalms are Hellenistic, and if it is true that none of those in the canonical Psalter originated after the Persian period, it may well be contended that (one of) the reason(s) for the exclusion of the apocryphal Psalms from the canonical Psalter is due to the fact that the rabbis did recognize the late origin of these compositions. This is however a question that can be clearly and unequivocally decided only on the basis of new facts and the discovery of further apocryphal writings.

Bibliography: J. A. Sanders, *Psalms Scroll of Qumrân Cave 11* (1965); idem, *Dead Sea Psalm Scroll* (1967), incl. detailed bibl. (pp. 151–3); Yalon, in: *Molad*, 22 (1964), 463–5; B. Uffenheimer, *ibid.*, 69–81, 328–42; Talmon, in: *Tarbiz*, 35 (1965/66), 214–34; idem, in: *Textus*, 5 (Eng., 1965), 11–21; Goschen-Gottstein, *ibid.*, 22–23; A. Hurvitz, in: *Eretz Israel*, 8 (1967), 82–87.

[Av.H.]

PSALMS, BOOK OF. This article is arranged according to the following outline:

Title
Place in the Canon
Number of Psalms
Verse Division
Division into Books
Composition of the Psalter
Date of the Psalter
Ascription to David
Types of Psalms
Psalms and the Cult
The Text
Superscriptions and Technical Terms
  Those Containing Personal Names (with affixed *lamed*)
  Titles with Liturgical Application
  Technical Terms in the Headings
  Technical Terms Within the Psalms
In the Talmud and Midrash
In the Liturgy
  Statutory Prayers
  Non-Statutory Prayers
  Various
In the Arts
  In Literature
  In Art
  In Music
Musical Rendition in Jewish Tradition
  Historical Sources
  Melody
  Performance

TITLE

The English name Psalms is derived from the Latin Vulgate *Liber Psalmorum* or *Psalmi* for short. The Latin, in turn, was borrowed from the Greek ψαλμοί which is the title found in most Greek manuscripts and by which the book is cited in the New Testament (Luke 20:42; 24:44; Acts 1:20). It meant "a song sung to a stringed instrument" and seems to be a translation of the Hebrew term *mizmor* which occurs 57 times in the individual Hebrew captions of the book. A variant title, derived from the same Greek root, is ψαλτήριον, found in the fifth-century Codex Alexandrinus (G^A), which is the source of the Latin *Psalterium* and the English Psalter. No Hebrew name which might have served as the origin of the Greek is known, but there is evidence of a Palestinian practice to refer to all psalms as *mizmorot*, even when the technical term *mizmor* is absent (cf. TJ, Ber. 4:3, 7d–8a; Shab. 16:1, 15c; Ta'an. 2:2, 65c). Closest to this is the Syriac title of the book, *Kēthaba de-mazmūrē*.

The Hebrew Bible does not preserve any original title for the compilation as a whole. The editorial note, Psalm 72:20, would indicate that at some period "The Prayers of David son of Jesse" designated a smaller collection of psalms, although the Hebrew term *tefillah* in its usual supplicatory meaning would be inappropriate to much of the contents of the present Books I and II. Perhaps it was used in a more generalized sense of the articulated communication of man with God (cf. I Sam. 2:1; Hab. 3:1).

The universally accepted Hebrew name for the book in rabbinic and subsequent literature is סֵפֶר תְּהִלִּים (*Sefer Tehillim;* cf. BB 14b), often contracted to תִּלִּים (*Tillim;* Av.

Figure 1. David the psalmist entering the house of the Lord. Ivory relief illustrating Psalm 27, executed by the Liuthard group at the court of Charles the Bald, c. 870; and presumed to have decorated the binding of the emperor's prayer book, $4\frac{1}{2}\times3\frac{1}{2}$ in. (11.2×8.8 cm.). Zurich, Swiss National Museum.

Zar. 19a; TJ, Suk. 3:12, 53d; Ket. 12:3, 35a) or תִּלֵּי *(Tille)* and reflected in the transliterations of the Palestinian Church Fathers as Σφαρ Θελλείμε (Origen, in Eusebius, *Historia Ecclesiastica,* 6:25) and *Sephar Tallim* (Jerome, *Psalterium juxta Hebraeos*).

This Hebrew title poses several difficulties. In the first place, there is the use of the normally masculine plural ending *-im* for a feminine noun as against the regular feminine plural *-ot* (i.e., *tehillot*), which the word *tehillah* takes in the Bible (cf. Ps. 22:4; 78:4; cf. Ex. 15:11; Isa. 60:6; 63:7). Then, only a single psalm (145) is actually entitled *tehillah* and this, curiously, is replaced by *tefillah* in the Qumran scroll (11QPs[a] 16:1, 7). Lastly, a title based on *tehillah,* a song of praise, would seem to be applicable only to a selection of the compositions that make up the collection.

The oft-repeated assumption that *Tehillim* was artificially coined to differentiate the title of the canonical book (i. e., Psalms) from the ordinary plurality of *tehillah* (i. e., psalms) must now be discarded in view of the presence of *tehillim* in the aforementioned Qumran scroll (11QPs[a] 27:1, 4) in the simple sense of liturgical compositions. It must be supposed that the masculine plural form represents an internal, post-biblical Hebrew development parallel to the development of *tefillim/n* as the plural of *tefillah* in the sense of "phylactery." In any case, medieval Hebrew writers such as Mishael b. Uzziel *(Kitāb al-Khilaf)* and Abraham ibn Ezra (*Iggeret ha-Shabbat,* 3) refer to the book as *Sefer Tehillot,* though whether they do so by some tradition or out of a desire to preserve the biblical Hebrew form, it is difficult to tell.

The Hebrew title itself was selected or emerged doubtless because the root *hll* in biblical usage is overwhelmingly characteristic of the language of psalms and, in fact, seems to have acquired in the post-Exilic books the specialized connotation of "Temple worship" (cf. Ezra 3:10–11; Neh. 5:13; 12:24; I Chron. 16:4, 36; 23:5, et al.). The popular liturgical refrain *Hallelujah, which is exclusive to the Book of Psalms, was probably an additional influence, as was the fact that the hymn plays a leading role among the categories of psalms (see discussion of technical terms, below).

PLACE IN THE CANON

According to an anonymous tannaitic source, the proper place of Psalms in the corpus of *Ketuvim* is second, following Ruth and succeeded by Job and Proverbs (BB 14b; see *Bible). The source does not give any explanation for the sequence, but the precedence of Ruth is undoubtedly due to the closing genealogy of David (Ruth 4:18–22), the reputed author of Psalms. For an exploration of the other features of the arrangement, see *Job, beginning. The importance of the book in the canon may be gauged by the fact that despite the great variety in the order of the books of the *Ketuvim* exhibited by the manuscripts, Psalms invariably either heads the list or is preceded only by Ruth and/or Chronicles. In the early printed editions the book always comes first and this has become the universal practice in Hebrew printed Bibles (see *Bible, table 2, cols. 829–30).

It is quite likely that this represents the oldest order of the *Ketuvim* for II Maccabees 2:13 refers to "books about the kings and prophets and the writings of David ...," and Philo similarly speaks of "Laws and oracles delivered by prophets and hymns and other writings" (Cont. 25). The New Testament likewise invokes "the law of Moses and the prophets and the psalms" (Luke 24:44). It is reasonable to infer from this early testimony that the Psalter was looked upon as being the most important among the books of the *Ketuvim.*

NUMBER OF PSALMS

Current editions of the Psalter universally contain 150 psalms. The ancient Greek version of the Jews of Alexandria has the same number even though it exhibits some different internal divisions, combining into single psalms the Hebrew 9–10 and 114–115, while dividing the Hebrew 116 and 147 each into two psalms. The Hebrew-Greek correspondences are as follows:

MT	LXX
1–8	1–8
9–10	9
11–113	10–112
114–115	113
116:1–9	114
:10–19	115
117–146	116–145
147:1–11	146
:12–20	147
148–150	148–150

The coincidence of 150 psalms in the two versions, despite the differences, would seem to be significant, particularly since the Greek contains an additional composition which it designates as "supernumerary," thereby exhibiting a conscious desire to limit the canonical psalms to 150.

On the other hand, there is a wealth of evidence for the existence of widely varying traditions. A Psalter of 147 chapters is mentioned as early as amoraic times (TJ, Shab. 16:1, 15c; cf. Sof. 16:11; Mid. Ps. to 22:4) and is to be found in manuscripts (C. D. Ginsburg, in bibl., 18, 777) and in the first edition of the *Yalkut Shimoni* (Salonica, 1521–26; cf. also Jacob b. Asher, *Ba'al ha-Turim,* Gen. 47:28). The Leningrad Codex B and the Brescia (1494) and Naples (1491–94) Bibles all feature a division into 149 psalms, an arrangement also known to Mishael b. Uzziel *(Kitāb al-Khilaf)* and to Samuel ha-Nagid (J. H. Schirmann, in bibl.) and present in some Hebrew manuscripts (I. Joel, in bibl.). Others comprise divisions of 148 *(ibid.),* 151, 159, and even 170 psalms (C. D. Ginsburg, in bibl., 583, 536, 725).

These variations have nothing to do with the content of the Psalter which remains the same in all the editions. They merely register differences in the divisions and combinations of psalm units. That our Psalms 1 and 2 were very early conjoined is explicitly attested in rabbinic sources (Ber. 9b–10a; TJ, Ber. 4:3, 8a; Ta'an. 2:2, 65c) and in New Testament manuscripts (Acts 13:33) and may possibly also be reflected in a Qumran scroll (4Q 174 col. 1). The truncated alphabetic acrostic that spans Psalms 9–10 shows that the two originally constituted a single psalm in the Hebrew just as they do in the Greek. It is very likely that such a combination is behind a Palestinian *amora's* citation of Psalm 20:2 as belonging to the 18th psalm (TJ, Ber. 4:3, 8a; Ta'an. 2:2, 65c), thus showing that a pair of our short units apart from 1 and 2 must have counted as a single entity in his Psalter.

Other documented examples of the conjoining in earlier times of what appear in our texts as individual psalms are 42–43 (cf. 42:6, 12; 43:5; Yal., Ps. 745; C. D. Ginsburg, in bibl., 725); 53–54 *(ibid.);* 70–71 (*ibid.,* 18, 777); 93–94 (I. Joel, in bibl.); 94–95, 104–105, 114–115, 116–117, 117–118:4 (C. D. Ginsburg, in bibl., 18, 536, 777, 853, 873). In the case of 117, the idea of a two-versed psalm seemed preposterous (cf. Tos. to Pes. 117a) and led to its merging with either the preceding or following psalm. On the other hand, just as the Greek displays the breakdown of 116 and 147 each into two separate compositions, so there are manuscripts in which 118 and 119 are subdivided (C. D. Ginsburg, in bibl., 536–7, 583, 725–6).

All in all, it is quite clear that no fixed and uniform system of chapter divisions existed in ancient times. Except where a superscription intervenes, the manuscripts frequently do not in any way mark the transition from one psalm to another, thus easily permitting varieties of verse groupings. What is not clear is the significance to be attached to the variant numbers of the psalms. The most plausible explanation is that which relates them to the custom of reading the Torah each Sabbath in the Palestinian synagogues in a triennial cycle (cf. Meg. 29b). It is presumed that there also existed a similar cycle of weekly Psalter readings in association with the Torah and prophetical readings. Since the latter were not stable, but varied from community to community, this would account for the diversity in the numeration of the psalms.

VERSE DIVISION

In the Qumran scroll (11 QPs^{a}), all the psalms are written in prose form with nothing to indicate verse division, except for Psalm 119 where the alphabetic arrangement provides a natural indication. However, the verse division must be quite early. Other Qumran Psalms manuscripts, especially from cave 4, do reflect a practice of transmitting the text in a form in keeping with the verse structure.

According to a tannaitic report, the number of verses in the Psalter is 5,896 (Kid. 30a). This is over twice the sum of 2,527 specified in the western masorah's note at the end of the book. The eastern masorah details only three fewer due to the combination of each of the following two verses into one: 22:5–6; 52:1–2; 53:1–2; and 129:5–6, and the division of verse 1 in Psalm 90 into two (C. D. Ginsburg, in bibl., 101; Lewin, in bibl., 84). The great discrepancy between the masoretic and tannaitic traditions is to be explained by varying concepts of "verse." The former enumerates the larger poetic unit which may contain two or three stichs and which is marked off by a major stop or caesura; the latter is most likely based on a peculiar mode of writing biblical poetry in which the spacing of words and their alignment, column by column, was important (cf. Meg. 16b; TJ, Meg. 3:8, 74b; Sof. 12:9). The *tannaim* evidently counted as a "verse" each compact cluster of words and even a caption of one or two words (S. D. Luzzatto, in bibl., 281–2). In this connection, incidentally, it should be noted that our printed editions, following the pattern fixed in the Torah (cf. Gen. 26:6), may accept three words, but not less, as a separate verse, so that a superscription of three words or more receives a separate enumeration. This is never the case in the English versions and accounts for the frequent difference of one between the Hebrew and English verse numberings.

One other distinction between the talmudic and masoretic traditions lies in the location of the middle verse of the book which is stated by the note at the end of the Psalter to be Psalm 78:36, but two verses ahead in the rabbinic computation (Kid. 30a).

DIVISION INTO BOOKS

The Psalter is divided into five books, each of the first four being marked off by a doxology, or formulaic expression of praise to God, as follows:

Book I, Ps. 1–41
41:14 Blessed is the Lord, God of Israel,
From eternity to eternity.
Amen and Amen.
Book II, Ps. 42–72
72:18–20 Blessed is the Lord God, God of Israel,
Who alone does wondrous things;
Blessed be His glorious name for ever,
And let His glory fill the whole world.
Amen and Amen. End of the prayers of David son of Jesse
Book III, Ps. 73–89
89:53 Blessed be the Lord to eternity.
Amen and Amen.
Book IV, Ps. 90–106
106:48 Blessed is the Lord, God of Israel,
From eternity to eternity.
And let all the people say
Amen, Hallelujah.
Book V, Ps. 107–150.

This last book bears no closing formula. It is likely that Psalm 150 was regarded as a doxology for the entire Psalter.

These liturgical formulas which distinguish the various books that now make up the Book of Psalms are present in the Greek and are therefore at least as old as the second half of the second century B.C.E., by which time that translation was certainly completed. They are also definitely post-Exilic in origin as can be determined by some stylistic and terminological peculiarities (e.g. ברוך שם (ה׳) לעולם, עד עולם להשתבח (A. Hurvitz), in bibl.). Indeed, three of the four doxologies are not integrated with the psalms to which they are attached, but form an appendage to them. It is thus reasonable to assume that they signify the close of what were once independent collections. Further support for this inference may be derived from the colophon to Book II. It is hardly conceivable that an editor who was aware of the 18 psalms attributed to David in the subsequent books would have written that "the prayers of David son of Jesse" had come to an end (Ps. 72:20; cf. Jer. 51:64; Job 31:40). It is also unlikely that a single compiler would have duplicated individual psalms. If Psalm 14 appears again in Book II (Ps. 53) which also repeats Psalm 40:14–18 (Book I) in the form of Psalm 70, and if parts of two psalms of Book II (57:8–12; 60:7–14) become Psalm 108 in Book V then it should be conceded that the various books existed at some time or other as independent entities. In other words, the division of the Psalter into books may represent successive stages in the growth of the work as a whole.

There are good reasons for believing, however, that the doxology to Book IV (Ps. 106:48) constitutes the exception to the rule and that the division between Books IV and V is artificial. These books share in common certain characteristics which put them in contrast with the preceding ones. Eighteen of their 61 psalms bear no superscriptions as opposed to only six psalms without superscriptions in all the foregoing 89 psalms. Strangely, not a single musical reference is to be found in the headings, while such otherwise characteristically technical terms as *La-Menazze'aḥ* and *Selah* are almost totally absent, the former occurring only three times and the latter four. On the other hand, Hallelujah appears exclusively in these two collections. In addition, the subject matter of the two is very much alike; they contain predominantly praise and thanksgiving psalms suitable for the public service in the Temple. Most telling is the fact that the doxology of Book IV seems really to be an integral part of the last psalm and need not originally have applied to the entire collection. The first and last two verses of Psalm 106 are cited in I Chronicles 16:34–36 together with the peculiar invocational rubric. Since the latter fits naturally into the situation there described it is likely that the presence of the rubric, slightly varied, at the end of Psalm 106 has been due to the influence of the Chronicles passage.

The cumulative effect of the evidence here presented is to cast grave doubt upon the originality of the book division after Psalm 106. In this connection it is of interest that the Qumran scroll (11QPs^{a}) intersperses in Book V selections from Book IV, although in an order differing slightly from ours. While it is not at all certain that the scroll is not a sectarian liturgy or hymn book, rather than a canonical Psalter, the phenomenon may reflect a period of time before the division of Psalms 90–150 into two. At any rate, the extension of a fourfold into a pentateuchal arrangement was probably suggested by the analogy of the Torah, and may have been the result of the reading of the Psalms, week by week, in association with the triennial cycle of Torah readings. An echo of this is to be found in the rabbinic observation that "Moses gave the five books of the Torah to Israel, and David gave the five books of the Psalms to Israel" (Mid. Ps. to 1).

At all events, the liturgical character of the doxologies would seem to prove that the book divisions were originally fixed for purposes of public worship, and it can hardly be accidental that the Book of Psalms opens with a reference to the study of the Torah.

COMPOSITION OF THE PSALTER

From the foregoing data it becomes evident that the present pentateuchal division is only the crystallization of a long and complex history involving the emergence of several small collections and their combination into larger units. The process of development can only be partially discerned and any reconstruction must of necessity remain conjectural to a certain extent.

The earliest collection is undoubtedly Book I, or rather Psalms 3–41 within it. Except for Psalms 10 and 33 which are anonymous, every unit is "Davidic." As has been pointed out above (on the number of psalms) the alphabetic arrangement, supported by contextual and stylistic considerations, confirms the tradition of the rabbis, the Greek translation, and several Hebrew manuscripts, that Psalms 9 and 10 originally were one. Psalm 33 has a "Davidic" superscription in the Greek which may have gotten lost in the Hebrew, although it is more likely that the psalm was inserted into Book I at a later date. (Perhaps it was influenced by the similarities between 32:11 and 33:1; כֹּנֵס (33:7) is a vocable characteristic of post-Exilic Hebrew and a late composition for Psalm 33 is also suggested by the fact that the summons to sing a new song to the Lord is put off to verse 3 instead of coming at the beginning as in Psalms 96, 98, etc.). The "Davidic" psalms would thus constitute the very first stage in the compilation of the Psalter.

The second collection is the group comprising Psalms 42–83 which is distinguished by the rarity of the use of YHWH and the frequency of the appearance of *ʾElohim* (in its absolute or suffixed forms) in its place, in striking contrast to the situation in the rest of the Psalter. Within this group of 42 psalms, the Tetragrammaton occurs some 45 times and *ʾElohim* 210 times. However, in the remaining 118 psalms (1–41, 84–150) *ʾElohim* appears only 94 times altogether, while YHWH occurs 584 times. This overwhelming preference for *ʾElohim* is so consistent that it even influences two psalms of Book I as they reappear in a second recension in this group. YHWH in Psalm 14:2,4,7 becomes *ʾElohim* in Psalm 53:3, 5, 7 and the same switch occurs between Psalm 40:14a, 17 and Psalm 70:2a, 5 (cf. also Ps. 50:7 with Ex. 20:2; Ps. 68:2, 8–9 with Num. 10:35 and Judg. 5:4–5). Furthermore, such otherwise unknown combinations as *ʾElohim ʾElohai* (אֱלֹהִים אֱלֹהָי; Ps. 43:4) and *ʾElohim ʾElohekha* (אֱלֹהִים אֱלֹהֶיךָ; Ps. 45:8; 50:7) make their appearance.

Since this phenomenon is restricted to Books II and III (up to Ps. 83), it is evident that the "elohistic" Psalms 42–83 once constituted an independent collection. Their superscriptions show, however, that this development resulted, in turn, from the combination of smaller "elohistic" groupings. Psalms 51–65 and 68–70 make up a second "Davidic" collection which quite probably once followed the first and to which the subscription of Psalm 72:20 was attached. Insofar as no additional psalms are ascribed to David in the "elohistic" Psalter, the colophon is accurate. The other constituents are the "Korahite" Psalms 42–49 (42–43 were originally a unit) and the "Asaphic" Psalms 50, 73–83, both collections internally arranged according to the technical terms of the superscriptions. Four other psalms (66, 67, 71, 72) belong to the "elohistic" Psalter, three of which are anonymous in the received Hebrew text; Psalm 67 is ascribed to David in some Greek manuscripts; Psalm 71 is conjoined with Psalm 70 to form one psalm in many Hebrew manuscripts, but is "Davidic" in the Greek; Psalm 72 is "Solomonic." The presence of the colophon at the end of Psalm 72 naturally influenced the bisection of the "elohistic" Psalter so that it marked off Book II and received a doxology. To the rest of the "elohistic" group was added an appendix (Ps. 84–89) consisting of four more "Korahite" psalms, one "Davidic" psalm, and one attributed to "Ethan" to complete Book III.

The distinguishing characteristics of Psalms 90–150 and their artificial bisection into Books IV and V have been discussed earlier. Here it may be added that this group of psalms must postdate the "elohistic" Psalter because Psalm 108 is constituted from it (Ps. 57:8–12; 60:7–14) and still retains its "elohistic" character despite its presence in a collection otherwise differentiated by the preferred use of YHWH as the divine name. Within the group of Psalms 90–150 some originally smaller collections are still discernible. The most obvious example is that comprising 15 psalms (120–134) entitled *Shir ha(la)-Maʿalot* (שִׁיר הַ(לְ)מַּעֲלוֹת). There also seems to have existed still another "Davidic" collection from which were extracted Psalms 101, 103, 108–110, and 138–145. On the other hand, Psalms 90–100 are practically all anonymous and although some of them have features in common, they can hardly be said to derive from a recognizable source. Whether the "Hallelujah" psalms (104–106, 111–117, 135, 146–150) were once a separate hymnbook is a question impossible to decide with any degree of confidence.

It is extremely improbable that Psalm 1 or Psalm 2 originally formed part of Book I, if only for the reason that they are anonymous. It is far more likely that when Psalm 2 came to be messianically interpreted and associated with David it was affixed to the "Davidic" collection, just as Ruth was placed immediately before Psalms in many orders of the *Ketuvim* because of its concluding Davidic genealogy (see discussion on place in Canon, above).

After the Psalter had been completed, Psalm 1 was added as a sort of introduction to the entire work, for a combination of various factors made it an ideal choice for the purpose. In the first place, the psalm affirms the governance of the world by a divinely ordained moral order so that the operation of providence is both inevitable and effective. It thus gives expression to the fundamental and indispensable presupposition for all meaningful communication with God, in the biblical view. At the same time it formulates the basic Pharisaic notion of the preoccupation with Torah as the response of Israel to the Divine demand, with the consequent interdependence of study and piety.

The selection of what became Psalm 1 also proved to be felicitous from an external literary viewpoint, for it exhibits striking verbal associations with both Psalm 2 (Table 1) and Psalm 41 (Table 2). It could simultaneously be unified with the former, if need be (see discussion on the number of psalms above), and serve with Psalm 41 as a literary framework to Book II.

Table I

Ps. 1	verse	1	אַשְׁרֵי
		2	תּוֹרָה
		2	יֶהְגֶּה
		6	דֶּרֶךְ... תֹּאבֵד
Ps. 2	verse	12	אַשְׁרֵי
		7	חֹק
		1	יֶהְגּוּ
		12	תֹאבְדוּ דֶרֶךְ

Table II

Ps. 1	verse	1	אַשְׁרֵי
		2	חֶפְצוֹ
		5	לֹא־יָקֻמוּ
		6	תֹּאבֵד
Ps. 41	verse	2	אַשְׁרֵי
		12	חָפַצְתָּ
		9	לֹא־יוֹסִיף לָקוּם
		6	אָבַד

DATE OF THE PSALTER

Critical scholarship in the 19th century generally regarded the Psalms as the product of the Maccabean-Hasmonean era. This view was grounded in the conviction of the late development of pure monotheism in Israel with its concomitant that the Psalms postdated the prophets. The numerous traces of Psalms' language in the prophetic literature were explained by the influence of the latter on the former, while the extremely individualistic consciousness that is mirrored in the psalms was taken as sure evidence for a highly developed, and hence late, stage in the history of the religion of Israel. Granted these assertions, it was not difficult to interpret allusions to historic events in the Psalter as reflections of internal and external affairs in Judea in the course of the second century B.C.E.

The 20th century has witnessed the almost complete abandonment of this position on the part of biblical scholars for whom the convergence of several lines of independent evidence has meant a far more conservative reevaluation of the problem of the age of the Psalter.

In the first place, renewed attention has been paid to the testimony provided by the Greek version. The unchallenged prestige and prominence of the Psalter among the books of the Hagiographa (cf. II Macc. 2:13; Philo, Cont., 25; Luke 24:44) would of itself have been a factor in its early translation into Greek. In addition, the known fact that this version was made in response to the needs of the synagogue worship makes it virtually certain that the Psalms were turned into the vernacular in Alexandria even before much of the Prophets. Ben Sira itself amply attests a knowledge of the Psalms and it may be taken for granted that his grandson, writing around 132 B.C.E., had in mind a Greek Psalter when he referred to the translation into that language of "the law, the prophecies, and the rest of the books." Since the Greek Book of Psalms is identical in order and number with the received Hebrew, the canonization of the corpus must have taken place well before the beginning of the second century B.C.E., by which date the Greek translation is now generally agreed to have existed. It is apparent, moreover, that the translators often encountered difficulty with the original language and were quite ignorant of the meaning of the Hebrew technical terminology which had become completely obsolete. This loss of the living tradition presupposes a considerable passage of time between the composition of the psalms and their rendition into Greek. It is significant that whereas Daniel 3:5ff. contains a list of characteristic musical instruments of the Hellenistic period, not one of these appears among the more than ten instruments referred to in the psalms.

All this, of course, precludes the possibility of any Maccabean psalms, influences, or historical references. In fact, the Hebrew Psalter is completely free of Greek linguistic influences and its theology is wholly devoid of Hellenistic concepts.

This conclusions fits in precisely with the evidence to be derived from various types of literature recovered from the Judean Desert. A second-century B.C.E. Psalter (4QPs[a]), although fragmentary, clearly demonstrates that at least Books I and II of the Hebrew Psalms collection had been fixed by Hasmonean times. In fact, the Psalter had gained such wide currency that it had generated an imitative literature in the form of psalms (or hymns) of thanksgiving (4QH) which are replete with the phraseology of the canonical Psalter. Nevertheless, linguistic, stylistic, structural, thematic, and theological differences between the two bodies of literature are so large as to leave no doubt of the far greater antiquity of the biblical Psalms. Moreover, the recovery of parts of the original Hebrew version of the Ben Sira from Qumran and Masada has clearly shown that the style of the Psalms belongs to a much earlier stratum of the language than that of an educated Jew of approximately 200 B.C.E.

As to historic allusions, explicit references to national events are to be found in but a handful of psalms, and with the exception of the Babylonian Exile (Ps. 126?, 137), no occurrence later than the period of the Judges is recalled (Ps. 78, 81, 83, 95, 105, 106, 135). Of the Judahite or Israelite kings, David alone is favored with a mention in the body of a psalm (Ps. 18:51; 89:4, 36, 50; 132:1, 11, 17). Otherwise, there are allusions to foreign invasions of Israel (cf. Ps. 2, 48, 74, 79, 83, 89), but no way of pinpointing the specific event nor any reason to assume a reference to post-Exilic developments exists. Similary, the picture of internal corruption and social injustice reflected in many of the psalms could as well mirror the same conditions inveighed against by the literary prophets as the state of affairs in Second Temple times.

Above all, it is in the realm of the religious ideas of the Psalter, or rather in the inexplicable omission of certain concepts, that a late date for the collection becomes highly dubious. There is no clear notion of eschatological judgment upon the wicked and no trace of the characteristic eschatological terminology such as "the end of days," "the day of the Lord," "in that day." The motif of national sinfulness is lacking, and the theme of the absolute supremacy of morality over the cult, which has no intrinsic worth without morality, does not find unambiguous expression. There are no prayers for the restoration of the Davidic line or for the ingathering of the exiles. Were the prophetic activities and teachings indeed the source of inspiration for the psalmist, and if he composed during the life of the Second Temple, then the absence of all these would be very strange, especially since they all appear as characteristically dominant features of the known literature of the period. There is an exception which proves the rule. The lateness of the Books IV and V of Psalms was stressed above; and near the very end of Book V it is found that Psalm 147, which, among other signs of lateness, borrows extensively from older psalms is also replete with echoes of Deutero-*Isaiah, including, at the beginning, praise of the Lord for rebuilding Jerusalem (cf. Isa. 44:28) and for healing the brokenhearted (cf. Isa. 57:15, 18; 61:1). But even when the other echoes from Deutero-Isaiah are added they fall far short of the extent to which Deutero-Isaiah and other prophets make use of various psalms, which are thereby proved to antedate them (see, e.g., Ginsburg, in bibl.).

Finally, the argument concerning the supposedly late

date of the highly individualistic and personal spirit that animates the religion of Psalms has increasingly lost its validity in the wake of the progressive discovery of a huge psalms' literature of the Ancient Near East. Most of it antedates by far the appearance of Israel on the scene of history, yet it exhibits exactly the same individualized and personal qualities as does the Hebrew Psalter.

ASCRIPTION TO DAVID

The Book of Psalms contains neither superscription nor colophon and nowhere in the Hebrew Bible is there any indication of its Davidic authorship. Seventy-three of 150 psalms are designated *le-David,* but the precise connotation of this term is uncertain. It could well have reflected a tradition of authorship ("by David"); it might equally have related to some tradition connecting the content with an event in the life of David ("concerning David;" cf. *la-Nevi'im* in Jer. 23:9 and the headings of Jer. 46:2; 48:1; 49:1,7,23,28). The existence of such exegesis is apparent in the superscriptions to Psalms 3, 7, 18, 34, 51, 52, 54, 56, 57, 59, 60, 63, and 142. That it was once more widespread is evident from the headings in the Greek version of Psalms 27, 71, 97, 143 and 144. However, such an interpretation of *le-David* might be of secondary origin and in any case does not of itself preclude an original understanding of the phrase as implying Davidic authorship of the individual psalms involved. Other possibilities include a dedication to David, a tune or style supposedly Davidic in origin, or a composition taken from the repertoire of a Davidic guild of singers.

If *le-David* indeed originally indicated authorship, then it is of interest that the form is unique to the psalms' literature (cf. Hab. 3:1) for the ascription of no other biblical book to a historic personality ever involves the use of the *lamed* formula (cf. Song, Proverbs). On the other hand, the Psalter is internally consistent in its employment of the same construction with other names such as the Korahites (Ps. 42, et al.), Asaph (Ps. 50, et al.), Solomon (Ps. 72), Heman (Ps. 88), Ethan (Ps. 89), and Moses (Ps. 90).

Whatever its original meaning, there cannot be any doubt that *le-David* was very early interpreted in the sense of authorship. This can be demonstrated by the heading of Psalm 18 which explicitly declares that David "addressed the words of this song to the Lord" (cf. the parallel in II Sam. 22:1 which lacks *le-David*). Another proof is provided by the editorial colophon to the second book of Psalms (72:20): "End of the prayers of David son of Jesse." Since 56 of the 73 occurrences of the formula appear in the first two books, it must be assumed that this remark is a sure indication of how that term was understood very early in the history of the development of the canon of Psalms.

In the course of time, the claim for Davidic composition was extended to the entire Psalter. II Maccabees 2:13 mentions "the writings of David," apparently in reference to the Book of Psalms. The Greek version extends the Davidic heading to psalms not so marked in the received Hebrew text (viz., 33, 43, 71, 91, 93–99, 104, 137). How the idea of Davidic authorship could be applied to the entire collection can now be illustrated by the epilogue of the large Qumran scroll ($11QPs^a$, 27:4–5, 9–10) which ascribes to David a library of 3,600 "psalms" *(tehillim)* and 450 "songs" *(shirim),* although its use of the Davidic superscription does not differ greatly from that of the standard Hebrew text. The first explicit claim to the Davidic origin of the entire Psalter is to be found in rabbinic literature which draws a comparison between the five books of Davidic psalms and the Pentateuch of Moses and was not perturbed by the incidence of other names in the headings (Mid. Ps. to 1:2; BB 14b, 15a; cf. Pes. 117a).

There can be no doubt that the association of David with psalmody rests upon very ancient traditions. The king had a reputation as a skillful player on the lyre in his early youth (I Sam. 16:16–23), an inventor of musical instruments (Amos 6:5; Neh. 12:36; I Chron. 23:5; II Chron. 29:26–27), as a composer of dirges (II Sam. 1:17; 3:33), and as a "sweet singer of Israel" (II Sam. 23:1; cf. 6:5). His role in the establishment of Jerusalem as the supreme, national, religious center (6:2–17; I Chron. 13:3–14; 15:1–16:2) is beyond dispute, and although the sources making David responsible for the organization of the guilds of Temple singers and musicians and for the institution of the liturgy are post-Exilic (Neh. 12:24; I Chron. 6:16 ff.; 16:4–7, 41–42; 25:1, 5; II Chron. 7:6; 8:14; 23:18; 29:26–27, 30), there is every reason to believe that they rest upon a solid kernel of historical fact.

TYPES OF PSALMS

The Psalter presents a picture of unusual variety and complexity in its literary typology. Any attempt, however, to effect a systematic generic classification based upon considerations of a commonality of theme, mood, occasion, and style is bound to be more an exercise in convenience than precision. The choice of categories will be influenced by subjective or exegetical factors; sometimes the lines between one class and another cannot be clearly drawn; sometimes a single psalm can be simultaneously subsumed under more than one heading; many psalms are a fusion of two or more types; many are susceptible of diverse interpretations; the tense system, for example, is still imperfectly understood and it is difficult at times to decide whether one is dealing with a prayerful description of present troubles or grateful enumeration of afflictions now happily over; lastly, external criteria might favor one arrangement, whereas a determination of the original life-setting *(Sitz im Leben)* of a psalm might disclose an unsuspected generic affinity with other compositions.

The leading genre is the hymn. Broadest in scope, it invades other groups as well and its preeminence helped provide the most popular title of the book (see discussion on title, above). In essence, it is a poem of praise celebrating the majesty, greatness and providence of God. Examples of such include Psalms 8, 19a, 29, 33, 65, 66, 92, 100, 104, 113, 114, 117, 135, and 145–150. Several psalms specifically extol God's royal role in the universe and so may be regarded as forming a special category within the hymn (Ps. 47, 93, 96–99). They are often referred to as "enthronement psalms." Another group (Ps. 46, 48, 76, 84, 87, 122) glorifies God's city, His holy mount in which He has placed His abode, and is thus designated "Zion Songs." Two psalms (19b, 119; cf. 1) acclaim God's Torah and laud its attributes and its beneficial effects on those who study and observe it.

About one third of the Psalter is given over to laments in which the speaker may be either the individual or the community. The latter type bewails situations of national oppression or misfortune (e. g., Ps. 44, 60, 74, 79, 80, 83, 89c, 94); the former comprises about 40 psalms in all and is distinguished by personal complaints of bodily or mental suffering which may frequently be accompanied by protestations of innocence and integrity and are usually coupled with a strong plea for divine help (Ps. 3, 5, 6, 7, 9–10, 13, 17, 22, 25–28, 31, 35, 36, 38, 39, 41, 42–43, 51, 52, 54–57, 59, 61, 63, 64, 69, 71, 77, 86, 88, 102, 120, 123, 130, 140–143). A distinctive feature of many of the laments is the expression by the worshiper of the absolute certainty that His prayers will be heard. These "psalms of confidence" may be both collective (e. g., Ps. 46, 125, 129) or individual in nature, the latter being more frequent (e. g., Ps. 4, 11, 16, 23, 27, 62, 91, 121).

Closely related to the hymn and the lament is the genre of thanksgiving psalms. Here, again, community songs are relatively rare (e. g., Ps. 66, 67, 118, 136). This may be due to the fact that many of the hymns may have had their origin in a national song of thanksgiving. Psalms in which the speaker is an individual are 9–10, 18, 30, 34, 40, 111, and 138. In Psalm 107 it is difficult to know whether the speaker is a single worshiper or the congregation as a whole. Similarly, in Psalm 144 the speaker employs both the singular and plural forms of address. Many psalms of thanksgiving also contain descriptions of the original misfortune which has now given way to new circumstances. They thus combine two or more types of psalmody into a cohesive union (e. g., 6, 13, 22, 28, 30, 31, 36, 41, 54, 55, 56, 61, 63, 64, 69, 71, 86, 94, 102, 130).

A class in itself is the "royal psalms" in which the center of attention is the anointed one of God, the earthly king of Israel. His relationship to God, his ideal qualities, the misfortunes that befall him, and the woes that afflict him may all be the themes of the song (Ps. 2, 18, 20, 21, 45, 72, 89, 110, 132, 144, cf. 28, 61, 63, 84). Psalms 44 and 101, which contain no direct reference to the reigning monarch but which appear to have been liturgies recited by him, probably belong within this same category.

One other major category is provided by those compositions which betray the influence of wisdom literature or which have a distinctly pedagogic function or character. They may be reflective or sententious (Ps. 1, 34, 36, 37, 49, 73, 78, 112, 127, 128, 133) or descriptive of the kind of conduct pleasing to God (Ps. 15, 24, 32, 40, 50). They may also be historical retrospects which either directly or inferentially project the lessons to be derived from the past and which are deemed to be relevant to the occasion of the psalm (Ps. 78, 81, 105, 106, 114).

PSALMS AND THE CULT

The religious act in pagan cults consisted of an inextricable combination of prayer and ritual, the one being the complement of the other. In contrast, the detailed and elaborate prescriptions of the Pentateuch's Priestly Code contain no reference to any recitations by the priest or the worshiper in the course of the performance of the daily and festival rituals. In the same way, none of the psalms provides any explicit information on the type of cultic priestly ceremony to which it might have been attached. This mutual silence is expressive of a significant departure of the Israelite cult from that of its contemporary world in that the spoken word, what was elsewhere the indispensable incantatory ingredient, was not an essential part of the cult of the First Temple. It also means that the origins of Israelite psalmody must lie in an independent creation of the religious spirit outside priestly circles.

This conclusion is supported by the Chronicler as well as by the Psalter itself. The former carefully and consistently differentiates the origin of the sacrificial system which he ascribes to Moses, from the institution of its musical-recitative accompaniment which is attributed to Davidic innovation (II Chron. 23:18; see section on ascription to David, above). The Psalter, significantly, never associates any psalm with the Aaronide priests. This fits in exactly with the non-priestly genealogies of the Temple singers in Chronicles and Ezra.

On the other hand, there is ample evidence to show that the verbal element did constitute an aspect of the worship of the pre-Exilic period. The priestly benediction (Num. 6:22–26) is one example, the cultic liturgy of the firstfruits offering (Deut. 26:1–11) is another. Hannah's personal prayer in the Sanctuary at Shiloh (I Sam. 1:10–13) could not have been exceptional. Solomon's Temple dedication address repeatedly refers to "prayer and supplication" (I Kings 8:28ff.), and Isaiah shows the Temple to have been, indeed, a place of a multitude of prayers (Isa. 1:15; cf. 56:7). Amos (5:23) makes it quite clear that song set to musical accompaniment was part of the cult at the temple at Beth-El. It is not regarded as illegitimate as such, and there is no reason to believe that it was unique to this place. Jeremiah describes the chanting of a well-known refrain during the bringing of the *todah* offering to the Jerusalem Temple (Jer. 33:11; cf. Ps. 100:1, 4–5; 107:1; 118:1, 29; 136:1ff.). The prophet of the late Babylonian Exile describes the Temple as "a house of prayer" (Isa. 56:7).

All this suggests a close and ancient connection between cult and liturgy even if the role of the latter was subordinate. In fact, without some association between the two it would be extremely difficult to account for the preservation and transmission of the individual compositions over long periods of time until they became gathered into collections and ultimately canonized as a corpus.

Two basic forces operated simultaneously in anchoring the psalms to the cult. First, most of them clearly answer to specific situations in the life of the individual or the community. The ability to categorize them according to a relatively few major and minor types (see above) and to recognize a recurrent use of a limited number of fixed patterns and conventional modes of expression strongly suggest standardized liturgies available for recitation, when the need arose, either at the central Temple or at the provincial shrines that existed throughout most of the period of the Monarchy. The great national festivals which were fundamental to the religious life of Israel would have been the natural occasions for the public recitation of many of the psalms.

Once a liturgical tradition is assumed within the Israelite cult, and it must be so assumed, then the analogy of Near Eastern temples can be drawn upon. In Egypt, Mesopotamia, Ugarit, and Canaan, guilds of singers and musicians connected with the temples enjoyed official status and were highly organized. There is good reason to believe that similar guilds existed in Israel, and there is ever-increasing evidence to support the view that the Davidic date for their establishment as claimed by the Chronicle may not be very wide of the mark (I Chron. 6, 15, 16, 25, 29; II Chron. 35:15).

Proof for the well-rooted and extensive tradition of music and psalmody in Israel in the period of the First Temple comes from several sources. King Hezekiah of Judah included male and female musicians among the tribute he paid to Sennacherib of Assyria (c. 701 B.C.E.; Annals of Sennacherib, 3:46–48; Pritchard, Texts, 288) and no less than 200 lay singers of both sexes were among those who returned from the Babylonian Exile with Zerubbabel (Ezra 2:65, 70), apart from the 148 Asaphites (Ezra 2:41; Neh. 7:44). The latter are connected with several psalms (Ps. 50, 73–83) and are said to have been appointed by David to be in charge of the service of the song in the Temple at Jerusalem (I Chron. 6:16, 24). At any rate, their presence in the list of returnees can prove that they had functioned as professional singers in the First Temple. Another guild of Temple servitors from the same period is called "the Korahites" (I Chron. 6:7, et al.) and their name, too, appears in the superscriptions of several psalms (Ps. 42, 44–49, 84–85, 87–88). Their existence as Temple functionaries, in the times of the late Monarchy at least, is now attested by the appearance of their name among the inscribed Hebrew ostraca discovered in the temple of Arad.

There can be no doubt of the involvement of musical guilds in the public worship of Israel in the days of the kings. Inevitably, each guild would develop its own liturgical repertoire and thus constitute another important factor in the presentation and transmission of Hebrew psalmody, rooted in the cult as it naturally was anyway.

THE TEXT

It is unlikely that the standard Hebrew text is free of the corruptions that inevitably beset all ancient literature in the course of scribal transmission. Hundreds of years elapsed between the editio princeps of a given psalm and its earliest witnesses, and while the special circumstances of its connection with the cult must certainly have reduced its susceptibility to gross error, it cannot be gainsaid that many of the textual cruxes owe their origin to the carelessness of intermediaries. At the same time, so long as no autograph is available there can be no way of knowing the extent, if any, of editorial activity behind the smoothest text. That such occurred is the inescapable conclusion from a comparison of Psalms doublets (Ps. 14=Ps. 53; Ps. 18=II Sam. 22; Ps. 31:2–4=Ps. 71:1–3; Ps. 40:14–18=Ps. 70; Ps. 57:8–12= Ps. 108:2–6; Ps. 60:7–14=Ps. 108:7–14).

On the other hand, there can also be no doubt that the consonantal text of Psalms has proved to be far more reliable than an earlier age of textual criticism had judged. Northwest Semitic inscriptions and comparative Near Eastern literature have opened up new vistas in the understanding of the biblical poetic idiom and in ancient Hebrew orthography, lexicography, grammar, and syntax. The result has been a considerable diminution in the number of instances previously deemed to be corruptions of the text.

This conclusion intermeshes with the observation that, unlike the case with some other biblical books, a comparison of the received Hebrew of Psalms with the Greek, Latin, Aramaic, and Syriac version shows that all known witnesses to the text basically constitute a single recension. This conclusion is, in turn, in perfect agreement with the evidence from the scrolls of the Judean Desert. About 30 exemplars in various stages of preservation have been uncovered in the library of Qumran, more copies than of any other part of the Scriptures. While numerous variations from the standard Hebrew text may be registered, the overwhelming number are merely orthographic in character and very rarely present significant differences in meaning or interpretation. In no instance can a recension different from that of the earlist Ben Asher manuscripts be detected. The text of the Massadah Scrolls is, in fact, virtually identical in content and orthography with the received Hebrew text.

It is clear that this latter enjoys a traceable history of over 2,000 years. Its great prestige and constancy must derive from its use in the liturgy of the Second Temple times, a powerfully conservative factor in the preservation of a text.

SUPERSCRIPTIONS AND TECHNICAL TERMS

Only 24 psalms have no headings of any sort. Psalms 1, 2, 10, 33, 43, 71, 93–97, 99, 104, 105, 107, 114–119, 136, and 137 may thus be termed "orphan psalms" (Av. Zar. 24b). In each instance, the LXX repairs the Hebrew deficiency, though in Psalms 105, 107, 114–119, and 135 the addition consists solely of an initial "Hallelujah." In all but Psalms 115 and 118 this term belongs in the Hebrew to the preceding composition.

The titles of the psalms are for the most part obscure. For the sake of convenience they may be classified as follows:

Those Containing Personal Names (with affixed lamed). Usually the preposition *le* must indicate either authorship or a collection identified with a guild. However, in Psalm 72 it must mean "about" or "dedicated to," and Psalm 102 *le-ʿani* can only mean, "for [recitation by] the afflicted man."

David. Seventy-three psalms are connected with the name David, distributed as follows:

Book I, 37 (3–9, 11–32, 34–41).
Book II, 18 (51–65, 68–70).
Book III, one (86).
Book IV, two (101, 103).
Book V, 15 (108–110, 122, 124, 131, 133, 138–145).

The LXX omits the Davidic reference in Psalms 122, 124, 131, and 133, but adds it to Psalms 33, 42 (G^A), 43, 67, 71, 91, 93–99, 104, and 137. It is of interest that 96, 105, 106, and 107 are connected with Davidic activity in I Chronicles 16, yet they do not have Davidic superscriptions in the Hebrew text.

A unique feature of the Davidic ascription is the tendency, found 13 times, to connect a psalm with some event in the life of that king: Psalms 3 (II Sam.15–19); 7 (? II Sam. 18:21), 18 (II Sam. 22), 34 (I Sam. 21:14), 51 (II Sam. 11–12), 52 (I Sam. 22:9), 54 (I Sam. 23:19; 26:1), 56 (? I Sam. 21:11; 27:2), 57 (I Sam. 22:1; 24:3), 59 (I Sam. 19:11), 60 (II Sam. 8:13; I Chron. 18:1–12), 63 (I Sam. 23:14; 24:1; 26:2), 142 (I Sam. 22:1; 24:3). Here, again, the LXX extends this practice by connecting Psalms 27, 71, 97, 143, and 144 with David's biography, but apart from 144 (cf. I Sam. 17) the references are indeterminate.

It should be noted that in some instances the connection between the Hebrew superscription and the body of the psalm is very tenuous. It is possible that the reference may often be to some tradition rooted in a biography of David not included in the biblical narratives and now lost.

Asaph. Twelve psalms are associated with Asaph (50, 73–83). If the reference is to Asaph rather than to the Asaphites (Ezra 2:41; 3:10, et al.) it is probably because he was a contemporary of David, appointed by him to a prominent position in the leadership of the Temple (Neh. 12:46; I Chron. 6:24; 15:19, et al.).

The Korahites. There are 11 Korahite psalms (42, 44–49, 84–85, 87–88). The Korahites (cf. Num. 26:11) are first recorded as participating in the public worship of the Temple in the time of Jehoshaphat (II Chron. 20:19). They are not listed among the returnees from Babylon (Ezra 2; Neh. 7), so that they operated only during the First Temple period. The appearance of the Korahites among the ostraca of Arad confirms the existence of the guild in the Monarchy period.

Heman, Ethan. Only one psalm each is assigned to Heman and Ethan (Ps. 88, 89). Both are entitled "Ezrahite" (LXX, "Israelite"). They are both leaders of the Temple musicians under David (I Chron. 2:6; 6:18, et al.). Both names are otherwise mentioned as personages famous for their wisdom (I Kings 5:11). Psalm 88 is also ascribed to the Korahites, indicating a double tradition.

Solomon. It appears that in the case of Psalm 72 the reference to Solomon is to the content rather than the authorship and was so understood by the Greek translators. In Psalm 127 the presence of "Solomon" in the title (omitted in LXX) was conditioned by the mention of "the building of the house."

Moses. The attribution to Moses in Psalm 90 is probably based on the affinities between verse 1 and Deuteronomy 33:27, verse 10 and Exodus 7:7, and verse 13 and Exodus 32:12.

Jeduthun. At first sight Psalms 39, 62, and 77 appear to be ascribed to Jeduthun who was a levitical singer in David's time (I Chron. 16:38, 41, 42; 25:1, 3, 6; II Chron. 5:12). However, not only are the first two also attributed to David and the third to Asaph, implying a combination of variant traditions, but the preposition *ʿal* (62–77) is difficult to reconcile with a personal name. It is possible, therefore, that a musical instrument is intended.

Another interpretation connects the term with the verb *ydh*, "to confess," and presumes some confession liturgy or ritual.

Eight names are listed, at most, to which the Septuagint adds "Zechariah" in Psalm 137 and "Haggai and Zechariah" in Psalms 146, 147:1, 147:12, and 148.

Titles with Liturgical Application. The heading of Psalm 30 mentions "the dedication of the Temple" which must be an allusion to the occasion of its public recitation. The identification of the reference, however, is not clear (cf. Sof. 18:2). Psalm 100 implies a liturgy for the *todah* offering (cf. Jer. 33:11). Psalm 92 indicates a Sabbath reading. The Greek Psalter further reflects liturgical traditions by affixing additional superscriptions indicating that Psalms 24, 48, 94, and 93 were read, respectively, on the first, second, fourth, and sixth days of the week (cf. Tam. 7:4; RH 31a). It also, strangely, designates Psalm 38 "for the Sabbath" and appends to Psalm 29 the notice, "on the going forth of the Tabernacle," perhaps a reference to a custom of reading this hymn on the last day of the Feast of Tabernacles. However, the rubric may also allude to a tradition connecting Psalm 29 with David's bringing of the ark to Jerusalem, since the verses supposedly sung on that occasion (I Chron. 16:28–29) betray a close affinity with verses 1–2. Another possibility in explanation of the Greek annotation may be that the original Hebrew rubric containing the term *ʿaẓeret* was mistakenly identified with the eighth day of Tabernacles (cf. Lev. 23:36), whereas it is the rabbinic term for Pentecost. Indeed, the reading of Psalm 29 on this festival is attested (Sof. 18:3).

The Greek rubric to Psalm 96, "when the house was built after the captivity," would imply some tradition not otherwise known. Totally obscure is the Septuagint annotation to Psalm 97, "when the land was established.

Technical Terms in the Headings. The superscriptions are remarkably rich in the number and variety of technical terms, most of which are shrouded in obscurity. Their meanings were already lost in early times for the Greek translators were generally ignorant of them, even in the days of the Second Temple, and rabbinic literature and medieval commentators present an assortment of interpretations. The explanation for this severance of tradition may lie, at least partially, in the fact that the terminology was rooted in the technical jargon of the different guilds of singers and musicians who jealously guarded their professional secrets until they, themselves, went out of existence (cf. Yoma 3:11).

Mizmor (Heb. מִזְמוֹר). The term *mizmor* appears exclusively in the Book of Psalms, always as a title and never in the body of a psalm. It is never attached to those psalms found elsewhere in biblical literature. With a single exception (Ps. 98:1, but LXX adds "of David") it is always used in conjunction with a proper name preceded by *lamed.* Why it is restricted to 57 psalms cannot be known. It was translated *psalmos* by the Septuagint and by Theodotion and so came down in English as "psalm" lending its name to the entire book (see discussion on title, above). The verbal form appears outside Psalms only in Judges 5:3, II Samuel 22:50 (=Ps. 18:50), Isaiah 12:5, and I Chronicles 16:9 (=Ps. 105:2) and always in a liturgical context (cf. Isa. 51:3). It appears 44 times alone, 13 times together with *shir,* and also frequently in parallelism with that term (cf. Ps. 21:14; 27:6; 57:8; 68:5, 33; 104:33; 108:2; Judg. 5:3; Amos 5:23). It is also used in connection with the lyre (Ps. 71:22; 98:5; 147:7; 149:3), the harp (33:2; 144:9; cf. Amos 5:23), and the timbrel (81:3; 149:3). There can be no doubt that *mizmor* refers to liturgical music.

La-Menaẓẓe'aḥ (לַמְנַצֵּחַ). The title *la-menaẓẓe'aḥ* occurs in 55 psalms invariably in the initial position. Outside the book it appears only in Habakkuk 3:19, also a liturgy. Its absence from II Samuel 22 and its presence in Psalm 18 shows that it has to do with the liturgical performance. Medieval Jewish commentators generally point to the verbal usage in the sense of overseeing labor (Ezra 3:8, 9; I Chron. 23:4; II Chron. 2:1, 17; 34:13) and so understand the term to mean "director, overseer, choirmaster" or the like. Its connection with music is established by I Chronicles 15:21 and II Chronicles 34:12. However, the Septuagint took it to mean "eternity" (cf. Heb. *la-neẓaḥ*), the other Greek versions and Jerome connecting it with victory (cf. Heb. *niẓẓaḥon*). The Targum understood it to mean "to praise."

Shir (שִׁיר). Thirty psalms are entitled *shir.* The feminine *shirah* appears but once (Ps. 18:1; cf. Ex. 15:1; Num. 21:17; Deut. 31:19, et al.). *Shir* is not restricted to psalms and may be used of secular as well as religious songs (cf. Isa. 23:16). However, the invocation "sing ye!" *(shiru)* is exclusively liturgical. The term *shir,* unlike *mizmor,* may also appear in the body of the psalm itself (Ps. 18:1; 28:7; 33:3, et al.). Only in Psalm 46 is it found alone. In five instances it is followed by *mizmor* (Ps. 48, 66, 83, 88, 108) and in seven (or eight) others the order is reversed (30?, 65, 67, 68, 75, 76, 87, 92). The significance of the sequence is unknown. The emphasis in its use would be on the words set to a rhythm since the Hebrew uses the phrase "to speak a song" (Judg. 5:12; cf. 11QPs[a] 27:9, 11), but whether it indicates a special mode of presentation is a matter of conjecture.

Shir ha-Maʿalot (שִׁיר הַמַּעֲלוֹת). *Shir ha-Maʿalot* appears at the head of a cluster of 15 psalms (Ps. 120–134; Ps. 121 *la-ma ʿalot*). LXX and Jerome translate it "degrees" (cf. II Kings 20:9–11), but what was understood by that is not clear. Some assume a reference to some peculiar gradational style of musical execution. The rendering "ascents" assumes a connection with the return from Babylon (cf. Ezra 7:9), but only Psalm 126 would be suitable to such a context for in Psalms 122 and 134 the Temple is still standing. Similarly, only Psalm 122 would be appropriate to a "pilgrim psalm" interpretation which would better fit other psalms (e.g., 15, 24, 43, 84) not so designated. The Mishnah appears to understand *maʿalot* as "steps" (cf. Ex. 20:26 [23]; I Kings 10:19, 20) and to find a connection with the 15 steps joining the court of the Israelites to the court of women in the Second Temple on which the levitical musicians used to stand during the ceremony of the "drawing of water" on Sukkot (Suk. 5:4; Mid. 2:5). These psalms may also have derived their designation from their use in some festal procession.

Maskil (מַשְׂכִּיל). Featured in the headings to 13 psalms, *maskil* never appears without a proper name with a prepositional *lamed* (Ps. 32, 42, 44, 45, 52–55, 74, 78, 88, 89, 142). The LXX understood it to mean "instruction" (cf. Ps. 32:8). It must be assumed to refer to some special skill required in the manner of musical performance (cf. Ps. 47:8). From the context of Amos 5:13 and the contrast between the *maskil* and the mourning rites (5:16–17), the term might well indicate some type of song.

Neginot (נְגִינ(וֹ)ת). The term *neginot* appears six times (Ps. 4, 6, 54, 55, 67, 76) preceded by *la-menaẓẓe'aḥ* and with the preposition *be-* (cf. Hab. 3:19), and once in the singular preceded by *ʿal* (Ps. 61). From I Samuel 16:16, 23 it would clearly seem to indicate stringed instruments (cf. Ps. 68:33; Isa. 23:16; Ezek. 33:32).

Mikhtam (מִכְתָּם). All six appearances of the term *mikhtam* are attached to *le-David* (Ps. 16, 56–60). LXX and Theodotion rendered it *stēlographia* which most likely represents its original meaning as "an inscription upon a slab." It is probably interchangeable with the title *mikhtav* in Hezekiah's thanksgiving psalm (Isa. 38:9). Some connect the word with an Akkadian root meaning "to cover" and assume a connection with some purificatory or atonement rite.

Tefillah (תְּפִלָּה). Despite the epilogue to the second book of Psalms (72:20) which speaks of "the prayers *[tefillot]* of David" and the more than a score of appearances in the body of the psalms, the term *tefillah* is found only in the superscriptions to five psalms (17, 86, 90, 102, 142) and to Habakkuk 3.

ʿAl Shoshannim (עַל־שֹׁשַׁנִּים), *Al Shushan ʿEdut* (עַל־שׁוּשַׁן עֵדוּת), *ʾEl Shoshannim ʿEdut* (אֶל־שֹׁשַׁנִּים עֵדוּת). *ʿal-Shoshannim* may be translated "On the lilies" (Ps. 45, 69), *ʿal shushan ʿedut* "On the lily of testimony" (Ps. 60), and *ʾel-shoshannim ʿedut* "To the lilies of testimony" (Ps. 80). They may be cue-words, i.e., the incipits or titles of some well-known songs to the tune of which the psalm was sung. The reference may also be to a six-stringed or six-bell instrument shaped like the lily.

ʾAl Tashḥet (אַל־תַּשְׁחֵת). Found in the headings of Psalms 57–59, *ʾal-tashḥet* means "do not destroy" and may be an incipit, perhaps of some old vintage song (cf. Isa. 65:8). Since it is accompanied by *mikhtam* (see above) in three of its four occurrences, it has been suggested that it may be an adjuration against altering or destroying inscriptions.

ʿAl ha-Gittit (עַל הַגִּתִּית). The ancient versions generally connect the term *ʿal-ha-gittit* in Psalms 8, 81, 84 with the winepress *(gat).* It may indicate a tune sung by the grape treaders (cf. Isa. 16:10; Jer. 25:30), or it may be a musical instrument derived from the Philistine city of Gath (so Targum).

ʿAl ha-Sheminit (עַל־הַשְּׁמִינִית). Meaning literally, "on the eighth," *ʿal-ha-sheminit* may refer to an eight-stringed instrument in Psalm 6, 12 (cf. Ar. 13b; Tosef., Ar. 2:7). It cannot mean an octave as the division into eight modes was unknown. The reference in I Chronicles 15:21, "with lyres on the *sheminit*" in parallel with verse 20, "with harps on *ʿalamot*" (see below) has suggested a quality of the voice, perhaps a low bass.

Lehazkir (לְהַזְכִּיר). The appearance of the term *lehazkir* in I Chronicles 16:4 in a context of public worship strongly suggests a liturgical or cultic meaning in the headings of Psalms 38, 70. However, the precise circumstances cannot be determined for the verb is elsewhere used of invoking the divine name (cf. Ex. 20:21; Isa. 26:13; 48:1; 62:6; Amos 6:10; Ps. 20:8), of recalling sinfulness (cf. Gen. 41:9; Num. 5:15; I Kings 17:18; Ezek. 21:28, 29; 29:16), and in connection with the meal offering or incense burning (cf. Lev. 2:2; 24:7; Num. 5:15, 26; Isa. 66:3).

ʿAl Maḥalat (עַל־מָחֲלַת). If *ʿal-maḥalat* is not a cue-word identifying the tune to which Psalms 53, 88 were to be sung, it may indicate a wind instrument (cf. I Kings 1:40, et al.) or some choreographic direction (cf. Judg. 21:23, et al.). It might also be translated, "for sickness" (cf. I Kings 8:37) and imply some accompanying ritual.

ʿAl ʿAlamot (עַל־עֲלָמוֹת). The term *ʿal-ʿalamot* is found as a heading only once (Ps. 46). However, another occurrence of *ʿal-ʿalamot* may be the obscure *ʿal-mut* in our received Hebrew text of Psalm 48:15, which might belong to the next psalm, as well as in the title of Psalm 9 (see below *ʿal-mut la-ben*). Its connection with public worship is attested by I Chronicles 15:20. It could refer to a musical instrument such as a small flute or pipe (cf. Greek Ἔλυμος) or express a quality of the voice, i. e., "youthful" (cf. *ʿalmah,* "a maiden"), perhaps high pitched or soprano.

ʿAl Mut la-Ben (עַל־מוּת לַבֵּן). *ʿAl-mut la-ben* could either mean "male soprano" or be a cue-word in its single appearance (Ps. 9).

ʾEl ha-Neḥilot (אֶל־הַנְּחִילוֹת). Either a wind instrument (cf. *ʿal-maḥalat* above) or a cue-word could be intended by *ʾel ha-neḥilot* in Psalm 5. The variant *ʾel* for the frequent *ʿal* cannot be explained.

ʿAl ʾAyyelet ha-Shaḥar (עַל־אַיֶּלֶת הַשַּׁחַר). *ʿAl ʾayyelet ha-shaḥar* is almost certainly a cue-word, the psalm (22) being set to the tune of a well-known song entitled, "On the hind of the morning."

ʿAl Yonat ʾElem Reḥoqim (עַל־יוֹנַת אֵלֶם רְחֹקִים). *ʿAl yonat ʾelem reḥoqim* too (Ps. 56) must be a cue-word that may be translated, "On the speechless dove far-off," or, "On the dove of the far-off terebinths *[ʾelim].*" The Septuagint seems to have understood "dove" as an epithet for the people of Israel and have read *ʾelim,* meaning "gods" or "holy beings."

Shir Yedidot (שִׁיר יְדִידֹת). The title *shir yedidot,* "a love song," is appropriate to the occasion of Psalm 45 which celebrates the marriage of an Israelite king to a Tyrian princess.

Lelammed (לְלַמֵּד). *Lelammed* means literally "to teach." Its use in Psalm 60 is reminiscent of the similar introductions to songs in Deuteronomy 31:19 and II Samuel 1:18.

Leʿannot (לְעַנּוֹת). The meaning "to afflict" indeed connects with the theme of Psalm 88. *Leʿannot* might refer to some ritual of penance (cf. Lev. 23:27, 29). It could also be an intensive form of the verb *ʿanah* ("to chant"; cf. Ex. 15:21; 32:18), and might indicate some antiphonal arrangement in the performance of the psalm.

Shiggayon (שִׁגָּיוֹן). *Shiggayon* (Ps. 7) also appears in the plural form in the heading to Habakkuk 3. On the basis of the Akkadian *šegu,* "to howl, lament," it has been understood as meaning a psalm of lamentation.

Tehillah (תְּהִלָּה). The term *tehillah,* which gave the book its most popular Hebrew title, occurs only in Psalm 145 (see discussion on title, above).

Hallelujah (הַלְלוּיָהּ). Ten psalms begin with the term Hallelujah (106, 111–113, 135, 146–150) which is not strictly a title but an invocation (see *Hallelujah).

Technical Terms Within the Psalms. Two terms appear within the body of the psalms themselves.

Selah (סֶלָה). The term *selah* occurs 71 times in 39 psalms mainly in the "elohistic" psalms, and three times in Habakkuk 3 (verses 3, 9, 13). In 31 of these psalms *la-menazzeʾaḥ* also appears, as it does in Habbakkuk 3. It is never to be found at the beginning of a verse, but occasionally comes in the middle (Ps. 55:20; 57:4; cf. Hab. 3:3, 9). Otherwise, its position is at the end of the verse and four times even at the end of the entire psalm (Ps. 3, 9, 24, 46). It may appear more than once in the same psalm (Ps. 3, 32, 46, 66, 68, 77, 89, 140). The LXX adds *selah* also at Psalms 34:11; 39:8; 50:15; 80:8; 94:15.

There is no agreement among the ancient versions and medieval Jewish commentators as to its meaning and function. There is no certainty that its current position in a psalm is always original and not sometimes the work of a later scribe or editor. The etymology is obscure and even the masoretic vocalization seems to be secondary.

The Septuagint, Theodotion (usually), and Symmachus all translated *selah* as διάψαλμα. However, the meaning of the Greek is as enigmatic as the Hebrew, and the usual rendering "interlude" is not at all sure. The Targum, Aquila, and Jerome all understood it as part of the text of the preceding verse in which it appears and rendered it as "always," or "for eternity." The present vocalization of the Hebrew word seems to reflect this tradition for it is the same as that of the usual word for eternity *(neẓaḥ),* and the accentuation connects the term with the preceding. The same interpretation is to be found in the Talmud (Er. 54a), and in the employment of *selah* in the Hebrew prayer book. It also finds support in the comments of Saadiah, Jonah ibn Janaḥ, and Rashi.

A different explanation is given by Kimḥi *(Sefer Shorashim)* who connects it with the use of the Hebrew root *sll* in the sense of raising up (cf. Isa. 57:14; Ps. 68:5). The term would then be an instruction for the singers or musicians. Abraham ibn Ezra (to Ps. 3:3) believes it to be a liturgical response on the part of the worshipers, affirming the truth of the sentiments previously stated in the psalm.

Some scholars have suggested a derivation from *sal* ("basket"), concluding that at certain points in the service a basket-shaped drum was beaten. Others believe the term to be an acrostic. No solution to the enigma of *selah* is possible in the present state of our knowledge.

Higgayon (הִגָּיוֹן). The term *higgayon* appears together with *selah* in Psalm 9:17 and with a musical instrument in Psalm 92:4. It is found as part of the text in Psalm 19:15 where it implies "utterance," or "musings." The basic root meaning seems to be "to make a sound" (cf. Isa. 16:7; 31:4; 39:14). *Higgayon* may therefore be an instruction to the musicians to produce a murmuring glissando or a flourish. [N.M.S.]

IN THE TALMUD AND MIDRASH

The rabbis reduced the traditional number of psalms to 147 (Mid. Ps. 22:19; 104:2) merely for homiletical purposes as is evident from the passage in *Berakhot* 9b–10a. The Talmud explains that Psalm 19:15 was instituted to be recited after the 18 benedictions of the **Amidah* since it comes at the end of the 18th Psalm. Whereupon the Talmud asks, "But this is the 19th Psalm, not the 18th," and answers that Psalms 1 and 2 constitute one psalm. It brings evidence for this in the statement that David first uses the word Hallelujah at the end of the 103rd Psalm, where in fact it is in Psalm 104:35. It is therefore evident that at that time Psalms 1 and 2 normally constituted two psalms, and Psalms 19 and 104 were numbered as they are today. That homiletical purpose seems clear. It is reflected in the statement "Moses gave the five books of the Torah to Israel, and corresponding to them, David gave the five books of the Psalms to Israel" (Mid. Ps. 1:2). In order to emphasize this relationship, the number of psalms was reduced to 147, probably in order to make it correspond to the number of *sedarim* in the Bible according to the triennial cycle current in Ereẓ Israel. The other two cases of two psalms which were combined in one were probably 114 and 115 (see Kimḥi in loc.) and 117 and 118 (see Buber in Mid. Ps. 22 note 88).

The Book of Psalms includes the compositions of ten earlier authorities, Adam, Melchizedek, Abraham, Moses, Heman, Jeduthun, Asaph, and the three sons of Korah (BB 14b, 15a, variants are given in Eccles. R. 7:19.4). Nevertheless the Book of Psalms was called after David because "his voice was pleasant" (Songs R. 4:4 no. 1 referring to II Sam. 23:1). All the psalms were inspired (Pes. 117a) and music helped to bring the inspiration: "A harp was suspended above the bed of David. When midnight came the north wind blew on it and it produced music of its own accord. Immediately David arose and occupied himself with Torah." That "Torah" consisted of songs and praises, however, since "until midnight he occupied himself with Torah; and from then with songs and praises" (Ber. 3b). The psalms are both individual and general; those in the singular are personal, those in the plural are of general application (Pes. 117a).

Various psalms and groups of psalms are singled out for special mention in the Talmud. They are the **Hallel,* Psalms 113–118, the only psalms which formed part of the liturgy in talmudic times (see below; Psalms in Liturgy) and also known as the "Egyptian *Hallel*" (Ber. 56a), to distinguish it from Psalms 145–150 and Psalm 136 which are also variously referred to as *Hallel* (Shab. 118b), or, the latter, *Hallel ha-Gadol* (Pes. 118a); the seven psalms which were "the psalms which the levites used to recite in the Temple" (Tam. 7:4) and which have been included in the liturgy; and the Fifteen Songs of Degrees 120–134 *(shir ha-maʿalot).* Such importance was attached to the alphabetical Psalm 145, that it was stated that "he who recites it three times a day is certain to be vouchsafed the world to come" (Ber. 4b). Psalm 16 compresses into 11 principles the whole of the Torah (Mak. 24a). The *Tamnei Appei* (lit. "eight faces"), i.e., Psalm 119, the eightfold alphabetical acrostic psalm which in later ages is given a special importance (see below), is only mentioned en passant *(ibid).*

The almost complete neglect of the psalms in the liturgy during talmudic times may give a wrong impression of the enormous importance with which the psalms were invested by the rabbis. A suggestion has been made that in some places there was a triennial cycle of the reading of psalms, corresponding to the triennial cycle of the reading of the Pentateuch, which would explain, *inter alia,* the comparison made between the Five Books of Moses and the Five Books of Psalms, and the equalization of the number of psalms with the pericopes of the Pentateuch. It was, however, in their homilies and preaching that the psalms were most heavily relied upon. The Midrash states that Ben Azzai "strung together [as a row of pearls] the words of the Pentateuch with those of the prophets, and of the prophets with the Hagiographa, and words of Torah rejoiced as on the day they were given at Sinai" (Lev. R. 16:4). Although it refers to the Hagiographa in general, there is no doubt but that Psalms was the favorite book of that section of the Bible employed. This method of "stringing together" the verses of Psalms with those of the Pentateuch is reflected in the proems to the classical Midrashim (see *Midrash), the overwhelming majority of which are expositons of verses of the psalms which are linked with the pentateuchal verse under discussion. As a result, even disregarding **Midrash Tehillim (Midrash Psalms),* which is a running commentary on the whole Book of Psalms, and which in any case is largely a compilation based on earlier material, there is not a single chapter of Psalms and hardly a single verse which is not expounded in the Talmud and Midrash (cf. A. Lavat, *Beit Aharon ve-Hosafot,* 1881).

IN THE LITURGY

The penetration of the psalms into the liturgy represents a gradual process extending over the centuries, the effect of which can be seen in the fact that whereas in the talmudic period the statutory prayers included no psalms whatsoever on Sabbaths and weekdays, and the only psalms recited were the *Hallel* on the three Pilgrim Festivals and Ḥanukkah, and later, despite a specific rubric to the contrary (Arukh 10a), on the *New Moon, the authorized Daily Prayer Book of the United Hebrew Congregation of England (Singer) gives an index of 73 psalms and part of another included in the various services. In part, at least, this inclusion of the psalms into the liturgy came as a result of popular demand. Of the Daily Psalm, for instance, there is the statement that "the people have adopted the custom of including it" (Sof. 18:1) and with regard to the choice of Psalm 136 as the psalm for the Passover "the people have adopted the custom of reciting this psalm, though it is not the best choice" (*ibid.,* 18:2).

Statutory Prayers. The process whereby the recitation of psalms became an integral part of the statutory prayers consisted of regarding every reference to the recitation of psalms in the Talmud, either as acts of special piety performed by individuals, or as part of the Temple service, as a justification for making them part of the statutory service. To this class belong the **Pesukei de-Zimra* and the Daily Psalm. The *Pesukei de-Zimra* consisted originally only of the six last psalms, the Hallelujah Psalms 145–50. The process of inclusion is clearly seen in the fact that whereas their recitation is mentioned in the Talmud by R. Yose as an act of especial piety (Shab. 118b; and it is the later authorities who decide that the *Hallel* to which he refers are those psalms), in the post-talmudic tractate **Soferim,* they are called simply "the six daily psalms" which are already part of the statutory service (Sof. 17:11). Both these passages, however, confine the *Pesukei de-Zimra* to those six psalms. On the principle, however, that there was more leisure on Sabbaths and festivals, both the Ashkenazi and Sephardi rites add a considerable number on those days: the former adds nine (19, 34, 90, 91, 135, 136, 33, 92 and 93) and the Sephardi 14 (103, 19, 33, 90, 91, 98, 121–124, 135, 136, 92, 93; some rites include the first two in the weekday service).

The same process is seen with regard to the Daily Psalm. They are mentioned in the Midrash as "the psalms which the levites used to sing in the Temple" (Tam. 7:4). By the time of *Soferim* they are already part of the daily prayers, "the people having adopted the custom" (18:1). However, here again, once the transfer was made to the synagogue, it was extended to special psalms for every festival (for the text see *Soferim* 18 and 19 and for a variant, Baer, *Avodat Yisrael,* last unnumbered page). In the course of time a large number of individual psalms were added: Psalm 30 before the *Pesukei de-Zimra,* Psalm 100 on weekdays in the *Pesukei de-Zimra,* Psalm 6 in the supplicatory prayers, Psalm 24 on weekdays when the *Sefer Torah* is returned to the ark, and 29 on Sabbaths and festivals. Psalm 20 was included in the last portion of the daily service. Some rites have psalms added to the evening service parallel to the Daily Psalm in the morning (see Singer 133–40). Psalm 27 was instituted for the penitential period from the second day of Elul to *Hoshana Rabba, 144 and 67 for the Service of the Termination of the Sabbath, etc.

Two groups of psalms have to be mentioned: Psalms 104 and the Fifteen Songs of Degrees, included in the Sabbath afternoon sevice during the winter months, instituted in the 12th century, and the latest addition of all, which spread with remarkable rapidity, Psalms 95–99 and 20, for the Inauguration of the Sabbath. Instituted by the kabbalists of Safed in the 16th century—although the author of the liturgical work *Matteh Moshe* published in 1615 makes no mention of it, and fifteen years later the author of *Yosef Omeẓ,* while praising it as "a good and beautiful custom," refers to it as "a new one, lately come up"—it has become standard in all Ashkenazi services (most Sephardi rites confine themselves to 29). This list, however, though incomplete, does not exhaust the inclusion of Psalms in the statutory service. Some of the prayers consist merely of a mosaic of single verses from Psalms of which the most notable are two passages which precede the Psalms of the *Pesukei de-Zimra,* called by their opening words *Romemu* and *Yehi Khevod.* Both consist entirely of verses from Psalms (except for one verse from Prov. 19:21 and one composite verse *(Adonai Melekh)* consisting of three parts, two of which are from Psalms) and of verse selected from the five books into which Psalms is divided. Only the second book has no verse in the *Yehi Khevod,* but the Yemenite rite adds Psalm 46:12 from this book, and this is probably the original version, already mentioned in *Soferim* (17:11). It would appear that this selection is deliberate. In all, no less than 250 individual verses from Psalms are thus added to the liturgy (A. Berliner, *Randbemerkungen,* p. 9).

Non-Statutory Prayers. It can safely be said that there is no special or non-statutory service which does not include one or more psalms. They include the introduction to the grace after meals, prayers for drought (Baer, appendix, p. 87), before going on a journey, the night prayer before retiring to rest, prayers for and by the sick, the burial service, the prayer in the house of mourning, the memorial service for the dead, and the service at the consecration of a tombstone which, apart from the memorial prayer, consists of a selection of psalms. The custom has been followed in all forms of service added in recent years, of which Singer includes service on the occasion of making collections for hospitals, of thanksgiving of a woman after childbirth, and on the consecration of a house. They are naturally included in the prayers for Independence Day. Custom has developed, under the influence of the Kabbalah, especially in Israel, with regard to Psalm 119, the eightfold alphabetical psalm. At memorial services the verses are recited which make up the name of the deceased and his father, with the addition of the verses the letters of which form the word *neshamah* ("soul").

Various. The regular reading of Psalms was not confined to services. The recital of the whole Book of Psalms is widespread, whether as an act of piety by saintly individuals, or by groups of unlearned people. For this purpose "societies of reciters of psalms" *(ḥevrot tehillim)* were formed, and in recent times a special society has been formed in Jerusalem whereby two separate groups recite the whole Book of Psalms daily at the Western Wall. The psalms are included in their entirety in all large prayer books. A prayer has been composed to be recited prior to and at the conclusion of each of the five books as well as for its reading on Hoshana Rabba which specifically equates them with the Five Books of Moses (Baer, Introduction to Psalms in *Avodat Yisrael,* pp. 5–8). Baer concludes with a list of psalms which it is customary to recite on Sabbath to correspond with the weekly portion "in the manner of the *haftarah,*" thus "stringing together" Pentateuch, Prophets, and Psalms (last page, unnumbered). [L.I.R.]

IN THE ARTS

In Literature. From the early Middle Ages the Book of Psalms has had an incalculable influence on literature, art, and music. Its impact has, perhaps, been greatest on writers. J. G. *Herder stated that "it is worth studying the Hebrew language for ten years in order to read Psalm 104 in the original" and Israel *Zangwill even claimed that the psalms "are more popular in every country than the poems of the nation's own poets. Besides this one book with its infinite editions... all other literatures seem 'trifles light as air'..." (1895). Literary treatment of Psalms has taken several forms: translation and paraphrase in verse and prose, imitation, and the composition of hymns and epics inspired by the themes and style of the original. Many of the first European translations of Psalms possess considerable literary merit and importance and some helped to mold the languages in which the sense of the Hebrew was conveyed. Among the earliest known are the versions in Anglo-Saxon (eighth century), Old Church Slavonic (ninth century), and Old High German (tenth century). During the 13th–15th centuries many more versions of the Psalter appeared in lands throughout Europe; and translations of Psalms were among the first books printed in some countries, notable examples being Jacques Lefèvre d'Etaples' French Psalter (1509), Jan Kochanowski's *Psałterz Dawidów* (1578) and Maciej Rybiński's *Psalmy monarchy i proroka świątego Dawida* (1598) in Poland, and the Psalter of the Brasov friar Coresi (1578–80) in Rumania. Together with other portions of the Old Testament, the Psalms were translated from the Hebrew by 15th-century Judaizing sects in Russia, and a version in Yiddish was published in Venice by the pioneer Hebrew grammarian and author Elijah *Levita (1545).

From the early 16th century the Psalms inspired the highest degree of literary creativity in England and France. Thomas Sternhold headed a team of scholars who published *The Whole Booke of Psalmes; collected into Englysh metre... conferred with the Ebrue...* (London, 1551[2], 1562), which ran to literally hundreds of editions during the 16th-18th centuries; and this version was first used for the Church of Scotland's metrical *Psalms of David* (Edinburgh, 1650), which has remained one of the standard collections for Protestants throughout the English-speaking world. Another verse translation of the 16th century was that by Sir Philip Sidney and his sister, Mary Herbert, Countess of Pembroke, whose *Psalmes of David* was, however, only published in 1823. The pioneering French translation was that prepared by the poet Clément Marot (later in collaboration with the Geneva Reformer Théodore de Bèze): *Trente Pseaulmes de David mis en francoys* (1541) and *Cinquante Pseaulmes de David* (1543), which ran to dozens of editions from 1560 onward. Marot's version, with its "sober, solemn music," became an integral part of the French Protestant liturgy and enjoyed an extraordinary vogue, not only at the Protestant court of Navarre but even at the Catholic French court, where it was officially banned by the Sorbonne. French writers who paraphrased or reinterpreted the Book of Psalms include Agrippa d'Aubigné, Jean Antoine de Baïf, Jean Bertaut, Honorat de Bueil, Jean de la Ceppède, Jean Baptiste Chassignet, Philippe Desportes, Guy *Le Fèvre de la Boderie (whose works include many verse paraphrases from the Hebrew), and François de Malherbe.

During the 17th century, too, the Psalms retained their fascination for many writers. They inspired German hymns by Paul Gebhardt; the so-called *Teitsch-Hallel,* a Yiddish compositon based, at least in part, on contemporary Protestant hymnology; and the first important work printed in New England, the *Bay Psalm Book* (Cambridge, 1640), a metrical (and highly literal) translation from the Hebrew for those who wished to "sing in Sion the Lord's songs of prayse according to his own wille." In the 18th century a Spanish verse paraphrase (*Espejo fiel de Vidas que contiene los Palmos de David in Verso,* London, 1720) was published by the ex-Marrano Daniel Israel Lopez *Laguna; and a German Jewish translation was prepared by the philosopher Moses *Mendelssohn (1783). Directly and indirectly many writers of the 19th and 20th centuries have been influenced by the Book of Psalms. Thomas Carlyle maintained that the Psalms of David "struck tones that were an echo of the sphere-harmonies." Even greater praise was expressed by the British statesman William Ewart Gladstone, who unfavorably contrasted "all the wonders of Greek civilization" with "the single Book of Psalms," claiming that the "flowers of Paradise ... blossomed in Palestine alone" (*The Place of Ancient Greece,* 1865). The same source has provided perennial inspiration for Jewish writers, including Penina *Moise, whose metrical renderings of the Psalms were adopted by U. S. Reform congregations; Heinrich *Graetz; and Samson Raphael *Hirsch, whose German neo-Orthodox edition of the Book of Psalms appeared in 1882. Jewish writers of the 20th century who dealt with the same theme included Nachman *Heller, who published an edition of the Psalms together with a rhymed Hebrew paraphrase, English and Yiddish translations, and English notes (1923); Izak *Goller, whose original verse translation of Ps. 113–118, *Hallel—Praise,* was published in 1925; and the U.S. rabbi Gershon Hadas who published a new translation for "the modern reader" (1964). [G.E.S.]

In Art. Among Christians of the Middle Ages the Book of Psalms was the most popular section of the Hebrew Bible and it was frequently illustrated in illuminated manuscripts such as Psalters, Bibles, breviaries, and Books of Hours. A particularly popular subject was King David the Psalmist playing on his harp

Figure 2. Psalm 118, in the *Hallel* prayers from the *Rothschild Miscellany,* Italy (Ferrara?), c. 1470. The passage, "Out of the straits I called upon the Lord," is illustrated with David hiding from Saul. Jerusalem, Israel Museum, Ms. 180/51, fol. 163a. Photo David Harris, Jerusalem.

Figure 3. David depicted composing the Psalms in a Psalter of 1274 C.E. Sinai Peninsula, St. Catherine's Monastery, Ms. 61, fol. 2v.

or, occasionally, on other instruments. In the English 13-century Rutland Psalter he is shown playing the organ. Carolingian Psalters and Bibles and manuscripts of the following two centuries often depict David surrounded by Asaph, Heman, Ethan, and Jeduthun, his four musicians, symbolizing Jesus with the four evangelists. A charming representation of David the Psalmist is the introductory miniature to a 15th-century north Italian Book of Psalms, part of a Hebrew miscellany volume in the Israel Museum, Jerusalem. The king is shown seated in a garden near a wood from which deer emerge, charmed by his playing. The subject was revived in northern Europe in the 17th century. There are paintings by Rubens (Staedelmuseum, Frankfort), Pieter Lastman (Gallery Brunswick) and *Rembrandt (Kaplan Collection, New York). Modern works include those by Dante Gabriel Rosetti (Llandaff Cathedral) and by Jozef *Israels (Stedelijk Museum, Amsterdam).

The Middle Ages have also left manuscript illuminations of other subjects taken from the Psalms; and these are often extremely literal in interpretation. Some illustrations to Psalm 27:1 ("The Lord is my light") show David turning toward Jesus or the hand of God, and pointing to his own eyes. Psalm 53:2 ("The fool hath said in his heart: 'There is no God'...") is illustrated by a half-naked medieval jester with a bauble in his hand or wearing a jester's long-eared cap. Sometimes he swallows a stone or bites a dog by the tail. In the 16th-century *Henry VIII Psalter* (British Museum) David is shown as Henry and the fool as his court jester. In some cases, however, the fool is David himself feigning madness before Abimelech. Psalm 69:2–3 ("Save me, O God; For the waters are come in even unto the soul ... ") takes the form of a naked crowned monarch submerged up to the waist or shoulders, his hands raised in supplication. Psalm 81:2 ("Sing aloud unto God, our strength") is illustrated by David striking on bells with a hammer, playing his harp, or dancing before the ark. Psalm 137 ("By the rivers of Babylon") likewise formed the subject of manuscript illustrations, but also of paintings by the 19th-century French Romantic artist Eugène Delacroix (in the dome of theology of the Palais Bourbon, Paris) and the German academician Eduard Bendemann (Wallraf-Richartz Museum, Cologne). Psalm 150:1 ("Praise God in His sanctuary") inspired the bas-reliefs of choristers by Luca della Robbia (15th century; Florence Cathedral).

[ED.]

In Music. The singing of psalms was the chief medium of personal and communal devotion during the formative period of Christianity and has retained an important position in its liturgy ever since. In both the old Eastern and Western denominations, as in Jewish traditions, the melodies of the psalms are built on the principle of psalmody and show many similarities (see Musical Rendition, below). In the Christian traditions they are correlated with a rigid system of melodic theory, that of the Eight Modes or Tones, i. e., eight basic melodic-scalar patterns. The roots of this system also lie in the Near East; the psalmodic patterns have been the least affected by changes in style or creative initiative, since they were to all effect "canonized" no less than the liturgical texts. Their earliest notation in the West is found in the anonymous treatise, *Commemoratio brevis de tonis et psalmis modulandis*, dating from about the second half of the ninth century, and their final forms, preserved thereafter by notation and usage, are those established shortly after the turn of the first millennium. As in Jewish tradition, the performance of the Psalms in the Christian liturgies shows many forms of responsorial and antiphonal divisions (soloist-group, group-group) and various relationships and means of musical linkage with the hymns and prayers of the service. An important feature is the florid rendition of the *Alleluia*, interpolated between the half clauses or the verses (cf. *Hallelujah), often spun out into a long, wordless melisma on the final *a*, the so-called *Jubilus*, and the extension of the psalmodic principle to form the very melismatic chants of the *Tractus* ("drawn-out") category. Special psalmodic formulas are also used for the rendition of certain hymns from the Bible and the New Testament, such as the Songs of Moses—*Audite coeli* (*Ha'azinu*, Deut. 32:1–43)—and the Song of Mary—the *Magnificat* (Luke 1:46–55).

The Protestant Reformation and its related movements, basing its liturgy on the vernacular, created rhymed paraphrases of the Psalms, which were furnished with new melodies, i.e., newly composed, taken over from secular songs, or reshaped to the meter from a traditional ("Gregorian") melody. The major composers who took part in the creation of this new tradition were Loys Bourgeois (c. 1510–c. 1561), Claude Le Jeune (1528–1600), and Claude Goudimel (c. 1515–1572), in France and Switzerland, for the psalm paraphrases by Marot and Calvin; Jacobus Clemens Non Papa (c. 1510–c. 1556) in Holland, with his three-part arrangements of folk tunes to the Dutch rhymed Psalter (the *Souterliedekens*—"little Psalter songs"); and Martin *Luther and the members of his circle for the psalm paraphrases among the German chorales. The continental tunes were largely taken over into the English and Scottish repertoire (Sternhold Psalter, 1563), and then with local additions, migrated with the Puritans to North America, where the earliest book of music instruction published was *A very plain and easy introduction to the whole Art of Singing Psalms* by John Tufts (1712, 1744[11]). Almost from the outset, the Protestant and related movements linked their psalm and hymn collections with art music (and no doubt also popular harmonizing practices) by publishing them in three- or four-voice part settings, a practice which still continues.

Art music compositions for the Psalms appear much later than for the other parts of the service, in the early 15th century, since most of the Psalm texts appear in those parts of the service which are less frequently the occasion for artistic elaboration, such as Vespers. The polyphonic settings of the Psalms "do not constitute a musical category, but are the sum of all those musical categories and forms which stand in any relationship to the biblical Psalms, to their text (original, translated, paraphrased, rhymed, reinterpreted, or taken as the base for an instrumental interpretation), or, in a more narrow sense, to their liturgical melodies" (L. Finscher). It is therefore hardly possible to trace the history of these compositions separately from the mainstream of European art music, from the strictly liturgical-functional harmonizations of the Psalm tones, through the golden ages of the continental motet and the English verse anthem (16th–17th centuries), to the free settings of modern composers. The Psalms have always appealed to composers not only as the "essence of sacred music" but also through their balance of the individual and communal expression of joys and sorrows, which challenges each composer anew. Psalm settings are found in the works of almost all major composers from the 16th century onward. The tradition has been continued by such works as Igor Stravinsky's *Symphony of Psalms* (1930, to the Latin text), and Leonard *Bernstein's *Chichester Psalms* (1965, specified by the composer to be sung only in Hebrew). [B.B.]

MUSICAL RENDITION IN JEWISH TRADITION

Historical Sources. It is most probable that some of the components of the so-called psalm titles, i.e., the verses or half verses prefaced to many of the psalms, indicate certain musical aspects: *shir, mizmor* and their combinations (see above; see also *Music). The simple recurring response *ki le-olam ḥasdo* ("For His mercy endures forever") in Psalms 136, 118:1–4, 106:1, etc., may have been sung to an equally simple melodic formula (by the levitic choir or by the public) after the more elaborate rendition of the first part of the verse by a soloist or by the choir. The refrain or response verses did not have to be written out explicitly if the performers and the public knew them by tradition, and the same was true for the practice of interjecting the praise Hallelujah, once, or several times, after each verse or group of verses. Present-day traditional usages show many instances of the use of one verse as response or refrain, the intercalation of extraneous sentences as refrains, and the addition of Hallelujah in both Jewish and Christian traditions.

The version of Psalm 145 found in Cave 11 at Qumran (11QPs^{a}) may be an early documentation of the practices. A refrain-like clause ("Blessed be God and blessed be His Name forever and ever"), not found in the masoretic text or in the versions, is added after each verse. This refrain is obviously related to verse 1 and could have been intoned as a response. The talmudic sources offer a number of fairly detailed references to psalm singing. Especially important are those references that refer to the various possible divisions of performance between soloist and choir (or public) in the *Hallel* (Sot. 5:4 elaborated in Tosef., Sot. 6:2; TJ, Sot. 5:6, 20c; Sot. 30b; Mekhilta Shirata 1). The discussion centers upon the rendition of the Song of the Sea which is said to have been performed "as the *Hallel* is sung." The information may therefore be applied to the contemporary performance of the *Hallel.*

The historical notated sources begin rather late, as compared to the notations of masoretic cantillation (see *Masoretic Accents). A specimen of psalm-cantillation motives according to the masoretic accents was notated sometime during the first half of the 17th century by Jacob Finzi, cantor in Casale Monferrato. Four psalm melodies—three Italian-Sephardi and one Italian-German—were among the 11 synagogal melodies notated by Benedetto Marcello in Venice and published in his *Estro poetico armonico* (1724–27 and subsequent editions). More than half of the composition in Salamone de'*Rossi's *Ha-Shirim asher li-Shelomo* (Venice 1622–23) are settings of psalms (for three or more voices) with Psalms 92 and 111 set for a double choir of four-plus-four voices. Many freely composed settings of *Hodu* (Ps. 136) appear in the early cantor's manuals, beginning with the manuscript of Juda Elias of Hanover (1740). Similar to Rossi's works, these also belong to the province of art music; but the cantoral specimens frequently feature the

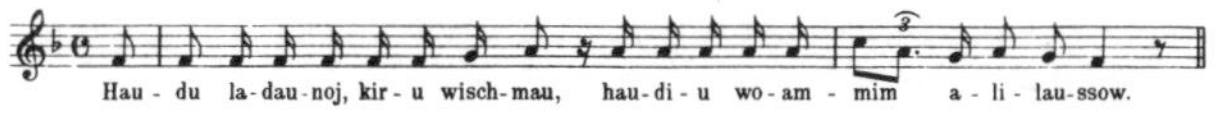
Hau - du la-dau-noj, kir - u wisch-mau, hau-di - u wo-am - mim a - li - lau-ssow.

EXAMPLE 1. Simple psalmody, Ps. 105, Frankfort tradition. From F. Ogutsch and J. B. Levy, *Der Frankfurter Kantor,* 1930, p. 4.

beginning of the traditional intonation as a point of departure for their late-baroque flights of fancy.

Since the practice of psalm singing was taken over by Christianity from the synagogues of the surrounding Jewish communities in the Near East (and not from the art music of the Second Temple), many fruitful—and often problematic—attempts have been made to discover the "common heritage" by comparative methods. A survey of the oral traditions shows that the melodic content of psalm singing is extremely varied. On the other hand, all the truly traditional styles and practices of psalm singing do fall into a very limited number of categories as regards the melodic structure, relationship between melody and text, response and refrain, usages, and the influence of external musical and non-musical factors.

Melody. About 90% of the existing melodies follow the pattern which musicologists call psalmody (Gr. Πσαλμῳδια, "singing of psalms"), i.e., a simple two-wave melodic curve corresponding to the parallel-clause structure of the majority of the psalm verses (two hemistichs). According to the still accepted definition established by medieval European church-music theory, psalmody consists of the following: *initium,* the opening rise; *tenor* (or *tonus currens,* or *tuba*) the holding tone for the recitation of the main parts of the verse; *mediant* (or *flexa*), the midpoint "dip" between the two hemistichs, with a kind of secondary *initium* leading to the reappearance of the *tenor* for the second hemistich; and *finalis* (or *punctum*), the closing formula (see ex. 1). The tenor may be repeated for as long as necessary to cover a varying number of words, and the system is applied with enough flexibility to cover even those psalm verses which are actually not bipartite but tripartite. The realization of the psalmodic principle in the Jewish traditions is frequently more complex than in the Christian ones in several respects: (1) many melodies have not one but two tenors, and there are also some "double" melodic formulas (see ex. 2); (2) the tenor, or tenors, are often covert, appearing as one or several long notes, or as the axis of a series of melismatic movements, or otherwise hidden beneath a florid elaboration; (3) in the second half of the verse, the structure is often disturbed by subtraction, addition, or other departures from the pattern; the ending, however, will always come to obey the convention of the *finalis* (see ex. 3). On the other hand, there are also many very simple and presumably archaic melodies which follow the psalmodic pattern faithfully: examples are known from Tunisia, Morocco, Persia, Yemen, and even Europe.

The character and complexity of the melody are linked with the liturgical function. A certain psalm may thus be sung to various melodies. The exceptions are the two psalms of national mourning,

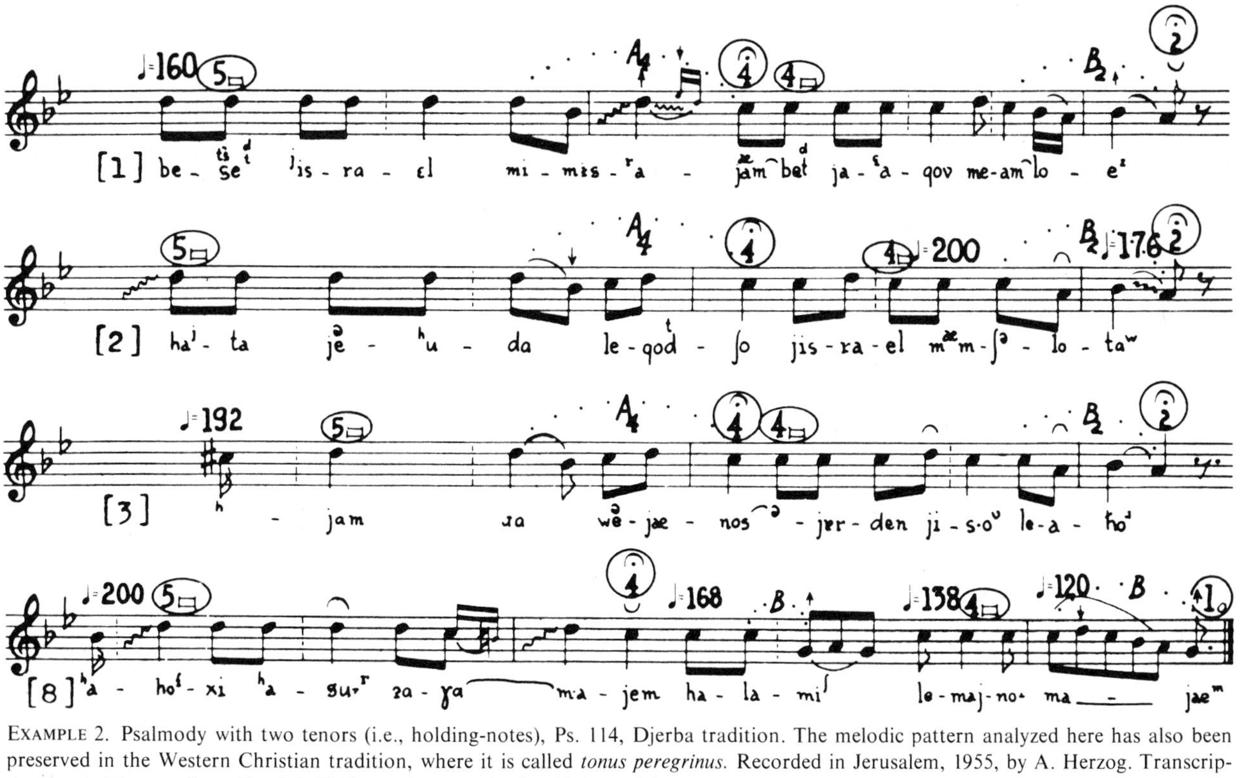

EXAMPLE 2. Psalmody with two tenors (i.e., holding-notes), Ps. 114, Djerba tradition. The melodic pattern analyzed here has also been preserved in the Western Christian tradition, where it is called *tonus peregrinus.* Recorded in Jerusalem, 1955, by A. Herzog. Transcription by A. Herzog, from *Yuval 1,* 1968, music examples booklet, no. 14.

Asaph, O God the heathen are come into Thine inheritance"), and Psalm 137 ("By the rivers of Babylon") and Psalm 79 ("A psalm of often Psalm 91 ("Psalm of the afflicted individual"). The traditional intonations these have acquired in each community are so strongly associated with their contents that they cannot be transferred to the more joyful and festive texts of other psalms. The daily reading in the synagogue, or in private devotions, is the simplest and most closely follows the principle of psalmody. For the group of psalms sung in the morning prayer *(Pesukei de-Zimra)*, different melodies are chosen for weekdays, Sabbath, and feasts. With the increasing festiveness of the occasion, the melodies tend to become more elaborate, especially when the rendition is given to the *ḥazzan*. Examples are the *Hallel* in the synagogue and psalms sung at weddings (especially Ps. 45). On extraordinarily festive occasions, the ritual will consist mostly of appropriately chosen psalms, and here virtuoso composition and performance are given the freest rein—as in a festive prayer for the sovereign (which will feature Ps. 21 and similar texts) and in the ceremony for the dedication of a new synagogue (where Ps. 118 is prominent).

In home rituals, such as in the *Hallel* sung at the *seder*, or for those parts of the above-mentioned ceremonies in which the congregation is expected to participate the simplest psalmodic melodies will retain their place by the force of tradition and for obvious practical reasons (cf. Volunio Gallichi's manuscript score for the inauguration of the Siena synagogue in 1786 (ed. I. Adler,

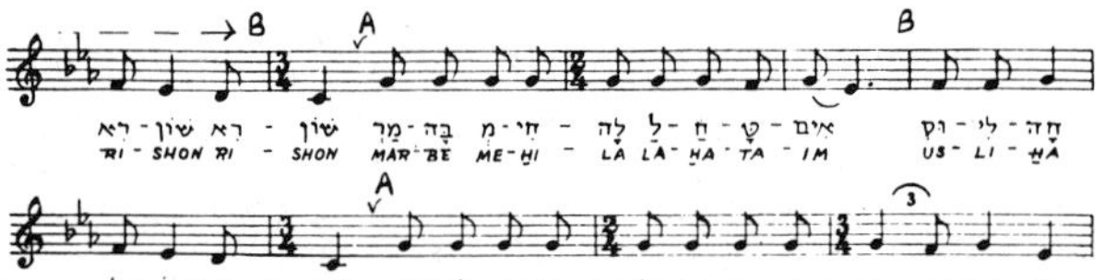

EXAMPLE 3. Psalmody with free expansion of the second half-clause. Ps. 95, East Ashkenazi tradition for the Friday evening service. Verses 1–9 and the first half-clause of verse 10 are sung to the strict psalmodic pattern. The melody then takes over elements of the *Adoshem malakh *shtayger*, but returns to the psalmodic closing-formula. From Idelsohn, *Melodien*, vol. 8, no. 27.

1965)) which, in addition to an elaborate composition of *Open to me the Gates of Righteousness* (Ps. 118) and of various poems, has also preserved the traditional intonation for the "obligatory" prayers of the ceremony, including those for Psalms 32 and 95 *(Lekhu nerannenah)*.

The psalmodic pattern may be overlaid by non-psalmodic

EXAMPLE 4. End of Ps. 117 and beginning of Ps. 118, as sung during the waving of the palm branches on Hoshana Rabba, Djerba tradition. Recorded at moshav Berekhyah, 1955, by A. Herzog. Parallel strict and simple transcription. From A. Herzog, *Renanot*, 10, 1963, p. 8.

elements as an effect of liturgical function. In the Ashkenazi *Lekhu nerannenah*, for example, the original psalmody seems to have been stretched by successive generations of *ḥazzanim* toward the *nusaḥ* of the "Reception of the Sabbath" (cf. Idelsohn, Melodien 8, no. 27, and A. Baer, *Ba'al T'fillah*, no. 320). "If . . . a psalm was used as an introduction to or interlude between prayers in a certain mode, that mode was, as a rule, transferred also to the Psalms—a procedure called by the precentors *me-inyana* [מעניינא—"of the relevant subject," a talmudic technical term]" (Idelsohn, Music, p. 60). The all-important end clause in the Ashkenazi **nusaḥ* intonation is truly psalmodic and it has been maintained that the *nusaḥ* system itself developed out of psalmody. Another instance of *me-inyana* is the singing of Psalms 92 and 93 in Yemen at the onset of the Sabbath, in the intonation of the study of the Mishnah, since the mishnaic passage *Ba-Meh Madlikin* is read there, as in many other communities, immediately preceding, as a kind of bridge between the afternoon and evening prayer.

Psalmodic melodies are also used for texts which are not psalms, as in the **Seliḥot* (of all communities) and in various prayers for Rosh Ha-Shanah and the Day of Atonement (among the Ashkenazim). Some of these may be better classified as a litany, which is an even simpler form than psalmody but closely related to it. In any case this again supports the contention of the relationship between prayer and psalmody.

Although the psalms are furnished with accents in the masoretic texts, the question, whether they were ever, or still are, sung according to the accents is still moot. Even the 17th-century Italian notation of accent motives for Psalms and the claims of present-day informants that they sing according to the accents are not conclusive. Most scholars think that the system of the accents is too sophisticated to be followed precisely or that there was a "lost art" of psalm cantillation. It may even be that some present-day practices of following the accents approximately are a back-formation phenomenon: since the accents were there, it was felt that they had to be obeyed somehow, and after many generations some characteristic motives became attached to the accent-signs in coexistence with the overall psalmodic line. Some modifications, such as those which occur in *Mizmor Shir le-Yom ha-Shabbat* (Ps. 92) in many communities, can only be explained by the influence of the accents.

Performance. In traditional group singing the psalm is sung in unison (or, as in Yemen, in the *organum*-like folk polyphony of that community). In most non-Ashkenazi communities the text is "metricized" in a precisely proportioned succession of the short and long syllables, as done with almost all prose or prose-like liturgical texts when sung by the congregation. As the oldest sources attest and contemporary practices still show, the psalms are also frequently sung in various forms of alternation: solo and group (responsorial psalmody), alternating or succeeding soloists, group against group (antiphonal psalmody), with response and refrain verses and intercalations of Hallelujah between the verses or even after each half clause (see *Music, ex. 4). The point of alternation is not always at the end of the verse or after each half clause: often the performers alternate only at the half-clause point, apparently disregarding the primary verse divisions. In some cases a singer will end his part with the word bearing a masoretic accent of major divisive status inside the verse (not the *etnaḥta* at the half clause). For the waving of the *lulav* (palm branch) on *Sukkot, verses of Psalm 118 are sung to an extended melody to allow for the waving in six directions (cf. Suk. 37b; A. Baer, *Ba'al T'fillah,* no. 814ff., for the Western and Eastern Ashkenazi melodies; and ex. 4 a melody from Djerba).

Some communities are particularly rich in psalm melodies: Yemen, Morocco, Tunisia, Cochin, Syria, Turkey, Italy, and the "Portuguese communities" of Western Europe. In Yemen groups of psalms are sung most artistically in the prayer meetings called *ashmorot* (at dawn on the Sabbath), very similar to the singing of hymns by the Near Eastern communities in the **bakkashot.* The Egyptian repertoire is less varied, but many of the melodies are extremely florid and linked to the **maqāma* system; it is a moot point whether the practice is rooted in the same old tradition from which Christianity derived its extended "Jubilus" (the wordless prolongation of Hallelujah) or acquired more recently from Arabic art song. Among the Ashkenazi communities hardly any true psalmodies have survived, and the home rituals for the singing of the psalms have absorbed many folk tunes from the surrounding cultures. In the realm of the ḥasidic *niggun,* psalm verses furnish some of the texts, with no particular distinction as to the choice of melody (cf. the well-known "neo-ḥasidic" *Yismeḥu ha-Shamayim*).

In the "ordered *ḥazzanut*" of the 19th century in Western Europe, the psalms were set to music in a manner not different from the style of the prayers and often as showpieces for the choir, somewhat in the manner of the Anglican anthem. In Reform Judaism where the text was paraphrased as a rhymed poem in Western meters, the result followed the precedents of the Protestant chorale and even utilized its tunes. At this stage the survey of the traditions of the musical rendition of the Psalms passes into the history of musical composition, discussed under Psalms in the arts (see above). [Av.He.]

Bibliography: General: Kaufmann Y., Toledot, 2 (1947), 200–6, 646–727; A. R. Johnson, in: H. H. Rowley (ed.), *The Old Testament and Modern Study* (1951), 162–209; S. Mowinckel, in: VT, 5 (1955), 13–33; M. H. (Z.) Segal, *Mevo ha-Mikra,* 4 (1955), 517–85; A. S. Kapelrud, in: *Annual of the Swedish Theological Institute,* 4 (1965), 74–90; H. H. Rowley, *Worship in Ancient Israel* (1967); N. M. Sarna, in: M. Buttenwieser, *The Psalms* (1969), xiii-xxxviii. Title: B. Jacob, in: ZAW, 16 (1896), 162–3. Place in Canon: C. D. Ginsburg, *Introduction to the Massoretico-Critical Edition of the Hebrew Bible* (1966), 1–8. Number of Psalms: Schirmann, Sefarad, 1 (1954), 92, 101; I. Joel, in: KS, 38 (1962), 125; J. Heinemann, in: *Tarbiz,* 33 (1963/64), 362–8; C. D. Ginsburg, *Introduction* . . . (1966), 18, 777. Verse Division: S. D. Luzzatto, *Peninei Shadal* (1888), 281–2; Lewin, Oẓar, 9 (1939), 84; P. W. Skehar, in: VTS, 5 (1957), 153–5. Division into Books: I. Abrahams, in: JQR, 16 (1903–04), 579; H. St. J. Thackeray. *The Septuagint and Jewish Worship* (1921); A. Hurwitz, *The Identification of Post-Exilic Psalms by Means of Linguistic Criteria* (1966); J. A. Sanders, *The Psalms Scroll of Qumran Cave 11 (11QPs^a)* (1965); idem, *The Dead Sea Psalms Scroll* (1967). Composition of the Psalter: R. G. Boling, in: JSS, 5 (1960), 221–55; W. F. Albright, *Yahweh and the Gods of Canaan* (1968), 31–33. Date of the Psalter: C. L. Feinberg, in: *Bibliotheca Sacra,* 104 (1947), 426–40; M. Tsevat, *A Study of the Language of the Biblical Psalms* (1955); S. Holm-Nielson, *Studia Theologia,* 14 (1960), 1–53. Ascription to David: Albright, Arch Rel, 121–5. Types of Psalms: H. Gunkel and J. Begrich, *Einleitung in die Psalmen* (1933); S. Mowinckel, *The Psalms in Israel's Worship,* 1–2 (1962); C. Westerman, *The Praise of God in the Psalms* (1965). Psalms and the Cult: H. L. Ginsberg, in: BASOR, 72 (1938), 13–15; idem, in: *L. Ginzberg Jubilee Volume* (1945), 159–71; W. F. Albright, in: *A. Marx Jubilee Volume* (1950), 66; Albright, Arch Rel, 121–5; A. Weiser, *The Psalms* (1959), 23–35; H. J. Kraus, *Worship in Israel* (1966); Y. Aharoni, in: BA, 31 (1968), 11; idem, in: IEJ, 17 (1967), 272; J. Liver, *Perakim be-Toledot ha-Kehunnah* . . . (1968). Superscriptions and Technical Terms: B. Jacobs, in: ZAW, 16 (1896), 129–82; R. B. Y. Scott, in: *Bulletin of the Canadian Society of Biblical Literature,* 5 (1939), 17–24; R. Gyllenberg, in: ZAW, 58 (1940–41), 153–6; H. G. May, in: AJSL, 58 (1941), 70–83; H. L. Ginsberg, in: *L. Ginzberg Jubilee Volume* (1945), 169–71; N. H. Snaith, in: VT, 2 (1952), 43–56; A. Guilding, in: JTS, 3 (1952), 41–55; H. D. Preuss, in: ZAW, 71 (1959), 44–54; W. Bloemendaal, *The Headings of the Psalms in the East Syrian Church* (1960); S. Mowinckel, *The Psalms in Israel's Worship,* 2 (1962), 207–17; J. J. Glueck, in: *Studies on the Psalms* (1963), 30–39; L. Deleket, in: ZAW, 76 (1964), 280–97; S. E. Loewenstamm, in: VT, 19 (1969), 464–70; J. Blau and J. C. Greenfield, in: BASOR, 200 (1970), 11–12. In the Talmud and Midrash: L. Rabinowitz, in: JQR, 26 (1935/36), 350–68; idem, in: HJ, 6 (1944), 109–22; K. Kohler, *Studies, Addresses and Personal Papers* (1931). Musical Rendition in Jewish Tradition: Sendrey, Music, nos. 982–1058, 1079–1297, 6760–6912; Idelsohn, Music, 58–64; E. Gerson-Kiwi, in: *Festschrift Bruno Stablein* (1967), 64–73; Adler, Prat Mus, 36, 48, 49, 256; A. Herzog, in: M. Smoira (ed.), *Yesodot Mizraḥiyyim u-Ma'araviyyim ba-Musikah be-Yisrael* (1968, 27–34; E. Werner, in: MGWJ, 45 (1937), 319–416; idem, in: HUCA, 15 (1940), 335–66; idem, in: *Review of Religion,* 7 (1943), 339–52; H. Avenary, in: *Tatzlil,* 5 (1965), 73–78; idem, in: *Musica Disciplina,* 7 (1953), 1–13; A. Herzog and A. Hajdu, in: *Yuval,* 1 (1968), 194–203; L. Levi, in: *Scritti sul' Ebraismo in memoria di Guido Bedarida* (1966), 105–36; *Dukhan,* 5 (1954), papers of conference devoted to Psalms.

PSANTIR, JACOB (1820–1902), historian of Rumanian Jewry. Born in Botosani, Rumania, Psantir was orphaned in childhood and received no formal education apart from a few years in a Jassy *talmud torah.* He earned a meager living in a variety of occupations, including that of singer in a gypsy band. In this way he traveled throughout Rumania and several other Balkan countries, and his great desire for knowledge coupled with an acute sense of observation enabled him to fill the gaps in his education. In his wanderings Psantir learned about the life of Jewish communities at first hand, investigating their history, their organization, their means of livelihood, and their relations with their non-Jewish neighbors. He supplemented his findings from communal and municipal archives and by deciphering inscriptions on gravestones. The results of his research are contained in two books written in Hebrew,

Jacob Psantir, historian of Rumanian Jewry. Courtesy Yad Vashem Archives, Jerusalem.

Divrei ha-Yamim le-Arẓot Rumanyah ("Chronicles of the Lands of Rumania," 1871) and *Korot ha-Yehudim be-Rumenyen* ("History of the Jews in Rumania," 1873), and the Yiddish *Sefer Zikhroynes* ("Memoirs," 1875).

Although Psantir's work lacks any scientific discipline, being the product of a self-taught writer whose imagination exceeds his critical faculty, it has important historical value because the sources completely disappeared after the Nazi Holocaust.

Bibliography: M. A. Halevi, in: YIVOA, 7 (1952), 204–11. [I.BE.]

PSEUDO-PHOCYLIDES, a Hellenistic Jewish didactic poet, author of 230 hexameters falsely ascribed to the sixth-century B.C.E. Greek lyric poet Phocylides. The few fragments of Phocylides that have survived suggest a reputation for moral wisdom which Pseudo-Phocylides seems to have drawn upon to lend authority to his own moral apothegms. The poem of Pseudo-Phocylides was apparently considered an authentic work of the Greek poet from the time of its earliest citation in Stobaeus (fifth century C.E.). In the later Byzantine Empire this poem became quite popular and it was widely distributed as a school textbook in the period of the Reformation. There are many Byzantine manuscripts; the first printed edition is of 1495; there are many 16th-century translations and reprints. In 1856 Jacob *Bernays wrote a definitive study on the subject demonstrating that the author was Jewish and dependent on the Bible. Since then others have argued for Christian elements in the poem (A. Harnack), pagan elements (A. Ludwich, W. Kroll), and that the work is by a convert to Judaism (M. Roissbroich).

The contents are primarily ethical maxims of such general content that they might easily be taken to be the work of a non-Jew. Their Jewishness can be recognized occasionally as, for example, in the injunction to let the mother bird escape and keep only the young when a nest is taken (84ff.; cf. Deut. 22:6ff.) or the prohibition against eating the flesh of an animal killed by a beast of prey (147ff., cf. Ex. 22:30 and 139, cf. Deut. 14:21). Most of the poem, however, preaches a universal moral code rather than a particular theology or ceremonial law. Even though many parallels can be made between passages in Pseudo-Phocylides and the Pentateuch, the spirit of the poem as well as some of its phraseology is more akin to the wisdom literature in the Bible and the Apocrypha, especially the Apocryphal books of *Ben Sira* and *Wisdom of Solomon.*

Absent from the poem is any specific attack on idolatry, which Bernays ascribes to the cowardice or indifference of the author. There is also little or nothing which can be considered as anti-Christian, thus placing it in the period before the anti-Christian polemics, i.e., before 70 C.E., if it is assumed that the author was a Jew. Some verses (103ff.) speak of physical resurrection and say that "those who rise up again afterward become gods." This is taken to be a Christian reference (Harnack), or a pagan reference (Kroll). Little else can be distinctly identified with any specific religious view. There are similarities between the moral admonitions of Pseudo-Phocylides and a moral manual of the early Church known as the *Didaché.* Rendel Harris, in his edition of the *Didaché* (1887, p. 46), suggests the possibility that both Pseudo-Phocylides and the *Didaché* go back to an earlier Jewish manual of morality. Part of Pseudo-Phocylides (5–79) was excerpted, with few variants and omissions, and incorporated into the **Sibylline Oracles* (2:56–148). Since the text is sometimes dependent on the Septuagint, the dating of the work would be in the second or first century B.C.E. (or, if Christian, in the first century C.E.). The metrics and the poetry are not very inspiring and the corruption of the text presents many problems. An exaggerated importance has been attached to the work.

Bibliography: T. Bergk (ed.) *Poetae Lyrici Graeci,* 2 (1882[4]), 74–109 (critical edition of the Greek text); J. Bernays, *Ueber das Phokylideische Gedicht* (1856); M. Roissbroich, *De Pseudophocylideis* (1910); Schuerer, Gesch, 3 (1909[4]), 617–22; W. Kroll, in: Pauly-Wissowa, 39 (1941), 506–10; *Anglican Theological Review,* 14 (1932), 222–8 (translation by B. S. Easton). [M.S.H.]

°**PSEUDO-SCYLAX** (fl. c. 350 B.C.E.), pseudonym of the Greek author of a seafarers' manual *(Periplus),* which includes a description of the Mediterranean and Black Sea coastlines. The work, entitled "Periplus of the sea of inhabited Europe, of Asia, and of Libya," refers to Scylax of Caryanda, a contemporary of Darius I (521–485 B.C.E.). However, the work was composed about the middle of the fourth century B.C.E. It has survived in almost complete form. The author charts, inter alia, the coastal cities of Palestine and Syria, such as Joppa (Jaffa), Doris (Dora), and Ascalon (Ashkelon). The latter two are described, respectively, as a city of the Sidonians and as a royal city of the Tyrians. He also mentions a mountain and temple of Zeus, which seems to refer to Mt. Carmel. He describes the boundaries of "Coele-Syria" as extending from Ascalon to the river Thapsacus, and states the distance between them.

Bibliography: C. Mueller, *Geographi Graeci Minores,* 1 (1855): A. Baschmakoff, *La Synthèse des Périples Pontiques* (1948), text and French translation. [S.RA.]

PSYCHIATRY.

The Biblical Period. References to states of mental disturbance are frequently found in the Bible. Deuteronomy 28:28, 34 views madness as punishment for disobeying the commandments. The tragedy of Saul's last years is ascribed to an evil spirit that troubled Saul when the Lord departed from him. Saul's paranoidal fears and jealousy of David could not be assuaged by David's attempts to help and reassure him by playing the harp (I Sam. 16:14–23; 18:10ff.; 19:9–10). Later, David himself, in order to escape from Achish, simulated insanity, "scribbling on the doors of the gate and letting his spittle fall upon his beard" (21:11–16). The Bible does not speak of treatment of mental illness or recognize insanity as illness. On the contrary, it was enjoined that the person who was seen to be possessed by spirits should be stoned to death (Lev. 20:27); yet the Bible abounds in counsel for mental health, usually with an ethical intention. In Proverbs it is held that understanding is "a wellspring of life" (16:22) and that "a merry heart doeth good like medicine" (17:22).

In the Talmud. In the Talmud mention of mental illness is generally of a legal nature. The episodic nature of mental illness is taken into account on several occasions and there are references to periods when the person is of lucid or of unsound mind. There are also suggestions of a possible classification of mental illness such as a mental defect, confusion, acute and cyclical psychoses, and those which result from physical illness. The Talmud recognizes mental illness and is chary of accepting popular definitions such as: "he who goes out alone at night, who sleeps in the cemetery and tears his clothes" (Tosef., Ter. 1:3, and cf. Ḥag 3b). The word *shoteh* which contains the idea of walking to and fro without purpose is used to describe the mentally ill. The legal and social implications of insanity are frequently referred to in the Talmud. The mentally ill are not responsible for the damage they cause and those who injure them must bear the responsibility; the insane are not responsible for the shame they cause. They may not marry but, contrary to Greek concepts, in periods of lucidity the individual is considered healthy and capable from every other point of view. The Talmud sets very little store by magical medicines and cures for mental illness which were then current among the nations and were frequently found among Jews in the Middle Ages. It prefers to admit frankly the lack of effective treatment.

The Medieval Period. In the Middle Ages Jewish physicians no less than others were dependent on the humoral theories of Greek and Roman medicine (Hippocrates and Galen). Some Jewish physicians made original discoveries and contributions. *Asaph, the earliest Jewish physician known by name who lived apparently in the sixth or seventh century, felt that that the heart is the seat of the soul and vital spirit. In his work, *The Book of Medicines,* he refers to the disturbed behavior of epileptics and to psychosis—phreneticus. Shabbetai *Donnolo, who lived in the tenth century, wrote in one of his medical books an analysis of the psychiatric conditions of melancholia and of nightmare. His description of mania contains a complex of conditions and undoubtedly included schizophrenia. Donnolo's psychiatric views while avoiding the magical element are derivative from the humoral theory of the Greeks. Nevertheless, though some of his explanations could be termed psychological his treatment was almost purely medicinal.

*Maimonides in the 12th century added to the genius of exegetical and philosophic work the brilliant practice of medicine and the exposition of it. His work *Pirkei Moshe* ("The Aphorisms of Moses") distinguishes clearly between motor and sensory nerves and voluntary and automatic activity. This book also deals with the anatomy of the brain and organic conditions such as epilepsy, weakness, contractions, and tremor. Maimonides' view of the influence of emotion on bodily function, in producing illness and retarding cure, was unique in his time. He was thus the father of psychosomatic medicine. In *Hanhagat ha-Beri'ut* ("The Regimen of Health") he sets out these views and instructions for attention to and the mitigation of the emotional state of the patient. He does, however, recognize the limitations of psychiatric care. *Sefer ha-Nimẓa,* which deals with mental illness, is questionably attributed to him. The *"Sefer Madda"* in Maimonides' Code sets out clearly his views on the promotion of individual mental health. His orientation to it is, of course, profoundly ethical, yet he relates mental health no less to the pragmatic functioning of the body and its appetites and effects. In essence this view recommends the middle road between indulgence and asceticism. He abjures all magical procedures.

The medieval flowering of Jewish medicine was followed by a prolonged period of folk medicine practiced by peripatetic healers. They acquired a reputation for healing as wonder-workers through incantations, *amulets, etc. They treated mental patients as if they were afflicted by spirits, devils, and impure influences. The founder of the ḥasidic movement *Israel ben Eliezer, in the 18th century, acquired his medical reputation by a rapid cure of a mental case. After him there ensued a further period of decadence in which the healers encouraged and exploited superstition.

The Modern Period. The reconstruction of psychiatry as a moral practice and a rational system after medieval times was accomplished in Europe only after a prolonged struggle against the demonological beliefs of the Church and the people. Phillipe Pinel's work in France after the Revolution was a turning point. The 19th century saw the progressive definition and classification of mental illness, of the psychoses and the neuroses, and the humanization of treatment in hospital. The first Jewish medical psychologist to join this European movement was Cesare *Lombroso who in 1864 published his *Genius and Insanity.* He described the delinquent personality carefully and related it to anatomical phenomena and genetic causes rather than moral factors. He thus became a pioneer in human and rational corrective measures for criminal behavior. His work also contributed much to the promotion of scientific thought and methods in psychiatry. Hippolyte *Bernheim's name is linked with the investigation of the neuroses which took precedence in the last two decades of the century. Although a careful observer, his interest was not in theory but in the cure of the patient. He was the first psychologist to advocate the principle of the "irresistable impulse" in legal medicine.

In 1889 Sigmund *Freud was a spectator of Bernheim's astonishing experiments in the treatment by hypnosis of mental hospital patients. Freud decided to use hypnosis in the treatment of neurotic patients and was associated in this task with Josef *Breuer, a practitioner in Vienna. In 1895 their epoch-making book, *Studien ueber Hysterie,* appeared. This work embodied the discovery of the unconscious. Freud soon found that he could dispense with hypnosis by letting the patient talk at random and obtained better therapeutic results. This new method Freud called free association. With the publication in 1900 of his *Interpretation of Dreams,* Freud invaded the field of normal psychology, and the borderland between abnormal and normal psychology began to disappear. Freud's theory and technique of psychoanalysis, after much resistance, not only revolutionized psychiatric therapy but was the final and decisive medium in which education, child care, and the treatment of criminals was humanized and made rational.

Alfred *Adler challenged the validity of Freud's concepts of basic sexual drives and repression as prerequisites for neurotic symptom formation. In 1912 he coined the term "individual psychology." He reduced the significance of childhood sexual factors to a minimum. For the school which developed around Adler, neurosis stems from childhood experience of over-protection or neglect or a mixture of both. This leads to a neurotic striving for superiority. His intuitive thinking may have been confirmed by thinkers subsequently who have defined the interaction between the goals of the individual and his social group and environment. Sandor *Ferenczi made a singular contribution to psychoanalysis which has been considered second only to that of Freud with whom he was associated. He attempted to correlate biological and psychological phenomena in his scientific method—bioanalysis. Karl *Abraham, one of the founders of psychoanalysis, contributed greatly through his researches to the clinical understanding of the neuroses and the psychoses especially of manic-depressive insanity. A. A. *Brill was responsible for the introduction of psychoanalysis into the United States and into the practice of psychiatry there. Max *Eitingon founded the first psychoanalytic training institute and polyclinic in Berlin in 1920. This became the model for all psychoanalytic training. He settled in Palestine in 1933 where he founded the psychoanalytic society and institute. Freud's inner circle or "Committee" by 1919 comprised Ferenczi, Abraham, Eitingon, Otto *Rank, Hans *Sachs, and the only non-Jew among them, Ernest Jones. Jones has commented on the effect of Freud's Jewishness on the evolution of his ideas and work; he attributed the firmness with which Freud maintained his convictions, undeterred by the prevailing opposition to them, to the "inherited" capacity of Jews to stand their ground in the face of opposition and hostility. That also held true for his mostly Jewish followers. Freud believed that the opposition to the inevitably startling discoveries of psychoanalysis was considerably aggravated by anti-Semitism. Early signs of anti-Semitism appeared in the Swiss analytic group. Freud felt that it was easier for Abraham to follow his thought than for Jung, because Jung as a Christian and the son of a pastor could only find his way to Freud through great inner resistance. Hans Sachs joined Freud in 1909. He abandoned law for the practice of psychoanalysis. Sachs was an editor and trained analyst whose main work was in the application of psychoanalysis to understanding the creative personality.

There were several other Jewish psychiatrists and lay psychoanalysts associated with the earlier phases of the development of psychoanalysis. Among them was Paul *Federn who met Freud in 1902 and was the fourth physician to become an analyst. Theodor *Reik was associated with Freud from 1910. Probably his major theoretical contribution was in the field of masochism. Helene *Deutsch as a psychiatrist and analyst made the pioneer exploration of the emotional life of women and constructed a comprehensive psychology of their life cycle. Melanie *Klein and Anna *Freud, both lay analysts, were originators of the psychoanalytical treatment of children, which they carried from the Continent to England.

In the United States, Erik Homberger *Erikson developed concepts of the development of the identity of the individual and his effort to maintain its continuity while seeking solidarity with group ideals and group identity. Margaret *Mahler added to the understanding of normal development in earliest infancy, describing the separation process from the mother. Perhaps the greatest contribution to child psychiatry was made in the United States by Leo *Kanner who, in 1943, first described and named the infantile psychosis, "early infantile autism." Lauretta *Bender believed that genetic factors determine the infants' vulnerability to a schizophrenic type of disorder and further related the onset of the psychosis to a biological crisis. Her visual Motor Gestalt Test was widely used to reveal organically based problems. Moritz *Tramer, the Swiss child psychiatrist, maintained that childhood schizophrenia exists as a hereditary entity in childhood and runs its course into the adult form. The psychoanalyst Paul *Schilder's dynamic concept of the "body image" contributed much to psychological thinking in the study of schizophrenia, especially in children. Beata Rank, while stressing the hereditary and constitutional factors in atypical emotional development, in therapy treated the early parent-child relationship. Rene *Spitz, a psychoanalyst, made important contributions in his studies of emotionally deprived infants and those separated from their mothers.

Many Jewish psychoanalysts, psychiatrists, and psychologists have been involved in the further development of child psychiatry and therapy especially in the United States. These include: Phyllis *Greenacre, Herman *Nunberg, Ruth Eissler, Edith Buxbaum (c. 1895–), Bertha Bornstein (c. 1890–), Marianne R. Kris, William Goldfarb (1915–), David Levy (1892–), Stella Chess (1914–), Augusta Alpert, S. R. *Slavson, Peter B. Neubauer (1913–), Reginald Lourie, Fritz *Redl, and Martin Deutsch (1923–).

The effect of analytic theory and practice on psychiatry in the United States received an historic impulse after the Nazi accession and the transplantation of the psychoanalytic centers and practitioners from Europe. Franz *Alexander from Berlin had already added much to ego psychology and that of the criminal before developing, in his Chicago School, concepts of psychosomatic medicine and modifications of psychoanalytic treatment methods. Sandor *Rado, who had studied drug addiction and developed "ego analysis" in New York, developed his modifications of it in "adaptational psychodynamics." Heinz *Hartman laid the foundations for the theoretical understanding of the interaction of the ego with personal, biological, and social reality. With Ernst *Kris and Rudolph *Loewenstein he explored the ways in which cultural differences produced variations of behavior. Géza *Roheim applied psychoanalytic principles to anthropological research. Otto *Fenichel is remembered as a teacher of psychoanalysis. Ernst *Simmel was noted for his contribution on war neuroses and on anti-Semitism. Wilhelm *Reich made a basic contribution in his analysis of character before his defection from psychoanalysis. Sander Lorand is noted for his teaching in technique. Kurt *Lewin made a notable contribution to the understanding of personality within its psychological environment; Erich *Fromm to the appreciation of the passions and behavior of men as determined by the creativity and frustrations of society; Kurt *Goldstein's studies have applied principles of perception and reaction of Gestalt psychology.

Among the U.S. psychiatrists and others who have contributed much to psychiatry the following should be mentioned here: F. J. Kallmann, for his genetic studies; Jules *Masserman, for his "biodynamic" methods; David *Rapaport, in his psychological researches; Melitta Schmideberg, for her treatment of major criminals; Manfred *Sakel who discovered insulin therapy; Roy *Grinker, for his integrative approach; and Nathan *Ackerman, for his family therapy. Other notable practitioners, teachers, and researchers were Eduardo Weiss, Milton Greenblatt (1914–), Paul Lemkau (1909–), Felix *Deutsch, Greta L. Bibring (1899–), Melvin Sabshin (1925–), Lewis *Wolberg, Theresa *Benedek, Lawrence S. Kubie (1896–), Leon Salzman (1915–), David A. Hamburger (1925–), David Shakow (1901–), Abraham *Kardiner, Frieda *Fromm-Reichman, Theodore Lidz (1910–), Thomas Szasz, Samuel Beck (1896–), Bruno *Bettelheim, David Wechsler (1896–), J. S. Kasanin (1897–1946), Samuel Ritvo, Ralph Greenson (1911–), Rudolf Ekstein (1912–), Milton Rosenbaum (1910–), Eugen Brody (1921–), Eric D. Wittkower (1899–), Iago Galdston (1895–), M. Ralph Kaufman (1900–), Howard P. Rome (1910–), J. R. Linton (1899–), Frederick Redlich (b. 1910), and J. L. *Moreno who developed psychodrama.

Social scientists who contributed to mental health were: Marvin and Morris *Opler, Melford Spiro (1920–), Leo Srole (1908–), Morris and Charleen Schwartz, Bert Kaplan (1919–), and Daniel Lerner (1917–).

In England the psychoanalytic approach was represented by Michael *Balint, Kate *Friedlander, Willie *Hoffer, Susan *Isaacs, August Bonnard, Joseph J. Sandler (1927–), W. G. Joffe, and Liselotte Frankl. Erwin Stengel (1902–) made remarkable contributions on suicide and M. D. *Eder, an early member of the movement, was also a devoted Zionist. Jews in psychiatry are ably represented by Sir Aubrey *Lewis, W. Mayer-Gross, Emanuel *Miller (1894–1970), and H. J. Eysenck (1916–), who represents the school of "behavior therapy" and psychology. In South Africa, Wulf Sachs (1893–1949) pioneered psychoanalysis and analyzed the first African subject. In France, Eugene *Minkowski was a pioneer in psychiatry and existentialist psychotherapy. In the Soviet Union L. M. Rozenshteyn developed preventive methods in neuropsychiatry. M. O. Gurevich (1906–) shared the writing of a well-known textbook of psychiatry. The noted Soviet psychiatrist T. I. Yudin wrote an outline of the history of Russian psychiatry, O. B. Feltsman tried to popularize psychoanalysis between 1910 and 1914 through a psychotherapy journal, and Moshe *Woolf attempted this through his activities. The psychologist L. *Vygotski and his co-worker Luria contributed fundamentally to the understanding of disturbed thought processes.

Psychoanalysis was brought to Palestine in 1933 by Eitingon, Moshe Woolf, and Ilya Shalit (d. 1953). Its influence was extended into the practice of psychiatry by Henri *Winnik, Ruth Jaffe (1907–), Eric Gumbel (1908–), and Shmuel Nagler (1914–). The establishment of the State of Israel led to a rapid expansion of psychiatric facilities, initially in the army and later in communities. Notable contributions were made in this respect and in others by Yeshayahu Baumatz (1897–1964), Erich *Neumann, Shmuel Golan (1901–1966), Janus Schossberger (1914–), Shlomo Kulcar (1901–), Abraham Weinberg (1891–1972), Julius Zellermayer (1910–), F. S. *Rothschild, Franz Bruell (1904–), Ludwig Tramer (1923–), Miriam Gay (1917–), Phyllis Palgi (1917–), and Nehama Barzilai (1918–).

The impact of Jews in modern Western psychiatry probably relates to their personal analytic gifts fostered by their own historic culture. Two events of the last century contributed to their entry into psychiatry in this century: the political emancipation of Jews in Europe which permitted their entry into the universities and into the valued profession of medicine in which they had been involved in medieval times; and the freeing of psychiatry from its cloak of irrationality and prejudice, speeded by the discoveries of Freud. Ernest Jones has remarked that historically psychoanalysis was not a particularly Jewish movement in England. Neither psychoanalysis nor psychiatry in England are so even today. Psychoanalysis was not essentially attractive to Jews in the United States until the displacement to the U.S. of the largely Jewish Viennese and German schools and their attraction of Jews there to the profession. In psychiatry in Western countries, Jews were on the whole under-represented but they are especially today well represented in the U.S.

See also *Psychology and list at end.

Bibliography: J. M. Leibowitz, in: *Harofe Haivri,* 1 (1961), 167–75; D. Margalit, *Ḥakhmei Yisrael ke-Rofe'im* (1962); G. Zilboorg, *History of Medical Psychology* (1941), 484–570.

[Lo.M.]

PSYCHOLOGY, the science of the mind or of mental phenomena and activities.

Psychological Concepts in the Bible. "Psychology has a long past, but only a short history" (H. Ebbinghaus, *Abriss der Psychologie,* 1908). Nowhere is this aphorism better exemplified than in the many centuries during which Jewish physicians and thinkers dealt with the problems of behavior and behavior disorders. Many current notions on classification and therapy were foreshadowed in biblical and talmudic literature, and Jewish philosophers wrestled with the same psychological concepts that still occupy attention today.

The Jewish art of healing always emphasized mental as well as physical health. Behavior disorders were well known to the early Hebrews, who were noteworthy for their observance of the laws of preventive medicine and hygiene. From the beginning Jewish monotheism excluded all kinds of magic practices. The Bible opposed occult healing as "Amorite customs" and prescribed as therapy for all mental and physical ills prayer to "God your healer" (Ex. 15:26) and the use of medicine (Ex. 21:19; I Kings 17:21; II Kings 4:32–35; Ezek. 30:21).

Cases of mental disorder described in the Bible include King Saul's paranoia, depression, and epileptic seizures, treated by music therapy, and Nebuchadnezzar's lycanthropy. Various types of insanity are cited in the Pentateuch, such as phobia and panic (Lev. 26:17).

Post-Biblical and Talmudic Period. The talmudic description of *shoteh* ("the mentally insane") approaches the symptomatology of several psychoses (Ḥag. 2b; Sanh. 65b; Nid. 17a). The rabbis saw in the act of transgression a *ru'aḥ shetut* ("a mental deviation," Sot. 3a). Other psychological conditions mentioned are: epilepsy (Yev. 64b); hysteria (Ḥag. 3a); phobias (Git. 70a); hereditary traits (Bek. 8a; Yev. 64b) versus environment (Suk. 56b), melancholia (Shab. 2:5; see Maim.), defense mechanisms such as repression, sublimation, and projection (Meg. 25b; Kid. 70a), and the concept of catharsis cited in both the Bible (Prov. 12:25) and the Talmud (Sanh. 100b). Talmudic and midrashic literature also discussed ideas related to individual and social behavior, attitudes and values, systems of learning, discipline, and punishment. The need for "group belongingness" in the spirit of Hillel (Avot 2:4) was always stressed, and social acceptance was considered an indicator of divine approval (Avot 3:10). In the realm of education, the Talmud approached the training of children in the light of an awareness of differing learning abilities and the relation of learning to stages of development (Ber. 28a; Kid. 30a; Yoma 27a; Avot 5:12). The Talmud understood and stressed such principles as the need for psychological understanding of the mentally sick, individual differences in personality assessment (Sanh. 38a; ARN[1] 4, 17), and the role of habit formation (Yoma 27a).

*Dreams were regarded as being of divine provenance. In antiquity Jews were famous as "dream interpreters," from Joseph to Daniel, and later the Essenes. The Talmud considers the dream "a sixtieth part of prophecy," that also contained irrelevant material, which "if not interpreted is like a letter which was not opened" (Ber. 55a). Halakhic literature deals with dreams related to oaths and promises, and with anxiety over a "bad dream," for which one is permitted to fast a *ta'anit ḥalom* even on the Sabbath (Shab. 11a). Hebrew "dream books" similar to those of the old Egyptians and Greeks were written by R. *Hai.

The nature and function of the *soul, reason, and intellect were treated by Jewish philosophers (under Greek influence) and in the Kabbalah. Judaism believes that the soul and the body comprise the total personality in the divine image and do not represent an essential duality. Although the biblical terms *ru'aḥ, nefesh,* and *neshamah* are used synonymously, the rabbis identified the *neshamah* as the human psyche—the higher spiritual substance. In recognizing the conflict between the *yeẓer ha-ra* (the orgiastic drive to sin) and the *yeẓer ha-tov* (the positive inclination to control it), Judaism believes in the *liber arbitrum* (the principle of free choice), whereby man can master the id forces of the destructive *yeẓer ha-ra* (Suk. 52a) for the sake of the emergence of a healthy ego. *Maimonides attributed to the divine soul five different faculties: the nutritive, the sensitive, the imaginative, the emotional, and the rational (*Shemonah Perakim,* 1), the last being the distinctive, discriminating trait of man enabling him to apprehend and create ideas (*Guide* 1:70).

Medieval Period. Medieval Jewish philosophers who wrote on psychology included the eclectic Isaac b. Solomon Israeli who wrote *Sefer ha-Yesodot* ("The Book of Elements"), and discussed the interaction of mind and body and identified epilepsy and melancholia with insanity; Baḥya b. Joseph ibn Paquda; Solomon ibn Gabirol; Joseph ibn Ẓaddik; Judah Halevi; Abraham ibn Daud; and the rationalist Maimonides.

The Jewish share in the spread and development of medieval culture and the sciences is well known. Jewish works in medicine and science became the ultimate source of European medicine in the schools of Salerno and Montpellier. *Asaph's earliest medical work in Hebrew contains the first medical notice of the hereditary character of mental diseases and of psychosomatics. A description of mania was given by the earliest Italian physician Shabbetai Donnolo who was born in 913 C.E. Although ideas about psychological illness were historically attributed to Ḥibat Allah ibn Jumay (c. 1180), who was the Jewish physician to Saladin, Jewish genius in this field really begins with that remarkable physician of mind and body, Moses Maimonides, the most modern in approach of all medieval physicians.

Maimonides advocated research through experiment. He emphasized the high regard a physician should have for the human mind, and stressed the psychosomatic approach in therapy (*Regimen Sanitatis,* 3:13). He also differentiated between constitutional and environmental sources of behavior, urging the mentally sick to avail themselves of a "physician of the mind" (Code, 1:2). He warned against excessive use of tranquilizers or any radical changes in behavior (*Shemonah Perakim,* 1). Quite modern from the psychotherapeutical point of view, Maimonides insisted on complete psychological harmony between couples during sexual union for the benefit of the offspring, and viewed "physical health as a prerequisite to mental health and excellence" (Code, 1:4). In his treatise on the manic-depressive state Maimonides proposed "a strict hygiene of the soul" based on self-discipline and mental calm (*Shemonah Perakim*, 3).

The 13th-century rabbi Gershon b. Solomon of Arles identified the brain as the center of motility and not the heart. He is said to have experimented by removing the heart of a monkey and to have made similar tests on birds. In the same century Shem Tov b. Joseph *Falaquera wrote *Battei Hanhagat Guf ha-Bari ve-ha-Nefesh* and *Sefer ha-Nefesh* dealing with the psychic forces. Philosophical and physiological psychology is treated by *Hillel b. Samuel of Verona in *Tagmulei ha-Nefesh* ("Rewards of the Soul"). Moses Narbonni (11th century) and Nathan b. Joel Falaquera wrote on mental hygiene. Sleep was analyzed by the tenth-century Karaite Jacob al-*Kirkisani, and later by Jedaiah (ha-Penini) Bedersi as "a state when the sense of comprehension comes to a standstill" (*Ketav ha-Da'at*, "Treatise of the Intellect"). The medical works of *Amatus Lusitanus (16th century) and of Jacob *Ẓahalon (17th century) contain ample references to psychological issues.

Responsa Literature. The responsa literature also deals with mental diseases, in connection with matrimonial suits. Among the topics discussed were: melancholia, hysteria, "lunacy," manic-depressive states, megalomania, and character disorders. Isaac Lampronti of Ferrara permitted the desecration of the Sabbath "to prevent a state of emotional anxiety" (Resp. *Naḥalat Shivah*, 83). Music therapy, already used by King Saul and later treated separately by both Saadiah Gaon and Maimonides, is discussed by Ḥ. J. D. *Azulai in the Responsum *Ḥayyim Sha'al* (53), while hypnotism was noted by R. Jacob Ettlinger (d. 1871) in *Binyan Ẓiyyon* (67). Prison psychology was first introduced by the 18th-century Marrano Ribeira Sanchez. Jewish religious law requires strict consideration and good care for the mentally deficient (Sh. Ar., YD 240:10; Sh. Ar., EH 119:6). Even before Pinel's pioneering work in France, Jewish law required communal care for the insane, who "are not held reponsible for their actions, yet, injuring them is legally prohibited" (Sh. Ar., ḤM 924:8). Suggestive therapy "to pacify a patient's mind" is permitted by Maimonides and Caro on psychological grounds (Sh. Ar., YD 179:6).

Ḥasidism. The ḥasidic movement of the 18th century again introduced suggestive therapy. Mental disorders were often treated by early *ẓaddikim*. The Ḥasid's identification with his ego-ideal, the *ẓaddik*, a humane, divinely inspired messenger, and the strong belief in this spiritual leader, had phenomenal therapeutic effects. Much psychological insight is to be found in the writings of R. Israel Ba'al Shem Tov, R. Dov Baer, the Maggid of Mezhirech, R. Naḥman of Bratslav, R. Shneur Zalman of Lyady, and their disciples. Ḥasidic teaching with its kabbalistic overtones and its strong emotional appeal and emphasis on the humane and mystical factors is the most psychologically oriented of all the expressions of Judaism. [M.M.BR.]

Modern Period. Psychology as a science and a profession emerged in the second half of the 19th century. Before the birth of psychology as an independent discipline, there had been a long period during which the subject matter of psychology—mental activity, human nature, and the relationship of mind and body—had been the province of philosophy. Jewish thinkers, ranging from Philo, who attempted to reconcile Greek and Hebrew thought, to the Jewish philosophers in the Arab countries during the Middle Ages, and from *Spinoza and his laws of the mind to *Husserl and his phenomenology, played an important role in this history. But modern, scientific psychology could only come into being when the progress of physiology had provided the biological basis and physics, the methods to make psychology an experimental science.

PSYCHOLOGICAL PIONEERS. The last two decades of the 19th century saw the founding of academic departments of psychology in most major universities in Europe and the United States. As it was difficult for Jews to obtain university appointments because of official and unofficial discrimination, there were relatively few Jewish pioneer psychologists involved in the founding of laboratories. G. F. *Heymans participated in the establishment of a laboratory at Louvain in Belgium in 1891 and went on to found the first Dutch laboratory at Groningen in 1892. Hugo *Muensterberg founded the laboratory at Freiburg in Breisgau, Germany, and was called to Harvard in 1892 to reactivate and take charge of the laboratory there. Joseph *Jastrow received the first doctorate in psychology granted in the United States, at Johns Hopkins University in 1886. Doubly handicapped by the absence of academic departments and the fact that he was Jewish, he circularized the major university departments with his proposals for a psychology curriculum. He was successful in gaining an appointment at the University of Wisconsin, thus founding the second psychological laboratory in the U.S. in 1888. In England, where resistance to the new experimental psychology was especially strong, C. S. * Myers was the first psychologist to be in charge of the laboratory at Cambridge.

THE SCHOOLS. After its initial phase, psychology passed through a period in which various schoools advanced their claims to be its true representative.·Although most psychologists remained eclectic, it was the schools which provided the chief directions for the development of psychological theory. Joseph Jastrow of Wisconsin was typical of this trend. Otto *Selz was a prominent member of the so-called "Wuerzburg" school which investigated the psychology of thinking processes. The next generation of psychologists rejected many of the theoretical concepts and experimental techniques of the older schools. The European movement, in opposition to the older schools, successfully challenged the earlier elementaristic concepts, substituting an emphasis on relationships and phenomenological methodology. It was influenced by the work of David *Katz and Edgar *Rubin on perception. The founders of the new school, known as Gestalt psychology, were Max *Wertheimer and his associates, including Kurt *Koffka. Other important early members of this school were Kurt *Goldstein and Kurt *Lewin. Gestalt psychology was particularly affected by the fact that most of its founders were Jewish. It was originally primarily a European school, but the forced emigration of most of its important contributors to the U.S. (including Koehler, who was not Jewish, but in sympathy with his Jewish colleagues) with the advent of the Nazis, introduced it into U.S. psychology. There it gained further support through the work of Hans Wallach in perception, Abraham Luchins in problem solving, and Solomon Asch in social psychology. In the 1920s and 1930s the acceptance of psychoanalytic and allied concepts in psychology grew rapidly and the ideas of Sigmund *Freud began to penetrate all facets of psychology, as well as literature, history, and the arts. The development of clinical psychology as a field of study and treatment of personality disorders can be traced primarily to the influence of psychoanalytic thinking. (See also *Psychiatry.)

Contemporary Period. Contemporary psychology has discarded the approach of the schools, with their attempt to bring all of psychology into one harmonious framework. It has substituted, in its systematic part, an emphasis on specific theories and models, and in its work, an emphasis on the investigation of specific problems and their applications. Many of the ideas of the schools have been incorporated into these modern approaches. Jewish psychologists have significantly contributed to the development of these theories. German and Austrian psychology was practically destroyed by the measures adopted by the Nazi regime, many of the displaced psychologists emigrating to the U.S. and making their contribution through teaching and research. Besides the Gestalt psychologists already mentioned, these included such important figures as Charlotte *Buhler, William *Stern, Heinz *Werner, Werner *Wolff, Erich *Fromm, Adhémar Gelb, and Else Frenkel-Brunswik (see Albert Wellek, "The impact of the German immigration on the development of American psychology," in *Journal of the History of the Behavioral Sciences*, 4 (1969), 207–29). A selective sample of prominent Jewish contributors to the development of present-day theoretical positions shows that practically all the psychological specialities are represented. Abram Amsel,

Howard Kendler, Joseph Notterman, Leo Postman, William Schoenfeld, and Richard Solomon engaged in the study of learning with human and animal subjects. In the field of perception and sensory functions, leading names include Julian Hochberg, Hershel Leibowitz, Carl Pfaffman, and Irvin Rock. Comparative and physiological psychology are represented by Daniel Lehrman and David Krech, and by Murray Jarvik in the allied field of psychopharmacology. Jerry Hirsch made important contributions to psychogenetics, and Joshua Fishman and Kurt Salzinger to the study of language. Melvin Marx worked in the field of learning, but is better known for his contribution to systematics. Abraham *Maslow figured prominently in the development of a humanistic psychology. The social field includes Leonard Berkowitz, Morton Deutsch, Leon Festinger, Otto Klineberg, and Daniel *Katz, with George Katona working in the allied area of the relation of economics and psychology.

Saul Rosenzweig, after work in personality and projective testing, became primarily interested in the history of psychology, as did Benjamin Wolman. In the development of projective testing Samuel Beck and Bruno Klopfer became known as experts on the Rorschach test. Personality theory has gained through the work of Milton Rokeach. David Wechsler originated the standard tests of intelligence named after him, while Boris Levinson used intelligence tests to discover the characteristic patterns of the mental development of Jewish children. Joseph Zubin attempted to devise objective tests of abnormal behavior. Jewish psychologists constitute a large segment of the U.S. clinical field. Their various contributions to theory and practice can be exemplified by the work of Perry London, Emanuel Schwartz, and Hans Strupp in clinical psychology, and Morton Seidenfeld in counseling.

The Jewish contribution to all branches of psychology has been very important from the start, and Jews make up a disproportionate number of the profession. The diversity of viewpoints and the distribution of psychologists in the past indicate that psychology has attracted Jewish professionals because it presented an opportunity for intellectual advancement that was denied in some of the better-established fields. Without the Jewish contribution it may safely be said that psychology would not have reached its present state of development and would be seriously handicapped in its future course.

See also *Psychiatry. [H.E.A.]

Bibliography: J. Preuss, *Biblisch-talmudische Medizin* (1911); M. Perlmann, *Midrash ha-Refu'ah,* 3 vols. (1926–34); H. J. Zimmels, *Magicians, Theologians, and Doctors* (1952); M. M. Brayer, in: *Harofe Haivri,* 1 (1964), 285–98; 2 (1965), 248–54; E. G. Boring, *History of Experimental Psychology* (1950²); H. Misiak and V. S. Sexton, *History of Psychology: An Overview* (1966); A. A. Roback, *History of American Psychology* (1952); R. I. Watson, *Great Psychologists* (1968²); M. Wertheimer, *Brief History of Psychology* (1970); B. Wolman (ed.), *Historical Roots of Contemporary Psychology* (1968); R. S. Woodworth and M. R. Sheehan, *Contemporary Schools of Psychology* (1964³).

Noted Jewish Psychologists and Psychiatrists. The individuals whose names are marked with an asterisk in the list below form the subjects of articles in their appropriate alphabetical position in the Encyclopaedia.

***ADLER, ALFRED** (1870–1937), Austrian psychiatrist.

BAKAN, DAVID (1921–), U.S. psychologist. Born in New York, Bakan held several university positions, from 1961 at Chicago. In his *Sigmund Freud and the Jewish Mystical Tradition* (1958) he attempted to trace the roots of early psychoanalytic concepts and methods in the Kabbalah, the Zohar, and talmudic interpretations. His *Duality of Human Existence: an Essay on Psychology and Religion* (1966) made important contributions to the history of psychology especially in relation to the problem of introspection, research methodology, and the psychology of religion.

***BENDER, LAURETTA** (1897–), U.S. research psychiatrist.

***BERNSTEIN, JULIUS** (1839–1917), German physiologist and medical educationist who laid the foundations of neurophysiology.

BLUMENFELD, WALTER (1882–1967), German psychologist. Born in Neuruppin, Silesia, Blumenfeld became professor at the Technische Hochschule in Dresden. Leaving Germany in 1936, he was appointed professor at the University of San Marcos, Lima, Peru, and director of the Institute of Psychopedagogy. He is known for the "Blumenfeld alleys," an apparatus he invented to measure the perceptual relationship between size and distance.

***BONAVENTURA, ENZO JOSEPH** (1891–1948), psychologist.

***BUHLER, CHARLOTTE** (1893–), child psychologist.

CHEIN, ISIDOR (1912–), U.S. psychologist. Chein was a research worker in the psychological aspects of social problems such as intergroup relations and narcotic addiction. He wrote *The Road to H: Narcotics, Delinquency, and Social Policy* (1964). His articles on the adverse effects of segregation were quoted by the U.S. Supreme Court in its desegregation decision of 1954. Chein was director of the commission on Community Interrelations of the *American Jewish Congress (1946–52).

***ERIKSON, ERIK HOMBERGER** (1902–), U.S. psychoanalyst.

FERNBERGER, SAMUEL (1887–1956), U.S. psychologist. Born in Pennsylvania, Fernberger served as professor at Clark University for eight years, and then at the University of Pennsylvania from 1920. He is best known for his work in psychophysics, sensation, perception, and the history of psychology.

FEUERSTEIN, REUVEN (1921–), Rumanian psychologist. Born in Botosani, Rumania, Feuerstein worked in Bucharest as a teacher of disturbed children. He directed the psychological services of Youth Aliyah in Europe (1951–55) after having worked in Israel with Youth Aliyah from 1945, and was appointed director of its child guidance clinic and the Canadian Hadassah-Wizo Research Institute in Jerusalem. His work is set forth in his book (with M. Richelle and the collaboration of Z. Rey) *Children of the Mellah* (*Yaldei ha-Melaḥ;* The Szold Foundation and Youth Aliyah, Jerusalem, 1963).

FINGERMAN, GREGORIO (1890–), Argentinian psychologist. Born in Bogopol, Russia, and taken to Argentina as an infant, Fingerman trained in medicine and then turned to education and finally to psychology. He was head of the National Institute for Secondary Education in Buenos Aires, and in 1934 was appointed director of the Institute of Professional Orientation. He also served as professor of psychology at the Escuela Superior de Comercio de la Nación. Among his several books are *Lecciones de Logica* and *Lecciones de Psychologia.* He was drama critic for *La Nación* and was a frequent contributor to the Jewish press in Buenos Aires.

***FOX, CHARLES** (1876–1964), British psychologist.

***FREUD, SIGMUND** (1856–1939), Austrian psychiatrist, creator of psychoanalysis.

***FRIEDLANDER, KATE** (1902–1949), English criminologist and psychiatrist.

***FROMM, ERICH** (1900–), U.S. psychoanalyst.

GOLDSCHMIDT, RICHARD HELLMUTH (1883–), German psychologist. Born in Posen, Goldschmidt became professor of psychology at Muenster in 1919. Just before World War II he managed to leave for England, where he was a fellow of Oxford University's Institute of Psychology from 1939 to 1945. He returned to the university at Muenster in 1949, remaining for the rest of his career. His early research dealt with the psychology of visual perception with regard to color schemes. He published *Postulat der Farbwandelspiele* (1928), and later wrote *Ahnung und Einsicht* (1967). Other areas of Goldschmidt's scientific interest were the psychology of religion and aesthetics.

***GOLDSTEIN, KURT** (1878–1966), neurologist and psychiatrist.

***HELLER, THEODOR** (1869–c. 1935), Austrian psychologist.

***HEYMANS, GERARDUS F.** (1857–1930), Dutch psychologist and philosopher.

***ISAACS, SUSAN SUTHERLAND** (1885–1948), English educator.

***KANTOR, JACOB ROBERT** (1888–), U.S. psychologist and academician.

***KARDINER, ABRAM** (1891–), U.S. psychoanalyst.

KATZ, DANIEL (1903–), U.S. psychologist. Born at Trenton, New Jersey, in 1943 he joined the Office of War Information as a research director. A leader in social psychology and public-opinion research, Katz served on the editorial boards of many journals in his field. He coauthored with R. L. Schanck *Social Psychology* (1938), and *The Social Psychology of Organizations* (with R. L. Kahn, 1966).

***KATZ, DAVID** (1884–1953), German psychologist.

***KOFFKA, KURT** (1846–1941), U.S. psychologist.

***LAZARUS, MORITZ** (1824–1903), German philosopher and social psychologist.

***LEWIN, KURT ZADEK** (1890–1947), psychologist and author.
***LIPMANN, OTTO** (1880–1938), German psychologist.
***LOMBROSO, CESARE** (1835–1909), Italian physician and criminologist.
***LURIA, ALEXANDER ROMANOVICH** (1902–), Russian psychologist.
***MALLER, JULIUS B.** (1901–1959), U.S. educator and sociologist.
***MASLOW, ABRAHAM** (1908–), U.S. psychologist.
***METZGER, ARNOLD** (1892–), German scholar and author.
***MUENSTERBERG, HUGO** (1863–1963), German psychologist.
***MYERS, CHARLES SAMUEL** (1873–1946), English psychologist.
***REDL, FRITZ** (1902–), child psychologist.
***RÉVÉSZ, GÉZA** (1878–1955), European (Hungarian?) psychologist.
***RUBIN, EDGAR** (1886–1951), Danish psychologist.
***SCHILDER, PAUL FERDINAND** (1886–1940), Austrian psychiatrist and psychoanalyst.

SEIDENFELD, MORTON (1906–), U.S. psychologist. Born in Spokane, Washington, Seidenfeld was educated at the University of Pennsylvania. During World War II, he served as a psychologist in the U.S. Army. From 1961 he served as the assistant chief, Division of Research Grants, Veterans Rehabilitation Administration. He taught at Yeshiva University. Among his important contributions was research in psychological aspects of physical disability.

***SELZ, OTTO** (1881–1944?), German psychologist.
***SPIRO, MELFORD ELLIOT** (1920–), U.S. anthropologist.
***STERN, WILLIAM LOUIS** (1871–1938), German psychologist.
***VYGOTSKI, LEV SEMYONOVICH** (1896–1934), Soviet psychologist.
***WECHSLER, DAVID** (1896–), U.S. psychologist.
***WEISS, ALBERT PAUL** (1879–1931), psychologist and social philosopher.
***WERNER, HEINZ** (1890–1964), U.S. psychologist.
***WERTHEIMER, MAX** (1880–1943), psychologist.

WOLFF, WERNER (1904–1957), U.S. existential psychologist. Born in Berlin, Wolff was one of the first to introduce existentialist psychology in the U.S. In 1933 he left Germany, spent three years at the University of Barcelona and then settled in the United States. He worked at Columbia (1940–42) and served as professor at Bard College in New York from 1942 onward. He studied the expression of personality in complex movements, in children's drawings, and in handwriting, and wrote books on his findings.

***WRESCHNER, ARTHUR** (1866–1932), psychologist.

PTOLEMY, the common name of monarchs of the Macedonian (or Thirty-First) Dynasty who ruled in Egypt from 323 to 30 B.C.E. It is unclear precisely how many such sovereigns there actually were; some scholars give a total of 14 and some 16. Most important for Jewish history were: PTOLEMY I (called Soter), reputed son of Lagus, founder of the dynasty. Ruler of Egypt as satrap from 323 B.C.E., he assumed the title of king in 305 and remained in power until his death in 283. Josephus states (Apion, 1:209ff., and cf. Ant. 12:2ff.) on the authority of Agatharchides of Cnidus that Ptolemy, after gaining admittance to Jerusalem on the pretext of wishing to make a sacrifice, captured the city on the Sabbath day when the Jews did not fight (320 B.C.E.). Agatharchides comments derisively that the Jews "persevering in their folly" of not defending their city on this day, were given over to a "harsh master." The second part of his statement is of especial interest, for scholars differ over whether Ptolemy was indeed a "harsh" master or whether his attitude toward the Jews was essentially benevolent. Whether the Jews in Egypt during his reign were indeed granted equal rights with Macedonian *clerouchoi* ("settlers") must remain an open question.

PTOLEMY II (called Philadelphus) reigned from 283 to 245 B.C.E. According to the Letter of *Aristeas he was responsible for two important actions, the one of immediate and the other of lasting consequence: he freed numerous Jewish slaves (themselves evidence of his father's military actions in Palestine) and initiated the Greek translation of the Bible—the *Septuagint. Both the foregoing statements may well have a historical basis. Philadelphus' literary interests are attested from other sources, and the Bible project may conceivably have been begun during his reign. The construction of several cities in Ereẓ Israel must also be attributed to his reign, including Philoteria (near Lake Kinneret) and Ptolemais, near present-day Acre (Arist. 115) as well as Philadelphia in Transjordan. He gained important victories in the first Syrian war against the Seleucid sovereign, *Antiochus I, and gave his daughter Berenice's hand in marriage to Antiochus II upon completion of the second Syrian campaign (c. 253 B.C.E.).

PTOLEMY III (called Euergetes) reigned from 246 to 221 B.C.E. Some scholars identify this Ptolemy with the king of that name mentioned by Josephus with regard to Joseph the Tobiad (Ant. 12:154ff.), while others are of the opinion that it was Ptolemy V (Epiphanes). If the king was Euergetes, then he must be credited with a favorable attitude toward his Jewish subjects. Josephus goes so far as to claim that after Euergetes' great victory over the Seleucids during the third Syrian war (246–241 B.C.E.) he offered incense at the Temple in Jerusalem. A possible reference to some of the king's actions during and after his campaigns in the Seleucid realm may be found in Daniel 11:7–9 where it is related that the Egyptian king removed idols from the conquered territories and restored them in his own country.

PTOLEMY IV (called Philopator) reigned from 221–203 B.C.E. A "wretched debauchee" according to E. Bevan, this monarch has fared less well than his predecessors in Jewish annals. Philopator is often associated with the following events described in III Maccabees: On the conclusion of the (fourth Syrian) war and his victory over Antiochus at Raphia (present-day Rafa) in 217 B.C.E., Philopator paid a visit to Jerusalem with the intention of entering the Temple. God intervened and he was felled to the ground. As revenge, when he returned to Egypt he ordered the Jews to be massacred in the Alexandrian arena by a horde of elephants, but the beasts turned on the royal troops instead. The day of deliverance was commemorated by the Jews as an annual feast day, which seems to be the only historically verifiable aspect of the story, though Josephus places it in a later context.

PTOLEMY V (called Epiphanes) reigned from 203 to 181 B.C.E. This monarch irretrievably lost the whole of Palestine to Antiochus III at the battle of Paneas (present-day Banias) c. 200 B.C.E.

PTOLEMY VI (or VII; called Philometor) reigned from 181 to 145 B.C.E. (from then on until the death of the last of the Ptolemies in 30 B.C.E., dates of birth and regnal years become increasingly uncertain). Philometor appears to have been generally well disposed toward the Jews, though he invaded Palestine to intervene in the disputes over the succession to the Syrian throne. His relations with *Jonathan the Hasmonean were cordial. II Maccabees 1–10 states that Philometor's mentor was a Jewish philosopher and biblical exegete, *Aristobulus by name. Under this same ruler the high priest *Onias IV, having fled from Jerusalem, built a temple at Leontopolis (c. 161 B.C.E.), while Philometor's military garrisons were commanded by two Jews, Onias and Dositheus.

PTOLEMY VII (or IX; called Euergetes II) reigned from 145 to 116 B.C.E. According to Josephus the Jews were persecuted during his rule, yet a synagogue was dedicated to him by the Egyptian Jewish community. It was in the 38th year of Euergetes' reign that the grandson of *Ben Sira went to Egypt where he translated his grandfather's work into Greek.

PTOLEMY VIII (or X; called Lathyrus and Soter II) reigned intermittently from 116 to 80 B.C.E. He launched an attack on the Hasmonean Alexander *Yannai shortly after the latter had come to the throne, only to be driven back by his mother, *Cleopatra III, who, with his brother Ptolemy IX (or XI; called Alexander I), later planned their own assault on Yannai.

Bibliography: A. Bouché-Leclercq, *Histoire des Lagides,* 4 vols. (1903–07), passim; Schuerer, Gesch, 3 (1909[4]), 24–52; E. R. Bevan, *A History of Egypt...* (1927), passim; Schalit, in: *Scripta Hierosolymitana,* 1 (1954), 64–77; J. Gutman, *Ha-Sifrut ha-Yehudit-ha-Hellenistit,* 1 (1958), 115ff.; V. Tcherikover, *Hellenistic Civilization and the Jews* (1959), index; M. Stern, *Ha-Te'udot le-Mered ha-Ḥashmona'im* (1965), 11–27; W. W. Tarn and G. T. Griffith, *Hellenistic Civilization* (1966[3]), passim. [DA.S.]

PTOLEMY (c. 135 B.C.E.), son of Ḥabub (Abubus) and son-in-law of *Simeon b. Mattathias (the Hasmonean). Ptolemy was *strategos* (i.e., military and local commander) at Jericho. Plotting to overthrow the Hasmonean House in 135 B.C.E., he invited Simeon and his entourage to a banquet while they were on a visit to the Jericho area, and treacherously murdered him and later two of his sons. He then sent messengers to Gazara (Gezer) to kill Simeon's other son John *Hyrcanus. At the same time, he set out to capture Jerusalem, dispatching a message to the Syrian king, Antiochus Sidetes, to inform him of the developments and to enlist his aid. Hyrcanus succeeded, however, in killing his assailants and hastened to Jerusalem where he won the trust of the people, who remained loyal to the Hasmonean dynasty. Having ensured his succession, Hyrcanus pursued Ptolemy and besieged him in a fortress in the vicinity of Jericho to which he had retreated. Ptolemy was able to defy Hyrcanus by holding his mother as a hostage. Eventually Hyrcanus had to lift the siege as a result of the onset of the Sabbatical year which led to a food shortage. Ptolemy fled to Philadelphia (Rabbath Ammon), after putting Hyrcanus' mother to death, and he is not heard of again.

Bibliography: I Macc. 16; Jos., Ant., 13:228–35; Jos., Wars, 1:54–60; Schuerer, Hist, 66–68. [L.RO.]

°**PTOLEMY (Son of Mennaeus),** king of Chalcis, in the region of the Lebanon (c. 85–40 B.C.E.). *Josephus relates that the inhabitants of Damascus despised Ptolemy, and preferred as king of Coele-Syria the Nabatean king, Aretas. Ptolemy's position in the area, however, was firmly established, and the Judean queen *Alexandra's armed attempt to weaken that influence brought no results. During Pompey's campaign in Syria, the territory under Ptolemy was devastated, but Ptolemy held fast to his principality though he was compelled to pay a ransom of 1,000 talents to the Roman conqueror. Following the Roman conquest of Judea, Ptolemy assumed guardianship over *Antigonus, the son of the Hasmonean prince, Aristobulus, and his sisters. They were brought to Ptolemy at Ashkelon by his son, Philippion, who eventually married one of the princesses, Alexandra. Philippion, however, was subsequently slain by his father on account of Alexandra, after which Ptolemy married the princess himself. Meanwhile, with the gradual subjugation of Judea under Herod, Antigonus gathered an army and with Ptolemy's assistance returned to his country, only to be defeated by Herod and again driven out of Judea. Ptolemy was succeeded as king of Chalcis by his son, Lysanias, who continued to support Antigonus.

Bibliography: Klausner, Bayit Sheni, 3 (1950[2]), 169f., 257f.; Schuerer, Hist, 112; A. Schalit, *Koenig Herodes* (1969), 819f. (index), s.v. *Ptolemaios, Sohn des Mennaios.* [I.G.]

°**PTOLEMY MACRON,** a general under *Antiochus IV (Epiphanes). The author of II Maccabees (10:12) explicitly states that Ptolemy "had taken the lead in preserving justice" for the Jews. As a result, he was accused before *Antiochus V (Eupator) and eventually took his life by poison. Some commentators accept the fact that the Ptolemy in question is synonymous with the Ptolemy son of Dorymenes, mentioned by Josephus (Ant. 12:298), in I Maccabees 3:38 and II Maccabees 4:45. The difficulty lies in equating this benevolent reputation with that in the foregoing passages (and cf. II Macc. 8:8–11). In these he is depicted as taking the field against *Judah Maccabee and being instrumental in the execution of a three-man Jewish deputation which had leveled charges against the Hellenizer *Menelaus. Polybius (27, 13) and Suidas (s.v. Πτολεμαῖος) refer to Ptolemy as former governor of Cyprus under Ptolemaic rule. He was later awarded the governorship of Coele-Syria and Phoenicia by the *Seleucids.

Bibliography: Meyer, Ursp, 2 (1921), 161f.; H. Bévenot, *Die beiden Makkabaeerbuecher* (1931), 30, 75, 218f.; Pauly-Wissowa, 46 (1959), 1763–65, nos. 48 and 49. [DA.S.]

PUBERTY. It was estimated that puberty, defined by the appearance of two pubic hairs, began in women early in the 13th year, and in men about the start of the 14th year, and for that reason maturity was regarded as beginning legally from the age of 12 years and one day in the case of females and 13 and one day in the case of males (Nid. 5:6; Nid. 52a). The rabbis reckoned religious responsibility to begin with the onset of puberty. From this period onward one was recognized as an adult, responsible for the observance of the precepts and the discharge of communal obligations. In the case of females, the rabbis delineated several distinct stages: *ketannah* ("minor"), from the age of three to the age of 12; the *na'arah* ("young woman"), for six months following the initial period; and the *bogeret* ("adult"), which begins at the expiration of these six months (Nid. 5:7). No such distinctions were made for the males who were simply *ketannim* ("minors") before 13 and *gedolim* ("adults") after their 13th birthday.

The attainment of the age of maturity did not automatically render one an adult, since the physical characteristics of puberty were also necessary in order to establish adulthood. However, when an examination for the signs of puberty was not made, it was presumed that a minor who reached the age of maturity had also developed the necessary signs (Nid. 46a). A young man past his *bar mitzvah is therefore counted for a **minyan* even without an examination (Isserles to Sh. Ar., OḤ 55:5). A woman's maturity was deemed sufficiently established if she bore a child (Yev. 12b). In the event that signs of puberty did not appear by the age of maturity, the person retained the status of a minor until the age of 20. After that age, if signs of impotence developed, thus accounting for the absence of secondary sex characteristics, the person was considered an adult (Nid. 5:9). If such signs did not develop, the person retained the status of a minor until the age of 35, which was considered the major portion of a person's life-span (Nid. 47b).

After attaining the age of maturity, young adults were held responsible in ritual, civil, and criminal matters, and were held punishable by the courts for their transgressions or breaches of contract. It was believed, however, that heavenly punishment was not forthcoming for sins committed before the age of 20 (Shab. 89b, cf. BB 121b) and only those above the age of 20 were liable for military service (Num. 1:3) or obligated to pay the half-shekel when the people were counted (Ex. 30:14).

See also *Legal Capacity and *Vows. See *Child Marriage for marriages entered into by minors or arranged for them.

Bibliography: Krauss, Tal Arch, 3 (1911), 23f., 449f.; J. Preuss, *Biblisch-talmudische Medizin* (1923³), 146–8; M. Perelman, *Midrash ha-Refu'ah*, 1 (1926), 36–38; ET, 5 (1953), 137–52, 168–79.

[A.Ro.]

PUBLIC AUTHORITY, in the context of this article, a term referring to an authoritative body composed of representatives of the public—whether appointed or elected by the latter—and entrusted with the duty and power to arrange various matters of common concern to this public. (For particulars concerning a personal authority, see *King and Kingdom; **Nasi;* *Exilarch.) It has been stated that "the foundations of the community, as they remained in existence until the modern Enlightenment, were laid mainly in the first generations of the Second Temple period" (Y. Baer, in: *Zion,* 15 (1950), 1). Attributable to this early period are a number of tannaitic sources incorporating *halakhot* concerning the "townspeople " (*benei ha-ir* or *anshei ha-ir,* Shek. 2:1; BB 1:5), as well as certain *beraitot* concerning the authority of the townspeople to compel each other toward the satisfaction of public needs in various fields (Tosef., BM 11:23ff.; BB 8a). At the head of such public authority stood the "seven good [elder] citizens" (*tovei ha-ir,* Jos., Ant., 4:214; TJ, Meg. 3:2, 74a; Meg. 26a). However, it was only with the rise of the Jewish community in various parts of the Diaspora from the tenth century onward that Jewish law came to experience its main development in the field of the laws concerning a public authority. This article deals with aspects of a public authority such as its legal standing, composition and powers, the legal relationship between itself and individual members of the community, and so on. For further particulars concerning the legislative institutions of the community and the related administration of the law, see **Takkanot ha-Kahal;* as regards the legal aspects of communal administration in fiscal and financial matters, see *Taxation; **Hekdesh.*

Qualifications, Duties, and Standing of Communal Leaders. The qualifications and duties of public representatives are discussed in the Bible and in the Talmud, mainly from the social, moral, and ideological aspects. The ways of the Patriarchs and other leading Jewish figures—such as Moses, Aaron, Samuel, and David—in dealings with the people serve as a basic source of guidance for the relationship between the people and their leaders, between the citizen and the public authority. It has been stated that appointment of "a good public leader *[parnas tov]* is one of the three things proclaimed by the Almighty Himself" (Ber. 55a; Kal. R. 8); that the Almighty had already shown to Adam "every generation with its leaders" (*dor dor u-farnasav,* Av. Zar. 5a), and to Moses, "all the leaders destined to serve Israel from the day of its leaving behind the wilderness until the time of the resurrection of the dead" (Sif. Num. 139); that in time to come, "when the Almighty shall renew His world, He shall stand Himself and arrange the leaders of the generation" (Yal., Isa. 454).

The requirements demanded of the leader representing a public authority are many and stringent: "In the past you acted only on your own behalf, from now on [i.e., upon appointment] you are bound in the service of the public" (Yal., Deut. 802); "a leader who domineers over the public" is one of those "whom the mind does not tolerate" (Pes. 113b) and over whom "the Almighty weeps every day" (Ḥag. 5b). It is not only forbidden for a leader to impose undue awe on the community if not intended "for the sake of Heaven" (*le-shem shamayim;* RH 17a), but he must himself stand in awe of the public (Sot. 40a). The scholars described in various ways the mutual interdependence between the citizen and the public authority: "A leader shall not be imposed on the public unless the latter is first consulted " (Ber. 55a), but once appointed, "even the most ordinary ... is like the mightiest of the mighty" (RH 25b), to whom the public owes obedience and honor. This interdependence is illustrated in the difference of opinion between Judah Nesi'ah (grandson of Judah ha-Nasi) and other scholars as to whether the stature of a leader follows that of his generation—*parnas le-fi doro*—or whether the generation is influenced by its leaders—*dor le-fi parnas.*

These, and other similar concepts scattered in halakhic and aggadic literature, guided the halakhic scholars in their determination of the principles of Jewish administrative law. A person engaged in public affairs is as one studying the Torah (TJ, Ber. 5:1). Moreover, "If he be engaged in studying the Torah and the time comes for recital of the *Shema* ["morning prayers"], he shall leave off studying and recite the *Shema* ... if he be engaged in the affairs of the public, he shall not leave off but complete this work, and recite the *Shema* if there remain time to do so" (Yad., Keri'at Shema 2:5; Sh. Ar., OḤ 70:4; based on Tosef., Ber. 1:4, 2:6; see also Lieberman, *Tosefta ki-Feshutah,* Berakhot, p. 3). Hence it followed that it was not merely a privilege to represent the public but also a duty. Thus in a case where a member of the community was elected to public office, contrary to his own declared wishes in the matter (namely, appointment as a tax assessor; see *Taxation), it was decided that "no person is free to exempt himself ... since every individual is bound in the service of the public in his town ... and therefore anyone who has sought to exclude himself from the consensus has done nothing and is bound to fulfill the duties of his office because the community has not agreed that he be excluded" (Resp. Rashba, vol. 3, no. 417; cf. also vol. 1, no. 769; vol. 7, no. 490; *Tashbeẓ,* 2:98).

In post-talmudic times the legal standing of a public authority was given precise definition based on the central legal doctrine accepted by the scholars of this period as the source of the community's standing and authority to make enactments; namely, that the standing of the communal leadership is assimilated to that of a court (*bet din;* see **Takkanot ha-Kahal*). In a certain case a person sought appointment to a public office; he had previously sworn a false oath with regard to his tax declaration, was fined for so doing, and came to an arrangement with the community concerning this tax payment. It was held by Israel *Isserlein (15th-century scholar of Vienna) that since such a person was unfit for appointment as a *dayyan,* he was also unfit to be numbered among the leaders of the community: "the leaders of the community fulfill the role of a court when they sit in supervision over the affairs of the public and private individuals" (*Pesakim u-Khetavim,* no. 214). This principle set a guide standard for the qualifications required of communal leaders (see, e.g., *Terumat ha-Deshen,* Resp. no. 344): "communal leaders appointed to attend to the needs of the public or private individuals are like *dayyanim,* and it is forbidden to include among them anyone who is disqualified from adjudicating on account of his own bad conduct" (*Rema,* ḤM 37:22). A further reason given by the scholars for assimilating the standing of communal leaders to that of *dayyanim* is that the duties of the former are largely concerned with providing for the social needs of the community, determination of the measure of support and relief for each being a task of a judicial nature (BB 8b and Rashi thereto; Sh. Ar., YD 256:3; *Mishpetei Uziel,* ḤM no. 4).

The assimilation of the communal leader's standing to that of *dayyan* is naturally limited to such powers as he enjoys in his official capacity only. Hence communal leaders who have been empowered to elect a body to supervise public affairs must do so themselves, since they have no power to delegate this authority to others (see below), even though an ordinary court has authority to appoint an agent and entrust him with the execution of certain tasks (Resp. Ribash no. 228).

The Public Authority and Laws of Property and Obligation. The aforementioned assimilation facilitated the solution of a number of problems arising in Jewish law with regard to legal relations between the public authority and the individual. Thus, for instance, the general requirement in Jewish law of a formal act of *kinyan* (see *Acquisition; *Contract) in order to lend a transaction legal effect would normally have constituted a serious obstacle to the efficient administration of a public authority's multiple affairs. However, beginning in the 13th century, the new legal principle of the validity of any legal transaction effected by a public authority, even without a *kinyan,* came to be recognized. Apparently this was first laid down by *Meir b. Baruch of Rothenburg in a case concerning the hire of a teacher by the community (quoted in *Mordekhai,* BM 457. 8). Normally the parties would have been entitled to retract, since no formal *kinyan* had been effected and the teacher had not yet commenced his work (see *Labor Law), but Meir of Rothenburg decided that there could be no retraction from the contract of hire "because a matter done by the public requires no *kinyan*—although this would be required in the case of an individual." He based this innovation on a wide construction of a number of talmudic rulings from which it may be inferred that the public has to be regarded differently from the individual, even though these contain no suggestion whatever that a *kinyan* might be dispensed with in a transaction effected by a public body (Meg. 26a; Git. 36a); in addition he compared the case of a transaction effected by a public body to that of a small *gift, although in this case withdrawal from the transaction is prohibited as amounting to a breach of faith and not because the transaction has full legal validity (i.e., when effected without a formal *kinyan;* BM 49a; Yad, Mekhirah 7:9; Sh. Ar., ḤM 2; see also *Contract). He further decided that a *suretyship for the fulfillment of the contract of employment between the community and the teacher was valid, even though it had been undertaken without a *kinyan* and in a manner in which the suretyship would otherwise be of no legal effect *(ibid.).* This decision is also given as the source of the rule that a gift by a public body is fully valid even if it is made without a formal *kinyan* (Sh. Ar., ḤM 204:9, and see also *Ha-Gra* thereto, n. 11). The law was similarly decided in regard to other legal matters affecting the public (see, e.g., Resp. Ribash no. 476; *Rema,* ḤM 81:1). This principle took root in the Diaspora: "The custom is widespread that whatever the communal leaders decide to do is valid and effective . . . and neither *kinyan* nor deed is required" (Resp. Rosh 6:19 and 21); similarly, in Constantinople in the 15th century it was held: "The widely accepted *halakhah* is that all matters of the public and anything that is done by or before the public is valid, even without *kinyan,* nor do the laws of alienation and acquisition *[hakna'ah]* apply in respect of such transactions" (*Mayim Amukkim,* no. 63); it was likewise decided by Isserles that "All matters of the public require no *kinyan*" (*Rema,* ḤM 163:6).

Other fundamental requirements of the law of *kinyan* were also relaxed with reference to a public authority. It was thus laid down, e.g., that the public may validly acquire something not yet in existence and alienate to someone not yet in existence (*Mayim Amukkim,* no. 63; see also *Acquisition, Modes of; *Contract); and also that in a public matter **asmakhta* constitutes no defect (Resp. Mabit, vol. 2, pt. 2, no. 228). One of the explanations given for this fundamental innovation was that it had to be assumed that in any transaction with which the public was connected the parties would make up their minds absolutely *(gemirut ha-da'at),* even without a *kinyan* and notwithstanding the fact of *asmakhta* and so on (see, e.g., Resp. Ribash no. 476; *Rema,* ḤM 81:1; *Sma,* ḤM 204, n. 14); However, the main explanation given for this innovation is the fact that the legal standing of a public authority has to be assimilated to that of a court, that is "because it is influenced by the rule of **hefker bet din* . . . and a public authority, in its dealings with the public, is as a court for the whole world" (Resp. Rashbash no. 566, also no. 112; cf. the statement of Meir of Rothenburg quoted in *Mordekhai,* BM 457–8; idem, Resp., ed. Prague, no. 38). For the same reason it was held that a public body might not plead that it had not seriously intended a particular transaction, nor that it had erred and not properly understood the nature thereof (Rashbash, loc. cit.).

Relaxation of the requirements of the law of *kinyan,* of the rule of *asmakhta,* and so on, in the case of public matters naturally extended not only to the public body but also to the individual transacting with that body, so that he too was not free to withdraw from the transaction, even if it was effected without a *kinyan,* etc. (Resp. Rashbash no. 112; *She'ot de-Rabbanan,* no. 14; *Ba'ei Ḥayyei* ḤM, pt. 2, no. 81; PDR 6:172f., 180f.).

The Public Authority and the Exercise of its Own Discretion. A basic question of administrative law concerning the power of a public authority to delegate authority in a matter requiring the exercise of its own discretion was extensively dealt with in a responsum of *Isaac b. Sheshet Perfet (Resp. Ribash no. 228). A certain Catalonian community was granted a royal privilege in terms of which three communal trustees, together with the court, were authorized to nominate 30 persons to supervise the affairs of the community, particularly tax matters. The trustees and the court were unable to reach agreement on the execution of their task and instead agreed to elect two persons and delegate to them authority to appoint the 30 communal leaders. When this was done, a section of the community objected on the ground that authority could not be delegated by a body required to exercise its own discretion. In upholding this objection Isaac b. Sheshet held that even if in general an agent could delegate his authority to another—in circumstances where it could be assumed that the principal was not particular about the matter (see *Agency, Law of)—this was not so in the case of a public authority, even though the latter is in a sense an agent of the public. The explanation offered is that no express power to delegate authority was given in the royal privilege, and the matter was of great importance since all the affairs of the community depended on selection of its 30 leaders, and those responsible for their selection had to choose leaders possessing suitable qualities; wise, just, and peace-loving persons, knowledgeable in the affairs of the community: "it is not the intention of the community that those who have to select them [the 30] shall be able to appoint others to act in their own place, even if these others equal them in wisdom and standing"; if, however, the responsible parties had been given express authority to delegate their powers, "then it would be as if the community itself had chosen these two."

In the same matter Isaac b. Sheshet went on to give an important ruling concerning resort to the law of the land in the interpretation of the royal privilege. In his opinion, even if it were to be said that the privilege had been given with the intention that it be construed "only according to the law of the land," and even if according to this "anyone entrusted with a matter may in turn entrust this matter to anyone he chooses," yet in the case under consideration the delegation of authority remained invalid, because the rules of administrative law, so far as the Jewish community was concerned, derived their authority from Jewish law also, which did not allow for the delegation of authority in the case at hand. This ruling also involved no conflict with the law of the land in accordance with which the privilege had been given, since the general authorities were not concerned if the Jewish public failed to avail itself of the powers given under the law of the land, but were only concerned when the Jewish collective interpreted the privilege in such a manner as to lend itself wider authority than was available under this law: "the king is only particular about an extension of authority, not about a narrowing of it" *(ibid.).*

The Public Authority as an Employer. The great development of Jewish public law that followed on the rise of the Jewish community also made itself felt in the field of master and servant, in relation to employment by a public body. Special requirements relating to a public-service contract had already been emphasized in talmudic law. Thus, it was laid down that if a public-bath attendant, barber, or baker was the only one available and a festival was approaching, he could be restrained from leaving his employment until he provided a replacement (Tosef., BM 11, 27; see also *Contract). In addition, in order to avoid harm to the public, it was laid down that an individual fulfilling his duties to the public in a negligent manner might be dismissed immediately, as in the case of a public gardener, butcher, or bloodletter, a scribe, a teacher of young children, "as well as other like artisans who may cause irretrievable harm, may be dismissed without warning, since they are appointed by the public for as long as they carry out their duties in a proper manner" (Yad, Sekhirut 10:7, based on BM 109a and BB 21b). The majority of the *rishonim* interpret the rule of the *Gemara* as also extending to a private servant, considering that he too may be dismissed during the duration of his service contract if he has caused irretrievable damage (*Hassagot Rabad,* Sekhirut 10:7; *Beit ha-Beḥirah,* BM 109a; Tur and Sh. Ar., ḤM 306:8; *Rema* thereto; *Sma* thereto, n. 19). It was, however, laid down that a servant might not be dismissed without proper warning unless he was continually guilty of slackness in his work, and it must also be proved in the presence of the worker that he was indeed failing in his duties (*Rema* loc. cit.; *Maggid Mishneh,* Sekhirut 10:7; *Nimmukei Yosef,* BM 109a; see also below).

In post-talmudic times the halakhic scholars had to contend with the converse question: namely, whether it was permissible for a public authority to dismiss its servant without justifiable reason, on expiry of the agreed period of service, in the same way as could a private employer, who is free to refrain from renewing his servant's employment. (In modern times Jewish law has come to recognize the master's duty to pay severance pay to his servant on his dismissal: see **Ha'anakah.*) The talmudic rule that the high priest may not be dismissed from his office (TJ, Sanh. 2:1) did not serve as an analogy for public servants in general (see Assaf, *Mi-Sifrut ha-Ge'onim,* 73f.; *Sha'arei Teshuvah,* nos. 50, 51). From the 12th century, Jewish law consistently tended toward recognition of the principle that a public servant may not be dismissed from his employment except for justifiable reason. Maimonides laid down the general rule: "a person is not removed from a public position in Israel unless he has offended" (Yad, Kelei ha-Mikdash 4:21); also that "it is not proper to dismiss any officeholder from office on account of mere rumors concerning him; this cannot be done even if he has no enemies, all the less so if there are people in the town who are his enemies and have ulterior motives" (his Resp. (ed. Blau) no. 111; this was also the view of Meir ha-Levi and R. *Yom Tov b. Abraham Ishbili (Ritba), see Nov. Ritba to Mak. 13a). This principle was explained on the ground of "avoiding suspicion," that is, termination of the servant's employment with the public may arouse suspicion that the servant is being dismissed on account of his improper conduct (Resp. Rashba, vol. 5, no. 283; quoted also in *Beit Yosef,* OḤ 53, conclusion).

At the same time, it is held to be permissible to dismiss a public servant whenever it is customary to appoint people in charge of public matters for a fixed period, "so that at the end of it these men depart and are replaced by others, whether they be appointed in charge of food supplies, the charity fund, tax, or any other public service, and whether or not they receive any remuneration for their service; even if no fixed period of service be stipulated for them, the terms of their appointment shall be similarly in accordance with the custom . . . because of their practice to replace [officials], the suspicion mentioned above is eliminated" (Rashba loc. cit.). In his responsum Solomon ibn Adret confirmed that such was in fact the custom in his time: "that the competent in each generation carry out tasks on behalf of the public, and thereafter depart to be replaced by others." The statement of this twofold principle—that a public servant may not be dismissed without justifiable cause except when it is the custom to hold office for a fixed period only—was accepted as *halakhah* in the Shulḥan Arukh (OḤ 53:25–26) and was applied in the different centers of Jewish life in respect of all persons employed by a public authority (*keneset ha-gedolah,* OḤ 53, *Beit Yosef; Arukh Ha-Shulḥan,* OḤ 53:26; *Mishnah Berurah,* OḤ 53, no. 73ff.; *Even ha-Ezer,* Sekhirut 10:7). In modern times attempts have been made to distinguish between different categories of public servants, although there is no apparent justification for this in the halakhic sources (see PDR 3:94ff.).

The discussions concerning dismissal of a public servant also embraced the related and more far-reaching proposition that a public office be transmitted from father to son by way of inheritance. In this respect too there was already the tannaitic rule, on the analogy of a king succeeded by his son (Deut. 17:20), that "all the leaders *[parnasim]* of Israel have their places taken by their sons" (Sif. Deut. 162; cf. Sifra Ẓav 5). Also Maimonides laid down that "Not only the kingship, but all offices and appointments in Israel are an inheritance from father to son for all time" (Yad, Melakhim, 1:7; Kelei ha-Mikdash, 4:20). In later times a trend toward restriction of this widely stated rule asserted itself. Thus, some scholars held that the rabbinate too was an office that could be passed by inheritance (Resp. Ribash no. 271; *Rema,* YD 245:22). Others disagreed, taking the view that "the crown of Torah is not an inheritance" (Resp. Maharashdam, YD, no. 85; Shneur Zalman of Lyady, Sh. Ar., OḤ 53:33, et al.). This was also Moses Sofer's original opinion, which he later reversed (Resp. Ḥatam Sofer, OḤ 12 and 13). It was laid down that local custom concerning inheritance of an office was to be followed (*Rema* loc. cit.). A son can in no event inherit a public office unless he is qualified for it and worthy of doing so (Sifra, loc. cit.; Maim. Yad, Melakhim, 1:7; *Rema,* Sh. Ar. YD 245:22; Ḥatam Sofer loc. cit.; for further details see OPD 46, 112; PDR 4:211; see also *Labor Law).

Election of Public Officeholders. Questions such as the nomination of candidates, their number, their manner of election, etc., are extensively dealt with in post-talmudic halakhic literature (see **Takkanot ha-Kahal;* *Taxation). In modern times, with the renewal of Jewish autonomy in Ereẓ Israel and the establishment of the State of Israel, halakhic discussion has been resumed in relation to various problems arising in connection with the election of officeholders to representative state and municipal bodies. The primary sources relied upon in this discussion are found in the post-talmudic halakhic literature dealing with the leadership and administration of the community and its institutions; sometimes, when these sources do not deal specifically with the subject discussed by modern scholars, a conclusion is reached by way of analogy.

MAJORITY AND MINORITY. The principle of electing a public representative by majority vote was based by the scholars on the doctrine of *Aḥarei rabbim le-hattot* ("to follow a multitude": Ex. 23:2; see *Majority Rule), which was interpreted to mean "that in all matters to which the community consents the majority is followed" (Resp. Rosh 6:5; in talmudic *halakhah* the doctrine was interpreted as pertaining to a majority of the court in giving its decision, or to the concept of majority as a legal presumption; see **Takkanot ha-Kahal; *Ḥazakah*). At various times extensive discussions and sharp disputes centered around the question of the weight to be attached to the vote of individual members of the community. Many scholars objected to a scale graded in accordance with social and economic standing: "and it makes no difference whether this majority was composed of rich or poor, of scholars or the common people" (Resp. Re'em no. 53). An illiterate person was held to be eligible even for certain public appointments (Resp. Rashba, vol. 3, no. 399).

An informative description of some such disputes is to be found in a responsum of Menahem Mendel *Krochmal (mid-17th-century leader of Moravian Jewry; *Ẓemaḥ Ẓedek* no. 2). It had been the custom in a certain community for all taxpayers, regardless of their financial standing or education, to participate in the election of communal leaders and the appointment of public officials. Some of the "respected citizens" sought to depart from this custom and to have it laid down that only a person paying tax in excess of a certain rate, or a *talmid ḥakham* ("at least qualified as a **ḥaver*"), could participate in the elections. Krochmal mentions that the "respected citizens" supported their demand with the argument that "most of the needs and affairs of the public involve the expenditure of money; how is it likely that the opinion of a poor man shall be as weighty as that of a rich man, or the opinion of an *am ha-areẓ* who is not wealthy be considered in the same way as that of a *ḥaver.*" They further contended that what they were seeking was anyhow customary in "large and important communities." The rest of the community objected to such a change in the system: "the poor, the masses of the people cry out against the derogation of their rights, since they also pay tax and contribute their share, and even if the rich pay more, the poor at any rate find the little they pay to be a greater burden than do the rich in paying much more."

In his decision Krochmal strongly condemned the discriminatory nature of the proposed change in the election system and held that—at the very least—"the little of the poor is balanced against the much of the rich." He nevertheless upheld the custom prevailing in most of the communities of striking a balance between a majority based on the number of souls and a majority based on financial contribution. He also rejected the proposition that those lacking in knowledge of the Torah be deprived of their vote, "lest they separate themselves from the public . . . which will lead to increased strife in Israel." A change involving discrimination against any section of the public was forbidden except with the unanimous consent of all members of the community, and, added Krochmal, in communities where there was such discrimination it had to be assumed that this had been instituted with the unanimous approval of the entire community. In recent times halakhic scholars have accepted as binding the view that every vote is to carry equal weight (see, e.g., *Mishpetei Uziel,* ḤM no. 3).

Eligible Age. The question of the age at which the right to elect and be elected to public office is acquired has in recent times come to be discussed by analogy with the criterion of age in other fields of the law. The general view is that the usual age of legal capacity—namely 13 years and one day for a man and 12 years and a day for a woman—is not to be relied upon as decisive with regard to the right to participate in elections, since in Jewish law the age of legal capacity is dependent on the specific nature of the legal act involved (see Elon, ILR, 1969, p. 121ff.) and exercise of the voting right carries with it legal consequences affecting the public as a whole—a factor calling for greater maturity on the part of the voter. According to one view, the active right to elect is acquired at 18 years: at this age a person has legal capacity to adjudicate in matters of civil law (*dinei mamonot*; Sh. Ar., ḤM 7:3) and to perform public religious duties, for instance as a ritual slaughterer (*Rema,* YD 1:5). Another view is that the right to vote is acquired from the age of 20, paralleling the biblical military age (Ex. 30:14; Num. 1:3) and the age of full majority, for instance for the purpose of the sale of paternal land which has been inherited (Yad, Mekhirah, 29:13; Sh. Ar., ḤM 235:9).

In the case of the passive right to be elected, the general view is that the minimal age is 20 years and over. At this age a person has the right to adjudicate in matters of criminal law (*dinei nefashot*; TJ, Sanh. 4:7) and even—for the purpose of permanent appointment as a *dayyan*—in matters of civil law (*Pitḥei Teshuvah,* ḤM 7, n. 4). Other scholars arrive at this age (20) following the minimal age for permanent appointment as a cantor (Sh. Ar., OḤ 53:8) or as an *apotropos (cf. Resp. Ribash no. 20). There is also an opinion that distinguishes between a person elected to a state body, such as the Knesset (by virtue of whose far-reaching substantive powers the function of its representatives is held to be analogous to that of a *dayyan* adjudicating in matters of the criminal law), and a person elected to a municipal body (whose function is held to be analogous to that of the *dayyan* adjudicating in matters of the civil law, and who is therefore eligible from the age of 18 years).

Women. A woman's right to elect and be elected to public office has been the subject of much halakhic discussion in recent times. In particular a great deal of opposition has been expressed to granting women the passive right to be elected, such opposition being based on tannaitic and amoraic law (Sif. Deut., 157 and Ber. 49a, respectively): "A woman is not appointed to the kingship, as it is said, 'set a king over thee' (Deut. 17:15) and not a queen; similarly for all offices in Israel none but men are appointed" (Yad, Melakhim 1:5). Some scholars took a different view, basing themselves on the fact that Deborah "judged Israel" (Judg. 4:4), i.e., that she functioned not only as a judge but was also the leader of the people. The *rishonim* had already commented on the contradiction between the fact of Deborah's leadership and the rule excluding women from public office, a contradiction they sought to reconcile by the qualification that the objection to a woman's leadership is eliminated when she is accepted by the will of the people (Nov. Rashba and Ran, Shevu. 30a; cf. also Tos. to BK 15a and Nid. 50a). On this basis some latter-day scholars have decided that a woman is entitled to elect and be elected (see, e.g., *Mishpetei Uziel,* ḤM no. 6), their conclusion being influenced by the consideration that under existing social conditions "men and women meet daily in business transactions" *(ibid.).* Although at the time he gave this decision (in the 1940s) R. Uziel wrote that it was of a purely theoretical nature and was not to be applied in practice (*ibid.* and see p. 292), it has nevertheless been accepted in practice in the state of Israel by the decisive majority of religious Jewry so far as concerns Knesset and municipal elections.

Period of Residence. The period of residence qualifying a person to elect and be elected has generally followed the period laid down for tax liability (see *Taxation; see also Resp. Maharit, vol. 1, no. 569; *Mishpetei Uziel,* ḤM no. 3).

Proportional Representation. In detailed decisions, scholars such as Rabbi *Kook, Jacob *Meir, and Ḥayyim *Brody expressed the opinion that the system of elections on a proportional basis answers the requirements of Jewish law, one of their main reasons being that in this way representation in the government of the state and its institutions is offered to all sections of the people (see *Sinai,* 14 (1943/44), 100–14).

In the State of Israel. In the Supreme Court. A number of Jewish law principles, concerning the legal standing of a public body and the relationship between the latter and its employees, have been considered and relied upon in decisions of the Supreme Court of Israel. In one case a municipal employee who had been dismissed on a charge of improper conduct applied to the Supreme Court—sitting as a high court of justice—to have his dismissal set aside on the ground that he had been given no opportunity to make himself heard and to answer the charge against himself prior to his dismissal. The court rejected the municipality's plea that in terms of the municipalities ordinance it had been under no obligation to hear the employee prior to his dismissal and upheld the employee's application, relying mainly on the following principles of Jewish law: (1) a person appointed to a public office, or holding a position with a public institution, may not be dismissed without a reasonable cause; (2) municipal councillors are as judges and therefore may not act arbitrarily but must consider a case on its merits; (3) since the councillors are like judges they have to follow a procedure that accords with natural justice, and a basic principle of Jewish law is that a person subjected to an inquiry must be enabled to appear and state his case (see PD 20, pt. 1 (1966), 29; cf. Resp. Rema no. 108). In another case the court applied the Jewish law principle that—for the good of the public—there is an obligation to dismiss a public servant who is proved to have neglected his duties after he has been given due warning (see PD 20, pt. 1 (1966), 41). In another instance the court, relying on the principle that a member of a public body is as a judge, concluded that no fault was to be found with a publicly elected official for not always following the opinions of those by whom he had been elected, since he has to act as a judge seeking the truth of a matter (PD 21, pt. 1 (1967), 59), provided only that he does so upon mature consideration and does not irresponsibly and often change his views (PD 20, pt. 1 (1966), 651). Another principle of Jewish law which the court has applied precludes a judge from adjudging a matter from which he stands to derive personal benefit, and in terms of this the court set aside the decision of a local council which had been taken with the participation of a councillor who had a personal interest in the matter (*ibid.*, 102; see also PD 19, pt. 3 (1965), 393).

IN THE RABBINICAL COURTS. There is among others a decision of the rabbinical court on a basic problem that has arisen in recent years, touching on the above-mentioned rules of Jewish administrative law (the court in this instance sitting as an arbitral body since its jurisdictional authority is confined to matters of personal status; see **Mishpat Ivri*). Three political parties entered the municipal elections under a joint list, having agreed that if only two of their candidates were elected then the second one on the list resign in favor of the next candidate on the list; only two candidates were elected and the second one refused to resign as agreed. It was contended before the court that the agreement was invalid because it had not been effected by means of a *kinyan,* because it related to something not yet in existence (the agreement having been concluded prior to the elections), and because it was defective on account of *asmakhta* (i.e., since the parties had been confident that more than two of their candidates would be elected, there had been no *gemirut ha-da'at*). The court rejected all these contentions and upheld the validity of the agreement, relying on the principles discussed above governing a public authority. The court emphasized that these principles applied not only to a public authority administering municipal affairs, but also to the public constituting a political party: "If it is the rule that in public matters there is no need for a *kinyan,* and the power of the public in its doings is so great that it is not restricted by the limitations imposed on the legal act of an individual—for instance as regards something that is not yet in existence, *asmakhta,* etc.—then there is no matter that is more eminently of a public nature than the matter under consideration, namely the composition of the public leadership" (PDR 6:176). It was accordingly held that the second one of the elected representatives was obliged to resign, as undertaken in the agreement. The decision was confirmed on appeal (*ibid.* 178ff.) and in addition the following guiding principle in the field of Jewish administrative law was laid down: "We have to add and say to the litigants that public leaders should not, in the course of their public duties, avail themselves of the plea that they are not bound by their own undertakings because of their questionable legal validity. Statements and undertakings, particularly in public affairs, are sacred matters which have to be observed and fulfilled wholeheartedly, in letter and spirit . . . for the public is always bound by its statements and may not retract" *(ibid.)*.

Bibliography: T. S. Zuri, *Mishpat ha-Talmud,* 8 (1922), 52–60; idem, *Toledot ha-Mishpat ha-Ẓibburi ha-Ivri,* 1 (1931), 301ff.; E. J. Waldenberg, *Ẓiẓ Eli'ezer,* 2 (1947), no. 24; Z. Warhaftig, in: *Sinai,* 23 (1948), 24–49; M. Findling, in: *Yavneh,* 3 (1949), 50–56, 63; A. Karlin, in: *Ha-Torah ve-ha-Medinah,* 1 (1949), 58–66; J. Pilz, *ibid.,* 2 (1950), 55–58; J. H. Asafi, *ibid.,* 4 (1951), 241–3; N. Z. Friedmann, *ibid.,* 7–8 (1954/57), 63–71; T. A. Agus, in: JQR, 43 (1952/53), 153–76; M. Feinstein, in: *Ha-Ma'or,* 12 (1960), issue 2 (English numbering: 10 (1960), issue 10), 4–7; M. Amsel, *ibid.,* 7–10; M. Vogelmann, in: *Sinai,* 48 (1960/61), 196–203; M. Elon, in: *Meḥkerei Mishpat le-Zekher Avraham Rosenthal* (1964), 1–54; idem, in: *Fifth World Congress of Jewish Studies,* 3 (1969), 90f. (Eng. Abstract). [M.E.]

PUBLIC RELATIONS. Public relations as a profession developed in the 20th century, mainly in the U.S. Until the beginning of the 20th century public relations was a refined form of propaganda employed almost exclusively to defend a movement, cause, or individual or institution, regardless of merit or social significance. Among the first Jews in the field were Moses Lindo of South Carolina, who made skillful use of publicity to promote the export of American indigo in the years before the Revolution, and Henry Castro, a French Jew who publicized Texas among European Jews in 1844 as an agent of the Republic of Texas. Henry Zeltner was a U.S. government press agent in New York City during and after the 1863 draft riots. Twenty years later his son, Louis, served as publicity man for Theodore Roosevelt when he was police commissioner of New York City. The country's first financial publicity agency was founded by Albert Frank in 1872 to obtain free newspaper space for stockbrokers. Rudolph Guenther set up a similar agency in 1892, and later the Albert Frank-Guenther law firm became the leading financial publicity organization. Gus J. Karger (1866–1924), a vice-president of the firm, was the press chief of William Howard Taft's 1908 presidential campaign and director of the Republican Party's press bureau in the 1912 presidential election.

Modern public relations took shape during World War I with the formation of the U.S. Committee on Public Information. This first organized use of all the tools and techniques of publicity as an offensive measure for mobilizing the power of mass opinion demonstrated to business, industry, government, and private institutions the value of public relations. This committee was the training ground for two young men, Carl Byoir (1888–1957) and Edward L. *Bernays, who became major forces in raising public relations to a profession. Byoir helped distribute 40,000,000 of the famous red, white, and blue texts on war aims abroad, publicized the draft, interpreted American war objectives throughout the world, and was on Woodrow Wilson's press staff at the Versailles Peace Conference. He also served as public relations adviser to Thomas G. *Masaryk, first president of Czechoslovakia. He was the originator of the Franklin D. Roosevelt birthday balls that raised millions for polio victims and led to the establishment of the National Foundation for Infantile Paralysis.

It was Bernays who coined the term "public relations counselor" and gave the profession its first code and set of principles. He also wrote the first book on the subject, *Crystallizing Public Opinion,* in 1923, and taught the first college course in public relations at New York University in 1930. Before his retirement in the late 1950s, Bernays represented some of the nation's largest corporations and newspapers as well as government agencies and social and health organizations.

The Europe of World War I was also the training ground for Benjamin Sonnenberg (1901–), who began his flamboyant career as a writer of publicity stories for the *American Joint Distribution Committee. He launched his own firm in 1924 and became a highly successful adviser to corporations, entertainment and literary personalities, and big businessmen. George Weissman (1919–), who rose from public relations director to president of the Philip Morris Co., learned the art in the Sonnenberg office. Out of the Byoir firm came Kalman Druck, later head of his own firm, and Edward Gottlieb. Druck was one of the key figures in uniting the Public Relations Society of America and the American Public Relations Association (APRSA) into a single professional organization. He headed the committee that developed the system for accrediting practitioners. Gottlieb, famed for coining the permanent-wave slogan

"Which twin has the Toni?" was responsible for popularizing French champagne in the U.S.

Public Relations in Entertainment and Sport. In the 1920s and 1930s, most Jews in public relations were not in industry but in the world of entertainment, in the film industry. One of the earliest motion picture press agents was Mike Newman, promotion director for Columbia Pictures, who made Mary Pickford an international celebrity. Howard Dietz was the publicity agent who in 1917 devised Leo the Lion as the Metro-Goldwyn-Mayer trademark. He spread the malapropisms of Samuel *Goldwyn for many years before becoming press chief for *Loew's. Another film public relations pioneer was Charles Einfeld (1901–) of Warner Brothers, who trained scores of people in motion picture promotion. He introduced the movie trailer and the premiere junket. Harry Reichenbach was an outstanding press agent from 1915 to 1930, as was Irving Strouse in the 1930s. Bernard Sobol was the man who made Flo *Ziegfeld's Follies a national institution before World War II. Sydney Eiges and Sid Garfield were publicity chiefs for the National Broadcasting Company and Columbia Broadcasting System respectively. Many of the leading stage and movie personalities were represented by Henry C. Rogers of Hollywood. The public relations resourcefulness of Henry Meyer converted Miami Beach from a winter playground for the rich to a year-round resort for people of modest means. The bathing beauty contests that became internationally famous were Meyer's brain children. Hal Cohen, Meyer's successor, built up the Florida resort even more.

Many of the best-known professional sports enterprises had Jewish public relations directors. Haskell Cohen was the public relations chief of the National Basketball Association. Robert Fishel and Harold Weisman were the public relations directors of the New York Yankees and the New York Mets respectively. Joe Goldstein, who promoted Roosevelt Raceway, began as a publicity man at the old Madison Square Garden. Irving Rudd, who handled public relations at Yonkers Raceway, grew up in small-time boxing club publicity. Harry Markson was for years the public relations man for Mike Jacobs, the leading fight promoter of Madison Square Garden. Joe Reichler handled public relations for the Baseball Commissioner of America.

Public Relations in Politics and Public Affairs. Events flowing from the depression of the 1930s and the New Deal, and later from World War II, were responsible for the immense expansion of public and private public relations in which Jews came to play an increasingly significant role. Charles Michelson (1869–1947), brother of the scientist Albert A. *Michelson, who became press director of the Democratic National Committee in 1929, was the ablest political publicist of his time. Mike Straus, who went to Washington with the New Deal, was the highly effective public relations director of the Department of the Interior under Harold C. Ickes.

One of the founders of the American College Public Relations Association in 1917 was Bernard Sobel, information director of Purdue University. An early president of this oldest organized group of publicists was Louis Boochever, public relations director of Cornell University in the 1920s, and later national public relations director of the American Red Cross. George Hecht, publisher of *Parents Magazine,* was the founder in 1919 of *Better Times,* the first publication to publicize social work. Six years later he established the Social Legislation Information Service as a public relations lobby. Louis Resnick (1892–1941), for 15 years public relations director of the National Society for the Prevention of Blindness, set many of the standards used in social welfare publicity during his years as information director of the National Safety Council. In 1935 he became the first information director of the newly established U.S. Social Security Administration. Harold Levy, for many years on the staff of the Russell Sage Foundation, was one of the pioneers of social work publicity. Irving Rimer was the third executive director of the National Public Relations Council on Health and Welfare, and his successor was Harold Weiner. Rimer later became public relations director of the American Cancer Society. Sol Lifson was for a long time director of public information for the National Tuberculosis and Respiratory Diseases Association. Another pioneer in social work publicity was Viola Paradis, who headed public relations for the *National Council of Jewish Women. Bernard Roloff introduced the "crusade for mercy" theme as public relations director of the United Fund for Chicago, one of the largest community chests. Victor Weingarten made the Child Welfare League widely known. From 1923 to 1936 Herbert Seligman was public relations director of the National Association of Colored People, and Frances Adlerstein directed public relations for the Travelers Aid Association.

Anna *Rosenberg, who served as assistant secretary of defense under President Truman, later became a highly successful public relations expert for big business. When he retired from newspaper work, Herbert Bayard *Swope, the renowned managing editor of the *New York World,* was public relations adviser to Bernard M. *Baruch and to many government agencies and business firms. In the 1950s, Sydney S. Baron was the publicity director of Tammany Hall. The C.I.O. Political Action Committee's public relations director was Allan Reitman, and David B. Charney had the same post with the International Teamsters' Union. Frank Mankiewicz was the press director for Senator Robert F. Kennedy, and held the same post in the unsuccessful effort of Senator George McGovern to win the 1968 Democratic presidential nomination.

Public Relations in the Jewish Community. The rise of the public relations man in Jewish communal life was a post-World War I phenomenon directly attributable to major events and developments in Jewish history. The relief campaigns on behalf of war-stricken European Jewry, the struggles against the anti-Semitism of Henry Ford and the Ku Klux Klan in the 1920s, the growth of national membership organizations and Jewish federations, the building-fund campaigns for synagogues, Jewish community centers, old folks homes and institutions of Jewish higher learning, the fight against Nazism, and the dramatic efforts to establish the State of Israel, all called between 1917 and 1948 for the unprecedented mobilization of Jewish public opinion as well as the winning of support from the general population.

The first public relations bureau serving the Jewish community was formed in 1919 by Louis Popkin (1894–1943) and his wife Zelda (née Feinberg). A reporter on the *American Hebrew,* Popkin had been drafted in 1914 to handle publicity for the newly-organized American Joint Distribution Committee. In 1917 he took on the same job for the wartime National Jewish Welfare Board. After the war the Popkins established Planned Publicity Service, which did public relations for a number of Jewish organizations. Their first assignment was the drafting of the cable to Woodrow Wilson at the Versailles Peace Conference asking for the protection of Jewish rights. For the New York Federation of Jewish Philanthropies they set up the first organized permanent public relations department in any Jewish agency. In 1922 Abraham H. Fromenson (1874–1935), editor of the English page of the Yiddish-language daily, the *Tageblatt,* who had been publicity head of the Zionist Organization of America when Louis D. *Brandeis controlled it, joined the Popkin firm, which trained many of the people who later became the first public relations directors of major Jewish organizations. David A. Brown, the Detroit business executive who turned into the leading Jewish fund-raiser of the 1920s and 1930s, pioneered many of the public relations techniques on which later public relations experts built.

As public relations chief of the Federation of Jewish Philanthropies from 1934 to 1945, Elliott Cohen, founder of **Commentary,* introduced to the field of public relations people of professional competence and familiarity with Jewish life and traditions, who were able to interpret health and welfare with intelligence, style, and clarity. He established the high standards of production and art that set the pattern of fund-raising literature for the whole Jewish community. One of Cohen's predecessors was Isidore Sobeloff (1899–), who went on to become a Federation executive in Detroit and Los Angeles.

Henry *Montor (1905–) became publicity director of the United Palestine Appeal in 1931, and was a genius in persuading American Jewish communities to provide unprecedented sums for Palestine by the use for the first time of all the tools and techniques of modern public relations. In 1939, when the JDC and UPA joined forces in the United Jewish Appeal, Montor was elevated to national campaign director. He and his successor, Meyer Steinglass, broke new ground by running full-page advertisements in the daily press and using radio for campaign publicity. When Montor left UJA to assume direction of the Bonds for Israel campaign, Steinglass went with him as public relations director. Raphael Levy and Ben Hanft, Steinglass' successors at UJA extended their methods to television and films.

The public relations techniques first tested by UJA and Bonds for Israel were adapted with some modifications but equal success by the American offices of Israel organizations as well by virtually every other national Jewish agency. The American Jewish Committee, the Anti-Defamation League, and the American Jewish Congress varied in approach and emphasis, but they all saw public relations as a significant element of their overall educational role in bringing to public attention the nature of prejudice, the evils of anti-Semitism and bigotry, and the importance of understanding among men of all races and ethnic groups.

A unique public relations instrument created by the Jews of America was the Jewish Welfare Board Public Relations Committee, formed during World War II by the American Jewish Committee, the Anti-Defamation League, the American Jewish Congress, the Jewish War Veterans, and the Jewish Labor Committee. This combined operation developed within the Jewish community an understanding of the war issues, and built up support for a program of religious and morale services to Jewish military personnel.

Through public relations of the most dignified character, the Jewish Theological Seminary of America helped establish Judaism as one of the major religious traditions in America. The Seminary's radio and TV program, "The Eternal Light," was a highly effective public relations instrument. Skilled public relations played significant roles in the expansion of Yeshiva University, Albert Einstein College of Medicine, Brandeis University, the growth of mass Jewish membership organizations such as Hadassah and B'nai B'rith, and the raising of hundreds of millions of dollars for new synagogues, community centers, hospitals, and other communal institutions.

By 1940 there were enough people professionally employed as public relations specialists by Jewish organizations to warrant the organization of the Jewish Publicity Directors Council. In 1956 this was reorganized as the American Jewish Public Relations Society. In 1968 it was estimated that more than 500 people were engaged in some phase of public relations for local and national American Jewish organizations and by international Jewish agencies with offices in the U.S. In the 1960s a number of commercial public relations firms headed by Jews were called in as short-or long-term consultants by several Jewish organizations. Ruder and Finn served the Jewish Theological Seminary in this capacity, while Kalman Druck's firm took over full public relations responsibility at UJA in 1968. Of the more than 15,000 public relations firms operating in the U.S. in 1968, some twenty percent were reported to be Jewish in ownership or management. [B.P.]

In Israel. The Public Relations Association of Israel was established in 1958 in Tel Aviv as the Public Relations and Tourism Coordinators. Each of the three major cities set up their own organization designed to serve the special interests in that area. Jerusalem members called their organization "The Spokesmen's Circle" and limited membership to government public relations and information officers.

In 1961 it was decided to create a national organization with all three branches maintaining a special autonomous status covered by a new constitution and the national body run by an Executive Committee drawn from all three branches. There are national conventions every year, professional activities on both a local and national scale, courses either sponsored or controlled by the organization, and in 1970 the Israel Association was host to the Fifth Public Relations World Congress. There are over 200 members in the Public Relations Association of Israel. [Z.H.Z.]

PUBLISHING. This entry is arranged according to the following outline:

General Publishing
- The "Dutch Jerusalem"
- In Germany and Austria
- In Scandinavia
- In Italy
- In France
- In Czechoslovakia
- In Yugoslavia
- In Rumania
- In Hungary
- In Poland
- In Russia
- In Spain and Latin America
- In Great Britain
- In the United States
  - Book Clubs, Reprints, and Children's Literature
  - Publishing of Hebraica and Judaica
    - Central and Western Europe
  - Non-Jewish Publishers of Judaica
- In Great Britain
- In Eastern Europe
- In the United States

In Israel
- New Developments
  - New Methods

GENERAL PUBLISHING

Little more than three decades after their pioneering efforts European publishing industry, notably in Italy, Spain, and Portugal. The first recorded Jewish printer of non-Hebrew books (possibly *Abraham b. Garton of Reggio di Calabria) published the outstanding fourth edition of Dante's *Divina commedia* (Naples, 1477), as a result of which he was bitterly attacked by a Christian rival who appended *Erubescat Judeus infelix* ("Let the unhappy Jew blush for shame") to his own edition of the *Purgatorio* (c. 1478). By this time Jews were evidently active in the Naples book trade, as they had been for some years as Hebrew printers in Italy as a whole. In its early stages, the printing industry was combined with book publishing, printers accepting, printing, and selling their works in one commercial venture. Prior to the expulsion from Spain (1492), Jews probably played an equally important part in printing there. During the 1470s, Juan de Lucena issued a prayer book (*cituri,* i.e., *siddur*) in Spanish, for which he was years later (as a New Christian) persecuted by the Inquisition. A more significant publishing achievement was that of Solomon b. Maimon *Zalmati of Jativa, who in 1483 entered into partnership with two Christian printers with the aim of producing Christian theological works for the general market. They subsequently published Jaime Perez's commentary on Psalms (Valencia, 1484) and other works by the same writer, including his anti-Semitic *Tractatus contra judaeos* (1485). In neighboring Portugal, Jewish printer-publishers also attained eminence as pioneers before the general expulsion of 1497. Samuel de Ortas issued *Tabulae tabularum coelestium motuum: sive almanach perpetuum* (Leiria, 1496), a classic by the great astronomer Abraham *Zacuto.

Jewish activity in the sphere of general publishing was centered in Italy from the beginning of the 16th century. The *Soncino family, famous in early Hebrew printing, also produced a host of works in other languages. Gershom Soncino the elder, who studied the art of printing in Mainz, published a series of books in Latin and Italian from 1502 and for 25 years thereafter issued about 100 titles—about as many as he published in Hebrew over a longer period. As Hieronymus Soncinus, he produced only non-Hebrew works in Ancona and Cesena. Gershom's new edition of Petrarch (Fano, 1503) was dedicated to Cesare Borgia, and his literary editor, the humanist Lorenzo Abstemio (Bevilaqua), urged other Italian scholars to patronize the Soncino press. Gershom Soncino later published the statutes of the cities of Fano (1508), Jesi (1516), and Rimini (1525), as well as many other works for Christians, including the "Rules of the Franciscan Order" (Pesaro, 1507). Gershom Soncino produced his non-Hebrew books for non-Jewish readers. He was, however, compelled to abandon this activity in about 1527.

From the early 1550s onward, Yom Tov b. Levi *Athias (Jeronimo Vargas) published Spanish versions of Jewish liturgical works at Ferrara and, in collaboration with Abraham *Usque, issued the famous Ferrara Bible (1553) which appeared in separate editions for Jews and Christians. Abraham Usque later published other liturgical books for Jewish immigrants as well as works by Bernardim *Ribeiro, Alfonso de la *Torre, and his kinsman Samuel *Usque. The self-imposed Jewish censorship of Hebrew books after the burning of the Talmud in Rome (1553), the temporary persecution of newly arrived Marranos, and Church interference in Jewish affairs all led to the eventual abandonment of vernacular publishing by Italian Jews. However, the physician Jacob Marcaria, who operated a Hebrew press in Riva di Trento (1558–62), was the unofficial publisher of speeches and works by many of the churchmen assembled at the Council of Trent (1545–63). The scene of Jewish activity in general publishing thereafter shifted to Amsterdam, where a host of works in Spanish and Portuguese was written and published from the beginning of the 17th century.

The "Dutch Jerusalem." The earliest Jewish vernacular publications in the Netherlands were written in Spanish for Marrano immigrants unfamiliar with Hebrew and often took the form of translations of biblical and liturgical texts. The first work of this type was a reissue of Yom Tov Athias' Ferrara prayer book (1552), published at Dordrecht ("Mainz") in 1584 and evidently intended for the crypto-Jewish community of Antwerp. The first work in Spanish to appear in Amsterdam dates from 1612 and during the next two centuries hundreds of books in Spanish and Portuguese were issued by the city's Jewish publishers. These included *Manasseh Ben Israel, whose press, founded in 1626, produced books in Spanish and Portuguese as well as Hebrew; Joseph *Athias; and Isaac Cohen de *Lara, a leading bookseller. The messianic frenzy roused by the claims of *Shabbetai Ẓevi led to a spate of publications in Spanish in 1666. Spanish substituted for Hebrew as the language of study and prayer among Marranos, while Portuguese was reserved for poetry and other secular literature.

In time, however, Dutch Jews began writing and publishing works in the vernacular. Two of the oldest Jewish publishing houses of Amsterdam, both noted for their Hebrew printing, also engaged in producing books in Dutch for the Jewish reader: the firms of the brothers *Proops, which flourished during the 18th–19th centuries, and J. L. Joachimsthal, which was still active in the 1970s and issued the Dutch Jewish weekly *Nieuw Israëlietisch Weekblad.* The bookseller L. Simons (1862–1932) founded the *Wereldbibliotheek,* while Isaac *Keesing established the firm of N. V. Keesing, noted for its production of reference books and archive material. Another Amsterdam Jewish publisher was the minor writer Emmanuel Querido (1871–1943), a victim of the Nazis, whose brother was the novelist Israël *Querido. [G.E.S.]

In Germany and Austria. During the Middle Ages, Jews played an active part in the European book trade, which assumed increasing importance in the German-speaking lands after the introduction of printing. From the 16th century onward, Jews naturally promoted Hebrew publishing, of which Frankfort became the principal center, and from the early 19th century they were active in the general sphere of German book production (Berlin, Breslau, Frankfort, Koenigsberg, Leipzig, Prague, and Vienna). Probably the earliest such enterprise was the Prague firm of Taussig (founded in 1783), which ceased its activities under the Nazis. Other pioneering firms were those of Julius Eduard *Hitzig (Berlin, 1808–14); Friedrich Cohen (Bonn, 1829); Joseph and Felix Lehmann (1832); and Moritz *Veit, president of the Berlin Jewish community, whose scientific publishing house, Veit & Co., flourished between 1834 and 1858. Also prominent in Berlin was the Schlesinger'sche Buch- und Musikalienhandlung (1810), headed by Adolf Martin Schlesinger (1768–1848), which issued some of the compositions of Beethoven.

In general publishing, however, Jews only achieved real importance from about 1835 during the heyday of the *Jung Deutschland* literary group. The leading literary publisher of this era was Karl (Zacharias) Loewenthal, who changed his name to Loening after abandoning Judaism. A close friend and admirer of Karl Gutzkow, the leader of *Jung Deutschland,* Loewenthal founded his publishing house in Mannheim in 1835 and published Gutzkow's periodical *Deutsche Revue* and his novel *Wally, die Zweiflerin* (1835). When the works of the *Jung Deutschland* group, including those of Heinrich *Heine, were proscribed and their authors and publisher brought to trial, Loewenthal did not abandon his friends, despite anti-Semitic slanders. In 1844 he moved to Frankfort and, together with the apostate author Joseph Jacob Ruetten (Rindskopf, 1805–78), reestablished his firm under the name of Rueten und Loening, producing philosophical and sociological books as well as fiction. The firm still operated in Munich in the 1970s. Other 19th-century enterprises included those of R. Levi (Stuttgart, 1840), J. Guttentag (Berlin, 1842), Moritz Perles (Prague, 1844; later moved to Berlin and Vienna), M. Glogau (Hamburg, 1850), J. Taubeles (Prague, 1861), Albert Goldschmidt (Hamburg, 1863), S. Cronbach (Berlin, 1867), R. L. Prager (Berlin, 1872), and the Enoch Brothers (Hamburg, 1875). In Vienna, a literary firm was established by Leopold Rosner (1838–1903).

During the 1880s, the champion of the school of realism was Otto *Brahm, who in 1889 founded the Freie Buehne, which later became the literary periodical *Die Neue Rundschau.* Closely connected with this new literature was the Berlin publishing house of Samuel *Fischer. The S. Fischer Verlag (1886) rapidly became a center of avant-garde literary life. Under the Nazis, this publishing house moved overseas but after World War II reopened in Frankfort. In 1895 George Bondi (1865–1935) established a firm in Berlin specializing in works by members of the Stefan George circle, such as Friedrich *Gundolf, Ernst Bertram, and Ernst Kantorowitsch (*Blaetter fuer die Kunst*). When George decided to make his own poetry available to the general public, Bondi became his publisher. Paul *Cassirer founded a publishing house in 1908 as a branch of his art gallery. He issued books mainly about modern artists (Herman *Struck, Ernst Barlach, Max Pechstein, Oskar Kokoschka), but also published literary works by Else *Lasker-Schueler, Ernst Barlach, Walter *Hasenclever, René Schickelé, and Kasimir Edschmid. Another field in which Cassirer became interested was cultural socialism, represented by the works of Ferdinand *Lassalle, Kurt *Eisner, and Gustav *Landauer. His cousin Bruno Cassirer (1872–1942) also founded a publishing house in 1898. Bruno Cassirer's book production, which was of the highest intellectual standard, ranged through art, philosophy, and literature. His art books were written by leading historians and critics of the fine arts; his journal, *Kunst und Kuenstler,* edited by Karl Scheffler, became the leading German art journal during the early 20th century. Bruno Cassirer also published all the writings of another cousin, the eminent philosopher Ernst *Cassirer. He issued the complete edition of Kant's works, edited by Ernst Cassirer, and those of Hermann *Cohen, the founder of neo-Kantianism. During the years before the rise of Hitler, he turned to modern fiction, where he was assisted by Max *Tau, who introduced several modern Scandinavian authors to the German reader. Bruno Cassirer finally emigrated to England. His publishing house, refounded in Oxford, now specializes in illustrated books about foreign countries.

Erich Reiss founded his Berlin publishing house in 1908 and was a keen enthusiast of the beautiful, well-printed book. He published German editions of Jonathan Swift's works, the writings of Georges *Brandes, and the political essays of Maximilian *Harden. For a time Reiss also issued Siegfried *Jacobson's periodical *Die Schaubuehne* (later *Die Weltbuehne*) and *Blaetter des deutschen Theaters*. After 1933 he tried to publish books of Jewish interest only, but soon abandoned the project and emigrated to New York.

All attempts to make Vienna a center of the publishing trade on a par with Leipzig and Berlin failed until Paul von Zsolnay established the Paul Zsolnay Verlag in 1924. In a very short time, this firm assembled the works of some of the most distinguished European novelists, including Sholem *Asch, Henri Barbusse, Max *Brod, John Galsworthy, Heinrich Mann, and Franz *Werfel. After the *Anschluss* of 1938, Zsolnay emigrated to England; his firm was refounded in Vienna after World War II. The Austrian capital was also the home of the Internationaler Psychoanalystischer Verlag, established by the *Freud family and later transferred to London, and of E. P. Tal (1919), a firm specializing in modern German and foreign literature.

Bela Horovitz (1898–1955), who was devoted to the study of Greek, Roman, and Jewish antiquity, established his Phaidon Verlag in Vienna (1923) with the aim of popularizing works on the ancient world. His publications included Plato, Petrarch, Shakespeare, Klabund, Friedell, and Unamuno. In later years, the Phaidon Verlag republished illustrated editions of the great German historians, such as Mommsen, Grimm, and Ranke. Assisted by Ludwig Goldscheider, Horovitz also issued many low-price art books which appeared in several languages and made Phaidon known in many countries. After 1938 he established the Phaidon Press in London, following the same line as in Vienna. The Nazi onslaught on the Jews led him to establish a new publishing house in London, the East and West Library, entirely devoted to Jewish literature. From 1955 onward, his family continued to run both publishing houses until these were sold to other companies in the late 1960s.

Other firms active between the world wars were Ernst Salter's literary Verlag die Schmiede in Berlin, which introduced Marcel *Proust to the German public; Erich Lichtenstein's Weimar house, devoted especially to new editions of classic writers (e.g., Annette von Droste-Huelshoff); and Victor Fleischer's Frankfurter Verlags-Anstalt, which published books on literary criticism and history.

Salman *Schocken, who headed a chain of department stores, founded the Berlin Schocken Verlag in 1931. This firm's publications dealt largely with Jewish philosophy, theology, Hebraica, and poetry, but also included the works of Franz *Kafka and Alfred *Mombert. Wide popularity was achieved by the "little Schocken books" and the works of Martin *Buber, particularly his German Bible. In 1933, Schocken, a leading German Zionist, emigrated to Jerusalem and his publishing house now operates in New York and in Tel Aviv, where it published, among others, the works of the Nobel Prize winner S. Y. *Agnon. In scientific publishing, firms like Carl Heymann (1815), Julius Springer (1842), S. Karger (1890), and the Akademische Verlagsbuchhandlung (1906) were in Jewish hands.

The Jewish publishers of the great liberal newspapers such as the *Frankfurter Zeitung* and the *Berliner Tageblatt* also entered book publication. Rudolf *Mosse established his firm in 1867 and, apart from his newspaper empire (*Berliner Tageblatt, Berliner Volkszeitung, 8-Uhr Abendblatt*), produced books of a popular character. The entire business was confiscated by the Nazis. Leopold *Ullstein founded the Ullstein Verlag in 1877. Besides a vast number of newspapers and magazines, the firm published popular fiction. Ullstein's Propylaeen Verlag (1919), under the direction of Emil Herz, who later emigrated to the United States, grew into a versatile publishing house of the highest standard, publishing an edition of Goethe's works in 45 volumes. It also issued the serialized *Klassiker des Altertums, Propylaeen-Weltgeschichte, Werke der Weltliteratur,* and *Klassiker des Altertums,* as well as the works of Brecht, Remarque, and *Zuckmayer. After World War II the corporation returned to family ownership, but it was eventually sold to Axel Springer in 1960. The Frankfurter Societaetsdruckerei, publishers of the liberal *Frankfurter Zeitung,* which was founded in 1856 by the democratic Jewish politician Leopold *Sonnemann, also published works by modern German writers. [R.K./ED.]

In Scandinavia. The only major house in Scandinavia was the Albert Bonniers Förlag of Stockholm (established in 1837). Its founder, Albert Bonnier (1820–1900), was the son of a Dresden Jew who settled in Copenhagen. Albert and his brother Adolf moved to Sweden, where they set up a publishing and printing enterprise that became the largest in the country. It was subsequently run by Albert's son, Karl Otto Bonnier (1856–1941), and, with associated firms, remained under family control. In Denmark, the Gad publishing house of Copenhagen specialized in Judaica, while Norway's leading publishers included the German refugee Max Tau, who began his career with Bruno Cassirer in Berlin.

In Italy. As mentioned above Italian Jews were among the pioneers of general publishing activity in the country, but Jewish participation in the trade declined sharply from the mid-16th century. It was not until the 1840s that Jews again became prominent in the general sphere, with the establishment of the Florence publishing house of Felice Paggi (1823–1895) and his brother Alessandro (1818–1893). This issued many works of popular education and other books by leading authors, including Carlo (Lorenzini) Collodi's children's classic, *Pinocchio* (1880). The firm was joined by Alessandro Paggi's son-in-law, Roberto Bemporad (d. 1891), whose son, Enrico *Bemporad, eventually assumed control, changing its name to R. Bemporad & Figlio. Under his direction it soon became one of the most important publishing houses in Italy. A firm associated with Bemporad was that founded by Simone Lattes in Turin.

Italy's greatest publishing house, however, was that established in Milan by Emilio *Treves and his brother Giuseppe (1838–1904). Fratelli Treves (1864) published newspapers and works by leading Italian and foreign authors. In 1886, Leo S. Olschki (1861–1944), a Prussian immigrant, established himself in Florence, where he later became the leading antiquarian bookseller and publisher of scholarly works in Italy. After his death the business remained under family control. Jews continued this close association with Italian publishing during the 20th century. Among them was Angelo Fortunato *Formiggini, a staunch anti-Fascist, whose firm was first established in Bologna (1908) and who published Italy's first "Who's Who." Luciano Morpurgo (b. 1886) founded his Casa Editrice Dalmatia in 1928, and this publishing house was still operating under the name in 1970.

In France. Jews only began to achieve prominence in the field of general publishing toward the middle of the 19th century. The two pioneering firms were those established by the *Alcan and *Lévy (Calmann-Lévy) families. Moyse Alcan's publishing house was active in Metz from about 1840 and was later headed by his son Félix, who specialized in works on philosophy. The brothers Michel, Alexandre-Nathan, and Calmann Lévy founded their enterprise in Paris in 1842 and, as Michel Lévy Frères, succeeded in building up one of the leading French publishing firms, issuing the works of writers such as Balzac, Dumas, Heine (in translation), and *Renan. From 1875 the business changed its name to Calmann-Lévy. Paul Ollendorf, the Paris-born son of a Polish immigrant, published *Gil Blas,* a political and literary newspaper that flourished between 1880 and World War I. In 1881 Fernand Nathan established a firm (still under family management) specializing in classics, reference works, and educational and children's books. Four other modern firms were Rieder (Crémieux), Bernheim-Jeune, Camille Bloch, and Fernand Hazan (1945). [G.E.S.]

In Czechoslovakia. Although, compared with Germany and Austria, Jewish publishing firms in what is now Czechoslovakia were few and limited in scope, they included some pioneering enterprises, such as Taussig und Taussig (see Germany and Austria, above). The first Jewish bookseller and antiquarian in Prague was Wolf (Ze'ev) *Pascheles, who founded S. Pascheles & Son in 1836. A branch of this famous house was established in Breslau (1899) by his son-in-law, Jacob B. Brandeis (relative of Louis D. *Brandeis). Both firms specialized in Judaica, but also published biographies and fiction in German (Sacher-Masoch, M. G. Saphir, M. Rosenfeld, etc.) under the imprint of the Juedische Universal-Bibliothek. Also active in Prague was the firm of Josef Flesch, which produced scholarly works between the world wars, while Julius Fuerth (1897–) managed the Melantrich publishing house and the liberal paper *Lidové noviny* at about the same period, later transferring his interests to London. Outside of Bohemia, the influence of German diminished, and most Jewish publishing enterprises were founded only from the late 19th century onward.

In Yugoslavia. The first translations and editions of world classics issued in Croatia were by the pioneer Jewish publisher and bookseller Lavoslav Hartmann (1813–1881). The Yugoslav book trade was later revolutionized by Geca Kon (1873–1941) of Belgrade, who headed the country's greatest publishing house between the world wars. [ED.]

In Rumania. From about 1880 until 1940 Jews made an outstanding contribution to the development of the Rumanian publishing industry. In Jassy, Elias Şaraga established an important firm, in partnership with his brother Samuel, in 1878. Three other Jewish publishing houses in the same town were those of A. Berman, Cuperman, and H. Goldner. The family business of Samitca in Craiova (c. 1895) specialized in low-cost editions and books of Jewish interest. In Bucharest, low-price books were also produced by Leon Alcalay (1900–34). Other firms included Simon Benvenisti, I. Ciornei, H. Steinberg, Carol Segal, and Emmanuel Ocneanu. Literary works were also published by the house of Virgil Montaureanu, which later transferred its activities to Israel. [ED.]

In Hungary. Jews played an important part in the Hungarian publishing industry from its very inception. A pioneer in the field was Sámuel Révai (Rosenberg; 1833–1908), who began trading as a bookbinder and later as a bookseller in Eperjes (now Prešov, Czechoslovakia). In 1869, he and his brother Leó established the Budapest publishing house of Révai Testvérek, which was later run by Sámuel's sons. In time, this became one of the leading firms in Hungary, its publications including the works of such eminent writers as Mór Jókai and Kálmán Mikszáth and an important reference work, *Révai Nagy Lexikona* ("Révai's Great Encyclopedia"). Earlier still, the Wodianer family, late 18th-century immigrants from Wodian, in Moravia, had achieved prominence when Fülöp Wodianer, a printer turned publisher, became the official publisher of the revolutionary government of Kossuth in 1848. He acquired the R. Lámpel firm in 1874 and was ennobled for his services to the state. Wodianer's business remained under family control after his death, the Lámpel house issuing books on a wide variety of subjects and publishing various newspapers. A firm specializing in the publication of musical works and scores was that founded by Gyula Rózsavölgyi (1822–1860), whose father was the eminent composer Márk Rózsavölgyi. Other leading Jewish publishers were József Wolfner, Lipót Hirsch de Örményes, and Andor Miklós, who took over the Athenaeum publishing house, which issued books by modern Hungarian writers. One of Athenaeum's directors was Viktor Ranschburg (1862–1930), who later moved to the firm of Pantheon. His brother, Gusztáv Ranschburg, was the editor of the Müveltség Könyvtára ("Library of Culture") and of the Athenaeum Könyvtár ("Athenaeum Library"). Izidor Kner (1860–1935) of Gyoma specialized in belles lettres and was awarded the gold medal at the Leipzig Exhibition of 1914 for his publications, mostly works by contemporary writers. His son, Imre Kner (1890–1944), a victim of the Nazi Holocaust, published the historical series *Monumenta Litterarum,* as well as other Hungarian and European classics, and gained first prize at the Paris Exhibition of 1937. As in Rumania, Jewish publishers in Hungary were subjected to increasing restrictions from the late 1930s onward. [B.Y.]

In Poland. One of the earliest Jewish influences in Polish literary life from the first quarter of the 19th century was the activity of Jewish, or converted Jewish, publishers. Side by side with the Jews who pioneered the printing and publishing of Hebrew and Yiddish works, there were a few who achieved distinction in the general field, notably Nathan Gluecksberg (1780–1831) and sons, Samuel Orgelbrand (1810–1868) and son, and S. Lewental. Orgelbrand is mainly remembered for the first modern Polish encyclopedia, which he issued in 28 volumes (1859–68). In the 20th century, particularly between the world wars, Jews made an increasingly important contribution to the Polish publishing industry with firms such as those headed by H. Altenberg, M. Arct, J. Mortkowicz, J. Przeworski, K. Wild, and W. Zukerkandel. Others, notably the well-known firm of Rój, had important Jewish managing interests, although they did not bear recognizably Jewish names. Even after the Communist takeover following World War II, there were Jews among the founders and directors of state publishing houses, of whom J. Borejsza of Czytelnik was one of the most prominent. [MO.A.]

In Russia. During the last decades Jews published on specifically Jewish topics in Russian, as well as Hebrew and Yiddish. After the Bolshevik Revolution, these activities tended to be transferred overseas. In the general sphere of prerevolutionary Russian publishing, the outstanding names were the brothers I. N. and A. N. Granat, who issued an important encyclopedia, and Ilya Abramovich *Efron, who began his activity in 1880. Efron's enterprise, which became one of the largest in Russia, mainly produced scholarly works and is best remembered for its massive 86-volume *Novy entsiklopedicheskiy slovar* (1907) and for the 16-volume Russian-Jewish *Yevreyskaya Entsiklopediya* (1907–13), in which the publisher himself took an active interest. [G.E.S.]

In Spain and Latin America. Despite the numerical insignificance of Spain's Jewish population in the 20th century, Jewish activity in the book trade was seen in the establishment of the Madrid firm of Aguilar (1923), which also operated in Latin America. It was only after World War I that Jews began to figure in the Latin American publishing industry (mainly in Argentina, Brazil, and Mexico). In Argentina, the Buenos Aires firm of Candelabro, established by Abrahám Mibashán and specializing in Judaica, was taken over by José Mirelman and Máximo G. Yagupsky, who also controlled the firm of Israel. Jews have played a more important role in the general publishing life of Brazil. Here the major names were Aizen, Bloch, Iussim, Koogan, and Waissman, with Adolfo Aizen publishing comic books and strip cartoons *(Brasil, América),* Nathan Waissman heading the Rio de Janeiro publishing house of Guanabara, and Henrique Iussim (who was also a writer) controlling the Biblos firm. Abrahão Koogan published literary, medical, and scientific books and, through the firm of Delta, world classics and encyclopedias. Almost all of the Jewish enterprises were based in Rio de Janeiro, one exception being Perspectiva of São Paulo. The largest Brazilian publishing firm under Jewish control was run by the Bloch family (Adolfo, Arnaldo, and Boris Bloch) and incorporated Fatos & Fotos and Manchete. It was later managed by Oscar Bloch Sigelman, Pedro Jack Kapeller, and H. W. Berliner. [ED.]

In Great Britain. Three 19th-century pioneers were Samuel Lewis (d. 1865), who published topographical dictionaries and atlases; John Wertheimer (1799–1883); and William Swan Sonnenschein (1855–1931). The latter, son of a refugee Hungarian revolutionary, founded Swan Sonnenschein & Co. (1878), which specialized in reference books, and also traded under his non-Jewish mother's name of Stallybrass, becoming senior managing director of the Routledge publishing firm. The Franklin family subsequently obtained a controlling interest in Routledge's (George Routledge and Kegan Paul, 1934).

Two prominent figures, both with marked Socialist leanings, were Leonard *Woolf and Sir Victor *Gollancz. Woolf co-founded the Hogarth Press (1917), which issued works by modern writers (including his wife, Virginia Woolf); while Gollancz, who established the firm bearing his name in 1928, also co-founded the Left Book Club (1936) and helped to stimulate the production of low-cost quality literature. Gollancz specialized in modern fiction and religious books and threw his prestige behind several unpopular causes. Oliver Simon (1895–1956), the typographer, was a director of the Soncino Press and managed another house, Curwen Press, from the 1930s until his death. He was succeeded by his brother Herbert Simon (c. 1899–). Another printer and publisher was Ellis Paul Howe (1910–). Among those who established publishing firms between the world wars were John *Rodker (Ovid Press, Imago Press), who issued works by Freud, T. S. Eliot, and Ezra Pound; Frederick Muller (1933); Michael Joseph (1935), a specialist in general fiction and mysteries; and Martin Secker and F. J. Warburg (1936).

Soon after World War II Jewish activity in the British publishing world increased with the establishment of many new publishing houses catering for a wide variety of interests. André Deutsch (1917–), who had immigrated from Hungary as a youth, entered the trade in 1942 and, after operating as Allan Wingate (1945–50), founded his own company in 1951, specializing in history, biography, and paperback editions. Deutsch founded African publishing firms in Nigeria (1962) and Kenya (1964). Sir George

*Weidenfeld, an Austrian refugee, founded *Contact* (1945), a journal of contemporary affairs and arts, and three years later established the firm of Weidenfeld and Nicolson in association with Nigel Nicolson. Weidenfeld, a keen Zionist, published many books by Israel writers and founded a subsidiary company in Jerusalem (1969). His firm specialized in books on literature, art, and archaeology (many in illustrated editions). Another postwar publisher of importance was Anthony Blond (1930–), who established his publishing house in 1958, specializing in new writers, paperbacks, and works for young people. Other names in postwar British publishing were Sidney Bernstein (1899–), the television pioneer, whose enterprises included the Granada Publishing company; the Labor M. P. Robert Maxwell, who headed Pergamon Press (1948); and Paul Hamlyn (1926–), who controlled Ginn & Co., Newnes, Odhams, and Spring Books, Temple Press, the Paul Hamlyn "coffee table books," and (in association with E. M. I.) Music For Pleasure Records. Other British publishing firms under Jewish management or with important Jewish interests include H. Pordes (1947), Thomas Yoseloff, W. H. Allen, Frank Cass, Peter Owen, Paul Elek, and a large group containing Cresset Press, Barrie and Rockliff, and Hammond, Hammond. [G.E.S.]

In the United States. Before the 20th century, Jews played an insignificant part in the general book publishing industry of the United States. In 1897 the bookselling firm founded by August *Brentano in 1858 started a publishing division. Brentano was the original U.S. publisher for the plays of George Bernard Shaw, but the firm discontinued publishing in 1933. Another pioneer, Ben[jamin] W. Huebsch (1873–1964), son of Adolph *Huebsch, began publishing under his own imprint from 1900 and introduced the writings of Hauptmann, Strindberg, Chekhov, and Gorki to the American public. He also published works by James Joyce and Sherwood Anderson. In 1925 his firm merged with the Viking Press. Alfred A. *Knopf began publishing in 1915 and quickly established a reputation for excellence in design and materials. His list featured many prominent authors, both foreign and American. The firm merged with Random House in 1960. Boni and Liveright was established by Albert Boni (1892–) and Horace Briabin Liveright (1896–1933). Their most successful project was the Modern Library, a reprint series now issued by Random House. Boni soon left the firm, but the original name was retained until 1928. In 1923 Boni became a partner in Albert and Charles Boni, a pioneer of paperback books. Albert Boni, who founded the Washington Square Players (now the Theatre Guild), invented Microprint and the Readex reading projector and from 1940 was president of the firm that produced these devices. Horace Liveright was a lavish promoter of authors such as Theodore Dreiser and Eugene O'Neill, but later worked mainly as a stage producer.

Men who had worked for Boni and Liveright established several important publishing firms. Thomas Seltzer formed his own firm in 1920 and Richard L. Simon organized Simon and Schuster with M. Lincoln *Schuster in 1924. In 1925 Liveright sold the Modern Library to Bennett A. *Cerf and Donald S. Klopfer. Two years later they and Elmer *Adler formed Random House. In 1965 when Cerf became chairman of the board, the presidency was assumed by Robert L. Bernstein. The poet and literary critic Joel Elias *Spingarn was a founder of Harcourt, Brace & Co. and the firm's literary adviser from 1919 to 1932.

Other book publishing firms established by Jews in the 1920s and 1930s included that of Greenberg Publisher (1924) by Jacob Walter Greenberg (1894–); Viking Press (1925); and the short-lived Covici-Friede, which specialized in limited editions. When this last firm was dissolved, Donald Friede joined the World Publishing Company as a senior editor, and Pascal Covici became an editor for Viking Press. William Bernard Ziff (1898–1953), a founder of the Ziff-Davis Publishing Company (1933), was also president of the Zionist Revisionist Organization of America. From Greenberg, Nat Wartels and Robert Simon bought the Outlet Book Company, which disposed of publisher's overstocks, and they began publishing under the imprint of Crown Publishers. Max Salom of the Harlem Book Company, who pioneered the sale of publishers' overstocks through drugstores, acquired the Dial Press in 1934. George W. Joel was editor-in-chief of Dial Press (1939–51) and president and publisher from 1951 until his death in 1959. Stanley Burnshaw (1906–) was founder, president, and editor-in-chief of Dryden Press (1936).

Several other publishing houses were established by Jews or had Jews in leading managerial positions. Roger W. Straus was president of Farrar, Straus, and Giroux (1945); Abelard-Schuman was headed by Lew Schwartz; Arthur J. Rosenthal was president and editor-in-chief of Basic Books, Inc. (1952); Oscar Dystal was president of Bantam Books, a subsidiary of Grosset and Dunlap whose president from 1944 was Manuel Siwak; Joseph Gaer (1897–) served as editor-in-chief of the Federal Writers Project. With Charles Boni, Gaer formed Boni and Gaer (1946), which soon changed its name to Gaer Associates. Jeremiah Kaplan, an executive of the Free Press of Glencoe from 1947, became president of the Macmillan Company in 1965. Harry N. Abrams, Inc., specialized in art books. Robert Salomon headed Citadel Press; Paul Steiner, Chanticleer Press; Arthur B. Frommer headed Arthur Frommer, Inc.; Harold H. Hart, Hart Publishing Co.; A. L. Furman, Lantern Press; Philip F. Cohen, Oceana Publications; Jacob Steinberg, Twayne Publishers; Milton Gladstone, Arco Publishing Co.; Richard L. Grossman, Grossman Publishers; and Sol Stein, Stein and Day.

The decades in which American Jews became active in book publishing saw tremendous changes in the book world in the United States. Alfred A. Knopf and Simon and Schuster did much to invigorate book promotion and advertising. Huebsch, Knopf, Seltzer, and their successors introduced many new European authors, but at the same time sought fresh American and British talents. The new publishers had high production standards, Knopf and Viking in particular insisting on attractive, well-made books.

BOOK CLUBS, REPRINTS, AND CHILDREN'S LITERATURE. Three publishing developments during the first half of the 20th century greatly expanded the market for books and in these Jews were prominent. The basic idea of membership in a club for the publication and distribution of books was not new. The *Jewish Publication Society of America (1888) was the successor to at least two earlier membership schemes, and several other groups had been established to publish special editions for members. Harold K. *Guinzburg, founder of the Viking Press (1925), was impressed by the popularity of recently-formed book clubs in Germany. He developed a plan for an American book club, The Literary Guild, which began active operations in 1927; it was sold to Doubleday in 1934. Harry Scherman (1887–1969), who was born in Montreal, Canada, had successfully promoted the Little Leather Library (1916), a mail-order firm, and felt that people living far from bookshops would subscribe to books as to magazines. With Robert K. Haas (1890–1964) and Maxwell B. Sackheim, he organized the Book-of-the-Month Club (1926), which by 1970 had distributed 250 million books. In 1929 George Macy started the Limited Editions Club, limited to 1500 members; and he also founded several others (Heritage Club, Junior Heritage Club, Readers Club). Thomas Yoseloff (1913–) has operated many book clubs, including the Jewish Book Guild, Military Science Book Club, Natural History Book Club, Book Collectors' Society, Art Book Guild, and the Science Book Club. He also established or bought several publishing houses (Beechurst Press, A. S. Barnes and Co., Sagamore Press, Thomas Yoseloff, Inc.) and was the U.S. publisher of the Ben-Yehuda Hebrew dictionary.

Another important development was in the area of low-price reprints, many publishers issuing inexpensive editions of popular works with several firms specializing in this field. The Modern Library was a notable addition to the hard-cover reprint world, and the World Publishing Co. of Cleveland, founded by Alfred Cahen as the Commercial Book Bindery (1905), became prominent, particularly after Benjamin David Zevin (1901–) joined the firm. However, the revolution in the industry really began with paperback books. As editor and publisher of Little Blue Books, Emanuel Halderman-Julius (1889–1951) had issued and distributed millions of small paperbound books through the mail for as little as five cents a copy. Occasionally, too, Simon and Schuster had issued a book in paper binding, while the paperbacks published by Albert and Charles Boni and by the *New Republic*, though praised for their content and format, made little impact on sales. In 1939, Pocket Books Inc. was organized by Robert F. de Graff, an expert in the cloth reprint field, with H. Lincoln Schuster, Leon Shimkin, and Richard L. Simon (1899–1962). The first printing of each of the ten titles in the initial list was about 10,000 copies. Twenty years later, 1,000,000 paperbacks a day were sold in the United States. By 1957 only Leon Shimkin remained active in Pocket Books. Others who entered the field were Joseph Meyers, who founded Avon Publications in 1940, and Ned L. Pines, who published under the Popular Library imprint. Doubleday opened a new era in paperback publishing in 1953 with its Anchor Books. The first editor of this serious fiction and non-fiction series was Jason Epstein, later an editor with Random House. Other higher-priced, serious paperback series were the Viking Press's Compass Books and those issued by Schocken Books.

During the 20th century, children's books became one of the most important divisions of American publishing. Knopf, Viking, and Random House were all leaders in the field, but the establishment by Simon and Schuster of Little Golden Books in 1942 brought low-cost books to young people for the first time. More than 400,000,000 Golden Books were sold in the first 13 years. Golden Press Inc., headed by Albert R. Leventhal (1907–), formerly a Simon and Schuster executive, became a division of Western Printing Co.

[I.So.]

PUBLISHING OF HEBRAICA AND JUDAICA

Central and Western Europe. The first publishers—in the modern sense—of Judaica were in Germany, which for a long time remained the center of Jewish (mainly non-Hebrew) publishing. The pioneer was W. *Heidenheim, who was succeeded by M. Lehrberger, in Roedelheim, the producer of famous editions of the Jewish liturgy. In the first half of the 19th century Jewish bookshops were opened in the larger towns and many of their owners later became publishers. M. W. Kaufmann established himself in Leipzig in 1828, later specializing in publishing synagogue music. J. *Kaufmann established himself in Frankfort on the Main in 1832 and his firm was the leading Jewish publisher (and bookseller) in Germany for three generations, taking over Lehrberger in 1899. In Prague W. Pascheles was active from 1836. Several firms were established in Berlin in the course of the 19th century, some of which, like *Asher and Co., later gave up Jewish publishing; others did not stay the course (A. Cohn, J. Sittenfeld, Springer and Co., Veit and Co., and others). M. Poppelauer (est. 1860) and C. Boas (est. 1863) remained of importance for some decades. The firm of B. L. Monasch was active in Krotoschin from 1835 to 1910 and that of Zirndorfer published works in Fuerth.

In the 20th century the most important publishing house became the *Juedischer Verlag, which not only produced Zionist literature but also a great variety of Hebrew and Yiddish works in the original and in translation. After World War I the concentration of Jewish writers and scholars from Eastern Europe in Germany, in Berlin in particular, produced a Jewish intellectual revival, and many publishing houses sprang up, producing both Hebraica and Judaica. Louis Lamm was already established in 1903; the Weltverlag followed it in 1919. The *Philo Verlag (1919–38), the publishing arm of the *Centralverein deutscher Staatsbuerger juedischen Glaubens, fought against the rising anti-Semitism, but its activities covered a wide range of Jewish literature, including the publication of periodicals like *Der Morgen* and *Zeitschrift fuer die Geschichte der Juden in Deutschland.* The Akademie Verlag was a branch of the Akademie fuer die Wissenschaft des Judentums. The Eschkol Verlag published the *Encyclopaedia Judaica* in German (10 vols., to 1934 unfinished) and in Hebrew (2 vols., 1929–32, also unfinished) and other important works such as J. Klatzkin's *Thesaurus Philosophicus Linguae Hebraicae* (4 vols., 1928–33). Other firms included Reuben Mass in Berlin, who later continued publishing in Jerusalem; Schocken Verlag, also in Berlin (see above); Saenger und *Friedberg (the bibliographer) in Frankfort; the Hermon Verlag, which was connected with the Orthodox weekly *Israelit; the Juedischer Verlag (1901); and the *Soncino Gesellschaft (1924). After 1938 Schocken Verlag published in Israel and the U.S. Some Hebrew publishers, like *Devir, *Moriah, and *Stybel, transferred to Germany, later moving to Ereẓ Israel or the U.S. Similarly, the Omanut Hebrew publishing house, established in Moscow in 1917 by H. *Zlatopolski and his daughter Shoshannah *Persitz, moved to Odessa in 1918, Homburg (near Frankfort) in 1920, and Tel Aviv in 1928. Other firms include Chorev, which published small-size reproductions of the great rabbinic texts, Yavneh, Ayyanot, and Yuval, the latter specializing in Jewish music. Klal and Vostock published Yiddish literature. The economic conditions in post-World War I Germany led to the closing of several smaller firms.

In Vienna Benjamin Harz republished, among other works, L. Goldschmidt's Talmud edition and German translation. The firm of R. Loewitt, active there from 1833, later issued mainly Jewish belletristic works. Joseph Schlesinger founded his firm in 1858—with a branch in Budapest at a later date—and became a leading publisher of prayer books and other items, supplying several European countries as well as North Africa.

In Leghorn, Italy, the house of *Belforte was active from 1838 to 1939 as publishers of liturgical literature for the Italian, North African, and Levantine market. In France (Paris), E. Durlacher and M. Lipschuetz published Hebraica and Judaica; the former was still active in 1970.

Non-Jewish Publishers of Judaica. In pre-Hitler Germany a number of non-Jewish publishers were responsible for some works of Hebraica and Judaica: the Insel Verlag (Brody-Wiener's *Anthologia Hebraica,* 1924), Langenscheidt (Eliezer Ben-Yehuda's *Thesaurus*), O. Harrassowitz in Leipzig, Toepelmann, Giessen, and others. In Holland the house of Brill in Leiden has been active for nearly 100 years. In France some general publishing houses published books dealing with Jews and Judaism, e.g., F. Rieder, Fernand Nathan, Albin Michel, Payot, Au-bier Montaine, Flammarion, and Presses Universitaires de France.

[Ed.]

In Great Britain. The pioneers of Jewish publishing in Great Britain were members of the London Sephardi community who issued works on philosophy, literature, and Jewish liturgy in Spanish and Portuguese from the early 18th century onward. Daniel Israel Lopez *Laguna's *Espejo Fiel de Vidas* ("Faithful Mirror of Life"), a Spanish metrical version of Psalms planned in the cells of the Inquisition and completed in Jamaica, was published in London in 1720. Long after Marrano immigration had virtually come to an end, Spanish and Portuguese remained the official languages of the Sephardim, with the result that Isaac *Pinto's English translation of the prayer book had to appear in New York (1761–66) because of the disapproval of the London *mahamad.* One of the first Anglo-Jewish publishers whose name has survived was Alexander b. Judah Loeb Alexander (d. 1807), who issued a *Haggadah* (1770) and a Sephardi prayer book with English translation (1788), as well as other works of a liturgical nature. This activity was maintained by his son, Levy Alexander (1754–1853), who also proved to be an indifferent translator with his pioneering, but defective, Hebrew-English Bible (1824). Levy, however, did not confine himself to religious publications, producing an account of Anglo-Jewish social scandals in 1808.

By about the middle of the 19th century Jews were becoming more prominent in the general field of publishing, founding several important family business concerns. Isaac Vallentine (1793–1868), the Belgian-born son of a rabbi, was a leading communal figure as well as a printer, publisher, and bookseller of note. In 1841 he founded the predecessor of the weekly *Jewish Chronicle* and also established *The Hebrew Almanack and Calendar* (1848), a forerunner of the *Jewish Year Book.* The firm of Vallentine & Co. later underwent a merger, becoming the bookselling and publishing firm of Shapiro, Vallentine, which remained in business until 1971.

[G.E.S.]

Other Jewish publishers of Hebraica and Judaica, who became active from the late 19th century included the booksellers M. Cailingold, R. Mazin (later Jack Mazin), and Edward Goldston. In the 1920s Jacob Davidson founded the Soncino Press, which was responsible for the publication of classic Jewish texts in English. They issued (35- and 11-volume editions) the Talmud edited by I. *Epstein, Midrash Rabbah (10 vols.), Zohar (5 vols.), the Bible (text, translation, and commentary, 13 vols.), a one-volume edition of J. H. Hertz's Pentateuch and Haftarot, the minor tractates of the Talmud (2 vols.), a collection of S. R. Hirsch's essays (2 vols., edited by I. *Grunfeld), and Hirsch's *Horeb* (2 vols.; also edited by I. Grunfeld). From the 1930s onward the East and West Library (see above) brought out a series of Jewish classics. In the 1940s and 1950s a number of books in Hebrew and Yiddish, as well as the journal *Metsudah,* were produced by the Ararat Publishing Company. Since World War II the firm of Valentine Mitchell (associated with the *Jewish Chronicle*) has published a large variety of books of Jewish interest. Literature pertaining to Anglo-Jewish history was published by the *Jewish Historical Society of England.

General publishing firms as well, some of them owned by Jews, have published Hebraica and Judaica. George Routledge and Sons published the Davis-Adler *Maḥzor* (6 vols., 1904), which has gone through many editions and reprints, and other books of Jewish interest. Eyre and Spottiswoode have issued the popular Singer's *Prayer Book* since 1890; it has sold over half a million copies. [ED.]

In Eastern Europe. In Eastern Europe publishing gradually emerged as distinct from Hebrew printing. Great printing houses signed contracts with authors, e.g., Romm in Vilna with I. M. *Dick and K. *Schulman. Important booksellers also began to publish works, e.g., A. Zuckermann and A. J. Shapiro in Warsaw; I. Ginzburg in Bobrisk; and Rawnitzki in Odessa. Newspaper owners, learned societies, and patrons published works, hitherto in manuscript or unsatisfactory editions. The first noncommercial publishing house was Aḥiasaf, founded in Warsaw in 1892–93 on the initiative of the *Bnei Moshe and under the direction of E. E. Kaplan and the guidance of *Aḥad Ha-Am. Aḥi'asaf, which was active until 1923, published works of modern Jewish scholarship and youth literature as well as the annual *Lu'aḥ Aḥi'asaf* and the periodicals *Ha-Shilo'ah* and *Ha-Dor.* One of the founders of Aḥi'asaf, A. Ben-Avigdor, set up the Tushiyyah company in 1895, which extended its activities to Hebrew belles lettres, both original and translated, works in the natural and social sciences, and modern school books.

In 1899, in Warsaw, J. Lidzki founded the "Progres" publishing firm for Yiddish literature. B. Schimin, also in Warsaw, brought out books both in Hebrew and Yiddish as did S. Scherberk in Vilna (established 1901–02), who published the popular Bible commentary *Mikra Meforash.* In order to further original Hebrew literature P. Lachower set up the Sifrut company in Warsaw in 1908. In 1910 in Vilna B. Klatzkin began to publish scientific books, as well as original and translated literature in Yiddish. A year later Tushiyyah, Progres, Schimin, and Scherberk merged under the name of Merkaz ("Zentral"). In 1901 Ḥ. N. Bialik, S. Ben-Zion, and Yehoshua Ḥana Rawnitzki founded the *Moriah publishing house in Odessa for classical Hebrew literature and textbooks for schools, while Turgeman concentrated on translations from other languages.

World War I brought with it a severe crisis in the Jewish book market in Russia, which was aggravated by an edict in 1915 prohibiting all printing in Hebrew types. After the March 1917 revolution two Hebrew publishing houses were set up in Moscow: *Stybel, under the direction of D. *Frischmann, for classical world literature in Hebrew, and Omanut (see above). Moriah also renewed its activities. After the October Revolution and the subsequent anti-Jewish measures of the Soviet government, all these ceased. Stybel moved to Warsaw and later to Berlin, New York, and finally Tel Aviv. In the early years of the Soviet regime some private Yiddish publishing continued, e.g., by the Kultur-Lige (founded in 1917 in Kiev), but these businesses were soon absorbed by the state corporation Der Emes in Moscow; the Ukrainian state publishers and the Belorussian state publishers year after year issued many hundreds of Yiddish books, most of them propagating communist ideology. With the outbreak of World War II this output was severely reduced, ceasing altogether with the liquidation of Jewish writers in the years 1942–48. From 1958 onward only very few books in Yiddish were published in Soviet Russia.

In Poland the centers of Jewish publishing between the two world wars were Warsaw and Vilna. In Warsaw "Zentral" continued its activities; S. L. *Gordon published his Bible commentary, and Stybel *Ha-Tekufah,* and hundreds of books. A Kultur-Lige, founded in 1921, issued the best of Yiddish literature, school books, and Dubnow's "World History of the Jewish People." B. Klatzkin moved from Vilna to Warsaw and expanded its activities. Other publishers include A. Gitlin, H. Bzoza, S. Goldfarb, Katzenellenbogen, and Armkraut and Freund (Przemysl). The brothers Lewin-Epstein, who had published religious literature from 1880, began to issue belles lettres in Hebrew as well as in Yiddish. In Vilna "Tomor" produced I. Zinberg's history of Jewish literature. The various political parties also published books, as did newspapers *(Literarishe Bleter)* and scholarly societies such as *YIVO. With the invasion of Poland by Nazi Germany this activity came to an end. After the war a state corporation under the control of Jewish communists, Dos Yidishe Bukh, produced some important studies on the Holocaust. [Y.S.]

In the United States. Until the early 19th century, Jews in the United States imported books of specifically Jewish interest (chiefly Bibles, prayer books, and instructional material for the young) from Europe. However, a Hebrew Bible, a reprint of Joseph *Athias' unpointed text, was printed in Philadelphia in 1814. In 1845 Isaac *Leeser established the American Jewish Publication Society for the dissemination of Jewish literature. Fourteen books were published under the general title "Jewish Miscellany," but the society collapsed in 1851 when a fire destroyed the building in which the books and plates were stored. The firm now known as the Bloch Publishing Co. was founded in Cincinnati in 1854 by Isaac M. *Wise and Edward Bloch (1816–1881) to print and publish books on Jewish subjects. The *Bloch family has retained control of the firm, which has been in New York since 1901. Edward H. Bloch (1899–), grandson of the founder, was president from 1940, and Solomon Kerstein (1901–1969), a founder of the Jewish Book Council, was vice-president from 1947 onward. By 1970 over 1,000 titles had appeared on the firm's catalogs. The Hebrew Publishing Company came into being in New York in 1883, when Joseph L. Werbelowsky and some associates began to publish prayer books and school texts. In 1901 the firm was known as Rosenbaum and Werbelowsky, Inc. Menahem Menschel (1894–), an agent for the Stybel (Hebrew) Publishing House and a partner in the Jewish bookselling firm of Reznick, Menschel and Co., was manager from 1938. The firm published new Hebrew-English editions of the *siddur* and the *maḥzor* by Philip *Birnbaum. The third of these pioneering Jewish publishing houses, the Jewish Publication Society, was established in Philadelphia in 1888, and its many titles include authoritative translations of the Bible (1917; 1963–). Unlike the others, this is a membership organization with many features of the modern book clubs. The *Jewish Encyclopedia* (1901–06) was issued by the non-Jewish publishing house of Funk and Wagnall (see Jewish *Encyclopedias).

National Jewish organizations in the United States have sponsored various publication programs. The *Union of American Hebrew Congregations (Reform) developed an extensive program under its own imprint. Emanuel *Gamoran, educational director of the UAHC and its Commission on Jewish Education (1923–1958), developed text and reference books catering for all age groups. The Conservative movement (*United Synagogue of America) also established its own publishing divisions. Burning Bush Press and the United Synagogue Book Service serve the needs of the affiliated synagogues and schools. The *Union of Orthodox Jewish Congregations of America has also published text materials, while many works for both adults and children have appeared under the imprint of the Ḥabad ḥasidic Merkos l'Inyonei Chinuch of New York. The viewpoint of *Reconstructionism is presented in the bound books and paperbacks of the Reconstructionist Press. The Herzl Press has issued Zionist classics, handbooks, and yearbooks. In 1967 the *B'nai B'rith Commission on Adult Education contracted with the W. W. Norton Co. for a 50-book series of "Jewish Heritage Classics."

The Anti-Defamation League of B'nai B'rith usually employs a general publisher for its major works, pamphlets and shorter publications normally appearing under the organization's own imprint. The B'nai B'rith Hillel Foundation has also published books and pamphlets, while *Commentary,* the monthly sponsored by the American Jewish Committee, operates its own book club. Other publishers active in the field include Pardes, the Jewish Agency, various Zionist bodies (Z.O.A., Farband, Mizrachi) and university presses (Dropsie College, H.U.C., J.T.S., Yeshiva University, Brandeis) and the National Jewish Welfare Board. The *Histadrut Ivrit publishes Hebrew literature and *YIVO, the Yiddish Scientific Institute, has issued several important Yiddish works. Several regional educational bodies have also entered publishing. The J.E.C. Press of the Jewish Education Committee of New York has issued a library of Hebrew story books for American children, while the bureaus of Jewish education of Chicago and Cleveland also have their own publishing divisions.

Establishing these institutional publishing firms or the sponsoring of individual books under the imprint of a general publisher has tended to discourage privately owned publishing houses from specializing in the Jewish field. Indeed, practically all the privately owned Jewish publishing firms also run bookshops where Jewish books under various imprints are sold. They include Behrman House (1920), founded by Louis Behrman and later directed by his son, Jacob; the Ktav Publishing House, which issued text and story materials from 1924 (with Asher Scharfstein as president), and which has latterly published and reprinted serious scholarly works; the Furrow Press (1933), which issued festival plays and literature for Jewish schools; and the U.S. branch of Schocken Books (1945), known particularly for its serious paperback program. Other privately owned firms specializing in Judaica are Shengold Publishers (Moshe Sheinbaum); the Jonathan David Publishing Co. (Alfred J. Kolatch); Philipp Feldheim, which published English translations of the works of Samson Raphael *Hirsch; and Hermon press. The established firm of Shulsinger Brothers also prints Jewish publications. Morris *Silverman, a Conservative rabbi in Hartford, edited and published a series of Conservative prayer books with English translations under the Prayer Book Press imprint. Most publishers active in the Jewish field belong to the Association of Jewish Book Publishers. The chief publication of Yiddish works include *YIVO, *Congress for Jewish Culture, and Der Kval, a private firm.

Several general publishers have displayed continuous interest in Jewish books and their authors. Rinehart (now Holt, Rinehart, and Winston) issued a series of Jewish anthologies edited by Leo W. Schwarz, and Abelard-Shuman operates a separate division, Ram's Head Books, for Jewish books. Maurice *Samuel's books have been published by Knopf, and those of Isaac *Bashevis Singer and Bernard *Malamud by Farrar, Straus, and Giroux. Meridian Books (established by Arthur A. Cohen) first distributed the paperbacks of the Jewish Publication Society, a function later performed by Harper and Row. Another area of cooperation is the joint issue of a title by a Jewish and a general publisher. Many J.P.S.A. titles appear under the joint imprint of the Society and a general publisher. Thus Columbia University Press collaborated in Salo W. *Baron's multivolume *Social and Religious History of the Jews,* while Herzl Press and Doubleday have also cooperated on several publications.

In 1925, Fanny *Goldstein, a librarian, organized a Jewish Book Week in Boston. The movement grew gradually, and the Jewish Book Council, sponsored by the *National Jewish Welfare Board, was established in 1943. Jewish Book Week was later expanded to Jewish Book Month. Twenty-seven volumes of the *Jewish Book Annual* had been issued by 1969/70 and a series of annual prizes for authors in the Jewish field was established. [S.KE.]

IN ISRAEL

Printing and publishing developed slowly in Ereẓ Israel. Eliezer ben Isaac *Ashkenazi, a Hebrew printer from Prague, established the first printing shop in Safed in 1577 in partnership with his brother Abraham. Their first book, *Lekaḥ Tov* ("Good Doctrine"), a commentary on the Book of Esther, by R. Yom Tov Ẓahalon, was also the first book to be printed in western Asia. The Ashkenazi press remained in Safed for about a decade, but only five books were printed during that time, and in 1605 the Hebrew type was sold to a Damascus printer. Almost two-and-a-half centuries later, in 1831, Israel *Bak set up business in Safed, where he printed six books before moving to Jerusalem, establishing the first Hebrew printing press there. The Bak family continued to print in Jerusalem until 1878. During the second half of the 19th century, Jerusalem developed into a center for the printing of Hebrew religious works. By 1900, more than a dozen printers in Jerusalem were producing Hebrew books and periodicals. These printers were usually also publishers and booksellers. During the second half of the 19th century Jerusalem was also the center of the literary revival of Persian Jewry and of its printing and publishing activities, in which Simon *Ḥakham played a leading role (see *Judeo-Persian Literature).

Book publishing in Palestine in the modern sense began in the 20th century. The Histadrut ha-Morim published some school texts in Hebrew. The periodical *Ha-Po'el ha-Ẓa'ir* introduced the writings of Asher *Barash, A. D. *Gordon, Moshe *Smilansky, and others and issued a series of books, The People's University Library, edited by Joseph *Sprinzak. In time Hebrew publishing firms from Central Europe moved to Ereẓ Israel. Moriah, established in 1911 in Odessa by Ḥayyim Naḥman Bialik, Yehoshua Ḥana Rawnitzky, and others, was merged in 1923 with the *Dvir Publishing Co., which had been founded by Bialik, Rawnitzki and Shemaryahu *Levin in Berlin (1922). After 1924 Dvir, which specialized in Judaica, and the works of modern Hebrew authors, on a wide range of subjects, was located in Tel Aviv. Shlomo Srebrek was a publisher in Vilna and Warsaw before he settled in Palestine in 1933, and the Izreel Publishing House was later headed by his son Alexander. The Omanut Company (see above) largely publishes children's books. Rubin Mass, who founded his firm in Berlin in 1927, moved to Jerusalem in 1933. The Schocken Publishing Company, also established in Berlin in 1927, was transferred to Tel Aviv in 1938.

At the same time new publishing enterprises were being established in Palestine. Three veterans of the Jewish Brigade, Joshua Chachik, Mordecai Newman, and Joseph Srebrek, became booksellers in Jerusalem. From 1925 they combined to publish books under the Mizpeh imprint, but in 1944 they separated, each partner establishing a firm under his own name. A Tel Aviv pioneer, Naḥum Twerski, established his own firm in 1930, and S. Zack and Co. began to publish texts and reference books in Jerusalem in the same year. Joshua Orenstein issued books in Tel Aviv under the Yavneh imprint since 1932. Massadah Publishing House was established by Meir Peli (1894–1958) and his wife Berakhah (1893–) in 1931, and became a large Israel publishing complex, with its own chain of bookstores. Its most ambitious project is the multivolume *Ha-Enẓiklopedyah ha-Ivrit,* of which Alexander Peli (1915–) is a managing director. In 1933, Schachna Achiasaf began publishing books in Jerusalem; his firm is now located in Tel Aviv. Kirjath Sepher, publishers of the Even-Shoshan Hebrew dictionary, was also founded in 1933, and the Sivan Press is its printing division. Moshe Spitzer, a former manager of Schocken in Berlin, established Sifrei Tarshish in Jerusalem in 1940; and the Amiḥai Publishing House has been in business since 1948.

The various kibbutz movements have been operating their own publishing firms since 1939. Ha-Kibbutz Ha-Me'uḥad Publishing House Ltd., affiliated with the kibbutz organization of the same name, has an extensive publishing program presenting original works and translations. Sifriat Poalim is the publishing arm of Ha-Kibbutz ha-Arẓi (1942). Am Oved Publishers, noted for its art books and paperbacks (some of them reaching distribution of 25,000), was founded by the Histadrut. Tarbut ve-Ḥinnukh Publishers is another Histadrut firm specializing in texts.

Two houses specializing in Yiddish literature are the I. L. Peretz Publishing Co. (1956) and Ha-Menorah Publishers (1958). Dar e Nashir el Arabi (Tel Aviv), the Arabic publishing house of the Histadrut, issues many translations of Hebrew books, and El Jalil of Acre is a widely read independent Arabic firm.

Other firms include Karni (1951); Carta, established by Emanuel Hausman in 1958 and specializing in maps and atlases; Eked (1959), specializing in poetry; M. Mizrachi (1960); and Koren (1962). Many educational works were also published by the Jewish Agency and the World Zionist Organization. Steimatzky's Agency operates a chain of bookstores, imports books from abroad, and prints and publishes popular works. Am Ha-Sefer (1955) also publishes the literary quarterly, *Keshet.*

New Developments. Significant publishing projects have been developed by firms established by Israel public bodies. One of the biggest Hebrew publishing firms is Mossad Bialik ("Bialik Institute"), which was established in Jerusalem by the World Zionist Organization in 1935. Its major publications have included *Enẓiklopedyah Mikra'it* (5 vols. by 1968), *Enẓiklopedyah Ḥinnukhit* (1959–69, 5 vols.), and the *Atlas Ereẓ-Yisre'eli.* Its program includes a series of world classics in Hebrew translation (including the paperback series *Dorot*) as well as original Hebrew books and the periodical *Beḥinot.*

The religious institution Mosad ha-Rav Kook ("Rabbi Kook Institute"), founded by R. Judah Leib ha-Kohen *Maimon in

Jerusalem under the Jewish Agency and Mizrachi organization in 1937, published books on many aspects of Judaism, some in Hebrew, particularly of Maimonides' works. It also produces the monthly *Sinai* (founded 1938) on Torah and Judaism. The Magnes Press of the Hebrew University has issued works by faculty members, as well as the scholarly quarterly, *Tarbiz,* and the bibliographical quarterly *Kirjath Sepher.* Scholarly publications have also been sponsored by other Israel universities and learned bodies. Keter Publications and Israel Universities Press are divisions of the *Israel Program for Scientific Translations (1959), the State's largest publisher and exporter, established originally as a government company but in 1969 sold to private investors. The "Misrad ha-Bittaḥon Hoẓa'ah la-Or" ("Ministry of Defense Publishing House"), founded in Tel Aviv in 1959, publishes educational and scientific books for the forces as well as short novels.

Most Israel publishers are members of the Book Publishers' Association of Israel, organized in 1939, which helps its members through cooperative purchasing of paper and advertising. It sponsors *Hebrew Book Week,* for which it prints a special sales catalog and also prepares the annual *Joint Book Catalogue,* in which catalogs of member firms are supplemented by title, author, and subject indexes. Many association members are also stockholders in Yachdav United Publishers Co., which publishes university texts in Hebrew that would not be economical for a single firm to produce.

For many years, book publishers in Israel faced many serious problems. All paper had to be imported until the establishment of the American Israeli Paper Mills at Haderah in 1955. In the early days, Hebrew type, generally old and worn, had to be set by hand; printing presses were generally old and inefficient; and bindings were poor. In time these faults were corrected, and Israel now has printing plants capable of manufacturing well-made volumes that meet international standards. Central Press, Israel Program for Scientific Translations, Jerusalem Academic Press, and Sivan Press, as well as the Government Printer, are all located in Jerusalem. In the Tel Aviv area are E. Lewin-Epstein Printers, Peli Printing Works, Japheth Press, and United Artists.

From the early 1960s, Israel publishers expanded their markets through copublishing ventures with overseas firms. Massadah pioneered in this field and others active in copublishing were IPST and Sabra Books, the imprint used by the American-Israel Publishing Co., a partnership of E. Lewin-Epstein and American Israeli Paper Mills, now known as Amis Publishing Co., a wholly-owned subsidiary of the paper mill. In December 1969 Weidenfeld and Nicolson Jerusalem Ltd. began operation as an overseas company of Weidenfeld & Nicolson Ltd. of London. The Jerusalem firm is producing books in Israel by Israel authors for the world market. The firm is also producing Hebrew editions of many of these as well as Hebrew translations of books published abroad. It also serves as Israeli representative of major British and American publishers. The Jerusalem International Book Fair, held biennially since 1963, has brought prominent foreign publishers to Israel, and the Book and Printing Center of the Israel Export Institute has helped publishers develop foreign markets. It publishes a combined catalog, *Books From Israel,* for distribution to foreign publishers and booksellers. Since 1970, it also publishes a quarterly in English, *Israel Book World.* A network of printing schools has been training workers for this expanding field. A quarterly, *Olam ha-Defus,* presents technical and cultural articles.

In 1969/70 Israeli publishers issued 3,158 titles; the average number of titles published for the preceding four years was 2,600. By the end of 1970 printing and publishing in Israel employed about 9,600 people. Exports for 1970 reached a record value of $5,733,000. [I.So.]

New Methods. The invention of photo-mechanical processes of book reproduction has led in recent times to the extensive republishing of Hebraica and Judaica. In the 1920s in Berlin Sefarim issued facsimiles of the first Venice editions of the Palestinian Talmud, the halakhic Midrashim, and the *She'iltot.* A number of famous Passover *Haggadot* (both manuscript and printed) have also been reproduced in facsimile. Firms more recently engaged in this kind of publishing include Ktav and Hermon Press (U.S.), Gregg International (England), Philo (Holland), Olms (Germany), and Makor (Israel).

Bibliography: F. Kapp and J. Goldfriedrich, *Geschichte des deutschen Buchhandels,* 4 vols. (1886–1913); R. Hamburger, *Rudolf Mosse* (1928); A. M. Hyamson, in: *Anglo-Jewish Notabilities* (1949), 4–73; H. Lehmann-Haupt, *The Book in America* (1951²); Y. Pograbinsky, in: *Ha-Sefer ha-Ivri,* 9 (1951), 37–56; 10 (1952), 37–53; K. Schottenloher, *Buecher bewegten die Welt,* 2 vols. (1952); A. Levinson, *Toledot Yehudei Varshah* (1953), 306–10; S. Z. Sreberk, *Zikhronot* (1954); A. Litai, in: *He-Avar,* 3 (1956), 51–54; C. Roth, *Jews in the Renaissance* (1959), 165–85; Roth, Marranos, ch. 13, 269, 322ff.; idem, in: JJS, 4 (1953), 116–30; J. Toury, in: BLBI, 3 (1960), 58–69; Ch. Shmeruk, *Pirsumim Yehudiyyim bi-Verit ha-Mo'aẓot* (1960); S. H. Steinberg, *Five Hundred Years of Printing* (1961²); S. Kaznelson, *Juden im deutschen Kulturbereich* (1962³), 131–46; H. G. Adler, *Juden in Deutschland* (1962); G. Berman-Fischer, *Der Fischer Verlag* (1967); M. Faeber, in: *Jews of Czechoslovakia,* 1 (1968), 532–8; A. M. Habermann, *Ha-Sefer ha-Ivri be-Hitpatteḥuto* (1968), incl. bibl.

PUERTO RICO, see Supplementary Entries.

PUGLIESE, EMANUELE (1874–), Italian soldier. His military career began when he took part in the Italo-Turkish war (1911–12). With the entry of Italy into World War I, Pugliese rose rapidly. In 1917, he took part in the battle of Vittorio Veneto. At the end of the war, he became a divisional commander and as such he fought in the war in Albania in 1920. In 1931, he was appointed military commander of Sardinia and in 1934 reached the rank of lieutenant general and corps commander. Pugliese received the highest military decoration of his own country and many foreign honors. [Mo.K.]

PUKHACHEWSKY, MICHAEL ZALMAN (1863–1947), pioneer of Jewish agriculture in Ereẓ Israel. Born in Brest-Litovsk in 1885. Pukhachewsky was one of six young men chosen by Ḥovevei Zion in Russia (at Baron Edmond de *Rothschild's suggestion) to specialize in agriculture in the Baron's settlements and become agricultural instructors for settlers. He established a farm in Rishon le-Zion and worked for many years as an agricultural instructor, specializing in viticulture in the Jordan Valley, the Jezreel Valley, and other areas. He published articles in Palestinian agricultural journals and wrote his memoirs on the early days of Jewish settlement (*Bustanai,* 1 (1929/30), nos. 6–44). His wife, Neḥamah (1869–1934), was a writer active in the public life of Palestine. She joined Ḥovevei Zion at the age of 17 and went to Ereẓ Israel together with her husband. She wrote essays under the pen name Nefesh.

Bibliography: Tidhar, 3 (1958), 1281–82. [Y.S.]

PUKHOVITSER, JUDAH LEIB (c. 1630–after 1700), rabbi, scholar, and preacher in Lithuania, Poland, and Germany. His father had settled in Pinsk by the end of the 1620s. Judah Leib studied under Naphtali b. Isaac Katz, the rabbi of Pinsk (1639–44). His surname appears to have been derived from the townlet of Pukhovichi, near Minsk. In 1659, when he was rabbi of *Bykhov, he was an eyewitness to the conquest of the town by Muscovite soldiers, who massacred the Jews and killed one of his daughters. After 1667 Pukhovitser returned to his native Pinsk where he acted as rabbi and preacher. From time to time he left Pinsk, preaching in the communities of Pinsk province and the large communities of Lithuania and Poland. In 1681–82 he stayed in Frankfort on the Oder, where he published his homiletic works in two parts, *Keneh Ḥokhmah* and *Derekh Ḥokhmah.* His work *Divrei Hakhamim* (in two parts) on Shulḥan Arukh was published in Hamburg (1692–93), and *Kevod Ḥakhamim* in Venice (1699–1700). Leaving Venice, he went to Jerusalem, where he died after 1700.

Pukhovitser lived during a period which saw tremendous changes in the lives of the Jews of Poland and Lithuania as a result of the massacres of 1648–49 and 1666–67. One of the fundamentals of his homiletic teaching is that the study of the Torah for its own sake must lead to good deeds and repentance. In his sermons, he urged that *battei midrash* in which Torah would be permanently studied should be maintained and every Jew obliged to fix regular times for Torah study; he thus gave a great impetus to the formation of study groups in Lithuania. Criticizing the prevailing methods of study in the *ḥadarim* and yeshivot, he called for a gradual progression from easier subjects to more difficult ones. He also attacked the situation which prevented the poor from studying in the yeshivot and demanded that several well-established members of the community provide for the upkeep of a Torah student. At the same time he condemned the method of study based on *pilpul*. Pukhovitser's works are imbued with kabbalistic motifs, containing many Lurianic elements. In a letter to the scholars of Jerusalem (Hamburg, 1692), he developed the idea that the future redemption of Israel would be effected by the community of Jerusalem when it had reached the degree of *kenishta ḥada* ("a unified community").

Bibliography: E. Pines, *Tanna de-Vei Eliyahu* (1753); Ḥ. N. Dembitzer, *Kelilat Yofi*, 1 (1888), 49–50; 2 (1893), 122; Frumkin-Rivlin, 2 (1928), 88ff.; A. Ya'ari, *Meḥkerei Sefer* (1958), 102–3; idem, *Ta'alumat Sefer* (1954), 17–21; G. Scholem, in: *Beḥinot*, 8 (1955), 79–95; A. Shochat, in: *Ha-Ḥinnukh*, 28 (1956), 410–2; M. Benayahu, in: *Sefunot*, 3–4 (1960), 134; I. Tishby, *Netivei Emuna u-Minut* (1964), 110ff.

[M.NA.]

PULAWY (Pol. **Puławy;** Yid. **Pilev;** Rus. **Novaya Aleksandriya**), a town in Lublin province, Poland. The first Jews to settle in Pulawy came from the neighboring townlets (mostly Włostowice) at the beginning of the 19th century when the area developed rapidly upon the initiative of its owner, Prince A. K. *Czartoryski. There was an organized Jewish community in Pulawy from 1820. In 1897 it numbered 3,883 (about 73% of the population). The principal Jewish occupations were shoemaking, gardening, furniture-making and shopkeeping. From the middle of the 19th century, the influence of Ḥasidism became widespread among the Jews of Pulawy; they were attached to the ḥasidic courts of *Lublin and *Kotsk and later to those of Gur (*Gora Kolwariya) and *Sokolow. From 1875 to 1884 the rabbinical seat of Pulawy was held by Elijah Lerman, the author of *Devar Eliyahu* (1884). In 1888, Ḥayyim Israel Morgenstern, the grandson of *Menahem Mendel of Kotsk, founded a ḥasidic court in Pulawy. At the close of the 19th century, enterprises established by Jewish initiative included iron industries, machinery and shoe manufacture. Jewish workers found employment in them and organized themselves into trade unions. From 1875 Jewish students studied at the Higher Institute of Agriculture of Pulawy; many of the students participated in revolutionary social democratic activities. From 1907 a Jewish cooperative bank functioned in Pulawy with much success. In 1910 there were 6,111 Jews (61% of the population). During World War I, the Jewish population of the town decreased because of persecutions and a fire. From 1917 branches of all parties then active on the Jewish scene were organized in Pulawy. At first, the *Bund and *Agudat Israel wielded the greatest influence, but *Po'alei Zion circles, other Zionist parties, and communists soon grew strong. Jewish craftsmen and merchants established unions in 1920. In 1921 there were 3,221 Jews (45% of the population) living in the town. Between the two world wars there was a private Hebrew secondary school, as well as *Tarbut, Yavneh and Beth Jacob schools, and a Jewish library.

[A.CY.]

Holocaust Period. At the outbreak of World War II there were 3,600 Jews in the town. At the end of October 1939, an open ghetto was established. On Dec. 29, 1939 the entire Jewish population was expelled to the nearby town of Opole Lubelskie, where all were in turn deported to the *Sobibor death camp in May 1942 and exterminated. No Jewish community was reconstituted in Pulawy. [S.KR.]

Bibliography: B. Wasiutyński, *Ludność żydowska w Polsce*... (1930), 34, 63, 72, 77, 78; *Słownik geograficzny Królestwa Polskiya*, 9 (1888), 287–9; 13 (1895), 720; N. Gasiorowska (ed.), *Zródła do dziejów klasy robotniczej na ziemiach polskich* (1962), nos. 354, 376, 377; J. Bernstein, *Yisker Bukh Pulav* (1964); R. Bender, in: BZIH, 34 (1960), 45–46.

PULITZER, JOSEPH (1847–1911), American editor and publisher who bought declining newspapers and restored them to national influence. Born in Mako, Hungary, son of a Jewish father and a Roman Catholic mother, Pulitzer emigrated to the U.S. at the age of 17 to serve in the Union Army during the Civil War. Discharged from the cavalry in 1865, he went to St. Louis and in 1868 became a reporter for the German-language daily *Westliche Post*. Three years later he bought an interest in the paper, became managing editor, and sold back his shares at a vast profit. In 1878 Pulitzer took his first big step toward creating a newspaper empire when he bought the St. Louis *Dispatch* at an auction for $2,500 and merged it with the St. Louis *Post* into the *Post-Dispatch*. By 1881 it was yielding profits of $85,000 a year. He left for New York in 1883 and bought *The World* from Jay Gould, the financier, for $ 346,000. Three years later, revived by Pulitzer's innovations in mass appeal journalism, *The World* was earning more than $ 500,000 a year. He established a sister paper in New York, the *Evening World*, in 1887. All three newspapers succeeded on a formula of vigorous promotion, sensationalism, sympathy with labor and the underdog, and innovations in illustration and typography. In 1869 Pulitzer served in the lower house of the Missouri legislature, and in 1885 was elected to the U.S. House of Representatives from New York, but served only briefly. A man of intellect and energy, he worked himself into a condition which compelled him to live his last years as a totally blind invalid. However, he still directed his newspapers. He endowed the Pulitzer School of Journalism at Columbia University and the famous Pulitzer Prizes for journalism. His son, JOSEPH JR. (1885–1955), continued the policies of his father with success as the publisher of the St. Louis *Post-Dispatch*, but under his other two sons, Ralph (1879–1959) and Herbert (1897–1957) the two New York papers declined and were sold in 1931 to Scripps-Howard.

Bibliography: W. A. Swanberg; *Pulitzer* (1967); K. Stewart, *Makers of Modern Journalism* (1952), 86–102.

[I.R.]

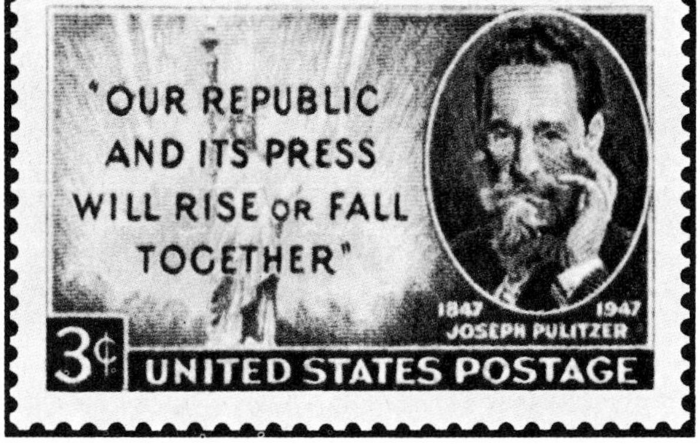

Joseph Pulitzer centenary stamp issued by the U.S. Post Office in 1947. Jerusalem, B. M. Ansbacher Collection.

PULKAU, small town in Lower Austria; it became notorious in the 14th century as the scene of a *Host desecration libel, which was followed by a wave of massacres of the Jews. A bleeding Host was allegedly found concealed in front of a Jew's house on Easter Sunday, April 12, 1338, the day following the last day of Passover. Rumors spread that the Host had performed miracles; crowds came to venerate it, and on April 23 they burned the Jews at the stake and plundered their property. The disorders spread, and Jews were massacred in 27 localities as far away as *Jindrichuv Hradec (Neuhaus) in Bohemia, *Trebic (Trebitsch) in Moravia, and St. Poelten. Duke *Albert II expressed his doubts about the accusation and asked Pope Benedict XII for an investigation. The pope ordered the bishop of Passau to conduct an inquiry, but its results are unknown. A church called "Zum Heiligen Blut" ("The Holy Blood") was built on the site; decorated with representations of the alleged occurrence, it attracted many worshipers throughout the years. The pictures were later painted over. The site where the Jews were burned is well marked. At the time of the massacres Jewish books were confiscated; possibly some of the parchment manuscripts confiscated in 1338 were utilized for binding city records in 1622 and 1623.

Bibliography: J. E. Scherer, *Rechtsverhaeltnisse der Juden*, 2 (1968), 363–9; Germ Jud, 2 (1968), 665–7. [M.LA.]

PULTUSK (Pol. **Pułtusk**), town in Warzawa province, Poland. Although there were some Jews in Pultusk in 1486 a settlement as such did not develop because of the privilege *de non tolerandis Judaeis* granted to the Masovia region during the 16th century by the Polish king, Sigismund II Augustus. Even temporary residence for Jews was authorized only by special permit. The prohibition was temporarily abrogated after the Grand Duchy of Warsaw was created in 1807 but renewed with the establishment of the Polish kingdom in 1815, according to the decision of the Congress of Vienna. The decree was finally abolished in 1866. During the 19th century the Jewish population increased; there were 118 Jews in 1810 (5.1% of the total population), 4,769 in 1856, and 6,950 (45.7%) in 1909. During World War I many Jews fled to Warsaw, so that by 1921 the number had decreased to 5,919 (about 46% of the total population). In independent Poland the Jewish population rose again and by 1931 there were 8,300 Jews (49.2% of the total) in the town.

Despite its proximity to Warsaw, Pultusk did not develop as a center of commerce and crafts mainly because it was removed from railway junctions. Nevertheless, a considerable number of Jews were craftsmen, particularly tailors. Because of the surrounding forests, there were a number of sawmills so that carpentry as well as trade in wood and furniture developed. However, economic difficulties led many Jews to emigrate. In 1894 many wealthy Jews left when a cholera epidemic broke out. During the 19th century the community supported various activities, the most important of which was social relief to the needy. Between the two world wars a Jewish educational program was developed. It attracted most of the community's elementary and secondary school students. Jews were represented in the municipal administration; about one-half of the delegates elected in 1922 and 1927 were Jews. The leadership of the Jewish community itself was elected democratically for the first time in 1927. The oldest synagogue was erected between 1805 and 1815. It burnt down and was rebuilt in 1854. Of the rabbis of Pultusk, the most renowned were R. Joshua *Trunk (from 1853 to 1861), R. Ḥanokh Zundel b. Jacob Grodzinski, who belonged to the **Mitnaggedim* (appointed in 1878), and R. Ḥayyim Meshullam ha-Kohen (1909–1929), known for his Zionist tendencies. The last rabbi of Pultusk was R. Israel Ber Lowenthal, who emigrated to Palestine at the outbreak of World War II and died there in 1942. [SH.L.K.]

Holocaust Period. The city was captured by the Germans on Sept. 7, 1939, and by September 11, 14 Jews had been shot. During the holiday of Sukkot, 1939, the Germans deported all the Jews to the other side of the Narev River, in the Soviet zone of occupation. All Jewish property was looted, and on the way to the border Jews were maltreated and many were killed. Many of the deportees found temporary shelter in Bialystok and surrounding cities under the Soviet administration, where they were subjected to administrative restrictions and met with difficulties in finding housing and work. In the summer of 1940 many were deported to the Soviet interior. [AR.W.]

PUMBEDITA, town in Babylonia. Pumbedita was situated on the bank of the River Euphrates on the site of the Shunya-Shumvata (Git. 60b), the most northerly of the canals joining the Euphrates and the Tigris. A canal called Nehar Papa also passed through Pumbedita itself (Yoma 77b), and situated near it was the town of Peruz-Shavur. The area had an exceptionally abundant water supply and a pleasant climate, and commerce flourished there, the caravan route to Syria passing nearby. Crops included cereals and fruits, dates being especially plentiful (Pes. 88a), and the flax grown there (Git. 27a; BM 18b) was the basis of the local textile industry. The Jewish settlement in Pumbedita apparently already existed during the period of the Second Temple and was included by Sherira Gaon among those settlements which were centers of the study of Torah during that period (*Iggeret Rav Sherira Ga'on*, ed. by B.M. Levin (1921), 40). However, its importance as a communal and religious center dates only from the middle of the third century C.E. In 259, after Nehardea was destroyed by Papa b. Naser (see *Odenathus and Zenobia), commander in chief of Palmyra, Judah b. Ezekiel founded an academy there. This academy and its *bet din* were the central religious authority for Babylonian Jewry until the middle of the fourth century C.E. During that period some of the best known **amoraim* of Babylonian Jewry headed the academy—Rabbah b. Nahamani, Joseph, Abbaye, and Rava. During the time of Rava the academy was transferred to Maḥoza, where Rava resided. During this period, when the academy began to flourish, exceptionally strong ties were established between it and its sister academy at Tiberias through the medium of the **neḥutei*. The aforementioned heads of the academy, with the exception of Joseph, were distinguished for their teaching methods which were marked by acumen and even casuistry (Hor. 14a; BM 38b). As a result of this intellectual acumen, which in their opinion was an efficient method to discuss *halakhah* and arrive at correct decisions, they came to be called "uprooters of mountains," and it was said of them that "they could draw an elephant through the eye of a needle" (BM 38b).

From the death of Rava in 352 until the first half of the geonic period, the Pumbedita academy did not occupy a central place in the scholastic and halakhic world. It was subordinate to *Sura, which was granted more privileges than Pumbedita. Life in a large, bustling, commercial city full of connections with foreign merchants had a deleterious influence on the character of the Jews of Pumbedita. The Babylonian Talmud has preserved many adverse evaluations of their moral character. Mention is made of the cheating by workers (BB 46a; Ḥul. 127a), and Rava refers to the thieves who would come to the city, as well as the resident thieves (Av. Zar. 70a). In fact, the dishonest practices of the people of Pumbedita became a byword among the Jews of Babylon (Ket. 82a), and it is therefore not surprising that scholars were not popular among them, since the scholars rebuked them for their deeds (Shab. 153a). One scholar advised his son not to dwell in affluent Pumbedita (Hor. 12a). [M.Be.]

During the Post-Talmudic Period. Sherira Gaon related that as the result of religious persecution under Persian rule, the Pumbedita academy was transferred to Peruz-Shavur, in the vicinity of Nehardea. It remained there during the period of the **savoraim;* when the Arabs conquered Babylonia (c. 634 C.E.), it returned to Pumbedita. R. Isaac, the *gaon* of Pumbedita, who lived in Peruz-Shavur, went out to welcome the conquering caliph ʿAli ibn Abi Ṭāleb. During the Arab period Pumbedita was known as Anbar, and the academy was called *yeshivah shel ha-golah* ("academy of the Diaspora"). Until the beginning of the ninth century Pumbedita was overshadowed by *Sura. During the 830s the *ḥakhamim* of the Pumbedita academy backed the candidacy of David b. Judah as exilarch against Daniel, who had the support of the *ḥakhamim* of Sura. The former's election as exilarch also resulted in the consolidation of the Pumbedita academy. From his time the Jews gathered in Pumbedita on the occasion of the *Shabbeta de-Rigla* (*Iggeret R. Sherira,* p. 93). In an extant letter of his son, the exilarch Judah, he seeks contributions for the academy, which is described "as having many **allufim, ḥakhamim,* elders, Mishnah scholars, Talmud scholars, and *tannaim:* there are seven *allufim* . . ." (Abramson, Merkazim, 18).

An important head of the academy in this period was *Paltoi b. Abbaye (842–52), the first to be styled *gaon* of Pumbedita, who maintained contacts with the communities of Spain and North Africa. From Spain, they turned to him "to write the Talmud and its interpretation down for them, and upon his order it was written for them" (Sherira Gaon, *Iggeret . . .,* ed. by M. N. Adler (1907), xxiii (2nd Roman pagination)). During his son *Ẓemaḥ's (872) lifetime these ties were strengthened and the status of the academy surpassed that of Sura. In the *Kaddish* the name of Ẓemaḥ b. Paltoi was mentioned before that of the *gaon* of Sura, *Ẓemaḥ b. Ḥayyim.

During the days of the *gaon* *Hai b. David (890–98), who had previously been a *dayyan,* the academy was transferred to Baghdad. In the first half of the tenth century contributions to the academy decreased—the centers of the Diaspora established their own Torah institutions and their attachment to the Babylonian center was thus weakened. The contest for the gaonate between R. *Aaron Sargado and R. *Nehemiah b. Kohen Ẓedek from the 940s to 960s and the dispute between the latter and R. Sherira were also responsible for the decline in the status of the academy. The situation changed under *Sherira Gaon, a powerful personality, who renewed the contacts with the communities of North Africa and called upon them to support his academy. The period of office of Sherira Gaon (968–98) and that of his son *Hai Gaon (998–1038) was the period of Pumbedita's efflorescence. The greatest number of extant responsa to the Diaspora, especially to the communities of North Africa (e.g., Kairouan, Fez, etc.), was written by these two *geonim.* Students came from abroad to study with R. Hai and later went on to hold important positions. These included *Shemariah b. Elhanan of Egypt, who was "the first in the 'great' [first] row of the three rows of the academy"; *Maẓliaḥ b. Albaẓak of Sicily; the *gaon* Solomon b. Judah's son from Palestine; and students from Byzantium and Italy. After R. Hai's death the exilarch *Hezekiah b. David headed the Pumbedita academy for 20 years (until 1058).

According to sources found in the Cairo *Genizah,* the *divan* of Eleazar b. Jacob ha-Bavli, and Arab sources, it appears that the Baghdad academy continued in existence until the 13th century. The names of nine *geonim* who lived during the 12th and 13th centuries and considered themselves the heirs of the Pumbedita academy are known. The last *gaon* was Samuel b. Daniel ha-Kohen (1288). According to Benjamin of Tudela, who visited Babylonia in the 1170s, there were about 3,000 Jews in Pumbedita. Even though this number seems to be exaggerated, it appears that an important community still existed there.

For futher information see *Academies; *Gaon (includes table of *geonim* of Pumbedita). [M.Be./El.B.]

Bibliography: Talmud: Neubauer, Géogr, 349; A. Berliner, *Beitraege zur Geographie und Ethnographie Babyloniens im Talmud und Midrasch,* 57f., in: *Jahres-Bericht des Rabbiner-Seminars zu Berlin pro 5643* (1882/83); J. Obermeyer, *Die Landschaft Babylonien* (1929), 226–42; M. D. Yudilewitz, *Yeshivat Pumbedita bi-Ymei ha-Amora'im* (1932); idem, *Ha-Ir Pumbedita bi-Ymei ha-Amora'im* (1939). Post-Talmudic: S. Schechter, *Saadyana* (1903), 117–21; L. Ginzberg, *Geonica,* 1 (1909), 14–22, 62–66; G. Margoliouth, in: JQR, 14 (1901/02), 307–11; A. Cowley, *ibid.,* 18 (1905/06), 399–403; 19 (1906/07), 104–6; J. Mann, *ibid.,* 8 (1917/18), 341–62; 9 (1918/19), 139–47; 11 (1920/21), 419–21; idem, in: *Tarbiz,* 5 (1933/34), 148–79; Mann, Texts, 1 (1931), 75–145, 179–201; B.M. Lewin (ed.), *Iggeret R. Sherira Ga'on* (1921), 99–100, 109–14, 119–22; Dinur, Golah, 1 pt. 2 (1961[2]), 106–9; Abramson, Merkazim, index; S. Assaf, in: *Ha-Shilo'aḥ,* 39 (1921), 218–20; Assaf, Ge'onim, 42–70, 261–78; B.M. Lewin (ed.), *Ginzei Kedem,* 2 (1923), 46–48; H.Z. Taubes, in: *Sefer Zikkaron li-Shelomo S. Mayer; Kovez le-Toledot Yehudei Italyah* (1956), 126–41; Benjamin of Tudela, *Masa'ot . . .,* ed. by M. N. Adler (1907), 34, 46 (Heb. pagination); Neusner, Babylonia, passim.

PUNISHMENT. While there is no modern theory of punishment that cannot, in some form or other, be traced back to biblical concepts, the original and foremost purpose of punishment in biblical law was the appeasement of God. God abhors the criminal ways of other nations (Lev. 20:23) whose practices the Israelites must not follow *(ibid.)* and from whose abominations they must not learn (Deut. 20:18); by violating His laws, His name is profaned (Lev. 22:31–32); and not only are criminals abhorrent to God (Deut. 18:12; 22:5; 25:16; 27:15), as well as crimes (Lev. 18:27–29), but God's own holiness obliges man to be holy like Him (Lev. 19:2). By taking "impassioned action" (Num. 25:13) to punish violators of His laws, expiation is made to God and God's "fierce anger" (Deut. 13:18) turned away from Israel (Num. 25:4). Closely related to the appeasement of God is another expiatory purpose of punishment: a crime, and more particularly the shedding of blood, pollutes the land—"and no expiation can be made for the land for the blood that is shed therein but by the blood of him that shed it" (Num. 35:33). Excrement must be covered because the land being holy demands that "thy camp be holy, . . ." (Deut. 23:15), so that God would "see no unseemly thing" occurring there *(ibid.).*

Still another aspect is reflected in the talionic punishment of death for *homicide, as originally formulated: "Whoso sheddeth man's blood, by man shall his blood be shed; for in the image of God made He man" (Gen. 9:6). Man being created in the image of God, it is an affront to God to kill him and killing the killer is the only acceptable expiation to God. Similarly, purging Israel of the blood of the innocent (Deut. 19:13) by killing the killer appears to be necessary in order to avoid blood guilt attaching to the land and to the people forever (cf. Deut. 21:9; 19:10); and it is for this reason that a murderer must be taken even from God's very altar to be put to death (Ex. 21:14).

All talionic punishment as such reflects its underlying purpose, namely the apparent restitution of the *status quo ante* by inflicting on the offender the injury inflicted by him (Lev. 24:20) and by doing to him what he had done to another (Lev. 24:19). This sort of sanction (see *Talion), where the character and measure of punishment is precisely commensurate with those of the crime, is intended to represent exact justice. It was, indeed, by proving that this kind of "exact justice" necessarily involved unavoidable injustice, that some talmudical jurists justified the abolition of talionic punishment except for murder (BK 84a). And while they did not abolish it for murder, whether by reason of the many express biblical injunctions that murderers must be killed (especially Num. 35:31), or in order to retain the deterrent effect of the death penalty, many of them held that judges must do everything in their power to avoid passing death sentences (cf. Mak. 1:10), e.g., by rigorously cross-examining the witnesses long enough to have them contradict themselves or each other in some particular (Mak. 7a) and thus render their evidence unreliable (see *Evidence, *Witness). The warning was already sounded then that any reticence in imposing capital punishment would result in an increase of crime and bloodshed (Mak. 1:10). Maimonides comments on the talmudical discussion, that while it was true that the courts must always satisfy themselves that the incriminating evidence was credible and admissible, once they were so satisfied, they ought to order the execution even of a thousand men, day after day, if that is what the law (the Torah) prescribes (his commentry to the Mishnah, Mak. 1:10).

The most common purpose of punishment, as found in the Bible, is "to put away the evil from the midst of thee" (Deut. 17:7, 12; 19:19; 21:21; 22:24; 24:7). While such "putting away" is applied in the Bible to capital punishment only (which indeed constitutes the only effective total elimination), the principle underlying the elimination of evil, as distinguished from that of the evildoer (cf. Ps. 104:35 and Ber. 10a), provides a theory of punishment of universal validity and applicable to all criminal sanctions. It means that the act of punishment is not so much directed against the individual offender—who is, however, unavoidably its victim—as it is a demonstration of resentment and disapproval of that particular mode of conduct. By branding that conduct as worthy of, and necessitating, judicial punishment, it is outlawed and ostracized. Similarly, punishment is inflicted on the offender not so much for his own sake as for the deterrence of others: that all people should hear and be afraid (Deut. 17:13—rebellious elder; 19:20—perjury; 21:21—rebellious son). From the point of view of criminal law enforcement policies, the deterrent aspect of punishment in Jewish law is already the most important of all: people who hear and see a man heavily punished for his offense are supposed to be deterred from committing the offense and incurring the risk of such punishment (they "will do no more presumptuously"—Deut. 19:20). Hence the particular injunction to have the offender impaled on a stake after having been put to death (Deut. 21:22), so as to publicize the execution as widely and impressively as possible; but note that the corpse must be taken off the gibbet before nightfall, "for he that is hanged is a reproach to God" and defiles the land (Deut. 21:23)—and no concession made to policies of law enforcement can derogate from the affront to God involved in killing and impaling a human being.

It is not only the principle known in modern criminology as "general prevention," the deterrence of the general public, but also that of "special prevention," the prevention of the individual offender from committing further crimes, that is reflected in Jewish law. It has been said that the imposition of capital punishment on such offenders as the rebellious son (Deut. 21:18–21), the rebellious elder (Deut. 17:12), the abductor (Ex. 21:16), and the burglar (Ex. 22:1) is justified on the ground that these are all potential murderers (cf. Maim., Guide 3:41); and rather than let them take innocent human lives, they should themselves be eliminated. That the deterrent effect of punishment on the offender himself was a consideration which weighed heavily with the talmudical jurists is illustrated also by the rule that where punishment had proved to have had no beneficial deterrent effect on the offender and he has committed the same or some similar offenses over and over again, he would be liable to be imprisoned and "fed on barley until his belly bursts" (Sanh. 9:5).

The talmudical law reformers also achieved the substitution for the ever-threatening divine punishment by the judicial punishment of *flogging, making it clear that whoever underwent judicial punishment would not be visited with any further *divine punishment (Mak. 3:15). They went so far as to lay down that even though God had Himself expressly proclaimed that a criminal would not be "guiltless" and escape divine wrath (Ex. 20:7; Deut. 5:11), the judicial authorities in imposing the flogging were authorized by the Torah itself to clear him: if God would never clear him, a court of justice could (Shevu. 21a). The measure of punishment must always conform to the gravity of the offense on the one hand, and the blameworthiness of the individual offender on the other: "according to the measure of his wickedness" (Deut. 25:2). Even here the talmudical law reformers found cause for some mitigatory improvement: they interpreted "wickedness" as the yardstick for the measure of punishment, as including also the physical capacity of the offender to undergo and suffer punishment (cf. Maim., Comm. Mak. 3:10 and Yad, Sanhedrin 17:1). In several instances, the particular turpitude of the offense is expressly stressed as reason for heavy penalties (e.g., "because she hath wrought a wanton deed in Israel"—Deut. 22:21; "it is wickedness"—Lev. 20:14); and in post-talmudic times, the imposition of severe punishments (such as *capital punishment) was always justified by stressing the severity of the particular offense and the public danger of mischief thereby caused.

Maimonides laid down that the gravity and measure of punishment are to be determined, first, by the gravity of the offense: the greater the mischief caused, the heavier must be the penalty; second, by the frequency of the offense: the more widespread and epidemic the offense, the heavier must the penalty be; third, the temptation prompting the offense: the more easily a man is tempted to commit it, and the more difficult it is for him to resist the temptation, the heavier must the penalty be; and fourth, the secrecy of the offense: the more difficult it is to detect the offense and catch the offender, the more necessary is it to deter potential offenders by heavy penalties (Maim., Guide 3:41).

[H.H.C.]

In the Framework of Jewish Autonomy. Within the framework of the Jewish *autonomy structure, a great variety of penalties could be imposed on wrongdoers, including *fines, *imprisonment, **ḥerem,* and—extremely rarely—capital punishment, according to judgment passed by a *bet din* under the ordinances of the community or a **ḥevrah.* New and previously unknown penalties were resorted to in the Middle Ages, sometimes for crimes not provided for in talmudic law. This development was especially evident in Muslim and Christian Spain. Capital punishment was openly imposed in Spain with the sanction of the state authorities, and somewhat clandestinely in other countries on rare occasions; the death penalty was reserved mainly for *informers, and it was imposed with the

Purim

LATE 1. *Megillah,* China, early 19th century. Scroll made for the survivors of the "lost" community of Kai-Feng-Fu. The archer, who represents the ecutioner, is flanked by a list of Haman's sons. Cecil Roth Collection. Photo David Harris, Jerusalem.

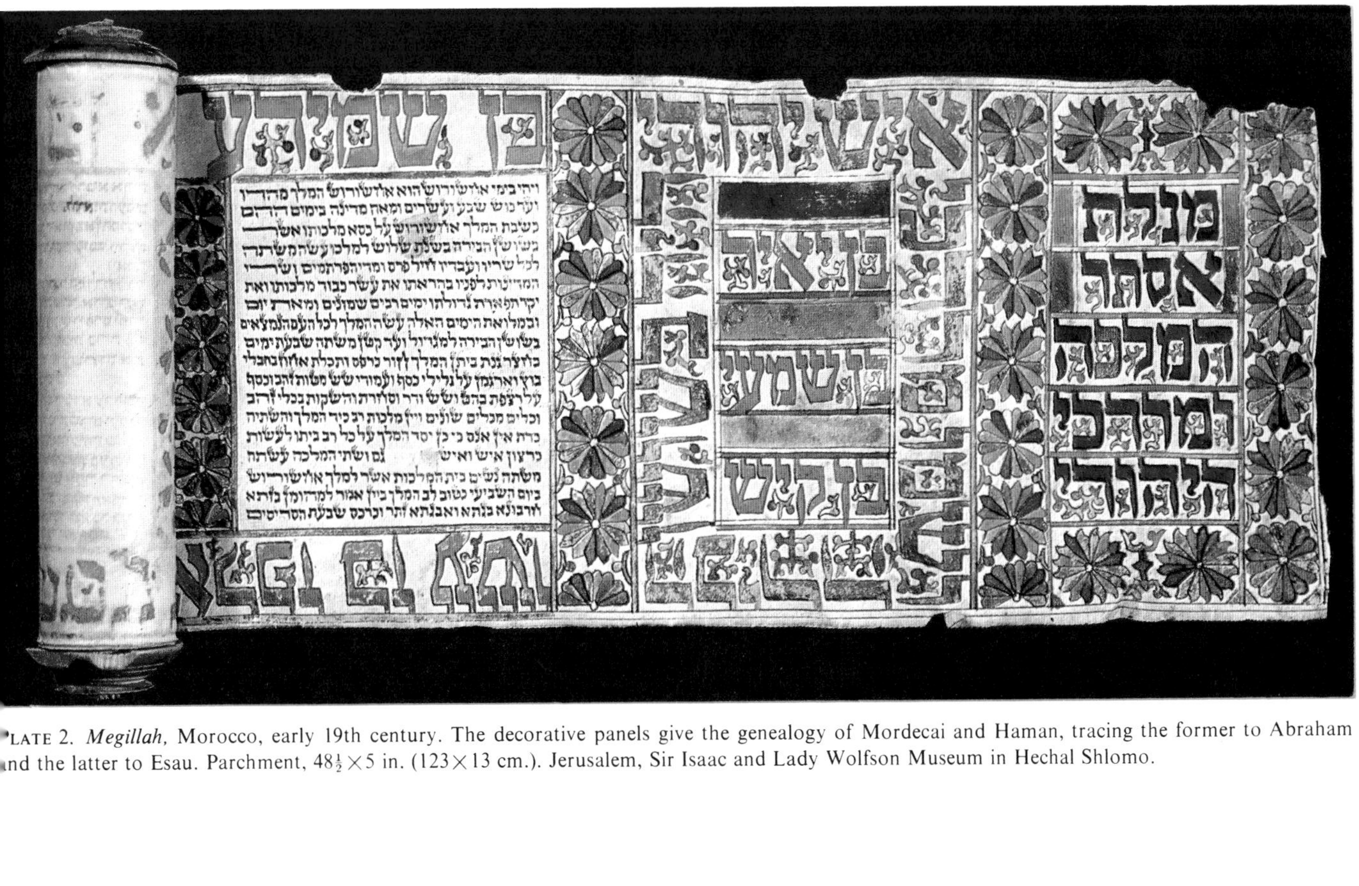

LATE 2. *Megillah,* Morocco, early 19th century. The decorative panels give the genealogy of Mordecai and Haman, tracing the former to Abraham nd the latter to Esau. Parchment, 48½×5 in. (123×13 cm.). Jerusalem, Sir Isaac and Lady Wolfson Museum in Hechal Shlomo.

PLATE 3. *Megillat ha-Melekh*, Italy, 18th century. A "king's scroll" is so designed that every column begins with "the king." In this example, the scenes from the Purim story are in Italian Renaissance style. Parchment, 10½ in. (27 cm.). Formerly New York, Michael Zagaysky Collection. Photo Malcolm Varon, New York.

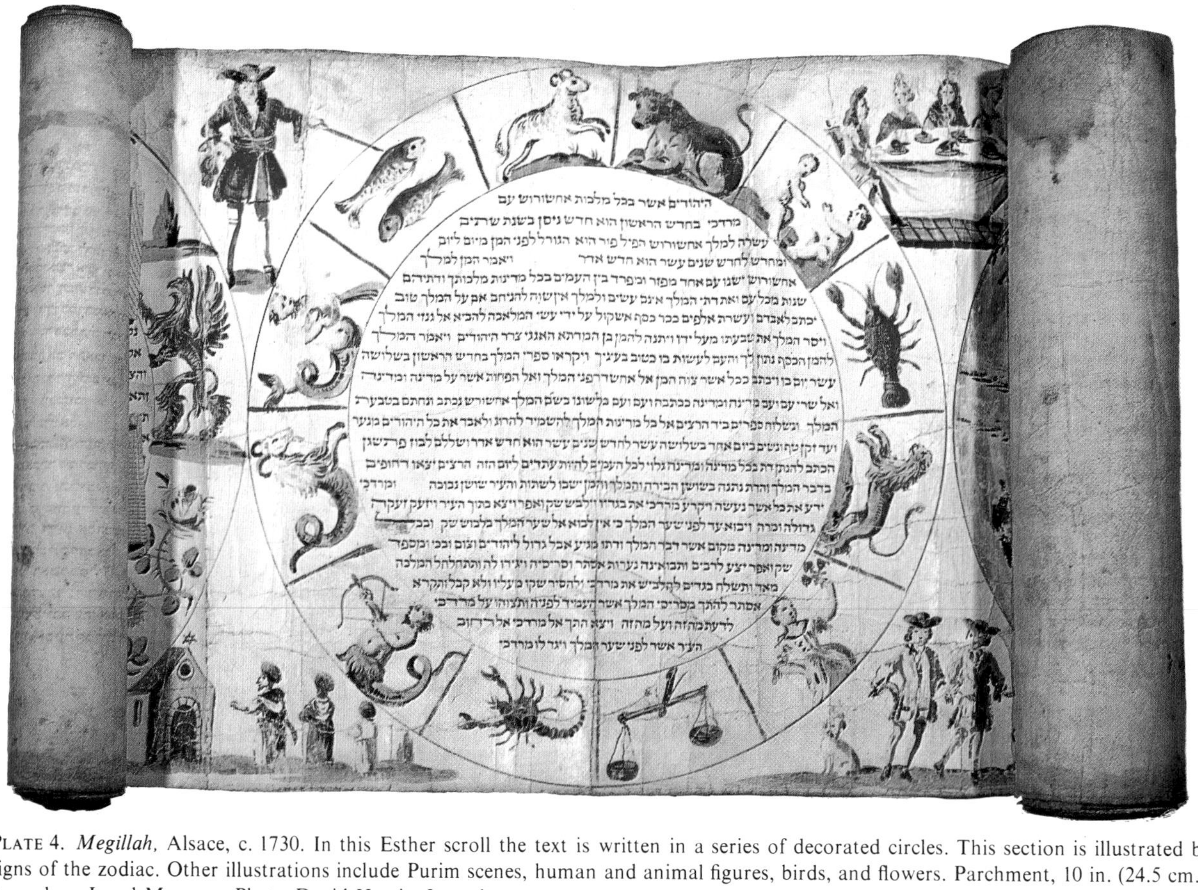

PLATE 4. *Megillah*, Alsace, c. 1730. In this Esther scroll the text is written in a series of decorated circles. This section is illustrated by signs of the zodiac. Other illustrations include Purim scenes, human and animal figures, birds, and flowers. Parchment, 10 in. (24.5 cm.). Jerusalem, Israel Museum. Photo David Harris, Jerusalem.

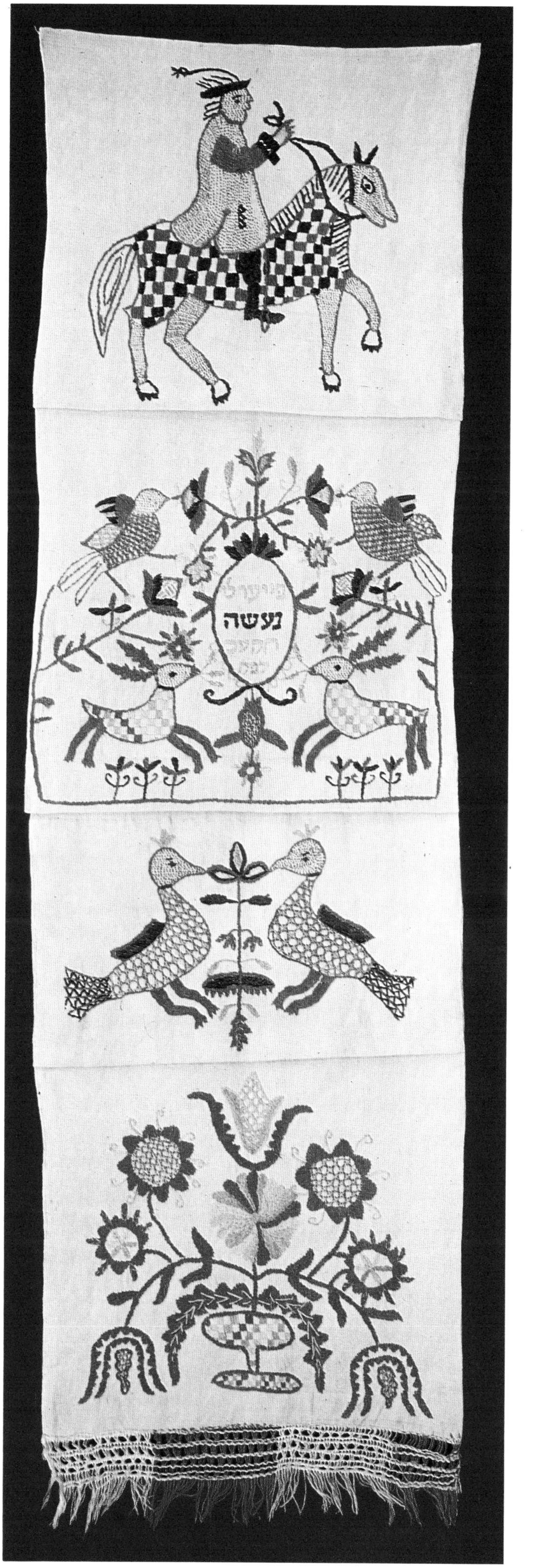

PLATE 5. Embroidered linen hand towel for use at the Purim meal. South Germany, 1812. Jerusalem, Israel Museum. Photo David Harris, Jerusalem.

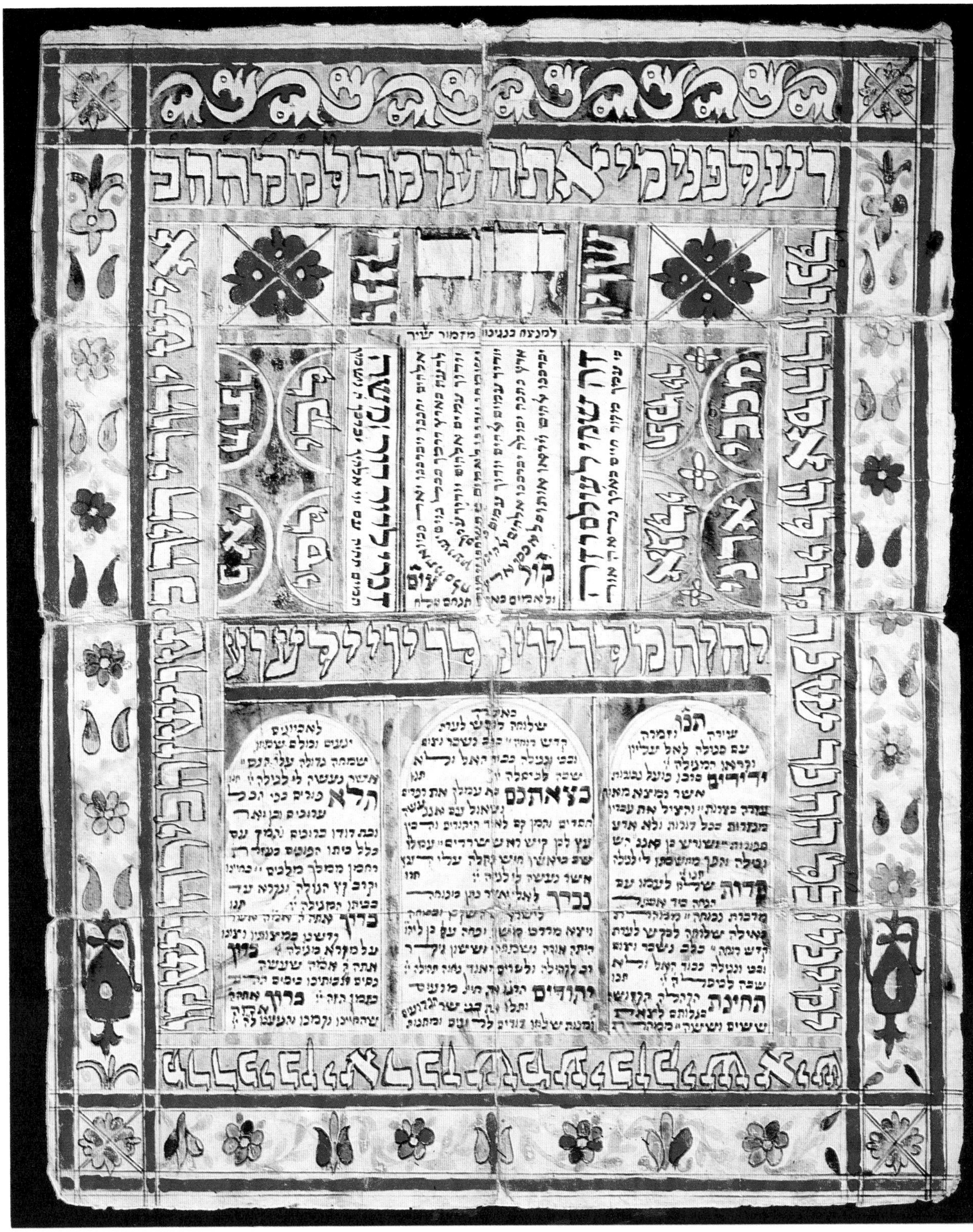

PLATE 6. Purim *shivviti,* Iran, c. 1800. This synagogue plaque contains the normal *shivviti* texts, as well as prayers, blessings, and quotations relating to Purim. Paper, 13×17 in. (33×43 cm.). Jerusalem, Michael Kaufman Collection. Photo David Harris, Jerusalem.

PLATE 7. *Megillah,* Lisbon, 1816. Parchment and wood. Jerusalem, Sir Isaac and Lady Wolfson Museum in Hechal Shlomo. Photo David Harris, Jerusalem.

aid and often the urging of the very authorities to whom the denunciation had been made. The manner of execution usually followed that obtaining in the host country, such as bloodletting from an arm, drowning, strangulation, or stoning. Some of the talmudic rules of evidence were waived. In 1380 the Jews of Castile were denied the right of capital punishment. Other bodily penalties—again mainly in Spain—were amputation and mutilation of limbs (mainly for sexual offenses), cutting off the nose and ears, cutting out the tongue (in the case of informers), gouging out the eyes, shaving of head and beard, and stripes. Flogging was most common, particularly in lands like Germany where capital punishment was not resorted to. There were two kinds of lashes: the biblical statutory 39 stripes and the discretionary rabbinic penalty, which could be severe or very light, aimed at inflicting not pain but rather public shame. In Babylonia the person punished in this way had his hands and feet tied as he lay on a bench in the courtroom. More customary was the symbolic penance at the threshold of the synagogue between the afternoon and evening daily services. Shaving the head or beard, which was dreaded more than bodily mutilation, was reserved mainly for assault and battery, adultery, or fornication with a gentile maiden.

The most severe social penalty was the *ḥerem,* with its associated "donkey's burial," interment by the fence of the cemetery, far from respectable graves. Another punishment was expulsion—most customary in Spain and Poland-Lithuania—from the town or even from the country for a stated period or permanently. Sometimes a man's entire family was banished with him. This penalty was imposed on suspected murderers who had only one witness to testify against them, for assault and battery resulting in death, for wife-beating, fornication, stealing, and forgery. The **Ma-hamad* community council of the Sephardi Jews of Hamburg expelled moral or business offenders for several years to Amsterdam or elsewhere. For card-playing and similar offenses German Jewry was accustomed to banish the recalcitrant from the local synagogue. A bankrupt was sometimes ordered to sit for three years behind the *almemar.* For libeling a friend, a woman was ordered to change her seat periodically in the women's gallery of the synagogue. Various penalties involving loss of title or prestige were imposed. For insulting a fellow Jew the culprit would be denied the title of *morenu* or *ḥaver* in Ashkenazi Jewry. The right to be called to the reading of the Torah was withdrawn in certain cases. Often an announcement would be made in all synagogues that for a stated offense a person could not be trusted as a witness or to take an oath.

Institutionally imposed punishment ran parallel to punishment self-inflicted by people who wanted to do penance for their sins. The *Ḥasidei Ashkenaz, in particular Eleazar b. Judah of Worms, developed a detailed and exacting system of penance, the *teshuvat ha-mishkal.* Throughout the Middle Ages and early modern times such offenders as mothers who smothered their infants in sleep, people who killed unwittingly, or persons who committed undetected sexual transgressions would ask the rabbi to impose on them strict penances, which included public confession and self-vilification. Denial of participation in and benefit from communal and religious services was considered a severe penalty. The sinner could also be deprived of certain citizenship rights, such as membership in the plenary assembly and the right to vote. Most damaging socially and economically—especially in Eastern Europe—was expulsion from a *ḥevrah* by the *kahal,* since expulsion from a guild could also mean the loss of livelihood. The *kahal* was especially strict with its own employees or other communal functionaries. A **badḥan* ("jester") would be forbidden to perform at weddings and musicians to solicit their customary holiday gifts. The *kahal* possessed much more serious weapons against persons who refused to cooperate: exorbitant taxes, frequent billeting of troops, and, in Russia during the *Cantonist troubles, drafting the son into military service. Fines and confiscation of property were very common.

With the weakening of Jewish autonomy in modern times these penalties became, in various stages in different countries, obsolete and inoperative.

See also *Banishment; *Reward and Punishment. [I.L.]

Bibliography: E. Goitein, *Das Vergeltungsprincip im biblischen und talmudischen Strafrecht* (1893); S. Gronemann, in: *Zeitschrift fuer vergleichende Rechtswissenschaft,* 13 (1899), 415–50; J. Wohlgemuth, *Das juedische Strafrecht und die positive Strafrechtsschule* (1903); J. Herrmann, *Die Idee der Suehne im Alten Testament* (1905); I. S. Zuri, *Mishpat ha-Talmud,* 6 (1921), 1–27; A. Pomeranz, in: *Ha-Mishpat,* 3 (1928), 23–27; A. Buechler, *Studies in Sin and Atonement in the Rabbinic Literature* (1928); J. Lipkin, in: *Haolam,* 16 (1928), 281–3; T. Ostersetzer, in: *Sefer ha-Shanah li-Yhudei Polanyah,* 1 (1938), 35–60; H. H. Cohn, in: ILR, 5 (1970), 53–74. In the Framework of Jewish Autonomy: S. Assaf, *Ha-Onshin Aḥarei Ḥatimat ha-Talmud* (1922); Dubnow, Hist Russ, index, s.v. *Kahal Courts;* I. Levitats, *Jewish Community in Russia* (1943), 198–217; Baron, Community, index; Baer, Spain, index s.v. *Criminal Jurisdiction of Jewish Community.*

PUNON (Heb. פונן), encampment of the Israelites in Edom, between Zalmonah and Oboth (Num. 33:42–43). It is identified with Khirbat Faynān, the Greek Phainon, in the Arabah. Remains of ancient copper mines abound in the area, the richest being at Umm al-ʿAmad. The copper ore of Punon was exploited from Chalcolithic times onward. There is evidence of extensive settlement at the end of the Early Bronze Age and in Iron Age I. The name of the Edomite prince Pinon (Gen. 36:41; I Chron. 1:52) may be connected with the locality. The mines were reopened in Nabatean times and continued to be exploited throughout the Roman and Byzantine periods. They were worked by condemned criminals, as well as Christian martyrs and bishops. Remains at the site include the foundations of a basilica and an inscription mentioning a bishop Theodorus. According to the Madaba map, the place where the Israelites were saved by the *copper serpent was located near Punon. The place was included in the fortifications of the Roman *limes,* Ala Prima miliaria Sebastena being stationed there (*Notitia dignitatum,* 73:32).

Bibliography: Frank, in: ZDPV, 57 (1934), 218–19, 221–24; Alt, in: ZDPV, 58 (1935), 6ff.; Glueck, in: AASOR, 15 (1935), 32–35.

[M.A.-Y.]

PURIM (Heb. פורים), the feast instituted, according to the Book of *Esther (9:20–28), by *Mordecai to celebrate the deliverance of the Jews from *Haman's plot to kill them. Purim (Akk. *pūrū,* "lots") is so called (Esth. 9:26) after the lots cast by Haman in order to determine the month in which the slaughter was to take place (Esth. 3:7). Purim is celebrated on the 14th of Adar, and in Hasmonean times it was known as the "Day of Mordecai" (II Macc. 15:36). The Jews of Shushan celebrated their deliverance on the 15th of Adar (Esth. 9:18), and this day became known as Shushan Purim. Out of respect for Jerusalem, it is said, the day is still kept by Jews living in cities which had a wall around them "from the days of Joshua" (Meg. 1:1). Thus in present-day Israel Purim is celebrated in Jerusalem on the 15th, but in Tel Aviv on the 14th. In leap years Purim is celebrated in the second month of *Adar.

The chronological difficulties such as the identity of King

*Ahasuerus and the absence of any reference in the Persian sources to a king having a Jewish consort; the striking resemblance between the names Mordecai and Esther to the Babylonian gods Marduk and Ishtar; the lack of any reference to Purim in Jewish literature before the first century B.C.E.; the language of the Book of Esther, which suggests a late date—all these have moved the critics to look elsewhere than the account in Esther for the true origin of the festival. Various conjectures have been made (see *Scroll of Esther) but the problem still awaits its solution. In any event the festival had long been established by the second century C.E. when a whole tractate of the Mishnah (*Megillah) was devoted to the details of its observance, especially to the rules governing the reading of the Scroll of Esther, called in the rabbinic literature the *megillah* ("scroll"). Purim is a minor festival in that work on it is permitted, but it has been joyously celebrated in Jewish communities as a reminder of God's protection of His people. However, the widespread acceptance of the festival as only minor is reflected in the popular Yiddish saying that as a high temperature does not denote serious illness neither is Purim a festival.

Figure 1. Poster advertising a Purim fete in New York, 1863. Courtesy Leon J. Obermayer, Philadelphia, Pa.

The main feature of Purim is the reading of the Book of Esther, the *megillah*, with a special cantillation. *Megillot* are frequently decorated, sometimes with scenes from the narrative. Since according to the midrashic interpretation the word *ha-melekh* ("the king"), when it is not qualified by Ahasuerus, refers to the King of the universe, some *megillot* are so written that each column begins with this word. It would seem that originally the *megillah* was read during the day, but eventually the rule was adopted to read it both at night and during the day (Meg. 4a). It is customary to fold the *megillah* over and spread it out before the reading since it is called a "letter" (Esth. 9:26, 29). The four verses of "redemption" (2:5; 8:15–16; and 10:3) are read in louder voice than the other verses. The custom of children to make a loud noise with rattles and the like whenever the name of Haman is read, in order to blot out the "memory of Amalek" (see Deut. 25:19; and Esth. 3:1 and I Sam. 15:8–9 for Haman was a descendant of Amalek) is ancient and still persists, though frowned upon as undecorous by some authorities. It is the practice for the reader to recite the names of the ten sons of Haman (Esth. 9:7–9) in one breath (Meg. 16b) to show that they were executed simultaneously. The custom has also been seen, however, as a refusal by Jews to gloat over the downfall of their enemies (C.G. Montefiore and H. Loewe (ed.), *A Rabbinic Anthology* (1938), 53). The Torah reading for Purim morning is Exodus 17:8–16.

The Book of Esther (9:22) speaks of "sending portions" (*mishlo'aḥ manot*—abbreviated to *shelakhmones*) to friends on Purim and of giving gifts to the poor. The rule is to send at least two "portions" of eatables, confectionery, and so forth, to a friend and to give a present of money to at least two poor men. A special festive meal is eaten on Purim afternoon toward eventide. Among the special Purim foods are boiled beans and peas, said to be a reminder of the cereals Daniel ate in the king's palace in order to avoid any infringement of the dietary laws, and three-cornered pies known as *hamantashen* ("Haman's ears"). There has been much discussion around the saying of the Babylonian teacher Rava (Meg. 7b) that a man is obliged to drink so much wine on Purim that he becomes incapable of knowing whether he is cursing Haman or blessing Mordecai. The more puritanical teachers tried to explain this away, but the imbibing of alcohol was generally encouraged on Purim and not a few otherwise sober teachers still take Rava's saying literally (see, e.g., H. Weiner: $9\frac{1}{2}$ *Mystics* (1969), 207). The laws of Purim and the reading of the *megillah* are codified in Shulḥan Arukh, OḤ 686–97. Various parodies of sacred literature were produced for Purim, the best known of which, *Massekhet Purim*, is a skillful parody of the Talmud with its main theme the obligation to drink wine merrily and to abstain strictly from water. The institution of the Purim rabbi, a kind of lord of misrule,

2a

2b

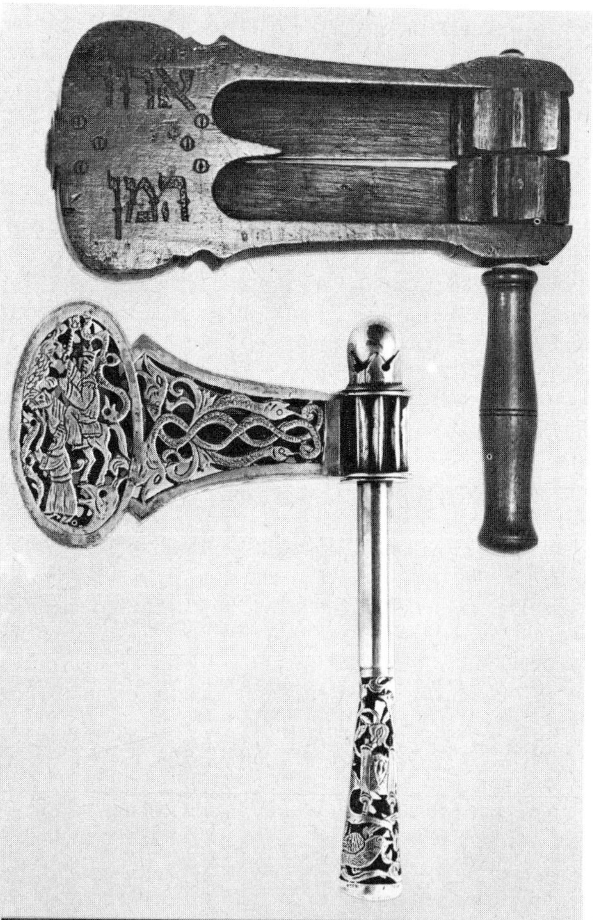

2c

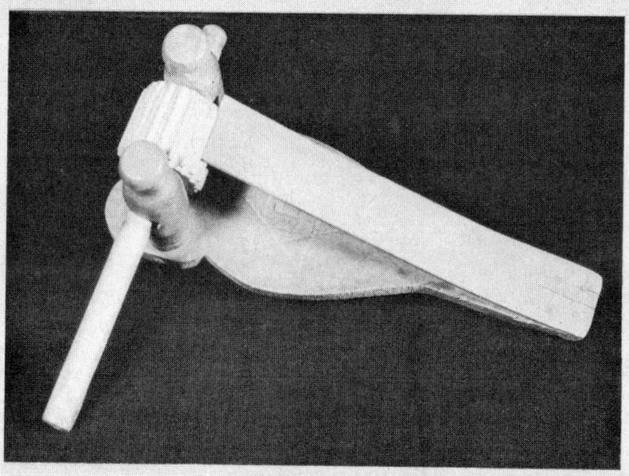

3

4

5a

5b

5c

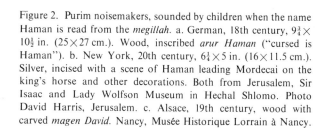

Figure 2. Purim noisemakers, sounded by children when the name Haman is read from the *megillah*. a. German, 18th century, $9\frac{3}{4}\times 10\frac{1}{2}$ in. (25×27 cm.). Wood, inscribed *arur Haman* ("cursed is Haman"). b. New York, 20th century, $6\frac{1}{4}\times5$ in. (16×11.5 cm.). Silver, incised with a scene of Haman leading Mordecai on the king's horse and other decorations. Both from Jerusalem, Sir Isaac and Lady Wolfson Museum in Hechal Shlomo. Photo David Harris, Jerusalem. c. Alsace, 19th century, wood with carved *magen David*. Nancy, Musée Historique Lorrain à Nancy.

Figure 3. Silver plate for *mishlo'aḥ manot* ("sending gifts") on Purim. The fish form symbolizes the month of Adar. Austria, 19th century, $15\frac{3}{4}$ in. (40 cm.). Jerusalem, Israel Museum. Photo David Harris, Jerusalem.

Figure 4. "The Masked Ball," engraving after a drawing by P. Wagenaar, Holland, 1780, showing Portuguese Jews of Amsterdam dancing against a background of special tapestries illustrating the Purim story. Jerusalem, Israel Museum. Photo David Harris, Jerusalem.

Figure 5. Wooden Purim pastry forms. a. Holland, 18th century. Jerusalem, Israel Museum. Photo David Harris, Jerusalem. b. and c. Central Europe, 19th century. Jerusalem, Sir Isaac and Lady Wolfson Museum in Hechal Shlomo. Photo David Harris, Jerusalem.

Figure 6. Reading the Purim *megillah* (Scroll of Esther) at Yavneh, a religious kibbutz in southern Israel, 1970. Courtesy Government Press Office, Tel Aviv.

who recites Purim Torah, the frivolous manipulation of sacred texts, was the norm in many communities. Some have seen in all this an annual attempt to find psychological relief from what otherwise might have become an intolerable burden of loyalty to the Torah (Druyanow, *Reshumot,* 1 and 2). Under the influence of the Italian carnival it became customary for people to dress up on Purim in fancy dress, men even being permitted to dress as women and women as men. The *Adloyada carnival in Tel Aviv has been a prominent feature of Purim observance in modern Israel.

In the kabbalistic and ḥasidic literature much is made of Purim as a day of friendship and joy and as the celebration of God at work, as it were, behind the scenes, unlike Passover which celebrates God's more direct intervention. (God is not mentioned in the Book of Esther.) The "lots" of Purim are compared with the "lots" cast on the Day of Atonement (Lev. 16:8), what human beings call "fate" or "luck" being, in reality, only another manifestation of God's providential care. So highly did the kabbalists esteem Purim that they reported in the name of Isaac Luria that the Day of Atonement is "like Purim" *(Yom ke-Furim).*

While some Reform congregations abolished Purim, others continued to celebrate it as a day of encouragement and hope, some even arguing that it helped Jews to express their aggressive emotions and to sublimate their feelings of wrath and hatred (W. G. Plaut, *The Growth of Reform Judaism* (1965), 224).

Bibliography: N. S. Doniach, *Purim* (Eng., 1933); S. Zevin, *Ha-Mo'adim ba-Halakhah* (1963[10]), 188–214; J. D. Epstein, *Oẓar ha-Iggeret* (1968); P. Goodman, *Purim Anthology* (1960), incl. bibl.; J. L. Fishman, *Ḥagim u-Mo'adim* (1944), 119–68: J. H. Greenstone, *Jewish Feasts and Fasts* (1945), 135–78; H. Schauss, *Jewish Festivals* (1938), 237–71. [L.J.]

PURIM KATAN (Heb. פּוּרִים קָטָן; "minor Purim"), the name given to the 14th and 15th days of the first month of *Adar in a leap year, when *Purim is celebrated during the second month of Adar. (The Karaites were the only sect to celebrate Purim during the first Adar in a leap year.) According to talmudic tradition, Purim should be celebrated in the second Adar because that was the date of the original Purim (which occurred in a leap year). The rabbis also wanted to bring the period of the redemption of Esther closer to that of the redemption of the Israelites from Egypt celebrated in the following month of Nisan (Meg. 6b). Purim Katan has none of the ritual or liturgical features of Purim: the *megillah* is not read, and no gifts are sent to the poor (Meg. 1:4). The **Al ha-Nissim* prayer is not said, but fasting and funeral eulogies are prohibited (Meg. 6b). Also, **Taḥanun* is not recited on these days, which are considered a minor occasion of rejoicing (Sh. Ar., OḤ 697:1).

Bibliography: Eisenstein, Dinim, 337; G. Ki-Tov, *Sefer ha-Toda'ah,* 1 pt. 1 (1958), 297. [Ed.]

PURIMS, SPECIAL. Following the talmudic injunction that one must recite a special thanksgiving benediction on returning to the place where one was once miraculously saved from danger (Ber. 54a), the custom evolved for Jewish communities or families to celebrate the anniversary of their escape from destruction by reciting special prayers and with a ritual similar to that of Purim. (See: A. Gumbiner's note to Sh. Ar., OḤ 686.) These special communal Purims are called *Purim Katan ("minor Purim"), or Mo'ed Katan ("minor holiday") or Purim . . . (followed by the name of the community or the special event). In many cases special Purims were preceded by a fast comparable to the Fast of *Esther. In addition, on the Purim Katan itself the story of the personal or communal salvation was often read from a scroll *(*megillah)* in the course of a synagogue service in which special prayers of thanksgiving, in the style of *piyyutim,* were offered. Sometimes the **Al ha-Nissim* prayer and the **Hallel* were inserted into the ritual. The traditional Purim observances of enjoying a festive meal and giving charity to the poor were also applied to special Purims.

Bibliography: C. Roth, in: HUCA, 10 (1935), 451–82; 12–13 (1937–1938), 697–99; Y. T. Lewinski (ed.), *Sefer ha-Mo'adim,* 6 (1956), 297–321; M. Steinschneider, in: MGWJ, 47 (1901–21) ff.; A. Danon, in: REJ, 54 (1907). [Ed.]

PURIM-SHPIL (Yid. lit. "Purim play"), monologue or group performances given at the traditional festive family meal held on the festival of *Purim. There is definite evidence that use of the term *Purim-shpil* was widespread among all Ashkenazi communities as early as the mid-16th century. The earliest written record in which the term

LIST OF SPECIAL PURIMS

Purim of . . .	Observed on	Established in	Reason for Observance
Algiers (called Purim Edom)	4th Ḥeshvan	1540	Saved from destruction in Spanish-Algerian wars of 1516–1517 and 1542
Algiers (called Purim Tammuz)	11th Tammuz	1774	Saved from danger.
Alessandria Della Paglia (Italy)	25th Av	1779	Saved from massacre.
Ditto	2nd Ḥeshvan	1797	Saved from riots during revolutionary war.
Ancona	21st Tevet	1690	Saved from earthquake.
Ancona	15th Tishri	1741	Synagogue escaped destruction by fire.
Ancona	24th Adar	1775	Jewish quarter saved from conflagration.
Ancona	12th Shevat	1797	Saved from riots in revolutionary war.
Angora/Ankara/(called: Purim Angora or Purim Sari-Kiz)	21st Elul	?	Saved from blood libel accusation.
Angora, called Purim Abazza	11th Iyyar	?	?
Angora, called Purim de la Turquito	14th Tammuz	1775	Saved from blood libel accusation.
Avignon	24th Tammuz	?	?
Avignon	28th Shevat	1757	Escaped dangers of a riot.
Baghdad	11th Av	1733	Relieved from Persian oppression.
Belgrade	19th Sivan	1822	Saved from destruction during Turko-Serbian war.

Purim of . . .	Observed on	Established in	Reason for Observance
Breche (Champagne, France)	14th Adar	1191	Chief Jew-baiter executed
Cairo	18th Shevat	?	?
Cairo, called Purim Miẓrayim	28th Adar	1524	Saved from extermination.
Candia (Crete)	18th Tammuz	1583	Saved from collective punishment for treason, during Turco-Venetian conflict
Carpentras	16th Kislev	1512	Saved from riot.
Ditto	9th Nisan	1692	Saved from annihilation.
Ditto, called Yom va-Yosha	21st Nisan	1651	Saved from threat of massacre.
Casablanca, called Purim Hitler	2nd Kislev	1943	Escape from riot and Nazi occupation.
Castille (Spain) called Purim Martinez	1st Adar	1339	Saved from annihilation following accusations by Jew-baiter Gonzales Martinez, king's adviser.
Cavaillon (Provence)	25th Iyyar	1631	Plague ended.
Ditto	29th Sivan	1677	Saved from blood libel accusation.
Cento (Italy)	12th Av	1820	Escaped from fire.
Chieri (Italy)	1st Av	1797	Saved from danger of war.
Chios (Greece), called Purim de la Senora ("Purim of the Good Lady")	8th Iyyar	1595 (or 1820)?	Saved from death during Franco-Turkish war.
Cuneo (Italy)	5th Kislev	1799	Synagogue saved from destruction by shell.
Ettingen (Germany)	18th Iyyar	1690	Saved from destruction by enemies.
Ditto	29th Sivan	1713	?
Ferrara	24th Kislev	?	Saved from destruction by fire.
Ditto	18th Iyyar	1799	Escaped war riots.
Fez	22nd Kislev	1840	Saved from destruction.
Florence	27th Sivan	1791	Escaped sacking and riots.
Fossano (Italy)	18th Nisan	1796	Saved from bomb explosion during war.
Frankfort on the Main, also called: Purim Winz or Purim Fettmilch	20th Adar	1616	Expelled Jews readmitted to town and chief Jew-baiter, Fettmilch, executed.
Fulda	15th Elul	?	?
Gumeldjina (Thrace) called: Purim de los ladrones ("Purim of the thiefs")	22nd Elul	1786	Saved from collective punishment for allegedly instigating robbers to sack town.
Hebron	1st Av	?	Saved from collective punishment and execution by Ibrahim Pasha.
Ditto, called Purim Takka ("Window Purim")	14th Tevet	1741	Saved from annihilation by miraculous find of ransom money on the windowsill of synagogue
Ivrea (Italy)	1st Shevat	1797	Escaped plundering during revolutionary war.
Komotini (Gumurjina, Gumuldjina) (Greece)	22nd Elul	1768	Saved from destruction during Turkish suppression of Greek revolt.
Kovno	7th Adar (II)	1783	Privileges of civic freedom granted by King Poniatowski.
Leghorn	12th Shevat	1742	Saved from destruction in earthquake.
Ditto	25th Tevet	1810	Plague ends.
Ditto	16th Adar	1813	?
Lepanto (Greece)	11th Tevet	1699	Saved from destruction during Turkish war.
Medzibezh (Poland)	11th Tevet	1648 or 1649	Saved from annihilation by Chmielnicki's bands.
Morocco	13th Nisan	1771	Saved from annihilation.
Mstislavl (Russia)	4th Shevat	1744	Saved from slaughter by Cossacks.
Ditto	3rd Kislev	1844	Saved from collective punishment for alleged rebellion against authorities.
Narbonne	20th Adar	1236	Saved from riots.
Oran	6th Av	1830	Saved from massacre before arrival of French troops.
Ostraha	23rd Nisan		
Ditto	7th Tammuz	1734 or 1768	Saved from pogrom.
		1792	Saved from destruction during Russo-Polish war.
Padua called Purim di fuoco ("Fire Purim")	11th Sivan	1795	Saved from fire.
Ditto, called Purim di Buda	10th Elul	1684	Saved from massacre during Austro-Turkish war (in Budapest).
Ditto, called Purim dei Sassi (?)	Shabbat "Bo"	1748	?
Pesaro/see also: Urbino and Senigallia	?	1799	Escaped damages of war.
Pitigliano (Italy)	15th Tammuz	1757	Collapse of school roof, no casualties.
Ditto	15th Sivan	1799	Saved from damages during revolutionary war.
Posen	1st Ḥeshvan	1704	Saved from death during Polish-Swedish war.
Prague	14th Ḥeshvan	1620	Saved from sacking and riots by protection of Emperor Ferdinand II.
Ditto, called Vorhang Purim ("Curtain Purim")	22nd Tevet	1622	Beadle of synagogue saved from hanging for keeping stolen curtains.
Purim Byzanc (observed by Jews of Thrace)	14th Adar	1574	Saved from extermination.
Ragusa	?	1631	Saved from accusation of blood libel.
Rhodes	14th Adar	1840	Saved from annihilation.
Ritova (Lithuania) called Purim Jeroboam b. Nebat	14th Adar	1863	Jew-baiter Count Aginsky died.

Purim of . . .	Observed on	Established in	Reason for Observance
Rome	1st Shevat	1793	Ghetto saved from assault and fire.
Sa'na	18th Adar	?	Saved from extermination.
Sarajevo	4th Ḥeshvan	1819	10 leaders of Jewish community freed from prison and saved from execution.
Senigallia (Italy)/see also: Urbino and Pesaro	15th Sivan	1799	Saved from annihilation during war by escaping to Ancona.
Sermide (Italy)	25th Tammuz	1809	Saved from earthquake.
Shiraz, called Purim Mo'ed Katan	2nd Ḥeshvan	1200 or 1400	Permitted to practice Judaism after having been forced to convert to Islam.
Sienna	15th Sivan	1799	Saved from destruction during revolution.
Spoleto	21st Sivan	1797	Saved from annihilation during revolutionary war.
Ditto	7th Adar	?	?
Syracuse (Sicily), called Purim Saragossa	17th Shevat	1425	Saved from destruction for alleged treason by honoring King Alfonso with empty cases of Torah Scrolls.
Tetuan and Tangiers, called Purim de las bombas, or Purim de los Christianos,	2nd Elul	1578	Saved from destruction during Moroccan-Portuguese war.
Tiberias	7th Elul	1743	Saved from danger of war.
Ditto	4th Kislev	?	?
Trieste	14th Adar	1833	Leading Jew-baiter died.
Tripoli and Tunisia	25th Shevat	?	?
Ditto, called Purim Sheriff or Purim Kadebani ("False Purim")	24th Tevet	1705	Saved from destruction by hostile ruler, Khalil Pasha.
Ditto, called Purim Borghel	29th Tevet	1793	Saved from destruction during occupation by Borghel Pasha of Turkey.
Tunisia, called: Purim Sheleg ("Purim of Snow")	24th Tevet	1891	Jewish quarter saved from natural disaster.
Tunisia	15th Shevat	?	?
Turino	1st Av	1797	Saved from war and sacking.
Urbino	11th Sivan	1799	Saved from war and riots.
Verona	20th Tammuz	1607	Permission granted to lock ghetto gates from inside instead of from outside.
Vidin, Bulgaria, called Purim de los borrachones ("Purim of the Drunken")	4th and 5th Heshvan or 9th–10th	1806	Saved from annihilation following accusation that the ruler had been poisoned by his Jewish physician.
Ditto	2nd Adar	1878	Saved from destruction during Russo-Turkish (Balkan) war.
Vilna	15th Av	1794	Saved from destruction during Russo-Polish war.
Zborow (Galicia)	12th Tevet	?	Saved from annihilation because of blood libel accusation.

Family purims

Altschul family of Prague	22nd Tevet	1623	Head of family, Ḥanokh Moses, saved from death.
Brandeis family of Jungbunzlau (Bohemia), called Povidl Purim "Plum Jam Purim"	10th Adar	1731	David Brandeis and family saved from accusation of having killed gentiles by poisoning plum jam.
Danzig family of Vilna, called Pulverpurim ("Powder Purim")	15th Kislev	1804	Family of Abraham Danzig, author of *Ḥayyei Adam,* saved from explosion of magnesium.
Elyashar family of Jerusalem	2nd Nisan	?	Saved from death.
Heller family of Prague	1st Adar	1629	Head of family, Yom Tov Lipmann, rabbi of Prague saved from death sentence.
Jonathan ben Jacob of Fulda (Germany)	17th Tammuz	?	?
Maimon family of Lithuania	?	1750	Grandfather of Solomon Maimon saved from death sentence for blood libel.
Meyuḥas family of Jerusalem	16th Adar	1724	Head of family, Raphael Meyuḥas, escaped death by highwaymen.
Samuel Ha-Nagid of Spain	1st Elul	1039	Saved from death plot of conspirators.
Segal family of Cracow	1st Iyyar	1657	Family saved from drowning in river while escaping from pogrom.
Treves family (?)	Shabbat "Va-Yeẓe"	1758	Escaped from fire.

The Karaites observe a special Purim on 1st Shevat, in memory of the release from prison of one of their leaders, Yerushalmi. The exact date of the event is unknown.
The followers of *Shabbetai Ẓevi observed a special Purim on 15th Kislev, because on this day in 1648, Shabbetai Ẓevi proclaimed himself Messiah.

Figure 1. Masked Purim players in a woodcut from the *Venice Minhagim Book*, 1601(?). Jerusalem, J.N.U.L.

appears is at the beginning of a lengthy poem relating the events of the Book of Esther with the aid of appropriate midrashic material, composed about 1555 in Venice by a Polish Jew (*Lieder des Venezianischen Lehrers Gumprecht von Szczebrszyn*, ed. by Moritz Stern (1922), 18). From the context it appears that the poem was intended as a *Purim-shpil.* However, there are extant manuscripts of Yiddish poems on the Purim story dating from at least the 15th century, and from the start of the 16th century printed versions began to circulate. Well into the 19th century this type of poem continued to be defined as a *Purim-shpil* (e.g., *Purim-Shpil,* Warsaw, 1869 and 1874). At first the term *Purim-shpil* was used to define a monologue during which the performer sometimes appeared in costume. The monologues were mostly rhymed paraphrases of the Book of Esther, as well as parodies on liturgical and other holy texts, such as a "kiddush" or a "sermon" for Purim, composed to entertain the audience. Together with the more complex forms, the monologue form of *Purim-shpil* continued to appear in Eastern Europe until World War II.

Manuscript fragments and other evidence from the second half of the 16th century attest the gradual enlarging of the *Purim-shpil* to include presentations by several performers. One such fragment includes a contest between cantors from Poland, Italy, and Germany; it may be assumed that this is a combination of three earlier satirical monologues. Other fragments show evidence of growing complexity in dramatic expression blended with the traditional parody. Judging from the extant material it is probable that during the 16th century and until at least the mid-17th century, the subject matter of the *Purim-shpil* was drawn from contemporary Jewish life and was based on well-known humorous tales. This type of *Purim-shpil* also survived in Eastern Europe until World War II (16 *Purim-shpil* texts of this non-biblical type were published in the collection, *Yidisher Folklor* (1938), 219–74). In its initial and developing stages, the *Purim-shpil* often parallels the German *Fastnachtspiel,* as evidenced from texts of the 15th and 16th centuries. The *Purim-shpil* in all its varieties was usually presented in private homes during the festive family meal; the performers, who wore masks or primitive costumes, were generally recruited from among yeshivah students. In the course of time the *Purim-shpil* became the object of competition between groups of performers recruited not only from among students but also from among apprentices, craftsmen, and mendicants; even professional entertainers saw in the *Purim-shpil* a field for their activity. By the 16th century, the prologues to the *Purim-shpil* had developed a conventional form, which included blessings for the audience, an outline of the contents of the performance, and an introduction of the actors; conventional epilogues had also developed, including parting blessings and appeals for an ample reward. (One of the shorter prologues reads in part: "Good Purim, good Purim, my worthy audience! And do you then know of Purim's significance? . . ." And an excerpt from an epilogue reads: "Today Purim has come in, tomorrow it goes out. Give me then my single groschen and kindly throw me out! . . .") Like the *Fastnachtspiel,* the Purim performance was introduced, conducted, and concluded by a narrator (leader of the performance), traditionally called *loyfer, shrayber,* or *payats,* and, as in the *Fastnachtspiel,* profanity and obscenity of an erotic nature are outstanding elements of the humorous effects.

Well-developed texts on biblical themes presented as *Purim-shpils* began to appear in the late 17th century. Naturally, the subject of the oldest surviving text of this type, a manuscript of 1697, is the story of the Book of Esther, popularly known as the *Akhashverosh-shpil.* In the 18th century the repertoire expanded to include *The Selling of Joseph* and *David and Goliath,* and in the 19th and 20th centuries East European performers presented *The Sacrifice of Isaac, Hannah and Penninah, The Wisdom of Solomon,*

Figure 2. Three Purim jesters with musical instruments and a jug of wine, from a *minhagim* book, printed in Amsterdam by Proops, 1707. Jerusalem, J.N.U.L.

Figure 3. "Purim at Home," a painting by Moritz Oppenheim, Germany, 19th century, depicting a family being entertained by Purim players. New York, Oscar Gruss Collection. Photo Frank Darmstaedter, New York.

etc. (A collection of this genre of *Purim-shpil* was edited by Noah Prylucki in *Zamlikher far Yidishn Folklor* (1912), 125–88; (1917), 143–5.) Most of these biblical works retain the conventional form of *shpil* with prologues, epilogues, parodies, vulgar language, the traditional narrator, and, often, stories unconnected with any biblical theme. These older forms are very apparent in the above-mentioned text of 1697 and in a similar version of an *Akhashverosh-shpil* printed at Frankfort in 1708 (which appears in J. J. Schudt's *Juedische Merckwuerdigkeiten,* 3 (Frankfurt and Leipzig (1714), 202–25). The printed version of the *Akhashverosh-shpil* was burned by the city fathers of Frankfort presumably because of the play's indecent elements. This was probably the reason for a public notice of 1728 in which the leaders of the Hamburg community banned the performance of all *Purim-shpils.* To assure compliance with the ban, fines were threatened and special investigating officers were posted.

As early as the beginning of the 18th century, the biblical *Purim-shpil* reflected many trends of the contemporary European theater in its literary style, choice of subject, and scenic design. Previously marked by extreme brevity, not exceeding a few hundred rhymed lines, and by the limited number of performers, the *Purim-shpil* became a complex drama with a large cast, comprising several thousand rhymed lines performed to musical accompaniment in public places for a fixed admission price. Nonetheless, the plays maintained a connection with Purim and were performed during the appropriate season. From the early 18th century there are extant texts of such plays and evidence of performances in Frankfort, Hamburg, Metz, and Prague, and, later in the century, in Amsterdam and Berlin. Although there is an historical tie between the traditional *Purim-shpil* and the more developed biblical dramas of a later era, the term *Purim-shpil,* if strictly applied, refers only to those early, short performances at family gatherings.

[CH.SH.]

Figure 4. "Purim-shpil" by Yankel Adler, 1931. Oil, 49×69 in. (124×175 cm.). Tel Aviv Museum.

PURITY AND IMPURITY, RITUAL (Heb. טֻמְאָה וְטָהֳרָה, *tumah ve-toharah*), a concept that a person or object can be in a state which, by religious law, prevents the person or object from having any contact with the temple or its cult. The state is transferable from one object to another in a variety of ways, such as touching the object or being under one roof with it, and is independent of the actual physical condition. The state of impurity can be corrected by the performance of specified rituals, mainly including ablution, after which the person or object becomes pure once more until impurity is again contracted.

The concept of purity and impurity is by no means exclusive to the Jewish religion; indeed it was a central and integral feature of most, if not all, ancient religions (see below). It is generally believed that the concept is a concurrent of the belief in evil spirits and a part of the taboo concept. The Hebrew terms are also used for animals forbidden or permitted for consumption, but for that usage see *Dietary Laws.

In the Bible. The main source for biblical laws of purity and impurity is Leviticus 11–17 and Numbers 19. In both these books various other specific laws are also scattered (Lev. 5:2–3; Num. 31:19–20 etc.) and further sources are to be found in Deuteronomy (14:3–21; 23:10–15; 24:8; 26:14). The state of impurity is considered hateful to God, and man is to take care in order not to find himself thus excluded from His divine presence (cf. Lev. 11:43–47). There is not, however, any theoretical definition of purity and impurity in the Bible nor any indication as to why the state of impurity is undesirable or harmful.

Three main causes of impurity are apparent: *leprosy, issue from human sexual organs, and the dead bodies of certain animals, and particularly human corpses.

"LEPROSY" (a conventional, (inexact) rendering of *ẓaraʿat*, צָרַעַת). Three types are distinguishable: of man, of clothes, and of buildings. Leprosy of human beings is further subdivided: one type is immediately declared as unclean, another as clean (including a case where the symptoms appear over the whole body), while a third type requires isolation for a week or a fortnight, and if there is no deterioration the bearer is considered clean. Leprosy of clothes and buildings always requires them to be isolated for a week or a fortnight and only following this period is it decided whether they are clean or not. The leper observes all the customs of one under a ban (Lev. 13:45–46). The purification ritual for the leper, carried out by the priest, is more intricate and complicated than for others, and bears certain similarities to the *Azazel (scapegoat) ceremony on the Day of Atonement (Lev. 16:5–11). It is held that biblical leprosy is not identical with the condition as medically diagnosed.

ISSUE FROM THE SEXUAL ORGANS. The **niddah* (woman at the time of her menstruation), besides being required to refrain from sexual relations (Lev. 18:19), is also considered impure for seven days as from the beginning of the menstrual flow, and the impurity can be transferred to persons, utensils, clothes, all of which cause a further transference on being touched (Lev. 15:19ff.). These secondary degrees of impurity continue only till the evening *(ibid.)* except for cohabitation with a *niddah* where the impurity lasts for a week (Lev. 15:24). No purity ritual for the *niddah* is prescribed in the Bible, not even bathing in water (but see **Niddah*). A woman who menstruates at any time other than her period is called a *zavah* and her uncleanness terminates only after seven "clean" days (Lev. 15:25ff.). For the final purity ritual she is required to bring a sacrifice (Lev. 15:29ff.) but there is no mention of bathing in water. Similar is the law of the *zav* (a man suffering an excretion from his sexual organs) except that he is required to bathe in living waters (*mayim ḥayyim;* Lev. 15:13). Ordinary cohabitation renders both the man and the woman impure until the evening. They must bathe in water as must also he who has an issue of semen (Lev. 15:16–18). A man with a flux is sent outside the camp as is also one with an issue of semen (Num. 5:2–3). A woman is unclean for a period of seven days after giving birth to a male child and 14 after a girl (Lev. 12:2, 5). For 33 additional days after a boy and 66 after a girl (Lev. 12:4, 5), she is forbidden to enter the Temple or to touch hallowed things. Her purification is completed on the bringing of a sacrifice (Lev. 12:6ff.).

DEAD BODIES. The carcasses of all beasts are impure except those permitted to be eaten when properly killed by man; of the reptiles eight are listed as being unclean when dead. On touching them one becomes impure until nightfall (Lev. 11:24ff.). There is no instance in the Bible of a living being becoming impure except man. The highest degree of impurity is that of the corpse, which conveys uncleanness on touch, and to everything in the same tent with it (Num. 19:14ff.). The Bible does not differentiate between the various substances as to their susceptibility to become unclean. A person becoming unclean through a corpse is sent outside the camp for seven days and has to undergo the purity rite with the sprinkling of the *red heifer's ashes (Num. 19:11ff.). He who has become unclean through a corpse transfers the uncleanness, but in a lesser degree, which passes in the evening after bathing. Food also becomes unclean provided it has first been in contact with water (which makes it "receptive" to uncleanness; Lev. 11:34).

Purity Ritual. Common to all purity rituals is the time factor: until the evening for the lesser degrees of impurity (e.g., Lev. 11:24, 25, 27) and seven days for the greater degrees (e.g., Lev. 12:2; with certain exceptions—the purity of the leper is dependent on his complete recovery). Bathing is also common to all purity rituals, even where it is not expressly specified. Greater degrees require the washing of the clothes of the unclean person (e.g., Lev. 11:25, 28) and still greater degrees, the offering of a sacrifice (Lev. 5:6ff.). Those unclean through a corpse also require sprinkling with the red heifer's ashes (Num. 19). The leper is sprinkled with a mixture of water and blood, and the unclean through a corpse with water and red heifer ashes. The priest who sprinkles becomes unclean himself as a result. The purity ritual for utensils made impure through a corpse was by passing through fire and for those unable to stand the heat—by water (according to the plain sense of the text in Numbers 31). Earthenware vessels cannot be purified but must be broken, as must even stoves and ovens. A spring or a cistern cannot become impure at all. According to the literal sense of the text it seems that the purity ritual was considered imperative and that one of the reasons for the purity ritual on the *Day of Atonement was to cleanse the Tabernacle (Lev. 16:16; see **Kipper*).

General. From various allusions in the Bible it is clear that other things were also considered impure: the uncircumcised (Isa. 52:1 etc.); countries other than Ereẓ Israel (Josh. 22:19; Hos. 9:3; Amos 7:17); and idols (Gen. 35:2; Isa. 30:22).

The terms "pure" and "impure" are also applied in the Bible to serious transgressions, especially sexual, which caused the land to become impure (Lev. 18:27–28, etc.). The prophets, especially Ezekiel, stress the uncleanness caused to the land by idolatry and bloodshed, but it seems that any sin is thought of as causing impurity and expressions taken from the purity ritual passages serve figuratively in the Bible as symbols for atonement and repentance (Ezek. 36:25; Ps. 51:4 et al.). The two terms of atonement and purification tend therefore to merge. The term for purification is sometimes used for holiness, but generally the difference between the two is apparent.

Several scholars have stressed the similarity between the laws of purity and impurity in the Bible and those of the ancient Near East—Egypt, Mesopotamia, and the ancient Hittites. According to Herodotus (1:198) it was customary in Babylon to bathe in water after cohabitation and it was forbidden to touch any utensil prior to this. According to an ancient Babylonian text a man touching a menstruant woman was unclean for six days. The pig was considered unclean—although it was not considered forbidden food. In Egypt it was forbidden for a man to enter the temple after cohabitation unless he first bathed, and the priests bathed twice daily and twice nightly. The king of Egypt purified himself every morning (cf. Ex. 7:15). Among the Hittites a corpse was considered impure and there is evidence of a detailed ritual for the purification of a mother after giving birth. Others, however, argue that the biblical purity laws are aimed against idol worship and that those connected with corpse impurity are especially aimed against the cult of the dead. Despite the great similarities between the various rites there is a decisive difference: in the ancient Near East the purity and impurity laws are part of a magic cult or medicine rite. It is not always clear whether the purity ritual in Egypt was secular to insure cleanliness or health, or for magic or cult purposes. In Babylon the purity rituals were accompanied by incantations whose purpose was to heal illness or prevent it, or to drive bad spirits out of the temples. In the Bible, however, there is no indication of any such intention and in the case of leprosy impurity, for example, the priest takes no measures for healing the illness.

In Halakhah. The laws of ritual impurity and purity are explained, defined, and extended in the *halakhah*. Twelve complete tractates in the Mishnah and the Tosefta, scores of *mishnayot* in other tractates, and many *beraitot* in the halakhic Midrashim and in the two Talmuds, as well as the studies of *amoraim* connected with them, are devoted to these *halakhot*.

THE CATEGORIES OF IMPURITY. These differ both as to their causes and to their degree and potency. The impurities mentioned in the Pentateuch are regarded as fathers of impurity (Heb. *avot ha-tumah*). In addition the sages decreed impurity at the level of a father of impurity upon a number of other things such as: idolatry, gentile countries, and a burial area (see below). Those rendered impure by fathers of impurity are called children (Heb. *veladot*) or offspring of impurity (*toledot ha-tum'ah*); those rendered impure by a father become impure in the first degree; and those rendered impure by a first degree become impure in the second degree of impurity. With regard to secular produce (not *terumah*) a second degree is impure but cannot pass on the impurity, while for the purposes of *_terumah_ the second gives rise to a third degree, and with sacred produce (dedicated to Temple use) the third degree to a fourth (Sot. 5:2; Toh. 2:3–5; Maim. Yad, Avot ha-Tumah 11:1–4). The exception to this descending series is that which became impure from a corpse, which itself becomes a father of impurity. In order to differentiate between them the corpse itself is called by Rashi (Pes. 14b, 17a, et al.) and other commentators (R. Samson to Kel. 1:1; Oho. 1:2): a "father of fathers" (*avi avot*) of impurity. The father of impurity renders men, garments and utensils impure, but the offspring of impurity only renders foods and liquids impure (BK 2b; Yad, Tumat Met 5:7).

METHODS OF CONTRACTING IMPURITY. The conveying of impurity from the fathers to the offspring can occur in various ways: by contact with the impure object, by carrying it even without moving it, by overshadowing (Heb. *ohel*) and others. Impurity by overshadowing (Kelim 1:4) is caused whether the corpse overshadows the person or utensil, these overshadow the corpse, or something a handbreadth wide overshadows both the corpse and the object (Oho. 3:1; Naz. 53b; Maim. Yad, Tumat Met 1:10). If a leper puts his head and the greater part of his body into a house, or similarly, if an olive's bulk of a leprous garment is put into it, the house becomes impure, even if they do not actually touch it (Neg. 13:8). A leprous house renders impure anyone who puts his head and the greater part of his body into it, as well as a garment brought into it. An olive's bulk of stone or wood or earth from a leprous house renders man and vessels impure by contact, carrying, and entering into the house in which they are (Neg. 13:6; Tosef., Neg. 6:11; Maim. Yad, Tumat Zara'at 16:1). Carrion of a clean bird renders impure neither by contact nor by being carried but only by being eaten and only when it enters the gullet (Toh. 1:1; Zav. 5:9; Maim. Yad, Avot ha-Tum'ah 3:1).

Things susceptible to impurity are: man, utensils, food, and drink. By man only an Israelite is meant. A gentile cannot contract corpse uncleanness (Naz. 61b; Maim. Yad, Tumat Met. 1:13), although a dead gentile renders impure by contact and carrying (Yev. 61a; Maim. *ibid.,* 1:12) and even, in one view, by overshadowing (Oho. 18:7). Similarly leprous impurity applies neither to gentiles nor to resident aliens (Neg. 3:1). All utensils except those made of stone, unfired clay, or dung, are susceptible to impurity no matter what their shape. Some, however, such as flat wooden or bone utensils, contract impurity by rabbinic law only (Men. 69b; Kelim 11:1; 15:1; Maim. Yad, Kelim 1:6, 10). Glass vessels are the subject of a special decree (Shab. 14b, 15a, 16b; Maim. *ibid.,* 1:15). Utensils can contract impurity only when they are completed and the sages defined what stage of manufacture marks completion for the different types of vessels. Broken vessels likewise are not susceptible to impurity but some, on being repaired or reassembled, revert by a special rabbinic decree to their original impurity (Shab. 16b).

FOOD. All foods set apart for human consumption can contract impurity, once they are detached from the ground and have been made susceptible through being moistened, to the satisfaction of their owners, by one of the seven liquids—water, dew, oil, wine, milk, blood, honey (Uk. 3:1; Makhsh. 1:1; 6:4). These liquids themselves also contract impurity (Maim. Yad, Tumat Okhelim 1:4 and commentaries), in an even stricter degree than foodstuffs (Par. 8:7; Toh. 2:6, Maim. Yad, Avot ha-Tumah 10:10).

FATHERS OF IMPURITY ON THE AUTHORITY OF THE SCRIBES. Some sources of impurity are regarded as innovations of the rabbis, although in some cases they were already current in ancient times and are even alluded to in the Bible itself. That objects of idolatry are impure is already suggested in Genesis (25:2): "Put away the strange gods that are among you, and purify yourselves and change your garments" (see comm. Naḥmanides ad loc.). The nature and degree of this impurity is disputed: some sages held that the idol itself renders impure by contact like a reptile, while, on the other hand, Akiva gave it the same degree of impurity as a menstruant (Av. Zar. 3:4; Shab. 9:1). According to another view, objects of idolatry were given the same degree of impurity as flux and leprosy (TJ, Pes. 9:1, 36c; see also Tosef., Av. Zar. 5:7). In the case of idolatrous offerings the law is even stricter and Judah b. Bava says that it conveys impurity by overshadowing, as does a corpse. The law that one passing under an *Asherah (idolatrous tree) becomes impure (Av. Zar. 3:8) was explained in conformity with this view, viz, it is impossible that there should be no idolatrous offering beneath it (*ibid.* 48b).

Gentile Countries. The idea of the impurity of gentile lands originated in early times (cf. Josh. 22:19; Amos 7:17) and became a *halakhah* by the decree of Yose b. Joezer and Yose b. Johanan (Shab. 14b; see Tosef., Par. 3:5). The conjecture that the purpose of this decree was to discourage leaving Ereẓ Israel following the persecutions and exterminations in the time of Antiochus has no basis in the sources. The decree, however, was not in operation in all periods, for not only do we find scholars in Alexandria—Joshua b. Peraḥya and Judah b. Tabai—but the Mishnah takes it as understood that people could legitimately be in foreign countries. Frequent contact with various countries and the existence of Jewish settlements outside Ereẓ Israel made the observance of this decree a burden and in consequence it was lightened in various ways (Tosef., Oho. 18:2; Maim. Yad, Tumat Met 11:6). The paths taken by the pilgrims from Babylon on their festival pilgrimages even in gentile lands are clean (Tosef., Oho. 18:3; Maim. *ibid.*, 11:12; see Maim. comm. to Oho. 18:7). Gentile towns that were included in Ereẓ Israel (Tosef., *ibid.*, 18:4; Maim. Yad. *ibid.*) were also declared free from impurity. The degree of impurity of gentile countries, however, is not explicit in the halakhic sources (see Maim. Yad, Tumat Met 2:16; Rashi, Shab. 14b s. v. *Al ha-Areẓ*).

Burial Area (Heb. *Bet ha-Peras*). A burial area is a locality where the existence of impurity is suspected. The Mishnah distinguishes three kinds of burial area: where a grave has been plowed over and a bone may have been thrown up by the plowshare; a field in which the site of the grave is no longer known; and a grave of mourners—Hebrew *bokhim* (or *kukhim*—grave niches), i.e., the field in which biers are rested in order to lament the dead. These fields have special laws for building, sowing, planting, and removing the impurity (Oho. 17:1, 18:1–5; Tosef., Oho. 17:1–2).

Gentiles. That gentiles were regarded as impure can be inferred from many places in the Mishnah (Toh. 7:6; Nid. 10:4; et al.), the Tosefta (Pes. 7:13), Josephus (Ant. 14:285; 18:93–94) and in the Acts of the Apostles. This impurity "of scribal origin" (Nid. 69b), was not imparted to gentiles from an external source and is unconnected with the impurities explicit in the Pentateuch (cf. Tosef., Zar. 2:1; Nid. 34a). There is a tradition from which it might be inferred that gentile impurity is one of the 18 decrees promulgated close to the time of the destruction of the Temple (TJ, Shab. 1:7, 3c; Shab. 17b), and some scholars believe that it was a political decree intended to segregate the Jews from the Romans and the neighboring peoples during the time of the war. There is, however, evidence that gentile impurity was current a long time before the revolt. Gentiles were forbidden entry to the Temple rampart, because of impurity (Kelim 1:8). This prohibition is attested to by both internal and external sources, and preceded the Hasmonean era (I Macc. 9:34; Mid. 2:3; Philo, *Legatio ad Gaium*, 212; Jos., Ant., 12:145; see also Tosef., Yoma 4 (3): 20). It seems that in the case of gentile impurity—as in the case of the impurity of gentile lands—an ancient law was renewed.

Impurity of Hands. The sages in a number of cases decreed impurity upon the hands of a person although he was not impure. The origin of this decree is connected with the Temple cult. The decree was meant to prevent hallowed things becoming impure (see also Tosef., Maas. Sh. 1:9) and thus—to prevent the loss of sacred meats—it was said that hands do not render impure in the Temple (Pes. 19a–b, Rashi; Maim. Yad, Avot ha-Tumah 8:6). It was similarly decreed that all the sacred writings and **tefillin* with straps render hands impure (Maim. *ibid.*, 3:3–5: and see Kelim 15:6). Of the sacred writings, Johanah b. Zakkai said: "their importance is the cause of their impurity, that they be not made into covers for animals" (Tosef., Yad. 2:19 and cf. Shab. 14a). The concept of impurity of hands was current in early times and indeed the *baraita* teaches: "Shammai and Hillel decreed the impurity of hands" (TJ, Shab. 1:7, 3d; Shab. 14b); the degree and extent of this decree is not, however, explained in that source. The tradition about the excommunication of Eleazar b. Enoch, who cast doubt on the idea (Eduy. 5:6) is also vague as neither the identity of the doubter nor the connection of the cleansing of hands with the Temple cult is known. The Babylonian Talmud assumes the origin of impurity of hands in hallowed things to be earlier than Hillel and Shammai (the regulation requiring washing the hands is ascribed to Solomon—Shab. 14b; Er. 21b), and explains that these extended it to *terumah* (Shab. 15a). In its view, however, hands in general were meant even if it is not known whether they have contracted impurity since they are presumed to be impure "because hands are fidgety" (i.e., touch a great number of things; *ibid.* 14a). This assumption, however, is not compatible with the aforementioned sources (see Rashi, *ibid.*). On the other hand, there are also decrees of *tannaim* requiring the washing of hands before eating *terumah* (Sif. Num. 116; cf. Bik. 2:1 and Er. 1:10) and even for common food (Ḥag. 2:5; TJ, Ḥag. 78b; Ḥag. 18b). From the fact that Bet Shammai and Bet Hillel differ on the washing of hands at the meal it follows that this *halakhah* was current in their time (Ber. 8:2; but cf. Tosef., *ibid.* 6(5):3, and S. Lieberman, *Tosefta ki-Feshutah*, ad loc.). Washing the hands before a meal is also referred to in Matthew (15:2) as a "tradition of the elders." It is possible that the ancient Greek custom of pouring water over the hands before a meal (see Yad. 1:2 and Tosef., Yad. 1:12) also took root in Ereẓ Israel, mainly in the circles of the wealthy and of the priests. The rabbis thereupon decreed impurity upon hands as if to say that the washing of hands is not merely for cleanliness (Ḥul. 106a). It seems then that the decree of Hillel and Shammai was only on hands that had become impure, but that the pious regarded hands in general as impure even for common food. (Jos., Wars, 2:129 relates that the Essenes were wont to bathe before their meal).

The Consequences of Impurity. The laws of impurity and purity have no relevant consequences of any substance except for priests and the affairs of the Temple and its hallowed things. This view has been summarized in the words of Maimonides (Yad, Tumat Okhelim 16:8–9): "Whatever is written in the Torah and in traditional teaching about the laws relating to things impure and pure is relevant only to the Temple and its hallowed things and to heave-offering and second tithe, for it warns those impure against entering the Temple or eating anything hallowed, or heave-offering, or tithe. However, no such prohibition applies to common food, and it is permitted to eat common food that is impure and to drink impure liquids ... Similarly, it is permissible to touch things that are impure and to incur impurity from them, for Scripture warns none but the sons of Aaron and the Nazirite against incurring impurity from a corpse, thereby implying that for all others it is permissible, and that even for priests and Nazirites it is permissible to incur impurity from other impure things, but not from a corpse." In conformity with this view, the command of sending the impure out of the camp was understood as meaning the area of Jerusalem and the Temple Mount (Kel. 1:8–9). The camp of Israel is "from the entrance of Jerusalem to the Temple Mount" (Sif. Num. 1). Lepers too are only sent out of walled cities (Kel. 1:7) but "they may go throughout the land" (Sif. Zut. to 5:2). The verse (Lev. 11:8): "of their flesh ye shall not eat, and their carcasses ye shall not touch; they are unclean unto you," directed to all Israel, is explained as referring only to the time of the festivals (Sifra, Shemini 4, 9; RH 16b), "since they must be ready to enter the Temple and eat of the hallowed things" (Yad, Tumat Okhelim 16:10). In Jerusalem precautions were taken to guard the hallowed things and the priests from impurity. No burials were permitted there, and corpses were not allowed to be kept there overnight. As a precaution against impurity it was forbidden to maintain refuse heaps or rear chickens in Jerusalem (Yad, *ibid.*; BK 82b). Impure persons themselves too took care not to impart impurity to the people of Jerusalem. In consequence: "Any spittle found in Jerusalem may be deemed free from impurity excepting what is found in the upper market" (Shek. 8:1). Priests were especially strict about the purity of the Temple. If a dead reptile was found in the Temple "a priest may remove it with his girdle even on the Sabbath" (Er. 10:15). "If a priest served [at the altar] in a state of impurity, his fellow priests did not bring him to the *bet din*, but the young priests took him outside the Temple court and split open his brain with clubs" (Sanh. 9:6; cf. Tosef., Kelim 1:6). They were so zealous that it was said of them "that to render a knife impure was more serious to them than bloodshed" (Tosef., Yoma 1:12). Alongside this tradition there is considerable evidence that the prohibition against contracting impurity and the obligation of purity extend also to all Jews and to all localities. A **ḥaver* was obliged to undertake "to eat [even] common food in purity" (Tosef., Dem. 2:2). This *halakhah* might be regarded as merely the custom of individuals who were strict with themselves, something like the report of Johanan b. Gudgada that "he always ate [even common food] in accordance with the purity of hallowed things" (Ḥag. 2:7; cf. Tosef., Ḥag. 3:2–3). This view, however, does not conform with the sources that teach the *halakhot* of common food purity with no differentiation between *ḥaverim* and others (Ḥul. 2:5; Tosef., Ber. 6:2–4; et al.), and the fact that the prohibition against causing impurity to common food in Ereẓ Israel is also taught as incumbent upon all people (Tosef., Makshsh. 3:7). Taking account of the inherent difficulties it is certain that the *halakhot* of purity were not observed in all their minutiae at all times. Apart from their impact on the eating of common food, certain impurities had an effect in regard to Torah study and prayer (Ber. 3:4–5; Ter. 1:6). On the origin of this prohibition opinions differ; some regard it as a regulation of Ezra (BK 82a), while others connect it with the pupils of Shammai and Hillel (TJ, Shab. 1:7, 3c). Various reasons have been suggested for it (TJ, Ber. 3:4, 6c; Ber. 22a; and L. Ginzberg, *Perushim ve-Ḥiddushim ba-Yerushalmi*, vol. 3, p. 221ff.). The idea that it arose under the influence of "the morning bathers" (see *Ablution and below) is not satisfactory. Although the Tosefta (Ber. 2:13) states explicitly, "males and females who have flux, menstruants and women after childbirth are permitted to read the Torah, and to study Mishnah and Midrash," some were stricter and maintained the prohibition of prayer and Torah study even in the case of other impurities, in addition to the issue of semen. The prohibition against praying where there is corpse impurity is inferred from the *baraita*, "If he were busy with a dead body in a grave and the time of reading the **Shema* arrives, he removes himself to a pure place, puts on **tefillin*, reads the *Shema* and says his prayers" (TJ, Ber. 2:3, 4c). Also the prohibition against a menstruant praying or entering the synagogue or of blessings being recited in her presence, explicitly stated in a late source (*Baraita de-Messekhta Niddah*, ed. Horowitz pp. 3 and 17; and see **Baraita de Niddah*; **Niddah*), is apparently of ancient origin. The words of the Mishnah (Nid. 7:4) on "places of uncleanness" point to a custom in tannaitic times of isolating menstruants in special places. It seems that there were two purposes in this extension of the laws of impurity and purity; to extend the idea of the Temple, including in it the synagogue and likening prayers to the sacrifices, and to extend the sanctity of the priesthood to all Israel.

Purification. Methods of purifiying the impure vary and match the grades of impurity and their categories. One with a flux counts seven pure days and then has to bathe in living waters, i.e., a spring (Mik. 1:8). A leper whose signs of impurity have disappeared brings two birds that have lived in freedom, and the priest (or in another view, any person) slaughters one over a new earthenware bowl, then takes cedar wood, hyssop, and scarlet wool and binds them together. He then brings the tips of the wings and the tail of the second bird near to them, dips them in the blood and sprinkles it seven times on the back of the hand (and some say also on the forehead) of the leper. After sending away the living bird the priest shaves the leper. After seven days, during which the leper may enter within the wall of Jerusalem but is still regarded as a father of impurity, the priest shaves him a second time and the leper must then wash his garments and bathe (Neg. 14:1–2; Maim. Yad, Tumat Ẓara'at 11:1–2). He who contracts impurity from a corpse is sprinkled on the third and seventh days of his impurity with sin-offering water, and after the sprinkling on the seventh day is obliged to bathe. It is sufficient for all others who are impure and can be purified to bathe. Wherever bathing is mentioned in connection with those impure, except in the case of one with a flux, it is in a **mikveh*. The purification of the impure is completed at the going down of the sun (Lev. 22:6–7). On the day he bathes he is called a **tevul yom* (immersed that day) and disqualifies *terumah* and hallowed things. The bathing of the hands for (the eating of) hallowed things also requires a *mikveh*. Otherwise those needing to wash their hands must pour a quarter *log* of water (about a quarter liter) over the hands (see *Ablution). Those ritually pure are obliged to immerse themselves only in connection with the Temple: "None may enter the Temple court for the service, even though he is clean, until he has immersed himself" (Yoma 3:3; TJ, Yoma 40b). The priest who was to burn the red heifer and the high priest who was to serve on the Day of Atonement were separated from their households seven days beforehand and sprinkled with the sin-offering water (Par. 3:1). The duty of every Israelite to purify himself for the festival (Sifra, Shemini 4; RH 16b) is also because of the pilgrimage to the Temple (Yad, Tumat Okhelim 16:10). On the other hand, there were sects that habitually immersed themselves even though they were not impure. According to Josephus (Wars, 2:129), the Essenes used to immerse their bodies in cold water before their communal meals at noon and in the evening. The immersion of the "morning bathers" too was unconnected with seminal impurity, but was a regular daily immersion. The Pharisees opposed this custom, and to the complaint of the morning bathers that "they mention the Divine Name in the morning without immersion," replied, "I complain against you morning bathers who mention the Divine Name out of a body in which impurity resides."

Impurity and Purity at the Present Time. The cessation of most of the *halakhot* of impurity and purity at the present time is the consequence of a prolonged process, which is only in part connected with the destruction of the Temple. The law of a leprous house was already not in practice halakhically in the time of the *tannaim*. This is clear not only from the *baraita* that teaches, "There has never been and never will be a leprous house," but from testimonies about a place in the Gaza region "which they were wont to call a leprous ruin," and a place in Galilee of which it was said, "leprous stores were removed thither" (Tosef., Neg. 6:1; Sanh. 71a) which point to an early period. Though indeed even in the laws regarding persons a clear trend to limit and lighten their impact is noticeable (Neg. 3:1–2; 5:1; "Any condition of doubt in leprous signs is deemed pure," in opposition to the rule: "Doubts in Torah law are decided stringently" cf. 7:4), it is certain that they were not completely abrogated. The law that when a leper enters the synagogue "they must make for him a partition ten handbreadths high and four cubits wide; he must enter first and come out last" (Neg. 13:12 and cf. Tosef., Neg. 8:2) is not directed especially to the era of the Temple. The laws of lepers were not in force in Babylon in the geonic era, as can be inferred from the summary of an unknown *gaon:* "Nowadays if a disciple or scholar is leprous he is not thrust forth from the synagogue or *bet midrash,* for there is not now the law that thy camp shall be holy" (*Sha'arei Teshuvah,* no. 176 and S. Assaf (ed.), *Teshuvot ha-Ge'onim* (1942), 123). The law that impurity arising from a flow of semen prevented Torah study and prayer was disputed in the tannaitic era in the generation of Usha, and then, later, in the time of the *amoraim* (cf. Ber. 22a). In Ereẓ Israel the common people—among them even transgressors—both men and women, were strict about bathing after cohabitation and when they wished to curtail it "because of the women of Galilee who became barren from the cold, Joshua b. Levi said to them, 'Do you want to curtail that which has guarded Israel from transgression?' " and Jacob b. Avun even said that "this immersion was instituted solely that Israelites shall not behave like fowls who cohabit, get up and go and eat" (TJ, Ber. 3:3, 6c; see Ginzberg, op. cit., pp. 231ff.). It is certain that the sages of Ereẓ Israel did not treat this immersion lightly and some were even meticulously careful to comply with bathing before their learning, so that Ḥanina who came from Babylon ridiculed them with the title "morning bathers" after the ancient sect (TJ, *ibid.*). During the geonic era it was considered a point of difference between Ereẓ Israel and Babylon (M. Margalioth, *Ha-Ḥillukim she-Bein Anshei Mizraḥ u-Venei Ereẓ Yisrael,* pp. 78 and 108ff.). Under the influence of the Arabs who were accustomed to bathe before every prayer, the *geonim* in Babylon were also strict "because of cleanliness and in order to sanctify the Name before gentiles" (*Sha'arei Teshuvah,* no. 298). It became "the common custom in Shinar and Spain that none from whom semen issues prays before washing his whole body in water" (Yad, Tefillah 4:6). The custom was not followed in Christian Europe "and all Jews among the uncircumcised are not accustomed to wash" (*Teshuvot ha-Ramban* (Leipzig, 1859), no. 140; see Tur., OḤ 88 and 613); some were strict, however, even in those countries and required bathing at least for the reader and the priest reciting the *priestly blessing (Resp., Maharam of Rothenberg (Berlin, 1841), 137). The Ḥasidim reintroduced the duty of bathing for one from whom semen issues (see *Ablution).

Purification from corpse impurity was possible as long as there was sin-offering water. Some of the ashes of the red heifer were distributed to each of the priestly courses (*mishmarot*—Par. 3:11) and Israelites were sprinkled with it (Tosef., *ibid.,* 3:14). In Galilee there was sin-offering water even in the time of the *amoraim* (Nid. 6b). With the cessation of sin-offering water all Israel are assumed to have incurred corpse impurity. Priests are forbidden to contract corpse impurity even nowadays (Sh. Ar., YD 369), but even so they are not pure, since they cannot guard against impurity from a metal utensil overshadowed by a corpse (see comm. Samson of Sens to Ḥul. 4:8). These facts have consequences also in the *halakhot* of *terumah* and **ḥallah* (*ibid.;* Sh. Ar., YD 322:4), and are the reason for the prohibition against entering the Temple area even nowadays (*Yere'im ha-Shalem,* no. 297; Magen Avraham to Sh. Ar., OḤ 561:2).

Reasons for Purity and Impurity. The reasons for impurity and purity are not given in the Torah, and there is not a great deal of discussion on the subject in rabbinic literature. It is certain that the rabbis did not regard the impurities as infectious diseases or the laws of purification as quasi-hygienic principles, for otherwise they would not have excluded gentiles from various impurities (see above). The statement of Johanan giving dietetic and hygienic reasons for the absence of lepers in Babylon—"Because they eat beet, drink beer, and bathe in the waters of the Euphrates" (Ket. 77b)—is exceptional. The mainstream opinion was that leprosy is a punishment for various transgressions (see Lev. R. 15:5 and 17:3). Johanan himself said of those guilty of the seven abominable acts of Proverbs 6:16–19, "they are punished by leprosy" (Lev. R. 16:1). This view is bound up with biblical theology and is reiterated in statements of the *tannaim* to the effect that sins make the world impure (Mekh., Shabbat 1: "seeing that murder which makes the land impure ..." and Ba-Ḥodesh 9: "anyone who is arrogant causes the land to become impure"), as well as the person transgressing (Yoma 38b). The sages did assume the existence of an "impure spirit" (Sanh. 65b) and of "impure art" (*ibid.,* 91a) as the source of witchcraft, yet we do not find them connecting the laws of impurity with them. Johanan b. Zakkai indeed referred to the magical practices used to drive out an evil spirit in order to explain to a gentile purification of corpse impurity through the sprinkling of sin-offering water, but said to his own pupils, "By your lives! The corpse does not cause impurity, nor do the waters purify, but it is a decree of the Supreme King of Kings" (PdRK 40a–b).

Purity is a religious ideal. It is said of the patriarch Abraham that he ate common food in purity (BM 87a). In describing the ideal era of the time of King Hezekiah, Isaac Napaha says, "Search was made... from Gabbat to Antipris and no boy or girl, man or woman, was found who was not well versed in the laws of impurity and purity" (Sanh. 94b).

Purity is one of the grades on the way to the spirit of holiness (Av. Zar. 20b). Repentance and good deeds are conducive to purity and holiness (Yoma 8:9; Ber. 17a). On the one hand man is required to study Torah in purity (Yoma 72b), to hallow his thoughts "that he meditate not by day in a manner conducing to impurity at night" (Ket. 46a), while on the other hand the Torah itself becomes a purifying factor: just as water purifies from ritual impurity so does the Torah purify the impure from his impurity (Song R. 1:2, no.3).

Bibliography: N. Brill, in: *Beit Talmud,* 2 (1881/82), 315–20, 325–33, 368–74; 3 (1882/83), 23–26, 49–52; M. Friedmann, in: *Ha-Goren,* 2 (1899), 66–74; 3 (1901), 30–39; J. L. Katzenelson, *Ha-Talmud ve-Ḥokhmat ha-Refu'ah* (1928), 304–82; idem, in: MGWJ, 43 (1899), 1–17, 97–112, 193–210; 44 (1900), 385–400, 433–51; W. Brandt, *Die juedischen Baptismen oder das religioese Waschen im Judentum...* (1910); idem, *Juedische Reinheitslehre und ihre Beschreibung in den Evangelien* (1910); A. Buechler, in: REJ, 62 (1911), 201–15; 63 (1912), 30–50; idem, in: JQR, 17 (1926), 1–81; J. Preuss, *Biblisch-talmudische Medizin* (1923), 369–413, 595–600; Alon, *Meḥkarim,* 1 (1953), 121–76; P. Reymond, *L'eau, sa vie, et sa signification dans l'ancien testament* (1958), 228–34; S. Weinfeld, *Mappat ha-Tohorah* (1965), explanatory diagram with notes.

[EH/ED.]

PUT (Heb. פּוּט), one of the sons of Ham son of Noah. In the Table of Nations, Put is mentioned, along with Cush, Egypt, and Canaan (Gen. 10:6; I Chron. 1:8). However, whereas the genealogies of the other three are recorded, nothing further is said of Put. However, the people is mentioned several times in the prophetic literature. Referring to the impending conquest of Egypt by Nebuchadnezzar, Jeremiah mentions the "men of Cush and Put, who handle the shield, men of Lud, skilled in handling the bow" (Jer. 46:9). Ezekiel mentions Put along with Persia and Lud as serving in the army of Tyre (Ezek. 27:10). In his prophecy against Egypt, he cites Put, together with Ethiopia (Cush), Lud, Arabia, and Cub (Gr. Libya), as doomed to fall by the sword (Ezek. 30:5), and in his oracle against Gog, he again places Put alongside Persia and Cush (Ezek. 38:5). From the passages cited the exact identity of Put cannot be decided, but an African location is strongly suggested. In all the prophetic passages cited above, except Ezekiel 30:5, the Septuagint translates Put by "Libyans." It would seem then that Put was identified with Libya or possibly some neighboring area such as Cyrene.

Bibliography: A. Reuveni, *Shem, Ḥam ve-Yafet* (1932), 85–87; U. Cassuto, *A Commentary on the Book of Genesis* (1964), 200ff.

[SH.BA.]

PUTIEL (Heb. פּוּטִיאֵל). The name Putiel occurs only once in the Bible (Ex. 6:25), where it is stated that Eleazar the son of Aaron married one of Putiel's daughters, and that their son was Phinehas.

The rabbis identify Putiel with Jethro and give two homiletical interpretations of the name, one praiseworthy and the other derogatory. The first one, connected with the view that he became converted to Judaism, is that he "emancipated" *(patar)* himself from idolatry (Mekh., Amalek 1) and the other that he fattened *(pittem)* calves for the purpose of idolatrous worship. The same passage, however, also makes it refer to Joseph, who overcame *(pitpet)* his passion, and concludes that Phinehas was descended from both (Sot. 43a). It has been suggested that Putiel is in fact a Hebraized version of Poti-Phera, the "priest of On" whose daughter Joseph married (Gen. 41:45), "ph" being the definite article in Egyptian, and Ra the Egyptian god.

Bibliography: Kohut, Arukh, 6 (1926^2), 310f.

[ED.]

PUTTERMAN, DAVID (1903–), U.S. cantor. Born in New York, Putterman was one of the first American-trained cantors to establish a reputation for himself. In his youth he sang and studied with the leading cantors of the time, including Zeidel Rovner (Jacob Samuel *Morogowsky) and Josef *Rosenblatt. From 1921 to 1933 he was cantor of Temple Israel, Washington Heights, New York, and then moved to the Park Avenue Synagogue. He had a pleasing tenor voice and was a popular soloist in concert and radio programs. Putterman strove to interest Jewish and non-Jewish composers alike in composing for the synagogue, and commissioned a series of "Services of Contemporary Liturgical Music." An anthology of 38 of these works, *Synagogue Music by Contemporary Composers,* was published in 1951 and includes compositions by Leonard *Bernstein, Darius *Milhaud, Morton Gould, Kurt *Weill, Mario *Castelnuovo-Tedesco, Alexander Gretchaninoff, Roy Harris, and the Afro-American composer William Grant Still. Putterman was also instrumental in the establishment of the Cantors Assembly of the United Synagogue of America and the Cantors Institute of the Jewish Theological Seminary.

Bibliography: Jewish Ministers Cantors' Association of America, *Di Geshikhte fun Khazzones* (1924), 165; *Cantors' Voice* (Dec. 1952), 7; I. Rabinovitch, *Of Jewish Music* (1952), 306–7.

[D.M.L.O.]

PUY (-EN-VELAY), LE, town in the department of Haute-Loire, S. France. The Jewish quarter of Le Puy, on the site of the Rue de la Juiverie, is first mentioned in 1212. There is no other information available on the early medieval community there. Following the return of the Jews to the kingdom in 1315 after the expulsion of 1306, a Jew of Le Puy was accused in 1320 of having killed a chorister of the church of Notre-Dame, the murder having been revealed by a miracle. The accused was murdered by the populace, and the other Jews were banished from Le Puy. In 1325 Charles IV granted the choristers of Le Puy the jurisdiction over any Jew found within the town.

Bibliography: Theodore, *Histoire angél... du Puy* (1693), 316ff.; M. Schwab, in: REJ, 33 (1896), 277–82; A. Jacotin, *Nomenclature historique... des rues du Puy* (1928).

[B.BL.]

PYRRHUS, DIDACUS (originally **Diogo Pires;** also known as **Pyrrhus Lusitanus** and, from his birthplace, Évora, as **Flavius Eborensis;** 1517–1607), Portuguese Marrano poet. He is not to be confused with the more famous Diogo Pires (Solomon *Molcho) who was martyred in 1532. In order to escape the Portuguese Inquisition, Pyrrhus left Évora for Salamanca in Spain, where he began to study medicine in 1535 and eventually qualified as a physician. His movements during the following two decades are relatively confused, but he is known to have fled to Antwerp in about 1540. From there he made his way to Venice and Ferrara, and then lived for a time in Ancona; but the persecution of the local Marrano colony in 1555 obliged him to take refuge in the Dalmatian town of Ragusa (Dubrovnik), where he formally reverted to Judaism under the name of Isaiah Kohen. Pyrrhus, who had first achieved literary distinction with his volume of *Carmina* (Ferrara, 1545), spent about 50 years of his life in Ragusa, then a center of Neo-Latin poetic culture, and was mainly active as a teacher and writer. According to some authorities, Pyrrhus made a pilgrimage to Jerusalem in his last years before returning to Ragusa, where he died.

He published two humanistic works in praise of his new home: *De illustribus familiis quae hodie Rhacusae exstant* (Venice, 1582; 1709^2) and *Excerpta ex Flavii Jacob Eborensis Carminibus ad Historiam Sacram Rachusinam aliquo modo facientibus* (1596); *Cato Minor* (Venice, 1592), moralizing verse for children; and *Jacobi Flavii Eborensis seu Didaci Pirrhi Lusitani Elegiarum Libri Tres...* (Venice, 1596). Pyrrhus ranks among the outstanding Neo-Latin poets of the Renaissance. One of his rare works of Jewish interest was a Latin elegy composed for the tombstone of *Amatus Lusitanus in Salonika, but unfortunately no trace of it survives.

Bibliography: A. Ribeiro, *Portugueses das sete partidas* (1950), 223–85; M. Gruenwald and A. Casnacich, *Didacco Pyrrho... ein Lebensbild* (1883); JE, s.v. *Flavius Eborensis;* Roth, England, 137–8; Roth, Marranos, 298; idem, *Jewish Contribution to Civilization* (1940), 113; (1956^3), 82n.; idem, *Jews in the Renaissance* (1959), 109–10.

[ED.]

°**PYTHAGORAS** (late sixth century B.C.E. (?)), Greek philosopher. Pythagoras founded a religious community incorporating strict rules of ritual and ethical purity. This perhaps led ancient Jewish, Christian, and pagan authors to claim that he owed his theories to the Jews and other Eastern peoples with whose teachers he had studied during his travels. The idea seems to have originated with *Hermippus of Smyrna (late third century B.C.E.), who only referred to the Jews. The idea that Greek philosophers were indebted to the East for their views was popular in Hellenistic times. Conversely, it has been suggested by Levy that the legends surrounding the life of Pythagoras influenced the account of Moses' life found in *Philo and *Josephus. Influence of the Pythagorean brotherhood on the Essenes and on the Dead Sea Sect have likewise been postulated. The five-pointed star found on some Pythagorean coins and in some Jewish inscriptions probably derives from a common Babylonian source.

Bibliography: I. Levy, *Recherches sur les sources de la légende de Pythagore de Grèce en Palestine* (1927); C. J. de Vogel, *Pythagoras and Early Pythagoreanism* (1966), 28–51.

[D.E.G.]

Initial letter "Q" for *Quomodo* at the beginning of Lamentations, from a Latin Bible, N. France, c. 1200. Within the letter is Jeremiah mourning Jerusalem. Amiens, Bibliothèque Municipale, Ms. 21, fol. 132v. Photo Caron, Amiens.

QALʿAT ḤAMMĀD, city formerly situated S.W. of Constantine, Algeria. It was founded in 1007 by a branch of the Banu Zīrī who reigned in Kairouan. Its population included Christians, Jews, and members of the Jerāwa tribe, Berbers formerly converted to Judaism. Qalʿat Ḥammād received the majority of the inhabitants of Kairouan when that city was sacked by Arab nomads in 1057, and inherited the importance of the former metropolis. As capital of a vast kingdom in the 11th century, it possessed a Jewish elite among whom was Solomon ha-Dayyan b. Formash. Abraham *ibn Daud knew of Solomon and also reported the tradition which stated that Isaac *Alfasi was born in Qalʿat Ḥammād. The city was completely destroyed by the Almohads in 1152.

Bibliography: Neubauer, Chronicles, 1 (1887), 73, 75; L. M. E. de Beylie, *La Kalaa des Beni-Hammad* (1909); Poznański, in: REJ, 58 (1909), 297–8; Hirschberg, Afrikah, 1 (1965), 167, 259. [D.Co.]

QAṢR IBN HUBAYRAH (Kaṣr ibn Hubayrah), town that was situated S. of the ruins of ancient Babylon, W. of the Euphrates (i. e., then its eastern arm which was known as the Sura River). Qaṣr ibn Hubayrah was founded by Omar ibn Hubayrah, the last governor of Babylonia appointed by the Ummayyad caliphs; the town bears his name. A report by the Arab geographer al-Mukaddasi, dating from the end of the tenth century, states that Qaṣr ibn Hubayrah had a large Jewish community. According to *Nathan ha-Bavli, it was the original home of *David b. Zakkai, the exilarch who had a bitter controversy with R. *Saadiah Gaon. At the beginning of the 12th century, when the town of *Ḥilla was founded and became a transit point for the district's caravans and its trade center, Qaṣr ibn Hubayrah lost its importance and eventually fell into a state of ruin.

Bibliography: G. Le Strange, *The Lands of the Eastern Caliphate* (1930), 70f., 83. [E.A.]

QAYNUQĀʿ (Ar. بنو قينقاع ; **Qaynuqāʿ, Banu Qaynuqāʿ**), one of the three Jewish tribes (the others *Nadīr and *Qurayẓa) in ancient *Medina (Yathrib). Some hold that the Qaynuqāʿ originally were of Idumean, rather than Judean descent. Owning no land—unlike the other Jewish tribes who engaged in agriculture—the Qaynuqāʿ were mostly goldsmiths and manufacturers of weapons. They concentrated in the center of town and were clients of the Arab tribe of Khazraj. (The other two Jewish tribes were clients of the Aws.) The Koran (Sura 2:79) alludes to rivalry between them and the other Jewish tribes. The Qaynuqāʿ were the first of the tribes to suffer at the hands of Muhammad. They actively opposed Islam, thus breaking their agreement with Muhammad. Muhammad's siege and the expulsion of Qaynuqāʿ in 622–23 were accomplished in 15 days. Although there were several hundred in number, they lacked the necessary support of their Arab allies. They were granted three days in which to collect their debts and given permission to take some possessions, with the exception of tools of their trade. Some Arabs opposed their expulsion. The Qaynuqāʿ wandered north toward the desert and the Persian Gulf area. Several became prominent converts to Islam, including *ʿAbdallah ibn Salām.

Bibliography: M. Ibn Isḥāq, *Life of Muhammad*, tr. by A. Guillaume (1955), index; H. Z. Hirschberg, *Yisrael be-Arav* (1946), index; W. M. Watt, *Muhammad at Medina* (1956), 208f.; de L. E. O'Leary, *Arabia Before Muhammad* (1938), 192f.; EIS, 2 pt. 2 (1924), 645–6. [Ed.]

QAZZĀZ, MANASSEH BEN ABRAHAM IBN (AL-) (tenth century, also known as **Menashe b. al-Farrār**), Jewish governor in Damascus from 990 to 996. In the year 980 he engaged in administering Yaʿqūb ibn Killis' property. He must have played a leading part in the military administration of Syria. Al-Qazzāz was appointed by the Fatimid caliph al-ʿAzīz (975–96) as deputy to the Coptic Christian vizier ʿĪsā b. Nestorius (995–96), whose seat was in Cairo These two high officials made use of their positions for the benefit of their coreligionists. The discontented Muslims complained to the caliph, and he imprisoned the two officials and their subordinates. After some time the Christian vizier was reinstated. The fate of al-Qazzāz is unknown. A poem discovered in the *genizah* praises his son, ʿAdiya (d. after 1037). It describes the exalted position of Manasseh and his activities, including his support of the Palestinian *geonim* and the exilarchs. Another source mentions that he was one of the opponents of the Jerusalem *gaon* R. *Salomon b. Judah. Al-Qazzāz' son ʿAdiya, who also held an important position in Damascus and protected his coreligionists, was employed as government secretary (*kātib*). ʿAdiya's sons Samuel and Ishmael held the position of *nagid*.

Bibliography: Mann, Egypt, 1)1920), 19–23; 2 (1922), 11–13; idem, in: HUCA, 3 (1926), 257–8; Fischel, Islam, 62–64; S. Assaf and L. A. Mayer (eds.), *Sefer ha-Yishuv*, 2 (1944), 51, 73–75; Ashtor, Toledot, 1 (1944), 29. [A.D.]

°**QUADRATUS, UMMIDIUS CAIUS,** Roman governor of Syria (50–60 C.E.). During the administration of Quadratus a series of disturbances erupted between the Jews and Samaritans of Palestine. *Cumanus, the Roman procurator of Judea at the time, was unable to cope with the situation, and the leaders of both camps presented their arguments before the Syrian governor at Tyre. Whereas the Samaritans accused Jewish bands of sacking their villages and thus taking the law into their own hands, the Jewish delegation, including the high priest *Jonathan b. Anan, alleged that Cumanus had been bribed by the Samaritans to ignore the murder of Jewish pilgrims on their way to Jerusalem through Samaritan territory. According to Josephus, Quadratus at first deferred judgment. He subsequently proceeded to Caesarea where he crucified the prisoners taken by Cumanus from both sides. From there he went to Lydda and granted a second hearing to the Samaritan case. As a result of this, several Jews, including Doetus, were executed for their part in the rising. Numerous Samaritan and Jewish dignitaries, among them the high priest *Ananias, were ordered to appear before the emperor Claudius and account for their actions. Quadratus then left for Jerusalem, found the people peaceably celebrating Passover and returned to Antioch (52 C.E.).

Bibliography: A. Schalit, *Namenwoerterbuch zu Flavius Josephus* (1968), 39, s.v. 4 Δοσίθεος. [I.G.]

QUAIL (Heb. שְׂלָו), the bird *Coturnix coturnix*, the smallest of the pheasant family. The quail is approximately seven inches (about 18 cm.) long and weighs some 3½ ounces (100 gr.). The color of its plumage is like that of the house sparrow, a fact indicated in the Talmud, which also states that the quail is one of four species of pheasant (the other being the *pheasant and two species of *partridge), that its flesh is very fatty and its taste inferior to that of the other species (Yoma 75b). Large flocks of quail provided food for the Israelites in the wilderness having been blown across the sea by a wind which "let them fall by the camp, about a day's journey on this side, and a day's journey on the other side, round about the camp, and about two cubits above the face of the earth." Some were eaten fresh, the rest being spread out on the ground to dry in the sun (Num. 11:31–33; cf. Ex. 16:3–4; Ps. 78:26–27; 105:40). According to Josephus, flocks of quails from the Arabian gulf "came flying over this stretch of sea, and, alike wearied by their flight and withal accustomed more than other birds to skim the ground, settled in the Hebrews' camp" (Ant. 3:25). This description is factual. The phenomenon repeats itself in spring and in fall when large flocks of quail pass over the Mediterranean Sea on their migration from northern countries to Africa in fall and on their return in spring. Weary from their lengthy flight, the flocks settle on the southern coast of the country (between Gaza and El-Arish), to be caught in nets spread out before they settle, into which they fall exhausted. The local population eats them, selling most of them in city markets. Until the 1930s and 1940s millions of quails were caught in this way at these seasons but their number has since decreased. In addition to the migratory flocks of quails, some of them breed in cereal and fodder fields in various regions of Israel, building their nests on the ground. Their grayish-brown color conceals them from human sight and only when approached do they rise in noisy flight, coming to rest in a nearby field, since their comparatively short wings make it difficult for them to fly high.

Bibliography: Lewysohn, Zool, 210f., no. 260; F. S. Bodenheimer, *Animal and Man in Bible Lands* (1960), 59; J. Feiks, *Animal World of the Bible* (1962), 56. [J.F.]

°**QUARESMIUS, FRANCISCUS,** a 17th-century Franciscan friar. Quaresmius was born at Lodi, Italy, and from 1619 to 1626 was custodian and apostolic commissary for the Holy Land. He later served as the general procurator of the Franciscan Order and from 1637 as custodian of St. Angelo, Milano.

He was the author of two folio volumes *Elucidatio Terrae Sanctae historica, theologica et moralis* (1639) which contain the most complete survey of the remains and legends of the Holy Land as accepted in Catholic circles. Quaresmius painstakingly copied inscriptions and used the archives of the Mt. Zion monastery for his description of the traditions and monastic institutions of 17th-century Palestine.

[M.A.-Y.]

QUASTEL, JUDAH HIRSCH (1899–), British biochemist. Quastel, who was born in Sheffield, was a fellow of Trinity College, Cambridge (1924). He was director of research at the Cardiff City Mental Hospital from 1929 to

1941, and director of the soil metabolism unit of the Agricultural Research Council from 1941 to 1947. In 1947 he went to Canada to become professor of biochemistry at McGill University and director of the McGill-Montreal General Hospital Research Institute. In 1966 he became professor of neurochemistry and biochemistry in the University of British Columbia, Vancouver. Quastel's fields of research were the chemistry of enzymes, microorganisms and soils, phytobiochemistry, and the biochemistry of mental disorders.

He was editor and coauthor of Neurochemistry (1955, 1962[2]), *Methods in Medical Research*, vols. 8–9 (1960–61), *Metabolic Inhibitors*, vols. 1–2 (1963–64), and coauthor of *The Chemistry of Brain Metabolism in Health and Disease* (1961). Quastel was a fellow of the British Royal Society and of the Royal Society of Canada, and president of the Canadian Biochemical Society. He was on the Board of Governors of the Hebrew University of Jerusalem from 1950 and honorary secretary of the Canadian Friends of the Hebrew University for 19 years. [S.A.M.]

QUE, the Assyrian *(Quwe)* and biblical Hebrew (קְוֵה, קְוֵא), name of Cilicia, the classical name of the Mediterranean littoral south of the Taurus Mountains in Turkey, from Paphlagonia in the west to the Amanos Mountains in the east. At its eastern end, this littoral broadens into a fertile valley watered by the rivers Pyramus (Ceyhan), Sarus (Seyhan), and Cydnus (Tarsus); this portion was known in classical times as *Cilicia Pedias* or *Campestris,* or simply *Cilicia* proper, to the Egyptians as *Kode* or *Qedi,* to the Hittites as *Kizzuwatna (Kizwatna),* and to the neo-Babylonians as *Ḫume.* According to some Egyptologists, the western portion of Cilicia (*Cilicia Aspera* or *Tracheia*) was called *Keftiu* (the biblical Caphtor), though this name is more generally held to designate Crete and perhaps the Aegean coasts as well. The name Cilicia is probably derived from that of the Ḫilakkû people who were the dominant ethnic group in the neo-Assyrian period (as identified by Herodotus). Like much of the surrounding littoral, Que was an important link in the trade routes of the Ancient Near East and subject to influences, by land and sea, from all its neighboring cultures (see below).

Political History. The political history of Que begins in about 1650 B.C.E. Kizzuwatna, eastern Que, was clearly under Hittite control, for Ḫattušili I and Muršili I, the outstanding Old Hittite kings, seem to have moved freely down the Pyramus River (Hittite *Purna*) on their campaigns into Syria. However, with the death of Muršili about 1590 B.C.E., the Hurrians asserted themselves in Que, as elsewhere, and Que enjoyed two precarious centuries of independence. The first attested king of Que, Išputaḫšu, son of Paria-watri, is known both from his own inscription and from a Hittite record. His bilingual bull from Tarsus proclaims him a "great king." In the time of Arnuwanda I (c. 1440–1420 B.C.E.), Kizzuwatna even expanded beyond the borders of Que as far east as Uršu and Wašukanni (see *Hittites). However, the increasing power of the new Hittite Empire and the rise of rival Hurrian states, particularly Mitanni, soon put an end to these pretensions.

An interesting light is thrown on western Que at this time. Texts from *Ugarit in the 14th and 13th centuries mention a number of merchants from Ura, the capital of the later Pirindu (see below). One in particular regulated their status at Ugarit, where they apparently enjoyed "extra-territorial" rights under Hittite protection.

Que After Hittite Times. With the collapse of the Hittite Empire under the onslaught of the Sea Peoples (c. 1200 B.C.E), Que too was plunged into obscurity. It is conceivable that as the remnants of Hittite culture and population sought refuge in northern Syria, those of Kizzuwatna migrated into Anatolia, and that the later name Katpat-uka (Cappadocia) preserves the ancient tribal name of Kizwatna. Que-Cilicia (or better, a part of it) reemerged into history at first through biblical sources. I Kings 10:28 and II Chronicles 1:16 state that royal merchants imported, and perhaps even transported and resold, horses from Que and *Miẓrayim* (= Muṣri, a neighbor of Que) for the king's personal use and for the other northern kings of Aram and of the Hittites (the petty successors of the Hittite Empire; cf. II Kings 7:6). The word *mi-qweh* ("from Que") in these passages was generally misunderstood. From the ninth century on, Que and the other parts of Cilicia are taking part in northern coalitions against Assyria. At this period, Que appears to have been settled by new ethnic elements, known to the Assyrians collectively as Ḫilakkû, though many individuals, including particularly the petty princes who ruled various parts of the area, still bore Luwian names comparable to those of the second millennium. The name of Kizzuwatna survived in the name of the city Kisuatni, but the principal site of Que in this period is Karatepe at Ceyhan (classical Pyramus in the Amanus mountains). According to the monumental bilingual inscriptions of Azittawdda the contemporary king in Phoenician and Hittite hieroglyphics, this site was the capital of Awar(a)ku king of the Danunites (Homer's Dannaeans?) of Que (identical with the Urikki king of Que in Tiglath-Pileser III's annals). The growing involvement of Que with Assyria began in Shalmaneser III's time, when the northern coalition was crushed by him. On the other hand, Que did not participate in the southern coalition (see *Karkar where the corrected lines of the inscription are cited). Que's connections with Assyria continued through *Esarhaddon's time down to that of Neriglissar.

Bibliography: E. D. Forrer, in: *Klio,* 30 (1937), 135–86; H. Goldman, in: R. W. Ehrich (ed.), *Relative Chronologies in Old World Archeology* (1954), 69–82; C. H. Gordon, in: JNES, 17 (1958), 28–31; A. Goetze, in: JCS, 16 (1962), 48; M. J. Mellink, in: *Bibliotheca Orientalis,* 19 (1962), 219–26; H. Tadmor, in: JEJ, 11 (1961), 143–50.

[ED.]

QUEBEC, largest of the ten provinces of Canada; total area of 594,860 sq. mi., total population 5,259,211 (1961); Jewish population 125,000 (1971). Quebec was founded in 1608 as a French colony and was called New France until its conquest by the British in 1759–60; it then became part of British North America (1763). By the North America Act of 1867 it was joined to the colonies of Ontario, Nova Scotia, and New Brunswick to form the Dominion of Canada, later joined by Prince Edward Island (1873), British Columbia, and the newly formed provinces of Manitoba (1870), Saskatchewan (1905), Alberta (1870), as well as Newfoundland (1949).

Jews were not allowed to live in Quebec under the French regime and first came to Canada in 1760 with the British army as commissary officers, soldiers, and settlers. In the first offical census of Canada in 1831 the Jewish population of Quebec numbered 107; it increased to 989 by 1881. The Russian pogroms in the 1880s and anti-Semitic discrimination in Rumania in that period caused an influx of Jewish immigrants from Eastern Europe, which increased the Jewish population of Quebec to 7,607 by 1901 and 30,758 by 1911. It continued to rise rapidly to 60,087 in 1931; 82,700 in 1951; 104,727 in 1961; and was estimated at 125,000 in 1971. Jews formed 2% of the total population of Quebec in each of the Canadian censuses from 1921 to 1961.

In 1961 there were 103,234 Jews living in the three metropolitan areas (*Montreal, *Quebec, Chicoutimi). There were an additional 1,493 Jews living in the smaller cities and towns of the province, and outside the boundaries of Metropolitan Montreal and Metropolitan Quebec there were only two towns in the rest of Quebec province in 1961 with more than 100 Jewish residents, Sherbrooke (181 Jews) and Ste. Agathe des Monts (110 Jews), and there were 25 towns and villages with only one Jewish resident.

Of the total Jewish population of Quebec province in 1961, 34.2% reported Yiddish as their mother tongue compared with 79% in 1941, and 90% in 1931, while 53.7% in 1961 reported English as their mother tongue compared with 16.5% in 1941 and less than 1% in 1931. In the census of 1961, 51.3% of the foreign-born Jewish population in Quebec reported Yiddish as their mother tongue, as compared with only 14.4% of the Canadian-born Jewish population. Quebec is the only province in Canada in which the majority of its total population, 80.6% in 1961, was of French ethnic origin, but no single ethnic group formed the majority in Canada as a whole nor in the provinces of Manitoba, Saskatchewan, and Alberta; the population of Anglo-Celtic origin formed the majority of the population in the provinces of Ontario, British Columbia, Nova Scotia, New Brunswick, Newfoundland, and Prince Edward Island. Although both English and French have equal status as the official languages in Quebec, in 1961 only 25.4% of Quebec's total population spoke both English and French; 36.5% of the Jewish population spoke both English and French, as compared with 28.7% of the population of Anglo-Celtic origin and 24.4% of the population of French origin.

For further information, see *Canada; *Montreal.

Bibliography: B. G. Sack, *History of the Jews in Canada* (1965); S. Rosenberg, *Jewish Community in Canada* (1970). [L.Ros.]

QUEBEC, capital city of the Canadian province of the same name. Under the French regime prior to the British conquest in 1759, Jews and Protestants were not permitted to settle in Quebec or any part of New France. The first Jews known to have lived in the city of Quebec were Abraham Jacob Franks and Eleazer Levy who settled there in 1767, and by 1784 they were joined by Elias Solomon, David Jacobs and Hyman Myers. John Franks, a Jew, was appointed the first chief of the Quebec Fire Brigade in 1790, a position which he held until his death in 1799.

Abraham Joseph (1815–1886), son of Henry Joseph, a fur trader and one of the founders of Canada's merchant marine, moved to Quebec after the death of his father in 1832. He was elected a member of the Quebec City Council, and was the president of the Quebec Board of Trade, president of the Stadacona Bank, and one of the founders of the Banque Nationale. His sons and grandsons played a prominent part in the commercial and cultural life of the city. Sigismund Mohr (1827–1893), an electrical engineer who went to Quebec from Germany in 1871, was the pioneer of hydroelectric development in Canada, harnessing Montmorency Falls to light the city of Quebec.

The Jewish population of Quebec City was very small prior to 1901, ranging from 40 in 1851 to 110 in 1861, decreasing to 45 in 1891, and increasing gradually from 302 in 1901 to 436 in 1931 and 495 in 1961. In 1970 most of the Jewish population of Quebec City were the children and grandchildren of Jewish immigrants from Eastern Europe who came to Quebec during the period from 1890 to 1921. The majority (63.6%) of the Jewish population of the city of Quebec in 1961 were Canadian-born and of those who were not born in Canada more than 65% settled in Quebec before the outbreak of World War II in 1939. Approximately 80% of the Jews in the city in 1969 were merchants, and a few were clothing manufacturers, lawyers, doctors, and professors at Laval University. Maurice Pollack, founder and proprietor of the city's largest department store, settled in Quebec in the first deade of the 20th century, and was a generous supporter of Jewish institutions in Canada and Israel, and of Laval University, the French Catholic university in Quebec.

A Jewish cemetery was consecrated in 1853, but it was not until 1892 that the first synagogue was built in the Lower Town section of the city. In 1945, following much opposition, including legal action from the city council, a synagogue building was consecrated in the newer residential area in the Upper Town section of the city. [L.Ros.]

QUEEN OF SHEBA. The biblical account of the queen of *Sheba (I Kings 10:1–10, 13; II Chron. 9:1–9, 12) describes how when the queen of Sheba heard of the fame of Solomon, she went to Jerusalem with a great train of camels, bearing spices, gold, and precious stones, "to prove him with hard questions," all of which Solomon answered to her satisfaction. They exchanged gifts, after which she returned to her land.

For details see *Solomon.

In the Aggadah. Talmudic references to the queen of Sheba are sparse. A most elaborate account, however, is given in *Targum Sheni* to Esther which can be supplemented by details found in the Alphabet of Ben Sira and Josephus (Ant. 8:165–73). A hoopoe informed Solomon that the kingdom of Sheba was the only kingdom on earth not subject to him and that its queen was a sun worshiper. He thereupon sent it to Kitor in the land of Sheba with a letter attached to its wing commanding its queen to come to him as a subject. She thereupon sent him all the ships of the sea loaded with precious gifts and 6,000 youths of equal size, all born at the same hour and clothed in purple garments. They carried a letter declaring that she could arrive in Jerusalem within three years although the journey normally took seven years. When the queen arrived and came to Solomon's palace, thinking that the shining floor was a pool of water, she lifted the hem of her dress, uncovering her legs. Solomon informed her of her mistake. When she arrived she asked him three (Targ. Sheni to Esther 1:3) or, according to another source, 19 riddles to test his wisdom. [Ed.]

In Islam. In later Arabic literature, under the influence of her name given by Josephus as Nikaulis, the name of the queen of Sheba (Saba) is given as Bilqis. The story in the Koran (Sura 27, 17–45) closely follows that given in the Targum Sheni, including the story of the hoopoe *(hudhud)* and the shining floor of the palace which she mistook for a pool of water (see above) though some details probably derive from Christian legends. Solomon acted on the advice of his counselors, among whom, according to the commentators, was his vizier Asaf, in inviting her to visit him. The queen failed to recognize her throne, which had been brought to Jerusalem with the help of Allah, by one of the "scholars" (Āsāf?). Realizing the greatness of Allah, she repented. Muhammad speaks of the location of Saba and the sins of its inhabitants in Sura 34:14–17. In Ethiopian tradition an important place is reserved for the marriage of Solomon and Makeda, the queen of Sheba, whose son was King Menelik I. The long version of the story is found in the Kebra Nagest. The royal house of Ethiopia claims to trace its ancestry back to this union (see *Ethiopia; *Falashas). [H.Z.H.]

Bibliography: In the Aggadah: Ginzberg, Legends, 3 (1911), 411; 4 (1913), 143–9; (1928), 288–91. In Islam: Thaʿlabī, *Qiṣaṣ* (1356 A.H.), 262–4; Kisāʾī, *Qiṣaṣ* (1356 A.H.), 285–92; G. Weil, *The Bible, the Koran, and the Talmud*... (1846); M. Gruenbaum, *Neue Beitraege zur semitischen Sagenkunde* (1893), 211–21; H. Speyer, *Die biblischen Erzaehlungen im Qoran* (1931, repr. 1961), 390–9; EIS, s.v. *Bilḳis*.

QUERIDO, ISRAËL (1872–1932), Dutch novelist and author. He belonged to an Amsterdam Sephardi family and displayed a generally ambivalent attitude toward his Jewish background. In an early novel, *Levensgang* ("Life," 1901), he vividly portrays the diamond workers and merchants of Amsterdam and contrasts virtuous Christians with venal

The Queen of Sheba meeting Solomon. Fresco by Piero della Francesca, 1452–66. Arezzo, Basilica of S. Francesco. Photo Alinari, Florence.

Jews. His autobiographical novel *Zegepraal* ("Triumph," 1904) was less successful. *Aron Laguna* (1916) is a lively recreation of Sephardi life which preserves the everyday speech of Sephardi Jewry of his generation.

His most important work was the cycle of novels published as *De Jordaan* (4 vols., 1912–25), a study of life in an Amsterdam working-class neighborhood. He wrote a number of novels and plays on biblical themes, including the lyrical drama *Saul en David* (1914) and a trilogy entitled *De oude waereld* ("The Old World"), which comprises three novels: *Koningen* ("Kings," 1918), *Zonsopgang* ("Sunrise," 1920), and *Morgenland* ("The Orient," 1921). Another biblical work was the novel *Simson* ("Samson," 2 vols., 1927–29). Toward the end of his life Querido published another novel cycle dealing with the Sephardim. It consisted of two books, *Van armen en rijken* ("Of the Rich and the Poor," 1931) and *Menschenharten* ("Human Hearts," 1932). They reappeared together as *Het volk Gods* ("God's People," 2 vols., 1932). Other works by Querido include *Misleide Majesteit* ("Misled Majesty," 1926), an animal story based on an Indian epic, and volumes of criticism.

His brother, the publisher EMANUEL QUERIDO (1871–1943), wrote a semi-autobiographical novel dealing with the development of Amsterdam during the years 1880–1910. This work, *Het geslacht der Santeljano's* ("The Santeljano Family," 10 vols., 1918–29), contains much important biographical material on his brother. After the Nazi occupation Emanuel Querido was deported and died in the Sobibor death camp.

Bibliography: J. L. Boender, *Israël Querido en het begrip literatuur* (1927); A. M. de Jong, *Israël Querido, De mens en de kunstenaar* (1933). [G.A.-T.]

QUERIDO, JACOB (c. 1650–1690), Shabbatean leader in Salonika. The son of R. Joseph Filosof, he was later generally known as Jacob Querido (Sp. "the beloved"). His sister became *Shabbetai Ẓevi's last wife. When she returned to Salonika after Shabbetai's death in 1676, she allegedly claimed that her brother was the recipient of her late husband's soul. Querido's father and R. Solomon Florentin supported his assertions which led, in 1683, to the mass apostasy of a large group of Salonika families. Together with the earlier converts to Islam among Shabbetai's followers, this group formed the nucleus of the *Doenmeh sect. Taking the Turkish name Abdullah Yacoub, Querido became the most prominent leader of the sectarians. An apocryphal letter attributed to Shabbetai confirmed his claims. His extravagant leadership led to dissension within the group as earlier converts had become dissatisfied with his innovations and therefore opposed his leadership. Insisting on outward demonstration of strict Muslim piety, he undertook a pilgrimage to Mecca in 1688, accompanied at least by one of his leading followers, Mustafa Effendi. Returning from Mecca, he died in Egypt, in either Alexandria or Bulak. When his companion returned, the schism among Querido's followers became final; according to tradition 43 families formed a subsect called Jacobites. As Querido had no male children, his adherents were led by chiefs who maintained a very strong control over the affairs of their group. They treasured several relics of Shabbetai Ẓevi and Querido and administered the personal fortune left by Shabbetai. The members of their subsect were mostly merchants and lower officials. No writings by Querido and his followers have survived, but one of the pamphlets written against him by another apostate between 1690 and 1695 is extant. Querido's followers took no part in the further divisions within the Doenmeh sect that led to yet another schism. Their organization existed down to the 20th century.

Bibliography: Tobias Rofe, *Ma'aseh Toviyyah* (Venice, 1707); A. Struck, in: *Globus*, 81 (1902), 221–2 (Ger.); J. Nehama, in: *Revue des écoles de l'Alliance Israélite* (1902), 308–9; A. Galanté, *Nouveaux documents sur Sabbetai Sevi* (1935), 58–62; G. Scholem, in: *Zion*, 7 (1942), 14–20 (on the apostasy in 1683); idem, in: *Sefunot*, 9 (1965), 195–207. [G.SCH.]

QUETSCH, SOLOMON (1798–1856), Moravian Orthodox rabbi. A native of *Mikulov (Nikolsburg) and pupil of Mordecai *Banet, he officiated as rabbi at Piesling and *Lipnik (1832–54). He was the last representative of the old Orthodoxy and the chief opponent of Samson Raphael *Hirsch as Moravian **Landesrabbiner*. In May 1855 he became rabbi of Mikulov, but the position was not combined with that of *Landesrabbiner*. His death in January 1856 caused the closing of the Mikulov yeshivah.

A few of his novellae were published as *Ḥokhmat Shelomo* together with the Prague edition of Mordecai Banet's *Har ha-Mor* (1862). S. J. Rapoport wrote a commemorative poem on him in *Kokhevei Yiẓḥak* (22 (1856), 3).

Bibliography: A. Schnitzer, *Juedische Kulturbilder* (1904), 38–56. [M.LA.]

°**QUIETUS, LUSIUS** (second century C.E.), Roman general. Quietus, who was of Moorish origin, was commander of the Moorish cavalry in the Roman army as early as the time of Domitian. He especially distinguished himself in the wars during Trajan's reign and was one of his principal commanders in the Parthian campaign. Among his activities in Mesopotamia was the subduing of the Jews there, who were hostile to Rome. Trajan ordered Lusius Quietus to crush them. He conducted the attack craftily, killing many. As a reward for this success he was appointed ruler of Judea in 117 C.E. (Eusebius, *Historia Ecclesiastica,* 4:2). Apparently Quietus also subdued the Jews in Judea who revolted against Rome. Details are lacking of this action, but a reference to them has been preserved in the talmudical accounts of "the war of Quietus." When Hadrian became emperor he removed Quietus from his command of the Moors and from the army, and shortly after he was executed for participating in a conspiracy against the emperor.

Bibliography: Schuerer, Hist., 277f., 292f.; Pauly-Wissowa, 26 (1927), 1874–90, no. 9; Allon, Toledot, 1 (1958[3]), 255ff.; E. M. Smallwood, in: *Historia,* 11 (1962), 500–10; S. Appelbaum, *Yehudim vi-Yvanim be-Kirini ha-Kedumah* (1969), 255–61, 273–4. [U.R.]

QUINCE, name of both a tree, *Cydonia oblonga,* and its fruit. It is not mentioned in the Bible, but in rabbinic literature it is referred to under three names: *ḥavush, parish,* and *aspargal. Ḥavush* (Aram. *ḥavusha*) is mentioned as being given to the sick (Tosef., Ter. 7:13). It is an aromatic fruit and is enumerated together with the *etrog* among the fruits over whose fragrance a blessing should be recited (Ber. 43b). The name *parish* is found in a discussion as to the permissibility, in time of emergency, of substituting some other large and beautiful fruit for the *etrog* in order to fulfill the precept of the *Four Species, and it was decided in the negative (Tosef. Suk. 2:9, 31a–b). According to the Jerusalem Talmud (Kil. 1:3, 27a), it was so called because it is the only fruit reserved *(parush)* for the pot, i.e., it is inedible in its raw state and must be cooked. The same passage notes that its Aramaic name is *aspargal* which is the Arabic name for the quince. The Mishnah lays down that the quince belongs to the same species as the hawthorn *(uzrar).* Apparently the ancients took the latter to be a degenerate quince.

Bibliography: Loew, Flora, 3 (1924), 240ff.; J. Feliks, *Kilei Zera'im ve-Harkavah* (1967), 93–96. [J.F.]

°**QUINTILIUS VARUS** (d. 9 C.E.), Roman consul in 13 B.C.E. and governor of Syria from 6 to 4 B.C.E. Varus first appeared in Judea during the last years of *Herod the Great, and on that occasion he participated in the king's trial of his son Antipater, accused of attempted patricide. After hearing lengthy denunciations of the prince and verification that the poison allegedly prepared for the plot was in fact potent, Varus went into private consultation with Herod, drafted a report to Augustus, and departed for Antioch. Antipater was put into chains, and it was assumed by the populace that Herod in so doing was acting upon the advice of the Syrian governor, although Antipater was eventually executed. With the death of Herod in 4 B.C.E., his primary heir Archelaus was unable to control the serious disturbances that broke out throughout the country. Following a bloody attempt on Passover at quieting the unrest, Archelaus departed for Rome and disturbances reached a new peak with the appearance of Sabinus, finance officer (procurator) of Syria, for the purpose of taking charge of Herod's estate. During the festival of Pentecost the Jews in Jerusalem rose up in open rebellion, which eventually spread to all of Palestine. Sabinus, realizing his inability to cope with the situation, was forced to appeal to Varus for help. The Syrian governor appeared at Acre with the three legions at his disposal, together with auxiliary troops supplied by the citizens of Berytus, and from there proceeded to subdue the whole country. Cities such as Sepphoris and Emmaus were reduced to ruins, and thousands of rebels were crucified. The invasion under Varus was so devastating that Josephus lists it together with the wars of Antiochus Epiphanes, Pompey, and Vespasian (Apion 1:34). The rabbinic chronology *Seder Olam Rabbah* also cites a *pulmus shel Asveiros* taking place 80 years before the war of Vespasian, and since Graetz historians have interpreted this as "the war of Varus." Varus was eventually killed by the Germans at the battle of the forest of Teutoburg.

Bibliography: Jos., Wars, 1:617ff., 2:16ff.; Jos., Ant., 17:89ff., 221ff.; Schuerer, Gesch, 1 (1901[4]), 322, 420f., 3 (1909[4]), 296. [I.G.]

°**QUIRINIUS, P. SULPICIUS,** Roman commander and administrator at the beginning of the first century C.E. Quirinius did not belong to an aristocratic family; his rise to power was due to his own abilities and the support of Augustus and his stepson Tiberius with whom he enjoyed a relationship of unwavering friendship. He achieved his reputation as a result of his military exploits in Africa and Asia Minor. He reached the peak of his public career in the year 6 C.E. when he was appointed governor of Syria. He was responsible for laying the foundations of the organization of the new province of Judea, after *Archelaus, son of Herod, had been dismissed from the post of ethnarch of Judea. Quirinius himself accompanied by Coponius, newly appointed governor of Judea, arrived in order to conduct a general census of property in the new province, and to deal with the possessions of Archelaus (Jos., Ant., 18:1ff.). The census aroused widespread opposition among the Jews, but thanks to the influence of the high priest, *Joezer b. Boethus, it was carried out without serious disturbances. However, extremist circles, headed by *Judah the Galilean and *Zadok the Pharisee, who incited the people to rebellion maintained that the institution of the census symbolized servitude to the Romans. Quirinius also introduced changes into the high priesthood. He dismissed Joezer b. Boethus and replaced him by *Anan b. Seth (Jos. Ant., 18:26), the first high priest of the house of Anan. Scholars dispute the passage in Luke 2:1–2 where the census of Quirinius is mentioned in connection with the birth of Jesus. An inscription discovered in Tibur Tivoli, Italy, has been regarded as referring to Quirinius and as a result an attempt has been made to maintain that Quirinius served twice as governor of Syria, the first time being during Herod's lifetime. But even if the inscription refers to Quirinius, it fails to prove that he served twice as governor of Syria.

Bibliography: T. Mommsen, *Res gestae Divi Augusti* (1865), 115ff.; Schuerer, Hist, 197; R. Syme, *The Roman Revolution* (1939), 399; Roos, in: *Mnemosyne,* 9 (1941), 306–18; H. Dessau, *Inscriptiones Latinae Selectae* 1 (1892), no. 918; D. Magie, *Roman Rule in Asia Minor,* 2 (1950), 1322–23; E. Gabba, *Iscrizioni greche e latine per lo studio della Bibbia,* no. xviii, 52–61.

[M.St.]

°**QUISLING, VIDKUN ABRAHAM LAURITZ** (1887–1945), Norwegian who openly met the conquering Nazis as their collaborator; since he was the first to do so, the British press used his name as the symbol of all collaborators and traitors during World War II. Born in Fyresdal (southern province of Telemark), where his father was a priest, he graduated with distinction from the military academy of Norway and served as an officer in the General Staff (1911–18). His special interest in Russia—and his fluent Russian—brought about his appointment as military attaché to the Soviet Union and a diplomatic post in Helsinski (1919–21). He became assistant to Fridtjof Nansen fighting starvation in the Ukraine in 1922 and after fulfilling humanitarian tasks on behalf of the League of Nations returned to Norway after Nansen's death in 1930. In his politics he veered from the Soviet-oriented left to the fascist right. He was minister of defense in 1931 in the government of the Farmers' Party. In 1930 Quisling founded his own party, Nasjonal Samling (National Union), which never gained popular support. The Nazi leaders took an interest in him while the invasion into Norway was planned, when he was received by Hitler on whom he made a favorable impression. On the day of the invasion he declared himself prime minister but was removed six days later by the German authorities, who installed Josef Terboven as a military police governor. In February 1942 Quisling succeeded in being named prime minister, but although his influence was nil, he committed enough crimes, including the preparations for the deportation of the Jews, to be condemned to death by a Norwegian tribunal in 1945, and was executed on October 24.

[L.Y.]

QUMRAN, region on the northwest shore of the Dead Sea, which has become famous since 1947 as the site of the discovery of the *Dead Sea Scrolls. The name belongs more particularly to Wadi Qumran, a precipitous watercourse which runs down to the sea from the west, and to Khirbet Qumran, a ruin standing less than a mile west of the sea on the marl terrace north of the wadi. Visitors to the region in earlier days, impressed by the fortuitous similarity of names, thought that Khirbet Qumran might be all that was left of Gomorrah. In 1873 C. S. *Clermont-Ganneau inspected the ruin, but was more interested in a cemetery lying between it and the sea. He came to no positive conclusions as a result of his inspection.

Occupation of Khirbet Qumran. In 1949, the possibility was raised of a connection between the discoveries in the first manuscript and Khirbet Qumran. A trial excavation was made on the site, but nothing was found which suggested any connection. In November and December 1951, three rooms were excavated. In the floor of one of them was found a jar of the same type as those in which the scrolls in Cave 1 had been placed, and along with it was a coin bearing a date equivalent to 10 C.E. Systematic campaigns of exploration were mounted in 1953, 1954, 1955, and 1956, in which the Jordan Department of Antiquities, the Palestine Archaeological Museum, and the French Dominican Ecole Biblique collaborated.

It soon became evident that the building complex had formed the headquarters of a fairly large and well-organized community. R. de Vaux, soon after the excavations began, expressed the belief that these were the headquarters of the *Essenes referred to by *Pliny the Elder in his *Natural History* (5:73), partly on the ground that nothing else in that region could correspond to Pliny's description. Pliny says that "below" the Essene headquarters lies *En-Gedi; since he is describing the Jordan Valley and Dead Sea region from north to south he may mean that En-Gedi lies south of the Essene headquarters; En-Gedi in fact lies some 22 miles (34 km.) south of Khirbet Qumran. But the identification of the community or *Yaḥad that occupied Khirbet Qumran cannot be determined on archaeological grounds alone.

The cemetery to the east of Khirbet Qumran proved to contain about 1,200 graves, laid out in parallel rows lying north and south, with the head to the south. The burials were as simple as possible; the bodies were neither placed in coffins nor accompanied by funeral offerings. In an eastern extension of the cemetery, skeletons of four women and one child were found. Skeletons of women and children were also identified in two subsidiary cemeteries lying north and south respectively of Wadi Qumran. Pottery in the earth-filling of the graves indicated that the burials belonged to the same general period as the community occupation of Khirbet Qumran.

The site of Khirbet Qumran had been occupied at various times in antiquity. At a low level were found the remains of walls and pottery of Iron Age II (8th–7th centuries B.C.E.). A potsherd inscribed with Phoenician characters and a royal seal stamped on a jar handle belonged to this period, as did also a deep circular cistern which, centuries later, was incorporated in an elaborate system of aqueducts and reservoirs. This phase of occupation may be correlated with the statement that Uzziah king of Judah (c. 790–740 B.C.E.) "built towers in the wilderness and hewed out many cisterns" (II Chron. 26:10). M. Noth has suggested that at this period the site was known as Ir ha-Melaḥ ("city of salt," Josh. 15:61). At the nearer end of the record there is evidence of brief and sporadic occupation during the Arab period.

Chief interest attaches to the abundant evidence for the occupation of the site in the Greco-Roman period. In this period archaeologists have distinguished the following phases of occupation: Ia. Occupation (c. 130 B.C.E.) by people who cleared the circular cistern, built two rectangular cisterns beside it, constructed a few rooms around these, and installed two pottery kilns in the Iron Age enclosure. Ib. Occupation of a much enlarged area, with two- and three-storey buildings, and an elaborate system of cisterns (incorporating the earlier ones) connected by channels and supplied by an aqueduct from a dam built to store the water which runs down Wadi Qumran in the rainy season. This phase began shortly before 100 B.C.E.; its termination is marked by an extensive fire followed by a severe earthquake (probably that otherwise attested for 31 B.C.E.). II. Occupation of a restored building complex, which in general followed the lines of phase Ib but was reinforced at various points against earthquake damage. This phase came to an end during the war of 66–73 C.E. III. Occupation by a Roman garrison for some 20 years until c. 90 C.E. IV. Occupation by Jewish freedom fighters in the second war against Rome, 132–135 C.E.

Description of Khirbet Qumran. The main building of the complex in phases Ib and II was roughly 37 meters square, of large undressed stones, with a strong tower at the northwest corner. There were several large rooms suitable for assembly rooms or refectories. Adjoining the largest of these rooms (on the south side of the building) was a smaller room containing over 1,000 earthenware vessels—all the varieties necessary for kitchen and refectory use. They may have been manufactured on the spot, since the excavations brought to light the best preserved pottery factory thus far found in ancient Palestine, complete with kilns and levigating pit. A first-storey room in the southwest part of the building was evidently furnished as a writing-room *(scriptorium)*. Flour mills, storage bins, ovens, a laundry, a stable, smelting furnaces, and workshops with metal implements were also uncovered. The occupants apparently aimed at being as self-sufficient as possible. The building complex does not seem to have included sleeping quarters; tents or the neighboring caves may have served the occupants for rest and shelter.

The elaborate series of cisterns, designed to ensure a plentiful water supply, has excited special interest; there has been a tendency to relate these to the prescriptions regarding cleansing in water laid down in the *Manual of Discipline found in the Qumran caves. But it is not certain that the water supply was used for ceremonial purposes; these might have been served more acceptably by the running water of the Jordan or the spring-water of Ein Feshkha. Water reservoirs like those of Khirbet Qumran, with steps leading down into them, are known from other Palestinian sites. It is especially in some of these cisterns that the damage from the earthquake is still most clearly visible. The 14 stone steps of the largest cistern, to the east of the site, show a central crack running down from top to bottom, so that their eastern half has sunk nearly half a meter below the level of the western half. When the site was reoccupied some 30 years after the earthquake, this cistern could not be used as it no longer held water; a new one was excavated southeast of the building. Other major repairs were effected at the same time: the walls were strengthened and the northwestern tower reinforced.

Chronology of Khirbet Qumran. The record of the phases of the occupation of Khirbet Qumran is indicated most clearly by the coins found in the course of excavations on the site. About 650 coins of the Greco-Roman period have come to light. The coin record starts with Antiochus VII of the Seleucid dynasty (139–129 B.C.E.) and his contemporary John Hyrcanus (135–104 B.C.E.) and goes on without a break to Antigonus, the last Hasmonean king (40–37 B.C.E.). Coins of Alexander Yannai (103–76 B.C.E.) are especially frequent. Only five coins from Herod's reign (37–4 B.C.E.) have come to light. The record is resumed with coins of Archelaus (4 B.C.E.–6 C.E.) and continues with those of the procurators and a particularly large number of Herod Agrippa's coins (37–44 C.E.). There are 73 coins from the second year of the war against Rome (67–68 C.E.) and several from the following year, contemporary with these are coins minted in the coastal cities of Caesarea, Dora, and Ashkelon; later are a coin of Agrippa II (86 C.E.), one of Vespasian (69–79 C.E.), three of Trajan (98–117 C.E.), one of the type struck by the liberation leaders during the second revolt. It is doubtful whether a hoard of 563 silver coins hidden in three pots in a floor to the west of the building can be related to the occupation of Khirbet Qumran. The hoard

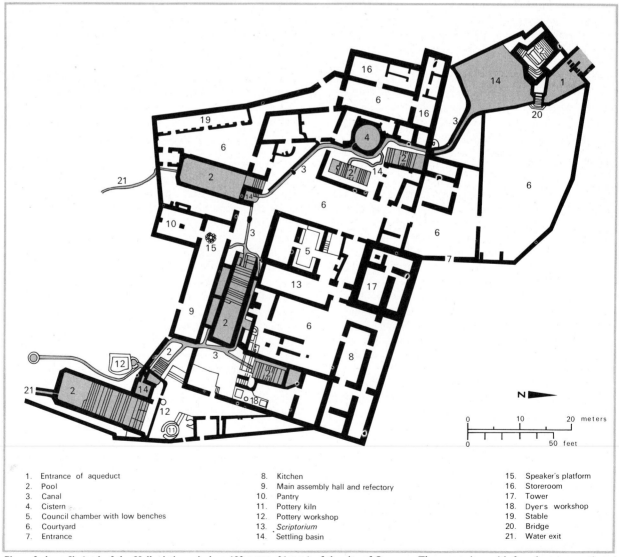

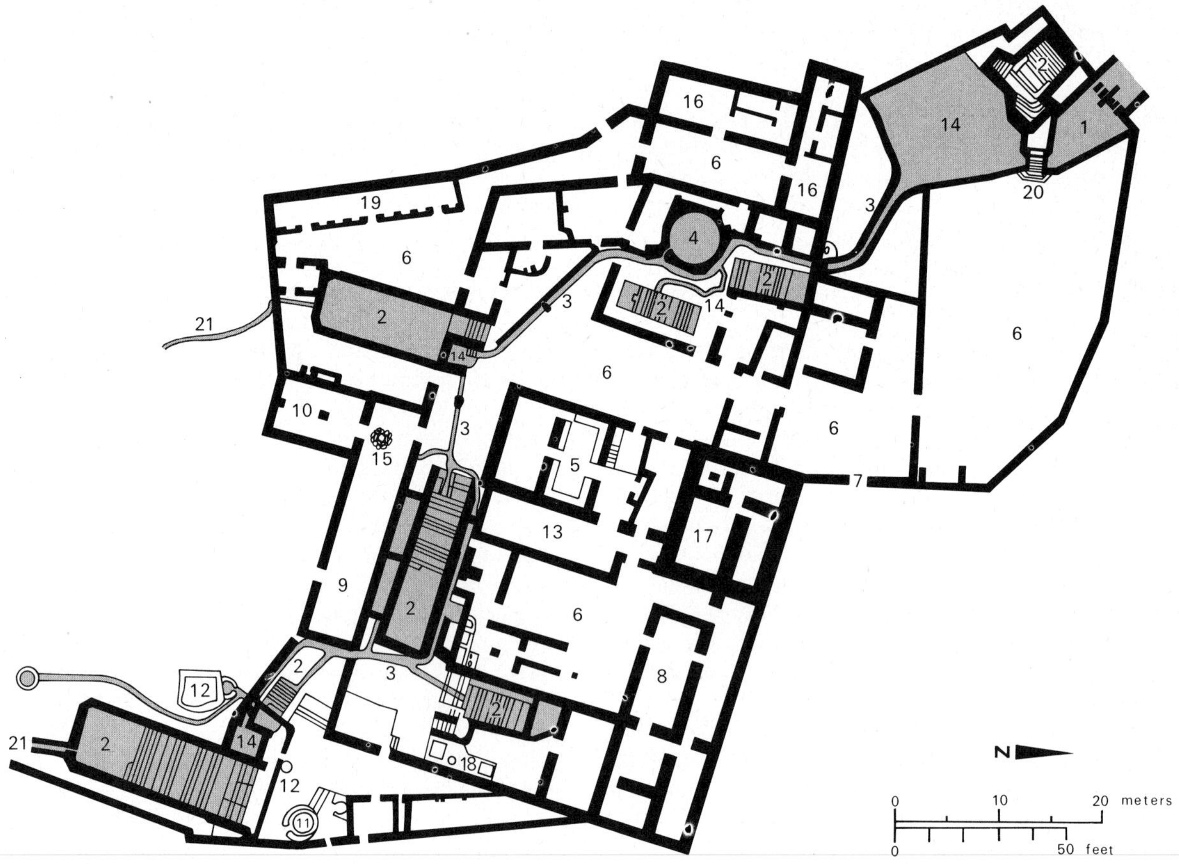

1. Entrance of aqueduct
2. Pool
3. Canal
4. Cistern
5. Council chamber with low benches
6. Courtyard
7. Entrance
8. Kitchen
9. Main assembly hall and refectory
10. Pantry
11. Pottery kiln
12. Pottery workshop
13. *Scriptorium*
14. Settling basin
15. Speaker's platform
16. Storeroom
17. Tower
18. Dyer's workshop
19. Stable
20. Bridge
21. Water exit

Plan of phase Ib (end of the Hellenistic period, c. 103 B.C.E.–31 C.E.) of the site of Qumran. The same plan, with few changes, continued until the last settlement c. 70 C.E.

Eastern view of the excavated settlement of Qumran, showing Wadi Qumran (1), the caves in which the scrolls were found (2), Khirbet Qumran (3), and the community's cemetery (4). Photo Werner Braun, Jerusalem.

was comprised of coins of Antiochus VII and tetradrachms of Tyre, the latest of which was dated 9 B.C.E. These coins may have been hidden there toward the end of the period when the building was unoccupied between Phases Ib and II.

A sample of charcoal from the room where the large number of earthenware vessels was found was subjected to the radiocarbon test, which yielded a date of 16 C.E. (with a margin of deviation of 80 years either way) for the age of the wood, and a date of 66 C.E. (with a similar margin of deviation) for the burning. Phase II of the occupation of Khirbet Qumran was brought to an end not by earthquake but by fire and sword. The destruction was much more thorough than that caused by the earthquake 100 years earlier. The walls were demolished, a layer of black ash covered the site, and a quantity of arrowheads added their silent testimony to the picture. It can hardly be doubted that the building was attacked and stormed by the Romans in the course of the war of 66–73.

A few rooms were built over the ruins and occupied by a Roman garrison which appears to have been stationed there for some 20 years. The brief occupation of the site by an insurgent garrison during the second revolt was followed by the complete destruction of its surviving fortifications.

The chronology of the occupation of Khirbet Qumran, archaeologically established, agrees remarkably well with that of the nearby manuscript caves and their contents, paleographically established. (The paleographical evidence is supplemented by the application of pottery dating to the jars in which the manuscripts of Cave 1 were placed and by the application of the radiocarbon test to some of the linen in which these manuscripts were wrapped before being placed in the jars, although the radiocarbon test involves too large a margin of deviation to be helpful when precise dating within decades is required.) A close connection between the occupants of the building and the manuscripts in the caves is cogently indicated; the community described in the "community documents" and the community which manifestly occupied Khirbet Qumran must have been one and the same community; at least, it would require specially conclusive arguments to make it probable that they were two separate communities. A discussion of the Qumran community is given under *Yaḥad.

Bibliography: Barthélemy-Milik (1955–); R. de Vaux, *L'Archéologie et les manuscrits de la mer morte* (1961); J. van der Ploeg, *The Excavations at Qumran* (1958); J. T. Milik, *Ten Years of Discovery in the Wilderness of Judaea* (1959); Zeuner, in: PEFQS, 92 (1960), 27ff.

[F.F.B.]

QUNAYṬIRA, AL- (**Kuneitra,** Ar. القنيطرة), central town in *Ramat ha-Golan, at the crossroads where the highway connecting the Benot Ya'akov bridge with Damascus intersects roads to Mt. Hermon and Lebanon, to Sheikh Miskīn and the southern Bashan, and to *Ḥammat Gader on the Jarmuk River. The town lies in a shallow valley, approximately 2,950–3,100 ft. (900–950 m.) above sea level. Remains from the Byzantine period were found there, e.g., a granite column and three tombstones with legends in Greek. An archaeological survey in 1968 revealed additional Greek inscriptions, some of which testify to a Jewish population there in the Byzantine period, e.g., the legend "Archelaus ben Hananiah" on a tombstone. Until the mid-19th century al-Qunaytira was only a wayfarers' inn *(khān).* With the settlement of Circassians in Golan the town became a regional center, and by the end of the 19th century had 1,800 inhabitants, almost all Circassian Muslims. Water from a spring was collected in a reservoir dating from the Byzantine period and conducted to ponds at several places in the town, and the houses were built along broad, paved roads. The Circassians regarded al-Qunayṭira as their national center. The economy was based on administrative services, commerce, small workshops, and auxiliary farming. In the 1950s, when the town belonged to Syria, it began to lose its Circassian character as Arab merchants settled there. In the 1960s al-Qunayṭira was made the district town of Golan, when the population approached 15,000 and the economy was increasingly geared to the Syrian military installations. A large headquarters for the "Palestinian Front" was erected at the town's western entrance. The Circassians by then constituted no more than 15–20% of the total population. When al-Qunayṭira was captured by Israel forces on the last day of the *Six-Day War (June 11, 1967), it was found abandoned by almost all its inhabitants. According to the Israel census (1967), there were still 206 people, but they subsequently left. Kibbutz Merom Golan was established at the town's western entrance. Al-Qunayṭira has a place in Theodor *Herzl's prophetic novel *Altneuland.* The town, which he envisioned as accessible by an electric train rising from the shores of Lake Kinneret, became a junction of Transjordanian railways.

Al-Qunaytira, November 1967. Courtesy Government Press Office, Tel Aviv.

[Mo.N.]

QURAYẒA (**Banu Qurayẓa** قريظة), one of the three important Jewish tribes in ancient *Medina. The Qurayẓa were related to the *Naḍīr tribe, both calling themselves *kāhinān,* implying priestly descent. The two branches of the tribe were the Banu Kaʿb and the Banu ʿAmr; they were clients of the Arab tribe of the Aws, with whom they appear in Muhammad's constitution (see *Muhammad). They engaged primarily in agriculture. The Qurayẓa are best known for the tragic massacre of their men and the sale of their women and children into slavery at Muhammad's command, a much more drastic punishment for their rejection of Islam than that suffered by the Naḍīr or the *Qaynuqāʿ. According to Islamic tradition, Muhammad was visited by the angel Gabriel, who warned him against laying down his arms before the Qurayẓa would be annihilated. Other reports mention the (doubtful) existence of a special treaty between Muhammad and the Qurayẓa, which was broken by their chief *Kaʿb ibn Asad in order to join the unsuccessful attack on Medina led by the Arab tribes of Quraysh and Ghaṭafān in 627. In any case, whether sympathetic or hostile to Muhammad, the Qurayẓa were surrounded and defeated within two weeks. Aware of their impending fate, they turned to their allies, the Aws, and surrendered their weapons. Apparently Muhammad let the Aws' chief Saʿd ibn Muʿādh decided the fate of the Qurayẓa. Presented with the choice of conversion to Islam or death, only four chose the former. Approximately 600–750 males were martyred and the women and children were sold as slaves. A young woman, Rayḥāna, was purchased by Muhammad. The defenselessness of the tribe, their betrayal by the Aws' chief who is glorified in Islamic tradition, and their tragic slaughter brought an end to Jewish life in Medina. The massacre of the heroic Qurayẓa, briefly alluded to by Maimonides in *Iggeret Teiman,* was the subject of Saul Tchernichowsky's poem *"Ha-Aḥaron li-Venei Kuraita"* ("The Last of the Banu Qurayẓa").

Bibliography: Baron, Social², 3 (1957), 79; H. Z. Hirschberg, *Yisrael be-Arav* (1946), 145f.; W. M. Watt, in: *Muslim World,* 42 (1952), 160f.; idem, *Muhammad at Medina* (1956), 208f.; S. Tchernichowsky, *Shirim,* 1 (1966), 63–65; M. Ibn Isḥāq, *Life of Muhammad,* tr. by A. Guillaume (1955), index; EIS, 2 pt. 2 (1924), 1127–28.

[Ed.]

Initial letter "R" of *Recordare,* the first word of a prologue to the apocryphal book of Baruch, in a Latin Bible written and illuminated in France, c. 1300. Princeton University Library, Med. and Ren. Mss., Garrett no. 29, vol. II, fol. 79v.

RAAB (Ben-Ezer), JUDAH (1858–1948), pioneer and one of the first Jewish guards in Ereẓ Israel. Born in the village of Szent István in western Hungary into a farming family which had contacts with the Jewish community in Ereẓ Israel, Raab went to Ereẓ Israel with his father in 1876. He joined the group of Jerusalemites who founded Petaḥ Tikvah and plowed the first furrow in its fields in 1878. He was one of the first guards and was responsible for the settlement's security during its early years. When Petaḥ Tikvah was abandoned during the sabbatical year *(shemittah)* of 1882, Raab became an instructor for new settlers in Rishon le-Zion and the Bilu settlers. In 1883, when Petaḥ Tikvah was resettled, he returned and instructed new immigrants ("the Byalistokites") in agricultural techniques. Raab was appointed a foreman by Baron de *Rothschild's officials and struggled to maintain the agricultural character of Petaḥ Tikvah. His memoirs, *Ha-Telem ha-Rishon* (1956) recorded by his son, B. Ben-Ezer, constitute valuable material on the early history of Jewish settlement in Ereẓ Israel. His daughter ESTHER (1899–) was born in Petaḥ Tikvah and joined kibbutz Deganyah in her youth. After her marriage she lived in Egypt for five years and then in Tel Aviv, returning afterward to Petaḥ Tikvah. Her lyric poetry, characterized by its descriptions of the landscape of Ereẓ Israel, is collected in *Kimshonim* (1930). Later poems were published in *Shirei Esther Raab* (1963).

Judah Raab, a founder of Petaḥ Tikvah, and his daughter, Esther Raab, poet.

Bibliography: Y. Yaari and M. Ḥarizman, *Sefer ha-Yovel shel Petaḥ Tikvah* (1929), 126–9, 187–92; Tidhar, 1 (1947), 119–21.

[Y.S.]

RA'ANANNAH (Heb. רַעֲנָנָה), urban community with municipal council status in central Israel, N.E. of Herzliyyah. Ra'anannah was established in 1922 as a village (moshavah) by a group of American Jews who founded Aḥuzzat New York A Inc. (1912). The land was bought through the Palestine Land Development Company. Initially there were many economic difficulties. An attempt was made to raise cattle as the mainstay of the economy. Ra'anannah progressed in the later 1920s and in the 1930s when a rich groundwater table was tapped, the citrus branch introduced, and middle-class immigrants of the Fourth Aliyah and later newcomers were absorbed. With the crisis in the citrus branch during World War II, the settlers changed over to mixed farming and made beginnings in industry. In the 1940s, two housing quarters for Yemenite and other immigrants were built with contributions from Zionists in the United States and South Africa. In 1947, Ra'anannah had 3,800 inhabitants and grew quickly after the War of Independence (1948) when *ma'barot* inhabitants were given permanent housing (1953—9,000 inhabitants; 1968—11,900). Ra'anannah belongs (1970) to the outer ring of the Tel Aviv conurbation and has developed various industries as well as agriculture. [E.O.]

RABB, MAXWELL MILTON (1910–), U.S. attorney, government official, and Jewish community leader. Rabb, who was born in Boston, was admitted to the Massachusetts bar in 1935, and subsequently became an administrative assistant to Senators Henry Cabot Lodge (1937–43) and Sinclair Weeks (1944). After naval service, Rabb became a legal and legislative consultant to Secretary of the Navy James Forrestal in 1946. He later served as associate counsel to President Dwight Eisenhower (1953–54), and was secretary to Eisenhower's cabinet from 1954 to 1958. Rabb was sent as chairman of the U.S. delegation to the tenth session of UNESCO in Paris in 1958, later serving on the executive committee of the United States Committee for UNESCO (1959–60).

Among other posts, Rabb was a director of several corporations and a member of the board of directors of the NAACP Legal Defense and Educational Fund. Active in Jewish community affairs, he was chairman of the government division of the UJA (1953–57), a member of the board of governors of the Hebrew Union College-Jewish Institute of Religion, and vice-chairman of the New York executive committee of the anti-Defamation League, among many other posts. Rabb was a member of the New York law firm of Stroock, Stroock and Lavan from 1958. [Ed.]

RABBA, MENAHEM (16th century), preacher in Padua. Rabba wrote *Beit Mo'ed* (Venice, 1605), a homiletic work containing sermons for every religious occasion during the year. A large number of his sermons deal with the concept of repentance *(teshuvah)* to which he ascribes a metaphysical dimension. Although the work exhibits certain philosophic influences, no specific philosophic thought is dominant. The book was published posthumously by Rabba's son, Elijah, who in the introduction lists other works of his father similar in style to *Beit Mo'ed: Ot ha-Berit, Ḥavvat Rabba, Netivot Olam, Kelil Tekhelet, Ma'aneh Rakh,* and *Kiryat Arba,* none of which was published. [Ed.]

RABBA BEN MATNAH (late fourth–early fifth century), Babylonian *amora.* He was a pupil of *Rabbah and *Sheshet and a colleague of *Abbaye b. Avin and *Ḥanina (Pes. 34a). On the death of R. Joseph he was a candidate, together with Abbaye, Rava, and Zera II, for the post of head of the Pumbedita academy. They decided on a contest to see which of them could make a statement that the others could not refute. Abbaye succeeded and was appointed. The rabbis, in discussing the relative merits of the intellectual characteristics of Zera and Rabba, described the former as "keen-witted, but indecisive," whereas Rabba was "slow, but able to arrive at conclusions" in deciding a law (Hor. ad fin). Strangely enough, though he was clearly a very great scholar, none of his teaching has survived. However if he is to be identified with R. Abba II much of his wisdom has been recorded under the latter name.

Bibliography: Halevy, Dorot, 2 (1923), 460–1; Hyman, Toledot, s.v. [Ed.]

RABBAH (Ha-Rabbah; Heb. הָרַבָּה, רַבָּה). (1) An abbreviation for Rabbath-Ammon (see *Rabbath-Ammon). (2) A town in Judah mentioned with Kiriath-Jearim as part of the inheritance of the tribe of Judah in the hill country (Joshua 15:60). It is probably identical with a city called *Rbt* near Gezer in Thutmosis III's list of Canaanite cities (no. 105). it may also be mentioned in a cuneiform letter found at Taanach. According to two el-Amarna letters (289, 290) sent by the king of Jerusalem to the pharaoh, Milkilu the king of Gezer together with Shuwardata captured Rubutu with the aid of mercenaries. The name appears for the last time in Shishak's list of conquered towns, after Gezer and before Aijalon. Some scholars, following the Septuagint, identify Rabbah with Soba (Ar. Ṣūbā) near Jerusalem, but the recently discovered site of Khirbat Bīr (Bi'r) al-Ḥilū fits the descriptions in the ancient sources remarkably well. (3) An abbreviation for the city of Rabbath-Moab, now Khirbat al-Rabba, 14 mi. (c. 22 km.) south of the River Arnon. Alexander Yannai conquered it with other cities in Moab; after his death it was restored to the Nabateans by Hyrcanus II (Jos., Ant., 14:18). It is called Rabbathmoba by Ptolemy (5:16, 4) and appears thus on the coins of his time. Rabbah appears as a district capital in one of the Babatha letters found in the Naḥal Hever in 1961. Eusebius refers to it as Areopolis, the town of the war god Ares (Onom. 124:15 ff.). In the fourth century it was identified with the Ar of Moab of Numbers 21:28; recently, the remains of a Canaanite-Moabite city (Early and Late Bronze ages) were found at al-Mishna in the vicinity of Khirbat al-Rabba. In late Roman times, Rabbah was a post of the Equites Mauri Illyriciani (*Notitia Dignitatum* 80:5); remains of a temple, walls, and a citadel have been noticed here. A sumptuous Jewish synagogue was destroyed there in the fifth century by the fanatical monk Bar-Sauma. After the Arab conquest, Rabbah, sometimes called Moab by Arab geographers, continued in existence. It is mentioned in 1321 as a village in the district of Karak and as a station on the Damascus-al-Karak road.

Bibliography: Glueck, in: AASOR, 14 (1934), 62; Press, Ereẓ, s.v.; Abel, Geog, 2 (1938), 23–5; Aharoni, Land, index; idem, in: VT (1969). [M.A.-Y.]

RABBAH (Mar-Rava), *gaon* of Pumbedita from 651, contemporary of *Huna, *gaon* of Sura. Rabbah and Huna were jointly responsible for one of the earliest and most important of post-talmudic *takkanot,* the *takkanah* of the *Moredet* ("the obstreperous wife"). According to the Talmud, a Jewish wife could demand a divorce only in certain exceptional cases specified in talmudic law (as for instance when her husband was stricken with a repulsive disease). The new *takkanah* extended the reasons and made it possible for some women to obtain dissolution of their marriages by the local courts obliging the husband to issue a divorce, without her forfeiting the amount of her *ketubbah* or suffering any loss of property which she had brought into the marriage. Moreover, the period of waiting was reduced from the usual 12 months to as short as one to four weeks.

Bibliography: Baron, Social[2], 6 (1958), 132f.; Ḥ. Tykocinski, *Takkanot ha-Ge'onim* (1960), 11–29. [M.H.]

RABBAH BAR BAR ḤANA (second half of the third century), *amora.* As his father's name was also Rabbah, it is thought his patronymic referred to his grandfather (see *Rabbah bar Ḥana). Born in Babylonia, he went to Ereẓ Israel to study in the academy of R. Johanan, and many years after returned to his native land, where he disseminated the teachings of Johanan, transmitting in his name close to 200 *halakhot* in all spheres. The heads of the Babylonian academies, such as R. Judah of Pumbedita and his distinguished disciples, Rabbah, and R. Joseph, transmitted in his name *halakhot* they had learned from him. He suffered from the persecutions of the Sassanids who even broke into his house, and he complained: "Merciful One! Either in Thy shadow or in the shadow of Esau [= Rome]" (Git. 17a). It is possible that in consequence of these sufferings he decided to return to Ereẓ Israel (Pes. 51a), but there is no evidence that he did so.

Rabbah achieved great renown for his remarkable legends (known as the "*aggadot* of Rabbah bar Bar Ḥana" and chiefly found in the tractate *Bava Batra* (73a–74a). These tales purport to relate what he saw and heard during his many journeys by sea and land. They are marked by hyperbole, and excited the wonder of contemporary scholars. Some of them spoke out sharply against him: "Every Abba is an ass and every bar Bar Ḥana is a fool" (BB 74a). Rabbah ascribes some of his stories to sailors and Arabs, but begins most of them with the words, "I myself saw." The following is a typical one: "We were once traveling in a desert and an Arab joined us . . . He said to me: 'Come and I will show you where the men of Korah were swallowed up' (cf. Num. 16:23ff). I saw two cracks that emitted smoke. I took a piece of clipped wool, dipped it in water, attached it to the point of a spear, and inserted it there, and when I took it out it was singed. He said to me: 'Listen carefully! What do you hear?' I heard them crying out: 'Moses and his Torah are true and we are liars!' The Arab said to me 'Every 30 days Gehenna returns them here as meat turns on a spit,' and they cry out: 'Moses and his Torah are true and we are liars'" (BB 74a).

The expositors of the Talmud, aware of the strangeness of these stories, sought to rationalize them. Yom Tov b. Abraham *Ishbili stated: "The stories in this chapter deal with subjects that are strange to people because they are unfamiliar with them, but they are very plausible to those with a knowledge of nature, such as the size of sea monsters and the size of waves in a storm. They also contain allusions to matters which were not seen with the eye but in a vision. For when the sages went on ocean voyages they saw there God's wonders . . . and during their sleep they experienced remarkable visions in the context of their meditations. The *geonim* wrote that wherever the words 'I myself saw' occur, it was in a dream while on a voyage." Some regard these tales and *aggadot* as ethical and national allegories, while others see them as intimations and cryptic sayings (see Maharsha (Samuel Eliezer b. Judah *Edels), ad loc.).

Bibliography: Hyman, Toledot, 1076–78; Bacher, Bab Amor, 87–93; idem, *Ergaenzungen und Berichtigungen* . . . (1913), 10; Bacher, Trad, 699, s.v. [A.AR.]

RABBAH BAR ḤANA (TJ, **Abba bar Ḥana,** e.g., in BM 5:5; early third century), Babylonian *amora.* In Babylon Rabbah studied under his uncle, Ḥiyya (MK 16b), whom he subsequently accompanied to Ereẓ Israel (MK 21a). Before they left to return to Babylon, Ḥiyya asked the *nasi* to give Rabbah permission to decide matters of ritual law, monetary cases, and defects in a firstborn animal which could render its slaughter permissible. Although such permission was rarely granted, the *nasi* acceded to the request (Sanh. 5a). Rabbah's closest colleague was Rav (TJ, BM 5:7, 10c), in whose company he is found both in Ereẓ Israel and in Babylon (MK 21a; Ḥul. 44b), with whom he held halakhic discussions (Ḥul. 8b), and in whose name he transmitted teachings (Shab. 50a; Nid. 47a). It is related that when Rabbah was once in mourning and thought that he ought not to give his regular lecture, Rav said, "We have learned, 'if the public have need of him, he does not refrain'" (MK 21a). Little is known of Rabbah's personal life, other than that he traded in wine (BM 83a, see Dik. Sof. *ibid.*) and that his wife died before him (BB 52a). His only known pupil was Hananel (MK 19a). Rabbah b. Ḥana is frequently confused with *Rabbah b. Bar Ḥana who, some believe, was his son. They can be distinguished only by context and chronology.

Bibliography: Hyman, Toledot. [ED.]

RABBAH BAR HUNA (in TJ, **Abba bar Huna** or **Bar bar Huna;** d. 322 C.E.), Babylonian *amora.* Rabba was a disciple of both Samuel (Er. 49a), and Rav (BB 136b), in whose names he transmitted sayings and decisions (Ber. 25a; Shab. 97a). His main teacher, however, was his father, Huna (Me'il. 15b), the head of the academy at Sura (cf. Git. 35a). His father urged him to attend Ḥisda's lectures diligently. Initially, however, Rabbah found some of the matters discussed (such as personal hygiene) alien to his earnest nature (Shab. 82a). Only in later life did he develop a close association with Ḥisda, and served with him as a judge (Shab. 10a). Indeed, his eventual respect for Ḥisda was such that he accepted his advice not to introduce the Decalogue in the statutory daily prayers (Ber. 12a; see Dik. Sof. thereto). He publicly acknowledged Ḥisda's correction of another of his decisions, instructing his *amora* to deliver a discourse on the theme that "no one can fully understand the words of the Torah until he has been mistaken in their interpretation" (Git. 43a). The two are also known to have studied *aggadah* together (Pes. 110a; 117a; Sot. 39a).

After Ḥisda's death Rabbah was appointed head of the academy of Sura (*Iggeret Sherira Gaon,* p. 82). Rabbah was particularly friendly with the exilarch, frequenting his home (Shab. 157b, Suk. 10b, etc.), and the exilarch used to address halakhic queries to him (Shab. 115b). Nevertheless, Rabbah insisted on his complete independence of him, and in a dispute with the members of the exilarch's household, he emphasized that he had received authority to act as judge from his father and not from the exilarch, and was therefore not bound by their views (Sanh. 5a). Rabbah was distinguished by his piety (Shab. 31a–b), and by his modesty which his colleague Rava once prayed that he might emulate (MK 28a). Among his maxims and sayings are many which stress this virtue: "An insolent person is considered a transgressor" (Ta'an. 7b). He also taught that he who possesses knowledge of the Torah but is without the fear of God is like a steward who, although in possession of the inner keys of the treasure house, is unable to gain access to it, because he does not possess the outer keys (Shab. 31a–b). He also said: "When a man loses his temper, even the Divine Presence is unimportant in his eyes" (Ned. 22b). Rabbah died in Babylon, but his remains were taken to Ereẓ Israel, where funeral orations were delivered for him (MK 25b).

Bibliography: Bacher, Bab Amor, 62f.; Hyman, Toledot, 1071–74. [ED.]

RABBAH BAR NAḤAMANI (c. 270–330; d. 321/22 according to *Iggeret R. Sherira Ga'on,* ed. by B. M. Lewin (1921), 87; according to Hyman c. 260–340), Babylonian *amora.* Rabbah was the scion of a priestly family, which traced its lineage to the high priest Eli (RH 18a). He studied under *Huna at Sura, and under *Judah b. Ezekiel at Pumbedita (Er. 17a). To such an extent did Huna respect him that he seldom decided a question of importance without consulting him (Git. 27a; BM 18b; BB 172b, et al.). On one occasion his contemporaries in Ereẓ Israel suggested that he join them and study under *Johanan, maintaining that he would learn more with a guide than by studying by himself (Ket. 111a). From *Nedarim* 59a, it would appear that he took their advice, although Bacher maintains that he never left Babylonia. He certainly spent most of his life in Babylonia, where his most constant colleague was Joseph (BB 114a). Rabbah's main interest was in the *halakhah,* and he was renowned for his interpretation of the Mishnah and for his elucidation and clarification of the apparent contradictions contained in various texts. He was particularly versed in the regulations concerning ritual purity, in which he was regarded as an authority (BM 86a). Whereas Joseph's encyclopedic knowledge of traditions earned him the title "Sinai," Rabbah was known as *oker harim* ("uprooter of mountains"), for his exceptionally skillful dialectic ability (Ber. 64a.). Only ten aggadic sayings are quoted in his name ((e.g., Shab. 64a; Pes. 68b; Meg. 15b; et al.), and there is no foundation for the statement of Abraham ibn Daud in the *Sefer ha-Kabbalah* that he was the author of such aggadic compilations as *Genesis Rabbah.*

Judah's death left the post of the head of the academy of Pumbedita vacant. Joseph declined the office, whereupon Rabbah was elected. He held the post for 22 years, until his death (Ber. 64a; *Iggeret R. Sherira Ga'on,* 85–86), and under his leadership the academy achieved its greatest renown. The number of regular students rose to 400 (Ket. 106a), and during the **kallah* months of Adar and Elul, the audiences numbered 12,000 (BM 86a). Rabbah's own contribution as a teacher was significant. He used to put his audience in a receptive mood by beginning his lectures with witty aphorisms and interesting anecdotes (Shab. 30b), and he would frequently invite comment on paradoxical *halakhot* and deliberately captious decisions (Ber. 33b). However, although highly esteemed by scholars, he was intensely disliked by the members of the Pumbedita community, whose behavior he frequently and severely denounced (Shab. 153a and Rashi *ibid.*).

Little is known of his private life other than that he was poor. The Talmud explicitly contrasts his poverty with Ḥisda's comfortable economic position (MK 28a). Rabbah died in tragic circumstances. Charged with aiding his large audiences to avoid paying poll tax during the *kallah* months, Rabbah was forced to flee the bailiffs who had been sent to seize him. He wandered about in the vicinity of Pumbedita, and it was there, in a thicket, that his body was ultimately found (BM 86a; *Iggeret R. Sherira Ga'on*, 78–87). According to the *aggadah*, it was on that day that the Heavenly Academy was debating whether, if the bright spot appeared after the white hair (cf. Lev. 13:1–3), the leper was clean or unclean. The Almighty maintained that he was clean, the Heavenly Academy that he was unclean. Rabbah was asked for his opinion, and, as he called out "Clean, clean," he expired. At that moment, a heavenly voice was heard to declare, "Happy art thou, O Rabbah b. Naḥamani, whose body is pure, and whose soul has departed in purity" (BM 86a). According to *Rosh Ha-Shanah* 18a (MK 28a) he was only 40 years old at his death. However, this figure is unacceptable on chronological grounds and has generally been emended to 60. He was survived by a son also called Rabbah (Shab. 123a). *Abbaye, who grew up in his house (Ber. 48a), was his nephew and pupil.

Bibliography: Halevy, Dorot, 2 (1923), 435–40; Hyman, Toledot.

[Ed.]

RABBAH BEN AVUHA, Babylonian *amora* of the second half of the third century C.E. Rabbah's first teacher was Rav, in whose name he transmitted many sayings (Shab. 129b; Er. 85a). After the latter's death, he continued his studies at Samuel's academy at Nehardea. When Nehardea was destroyed in 259 by the Palmyrenes, he moved to Maḥoza, where he was appointed a judge (Yev. 115b) and head of the academy (Shab. 59b). According to Sherira Gaon he was of the family of the exilarch, and Sherira himself claimed to be a descendant of his (*Iggeret R. Sherira Ga'on*, ed. by B. M. Lewin (1921), 82). The Talmud (Ber. 21a; BM 91b), records halakhic decisions in his name. He, however, stated that his knowledge extended only to four orders of the Mishnah (according to Rashi, *Mo'ed, Nashim, Nezikin,* and *Kodashim;* not *Zera'im* and *Tohorot;* but according to *tosafot*, the reference is to those four orders in the Tosefta; BM 114b). A legendary account is given of the manner in which Rabbah was miraculously relieved of his poverty. He was privileged to meet the prophet Elijah, and to discuss *halakhah* with him. Elijah gave him some leaves from paradise which, although discarded by Rabbah (in order not to consume his portion in the world to come), left such a pleasant fragrance on his robe, that he sold it for 12,000 denarii (BM 114a–b).

He had a son named R. Kamma (Er. 3a); however his main pupil and (probably) his son-in-law was R. Naḥman (b. Jacob), who transmits many of his sayings (Yev. 80b). Among his teachings were that the commandment to love one's neighbor as oneself (Lev. 19:18) applies even in the execution of a criminal, and is fulfilled by granting him as easy a death as possible (Ket. 37b).

Bibliography: Hyman, Toledot, 1070–71. [Ed.]

RABBAH BEN SHILAH (fl. late third early fourth century C.E.), Babylonian *amora*. His teacher was Ḥisda (Shab. 81a). Because of his aversion to bribery, Rabbah declared a judge unfit to try a case involving neighbors from whom he had borrowed anything (Ket. 105b). He was quick to defend others. According to an *aggadah*, Elijah appeared to Rabbah on one occasion, and told him that God mentions *halakhot* in the name of the sages but not in that of R. Meir, because he had been taught by *Elisha b. Avuyah who had denied the existence of God. Rabbah said to Elijah: "Meir found a pomegranate, ate the fruit, and threw away the peel," i.e., he had extracted only what was good from Elisha's teachings, whereupon Elijah replied that henceforward God would mention Meir's name (Ḥag. 15b).

Bibliography: Hyman, Toledot, 1083–84; Bacher, Bab Amor, 140–1.

[M.Be.]

RABBAH TOSFA'AH (middle of the fifth century), Babylonian *amora*. He was a pupil of *Ravina (I) (Suk. 32a; BK 119a), and a colleague of the latter's nephew, *Ravina (II) (Yev. 75b; MK 4a). He succeeded Mar Bar Rav Ashi as head of the Sura Academy, a position he held for six years until his death in 474 (Ibn Daud, *Book of Tradition*, 36). Although among the last of the *amoraim*, he still gave original rulings. He declared a child legitimate although born to a woman whose husband had gone overseas 12 months before the birth, assuming that a pregnancy may extend as long as that period (Yev. 80b; for another example see Ber. 50a). His main work was in putting the finishing touches to the compilation of the Talmud begun by Rav Ashi. Through additions of brief, explanatory remarks, he clarified talmudic themes and decided between the conflicting opinions of earlier *amoraim*. His name, Tosfa'ah ("the amplifier") was attributed to this activity (Halevy, Dorot, 3 (1923), 19; but see Ḥ. Albeck, in: *Sinai, Sefer Yovel* (1958), 72). He is mentioned by name in the Talmud only in nine places.

Bibliography: Hyman, Toledot, 1086f.; Ḥ. Albeck, *Mavo la-Talmudim* (1969), 448.

[A.Ro.]

RABBANITES, name and definition current from approximately the tenth century applied to Jews accepting the Oral Law *(Torah she-be-al peh)* as binding and normative in the same degree as Scripture *(Torah she-bi-khetav)*. As with many party definitions the term is used with pride by the Rabbanites themselves and with derision and contempt by their opponents the *Karaites. [Ed.]

RABBATH-AMMON (**Rabbah;** Heb. רַבָּה, רַבַּת בְּנֵי עַמּוֹן), the capital of the Ammonites, present-day Amman, capital of the Hashemite kingdom of *Jordan. The earliest settlement, dating from the Chalcolithic period until the end of the early Bronze Age (c. 2200 B.C.E.), was centered around a sacred rock on the acropolis. After a gap, occupation was resumed with the establishment of the Ammonite kingdom. Its strong fortifications prevented its capture by the Israelites (Josh. 13:25). The bedstead of the giant *Og, king of Bashan, in Rabbath-Ammon is mentioned in the Bible (Deut. 3:11). In the time of David, Joab captured the "royal city" and the "city of waters" (probably the acropolis and the water installations in the valley below), but he postponed conquest of the entire city till David's arrival (II Sam. 11–12; cf. I Chron. 20:1). Shobi, the son of Nahash (an Ammonite king) of Rabbath-Ammon, succored David when he fled before Absalom (II Sam. 17:27–29). Soon after David's death, however, the city again became the capital of an independent kingdom, and it is denounced as such by the prophets Amos (1:14), Jeremiah (49:2–3), and Ezekiel (21:25; 25:5). Remains of tombs and temples containing figurines and seals inscribed in Ammonite have been found there. The main temple was erected over the "sacred" rock on the acropolis.

In the Hellenistic period, Rabbath-Ammon was again a flourishing city and was known as Philadelphia in honor of Ptolemy II and his wife Arsinoe. It was besieged and taken by Antiochus III in 218 B.C.E. by a stratagem similar to that used earlier by *Joab (see I Chron. 19:10ff.). The city successfully resisted Alexander Yannai under its ruler Zeno Cotylas. It became a city of the *Decapolis in Roman times and later developed into a great and prosperous center of the caravan trade in Provincia Arabia. It was captured by the Arabs in 635 and became the capital of the Belqa' district. A Jewish community existed there in the 11th–12th centuries, as is known from the Scroll of *Abiathar. In the time of the Crusaders, Rabbath-Ammon, then known as Ahamant, was temporarily in the possession of the prince of Transjordan. It was subsequently abandoned until resettled by Circassians in 1878. In 1921 it became the capital of the emirate of Transjordan and later the kingdom of Jordan. An Italian expedition excavated there in 1927–37. Its 1970 population, greatly increased by refugees, numbered approximately 200,000.

Bibliography: H. C. Butler, *Architecture* (1909), 34ff.; Avi-Yonah, Geog, index; L. Harding, in: QDAP, 11 (1945), 67ff.; 14 (1950), 44ff.; idem, in: ADAJ, 3 (1956), 80; Maayah, *ibid.*, 4–5 (1960), 114–5; Ward, *ibid.*, 8–9 (1964), 47ff. [M.A.-Y.]

RABBI, RABBINATE. The title rabbi is derived from the noun *rav*, which in biblical Hebrew means "great" and does not occur in the Bible; in its later sense in mishnaic Hebrew, however, the word *rav* means a master as opposed to a slave (e.g., "does a slave rebel against his *rav*"—Ber. 10a; "It is like a slave who filled a cup for his *rav* and he poured the water over his face"—Suk. 2:9). It was only during the tannaitic period, in the generation after Hillel, that it was employed as a title for the sages. The passage in the New Testament (Matt. 23:7) in which the Scribes and Pharisees are criticized because they "love . . . to be called of men, Rabbi, Rabbi" probably reflects the fact of its recent introduction. The word "rabbi" therefore means literally "my master," although the Sephardim point it and pronounce it *ribbi*, the suffix therefore not being a pronominal one. In any case it lost its significance, and rabbi became simply the title accorded to a sage. Since the title was accorded only to those who had been properly ordained, and such ordination was not granted in talmudic times outside Ereẓ Israel (see **Semikhah*), it was not borne by the Babylonian sages (the **amoraim*) who adopted, or were granted, the alternative title of *rav*. In the Talmud, therefore, the title rabbi refers either to a *tanna* or to a Palestinian *amora*, while *rav* refers to a Babylonian *amora*. The rabbi of the Talmud was therefore completely different from the present-day holder of the title. The talmudic rabbi was an interpreter and expounder of the Bible and the Oral Law, and almost invariably had an occupation whence he derived his livelihood. It was only in the Middle Ages that the rabbi became—in addition to, or instead of, the interpreter and decisor of the law—the teacher, preacher, and spiritual head of the Jewish congregation or community, and it is with this meaning of the word that this article deals. For the talmudic rabbi see *Sages. In modern usage the word "rabbi" in Hebrew has sometimes become the equivalent of "mister." Thus every Jew called up to the reading of the Torah is invited to do so as "Rabbi So-and-So the son of Rabbi So-and-So," and for the rabbi as spiritual head the title *ha-rav* is employed. [L.I.R.]

Middle Ages. In medieval times, the title *ha-rav* denoted great scholarly standing and social reputation unconnected with the hierarchical structure of the *yeshivot* and *geonim*. In this sense it appears, for example, in various letters of the 10th–12th centuries, and in the Chronicle of *Ahimaaz is used to describe the mysterious Aaron, while the chronicler Abraham *ibn Daud employs these terms and their derivatives to define the generations of scholars—*rabbanim*—after the death of *Hai Gaon. Relatively early in these centuries, the term *rabbanim* (now translated into English as *Rabbanites) came to designate the mainstream of Orthodoxy in Judaism, which based itself on the authority of the Talmud and the *geonim*, as against the minority of the *Karaites. Centralistic tendencies in the leadership of the gaonate and *exilarchs are revealed in the tendency for one of these institutions to appoint from above the scholar who led the local community and in the main carried out the functions of judge *(dayyan)*, bringing with him as his letter of appointment a "writ of judgeship" *(pitka de-dayyanuta)*. What is known of their actual functioning, however, shows both that such appointees were in reality much more than judges only and that in fact local opinion had a say in their appointment. By the end of the 10th and beginning of the 11th century there were more and more cases of open local election by the community of a spiritual and moral leader.

Through their social functions rabbi and rabbinate carried over into the Middle Ages a medley of concepts and attitudes, the active elements being scholarship, judgeship, social-spiritual leadership, and example. A certain measure of religious authority attached to the concept of rabbi and to his person, deriving from the authority invested in the geonic academies and the outlook of their scholars, and also from the distant memories of the supreme authority of the mishnaic rabbi ordained by **semikhah*—the ordination of ancient times. These titles and designations never carried with them priestly or semi-priestly authority or functions. Prayer and leading in prayer, blessing of the people, and officiating in marriage and burial ceremonies never became an integral part of the conception of rabbinical office until the beginning of the 19th century, with the *Reform movement. Some rabbis led in prayer and blessed the people, but until modern times this was no more than a matter of personal inclination. The supervision of marriage, and even more so of divorce proceedings, became an integral part of the rabbinic office, both because the payment for performing such functions became part of the stipend of the local rabbi, and because legal acumen was required, especially in the case of divorce. It would seem that from its earliest days *preaching to the people was an integral part of the rabbinic function, the rabbi being both the authoritative scholarly expositor of law and morals, and the moral and spiritual leader of the people. At certain times and in certain regions scholarly exposition was regarded as the main part of preaching, while in others moral exhortation was seen as its main burden; both elements were always present in rabbinical preaching, though in varying proportions.

The weakening of centralistic institutions, as well as the continuing growth of Jewish communities in countries which had never known such leadership, increasingly augmented the importance of the local rabbi. Although the activities of many rabbis are known, in most cases neither income nor status are clearly apparent. Over the years the ideal has developed of the scholarly charisma of the rabbi asserting itself without recourse to official definitions. Ideally all rabbis are equal as officeholders; the only hierarchy ideally obtaining between them is that of personal intellectual and moral preeminence.

The office of rabbi was originally an honorary one on the principle that the Torah had to be taught free of charge. It was not until the 14th century that there is the first clear evidence of a rabbi receiving emoluments. When Simeon b. Ẓemaḥ *Duran fled from the anti-Jewish riots in Spain in 1391 and arrived in Algiers the local community wished to appoint him as rabbi. He pleaded inability to accept as he was penniless and had to earn a livelihood. In order to enable him to accept the position, a formula was worked out whereby instead of a salary for his services he was to receive *sekhar battalah,* i.e., compensation for loss of time due to his preoccupation with his rabbinic office. This remained the legal basis in Jewish law for a rabbi receiving a salary, even though in the modern period the rabbi's salary is generally regarded as in the category of a professional wage with contracts written between rabbis and their congregations.

In outward recognition of such preeminence, the various communities applied to a particular local rabbi for his personal *responsa on different legal and theoretical matters. He would thus be given, de facto and personally, the authority vested in the *geonim* ex officio.

In both Ashkenazi and Sephardi centers rulers became aware relatively early of this new development in Jewish society. In the story of the *Four Captives, Abraham ibn Daud describes the satisfaction of a local ruler in late tenth-century Muslim Spain, at having a scholarly Jewish authority in his country, independent of the *geonim* in Baghdad. The office of the *rab de la corte* in Castille and **Arraby moor* in Portugal, as well as appointments known from the 13th century of a Jewish *Hochmeister* for some regions of the German Empire (see, e.g., *Meir Baruch of Rothenburg), and also similar appointments in France—all are related phenomena. They are manifestations both of the gradual institutionalization of the office of rabbi, and of the attempts by rulers and community leaders to structure a formal and fixed hierarchy out of fluid relationships based on scholarly and personal charisma. The responsa of the Sephardi *Isaac b. Sheshet Perfet disclose a conflict surrounding the appointment to the office of rabbi of France in the 14th century, while other contemporary writings reveal the views of the Ashkenazi scholar Meir ha-Levi of Vienna on the nature of the rabbinate. All demand proven and attested knowledge, as well as integrity and excellence in character and conduct; and on these grounds candidates are approved and disqualified. The Ashkenazi scholar reveals a conception of a well-defined written diploma attesting to the knowledge and qualifications for a rabbi—the so-called *semikhah* diploma. For about a century—mainly in the 15th—Ashkenazi rabbis were titled *manhig* ("leader"), which shows their centrality in community life at that time. Sephardi society had its own ways of attesting these qualifications, without instituting such a diploma (see below). When Sephardim and Ashkenazim came in close contact after the expulsion from the Iberian Peninsula (1492–97), the institution of this diploma became a bone of contention, as is evidenced in the writings of Isaac *Abrabanel. Ironically enough, the abortive attempt to resurrect the *semikhah,* made in 1538 by Jacob *Berab and enthusiastically accepted by Joseph *Caro, served to strengthen the Ashkenazi type of *semikhah* diploma and the medieval line of development of the office of rabbi, and also gave impetus to the development of the Shulḥan Arukh, the combined work of Joseph Caro and the Ashkenazi-Polish Moses *Isserles (who was himself a royal appointee to the central rabbinate in Poland).

From the 14th century onward there emerged the concept of one rabbi for one locality—the *mara de-atra* ("the master of the locality"). Other scholars in his community were to submit to his authority, ex officio, a concept that took a long time to establish. In Poland-Lithuania of the 16th–17th centuries rabbinical office was linked to being a *rosh yeshivah,* thereby deriving much of its authority and prestige. In its main outline, though with various changes in details, this conception of the rabbi and his office remains to the present day that which in fact dominates the society and communities of *Mitnaggedim* wherever they are found, the religious establishment in the State of Israel, and communities of Hungarian and German Orthodoxy and Neo-Orthodoxy. In these circles the office and conception of the rabbi are those which have emerged from the Middle Ages: he is seen as scholar and teacher, judge and spiritual leader. His livelihood comes either from a fixed salary or from payments for functions performed, or from a combination of both. His rights and duties are often defined in a *ketav rabbanut* (letter of appointment to and acceptance of the rabbinic office, sometimes written as two separate documents), a custom deriving from the late Middle Ages. In the frame of this traditional rabbinate there have appeared in modern times centralistic trends, manifested, e.g., in the British office of *chief rabbi for the U.K. and the dominions and the Chief Rabbinate in Ereẓ Israel. On the other hand, in the huge concentrations of Jewish population in modern cities, in the U.S. in particular, the concept of the *mara de-atra* is on the point of vanishing and the rabbi there is mainly the rabbi of a synagogue congregation. In regions and communities where *Ḥasidism prevails, the status and function of the rabbi as such have in many ways become subordinate to those of the **zaddik*.

The Reform movement, with its progressive rejection of traditionally received **halakhah,* has changed the very concept of rabbi. The Reform rabbi is judge no longer: he has become to a large degree, for the first time in the history of the rabbinate, a priest ordering the prayer service and leading it. In the U.S. in particular he is also becoming the social and even the socialite director of his synagogue congregation. The *Conservative wing of Judaism, in particular in the U.S., is trying to combine both concepts of the rabbinate. [Ed.]

The Jewish Religious Leadership in the Muslim East. There is a scarcity of information concerning the religious leadership of the early Middle Ages in eastern lands. Extant fragments of records pertaining to such leadership date back only to the 12th century. Sources become more extensive beginning in the 16th century, after the expulsion of the Jews from Spain, and are found in the responsa of the eastern lands, especially from the Ottoman Empire. In this section the religious leadership will be discussed starting with the geonic era, although the title of "rabbi," in its usual sense of a scholar appointed over a community to decide and teach its religious regulations, was not used until the 12th century.

The *geonim* served as spiritual heads of the Babylonian or Palestinian communities, and in Babylonia they ruled alongside the exilarchs, who served as secular heads. The authority of the *geonim* extended over the borders of the Arabian caliphate due to their religious authority. Previously the exilarch had reserved the right to appoint judges, either alone or in consultation with the *gaon.* But during the decline of the exilarchate, the *geonim* appointed judges for most of Babylonia, granting them a "certificate of justiceship" *(pitka de-dayyanuta).*

In Ereẓ Israel the religious head of a community was known as a *ḥaver* (associated member of the Academy) and was ordained in the Palestinian academy. The *ḥaver* served as head of the community's rabbinical court once he had been empowered by the head of the academy. The Palestinian academies granted to ordained scholars the title of *ḥaver be-Sanhedrin ha-Gedolah* (member of the Great Sanhedrin); in Babylonia it was customary to call similar appointees **alluf*. At the same time the title of *rav* (rabbi) was common in Egypt, North Africa, and Spain.

The decline of the gaonate and the Palestinian Academy in the 11th century created some confusion regarding the rabbinate as a communal institution. There was no sufficient religious authority capable of continuing the traditional ordination (**semikhah*) or appointment of judges. Consequently, ordination was discontinued. In Spain, however, some religious heads of communities would grant their students a "writ of ordination" (*ketav masmikh*). *Judah ben Barzillai al-Bargeloni declared in his *Sefer ha-Shetarot* that this writ was only reminiscent of the ancient ordination and that no actual *semikhah* could be given outside Ereẓ Israel. This type of document, he maintained, was awarded only for the purpose of encouraging students.

In the 1130s R. Joseph *ibn Migash ordained Joseph ben Mamal by means of a *ketav minnui* (writ of appointment). Maimonides opposed the institution of the professional rabbi in the sense of a paid official; he preferred the ideal of the scholar who earns his living independently but serves as a communal teacher. Even in the geonic period in North Africa, there were scholars who received "appointments" to the rabbinate. R. *Ḥushi'el b. Elhanan of Kairouan ordained his son *Hananel and *Nissim b. Jacob b. Nissim (Ibn Shahin). Abraham *ibn Daud mentioned in his *Sefer ha-Kabbalah* that after the deaths of *Hananel and Nissim b. Jacob the tradition was discontinued, although judges officiated in Mahdia and Qalʿat Ḥammād without ordination. In the geonic period the title of *ha-rav ha-rosh* (chief rabbi) was widespread in North Africa. It was awarded by the academy in Pumbedita to designate the head of a famous rabbinical court.

In Spain the rank of *dayyan* (judge) was higher than that of rabbi. Certain individuals were empowered to punish offenders and bore the right to judge alone. Important authorities, such as Maimonides and his father Maimon, were called *dayyan*. The position of *dayyan* was more highly regarded in Spain than in the eastern lands after the expulsion. In those countries the *ḥakham* ("scholar") gained prominence, although the *dayyan* reserved the right to appoint a *ḥakham* or to empower even ordinary individuals with the right to judge. Two examples are known of appointment of rabbis by the government in the 14th and 15th centuries: Joseph Sasportas who was invested with judicial powers in the kingdom of *Tlemcen and Isaac b. Sheshet Perfet, who was appointed by the government of Algiers. Isaac b. Sheshet Perfet (second half of the 14th century) wrote that in Germany, as well, it was customary to award a "writ of ordination," although in Spain it was considered sufficient if a teacher gave permission to his student to act as congregational religious leader.

The arrival of Spanish and Portuguese refugees in eastern lands aroused a serious conflict concerning "ordination" as practiced by the native *Ashkenazim and *Romaniots. An example of this was the controversy about Messer David ben Judah *Leon, an "ordained" scholar and leader in Jewish education in Avilona (Valona), Albania, in the early 16th century. Rabbi David Cohen of Corfu supported Leon and stated that the method of ordination in use at least served to deter those not fit to decide the *halakhah*. David Cohen himself had received "ordination." Elijah *Mizraḥi opposed the Sephardi refugees who claimed that no one could ordain once the Sanhedrin no longer existed. Nonetheless, the Ashkenazim did influence some Eastern Sephardi communities to practice "ordination." However the significance of the ordination was completely different from the Ashkenazi ordination. The responsa cite several examples of writs of appointment containing the phrase *"yoreh, yoreh, yadin, yadin"* ("he will teach, he will judge"), sometimes adding *"yattir, yattir"* ("he will permit"); this was the text of ordination customary in the talmudic period. One factor which soothed the conflict was the public's reluctance to accept Ashkenazi ordination as an automatic qualification for communal leadership. The idea of reinstituting the traditional ordination as known in ancient times continued to excite scholars until the 16th century, when Jacob Berab relied on the words of Maimonides in his attempt to ordain certain scholars. This act aroused negative reactions and a fresh conflict continued for two generations.

When the Spanish and Portuguese refugees reached the Ottoman Empire, they organized communities according to their origins, each preserving its own traditions. Due to the absence of ordination, the spiritual leader in these communities was mainly called *ḥakham* or *marbiẓ-Torah* ("teacher of the Torah"). Other titles in use were *dayyan, ḥaver beit ha-din, kaẓin ve-rosh, moreh ẓedek*, and *moreh hora'ah;* these titles were not limited to congregational leaders in the strict sense. In Ereẓ Israel, Egypt, and Syria, however, the title *marbiẓ Torah* was replaced by *ḥakham* and in North Africa by *moreh ẓedek*. A rabbi in charge of all or most congregations in a city was called *ha-rav ha-kolel* ("the 'supreme' rabbi").

The *marbiẓ Torah* or *ḥakham* was the highest religious authority in his district. To qualify for his office he had to be expert in all fields of *halakhah*. He preached publicly on Sabbaths and holidays. Frequently he acted as chief controller over foundations and bequests and organized the redemption of hostages. In small communities he often served as a scribe or notary. The *marbiẓ Torah* judged in matters of marriage, divorce, *ḥaliẓah*, and monetary disputes generally alone but sometimes joined by two laymen to strengthen the verdict as having been passed in a court of three. Claims between people of different communities were judged by the *marbiẓ Torah* of the defendant's community. He was also responsible for judging in matters of ritual fitness and maintaining standards of morality in the city. Generally, his office was not inherited.

The *marbiẓ Torah* was usually treated with respect and admiration. He was paid an ample wage and honored with set marks of etiquette; the congregation stood when he entered and allowed him to pass first through the synagogue or street. He occupied a fixed seat in the synagogue and when he died he was buried with special marks of honor. Certain congregations purposely left the late leader's office vacant for a considerable period to show deference to their loss.

On the other hand there is record of conflicts between the *marbiẓ Torah* and members of his congregation. Sometimes his knowledge of *halakhah* was questioned or sometimes competition between two scholars for the same office would cause conflicts or a split in the community; many *marbiẓei Torah* are known to have been dismissed from their positions. A *ḥakham* who was disregarded or dishonored could excommunicate his opponents, and sometimes members of his congregation took measures to curb his powers of excommunication if used too freely.

From the late 15th century the Eastern communities felt the need for a central rabbinate that would assume the overall religious and administrative leadership that lay beyond the province of the local *marbiẓei Torah*. In the late 15th and early 16th centuries this office had already been filled by the two chief rabbis of the Romaniots, Moses *Capsali and Elijah Mizraḥi, both in Constantinople, who were called *rav kolel, ha-rav ha-manhig* ("leading rabbi"), or *ha-rav ha-gadol* ("grand rabbi"). They were appointed by the government and given a permit known as the *hurman* to collect Jewish taxes. For the privilege of maintaining this office, the community had to pay a special tax, known as *rav aqchesi* ("white (i.e., silver) coin for the permit to have a rabbi"). This tax had to be paid even in the 17th century long after the office of chief rabbi had been discontinued. After the death of Elijah Mizraḥi, there was no longer any one figure who filled this position; rabbinical councils, however, frequently met in various cities on important matters. At this time there was a growing feeling among the Sephardim to grant high office to great rabbis of the generation. Samuel de *Medina was recognized as chief rabbi in Salonika, and Jacob Berab filled the same office in Safed. In almost every large community there was a *rav kolel* who was not appointed by the government but by the Jews themselves. The *rav kolel* performed all tasks of the *marbiẓ Torah* and was also head of the rabbinical court or of a yeshivah. Often he was called *reish mata* (Aramaic: "head of the city"). In Izmir (Smyrna) it was customary for two chief rabbis to serve simultaneously, one in charge of civil law, the other in charge of ritual; both were called *ha-rav ha-gadol.* Their subordinate rabbis were called *morei ẓedek*. In this city there was a time when four chief rabbis ruled simultaneously. The *ḥakhamim* devoted all their time to the study of Torah and as such were exempt from taxes; an ordinance which fixed this exemption was drafted in Jerusalem in the early 16th century. The exemption applied to any *ḥakham rashum* ("recorded rabbi") who served as *marbiẓ Torah* or filled a spiritual position.

In other eastern countries, additional titles were awarded attesting the outstanding scholarship or eminence of the leader. The names *navon* ("understanding") or *maskil* ("wise, erudite") were used generally for young scholars who had acquired a fair knowledge of *halakhah.* The term *ḥakham vatik* ("senior" or "conscientious scholar"), despite its literal meaning, was also used for younger leaders. The name *he-ḥakham ha-shalem* was used to distinguish well-known important rabbis, *marbiẓei Torah,* heads of academies, and rabbinical courts.

Beginning in 1836 the Ottoman regime established the office of **ḥakham bashi* (head of the rabbis) in Constantinople. The incumbent had to be a citizen of the empire. Eventually similar offices were established in the capitals of big provinces. The exact duties and privileges of the *ḥakham bashi* were fixed in 1864. The *ḥakham bashi* of Constantinople exercised authority over all other rabbis in the empire (including the *rishon le-Zion* in Ereẓ Israel). In Egypt the *ḥakham bashi* was the only authority to decide ritual matters and was accompanied by a judge who had the right to sit alone. The Jewish community in Ereẓ Israel appointed a chief rabbi known as the *rishon le-Zion* ("first of Zion"). Although this title existed from the 17th century, it was not officially recognized until 1842, when the incumbent *rishon le-Zion* was named *ḥakham bashi* of Ereẓ Israel. In 1874 a *ḥakham bashi* was appointed in Tripoli (North Africa) and soon the title became so popular that almost every North African community had its *ḥakham bashi.*

There were also chief rabbis who were heads of rabbinical courts in Tunis, Djerba, in Algeria and Morocco.

In smaller cities in Morocco, which did not possess rabbinical courts, a *rabbin délégué* was appointed who acted as a one-man court and a community representative before the government. In Morocco there were some families who reserved the dynastic right *(serarah)* to serve as rabbis and judges. No parallel custom is found in any other land. Soleiman *Kareh was appointed in 1872 *ḥakham bashi* of Yemen by the Turkish regime. In that country the *ḥakham bashi* was the highest legal and religious authority. After Kareh the position of *ḥakham bashi* was held intermittently and for short durations. In each village and town in Yemen, the *mōrī* served as rabbi, judge, and teacher. The Yemenite rabbis earned their livings mainly as slaughterers, goldsmiths, and teachers. [L.Bo.]

Modern Period. Since the emancipation era, the functions of the rabbi, particularly in Western countries, have undergone a radical change to which various factors contributed. In the first place, the governments of the various countries abolished the right of jurisdiction previously granted to the Jews in civil law, in consequence of which the function of the rabbi as judge in civil litigation and the need to study *Ḥoshen Mishpat* (the Jewish civil code) for practical purposes no longer existed. Moreover, even matters of ritual and matrimonial law which remained within the sphere of Jewish jurisdiction were dealt with, in these countries, not by the individual rabbi, but by a central *bet din,* these functions being fulfilled by the **dayyan.* In the second place, with the entry of the Jews into general life the need became increasingly felt for the rabbis to be equipped with a wider knowledge than was regarded as necessary for the medieval rabbi in the Jewish community, in both Jewish spheres—Jewish history, literature, homiletics, and *Juedische Wissenschaft* generally—and in purely secular branches. This need, felt internally, was powerfully reinforced when the governments of various countries, commencing with Emperor Franz Joseph in Austria in 1848 and extending to other countries, demanded a certain standard of general education as a condition of recognizing rabbis. When the existing *yeshivot refused to countenance any change in their traditional syllabus, which was almost wholly confined to Talmud and the codes, the need was met by the establishment of *rabbinical seminaries which provided a comprehensive curriculum of Jewish studies (with a lessened stress on Talmud and codes), which was generally supplemented by a university education. The modern rabbi, whether Orthodox, Conservative, or Reform, was largely the product of these institutions.

FUNCTIONS OF THE RABBI. The function of the modern rabbi varied somewhat in the various countries according to local conditions. Thus in England he approximated until recently more to the cantor than in any other country. His official title in the United Synagogue was "minister-preacher," while his colleague was the "minister-reader," both sharing the conduct of the weekly and Sabbath services and the reading of the Torah. In England, France, and Germany the wearing of canonicals was obligatory, while in France the organizational aspects of the rabbinate was largely determined by the *Consistory. Nevertheless there are general lines of similarity which applied equally to all. Preaching, of course in the vernacular, occupied a place of prime importance, out of all proportion to the old-fashioned rabbi who generally limited his public discourses to two halakhic-aggadic addresses per year (see *Preaching). The modern rabbi was expected to devote much of his time to pastoral work, establishing a personal bond between himself and his congregants, visiting the sick, officiating at bar mitzvahs, marriages, funerals, and houses of mourning as a matter of course. He was expected to take part in all social, educational, and philanthropic activities of the congregation. Above all he was looked to as the spokesman of the Jewish community to the larger community, though the extent of this participation varied in different countries, being most extensive in the United States. The influence of the larger denominations, particularly the Protestant Church, was marked. Until recent times in England it was de rigueur for the rabbi to wear a clerical collar, while the garb of the French rabbi in synagogue was identical with that of the Protestant pastor. In England Chief Rabbis Adler and Hertz donned the gaiters and the silk hat with cockade of the Anglican bishop at official functions. Recent years have witnessed a departure from those models to a considerable extent, and a closer proximation to those of the old school, partly under the influence of the yeshivot and the revival of Orthodoxy.

In England particularly, as in the countries which constituted the British Empire for which it served as a model, it was not even regarded as essential that the rabbi should acquire the rabbinical diploma (it was actually forbidden by Chief Rabbi Herman Adler, who essayed to establish the principle that he was the only rabbi for the British Empire) and the title "reverend" was coined for them. This situation changed considerably, but a student of *Jews College still graduates and is qualified to accept a position on obtaining the minister's diploma, which is less than the rabbinical diploma and carries with it the title "reverend." In all other countries, without exception, and among Reform and Conservative, as well as Orthodox, the only title borne by the spiritual leader is rabbi, apart from the Sephardi congregations where he is called Haham *(ḥakham)*. In England, France, and South Africa, in which the various congregations are united in one roof organization, the rabbi tended more and more to become a local congregational functionary, the chief rabbi alone representing the community as a whole both in religious matters and vis-à-vis the non-Jewish world. In the United States (see below) and Canada, where the tendency is for each congregation to be an independent unit, his sphere of activities was much wider. In the United States, Canada, and England, and in other countries where yeshivah education developed, a return to the old conception of the classic Eastern European rabbi in appearance, outlook, and function is apparent within limited pockets of strict Orthodox Judaism. [L.I.R.]

GERMANY. Some special features characterized the German rabbinate until the Holocaust. In the debates on emancipation the question of the training and functions of the rabbis played an important part. In Prussia, which had the largest number of Jews, successive legislation beginning with the "Religionsedikt" of 1788 to the community law of 1847, had more or less ignored the position of the rabbi, leaving it to the communities whether to appoint rabbis at all, and if they did, they were shorn of their traditional authority, becoming mere functionaries, whose opinion in religious matters could be ignored by the lay leaders. Opinions given by prominent Jews such as Gumpert, Muhr, Rubo, and even Zunz had declared the rabbinical office to be altogether dispensable; rabbis were considered mere "Kauscherwaechters" (Kashrut Supervisors) and protests to the contrary remained ineffective. Their rabbinical jurisdiction had been abolished in 1811 (in Altona-Schleswig-Holstein as late as 1863) and when the last chief rabbi of Berlin, Hirschel *Lewin, appointed under the "General Juden Reglement" of 1750, died in 1800, his position was not filled again. Yet rabbis of the old school were in positions of religious authority to the middle of the century, such as Akiva Eger (d. 1837) and his son Solomon (d. 1852) in Posen. The Law of 1847 required government confirmation of rabbinical appointments, though they were not considered public functionaries. The constitution of the Bismarckian Reich gave rabbis equal status with Christian clergy in some respects. States like Hanover, Electoral Hesse, and Schleswig-Holstein, which were later incorporated in Prussia, retained their previously adopted Jewish community organization in which rabbis had the official status of Landrabbiner, Provinzialrabbiner, etc. Even where rabbis possessed no legal status, they were in fact recognized as the representatives and spokesmen of the Jewish faith and community, sat on the advisory educational boards, were given chaplaincy commissions, etc. In most other German states the new laws regulating the life of Jewish communities (Bavaria, 1813; Wurtemberg, 1828; Baden, 1809; grand-duchy of Hesse, 1841) recognized the official position of rabbis providing for offices of Landrabbiner, Konferenzrabbiner, Bezirksrabbiner or just local rabbis, regulating their qualifications, duties, emoluments, garb, etc. In several of these states they had to face examinations before specially appointed government boards. The new type of rabbi who emerged spoke High German and possessed besides rabbinical training a higher and often university education. This was not limited to Liberal and Reform rabbis; it applied to the Orthodox rabbinate as well as exemplified by such men as J. *Ettlinger, I. *Bernays, M. *Sachs, S. R. *Hirsch, and A. *Hildesheimer. The transition from the new to the old was not without struggle as shown by the controversy about A. *Geiger's appointment in Breslau. The emerging *Wissenschaft des Judentums was both creative of and created by this modern type of rabbi. At first, at least, their individual and collective authority within the community was paramount, while rabbinical conferences and synods were shaping a new non-Orthodox Judaism. *Rabbinical seminaries of the three main religious trends (Breslau, Hildesheimer, and Hochschule) trained these modern rabbis. Their students could not always be clearly classified. Orthodox ones could be found at Breslau and the Hochschule, while some non-Orthodox rabbis qualified at the Hildesheimer Seminary. A large part of the future rabbis hailed from Germany's eastern provinces or from East European countries where they had received the traditional yeshivah training. Toward the end of the 19th century and after World War I new yeshivot (the last of the old yeshivot was closed in 1865) were established in Germany itself, while some rabbinical students enrolled in eastern yeshivot. This raised both the qualifications and standing of the Orthodox rabbinate.

With this went a general lowering of their status and authority, with the lay leadership, qualified by mere professional or financial success, in the ascendancy. Most rabbis were no longer given a "call," but had to apply for advertised positions. They were now officials rather than leaders, without a vote and even a voice on their communities' administration. Even by 1922 there was only one congregation in Germany on whose board the rabbi had a seat and later became its chairman. Vigorous protests from within the rabbinate were of no avail. Only the Nazi persecutions brought about some belated change.

The rabbi usually taught at the community's religious school as well as to Jewish pupils in the state high schools. Adult education emerged gradually after World War I and became an important function in the Nazi period. Public relations with the non-Jewish community, such as lecturing, participation in public functions and social and educational work in general, occupied a considerable part of the rabbi's time. His relations to his congregation were regulated by private contract; his salary was usually adequate for maintaining a middle-class standard of living, incidental fees being paid into the community's funds.

In the larger communities with several synagogues a division developed between the community rabbi and the synagogue rabbi. In many parts of Germany, where rural, rabbi-less communities survived in great number, district rabbis, with their seat in state or provincial capitals, were in charge of their religious needs. Even after 1918, when the separation of church and state had led to the abolition of the 19th-century laws, the titles of Oberrabiner, Landesrabbiner, or Provinzialrabbiner survived as a historical relic, without much significance, unless it meant the care of rural communities. There was at no time a German chief rabbi. When, under the Nazis, Leo *Baeck became president of the *Reichsvertretung der deutschen Juden, his being a (liberal) rabbi was incidental.

From the Franco-Prussian War of 1870 until World War I, many German rabbis served as army chaplains. The needs of German Jewry under the Nazi regime produced the office of Youth Rabbi; the social—and educational—responsibilities of the rabbi in this tragic period increased manyfold.

In 1884 German rabbis united in the "Verband der Rabbiner Deutschlands" which in 1896 became the "Allgemeiner Rabbinerverband in Deutschland," though some Orthodox rabbis refused to join. The Orthodox, on their side, established in 1897 their own "Vereinigung traditionell-gesetzestreuer Rabbiner" while an "Orthodoxer Rabbinerverband" excluded those rabbis who served in "mixed" Reform-Orthodox communities. Another source of controversy was emerging Zionism; the great majority of German Jews were anti-Zionist and their assimilated leaders even more so; a great number of rabbis had signed the famous protest against the holding of the First Zionist Congress (see *Protestrabbiner). This led to a head-on conflict with some of the younger rabbis who had embraced Zionism, as in the case of Emil Bernard *Cohn, who was dismissed from his post by the Berlin Jewish community board for propagating Zionism. [A.C.]

In the U.S. The status and role of the contemporary rabbi in North America exhibit some unique features which can best be understood in the light of the historical development of the synagogue as the central institution in the Jewish community.

The North American cultural and social development accepted the concept of differences based on faith, but has resisted differences based on other criteria. A full treatment of this sociological phenomenon can be found in W. Herberg's *Protestant-Catholic-Jew* (1955). The Eastern European community, from which most North American Jews and their ancestors emigrated, was based on ethnic and other national minority differences. In the "melting pot" process, allowances were made for such concepts as Jewish nationality on the one hand, while on the other various ethnic minorities that make up the North American community (with the possible growing exception of the French-Canadian and the Black-American separatists) assimilated to a cultural climate in which only differences of faith are recognized and where each community is given equal status and dignity unrelated to the number of its adherents.

Insofar as earlier immigrant generations attended churches and synagogues, they probably preferred those where the language and customs of their countries of origin were used in worship and pulpit. Norwegian Lutherans attended churches where Norwegian was used, Italian Catholics where Italian was used. Their children and grandchildren however chose to affiliate with a place of worship which was American in loyalty and composition. The place of worship became a center around which gravitated social and cultural activities which previously had been the functions of societies and clubs of a strong ethnic flavor. In the Jewish community particularly, many of the functions previously performed by Hebrew communal schools, Zionist youth movements, philanthropic activities, and social action committees, became increasingly centered in the synagogue which developed into the comprehensive Jewish Center. The latter often was the only functioning Jewish institution in the community with adequate building, constituency, and professional leadership. Besides being spiritual leader, interpreter of Jewish law, and preacher, the rabbi tended more and more to become the senior Jewish professional in the community. This was equally true of the rabbi of a Conservative, Orthodox, Reform, or unaffiliated congregation. He came to interpret the Jewish tradition not only to the members of his congregation, but also to their Christian neighbors. He had to assume responsibility for all aspects of Jewish education. National and international Jewish organizations looked to him for influence. During the first decades of this century, the Reform rabbi tended to represent the total Jewish community to its neighbors. This function later came to be performed by rabbis of all denominations. The field of counseling has become a part of the modern rabbi's schooling. In the U.S. both the Reform and Conservative rabbinical training schools include courses in pastoral psychiatry for their students. These institutions also maintain pastoral psychiatry centers for research, marriage counseling, etc.

In recent years, the modern rabbi has played an increasing role in the general field of human relations or civil rights, and organizations dealing with them as a general rule increasingly tend to have a rabbi either on their staff or as an elected president. For example, the *American Jewish Congress has almost invariably elected a rabbi as president, after the election of Stephen Wise, its first rabbi president. One of the reasons is that when they participate in government or communal affairs, they often prefer that a rabbi represent them since their counterparts are likely to be Protestant or Catholic clergymen. The modern rabbi tends to model himself after the paradigm (and often the founders) of his rabbinical seminary and professional associations, e.g., Sabato Morais and Isaac Meyer Wise, the first presidents of the Jewish Theological Seminary and the Hebrew Union College respectively, who took forthright, if different, positions on the merits of the American Civil War. Alumni of all the American Jewish seminaries played central roles as social activists, Zionists or anti-Zionist leaders.

The status of the modern rabbi is probably best reflected in the number of institutions established by the different Jewish denominations to educate future rabbis (see *Rabbinical Seminaries). [W.Ke.]

In Israel. The rabbinate and the functions of the rabbi in modern Israel differ fundamentally from their counterparts in any other part of the Jewish world, whether ancient or modern. A number of factors have contributed toward this unique state of affairs. In the first place there is the law of the State of Israel which establishes the *halakhah* as state law in all matters affecting personal status, which includes marriage, divorce, legitimacy, and conversion and affords the rabbinical courts the status of civil courts of law within that wide sphere. This, coupled with the fact that the Ministry of Religious Affairs was, apart from one brief interregnum, the prerogative of the (Orthodox) National Religious Party, has had the effect of making Orthodox Judaism to all intents and purposes the "established church" of the state, to the virtual exclusion of other religious trends in Judaism, Conservative and Reform, which have only a handful of congregations, mostly composed of recently arrived immigrants belonging to those trends in the countries of their origin.

A second factor determining the complexion and the functions of the rabbinate is the establishment of the twin Orthodox chief rabbinate (Ashkenazi and Sephardi) which are state appointments, and similar twin chief rabbinates in the larger cities. These local rabbinates and chief rabbinates are administered by the local religious councils, which are nominated through a complicated system of political party representation and the Ministry of Religious Affairs, and it is to all intents controlled by the ministry. These councils consist of Orthodox Jews. All appointments of rabbis must be confirmed by the chief rabbis and the Ministry of Religious Affairs.

A third factor is the fact that almost without exception the *rashei yeshivot,* who exercise a powerful influence in Israel, as well as the other rabbis who belong to the *Agudat Israel (to which the *rashei yeshivot* also mostly belong), regard the National Religious Party and the chief rabbis who owe their appointments to their support as tending toward heterodoxy, a charge which they are at great pains to disprove or dispel. As a result, they are unduly apprehensive of any move which might be regarded as progressive or "reform." To these considerations must be added two others. The Ashkenazi rabbinate continues wholly the tradition of the classical Eastern European rabbinate, and the new incumbents to the rabbinate are wholly the products of the yeshivot, while the Sephardi rabbinate equally continues in their old traditions. Lastly, the synagogue in Israel is, with only a handful of exceptions, not a congregational entity with fixed membership but a place for worship and study.

All these factors add up to the distinctive features of the rabbinate and the functions of the rabbis in Israel. Next to the chief rabbis the hierarchy consists of the *dayyanim* of the Supreme Bet Din of Appeal, followed by the *dayyanim* of the district courts. They are classified as civil judges with the emoluments and privileges of judges, and their functions are wholly judicial and not pastoral. Next in importance, and in receipt of salaries from the religious councils, are a host of rabbis who act as religious functionaries with specific and limited duties such as inspection of *kashrut,* of *mikva'ot,* of the *eruv,* of the adherence to the various agricultural laws, etc. They also, by nature of their functions, perform no pastoral duties. Next in the scale come district rabbis, also appointed by the religious councils. In theory they are charged with the welfare of the community within the district over which they have been appointed, but with few exceptions they regard their position as a sinecure. Lowest on the scale come, what in theory is the nearest approach to the Western rabbi, the rabbi of a synagogue. In the absence of a regularly constituted congregation, however, and with no official source of income, they are financially the least rewarded. Few synagogues pay anything approaching a living wage to these rabbis. They mostly depend upon one of the other rabbinic functions referred to for their livelihood, and their appointments largely commence as de facto ones which sometimes develop into uneasy de jure ones. In the absence of the congregational unit with its duly paid-up membership, and the consequent lack of personal bond between rabbi and worshiper, there is nothing in the rabbinate in Israel which approaches the pastoral aspect of the work of the modern rabbi. Marriages are performed by duly appointed officials of the local religious councils, funerals by the various *ḥevra kaddisha* organizations. Visiting the sick is not regarded as the function of the rabbi of a synagogue; cultural activities apart from the *shi'urim* in rabbinics are undertaken by other agencies, as is youth work and philanthropic activity. The virtual nonexistence of regular preaching should be noted.

The cumulative effect of this situation is that the Western-trained rabbi even of Orthodox Jewry finds it hard to find a place in the rabbinate in Israel. Of all those who have immigrated few have been appointed to a rabbinical position in Israel, and most find their livelihood in other spheres. [L.I.R.]

Bibliography: MIDDLE AGES: Baron, Community, index; Baron, Social[2], index volume to vols. 1–8 (1960), 126; S. Assaf, in: *Reshumot,* 2 (1927), 259–99; Neuman, Spain, 2 (1942), index; Finkelstein, Middle Ages; S. Schwarzfuchs, *Études sur l'origine et le developpement de Rabbinat au Moyen-Age* (1957); H. H. Ben-Sasson, *Hagut ve-Hanhagah* (1959), 160–228; J. Katz, *Masoret u-Mashber* (1958), index, s.v. *Rav, Rabbanut;* idem, in: *Sefer Zikkaron . . . B. de Vries* (1968), 281–94; S. Spitzer, in: *Bar Ilan Sefer ha-Shanah,* 7–8 (1970), 261–79. MUSLIM EAST: Rosanes, Togarmah; Mann, Texts; Mann, Egypt; idem, in: JQR, 7 (1916/17), 457ff.; D. Revel, in: *Horeb,* 5 (1939), 1–26; H. Z. Hirschberg, in: *Religion in the Middle East,* 1 (1969), 119–225; Hirschberg, Afrikah, index; Baer, Spain, index; Baer, Urkunden, 2 (1936), index; H. H. Ben-Sasson, *Toledot Am Yisrael bi-Ymei ha-Beinayim* (1969); Neuman, Spain, index; M. Benayahu, *Marbiẓ Torah* (1953); idem, in: *Sefer . . . Baer* (1961), 248–69; S. Assaf, *Le-Korot ha-Rabbanut* (1943); idem, *Battei ha-Din . . .* (1924); Assaf, Geonim; Neubauer, Chronicles; Ibn Daud, Tradition; J. M. Landau, *Ha-Yehudim be-Miẓrayim ba-Me'ah ha-Tesha Esreh* (1967); A. Elmaleh, *Ha-Rishonim le-Ẓiyyon* (1970); *Saloniki Ir va-Em be-Yisrael* (1967); I. S. Emmanuel, *Maẓẓevot Saloniki,* 2 vols. (1963–68); Ashtor, Korot; Ashtor Toledot; A. Ben-Jacob, *Yehudei Bavel* (1965); M. S. Goodblatt, *Jewish Life in Turkey in the XVIth Century . . .* (1952); M. Zadoc, *Yehudei Teiman* (1967); S. D. Goitein, *Sidrei Ḥinnukh* (1965). MODERN PERIOD: *Sulamith,* 2 (1809), 300–5; S. Holdheim, *Ueber die Autonomie der Rabbiner . . .* (1847[2]); L. Auerbach, *Das Judentum und seine Bekenner* (1890), 284ff.; B. Jacobs, *Die Stellung des Rabbiners* (1910); *Paul Lazarus Gedenkbuch* (1961); M. S. Gelber, *Failure of the American Rabbi* (1962); M. M. Berman, *The Role of the Rabbi, What Was, What Is, and What Shall the Rabbi Be* (1941); A. Y. Feldman, *The American Reform Rabbi* (1962); L. M. Franklin, *The Rabbi, the Man and his Message* (1938); R. Hertz, *The Rabbi Yesterday and Today* (1943).

RABBI BINYAMIN (pseudonym of **Yehoshua Radler-Feldmann;** 1880–1957), Hebrew journalist. Born in Zborov, Galicia, Rabbi Binyamin published his first essay in 1903, and in 1906 moved to London, where he joined J. Ḥ.

Rabbi Binyamin, Ereẓ Israel journalist. Jerusalem, J.N.U.L., Schwadron Collection.

*Brenner in the publication of *Ha-Me'orer.* Arriving in Palestine in 1907, he first worked as a laborer in Petaḥ Tikvah, then as secretary of Herzlia, the first Hebrew high school in Tel Aviv. He left this position to join in the founding of kevutzat *Kinneret. In 1910 he moved to Jerusalem, taught at the Reḥavyah Hebrew high school, and later at the Taḥkemoni religious school. After World War I he was active in the Mizrachi Party and edited the religious national monthly *Ha-Hed* (1926–53). In 1925 he was among the founders of the *Berit Shalom association, which advocated a binational state for Arabs and Jews.

Rabbi Binyamin published thousands of articles and essays, often expressing individualistic viewpoints. He did much to introduce Brenner and Agnon to the Hebrew reading audiences. His critical essays include surveys and analyses of the great figures of ancient and modern European civilization, Asian cultures, and modern Hebrew literature. His works include *Al ha-Gevulin* (1923) and *Parzufim* (2 vols., 1934, 1936), a volume of memoirs, *Mi-Zborov ve-ad Kinneret* (1950), and essays on writers and scholars, *Mishpeḥot Soferim* (1960) and *Keneset Ḥakhamim* (1961).

Bibliography: *Rabbi Binyamin, Zikhrono li-Verakhah* (1958), contains bibliography and a collection of evaluations; Waxman, Literature, 4 (1960), 427–9; I. Cohen, *Demut el Demut* (1949), 225–33; D. Sadan, *Bein Din le-Ḥeshbon* (1963), 358–63; J. Fichmann, *Ruḥot Menaggenot* (1952), 285–311; Kressel, Leksikon, 2 (1967), 831–3. [G.K.]

RABBINER-SEMINAR FUER DAS ORTHODOXE JUDENTUM, the Rabbinical Seminary for Orthodox Judaism, founded in 1873 in Berlin by Azriel (Israel) *Hildesheimer to promote *Torah im Derekh Erez* (the combination of loyalty to Judaism with awareness of modern culture and method). For the next seven decades rabbinic and lay leaders emerged from that institution whose influence extended over four continents. Throughout his career Hildesheimer had to fight opponents from the left and the right. He inspired his disciples by his life and learning. After having headed the seminary for 26 years, Hildesheimer was followed by David *Hoffmann, Joseph *Wohlgemuth, and Jehiel Jacob *Weinberg. The students attended classes both at the seminar and at the university, and the curriculum included Bible, Talmud, Jewish philosophy, and other subjects. Hildesheimer's faculty was made up of distinguished scholars. Among them were Jacob *Barth, Abraham *Berliner, Hirsch *Hildesheimer (son of the founder), Simon *Eppenstein, Moses Auerbach, and Samuel *Gruenberg. The seminary's annual reports (*Jahresberichte*, 1873–1915; 1935–36) contained a series of important scholarly studies by the members of its teaching staff. The seminary was the center of modern Orthodoxy, which combined loyalty to traditional Judaism with the recognition of the need for scientific method (most of the graduates obtained a doctorate in philosophy). Many graduates, among them Joseph *Carlebach and Leo *Deutschlander, attained continental fame through their educational work in Eastern Europe, while many others built *Torah im Derekh Erez* congregations in Germany, France, and beyond their frontiers. The seminary, which started as a German-Hungarian enterprise, was greatly enriched in its last two decades by two Lithuanian scholars on its faculty: Abraham Elijah *Kaplan, who died at a young age, and Jehiel Jacob Weinberg, a great talmudist. In 1934 plans were prepared to transfer the seminary to Palestine but the proposal had to be abandoned owing to the opposition of extreme Orthodox elements there to the concept of a modern rabbinical seminary. The institution closed in November 1938 shortly after the *Kristallnacht* pogrom. The greater part of its library was transferred to Tel Aviv. The principal fruits of the seminary's work was the training of German rabbis who were trained to counter the tide of religious liberalism.

Bibliography: S. Goldschmidt, in: *Jeschurun*, 7 (1920), 216–55; J. Wohlgemuth, *Das Rabbiner-Seminar zu Berlin* (1923); H. Schwab, *History of Orthodox Jewry in Germany* (1950), 54–57; M. A. Shulvass (Szulvas), in: S. K. Mirsky (ed.), *Mosedot Torah be-Eiropah* (1956), 689–713; Y. Aviad (Wolfsberg), *Deyokena'ot* (1962), 40–51; I. J. Eisner, in: YLBI, 12 (1967), 32–52. [L.Ju.]

RABBINICAL ALLIANCE OF AMERICA, association of Orthodox rabbis. Founded in 1944, the Rabbinical Alliance "seeks to promulgate the cause of Torah-true Judaism through an organized rabbinate that is consistently Orthodox." In its first years the organization was connected with the Yeshivah Torah Vodaath (Brooklyn). It brought within its ranks U.S.-trained rabbis for whom the Orthodoxy of the preexisting *Rabbinical Council of America was insufficiently strict. In 1965 a membership figure of 250 was given, of whom 100 were active in the rabbinate. Many of the latter were also said to be members of the Rabbinical Council. [S.D.T.]

RABBINICAL ASSEMBLY, the official organization of *Conservative rabbis, founded in 1901 in New York as an alumni association for graduates of the rabbinical school of the *Jewish Theological Seminary of America. Soon after, it opened its membership to rabbis of other accredited theological schools who accepted the tenets of *Conservative Judaism. Its membership of 876 in 1968 served congregations in the United States, Canada, South America, Europe, and Israel. The organization strives to promote Conservative Judaism—to further the welfare of its members, and to promote the cause of Jewish learning. It works closely with the Jewish Theological Seminary of America and the *United Synagogue of America.

The Joint Placement Commission helps to provide rabbis with positions and constituent congregations to find rabbis. Its highly centralized procedures exert substantial discipline, as well as considerable control over the availability of rabbis for different positions. From World War II until 1968 the Rabbinical Assembly operated a self-draft system to supply Jewish men in the armed forces with chaplains. The organization has likewise helped its members to secure a greater measure of economic security by encouraging congregations to meet minimum standards in regard to salary, pensions, and tenure of rabbis.

A major concern of the Rabbinical Assembly has been to further traditional Jewish practice by interpreting it in accordance with the canons of Conservative Judaism. Its Committee on Jewish Law and Standards has particularly concentrated on this assignment. As a result of its deliberations a large collection of responsa has emerged dealing with such issues as the Sabbath, *kashrut*, conversion, marriage rites, and burial procedures. The task of the committee has been complicated by considerable diversity of opinion on religious questions within the membership of the Rabbinical Assembly. Consequently, it has customarily reported both majority and minority opinions on all matters of Jewish law referred to it by the members.

The Rabbinical Assembly has published revised editions of the Jewish prayer book. Its other publications include annual convention proceedings, a quarterly magazine, *Conservative Judaism*, and a volume on the philosophy of Conservative Judaism, entitled *Tradition and Change*.

Bibliography: A. Karp, *A History of the United Synagogue of America, 1913–1963* (1964); Rabbinical Assembly, *Bulletin* (1937–), and *Proceedings* (1937–); M. Davis, *The Emergence of Conservative Judaism* (1964), index. [A.K.]

RABBINICAL CONFERENCES. The idea of a *synod to provide authoritative guidance and meet the current needs of Jews in the era of *Emancipation led to the holding of rabbinical conferences in Germany in the mid-19th century. A convention was called by Abraham *Geiger in Wiesbaden in 1837 to discuss his proposals for *Reform, but had no practical results. Subsequently a conference initiated by Ludwig *Philippson met in Brunswick in 1844, and was attended by 25 Reform rabbis, including Geiger and Samuel *Holdheim. However, no substantial resolutions were passed, and the conference was attacked by all sectors: the Orthodox protested against the rejection of Jewish tradition, Philippson regretted the theorizing instead of practical solutions, and Zacharias *Frankel criticized the discussions and results. Following the conference 116 Orthodox rabbis declared that nobody could "abrogate the least of the religious laws." In 1845 31 rabbis, this time including Frankel, met at Frankfort on the Main. As laid down in a memorandum delivered to the Frankfort conference by three representatives of the *Reform Association of Berlin, their stated purpose was to strengthen Judaism by rescuing it from legalistic stagnation and adapting it to modern needs, thus making it attractive to the new generation. When Frankel was overruled on the retention of Hebrew prayers, he withdrew. Heinrich *Graetz expressed a similar view. Other proposed reforms referred to the messianic portions of the prayers, the supplication for the restoration of sacrifices, the triennial cycle of Torah readings, and the use of the organ in the synagogue. A third conference took place in 1846 at Breslau, attended by 25 rabbis only. While Holdheim suggested that the Sabbath should be transferred to the civil day of rest, the majority was satisfied with minor reform in Sabbath observance, and the abolition of the second day of holidays and many mourning customs. Several resolutions dealt with the supervision of circumcision from the hygienic aspect. A number of radical reformers, dissatisfied with the conservative line taken by the conference, demanded that laymen should participate in future meetings.

In 1868 24 rabbis met in Kassel to prepare such a "synod" and to decide on a number of liturgical reforms. The "synod" assembling at Leipzig in 1869 consisted of 49 lay and 34 rabbinical delegates from 60 communities. Presided over by Moritz *Lazarus, it dealt with Jewish education, liturgical reforms, and other questions. The Orthodox and Frankel's sympathizers were not represented. Two years later, the "synod" of Augsburg was attended by representatives from only 30 communities. Its resolutions dealt with marriage, *ḥaliẓah,* and other subjects, but the stand taken on the Sabbath was more conservative than before. Again, 133 Orthodox rabbis published a strong protest, asserting that the participants were unfit to hold religious office. Neither "synod" came up to the expectations of its own promoters, and no further meeting of this kind was convened in Germany. [Z.F.]

Nevertheless, agitation for synods continued especially in America, by Isaac Mayer *Wise in 1881, and at three sessions of the Central Conference of American Rabbis in 1904–06. Solomon *Schechter, leader of U.S. *Conservative Jewry, opposed synods as encouraging sacerdotalism and creating the danger of a schism within Orthodoxy. The Reform movement in the United States, nevertheless, adopted in 1887 its *Pittsburgh Platform, laying down the principles of classic Reform. It reversed its stance in 1937 in Columbus, when it reaffirmed its adherence to Hebrew, Zionism, and other traditional values. In 1961 the Federation of *Reconstructionist Congregations and Fellowships, at a conference of lay and rabbinic delegates, adopted a guide for Jewish ritual in line with their humanist philosophy of Judaism. Among certain Orthodox circles there has been agitation for a Sanhedrin to legislate for world Jewry, but the difficulties involved appeared insuperable.

See also *Bet Din,* *Chief Rabbi, *Synods. [I.L.]

Bibliography: D. Philipson, *Reform Movement in Judaism* (1931[2], repr. 1967), 140–224; W. G. Plaut, *Rise of Reform Judaism* (1963).

RABBINICAL COUNCIL OF AMERICA (RCA), the rabbinical authority of the *Union of Orthodox Jewish Congregations. Founded in 1923 (as the Rabbinical Council of the Union of Orthodox Jewish Congregations), in 1935 the RCA merged with the Rabbinical Association of the Rabbi Isaac Elchanan Theological Seminary (Yeshiva University) and took its present name. Over half its members are graduates of *Yeshiva University and approximately 15 percent more are graduates of the Hebrew Theological College, Chicago. Over two-thirds of the members are in the active rabbinate, and the majority of the remainder are in Jewish education. The RCA had over 900 members in 1970. The RCA maintains a *bet din* which concerns itself primarily with family problems, and is engaged in developing extensive records on Jewish marriage and divorce. Its purpose is to render authoritative decisions in areas which are either halakhically or emotionally too complex for any one rabbi to handle. The RCA also has a *halakhah* commission (chaired by Rabbi Joseph *Soloveitchik) which rules on religious policy for the organization. The RCA conducts welfare activities on behalf of its members, adopts policy positions, and publishes the quarterly *Tradition* (1958–) and a halakhic journal in Hebrew, *Hadorom* (1957–). It sponsors two schools in Israel, Yeshivat ha-Darom, a high school and teachers seminary in *Reḥovot, and Yeshivat Aḥuzzat Ya'akov, a trade high school in *Yavneh. The executive vice-president of the RCA from 1949 was Rabbi Israel Klavan.

Leaders of the Rabbinical Council of America at a special convention in New York in honor of the Israel Ashkenazi chief rabbi, Isser Yehuda Unterman, June 1966. Left to right, Rabbi Israel Klavan, executive vice-president; Shlomo Zalman Shragai, former mayor of Jerusalem; Rabbi Joseph B. Soloveitchik; Chief Rabbi Unterman; Rabbis Israel Miller and Pesach Z. Levovitz, former presidents; publisher of the Jewish Day—Morning Journal, Arthur L. Jacobs; Rabbi Sholem B. Kowalsky, former vice-president; Rabbi Bernard Twersky, director of public relations.

Bibliography: Leibman, in: AJYB, 66 (1965), 21–97; Davis, in: L. Finkelstein, *The Jews: Their History, Culture, and Religion,* 1 (1960[3]), 559f. [C.S.L.]

RABBINICAL LITERATURE, a modern scientific term used to describe the literature of *halakhah* which is based upon the Oral Law, its traditions and methodology in its different periods, its changing languages, and its varied forms. This definition excludes from its purview such sacred literature as liturgy, *piyyutim,* and other liturgical compositions, pure Kabbalah works, philosophical bible exegesis, theology, and grammar. On the other hand it frequently includes what appear at first sight to be purely secular topics, such as the works on astronomy—inasmuch as their aim is to clarify topics connected with the calendar, such as laws of the determination of the New Moon and its intercalation; "chronologies of the *tannaim* and *amoraim,*" which are strictly chronographies, but whose main purpose is to determine according to which authority the *halakhah* is to be established; homiletic ethical and aggadic works, which aim at giving the practical *halakhah* and guidance for everyday living, and other similar works. Despite this, or perhaps because of this, the term also includes books on the laws of the Temple and its appurtenances, the laws of ritual cleanness and uncleanness, which will be actual only in the messianic future, since their purpose was regarded as "practical" in view of the ever-present faith in the imminent redemption. Combined with this was the concept of "interpret and receive reward," i.e., the study of Torah for its own sake without regard to its application to practical life, as an independent discipline which was part of the concept of *talmud torah,* and therefore this literature too is included in the term "rabbinical literature." It must be clearly emphasized that, despite the formal name, the term does not indicate books written by rabbis but works whose subject matter and aim belong to the sphere that concerns rabbis in their function as teachers of Judaism. Works on grammar may have an important halakhic bearing, for instance in connection with the laws of reading the Torah, but in most cases such was not the intention of their authors, whose purpose was primarily to teach grammar for its own sake or as an aid to biblical exegesis. These books are therefore not included in the term "rabbinical literature." The name rabbinical literature is also used in an entirely different sense since it also describes literature written by Rabbanites against the *Karaites in all eras—even if it deals with theology or other non-halakhic topics.

Rabbinical literature can be divided, according to its contents, into several basic categories: exposition of the *Talmud; *responsa; codes and their commentaries; *minhagim;* halakhic monographs; rules of conduct and ethical wills, and the like. This formal division, however, was adopted in practice long after the inception of this literature. The term is commonly accepted to indicate every category of this literature as defined above, from *Saadiah Gaon, who was the first rabbinical scholar to write "books" in the present sense of the word. According to this usage rabbinical literature constitutes a stage following the period of talmudic and midrashic literature, which, as is usually accepted, came to a close at the end of the geonic period. No books in the present sense of the word were written, however, from the close of this period until Saadiah, with the possible sole exception of the *She'iltot* of *Aḥa of Shabḥa. Saadiah was also a very prolific writer, and the many fragments extant of his various works bear evidence to his creativity in every branch of rabbinical literature.

The formal division begins to emerge in the 11th and 12th centuries, and, with the general development of literary expression, it became progressively more refined and defined. In its historical development rabbinical literature may be divided into three periods: (1) The geonic period; (2) The period of the *rishonim;* (3) The period of the *aḥaronim* (the subdivisions of each period are dealt with under their separate headings). In its fate and its preservation in manuscripts in libraries or in the *genizah,* there is not much difference between rabbinical literature and other branches of Jewish literary creativity. It is likewise very difficult to indicate lines of development which are unique or specially characteristic of it. Research into rabbinical literature, as a branch of the study of Jewish literature in general, is still in its infancy, and the basic groundwork toward it has not yet been done. There are as yet no reliable and comprehensive catalogs of Hebrew manuscripts in the different libraries and erroneous identification of books belonging to it is still widespread. [I.T-S.]

RABBINICAL SEMINARIES. Until the first quarter of the 19th century the only source for the training of rabbis was the *yeshivot. These were not rabbinical training institutions in the strict sense, but institutions of higher rabbinic learning designed for the education of the people as a whole. The curriculum was thus strictly limited to Talmud and its commentaries and the codes. A student wishing to enter the rabbinate obtained *semikhah* and thus became an ordained rabbi.

With the advent of the era of emancipation and the consequent demolition of the ghetto walls in Western Europe, and under the influence of the *Haskalah and the development of the *Wissenschaft des Judentums, the demand became increasingly heard for the establishment of institutions specifically for the training of rabbis. These institutions would produce a new type of modern rabbis, equipped with a thorough mastery of the vernacular and a knowledge of both secular and extra-talmudic Jewish subjects. An added incentive to the establishment of such institutions was the regulation enacted by Franz Joseph I of Austria-Hungary in 1848 requiring secular knowledge of an academic standard for rabbis in his country.

The proposed seminaries were bitterly contested by the rabbis and heads of the yeshivot of the old school as a dangerous innovation, with the result that where they dominated the religious life of the community these seminaries never struck root and consequently they played no significant part in Russia and Poland. This opposition, which still exists, is the cause of the curious fact that in Israel there is no institution specifically set up for the training of rabbis. It was only in Central and Western Europe and in the United States that such seminaries flourished.

The first rabbinical seminary was the Instituto Convitto Rabbinico, established in Padua by I. S. *Reggio in 1829, in which Lelio *Della Torre and Samuel David *Luzzatto were the first teachers. It served as the model for all future seminaries. It was closed in 1871 but reopened in 1887 in Rome as the Collegio Rabbinico Italiana. In 1899 it moved to Florence where it remained until 1932, when again it moved to Rome remaining there until it was closed down under the Fascist regime in 1939. In 1928 a branch was established for Sephardi communities on the Island of Rhodes, but it was also closed down at the outbreak of World War II.

The Ecole Centrale Rabbinique was established in Metz in 1830 and a year later it received a state subsidy. It moved to Paris in 1859 as the Seminaire Israelite de France and later was given the name of the Ecole Rabbinique. Probably the most famous rabbinical seminary in Europe was the Juedisch-Theologisches Seminar of Breslau founded by Zacharias *Frankel in 1854. Among its professors were H. *Graetz, Immanuel *Loew, J. *Gutman, and Yiẓḥak *Heinemann. Jews' College was founded in London in 1855. Its most prominent principals were Michael *Friedlaender (1865–1907), Adolph *Buechler (1907–39), and Isidore *Epstein (1948–62). In Berlin the Juedische Hochschule was established in 1872. Its name was changed to the Lehranstalt fuer die Wissenschaft des Judentums in 1883, but it resumed its old name in 1920. A year after the establishment of the Hochschule the strictly Orthodox Rabbiner Seminar fuer das Orthodoxe Judentum was established in Berlin by Azriel *Hildesheimer, and is usually referred to as Hildesheimer's Seminar.

The bitter opposition of Hungarian Orthodox circles to the establishment of a rabbinical seminary in that country caused a delay in its opening for over a quarter of a century. In 1850 the Emperor Franz Joseph I devoted a million talers, derived from the fine imposed upon the Jews of Hungary for their participation in the rebellion of 1849, to a fund for Jewish education, but the rabbinical seminary was not established until 1877 in Budapest. Among its prominent teachers were Wilhelm *Bacher, M. *Guttmann, and I. *Goldziher. The Israelitisch-theologische Lehranstalt of Vienna, established by A. *Jellinek in 1862, did not make much progress until 1893 when it moved to the Jewish quarter of Leopoldstadt and Adolph Schwarz was appointed its rector.

An outstanding example of the complete failure of a rabbinical seminary was provided by Poland. Established in 1826 and strongly supported by the government, in the 36 years of its existence, it did not produce a single rabbi. The fact is not surprising since both its principal, A. *Eisenbaum, and its main teacher, A. *Buchner, were pronounced assimilationists. Buchner actually published a book, *Der Talmud in seiner Nichtigheit* ("The Worthlessness of the Talmud," 1848). Not much more successful was the Russian seminary which was opened in 1847 in Vilna and in Zhitomir. It was regarded with suspicion by the Jews as an instrument of the government's anti-Jewish educational policy and was closed down in 1873.

On the other hand the *Makhon le-Ḥokhmat Yisrael,* whose name was later changed to the *Makhon le-Madda'ei ha-Yahadut,* established by M. *Schorr, the chief rabbi of Warsaw and its first principal, served as the rabbinical seminary for Poland until the outbreak of World War II.

The United States has rabbinical seminaries for all three trends in religious Jewry. The first to be established, the Reform Hebrew Union College, was founded by Isaac Mayer *Wise in Cincinnati in 1875. In 1922 Stephen *Wise established the Jewish Institute of Religion in New York which merged with the Hebrew Union College in 1950.

The rabbinical seminary of the Conservative movement, the Jewish Theological Seminary, was established in 1886. Orthodox seminaries are represented by the Rabbi Isaac Elchanan Theological Seminary, later a unit of the *Yeshiva University, established in 1897; and the Talmudical College of Chicago, in 1922. As a result of the Holocaust, all the seminaries in Central and Eastern Europe, with the exception of the Budapest seminary have ceased to exist. The only seminaries still functioning in Europe are the Ecole Rabbinique, Jews' College, and the Reform Leo Baeck College in London.

See also *Yeshivot, *Rabbi, and the articles on the individual seminaries.

Bibliography: D. Prato, in: *Relazione sul biennio 1899–1900* (1901); A. Toaff, in: RMI, 12, nos. 7–9 (1937/38), 194f.; *Jews' College Jubilee Volume* (1906); P. Smolenskin, in: *Ha-Shaḥar,* 9 (1876/77), 57–61; *Sefer ha-Zikkaron le-Veit-ha-Midrash le-Rabbanim be-Vinah* (1946); *Sefer ha-Yovel li-Melot 50 Shanah le-Veit-ha-Midrash ha-Rabbanim be-Budapest* (partly in Ger. and Hung.; 1927); A. Geiger, in: WZJT, 2 (1836), 1–21; M. Brann, *Geschichte des juedisch-theologischen Seminars ... in Breslau* (1904); J. Elbogen, in: *Festschrift ... der Hochschule fuer die Wissenschaft des Judentums in Berlin* (1922), 101–44; J. Bauer, *L'Ecole rabbinique de France 1830–1930* (1930); J. Heinemann, in: *Bericht des juedisch-theologischen Seminars ... in Breslau* (1929), 34–48; *Festschrift zum 50-jaehrigen Bestehen des Rabbinerseminars zu Berlin 1873–1923* (1924); G. Kisch (ed.), *Das Breslauer Seminar* (partly in Heb. and Eng.; 1963). IN THE U.S.: M. Davis, in: L. Finkelstein (ed.), *Jews, Their History, Culture, and Religion,* 1 (1960^3), 488–587.

[L.I.R.]

RABBINOVICZ (Rabinovitz), RAPHAEL NATHAN NATA (1835–1888), talmudic scholar. Born in Novo-Zhagory, district of Kovno, at the age of 16 he wrote a bibliographical treatise, *Siftei Yeshenim Gimmel.* Several years later he gave it to the bibliographer Isaac *Benjacob, who used it in compiling his *Oẓar ha-Sefarim.* Rabbinovicz lived for a time in Lemberg, Galicia, where he published a volume of responsa by R. Meir of Rothenburg (1860) and *Ge'on Ya'akov* (1863), novellae on the tractate of *Eruvin* by R. Jacob Kahana of Vilna. Moving on to Pressburg, he published *Kunteres Ikkarei ha-Avodah* (1863) by his teacher R. Joseph b. Israel Issar of Vilkomir. About that time he learned from Adolph *Jellinek in Vienna of the 14th-century manuscript of the Babylonian Talmud preserved in the Royal Library of Munich. He proceeded to that city, and with the encouragement of R. Joseph Saul *Nathanson, the

Raphael Nathan Rabbinovicz, talmudic scholar. Jerusalem, J.N.U.L., Schwadron Collection.

rabbi of Lemberg, devoted himself to copying the variant readings in order to publish them. In 1864 he published a small booklet, *Alim le-Mivḥan* (lithographed from his handwriting), containing samples of the variant readings found in the Talmud manuscript. The following year he published a similar, but more detailed, treatise, *Kunteres Dikdukei Soferim,* in the Hebrew weekly *Ha-Maggid.*

Between 1867 and 1886 he published 15 volumes of *Dikdukei Soferim,* containing the variant readings on all the tractates of the orders of *Zera'im, Mo'ed,* and *Nezikin,* and on the tractates of *Zevaḥim,* and *Menaḥot.* The variant readings are accompanied by explanatory notes in which readings found in other manuscripts—in the writings of early authorities and in old printed editions—are recorded. In his introduction to *Dikdukei Soferim* Rabbinovicz gave a history of the printing of the Babylonian Talmud. A revised and much enlarged version of this essay *Ma'amar al Hadpasat ha-Talmud* appeared later in volume 8 (1877). In the course of his work he traveled widely to consult manuscripts and early printed editions in various libraries. He was aided greatly in his efforts by the Munich Jewish banker Abraham *Merzbacher, who supported him materially and permitted him to buy at his expense all the books and manuscripts he needed. After the death of Merzbacher, Rabbinovicz compiled, at the request of the banker's son, a catalog (*Ohel Avraham,* 1888) of the rich library he had amassed for his father. Its treasures included 156 manuscripts and 43 incunabula.

Despite the material support he received, Rabbinovicz was forced to engage in the selling of books and manuscripts. He died in Kiev, while on one of his business journeys to Russia. Shortly before his death he began printing *Dikdukei Soferim* on the tractate of *Ḥullin.* The work on the volume was completed by Heinrich Ehrentreu and appeared in 1897.

Rabbinovicz also wrote *Moreh ha-Moreh* (1871), a critique of D. B. *Zomber's *Moreh Derekh,* about Rabbenu Gershom's and Rashi's commentaries on the tractate *Mo'ed Katan,* and published a small part of the medieval *Yiḥusei Tanna'im va-Amora'im* (1874). He also contributed to *Ha-Maggid,* where his notes on Jehiel M. Zunz's *Ir ha-Ẓedek* appeared (vols. 19–20, 1875–76).

Bibliography: R. N. Rabbinovicz, *Ma'amar al Hadpasat ha-Talmud,* ed. by A. M. Habermann (1952^2), 261–7; A. Schischa, in: *Aresheth,* 3 (1961), 376–91; Y. Raphael, *ibid.,* 392–4. [T.P.]

RABBINOWICZ, ISRAEL MICHEL (1818–1893), writer and scholar. Born in Gorodets, Lithuania, Rabbinowicz, whose father was rabbi in Gorodets and from 1828 in Antopol, received a traditional education. His brother, Joshua Jacob, also rabbi in Gorodets, was the author of several talmudic works. At the yeshivah in Brest-Litovsk

Rabbinowicz began his study of the philosophers, especially Maimonides. Deciding to widen his field of study, he learned German in Brody and Greek and Latin (with D. Chwolson) in Breslau, where he subsequently entered the university as a student of philology. In 1851 he published a Hebrew grammar, *Hebraeische Grammatik nach neuen, sehr vereinfachten Regeln und Grundsaetzen,* followed by *Hebraeische Schulgrammatik* . . . in 1853 (French translation by J. J. Clement-Mullet, 1862–), selling the books himself in order to earn a living. Later he took up medicine and in 1854 went to Paris, where he continued his studies in hospitals until 1865. In that year he obtained his M.D. with his *Etudes historiques de l'empoisonnement,* which consisted in the main of a translation of Maimonides' "Treatise on Poisons." However, he rarely practiced medicine, preferring to devote himself, in solitude and poverty, to scholarship. Too poor to heat his room, he wrote his books in a café. As well as extending his grammatical methods to other languages (*Nouveaux principes comparés de la prononciation Anglaise* . . . , 1874; *Vergleichende Grammatik der polnischen Sprache,* 1877; *Grammaire de la langue française d'après de nouveaux principes* . . . 1886, 1889²), he defended Jewish tradition against its detractors, publishing *Le rôle de Jésus et des apôtres* (1866), a critique of Renan; *La religion nationale des anciens Hébreux* (1873), a criticism of Jules Soury; and *Histoire Sainte: Ancien Testament* (1877). However his main work was his condensed translation, with commentary, of talmudic legislation, *La législation criminelle du Thalmud* (1876) and *La législation civile du Thalmud* (1–5, 1877–80). A Zionist from the early days of the movement, he took part in the Kattowitz Conference of 1884 and presided over the Benei Zion of Paris. He went to Russia in 1889 with the intention of trying to have his books republished, and subsequently lived in London, where he was assisted until his death by Chief Rabbi N. M. Adler and other benefactors.

Bibliography: *Ha-Maggid,* 32 (1888), 153–5; Reines, in: *Ozar ha-Sifrut,* 5 (1896), 117–23; M. Schwab, *Le Docteur I. M. Rabbinowicz* (1903). [M.C.]

RABBINOWITZ, SARAH (**Sonia:** married name—**Margolin;** 1880–1918), publicist, daughter of S. P. *Rabbinowitz. Born in Berezin, province of Minsk, Sarah graduated in Germany in 1902 as a doctor of social sciences, her thesis dealing with the organization of the Jewish working class in Russia. In 1903 she was sent to Galicia on behalf of women's organizations against white slavery and together with Bertha *Pappenheim she wrote a study on the situation of the Jewish population in Galicia. During 1904–05 she organized illegal political activities by workers against the military in Odessa and was arrested. Released after a short time, she left for Germany where she continued her political and publicistic work, writing in Russian, German, and Yiddish. Her writings include: "Trade and Handcraft Classes in the Works of I. L. Peretz" in *Yevreyski Mir* (1909); *"Die Heiraten der Juden in Russland von 1867 bis 1902,"* in *Zeitschrift fuer Demografie und Statistik der Juden* (5 (1909), nos. 10, 11, 12); *"Zur Statistik der juedischen Schulen in Russland," ibid.* (7 (1911), [nos. 9, 121–30).] During World War I Sarah was active in the German Independent Labor Party and was again arrested. In a seizure of depression she committed suicide in prison.

Bibliography: Rabbinowitz, in: *Yidishe Shriftn,* 3 (1939), 345–6. [Ed.]

RABBINOWITZ, SAUL PHINEHAS (acronym, **SHePHeR;** 1845–1910), East European Hebrew writer and historian. Rabbinowitz, who was born in Tavrogi, Lithuania, to a family of rabbis, received *semikhah* from Israel Salanter (Lipkin), while also becoming interested in Haskalah and teaching himself German and Russian. Rabbinowitz first worked as a private tutor in Vilna and other Lithuanian towns before settling in Warsaw in 1875 where he wrote for the Hebrew press. During this period he inclined toward socialist cosmopolitanism, which brought him into contact with A. S. *Liebermann's circle of Jewish Socialists. In 1881 Rabbinowitz was among those who reported on the Russian pogroms to Western Jewry. He accompanied S. *Mohilever to Brody, where they organized help for the refugees; he also took part in the St. Petersburg Conference of Notables (1882), calling for mass emigration from Russia. At first, Rabbinowitz advocated emigration to the U.S. but he soon joined Ḥovevei Zion, became secretary of the important Warsaw branch, and attended the Kattowitz Conference (1884). During 1886–88 he published the annual *Keneset Yisrael,* an organ for national revival and Ḥibbat Zion, and published documents on the history of Russian-Polish Jewry in a supplement *(Orot me-Ofel).* In 1890 he was among the founders of the Warsaw office of Aḥad Ha-Am's order *Benei Moshe and tried to defend the interests of religious tradition within its ranks. In 1891 he joined an abortive Ḥovevei Zion mission to the West. A member of the Zionist movement, Rabbinowitz attended the first Zionist Congresses, although he criticized aspects of the movement in *Al Ẓiyyon ve-al Mikra'eha* (1898).

Rabbinowitz's great scholarly achievement was his Hebrew translation of H. Graetz's *History of the Jews* (1890–99), in which the author had given him a free hand. Rabbinowitz introduced many changes in the text, also omitting passages that might offend the Orthodox and the Russian censors. The translation includes his own notes and those of A. Harkavy and other scholars. Rabbinowitz's work, which was in fact a new "Graetz," had a tremendous impact on Eastern Jewry, despite its *meliẓah* style, and was reprinted in many editions. Other writings by Rabbinowitz include biographies of L. *Zunz (1896), Z. *Frankel (1898), and *Joseph (Joselman) of Rosheim (1902), and a study on the Jews expelled from Spain, published on the 400th anniversary of the Expulsion (*Moẓe'ei Golah,* 1894). He contributed articles to the newly founded (1896) Hebrew periodical *Ha-Shilo'aḥ,* participated in the early *Eshkol* Hebrew encyclopedia (1888), and completed S. J. *Fuenn's Hebrew dictionary *Ha-Oẓar* (1900–03).

Beset by poverty and family misfortunes, and having suffered great hardship during and after the 1905 revolution, Rabbinowitz left Russia for Frankfort where, however, he found little recognition and had to live on charity. His proposed three-volume modern Jewish history did not advance beyond the publication of a few chapters. His biography was written by his son-in-law, the historian J. *Meisl.

Bibliography: J. Meisl, *Rabbi Sha'ul Pinḥas Rabbinowitz (Shefer); ha-Ish u-Fo'olo* (1943), incl. bibl.; A. Druyanow (ed.), *Ketavim le-Toledot Ḥibbat Ẓiyyon* 1–3 (1919–32), index. [J.S.]

RAB DE LA CORTE ("court rabbi"), an office common in Navarre and Castile until the expulsion of the Jews from Spain in 1492. He was appointed by the crown to supervise the Jewish communal leadership and the apportionment of taxes among the communities. Because of this task he is referred to as *repartidor de todas las aljamas* and was considered "Judge in Chief" of the Jewish communities. The office was established in these kingdoms during the middle of the 13th century. Attempts to introduce it into Aragon, Catalonia, and Valencia, mainly at the end of the 13th century, failed. The beginnings of this office are unknown. As judge in chief, *juez mayor* ("chief justice"), he served as a kind of a court of appeals for the Jews. Generally those appointed to this position were Jews close to the kings or crown princes, serving as physicians, interpreters, or fiscal agents. The majority were not distinguished for their learning, and Solomon b. Abraham ibn *Adret complained that "in our country there are rabbis appointed by the king who do not know how to read properly." Some, however, were scholars, for instance Abraham *Benveniste. The Rab de la Corte presided over meetings of representatives of the communities who were convened when necessary and supervised the drafting of the *askamot* ("communal regulations") and the tax apportionment. Sometimes, he acted as arbitrator in intercommunal disputes. The last Rab de la Corte in Castile was Abraham *Seneor, who became converted to Christianity shortly before the expulsion. The office of *Arraby Mor in Portugal largely corresponds to that of Rab de la Corte.

Bibliography: Baer, Spain, index; Baer, Urkunden, index; Neuman, Spain, index; Suárez Fernández, Documentos (1964), 108–9, 162–3, 243–5, 246–7, 297–9, 375–7. [ED.]

RABI, ISIDOR ISAAC (1898–), U.S. physicist and Nobel Prize winner. Rabi was born at Rymanow, Austro-Hungary, and taken to the United States when he was a year old. He became a tutor in physics at City College, New York, and won fellowships to various European universities. In 1937 he returned to lecture at Columbia, where he was appointed a full professor in 1950. Meanwhile, he continued his own researches in nuclear physics, quantum mechanics and magnetism. He realized that the essential step was to determine the nature of the force that holds together the protons within the nucleus of the atom, overcoming the mutual repulsion that must exist between them, as all are positively charged. When Otto *Stern discovered how to measure this force by means of a "molecular beam," Rabi followed up the discovery, which he found more effective than fission for elucidating the structure of the atom. His most distinguished work was the development of a method of receiving and interpreting such beams, and it was this that won him the Nobel Prize for physics in 1944, four years after he had become associate director of the radiation laboratory at the Massachusetts Institute of Technology. During the remainder of World War II Rabi served as a civilian investigator for the Office of Scientific Research and Development. From 1953 he was chairman of the general advisory committee of the Atomic Energy Commission, but he was active among those

Isidor Isaac Rabi, U.S. physicist and Nobel Prize winner. Courtesy Columbia University, New York.

opposing the strict military control of atomic energy proposed by Congress, and he deplored what he saw as a tendency for pure science to be subordinated to industrial needs. He was involved with building the cyclotron as well as with other work at the Brookhaven National Laboratory for Atomic Research. Rabi was a member of the U.N. Science Committee and on the Atomic Energy agency, among other international agencies. He was a member of the board of governors of the Weizmann Institute in Israel. Two autobiographical lectures, published under the title *My Life and Times as a Physicist*, appeared in 1960.

Bibliography: T. Levitan, *Laureates, Jewish Winners of the Nobel Prize* (1960), 89–92; *Current Biography Yearbook 1948* (1949), 509–10. [J.E.H.]

RABĪʿ IBN ABI AL-ḤUQAYQ (end of the sixth century), Jewish poet from the Naḍīr tribe in Yathrib (*Medina) in the generation before Muhammad. Rabīʿ was a contemporary of al-Nābigha al-Dhubyānī, one of the foremost poets in pre-Islamic Arabia. Tradition relates that in a contest between the two in the *sūq* (market) of the Banu *Qaynuqāʿ in Yathrib, Nābigha admitted the greatness of his rival. Rabīʿ took part in the famous Buʿāth battle between the two foremost Arab tribes in Yathrib as a partisan on the side of the Aws tribe. His sons participated in battles against Muhammad.

Bibliography: H. Z. Hirschberg, *Yisrael ba-Arav* (1946), 129, 172, 250–1. [H.Z.H.]

RABIN, family of scholars. ISRAEL ABRAHAM RABIN (1882–1951) was born in Proskurov, Ukraine. After the *Kishinev pogrom of 1903, he was entrusted to accompany the orphans to Austria (in the post-World War I Ukrainian pogroms his own parents were murdered). From 1909 he taught at the Ezra teachers' seminary in Jerusalem, and in 1911 was called to head the Odessa Rabbinical Seminary. Detained in Germany by the outbreak of World War I, he subsequently took up a teaching position in post-biblical Jewish literature and history at Giessen University, taught at Frankfort University (1918–21), and at the Jewish Theological Seminary, Breslau. From 1929 Rabin also taught Semitics and post-biblical literature at Breslau University. In 1935 he left Nazi Germany for Palestine where he headed a Mizrachi elementary school at Haifa, and was chairman of the Haifa Religious Council. Rabin was an early supporter of religious Zionism (Mizrachi) and as its delegate attended all Zionist Congresses from the sixth—at which he voted against acceptance of the Uganda offer—to the twenty-first. While teaching at Jerusalem (1909–11), he was among the members of the *Academy of the Hebrew Language.

Rabin's published work ranges over a wide field of Jewish scholarship. His historical studies are devoted to the Jews of Silesia (*Beitraege zur Rechts- und Wirtschaftsgeschichte*... 1, 1932; *Rechtskampf der Juden in Schlesien*, 1927; *Juden in Dyhernfurth*, 1929; in *Zuelz*, 1926) and also deal with general problems of historiography (*Stoff und Idee*..., in *Festschrift*... *Dubnow*, 1930, 41–56). His *Studien zur Vormosaischen Gottesvorstellung* (*Festschrift zum 75 jaehrigen Bestehen des Juedisch-Theologischen Seminars*, 2, 1929) deal critically with the hypotheses of higher biblical criticism and anticipate some of the ideas on Israel's monotheism later developed by Y. *Kaufmann. Of special importance to rabbinics is the critical edition of *Mekhilta*, prepared by S. Horovitz but completed and published by Rabin (1931, repr. 1960).

His son, CHAIM MENACHEM RABIN (1915–), Hebraist and linguist, was born in Giessen, Germany, and studied at the Hebrew University, London University, and at Oxford where he lectured in post-biblical Hebrew (1942–56). In 1956 he was appointed professor of Hebrew at the Hebrew University. He was a member of the Hebrew Language Academy; philological editor of the *Enzyklopedia Mikra'it;* and a consulting editor of the *Encyclopaedia Judaica*.

Rabin's published work includes many textbooks in Hebrew and Arabic (*Everyday Hebrew*, 1944; *Hebrew Reader*, 1949; *Everyday Arabic*, with H. M. Nahmad, 1940; *Arabic Reader*, 1947;

a Hebrew thesaurus, *Oẓar ha-Millim* 1 (1970), letters A-M with Z. Raday). On the topic of the *Dead Sea Scrolls Rabin's writings include *Zadokite Document* (1958²) and *Qumran Studies* (1957). He translated an abridged edition of Maimonides' *Guide* from Arabic into English (1952). His work in Semitic linguistics includes *Ancient West-Arabian* (1951) and studies on etymology and borrowing. He was a member of the editorial board of the Hebrew University Bible project.

Israel's younger son, MICHAEL OSER RABIN (1931–), was born in Breslau and taught mathematics at the Hebrew University from 1958 (professor, 1961; rector, 1972). He did important work on mathematical logic, theory of computers, and theory of games. [ED.]

RABIN, YIẒHAK (1922–), Israel military commander and diplomat. Born in Jerusalem, Rabin was graduated from Kadoorie Agricultural College. He joined the *Palmaḥ when it was founded in 1940 and participated in the Allied

Yiẓhak Rabin, Israel chief of staff and diplomat. Courtesy Government Press Office, Tel Aviv.

invasion of Syria in 1941. In 1944, as second in command of a Palmaḥ battalion, he took part in underground actions against the British Mandatory regime and on June 29, 1946—"Black Saturday"—he was arrested and imprisoned in the Rafah detention camp for six months. In 1947 he was appointed deputy commander of the Palmaḥ. In 1948, during the *War of Independence, he was appointed commander of the Harel Brigade, which was prominent in the fight for Jerusalem. Later that year he became deputy to Yigal *Allon during the operations in the Lydda-Ramleh area. His next appointment was chief of operations of the Southern Command until the Armistice Agreement with Egypt, being himself a member of the Israel truce delegation to the Rhodes armistice talks. After the War of Independence Rabin was given various assignments and graduated from the British Staff College in 1953. After he served as C.O. Northern Command from 1956 to 1959, he was appointed head of the General Staff Branch and, in 1961, deputy chief of staff. He became the seventh chief of staff on January 1, 1964. During his term of duty, the Israel Defense Forces were victorious in the *Six-Day War of 1967. After the war he was awarded an honorary degree by the Hebrew University at a ceremony on Mount Scopus and delivered an address which made a deep impression by virtue of its humanistic tone. He retired from the army on January 1, 1968, to become Israel ambassador to the U.S. [J.WA.]

RABINOFF, GEORGE W. (1893–1970), pioneer of U.S. professional Jewish communal service. Rabinoff, born in New York City, graduated from the New York School of Social Work (1914), one of the first trained Jewish social workers. After serving various Jewish communities and the Jewish Welfare Board, he became associate executive director of the Bureau of Jewish Social Research (1928–32), where he was instrumental in founding the Council of Jewish Federations and Welfare Funds, serving as its first executive (1932–35) and, after the merger of the Council and the Bureau, as its associate director. He was associate director of Chicago's Jewish Charities and Jewish Welfare Fund during World War II and served UNRRA as deputy director of the Division of Welfare and Displaced Persons in Europe. From 1947 to 1951 he directed the training bureau for Jewish Communal Service, reflecting his concern for Jewish communal professionalism. He then became associate director of the National Social Welfare Assembly (1951–61), afterward spending a year aiding the development of social work in Australia. Throughout his career Rabinoff was a leader of the National Conference on Jewish Communal Service, serving as secretary (1929–33) and president (1949). His influence on Jewish communal service and its professional practitioners was extensive.

Bibliography: Bernstein, in: *Journal of Jewish Communal Service*, 46 (1970), 351–3. [R.S.G.]

RABINOVICH, ISAIAH (1904–1972), teacher and essayist. Born in the Ukraine, Rabinovich taught in Canada from 1924, and from 1960 to 1969 he lectured in modern Hebrew literature at the College of Jewish Studies in Chicago. He published critical essays on literature in the Tel Aviv daily *Davar* and contributed to literary forums in Israel, the U.S., and other countries.

His works, of essays on Hebrew and general literature, are: *Ha-Sifrut be-Mashber ha-Dor* (1947); *Yeẓer vi-Yẓirah* (1951); *Be-Ḥevlei Doram* (1959); *Shorashim u-Megammot* (1967); a collection of stories in autobiographical style, *Ner Dolek* (1954); and *Ha-Sipporet ha-Ivrit Meḥappeset Gibbor* (1967; *Major Trends in Modern Hebrew Fiction*, 1968). [G.K.]

RABINOVICH, JOSEPH (1837–1899), missionary in *Kishinev, Bessarabia, and founder of a Jewish-Christian sect. Born into a ḥasidic family, Rabinovich was attracted by the *Haskalah movement. During the early 1880s he joined the *Ḥibbat Zion movement and visited Palestine. He returned disappointed in the new movement and at the end of 1883, under the influence of a missionary named

Joseph Rabinovich standing on the Mount of Olives, overlooking Jerusalem. Double-page illustration from his tract on unrest in Russian Jewry, *De Bewegung on der Joden in Rusland*, published by the Dutch Society for Israel. Jerusalem, J.N.U.L.

Faltin, he founded a new sect called "The Children of Israel of the New Testament" (this sect should not be confused with the sect called Novy Izrail (*New Israel) founded by Jacob Priluker of Odessa). Adherents of the sect were to accept the basic precepts of Christianity, while at the same time retaining their Jewish nationalism and observing Jewish traditions such as circumcision, the Sabbath, Jewish festivals, etc. On Christmas Day, 1884, a prayer house "Bethlehem," in which prayers were recited in Hebrew and sermons delivered in Yiddish, was opened in Kishinev. In 1885 Rabinovich converted to Protestantism and continued his work in Kishinev with the support of Protestant missionaries whose funds allowed him to open a small printing press where he published prayer books and sermons. Among his publications were *Tefillah ve-Ikkerei Emunah li-Venei Yisrael Benei Berit Ḥadashah* ("Prayers and Principles of Faith of the Children of Israel of the New Testament," 1892), and *Divrei Niḥumim* ("Words of Comfort," 1897). His activities had no influence on Russian Jewry and he remained an inefficient instrument in the hands of the German Protestant mission.

Bibliography: J. Dunlop, *Memories of Gospel Triumphs among the Jews* (1894), 445–8; J. Rabinowitsch, *Neue Dokumente der suedrussischen Christentumbewegung* (1887), includes autobiography. [Y.S.]

RABINOVICH, OSIP ARONOVICH (1817–1869), Russian author and publicist, founder and editor of **Razsvet,* the first Jewish journal in Russian. Born in Kobelyaki, Ukraine, the son of a well-to-do businessman, he studied both Jewish and secular subjects under private tutors. He settled in Odessa in 1845 and developed a successful practice as an adviser and pleader at the commercial court, and later, as a notary. Rabinovich's literary career also began in Odessa. In 1847 he translated Jacob *Eichenbaum's Hebrew poem on chess, *Ha-Kerav,* into Russian and contributed articles and feuilleton-type fiction to local publications. Later his works were published by leading Russian journals. Although published after the abolition of certain laws regarding recruitment of Jews into the Russian army, his story, *"Shtrafnoy"* (in *Russkiy Vestnik,* 1859), was considered a bitter reflection of the abuse perpetuated on Jews under the rule of *Nicholas I. It was a tale of the anguish suffered by a fine, public-spirited, middle-aged Jew recruited for a lifetime into the Russian army in partial payment for communal indebtedness. In 1860–61 Rabinovich published *Razsvet.* He was the mainstay of the journal, writing articles and stories for it and setting its tone by his weekly editorials. Maintaining a high standard, Rabinovich concentrated in the journal on the relationship of Jewish life

Osip Aronovich Rabinovich, journalist and publisher of Russia's first Jewish journal. Jerusalem, J.N.U.L., Schwadron Collection.

to outside forces, i.e., to Russian society, and in particular to the Russian authorities. He relegated to others the concern for the inner aspects of Jewish life. He pleaded for the recognition of Jews as Russian citizens and for their integration step by step into Russian society as useful, contributing human beings. If inner reforms were needed to prepare Jews for their role in society, it was no less important to rid them of the outward vestiges of medieval segregation and discrimination they were suffering in Russia. Rabinovich felt that a first step must be the removal of such vestiges from the law and from state and public institutions. As Rabinovich saw it, the major obstacle toward citizenship for Jews was the *Pale of Settlement. He contended that not only Jews but the country as a whole suffered from this system which closed off most of the state from Jewish settlement. He believed that the humanist and reformist tendencies during the early years of the reign of *Alexander II, which culminated in the abolition of serfdom (1861), should also lead to reforms for Russian Jews, enabling them to emulate the progress of Western Europe. Rabinovich insisted that the coercive administrative measures sometimes urged by westernizers would not help to better the conditions of the Jewish masses and should not be applied. He believed that a progressive modernization among the Jews would be evoked primarily by improving social and legal conditions. Full equality was due to Jews as human beings, irrespective of the degree to which they might be considered modern, i.e., westernized. Under oppressive Russian censorship, Rabinovich decided to discontinue the publication of *Razsvet.* He died in Merano, Italy. His complete works were published in three volumes in 1880–88.

Bibliography: Yu. I. Gessen, *Gallereya yevreyskikh deyateley,* 1 (1898), 5–72; N. A. Buchbinder, *Literaturnye etyudy* (1927); Perlmann, in: JSOS, 24 (1962), 162–82; Waxman, Literature, index. [M.Pe.]

RABINOVICH, YEHUDAH LEIB (Leon) (1862–1937), Hebrew writer, editor, and physicist; known by his pen name, Ish Yehudi. Born in Brestovitz, Russia, Rabinovich studied medicine and physics. In 1887 he began to write popular articles on science etc. in **Ha-Meliẓ* and *Keneset Yisrael.* In 1890 he won a gold medal at the Paris Exhibition for his inventions.

A collection of his articles appeared in *Ha-Yerushah ve-ha-Ḥinnukh* (1903), and *Yesod Leshon ha-Mikra* (1939). In 1903 he published a Yiddish newspaper *Bleter fun a Togbukh.* Later he served as editor of *Ha-Meliẓ* but was unable to adapt it to the spirit of the times, and had to discontinue it in 1904. In his later years he lived in poverty in Leningrad and contributed articles to the Jewish press in the United States. His memoirs appeared in *Hadoar,* 3 (1924), no. 1, pp. 7–8; no. 3, pp. 5–6).

Bibliography: Kressel, Leksikon, 2 (1967), 816–7; R. Malachi, in: *Hadoar,* 17 (1938), 182–3. [Y.S.]

RABINOVITZ, ALEXANDER SISKIND (known by acronym **Azar;** 1854–1945), Hebrew author. Born in Lyady, Belorussia, Rabinovitz became affiliated with the *Ḥibbat Zion movement during a stay in Moscow. In 1888 he became a teacher in Poltava, where his pupils included D. B. *Borochov and Izhak *Ben-Zvi. It was in Poltava that he was elected a delegate to the First Zionist Congress (1897). Settling in Ereẓ Israel in 1906, he alternately taught and worked as a librarian.

From 1888 the Hebrew language was his medium of expression, although he also wrote occasionally in Yiddish. He contributed articles to *Ha-Meliẓ* (1899) and to *Sefer ha-Sharon* (1891), a children's book. From that time on, he concentrated on storywriting, and was among the first to write stories of social content in Hebrew. These were published successively in the books *Be-Ẓel ha-Kesef* (1894), *Ḥattat ha-Ẓibbur* (1896), *Bat he-Ashir* (1898), and in various Hebrew literary journals, such as *Ha-Shilo'aḥ* and *Lu'aḥ Aḥi'asaf.* His writings were a synthesis of his affinity with the common people, his interest in socialism and Russian literature, and of his strong attachment to the Jewish tradition and its cultural values—an attachment which, upon his arrival in Ereẓ Israel, expressed itself both in his personal ties with Rabbi A. I. *Kook and in his own inclination to religious observance.

Alexander Siskind Rabinovitz, Hebrew writer. Jerusalem, J.N.U.L., Schwadron Collection.

In its entirety, Rabinovitz's prolific and varied output numbers over 100 books and pamphlets, including original works, translations, and adaptations. He popularized scientific subjects in Hebrew, and for many years also wrote *"Hirhurim,"* a regular column in *Kunteres* and *Davar,* which dealt with matters of concern to the labor movement. The first collection of his stories and articles was published in 1904; the second and third volumes were published, in Ereẓ Israel, in 1914–22. Some of his stories were also published separately at various times. Among his monographs are *Jean Jacques Rousseau* (1899); *Keter Torah* (1911), on Rabbi Kook; *Yosef Ḥayyim Brenner* (1922); and *Ḥayyei L. N. Tolstoi* (1924). He also wrote *Toledot ha-Sifrut ha-Ivrit li-Venei ha-Ne'urim* (1906–10), a literary history for youth; *Toledot ha-Pedagogikah* (1913) a history of pedagogy from early times to the present; textbooks for Jewish history; original and translated books for children and youth; and *Ha-Islam* (1927) and *Ha-Inkvizizyah* (1930), popular histories. Encouraged by Bialik, he worked for many years on the translation of the works of W. Bacher, among them *Aggadot ha-Tanna'im* (3 vols., 1920–23) and *Aggadot Amora'ei Ereẓ Yisrael* (1916–17, 2 pts.; 1925–30², 5 vols.). In addition he edited several literary collections, notably *Yizkor* (1912), commemorating Jewish laborers who fell in the course of their work in Ereẓ Israel. On his 80th birthday his collected works were published in five volumes (1934–36).

Bibliography: Z. Fishman, in: *Sefer Zikkaron le-Yovel ha-Shivim shel A. S. Rabinovitz* (1924), 3–23 (incl. bibl.). [G.K.]

RABINOWICZ (Kwasnik), OSKAR K. (1902–1969), financier, author, and Zionist. Born in Aspern, Austria, Rabinowicz studied at Brno, Prague and Berlin, later engaging in the gold business. He was active in the Zionist Revisionist movement and after 1933 became chairman of the Czechoslovak committee to boycott Nazi Germany. When the Germans occupied Prague in 1939, he barely managed to escape, though he had helped 3,000 Jews leave Czechoslovakia for Palestine; he went to England, living mainly in London, and became active in communal life, being on the councils of Jews' College and the Jewish Historical Society. He was director of the Anglo-Federal Banking Corporation from 1946 to 1956. In 1956 he settled in the U.S., where he was active in communal affairs, particularly in the Jewish Theological Seminary and the Jewish Publication Society of America.

In his Prague period Rabinowicz wrote, among other works, *Einleitung in die Probleme des rituellen Schlachtens* (1937), in defense of *sheḥitah* and edited his father's *Makor Niftaḥ* (1938), a lexicographical Bible index. In England he wrote *Vladimir Jabotinsky's Conception of a Nation* (1946), submitted Chaim *Weizmann's autobiography *Trial and Error* to a searching factual criticism in his *Fifty Years of Zionism* (1950), and championed Herzl as the great figure in Zionism in his *Herzl, Architect of the Balfour Declaration* (1958). Among his other works is *Winston Churchill on Jewish Problems* (1956, 1960²). He left an unpublished manuscript, entitled "Arnold Toynbee and the Jews." He was one of the initiators of the Society for the History of Czechoslovak Jews and coeditor of *The Jews of Czechoslovakia* (vol. 1, 1968). His literary work was based on his extensive library, which was particularly rich in periodicals and works on Zionist and contemporary history. This was bequeathed to the National and University Library, Jerusalem. Rabinowicz was a departmental editor of the *Encyclopaedia Judaica* for Czech Jewish history.

His son, THEODORE K. RABB (1937–), was associate professor of history at Princeton, specializing in 16th- and 17th-century European history. His works include *Enterprise and Empire* (1967), a study of merchant and gentry investment in early English maritime ventures, and he co-edited *Action and Conviction in Early Modern Europe* (1969).

Bibliography: A. Hertzberg, in: JSOS, 32 (1970), 99–100. [C.R.]

RABINOWITCH, EUGENE (1901–), U.S. biochemist and biophysicist. Born in St. Petersburg, Russia, Rabinowitch worked in the Kaiser Wilhelm Institute of Physical Chemistry at Dahlem, Berlin (1926–29), and at the University of Goettingen until the Nazis came to power. In 1933 he was Rask-Orsted Fellow of the Royal Academy of Sciences in Copenhagen and from 1934 worked in London. In 1939 he went to the United States, where he was attached to the Massachusetts Institute of Technology and associated with the Manhattan Atomic Bomb Project. In 1947 he became professor of botany at the University of Illinois, and in 1960 professor of biophysics. In 1968 he was appointed professor of chemistry and biology, and adviser to the Center for Science and Human Affairs, at the State University of New York (Albany). His major scientific papers were on photochemistry, photobiology and reaction kinetics.

He wrote *Periodisches System* (1930) and *Photosynthesis and Related Processes* (3 vols., 1945–56), edited *The Bulletin of Atomic Scientists* (1945–); *Minutes to Midnight* (1950); *The Chemistry of Uranium* (1951); and *Dawn of a New Age* (1963), and co-edited *The Atomic Age* (1963). [S.A.M.]

RABINOWITZ, ELIAHU WOLF (1853–1932), Hebrew writer. Born in Stawiski, Poland, he went to Germany in his youth. Rabinowitz joined the Socialist movement, was also involved in the Hebrew Socialist Circle and became friendly with Morris *Vinchevski. In 1876, after contributing to the journal *Ha-Shaḥar,* he became the assistant of M. L. *Rodkinson, owner of *Ha-Kol.* As a result of the persecution of German Socialists he moved to Paris and then to London (1880). A member of Ḥibbat Zion from its early days, he conducted a correspondence with Judah L. *Levin regarding the social prospects of Palestinian settlement in Ereẓ Israel (*Ha-Maggid* (1883), no. 20). In his later years he published chapters from his memoirs, in: *Haolam* (1927), nos. 52, 53, and in *Iyyim,* 1 (1927). His autobiographical notes appeared in *Davar* (July 7, 1933).

Bibliography: S. L. Zitron, *Drey Literarishe Doyres,* 2 (1921), 129–32; Klausner, Sifrut, 6 (1958²), index. [Y.S.]

RABINOWITZ, JOEL (1828–1902), one of the first Jewish ministers in South Africa. Born in Lublin, Poland, Rabinowitz was second minister to the synagogue in Birmingham, England. He came to Cape Town in 1859, when the congregation was struggling to keep alive. Largely as a result of Rabinowitz' efforts, the congregation was able to erect its first synagogue in 1863, which still stands. Taking the small Jewish communities scattered over the whole *Cape Province and beyond as his parish, Rabinowitz corresponded with outlying families and traveled long distances by post-cart to officiate at marriages or circumcisions, thus contributing greatly to the preservation of Judaism. He was also a tireless collector for charitable causes, Jewish or non-Jewish, at home and abroad.

After serving the Cape Town community for 23 years he returned to England, but was back in Cape Town in 1886. His modest investments having failed because of a depression at the Cape, he took a course in metallurgy at the South African College in Cape Town and opened an assay laboratory on the Witwatersrand. He remained involved in communal life, raised funds for building the first synagogue in *Johannesburg and officiated at High Holy Day services. Two years later ill health forced him to retire to Cape Town, where he continued to devote himself to communal affairs. Rabinowitz wrote a series of articles about the early Jewish settlers in South Africa for the London *Jewish Chronicle* (1895).

Joel Rabinowitz, one of the first Jewish ministers in South Africa. From *Transactions of the Jewish Historical Society of England,* vol. 10, London, 1924.

Bibliography: L. Herrman, *History of the Jews in South Africa* (1935), index; G. Saron and L. Hotz, *The Jews in South Africa* (1955), index; I. Abrahams, *The Birth of a Community* (1955), index. [L.S.]

RABINOWITZ, LOUIS ISAAC (1906–), rabbi. Born in Edinburgh, he served as rabbi in the London communities of Shepherd's Bush, South Hackney, and Cricklewood, successively. During World War II he was senior Jewish chaplain with the British army in the Middle East and Normandy. In 1945 he became chief rabbi of the United Hebrew Congregation of Johannesburg and the Federation of Synagogues of Transvaal and the Orange Free State. He was appointed professor of Hebrew at the University of Witwatersrand and head of the Johannesburg *bet din.* In 1947, in protest against British policy in Palestine, he discarded his war decorations in public. An eloquent preacher, he was also outspoken in his criticism of the South African government's apartheid policy. Retiring in 1961, he settled in Israel and became deputy editor in chief of the *Encyclopaedia Judaica.* He was also a *Gaḥal* representative in the Jerusalem municipality from 1969.

Rabinowitz is the author of *The Social Life of the Jews of Northern France* (1938), *Ḥerem Hayyishub* (1945), and *Jewish Merchant Adventurers* (1948). His other books include *Soldiers from Judea* (1942), *Far East Mission* (1952), and volumes of sermons. [L.S.]

RABINOWITZ, LOUIS MAYER (1887–1957), U.S. manufacturer and philanthropist. Rabinowitz, who was born in Rosanne, Lithuania, immigrated to the U.S. in 1901. In 1916 he established a corset manufacture company in New York. Rabinowitz subsequently became chairman of the corset industry (1934) and director of the Business Men's Council (1935).

Active in Jewish community affairs, he was vice-president of the Hebrew National Orphan Home (1921), the Jewish Hospital of Brooklyn, the American Jewish Historical Society, the New York chapter of the America-Israel Society, and director of the Federation for the Support of Jewish Philanthropic Societies of New York City (1935). A collector of books, manuscripts, and paintings, he gave much of his collection to the New York Public Library, Library of Congress, Jewish Theological Seminary, and Yale University. Donating the Rabinowitz Fund for Judaica Research at Yale, he established a chair there in Semitic languages and literature (1955). Rabinowitz served as director of the Yale University Association of Fine Arts and as honorary trustee of the Yale Library Associates. A director of the Jewish Theological Seminary, he established the Louis M. Rabinowitz Institute for Research in Rabbinics at the seminary in 1951 and donated many rare books to its library. The Louis M. Rabinowitz Foundation (1953) sponsored a five-year archaeological exploration in Israel in conjunction with the Hebrew Union College of Cincinnati. [Ed.]

Louis M. Rabinowitz, U.S. manufacturer and philanthropist. From *American Jewish Historical Society Quarterly,* Vol. 45, New York, 1956.

RABINOWITZ, SAMUEL JACOB (1857–1921), Lithuanian rabbi and Zionist leader. Born in Kelme, Rabinowitz held rabbinical posts at Ivye, Aleksot, and Sopotskin and was esteemed as a writer of responsa and novellae, some of which were collected in his *Sefer Oraḥ Yashar* (1903). An early member of the Ḥovevei Zion, Rabinowitz attended the Second Zionist Congress, where he made a deep impression on both Theodor Herzl and the delegates; he was elected to the Zionist General Council, later serving as one of the first directors of the *Jewish Colonial Trust. In 1899 Rabinowitz led the Lithuanian Zionists in their battle against the Lishkah Sheḥorah, a group of violently anti-Zionist rabbis. As a result of his vigorous efforts, over 100 East European rabbis wrote letters in support of the Zionist movement. His own essays on the religious aspects of Zionism appeared in *Ha-Dat ve-ha-Le'ummiyyut* (1900). After the Fourth Zionist Congress Rabinowitz accompanied Isaac J. *Reines on a mission to the Warsaw area, where their efforts to gain the support of leading ḥasidic rabbis for the Zionist cause met with some success.

In 1906 Rabinowitz was appointed rabbi of Liverpool, where he did much to promote traditional observance and communal harmony, despite the early hostility of more Anglicized members of the local community. Together with Reines, he founded the *Mizrachi world movement of religious Zionists in 1902, and he maintained his Zionist activity in England, being elected president of the British Mizrachi organization at its first conference in 1918.

A volume of his essays and addresses, *Li-Tekufot ha-Yamim* ("The Cycle of Seasons," 1918), was sponsored by *Aḥad Ha-Am, and a supplementary work, *Sefer Yashresh Ya'akov* (1925), appeared as Liverpool Jewry's memorial tribute, with a preface written by Rabinowitz's successor, Isser Yehudah *Unterman. He inspired the character of "Reb Shemu'el" in Herzl's novel *Altneuland.*

Bibliography: JC (June 17 and 24, 1921); G. Kressel, in: *Kaẓir* (1964), 123–39; J. L. Maimon, *Sarei ha-Me'ah,* 6 (1956), 217–21; L. P. Gartner, *Jewish Immigrant in England* (1960), 193–6, 216, 249; G. E. Silverman, in: *Jewish Review* (May 31, 1961); idem, in: *Niv ha-Midrashiyyah* (Spring, 1970), 74–81 (Eng. section). [G.E.S.]

RABINOWITZ, YA'AKOV (1875–1948), Hebrew journalist and author. Born in Volkovysk, Poland, Rabinowitz, after teaching for several years in Vitebsk, left in 1900 for Switzerland, where he started to write. Upon his return to Russia in 1904, he became active in Zionist affairs and began his long career as journalist and author. From 1907 until his departure for Erez Israel in 1910, he was active in the *Odessa Committee, becoming M. M. *Ussishkin's principal aide. In Ereẓ Israel he first settled in Petaḥ Tikvah, but moved to Tel Aviv in 1923.

Rabinowitz became a regular contributor to *Ha-Po'el ha-Ẓa'ir.* Together with A. *Barash he founded the literary journal *Hedim* (1922), which became a forum for both the old and young generations of writers and an outstanding expression of the literary milieu in Ereẓ Israel from the time of the Third Aliyah. His own contributions consisted of monographs on various authors. In addition, he wrote a regular column for *Davar,* contributed to many literary periodicals, and published translations. Among Rabinowitz' books are *Be-Ein Shoresh* (1914), a historical novel; *Or va-Ed* (1922), stories; *Setav* (1926), poems; *Nedudei Amasai ha-Shomer* (2 vols., 1929), a story of the Second Aliyah period; *Neveh Kayiẓ* (1934), a novel; and *Hassagot* (1935), articles and essays.

Bibliography: Kressel, Leksikon, 2 (1967), 817–8. [G.K.]

RABINOWITZ, ẒEVI HA-COHEN (1832–1889), science popularizer. Born in Linkavo, in the Kaunas district of Lithuania (then Russia), Rabinowitz early showed an inclination for mathematics and physics, and from 1852 began to prepare a comprehensive Hebrew work which was to encompass all the fields of physics, with his own notes.

Because of financial difficulties, he only published one volume, *Sefer ha-Menuḥah ve-ha-Tenu'ah* (1867). He later wrote other books on mathematics, magnetism, chemistry, and steam engines, thus enriching Hebrew terminology in these fields and bringing them to the attention of Hebrew readers. He also published many articles on these subjects in *Ha-Meliẓ,* and in Russian in several newspapers and periodicals which he edited and published between the late 1870s and 1885. Even after the pogroms of the 1880s he remained convinced that education was the solution to the Jewish problem in Russia. He died in St. Petersburg.

Bibliography: Kressel, Leksikon, 2 (1967), 821; Waxman, Literature, 3 (1960[2]), 331. [G.K.]

RABINOWITZ, ZINA (1895–1965), Hebrew writer. Born in Bendery, Bessarabia, she went to Ereẓ Israel in 1913. With the outbreak of World War I she returned to Bessarabia and later continued her studies at Moscow University. After living in the U.S., Canada and Palestine, she permanently settled in Israel in 1961.

Her poems and stories first appeared in *Ha-Shilo'aḥ* during World War I, after which she continued to publish stories and travel articles in Hebrew and Yiddish. Her books include *Ma'aseh be-Makkel* (1960), *Ba-Derekh la-Ḥerut* (1962), and *Be-Ahavatam Nitgallu* (1963).

Bibliography: Kressel, Leksikon, 2 (1967), 816. [G.K.]

RABINOWITZ-TEOMIM, ELIJAH DAVID BEN BENJAMIN (ADeReT; 1842/43–1905), Ashkenazi chief rabbi of Jerusalem. Elijah David was born in Pikeln, Lithuania. His father Benjamin Rabinowitz, who was rabbi of Zamosc and later of Wilkomierz, was called "Benjamin the righteous" because of his great piety; it was said that he never slept the night through and never ate a meal before completing the study of a tractate. As Elijah David was a twin, his brother being Ẓevi Judah, the name Teomim ("twins") was added to the family surname. Elijah David was known from his youth as an unusual genius and in 1874 was chosen rabbi of the community of Ponevezh. In 1893 he was appointed rabbi of Mir which, though smaller than Ponevezh, was renowned for its large yeshivah. His decision to move to Mir started a controversy, and the leaders of Ponevezh sent "an open letter" to Mir asking that their rabbi be "freed," but the appeal was ignored. His period at Mir was regarded as the creative period of his life. There he published the most notable of his works, as well as articles which appeared in many periodicals—*Ha Tevunah, Ha-Me'assef, Kevod ha-Levanon, Ha-Ẓofeh, Ha-Maggid, Keneset Ḥakhmei Yisrael, Ittur Soferim, Keneset ha-Gedolah,* etc. In Mir he wrote no less than a hundred works, especially notes and glosses to the Talmud, Maimonides' *Mishneh Torah,*

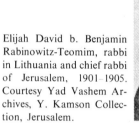

Elijah David b. Benjamin Rabinowitz-Teomim, rabbi in Lithuania and chief rabbi of Jerusalem, 1901–1905. Courtesy Yad Vashem Archives, Y. Kamson Collection, Jerusalem.

the *Tur* of Jacob b. Asher, the Shulḥan Arukh, and responsa. His novellae and glosses on the Jerusalem Talmud entitled *Tuv Yerushalayim* appeared in the Romm-Vilna edition (1922) and those on the *Tur Ḥoshen Mishpat* entitled *Et Devar ha-Mishpat* in the *El ha-Mekorot* (1959) edition of the *Turim.* His extraordinary erudition is discernible in his novellae and notes, and his great knowledge of historical matters from his correspondence on these subjects with Jacob Reifmann, Isaac Hirsch Weiss, and others.

The following of his works may be mentioned: *Oholei David, Matta'ei Hadar,* and *Heshiv Davar,* responsa; *Gefen Adderet,* on the Babylonian and Jerusalem Talmud; *Seder ha-Mo'adot,* on the festivals and special seasons; *Ma'as la-Melekh,* on Maimonides' *Mishneh Torah; Ẓiyyunim la-Torah,* source references; and *Kelei ha-Ro'im,* on the *aggadot* of the rabbis. Among his published works are: *Zekher le-Mikdash* (1889), on *Hakhel; Aḥarit ha-Shanim* (1893); *Over Oraḥ,* appended to N. Cahana, *Orḥot Ḥayyim* (pt. 2, 1898); notes and glosses on the *Mishneh Torah* of Maimonides (1900); *Teshuvah mi-Yirah* (1906), on all topics in which Maimonides employs the phrase *Yireh Li* ("it seems to me"); *Zahav Sheva* (appended to *Tosefot ha-Rashba,* 1956), notes on the *tosafot* to *Pesaḥim* by Samson b. Abraham of Sens.

In 1899 a new period of his life commenced. When Samuel *Salant reached an advanced age and asked for a successor to be appointed chief rabbi of Jerusalem, extended negotiations with rabbis of the Diaspora began. At the recommendation of Ḥayyim Ozer *Grodzinski of Vilna, Elijah David was officially appointed in 1901. He succeeded in uniting the Jerusalem community, which was split into various *kolelim and suffered from inner dissension between the *perushim* (the non-ḥasidic Ashkenazi community) and the *Ḥasidim,* and in forming a single organization for *sheḥitah.* He was also active in many communal spheres. He was the first treasurer of the Bikkur Ḥolim hospital, made regulations for institutions of learning and charity—particularly in the yeshivah Eẓ Ḥayyim, and arranged strict supervision of shops and merchants. His local regulations and customs are still in force, included in the annual calendar which is published by the Eẓ Ḥayyim yeshivah. The most famous of his sons-in-law, Abraham Isaac ha-Kohen *Kook, published a special brochure entitled *Eder ha-Yakar* (1906, 1967[2]) describing his father-in-law's personality and quoting his testament, which shows the extraordinary humility and modesty of its author, and 20 of his letters.

Bibliography: A. I. Kook, *Eder ha-Yakar* (1906, 1967[2]); J. Gelis, *Mi-Gedolei Yerushalayim* (1967), 116–35. [Y.AL.]

RABON (Rubin), ISRAEL (1900–c. 1943), Yiddish poet and novelist. Born in a village near Radom, Poland, Rabon lived most of his life in Lodz. During World War II he moved to Vilna, where he was killed by the Nazis.

His published works include two books of poetry, *Hintern Ployt fun der Velt* (1928) and *Groer Friling* (1933), and two novels, *Di Gas* (1928), and *Balut, Roman fun a Forshtot* (1934). Rabon is a neglected writer of raw power and imaginative force.

Bibliography: J. J. Trunk and A. Zeitlin (eds.), *Antologie fun der Yidisher Proze in Poyln* (1946), 611–8, 637; Fuks, in: *Fun Noentn Over* (1957), passim; Shnapper, in: *Literarishe Bleter* (Jan. 1, 1938).

[L.P.]

RABOY, ISAAC (1882–1944), U.S. Yiddish novelist. Born into a ḥasidic family in the Ukraine, he emigrated to the United States in 1904. His autobiography, published posthumously (*Mayn Lebn,* 2 vols., 1945–47), related the story of his flight from Bessarabia and his first impressions of New York. For four years he worked in a hat factory, where he met David *Ignatoff. The latter introduced him to the literary group Di *Yunge, in whose anthologies Raboy published his first stories. In 1908, weary of the sweatshop and of New York's literary coteries, he enrolled in the Jewish Agricultural School near Woodbine, N.J. Upon graduation two years later, he worked on a ranch in North Dakota. These were happy years, marred only by the anti-Semitic prejudices of his employer and fellow workers. On his return to the East in 1913, he failed in a Connecticut farming venture and was compelled to work in New York factories for the rest of his life. Only at night and during periods of unemployment could Raboy devote himself to literature.

His experiences on farms gave him the subject matter for his short stories and for his two best novels *Her Goldenbarg* (1923), and *Der Yidisher Cowboy* (1942). The former novel, which was adapted for the stage and produced in 1926 by Peretz Hirschbein, introduced the Yiddish rancher of the prairies whose heart went out to horses and cows. The latter novel contrasted the beauty of the prairies with the cruelty of man. Raboy is a lyricist in prose, depicting open spaces with ardent affection.

Bibliography: Rejzen, Leksikon, 4 (1929), 1–8; D. Ignatoff, *Opgerisene Bleter* (1957), 52–56; C. Madison, *Yiddish Literature* (1968), 300f.; Jeshurin, in: Y. Y. Schwarz and A. Raboy (eds.), *Pionern in Amerike* (1963), bibl; S. Liptzin, *Maturing of Yiddish Literature* (1970), 5–9. [S.L.]

RAB-SARIS AND RAB-MAG (Heb. רַב־סָרִיס; רַב מָג), titles of high ranking Assyrian and Babylonian officials. An economic bilingual document in Akkadian and Aramaic attests the title Rab-Saris as held by an Assyrian eponym. In that document, however, the corresponding Akkadian term is absent and it is as yet unattested elsewhere. Further a מרסרס of Sargon is found in Aramaic. The meaning of all these is "chief of the king's attendants." Though the *saris*—in Akkadian *ša rēši*—was often a *eunuch (in contradistinction to the *ša ziqni,* "the bearded one"), there is no indication that the Rab-Saris was always castrated. In the story of Daniel, the Rab-Saris Ashpenaz trained certain aristocratic Jewish youths for service in the court of Nebuchadnezzar (Dan. 1:3ff.). The Rab-Saris is among the Assyrian officials leading the siege of Jerusalem in the days of Hezekiah (II Kings 18:17). In Jeremiah 39:3–13, the Rab-Saris Nebushazban is mentioned together with other Babylonian officials. Among these was Nergalsharezer the Rab-Mag. In late Assyrian and late Babylonian texts the *rab-mugi* (or *rab-mungi*) is described as a high official who performed military, administrative, and diplomatic duties, although the precise significance of the title is unclear.

Bibliography: M. Sprengling, in: AJSLL, 49 (1932), 53–54; E. Weidner, in: AFO, 17 (1954–56), 293; J. Nougayrov, *Le Palais royal d'Ugarit,* 3 (1955), 16:162; H. Tadmor, in: BIES, 31 (1967), 77. [D.Sp.]

RAB-SHAKEH (Heb. רַבְשָׁקֵה; Akk. *rab šāqî*), title of a high Assyrian and Babylonian official. Akkadian texts indicate that he was in charge of territories. In the Assyrian eponym succession, this official was fourth in line from the king. In Middle Assyrian texts the *šāqû* ("butler") is mentioned as a member of the domestic staff of the palace. The *rab-šāqî* was thus originally "chief butler." The development calls to mind the English "chamberlain." At the siege of Jerusalem by Sennacherib the Rab-Shakeh addresses the leaders and the people in an effort to secure their surrender (II Kings 18:19; Isa. 36–37).

Bibliography: L. Waterman, *Royal Correspondence of the Assyrian Empire* (1930), pt. 1, 353, r. 9; E. Weidner, in: AFO, 17 (1954–56), 290; R. Labat, in: *Fischer Weltgeschichte,* 5 (1970), 36.

[D.Sp.]

RACAH, GIULIO (Yoel; 1909–1965), Israel physicist, born in Florence, Italy. On his mother's side, Racah's family claimed to trace its ancestry in Italy back to the destruction of the Second Temple. Racah studied in Rome under Enrico Fermi and in Pisa under Wolfgang Pauli. At the age of 28 he was appointed professor at the University of Pisa. An ardent Zionist, he placed his farm outside Pisa for use by the Zionist Organization as an agricultural training center. He first visited Palestine in 1934, and on settling in Jerusalem in 1939 headed the department of theoretical physics of the Hebrew University. Here, Racah began his studies of atomic spectroscopy which gained the department an international reputation. During the Israel War of Independence he served as deputy commander of the Haganah on Mount Scopus, and led research on munitions that could be produced from the raw materials available in the besieged city. The "Racah method" of spectroscopy has been recognized as one of the most effective methods of studying all types of nuclear structure. His "Racah coefficient W" has wide application in research on nuclear radiations, and is the basis of books of tables published by many of the world's leading scientific institutions. In 1958 Racah was awarded the Israel Prize for natural sciences. His reputation attracted notable scientists to Israel, and the department of nuclear physics at the Weizmann Institute of Science was built up mainly by graduates trained by Racah.

Giulio Racah, Israel physicist. Courtesy G. Y. Racah, Jerusalem. Photo David Harris, Jerusalem.

In 1961 Racah was elected rector of the Hebrew University. He died while visiting Florence.

Bibliography: PIASH, section of sciences, no. 2 (1966); I. Talmi, in: *Nuclear Physics,* 83 (1966), 1–8, incl. bibl.; *Journal of the Optical Society of America,* 56 (Feb. 1966), 268. [Ed.]

RACCAH, MAS'ŪD BEN AARON (1690–1768), rabbi in Tripoli. Raccah appears to have been descended from the Venetian Raccah family. Isaac Raccah, whose daughter he married, and Solomon Raccah, wealthy uncles of his, and his brother-in-law Mas'ūd lived in Venice. These relatives encouraged him and lent him their support. He studied principally in Smyrna under R. Ḥayyim Abulafia the Elder and R. Isaac ha-Kohen Rapoport, the author of *Battei*

Kehunnah. Raccah immigrated to Ereẓ Israel, settled in Jerusalem, and was sent from there as an emissary to Tripoli. The leaders of the Tripoli community invited him to become their spiritual leader. Accepting their proposal, he was appointed *av bet din*. During his stay in Tripoli he founded a yeshivah and trained many disciples who later became rabbis and community leaders. They included R. Shalom Flus, R. Moses Lahmias, R. Nathan Adadi, who married his daughter, R. Benjamin Vaturi, and others. During the years 1731–36 he appears to have been in Leghorn, where he corresponded on halakhic matters with the rabbi of Leghorn, R. Abraham Rodriguez. While there, he gave his *haskamah* ("approval") in 1736 to the responsa of R. David b. Zimra, which were then published there.

Raccah wrote the following works: (1) *Ma'aseh Roke'aḥ* ("Works of the Apothecary," a pun on his own name), a commentary in four parts on Maimonides' *Mishneh Torah* (parts 1–2, Venice, 1742; part 3, Leghorn, 1863; part 4, Tel Aviv, 1964). In this work he compares the texts of the various editions of *Mishneh Torah* in order to determine the correct version; (2) *Divrei ha-Baraita* ("Words of the *Baraita*"), commentaries on the *beraitot*, which is extant in manuscript; (3) various sermons which are extant in manuscript; (4) a commentary on the Five Scrolls; and (5) a collection of commentaries on several of the tractates of the Talmud.

Bibliography: R. Attal, in: *Sefunot*, 9 (1965), 384ff., incl. bibl.; Va'ad Kehillot Luv be-Yisrael, *Yahadut Luv* (1960), 67 and passim; M. Raccah, *Ma'aseh Roke'aḥ*, ed. by S. A. Schlesinger, 4 (1964), introd.

[HA.BE.]

RACE, THEORY OF. Nowadays, although anthropologists differ over the exact number and subdivisions of the races of humanity, most are agreed that the characteristics which distinguish races are limited to physical features (see *Anthropology, Physical). This conclusion is, however, of comparatively recent date. In the 18th century the "founding fathers" of anthropology almost all believed that the human races differed in innate intelligence, or even in virtue. Obviously the idea of such racial differences is far older than the first attempts at their scientific classification.

Early Beliefs. Primitive tribes who laid claim to particular genealogies, going back to legendary ancestors, developed these ideas in their own way. In classical Greece philosophers like Plato and Aristotle were "racists" in the modern sense of the word: according to Aristotle, the Greeks were born to be free while the Barbarians were slaves by nature. However, in the melting pot of Alexander's empire and later in the Roman empire, belief in ethnocentrism faded; this was especially true of Stoic philosophy. The Jewish tradition, with its majestic story of Adam which furnished all men with a common ancestor, can be considered the first historical example of a fundamentally "anti-racist" conception. On this subject the Talmud states: "for the sake of peace among creatures, the descent of all men is traced back to one individual, so that one may not say to his neighbor, my father is greater than yours" (Sanh. 4:5). Belief in a common descent from Adam was taken over by Christianity and became one of the fundamentals of the Christian principle of the equality of all men before God. However, at the same time, medieval society was divided into three estates—commoners, clergy, and nobility—superiority being ascribed to the "blue blood" of the latter. As most of Europe's reigning monarchs were of Germanic origin, there was a tendency apparent from the earliest days to accord a measure of preeminence to "Germanic blood." Conflicts between such conceptions of degree and the Christian universalist principle were particularly acute in the 16th-century Spanish empire. It was only after lengthy struggles and theological discussions that the Spaniards recognized the native races they found in America as men endowed with souls. At the same time, through statutes dealing with racial purity (*limpieza de sangre*), a system of racial discrimination was instituted in Spain, applying to the descendants of Jews and Moors who had been converted to Christianity. In spite of their baptism, the blood of these "new Christians" was considered impure and their race inferior.

Eighteenth-Century Anthropological Theories. So, during the whole of European history, it is possible to speak of latent, or even open, racial prejudice. The establishment of the anthropological sciences in the 18th century enabled these prejudices to be expressed systematically, and the systems of classification worked out by the scientists Buffon and Linné were typical in this respect. Both men coupled features (color of skin, type of hair, etc.) with mental and moral characteristics, which were interpreted in favor of the white man of Europe. Buffon, whose system was more overtly racial than Linné's, even considered the white man as the norm, the "king of the creation," and colored men as members of degenerate races. The tendency to regard the white race as superior characterized the majority of anthropological systems elaborated during the 18th and 19th centuries. The rejection of biblical anthropology favored this trend, because then it became possible to attribute different origins to different races. Thus, according to *Goethe, Adam was the ancestor of the Jews only, while *Voltaire believed that black men were an intermediate species between white men and apes. In the 18th century the major systems of classification (of which the best known and least marred by racial value judgments was that of Blumenbach) distinguished between only four or five principal races. The Jews were usually included in the white race, in whose midst they were supposed to form a nation *sui generis*. But at the beginning of the 19th century, with the emergence of nationalistic struggles, writers began to multiply the number of races, to distinguish between different European races and even to set one against the other. There was continuous interaction in this field between the mental climate of the time, itself closely related to political upheavals, and the current intellectual theories.

Nineteenth-Century Nationalism. From then on racist or quasi-racist notions took root, especially in Germany where nationalist agitators like E. M. Arndt and F. L. Jahn extolled the merits and qualities of the Teutonic race. The philosopher *Fichte elaborated a patriotic theory postulating that German was the original language of Europe (*Ursprache*) and the Germans its original people (*Urvolk*). After 1815, many German students and academics propounded these opinions as part of the Pan-Germanic movement. Ideas of the same type also spread in other countries. After the restoration of the monarchy in France some bourgeois intellectuals, reacting against the pretensions of the "Frankish" nobility, claimed to belong to the native "Gallic" race. In Britain "Germanism" or "Teutonism" found influential supporters in Carlyle and Thomas Arnold. In more enlightened English circles the "Hebrew race," which had given the West its spiritual values, was championed by Benjamin *Disraeli: "All is race, there is no other truth" was his maxim. In that age the concept of "race" was espoused by numerous authors as a substitute for divine providence as the determining factor in history. Germany continued to be the principal nursery of racist theories reinforced by scientific pretensions, partly because its political divisions before 1871 stimulated nationalist fervor, and partly because according to the most prevalent notions the Germans were the only European nation who could claim to be a wholly "pure" race, that is, purely Teutonic. Heinrich *Heine commented ironically: "We Germans are the strongest and wisest race; descendants of our princely house sit on all European thrones; our Rothschilds control all the world's stock markets; our scholars lead in all sciences; we know it all."

"Aryan" and "Semite." It is obvious that from then on the Jews were considered as a race apart, an oriental one, and the spectacle of their success in all walks of life after emancipation strengthened the tendency to attribute to them certain specific—and detrimental—racial characteristics. In intellectual spheres the racist theories of the 19th century received a powerful impetus and gained a new orientation from the linguistic discovery of the Indo-European group of languages. A confusion arose between languages and races, a mistake which had grave consequences. It was believed that the nations who spoke European languages, which were thought to have derived from Sanskrit, belonged to the Indo-European or "Aryan" race. In opposition to them was a "Semitic" race, represented by the Jews and the Arabs. Typically enough, German scholars used the term "Indo-Germanic" instead of Indo-European. Of course it was also taken for granted that the "Aryan" race was morally superior to the "Semitic" one. Thus, according to the famous oriental scholar Lassen, "the Semites do not possess that harmonious equilibrium between all the powers of the intellect which characterized the Indo-Germans." His well-known French colleague Ernest *Renan spoke of the "appalling simplicity of the Semitic mind." All original creations of the human spirit—with the possible exception of religion—were attributed to the "Aryans." Moreover, many authors considered that, to preserve their special qualities, the Aryan nations must avoid intermingling with the people of an "inferior race." They accorded the Germans the distinction of being the purest Aryans.

Such were the opinions, which, pushed to their limits, were developed and popularized by Comte de *Gobineau in his infamous *Essai sur l'Inégalité des Races Humaines* (1853–55). The racial theories of the 19th century tended to establish a double hierarchy: the superiority of the "Aryans" over "Semites" and other "inferior races"; and the superiority of the "Germans" over other "Aryans." The political and economic success (especially after 1871) of the nations who spoke Germanic languages and who therefore considered themselves as belonging to the Teutonic race helped to sanction these opinions. In Latin countries efforts were made to set up a rival hierarchy (which gave rise to the myths of "Latinity" and "Celticity") or, especially in France, to proclaim the superiority of a "racial mixture" over "racial homogeneity." Similarly, in the United States, the adherents of the "melting-pot" conception of the country (limited to the white race) were in conflict with the acolytes of the "Anglo-Saxon race." All these notions continued to be based on the tenacious confusion, typical of the materialist orientation of anthropological science in the 19th century, between "races" and languages or cultures.

However, during the same century, progress in anthropology, ethnography, and prehistory made most specialists gradually abandon these simplified conceptions. Thus the distinguished philologist Max Mueller, although he had previously supported such theories, announced in 1871 that it was absurd to speak of an "Aryan race" or of a "grammar based on the size of the head." However, the "Aryan theory" continued to gain adherents among the general public. It was propagated in every country in school textbooks, which usually summarily repeated ancient opinions and classified Europeans as "Aryans," all except the "Semitic" Jews. The anti-Jewish campaigns, from then on styled "anti-Semitic," made their contribution to the spread of the theory. As a result of all this, by 1900 the existence of an "Aryan race" was firmly established in the public mind as a scientific truth. Usually, this only implied a vague belief in the intellectual or moral superiority of the "Aryans" over the "Semites," and a more marked superiority of the "Whites" over the "Yellows" and especially the "Blacks." But in the arena of the violent anti-Semitic campaigns of the time, some fanatics worked out elaborate eschatological systems in which the struggle between the Aryan and Semitic races was the counterpart of the final struggle between Good and Evil. The most influential of these writers was the Anglo-German Houston Stewart *Chamberlain, who stated that the original sin of the Jews was that from ancient times they had been a mixed race opposed to Aryan purity. Ingenuously, in the time of King Cyrus, the Aryans had committed the fatal blunder of protecting the Jews: "... under the protection of Aryan tolerance was planted the seed from which Semitic intolerance spread its poison over the earth for thousands of years, a curse on all that was noble and a shame to Christianity."

From the second quarter of the 20th century scientific anthropology rid itself almost entirely of the dangerous error of dividing the human races into "superior" and "inferior," or even "good" and "bad." At that same time, however, in a defeated and disoriented Germany, gripped by unemployment, this same error helped to weld a political party and then grew into a state dogma. Thus, from 1933 the theory of race was nothing but a kind of totemistic mythology, serving to justify an imperialistic and murderous expansionism.

However, the racial tensions occasioned in the United States by the struggle of blacks for increased rights did again raise the issue of race, on theoretical grounds, in the 1960s. At least two serious scholars, Carleton S. Coon and Arthur R. Jensen, argued on the basis of statistical evidence that the physical and mental characteristics of blacks differed from those of whites and that the capacity of blacks to absorb education was different from that of whites. Against such notions other scholars argued that the tests used to determine intellectual capacity were themselves biased in favor of western, bourgeois, cultural norms. The presumption that there is any important reality to racial differences continued to be denied by the bulk of American scholarship, largely on the moral ground that to take such differences seriously and to presume that change in environment and increased educational opportunity could not ultimately give individuals of all the races equality of personal opportunity was an offense to democracy. Nonetheless the discussion of racial difference, which was completely taboo in the U.S. in the generation which had witnessed Hitler and which looked to a peaceful and gradualist solution of the "Negro problem," is now again a matter of debate. See also *Anthropology, Physical; *Anti-Semitism; *Fascism; *Genocide Convention; *Holocaust; *Hitler; *Judenrein; *Legislation, Anti-Jewish.

Bibliography: M. F. Ashley Montagu, *Man's Most Dangerous Myth: The Fallacy of Race* (1942); H. Kohn, *Idea of Nationalism* (1944); G. W. Allport, *Nature of Prejudice* (1954); UNESCO, *Race Question in Modern Science* (1957); L. L. Snyder, *Idea of Racialism* (1962); L. Poliakov, *Histoire de l'Antisémitisme de Voltaire à Wagner* (1968); S. Conn and E. E. Hunt, *Living Race of Man* (1965); idem, *The Origin of Races* (1962); idem, *The Races of Europe* (1939); idem, *The Story of Man* (1962²); A. R. Jensen, in: *Harvard Educational Review*, 39, no. 1 (Winter 1969), 1–123; 39, no. 2 (Spring 1969), 273–356; L. Edson, in: *The New York Times Magazine* (August 31, 1969), 10–11; M. Deutsch, in: *Harvard Educational Review*, 39, no. 3 (Summer 1969), 523–57. [L.Po.]

RACHEL (Heb. רָחֵל), matriarch of Israel, wife of *Jacob and the mother of *Joseph and Benjamin. She was the younger daughter of *Laban, brother of Rebekah.

Rachel first appears as a shepherdess who happened to come in sight just when Jacob had arrived at a well near Haran in his flight from his brother Esau. The two seem to have fallen in love at once, and Jacob made an agreement with his uncle to work for him for seven years in return for receiving Rachel in marriage. However, when the time of the nuptials arrived, Laban cheated Jacob and gave him Leah, his older daughter, instead. Laban, however, agreed to deliver Rachel in advance if Jacob undertook to serve him for another seven years as the bride-price for Rachel (Gen. 29:4–30).

Rachel is described as "shapely and beautiful" (29:17) and was more beloved of Jacob than Leah (29:30). She was, however, barren and became very jealous of her sister's fecundity. In her desperation, she resorted to the device of concubinage, used earlier by Sarah under similar circumstances (16:2–4; see *Patriarchs). She gave her maid Bilhah to Jacob and looked upon the offspring of the union, Dan and Naphtali, as her own children (30:1–8). On one occasion, she yielded her conjugal rights to Leah in return for some mandrakes that Reuben had collected (30:14–16), apparently sharing the widespread belief that this "love apple" could cure barrenness in women. It was only after Leah had borne seven children that Rachel finally gave birth, naming her son Joseph, noting with satisfaction that God had taken away *('asaf)* her disgrace and expressing the wish that the Lord might give her an additional *(yosef)* son (30:22–24).

Jacob consulted with Rachel and her sister about his plan to return to his homeland and he received their consent. Before the family's precipitate flight, Rachel stole her father's household idols, unbeknown to her husband. The exact significance of this act is uncertain (see *Teraphim). Three days later, Laban caught up with Jacob and searched his effects. Rachel, however, managed to outwit her father and to conceal the idols (31:4–35).

When Jacob prepared for the encounter with Esau on his return home, he took care to place Rachel and Joseph last in the receiving line (33:1–7), apparently to ensure that they would have a chance to escape should the meeting prove to be hostile.

Rachel died in childbirth on the way from Beth-El to Ephrath. As she lay dying she named her son Ben-Oni, "son of my suffering," although her husband called him Benjamin. Jacob did not bury her in the ancestral, patriarchal vault at Machpelah, but interred her at the place of her death and set up a monument over the grave (35:16–21; cf. 48:7).

Rachel appears again only twice in biblical literature. She is mentioned, together with Leah, as a matriarch of Israel, in the marriage blessing of Ruth (Ruth 4:11), and Jeremiah poetically visualizes her weeping in Ramah for her children (the tribes of Ephraim and Manasseh descended from Joseph), who are in exile (Jer. 31:15).

The traditions about Rachel in Genesis are generally regarded as reflections of Israelite tribal history—though there is no unanimity as to the period involved. It is assumed that at some stage in the development of the twelve-tribe league, the tribes associated with Rachel (Benjamin, Ephraim, and Manasseh) and Bilhah (Dan and Naphtali) constituted a distinct confederation. The territory of Benjamin is, as a matter of fact, contiguous with that of Ephraim. The attribution of two tribes to the concubine Bilhah probably reflects their inferior status within the smaller confederation, while the birth of Benjamin in Canaan would imply a late association of that tribe with the others in the group. The very name can be interpreted as "son of the south," which correctly describes the location of Benjamin's territory in Israel in relation to that of the other members of the groups. [N.M.S.]

In the Aggadah. Rachel warned Jacob that her cunning father would try dishonestly to wed her elder sister, Leah, to him. Jacob and Rachel therefore agreed upon a sign by which he would recognize her on the nuptial night. Nevertheless, when Laban actually sent Leah into the bridal chamber, Rachel revealed the sign to her sister lest she be put to shame. As a reward for this act, Rachel was vouchsafed to be the ancestress of King *Saul (Meg. 13b).

Rachel began to envy her sister after Leah had borne Jacob four sons because she attributed this good fortune to her sister's piety (Gen. R. 71:6). After she implored Jacob to pray for the termination of her barrenness, he hinted that Sarah was only

Figure 1. "Meeting of Jacob and Rachel," drawing by the Flemish artist, Hugo Van der Goes (1440–82). Oxford, Christ Church.

blessed with Isaac because "she brought her rival [Hagar] into her home." Rachel thereupon gave her maidservant, Bilhah, to Jacob (Gen. R. 71:7). When she finally bore a son, she was doubly thankful because she had feared that Laban would permit only Leah to accompany Jacob to Ereẓ Israel, and would detain the childless wife (Gen. R. 73:3). She was a prophetess and thus knew that Jacob was destined to have only 12 sons. Since Joseph was the 11th, she prayed for only one more son (Tanḥ. Va-Yeẓe, 20). One opinion is that she stole her father's teraphim in order to conceal the knowledge of Jacob's flight (PdRE 36); another is that the purpose was to turn her father away from idolatry (Gen. R. 74:5). Jacob's unintentional curse against her on that occasion caused Rachel's premature death. The curse would have taken effect at once were it not that she was destined to bear Jacob his youngest son (Gen. R. 74:9; PdRE 36).

She was not vouchsafed burial next to her husband in the cave of Machpelah because of her indelicate request to Leah in the mandrake incident (Gen. R. 72:3). Jacob buried her at Ephrath because he foresaw that the exiles would pass this place when they were exiled to Babylon. As they passed, Rachel would entreat God's mercy for them (Gen. R. 82:10). Indeed, it was only Rachel who was able to obtain God's promise that Israel would ultimately be restored after she pleaded with Him to recall her kindness to Leah on the night that should have been her own nuptial celebration (Lam. R., Proem 24). [A.Ro.]

Tomb of Rachel. According to Genesis (35:19–20), Rachel was buried "on the road to Ephrath, which is Beth-Lehem"; according to I Samuel (10:–2) the tomb of Rachel was situated "within the border of Benjamin, in Zelzah." The words of the prophet Jeremiah (31:15) allude to the tomb of Rachel as being in the portion of Benjamin. The rabbis who sought to correct this contradiction saw an error in the order of the words in the construction of the verse in the Book of Samuel. Among others, they suggested the following correction: "When thou goest from me today to the border of Benjamin, to Zelzah, thou shalt find two men by the tomb of Rachel" (Gen. R. 82:10; Tosef., Sot. 11:11; Sif. Deut. 352). Some modern scholars read: "When thou goest from me today, thou shalt find two men within the border of Benjamin, in Zelzah, and they shall say to thee: the she-asses which thou went to seek by the tomb of Rachel have been found."

Figure 2. The tomb of the matriarch Rachel, outside Bethlehem. Courtesy Ministry of Tourism, Jerusalem. Photo David Harris, Jerusalem.

The tombstone near Beth-Lehem is mentioned by the first Christians, e.g., Eusebius; the most ancient Jewish source on the tomb of Rachel is the *Guide to Jerusalem* of the tenth century, which was found in the Cairo **Genizah*. According to the descriptions of Jewish travelers, from R. Benjamin of Tudela (c. 1170) until the 18th century, the tombstone consisted of 11 stones which were laid by the 11 sons of Jacob on the grave; a large stone was placed over them, that of Jacob. The tomb was roofed over with a dome which was supported by four pillars. At the end of the 18th century the tomb was surrounded by a closed structure. In 1841 this structure was renovated with funds which were supplied by Sir Moses Montefiore. This is attested by an inscription engraved on a marble tablet inside the structure.

The tomb is especially visited on the new moons, during the whole of the month of Elul, and on the 14th of Ḥeshvan, the traditional anniversary of the death of "Our Mother Rachel." Jews donated oil, sacred curtains, and charity for the tomb structure. They were also accustomed to inscribing their names on the tombstone and measuring it with red woolen threads, which were tied onto children and the sick as a remedy for good health and healing. During the Jordanian occupation, the area around the tomb was converted into a Muslim cemetery. After the Six-Day War, the structure was renovated by the Israel Ministry of Religions and adapted to mass pilgrimage. A picture of the Tomb of Rachel was commonly used as a decoration in Jewish homes throughout the world. [Jo.Br.]

In the Arts. Of the four matriarchs Rachel has inspired the most original work in literature and art. In many instances she figures largely as the wife of Jacob, but in others she appears as the central character, often in connection with the theme of Jeremiah 31:15—"A voice is heard in Ramah, Lamentation, and bitter weeping, Rachel weeping for her children; She refuseth to be comforted for her children, Because they are not." The account of Rachel's marriage to Jacob forms the basis of three early literary works, the German dramatist Christian Weise's *Jacobs doppelte Heyrath* (1683), the Swiss German Johann Jacob Bodmer's epic *Jacob und Rachel* (1752), and an anonymous Spanish allegorical play, *La mas hermosa Rachel pastora de las almas* (c. 1780). Probably the outstanding 19th-century treatment of the subordinate theme was *Rachel* ("Rachel's Lament," 1851), a verse allegory of the fate of his homeland by the Hungarian nationalist poet János Arany. Among works on the subject written in the 20th century are *Plach Rakhili* ("Rachel's Lament," c. 1923), by the Russian writer Nikolai Alexandrovich Krasheninnikov; "Rahel," a lyrical ballad by the German poet Max Barthel, who later became sympathetic to the Nazis; and *Jacob's Ladder,* one of Laurence Housman's *Old Testament Plays* (1950), in which Rachel and Leah unendearingly squabble over their claims to Jacob's affection. A Jewish treatment was that by the Hebrew poet *Raḥel, whose *Shirat Raḥel* ("Song of Rachel," 1935) includes the phrase "Her voice sings in mine . . ." In medieval Christian iconography, the two wives of Jacob, Leah and Rachel, were associated with the New Testament figures of Martha and Mary (representing the active and the contemplative life), since Rachel was preferred by Jacob as Mary was preferred by Jesus. However, Rachel was not a popular subject among artists of the Middle Ages. Interest revived in the 15th century, when the meeting of Jacob and Rachel (Gen. 29:10ff.) was the subject of a pen-and-wash drawing by the Flemish painter Hugo van der Goes (Christ Church, Oxford). During the Renaissance, Palma Vecchio painted Jacob kissing Rachel (Gen. 29:11), and there is a study of Jacob and Rachel by Raphael in the Loggia of the Vatican. A painting by Hendrik Terbrugghen (National Gallery, London) shows Jacob asking Laban for Rachel's hand (Gen. 29:18). Claude Lorrain painted an idyllic landscape with Jacob and Rachel (Hermitage, Leningrad). The robust nude by *Rembrandt, known as *Danaë* (Hermitage, Leningrad), may have been intended to represent Jacob's unintended marriage to Rachel's sister, Leah. Jacob's appropriation of Laban's household idols, which were taken and hidden by Rachel (Gen. 31:30–35), is depicted in the seventh-century *Ashburnham Pentateuch* (Bibliothèque Nationale, Paris). This subject later appeared in the Vatican Loggia frescoes by Raphael and in a tapestry by Barend van Orley, one of a series recounting the story of Jacob. It was also a popular subject in the 17th century. There are examples by the French painter Sébastien Bourdon (Louvre), by the Spanish master Murillo (Duke of Westminster Collection, London), by the Dutch genre painter Jan Steen, and by Rembrandt's teacher Pieter Lastman. Among works of the 18th century is a painting by Gabriel de Saint-Aubin in the Louvre; and the subject was included by Tiepolo in his wall paintings for the archbishop's palace at Udine, Italy. [ED.]

In Music. Rachel has attracted rather less attention in music, although she and Jacob have together inspired some compositions, notably a 16th-century motet by Joachim à Burck (1599), some 17th-century Spanish songs, and a comic opera by Johann Philipp Krieger (1649–1725). The oratorio *Rachel* was composed by Jean François Lesueur (1760–1837), and in the 20th century Lazare *Saminsky wrote a ballet on the theme. *Raḥel Mevakkah al Baneha* (Jer. 31:15–17) has been a favorite subject for composers of cantorial music, and settings have been recorded by several leading *ḥazzanim*, including Josef (Yossele) *Rosenblatt; there are also modern interpretations by singers such as Jan Peerce and Richard Tucker. David Roitman's extended version of *Raḥel Mevakkah al Baneha* (Jer. 31:15; Jer. 25:30; Isa. 20:12; Lam. 1:16; and Isa. 33:7) was arranged for voice and piano by A. W. Binder (1930).

See also: *Jacob in the Arts. [B.B.]

Bibliography: B. Stade, in: ZAW, 1 (1881), 112–4; B. Luther, *ibid.*, 21 (1901), 37ff.; C. H. Gordon, in: RB, 44 (1935), 35, 36; J. Bright, *Early Israel in Recent History Writing* (1956), 115ff.; for further bibliography see *Genesis, *Patriarchs. IN THE AGGADAH: Ginzberg, Legends, index. TOMB OF RACHEL: Eshtori ha-Parḥi, *Kaftor va-Feraḥ*, ed. by A. M. Luncz (1897), 221, 229, 299; J. Schwarz, *Tevu'ot ha-Areẓ*, ed. by A. M. Luncz (1900), 131–5; A. Yaari, *Masot Ereẓ Yisrael* (1946), index; A. Schlesinger, in: *Sefer Neiger* (1959), 19–26; Z. Vilnay, *Maẓẓevot Kodesh be-Ereẓ Yisrael* (1963²), 98–107; J. Braslavi, in: *Eretz-Israel*, 7 (1964), 76.

RACHEL (first century C.E.), wife of R. *Akiva. The daughter of *Kalba Savua, one of the three richest men of Jerusalem, Rachel secretly married Akiva, who was ignorant and her father's shepherd, because she saw in him a man of modest and noble character. When her father found out about the secret betrothal, he took a vow against her deriving any benefit from his estate. Akiva and Rachel lived in straitened circumstances, but Akiva promised her a gift of a golden ornament with an engraving of Jerusalem on it. According to legend, the prophet *Elijah once came to them disguised as a poor man and begged them for some straw for a bed for his wife who had just given birth, in order to make them realize that there were people worse off than they (Ned. 50a). Akiva later decided to study Torah. Encouraged by Rachel he stayed away for 24 years (Finkelstein assumes that this absence did not last more than three years). He returned home with 24,000 disciples to whom he said, "mine and yours are hers," i.e., the credit for all our achievements is hers. When Akiva was able to fulfill his promise and give Rachel the "Jerusalem of Gold," Rabban *Gamaliel's wife envied her and told her husband of Akiva's generosity. He replied, "Did you do what she did, selling her hair in order that he might study?" (TJ, Sot. 9:16, 24c). Akiva's love for Rachel is reflected in his saying, "who is wealthy? . . . He who has a wife comely in deeds" (Shab. 25b).

When Akiva's daughter became secretly betrothed to Simeon *ben Azzai, the Talmud concluded that this was indeed an illustration of the proverb "Ewe (Heb. *raḥel*) follows ewe; a daughter acts like her mother" (Ket. 63a). Two major traditions are preserved in the Talmud about Rachel. One is that it was she who encouraged Akiva to study (Ket. 62b, 63a; see also Ned. 50a, which is a more legendary source), while the other presents the stimulus as coming from himself and his gift to his wife as a compensation for her suffering during his absence (ARN[1] 6, 29).

Bibliography: L. Finkelstein, *Akiba; Scholar, Saint, and Martyr* (1936), 22ff., 79ff. [ED.]

RACHEL, the stage name of **Eliza Rachel Felix** (1821–1858), French actress and one of the world's greatest tragediennes. Born in Switzerland, Rachel was the daughter of a peddler, Jacob Felix, who took his large family to

Engraving of Rachel, the French actress, 1851, Jerusalem, J.N.U.L., Schwadron Collection.

Paris. She was singing with her sisters in the streets when she was heard by the singing master, Etienne Choron, who undertook to give her free instruction. Under his sponsorship, she attended drama classes and the conservatoire, and at the age of 17 played at the Théâtre Gymnase. The leading Paris critic, Jules Janin of the *Journal de Débats*, was the only one to perceive her quality, and saw his enthusiasm vindicated when, in 1838, she entered the Comédie-Française and achieved success in Corneille's *Horace*. Thereafter her career was one of fame and notoriety. Rachel was slight of build and by some considered plain; but on the stage she had beauty, charm, and power. Though she had little formal education, her supreme dramatic achievement was in the French classics, especially Corneille and Racine, in which she replaced the declamatory style of the period with vitality and passion. She appeared in some contemporary plays, including *Adrienne Lecouvreur*, written for her by Legouvé and Scribe. Her greatest performance was in Racine's *Phèdre;* it was described as "an apocalypse of human agony."

The notoriety attending Rachel's name arose from her private life. She never married, but she had two children, one by Count Colonna-Walewski, an illegitimate son of Napoleon. She was also the mistress at different times of the poet Alfred de Musset, the Prince de Joinville, and a nephew of Napoleon, Prince Jerome. She first appeared in London in 1841 and subsequently toured the Continental capitals, including St. Petersburg. Her tour of the United States in 1855 proved to be the end of her career, for the tubercular condition from which she suffered became worse, and she never acted again. At her funeral, the chief rabbi of the Consistory of Paris delivered an oration in Hebrew.

Rachel's brother RAPHAEL (1825–1872), and her sisters SARAH (1819–1877), LIA (1828–1908), REBECCA (1829–1854), and DINAH (1836–1909) all had theatrical careers of varying success.

Bibliography: J. E. Agate, *Rachel* (Eng., 1928); B. Falk, *Rachel the Immortal* (1936); J. Richardson, *Rachel* (Eng., 1956). [R.BR.]

RACHMILEWITZ, MOSHE (1899–), Israel hematologist. Born in Mstislavl (Russia) and educated in Berlin, he reached Palestine in 1926. He joined the Hadassah Department of Internal Medicine in Jerusalem in 1931 and became its head in 1939. One of the architects of the Hebrew University–Hadassah Medical School, he became professor in 1950 and served as dean from 1957 to 1961. From 1960 he headed the Israel Association for Hematology and Blood Transfusions and in 1964 was president of the first Congress of the Asian and Pacific Society of Hematology to be held in Israel. His research work has centered on the metabolism of vitamin B-12 and folic acid, Mediterranean fever, liver diseases, the mechanisms regulating blood creation, and nutritional anemia. He made a significant contribution to the formulation of Israel's health policies as vice-chairman of the National Health Council, and internationally as a member of the World Health Organization's Expert Committee on Nutritional Anemia. In 1964, he was awarded the Israel Prize in Medicine. [L.Ha.]

°**RACINE, JEAN** (1639–1699), French tragic dramatist. Racine's reputation rests on nine tragedies in Alexandrine verse written between 1667 and 1691. There is no record of his having any personal knowledge of Jews, but the heroine's speech in *Esther* (1689) makes his sympathy for them clear enough. A reference in the preface to *Esther* to the modern celebration of Purim also shows an awareness of Jewish customs. Racine's profound knowledge of the Scriptures and its application to his work can be traced to his Jansenist education at Port-Royal (1655–58), where he first met Blaise *Pascal and enjoyed semiprivate tutoring by such scholars as Louis-Isaac Le Maître de Saci (1615–84), the translator and Bible commentator, and Jean Hamon (1618–87), author of a four-volume commentary on the *Song of Songs* (1708). Racine obtained the most thorough grounding in the Scriptures then available in France, but did not learn Hebrew. His knowledge of *Midrash* and *Targum* and Jewish traditions were derived from the works of the contemporary Christian Hebraists Matthew Poole, John *Lightfoot, and Richard *Simon. Racine's *Phèdre* (1677), though based on classical myth, involves Judeo-Greek syncretism. Phaedra's pangs of conscience can only be understood within the framework of biblical law and a biblical conception of man's relationship to the Deity. The biblical tragedies (*Esther,* 1689; *Athalie,* 1691) are less religious in implication than *Phèdre,* and partake of the rationalist spirit that pervaded French intellectual society at the end of the 17th century. Like most of Racine's plays, *Esther* depicts only the last part of the story, stressing midrashic, apocryphal, and original elements—Ahasuerus' dream, Esther's prayer, and an intimate conversation between Haman and his wife. Haman's pathetic supplication to the queen, Esther's refusal of pardon, and her silence when the king falsely accuses Haman of attempting to rape her are given far more emphasis in Racine's play than in the biblical narrative. David *Franco-Mendes, who pointed out that Racine's last great tragedy supports Queen Athaliah in her struggle against God, intended his Hebrew melodrama *Gemul Atalyah* (Amsterdam, 1770) as a reply to the French author. Racine makes the high priest Joad (the biblical Jehoiadah) a prophet of heroic faith, who foresees on stage the criminal career of his Davidic protégé, yet unflinchingly sacrifices his own son to his messianic hopes.

A Hebrew verse translation of *Esther* by Solomon Judah *Rapoport, entitled *She'erit Yehudah,* was published in Vienna in 1827 in *Bikkurei ha-Ittim,* 7, 171–254. *Athalie* was twice translated into Hebrew, first by Meir ha-Levi *Letteris (1835), and a century later by Elijah Meitus (1950). A two-volume English translation by Samuel Solomon of Racine's complete plays appeared in New York in 1968.

Bibliography: L.-C. Delfour, *La Bible dans Racine* (1891); J. Lichtenstein, *Racine, poète biblique* (1934); G. Spillebout, *Le vocabulaire biblique de Racine* (1968); Salomon, in: *Cahiers raciniens,* 15 (1964); 23 (1968); idem, in: *Etudes françaises,* 1 (June 1965), 131–5; C. Lehrmann, *L'Elément juif dans la littérature française,* 1 (1960²), 97–113; J. M. Cohen, *History of Western Literature* (1956), 190–5; L. Goldmann, *Le Dieu Caché* (1955); idem, *Jean Racine dramaturge* (1956).

[H.P.S.]

RACKMAN, EMANUEL (1910–), U.S. Orthodox rabbi, educator, and author. Rackman was born in Albany, New York, and studied at Columbia University and the Rabbi Isaac Elchanan Theological Seminary (see *Yeshiva University) where he was ordained in 1934. He served congregations in Glen Cove (1930–36) and Lynbrook (1936–43), New York, and was a chaplain in the U.S. Air Force (1943–46), later attaining the rank of colonel in the reserves. In 1946 he became the rabbi of Congregation Shaarey Tefila of Far Rockaway, New York, and in 1967 succeeded to the rabbinate of Manhattan's Fifth Avenue Synagogue. Rackman was prominently identified with the modern Orthodox group within American Orthodoxy, and was particularly concerned with understanding the meaning of the *halakhah* in order to find contemporary applications. He took issue with those who he claimed have frozen Jewish law and refuse to solve current problems within its

Emanuel Rackman, U.S. Orthodox rabbi. Courtesy Fifth Avenue Synagogue, New York. Photo Fred Marcus Inc., N.Y.

framework. Rackman also held that Orthodox rabbis and institutions should cooperate with the non-Orthodox and could participate in organizations which contained all the divisions of American Jewry. Rackman was also a leading figure in the Far Rockaway Jewish community and was instrumental in making it an important center for Orthodoxy. He also taught political science and served as assistant to the president of Yeshiva University (1962–1970), and professor of Jewish studies at the City University of New York (1971–). Rackman was president of the New York Board of Rabbis (1955–57) and the Rabbinical Council of America (1958–60), and a member of the executive of the Jewish Agency. He was the author of *Israel's Emerging Constitution* (1955) and *One Man's Judaism* (1970), which included all his previously published essays.

Bibliography: D. Rackman, *Kiryat Ḥannah David* (1967), 29–33; C. Liebman, in: AJYB, 66 (1965), 48–49; 69 (1968), 70, 74.

[A.Ro.]

°**RAD, GERHARD VON** (1901–1971), German Bible scholar. Born in Nuremberg, Von Rad was a disciple of A. Alt. He was professor in Jena (1934), Goettingen (1945), and Heidelberg (from 1949).

His earliest research was concerned with the theological aspects of certain books of the Bible (*Das Gottesvolk im Deuteronomium,* 1929; *Das Geschichtsbild des chronistischen Werkes,* 1930; *Die Priesterschrift im Hexateuch,* 1934). Later he applied the form-critical method to the entire Hexateuch, whose nucleus he saw in confessional summaries of the Exodus and the entrance into Canaan, like Deuteronomy 26:5–9 ("short historical credo"), which had their

"*Sitz im Leben*" in the cult (*Das formgeschichtliche Problem des Hexateuchs*, 1938). His *Theologie des Alten Testaments* (2 vols., 1957–60) tries to let the biblical texts speak for themselves (*"Nacherzaehlung"*), and traces a history of the tradition, in continuity and discontinuity, through to the New Testament. Von Rad was particularly concerned with Wisdom Literature, in which he found a possible relevance to contemporary thought (*Weisheit in Israel*, 1970).

Bibliography: *Probleme biblischer Theologie* (1971), jubilee volume in honor of G. Von Rad's 70th birthday. [R.SM.]

RADANIYA (Radhanites), Jewish merchants of the ninth century C.E., who, according to the contemporary report of the Arab geographer Ibn Khurradādhbih, spoke Arabic, Persian, Greek, Frankish, Spanish, and Slavonic, and traveled from the farthest west to the farthest east and back again. Their starting point is stated to have been in Spain or France. They crossed the Mediterranean to Egypt, and transferred their merchandise on camelback across the isthmus of Suez to the Red Sea, whence by ship they eventually reached India and China. They returned by the same route with musk, aloeswood, camphor, cinnamon, and other products of the oriental countries. From the west they brought eunuchs, slave girls and boys, brocade, beaver and marten skins, and swords. Some of them sailed to Constantinople to sell their goods. Others visited the residence of the Frankish king for the same purpose. Sometimes, instead of using the Red Sea route to the East, they disembarked at Anṭākiya (Antioch) and crossed Syria to the Euphrates, whence they passed to Baghdad. Then they descended the Tigris to the Persian gulf, and so reached India and China. These journeys could also be made by land. Thus the Jewish merchants might proceed to the east via Tangier, Kairouan, and the other North African towns, reaching Cairo, Damascus, Kufa, Basra, Ahwaz, Persia, and India, and finally, as before, attaining by this land route their destination in China.

Another of their routes lay across Europe, "behind Rome," through the country of the Ṣaqāliba (Slavonians) to Khamlīj, the capital of the *Khazars, another name for *Atil. Thence they passed to the sea of Jurjan (i.e., down the Volga to the Caspian), then to Balkh and Transoxiana, and so to the Far East. Since Ibn Khurradādhbih relates that the Russian merchants, when passing through the Khazar capital, were tithed by the Khazar ruler, the Radaniya in similar circumstances were no doubt also liable.

The name occurs in two forms: Rādhāniya (as recorded by Ibn Khurradādhbih) and Rāhdāniya (by Ibn al-Faqīh). Since the researches of J.-T. Reinaud it has been customary to explain the latter form as Persian, from *rāhdān*, "knowing the way," but it is not certainly the more original. Other suggestions have been that the name is connected with Latin Rhodanus, i.e., the river Rhone, and that in the Letter of Ḥasdai (see *Khazars) the people called *sheluḥei Ḥorasan ha-soḥarim*, apparently "merchant-envoys of Khurasan" (not very probably), are the Radaniya.

Bibliography: *Bibliotheca Geographicorum Arabicorum*, 5 (1885), 270ff.; 6 (1889), 153–5 (Ar. section), 114ff. (Fr. section); L. Rabinowitz, *Jewish Merchant Adventurers* (1948), bibl. 202–4; Dunlop, Khazars, 138ff.; M. I. Artamonov, *Istoriya Khazar* (1962), 404; Baron, Social², 4 (1957), 328–9; C. Cahen, in: REJ, 123 (1964), 499–505. [D.M.D.]

RADAUTI (Rum. **Rădăuţi,** Ger. **Radautz**), city in Bukovina, N. Rumania, near the Ukrainian border. The first Jews to settle there came from Bohemia in the late 18th century and were later joined by others from Galicia and Russia. Three Jewish families were listed in the tax register of 1807. The Jews of Radauti were at first affiliated to the community of the district capital *Suceava. They opened their own synagogue in 1830, when a *talmud torah* was also founded. Subsequently land for a cemetery was acquired (until then the cemetery at *Siret had been used). After Radauti became an independent community it established its own institutions. The Jewish population numbered 3,452 in 1880 (30.9% of the population), and 6,000 in 1914. In 1888 there were in Radauti eight prayer-houses (*shtiblekh*) in addition to the central synagogue. In that year 523 heads of families were registered in the community.

Ḥasidism had a strong influence on Jewish life in Radauti, especially the *Vizhnitz, *Bojan, and *Sadagora dynasties. The Ḥasidim held services in their own *kloyzen* and were frequently the cause of local disputes in their opposition to Zionism. There had been adherents of Zionism in Radauti from the beginning of the *Bilu movement, and in 1892 a local group Ahavat Zion was founded. The movement gained headway in the early 20th century. When the city was incorporated in Rumania (1918) the Zionist parties began to exert an active influence on municipal and communal affairs. Members of the *Bund were also active on the municipal and community councils. A Hebrew school, which maintained a kindergarten and adult courses, was supported by the community. From 1919 to 1926 a private Jewish high school also functioned in Radauti. In 1930 the community numbered 5,647 (about 31% of the total population). Among rabbis of Radauti were Eliezer Lipmann Kunstadt (officiated 1894–1907); Jacob Hoffmann (1912–23); and the Hebrew author and scholar Jacob Nacht (1925–28).

Holocaust and Contemporary Periods. Rumanian anti-Semites increased their agitation in 1939, and in October 1941 the Jews of Radauti, numbering 4,763 (32% of the total population), were deported to death camps. In 1942 there were only 42 Jews remaining in the city.

Some survivors made their way back in 1944, and by 1947 there were as many as 6,000 Jews living in the city. The Zionist movement regained strength after World War II (until the government decided to dissolve it in 1949). New communal and welfare institutions were established with the aid of overseas organizations, such as *OSE, the *American Jewish Joint Distribution Committee, and the *World Jewish Congress, but their activities gradually decreased. From 1948 the community dwindled through emigration to Israel and other countries. In 1971 only 700 Jews remained in the city (3.5% of the total population). Some communal activity continued, however, including the holding of Sabbath and holiday services in the central synagogue.

Bibliography: H. Gold (ed.), *Geschichte der Juden in der Bukowina*, 2 vols. (1958–62), index. [Y.M.]

RADEK (Sobelsohn), KARL (1885–1939?), Russian revolutionary and publicist. Born in Lemberg, Radek was a member of the Polish Social Democratic Party, for which he wrote many articles. Before World War I he was also active as a publicist for the left wing of the German Social Democratic Party. During the war he played a prominent part in the Zimmerwald and Kintal pacifist conferences. After the Russian Revolution broke out in February 1917, Radek was one of those who accompanied Lenin on his famous journey from Switzerland through Germany to Sweden in a sealed wagon. He remained in Sweden as a representative of the Bolshevik Party, but after the October Revolution he returned to Russia and became head of the Central European section of the Foreign Affairs Commissariat. In 1918, when revolution broke out in Germany, Radek entered the country secretly and helped to organize the first congress of the German Communist Party. He was arrested in February 1919 but was released at the end of the year. He returned to the U.S.S.R. and in 1922 became a leading official of the Communist International. In this capacity he maintained contact with communist-oriented Zionists of the "left *Po'alei Zion faction" who applied for admission into and recognition by the Communist International. In 1924, however, he joined the Trotskyite opposition and in 1927 was expelled from the party and banished to the Ural mountains. He was readmitted in 1930 on renouncing his adherence to the Trotskyists. Just before his banishment he had served for a year as rector of the Sun Yat-Sen University for Chinese students in Moscow.

In the 1930s Radek was an influential writer and speaker on international affairs and was a regular contributor to *Pravda* and *Izvestia*. He was the coauthor of the draft of the so-called "Stalin constitution" of the U.S.S.R. (1936). Radek's writings include *In den Reihen der deutschen Revolution 1909–1919* (1921) and many articles on literature and the theater. In 1937 Radek was arrested and charged with complicity in plots against the Soviet government. At a show trial which received worldwide publicity, with the prisoners compelled to make dramatic and abject confessions, he was convicted of being "an enemy of the people" and was sentenced to ten years' imprisonment. There are conflicting accounts of his subsequent fate, and the date of his death is thus a matter of conjecture. A selection of his works, *Portraits and Pamphlets,* appeared in 1935.

Bibliography: L. Schapiro, *The Communist Party of the Soviet Union* (1960), index; E. H. Carr, *The Bolshevik Revolution 1917–1923,* 3 (1966^{3}), index; idem, *Socialism in One Country,* 3 pt. 2 (1964), index; D. Collard, *Soviet Justice and the Trial of Radek and Others* (1937); R. Conquest, *Great Terror* (1968), index. [Ed.]

°RADEMACHER, FRANZ (1906–), German diplomat; from 1940–43 head of Section Deutschland III of the German Foreign Office, which dealt with "Jewish Affairs" and cooperated closely with *Eichmann. Rademacher wrote a memorandum on the "*Madagascar Plan" and exerted personal influence on the German representatives in the satellite states to facilitate the "Final Solution" (see *Holocaust, General Survey). In the autumn of 1941 he was sent to speed up the killing of 8,000 Serbian Jews (see *Yugoslavia). After the war he was sentenced to only five months' imprisonment by a German court in 1952, but skipped bail and escaped to Syria. In 1966 he returned to Germany and was sentenced in May 1966 to five years' imprisonment for aiding in the murder of Rumanian, Bulgarian, and Yugoslav Jews, but was released from prison for medical reasons.

Bibliography: G. Reitlinger, *Final Solution* (1968^{2}), index; L. Poliakov and J. Wulf, *Das dritte Reich und seine Diener* (1956), passim; Billig, in: *Le Monde Juif,* 24 no. 50 (1968), 27–36; R. Hilberg, *Destruction of the European Jews* (1967^{2}), index s.v. *Rademacher, Karl.* [Y.Re.]

RADIN, ADOLPH MOSES (1848–1909), U.S. rabbi and communal worker. Radin, born in Neustadt-Schirwindt, Lithuania, served as rabbi in Prussia and Poland, and then emigrated to the United States in 1886, becoming rabbi in Elmira, New York. There he was appointed visiting Jewish chaplain of the State Reformatory, but soon accepted a position as rabbi of Congregation Gates of Hope in New York City. A pioneer among American rabbis in working with Jewish inmates, Radin was named chaplain of all penal institutions in New York and Brooklyn (1890), serving until his death. In 1905 he assumed the pulpit of the People's Synagogue of the Educational Alliance, from which he assisted immigrants on the Lower East Side, and founded the Russian American Hebrew Association, which he considered his greatest achievement. Radin was an active philanthropic fund raiser and a champion of Zionism.

He wrote *Offener Brief eines polnischen Juden an Heinrich von Treitschke* (1885^{3}); *Asirei Oni u-Varzel* (1893), a report on the Jews in New York prisons; and other works, and contributed to Hebrew, German, Polish, and American Jewish periodicals.

Bibliography: S. A. Neuhausen, *Telishat Asavim al Kever A. M. Radin* (1910); AJYB, 5 (1903/04), 87; CCARY, 19 (1909), 424–31. [Ed.]

RADIN, MAX (1880–1950), U.S. jurist, teacher, and legal historian. Son of Adolph *Radin, he was born in Kempen, Russian Poland. He taught in public schools and then at Columbia University (1918–19). He was professor of law at the University of California at Berkeley from 1919 to 1948. Among his many offices and positions, he was Commissioner on Uniform State Laws for California 1941–48. Upon his death his library went to the Hebrew University of Jerusalem. Radin's work as a scholar and teacher ranged through law, philosophy, history, linguistics, anthropology, and literature. He was known as one of the chief proponents of "legal realism."

The principal works in which he propagated his views are: *The Law and You* (1947); *Stability in Law* (1944); *Law as Logic and Experience* (1940); and *The Law and Mr. Smith* (1938). His first interest was in the relationship of morals and ethics to commercial occupations. One of his first publications was *The Legislation of the Greeks and Romans on Corporations* (1909). Related works are *Lawful Pursuit of Gain* (1931) and *Manners and Morals of Business* (1939). Radin was deeply concerned with the political events of his time. In *The Day of Reckoning* (1943), he expounded his thoughts on the war crimes trials, then in the planning stage, and he also wrote on the treatment of the Nisei (American-born citizens of Japanese descent) of California during World War II. His pervasive interest in legal history found expression in his *Handbook of Anglo-American Legal History* (1936) and *Handbook of Roman Law* (1927), and numerous works on Jewish law and history, including: *The Life of the People in Biblical Times* (1929), *The Trial of Jesus of Nazareth* (1931), and his unpublished *Bibliography of Jewish Law.*

Bibliography: *American Historical Review,* 56 (1950), 58. [A.A.E.]

RADIN, PAUL (1883–1959), U.S. anthropologist. Born in Lodz, Russian Poland, Paul Radin was the youngest son of Adolph *Radin, a rabbi, and brother of Herman, a physician, and of Max *Radin, an eminent legal scholar. He studied first in Europe, then in New York, coming to anthropology via zoology and history. A student of Franz Boas and James Harvey Robinson, he did his first field work with the Winnebago Indians, and during the next five decades explored this group intensively. He advocated the outlook of a natural scientist for the study of human cultures. Like his mentor Boas, he represented the humanistic approach to the understanding of preliterate societies.

A member of the Boas School, he differed from it principally in holding that Boas' quantitative and distributional treatment of culture data leads to inadequate and faulty histories of the societies concerned. With his historicist perspective, Radin interpreted Boas' work in terms of the latter's intellectual antecedents, showed how changes in Boas' intellectual perspective influenced his interpretation of the primitive, and how his positions became the framework and presupposition for subsequent American anthropology. Radin taught at various universities including Cambridge, Chicago, Brandeis, and California.

His contributions to linguistics are impressive, comprising texts of Winnebago and various other American Indian languages, and work in historical linguistics (*The Genetic Relationship of the North American Indian Languages,* 1919). He also endeavored to produce a systematic ethnological theory in such works as *The Method and the Theory of Ethnology* (1933, 1966^{2}).

Radin's life style was that of a liberated cosmopolitan intellectual, and evinced humanistic skepticism toward our culture-bound arrogance vis-à-vis the primitives. His Enlightenment perspective stimulated his immersion in the intellectual world of the primitive and his defense of the primitive mentality as against denigration of it by *Levy-Bruhl as "prelogical." While admitting, in *Primitive Man as Philosopher* (1927), that primitive mentality differs in degree, he noted that its reaction patterns evince regularity, uniqueness, individuality, and depth, and betray neither linguistic nor conceptual inadequacy. He devoted much study to the phenomena of religion, especially the God concept among primitives, as in *Primitive Religion* (1937) and *The Trickster: A Study in American Indian Mythology* (1956).

His synthesis of the objective and subjective worlds of the primitive culminated in an apologia for pristine civilizations, and he stressed the virtues found therein—viz., their respect and concern for the individual and their impressive social and political organization.

His deeply felt insight that the universal human drama is enacted in primitive societies was set forth in *The Road of Life and Death: A Ritual Drama of the American Indians* (1945) and in his other studies of the Winnebago Indians.

Bibliography: S. Diamond (ed.), *Culture in History, Essays in Honor of Paul Radin* (1960). [E.Fi.]

RADISH, a vegetable, the *Raphanus raphanistrum;* not mentioned in the Bible, despite the fact that it is one of the ancient plants of the Mediterranean region. Herodotus reports that the large sum spent on radishes for the pyramid workers was inscribed on the pyramid of Cheops. In Israel it is found as a weed. In the Mishnah it is called *ẓenon* and in the *Gemara* it is called *pugla* (Akk., *puglu*). The radish tuber was regarded as a healthy vegetable but its leaves as harmful (Er. 56a). It is a winter plant difficult to grow in Israel in the summer, and it is therefore related of the emperor Antoninus and Judah ha-Nasi that radish was not absent from their tables even in summer (Ber. 57b). From the radish seeds an oil was extracted which the Mishnah (Shab. 2:2) declares invalid as fuel for the Sabbath lamp. In the Tosefta *(ibid.)* however, a *tanna* contends against those forbidding its use: "What shall the people of Alexandria do who possess only radish oil?" The radish is very like the rape, called *nafos* or *nafoẓ* in the Mishnah. According to the Jerusalem Talmud (Kil. 1:5, 27a) they are regarded as belonging to different species in spite of their similarity.

Bibliography: Loew, Flora, 1 (1926), 511-5; J. Feliks, *Kilei Zera'im ve-Harkavah* (1967), 76-79. [J.F.]

RADNÓTI, MIKLÓS (1909–1944), Hungarian poet. Radnóti, born in Budapest and an orphan from childhood, was converted to Christianity. He trained to become a teacher, but because of his Jewish origin was prevented from taking up a post. He spent his last years in Hungarian army labor camps. Radnóti's writings are overshadowed by World War II and the social crises of the Horthy regime. His early poetry is filled with surrealistic influences, but over the years, as the atrocities of the Holocaust increased, it became pure enough to be defined as neoclassicist.

His verse collections include *Pogány köszöntő* ("Pagan Salute," 1930), *Újhold* ("New Moon," 1935), *Meredek út* ("Steep Way," 1938), and the autobiographical *Ikrek hava* ("Under the Sign of Gemini," 1940). Two verse collections that appeared after World War II were *Radnóti, Miklós versei* ("The Poems of Miklós Radnóti," 1948), and *Radnóti, Miklós összes versei és műfordításai* ("Translations and Poems of Miklós Radnóti," 1963).

His last *Tajtékos ég* ("Stormy Skies"), published in 1946, contains poems found in his pocket as he lay in a mass grave at Abda. They accurately prophesy the circumstances of his death. Radnóti, who has come to be considered one of the most important Hungarian lyric poets, was also a skilled translator.

Bibliography: *Magyar Irodalmi Lexikon*, 2 (1965), 543–9; L. Madácsi, *Radnóti Miklós* (Hung., 1954). [I.Y.-K.]

RADO, SANDOR (1890–), psychoanalyst. Born in Hungary, Rado became secretary of the Hungarian Psychoanalytic Society in 1913 during the presidency of Sándor *Ferenczi. In 1922 he was analyzed by Karl *Abraham in Berlin and from 1926 to 1930 was secretary of the German Psychoanalytic Society, playing an active part in organizing the training curriculum there. Sigmund *Freud appointed him managing editor of the *Internationale Zeitschrift fuer Psychonalyse* in 1924 and three years later managing editor of *Imago*. In 1931, at the invitation of A. A. *Brill, Rado moved to the U.S., where he organized the New York Psychoanalytical Institute on the Berlin model. In 1944 Rado was appointed professor of psychiatry and head of Columbia University's pioneering psychoanalytic institute. He was subsequently professor of psychiatry at New York State University (1956–58) and from 1958 he organized a progressive teaching program in the New York School of Psychiatry.

Rado's contributions to psychiatry were threefold: in the sphere of classical psychodynamics, the quest for a basic conceptual system of mind, and the development of adaptational psychodynamics. In his early writings, which included two works on the problem of melancholia, Rado revealed his search for psychological realities rather than abstractions. His research into drug addiction developed the concept of "alimentary orgasm" (later, "narcotic elation") replacing genital satisfaction. During the years 1933–45, in his search for generally valid conceptual schemata, Rado wrote papers on the fear of castration in women (*Die Kastrationsangst des Weibes*, 1934) and the concept of bisexuality. His work culminated in his writings on adaptational psychodynamics. Rado questioned the therapist's exclusive preoccupation with the patient's past. He felt that the exploration of the past should be the beginning of an "emotional reeducation" of the patient in relation to his past and his adaptation to present reality. His *Collected Papers (Psychoanalysis of Behavior)* appeared in 1956 and 1962. Rado also co-edited *Changing Concepts of Psychoanalytic Medicine* (1956).

Bibliography: F. Alexander, in: F. Alexander et al. (eds.), *Psychoanalytic Pioneers* (1966), 240–8 (incl. bibl.); *New Perspectives in Psychoanalysis: Sandor Rado Lectures 1957–1963* (1965), vi–viii. [Lo.M.]

RADOM, city in Kielce province, Poland. The first Jews to visit Radom mainly traveled there as representatives of the Jewish communities at the sessions of the Polish Sejm (Diet) or to negotiate with the tribunal of the treasury, which met at Radom between 1613 and 1764. Jewish residence in the city was banned in 1633, 1724, and 1746; a few Jews settled in the suburbs and numbered 67 by 1765. They were later permitted to reside in a special quarter. The settlement began to develop after 1814, and an organized community was formed; a cemetery was established in 1831 and the first synagogue built in 1884. The community increased from 413 in 1815 (about 16% of the total population) to 1,495 in 1856 (23%); 11,277 in 1897 (37.6%); 24,465 in 1921 (39.7%); and 25,159 in 1931 (23.3%). Before World War I and during the period between the two world wars Jews played a considerable role in the development of commerce and industry in Radom, both as entrepreneurs and employed workers. Jewish organizations in 1925 included a merchants' and artisans' bank and trade unions; there were numerous welfare institutions, including the hospital, founded in 1847, and an old age home, founded in 1913. Religious and secular educational and cultural needs were met by yeshivot, the first founded in 1908, the *talmud torah*, and prayer houses *(shtiblekh)* for the ḥasidic community, as well as schools of various types, including a high school, and five libraries. Periodicals published in Radom during the inter-war period were the Yiddish daily *Radomer Tsaytung* until 1925; the weekly *Radomer Lebn*, later *Radomer-Kelt-ser Lebn; Radomer Shtime;* and *Trybuna* (in Polish). The first rabbi of the community officiated at the beginning of

Synagogue of the old people's home in Radom, Poland. From *Sefer Radom*, Jerusalem, 1961.

the 19th century. Rabbis of note were Samuel *Mohilewer and Simḥah Treistman (1904–13), later rabbi of Lodz. [W.G.]

Holocaust Period. In 1939 over 30,000 Jews, comprising 30% of the total population, lived in Radom. During the German occupation it was the capital of the Radom District in the General Government. The German army entered the city on Sept. 8, 1939, and immediately subjected the Jewish population to persecution. During the first months of German occupation, about 2,000 Jews from the Poznan and Lodz provinces were expelled to Radom. In turn, 1,840 Jews from Radom were expelled to the smaller towns in the Kielce Province (December 1939). In August about 2,000 young men and women were deported to slave labor camps, where almost all of them perished. In March 1941 a decree for the establishment of the ghetto was issued and by April 7, 1941, the entire Jewish population was concentrated in two separate ghettos. At the beginning of 1942 the Nazis conducted a number of terror actions within the ghettos, among them an action of February 19 ("bloody Thursday") when 40 men were shot, and on April 28, when 70 men were killed and hundreds deported to the concentration camp in *Auschwitz. On Aug. 5, 1942, the smaller ghetto was liquidated and its inhabitants (almost 10,000 people) were deported to *Treblinka death camp. On Aug. 6–17, 1942, the larger ghetto was liquidated and its 20,000 Jews dispatched for extermination. Within the part of the ghetto which was transformed into a slave labor camp (the "small ghetto"), only about 4,000 Jews remained. On Dec. 4, 1942, about 800 inmates of this camp were deported to Szydlowiec and afterward exterminated. On Jan. 13, 1943, another 1,500 prisoners were deported to Treblinka. On Nov. 8, 1943, the prisoners of the "small ghetto" were transferred to the newly established forced labor camp in the town. On July 26, 1944, all but 300 prisoners were deported to Auschwitz, where only a handful survived. The last 300 prisoners were liberated on Jan. 16, 1945.

At the time of the mass deportations in August 1942, hundreds of Jews fled to the forests to organize guerrilla units. Such units were composed mostly of persons who escaped from Radom. All the partisans fell in battles with the Germans. Many who escaped from Radom reached Warsaw and took part in the Polish Warsaw uprising (August 1944). In the whole Radom District 380,000 Jews lost their lives during the German occupation, according to figures of the Radom Regional Commission to investigate Nazi Crimes. A few hundred Jews settled in Radom for a short time after World War II, but soon left due to the hostility of the Polish population. Organizations of former Radom residents exist in Israel, the United States, Canada, France, and Australia. There were seven Jews living in Radom in 1965. [S.Kr.]

Bibliography: Halpern, Pinkas, index; A. Rutkowksi, in: BZIH, 15–16 (1955), 75–182; 17–18 (1956), 106–8; *Sefer Milḥamot ha-Getta'ot* (1954²), index; *Sefer Radom* (1961), a memorial book published in Heb. and Yid.

RADOMSKO (Radomsk), town in Lodz province, S. central Poland. In 1643 King Ladislaus IV granted the city the privilege *de non tolerandis Judaeis* excluding Jews from its bounds, which remained in force until 1862. Although the city council complained about the presence of Jews on the nobles' estates and in neighboring villages during the 17th and 18th centuries Jewish settlement there continued. The establishment of a Jewish cemetery in the city was permitted in 1816, and by 1822 a synagogue committee existed which levied taxes for the engagement of religious functionaries. The census of 1827 recorded 369 Jews of the total 1,792 inhabitants. In 1834 the community engaged Solomon ha-Kohen Rabinowich of Włoszczowa as rabbi and *av bet din,* who in 1843 established a ḥasidic court and founded the *Radomsko ḥasidic dynasty.

After the opening of the Vienna-Warsaw railroad in 1846 the community developed rapidly. By 1857 there were 1,162 Jews living in Radomsko (about 39% of the total population). The 1897 census showed 5,054 Jews (43%). They were mainly occupied in carpentry, weaving, and dealing in timber and grain. Well-to-do Jews established factories, hotels, and restaurants which employed some 500 Jews. In this period the community expanded its activities in all spheres. Ḥovevei Zion (see *Ḥibbat Zion) groups formed Zionist parties. In 1899 the Great Synagogue was completed. Jewish workers organized in the *Po'alei Zion, *Bund, etc., from 1905 to 1907. In 1906 the Jews in Radomsko organized *self-defense against pogroms.

During World War I the Jews in Radomsko suffered from the depredations of Russian soldiers and economic depression. The historian M. *Balaban visited the city in 1916 and established a Jewish youth group, Kultura.

In 1919, after Poland became independent, there were attempts at pogroms, but they were prevented by the Jewish self-defense organization. The Jewish population rose from 7,774 in 1921 (41.5%) to 12,371 in 1935 (55%). During this period the number of Jewish workers doubled in the large industrial plants for furniture, metal goods, and printing. Of the 24 members of the city council elected in 1926, eight were Jews. Jewish educational institutions included a high school (from 1916), two *talmud torah* schools, the Keter Torah yeshivah, a *bet midrash,* and two government elementary schools. There were also guilds of craftsmen and small businessmen, and a cooperative commercial bank. In 1926 a library named for *Shalom Aleichem was opened, and there were Ha-Po'el and Ha-Ko'aḥ sports clubs. In 1930 a commune preparing for emigration to Ereẓ Israel was established named Vitkinyah. [A.Cy.]

Holocaust Period. Under the German occupation Radomsko was incorporated into the *Radom district of the General Government. When the German army entered the city on Sept. 3, 1939, they immediately began a campaign of terror against the Jewish population. On Dec. 20, 1939, a decree was issued establishing a closed ghetto in Radomsko into which all the Jews from the surrounding districts were also concentrated. In consequence, the Jewish population of the Radomsko ghetto increased despite the high mortality due to starvation and epidemics. Two especially severe epidemics of typhus broke out during the early winter of 1940 and in January 1941. In June 1941 the authorities reduced the area of the ghetto, thus aggravating the living conditions there. On Oct. 9, 1942, an *Aktion* was carried out, and in the course of the following three days almost the entire Jewish population was deported to *Treblinka death camp where they perished. About 500 Jews and seven houses remained in the Radomsko ghetto (including some 200 Jews there "illegally"). During the deportations hundreds of Jews from Radomsko and thousands from the surrounding districts escaped to the forests, among Jewish guerrilla groups which rapidly organized. They encountered severe obstacles: lack of arms, an inimical local peasant population, and no possibility of a food supply for the great number of Jews who had escaped. In November 1942 the Germans established a "second ghetto" in Radomsko, and promised security for all who voluntarily left the forests. About 4,500 Jews unable to survive the winter there returned to resettle in the ghetto. On Jan. 5, 1943, the Germans liquidated the ghetto in a surprise *Aktion;* hundreds of Jews who resisted were murdered on the spot while the rest were deported to Treblinka. A number of Jews who escaped from Radomsko were active in partisan units and resistance organizations. Some of them won recognition for bravery, including Tuvia Borzykowski, who became a member of the staff of the Jewish Fighting Organization in the *Warsaw ghetto; the three brothers Sabatowski (Ḥayyim, Mordekhai, and Herzke) who fought together in a guerrilla unit in the Konskie forest (all three were murdered in a treacherous attack by anti-Semitic Polish nationalists); and Rosa Szapiro, who managed to make her way out of Radomsko to the Yugoslav partisans under Tito.

After the war the community was not renewed in Radomsko. Organizations of former Radomsko residents were formed in Israel, Argentina, the United States, Canada, and France. A memorial book, *Sefer Yizkor li-Kehillat Radomsk ve-ha-Sevivah,* was published in 1967 (Heb. and Yid.). [S.Kr.]

Bibliography: B. Wasiutyński, *Ludność żydowska w Polsce w wiekach XIX i XX* (1930), 29, 51, 52, 71, 75, 78; *Almanach gmin żydowskich w Polsce* (1939), 209–11; *Novoradomsker Almanakh* (1939); Gelber, in: *Beit Yisrael be-Polin,* 1 (1948), 110–27.

RADOMSKO (Radomsk), SOLOMON HA-KOHEN RABINOWICH OF (1803–1866), ḥasidic *ẓaddik.* Solomon studied in the yeshivah of Piotrkow under Abraham Ẓevi, author of the responsa *Berit Avraham* (1819). His father educated him in Ḥasidism. In his youth he joined Meir of *Apta, leader of the popular trend in Polish Ḥasidism after the death of *Jacob Isaac ha-Ḥozeh ("the Seer") of Lublin. In 1834 Solomon was appointed rabbi of Radomsk, and from 1843 he was accepted as a ḥasidic rabbi. Solomon's teachings were in the spirit of the popular trend of Polish Ḥasidism. He engaged in public affairs and worked on behalf of the poor of his town. His striking personality, his enthusiastic way of praying, and his witty sayings attracted to him many disciples, among them the Ḥasid and philosopher Aaron *Marcus (Verus) and the physician Ḥayyim David Bernard of Piotrkow. Solomon's book, *Tiferet Shelomo* (1867–69), is considered one of the classic works of Polish Ḥasidism. His successor was Abraham Issachar ha-Kohen (d. 1892), author of *Ḥesed le-Avraham* (1893–95), who in turn was succeeded by his son Ezekiel ha-Kohen (d. 1911), author of *Keneset Yeḥezkel* (1913). The last of the ḥasidic rabbis of Radomsk in Poland before the Holocaust was Solomon Enoch ha-Kohen (d. 1942), famous for his establishment of a network of yeshivot called Keter Torah. He was murdered in the Warsaw ghetto. His novellae and those of his son-in-law David Moses, who was killed at the same time, were collected in the book *Shivḥei Kohen* (1953).

Bibliography: I. M. Rabinowitz, *Ohel Shelomo* (1924); idem, *Ateret Sholomo* (1926); A. Marcus (Verus), *Der Chassidismus* (1901), 363–5; *Sefer Yizkor le-Kehillat Radomsk ve-ha-Sevivah* (1967), 22–26, 75–106, 110–4. [Z.M.R.]

RADOMYSHL, city in Zhitomir oblast, Ukrainian S.S.R. The Jewish community of Radomyshl was established in the 18th century. In 1797 it numbered 1,424 (80% of the total population), in 1847, 2,734, and it increased to 7,502 (67%) in 1897. The district of Radomyshl included the communities of *Chernobyl near *Korostyshev (4,160), Brusilov (3,575), Malin (2,547), and others. The entire region was influenced by the teaching of the ḥasidic rabbis of Chernobyl. In the spring of 1919 bands of peasants of the *hetman* Sokolovski organized pogroms in the Jewish communities of Radomyshl and neighboring towns. Hundreds of Jews were massacred and many others fled to the big cities. Under the Soviet regime, Jewish community life stopped and the town declined. In 1926 there were 4,637 Jews (36% of the total population) in Radomyshl. When the Nazis invaded Russia (1941) all the Jews who remained in Radomyshl were exterminated. Six mass graves mark the murder of Jews in the vicinity. Later, Jews were prohibited from gathering at the graves, since the militia claimed that for them to do so was to cause a "demonstration." Jews were also forbidden to erect a monument to the dead. In 1970 the Jewish population was estimated at about 250.

Bibliography: *Yidishe avtonomye un der Natsyonaler Sekretaryat in Ukraine* (1920), 176, 180; E. Tcherikower, *Di Ukrainer Pogromen in Yor 1919* (1965), 220–3. [Y.S.]

RADOSHITSER (of Radoszyce), ISSACHAR BAER (1765–1843), ḥasidic *ẓaddik* whose popularity is attested by his nickname, "the holy old man"; famous as a miracle healer. At first he lived in great poverty as a village schoolmaster *(melammed)* in Checiny (Chantchin) and Chmielnik. He frequented the courts of numerous *ẓaddikim* and was among the disciples of *Jacob Isaac ha-Ḥozeh (The Seer) of Lublin, Jacob Isaac "the holy Jew of *Przysucha," Joshua Heshel of *Apta, and Israel the *maggid* of *Kozienice. From 1815 he became a *ẓaddik* in his own right in Radoszyce. He was a *tärnik,* i.e., one of those who believed that 1840 (ת״ר) would be the year of the redemption.

Bibliography: R. H. Tshernoḥa, *Nifla'ot ha-Sava Kaddisha* (1937); I. Alfasi, *Ha-Sava ha-Kadosh mi-Radoshitz* (1957); M. Buber, *Tales of the Hasidim,* 2 (1966), 200–5; R. Mahler, *Ha-Ḥasidut ve-ha-Haskalah* (1961), 303–5, 307–11. [E.Z.]

RADOSHKOVICHI (Pol. **Radoszkowice**), town in Belorussian S.S.R.; within Poland until the partitions and between the two world wars. The Jewish community was established in the 16th century. The Jews numbered 455 in 1765; 1,701 in 1847; 1,519 (58.9% of the total population) in 1897; and 1,215 (49.4%) in 1921. The Jews earned their livelihood from trading at the annual fair, dealing in wood and cereals (exported to Germany and even Hungary), local retail trade, and crafts. In the town there was also a brewery, a brick factory, flour mills, and small tanneries. Many families earned their living from cultivating orchards on behalf of non-Jewish farmers and landowners. In the 1920s and 1930s the Jewish economy suffered and there was considerable poverty as a result of the poor returns, the heavy taxes, and the competition of non-Jews who were supported by the Polish government. The local Jewish people's bank made considerable efforts to assist the community in its economic struggle. The members of the community were largely **Mitnaggedim*, but local Ḥasidim had two prayer rooms. Pioneers from Radoshkovichi were among the first members of the Third *Aliyah. After World War I, Zionist youth movements were very active and a *He-Ḥalutz training farm was established. In 1921–22 Radoshkovichi (then on the Polish-Russian border) was a transit station for the Jewish refugees returning from Soviet Russia to their homes in Poland. Communal institutions included a *Tarbut school, and a Hebrew library named after the poet Mordecai Ẓevi *Manne, a native of Radoshkovichi. Among the community's rabbis were Abraham b. Judah Leib *Maskileison, Meir b. Joshua Ẓevi Rabinsohn, who settled in Palestine in his old age, and his son, Joseph Zundel, the last rabbi of Radoshkovichi. Notable natives of the town included Israel Rivka'i-Rubin, educator and author; Mordecai Rabinsohn, Hebrew critic; and Naphtali Maskileison, poet and Talmud scholar. [D.R.]

Holocaust Period. On the outbreak of World War II there were about 1,200 Jews in Radoshkovichi. On Sept. 18, 1939, the Red Army entered the town and a Soviet administration was established there. The Germans occupied the town on June 25, 1941. An *Aktion* took place on March 11, 1942, when 850 Jews were killed. After this *Aktion,* a ghetto was established for the remaining 350 Jews. The Jewish community was liquidated on March 7, 1943, when the remaining 300 Jews were killed in the ghetto. During the liquidation, about 50 Jews succeeded in escaping to the nearby forests, where they joined the partisan unit, "the Revenge." After the war the Jewish community of Radoshkovichi was not reconstituted. [ED.]

Bibliography: I. Rubin and M. Rabinsohn (eds.), *Radoshkovich, Sefer Zikkaron* (1965); *Unzer Hilf* (1932).

RADUN (Pol. **Raduń;** Yid. **Radin**), village in Grodno oblast, Belorussian S.S.R. Originally a Polish royal estate, Radun became important in the 16th century because it was situated on the main road between Cracow and Vilna. Jews were still forbidden to live there in 1538 and Jewish farmers who cultivated lands in the vicinity exerted their influence to have Radun granted municipal status so that they would not be expelled. In 1623 the Council of the Province of Lithuania (see *Councils of the Lands) made the Radun community subordinate to that of Grodno. In 1765 there were 581 poll tax paying Jews in Radun and district; in the town itself there were 283 Jews in 1847; 896 (53.3% of the total population) in 1897; and 671 (53.5%) in 1921. The center of Radun spiritual life was the yeshivah founded in 1869 by *Israel Meir Kohen (the Ḥafez Ḥayyim). Its fame was widespread and the 300 students came from far and near. The Jews of Radun earned their livelihood from commerce, crafts, and agriculture; in the 1920s, 12% of the 200 members of the Jewish cooperative bank were farmers. In 1922 the *Yekopo relief society in Vilna gave loans to 19 farms, covering an area of 420 dessiatines (1,134 acres). [D.R.]

Holocaust Period. Before the outbreak of World War II, there were about 800 Jews in Radun. In September 1939 the Red Army entered the town and a Soviet administration was established there until the outbreak of the German-Soviet war. The Germans occupied the town on July 1, 1941. A large-scale *Aktion* took place on May 10, 1942, when 2,000 Jews from Radun and its vicinity were killed. The Jewish community was liquidated on Aug. 9, 1942, when most of the Jews were killed; some escaped to the nearby forests and joined the partisan units. After the war the Jewish community of Radun was not reconstituted. [ED.]

Bibliography: S. Dubnow (ed.), *Pinkas ha-Medinah* (1925), 17–18; A. Rivkes, in: *Life,* 1 (1951), 653; *Unzer Hilf,* 1–3 (1921–23); *Yahadut Lita,* 3 (1967), 57–58.

RADYMNO (Yid. **Redem**), town in Rzeszow province, S.E. Poland; between the two world wars in the province of Lvov. The town was founded in the 14th century by the Polish king Casimir the Great. In 1640 King Ladislaus IV granted it the privilege *de non tolerandis Judaeis,* excluding

The former synagogue of Radymno, Poland, now a factory.

Jews from the town. Subsequently Jewish settlement was discontinued until the first partition of Poland and the incorporation of Radymno into Austria in 1772, although during this period a few Jews were granted the right of residence. In 1644 the Jew Benko was granted the right by the owners of the town to settle in Radymno with his family and trade there. When a survey of the population carried out in 1711 showed some Jews living there, they were expelled on the demand of the townsmen. Jews who settled in the town from the close of the 18th century engaged in commerce. The Jewish population gradually increased, and around 1880 numbered 898 (46.8% of the total population). During World War I the number declined, and in 1921 there were 808 (42.3%). After World War I and the incorporation of Radymno into independent Poland, it lost its importance. The Jewish population became impoverished, Jewish communal activities, particularly in the sphere of social relief, began to wane. Elections to the community council were held in 1927, and Jews also took part in the municipal elections of 1934. The community came to an end during the Holocaust. [SH.L.K.]

RADZINOWICZ, SIR LEON (1906–), British criminologist. Born in Poland, Radzinowicz lectured at the University of Geneva from 1928 to 1931. In 1932 he began teaching at the Free University of Warsaw and in 1936 was appointed an assistant professor. Two years later he made a study of the English penal system on behalf of the Polish Ministry of Justice. In 1946 he was named assistant director of research at the University of Cambridge and in 1949 director of the department of criminal science, a post he held for ten years. From 1959 he was professor of criminology at Cambridge, and from 1960 was director of the Institute of Criminology which he had founded.

Radzinowicz held many important offices in the field of law and criminology, among them, head of the Social Defense Section of the United Nations and a member of the Royal Commission on Capital Punishment in the Advisory Council on the Penal System of the Home Office and president of the British Academy of Forensic Sciences (1960–61). He was knighted in 1970. Radzinowicz made a major contribution by his research in the trends of legal thought which led to modern concepts in the administration of justice which were adopted in many of the democratic countries. Among his most significant works are *History of English Criminal Law* (4 vols. 1948–68); *In Search of Criminology* (1961); *The Need for Criminology* (1965) and *Ideology and Crime* (1966). He was the editor of *English Studies in Criminal Science,* called later *Cambridge Studies in Criminology* (1940–). Radzinowicz converted to Christianity prior to World War II. [ED.]

RADZIWILLOW (since 1940, **Chervonoarmeisk**), town in Volyn oblast, Ukrainian S.S.R. A Jewish community existed in Radziwillow from the early 18th century. In 1787 the owner of the town, K. Miączyński, obtained permission from King Stanislaus II Augustus (Poniatowski) to establish a printing press for Hebrew books. At that time Jewish merchants and contractors founded an explosives factory in the town. From 298 Jews who paid poll tax in 1765, the community increased to 3,064 in 1857 and 4,322 (59% of the total population) in 1897. The majority were shopkeepers, tailors, and furriers, but some Jews also engaged in tanning, joinery, manufacture of building materials, and transportation; the wealthy traded in timber and grain. Branches of the Jewish labor movement and of the Zionist movement were first organized in 1905/06. The Jewish population of Radziwillow suffered heavily during World War I and the civil war between Ukrainian nationalists and Bolsheviks. In 1920 the town was incorporated into independent Poland. By 1921 the number of Jews had declined to 2,036 (48%). Jewish cultural and educational institutions functioned until 1939. [A.CY.]

Holocaust Period. In 1939 the Jewish population numbered more than 3,000. As a result of the Soviet-German partition of Poland, the Red Army entered the city on Sept. 19, 1939. The Soviet authorities conducted a survey to determine how many of the refugees wished to return to the German-occupied zone. All those who declared that they wished to do so were deported in the summer of 1940 to the Soviet interior. After June 22, 1941, when war broke out between Germany and the U.S.S.R., groups of Jews retreated with the Red Army, but were turned back by the Soviet border patrol at the old Soviet-Polish border. Most of these Jews returned to Radziwillow.

On June 29, 1941, the city was captured by the Germans. In the first few weeks the Jewish population suffered damage to life and property at the hands of the Ukrainian police and population. On July 15, 1941, 28 Jews were killed for being "dangerous Communists." The following day the Germans set the synagogue aflame and burned the Torah scrolls. On April 9, 1942, a ghetto was established and divided into two categories: "fit" and "unfit" for labor. Only about 400 persons were found to be "fit." On May 29, 1942, an *Aktion* took place and some 1,500 persons were killed near the city. After this *Aktion* the youth attempted to organize; at the head of one of these underground organizations was Asher Czerkaski. A second *Aktion* took place on Oct. 5, 1942, and hundreds of persons were killed in Suchodoly. Under the assumption that this was a final *Aktion* mass suicides were committed and some 500 Jews broke out of the ghetto and succeeded in reaching the forests, but only 50 of them survived; some reached Brody, where a ghetto still existed, but later they also perished. [AR.W.]

Bibliography: B. Wasiutyński, *Ludność żydowska w Polsce w wiekach XIX i XX* (1930), 85; I. Schiper, *Dzieje handlu żydowskiego na ziemiach polskich* (1937), index; *Radzivilov; Sefer Zikkaron* (Heb. and Yid., 1966).

RADZYMIN (Rus. **Radimin**), town in Warszawa province, E. central Poland. Founded during the middle of the 17th century as a private town by a privilege granted by King Ladislaus IV of Poland, it grew rapidly during the 19th century as a result of Jewish enterprise. The synagogue was erected in 1840. There were 432 Jews (about 33% of the total population) in Radzymin in 1827, 1,278 (c. 70%) in 1856, 2,133 (c. 53%) in 1897, 2,209 (55% of the population) in 1921, and 3,559 (52.6%) in 1931. Radzymin was a center of Ḥasidism, and during the 19th century it was the home of Jacob Aryeh Guterman, founder of the *Radzymin dynasty of *ẓaddikim*. A yeshivah which gained renown was also established by the dynasty in Radzymin. Zionists played an important role in the public life of the town and in the municipal elections of 1927 they won seven of the ten seats reserved for Jews. The community council, elected in 1931, included six Zionists and two members of Agudat Israel. Among religious, educational, and charitable institutions in Radzymin was the *Linat ha-Ẓedek* ("Hospice for the Poor") established in 1910. [SH.L.K.]

Holocaust Period. Before the outbreak of World War II there were 3,900 Jews living in Radzymin. The Jewish community was liquidated on Oct. 3, 1942, when all the Jews were deported to *Treblinka death camp. After the war the Jewish community was not reconstituted. [ED.]

RADZYMIN, dynasty of ḥasidic *ẓaddikim* in central Poland. The founder of the dynasty, JACOB ARYEH BEN SOLOMON GUTERMAN OF RADZYMIN (1792–1874), was a pupil of the *ẓaddikim* *Simḥah Bunem of Przysucha and Isaac Kalish of Worky (*Warka). Jacob Aryeh was rabbi in Rychwal and Radzymin. He became famous as a miracle-worker and attracted a large ḥasidic followership. His teachings were published in *Divrei Aviv* (1924) and *Bikkurei Aviv* (1936). Jacob Aryeh's son, SOLOMON (d. 1903), followed his father in the rabbinate of Radzymin and in the ḥasidic leadership. The third *ẓaddik* of the Radzymin dynasty was AARON MENAHEM MENDEL (d. 1934). During World War I he moved to Warsaw, where he also remained after the war. He was active in Jewish communal affairs in Poland. He visited Ereẓ Israel in 1929 and on his initiative a separate section for women was established at the Western Wall. This served as a pretext for the Arabs in the bloody anti-Jewish riots which occurred in 1929. Aaron Menahem Mendel was the author of *Ḥinnukh ha-Banim* (1913) and *Alim li-Terufah* (1936). [A.RU.]

RADZYN (Pol. **Radzyń-Podlaski;** Rus. **Radin**), district capital in the province of Lublin, E. Poland. Founded in 1468, the town was first named Koźirynek. Although no reliable evidence is available, it has been assumed that Jews lived in Radzyn from its foundation. In 1765 there were 537 Jews living there. The town developed during the 19th century. There were 1,301 Jews (about 53% of the total population) by 1856 and 2,853 (53.5% of the total population) in 1897. During World War I the general population decreased, but in 1921 there were still 2,895 Jews (59.7%) in Radzyn, and an estimated 3,000 on the eve of World War II.

The synagogue, a single-story stone building, was erected

at the beginning of the 19th century. Among the outstanding personalities of the community was Gershon Ḥanokh Leiner, founder of the Radzyn dynasty of Ḥasidim, who reintroduced the interweaving of the blue thread among the *ẓiẓit* and established a laboratory for producing the proper color. His grandson, Samuel Solomon Leiner, also a leader of the Radzyn Ḥasidim, perished in the Holocaust. Prominent rabbis of Radzyn were Simeon Deutsch, who held office during the first half of the 19th century, and Ḥayyim Fein (d. during World War II). Jewish economic life was affected by a fire which destroyed many homes in 1929, and many Jewish families became dependent on support from their coreligionists in other communities. During the 1930s an economic crisis and the anti-Jewish economic *boycott proclaimed by Polish anti-Semites also undermined Jewish economic life. In the democratic elections to the community's council (1931) two Zionists, two Ḥasidim, two representatives of the craftsmen, one of the socialist craftsmen, and two representatives of the *battei midrash* were elected. [Sh.L.K.]

Holocaust Period. On Sept. 9, 1939, the Jewish quarter of Radzyn was heavily bombarded by the German air force. At the end of the month, just before the German army entered the town, several hundred Jews, mostly young men and women, left for Soviet-occupied territory. In December 1939 the Germans sent most of the Jews to Sławatycze and Miedzyrzec, but after a few months most returned to Radzyn. In the summer of 1940 an open ghetto was established in Radzyn. Considerable underground activites were conducted, mainly by *Ha-Shomer ha-Ẓa'ir, which organized several smaller partisan groups. On Aug. 20, 1942, the first deportation of Jews to the *Treblinka death camp took place, and on Dec. 20, 1942, the second, when the Jewish community was "liquidated."

Bibliography: *Sefer Radzyn* (Heb. and Yid., 1957). [S.Kr.]

RAFA (Ar. **Rafah;** Heb. **Rafi'aḥ**), town, near the Mediterranean coast, 22 mi. (35 km.) S. of Gaza. Rafa is first mentioned in an inscription of the pharaoh Seti I (c. 1300 B.C.E.) as Rph; it also appears in other Egyptian sources, in Papyrus Anastasi I and in the inscription of Shishak. As a border town on the way to Egypt and a point of sharp transition from desert to cultivated land, it is frequently referred to as the site of conflicts between the armies of Egypt and its neighbors. In 721 B.C.E. Sargon of Assyria defeated at Rapihu (Rafa) Sib'e of Egypt and Hanno of Gaza; the Assyrians burned the city and deported 9,033 inhabitants. Rafa does not appear in the Bible; the Targums (on Deut. 2:23) identify it with Hazerim. It was the center of important operations in the Hellenistic period during the wars of the Diadochi. Antigonus attacked it in 306 B.C.E. and in 217 B.C.E. Antiochus III of Syria was defeated there by the army of Ptolemy V of Egypt (Polybius 5:82–86). The town was conquered by Alexander Yannai and held by the Hasmoneans until it was rebuilt in the time of Pompey and Gabinius; the latter seems to have done the actual work of restoration for the era of the town dates from 57 B.C.E. Rafa is mentioned in Strabo (16:2, 31), the Itinerarium Antonini, and is depicted on the Madaba Map. It was the seat of worship of Dionysius and Isis (*Papyrus Oxyrrhynchus*, 1380). A Jewish community settled there in the geonic period; it flourished in the ninth to tenth centuries and again in the 12th, although in the 11th century it suffered a decline and in 1080 the Jews of Rafa had to flee to Ashkelon. A Samaritan community also lived there at this period. Like most cities of southern Ereẓ Israel, ancient Rafa had a landing place on the coast (now Tell Rafāḥ), while the main city was inland. [M.A.-Y.]

Modern Period. Between 1905 and 1913 Ereẓ Israel Jews and Zionist groups in Central and Eastern Europe made repeated but futile attempts to buy land and establish settlements in the area. The town was reestablished in the 1920s under the British Mandate, and built for the most part on the Palestinian side but also on the Egyptian side of the border. Rafa's population grew around the time of World War II, when the British army established large military camps there, providing the Arab inhabitants with employment. In the late 1940s, before the *War of Independence, members and leaders of Jewish settlements, *Haganah, *Irgun Ẓeva'i Le'ummi, and the *yishuv* were detained in British detention camps at Rafa. After the battles of 1948 Arab refugees settled in the former British camps at Rafa, which was under Egyptian administration in the *Gaza Strip. Taken by Israel forces in the Sinai Campaign (1956), Rafa was evacuated by them in March 1957. During the *Six-Day War, on June 5, 1967, Israel again took the town. In 1931 the town had 1,400 inhabitants, in 1945 2,500, and according to the Israel census of the fall of 1967, 49,812, almost all Muslim Arabs, 39,000 of whom lived in refugee camps. In 1971 many inhabitants worked as farm laborers and in small trades, but the percentage of those subsisting on relief was particularly high. [E.O.]

Bibliography: J. Mann, *The Jews in Egypt*, 2 (1922), 71–72; S. Klein (ed.), *Sefer ha-Yishuv* (1939), s.v.; Abel, in: RB, 49 (1940), 73ff.

RAFES, MOSES (1883–1942), leading member of the Russian Bund. Rafes, born into a family of merchants, was associated in his youth with revolutionary circles and in 1902–03 joined the *Bund in Vilna, where he had some connection with the terrorist act of Hirsch *Lekert. He was also active in *Gomel (1906) and St. Petersburg and was a Bund delegate to the London convention of the Social Democratic Workers' Party of Russia (1907). In 1912 he was co-opted to the central committee of the Bund. During World War I he supported the "defensist" wing of the Social Democrats, which preferred the victory of Russia. Together with H. *Erlich he represented the Bund on the "industrial war committees." After the revolution of February 1917 he was a member of the Executive Council of the Petrograd Soviet and was later active within the Ukrainian Bund. He was at first an extremist of the right and anti-Bolshevist wing, then turned toward the center, and after the revolution in Germany made a sharp turn toward communism. He played a central role in the divisions in the Bund and the amalgamation of its majority with the Communist Party in Soviet Russia, and he was then also sent to work for the liquidation of the Bund in Poland. He acted with particular energy in the "Liquidation Committee for Jewish Affairs" of the *Yevsektsiya, subsequently adhering to the assimilationist trend and abandoning Jewish activities. After having served as a commissar in the Red Army, he worked in the government in Moscow, and also for the Comintern and the Soviet Foreign Service (Chinese affairs). He was finally transferred to the sphere of cinema work and escaped the "purges."

Before World War I, he contributed to the Bundist press and continued to write from time to time in the Soviet Yiddish press. He published some works on the history of the Bund which, in spite of their bias, are of some historiographic value. These include (in Russian): "Two Years of Revolution in the Ukraine" (1920) and "Chapters on the History of the Bund" (1923). He edited the anthology *Der Yidisher Arbeter* (4 vols., 1925–28) of A. *Kirzhnitz.

Bibliography: Ch. Shmeruk (ed.), *Pirsumim Yehudiyyim bi-Verit ha-Mo'azot* (1961), index; Rejzen, Leksikon, 4 (1929), 237–43; I. S. Hertz et al. (eds.), *Geshikhte fun Bund* 1–3 (1960–66), index; M. Altschuler (ed.), *Russian Publications on Jews and Judaism in the Soviet Union* (1970), index. [M.M.]

RAFFALOVICH, ARTHUR GERMANOVICH (1853–1921), Russian economist. Born in Odessa, Raffalovich lived in Paris where his lucid and pertinent explanations of, and comments on, contemporary economic issues such as cartels and other commercial agreements, brought him in close contact with leading French publications and journalists. He became a regular contributor to *Le Temps* and *Le Journal des Débats.* Having acquired the confidence of the Russian authorities particularly of Prime Minister Witte and Finance Minister Kokovtsev, whom he successfully advised on commercial and financial affairs, he became the major Russian publicity agent in France, and was particularly concerned with press relations and their effect on the placement of Russian government bonds in France. His assignment included guidance to the Russian authorities on the allocation of advertising in the French press. This exposed him to the charge of bribery. After having attacked Bolshevism, Raffalovich became the object of relentless charges by *L'Humanité,* the Communist daily, which published his confidential reports to St. Petersburg after their release by the Soviet government. Most of these publications, however, did not prove conclusively the bribery charge. [J.O.R.]

RAFFALOVICH, ISAIAH (1870–1956), rabbi and author who promoted the development of Brazil's Jewish community. Born in Bogopol, Podolia, Raffalovich was taken in 1882 by his parents to Ereẓ Israel. He became interested in Jewish settlement schemes on both sides of the Jordan and worked for nine months at Es-Salt in Transjordan, trying to encourage young Jews in Jerusalem to follow his example. Together with M. E. Sachs, he published an album of his own photographs, *Views from Palestine and its Jewish Colonies* (1898). Raffalovich left for Europe, where he studied in Berlin and London, obtaining his rabbinical diploma at the Hildesheimer Seminary in Berlin. He served congregations in Manchester and Wales and the Hope Place Synagogue in Liverpool (1904–24).

While on a mission to South America in 1923, he was invited by the *Jewish Colonization Association (ICA) to go to Brazil as its representative, promote immigration to that country, and serve as a spiritual guide to the Jewish community. In this capacity he toured the country, established welfare institutions and improved already existing ones, and helped the newly established communities and synagogues. Raffalovich appealed to the common heritage of the Ashkenazi and Sephardi immigrants in working for the coordination of Jewish life in Brazil, and it was through his personal efforts that more than 30 Jewish schools and teachers' training courses were firmly established. His publications include: *Rudiments of Judaism* (1906); *Anglo-Hebrew Modern Dictionary* (1926); and *Our Inheritance* (1932), a volume of sermons and addresses. He also published in 1927 a Portuguese version of Paul *Goodman's popular short *History of the Jews* (1911) and the first Jewish sermons in Portuguese printed in modern times, *Rudimentos de judaismo* (1926²). In 1935 he retired to Ereẓ Israel and five years later was appointed senior Jewish chaplain to the British forces in the Middle East. A Hebrew edition of his collected sermons *(Ma'gelei Yosher)* appeared in 1950 and his autobiography, *Ẓiyyunim ve-Tamrurim,* in 1952. His brother Samuel Refaeli (1867–1927), a numismatist, was director of the numismatic department of the Department of Antiquities in Palestine (under the British) and left his coin collection to the Bezalel Museum.

Bibliography: Tidhar, 1 (1947), 216–7; JC (June 8, 1956); G. E. Silverman, in: *Niv ha-Midrashiyyah* (Spring, 1970), 74–81, Eng. section. [G.E.S.]

RAFI (abbreviation of Heb. *Reshimat Po'alei Yisrael,* "Israel Labor List"), founded in 1965 as the result of a split in *Mapai. The original split was the outcome of *Ben-Gurion's political fight against Levi *Eshkol over the *Lavon Affair and of the struggle for succession to the leadership between a group of younger men, headed by Moshe *Dayan and Shimon *Peres, supported by Ben-Gurion, and the party veterans, headed by Levi Eshkol and Golda *Meir. At the Mapai convention in February 1965, the rebels supported Ben-Gurion's demand for an inquiry into the Lavon Affair and opposed the proposed political alignment with Aḥdut ha-Avodah. After their defeat at the convention, they proposed Ben-Gurion's return to the premiership in place of Eshkol. In July, seven Mapai Knesset members (later joined by Dayan) formed a new list, called Rafi, which obtained 12% of the votes at the Histradrut elections in September and ten Knesset seats in November.

At its founding convention in May 1966, representing 23,000 members, Rafi called for electoral reform, self-reliance in the field of defense, national health insurance, free secondary education, and modernization of the economy, with particular emphasis on the full utilization of science. It became part of the parliamentary opposition, especially in defense and foreign affairs, sometimes cooperating with *Gaḥal. In May 1967, during the prewar tension and the discussions on the appointment of Dayan as minister of defense, Rafi offered to return to Mapai bodies and when the government was re-formed after the 1969 elections Peres joined it. The elections were also contested by the State (or National) List *(Reshimah Mamlakhtit),* headed by Ben-Gurion, which consisted mainly of Rafi supporters and won four seats. In February 1971 (after Ben-Gurion's resignation from the Knesset) it decided to call itself Rafi-State List. Negotiations after the *Six-Day War led to agreement between Mapai, Rafi, and Aḥdut ha-Avodah. When the united Israel Labor Party was formed on Jan. 21, 1968, Rafi received 21½% of the places on its governing bodies. [M.L.]

RAGOLER, ABRAHAM BEN SOLOMON (18th century), Lithuanian rabbi and preacher, brother of *Elijah b. Solomon Zalman Gaon of Vilna. Abraham was born in Vilna, but because of the controversy between *Ḥasidim and *Mitnaggedim* he moved to Ragola and was thereafter called Abraham of Ragola or "the Ḥasid ("righteous one") of Ragola." He was appointed preacher in Shklov.

He was the author of the *Ma'alot ha-Torah* (1828), a collection of rabbinic dicta dealing with the virtue of those who occupy themselves with the study of Torah. While explaining in detail the precepts of Torah study, he stressed that it is not sufficient "merely to study the text superficially, but it is also essential to carry it out in practice." He left in manuscript a kabbalistic commentary to the tractate *Megillah* and a commentary to the Book of Esther.

Bibliography: S. J. Fuenn, *Kiryah Ne'emanah* (1915²), 206; S. M. Chones, *Toledot ha-Posekim* (1929), 53; *Yahadut Lita,* 1 (1959), 355; 3 (1967), 24; E. Landau, *Toledot u-Mifalot ha-Gra u-Mishpaḥto,* in: *Minḥat Eliyahu* (1927). [Y.Ho.]

RAGOLER, ELIJAH BEN JACOB (1794–1850), Lithuanian talmudist. Ragoler was born in Sogindat in the Zamut region. His only teacher was his father Jacob, a distinguished scholar and wealthy merchant. In his youth Elijah acquired a comprehensive knowledge of the Talmud, the *rishonim,* and the *posekim*—which he regarded as the essential elements of study in contrast to the prevalent methods of *pilpul* and hairsplitting unconnected with the definitive *halakhah.* He was renowned throughout Lithuania for his encyclopedic talmudic knowledge, and his contemporaries said of him that he had gone over the whole of the Talmud more than 400 times. He devoted himself to considerable study of the Kabbalah, in which he also became renowned. Nevertheless, he refused throughout his life to have any dealings with mystic exercises, despite the many appeals for prayers, amulets, etc. made to him by scholars and the common people. In his youth he spent some months with Isaac of *Volozhiner for the purpose of learning Kabbalah from him in accordance with the traditions which Isaac had received from *Elijah of Vilna. When, however, he lost hope of this he returned home. At that time, his father and father-in-law failed in business and Elijah was compelled to accept a rabbinical post. He first served as rabbi of the small town of Schatt near Keidany. From 1821 to 1824 he was rabbi of Ragola (Eiragola) where he gained his main reputation and from which he derived his name. From 1824 to 1840 he was rabbi of Slobodka and from 1840 until his death rabbi of Kalisz in Poland.

In addition to his great reputation as a *posek* and scholar in *halakhah* and Kabbalah, Elijah was distinguished for his diligence and application, and for his shrewdness and sincerity. During his last years he suffered from ill health as well as from the opposition of a group of members of the Kalisz community to whom the Lithuanian ways of their rabbi were strange. Despite this he did not hesitate to take a decisive attitude in his leadership of the community, and sided with Akiva *Lehren of Amsterdam in his violent opposition to the Reform conference of Brunswick (1844), organized by A. *Geiger. Ragoler's letter to Lehren differs from the many other letters of contemporary Orthodox rabbis in its exceptionally moderate tone. In contrast to them, Elijah held that the weapon of excommunication, prohibition of marriage, etc., should not be followed because of the grave danger it held for the whole of the Jewish community. In his view a sharp and unequivocal dissociation from the path of reform, and a warning to the public against it were necessary, but not a "war of destruction."

Ragoler left many manuscripts in all spheres of Torah study. According to the members of his family their number exceeded 35. Of these only one has been published: *Yad Eliyyahu* (1900), pt. I, 120 responsa and a methodology of the Talmud in alphabetical order, pt. II, talmudic novellae. Among his pupils were many great Lithuanian talmudists, including Mordecai Eliasberg and Joshua Heshel *Lewin. Many of his novellae are to be found in the works of other scholars, particularly in those of his pupils, including the *Ilana de-Ḥayyei* (1860–65) of Gershon Tanḥum. The *Keneset ha-Gedolah,* pt. 4 (1892), of Isaak *Suwalski cites many of his sayings on prayer.

Ragoler's brother, Samuel Kelmer, was also a renowned scholar who went to Ereẓ Israel in the closing years of his life. Samuel was the father of Aryeh Leib *Frumkin.

Bibliography: A. L. Frumkin, *Toledot Eliyyahu* (1900); Urbach (ed.), in: *Koveẓ al Yad,* 6 (16) pt. 2 (1966), 535–53. [I.T.-S.]

RAHAB (Heb. רָחָב), the prostitute (Heb. *zonah*—see below), mentioned in the Book of Joshua as a central figure in Joshua's conquest of Jericho (Josh. 2–6). When Joshua sent two of his men to Jericho on a reconnaissance mission, they came to the house of Rahab and spent the night there (2:1–2). When the king of Jericho learned about the two spies, he sent word to Rahab ordering her to surrender them (2:3). However, she hid them on the roof under stalks of flax, and declared that they had already left (2:4–6). In

Rahab inviting the two Israelite spies into her house. Illustration from a 12th-century Greek Octateuch. Vatican Library, Ms. Gr. 746.

return for the kindness that she had shown them and her promise to keep the entire affair confidential, the spies took an oath that she and her family would be spared when Joshua conquered the land (2:12–14). They further stipulated that when the conquest began, she was to gather her entire family into her home and bind a cord of crimson thread in the window, which would serve to identify her house (2:17–21). This cord of crimson thread was the same one which had been used to let the spies down through the window when they left Rahab's house (2:18). Rahab did as she was bidden, and so when Joshua did conquer the land, she and her entire family were saved (6:22–23, 25). After the total destruction of Jericho, it is stated that Rahab and her family elected to reside with the Israelites, who accepted her into their camp (6:25).

There are two somewhat conflicting Jewish traditions concerning Rahab's profession and later life among the Israelites. The first (e.g., Meg. 14b; Ginzberg, Legends, 4 (1954), 5–8) maintains that she married Joshua after becoming a proselyte, and became the ancestress of eight prophets and priests among whom were the prophet Jeremiah and the prophetess Huldah. According to this tradition, the fact that a proselyte and former prostitute could achieve such a name for herself in the annals of Jewish history proved that repentance can work salvation for anyone no matter how great his past sins. The second tradition contends that Rahab was not a prostitute at all but an innkeeper. This tradition (e.g., Rashi on Josh. 2:1) is based on the Targum's rendering of *zonah* as *pundekita (pundeqita),* the assumption being that this word means, like *pundakit (pundaqit)* in Hebrew, "hostess, innkeeper," and the derivation of the word *zonah* (normally "prostitute") from the same stem as *mazon* (מָזוֹן, "food"). If Rahab had been merely an innkeeper, then the shame of considering a former prostitute to be the ancestress of some of Israel's most important figures would cease to be a problem. However, as first noted by Kimḥi (on Josh. 2:1), the adherents of this theory simply misunderstood the Targum, for the Targum to the Prophets in various passages also renders *zonah* by *pundeqētā,* plural *pundeqāyān* or *pundeqā'ān* (e.g., I Kings 3:16; Ezek. 23:44), in which it cannot possibly have been understood to mean anything but "prostitute." Therefore, the Targum's rendering of Hebrew "prostitute" with Aramaic "innkeeper" is to be understood either as a euphemism or as an intended double entendre, implying that there is a connection between bars or inns and prostitutes. [H.Co.]

In the Aggadah. Rahab was one of the four most beautiful women in history. The mere mention of her name sufficed to excite desire (Meg. 15a). At the age of ten Rahab became a prostitute. There was not a prince or ruler who did not have relations with her. Because of this, she was well informed about events outside of Jericho (Zeb. 116b). Rahab became a righteous proselyte and married Joshua. She was the ancestress of eight prophets, among them Jeremiah, who were also priests, and of the prophetess Huldah (Meg. 14b). Her conversion is regarded as more complete than that of Jethro and Naaman for, unlike them, she acknowledged that the God of Israel is the only God both in heaven and on earth (Deut. R. 2:26–27). [Ed.]

Bibliography: Y. Kaufmann, *Sefer Yehoshu'a* (1959). In the Aggadah: Ginzberg, Legends, index.

RAHABI, EZEKIEL (1694–1771), merchant and community leader in *Cochin, India. In 1726, after the death of his father, Rahabi was appointed by the Dutch East India Company as "chief merchant and agent," and invested with a monopoly of the trade in pepper and other commodities in Malabar. He rose to a position of remarkable influence and prestige; for almost 50 years he was connected with all the company's major financial transactions in Malabar, and undertook for it diplomatic assignments to the king of Travancore (1734–42), to the zamorin of Calicut (1751), and to other native rulers.

Rahabi was also an outstanding leader of the Jewish community. He purchased land for the Black Jews near Cranganore and in 1756 built a synagogue there for ten Jewish families, supporting it until it was closed in 1761; improved and embellished the Parathesi synagogue of the White Jews in Cochin; and imported Hebrew books from Holland. Through his efforts to decipher the ancient copperplate inscriptions in Cochin, Ezekiel Rahabi also became the historian of his community. His letter of 1768 to the Dutch banker Tobias Boas remains a major source of information about Cochin Jewry. Rahabi's tombstone is preserved in the courtyard of the Parathesi synagogue. The changed economic and political conditions in Malabar after the English occupation of Cochin (1795) caused the decline of the Rahabi family and the Jewish community as a whole.

Bibliography: S. S. Koder, in: *Journal of the Rama Varma Archaeological Society*, 15 (1949), 1–6; W. J. Fischel, *Ha-Yehudim be-Hodu* (1960), 97–111; idem, in: PAAJR, 30 (1962), 37–59; A. Das Gupta, *Malabar in Asian Trade* (1967), index. [W.J.F.]

RAHABI (Raby), NAPHTALI ELIAHU (1863–1951), "white" Jewish scholar of *Cochin. He is the author of *Divrei Yemei ha-Yehudim be-Cochin* ("History of the Jews of Cochin"; Sasson Ms. 268), and of *Toledot Beit Rahabi be-Cochin* ("History of the Rahabi Family"), both unpublished. He edited *Ḥuppat Ḥatanim* (1917), a collection of songs and hymns for weddings, etc. Like many Cochin leaders, Rahabi had strong Zionist sympathies.

Bibliography: D. S. Sassoon, *Ohel Dawid*, 1 (1932), 370; 2 (1932), 844, 967; A. Yaari, *Ha-Defus ha-Ivri be-Arẓot ha-Mizraḥ*, 2 (1940), 70; W. J. Fischel, *Ha-Yehudim be-Hodu* (1960), 97–111; idem, in: *Herzl Yearbook*, 4 (1961–62), 309–28. [W.J.F.]

RAḤBAH, AL- town situated on the W. bank of the Euphrates, S. of Kirkisiya. Founded in the first third of the ninth century by Mālik ibn Ṭauq, al-Raḥbah was named Raḥbat Mālik ibn Ṭauq to differentiate it from other towns bearing the name Al-Raḥbah. Onkelos, and after him R. Saadiah Gaon, identify the town with the biblical Rehoboth by the River (Gen. 36:37), while the Arab geographer Yākūt reports an ancient tradition, according to which Al-Raḥbah was founded by Namrūd (Nimrod) b. Kush. It was, at any rate, one of the large cities on the Euphrates—as confirmed by another Arab geographer, al-Mukaddasi, writing at the end of the tenth century—and it had a large Jewish community. Obadiah the proselyte was in this town at the beginning of the 12th century. *Benjamin of Tudela, the 12th-century traveler, found a Jewish community of 2,000 there. In a letter *(iggeret)* written by R. *Samuel b. Ali, head of the Baghdad academy, in 1191, Al-Raḥbah heads the list of the communities of northern Babylonia and Syria. There were also Karaites living in the town, as is known from a list appearing at the end of a manuscript of Japheth b. Ali's commentary on Numbers, dedicated by Moses b. Japheth al-Raḥbi to the Karaite community in Jerusalem. By the 14th century the ancient town had been destroyed and its site had been moved further to the west. At the time that the town was included within the Mamluk kingdom, Jews still lived there, as may be inferred from an inscription found in the synagogue of Tadef (a village near Aleppo), dating apparently from about 1400, which mentions the name "Obadiah b. Moses . . . b. Abraham al-Raḥbi." During Turkish rule Jews from al-Raḥbah moved to India, and some of them (e.g., a prominent family which lived in Cochin in the 18th century), bore the name of their ancient home.

Bibliography: Yaqut, *Mu'jam al-Buldān* s.v.; J. Obermeyer, *Die Landschaft Babylonien* (1929), 36f; Mann, Texts, 2 (1935), 28f; Ashtor, Toledot, 1 (1944), 278; 2 (1951), 120; S. D. Goitein, in: JJS, 4 (1953), 83; A. Ben-Jacob, *Yehudei Bavel* (1965), 56. [E.A.]

RAḤEL (pseudonym of **Raḥel Bluwstein,** 1890–1931), Hebrew poet in Ereẓ Israel. Raḥel was born in Saratov, on the Volga in northern Russia, and raised in Poltava. She began writing poetry in Russian at the age of 15 and also studied painting. In 1909 she emigrated to Ereẓ Israel, settling in Reḥovot. She abandoned her native Russian idiom and learned Hebrew. Under the influence of the pioneer Zionist Hannah Maisel (Shoḥat) she became a pioneer and was one of the first trainees at the young women's training farm at Kinneret. At Kinneret she met Aaron David *Gordon, the philosopher of Zionist agrarianism, and to him she dedicated her first Hebrew poem, *"Halokh Nefesh"* ("Mood"), in *Ha-Shilo'aḥ*, 37 (1920). Having decided on an agricultural life, she studied agronomy at the University of Toulouse (1913). Unable to return to Ereẓ Israel because of World War I, she went to Russia, where she taught Jewish refugee children. After the war she settled in Deganyah. However, having contracted tuberculosis during the war, she soon became too ill for farm life and had to spend the rest of her life in hospitals and sanatoria.

Raḥel is among the first modern Hebrew poets who wrote in a conversational style. Her knowledge of Hebrew was drawn from both the developing spoken idiom and the

The poet Raḥel (Raḥel Bluwstein). Drawing by Alexander Bogen. Courtesy Genazim, Tel Aviv.

Bible. She was also influenced by the conversational school which then prevailed in Russian poetry (Blok, Akhmatova, and Yesenin). Her poems are characterized by a clear, uncomplicated lyrical line and a musicality, then rare in

Hebrew poetry. Invariably short, her poems are elegiac and nostalgic in tone, many of them reflecting the pessimism of a young writer on the brink of death. These qualities made her writings very popular with younger Hebrew readers and with the general public. Many of the poems, including the widely sung *"Kinneret,"* have been put to music. Raḥel also translated Russian, Yiddish, and French poetry and wrote occasional pieces of criticism. Two volumes of her verse appeared in her lifetime: *Safi'aḥ* ("Aftergrowth," 1927), *Mi-Neged* ("From Opposite," 1930), and one posthumously, *Nevo* (1932). These were collected in *Shirat Raḥel* ("The Poetry of Raḥel," 1935), the eighth edition (1961) of which also contains her other works as well as a biography by Bracha *Ḥabas and a bibliography of her poems and their translations.

Bibliography: Kressel, Leksikon, 1 (1965), 243–4; R. Wallenrod, *Literature of Modern Israel* (1956), 54–59; Goell, Bibliography, for list of her poetry translated into English. [E.Sp.]

RAILROADS. Jewish financiers played a considerable role in the construction of railroads in France and in Central and Eastern Europe from the 1830s until the beginning of the 20th century. These Jewish financiers were the only investors—besides the British—among the private bankers dominant in Europe until the second half of the 19th century (see also *Banking) who were prepared to risk their capital in the pioneer stage of railroad construction. In the second half of the 19th century, when large banking joint-stock firms sprang up and expanded, private banks were increasingly pressed into the background, and the share of private Jewish capital in railroad investment diminished accordingly. In the majority of European countries this tendency became linked to nationalization of the railroads when financial crises occurred in private railroad companies. The nationalization of Prussian railroads was organized on the financial side by Bismarck's adviser Gerson von *Bleichroeder. In the 19th-century era of "railroad fever" former *court Jews who had become private bankers with considerable funds took part in furthering the industrial revolution through their investments in railroad construction.

The *Rothschilds were urged by Nathan Mayer Rothschild soon after the opening of the first successful railroad in England (1825) to invest money on the continent in railroad construction. Salomon Rothschild of Vienna sent Professor F.X. Riepel from the Vienna Institute of Technology to England to study the new means of transportation with Rothschild's secretary Leopold von Wertheimstein. Subsequently they proposed the construction (1829) of a first line to run straight through the Hapsburg Empire, connecting Vienna with Galicia and Trieste. The July Revolution postponed the execution of Rothschild's plans. It was only in 1836, after overcoming many obstacles (especially the rivalry of the Viennese banking houses of *Arnstein and *Eskeles) that he began construction of the northern line from Vienna to Bochnia, in Galicia. The railroad was only completed in 1858. The house of Rothschild sold the shares on the stock market mainly to small investors.

James Rothschild of Paris was encouraged to construct the local line between Paris and St. Germain (opened in 1837) by Emile *Pereire. Emile Pereire and his brother Isaac viewed the railroad as the salvation of the future, producing work for the masses, connecting nations, and conducive to world welfare and peace. The two brothers could later boast that through their efforts more than 6,000 miles (10,000 km.) of railroads had come into existence. In the 1840s they were the rivals of the Rothschilds in this field.

After the success of the Paris-St. Germain line, James Rothschild and the *Fould brothers (apostate Jews), were eager to receive the concession for the Paris-Versailles line. The government eventually approved two plans, so that Rothschild constructed his line on the left bank of the River Seine and the Foulds on the right bank. In 1839 the railroad was opened, and in 1840 the two companies merged. This did not diminish the rivalry between them and the Pereire brothers. James Rothschild also succeeded in obtaining the concession for the construction of a northern line connecting Paris with England and the industries of northern France. The financial means of the Rothschilds were thereby severely strained, but the line was at last opened in 1846.

Nathan Mayer Rothschild and his sons helped finance the state-constructed railroad network in Belgium in the years 1834 to 1843. The Antwerp-Ghent line was built by the first private railway company in Belgium formed by Leopold *Koenigswarter. The Rothschilds were the chief financiers of the world-spanning railroad politics of Leopold I. They also raised funds for building railroads in Italy, Spain, and Brazil.

The Pereire brothers were second only to the Rothschilds in the first stage of railroad network development on the continent until 1869. The first half of their organizational activity was spent on a substantial part of the French railroad network. While the Rothschilds constructed the "northern" line in the 1840s, the Pereires were responsible for the "southern" one. The 1848 revolution plunged the railroads into a severe crisis (the "southern" line, managed by Isaac Pereire, was also financially ruined). The Pereire brothers wished to overcome this crisis by diverting to plans for a "railroad bank," a bank that would solve all the current financial difficulties of the French economy. The Crédit Mobilier (1852) also was intended not only to finance railroad construction but also heavy industry. Pereire introduced a new type of railroad security, the 500-franc capital bond *(obligation)*, paying 15 francs annual interest and issued at whatever the market would bring, generally between 300 and 400 francs. With interest guaranteed by the state these bonds were ideally suited to the investor of moderate means. They quickly replaced other types of railroad borrowing and greatly facilitated railroad finance.

In the first years of its establishment the Crédit Mobilier financed (through advance payments and increased circulation of bonds) the "southern" line, the "grand central," the French "eastern" line, and many others in their first years. Through its contribution the railroad network expanded from 2,000 miles (3,600 km.) in 1852 to 11,000 miles (18,000 km.) in 1870. The Pereire brothers did not neglect to finance railroad construction and industrial ventures abroad. They contributed to the predominance of French finance in the development of foreign railroads in the post-1850 decade: in Austria, where there was fierce competition between the Pereires and the Rothschilds, the Pereires founded the important Austrian State-Railroad Company, in conjunction with Sina, Arnstein, and Eskeles, while the Rothschilds were successful in buying the Lombard-Venetian and the Central Italian Railway (1856). In Spain there was lively rivalry between the Rothschilds, Pereires, and Jules Isaac *Mirès; and in Hungary they built the "Franz-Joseph" line (1857). The Crédit Mobilier also financed Swiss railroads.

The importance of railroads was grasped in Russia only after its defeat in the Crimean War. The Grande Société des Chemins de fer Russes (1857) had, besides the Pereires, other Jewish bankers as founders: Alexander *Stieglitz of St. Petersburg, S. A. Fraenkel of Warsaw, and the *Mendelssohns of Berlin. An important figure in Russian railroad construction in the 1860s and 1870s was Samuel *Polyakov. He built railroads of supreme importance for the Russian grain export trade, and also wrote on the political aspect of railroad construction. He and other Jewish entrepreneurs succeeded in attracting foreign capital (Leopold *Kronenberg, J. J. Sack, Gerson von Bleichroeder, Sulzbach Brothers, etc.) without which their plans would have been unattainable. Railroad construction by Jewish bankers in Russia created employment for numbers of Jews, who filled technical and administrative posts. The advent of the railroad brought many changes in Jewish economic and social life, described, for instance, in the poem *Shenei Yosef ben Shim'on* of J. L.*Gordon.

Bethel Henry *Strousberg started by working for English firms, and when he had accumulated enough capital, founded railway companies in Prussia and later in Hungary. He also acquired locomotive factories and rolling mills for rails, and subsequently coal mines. A careless venture into Rumanian railroad construction ruined his enterprise. His bankruptcy influenced public opinion in favor of nationalization of railroad lines in Germany. It also revealed malpractices and bribery, which were given a prominent place in anti-Semitic propaganda.

Jewish bankers were large-scale investors in railroad construction outside Europe. Baron Maurice de *Hirsch bought, in 1869, the concession for railroad building in Turkey from the bankrupt International Land Credit Company. His connection by marriage with the Jewish banking enterprise Bischoffsheim and Goldschmidt aided him initially. In 1869 he began the first stage of extending the Austro-Hungarian lines southward. However, before beginning construction on the Oriental Railroad, he took steps to secure financial backing, and chose a new type of 3% government loan. "Turkish lottery bonds," which attracted small investors in France and Germany, were offered on the general market. Hirsch concluded his project in 1888.

At first Jewish financiers, mainly of German origin, acted as intermediaries between foreign finance and the United States. When the Civil War broke out in 1861, railway bonds, mainly distributed by Jewish bankers in Europe, served as a means of payment for munitions bought in Europe. The Speyer, Stern, and *Seligman New York banking houses all dealt in railway shares. A leading personality in late 19th and early 20th century American financing was Jacob H. *Schiff. In 1875 he became a member of the banking firm of Kuhn, Loeb & Company (a firm long engaged in railroad financing) which he eventually dominated. In 1897 he reorganized the Union Pacific Railroad, which was described in the period as being "battered, bankrupt and decrepit." According to financial authorities the Harriman-Schiff railway combination became the most powerful and most successful that America had ever known. Schiff was one of the first supporters and associates of James Hill, who, by building the Great Northern Railway, virtually became the founder of a vast empire in the northwest. His firm aided other railroads by financial operations until the end of World War I. Schlesinger-Trier in Berlin, together with other Jewish banks, imported the shares of the Canadian Pacific railroad and offered them on the Berlin stock market.

A position similar to that of Schiff in financing railway companies in the United States was held by Sir Ernest *Cassel in England. He had a share in developing Swedish, American, and Mexican railway companies. The Vickers and Central London Railway Company was connected with his name.

Bibliography: K. Grunwald, in: YLBI, 12 (1967), 163–212; 14 (1969), 119–61; idem, *Tuerkenhirsch* (1966); R.E. Cameron, *France and the Economic Development of Europe, 1880–1914* (1961); E. C. Corti, *Rise of the House of Rothschild* (1928); idem, *Reign of the House of Rothschild* (1928); P. H. Emden, *Money Powers of Europe* (1937); J. Plenge, *Gruendung und Geschichte des Crédit Mobilier* (1903); AJYB, 23 (1921).

[M.GRA.]

RAIN (Heb. גֶּשֶׁם, מָטָר). The large number of quotations referring to rain in the biblical and talmudic sources may be attributed to the fact that rain is the most important climatic element for the agriculture of Israel, particularly in nonirrigated areas. In comparing these quotations with modern knowledge of rainfall in Israel it is evident that although part of the quotations are in the realm of folklore, many of them are valid and correspond to contemporarily measured data, although the descriptions of rain in the Bible and talmudic literature are mainly qualitative. This correspondence not only shows the keen observations of weather phenomena made in ancient times, but also indicates that during the last 3,000 years there were fluctuations but not fundamental changes in the climate of Israel. The importance of a normal rainfall regime, i.e., an appropriate seasonal distribution of rainfall, for the success of agricultural crops is clearly stated in the Bible on several occasions (Lev. 26:4; Deut. 28:12; Ezek. 34:26), sometimes with special emphasis on the first and last rains of the season (the *yoreh* and the *malkosh*) whose importance for agriculture is particularly great (Deut. 11:14; Jer. 5:24). The local nature of rainfall, expressed in Ereẓ Israel particularly at the beginning and end of the rainfall season, is also mentioned (Amos 4:7; cf. Ta'an. 6b). An impressive description of the results of droughts is available in Jeremiah 14:1–6. Late and strong rains at the beginning of June are as rare and notable nowadays as they were at the time of Samuel (I Sam. 12:16–18). Similarly, three consecutive drought years in the region of Samaria are as rare and notable in the last 50 years of rainfall measurements (1931/32, 1932/33, and 1933/34) as they were at the time of Elijah and Ahab (I Kings 18:1).

In the Talmud and Midrashim. Rain is referred to on many occasions in the Talmud and midrashic literature, particularly in tractate *Ta'anit* (Mishnah, Tosefta, and the Babylonian and Jerusalem Talmuds). In the Mishnah there is a quantitative definition of drought (Ta'an. 3:1). The following references are examples of keen observations of weather phenomena: R. Eleazar b. Perata paid attention to the variations from year to year in both amounts and times of rain occurrence (Ta'an. 19b). R. Johanan and R. Papa determined that thin clouds under thick clouds are a sign of rainfall (*ibid.* 9b); the ragged fragments of low cloud, known as scud (nautical term) or stratus fractus (meteorological term), often moving rapidly below rain clouds, indicate rainy weather (which is also the case today). On the same page in the Babylonian Talmud a weather forecast is given by R. Ulla, using the above-mentioned sign. Even a forecast for the rainfall of a whole year is given in the Jerusalem Talmud (Ta'an. 2:1, 65b). The dates of the beginning and end of the rainfall season in Israel also fit modern conditions (Ta'an. 1:1; Ned. 8:5; see also Yal., Num. 29). As for rain intensities, there are various expressions for slight, moderate, and heavy rains in the Bible (e.g., I Kings 18:45; Ezek. 13:11; 34:26; Ps. 68:10; Prov. 28:3; for the Mishnah see Ta'an. 3).

In Contemporary Israel. Israel is situated on the boundary of two different climatic regions: its northern half belongs to the southern part of a region having the so-called "Mediterranean" type of climate, whose main feature is that the greatest part of the annual rainfall occurs during the moderately cold winter months, while in the warm summer practically no rain falls; the southern half of Israel, the Negev, is situated on the northern boundary of a hot desert. Like every country with a Mediterranean climate Israel also lies near the limit of the cyclonic rains. Most of the rain-bearing cold lows (barometric depressions) arriving or

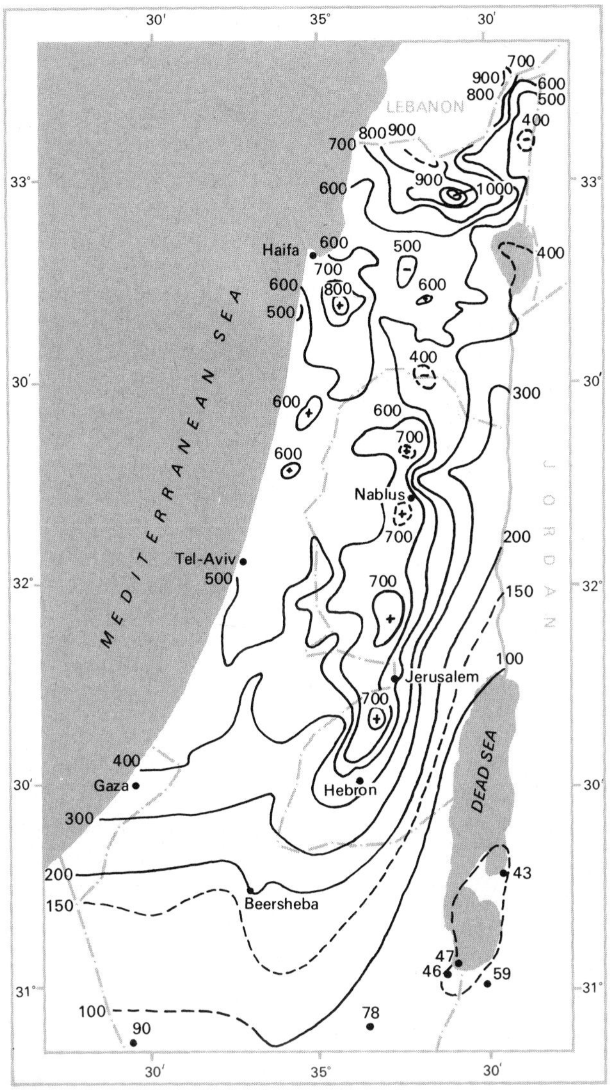

Map 1. Average annual rainfall, amounts in mm. (1921–1950).

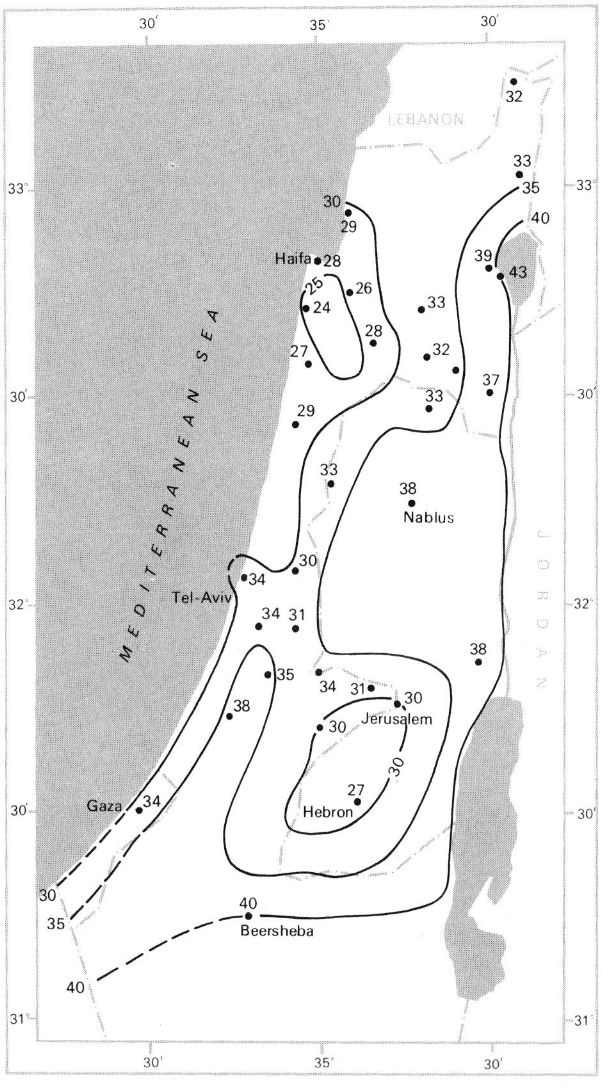

Map 2. Interannual variability of rainfall amount, as a percentage of the average for the period 1921/22–1950/51.

forming in the eastern Mediterranean during the rainfall season are situated in the northeastern part of this sea (the "Cyprus Low"). Such a depression in the lower layers of the atmosphere is generally associated with a cold barometric trough in the higher layers (upper trough). The great majority of rainfall in Israel is due to this combination, even in the southern Negev—which is far away from the center of the Cyprus Low. Rains usually fall in Israel when cold air masses arrive mainly from Russia, the Balkans, or Turkey. These air masses are cold and dry, but in passing over the relatively much warmer waters of the Mediterranean they are heated in their lower layers, absorb much moisture, and reach Israel in a state of marked instability. Then, the land areas of Israel serve as a "trigger" to induce rainfall.

Regional Distribution of Rainfall. For the areal distribution of rainfall over Israel four rules can be stated: (1) rainfall decreases with increasing distance from the sea, i.e., from west to east (continental effect); (2) rainfall increases with increasing elevation (orographic effect); (3) rainfall depends on exposure: of two localities at the same elevation, other conditions being equal, the windward slope facing ascending air (anabatic effect) receives more rainfall than the leeward slope with descending air (katabatic effect); (4) rainfall decreases from north to south, i.e., with increasing distance from the Cyprus Low and decreasing distance from the planetary desert. A good example for the first rule is the Valley of Jezreel where the average annual rainfall decreases gradually from west to east (650 mm.–400 mm.), and for the fourth rule—the Coastal Plain (650 mm.–200 mm., north to south). In each of these regions there are no significant differences in elevation. The second and third rules are clearly demonstrated on the Carmel range (600 mm.–850 mm.), where the isolines of rainfall (isohyets) are somewhat similar to those of elevation (isohypses), demonstrating the importance of the height factor. The same applies to two other compact and continuous ranges, namely, Upper Galilee, which is the highest and most northerly region in Israel and therefore the rainiest one (600 mm.–1000 mm.), and the Judean Hills (450 mm.–700 mm.); whereas the Samarian Hills and those of Lower Galilee are broken up and scattered, so that their isohyets do not take a markedly topographic course. The Samarian Hills, which generally become higher from north to south, demonstrate the prevalence of height over latitude when the latter factor is opposed to the former: this is the only region in Israel where rainfall increases from north to south (500 mm.–700 mm.). In the Jordan Rift Valley, on the other hand, the combined influence of southward progress and falling elevation is seen in the rapid decrease of the average annual rainfall from 570 mm. in the northern part of the Ḥuleh Area to 90 mm. at the northern edge of the Dead Sea. Further south, the Arabah between the Dead Sea and the Gulf of Eilat, forming the eastern border of the Negev, is the driest region in the country (25mm.–50mm.). Even the highest hills of the Negev do not enjoy 100 mm. while the northwestern Negev receives 200 mm. as an annual average.

Seasonal Distribution or Regimen of Rainfall. In effect rains fall in Israel only during the period October through May, which is called "the rainfall season." The three central rainy months—the "winter" of the temperate climates, December, January, and February—contribute two-thirds to three-quarters of the annual rainfall in most regions of the country. The remaining 30% is distributed among the first and last months of the rainfall season: the "autumn" months October and November and the "spring" months March, April, and May, although in the Coastal Plain the percentage of rainfall in autumn is greater than in the hill region, while in the hills and other regions of the interior the percentage of spring rains is larger than near the coast. In addition to this west-east variation of the rainfall regime there is a north-south variation: while the northern half of the country has a Mediterranean rainfall regime with the characteristic steep increase from the beginning of the season toward the peak month and a rapid decrease from then to the end of the season, no specific month can be singled out in the central and southern Negev as having a marked maximum, and the curve typical for the Mediterranean regime becomes ill-defined. All the preceding facts are true with respect to a normal rainfall regime, i.e., a seasonal distribution of rainfall in which each month receives its average value. But in fact there are large variations from year to year in the seasonal rainfall, and particularly in its monthly distribution, so that it is difficult to find a season in which each of its months has even approximately received its average amount.

VARIABILITY OF RAINFALL. There are several statistical methods for measuring quantitatively the variations of annual rainfall from year to year. One measure, called Relative Variability, is defined as the percentage ratio between the mean deviation of individual annual totals from their average and the average; another measure, Relative Interannual Variability, relates, in percent, the mean value of absolute differences between successive annual totals to the average. The values of each of these measures of variability are relatively low (20%–26% RV; 25%–37% RIV) in regions with much rainfall (the hill region and Coastal Plain) and higher ($\geq$ 27% RV; $\geq$ 38% RIV) in regions with less rainfall (the Jordan Valley and Negev). This property is of important consequence to nonirrigated areas in the eastern and southern parts of Israel in drought years. For charts, tables, and further details see bibliography.

See *Rain, Prayer for; *Israel, Land of (climate).

Bibliography: D. Ashbel, in: *Aklim Ereẓ Yisrael la-Azoreha* (1951); idem, in: *Leksikon Mikra'i,* 1 (1965), 94–103; N. Shalem, in: *Desert Research* . . . (1953), 153–64; N. Rosenan, in: IEJ, 5 (1955), 137–53; idem, in: UNESCO (ed.), *Symposium on Changes of Climate* . . . (1963), 67–73; idem, in: *Atlas of Israel* (1970), sheet IV/2; J. Katsnelson, in: *Archiv fuer Meteorologie, Geophysik und Bioklimatologie,* 13 (1963/65), 163–72; idem, in: *Ha-Enẓiklopedyah le-Ḥakla'ut,* 1 (1966), 27–62; idem, in: *Gishmei Ereẓ Yisrael ke-Gorem Yesod be-Meshek ha-Mayim shel ha-Areẓ* (1968/69).

[J.KAT.]

RAIN, PRAYER FOR (Heb. תְּפִלַּת גֶּשֶׁם, *Tefillat Geshem* (Ashkenazi); תִּקּוּן הַגֶּשֶׁם, *Tikkun ha-Geshem* (Sephardi)), prayers offered on various occasions, in which God is acknowledged as the power causing rain and the change of seasons, and which contain petitions for the fertility of the fields and for preservation from famine.

The principal prayer for rain is recited during the *Musaf* service on the eighth day of Sukkot (*Shemini Aẓeret) as part of the second benediction in the reader's repetition of the **Amidah* (Ashkenazi tradition). The Sephardim recite it before the Additional Service. The *piyyutim* of which this prayer is composed vary according to the different rites. Those in the Ashkenazi rite are by Eliezer *Kallir; the last of the six *piyyutim* invokes the remembrance of Abraham, Isaac, Jacob, Moses, Aaron, and the Twelve Tribes, and culminates in the invocation: "In their merit favor us with abundant water (rain) . . . For a blessing and not for a curse, for life and not for death, for plenty and not for famine. Amen." From this service on Shemini Aẓeret until that of the first day of Passover when the prayer for *dew is said, the sentence *mashiv ha-ru'aḥ u-morid ha-geshem* ("cause the wind to blow and the rain to fall") is included in every *Amidah* prayer at the beginning of the second benediction (Sh. Ar., OḤ 114). This insertion is called by the Mishnah (Ta'an. 1:1) *gevurot* (meaning "the Powers of God"). In traditional synagogues following the customs of Eastern Europe the *ḥazzan* officiates in the *kitel at the *Musaf* service when the prayer for rain is read as on the Day of Atonement, and recites the *Kaddish* before the *Musaf* service to a solemn melody. In Israel, the *Tefillat Geshem* is recited after the Torah scrolls have been returned to the ark and before the *Musaf* service so as to avoid an "interruption" in the statutory *Amidah;* however, the ḥasidic rite in Israel recites it in the reader's repetition of the *Amidah.* The *Tefillat Geshem* (like the prayer for dew) is part of the service in all Jewish rituals including the *Conservative and *Reform where it appears in a shortened version.

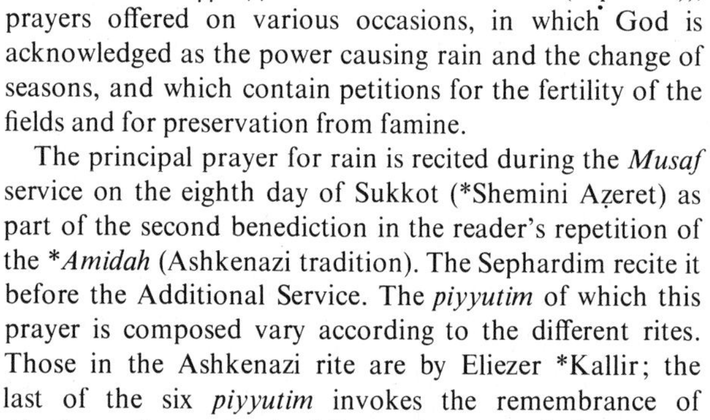

Plaque from a Hamburg synagogue to remind the congregation to recite the prayer for dew and rain during the winter season. Carved walnut with colored trimming, 18th century. Hamburg, Altonaer Museum.

Another prayer for rain is the petition *(she'elah)* "and give dew and rain for a blessing" (*ve-ten tal u-matar li-verakhah;* in the Sephardi rite this is a different and longer petition) inserted in the ninth benediction of the **Amidah* for weekdays. This petition is recited only from a date two weeks or more after the *Tefillat Geshem* on Shemini Aẓeret because the pilgrims in Temple times had to return from Jerusalem to their homes and traveling during a rainy season would have caused them hardship. Thus, in Ereẓ Israel the insertion is made from the evening prayer of the seventh of Ḥeshvan (Ta'an. 1:3; Ta'an. 4b); elsewhere, from the 60th day after the autumnal equinox, that is, from the fifth or sixth of December. This petition for rain appears in the ninth benediction (the "Blessing of the Years"), rather than in the second benediction of the *Amidah,* because the first three benedictions of the *Amidah* should contain the praise of God only and no petitions.

Prayers for rain are among the earliest liturgical texts and withholding of rain is regarded in the Bible as a punishment from God (cf. Deut. 11:11–17; I Kings 17:1). In the time of the Second Temple, the high priest recited a special prayer for rain on the *Day of Atonement (Yoma 53b) based upon Solomon's prayer (I Kings 8:35–36; II Chron. 7–13). During periods of drought, special prayers and supplications combined with fasting (see *Fast Days) were ordained (Ta'an. 1:4–3:9). These prayers entered the liturgy as it evolved in the time of the Mishnah and thereafter.

The dates for the special fasts and prayers for rain were fixed by the rabbis with a view to the climate and agricultural needs of Palestine; later rabbinic authorities decreed that wherever rain is beneficial during the summer, appropriate prayers for rain may be inserted, even during this season, in the 16th benediction of the *Amidah, Shome'a Tefillah* (Ta'an. 14b; Maim. Yad, Tefillah, 2:17; Sh. Ar., OḤ 117:2).

Bibliography: Elbogen, Gottesdienst, 44–45, 214–5; Davidson, Oẓar, 1 (1924), 322 (no. 7091), 324 (no. 7128), 337 (no. 7419); 2 (1929), 209 (no. 91), 418 (no. 3466); 3 (1930), 528 (no. 267); *Union Prayer Book,* 1 (1927²), 268–9 (Reform); Silverman, Prayer, 210–1 (Conservative); E. Levy, *Yesodot ha-Tefillah* (1952²), 161–2; ET, 5 (1953), 65–79.

[ED.]

RAINBOW, "bow" (Heb. קֶשֶׁת), "in the cloud" (Gen. 9:13–14, 16; Ezek. 1:28). In the sequel to the Flood Story (Gen. 9:8–17) God sets His bow in the clouds as a sign to the people and as a reminder to Himself that no deluge shall again destroy the earth. According to the rabbis this rainbow was created during the eve of the Sabbath of

The rainbow seen by Noah and his sons, in an illumination from the sixth-century Byzantine *Vienna Genesis*. Vienna, Austrian National Library, Vindobon Theol. Gr. 31, p. 5.

Creation at twilight (Pes. 54a). Naḥmanides similarly explained that the rainbow had existed previously but was now designated to serve as this symbol (to Gen. 9:12). However, Ibn Ezra held that the bow was first created by God after the Flood (to Gen. 9:13). The bow symbolized that God's wrath had ceased since the end of the bow pointed downward just as the warrior lowers his bow on declaring peace (Naḥmanides to Gen. 9:12).

The rabbis held that the rainbow need not appear in the lifetime of a saint whose merit alone is sufficient to save the world from destruction (Ket. 77b and Rashi ad. loc.). Since the rainbow was the reflection of "the glory of the Lord" (Ezek. 1:28), it was considered injurious to gaze directly at it (Ḥag. 16a). It was reported that R. Joshua b. Levi declared that upon seeing the rainbow one should fall on his face as did Ezekiel (Ezek. 1:28). Nevertheless, in Ereẓ Israel, the rabbis disapproved of such action since it appeared as if the person was bowing down to the rainbow. They, however, approved of reciting a blessing upon the rainbow's appearance. The text of this blessing as it is today recited is: "Blessed are Thou O Lord our God, King of the Universe, Who remembers the Covenant, is faithful to His Covenant, and keeps His promise" (Ber. 59a; Sh. Ar. OḤ 229:1). The blessing is to be recited even if a rainbow is seen twice within 30 days (*Mishnah Berurah* to Sh. Ar., loc. cit.).

Bibliography: Idelsohn, Liturgy, 126, note j; ET, 4 (1952), 358.

[Ed.]

RAISIN, JACOB ZALMAN (1877–1946), rabbi and writer. After emigrating from Poland to the United States, he served as a Reform rabbi in Charleston, South Carolina, for many years (1915–44).

An author of Hebrew poems and articles on English literature in Hebrew, his books—in English—include *Sect, Creed and Custom in Judaism* (1907), *Centennial Booklet Commemorating the Introduction of Reform Judaism in America* (1925), and the posthumously published *Gentile Reactions to Jewish Ideals* (1953). His volume *The Haskalah Movement in Russia* (1913) is still an important contribution to the literature of Haskalah.

Bibliography: M. Raisin, *Mi-Sefer Ḥayyai* (1956), 117–20; Lefkowitz, in: *Central Conference of American Rabbis Yearbook*, 56 (1946), 267–8.

[Ei.S.]

RAISIN, MAX (1881–1957), rabbi and author, the younger brother of Jacob *Raisin. Born in Poland, he arrived in the United States as a boy of 12. He was ordained as rabbi at the Hebrew Union College in Cincinnati in 1903. He served as rabbi of Congregation B'nai Jeshurun of Paterson, New Jersey (1921–53).

A prolific writer in Hebrew, English, and Yiddish, Raisin dealt with contemporary problems, with the history of the Reform movement, and with Hebrew literature, on both a popular and a scholarly level. His books included *Mordecai Manuel Noah: Zionist, Author and Statesman* (1905); *John Milton* (1924); *Israel in America* (1947); and *A History of the Jews in Modern Times* (1919) which was published as a supplement to *Graetz's *History of the Jews*. An ardent Zionist when Zionism was unpopular in the Reform movement, his views were influenced by *Aḥad Ha-Am. A number of his works were autobiographical: *Dappim mi-Pinkaso shel Rabbi* (1941); *Out of My Life* (1956); and *Great Jews I have Known* (1959).

Bibliography: Morgenstern, in: Central Conference of American Rabbis, *Yearbook*, 67 (1957), 154f.; Kressel, Leksikon, 2 (1967), 861f.

[Ei.S.]

RAISMAN, SIR ABRAHAM JEREMY (1892–), British economist and banker. Born in Leeds, in 1916 he entered the Indian Civil Service, first in Bihar and Orissa, then with the customs department in Bombay and Calcutta, and as commissioner for income tax in the Punjab and the Northwest Frontier Province. In 1931 he joined India's central government as joint secretary in the Commerce Department. In 1938 he was appointed secretary to the Finance Department, and a year later became finance member of the government of India. In 1944 he led India's delegation to the International Monetary Conference at Bretton Woods (New Hampshire) which resulted in the formation of the International Monetary Fund and the International Bank for Reconstruction and Development. In 1939 he was knighted, and in 1945 resigned from service in India, where he had been helpful to many Jewish refugees from Europe. After his retirement he served as an adviser to several newly independent countries including Pakistan, Rhodesia, Nigeria, and East African countries. [J.O.R.]

RAISZ, ERWIN J. (1893–1968), U.S. geographer and authority on cartography. Raisz was born in Hungary, where he studied architecture and engineering. He settled in New York City in 1923 and studied geology at Columbia University. From 1925 to 1931 he was an instructor in this field, but during this period turned his attention to geography and cartography. He instituted Columbia's first course in cartography. From 1931 to 1950 he was a lecturer at the Institute of Geographical Exploration at Harvard. In 1945 he founded the cartography group of the Association of American Geographers and was its chairman until 1952.

Raisz was the author of *General Cartography* (1938); the *Atlas of Global Geography* (1944); *Mapping the World* (1956); *Principles of Cartography* (1962); and *Atlas of Florida* (1964).

Bibliography: *New York Times* (Dec. 5, 1968).

[Ed.]

RAJPURKAR, JOSEPH EZEKIEL (1834–1905), scholar of the *Bene Israel community in Bombay. After studying at the Free Assembly School, he became a teacher in the David Sassoon Benevolent Institution, Bombay, in 1856 and after five years its headmaster, a post which he occupied for 40 years. In 1871 he was appointed Hebrew examiner at the University of Bombay, which elected him a fellow in 1879. A master of Hebrew as well as of Marathi, the vernacular of Bombay, he translated over 20 works of the Hebrew liturgy and many English works of Jewish interest into Marathi.

His translations of Hebrew liturgical works include the Daily Prayer Book (1889, 1924), the *maḥzor, piyyutim,* and *seliḥot*. In 1887 he published *Kuttonet Yosef*—a handbook of Hebrew abbreviations, a Hebrew grammar in Marathi, a Hebrew primer for children, and prayers for various occasions.

Bibliography: H. S. Kehimkar, *History of the Bene Israel of India* (1937); *The Israelite*, 9 (1925), 97ff.; A. Yaari, *Ha-Defus ha-Ivri be-Arẓot ha-Mizraḥ*, 2 (1940), 54n, 73–79, 82.

[W.J.F.]

RÁKOSI, MÁTYÁS (1892–1971), Hungarian Communist dictator. Born in Ada (then Hungary), Rákosi was the son of a small shopkeeper. He completed his studies at the Budapest Oriental Academy and after working as a bank clerk in Budapest and Hamburg, went to England where he became active in the socialist movement. During World War I he fought in the Austro-Hungarian army until 1915 when he was taken prisoner by the Russians. Following the October Revolution of 1917, Rákosi joined the Red Army and the Communist Party and returned to Hungary with Béla *Kun. He was made deputy commissioner of trade in Kun's Hungarian soviet republic (1919) and with the suppression of the regime in the same year, fled to the Soviet Union. He returned to Hungary secretly in 1924 to organize the illegal Communist Party, and was arrested and sentenced to death. Following the intervention of leading intellectuals abroad such as Romain Rolland his sentence was commuted to life imprisonment. In 1940 he was released and settled in the Soviet Union where he became the leading figure and propagandist among the Hungarian exiles in Moscow.

Rákosi returned to Hungary in 1944, and reorganized the Hungarian Communist Party. Between 1945 and 1948 he served as deputy leader of a coalition government, but step by step he removed the other parties from political life and assumed dictatorial powers. From 1949 he removed all traces of the former regime, among them leaders of the Catholic Church, Social Democrats, and even Communists and secret police chiefs. Rákosi conducted his policy in strict conformity with the Stalinist line. After Stalin's death (1953) he was summoned to Moscow and severely criticized for the failure of his economic policy. He resigned but was recalled to the premiership in the following year and remained in power until the summer of 1956, shortly before the outbreak of the Hungarian revolution. Once again, he was obliged to flee to the Soviet Union but after the rebellion's suppression did not return to Hungary until shortly before his death. Rákosi did not take any interest in Jewish affairs and tried to hide his Jewish origins. His policy of trials against Zionists, the confiscation of private enterprises, and the transfer of populations from the large cities caused great suffering to many Jews.

Bibliography: M. M. Drachkovits and B. Lazitch (eds.), *The Comintern: Historical Highlights* (1966); T. Aczél and M. Méray, *The Revolt of the Mind* (1959). [B.Y.]

RAKOUS, VOJTĚCH (pseudonym of **Vojtěch Oesterreicher;** 1862–1935), Czech author. He published some short stories in a serious vein, such as *Na rozcestí* ("At the Crossroads") and *Strýc Václav* ("Uncle Wenceslas"), but is best remembered as a writer with a sense of comedy.

In the four volumes of humorous tales entitled *Vojkovičtí a přespolní* ("Those from Vojkovice and Those from Elsewhere," 1911), Rakous vividly portrayed Jewish life in the Czech villages. The volume featuring the **schlemiel*, Motke, and his domineering wife, Rézi, became a popular classic and was later dramatized and filmed. The stories also shed important light on Jewish-Christian relations in Czech villages at the turn of the century.

Bibliography: O. Donath, *Židé a židovství v české literatuře* (1930); F. Kafka, in: *Židovská ročenka* (1967/68), 106–15. [Av.D.]

RALL, YISRAEL (1830–1893), Hebrew writer and translator. Born in Brody, Galicia, he became interested in the Haskalah and studied classical and European languages. He lived for many years in Odessa where he published a collection of translations from classical Latin poetry, *Shirei Romi* (1876), which established his reputation. After years of wandering in Western Europe he settled in Lemberg, where he founded the periodical *Shem ve-Yafet* (1887). He also published booklets in German and French in which he rebutted anti-Semitic libels. Rall contributed to **Ha-Meliẓ*, **Ha-Maggid*, and also to the German press.

Bibliography: Lachower, Sifrut, 2 (1963), 171–6; Waxman, Literature, 3 (1960[2]), 262. [Y.S.]

RĀMA, AL-(Arab. الرامة), Christian-Arab and Druze village in Upper Galilee, Israel, at the foot of Mt. Ha-Ari. Reported uninhabited and in ruins in 1729, the village thrived in the 20th century, and as in antiquity, is one of the principal olive-growing centers in the country. In the Israel *War of Independence, al-Rāma fell to Israel forces in October 1948. The number of inhabitants increased from about 1,100 in 1947 to 3,570 in 1968, with a majority of Christians (mostly Greek-Orthodox and Greek-Catholic), and about one third Druze. [E.O.]

RAMAH or **HA-RAMAH** or **HA-RAMATHAIM-ZOPHIM** (Heb. רָמָה, הָרָמָה, הָרָמָתַיִם–צוֹפִים ; "height"), the designation of several places located on high ground (see also Ramoth).

(1) A town in the territory of Benjamin, mentioned together with Gibeon and Beeroth in Joshua 18:25 and with Gibeah on the main road north of Jerusalem in Judges 19:13, Isaiah 10:29, and Hosea 5:8. Baasha, king of Israel, tried to fortify the place against Judah, but Asa of Judah dismantled the fort and used the materials to strengthen Gebah and Mizpeh (I Kings 15:17ff.; II Chron. 16:1, 5–6). Jeremiah, following the tradition of the north, located the tomb of Rachel in Ramah (31:15). There the Babylonians concentrated the captives taken from Jerusalem before exiling them (Jer. 40:1). After the return from exile, the place was resettled by Judeans (Ezra 2:26; Neh. 7:30; 11:33). Later authors place it 6 mi. (c. 9 km.) north of Jerusalem (Eusebius, Onom. 144:14; Jerome, Hosea 5:8, and Zephaniah 1:15), a location corresponding to the village of al-Rām, which was a fief of the Holy Sepulcher in the Middle Ages.

(2) A town in the territory of Naphtali, mentioned together with Adamah and Hazor in Joshua 19:36. It is identified with Khirbet al-Jūl, near al-Rāma in the valley of Beth-Cherem in Galilee. In 1933 I. Ben-Zvi discovered a synagogue lintel with an Aramaic inscription there.

(3) A town in the territory of Asher (Josh. 19:29). Its identification with Rāmiya, southeast of Tyre, is controversial.

(4) The hometown of Samuel (I Sam. 1:1; as Ramathaim-Zophim) and possibly the residence of Deborah (Judg. 4:5). There Samuel judged Israel (I Sam. 7:17; 8:4) and was later buried (I Sam. 25:1; 28:3); his school

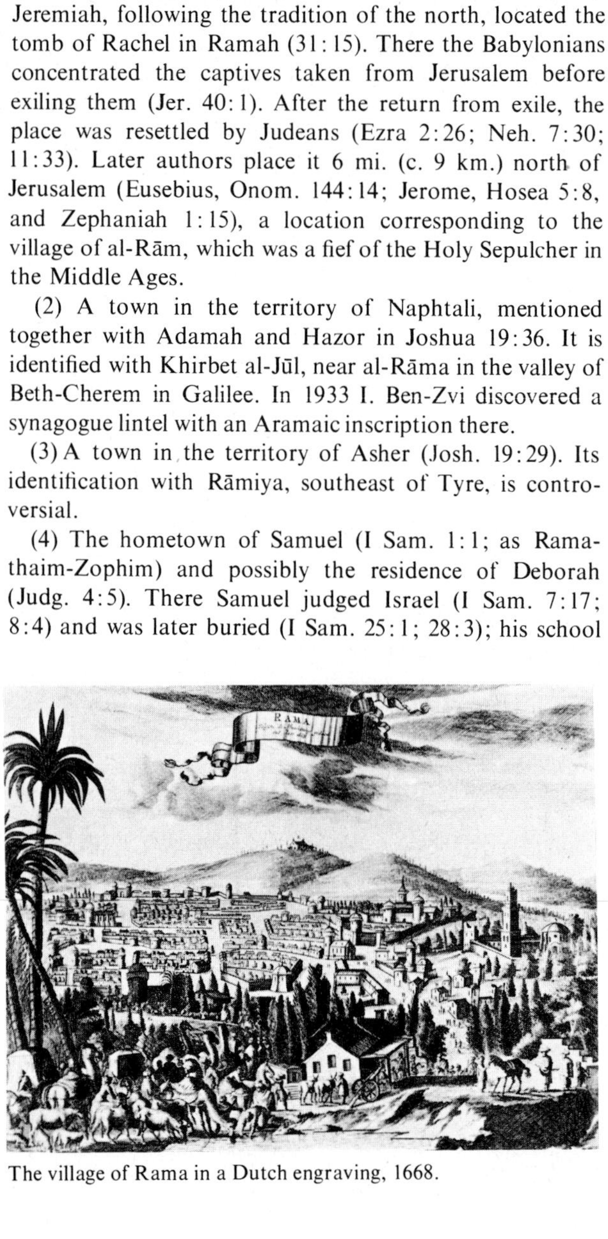

The village of Rama in a Dutch engraving, 1668.

of prophets was located in Naioth in Ramah (I Sam. 19:22–24). In the Septuagint, it is identified with ha-Ramatha or Arimathea, which is described in I Maccabees 11:34 as the headquarters of a Samaritan toparchy transferred to Judea in 145 B.C.E.; this place was the home town of Joseph, a Jerusalem councilor, in whose tomb Jesus was buried (Matt. 27:57, et al.). It was called Remphthis by Eusebius (Onom. 144:28) and is the present-day Rantis, northeast of Lydda. However, the identification of this site with Samuel's birthplace is controversial. Various scholars view Ramathaim-Zophim as identical with (1) above, assuming that both names refer to the settlement of the family of Zuph on the border of the territories of Benjamin and Ephraim (I Sam. 1:1; 9:4).

Bibliography: Abel, Geog, 2 (1938), 427; Abel and Ben-Zvi, in: JPOS, 13 (1933), 94ff.; Alt, in: PJB, 24 (1928), 70; Aharoni, Land, index.

[M.A.-Y.]

RAMALLAH (**Rām Allāh**; Ar. رام الله and **al-Bīra** البيرة), twin towns in the northern Judean Hills, 9 mi. (15 km.) N. of Jerusalem. While al-Bīra is supposed to stand on the site of biblical *Beeroth, Ramallah is generally

The pottery market in Ramallah, 1967. Jerusalem, Jewish National Fund.

identified with *Ramah. The twin towns occupy a strategical position at 2,854 ft. (870 m.) above sea level, where the Judean upfold broadens, and at a crossroads. During the British Mandate, Ramallah was preponderantly Christian-Arab with 4,710 Christian and 650 Muslim inhabitants in 1946. The proportion was reversed in al-Bīra, then a village with 2,100 Muslims and 150 Christians. Because of Ramallah's elevation, the authorities chose it as the site for the country broadcasting transmitters. The clear, brisk climate encouraged the development of the town as a summer resort, which gained impetus under Jordanian rule when wealthy citizens built summer houses there and tourists came from other Arab countries to spend the summer. In the *Six-Day War, Ramallah was taken by Israel forces. The census taken by the Israel authorities in the fall of 1967 revealed that the population of both towns had greatly increased since 1948, mainly through the opening of refugee camps, while the relative strength of the Christian communities had diminished. Ramallah in 1967 had 12,134 inhabitants, of whom 6,966 (57.4%) were Christians, while al-Bīra, with a population of 13,037, was larger than Ramallah and was almost exclusively Muslim.

[E.O.]

RAMAT DAVID (Heb. רָמַת דָּוִד), kibbutz in northern Israel, near Nahalal, affiliated with Iḥud ha-Kevuẓot ve-ha-Kibbutzim, founded in 1926 by two groups of Third Aliyah pioneers, "Ayanot" and "Ha-Sharon," from Eastern Europe. The kibbutz economy is based on field and fodder crops and dairy cattle. The village is named after David *Lloyd George who was prime minister of the British War Cabinet which issued the *Balfour Declaration.

[E.O.]

RAMAT GAN (Heb. רָמַת גַּן; "Garden Height"), city in central Israel adjoining Tel Aviv and fourth in rank among the country's cities. In 1914, 20 settlers from Eastern Europe formed a group called Ir-Gannim ("garden city"); they envisaged a garden suburb where they could enjoy a country-like life without having to relinquish the amenities of a city. The group resolved to carry out the building without the use of any hired labor and forbade the establishment of factories within the settlement's boundaries. The project became feasible only in December 1921. The proximity of Jaffa and expanding Tel Aviv engendered Ramat Gan's quick growth. In 1922 it had 140 inhabitants, but in 1926 already rated municipal council status with A. *Krinitzi as its first mayor. In the 1930s relatively large industrial enterprises, instead of choosing Tel Aviv, preferred to establish themselves in Ramat Gan where land prices were cheaper. In 1939, the community had 5,000 inhabitants and grew vigorously. In 1948 its population was 19,000. Care was taken to preserve the design of the town. Avenues of trees were planted and many public gardens were laid out, utilizing mainly the slopes of the low sandstone hills. In 1948 the municipal area covered about 3 sq. mi. (7.92 sq. km.). After 1948 Ramat Gan's growth accelerated and city status was obtained in 1950. Population growth was most rapid in the early 1950s (in 1953 there were 42,000 inhabitants, in 1958, 71,500, and by 1963, 95,800), and by 1968 the city's population, together with that of *Bar Ilan University lying within the municipal boundary, totaled 106,800.

Bordering on Tel Aviv in the west and north, on Givatayim in the southwest, on Bene-Berak in the east and on Ramat ha-Sharon in the northeast, Ramat Gan, whose municipal area expanded to about 5.8 sq. mi. (15 sq. km.) in 1968, occupies a central position in the country's largest conurbation. The city is one of Israel's foremost manufacturing centers (food preserves, chocolate, cigarettes, textile spinning, weaving, dyeing and finishing, metals, building materials, and wood). In 1968 the Israel Diamond Bourse was opened in Ramat Gan. Hotels and recreation homes constitute another branch

The National Park at Ramat Gan. Courtesy Government Press Office, Tel Aviv.

of the city's economy. The largest of the city's network of gardens was the 494 acre (200 ha.) national park to the south with tropical tree species, a rose garden, and a large artificial lake with boating facilities. Ramat Gan has the country's largest sport stadium with a capacity of 60,000 and Israel's most important sports center. Makkabiah Village and many other installations and children's playgrounds belong to its municipal area. It has many cultural institutions (municipal library, museum, and lecture halls), and a chamber orchestra. [E.O.]

RAMAT HA-GOLAN (Heb. רָמַת הַגּוֹלָן; the "Golan Heights" or "Plateau"), comprises practically the whole Golan region of N. Transjordan which forms the western section of the *Bashan. Ramat ha-Golan borders on the upper Jordan Rift Valley and Lake Kinneret in the west, on the Yarmuk Valley in the south, on the Ruqqād stream in the east, and on the Hermon Massif in the north. In the last stage of the Six-Day War (1967), nearly the entire region was occupied by the Israel army and came under Israel administration. Together with the southeast portion of Mount Hermon—also occupied by Israel forces—it measures about 480 sq. mi. (1,250 sq. km.). The origin of the name Golan is not clear; A. J. Brawer proposes that it is derived from *golah* ("exile") as the biblical "Golan in Bashan" (Deut. 4:43; I Chron. 6:56) was a city of refuge for expatriates.

Two subregions are distinguished: the Lower Golan in the south, with altitudes between 600 and 1,900 ft. (185–600 m.) above sea level, and the Upper Golan in the north, rising to altitudes of 2,000–3,000 ft. (600–900 m.), with a number of hilltops attaining 3,600–4,040 ft. (1,100–1,226 m.). The dominant characteristics of the Golan's topography were created through volcanism, which continued into the Middle Pleistocene period, i.e., until approximately 500,000 years ago, with lava pouring out from fissures and craters and covering the plateau with a continuous layer of basalt and strings of volcanic cones, the largest being Tel Avital (Tell Abu al-Nadā', 1,204 m.). The plateau rises gently from south to north and dominates the rift valley to the west and south with abrupt escarpments. Stream courses, mainly in the southern section, have cut deep ravines, laid bare light-colored chalks, marls, and limestones underneath the black basalt, and separated small portions of the plateau from each other. Soils are mostly dark, fertile, and deep grumusols and are covered with basalt boulders in the north.

The northern Golan's climate is perceptibly cooler than that of other parts of Israel. While annual precipitation near the southern border of the Golan averages 16 in. (400 mm.), it amounts to 36–40 in. (900–1000 mm.) and more in the north. The Lower Golan has been farming country throughout most of its historic past, with grain crops as the principal branch; the ample rainfall and resulting stronger erosion make the Upper Golan a region of brush, forest, and pastures, rather than tilled fields, and biblical expressions such as the "cows" or "cattle of Bashan" (Amos 4:1; Ezek. 39:18) and "oaks of Bashan" (Isa. 2:13; Ezek. 27:6) seem to refer to this section. Deforestation by man has left only stunted remnants of ancient forests in the northern Golan; flocks of sheep and herds of cattle, however, continued to be the region's economic mainstay until the recent past. [E.O.]

Figure 1. The Yarmuk River flowing through the southern hills of the Golan Heights. Photo Zev Radovan, Jerusalem.

Figure 2. Remains of a synagogue at Khirbat Kânif, with the original corner and entrance intact. Courtesy M. Neistadt.

Archaeological Finds. The archaeological and geographical explorations of Ereẓ Israel in the late 19th and early 20th centuries almost completely overlooked the Golan. In 1884–86 the German engineer G. Schumacher prepared the first map of the Golan under the auspices of the Palestine Exploration Fund. During his cartographic work, he visited hundreds of sites and recorded all the surface finds, thus carrying out the first archaeological survey of the Golan. He discovered about a dozen sites containing typical Jewish symbols, such as the seven-branched *menorah* and other motifs, which he attributed to remains of ancient synagogues. These sites include Fīq, Umm al-Qanāṭir, Khan-Bandaq, Lawiyya, al-Dikkī (Dikke), al-Rafīd, al-Aḥmadiyya, al-Burayka, etc.—most of them in southwestern Golan near the shores of Lake Kinneret. In the village of Fīq (apparently Aphek, mentioned in I Kings 20:26), a basalt column was found engraved with a seven-branched *menorah* and under it an Aramaic inscription: "I, Judah, the cantor."

In 1885 L. Oliphant discovered the remains of a synagogue at Khirbat Kānif and a lintel with an incomplete Aramaic inscription: "... remembered be for good Yose son of Ḥalfu son of Ḥana[n]." In excavations at Ḥammat Gader in 1932, E. L. Sukenik found the remains of a synagogue. The main hall was paved with mosaics and contained four Aramaic inscriptions in honor of Jewish donors from Susita, Kefar Akavyah (on the northeastern shore of Lake Kinneret), Kefar Naḥum, and Arbel. Israel surveys, begun in July 1967, have explored more than 100 sites and uncovered carved stones from the talmudic period with Jewish motifs typical of the Golan (and of the Bashan in general). Some 100 inscriptions, the majority in Greek and containing Hebrew names, were also found. The large amount of objects surviving in the Golan is due to the durability of basalt stone, which is characteristic of the area. In addition to the seven-branched *menorah*, the typical Jewish ornamental motifs include bunches of grapes, vine leaves, palm and pine branches, fish, doves, and eagles. Walls and stone courses of buildings have also been well preserved thanks to the basalt stone.

In 1970 a site was discovered on the ridge of Wadi al-Dāliya, near the village of Deir Krūḥ which the surveyors have identified with the village of *Gamala, mentioned by Josephus. At the village of Dabbūra in the western Golan above the Ḥuleh Valley, a wealth of objects were discovered, including a Hebrew lintel inscription that attests to the existence of a *bet midrash* in the settlement. On either side of the inscription stands a bird, either a dove or an eagle, which grasps in its beak the end of a wreath that encircles the inscription: "This is the *bet midrash* of the rabbi." To the right and left of the wreath are the words "Eleazar ha-Kappar." This personage belonged to the fifth generation of *tannaim,* i.e., the second century. In addition, five Aramaic inscriptions found there can be related to the existence of a *bet midrash* or synagogue during the talmudic period. Dabbūra should perhaps be identified with the biblical city of refuge "Golan in Bashan" (Deut. 4:43). A seven-branched *menorah* and other stones carved in relief found at al-Yahūdiyya undoubtedly belonged to a synagogue not yet uncovered. It has been proposed to identify al-Yahūdiyya with Sogane, which was fortified by Josephus before the Jewish War (66–70/73). A Jewish community lived at Yahūdiyya up to the 13th century and Jewish travelers of the Middle Ages used to visit the local synagogue.

Stones engraved with Jewish symbols have also been found in the villages of ʿAyyūn, Kafr Ḥārib (Kefar Ḥaruba in the Mishnah), Khasfīn (Ḥasfiyah), and Nāb (Nob) in the southwestern Golan. The names of these four villages are included among the nine villages in the territory of Susita, which are considered as lying within the boundaries of Ereẓ Israel (TJ, Dem. 1:2, 22d). Scores of stone houses from the talmudic period have survived almost intact at al-Rafīd, al-Ruthmāniyya, and Furayj. These houses have been used as dwellings up to the present. Some lack ceilings, but most of them are preserved together with walls, ceilings, doorsills, and partitions, just as they were built in the fourth to fifth centuries.

The discoveries in the Golan clearly attest the existence of a dense Jewish population in the talmudic period, which, despite changes of fortune, survived for more than 600 years from its inception in the time of Herod, who established Jewish settlement in northern Transjordan, up to the Arab conquest. Important Christian remains in the Golan were excavated in 1970 at Kursī, on the eastern shore of Lake Kinneret at the mouth of Wadi al-Samak. This was the site of the city of Gerasa sacred to Christians as the place where Jesus performed the miracle of driving devils out of man and sending them into a herd of swine (see also *Gadara). Inside an enclosure fortified by a wall 492 x 426 ft. (150 x 130 m.) were the ruins of a large church from the fifth to sixth century. Nearby were remains of a chapel with mosaic pavement, pulpit, fragmentary chancel screen with a cross carved on it, and a Greek inscription that mentions the name of the bishop. A series of rooms belonging to the church complex were paved with a colored mosaic floor.

In 1967 when the Israel Archeological Survey Society organized a survey in the Golan it discovered in Qaṣrayn the remnants of a large synagogue dating from the talmudic period, and near it a massive doorpost on which were reliefs of a *menorah* and a peacock. During excavations organized in 1971 part of a synagogue was uncovered. Its area measured 59 ft. (18 m.)×50 ft. (15.4m.) in a north-south direction. Along the length of its walls was a bench about 1 ft. 4 in. (40 cm.) high made of smoothed basalt blocks. In the northern wall, constructed from large hewn basalt stones, a wide gate (1.90 m.:6 ft.; see figure 4) was uncovered, adorned with the traditional embellishments of a synagogue of the talmudic period. North of this wall was laid bare a large square built in a later era. On one of the capitals an engraved depiction of a three-branched *menorah* was uncovered. Below the square two additional levels of paved streets were discovered belonging evidently to the earlier stages of the synagogue. Around the synagogue extending over a large area many old buildings were found that testify to the existence in early times of a large community in the place. [Mo.N.]

Modern Period. One of Syria's backward provinces, Golan entered modern history in the 1880s, when the

Figure 3. Lintel from the *bet-midrash* at Dabbûra, bearing the name of the second-century sage, Eleazar ha-Kappar. Courtesy D. Urman, Israel Archeological Survey.

Figure 4. Portal and remains of the north wall of the synagogue at Qaṣrayn. Stone relief decoration on the lintel includes a wreath and pomegranates. Courtesy D. Urman, Israel Archaeological Survey.

Turkish authorities settled Circassians there to ward off Bedouin robbers. The regional center, al-*Qunaytira, came into being at that time. Shortly afterward, Jews made attempts to found settlements in the Golan, initially at Rumsaniyya, south of al-Qunaytira; then at *Benei Yehudah east of Lake Kinneret; and finally, in 1908, in the Bet Ẓayyada (al-Buṭayḥa) Valley (a much larger enterprise, at Benei Binyamin and Jilīn, was undertaken with Baron E. de Rothschild's aid in the Bashan, further east). Prior to 1967, the Golan's population included Sunnite Muslims, as well as Circassians, Druze, Alawids (Nusayris), a small Christian minority, and others. In the 1950s and 1960s, the Syrians covered the Golan with a network of artillery positions and fortifications to harass Israel settlements in Upper Galilee and the Lake Kinneret area, and geared the region's entire economy to military needs. In the last two days of the Six-Day War (June 9–10), almost the entire population took to flight together with the Syrian army, with the exception of the Druze who stayed on in six villages in the north (in the September 1967 census they numbered over 6,000). The remaining Druze villagers in the area quickly made contact with their kinsmen in Israel and developed friendly relations with the Israel administration and their new Jewish neighbors.

The first initiative for new Jewish settlement in the region was taken in July 1967 by a group of Ha-Kibbutz ha-Me'uḥad, which founded the village Merom Golan. By 1970 the number of Golan settlements had increased to 12, including Ramat Banias (Senir; of Ha-Shomer ha-Ẓa'ir), Merom Golan and Ein Zivan (Ha-Kibbutz ha-Me'uḥad) in the north; Naḥal Geshur (Ha-Shomer ha-Ẓa'ir) in the center; Ramot Magshimim (moshav shittufi of Ha-Po'el ha-Mizrachi), Givat Yo'av (Tenu'at ha-Moshavim), Ne'ot Golan (moshav shittufi of Ha-Oved ha-Ẓiyyoni), El Al (Tenu'at ha-Moshavim), Mevo Ḥammah (Iḥud ha-Kibbutzim), Naḥal Golan, and Ramot (Tenu'at ha-Moshavim) in the south Hermon. After 1967, land reclamation was carried out on a large scale and the first storage ponds were installed to retain runoff and ease the problem of water shortage, which is serious despite the relatively ample rainfall. For the northern Golan, deciduous fruit, particularly nuts (dependent on winter cold), are viewed as promising, while near Lake Kinneret preference is given to subtropical species (e.g., avocado).

See also *Bashan. [E.O.]

RAMAT HA-KOVESH (Heb. רָמַת הַכּוֹבֵשׁ), kibbutz in central Israel, N.E. of *Kefar Sava, affiliated with Ha-Kibbutz ha-Me'uḥad. It was founded in 1932 by pioneers

from Eastern Europe who, before setting up their own kibbutz, had worked in Kefar Sava's citrus groves. In the 1936–39 Arab riots, the kibbutz was the easternmost outpost of Jewish settlement in the southern Sharon and suffered attacks, losing 15 of its members. Similarly, the kibbutz found itself in the front line during the Israel *War of Independence (1948), and again suffered losses. In 1970 Ramat ha-Kovesh had 520 inhabitants. Its economy is based on citrus groves and irrigated crops etc., as well as on a large bakery. The name, "Height of the Conqueror," symbolizes the settlers' early history as "conquerors of labor" in Kefar Sava. [E.O.]

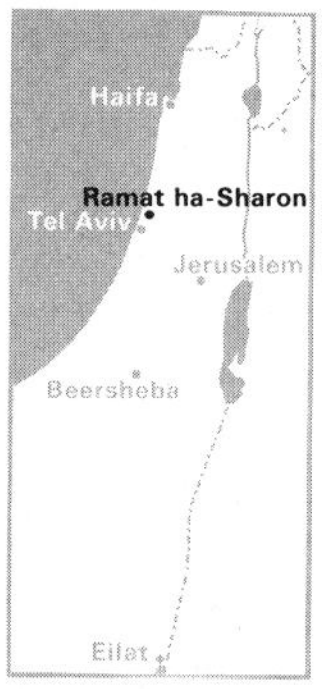

RAMAT HA-SHARON (Heb. רָמַת הַשָּׁרוֹן; "Sharon Height"), urban community with municipal council status, in central Israel, N. of Tel Aviv. Ramat ha-Sharon was founded in 1923 as a middle-class village (moshavah) primarily based on citriculture. Following the crisis in citrus exports during World War II, the settlers turned to other branches, including vegetable growing. In the late 1940s, industrial enterprises were opened. By 1947 the population reached 1,150. After the War of Independence (1948), a large *ma'barah* was included in Ramat ha-Sharon's area which covers 4,250 acres (1,700 ha.). The population increased quickly as the *ma'barah* inhabitants were gradually transferred to permanent housing and numerous veteran Israelis settled in Ramat ha-Sharon. It became a town within the Tel Aviv conurbation. The number of inhabitants grew to 8,200 in 1958, and 17,600 in 1970. The town has a number of large- and medium-sized industrial businesses, e.g., cooking-gas plants, and metal and machinery factories. Many of the inhabitants work in Tel Aviv and its surroundings. [E.O.]

RAMAT HA-SHOFET (Heb. רָמַת הַשּׁוֹפֵט), kibbutz in central Israel, on the Manasseh Hills near Ein ha-Shofet, affiliated with Kibbutz Arẓi ha-Shomer ha-Ẓa'ir. It was founded by pioneers from Lithuania, Poland, Hungary, and Bulgaria in 1941, with the aim of reinforcing the "bridge" of Jewish settlements between the Sharon and the Jezreel Valley. In 1970 the kibbutz had 530 inhabitants. Its economy is based on field crops, deciduous fruit orchards, vineyards, and dairy cattle. The kibbutz also produces bruce boxes for citrus packing. The Bet Aḥim youth hostel is located at Ramat ha-Shofet. The name, meaning "Height of the Judge," commemorates Judge Julian W. Mack, U.S. Zionist leader. [E.O.]

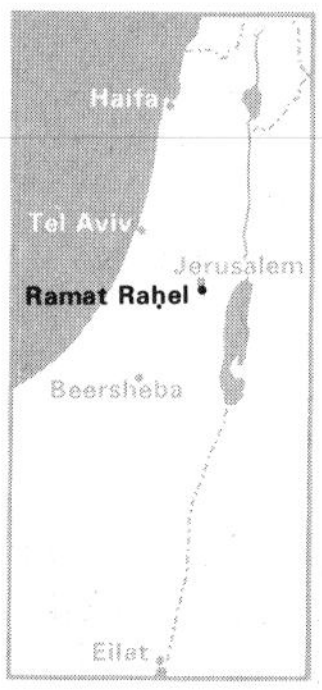

RAMAT RAḤEL (Heb. רָמַת רָחֵל), an ancient tell (Khirbat Ṣāliḥ) situated on the lands of a kibbutz by the same name in the southern outskirts of Jerusalem. The tell contains remains from the First Temple period to the early Arab period. The Hebrew University and the University of Rome conducted five seasons of excavations there (1954–62) under the direction of Y. Aharoni. The finds include especially important discoveries concerning the Judean kingdom and post-Exilic periods and indicate that the site should probably be identified with ancient *Beth-Cherem. Seven periods of occupation were uncovered during the excavations: (1) The site was first settled at the time of the kings of Judah in the ninth or eighth century B.C.E. (Stratum VB), when a royal fortress was apparently built, as evidenced by fragments of walls of ashlar stones and a large number of handles of storage jars stamped with royal seal impressions found in this stratum. This fortress was possibly a house located in the king's vineyards (hence the name Beth-Cherem, "House of the Vineyard"); private dwellings, perhaps belonging to tenant farmers, were built around it. In one of these houses were found seal impressions of "Shebnah [son of] Shaḥar," which have also been discovered at Lachish and Mizpeh. (2) In the following stratum (VA) one of the last kings of Judah erected an imposing palace surrounded by a lower citadel extending over an area of about 20 dunams. This is the first palace of a Judean king found thus far in archaeological excavations, and judging from its late date it was probably built by *Jehoiakim son of Josiah (608–598 B.C.E.), whose palace is described by Jeremiah (22:13–19). The palace walls were constructed of ashlar blocks, similar to Ahab's palace at Samaria, and it was decorated with proto-Aeolic capitals, found here for the first time in Judah. Among the other main finds were window balustrades of the palace (cf. Jer. 22:14), a painted potsherd depicting a king seated on his throne (or chariot?), and a seal impression of "Eliakim, steward of Yokhan," also known from Beth-Shemesh and Tell Beit Mirsim and attributed to an official of Jehoiachin (Yokhan) son of Jehoiakim. (3) In the next settlement (Stratum IVB), dating to the post-Exilic period, a new citadel was erected. The many seal impressions found from the Persian period indicate that the site then served as an administrative center and also strengthen its identification with Beth-Cherem, which is mentioned in the Bible as a district capital in the time of Nehemiah (3:14). In addition to the numerous seal impressions inscribed "Yehud" and "Jerusalem," others were stamped with the names of two royal officials, Jehoezer and Ahzai, who were apparently Jewish governors previously unknown. (4) After the destruction of this citadel in about the third century B.C.E. an unwalled settlement (Stratum IVA) took its place and continued to exist until the end of the Second Temple period. Tomb caves dating to this period contained ossuaries with Jewish names written in Aramaic and Greek. (5) After the fall of the Second Temple, buildings were erected on the hill for the Tenth Roman Legion (Stratum III), as evidenced by bricks

Figure 1. Ashlar masonry of the inner casemate wall of the palace built by one of the last kings of Judah, c. 600 B.C.E. Stratum VA of the Ramat Raḥel excavations. Courtesy Y. Aharoni, Tel Aviv University.

Figure 2. Brick with the stamp of the tenth Roman legion LEG(10)× FRE(TENSIS), found in Stratum III of the Ramat Raḥel excavations. Courtesy Y. Aharoni, Tel Aviv University.

stamped LXFR *(Legio X Fretensis).* A Roman-style house and well-built bathhouse were also found. (6) In the fifth century a Christian church was built on the tell with an attached monastery complex (Stratum II). This is the church of the "Kathisma" ("the Seat") often mentioned in Byzantine sources on the way from Jerusalem to Bethlehem. According to Christian tradition, Mary, mother of Jesus, rested there during her journey to Bethlehem where she gave birth. (7) In the early Arab period (Stratum I), the settlement consisted of poorly built structures (seventh century C.E.). This was the last occupation of the tell. [Yo.A.]

Modern Period. The founders of kibbutz Ramat Raḥel originated from Eastern Europe. They came with the Third Aliyah to the country and belonged to *Gedud ha-Avodah ("Labor Legion"). In 1921 they were sent to Jerusalem as an "urban work group" and set up a temporary camp on the site of Jerusalem's Reḥavyah quarter. The first houses in this quarter were built by the work group, who became construction workers and stone dressers. In 1926 the kibbutz was transferred to its present site on a dominating hill overlooking a wide expanse of the Judean Desert to the east, *Herodium, and the town of *Bethlehem with Rachel's Tomb to the south (from which the settlement took its name). Ramat Raḥel joined Ha-Kibbutz ha-Me'uḥad at the end of the 1920s. In the 1929 Arab riots a large armed mob stormed Ramat Raḥel and completely destroyed it. The kibbutz was rebuilt in 1930. Ramat Raḥel again came under repeated attacks in the 1936–39 Arab riots. As the settlement's cultivable area was then severely limited, its economy was partly based on outside work in which the members performed important pioneering tasks, e.g., in the potash works near the Dead Sea, the railway service, and in enterprises established in the kibbutz, notably a laundry and bakery for Jerusalem customers. In 1946 additional land was allocated and the deciduous fruit orchards and vegetable gardens were enlarged. In the Israel *War of Independence (1948), Ramat Raḥel constituted one of Jewish Jerusalem's forward defense positions and the battles around it were decisive for the city's fate. In May 1948 the kibbutz was attacked by the Arab Legion and irregulars advancing from the east and by an Egyptian tank force simultaneously attacking from the Bethlehem road in the west. In the following battles, the place changed hands several times and was completely destroyed, but finally remained in Israel hands. The armistice border was drawn around it to the east, south, and southwest. The village was rebuilt and received farmland in the nearby demilitarized zone around the former high commissioner's palace and in the Coastal Plain. A seminary was opened at the kibbutz. In the 1951–52 split in Ha-Kibbutz ha-Me'uḥad, Ramat Raḥel joined Iḥud ha-Kevuzot ve-ha-Kibbutzim, while a part of its members went to Ein Karmel. In the autumn of 1956 nearby Jordanian positions opened fire on a party of the Israel Exploration Society congress visiting the local excavations and killed four persons. In the *Six-Day War (1967), the kibbutz again found itself in the front line, when the way to Bethlehem and the Hebron Hills was opened by Israel forces on June 6–7, by the capture in a hard battle of fortifications around the nearby monastery of Mar Elias. [E.O.]

Bibliography: Y. Aharoni, *Excavations at Ramat-Rahel,* 2 vols. (1962–64); idem, in: *Eretz Israel,* 6 (1960), 56–60; idem, in: BIES, 19 (1955), 147–74; 20 (1956), 44–48; 24 (1960), 73–119; B. Maisler and M. Stekelis, in: *Masie Jubilee Volume* (1934–35), 4–40 (Heb.).

RAMAT RAZIEL (Heb. רָמַת רָזִיאֵל), moshav in Israel's Judean Hills, on the Ẓobah-Eshtaol road, affiliated with the Ḥerut movement. Ramat Raziel was founded in 1948 as one of the first settlements designed to secure the Jerusalem Corridor that had been opened in the fighting in the Israel *War of Independence in the preceding months. The terrain conditions were particularly difficult and all the farming land had to undergo heavy reclamation. Ramat Raziel was therefore included in the work village scheme. The population, in spite of this scheme, changed several times. In 1970 the moshav had 135 inhabitants. Its farming is based on deciduous fruit orchards, vineyards, and poultry. The village bears the name of David *Raziel, the *Irgun Ẓeva'i Le'ummi commander. [E.O.]

RAMAT YISHAI (Heb. רָמַת יִשַׁי), semi-rural settlement in N. Israel, in the Tivon Hills. It was founded in 1925 by industrialists from Poland as a textile center. Abandoned with the outbreak of the Arab riots in 1936, Ramat Yishai was resettled in 1943. In 1970, it had 800 inhabitants and medium-size factories for textiles and leather. It is named after the writer and teacher Yishai Adler, whose contribution was instrumental in rebuilding the settlement in 1943. [E.O.]

RAMAT YOḤANAN (Heb. רָמַת יוֹחָנָן), kibbutz in N. Israel, in the Haifa Bay area, E. of Kiryat Ata, affiliated with Iḥud ha-Kevuẓot ve-ha-Kibbutzim, founded in 1932 by pioneers from Eastern Europe. In 1939 an ideological split brought about an exchange of members with *Bet Alfa, with those in favor of Ha-*Shomer ha-Ẓa'ir concentrating in the latter kibbutz, while the members who supported the *Mapai Party stayed in Ramat Yoḥanan. In the Israel *War of Independence, the kibbutz was attacked by a strong unit of Druze irregulars, but held out and counterattacked successfully (April 13–16, 1948). After this battle, the Druze in Israel ceased to side with the Arabs. In 1970 Ramat Yoḥanan had 500 inhabitants. The kibbutz' economy is based on highly intensive and fully irrigated farming and on a food and a plastics factory. Ramat Yoḥanan has among its members several painters and writers. The ancient tradition of gathering the *omer* ("sheaf") during the Passover week was first renewed in Ramat Yoḥanan. The name, "Height of Yoḥanan," commemorates Gen. Jan (Yoḥanan) *Smuts. [E.O.]

RAMAT ẒEVI (Heb. רָמַת צְבִי), moshav in N. Israel, on the Kokhav Plateau of Lower Galilee, affiliated with Tenu'at ha-Moshavim. It was founded in 1942 by a group of veteran farm laborers, who had previously set up a temporary settlement, based on auxiliary holdings at Shimron, near Nahalal. They were later joined by demobilized soldiers from World War II. After 1948 the population changed when most of the veteran settlers left and were replaced by new immigrants. Farming at Ramat Ẓevi consists mainly of field crops and dairy cattle. The village is named after Ẓevi (Henry) Monsky, B'nai B'rith president. Its population in 1970 was 180. [E.O.]

RAMBERT, DAME MARIE (1888–), British ballet teacher and founder director of the Ballet Rambert. Born in Warsaw as Miriam Rambach, she studied eurythmics and was invited by Serge Diaghilev to teach in his company. While she influenced Diaghilev's most famous dancer,

Dame Marie Rambert, founder of the Ballet Rambert. Photo Niki Ekstrom, New York.

Nijinsky, in his choreographic work, she was herself won over to classical ballet, became a pupil of Enrico Cecchetti, the Italian ballet dancer and teacher, and followed his principles when she opened a school in London in 1920. By 1930 the school had developed into the Ballet Club which, as the Ballet Rambert, became famous for its performances at the Mercury Theater, a former parish hall at Notting Hill rebuilt by Rambert's husband, the author, Ashley Dukes. Rambert had a great flair for discovering new talent and inspired choreographers, designers, and dancers. She was the first to present a whole group of young dancers under British names, and she drew the public with ballets like *A Tragedy of Fashion, Lilac Garden, Lady into Fox,* and *Death and the Maiden.* In 1966 she became co-director with Nathan Morrice of the New Ballet Rambert Company. She was made a Dame of the British Empire in 1962.

Bibliography: W. Gore (ed.), *Ballet Rambert 1926–1946* (Eng., 1946); L. J. H. Bradley, *Sixteen Years of Ballet Rambert* (1946); M. Clarke, *Dancers of Mercury* (1960); Haskell, in: *Ballet* (Eng., 1938), 137–41. [L.S.]

RAMERUPT, village in the Aube department, N.E. central France. No single extant non-Jewish source confirms the existence of a Jewish community in Ramerupt during the Middle Ages, but Jewish sources mention a community which existed from at least around 1100 until the latter half of the 12th century. It was renowned for its yeshivah, headed by *Meir b. Samuel, Rashi's son-in-law, who was succeeded by his sons, Jacob *Tam and *Samuel b. Meir. The chronicle of *Ephraim b. Jacob of Bonn records an attack made by crusaders on the community of Ramerupt on the second day of Shavuot, 1147, but only describes in detail the ill-treatment of R. Jacob Tam. His house was looted, a Torah Scroll was desecrated, and he would have been murdered in the fields had not a passing nobleman tricked the crusaders into releasing him.

Bibliography: Gross, Gal Jud, 634–8; A. M. Habermann, *Sefer Gezerot Ashkenaz ve-Ẓarefat* (1946), 121. [B.Bl.]

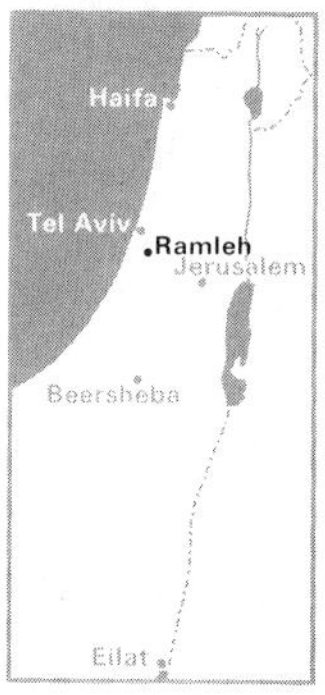

RAMLEH (Ramlah; Heb. רַמְלָה), city in Israel, situated on the Jerusalem-Tel Aviv highway, approximately 28 mi. (45 km.) from Jerusalem.

The Old City. Ramleh was founded in 716 by the Umayyad caliph Suleiman ibn ʿAbd al-Malik and is the only city in the country established by Arabs. The name means "sand" in Arabic and refers to the sandy ground on which the city arose. Ramleh was the administrative capital of the country under the Umayyads and the Abbasids. Although originally founded as a town for Muslims, it had from the beginning a large population of Christians, Jews, and Samaritans. Hārūn al-Rashīd, the Abbasid ruler in the late eighth century, increased the Samaritan farming population. Due to its advantageous location on the crossroads of the Egypt-Damascus and Jerusalem-Jaffa highways, the city prospered till the time of the Crusades.

Among the Jewish community, Ramleh was called Gath or Gath-Rimmon or Ramathaim-Zophim, after the biblical towns with which it was identified. The temporary transfer of the Jerusalem academy to Ramleh in the tenth century greatly strengthened the Jewish population. At that time, a Karaite and a Rabbanite community, the latter divided into Palestinians and Babylonians, existed in the town; there were also synagogues for the Jerusalemites and the Damascenes. In the 11th century the flourishing communities of Ramleh suffered from a series of blows: a disastrous Bedouin raid in 1025 and two devastating earthquakes in 1033 and 1067 (in the latter, 25,000 people reportedly perished). During the Crusader occupation, beginning in 1099, the Jewish and Samaritan communities were dispersed. When Benjamin of Tudela visited there in 1170–71, he recorded a Jewish population of only three dyers, living in the midst of extensive cemeteries.

During the 12th and 13th centuries, the city was often attacked by Muslims. It was finally captured by the Mamluk sultan Baybars and as the capital of a province, it regained some of its former importance. By the 14th century, it was again the largest town in Palestine and a Jewish community was reestablished there. With the Ottoman conquest, it once more declined, although most pilgrims passed through the town, at the time called Rames, on their way to Jerusalem. The tax records for 1690–91 show no Jews living there. The main buildings of the early city which still stand are the Cathedral of St. John (now the Great Mosque), the White Mosque and its minaret (completed in 1318) and the ʿUnayziyya cistern (dating from the eighth century). [M.A.-Y.]

The New Town. In 1890 Ramleh had 9,611 inhabitants, the majority of whom were Muslim Arabs, with a sizable

The ʿUnayziyya cistern, also known as the pool of St. Helena, in Ramleh, built during the rule of Hārūn al-Rashīd, late eighth century C.E. Photo Werner Braun, Jerusalem.

minority of Arab and non-Arab Christians, and a small Jewish community of 66 people. Under the British Mandate (1917–48), the town's economy benefited only slightly from its location near a principal highway. Christian institutions helped raise the local educational level. In the 1930s Ramleh still had five Jewish families; they left, however, in 1936, with the outbreak of the Arab riots.

During the Israel *War of Independence, when Ramleh was occupied by Israel forces in July 1948, most of the town's Arabs abandoned it, causing the population to shrink to 1,547 persons by the November 1948 census. At the beginning of the 1950s the town absorbed a large number of Jewish immigrants from various countries, raising the population to 20,548 in 1961. Initially the newcomers were housed in three *ma'barot* ("transitory immigrant camps"); but, with housing construction proceeding rapidly, Ramleh's built-up area expanded, principally to the west and southwest. in 1969 about 4,200 families lived in its new sections, compared to 3,000 in the town's older areas, where numerous structures are earmarked for leveling and reconstruction. Of its 30,800 inhabitants in 1970, 27,000 were Jews and 3,800 Arabs. The Arabs are mostly well integrated in the city's economic life, employment, and local cultural activities. Good social relations exist between the Jewish and Arab communities, and the town has a Jewish-Arab Friendship League. The city's economy is based mainly on industry, which benefits from its location at one of the country's major highway and railroad junctions and its relative proximity to the port of Ashdod. In 1969, 23 of the larger industrial enterprises employed about 2,000 workers. Some items manufactured are cement (the country's largest factory of this kind is situated here), wood products, metal pipes, motors, refrigerators and miscellaneous metal products, prefabricated houses, and canned foods. There are two industrial zones. Until June 1971, the Tel-Aviv-Jerusalem traffic artery intersected the town from northwest to southeast, and the number of vehicles passing through Ramleh averaged 17,000 daily in 1969. The local market mainly services rural settlements around Ramleh, and provides an outlet for its farming produce. From Ramleh health services are extended to the villages in the vicinity. [S.H.]

Bibliography: B. Segal, in: *Zion*, 5 (1933), 12–18; S. Klein, *Toledot ha-Yishuv ha-Yehudi be-Ereẓ Yisrael* (1935), index; S. Assaf and L. A. Mayer (eds.), *Sefer ha-Yishuv*, 2 (1944), 56–63; Mayer-Pinkerfeld, *Principal Muslim Religious Buildings in Israel* (1950), 25–30; J. Braslavski, *Le-Ḥeker Arẓenu* (1954), index; Hirschberg, in: *Yerushalayim*, 4 (1953), 123–8; Shapira, *ibid.*, 118–22; J. Kaplan, in: *ʿAtiqot*, 2 (1958), 106–15; Z. Vilnay, *Ramleh* (1961); I. Ben-Zvi, *She'ar Yashuv* (1965), 316–21; Ben-Zvi, Ereẓ Yisrael, index; M. Rosen-Ayalon, in: IEJ, 16 (1966), 148–50.

°**RAMÓN LULL** (**Raimundus Lullus;** c. 1234–1315), Catalan Christian preacher, mystic, and philosopher. As a youth Lull grew up in *Majorca, where a substantial Muslim majority had remained even after this island's conquest (1229–32) by King James I. This enabled him, besides the traditional education imparted to the sons of Spanish nobility, to familiarize himself with Muslim culture and the Arabic language. When he was 30, Lull turned to ascetic life. Besides his immersion in mystical contemplation, he considered it his vocation to preach and propagate Christianity among nonbelievers, Muslims, and Jews in Aragon and, chiefly, in Majorca. To this end, Lull devoted many years to the study of Arabic language, philosophy, and theology, and some of his initial works were written in that language. In comparison, his knowledge of Judaism was scant and superficial, some works by Jewish thinkers being known to him through Arabic philosophy, or from Maimonides' *Guide of the Perplexed.* In about 1272 Lull wrote in Arabic and translated into Catalan the widely circulated *Libre del gentil e los tres savis,* which was subsequently translated into Latin, French, and probably Hebrew. It is a work of apologetic character, drawn up in a form frequent in those times. A man, either a nonbeliever or a pagan, consults three sages—a Jew, a Christian, and a Muslim—and asks them the basic principles of their respective creeds. This furnishes the starting point of a peaceful debate between the three, which finally remains inconclusive, although the author does not conceal his sympathy for the Christian. There has been speculation as to the possible influence of *Judah Halevi's *Kuzari* over this work, but there is nothing to warrant it. In 1305 Lull wrote a second apologetic work chiefly directed against the Jews, *Liber de Trinitate et Incarnatione adversus Judaeos et sarracenos,* better known under its shorter appellation *Liber Predicationis Contra Judaeos* (scholarly edition published in Madrid-Barcelona, 1957). The book comprises 52 sermons, one for each week of the year, preceded by a verse from the Bible. In these Lull strives to demonstrate, against Jewish and Muslim arguments as to the irrationality of Christianity, that the Christian truth is not only rational but also borne out by common sense.

Lull was also active as a preacher. In 1299 James II (1291–1327) allowed him to give sermons on Saturdays and Sundays in the synagogues and on Fridays and Sundays in mosques. In his important *Ars Magna* (c. 1274) Lull reduces all knowledge to a few basic metaphysical principles. The theory of the attributes of God occupies the central part of this work and it is interesting to compare the *dignitates* of Lull with the *Sefirot* of the kabbalists. The similarity between the two categories possibly stems from Neoplatonic influence common to the kabbalists and to Lull; the latter maintained friendly relations with a circle of Jewish religious thinkers in Catalonia, such as Solomon b. Abraham *Adret and R. Aaron ha-Levi of Barcelona, author of *Sefer ha-Ḥinnukh;* Lull presumably learned about the foundations of *Kabbalah from them.

Bibliography: Baer, Spain, index; J. M. Millás Vallicrosa, in: *Sefarad*, 18 (1958), 241–53; idem, in: S. Ettinger et al. (eds.), *Sefer Yovel le-Yiẓhak Baer* (1961), 186–90; R. J. Z. Werblowsky, in: *Tarbiz*, 32 (1962/63), 207–11; A. Llinares, *Raymond Lulle* . . . (Fr., (1963), bibl.: 455–81. [J.M.M.-V.]

RAMOTH (Heb. רָאמוֹת), levitical city in the territory of Issachar (I Chron. 6:58), called Jarmuth in one of the lists apportioning territory to the levites (Josh. 21:29). In the

city list of Issachar, the town is called Remeth (Josh. 19:21). It seems to have been the center of the mountainous district of Yarmutu, which was inhabited by Ḥabiru even before the Israelite conquest; Seti I, in one of his stelae found at Beth-Shean, describes his victory over them in approximately 1300 B.C.E. The suggested identification is with Kokhav ha-Yarden (Ar. Kawkab al-Hawā, the Crusader "Belvoir"), a dominating height (895 ft., 275 m.) overlooking the Jordan Valley; it is possibly identical with the fortress of *Agrippina. The topographical position of the site justifies the name Ramoth ("the Heights").

Bibliography: Abel, Geog, 2 (1938), 435; Aharoni, Land, index.

[M.A.-Y.]

RAMOT HA-SHAVIM (Heb. רָמוֹת הַשָּׁבִים; "Heights of the Returning"), moshav with municipal council status, in central Israel, near Hod ha-Sharon, affiliated with Ha-Mo'eẓah ha-Ḥakla'it. It was founded in 1933 by middle-class immigrants from Germany, who chose to become farmers although they had been merchants and members of the free professions abroad. As the area initially available for farming was extremely limited, poultry breeding became their principal farming branch. In 1970, Ramot ha-Shavim had 450 inhabitants. [E.O.]

RAMOTH-GILEAD (Heb. רָמוֹת גִּלְעָד), levitical city of refuge in the territory of the tribe of Gad in N. Transjordan, which was held by the family of Merari (Deut. 4:43; Josh. 20:8; 21:38). Ramoth-Gilead was chosen by Solomon as the capital of his sixth district, which included the villages of Jair and the region of Argob in Bashan (I Kings 4:13), thus strengthening the assumption that the levitical cities served as administrative centers from the time of David. Its fall to the Arameans in the days of the divided monarchy was regarded as a grievous blow. Ahab, king of Israel, tried to retake it with the help of Jehoshaphat, king of Judah, but fell in the battle (I Kings 22; II Chron. 18); his son Joram was wounded in another attempt (II Kings 8:28ff.; II Chron. 22:5ff.). Jehu was anointed and proclaimed king by a messenger of the prophet Elisha in the camp before Ramoth-Gilead (II Kings 9). Josephus calls the city Arimanon or Aramatha(h) (Ant., 4:173; 8:399; 9:105). Eusebius identified it with the village al-Rāmm on the Jabbok (Onom. 144:4). Modern scholars locate it at Ḥuṣn ʿAjlūn or at Tell Ramīth south of Edrei, near the village of al-Ramta. A fortress of the Israelite period was discovered at the latter site in recent excavations.

Bibliography: Abel, Geog, 2 (1938), 430–1; Aharoni, Land, index; N. Glueck, in: AASOR, 25–28 (1951), 96ff.; H. J. Stoebe, in: ZDPV, 82 (1966), 27.

[M.A.-Y.]

RAMOT MENASHEH (Heb. רָמוֹת מְנַשֶּׁה; *ramot*, "heights"), kibbutz in the Manasseh Hills, Israel, affiliated with Kibbutz Arẓi ha-Shomer ha-Ẓa'ir. It was founded in 1948 by young immigrants from Poland, including ghetto fighters of World War II, and Bulgaria. Later, immigrants from Chile and Uruguay joined the kibbutz and became the majority among the settlers. In 1970 the kibbutz had 500 inhabitants. Its economy is based on partly intensive farming and on a food-processing factory. Ramot Menasheh is also a partner in a metal factory at nearby *Daliyyah. [E.O.]

RAMOT NAFTALI (Heb. רָמוֹת נַפְתָּלִי; *ramot*, "heights"), moshav E. of the Israel-Lebanese border, Israel, affiliated with Tenu'at ha-Moshavim. It was founded by a group of veteran soldiers called "Irgun Wingate." Originally a moshav shittufi, Ramot Naftali was the first settlement of demobilized soldiers from World War II. In the *War of Independence (1948), the settlers were in a highly dangerous position and in one instance drove off Lebanese attacking forces after they had already broken into the settlement's perimeter. Although after the war moshav-born youth, and later new immigrants joined the village, it made little progress, due to a number of difficulties: access to the site, the pumping of water, and reclamation of the mountainous terrain for farming. Deciduous fruit trees and vineyards constitute its prominent agricultural branches. Large areas in the vicinity have been afforested. [E.O.]

RAMSES (**Raamses, Rameses**; Heb. רַעַמְסֵס, רַעְמְסֵס), ancient city in Lower Egypt. The second but the more important of the two treasury cities which the Hebrews built in Egypt (Ex. 1:11), Ramses is mentioned four further times in the Bible (see also *Pithom). In Genesis 47:11 *Joseph established his family in the land (i.e., region) of Ramses, and in Exodus 12:37 and Numbers 33:3, 5. Ramses was the Israelites' point of departure from Egypt. Ramses can be hardly any city other than the Delta residence of the Ramessid kings of the Egyptian 19th dynasty, Per-Rameses-Miʿamun-pa-ka-aʿo-en-preʿ-Ḥorakhty ("The House of Rameses-Beloved-of-Amun, the-Great-Ka-Soul-of-Re-Ḥorakhty"), the identification of which was long a subject of controversy among modern scholars. Since it was certainly situated

The building of Pithom and Ramses by Hebrew slaves in an illustration from the *Barcelona Haggadah*, Spain, 14th century. London, British Museum, Ms. Add. 14761, fol. 43r.

within the eastern Delta, its exact location would shed light on the possible route of the Exodus. It was first thought to have been Pelusium, but the identification was then narrowed down to either Tanis (biblical *Zoan) or Qantir, with the weight of scholarly opinion favoring the latter.

Bibliography: E. P. Uphill, in: JNES, 27 (1968), 291–316; 28 (1969), 15–39. [AL.R.S.]

RAMSES (Egyptian **Rʿ-ms-sw**; "Re is he that has borne him"; name of several Egyptian rulers of the 19th and the 20th dynasties. Connected with the sun god of Heliopolis, the name is significant for the orientation toward Lower Egypt that accompanied the attempt to regain power over Asia, which had been lost in the Amarna period.

Ramses I (c. 1306–1305 B.C.E.) rose to become founder of the 19th dynasty from a non-royal position as vizier. It was left to his grandson Ramses II (c. 1290–1223 B.C.E.) to restore Egypt to her former greatness. His long reign, splendid building activities (additions to the Karnak and Luxor temples, the Ramesseum, the monumental rock-cut temple at Abu Simbel), and numerous offspring (over 100 children) made him a legendary figure for later times. The enlargement of his residence at Tanis, renamed Per-Ramses in his honor, agrees with the biblical record (Ex. 1:11) of the building of *Ramses and *Pithom (Tell el-Maskhouta in the eastern Delta) by the Israelites, and makes him the probable *pharaoh of the Exodus. A battle with the Hittites at Kadesh in his fifth year ended in a stalemate. Campaigns in Palestine, southern Phoenicia, and Edom are attested for the following years. In year 21 of his reign a treaty with Hatti was drawn up in the face of the new common menace embodied in the advancing Sea Peoples. The full impact of these peoples fell on Ramses III (c. 1188–1157 B.C.E.), the son of the founder of the 20th dynasty. He warded off their attack in his eighth year, after they had overrun the Hittites. He also managed to check the Libyans and maintained authority over Palestine. However, after his death by a harem intrigue, Palestine, now settled by Philistines and the Israelites, was forever lost to Egypt. A list of his temple donations shows that increasing wealth accumulated in the hands of the priests of Amun at Thebes. Under his successors (Ramses IV–XI, c. 1157–1085 B.C.E.), political influence was also taken over by the priests, while the might of the rulers steadily declined in a country lacking foreign influence and troubled by poverty and inflation.

Bibliography: M. B. Rowton, in: *Journal of Egyptian Archaeology*, 34 (1948), 57–74; J. A. Wilson, *The Burden of Egypt* (1951), 239ff.; P. Montet, *Géographie de l'Egypte ancienne*, 1 (1957), 214; O. Eissfeldt, in: CAH², vol. 2, ch. 26, 17–19; R. O. Faulkner, *ibid.*, ch. 23. [I.GRU.]

RANK, OTTO (original surname—**Rosenfeld,** 1884–1939), psychoanalyst. Born in Vienna, Rank met *Freud in 1906 and became a member of his inner circle. Rank edited with H. *Sachs the psychoanalytic journal *Imago* and with S. Ferenczi and E. Jones *International Zeitschrift fuer Psychoanalyse* (1912–24). He founded and directed the Internationale Psychoanalytische Verlag (1919–24). He had an especial flair for interpreting myths, legends, and dreams. His vast erudition was evident in his great work on incest myths, *Das Inzest Motiv in Dichtung und Sage* (1912). He spent the war years in Cracow. E. Jones notes the change that had occurred in him as a reaction to the melancholia he suffered there. He later eventually broke with Freud after his book *Das Trauma der Geburt* (1923; *The Trauma of Birth,* 1929) appeared. Freud opposed what he finally considered to be Rank's error in attributing to birth trauma the determination of anxiety and his underemphasis of the role of incest drives and the Oedipus complex. After the split with Freud he left Vienna, finally settling in the U.S. in 1935. Rank applied psychoanalytic theory to the arts and to mythology in his works *Der Kuenstler* (1907; *Art and Artist,* 1932) and *Der Mythus von der Geburt des Helden* (1909; *The Myth of the Birth of the Hero,* 1914).

Bibliography: E. Jones, *Sigmund Freud,* 3 (1957), 45ff. [LO.M.]

RANSCHBURG, BEZALEL BEN JOEL (1760–1820), rabbinical author. In accordance with the imperial decree of 1787 (see *Names) he adopted the name "Daniel Rosenbaum" but was later called Ranschburg, the Yiddish pronunciation of the town Ronsperg, the German name for *Pobezovice where he was born. He attended yeshivot at Schwabach, Fuerth, and Prague, where he was a pupil of Leib Fischels and also studied under Ezekiel *Landau. He never held an official appointment and was supported by his wife and her father, but acted as *rosh yeshivah* in Prague. Ranschburg fought Reform (Resp. Ḥatam Sofer). Among his pupils was Zacharias *Frankel (MGWJ, 45 (1901), 220).

He devoted himself to commenting on those tractates of the Talmud on which there are few commentaries, such as his *Horah Gever* on *Horayot (Prague, 1802) and *Pitḥei Niddah* (1957; published in Jerusalem 1928 under the title *Ḥokhmat Beẓalel*). His *Sedeh Ẓofim* on *Asher b. Jehiel's *halakhot* was appended to the Prague Talmud edition (1839–46). His *Ma'aseh Rav* (Prague, 1823) deals partly with tractate *Nazir.* **Haggahot* based on it are included in all subsequent editions of the Talmud. Many letters on halakhic subjects which he wrote to the censor Carolus Fischer (partly signed "Ilan Shoshan") are preserved in the Prague University Library (MGWJ, 62 (1918), 49–56).

Bibliography: B. Ranschburg, *Horah Gever* (1802), introd.; idem, *Ma'aseh Rav* (1823), introd.; S. Kauder, *Ahavat Emet* (1828), 47b–50b; O. Muneles, *Bibliographical Survey of Jewish Prague* (1952), index. [M.LA.]

RANSOM (Heb. כֹּפֶר, *kofer*), the compensation required to avoid bodily punishment or to free one's self from an undesirable state or condition (Isa. 43:3). The term *kofer* is related to the Akkadian *kapāru* ("to wipe off") or *kuppuru* ("to expiate"). The substitution of a penal sum for corporal punishment was widespread in the ancient world. Thus, the Hittite Code provides for fixed damages for bodily harm; and the Bedouin, too, allowed for ransom as an alternative to blood vengeance. Except in the case of murder (Num. 35:31–34), the Israelites followed this practice too, though fixed sums do not seem to have existed in early times. Instead the principle of "measure for measure" was employed (Ex. 21:36; Lev. 24:18), together with specific standards for determining the compensation (Ex. 21:19; 22:16). Later, set amounts were established (Deut. 22:29), such as the "redemption" fees for those consecrated to YHWH (Lev. 27). To be distinguished from *kofer* in the sense of "ransom," which is paid to an aggrieved party, is *kofer* in the sense of "bribe," which is paid to a judge in the hope of influencing his decision (I Sam. 12:3; Amos 5:12).

See also *Captives, Ransoming of.

Bibliography: Pedersen, Israel, 1–2 (1926), 398–9; Pritchard, Texts, 189–90; E.A. Speiser, in: JBL, 182 (1963), 301–6. [D.L.L.]

°**RAOUL** (**Rodulphus**) **GLABER** (before 1000–1049?), Benedictine chronicler. In his very comprehensive account of the anti-Jewish persecutions perpetrated in France (and in Germany) at the beginning of the 11th century, Glaber confirms or completes many details of the Hebrew report concerning the same events, in which Jacob b. Jekuthiel of Rouen had become involved. His narrative gives a clearer insight than the Hebrew report as to what extent this persecution gave rise to the idea of the *Crusades. He is also the source of information on a Judaizing movement promoted by Raynaud, Duke of Sens, from 1009, and a similar Judaizing heresy in Lombardy in 1024.

Bibliography: B. Blumenkranz, *Auteurs chrétiens latins*... (1963), 256–9. [B.BL.]

RAPAPORT, DAVID (1911–1960), U.S. clinical psychologist. Born in Hungary, he interrupted his studies in 1933 and for two years lived in a kibbutz in Palestine. He moved to the U.S. and from 1940 to 1948 was a leading figure at the Menninger Foundation, Topeka, Kansas, first as chief clinical psychologist and then as director of research. From 1948 he worked at the Austen Riggs Center, Stockbridge, Massachusetts.

He wrote *Emotions and Memory* (1950) which reflects his continuous attempts at demonstrating the close interaction between the affective and cognitive spheres in mental functioning; *Diagnostic Psychological Testing* (with M. M. Gill and R. Schafer, 2 vols. 1948–49; rev. ed. 1968) presenting his pioneering work in clinical psychology and reflecting the revolutionary transition of psychologists from psychometricians to clinicians; and *Organization and Pathology of Thought* (1951), a monumental annotated source book, in which his copious critical footnotes to excellent translations into English of important contributions to psychology and psychiatry from Europe attempted to create a conceptual framework linking ideas and findings of different thinkers. A visit to Israel in 1953 resulted in his paper "Study of Kibbutz Education and its Bearing on the Theory of Development" (1957). His works extend from clinical research on the etiology of the psychosis of dementia paralytica to the analysis of different psychodiagnostic instruments. His attempt at systematization of psychoanalytic theory appeared as *The Structure of Psychoanalytic Theory: A Systematizing Attempt* (1960). He was also concerned with the professional status of the clinical psychologist and his training. With David Shakow he wrote *The Influence of Freud on American Psychology* (1964). His collected papers, edited by M. M. Gill, were published in 1967.

Bibliography: R. P. Knight, in: *Psychoanalytic Quarterly*, 30 (1961), 262–4; M. M. Gill, in: *Rapaport, Collected Papers* (1967), 3–7; M. M. Gill and G. S. Klein, *ibid.*, 8–31, incl.bibl. [Av.A.W.]

RAPAPORT, DAVID HA-KOHEN (second half of 17th century), rabbi and Jerusalem emissary. Rapaport's family originated in Lublin. He emigrated to Ereẓ Israel and settled in Jerusalem, where he served as a *dayyan* in the *bet din* of Moses *Galante. A responsum to a halakhic query from Mordecai ha-Levi, chief rabbi of Egypt, signed by Rapaport, Abraham *Amigo, and Moses ibn Ḥabib, is mentioned in Ha-Levi's *Darkhei No'am* (*Even ha-Ezer*, no. 18), where he refers to Rapaport as "one of the three great men of Ereẓ Israel" (*ibid.*, 17, 31). In 1679, apparently, Rapaport went as an emissary to Germany, and his mission seems to have terminated in 1682. When he passed through Belgrade he appended his signature in approval to two rulings of Joseph b. Isaac *Almosnino (see *Edut bi-Yhosef*, pt. 1 (Constantinople, 1716), nos. 1 and 3), who refers to him in the most laudatory words, stating that "his decision is final since the *halakhah* is according to him" (*ibid.*, no. 23).

His responsum on the subject of a will in the town of Arta in 1675 is no longer extant, but it was seen by Moses b. Jacob Shilton of Constantinople, who agreed with his decision (Resp. *Benei Moshe* (Constantinople, 1712), no. 4). Rapaport's responsum is also mentioned in *Shenei ha-Me'orot ha-Gedolim* of Elijah Covo (Constantinople, 1739), pt. 1, nos. 21–22). In 1700 Rapaport signed in Jerusalem the authentication of a Safed bill of debt (*Mishkenot ha-Ro'im* of Uzziel Al-Haïk, 1860, 153c). He was the author of *Da'at Kedoshim* (Leghorn, 1809), source references to the *posekim*—both *rishonim* and *aḥaronim*—on the four sections of the Shulḥan Arukh, arranged alphabetically and published by his grandson Jacob David Jekuthiel, who added his own commentary, entitled *Shelal David*. Rapaport's novellae together with the sermons and memorial addresses he delivered on various occasions were published under the title *Ben He He* (Leghorn, 1821).

His son JACOB was rabbi of Safed. His daughter married her relative Judah ha-Kohen Rapaport of Lublin, who emigrated to Jerusalem. Their son ISAAC HA-KOHEN, author of the *Battei Kehunnah*, was rabbi of Smyrna.

Bibliography: Azulai, 2 (1852), 30, no. 36; Frumkin-Rivlin, 2 (1928), 86f.; 3 (1929), 61; S. M. Chones, *Toledot ha-Posekim* (1910), 165; Rosanes, Togarmah, 4 (1934–35), 320; Yaari, Sheluḥei, 299f., 705. [Y.Ho]

RAPE (Heb. אֹנֶס, *ones*), sexual intercourse with a woman against her will. Unless the contrary be proved by the testimony of witnesses, intercourse with a woman in a place where no one could have come to her aid even if she had cried out ("in the open country," Deut. 22:25, 27) will be presumed to have occurred against her will. If, however, it happened in a place where she could have summoned help ("in the town," Deut. 23), but there are no witnesses to testify that she did so, she will be presumed to have been seduced, i.e., to have consented to intercourse (*ibid.* and Sif. Deut. 242:5 and commentaries; Yad, Na'arah Betulah 1:2 and *Hassagot Rabad* thereto). If intercourse took place while she was asleep and thus unaware, she is considered to have been raped because of the absence of her free will. Intercourse with a female minor is always regarded as rape since she has no will of her own (Yev. 33b, 61b; Sh. Ar., EH 178:3 and Beit Shemu'el n.3, thereto). If intercourse began as a forcible violation but terminated with the woman's consent, she will nevertheless be regarded as having been raped since in such circumstances her passions and nature have compelled her to acquiesce (Ket. 51b; Yad, Issurei Bi'ah 1:9).

Legal Consequences. IN CIVIL MATTERS. A person who violates a virgin *na'arah* (between the ages of 12 years and one day and 12 years and six months) must pay a fine at the fixed amount of 50 shekels of silver (Deut. 22:28–29), as well as compensation for pain and suffering, shame, and blemish, which is to be assessed according to the circumstances in each case (Yad, Na'arah Betulah 2:1–6; see *Damages). If the *na'arah* is seduced, the seducer is liable to pay the same fine and compensation, but in view of her consent is not liable for compensation for pain and suffering (*ẓa'ar; ibid.*). Since when laying down the liability for the fine the pentateuchal law speaks of a *na'arah* only, there is no liability for a fine upon the rape or seduction of a *bogeret* i.e., a girl above the age of 12 years and six months (Yad, *ibid.* 1:8), but compensation for pain and suffering, shame, and blemish is due if she was raped (Tur, EH 177, contrary to Yad, *ibid.* 2:10, 11). The seducer of a *bogeret* is exempt from all financial liability toward her since, having consented to the intercourse, she is presumed to have waived all such claims (Ket. 42a; Yad, *ibid.*; *Beit Yosef*, EH 177).

IN PERSONAL LAW MATTERS. In addition to the financial liabilities mentioned above the violator of a *na'arah* is compelled to marry her, "She shall be his wife... he cannot put her away all his days" (Deut. 22:29), unless marriage between them is prohibited by the pentateuchal or rabbinic law (see *Marriage, Prohibited). However, for the reasons set out above concerning the fine, this obligation does not apply if the victim is a *bogeret* (Ket. 39a; Yad, *ibid.* 1:3; 5:7; Resp. Radbaz, no. 63; Glosses (*haggahot*) of Akiva Eger to Sh. Ar., EH 177:2). The *na'arah* or her father may refuse her marriage to the violator, in which event the transgressor will be exempt from the obligation to marry her and be liable only for the fine and the other payments (Yad, *ibid.* 1:3; Sh. Ar., EH 177:3). A person who seduces a *na'arah* has no obligation to marry her (Yad, *ibid.*). A married woman who has been raped does not become prohibited to her husband unless he is a priest, in which case he must divorce her (Yev. 56b; Yad, Ishut 24:19, 21; Sh. Ar., EH 6:10, 11; see also *Marriage, Prohibited). The outraged wife's pecuniary rights toward her husband, in particular her **ketubbah*, remain unaffected in both cases since there is no blameworthiness on her part (Yad, *ibid.* 24:22; Sh. Ar., EH 115:6).

In suits concerning matters of rape and seduction the court must be composed of three competent ordained judges *(mumḥim semukhim)*, and, therefore, in strict law the fine (see above) is no longer recoverable since today there are no *semukhim* (see **Bet Din*); in various *takkanot*, however, the scholars have nevertheless regulated for recovery of the fine, "lest the sinner be rewarded" (Tur, EH 177; Sh. Ar., EH 117:2; Resp. Radbaz, no. 63; see also *Fine).

In the State of Israel. Of practical significance is the *halakhah* concerning the effect of rape on the marital relationship between the victim and her husband, since this is a matter of personal law which for Jews is governed by Jewish law. The purely civil-law aspects, such as the question of compensation, are governed before the civil courts by the general law of the state, i.e., the Civil Wrongs Ordinance, 1946 (N. V. 1968). The provision that a person must marry the *na'arah* he has violated is rendered unenforceable by the provisions of the Marriage Age Law, 1950, as amended in 1960.

See also *Sexual Offenses; *Penal Law.

Bibliography: ET, 1 (1951[3]), 166–72; 2 (1949), 60–63, 295f.; B. Schereschewsky, *Dinei Mishpaḥah* (1967[2]), 49–51, 316. [B.-Z.SCH.]

RAPHAEL, one of the chief angels. The name occurs in the Bible (I Chron. 26:7) but not yet as an angelic name, first appearing as such in the Apocrypha (Tob. 12:15 and I En. 20:3), where he is one of the seven archangels. In angelological systems built upon four archangels, he is one of the four; the others are *Michael, Gabriel, and *Uriel or Suriel (I En. 9:1–3). He defeats the demon Asmodeus (Tob. 3:17) and binds *Azazel, chief of the demons, throwing him into the abyss (I En. 10:4). As his name implies ("God is healing"), he is the angel set over all kinds of healing and this is his main function. The Talmud (Yoma 37a; BM 86) knows of him as one of the three angels who came to visit Abraham after he had circumcised himself. From the second century on, Jewish traditions referring to Raphael were taken over by both Christian angelology and syncretistic magic. His name occurs frequently in magical papyri in Greek and Coptic, on amulets, and in many Jewish and Mandean incantations. As a planetary angel he governs the sun, and in the division of the four corners of the world he commands the west. He is one of the four angels of the Presence who stand on the four sides of God, a notion taken over into the prayer at bedtime: "to my right Michael and to my left Gabriel, in front of me Uriel and behind me Raphael, and over my head God's *Shekhinah* ["the presence of God"]." According to esoteric Midrashim, his original name was Laviel or Buel but the name was changed to Raphael when he defended against the other angels God's decision to create man. In kabbalistic literature he keeps his high rank and is credited with many missions and functions. Among the four elements he governs earth; in the colors of the rainbow he represents green. M. Recanati even sees him as the angel who governs primordial matter before it divides up into the four elements. According to others, he commands the host of angels known as the *ofannim*. He is also ordained over one of the four rivers coming out of paradise. In the Zohar he is the angel who dominates the morning hours which bring relief to the sick and suffering.

Bibliography: M. Schwab, *Vocabulaire de l'angélologie* (1897), 10, 249; A. Kohuth, *Die juedische Angelologie* (1866), 35; C. Preisendanz, *Papyri graecae magicae*, 3 (1928), index; G. Davidson, *A Dictionary of Angels* (1967), 240–2; R. Margolioth, *Malakhei Elyon* (1945), 184–92. [G.SCH.]

RAPHAEL, ALEXANDER (1775–1850), English merchant. Born in Madras (India) of Persian Jewish parentage, Raphael settled in England and built up a considerable fortune. Having become converted to Roman Catholicism, he was sheriff of London in 1834 and was elected to the House of Commons in 1835 and again in 1847–50. He was one of the two Roman Catholic M.P.s who opposed Jewish emancipation, notwithstanding the fact that their own religious disabilities had been removed so recently. Although he was not the first person born a Jew to be elected to the English parliament, his career is of interest as typifying the assimilatory potentialities of even an oriental Jew in early-19th-century England.

Bibliography: A. M. Hyamson, in: JHSET, 16 (1952), 225–6. [C.R.]

RAPHAEL, FREDERIC (1931–), English novelist and scriptwriter. Born in Chicago of an American mother and a British father, Raphael was taken to England by his parents in 1938. His first novel, *Obbligato*, was published in 1956 and *The Earlsdon Way*, a study of suburban life, in 1958. Later books included *Orchestra and Beginners* (1967) and *Like Men Betrayed* (1970).

Jewish themes dominate two of Raphael's novels, *The Limits of Love* (1960) and *Lindmann* (1963). The former traces the development of three children of a lower-middle-class London Jewish shopkeeper from the years immediately after World War II up to the Suez Campaign and the Hungarian Revolt in 1956. A family chronicle in form, this novel touches vividly upon a number of social themes. *Lindmann* is different in form and conception. It is a brilliant tour de force, based on the tragic fate of the S.S. Struma which sank in Turkish waters with its cargo of "illegal" immigrants during 1941.

Bibliography: F. P. W. McDowell, in: *Novel* (Brown University), 2 (1969), 288–90. [S.NA.]

RAPHAEL, RALPH ALEXANDER (1921–), British organic chemist. Born in London, Raphael worked with a leading chemical firm from 1943 to 1946 and then as research fellow at Imperial College in London (1946–49), and at Glasgow University (1949–54). He was professor of organic chemistry at Queens University, Belfast, from 1954 to 1957 and from 1957 professor of chemistry at Glasgow University.

Raphael's research was mainly on the chemistry of acetylenic and allylic compounds, and on the synthesis of natural products. He wrote Volume IIA of *The Chemistry of Carbon Compounds* (1953), and *Acetylenic Compounds in Organic Synthesis* (1955). He was a fellow of the Royal Society. [S.A.M.]

RAPHAEL (Werfel), YIZHAK (1914–), Israel politician. Born in Sasov, East Galicia, Raphael moved to Lvov in 1929. He was one of the founders of the *Benei Akiva movement and a member of the Torah va-Avodah leadership. He settled in Palestine in 1935. Raphael was a member of the Jerusalem Committee during the *War of Independence (1948) and a member of the *Jewish Agency Executive and head of its Aliyah Department during the period of mass immigration (1948–54). A member of *Ha-Po'el ha-Mizrachi (later *National Religious Party) and of the Knesset (first elected to the Second Knesset), Raphael also served as deputy minister of health from 1961 to 1965. During this period an official of his department was sentenced to imprisonment on charges of extorting contributions to a public enterprise in connection with the building of the Tel Gibborim Hospital. Raphael was named and involved in a judicial report on the affair. He resigned from his post in 1965 but was acquitted of complicity by the Tel Aviv District Court. He was chairman of Mosad ha-Rav Kook and Yad ha-Rav Maimon, and a member of the party executive and of the world center of Ha-Mizrachi Ha-Po'el ha-Mizrachi.

His studies on Ḥasidism include *Ha-Ḥasidut ve-Ereẓ Yisrael* (1940) and *Sefer ha-Ḥasidut* (1947, enlarged edition 1955, 1962[3]). He also edited various collections and the weekly *Ba-Mishor* (1940–46), was chief editor of the *Enẓiklopedyah shel ha-Ẓiyyonut ha-Datit* ("Encyclopedia of Religious Zionism," 3 vols., 1958–65), and from 1963 was editor of *Sinai*, a monthly on Judaica.

Bibliography: Kressel, Leksikon, 2 (1967), 871–3; Shunami, Bibl, 949f. [Y.Go.]

RAPHAEL OF BERSHAD (d. between 1816 and 1826), ḥasidic *ẓaddik*. Raphael was a close disciple and successor of Phinehas of *Korets, who thought highly of him. After Phinehas' death many of his followers became Raphael's disciples. He introduced several customs and liturgical elements ("the Bershad liturgy") that differed from the accepted ḥasidic style and came closer to the Ashkenazi rite. His followers remained a distinct group after his death, although he had no successor. There are many legends about him and some of his sayings were published in *Midrash Pinḥas* (1872), most of which is still in manuscript.

Bibliography: Horodezky, Ḥasidut, 1 (1951[3]), 150, 155f.; N. Huberman, *Bershad* (Heb., 1956), 8, 21, 23–39. [A.St.]

RAPHALL, MORRIS JACOB (1798–1868), rabbi. Raphall, who was born in Stockholm, Sweden, settled in England in 1825. He quickly became prominent in British Jewry and one of its chief exponents to the Christian world, fighting for the political rights of Jews and against defamations of Judaism. He published *Hebrew Review and Magazine of Rabbinical Literature* (3 vols., October 1834—July 1836), the first Jewish periodical in England, and, with

Morris J. Raphall, anti-abolitionist rabbi in the U.S. From J. Goldstein, *Century of Jewry in New York*, 1930.

David Aaron de *Sola, he produced the first translation of parts of the Mishnah into English, *Eighteen Treatises from the Mishna* (1843; 1845[2]). In 1849 Raphall went to the U.S. to serve as rabbi of B'nai Jeshurun Synagogue in New York. There he associated himself with Isaac *Leeser and S. M. *Isaacs and preached against Reform. His lectures on Jewish history attracted large crowds, including many Christians. In 1860 he gave the first invocation by a rabbi before the House of Representatives.

At the peak of the secession crisis, on Jan. 4, 1861, a day President Buchanan had proclaimed a National Fast Day, Raphall delivered what became the most highly publicized rabbinical statement on the "Bible and Slavery." Placing Judaism squarely in opposition to abolitionism, he denied that any statement in the Bible could be interpreted to prohibit slavery, and insisted that, on the contrary, biblical law granted the right to own slaves. He did distinguish between biblical slavery and the southern system; the Bible, he said, regarded the slave as a person, whereas Southerners treated the slave as a thing. But he directed his major attack against the abolitionists for their misrepresentation of the Bible and their agitation against the legitimate right of slaveholding. The sermon was widely reprinted, drawing praise throughout the South and criticism from Jewish and non-Jewish abolitionists in the North. A notable reply came from the Reform leader and abolitionist Rabbi David *Einhorn.

An active fund-raiser on behalf of the needy, Raphall was particularly concerned for the poor of Palestine. His books include *Ruhama: Devotional Exercises for the Use of the Daughters of Israel* (1852), *Post-Biblical History of the Jews* (2 vols., 1855), and *Path to Immortality* (1859).

Bibliography: DAB, s.v.; I. Goldstein, *Century of Judaism in New York* (1930), 111–5, 148–53; H. S. Morais, *Eminent Israelites of the Nineteenth Century* (1880), 287–91; E. M. F. Mielziner, *Moses Mielziner* (Eng., 1931), 212–50; M. Davis, *Emergence of Conservative Judaism* (1963), 356–58. [J.Ri.]

RAPKINE, LOUIS (1904–1948), biochemist. Rapkine was born in Russia, taken to Canada in 1911, and settled in France in 1924. As early as 1932 he became involved with the plight of European victims of racial and political discrimination and in 1934 set up in France the "Comité d'accueil des savants étrangers" to find work for academic refugees. During the war he went to the United States, where he worked tirelessly and managed to rescue a group of men of science and their families. When American legislation made it difficult for this group of foreign scientists to work for the allied war effort, Rapkine arranged for them to be transferred to the United Kingdom, where he became head of a French Scientific Mission. In 1946 he followed his group back to France to continue his research in a department of cellular chemistry created for him at the Pasteur Institute. He also devoted much of his energy to getting French science back on its feet.

Bibliography: Crowther, in: *Nature*, 163 (1949), 162–3, 458–9. [Ed.]

RAPOPORT (**Rappoport;** also **Rapaport** or **Rappaport**), common surname among Jews in Italy, Germany, Poland, and Russia. The family was descended from Abraham Menahem b. Jacob ha-Kohen Rapa who lived in Porto, Italy, at the beginning of the 16th century. The name Rapa originated in the German *Rabe* (*Rappe* in Middle High German), i.e., a raven. In order to distinguish themselves from other members of the Rapa family, the members of this family added the name of the town of Porto, and thus the name Rapoport was formed. (According to another version, this came about by a marriage between the Rapa and Porto families.) The family escutcheon of Abraham Rapa of Porto shows a raven surmounted by two hands raised in blessing (indicating the family's priestly descent). In the course of time other families, including some who were not *kohanim*, took the name of Rapoport.

Known from the 17th century were David ha-Kohen *Rapaport of Lublin and Solomon ben Naḥman ha-Kohen, who officiated as a rabbi in Dubno, Grodno, and Lublin. In the 18th century there were Ḥayyim ben Simḥah ha-Kohen Rapoport (c. 1700–1771), rabbi in Slutsk and Lvov, who took part in the disputation with the Frankists in Lvov in 1759 and was the author of *Zekher Ḥayyim* (Lemberg, 1865), responsa and funeral orations. His brother, Benjamin ben Simḥah ha-Kohen Rapoport, a *maggid* in the community of Brzezany (Berezhany), Galicia, wrote *Gevulot Binyamin* (Lemberg, 1789), containing novellae on the Torah, and a commentary on the Passover *Haggadah*. Isaac ben Judah ha-Kohen *Rappaport officiated

הָעוֹרְבִים

כִּי יִשְׁאָלְךָ בִּנְךָ מָחָר
עַל מָה אֲנַחְנוּ עוֹרְבִים
תֹּאמַר אֵלָיו עַל מִבְחַר
הַסַאְטְרִים זֶה נִקְרָא הָעוֹרְבִים:

פרק א

בני כעורבים לעשפמותס, רפא, לפאפורט, ופורט רפא.

הציור הזה מצאחי בסוף ספר מנחה בלולה, פירוש על חמשה
חומשי תורה, יסרו וגם חברו החכם השלם רבי אברהם מנחם כ"ר
יעקב הכהן רפא ז"ל מפורטו, אשר אליו מתיחשים בני רפאפורט.

Escutcheon of the family of Abraham b. Jacob ha-Kohen Rapa of Porto, otherwise known as Abraham Menahem Rapoport, d. 1596. From E. Carmoly, *Ha-Orevim u-Venei ha-Yonah*, Redelheim, 1861.

as rabbi at Smyrna. He died in Jerusalem, having published responsa and homilies *Battei Kehunnah* (Smyrna, 1736; Salonika, 1754²). In the 19th century Benjamin Ze'ev Wolf ha-Kohen ben Isaac *Rapoport (1754–1837) officiated as rabbi in Papa, Hungary. He was known for the lenient decisions in his responsa, which caused the extreme Orthodox Mordecai *Banet and Moses *Sofer to demand his dismissal. He opposed Kabbalah and Ḥasidism. He wrote *Simlat Binyamin* (Dyhernfurth, 1788), *Simlah Sheniyyah* (Vienna, 1800), and responsa *Edut le-Yisrael* (Pressburg, 1839).

The most important member of the Rapoport family in the 19th century was Solomon Judah Leib *Rapoport ("Shir"). His grandson, ARNOLD RAPOPORT (b. 1840), a leader of the assimilationists in Galicia, was a deputy of the Austrian Reichsrat from 1879 to 1907 representing the Polish party. He was popular among the Jewish masses in Galicia for founding relief organizations. In 1890 he was ennobled, receiving the title von Porada.

Members of the family well known in Russia in modern times were the Russian-Yiddish journalist SIMON RAPAPORT, the author and folklorist Solomon Zainwil Rapoport (S. *An-ski), and the socialist leader and writer Charles *Rappoport. ALEXANDER RAPOPORT (1862–1928), a publisher in Russia, was the last owner of the Hebrew newspaper *Ha-Meliz,* as well as the publisher of *Der Fraynd,* the first Yiddish daily in Russia.

See also *Porto.

Bibliography: E. Carmoly, *Ha-Orevim u-Venei ha-Yonah* (1861); J. Reifmann, in: *Ha-Shaḥar,* 3 (1872), 353–76; I. T. Eisenstadt and S. Wiener, *Da'at Kedoshim* (1897–98), 135–81.
[Y.S.]

RAPOPORT, ABRAHAM BEN ISRAEL JEHIEL HA-KOHEN (1584–1651), Polish talmudist and halakhic

authority. Abraham was born in Cracow, and studied in the yeshivah there under Meshullam Feivush of Zbarazh. He married the daughter of Mordecai Schrenzilsh, a wealthy man of distinguished ancestry from Lvov, and adopted his surname, becoming known as Abraham Schrenzel of Schrenzilsh. In Lvov he studied under Joshua ben Alexander *Falk. Although one of the outstanding scholars of his time, Abraham did not take up a rabbinical position, and taught in a voluntary capacity for more than 40 years in the yeshivah of Lvov. He was prominent in the *Council of the Four Lands, and was placed in charge of the collection of funds for the needy in Ereẓ Israel.

Rapoport's most important work is his *Eitan ha-Ezraḥi,* published by his grandson Abraham, the rabbi of Baslov (Ostrow, 1796). It is divided into two parts, the first containing more than 50 responsa, and the second including sermons arranged according to the weekly sections of the Pentateuch, together with a commentary on the Five Scrolls and parts of Psalms and Proverbs. Rapoport's genealogy appears at the end of the work. In addition to its halakhic value, *Eitan ha-Ezraḥi* contains much important historical material, biographies of rabbis and heads of yeshivot, and details of the economic and moral state of the Polish communities of the time. Some responsa shed light on the Chmielnicki massacre (1648–49) which occurred during his lifetime. From the introduction to *Eitan ha-Ezraḥi* it appears that Rapoport left many writings in manuscript, which were destroyed during various upheavals which occurred after his death.

Bibliography: A. Harkavy, *Ḥadashim Gam Yeshanim,* 2, pt. 3 (1899), 40f.; Rubashov (Shazar), in: *Historish Shriftn,* 1 (1929), 172f.; Halpern, Pinkas, 67, 74 n. 6, 220; Markon, in: *Festschrift . . . J. Freimann* (1937), 93–104 (Heb. section).   [S.E.]

RAPOPORT, BENJAMIN ZE'EV WOLF HA-KOHEN BEN ISAAC (1754–1837), Hungarian rabbi. His father Isaac and his grandfather came from Fuerth in Germany to Nikolsburg, where Benjamin was born. In 1771 Rapoport went, as was the custom with many Moravians, to nearby Hungary in order to evade the ban on Jewish marriages of other than the eldest son in force at the time in Moravia (see *Familiants Laws). He settled in Obuda (now part of Budapest) and married the daughter of David Boskovitz, one of the leaders of the community. He lived with his father-in-law for ten years, engaging in studying and teaching. In 1781 he was appointed rabbi of the community of Pápa in Hungary, where he served until his death. This community, founded in 1749, made considerable progress during the period of his office. Because of his comparatively liberal attitude, differences between him and the influential rabbis of the time, particularly Moses *Sofer and Mordecai *Banet, increased. These two rabbis were opposed to his methods of study and teaching as well as to his halakhic rulings, even attempting to oust him from his rabbinic office. Rapoport was opposed to *Ḥasidism and to the study of *Kabbalah. A dispute, which exercised Jewish communities in Central Europe for many years, also developed between him and Moses Sofer with regard to Jonathan Alexandersohn, rabbi of Hejőcsaba in Hungary. Like R. *Schwerin-Goetz, Rapoport supported the attacked Alexandersohn, while Moses Sofer was opposed to him, even invoking the secular government, but his community supported him.

Rapoport published during his lifetime, *Simlat Binyamin u-Vigdei Kehunnah* (Dyhrenfurth, 1788) on the Shulḥan Arukh *Yoreh De'ah,* but he left a number of works in manuscript, some of which were published after his death, among them *Edut le-Yisrael* on tractate *Makkot* with additions by his son (Pressburg, 1839). It constitutes the third part of his *Masat Binyamin.*

Bibliography: E. Carmoly, *Ha-Orevim u-Venei ha-Yonah* (1861); P. Z. Schwartz, *Shem ha-Gedolim me-Erez Hagar* 1 (1914), 28bf., no. 13.   [Y.M.]

RAPOPORT (Rappaport), SAMUEL (1871–1943), rabbi, folklorist, and religious Zionist. Born in Lemberg, Rapoport studied in Germany and then returned to Galicia where he managed the family estate at Kalinka near Zloczow. An ardent (pre-Herzlian) Zionist from his youth, he was active and prominent in the Zionist movement from its beginning, participating in Zionist Congresses from 1898. Rapoport was co-founder of the *Mizrachi and the leader of its East Galician branch. During World War I, the Austrian government appointed him honorary rabbi of Zloczow, in which post he remained to the end. He was a victim of the Holocaust. His scholarly interests were in Jewish folklore, Ḥasidism, and Kabbalah.

In 1906 he published in Polish a work on the psychology of Ḥasidism, and also wrote a historical study in German on the Ḥanukkah festival (1912). His main work, *Werdegang und Charakteristik des religioesen Lebens der Ostjuden,* was not completed, but a number of chapters appeared in M. Buber's *Der Jude* from 1917–23. These gave western Jews an insight into the rich religious and cultural life of Eastern Jewry. Rapoport also wrote the articles on Jewish folkore for the *Juedisches Lexikon.*

Bibliography: N. M. Gelber, in: S. K. Mirsky (ed.), *Ishim u-Demuyyot be-Ḥokhmat Yisrael*... (1959), 353–6. [Ed.]

RAPOPORT (Rappaport), SOLOMON JUDAH LEIB (known by his acronym **Shir;** 1790–1867), rabbi and scholar, pioneer of Haskalah and *Wissenschaft des Judentums. Rapoport, born in Lemberg, Galicia, received a traditional education and became known for his brilliance as a talmudist. Under the influence of Nachman *Krochmal he took an early interest in Haskalah and secular learning, studying classical, Semitic, and modern languages, as well as science. Supported at first by his father-in-law Aryeh Leib *Heller, who was one of the leading talmudists of his time, Rapoport later had to take the position of a manager of the government kosher-meat tax. Without income again in 1832, Rapoport tried unsuccessfully to obtain a rabbinical position in Berlin and in Italy through recommendations by L. Zunz and S. D. Luzzatto, but his German was poor and he had no university education. After a period in business in Brody, he became rabbi of Tarnopol (1837), where he had to contend with the violent opposition of the

Solomon Judah Leib Rapoport, Prague rabbi and scholar. Jerusalem, J.N.U.L., Schwadron Collection.

Ḥasidim, whom he had attacked in a pamphlet (*Ner Mitzvah,* in: *Naḥalat Yehudah,* 1868) in defense of Haskalah in 1815 (see also his introduction to *She'erit Yehudah,* in: *Bikkurei ha-Ittim,* 8, 1827). Rapoport was appointed chief rabbi of Prague in 1840, successfully opposing the candidacy of Ẓevi Hirsch *Chajes for the same position.

After some youthful efforts at poetry and drama, including a paraphrase of Racine's *Esther* entitled *She'erit Yehudah* ("The Remnant of Judah," first published in *Bikkurei ha-Ittim,* 8, 1827), Rapoport turned to Jewish scholarship, publishing articles in *Bikkurei ha-Ittim* and *Kerem Ḥemed.* Dealing with biblical subjects, he considered the Book of Judges a composite work, certain Psalms to be post-Davidic, and some chapters in Isaiah as belonging to a later prophet. His real mark on Jewish scholarship was made in a series of bibliographical studies of the geonic leaders Saadiah, Hai, Hananel b. Ḥushi'el, Nissim b. Jacob, and Ḥefeẓ b. Yaẓli'aḥ, and of Eleazar ha-Kallir and Nathan b. Jehiel of Rome, author of the *Arukh* (published in *Bikkurei ha-Ittim,* 1828–31; and also separately and posthumously under the title *Yeri'ot Shelomo,* 1904, repr. 1913 and 1960). These studies illuminated a relatively obscure period of Jewish history and paved the way for later research; moreover, they set a new standard of critical methodology to be applied to the history of rabbinics. In them Rapoport traced the migration of rabbinic scholarship and tradition from Ereẓ Israel through Italy to Central and Western Europe, and from Babylonia through North Africa to Spain.

Of importance, too, was his *Erekh Millin,* a talmudic encyclopedia dealing mainly with historical and archaeological aspects of the Talmud (vol. 1 (1852); the rest, 1914). Rapoport also wrote an introduction to Abraham b. Ḥiyya's ethical treatise *Hegyon ha-Nefesh* (ed. by Freimann, 1860, reprint 1967). Rapoport wrote articles for Abraham Geiger's *Wissenschaftliche Zeitschrift,* Julius Fuerst's *Orient,* and Zacharias Frankel's *Zeitschrift fuer die religioesen Interessen des Judentums* and became editor of **Kerem Ḥemed.* He was in close contact with these and other leading figures of the Wissenschaft des Judentums (see his correspondence in A. Harkavy, *Zikkaron la-Rishonim* (vol. 2, pt. 1, 1881); *Iggerot Shir,* ed. by S. E. Graeber (1885); M. S. Ghirondi, *Peletat Soferim* (1890); and B. Z. Dinaburg-Dinur (in KS, 3 (1927), 222–35; 306–19). Rapoport took a moderate line against radical writers such as Geiger (see his *Or Torah,* a detailed criticism of the latter's *Urschrift,* in: *Naḥalat Yehudah,* published posthumously in 1868 by Rapoport's son David). He strongly opposed the decisions of the Rabbinical Conferences held by the German Reform rabbis (1844–46), both for the divisive character of the proposed reforms and for the assimilationist tendencies which inspired them, but even so did not exclude the reformers from the Jewish people as long as they considered themselves Jewish (*Tokhaḥat Megullah,* with German translation by R. Kirchheim, 1845). Like Krochmal and Luzzatto, he wanted to see the national character of Judaism preserved. When Frankel's *Darkhei ha-Mishnah* was attacked by Samson Raphael *Hirsch and others on dogmatic grounds, Rapoport came to his defense (*Divrei Shalom ve-Emet,* 1861, repr. 1969; see Hirsch's reply in his *Gesammelte Schriften,* 6, 419–34).

Bibliography: I. E. Barzilay, *Shelomo Yehudah Rapoport* (Eng., 1969), incl. bibl.; A. Kurlaender, *Biographie S. J. Rapoports*... (1878[3]); S. Bernfeld, *Toledot Shir* (1899); Kressel, Leksikon, 2 (1967), 874–6, incl. bibl.; Waxman, Literature, index. [V.A.M.]

RAPPAPORT, ISAAC BEN JUDAH HA-KOHEN (d. 1755), rabbi in Jerusalem and Smyrna, and rabbinic emissary of Safed. His father emigrated from Lublin to

Jerusalem, where Isaac studied at the yeshivah Beit Ya'akov Pereira, headed by *Hezekiah da Silva. Because of the difficult circumstances then prevailing in Jerusalem, Isaac accepted the assignment of rabbinic emissary of Safed to Turkey and the Balkans (1702–12). Arriving in Constantinople in 1709, he joined Abraham *Yiẓḥaki, who was there as the emissary of Jerusalem, in issuing a proclamation against the Shabbatean, Nehemiah Ḥiyya *Ḥayon, and engaged there in halakhic discussions with Aaron *Alfandari. He arrived in Salonika in 1712. At the conclusion of his mission, because of the straitened circumstances in Jerusalem, he accepted the position of rabbi at Smyrna, a position he held for 36 years, though he originally intended to stay only a short time. In this capacity, he greatly assisted Ereẓ Israel emissaries who visited Smyrna, and in 1732–33 saw through the press in Constantinople and Smyrna *Zera Abraham*, responsa by Abraham Yiẓḥaki, then the chief rabbi in Jerusalem. In 1749 he returned to Jerusalem, where he became the chief rabbi. Unable to trace the old record book of the local *takkanot*, he published many of them from memory, but was unwilling to issue new ones of his own accord. A collection of his responsa, novellae, and homilies, entitled *Battei Kehunnah*, was published in two volumes, the first in Constantinople, 1736, and the second at Salonika, 1754.

Bibliography: Rivkind, in: *Reshummot*, 4 (1925), 341–2; Frumkin-Rivlin, 3 (1929), 61–4; Yaari, Sheluḥei, 423–5. [A.Ya.]

RAPPOPORT, CHARLES (1865–1941), Socialist politician and writer. Born in Doukshty (Dukštos), Lithuania, Rappoport joined the social revolutionary movement in Vilna as a youth. In 1887 he took part in a conspiracy together with Lenin's brother Alexander Ulyanov, to assassinate Czar Alexander II. Ulyanov was apprehended and hanged. Rappoport fled to France where he joined the Socialist Party and became a prominent Marxist, in opposition to the moderate doctrines of the Socialist leader, Jean Jaurès (1858–1914). Rappoport opposed France's participation in World War I and was present at the left-wing anti-war conferences at Kienthal and Zimmerwald and was arrested in 1917 on charges of making defeatist speeches. Sentenced to three months' imprisonment, his pamphlet *Devant les juges militaires*, describing how he conducted his own defense, created a sensation. In 1921 Rappoport joined the French Communist Party and edited the *Revue Communiste* and the official party organ *Humanité*. Already disillusioned by the evolution of communism in Russia, and shocked by the Moscow trials, Rappoport resigned from the Communist Party in 1938. He condemned the Munich pact and expressed his great sympathy for the Jewish victims of Nazism, regretting that he had not fought more often for Jewish rights.

Rappoport published several works on politics and history including: *La Philosophie de l'histoire comme science de l'évolution* (1925²), *Jean Jaurès, L'homme, le penseur, le socialiste* (1916, 1925) and *La revolution mondiale* (1921). His autobiography was published in the Paris Yiddish newspaper, *Arbeter Shtime*.

Bibliography: A. Kriegel, *Aux origines du communisme français*, 2 vols. (1954), index. [Ed.]

RAQQA (al-), city on the Euphrates in N.E. Syria, founded in 722 by the Abbasid caliph al-Manṣūr. The Jews identified al-Raqqa with the Calneh of Genesis 10:10. According to the Arab geographer al-Muqaddasi (late 10th century) the city was an important commercial center during his lifetime. Throughout the period of caliphal rule there was a large Jewish community in al-Raqqa and its environs. The philosopher David *al-Mukammiṣ was from this city. An 11th-century letter from a *ḥaver* (rabbi) to a *rosh yeshivah* in Jerusalem is extant which states that he will go to Calneh the following day to pacify the community, where a dispute had arisen over the appointment of a successor to the deceased *dayyan*. The Jewish community of al-Raqqa also prospered during the period of the Crusades. In the latter half of the 12th century the traveler *Benjamin of Tudela found about 700 Jews there. In 1191 the head of the Baghdad academy, Samuel b. Ali, addressed an *iggeret* ("letter") to al-Raqqa and other important communities in northern Babylonia and Syria. A letter from the last decade of that century, from a Jewish scholar in al-Raqqa to Cairo, is extant; he sends greetings to Maimonides and tells about his contacts with the Jews of Aleppo. At the beginning of the 13th century Judah *al-Ḥarizi visited the city and complained about the miserliness of the Jews living there, deriding them bitterly.

Bibliography: Harizi, Juda b. Solomon, *Taḥkemoni*, ed. by A. Kaminka (1899), 189, 367, 399, 411, 417, 453; Mann, Egypt, 1 (1920), 201, 245f.; Assaf, in: *Tarbiz*, 1 pt. 1 (1930), 102–30; 1 pt. 2 (1930), 43–84; 1 pt. 3 (1930), 15–80. [E.A.]

RASEINIAI (Rus. **Rossieni**), city in W. central Lithuanian S.S.R. The community there, which included *Karaites, numbered 4,247 in 1797, 2,649 in 1847, and 3,484 in 1897 (46.7% of the total population). Raseiniai was one of the centers of the *Haskalah movement in Lithuania. Abraham *Mapu and Senior *Sachs lived there. According to the 1923 census there were 2,305 Jews living in Raseiniai (43.7% of the total), most of whom were occupied in small trade and crafts, with a number in business on a larger scale. The Jewish People's Bank had 600 members. Communal institutions included a Yavneh primary school, a Hebrew secondary school, and a yeshivah. Raseiniai was occupied by the Germans a few days after the outbreak of the German-Soviet war in 1941. The more prominent Jews were murdered first, followed by the men, and ultimately the women and children. A few families who managed to escape survived until the liberation.

Bibliography: Z. Kadish, in: *Lite*, 1 (1951), 1383–86; N. Ben-Ḥayyim, *ibid.*, 1576–77; *Lite*, 2 (1965), index; *Yahadut Lita*, 1 (1959), index; 2 (1967), 359–60. [Jo.Ga.]

RASHI (**Solomon ben Isaac**; 1040–1105), leading commentator on the Bible and Talmud.

His Life. Rashi was born at Troyes, France. His mother was the sister of the liturgical writer, *Simeon b. Isaac. His father was a scholar whom Rashi quoted in his writings (Av. Zar. 75a). Few facts are known about his early life, although many legends are told about this period. A legend tells that his father cast a precious gem into the sea rather than surrender it to Christians who desired it for idolatrous purposes. A heavenly voice then foretold the birth of a son who would enlighten the world with his wisdom. It is also related that his mother was imperiled in a narrow street during her pregnancy. She pressed against a wall which formed a niche to rescue her.

Troyes was then the capital city of Champagne which attracted merchants from many countries. Rashi learned about different currency standards, banking, and trade. He knew of soldering, engraving, weaving figures into material, and the embroidering of silk with gold. He also learned much about agriculture and husbandry. After his initial education in Troyes, Rashi was attracted to the great academies of Mainz and Worms where he studied after his marriage. His main teachers were *Jacob b. Yakar and *Isaac b. Judah at Mainz, and *Isaac b. Eleazar ha-Levi at Worms. At about the age of 25, Rashi returned to Troyes. He maintained close relations with his teachers, occasionally returning to the academies to discuss unclear talmudic texts with them.

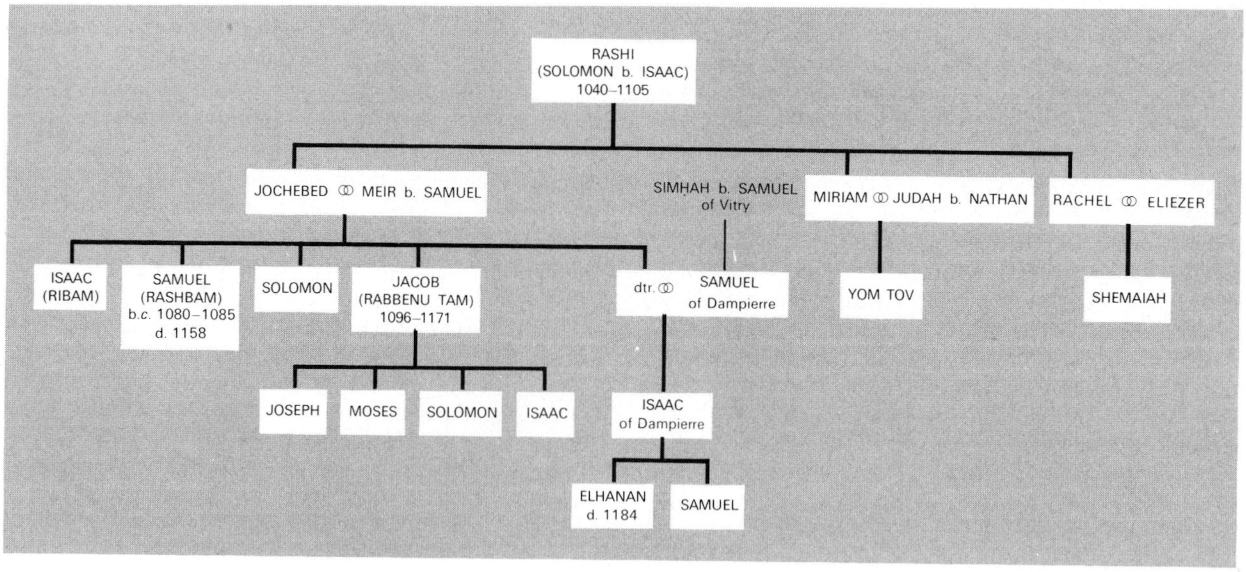

Rashi's return to Troyes was notable, since, due to his influence, henceforth the schools of Champagne and northern France were destined to rival and finally supplant those of the Rhenish provinces. Around 1070, he founded a school which attracted many pupils and became even more important after the death of his own teachers. His most gifted pupils were his relatives, *Simḥah b. Samuel of Vitry, *Shemaiah, Judah b. Abraham, Joseph b. Judah, and *Jacob b. Samson. Although he had no sons, Rashi had three daughters, who married prominent scholars. One of them, Jochebed, married R. *Meir b. Samuel who attended the Mainz academy with Rashi. Four sons were born to Jochebed and Meir and they all became famous scholars: *Isaac, *Samuel, *Solomon, and the youngest but greatest of them, Jacob, popularly known as Rabbenu *Tam. They all belonged to the outstanding group of French scholars of the following generation who founded the school of **tosafot*. Another daughter, Miriam, was married to *Judah b. Nathan, whose commentary to the end of *Makkot* is included in all editions of the Talmud (19b–24b). This couple also had a learned son, Yom Tov, and a daughter. A third daughter whose name may have been Rachel was the mother of Shemaiah.

Rashi's last years were aggrieved by the massacres committed at the outset of the First Crusade (1095–96), in which he lost relatives and friends. Tradition relates that he foretold the defeat of the expedition of Godfrey of Bouillon, correctly predicting that Godfrey would return to his native city with only three horses remaining from his entire massive army. It is only a legendary tradition that during this period Rashi transferred his school to Worms; there the house called his *bet ha-midrash,* which was located next to the city's synagogue, is a construction of the 16th century. He is reported to have died while writing the word "pure" in his commentary to *Makkot,* (19b) on 29 Tammuz. His burial place is not known. [A.Ro.]

Biblical Exegesis. Rashi commented on most, if not all, the books of the Bible. The comments ascribed to him on Job, from 40:25, on Ezra, Nehemiah, and Chronicles are not his, being different in style and method of exegesis. According to Poznański, Rashi did not manage to comment on these, since in writing his commentary he followed the order of the books in the Bible. Lipschuetz, however, contends that the exegesis on these books is substantially Rashi's but was recast and augmented by his pupils. Comments of pupils of Rashi, who studied with him, are embodied in his biblical commentary, which contains (1) explanations that Rashi himself accepted and included in his commentary, and (2) annotations written alongside Rashi's commentary by others, and later interpolated into the text by copyists. Rashi incorporated in his comments that of *Samuel b. Meir (Rashbam) on Exodus 15:6 ("Thy right hand, O Lord, glorious in power"), even referring to this and other verses expounded by the latter as "the verses of Samuel" (Tosafists' Commentary on the Pentateuch, in Ms.). Writing to the rabbis of Auxerre in connection with his commentary on Ezekiel, Rashi declared: "At all events I made a mistake in that comment . . . I have now gone through it with our brother Shemaiah and have corrected it" (A. Geiger, *Melo Chofnajim* (1840), Heb. pt. 36). A third pupil whose explanations are embodied in Rashi's commentary is Joseph *Kara (the passages are enumerated by A. Berliner in *Peletat Soferim* (1872)). There is evidence that the latter two, Shemaiah and Joseph Kara, studied the Book of Ezekiel under Rashi, while he was writing his commentary to it. The copyists' interpolations, now part of Rashi's commentary, can be identified by the aid of manuscripts, in which these are written between the lines, accompanied by the word "addition."

Main Characteristics of His Commentary. The main distinguishing characteristic of Rashi's commentary is a compromise between the literal and the midrashic interpretations; to the latter, which was the principal method of exposition in French biblical exegesis, he added the former. At least three-quarters of Rashi's comments are based on rabbinic sources. The few that are original are mainly philological explanations. When basing his comment on the Midrashim, Rashi chose from the available material those that were closest to the literal interpretation of the biblical text, or solved the difficulties presented by it. Thus, for example, in commenting on Leviticus 19:3 ("Ye shall fear every man his mother, and his father"), Rashi, instead of using the *Sifra,* the halakhic Midrash on Leviticus, as he had done in interpreting the preceding verses, now resorted to the *Mekhilta,* the halakhic Midrash on Exodus. The latter explains the twofold difficulty in the verse, namely, the prior mention of the mother and the use of the verb "fear" rather than "honor" as in the Ten Commandments, whereas the *Sifra* explains only the first difficulty.

Another characteristic aspect of Rashi's exegesis is the manner in which he formulated his comment. In many instances he did not quote a Midrash literally but either augmented or abridged it, or even altered its wording (cf. Gen. 1:5, 6, 7 with Gen. R.), his aim being to make for easier understanding and lucidity, and to adapt the language of the Midrash to that of the text. In this way Rashi obviated a patchwork impression and instead achieved a uniform style. The criterion on which he based his choice of comment is clearly stated by him: "As for me, I am only concerned with the literal meaning of the Scriptures and with such *aggadot* as explain the biblical passages in a fitting manner" (Gen. 3:8). In many instances where he departs from this latter principle he adds the comment that these *aggadot* do not give the literal interpretation. But it is not to be assumed that where he failed to add this comment he regarded such Midrashim as providing a literal exposition of the text (thus, for example, the Midrash quoted without this comment in his explanation on Gen. 1:6 ("Let there be a firmament") does not accord with his exegesis of Gen. 1:1). While Rashi based his comment on the halakhic part of the Pentateuch on talmudic literature, his purpose was not to lay down the *halakhah*, and he therefore quoted only some of the many *halakhot* dealing with the subject in question. Sometimes he states that the halakhic Midrash does not give the literal interpretation of a passage (Ex. 16:29, 22:8); at others he interprets a verse contrary to the decided *halakhah* (Lev. 13:6). His partiality for the literal explanation is further attested by the fact that, having revised his commentary several times, he wished at the end of his days to improve it "on the basis of the plain meanings which appear daily" (Rashbam, to Gen. 37:2).

Generally, Rashi did not state his sources but these have been given in detail by Zunz in his book on Rashi, the most important of his sources being the Targums. In his Pentateuch commentary, Rashi derived much help from Targum Onkelos. Not only did he expound many verses according to it, but on occasion dwelt at length on its rendering (Gen. 49:24; Ex. 24:14); interpreted the words of Targum Onkelos; quoted from the Talmud in support of them, and dealt with the etymology of some Aramaic word in the Targum (Deut. 14:5). He laid down general rules explaining Onkelos' choice of words (Gen. 43:15), but in many instances rejected his translation where he found this unacceptable (Gen. 15:11). On several passages Rashi had a different version of Targum Onkelos (Gen. 27:36; Ex. 23:27), which was subsequently emended by publishers in accordance with his version. In his commentary on the Prophets and the Hagiographa he made much use of Targum Jonathan and even quotes Targum Sheni on Esther but apparently did not know the Palestinian Targum on the Pentateuch nor the Targum on the Hagiographa. Some of his sources he heard from others (Deut. 29:3). On one occasion he even declared: "I have had no one to help me, nor a teacher, in all this edifice, but it is as revealed to me from Heaven." [Av.G.]

The so-called Rashi *bet ha-midrash* adjoining the Old Synagogue of Worms, photographed before 1938. Photo Kulturinstitut, Worms.

Rashi as Grammarian. Rashi centers his commentaries on meticulous analysis of the language of the text. He was both philologist and linguist and derived his grammatical principles from rabbinic literature and the Hebrew works of the Spanish grammarians, *Menahem b. Jacob ibn Saruq and *Dunash b. Labrat (Ps. 39:7, 55:22). Since he knew no Arabic, Rashi never learned of Judah b. David *Ḥayyuj's and Jonah *ibn Janaḥ's work on tri-consonantalism. Like Menahem, Rashi sometimes assumes the existence of roots of one consonant (like *hoga*), although, following Dunash, he generally regards the verbs primae *waw* as being tri-consonantal. Verbs tertiae *he* are in his view bi-consonantal. To support this view Rashi calls attention to the nominal derivation from the root (such as *ẓadah-ẓedi'ah* in Ex. 21:13). Verbs primae *nun* are bi-consonantal (e.g., *niḥatu*, Ps. 38:3), as are those mediae *waw* as the middle letter, and the geminates like *yegudennu* (Gen. 49:19). By turns, he utilizes the terms *yesod, ikkar*, and *shoresh* to indicate the root; *yesod nofel* (omitted root) to represent a consonantal root which falls away in conjugation; and *pa'ol* and *asoh* to indicate the conjugation of the verb. For the names of vowels he utilizes *pathaḥ* (a), *pathaḥ qatan* or *segol* (ε (or: ae)), *ḥireq* (i), *qameṣ* or *qameṣ gadol* (a), *ṣereh* (e), *melopum* (o), *šuruq* (u). Scattered throughout his commentaries are many remarks on syntax, tenses, moods, conjugations (such as the privative use of the *pi'el*—Ex. 27:3), collective nouns (Gen. 32:6), deletion of parts of the sentence, prepositions required by certain verbs (Judg. 6:32), and changes in word order (Gen. 2:19). Occasionally he formulates rules on linguistic usage (Jer. 51:12), and discusses the shades of meaning of various synonyms (Gen. 1:11, Micah 5:7). He discriminates clearly between biblical Hebrew and mishnaic Hebrew (e.g., Ps. 76:11), even though he sometimes interprets the verse in accordance with the rabbinic literature (Ex. 12:7), for which he was criticized by his grandson, Samuel b. Meir. Rashi often resorts to the vernacular French in order to explicate difficult words and phrases, for example, about 1,000 such words and phrases are so explained in his commentary on the Bible. This practice has proven invaluable for the study of Old French glosses (see *La'az). He wrote a small number of glosses in German. However, some of the existing German glosses, and all of the Slavonic glosses, were added by other scholars in subsequent generations (I Kings 6:7). [M.Z.Ka.]

His language is concise and straightforward. At times his terseness is due to his assuming that the reader is fully acquainted with the relevant details (Deut. 1:3, 18), and it is therefore a mistake to hold, as some do, that his commentary was intended for the masses. He explained many difficult problems with a word or a mere hint. Thus, for example, he did not deal explicitly with the difficulty raised (in view of the belief in the giving of the Torah at Mt. Sinai) by the passage "And the Canaanite was then in the land" (Gen. 12:6), but contented himself with the brief comment: "He [i.e., the Canaanite] was increasingly conquering Ereẓ Israel from the descendants of Shem." In many instances he even refrained from entering into the detailed proof of his comments hinted at in the verses he cites. A thorough study of his statements is thus necessary to reveal the problems that faced him, his manner of solving them, and the support for his comments that he derived from scriptural verses and rabbinic sources. His honesty led him in many instances to declare: "I do not know what it is" (Ex. 22:28; Is. 13:21).

Other Characteristic Aspects of Rashi's Commentary. (1) He placed great reliance on the cantillation signs: "Had I not seen the accent *zakef gadol* on the word *u-feneihem*, I would not have been able to explain it" (Ezek. 1:11), but also on occasion he disagreed with them (Gen. 20:16). (2) Sometimes he combined verses (Deut. 4:44), or explained apparently superfluous details in order to throw light on events mentioned elsewhere (Ex. 13:18), two methods that were later developed and elaborated by his French pupils in their exegesis. (3) On occasion, as at the beginning of his commentary on Zechariah and Song of Songs, he prefaced his comments with the principles underlying his exegesis, or added illustrations for greater clarity (I Kings 6:31), some of which were omitted by copyists and publishers (*Rashbam* Num. 34:2: "Our teacher, my grandfather, explained and made a drawing of the borders"). (4) He refrained from dealing with problems associated with philosophy which had not penetrated into German Jewish culture, and thus the question of reconciling philosophy with the biblical concept of the universe did not arise. In many instances he did not even deal with moralistic appreciations of the Patriarchs' actions, e.g., the driving out of Hagar), nor was he concerned with mysticism. (5) On various occasions he referred to contemporary events (Ex. 28:41; Job 19:24). Here and there one can detect in his comments an echo of the persecution of the Jews in his day (Isa. 53:9; Ps. 38:18). He also disputed the christological interpretation of biblical passages (e.g., Isa. 9:6), a course also adopted by his pupils in Germany in their exegesis.

Rashi's commentary on the Bible, and particularly that on the Pentateuch, enjoyed an enormous circulation. More than 200 supercommentaries were written on his Pentateuch commentary, some even by distinguished halakhists, such as, for example, Joseph *Caro, the author of the Shulḥan Arukh. Of particular importance is Elijah Mizraḥi's supercommentary. The study of Rashi's commentary spread to such an extent that he was accorded the title of "Parshandata" ("the expounder of the law," "the commentator par excellence," a pun on Esther 9:7). It was even laid down in the *halakhah* that the reading of the weekly portion with his commentary could take the place of the obligatory reading "twice in the original and once in the Targum." Christian scholars were also influenced by his commentary. As early as the 12th century Nicholas of Manjacoria mentions him. Nicholas de Lyra (1279–1340) in particular was so greatly influenced by him that his critics called him "the ape of Rashi." This interest of Christian scholars in Rashi grew in the 15th century, and from the 17th century onward his commentary began to be translated into other languages. Rashi's commentary on the Pentateuch is the first known Hebrew work to have been printed (1475), and since then hardly an edition of the Hebrew bible for Jewish use has appeared without his commentary. An excellent edition has been issued by A. Berliner (1905^2) who examined more than a hundred manuscripts and printed books, indicated Rashi's sources, and added annotations of his own. Part of Rashi's commentary to the Prophets and Hagiographa was edited by I. Maarsen, Isaiah (Jerusalem, 1933), the Minor Prophets (Amsterdam, 1932), and Psalms (Jerusalem, 1936). I. Elbogen published fragments from his commentary to Ezekiel from manuscripts in the S. Poznański jubilee volume (Warsaw, 1927) and by A. Levy in Rashi's commentary on Ezekiel (Philadelphia, 1931). J. Rosenthal edited his commentary to Song of Songs, on the basis of manuscripts and various printed versions (S. Mirsky jubilee volume (New York, 1958), 130–88). An English translation of Rashi's commentary on the Pentateuch was made by M. Rosenbaum and A. M. Silbermann (5 vols., London, 1929–34).

Commentary to the Babylonian Talmud. The summit of Rashi's creative work was his commentary to the Babylonian Talmud. His commentary on most of the tractates of the Talmud has been preserved, but those to tractates *Ta'anit, Nedarim, Nazir,* and *Horayot* ascribed to him are not his. The commentary to *Mo'ed Katan* which bears his name is not by him, but his commentary to this tractate has been published by A. Kupfer (1961). His commentary to *Bava Batra* was completed by his grandson and pupil, Samuel b. Meir (Rashbam), and to *Makkot* by his pupil, *Judah b. Nathan. Rashi's commentary to the Talmud was published with the first printed edition of the Talmud, and except for modern editions of a few tractates no edition of the Talmud has appeared without it. There are extant whole or fragmentary manuscripts of his commentary on most tractates but no critical and scientific edition of his commentary to even one tractate had appeared by the end of the 1960s. Rashi's commentary on the Talmud had been preceded by others, both of the Franco-German school, including his own teachers, and of other centers. His commentary, however, superseded them all and caused them to be virtually forgotten. The language of his commentary is variegated but nevertheless accurate. In his explanations of words he does not confine himself to dry lexicographical data; his explanation is often colorful and the commentary is replete with realistic concrete descriptions. He adduces reasons for *halakhot* and talmudic argumentations, and often provides psychological and realistic backgrounds to talmudic times. In manifold ways he aids the student in the understanding of the text. He provides introductions to themes, intersperses the commentary with the words of the text, and combines recurring statements. With an excellent feeling for the methodology of the Talmud, he points out difficulties in the construction of the passages and unusual terminology. In all this his commentary is unique. In Rashi's view, the only acceptable explanation of the Mishnah is that given to it by the *Gemara* (see BM 33a and b et al.), with the result that he does not give an independent explanation of the Mishnah. Rashi did not write commentaries to those tractates that have no Babylonian Talmud (the commentary to *Avot* ascribed to him is not his).

Although carefully planned, the linguistic variety led many scholars to point to inconsistencies and contradictions, but most of these have no real substance and can be explained against the background of his methods. From the statements of medieval scholars it is known that Rashi emended his commentary here and there after it had already been issued. However, there are only a few emendations which are definitely from Rashi's pen and an examination of the manuscripts proves that Rashi did not write his commentary more than once, i.e., there were no revised editions of it. The commentary circulated rapidly, and from the beginning of the 13th century almost every talmudic scholar made use of it and pointed out difficulties which he answered or explained. Some even worked over his commentary to various tractates, e.g., to *Sukkah, Ketubbot, Bava Kamma,* and *Sanhedrin.* Rashi's corrections of the Talmud text were for the most part introduced into the standard editions and became the accepted text. [Jo.Fra.]

As a Halakhist. Despite the fact that Rashi's main aim in his commentary to the Talmud was not to determine the *halakhah*, practical halakhic rulings are scattered here and there, and at times even at length, and he was regarded as a halakhic authority of the first rank in Germany during a very long period. In the same way as his commentary on the Talmud became the basis for all later literary activity in this field in France and Germany, even though his pupils and their pupils did not hesitate to query his comments, disagree with them, and suggest alternatives, so with regard to his halakhic rulings. They based themselves upon his oral teachings and his practices as testified to by those who witnessed them, though they did not hesitate to differ from him in practice from time to time. His grandson Jacob already disagreed with him on *halakhah*, and did not even refrain from criticizing him sharply (cf. *Sefer ha-Yashar*, novellae no. 449). To such an extent was he regarded as a halakhic authority that shortly after his death his responsa, teachings, communications, and practices were assembled in different collections. This literature, the greater part of which has survived, both published and in manuscript, is very ramified, and has acquired the general title of "the school of Rashi." The published collections are: *Sefer ha-Pardes* (Constantinople, 1807, ed. by H. L. Ehrenreich, 1924), *Sefer ha-Orah* (ed. by S. Buber, 1905), *Siddur Rashi* (ed. by S. Buber, 1911), *Maḥzor Vitry* (ed. by S. Hurwitz, 1923²), *Likkutei ha-Pardes* (Venice, 1519), *Sefer Issur ve-Hetter* (printed in part c. 1925), and the one published by Urbach (see bibl.). The connection of the *Sefer ha-Sedarim* (ed. by S. Elfenbein, in: *Horeb*, 11 (1951), 123–56) with Rashi is very much closer. Apart from all these there are extant about 350 of Rashi's responsa, collected from various sources by S. Elfenbein (1943). On the other hand, the works of "the school of Rashi" include additions of a very varied and diversified nature, from the teaching of the *geonim*, from the great Spanish scholars (chiefly in accordance with the *Sefer ha-Ittim* of *Judah b. Barzillai al-Bargeloni), as well as from the early teaching of Ereẓ Israel. It is still somewhat of a riddle how the teaching of Ereẓ Israel was preserved and in what manner it found its way into various works of "the school of Rashi."

The special character of the books of "the school of Rashi" as halakhic collections caused them to pass through many hands, involving additions and omissions, so that the traditions and the practices have become confused. The many parallels existing among these books themselves show considerable differences. Rashi's influence as a ruling authority is also discernible upon the Italian authorities, both among the pupils of *Isaiah di Trani I and also upon Zedekiah *Anav, whose *Shibbolei ha-Leket* depends upon the work of Rashi and his school. [I.T.-S.]

Bibliography: A. Marx, in: *Rashi Anniversary Volume* (1941), 9–30; A. Owen, *Rashi, his Life and Times* (1952); H. Hailperin, *Rashi and his World* (1957); M. W. Glenn, in: *Rashi, his Teachings and Personality*, ed. by S. Federbush (1958), 131–55; S. A. Poznański, *Mavo al Ḥakhmei Ẓarefat Mefareshei ha-Mikra*, in: idem (ed.), *Perush al Yeḥezkel u-Terei Asar le-Rabbi Eliezer mi-Belganẓy*, introd. (1913), xiii–xxii (extensive bibl. in xiii n. 2); Sonne, in: HUCA, 15 (1940), Heb. pt. 37–56; M. Liber, *Rashi* (Eng., 1906); E. M. Lipschuetz, *R. Shelomo Yiẓḥaki* (1912); J. L. Maimon (Fishman) (ed.), *Sefer Rashi* (1940¹, 1956²); (American Academy for Jewish Research), *Rashi Anniversary Volume* (1941); M. Waxman, in: S. Federbush (ed.). *Rashi, his Teaching and Personality* (1958), 9–47; J. Bloch, *ibid.*, 49–61; H. Englander, *Rashi's View of the Weak* ע״ע *and* פ״ן *Roots*, in: HUCA, 7 (1930), 399–437; idem, *Grammatical Elements and Terminology in Rashi's Biblical Commentaries*, in *ibid.*, 11 (1936), 367–89; 12–13 (1937–38), 505–521; 14 (1939), 387–429; N. Šapira, *Die grammatische Terminologie des Solomon be Isaak (Raschi)* (1930?); J. Pereira-Mendoza, *Rashi as Philologist* (1940); Ḥ. Yalon, in: *Sefer Rashi* (1956), 515–22; Urbach, *ibid.*, 322–65; I. Schapiro in: *Bitzaron*, 2 (1940), 426–37 (published separately with additions, same year); D. S. Blondheim, in: REJ, 91 (1931); Epstein, in: *Tarbiz*, 4 (1933), 189–92; Shunami, Bibl. 755–757; J. Fraenkel, *Rashi's Methodology in his Exegesis of the Babylonian Talmud* (Ph.D. thesis, Hebrew University, Jerusalem, 1969); S. N. Blumenfeld, in: S. Noveck (ed.), *Great Jewish Personalities in Ancient and Medieval Times* (1959), 233–52; H. Hailperin, *Rashi and the Christian Scholars* (1963); Y. Avineri, *Heikhal Rashi* (4 vols. 1940–60).

RASHĪD AL-DAWLA (al-Dīn; 1247–1318), physician, historian, and vizier in Persia. Known in Muslim sources as Faḍl Allah ibn Abi al-Khayr ibn Ali al-Hamadhānī, he was born of Jewish parents, and served as chief minister of the Persian empire under Īl-Khān rule from 1298 until his death. His spectacular rise to political power was accompanied by unique scholarly achievements. Author of many medical and scientific treatises in Persian, he made Tabriz and Sulatniya, the residences of the Īl-Khān dynasty, into centers of learning known throughout the oriental and Islamic world. His most important work was his *Jamiʿ al-Tawārīkh* ("Collection of Chronicles"), which he wrote on the command of the emperor in 1302. It is the first systematic attempt to deal with the history of all great peoples of the known world, the first medieval "world history." It included a special chapter on "The History of the Children of Israel," the first account written in Persian, which shows his knowledge of Hebrew and thorough acquaintance with the Bible.

Though Rashīd al-Dawla was converted to Islam in 1277, his enemies at court made use of his Jewish origin to plot against him. In 1316 he was accused of having caused the death of the emperor Ūljāʾitū Khān through prescribing the wrong treatment. At his trial he asked in his defense: "How could I, a simple Jew, son of a druggist of Hamadhān, who rose to power in the service of the Īl-Khān, have done this thing?"; but the tribunal sentenced him to death. Together with his son Ibrahim he was executed on July 13 near Tabriz. His head was severed from his body, and carried around the city as the head of an "Infidel Jew." Even in his grave Rashīd al-Dawla found no rest. In 1407 Mīrānshāh, the mad son of Tamerlane, ordered the exhumation of his bones and transferred them from the Muslim cemetery to a Jewish cemetery in Tabriz.

Bibliography: K. Jahn (ed.), *Rashid al-Din's History of India* (1965); B. Spuler, *Die Mongolen in Iran* (1968³); Fischel, Islam, 118–25; idem, in: PAAJR, 22 (1953), 1–21. [W.J.F.]

RASKIN, SAUL (1886–1966), artist. Born in Nogaisk, Russia, Raskin studied painting at different art schools in Europe and in 1904 went to the U.S. Raskin worked in many media and was known for his draftsmanlike attention to detail and his realistic approach. He painted mostly scenes of Jewish life and lore, especially Jewish life on the East Side of New York. His trips to Palestine yielded a series of paintings of Jewish life there, among them 20 lithographs on Jerusalem. Raskin also illustrated many Hebrew texts, e.g., *Pirkei Avot* (1940); the *Haggadah* (1941); Psalms (1942); the *Siddur* (1945); the Kabbalah, called *Kabbalah in Word and Image* (1952), and other works of Jewish context, such as *Hebrew Rhapsody* (1959). [Ed.]

RASMINSKY, LOUIS (1908–), Canadian economist and central banker. Born in Montreal, he joined the Economic and Financial Section of the League of Nations in 1930 and remained there until 1939. Upon his return to Canada, following a short visit to Mexico on behalf of the League, he joined the staff of the Bank of Canada and organized the statistical and economic research section of Canada's Foreign Exhange Control Board. Subsequently he became assistant to the chairman of this board (1941), and then alternate chairman (1942). While serving on the Exchange Control Board, he was also executive assistant to the governor of the Bank of Canada, in which position he represented Canada at the 1944 Bretton Woods Conference where he served as chairman of the drafting committee on the articles of agreement of the International Monetary Fund. He represented Canada on the executive boards of both the Fund and the International Bank for Reconstruction and Development from their inceptions. In 1961 he was appointed governor of the Bank of Canada. He also

Louis Rasminsky, governor of the Bank of Canada. Photo Paul Horsdal, Ottawa.

represented his government at the United Nations in 1945, at Commonwealth prime ministers' conferences, and many other international meetings.

Bibliography: *Current Biography Yearbook, 1961* (1962), 382–4.

[J.O.R.]

RASSEGNA MENSILE DI ISRAEL, LA, Italian Jewish review founded by Alfonso *Pacifici in 1925 as a monthly supplement to the weekly newspaper *Israel.* It dealt with Jewish history and contemporary Jewish life from the traditional point of view. Its editor until 1938 was Guido *Bedarida, but it became most effective under the direction, until 1965, of Dante *Lattes. From 1965 the review was directed by Yoseph *Colombo. The *Rassegna* was closed by the Fascist government in 1938, but reappeared in 1948 and in time regained its importance. For the centenary of Samuel David *Luzzatto in 1966, a special number of 300 pages was issued.

Bibliography: I. Zolli, *Il giornalismo israelitico in Italia* (1924); A. Milano, in: RMI, 12 (1937/38), no. 7–9. [Y.C.]

RAT (Heb. חֹלֶד, *ḥoled,* mod. Heb. חֻלְדָּה, *ḥuldah,* JPS and AV "weasel"), rodent. Two species of rat are found in Israel, *Rattus rattus* and *Rattus norvegicus.* The second only reached the country in approximately the 18th century. *Ḥuldah* occurs as the name of a prophetess (II Kings 22:14, the same verse including two other names taken from the world of fauna: *shafan* ("coney") and *akhbar* ("mouse")). In Torah *ḥoled* is mentioned with the *akhbar* among the unclean creeping things, from which it seems that *ḥoled* is the same as *ḥuldah* (so rendered by Onkelos) where the Palestinian Targum (cf. Meg. 14b) has *kirkushta,* "rat." The name *ḥuldah* is derived from *ḥalod* ("to undermine"); "*ḥuldah* that undermines the foundations of the houses" (Pes. 118b in Ms. Munich). The *ḥuldah* is frequently mentioned in rabbinic literature. It is said to drag food into its nest for storage (Pes. 1:2; TJ, Shab. 14:1, 14c; Lev. R. 6:2). There is a well-known legend of "the rat *[ḥuldah]* and the pit," in which the *ḥuldah* bit the child of a man who did not keep faith with a maiden and married another (see Rashi, Ta'an. 8a). These characteristics do not apply to the cat or the polecat *(Mustela nivalis),* with which some have identified the *ḥuldah.* The polecat is not found in Israel, neither does it store up its food.

See also *Mole.

Bibliography: Lewysohn, Zool, 101f. (no. 135), 107f. (no. 139); F. S. Bodenheimer, *Animal and Man in Bible Lands* (1960), 227 (index), s.v. *Rattus;* J. Feliks, *Animal World of the Bible* (1962), 42; M. Dor, *Leksikon Zo'ologi* (1965), 122. [J.F.]

RATH, MESHULLAM (1875–1963), talmudist and rabbinic authority. Rath's father and earlier forebears had occupied the rabbinate of Kolomyya for 150 years consecutively. Rath, who had a remarkable memory and a rapid grasp of essentials, was ordained at the age of 12 by Isaac *Shmelkes and Jacob Teomim. In 1895 he was appointed rabbi of Molniza and in 1899 rabbi to his native town Horoskov and then to Ushbuza. Rath was an active community leader. He founded a yeshivah for outstanding students, was elected to the Rumanian senate, and was one of the first rabbis to join the Mizrachi movement openly. He spent part of World War I in Vienna, where his renown spread. On returning to Galicia after the war, he was considered for the Lvov rabbinate but withdrew his candidacy when asked to give up his Zionist work. He was then appointed rabbi of Chernovtsy. In 1944 he settled in Ereẓ Israel and became a member of the chief rabbinate. There he was consulted by the Supreme Rabbinic Court, and examined candidates for the post of *dayyan.*

Some of his responsa were published under the title *Kol Mevasser* (2 vols., 1955–62). These deal with such topical matters as the permissibility of a bat mitzvah ceremony for girls and of the wording of the *ketubbah* in Hebrew instead of Aramaic. He ruled that *Hallel* with blessings and the *She-Heḥeyanu* should be recited on Israel Independence Day.

Bibliography: O. Feuchtwanger, *Righteous Lives* (1965), 98–101; S. N. Gottlieb, *Oholei Shem* (1912), 407; Kaniel, in: *Shanah be-Shanah* (1963), 493–7. [Mo.Ha.]

RATHAUS, KAROL (1895–1954), composer. Born in Poland, Rathaus studied composition in Vienna and in Berlin, where he taught at the Hochschule fuer Musik. In 1934 he moved to London, and in 1938 to New York. He taught at Queen's College, New York, from 1940 until his death.

His music was very individual in style. It was atonal and intellectual, showing skill in contrapuntal development and at the same time brooding and romantic. Among his works are: three symphonies; an opera *Fremde Erde* describing the modern American city; a ballet; chamber and piano music; incidental music to films, a setting of Psalm 23; and stage music, including, for the Habimah Theater, the music for *Uriel Acosta, Jacob's Dream,* and *Herod and Mariamne.*

Bibliography: Riemann-Gurlitt; Grove, Dict; MGG, incl. bibl.; Baker, Biog Dict, incl. bibl.; Sendrey, Music, index. [Ed.]

RATHENAU, EMIL (1838–1915), German industrialist and engineer, founder of the electrical corporation A.E.G., born in Berlin. His efforts to introduce the telephone

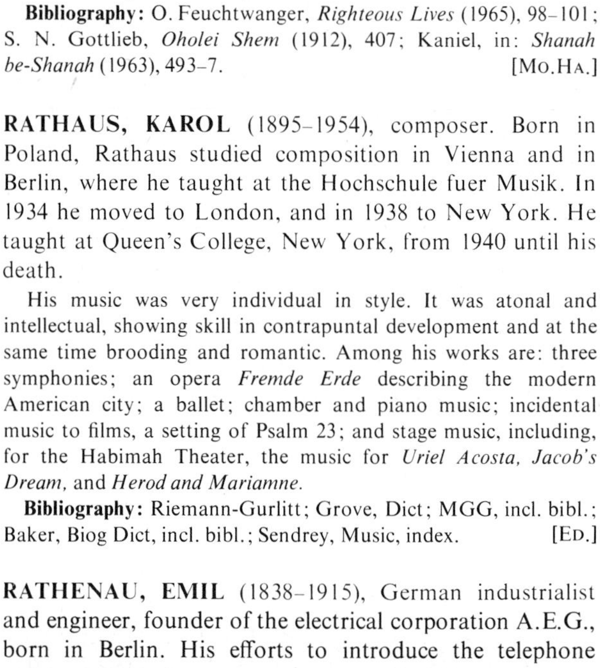

The funeral of Emil Rathenau, from an A.E.G. memorial album, Berlin, 1915. Jerusalem, J.N.U.L.

into the postal service in Germany were at first opposed by the postmaster general, but shortly afterward he was commissioned to set up a telephone exchange for Berlin. Following the Paris Electrical Exhibition of 1881, Rathenau developed an improved version of Edison's incandescent lamp, and for its manufacture established the Deutsche Edison Gesellschaft, which in 1887 became the Allgemeine Elektrizitaets-Gesellschaft (AEG). Under the management of Rathenau and his son Walther *Rathenau, the AEG grew into one of Europe's leading electrical concerns and by the time of Emil Rathenau's death employed more than 70,000 people.

Rathenau was also responsible for other important electrical inventions. He developed the rotary (multiphased) current process which was capable of sending high-tension current to any distance, and made improvements in wireless telegraphy, rapid electrical communications, the steam turbine, and the automobile aeration motor.

Bibliography: F. Pinner, *Emil Rathenau und das elektrische Zeitalter* (1918). [J.O.R.]

RATHENAU, WALTHER (1867–1922), German statesman, writer and industrialist; son of Emil *Rathenau, head of the A.E.G. (Allgemeine Elektrizitaets-Gesellschaft). Walther Rathenau studied electrical engineering and after working independently in Switzerland for 11 years, joined the board of the A.E.G., leading a drive for diversification and expansion, particularly through finance banking. He became the head of the A.E.G. after his father's death in 1915.

Rathenau evolved his own characteristic eclectic philosophy on which he wrote a series of books that had great impact and were translated into many languages. The most popular were *Zur Kritik der Zeit* (1912) and *Von kommenden Dingen* (1917). His *Zur Mechanik des Geistes* (subtitled *Vom Reich der Seele,* 1913) proclaimed a new moral system of social values. He condemned the contemporary faith in technology, rationalism, and materialism and advocated a return to transcendental values. At the same time, he called for international cooperation and the organized distribution of goods. His vision of a cooperative state and a controlled and planned mechanized economy, led by an intellectual elite was paradoxically combined with political liberalism and ethical individualism. He also expressed these views in numerous newspaper articles, especially in the Austrian *Neue Freie Presse,* in periodicals, and in pamphlets, until 1911 mostly anonymously.

Rathenau's attitude toward Judaism was equivocal. His first literary effort, a pseudonymous piece, *"Hoere, Israel"* in Maximilian *Harden's journal *Zukunft* (1897), was a vehement plea for total assimilation, calling the Jews "ein Furchtvolk" ("a people of fear") who developed their intellectual faculties for their own protection. Later he

Walther Rathenau, German statesman. Detail of engraving by Kauffman-Miller. New York, Leo Baeck Institute.

showed respect for the intellectual, ethical, and economic achievements of the Jews, but only because of their general value for humanity. He always expressed contempt for Jews who converted to Christianity out of social and economic interests. He conducted an eight-year correspondence with Wilhelm Schwaner (1863–1941), a rabid anti-Semite and propagator of racist and *"voelkisch"* ideas, whom he considered to be the last person in his life (in 1915) for whom he had any genuine feelings.

The outbreak of World War I threw Rathenau into despair and depression because he anticipated a catastrophe. Nevertheless, he entered the War Ministry and set up a raw material supply department which he successfully headed for six months, introducing controlled economy. While advocating state centralization, nationalization and planning, and control of consumption and production, he grew increasingly critical of German policy and publicly opposed unrestricted submarine warfare. He stated in November 1918 that Germany could still avoid defeat and the armistice. At the start of the Weimar Republic, Rathenau remained politically isolated, but Chancellor Josef Wirth installed him—against much opposition—as economic adviser and negotiator on the war reparations (July 1919). In 1921 he served Wirth for six months as minister of reconstruction, trying to obtain a moratorium on Germany's obligations. Against the advice of friends and the foreboding misgivings of his mother, he became foreign minister in February 1922. In April 1922, while negotiating with the suspicious Western allies in Genoa, he signed the Rapallo Treaty with Soviet Russia. Rathenau had long been the target of anti-Semitism. An article he wrote in 1909 in the *Neue Freie Presse* ("Unser Nachwuchs") had contained the sentence: "Three hundred men, each of whom knows all the others, are guiding the economic fate of the continent [i.e., Europe] and are choosing their successors from their circle." This sentence was interpreted by anti-Semites as a proof for the *Protocols of the *Elders of Zion.* When serving as minister Rathenau realized that his life was in danger, but he refused to allow his being a Jew to deter him from leading Germany's foreign policy. Ultimately a group of young conspirators fulfilled what many extreme right-wing elements had openly demanded and assassinated Rathenau on June 24, 1922. The resulting storm of indignation bolstered the young Weimar Republic. Some of his assassins were caught and sentenced. Rathenau's mother wrote a letter of condolence to the mother of one of the murderers who had been publicly insulted. Rathenau had a many-sided and complicated personality. His practical and intellectual abilities were outstanding; he was also artistically gifted, sensitive, and had mystical inclinations. He never married. He had a wide circle of friends and acquaintances, even though most of his close relationships ended in violent quarrels. His correspondence of some 1,500 letters includes exchanges with the leading writers of his time, Gide, Hesse, Rilke, Stefan *Zweig, and Gerhardt Hauptmann, with whom he was especially friendly. He had close relationships with several Scandinavians, among them the painter Edward Munch, who made an important portrait of Rathenau, while in literature he is portrayed by Robert Musil in his *Man without Qualities.*

Bibliography: G. Gottlieb, *Walther Rathenau—Bibliographie* (1929); P. Berglar, *Walther Rathenau* (1970); J. Joll, *Intellectuals in Politics* (1960), 59–129; H. Graf Kessler, *Walther Rathenau, sein Leben und sein Werk* (1928); S. Liptzin, *Germany's Stepchildren* (1944), 139–51; E. Rosenbaum, in: YLBI, 4 (1959), 260–4; 13 (1968), 132–4; W. O. Henderson, in: *Economic History Review,* 4 (1951/52), 98–108; E. C. Kollmann, in: *Journal of Modern History,* 24 (1952), 127–42; E. Hyams, *Killing no Murder* (1969); R. A. Pois, in: YLBI, 13 (1968), 120–31. [H.W./L.Y.]

RATISBONNE BROTHERS, two French Jews who converted to Christianity and who became prominent in the Catholic Church in the 19th century. The Ratisbonne brothers were sons of a Strasbourg Jewish banker who was president of the Consistoire of Alsace. His second eldest son, THEODORE RATISBONNE (1802–1884) was born in Strasbourg and practiced law in his native city. He devoted much of his time to the improvement of the social and economic plight of the Jews in the Strasbourg ghetto. However, his study of the Bible and church history led him to be baptized secretly. He adopted the name Marie and was hereafter known as Marie Théodore Ratisbonne. After being ordained a priest in 1830 he taught at a church school in Strasbourg and in 1840 went to Paris to work for the archconfraternity of the parish Notre-Dame des Victoires. In 1843, together with his brother Alphonse, he founded the Congregation of Notre Dame de Sion for women and in 1852 the Fathers of Zion. Marie Théodore Ratisbonne's avowed aims in founding these religious societies were to bring about a better understanding between Jews and Christians and to convert Jews. He wrote profusely, and among his principal works are: *Histoire de Saint Bernard et de son siècle* (2 vols., 1840; 1903[11]) *Manuel de la mère chrétienne* (1859; 1926[22]).

ALPHONSE RATISBONNE (1812–1884), the ninth child of the family, was also born in Strasbourg and began his career as a lawyer and banker. Like his brother Théodore he was filled with fervor to help his fellow Jews. At first he found it difficult to forgive his brother's conversion and felt hatred toward Christendom for its persecution of Jews. However, an experience during a visit to a church in Rome in which he reportedly saw a vision of Mary (January 20, 1842) moved him so powerfully that he had himself baptized eleven days later. He took the name of Marie, became a Jesuit, as Marie Alphonse Ratisbonne, and in 1848 was ordained a priest. He left the Society of Jesus in 1852 to collaborate with Théodore in Paris, but in 1855 went to Palestine, where he spent the rest of his life working for the conversion of Jews and Muslims. In 1856 he established the Ecce Homo convent for the Sisters of Zion in the Old City of Jerusalem and, subsequently, two orphanages. He wrote *Monument à la gloire de Marie* (1847). [ED.]

The Ratisbonne Congregations. The Sisters of Zion benefited from the fact that in the middle of the 19th century there was a prodigious development in the education of girls, particularly in France, and that the French teaching congregations were spreading throughout the world. A congregation whose aim was the conversion of the Jews would have attracted a very limited number of candidates, whereas the movement toward teaching and the establishment of boarding schools made it possible to reach young ladies attracted to religious life. The development deflected the primitive orientation of the congregation: if in their life of prayer their objects remained unchanged the sisters made no efforts at proselytizing. The Fathers of Zion who did not constitute a canonically erected religious congregation during the lifetime of the Ratisbonne brothers were at the beginning primarily chaplains and spiritual directors to the Sisters and their pupils. Until the end of World War I both congregations had little contact with Jews and Judaism. With the rise of Hitlerism Fathers and Sisters were among its most prominent opponents on the Catholic side, and insisted in their publications on the necessity of common action by Jews and Christians against neo-paganism. In the countries occupied by Nazi Germany Sisters and Fathers made efforts to provide Jews with shelter and a passage to safety, although they themselves were closely observed by the Gestapo. After World War II they were active in the development of the mentality which led to the Declaration *"Nostra Aetate"* by the second Vatican Council. Both Congregations now hold that proselytizing must be entirely abandoned and they considered themselves pioneers of a new era of Jewish-Christian understanding. The Sisters and Fathers of Zion have taken a positive attitude toward the State of Israel. [M.J.S.]

Bibliography: J. Guitton, *Le conversion de Ratisbonne* (1964); L. M. Leggatt (tr.), *A Nineteenth Century Miracle* (1922); M. J. Egan, *Our Lady's Jew, Father M. A. Ratisbonne* (1953); idem, *Christ's Conquest: The Coming of Grace to Theodore Ratisbonne* (1945).

RATNER, DOV BAER (1852–1917), Lithuanian talmudic scholar. Born in Kalvarija, Lithuania, Ratner studied at the yeshivot of Mir and Volozhin, and acquired a wide secular knowledge by independent study. In St. Petersburg and Vilna he engaged in commerce, but later devoted himself entirely to scholarly research.

Having made his literary debut at the age of 16, he contributed studies, learned notes, and book reviews to a variety of publications, particularly to *Ha-Meliẓ*. In 1894 his *Mavo le-Seder Olam Rabbah* appeared in Vilna and was followed three years later by a critical edition of the text of the *Seder Olam Rabbah*. From 1901 until his death, he published 12 parts of *Ahavat Ẓiyyon vi-Yrushalayim*, on the entire orders of *Zera'im* and *Mo'ed* of the Jerusalem Talmud, except for the tractate *Eruvin*, containing variant readings and explanations culled from the writings of early authorities. Selections from this work were subsequently included in the Vilna (Romm) edition of the Jerusalem Talmud. An early adherent of the Zionist movement, Ratner was among the Vilna community notables who welcomed Theodor Herzl on his visit to the city in 1903. He left his books to the Straschun Library of Vilna, of which he had been a director.

Bibliography: L. Slonimski, in: *Vilner Zamelbukh*, 2 (1918), 186–91; T. Preschel, in: D. B. Ratner (ed.), *Midrash Seder Olam* (1966), bio-bibliography.

[T.P.]

RATNER, LEONARD (1896–), U.S. business executive and Jewish community leader. Ratner, who was born in Bialystok, Poland, went to the U.S. and settled in Shaker Heights, Ohio. He was founder and chairman of the board of directors of Forest City Enterprises, Inc., a national real estate development firm with interests in retail stores and building materials.

Ratner served a wide variety of community organizations and educational institutions in the United States and Israel. He was a member of the board of overseers of the Jewish Theological Seminary from 1953, a member of the board of the American Committee for the Weizmann Institute of Science in Israel, and former vice-president and board member from 1965 of the American Friends of the Hebrew University. He worked for many charitable organizations, including the Jewish Community Federation of Cleveland, the UJA, and the American Jewish Joint Distribution Committee. [ED.]

RATNER, MARC BORISOVICH (1871–1917), Russian lawyer and socialist. Born in Kiev, Ratner was brought up in an assimilated environment. He was expelled from high school because of clandestine Socialist activities. As a law student he was arrested and exiled for two years, but later graduated as a lawyer. In his student days he attracted attention with his articles in *Russkoye Bogatstvo* on the agrarian problem, Marxism, political economy, and labor legislation. He appeared as counsel for the defense in political trials and as civil prosecutor in the pogrom trials. The Kishinev pogrom brought him closer to Jewish affairs. He was among the leaders of the *Vozrozhdeniye and later the *Jewish Socialist Workers' Party, in which, with Chaim *Zhitlowsky, he represented the populist socialist-revolutionary trend. He fought for the inclusion of Yiddish in the curriculum of the *Society for the Promotion of Culture among the Jews of Russia, and was a candidate to the second *Duma. As a result of his activities during the 1905 revolution, he was compelled to leave Russia. Ratner was the initiator of the convention of the socialist parties of oppressed nations in Russia (1907). He represented the Jewish Socialist Workers' Party at the Congress of the Socialist International in Copenhagen (1910) and initiated the campaign for the recognition of a Jewish section of the International. The hardships of emigration (Switzerland, Vienna) ruined his health. A short while before his death he settled in Jassy, Rumania.

In his works on the national question he rejected assimilationism and supported the idea of a national-personal, exterritorial, autonomy. Noteworthy are his *"Evolyutsiya natsionalno-politicheskoy mysli v russkom yevreystve"* ("The Evolution of National-Political Thought among Russian Jewry," in *Serp*, vol. 2, 1907); *"Natsionalny vopros v svete sotsialisticheskago mirovozzreniya"* ("The National Question in Light of the Socialist Weltanschauung," in *Russkoye Bogatstvo*, nos. 2–5, 1908); and articles on autonomism in *Yevreyskiy Mir*, nos. 6, 9, and 10 (1909).

Bibliography: Rejzen, Leksikon, 4 (1929), 187–93; O. I. Janowsky, *Jews and Minority Rights* (1933), index; *Kniga o russkom yevreystve* (1960), index; B. Borochov, *Ketavim* . . . 2 (1958), index. [M.M.]

RATNER, YOHANAN (1891–1965), Israel architect and a commander in the *Haganah and the *Israel Defense Forces. Born in Odessa into an assimilated family, Ratner completed university studies in Germany and served in the Czar's army during World War I and, despite being a Jew, was employed in planning campaigns

Yohanan Ratner, Israel architect and soldier. Courtesy Technion, Haifa.

on various fronts. Ratner went to Palestine in 1923 and was appointed a professor at the *Technion in Haifa. He played an important role in establishing the faculty of architecture, which he headed from 1930 until his retirement in 1963. Parallel to his career as a teacher, Ratner worked as an architect and drew up the plans for many public buildings, including the *Jewish Agency building in Jerusalem, the Eden Hotel, Jerusalem, the aeronautics building for the Technion in Haifa, the Kefar ha-Yarok Agricultural School, and Bet Berl at *Ẓofit.

Ratner joined the Haganah upon arrival in Palestine, became a member of the Haganah Committee in Haifa, and participated in the defense of Jerusalem during the riots of August 1929. He supported a more efficient and compact organization of the Haganah, and when the decision was made to appoint a head of the territorial command of the Haganah, Ratner was the first to occupy the position, which he held in 1938–39. During the German advance on Egypt (1941–42), he was among the creators of the "Carmel Plan," the main aim of which was to concentrate the Jewish armed forces in the Haifa region to fight the invaders. In 1947 Ratner became a member of the Haganah's high command, and, when the Israel Defense Forces were formed, became head of a department of general headquarters with the rank of *alluf* ("brigadier general"). In 1948 he was appointed military attaché to the Israel embassy in Moscow and filled the post until 1951.

Bibliography: Dinur, Haganah, 2, pt. 3 (1963), index. [Y.S.]

RATOSH, YONATHAN (originally **Uriel Halperin;** 1908–), Hebrew poet and journalist. Born in Russia, the son of Yehiel *Halperin, he was brought up in an exclusively Hebrew-speaking environment. Ratosh went to Palestine in 1921. In the mid-1930s, he worked on the staff of two daily newspapers, first *Haaretz* and then the right-wing *Ha-Yarden*. In 1938 he left the country to avoid imprisonment by the Mandatory authorities for his political activities, but returned with the outbreak of World War II.

Ratosh published several volumes of poetry; the first, *Ḥuppah Sheḥorah* ("Black Canopy," 1941), caused a scandal because of its sensuality, its innovations of language, and the *Canaanite motifs intrinsic to the writer's political-cultural thought. He translated many books into Hebrew, including such classics as *Cyrano de Bergerac* (1965) and the *Fables* of La Fontaine. Ratosh founded a political movement, originally called the Young Hebrews, but dubbed the "Canaanites" by its opponents, and he published articles on politics. He coined many new Hebrew words, worked in Hebrew literature and linguistics, and advocated the use of the Latin alphabet for Hebrew.

Ratosh was distinguished by his political-cultural philosophy. His insistence on being defined as a "Hebrew" rather than as a "Jew" reflects his conviction that the population developing an identity in Palestine/Israel is a new nation—as the descendants of immigrants in a country of immigration invariably become. Through its choice of the Hebrew language and culture, the new nation is defining itself as the cultural descendant of the ancient Hebrew-Canaanite nation, indigenous to what is generally known as the Fertile Crescent, which produced such cultural documents as the Ugaritic tablets and the body of literature that, extensively and tendentiously edited, has come down as the Hebrew Bible. The terms "Jew" and "Jewish" are, in Ratosh's opinion, to be reserved for the adherents of the religion of that name, developed by a group of Judean emigrés during the Babylonian Exile and imposed on the people of the land when part of them returned there in the time of Ezra and Nehemiah. To apply the term now as a national determinant is in his view a distortion, and the resulting identification between the old-new Hebrew nation and the Jewish communities of different persuasions in the rest of the world runs counter to history. In addition, Ratosh believed that the identification is injurious to the Hebrew nation and to the role that it must play in the national revival of the lands of the Euphrates. Ratosh had considerable influence on contemporary Hebrew poetry. The vicissitude of his early work, which provoked violent opposition when it first appeared, and was accepted ten years later and held up as a standard 20 years later, is perhaps characteristic. Devices and principles which he was the first to use were later taken for granted as part of the Hebrew poet's tools. This is true at all levels, from such purely technical matters as the use of an indention and dash pattern instead of punctuation, to structural techniques such as the near-repetition of phrases and refrains to obtain a counterpoint effect, to the recourse to local mythology as a vivifying poetic element. It seems likely that later works, particularly his verse in *Ha-Holkhi ba-Ḥoshekh* ("Who Walketh in Darkness," 1965) will, in time, be found to have had a similar influence. For English translations of Ratosh's works see Goell, Bibliography.

Bibliography: D. Meron, *Arba'ah Panim ba-Sifrut ha-Ivrit Bat Yameinu—Iyyunim bi-Yẓirot Alterman, Ratosh, Yizhar, Shamir* (1962); S. Burnshaw et al. (eds.), *Modern Hebrew Poem Itself* (1966), 92–105. [Da.Sa.]

RATSHESKY, ABRAHAM CAPTAIN (1864–1943), U.S. banker and civic leader. Ratshesky was born in Boston. He became a state Republican leader and was state senator in 1892–94. In 1895 he left career politics and founded the U.S. Trust Company, of which he served as president and board chairman. Subsequently, Ratshesky held numerous civic posts, including Massachusetts food administrator during World War I and U.S. minister to Czechoslovakia (1930–33). He was chairman of the Massachusetts Department of Public Welfare for ten years.

Ratshesky served as first president of the Federated Jewish Charities of Boston (1909–19), and was prominent in many civic and Jewish endeavors. He formed the A. C. Ratshesky Charity Foundation in 1916. [E.GR.]

RAU, HEINZ (1896–1965), Israel architect. Rau was born in Berlin, where he specialized in interiors, among which were several for Berlin University. When Hitler came to power in 1933 he emigrated to Ereẓ Israel, where he entered the office of Richard *Kaufmann. From 1949 to 1953 he

The synagogue of the Hebrew University of Jerusalem, designed by Heinz Rau and David Reznik, dedicated 1957. Courtesy Government Press Office, Tel Aviv.

worked for the Israel Government Planning Department. In 1962 he went to England to become assistant professor in the Department of Town and Country Planning, Manchester. Among Rau's designs in Jerusalem were the Hebrew Union College, the Mathematics Institute, and the domed synagogue at the Hebrew University of Jerusalem (in collaboration with Reznik). A feature of his buildings in Israel is the small intake of light, which he regarded as most suited to the climatic conditions. [ED.]

RAUH, FRÉDÉRIC (1861–1909), French philosopher. He was born at St. Martin-le-Vinoux, was professor at Toulouse and later (1901) at the Sorbonne (where he replaced *Bergson) and at the Ecole Normale Supérieure.

His main philosophical interest was in morality, which he treated apart from metaphysics and empirical facts. He held that moral thought is like invention, and finds its verification in action. Moral certitude is possible, and man's true guide is reflection upon instinct, rather than either just reflection or just instinct. Individual conscience in which active moral belief manifests itself is all important. His main works were *Essai sur le fondement métaphysique de la morale* (1890); *L'experience morale* (1903); *Psychologie appliquée à la morale et à l'éducation*, with R. d'Allones (1900–17); and *Etudes de Morale* (posthumous, 1911). He was a brilliant teacher. He was actively involved in the Dreyfus case.

Bibliography: L. Brunschwicg, in: *Revue Philosophique* (1928), 5–32; H. Daudin, in: *Revue de Métaphysique et de Morale* (1910), 185–218, 318–44 (contains complete bibliography); R. Junod, *Frédéric Rauh, Essai de biographie intellectuelle* (1932). [R.H.P.]

RAUH, JOSEPH L. (1911–), U.S. lawyer. Rauh, who was born in Cincinnati, Ohio, was law secretary to U.S. Supreme Court Justice Cardozo and as counsel to various government agencies, including the Wage and Hour Administration and the Federal Communications Commission (1935–42). Rauh served in the U.S. army during World War II and was discharged with the rank of lieutenant colonel. He was a founder of the Americans for Democratic Action in 1947, which presented a liberal, non-Communist alternative to the then-conservative domination of both the Republican and Democratic parties. He was chairman of the ADA executive committee (1947–52), vice-chairman (1952–55 and 1957), and national chairman (1955–57). Rauh was a delegate to all Democratic National Conventions from 1948, when he fought for the inclusion of the first strong civil rights plank in that party's platform, through 1964, when he strongly advocated seating the Negroes of the Mississippi Freedom party as the official Democratic delegation from that state. Rauh was the Washington counsel (1951–63, 1966–) and general counsel (1963–66) for the United Automobile Workers. He also served as attorney for the insurgent United Mineworkers Union group led by Joseph Yablonski, who opposed incumbent Tony Boyle for the union's presidency in 1969. [ED.]

°**RAUTER, HANNS ALBIN** (1895–1949), Austrian *SS officer and *Himmler's principal representative in the occupied *Netherlands. One of the founders of the fascist Steirischer Heimatschutz ("Styrian Homeguard"), he became its chief. In 1933 he adhered with his organization to the Austrian branch of the Nazi Party. Himmler appointed him in 1940 Higher SS and Police leader in the Netherlands. In this capacity he won Himmler's praise for precisely and zealously carrying out the persecution of Dutch Jewry and their deportation to the camps in Poland. Rauter was considered the chief executor of the "Final Solution" (see *Holocaust, General Survey) of the Jews of the Netherlands. He was sentenced to death by a Dutch court and executed in 1949.

Bibliography: *Het proces Rauter* (Dutch, 1952); J. Presser, *Ashes in the Wind* (1968); G. Reitlinger, *Final Solution* (1953), index.

[Y.RE.]

RAV (third century C.E.), leading Babylonian *amora* and founder of the academy at *Sura. His name was Abba b. Aivu, but he was also called Abba Arikha ("Abba the Tall") because of his tall stature (Nid. 24b). He is generally known as Rav by reason of being "the teacher *[rav]* of the entire Diaspora" (Beẓah 9a, and Rashi thereto). Born at Kafri in southern Babylonia in the latter half of the second century C.E., he belonged to a very distinguished family; he was related to Ḥiyya through both his parents (Sanh. 5a; Pes. 4a and Rashi) and traditionally was descended either from Shimei, brother of David (Ket. 62b), or from Shephatiah, the son of Abital and David (TJ, Ta'an. 4:2, 68a). It is not known who were Rav's teachers in Babylonia, but he immigrated to Ereẓ Israel and studied under his uncle Ḥiyya (MK 16b), was a member of his household (Shab. 66b), and assisted him in his business affairs (TJ, BM 6:1, 10d). Ḥiyya introduced him into the home of Judah ha-Nasi (Ber. 46b), where he discussed *halakhah* under Ḥiyya's guidance (Ḥul. 16a). Extremely diligent in his studies (cf. Suk. 26b), Rav joined the academy of Judah ha-Nasi, with whom he debated halakhic topics (Ḥul. 137b) and whose *bet din* he joined (Git. 59a). He knew and entered into halakhic discussions with the greatest of the last generation of *tannaim*, being in contact with Ishmael b. Yose (Pes. 112b, according to R. Hananel's version; see Dik. Sof. *ibid.*), Symmachus (Ket. 81a), Bar Kappara (Yoma 87b), Eleazar b. Simeon (Zev. 102b), as well as with Levi (Beẓah 24b) and Ḥanina b. Ḥama (Yoma 87b).

He learnt the Torah of Ereẓ Israel, and prior to leaving the country was ordained by Judah ha-Nasi and was authorized to give decisions in ritual law and in civil cases (Sanh. 5a–b; TJ, Ḥag. 1:8, 76c). Some hold that after going back to Babylonia, he returned several times to Ereẓ Israel (see TJ, Pe'ah 6:3, 19c) before finally deciding to settle in Babylonia, apparently in 219 C.E. (*Iggeret R. Sherira Ga'on,* ed. by B. M. Lewin (1921), 78). He encountered some difficulties in Nehardea (Shab. 108a), which was an important center of sages and Torah, and where Shila, Samuel, and Karna flourished at the time. Rav first served as an interpreter in Shila's *bet midrash* (Yoma 20b), and subsequently the exilarch appointed him *agoranomos* ("market commissioner," TJ, BB 5:11, 15a), whose duties in Babylonia comprised superintending market measures and prices; in keeping with the prevailing *halakhah* in Ereẓ Israel, however, he refused to regulate prices. Compelled to resign his position, he left Nehardea and went to Sura, whose inhabitants were not distinguished for their knowledge of the Torah (Ḥul. 110a); there he established a *bet din* and academy which in time attained such eminence that it was regarded as "a little sanctuary" (Meg. 29a) and attracted hundreds of pupils from Sura and its neighborhood. Its permanent pupils numbered 1,200 (Ket. 106a).

The Jews of Sura and its neighboring towns accepted his religious leadership and jurisdiction (*ibid.* 54a). Not only the Babylonian sages, foremost among them Samuel, acknowledged his considerable religious authority (Git. 36b), but Johanan, the head of the academy at Tiberias and one of the outstanding sages of Ereẓ Israel at the time, counted Rav as his teacher in *halakhah* (Ḥul. 95b). Perhaps the most conspicuous recognition of his signal religious authority is the statement: "Rav is a *tanna* and differs" (Ket. 8a), that is, Rav has the right to differ from a *tanna* without sustaining or basing his view on that of another *tanna*, a privilege accorded only to him among all the Babylonian sages of that generation. Returning to Babylonia equipped with the teachings of Judah ha-Nasi and with a profound, comprehensive knowledge of the Torah of Ereẓ Israel, Rav introduced into Babylonia several *halakhot* previously not practiced there. Thus Huna, one of Rav's distinguished pupils, declared: "From the time Rav arrived in Babylonia, we in Babylonia have put ourselves on the same footing as Ereẓ Israel with regard to the breeding of small cattle" (which was prohibited there; BK 80a), as well as "with regard to bills of divorce" (the bearers of which in Ereẓ Israel were exempted from stating, "In my presence it was written and in my presence it was signed"; Git. 6a). Rav enacted regulations relating to matrimony (Yev. 52a; Kid. 12b) and the education of children (Ket. 50a), and frequently visited different communities in Babylonia to institute various ordinances there and to raise their religious and social standard (the sources have been collected by J. Umanski, notes 140/1).

That he relied on his independent judgment, unrestrained by other authorities, when issuing regulations and arriving at decisions, shows the extensive authority enjoyed by him in Babylonia and recognized, according to all indications, also by the exilarch and his officials. Rav was a member of the exilarch's *bet din* (Kid. 44b) and his daughter married into the exilarch's family (Ḥul. 92a). The fact that Rav was economically independent (Ber. 57b), owning landed property (Kid. 59a) and enjoying an income from the manufacture and sale of beer (Pes. 107a), helped to sustain his eminent status. Although there is evidence that he was in some contact with Artabanus V, the last of the royal Arsacid dynasty (Av. Zar. 10b), unlike Samuel, he did not maintain close relations with the authorities or with non-Jews, his chief activity being directed to internal affairs, to the religious welfare of the members of the Babylonian Jewish community. In addition to his labors in his *bet din* and the academy, Rav was one of the most eminent and prolific Babylonian aggadists and frequently delivered public discourses. In his addresses, greatly influenced by the Ereẓ Israel *aggadah*, he urged his audiences to observe the *mitzvot* and to study the Torah.

In explaining the reason for the *mitzvot* and for their observance he declared: "The *mitzvot* were given only as a means of refining men. For what difference does it make to God whether one slaughters an animal from the front or from the back of the neck?" (Gen. R. 44:1). Of the study of the Torah he said that it "is more important than the offering of the daily sacrifices" (Er. 63b), that it "is superior to the building of the Temple" (Meg. 16b), that "whoever departs from the words of the Torah is consumed by fire" (BB 79a), and that "he who says, 'I shall rise early to study this chapter or this tractate,' has vowed a great vow to the God of Israel" (Ned. 8a). In his solicitude for the status and dignity of scholars he asserted that anyone who insults a scholar is a heretic (*eppikoros;* Sanh. 99b) and "has no remedy for his wounds" (Shab. 119b). Urging scholars to be diligent in teaching the Torah, he declared that "whoever withholds a *halakhah* from a disciple is as though he has robbed him of his ancestral heritage" (Sanh. 91b), and "that whoever teaches Torah to his neighbor's son will be privileged to sit in the Heavenly Academy. . . . if he teaches it to an ignorant man's son, even if the Holy One blessed be He decrees adversely, He annuls it for his sake" (BM 85a). From the examples quoted and their emphasis, it is evident that Rav regarded the teaching of the Torah and the spreading of the knowledge of the Torah as one of the most important spheres of his communal activities.

Of the Jews of Babylon who had refused to grant a certain Shabbetai b. Marinus facilities for earning a livelihood and had not given him any food either, Rav said: "These are the descendants of the 'mixed multitude' (Ex. 12:38), for it is written (Deut. 13:18). 'And [He will] show thee mercy, and have compassion upon thee.' Whoever is merciful to his fellowmen is decidedly of the children of our father Abraham, and whoever is not merciful to his fellowmen is decidedly not of the children of our father Abraham" (Beẓah 32b). Rav warned his audiences against quarreling (Sanh. 110a), against slander and its grave consequences (BB 164b), against paying heed to slander (Shab. 56b), and against boastfulness (Pes. 66b), and was solicitous for the position and welfare of workers (BM 83a).

In some of Rav's homilies a tendency to a certain mystical thinking is discernible. Describing, for example, the difference between this and the next world, he said: "In the future world there is no eating nor drinking, no propagation nor business, no jealousy nor hatred nor competition, but the righteous sit with their crowns on their heads feasting on the Divine Glory" (Ber. 17a). Rav expounded God's names and their pronunciation (Kid. 71a), the purpose of creation (Shab. 77b) and the process of creation (Ḥag. 12a), the divine providence of the world and its creatures (Sot. 2a; Ḥag. 5b), and warned against criticizing God's attributes (Men. 29b). Rav composed several prayers, the best known being *Teki'ata de-Rav* which is recited during the *Amidah* on Rosh Ha-Shanah (TJ, RH 1:3, 57a) and whose contents express his outlook on God's providence over the nations and of Israel.

Opposed to a life of abstinence and mortification, Rav asserted: "Man is destined to render an account for all that his eye has seen and he has not eaten" (TJ, Kid. 4:12, 66d). To *Hamnuna he declared: "My son, if you have anything, derive what benefit you can from it, for there is no enjoyment in the grave nor does death delay. And should you say, 'I would leave a portion for my children,' who will tell you in the grave? The children of men are like the grasses of the field, some blossom and some fade" (Er. 54a, based on Ecclus. 14:12–14). The Jews of Babylonia had great esteem for Rav and grieved deeply at his death. Samuel rent his garments (MK 24a), as did Rav's pupils (Ber. 42b–43a) who mourned him for a long time (Shab. 110a). People took earth from his grave for medicinal purposes (Sanh. 47b). Rav and Samuel are the founders of the Babylonian Talmud, and their discussions and debates both in *halakhah* and *aggadah* are one of its prominent features. Where Samuel, who probably never visited Ereẓ Israel, and his academy in Nehardea reflect the Babylonian tradition, Rav and the academy of Sura which he founded reflect that of Ereẓ Israel.

Bibliography: Bacher, Bab Amor; Hyman, Toledot, 15–42; Kohut, Arukh, 1 (1926²) 6–10; 7 (1926²), 236–9; Weiss, Dor, 3 (1904⁴), 129–43; Halevy, Dorot, 2 (1923), passim; Graetz-Rabbinowitz, 2 (1893), 350–6; I. S. Zuri, *Rav* (Heb., 1925); J. Umanski, *Ḥakhmei ha-Talmud, Sefer Rav* (1931); M. Beer, in: *Divrei ha-Congress ha-Olami ha-Revi'i le-Madda'ei ha-Yahadut*, 1 (1967), Heb. pt., 99–101; Epstein, Mishnah, 1 (1948), 166–211; S. Rosenthal, in: *Sefer H. Yalon* (1963), 281–337; H. Albeck, *Mavo la-Talmudim* (1969), 170f. [M.BE.]

RAVA (d. 352 C.E.), Babylonian *amora*. Rava is an abbreviation of R. Abba, and his full name was R. Abba b. Joseph b. Ḥama (Er. 54a). He lived at *Maḥoza. His teachers were *Ḥisda, the head of the academy at Sura, whose daughter he married (BB 12b), but principally *Naḥman b. Jacob (Shab. 4a) and R. Joseph, head of the academy at Pumbedita (Ḥul. 133a). His main halakhic discussions were with his companion *Abbaye, and their statements and controversies are found throughout the Babylonian Talmud. In their many debates the *halakhah* follows Rava's view except in six instances (for which the mnemonic יע״ל קג״ם was given) in which the *halakhah* is according to Abbaye (BM 22b). After R. Joseph's death in 323 (*Iggeret Sherira Ga'on*, ed. by B. M. Lewin (1921), 85–86), Abbaye was chosen in preference to the other candidates (Rava, Zera, and Rabbah b. Matna) as the head of the Pumbedita academy. Rava thereupon left that city and returned to Maḥoza, where he established a *bet midrash* which attracted many pupils (BB 22a). Rava ascribed overriding weight to logical reasoning and inference in the study and comprehension of the Torah; this approach is reflected in his statement that "one grain of pungent pepper is better than a basketful of pumpkins" (Ḥag. 10a) and in his assertion that he was "like Ben Azzai," who was noted for his mental keenness (Er. 29a). His educational approach was popular with Rava's pupils, one of whom, addressing the pupils of Abbaye, who in his teaching preferred a thorough knowledge and comprehension of halakhic discussions, said: "Instead of gnawing bones in the school of Abbaye, why do you not eat fat meat in the school of Rava?" (BB 22a). Those who had studied under Rava found no great satisfaction in other sages' discourses (Ta'an. 9a). Rava's academy became the principal one after Abbaye's death in 338, the sages and pupils of Abbaye's academy moving to Maḥoza (*Iggeret Sherira Ga'on* pp.88–89).

For 14 years, until his death, Rava was the head of the academy, during which time his intellectual powers and economic position so expanded as to enable him to assert that he had been granted the wisdom of *Huna and the wealth of Ḥisda, though not the modesty of *Rabbah b. Huna (MK 28a). He owned fields and vineyards (BM 73a) and traded in wine (Ber. 56a), cooperated in public and administrative matters with the exilarch's officials (BB 22a; Git. 31b), and negotiated with the Persian authorities. He was on friendly terms with the exilarch (Beẓah 21b; Ber. 50a; Pes. 74b), and there is illuminating information on his contacts with *Shapur II. When the sages of the academy complained that Rava had established too close relations with the royal court, he replied by telling them what he had to endure there and the large sums with which he bribed the court (Ḥag. 5b). Apparently much money was demanded from the Jews, as from the rest of the population, to finance Shapur's wars against the Romans. Rava also maintained close ties with Ifra Hormuz, the king's mother, who sent him money for distribution among the poor (BB 10b) and a calf to be sacrificed on her behalf (Zev. 116b). She told her son of Rava's greatness when the king wished to punish him for having sentenced a man to flogging which proved fatal (Ta'an. 24b). Maḥoza's geographic proximity to Be-Ardashir, one of the country's capitals, may have facilitated Rava's contacts with the authorities there.

Rava's main activity, however, lay in teaching and in spreading knowledge of the Torah. He instituted various regulations for the people of Maḥoza (Beẓah 30a; Er. 40a; MK 22a; Nid. 66b). He denounced for their pursuit of pleasure (RH 17a), many among the well-to-do (BK 119a) who ate and drank to excess (Shab. 109a) and whose wives did no work (Shab. 32b–33a). On the other hand, he praised the industry of the workers of Maḥoza (BM 77a). Large audiences gathered on Sabbaths to hear Rava's discourses (Er. 44b), and in numerous statements he stressed the signal religious value of studying the Torah. Once, when he noticed a disciple of the sages praying at great length, he said: "They forsake eternal life and occupy themselves with temporal life" (Shab. 10a). He declared that whoever occupies himself with the study of the Torah has no need of sacrifices (Men. 110a) and is superior to a high priest who enters into the innermost part of the sanctuary (Sot. 4b), that the Torah is an antidote to the evil inclination (BB 16a), that suffering comes upon a man for neglecting the study of the Torah (Ber. 5a), and that King Asa was punished for having imposed forced labor on the disciples of the sages who were thus compelled to neglect the study of the Torah (Sot. 10a). He claimed exemption from government taxes for disciples of the sages (Ned. 62b), to whom he gave the right to sell their goods in the market (BB 22a). To uphold their honor and prevent them from wasting their time, which should be devoted to the study of the Torah, he allowed them to disclose that they were disciples of the sages so that they might be judged or give evidence without having to wait for the cases of others to be finished (Ned. 62a). But he also demanded of them that they be worthy of the name, declaring that "any disciple of the sages whose inside is not like his outside is not a disciple of the sages" (Yoma 72b).

Yet despite its great importance Rava did not regard the study of the Torah as an end in itself. Thus a favorite saying of his was, "The goal of wisdom is repentance and good deeds, so that a man should not study the Torah and Mishnah and then despise his father and mother, his teacher, and his superior in wisdom and rank" (Ber. 17a). In like manner, when describing what is demanded of man in this world, he said: "When man is brought in for judgment [in the next world] he is asked, 'Did you deal faithfully, fix times for studying the Torah, did you engage in procreation, hope for salvation, did you search after wisdom, infer one thing from another?' Yet, even so, if 'the fear of the Lord is his treasure' (Isa. 33:6) it is well; if not, it is not well" (Shab. 31a). Rava's special outlook can be better comprehended when compared with Hamnuna's statement that "the first matter for which a man is called to render account in the hereafter is with regard to the study of the Torah" (Sanh. 7a). Rava likewise said: "Jerusalem was destroyed only because men of integrity ceased therein" (Shab. 119b). An illuminating view of his is that "length of life, children, and sustenance depend not on merit but on luck" (MK 28a). He had many affinities with mysticism and performed miracles (see Sanh. 65b). On one occasion he even wished to discourse in the *bet midrash* on the mystery of the Tetragrammaton but was stopped by a certain old man (Pes. 50a). On Rava's death the academy at Maḥoza was divided in two, *Naḥman b. Isaac, the head of the **kallah* at Maḥoza, succeeding Rava as head of the academy there, while R. *Papa, a pupil of Rava, established one at Naresh.

Bibliography: Bacher, Pal Amor; Hyman, Toledot, s.v.; Ḥ. Albeck, *Mavo la-Talmudim* (1969), 374–6. [M.Be.]

RAVA, MAURIZIO (1878–after 1935), Italian colonial administrator and traveler. Born in Milan, Rava studied painting. Due to poor health he moved to warmer climates, traveling in Africa and Asia. He published his impressions in Italian magazines and geographical periodicals. In 1909 he founded *Il Carrocio,* a political literary periodical, staunchly supporting the new Italian Nationalist Party. Rava strongly advocated Italian colonial expansion. He served in the Libyan campaign and was decorated for valor. In 1927 Rava was appointed secretary-general of the Tripoli government and from 1932 to 1935 was governor of Italian Somaliland. Rava published many studies on Italian administration in Libya, East Africa, and Ethiopia. [Ed.]

RAVAYA (Ravalia, Ravaylla), family of courtiers in 13th-century Spain, originating from Gerona in Aragon. Its prominent members included Astrug Ravaya, bailiff of Gerona from 1276 to 1281. In the 1260s Astrug and his son Joseph (d. 1282) loaned large sums to King James I, and also farmed the royal revenues. Joseph was the treasurer of King Pedro the Great (1276–85). In the reign of Pedro's father, James I, Joseph had served as the infante's banker and for a time managed all the latter's property. From 1268 Joseph was bailiff of Besalú and from 1271 also of Gerona and district. Apart from the king and the infante, Joseph was the only person in the kingdom of Aragon whose functions enabled him to act in the three states of the crown (Aragon, Catalonia, and Valencia). The general local bailiffs as well as various other officials were all subordinated to his authority. Muça de *Portella, Aaron Abinafia, and Joseph's brother, Moses (see below), served under him as district commissioners, their functions being similar to those of the general bailiffs in later periods. As king's treasurer, Joseph had to supervise the royal accounts and manage the crown revenues. In 1279 he is mentioned by the title *thesaurarius* ("treasurer"). Joseph had a part in the appointment or dismissal of royal officials and often served Pedro in an advisory capacity. He accompanied the king at the siege of Balaguer against the rebel Catalonian nobles (1280) and during the campaign against Sicily (1282). Various state documents contain Joseph's signature in Hebrew and other administrative notes in this language.

Joseph's brother, Moses, headed the crown administration of Catalonia until his dismissal (before February 1283). In that year, when he was about to inherit his brother's office in charge of the three states of the kingdom, the king ordered that Moses' functions should be restricted to Catalonia only, while for the first time Christian officials were appointed to these posts in Aragon and Valencia. Moses also continued his activities under Alfonso III (1285–91), despite the laws of 1283 which barred Jews from holding public office in the kingdom.

Bibliography: Baer, Spain, index; *Sefarad,* index; D. Romano, *Los funcionarios judíos de Pedro el Grande de Aragón* (1970). [Ed.]

RAVEN (Heb. עוֹרֵב), bird. Mentioned in the Pentateuch among the unclean birds is "every raven after its kind" (Lev. 11:15). The reference is to the genus *Corvus* of which four species are found in Israel, three black (cf. Song 5:11) and one, very prevalent near inhabited areas, the hooded crow, *Corvus corone,* which has a gray back and belly and a black head and wings. It is commonly found in Jerusalem where it nests in high trees. Metal spikes were placed on the roof of the Temple to prevent ravens, undoubtedly attracted by the remains of sacrifices, from sitting on these (Mid. 4:6) and disturbing the Temple service with their raucous cries. These sounds are particularly strident during hot spells at the beginning of summer, when the "young ravens" leave the nest. Although already grown, the young are incapable of finding food, and since they have a voracious appetite their parents fly to and fro in search of food for them, the air being filled with their cries, and hence the description: "He giveth to the beast his food, and to the young ravens which cry" (Ps. 147:9). These young ravens cry, as it were, to God to satisfy their hunger, as it says in Job (38:41): "Who provideth for the raven his prey, when his young ones cry unto God . . . ?" The hooded crow is found in flocks which with great devotion defend their companions and especially the young, and hence the saying: "Three love one another, proselytes, slaves, and ravens" (Pes. 113b). The black raven, *Corvus corax,* preys on small animals and feeds on carcasses and corpses (cf. Prov. 30:17). Although folklore represents the raven as presaging evil (cf. Isa. 34:11), it is once mentioned in a favorable context, ravens having fed *Elijah when he hid in the brook *Cherith (I Kings 17:2–6). The raven is endowed with a highly developed sense of orientation, and in eastern countries mariners took with them ravens to direct them to dry land; the story of the raven in the ark (Gen. 8:7) is reminiscent of this.

Bibliography: Lewysohn, Zool, 172–5, nos. 205–8; F.S. Bodenheimer, *Animal and Man in Bible Lands* (1960), 57; J. Feliks, *Animal World of the Bible* (1962), 88. [J.F.]

RAVENNA, city in N. central Italy. There is evidence that a Jewish settlement existed in Ravenna in the third and fourth centuries, probably the earliest Jewish community in the region. Around the beginning of the sixth century Ravenna became the capital of the kingdom of the Ostrogoths under *Theodoric, who was well disposed toward the Jews. Thus in 519, after the Christian populace incited by the clergy burnt down the synagogue in Ravenna, Theodoric ordered that those responsible should pay compensation: persons who refused were to be publicly flogged. The early medieval Jewish community probably consisted of merchants engaged in overseas commerce. A number of Jews continued to reside there in the 13th century, after Ravenna had been displaced by the maritime power of Venice. The vigilance committee of the Italian Jewish communities met at Ravenna in 1443 to consider measures to counteract the restrictive papal bull recently issued. The original nucleus had by now been joined by loan-bankers, whose lucrative activities continued until 1492 when a public loan-bank (*Monti di Pietà) was opened. The previous year the synagogue had been destroyed by the populace incited by the preachings of the *Franciscans, and the Jews had been attacked. Since Ravenna was now under the sovereignty of the Church, the anti-Jewish regulations issued by the popes in the second half of the 16th century were all enforced, and the Talmud was burned in 1553. In 1569, when Pope *Pius V ordered the Jews to leave the minor centers of the Papal States, the Jews were expelled from Ravenna. Thirty loan-bankers returned following the concessions made by *Sixtus V in 1587. In 1593, the Jews were again expelled by Clement VIII.

Bibliography: L. Ruggini, *Ebrei e orientali nell'Italia settentrionale . . .* (= *Studia et Documenta Historiae et Juris,* 25 (1959), 186–308), index; A. Balletti, *Gli ebrei e gli Estensi* (1930²), 18ff.; Roth, Italy, index; Milano, Italia, index; Loevinson, in: REJ, 94 (1933), 173–5. [A.To.]

RAVENSBRUECK, Nazi concentration camp for women. This camp, the only one of its kind, was located near Fuerstenberg in Mecklenburg (today East Germany). Its construction by prisoners from *Sachsenhausen, begun in the fall of 1938, was completed in the spring of 1939. The first camp commandant, Max Koegel, was replaced in 1942 by Fritz Suhren, who remained in charge until the evacuation of the camp (April 30, 1945). The key posts were held by men, but the *SS staff was mostly female and excelled in its cruel treatment of the inmates. On May 15, 1939 the first prisoner transport arrived from Lichtenburg, formerly a concentration camp for women. The women were "Bibelforscher" (Jehovah's Witnesses) or criminals. On May 18, 1939, 867 women, some of whom were political prisoners (some Jewish), arrived from Germany and Austria. In the summer of 1939 a transport of gypsies arrived from Austria. After the outbreak of World War II, thousands of Polish women (many with their children) and Czech women were imprisoned in Ravensbrueck. Later on other prisoners came, especially resistance fighters from all over Europe. The outbreak of the war brought about a swift deterioration in living conditions due to overcrowding, malnutrition, and hard labor. A clothing industry, especially for furs, operated in the camp. In 1941 the sick prisoners were included in the *Euthanasiaaktion* involving the killing of the mentally ill. The steadily growing death rate was caused by overwork and deteriorating living conditions. In the fall of 1944 a gas chamber was constructed (until then prisoners had been sent for gassing to other camps). Ravensbrueck prisoners served as guinea pigs for pseudomedical experiments carried out by the *Auschwitz physicians, August Horst and Karl Clauberg. The surviving victims were cripples for life. The rising number of Jewish inmates were concentrated in a special Jewish block, where the worst living conditions prevailed. In October 1942 all Jewish prisoners were sent to Auschwitz or *Majdanek. In the summer of 1944 Hungarian Jewish women arrived, followed later by others from other camps. Due to the intervention of Himmler's favorite, the Finnish Dr. Kersten, and of the representatives of the World Jewish Congress in Sweden, together with the activities of *Bernadotte, on April 21 Himmler gave his consent to release thousands of women from Ravensbrueck and two other camps nearby. They were transferred by the Red Cross to Sweden and Denmark. Among them were at least 1,000 Jewish women. This rescue action had been decisively influenced by the personal intervention of Norbert Masur, a member of the Swedish section of the World Jewish Congress, who flew with Kersten to Berlin on April 19 and conferred with Himmler in a meeting arranged by Kersten, during the night of April 20 to 21. With the approach of the Soviet army, evacuation of Ravensbrueck was ordered by *Himmler. Up to this time, 132,000 women and children had passed through the camp, of whom 92,000 succumbed to camp conditions. The camp ceased to exist on April 30, 1945.

Bibliography: W. Machlejd (ed.), *Experimental Operations on Prisoners of Ravensbrueck Concentration Camp* (1960); M. Buber-Neumann, *Under Two Dictators* (1950), passim; IMT, *Trial of the Major War Criminals*, 23 (1949), index s.v. *concentration camps;* E. N. Masur, *En Jude Talar med Himmler* (1945); L. Yahil, in: *Yad Vashem Studies*, 6 (1967), 210–20; E. Buchmann (ed.), *Die Frauen von Ravensbrueck* (1959); D. Dufournier, *Ravensbrueck: the Women's Camp of Death* (1948); M. Maurel, *An Ordinary Camp* (1958); *Ravensbrueck: German Concentration Camp for Women* (1961). [Y.Re.]

RAVENSBURG, city in Wuerttemberg, W. Germany. A Jewish community existed there in the first half of the 14th century and had a synagogue. From 1330 to 1343 ten Jews are listed in the burgher rolls, including a rabbi or teacher (referred to as Ysak *scholasticus*) and a miller. The Jewish *oath (a brief dignified formula) was administered in the synagogue. The Jews' street was near the northern wall. During the *Black Death persecutions the Jews fled to the imperial bailiff's castle, where most of them were burned to death by the populace early in 1349. A survivor was admitted as a burgher in *Esslingen in 1385. Jews again appear in Ravensburg in 1380; in 1385 two Jewish masons are mentioned. In 1427 a Jew was imprisoned on charges of forgery but released upon proving his innocence. In 1429, when a young lay brother's body was found hanging from a tree in a nearby wood, two Jewish couples, one of them with their son, were accused of murder and imprisoned; they made a public declaration of innocence, which was signed by the Swabian imperial bailiff, his deputy, and others. However, the social unrest in the area caused the *blood libel to spread, and Jews in the communities on Lake *Constance were also arrested. In 1430 the imprisoned Jews in Ravensburg were burned to death and the rest banished from the city. The decision was reaffirmed by King Ferdinand I in 1588. Both King Sigismund II at the end of 1430 and Bishop Henry of Constance in 1441 vigorously opposed attempts to venerate the dead boy. Nevertheless, in local tradition the blood libel fable prevailed, as crystalized in a chronicle written c. 1770.

In the 18th century some Jews attended fairs held in Ravensburg, and by 1835 a few Jews had moved to the city. They numbered 44 in 1900 and 28 between 1925 and 1933. Of these 12 emigrated, five moved elsewhere, and 13 were deported to death camps in Eastern Europe in 1941–42. There were 32 liberated Jewish survivors of the Holocaust living in Ravensburg by 1947–48; 17 Jews remained by 1965. In 1968 eight Jews were affiliated with the *Stuttgart community.

Bibliography: M. Stern, in: ZGJD, 1 (1887), 301 (15a), 303 (2), 307 (16); 7 (n.s. 1937), 248; *Der Israelit*, 50, nos. 30, 31, 33 (1909); H. Maor, *Ueber den Wiederaufbau der juedischen Gemeinden in Deutschland seit 1945* (1961), 59; A. Dreher, in: *Wuerttembergisches Staedtebuch* (1962), 407; idem, in: *Zeitschrift fuer Wuerttembergische Landeskunde*, 12 (1962), 453–5; P. Sauer (ed.), *Dokumente ueber die Verfolgung der juedischen Bevoelkerung in Baden-Wuerttemberg 1933–1945* (1966), index; Stadtarchiv Ravensburg: Urkunden nos. 943, 945. Reportorium, vol. 2, 92d, 864f., 23a; Germ Jud, 2 (1968), 676–8. [T.O.]

RAVIKOVITCH, DALIA (1936–), Hebrew poet, writer, and translator. Born in Ramat Gan, she first published poems in *Orlogin*. Subsequently her poems as well as articles on literature and art appeared in various newspapers and journals in Israel.

Her volumes of poetry include *Ahavat Tappu'aḥ ha-Zahav* (1959, 1963²); *Ḥoref Kasheh* (1964, 1967²); *Dalia Ravikovitch; Mivḥar Shirim u-Devarim al Yeẓiratah* (1962), a collection of poems with an introduction by Dan Zelkah; and *Ha-Sefer ha-Shelishi* (1969). She wrote a number of children's books, including *Mekhonit ha-Kesamim* (1959); *Mi-Sippurei Ḥevrat ha-Lev ha-Ammiẓ* (1961); *Mikhah u-Mekhabbei ha-Esh* (1962); and *Mesibbah Mishpaḥtit* (1968), which contains some of her own poetry and that of her father, Levi Ravikovitch. She also translated several children's books into Hebrew.

Bibliography: R. Gurfein, *Mi-Karov u-me-Raḥok* (1964), 247–50; A. Cohen, *Soferim Ivriyyim Benei Zemannenu* (1964), 296–7; G. Yardeni-Agmon, in: *Haaretz* (Jan. 30, 1970), 14–15.

RAVINA (abbreviation of **Rav Avina**), the name of several Babylonian *amoraim*, some of whom are mentioned with their patronymics and some without. At times it is difficult to identify the particular Ravina. The two best known are: Ravina I (d. 422), who studied under Rava (Ber. 20b; 38a, et al.), and also maintained contact with Rava's other pupils, Naḥman b. Isaac, Papa, and Huna b. Joshua (Pes. 105a; BM 74b; Sanh. 69a). He had frequent discussions with R. Ashi, who was his junior. He attended his academy in *Mata Meḥasya and referred to himself as a pupil-colleague of Ashi (Er. 63a; et al.). He gave rulings on various occasions (Er. 40a, 63a). The statement, "Ravina and R. Ashi conclude the [authoritative] teaching [of the Talmud]" (BM 86a), may refer to him (Ravina's name occurs before that of Ashi in many manuscripts and early sources; see bibl., *Sinai Sefer Yovel,* 60, n. 6). He was renowned for his devotion to study and it was said of him that "he made nights as days in study of the Torah" (MK 25b; see Dik. Sof., *ibid.*). He had a son and daughter (BM 104b; Nid. 66a), and lived to an advanced age (*"Seder Tanna'im ve-Amora'im"* in *Maḥzor Vitry,* p. 483). Lavish eulogies were delivered at his death (MK 25a).

Ravina II (d. 499), Ravina b. Huna, apparently a nephew of Ravina I (Ket. 100b). His father, who was a scholar since he transmitted sayings of R. Papi (Ned. 90a) and of R. Joseph (Ned. 60b), died while Ravina was still young and his mother reported some of his father's customs in a number of *halakhot* that were in dispute (Ber. 39b; Men. 68b). Maremar was his main teacher and Ravina frequently discussed halakhic problems with him (Shab. 81b; et al.). Ravina served as *dayyan* in Mata Meḥasya and helped Ashi's daughter collect the portion of her father's property that was her due from the property of her brother Mar (Ket. 69a). On the death of Rabbah Tosfa'ah in 474, Ravina succeeded him as head of the academy of Sura (*Iggeret R. Sherira Ga'on,* ed. by B. W. Lewin (1921), 95; and see Abraham ibn Daud, *Sefer ha-Kabbalah—Book of Tradition,* ed. by G. D. Cohen, 1942). During that period the Babylonian government issued harsh decrees against the Jewish community; synagogues were closed and Jewish children compelled to apostasize (*Iggeret R. Sherira Ga'on,* p. 97). According to Sherira Gaon it is this Ravina who together with Ashi "concluded the teaching" (see above). The death of Ravina marks the end of the era of *amoraim* in Babylonia and the beginning of the age of the *savoraim.*

Bibliography: Halevy, Dorot, 2 (1923), 536–51; 3 (1923), 74–85; Hyman, Toledot s.v.; B. M. Lewin, *Rabbanan Savora'im ve-Talmudam* (1937), 2–6; S. Albeck, in: *Sinai Sefer Yovel* (1958), 57ff.; Ḥ. Albeck, *ibid.,* 73 ff. [M.Be./Y.D.G.]

RAVITCH, MELECH (pseudonym of **Zekharye Khone Bergner;** 1893–), Yiddish poet and essayist. Born in Radymno, East Galicia, Ravitch left his home at 14, and lived in various cities, including, for long periods, Vienna and Warsaw. In 1941 he settled in Montreal.

Ravitch's earliest lyrics appeared in *Oyf der Shvel* (1912). His *Spinoza* (1918) is a tribute to the philosopher whom he ranked with Moses and Jesus. In Vienna he felt the impact of expressionistic poets such as F. *Werfel and E. *Lasker-Schueler and began to experiment with expressionistic technique. In his *Nakete Lider* ("Naked Songs," 1921), he gave up rhyme, regular metric lines, and stanzas.

Impressed by the Yiddish revival in postwar Poland, he settled in Warsaw in 1921. There he joined Uri Ẓevi *Greenberg and Peretz *Markish, a triumvirate branded the *Khaliastre ("Gang"), in the struggle against realism in art. Ravitch reached the climax of his expressionistic striving in his *"Dos Gezang tsum Mentshlekhn Kerper," "Gezang tsu der Zun," "Dos Gezang fun Has un Libe tsum Yidishn Folk"* and *"Efntlekher Mishpet Ibern Toyt."* All four, having appeared in periodicals, were published in book form: *Di Fir Zaytn fun Mayn Velt* (1929). Ravitch's retreat from expressionism was reflected in the song and ballads of *Kontinentn un Okeanen* (1937), a volume which embodied his moods and experiences of the restless decade that preceded his two years at Melbourne (1936–37). Instead of trying to shock and mystify his readers, he aimed at maximum clarity. He proclaimed himself a citizen of the world, a poet beyond nationalism.

Melech Ravitch, Yiddish poet and essayist. Courtesy Y. Bergner, Tel Aviv.

In 1946 he and his brother H. *Bergner published the memoirs of their family as recorded by their mother Hinde Bergner (1870–1942) on the eve of World War II. *Di Lider fun Mayne Lider* (incl. bibl.) was published in 1954. In Montreal he served as a catalyst of Yiddish literary, educational, and cultural activities. There he completed four additional volumes of verse as well as a volume of essays, two autobiographic volumes *Dos Mayse-Bukh fun Mayn Lebn* (1962–64), and three encyclopedic volumes on Yiddish writers, *Mayn Leksikon* (1945–58).

Bibliography: Rejzen Leksikon, 4 (1929), 84–90; I. Biletzki, *Essays on Yiddish Poetry and Prose Writers* (1969), 147–58; A. Tabachnik, *Dikhter un Dikhtung* (1965), 339–49; S. Liptzin, *Maturing of Yiddish Literature* (1970), 142–9. [S.L.]

RAVITZ, SHELOMO (c. 1885–), *ḥazzan* and composer. Born in Novogrudok, Russia, Ravitz studied music from the age of 15 and received his diploma in Vienna. He officiated in various European communities, including Riga, and in Johannesburg before moving to Ereẓ Israel in 1932. He became *ḥazzan* of the Ohel Shem Synagogue in Tel Aviv and his reputation spread through his singing together with his own choir, at the weekly *oneg shabbat* organized there by Ḥ. N. *Bialik. He subsequently became *ḥazzan* of the Tel Aviv Great Synagogue, where his expressive, yet unexaggerated, style of singing brought him admiration and popularity. As director of the Selah Seminary for *ḥazzanim,* Ravitz was the teacher of many present-day *ḥazzanim.*

His compositions and arrangements of traditional melodies were published in *Yalkut Zemirot* (1954) and *Kol Yisrael,* 2 vols. (1964), edited by M. S. Geshuri. Ravitz also edited the music section in each volume of Y. L. Baruch and Y. T. Levinsky (eds.), *Sefer ha-Mo'adim,* 8 vols. (1946–67), which serves as a popular source of Jewish musical tradition in Israel homes and schools.

Bibliography: M. S. Geshuri (ed.), *Kol Yisrael,* 1 (1954), xxii–xxv; idem, in: *Dukhan,* 3 (1962), 31–38; *Yedi'ot ha-Makhon ha-Yisre'eli le-Musikah Datit,* 5 (1963), 23–25; S. Samet, in: *Haaretz* (April 10, 1970), 18. [D.L.M.O.]

RAWICZ (Ger. **Rawitsch**), town in Poznan province, W. Poland. The first settlement of Jews in Rawicz took place soon after the founding of the town in 1639. In 1648 complaints were lodged against Jewish merchants who were then expelled. They returned soon thereafter, only to be expelled again in 1674. By 1698 an organized community was in existence and in 1719 it received a *Freibrief* ("letter of privileges") regulating the rights and taxes of its members. By then the community totaled 12 families. A *ḥevra kaddisha* was founded in 1728 and the first rabbi, Menahem Mendel Gradenwitz, was appointed in 1755. Its *bet din* was headed by learned talmudic authorities, including R. Solomon b. Dov Baer (1786–93), later to be the community's rabbi. In 1774 a *bet midrash* was founded. Services were held in a private house until a synagogue was built in 1783. The community (35 families in 1739) flourished, and after a fire in *Leszno (1790) absorbed many refugees, including R. Akiva *Eger, who lived there for one year. The local Jews were mainly shopkeepers, tailors, livestock merchants, and artisans. In 1797 the community had 198 families, and by 1835 there were 401 families (a total of 1,574 persons, or about 50% of the total population). A new synagogue was built in 1889 when the community was at its economic peak and served by a long line of scholarly rabbis, including its last one, the scholar John Cohn (1893–1920). The Jewish population subsequently declined to 363 in 1905. The town suffered during World War I, and under Polish rule the community was subjected to discrimination which induced many to leave for Germany; only 15 remained in 1933. The cemetery and synagogue were both destroyed by the Nazis during World War II. Markus *Brann, the historian, and Arthur *Ruppin, the Zionist leader, were both born in Rawicz.

Ark of the Law of the Rawicz synagogue, built in 1889 and destroyed by the Nazis during World War II. Courtesy Israel Museum Photo Archives, Jerusalem.

Bibliography: J. Cohn, *Geschichte der juedischen Gemeinde Rawitsch* (1915); A. B. Posner, *The Annals of the Community of Rawitsch* (Heb. and Eng., 1962). [Ed.]

RAWIDOWICZ, SIMON (1897–1957), Hebrew writer and thinker. Born near Bialystok, Poland, Rawidowicz received a traditional Jewish education in the house of his father who was a fervent Zionist. From 1919 he lived and studied in Berlin. From 1933 on he resided in London, and in 1941 became professor of Jewish philosophy at Leeds University, England; in 1947 he left for the United States where he taught first at the College of Jewish Studies at Chicago and then headed the Department of Near Eastern and Judaic Studies at Brandeis University. He was noted as an editor,

Simon Rawidowicz, Hebrew writer and scholar. Courtesy Dr. Esther Rawidowicz, Waltham, Mass.

historian of Jewish thought, philosopher of Jewish history, and teacher. During the 1920s he founded the publishing house Ayanot which issued a number of Hebrew texts, some of which he edited; became coeditor of the Hebrew periodical **Ha-Tekufah;* and edited volume 7 of the projected new edition of the writings of Moses Mendelssohn. In 1941, during the darkest hours of World War II, he founded the Ararat Publishing Society of London, as an affirmation of faith in the future of Hebrew literature in the Diaspora. He published and edited seven volumes (in five books) of the scholarly and literary Hebrew miscellany *Metsudah* and also a Festschrift, *Sefer Shimon Dubnov* (1954) in memory of the historian *Dubnow.

In his role as historian of Jewish thought, he published his edition of Naḥman *Krochmal's major work accompanied by a lengthy study of Krochmal's life and thought. He also wrote extensively on medieval and modern Jewish philosophy. In the field of general philosophy his *Ludwig Feuerbachs Philosophie: Ursprung und Schicksal* appeared in 1931 (rep. 1964). From the 1920s on, Rawidowicz concentrated on the idea of the unity of the Jewish people, both in Palestine and in the Diaspora. He objected to the ideology of the negation of the Diaspora, and formulated the idea of partnership between the Jewish state and the Jewish people in the Diaspora. In his *Bavel vi-Yrushalayim* (1957) he elaborated his conception of Jewish history and considered the impact of the founding of the State of Israel on modern Jewish history.

Bibliography: S. Rawidowicz, *Iyyunim be-Maḥashevet Yisrael*, ed. by B. Ravid, 1 (1969), incl. bibl. and biography, 2 (1971). [L.V.B.]

RAWNITZKI, YEHOSHUA ḤANA (1859–1944), Hebrew journalist and publisher. Born in Odessa, Rawnitzki began his journalistic career—in which he continued for most of his life—in 1879, by contributing first to *Ha-Kol*, and then to other periodicals. His articles, first in Hebrew and later in Yiddish, were largely the result of his activities in the *Ḥibbat Zion movement. He was the editor and publisher of the literary collection *Pardes* (3 vols., 1892–96), a forum for the outstanding Hebrew writers of the time and a forerunner of **Ha-Shilo'aḥ*. With his publication of Ḥ. N. *Bialik's first poem, *"El ha-Ẓippor,"* in *Pardes*, Rawnitzki became Bialik's first patron, thus initiating a lifelong association with the poet. Some of his own works appeared in *Pardes* and subsequently in *Ha-Shilo'aḥ*, as well as other periodicals. Special recognition was aroused by a series of feuilletons, *"Kevurat Soferim"* ("The Burial of Writers"), which were written with Shalom Aleichem under the pseudonyms of Eldad (Shalom Aleichem) and Medad (Rawnitzki). As a result of his teaching experience and interest in pedagogical problems, he established the Moriah

Yehoshua Ḥana Rawnitzki (right), Hebrew journalist and publisher, with Ḥayyim Naḥman Bialik. Jerusalem, J.N.U.L., Schwadron Collection.

publishing house in Odessa in 1901, together with S. *Ben-Zion and Bialik, having influenced the latter to move to Odessa. The publishing house, the first of his joint endeavors with Bialik, began with the publication of textbooks (e.g., *Sippurei ha-Mikra,* 1903–05), followed by the influential aggadic anthology *Sefer ha-Aggadah* (1908–11), and many other books. This partnership between the two continued until the poet's death. Bialik frequently complained that Rawnitzki's role was not sufficiently appreciated. Settling in Ereẓ Israel in 1921, Rawnitzki, together with Bialik and S. *Levin, founded the Devir publishing house, where he published the works on which he and Bialik had co-operated (e.g., the commentary on the poems of Moses *ibn Ezra and Solomon ibn *Gabirol).

Later, he published *Dor ve-Soferav* (2 vols., 1926–37), a collection of his articles and memoirs on Bialik, Mendele Mokher Seforim, and other writers of his time, and *Mikhtavim le-Vat Yisrael* (2nd ed., 1923), on educational problems. A collection of his articles, *Be-Sha'arei Sefer* (1961), was published by S. Kremer, together with a comprehensive introduction by the editor. Rawnitzki also published Yiddish books and edited various Yiddish periodicals.

Bibliography: Kressel, Leksikon, 2 (1967), 828–9. [G.K.]

RAY, MAN (1890–), French photographer and painter. Ray is known as a founder of the dadaist-surrealist movement in painting, and in photography circles he is famous for his abstract prints made in the darkroom without a camera, to which he gave the name of "Rayograph."

Ray added beams and moving pencils of light to the original technique of spreading objects on photographic sensitized papers which were exposed and then developed. He also contributed other facets to creative photography, making effective use of solarization by giving a momentary second exposure to his negative before developing it. The prints he produced from film treated this way showed strong secondary black lines along the major contours of the subject. Ray's portfolio of portraits records the celebrities of the 1920s. Ray fled from France in 1940 on the Nazi invasion and went to Hollywood where he remained for the duration of World War II, after which he returned to Paris. His autobiography, *Self Portrait* (1963), explains a great deal of his artistry and his personality.

Bibliography: *Current Biography Yearbook 1965* (1965), 336–8; J. I. H. Baur (ed.), *New Art in America* (1957), 88–91. [P.P.]

°**RAYMOND de PENAFORTE** (d. 1275), Dominican monk, one of the initiators of anti-Jewish activities in Catalonia during the reign of James I (1213–76). Raymond was born in Peñaforte, Catalonia, and studied law at the University of Bologna, completing his studies in 1216. In 1222 he founded the Dominican monastery of Barcelona. He was a favorite of Pope *Gregory IX and, among other duties, he served as the Pope's confessor beginning in 1230. When the heresy of the *Albigenses spread to northern Catalonia from Provence, Raymond influenced the king of Aragon to establish the Papal *Inquisition in the district of *Tarragona. As initiator of missionary activities in his order, he made great efforts to convert Jews to Christianity, founding Hebrew and Arabic schools for this purpose. He was the moving spirit of the anti-Jewish legislation of James I in 1228. He was also among the initiators and most prominent participants of the *Barcelona disputation of 1263. The accusation before the royal tribunal of Barcelona against *Naḥmanides, in 1265, that he had "blasphemed Christianity," was also instigated by Raymond and the Christian anti-Jewish literature written after the disputation of Barcelona was a product of his school. He was canonized in 1601.

Bibliography: Baer, Spain, 1 (1961), 152, 156f., 161; F. Valls-Taberner, *San Ramón de Penyafort* (1953), incl. bibl., 372–80. [Ed.]

RAYNAL, DAVID (1841 – 1903), French politician. Born in Paris, Raynal founded the firm of Astruc and Raynal in Bordeaux in 1862 and there made the acquaintance of the French leader, Léon Gambetta. He was elected deputy for Bordeaux in 1879 and two years later became minister of works in the government of Gambetta. From 1883 to 1885 Raynal was again minister of public works, from 1893 to 1894 he was minister of the interior. While in office he was accused of underhand dealings in his handling of the railways, but his successful libel action against the journal *La Cocarde* in 1893 cleared him of all suspicion. He was made a senator in 1897 and was president of a commission to reform the merchant navy. [S.C.]

RAYNER, ISIDOR (1850–1912), U.S. lawyer and politician. Rayner was born in Baltimore, where his Bavarian immigrant father William Solomon Rayner had been one of the founders of the Har Sinai Congregation. He studied law at the University of Virginia and was admitted to the Baltimore bar in 1870. After several years of legal practice he entered Democratic Party politics and was elected to the Maryland state legislature in 1878 and to the state senate in 1885. In 1886 he was elected to the first of three terms in the U.S. House of Representatives, and after serving a term as Maryland attorney general (1899–1903), he was elected to the U.S. Senate in 1904 and again in 1910. Politically, Rayner was a moderate liberal. While still in the state legislature, he was a vigorous opponent of Negro disenfranchisement laws and Jim Crow, and his 1904 senatorial campaign was undertaken in defiance of the corrupt Democratic machine. In the Senate Rayner was particularly active on the Foreign Relations Committee, which he used as a forum to eloquently criticize President Theodore Roosevelt's imperialist policies toward Latin America. He also helped lead successful Senate efforts to abrogate the treaty with Russia in 1911 in protest against czarist anti-Semitism and discrimination against U.S. Jewish travelers. A nominal member of his father's congregation, Rayner married a Christian and was buried in a Unitarian ceremony. [H.H.]

RAYSS, TSCHARNA (1890–1965), Israel botanist. Born in Vinnitsa, Russia, Rayss was in charge of research at the department of botany at the universities of Odessa and Bucharest, 1918–29, and deputy director of the phytopathology department of the Institute for Agricultural Research, Rumania. An enthusiastic Zionist she joined the newly formed botany department of the Hebrew University in Jerusalem in 1934 and was appointed professor in 1951.

Her research on the lower plants dealt with the taxonomy and ecology of algae of the Mediterranean and the Red Sea; mycoflora of Israel; taxonomy and biology of fungi in Rumania, France, and Israel, with special emphasis on their pathogenicity to crops and wild plants. She built up the herbarium and library of cryptogamic plants in the Hebrew University.

Bibliography: Viennot Bourgin, in: *Bulletin de la Société Mycologique de France,* 81 no. 2 (1965), 113–5. [SHI.B.]

RAZA RABBA, SEFER (Aram. סֵפֶר רָזָא רַבָּא; "The Book of the Great Secret"), a work of *Merkabah mysticism which is no longer extant as a separate entity. That it existed, however, cannot be doubted. Several Near Eastern, Palestinian, and Babylonian authors of the ninth, tenth, and 11th centuries who attest to its existence were discovered by Jacob Mann (Mann, Texts, 2 (1935), 74–83). In the polemical works of the leading Karaite sage of Jerusalem, *Daniel b. Moses al-Qumisi (late ninth century), the work is described as having magical content. Another Karaite author writes about the magical acts described in the book: "for love and hate, miraculous shortcuts, and questions in dreams." *Raza Rabba* is also mentioned in a responsum of *Hai Gaon (B. M. Lewin (ed.), *Oẓar ha-Ge'onim,* on *Ḥagigah* (1931), 21). In *Sefer Raza Rabba* magical content is intertwined with an exposition on the Merkabah, including speculations on the names of angels and demons known from magical literature on oaths, formulations of amulets by Babylonian Arabs from the fifth to eighth centuries, and *gematriot* which afterward passed on to the *Ḥasidei Ashkenaz.

Raza Rabba differs in character from Midrashim written in France and in Narbonne and apparently derived from an Eastern or Babylonian source which reached Germany and groups of Ḥasidim. However, it is not clear whether either *Judah he-Ḥasid or *Eleazar of Worms knew the work.

Portions of *Raza Rabba* were found in a manuscript of a commentary on *Sefer *Shi'ur Komah* written in the late 13th century by Moses (Azriel) b. Eleazar ha-Darshan ("the preacher"), son of Moses ha-Darshan (the husband of Judah b. Samuel he-Ḥasid's granddaughter in Wuerzburg), and have been published by G. *Scholem. Moses cites a work which he calls *Ha-Sod ha-Gadol* ("The Great Secret") and quotes other works which leave no doubt that he saw several versions of *Raza Rabba* or parts of it; he cites *Sefer ha-*Bahir* as a separate source.

In contrast to extant visionary Merkabah texts, *Raza Rabba* was a Merkabah Midrash and some elements in it are clearly and unquestionably linked to *Sefer ha-Bahir,* although they appear in different versions. While *Raza Rabba* contains no definitely Gnostic homilies, the *Sefer ha-Bahir* develops the same motifs in a new direction, a kabbalistic-Gnostic one. *Sefer ha-Bahir* contains the oldest enumeration of the ten *Sefirot* interpreted kabbalistically; an older, though incomplete, list is found in *Raza Rabba,* which was one of the literary sources for the editing of the *Bahir.* The homiletic symbolism of the *Sefirot* developed in the *Bahir* does not occur in *Raza Rabba.* Other matters treated in the *Bahir,* such as **gilgul,* are not present in the extant portions of *Raza Rabba.*

Bibliography: G. Scholem, *Reshit ha-Kabbalah* (1948), 195–238; idem, *Ursprung und Anfaenge der Kabbala* (1962), 94–109. [E.Z.]

RAZIEL, an important angel who, according to his name, is connected with "the mysteries of God." In midrashic and magical literature he is mentioned only in sources going back to the esoteric teachings of the talmudic period, where he appears in three sources. When Moses is ascending to heaven in order to receive the Torah, he encounters on his way the angel Galliẓur ("he who reveals the hidden reasons of the Rock"; i.e., God), who is also called Raziel because he hears from behind the divine curtain all that is going to happen in the world, and this he reveals to Elijah, who "spreads the voice" over all the world. The angel Raziel also appeared to Adam three days after he had been expelled from paradise and had fallen into despair. Then Raziel revealed to him a magical textbook containing the mysteries of the workings of creation. This version of an old esoteric *aggadah* was incorporated into a collection of cosmological and angelological material culled mainly from the writings of *Eliezer b. Isaac of Worms and some other 13th-century kabbalists, and published in Amsterdam in 1701 under the title, "This is the book of the first Adam which the angel Raziel delivered to him," commonly called *"Sefer Razi'el"* (see below). It had a wide circulation, being reprinted nearly 40 times. The third source is the apocryphal *Sefer ha-*Razim,* known in manuscript form in post-talmudic times. This purported to be the book of mysteries which the angel Raziel taught to Noah in the year he entered the ark and which Noah later wrote down on tablets of sapphire. It is a handbook of magic, both Jewish and syncretistic, giving a detailed account of the angels in the seven heavens and the magical practices connected with them and their conjuration. Whereas the first part is of a strictly Jewish character, the magical practices contain strong pagan elements. In the opinion of the editor, Mordecai Margalioth (1966), the text goes back to the talmudic period, perhaps even to the earlier part, especially because of its close connection with some texts in the Greek magical papyri. The age of the book is still a matter of controversy. According to the Zohar, Adam received his book while he was still in paradise, and the angel Raziel was none other than the archangel *Uriel who revealed the deep mysteries of the Torah. The numerical value of the Hebrew name is 248, corresponding to the number of the positive commandments of the Torah and the name Abraham. The kabbalist Abraham b. Samuel *Abulafia used this name as a pseudonym in several of his books.

Bibliography: M. Margalioth, *Sefer ha-Razim* (a newly recovered book of magic from the talmudic period) (1966[0]); M. Schwab, *Vocabulaire de l'angélologie* (1897), 246; R. Margalioth, *Malakhei Elyon* (1945), 280–2; J. Dan, in: Tarbiz, 37 (1967/68), 208–14; F. Secret, in: REJ, 128 (1969), 223–45.

[G.SCH.]

RAZIEL, BOOK OF, collection of mystical, cosmological, and magical Hebrew works and portions of works. First printed in Amsterdam in 1701, it was reprinted many times, because of the popular belief that the book protected its owner's home from fire and other dangers. There are some manuscripts of, at least, parts of this work which date back to the 16th century. However, in its printed form, it was not compiled much earlier than the 17th century. Many manuscript collections of material of the same sort are extant, and *Raziel* is not unique among them in any way. The material included in the collection can be divided into three distinct categories or strata:

(1) Works, or parts of works, which belong to *Heikhalot* and *Merkabah mysticism, the mystical and cosmological literature of the talmudic and geonic periods. Of these, *Raziel* contains a version of the *Sefer ha-Malbush,* a magical work; *baraita* of *Ma'aseh Bereshit,* a cosmological and astrological description of the Creation, which has some mystical overtones; and a major part of the *Sefer ha-Razim* ("Book of Magical Secrets"), which is a collection of magical formulas and angelological material from talmudic times. The introduction to *Sefer ha-*Razim* probably gave the whole collection its name. In this introduction, the angel Raziel is claimed to have revealed the secrets described to Adam. In this category, there is some importance to

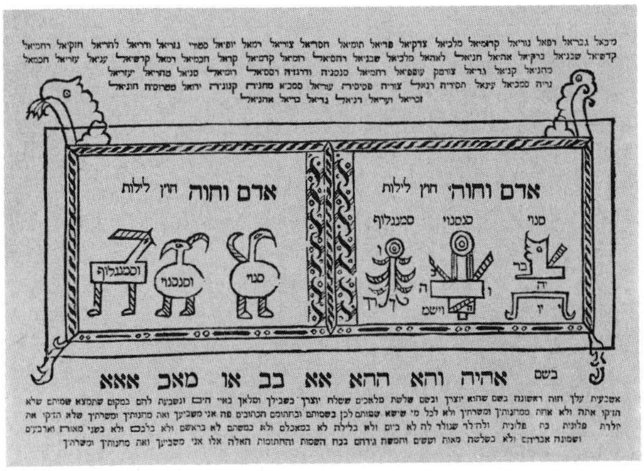

Page from the *Book of Raziel* with an illustration of an amulet to be worn by pregnant women. Amsterdam, 1701.

a long version of the early anthropomorphic work, the **Shi'ur Komah,* describing the members and secret names of the Creator. (2) Material which belongs to literature of the 13th-century *Ḥasidei Ashkenaz. To this category belong the introduction and the first half of *Eleazar of Worms' work, *Sod Ma'aseh Bereshit* ("The Secret of the Creation"), which formed the first part of his *Sodei Rezaya.* Some exegetical works on the Holy Names of God, and some magical formulas which conclude the collection, also belong to the literary heritage of the Ḥasidei Ashkenaz. (3) A few portions of kabbalistic literature, descriptions of the *Sefirot* and exegeses of Holy Names, mostly reflecting kabbalistic theology of pre-Lurianic periods. A critical analysis of the work by Elyakim Melsack (Milzahagi) is preserved in a manuscript in Jews' College, London.

Bibliography: M. Margalioth, *Sefer ha-Razim* (1966), introduction; J. Dan, *Torat ha-Sod shel Ḥasidei Ashkenaz* (1968), 83, 208.

[Y.D.]

RAZIEL, DAVID (1910–1941), commander of the *Irgun Ẓeva'i Le'ummi (I.Ẓ.L.). Born in Smorgon, near Vilna, Raziel was taken to Ereẓ Israel at the age of three by his parents. From an early age he displayed literary ability, writing essays and plays on biblical themes. During the 1929 Arab riots he joined the *Haganah, becoming one of the first members of the I.Ẓ.L., which seceded from the Haganah in 1931. He soon became known as a gifted instructor and leader and produced manuals of military instruction. About a year after the first split in I.Ẓ.L. (1937), he became commander of the organization, and during that tense year led it in its reprisal activities against the Arabs. On May 19, 1939 he was captured by the British authorities, and sent to a prison camp, from which he was re-

David Raziel, commander of the Irgun Ẓevai Le'ummi. Courtesy Shoshana Raziel, Jerusalem.

leased at the end of October as a result of the outbreak of World War II and the I.Ẓ.L.'s readiness to cooperate in the war effort against the Axis. He continued to serve as commander of the I.Ẓ.L. and leader of *Betar in Palestine even after the June 1940 split in I.Ẓ.L. On May 17, 1941, in cooperation with British Army intelligence, he led a group of I.Ẓ.L. members to Ḥabbāniyya, Iraq, to sabotage the oil depots on the outskirts of Baghdad, which were serving the German Luftwaffe; but on May 20 in a German bombing attack the car in which he was traveling was hit and he and a British officer were killed. Buried in the British military cemetery at Ḥabbāniyya, his remains were transferred to Nicosia, Cyprus, in 1955 and finally interred on Mount Herzl in Jerusalem in 1961. Ramat Raziel, a moshav in the Judean Mountains, is named after him.

Bibliography: S. Katz, *Days of Fire* (1968), index; Jabotinsky Institute in Israel, *David Raziel* (Heb., 1956); D. Niv, *Ma'arekhot ha-Irgun ha-Ẓeva'i ha-Le'ummi,* 3 (1967), index; Dinur, Haganah, 2 pt. 3 (1963), index.

[D.N.]

RAZIM, SEFER HA- (Heb. סֵפֶר הָרָזִים; "Book of Secrets"), early work of Jewish mystical literature. *Sefer ha-Razim* is remarkable for its systematic treatment of magic, witchcraft, incantations, and supernatural remedies, on which no special works have otherwise been preserved in Hebew literature. In the midst of deliberations on the angels, their names, and their functions in the six heavens which precede the supreme heaven, the book interweaves about 30 magical counsels for suppliants—who might include those seeking to know the future, to sway the hearts of the great, to have their enemies overtaken by misfortune, to be healed, to have their dreams interpreted, to overcome an enemy or a wild animal, to see the sun during the day or the night, or to speak with the moon and the stars. The general contents of this work have long been known, especially from the extracts scattered in *Sefer *Razi'el,* but most of its magical terms became known only through Mordecai Margalioth's discovery, as he probably succeeded in restoring *Sefer ha-Razim* to its original form. On the basis of fragments from the *genizah* and Hebrew, Latin, and Arabic manuscripts, he organized the work into a preface and seven short chapters describing the Seven Heavens. The work is relatively short (about 800 lines), but it is of considerable literary and historic interest. Written in a beautiful midrashic Hebrew containing hardly any Aramaic, it is however inlaid with transliterated Greek words—some of which are *termini technici* of Greek magic—as well as a short Greek prayer. The names of about 700 angels are listed (some having a Greek etymology); several have specified "characters" (symbolic figures, which form a quasi-magical alphabet). The chapter on the Seventh Heaven, dealing with the Divine Throne, the Throne of the Great Light, praises God in an exalted liturgical style. The chapters dealing with the heavens are skillfully constructed to form one unit (but it cannot be ascertained if the preface in the Margalioth edition belongs to the work because it differs widely in content from the seven chapters). Nor is it at all certain that the original name of the work in its original context was *Sefer mi-Sifrei ha-Razim.* It may perhaps have been entitled *Razi'el ha-Malakh* or possibly *Razei Ḥokhmah,* or some other name.

In this work, Raziel is mentioned as the angel who stands on the seventh step of the Second Heaven. Scholars differ on the extent of the role and influence which mystical doctrines wielded over the rabbis and their schools, but it may definitely be assumed that these doctrines, which were accepted in the Orient as well as by the Greeks and Romans, were not basically foreign to the Jews of Palestine during the Second Temple period and the generations which followed the destruction of the Temple. According to *Origen (third century), such Hebrew names as Ẓeva'ot, Eloha, etc. were mentioned along with the names of the archons, and Gabriel, Raphael, Michael, and Soriel with the demons of the Gnostic sect of the Ophites (*Contra Celsum* I, 22, 26; II, 6; IV, 33–34; V. 9, 42, 45, etc.). Those engaged in magic recited the prayer to the God of Abraham, Isaac, and Jacob while invoking demons (*Contra Celsum,* IV, 33). Greek amulets which have been preserved show a marked relation to Jewish concepts. The pagans even attributed the worship of the sun and the moon to the Jews, but Origen pointed out their error. Some of the themes of the *Sefer ha-Razim* are also discussed in the apocryphal books of the Bible, especially in II *Enoch (the Slavonic version), and in the Apocalypse of *Baruch: others are mentioned in talmudic literature (Seven Heavens, dreams, amulets in Shab. 8:2; remedies in Ber. 40a; and "Hezekiah burned the Book of Remedies" in Pes. 4:8), while parallels to them can be found in various Midrashim, *Heikhalot,* *Merkabah, and *Ma'aseh Bereshit* literature.

On the grounds of contents and style, his work should be dated to no later than the talmudic period, a dating corroborated by the chronology of Greek kings mentioned in it, which A. S. Rosenthal explained as referring to the *Indictio* of the middle or possibly the beginning of the fourth century. However, further study may perhaps reveal the later inclusion of Greco-Egyptian magical texts to eighth-century Arabic literature.

Bibliography: M. Margalioth (ed.), in: *Sefer ha-Razim* (1966), 1–62; H. Merhavia, in: KS, 42 (1967), 297–303; E. E. Urbach, in: *Studies in Mysticism and Religion presented to G. G. Scholem* (1968); G. Scholem, *Jewish Gnosticism, Merkabah Mysticism and Talmudic Tradition* (1965[2]), 101–17; idem, *Kitvei Yad be-Kabbalah* (1930), 12; J. Dan, in: *Tarbiz,* 37 (1968), 208.

[CH.M.]

RAZOVSKY (Davidson), CECILIA (1891–1968), U.S. social worker and expert on immigration. Born in St. Louis, she worked there as a volunteer at the Jewish Educational Alliance, teaching English to foreigners. In 1917 she moved to Washington, D.C. and served as an inspector in the U.S. Children's Bureau. She was secretary in the immigration department of the National Council of Jewish Women and in 1932 became associate director of the council. Razovsky traveled widely to study the conditions of Jewish refugees, and in Cuba she set up a social service program for the refugees.

Razovsky was head of a group of experts assigned by Secretary of Labor Perkins to study conditions on Ellis Island and was on several U.S. immigration committees. She also served as assistant to the executive director of the National Refugee Service.

From 1922 to 1930 she was editor of *The Immigrant* and she wrote articles, plays, and pamphlets on immigration. Her pamphlet *Handicaps in Naturalization* (1932) investigated the effects of the 1929 amendment to the Naturalization Law, raising the fee from five to twenty-five dollars. Her *Making Americans* (1938), a manual prepared for the National Council of Jewish Women, contains information on the naturalization process and suggests ways of organizing communal naturalization aid programs.

[ED.]

RAZSVET (Rus. "Dawn"), name of four Russian-Jewish weeklies that appeared in Russia and abroad.

(1) The first *Razsvet* was published in Odessa (May 1860–May 1861). The first Jewish periodical in Russian, it was founded in an era when knowledge of the Russian language was rare even among "enlightened" Jews. Although a few *maskilim* in Vilna and Minsk regarded the promotion of Russian among the Jews as a step toward social integration in Russia (see *Haskalah), Odessa was the only Russian-speaking Jewish community of any considerable size. Among the founders of *Razsvet* were Osip *Rabinovich and Joachim (Ḥayyim) *Tarnopol, who in

Abraham Idelson (seated, center), editor of the third *Razsvet,* with his staff. Seated on his left and right are Vladimir Jabotinsky and Max Soloveichik (Solieli); standing, left to right, are Shlomo Gepstein, Alexander Goldstein, and Arnold Seidenman. Courtesy A. Raphaeli-Zenziper, Archive for Russian Zionism, Tel Aviv.

1856 appealed to the ministry of education through N. I. Pirogov, inspector of education for the Odessa region, to allow them to publish a weekly. The purpose of this weekly was to spread Russian among the masses, thus helping to eliminate prejudices and enlighten the Jews. Rabinovich and Tarnopol also claimed that the periodical would serve to clarify Jewish problems to the Russian public and combat defamation of the Jews and attacks against them. After considerable effort permission was received to publish the weekly. Soon after the first issues a disagreement arose among the founders as to whether *Razsvet* should include Jewish self-criticism and a public airing of internal Jewish problems. It was feared that a lack of discretion might provoke anti-Semitic reaction. Those who opposed self-criticism, led by Tarnopol, left the staff, and Rabinovich remained as sole editor. Among those who contributed to *Razsvet* were the writer L. *Levanda, the physician and communal leader E. Soloveychik, and the jurist and historian Hermann *Baratz, as well as the Russian professor A. I. Georgiyevski and the German-Jewish historian I. M. *Jost. From the outset *Razsvet* encountered difficulties from the censors, who forbade all reference to emancipation for the Jews, and from the apathy of the Jewish public toward the Russian language. The number of subscribers never exceeded 640. After a year's publication, Rabinovich was forced to relinquish editorship to L. *Pinsker and Soloveychik, who for technical reasons changed the periodical's name to *Sion. Razsvet* was a first step in an effort to encourage an active Russian-speaking Jewish intelligentsia and a Jewish literature in Russian.

(2) The second *Razsvet,* published in St. Petersburg (September 1879–January 1883), was founded by a group of young intellectuals seeking ways to attract more enlightened Jews back to their national values. Publication rights were acquired from the journalist Alexander *Zederbaum, who had been granted them by the authorities. The editors were Jacob *Rosenfeld and G. I. *Bogrov, and the staff was filled by such writers as S. *Wengeroff, L. *Slonimski, A. Tenenbaum, S. Z. Luria, A. *Volynski (A. L. Flexer), and M. B. H. Ha-Kohen, and the poets N. *Minski (Vilenkin) and S. *Frug. *Razsvet* called for Jewish patriotism and the development of Jewish literature in Russian, closer association with the Jewish masses, and a positive approach to Jewish national values, the Jewish religion, the Hebrew language, and the settlement of Ereẓ Israel. The solution of the Jewish problem would be for large numbers of Jews to

take up agriculture. The publication soon attained a circulation of 3,400. However, the wave of pogroms and anti-Semitism in 1881 caused severe disillusionment among the staff, and after several weeks of indecision they reached the conclusion that the sole solution to the Jewish problem was emigration. Hence *Razsvet* became the outstanding spokesman for organized emigration and the proponent of the *Ḥibbat Zion movement. The January 16, 1882 edition of *Razsvet* contained an interview between a staff member, I. Orshanski, and the minister of the interior, N. Ignatiev, in which the latter announced that "the western borders were open to the Jews." The Zionist writings of Levanda and M. L. *Lilienblum appeared in *Razsvet*, as well as a translation of Pinsker's *Autoemanzipation*. Bogrov left the staff, and Rosenfeld departed for Constantinople to examine the possibilities of Jewish immigration into, and settlement in, Ereẓ Israel. Opponents of mass emigration sought all possible ways to fight *Razsvet's* policies. The two other Russian-Jewish periodicals, *Russky Yevrey* and **Voskhod*, attacked *Razsvet*, and letters were sent to the provinces to discourage further subscriptions; by 1883 circulation fell to 900. Financial support was not forthcoming and *Razsvet* closed down. Its staff dispersed, some withdrawing from public life and some joining Ḥibbat Zion; others turned their attention from Jewish affairs to find their places in Russian literature and public activity. Despite its brief existence *Razsvet* opened up a new direction in Jewish life and thought in Russia, especially among the intellectuals.

[Y.S.]

(3) The third *Razsvet* was a weekly journal of topical political and literary content, published in St. Petersburg by the Zionist Organization of Russia from 1907, when it replaced the weeklies *Khronika Yevreyskoy Zhizni* ("Chronicle of Jewish Life") and *Yevreyskiy Narod* ("The Jewish People"), which had been suppressed by the czarist administration. The editor of *Razsvet* was A. D. *Idelson, assisted by an editorial staff consisting of S. Gepstein, A. *Goldstein, V. *Jabotinsky, A. Seidenman, and M. Soloveichik (*Solieli). Questions of major policy were decided upon by the Zionist Central Committee. *Razsvet* played an outstanding part in molding and disseminating the ideology and program of the Zionist movement in Russia. Strictly adhering to Herzl's political Zionism, the journal also advocated immediate practical colonizing work in Ereẓ Israel and active Zionist participation in the defense of the rights and interests of the Russian-Jewish community. It laid the foundation of what later became known as "synthetic Zionism" a concept which harmoniously combined the traditional Zionist negation of *Galut with the struggle for Jewish survival and national organization in the countries of dispersion. *Razsvet's* militant nationalist crusade against all forms of assimilation contributed essentially to the defeat of assimilationist tendencies and groups in Russian Jewry and made it the most widely read Jewish publication in the Russian language. Early in its career its circulation reached 10,000. In July 1915 the weekly was closed down, and in its stead appeared in Moscow the *Yevreyskaya Zhizn*. In July 1917 *Razsvet* again appeared in Petrograd, and its circulation rose to 25,000. After the Bolshevik Revolution of November 1917, the Zionist press was allowed to exist for a time. But in September 1918 *Razsvet* was closed by the Cheka. In its place appeared the *Khronika Yevrevskoy Zhizni*, edited by Y. Klebanov, which was also closed down on July 18, 1919.

(4) The fourth *Razsvet* reappeared in 1922 in Berlin as the organ of the Federation of Russian-Ukrainian Zionists in exile. It was headed by an editorial board nominated by the Federation and consisting of S. Gepstein (editor), J. *Schechtman (secretary), M. Aleinikov, Ḥayyim *Greenberg, M. Hindes, and V. *Jacobson. Soon after V. Jabotinsky's resignation from the Zionist executive (February 1923), *Razsvet* endorsed his criticism of the official Zionist political line and his concept of an activist Zionist policy; it strongly disapproved, however, of Jabotinsky's later decision to leave the World Zionist Organization. Soon Jabotinsky, J. *Brutzkus, Y. Klinov, M. Schwartzman, and I. Trivus joined the reconstructed editorial board and *Razsvet* became the spokesman of the Zionist Revisionists. Financial difficulties led to the periodical's brief discontinuance in May 1924, but by the end of the year publication was resumed in Paris, with Jabotinsky as editor-in-chief and M. Berchin and J. Schechtman as acting editors. The first issue of the Paris edition sold 1,000 copies; the tenth issue, 2,500. The ideology, program, and tactical line of the Zionist-Revisionist World Union, founded in April 1925, was largely molded by the *Razsvet* group. Although the readership of the journal largely consisted of Jewish émigrés from Russia in West European countries and groups in Ereẓ Israel, and of the Jewish communities in east and southeast Europe which had a Russian cultural background, *Razsvet's* influence reached far beyond its immediate audience. Its articles were frequently translated and reprinted in other periodicals and widely commented upon by Zionists and non-Zionists alike. Stressing that *Razsvet* was the only Russian-language journal serving the Russian-Jewish diaspora, a group of noted non-Revisionist and non-Zionist émigré leaders in Paris, headed by Henry *Sliozberg, and including I. *Naiditsch, M. Goldstein, G. Vishnyak, and the sculptor N. *Aronson, formed in the spring of 1933 the "Society of Friends of Razsvet." The editorial policy in Zionist affairs remained unaffected by the agreement between the editorial board and the "Friends," but the coverage of matters of general topical Jewish interest—cultural, economic, and political—was expanded. The financial position of the paper steadily deteriorated, however, as the circle of the Jewish Russian-reading public shrank. *Razsvet* had to be converted from a weekly to a biweekly, and even in this form it appeared irregularly; the periodical was discontinued in 1935. [J.B.SCH.]

Bibliography: M. L. Lilienblum, *Derekh La'avor Ge'ulim* (1899); M. Kagan, in: *Perezhitoye*, 3 (1911), 151–7; M. Ha-Kohen, *Olami*, 1 (1927), 112–206; 2 (1927), 42–46; S. Zinberg, *Istoriya yevreyskoy pechati* (1915); S. Ginzburg, *Amolike Peterburg* (1944), 155–69; B. Shochetman, in: *He-Avar*, 2 (1954), 61–72; J. B. Schechtman, *The Vladimir Jabotinsky Story*, 1 (1956), index; M. Perlmann, in: JSOS, 24 (1962), 162–82; idem, in: PAAJR, 33 (1965), 21–50; J. Slutsky, *Ha-Ittonut ha-Yehudit-Rusit ba-Me'ah ha-19* (1970), 102–15, 122–7.

RAZUMNI, EPHRAIM ZALMAN (Solomon; 1866–1904), *ḥazzan* and composer. Born in Nikolayev, Russia, Razumni became *ḥazzan* there at the age of nineteen. After serving in Kishinev, he moved to Odessa where he spent the rest of his life. An unpredictable character, Razumni was a lyric tenor with an unusually fine faculty for improvisation. He officiated as guest cantor in many communities and gave concerts throughout Eastern Europe, gaining a huge popular following and becoming a legend in his own lifetime. His rendition of **El Male Raḥamim* after the *Kishinev pogrom became the standard musical version of the prayer in the East European Ashkenazi area and its sphere of influence. A collection of his recitatives, *Shirei Razumni*, was published by S. *Alman in 1930.

Bibliography: Y. Icht, in: *Khazonim Velt* (March, 1934), 11–12, 23; H. H. Harris, *Toledot ha-Neginah ve-ha-Ḥazzanut be-Yisrael* (1950), 448–9. [D.M.L.O.]

READING, family of British statesmen and lawyers. RUFUS DANIEL ISAACS (1860–1935), first marquess of Reading, British statesman, advocate and lord chief justice. Born in

Figure 1. Rufus Isaacs, first marquess of Reading, as viceroy of India.

London into a family of wealthy merchants, Isaacs went to sea as a ship's boy at the age of 16. He returned to England two years later and in 1879 went into the London Stock Exchange in an attempt to make his fortune. In 1884, however, he was unable to meet his obligations and was "hammered" (suspended from the exchange). Isaacs planned to sail to Panama to recoup his losses but was persuaded by his mother to study for the bar instead and was admitted in 1887. His knowledge of the commercial world enabled him to establish himself as a leading commercial counsel and in 1898 he was made a queen's counsel. Subsequently he was involved in a series of cases which brought him before the public eye. His ability to master complicated facts and his magnificent cross-examination of the financier Whittaker Wright on charges of fraud and of Frederick Seddon on charges of murdering his lodger won him the reputation as one of the greatest advocates of all time. Isaacs' success at the bar was phenomenal. He amassed a considerable fortune and honors were heaped upon him. He was elected to parliament as a Liberal Imperialist in 1904 and was made solicitor-general in 1910. In the same year Isaacs was given a knighthood and appointed attorney-general. Nevertheless, he was passed over for the appointment of lord chancellor because of his involvement in the Marconi scandal in which he was one of four ministers accused of attempting to make financial gain out of a government contract with the English Marconi Company. In 1913 Isaacs was made lord chief justice of England, the only Jew ever to hold this post, and took the title of Lord Reading. He presided over several famous criminal cases, among them the trial of the Irish nationalist, Roger Casement, on charges of treason. Yet although he was well known for his humanity and impartiality he was not considered a great judge.

Following the outbreak of World War I, Isaacs became increasingly involved in problems of government finance and introduced the scheme by which the state guaranteed all bills of exchange, thereby preventing a panic in the London bill market. In 1915 he went to the United States as president of the Anglo-French mission and secured a loan of 500 million dollars. Isaacs returned to the U.S. two years later as special envoy with the object of persuading America to join the Allies. In the following spring he went to the U.S. for a third time as high commissioner and special ambassador to convince the American government to send half a million American troops to France immediately. Isaacs remained lord chief justice until 1920 when he was made viceroy of India, ruler of India on behalf of the British crown. His appointment was hailed as a move to reconcile warring factions in India and also to assuage the growing hostility toward British rule. Isaacs succeeded in initiating the widespread reforms embodied in the Montagu-Chelmsford report (1918), establishing a form of self-government in most of the Indian provinces and introducing improvements in agriculture and housing. He was much admired for the genuine sympathy he and his wife showed for the people of India but he failed, nevertheless, to obtain the cooperation of Mahatma Gandhi and the Hindu nationalists and was eventually obliged to arrest Gandhi for incitement to civil disobedience and to call in the army to keep order. Isaacs returned to England in 1926 and was given the title of marquess, the only Jew to be so honored. He held numerous company directorships and remained a prominent figure in the Liberal Party, representing the party at the Indian Round Table Conference of 1930. For a short period in 1931 he was foreign secretary in the national government headed by J. Ramsay MacDonald and he retired in 1934 from public life with the honorary post of lord warden of the Cinque ports.

Rufus Isaacs was one of the outstanding figures of his age and in Anglo-Jewish history. He showed considerable interest in Jewish and Zionist affairs toward the end of his life and in 1926 became chairman of the Palestine Electric Corporation. He visited Palestine in 1932 and associated himself with various Zionist projects. After the advent of Hitler, Isaacs resigned the presidency of the Anglo-German Fellowship and spoke in the House of Lords against the persecution of the Jews in Germany.

GERALD RUFUS ISAACS (1889–1960), second marquess of Reading, British statesman and lawyer. Born in London, he was the only son of Rufus Isaacs and succeeded to his father's titles in 1935. He was admitted to the bar and was a bencher of the Middle Temple from 1936, becoming treasurer in 1958. Isaacs was chairman of several government committees and was undersecretary of state for foreign affairs from 1951 to 1953. He served as minister of state for foreign affairs from 1953 until his retirement in 1957. Isaacs was active in Jewish affairs as chairman of the Council for German Jewry and president of the London Jewish Hospital.

EVA VIOLET, MARCHIONESS OF READING (1895–), English social worker. The daughter of Alfred *Mond, first

Figure 2. Gerald Rufus Isaacs, second marquess of Reading, and Eva, marchioness of Reading.

Lord Melchett, she married Gerald Rufus Isaacs in 1914. Eva Reading devoted her life to problems of nursing and child care and was adviser to the ministry of health on child care during World War II. From 1957 to 1959 she was president of the National Council of Women. Though brought up as a Christian, Eva Reading reverted to Judaism in the 1930s and became a staunch Zionist; she toured the United States on behalf of the *United Jewish Appeal in 1939, and later served as chairman of the British section of the *World Jewish Congress.

Bibliography: H. M. Hyde, *Lord Reading; the Life of Rufus Isaacs, First Marquess of Reading* (1968); D. Walker Smith, *Lord Reading and his Cases* (1934); L. Broad, *Advocates of the Golden Age; Their Lives and Cases* (1958); P. H. Emden, *Jews of Britain* (1943), 295–316; N. B. Birkett, *Six Great Advocates* (1962); I. Butler, *The Viceroy's Wife* (1970). [ED.]

REBEKAH (Heb. רִבְקָה), wife of *Isaac, daughter of Bethuel, and granddaughter of Nahor, a brother of *Abraham (Gen. 22:23; 24:15, 24, 47). Rebekah is also described as "the sister of *Laban" (24:29, 50; 25:20). When Abraham sought a wife for his son he sent his servant to his homeland, Aram-Naharaim, for he wanted to avoid intermarriage with the Canaanites. The episode is described in detail in Genesis 24, which makes clear the providential nature of the union of Isaac with Rebekah (verses 7, 14, 27, 48, 50).

The text provides an insight into her character by stressing her hospitality to strangers and her kindness to animals (verses 14, 18, 20), as well as her beauty and chastity (24:16; 26:7). On one occasion Isaac felt that his life was in danger because of Rebekah's great beauty and he felt constrained to claim that she was his sister (26:6–11). Isaac's age at the time of the marriage is given as 40 (25:20); Rebekah's is not recorded. She is said to have remained childless for 20 years until, in divine response to her husband's prayers, she gave birth to twins: Esau and Jacob. During a difficult pregnancy, she received an oracle about the future relationships between, and destinies of, her unborn children (25:21–26). This experience may account for the favoritism she displayed toward Jacob (25:28).

Figure 2. Illumination from a 14th-century Spanish *Haggadah* showing (upper register) Rebekah giving birth to her twin sons. At left are Jacob, the scholar, and Esau, the hunter. Below, Rebekah watches as Isaac blesses Jacob. Sarajevo, National Museum, *Sarajevo Haggadah*, fol. 9v.

Figure 1. The marriage of Rebekah and Isaac, from a 16th-century Greek manuscript. Sinai Peninsula, Monastery of St. Catherine, Ms. 1187, fol. 100r.

When Isaac in his old age expressed his intention of bestowing his farewell blessing on Esau, Rebekah skillfully induced Jacob to supplant his brother so as to obtain it for himself. When Esau, in his bitter disappointment, threatened to kill Jacob, Rebekah arranged Jacob's flight to the house of Laban in Haran (Gen. 27), using as a pretext her bitterness and disgust over Esau's marriage to local women and her determination that Jacob marry within the family (26:34–35; 27:46; 28:1).

The death of Rebekah is not recorded in the Bible, but only the fact that she was buried in the cave of Machpelah together with the Patriarchs and *Sarah and *Leah (49:31). [N.M.S.]

In the Aggadah. The description of Rebekah as the "daughter of Bethuel the Aramean, of Padan-Aram, the sister of Laban the Aramean" (Gen. 25:20) is taken to indicate her righteousness. Despite the fact that her father and brother were scoundrels and she came from a land where deceit was rife, she succeeded in being pious (a play on the Hebrew *arammi* which by a transposition of letters is read as *ramai*, "scoundrel" or "cheat"; Gen. R. 63:4). Eliezer immediately perceived her greatness since the water of the well rose to greet her when she came to draw water (Gen. R. 60:5). The blessings of her mother and brother when she left with Eliezer were not sincere, and they were considered the "blessings of the impious which are curses." This caused Rebekah to remain barren for years (60:13). Rebekah was either three or fourteen years old at the time of her marriage (Tos. to Yev. 61b). When she entered

Sarah's tent, the divine cloud that had overhung it during Sarah's lifetime immediately reappeared (Gen. R. 60:16). Nevertheless, their marriage was not entirely happy, as a result of Rebekah's barrenness. Together they prayed for children. Finally, God acceded to the prayers of Isaac since the prayer of a pious man who is the son of a pious man is far more efficacious than the prayer of one who descends from a godless father (Yev. 64a). While pregnant, Rebekah suffered agonizing pains because her twin sons had already begun their lifelong quarrel in her womb. If she walked near a synagogue, Jacob tried to break forth from her womb, while Esau attempted to get out when she passed an idolatrous temple (Gen. R. 63:6). Finally she went to consult in the *bet midrash* of Shem and Eber where she was informed that two opposing nations were in her womb (63:6, 7).

When children Esau and Jacob seemed alike, yet Rebekah already perceived Jacob's greatness. The more often she heard his voice (engaged in study), the deeper grew her affection for him (63:10). Rebekah was not present when Isaac requested Esau to bring him savory food so that he would bless him; Isaac's charge was revealed to her through the holy spirit since she was a prophetess (67:9). She thereupon insisted that Jacob receive Isaac's blessing. She was not only actuated by love for Jacob, but also by the wish to keep Isaac from committing a detestable act by blessing the wicked Esau (65:6). She agreed to bear the possible imprecation of Isaac just as the curse of Adam fell upon "his mother," the earth (65:15). Rebekah died a short time after the death of her nurse Deborah. Her death was not mentioned explicitly in the Scripture, but is implied by the words *allon bakhut* (Allon-Bacuth; Gen. 35:8) which the Midrash renders "weeping for another," *allon* being connected with the Greek *ἄλλον* "another" (Gen. R. 81:5). There was no public mourning for Rebekah. Since Abraham was dead, Isaac blind, and Jacob away from home, only Esau remained to represent the family in public. It was feared that onlookers might say, "Cursed be the breasts that sustained thee." To avoid this, Rebekah was buried at night (PdRK 23; PR 12:48b). [Ed.]

Bibliography: Noth, Personennamen. 10; H. Bauer, in: ZDMG, 67 (1913), 344; idem, in: ZAW, 48 (1930), 78; See Commentaries on *Genesis. In the Aggadah: Ginzburg, Legends, index.

REBELLIOUS SON. "If a man have a stubborn and rebellious son, that will not hearken to the voice of his father and [not "or"] the voice of his mother and though they chasten him, will not hearken unto them, then shall his father and his mother lay hold of him and bring him out unto the elders of his city . . . They shall say unto the elders of his city: This our son is stubborn and rebellious, he doth not hearken to our voice, he is a glutton and a drunkard. And all the men of his city shall stone him with stones that he die; so shalt thou put away the evil from the midst of thee; and all Israel shall hear, and fear" (Deut. 21:18–21).

It appears that this law was intended to limit the powers of the *pater familias:* the head of the household could no longer punish the defiant son himself, according to his own whim, but had to bring him before the elders (i.e., judges) for punishment. In earlier laws (eg., Hammurapi Code, nos. 168, 169) only the father had to be defied; in biblical law it must be both father and mother, and the father cannot act without the mother's concurrence. If either was dead (Sif. Deut. 219) or refused to join in the prosecution, the son could not be indicted (Sanh. 8:4), but it was not necessary that father and mother should be validly married to each other (Sanh. 71a).

There is no record of a rebellious son ever having been executed, except for a dictum of R. Jonathan stating that he had once seen such a one and sat on his grave (Sanh. 71a). However, it is an old and probably valid tradition that there never had been, nor ever will be, a rebellious son, and that the law had been pronounced for educational and deterrent purposes only, so that parents be rewarded for bringing their children up properly (*ibid.;* Tosef. Sanh. 11:6).

Interpreting every single word of the biblical text restrictively, the talmudic jurists reduced the practicability of this law to nil. The "son" must be old enough to bear criminal responsibility, that is 13 years of age (see *Penal Law), but must still be a "son" and not a man: as soon as a beard grows ("by which is meant the pubic hair, not that of the face, for the sages spoke euphemistically") he is no longer a "son" but a man (Sanh. 8:1). The period during which he may thus be indicted as a "son" is three months only (Sanh. 69a; Yad, Mamrim 7:6), or, according to another version, not more than six months (TJ, Sanh. 8:1). The term "son" excludes a daughter (Sanh. 8:1; Sif. Deut. 218), though daughters are no less apt to be rebellious (Sanh. 69b–70a).

The offense is composed of two distinct elements: repeated (Sif. loc. cit.) disloyalty and defiance, consisting in repudiating and reviling the parents (Ex. 21:17), and being a "glutton and drunkard." This second element was held to involve the gluttonous eating of meat and drinking of wine (in which sense the same words occur in Prov. 23:20–21), not on a legitimate occasion (Sanh. 8:2), but in the company of loafers and criminals (Sanh. 70b; Yad, Mamrim 7:2) and in a ravenous manner (Yad, Mamrim 7:1). There are detailed provisions about the minimum quantities that must be devoured in order to qualify for the use of the term (cf. Yad, Mamrim 7:2–3). As no "son" can afford such extravagance, the law requires that he must have stolen money from his father and misappropriated it to buy drinks and food (Sanh. 8:3, 71a; Yad, Mamrim 7:2). "Who does not heed his father and mother" was interpreted as excluding one who does not heed God: thus, eating pork or other prohibited food, being an offense against God, would not qualify as gluttony in defiance of parents *(ibid.)*. But it was also said that one who in his use of the stolen money performed a precept and thus heeded his Father in heaven could not be indicted (TJ, Sanh. 8:2).

As father and mother have to be "defied," to "take hold of him," to "say" to the elders, and to show them "this" is our son, neither of them may be deaf, dumb, blind, lame, or crippled, or else the son cannot be indicted as rebellious (Sanh. 8:4; Sif. Deut. 219). Either of them could condone the offense and withdraw the complaint at any time before conviction (Sif. Deut. 218; Sanh. 88b; TJ, Sanh. 8:6; Yad, Mamrim 7:8).

The son had first to be brought before a court of three judges (see *Bet Din*) where, when he was convicted, he would be flogged and warned that unless he desisted from his wanton conduct he would be indicted as a rebellious son and liable to be stoned; if he did not desist, he would be brought before a court of 23, including the three judges who had warned him (Sanh. 8:4; 71b; Mid. Tan. to 21:18; Yad, Mamrim 7:7). If he escaped before sentence was passed, and in the meantime his hair had grown, he had to be discharged; but if he escaped after sentence, he would be executed if caught (Sanh. 71b; Yad, Mamrim 7:9).

The sentence passed upon a rebellious son had to be published far and wide, so that "all Israel will hear and be afraid" (Sanh. 89a; Mid. Tan. to 18:21). According to one view, the sentence was to be passed and executed at Jerusalem, at the time of mass pilgrimages, when all the people would be there to see and to hear (Tosef. Sanh. 11:7). It is said that the rebellious son is executed, not because of what he has actually done, but because of what he was foreseen to be prone to do were he allowed to live. His conduct showed that eventually he would have ruined his parents and become a robber and murderer (Sanh. 72a; TJ, Sanh. 8:7), so God considered it better for him to die innocent than to die guilty (Sanh. 8:5).

"In our times, we pay no attention to gluttonous and defiant sons, and everybody covers up the sins of his children; even where they might be liable to flogging or to capital punishment under the law, they are not even reprimanded. Many such children are leading purposeless lives and learn nothing—and we know that Jerusalem was destroyed because children loafed around and did not study" (Shab. 119b; Samuel Eliezer Edels, *Ḥiddushei Halakhot ve-Aggadot*, Sanh. 71a).

Bibliography: J. S. Zuri, *Mishpat ha-Talmud*, 6 (1921), 88; ET, 3 (1951), 362–7; A. Ch. Freimann, in: EM, 2 (1954), 160–2.

[H.H.C.]

REBREANU, village in Transylvania, central Rumania. Jews settled in the villages of Lusça and Entrádám which later became part of Rebreanu. There was a Jewish community in Lusça dating from the early 18th century, while the population of Entrádám was entirely Jewish and its Rumanian name was Jidoviţa, from the Old Rumanian word *jidov* ("Jew"). The Jews engaged mainly in commerce and agriculture and operated water mills. With the abolition of the settlement restrictions in Transylvania in 1848 many Jews from Entrádám moved to the nearby city of Nasaud, founding the community there. The population of the village was almost wholly Jewish in 1900. In 1930 the 135 Jews formed over 60% of the total population. The administration of the village remained in Jewish hands, and Rebreanu was popularly known as "Klayn Ereẓ Israel" ("little Ereẓ Israel"). The community was Orthodox with a strong ḥasidic influence.

During World War II, in 1944, the Jews were moved by the Hungarian Fascists first to Nasaud, then to Bistrita, then finally deported to *Auschwitz. In 1947 there were 17 Jews living in Rebreanu, but they left soon afterward.

[Y.M.]

REBUKE AND REPROOF (Heb. *tokhaḥah*), admonition and chastisement for the purpose of restraint or correction. The biblical source for the duty to rebuke the wrongdoer is: "You shall not hate your kinsman in your heart. Reprove your neighbor, but incur no guilt because of him" (Lev. 19:17). In the view of the rabbis the duty to reprove one's neighbor has two applications: the first, to confront one's fellow with personal grievances held against him, and the second, to chastise evildoers in the hope of bringing about their regeneration (Maim. Yad, De'ot 6:6, 7). The duty to openly confront one's neighbor with personal grievances is entailed in the injunction against hatred of one's brother, insofar as the silent harboring of resentments leads to hatred (Ch. B. Chavel (ed.), *Sefer ha-Ḥinnukh* (1961), 297). Thus the behavior of Absalom toward his brother Amnon ("Absalom spoke unto his brother Amnon neither good nor bad, for Absalom hated Amnon . . .," II Sam. 13:22) is cited as an example of the wickedness of bearing unexpressed grievances (see Gersonides on this verse; and also Yad, De'ot 6:6, 7). The duty to chastise sinners and wrongdoers stems from the view that everyone is charged with the responsibility of bringing about the correction of the sins of his fellowman. Failure to discharge this responsibility is tantamount to bearing the same sins and faults (cf. Targum Onkelos and commentary of Naḥmanides on Lev. 19:12).

Because the intention behind the rebuking of the evildoer is his rehabilitation, a number of qualifications are imposed upon this commandment. One is prohibited from rebuking another to the point of embarrassment (Ar. 16b). According to Maimonides, admonition must be carried out in private (Yad, De'ot 6:7). In fact, rebuke must be effected with such delicacy that R. Eleazar b. Azariah doubted that there were any in his generation sufficiently capable in this regard (Ar. 16b). Furthermore, the Talmud, in accordance with the dictum "Reprove not a scorner lest he hate thee" (Prov. 9:8), prohibits admonition where there is a foregone conclusion that it will be rejected and merely increase enmity (Yev. 65b). Certain later rabbinic authorities maintain that in cases where it may safely be assumed that rebuke will be disregarded, it is preferable not to rebuke people for violating prohibitions that are not explicit in the Torah, for it is preferable that they transgress unknowingly rather than deliberately (Sh. Ar., OḤ 608:2).

Procedures of Rebuke. It is not sufficient to rebuke the wrongdoer once, rather one must rebuke him incessantly so long as he is recalcitrant. According to R. Johanan, a person should persist in rebuking his neighbor until the wrongdoer insults him; according to Samuel, until he curses him; and according to Rav, until he is ready to strike him (Ar. 16b). The obligation to rebuke one's neighbor falls even upon one who is generally intellectually and morally inferior to the person at fault, so that the disciple, for instance, must rebuke his teacher where necessary (BM 31a). Every community must appoint a wise and respected person whose function it is to publicly chastise wrongdoing and call for repentance (Yad, Teshuvah 4:2).

The role of admonition is central in Jewish ethical thought. The rabbis proclaim that there exists no love or peace where there is no admonition, citing as an example the peace covenant between Abimelech and Abraham which resulted from Abraham's reproving Abimelech (Gen. R. 54:3). The duty of admonition extends not only to individuals, but to the community at large, and even to the entire world, to the extent that if one does not fulfill the commandment of rebuke, the guilt of all those he might have reformed accrues to him (Shab. 54b). Some rabbis of the Talmud maintain that the Second Temple was destroyed, despite the presence of the righteous, because the righteous did not fulfill their obligation to rebuke the wrongdoers of their time, and thus shared their guilt (Shab. 119b). In the opinion of Judah ha-Nasi, the most righteous course for a man to choose is the love of admonition: "As long as there is admonition in the world there is satisfaction, goodness, and blessing in the world . . . as it is written [Prov. 24:25] 'To them that rebuke shall be delight, and a good blessing shall come upon them' " (Tam. 28a).

Bibliography: Ḥ. N. Bialik, and Y. Ḥ. Rawnitzki (eds.), *Sefer ha-Aggadah*, 2 (1960), 541–3; J. D. Eisenstein, *Oẓar Musar u-Middot* (1941).

[J.H.Sh.]

RECANATI, town in the Marches, central Italy. Already by the 13th century there was a Jewish community in Recanati, trading in wine, oil, and cereals. Around the end of the following century Jewish loan-bankers settled in Recanati. In the 15th and 16th centuries Recanati became the most important Jewish center in the Marches, and in 1448 delegates of the Jewish communities in the region were summoned to assemble there to consider ways of defending themselves against the prevailing anti-Jewish agitation. Other meetings took place in 1480, 1509, and 1515. In 1558 the apostate Fra Filippo (formerly Joseph Moro) burst into the synagogue during the Day of Atonement service and profaned the Ark. After he had been driven out of the synagogue by the furious congregation, he appealed to the ecclesiastical authorities and obtained a severe sentence against the Jewish community. In 1569, following a bull by Pius V, the Jews were expelled from Recanati, as they were from all other centers in the Papal States, except Rome and Ancona. They returned for a brief period under *Sixtus V (1587) and opened loan-banks once again until 1593. The famous mystical exegete, Menahem (of) *Recanati, may have lived here in the 14th century.

Bibliography: Kaufmann, in: REJ, 23 (1891), 249–55; Servi, in: *Vessillo Israelitico*, 47 (1899), 79–81, 117f.; Ghetti, in: *Atti e memorie della Regia deputazione di storia patria delle Marche*, 4 (1907), 11–39; Milano, Bibliotheca, index; A. Bravi, *Reminiscenze recanatesi* (1878), 71–78.

[A.To.]

RECANATI, Italian family, originally from Spain, which produced scholars, physicians, merchants, and financiers. The name derives from the town of *Recanati. The family rose into special prominence in the 17th century, but earlier members of the family are Menahem *Recanati in the 13th century and AMADEO (Jedidiah) in the 16th century who translated Maimonides' *Guide of the Perplexed* into Italian, under the title *Erudizione dei Confusi*, which he dedicated to Menahem Azariah da *Fano.

The main branch of the family begins with SHABBETAI ELHANAN (early 17th century), rabbi of Ferrara when the ghetto was established there (1624). He founded a dynasty of rabbis that continued for at least six generations. MENAHEM, his son, succeeded him as a rabbi in Ferrara. He wrote a number of responsa. Some of these are included in *Piskei Recanati ha-Aḥaronim* of Jacob Ḥayyim Recanati (nos. 4, 6, 33; see below). JUDAH ḤAYYIM (late 17th century), Menahem's son, was rabbi of the Sephardi community of Ferrara. He wrote a number of responsa and his name appears often with the other rabbis of the city on rabbinical decrees. One of his responsa appears in *Piskei Recanati ha-Aḥaronim* (no. 5). SHABBETAI ELHANAN (d. 1738), his son, continued as rabbi of the Sephardi community of Ferrara. He was a contemporary of Mordecai *Ẓahalon and his name appears often together with Ẓahalon's and those of the other rabbis of Ferrara on regulations *(takkanot)* and approvals *(*haskamot)*. He wrote responsa at a very early age. One of them is found in *Devar Shemu'el* (p. 280) of Samuel Aboab. He is mentioned in the *Paḥad Yiẓḥak* of Lampronti, *Reshit Bikkur Kaẓir* of Jacob Daniel Olmo, and *Shemesh Ẓedakah* of Samson Morpurgo. His son MOSES was also a rabbi in Ferrara as early as 1730.

JACOB ḤAYYIM BEN ISAAC SAMUEL (1758–1824), his grandson, was born in Pesaro. At first an elementary school teacher in Ferara, he later served as rabbi in Siena, Acqui, Moncalvo, Finale, Carpi, Verona, and Venice. In Verona he also acted as head of a rabbinical school. He is best known for his *Piskei Recanati ha-Aḥaronim* (Leghorn, 1813) a collection of responsa, and for *Ya'ir Nativ* (Dessau, 1818) a responsum on the Hamburg Temple and its use of an organ. He was one of the four rabbis who took the liberal view. He was a man of wide interests, being also a grammarian and mathematician, poet and preacher. He published a treatise on arithmetic at Siena. Unpublished are books of sermons entitled *Afikei Mayim, Oholei Ya'akov*, and *Neveh Ya'akov*. He also wrote a compendium on Judaism (Verona, 1813), a number of Hebrew poems, and *Har ha-Tov*, quotations from *Ein Ya'akov*. EMANUELE (Menahem; 1796–1864), the son of Jacob Ḥayyim, was physician in Verona. He wrote *Grammatica Ebraica in Lingua Italiana* (Verona, 1842); and *Dizionario Ebraico-Caldaico ed Italiano e Italiano ed Ebraico* (2 vols., *ibid.*, 1854–56). Other branches of the family are found in various Italian cities. In the 20th century branches of the family spread to Greece, Israel, and the U.S.

[IS.KL.]

In Greece, YEHUDAH LEIB RECANATI (1890–1945) was a noted banker. Born in Salonika, Recanati was a leader of Greek Jewry for many years and became the president of the Greek communities in 1934, representing them on the Jewish Agency council. In 1935 he settled in Tel Aviv and established the Discount Bank of which he became chairman of the board of directors. This bank became one of the largest in the country and contributed substantially to the economic development of Israel. Recanati was the chairman of the Sephardi community council in Tel Aviv and was active in a large number of public institutions and bodies. His sons, HARRY RAFAEL (1918–) and DANIEL (1921–), were both directors of the Discount Bank and developed wide banking and commercial interests in Israel and elsewhere. They were dedicated to public and social needs in Israel (see *Israel: Banking). [B.J.]

Bibliography: Ghirondi-Neppi, 127, 155–7, 225–7, 319, 335; I. Sonne, in: *Horeb*, 6 (1941), 79–95.

RECANATI, MENAHEM BEN BENJAMIN (late 13th–early 14th centuries), Italian kabbalist and halakhic authority. No information whatsoever is available on Recanati's life, although according to family tradition mentioned in *Shalshelet ha-Kabbalah* he was once an ignorant man who miraculously became filled with wisdom and understanding.

He wrote three kabbalistic works: *Perush al ha-Torah* (Venice, 1523); *Ta'amei ha-Mitzvot* (Constantinople, 1544); and *Perush ha-Tefillot* (*ibid.*, 1544); and one halakhic work, *Piskei Halakhot* (Bologna, 1538). Two commentaries on the *Perush al ha-Torah* were written during the 16th century: one by Mattathias Delacrut (Neubauer, Cat, nos. 1615, 1623, 3); and *Be'ur Levush Even Yekarah* by Mordecai Jaffe (Lublin, 1605; Lemberg, 1840–41). An important part of the *Ta'amei ha-Mitzvot*, in which Recanati deals with the problem of the nature of the *Sefirot*, still remains in manuscript. According to Recanati, the *Sefirot* are not the essence of God but coverings in which God enfolds Himself and instruments through which He acts. This entire extract is quoted by Judah *Ḥayyat in his commentary to **Ma'arekhet ha-Elohut*, and in their discussions of this question other 16th-century kabbalists (notably Isaac Mor Ḥayyim, Elhanan Sagi Nahor, Solomon *Alkabeẓ, and Moses *Cordovero) refer to Recanati's views. Even those who oppose his theory refer to him with admiration and respect, with the exception of David Messer *Leon, who attacks him harshly in *Magen David* (MS Montefiore 290).

With the exception of his discussion on the essence of the *Sefirot*, where his conclusion is the result of his own speculations, Recanati's doctrine is drawn mainly from written sources. He cannot be regarded as the recipient of "revelations from heaven" (despite Guedemann; see bibl.), and in few places indeed does he tell of his dreams and visions. Thanks to him the doctrines of many kabbalists whose writings are otherwise unknown have been preserved. He made use of many sources, which he usually does not mention by name, and was especially indebted to *Naḥmanides, whom he refers to as "the great rabbi." Another kabbalist he mentions frequently is R. Ezra (whose name is occasionally changed to R. Azriel), and he made use of the writings of Jacob b. Sheshet Gerondi, *Asher b. David, Joseph *Gikatilla, and *Moses b. Shem Tov de Leon. Recanati was acquainted with two large works on the reasons for the precepts which were written during his lifetime: one by R. Joseph from Shushan (then attributed to Isaac ibn Farḥi) and another by an unknown author. An important part of his commentaries on Naḥmanides' esoteric mysticism derives from *Keter Shem Tov* by Shem Tov *ibn Gaon. Other important sources were *Sefer ha-*Bahir* and the Zohar, which he quotes often although he had access to only a limited number of sections.

Bibliography: Zunz, Lit Poesie, 369ff.; Guedemann, Gesch Erz, 2 (1884), 180–2; I. Sonne, in: KS, 11 (1934/35), 530; G. Scholem, *ibid.*, 185; Scholem, Mysticism, index s.v. *Menahem of Recanati*; idem, *Ursprung und Anfaenge der Kabbala* (1962), index; idem, *Von der mystischen Gestalt der Gottheit* (1962), index; idem, *On the Kabbalah and its Symbolism* (1965), index; Y. Nadav, in: *Tarbiz*, 26 (1956/57), 440–58; J. Ben-Shelomo, *Torat ha-Elohut shel R. Moshe Cordovero* (1965), index; E. Gottlieb, *Ha-Kabbalah be-Khitvei Rabbenu Baḥya ben Asher* (1970), 259–63. [E.G.]

°**RECCARED,** Visigothic king of Spain (586–601). He succeeded his father Leovigild and shortly thereafter converted from Arianism to orthodox Christianity. This conversion was followed in 589 by the Third Council of

Toledo, where it was decreed that all Arians must become orthodox. His preoccupation with religious matters seems to have led Reccared to reaffirm and modify existing anti-Jewish legislation. He forbade Jews to own Christian slaves and decreed that if a Jew circumcised a Christian slave, the latter was to be set free and the owner was himself to be enslaved. Jews were further forbidden to have Christian wives or mistresses and any children born from such a union were to be baptized. This is the earliest example of compulsory conversion of Jews in Visigothic Spain. Aside from the enactment requiring the forced baptism of offspring from mixed marriages, Reccared's legislation did not go beyond that which had existed under his Arian predecessors. In fact the punishment for converting one's own slaves was reduced from death to slavery. Like his predecessors, moreover, Reccared was lax in enforcing the anti-Jewish laws. Not only did Jews continue to own and trade Christian slaves, but the pope felt compelled to indicate his wrath at this state of affairs. This had little effect, however, and the Jews seem to have been little bothered by Reccared's legislation against them.

Bibliography: S. Katz, *Jews in the Visigothic and Frankish Kingdoms of Spain and Gaul* (1937), index; B. Blumenkranz, *Juifs et Chrétiens dans le monde occidental, 430–1096* (1960), index; E. A. Thompson, *The Goths in Spain* (1969). [B.BA.]

RECHAB AND BAANAH (Heb. רֵכָב, "rider"; and בַּעֲנָה, cf. Ugaritic *bnᶜna,* "son of Ana"), sons of Rimmon from Beeroth, one of the four cities which constituted the Gibeonite (or Hivite) league, and which has been identified as the site of el-Bire, lying northwest of Jerusalem just outside the territory of the tribe of Benjamin. Rechab and Baanah, captains of the army of Saul's son Ish-Bosheth (II Sam. 4:2), murdered their king (verse 7). Entering Ish-Bosheth's house undetected, they decapitated him while he was sleeping (verse 7) and took his head to David, claiming to have carried out the will of God (verse 8). David, anxious to clear himself of the suspicion of complicity, had them summarily executed, reminiscent of the way he treated the man who brought the news of Saul's suicide. The assassins' bodies were mutilated and hanged beside the pool in Hebron, while the head of Ish-Bosheth was honorably buried in Abner's grave in the same town (verse 12). Several possible motives may explain the captains' regicide: the hope of being rewarded by David; the desire to realize Abner's plan for a united kingdom with David as king, by eliminating David's most dangerous opponent; and revenge for Saul's conquering the confederacy of the Hivite cities (cf. Josh. 9:17).

Saul's conquering of the confederacy explains why the Beerothites, including the sons of Rimmon, fled to Gittaim, where they lived as aliens (II Sam. 4:3). In the course of time the sons of Rimmon became officers of Ish-Bosheth and at an opportune moment murdered him as an act of blood revenge.

Bibliography: M. H. Segal, in: JQR, 8 (1917/18), 98–99. [ED.]

RECHABITES (Heb. בְּנֵי הָרֵכָבִים), a small religious sect first identified as such in Jeremiah 35 in an incident dated in the reign of *Jehoiakim, but tracing their descent to Jonadab son of Rechab, who was a contemporary of *Jehu (II Kings 10:15–17 where he is called Jehonadab; see below). Jeremiah was commanded by God to take the Rechabites to one of the chambers in the Temple and serve them wine. The Rechabites, however, refused to drink the wine, citing the charge of their ancestor Jonadab son of Rechab, which forbade them to drink wine, to cultivate or even to own fields or vineyards or to build houses. They had remained pastoral tent-dwellers until the invasion of Nebuchadnezzar, when they had taken refuge in Jerusalem. It is not known whether this was when Nebuchadnezzar merely occupied the West and Jehoiakim became his vassal (604 B.C.E.) or during Jehoiakim's rebellion (601–598), nor whether the Rechabites had been able to continue to dwell in tents while residing in Jerusalem, but at any rate they continued to abstain from wine. Jeremiah, while he did not necessarily demand this Nazirite-like asceticism, extolled their strict observance of these commandments, contrasting it with the evil ways of the people of Judah. He promised the Rechabites that they would continue to serve before God: "Jonadab son of Rechab shall never lack a man to stand before me" (35:19).

"Ben Rechab" may mean not literally "son of Rechab" but "Rechabite," in which case Jonadab may have won over his clansmen as well as his descendants to his way of life. He was not necessarily the physical ancestor of all the Rechabites of Jeremiah's day, but he was in any case their lawgiver and spiritual ancestor. Whether the Rechabites had peculiar religious observances (e.g., letting the hair grow) other than those enumerated above is not known.

Opposition to the Monarchy of Omri. Jonadab son of Rechab sided with Jehu against the House of Ahab. From a fragmentary text (II Kings 10:15–17) it appears that Jonadab, riding in Jehu's chariot from Jezreel to Samaria, gave his blessing to the slaughter of the royal family, and that Jehu was interested in proving to him his zealousness on behalf of God. Jonadab also participated at Jehu's side in the slaughter of the prophets of Baal in the House of Baal in Samaria (II Kings 10:23). There is no evidence in the text that other men of the family of Rechab participated with Jonadab or that he acted as a representative of the sect. However, although Jonadab was accepted by Jehu on the strength of his personality, it may be assumed that his reputation as a zealous supporter of the God of Israel, who would tolerate no compromises, derived from his position as a head of a family that was completely opposed, because of its zealous faith and unique social charcter, to the rule of the House of Omri. Jonadab may have promulgated his rules as a reaction to the policies of Ahab, which notoriously provoked the opposition of the prophets and the sons of prophets headed by *Elijah and *Elisha. It appears that even at that time the Rechabites were distinguished from the prophets by their asceticism and extreme zealousness on behalf of the God of Israel (there is no sign that the prophets also participated in the slaughter of the worshipers of Baal in Samaria).

Origin of the Group. There is no definite information concerning the origins of the Rechabites. From a vague verse in I Chronicles 2:55— "These are the Kenites who came from Hammath, the father of the house of Rechab" —it follows that the house of Rechab (as far as it is possible to identify it with "the house of the Rechabites" in Jer. 35 and "the son of Rechab" in II Kings 10) was related to the *Kenites. This verse mentions the Rechabites only in passing, in connection with the lineage of the Kenites. It goes on to say that the Kenites, or at least some of them, were among the inhabitants of Jabez, implying that they established a permanent settlement there, which cannot of course refer to the Rechabites. Even if "the house of Rechab" is also a place-name, identical with the name of the family, as is usually the case in the genealogies of Chronicles, there is no proof that it refers to a permanent settlement. If preference is given to the text of the Septuagint: "these are the men of Rechab," over that of I Chronicles 4:12: "these are the men of Recah," it is seen that, in accordance with the genealogical context in I Chronicles 4:11–15, the Rechabites were related to the Kenazites and the Calebites. Indeed, if these above verses reflect the process of settlement of the desert tribes in Judah in the period of the united monarchy in Israel, it may be estimated that the Rechabites were known, many years before Jonadab, as a special family in Judah. It is reasonable to suppose that, like the Kenites and the Kenazites, the Rechabites were absorbed in Judah at the time of the united monarchy, and in any case their territory was adjacent to the permanent settlements in the hill country of Judah. But their character as a religious sect dates only from the time of Jonadab.

Seminomadic Shepherds. Not engaging in agriculture and living in tents, the Rechabites must have subsisted by raising sheep and goats (cf. Gen. 4:20; 25:27). It follows that the Rechabites were among the nomads and herdsmen who dwelt in proximity to the permanent settlements in Israel and Judah, and even wandered further to the Wilderness of Judah. From the verses describing the meeting between Jonadab and Jehu—which took place between Jezreel and Samaria—it may be inferred that Jonadab's settlement was in the neighborhood of the cities in Israel. But their wanderings in the different periods ranged over Israel and Judah.

Relation to Society at Large. It appears that, in contrast to the deeds of Jonadab in the days of Jehu, the Rechabites in the following generations did not participate in the practical life of the kingdom and were essentially not a rebellious sect. The impression is that they did not set out to preach a way of life to the whole people, but, as is generally the case with a separatist group unified by family ties and stringent communal restrictions, it served in its very existence as a challenge to the conventions of the agrarian society and culture; in this respect it was analogous to some of the ascetic sects in the Wilderness of Judah in Second Temple times.

Second Temple Period. There are allusions to the existence of the family of the Rechabites in the days of the Second Temple. In Nehemiah reference is made to Malchijah son of Rechab, officer of the district of Beth-Cherem who held the Dung Gate (3:14), but there is no mention of his being unique among the other officers. Diodorus Siculus (19:9), in the name of Jerome of Cardia, speaks of the asceticism of the early Nabateans at the end of the fourth century B.C.E. in terminology almost exactly like that which Jeremiah used in describing the Rechabites, and he too placed special emphasis on the prohibition against drinking wine. There is no way of knowing of any connection between the Rechabites and the Nabateans, but it is probable that there were parallels to biblical asceticism, such as that of the house of Rechab, among other ethnic groups that settled in the south and Transjordan. According to the Mishnah (Ta'an. 4:5), "the children of Jonadab son of Rechab" had (in Second Temple times) a fixed day in the year for bringing wood for the altar of the Temple. They were probably descended from the tent-dwelling Rechabites, but they hardly constituted a separate sect. There were "water-drinking" sacrificers, and the Midrash traces their descent to Jonadab (Gen. R. 98:10; Sif. Num. 78, 81, et al.; cf. Ta'an. 28a; TJ, Ta'an. 4:2, 68a), but this merely indicates that sects of teetotalers existed in the Second Temple period. The designation which connects them with the pre-Exilic Rechabites may very well be typological rather than truly genealogical.

Bibliography: E. Meyer, *Die Israeliten und ihre Nachbarstaemme* (1906), 40–409, 444ff.; J. W. Flight, in: JBL, 42 (1923), 158–226 (incl. bibl.); S. Klein, in: *Ẓiyyon Me'assef*, 2 (1927), 9; J. A. Montgomery, in: JBL, 51 (1932), 183–213; H. Schmoekel, *Jahwe und die Fremdvoelker*... (1934), 212–22; S. Talmon, in: *Eretz Israel*, 5 (1958), 111–3; N. Glueck, *Rivers in the Desert* (1959), 142–5; Kaufmann Y., Toledot, 2 (1960), 232, 338, 625–6; S. Abramsky, in: *Eretz-Israel*, 8 (1967), 255–64, incl. bibl. For the Rechabites in the Second Temple period see: Y. Baer, *Yisrael ba-Ammim*, 1 (1955), 45, 125.
[SH.AB.]

RECHITSA, city in Gomel oblast, Belorussian S.S.R. Rechitsa had one of the oldest Jewish communities in Belorussia. In 1648 the rampaging Cossacks murdered many of its Jews. The Jewish population in 1766 numbered 133, increasing to 1.268 in 1800 (two-thirds of the total population), and 2,080 in 1847. The city was a center for *Ḥabad Ḥasidism. At the end of the 19th century Rechitsa had a yeshivah and was the residence of the ḥasidic leader, R. Shalom Dov Ber *Schneersohn. Rechitsa's Jews were merchants in lumber and agricultural produce. In 1897 the 5,334 Jews of Rechitsa constituted 57% of the population. In October 1905 the peasants of the surrounding area participated in a pogrom which killed more than 50 Jews, among them members of the Jewish self-defense force. On the eve of World War I the Jewish population numbered about 7,500. Jewish communal and religious life began to decline under Soviet rule. In 1926 there were 7,386 Jews. On November 25, 1941, the Nazi invaders murdered about 3,000 Jews who had remained in the city. A few Jews returned after the war. They had no synagogue and in 1970 the Jewish population was estimated at about 1,000.

Bibliography: I. Halpern, *Sefer ha-Gevurah*, 3 (1950), 186–90; *Die Judenpogrome in Russland*, 2 (1909), 465–7; *Prestupleniya nemetsko-fashistskikh okkupantov v Belorussii* (1963), 268–71.
[Y.S.]

RECHTER, Israel architects. ZE'EV RECHTER (1899–1960) was born in Russia and went to Palestine in 1919. He worked for many years as a draughtsman and surveyor, later studying architecture and engineering in Italy and France. He had a considerable influence in formulating the types of urban dwelling houses in Israel as a whole, and in Tel Aviv in particular. He introduced the house built on piles, with the lower floor open to the street, which determined the look of residential streets in Tel Aviv and other towns. The first building of this type was Bet Engel in the Rothschild Boulevard in Tel Aviv built by Rechter in 1934–36. Among other public buildings built or designed by Rechter are Binyenei ha-Ummah in Jerusalem, the Meir Hospital at Kefar Sava, the Elisha Hospital in Haifa, and the Tel Aviv lawcourts (in partnership with Dov *Karmi).

His son, YA'AKOV RECHTER (1924–), was born in Tel Aviv and served as an officer during the War of Independence. In 1951 he became partner in his father's firm. He worked on a number of private buildings and public projects such as the F. R. Mann Auditorium in Tel Aviv (in col-

Rest home in Zikhron Ya'akov, designed by Israel architect Ya'akov Rechter. Photo Isaac Percal.

laboration with D. Karmi). On the death of his father, designs emerging from the reorganized office seem to shift from a solid sobriety to lively sculptural forms. In the Zikhron Ya'akov Rest Home, Rechter repeated the cellular pattern of his Tel Aviv Hilton. In a different mood, Rechter experimented with concrete and glass at the Polyclinic in Haifa. Rechter worked on a town-planning scheme for the development of the Tel Aviv seafront. [A.E.]

RECIFE, city in N.W. *Brazil, capital of the state of Pernambuco. When Recife became a prosperous center for sugar production in the 16th and 17th centuries, Portuguese settlers of Jewish descent and *New Christians or Marranos were already living in the city and its environs. They gave impetus to sugar production and commerce. The large number of New Christians in Recife (including the first historian of Brazilian economic life, Ambrosio Brandão), took part in a variety of activities, and bound themselves through intermarriage to prestigious Old Christian families. Denunciations on the part of inquisitional officers and of "friends of the Holy Office" acquainted the inquisitors with a great number of Portuguese—for the most part New Christians—who did not conform to the fixed patterns of behavior imposed by the church. Thus the New Christian Diego Fernandez, the greatest expert in sugar plantations, was accused by the Inquisition of being a "Judaizer." The Inquisition dispatched an official inspector *(visitator)* for the purpose of seizing and confiscating the suspects' possessions, and an inquisitional commission was established in 1593 in Olinda, the port of Recife. New Christians were tried and arrested; some were taken to Lisbon and handed over to the inquisitional tribunal. After the inspector had left, surveillance of New Christians was continued by the bishop of Brazil, with the assistance of the local clergy and Jesuits.

In 1630 Pernambuco was occupied by the Dutch, and it remained in their hands until 1654. This was an important period in Jewish history in Latin America, as Brazil was the only region—during colonial times—where Jews were permitted to practice their religion openly and establish an organized community. Its members were mainly Jews from Holland, joined by New Christians already living in the colony. The Jews of Recife were known as financiers, brokers, sugar exporters, and suppliers of Negro slaves. Their congregation, Ẓur Israel, maintained a synagogue, the religious schools Talmud Torah and Eẓ Ḥayim, and a cemetery. In 1642 the first rabbi of the New World, Isaac Aboab da Fonseca, arrived from Holland, accompanied by the *ḥakham* Moses Rafael de Aguilar and a large number of immigrants. The synagogue's cantor was Josue Velosino, and notables included David Senior Coronel, Abraham de Mercado, Jacob Mocatta, and Isaac Castanho. According to the minute books of the congregation, there were approximately 1,450 Jews in Dutch Brazil in 1645; the number diminished to 720 in 1648 and to 650 in 1654. The majority lived in Recife and its environs. Despite official tolerance, however, the Jews were victims of hostility and discrimination at the hands of Calvinists and Catholics.

With the start of the Reconquest, the Jews were victimized by both the Dutch and the Portuguese, and in 1645 various Jewish prisoners were executed as allies of the Dutch; others were sent to Lisbon and handed over to the Inquisition; still others returned to Holland. After several years of fighting, the Portuguese succeeded in reconquering the territory thanks to the creation of the Commercial Company for Brazil (in Lisbon), most of whose capital came from New Christians. After the fall of Recife, the Jewish community disintegrated, and those who had openly professed their Judaism left Brazil together with the Dutch. These emigrants developed the sugar industry of the Antilles. After many difficulties, 23 of these Jewish emigrants arrived in New Amsterdam, where they founded the first Jewish community of what later became the City of New York.

New Christians continued to live in Recife, some as Crypto-Jews. Two decades after the departure of the Dutch, the Inquisition was also acquainted with and persecuted the New Christians who had converted to Judaism during the Dutch occupation and had remained in Pernambuco. Many reports reached the Lisbon Inquisition in the second half of the 17th century and during the 18th century regarding their clandestine observance of Jewish rituals. Portuguese policy in the middle of the 18th century eventually enabled the New Christians to mingle with the rest of the population, until their traces disappeared as they became completely assimilated.

The present-day Jewish community in Recife was founded by immigrants from Eastern Europe, particularly Russia, Rumania, and Poland, who settled there in the second decade of the 20th century. They number 350 families (1,600 persons) and maintain a Centro Israelita, a high school *(colegio)*, whose 350 pupils constitute 90% of all Jewish pupils attending schools, a synagogue, and various Jewish organizations.

Bibliography: A. Wiznitzer, *Jews in Colonial Brazil* (1960); C.R. Boxer, *Dutch in Brazil 1624–1654* (1957); H. F. de Mendonca, *Primeira Visitacão do Santo Ofício as partes do Brasil—Denunciaçoes de Pernambuco 1593–1595*(1929); J. G. de Mello, *Tempo dos Flamengos* (1947); H. Kellenbenz, *Sephardim an der unteren Elbe* (1958); A. Novinsky, in: *Comentario*, 10 (July–Sept. 1963), 231–42.
[A.No.]

RECKENDORF, HERMANN SOLOMON (1863–1923), German orientalist. Reckendorf's father, also named HERMANN (Ḥayyim Ẓevi; 1825–1875), taught Semitic languages at Heidelberg University, and wrote a Hebrew translation of the Koran (1857). Inspired by E. Sue's *Les Mystères de Paris*, he also wrote *Die Geheimnisse der Juden* (5 vols., 1856–57), a fictionalized recounting of Jewish history. Several Hebrew versions of this work were published; the one by A. S. Friedberg (*Zikhronot le-Veit David*, 1893–1900) is still popular with Israel youth. Hermann Solomon Reckendorf studied Semitics under T. Noeldeke and at the Berlin rabbinical seminary, but later abandoned Orthodoxy. Reckendorf became professor at Freiburg University, specializing in Arabic syntax.

His *Die syntaktischen Verhaeltnisse des Arabischen* (1895–98) outlines the problems of Arabic syntax; his *Arabische Syntax* (1921) is important for its collection of material. The two works remain outstanding. In his *Ueber Paronomasie in den semitischen Sprachen* (1909) Reckendorf covers a wider field, dealing with a well-defined syntactic phenomenon in most Semitic languages. Another of his works is *Mohammed und die Seinen* (1907).

Bibliography: J. Fueck, *Arabische Studien in Europa* (1955), 312–3.
[J.L.BL.]

RECKLINGHAUSEN, town in Westphalia, W. Germany, where the presence of Jews is attested as early as 1305. The financier, Gottschalk of Recklinghausen, who carried on extensive business from Lochern (in Dutch Gelderland), was killed during the disturbances caused by the Black Death in 1349–50. No organized community, however, came into being in medieval times, and there is no record of one in Recklinghausen until 1828. In the course of time an active Jewish life developed and the community established a synagogue, communal center, elementary school, *mikveh*, and a variety of Jewish societies. Eastern European immigrants founded their own society and *minyan*. The Jewish population of Recklinghausen grew from 72 in 1880 to 298 in 1905. It dropped to 280 (5% of the total population) in 1933. From 1903 until 1922 and again from 1934 to 1938, Recklinghausen was the seat of a district rabbi. The last incumbent was Selig Auerbach who later emigrated to the U.S. During the Nazi persecutions many members of the community succeeded in emigrating from Recklinghausen, principally to Holland. On Nov. 9–10, 1938 the synagogue was destroyed, and subsequent deportations of the remaining Jews brought the community to an end. A new community of 52 Jews was established in Recklinghausen after World War II in conjunction with *Bochum and Herne, numbering 76 persons in 1962. In 1960 and 1961 the "Synagoga" exhibition of Jewish art and folklore was held in Recklinghausen and was subsequently shown throughout Germany.

Bibliography: H.C. Meyer (ed.), *Aus Geschichte und Leben der Juden in Westfalen* (1962), 125–33, 165, 187, 255; Germ Jud, 2 (1968), 678–9; *Monumenta Judaica*, 2 (1963), 369, 379, 653. [Ed.]

RECONSTRUCTIONISM, an ideology and a movement in U.S. Jewish life. Both the idea and the movement owe their inspiration to Mordecai Menahem *Kaplan. Kaplan argues that with the breakdown of certain traditional beliefs, Jewish identity had become attenuated. Jews remain loyal to their faith despite hardship and suffering because they believe that adherence to Judaism assures them of salvation in the next world. But in Kaplan's view, this is no longer credible. Consequently, Judaism must transform itself from a civilization orientated toward the life hereafter into one which can help Jews to attain salvation in this world. Belief in the possibility of this salvation is crucial to Kaplan's thought. It means the progressive improvement of the human personality and the establishment of a free, just, and cooperative social order. Kaplan maintains that there are adequate resources in the world and capacities in man to achieve such salvation. He defines God as the "power that makes for salvation." This notion of God conforms to our experience, since man senses a power which orients him to this life and elicits from him the best of which he is able.

Some Reconstructionists, Milton *Steinberg probably being the best example, refused to accept Kaplan's theology. A more popular notion of Kaplan's was his definition of Judaism as an evolving religious civilization whose standards of conduct are established by the Jewish people and whose common denominator is neither beliefs, tenets, nor practices, but rather the continuous life of the Jewish people. The Jewish religion, said Kaplan, exists for the Jewish people, not the Jewish people for the Jewish religion. Judaism, like any other civilization, comprises a history, a language, a religion, a social organization, standards of conduct, and spiritual and social ideals. Under the influence of the early French sociologist, Emile Durkheim, Kaplan stated that whatever is an object of collective concern takes on all the traits of a religion, which in its turn functions in order to hold up to the individual the value of the group and the importance of his complete identification with it. Religion, therefore, lies at the very heart of every civilization.

Many Jewish intellectuals were attracted to Kaplan's program for a Jewish life. Since Judaism is, in his view, a civilization, its parts can only function in interrelationship with one another. He argued for what he called an "organic community" in which the basic unit of Jewish life would be the entire aggregate of synagogue, educational institutions, Zionist organizations, and defense and fraternal bodies, linked into a single community with a democratically elected leadership. Kaplan was also among the first to maintain that the synagogue must function as a Jewish center where an individual might find expression for virtually all Jewish and related activities.

The founding of the Reconstructionist movement may be dated from the establishment of the Society for the Advancement of Judaism (SAJ) in January 1922. The society served both as a synagogue center and as a forum for Kaplan's ideas. In 1935 he launched the magazine *Reconstructionist* in collaboration with his closest associates, of whom Milton Steinberg, Eugene *Kohn, and Kaplan's son-in-law, Ira *Eisenstein, formed the nucleus. In 1941 the *New Haggadah* and the *Guide to Jewish Ritual* were published. In the *Guide* ritual was viewed not as law but a means to group survival and the spiritual growth of the individual Jew. The individual was to be the arbiter of which rituals or folkways should or should not be practiced, though when making his choice, he was recommended to strike a balance between his own needs and those of the group. In 1945 the Reconstructionist *Sabbath Prayer Book* appeared, against which a ban *(ḥerem)* was proclaimed by the Aguddat ha-Rabbanim and an adverse "statement of opinion" *(gillui da'at)* was issued by Louis Ginzberg and Alexander Marx (*Hadoar*, 24 (1945), 904f.). In accordance with Kaplan's ideology, it excised references to the Jews as a chosen people, and to such concepts as God's revelation of the Torah to Moses and a personal Messiah. Some passages of the traditional prayer book were retained despite Kaplan's rejection of the concepts which lay behind them. In such cases the editors suggested to the reader how the passages were to be understood. Thus, prayers for the restoration of Israel were retained, but readers were told this should not be construed as the return of all Jews to Palestine. Kaplan was a Zionist of the American school, ardent in his support for the colonization of Palestine, but opposed to concepts implying the "negation of the Diaspora" and to emphasis on the necessity of *aliyah*.

Kaplan's greatest success was in his impact on Jewish educators, social workers, and rabbis, especially students of the Jewish Theological Seminary, where he taught from 1909 to 1963. He left an indelible mark upon many of the leaders of the Jewish community. The movement was, however, less successful in recruiting a mass following. In 1970 there were ten congregations affiliated to the Federation of Reconstructionist Congregations and Fellowships and about nine *ḥavurot* (small groups who meet once every week or two for study and/or to observe the holidays together). The Federation affiliates have a combined membership of about 2,300 families. However, not all members think of themselves as Reconstructionists any more than all members of Orthodox, Conservative, or Reform synagogues think of themselves as Orthodox, Conservative, or Reform Jews. A more unreservedly Reconstructionist organization, the Reconstructionist Foundation, whose membership is open to any Jew (including Federation members), has approximately 1,000 members. Reconstructionist influence, however, is far greater than these numbers might suggest. It was greatly enhanced—it might even be said that a turning point in the movement's history was reached—when in 1968 the Reconstructionist Rabbinical College was established in Philadelphia. Students are expected to complete a doctoral program in religious or cognate studies at neighboring institutions in Philadelphia (primarily Temple University) at the same time as preparing for rabbinical ordination at the college.

After Kaplan, the leader of Reconstructionism has been Ira Eisenstein, who has served as president of the Reconstructionist Foundation and of the college, editor of the magazine *Reconstructionist*, and de facto editor of the Reconstructionist press.

Bibliography: C. S. Liebman, in: AJYB, 71 (1970), 3–100; M. M. Kaplan, *Judaism as a Civilization* (1934); idem, *The Future of the*

American Jew (1948); idem, *The Meaning of God in Modern Jewish Religion* (1937); *The Reconstructionist* (1935ff.); M. Ben Horin, *Common Faith—Uncommon People: Essays in Reconstructionist Judaism* (1970). [C.S.L.]

RECORDS, PHONOGRAPH. The earliest "talking machine" was patented by Thomas A. Edison in 1878 as a vertical cylinder device. In 1887 Emile *Berliner produced a lateral flat disc mechanism, bringing the disc "gramophone" into competition with the cylinder "phonograph." By 1891 recordings were introduced to public entertainment as coin-in-slot machines, and soon included some Jewish monologues, skits, and songs.

One of the most widespread Jewish subjects on recordings was cantorial music. Gershon *Sirota was the first cantor to record liturgicals commercially. He was widely criticized because recordings were played in cabarets and on Sabbath. Then Zavel *Kwartin recorded and other cantors followed in a "golden cantorial age." In the 1920s such favorites as Mordecai *Hershman, David *Roitman, and Berele *Chagy were presented on discs and cylinders. Cantor Josef (Yossele) *Rosenblatt put 82 different liturgical selections on ten labels. Since World War II revival of interest in European-style cantorials has resulted in re-pressings and reissues of old liturgical performances, as well as recordings of modern cantors such as Moshe *Koussevitzky and Leib *Glantz, and the cantorial records of such prominent concert and opera artists as Jan *Peerce and Richard Tucker. In the U.S. congregations have honored their own cantor with a recording issue of his performances. In the 1960s recordings of the devotional music of ḥasidic groups, such as the Lubavicher, Modzhitzer, and Gerer, on their own labels or Jewish companies, added to the number of Jewish liturgical recordings.

Theatricals. Edison cylinders early captured such voices as the Yiddish artist Madame Regina Prager (1874–1949) and the Jewish entertainer Sophie *Tucker. Among the Jewish performances early in this century on single-side small discs were a folk melody *Min ha-Meẓar* and a popular ditty *Kum Yisrulik, Kum Aheym.* Shalom Aleichem read his works for cylinders, and the comic monologuist, Ikey Eisenstein, was a great favorite on discs. Especially in the U.S. dance music recordings sold well, particularly of Jewish wedding *freylekhs, shers, kazatskis,* and *horas.* By the end of World War I every recording company had a roster of all types of Jewish performers. With the rise of radio in the 1920s, records dropped in sales. Jewish records especially lost their audiences with the changing tastes of the U.S. Jewish public for "Anglicized" entertainment and with the appearance of Jewish "stars" on the general stage, in radio, and "talking pictures." Some recordings include Yiddish theatrical personalities of the era between the two world wars, such as Joseph Rumshinsky (1881–1956), Aaron Lebedeff (1873–1960), Ludwig Satz (1891–1944), Moishe Oysher (1907–1958), and Menasha Skulnick (1892–1970). The aftermath of the Holocaust in Europe and the establishment of the State of Israel stimulated wider interest for popular performances of Yiddish and Hebrew folk music. Prominent among recorders of this postwar Jewish expression have been the actor-singer Theodore Bikel, the ḥasidic performer Shlomo Carlebach, the Israel entertainer Shoshana Damari, and the Yiddish actress Molly Picon. With the rise of the "youth market" in the 1960s, such phenomena as folk-rock liturgicals and rock-ballads in Hebrew with electronic instrumentation have appeared in the U.S. and Israel.

At the turn of the century, in St. Petersburg, Russia, the Jewish proprietor of Rappaport's "listening shop" encouraged and assisted his supplier of discs to present in 1902 a roster of higher quality selections on a special "red seal" label. The entire industry followed over the next decade with "quality labels" on larger double-side discs, upon which were available the performance of concert artists, many of them Jewish. In the worldwide growth of better quality recordings over the decades to the 1970s, Jewish participation has been outstanding. In 1969 the *Service Technique pour l'Education* (STE) of the Alliance Israélite Universelle in Paris published a selective listing of all types of Jewish recordings available on the Continent at the time.

Folk Music. Use of cylinder recording for collection of Jewish folk materials was made at the turn of this century by collectors in Russia. Before World War I the Jewish musicologist Abraham Ẓevi *Idelsohn made use of recording apparatus in assembling liturgical materials in Jerusalem for his ten-volume *Thesaurus of Hebrew-Oriental Melodies.* Such scholars in Israel and America as Edith *Gerson-Kiwi and Johanna *Spector used recording equipment in their work among groups in the field.

Jewish Recording Companies. By 1920 there were about thirty different companies each issuing several labels, all of which had some Jewish materials in addition to rosters of Jewish performers. The decade of the 1920s was an era of consolidation into "big business" concerns in the recording industry, as well as much technological expansion. The oldest continually operating record shop into 1971 has been the Metro Music Shop, which was established in 1918 on the Lower East Side of Manhattan in the Yiddish theatrical area of Second Avenue by Henry Lefkowitch (1892–1959), a composer and publisher of Jewish music. A number of specifically Jewish recording companies have been formed since World War II. In 1939 Moses Asch formed Asch Record Company to supply Jewish recordings for the all-Jewish radio station WEVD in New York. Expanded to Ethnic-Folkways Records in 1947, its scope of Jewish materials was broadened to include recordings of Sephardim, Falashas, Yemenites, and other Oriental Jewish groups, much of it based on field collections by researchers, in addition to folk music in Yiddish and Hebrew Zionist songs. Formed after the war, Banner Records has made a speciality of Jewish variety and theatrical presentations by more recent artists. Ḥasidic music has been issued by smaller companies as well as by the larger Jewish companies. Menorah Records features recordings for children, holiday albums, and other educational releases. Since 1947, Tikva Records has manufactured and distributed a wide variety with an active market catalog of about 130 different issues. It has been especially successful in presenting Jewish folk dance records with instructions for the performances of the dances. In 1962 Greater Recording Company was formed to locate and re-issue on long-playing records rare Jewish performances done originally in the early decades of this century on cylinders and discs. Some recent performances of ḥasidic music and cantorials are included in its roster. Benedict Stambler (1903–1967) formed Collectors Record Guild and began in 1955 to re-press for commercial sale many of the old Jewish recordings from his large personal collection. He also produced new ḥasidic recordings. In 1971 the Stambler collection of recorded Jewish music, comprising 4,000 different selections, was donated to the Rogers and Hammerstein Archives of Recorded Sound, housed in the New York Public Library at Lincoln Center. This collection, recorded on approximately 150 labels and starting with materials from 1902, is available for study on the library premises. Among the leading Israel recording companies are: Hed Arẓi, for light Israel entertainers and folk ensembles; Ha-Taklit, with folk music presentations; Israeli Music Foundation, for serious compositions as well as folk dances; and, the largest, CBS-Israel, which produces light popular, classical, musical and drama, educational material, and "small disc specials" for children.

Bibliography: R. Gelatt, *Fabulous Phonograph: From Edison to Stereo* (1966[2]); S. Rosenblatt, *Yossele Rosenblatt* (1954); Catalogs of: Folkways, Banner, Tikva, Menorah, Greater Recording, Collectors Record Guild, CBS, Hed Arẓi, Ha-Taklit; *Schwann Record and Tape Guide* (1971–); Alliance Israélite Universelle, *Service Technique pour l'Education,* Catalogs (1961; 1969). [I.He.]